South America

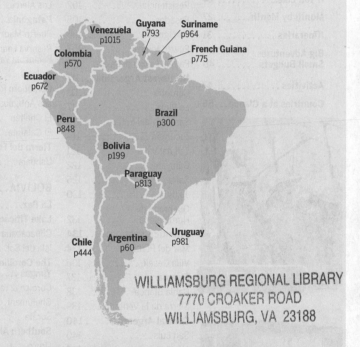

Venezuela p1015

Guyana p793

Suriname p964

French Guiana p775

Colombia p570

Ecuador p672

Peru p848

Brazil p300

Bolivia p199

Paraguay p813

Chile p444

Argentina p60

Uruguay p981

Regis St Louis, Isabel Albiston, Celeste Brash, Brendan Sainsbury,
Robert Balkovich, Jade Bremner, Cathy Brown, Gregor Clark,
Alex Egerton, Michael Grosberg, Anthony Ham, Mark Johanson,
Anna Kaminski, Brian Kluepfel, Tom Masters, Carolyn McCarthy,
MaSovaida Morgan, Anja Mutić, Kevin Raub, Adam Skolnick,
Paul Smith, Andy Symington, Phillip Tang,
Luke Waterson, Wendy Yanagihara

Contents

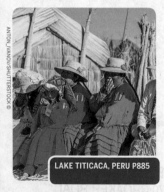

LAKE TITICACA, PERU P885

ANTON_IVANOV/SHUTTERSTOCK ©

FOZ DO IGUAÇU, BRAZIL
P358

JIXIN YU/SHUTTERSTOCK ©

ON THE ROAD

Contents

ON THE ROAD

Contents

Welcome to South America

Andean peaks, Amazonian rainforest, Patagonian glaciers, Incan ruins, colonial towns and white-sand beaches: the wonders of South America set the stage for incredible adventures.

Captivating Landscapes

From the snow-capped peaks of the Andes to the undulating waterways of the Amazon, South America spreads a dazzling array of natural wonders. This is a continent of lush rainforests, towering volcanoes, misty cloud forests, bone-dry deserts, red-rock canyons, ice-blue glaciers and sun-kissed beaches. As landscapes go, there aren't many other places on earth that offer so much variety.

Big Adventures

You can hike past ancient temples first laid down by the Incas, contemplate the awe-inspiring power of Iguazú Falls, or spend the day watching wildlife from a dugout canoe on one of the Amazon's countless *igarapés* (narrow waterways). You can barrel down Andean roads by mountain bike, go whitewater rafting on Class V rivers and surf amazing breaks off both coasts. And once you think you've experienced it all, head to the dramatic landscapes in Tierra del Fuego, go eyeball to eyeball with extraordinary creatures in the Galápagos, and take in a wondrous array of wildlife in the Pantanal (aka the world's largest wetlands).

Cultural Treasures

South America's diversity doesn't end with landscapes. You'll find colonial towns where cobblestone streets lead past gilded churches and stately plazas little changed since the 18th century. You can haggle over colorful textiles at indigenous markets, share meals with traditional dwellers of the rainforest and follow the pounding rhythms of Afro-Brazilian drum corps. South America is home to an astounding variety of living and ancient cultures, and experiencing it firsthand is as easy as showing up.

La Vida Musical

This is one of the world's great music destinations. Nothing compares to hearing the rhythms of Colombian salsa, Brazilian samba, Argentine tango and Andean folk music in the place where they were born. Buenos Aires' sultry *milongas* (tango clubs), Rio's simmering *gafieiras* (dance halls), Quito's *salsotecas* (salsa clubs) – all great places to chase the heart of Saturday night. Yet this is only the beginning of a great musical odyssey that encompasses Peruvian *trovas*, soulful Ecuadorian *pasillos*, fast-stepping Brazilian *forró*, steel-pan Guyanese drumming, Paraguayan harp music and more. Simply plunge in – though you might want to take a dance class along the way!

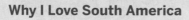

Why I Love South America

By Regis St Louis, Writer

Be mindful of what you're getting into: South America can be a lifetime addiction. I didn't real-ize this when I first hiked Andean trails and visited pre-Columbian sites more than 15 years ago. Like other travelers who shared the journey, I was hooked. I fell hard for the incredible wonders of this continent: its mist-covered peaks, thundering falls and vast rainforests. Add to this the human-made treasures: buzzing indigenous markets, picturesque colonial towns and vibrant cityscapes. This is just the beginning, and in South America there really is no end. It's the reason I've returned so many times, but know there is still much more to discover.

For more about our writers, see p1088

Above: Carnaval (p311), Rio de Janeiro

South America

Cartagena
A salsa-loving colonial beauty (p610)

Otavalo Market
Vast Andean handicrafts market (p698)

Machu Picchu
The ancient Inca citadel (p906)

Lake Titicaca
Island-hopping and indigenous cultures (p885)

Central Suriname Nature Reserve
Explore Maroon culture (p975)

The Amazon
The fabled rainforest (p424)

HONDURAS
NICARAGUA
COSTA RICA
PANAMA

PACIFIC OCEAN

ATLANTIC OCEAN

Equator

Galapagos Islands (ECUADOR)
Puerto Ayora

Santa Marta
Ciudad Perdida
Barranquilla
Cartagena
Maracaibo
Coro
Puerto la Cruz
Saint Vincent & the Grenadines
Cumaná
Barcelona
CARACAS
Maracay
Tucupita

Medellín
Cali
Popayán
Esmeraldas
Manta
QUITO
ECUADOR
Otavalo
Coca
Latacunga
Riobamba
Cuenca
Loja
Guayaquil
Machala

Santa Ciudad
Mérida
Cúcuta
Bucaramanga
Tunja
BOGOTÁ
COLOMBIA

Río Cauca
Río Magdalena

VENEZUELA
Río Orinoco
Ciudad Bolívar
Puerto Ayacucho
Río Guaviare

GEORGETOWN
PARAMARIBO
Cayenne
FRENCH GUIANA (FRANCE)
SURINAME
GUYANA
Kaieteur Falls
Roraima (2810m)
Santa Elena de Uairén
Boa Vista
Río Branco

Río Negro

Macapá
Ilha de Marajó
Belém
São Luís
Fortaleza
Natal
João Pessoa
Recife
Maceió

BRAZIL

Santarém
Manaus
Río Amazonas
Río Solimões
Leticia
Río Japurá

Río Tapajós
Río Xingu
Río Tocantins
Río Araguaia

BRASÍLIA
Goiânia

Río São Francisco

Salvador
Ilhéus
Porto Seguro

Piura
Chiclayo
Trujillo
PERU
Huaraz
LIMA
Pisco
Ica
Ayacucho

Río Marañón
Río Napo
Río Ucayali
Pucallpa
Parque Nacional Manú
Machu Picchu

Porto Velho
Río Madeira
San Matías
Cuiabá

Puerto Maldonado
Parque Nacional Madidi
Rurrenabaque
Trinidad
BOLIVIA
LA PAZ
Cochabamba
Santa Cruz
Oruro
Lago Titicaca
Moquegua

Equator

10°N
10°S

80°W
70°W
60°W
50°W
40°W

Rio de Janeiro
Beaches, caipirinhas and samba (p304)

Iguazú Falls
One of earth's mightiest falls (p110)

Encarnación
Paraguay's most captivating city (p825)

Colonia del Sacramento
Photogenic 18th-century charmer (p993)

Glaciar Perito Moreno
Massive, dramatically set glacier (p179)

Torres del Paine
Granite peaks soaring over Patagonia (p552)

Salar de Uyuni
Otherworldly salt flats (p242)

Atacama Desert
Canyons, geysers and pink flamingos (p490)

Buenos Aires
Blazing nightlife and colorful neighborhoods (p63)

ATLANTIC OCEAN

PACIFIC OCEAN

Belo Horizonte
Ouro Prêto
Rio de Janeiro
São Paolo
Curitiba
Florianópolis
Caxias do Sul
Porto Alegre
Campo Grande
Ciudad del Este
Foz do Iguaçu
Puerto Iguazú
Encarnación
Posadas
PARAGUAY
ASUNCIÓN
Corrientes
Santa Fe
Rosario
URUGUAY
MONTEVIDEO
Punta del Diablo
Punta del Este
Pelotas
Mar del Plata
BUENOS AIRES
Río Paraná
Río Uruguay

Iquique
Calama
Tupiza
Tarija
Villazón
Antofagasta
San Salvador de Jujuy
San Pedro de Atacama
Salta
Tucumán
ARGENTINA
Córdoba
Mendoza
SANTIAGO
Viña del Mar
Valparaíso
La Serena
Archipiélago Juan Fernández (CHILE)

Concepción
Chillán
Temuco
Pucón
Valdivia
Bariloche
Osorno
El Bolsón
Puerto Montt
Ilha Grande de Chiloé
CHILE
Coyhaique
Puerto Madryn
Parque Nacional Los Glaciares
El Calafate
Parque Nacional Torres del Paine
Puerto Natales
Río Gallegos
Punta Arenas
Ushuaia
Falkland Islands (Islas Malvinas)
Stanley

Tropic of Capricorn

20°S
30°S
40°S
50°S

30°W
40°W
50°W
60°W
80°W
90°W
100°W

Rapa Nui (Easter Island)

Rapa Nui (CHILE)

South America's
Top 15

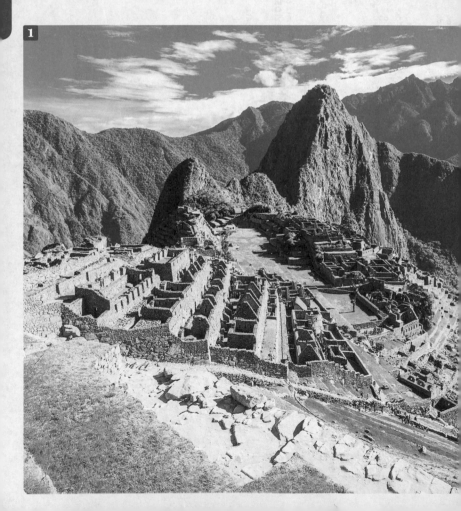

Machu Picchu

1 A fantastic Inca citadel, a secret held by local Quechua people until the early 20th century, Peru's Machu Picchu (p908) stands as a ruin among ruins. With its emerald terraces and steep peaks that echo on the horizon, the sight simply surpasses the imagination. This marvel of engineering has withstood half a dozen centuries of earthquakes, foreign invasion and howling weather. Discover it for yourself, wander through its stone temples and scale the dizzying heights of Wayna Picchu.

The Amazon

2 Home to the greatest collection of plant and animal life on earth, the awe-inspiring Amazon (p424) encompasses more than 7 million sq km. There are countless ways to experience its astounding biodiversity: trekking through dense jungle, visiting indigenous villages, flying over the vast green expanse of undulating waterways, slow-boating between river towns or lounging in a jungle lodge after a day spent wildlife-watching. Nine countries share a bit of the famous rainforest, all of which have excellent bases to experience it firsthand. Below: Jaguar

SAIKO3P/SHUTTERSTOCK ©

RICHARD CONSTANTINOFF/SHUTTERSTOCK ©

3

Rio de Janeiro

3 Few cities in the world enjoy more seductive charm than Brazil's *Cidade Maravilhosa* (Marvelous City), but calling Rio (p304) merely marvelous doesn't quite cut it. On privileged real estate flanked by striking Atlantic-blue waters, sugary-white sands and a mountainous backdrop of Crayola-green rainforest, Rio's cinematic cityscape has few rivals. And once its soundtrack kicks in – a high-on-life siren's song of bossa nova and samba – Rio's raw energy seizes you with the come-hither allure of a tropical fantasy. You'll have no choice but to follow. Above: Cristo Redentor (p307)

Buenos Aires

4 Whip together a beautiful Argentine metropolis with gourmet cuisine, awesome shopping, frenzied nightlife and gorgeous locals, and you'll get Buenos Aires (p63). It's a European-like, cosmopolitan city encompassing both slick neighborhoods and downtrodden ghettos, but that's the appeal. You can experience classic cafes, amazing steaks, surprising architecture, energizing *fútbol* games and – of course – that sultry tango. Buenos Aires is elegant, seductive, emotional, confounding, frustrating and chock-full of attitude – and there's absolutely no other place like it in the world. Above right: Tango (p71)

Lake Titicaca

5 Less a lake than a highland ocean, Lake Titicaca (p219) is the highest navigable body of water in the world. In Andean tradition it's the birthplace of the sun. Here, banner blue skies turn to bitterly cold nights. Among the fantastical sights of this lake spread across Peru and Bolivia are the surreal floating islands crafted entirely of tightly woven *totora* reeds. Enthralling and in many ways singular, the shimmering deep-blue Titicaca is the longtime home of highland cultures steeped in the old ways. Below right: Islas Uros (p890)

4

5

Iguazú Falls

6 The thunderous roar, the dramatic cascades, the refreshing sprays, the absolute miraculous work of Mother Nature – nothing prepares you for that flooring first moment you set eyes upon Iguazú Falls (p110). On the Brazilian side, the wide-eyed view of the whole astounding scene stretches out before you in all its panoramic wonder. In Argentina, get up close and personal with the deafening Devil's Throat, which provides the fall's single most mind-blowing moment. In all, some 275 falls deliver one of the world's best wows in unforgettable fashion.

Atacama Desert

7 You'll feel like you've arrived in another world in this bone-dry desert framed by soaring mountain peaks in northern Chile. Days are spent taking in Mars-like rock formations, floating on salt lakes and wandering through a spurting geyser field, followed by evenings gazing at some of the clearest night skies on the planet. Uncommon adventures abound, from sandboarding and mountain-bike rides to scenic hikes through red-rock canyons, or simply watching pink flamingos and other animal life. Gateway to it all is the traveler hub of San Pedro de Atacama (p488).

Salar de Uyuni

8 Who knew feeling this cold could feel so good? While the three- to four-day jeep tour through the world's largest salt flat (p242) will leave your bones chattering, it quite possibly could be the singular experience that defines your South American adventure. The Bolivian salt flat in its vastness, austerity and crystalline perfection will inspire you, while your early morning exploration of rock gardens, geyser fields and piping hot springs along with the camaraderie of three days on the road with your fellow 'Salterians' will create a kinship not likely to fade anytime soon.

9

10

Central Suriname Nature Reserve

9 Cascading rapids rush past smooth boulders and forested islands lined with white-sand beaches. The sun-dappled jungle is hot and muggy, but the beauty of the foliage, birdsong and musky scents outweigh the discomforts. In Central Suriname Nature Reserve (p975), one of Suriname's largest reserves, you can trek to plateaus with views over never-ending pristine forest, then cool off in a waterfall at the end of the day. At night dance to African drums before gazing at shooting stars in the deep-black sky.

Otavalo Market

10 Every Saturday the world seems to converge on the bustling Ecuadorian town of Otavalo in the Andes, where a huge market (p698) spreads from the Plaza de Ponchos throughout the town. While the crowds can be a drag and the quality is immensely changeable, the choice is enormous and you'll find some incredible bargains here among the brightly colored rugs, traditional crafts, clothing, Tigua folk art and quality straw hats. Nearby, the squawks and squeals of livestock drown out the chatter of Kichwa-speaking farmers at Otavalo's equally famous animal market.

Cartagena

11 Stroll through the perfectly preserved streets of Cartagena's Old Town (p610) and be swept away by the grace, romance and legend of one of the continent's finest colonial settlements. Inside its imposing walls, much of the Colombian city still looks as it did during Spanish rule – pastel-hued mansions boast elegant wooden balconies, which open onto majestic plazas shaded by magnificent churches. Throw away the map, get lost in the maze of narrow cobblestone streets and discover why this magical place has seduced travelers for centuries

Glaciar Perito Moreno

12 Possibly the world's most dynamic glacier, the Perito Moreno (p179) in Argentina advances up to 2m per day, which means plenty of exciting, spine-tingling calving. It's supremely accessible, too – you can get very close to the action via a complex network of steel boardwalks, perfectly situated near (but not too near!) the glacier's face. Everyone stands there, watching in suspense, for the next building-size chunk to sheer off and slowly tip into the water below, creating thunderous crashes and huge waves. Trust us, it's awesome.

Torres del Paine

13 The wind is whipping and dark clouds form overhead as the hiking trail suddenly opens to reveal a stunning vista of rugged granite spires soaring high over the Patagonian steppe. These are the Torres del Paine (p552), the proud centerpiece of Chile's famous national park. Trekking through this Unesco Biosphere Reserve isn't for the faint of heart – guides say the park sees all four seasons in a single day – but hiking the 'W' remains a rite of passage for generations of adventurous travelers.

Colonia del Sacramento

14 Take a step back in time as you explore the gracious 18th-century cobbled streets and fascinating history of former smugglers' haven, Colonia del Sacramento (p993) in Uruguay. Then check out the great bar and restaurant scene and the gorgeous position on a peninsula of the Río de la Plata. All this and its super-accessible location a short hop away from both Montevideo and Buenos Aires make 'Colonia' a classic tourist town, but even on weekends it's worth dodging the crowds and letting yourself get seduced by the town's eternal charms.

Encarnación

15 With its new beach, sparkling coastal promenade and wildly energetic Carnaval (pictured left), Paraguay's 'Pearl of the South' (p825) is billing itself as the local answer to Rio de Janeiro. Though that might be a bit ambitious, there is no doubt that Encarnación's unique take on Carnaval is a whole lot of fun, where the crowd dances as much as the participants, spray snow fills the hot summer air and the party goes on well into the early hours of the morning.

Need to Know

For more information, see Survival Guide (p1033)

Visas
Visas are sometimes required, or in some cases other charges must be paid, for example for reciprocity fees or tourist cards.

Money
ATMs are available in major towns and cities; stock up on funds before visiting remote areas. Credit cards are widely accepted.

Cell Phones
Local SIM cards can be used in unlocked European and Australian (GSM) phones. Or you can purchase a phone when you arrive (a cheap one costs about US$30).

Time
South America has five time zones, ranging from GMT minus two hours (Fernando de Noronha off Brazil's east coast) to GMT minus six hours (Easter Island and the Galápagos, off South America's west coast)

When to Go

Quito
GO May–Sep

The Amazon
GO Jul–Nov

Cuzco
GO May–Sep

Rio de Janeiro
GO Year-round

Buenos Aires
GO Nov–Apr

- Dry climate
- Tropical climate, wet & dry seasons
- Mild to hot summers, cold winters
- Tropical climate, rain (year–round)
- Cold climate

High Season
(Dec–Mar)

➜ It's high season in Brazil and the Atlantic coast; beaches and festivals (such as Carnaval) are big draws.

➜ The best time to visit Patagonia, though expect higher prices.

Shoulder
(Oct–Nov)

➜ It's dry season in the Amazon, making for fine wildlife-watching.

➜ Fewer crowds and lower prices make this a good time to visit Buenos Aires, Rio and other coastal destinations.

Low Season
(Jul–Aug)

➜ In Chile and Argentina, many services close at beach resorts, and mountain passes can be blocked by snow.

➜ Less rain and warm clear days make it an excellent time for visiting the Andean highlands in Peru, Ecuador and Bolivia.

Daily Costs

Budget:
less than US$30

➡ Dorm beds: from US$10

➡ Double rooms: from US$25

➡ Shopping at markets, eating inexpensive set meals: from US$5

Midrange:
US$30–90

➡ Budget jungle lodge in the Amazon per day: US$50–80

➡ Hiking and cycling tours per day: from US$50

➡ 3½-day Manaus–Belem boat trip (hammock fare): from US$100

Top end:
more than US$90

➡ Hiking the Inca Trail (four-day trek) per person: US$600

➡ Multiday Galápagos cruise per day: around US$200

Useful Websites

Lonely Planet (www.lonely planet.com/south-america) Destination information, hotel bookings, traveler forum and more.

Latin American Network Information Center (www.lanic. utexas.edu) Links to all things Latin American.

UK Foreign Travel Advice (www.gov.uk/foreign-travel-advice) Travel advisories.

US State Department (www. state.gov) Travel advice and warnings.

Thorn Tree (lonelyplanet.com/thorntree) Get trip recommendations and destination tips from other travelers.

Arriving in South America

Aeropuerto Internacional Ministro Pistarini (Buenos Aires) Frequent shuttle buses head downtown (AR$240); taxis cost around AR$1200.

Aeropuerto Internacional Jorge Chávez (Lima) Fast and safe Airport Express shuttle buses (S25) operate hourly services with stops throughout Miraflores. A taxi is around S60.

Aeropuerto El Dorado (Bogotá) Take a shuttle buses to Portal El Dorado and transfer to Trans-Milenio bus (COP$2300). Taxis cost about COP$30,000.

Getting Around

Bus Extensive services throughout the continent, except for the Amazon. You'll find reclinable seats (and super-powered air-conditioning on long hauls).

Plane Useful for crossing immense distances; can save days of travel; prices are generally high, but airfare promotions are frequent.

Car Useful for traveling at your own pace, though cities can be difficult to navigate and secure parking is a must.

Boat Slow, uncomfortable, but brag-worthy transport between towns in the Amazon, with trips measured in days rather than hours. You'll need a hammock, snacks, drinking water and a high tolerance for boredom.

Train Limited networks, generally geared toward tourists.

Get Inspired

Literature

Gabriel Garcia Marquez Marquez (*Love in the Time of Cholera*) and **Mario Vargas Llosa** (*War of the End of the World*) – Nobel Prize winners and sometime rivals – are considered the continent's modern living writers.

Jorge Luis Borges This giant of modern literature is best known for his labyrinthine tales, and playful melding of myth and truth, such as in *Ficciones*.

Jorge Amado Colorful, ribald stories set in Bahia such as the classic *Dona Flor and Her Two Husbands*.

Ernesto Che Guevara Breezy travelogue *The Motorcycle Diaries* was written by this Argentine-born revolutionary.

Bruce Chatwin Poignant and beautifully written travel narrative, *In Patagonia*, blends fact and fable.

Music

África Brasil (Jorge Ben Jor) Celebratory album from the 1970s that blends funk, samba and blues.

Amanecer (Bomba Estéreo) A blend of African, indigenous and vibrant dance beats by an inventive Colombian band.

Lunático (Gotan Project) Brilliant fusing of tango with electronic grooves.

Roots of Chicha (various artists) Wild Peruvian cumbias that channel psychedelic, rock and melodic sounds.

Tropicália ou Panis et Circencis A famed Brazilian collaboration between Gilberto Gil, Caetano Veloso, Gal Costa and Tom Zé.

For much more on **getting around**, see p1042

First Time South America

For more information, see Survival Guide (p1033)

Checklist

➡ Ensure your passport is valid for six months past your arrival date.

➡ Apply for visas well in advance.

➡ Organize travel insurance.

➡ Medical check-up and vaccinations.

➡ Stock up on contact lenses and prescription medicines.

➡ Inform banks of travel plans.

➡ Scan key documents (passports, visas, credit cards) and email them to yourself in case of loss.

What to Pack

➡ A week's worth of clothes

➡ Rain gear (jacket, dry pack for electronics)

➡ Hat (for sun and rain)

➡ Good walking shoes

➡ Small flip-flops (for beaches and dodgy showers)

➡ Earplugs

➡ Medicine/first-aid kit

➡ GSM cell phone

➡ Refillable water bottle

➡ Sunscreen

➡ Tissues (for public toilets)

Top Tips for Your Trip

➡ Don't be shy. Talk to locals, who are often happy to share insights into their culture.

➡ Be prepared. Read up on destinations before you arrive; know the exchange rate. Have a map handy when arriving in a new town.

➡ Slow down. Don't be in such a hurry to tick off sites that you miss the beauty in front of you.

➡ Learn some Spanish and Portuguese. Don't expect to rely just on English.

➡ Prepare for crazy driving. Pedestrians have no rights.

➡ Carry valuables in a hidden money belt to prevent theft.

➡ Don't cram the whole continent into a month. Pick a country or two, and get to know it.

➡ Prepare for huge contrasts in weather and terrain.

➡ Get your vaccines in order — especially yellow fever!

➡ Acclimatize! Give yourself ample time to adjust to the Andean heights and heat/humidity of the tropics.

What to Wear

In general, lightweight, loose-fitting clothes will be the most comfortable options. Bring a jacket for cool highland temperatures and over-air-conditioned buses. Pants and long-sleeve shirts are handy insect protection for jungle hikes.

Sleeping

Book well in advance when visiting during big festivals (particularly Carnaval time anywhere in Brazil).

Hostels Dorm rooms provide cheap and social lodging for solo travelers.

Hotels A wide range of options, from boxy cells to flashy boutiques.

Guesthouses Often family-owned, guesthouses run the gamut from bare bones to lavish.

Homestays Live like a local in a family home.

Safety

The dangers of traveling in South America are greatly exaggerated, often by people who've never been here. While there are threats, traveling sensibly will reduce your risk of becoming a victim.

➡ Carry only the minimum cash you need when out for the day.

➡ Dress down and don't flash iPhones, designer sunglasses and other expensive gear.

➡ In urban areas, take a taxi after dark.

➡ Be mindful walking in deserted areas.

➡ Use ATMs inside buildings. Before doing so, be very aware of your surroundings.

➡ Don't take valuables to the beach or leave them lying around your guestroom.

➡ Don't accept food and drink from strangers. Druggings can occur.

Bargaining

Bargaining is common practice at markets and when arranging long-term accommodations.

Tipping

Restaurants In some countries (such as Brazil and Chile), a 10% service charge is typically included.

Tours When booking tours (such as to the Galápagos or the Amazon), it's customary to tip your guide – from a few dollars per day to 15%, depending on service.

Taxis Not expected, though you can round up the bill.

Bars Not expected.

Language

Spanish is the first language of most South American countries, followed by Portuguese, which is spoken in Brazil. Without a basic knowledge of Spanish, travel in South America can be difficult and your interaction with local people will be limited. Consider taking a crash course in *español* during your trip. French is spoken in French Guiana, Dutch and English are spoken in Suriname, and English is spoken in Guyana.

Lonely Planet publishes the handy, pocket-size *Latin American Spanish* and *Brazilian Portuguese* phrasebooks

 Can you recommend private lodgings?
¿Puede recomendar una casa particular?
pwe·de re·ko·men·dar oo·na ka·sa par·tee·koo·lar

Staying with locals will give you a true Cuban experience and an opportunity to sample hearty home-cooked dishes.

 I'd like the fixed-price menu, please.
Quisiera el menú del día, por favor.
kee·sye·ra el me·noo del dee·a por fa·vor

Eateries in Guatemala and Mexico usually offer a fixed-price meal which may include up to four courses and is great value.

 Where can I get a shared taxi/minibus?
¿Dónde se puede tomar un colectivo?
don·de se pwe·de to·mar oon ko·lek·tee·vo

Cheap transport options in Peru and other countries are shared taxis or minibuses – ask locally as there are no obvious stops.

 Where can we go salsa/tango dancing?
¿Dónde podemos ir a bailar salsa/tango?
don·de po·de·mos eer a bai·lar sal·sa/tan·go

In dance-crazy Colombia and Argentina you won't be lacking in dance-hall options, but you may want a local recommendation.

5 **How do you say ... in your language?**
¿Cómo se dice ... en su lengua?
ko·mo se dee·se ... en su len·gwa

Among hundreds of indigenous languages in Latin America are Quechua, Aymara, Mayan languages, Náhuatl and Guaraní.

Etiquette

Greetings In Spanish-speaking countries, greet people with *buenos días* (good morning), *buenas tardes* (good afternoon) or *buenas noches* (good evening). Use *bom dia*, *boa tarde* and *boa noite* in Brazil.

Cheek kissing When meeting people socially, give *besos* (kisses) on the cheek (both cheeks for Brazilians). Men shake hands.

Shorts Dress for the occasion; for example, only tourists and athletes wear shorts in Buenos Aires.

Photographs Ask before photographing people, particularly in indigenous communities – payment may be requested.

If You Like...

Colonial Splendor

South America has a stunning array of architectural wonders, where cobblestone streets lead past magnificent cathedrals, photogenic plazas and brightly painted townhouses – some of which date to the 16th century.

Quito Wandering the buzzing streets of the *centro histórico* (old town) presents dramatic scenery with every turn you take. (p676)

Colonia del Sacramento Uruguay's delightfully picturesque riverfront town is just a short ferry ride from Buenos Aires. (p993)

Ouro Prêto One of Brazil's most alluring colonial towns, hilly Ouro Prêto is packed with 18th-century treasures. (p344)

Cartagena Colombia's comeliest coastal town has a beautifully preserved center scenically set on the Caribbean. (p610)

Arequipa A Peruvian charmer with striking colonial *sillar* architecture and spicy salt-of-the-earth eateries. (p875)

Paramaribo A strange and exotic blend of colonial Dutch buildings and grassy squares in oft-overlooked Suriname. (p967)

Big Cities

South America's cities are home to first-rate museums, top-notch restaurants and rocking nightlife. You can shop at atmospheric markets, cozy up at an art-filled cafe or spend the day exploring charming neighborhoods.

Rio de Janeiro The *Cidade Maravilhosa* (Marvelous City) lives up to its name with lovely beaches, samba-fueled nightlife and jaw-dropping scenery. (p304)

Buenos Aires A place that's hard to leave, with colorful neighborhoods, late-night dining, old-world cafes, sultry tango clubs, and French and Italianate architecture. (p63)

Lima Sure, it's chaotic, but Lima is a great place for seafood feasts and late-night bar-hopping in bohemian Barranco. Its museums also house Peru's best pre-Columbian collections. (p852)

Bogotá The Colombian capital has salsa-fueled nightclubs, a bicycle-loving culture and an intriguing colonial center – plus fascinating nearby sights such as the surreal underground salt cathedral at Zipaquirá. (p574)

Valparaíso A bohemian city and Unesco World Heritage Site that's often considered Chile's cultural capital. (p465)

Ancient Ruins

Pre-Columbian peoples left behind a wide-ranging legacy: the awe-inspiring monuments and artfully crafted works in ceramic, gold and stone comprise but a fraction of the great works in existence before the Europeans arrived.

Machu Picchu The godfather of great ruins, this mountaintop Inca citadel is best enjoyed as the finale of a multiday trek. (p906)

Cuzco The continent's oldest continuously inhabited city, where you can still find flawless Inca-built walls lining cobblestone streets. (p890)

Kuélap Perched atop a limestone mountain, this monumental stone-fortified city is a relic of a fierce cloud-forest-dwelling civilization. (p939)

San Agustín In southwest Colombia, the mysterious San Agustín culture left behind hundreds of statues carved from volcanic rock. (p647)

Rapa Nui Better known as Easter Island, this Polynesian outpost is home to utterly mystifying *moai* statues. (p556)

Nazca Lines Mysterious carvings in the sand spread across hundreds of square kilometers; scenic flights are the best way to see them. (p872)

Top: *Moai* statue, Rapa Nui (Easter Island; p556)

Bottom: Frigate bird, Galápagos Islands (p753)

Beaches

Shimmering beaches wedged between tropical rainforest and deep blue sea: South America has many seaside enticements, including remote island getaways, party-loving surf towns and glittering sands amid big-city allure.

Arraial d'Ajuda Brazil is spoiled for choice when it comes to world-class beaches; this peaceful town in the northeast is gateway to some of Bahia's prettiest coastline. (p386)

Punta del Diablo Forget the over-hyped mayhem of Punta del Este; Uruguay's more tranquil summertime getaway is this coastal beauty just south of the Brazilian border. (p1007)

Parque Nacional Natural Tayrona Fronting the Caribbean Sea, this pristine national park in Colombia has gorgeous beaches and does a fine imitation of paradise lost. (p603)

Baía do Sancho On the island of Fernando de Noronha, this is easily one of Brazil's most gorgeous beaches. (p392)

Outdoor Adventures

Adrenaline junkies can get their fix negotiating snow-capped peaks, rushing rivers and pounding surf. Rafting, rock climbing, mountain biking, hang-gliding, sandboarding and ziplining: there are hundreds of ways to get your heart racing.

Whitewater rafting Heart-thumping rivers – from turquoise to crystalline – draw rafters and kayakers to the Chilean south. Tena in Ecuador is another major rafting spot. (p53)

Mountain biking The World's Most Dangerous Road: the name says it all. This 64km mountain-bike trip outside La Paz takes in perilous descents. Make sure your brakes (and travel insurance!) are top notch. (p204)

Hang-gliding Sail high above the forest-covered hills of Rio to a beachside landing on a fantastic tandem flight. (p308)

Mountain climbing Strap on your crampons and make your way up 5897m Volcán Cotopaxi, one of Ecuador's most popular climbs. (p704)

Paragliding Get airborne in Bucaramanga and Colombia's adventure capital of San Gil. (p598)

Dramatic Scenery

Thundering waterfalls, cone-shaped volcanoes and red-rock canyons – the only things missing are the pterodactyls. When gazing upon these natural wonders, you might feel like you've stepped back a few million years.

Parque Nacional da Chapada Diamantina Head to Brazil's northeast to hike across dramatic plateaus and swim in refreshing waterfalls. (p381)

Iguazú Falls Spread between Argentina and Brazil, these are some of the most spectacular waterfalls on earth. (p110)

Salar de Uyuni The world's largest salt flats are a dazzling remnant of a vast prehistoric lake. (p242)

Parque Nacional Torres del Paine In southern Patagonia, sparkling glaciers, topaz lakes and sheer granite cliff-faces defy the imagination. (p552)

Kaieteur Falls Visit the world's highest single-drop waterfall

in the middle of the Guyanese rainforest. (p802)

Festivals & Events

Whether you prefer the pageantry of *Semana Santa* or the revelry of Carnaval, the continent has you covered. From traditional to surreal, here are a few events worth planning a trip around.

Carnaval Many towns in Brazil throw a wild pre-Lenten bash, but Salvador and Rio are the best places to enjoy a few sleepless nights. Bolivia's Oruro and Paraguay's Encarnación also stage legendary parties. (p27)

Mama Negra This Ecuadorian fest features processions, witches, whole roast pigs, a bit of cross-dressing and plenty of alcohol. (p705)

Tango BA Festival y Mundial Learn some new moves at this massive tango festival in Buenos Aires in August. (p72)

Virgen de la Candelaria In Puno, Peru gives a thunderous street party for its patron saint. (p887)

Fiesta de Moxos One of Bolivia's biggest bashes includes fireworks, dancing, feasts and wild costumes. (p283)

Hiking & Trekking

Against a backdrop of Andean peaks, misty cloud forests and Amazonian jungle, trekking here is world class. Whether you're out for a short day hike or a multiday journey, you'll find limitless options.

Quilotoa Avid walkers shouldn't miss this scenic multiday Ecuadorian journey, overnighting at simple village guesthouses along the way. (p706)

El Chaltén In Argentine Patagonia, El Chaltén offers unparalleled trekking amid glaciers, alpine lakes and craggy mountains. (p173)

Ciudad Perdida Like a scene torn from an *Indiana Jones* film, the trek to Colombia's 'Lost City' is a challenging four-day (return) journey to the overgrown ruins of a large pre-Columbian town. (p606)

Wildlife

South America is home to more plant and animal species than any other place on earth. There are countless settings to watch wildlife.

The Amazon Manaus is still one of the top gateways for a journey into the mother of all rainforests. (p424)

The Pantanal At these wildlife-rich wetlands, you're likely to see even more animal species than in the Amazon. Cuiabá is one of the top spots to plan a trip. (p364)

The Galápagos These volcanic islands are home to creatures so tame, you'll practically be tripping over all the sea lions. (p753)

Cloud forests With more than 400 recorded bird species in the area, Mindo's cloud forests are a mecca for birders. (p696)

Parque Nacional San Rafael Paraguay's verdant strand of Atlantic Forest has refreshing lakes, forest paths and superb bird-watching. (p830)

Parque Nacional Madidi Encompassing mountains and dense rainforests, this Bolivian jewel is one of the world's great biodiversity hotspots. (p281)

North Rupununi Lodges in Guyana make a fine base for exploring the amazingly rich wildlife found here. (p804)

Month by Month

January

It's peak season in Brazil and Argentina. Expect higher prices, bigger crowds and sweltering temperatures as city dwellers head to the coast. This is also the most popular time to travel to Patagonia.

☆ Santiago a Mil

This long-running theater and dance fest features dozens of shows and events around the Chilean capital, staged by international and local companies. The 17-day event begins in early January and is held throughout the city, including in free outdoor venues. (p452)

☆ Festival Nacional del Folklore

Near the city of Córdoba, the town of Cosquín hosts Argentina's National Festival of Folk Music during the last week of January. It's the country's largest and best-known folk festival. (p117)

February

The sizzling summer is still in full swing in the southern half of the continent, with exorbitant prices and sparse accommodations during Brazilian Carnaval. Elsewhere, it's fairly wet in the northern Andes and the Amazon region.

☆ Fiesta de la Virgen de Candelaria

Celebrated across the highlands in Bolivia and Peru, this festival features music, drinking, eating, dancing, processions, water balloons (in Bolivia) and fireworks. The biggest celebrations take place in Copacabana (Bolivia) and Puno (Peru). The big day is February 2.

☆ Carnaval

The famous bacchanalian event happens across South America, though the pre-Lenten revelry is most famous in Brazil. Rio and Salvador throw the liveliest bashes, with street parades, costume parties and round-the-clock merriment.

Carnaval runs from Friday to Tuesday before Ash Wednesday in February or early March.

☆ Carnaval Encarnaceno

Although its northern neighbor hogs all the attention, Paraguay is also a great place to celebrate Carnaval – especially in Encarnación, which throws a riotous fest on every weekend in February. Come for the costumed parades, pounding rhythms and partying through the late hours (www.carnaval.com.py; p823)

☆ Festival de Viña

One of the largest and most important music fests in Latin America, this Chilean blockbuster has been going strong since 1960. Expect to see top stars as well as rising talents on the international scene – Shakira was one of many who came to fame during the event. It kicks off in late February in Viña del Mar (www.festivaldevina.cl).

March

While the weather is still warm in the south, the crowds thin and prices fall a bit at beach destinations. It's still rainy in the northern Andes.

Semana Santa

Throughout Latin America, Holy Week is celebrated with fervor. In Quito (Ecuador), purple-robed penitents parade through the streets on Good Friday, while Ouro Prêto (Brazil) features streets 'painted' with flowers. Ayacucho hosts Peru's most colorful Semana Santa, culminating in an all-night street party before Easter. (p913)

Pujillay

Celebrated in Tarabuco (Bolivia) on the second Sunday in March, hordes of indigenous folks gather to celebrate the 1816 victory of local armies over Spanish troops with ritual dancing, song, music and *chicha* (corn beer) drinking.

Fiesta Nacional de la Vendimia

In Argentina's wine country, Mendoza hosts a renowned five-day harvest festival with parades, folkloric events, fireworks, the blessing of the fruit and a royal coronation – all in honor of Mendoza's intoxicating produce. (p140)

Semana Criolla

After Carnaval, this is Montevideo's liveliest fest, and is essentially a celebration of *gaucho* culture – those tough-looking, leather boot-wearing cowboys from Uruguay's interior who manage to make oversized belt buckles look cool. Come for rodeo events, concerts, open-air barbecues and craft fairs.

☆ Lollapalooza Chile

Chile's rock fest kicks off in Santiago in late March or early April, and features an impressive line-up of homegrown and international groups on par with the North American version of Lollapalooza. Buy tickets early for the best deals. (p453)

◉ Lethem Rodeo

In Lethem (Guyana), Easter weekend means good fun at the rodeo. Some 10,000 visitors come to watch the blend of Wild West meets indigenous traditions. There's roping, saddle- and bareback riding (broncos, bulls) and a beauty pageant (www.visitrupununi.com/event/rupununi-rodeo).

May

Buenos Aires and Rio head into low season, with cooler weather and lower prices; the rain begins to taper off in the Andes, making it a fine time to go trekking.

Diablos Danzantes

In Caracas, Diablos Danzantes (Dancing Devils) features hundreds of diabolically clothed dancers parading through the streets to the sounds of pounding drums. The Venezuelan fest, which blends Spanish and African traditions, takes place on Corpus Christi, 60 days after Easter (May or June).

🏃 Q'oyoriti

A fascinating indigenous pilgrimage to the holy mountain of Ausangate, outside Cuzco, takes place around Corpus Christi (May or June). Though relatively unknown outside Peru, it's well worth checking out. (p895)

June

High season in the Andean nations corresponds with the North American summer (June to August), when the weather is also sunniest and driest. Book major tours (such as hiking the Inca Trail) well in advance.

Inti Raymi

This millennia-old indigenous celebration of the solstice and harvest is celebrated in many Andean towns. In Cuzco it's the event of year, attracting thousands of visitors for street fairs, open-air concerts and historical reenactments. In Ecuador, Otavalo is the place to be.

Bumba Meu Boi

This traditional fest, celebrated across Brazil's Maranhão region in late June, blends African, indigenous and Portuguese traditions. Hundreds of troupes take to the streets in São Luís, dancing, singing and reenacting one of the region's great creation myths. (p406)

☆ Sao Paulo Pride

It's official: São Paulo throws the largest gay-pride parade on the planet, attracting some three million people. There are street fairs, concerts, film screenings and exhibitions in the days leading up to the big parade – which usually happens on Sunday in mid-June. (p335)

🎎 San Juan

The feast of San Juan is all debauchery in Iquitos, Peru, where dancing, feasting and (unfortunately) cockfights go until the wee hours on the eve of the actual holiday of June 24. (p947)

July

July is one of the coldest months in the far south (not a good time to visit Patagonia or Buenos Aires). It is, however, a great time to plan a wildlife-watching trip in the Pantanal.

🎎 Founding of Guayaquil

Street dancing, fireworks and processions are all part of the celebration on the nights leading up to the anniversary of Guayaquil's founding (July 25). Along with the national holiday on July 24 (Simón Bolívar's birthday), Ecuador's largest city closes down and celebrates with abandon.

🎎 Fiesta del Santo Patrono de Moxos

Running from July 22 to the end of the month, this spirited festival transforms Bolivia's sleepy San Ignacio de Moxos into a hard-partying town. Expect processions, outrageous costumes (including locals dressed as Amazon warriors), fireworks and plenty of drinking.

August

It's dry in many parts of the continent, making August a fine time to visit the Amazon, the Pantanal or the Andes. It's chilly to freezing south of the Tropic of Capricorn.

🎎 El Día de La Virgen del Cisne

In Ecuador's southern highlands, thousands of colorfully garbed pilgrims take to the roads each year around August 15 in the extraordinary 70km procession to Loja, carrying the Virgen del Cisne (Virgin of the Swan).

☆ Tango BA Festival y Mundial

World-class tango dancers perform throughout Buenos Aires during this two-week festival. Competition is fierce for the title of 'world's best tango dancer.' You can also hone your own moves at classes and workshops. (p72)

🎎 Feria de las Flores

The Flower Festival brings sweet smells to the Colombian city of Medellín. Highlights include concerts, a gastronomy fair, a horse parade, orchid exhibits and the Desfile de Silleteros, when farmers parade through the streets laden with enormous baskets of flowers. (p625)

☆ Festival de Música del Pacífico Petronio Álvarez

In Cali, one of Colombia's best fests celebrates Afro-Colombian music and culture over five days in mid-August (http://petronio. cali.gov.co), when more than 100 groups light up the city. You'll find infectious rhythms and welcoming, dance-happy crowds.

September

The weather remains dry and sunny (but chilly) in the Andes, though you'll find fewer crowds. September is also a good (less rainy) time to visit the Amazon.

🎎 Fiesta de la Mama Negra

Latacunga (Ecuador) hosts one of the highlands' most famous celebrations, in honor of La Virgen de las Mercedes. La Mama Negra, played by a man dressed as a black woman, pays tribute to the 19th-century liberation of African slaves. (p705)

☆ Bienal de São Paulo

One of the world's most important arts events showcases some 3000 works by more than 100 artists from across the globe. It runs from September to December in even-numbered years, and is mainly based in Parque do Ibirapuera.

October

Heavy rains make for tough traveling in Colombia, while the Andes generally have milder weather. In Bolivia, Brazil, Chile and Argentina, temperatures are mild, making it a pleasant time to visit.

 Cirio de Nazaré

Belém's enormous annual event brings one million to the streets to take part in the procession of one of Brazil's most important icons. Fireworks, hymns and one massive flower-bedecked carriage creaking through the throngs are all part of this wild spiritual gathering. (p412)

Oktoberfest

Celebrating the historical legacy of Brazil's substantial German immigrant population, Oktoberfest features 17 days of folk music, dancing and beer drinking. It's considered the largest German fest in the Americas and goes down in mid-October in Blumenau (www.oktoberfestblumenau.com.br).

November

Rainier days are on the horizon in the Amazon. Generally November nets better prices, good weather and fewer crowds than December in most parts of South America.

Puno Day

The traditional city of Puno in Peru hosts dozens of colorful fiestas throughout the year. One of the best is Puno Day, where costumed dancers, military parades and folk bands celebrate the legendary emergence of the first Inca, Manco Cápac, from Lake Titicaca.

Hmong New Year

For something completely different, head to the small village of Cacao (French Guiana) to celebrate the Hmong New Year with a thriving community of Laotians. Traditional singing and dancing, Laotian cuisine and beautifully embroidered costumes are all part of the experience. Held in November or December.

International Film Festival

Launched in 1950, this cinematic event is one of the most important film festivals in Latin America. Running for nine days in mid-November, the fest screens an international lineup of features, shorts, documentaries and experimental works. (p135)

Buenos Aires Jazz Festival Internacional

BA's big jazz festival (www.buenosairesjazz.gob.ar) showcases the talents of more than 200 musicians to play in 70 different concerts around town. Jazz musicians of all kinds are featured – emerging and established, avant-garde and mainstream, national and international.

Fiesta de la Tradición

San Antonio de Areco celebrates Argentina's *gaucho* culture in this lively mid-November fest, with live music, crafts, regional foods and impressive displays of horsemanship. (p87)

December

December marks the beginning of summer, with beach days (and higher prices) on both the Atlantic and Pacific coasts. It's fairly rainy in the Andes.

Founding of Quito Festival

Quito's biggest bash is a much anticipated event, with parades and street dances throughout the first week of December. Open-air stages all across town fill the Ecuadorian capital with music, while colorful *chivas* (open-sided buses) full of revelers maneuver through the streets.

Carnatal

Brazil's biggest 'off-season Carnaval' is this Salvador-style festival held in Natal in December. It features raucous street parties and thumping *trios elétricos* (amplified bands playing atop mobile-speaker trucks). You can get in on the fun by joining one of the *blocos* (drumming and dancing processions). (p397)

Reveillon

There are many great spots in South America to celebrate New Year's Eve, but Rio is a perennial favorite. Some two million revelers, dressed in white to bring good luck, pack the sands of Copacabana Beach to watch fireworks light up the night sky.

Itineraries

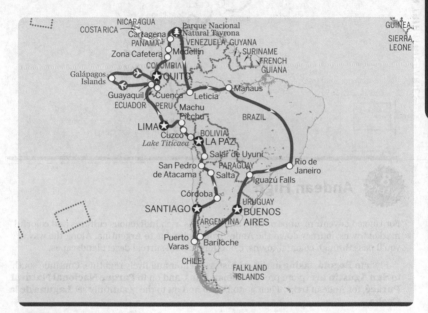

The Big Loop

20 WEEKS

This classic South American journey takes in some of the continent's most famous sites, including Andean peaks, Amazonian rainforest, Machu Picchu, Iguazú Falls and the Galápagos Islands.

Start off in **Buenos Aires**. Spend several days exploring the mesmerizing Argentine capital. Go west to **Bariloche** for spectacular scenery then head to Chile's verdant Lake District at **Puerto Varas**. Continue north to **Santiago**, then cross back into Argentina to **Córdoba** and gorgeous **Salta** before re-entering Chile at the desert oasis of **San Pedro de Atacama**. Head into Bolivia to experience the surreal **Salar de Uyuni**. Continue to **La Paz** and on to Peru via **Lake Titicaca**. Linger at ancient **Cuzco** and **Machu Picchu** before going to **Lima** and on to Ecuador.

From **Guayaquil**, fly to the **Galápagos Islands**. Back on the mainland, visit colonial **Cuenca** and historic **Quito**. Pass into Colombia to the lush **Zona Cafetera** and bustling **Medellín**, then go to **Cartagena** for Caribbean allure. See beautiful **Parque Nacional Natural Tayrona**, then head towards **Leticia** and cross into Brazil. Head to **Manaus** for a jungle trip. Afterwards fly down to **Rio de Janeiro** for beaches and nightlife. Visit thundering **Iguazú Falls** and return to Buenos Aires.

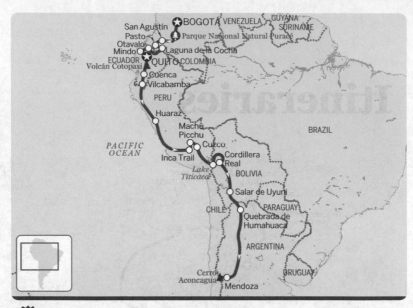

8 WEEKS Andean High

For rugged adventure, unparalleled alpine vistas, rich indigenous cultures and colorful market towns, journey down the Andes from Colombia to Argentina. Along the way, you'll pass through colonial towns, cloud forests and surreal desert landscapes.

Fly into **Bogotá**, taking in the old historic center and lively nightlife. Continue south to **San Agustín** to explore pre-Columbian ruins, and on to **Parque Nacional Natural Puracé**, for Andean treks. Then go to **Pasto** and on to the beautifully set **Laguna de la Cocha**.

Cross into Ecuador and visit **Otavalo** for markets and day trips to alpine lakes. Head west to **Mindo** for misty cloud-forest adventures. Continue south through **Quito** and on to **Volcán Cotopaxi** for hikes and majestic scenery.

Visit colonial **Cuenca**, relax in laid-back **Vilcabamba**, then continue into Peru and down to **Huaraz** for trekking in the Cordillera Blanca.

Spend a few days in **Cuzco**, then hike the **Inca Trail** to **Machu Picchu**. Head across shimmering **Lake Titicaca** into Bolivia for more hiking in the **Cordillera Real**. Continue south to the **Salar de Uyuni**, before crossing to Argentina by way of the spectacular **Quebrada de Humahuaca**. In Argentina end the trip at enchanting **Mendoza**, near massive **Cerro Aconcagua**, the western hemisphere's highest peak.

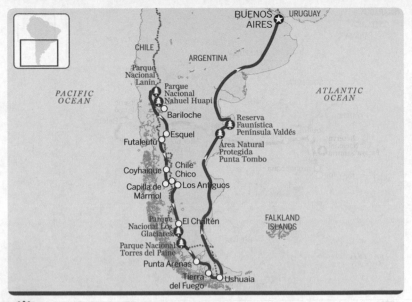

6 WEEKS Patagonian Pilgrimage

Mysterious, windswept, glacier-riddled Patagonia is one of South America's most magical destinations. Patagonia – and the archipelago of Tierra del Fuego – is best visited November through March, and you can see more for less money if you camp.

Start in the outdoors-loving town of **Bariloche**. Take in the stunning **Parque Nacional Nahuel Huapi** and **Parque Nacional Lanín**. Head south to **Esquel**, for a taste of the Old Patagonian Express.

Travel west into Chile to the Andean hamlet of **Futaleufú** for outstanding rafting. Take the scenic Carretera Austral to **Coyhaique** and visit the caves of **Capilla de Mármol**. Head to windswept **Chile Chico** on Lago General Carrera, then cross into Argentina to **Los Antiguos**.

Bounce down to **El Chaltén** in spectacular **Parque Nacional Los Glaciares**, home of the wondrous Glaciar Perito Moreno, near El Calafate.

Cross back into Chile at Puerto Natales to hike beneath the granite spires of **Parque Nacional Torres del Paine**. Head to **Punta Arenas**, then south into Argentina's **Tierra del Fuego** and bottom out at edge-of-the-earth **Ushuaia**.

Travel north along the Atlantic, stopping for penguins in **Área Natural Protegida Punta Tombo** and whales in **Reserva Faunística Península Valdés**. End the trip in **Buenos Aires**.

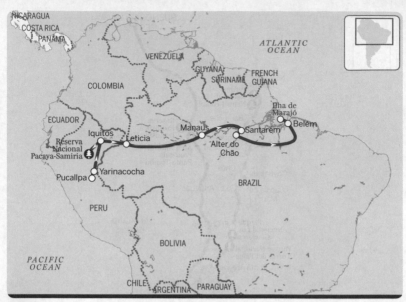

6 WEEKS Sailing the Mighty Amazon

This tough but rewarding journey travels the length of the fabled Amazon, incorporating wildlife-watching, historic cities and beautiful river beaches.

Start in **Pucallpa**, Peru (a flight or bus ride from Lima). Before hitting the river, spend the night in nearby **Yarinacocha**, a lovely oxbow lake ringed by tribal villages. From Pucallpa, begin the classic slow riverboat journey north along the Río Ucayali to **Iquitos**. This northern jungle capital has a buoyant cultural scene and a bustling port, where you can catch a more comfortable cruise into Peru's largest protected space, **Reserva Nacional Pacaya-Samiria**. From Iquitos, get a boat to the tri-border region of Peru, Colombia and Brazil, and take a break in Colombia's **Leticia**.

From Leticia, it's three more arduous days to the bustling city of **Manaus**, which is famed for its 19th-century opera house and buzzing markets. This is also a great base for jungle excursions.

Chug east to **Santarém**, where you can visit the white-sand beaches of **Alter do Chão**. Another 3½ days further, and you'll reach culturally rich **Belém**, a good spot for sampling traditional Amazonian cuisine.

From here, cross over to **Ilha de Marajó**, a massive river island dotted with friendly towns, wandering buffaloes and pleasant beaches.

Top: Iquitos (p947), Peru

Bottom: Traditional cuisine, Belém (p413), Peru

DADO PHOTOS/SHUTTERSTOCK ©

PLAN YOUR TRIP ITINERARIES

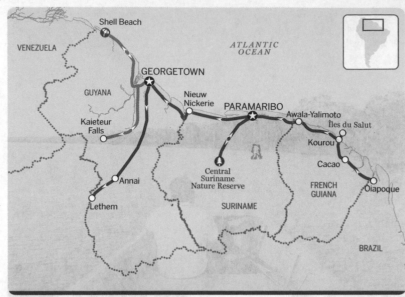

4 WEEKS: Exploring the Guianas

They're expensive, they're hard to reach, they're largely unpopulated, and they can be very, very captivating. And they're *definitely* off the beaten path. Where you start depends on where you're coming from: Guyana via New York, Cayenne via Paris or Paramaribo via Amsterdam. For the sake of argument, let's say you're traveling overland from Brazil.

From **Oiapoque** in Brazil, cross the border via the new bridge spanning the Rio Oiapoque into French Guiana. You're now officially off the beaten track. Make your way by bus across the verdant, forgotten landscape (complete with burned-out cars along the roadside) to **Cacao**. From here, embark upon the two-day hike along **Sentier Molokoï** for some wildlife-spotting fun. Then make your way up to **Kourou**, where you can witness rockets blast off from South America's only satellite launcher. Take a ferry (or a more comfy catamaran) across shark-infested waters to the **Îles du Salut**, a former island prison where you can sling up a hammock in the old prison dormitories! Back on the mainland, head up the coast and watch the turtles nesting (April to July only) at **Awala-Yalimopo** before crossing into Suriname. Hang out for a few days in weirdly wonderful **Paramaribo**, and set up a tour into the majestic **Central Suriname Nature Reserve**. From Paramaribo, continue west to **Nieuw Nickerie**, where you cross into Guyana. Head up to **Georgetown**, and make a detour by boat up to isolated **Shell Beach** or to see the spectacular **Kaieteur Falls**. Back in Georgetown, get a bus south across the majestic Rupununi Savannas, stopping in **Annai** and **Lethem** to savor the vast isolation.

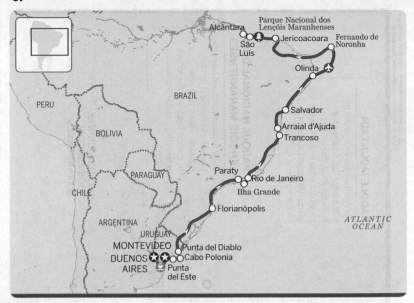

The Atlantic Coast

Colonial towns, Afro-Brazilian culture, gorgeous beaches and buzzing nightlife set the stage for an epic 7400km ramble up the Atlantic coast. Surfing, snorkeling, forest treks and urban exploring are all essential experiences along the way.

Start off in Argentina, spending a few days taking in the charms of **Buenos Aires** before ferrying over to historic **Montevideo**. Follow Uruguay's coastline north through glitzy **Punta del Este**, dune-fringed **Cabo Polonio** and the laid-back beach town of **Punta del Diablo**.

Make your way to **Florianópolis**, gateway to secluded beaches and stunning scenery, then head up to the scenic colonial town of **Paraty**, and rainforest-covered **Ilha Grande**. Continue to **Rio de Janeiro** for pretty beaches, lush scenery and samba-fueled nightlife.

Fly to Porto Seguro and continue to **Trancoso** and **Arraial d'Ajuda** – both enticing, laid-back towns near cliff-backed beaches. Spend a few days in **Salvador**, Brazil's mesmerizing Afro-Brazilian gem. Further up the coast, visit pretty **Olinda**, then catch a flight from Recife to the spectacular **Fernando de Noronha**.

Back on the mainland, travel north, stopping at the backpackers' paradise of **Jericoacoara** and the surreal dunes of **Parque Nacional dos Lençóis Maranhenses**. The final stops are reggae-charged **São Luís** and colonial **Alcântara**.

South America: Off the Beaten Track

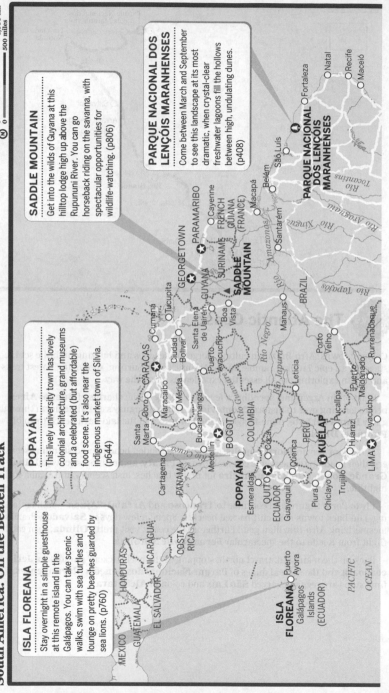

ISLA FLOREANA

Stay overnight in a simple guesthouse at this remote island in the Galápagos. You can take scenic walks, swim with sea turtles and lounge on pretty beaches guarded by sea lions. (p760)

POPAYÁN

This lively university town has lovely colonial architecture, grand museums and a celebrated (but affordable) food scene. It's also near the indigenous market town of Silvia. (p644)

SADDLE MOUNTAIN

Get into the wilds of Guyana at this hilltop lodge high up above the Rupununi River. You can go horseback riding on the savanna, with spectacular opportunities for wildlife-watching. (p806)

PARQUE NACIONAL DOS LENÇÓIS MARANHENSES

Come between March and September to see this landscape at its most dramatic, when crystal-clear freshwater lagoons fill the hollows between high, undulating dunes. (p408)

ATLANTIC OCEAN

Salvador
Ilhéus
Porto Seguro

BRASÍLIA

Belo Horizonte

Rio de Janeiro

São Paulo

Goiânia

Curitiba

Florianópolis

Rio Paraná

Campo Grande

Cuiabá

Trinidad

Santa Cruz

SUCRE

PARAGUAY • THE CHACO

Ciudad del Este

Puerto Iguazú

Caxias do Sul

Porto Alegre

Pelotas

Punta del Diablo

MONTEVIDEO

URUGUAY

PARQUE NACIONAL DE APARADOS DA SERRA

In the south of Brazil, this stunning national park is home to a jagged canyon with waterfalls, scenic lookouts and memorable hiking trails. (p353)

San Salvador de Jujuy

ASUNCIÓN

Encarnación

Santa Fe

Rosario

Córdoba

ARGENTINA

BUENOS AIRES

Mar del Plata

Tucumán

Tarija

Oruro

LA PAZ

Moquegua

Iquique

Antofagasta

La Serena

SANTIAGO

Santa Cruz

Mendoza

Concepción

Temuco

Valdivia

Puerto Montt

CHILE

Bariloche

El Bolsón

Coyhaique

Puerto Madryn

FALKLAND ISLANDS

Stanley

Río Gallegos

Punta Arenas

El Calafate

Puerto Natales

Ushuaia

PARQUE NACIONAL PATAGONIA

Pisco
Ica

KUÉLAP

Escape the Machu Picchu crowds at this stunning pre-Columbian citadel in the north of Peru. You can make the most of the experience by overnighting at one of the basic guesthouses here. (p939)

THE CHACO

Paraguay's wild, dusty west teems with animal life. You can camp out under star-filled skies and spend your days spying macaws, otters, tapirs and countless other creatures. (p835)

PARQUE NACIONAL PATAGONIA

This gem of restored grasslands, rushing rivers and snowbound peaks is home to guanacos, flamingos, foxes and pumas, and has great infrastructure for camping and hiking. (p543)

Brazilian Amazon (p424

Plan Your Trip
Big Adventures, Small Budgets

In South America there are plenty of memorable experiences to be had even if you're traveling on a tiny budget. Frolicking on beaches, wildlife-watching and exploring captivating towns are some of the ways to enjoy the continent on a shoestring. While deep pockets aren't necessary, a bit of planning can help make the most of the grand journey.

Planning & Costs

Planning Timeline

Twelve months before Calculate a trip budget and start saving.

Six months Pick which countries to visit, when and for how long.

Eight weeks Book flights. Renew your passport if it's expired or about to soon.

Six to four weeks Get vaccinations and travel insurance.

Four weeks Make visa and passport arrangements. Book specialty tours/accommodation (Amazon jungle lodges, Galápagos cruises).

Two weeks Reserve high-season accommodation for popular destinations.

One week Book accommodation for international arrival city; start packing.

Average Costs

Bottle of beer US$2–4

Fixed-price market lunch special US$5–8

Dorm bed US$10–20

Guesthouse bedroom for two from US$25

Long-distance bus ticket around US$1–2 per hour of travel

One-hour domestic flight from US$100

Cable-car ride up Pão de Açúcar US$28

Whitewater rafting on the Upper Napo River US$65–90

When to Go

Before penciling in dates for your trip, take into consideration the regions you want to visit, and what you want to see when you're there. Rainy months in the Amazon and Pantanal should be avoided when planning a wildlife-watching expedition for instance. And once you get below the tropic line, you'll see much more dramatic seasonal fluctuations, with a very cold winter in Chile and Argentina (and even southern Brazil) and very hot summers.

Festivals & Holidays

Even if you're not planning a trip around a major festival, these events can affect your travel plans, so keep them in mind when designing your itinerary. The big one is Carnaval, which happens on the four days preceding Ash Wednesday. The biggest celebrations happen in Brazil, and you should pick where you want to be for a few days when it all goes down. Flights are expensive then, bus services crowded (with fewer runs), and banks and many other businesses will close. You'll also pay a premium for accommodations, with some places requiring minimum stays (four days is common). Brazil aside, Carnaval is celebrated in pretty much every other part of South America.

Another big event in the South American calendar is Semana Santa (Holy Week – the week leading up to Easter Sunday), when many people go on holiday. Students also have a two-week break in July, and many families travel at this time.

Beaches

It can be a challenge figuring out the perfect time to plan a beach getaway: getting warm weather (but not stiflingly hot) while still avoiding the worst of the crowds. Try to visit during shoulder seasons, which bookend the hot, busy summer season. November and March (after Carnaval) can be great times to enjoy the beach with fewer crowds and lower prices.

In Brazil, the beaches in the far south (in the states of Santa Catarina and Rio Grande do Sul) have chilly weather, not conducive to swimming. Elsewhere, you'll find beach weather throughout the year. Rio has a handful of cooler, wintery days, but is mostly sunny and warm even in July (winter). The northeast has no winter (it's too hot!).

Jungle Trips

If you're heading into the Amazon, be mindful of the wet and dry seasons. Although it rains year-round (it's not called a 'rainforest' for nothing), the heaviest, longest downfalls happen from January to May. The dry season (and best time to visit) is from July to October. The Pantanal, which also has spectacular wildlife-watching opportunities, has nearly identical seasons, with the winter dry season from July to

October and the heaviest rains from January to March. The Orinoco Basin of Venezuela has different wet and dry periods. The drier months from January to May are best for seeing wildlife.

Mountain Treks

In the Andes, the wettest months are from November to March. February can be the worst (and the Inca Trail is closed). May through August are considered the best months for hikes in the Andes, with June and July being particularly pleasant – that said, they're also the busiest months, so consider coming in April, May, September or October.

The Galápagos

The islands have two distinct seasons, though the tourism high season is generally December to April, and July and August.

The warm and wet season runs from January to May, and is characterized by sunny days with strong but short periods of rain. The cool and dry season runs June to December. It's often known as the *garúa* for the misty precipitation that affects the highlands. While the air temperature is pleasant (averaging 22°C), the water is colder.

Surfing

In Brazil you can surf all year round, though you'll have to chase the waves. In the north, you'll catch northern swells and the best conditions from November to March, particularly in Fernando de Noronha. In the south, April to November brings the best waves, when offshore winds and South Atlantic storms drive the swell to fine conditions all along the coast. In Argentina, the best waves are from April to June. Uruguay gets decent waves year-round, with waves the biggest in winter from June to August (although you'll need a good wetsuit then!).

On the Pacific side, things are a little different. All along Chile's coast you'll find excellent breaks, which are consistent all year long. Peru, meanwhile, gets its best waves in the winter months, with sizable swells from March through November.

Skiing

To take advantage of the great powdery runs of the southern Andes, plan to visit Chile and Argentina during the ski season

The Quilotoa Loop (p706), Ecuador

running from mid-June to mid-October. If you have to pick just one month, come in August, when the skiing is at its finest.

Budget Guide

Western currencies enjoy a favorable exchange rate in South America, giving you greater purchasing power. The cost of living is noticeably cheaper in most parts of the continent, and shoestringers can skimp their way to a budget of about US$40 a day. In the Andean countries, you might be able to get by on as little as US$30 a day, but in pricier Chile and French Guiana, you may struggle to keep the daily budget below US$50. This covers the basics: food, shelter, local transportation and a few beers. This budget will vary not only by country but even regionally within a country (eg southeast Brazil vs cheaper northeast Brazil), the popularity of the destination and the time of year (high versus low season).

In addition to this base rate, factor in the costs of long-distance travel – by bus, boat or air. Add any special activities, such

Córdoba (p111), Argentina

as diving, mountain biking, jungle trekking or a sightseeing tour. Then allow for unexpected expenses, such as increased costs for transportation or accommodations due to holidays or having to pay for a pricier room if the budget accommodations are booked up.

Accommodation costs occupy the largest portion of your budget. Generally, the continent has ample simple lodging options that charge low prices. The more creature comforts (air-con, hot water, en suite) you can forsake, the more money you'll save. Bus and river transportation within each country is generally affordable. Costs rise with air travel and wherever road conditions are rough, or require unique forms of transportation (dune buggies in parts of northeast Brazil, for instance).

Budget Tips

There are many ways to rack up some great memories in South America without putting a big ding in the budget. Travel is cheapest in Bolivia, Ecuador and Colombia. This country-by-country list gives a few places for you to start:

Argentina With its fascinating blend of old and new, Córdoba makes for some worthwhile exploring. Grand architecture, free churches and galleries, affordable lodging options and cheap market dining all add to the appeal.

Bolivia There are many great DIY adventures to be had in this enchanting country. For a fun, cheap experience in La Paz, the Botanical Garden is an oasis of quiet, while the *teleférico* (aerial cable car) provides fabulous views. People-watching in Plaza Murillo or Plaza Avaroa is of course free. You can also talk to a shoe-shine kid and arrange a cheap tour around the community.

Brazil Rio de Janeiro doesn't have to be an expensive destination. There are hostels aplenty (from US$15 per night), cheap *caipirinhas* served right on the beach, and plenty of free amusements (live music at sidewalk cafes, free exhibitions at Centro Cultural Banco do Brasil and great people-watching at the outdoor street party in Lapa on weekends).

Chile It's easy to fall for the bohemian charms of Valparaíso. There are fascinating cobblestone neighborhoods to explore, with great bay views lurking around every corner. This student-loving town also has great eating and drinking spots that are quite budget-friendly.

Valparaíso (p465), Chile

Colombia It's hard to beat the beauty of the Caribbean coast, especially around Parque Nacional Natural Tayrona. You can sleep in a hammock near Arrecifes and spend the day scouting gorgeous coves and sparkling beaches. Colombia has a massive cycling culture, with great road-biking as well as a growing mountain-biking scene – particularly near San Gil.

Ecuador In Baños, you can take a scenic DIY bike ride from highland to jungle, stopping at waterfalls along the way. In the evening, recover with a soak in the hot springs followed by dinner and microbrews at one of the town's enticing eateries.

French Guiana In Cayenne you'll need to eat very cheaply to keep to a budget, as hotel costs are high. Don't miss the buzzing central market with its mishmash of African, indigenous and European elements. Vietnamese vendors serve up the best *pho* on the continent.

Guyana Base yourself in the Africa-like savanna of North Rupununi. You can stay in a rustic hut on a jungle island and visit indigenous villages, and go forest trekking, fishing and caiman-spotting.

Paraguay A city on the make, Encarnación has a lovely waterfront promenade, an enticing river beach, and cheap and tasty *lomito Arabe* – a kind of Paraguayan-style kebab.

Peru If you've been traveling hard for a few weeks, Cuzco is a great place for some R&R. Walking the ancient streets past stunning Inca architecture and taking in its grand plazas and picturesque views won't cost a penny. It's also an excellent town for meeting other travelers. Well-prepared adventure seekers can take on the three- to four-day Santa Cruz trek in the Cordillera Blanca; this can be done without guides or permits.

Suriname Take in Paramaribo's wooden Dutch colonial architecture then feast on delicacies from the East (thanks to Suriname's immigrants): try Javanese rice dishes, Chinese dumplings and Indian roti – plus hearty, rich Creole cooking.

Uruguay One of the prettiest beach towns on the Atlantic Coast, the Punta del Diablo has an easygoing vibe and laid-back guesthouses, beachfront bars and fireside parties on the sands.

Sticking to a Budget

➡ Slow down: stick around and enjoy a place rather than rushing off to the next destination. The further and faster you go, the more you'll have to pay.

➡ Eat like a local at street stalls or markets.

➡ Opt for dorm rooms or share a room with a buddy.

➡ Stay in fan (non-air-con) rooms with shared bathroom.

➡ Travel overland instead of flying.

➡ Book flights online (and bus tickets where possible) rather than paying a travel agent's commission.

➡ Snorkel instead of dive.

➡ Stick to small towns instead of big cities.

➡ Be discriminating about which sites and national parks to visit.

➡ Factor in more free days: on the beach and exploring neighborhoods.

➡ Avoid package deals (transportation, lodging, touring).

➡ Know how much local transportation should cost and bargain accordingly.

➡ Avoid surprises by negotiating taxi fares before getting inside.

➡ Don't forget to factor in the costs of visas.

➡ Do souvenir shopping at the end of your trip with surplus funds.

➡ Track all of your daily expenses so you know your average costs.

Top: Baños (p707), Ecuador

Bottom: Encarnación (p825), Paraguay

MATYAS REHAK/SHUTTERSTOCK ©

Accommodation Tips

Lodging will be one of your biggest expenses. Here are some tips for keeping sleeping costs down:

➡ If the price is too high, ask if the hotel or guesthouse has anything cheaper.

➡ Unless it is the low season, most rates are non-negotiable – though it never hurts to ask for a discounted price.

➡ Once you've paid for a room, there is little chance of a refund, regardless of the size of the cockroach that scurried across the floor.

➡ Pay for the first day rather than for multiple days all at once. This gives you the option of changing hotels if the conditions are unsuitable.

➡ However, if you do decide you are going to stay for a few days, ask for a discount. Some hotels will give better rates if you're staying more than a couple of nights.

➡ Advance reservations (especially with advance deposits) are generally not necessary.

➡ If you do make a booking, don't rely on an agent, who will charge a commission.

Packing

Take as little as possible because you're going to have to carry it everywhere. Pack your bag once and then repack it with a third less stuff. Repeat until your pack is small enough to fit into the aircraft's overhead locker. The smaller your pack the easier it will be to climb on and off public transportation (which doesn't always come to a complete stop), the easier it will be to walk if taxi drivers are asking for too much money, and you'll look like less of a target for touts and hustlers.

Going with Gadgets

Many travelers hit the road with multiple gadgets – phones, tablets, laptops, cameras – but the risk of theft or damage is high. South America poses a mix of hot and icy temperatures, bags get dropped or tossed, thieves and pickpockets want what you have, and you or your stuff could easily get caught in a rainstorm long enough for a short-circuit.

However, it is wise to travel with at least some form of wi-fi–enabled device so you can communicate with people back home. Don't rely on internet cafes, which have largely disappeared from South American towns and cities.

Here are some tips for traveling smart with technology:

➡ Limit yourself to one or two versatile devices: a tablet or iPad that can read books and check emails or a smartphone that can do it all.

➡ Store your electronics in dry packs and separate the batteries in case of rain.

➡ Get a travel-insurance policy that covers theft or damage to your equipment.

➡ Sign up for WhatsApp so you can communicate with locals and travelers you meet on the road.

Altiplano (Andean high plain; p564)

Plan Your Trip
Activities

There's a whole range of adventures awaiting in South America. You can go hiking amid the soaring peaks of the Andes, go rafting along rushing jungle-lined rivers and overnight in a rainforest lodge with the sounds of the Amazon all around you. And you'll find many more astounding options in every country on the continent.

Best Outdoors

Exploring the Atacama, Chile
Scale massive dunes, admire petroglyphs and question the shimmering visions of oases.

Climbing a volcano, Ecuador
Volcán Cotopaxi (5897m) provides a fantastic view for those fit enough to make the summit.

Hiking Cañón del Colca, Peru
Andean condors glide over this rugged canyon in Peru, the second deepest in the world.

Wildlife-watching in the Amazon
Seeing monkeys, macaws, capybaras, caimans, toucans and dozens of other species while based in a jungle lodge (such as Brazil's Mamirauá Reserve).

Trekking to the Lost City, Colombia
This fabulous multiday journey through the jungle leads to the remarkably preserved ruins of the lost city of Tayrona.

Mountain biking the World's Most Dangerous Road, Bolivia
The name says it all in this dramatic Andean descent. Check your brakes before departing!

Whitewater rafting, Chile
Rushing down thundering rapids in Patagonia's Futaleufú River.

Hiking

The opportunities for hiking are practically limitless. Stunning scenery is a guarantee wherever you go, with snow-covered peaks, cloud forests and verdant lowland jungle setting the stage for hiking and wildlife-watching.

The Andean countries are famous for their old Inca roads, which are ready-made for scenic excursions. The overtrodden, four-day tramp along the Inca Trail to Machu Picchu is, of course, the classic, but alternative routes are more highly recommended because they are cheaper, less traveled, more scenic and less destructive. Other possibilities around Cuzco include the spectacular six-day trek around the venerated Ausangate (6372m), which will take you over 5000m passes, through huge herds of alpacas and past tiny hamlets unchanged in centuries.

There are other treks along Inca trails as well, including Ecuador's lesser-known Inca trail to Ingapirca, and numerous trails along ancient Inca routes through Bolivia's Cordilleras to the Yungas. Ecuador also offers memorable hikes amid its volcanic peaks.

There are lots of great places to hike in Brazil, both in the national and state parks and along the coastline. In Bahia, the Parque Nacional da Chapada Diamantina has spectacular day hikes and multiday treks; Lençóis is a good base. Other highlights are the parks around Cambara do Sul, and the Chapada Guimarães and Chapada Veadeiros.

Colombia has some outstanding trekking opportunities. The casual hiker looking for good one-day walks also has many options to choose from – most of which, such as Laguna Verde and Valle de Cocora, can be done independently without a guide. You can also undertake some great day hikes in Parque Nacional El Cocuy.

The national parks of southern South America, including Chile's Torres del Paine, those within the Argentine Lake District, and even Argentina's storm-pounded but spectacular Fitz Roy range, are superb and blessed with excellent trail infrastructure and accessibility. And for getting well off the beaten path, northern Patagonia in Chile has some excellent treks.

Lesser-known mountain ranges, such as Colombia's Sierra Nevada de Santa Marta (for the Ciudad Perdida) have great potential.

Top Hiking Destinations

Peru The main trekking centers are Cuzco and Arequipa in the southern Andes, and Huaraz in the north. Hikers will find many easily accessible trails around Peru's archaeological ruins, which are also the final destinations for more challenging trekking routes. From Arequipa, you can get down in some of the world's deepest canyons – the world-famous Cañón del Colca and the Cañón del Cotahuasi. Outside Huaraz, the Cordillera Blanca can't be beaten for vistas of rocky, snowcapped mountaintops, while the remote and rugged Cordillera Huayhuash is similarly stunning. The classic and favorite trekking route is the four-day journey from Llanganuco to Santa Cruz, where hardy mountaineers climb the 4760m Punta Union pass, surrounded by ice-clad peaks.

Argentina The Lake District offers outstanding day and multiday hikes in several national parks, including Nahuel Huapi and Lanín. For Patagonia, El Bolsón is an excellent base for hiking both in the forests outside of town and in nearby Parque Nacional Lago Puelo. Parque Nacional Los Glaciares offers wonderful hiking in and around the Fitz Roy Range; base yourself in El Chaltén and wait out the storms.

Chile Head to Parque Nacional Torres del Paine in Patagonia for epic hiking. For awe-inspiring isolation, Tierra del Fuego's Dientes de Navarino hiking circuit is stunning but harder to access. Other parts of Chile also have spectacular hikes. You can set off from Santiago on a trek through some of the highest mountains in the world outside Asia. Middle Chile is full of amazing, off-the-beaten-path trekking circuits, as is the Lakes and Volcanoes district, where you can hike up volcanoes and through dense Valdivian forests.

Colombia On the Caribbean coast, the long trek to the Ciudad Perdida (Lost City) involves a sweaty, multiday hike through the jungle and across waist-high rivers. In Parque Nacional Natural (PNN) El Cocuy, you'll find a dozen 5000m-high peaks and phenomenal high-altitude landscapes. PNN Tayrona offers accessible short hikes through tropical dry forest with the opportunity to eat, drink and swim along the way.

Ecuador Near the dramatic topaz crater lake of Quilotoa there are some excellent hikes, including village-to-village trips and a few shortcuts through high-altitude canyons. One excellent DIY route goes from Quilotoa to Isinliví, overnighting in Chugchilán along the way.

Tucan, Amazon

at a jungle lodge in the Amazon. Odds are higher that you'll see even more species in the Pantanal, an extensive wetlands area that can also be accessed from Bolivia or Paraguay.

Speaking of Bolivia, Parque Nacional Madidi harbors over 1000 bird species as well as wildlife endemic to the majority of Bolivia's ecosystems, from tropical rainforest and savanna to cloud forest and alpine tundra. Agencies, often run by scientists or environmentalists, run nature trips out of

Wildlife-Watching

The number of creatures great and small reaches epic proportions in the land of cloud forests, Andean mountains and Amazon rainforest. Whether you're an avid bird-watcher or just want to see monkeys in the wild, South America is hard to top. Its biodiversity is staggering.

Brazil has superb places for seeing wildlife. You can look for toucans, sloths, river dolphins and various monkey species

HIKING PREPARATION

Many trails in South America are poorly marked or not marked at all. Trekkers should always inquire ahead, as navigation may be a major component of hiking and many travelers come unprepared. When it comes to packing, quality mountain gear is a must. Even in summer the Andes can have extreme temperatures – summer sleeping bags and nonwaterproof gear will not work!

FEDOR SELIVANOV/SHUTTERSTOCK ©

Rio de Janeiro (p304), Brazil

Santa Cruz, Cochabamba and Samaipata and, to a lesser extent, La Paz.

Peru boasts a spectacular variety of plant and animal life. In the expansive Parque Nacional Manu, jaguars, tapirs and monkeys inhabit one of the continent's wildest rainforest reserves. On the Islas Ballestas, colonies of honking sea lions and penguins claim rocky Pacific outcrops off Peru's south coast.

Clocking in at over 1900 bird species, Colombia is the world's number-one country in bird diversity and easily holds its own against Peru and Brazil in endemic species. The Andean mountains are full of hummingbirds (more than 160 species); the Amazonian jungle is full of toucans, parrots and macaws; and Parque Nacional Natural (PNN) Puracé, near Popayán, is home to condors. The single best bird-watching spot in the country is Montezuma Peak, located inside Parque Nacional Natural (PNN) Tatamá in the Cordillera Occidental.

Despite its small size, Ecuador has amazingly diverse wildlife. Bird-watchers should head to the cloud forests around Mindo. The lower Río Napo region of the Amazon has even more biological diversity.

And of course, the Galápagos are simply extraordinary in every way.

Mountain Biking

From a leisurely ride around enchanting lowland scenery to bombing down smoldering volcanoes, South America has some exciting destinations for mountain bikers. The Andes are blessed with some of the most dramatic mountain-biking terrain in the world, and offer relatively easy access to mountain ranges, magnificent lakes, precolonial ruins and trails, and myriad eco-zones connected by an extensive network of footpaths and jeep roads. Mountain bikes are widely available for hire, though quality varies considerably. Make a thorough inspection of key components (brakes, tires, gears) before committing. For longer multiday trips, it's better to bring your own bike.

Peru There is no shortage of incredible terrain. Single-track trails ranging from easy to expert await mountain bikers outside Huaraz, Arequipa and even Lima. If you're experienced, there are incredible mountain-biking possibilities around the Sacred Valley and downhill trips to the Amazon jungle, all accessible from Cuzco. Easier cycling routes include the wine country around Lunahuaná and in the Cañón del Colca, starting from Chivay.

Colombia Mountain biking is most popular in San Gil and Villa de Leyva, where several adventure companies and bike-rental shops can facilitate your adrenaline fix.

Bolivia One of the world's longest downhill rides will take you from Parque Nacional Sajama down to the Chilean coast at Arica. More famous is the thrilling 3600m trip down the World's Most Dangerous Road from La Cumbre to Coroico. Another popular route near La Paz is the lush Zongo Valley ride, which can be started from Chacaltaya (5395m).

Chile A favorite mountain-biking destination in the north is San Pedro de Atacama. Fabulous trips in the Lakes District access pristine areas with limited public transportation. The bike lane around Lago Llanquihue is very popular, as is the Ojos de Caburgua loop near Pucón. In the south, the Carretera Austral remains one of the most popular biking destinations in South America. From December to March the road is packed with cyclists.

Argentina At outdoor hot spots you can rent a mountain bike for a day of independent pedaling or for guided rides. Good bases include San Martín de los Andes, Villa la Angostura, Bariloche and El Bolsón in the Lake District; Esquel in Patagonia; Mendoza and Uspallata in Mendoza province; Barreal in San Juan province; Tilcara in the Andean Northwest and Tandil in La Pampa province.

Ecuador It's hard to beat the adrenaline-charged downhills on the flanks of Cotopaxi and Chimborazo. From Baños, you can travel 'La Ruta de las Cascadas' (Highway of the Waterfalls), a 61km (mostly) downhill ride to Puyo, with some refreshing dips in waterfalls along the way.

Mountaineering

On a continent with one of the world's greatest mountain ranges, climbing opportunities are almost unlimited. Ecuador's volcanoes, the high peaks of Peru's Cordillera Blanca and Cordillera Huayhuash, Bolivia's Cordillera Real and Argentina's Aconcagua (6960m; the Western Hemisphere's highest peak) all offer outstanding mountaineering opportunities. Despite its relatively low elevation, Argentina's Fitz Roy Range – home to Cerro Torre, one of the world's most challenging peaks – chalks in as a major climbing destination, while the mountains of Parque Nacional Nahuel Huapi offer fun for all levels.

The Andes are a mountaineer's dream, especially in the San Juan and Mendoza provinces, where some of the highest peaks in the Western Hemisphere are found. While the most famous climb is Aconcagua, there are plenty of others that are more interesting and far more technical. Near Barreal, the Cordón de la Ramada boasts five peaks over 6000m, including the mammoth Cerro Mercedario, which tops out at 6770m. The region is less congested than Aconcagua, offers more technical climbs and is preferred by many climbers. Also near here is the majestic Cordillera de Ansilta, with seven peaks scraping the sky at between 5130m and 5885m.

Surfing

Brazil is South America's best-known surfing destination, with great breaks near Rio and in the southeast, and sprinkled all along the coast from Santa Catarina to São Luís. If you've got the cash, the surfing in Fernando de Noronha is spectacular.

In Peru, national championships are held at Punta Rocas as well as Pico Alto, an experts-only 'kamikaze' reef break with some of the largest waves in the country. Peru's north coast has a string of excellent breaks. The most famous is Puerto Chicama, where rides of more than 2km are possible on what's considered the longest left-hand break in the world.

With breaks lining the long Pacific Coast, Chile nurtures some serious surf culture, most active in middle and northern Chile. Matanzas is major surf destination (and a favorite among wind surfers). Keep in mind, you'll need a wetsuit. With big breaks and long left-handers, surf capital Pichilemu hosts the national surfing championship. Pilgrims crowd the perfect left break at Pichilemu's Punta de Lobos, but beginners can also have a go nearby at La Puntilla. The coastal Ruta 1 is lined with waves.

Ecuador's best breaks are off Isla San Cristóbal in the Galápagos. On the mainland, Montañita has a fast, powerful reef

Top: Futaleufú (p540), Chile

Bottom: Iquique (p493), Chile

break that can cough up some of the mainland's best barrels.

You'll also find good waves in Mar del Plata (Argentina) and Uruguay. In Venezuela, there's great kitesurfing in Adicora and Margarita.

Wind Sports

Paragliding and hang-gliding have their followers. Top destinations include Iquique (Chile), La Paz (Bolivia) and Medellín, San Gil and Bucaramanga (Colombia). You can even fly from urban locations like Miraflores in Lima and Pedra Bonita in Rio de Janeiro.

River Rafting

You'll find churning white water all over the continent. The settings are spectacular: splashing through deep canyons or pounding down the forest-lined banks of a Class IV rapid.

Ecuador boasts world-class river rafting and kayaking. Some of the rivers offer up to 100km of continuous Class III to Class IV white water before flattening out to flow toward the Pacific on one side of the Andes and into the Amazon Basin on the other. Tena is Ecuador's de-facto white-water capital, with the nearby upper Río Napo (Class III+) and the Río Misahuallí (Class IV+) among the country's best-known rivers.

The wealth of scenic rivers, lakes, fjords and inlets in southern Chile make it a dream destination. Chile's rivers, raging through narrow canyons from the Andes, are world class. Northern Patagonia's Futaleufú River offers memorable Class IV and V runs. Less technical runs include those outside Pucón and the beautiful Petrohué, near Puerto Varas, as well as Aisén's Río Simpson and Río Baker. Near Santiago, the Cajón del Maipo offers a gentle but enjoyable run.

In Peru, Cuzco is the launch point for the greatest variety of river-running options. Choices range from a few hours of mild rafting on the Urubamba to adrenaline-pumping rides on the Santa Teresa to several days on the Apurímac, technically the source of the Amazon. A river-running trip on the Tambopata, available from June through October, tumbles down the eastern slopes of the Andes, culminating in a couple of days of floating in unspoiled rainforest. River running is also possible on the Río Cañete south of Lima, and in the canyon country around Arequipa, in Peru.

In Argentina, several rivers around Bariloche and Mendoza are worth getting wet in. In Colombia, the Río Suárez near San Gil has decent runs.

ALTERNATIVE ADVENTURES

If you can dream it up, you can probably make it happen in South America. Whether you want to hang-glide over rainforest or board down towering sand dunes, the continent has you covered.

Sand-boarding Be prepared to get sand in places you never imagined possible. Try it in Chile at San Pedro de Atacama or Iquique, or in Peru around Nazca.

Whale-watching With an annual population of humpback whales of around 400, Puerto López (Ecuador) is considered the epicenter of whale breeding grounds. Numerous boat operators ply the waters from June to September.

Hang-gliding The 10-minute descent from Pedra Bonita to a beachside landing in Rio de Janeiro is pure magic (or terror, depending on your fear threshold).

Horseback riding In San Agustín (Colombia) you can travel between remote pre-Columbian monuments in stunning natural settings.

Dog sledding You can't say you've done it all until you've tried dog sledding. Argentina is a great place to start, with operators near Caviahue, San Martín de los Andes and Ushuaia.

Land sailing Near Barreal (Argentina) you can zip across a dry lake bed beneath Andean peaks in so-called sail cars.

Valle Nevado (p464), Chile

Skiing & Snowboarding

Powder junkies rejoice. World-class resorts in the Chilean and Argentine Andes offer myriad possibilities for skiing and snowboarding. Don't expect too many bargains; resorts are priced to match their quality. The season is roughly June to September.

Most resorts in Chile are within an hour's drive of Santiago, including a wide variety of runs at family-oriented La Parva, all-levels El Colorado, and Valle Nevado, with a lot of terrain and renowned heliskiing. Legendary Portillo, the site of several downhill speed records and the summer training base for many of the Northern Hemisphere's top skiers, is northeast of Santiago near the Argentine border crossing to Mendoza.

Termas de Chillán, just east of Chillán, is a more laid-back spot with several beginners' slopes, while Parque Nacional Villarrica, near Pucón, has the added thrill of skiing on a smoking volcano. On Volcán Lonquimay, Corralco has novice and expert terrain, plus backcountry access. Volcanoes Osorno and Antillanca, east of Osorno, have open terrain with incredible views.

Argentina has three main snow-sport areas: Mendoza, the Lake District and Ushuaia. Mendoza is near Argentina's premier resort, Las Leñas, which has the best snow and longest runs; the resort Los Penitentes is also nearby. The Lake District is home to several low-key resorts, including Cerro Catedral, near Bariloche, and Cerro Chapelco, near San Martín de los Andes.

Countries at a Glance

Thirteen countries strong, South America is home to astounding natural and cultural wonders. The challenge is deciding where to begin. Peru, Bolivia, Ecuador and Colombia offer affordable adventures: climbing Andean peaks, trekking through cloud forests and visiting remote indigenous villages. Brazil is the land of magnificent beaches, outstanding nightlife and unforgettable journeys, from slow-boating down the Amazon to dune buggy rides across the northeast. Chile and Argentina harbor fantastic alpine adventures, picturesque coastlines and the rugged wilderness of Patagonia. For off-the-beaten-path travel, explore the jungle-lined interior of the Guianas. All over the continent you'll find colonial towns and laid-back seaside villages – just the antidote after a few days (or weeks) of taking in South America's jaw-dropping sights.

Argentina

Big Cities
Scenery
Outdoors

Urban Allure

Buenos Aires is a scintillating metropolis of steamy tango halls, old-world cafes and hip boutiques. Córdoba boasts a flourishing arts scene, while Mendoza draws adventure-seekers.

Natural Wonders

The Moreno glacier is awe-inspiring. The Península Valdés is home to whales, penguins and other wildlife. Witness spectacular rock formations in Quebrada de Humahuaca and nature's raw power at Iguazú Falls.

Outdoor Adventures

You'll find magnificent hiking in Patagonia, the Mendoza area and the Lake District, whitewater rafting near Bariloche and Mendoza, and skiing at Las Leñas and Cerro Catedral.

p60

Bolivia

Scenery
Trekking
Wildlife

Stunning Vistas

As you travel across this remarkable remote wilderness, you'll marvel at the world's largest salt flat, whimsical rock formations, cactus-encrusted valleys straight out of the Old West, volcanic peaks, Technicolor lakes and a sky that seems to stretch forever.

Inca Trails

For long hauls and shorter day trips along ancient Inca paving, down cloud-encased valleys and through vast swaths of wilderness, you can't beat Bolivia's treks.

Wild Explorer

Nature is everywhere, making Bolivia a hands-down favorite for nature lovers. A series of large national parks and nature reserves protect (to a certain degree) the country's endemic and at-risk species.

p199

Brazil

Beaches
Wildlife
Culture

Captivating Coastlines

Synonymous with paradise, Brazil boasts nearly 7500km of perfect-palmed coastline to prove it. For idyllic sands, start with Fernando de Noronha, Bahia and Ceará.

Unrivaled Biodiversity

The world's most biodiverse country is home to a lifetime's worth of wildlife, most famously found in the Amazon and the Pantanal, but from Bonito to Belém, you'll be floored.

The Melting Pot

Portuguese colonists; Japanese, African, Arab and European immigrants; and a healthy indigenous population shaped the Brazil melting pot. From food to film, *isso é Brasil* (this is Brazil)!

p300

Chile

Outdoors
Landscapes
Wine & Pisco

Trekking in Chilean Patagonia

Strong winds, sudden rain, rustic *refugios* (shelters) and striking landscapes – hiking the classic 'W' is an unforgettable adventure in Torres del Paine.

Dreamy Desertscapes

The driest desert in the world, the Atacama is an otherworldly place of salt caves, eerie moonlike surfaces and powerful geysers circled by snow-tipped volcanoes.

House of Spirits (and Wine)

Chile is still battling Peru over the ownership of *pisco*; here, the potent grape brandy is produced in the Elqui Valley. But no one can contest Chile's mastery of Carmenere, a full-bodied red wine – it's the toast of the nation.

p444

Colombia

Landscapes
Outdoors
Coffee

Nature's Bounty

From the towering sand dunes near Punta Gallinas to the glaciers of Parque Nacional El Cocuy and the flooded forests of the Amazonas, Colombia's phenomenal landscapes make for your very own nature documentary.

Outdoor Adventure

The small city of San Gil is a one-stop adventure playground with rafting, climbing, paragliding and more – just a fraction of the adventures on offer around the country to keep your adrenaline pumping.

Black Gold

Learn to pick and grade coffee beans (and sample the final product) at award-winning plantations around Manizales and Armenia in the Zona Cafetera.

p570

Ecuador

Architecture
Landscapes
Ecotourism

Art & Architecture

The picturesque colonial centers of Quito and Cuenca are packed with architectural treasures. Quito and Guayaquil have outstanding collections of pre-Columbian art and modern works by Oswaldo Guayasamín.

Scenery

Get a taste of the Amazon in jungle lodges, and stunning Andean scenery in Quilotoa. If money allows, take a cruise around the otherworldly Galápagos.

The Great Outdoors

Top ways to experience the great outdoors include climbing Andean peaks (Cotopaxi is popular), mountain biking down them (try Chimborazo), ecotourism in the cloud-forests of Mindo and whitewater rafting near Tena.

p672

French Guiana

History
Cuisine
Wildlife

Haunted Prisons

Between 1852 and 1938 around 70,000 prisoners were sent to French Guiana from France. Today, the old structures are eerily crumbling into the jungles; the most interesting are offshore on the relaxing Îles du Salut.

Spicy Mix

African, Hmong, French, Javanese and Brazilian culinary traditions plus local spices and fresh jungle produce equals the most interesting food in the region.

Turtles, Birds & Caimans

Look for caimans and the brilliant scarlet ibis on a wildlife-watching tour in the Kaw Nature Reserve. Or take a trip to the coast in turtle season to watch crowds of turtles laying eggs in the sand.

p775

Guyana

Wildlife
Culture
Architecture

Amazonian Monsters

You want big? Track the world's largest scaled freshwater fish (arapaima), ant-eaters, caimans and more. The best part: they're all relatively easy to find.

Indigenous Eco-Trail

Hop from one indigenous village–run lodge to the next through the Rupununi savannas. Bird-watch and learn to shoot a bow and arrow while supporting sustainable businesses.

Dilapidated Gems

Nothing is shined up in colonial Georgetown, but that's part of its charm. Marvel at the ingenious natural cooling system even as the paint seems to chip off before your eyes.

p793

Paraguay

History
Culture
Wildlife

Colonial Relics

The Jesuit revolution began and ended in the jungles of eastern Paraguay, and though the social experiment is long gone, the wonderful churches the Jesuits left behind stand in silent testament.

Indigenous Influences

Paraguayan culture has been shaped by a history of corrupt dictatorships and a strong indigenous influence, a cultural cocktail that makes it a strange and fascinating country to explore.

Biodiversity in the Chaco

Paraguay's arid Chaco positively teems with wildlife, and though the dusty surroundings look inhospitable, it's arguably the best place to see big animals like tapir, puma and the endangered Chaco peccary.

p813

Peru

Culture
Ruins
Landscapes

Indigenous Lore

In Peru, culture isn't something you enter a dusty museum to find. It's all around you. The strong traditions of indigenous cultures are easily witnessed in many religious or seasonal festivals.

Civilization of the Incas

From the heights of Machu Picchu to the cloud forest of Kuélap, Peru's ruins garner due fame, but that doesn't always mean crowds. Many are reached by gorgeous hikes, attractions in their own right.

Hiking & Trekking

From the ample sands of the coast to verdant Amazonian rainforest, lost-canyon villages and the majestic peaks of the Cordillera Blanca, Peru offers some of the best trekking and hiking on earth.

p848

Suriname

Culture
Wildlife
Architecture

Maroon Adventures

Boat down the Upper Suriname River to find myriad lodges run by Maroon tribes who have retained a distinctive African-Amazonian culture. Lodging ranges from luxurious bungalows to simple hammock shelters.

Vast Jungles

Deep in the Central Suriname Nature Reserve you'll see troupes of monkeys, tons of birds, caimans and maybe even a jaguar or harpy eagle.

Unesco City

Paramaribo's heritage district is unlike anywhere else in the world. Imagine colonial Dutch lines in a Wild West setting doused in all the colors and culture of the Caribbean.

p964

Uruguay

Beaches
Architecture
Landscapes

Sun, Sand & Surf

With over 300km of quality coastline, Uruguay pretty much guarantees you'll find a spot to lay your towel.

Colonial Riches

Colonia del Sacramento is the superstar, of course, and Montevideo's Old Town has its fans, too. But visit pretty much any plaza in the country for gorgeous Spanish-influenced streetscapes.

Inland Adventures

While everyone's chuckling it up beachside, those in the know head for Uruguay's interior – a beautiful rolling hillscape that's the epitome of getting off the Gringo Trail.

p981

Venezuela

Inaccessible

Venezuela is home to abundant wildlife in the Orinoco Delta, Caribbean beaches and colorful colonial villages – not to mention South America's highest waterfalls (Salto Ángel). Unfortunately, owing to security concerns, we cannot recommend traveling here at present. There is a basic lack of services for the ordinary citizen – food, healthcare and personal security – so a traveler with no knowledge of the lay of the land could find themselves seriously out of their depth in a hurry. Travelers should also be mindful traveling in areas bordering Venezuela, where towns are straining to deal with the flood of refugees fleeing a crisis situation.

p1015

On the Road

Argentina

POP 44 MILLION

Best Places to Eat

➡ Chirimoya (p127)

➡ Pistach' (p157)

➡ Crucoli Caffe (p135)

➡ Morphen (p155)

Best Places to Stay

➡ Adventure Bed & Bike (p154)

➡ Portal del Sur (p73)

➡ Espacio Mundano (p127)

➡ Bonita Lake House (p159)

Why Go?

With its gorgeous landscapes, cosmopolitan cities and lively culture, Argentina is a traveler's paradise. It stretches almost 3500km from Bolivia to the tip of South America, encompassing a wide array of geography and climates. Nature-lovers can traverse the Patagonian steppe, climb South America's highest peak, walk among thousands of penguins and witness the world's most amazing waterfalls. Hikers can sample the stunning scenery of the lush Lake District – with its glorious lakes and white-tipped mountains – and revel in Patagonia's glacier-carved landscapes and painted Andean deserts. City slickers will adore fabulous Buenos Aires, where they can dance the sexy tango, shop for designer clothes, sample a wide range of ethnic cuisine and party at nightclubs till dawn.

Beautiful, defiant and intense, Argentina is strikingly seductive. Now is a great time to visit, so get your spirit in gear and prepare for an unforgettable adventure!

When to Go
Buenos Aires

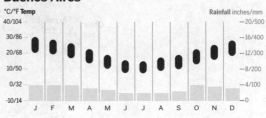

Dec–Feb Warmer temperatures and longer daylight hours in Patagonia. Buenos Aires and the north are hot.

Mar–May & Sep–Nov Mild weather means its a great time to visit Buenos Aires, the Lake District and Mendoza.

Jun–Aug Peak ski season. A good time to visit the north. Beaches shut down.

Entering the Country

Buenos Aires is linked by air to most other country capitals in South America. Overland, there are numerous border crossings from neighboring Bolivia, Brazil, Chile, Paraguay and Uruguay. Border formalities are generally straightforward as long as all your documents are in order. When crossing into Chile by air or land, don't take fresh fruits or vegetables (even in sandwiches), dairy products or meat; fines are steep.

FOUR-WEEK ITINERARY

Spend your first few days taking in Buenos Aires, then head to Mendoza (for wine-tasting and outdoor adventures) and Bariloche (for hiking in summer and skiing in winter). If you love summertime hiking make the Patagonian hamlet of El Chaltén your priority; once here you can't miss El Calafate for its amazing Perito Moreno glacier.

Seeing all of Argentina in one month will likely require a few key flights. Or, depending on the season, concentrate on the north or south. First, take a few days to explore the wonders of Buenos Aires. Spectacular Iguazú Falls is worth a couple of days any time of year. Colonial Salta is best April to November, while Córdoba, Mendoza and the Lake District can be visited year-round. Some Patagonian destinations, such as El Chaltén and Ushuaia, have limited services from June to August (except for skiing).

Essential Food & Drink

Beef Argentines have perfected the art of grilling steaks.

Wine From the malbecs of Mendoza to the syrahs of San Juan.

Mate This bitter, grassy tea is an important social bonding experience.

Dulce de leche Milk and sugar magicked into the world's best caramel sauce.

Top Tips

➡ Book regional flights from the capital's Aeroparque Jorge Newbery – it's closer to the city center and it's easier to access.

➡ Install WhatsApp on your phone for easy wi-fi contact with hotels and local businesses.

➡ Seasonality plays a big part in Patagonia. If going in low season research what's open; plan extra days for poor weather.

➡ Dress to explore Buenos Aires on foot.

➡ Accept *mate* when offered. It's the best way to make friends.

➡ ATMs generally have very low withdrawal limits. Ask ahead whether hotels and restaurants take credit or debit cards.

➡ In touristy provincial areas ATMs can run out, particularly on weekends. Get cash before the need becomes urgent.

ARGENTINA

FAST FACTS

Currency Argentine peso (AR$)

Visas Generally not required; some nationalities pay a reciprocity fee

Money ATMs widespread; credit cards accepted at higher-end places

Time GMT minus three hours

Capital Buenos Aires

Emergency 101

Language Spanish

Exchange Rates

Australia	A$1	AR$25.67
Canada	C$1	AR$27.22
Chile	CH$100	AR$5.18
Euro	€1	AR$40.75
Japan	¥100	AR$31.67
NZ	NZ$1	AR$23.76
UK	UK£1	AR$46.43
Uruguay	UR$1	AR$1.09
USA	US$1	AR$35.68

For current exchange rates see www.xe.com.

Daily Costs

➡ Dorm bed: US$15–22; double room in a midrange hotel: US$75–150

➡ Cheap main dish: under US$11; average main: US$10–16

Resources

Argentina Independent (www.argentinaindependent. com)

The Bubble (www.the bubble.com)

Ruta 0 (www.ruta0.com)

Pick up the Fork (http://pickupthefork.com)

Lonely Planet (www.lonely planet.com/argentina)

Argentina Highlights

❶ Buenos Aires (p63) Eating, shopping, dancing, and partying all night long in Argentina's sophisticated capital.

❷ Iguazú Falls (p110) Taking in the world's most amazing waterfall, stretching almost 3km long.

❸ Córdoba (p111) Exploring Argentina's second-largest city, an attractive destination with alternative culture.

❹ El Chaltén (p173) Hiking, camping and gazing at the vistas to your heart's content.

❺ Bariloche (p157) Fishing, skiing, hiking or whitewater rafting among gorgeous mountains and lakes.

❻ Mendoza (p140) Sipping world-class wines and partaking in outdoor adventures.

❼ Parque Nacional Los Glaciares (p179) Checking out the amazing and constantly calving Perito Moreno glacier.

❽ Península Valdés (p170) Ogling whales, elephant seals and penguins at this wildlife mecca.

❾ Quebrada de Humahuaca (p132) Setting your sights on lovely, vivid and harsh cactus-dotted mountainscapes.

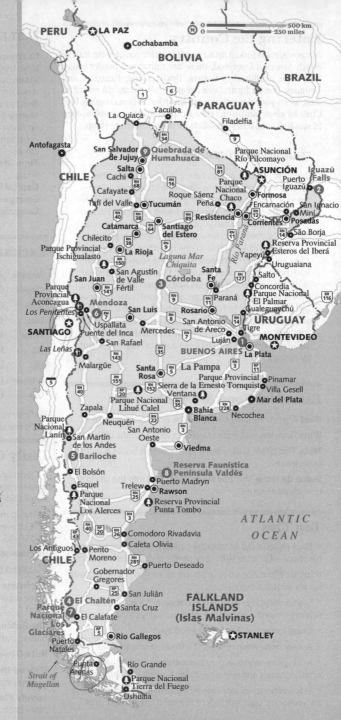

BUENOS AIRES

📞 011 / POP 13 MILLION (GREATER BA)

Believe everything you've heard – Buenos Aires is one of South America's most electrifying cities, graced with European architecture, atmospheric neighborhoods and bustling nightlife. BA's passionate residents are proud and even haughty, but once you get to know them they'll bend over backward to help.

After Argentina's economic collapse in 2002, BA bounced back and created a renaissance that's still keeping the city aglow today. Argentines found the 'outside' world prohibitively expensive, so turned their energy inward, with impressive results. New restaurants, boutiques and businesses keep popping up, not only to serve the locals and their pesos, but also to cater to the influx of foreign tourists bringing hard currency.

Yet every great metropolis has a poorer side. Cracked sidewalks, ubiquitous graffiti and rough edges – even in the wealthiest neighborhoods – speak volumes about this city. Poverty and beggars exist, and there's a deep melancholy here: an acknowledgement of Argentina's riches coupled with the despair of not realizing its full potential. The undeniable reality is that BA comes with a darker side.

So throw yourself into this heady mix and hold on tight, 'cause you're going for a wild ride. Don't be surprised if you fall in love with this amazing and sexy city – you won't be the first, or the last.

⊙ Sights

At Buenos Aires' heart is its *microcentro*, which holds many of the city's historical buildings and museums. To the north lies upper-crust Recoleta, with its famous cemetery, and park-filled Palermo, home to many great restaurants and bars. Down south is where the blue-collar class hangs: this includes the tango neighborhood of San Telmo and colorful, roughhousing La Boca. There's enough bustle in this city to keep you trotting around all day and all night.

⊙ City Center

Buenos Aires' *microcentro* holds many 19th-century European buildings, which surprises travelers expecting a more Latin American feel. The liveliest street here is pedestrian Florida, packed with masses of businesspeople, tourists, leather salespeople and money changers. Make sure to stop at Galerías Pacífico, one of BA's most gorgeous shopping malls and home to some amazing ceiling paintings.

Florida intersects busy Av Corrientes, and if you head west on this thoroughfare you'll cross super-wide Av 9 de Julio. It's decisively punctuated by the famously phallic Obelisco, a major symbol of Buenos Aires. Just beyond is the city's traditional theater district, also full of cheap bookstores.

East of the city center is BA's newest barrio, Puerto Madero. This renovated docklands area is lined with pleasant pedestrian walkways, expensive lofts, trendy restaurants and bars, and some of the city's priciest hotels.

★**Plaza de Mayo** PLAZA

(Map p66; cnr Av de Mayo & San Martín; ⑤ Línea A Plaza de Mayo) Surrounded by the Casa Rosada, the Cabildo and the city's main cathedral, Plaza de Mayo is the place where Argentines gather in vehement protest or jubilant celebration. At the center is the **Pirámide de Mayo**, a white obelisk built to mark the first anniversary of independence from Spain.

If you happen to be here on Thursday at 3:30pm, you'll see the Madres de la Plaza de Mayo gather and circle the pyramid, holding photographs of their missing children. These mothers of the 'Disappeared' (Argentines abducted by the state during the military dictatorship of 1976 to 1983) continue to march as a reminder of the past and for other social justice causes.

★**Casa Rosada** NOTABLE BUILDING

(Pink House; Map p66; 📞 011-4344-3804; https://visitas.casarosada.gob.ar; Plaza de Mayo; ⊗ tours in Spanish 10am-6pm Sat & Sun, in English 12:30pm & 2:30pm Sat & Sun; ⑤ Línea A Plaza de Mayo) **FREE** On the eastern side of Plaza de Mayo stands the Casa Rosada, named for its distinctive color. It was from the balcony here that Eva Perón famously addressed the throngs of impassioned supporters packed into Plaza de Mayo. The building houses the Argentine President's offices; the presidential residence is in the suburb of Olivos, north of the center. Free hour-long guided tours are given at weekends and must be booked online in advance; bring ID.

Museo Casa Rosada MUSEUM

(Map p66; 📞 011-4344-3802; cnr Av Paseo Colón & Hipólito Yrigoyen; ⊗ 10am-6pm Wed-Sun; ⑤ Línea A Plaza de Mayo) **FREE** Behind the Casa Rosada you'll notice a glass wedge that's the roof of this bright and airy museum, housed within

Greater Buenos Aires

Greater Buenos Aires

◎ Top Sights
1 El Caminito D4
2 Museo Benito Quinquela Martín D4
3 Museo Nacional de Bellas Artes C2
4 Reserva Ecológica Costanera Sur D3

◎ Sights
5 Fundación Proa D4
6 Museo de la Pasión Boquense D4
Museo Histórico Nacional ....(see 7)
7 Parque Lezama D4

⦿ Activities, Courses & Tours
8 Parque Norte B1

⊗ Eating
Proa Cafe ....(see 5)

⦿ Drinking & Nightlife
9 Doppelgänger C4
On Tap ....(see 10)

⦿ Entertainment
10 Centro Cultural Torquato Tasso.......... C4
11 El Monumental................................. A1
12 La Bombonera Stadium..................... D4
13 Usina del Arte................................. D4

the brick vaults of the old *aduana* (customs house). Head down into the open space, which has over a dozen side rooms, each dedicated to a different era of Argentina's tumultuous political history. There are videos (in Spanish) and a few artifacts to see, along

with an impressive restored mural by Mexican artist David Alfaro Siqueiros.

Catedral Metropolitana　　　　CATHEDRAL
(Map p66; ⊘ 7:30am-6:30pm Mon-Fri, 9am-6:45pm Sat & Sun, museum 10am-1:30pm Mon-Fri; Ⓢ Línea D Catedral) This cathedral was built on the

site of the original colonial church and not finished until 1827. It's a significant religious and architectural landmark, and carved above its triangular facade and neoclassical columns are bas-reliefs of Jacob and Joseph. The spacious interior is equally impressive, with baroque details and an elegant rococo altar. There's a small museum dedicated to the cathedral's history. For Pope Francis souvenirs, visit the small gift shop near the entrance.

Cabildo
MUSEUM
(Map p66; ☎011-4342-6729; https://cabildo nacional.cultura.gob.ar; Bolívar 65; ⊙10:30am-5pm Tue, Wed & Fri, to 8pm Thu, to 6pm Sat & Sun; ⑤Línea A Perú) FREE This mid-18th-century town hall building is now an interesting museum largely dedicated to the revolution of May 1810, when Argentina declared independence. Exhibits cover the history of the Cabildo during colonial times (when it was also a prison) through to the British invasions of 1806 and 1807 and independence three years later. There are good views of Plaza de Mayo from the 2nd-floor balcony.

★ Teatro Colón
THEATER
(Map p66; ☎011-4378-7100; www.teatrocolon.org. ar; Tucumán 1171, Cerrito 628; tours AR$500-600; ⊙tours 9am-5pm; ⑤Línea D Tribunales) This impressive seven-story building is one of BA's most prominent landmarks. It's the city's main performing-arts venue and a world-class forum for opera, ballet and classical music, with astounding acoustics. Occupying an entire city block, the Colón can seat 2500 spectators and provide standing room for another 500. The theater's real beauty lies on the inside, so if you can't get hold of tickets to a performance, take one of the frequent 50-minute backstage tours to view the stunning interior.

★ Centro Cultural Kirchner
CULTURAL CENTER
(Map p66; ☎0800-333-9300; www.cultural kirchner.gob.ar; Sarmiento 151; ⊙1-8pm Wed-Sun; ⑤Línea B Alem) FREE It was former president Néstor Kirchner who, in 2005, first proposed turning the abandoned former central post office into a cultural center. He died in 2010 before the project was completed, but the breathtaking cultural center was named in his honor. Within the vast beaux-arts structure – which stands eight stories tall and takes up an entire city block – are multiple art galleries, events spaces and auditoriums. The highlight,

however, is the Ballena Azul, a concert hall with world-class acoustics that seats 1800.

Colección de Arte Amalia Lacroze de Fortabat
MUSEUM
(Museo Fortabat; Map p66; ☎011-4310-6600; www. coleccionfortabat.org.ar; Olga Cossettini 141; adult/child AR$100/50; ⊙noon-8pm Tue-Sun, tours in Spanish 5pm; ⑤Línea B Alem) Prominently located at the northern end of Puerto Madero is this stunning art museum showcasing the private collection of the late billionaire, philanthropist and socialite Amalia Lacroze de Fortabat. There are works by Antonio Berni and Raúl Soldi, as well as pieces by international artists including Dalí, Klimt, Rodin and Chagall; look for Warhol's colorful take on Fortabat herself in the family portrait gallery.

★ Reserva Ecológica Costanera Sur
NATURE RESERVE
(Map p64; ☎011-4893-1588; visitasguiadas_recs@ buenosaires.gob.ar; Av Tristán Achaval Rodríguez 1550; ⊙8am-7pm Tue-Sun Nov-Mar, to 6pm Apr-Oct; ☐2) FREE The beautifully marshy land of this 350-hectare nature reserve has become a popular site for weekend picnics, walks and bike rides. Bring binoculars if you're a birder – over 300 bird species can be spotted, along with river turtles, iguanas and nutria. At the eastern shoreline of the reserve you can get a close-up view of the Río de la Plata's muddy waters.

The park has a **second entrance** (Map p66; cnr Mariquita Sánchez de Thompson & Av Intendente Hernán M Giralt; ☐92, 106) at the other end of the Costanera, from where free guided tours (in Spanish) depart at 9:30am and 4pm on Saturday and Sunday, November to March. From April to October tours depart at 10:30am and 3:30pm on Saturday and Sunday. Free night tours are also held one Friday per month (call for the latest schedule; reserve ahead).

Manzana de las Luces
NOTABLE BUILDING
(Block of Enlightenment; Map p66; ☎011-4342-6973; Perú 222; ⊙10am-7:30pm Mon-Fri, 2-8pm Sat & Sun; ⑤Línea E Bolívar) FREE In colonial times, the Manzana de las Luces was Buenos Aires' most important center of culture and learning, and today the block still symbolizes education and enlightenment. Two of the five original buildings remain; Jesuit defensive tunnels were discovered in 1912. Free tours in Spanish are given at 2pm from Monday to Friday, but you can go inside and see the main patio area without taking a tour.

Central Buenos Aires

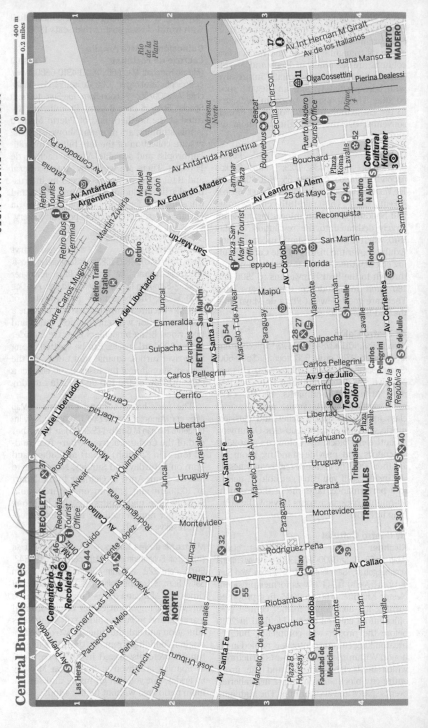

400 m
0.2 miles

PUERTO MADERO

Río de la Plata

Av Int Hernan M Giralt
Av de los Italianos

Juana Manso

17

11

OlgaCossettini
Pierina Dealessi

Dique 4

Cecilia Grierson

Seacat

Centro Cultural Kirchner

52

Buquebus

Puerto Madero Tourist Office

Av Antártida Argentina

Dársena Norte

Manuel Tienda León

Laminar Plaza

Bouchard

Plaza Roma

3

Av Eduardo Madero

Av Leandro N Alem

25 de Mayo

47 42

Leandro N Alem

Sarmiento

Retiro Tourist Office

Av Antártida Argentina

Martin Zuviria

Reconquista

Retiro

San Martín

Plaza San Martín Tourist Office

San Martín

50

Florida

Av Córdoba

Florida

Av Comodoro Py

Letonia

Retiro Bus Terminal

Retiro Train Station

Padre Carlos Mugica

Av del Libertador

Juncal

Maipú

Viamonte

Tucumán

Lavalle

Av Corrientes

Esmeralda

San Martín

Av Santa Fe

Marcelo T de Alvear

Paraguay

Suipacha

21 28 27

9 de Julio

RETIRO

Arenales

Suipacha

54

Carlos Pellegrini

Carlos Pellegrini

Av del Libertador

Carlos Pellegrini

Av 9 de Julio

Cerrito

Plaza de la República

Posadas

37

RECOLETA

Cerrito

Cerrito

Libertad

Teatro Colón

8

Montevideo

Libertad

Libertad

Talcahuano

Plaza Lavalle

Cementerio de la Recoleta

2

Recoleta Tourist Office

46

Av Callao

Guido

Vicente López

44

41

Av Quintana

Av Alvear

Rodríguez Peña

Av Santa Fe

Arenales

Marcelo T de Alvear

Uruguay

Tribunales

TRIBUNALES

Uruguay

40

Juncal

Montevideo

Uruguay

49

Paraná

Montevideo

30

Junín

Ayacucho

Junín

BARRIO NORTE

Juncal

Rodríguez Peña

Callao

Av Callao

39

Av Callao

Av Pueyrredón

Las Heras

Larrea

Pacheco de Melo

Peña

French

Juncal

Av General Las Heras

José Uriburu

Arenales

55

Riobamba

Ayacucho

Av Córdoba

Viamonte

Tucumán

Lavalle

Plaza B Houssay

Facultad de Medicina

Av Santa Fe

32

Paraguay

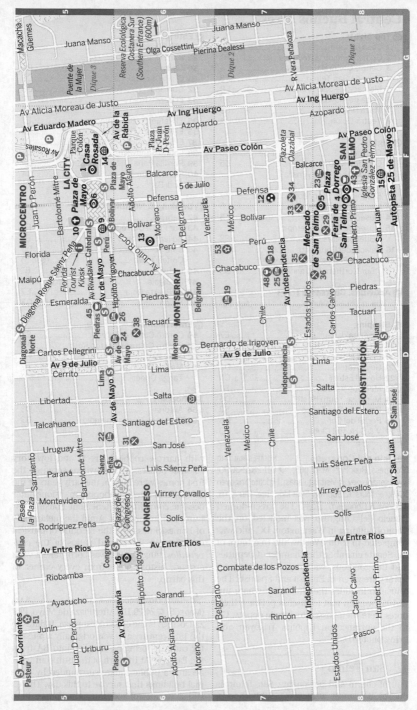

Central Buenos Aires

Palacio del Congreso   NOTABLE BUILDING
(Congress Building; Map p66; ☎011-2822-3000; www.senado.gov.ar/visitasguiadas; Hipólito Yrigoyen 1849; ⊙tours 12:30pm & 5pm Mon, Tue, Thu & Fri; Ⓢ Línea A Congreso) **FREE** The green-domed Palacio del Congreso was modeled on the Capitol Building in Washington, DC, and was completed in 1906. Worthwhile free tours of the Senate chamber, the Chamber of Deputies and the gorgeous, walnut-paneled Congress library are given in English and Spanish. The tour also includes the pink room where until 1951 women met to discuss policies; their notes were then passed to a male deputy. Go to the entrance on Hipólito Yrigoyen and bring photo ID.

◉ **San Telmo**

Full of charm and personality, San Telmo is one of BA's most attractive neighborhoods, with narrow cobbled streets and low-story colonial houses. This is where some of the first homes were built in the early years of the colony, and these elaborate mansions later became *conventillos* (tenement housing) for European immigrants. Amid the melancholy of homesickness and the merging of musical traditions in the shared patios of the *conventillos,* tango music was born. Take a walk around; history oozes from every corner of this barrio.

★ **Plaza Dorrego**   PLAZA
(Map p66; ☐ 24, 29, 111) After Plaza de Mayo, Plaza Dorrego is the city's oldest plaza. It dates to the 18th century and was originally a pit stop for caravans bringing supplies into BA from the Pampas. At the turn of the 19th century it became a public square surrounded by colonial buildings that survive to this day. There's still a wonderful old-time atmosphere here

as well as cafe-restaurants that will definitely take you back in time – if you can ignore the nearby chain coffee shops.

⭐ **Feria de San Telmo**   MARKET
(Map p66; Defensa; ⊙ 10am-6pm Sun; 🚌 10, 22, 29, 45, 86) On Sundays, San Telmo's main drag is closed to traffic and the street is a sea of both locals and tourists browsing craft stalls, waiting at vendors' carts for freshly squeezed orange juice, poking through the antique glass ornaments on display on Plaza Dorrego, and listening to street performances by myriad music groups. It runs from Avenida San Juan to Plaza de Mayo. It's a tight and crowded scene, so be prepared to bump into people, and watch your bag carefully.

⭐ **Mercado de San Telmo**   MARKET
(Map p66; btwn Defensa & Bolívar, Carlos Calvo & Estados Unidos block; ⊙ 8am-8:30pm; 🚇 Línea C Independencia) This market was built in 1897 by Juan Antonio Buschiazzo, the Italian-born Argentine architect who designed Cementerio de la Recoleta. It occupies the inside of an entire city block, though you wouldn't be able to tell just by looking at the modest sidewalk entrances. The wrought-iron interior (note the beautiful original ceiling) makes it one of BA's most atmospheric markets; locals shop here for fresh produce and meat. Peripheral antique stalls offer old treasures.

El Zanjón de Granados   ARCHAEOLOGICAL SITE
(Map p66; 📞 011-4361-3002; www.elzanjon.com.ar; Defensa 755; tours AR$350; ⊙ tours noon, 2pm & 3pm Mon-Fri, every 30min 11am-5:30pm Sun; 🚇 Línea C Independencia) One of the more unusual places in BA is this amazing urban architectural site. A series of old tunnels, sewers and cisterns (built from 1730 onwards) were constructed above a river tributary and provided the base for one of BA's oldest settlements, which later became a family mansion and then tenement housing and shops.

**Museo de Arte
Moderno de Buenos Aires**   MUSEUM
(MAMBA; Map p66; 📞 011-4361-6919; www.museodeartemoderno.buenosaires.gob.ar; Av San Juan 350; AR$30, Tue free; ⊙ 11am-7pm Tue-Fri, to 8pm Sat & Sun; 🚌 29, 24, 111) Housed in a former tobacco warehouse, this spacious, multistory museum shows off the works of (mostly) Argentine contemporary artists. Expect exhibitions showcasing everything from photography to industrial design, and from figurative to conceptual art. There's also an auditorium and gift shop.

Museo Histórico Nacional   MUSEUM
(Map p64; 📞 011-4300-7530; https://museohistoriconacional.cultura.gob.ar; Defensa 1600; ⊙ 11am-6pm Wed-Sun, tours in English noon Thu & Fri; 🚌 29) **FREE** Located in **Parque Lezama** (Map p64; cnr Defensa & Av Brasil; 🚌 29, 24, 111) is the city's national historical museum. It's mostly dedicated to Argentina's revolution of May 25, 1810, though there is also some coverage of precolonial times. There are several portraits of presidents and other major historical figures of the time, along with a beautifully lit generals' room. Peek into the re-created version of José de San Martín's bedroom – military hero and liberator of Argentina (along with other South American countries).

⊙ **La Boca**

Blue collar and raffish to the core, La Boca is very much a locals' neighborhood. Its colorful shanties are often portrayed as a symbol of Buenos Aires, while El Caminito is the barrio's most famous street, full of art vendors, buskers and tango dancers twirling for your spare change.

⭐ **El Caminito**   STREET
(Map p64; Av Don Pedro de Mendoza, near Del Valle Iberlucea; 🚌 33, 64, 29, 168, 53) **FREE** La Boca's most famous street and 'open-air' museum is a magnet for visitors, who come to see its brightly painted houses and snap photographs of the figures of Juan and Eva Perón, Che Guevara and soccer legend Diego Maradona, who wave down from balconies. (Expect to pay a few pesos to take pictures of tango dancers or pose with props.) Sure, it could be called a tourist trap, but don't let that put you off.

Fundación Proa   GALLERY
(Map p64; 📞 011-4104-1000; www.proa.org; Av Don Pedro de Mendoza 1929; AR$80; ⊙ 11am-7pm Tue-Sun; 🚌 33, 64, 29) Only the most cutting-edge national and international artists are invited to show at this contemporary art center, with its high ceilings, white walls and large display halls. The innovative installations utilize a wide variety of media and themes, while the rooftop terrace cafe (Map p64; 📞 011-4104-1003; www.proa.org/eng/cafe.php; mains AR$220-365; ⊙ cafe 11am-7pm, kitchen noon-3:30pm Tue-Sun; 🚌 33, 64, 29) is the most stylish place in La Boca for pausing for a drink or snack as you take in the spectacular views of the Riachuelo river.

★**Museo Benito**
Quinquela Martín MUSEUM

(Map p64; ☑ 011-4301-1080; www.buenosaires.
gob.ar/museoquinquelamartin; Av Don Pedro de
Mendoza 1835; AR$40; ⊘10am-6pm Tue-Fri,
11:15am-6pm Sat & Sun; ☐33, 64, 29) Once the
home and studio of painter Benito Quinquela Martín (1890–1977), this fine-arts museum exhibits his works and those of other
Argentine artists. Quinquela Martín used
silhouettes of laboring men, smokestacks
and water reflections as recurring themes,
and painted with broad, rough brushstrokes
and dark colors. Don't miss the colorful tiles
of his former kitchen and bathroom, his
hand-painted piano and the sculptures on
the rooftop terraces; the top tier has awesome views of the port.

Museo de la Pasión Boquense MUSEUM

(Map p64; ☑ 011-4301-1080; www.museoboquense.
com; Brandsen 805; museum AR$230, museum &
stadium tour AR$320; ⊘10am-6pm; ☐29, 53, 152)
This high-tech *fútbol* museum chronicles
the history of the boisterous neighborhood
of La Boca and its famous soccer team Boca
Juniors with displays on the club's idols,
championships and trophies and, of course,
the gooooals. There's a 360-degree theater in
a giant soccer-ball auditorium and a good
gift shop. It's worth paying the extra pesos
for the stadium tour, which includes the
chance to step onto the pitch. Located at La
Bombonera stadium, three blocks north of
El Caminito.

◉ **Recoleta**

It's easy to see how Buenos Aires could be
called the Paris of the South in this grand
neighborhood. Recoleta is where the rich
live in luxury apartments and mansions
while spending their free time sipping coffee
at elegant cafes and shopping in expensive
boutiques. Full of lush parks, grand monuments, art galleries, French architecture and
wide avenues, Recoleta is also famous for its
cemetery.

★**Cementerio de la Recoleta** CEMETERY

(Map p66; ☑ 0800-444-2363; visitasguiadas
recoleta@buenosaires.gob.ar; Junín 1760; ⊘7am-
5:30pm; ⑤ Línea H Las Heras) FREE This cemetery is perhaps BA's top attraction. You can
wander for hours in this incredible city of
the dead, where the 'streets' are lined with
impressive statues and marble mausoleums.
Peek into the crypts and check out the dusty

coffins and try to decipher the history of its
inhabitants. Past presidents, military heroes,
influential politicians and the just plain rich
and famous have made it past the gates here.

★**Museo Nacional**
de Bellas Artes MUSEUM

(Map p64; ☑ 011-5288-9900; www.mnba.gob.
ar; Av del Libertador 1473; ⊘11am-8pm Tue-Fri,
10am-8pm Sat & Sun; ☐130, 92, 63) FREE This
is Argentina's most important fine art museum and contains many key works by Benito Quinquela Martín, Xul Solar, Eduardo
Sívori and other Argentine artists, including
a whole room of works by Antonio Berni.
There are also pieces by European masters
such as Cézanne, Degas, Picasso, Rem-
brandt, Toulouse-Lautrec and Van Gogh.

◉ **Palermo**

Palermo's large, grassy parks – regally
punctuated with grand monuments – are
popular destinations on weekends, when
families fill the shady lanes, cycle the bike
paths and paddle on the peaceful lakes. The
sub-neighborhood of Palermo Viejo (itself
subdivided into Soho and Hollywood) is
home to dozens of restaurants, bars, nightclubs and shops, along with the city's largest
selection of boutique hotels.

★**Museo de Arte Latinoamericano**
de Buenos Aires MUSEUM

(MALBA; Map p76; ☑ 011-4808-6500; www.malba.
org.ar; Av Figueroa Alcorta 3415; adult/student Thu-
Mon AR$140/70, Wed AR$70/free; ⊘noon-8pm
Thu-Mon, to 9pm Wed; ☐102, 130, 124) Sparkling
inside its glass walls, this airy modern art
museum is one of BA's most impressive. It
displays the fine collection of Latin American art of millionaire and philanthropist
Eduardo Costantini, including works by
Argentines Xul Solar and Antonio Berni, as
well as pieces by Mexicans Diego Rivera and
Frida Kahlo. The temporary exhibitions here
are usually world class so it's worth checking
what's currently on offer. A cinema screens
art-house films.

★**Parque 3 de Febrero** PARK

(Map p76; cnr Avs del Libertador & de la Infanta
Isabel; ☐10, 34, 130) Also known as Bosques
de Palermo (Palermo Woods), this sweeping
open parkland abounds with small lakes
and pretty gazebos. Stands rent bikes and
in-line skates, and joggers and power walkers circle the ponds – if you don't have the

energy to join them, lie back under a tree and people-watch. There's also a monument to literary greats called El Jardín de los Poetas (the Garden of Poets), and the exquisite Rosedal (rose garden).

Jardín Japonés
GARDENS

(Map p76; ☑011-4804-4922; www.jardinjapones. org.ar; Av Casares 2966; adult/child AR$120/free; ⊙10am-6pm; ◻67, 102, 130) First opened in 1967, these well-maintained Japanese gardens are a peaceful spot for a stroll, unless you're averse to the gentle chimes of Japanese music that emanate from speakers around the grounds. Inside there's a Japanese restaurant along with ponds filled with koi and spanned by pretty bridges.

Museo Evita
MUSEUM

(Map p76; ☑011-4807-0306; http://web.museo evita.org.ar; Lafinur 2988; admission incl audio guide AR$180; ⊙11am-7pm Tue-Sun; Ⓢ Línea D Plaza Italia) Argentina's iconic first lady and wife of President Juan Domingo Perón has this fine museum devoted to her. Housed in a gorgeous 1923 mansion that from 1948 belonged to Eva Perón's social foundation, Museo Evita celebrates the Argentine heroine with videos, historical photos, books and posters. However, the prize memorabilia has to be her wardrobe: dresses, shoes, handbags, hats and blouses are all on display. Look for the picture of her kicking a soccer ball – in heels.

🏃 Activities

Porteños' main activities are walking, shopping and dancing tango. Those searching for greener pastures, however, head to Palermo's parks, where joggers run past strolling families and young men playing *fútbol*.

Safe cycling is possible in BA, and protected bike lanes have popped up on certain streets. Good places to pedal are Palermo's parks (weekend rentals on Av de la Infanta Isabel near Av Pedro Montt), and in the Reserva Ecológica Costanera Sur. Bike tour companies rent bikes and also do guided tours.

Unless you stay at a fancy hotel or join a gym, swimming pools are hard to come by; to cool off, try **Parque Norte** (Map p64; ☑011-4787-1382; www.parquenorte.com; Avs Cantilo & Guiraldes; adult/child Mon-Fri AR$195/105, Sat AR$230/135, Sun AR$250/135; ⊙pool 9am-8pm, park 8am-midnight; 🖫; ◻33, 42, 160), a fun water park. Soccer players should check out **Buenos Aires Fútbol Amigos** (BAFA; Map

p76; www.fcbafa.com; El Salvador 5301; per game AR$160; Ⓢ Línea D Plaza Italia), while yoga aficionados can try **Buena Onda Yoga** (Map p76; www.buenaondayoga.net; Thames 1916; class US$14; Ⓢ Línea D Plaza Italia).

Some companies like Tangol (p85) offer activities such as tango, kayaking, fishing and *estancia* visits, which often include horse riding. For something totally different, learn to play polo with **Argentina Polo Day** (☑011-15-6738-2422; www.argentinapoloday.com.ar; RP 39, Km11.2, Capilla del Señor; full day/half-day polo US$185/160).

🌿 Courses

Language

BA has become a major destination for students of Spanish. Good institutes are opening up all the time and private teachers are a dime a dozen. Cultural centers also offer language classes; the **Centro Cultural Ricardo Rojas** (Map p66; ☑011-5285-4800; www.rojas. uba.ar; Av Corrientes 2038; Ⓢ Línea B Callao) has an especially good range of offerings, including Japanese, Portuguese, Italian, German and French.

Most private language institutes organize social activities, private classes and (usually) volunteer opportunities. Homestay programs are also available but often cost more than finding a place yourself. Check websites for fees and schedules.

Tango

Tango classes are available everywhere – your own hostel may offer them. Many inexpensive classes are available at *milongas* (dance halls), which can put you in touch with private teachers, some of whom speak English. Cultural centers and dance academies often have affordable classes as well.

★**DNI Tango** DANCING
(Map p76; ☎011-4866-6553; https://dni-tango.com; Bulnes 1101; group class per person AR$130; ⑤Línea B Medrano) This excellent tango school offers group and private classes in English and Spanish for all levels. For those starting out, the Saturday afternoon *práctica* is a friendly place to dance with different partners without the pressure of taking to the floor at a more formal *milonga*. DNI is located in a beautiful old building in the neighborhood of Almagro.

⟲ Tours

If you want to take a tour, plenty of creative choices exist. Tangol (p85) is a travel agency that brokers many kinds of city tours, while www.LandingPadBA.com has some interesting options as well.

Graffitimundo TOURS
(☎011-15-3683-3219; www.graffitimundo.com; tours US$20-35) Excellent tours of some of BA's best graffiti are offered by this nonprofit organization that supports the local urban art scene. Learn artists' history and the local graffiti culture. Several tours available; stencil workshops too.

BA Free Tour WALKING
(☎011-4420-5897; www.bafreetour.com; by donation; ☉11am & 3:30pm Mon-Sat) Free walking tours given by enthusiastic young guides who love their city. Donations recommended. But if you can't give anything, you're still welcome to join.

Biking Buenos Aires CYCLING
(Map p66; ☎011-4300-5373; www.bikingbuenosaires.com; Perú 988; ☉9am-6pm; ⑤Línea C Independencia) Friendly American and Argentine guides take you on tours of Buenos Aires; tour themes include graffiti and architecture.

Tango Trips DANCING
(☎011-5235-4923; www.tangotrips.com; tour for 1/2/3 people US$160/190/240) Private tours to *milongas* with experienced and passionate *tangueros* (tango dancers). The venues visited depend on which is the best place to go on any particular night. Start with a private tango lesson to gain confidence before hitting the salons; if you're not a dancer, just sit back and watch tango danced in its most authentic form.

Parrilla Tour FOOD & DRINK
(☎011-15-4048-5964; www.parrillatour.com; per person US$85; ☉Palermo tour noon Tue, Fri & Sat, San Telmo tour noon Mon & Wed) *Choripan* (a traditional sausage sandwich), empanadas and ice cream are all on the menu on this tour of your knowledgeable guide's favorite haunts. You'll finish at a local parrilla (grillhouse).

✿ Festivals & Events

The following are a few of Buenos Aires' biggest celebrations.

Arte BA ART
(www.arteba.org; ☉May) Popular event highlighting contemporary art, introducing exciting new young artists, and showing off top gallery works. Held at **La Rural** (Map p76; www.larural.com.ar; Av Sarmiento 2704; ⑤Línea D Plaza Italia).

Tango BA Festival y Mundial DANCE
(http://festivales.buenosaires.gob.ar; ☉mid-Aug) Masterful tango performances, movies, classes, workshops, conferences and competitions in venues all over Buenos Aires. The final of the *mundial* (tango world cup) is held at **Luna Park** (Map p66; ☎011-5278-5800; www.lunapark.com.ar; cnr Bouchard & Av Corrientes; ⑤Línea B Alem).

Vinos y Bodegas WINE
(www.expovinosybodegas.com.ar; admission AR$350; ☉Oct) A can't-miss event for wine aficionados, offering vintages from over 100 Argentine bodegas (wineries). The entrance fee includes your own glass to use for tastings. Usually held at La Rural.

Marathon SPORTS
(www.maratondebuenosaires.com; ☉Sep) More than 10,000 runners cover the 42km route that begins in Palermo and passes some of BA's most iconic sights, including the Obelisco, Plaza de Mayo, La Boca and Puerto Madero.

☐ Sleeping

Buenos Aires' *microcentro* is close to many sights and services, though it's busy and noisy during the day. San Telmo is about 15 minutes' walk south and good for those seeking a colonial atmosphere, cobbled streets, proximity to some tango venues and a blue-collar flavor around the edges. Palermo Viejo is northwest of the center and about a 10-minute taxi ride. It's a pretty area full of wonderful old buildings and dotted with the city's best ethnic restaurants, trendiest boutiques and liveliest bars.

Private rooms in some hostels don't always come with private bathroom, though they can cost more than rooms in a cheap hotel. All hostels listed here include kitchen access, light breakfast and free internet; most have free wi-fi and lockers (bring your own lock). The bigger ones offer more services and activities, and many take credit cards.

BA has some good budget hotel choices. Most offer a simple breakfast and cable TV; some take credit cards (which might incur a fee of up to 10% – ask beforehand). All listings also have internet and/or wi-fi available for guests.

City Center

★ Portal del Sur
HOSTEL $

(Map p66; 011-4342-8788; www.portaldelsurba. com.ar; Hipólito Yrigoyen 855; dm from US$12, s US$35, d with/without bathroom from US$45/40; @; Línea A Piedras) Located in a charming old building, this is one of the city's best hostels. Beautiful dorms and hotel-quality private rooms surround a central common area, which is rather dark but open. The highlight is the lovely rooftop deck with views and attached bar. A relaxed but sociable place with plenty of activities on offer including *asados* (barbecues) and tango classes.

Milhouse Youth Hostel
HOSTEL $

(Map p66; 011-4345-9604; www.milhousehostel. com; Hipólito Yrigoyen 959; dm/r from US$12/40; @; Línea A Av de Mayo) BA's premiere party hostel, this popular spot offers a plethora of activities and services. Dorms are good and private rooms can be very pleasant; most surround an appealing open patio. Common spaces include a bar-cafe with pool table on the ground floor, a TV lounge on the mezzanine and a rooftop terrace. A gorgeous annex building nearby offers similar services.

Hostel Estoril
HOSTEL $

(Map p66; 011-4382-9684; www.hostelestoril3. com; Av de Mayo 1385, 1st & 6th fl; dm/s/d from US$10/20/32; @; Línea A Sáenz Peña) This well-run hostel occupies two floors in a beautiful old building. It's stylish and clean, with pleasant, good-sized dorms and hotel-quality doubles. There's also a decent kitchen for guests, but the hostel's biggest draw has to be the awesome rooftop terrace overlooking the Palacio Barolo and Av de Mayo; the owners organize regular *asados* and yoga classes.

V & S Hostel Club
HOSTEL $

(Map p66; 011-4322-0994; www.hostelclub.com; Viamonte 887; dm/d from US$12/33; @; Línea C Lavalle) This attractive, central hostel is located in a pleasant older building. The common space, which is also the dining and lobby area, is good for socializing, and there's a kitchen for guests. The spacious dorms are carpeted and the private rooms are excellent; all have their own bathroom. A nice touch is the tiny outdoor patio in back.

Goya Hotel
HOTEL $

(Map p66; 011-4322-9269; www.goyahotel. com.ar; Suipacha 748; s US$55-65, d US$60-85; @; Línea C Lavalle) This family-run hotel is a good budget choice with 42 modern, comfortable and carpeted rooms. 'Classic' rooms are older and have open showers; 'superior' rooms are slicker and come with bathtubs. There's a pleasant breakfast room with patio; good breakfast too.

San Telmo

★ América del Sur
HOSTEL $

(Map p66; 011-4300-5525; www.americahostel. com.ar; Chacabuco 718; dm/d from US$15/60; @; Línea C Independencia) This gorgeous boutique-like hostel – the smartest of its kind in BA – was built especially to be a hostel. Beyond the reception is a fine bar area with a large wood-decked patio. Sparklingly clean dorms with four beds all have well-designed bathrooms, while private rooms are tastefully decorated and better than those at many midrange hotels. A wide range of services is on offer.

Circus Hostel & Hotel
HOSTEL $

(Map p66; 011-4300-4983; www.hostelcircus. com; Chacabuco 1020; dm/r from US$11/40; @; Línea C Independencia) From the flash lounge at the front right through to the wading pool surrounded by wooden deck in back, this hotel-hostel exudes hipness. Dorms and private rooms, all small and simple, have basic furniture and their own bathrooms. There's a pool table and slick TV area, but no kitchen.

Art Factory Hostel
HOSTEL $

(Map p66; 011-4343-1463; www.artfactoryba. com.ar; Piedras 545; dm/d from US$8/25; @; Línea E Belgrano) Friendly and art-themed, this fine hostel offers more private rooms than most – and all feature huge murals, painted and decorated by different artists. Even the hallways and water tanks have colorful cartoonish themes, and the 1850s rambling mansion adds some charm. There's a large rooftop terrace with hammocks, and separate bar-lounge area with pool table.

Patios de San Telmo   BOUTIQUE HOTEL **$$**
(Map p66; ☑ 011-4307-0480; http://patiosdesan
telmo.com.ar; Chacabuco 752; r US$90-110;
❄ @ ⊠ ☎; ⑤ Línea C Independencia) Located
in an 1860 former *conventillo* (tenement
house) is this pleasant boutique hotel with 30
spacious, elegant rooms surrounding several
patios. There's a lovely 'library' room decorat-
ed with artwork, a back patio with hanging
basket chairs and a tiny rooftop pool with
wood deck.

Mansión Vitraux   BOUTIQUE HOTEL **$$**
(Map p66; ☑ 011-4878-4292; www.mansion
vitraux.com; Carlos Calvo 369; r from US$110;
❄ @ ⊠ ☎; ⑤ Línea C Independencia) Almost too
slick for San Telmo, this glass-fronted boutique hotel offers 12 beautiful rooms, all in
different designs. All have either flat-screen
or projection TV, and bathrooms have a contemporary design. The breakfast buffet is in
the basement wine bar. There is also a large
Jacuzzi, a sauna, an indoor pool and a slick
rooftop terrace with a second pool.

🛏 Palermo

★ **Reina Madre Hostel**   HOSTEL **$**
(Map p76; ☑ 011-4962-5553; www.rmhostel.com;
Av Anchorena 1118; dm US$11-17, s/d US$35/37;
❄ @ ☎; ⑤ Línea D Pueyrredón) This wonderful
hostel is clean, safe and well run. It's in an
old building that has plenty of personality,
with high ceilings and original tiles, and
all rooms are comfortable (and have share
bathrooms). There's a cozy living room and
small kitchen, plus lots of dining tables, but
the highlight is the wooden-deck rooftop
with parrilla (barbecue). There's a pet cat on
the premises.

★ **Palermo Viejo B&B**   GUESTHOUSE **$**
(Map p76; ☑ 011-4773-6012; www.palermoviejo
bb.com; Niceto Vega 4629; s US$55, d US$60-75, tr
US$85; ❄ @ ☎; 🖵 140) This friendly B&B is
located in a remodeled *casa chorizo* dating
from 1901 that was once the clothes factory
of the owner's father. The six rooms all front
a leafy outdoor patio and are decorated with
local artwork; two have lofts. All come with
a fridge and a good breakfast. Call ahead.

★ **Chill House**   GUESTHOUSE **$**
(Map p76; ☑ 011-4861-6175; www.chillhouse.com.
ar; Agüero 781; s US$38-43, d US$43-60, tr US$53-
60; @ ☎; ⑤ Línea B Carlos Gardel) This relaxed
and friendly guesthouse is in a remodeled
old house with high ceilings and a rustic artsy style, and has 10 private rooms (number

6, with a balcony and air-con, is especially
nice). There's also an awesome rooftop terrace where *asados* take place, with DJs and
occasional live music.

Mansilla 3935 B&B   B&B **$**
(Map p76; ☑ 011-4833-3821; Mansilla 3935; s/d
US$25/40; ❄ @ ☎; ⑤ Línea D Scalabrini Ortiz)
Family-run B&B in a homey, darkish house,
offering great value. Each of the two sim-
ple rooms comes with its own bathroom.
Ceilings are high, and a few tiny patios add
charm.

Eco Pampa Hostel   HOSTEL **$**
(Map p76; ☑ 011-4831-2435; www.hostelpampa.
com.ar; Guatemala 4778; dm/d from US$15/50;
@ ☎; ⑤ Línea D Plaza Italia) 🌱 Buenos Aires'
first 'green' hostel is this casual spot sporting
vintage and recycled furniture, low-energy
light bulbs and a recycling system. The rooftop is home to a small veggie garden, compost
pile and solar panels. Dorms are a good size
and each of the eight private rooms comes
with bathroom and flat-screen TV (most have
air-con). Also has a kitchen.

★ **Le Petit Palais**   B&B **$$**
(Map p76; ☑ 011-4962-4834; www.lepetitpalais-
buenosaires.com; Gorriti 3574; s US$75-85, d US$85-
95; ❄ ☎; ⑤ Línea D Agüero) Small but charming,
this French-run B&B offers just five simple but
pleasant rooms, all with private bathrooms.
The highlight is the pretty little terrace on the
2nd floor, where possibly BA's best breakfast is
served in warm weather – fresh yogurt, jams
and breads (all homemade), along with eggs,
medialunas (croissants) and cereals. Friendly
cats on the premises.

Hotel Clasico   HOTEL **$$**
(Map p76; ☑ 011-4773-2353; www.hotelclasico.com;
Costa Rica 5480; r US$125-165; ❄ ☎; ⑤ Línea
D Palermo) Attractive hotel with 33 tasteful
'classic' rooms, some with tiny balconies but
all with wood floors, modern conveniences
and earthy color schemes; a local photographer was specially commissioned to take the
photos of BA that adorn the walls. Go for
the penthouse with terrace for something
special. Creative elevator with one glass wall
facing an artsy mural.

Infinito Hotel   BOUTIQUE HOTEL **$$**
(Map p76; ☑ 011-2070-2626; www.infinitohotel.
com; Arenales 3689; r/ste US$70/95; ❄ @ ☎;
⑤ Línea D Scalabrini Ortiz) Starting at its small
lobby cafe-reception, this hotel exudes a
certain hipness. Rooms are small but good,

with flat-screen TVs, fridges, wooden floors and a purple color scheme, and there's a Jacuzzi on the sunny rooftop terrace. An effort is made to be ecologically conscious, mostly by recycling. Located near the parks but still within walking distance of Palermo's nightlife.

✕ Eating

Buenos Aires is overflowing with excellent food, and you'll dine well at all budget levels. Typical restaurants serve a standard fare of *parrilla* (grilled meats), pasta, pizza and *minutas* (short orders), but for something different head to Palermo, home to a large number of ethnic eateries. Another food-oriented neighborhood is Puerto Madero, but most of the restaurants here cater to the business set and are consequently very fancy and relatively expensive, and lean more toward steaks than stir-fries.

Vegetarians rejoice: unlike in the rest of Argentina, there is a good range of meat-free restaurants in BA – you just have to know where to look: Palermo is a good place to start. Most nonvegetarian restaurants offer a few pasta dishes, salads and pizzas, but not much else is meat-free.

✕ City Center

★ Pizzería Güerrín   PIZZA $
(Map p66; ☎ 011-4371-8141; www.facebook.com/pizzeriaguerrin; Av Corrientes 1368; pizza slices AR$35-45; ⊙ 11am-1am; ⑤ Línea B Uruguay) This much-loved pizza joint on Av Corrientes has been feeding the masses since 1932. For a quick pit stop (and the cheapest prices), order a slice of thick, doughy *muzzarella* at the counter and eat standing up at the benches with the rest of the crowd. Add a portion of *fainá* (chickpea-based flatbread) and wash it down with Moscato and soda.

Chan Chan   PERUVIAN $
(Map p66; ☎ 011-4382-8492; www.facebook.com/chanchanbsas; Hipólito Yrigoyen 1390; mains AR$100-710; ⊙ noon-4pm & 8pm-midnight; ⑤ Línea A Sáenz Peña) Thanks to fair prices and quick service, this colorful Peruvian eatery is usually packed with office workers devouring plates of ceviche (seafood cured in citrus) and *ajiaco de conejo* (rabbit and potato stew). There are also *arroz chaufa* (Peruvian-style fried rice) dishes, easily washed down with a tangy *pisco* sour or a pitcher of *chicha morada* (a sweet fruity drink).

Latino Sandwich   SANDWICHES $
(Map p66; ☎ 011-4331-0859; www.latinosandwich.com; Tacuari 185; sandwiches AR$85-120; ⊙ 8am-5pm Mon-Fri; ⑤ Línea A Piedras) Some of the best eateries in BA are holes-in-the-wall – and here's a case in point. This is the downtown place to grab sandwiches such as Argentine *milanesa* (breaded cutlet but with rocket and guacamole!), barbecue pork with cheddar cheese, or grilled zucchini and eggplant. There's only one communal table, as they cater to a mostly to-go business clientele.

180 Burger Bar   BURGERS $
(Map p66; ☎ 011-4328-7189; www.facebook.com/180burgerbar; Suipacha 749; burgers AR$130-160; ⊙ noon-4pm Mon-Fri; ⑤ Línea C Lavalle) Hankering for a hamburger? Then join the young crowd that will likely be lined up at this small diner. Choose a 'salsa' (mayochimi, tzatziki, barbacoa) and add cheese if you wish. Chow down within the confines of concrete walls, clunky furniture and blasting music.

Parrilla Peña   PARRILLA $$
(Map p66; ☎ 011-4371-5643; www.parrillapenia.url.ph; Rodríguez Peña 682; mains AR$250-520; ⊙ noon-4pm & 8pm-midnight Mon-Sat; ⑤ Línea D Callao) This simple, traditional, long-running *parrilla* is well-known for its excellent quality meats and generous portions. The service is fast and efficient and it's great value. Also on offer are homemade pastas, salads and *milanesas,* along with several tasty desserts and a good wine list.

✕ San Telmo

★ El Banco Rojo   INTERNATIONAL $
(Map p66; ☎ 011-4040-2411; www.elbancorojo.wordpress.com; Bolívar 866; mains AR$115-150; ⊙ noon-12:30am Tue-Sat, to 11:30pm Sun; ⑤ Línea C Independencia) A San Telmo youth magnet, this trendy joint serves up sandwiches, falafels, burgers and tacos, as well as a range of beers and spirits. Try the *empanada de cordero* (lamb turnover) if they have it. This place, Banco Rojo's new digs (one block over from the old one), has more space to eat in but the same grungy vibe.

Bar El Federal   ARGENTINE $
(Map p66; ☎ 011-4361-7328; Carlos Calvo 599; mains AR$185-420; ⊙ 8am-2am Sun-Thu, to 4am Fri & Sat; ⑧; ⑤ Línea C Independencia) Dating from 1864, this historical bar is a classic,

Palermo

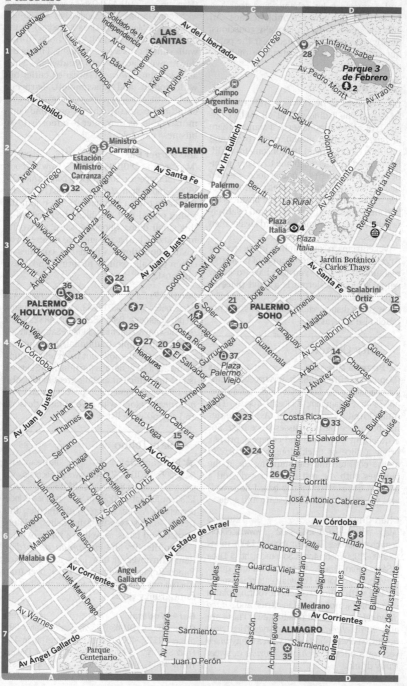

Palermo

with original wooden features, black-and-white floor tiles, and an eye-catching antique bar and cash register. The specialties here are sandwiches (especially turkey) and

DON'T MISS

DREAMY ICE CREAM

Cadore (Map p66; ☎011-4374-3688; http://heladeriacadore.com.ar; Av Corrientes 1695; ice cream from AR$100; ⏱11:30am-1am Mon-Thu, to 3am Fri-Sun; Ⓢ Línea B Callao), one of BA's classic *heladerías* (ice-cream parlors), was founded by the Italian Olivotti family in 1957 and gets busy with the post-theater crowds late into the night. Try the *dulce de leche* (milk caramel), made using a process that involves boiling sweetened milk for 14 to 16 hours.

picadas (shared appetizer plates), but there are also lots of pastas, salads, desserts and tall mugs of icy beer.

El Refuerzo Provisiones ARGENTINE $$
(Map p66; ☎011-4300-0023; www.facebook.com/refuerzoprovisiones; Estados Unidos 758; mains AR$250-450; ⏱6pm-2am Mon-Sat; Ⓢ Línea C Independencia) Grocery store–style restaurant serving wholesome pastas, casseroles, salads, cured meats and cheeses. Its sister restaurant, **El Refuerzo Bar Almacen** (Map p66; ☎011-4361-3013; www.facebook.com/elrefuerzobaralmacen; Chacabuco 872; mains AR$230-450; ⏱10am-2am Tue-Sun; Ⓢ Línea C Independencia), is just around the corner.

El Desnivel PARRILLA $$
(Map p66; ☎011-4300-9081; Defensa 855; mains AR$200-430; ⏱noon-1am Tue-Sun, 7pm-1am Mon; Ⓢ Línea C Independencia) This long-running, low-key *parrilla* joint packs in both locals and tourists, serving them treats such as *chorizo* (sausage) sandwiches and *bife de lomo* (tenderloin steak). The delicious smells from the sizzling grill out front are torturous as you wait for a table – get here early, especially on weekends.

🍴 Recoleta

⭐**El Sanjuanino** ARGENTINE $
(Map p66; ☎011-4805-2683; www.elsanjuanino.com.ar; Posadas 1515; empanadas AR$35; ⏱noon-4pm & 7pm-1am; 🚌130, 93, 124) El Sanjuanino is a long-running, cozy little joint that has some of the cheapest food in Recoleta. It attracts both penny-pinching locals and thrifty tourists. Order spicy empanadas, tamales or *locro* (a spicy stew of maize, beans, beef, pork and sausage).

Cumaná ARGENTINE $
(Map p66; ☎011-4813-9207; Rodríguez Peña 1149; mains AR$120-250; ⏱noon-1am; Ⓢ Línea D Callao) To sample Argentina's regional cuisine, check out this colorful, budget-friendly eatery with huge picture windows and an old-fashioned adobe oven. Cumaná specializes in delicious *cazuelas* – stick-to-your-ribs stews filled with squash, corn, eggplant, potatoes and meat. Also popular are the empanadas, *locro* and *humita* (stuffed corn dough, resembling Mexican tamales).

Rodi Bar ARGENTINE $$
(Map p66; ☎011-4801-5230; Vicente López 1900; mains AR$200-450; ⏱8am-1am Mon-Sat; 📶; Ⓢ Línea H Las Heras) A great option for well-priced, unpretentious food in upscale Recoleta. This traditional neighborhood restaurant with a fine old-world atmosphere and extensive menu offers something for everyone, from inexpensive combo plates to relatively unusual dishes such as marinated beef tongue.

🍴 Palermo

⭐**NoLa** CAJUN $
(Map p76; www.nolabuenosaires.com; Gorriti 4389; mains AR$140-160; ⏱12:30pm-midnight Sun-Thu, to 1am Fri & Sat; 🚌140, 141, 110) The brainchild of American Lisa Puglia is this small, popular place serving New Orleans Cajun cuisine. Everything is homemade, from the fried chicken sandwich to the *chorizo* gumbo and the spicy, vegetarian red beans and rice. The jalapeño cornbread and bourbon-coffee pecan pie are the bomb, as is the microbrewed beer. Happy hour until 8pm.

Sarkis MIDDLE EASTERN $
(Map p76; ☎011-4772-4911; Thames 1101; mains AR$120-290; ⏱noon-3pm & 8pm-1am; 🚌140, 111, 34) The food is fabulous and well priced at this long-standing Middle Eastern restaurant – come with a group to sample many exotic dishes. Start with the roasted eggplant hummus and *boquerones* (marinated sardines), then follow up with kebabs or lamb in yogurt sauce. Less busy at lunchtime; there's usually a wait for a table at dinner.

Chori ARGENTINE $
(Map p76; ☎011-3966-9857; www.facebook.com/Xchorix; Thames 1653; choripán AR$110-140; ⏱12:30pm-12:30am; 📶; 🚌55, 39) Elevating the humble Argentine *chori* (sausage) to new heights is this hip joint, its bright yellow walls decorated with smiling cartoon sausages.

The quality, 100% pork *choris* and *morcillas* (blood sausages) hang on display – choose from a range of gourmet toppings and home-made breads for a *choripán* sandwich.

Fukuro Noodle Bar   JAPANESE $
(Map p76; ☑011-4773-6810; www.fukuronoodle bar.com; Costa Rica 5514; noodles AR$260; ⊗8pm-midnight Tue-Thu, to 1am Fri & Sat; ⑤Línea D Palermo) For a change from all that meat, check out this comfort-food eatery. Four kinds of ramen are on offer, along with a good selection of *bao* (steamed buns) and *gyoza* (dumplings). Gluten-free noodles available, plus sake and microbrew draft beer. Counter seating only.

Burger Joint   BURGERS $
(Map p76; ☑011-4833-5151; www.facebook.com/ burgerjointpalermo; Jorge Luis Borges 1766; burg-ers AR$140; ⊗noon-midnight Sun-Thu, to 1am Fri & Sat; ⑤Línea D Plaza Italia) For some of the juiciest burgers in BA, head to this popular, graffiti-covered spot. NYC-trained chef Pierre Chacra offers just four kinds to choose from, but they're all stellar. Try the Mexican (jala-peños, guacamole and hot sauce) or Jamai-can (pineapple, cheddar and bacon) with a side of hand-cut fries.

El Preferido de Palermo   ARGENTINE $$
(Map p76; ☑011-4774-6585; Jorge Luis Borges 2108; mains AR$220-450; ⊗9am-11:30pm Mon-Sat; ⑤Línea D Plaza Italia) You can't get much more traditional than this atmospheric, family-run joint. Order tapas, meat platters, homemade pastas and seafood soups, or try one of its specialties – the tortillas, *milane-sas* and Cuban rice with veal and polenta. Hanging hams, jars of olives and high tables with blocky wood stools add to the charm.

Gran Dabbang   FUSION $$
(Map p76; ☑011-4832-1186; www.facebook.com/ grandabbang; Av Scalabrini Ortiz 1543; small plates AR$60-350; ⊗8pm-midnight Mon-Sat; ☐141, 15, 160) The rule-breaking, experimental fusion food conjured up by Mariano Ramón, one of the rising stars of the BA food scene, can be sampled in the small, packed dining room of this unassuming restaurant. Choose three small plates to share between two and get ready for a wild-eyed blend of Indian, Thai and Paraguayan flavors (among others), drawn from Ramón's travels.

Buenos Aires Verde   VEGETARIAN $$
(Map p76; ☑011-4775-9594; www.bsasverde.com; Gorriti 5657; mains AR$275-300; ⊗9am-midnight

Mon-Sat; ☑; ☐111, 140, 39) Long-running or-ganic, vegetarian restaurant serving wraps, salads, soups and sandwiches. Wash them down with a wheatgrass juice or fruit smoothie. Small grocery too.

Big Sur   BURGERS $$
(Map p76; ☑011-4806-7264; www.facebook.com/ BigSurBA; Av Cerviño 3596; mains AR$190-265; ⊗5pm-midnight Mon, noon-midnight Tue-Sun; ⑤Línea D Scalabrini Ortiz) This casual, industrial-style joint serves great hamburgers, fried chicken, hot dogs and fries in baskets, plus quality craft beer.

🍷 Drinking & Nightlife

Buenos Aires' nightlife is legendary. What else could you expect from a country where dinner rarely starts before 10pm? In some neighborhoods, finding a good sports bar, classy cocktail lounge, atmospheric old cafe or upscale wine bar is as easy as walking down the street. And dancers will be in heaven, as BA boasts spectacular nightclubs showcasing top-drawer DJs.

🍷 City Center

Café Tortoni   CAFE
(Map p66; ☑011-4342-4328; www.cafetortoni.com. ar; Av de Mayo 829; ⑤Línea A Piedras) BA's oldest and most famous cafe, Tortoni has become so popular with foreigners that the busloads of tourists detract from its charm. Still, it's practically an obligatory stop for any visitor to town: order a couple of *churros* (fried pas-try dough) with your hot chocolate and for-get about the inflated prices. There are also nightly tango shows – reserve ahead.

Milión   COCKTAIL BAR
(Map p66; ☑011-4815-9925; www.milion.com.ar; Paraná 1048; ⊗noon-2am Mon-Wed, to 3am Thu, to 4am Fri & Sat, 8pm-2am Sun; ⑤Línea D Callao) One of BA's most elegant bars, this sexy spot takes up three floors of a renovated old man-sion. The garden out back is a leafy paradise, overlooked by a solid balcony that holds the best seats in the house. Nearby marble steps are also an appealing place to lounge with a frozen mojito or basil daiquiri.

La Cigale   BAR
(Map p66; ☑011-4893-2332; www.facebook.com/ lacigalebar; 25 de Mayo 597; ⊗noon-3pm & 6pm-3am Mon-Fri, 9:30pm-3am Sat; ⑤Línea B Alem) This upstairs bar-restaurant is popular with office workers during the week, and fusion foods are served for both lunch and dinner.

Come on the second Monday of the month for the Buenos Aires Pub Quiz (www.buenos airespubquiz.com). Happy hour is from 6pm to 10pm.

Bahrein
CLUB

(Map p66; ☑ 011-4314-8886; www.bahreinba.com; Lavalle 345; ⊙ 11pm-7am Fri & Sat; ⑤ Línea B Alem) Attracting a good share of BA's tattooed youth, Bahrein is a hugely popular downtown club housed in an old bank (check out the 'vault' in the basement). On the ground floor is the lounge-like Funky Room where resident DJs spin house music and electronica. Downstairs is the Xss discotheque, an impressive sound system and a dance floor for hundreds.

 ## San Telmo

★ Bar Plaza Dorrego
CAFE

(Map p66; ☑ 011-4361-0141; Defensa 1098; ⊙ 8am-midnight Sun-Thu, to 3:30am Fri & Sat; ☐ 29, 24, 33) You can't beat the atmosphere at this traditional joint; sip your *submarino* (hot milk with chocolate) by a picturesque window and watch the world pass by, or grab an outdoor table next to the busy plaza. Meanwhile, traditionally suited waiters, piped-in tango music, antique bottles and scribbled graffiti on the walls and counters might take you back in time.

Doppelgänger
COCKTAIL BAR

(Map p64; ☑ 011-4300-0201; www.doppelganger. com.ar; Av Juan de Garay 500; ⊙ 7pm-2am Tue-Thu, to 4am Fri, 8pm-4am Sat; ☐ 29, 24) At this cool, emerald-hued corner bar you can count on being served a perfectly mixed martini. That's because Doppelgänger specializes in vermouth cocktails. The lengthy menu is full of creative concoctions: start with the journalist (a martini with a bitter orange twist) or go for the bar's best seller – an old fashioned.

Coffee Town
COFFEE

(Map p66; ☑ 011-4361-0019; http://coffeetown company.com; Bolívar 976, Mercado de San Telmo; ⊙ 8am-8:30pm; ⑤ Línea C Independencia) For some of BA's best coffee, drop by this coffee shop inside the Mercado de San Telmo (p69) – enter via Carlos Calvo. Experienced baristas serve up organic, fair-trade coffee derived from beans from all over the world – Colombia, Kenya, Sumatra and Yemen. A few pastries help the java go down.

La Puerta Roja
BAR

(Map p66; ☑ 011-4362-5649; http://lapuertaroja. com.ar; Chacabuco 733; ⊙ noon-5:30am; ⑤ Línea

C Independencia) There's no sign at this upstairs bar – just look for the red door. It has a cool, relaxed atmosphere with low lounge furniture in the main room and a pool table tucked behind. This is a traditional place, so you won't find fruity cocktails on the menu, but there is good international food including curries, tacos and chicken wings.

On Tap
CRAFT BEER

(Map p64; www.ontap.com.ar; Av Caseros 482; ⊙ 5pm-12:30am Sun, Tue & Wed, to 1:30am Thu, to 2am Fri & Sat; ☐ 29) Sample some of the 20 locally brewed craft beers at the San Telmo branch of On Tap.

Recoleta

Buller Brewing Company
MICROBREWERY

(Map p66; ☑ 011-4806-0556; www.bullerpub.com; Junín 1747; ⊙ noon-1am Mon-Wed, to 2am Thu & Sun, to 4am Fri & Sat; 🐾; ⑤ Línea H Las Heras) Six kinds of beer are brewed on the premises at this industrial-style microbrewery incongruously located opposite Recoleta Cemetery. If you can't choose between the stout, IPA, Hefeweizen, rubia, honey beer or amber, order a sampler of all six. There's a great outdoor patio in front and an extensive menu of snacks and sandwiches.

La Biela
CAFE

(Map p66; ☑ 011-4804-0449; www.labiela.com; Av Quintana 600; ⊙ 7am-2am Mon-Thu, to 3am Fri & Sat, 8am-2am Sun; ☐ 130, 62, 93) A Recoleta institution, this classic cafe has been serving the *porteño* elite since the 1950s – when racecar champions used to frequent the place. The outdoor front terrace is unbeatable for a coffee or beer on a sunny afternoon. Just know that the privilege of seating here will cost 20% more.

Palermo

★ LAB Training Center & Coffee Shop
CAFE

(Map p76; ☑ 011-4843-1790; www.labcafe.com.ar; Humboldt 1542; ⊙ 8am-8pm Mon-Fri, from 10am Sat; ☐ 111, 140, 39) The high ceilings, exposed brick wall and industrial aesthetic here are such hallmarks of a hipster cafe that the place borders on self-parody, but the coffee *is* excellent. Choose your house-roasted beans and have them run through a Chemex, Aero-Press, V60, Kalita, syphon or Clever Dripper. Mostly counter seating.

★ **Verne** COCKTAIL BAR
(Map p76; ☎ 011-4822-0980; http://vernecocktail club.com; Av Medrano 1475; ☺ 9pm-2am Sun-Tue, 8pm-2am Wed, 8pm-3am Thu, 8pm-4am Fri, 9pm-4am Sat; 🚇 160, 15) This upscale yet casual bar has a vague Jules Verne theme. Cocktails are the house specialty, whipped up by one of BA's best bartenders, Fede Cuco. A few tables, some cushy sofas and an airy outdoor patio offer a variety of seating options, but plant yourself at the bar to watch the mixologists work their magic.

★ **Uptown** BAR
(Map p76; ☎ 011-2101-4897; www.uptownba.com; Arévalo 2030; ☺ 8:30pm-2am Tue & Wed, to 3am Thu-Sat; Ⓢ Línea D Ministro Carranza) Descend the graffiti-strewn stairwell and step aboard the carriage of an actual New York subway train to reach BA's hottest bar, a cavernous underground space with DJs and dancing, and a smaller, cozier room styled as a pharmacy. It's a popular place; call ahead to put your name on the guest list.

★ **Niceto Club** CLUB
(Map p76; ☎ 011-4779-9396; www.nicetoclub.com; Niceto Vega 5510; ☺ Tue-Sat; 🚇 111, 140, 34) One of the city's biggest crowd-pullers, the can't-miss event at Niceto Club is Thursday night's Club 69, a subversive DJ extravaganza featuring gorgeously attired showgirls, dancing drag queens, futuristic video installations and off-the-wall performance art. On weekend nights, national and international spin masters take the booth to entertain lively crowds with blends of hip-hop, electronic beats, cumbia and reggae.

Benaim BAR
(Map p76; www.facebook.com/benaimBA; Gorriti 4015; ☺ 6pm-12:30am Mon-Thu, to 3am Fri, noon-3am Sat, noon-12:30am Sun; 🚇 140, 39, 99) Order a pint of IPA or golden ale from the caravan bar and drink it under the fairy lights and hanging plants in Benaim's attractive beer garden. There's also a kitchen serving good-value Jewish street food, such as hummus and falafel, kebabs and pastrami. Happy hour is from 6pm to 8pm.

Crobar CLUB
(Map p76; ☎ 011-4778-1500; www.crobar.com.ar; cnr Av de la Infanta Isabel & Freyre; ☺ 11:30pm-7am Fri & Sat; 🚇 10, 33, 111) Stylish and spacious Crobar remains one of BA's most popular clubs. On Friday international DJs mash up the latest techno selections, while on Saturday there's trance at Pixel in the main room,

as well as the gay party Rheo. Bring a full wallet – this is a top-end spot.

Kika CLUB
(Map p76; www.kikaclub.com.ar; Honduras 5339; ☺ 1am-late Tue-Sun; 🚇 111, 34, 140) Being so well located near the heart of Palermo's bar scene makes Kika's popular Tuesday-night 'Hype' easily accessible for those up for a party. It's a mix of electro, rock, hip-hop, drum and bass, and dubstep, all spun by both local and international DJs. Other nights see electronica, reggaeton, Latin beats and live bands ruling the roost.

Boticario COCKTAIL BAR
(Map p76; www.boticariobar.com; Honduras 5207; ☺ 8pm-3am Tue & Wed, 9pm-4am Thu-Sat; 🚇 55, 34) With walls draped in leafy vines and wooden shelves lined with glass bottles and jars, Boticario takes its inspiration from an old-time apothecary. The mixologists work their magic to create cocktails with botanical touches, like lemongrass and fresh mint. DJs spin the tunes at weekends.

☆ **Entertainment**

Buenos Aires never sleeps, so you'll find something to do every night of the week. There are continuous theater and musical performances, and tango shows are everywhere.

Every modern shopping center has its multiscreen cinema complex; most movies are shown in their original language, with subtitles.

Discount ticket vendors (selling tickets for select theater, tango and movie performances) include **Cartelera Vea Más** (☎ 011-6320-5319; Av Corrientes 1660, Local 2; ☺ 10am-7pm Mon-Wed, to 11pm Thu & Fri, noon-midnight Sat, 1-9pm Sun; Ⓢ Línea B Callao), **Cartelera Baires** (☎ 011-4372-5058; Av Corrientes 1382, Galería Apolo; ☺ 12:30-8pm Mon-Thu, 1:15-8:30pm Fri & Sat; Ⓢ Línea B Uruguay) and **Cartelera Espectáculos** (☎ 011-4322-1559; www.123info.com.ar; Lavalle 742; ☺ noon-9pm Mon-Sat, to 8pm Sun; Ⓢ Línea C Lavalle).

Ticketek (☎ 011-5237-7200; www.ticketek.com.ar; Av Santa Fe 4389; ☺ 8-8pm Mon-Sat, 1-8pm Sun; Ⓢ Línea D Plaza Italia) has outlets throughout the city and sells tickets for large venues.

Tango Shows

Most travelers will want to take in a tango show in BA, but it's a bit futile to look for 'nontouristy' shows – tango is a participatory dance and so shows are geared toward voyeurs. Less expensive shows tend to be more traditional. *Milongas* are where dancers strut their stuff, but spectators don't really belong there (though some *milonga* venues put on occasional spectator shows).

There are many dinner-tango shows oriented to tourists with cash to spend. Some have a Las Vegas–like feel and often involve costume changes, dry ice and plenty of high kicks. The physical dancing feats can be spectacular. Reserve ahead.

There are 'free' (donation) street tango shows on Sunday at San Telmo's antiques fair and on El Caminito in La Boca, and sometimes on Calle Florida near Lavalle.

★ Centro Cultural Borges   TANGO
(Map p66; ☑ 011-5555-5359; www.ccborges.org.ar; cnr Viamonte & San Martín; shows from AR$470; ⑤ Línea C Lavalle) This excellent cultural center has many quality offerings, including reasonably priced tango shows several times per week. Bien de Tango, on Friday and Saturday nights at 8pm, is especially good and comparable to other tango shows that are triple the cost. Check the cultural center website or stop in beforehand to see what's on and get an advance ticket.

★ La Catedral   MILONGA
(Map p76; ☑ 011-15-5325-1630; www.lacatedralclub.com; Sarmiento 4006; ⑤ Línea B Medrano) This grungy warehouse space is very casual, with unusual art on the walls, thrift-store furniture, dim, atmospheric lighting and the occasional cat wandering among the tables. It's very bohemian and there's no implied dress code – you'll see plenty of jeans. A great place for beginners since even non-expert dancers can feel comfortable on the dance floor.

Maldita Milonga   TANGO
(Map p66; ☑ 011-15-2189-7747; www.facebook.com/malditamilonga1; Perú 571, Buenos Ayres Club; ⊙ class 9pm, milonga 10:30pm Wed; ⑤ Línea E Belgrano) Maldita Milonga, held on Wednesday at Buenos Ayres Club, is a well-run and popular event, and one of the best places to see tango being danced by real couples. The highlight of the night is when the dynamic orchestra El Afronte plays at 11pm; at midnight there's a professional dance demonstration.

Tango Queer   TANGO
(Map p66; ☑ 011-15-3252-6894; www.tangoqueer.com; Perú 571, Buenos Ayres Club; ⊙ class 8:30pm, milonga 10pm-2am Tue; ⑤ Línea E Belgrano) On Tuesday night at Buenos Ayres Club, anyone can dance with anyone, leading or following as they choose, at this excellent gay tango class and *milonga*.

Live Music
Some bars have live music, too.

★ La Bomba de Tiempo   LIVE MUSIC
(Map p76; www.labombadetiempo.com; Sarmiento 3131, Ciudad Cultural Konex; AR$90; ⊙ 7-10pm Mon; ⑤ Línea B Carlos Gardel) One of BA's most unusual events takes place every Monday when the long-running percussion group La Bomba de Tiempo plays at Ciudad Cultural Konex (Map p76; ☑ 011-4864-3200; www.ciudadculturalkonex.org; Av Sarmiento 3131; ⑤ Línea B Carlos Gardel). You'll find it impossible not to dance to the rhythms when the drummers get into their stride.

Centro Cultural Torquato Tasso   LIVE MUSIC
(Map p64; ☑ 011-4307-6506; www.torquatotasso.com.ar; Defensa 1575; ☐ 29, 168, 24) One of BA's best-loved live-music venues, with top-name tango music performances – keep an eye out for Rodolfo Mederos and La Chicana. Attracts bands that mix genres, such as fusing tango or *folklórico* with rock.

Usina del Arte   CONCERT VENUE
(Map p64; www.buenosaires.gob.ar/usinadelarte; Agustín R Caffarena 1; ☐ 130, 86, 8) FREE This former power station has been transformed into a spectacular concert venue in an effort to regenerate a somewhat sketchy area of La Boca. It's a gorgeous red-brick building complete with scenic clock tower, and the two concert halls have top-notch acoustics. Nearly all the art exhibitions, concerts and dance performances here are free; check the website for upcoming events.

Spectator Sports
If you're lucky enough to witness a *fútbol* match, you'll encounter a passion unrivaled in any other sport. The most popular teams are **Boca Juniors** (Map p64; ☑ 011-5777-1200; www.bocajuniors.com.ar; Brandsen 805; ☐ 29, 53, 152) in La Boca and **River Plate** (Estadio Monumental; Map p64; ☑ 011-4789-1200; www.cariverplate.com; Alcorta 7597; museum admission AR$225-300; ⊙ museum 10am-7pm; ☐ 42, 29) in Belgrano, northwest of Aeroparque Jorge Newberry. The season runs from late August to late May.

Ticket prices ultimately depend on the teams playing and the demand. In general, however, *entradas populares* (bleachers) are the cheapest seats and attract the more emotional fans of the game; don't show any signs of wealth in this section, including watches, necklaces or fancy cameras. *Plateas* (fixed seats) are a safer bet. There are also tour companies such as Tangol (p85) that take you to games.

Polo in Buenos Aires is most popular from October to December, and games take place at Campo de Polo in Palermo. Rugby, horse racing and *pato* (a traditional Argentine game played on horseback) are some other spectator possibilities.

🛍 Shopping

Buenos Aires has its share of modern shopping malls, along with flashy store-lined streets like Calle Florida and Av Santa Fe. You'll find decent-quality clothes, shoes, leather, accessories, electronics, music and homewares, but anything imported (like electronics) will be very expensive.

Palermo Viejo is the best neighborhood for boutiques and creative fashions. Avenida Alvear, toward the Recoleta cemetery, means designer labels. Defensa in San Telmo is full of pricey antique shops. There are several weekend crafts markets, such as the hip *feria artesanal* in front of Recoleta's cemetery. The famous San Telmo antiques fair takes place on Sunday. Leather jackets and bags are sold in stores on Calle Murillo (599-600 blocks) in the neighborhood of Villa Crespo. For cheap imports, head to Av Pueyrredón near Estación Once (Once train station); you can find just about anything there.

★ Elementos Argentinos   HOMEWARES
(Map p76; ☑ 011-4832-6299; www.elementos argentinos.com.ar; Gurruchaga 1881; ⊙ 11am-7pm Tue-Sat; ⓢ Línea D Plaza Italia) 🥾 The high-quality carpets, rugs and blankets sold here are hand-dyed, hand-woven on a loom and fair trade; the owners work with cooperatives and NGOs to help the communities in northwestern Argentina where the textiles are produced. Larger items can be shipped home, or pick up a super-soft llama wool blanket to squeeze into your suitcase.

★ Autoría   ARTS & CRAFTS
(Map p66; ☑ 011-5252-2474; www.autoriabsas.com. ar; Suipacha 1025; ⊙ 9:30am-8pm Mon-Fri, 10am-6pm Sat; ⓢ Línea C San Martín) This gallery-like store, stocked with edgy art books, fashion, accessories, whimsical leather desk sculptures, original artworks and unique handmade jewelry, strives to promote Argentine designers. Especially interesting are the recycled materials – check out the bags made

of Tyvek, inner tubes, fire hoses or even old sails. Products are of high quality and prices are accessible.

★ El Ateneo Grand Splendid   BOOKS
(Map p66; ☑ 011-4813-6052; www.yenny-elateneo. com/local/grand-splendid; Av Santa Fe 1860; ⊙ 9am-10pm Mon-Thu, to midnight Fri & Sat, noon-10pm Sun; ⓢ Línea D Callao) This glorious bookstore in a converted theater continues to flourish in the age of the Kindle. The Grand Splendid theater opened in 1919 and was converted into a bookstore in 2000. Most of the seating was replaced with bookshelves, but the original features have been preserved, including the beautiful painted cupola and balconies.

Bosque   ARTS & CRAFTS
(Map p76; ☑ 011-4516-3052; https://bosque2. mitiendanube.com; Gorriti 5697; ⊙ 11am-8pm Mon-Fri, noon-8pm Sat; ⓢ Línea D Ministro Carranza) A charming range of arts and crafts with a botanical bent are sold in this tiny boutique. The woodland theme is evident in the forest scenes of the limited-edition illustrations, hand-painted decorative plates, ceramics and cushions, as well as geometric wooden lamps and decorative objects, all by independent local designers.

ℹ Information

DANGERS & ANNOYANCES
Buenos Aires is generally pretty safe and you can comfortably walk around at all hours of the night in many places, even as a solo woman. Some areas where you should be careful at night, however, are around Constitución's train station, the eastern border of San Telmo, some parts of Once and La Boca – where, outside tourist streets, you should be careful even during the day. Using your head is good advice anywhere: don't flash any wealth (including expensive jewelry), always be aware of your surroundings and look like you know exactly where you're going (even if you don't).

IMMIGRATION OFFICES
Immigration (☑ 011-4317-0234; www.mig raciones.gov.ar; Av Antártida Argentina 1355; ⊙ 8am-2pm Mon-Fri; ◻ 92, 106) Issues extensions to the 90-day tourist entry period.

INTERNET ACCESS
Wi-fi is available at nearly all hotels, hostels, restaurants, cafes and bars, and is generally fast and free.

Locutorios (telephone offices) with internet access are common; you can often find one by just walking a few blocks in any direction. Rates are cheap and connections are quick.

GETTING INTO TOWN

If you fly into Buenos Aires from outside Argentina, you'll probably land at Ezeiza Airport, about a 40-minute ride from downtown. Travelers from the US, Canada and Australia no longer have to pay a reciprocity fee to enter Argentina.

One way into town is the frequent, comfortable shuttle service by **Manuel Tienda León** (MTL; Map p66; ☎ 011-4315-5115; www.tiendaleon.com; Av Eduardo Madero 1299; ⓢ Línea C Retiro; AR$310); its booth is just outside customs. Another option is **Hostel Shuttle** (☎ 011-4511-8723; www.hostelshuttle.com.ar; US$13).

To catch a taxi, go past the transportation 'lobby' area immediately outside customs, walk past the taxi touts, and you'll see the freestanding city taxi stand with a blue sign saying **Taxi Ezeiza** (☎ 011-5480-0066; www.taxiezeiza.com.ar; from Ezeiza to Center AR$780; ⊙ 24hr).

Penny-pinchers can take public bus 8 (AR$8, two hours). Catch it outside Terminal B, or outside Terminal A (turn to the right and walk a couple minutes to the bus stop across from the Petrobras gas station). You'll need a SUBE card to pay for the bus; buy one at the *kiosko* across from check-in stand 25 (the sign says 'open 25 hours!').

Avoid the *cambios* (exchange houses) as their rates are generally bad. Instead, head to the nearby Banco de la Nación, which has fair rates and is open 24 hours. There are several ATMs in Ezeiza.

Most domestic flights land at **Aeroparque Jorge Newbery** (Map p64; ☎ 011-5480-6111; www.aa2000.com.ar; Av Rafael Obligado; ⊟ 33, 45), only a few kilometers north of the city center. Manuel Tienda León shuttles to the city center take 15 minutes and cost AR$60. Bus 45 also goes to the center; take it going south (to the right as you leave the airport). Taxis to downtown cost about AR$160.

Shuttle transfers from Ezeiza to Aeroparque cost AR$155.

Retiro bus station is about 1km north of the city center. You can take the Subte if your destination is near a stop, or head to one of the *remise* (a type of taxi) booths near the bus slots.

MONEY

Banks and *cambios* (exchange houses) are the safest places to change money, and US dollars are the best foreign currency to exchange. In December 2015 currency controls were abolished, decreasing demand for US dollars on Argentina's 'blue' (ie black) market, but you'll still hear people on pedestrian Av Florida call out '*cambio, cambio, cambio.*' These folks are best avoided.

Most transactions require ID, and lines can be long at banks. *Cambios* have slightly poorer exchange rates, but are quicker and have fewer limitations. You can get a pretty fair rate for US dollars at many retail establishments.

ATMs are commonplace, though there are withdrawal limits that depend on your banking system. Visa and MasterCard holders can get cash advances, but check with your bank before traveling.

POST

The more-or-less reliable **Correo Argentino** (www.correoargentino.com.ar) is the government postal service, with numerous branches scattered throughout BA. Essential overseas mail should be sent *certificado* (registered). For international parcels weighing over 2kg, take a copy of your passport and go to the **Correo Internacional** (Map p66; ☎ 011-4891-9191; www.correoargentino.com.ar; Av Antártida Argentina 1100; ⊙ 9am-4pm Mon-Fri; ⓢ Línea C Retiro) near the Retiro bus station. Check the website for prices.

Privately run international and national services are available including **Fedex** (Map p66; ☎ 0810-333-3339; www.fedex.com; Av Corrientes 654; ⊙ 9am-6pm Mon-Fri; ⓢ Línea B Florida) and **DHL** (Map p66; ☎ 0810-122-3345; www.dhl.com.ar; Av Córdoba 783; ⊙ 9am-7pm Mon-Fri; ⓢ Línea C Lavalle). **OCA** (Map p66; ☎ 011-4311-5305; www.oca.com.ar; Viamonte 526; ⊙ 8am-6pm Mon-Fri; ⓢ Línea C Lavalle) and **Andreani** (Map p66; ☎ 0810-122-1111; www.andreani.com.ar; Av Belgrano 1211; ⊙ 9am-7pm Mon-Fri, to 1pm Sat; ⓢ Línea C Moreno) are good for domestic packages; both have many locations around town.

TELEPHONE

The easiest way to make a call is from a *locutorio* (small telephone office), where you enter a booth and make calls in a safe, quiet environment. Costs are comparable to street telephones and you don't need change. Most *locutorios* offer reasonably priced internet services as well.

TOURIST INFORMATION

There are several tourist offices and kiosks in Buenos Aires. Staff speak English and can provide maps and information about free guided walks and other activities.

Ezeiza airport (☑ 011- 4480-0224; Terminal A arrivals, 1st fl, Ezeiza Airport; ☉ 8:15am-7:15pm)

Florida (Map p66; cnr Florida & Roque Sáenz Peña; ☉ 9am-6pm; ⑤ Línea D Catedral)

La Boca (Map p64; https://turismo.buenos aires.gob.ar; Av Don Pedro de Mendoza 1901; ☉ 9am-6pm; ☎; ☐ 33, 64, 29)

Plaza San Martín (Map p66; cnr Av Florida & Marcelo T de Alvear; ☉ 9am-6pm; ⑤ Línea C San Martín)

Puerto Madero (Map p66; Dique 4, Juana M Gorriti 200; ☉ 9am-6pm; ⑤ Línea B Alem)

Recoleta (Map p66; https://turismo.buenos aires.gob.ar; Av Quintana 596; ☉ 9am-6pm; ☐ 130, 62, 93)

Retiro (Map p66; Retiro Bus Station, Booth 83; ☉ 7:30am-4:30pm; ⑤ Línea C Retiro)

TRAVEL AGENCIES

Say Hueque (☑ 011-5258-8740; www.say hueque.com; Thames 2062; ☉ 9am-6pm Mon-Fri, 10am-1pm Sat; ⑤ Línea D Plaza Italia) This recommended independent travel agency specializes in customized adventure trips all around Argentina, and will also make air, bus and hotel reservations. It offers various BA tours as well.

Tangol (☑ 011-4363-6000; www.tangol.com; Florida 971, Suite 31; ☉ 9am-6pm Mon-Sat, 10am-7pm Sun; ⑤ Línea C San Martín) Does-it-all agency that offers city tours, tango shows, guides for *fútbol* games, hotel reservations, Spanish classes, air tickets and country-wide packages. Also offers unusual activities including helicopter tours and skydiving. Has another branch in **San Telmo** (☑ 011-4363-6000; www. tangol.com; Defensa 831; ☉ 9am-6pm Mon-Sat, 10am-7pm Sun; ⑤ Línea C Independencia).

ⓘ Getting There & Away

AIR

Most international flights arrive at Buenos Aires' **Aeropuerto Internacional Ministro Pistarini** (Ezeiza; ☑ 011-5480-6111; www.aa2000.com. ar), about 35km south of the Center. Ezeiza is a modern airport with ATMs, restaurants, a pharmacy and duty-free shops.

BOAT

There's a regular ferry service to/from Colonia and Montevideo, both in Uruguay. **Buquebus** (Map p66; ☑ 011-4316-6530; www.buquebus.com; Av Antártida Argentina 821; ⑤ Línea B Alem) and **Seacat** (Map p66; ☑ 011-4314-5100; www.seacat colonia.com; Av Antártida Argentina 821; ⑤ Línea B Alem) ferries leave from the same terminal in Puerto Madero. The terminal is a 15-minute walk from Alem Subte station on Línea B.

Colonia Express (Map p64; ☑ 011-4317-4100; www.coloniaexpress.com; Av Don Pedro de Mendoza 330; ☐ 130, 8, 86) is the cheapest company but has limited departures; book online in advance for the best prices. Its terminal is in an industrial neighborhood near La Boca; take a taxi.

BUS

Retiro (Retiro; Map p66; ☑ 011-4310-0700; www.retiro.com.ar; Av Antártida Argentina; ⑤ Línea C Retiro) is a huge three-story bus terminal with bays for 75 buses. Inside are cafeterias, shops, bathrooms, luggage storage, telephone offices with internet, ATMs, and a 24-hour information kiosk to help you navigate the terminal. There's also a tourist office and a booth where you can buy a SUBE card (p86).

The following lists are a small sample of very extensive services. Prices will vary widely depending on the season, the company and the economy. During holidays, prices rise; buy your ticket in advance. For current prices check www. omnilineas.com or www.plataforma10.com.ar.

Domestic Buses from Buenos Aires

DESTINATION	COST (AR$)	DURATION (HR)
Bariloche	1070-2410	24
Comodoro Rivadavia	1650-2750	27
Córdoba	570-1100	10
Mar del Plata	510-960	5½
Mendoza	830-2050	15
Puerto Iguazú	1820-2480	18
Puerto Madryn	1350-2300	19
Rosario	420-520	4
Salta	3000	21
Tucumán	1270-2230	15

International Buses from Buenos Aires

DESTINATION	COST (AR$)	DURATION (HR)
Asunción, Paraguay	1900-3200	18
Foz do Iguazú, Brazil	1820-2480	19
Montevideo, Uruguay	1200	8
Rio de Janeiro, Brazil	4000	42
Santiago, Chile	2200-2600	20
São Paulo, Brazil	3500	34

ℹ SUBE CARD

To use BA's public-transportation system, you'll need a **SUBE card** (🖳0800-
777-7823; www.sube.gob.ar; AR$60); it's
no longer possible to pay for buses
with cash. Purchase one at any of the
city tourist information booths, some
kioskos and Correo Argentino or OCA
post offices around the city; check the
website for locations or look for the
SUBE logo at businesses. To purchase
a SUBE card, you'll need your passport
or a copy of it. Charging the card itself is
easy, and can be done at many kiosks or
Subte stations.

TRAIN

With just a few exceptions, rail travel in Argentina is limited to Buenos Aires' suburbs and
provincial cities. It's cheaper than hopping on a
bus, but worth noting that it's not nearly as fast,
frequent or comfortable.

ℹ Getting Around

BICYCLE

For those comfortable with the trials of cycling in
a major city, bicycle is often the fastest and most
pleasant way of getting around Buenos Aires.
The city is almost completely flat, most streets
are one-way, and you can use the 130km network
of interconnected bike lanes. Just remember to
watch out for traffic; if in doubt, always give way,
be prepared for the occasional vehicle running
a red traffic light and be especially careful of
buses – assume they haven't seen you. If you are
cycling on one of the main, one-way avenues (eg
Av Corrientes), use the lane on the far left (but
watch out for motorcycles).

The city government has a free **city bike** (Eco-
Bici; 🖳0800-333-2424; www.buenosaires.gob.
ar/ecobici/sistema-ecobici/turistas; ⊙24hr)
scheme, called EcoBici, which tourists can use.
Complete the registration form online or via the
app – you'll need to upload a photo of your passport. Once you're registered, you can use the
EcoBici app to hire a bike by entering an access
code at any of the (unstaffed) bike stations.
You'll need data on your cell phone to use the
app while at the bike stations. The free bike hire
period is one hour on weekdays and two hours
at weekends.

Ask at any of the city tourist offices for a copy
of the city government cycle map (*mapa de
ciclovías de la Ciudad de Buenos Aires*), which
shows the bike lanes and location of city bike
stations and repair shops (*bicicletarías*). You can

also use CómoLlego (http://comollego.ba.gob.
ar) to plot your route.

You can also join city bike tours, which include
a bicycle and guide; heck out Biking Buenos
Aires (p72).

BUS

Buenos Aires has a huge and complex bus
system. Luckily the city government's website
CómoLlego (http://comollego.ba.gob.ar) helps
you plot your journey; there's also a free app you
can download to your smartphone.

To use the buses, you must have a SUBE card
– coins are no longer accepted.

Most bus routes (but not all) run 24 hours;
there are fewer buses at night. Seats up front
are offered to the elderly, pregnant women and
those with young children.

CAR & MOTORCYCLE

Driving in Buenos can be challenging. Problems
include aggressive drivers, unpredictable
buses, potholes, traffic, difficulty parking and
the fact that pedestrians cross the road haphazardly. Reconsider your need to have a car
in this city; public transportation will often get
you anywhere faster, cheaper and with much
less stress.

SUBTE (UNDERGROUND)

Buenos Aires' Subte is fast, efficient and cheap.
The most useful lines for travelers are Líneas
A, B, D and E (which run from the *microcentro*
to the capital's western and northern outskirts)
and Línea C (which links Estación Retiro and
Constitución).

Trains operate from 5am to around 8:30pm
Monday to Saturday and 8am to around 8pm
on Sunday and holidays, so don't rely on the
Subte to get you home after dinner. Service is
frequent on weekdays; on weekends you'll wait
longer.

TAXI & REMISE

Black-and-yellow cabs are ubiquitous on BA's
streets and relatively inexpensive. Tips are unnecessary, but rounding up to the nearest peso
is common.

It's generally safe to hail a street taxi, though
some drivers take advantage of tourists. Make
sure the driver uses the meter: it's good to have
an idea of where you're going, and make sure the
meter doesn't run fast (it should change every
200m, or about every three blocks). Finally,
watch your money as some drivers deftly replace high bills with low ones, or switch your real
bill for a fake one.

Remises (unmarked call taxis) are considered
safer than street taxis, since an established
company sends them out. Any business can
phone a *remise* for you.

AROUND BUENOS AIRES

Day trips to charming, cobbled Colonia del Sacramento in Uruguay are popular, and it's also easy to reach Montevideo (Uruguay's capital), and the beach resort of Punta del Este, only a few hours away from Buenos Aires.

Tigre

About an hour north of Buenos Aires is this favorite *porteño* weekend destination. You can check out the popular **riverfront**, take a relaxing boat ride on the **Delta del Paraná** and shop at **Mercado de Frutos** (a daily crafts market that's best on weekends).

Tickets for commuter boats that cruise the waterways can be purchased at the *estación fluvial;* the **tourist office** (☑ 011-4512-4080; www.vivitigre.gov.ar; Bartolomé Mitre 305; ⊘ 9am-6pm) here can recommend a destination.

The quickest, cheapest way to get to Tigre from BA is by taking the train 'Mitre-Ramal Tigre' from Retiro train station all the way to Tigre (with/without SUBE AR$13.25/26.50, 50 minutes, frequent). The most scenic way, however, is to take this same train to the suburb of Olivos, then transfer to the Tren de la Costa – a pleasant electric train that also ends up in Tigre. Buses 59, 60 and 152 also stop at the Tren de la Costa's Olivos station.

San Antonio de Areco
☑ 02326 / POP 20,000

Dating from the early 18th century, this serene village northwest of Buenos Aires is the symbolic center of Argentina's diminishing *gaucho* (cowboy) culture. It's also host to the country's biggest *gaucho* celebration, **Fiesta de la Tradición** (www.sanantoniodeareco.com; ⊘ Nov). There's a cute plaza surrounded by historic buildings, while local artisans are known for producing maté paraphernalia, *rastras* (silver-studded belts) and *facones* (long-bladed knives). Buses run regularly from BA's Retiro bus terminal (AR$119 to AR$225, two hours).

NORTHEAST ARGENTINA

From the spectacular natural wilderness of Iguazú Falls in the north to the chic sophistication of Rosario in the south, the northeast is one of Argentina's most diverse regions. Wedged between the Ríos Paraná and Uruguay (thus earning it the nickname Mesopotamia), the region relies heavily on these rivers for fun as well as its livelihood. In contrast, the neighboring Chaco is sparsely populated, and often called Argentina's 'empty quarter.'

The northeast was one of the Jesuits' Argentine power bases until their expulsion from the Americas in 1767, the legacy of which can be seen in the remains of the many missions in the region's northeast.

Rosario
☑ 0341 / POP 1.27 MILLION

So, you dig the vibe of the Buenos Aires, but its sheer size is sending you a little loco in the coco? Rosario may be the place for you.

Located just a few hours north, this is in many ways Argentina's second city – not in terms of population, but culturally, financially and aesthetically. Its roaring port trade and growing population even made it a candidate for national capital status for a while.

These days the city's backpacker scene is growing slowly, and the huge university and corresponding population of students, artists and musicians give it a solid foundation.

Nighttime, the streets come alive and the bars and clubs pack out. In the day, once everybody wakes up, they shuffle down to the river beaches for more music, drinks and lounging about.

It's not all fun and games, though. There's a good selection of museums and galleries, and Che Guevara fans will want to check out his birthplace.

⊙ Sights & Activities

⊙ Central Rosario

Museo de Arte Contemporáneo de Rosario GALLERY
(MACRO; www.castagninomacro.org; cnr Av de la Costa & Blvd Oroño; suggested donation AR$20; ⊘ 11am-7pm Tue-Sun) **FREE** In a brightly painted grain silo on the waterfront, this museum is part of Rosario's impressive riverbank renewal. It features temporary exhibitions, mostly by young local artists, and of varying quality, housed in small galleries spread over eight floors. There's a good view of river islands from the *mirador* (viewpoint) at the top and an attractive cafe-bar by the river.

Northeast Argentina

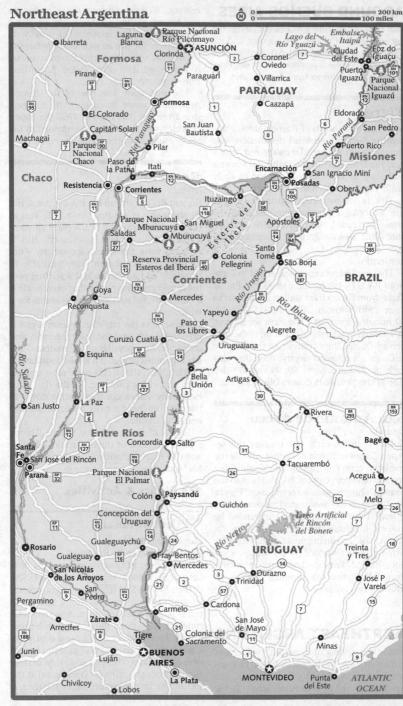

Museo de la Memoria
MUSEUM

(www.museodelamemoria.gob.ar; Córdoba 2019; suggested donation AR$20; ⊙1-7pm Tue-Fri, 3-7pm Sat & Sun) **FREE** A former army HQ, not far from where police held, tortured and killed people during the Dirty War, this museum seeks to remember the violence and victims. If you can read Spanish, you'll find it's a small but very moving display, with witness descriptions, photos of the 'Disappeared' and an attempt to look at the wider history of man's inhumanity. There are temporary exhibitions upstairs.

Monumento Nacional a La Bandera
MONUMENT

(www.monumentoalabandera.gob.ar; Santa Fe 581; elevator AR$20; ⊙9am-6pm Tue-Sun, 2-6pm Mon) Manuel Belgrano, who designed the Argentine flag, rests in a crypt beneath this colossal stone obelisk, built where the blue-and-white stripes were first raised. Even if rampant nationalism isn't your thing, it's worth taking the elevator to the top for great views over the waterfront, Paraná and islands. The attractive colonnade houses an eternal flame commemorating those who died for the fatherland.

★Museo Municipal de Bellas Artes
GALLERY

(www.castagninomacro.org; cnr Av Carlos Pellegrini & Blvd Oroño; suggested donation AR$20; ⊙11am-7pm Tue-Sun) **FREE** This gallery is worth a visit for its inventive displays of contemporary and 20th-century artworks from the MACRO (p87) collection, and its small collection of European works, which contains a couple of very fine pieces. Free guided tours at 5pm.

Museo Histórico Provincial
MUSEUM

(www.museomarc.gob.ar; Av del Museo, Parque Independencia; ⊙9am-6pm Tue-Fri, 3-7pm Sat & Sun) **FREE** The well-presented collection features plenty of post-independence exhibits plus excellent displays on indigenous cultures from many parts of Latin America. Particularly interesting is the collection of baroque religious art from the southern Andes. Information is in Spanish only. It's closed when Newell's Old Boys are playing at home in the adjacent stadium (p91).

⊙ Costanera

Rosario's most attractive feature is its waterfront, where what was once derelict warehouses and train tracks has been reclaimed for the fun of the people. It stretches some 15km from its southern end at Parque Ur-quiza to the city's northern edge, just short of the suspension bridge crossing into Entre Ríos province. It's an appealing place to wander and watch what's going on, from the plentiful birdlife and impromptu *fútbol* games to massive cargo ships surging past on the river.

Costanera Norte
WATERFRONT

In summer this strip beginning 5km north of downtown attracts crowds for its beaches. The mediocre public beach of **Rambla Catalunya** is backed by a promenade and bar-restaurants; beyond, the best beach is **Balneario La Florida** (AR$50; ⊙9am-8pm Oct-Apr), with services, a safe bathing area and picturesque stalls behind it selling river fish. The summer-only 'Linea de la Costa' bus heads here from Rioja/Roca. Otherwise take bus 153 Roja from the center which passes along the river bank.

Costanera Sur
WATERFRONT

The grassy zone below downtown includes plenty of space for jogging and courting, as well as the **Estación Fluvial** (La Fluvial; ☎0341-447-3838; www.estacionfluvial.com; ⊙9am-6pm) building, where you can find eating and drinking options and operators offering boat trips. Heading further north, you pass various cultural venues before reaching **Parque de España** (Paraná riverbank) and its mausoleum-like edifice. Beyond here is a zone of bars and restaurants that gets lively at weekends, and then the city's contemporary-art museum (p87).

Courses

Spanish in Rosario
LANGUAGE

(☎0341-15-560-3789; www.spanishinrosario.com; Catamarca 3095) Rosario is a great base for learning Spanish. This place offers enjoyable language programs and can arrange family stays and volunteer work placements.

Tours

★Rosario Kayak & Motor Boat Tours
TOURS

(Paseos en Lancha y Kayak; ☎0341-15-571-3812; www.paseosenlancharosario.com; Estación Fluvial) A friendly, professional, multilingual set-up with great boat trips around the Paraná delta (AR$450, one to 1½ hours) with an optional lunch stop on a delta island. You can also explore the islands by kayak. It also offers water-taxi service to the delta islands and rents bikes (AR$250 per day). Book by phone or at the Estación Fluvial.

Rosario

Rosario

Rosario Free Tour
WALKING

(☑0341-560-3789; www.rosariofreetour.com; cnr Maipú & Urquiza; ☺tours 10am Sat) Two-hour walking tours in Spanish and English. Meet on the steps of the old customs building at the end of Maipú. Though it's technically free, a donation is appropriate.

✱✱ Festivals & Events

Rosario packs out for the October 12 long weekend. Many hotels and hostels double their prices and fill up well ahead of time.

Semana de la Bandera
FIESTA

(☺Jun) Climaxing in ceremonies on June 20, the anniversary of the death of Belgrano, Flag Week is Rosario's major fiesta.

Fiesta de las Colectividades
CULTURAL

(☺Nov) A 10-day festival celebrating the cultural diversity of Rosario with groups representing immigrant communities presenting concerts, dances, workshops and culinary arts. It finishes with a major fireworks display.

🛏 Sleeping

There are dozens of hostels, but they're often block-booked by government workers. There's also a herd of average midrange hotels. Prices generally drop midweek.

Residence Boutique Hostel
HOTEL, HOSTEL $

(☑0341-421-8148; www.residenceboutique.com. ar; Buenos Aires 1145; dm/d US$13/57; ✳@🛜) Rather a special place, this early-20th-century building houses a serene, beautiful hotel and hostel. Public spaces are full of art-nouveau flourishes, and the compact, stylish private rooms offer great value for this level of comfort. Dorms are similarly upmarket, and the little garden patio and breakfast area are lovely places to relax.

La Casa de Arriba
HOSTEL $

(☑0341-430-0012; www.lacasadearriba.com.ar; Córdoba 2889; dm weekend/weekday US$12/16, d US$30; @🛜) A designer's flair has made a fabulous hostel from this old house. Exposed brick, creative use of space, modern shelf-style bunks and a welcoming attitude make this a comfortable, stylish Rosario base. Its distance from the center is offset by its relative proximity to bars and nightlife.

La Casa de Pandora
HOSTEL $

(☑0341-679-9314; www.lacasadepandora.com.ar; San Lorenzo 1455; dm/r US$10/25; @🛜) Arty and welcoming, this fine hostel has moved to expansive new digs in a classic older

FÚTBOL IN ROSARIO

Rosario has two rival *fútbol* teams with several league titles between them. Newell's Old Boys plays in red and black at **Estadio Marcelo Bielsa** (☑0341-425-4422; Parque Independencia) and has a long, proud history of producing great Argentine players. Rosario Central plays in blue-and-yellow stripes at **Estadio 'El Gigante de Arroyito'** (☑0341-421-0000; cnr Blvd Avellaneda & Génova). Buy tickets from the stadiums from two hours before the match.

building but it remains clean and comfortable with a relaxed vibe. Air-conditioned dorms are roomy and comfortable and the cafe out the front is a good place to hang out. Various workshops and events – yoga, dance, folk music – are held on-site.

Esplendor Savoy Rosario
HOTEL $$

(☑0341-429-6000; www.esplendorsavoyrosario. com; San Lorenzo 1022; standard/superior r US$125/150, ste US$180; P✳@🛜🏊) Even among Rosario's many elegant early-20th-century buildings, this art-nouveau gem is a standout. It's a flawless contemporary conversion; rooms feature modern conveniences that blend well with the centenarian features. An indoor pool, handsome cafe-bar and roof garden are among the attractions. It's popular during events, so don't expect a peaceful stay.

Catamarca Suites Land
HOTEL $$

(☑0341-440-0020; www.catamarcasuitesland. com.ar; Catamarca 1219; r US$65; ✳🛜) These spacious apartment-style doubles with breakfast bar, microwave and minibar have plenty of style, while big comfy beds and powerful showers add value. Rooms have a balcony looking down the street to the Paraná and there's a small roof terrace with a Jacuzzi. Breakfast is brought up to your room. Cash only.

🍴 Eating

If you feel like exploring, take a wander along Av Carlos Pelligrini between Maipú and Moreno. This is Rosario's restaurant strip – 10 blocks dedicated to the pillars of Argentina cuisine: pizza, *parrilla* (grill), pasta, *tenedores libres* (all-you-can-eat restaurants) and ice cream, sometimes all gloriously available in the one location. Otherwise,

LOCAL KNOWLEDGE

PICHINCHA

Between Oroño and Francia, and north of Urquiza, the barrio of Pichincha is the city's most interesting for nightlife. The leafy streets and wide pavements make it seem a sleepy suburb by day, but at night every corner seems to have a quirky bar or hipster restaurant. The city's best *boliches* are also found here.

there's a *confitería* (cafe-snack bar) on just about every street corner.

La Marina   SPANISH, SEAFOOD $
(www.facebook.com/restaurante.lamarina.39; 1 de Mayo 890; mains AR$80-140; ⊙noon-3pm & 8-11:30pm Mon-Sat) Just above the flag monument, this basement place decorated with faded Spanish tourism posters is a top spot for inexpensive and delicious seafood, like *rabas* (calamari) or succulent river fish on the grill. Wash it all down with a bottle of imported cider from Asturias. No bookings, so be prepared to wait, as it's deservedly popular.

Monreal   SANDWICHES $
(☑0341-421-9356; www.sandwichesmonreal.com. ar; cnr San Lorenzo & Entre Ríos; sandwiches AR$120-220; ⊙9am-10pm Mon-Fri, 8am-1pm & 6-10pm Sat, 6-10pm Sun; ☑) A Rosario institution, this no-nonsense corner place serves up a wide variety of delicious hot and cold sandwiches which are widely regarded as the best in town. It's more a take-out place than somewhere to hang out. Grab some for a picnic on the *costanera*.

Comedor Balcarce   ARGENTINE $
(www.comedorbalcarce.com.ar; cnr Balcarce & Brown; mains AR$160-310; ⊙noon-3pm & 8:15pm-midnight Mon-Sat) In business for decades, this typical corner *bodegón* (traditional diner) is one of a fast-disappearing breed. Home-style Argentine cooking comes in big portions. Quality is average to good, prices are great and it's an authentic, friendly experience. Don't let its affectionate nickname, El Vómito, put you off.

★**Zazpirak Bat**   BASQUE $$
(☑0341-421-7670; www.zazpirakbat.com; Entre Ríos 261; mains AR$160-380; ⊙8pm-12:30am Tue-Sat, 12:30-4pm Sun) From outside, this Basque cultural center gives few clues that there's a restaurant inside, and the menu seems a little humdrum at first glance. But

what a place this is. Fish and seafood are prepared to give maximum expression to the natural flavors; it's all delicious, quantities are enormous and the salads are particularly praiseworthy.

★**Escauriza**   SEAFOOD $$
(☑0341-454-1777; cnr Bajada Escauriza & Paseo Ribereño; mains AR$550; ⊙noon-3:30pm & 8pm-midnight) Backing Florida beach, this legendary place is one of Rosario's best spots for fish. The enormous indoor-outdoor dining area is redolent with the aromas of chargrilling river catch like surubí; start with some delicious seafood empanadas. Service, quality and quantity are all highly impressive. Book, get there at noon, or wait and wait at summer weekend lunchtimes. No credit cards. Awful coffee.

El Ancla   ARGENTINE $$
(☑0341-411-4142; Maipú 1101; mains AR$375-490; ⊙7am-1am Mon-Fri, 8am-4pm & 7pm-1am Sat, 10am-4pm & 7pm-1am Sun) One of Rosario's many beloved corner restaurants, this much-frequented local has an appealingly venerable interior and an authentic feel. The food – with lots of inexpensive single-plate meals – is reliably good and you always receive a friendly welcome.

🍷 Drinking & Entertainment

Rosario has a great number of *restobares,* which function as hybrid cafes and bars and generally serve a fairly standard selection of snacks and plates. Many are good for a morning coffee, an evening glass of wine – or anything in between.

There are regular tango events in Rosario; grab the monthly listings booklet from the tourist office and check www.rosario turismo.com.

★**Fenicia**   BREWERY
(Francia 168; ⊙noon-late Tue-Fri, 6pm-late Sat & Sun; 🛜) You can smell the malt at this brewpub, where the delicious ales are produced right beneath your feet. It's a fine place to start exploring this bar-rich nightlife zone, and it also does a handy line in quesadillas, burgers and salads. The roof terrace is good on a warm evening. It's northwest of the city center, near the train station.

El Diablito   PUB
(www.facebook.com/eldiablito.bar; Maipú 622; ⊙8:30pm-2am Wed & Thu, to 3am Fri & Sat) With a red-lit interior true to its origins as a brothel,

this place has an atmosphere all of its own. The soundtrack is 1970s and 1980s rock, and the decor is sumptuous, with stained-glass panels and age-spotted mirrors. A classic place to drink.

Bound CLUB
(www.facebook.com/boundoficial; Blvd Oroño 198; ⊙11pm-5am Sat) One of Rosario's fanciest *boliches* (nightclubs), this stylish spot is in the heart of the liveliest nightlife zone. It operates a pretty strict door policy, so think twice if the queue's long.

Distrito Siete LIVE MUSIC
(www.facebook.com/distritosie7e; Av Lagos 790; ⊙9am-1am Mon-Thu, 9am-4:30am Fri & Sat, 6pm-1am Sun; 🛜) This warehouse-like industrial space is run by the Giros local social movement and sees plenty of live acts as well as classes, activities, a cheap daily meal, and a bar where you can stop for a coffee or beer and see what's going on.

ℹ Information

The informative **tourist office** (📞 0341-480-2230; www.rosario.tur.ar; Av del Huerto; ⊙8am-7pm Mon-Fri, 9am-7pm Sat, 9am-6pm Sun) is on the waterfront. There's also a more **central branch** (Córdoba, near Av Corrientes; ⊙8am-7pm Mon-Fri, 9am-7pm Sat, 10am-6pm Sun) downtown.

Cambios along San Martín and Córdoba change money; there are many banks and ATMs on Santa Fe between Mitre and Entre Ríos.

The **post office** (www.correoargentino.com.ar; Córdoba 721; ⊙8am-8pm Mon-Fri, 9am-1pm Sat) is near Plaza Sarmiento.

ℹ Getting There & Away

AIR
The Aeropuerto Internacional Islas Malvinas is located 8km west of town; to get here take a *remise* (taxi), which costs AR$300. **Aerolíneas Argentinas** (📞 0810-2228-6527; www.aerolineas.com.ar; España 840; ⊙10am-6pm Mon-Fri) flies four times weekly to Buenos Aires, and also offers direct flights to Mendoza, Puerto Iguazú and Salta.

BUS
The modernized **long-distance bus terminal** (📞 0341-437-3030; www.terminalrosario.gob.ar; cnr Cafferata & Santa Fe) is 25 blocks west of downtown. To get there, any bus along Santa Fe will do the trick. To get into town from there, take a bus marked 'Centro' or 'Plaza Sarmiento.' It's about AR$100 to AR$120 in a taxi.

There are direct daily services to nearly all major destinations, including international services.

REMOTE NATIONAL PARKS IN NORTHEAST ARGENTINA

Northeast Argentina is home to some incredible parks that take some effort getting to, but are well worthwhile. Here are a few. For more information, visit www.parquesnacionales.gov.ar.

Parque Nacional El Palmar (📞 03447-493049; www.parqueelpalmar.com.ar; RN 14, Km 199; Argentines/foreigners AR$140/300) Home to capybara, *ñandú* (rhea; a large flightless bird resembling the ostrich) and poisonous pit vipers, this 85 sq km park protects the endangered yatay palm. The park also has cheap camping, good walking trails and swimming holes. It lies between Colón and Concordia, on the Uruguayan border; both are easily accessible from Gualeguaychú.

Parque Nacional Chaco (📞 03725-499161; www.parquesnacionales.gob.ar; ⊙8am-7pm) FREE This park protects 150 sq km of marshes, palm savannas and strands of the disappearing *quebracho colorado* tree. Birds far outnumber mammals – there are plenty of rhea, jabiru, roseate spoonbills, cormorants and common caracaras – but mosquitoes outnumber them all. Bring repellent. Camping is free, but facilities are basic. Capitán Solari (5km from the park entrance) is the nearest town, and is easily accessed from Resistencia.

Parque Nacional Río Pilcomayo (📞 03718-470-045; www.parquesnacionales.gob.ar; RN86; ⊙8am-4pm Mon-Fri, to 6pm Sat & Sun) FREE This 600-sq-km park is home to caiman, tapirs, anteaters, maned wolves and an abundance of birdlife, particularly around the centerpiece, Laguna Blanca (where piranha make swimming a bad idea). Access is via the small town of Laguna Blanca (9km east of the actual lagoon), which can be reached from Formosa.

ARGENTINA SANTA FE

Buses from Rosario

DESTINATION	COST (ARS)	DURATION (HR)
Buenos Aires	350-670	4
Córdoba	580-685	5½-7
Mendoza	690-1150	12-15
Santa Fe	295	2½-3½
Tucumán	1435	11-13

TRAIN

Slow air-conditioned trains leave from **Rosario Norte train station** (www.trenesargentinos. gob.ar; Av del Valle 2750; ☺ ticket office 8-2:30am Mon & Fri, 8am-1:30pm Tue-Thu, 5:30pm-1:30am Sat, noon-1:30am Sun) for Buenos Aires (1st/2nd class AR$360/300, seven hours, daily 12:15am) passing **Rosario Sur train station** (www.trenesargentinos.gob. ar; cnr San Martín & Battle y Ordóñez; ☺ ticket office 6pm-2am), 7.5km south of the city center, on the way. From Buenos Aires, trains depart at 4:40pm from Retiro.

Other less frequent services on the route between Buenos Aires and Córdoba, and Buenos Aires and Tucumán, call at Rosario Norte only. These services book out well in advance.

Bus 140 runs south down Sarmiento to the Rosario Sur station. Take bus 134 north up Mitre to a block from the Rosario Norte train station.

ℹ Getting Around

Rosario's public transportation system is efficient and comprehensive; once you learn the ropes there should be no need to take taxis.

Local buses run from the terminal on Plaza Sarmiento; see www.rosario.gov.ar for a journey planner. You can pay the AR$18 fare in coins, but unless you've broken a piggy bank, it's much easier to buy a rechargeable Tarjeta Movi card (AR$30) from the little booths at many major central bus stops. Trips then cost AR$16.80.

Santa Fe

📞 0342 / POP 569,100

Santa Fe would be a fairly dull town if not for the university population. Thanks to this, there's a healthy bar and club scene, and plenty of fun to be had during the day.

Relocated during the mid-17th century because of hostile indigenous groups, floods and isolation, the city duplicates the original plan of Santa Fe La Vieja (Old Santa Fe). But a 19th-century neo-Parisian building boom and more recent construction have left only isolated colonial buildings, mostly near Plaza 25 de Mayo.

◎ Sights & Activities

★ Convento y Museo de San Francisco   MONASTERY

(📞0342-4593303; Amenábar 2257; AR$30; ☺8am-12pm & 3:30-6:30pm Mon-Sat) Santa Fe's principal historical landmark is this Franciscan monastery and museum, built in 1680. While the museum is mediocre, the church is beautiful, with an exquisite wooden ceiling. The lovely cloister has a real colonial feel and is full of birdsong and the perfume of flowers. The monastery is still home to a handful of monks.

★ Museo Histórico Provincial   MUSEUM

(www.museobrigadierlopez.gob.ar; Av San Martín 1490; ☺8am-12:30pm & 4-8pm Tue-Fri, 5-8pm Sat & Sun Oct-Dec, 4-8pm Tue-Fri, 5-8pm Sat & Sun Jan & Feb) FREE In a lovable 17th-century building, this museum has a variety of possessions and mementos of various provincial governors and *caudillos* (provincial strongmen), as well as religious art and fine period furnishings, including a sedan chair once used to carry around the Viceroy of Río de la Plata. Opening hours are for summer: it doesn't close mid-afternoon the rest of the year, but shuts at 7pm.

Museo Etnográfico y Colonial Provincial   MUSEUM

(www.museojuandegaray.gob.ar; 25 de Mayo 1470; donation AR$5; ☺8:30am-12:30pm & 3-7pm Tue-Fri, 8:30am-12:30pm & 4-7pm Sat & Sun) Run with heartwarming enthusiasm by local teachers, this museum has a chronological display of stone tools, Guaraní ceramics, jewelry, carved bricks and colonial objects. Highlights include a set of *tablas* (a colonial game similar to backgammon) and a scale model of both original Santa Fe settlements. Afternoon opening hours vary.

Cervecería Santa Fe   BREWERY

(📞0342-450-2237; www.cervezasantafe.com. ar; Calchines 1401; ☺tours 4pm Tue-Sat) FREE This is the brewery that produces Santa Fe lager as well as Budweiser and Heineken under license. Numbers are limited on the free tours: come 15 minutes before to register or reserve online. You'll need to wear sturdy footwear and long pants for safety reasons.

Costa Litoral   BOATING

(📞0342-456-4381; www.costalitoral.info; Dique 1) From the redeveloped harbor area, a large catamaran runs trips around the river islands.

Santa Fe

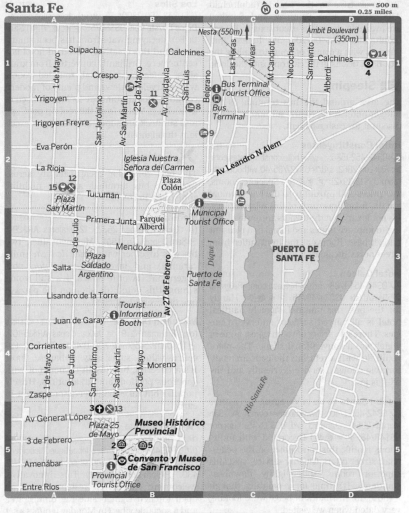

ARGENTINA SANTA FE

Two-hour trips to the islands (adult/child AR$320/180, 4pm Saturday and Sunday) are available, as well as excursions to Paraná (adult/child AR$400/200, 5½ hours, 2pm Sunday) with a couple of hours to explore the city. Book tickets in the cafe opposite the dock.

Sleeping

The area around the bus terminal is the budget-hotel zone. Nearly all hotels offer a discount for cash payment.

Hotel Constituyentes   HOTEL $
(☑0342-452-1586; www.hotelconstituyentes.com.ar; San Luis 2862; s/d/tr US$27/35/40, without bathroom US$13/19/21; ｐ✳@🗟) Spacious rooms, low prices and proximity to the bus terminal are the main drawcards of this relaxed place. It's not luxury, but the owners are always looking to improve things and it makes a pleasant budget base. Rooms at the front suffer from street noise. Breakfast is extra.

Hotel Galeón   HOTEL $
(☑0342-454-1788; http://hgaleon.com; Belgrano 2759; s/d/ste US$34/40/45; ｐ✳@🗟) Handy for the bus, this unusual, vaguely nautical hotel is all curved surfaces and weird angles. There's a variety of room types, none of which are a conventional shape. The place could do with a refit but the beds are comfortable enough, service is friendly and the wi-fi is fast.

Hostal Santa Fe de la Veracruz   HOTEL $
(☑0342-455-1740; www.hostalsf.com; Av San Martín 2954; standard s/d US$32/45, superior US$43/48; ｐ✳@🗟) Decorated with indigenous motifs, this retro hotel on the pedestrian street offers friendly service, spacious superior rooms and slightly downbeat standards. It's time for repainting though – those dozen shades of beige were looking very dated when we visited.

★Ámbit Boulevard   BOUTIQUE HOTEL $$
(☑0342-455-7179; www.ambithotel.com.ar; Blvd Gálvez 1408; superior/premium r from US$60/65; ｐ✳🗟🖩) An early-20th-century flour magnate's mansion has been converted into this compact, rather lovely hotel. Exquisitely decorated rooms were each designed as a charity project by different architects; all are charming. Premium-category rooms have high ceilings and venerable floorboards, while superior rooms are in the modern upstairs annex but don't lack charm. A little spa-style plunge pool sits between floors.

Los Silos   HOTEL $$
(☑0342-450-2800; www.hotellossilos.com.ar; Dique 1; r/ste from US$50/55; ｐ✳@🗟🖩) Santa Fe's decaying waterfront has been smartened, and this creatively designed hotel is a centerpiece. Brilliantly converted from grain silos, it features original, rounded rooms with marvelous views and plenty of modern comfort, though some are looking in need of a touch-up. Vistas from the rooftop pool, spa and sundeck are super, and service is excellent throughout.

✗ Eating

The best zones for cheap eats are across from the bus terminal, and the nightlife zone of La Recoleta.

Merengo   BAKERY $
(Av General López 2632; 12 alfajores AR$290; ⊙8am-10pm) In 1851, Merengo stuck two biscuits together with *dulce de leche* (milk caramel) and invented the *alfajor,* now Argentina's favorite snack. It's still going strong: this cute little shop on the plaza is one of several branches.

Makánun Diáafah   MIDDLE EASTERN $
(cnr Tucumán & 9 de Julio; dishes AR$15-100; ⊙11:30am-2:45pm & 7:30-11:45pm Tue-Sat) Excellent-value, super-tasty Lebanese food. It's a cheerful, brightly lit corner spot with generous portions and great prices. Hugely popular but takes no reservations, so get in early.

★La Boutique del Cocinero   INTERNATIONAL $$
(☑0342-456-3864; www.laboutiquedelcocinero.com; Yrigoyen 2443; 2-course set meals AR$245-430; ⊙9pm-1am Mon-Sat) This innovative, welcoming chef-driven restaurant has an open kitchen right beside the dining area and a sociable vibe. On Monday it offers a set house meal, while on Tuesday and Wednesday it serves a set Italian meal, including an appetizer, main plate and dessert. On other nights there is a small menu of high-quality dishes from various international cuisines. Great atmosphere.

Nesta   ARGENTINE $$
(☑0342-15-595-1983; www.facebook.com/nesta.restobar; Maipú 1964; mains AR$250-380; ⊙9pm-12:30am Tue-Sat; 🗟) The hippie decor and inviting rear patio of this handsome house in a quiet leafy barrio make a welcome evening retreat. A small but interesting menu of tacos,

salads, pizzas, vegetarian options and a couple of well-prepared gourmet takes on traditional meat dishes are all prepared with fresh, healthy ingredients. Meals are accompanied by reggae or chillout beats. Good drinks too.

El Quincho de Chiquito ARGENTINE $$
(☑ 0342-460-2608; cnr Brown & Obispo Principe; set menu AR$350; ☺ 11:30am-3pm & 8pm-midnight) This legendary local institution is *the* place for river fish, on the *costanera* 6km north of downtown. There are few frills and no choice: four or five courses of delicious surubí, sábalo or pacú are brought out, and you can repeat as often as you want. Drinks are extra but cheap.

It's around AR$160 each way in a taxi (staff will phone one to take you back) or catch bus 16 from any point on the waterfront road.

Drinking & Nightlife

Santa Fe's rock-steady nightlife once centered on the intersection of Av San Martín and Santiago del Estero, an area known as La Recoleta, but is now starting to spread through town.

Uh Lala BAR
(☑ 0342-455-7633; Tucumán 2832; ☺ cafe 8am-12:30pm & 5:30-8:30pm Mon-Fri, 7-8:30pm Sat, events 8:30pm-2am Thu-Sat) A chilled bohemian cafe-bar with friendly staff, Uh Lala is a good place to mix it with locals over a coffee or an evening drink. From Thursday to Saturday there's stand-up comedy and live music performances.

Patio de la Cervezaría BREWERY
(cnr Calchines & Lavalle; ☺ 6pm-1am Tue-Sun) Part of the Santa Fe brewery opposite, this picturesque beer garden has its lager piped across the road via a 'beerduct' bridge. It's a great outdoor setting for *liso*, as draft beer, traditionally served in 8oz cylindrical glasses, is known hereabouts; there's a menu of deli plates, sandwiches, salads etc to accompany it.

ℹ Information

The **Municipal Tourist Office** (☑ 0342-457-4123; www.santafeturismo.gov.ar; Dique 1, Puerto de Santa Fe; ☺ 7am-8pm Mon-Fri, 10am-4pm & 5-9pm Sat, 5-9pm Sun) is located under the old steel crane at the entrance to the port. There's also an office at the **bus terminal** (☑ 0342-457-4124; www.santafeturismo.gov.ar; Belgrano 2910; ☺ 7am-8pm Mon-Fri, 8am-8pm Sat & Sun).

ℹ Getting There & Around

Aerolíneas Argentinas (www.aerolineas. com.ar; 25 de Mayo 2287; ☺ 9:30am-5:30pm Mon-Fri) flies to Buenos Aires from the airport, located 7km south of town on RN 11. A *remise* (taxi) costs about AR$250.

From the **bus terminal** (☑ 0342-457-4124; www.terminalsantafe.com; Belgrano 2910) there are services throughout the country. Buses to nearby Paraná (45 minutes) are frequent but often oversubscribed: prepare for long queues. A *remise* costs AR$650.

BUSES FROM SANTA FE

DESTINATION	COST (AR$)	DURATION (HR)
Buenos Aires	420-1150	6-7½
Córdoba	400-715	5
Corrientes	620-1400	6½-8
Paraná	145-175	¾
Posadas	1255-1715	12
Resistencia	775-1325	6½-8
Rosario	295	2
Tucumán	820-1490	11½

Paraná

☑ 0343 / POP 367,792

Although less famous than Santa Fe, Paraná is, in many ways, a more attractive place. Built on the hilly banks of its namesake river, the historical center is largely intact, and the city boasts a couple of majestic plazas. As is the rule in this part of the world, fun seekers hit the riverbanks at night to choose from an array of restaurants, clubs and bars.

◉ Sights & Activities

From Plaza Primero de Mayo, the town center, San Martín is a *peatonal* (pedestrian district) for six blocks. Plaza Primero de Mayo has had an **Iglesia Catedral** since 1730, but the current building dates from 1885. When Paraná was capital of the confederation, the Senate deliberated at the **Colegio del Huerto**, at the corner of 9 de Julio and 25 de Mayo.

Museo Histórico de Entre Ríos MUSEUM
(cnr Buenos Aires & Laprida; ☺ 8am-12:30pm & 3-8pm Tue-Fri, 9am-noon & 4-7pm Sat, 9am-noon Sun) **FREE** Flaunting local pride, this modern museum on Plaza Alvear contains information on the short-lived Republic of Entre Ríos and the battle of Monte Camperos, as well as *mate* paraphernalia and numerous

solid wooden desks and portraits of former President Justo José de Urquiza. Much of it was the collection of a local poet.

★ Museo y Mercado
Provincial de Artesanías
HANDICRAFTS

(Av Urquiza 1239; ⊙ 8:30am-12:30pm & 4:30-8pm Mon-Fri, 8:30am-12:30pm Sat) 🖊 **FREE** Promoting handicrafts from throughout the province, this is a likable little place that is part museum, part shop. Ask the curator to explain things to you; you'll be amazed by the intricacy of some of the work, like the hats made from tightly woven palm fibers. Those items available for purchase are identified by a sticker.

Costanera
WATERFRONT

From the northern edge of downtown, Parque Urquiza slopes steeply downward to the banks of the Río Paraná. During summer, the waterfront fills with people strolling, fishing and swimming. There's a public beach, **Playa El Parque**, west of the Paraná Rowing Club's private strand, but a better strip of sand, **Playas de Thompson**, is 1km further east, beyond the port.

Costa Litoral
BOATING

(☑ 0343-423-4385; www.costalitoral.info; Buenos Aires 212) This outfit runs weekend one-hour cruises on the river in a large catamaran (AR$450 per person) in addition to one-way transportation across the river to Santa Fe. Trips leave from near the tourist office on the *costanera*.

GUALEGUAYCHÚ CARNAVAL

A mellow riverside town, Gualeguaychú is quiet out of season but kicks off in summer with the country's longest and flashiest **Carnaval** (www.carnavaldelpais. com.ar). Any weekend from mid-January to late February you'll find things in full swing. The main venue is the Corsódromo, where admission is AR$230 to AR$290 most nights.

There's a string of decent budget hotels along Bolívar between Bartolomé Mitre and Monseñor Chalup, and several hostels in town.

Gualeguaychú is easily reached by bus from Buenos Aires (3½ hours), Paraná and other Río Uruguay towns. Gualeguaychú is also a crossing point to Uruguay: Fray Bentos lies just across the bridge.

🛏 Sleeping

★ Las Mañanitas
HOTEL $

(☑ 0343-407-4753; www.lasmananitas.com.ar; Carbó 62; s/d US$24/35; 🅿❄️@🛜🏊) There's a summer-house feel about this delightfully relaxed little budget place, which has nine rooms alongside a courtyard and garden with pool. Colorful and comfortable rooms differ widely, from darkish duplexes to simpler, lighter chambers, but it's the grace and friendliness of the whole ensemble that makes this a winner.

Entre Ríos Apart Hotel
APARTMENT $

(☑ 0343-484-0906; Montevideo 55; d/t US$70/80; 🅿❄️🛜) Spotless, spacious apartments here have stove, microwave and fridge, as well as a fold-out sofa, decent bathroom and attractive bedroom. It's in a clean-lined modernized building and rates include breakfast and parking, making this a great deal.

🍴 Eating

★ La Pastelería
CAFE $

(☑ 0343-422-2339; 25 de Junio 100; snacks AR$90-250; ⊙ 8am-1pm & 4:30-9pm Mon-Fri, 8:30am-1pm & 4:30-9pm Sat) You might have to wait for a table at this popular little corner cafe where locals go for their *merienda* to plug the gap between lunch and the late Argentine dinner. Enjoy tasty light meals and big portions of delicious cakes and pastries as well as good coffee, milkshakes and fresh juices. The blueberry lassi is a winner.

Flamingo Grand Bar
CAFE $

(cnr Av Urquiza & José de San Martín; mains AR$160-350; ⊙ 8am-midnight; 🛜) Smart seats and a plaza-side location make this a favorite throughout the day, from morning croissants and juices through to *lomitos* (steak sandwiches) and lunch specials, to decent à la carte dishes and *picadas*. The menu includes some vegetarian and diet options. Service could be better.

Lola Valentina
ARGENTINE $$

(☑ 0343-423-5234; Mitre 310; mains AR$170-390; ⊙ noon-3pm & 8:30-11:30pm Wed-Mon; 🛜) Blending the cheerful vibe of a favorite corner eatery with formal service, this place offers great value for a long menu of Argentine classics, delicious homemade pastas, *parrilla* options and plenty of river fish choice. It fills fast, so get there early or book.

❶ GETTING TO BRAZIL

The small, largely uninteresting town of **Paso de los Libres** is the gateway to the Brazilian town of Uruguaiana. The border crossing is marked by a bridge about 10 blocks southwest of central Plaza Independencia. Buses to Uruguaiana (around AR$40) leave frequently, stopping on Av San Martín at Colón and opposite the bus terminal. The border is open 24 hours. Once in Brazil, the nearest town to the border we recommend is **Porto Alegre**.

Between Paso's bus terminal and the center are some very dodgy neighborhoods – it's well worth investing in the AR$12/90 bus/taxi fare to get you through.

Hotels include the basic, well-kept **Hotel Las Vegas** (☑03772-423490; hotellasvegas 2000@hotmail.com; Sarmiento 554; s/d US$20/32; ⓟ✳🛜) and the reliable **Hotel Alejandro Primero** (☑03772-424100; www.alejandroprimero.com.ar; Coronel López 502; s/d US$28/32; ⓟ✳@🛜✖). There are resto-bars all along Colón between Mitre and Sitja Nia. The best restaurant in town is **El Nuevo Mesón** (Colón 587; mains AR$140-320; ◷11:30am-3pm & 8pm-midnight; 🛜).

Moving on from Paso de los Libres, there are regular buses to Mercedes (AR$175, three hours), Buenos Aires (AR$940 to AR$1030, eight to nine hours), Corrientes (AR$545, five hours) and many other destinations.

🍷 Drinking & Nightlife

Paraná is quiet midweek, but gets busy at weekends. Most of the action is at the eastern end of the riverfront around Liniers Lineal.

❶ Information

The helpful **tourist office** (☑0343-423-0183; www.turismoparana.com.ar; Plaza 1 de Mayo s/n; ◷8am-8pm) on the central square has good brochures. There's another branch by the **Río Paraná** (☑0343-420-1837; Laurencena & San Martín; ◷8am-8pm) and in the **bus terminal** (☑0343-420-1862; ◷8am-8pm).

❶ Getting There & Around

The airport is located 6km south of town. It is accessible by bus 14, which leaves from in front of the **post office** (www.correoargentino.com.ar; cnr 25 de Mayo & Monte Caseros; ◷8am-8pm). A *remise* will cost around AR$300. Aerolineas Argentinas serves Buenos Aires.

The **bus terminal** (☑0343-422-1282; Ruiz Moreno 902-950) is eight blocks southeast of the central square. Buses 1, 4, 5 and 9 run downtown. There are two companies running the route to Santa Fe (AR$30, 40 minutes, 30 minutes); Etacera is more comfortable and has space for bags in the hold.

Parque Esteros del Iberá

Esteros del Iberá is a wildlife cornucopia comparable to Brazil's Pantanal in Mato Grosso. Aquatic plants and grasses, including 'floating islands,' dominate this wetlands wilderness covering 13,000 sq km. The most notable wildlife species are reptiles such as the caiman and anaconda, mammals such as the maned wolf, howler monkey, neotropical otter, capybara, and pampas and swamp deer, as well as more than 350 bird species.

Bird-watchers and nature nuts from all over the world converge on the village of **Colonia Pellegrini**, which is 120km northeast of Mercedes, to take advantage of the ease of access to the park (Colonia Pellegrini lies within the park's boundaries). It's a charming enough place in its own right: dirt roads, little traffic and plenty of trees. There's a **visitors center** across the causeway from Colonia Pellegrini with information on the reserve and a couple of short self-guided walking trails. The **tourist office** (☑03773-401575; www.ibera.gob.ar; RP 40; ◷8am-noon & 2-7pm) at the entrance to the village is helpful. Two-hour **launch tours** (per person AR$300-500), available everywhere, are good value. Horse tours (AR$350) are pleasant, but you'll see more wildlife from the boat.

Many hotel operators in **Mercedes** (the gateway town) will try to railroad you into buying a package tour with tales of overbooking, closed hotels and so on. If you want to book ahead and go all-inclusive, fine, but there's really no need to panic – there are way more beds available than there will ever be tourists and it's easy (and much cheaper) to organize your room, food and tours on the spot. The tourist office in Colonia Pellegrini has a complete list of accommodations and eateries in town.

Camping is possible at the municipal campground **Camping Iberá** (☑03773-15-412242; www.ibera.gob.ar; Mbiguá s/n; campsite

OFF THE BEATEN TRACK

YAPEYÚ

This delightfully peaceful place is no one-horse town: there are many horses, and the sound of their hooves thumping the reddish earth in the evening is one of the nicest things about it. Yapeyú is a great spot to relax with its tree-filled plaza and quiet grassy riverfront. It's the sort of place where locals will greet you on the street.

An hour north of Paso de los Libres by bus, Yapeyú was founded in 1626 as the southernmost of the Jesuit missions. It's also famous for being the birthplace of the great Argentine 'Liberator,' José de San Martín.

You can examine the Jesuit ruins – the **Museo de la Cultura Jesuítica** (Sargento Cabral s/n; ⏲8am-noon & 3-6pm Tue-Sun) FREE here has a comprehensive overview of all the missions – and admire the ornate **Casa de San Martín** (⏲8am-noon & 2-6pm) FREE, a pavilion that now shelters the ruins of the house where San Martín was born in 1778.

On the plaza between these, **Hotel San Martín** (☎03772-493120; Sargento Cabral 712; s/d US$16/27; P ❄ 📶) is a simple, welcoming place set around an echoey inner courtyard. Up a notch, **El Paraíso Yapeyú** (☎03772-493056; www.paraisoyapeyu.com.ar; cnr Paso de los Patos & Juan de San Martín; bungalows for 2/4 people US$32/43; P ❄ 📶 ≋) is a faded complex of bungalows with a nice riverside position. More upmarket options are on the highway west of town. **Comedor del Paraíso** (Gregoria Matorras s/n; mains AR$300; ⏲8pm-midnight) is a likeably simple central spot to eat with no menu, just a limited choice of what's available that day.

The **Terminal de Transporte** (Sargento Cabral s/n) is just two blocks from the main plaza. Four daily buses run to/from Paso de los Libres (AR$70, one hour), and to Posadas (AR$355 to AR$460, 4½ hours) in the other direction. More buses stop on the highway at the edge of the town.

per person 1st/subsequent days US$6/5, per vehicle US$3; P) in Colonia Pellegrini, which has excellent, grassy waterfront sites.

A number of *hospedajes* (basic hotels) offer rooms with private bathroom, the best of which is probably **Posada Rancho Jabirú** (☎03773-15-474838; www.posadarancho jabiru.com.ar; Yaguareté s/n; s/d/tr US$26/44/66; ❄ 📶). **Hospedaje Los Amigos** (☎03773-15-493753; cnr Guazú Virá & Aguapé; r per person US$9; ❄) is the budget-watchers' current favorite.

If you've got the budget and are looking for more comfort, **Rancho de los Esteros** (☎03773-15-493041; www.ranchodelosesteros.com.ar; cnr Ñangapiry & Capivára; per person incl full board & activities US$90; P ❄ 📶 ≋) has pretty much everything you could hope for.

Transport options alter regularly: check tourist information at the Mercedes bus terminal. The road from Mercedes to Colonia Pellegrini (120km) is drivable in a normal car except after rain.

Crucero del Norte runs one rickety bus a day between Pellegrini and Mercedes (AR$230, three hours). It leaves Pellegrini at 4am and returns from the terminal in Mercedes at 12:30pm. There's no terminal in Pellegrini – just tell the driver where you're staying and he'll drop you at the door. Heading back you'll need to arrange a pick-up in advance.

More expensive than the bus are the scheduled minibus/van services. Chartered transfers in 4WD pickups between the towns cost around AR$2000 from Mercedes for up to four people. If it hasn't been raining, you could also get a *remise*.

Iberá Bus TRANSFERS
(Mario Azcona; ☎03773-15-462836; cnr Aguará & Pindó) The most regular of the private transport operators. Leaves from the market on Pujol between Gómez and Alvear in Mercedes at noon to 12:30pm Monday to Friday and 9:30am Saturdays; the trip costs AR$350. Returns from Pellegrini 4am Monday to Saturday.

Corrientes

☎0379 / POP 398,163

Stately Corrientes sits below the confluence of the Paraná and Paraguay rivers, just across the water from its twin city, Resistencia. One of the nation's most venerable cities, it has elegant balconied buildings dating from the turn of the 20th century that lend a timeworn appeal to its colorful streets.

The *costanera* is everybody's destination of choice for strolling, eating ice creams, jogging or sipping maté with friends.

◉ Sights & Activities

Museo de Artesanías Tradicionales Folclóricas
MUSEUM

(https://museosdecorrientes.org/museo-de-artesanias; Quintana 905; ⊙8am-8pm Mon-Fri) FREE This intriguing museum in a converted colonial house has small displays of fine traditional *artesanía* (handicrafts) plus a good shop, but the highlight is watching students being taught to work leather, silver, bone and wood by master craftspeople. Other rooms around the courtyard are occupied by working artisans who will sell to you directly. Museum guides are enthusiastic, knowledgeable and friendly.

★ Experiencia Corrientes
KAYAKING

(📞0379-15-450-1702; www.experienciacorrientes.com) Adventure tour operator offering a variety of kayaking trips on the Río Paraná, ranging from short sightseeing jaunts and night tours to longer adventures. Also runs excursions in the Esteros del Iberá and Mburucuyá.

Turistas Con Ruedas
CYCLING

(cnr Costanera & 9 de Julio; ⊙8am-noon & 3-7pm) FREE Head down to the riverside tourist office with your passport, and grab a free bike to explore the *costanera*. You are restricted to the riverside areas and rentals are only for an hour, so you'll need to go back and check in again if you want to ride in both directions.

★☆ Festivals & Events

The once-moribund Carnaval Correntino is now one of the country's showiest, running over four consecutive weekends starting nine weeks before Easter.

⌷ Sleeping

Most hotels are located around Plaza 25 de Mayo or in the blocks between the center and the port. Many offer discounts for paying cash.

Bienvenida Golondrina
HOSTEL $

(📞0379-443-5316; www.hostelbienvenidagolondrina.com; La Rioja 455; dm/s/d US$12.50/20/30; P ❋ @ 🛜) Occupying a marvelous centenarian building, all high ceilings, stained glass and artistic flourishes, this hostel makes a great base a few steps from the *costanera*. Comfortable wide-berthed dorm beds have headroom, and common areas are inviting. Warmly welcoming management are helpful.

Ñanderoga
GUESTHOUSE $

(📞0379-443-9401; www.nanderogacorrientes.com.ar; Pellegrini 1765; d/tr US$35/45; ❋ 🛜) A short walk from the center, this small, quiet hotel has just a handful of spacious comfortable rooms set in a converted house. Beds and bathrooms are comfortable and the staff helpful. An attached tour office offers trips with a natural slant throughout the region.

La Rozada
BOUTIQUE HOTEL $$

(📞0379-443-3001; www.larozada.com; Plácido Martínez 1223; s/d/ste US$43/55/70; P ❋ 🛜) An excellent option near the riverfront, this hotel has commodious apartments and suites unusually set in a tower in the courtyard of an appealing 19th-century, battleship gray historic building. Fine views are on offer from most rooms. A balcony room is slightly more expensive. There's an attractive bar area and guests can use the pool at the nearby rowing club.

✖ Eating & Drinking

Look out for *mbaipú*, a traditional *correntino* dish of fried chicken and onions topped with toasted flour and cheese.

The *costanera* has plenty of action, with several bars and *boliches* (nightclubs) in the Costanera Sur zone south of the Resistencia bridge, and bars strung out north of it. Near the intersection of Junín and Buenos Aires, several bars and clubs pump along at weekends.

★ Martha de Bianchetti
CAFE, BAKERY $

(cnr 9 de Julio & Mendoza; pastries from AR$50; ⊙7am-1pm & 4-10pm Mon-Sat; 🛜) This old-fashioned Italian-style bakery and cafe serves delicious pastries and excellent coffee accompanied by *chipacitos* (little cheese scones). It's all warm when the doors open and the lovely smell wafts halfway down the block. Ice cream too.

Cristóbal del Puerto
ARGENTINE $$

(📞0379-442-4229; Martínez 1102; mains AR$120-250; ⊙5:30pm-4am; ❋) A popular restaurant near the port with a large air-conditioned dining room and a big bunch of tables out on the sidewalk. The place is famous for its *picadas* (shared appetizer plates). There are also crepes and tacos alongside the standard fare. The lively atmosphere makes it worth sticking around for drinks once the plates are cleared away.

Confitería Panambi
CAFE

(www.facebook.com/confiteriapanambi; Córdoba 932; ⊙7am-1pm & 4:30-9:30pm) This cozy cafe just off the Junín mall serves good coffee alongside a mouthwatering array of quality handmade chocolates and pastries. It's also a good spot for breakfast.

☆ Entertainment

★ Cantalicio   LIVE MUSIC
(☑ 3794-751-005; Chaco 1236; ⊙ 9:30pm-2am Thu-Sat) This welcoming traditional-style bar a couple of blocks off the *costanera* is the place to go to get to know *chamamé,* with live performances and a colorful, energetic crowd. The tables are packed in but the aficionados still manage to find places to dance once things heat up. Also serves meals with an emphasis on typical plates of the region.

❶ Information

There are various irregularly open tourist offices around town, including at the airport and bus terminal.

Municipal Tourist Office (☑ 0379-447-4733; www.ciudaddecorrientes.gov.ar; cnr Av Costanera & 9 de Julio; ⊙ 8am-9pm) The main municipal tourist office, though opening can be patchy.

Provincial Tourist Office (☑ 0379-442-7200; http://turismo.corrientes.gob.ar; 25 de Mayo 1330; ⊙ 7:30am-2pm & 4:30-8:30pm Mon-Fri) Helpful for information about the province.

Casa Ibera (www.parqueibera.com; Pellegrini 501; ⊙ 8am-1pm & 4:30-9pm) Offers assistance in organizing trips to the Esteros de Iberá wetlands.

❶ Getting There & Around

Aerolíneas Argentinas (☑ 0379-442-3918; www.aerolineas.com.ar; Junín 1301; ⊙ 8am-12:30pm & 4:30-8pm Mon-Fri) flies to Buenos Aires daily. Local bus 109 (AR$11.50) goes to the **airport** (☑ 0379-445-8684; RN 12, Km 10), which is about 10km northeast of town.

Frequent buses (AR$51) and shared taxis to Resistencia leave from the **local bus terminal** (cnr Av Costanera General San Martín & La Rioja). Shared taxis also leave from the corner of Santa Fe and 3 de Abril. Listed here are departures from the **long-distance bus terminal** (☑ 0379-447-7600; Av Maipú 2400).

Bus 103 runs between the local bus terminal and the long-distance bus terminal via downtown.

BUSES FROM CORRIENTES

DESTINATION	COST (AR$)	DURATION (HR)
Buenos Aires	990-2650	12-14
Córdoba	1050-1740	11-14
Mercedes	350	3-4

DESTINATION	COST (AR$)	DURATION (HR)
Paso de los Libres	430	5
Posadas	530-760	4-4½
Puerto Iguazú	1055-1255	9-10
Rosario	780-1700	9-11
Salta	1565	14
Santa Fe	620-1200	6½-8

Resistencia

☑ 0362 / POP 425,922

This provincial capital is perched on the edge of the barely populated Chaco, northern Argentina's 'outback.' It isn't the most likely candidate for the garland of artistic center of the north, yet its streets are studded with several hundred sculptures and there's a strong boho-cultural streak that represents a complete contrast to the tough cattle-and-scrub solitudes that characterize the province.

◉ Sights

At last count, more than 650 sculptures graced the city, a number that increases with every Bienal. The streets are packed with them, especially around the plaza and north up Avenida Sarmiento. Every Bienal, a brochure is printed with a sculpture walking tour around the city. Locals can buy pieces at a symbolic cost, but they have to display them streetside.

Download the CulturApp Resistencia app for smartphones for a self-guided tour of the artworks.

★ MusEUM   GALLERY
(www.bienaldelchaco.com; Av de los Inmigrantes 1001; ⊙ 9:30am-1:30pm & 4-8pm Mon-Sat) FREE The headquarters of the **sculpture Bienal** (www.bienaldelchaco.com) and the venue for it, the exhibition room and grounds house many of the most impressive pieces from past festivals. It's well worth a visit. It also distributes brochures in English and Spanish on sculptural walking tours in town. The avenue is a northward continuation of Wilde. If going by taxi, mention the adjacent Domo del Centenario.

Museo del Hombre Chaqueño   MUSEUM
(http://museohombrechaco.blogspot.com; JB Justo 280; ⊙ 8am-1pm & 3-8pm Mon-Fri) FREE This small but excellent museum is run by enthusiastic staff (some English spoken) who talk

you through displays covering the three main pillars of Chaco's population: indigenous inhabitants (there are some excellent ceramics and Toba musical instruments here); Criollos who resulted from interbreeding between the European arrivals and the local populations; and 'gringos,' the wave of mostly European immigration from the late 19th century onward. Best is the mythology room upstairs, where you'll get to meet various quirky characters from Chaco's popular religion.

El Fogón de los Arrieros   CULTURAL CENTER
(www.fogondelosarrieros.com.ar; Brown 350; ☺ 8am-8pm Mon-Fri, 9am-1pm Sat) FREE Founded in 1943, this is a cultural center and gallery that for decades has been the driving force behind Resistencia's artistic commitment. It's famous for its eclectic collection of objets d'art from around Chaco and Argentina. The museum also features the wood carvings of local artist and cultural activist Juan de Dios Mena. Check out the irreverent epitaphs to dead patrons in the memorial garden; it's called 'Colonia Sálsipuedes' (leave if you can).

🛏 Sleeping

Hotel Diamante   HOTEL $
(☎ 0362-443-2127; http://hoteldiamante.site; Belgrano 379; s/d/tr US$29/40/45) A cheap, well-run hotel offering a variety of small but clean rooms with flat-screen TVs, old school air-conditioners and mini-bars. The garish bright-blue paint jobs are not particularly attractive but the facilities are good for the price, especially if you snag one in the newer wing, where the beds are more comfortable.

Hotel Colón   HOTEL $
(☎ 0362-442-2861; www.colonhotelyapart.com; Santa María de Oro 143; s/d/apt US$25/33/42; 🕸 @ 🛜) Art-deco fans mustn't miss this 1920s classic, just south of the plaza. It's an amazingly large and characterful building with enticingly curious period features. Refurbished rooms are great; make sure you get one, as there are some far sketchier chambers with worn mattresses and dilapidated bathrooms that you will definitely not enjoy. Good-value apartments are available.

Hotel Covadonga   HOTEL $
(☎ 0362-444-4444; www.hotelcovadonga.com.ar; Güemes 200; s/d US$38/42; P 🕸 @ 🛜 🥽) With an excellent location close to Plaza 25 de Mayo, this upmarket hotel has fine facilities, including a pool, sauna and Jacuzzi, and personable staff. Public areas are slickly furnished, and the renovated rooms feature streetside balconies and attractive wooden floors.

★ **Amerian Hotel Casino Gala**   HOTEL $$
(☎ 0362-445-2400; www.hotelcasinogala.com.ar; Perón 330; s/d US$52/57; P 🕸 @ 🛜 🥽) The city's smartest choice, with various grades of room and slick service. Rooms are excellent for these rates: very spacious, and with a dark, elegant, vaguely Asian feel to the decor. As well as slot machines, there's a sauna, gym and self-contained spa complex. The huge outdoor pool with bar is a highlight.

🍴 Eating

No Me Olvides   ARGENTINE, BAR $
(www.facebook.com/nomeolvidesmilo; Laprida 198; mains AR$175-320; ☺ 7am-3am; 🛜) Huge windows and a high-ceilinged interior make this hip corner spot feel much larger than it is. Verve and color are added by vibrant paintings, paper lampshades and arty touches. As the heroic opening hours suggest, it does everything from breakfasts to late-night cocktails. The pasta, ciabattas and *lomitos* are really excellent.

Juan Segundo   ARGENTINE $$
(☎ 0362-443-4693; www.facebook.com/juansegundoresistencia; Av Paraguay 24; mains AR$220-390; ☺ noon-2:30pm & 9pm-12:30am Tue-Sat, noon-2:30pm Sun; 🛜) With a casually elegant chessboard-tiled interior and appealing outdoor tables in an upmarket zone of the city, Juan Segundo offers decent *parrilla* choices and salads, and even better fish and meat dishes with well-prepared sauces. There's a play area for kids but not many cheap choices on the short wine list.

Coco's Resto   ARGENTINE $$
(☎ 0362-442-3321;www.facebook.com/cocosresto; Av Sarmiento 266; mains AR$150-260; ☺ 12:30-3:30pm & 9pm-midnight Mon-Sat, 12:30-3:30pm Sun; 🛜) Stylishly occupying the front rooms of a house, this intimate, well-decorated restaurant is popular with suited diners from the nearby state parliament. A wide-ranging menu of pastas, meats soused in various sauces, river fish and a long wine list make this a pleasant Chaco choice. Some good options for vegetarian diners.

🍸 Drinking & Nightlife

Guana y Velasquez   BAR
(cnr French & Don Bosco; ☺ 8pm-late Tue-Sun) This groovy corner bar is an excellent place

NORTH TOWARD PARAGUAY

If you're heading to Paraguay, buses run from Resistencia to Asunción, Paraguay's capital, crossing in Argentina's far north at **Clorinda**, a chaotic border town with little of interest beyond bustling markets.

A better stop is baking-hot **Formosa**, a medium-sized provincial capital two hours' bus ride north of Resistencia. Hotels, restaurants and services can be found along Av 25 de Mayo, which links the sleepy plaza with the Río Paraguay waterfront – the best place to stroll once the temperatures drop. **Laguna Oca** offers good bird-watching 6km from town, but the rest of Formosa province has even more.

One good spot is Parque Nacional Río Pilcomayo (p93), 126km northwest of Formosa and 55km west of Clorinda. Daily buses connect these with **Laguna Blanca**, an easy-paced citrus town where you'll find inexpensive lodgings – **Residencial Guaraní** (☑ 03718-470024; www.hotel-guarani.com; cnr San Martín & Sargento Cabral, Laguna Blanca; r per person US$18; ✻) is the standout – and *remises* to the national park. The park's main feature is also called **Laguna Blanca**, where rangers can take you out in boats to spot caiman.

Formosa province's standout attraction is **Bañado la Estrella** (www.banadolaestrella. org.ar; ◎ 8am-6pm). This stunning wetland area, a floodplain of the Río Pilcomayo, harbors an astonishing range of birdlife, as well as alligators, capybaras, sizeable serpents and beautiful water plants. From the roads that cross this 200km-long finger-shaped area, it's easy to spot a huge variety of wildlife: pack binoculars.

The handiest town is Las Lomitas, 300km west of Formosa on RN81 with regular bus service (AR$565, 5½ hours). From here, paved RP28 heads north, cutting across the wetlands via a causeway, starting 37km north of Las Lomitas and extending for some 15km.

for some drinks. Head inside for wooden floors, mosaic walls and fashionably mismatched wooden chairs or pick a table outside under the trees beneath the murals. The music is as interesting as the decor, and a large Jim Morrison portrait keeps an eye over proceedings.

❶ Information

Centro Cultural Leopoldo Marechal (☑ 0362-445-2738; www.facebook.com/centrocultural marechal/; Pellegrini 272; ◎ 9am-2pm & 4:30-7:30pm Mon-Fri) Information about indigenous issues and visiting Toba communities. There's a small display of Toba handcrafts.

Terminal Tourist Office (www.chaco.travel; ◎ 7am-8pm Mon-Fri Sat, 7-9:30am & 6-8:30pm Sat & Sun) Useful office in the bus terminal. There's a municipal office opposite it.

City Tourist Office (☑ 0362-445-8289; Roca 20; ◎ 7am-noon & 2:30-8pm) On the southern side of Plaza 25 de Mayo.

❶ Getting There & Around

Aeropuerto San Martín is 6km south of town on RN11; a taxi costs around AR$230. Aerolíneas Argentinas (www.aerolineas.com.ar) flies to Buenos Aires daily.

The **bus terminal** (☑ 0362-446-1098; cnr MacLean & Islas Malvinas) is a AR$150 taxi from the center, or you can take bus 3, 9 or 110 from Santa María de Oro near Perón. Don't walk it: travelers have reported muggings. To ride the city buses you'll need to purchase a card (AR$60) at the office on the southern side of Plaza 25 de Mayo and then load it with credit. Each ride around town costs AR$11.

There's an urban bus service between Resistencia and Corrientes for AR$50. You can catch it on Av Alberdi just south of Plaza 25 de Mayo.

BUSES FROM RESISTENCIA

DESTINATION	COST (AR$)	DURATION (HR)
Asunción, Paraguay	350-550	6
Buenos Aires	990-2650	13-14
Córdoba	1260-1740	10-14
Formosa	270-380	3
Posadas	540-690	4½-5
Puerto Iguazú	1085-1290	10-11
Rosario	780-1740	9-10
Salta	1325-1430	12-13
Santiago del Estero	1030-1180	10
Tucumán	1290-1460	11-12

Posadas

☑ 0376 / POP 358,986

Capital of Misiones, and a base for visiting the Jesuit ruins after which the province is named, Posadas is a modern city that gazes across the wide Río Paraná to Encarnación in Paraguay. It's a stopover on the way north, and though it offers few in-town sights, it has a pleasant riverbank and an enjoyable vibe.

◎ Sights

The Jesuit missions are the area's big attraction in Posadas.

★ Costanera   WATERFRONT

In the afternoon, the *costanera* comes alive with joggers, cyclists, dog walkers, *mate* sippers, hot-dog vendors and young couples staring at Paraguay across the water. Pride of place goes to 'Andresito,' a huge stainless-steel sculpture of Guaraní provincial strongman Andrés Guazurary.

☞ Tours

Yacaré Tours   TOURS

(☑ 0376-442-1829; www.yacaretours.com.ar; Bolívar 1419) This operation offers half-day trips to Argentine (AR$1850 per vehicle) and Paraguayan (AR$2200 per vehicle) missions. Also has trips to *mate* plantations, Saltos del Moconá, Los Esteros del Iberá and more.

⎵ Sleeping

Posadeña Linda   HOSTEL $

(☑ 0376-4439238; www.facebook.com/hostel posadenalinda; Bolívar 1439; dm/r US$8/20; ❄ @ 🛜 ⛱) Run with a caring attitude, this narrow hostel a short walk from the plaza offers a genuine welcome, comfortable bunkrooms with bathroom, and a patio with a tiny plunge pool. En suite private rooms are a little musty but a decent deal. It's colorful and relaxing with a compact but OK kitchen. Despite the address, it's between 1411 and 1419.

La Misión   HOTEL $

(☑ 0376-445-1222; www.lamisionposadashotel. com; Av Quaranta 6150; s/d/tr US$40/48/55; ⛱) A fair way out of town but convenient for the bus terminal and airport, this modern hotel offers real value, with smart spacious rooms decked out with king beds and great bathrooms and an inviting pool area. A good option if you're just passing through and don't actually want to see Posadas. It's a AR$200 taxi from downtown.

★ Hotel Posadas Urbano   HOTEL $$

(☑ 0376-444-3800; http://alvarezarguelles.com/ hotel/hotel-urbano; Bolívar 2176; r/ste from US$65/105; 🅿 ❄ @ 🛜 ⛱) This smartly renovated hotel has rapidly become top dog with its wide array of facilities and great central location. Bright, very large, carpeted chambers all have gleaming bathrooms, balconies and big windows with views over town. Suites add space but little else. The atrium pool area, art exhibitions, gym and spa facilities, and appealing lounge add points.

✗ Eating & Drinking

A delicious specialty is *galeto* (chargrilled chicken pieces stuffed with bacon, red peppers and butter). A string of popular places along Bolívar west of the plaza do *lomitos* (steak sandwiches), sandwiches and other cheap eats.

Most weekend action is down at the *costanera*, where a knot of eateries, bars and clubs go loud and late.

★ La Tradicional Rueda   PARRILLA $$

(La Ruedita; cnr Arrechea & Av Costanera; mains AR$190-310; ⏱ 11am-3:30pm & 8pm-midnight; 🛜) Stylish and traditional in feel, with uniformed waiters and sturdy wooden seats, this two-level grillhouse has a prime riverside position: look for the wooden wheel outside. Quality meats and nice choice of salads and river fish put this a class above most *parrilla* places. If you go for *galeto*, make sure to get it encrusted with Parmesan. Service is excellent.

La Querencia   PARRILLA $$

(www.laquerenciarestaurante.com; Bolívar 1867; mains AR$290-360; ⏱ noon-2:30pm & 8pm-12:30am Mon-Sat, noon-2:30pm Sun; 🛜) This upmarket *parrilla* on the plaza specializes in delicious *galeto*. Also memorable are the brochettes (giant spikes with various delicious meats impaled upon them). Salads are also unusually well prepared. Service is great and the atmosphere a highlight.

⬛ Shopping

Fundación Artesanías Misioneras   GALLERY

(www.famercosur.com.ar; cnr Álvarez & Arrechea; ⏱ 8:30am-noon & 5-8pm Mon-Fri, 9:30am-12:30pm Sat) 🪶 Guaraní culture is strong in this part of Argentina, and particularly fine indigenous crafts are displayed and sold here. There's another branch on the *costanera* near the train station, which is open in the evenings and on weekends when the main branch is closed.

ℹ️ Information

Misiones Tourist Office (☑ 0376-444-7539; www.misiones.tur.ar; Colón 1985; ⊗ 7am-8pm) is the most efficient, but there are other tourist kiosks around town.

ℹ️ Getting There & Away

Aerolíneas Argentinas (☑ 0810-222-86527; Sarmiento 2280; ⊗ 8am-noon & 4-8pm Mon-Fri) flies daily to Buenos Aires.

A shiny modern rail service connects Posadas and Encarnación in Paraguay, leaving Posadas every 30 minutes from 7:15am to 6:15pm (AR$50, six minutes). You clear both Argentine and Paraguayan authorities at the **Apeadero Posadas station** (www.sofse.gob.ar). Buses depart Posadas for Buenos Aires, Puerto Iguazú and other destinations.

BUSES FROM POSADAS

DESTINATION	COST (AR$)	DURATION (HR)
Buenos Aires	1440-1950	12-14
Corrientes	530-610	4-4½
Paso de los Libres	425-700	5-6
Puerto Iguazú	465-480	4½-5½
Resistencia	540-660	4½-5
Rosario	1470-1750	14-15
San Ignacio	85	1
Tucumán	1855-2115	18

ℹ️ Getting Around

Posadas' bus terminal is 5km south of town and can be reached from downtown by bus 8, 15 (from Junín), 21 or 24 (AR$12). It costs about

ℹ️ GETTING TO PARAGUAY

Buses to Encarnación (AR$35, every 20 minutes), Paraguay, stop at the corner of San Lorenzo and Entre Ríos. With queues and border formalities, the trip can take more than an hour.

Everyone gets out to clear Argentine emigration. If the bus leaves without you, keep your ticket and catch the next one. The same happens on the Paraguayan side. There are fairly honest money-changers hanging out by Paraguayan immigration. Get small denominations: a 100,000 guaraní note is hell to change.

AR$150 in a taxi. From the bus terminal, catch local buses out in front or from the adjacent metropolitan terminal.

Bus 28 (AR$12) goes to the airport from San Lorenzo (between La Rioja and Entre Ríos). A *remise* costs around AR$250.

Buses 7 and 12 (AR$12) go to the Apeadero Posadas station.

San Ignacio

☑ 0376 / POP 6800

A mellow little town between Posadas and Puerto Iguazú, San Ignacio attracts most visitors for the large, well-preserved ruins of the Jesuit mission that gives the town its name. If you're staying here and have some time to kill, it's also well worth checking out the Casa de Quiroga. If you're just passing through, you can leave your bags in the ticket office at the bus terminal while you check out the ruins.

◉ Sights & Activities

★ **San Ignacio Miní** RUINS
(www.misiones.tur.ar; entrance Alberdi s/n; combined missions ticket foreigners/Latin Americans/Argentines AR$200/170/130; ⊗ 7am-5:30pm Apr-Oct, 7am-7pm Nov-Mar) These mission ruins are the most complete in Argentina: atmospheric and impressive for the quantity of carved ornamentation still visible and for the amount of restoration. There's a small museum and the ruins themselves feature interactive panels providing multilingual audio (although not all are in operation). Admission includes entry to nearby ruins at **Santa Ana** (www.misiones.tur.ar; combined missions ticket foreigners/Mercosur/Argentines AR$200/170/130; ⊗ 7am-6pm Apr-Oct, 7am-7pm Nov-Mar) and **Loreto** (www.misiones.tur.ar; combined missions ticket foreigners/Mercosur/Argentines AR$200/170/130; ⊗ 7am-5:30pm Apr-Oct, 7am-7pm Nov-Mar) and to **Santa María la Mayor** (RP 2, Km 43; combined missions ticket foreigners/Latin Americans/Argentines AR$200/170/130; ⊗ 7am-5:30pm Apr-Oct, 7am-7pm Nov-Mar) further afield. There's a worthwhile sound-and-light show (foreigners AR$200) at the ruins every nonrainy night.

Casa de Horacio Quiroga MUSEUM
(Av Quiroga s/n; AR$100; ⊗ 10am-6pm) Uruguayan writer Horacio Quiroga was a get-back-to-nature type who found his muse in the rough-and-ready Misiones backwoods lifestyle. He built his simple stone house at the southern end of town (a 30-minute walk) himself. Spanish-speaking guides will lead you through the sugarcane fields to the

house and inform you about Quiroga's deeply tragic life, so full of shotgun accidents and doses of cyanide it almost seems to be a thing of fiction.

🛏 Sleeping & Eating

Rivadavia, between the bus stop and the ruins, is lined with small restaurants serving *milanesas* (breaded cutlets), pizza and so on.

Adventure Hostel   HOSTEL $
(📱0376-447-0955; www.sihostel.com; Independencia 469; campsites per person US$7, dm US$10-12, d US$40; P❄@🕸🏊) This well-run, motivated place has comfortable dorms with either three beds or four bunk-berths, decent private rooms with renovated bathrooms, and excellent facilities. Added perks include pool (both kinds), ping-pong and spacious grounds. Tasty homemade breakfasts are included and the restaurant does decent pasta-pizza-type meals. There are also powered campsites.

Posada Madre America   GUESTHOUSE $
(📱0376-447-0778; Sarmiento 605; s/d/tr US$38/44/50, dm/s/d without bathroom US$12/16/32) Right in the middle of town, this welcoming new place has spacious but sparsely decorated hotel rooms with spotless bathrooms and cheaper hostel rooms with shared facilities. There's good fast wi-fi throughout and the staff are very obliging. It's set back from the road so is fairly tranquil.

La Misionerita   ARGENTINE $$
(📱0376-437-6220; RN 12; mains AR$150-280; ⏰5am-midnight; 🕸) On the highway opposite the town entrance, this place has impressive opening hours, friendly service and a decent range of burgers, *milanesas* and the like, along with grill options and river fish. One of the few evening options.

ℹ Getting There & Away

The **bus terminal** is on the main road near the town entrance. Services between Posadas (AR$65, one hour) and Puerto Iguazú (AR$220, four to five hours) are frequent.

Puerto Iguazú
📱03757 / POP 94,994

At the end of the road in Argentina, Puerto Iguazú sits at the confluence of the Ríos Paraná and Iguazú and looks across to Brazil and Paraguay. There's little feeling of community: everyone is here to see the falls or to make a buck out of them, and planning laws seem nonexistent as hotels go up on every street. Still, it's not unattractive and is quiet, safe and has good transportation connections; there are also many excellent places to stay and eat.

👁 Sights

Güirá Oga   ANIMAL SANCTUARY
(www.guiraoga.com.ar; RN 12, Km 5; adult/child AR$200/150; ⏰9:30am-6pm, last entry 4:45pm) 🍃 On the way to the falls, this is an animal hospital and center for rehabilitation of injured wildlife. It also carries out valuable research into the Iguazú forest environment and has a breeding program for endangered species. You get walked around the jungly 20-hectare park by one of the staff, who explains about the birds and animals and the sad stories of how they got there. The visit takes about 90 minutes.

Casa Ecológica de Botellas   ARCHITECTURE
(http://lacasadebotellas.googlepages.com; RN 12, Km 5; AR$100; ⏰9am-6:30pm) 🍃 About 300m off the falls road, this fascinating place is well worth a visit. The owners have taken used packaging materials – plastic bottles, juice cartons and the like – to build not only an impressive house, but furnishings and a bunch of original handicrafts that make unusual gifts. The guided visit talks you through their techniques.

🛏 Sleeping

Porämbá Hostel   HOSTEL $
(📱03757-423041; www.porambahostel.com; El Urú 120; dm US$7, r/tr US$21/24; ❄@🕸🏊) In a very peaceful location but an easy walk from the bus terminal, this is a popular choice for its variety of noncrowded dorms, private rooms with or without bathroom and small pool. It's a chilled place with a kitchen and a super laid-back atmosphere.

125 Hotel   HOSTEL $
(📱03757-422346; Misiones 125; dm/d US$15/52; ❄🕸🏊) With a fine location, a social vibe and friendly staff, this hostel is a decent budget base. Private rooms are a bit poky but they're modern, clean and good value. Dorms are some of the best in town, with each bunk sectioned off by curtains, and the shared bathrooms are well maintained. Has a good pool area.

Bambú Hostel   HOSTEL $
(📱03757-425864; www.hostelbambu.com.ar; cnr Avs San Martín & Córdoba; dm/r US$12/40) A

Puerto Iguazú

0 / 0   400 m / 0.2 miles

Puerto Iguazú

popular choice close to the bus station, this well-run hostel has friendly staff and a social vibe. Accommodations are just OK for the price: private rooms are comfortable but fairly plain and the dorms are a bit tight for space. However, there's an excellent, loungy street-side bar that is the perfect place to hang out in the evenings.

Hotel Lilian HOTEL $
(☎03757-420968; hotellilian@gmail.com; Beltrán 183; d/tr US$36/38; P❄🛜) Run by a hospitable family, which isn't out to rip off tourists, this friendly place offers plenty of value, with decent rooms around a couple of plant-filled patios. Most superiors – worth the small extra outlay – have a balcony and heaps of natural light. All bathrooms are spacious and spotless.

★ **Boutique Hotel de la Fonte** HOTEL $$
(☎03757-420625; www.bhfboutiquehotel.com; cnr Corrientes & 1 de Mayo; r/ste from US$65/100; P❄@🛜🏊) The mark of a good hotel is constant improvement, and this place adds great features so fast we can barely keep up. It's a secluded, enchanting spot, featuring characterful, individually decorated rooms and suites around a tree-filled courtyard garden that is romantically lit at night. One of the welcoming owners is an architect, and it shows in the numerous small decorative touches and artistic design.

★ **Jasy Hotel** HOTEL $$
(☎03757-424337; www.jasyhotel.com; San Lorenzo 154; d/q from US$60/80; P❄🛜🏊) Original and peaceful, these 10 two-level rooms, with a great design for family sleeping,

climb a hill like a forest staircase and are all equipped with a balcony gazing over plentiful greenery. Artful use of wood is the signature; you'll fall in love with the bar and deck area. Prepare to stay longer than planned. There's a decent restaurant open evenings.

Eating

★ Feria
MARKET $
(Feirinha; cnr Av Brasil & Félix de Azara; picadas AR$250-350; ⊙8am-midnight) A really nice place to eat or have a beer is this market in the north of town. It's full of stalls selling Argentine wines, sausages, olives and cheese to visiting Brazilians, and several of them put out *picadas*, grilled meats, other simple regional dishes and cold beer. There's folk music some nights and a good evening atmosphere.

La Misionera Casa de Empanada
EMPANADAS $
(☑03757-424580; P Moreno 228; empanadas AR$27; ⊙11:30am-midnight Mon-Sat) Excellent empanadas with a big variety of fillings, as well as a delivery option.

Lemongrass
CAFE $
(Bompland 231; light meals AR$95-210; ⊙8:30am-2:30pm & 5-9:30pm Mon-Sat; ☑) One of few decent cafes in Puerto Iguazú, this offers good fresh juices, good coffee, delicious sweet temptations, sandwiches, pizzas and tasty savory tarts. Beers, mojitos and caipirinhas are also available.

Color
PARRILLA, PIZZA $$
(☑03757-420206; www.parrillapizzacolor.com; Av Córdoba 135; mains AR$230-350, pizza AR$255-450; ⊙noon-midnight; ☎) This popular indoor-outdoor pizza 'n' *parrilla* packs them into its tightly spaced tables, so don't discuss state secrets. Prices are OK for this strip, and the meat comes out redolent of wood smoke; the wood-oven pizzas and empanadas are also very toothsome. You'll have to wait for a seat during high season, or reserve online.

🍷 Drinking & Nightlife

Tourism and Brazilians from Foz make Puerto Iguazú's nightlife lively. Action centers on Av Brasil, where a string of bars attract evening drinkers.

Quita Penas
BAR
(☑03757-458223; Av Brasil 120; ⊙6pm-late) A happening open-air bar in the middle of Puerto Iguazú's little nightlife strip, Quita Penas has an elevated deck and a variety of other spaces below. It serves good food and is a fine place to sink some beers and watch the action. Often has live music.

Cuba Libre
CLUB
(www.facebook.com/cuba.megadisco; cnr Av Brasil & Paraguay; ⊙11pm-late Wed-Sun) This unsubtle but fun nightclub just off the Av Brasil strip fills up with Brazilians looking for a big night out on the weak peso. The dance floor fills late but fast.

ℹ Information

The Brazilian Consulate (p193) here arranges visas in half a day, much better than the week it takes their Buenos Aires counterparts to do the same job.

Municipal Tourist Office (☑03757-423951; www.iguazuturismo.gob.ar; Av Victoria Aguirre 337; ⊙8am-2pm & 4-9pm)

Provincial Tourist Office (☑03757-420800; www.misiones.tur.ar; Av Victoria Aguirre 311; ⊙8am-9pm) The most helpful information office in town.

ℹ Getting There & Around

AIR

Aerolíneas Argentinas (☑03757-420168; www.aerolineas.com.ar; Av Victoria Aguirre 295; ⊙8am-noon & 3-7pm Mon-Fri, 8am-1pm Sat) flies daily to Buenos Aires.

Remises to the airport cost about AR$400. Various companies offer shuttle service for AR$90. Ask at your hotel.

BICYCLE

Near the bus terminal, **Jungle Bike** (☑03757-423720; www.junglebike.com.ar; Av Victoria Aguirre 262, Local 7 Galeria Plaza Pueblo; bike hire per hr/day AR$50/200, mountain bikes per day AR$350-400; ⊙9am-8:30pm) offers bikes for hire and arranges guided excursions.

ℹ GETTING TO BRAZIL & PARAGUAY

Buses to Foz do Iguaçu, Brazil (AR$25, one hour), leave regularly from Puerto Iguazú's bus terminal. The bus will wait as you complete immigration procedures. The border is open 24 hours, but buses only run in daylight hours.

Frequent buses go from Puerto Iguazú's bus terminal to Ciudad del Este, Paraguay (AR$30, one hour), and wait at the border as you complete customs formalities.

BUS

The **bus terminal** (cnr Avs Córdoba & Misiones) has departures for Posadas (AR$250, 5½ hours), Buenos Aires (AR$1200 to AR$1730, 20 hours) and intermediate points. Frequent buses also leave for Parque Nacional Iguazú (AR$50, 30 minutes).

Parque Nacional Iguazú

People who doubt the theory that the negative ions generated by waterfalls make people happier might have to reconsider after visiting the **Iguazú Falls**. Moods just seem to improve the closer you get, until eventually people degenerate into a giggling, shrieking mess. And these are grown adults we're talking about.

But sheer giddiness isn't the only reason to come here. The power, size and sheer noise of the falls have to be experienced to be believed. You could try coming early, or later in the day (tour groups tend to leave by 3pm), but you're unlikely ever to have the place to yourself. The **park** (☑ 03757-491469; www.iguazuargentina.com; adult foreigners/Mercosur/Argentines AR$600/480/310, child AR$150/120/100; ☺ 8am-6pm) quickly fills with Argentines, backpackers, families and tour groups – but who cares? Get up close to the Garganta del Diablo (Devil's Throat) and the whole world seems to drop away.

Guaraní legend says that Iguazú Falls originated when a jealous forest god, enraged by a warrior escaping downriver by canoe with a young maiden, caused the riverbed to collapse in front of the lovers, producing precipitous falls over which the maiden fell and, at their base, turned into a rock. The warrior survived as a tree overlooking his fallen lover.

The geological origins of the falls are more prosaic. In southern Brazil, the Río Iguazú passes over a basalt plateau that ends just above its confluence with the Paraná. Before reaching the edge, the river divides into many channels to form several distinctive *cataratas* (cataracts).

The most awesome is the semicircular Garganta del Diablo, a deafening and dampening part of the experience, approached by launch and via a system of *pasarelas* (catwalks). There's no doubt that it's spectacular – there's only one question: where's the bungee jump?

Despite development pressures, the 550-sq-km park is a natural wonderland of sub-tropical rainforest, with more than 2000 identified plant species, countless insects, 400 bird species, and many mammals and reptiles.

If you've got the time (and the money for a visa), it's worth checking out the Brazilian side of the falls too, for a few different angles, plus the grand overview.

◉ Sights

Before seeing Iguazú Falls themselves, grab a map, look around the **museum**, and climb the nearby **tower** for a good overall view. Plan hikes before the mid-morning tour-bus invasion. Descending from the visitors center, you can cross by free launch to **Isla San Martín**, which offers unique views and a refuge from the masses on the mainland.

Several *pasarelas* give good views of smaller falls and, in the distance, the **Garganta del Diablo**. A train from the visitors center operates regularly to shuttle visitors from site to site. At the last stop, follow the trail to the lookout perched right on the edge of the mighty falls.

🏃 Activities

Best in the early morning, the **Sendero Macuco** nature trail leads through dense forest, where a steep sidetrack goes to the base of a hidden waterfall. Another trail goes to the *bañado,* a marsh abounding in birdlife. Allow about 2½ hours return (6km) for the entire Sendero Macuco trail.

To get elsewhere in the forest, you can hitchhike (which Lonely Planet does not recommend, as it is never entirely safe) or hire a car to take you out along RN 101 toward the village of Bernardo de Irigoyen. Few visitors explore this part of the park, and it is still nearly pristine forest.

Iguazú Jungle Explorer   BOATING
(☑ 03757-421696; www.iguazujungle.com) This operation offers three adventure tours: most popular is the short boat trip leaving from the Paseo Inferior that takes you right under one of the waterfalls for a high-adrenalin soaking (AR$1000). The Gran Aventura combines this with a jungle drive (AR$1500), while the Paseo Ecológico (AR$400) is a wildlife-oriented tour in inflatable boats upstream from the falls.

Safaris Rainforest   JUNGLE TOUR
(☑ 03757-491074; www.rainforest.iguazuargentina.com) Using knowledgeable guides, this is the best option for appreciating Parque Nacional Iguazú's flora and fauna. It offers combined

driving-walking excursions: the Safari a la Cascada takes you to the Arrechea waterfall (AR$560, 90 minutes); better is the Safari en la Selva (AR$660, two hours), a trip in a less-touristed part of the park that includes explanations of Guaraní culture.

Full Moon Walks WALKING
(📲 03757-491469; www.iguazuargentina.com/en/luna-llena) For five consecutive nights per month, these guided walks visit the Garganta del Diablo. There are three departures nightly. The first, at 8pm, offers the spectacle of the inflated rising moon; the last, at 9:30pm, sees the falls better illuminated. Don't expect wildlife. The price (AR$1100) includes admission and a drink; dinner is extra (AR$500). Book in advance as numbers are limited.

❶ Information

Buses from Puerto Iguazú drop passengers at the **Centro de Informes**, where there's a small natural-history museum.

DANGERS & ANNOYANCES

The Río Iguazú's currents are strong and swift; more than one tourist has been swept downriver and drowned near Isla San Martín.

The wildlife is also potentially dangerous. Visitors should respect the big cats; in case you encounter one, it's important not to panic. Speak calmly but loudly, do not run or turn your back, and try to appear bigger than you are by waving your arms or clothing.

❶ Getting There & Away

Regular buses run to Puerto Iguazú (AR$130, 40 minutes).

NORTHWEST ARGENTINA

With a very tangible sense of history, the northwest is Argentina's most indigenous region, and the sights and people here show much closer links with the country's Andean neighbors than the European character of its urban centers.

Córdoba

📲 0351 / POP 1.391 MILLION

Argentina's second city is everything it should be – vibrant, fun, manageable in size and (in places) gorgeous to look at. Culture vultures beware: you may get stuck here. Music, theater, film, dance: whatever you want, you can be pretty sure it's going on somewhere in town. The city also rocks out with seven universities, and has a buzz that some say is unmatched in the entire country.

◉ Sights

To see Córdoba's colonial buildings and monuments, start at the **cabildo** (Independencia 30), on Plaza San Martín. At the plaza's southwestern corner, crowned by a Romanesque dome, the **Iglesia Catedral** (Independencia 80; ⊙ 8am-4pm & 5-8pm), begun in 1577, mixes a variety of styles.

South of the center is Córdoba's **Milla Cultural** (Cultural Mile) – 1.6km of theaters, art galleries and art schools. The highlights here are the **Paseo del Buen Pastor** (Av H Yrigoyen 325; ⊙ 10am-8pm) **FREE**, which showcases work by Córdoba's young and emerging artists; the **Museo Superior de Bellas Artes Evita** (Av H Yrigoyen 551; AR$50, Wed free; ⊙ 10am-8pm Tue-Sun, 10am-1pm & 6-9pm Jan), housing 400 works of fine art; and the **Museo Provincial de Bellas Artes Emilio Caraffa** (www.museocaraffa.org.ar; Av Poeta Lugones 411; AR$50, Wed free; ⊙ 10am-8pm Tue-Sun), which features a rotating collection of top-shelf contemporary art.

Museo Histórico de la Universidad Nacional de Córdoba MUSEUM
(Obispo Trejo 242; AR$20, Wed free; ⊙ 9:30am-6:30pm Mon-Sat Mar-Dec, 9am-1pm & 4-8pm Mon-Sat Jan & Feb, guided visits 11am & 3pm Thu-Tue) In 1613 Fray Fernando de Trejo y Sanabria founded the Seminario Convictorio de San Javier, which, after being elevated to university status in 1622, became the Universidad Nacional de Córdoba, the country's oldest. Today the building contains, among other national treasures, part of the Jesuits' Grand Library and the Museo Histórico de la Universidad Nacional de Córdoba.

Museo de la Memoria MUSEUM
(Pje Santa Catalina 1; ⊙ 1-7pm Tue-Fri, 3-7pm Sat & Sun) **FREE** A chilling testament to the excesses of Argentina's military dictatorship, this museum occupies a space formerly used as a clandestine center for detention and torture. It was operated by the dreaded Department of Intelligence (D2), a special division dedicated to the kidnapping and torture of suspected political agitators and the 'reassignment' of their children to less politically suspect families.

Northwest Argentina

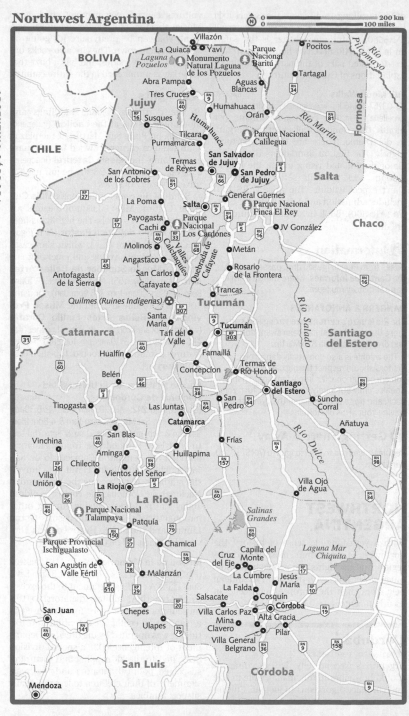

N 0   200 km
0   100 miles

ARGENTINA CÓRDOBA

Villazón
Yavi
La Quiaca
BOLIVIA
Laguna Pozuelos
Monumento Natural Laguna de los Pozuelos
Parque Nacional Baritú
Pocitos
Río Pilcomayo
Tartagal
Abra Pampa
Aguas Blancas
RN 34
Tres Cruces
RN 9
Humahuaca
Orán
Jujuy
RN 16
Susques
Humahuaca
Río Martín
RN 81
Formosa
Tilcara
Purmamarca
CHILE
San Salvador de Jujuy
RP 5
Termas de Reyes
San Pedro de Jujuy
Salta
San Antonio de los Cobres
RN 51
RN 66
RP 27
General Güemes
La Poma
Salta
RN 9
Parque Nacional Finca El Rey
Chaco
Payogasta
RP 17
Cachi
Parque Nacional Los Cardones
RN 34
RP 5
RN 16
JV González
RN 40
RP 33
Molinos
RN 68
Metán
RP 43
Angastaco
Valles Calchaquíes
Rosario de la Frontera
San Carlos
Quebrada de Cafayate
Antofagasta de la Sierra
Cafayate
Trancas
Quilmes (Ruines Indígenas)
RP 307
Tucumán
Santa María
RN 9
Tucumán
Catamarca
Tafí del Valle
RP 303
RN 40
Hualfín
Famaillá
RN 60
Termas de Río Hondo
Belén
Concepción
Santiago del Estero
RP 46
RN 38
Río Salado
RP 3
Las Juntas
San Pedro
RN 64
Santiago del Estero
RN 89
Tinogasta
RN 64
Suncho Corral
Catamarca
San Blas
Frías
Añatuya
Vinchina
RN 40
Aminga
Huillapima
RN 9
RN 98
RP 26
Chilecito
RN 38
Villa Unión
Vientos del Señor
RN 157
RP 5
La Rioja
Villa Ojo de Agua
RN 34
RP 26
RN 74
La Rioja
RN 60
RN 40
Parque Nacional Talampaya
Patquía
Salinas Grandes
RN 79
Parque Provincial Ischigualasto
RN 150
RP 27
Chamical
Capilla del Monte
Laguna Mar Chiquita
San Agustín de Valle Fértil
RN 38
Cruz del Eje
La Cumbre
RP 17
RP 28
Malanzán
Jesús María
RP 29
La Falda
RP 10
San Juan
RP 510
RP 20
Salsacate
Cosquín
Chepes
Villa Carlos Paz
Córdoba
RN 19
RN 40
Ulapes
RN 79
Mina Clavero
Alta Gracia
RN 141
Villa General Belgrano
Pilar
San Luis
RN 36
RN 9
RN 158
Córdoba
Mendoza
RN 9

📚 Courses

Able Spanish School
LANGUAGE

(📞0351-422-4692; www.ablespanish.com; Tucumán 443; ⊙9am-5pm Mon-Fri) Offers accommodations and afternoon activities at extra cost and discounts for extended study.

Tsunami Tango
DANCING

(📞0351-15-313-8746; Laprida 453) Tango classes and *milongas* (tango halls) on Monday (at 8pm), Tuesday (7:30pm), Wednesday (7:30pm) and Friday (10pm).

🛏 Sleeping

Hostel Rupestre
HOSTEL $

(📞0351-15-226-7412; http://rupestre.insta-hostel. com; Obispo Oro 242; dm/s/d from US$6.50/ 15.50/20; 🐱) A very well-appointed, stylish hostel just on the edge of Nueva Córdoba's party zone. The location is great and the whole setup is well thought out, with an indoor climbing gym, spacious dorms and friendly, enthusiastic staff.

Hostel Alvear
HOSTEL $

(📞0351-421-6502; www.hostelalvear.com; Alvear 158; dm/d US$8/27; @🐱) An excellent location and spacious dorms set in an atmospheric old building make this one of the better hostels in the downtown area.

★ Sacha Mistol
HOTEL $$

(📞0351-424-2646; www.sachamistol.com; Rivera Indarte 237; s/d/tr from US$60/70/80; ❄🐱🏊) This stylish and original hotel is a favorite with the artsy crowd. Rooms are spacious and comfortable, decorated with eclectic art and well-chosen furnishings. It's set in a carefully renovated classic house and features art exhibitions and a small lap pool, all in a quiet, central location on the pedestrian mall.

Yrigoyen 111
HOTEL $$

(📞0351-571-4000; www.y111hotel.com; Av H Yrigoyen 111; s/d US$70/85; ❄🐱🏊) A swank hotel with an unbeatable location at the heart of Nueva Córdoba, showcasing all the bells and whistles in its spacious, tastefully decked-out rooms with great city views from the upper floors. There's a rooftop pool and gym facilities too, and a cozy lounge bar downstairs.

🍴 Eating

La Vieja Esquina
ARGENTINE $

(📞0351-424-7940; Belgrano 193; empanadas AR$30, locro AR$140; ⊙11:30am-3pm & 7:30pm-1am Mon-Sat) A cozy little lunch spot with stools and window seating. Don't expect elaborate meals – it's mostly empanadas, *locro* (a spicy stew of maize, beans, beef, pork and sausage) and other mainstays – but they're tops when it comes to taste. Order at the bar.

Bruncheria
CAFE $

(www.facebook.com/bruncheriacafe; Rodriguez 244; breakfast AR$120-185, brunch for 2 people AR$435; ⊙10am-9pm; 🐱) Down in the hipster sector of Güemes, the Bruncheria offers a great mix of fresh decor, yummy food and cool music. It's a good spot for that second breakfast, in case the typical morning fare of coffee and croissant didn't fill you up. The sandwiches are winners too.

La Candela
ARGENTINE $

(📞0351-428-1517; Duarte Quirós 67; empanadas AR$22, locro AR$140; ⊙noon-4:30pm & 7:30pm-1am) Rustic and wonderfully atmospheric, La Candela is run by three cranky but adorable *señoras*. To match the vibe, the food is no-frills and honest.

Mercado Norte
MARKET $

(www.facebook.com/mercadonortecordoba; Oncativo 50; snacks & mains AR$50-300; ⊙7am-7:30pm Mon-Fri, to 2:30pm Sat) Córdoba's indoor market has delicious and inexpensive food, such as pizza, empanadas (baked savory turnovers) and seafood. Browsing the clean stalls selling every imaginable cut of meat, including whole *chivitos* (goat) and pigs, is a must. Saturday here is particularly lively.

Quadrata
ITALIAN $

(📞0351-421-1290; 9 de Julio 458; mains AR$35-90; ⊙11:30am-10:30pm Mon-Fri, to 3:30pm Sat) Tiny spot that churns out top-notch Italian food at low prices. The pizzas, pastas and panini are the real deal, made fresh daily. Great for a grab-n-go slice of pizza. Don't miss the tiramisu.

Alfonsina
ARGENTINE $$

(Duarte Quirós 66; mains AR$250-300; ⊙8am-1am Mon-Fri, 8am-4pm & 6pm-2am Sat, 7pm-midnight Sun; 🐱) In a rambling colonial town house at the historic heart of Córdoba, this bric-a-brac-filled restaurant-bar has a huge menu of favorites – pastas, pizzas, *locro* (a spicy meat, beans and maize stew), empanadas and steaks – and some regional mainstays such as *cabrito* (goat) stew. Though Alfonsina has a couple of other locations, this one wins on ambience. There's live music some nights.

Córdoba

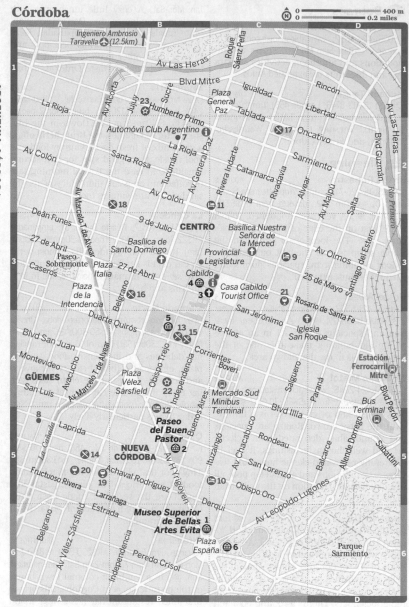

Drinking & Nightlife

Córdoba's drink of choice is Fernet, a strong, medicinal-tasting herbal liqueur from Italy. It's almost always mixed with cola.

Córdoba's nightlife divides itself into distinct scenes. All the bright young things

barhop in Nueva Córdoba – a walk along Rondeau between Avs H Yrigoyen and Chacabuco after midnight gives you a choice of dozens of bars, mostly playing laid-back (or ribcage-rattling) electronic music. Avenida Ambrosio Olmos, connected to Plaza España, also has a long strip of clubs for night owls.

Córdoba

El Mentidero de Güemes PUB
(www.facebook.com/elmentiderodeguemes; Fructuoso Rivera 260; ⊙8pm-5am Tue, from 6pm Wed-Sun) In the back of Muy Güemes, one of the district's buzziest courtyards, this fun pub with outdoor seating has great craft beer, cocktails and plates for sharing. It also hosts a range of events, from live blues, jazz and rock to theater performances.

Beer Joint CRAFT BEER
(www.facebook.com/beerjointguemes; Achaval Rodríguez 183; ⊙6pm-1am Mon-Wed, to 2am Thu-Sat, to midnight Sun) This chic hole-in-the-wall does the best happy hour (from 6pm to 9pm) in Güemes. Come for craft beer, free popcorn, cheap tacos and a local vibe.

Studio Theater CLUB
(www.facebook.com/studiotheateroficial; Rosario de Santa Fe 272; cover AR$200; ⊙11pm-6am Fri-Sun) One of Córdoba's coolest spots, this three-floor revamped theater still has its original box seats, pillars and columns. It's known for DJs spinning reggaeton, cumbia and *cuarteto* (Argentina's original pop music, with an arresting rhythm and offbeat musical pattern, and working-class lyrics) but also hosts live-music performances on the main stage.

☆ Entertainment

Cuarteto music (a Córdoba invention) is big here and played live in many venues. Unfortunately, it tends to attract undesirable crowds. **La Sala del Rey** (☑0351-422-0010; www.facebook.com/saladelrey; Humberto Primero 439; from AR$100; ⊙hours vary) is a respectable venue and the best place to catch a *cuarteto* show.

Cineclub Municipal Hugo del Carril CINEMA
(☑0351-434-1609; www.cineclubmunicipal.com; Blvd San Juan 49; Mon-Wed AR$60, Thu-Sun AR$100; ⊙1-11pm Mon-Fri, from 3pm Sat & Sun) For a great night (or day) at the movies, pop into this municipal film house, which screens everything from art flicks to Latin American award winners and local films. Stop by for a program. You can also catch live music and theatrical performances here.

❶ Information

Automóvil Club Argentino (☑0800-888-9888; Av General Paz 499; ⊙10am-5pm Mon-Fri)
Casa Cabildo Tourist Office (☑0351-434-1200; https://turismo.cordoba.gob.ar; Independencia 30; ⊙8am-8pm)

❶ Getting There & Around

AIR
Aerolíneas Argentinas (☑0810-2228-6527; www.aerolineas.com.ar; Av Colón 520; ⊙10am-6pm Mon-Fri, 9:30am-12:30pm Sat) has offices downtown and flies several times daily to Buenos Aires and Puerto Iguazú; there is also one daily flight to Neuquén. **Andes Líneas Aéreas** (☑0351-571-9970; www.andesonline.com; Tucumán 41, Galería Vía Nueva, Units 62 & 63; ⊙9am-1:30pm & 2:30-6:30pm Mon-Fri, 9am-1:30pm Sat) is a reliable airline with cheap flights to Buenos Aires, Puerto Madryn, Bariloche and other destinations in Argentina.

The **airport** (☎ 0351-475-0881; www.aa2000.com.ar/cordoba; Av La Voz del Interior 8500) is about 15km north of town. Bus 25 runs between the airport and Plaza San Martín (AR$17) or you can take the airport bus (AR$70), also to/from the plaza.

BUS

Córdoba's **bus terminal** (☎ 0351-421-2472; www.terminaldecordoba.com; Blvd Perón 380) is about a 15-minute walk from downtown.

In the new terminal (across the road, accessed by tunnel), several bus companies offer services to the same destinations as those offered at the **Mercado Sud minibus terminal** (☎ 0351-424-6775; Blvd Illía 155). Be aware that services leaving from the minibus terminal stop everywhere, often adding an hour to the journey time.

Several companies offer service to destinations in Chile, including Santiago (AR$1880, 18 hours), although some involve changing buses in Mendoza.

Buses from Córdoba

DESTINATION	COST (AR$)	DURATION (HR)
Buenos Aires	650-1250	10
Mendoza	830-1380	11
Montevideo, Uruguay (via Rosario)	1400-1990	14¼
Salta	1500-2155	11
Tucumán	800-1480	9

TRAIN

Córdoba's **Estación Ferrocarril Mitre** (☎ 0351-426-3565; www.sofse.gob.ar; Blvd Perón 600) has departures for Buenos Aires (AR$500 to AR$1750, 20 hours) via Rosario. Book tickets well in advance.

Trains to Cosquín (AR$11, 2½ hours, 8:25am, 10:40am and 11:40am daily) leave from Estación Alta Córdoba, 2km north of Plaza San Martín.

Around Córdoba

Jesús María
☎ 03525 / POP 26,800

After losing their operating funds to pirates off the coast of Brazil, the Jesuits produced and sold wine from Jesús María to support their university in colonial Córdoba. The town is located 51km north of Córdoba via RN 9.

If you're only planning on seeing one Jesuit mission, **Museo Jesuítico Nacional de Jesús María** (https://museojesuitico.cultura.gob.ar; Pedro de Oñate; ⊙ 8am-7pm Tue-Fri, 10am-6pm Sat & Sun) FREE should probably be it. Easily accessed, but in a peaceful rural setting, it's been wonderfully preserved and restored, and is crammed full of artifacts.

Buses run between Córdoba and Jesús María (AR$110, one hour).

Alta Gracia
☎ 03547 / POP 48,330

Only 35km southwest of Córdoba, the colonial mountain town of Alta Gracia is steeped in history. Its illustrious residents have ranged from Jesuit pioneers to Viceroy Santiago de Liniers, Spanish composer Manuel de Falla and revolutionary Ernesto 'Che' Guevara. The **tourist office** (☎ 03547-428128; www.altagracia.

QUIRKY TOWNS IN CÓRDOBA'S SIERRAS

For some reason, Córdoba's Sierras region is one of the quirkiest in Argentina. The great thing about traveling here is that every once in a while you stumble upon something truly wonderful and unexpected. Here are a few of our favorites:

Capilla del Monte This otherwise sleepy little hill town is world famous among UFO watchers, who come here in the hope of communing with the extraterrestrials from on top of the mystical Cerro Uritorco.

Villa General Belgrano (www.elsitiodelavilla.com/oktoberfest) The town's strong German heritage gives it a very European flavor, which really takes off when the beer starts flowing during Oktoberfest.

Villa Carlos Paz (www.villacarlospaz.gov.ar/turismo) Like a mix between Vegas and Disneyland, this lakeside getaway is dotted with theme hotels (the Great Pyramids, the Kremlin) and centered around a massive cuckoo clock.

Museo Rocsen (www.museorocsen.org) Near the tiny town of Nono, outside of Mina Clavero, the 11,000-plus pieces on display form probably the most eclectic collection of trash and treasure you're ever likely to see.

WORTH A TRIP

COSQUÍN

Up in the hills, 55km outside Córdoba, this sleepy little town springs to life once a year for the world-famous nine-day **Festival Nacional del Folklore** (www.aquicosquin.org; ⊙ late Jan), held every January since 1961. Aside from that, there's not a whole lot going on, but the **aerosilla** (www.aerosilla.com; return AR$200; ⊙ 9:30am-12:30pm & 2:30-7:30pm) up Cerro Pan de Azúcar (1260m), 15km out of town, gives some great views over the valley. A taxi there costs around AR$150, including waiting time.

Hotels in town include the basic **Hospedaje Petit** (✆ 03541-451311; petitcosquin@hotmail.com; Sabattini 739; d US$33; ☎) and the more comfortable **Hostería Siemprevende** (✆ 03451-450093; www.hosteriasiemprevende.com; Santa Fe 525; s/d US$40/50; ☎). Accommodation can get tricky during festival time – book early or consider commuting from Córdoba.

San Martín between the plaza and the stadium is lined with cafes, restaurants and *parrillas*. **La Casona** (cnr San Martín & Corrientes; mains AR$216-350; ⊙ 12:30-3pm Mon-Tue & Thu, noon-3am Fri-Sun) has good homemade pastas plus the standard *parrilla* offerings.

Frequent buses run to Córdoba (AR$117, 1¼ hours).

gob.ar; cnr Padre Viera & Calle del Molino; ⊙ 7am-8pm Mon-Fri, from 8am Sat & Sun), located in the clock tower opposite the museum Virrey Liniers, has a good town map.

◉ Sights

From 1643 to 1762 Jesuit fathers built the **Iglesia Parroquial Nuestra Señora de la Merced** (west side of Plaza Manuel Solares; ⊙ 9am-8pm) **FREE**; the nearby Jesuit workshops of **El Obraje** (1643) are now a public school. Liniers, one of the last officials to occupy the post of viceroy of the Río de la Plata, resided in what is now the **Museo Histórico Nacional del Virrey Liniers** (Padre Viera 41; ⊙ 9am-1pm & 3-7pm Tue-Fri, 9:30am-12:30pm & 3:30-6:30pm Sat & Sun) **FREE**, alongside the church.

Though the Guevaras lived in several houses in the 1930s, their primary residence was Villa Beatriz, which has now been converted into the **Museo Casa de Ernesto Che Guevara** (Avellaneda 501; AR$75; ⊙ 2pm-6:45pm Mon, 9am-6:45pm Tue-Sun). The museum focuses heavily on the legend's early life, and, judging by the photographs, Che was already a pretty intense guy by the time he was 16, and definitely had his cool look down by his early 20s. Particularly touching are some of Che's letters that he wrote to his parents and children toward the end of his life.

⊨ Sleeping & Eating

The **Alta Gracia Hostel** (✆ 03547-428810; Paraguay 218; dm/d/tr US$10/28/36; ☎) offers spacious, clean dorms a few blocks downhill from the clock tower.

The most comfortable digs in town can be found at **279 Boutique B&B** (✆ 03547-15-459493; www.279altagracia.com; Giorello 279; r US$75; ☎) 🕮, run by a vivacious New Yorker who is full of local info.

Parrillas and sidewalk cafes line Av Belgrano in the few blocks downhill from the *estancia* (ranch). The best restaurant in Alta Gracia by a long, long shot is **El Bistro del Alquimista** (www.facebook.com/elbistrodelalquimistaalquimiaescueladecocina; Castellanos 351; ⊙ 9pm-midnight Mon-Sat; ☎), with a rotating menu of excellent local and international dishes. Bakery **La Creación** (Prudencio Bustos 99; pastries AR$30-100; ⊙ 8am-1pm & 5-9pm) churns out the best bread you'll find in the entire province.

❶ Getting There & Away

Minibuses depart regularly for Córdoba (AR$64 to AR$75, one hour) from a block uphill from the *estancia*. The **bus terminal** (cnr Costanera & Esperanza) near the river also has departures for Córdoba.

La Rioja

✆ 0380 / POP 179,000

Encircled by the Sierra de Velasco's graceful peaks, La Rioja is quite a sight on a sunny day. And there are plenty of those: summer temperatures rise sky-high in this quiet, out-of-the-way, yet affluent provincial capital dotted with palm trees. It's an understated but quite charming place; even if you're on a short highlights tour, you might consider stopping off (it's halfway between Mendoza and Salta) to take a tour to Parque

Nacional Talampaya and Parque Provincial Ischigualasto.

◉ Sights

★ **Museo Folklórico**   MUSEUM
(Pelagio Luna 811; entry by donation; ☺9am-1pm & 5-9pm Tue-Fri, 9am-1pm Sat & Sun) This worthwhile museum is set in a wonderful early 17th-century adobe building, and has fine regional cultural displays. Themes include *chaya* (local La Rioja music), the Tinkunaco festival, weaving and winemaking. The guided tour is excellent if your Spanish is up to it.

Convento de San Francisco   CHURCH
(cnr 25 de Mayo & Bazán y Bustos; ☺7am-1pm & 5-9pm) The order of St Francis was on the scene very early and began building here in the late 16th century. Bad luck with construction and then an earthquake means the current church is only an early-20th-century neo-Gothic affair. It houses the image of the Niño Jesús Alcalde, a Christ-child icon symbolically recognized as the city's mayor, dressed in robes of office.

✿ Festivals & Events

★ **La Chaya**   CARNIVAL
(☺Feb) The local variant of Carnaval. Its name, derived from a Quechua word meaning 'to get someone wet,' should give you an idea of what to expect. In other words, welcome to the biggest and most joyous water fight in South America! The musical style associated with the festival is also called *chaya*.

🛏 Sleeping

Accommodation in La Rioja suffers from two problems: it's overpriced and often booked out. The tourist office keeps a list of homestays.

Gute Nacht   HOSTEL $
(☎0380-432-4325; www.facebook.com/gutenacht hostel; Catamarca 43; dm/d without bathroom US$18/44; ☎) A German-owned hostel with attached cafe and bar. It's rather well run, and well branded, with both shared and private rooms. All guests share spotless bathrooms. It's set in a restored row house, where rooms spill onto an attractive tiled courtyard with plenty of lounging space.

Wayra Hostel   HOSTEL $
(☎0380-15-435-4140; www.wayrahostel.com.ar; Escalada 1008; dm/d US$8/20; ❄☎) Pleasant, clean and friendly, this is a well-run place with a peaceful feel despite some main-road

noise. Pay the extra pesos for the downstairs dorm, which has plenty of space and is a little quieter. Private rooms are neat and decent value. The hostel picks you up for free from the bus terminal, rents out bikes and organizes paragliding tours.

🍴 Eating

Rivadavia east of Plaza 9 de Julio is lined with cafes, restaurants and *parrillas*.

Café del Paseo   CAFE $
(cnr Pelagio Luna & 25 de Mayo; light meals AR$90-200; ☺7:30am-3pm & 5:30pm-1am; ☎) This is your spot on the corner of Plaza 25 de Mayo to observe local life. Professionals mingle with families, and tables of older men chew the fat, burning just another slow-paced La Rioja day.

El Marqués   ARGENTINE $$
(☎0380-446-2461; Av San Nicolás de Bari 484; meals AR$190-320; ☺8am-1am Mon-Sat; ☎) This simple local eatery just off Plaza 25 de Mayo offers the full range, from sandwiches to traditional local dishes to pasta, pizza, omelets and grilled meats – all of it well prepared and fairly priced. The fruit *licuados* (shakes) are delicious.

La Stanza   ITALIAN $$
(☎0380-443-0809; www.lastanzaresto.com.ar; Dorrego 164; mains AR$225-360; ☺noon-3pm & 8pm-midnight Tue-Sat, noon-3pm Sun) One of the best places in town, this stylish restaurant has an upbeat, urban vibe and serves imaginative pasta dishes that are a cut above most places. Better still are the inventive main dishes, which feature delicious cuts of meat, accompanied by baked vegetable medleys.

ⓘ Information

Municipal Tourist Office (Plaza 25 de Mayo; ☺8am-1pm & 4-9pm Mon-Fri, 8am-9pm Sat & Sun) In a kiosk on Plaza 25 de Mayo.
Provincial Tourist Office (☎0380-442-6345; www.turismolarioja.gov.ar; ☺8am-8pm) On the roundabout next to the bus terminal in the south of town.

ⓘ Getting There & Away

Aerolíneas Argentinas (☎0380-442-6307; www.aerolineas.com.ar; Belgrano 63; ☺8am-1pm & 5:30-8:30pm Mon-Fri, 8:30am-12:30pm Sat) flies daily to Buenos Aires.

La Rioja's **bus terminal** (Av Circunvalación s/n) is an interesting, modern building 3km south from the center of town, with services to various destinations.

There's also a **minibus terminal** (📞 0380-446-8562; Artigas 750), from where you can board frequent departures to Catamarca and Tucumán.

BUSES FROM LA RIOJA

DESTINATION	COST (AR$)	DURATION (HR)
Buenos Aires (via Caucete)	1565-2615	19-21
Catamarca	240-275	2
Chilecito	150	3
Córdoba (via Tucumán)	1050-1655	6
Mendoza	965-1110	8½
Salta (via Tucumán)	580-1150	8-9
San Juan	695-800	5½
Santiago del Estero (via Tucumán)	620-865	7-8
Tucumán	590-680	5½-6½

Santiago del Estero

📞 0385 / POP 392,000

Placid, hot Santiago enjoys the distinction 'Madre de Ciudades' (Mother of Cities). Founded in 1553, this was the first Spanish urban settlement in what is now Argentina. Sadly, it boasts no architectural heritage from that period, but still makes a pleasant stop.

🛏 Sleeping & Eating

Hotel Savoy HOTEL $
(📞 0385-421-1234; www.savoysantiago.com.ar; Tucumán 39; s/d/ste US$25.50/38/47; P❄@🌐⛱) With a sumptuous entrance and gorgeous curving staircase, this place looks like a palace at first glance. Sadly, there are no four-poster beds or servants fanning you with ostrich feathers, but the remodeled rooms are comfortable enough, with decent showers, and the service is attentive. It's well located and has a heated outdoor pool.

Hotel Carlos V HOTEL $$
(📞 0385-424-0303; www.carlosvhotel.com; Independencia 110; s/d US$32/50; P❄@🌐⛱) This hotel has a great central location and spacious rooms with business-class facilities and large comfortable beds. Some rooms have a balcony. Superiors are larger and have table and chairs. There's a gym, sauna and indoor pool.

★ **Aladdin** LEBANESE $
(📞 0385-422-0300; Belgrano Norte 228; dishes AR$100-170; ⊙noon-3pm & 9pm-midnight; 📶) The marketing of this restaurant will look familiar to fans of the Disney film, but you've made the trek from the center of town for the authentic Lebanese fare. Think faithful hummus, baba ghanoush, falafel, kofta, kebabs, tabbouleh and a magnificent flakey, syrupy baklava. All of it well prepared in a family kitchen and served in an atmospheric arched dining room.

Itamae FUSION $$
(📞 0385-424-1539; www.facebook.com/itamaesushi santiago; Roca Sur 669; sushi AR$150-225; ⊙7pm-midnight; 📶) A sleek Nikkei (Japanese-Peruvian) spot in Santiago's popular dining district. It offers rolls, nigiri and ceviche, along with a range of cooked food, most of it featuring salmon or steak. It's a tasty splurge.

ℹ Information

The **tourist office** (📞 0385-421-3253; www.turismosantiago.gob.ar; Libertad 417; ⊙7am-9pm Mon-Fri, 10am-1pm & 5-8pm Sat, 10am-1pm Sun) is on Plaza Libertad. There's also an office at the **bus terminal** (⊙8am-9pm Mon-Fri, 10am-1pm & 5-8pm Sat & Sun).

ℹ Getting There & Away

Santiago del Estero's **airport** (📞 0385-434-3654; Av Madre de Ciudades) is 6km northwest of downtown. Aerolíneas Argentinas (www.aerolineas.com.ar) flies daily to Buenos Aires.

The **bus terminal** (📞 0385-422-7091; Chacabuco 550) has frequent departures to Tucumán (AR$185 to AR$482, two hours) and Buenos Aires (AR$1700 to AR$2150, 12 to 15 hours).

Santiago del Estero's twin town La Banda is on the line between Tucumán (four hours) and Buenos Aires' Retiro station (23 hours). Bus 117 does a circuit of Santiago's center before heading across the river to the station.

Tucumán

📞 0381 / POP 884,400 (URBAN AREA)

A big city with a small-town feel, Tucumán is definitely improving in terms of the backpacking scene. There are some good hostels, a pumping nightlife and some excellent adventures to be had in the surrounding hills. Independence Day (July 9) celebrations are especially vigorous in Tucumán, which hosted the congress that declared Argentine independence in 1816.

Sights & Activities

Tandem paragliding flights over the Yungas forests are possible here.

Casa de la Independencia MUSEUM

(Casa Histórica; ☎0381-431-0826; Congreso 151; ⏰10am-6pm) FREE Students and families descend from far and wide to visit this late-colonial mansion where a collection of Unitarist lawyers and clerics declared Argentina's independence from Spain on July 9, 1816. Portraits of the signatories line the walls of the room where the deed was done, and outside, in the courtyard, you'll find a bronze relief of the original *declaración*. There's plenty of information in Spanish on the lead-up to this seismic event, and free guided tours are available hourly.

There's usually a sound-and-light show nightly, although at research time the show was suspended for technical reasons. If the show is running, come to the museum between 11am and 6pm to get your free ticket, as there is limited space available.

Museo Folclórico Provincial MUSEUM

(☎0381-421-8250; Av 24 de Septiembre 565; ⏰9am-12:30pm & 3:30-7:30pm Tue-Fri, 10am-1pm & 3:30-7:30pm Sat, 3:30-7:30pm Sun) FREE Occupying a colonial house, this small but pleasant museum features a modest collection of traditional *gaucho* gear, indigenous musical instruments, weavings and pottery. There was a room on local singer Mercedes Sosa, one of Argentina's finest vocalists, at the time of research.

Antique Tour Experience SCENIC DRIVE

(☎0381-430-5445; www.antiquetour.com.ar; Crisóstomo Álvarez 467) A unique operator offering scenic drives between the cities of Tucumán, Salta and Jujuy in vintage Ford Model A vehicles dating from 1928 and 1929. The route is slow but the views from the back seat of these convertibles are splendid, and the guides are top-shelf.

Sleeping

A La Gurda HOSTEL $

(☎0381-497-6275; www.lagurdahostel.com.ar; Maipú 490; dm/d US$15/30; @ 🛜) Upstairs in a lovely old house, this pleasant hostel offers eight-bed dorms with lockers and OK-value private bunk rooms. There's a pool table and excellent bathroom facilities, bar service and a kitchen. Everything's spotless, although fan-cooled rooms do steam up in hot Tucumán. Management is helpful and friendly.

Casa Calchaquí GUESTHOUSE $

(☎0381-484-5949; www.casacalchaqui.com; Lola Mora 92, Yerba Buena; d/q US$39/80, s/d without bathroom US$33/37; ⏰Mar-Jan; P ❄ @ 🛜 ≋) Located 8km west of the center in the upmarket Yerba Buena barrio, Casa Calchaquí is a welcome retreat. Comfortably rustic rooms surround a relaxing garden space with hammocks, bar service and a minipool. Yerba Buena has plenty of restaurants and nightlife, but isn't central. To get here grab a taxi or bus 102 or 118 from opposite the bus terminal.

Posada Arcadia B&B $$

(☎0381-425-2214; www.posadaarcadia.com.ar; Güemes 480, Yerba Buena; d US$36-75; ❄ 🛜 ≋) Posada Arcadia has four charming rooms in a gorgeous home with a huge garden and pool in leafy Yerba Buena. The biggest of the bunch has a king-sized bed, walk-in closet, fireplace, flat-screen TV, tub and shower. The common room is cushy, and you'll snag a discount for stays of more than one night. It's 8km west of downtown. There's street parking.

Eating & Drinking

From Thursday to Saturday nights, the action is in the Abasto region, on Calle Lillo. Follow San Lorenzo west from the town center and you'll hit the middle of the zone. There are dozens of bars and nightclubs – take your pick. Other *boliches* (nightclubs) can be found in Yerba Buena, at least 6km west of the town center.

Black Pan BURGERS $

(www.facebook.com/blackpanburgers; 25 de Mayo 724; burgers AR$130-150; ⏰noon-midnight Sun-Thu, to 1am Fri & Sat) Black Pan is a hip spot, exceptionally well branded, and beloved by Tucumán's young and upwardly mobile. Its standard is a 120g burger with cheddar cheese, served on a brioche bun. But you can build yours as you like. In a nod to California's famous In-N-Out chain, it will even do your burger 'animal style' (with grilled onions, extra pickles and Thousand Island dressing).

El Portal ARGENTINE $

(☎0381-422-6024; Av 24 de Septiembre 351; empanadas AR$20, mains AR$130-240; ⏰noon-4pm & 8pm-midnight) Half a block east of Plaza Independencia, this rustic indoor-outdoor eatery is a true hole-in-the-wall. It has a tiny but perfectly formed menu, based around empanadas, *locro* (stew) and wood-fired meat. Delicious and authentic.

Shitake 2
VEGETARIAN $

(☑ 0381-422-1817; 9 de Julio 392; buffet AR$170, with juice AR$185; ⊙ 11:30am-4pm & 7:30pm-midnight; 🐶 🌱) You can expect the same tasty veggie buffet that made the **original branch** (9 de Julio 94; all you can eat AR$175; ⊙ 11:30am-4pm & 7:30pm-midnight; 🐶 🌱) a hit with locals. Platters and bowls piled with lentils, stir-fried vegetables and soy-based meat substitutes, roasted potatoes, quiches, pizzas and more, but with smaller crowds and even better execution.

Setimio
ARGENTINE $$

(☑ 0381-431-2792; Santa Fe 512; mains AR$300-500; ⊙ 10am-3pm & 6pm-1:30am Mon-Sat, 10am-3pm Sun; 🐶) Wall-to-wall bottles decorate this smart wineshop and restaurant, with a menu that features Spanish-style tapas, fine salads and well-prepared fish dishes among other gourmet delights. Wine is not offered by the glass, but you can pick any one of the hundreds of bottles from the shelves and uncork it for dinner.

❶ Information

The **tourist office** (☑ 0381-430-3644; www.tucumanturismo.gob.ar; Av 24 de Septiembre 484; ⊙ 8am-9pm Mon-Fri, 9am-9pm Sat & Sun) on Plaza Independencia is very helpful and staff knowledgeable. There's another office in the shopping center at the bus terminal with the same opening hours.

❶ Getting There & Around

AIR

Aeropuerto Benjamín Matienzo (☑ 0381-426-5072) is located 8km east of downtown; a *remise* (taxi) costs around AR$250 from the town center. **Aerolíneas Argentinas** (☑ 0810-222-86527; www.aerolineas.com.ar; 9 de Julio 110; ⊙ 9am-5pm Mon-Fri) and **LATAM** (☑ 0381-422-0606; www.latam.com; San Juan 426; ⊙ 9am-6pm Mon-Fri) fly daily to Buenos Aires; Aerolíneas also flies to Córdoba five times weekly.

BUS

Tucumán's **bus terminal** (☑ 0381-430-0452; Brígido Terán 350; 🐶) is a few blocks from the center, a decent walk if you don't want to stump up for a cab. It has a post office, *locutorios* (small telephone offices), a supermarket, bars and restaurants – all blissfully air-conditioned.

Aconquija services Tafí del Valle (AR$260, 2½ hours) and Cafayate (AR$385 to AR$430, 6½ hours).

Long-distance destinations include Santiago del Estero (AR$205 to AR$400, two hours), Córdoba (AR$800 to AR$1240, seven to nine hours),

Salta (AR$440 to AR$500, 4¼ hours) and Buenos Aires (AR$1960 to AR$2235, 15 to 18 hours).

TRAIN

Trains run from **Estación Mitre** (☑ 0381-430-9220; www.sofse.gob.ar; Plaza Alberdi s/n) to Buenos Aires (AR$700 to AR$2450, 19 hours, twice daily).

Tafí del Valle

☑ 03867 / POP 3400

Set in a pretty valley overlooking a lake, Tafí is where folks from Tucumán come to escape the heat in summer months. In the low season it's much mellower (which isn't to imply that there's any sort of frenzy here in summertime), but still gorgeous, and makes a good base for exploring the surrounding countryside and nearby ruins at Quilmes.

◎ Sights

Parque de los Menhires
MUSEUM

(Plaza s/n, El Mollar; AR$50; ⊙ 8am-noon & 5-8pm) At pretty El Mollar, at the other end of the valley from Tafí, you can visit the Parque de los Menhires on the plaza, where there is a collection of more than 100 carved standing stones, found in the surrounding area. They were produced by the Tafí culture some 2000 years ago.

🛏 Sleeping & Eating

Numerous *parrillas,* specializing in *lechón* (suckling pig) and *chivito* (goat), line Av Perón.

★ Estancia Los Cuartos
ESTANCIA $

(☑ 0381-15-587-4230; www.estancialoscuartos.com; Av Miguel Critto s/n; d US$53-62; 🅿 @ 🐶) 🌿 Oozing with character, this lovely spot with grazing llamas out front is two centuries old, and feels like a museum, with venerable books lining antique shelves and authentic rooms with aged wood and woolen blankets, but with great modern bathrooms. Newer rooms offer less history but remain true to the feel of the place.

Traditional cheeses are also made here. Don't confuse this place with nearby Hostería Los Cuartos.

Nomade Hostel
HOSTEL $

(☑ 03867-307-5922; www.nomadehostel.com.ar; Los Castaños s/n; dm/d US$13/45; 🅿 @ 🐶) 🌿 Relaxed, colorful, enthusiastic and welcoming, this hostel is an easy 10-minute walk from the bus terminal (turn right, go round the bend, veer right). It's got a lovely location with great

IT'S ALL DOWNHILL FROM HERE

One of the best day trips you can do from Tafí del Valle needs no guide at all. Rent a bike, and coast downhill past the lake and out onto the road to Tucumán. It's a 40km (mostly) downhill cruise, following the course of the Río Los Sosa, with hundreds of gorgeous swimming holes and picnic spots right by the roadside.

Once you lose sight of the river and houses start appearing, you know the best part of the ride is over. You can hail any Tafí-bound bus (make sure you choose a safe place for them to pull over), stash your bike underneath and ride home in style.

There's no food or water anywhere along this route, so come prepared. And check your brakes before leaving, too – you'll definitely be using them.

views from the spacious garden. Rates include breakfast and tasty home-cooked dinners, and the atmosphere here is excellent. It's best to book ahead in summer. Prices drop substantially in the low season.

★ **Descanso de las Piedras** CABAÑAS $$
(🖉0381-15-642-8100; www.descansodelaspiedras. com; Madre Teresa de Calcuta s/n; d from US$47, q from US$60; 🅿️ 🛜 🛏) 🏊 Welcoming and social, these orange riverside cabins and rooms, decked out with exquisite bathrooms and flat-screen TVs, surround a grassy area with a solar-heated pool, vegetable garden, a duck pen and a few wandering llamas. It's a relaxing retreat 20 minutes' walk from Tafí's center and a great option for families; cabins sleeping up to seven are available.

★ **Restaurante El Museo** ARGENTINE $
(Av José Silva s/n; dishes AR$70-220; ⊙noon-4pm) Set in the venerable adobe Jesuit chapel 1km from the center, this place makes an atmospheric venue for a lunch of traditional local specialties, such as *humitas*, tamales and empanadas. Just turn up and see what's cooking that day. It all smells divine!

Mi Abuela ARGENTINE $
(cnr Av Miguel Critto & Perón; empanadas AR$18, mains AR$65-170; ⊙8am-2pm & 5-8pm; 🛜) An endearing corner kitchen on the main drag, it does *humitas*, tamales, sandwiches and

chicken and beef empanadas. Grab lunch for the road!

Rancho de Félix ARGENTINE $$
(cnr Belgrano & Perón; empanada AR$25, mains AR$245; ⊙11:30am-3pm & 8pm-midnight; 🛜) Rancho de Félix is an expansive and warm thatched barn that's incredibly popular for lunch. Regional specialties such as *locro* and *humitas* are served; *parrilla* and pasta are also on offer. The quality is reasonably good and prices are fair. It may not open evenings if the town is quiet.

🛍 Shopping

★ **Ruta del Artesano** ART
(www.tucumanturismo.gob.ar/ruta-del-artesano/ 15770/230/ruta-del-artesano-tafi-del-valle; ⊙hours vary) Tafí's main diversion, aside from walks in the countryside, is this driving route to the home studios of area artisans, whose work includes ceramics, jewelry, musical instruments, art and more. The Casa de Turista (tourist office) will give you a map, or you can navigate an interactive Google map on the tourist office website.

ℹ Information

Casa del Turista (🖉0381-15-594-1039; www. tafidelvalle.gob.ar; Los Faroles s/n; ⊙8am-10pm) is on the pedestrian street.

ℹ Getting There & Around

Tafí's **bus terminal** (🖉03867-421025; Av Miguel Critto) is located in the town center. Departures include Cafayate (AR$275, 3½ hours) and Tucumán (AR$260, 2½ hours). Mountain bikes can be rented from Hostel Nomade.

Cafayate

🖉03868 / POP 13,700

Set at the entrance to the **Quebrada de Cafayate**, 1600m above sea level and surrounded by some of the country's best vineyards, Cafayate provides the opportunity to indulge in two of life's great pleasures: drinking wine and exploring nature. If you're pressed for time, you can combine the two and take a bottle out into the *quebrada* (gorge) with you, in which case we would recommend a local torrontés (dry white wine), provided you can keep it chilled.

◉ Sights & Activities

From 25 de Mayo, two blocks south of Colón, a 5km walk southwest leads you to the **Río**

Cafayate

Colorado. Follow the river upstream for about two hours to get to a 10m **waterfall**, where you can swim. Look out for hidden **rock paintings** on the way (for a couple of pesos, local children will guide you).

Several operators around the plaza offer tours of the *quebrada* for AR$600 per person. **Majo Viajes** (☏03868-422038; majo viajes@gmail.com; Nuestra Señora del Rosario 77) is straight-talking and reliable. Try to go in the late afternoon, when it's cooler and the colors and photo ops are better.

Museo de la Vid y El Vino MUSEUM
(www.museodelavidyelvino.gov.ar; Av General Güemes; foreigners/Argentines AR$100/80; ⊙9am-7pm Tue-Sun) This impressive museum gives a good introduction to the area's wine industry. The atmospheric first section, which deals with the viticultural side – the life of the vines – through a series of poems and images, is particularly appealing. The second part covers the winemaking side, and there's a cafe where you can try and buy. English translations appear throughout.

✨ Festivals & Events

Serenata a Cafayate
MUSIC

(www.serenata.todowebsalta.com.ar; ⊙ Feb) A worthwhile three-day *folklórico* festival.

Dia de la Cruz
RELIGIOUS

(⊙ May) A mass of devotees (what seems like the entire city – the young and old among them) make a pilgrimage 1000m up San Isidro mountain – aka Cerro de la Cruz – to the white cross erected above town decades ago. It's quite a hike and unlike any other you're likely to have experienced.

🛏 Sleeping

Rusty-K Hostal
HOSTEL $

(☑ 03868-422031; Rivadavia 281; d with/without bathroom US$20/18; @ 🛜) The peace of the vine-filled patio garden here is a real highlight, and the rooms are cozy too, with good-quality terra-cotta floors, beamed ceilings and a colorful accent wall. The warm service makes it terrific value. Book ahead.

Casa Árbol
GUESTHOUSE, HOSTEL $

(☑ 03868-422238, 03868-15-638434; http://casa arbolhostel.com; Calchaquí 84; dm US$8, d without bathroom US$23; 🛜) 🌿 There's something pleasant about this intimate, charming hostel with pretty, spotless rooms and a four-bed dorm. Everyone shares two bathrooms. There's lounging room to spare in the patio, breakfast area and garden. It also rents bikes (AR$150 per half-day).

El Hospedaje
GUESTHOUSE $

(☑ 03868-421680; elhospedaje@gmail.com; Salta 13; s/d US$65/75; P ❄ 🛜 ♨) On a corner just a block from Cafayate's plaza, this easygoing guesthouse is dotted with incongruent antiques – irons, radios, typewriters and cash registers. Rooms are simple, terra-cotta-tile affairs, and some are a bit dark. A good option for the price.

★ Portal del Santo
HOTEL $$

(☑ 03868-422400; www.portaldelsanto.com; Chavarría 250; s/d US$35/60; P ❄ @ 🛜 ♨) Cool white elegance is the stock-in-trade of this hospitable family-run hotel with arched arcades. Lower rooms open onto both the front porch and the inviting garden-pool-Jacuzzi area (reason enough to stay); top-floor chambers have mountain views and even more space. All have fridge and microwave; suites sleep four. The owners are helpful and put on a wonderful homemade breakfast.

🍴 Eating

On Rivadavia, between Calles San Lorenzo and 12 de Octubre, you'll find a string of no-frills grillhouses that make a worthwhile dinner escape.

Casa de las Empanadas
EMPANADAS $

(Mitre 24; 12 empanadas AR$160; ⊙ 11am-3pm & 8pm-midnight Tue-Sun; 🛜) Decorated with the scrawls of contented customers, this no-frills place has a wide selection of empanadas that are all delicious. Local wine in ceramic jugs, and *humitas* (stuffed corn dough, resembling Mexican tamales) and tamales can round

---

THE BACK ROAD BETWEEN CACHI & CAFAYATE

If you're in Cachi and heading toward Cafayate (or vice versa), buses reach Molinos and start again in Angastaco, leaving a 42km stretch of gorgeous, lonely road unserviced. Hitching is common in these parts, but traffic is rare and even the towns that have bus service have infrequent departures.

It's hard, but not impossible. The last thing you want to do is stand on the roadside with your thumb out. The best thing to do? When you hit town, start asking around literally everywhere – the police station, hospital, *kioskos* – to see if anybody knows anyone who is going your way. Somebody will and you won't be stuck for long. If you do get stuck, there are decent, cheap places to stay and eat in Molinos, Angastaco and San Carlos. Be very careful, as hitchhiking is never totally safe.

You may end up in the back of a pickup truck with the wind in your hair and the mountains in your face. But really, this is possibly the sort of adventure you had in mind when you booked your airfare.

Sound like too much? You can always ask at the *remisería* (*remise* office) in front of Cachi's bus terminal if there's a group going that you can join. *Remises* seat four passengers and cost between AR$1800 to AR$2300 from Cafayate to Cachi. The stretch from Molinos to Angastaco should cost about AR$500.

out the meal. If it's closed, head to its other **branch** (Nuestra Señora del Rosario 156; mains AR$130-145; ☺ 11am-3pm & 7-11pm).

★ **Pacha**   FUSION $$$
(☑ 03868-639002;   www.facebook.com/pacharestaurantecafayate; Guemes Sur 153; mains AR$270-490; ☺ 7pm-midnight Mon, 12:30-3pm & 5pm-midnight Tue-Sat) A lovely bistro, half a block off Cafayate's main plaza. The Buenos Aires–trained chef sources ingredients (and wines) carefully and crafts a menu with welcome departures from traditional Argentine fare. Hits include seafood risotto and pork ribs slathered with a whiskey barbecue sauce. He also bakes his own crusty sourdough bread with yeast he's been fermenting for years.

The kitchen will cater to vegetarian and vegan off-menu requests if you speak up.

ℹ Information

The **tourist office** (☑ 03868-422442; Av General Güemes s/n; ☺ 9am-7pm Tue-Sun), attached to the Museo de la Vid y El Vino, offers an invaluable printout of winery opening times.

ℹ Getting There & Around

For those without wheels, the new **bus terminal** (RN 40) is at the northern entrance to town, where you can connect to Salta (AR$215, four hours) and Angastaco (AR$81, two hours) via San Carlos (AR$23, 45 minutes). Buses also leave for Tucumán (AR$390 to AR$440, five to 6½ hours, two to four daily) via Amaicha and Tafí del Valle (AR$270, 2½ to four hours); others go via Santa María (AR$120, two hours). Counterintuitively, quicker buses can be cheaper.

Around Cafayate

Quebrada de Cafayate

From Cafayate, RN 68 slices through the Martian-like landscape of the Quebrada de Cafayate on its way to Salta. About 50km north of Cafayate, the eastern Sierra de Carahuasi is the backdrop for distinctive sandstone landforms such as the Garganta del Diablo (Devil's Throat), El Anfiteatro (Amphitheater), El Sapo (Toad), El Fraile (Friar), El Obelisco (Obelisk) and Los Castillos (Castles).

Other than car rental or organized tours, the best way to see the *quebrada* is by bike or on foot. Bring plenty of water and go in the morning, as unpleasant, strong winds kick up in the afternoon. At Cafayate, cyclists can load their bikes onto any bus heading to

Salta and disembark at the impressive box canyon of Garganta del Diablo. From here, the 50-odd kilometers back to Cafayate can be biked in about four hours, but it's too far on foot. When you've had enough, walkers should simply hail down another bus on its way back to Cafayate.

Valles Calchaquíes

In this valley north and south of Cafayate, once a principal route across the Andes, the Calchaquí people resisted Spanish attempts to impose forced labor obligations. Tired of having to protect their pack trains, the Spaniards relocated many Calchaquí to Buenos Aires, and the land fell to Spaniards, who formed large rural estates.

CACHI
☑ 03868 / POP 2600
Cachi is a spectacularly beautiful town and by far the most visually impressive of those along the Valles Calchaquíes. There's not a whole lot to do here, but that's all part of the charm. The **tourist office** (☑ 03868-491902; oficinadeturismo.cachi@gmail.com; Güemes s/n; ☺ 9am-9pm) is in the municipal building on the plaza. They have an atrocious city map but good info on hotels and attractions.

While you're here, definitely stop in at the **Museo Arqueológico** (☑ 03868-491080; Calchaquí s/n; AR$60; ☺ 9am-6pm Tue-Sun), a slickly presented collection of area finds, including an impressive array of petroglyphs.

Various companies offer excursions and activities in the surrounding hills. **Urkupiña** (☑ 03868-491317; www.urkupinatur.wix.com/cachi; Zorrilla 237) offers cycling trips, quad-bike excursions and reasonably priced transportation to Cafayate along the RN40.

For budget accommodations, check out the **municipal campground & hostel** (☑ 03868-491902; oficinadeturismo.cachi@gmail.com; campsite per person US$2.50, cabin US$24; P ☒) or **Viracocha hostel** (☑ 03868-15-491713; Ruiz de los Llanos s/n; dm US$9, d with/without bathroom US$42/22; ☏). One of the better hotels in town is **El Cortijo** (☑ 03868-491034; www.elcortijohotel.com; Av ACA s/n; d standard/superior US$120/140; P ❀ ☏ ☒), a reasonably priced boutique hotel on the edge of town.

Some cheap restaurants surround the plaza. The most interesting restaurant in town is vegetarian **Ashpamanta** (☑ 0387-576-4488; Bustamante s/n; set lunch AR$200, mains AR$150-230; ☺ noon-3pm & 7-10pm; ☑), just off the plaza, where all ingredients are locally grown; call ahead to check they are open for lunch.

Two to three daily buses run between Salta (AR$240, four hours) and Cachi: it's quite a ride!

Quilmes

This pre-Hispanic **pucará** (indigenous Andean fortification; adult/child AR$70/free; ⊘ 8am-6pm) in Tucumán province, 50km south of Cafayate, is Argentina's most extensive preserved ruin. Dating from about AD 1000, this complex urban settlement covered about 30 hectares and housed perhaps 5000 people. The Quilmes people abided contact with the Incas but could not outlast the Spaniards, who, in 1667, deported the last 2000 to Buenos Aires.

Quilmes' thick walls underscore its defensive functions, but evidence of dense occupation sprawls north and south of the nucleus.

Buses from Cafayate to Santa María pass the Quilmes junction; from there, it's 5km to the ruins.

Salta

☑ 0387 / POP 520,700

Salta has experienced a huge surge in popularity as a backpacking destination over the last few years, and rightly so – the setting's gorgeous, the hostels are attractive, the nightlife pumps and there's plenty to do in and around town.

⊙ Sights

Salta owes much of its reputation for beauty to the various churches scattered around the downtown area. The 19th-century **Iglesia Catedral** (www.catedralsalta.org; España 590; ⊘ 6:30am-12:30pm & 4:30-8:30pm Mon-Fri, 7:30am-12:30pm & 5-8:30pm Sat, 7am-1pm & 5-9:30pm Sun) guards the ashes of General Martín Miguel de Güemes, a hero of the wars of independence. So ornate it's almost gaudy, the **Iglesia San Francisco** (www.conventosanfranciscosalta.com; cnr Caseros & Córdoba; tours AR$40; ⊘ 9:30am-1pm & 2-6:30pm) is a Salta landmark. Only Carmelite nuns can enter the 16th-century adobe **Convento de San Bernardo** (Caseros s/n; ⊘ pastries for sale 9am-noon & 4-6pm Mon-Sat), but anyone can admire its carved *algarrobo* (carob wood) door or peek inside the chapel during Mass, held at 8am daily.

★ **Museo de Arqueología de Alta Montaña** MUSEUM
(MAAM; www.maam.gob.ar; Mitre 77; adult/student & senior AR$200/70; ⊘ 10am-6:30pm Tue-Sun) One of northern Argentina's premier museums, MAAM has a serious and informative exhibition focusing on Inca culture and, in particular, the child sacrifices left on some of the Andes' most imposing peaks. The centerpiece is the mummified body of one of three children (rotated every six months) discovered at the peak of Llullaillaco in 1999. It was a controversial decision to display the bodies and it is a powerful experience to come face-to-face with them.

Pajcha – Museo de Arte Étnico Americano MUSEUM
(www.museopajchasalta.com.ar; 20 de Febrero 831; AR$150; ⊘ 10am-1pm & 4-8pm Mon-Fri, 4-8pm Sat) This eye-opening private museum is worth seeing if you're interested in indigenous art and culture. Juxtaposing archaeological finds with contemporary and recent artisanal work from all over Latin America, it encourages a broad view of Andean culture and is an exquisite dose of color and beauty run with great enthusiasm. The collection is revealed on bilingual tours (with flair!) by the charming English-speaking management.

Cerro San Bernardo HILL
For outstanding views of Salta, take the **teleférico cable car** (www.telefericosanbernardo.com; 1-way/round-trip adult AR$150/75, child AR$80/40; ⊘ 9am-6:30pm) from Parque San Martín to the top of this hill, a 1km ride that takes eight minutes. Alternatively, take the trail starting at the **Güemes Monument**. Atop is a unique **wine bar** (☑ 0387-610-1590; www.facebook.com/winebikesalta; Cerro San Bernardo; ⊘ 11am-6pm), a watercourse and *artesanía* (handicraft) shops.

☞ Tours

Whitewater rafting outside of town is available with various tour companies along Buenos Aires, near the Plaza 9 de Julio. **Salta Rafting** (☑ 0387-421-3216; www.saltarafting.com; Caseros 177) can take care of all your rafting, ziplining, mountain biking, trekking and horse-riding requirements.

★ **Origins** TREKKING
(☑ 0387-431-3891; www.originsargentina.com; Zorrilla 171; ⊘ 9am-8pm Mon-Fri, to noon Sat) A highly rated, community-based tour operator that combines well-planned trekking, horseback-

riding and other active cultural itineraries with farm stays. Responsible tourism is its ethos, and the company can even help you learn Spanish. Guides speak English and French as well as Spanish.

Tren a las Nubes
TOURS

(www.trenalasnubes.com.ar; cnr Ameghino & Balcarce; bus & train AR$2850, train only AR$1850; ☺ Sat Apr–mid-Dec) The 'Train to the Clouds,' Argentina's most famous rail trip, heads from Salta down the Lerma Valley then ascends multicolored Quebrada del Toro, continuing past the Tastil ruins and San Antonio de los Cobres, before reaching a stunning viaduct spanning a desert canyon at La Polvorilla (altitude 4220m). Additional tours often run on Tuesday and Thursday; check the website for the schedule.

🛏 Sleeping

★ Espacio Mundano
B&B $

(☑ 0387-572-2244; www.espaciomundano.com.ar; Güemes 780; r US$40; ✳ ☎) An artistic oasis in the heart of Salta. The setting is a 200-year-old house, converted into an art studio and B&B that is a riot of color and imagination. Rooms have timber floors, are decked out with vintage vanities and wrought-iron beds, and open onto a leafy courtyard.

Posada de las Farolas
HOTEL $

(☑ 0387-421-3463; www.posadalasfarolas.com.ar; Córdoba 246; s/d/tr US$30/45/55; ℗ ✳ ☎) This place is good value for its neat, clean and air-conditioned rooms in the center, some of which look onto tiny garden patios. It's a spotless and reliable choice. A few extras such as big fluffy towels and hairdryers put it above most in its price band. Cash only.

Residencial El Hogar
GUESTHOUSE $

(☑ 0387-431-6158; www.residencialelhogar.com.ar; Saravia 239; d with/without bathroom US$33/20; ℗ ✳ ☎) Run with genuine warmth, this pleasing little place is on a quiet residential street with Cerro San Bernardo looming over it, and is still an easy stroll into the center. Attractive rooms with tasteful touches, helpful owners and a good breakfast make this a recommended base at a fair price.

Coloria Hostel
HOSTEL $

(☑ 0387-431-3058; www.coloriahostel.com; Güemes 333; dm US$9, d with/without bathroom US$30/20; ℗ ✳ ☎ ⛱) Upbeat, engaged staff and an open-plan common area that looks over the garden and small pool are the major highlights of this enjoyable central hostel. It's colorful and quite upmarket by Argentine hostel standards; cleanliness is good; and dorms, though there's not a huge amount of space, are comfortable. Private rooms are very tight.

Las Rejas
HOSTEL $

(☑ 0387-422-7959; www.lasrejashostel.com; Güemes 569; dm/d US$7/32; ☎) Occupying an older building with character to spare, this hostel has trendy exposed brick in the common areas, and two levels of rooms and dorms. The combination of the central location and a relaxed vibe works. Staff speak good English, and there are bike rentals on-site.

★ Design Suites
HOTEL $$

(☑ 0387-422-4466; www.designsuites.com; Pasaje Castro 215; r from US$80; ℗ ✳ @ ☎ ⛱) You may wonder whether the look of this place – all exposed concrete and urban-trendy design – works in colonial Salta, but its excellent, large and quiet rooms are undeniably attractive. They have hydromassage tubs and almost-floor-to-ceiling windows that offer super town views. The rooftop pool-and-spa space is another great spot to linger over splendid views of pretty, old Salta.

🍴 Eating

The western side of Plaza 9 de Julio is lined with cafes and bars that have tables out on the plaza; there are some great spots for coffee, snacks or a few drinks.

Dubai
MEDITERRANEAN $

(☑ 0387-431-6140; www.facebook.com/dubaicomida sarabes; Leguizamón 474; mains AR$110-250; ☺ noon-3pm & 9pm-midnight; ☎) Family-owned and set in a charming corner dining room, this Syrian kitchen offers a welcome break from *parrilla* fare. Expect solid falafel, hummus and baba ghanoush, shawarma, kebabs and much more served in tasteful upscale environs at fair prices. Free delivery to your hotel.

La Tacita
EMPANADAS $

(☑ 0387-431-8289; Caseros 396; empanadas AR$20; ☺ 8am-11pm Mon-Sat, 10am-11pm Sun) This basic little eatery offers some of the city's best empanadas, all baked, in a welcoming no-frills setting. Great for a quick stop while sightseeing.

★ Chirimoya
VEGAN $$

(☑ 0387-431-2857; www.facebook.com/chirimoya. vegetariano; España 211; mains AR$200-260; ☺ 9am-2:45pm & 8:30-11:15pm Mon-Sat; ☎ ☑) Colorful and upbeat, this artsy, world-class vegan restaurant is the most inventive and

Salta

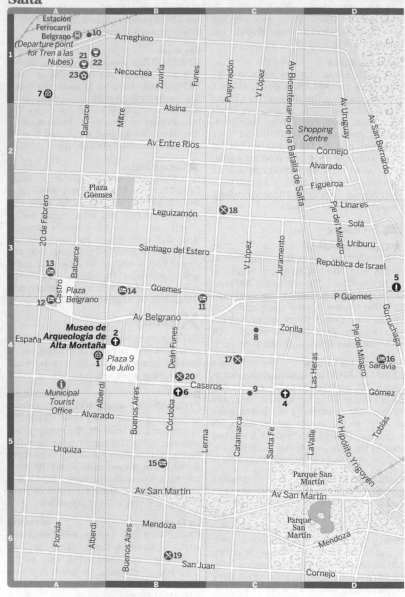

consistently excellent kitchen in the entire region. Here pasta is fashioned from zucchini, cannelloni are made from corn flour and stuffed with cauliflower florets, they make savory soups and meat-like quinoa patties, and turn mushrooms into high culinary art.

La Céfira   ITALIAN $$
(☎ 0387-447-6825; Córdoba 481; mains AR$190-240; ☺ 7pm-midnight Mon-Sat, noon-3pm Sun; 🛜♩) This cute hole-in-the-wall, well-lit and decorated with original art, is set a few blocks south of the center, but it's worth the

☕ Drinking & Entertainment

Peñas (folk music clubs) are the classic Salta nighttime experience. The two blocks of Balcarce north of Alsina, and the surrounding streets, are the main zone for these and other nightlife. Bars and clubs around here follow the typical 'boom/bust/reopen with new name' pattern, so just follow your nose.

★ Café del Tiempo   BAR
(www.facebook.com/cafedeltiempo; Balcarce 901; ⊙ 6pm-3am Mon-Sat, 8am-2am Sun; ⑧) Decked out to resemble a Buenos Aires cafe, this place has prices to match and offers a stylish terrace in the heart of the Balcarce zone; it's a top spot for a drink and makes a mean mojito. Expect some sort of performance or live music every night. The menu includes llama dishes and international offerings such as chop suey.

walk here for the menu of house-made pasta combined with inventive ingredients including squid ink, curried pumpkin, coconut milk and poppy seeds. There are some meat and fish dishes too, such as beef stuffed with figs and sun-dried tomatoes.

Macondo BAR
(www.facebook.com/macondo.barensalta; Balcarce 980; ⊗8pm-late Wed-Sun; 🛜) With all the *folklórica* music on this street, the mostly indie mix in this trendy bar might come as a relief. Popular with locals and tourists, it keeps it lively until late and has a good streetside terrace. There's live music most nights.

Nora Julia TRADITIONAL MUSIC
(Balcarce 887) This brick and adobe haunt is a good choice for *peña* music. The singers all wear traditional garb and a crew of dancers entertain as well. You'll need to buy drinks or dinner in addition to the cover charge.

ℹ️ Information

The **municipal tourist office** (Caseros 460; ⊗8am-9pm Mon-Fri, 9am-9pm Sat & Sun) gives out maps. It also has desks in the bus terminal and at the airport.

ℹ️ Getting There & Around

AIR

Aerolíneas Argentinas (📲0810-222-8652; www.aerolineas.com; Caseros 475; ⊗9am-5pm Mon-Fri) flies several times daily to Buenos Aires; it also serves Córdoba, Mendoza and Puerto Iguazú. **LATAM** (📲0-810-999-9526; www.latam.com; Caseros 476; ⊗8:30am-1pm & 4:30-8pm Mon-Fri) flies regularly to Buenos Aires. **Andes** (📲0387-431-3514; www.andesonline.com; Caseros 459; ⊗8am-1pm & 4:30-7pm Mon-Fri, 9:30am-1pm Sat) has flights to Buenos Aires with connection to Puerto Madryn. **BoA** (📲0387-471-1558; www.boa.bo; Mitre 37, Shop 24; ⊗9am-1pm & 3-6pm), with an office in a shopping arcade off the plaza, flies to Santa Cruz in Bolivia.

Bus 8A runs to Salta's **airport** (SLA; 📲0387-424-3115; RN 51, Km 5), 9.5km southwest of town, from San Martín by Córdoba. A taxi costs AR$180 to AR$220.

BUS

Salta's **bus terminal** (📲0387-431-5022; Av Hipólito Yrigoyen; ⊗information 6am-10pm) has ATMs, tourist information and left-luggage services.

Three companies run to San Pedro de Atacama, Chile (AR$700, nine to 10 hours, daily 7am), via Jujuy and Purmamarca. They continue to Calama (AR$850), Antofagasta (AR$900), Iquique (AR$1050) and Arica (AR$1150).

Buses from Salta

DESTINATION	COST (AR$)	DURATION (HR)
Buenos Aires	3000	18-22
Cafayate	390-440	4

DESTINATION	COST (AR$)	DURATION (HR)
Córdoba	750-2155	11-14
Jujuy	250	2
La Quiaca	430	7½
La Rioja	1400-1600	10
Mendoza	1880-3095	18-20
Resistencia	1325-1430	10-12
Salvador Mazza	850	6½
Santiago del Estero	400-1125	7
Tucumán	262-500	4¼

Jujuy

📲0388 / POP 258,000

If you're heading north, Jujuy is where you start to feel the proximity to Bolivia. You see it in people's faces, the chaotic street scenes, the markets that spill out onto sidewalks, and the restaurant menus that offer *locro*, *humitas* and *sopa de maní* (spicy peanut soup) as a matter of course, rather than as 'regional specialties.'

👁️ Sights

⭐**Culturarte** GALLERY
(www.facebook.com/culturarte.ccultural; cnr San Martín & Sarmiento; ⊗8am-8pm Mon-Sat) FREE An attractive modern space, Culturarte showcases exhibitions by a collective of 26 well-established Argentine contemporary artists. There's often work of excellent quality here, and it makes a fun place to check out the Jujuy scene. The downstairs cafe has a nice little balcony terrace overlooking the center of town.

Museo Arqueológico MUSEUM
(📲0388-422-1343; Lavalle 434; ⊗9am-1pm & 4-8pm Mon-Fri, 9am-noon & 4-8pm Sat) FREE The central exhibit here is a vivid 3000-year-old fertility goddess figure, depicted with snakes for hair and in the act of giving birth. She's a product of the advanced San Francisco culture in Las Yungas from about 1400 BC to 800 BC. There's also a selection of skulls with cranial deformities (practiced for cosmetic reasons) and mummified bodies.

🛏️ Sleeping

Hostelina HOSTEL $
(📲0388-424-8522; www.hostelina.com.ar; Alvear 529; dm US$8; 🛜) A simple, tasteful and

comfortable hostel set in a restored old building with original tiling, and modern art on the walls. You'll snooze in one of four dorms, set up with four to six beds each. There's nothing smashing here, but the price works.

D-Gira Hostel HOSTEL $
(📱0388-410-0877; www.facebook.com/dgira.hostel jujuy; JM Gorriti 427; dm/d US$7/19; @🌐) Located in an unfashionable but relatively central zone of the city, this place beats the downtown hostels on several points. First is the genuine welcome, then you can add the comfortable blond-timber bunks with their plump mattresses and decent bedding. Dorms all have en suite bathrooms and plenty of room, and there's one double room.

★ Posada El Arribo BOUTIQUE HOTEL $$
(📱0388-422-2539; www.elarribo.com; Belgrano 1263; r from US$50; P✱@🌐≋) An oasis in the heart of Jujuy, this impressive family-run place occupying a renovated 19th-century mansion is wonderful, with original floor tiles and high ceilings. There's plenty of patio space and a huge garden too, and the modern annex behind doesn't lose much by comparison. Still, go for an older room if you can.

✖ Eating

Jujuy's two lively markets, **Mercado del Sur** (Iglesia 1002-1060; meals AR$70-120; ☺8am-4pm) and **Mercado Central 6 de Agosto** (Alvear 885; ☺8am-6pm), are genuine trading posts where indigenous Argentines swig *mazamorra* (cold maize soup) and peddle *coca* leaves.

Madre Tierra BAKERY, CAFE $
(📱0388-422-9578; Belgrano 619; mains AR$80-140; ☺7am-10pm Mon-Sat; 🌐📱) This place is a standout. The design is creative and inviting, the vegetarian food (there's a daily set menu) is excellent, and the sandwiches and pizzas can be washed down with fresh juice or organic craft beer. There's lovely garden-patio seating, which is popular and fills up every evening. The bakery up front does wholesome breads.

Manos Jujeñas ARGENTINE $
(📱0388-424-3270; Av Pérez 379; mains AR$150-250; ☺11am-3pm & 7-11pm Tue-Sun; 🌐) 🍴 If you crave no-frills traditional slow-food cooking, make your way here for the *picante* – marinated chicken or tongue (or both) with onion, tomato, rice and Andean potatoes. That's the pride of the house. Takeout is also available.

★ Krysys ARGENTINE $$
(📱0388-423-1126; Balcarce 272; mains AR$185-295; ☺12:30-3pm & 8:30pm-12:30am Mon-Sat, 12:30-3:30pm Sun; 🌐) The best *parrilla* option in Jujuy is this central, upscale place offering your barbecued favorites in a relaxed atmosphere. But there's more on the menu, including tasty sauces to go with the meat, plus octopus, trout and paella. Prices are fair, and you'll get the meat cooked the way you want it.

ⓘ Information

Municipal Tourist Office (📱0388-402-0246; www.sansalvadordejujuy.gob.ar; cnr Alvear & Otero; ☺7am-10pm) Friendly and central. Hours vary depending on staffing.

Provincial Tourist Office (📱0388-422-1325; www.turismo.jujuy.gov.ar; Canónigo Gorriti 295; ☺7am-10pm Mon-Fri, 8am-9pm Sat & Sun) Excellent office on the plaza, with helpful brochures and staff.

ⓘ Getting There & Around

AIR
Aerolíneas Argentinas (📱0388-422-2575; www.aerolineas.com.ar; San Martín 96; ☺9am-5pm Mon-Fri) services Buenos Aires and Córdoba from **Aeropuerto Horacio Guzmán** (📱0388-491-1102), 33km southeast of downtown Jujuy. An **airport shuttle** (📱0388-15-432-2482; per person AR$250) leaves three times daily from the corner of Canónigo Gorriti and Belgrano to coincide with flights; alternatively it's AR$550 in a *remise* (taxi).

BUS
The new **bus terminal** is 6km southeast of the center. It has great facilities, including showers and a **tourist office** (☺7:30am-9:30pm Mon-Fri, 8am-1pm & 3:30-9:30pm Sat & Sun).

Daily buses going from Salta to Chile stop here.

Buses from Jujuy

DESTINATION	COST (AR$)	DURATION (HR)
Buenos Aires	2485-3135	20-23
Córdoba	1715-2235	12-16
Humahuaca	130	2
La Quiaca	200	4-5
Mendoza	2070-2380	21
Purmamarca	85	1¼
Salta	250	2
Salvador Mazza	575	7
Tilcara	85	1¾
Tucumán	700-795	5

Quebrada de Humahuaca

North of Jujuy, RN 9 snakes its way through the Quebrada de Humahuaca, a painter's palette of color on barren hillsides, dwarfing hamlets where Quechua peasants scratch a living growing maize and raising scrawny livestock. On this colonial post route to Potosí, the architecture and other cultural features mirror Peru and Bolivia.

Earthquakes leveled many of the adobe churches, but they were often rebuilt in the 17th and 18th centuries with solid walls, simple bell towers, and striking doors and wood paneling from the *cardón* cactus.

Tilcara

🖉 0388 / POP 4700

The most comfortable of the Quebrada towns, Tilcara is also one of the prettiest, and it hosts a number of fine eating and sleeping options.

Tilcara's hilltop *pucará,* a pre-Hispanic fortress with unobstructed views, is its most conspicuous attraction, but the village's museums and its reputation as an artists' colony help make it an appealing stopover.

◉ Sights & Activities

Pucará   RUINS

(🖉 0388-422-1325; entry incl Museo Arqueológico adult/student AR$100/25; ⊙9am-6pm) This reconstructed pre-Columbian fortification is 1km south of Tilcara's center, across an iron bridge. Its location is strategic, commanding the river valley both ways and, though the site was undoubtedly used earlier, the ruins date from the 11th to 15th centuries. There are great views and, seemingly, a cardón cactus for every soul that lived and died here. For further succulent stimulation, there's a botanic garden by the entrance.

Museo Arqueológico   MUSEUM

(Belgrano 445; entry incl Pucará adult/student AR$100/25; ⊙9am-6pm) This well-presented collection of regional artifacts in a striking colonial house has some pieces from the pucará (p132) just south of the center. Exhibits offer insight into the life of people living around the time of this fortification (from the 11th to 15th centuries). The room dedicated to ceremonial masks is particularly impressive.

🍴 Sleeping & Eating

Cheap places to eat line Belgrano and Lavalle between the bus terminal and Plaza Prado.

La Calabaza   CABAÑAS $

(🖉 0388-495-5169, WhatsApp 388-15-272442; www.calabazatilcara.com.ar; Sarahuaico s/n; d from US$35, 5-person cabin US$60; 🅿 🗟) Across the main road from Tilcara's center, this cute spot has a casual hippie vibe and friendly welcome. The view: just spectacular. There's a cabin with kitchen sleeping five, perfect for a family, and an adorable little double with views from the bed and tea/coffee facilities. There's a three-night minimum stay in summer. Breakfast is extra.

Albahaca Hostel   HOSTEL $

(🖉 0388-15-585-5994; www.albahacahostel.com.ar; Padilla s/n; dm/d US$8/20; 🗟) Albahaca is simple but well priced and friendly, with decent dorms, comfortable private rooms and a sociable roof terrace. A place to make friends.

★Antigua Tilcara   GUESTHOUSE, HOSTEL $$

(🖉 0388-527-3805; www.antiguatilcara.com.ar; Sorpresa 484; dm US$11, d US$40-45; @🗟) 🗹 A cute red adobe building, adorned with flowers, and set up a dirt road from the town center, where the roads seemingly disappear into the hills. Rooms here are wonderful, with ceramic-tile floors, exposed stone, wood furnishings and artistic accents, such as cactus-wood lanterns. The service is charming, relaxed and conscientious.

Khuska   ARGENTINE $

(🖉 0388-478-7356; Padilla 533; mains AR$90-200; ⊙6pm-midnight; 🗟🗹) Grab a table in this charming, rambling, creative dining room serving regional dishes including *humitas,* empanadas and *picadas Andinas,* along with some decent vegetarian options. Andean platters feature roasted local potatoes, sautéed quinoa and grilled goat cheese.

Ma'koka   CAFE $

(🖉 0388-15-509-5617; Belgrano s/n; sandwiches AR$80-115; ⊙8:30am-9pm; 🗟🗹) 🗹 With an eclectic music mix and interesting texts on the area and the Andes in general, this excellent bookstore-cafe also has the best coffee in town, tasty cakes and top sandwiches using bread made from *coca* or local corn varieties. There are great choices for celiacs too, with manioc bread and other treats. The owner is knowledgeable about indigenous Argentina.

★ **El Nuevo Progreso** ARGENTINE **$$**
(🖉 0388-495-5237; www.facebook.com/elnuevo progreso; Lavalle 351; mains AR$160-300; ☺ 6-11:30pm Mon-Sat; 🛜) An engaging, artsy ambience here is combined with delicious tourist-oriented cuisine. Think imaginatively prepared llama dishes, excellent meat plates, one interesting veggie option and great salads. The trout, steamed in spinach leaves and topped with roast pumpkin, is quite good. Service can be a bit standoffish. Book a table in advance on weekends.

ℹ Information

The **tourist office** (Belgrano 366; ☺ 8am-9pm Mon-Fri, 9am-1pm & 2-9pm Sat, 9am-1pm Sun) has information on walks. It's often open Sunday afternoons despite the official hours. Conversely, it's often not open when it's supposed to be.

ℹ Getting There & Around

The bus terminal is on the main street, Belgrano; further services stop on the highway nearby. There are buses roughly every 45 minutes to Jujuy (AR$85, 1½ hours) and north to Humahuaca (AR$45, 45 minutes) and La Quiaca (AR$205, three hours). Several daily buses hit Purmamarca (AR$20, 30 minutes) and Salta (AR$300, 3½ hours).

Humahuaca

🖉 03887 / POP 10,300

A popular stopover on the Salta–Bolivia route, Humahuaca is a mostly Quechuan village of narrow cobbled streets lined with adobe houses. There's plenty to do in the surrounding countryside, and the town provides some great photo opportunities.

◉ Sights & Activities

Built in 1641, Humahuaca's **Iglesia de la Candelaria** faces Plaza Gómez. Nearby, the lovably knobbly **cabildo** (Plaza Gómez) is famous for its clock tower, where a life-size figure of San Francisco Solano emerges at noon to deliver a benediction. From the plaza, a staircase climbs to the rather vulgar **Monumento a la Independencia**.

✖ Festivals & Events

Humahuaca observes February 2 as the day of its patron, the **Virgen de Candelaria**.

🛏 Sleeping & Eating

La Humahuacasa HOSTEL **$**
(🖉 03887-412-0868; www.humahuacasa.com.ar; Buenos Aires 740; dm/d US$11/22.50; 🛜) Artistic and personable, this hostel is central and offers cozy dorms around a small patio, with thick mattresses dressed in colorful blankets. It's a social place with a decent kitchen and a good vibe. Everything is very clean and well run. There's one private room – an en suite double.

Inti Sayana HOSTAL **$**
(🖉 03887-421917; www.intisayanahostal.com.ar; La Rioja 83; d from US$36; 🅿🛜) A central cheapie with spotless tiled rooms that sleep three, set around a courtyard and parking area. If you're toting a bag full of dirty clothes you'll want to take advantage of its inexpensive laundry service.

Ser Andino CAFE **$**
(🖉 03887-421659; Jujuy 393; mains AR$90-160; ☺ 9am-10pm) A homey cafe decked out with

---

ℹ GETTING TO BOLIVIA

Cold, windy **La Quiaca** is a major crossing point to Bolivia. It has decent places to stay and eat, but little to detain the traveler. If you arrive late at night, however, it's best to stay here as services are much better than across the border in Villazón.

Opposite the bus terminal, La Quica's **information kiosk** (Av España s/n; ☺ 10am-1pm & 4-8pm) offers decent info. Sweet **Copacabana Hostel** (🖉 03885-423875; www.hostelcopacabana.com.ar; Pellegrini 141; s/d US$10/18; @ 🛜) offers small, heated rooms serviced by amiable staff. The down-home **Frontera** (🖉 0388-542-5162; cnr Belgrano & Árabe Siria; mains AR$140-200; ☺ 10am-4pm & 7-11pm) has meat plates and decent *tallarines al pesto* (noodles with pesto), plus a set lunch.

From the **bus terminal** (cnr Belgrano & España), there are frequent connections to Jujuy (AR$200, five hours), Salta (AR$430, eight hours) and intermediate points, plus long-distance services.

The border is a 1km walk from the bus terminal. There is no public transportation, but there may be a taxi around. The border is generally open 24 hours, but this is subject to change – don't arrive at 2am without a plan B.

dried flowers and potted plants attached to a tour operator of the same name. Get coffee or tea, a hot meal or book a tour. You can do it all here. The cafe serves pasta, *cazuela de cabrito* (goat stew), breakfasts, tamales and more.

Aisito ARGENTINE $
(☑ 03887-488-6609; Buenos Aires 435; mains AR$80-150; ⊙ 11am-3pm & 7-11pm; 🛜) Well decorated and blessed with caring service, this is a pleasing option for good-priced local cuisine. Tasty baked empanadas take their place alongside decent stir-fries and tender llama. There's live music on weekends, and nightly in summer.

Mikunayoc ARGENTINE $
(☑ 03887-421442; cnr Corrientes & Tucumán; mains AR$60-130; ⊙ 11am-3:30pm) The wide-ranging menu here includes several interesting llama dishes, cordial service and a range of empanadas with intriguing fillings. The salads are also a good bet. It's a pleasant, colorful place so you'll forgive the odd lapses in service. Lunch only.

❶ Information

The **tourist office** (Plaza Gómez s/n; ⊙ 7am-9pm Mon-Fri, 9am-9pm Sat & Sun) is located in the *cabildo* (municipal building).

❶ Getting There & Away

The **bus terminal** (cnr Belgrano & Entre Ríos) is three blocks south of Humahuaca's plaza. There are regular buses to Salta (AR$345, 4½ hours), Jujuy (AR$130, 2¼ hours) and La Quiaca (AR$160, two to three hours).

ATLANTIC COAST

The beaches along the Atlantic coast form Buenos Aires' backyard, and summer sees millions of *porteños* pouring into towns such as Mar del Plata and Pinamar for sun and fun. The rest of the year, and in smaller towns, the pace of life rarely approaches anything resembling hectic.

Mar del Plata

☑ 0223 / POP 621,000
On summer weekends, the beach in Mardel (as it's commonly known) gets really, seriously, comically crowded. We're talking people standing shoulder to shoulder, knee-deep in water. During the week, and in the nonsummer months, the crowds disperse, hotel prices drop and the place takes on a much more relaxed feel.

Founded in 1874, this most popular of Argentine beach destinations was first a commercial and industrial center, then a resort for upper-class *porteño* families. Mardel now caters mostly to middle-class vacationers.

◉ Sights & Activities

★ **Puerto Mar del Plata** PORT
(www.puertomardelplata.net; ☎ 533, 581) Mar del Plata is one of Argentina's most important fishing centers. Its port area, 8km south of the city center, is worth a visit, though public access to the jetty – and its graveyard of ruined ships, half-sunken and rusting in the sun – is now restricted. You can still watch the fishing boats come and go from the **Banquina de Pescadores**, the port's scenic, rather aromatic and slightly touristy wharf.

Torreón del Monje HISTORIC BUILDING
(☑ 0223-486-4000; www.torreondelmonje.com.ar; cnr Viamonte & Paseo Jesús de Galindez; ⊙ 8am-10pm) Grand and castle-like, positioned on a cliff over the ocean, Torreón del Monje is hard to miss – look for the red domes and the stone footbridge straddling the oceanfront road. This classic landmark is a throwback to Mar del Plata's glamorous heyday. The Argentine businessman Ernesto Tornquist, intent on beautifying the area around his own summer getaway, had the medieval-style lookout tower built in 1904. Stop for the view, and perhaps a coffee break on the terrace.

Más Vida YOGA
(☑ 0223-495-1189; www.facebook.com/masvidayoga; Bolívar 2976; prices vary) A popular yoga space in the vibrant Plaza Mitre area offering Hatha, Ashtanga and aerial yoga classes. It can also arrange massages and yoga and SUP sessions in the summertime. The schedule is online, but call to confirm before turning up.

Bicicletería Madrid CYCLING
(☑ 0223-494-1932; Yrigoyen 2249; per hr from AR$90; ⊙ 9am-5:30pm Mon-Fri, 10am-6pm Sat) Bicycles can be rented here. Hours extend during the summer.

Acción Directa OUTDOORS
(☑ 0223-474-4520; www.facebook.com/acciondirecta.mdp; Av Libertad 3902; ⊙ 10am-1pm & 5-9pm Mon-Fri, 10am-1pm Sat) The rocky cliffs by the sea and the hills of Sierra de los Padres make for excellent climbing and rappelling. Acción Directa runs a school and

also offers mountain biking, canoeing and overnight active camping trips.

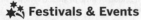 Festivals & Events

International Film Festival   FILM
(www.mardelplatafilmfest.com; ⊙Nov) Launched in 1950, the city's International Film Festival is considered South America's most important film festival.

🛌 Sleeping

Prices start climbing in November and December, peak in January and February, then drop off in March. Reserve ahead in summer. In the off-season, some accommodations close their doors. If you love Airbnb, seek an apartment near Plaza Mitre, a fashionable local district.

Che Lagarto Hostel   HOSTEL $
(📞0223-451-3704; www.chelagarto.com; Alberti 1565; dm/d/tr from US$10/22/33; ⊙Sep 15-Apr; @🛜) This popular branch of the Che Lagarto chain has it all: friendly staff, a central location close to Mardel's best nightlife and shopping, and squeaky clean, fan-cooled private rooms and dorms. There's also a guest kitchen and a pleasant living area and cocktail bar. It's closed in the Argentine winter.

Dodo   BOUTIQUE HOTEL $
(📞0223-451-1479; www.hoteldodo.com.ar; Güemes 3041; d US$45-60; ❄🛜) A cute boutique sleep in the heart of Mardel's fashionable Los Troncos district. Set in a three-story, white-washed brick walk-up, rooms are all dressed in creams and whites, with white leather headboards and wall-mounted flat-screen TVs. Great value for money here.

On Tap   B&B $
(📞0223-622-1394; www.ontap.com.ar; Alsina 2583; d US$32; ❄🛜) A popular *cervecería* with small, well-imagined rooms on the floor above. Fashioned from reclaimed wood and polished concrete, each has a private bath, cable TV and wi-fi, as well as access to bicycles to tool around town. In this case the 'B&B' means 'bed and beer'.

Hotel 15 de Mayo   HOTEL $$
(📞0223-495-1388; www.hotel15demayo.com; Mitre 1457; s from US$60, d from US$80-105; ❄🛜) Conveniently located between Plaza San Martín and La Perla beach, this modern, four-star hotel is great value for its spotless, decent-sized guest rooms, spa, professional service, breakfast buffet and fast wi-fi.

Eating

★ Crucoli Caffe   CAFE $
(📞0223-451-2386; Garay 1511; dishes AR$90-170; ⊙8:30am-8pm Mon-Sat, noon-8pm Sun) This dreamy little cafe in Los Troncos is like a portal into the brain of artist, designer and baker Maria Bertone. She has crafted or painted everything on the walls – the mermaids and sailors, the sailboat napkin dispensers and fishy place mats, as well as the mixed-media art.

Montecatini   ARGENTINE $
(📞0223-492-4299; www.montecatini.com.ar; cnr La Rioja & 25 de Mayo; mains AR$125-310; ⊙noon-3pm & 8pm-midnight; ❄🍴) For solid, good-value dishes, make like the locals and head to this large, modern and popular restaurant – one of three branches in town. There's something for everyone on the menu (meat, fish, pasta, *milanesas*, sandwiches) and portions are generous. The weekday lunch special (AR$255, including dessert and a drink) is a steal. Good for families and large groups.

La Marina   SEAFOOD $$
(📞0223-489-9216; 12 de Octubre 3147; mains AR$140-440; ⊙noon-4pm & 8pm-midnight Thu-Mon, noon-4pm Tue) You won't find seafood any fresher or more affordable than at this down-to-earth place a few blocks inland from the entrance to the port. In business since 1957, its specialty is the delicious *cazuela especial La Marina,* a seafood stew packed with fish, shrimp, squid and mussels simmered in white wine, cream and saffron.

🍷 Drinking & Nightlife

Many recommended venues are located in chic **Barrio Los Troncos** and the area along Irigoyen and LN Alem, between Almafuerte and Rodríguez Peña, a section of the city that's thick with cocktail bars and nightlife. Wander around the neighborhood for yourself and see what appeals.

Pueblo   BEER HALL
(www.facebook.com/pueblogalpondecervezas; La Rioja 2068; ⊙7pm-4am Tue-Sun) There's a youthful crowd and free-flowing *cerveza* at this stylish pub with a corrugated facade and a cool front door that rolls open to expose the pub directly to the street. There are surf videos on the flat-screen TVs, 11 beers on tap and a menu of pub grub on the blackboard.

ARGENTINA MAR DEL PLATA

Almacén Estación Central BAR
(www.facebook.com/estacioncentral.mardelplata; cnr Alsina & Garay; ☺6:30pm-4am Wed-Sun) This glitzy pub is set in a quaint and thoughtfully restored antique building – an old corner store where the former President of Argentina, Marcelo Torcuato de Alvear, reportedly did his shopping. Expect gourmet pub food, frequent happy-hour deals (even on weekends), and a mostly conservative crowd.

La Bodeguita del Medio BAR
(Castelli 1252; ☺6pm-4am) A classic rum-soaked dive, named after one of Hemingway's favorite haunts in Havana, serving famously delicious mojitos (choose among seven varieties), Cuban-inspired food and occasional live music.

ℹ Information

There are several branches of the city's official tourist office around town. The centrally located **tourist office** (☎0223-495-1777; www.turismo mardelplata.gov.ar; Blvd Marítimo 2270; ☺9am-5pm Mon-Fri, 10am-5pm Sat & Sun) is exceptionally helpful.

ℹ Getting There & Away

AIR

From Mardel's **Ástor Piazzolla International Airport** (☎0223-478-0744), 10km north of town, **Aerolíneas Argentinas** (☎0223-496-0101; www.aerolineas.com.ar; Moreno 2442; ☺9:30am-5:30pm Mon-Fri) has several daily flights to Buenos Aires.

BUS

Mardel's new bus terminal is adjacent to the train station. There are departures to Buenos Aires (AR$400 to AR$1055, 5½ hours), Pinamar (AR$220 to AR$545, 2½ hours) and Villa Gesell (AR$185 to AR$240, 1½ hours).

TRAIN

Trains with *primera*-class service (AR$615) run daily between Mar del Plata's **train station** (☎0223-475-6076; www.sofse.gob.ar; Av Luro 4700 at Italia; ☺6am-midnight) and Buenos Aires' Constitución station (six hours). Visit www.sofse.gob.ar for more information, and be sure to reserve tickets well ahead in summer.

ℹ Getting Around

The airport (p136) is 10km north of the city. Take bus 715 (AR$10, 30 minutes) from the corner of Blvd Marítimo and Belgrano. Taxis cost from around AR$200, depending on where you're going.

Despite Mar del Plata's sprawl, frequent buses reach just about every place in town. However,

most buses (including the airport bus) require *tarjetas de aproximación* (magnetic cards) that must be bought ahead of time at *kioscos* (newsstands) and charged up.

Visit www.cualbondi.com.ar/mar-del-plata for useful maps of all local bus routes. The tourist office can also help with transportation details.

Villa Gesell

☎02255 / POP 34,000

This laid-back dune community sleeps in the low season, but in summer it's a favorite for young *porteños*, who stream in to party the warm nights away. It's one of the prettiest coastal towns: small, with windy, sandy roads sporting charming summer cottages (and also grander retreats).

◉ Sights & Activities

Gesell's long **beach** and boardwalk draw swimmers, sunbathers and horse riders. There's year-round **fishing** from the pier.

Feria Artesanal MARKET
(Crafts Fair; Av 3 btwn Paseos 112 & 113) There's a nightly handicrafts fair in mid-December to mid-March. Expect lots of handmade jewelry, carved wood, paintings and souvenirs. The rest of the year it's a weekend-only event.

Windy Playa Bar SURFING
(www.windyplayabar.com.ar; cnr Paseo 104 & beach; ☺8am-dusk in summer) You can't miss it: just look for the faux pirate ship parked on the sand. At Windy, you can rent surf gear or sign up for lessons; you can also rent beach equipment or just grab some cold drinks and sandwiches with a view.

Casa Macca CYCLING
(Av Buenos Aires 449) For bicycle rentals, try Casa Macca. It's located between Paseo 101 and Av 5.

⊨ Sleeping

The most affordable *hospedajes* (basic hotels) are north of Av 3. It's important to book ahead in summer, especially in the second half of January, when prices rise even more.

La Deseada Hostel HOSTEL $
(☎02255-473276; www.ladeseadahostel.com.ar; cnr Av 6 & Paseo 119; dm/d from US$25/50; @☺) Teeming with young Argentines in January, and shuttered in the off-season, this homey hostel sits atop a sloping, evergreen-fringed lawn in a residential area between the bus terminal and the center, six blocks from the

beach. Eight-bed dorms are complemented by spacious common areas and a nice kitchen. Breakfast is served till 1pm.

★ Hostería Santa Barbara
BOUTIQUE HOTEL $$
(☑ 02255-463143; www.hosteriasantabarbara.com; Av 1, No 938; s/d from US$40/50; ⊘Oct-Apr; P 🔊) This four-floor walk-up offers a sparkling-clean, three-star habitat. Rooms aren't huge, but they are bright, and the best situated have balconies. The top floor *comedor* (dining room) where you'll have breakfast overlooks the sea, and there's a gorgeous brick *parrilla* here, too.

🍴 Eating

Like most beach resorts, there are plenty of popular kitchens churning out mass-market nosh to less-than-discerning clientele. Nevertheless, there are a few genuinely great restaurants in and around Villa Gesell.

Rancho Hambre
EMPANADAS $
(Av 3, No 871; empanadas AR$35; ⊘11:30am-3pm & 7-11pm) This main-street hot spot features 36 varieties of empanadas, from the humble (minced beef) to the more elaborate (arugula, parmesan and walnuts, or bacon with mozzarella and muscat-infused prunes). Pick up a dozen to go. There's a second location on the corner of Av 3 and Paseo 125.

El Náutico
ARGENTINE $$
(☑ 02255 46-8620; Paseo 102 & Playa; mains AR$300-350; ⊘8am-11pm daily Dec-Mar, Fri-Sun only Apr-Nov; 🔊) This charming jumble of wood festooned with fishing nets is set on the sand like a barge in dry dock. And though it looks like a fish house, it's actually known for its steaks, especially the *bife de chorizo*. It does burgers, sandwiches, salads and a lovely grilled fish, too.

❶ Information

The **tourist office** (☑ 02255-478042; http://turismo.gesell.gob.ar/; Paseo 107, btwn Avs 2 & 3; ⊘8am-8pm Mar-Dec, to midnight Jan & Feb) is conveniently located in the center. There's another branch at the bus terminal.

❶ Getting There & Away

The main **bus terminal** (cnr Av 3 & Paseo 140; ⊘5am-midnight mid-Dec–Easter, 8am-8pm rest of year) is south of town; local buses into the center (AR$10, 15 minutes) leave regularly from a shelter just across Av 3. Bus destinations include Buenos Aires (AR$760 to AR$865, 5½

hours), Mar del Plata (AR$185 to AR$240, two hours) and Pinamar (AR$75, 30 minutes).

Pinamar
☑ 02254 / POP 30,000

Rivaling Uruguay's Punta del Este in the fashion stakes, Pinamar and the surrounding towns are where wealthy Argentine families come to play in summertime.

⊙ Sights & Activities

Many places are only open on weekends and in summer, but at other times you can stroll peacefully in bordering pine forests and along the wide, attractive **beach** without being trampled by vacationers.

Bike hire is available from **Leo** (☑ 02254-488855; Av Bunge 1111; bike rental per hr AR$100; ⊘9am-9pm). There are many more activities on offer – especially in the summer months; look for brochures in the **tourist office** (☑ 02254-491680; www.pinamar.tur.ar; cnr Av Bunge & Shaw; ⊘8am-8pm Mon-Fri, 10am-8pm Sat, 10am-5pm Sun).

🎉 Festivals & Events

Pantalla Pinamar (www.facebook.com/pantallapinamaroficial; ⊘Mar), Pinamar's film festival, takes place in March, and there are concerts and parties on the beach around New Year.

🛏 Sleeping

Reservations are a must in January, when some places have a one-week minimum stay. The best options for the budget-minded are near the southern beaches of Ostende and Valeria, though you'll also find some cheaper hotels and *hospedajes* along Calle del Cangrejo, north of the tourist office.

Hotel Yarma
HOTEL $
(☑ 02254-405401; www.hotelyarma.com.ar; Del Tuyú 109; d US$40-50; P 🔊) The stone-and-stucco exterior helps this one stand out, and there's some interesting art on the interior walls, too. The rooms are a bit dated, yet they are super-clean and great value at this price.

Cabañas Pinaforet
CABAÑAS $$
(☑ 02254-409277; www.pinaforet.com.ar; cnr Apolo & Jason; cabañas from US$90; ❋🔊) This cluster of spacious log cabins set among piney grounds is only a handful of paces from the bus terminal, and within a few minutes' walk of the town center and beach. Each sleeps up to four people, making this a

great budget option in low season (despite the high weekly prices quoted in summer).

✖ Eating

Countless restaurants and food stands line the beachfront and Av Bunge; wander onto the side streets to find better deals (and fewer crowds).

★ Los Troncos   ARGENTINE $$
(☑ 02254 48-1784; cnr Eneas & Lenguado; mains AR$140-400; ⊙ noon-3pm & 8pm-midnight Thu-Tue; 🛜) In business for four decades, this beloved backstreet eatery is often packed with locals even in low season. There's a casual but convivial old-school ambience, and the menu includes everything from roast meats to seafood stews to homemade pastas, all well executed.

Nelson Resto Bar   PUB FOOD $$
(☑ 02254-517550; Bunge 68; mains AR$220-375; ⊙ noon-3pm & 6:30pm-midnight; 🛜) This vibrant, corrugated tin shack is packed with memorabilia, rocks with reggae and salsa, and serves gourmet burgers (including veggie burgers), tacos and pizza to vintage vinyl booths and tables made from reclaimed wood. Quirky and fun, with bars and dining areas inside and out, this place packs them in.

❶ Getting There & Away

Pinamar's **bus terminal** (☑ 02254-403500; Jason 2250) is about eight blocks north of the town center, just off Av Bunge. Bus destinations include Buenos Aires (AR$495 to AR$560, five hours), Mar del Plata (AR$220 to AR$545, 2½ hours) and Villa Gesell (AR$75, 30 minutes).

Bahía Blanca
☑ 0291 / POP 297,000

Mostly a stopover point for people headed elsewhere, Bahía Blanca is surprisingly cosmopolitan for its size, and boasts Argentina's worst-signposted museum.

◉ Sights

★ Museo Taller Ferrowhite   HISTORIC BUILDING
(☑ 0291-457-0335; http://ferrowhite.bahiablanca. gov.ar; Juan B Justo 3883; by donation; ⊙ 9am-noon Mon-Fri, 3-7pm Sat & Sun) Ferrowhite is the kind of ghostly landmark you see from far away and no matter how eerie, you can't stop yourself from inching closer and closer. The castle-like power plant, built by Italians in

the 1930s, sits beside massive grain elevators on the edge of the bay. There's a museum and cafe, but half the fun is strolling around the abandoned structure with its elegant architecture, shattered windows and purported paranormal activity.

Museo del Puerto   MUSEUM
(☑ 0291-457-3006; www.museodelpuerto.blogspot. com; cnr Guillermo Torres & Carrega; donation requested; ⊙ 8:30am-12:30pm Mon-Fri, 3:30-7:30pm Sat & Sun) Housed in a colorfully painted former customs building dating from 1907, this small but engaging museum is a tribute to the region's immigrants. The rooms include archives and photographs, and mock-ups of an old *peluquería* (barber shop) and bar. The historical collection starts in the yard outside, where a wooden fishing boat and other antique artifacts harken back to the port's intriguing past.

🛏 Sleeping & Eating

Hotel Muñiz   HOTEL $
(☑ 0291-456-0060; www.hotelmuniz.com.ar; O'Higgins 23; s US$20-37, d US$36-47, ste US$60; ❄@🛜) A downtown landmark, the Muñiz is located in a beautiful 90-year-old building. Note the vintage charm on the lobby level: B&W tiled floors, polished woodwork, an antique phone booth. Upstairs, three levels of guest rooms are linked by long hallways. Superior rooms are the largest and best of the bunch. Service is impeccable.

★ Gambrinus   ARGENTINE $$
(www.gambrinus1890.com; Arribeños 174; mains AR$120-310; ⊙ noon-3pm & 8pm-1am) Located in a lovely 19th-century corner building, on a side street a few blocks south of the main plaza, the menu features Spanish- and Italian-inspired Argentine classics. There's a good wine list and a number of beers on tap. The vivacious local crowd and walls plastered with vintage ads and Argentine basketball memorabilia contribute to the welcoming atmosphere.

Pelicano Bar   PUB FOOD $$
(☑ 0291-451-2758; Alsina 226; mains AR$150-270; 🛜) A popular, music-themed bar and cafe. Each booth has been assigned its own decade and the table is plastered in artwork and photographs from famous albums and bands of that era. It serves coffee, Argentine beer and wine, pizzas and hot sandwiches all day and night. Sports or music videos stream on four flat screens.

ℹ️ Information

Tourist Kiosk (☎ 0291-481-8944; www.bahia.
gob.ar/conoce/turismobahia; Drago 45, Municipalidad de Bahía Blanca; ⊗ 9am-6pm Mon-Fri,
10am-1pm & 3:30-6:30pm Sat)

ℹ️ Getting There & Around

AIR

Aerolíneas Argentinas (☎ 0291-456-0561;
www.aerolineas.com.ar; San Martín 298;
⊗ 9:30am-5:30pm Mon-Fri) and **LATAM**
(☎ 0810-999-9526; www.latam.com; Chiclana
344; ⊗ 9am-6pm Mon-Fri) offer flights from
Bahía Blanca's airport, 15km east of town. The
airport isn't connected to town by bus; it costs
around AR$300 by taxi.

BUS

The **bus terminal** (Brown 1700) is about 2km
southeast of Plaza Rivadavia; there are many
local buses heading into town (buy magnetic
cards from kiosks). A taxi costs around AR$100.
To avoid the trek out to the terminal you can
buy bus tickets at the kiosks around the south
end of Plaza Rivadavia. Destinations include
Buenos Aires (AR$1110 to AR$1660, nine hours),
Mar del Plata (AR$829 to AR$921, seven hours)
and Neuquén (AR$635 to AR$890, 7½ hours).
Condor Estrella (p139) runs three daily buses to
Sierra de la Ventana (AR$230, 2½ hours). Call
ahead to reserve a spot.

TRAIN

Trains run from the **Estación Ferrocarril Roca**
(☎ 0291-452-9196; www.sofse.gob.ar; Cerri 750)
to Buenos Aires' Constitución station several
days of the week (AR$750 to AR$2625, 14 hours).
Check www.sofse.gob.ar for more details on
routes and fare options, and to make reservations.

Sierra de la Ventana

☑ 0291 / POP 2200

Sierra de la Ventana is where *porteños* come
to escape the summer heat, hike around
a bit and cool off in swimming holes. The
nearby mountain range of the same name in
Parque Provincial Ernesto Tornquist attracts
hikers and climbers to its jagged peaks,
which rise over 1300m.

For a nice walk, go to the end of Calle
Tornquist and cross the small dam (which
makes a local **swimming hole**). On the other side you'll see **Cerro del Amor**; hike to
the top for good views of town and pampas.

El Tornillo (☎ 0291-15-431-1812; Roca 142;
bike rental per hr/day AR$30/120; ⊗ 10am-7pm,
closed in afternoons during hot weather) rents
quality mountain bikes.

🛏️ Sleeping & Eating

There are several free campsites along the
river, with bathroom facilities nearby at the
pleasant and grassy municipal swimming
pool. Some restaurants close one or more
days per week outside the December to
March summer months. Self-caterers will
find several supermarkets and artisanal
food shops on the main street.

Alihuen Hotel   HOTEL $
(☎ 0291-491-5074; www.lasierradelaventana.com.
ar/alihuen; cnr Tornquist & Frontini; d from US$36;
🅿️ 🛜 🏊) Sierra de la Ventana's mini–Grand
Budapest Hotel is 'an enchanted old ruin'
set about four blocks from the main drag
and strategically positioned on the banks
of the river. It's not exactly luxurious, with
creaky wood floors and simple furnishings,
but there is plenty of atmosphere at this
vine-covered Victorian building.

Cabañas Bodensee   CABAÑAS $$
(☎ 0291-491-5356; www.sierrasdelaventana.com.ar/
bodensee; Raycos 455, Villa La Arcadia; cabaña for
2/4 people from US$40/50; 🛜 🏊) This peaceful
complex of brick cottages, situated around an
appealing swimming pool, is a lovely respite
within easy walking distance of the town
center. Each cabin features a small kitchen
and a porch with a large *parrilla*. It's locat-
ed in the neighborhood of Villa La Arcadia,
just across the river from most of Sierra de la
Ventana's services.

El Molino de la Casa Azul   ARGENTINE $$
(☎ 0291-414-2322; San Martín 480; mains AR$225-
300; ⊗ noon-3pm & 8:30-11pm Thu-Sun; 🛜) A
slightly progressive kitchen set in a gorgeous,
historic blue house with a windmill (hence
the name). The interior is alive with art and
the menu offers creative takes on Argentine
classics. It's not cheap, but it is the most fun
dining room in town.

ℹ️ Information

The **tourist office** (☎ 0291-491-5303; www.
sierradelaventana.org.ar; Av del Golf s/n;
⊗ 8am-8pm) is located near the train station.

ℹ️ Getting There & Away

Condor Estrella (☎ 0291-491-5091; www.
condorestrella.com.ar) has buses to Buenos
Aires (AR$1020 to AR$1160, nine hours, six
times weekly) and Bahía Blanca (AR$230, 2½
hours, twice daily) leaving from a small office
on Av San Martín, a block from the YPF gas
station.

Around Sierra de la Ventana

Popular for ranger-guided walks and independent hiking, the 67-sq-km **Parque Provincial Ernesto Tornquist** (☑0291-491-0039; www.facebook.com/parqueprovincialtornquist cerroventana; entry/guided treks per person AR$100/200; ☉9am-5pm) is the starting point for the 1150m five-hour (round-trip) guided hike to **Cerro de la Ventana**. The climb offers dramatic views of surrounding hills and the distant pampas. Register with rangers before 9am at the trailhead, and take plenty of water and sun protection. That hike costs an additional AR$200 per person.

Condor Estrella (p139) serves Tornquist from Sierra de la Ventana (AR$90, one hour, three daily) – tell the driver you want to get off at the park entrance. For better timing, to catch the park opening, arrange a *remise* (taxi) to the park from Sierra de la Ventana or Villa Ventana.

CENTRAL ARGENTINA

Containing the wine-producing centers of Mendoza, San Luis and San Juan (which themselves comprise an area known as Cuyo), there's no doubt what Central Argentina's main attraction is. But once you've polished off a few bottles, you won't be left twiddling your thumbs – this is also Argentina's adventure playground, and the opportunities for rafting, trekking, skiing and climbing are almost endless.

San Luis

☑0266 / POP 204,000

San Luis is coming up as a backpacking destination, but it still has a long way to go. Most people come here to visit the nearby Parque Nacional Sierra de las Quijadas. The commercial center is along the parallel streets of San Martín and Rivadavia, between Plaza Pringles in the north and Plaza Independencia to the south.

The large, multibed dorms at **San Luis Hostel** (☑0266-424188; www.sanluishostel.com.ar; Falucho 646; dm/s/d/tr US$10/20/34/43; @⊚☜⛲) could be a bit more atmospheric, but the rest of the hostel is beautiful. Staff can arrange trips to Sierra de las Quijadas and tours of local gold mines.

Av Illia, which runs northwest from the delightful Plaza Pringles, is the center of San Luis' moderately hopping bar scene. There are plenty of fast-food options along this street. **Aranjuez** (Rivadavia 689; pizzas & sandwiches AR$100-220; ☉6:30am-12:30am; ☜) is a fairly standard plaza-side cafe-bar-restaurant that gets a mention for its sidewalk tables, a great place to take a breather.

The **tourist office** (☑0266-442-3479; www.sanluis.gov.ar; Av Illia 35; ☉8am-8pm Mon-Fri, 9am-1pm Sat, 9am-9pm Sun) has an almost overwhelming amount of information on San Luis' surrounding areas.

Aerolineas Argentinas (☑0266-442-5671; www.aerolineas.com.ar; Av Illia 472; ☉9am-1pm & 5-9pm Mon-Fri) flies twice daily to Buenos Aires. The bus terminal has departures to Mendoza (AR$240 to AR$700, four hours), San Juan (AR$485 to AR$750, four hours), Rosario (AR$1035 to AR$1580, 10 hours) and Buenos Aires (AR$930 to AR$2200, 11 hours).

Mendoza

☑0261 / POP 1.2 MILLION

In 1861 an earthquake leveled the city of Mendoza. This was a tragedy for the *mendocinos* (people from Mendoza), but rebuilding efforts created some of the city's most-loved aspects: the authorities anticipated (somewhat pessimistically) the *next* earthquake by rebuilding the city with wide avenues (for the rubble to fall into) and spacious plazas (to use as evacuation points). The result is one of Argentina's most seductive cities – stunningly picturesque and a joy to walk around.

Add to this the fact that it's smack in the middle of many of the country's best vineyards and that it's the base for any number of outdoor activities, and you know you'll be spending more than a couple of days here.

Mendoza's famous **Fiesta Nacional de la Vendimia** (National Wine Harvest Festival; www.vendimia.mendoza.gov.ar; Teatro Griego Frank Romero Day; ☉late Feb-early Mar) attracts big crowds; book accommodation well ahead. The surrounding countryside offers wine tasting, mountaineering, cycling and whitewater rafting. Many different tours of the area are available.

◉ Sights

Museo Fundacional　　　　　　MUSEUM
(museofundacional@ciudaddemendoza.gov.ar; cnr Alberdi & Videla Castillo; adult/child AR$50/23; ☉9am-5pm Mon-Fri) Mendoza's renovated

Central Argentina

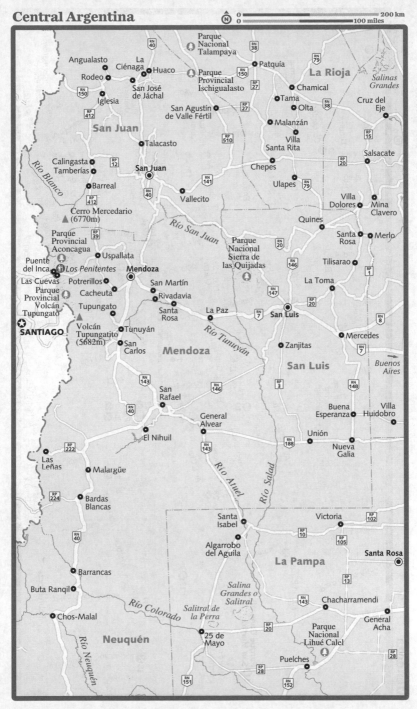

0 — 200 km
0 — 100 miles

RN 40 · Parque Nacional Talampaya · RN 38 · RN 79 · La Rioja · Salinas Grandes

Angualasto · La Ciénaga · Huaco · RN 150 · Patquía · Chamical

Rodeo · San José de Jáchal · Parque Provincial Ischigualasto · RP 27 · Tama · Olta · RN 38 · Cruz del Eje

RN 150 · Iglesia

RP 412 · San Agustín de Valle Fértil · RP 27 · Malanzán · RP 15

San Juan · Talacasto · RP 510 · Villa Santa Rita · Salsacate

Calingasta · RP 12 · San Juan · Chepes · RP 20

Tamberías · RN 40 · Vallecito · Ulapes · RN 79 · Villa Dolores · Mina Clavero

Barreal · RP 412 · Río San Juan · Quines · Santa Rosa · Merlo

Cerro Mercedario (6770m) · RP 39 · Parque Nacional Sierra de las Quijadas · RN 20 · Tilisarao · RP 1

Parque Provincial Aconcagua · Uspallata · RN 146 · La Toma · RP 20

Puente del Inca · Los Penitentes · **Mendoza** · RN 147

Las Cuevas · Potrerillos · San Martín · RN 7 · San Luis · RN 8

Parque Provincial Volcán Tupungato · Cacheuta · Rivadavia · La Paz · Mercedes · RN 7

SANTIAGO · Tupungato · Santa Rosa · Zanjitas · **San Luis** · Buenos Aires

Volcán Tupungatito (5682m) · Tunuyán · **Mendoza**

San Carlos · RP 3 · RN 148

RN 143 · RN 146 · Buena Esperanza · Villa Huidobro

San Rafael · RN 40 · General Alvear · Unión · Nueva Galia

RP 222 · El Nihuil · RN 143 · RN 188

Las Leñas · Malargüe · Río Atuel · Río Salad

RP 224 · Bardas Blancas · Santa Isabel · Victoria · RP 102

RN 40 · Algarrobo del Aguila · RP 10 · RP 105 · **Santa Rosa**

Barrancas · **La Pampa** · RP 13

Buta Ranquil · Salina Grandes o Salitral · RN 143 · Chacharramendi · General Acha

Chos-Malal · Río Colorado · Salitral de la Perra · RP 20 · Parque Nacional Lihué Calel · RP 28

Neuquén · 25 de Mayo · Puelches

Río Neuquén · RP 28 · RN 152 · RN 151

Mendoza

N
0   500 m
0   0.25 miles

Parque General
San Martín

Centro de
Información

Av Boulogne Sur Mer

Av Juan B Justo

Paso de los Andes

Grandaderos

Grandaderos

Peru

25 de Mayo

Chile

Eusebio Blanco

Barcala

España

Av Godoy Cruz

Av Mitre

Paz

Av Las Heras

Patricias Mendocinas

Plaza San
Martín

9 de Julio

Ferrocarril San
Martín (not
functioning)

Av Juan B Justo

L Aguirre

Avellaneda

Alvarez

Av E Civit

Liniers

Av E Civit

Necochea

Gutiérrez

25 de Mayo

Espejo

Peru

Plaza
Chile

Chile

Plaza
Independencia

Plaza
Italia

Rivadavia

Montevideo

San Lorenzo

Av Colón

Av Mitre

Chile

Av Pedro Molina

Av Belgrano

Chacras de
Coria (11km)

M Zapata

Av Arístides Villanueva

Rodríguez

Paso de los Andes

Olascoaga

Sobremonte

España

España Vargas

Av Sarmiento

Av Sarmiento

Amigorena

Av San Martín

Ministerio
de Turismo

Tourist
Kiosk

P de la Reta

ACA

Plaza
Pellegrini

Plaza
España

Don Bosco

Av José Vicente Zapata

Pardo

Intercultural
(150m)

Av LN Alem

Vicente
López

Don Bosco

Zuloaga

JF Moreno

Pedro Palacios

Av Acceso Este

Bus
Terminal

Information
Office

Alem

Plaza
Almirante
Brown

Bus to Airport
Garibaldi

Bus to
Malipú

Catamarca

Lavalle

Buenos Aires

Entre Rios

San Luis

Córdoba

La Rioja

San Juan

Av San Martín

Salta

Urquiza

Alberdi

Corrientes

Montecaseros

Plaza
José F Moreno

Plaza
Sarmiento

PB Palacios

Av R Videla

Albania

Saavedra

Parque
Bernardo
O'Higgins

Ituzaingó

Plaza del
Castillo

Black Sheep
(350m)

1 Parque General
San Martín

2 Plaza del Castillo

3

4

5

6

7 Plaza
Independencia

8

9

10 Plaza
Chile

11

12

13

14

15

16

17

18

19

20

21

22

23

24

25

Mendoza

ARGENTINA MENDOZA

Museo Fundacional protects excavations of the colonial *cabildo* (town council), destroyed by an earthquake in 1861. At that time, the city's geographical focus shifted west and south to its present location. A series of small dioramas depicts Mendoza's history, working through all of human evolution as if the city of Mendoza were the climax (maybe it was). The **Ruinas de San Francisco**, across the Plaza Pedro del Castillo, are the sole remaining remnants of the city prequake.

★ **Parque General San Martín**   PARK
Walking along the lakeshore and snoozing in the shade of the rose garden in this beautiful 420-hectare park is a great way to enjoy one of the city's highlights. Walk along Sarmiento/Civit out to the park and admire some of Mendoza's finest houses on the way. Pick up a park map at the **Centro de Información** (☎0261-420-5052; cnr Avs Los Platanos & Libertador; ⊙9am-5pm), just inside the impressive entry gates, which were shipped over from England and originally forged for the Turkish Sultan Hamid II.

🏃 Activities

Scaling nearby Aconcagua is one of the most popular activities here, but there are also plenty of operators offering rafting, climbing, mountain biking and trekking, among other things. Most hostels can organize these.

Ski rental places operate along Av Las Heras during winter.

★ **Mendoza City Tour**   BUS TOUR
(www.mendozacitytour.com; adult/child AR$280/170; ⊙10am-8pm) Double-decker hop-on, hop-off bus tour with 20 stops throughout the city, including ones in Parque General San Martín and Godoy Cruz, the suburb just to the south. The most central stop and ticket kiosk is on Plaza Independencia, across from the Park Hyatt Mendoza hotel. Guides provide commentary in Spanish; more spare narration is provided in English and Portuguese via headphones.

Argentina Ski Tours   SKI TOUR
(☎0261-423-6958; www.argentinaskitours.com; Av Belgrano 1194B; ski tours US$290; ⊙11am-8:30pm Mon-Fri, from 5:30pm Sat) Full-service ski tours, primarily to Los Penitentes, with transportation, breakfast, lunch, equipment rental and guiding included. Also rents ski outerwear to tour guests and nonguests alike, and brokers a range of on-mountain accommodations. Owned and operated by the very experienced and engaging Adam Stern, who also runs Mendoza Wine Camp (p144) out of the same office.

Andes Vertical   CLIMBING
(☎0261-476-0864; www.andes-vertical.com) Highly recommended operation running personalized climbing trips, of both mountain summits (including Aconcagua) and rock climbing in El Salto and Arenales in the Andean foothills. The former is ideal for beginners. Also mountain biking, rafting and horseback riding.

Inka Expediciones HIKING
(☎0261-425-0871; www.inka.com.ar; Av Juan B Justo 345, Mendoza; ⏰9am-6pm Mon-Fri, to 1pm Sat) Company with more than 1000 expeditions in the bank offering fixed and tailor-made expeditions.

Argentina Rafting ADVENTURE
(☎0261-429-6325; www.argentinarafting.com; Amigorena 86; ⏰9am-6pm Mon-Sat) Rafting, mountain biking, kayaking, paragliding and rock climbing, among other activities. While rafting is year-round, November to April are the best months for rafting on the Mendoza River near the Potrerillos dam.

Courses

Mendoza Wine Camp WINE
(☎0261-423-6958; www.mendozawinecamp.com; Av Belgrano 1194B; per day US$140-185; ⏰11am-8:30pm Mon-Fri, from 5:30pm Sat) American expat Adam Stern runs this company offering small-group English- and Portuguese-speaking wine tours with an emphasis on interaction and education. Also offers a great *asado* (barbecue grill) cooking-class day trip held at a chef's house in Luján de Cuyo – you learn to build a fire and drink *mate* as well.

Intercultural LANGUAGE
(☎0261-429-0269; www.intercultural.com.ar/en/spanish-school; República de Siria 241; ⏰9am-8pm Mon-Sat) Offers group and private Spanish classes and internationally recognized exams. Can also help find longer-term accommodation in Mendoza.

Sleeping

Note that hotel prices rise from January to March. Home-sharing services are more and more popular. Luján de Cuyo and Chacras de Coria are less urban options, but still close to the city.

Hostel Alamo HOSTEL $
(☎0261-429-5565; www.hostelalamo.com.ar; Necochea 740; dm US$9, d US$20-30; @🛜🏊) Reliable, conveniently located hostel housed in a colonial-style family residence with roomy four-bed dorms, great hangout areas and a wonderful backyard with a tiny plunge pool.

Hostel Lagares HOTEL $
(☎0261-423-4727; www.hostellagares.com.ar; Corrientes 213; dm/d US$10/40; ❄🛜) With friendly, helpful owners, spotlessly clean Lagares is a good choice if you don't mind being a very long walk away from the nightlife on Aristedes Villanueva. The breakfast is generous and there are a couple of charming indoor and outdoor common areas.

Hostel Lao HOSTEL $
(☎0261-438-0454; www.laohostel.com.ar; Rioja 771; dm US$10-12, r with/without bathroom US$43/40; ❄🛜🏊) English-owned converted family home, more of a B&B than hostel, with a variety of accommodations options, spacious lounge and outdoor garden (occasional communal *asados*) with hammocks and tiny plunge pool.

Punto Urbano Hostel HOSTEL $
(☎0261-429-5281; www.puntourbanohostel.com; Av Godoy Cruz 326; dm US$7-11, d US$25-35; @🛜)

REMOTE NATIONAL PARKS IN CENTRAL ARGENTINA

Central Argentina has an amazing range of landscapes, which is reflected in its national parks. For more information, log on to www.parquesnacionales.gob.ar. A couple of hard-to-reach but extremely worthwhile examples:

Parque Nacional Lihué Calel (☎02952-412800; www.parquesnacionales.gob.ar; ⏰8am-6pm) FREE In a desert-like landscape in the middle of the pampa, this 320-sq-km park is surprisingly biodiverse, playing host to puma, jaguarondi, armadillos and many birds of prey, such as the *carancho* (crested caracara), alongside flowering cacti and petroglyphs. Santa Rosa is the nearest town of any size – there are cheap hotels near the bus terminal and restaurants on the plaza, but it's still 226km away and access is complicated – and hiring a car is the best way to see the park.

Parque Nacional Sierra de las Quijadas (☎0266-444-5141; www.parquesnacionales.gob.ar; AR$280; ⏰8am-8pm Jan-Mar, 9am-7pm Apr-Dec) Covering 1500 sq km, this park features spectacular, surreal rock formations and dinosaur tracks and fossils. Hiking is excellent and camping is free, but be careful of flash flooding. The nearest town is San Luis; its park office can help with transportation and logistics.

Just north of the city center, this hostel maintains an air of intimacy despite its grand proportions. The dorms are basic, but the doubles are good value – roomy, with wide-screen TVs and tastefully decorated bathrooms. The large backyard – good for drinking, barbecuing and generally hanging out – is an added bonus, and the hostel schedules *asados,* happy hours and day trips.

★ **Hotel Bohemia** BOUTIQUE HOTEL **$$**
(☏0261-420-0575; www.bohemiahotelboutique.com; Granaderos 954; d from US$42; ✳@🖥🛜) Located on a quiet residential street around eight blocks west of the Plaza Independencia, this refashioned family home features a few stylish and charming common areas and comfortable, if ordinary rooms. Dinners made to order can be enjoyed outside in the small patio area next to the pool.

★ **B&B Plaza Italia** B&B **$$**
(☏0261-615-2357; www.plazaitalia.net; Montevideo 685; d US$100-115; ✳🛜) Comfortable and homey, a stay at this family-run B&B hits the right notes, combining personal intimacy and understated professionalism. Each of the five spacious rooms have comfy bedding, and a delicious breakfast is served in an elegant downstairs dining room. The English-speaking owners, including Javier, who runs customized wine tours, are lovely and can give you the lowdown on all things Mendoza.

🍴 Eating

Some of Mendoza's best restaurants, often with outdoor seating and lively young crowds, are along Av Arístides Villanueva, the western extension of Av Colón.

★ **Bröd** CAFE **$**
(☏0261-425-2993; www.facebook.com/brodbakery; Chile 894; sandwiches AR$100-190; ⊙8am-9pm Mon-Sat, 9am-4pm Sun; 🛜) There's no better spot in the city to pass a few hours on a sunny day than Bröd's whitewashed backyard patio. The pastries, sandwiches and egg dishes are done to exacting and delicious standards – unsurprising, since it's run by the former chef of an upscale wine lodge. There's even a *pétanque* court if you're looking for a little activity while enjoying brunch.

Mercado Central MARKET **$**
(cnr Av Las Heras & Patricias Mendocinas; mains from AR$90; ⊙8:30am-1pm & 5-9pm Mon-Sat, to 1pm Sun) Worth a visit for a quick meal, including pizza, pasta, sandwiches and empanadas, or

simply to wander the aisles of eateries and small shops primarily selling foodstuffs.

Heladeria Famiglia Perin ICE CREAM **$**
(www.facebook.com/famigliaperinheladados; Sarmiento 799; ice-cream cones AR$65-105; ⊙10am-2am; 🛜) Traditional-looking ice-cream parlor serving up classic gelato since 1947. Wide range of flavors and good espresso drinks as well.

Via Civit CAFE **$**
(☏0261-429-8529; Civit 277; mains AR$240-400; ⊙7am-10pm; 🛜) An old-school place popular with locals in an upscale neighborhood, convenient as a stop on the way to or from Parque General San Martín. The coffee and bakery are the draw, but there's a small brunch menu, sandwiches, salads and a few basic pasta and meat dishes. The grand entrance is framed with Roman columns and an oversized clock.

★ **Fuente y Fonda** ARGENTINE **$$**
(☏0261-429-8833; www.facebook.com/fuenteyfonda; Montevideo 675; meals to share AR$570-770; ⊙noon-3pm & 8pm-midnight) Take the menu's suggestion with a grain of salt. Mains are good for two if you're overworked gauchos, but are more manageable for three healthy appetites, especially the meat dishes. Most come with bread, salad, a side and dessert, all served in farmhouse dishware. The large, wooden family table in back is often occupied by big groups.

★ **Silla 14** CAFE **$$**
(www.silla14cafe.com.ar; San Lorenzo 656; mains AR$220-300; ⊙8am-9pm Mon-Fri, from 9am Sat; 🛜🍴) The priciest and finest coffee in the city is served at this elegant and sophisticated cafe. Silla 14 resembles the parlor of an upscale colonial-era home with contemporary touches, including suspendered waiters à la Brooklyn. Gourmet sandwiches and salads, healthy juices and pastries are on the menu.

El Mercadito ARGENTINE **$$**
(☏0261-463-8847; www.elmercaditoar.com; Av Aristedes Villanueva 521; mains AR$145-300; ⊙11am-1am; 🛜🍴) Charmingly rustic with a flowering outdoor patio and an equally discerning kitchen, it's no wonder El Mercadito is often packed with young locals. The menu runs the gamut from Thai noodles to vegetarian lasagna and lobster salad.

El Patio de Jesús María PARRILLA **$$**
(☏0261-429-6767; www.facebook.com/patiodejesus maria; cnr Villanueva & Boulogne Sur Mer; mains

THE GRAPE ESCAPE

It would be a crime to come to Mendoza and not visit at least one vineyard. Argentina's wines are constantly improving and, consequently, attracting international attention. Wine tasting is a popular activity at the many wineries in the area.

Depending on your budget and time frame, there are a few options:

➡ Bussing around Maipú and Luján.

➡ Bussing to Maipú, then renting a bike from **Mr Hugo** (☑ 0261-497-4067; Urquiza 2228, Maipú; bikes per day AR$300; ☺ 10am-6pm Mon-Sat) for a self-guided tour. Cyclists can consider biking a 40km circuit that would cover **Bodega la Rural** (☑ 0261-497-2013; www.bodegalarural.com.ar; Montecaseros 2625, Maipú; tour incl tasting AR$270; ☺ 9am-5:30pm Mon-Sat), **Trapiche** (☑ 0261-520-7666; www.trapiche.com.ar; Nueva Mayorga s/n, Maipú; ☺ 10am-6pm) and more. Call first to confirm opening hours. Tourist information offices in Mendoza also have area maps.

➡ A low-cost (around AR$800) tour, available through any hostel or tour operator. These are fine, but they can get crowded and rushed, and tastings certainly won't include any of the good stuff.

➡ A high-end wine tour with outfits such as **Trout & Wine** (☑ 0261-425-5613; www.troutandwine.com; Espejo 266; ☺ 8am-8pm Mon-Fri, noon-8pm Sat) or **Ampora Wine Tours** (☑ 0261-429-2931; www.mendozawinetours.com; Av Sarmiento 647; ☺ 9am-9pm Mon-Fri, 5-9pm Sat & Sun). These start at around US$175, but you'll be visiting some exclusive wineries in small groups and be getting samples of some of the finest wines that the region has to offer.

AR$230-540; ☺ noon-3:30pm & 8pm-12:30am) Heaped slabs of top-quality meat cooked over flaming wood chips. That's what makes this simple, low-frills restaurant one of Mendoza's favorite *parrillas*. *Chivito* (goat), *bife de chorizo* (similar to New York Strip) and *costillitas de ternera* (veal ribs) are specialties.

El Asadito   PARRILLA $$
(☑ 0261-205-8580; www.facebook.com/elasadito mza; cnr Av Juan B Justo & Granaderos; mains AR$230-445; ☺ noon-4:30pm & 8pm-2am) Deservedly popular cantina-style eatery that does juicy barbecue and meat sandwiches. Vegetarian options as well.

🍷 Drinking & Nightlife

Av Aristides Villanueva, west of the center, is ground zero in terms of Mendoza's happening bar scene. Going for a wander is your best bet, but here are a few places to get you started.

⭐ **Antares**   BAR
(www.facebook.com/antaresmendozaoficial; Av Aristedes Villanueva 153; ☺ 6pm-late) Nearly always packed, this hipster-heavy bar is the best place in the city for a wide selection of quality beer.

La Reserva   GAY
(Rivadavia 34; ☺ from 9pm Tue-Sat) This small, nominally gay bar packs in a mixed crowd and has outrageous drag shows at midnight

every night, with hard-core techno later. Some nights have a cover charge.

Black Sheep   SPORTS BAR
(☑ 0261-374-1230; Maipú 131; ☺ noon-4am; 🛜) Unpretentious pub with accompanying grub, like nachos and wings, and a good place to say no to vino and yes to a margarita or beer.

ℹ Information

Wine snobs and the wine-curious should pick up a free copy of the Wine Republic (www.winerepublic.com), an English-language magazine devoted to Mendoza's wining and dining scene.

ACA (Automóvil Club Argentina; ☑ 0261-420-2900; www.aca.org.ar; cnr Av San Martín & Amigorena; ☺ 24hr) Argentina's auto club; good source for provincial road maps.

Ministerio de Turismo (☑ 0261-420-2800; www.turismo.mendoza.gob.ar; Av San Martín 1143; ☺ 9am-9pm) Long counter with helpful staff, maps and regional information, housed in a grand building.

Tourist Kiosk (☑ 0261-420-1333; Garibaldi; ☺ 8am-6pm) This helpful kiosk near Av San Martín is a convenient information source; there's another at the **bus terminal** (☑ 0261-431-5000; ☺ 8am-8pm).

ℹ Getting There & Away

AIR

Flights to Mendoza arrive at **Francisco Gabrielli International Airport** (El Plumerillo; ☑ 0261-

520-6000; www.aa2000.com.ar; Acceso Norte s/n; 🐾). **Aerolíneas Argentinas** (📞 0810-222-86527; www.aerolineas.com.ar; Av Sarmiento 82; ⏰ 10am-6pm Mon-Fri) flies several times daily to Buenos Aires. **LATAM** (📞 0261-425-7900; www.latam.com; Rivadavia 256; ⏰ 10am-6pm Mon-Fri) flies twice daily to Santiago, Chile, and several times weekly to Lima, Peru.

BUS

The **bus terminal** (📞 0261-431-3001; cnr Avs de Acceso Este & Costanera) is about 10 blocks east of the town center.

Buses from Mendoza

DESTINATION	COST (AR$)	DURATION (HR)
Bariloche	2035-2350	19
Buenos Aires	1110-2350	14-17
Córdoba	1104-1650	11-12
Malargüe	360	6¼
Neuquén	1400-1850	10½-12¾
San Juan	320-440	2¼
San Luis	540-700	3¾
Tucumán	1550-1785	14
Uspallata	140	2
Valparaíso, Chile	500	8

ℹ Getting Around

The bus terminal is about 15 minutes' walk from the center; catch the Villa Nueva trolley if you don't feel like walking. Mendoza's airport is 6km north of the city. **Bus 60** goes from Calle Salta (between Garibaldi & Catamarca) straight there.

Local buses cost AR$11 – more for longer distances – and require a magnetic Redbus card, which can be bought at most kiosks.

Uspallata

📞 02624 / POP 1751M

In an exceptionally beautiful valley surrounded by polychrome mountains, 105km west of Mendoza at an altitude of 1751m, this crossroads village along RN 7 is a good base for exploring the surrounding area.

◉ Sights

Museo Las Bóvedas   MUSEUM
(www.facebook.com/museolasbovedas;   ⏰ 9am-5pm) FREE A kilometer north of the highway junction in Uspallata, a signed lateral leads to ruins and a museum at the Museo Las Bóvedas, a smelting site since pre-Columbian times.

Cerro Tunduqueral   ARCHAEOLOGICAL SITE
(RP 52; ⏰ 11am-6:30pm) FREE An easy 8km walk (or an easier drive) north of town brings you to Cerro Tunduqueral, where you'll find sweeping views and Inca rock carvings; *Seven Years in Tibet* scenes were shot here.

🍴 Sleeping & Eating

Hostel International Uspallata   HOSTEL $
(📞 0261-15-466-7240; RN 7 s/n, Km 1141; dm/d US$11/55; 🐾) Friendly hostel 7km east of town, with plain but comfortable rooms and a couple of sweet little cabins. Dinner is available. There's good hiking from the hostel and you can rent bikes and horses here. Ask the bus driver to drop you at the front before you hit Uspallata.

El Rancho   PARRILLA $$
(cnr RN 7 & Cerro Chacay; mains AR$190-460; ⏰ noon-3pm & 7pm-1am Tue-Sun; 🐾) Uspallata's most upscale restaurant has an open barbecue grill carved out of a wall in the center of the dining room. Meat, especially a good roasted *chivo* (goat), is the way to go; trout and salmon also available, as well as very ordinary pasta dishes and sandwiches.

ℹ Information

The **tourist office** (📞 0624-420009; RN 7 s/n; ⏰ 8am-9pm) is opposite the YPF station.

ℹ Getting There & Away

The bus terminal is tucked behind the new, rampantly ugly casino on the main drag. There are departures for Mendoza (AR$140, 2½ hours) and Puente del Inca (AR$80, one hour) and points in between. Santiago-bound buses will carry passengers to and across the border but are often full; in winter, the pass can close to all traffic for weeks at a time.

Around Uspallata

Los Penitentes

Both the terrain and snow cover can be excellent for downhill and Nordic skiing at **Los Penitentes** (http://skipenitentes.com; RN 7; lifts pass per day AR$690-980; ⏰ 9am-4pm), two hours southwest of Uspallata at an altitude of 2580m. Lifts and accommodations are very modern; the maximum vertical drop on its 21 runs exceeds 700m. The season runs from June to September.

The cozy converted cabin of **Hostel Campo Base Los Penitentes** (📞 0261-334-1150;

www.penitentes.com.ar; RN 7; dm from US$15) accommodates 38 in very close quarters, and has a kitchen, wood-burning stove and three shared bathrooms. Meals are available from AR$70, and dorm rates are halved in summer. The hostel offers Nordic- and downhill-skiing trips in winter and Aconcagua treks and expeditions in summer. If you're looking for a bit more comfort, the **Hotel Ayelén** (☑ in Mendoza 0261-428-4343; RN 7, Km 1212; d/tr from US$175/245; @) is open year-round; it offers good meals in its on-site restaurant.

From Mendoza, several buses pass daily through Uspallata to Los Penitentes (AR$170 to AR$210, 3¾ hours).

Puente del Inca

About 8km west of Los Penitentes, on the way to the Chilean border and near the turnoff to Aconcagua, is one of Argentina's most striking wonders. Situated 2720m above sea level, Puente del Inca is a natural stone bridge spanning the Río Mendoza. Underneath it, rock walls and the ruins of an old spa are stained yellow by warm, sulfurous thermal springs. You can hike into Parque Provincial Aconcagua from here.

The little, no-frills **Hostel El Nico** (☑ 0261-592-0736; www.facebook.com/hostelnico; RN 7, KM 1221, Puente del Inca; dm/d US$25/55) offers mountain climbing, glacier trekking and snowshoeing. There's a cheap restaurant and bar on the premises. Other restaurants are scattered around the car park.

Daily buses to Mendoza take about four hours (AR$170 to AR$210).

Parque Provincial Aconcagua

On the Chilean border, **Parque Provincial Aconcagua** (north of RN7; ☉10am-6pm) protects 710 sq km of high country surrounding the western hemisphere's highest summit: 6962m **Cerro Aconcagua**. There are trekking possibilities to base camps and refuges beneath the permanent snow line.

Reaching Aconcagua's summit requires at least 13 days, including some time for acclimatization. Potential climbers should get RJ Secor's climbing guide, *Aconcagua*, and check www.aconcagua.mendoza.gov.ar for more information.

From December to March, permits are mandatory for trekking and climbing. Fees vary according to the complex park-use seasons – check the government website for the latest information. Mid-December to late January is high season. Purchase permits in Mendoza from the main tourist office (p146).

Many adventure-travel agencies in and around Mendoza arrange excursions into the high mountains.

San Juan

☑ 0264 / POP 503,000

Life in this provincial capital with long, shaded avenues moves at its own pace, and the locals are humbly proud of their little town. In 1944 a massive earthquake destroyed the city center, killing more than 10,000 people – Juan Perón's subsequent relief efforts are what first made him a national figure.

No slouch on the wine-production front, San Juan's wineries are refreshingly low-key compared to the Mendoza bustle, and the province's other attractions are all within easy reach of the capital.

Rather than changing names as they intersect the central plaza (which is what happens in most Argentine towns), streets in San Juan keep their names but are designated by compass points, with street numbers starting at zero at the plaza and rising from there. Thus there will be two Laprida 150s – one Laprida 150 Este and one Laprida 150 Oeste.

◉ Sights & Activities

Museo de Vino
Santiago Graffigna   MUSEUM
(☑ 0264-421-4227; www.graffignawines.com; Colón 1342 Norte; ☉tours hourly 11:15am-4:15pm Thu-Sat) **FREE** Museo de Vino Santiago Graffigna is a wine museum housed in a handsome brick building, a reconstruction of what the winery looked like before the 1944 quake. It also has a wine bar where you can taste many of San Juan's best wines. The bodega produces both reds and whites; it's now owned by French beverage company, Pernod Ricard. Take bus 12A from in front of the tourist office on Sarmiento (AR$13, 15 minutes) and ask the driver to tell you when to get off.

★ **Las Marianas**   WINERY
(☑ 0264-463-9136; Calle Nuevo s/n; ☉10am-5pm Tue-Sat) **FREE** One of the prettiest wineries in the region, this one was built in 1922, abandoned in 1950 and reinstated in 1999. The main building is gorgeous, with thick adobe walls and a few examples of the original winemaking equipment lying around. The

mountain views out over the vineyard are superb.

🛏 Sleeping

San Juan Hostel — HOSTEL $

(☑0264-420-1835; www.sanjuanhostel.net; Av Córdoba 317 Este; dm US$9, s/d US$21/24, without bathroom US$15/18; ❄@�) A basic hostel with a variety of aging rooms in a residential neighborhood placed conveniently between the bus terminal and downtown. Good info on tours and local attractions, and a rooftop patio.

Del Bono Suites Art Hotel — HOTEL $$

(☑0264-421-7600; www.delbonohotels.com/suites. html; Mitre 75 Oeste; d/ste from US$50/85; ❄�🄬) Downtown's most contemporary hotel; with design features taking the edge off the corporate blandness, this is a good deal for the price, and the well-stocked kitchenettes and rooftop pool are added bonuses.

🍴 Eating

The pedestrian section of Rivadavia is crammed with sidewalk cafes and fast-food joints.

Soychú — VEGETARIAN $

(☑0264-422-1939; Av José Ignacio de la Roza 223 Oeste; mains from AR$100; ⊙noon-3pm & 8pm-midnight Mon-Sat, noon-3pm Sun; 🖉) Vegetarians rejoice! This simple restaurant – attached to a health-food store selling all sorts of groceries and a range of teas – has an excellent buffet with a wide range of tasty fare. Arrive early for the best selection, since it's very popular with locals ordering take-out for the office.

Tres Cumbres — CAFE $

(www.facebook.com/trescumbrescafe; Rivadavia 2; sandwiches AR$120; ⊙7:30am-10pm Mon-Fri, 8am-10pm Sat, 9am-1pm & 5-10pm Sun; ❄�) Centrally located modern coffee shop with windows looking out onto the city's main downtown plaza. Simple sandwiches, cookies, muffins, croissants and pies make it a good place to spend an afternoon.

ℹ Information

The **tourist office** (☑0264-421-0004; www. turismo.sanjuan.gob.ar; Sarmiento 24 Sur; ⊙8am-8pm) has helpful staff, with usually at least one English-speaker on the premises. There are good maps of the city and surroundings, plus useful info on the rest of the province, particularly Parque Provincial Ischigualasto.

ℹ Getting There & Away

Aerolíneas Argentinas (☑0264-421-4158; www.aerolineas.com.ar; Av San Martín 215 Oeste; ⊙8:30am-12:30pm & 5-7:30pm Mon-Fri) flies daily to Buenos Aires.

The **bus terminal** (☑0264-422-1604; Estados Unidos 492 Sur) has buses to Mendoza (AR$270 to AR$245, 2½ hours), Córdoba (AR$1104 to AR$1650, 8½ hours), San Agustín de Valle Fértil (AR$325, four hours), La Rioja (AR$965 to AR$1190, six hours) and Buenos Aires (AR$1050 to AR$2350, 14 hours).

For car rental, try **Classic** (☑0264-422-4622; www.classicrentacar.com.ar; Av San Martín 163 Oeste; ⊙9am-7pm). If you're heading to Ischigualasto, one of the cheapest ways to do it is to get a group together in your hostel and hire a car for the day.

Around San Juan

San Agustín de Valle Fértil

This relaxed, green little village is 250km northeast of San Juan and set amid colorful hills and rivers. It relies on farming, animal husbandry, mining and tourism. Visitors to Parques Ischigualasto and Talampaya use San Agustín as a base, and there are also nearby **petroglyphs** and the Río Seco to explore.

The **tourist office** (☑0264-642-0192; www. ischigualastovallefertil.org; General Acha 1065; ⊙9am-1pm & 5-9pm Mon-Fri, 9am-1pm Sat), on the plaza, can help set you up with tours of the area. There's camping and cheap accommodation, and a couple of good *parrillas*. Change money before you get here.

Buses roll daily to and from San Juan (AR$325, four hours).

Parque Provincial Ischigualasto

At every meander in the canyon of **Parque Provincial Ischigualasto** (Valle de la Luna, Valley of the Moon; ☑0264-422-5778; http://ischigualasto. gob.ar; admission AR$350; ⊙8am-5pm), a desert valley between sedimentary mountain ranges, the intermittent waters of the Río Ischigualasto have exposed a wealth of Triassic fossils and dinosaur bones – up to 180 million years old – and carved distinctive shapes in the monochrome clays, red sandstone and volcanic ash. The desert flora of *algarrobo* trees, shrubs and cacti complement the eerie moonscape, and common fauna include guanacos, condors, Patagonian hares and foxes.

Camping is (unofficially) permitted at the visitors center near the entrance, which also has a *confitería* with simple meals and cold drinks. There are toilets and showers, but water shortages are frequent and there's no shade.

Ischigualasto is about 80km north of San Agustín. Given its size and isolation, the only practical way to visit the park is by vehicle. After you pay the entrance fee, a ranger will accompany your vehicle on a two- or three-hour circuit over the park's unpaved roads, which may be impassable after rain.

If you have no transportation, ask the San Agustín tourist office about tours or hiring a car and driver, or contact the park. Tour operators in San Juan do tours here, but it's way cheaper to make your own way to San Agustín and line something up there. Some tours can be combined with **Parque Nacional Talampaya**, almost 100km northeast of Ischigualasto.

Malargüe

📞 0260 / POP 25,000

From precolonial times, the Pehuenche people hunted and gathered in the valley of Malargüe, but the advance of European agricultural colonists dispossessed the original inhabitants of their land. Today petroleum is a principal industry, but Malargüe, 400km south of Mendoza, is also a year-round outdoor activity center: Las Leñas offers Argentina's best skiing, and there are archeological sites and fauna reserves nearby, plus organized caving possibilities.

🛏 Sleeping & Eating

Several good *parrillas* can be found on the city's main thoroughfare.

★ **Eco Hostel Malargüe**   HOSTEL $
(📞 0260-447-0391; www.hostelmalargue.net; Finca 65, Colonia Pehuenche; dm US$15, d with/without bathroom US$60/45; 🐾) 🏠 Six kilometers south of town, this whimsically designed hostel and B&B is set on an organic farm and built using sustainable practices. Rooms are rustically simple but comfortable, the surrounds are beautiful, and breakfast (featuring farm produce) is a winner too.

★ **Hotel Malargüe Suite**   BOUTIQUE HOTEL $$
(📞 0260-4472-3001;   www.hotelmalarguesuite. com; RN 40 s/n; s/d from US$70/95; 🅿❄@ 🐾❄) At the northern edge of town, the most

luxurious hotel for kilometers around lays it all on – buffet breakfast, art gallery, indoor pool. Rooms are spacious and modern and come with hydromassage tubs, which are a welcome sight after a hard day on the slopes.

Café Tibet   CAFE $
(cnr RN 7 & Las Heras; mains AR$100-200; ⊙ 3:30-8pm Wed-Sat) The food is ordinary and the opening hours irregular, but the decor, comprising leftover props from *Seven Years in Tibet,* is curious enough to deserve a look-see.

★ **La Cima Restaurant & Parrilla**   ARGENTINE $$
(📞 0260-429-0671;   www.lacimarestaurant.com. ar; San Martín 886; mains AR$255-470; ⊙ noon-3pm & 8:30-11:30pm Tue-Sat, 8:30-11:30pm Sun & Mon; 🐾) The name, a holdover from when the restaurant was located at high altitude in Las Leñas, could refer to its status in the Malargüe dining scene, such as it is. It's at the top of the heap. Besides good-quality *asado,* there's rare variety on the menu, including salmon, trout, lasagna and a version of chop suey.

ℹ Information

The helpful **tourist office** (📞 0260-447-1659; www.facebook.com/TurismoMalargue/; RN 40, Parque del Ayer; ⊙ 8am-9pm) with facilities is at the northern end of town, on the highway. A small **kiosk** (⊙ 9am-9pm) also operates out of the bus terminal.

ℹ Getting There & Away

The **bus terminal** (cnr Av General Roca & Aldao) has regular services to Mendoza (AR$358, five hours) and Las Leñas (AR$76, 1½ hours). There is a weekly summer service across the 2500m Paso Pehuenche and down the awesome canyon of the Río Maule to Talca, Chile.

If you're heading south, there is a daily bus to Buta Ranquil (AR$592, five hours) in Neuquén province, with connections further south from there. Book at least a day in advance at **Transportes Leader** (📞 0299-445-3696; www.leader. com.ar), which operates out of the Club los Amigos pool hall.

Las Leñas

Wealthy Argentines and foreigners alike come to Las Leñas (📞 0260-447-1281; www.laslenas. com; 1-day ticket AR$1080-1590; ⊙ 8:30am-5pm mid-Jun–late Sep), the country's most prestigious ski resort, to look dazzling zooming down the slopes and then spend nights partying until the sun peeks over the snowy mountains.

Outside the ski season Las Leñas is also attempting to attract summer visitors who enjoy weeklong packages, offering activities such as mountain biking, horseback riding and hiking.

Only 70km from Malargüe, Las Leñas has 33 runs; slopes reach a peak of 3430m, with a maximum drop of 1230m. Prices for lift tickets can vary considerably throughout the ski season, depending how long you're staying.

Budget travelers will find regular transportation from Malargüe, where accommodation is cheaper. Buses from San Rafael (AR$200) take two hours.

THE LAKE DISTRICT

Extending from Neuquén down through Esquel, Argentina's Lake District is a gorgeous destination with lots of opportunities for adventure. There are lofty mountains to climb and ski down, rushing rivers to raft, clear lakes to boat or fish and beautiful national parks to explore. From big-city Bariloche to hippie El Bolsón, the Lake District's towns and cities each have their own distinct geography, architecture and cultural offerings. There's something fun to do every month of the year, so don't miss visiting this multifaceted region.

The Lake District's original inhabitants were the Puelches and Pehuenches, so named for their dependence on pine nuts from the *pehuén* (monkey puzzle tree). Though Spaniards explored the area in the late 16th century, it was the Mapuche who dominated the region until the 19th century, when European settlers arrived. Today you can still see Mapuche living around here, especially on national park lands.

Neuquén

📞 0299 / POP 231,200

Palindromic (forgiving the accent) Neuquén is a provincial capital nestled in the confluence of two rivers, the Limay and the Neuquén. It's the gateway to Patagonia and the Andean Lake District, as well as an important commercial and agricultural center. Neuquén isn't a major tourist magnet, but it isn't unpleasant either – and if you're interested in palaeontology, bones of the largest

---

DINOSAURS

Neuquén province has one of the world's richest concentrations of dinosaur bones, along with a couple of dinosaur museums highlighting gigantic specimens. A few hints: Plaza Huincul, Villa El Chocón and Centro Paleontológico Lago Barreales are all within a few hours' drive. The greater region also boasts lakes, a few *bodegas* (wineries), a notable bird sanctuary and some world-class fishing. Renting your own vehicle (about AR$1200 per day) is the way to go. For information and maps, visit the Neuquén tourist office (p153).

---

dinosaurs have been found in the surrounding countryside.

👁 Sights

Museo Nacional de Bellas Artes MUSEUM
(📞 0299-443-6268; www.mnbaneuquen.gov.ar; cnr Bartolomé Mitre & Santa Cruz; ⏰ 9:30am-8pm Mon-Sat, 4-8pm Sun) FREE An offshoot of the fine-arts museum in Buenos Aires, MNBA showcases fine arts from the region, as well as paintings representative of major European art movements and an excellent contemporary art section. It frequently hosts worthwhile temporary exhibitions.

🛏 Sleeping & Eating

Punto Patagonico Hostel HOSTEL $
(📞 0299-447-9940; www.puntopatagonico.com; Periodistas Neuquinas 94; dm/s US$14/40, d with/without bathroom US$50/35; @ 🕸) Neuquén's best hostel is a good deal: it's well set up with comfy dorms, a spacious lounge and a good garden area, with several restaurants and microbreweries just minutes away on foot.

Hotel Crystal HOTEL $
(📞 0299-442-2414; www.hotelcrystalneuquen.com.ar; Olascoaga 268; s/d from US$28/35; 🕸 🕸) The decor won't make your social media posts, but otherwise this friendly budget hotel has everything you need for a comfortable overnighter: air-con, mini-fridge, bug netting and good wi-fi. Restaurants and attractions are within walking distance, and there's a parking lot diagonally across the street from the hotel.

La Nonna Francesa INTERNATIONAL $$
(📞 0299-430-0930; www.facebook.com/lanonna francesca; 9 de Julio 56; mains AR$220-370;

The Lake District

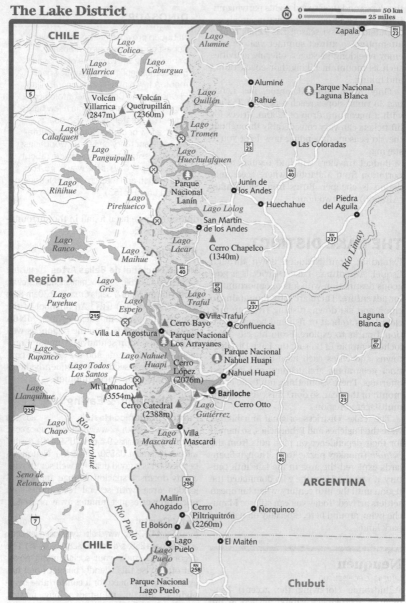

⊙ 11am-3pm & 8pm-midnight Mon-Fri, to 1am Sat, noon-3pm Sun; 🐾) Some of Neuquén's finest dining can be found at this French-Italian trattoria – the pastas are all extremely good, and dishes such as *fusilli al proscuitto* and lasagna are standouts. Service could be a tad more gracious, though.

🍷 Drinking & Nightlife

TresCatorce Bodegon Chic　　CRAFT BEER
(📞 0299-456-9102; 9 de Julio 63; ⊙ 8pm-2am Tue-Sun; 🐾) This chic eatery takes itself rather seriously, but it's a good spot to knock back a local craft beer or choose from a small but

well-selected range of boutique wines. Skip the food, though.

ℹ Information

The **provincial tourist office** (📞 0299-442-4089; www.neuquentur.gov.ar; San Martín 182; ⏰7am-9pm) has great maps and brochures. There's a more centrally located **kiosk** (⏰ 8am-8pm) in Parque Central.

ℹ Getting There & Around

Aeropuerto Internacional de Neuquén (📞0299-444-0525; www.anqn.com.ar; off RN 22) is west of town. There are at least six flights per day with Aerolíneas Argentinas (www.aerolineas.com.ar) to Buenos Aires, as well as several more with LATAM (www.latam.com).

Neuquén's modern bus terminal is about 3.5km west of the center. To get downtown take either a Pehueche bus (buy a ticket at local 41) or a taxi (about AR$120). Destinations include Bahía Blanca (AR$635 to AR$890, seven to 8½ hours), Buenos Aires (AR$1330 to AR$1800, 15 to 18¾ hours), Junín de los Andes (AR$695 to AR$881, six hours), Mendoza (AR$1400 to AR$1850, 11¼ to 12¾ hours), and Temuco, Chile (AR$1072 to AR$1355, nine hours).

Most local buses take magnetic cards, bought at the terminal or at some kiosks. Also note that taxis charge 20% more between 11pm and 6am.

Junín de los Andes

📞 02972 / POP 12,621

Cute and pleasant, Junín proclaims itself Argentina's 'trout capital' – and there are indeed some beautiful, trout-filled rivers in the area. It's a tranquil and slow-paced hamlet on the beautiful Río Chimehuín, 42km north of San Martín de los Andes. There's nothing much to do besides wander around, explore the river or mountains and visit gorgeous Parque Nacional Lanín. If you're into churches, visit the cathedral's Christ figure, who sports a Mapuche visage.

◉ Sights

Vía Cristi   LANDMARK
(off Av Antártida Argentina; ⏰24hr) Situated about 2km from the center of Junín de los Andes, near the end of Av Antártida Argentina, Vía Cristi contains a collection of 22 sculptures, bas-reliefs and mosaics as it winds its way up Cerro de la Cruz and vividly depicting the Conquest of the Desert, Mapuche legends, Christian themes and indigenous history.

Museo Mapuche   MUSEUM
(Domingo Milanesio 751; entry by donation; ⏰8:30am-12:30pm & 2-7pm Mon-Fri, 9am-12:30pm Sat) This small but interesting museum showcases Mapuche pottery, pipes, *piñon* (araucaria tree nut) grinders and musical instruments. Another display features dinosaur bones.

🛏 Sleeping & Eating

El Reencuentro   HOSTEL $
(📞02792-492220; www.elreencuentrohostel.blogspot.com; Illera 189; dm/s/d from US$10/11/21; 📶) A hostel that ticks all the right boxes – friendly, helpful hosts, four-bed dorms, good facilities and plenty of activities and information on offer.

Camping Laura Vicuña   CAMPGROUND $
(📞02972-491349; Ginés Ponte s/n; campsite per person US$7; 📶) You won't find a much more sublime location for an urban campground: perched on an island in between two burbling creeks, with fire pits and hot showers, plus fully equipped cabins. There's a three-night minimum.

Hostería Chimehuín   HOTEL $
(📞02972-491132; www.interpatagonia.com/hosteriachimehuin; cnr Coronel Suárez & 25 de Mayo; d US$40-44, tr US$56; 📶) This is a beautiful spot a few minutes from the center of town. Book early and you'll have a good chance of snagging a room with a balcony overlooking the creek. Either way, rooms are big, warm and comfortable and the whole place has a tranquil air about it.

Sigmund   ARGENTINE $$
(📞02972-492189; www.facebook.com/sigmund.restaurante.3; Juan M de Rosas 690; mains AR$170-290; ⏰noon-3pm & 8pm-midnight; 📶) A fabulous trendy eatery with colorful artsy decor, healthy food and a great *onda* (vibe). Choose from dozens of pizzas, pastas, sandwiches and salads, all delivered with friendly service.

ℹ Information

The **tourist office** (📞 02792-491160; www.junindelosandes.gov.ar; cnr Domingo Milanesio & Coronel Suárez; ⏰8am-9pm) has enthusiastically helpful staff. Fishing permits and a list of licensed fishing guides are available here.

ℹ Getting There & Away

Chapelco Airport (p156) is 19km south, toward San Martín de los Andes.

The **bus station** (☑ 02792-492038; cnr Olavarría & Félix San Martín) is three blocks west of the plaza. Destinations include San Martín de los Andes (AR$55, 45 minutes) and Neuquén (AR$565, six hours).

Parque Nacional Lanín

At 3776m, snowcapped Volcán Lanín is the dominating centerpiece of this tranquil **national park** (www.pnlanin.org; adult AR$300), where extensive stands of *lenga* (southern beech) and the curious monkey puzzle tree flourish. Pleistocene glaciers left behind blue finger-shaped lakes, excellent for fishing and camping. For more information and maps, contact the National Park Office in Junín or San Martín.

In summer (January and February) **Lago Huechulafquen** is easily accessible from Junín; there are outstanding views of Volcán Lanín and several worthwhile hikes. Mapuche-run campgrounds include **Raquithue** (RP 61; Km51; camping per person US$10) and **Bahía Cañicul** (☑ 02972-490211; www.facebook.com/campingbahia.canicul; RP 61, Km49; camping per person US$10). Free campsites around the park are also available; bring supplies from town. The forested **Lago Tromen** area also offers good hiking and camping.

From San Martín you can boat west on **Lago Lácar** to Paso Hua Hum and cross by road to Puerto Pirehueico (Chile); there's also bus service. Hua Hum has camping and hiking trails. Fifteen kilometers north of San Martín, serene **Lago Lolog** has good camping and fishing.

In summer, vans from Junín's bus station go all along Lago Huechulafquen to Puerto Canoa and beyond (AR$55, two to three times daily). There are also services to Lagos Tromen and Curruhué. Buses to Chile over the Hua Hum and Tromen passes can also stop at intermediate points, but in summer are often full.

San Martín de los Andes

☑ 02972 / POP 33,600

Attractive San Martín is a small, fashionable destination crowded with rowdy Argentines in summer. Nestled between two verdant mountains on the shores of Lago Lácar, the town boasts many wood and stone chalet-style buildings, many of them chocolate shops, ice-cream stores and souvenir boutiques. But behind the touristy streets

lie pleasant residential neighborhoods with pretty rose-filled gardens, and the surrounding area has wonderful forested trails perfect for hiking and biking.

◎ Sights & Activities

The 2.5km steep, dusty hike to **Mirador Bandurrias** ends with awesome views of Lago Lácar; be sure to take a snack or lunch. Tough cyclists can rent bikes at several shops in town and reach the *mirador* (lookout) in about an hour via dirt roads. **Playa la Islita** is a pleasant little beach located 2.5km further from the *mirador*.

Che Guevara fans can check out **La Pastera** (☑ 02972-411994; www.lapastera.org.ar; cnr Sarmiento & Roca; ◎ 9am-2pm & 5-8pm Mon-Sat) **FREE**, a small museum dedicated to this icon. In winter you can ski at **Cerro Chapelco** (☑ 02972-427845; www.chapelco.com; RP 19; ski day pass adult AR$1160-2660, child AR$930-1330; ◎ mid-Jun–late Sep), a ski center 20km away.

From the pier **Naviera** (☑ 02972-427380; https://lagolacarynonthue.com; Costanera MA Camino s/n; ◎ 10am-7:30pm) runs seven-hour boat tours to Paso Hua Hum on the Chilean border (round-trip AR$1550) to access walks and a waterfall. There's also boat transport to Quila Quina (round trip AR$600) for beaches and water sports.

⌕ Sleeping

Reserve ahead during the high seasons (January to March, Easter, and July and August).

★**Adventure Bed & Bike** HOSTEL $
(☑ 02972-413236; http://adventurebedandbike.com.ar; Atahualpa Yupanqui 289; dm US$26, d with/without bathroom US$75/65; ☏) On most days here, you'll find gregarious owner Indiana chatting with (predominantly cyclist) guests over ample breakfasts or in the chillout areas, advising them on the area's best routes. The wood-paneled rooms are cozy and you don't have to be a cyclist to stay here. Roughly halfway between San Martín and Lago Lolog, it's connected to town by shuttle buses.

El Oso Andaluz Hostel HOSTEL $
(☑ 02972-413010; www.elosoandaluz.com.ar; Elordi 569; dm/d US$12/46; ✳@☏) San Martín's coziest little downtown hostel has a good bed-to-bathroom ratio, atmospheric common areas and good-value private rooms.

Hotel Antiguos HOTEL $
(☑ 02972-411876; www.hotelantiguos.com.ar; Diaz 751; s/d/tr from US$44/50/65; ✳☏) Set just off

the main drag, the Antiguos indulges in San Martín's heavy-wood-and-stone fetish, and does it well. Some rooms have sweeping garden or mountain views; all are spacious and luxuriously appointed. The roaring fireplace in the lounge area makes for a welcome sight in winter.

★ La Raclette
HOTEL **$$**

(☑ 02972-427664; www.laraclette.com.ar; Coronel Pérez s/n; r US$96; @ 🕏) Inside this turreted residence, the narrow, low-ceilinged hallways lead on to spacious, comfortable rooms. What really tip the scales are the downstairs common areas – a lounge-bar area and cozy little conversation pit centered on a big open fireplace.

Hostería Las Lucarnas
LODGE **$$**

(☑ 02970-427085; www.hosterialaslucarnas.com; Coronel Pérez 632; r from US$42; ⊝ 🕏) Right off the main square, this heavy-timbered boutique inn combines excellent service with a couldn't-be-more-central location. Rooms are on the compact side, but are well furnished. The ample breakfast makes good use of regional produce.

Hostería Hueney Ruca
HOTEL **$$**

(☑ 02972-421499; www.hosteriahueneyruca.com.ar; cnr Obeid & Coronel Pérez; s/d US$75/85; 🕏) The big terra-cotta-tiled rooms at this araucaria-shaded property look onto a cute, well-kept little backyard. Beds are big and firm and bathrooms spacious, with glass-walled showers. The fireplace in the common area is a boon in colder months.

✗ Eating

Corazón Contento
CAFE **$**

(☑ 02972-412750; Av San Martín 467; mains AR$150; ⊙ 9am-11pm; 🕏) A cute little bakery-cafe serving up an excellent range of snacks, such as empanadas and quiches, as well as inexpensive daily specials. The salads are great and the freshly baked scones and muffins hit the spot.

★ Morphen
FUSION **$$**

(☑ 02972-422545; www.morphen.com.ar; Av San Martín 151; mains AR$275-425; ⊙ 8-11:30pm Tue-Sun; 🕏🍴) Enter Morphen, and you enter a wonderland of Banksy graffiti, surreal sculpture, swirling murals and strange mobiles suspended from the ceiling. The food is a pleasant deviation from the meaty standards touted by most of the town's restaurants. Feast on vegan 'hamburgers,' pizza-caccia

WORTH A TRIP

THE SEVEN LAKES ROUTE

From San Martín de los Andes, RN 40 follows an eminently scenic but rough, narrow and sometimes dusty route past numerous alpine lakes to Villa la Angostura. It's known as the **Ruta de los Siete Lagos** (Seven Lakes Route) and its spectacular scenery has made the drive famous. Sections of the 110km route close every year due to heavy snowfalls.

December to May is the best time to schedule this trip, but ask around for current conditions.

Full-day tours from San Martín, Villa la Angostura and Bariloche regularly do this route, but there's also a scheduled bus service and, with a little forward planning, it's possible to drive or cycle it yourself.

with pesto, and pumpkin ravioli with shrimp in curry sauce, and wash it all down with craft beer.

Pizza Cala
PIZZA **$$**

(☑ 02972-422511; www.facebook.com/pizzacalasanmartindelosandes; Av San Martín 1129; pizzas AR$250-350; ⊙ noon-1am; 🕏🍴) The local's choice for pizza is this well-established place near Plaza Sarmiento. You can choose between a one-person 'chica' or family-sized 'grande,' with almost three dozen different topping options, including 'gourmet' offerings such as smoked trout, spinach and eggplant. Empanadas and beer also feature on the menu.

★ Bamboo Brasas
PARRILLA **$$$**

(☑ 02972-420042; cnr Belgrano & Villegas; mains AR$310-450; ⊙ noon-3:30pm & 8pm-midnight; 🕏) As you'd expect, this upmarket *parrilla* does wonderful things with meat, from steaks to *morcilla* and chorizo. Some even claim that it serves the best meat in all of Argentina. We haven't tried all the meat in Argentina (yet), but judging from the way they cooked our sweetbreads, they know what they're doing.

ⓘ Information

ACA (Automóvil Club Argentino; ☑ 02972-429194; Av Koessler 2176; ⊙ 24hr) Good source for provincial road maps.

Lanín National Park Office (Intendencia del Parque Nacional Lanín; ☑ 02972-427233; www.

pnlanin.org; Plaza San Martín; ⊘8am-3pm Mon-Fri) Has limited maps as well as brochures and information on road conditions on the Ruta de los Siete Lagos (p155).

Tourist Office (☑02972-427347; www.san martindelosandes.gov.ar; cnr Av San Martín & M Rosas; ⊘8am-8:30pm) Provides surprisingly candid information on hotels and restaurants, plus excellent brochures and maps.

❶ Getting There & Away

There are regular flights from **Chapelco Airport** (☑02972-428388; RN 40) to Buenos Aires with Aerolíneas Argentinas.

The **bus station** (☑02972-427044; cnr Villegas & Juez del Valle) is a block south of RN 40 and 3½ blocks southwest of Plaza San Martín. Destinations include Junín de los Andes (AR$90 to AR$115, 45 minutes), Villa la Angostura (AR$290, 2¼ hours) and Bariloche (AR$440, four hours). There are departures to Chilean destinations such as Temuco (AR$1072, seven hours) from December to February; book these trips at least two days in advance.

Villa la Angostura

☑0294 / POP 11,063

Villa la Angostura is a darling chocolate-box town that takes its name from the *angosta* (narrow) 91m neck of land connecting it to the striking Península Quetrihué. There's no doubt that Villa is touristy, but it's also charming; wood-and-stone alpine buildings line the three-block-long main street. There's skiing at nearby Cerro Bayo in winter.

El Cruce is the main part of town and contains the bus terminal and most hotels and businesses; the main street is Arrayanes. Woodsy La Villa, with a few restaurants, hotels and a nice beach, is 3km southwest and on the shores of Lago Nahuel Huapi.

◉ Sights & Activities

The cinnamon-barked *arrayán*, a myrtle relative, is protected inside the small but beautiful **Parque Nacional Los Arrayanes** (www.parquesnacionales.gob.ar; adult/student AR$250/130; ⊘8am-7pm) 🍃 on the Península Quetrihué. The main *bosque* (forest) of *arrayanes* is situated at the southern tip of the peninsula; it's reachable by a 40- to 60-minute boat ride (one-way/round trip AR$95/170; several boat trips per day) or via hike on a relatively easy 12km trail from La Villa.

Experienced mountain bike riders (there are stairs and hills) should rent a bike to reach the *arrayán* forest. It's possible to

boat either there or back with your bike, hiking or biking the other way; buy your return boat ticket in advance. Take food and water; there's an ideal picnic spot next to a lake near the end of the trail.

At the start of the Arrayanes trail, near the beach, a steep 30- to 45-minute hike leads to a panoramic viewpoint over Lago Nahuel Huapi.

From the El Cruce part of town, a 3km walk north takes you to the **Mirador Belvedere** trailhead; hike another 30 minutes for good views. Nearby is **Cascada Inayacal**, a 50m waterfall, and a few hours' hike further on is **Cajón Negro**, a pretty valley; get a map and directions from the tourist office before you set out, as trails and shortcuts around here can be confusing.

🛏 Sleeping & Eating

The following are all in or near El Cruce. Reserve accommodation ahead in January and February.

★Hostal Bajo Cero   HOSTEL $
(☑0294-449-5454; www.bajocerohostel.com; Río Caleufu 88; s/d US$45/60; @ 🛜) A little over 1km northwest of the bus terminal is this gorgeous hostel, with large, well-designed rooms and lovely doubles with down comforters. It has a nice garden and kitchen, plus airy common spaces. Bicycles are available for rent.

Residencial Río Bonito   GUESTHOUSE $
(☑0294-449-4110; www.riobonitopatagonia.com.ar; Topa Topa 260; d/tr US$37/48; @ 🛜) Residencial Río Bonito has bright and cheery rooms in a converted family home a few blocks from the bus terminal. The big, comfortable dining-lounge area is a bonus, as are the friendly hosts and the kitchen for guest use.

Camping Cullumche   CAMPGROUND $
(☑0294-449-4160; http://turismo.uncuyo.edu.ar/camping-y-albergue-cullumche; Blvd Quetrihué s/n; campsite per person US$10) Well signed from Blvd Nahuel Huapi, this secluded but large lakeside campground can get very busy in summer, but when it's quiet, it's lovely.

La Roca de la Patagonia   BOUTIQUE HOTEL $$
(☑0294-449-4497; www.larocadelapatagonia.com.ar; Pascotto 155; s/d US$50/68; ❋ 🛜) A cute little place off the main drag, with just six rooms. It's set in a large converted house, so there are some great dimensions here. Decor is very Patagonian – lots of wood and stone,

and there are fantastic mountain views from the deck.

Gran Nevada
ARGENTINE $

(☑0294-449-4512; Av Arrayanes 106; mains AR$170-350; ☺noon-11:30pm) With its big-screen TV (quite possibly showing a soccer game) and big, cheap set meals (stews, grilled fish), this is a local favorite. Come hungry, leave happy.

★Pistach'
FUSION $$

(☑0294-449-5203; Cerro Inacayal 44; mains AR$280-450; ☺8-11:30pm Tue, noon-3pm & 8-11:30pm Wed-Sun; ☜☑) A feisty newcomer on a dining scene dominated by *parrillas* and pizzerias, Pistach' blends elegant surroundings with dishes inspired by the chef's heritage and travels and conjured from fresh market ingredients. Feast on shrimp and fish curry, homemade hamburgers, pad Thai and lamb slow-cooked in malbec.

Nicoletto
ITALIAN $$

(☑0294-449-5619; Pascotto 165; mains AR$190-310; ☺8:30-11:30pm Tue-Sat, noon-3pm Sun) The best pasta for miles around is to be found at this unassuming family-run joint just off the main street. It's all good – freshly made and with a fine selection of sauces – but the trout *sorrentino* with leek sauce comes highly recommended.

❶ Information

The **tourist office** (☑0294-449-4124; www.laangostura.com; cnr Avs Siete Lagos & Arrayanes; ☺8am-9pm) has info on the town and surrounds.

❶ Getting There & Around

From the **bus terminal** (☑0294-449-5104; cnr Av Siete Lagos & Av Arrayanes), one block north of Plaza Los Pioneros, buses depart for Bariloche (AR$155, 1¼ hours) and San Martín de los Andes (AR$290, 2¼ hours, sit on left for the best views). If heading into Chile, reserve ahead for buses passing through. Buses to La Villa (where the boat docks and park entrance are located) leave every two hours.

There are several bike-rental places in town.

Bariloche

☑0294 / POP 127,300

The Argentine Lake District's largest city, San Carlos de Bariloche attracts scores of travelers in both summer and winter. It's beautifully located on the shores of beauti-ful Lago Nahuel Huapi, and lofty mountain peaks are visible from all around. While Bariloche's center bustles with tourists shopping at myriad chocolate shops, souvenir stores and trendy boutiques, the real attractions lie outside the city. Parque Nacional Nahuel Huapi offers spectacular hiking, and there's also great camping, trekking, rafting, fishing and skiing in the area. Despite the heavy touristy feel, Bariloche is a good place to stop, hang out, get errands done and, of course, have some fun.

◉ Sights & Activities

The heart of town is the **Centro Cívico**, a group of well-kept public buildings built of log and stone; architect Ezequiel Bustillo originally adapted Middle European styles into this form of architecture, now associated with the Lake District area). The **Museo de la Patagonia** (☑0294-442-2309; Centro Cívico; by donation; ☺10am-12:30pm & 2-5pm Tue-Fri, 10am-5pm Sat), located here, offers a history of the area, along with good displays of stuffed critters and archaeological artifacts.

Rafting trips on the Río Limay (easy class II) or Río Manso (class III to IV) are very popular. **EXtremo Sur** (☑0294-442-7301; www.extremosur.com; Morales 765; ☺9am-6pm) and **Aguas Blancas** (☑0294-469-0426; www.aguasblancas.com.ar; Morales 564; ☺9am-1pm & 3-7pm) have good tours.

For kayaking, **Pura Vida Patagonia** (☑0294-441-4053; www.puravidapatagonia.com.ar) gets consistently good reviews. Other activities include hiking, rock climbing, biking, paragliding, horse riding, fishing and skiing.

Many agencies and hostels offer tours. **Historias de Bariloche** (☑0294-460392; www.historiasdebariloche.com.ar; Centro Cívico; 2hr tour AR$500) provides excellent themed walking tours that shed light on Bariloche's history, while **Bikeway** (☑0294-461-7686; www.bikeway.com.ar; Av Bustillo, Km12.5; per day around AR$250) rents bicycles and offers bike excursions.

❧ Courses

La Montaña
LANGUAGE

(☑0294-452-4212; www.lamontana.com; Elflein 251, 2nd fl; ☺9am-4pm Mon-Fri) This is a recommended Spanish-language school. An intensive Spanish crash course costs US$210 per week.

Bariloche

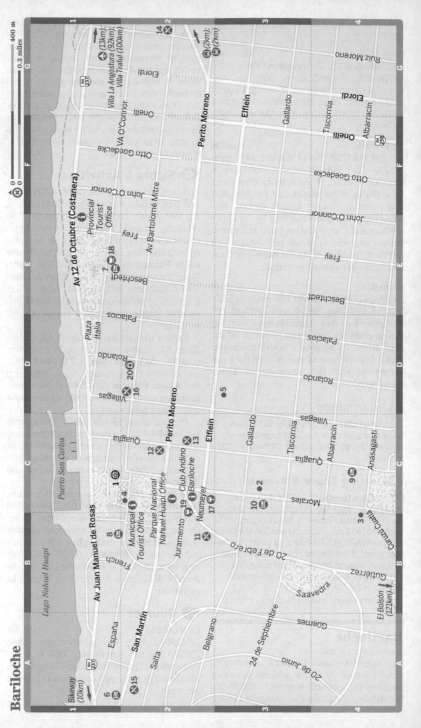

Bariloche

🛏 Sleeping

Make reservations from late December to February, July and August and during holidays (especially Easter).

★ Bonita Lake House   HOSTEL $
(☎0294-446-2561; www.bonitalakehouse.com.ar; Av Bustillo, Km 7.8; dm/d/bungalow US$14/47/80; P ⊜ ❀ 🖧) With its gorgeous lakefront setting, close to Playa Bonita, this friendly hostel is where international travelers mingle with locals looking for some R&R. There are common spaces in which to socialize, and nooks to retreat to for enjoying the tranquility. The fully equipped apartments are a boon for groups, and there's easy bus access.

★ Periko's   HOSTEL $
(☎0294-452-2326; www.perikos.com; Morales 555; dm US$9.50-17, d US$33-55, d without bath US$24.50-50; @🖧) An atmospheric little hostel set up on the hill overlooking Bariloche. Rooms are nicely situated around the kitchen, the social hub of the place, staff organize all manner of activities, and impromptu barbecues are frequent happenings. The DVD library and laundry service for your dirty togs are nice touches.

La Justina Hostel   HOSTEL $
(☎0294-452-4064; www.lajustinahostel.com.ar; Quaglia 726; dm US$10, d with/without bathroom US$35/25; 🖧) An intimate, colorful hostel with a roaring hearth in colder months and a garden in which to chill out in summer. A homey atmosphere reigns and owner Leo is very informative and helpful.

La Selva Negra   CAMPGROUND $
(☎0294-444-1013; www.campingselvanegra.com.ar; Av Bustillo, Km2.95; campsite per person from US$8) Located 3km west of Bariloche on the road to Llao Llao, this is the nearest organized camping area to town. It has good facilities and, in the fall, you can step outside your tent to pick apples. The backpacker section gets an AR$30 discount.

Hostel Los Troncos   HOSTEL $
(☎0294-443-1188; www.hostellostroncos.com.ar; San Martín 571; dm/d from US$18/50; 🖧) A step above some other hostels in Bariloche, the Troncos offers modern rooms with private bathrooms and cozy touches such as private reading lamps. There's also a range of supercomfy hang-out areas, an industrial-sized kitchen and a courtyard garden. A refurb wouldn't go amiss, though.

★ Posada Los Juncos   GUESTHOUSE $$
(☎0294-495-7871; www.posadalosjuncos.com; Av Bustillo, Km20.1; ste from US$80; P 🖧) Sitting on a tranquil piece of land, surrounded by ancient araucaria pines, this homey, luxurious guesthouse gets pretty much everything right. The personalized service is friendly yet unobtrusive, the suites are individually decorated to represent one of the four elements, the lake views are gorgeous and breakfast is ample.

Hotel Tirol   HOTEL $$
(☎0294-442-6152; www.hoteltirol.com.ar; Libertad 175; r with city/lake view US$90/100; @🖧) Right in the middle of Bariloche, this charming lodge offers comfortable, spacious rooms. Those out the back have spectacular views over the lake and to the mountain range beyond, as does the bright sitting/breakfast area.

Hotel Milan   BUSINESS HOTEL $$
(☎0294-442-2624; www.hotelmilan.com.ar; Beschtedt 128; s/d/tr US$50/60/75; P ⊜ 🖧) A

block from the lakeshore and a short walk from the heart of Bariloche, this smart hotel features spotless rooms in tranquil creams and beiges that come in a variety of shapes and sizes. Have a look at a few (the price is the same) and try to snag a lake view.

🗶 Eating

Regional specialties include *jabalí* (wild boar), *ciervo* (venison) and *trucha* (trout). Most bars serve food, too.

★ Helados Jauja   ICE CREAM $
(☑ 0294-443-7888; www.heladosjauja.com; Perito Moreno 48; ice cream from AR$60; ⊙ 10am-midnight) Ask Bariloche residents who serves the best ice cream in Bariloche and most will reply with one word: 'Jauja.' Of the 60 or so flavors, there are usually a couple dozen in rotation at any given time.

La Fonda del Tio   ARGENTINE $
(☑ 0294-443-5011; www.lafondadeltio.com.ar; Av Bartolomé Mitre 1130; mains AR$180-280; ⊙ noon-3:30pm & 8pm-midnight Mon-Sat; 🛜) No nonsense here – just big servings of homemade pastas and raviolis, along with a carefully chosen wine list.

Rapa Nui   ICE CREAM $
(☑ 0294-443-3999; https://chocolatesrapanui.com.ar; Av Bartolomé Mitre 202; ice cream from AR$60; ⊙ 8:30am-11:30pm Mon-Thu, 9am-midnight Sat, 9am-11:30pm Sun) Rapa Nui wears many hats and we love all of them. It's simultaneously a chocolate shop, an ice-cream parlor (with some of the best ice cream in Bariloche) and a bright and airy cafe. And if that weren't enough, there's a small ice rink in the back (open 2pm to 10pm) for you to practice your toe loops and triple axels.

★ La Parilla de Julián   PARRILLA $$
(☑ 0294-443-3252; www.laparrilladejulian.com; San Martín 590; mains AR$200-550; ⊙ noon-4pm & 8pm-midnight) This friendly, family-run *parrilla* (steak restaurant) is a long-standing local favorite and one of the few places open on Sunday. Waiters bustle about, bearing beautifully grilled cuts of beef, *cordero patagónico* (spit-roasted lamb), *morcilla* (blood sausage) and grilled provolone cheese. Portions are ample, and reservations are a good idea, particularly on weekends.

★ Alto El Fuego   PARRILLA $$
(☑ 0294-443-7015; www.facebook.com/altoelfuego patagonia; 20 de Febrero 451; mains AR$250-450; ⊙ 8pm-midnight Mon, noon-3pm & 8pm-midnight Tue-Sat; 🛜) The most frequently recommended *parrilla* (steak restaurant) in town, featuring the killer combination of great cuts of expertly seared meat and a well-chosen wine list. It's a small place – if you're coming for dinner, make a reservation. Or, if weather permits, go for lunch and take advantage of the breezy deck area.

La Casita   GERMAN $$
(☑ 0294-442-3775; www.facebook.com/lacasita restaurantebariloche; Quaglia 342; mains AR$200-380; ⊙ noon-3pm & 8-11:30pm Wed-Mon; 🛜) This snug restaurant puts a German spin on dishes crafted from local ingredients, so expect the likes of smoked pork chop with *chukrut* (sauerkraut), hearty goulash with spätzle (egg pasta) and venison casserole. Bring a friend to order *arróz de montaña* (mountain paella with wild mushrooms) and *morcilla* (blood sausage).

🍷 Drinking & Nightlife

Bariloche is at the epicenter of the region's craft-beer movement, and breweries and brewpubs are both numerous and excellent in quality.

★ Cervecería Manush   MICROBREWERY
(☑ 0294-442-8905; www.cervezamanush.com.ar; Neumeyer 20; ⊙ 5:30pm-3am; 🛜) Going strong since 2011, not only is Manush responsible for some of the region's best stout, brown porter, pale ale and kölsch, but it is the only brewpub where the quality of the tapas and *picadas* matches the beer – courtesy of the husband-and-wife-professional chef team. Go early or be prepared to wait; this place is super-popular!

Cervecería La Cruz   BEER GARDEN
(☑ 0294-444-2634; http://cervecerialacruz.com.ar; Nilpi 789; ⊙ 5:30pm-12:30am Tue-Sun; 🛜) This microbrewery-beer garden is almost a place of pilgrimage for local beer aficionados, who make their way nightly to Bariloche's suburbs for the world-class Workingman porter, the IPAs and the live music (on weekends).

La Estepa Cafe   COFFEE
(VA O'Connor 511; ⊙ 8am-8pm Mon-Sat; 🛜📶) The lattes, ristrettos and cappuccinos at this cafe are brought to you by a couple from Buenos Aires, bringing some big-city coffee-culture sophistication to the Lake District. The place is equally popular with the tablet-toting young crowd and with families (there's a creative corner for kids).

Aside from breakfast, you can also grab an empanada or a cookie.

Los Vikingos BAR
(www.facebook.com/losvikingosbar; cnr Juramento & 20 de Febrero; ⏰7pm-3am Mon-Sat) A laid-back little corner bar serving a good range of local microbrewery beers at excellent prices. The music is cool and the decor eclectic. DJs play on weekends.

Shopping

★ **Mamuschka** CHOCOLATE
(☑0294-442-3294; www.mamuschka.com; Av Bartolomé Mitre 298; ⏰8:30am-10:30pm) Quite simply, the best chocolate in Bariloche. Don't skip it. Seriously.

ⓘ Information

Club Andino Bariloche (☑0294-442-2266; www.clubandino.org; 20 de Febrero 30; ⏰9am-1:30pm & 3-7pm) Excellent, in-depth information on trekking routes and *refugios* in Parque Nacional Nahuel Huapi. Also sells excellent hiking maps.

Municipal Tourist Office (☑0294-442-3022; Centro Cívico; ⏰8am-9pm) Has many giveaways, including useful maps and the blatantly commercial but still useful *Guía Busch*, updated biannually and loaded with basic tourist information about Bariloche and the Lake District.

Parque Nacional Nahuel Huapi Office (☑0294-442-3111; San Martín 24; ⏰8am-6pm Mon-Fri year-round, plus 9am-3pm Sat & Sun Jan & Feb) Office for the nearby national park (p162).

Provincial Tourist Office (☑0294-442-3188, 0294-442-3189; secturrn@bariloche.com.ar; cnr Av 12 de Octubre & Emilio Frey; ⏰9am-7pm) Has information on the province, including an excellent provincial map and useful brochures in English and Spanish.

ⓘ Getting There & Around

AIR

The **airport** (☑0294-440-5016) is 15km east of town; take bus 72 (AR$28) from the town center or a taxi (AR$620).

There are at least a dozen flights daily to Buenos Aires with Aerolíneas Argentinas, GOL and LATAM.

BUS

The **bus terminal** (☑0294-443-2860) is 2.5km east of the center. Buses 70, 71 and 83 connect downtown with the bus terminal.

Some long-distance bus companies have a ticket office downtown, so you might be able to

---

ⓘ BARILOCHE BUS CARDS

Bariloche's local buses work with Sube magnetic cards (www.sube.gob.ar), available from kiosks at Av Bartolomé Mitre 91 and Moreno 480, and Moreno 69 and Morales 501, respectively. You can also pick up handy *horarios* (schedules) for all destinations from the bus terminal. Cards cost AR$60 (recharged with as much credit as you want). For most routes a ride will cost AR$19, with AR$42 being the highest fare. Some hostels loan cards to guests on payment of a deposit.

---

buy an advance bus ticket without going to the bus terminal.

During the peak months of December to February, **Chaltén Travel** (☑0294-442-3809; www.chaltentravel.com; Av Bartolomé Mitre 442; ⏰9am-1pm & 5-9pm Mon-Sat) runs buses along the legendary RN 40 as far south as El Calafate. There are a couple of weekly departures from Bariloche.

Buses from Bariloche

DESTINATION	COST (AR$)	DURATION (HR)
Buenos Aires	1790-2410	20½-24½
El Bolsón	195-245	2¼
Osorno, Chile	410-600	5¼
Puerto Montt, Chile	420-600	8
San Martín de los Andes	440	4
Villa la Angostura	90	1¼

CAR

There are plenty of car rental agencies in town; try **Andes** (☑0294-443-1648; www.andesrentacar.com.ar; San Martín 162; ⏰9am-6pm). Prices vary greatly depending on season and demand, but usually come in around AR$1200 per day, with unlimited mileage.

TRAIN

When it's running, the **Tren Patagonico** (☑0294-442-3172; www.trenpatagonico-sa.com.ar) leaves the **train station** (☑0294-442-3172), across the Río Ñireco, next to the bus terminal. It generally leaves Bariloche for Viedma (16 hours) at 5pm on most Sundays (and the occasional Monday); fares range from AR$930 in *primera* (1st-class seated) to AR$1795 in *camarote* (1st-class sleeper). Check departures with the tourist office beforehand.

ARGENTINA BARILOCHE

Parque Nacional Nahuel Huapi

Lago Nahuel Huapi, a glacial relic over 100km long, is the centerpiece of this gorgeous **national park** (☑0294-442-3111; www.parquesnacionales.gob.ar/areas-protegidas/region-patagonia/pn-nahuel-huapi; AR$300). To the west, 3554m Monte Tronador marks the Andean crest and Chilean border. Humid Valdivian forest covers its lower slopes, while summer wildflowers blanket alpine meadows.

The 65km **Circuito Chico** loop is a popular excursion. Every 20 minutes, bus 20 (from San Martín and Morales in Bariloche) heads along Lago Nahuel Huapi to end at Puerto Pañuelo, where boat trips leave a few times daily for beautiful **Puerto Blest**, touristy **Isla Victoria** and pretty **Península Quetrihué**. Bus 10 goes the other way, inland via **Colonia Suiza** (a small, woodsy Swiss community), and ends at Bahía López, where you can hike a short way to the tip of the peninsula Brazo de la Tristeza. In summer, bus 11 does the whole Circuito, connecting Puerto Pañuelos with Bahía López, but in winter you can walk the 8km stretch along the sleepy highway, with much of that being on a woodsy nature trail. There's a beautiful two-hour side hike to Villa Tacul, on the shores of Lago Nahuel Huapi. It's best to walk from Bahía López to Puerto Pañuelos rather than the other way around, since many more buses head back to Bariloche from Pañuelos. Be sure to confirm bus schedules in Bariloche's tourist office, as schedules vary from season to season.

Tough cyclists can hop a bus to Km 18.6 and rent a bike at **Bike Cordillera** (☑0294-452-4828; www.cordillerabike.com; Av Bustillo, Km18.6; per hour/day AR$200/450; ☺9am-6pm). This way you'll bike less, avoid busy Av Bustillo and take advantage of the loop's more scenic sections. Be aware this is a hilly, 25km ride, but you can extend it to visit area attractions. Call ahead to reserve a bicycle.

Skiing is a popular winter activity from mid-June to October. **Cerro Catedral** (☑0294-440-9000; www.catedralaltapatagonia.com; ☺mid-Jun–mid-Oct), some 20km west of town, is one of the biggest ski centers in South America. It boasts dozens of runs, a cable car, gondola and plenty of services (including rentals). The best part, however, is the view: peaks surrounding the lakes are gloriously visible.

Area hikes include climbing up **Cerros Otto**, **Catedral** and **Campanario**; all have chairlifts as well. The six-hour hike up Monte Tronador flanks to Refugio Meiling usually involves an overnight stay as it's a 2½-hour drive to the trailhead (Pampa Linda) from Bariloche. Summiting Tronador requires technical expertise.

If trekking, check with Club Andino (p161) or the National Park Office (p161), both in Bariloche, for trail conditions; snow can block trails, even in summer.

El Bolsón

☑0294 / POP 17,061

Hippies rejoice: there's a must-see destination for you in Argentina, and it's called El Bolsón. Within its liberal and artsy borders live alternate-lifestyle folks who've made their town a 'nonnuclear zone' and 'ecological municipality.' Located about 120km south of Bariloche, nondescript El Bolsón is surrounded by dramatically jagged mountain peaks. Its economic prosperity comes from a warm microclimate and fertile soil, both of which support a cadre of organic farms devoted to hops, cheese, soft fruits such as raspberries, and orchards. This, and El Bolsón's true personality, can be seen at its famous **Feria Artesanal** (Plaza Pagano; ☺10am-4pm Tue, Thu, Sat & Sun) ✐, where creative crafts – everything from wooden cutting boards and handcrafted *mate* gourds to jewelry, flutes and marionettes – and local food items are sold.

The competent **tourist office** (☑0294-449-2604; www.elbolson.gov.ar; off Plaza Pagano; ☺8am-8pm) is next to Plaza Pagano. It has a good town map and brochures, plus thorough information on accommodations, food, tours and services.

For summer activities like rafting on Río Azul, paragliding and horse riding, contact **Grado 42** (☑0294-449-3124; www.grado42.com; Av Belgrano 406; ☺8:30am-8:30pm Mon-Sat, 10:30am-1pm & 5-7pm Sun).

🛏 Sleeping

Surrounding mountains offer plenty of camping opportunities, plus *refugios*.

★**La Casona de Odile**   HOSTEL $
(☑0294-449-2753; www.odile.com.ar; dm/d US$8/40; @☜) ✐ Five kilometers north of the center, off Av San Martín, is one of the best hostels in Argentina. Traveler-run and sitting on 2 hectares of park-like riverside land, it's got all you could possibly want – good amenities, comfy dorms and private rooms, an on-

site microbrewery, yoga classes, massage, bike hire, and cheap, hearty dinners. Many come for days and stay for weeks.

★ **Earthship Patagonia**   BOUTIQUE HOTEL $
(📞 0294-448-3656;   www.earthshippatagonia.com; Azcuénaga 754; dm/d US$8/30; 🅿️😊🤝) 🍴 Its construction having involved earth-packed tires, recycled glass bottles, tin cans and solar panels, Earthship Patagonia is a labor of love. Brought to you by American transplants Trent and Natalie, it houses guests in stylishly decorated Mongolian yurts, with optional communal dinners including organic vegetables from the garden on offer, along with mountain biking and yoga retreats.

Even if you're not staying here, it's well worth attending a 4pm tour to learn how this marvel was created.

Cabañas Tulquelen   CABAÑAS $
(📞 0294-448-3251; www.cabanastunquelen.com; Feliciano 771; 2-person cabañas US$25; 🅿️😊🤝) Friendly owners preside over this clutch of cozy *cabañas,* just a couple of blocks from El Bolsón's main square. All come with kitchenettes and dining areas on the ground floor and snug sleeping lofts upstairs.

Camping Refugio Patagónico   CAMPGROUND $
(📞 0294-448-3888; www.refugiopatagonico.com.ar; Islas Malvinas s/n; campsite per person US$11, dm US$14; 🤝) Not bad as far as campgrounds go – basically a bare field, but a pleasant stream burbles alongside it. Services are good, including *asados* and a modern toilet block. If you're looking for a room, there are much better deals elsewhere.

Hostería La Escampada   BOUTIQUE HOTEL $$
(📞 0294-448-3905; www.laescampada.com; Azcuénaga 561; s/d from US$60/70; 🤝) Comprising just 10 rooms behind a salmon-colored facade, La Escampada delights with warm service and attention to detail. The beds are properly comfortable, the breakfast spread is excellent and the superior rooms come with whirlpool tubs.

🍴 Eating & Drinking

Food at the **feria artesanal** (Plaza Pagano; snacks from AR$35; ⏱️ 10am-4pm Tue, Thu, Sat & Sun) 🍴 is tasty, healthy and good value.

Jauja   CAFE, ICE CREAM $
(📞 0294-449-2448; www.heladosjauja.com; Av San Martín 2867; cones from AR$70; ⏱️ 8am-11pm; 🤝) The most dependable *confitería* (cafe offering light meals) in town serves up all your faves

with some El Bolsón touches (such as homemade bread and strawberry juice) thrown in. The daily specials are worth checking out – the risotto with lamb and wild mushrooms is divine. The attached ice creamery is legendary – make sure you leave room for a kilo or two.

La Salteñita   EMPANADAS $
(📞 0294-449-3749; Av Belgrano 515; empanadas from AR$25; ⏱️ 11am-3pm & 8-10pm) For spicy northern empanadas, try this cheap rotisserie.

★ **La Gorda**   INTERNATIONAL $$
(📞 0294-472-0559; 25 de Mayo 2709; mains AR$250-600; ⏱️ 7-11:30pm Tue-Sun; 🤝🍴) This is El Bolsón's don't-miss eating spot, with large portions of delicious, well-prepared food in relaxed, stylish surrounds. There are good vegetarian options, a couple of Asian dishes, beautifully cooked cuts of meat and some interesting sides. If it's a warm night, try for a garden table. Bookings highly recommended.

Patio Cervecero El Bolsón   BEER GARDEN
(www.facebook.com/patiocerveceroelbolsoncentro; Av San Martín 2400; ⏱️ noon-1am; 🤝) If you're a beer drinker, make for the patio here on a warm day and kick back with an IPA, a smoky *negra ahumada* (extra-dark bock), a pilsner-style *rubia* or one of the seasonal flavored beers. Inside, it's soccer on TV, a grungy rock soundtrack and half-decent pizzas and burgers to line your stomach.

Awka Cervecería   CRAFT BEER
(www.facebook.com/awka.cerveceria.5; cnr Perito Moreno & Dorrego; ⏱️ 6pm-3am; 🤝) Packed in the evenings with young locals and visitors alike, this is the place to enjoy locally brewed oatmeal stout, Belgian Tripel-style beer, a hoppy IPA or a skull-crushing barley wine.

ℹ️ Getting There & Around

There's no central bus terminal; several bus companies are spread around town, with **Via Bariloche** (📞 0294-445-5554; www.via bariloche.com.ar; cnr Onelli & Roca) having the most departures to and from Bariloche. See the tourist office for schedules. Destinations include Bariloche (AR$195 to AR$245, two hours), Esquel (AR$270 to AR$345, 2¼ to 3½ hours) and Buenos Aires (from AR$2500, 23 hours).

Around El Bolsón

The spectacular granite ridge of 2260m **Cerro Piltriquitrón** looms to the east like the back of some prehistoric beast. From the 1100m level ('plataforma'), reached by *remise,* a further 40-minute hike leads to **Bosque Tallado** (Sculpted Forest; off RN 40; Jan, Feb & Easter AR$100), a shady grove of about 50 figures carved from logs. Another 20-minute walk uphill is **Refugio Piltriquitrón** (☑ in El Bolsón 0294-448-3433; dm US$14, camping free), where you can have a drink or even sack down (bring your sleeping bag). From here it's 2½ hours to the summit. The weather is very changeable, so bring layers.

On a ridge 7km west of town is **Cabeza del Indio** (off RN 40; ⊙8am-6pm), a rock outcrop resembling a man's profile; the trail has great views of the Río Azul and Lago Puelo. There is also a **waterfall** (off RN 40; ⊙8am-6pm) about 10km north of town. These are all most accessible by bus in January and February.

A good three-hour hike reaches the narrow canyon of pretty **Cajón del Azul**. At the end is a friendly *refugio* where you can eat or stay for the night. From where the town buses drop you off, it's a 15-minute steep, dusty walk to the Cajón del Azul trailhead.

About 18km south of El Bolsón is windy **Parque Nacional Lago Puelo**. You can camp, swim, fish, hike or take a boat tour to the Chilean border. In summer, regular buses run from El Bolsón.

Esquel

☑ 02945 / POP 32,400

If you tire of the gnome-in-the-chocolate-shop ambience of Bariloche and other cutesy Lake District destinations, regular old Esquel will feel like a breath of fresh air. Set in western Chubut province's dramatic, hikeable foothills, Esquel is a hub for Parque Nacional Los Alerces and an easygoing, friendly base camp for abundant adventure activities. It's the perfect place to chill after hard travel on RN40.

🏃 Activities

EPA　　　　　　　　　　　　ADVENTURE
(Expediciones Patagonia Aventura; ☑ 02945-457015; www.facebook.com/epaexpediciones2; Av Fontana 484; ⊙9am-1pm & 5-8:30pm) EPA offers rafting, canyoning, horseback riding and trekking. Those whitewater rafting on Río Corcovado (90km away) can overnight at the recommended riverside hostel; canopy tours, horseback riding and trekking use the mountain center, an attractive wooden lodge in Parque Nacional Los Alerces. Guests have access to kayaks, and camping is also available.

Coyote Bikes　　　　　　　　　CYCLING
(☑ 02945-455505; www.coyotebikes.com.ar; Rivadavia 887; ⊙9am-12:30pm & 4-8pm Mon-Fri, 9am-12:30pm Sat) Has mountain-bike rentals and trail details in summer.

🛏 Sleeping

★**Sol Azul**　　　　　　　　　　HOSTEL $
(☑ 02945-695556; www.hostelsolazul.com.ar; Rivadavia 2869; dm US$15; @ 🛜) Resembling an attractive mountain lodge, this welcoming hostel ups the ante with a Turkish sauna and a fully decked-out kitchen with industrial stoves lined with spices. Occasional dinners using local products are served. Dorms are in a house at the back, with heated floors and small but tidy bathrooms. It's on the northern edge of town; take a taxi ride to the center.

Planeta Hostel　　　　　　　HOSTEL $
(☑ 02945-456846; www.planetahostel.com; Av Alvear 1021; dm/d incl breakfast US$13/37; 🛜) This old but boldly painted downtown house features friendly service but cramped rooms. Down comforters, a spotless communal kitchen and a TV lounge are a cut above the usual.

Sur Sur　　　　　　　　　　HOTEL $$
(☑ 02945-453858; www.hotelsursur.com; Av Fontana 282; d/tr incl breakfast US$45/50; 🛜) A popular option, this family enterprise delivers warmth and comfort. Small tiled rooms feature TV, fan and hairdryers, and the hallways are decked out with regional photos taken by former guests. Breakfast is served buffet-style.

Hostería La Chacra　　　　　　B&B $$
(☑ 02945-452802; www.lachacrapatagonia.com; RN 259, Km5; s/d incl breakfast US$60/70; @ 🛜 ♿) If you want a shot of local culture, nothing is better than this country lodging in a 1970s home with ample bright rooms, generous gringo breakfasts and thick down bedding. Owner Rini is a consummate host and expert on local Welsh history. It's located 6km southwest of Esquel; get here via shuttle, taxi or Trevelin bus – they pass hourly.

🍴 Eating & Drinking

Dimitri　　　　　　　　　　BAKERY $
(☑ 02945-15-584410; www.facebook.com/dimitri coffeehouse; Rivadavia 805; snacks AR$90-150; ⊙9am-8pm Mon-Sat) Overboard adorable, this pastel cafe serves big salads, baked goods and sandwiches with three kinds of home-

made bread on mismatched china. There's both beer and barista drinks in a cheerful, casual atmosphere.

Quillen VEGETARIAN $
(☑02945-400212; www.facebook.com/quillen restaurant; Av Fontana 769; mains AR$200-300; ⊙10am-2pm Mon, 10am-3pm & 8pm-midnight Tue-Sun, 8pm-midnight Sat & Sun; ✍) Serving organic pizza, pastas, fresh lemonade and artisan beer, Quillen might be more at home in Palermo, Buenos Aires, than the Andean foothills, but here it is. The light vegan and vegetarian options are a godsend for those fresh from the RN40.

Don Chiquino ITALIAN $$
(☑02945-450035; www.facebook.com/donchiquinoesquel; Av Ameghino 1641; mains AR$250-360; ⊙noon-3pm & 8pm-midnight) Of course, pasta is no novelty in Argentina, but the owner-magician performing tricks while you wait for your meal here is. The ambience is happy-cluttered and dishes such as *sorrentinos* with arugula prove satisfying.

Charlá Cafe CAFE
(☑02945-400714; 25 de Mayo 780; ⊙8am-9pm Mon-Fri, 9am-9pm Sat, 4-9pm Sun) This stylish cafe does real coffee with scones, homemade cakes and *alfajores* (cookie-type sandwiches usually stuffed with milk caramel) for those in the mood for a pick-me-up. There are outdoor tables, too.

Heiskel MICROBREWERY
(☑02945-15-507177; www.facebook.com/cerveceriaheiskel; Chacabuco 2311; ⊙6-11:30pm Tue-Sat) Simplicity is the name of the game at this tiny home bar – it serves a variety of decent beers made on-site (we liked the IPA), with meat and cheese boards. Large picture windows give views into the brewing room. It can get pretty crowded.

ℹ Information

The **tourist office** (☑02945-451927; www.esquel.tur.ar; cnr Av Alvear & Sarmiento; ⊙8am-8pm Mon-Fri, 9am-8pm Sat & Sun) is well organized, with an impressive variety of detailed maps and brochures, and has helpful, multilingual staff.

ℹ Getting There & Around

The **airport** (☑02945-451676) is 24km east of town (taxi AR$400). Aerolíneas Argentinas (www.aerolineas.com.ar) flies to Buenos Aires several times a week.

WORTH A TRIP

TEATIME IN TREVELIN

Historic Trevelin (treh-veh-lehn), from the Welsh for town (*tre*) and mill (*velin*), is the only community in interior Chubut with a notable Welsh character. Easygoing and postcard-pretty, it makes a tranquil day trip for afternoon tea. Conquer a platter of pastries at **Nain Maggie** (☑02945-480232; www.nainmaggie.com; Perito Moreno 179; ⊙3:30-8pm) or **La Mutisia** (☑02945-480165; www.casadetelamutisia.com.ar; Av San Martín 170; ⊙3:30-8:30pm), while keeping your ears pricked for locals speaking Welsh.

Half-hourly buses run from Esquel to Trevelin (AR$50, 30 minutes).

Esquel's modern **bus terminal** (http://terminalesquel.com.ar; cnr Av Alvear & Brun; ⊙6:30am-midnight) is close to the town center. Destinations include El Bolsón (AR$270 to AR$345, 2½ hours), Bariloche (AR$470 to AR$580, 4¼ hours), Puerto Madryn (AR$1100 to AR$1400, seven to nine hours) and Comodoro Rivadavia (AR$1000 to AR$1560, eight hours). Buses go to Trevelin (AR$50, 30 minutes) from the terminal, stopping along Av Alvear on their way south.

The narrow-gauge steam train **La Trochita** (☑02945-451403; www.latrochita.org.ar; AR$900) departs from the diminutive **Roca train station** (cnr Roggero & Urquiza; ⊙8am-2pm Mon-Sat). There's a weekly tourist-oriented service to Nahuel Pan. Confirm schedules online or via the tourist office.

Parque Nacional Los Alerces

Just 33km west of Esquel, this collection of spry creeks, verdant mountains and mirror lakes resonates as unadulterated Andes. The real attraction of the **park** (www.parquesnacionales.gob.ar/areas-protegidas/region-patagonia/pn-los-alerces; adult/child AR$300/70; ⊙south entrance 9am-5pm), however, is the alerce tree (*Fitzroya cupressoides*), one of the longest-living species on the planet, with specimens that have survived up to 4000 years. Lured by the acclaim of well-known parks to the north and south, most hikers miss this gem, which makes your visit here all the more enjoyable.

The receding glaciers of Los Alerces' peaks, which barely reach 2300m, have left nearly pristine lakes and streams with charming vistas and excellent fishing. Westerly storms drop nearly 3000mm of rain annually, but summers are mild and the park's eastern zone is much drier. **Intendencia** (☑02945-471015; ⊙8am-9pm summer, 9am-4pm rest of year) can help you plan excursions.

A popular five-hour boat tour sails from Puerto Chucao (on Lago Menéndez) and heads to **El Alerzal**, an accessible stand of rare alerces (AR$2380). A one-hour-plus stopover permits a walk around a loop trail that passes Lago Cisne and an attractive waterfall to end up at **El Abuelo** (Grandfather), a 57m-tall, 2600-year-old alerce.

Los Alerces has several full-service campgrounds, all of which have showers, grocery stores and restaurants on-site or nearby. Free (no services) and semi-organized campgrounds exist near most of these fee sites. Lago Krüger, reached by foot (17km, 12 hours) or taxi boat from near Villa Futalaufquen, has a campground, restaurant and expensive *hostería*. See Esquel's tourist office for a complete list of accommodation options.

From January to mid-March there are twice-daily buses from Esquel (AR$150, 1¼ hours); outside summer there are three buses per week.

PATAGONIA

Few places in the world inspire the imagination like mystical Patagonia. You can cruise bleak RN40 (South America's Route 66), watch an active glacier calve house-size icebergs, and hike among some of the most fantastic mountain scenery in the world. There are Welsh teahouses, petrified forests, quirky outpost towns, penguin colonies, huge sheep *estancias* and some of the world's largest trout. The sky is wide and the late sunsets nearly spiritual.

Patagonia is thought to be named after the Tehuelche people's moccasins, which made their feet appear huge – in Spanish, *pata* means foot. Geographically, the region is mostly a windy, barren expanse of flat nothingness that offers rich wildlife only on its eastern coast, and rises into the spectacular Andes way into its western edge. It has attracted an interesting range of famous personalities, from Charles Darwin to Bruce Chatwin to Butch Cassidy and the Sundance

Kid. Despite the big names, however, Patagonia maintains one of the lowest population densities in the world.

Puerto Madryn

☑0280 / POP 94,000

The gateway to Península Valdés, Puerto Madryn bustles with tourism and industry. It retains a few small-town touches: the radio announces lost dogs, and locals are welcoming and unhurried. With summer temperatures matching those of Buenos Aires, Madryn holds its own as a modest beach destination, but from June to mid-December the visiting right whales take center stage.

◉ Sights & Activities

★EcoCentro   MUSEUM

(☑0280-445-7470; www.ecocentro.org.ar; J Verne 3784; adult/child AR$400/300; ⊙5-9pm Wed-Mon, cruise-ship days 10am-1pm Dec-Feb, 3-7pm Wed-Sun Mar & mid-Jun–Nov, 3-7pm Thu-Sun Apr, closed May–mid-Jun) Celebrating the area's unique marine ecosystem, this masterpiece brings an artistic sensitivity to extensive scientific research. There are exhibits on the breeding habits of right whales, dolphin sounds and southern-elephant-seal harems, a touch-friendly tide pool and more. The building includes a three-story tower and library, with the top featuring glass walls and comfy couches for reading.

Observatorio Punta Flecha   WILDLIFE RESERVE

(⊙high tide) FREE Run by Fundación Patagonia Natural, this whale-watching observatory sits 17km north of Puerto Madryn on Playa el Doradillo. It offers tourist information and opens at high tide, when there are more whales and visitors at the beach.

Napra Club   WATER SPORTS

(☑0280-445-5633; www.napraclub.com; Bulevar Brown 860; ⊙9:30am-7:30pm) This rental shack offers bicycles (per day AR$300), stand-up paddle boards (per hour AR$450) and guided sea kayaking (per two hours AR$550) in sit-on-tops. If need be, you can also rent a wet suit. Located next to Bistro de Mar Nautico.

☞ Tours

Countless agencies sell tours to Península Valdés for around AR$2000; prices do not include the AR$520 park admission fee or whale watching. Most hotels and hostels also offer tours; get recommendations from fellow

Patagonia

0 — 200 km
0 — 100 miles

Aluminé
Parque Nacional Laguna Blanca
Choelle Choel
Río Negro
5
Parque Nacional Lanín
RN 237
RP 74
RP 6
RN 250
RN 251
Junín de los Andes
Río Limay
San Martín de los Andes
Piedra del Aguila
La Esperanza
RN 23
San Antonio Oeste
RN 250
RN 3
Viedma
Cerro Chapelco (1340m)
RP 67
RP 6
RP 8
Las Grutas
Parque Nacional Nahuel Huapi
Ingeniero Jacobacci
Río Negro
RP 1
Golfo San Matías
La Lobería
215
Monte Tronador (3554m)
Bariloche
RN 23
Sierra Grande
Cerro Catedral (2388m)
Puerto Montt
RN 258
Cerro Piltriquitrón (2260m)
El Bolsón
El Maitén
RP 76
Península Valdés
Punta Norte
Parque Nacional Lago Puelo
RP 13
Isla de los Pájaros
Reserva Faunística Península Valdés
Parque Nacional Los Alerces
Paso del Sapo
RP 4
Puerto Madryn
RP 2
Puerto Pirámides
Esquel
RN 25
Gaiman
Trelew
Punta Ninfas
Trevelin
Dolavon
RP 8
Tecka
RP 62
RP 12
Río Chubut
Las Plumas
RN 25
Rawson
Lago General Vintter
Área Natural Protegida Punta Tombo
José de San Martín
Paso de Indios
Chubut
RN 3
Cabo Raso
RP 40
RP 19
RP 1
RP 20
RP 30
Camarones
Lago Musters
Lago Colhué Huapi
Cabo Dos Bahías
Coyhaique
RN 26
Río Mayo
Sarmiento
Comodoro Rivadavia
Golfo San Jorge
7
RP 55
RN 26
RP 18
Las Heras
Lago Buenos Aires
Chile Chico
RP 43
Caleta Olivia
Perito Moreno
Río Deseado
Pico Truncado
Los Antiguos
Fitz Roy
Cueva de las Manos
Santa Cruz
RP 12
RP 49
RN 3
RN 281
Puerto Deseado
RP 39
Bajo Caracoles
Monumento Natural Bosques Petrificados
CHILE
Lago Pueyrredón
RP 40
RP 47
Villa O'Higgins
RP 12
Gobernador Gregores
ATLANTIC OCEAN
Lago Cardiel
RN 40
Candelario Mansilla
RP 25
Cerro Fitz Roy (3441m)
RN 288
Río Chico
San Julián
El Chaltén
524
Tres Lagos
Lago Viedma
Santa Cruz
Parque Nacional Los Glaciares
Río Santa Cruz
RP 9
Parque Nacional Monte León
Lago Argentino
El Calafate
RN 40
RN 3
Bahía Grande
RP 7
Esperanza
RP 5
Parque Nacional Torres del Paine
Villa Cerro Castillo
Río Turbio
Güer Aike
Puerto Natales
Río Gallegos
Río Gallegos
Punta Delgada
Región XII
RN 3
RP 1
Cabo Vírgenes
Strait of Magellan

Puerto Madryn

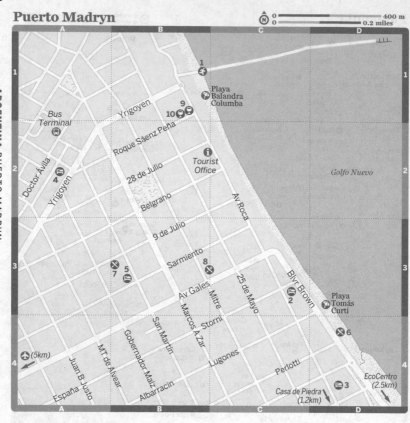

Puerto Madryn

Activities, Courses & Tours
Napra Club .... (see 6)
1 Regina Australe B1

Sleeping
2 Chepatagonia Hostel C3
3 Hi Patagonia Hostel D4
4 La Casa de Tounens A2
5 La Tosca B3

Eating
6 Bistro de Mar Nautico D4
7 La Milonga B3
8 Lupita B3

Drinking & Nightlife
9 James Beer B1
10 Margarita Pub B1

travelers before choosing. You can also take a tour to visit the elephant seals and penguins at Punta Ninfas.

Regina Australe   CRUISE
(📞0280-445-6447; www.reginaaustrale.com.ar; Muelle Piedra Buena; adult/4-12yr AR$800/600; ⏲ticket office 10am-1pm & 2-7pm) This 300-passenger ship cruises the Golfo Nuevo to Punta Lobo, departing conveniently from the town pier, where tickets are sold. The three-hour tour departs at 1pm on Saturday, Sunday,

Wednesday and holidays. The ship has three decks, a bar and fast food.

🛏 Sleeping

★ **Hi Patagonia Hostel**   HOSTEL $
(📞0280-445-0155; http://hipatagonia.com; Av Roca 1040; dm US$12, d with/without bathroom US$45/35; 📶) With wonderful service, this central hostel provides a congenial adventure base. Double-glazed windows ensure your rest, while a grassy backyard and barbecue

area create a social atmosphere. There are also bikes and cars for rent on-site, tour information, plus precise weather forecasts and tidal details from host Gaston.

La Tosca
HOSTEL $

(📞0280-445-6133; www.latoscahostel.com; Sarmiento 437; d US$50, dm/s/d without bathroom US$13/35/40; @🛜) A cozy guesthouse where the owners and staff greet you by name. The creation of a well-traveled couple, La Tosca is modern and comfy, with a grassy courtyard, good mattresses, and varied breakfasts with homemade cakes, yogurt and fruit. Double suites and a post-checkout bathroom with showers are wonderful additions. There's also bike rental.

La Casa de Tounens
HOSTEL $

(📞0280-447-2681; www.lacasadetounens.com; Passaje 1 de Marzo 432; d with bathroom US$50, dm/d without bathroom US$11/40; @🛜) A congenial nook near the bus station, run by a friendly Parisian-Argentine couple. With few rooms, personal attention is assured. There's a cozy stone patio strewn with hammocks, a living area with pool table, barbecue grill, and homemade bread for breakfast.

Chepatagonia Hostel
HOSTEL $

(📞0280-445-5783; www.chepatagoniahostel.com. ar; Storni 16; dm/d US$12/35; @🛜) This stylish and cheerful hostel is owned by a friendly couple who book tours for guests and fire up the grill for barbecues twice a week. Adding to the appeal are comfortable beds and the possibility of glimpsing whales from the hostel balcony. Guests can wash clothes and cook. There are also bikes for rent (AR$350 per day).

★Casa de Piedra
B&B $$

(📞0280-15-499-1611, 0280-447-3521; www.las piedrashosteria.com; Arenales 82; d/tr incl breakfast US$70/80; @🛜) 🗝 This wonderful B&B shines with warm and attentive service. The artisan owners have thoughtfully crafted every detail, from stone patterns in the walkway to wood details and an oversized rocking horse. Immaculate rooms with private entrances off a cement courtyard feature coffee-and-tea service, flat-screen TVs, lock boxes and mini-fridges.

✖ Eating & Drinking

La Milonga
PIZZA $

(📞0280-447-0363; 9 de Julio 534; pizzas AR$250; ⊘7pm-12:30am Tue-Sun) Locals flock to this retro pizzeria for its huge variety of clay-oven pizzas, with toppings like arugula and tapenade (marinated-olive spread).

Lupita
MEXICAN $

(📞0280-15-472-2454; www.facebook.com/lupita. taqueria; Av Gales 195; mains AR$150-320; ⊘8pm-1am) This tiny, colorful eatery serves up nachos and fajitas to travelers yearning for something spicy. While it's not straight out of Guadalajara, a valiant effort is made with homemade whole-wheat tortillas and house salsas.

Bistro de Mar Nautico
SEAFOOD $$

(📞0280-445-7616; www.cantinaelnautico.com. ar; Bulevar Brown 860; mains AR$250-550; ⊘7:30am-midnight) With unbeatable beachfront atmosphere and bustling old-school waiters, this busy cafe does the job. Seafood lovers can get grilled fish or crisp calamari. There are also burgers, pizzas and even breakfast, with gorgeous water views that few Madryn restaurants can boast. After 8pm there's a limited menu.

James Beer
CRAFT BEER

(www.facebook.com/jamesbeermadryn; cnr Av Roca & Roque Sáenz Peña; ⊘noon-4pm & 6pm-1am) With modern ambience and 12 microbrews from all over Argentina on tap, this hipster bar is the latest addition to Madryn's nightlife. It also serves pub food like burgers and sausages, as well as its own craft beer.

Margarita Pub
PUB

(📞0280-447-2659; www.margaritapub.com; Roque Sáenz Peña 15; ⊘7pm-4am) With a trendy edge, this low-lit brick haunt has a laundry list of cocktails, friendly bar staff and decent food, with popular sushi Wednesdays. On Friday and Saturday there's dancing after 1:30am.

❶ Information

The **tourist office** (📞0280-445-3504; https://madryn.travel; Av Roca 223; ⊘8am-9pm Dec-Feb, limited hours Apr-Nov) has helpful and efficient staff, and there's usually an English or French speaker on duty. Check the *libro de reclamos* (complaint book) for traveler tips. There's another helpful desk at the bus terminal (open 7am to 9pm in high season).

❶ Getting There & Around

Though Puerto Madryn has its own modern airport, **Aeropuerto El Tehuelche** (📞0280-445-6774), 10km west of town, most commercial flights still arrive in Trelew's Airport Almirante Marcos A Zar (p171), 65km south.

Regional airline **Andes** (📞0280-447-5877; www.andesonline.com; Belgrano 41; ⊘7am-7pm

Mon-Sat, noon-8pm Sun) has daily flights to Buenos Aires' Aeroparque. **Aerolíneas Argentinas** (☑ 0280-445-4318; 25 de Mayo 11, 2nd fl; ☺ 9am-12:30pm & 3-7pm Mon-Fri, 9:30am-1pm Sat) and **LADE** (☑ 0280-445-1256; Av Roca 119; ☺ 9am-4pm Mon-Fri) fly from Trelew, but each has a ticketing representative in Puerto Madryn.

From the **bus terminal** (☑ 0280-445-1789; www.terminalmadryn.com; cnr Ciudad de Nefyn & Dr Ávila), destinations include Puerto Pirámides (AR$130, 1½ hours), Trelew (AR$76 to AR$120, one hour), Comodoro Rivadavia (AR$745 to AR$900, six to eight hours), Río Gallegos (AR$2170 to AR$2470, 15 to 20 hours), Esquel (AR$1100 to AR$1400, nine hours) and Buenos Aires (AR$2200 to AR$2500, 18 to 20 hours).

Rental cars are available through **Hi Patagonia Rent-a-Car** (☑ 0280-445-0155; www.hipatagonia.com; Rawson 419; ☺ by reservation); basic vehicles run AR$2000 per day, with insurance and 200km included.

Reserva Faunística Península Valdés

☑ 0280

Home to sea lions, elephant seals, guanacos, rheas, Magellanic penguins and numerous seabirds, Unesco World Heritage site **Reserva Faunística Península Valdés** (☑ 0280-445-0489; http://peninsulavaldes.org.ar; adult/child AR$520/250; ☺ 8am-8pm) is one of South America's finest wildlife reserves. More than 80,000 people each year visit this sanctuary, which has a total area of 3600 sq km and more than 400km of coastline. The wildlife viewing is truly exceptional, though the undisputed main attraction is the endangered *ballena franca austral* (southern right whale). The warmer, more enclosed waters along the gulf become prime breeding zones for right whales between June and mid-December.

As you enter the sanctuary you'll pass the thin 5km neck of the peninsula. Squint northwards for a glimpse of **Isla de los Pájaros**. This small island inspired Antoine de Saint-Exupéry's description of a hat, or 'boa swallowing an elephant,' in his book *The Little Prince*. From 1929 to 1931, Saint-Exupéry flew the mail here. Watch for salt flats **Salina Grande** and **Salina Chico** (42m below sea level) – South America's lowest spots.

Caleta Valdés is a bay sheltered by a long gravel spit and favored by elephant seals. Just north of here lives a substantial colony of burrowing Magellanic penguins.

At **Punta Norte** a mixed group of sea lions and elephant seals snoozes, with the occasional orca pod patrolling.

The hub is **Puerto Pirámides**, a sandy, shrubby, one-street kinda town that's home to around 500 souls. You can stay here to be closer to wildlife attractions. Services are minimal: there's only one ATM in town (which may not work) and no car rentals. Scuba diving, horseback riding and mountain biking tours are available. Boat tours outside whale-watching season aren't really worth it unless you adore shorebirds and sea lions, though there's a chance of seeing dolphins. For information visit the **tourist office** (☑ 0280-449-5048; www.puertopiramides.gov.ar; 1era Bajada; ☺ 8am-8pm).

🛏 Sleeping & Eating

Accommodation and dining options are mostly clustered in and around Puerto Pirámides.

La Casa de la Tía Alicia   GUESTHOUSE $
(☑ 0280-449-5046; info@hosteriatiaalicia.com.ar; Av de las Ballenas s/n; d incl breakfast US$50; 🐾) 🍃 A cozy spot, this petal-pink house has just three cabin-style rooms in bright crayon-box colors around a cute garden area. There's in-room tea service, and management has a conscientious approach to recycling water and composting.

Hostel Bahía Ballenas   HOSTEL $
(☑ 0280-15-456-7104; www.bahiaballenas.com.ar; Av de las Ballenas s/n; dm US$12; ✳@🐾) A welcoming brick hostel with two enormous dorms; the 'Backpackers' sign will catch your eye. Guests get discounts on area tours. Rates include kitchen use; breakfast is extra.

Camping Municipal   CAMPGROUND $
(☑ 0280-15-420-2760; per person US$12) Convenient, sheltered gravel campsites with clean toilets, a store and hot pay showers, down the road behind the gas station. Come early in summer to stake your spot. Avoid camping on the beach: high tide is very high.

El Origen   CAFE $$
(☑ 0280-449-5049; Av de las Ballenas s/n; mains AR$200-350; ☺ 8:30am-7pm) If you're looking for a quick bite, this cute cafe does homemade sandwiches, salads and pizza. Organic coffee, loose-leaf tea or organic juice will satisfy your thirst. There's attention to health-conscious items too; try the dairy-free chia and coconut-milk dessert.

ℹ️ Getting There & Away

Buses from Puerto Madryn leave for Puerto Pirámides (AR$131, 1½ hours) once or twice daily in summer.

Trelew

📞 0280 / POP 98,600

Though steeped in Welsh heritage, Trelew isn't a postcard city. In fact, this uneventful midsized hub may be convenient to many attractions, but it's home to few. Trelew is the region's commercial center and a good base for visiting the Welsh villages of Gaiman and Dolavon. Also worthwhile is the top-notch dinosaur museum.

Eisteddfod de Chubut (☉late Oct) is a Welsh literary and musical festival.

◉ Sights

⭐**Museo Paleontológico Egidio Feruglio** MUSEUM
(📞0280-443-2100; www.mef.org.ar; Av Fontana 140; adult/child AR$220/160; ☉9am-7pm mid-Sep–mid-Mar, 9am-6pm Mon-Fri, 10am-6pm Sat & Sun mid-Mar–mid Sep) Showcasing the most important fossil finds in Patagonia, this natural-history museum offers outstanding life-size dinosaur exhibits and more than 1700 fossil remains of plant and marine life. Nature sounds and a video complement the informative plaques, and tours are available in a number of languages. The collection's most exciting addition is the Patagotitan, possibly the largest animal to ever walk the earth, discovered in 2013.

☞ Tours

Nievemar TOURS
(📞0280-443-4114; www.nievemartours.com.ar; Italia 20; ☉8:30am-12:30pm & 3:30-8:30pm Mon-Fri, 9am-1pm Sat) Offers conventional tours and trips to Punta Tombo.

🛏️ Sleeping

Hostel El Agora HOSTEL $
(📞0280-442-6899; www.hostelagora.com.ar; Edwin Roberts 33; dm/d US$18/45; ❋ @ 🛜) A backpacker haven, this brick house is sparkling and shipshape. Features include a tiny patio, a book exchange and laundry. It also does guided bicycle tours. It's two blocks from Plaza Centenario and four blocks from the bus terminal.

⭐**La Casa de Paula** B&B $$
(📞0280-15-435-2240; www.casadepaula.com.ar; Marconi 573; d/tr incl breakfast US$62/66; P ❋ 🛜)

A haven after a day of sun and wind, artist Paula's house beckons with huge king beds covered in down duvets and woven throws. An eclectic and warm decor fills this modern home, with jazz on the radio and cozy living areas stacked with fashion mags. There's also a lush garden and an outstanding breakfast with homemade jam.

🍴 Eating & Drinking

Sugar ARGENTINE $$
(📞0280-442-1210; 25 de Mayo 247; mains AR$180-300; ☉7am-1am; 🍴) Facing Plaza Independencia, this modern restaurant spices up a basic menu of classic Argentine fare with options like quinoa *milanesas,* stir-fried beef, grilled vegetables and herbed fish. There are salads and fresh juice on offer too. While it isn't gourmet, it's still a welcome change from the Argentine same-old, same-old.

Touring Club CAFE
(Av Fontana 240; ☉6:30am-2am) Old lore exudes from the pores of this historic *confitería* (cafe offering light meals), from the Butch Cassidy 'Wanted' poster to the embossed tile ceiling and antique bar back. Even the tuxedoed waitstaff appear to be plucked from another era. Service is weak and the sandwiches are only so-so, but the ambience is one of a kind.

ℹ️ Information

The helpful **tourist office** (📞0280-442-0139; www.trelew.gov.ar; cnr San Martín & Mitre; ☉8am-8pm Mon-Fri, 9am-9pm Sat & Sun; 🛜) is well stocked and has some English-speaking staff.

ℹ️ Getting There & Around

Trelew's **Airport Almirante Marcos A Zar** (📞0280-443-3443; www.aeropuertotrelew.com; RN 3, Km1450) is 5km north of town. The **Transfer Aeropuerto** (📞0280-487-7300; AR$300) service goes to Puerto Madryn. From the airport, a **taxi** (📞0280-442-0404) to downtown is AR$180. **Aerolíneas Argentinas** (📞0810-222-86527; Rivadavia 548; ☉9am-5pm Mon-Fri) flies to Buenos Aires.

Trelew's **bus station** (📞0280-442-0121; Urquiza 150) is six blocks northeast of downtown. Destinations include Puerto Madryn (AR$76 to AR$120, one hour), Gaiman (AR$35 to AR$65, 30 minutes), Comodoro Rivadavia (AR$650 to AR$780, five to six hours), Esquel (AR$1000 to AR$1325, nine hours) and Buenos Aires (AR$1500 to AR$2250, 18 to 21 hours).

Car-rental stands are at the airport and in town.

Around Trelew

Gaiman

📞 0280 / POP 9600

For a taste of Wales in Patagonia, head 17km west of Trelew to Gaiman. The streets are calm and wide and the buildings are non-descript and low; on hot days the local boys swim in the nearby river. The real reason travelers visit Gaiman, however, is to down pastries and cakes at one of several good Welsh teahouses. Two standout options are **Ty Gwyn** (📞 0280-499-1009; 9 de Julio 111; ☺ 2-7:30pm), in business for 30 years, and **Plas y Coed** (📞 0280-449-1133; www.plasycoed.com.ar; MD Jones 123; ☺ 2-7:30pm), run by the original owner's great-granddaughter. To get oriented visit the **tourist office** (📞 0280-449-1571; informes@gaiman.gov.ar; cnr Rivadavia & Belgrano; ☺ 9am-8pm Dec-Mar, to 6pm Apr-Nov; 🐱).

The small **Museo Histórico Regional Gales** (📞 0280-449-1007; cnr Sarmiento & 28 de Julio; AR$20; ☺ 3-8pm daily Dec-Mar, 3-7pm Tue-Sun Apr-Nov) details Welsh colonization with old pioneer photographs and household items.

Gaiman is an easy day trip from Trelew, but if you want to stay, try charming **Yr Hen Ffordd** (📞 0280-449-1394; www.yrhenffordd.com.ar; MD Jones 342; s/d incl breakfast US$27/35; 🐱), with simple but cozy rooms (and private bathrooms with great showers). Some teahouses also let rooms.

Frequent buses go to/from Trelew (AR$35 to AR$65, 30 minutes).

Área Natural Protegida Punta Tombo

Continental South America's largest penguin nesting ground, **Área Natural Protegida Punta Tombo** (adult/child AR$400/200; ☺ 8am-6pm Sep-Apr) has a colony of more than half a million Magellanic penguins and attracts king and rock cormorants, giant petrels, kelp gulls, flightless steamer ducks and black oystercatchers. Rangers accompany visitors on rookery visits.

Centro Tombo (Área Natural Protegida Punta Tombo; ☺ 8am-6pm) is an interpretive visitor center and the departure point for visits to the rookery, with a *confitería* on-site. To visit, arrange a tour in Trelew or Puerto Madryn or rent a car, a good option for groups.

Comodoro Rivadavia

📞 0297 / POP 177,000

Surrounded by dry hills of drilling rigs, oil tanks and wind-energy farms, tourism in the dusty port of Comodoro usually means little more than a bus transfer. What this modern, hardworking city does provide is a gateway to nearby attractions with decent services (cue the Walmart). Hotels run expensive.

🛏 Sleeping & Eating

Hotel Victoria   HOTEL **$$**
(📞 0297-446-0725; Belgrano 585; s/d/ incl breakfast US$44/50; 🅿🐱) The friendliest hotel on the block, with soothing, good-sized rooms with firm twin beds, desks and cable TV. If the aroma of baking pastries is any indication, it's worth taking breakfast. Parking is extra.

Hilario   CAFE **$$**
(📞 0297-444-2516; www.facebook.com/hilariocrd; Belgrano 694; mains AR$220-360; ☺ 10am-midnight Tue-Sat, from 5pm Sun) A modern cafe with brickwork and bare lightbulbs, it draws locals for stews served as pot pies with seeded crusts, pizza and mint-ginger lemonade. It's a good alternative to the traditional Argentine fare, with even quinoa on the menu.

ℹ Information

The **tourist office** (📞 0297-444-0664; www.comodoroturismo.gob.ar; Parque Soberania; ☺ 8am-8pm Mon-Fri, 9am-3pm Sat & Sun) is well stocked and well organized, and has friendly staff.

ℹ Getting There & Around

AIR

Aeropuerto General Mosconi (📞 0297-454-8190) is 9km north of town. **Aerolíneas Argentinas** (📞 0297-444-0050; www.aerolineas.com.ar; Av Rivadavia 156; ☺ 9am-5pm Mon-Fri) and **LATAM** (📞 0297-454-8160; www.latam.com; Airport) fly a couple of times daily to Buenos Aires. **LADE** (📞 0297-447-0585; www.lade.com.ar; Av Rivadavia 360; ☺ 8am-8pm Mon-Fri, 10am-5pm Sat) wings it to El Calafate, Río Gallegos, Trelew, Ushuaia, Buenos Aires and points in between.

BUS

The **bus terminal** (Pellegrini 730) is in the center of town. Destinations include Puerto Madryn (AR$745 to AR$900, six hours), Los Antiguos (AR$550, five hours), Esquel (AR$960, 10 hours), Bariloche (AR$1015 to AR$1200, 12 hours), Río Gallegos (AR$1150, 10 to 12 hours) and Buenos Aires (AR$2380, 24 hours).

Los Antiguos

♩ 02963 / POP 3360

Situated on the windy shores of Lago Buenos Aires, the agricultural oasis of Los Antiguos is home to *chacras* (small independent farms) of cherries, strawberries, apples, apricots and peaches. It makes an attractive crossing to Chile, and getting here via RN40 can be an adventure in itself.

With rodeos and live music, the **Fiesta de la Cereza** (cherry festival) occurs the second weekend in January. **Chelenco Tours** (♩ 02963-491198; www.chelencotours.tur.ar; Av 11 de Julio Este 584; ☉10am-1pm & 4:30-9:30pm) leads trips to Cueva de las Manos, with incredible rock art from 7370 BC, and Monte Zeballos, where there's trekking and mountain biking. The **tourist office** (♩ 02963-491261; www.losantiguos.tur.ar; Lago Buenos Aires 59; ☉8am-8pm) has information on other activities, including fishing and windsurfing. There's one bank with an ATM.

A 20-minute walk east of the center is the cypress-sheltered **Camping Municipal** (♩ 02963-491265; Av 11 de Julio Este s/n; campsite tent US$6 plus per person US$2, per person dm/cabin US$24/29), which also has cabins. **Hotel Los Antiguos Cerezos** (♩ 02963-491132; www.facebook.com/hotellosantiguoscerezos; Av 11 de Julio 850; s/d/tr US$35/55/65; ☏) offers sterile rooms, or upgrade to the plush **Hotel Mora** (♩ 0297-15-540-2444; www.hotelmorapatagonia.com; Av Costanera 1064; s/d/tr incl breakfast US$42/60/75; ☏) on the lakeshore. Espresso and good cafe fare are served at the chalet-like **Viva El Viento** (♩ 02963-491109; www.vivaelviento.com; Av 11 de Julio 477; mains AR$190-400; ☉11am-1am Mon-Thu, to 2am Fri & Sat, to 11:30pm Sun; ☏).

From mid-November through March, **Chaltén Travel** (♩ 0297-623-4882; www.chaltentravel.com; Av Tehuelches s/n, Los Antiguos) buses go daily to El Chaltén and El Calafate (AR$1600, 12 hours). Other bus destinations include Perito Moreno (AR$125 to AR$270, 40 minutes), Bariloche (AR$1490, 12 hours) and Comodoro Rivadavia (AR$640, seven hours). The tourist office has current bus schedules.

El Chaltén

♩ 02962 / POP 1630

This colorful village overlooks the stunning northern sector of Parque Nacional Los Glaciares. Every summer thousands of trekkers come to explore the world-class trails under the toothy spires of the **Fitz Roy range**.

ⓘ GETTING TO CHILE

For Chile, there is a border crossing from Los Antiguos to Chile Chico. At the time of research, public transportation across the border was suspended. Inquire locally, as this situation could likely change. It's 1.5km from Los Antiguos to the Argentine border, then 1km further to the Chilean border, with Chile Chico 5km beyond.

A Chilean ferry run by Somarco (p544) crosses Lago General Carrera daily from Chile Chico to Puerto Ingeniero Ibáñez almost daily, a big shortcut to Coyhaique.

Climbers from around the world make their bid to summit the premier peak **Cerro Fitz Roy** (3441m), among others. Pack for wind, rain and cold temperatures even in summer, when views of the peaks can be obscured. If the sun is out, however, El Chaltén is an outdoor-lover's paradise.

Note that El Chaltén is within national park boundaries, meaning rules regarding fires and washing distances from rivers must be followed. The area's river waters are potable without filtration – help keep them clean. El Chaltén mostly shuts down from April to October.

🏃 Activities

Laguna Torre   HIKING

Views of the stunning rock needle of Cerro Torre are the highlight of this 18km round-trip hike. If you have good weather – ie little wind – and clear skies, make this hike (three hours one-way) a priority, since Cerro Torre is the most difficult local peak to see on normal blustery days.

★ Laguna de Los Tres   HIKING

This hike to a high alpine tarn provides one of the most photogenic spots in Parque Nacional Los Glaciares. It's somewhat strenuous (10km and four hours one-way) and best for those in good physical shape. Exercise extra caution in foul weather as trails are very steep.

Lago del Desierto–Chile Trail   HIKING

Some 37km north of El Chaltén (a one-hour drive on a gravel road), Lago del Desierto sits near the Chilean border. At the lake a 500m trail leads to an overlook with fine lake and glacier views. A lake trail along the eastern side extends to Candelario Mansilla in Chile.

An increasingly popular way to get to Chile is by crossing the border here with a one- to three-day trekking/ferry combination to Villa O'Higgins, the last stop on the Carretera Austral. The route is also popular with cyclists, though much of their time is spent shouldering their bike and gear through steep sections too narrow for panniers. Plans have started to put a road in here, but it may take decades.

Spa Yaten   HEALTH & FITNESS
(☑ 02962-493394; spayaten@gmail.com; Av San Martín 36; 1hr massage AR$1750; ⊙ 10am-10pm) Spa Yaten has showers, robes and slippers, so sore hikers can come straight here off the trail. There are various therapies, massage, dry sauna and Jacuzzi tubs in a communal room. Reserve massages ahead.

☞ Tours

Zona Austral   TOURS
(☑ 02902-489755; http://zonaaustralturismo.com; Av MM de Güemes 173; half-day/full-day tour US$15.50/20) Offers sea kayaking and the Glaciar Vespignani tour at Lago del Desierto.

Casa de Guias   OUTDOORS
(☑ 02962-493118; www.casadeguias.com.ar; Lago del Desierto 470, El Chaltén; ⊙ 10am-1pm & 4:30-9pm) Friendly and professional, with English-speaking guides certified by the Argentine Association of Mountain Guides (AAGM). It specializes in small groups. Offerings include mountain traverses, ascents for the very fit and rock-climbing classes.

🛏 Sleeping

Prices listed are for late December through February, when you should arrive with reservations. Some accommodations include breakfast.

Albergue Patagonia   HOSTEL $
(Patagonia Travellers' Hostel; ☑ 02962-493019; www.patagoniahostel.com.ar; Av San Martín 376; incl breakfast dm/s/d/tr US$15/47/60/70; ⊙ Sep-May; @ 🛜) A gorgeous and welcoming wooden farmhouse with helpful staff. Dorms in a separate building are spacious and modern, with good service and a lively atmosphere. A B&B option features rooms with private bathrooms, kitchen use and a sumptuous buffet breakfast at Fuegia Bistro.

The hostel also rents bikes and offers a unique bike tour to Lago del Desierto with shuttle options.

Lo de Trivi   HOSTEL $
(☑ 02962-493255; www.lodetrivi.com; Av San Martín 675; dm US$10-17, d without bathroom US$25; 🛜) A good budget option, this converted house has added shipping containers and decks with antique beds as porch seating. It's a bit hodgepodge but it works. There are various tidy shared spaces with and without TV; best is the huge industrial kitchen for guests. Doubles in snug containers can barely fit a bed.

Rancho Grande Hostel   HOSTEL $
(☑ 02962-493005; www.ranchograndehostel.com; Av San Martín 724; dm/d/tr/q from US$16/57/70/90; @ 🛜) Serving as Chaltén's Grand Central Station (Chaltén Travel buses stop here), this bustling backpacker factory has something for everyone, from bus reservations to internet (extra) and 24-hour cafe service. Clean four-bed rooms are stacked with blankets, and bathrooms sport rows of shower stalls. Private rooms have their own bathroom and free breakfast.

Camping El Relincho   CAMPGROUND $
(☑ 02962-493007; www.elrelinchopatagonia.com.ar; Av San Martín 545; campsites per person/vehicle/motorhome US$9/3/5; 🛜) A private campground with wind-whipped and exposed sites, and an enclosed cooking area.

★ Nothofagus B&B   B&B $$
(☑ 02962-493087; www.nothofagusbb.com.ar; cnr Hensen & Riquelme; s/d/tr from US$35/41/55, without bathroom from US$30/33/44; ⊙ Oct-Apr; @ 🛜) 🌿 Attentive and adorable, this chalet-style inn offers a toasty retreat with hearty breakfast options. Practices that earn them the Sello Verde (Green Seal) include separating organic waste and replacing towels only when asked. Wooden-beam rooms have carpet and some views. Those with hallway bathrooms share with one other room. The owners, former guides, are helpful with hiking information.

Pudu Lodge   HOTEL $$
(☑ 02962-493365; www.pudulodge.com; Calle Las Loicas 97; d incl breakfast US$120; P @ 🛜) This comfy lodging with modern style and congenial service has 20 spacious rooms with good mattresses. It's great value for El Chaltén. Buffet breakfasts are served in the cathedral-ceilinged great room.

🍴 Eating & Drinking

Pack lunches are available at most hostels and hotels and at some restaurants.

Techado Negro
CAFE $

(☑ 02962-493268; Av Antonio Rojo; mains AR$120-220; ☉noon-midnight; ☑) 🍴 With local paintings on the wall, bright colors and a raucous, unkempt atmosphere in keeping with El Chaltén, this homespun cafe serves up abundant, good-value and sometimes healthy Argentine fare. Think homemade empanadas, squash stuffed with *humitas* (sweet tamale), brown-rice vegetarian dishes, soups and pastas. It also offers box lunches.

Cúrcuma
VEGAN $$

(☑ 02902-485656; Av Rojo 219; mains AR$320-380; ☉10am-10pm; ☑) With an avid following, this vegan, gluten-free cafe does mostly takeout, from adzuki-bean burgers to whole-wheat pizzas, stuffed eggplant with couscous and arugula. Salads, coconut-milk risottos and smoothies are as rare as endangered species in Patagonia – take advantage. Hikers can reserve a lunch box a day in advance.

★ Maffía
ITALIAN $$

(Av San Martín 107; mains AR$180-360; ☉11am-11pm) Bring your appetite. In a gingerbread house, this pasta specialist makes delicious stuffed *panzottis* and *sorrentinos,* with creative fillings like trout, eggplant and basil or fondue. There are also homemade soups and garden salads. Service is professional and friendly. For dessert, the oversize homemade flan delivers.

Estepa
ARGENTINE $$

(☑ 02962-493069; cnr Cerro Solo & Av Antonio Rojo; mains AR$120-350; ☉11:30am-2pm & 6-11pm) Local favorite Estepa cooks up consistent, flavorful dishes such as lamb with calafate sauce, trout ravioli or spinach crepes. Portions are small but artfully presented, with veggies that hail from the onsite greenhouse. For a shoestring dinner, consider its rotisserie takeout service.

La Vinería
WINE BAR

(☑ 02962-493301; Lago del Desierto 265; ☉2:30pm-3am Oct-Apr) Transplanted from Alaska, this tiny, congenial wine bar offers a long Argentine wine list accompanied by 70 craft-beer options and standout appetizers. With 50 wines sold by the glass, and an entire gin menu, enthusiasts might be tempted to sabotage their next day on the trail.

❶ Information

On the left just before the bridge into town, the **Park Ranger Office** (☑ 02962-493024, 02962-493004; pnlgzonanorte@apn.gob.ar; ☉9am-5pm Sep-Apr, 10am-5pm May-Aug) has maps and hiking information (and videos for rainy days); day buses automatically stop here. The helpful **Municipal Tourist Office** (☑ 02962-493370; www.elchalten.tur.ar; Bus Terminal; ☉8am-10pm) is at the bus terminal.

Bring extra Argentine pesos, since there are only two ATMs (one in the bus station). Few places take traveler's checks or credit cards and exchange rates are poor.

A decent selection of camping food and supplies is available at the small supermarkets in town. Gear like stoves, fuel, sleeping bags, tents and warm clothes can be bought or rented from several businesses on San Martín (the main drag). Bike rentals and mountain guide services are also available.

❶ Getting There & Away

The following schedules are for December through February; off-season services are less frequent or nonexistent. There are several daily buses to El Calafate (AR$530 to AR$800, 3½ hours). **Las Lengas** (☑ 02962-493023; Antonio de Viedma 95) has minivans to Lago del Desierto (AR$450 round-trip), stopping at Hostería El Pilar and Río Eléctrico.

Chaltén Travel (☑ 02962-493092; www.chaltentravel.com; Av MM de Güemes 7; ☉7am-noon & 5-9pm) goes to Bariloche on odd days of the month in high season (around AR$3000, two days), with an overnight stop (meals and accommodations extra).

Growing numbers of travelers are making the one-to-two day crossing to Villa O'Higgins, Chile (the end of the Carretera Austral) that's done via a hiking and ferry combination between November and March; see Argentina via the Back Door for details.

El Calafate
☑ 02902 / POP 21,130

Named for the berry that, once you eat it, guarantees your return to Patagonia, El Calafate hooks you with another irresistible attraction: Glaciar Perito Moreno, 80km away in Parque Nacional Los Glaciares. The glacier is a magnificent must-see, but its massive popularity has encouraged huge growth and rapid upscaling in once-quaint El Calafate. However, it's still a fun place to be and there's a range of traveler services available. The city's strategic location between El Chaltén and Torres del Paine (Chile) makes it an inevitable stop for those in transit.

El Calafate

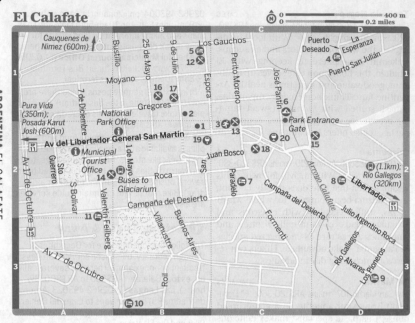

El Calafate

⊙ Sights

★ Glaciarium   MUSEUM
(📞 02902-497912; www.glaciarium.com; adult/child AR$480/200; ⊙ 9am-8pm Sep-May, 11am-8pm Jun-Aug) Unique and exciting, this gorgeous museum illuminates the world of ice. Displays and bilingual films show how glaciers form, along with documentaries on continental ice expeditions and stark meditations on climate change. Adults suit up in furry capes for the *bar de hielo* (AR$240 including drink), a blue-lit below-zero club serving vodka or fernet (an aromatic Italian spirit) and cola in ice glasses.

The gift shop sells handmade and sustainable gifts crafted by Argentine artisans.

Glaciarium also hosts international cinema events. It's 6km from Calafate toward Parque Nacional Los Glaciares. To get here, take the free hourly shuttle from 1 de Mayo between Av Libertador and Roca.

☞ Tours

★ Glaciar Sur   ADVENTURE
(📞 02902-495050; www.glaciarsur.com; 9 de Julio 57; per person US$250; ⊙ 10am-8pm) Get glacier-stunned *and* skip the crowds with these recommended day tours to the unexplored end of Parque Nacional Los Glaciares. Small groups drive to Lago Roca with an expert multilingual guide to view Glaciar Frias. The

adventure option features a four-hour hike; the culture option includes a traditional *estancia asado* (barbecue grill) and off-hour visits to Glaciar Perito Moreno. Trips run October through April, weather permitting.

Overland Patagonia   TOURS
(☑ 02902-491243, 02902-492243; www.glaciar. com; glacier tour US$52) Overland Patagonia operates out of both Hostel del Glaciar Libertador (p177) and **Hostel del Glaciar Pioneros** (☑ 02902-491243; www.glaciar.com; Los Pioneros 251; dm US$13-18, s US$34-45, d US$50-55; ☺ Nov-Mar; @☎), and organizes an alternative trip to Glaciar Perito Moreno, which consists of an *estancia* visit, a one-hour hike in the park and optional lake navigation.

🛏 Sleeping

Reserve ahead from late December through February.

America del Sur   HOSTEL $
(☑ 02902-493525; www.americahostel.com.ar; Puerto Deseado 151; dm from US$22, d US$150-200; @☎) This backpacker favorite has a stylish lodge setting with views and heated floors. Modern doubles make you rethink the limitations of a hostel. There's a well-staffed and fun social scene, including affordable nightly barbecues with salad buffet in high season. It also offers electric-bike rentals.

Hostal Schilling   GUESTHOUSE $
(☑ 02902-491453; http://hostalschilling.com; Paradelo 141; dm US$27, s/d without bathroom US$50/65, s/d/tr with bathroom US$65/80/105; ☎) Good value and centrally located, this friendly guesthouse is a top choice for travelers who value service. Much is due to the family owners, who look after guests with a cup of tea or help with logistical planning. Breakfast includes scrambled eggs, yogurt and cakes. There are also multiple living rooms, adult coloring books and games.

Hostel del Glaciar Libertador   HOSTEL $
(☑ 02902-492492; www.glaciar.com; Libertador 587; dm/s/d US$18/60/70; @☎) The best deals here are dorm bunk beds with thick covers. Behind a Victorian facade, the modern facilities include a top-floor kitchen, radiant floor heating, computers and a spacious common area with a plasma TV showing sports channels. Breakfast is extra for dorm users (AR$84).

Las Cabañitas   CABIN $
(☑ 02902-491118; www.lascabanitascalafate.com; Valentín Feilberg 218; incl breakfast 2-/3-person cabins US$60/70, 4-person apt US$80; ☺ Sep-May; @☎) A restful spot that has snug storybook A-frames with spiral staircases leading to loft beds and apartments, all with LED TVs. It's run by Eugenia, the helpful daughter of the original owner. Extra touches include a barbecue area, guest cooking facilities, and English lavender in the garden.

I Keu Ken Hostel   HOSTEL $
(☑ 02902-495175; www.patagoniaikeuken.com.ar; FM Pontoriero 171; dm from US$12, cabins per person incl breakfast US$50; @☎) With helpful staff, artisan beer and deck chairs on industrial springs, this quirky hostel has proven popular with travelers. Features include inviting common areas, a terrace for lounging and first-rate barbecues. Its location, near the top of a steep hill, offers views (and a workout); it's an AR$80 taxi ride to the bus terminal.

Bla! Guesthouse   HOSTEL $
(☑ 02902-492220; www.blahostel.com; Espora 257; dm from US$17, d US$90; ☎) If you're wondering where all the hipsters are, check out this tiny, mellow design hostel. While dorms are cramped, private rooms are comfortable, although walls are on the thin side.

Camping El Ovejero   CAMPGROUND $
(☑ 02902-493422; www.campingelovejero.com.ar; José Pantín 64; campsites per person US$7; @☎) El Ovejero has woodsy, well-kept (and slightly noisy) campsites with spotless showers that have 24-hour hot water. Locals say that the on-site restaurant is one of the best deals in town for grill food. Extras include private tables, electricity and grills. It's located by the creek just north of the bridge into town. Make reservations online.

Posada Karut Josh   B&B $$
(☑ 02902-496444; www.posadakarutjosh.com.ar; Calle 12, No 1882, Barrio Bahía Redonda; d US$85; ☎) Run by an Italian-Argentine couple, this peaceful aluminum-sided B&B features big, bright rooms and a lovely garden with lake views. Breakfast is abundant and satisfying meals (AR$280) are also available.

Cauquenes de Nimez   B&B $$
(☑ 02902-492306; www.cauquenesdenimez.com.ar; Calle 303, No 79; s/d incl breakfast from US$85/90; ✳☎) ✔ Both modern and rustic, this welcoming two-story lodge offers views of flamingos on the lake (from November through summer). Rooms decorated with corduroy duvets and nature photography also feature lock boxes and TVs. Personalized attention is

a plus, as is the complimentary tea time with lavender muffins, and free bikes (donations support the nature reserve).

Eating & Drinking

There's a range of eating establishments for all budgets. Small shops selling picnic provisions such as fresh bread, fine cheeses, sweets and wine are found on the side streets perpendicular to Libertador. Head to **La Anónima** (cnr Libertador & Perito Moreno; take-out AR$190; ⊙9am-10pm) for cheap take-out and groceries.

Olivia CAFE $
(☑02902-488038; 9 de Julio 187; snacks AR$90-180; ⊙11am-8pm Mon-Sat, 2-8pm Sun; 🔊) This adorable coffee shop does *croque monsieurs* (grilled ham and cheese), fresh donuts and espresso drinks in a loungy pastel setting. It also uses whole-bean Colombian coffee. Want to take the chill off? Try the cheese scones served hot with cream.

Viva la Pepa CAFE $
(☑02902-491880; Amado 833; mains AR$125-390; ⊙11am-11pm Mon-Sat) Decked out in children's drawings, this cheerful cafe specializes in crepes but also offers great sandwiches with homemade bread (try the chicken with apple and blue cheese), fresh juice and gourds of maté.

Morphi al Paso FAST FOOD $
(☑911-3143-6005; www.facebook.com/morfialpaso; 25 de Mayo 130; mains AR$150-250; ⊙noon-midnight Mon-Sat, 7pm-midnight Sun) For fresh *milanesas,* hot dogs and burgers in the off hours, this clean come-and-go counter flanked with stools is the way to go. *Morphi* means to chow down in Lunfardo, an Argentine slang derived from a dialect in Lombardy, Italy.

★**Buenos Cruces** ARGENTINE $$
(☑02902-492698; www.facebook.com/buenos crucesrestaurante; Espora 237; mains AR$150-310; ⊙12:30-3pm & 7-11pm Mon-Sat; 🖬) This dynamic family-run enterprise brings a twist to Argentine classics. Start with a warm beet salad with balsamic reduction. The nut-crusted trout is both enormous and satisfying, as is the guanaco meatloaf or the baked ravioli crisped at the edge and bubbling with Roquefort cheese. The service is excellent and there's a play area for children.

★**Pura Vida** ARGENTINE $$
(☑02902-493356; Libertador 1876; mains AR$130-290; ⊙7:30-11:30pm Thu-Tue; 🖊) Featuring the rare treat of Argentine home cooking, this offbeat, low-lit eatery is a must. Its longtime owners are found cooking up buttery spiced chicken pot pies and filling wine glasses. For vegetarians, brown rice and wok veggies or salads are satisfying. Servings are huge. Don't skip the decadent chocolate brownie with ice cream and warm berry sauce. Reserve ahead.

La Cantina ITALIAN $$
(☑02902-491151; Roca 1299; mains AR$140-220; ⊙noon-3pm & 7-11:30pm Mon-Sat) This friendly, family-run eatery specializes in *piadinas,* an Italian bread topped with cheese and fillings, taco-style. They're enormously filling, but you can order the smaller size. There's also worthwhile vegetarian *humitas* (corn tamales). The setting is casual bohemian, with vinyl on the record player and live blues on Thursday and weekends.

La Tablita PARRILLA $$
(☑02902-491065; www.la-tablita.com.ar; Rosales 24; mains AR$135-650; ⊙noon-3:30pm & 7pm-midnight) Steak and spit-roasted lamb are the stars at this *parrilla* that's popular beyond measure for good reason. For average appetites a half-steak will do, rounded out with a good malbec, fresh salad or garlic fries.

★**La Zorra** MICROBREWERY
(☑02902-490444; www.facebook.com/cervezala zorra; Av San Martín s/n; ⊙6pm-2am Tue-Sun) Long, skinny tables fill with both locals and travelers to quaff what we consider to be the best artisan beer in Patagonia, La Zorra. The smoked porter and double IPA do not disappoint. There's also pub fare such as fries and sausages.

Borges y Alvarez Libro-Bar BAR
(Libertador 1015; ⊙noon-9pm Mon-Thu, 3pm-midnight Fri & Sat; 🔊) Upstairs in the gnome village shopping complex, this bookstore-bar serves coffee, artisan beers as well as pricey cocktails. Peruse the oversized photography books on Patagonian wildlife or bring your laptop and take advantage of the free wi-fi. There's also 2nd-story deck seating.

ℹ Information

There are several banks with ATMs in town, though money can run out on busy weekends. If you're planning on visiting El Chaltén, withdraw enough money here.

Municipal Tourist Office (☑02902-491090, 02902-491466; www.elcalafate.tur.ar; Libertador 1411; ⊙8am-8pm) Has town maps and general information. There's also a kiosk at the bus terminal; both have some English-speaking staff.

National Park Office (📞 02902-491545; Libertador 1302; ⏰ 8am-8pm Dec-Apr, to 6pm May-Nov) Offers brochures and a decent map of Parque Nacional Los Glaciares. It's best to get information here before reaching the park.

ℹ Getting There & Around

The modern **Aeropuerto El Calafate** (📞 02902-491220) is 23km east of town. **Ves Patagonia** (📞 02902-494355; www.vespatagonia.com.ar; airport transfer AR$250) offers door-to-door shuttle services. **Aerolíneas Argentinas** (📞 02902-492816, 02902-492814; Libertador 1361; ⏰ 9:30am-5:30pm Mon-Fri), **LADE** (📞 02902-491262; Jean Mermoz 160) and **LATAM** (📞 0810-999-9526; www.latam.com) operate flights here. Book your flight to and from El Calafate well in advance.

Calafate's **bus terminal** (📞 02902-491476; Jean Mermoz 104; ⏰ 24hr) is a couple blocks above the main drag. Destinations include Río Gallegos (AR$580 to AR$680, four hours), El Chaltén (AR$530 to AR$800, 3½ hours) and Puerto Natales, Chile (AR$1100, five hours).

In summer, **Chaltén Travel** (📞 02902-492212; www.chaltentravel.com; Libertador 1174; ⏰ 9am-9pm) does the two-day trip from El Calafate to Bariloche via adventurous Ruta 40 (around AR$3000). For car rentals try **Servi Car** (📞 02902-492541; www.servicar4x4.com.ar; Libertador 695; ⏰ 9:30am-noon & 4-8pm Mon-Sat).

Parque Nacional Los Glaciares

Few glaciers can match the suspense and excitement of the blue-hued **Glaciar Perito Moreno**. Its jagged ice peaks shear off and crash with huge splashes and thunderous rifle-cracks, birthing small tidal waves and large bobbing icebergs – all while your neck hairs rise a-tingling. The highlight of **Parque Nacional Los Glaciares** (www.parquesnacionales.gob.ar/areas-protegidas/region-patagonia-austral/pn-los-glaciares; adult/child AR$600/150; ⏰ 8am-6pm Sep-Easter, 9am-4pm Apr-Aug), the Glaciar Perito Moreno measures 35km long, 5km wide and 60m high, constantly dropping chunks of ice off its face. While most of the world's glaciers are receding, Perito Moreno is considered 'stable.' And every once in a while, part of its facade advances far enough to reach the Península de Magallanes to dam the Brazo Rico arm of Lago Argentino. This causes tremendous pressure to build up, and after a few years a river cuts through the dam and eventually collapses it – with spectacular results.

The Glaciar Perito Moreno was born to be a tourist attraction. The Península de Magallanes is close enough to the glacier to provide glorious panoramas, but far enough away to be safe. A long series of catwalks and platforms gives everyone a great view. It's worth spending several hours just looking at the glacier (or condors above) and waiting for the next great calving.

Most tours from El Calafate charge AR$1300 and up for transport (sit on the left of the vehicle), guide and a few hours at the glacier. If you don't want a tour, negotiate a taxi trip or head to El Calafate's bus station; round-trip transport costs AR$540 and gives you several hours at the glacier. Consider visiting later in the afternoon, when crowds disperse and more ice falls after the heat of the day.

There are no hiking trails here. A cafeteria sells sandwiches and snacks on-site, but it's better to bring a lunch. The weather is very changeable and can be windy, so bring layers.

Boat tours to other glaciers are also available; the most adventurous option is to take a tour with **Hielo y Aventura** (📞 02902-492094, 02902-492205; www.hieloyaventura.com; Libertador 935) for optional glacier hiking or introductory ice climbing.

Río Gallegos

📞 02966 / POP 95,800

Hardly a destination for tourists, Río Gallegos is a coal-shipping, oil-refining and wool-raising hub. It's a busy port with few merits for travelers, though some of the continent's best fly-fishing is nearby. Traveler services are good, but most visitors zip through en route to El Calafate, Puerto Natales or Ushuaia.

🛏 Sleeping & Eating

Hostel Elcira HOSTEL $
(📞 02966-429856; Zuccarino 431; dm/d US$10/22; 📶) An impeccable yet kitschy family home with friendly hosts. It's far from the town center but just a 10-minute walk from the bus terminal.

★ La Lechuza ARGENTINE $$
(📞 02966-425421; Sarmiento 134; mains AR$220-350; ⏰ 11:30am-4pm & 8pm-midnight) This chic pizzeria and restaurant that first found success in El Calafate is hands down the most ambient eatery in Río Gallegos. The room is low-lit, with walls sheathed in old newspapers and wine crates. There's an encyclopedic list of pizzas, including spinach, caprese

and Patagonian lamb and mushroom. It also offers wines and other liquor.

❶ Information

Municipal Tourist Office (☎02966-436920; www.turismo.riogallegos.gov.ar; Av Beccar 126; ⊗7am-9pm Mon-Fri, 8am-2pm & 4-8pm Sat & Sun) Helpful office outside the downtown area. A desk at the bus terminal keeps sporadic hours.

Provincial Tourist Office (☎02966-437412; www.santacruzpatagonia.gob.ar; Av Kirchner 863; ⊗9am-3pm Mon-Fri) Most helpful, with maps, bilingual staff and detailed info.

❶ Getting There & Away

The **airport** (☎02966-442340; RN 3, Km8) is 7km from the center (a taxi costs AR$90). **Aerolíneas Argentinas** (☎0810-2228-6527; Av San Martín 545; ⊗9:30am-5:30pm Mon-Fri), **LADE** (☎02966-422316; www.lade.com.ar; Fagnano 53; ⊗8am-3pm Mon-Fri) and **LATAM** (☎02966-457189; www.latam.com) operate services.

The bus terminal is about 3km southwest of the city center. Destinations include El Calafate (AR$580 to AR$680, four hours), Ushuaia (AR$1300, 12 hours), Comodoro Rivadavia (AR$1375 to AR$1568, nine to 11 hours), Río Grande (AR$910, eight to 10 hours) and Buenos Aires (AR$2750, 36 to 40 hours). Buses to Punta Arenas, Chile (AR$540, five to six hours), run only twice weekly; try to buy your ticket in advance.

TIERRA DEL FUEGO

The southernmost extreme of the Americas, this windswept archipelago is alluring as it is moody – at turns beautiful, ancient and strange. Travelers who first came for the ends-of-the-earth novelty discovered a destination that's far more complex than just these bragging rights. Intrigue still remains in a past storied with shipwrecks, native peoples and failed missions. In Tierra del Fuego, nature is writ bold and reckless,

Tierra del Fuego

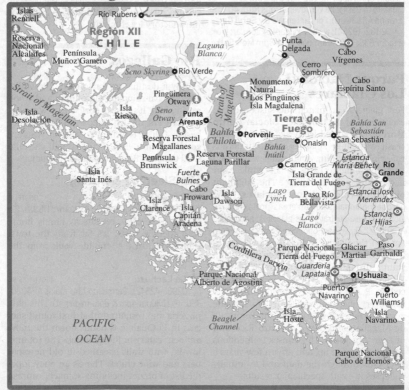

from the scoured plains, rusted peat bogs and mossy lenga forests to the snowy ranges above the Beagle Channel. Shared with Chile, this archipelago features one large island, Isla Grande, Chile's Isla Navarino and many smaller uninhabited ones.

In 1520 Magellan paid a visit while seeking passage to the Asian spice islands. Passing ships named Tierra del Fuego for the distant shoreline campfires that they spotted. Native inhabitants were Ona (or Selk'nam) and Haush, who hunted land animals, and fishing tribes Yámana and Alacalufe. The early 1800s, however, brought on European settlement – and the untimely demise of these indigenous peoples.

Ushuaia

02901 / POP 57,000

A busy port and adventure hub, Ushuaia is a sliver of steep streets and jumbled buildings below the snowcapped Martial Range.

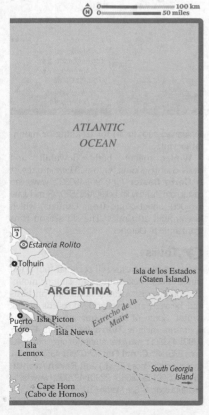

Here the Andes meet the southern ocean in a sharp skid, making way for the city before reaching a sea of lapping currents.

It's a location matched by few, and chest-beating Ushuaia takes full advantage of its end-of-the-world status as an increasing number of Antarctica-bound vessels call in to port. Its endless mercantile hustle knows no irony: the souvenir shop named for Jimmy Button (a native kidnapped for show in England), the ski center named for a destructive invasive species…you get the idea. That said, with a pint of the world's southernmost microbrew in hand, you can happily plot the dazzling outdoor options: hiking, sailing, skiing, kayaking and even scuba diving are just minutes from town.

⊙ Sights & Activities

The small but good **Museo del Fin del Mundo** (02901-4218603; https://mfm.tierradelfuego. gov.ar; cnr Av Maipú & Rivadavia; admission AR$200; 10am-7pm Nov-Mar, 10am-5pm Mon-Fri, 1-5pm Sat Apr-Oct) explains Ushuaia's indigenous and natural histories; check out the bone implements and bird taxidermy room. It has a nearby annex in a historical building at Av Maipú 465. The intriguing **Museo Marítimo & Museo del Presidio** (02901-437481; www. museomaritimo.com; cnr Yaganes & Gobernador Paz; adult/student/family AR$600/450/1350; 10am-8pm Mar-Dec, 9am-8pm Jan & Feb) is located in an old prison that held up to 700 inmates in 380 small jail cells. There are interesting exhibits on expeditions to Antarctica, plus stuffed penguins and an art gallery.

After seeing the Glaciar Perito Moreno in El Calafate, the **Glaciar Martial** here will seem like a piddly ice cube – but at least it's located in a beautiful valley with great views of Ushuaia and the Beagle Channel. Walk or shuttle to the base 7km northwest of town; from here it's about two hours' walk up to the glacier. There's a teahouse serving snacks and **canopy tours** (02901-503767; www.canopyushuaia. com.ar; Refugio de Montaña, Cerro Martial; long/short route AR$720/540; 10am-5pm Oct-Jun).

Hop on a **boat tour** to *estancias,* a lighthouse, Puerto Williams, bird island and sea lion or penguin colonies. Ask about the size of the boat and its covered shelter area, whether there are bilingual guides and if there are any landings; only **Piratour** (02901-15-604646, 02901-435557; www. piratour.net; Av San Martín 847; penguin-colony tour AR$2500, plus port fee AR$20; 9am-9pm) actually lands at the penguin colony, which

Ushuaia

ARGENTINA USHUAIA

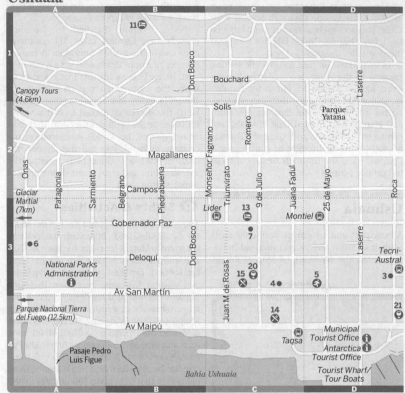

is active October through March. Tours run around AR$900; tickets are available at the pier, travel agencies and hotels.

Founded by missionary Thomas Bridges and located 85km east of Ushuaia, **Estancia Harberton** (✆ Skype estanciaharberton. turismo; www.estanciaharberton.com; entrance adult/child AR$240/free, dm US$50, s/d incl full board & activities US$325/580; ⊙10am-7pm Oct 15-Apr 15) was Tierra del Fuego's first *estancia*. This 200-sq-km ranch boasts splendid scenery and alluring history. There's a good museum, and you can take an optional boat trip to the area's penguin colony. Get here by taxi, rental car or boat tour. Overnight stays are possible.

Hiking and trekking opportunities aren't limited to the national park: the entire range behind Ushuaia, with its lakes and rivers, is a natural wonderland. Trails are poorly marked; you can hire a guide from **Compañía de Guías** (✆02901-437753; http://

companiadeguias.tur.ar) for trekking or mountaineering.

Winter offers both downhill and cross-country skiing options. The main resort is **Cerro Castor** (✆02901-499301; www.cerro castor.com; full-day lift ticket AR$1590; ⊙mid-Jun–mid-Oct), about 27km from Ushuaia, which has around 20 slopes. The ski season runs from June to October.

☞ Tours

Many travel agencies sell regional tours. You can go horseback riding, canoeing or mountain biking, visit nearby lakes, spy on birds and beavers, and even ride dogsleds during winter. Some of the better adventure tour operators include **Tierra** (✆02901-15-486886, 02901-433800; www.tierraturismo.com; office 4C, Onas 235) ✆, **Canal Fun** (✆02901-435777; www. canalfun.com; Roca 136; ⊛) and **Rayen Aventura** (✆02901-15-580517, 02901-437005; www.rayen aventura.com; Av San Martín 611).

0 ———— 200 m
0 ———— 0.1 miles

Ushuaia

◎ Sights

✪ Activities, Courses & Tours

🛏 Sleeping

✗ Eating

🍷 Drinking & Nightlife

bathroom might be on another floor. There's a fine backyard patio, though indoor shared spaces are scant. Discounts are given for stays longer than four nights.

Torre al Sur HOSTEL $
(📞02901-430745; Gobernador Paz 855; dm/d US$18/45; 🛜) The sister hostel to Cruz del Sur (p183) may not seem like much on the outside, but inside there's a welcoming, organized ambience, with colorful rooms, renovated bathrooms and a well-stocked kitchen. Marisa is the warm host.

Los Cormoranes HOSTEL $
(📞02901-423459; www.loscormoranes.com; Kamshen 788; dm US$23-28, d/tr US$70/110; @🛜) This friendly, mellow HI hostel is a 10-minute (uphill) walk north of downtown. Six-bed dorms, some with private bathrooms, have radiant-heated floors and face outdoor plank hallways. Doubles have polished-cement floors and down duvets – the best is room 10, with bay views. Linens could use an update, and common spaces are so-so. Breakfast includes DIY eggs and fresh-squeezed OJ.

🛏 Sleeping

Reservations are a good idea in December and January.

★ Antarctica Hostel HOSTEL $
(📞02901-435774; www.antarcticahostel.com; Antártida Argentina 270; dm US$20, d with/without bathroom US$75/55; @🛜) This friendly backpacker hub delivers with a warm atmosphere and helpful staff. The open floor plan and beer on tap are plainly conducive to making friends. Guests lounge and play cards in the common room and cook in a cool balcony kitchen. Cement rooms are clean and ample, with radiant floor heating.

Hostel Cruz del Sur HOSTEL $
(📞02901-434099; Deloquí 242; dm US$16; @🛜) This easygoing, organized hostel comprises two renovated houses (1920 and 1926), painted tangerine and joined by a passageway. Dorm prices are based on room capacity, the only disadvantage being that your

FUEGIAN FINE DINING

Creating quite a stir, tiny **Kalma Resto** (📞 02901-425786; www.kalmaresto.com.ar; Valdéz 293; ⏱ 7-11pm Mon-Sat) presents Fuegian staples like crab and octopus in a creative new context. Black sea bass wears a tart tomato sauce for contrast; there's stuffed lamb seasoned with pepper and rosemary; and the summer greens and edible flowers come fresh from the garden. It's gourmet at its least pretentious. Service is stellar, with young chef Jorge Monopoli making the rounds of the few black-linen tables.

★**Galeazzi-Basily B&B**　B&B $$
(📞 02901-423213; www.avesdelsur.com.ar; Valdéz 323; s/d without bathroom US$53/75, 4-person cabins US$140; @ 📶) The best feature of this elegant wooded residence is its warm, hospitable family of owners, who will make you feel right at home. Rooms are small but offer a personal touch. Since beds are twin-size, couples may prefer a modern cabin out the back. It's a peaceful spot, and where else can you practice your English, French, Italian and Portuguese?

Mysten Kepen　GUESTHOUSE $$
(📞 02901-15-497391, 02901-430156; http://mystenkepen.blogspot.com; Rivadavia 826; r from US$65; 📶) If you want an authentic Argentine family experience, this is it. Hosts Roberto and Rosario's immaculate two-kid home feels busy and lived in – in a good way. Rooms have newish installations, bright corduroy duvets and handy shelving for nighttime reading. Airport transfers and winter discounts are available.

✗ Eating & Drinking

★**Almacen Ramos Generales**　CAFE $
(📞 02901-424-7317; Av Maipú 749; mains AR$125-335; ⏱ 9am-midnight) With its quirky memorabilia and postings about local environmental issues, this warm and cozy former general store is a peek inside the real Ushuaia. Locals hold their powwows here. Croissants and crusty baguettes are baked daily. There's also local beer on tap, a wine list and light fare such as sandwiches, soups and quiche.

Freddo　ICE CREAM $
(Av San Martín 209; cone AR$65; ⏱ 9:30am-12:30am) One of Argentina's most-loved gela-

to shops has opened its doors in snowbound Ushuaia – and suddenly it's summer.

Cafe Bar Banana　CAFE $
(📞 02901-435035; www.facebook.com/bananaushuaia; Av San Martín 273; mains AR$150-225; ⏱ 8am-1am) Serving homemade burgers and fries, sandwiches, and steak and eggs, this is a local favorite for high-octane, low-cost dining with friends.

Bodegón Fueguino　PATAGONIAN $$
(📞 02901-431972; www.tierradehumos.com/es/bodegon-fueguino-restaurante; Av San Martín 859; mains AR$180-250; ⏱ noon-2:45pm & 8-11:45pm Tue-Sun) The spot to sample hearty home-style Patagonian fare or gather for wine and appetizers. Painted peach, this century-old Fuegian home is cozied up with sheepskin-clad benches, cedar barrels and ferns. A *picada* (shared appetizer plate) for two includes eggplant, lamb brochettes, crab and bacon-wrapped plums.

Volver　SEAFOOD $$$
(📞 02901-423977; www.facebook.com/restovolverushuaia; Av Maipú 37; mains from AR$290, tasting menu US$100; ⏱ noon-3pm & 7pm-midnight Tue-Sun) Self-promoted as serving up *ceviche de la puta madre* (politely translated as 'fantastic seafood'), this place is run by a charismatic chef loved by locals. The food is served simply but is of incredible quality. Those who think they don't like king crab should give it a second chance here: there are no added sauces and the crab is cooked to perfection.

Dublin Irish Pub　IRISH PUB
(📞 02901-430744; 9 de Julio 168; ⏱ 7pm-4am) Dublin doesn't feel so far away at this dimly lit pub. Popular with the locals, it's the scene of lively banter and free-flowing drinks. Look out for occasional live music and be sure to try at least one of its three local Beagle beers. Arrive by 9pm if you want to score a seat.

Viagro　BAR
(📞 02901-421617; www.facebook.com/viagropub; Roca 55; ⏱ 8pm-4am Tue-Sun) If you can get past the unfortunate name, this cocktail nook is the perfect low-lit rendezvous spot, with exotic concoctions and appetizing tapas to fuel your night out. There's dancing on Saturday nights.

ℹ Information

Municipal Tourist Office (📞 02901-437666; www.turismoushuaia.com; Prefectura Naval 470; ⏱ 8am-9pm) Very helpful, with English- and

BEYOND THE EDGE OF THE WORLD: ANTARCTICA

A trip to awe-inspiring Antarctica is a once-in-a-lifetime adventure. It's expensive but worth every penny, and so much more than just a continent to tick off your list. The land and ice shelves pile hundreds of meters thick with kilometers of undulating, untouched snow, while countless glaciers drape down mountainsides. Icebergs loom like tall buildings and come in shapes you didn't think possible. The wildlife is magnificent; you'll see thousands of curious penguins and a wide variety of flying birds, seals and whales.

For the average person, cruising is the easiest and best way to visit the White Continent. The season runs from November through March; peak-season voyages often get sold out. Last-minute tickets might be available later in the season, but sailings on reasonably small ships (fewer than 100 passengers) will still cost at least US$5000. Regular tickets start from around US$7000. Ask how many days you will actually spend in Antarctica – crossing the Southern Ocean takes up to two days each way – and how many landings will be included. The smaller the ship, the more landings per passenger (depending on the weather).

Thanks to its proximity to the Antarctic peninsula (1000km), most cruises leave from Ushuaia. Last-minute bookings can be made through **Freestyle Adventure Travel** (☑02901-609792, 02901-606661; www.freestyleadventuretravel.com; Gobernador Paz 866), a 1% for the Planet member that also offers discount Cape Horn trips, and **Ushuaia Turismo** (☑02901-436003; www.ushuaiaturismoevt.com.ar; Gobernador Paz 865). Other agencies offering packages include **Rumbo Sur** (☑02901-421139; www.rumbosur.com.ar; Av San Martín 350; ☺9am-7pm Mon-Fri), **All Patagonia** (☑02901-433622; www.allpatagonia.com; Juana Fadul 48; ☺10am-7pm Mon-Fri, to 1pm Sat) and Canal Fun (p182).

Check that your company is a member of **IAATO** (www.iaato.org), which has strict guidelines for responsible travel to Antarctica. For basic info in Ushuaia, visit the very helpful **Antarctica Tourist Office** (☑02901-430015; www.tierradelfuego.org.ar/antartida; Av Maipú 505; ☺with ship in port 9am-5pm) at the pier.

Lonely Planet's *Antarctica* guidebook is an indispensable guide to the region's history and wildlife.

French-speaking staff, a message board and multilingual brochures, as well as good lodging, activities and transport info. It also posts a list of available lodgings outside after closing time. There's a second office at the airport.
National Parks Administration (☑02901-421315; Av San Martín 1395; ☺9am-5pm Mon-Fri) Offers information on Parque Nacional Tierra del Fuego.

❶ Getting There & Around

In January and February, book your passage in and out of Ushuaia in advance.

Ushuaia's airport is 4km south of the center; a taxi costs AR$120. **Aerolíneas Argentinas** (☑0810-2228-6527; www.aerolineas.com.ar; cnr Av Maipú & 9 de Julio; 9:30am-5:30pm Mon-Fri) and **LADE** (☑02901-421123, in Buenos Aires 011-5353-2387; www.lade.com.ar; Av San Martín 542) have offices; LATAM sells tickets through travel agencies.

Ushuaia does not have a bus terminal, but the tourist office can help with transport options. **Taqsa** (☑02901-435453; www.taqsa.com.ar; Juana Fadul 126) and **Tecni-Austral** (☑02901-431408; Roca 157) have daily services to Río Grande (AR$330, 3½ hours) and Río Gallegos (AR$1300, 13 hours); both also go to Punta Arenas (AR$1427, 12 hours) a few times weekly. **Lider** (☑02901-436421, 02901-442264; Gobernador Paz 921) and **Montiel** (Transporte Montiel; ☑02901-421366; https://transporte-montiel-rio-grande.negocio.site; Gobernador Paz 605) head to Río Grande up to eight times daily. You can connect to Puerto Natales via Río Gallegos or Punta Arenas.

Taxis around town are available. Rental cars cost around AR$1800 per day with 200km free.

Parque Nacional Tierra Del Fuego

West of Ushuaia 12km lies beautiful **Parque Nacional Tierra del Fuego** (www.parquesnacionales.gob.ar; adult/child AR$420/70), which extends from the Beagle Channel in the south to beyond Lago Fagnano in the north. Only a small part of the park is accessible to the public, and despite a tiny system of short trails, the views along the bays, rivers and forests are wonderfully scenic. Keep your eyes peeled for *cauquén* (upland geese), cormorants and grebes. Commonly seen European rabbit and

North American beaver are introduced species that have wreaked havoc on the ecosystem. Foxes and the occasional guanaco might visit, while marine mammals are most common on offshore islands.

For information on the park's walks, get a map from the tourist office or National Parks Office in Ushuaia. There's also a nice **visitors center** (⊘ 9am-7pm, shorter hours Mar-Nov) in the park.

Minibuses to the park (AR$300 round-trip) leave hourly from the corner of Av Maipú and Fadul (9am to 6pm daily). For groups, taxis are cheaper. You can also take the **El Tren del Fin del Mundo** (☏ 02901-431600; www.tren delfindelmundo.com.ar; adult/child AR$1000/650) narrow-gauge steam train (first, taxi to the train station, 8km west of Ushuaia).

UNDERSTAND ARGENTINA

Argentina Today

In December 2015 Mauricio Macri, Buenos Aires' mayor since 2007, took over Argentina's presidency. In a surprising run-off election he beat the outgoing Cristina Kirchner's preferred candidate, Daniel Scioli, ending 12 years of Peronist-run government. Macri promised drastic economic changes, and he immediately started implementing them: currency controls over foreign currencies were abolished (essentially ending the 'blue market' for US dollars), export taxes were lowered to boost agricultural trade and thousands of redundant public sector jobs were eliminated.

His idea is to encourage economic growth and foreign investment (again) while reducing Argentina's immense deficit and, eventually, its unsustainable inflation rate. It's quite a difference from Kirchner's practices, which implemented heavy state intervention and used the country's central bank reserves to artificially prop up the peso. But within three years, a rapid fall in value of the peso against the dollar, along with a spike in utility prices (which had been previously heavily subsidized), led many Argentinians to feel the pinch. And considering the country has been through these cycles many times before, they had no choice but to take a ride on Argentina's economic roller coaster once again.

History

The Good Old Days

Before the Spanish hit the scene, nomadic hunter-gatherers roamed the wilds of ancient Argentina. The Yámana (or Yahgan) gathered shellfish in Patagonia, while on the pampas the Querandí used *boleadoras* (weights on cords) to snag rhea (ostrich-like birds) and guanaco (the llama's cousin). Up in the subtropical northeast, the Guaraní settled down long enough to cultivate maize, while in the arid northwest the Diaguita developed an irrigation system for crops.

In 1536 the Querandí were unfortunate enough to meet pushy Spaniards in search of silver. They eventually drove the colonists away to more welcoming Paraguay. (Left behind were cattle and horses, which multiplied and gave rise to the legendary *gaucho*). The Spanish were persistent, however, and in 1580 they returned and managed to establish Buenos Aires, though trade restrictions from Spain limited the new settlement's growth. The northern colonies of Tucumán, Córdoba and Salta, however, thrived by providing mules, cloth and foodstuffs for the booming silver mines of Bolivia. Meanwhile, Spaniards from Chile moved into the Andean Cuyo region, which produced wine and grain.

Cutting the Purse Strings

In 1776 Spain designated the bootlegger township of Buenos Aires as 'capital of the new viceroyalty of the Río de la Plata,' a nod to its strategic port location. A rogue British force, hoping to snag a piece of the trade pie, invaded in 1806 but was given the boot soon after. With newfound power, the confident colonists revolted against Spain; complete independence was their reward six years later in 1816.

Despite this unity, the provinces resisted Buenos Aires' authority. Argentina split allegiances between the inhabitants of Buenos Aires (Unitarists) and the country folk (Federalists). A civil war ensued, and the bloody, vindictive conflicts nearly exhausted the country.

In 1829 Juan Manuel de Rosas came into power as a Federalist, but applied his own brand of Unitarist principles to centralize control in Buenos Aires. He built a large army, created the *mazorca* (a ruthless secret police) and forced overseas trade through the port city. Finally, in 1852, Justo José de Urquiza led a Unitarist army that forced the dictator from power. Urquiza drew up a constitution and became Argentina's first president.

The Fleeting Golden Age

Argentina's new laws opened up the country to foreign investment, trade and immigration. In the following decades, sheep, cattle and cereal products were freely exported, while Spanish, Italian, French and other European immigrants came in search of a better life. Prosperity arrived at last, and Argentina became one of the richest countries in the world in the early 20th century.

The prosperity was tenuous, however, as global economic fluctuations brought about new international trade restrictions. After the 1880s poor immigrants continued flooding into the city, nearly doubling Buenos Aires' population to one million. The industrial sector couldn't absorb all the immigrants and their needs, and the gap between rich and poor widened. In 1929 the military took power from an ineffectual civilian government, but an obscure colonel – Juan Domingo Perón – was the first leader to really confront the looming social crisis.

The Peróns: Love 'em or Hate 'em

Today the Peróns have become Argentina's most revered – as well as most despised – political figures. Many people believe that Argentina never recovered, either economically or spiritually, following Perón's first presidency.

From a minor post in the labor ministry, and with the help of his charismatic soon-to-be wife, Eva Duarte (Evita), Juan Perón won the presidency in 1946. His social welfare and new economic order programs helped the working class, but his heavy control over the country was tinged with fascism: he abused his presidential powers by using excessive intimidation and suppressing free press. Dynamic Evita, meanwhile, had her own sometimes vindictive political ends, though she was mostly championed for her charitable work and women's rights campaigns.

Rising inflation and economic difficulties undermined Perón's second presidency in 1952; Evita's death the same year was another blow. After a coup against him in 1955, Perón retreated to Spain to plot his return. The opportunity came almost two decades later when Héctor Cámpora resigned the presidency in 1973. Perón won the elections easily, but his death in mid-1974 sucked the country back into the governmental coups and chaos that had plagued it since his exile. In 1976 military rule prevailed once again, and Argentina entered its darkest hour.

Dirty War (1976–83)

In the late 1960s, when antigovernment sentiment was rife, a left-wing, highly organized Peronist guerrilla group called the Montoneros was formed. The educated, middle-class youths bombed foreign businesses, kidnapped executives for ransom and robbed banks to finance their armed struggle and spread their social messages. On March 24, 1976, a bloodless military coup led by General Jorge Videla took control of the Argentine government and ushered in a period of terror and brutality. Euphemistically called the Process of National Reorganization (El Proceso), this movement began a period of state-sponsored violence and anarchy, and the primary target was the Montoneros.

Some estimate that up to 30,000 people died in the infamous Guerra Sucia (Dirty War). Zero tolerance was the theme: the dictatorship did not distinguish between revolutionary guerrillas or those who simply expressed reservations about the dictatorship's indiscriminate brutality. To 'disappear' meant to be detained, tortured and probably killed, without legal process. Ironically, the Dirty War ended only when the Argentine military attempted a real military operation, the repossession of the Islas Malvinas (Falkland Islands).

Falklands War

Argentina's economy continued to decline during military rule and eventually collapsed into chaos. El Proceso was coming undone.

In late 1981 General Leopoldo Galtieri took the presidential hot seat. To stay in power amid a faltering economy, a desperate Galtieri played the nationalist card and launched an invasion in April 1982 to dislodge the British from the Falkland Islands (Islas Malvinas).

The brief occupation of the islands, claimed by Argentina for 150 years, unleashed a wave of nationalist euphoria that lasted about a week. Then the Argentines realized that ironclad British prime minister Margaret Thatcher was not a wallflower, especially when she had political troubles of her own. Britain fought back, sending a naval contingent to set things straight, and Argentina's ill-trained forces surrendered after 74 days. The military, stripped of its reputation, finally withdrew from government. In 1983 Argentina handed Raúl Alfonsín the presidency.

Crisis...

Alfonsín brought democracy back to Argentina and solved some territorial disputes with Chile. He also managed to curb inflation a bit, but couldn't pull the long-struggling country back onto its feet.

Carlos Menem, president from 1989 to 1999, brought brief prosperity to Argentina by selling off many private industries and borrowing heavily. He also practically stopped inflation in its tracks by pegging the peso with the US dollar, but this was only a quick fix. After a few years the peso became so overvalued that Argentine goods weren't competitive on the global market. Toward the end of Menem's rule unemployment spiraled steadily upward.

In 1999 Fernando de la Rúa was sworn into office. He inherited an almost bankrupt government, which witnessed yet another economic downturn, even higher unemployment and a widespread lack of public confidence. By 2001 the economy teetered on the brink of collapse, and in December De la Rúa resigned. The country went through three more presidents within two weeks before finally putting Eduardo Duhalde in charge. Duhalde devalued the peso in January 2002, defaulting on AR$140 billion in debt.

...And Comeback

After some instability, the peso settled to around three to the US dollar, which, due to Argentina's suddenly cheap exports, created a booming economy. In 2003 the left-leaning Néstor Kirchner was handed the presidential reins and became an immensely popular leader. He kept the economy growing strong, paid some of Argentina's debts to the IMF and curbed corruption to a degree. Argentina was living high and there was optimism in the air.

In 2007 Kirchner's term was up, but he wasn't through with politics. His wife, Cristina Fernández de Kirchner, ran for and won the nation's highest office, becoming Argentina's first elected woman president. And despite a rocky first tenure that included the occasional corruption scandal and a major tax-hike conflict, Cristina easily won re-election in 2011 – possibly helped by the sympathy she gained after her husband passed away from a sudden heart attack in 2010.

Cristina administered generous social programs and liberal same-sex marriage laws, and addressed abuses of the military dictatorship (1976–83). But her presidencies were also plagued by high inflation and economic instability and mass protests. Her eventual unpopularity cut short lofty ambitions to repeal the two-tenure presidential limit. Mauricio Macri was elected president in December 2015.

Culture

Lifestyle

A quarter of Argentines are considered to be living in poverty. To save resources and maintain family ties, several generations often live under one roof.

Families are pretty close, and Sunday is often reserved for the family *asado* (barbecue). Friends are also highly valued and Argentines love to go out in large groups. They'll give each other kisses on the cheek every time they meet – even introduced strangers, men and women alike, will get a kiss.

Argentines like to stay out *late*. Dinner is often at 10pm, and finishing dessert around midnight on a weekend is the norm. Bars and discos often stay open until 6am or so, even in smaller cities.

The important culture of maté is very visible in Argentina; you'll see folks sipping this bitter herb drink at home, work and play. They carry their gourds and hot-water thermoses while traveling and on picnics. Consider yourself honored if you're invited to partake in a maté-drinking ritual.

Population

About 92% of the country's population lives in urban areas. Argentina's literacy rate is over 98%.

Nineteenth-century immigration created a large population of Italians and Spanish, though many other European nationalities are represented. Newer mixes include Japanese, Koreans and Chinese (rarer outside the capital), and other South American nationalities, such as Peruvians, Bolivians, Paraguayans and Uruguayans.

Indigenous peoples make up less than 1% of Argentina's population, with the Mapuche of Patagonia being the largest group. Smaller groups of Guaraní, Tobas, Wichi and Tehuelche, among others, inhabit other northern pockets. Up to 15% of the country's population is *mestizo* (of mixed indigenous and Spanish descent); most *mestizo* reside up north.

Religion

Most of Argentina's population is Roman Catholic (the official state religion), with Protestants making up the second biggest group. Buenos Aires is home to one of the largest Jewish populations outside Israel, and also claims what is likely Latin America's largest mosque.

Spiritualism and veneration of the dead are widespread: visitors to Recoleta and Chacarita cemeteries in Buenos Aires will see pilgrims communing with icons like Juan and Evita Perón and Carlos Gardel. Cult beliefs like the Difunta Correa of San Juan province also attract hundreds of thousands of fans.

Arts

Literature

Argentina's biggest literary name is Jorge Luis Borges, famous for his short stories and poetry. Borges created alternative-reality worlds and elaborate time circles with vivid and imaginative style; check out his surreal compendiums *Labyrinths* or *Ficciones*. Internationally acclaimed Julio Cortázar wrote about seemingly normal people while using strange metaphors and whimsical descriptions of people's unseen realities. His big novel is *Hopscotch*, which requires more than one reading.

Ernesto Sábato is known for his intellectual novels and essays, many of which explore the chasm between good and evil. Sábato's notable works include *Sobre héroes y tumbas* (On Heroes and Tombs), popular with Argentine youth in the '60s, and the startling essay *Nunca más*, which describes Dirty War atrocities. Other famous Argentine writers include Manuel Puig *(Kiss of the Spider Woman)*, Adolfo Bioy Casares *(The Invention of Morel)*, Osvaldo Soriano *(Shadows)*, Roberto Arlt *(The Seven Madmen)* and Silvina Ocampo (poetry and children's stories).

Contemporary writers include Juan José Saer, who penned short stories and complex crime novels, and novelist and journalist Rodrigo Fresán, who wrote the best-selling *The History of Argentina* and the psychedelic *Kensington Gardens*. Ricardo Piglia

and Tomás Eloy Martínez are other distinguished Argentine writers who, in addition to their important works, have taught at prominent American universities.

Cinema

In the past, Argentine cinema has achieved international stature through such directors as Luis Puenzo (*The Official Story;* 1984) and Héctor Babenco (*Kiss of the Spider Woman;* 1985).

More recent notable works by Argentine directors include Fabián Bielinsky's witty *Nueve reinas* (Nine Queens; 2000), Juan José Campanella's *El hijo de la novia* (The Son of the Bride; 2001) – which got an Oscar nomination for Best Foreign Language Film – and Lucrecia Martel's sexual-awakening film *La niña santa* (The Holy Girl; 2004). Carlos Sorín's *Bombón el perro* (Bombón, the Dog; 2004) is a captivating tale of man's best friend and changing fortunes.

Pablo Trapero is one of Argentina's foremost filmmakers. Among his works are the comedy-drama *Familia rodante* (Rolling Family; 2004) and *The Clan*, which won the 2015 Silver Lion award at the Venice international Film Festival. Daniel Burman is another bright directoral star whose most recent effort is *El Misterio de la felicidad* (The Mystery of Happiness; 2015), a warm comedy. Burman also co-produced Walter Salles' Che Guevara–inspired *The Motorcycle Diaries* (2004).

Other noteworthy films include Damián Szifron's hilarious *Tiempo de valientes* (On Probation; 2005) and Lucía Puenzo's *XXY* (2007), the tale of a teenage hermaphrodite. Mariano Cohn and Gastón Duprat's *El hombre de al lado* (The Man Next Door; 2009) is an award-winning moral drama that screened at Sundance Film Festival. At the time of writing, Argentina's most recent Oscar-winning film is Campanella's crime thriller *El secreto de sus ojos* (The Secret in Their Eyes; 2009).

In 2013 Puenzo directed *Wakolda* (The German Doctor), a true story about the family who unknowingly lived with Josef Mengele during his exile in South America. Szifron's black comedy *Relatos salvajes* (Wild Tales; 2014) was Oscar-nominated for Best Foreign Language Film. Martel received critical acclaim for her 2017 film *Zama*, a haunting adaptation of Antonio di Benedetto's novel about a Spanish colonial administrator stranded on a remote outpost on the Río Paraguay.

Music

Legendary figures like Carlos Gardel and Astor Piazzolla popularized tango music, and contemporaries such as Susana Rinaldi, Adriana Varela and Osvaldo Pugliese carry on the tradition. Recent tango 'fusion' groups include Gotan Project, BajoFondo Tango Club and Tanghetto.

Folk musicians Mercedes Sosa, Leon Gieco, Horacio Guarany, Atahualpa Yupanqui and Los Chalchaleros have been very influential in the evolution of Argentine *folklórica*, as have Mariana Baraj and Soledad Pastorutti.

Rock stars Charly García, Gustavo Cerati, Andrés Calamaro, Luis Alberto Spinetta and Fito Páez are some of Argentina's best-known musicians, while popular groups have included Soda Stereo, Sumo and Los Pericos.

Contemporary Argentine musical artists include wacky Bersuit Vergarabat, alternative Catupecu Machu, versatile Gazpacho and the multitalented Kevin Johansen.

Heavyweights in DJ-based club music scene include Aldo Haydar (progressive house), Bad Boy Orange (drum 'n' bass), Diego Ro-K ('the Maradona of Argentine DJs') and Gustavo Lamas (blending ambient pop and electro house). Award-winning Hernán Cattáneo has played at Burning Man.

Córdoba's edgy *cuarteto* is Argentina's original pop music, while coarse *cumbia villera* was born in shantytowns and fuses cumbia with gangsta rap, reggae and punk. Finally, *murga* is a form of athletic musical theater composed of actors and percussionists; they often perform at Carnaval.

Cuisine

Food

As a whole, Argentina does not have a widely varied cuisine – most folks here seem to survive on meat, pasta and pizza – but the country's famous beef is often sublime. At a *parrilla* or *asado* you should try *bife de chorizo* (thick sirloin), *bife de lomo* (tenderloin) or a *parrillada*. Ask for *chimichurri*, a tasty sauce of garlic, parsley and olive oil. Steaks tend to come medium *(a punto)*, so if you want it rare, say *jugoso*.

The Italian influence is apparent in dishes like pizza, spaghetti, ravioli and chewy *ñoquis* (gnocchi). Vegetarian fare is available in Buenos Aires and other large cities. *Tenedores libres* (all-you-can-eat buffets) are popular and good value. Middle Eastern food is common in the north, while the northwest has spicy dishes like those of Bolivia or Peru. In Patagonia lamb is king, while specialties such as trout, boar and venison are served around the Lake District.

Confiterías usually grill sandwiches like *lomito* (steak), *milanesa* (a thin breaded steak) and hamburgers. *Restaurantes* have larger menus and professional waiters. Cafes usually serve alcohol and simple meals.

Large supermarkets often have a counter with good, cheap takeout. Western fast-food chains exist in larger cities.

Breakfast is usually a simple affair of coffee or tea with *tostadas* (toast), *manteca* (butter) and *mermelada* (jam). *Medialunas* (croissants) come either sweet or plain.

Empanadas are baked or fried turnovers with vegetables, beef, cheese or other fillings. *Sandwichitos de miga* (thin, crust-free sandwiches layered with ham and cheese) are great at teatime. Commonly sold at kiosks, *alfajores* are cookie sandwiches filled with *dulce de leche* (a thick milky caramel sauce) or *mermelada* and covered in chocolate.

Postres (desserts) include *ensalada de fruta* (fruit salad), pies and cakes, *facturas* (pastries) and flan, which can be topped with *crema* (whipped cream) or *dulce de leche*. Argentina's Italian-derived *helados* (ice cream) are South America's best.

The usual *propina* (tip) at restaurants is 10%. At fancier restaurants, a *cubierto* (a service charge separate from the tip) of a few pesos is often included in the bill to cover bread and 'use of utensils.'

Drinks
ALCOHOLIC DRINKS

Argentines like to drink (but not to excess), and you'll find lists of beer, wine, whiskey and gin at many cafes, restaurants and bars. Quilmes and Isenbeck are popular beers;

ask for *chopp* (draft or lager). Microbrews are widely available in the Lake District.

Some Argentine wines are world-class; both *tintos* (reds) and *blancos* (whites) are excellent, but malbecs are especially well-known. The major wine-producing areas are near Mendoza, San Juan, La Rioja and Salta.

Argentina's legal drinking age is 18.

NONALCOHOLIC DRINKS

Soft drinks are everywhere. For water, there's *con gas* (carbonated) or *sin gas* (noncarbonated) mineral water. Or ask for Argentina's usually drinkable *agua de canilla* (tap water). *Licuados* are water- or milk-blended fruit drinks.

Argentines love their coffee, and you can order several versions. A *café con leche* is half coffee and half milk, while a *cortado* is an espresso with a little milk. A *café chico* is an espresso.

Tea is commonplace. You shouldn't decline an invitation for grass-like maté, although it's definitely an acquired taste.

Sports

Rugby, tennis, basketball, polo, golf, motor racing, skiing and cycling are popular sports, but *fútbol* (soccer) is an obsession. The national team has twice won the World Cup, in 1978 and 1986. Today Lionel Messi is Argentina's biggest *fútbol* star.

The game between River Plate and Boca Juniors is a classic match not to be missed, as the rivalry between the two Buenos Aires teams is intense.

Environment

The Land

Argentina is huge – it's the world's eighth-largest country. It stretches some 3500km north to south and encompasses a wide range of environments and terrain.

The glorious Andes line the edge of northwest Argentina, where only hardy cacti and scrubby vegetation survive. Here, soaring peaks and salt lakes give way to the subtropical lowland provinces of Salta and Santiago del Estero. To the south, the hot and scenic Tucumán, Catamarca and La Rioja provinces harbor agriculture and viticulture.

Drier thornlands of the western Andean foothills give way to the forked river valleys and hot lowlands of Formosa and Chaco

provinces. Rainfall is heaviest to the northeast, where swampy forests and subtropical savannas thrive. Densely forested Misiones province contains the awe-inspiring Iguazú Falls. Rivers streaming off these immense cataracts lead to the alluvial grasslands of Corrientes and Entre Ríos provinces. Summers here are very hot and humid.

The west-central Cuyo region (Mendoza, San Juan and San Luis provinces) pumps out most of Argentina's world-class wine vintages. Central Argentina has mountainous Córdoba and richly agricultural Santa Fe provinces. The Pampas is a flat, rich plain full of agriculture and livestock. Along the Atlantic Coast are many popular and attractive beaches.

Patagonia spans the lower third of Argentina. Most of this region is flat and arid, but toward the Andes rainfall is abundant and supports the lush Lake District. The southern Andes boasts huge glaciers, while down on the flats cool steppes pasture large flocks of sheep.

The Tierra del Fuego archipelago mostly belongs to Chile. Its northern half resembles the Patagonian steppe, while dense forests and glaciers cover the mountainous southern half. The climate can be relatively mild, even in winter (though temperatures can also drop below freezing). The weather in this region is very changeable year-round.

Like several other countries, Argentina lays claim to a section of Antarctica.

Wildlife

The famous Pampas are mostly sprawling grasslands and home to many birds of prey and introduced plant species. The northern swamplands are home to the odd-looking capybara (the world's largest rodent), swamp deer, the alligator-like caiman and many large migratory birds.

The main forested areas of Argentina are in subtropical Misiones province and on the eastward-sloping Andes from Neuquén province south, where southern beech species and coniferous woodlands predominate; look for the strange monkey-puzzle tree (*Araucaria araucana* or *pehuén*) around the Lake District. In the higher altitudes of the Andes and in much of Patagonia, pasture grasses are sparse. Northern Andean saline lakes harbor pink flamingos, and on the Patagonian steppe you're likely to see guanacos, rheas, Patagonian hares, armadillos, crested caracaras and gray foxes. Pumas and condors live in the southern Andean foothills, but sightings are rare.

Coastal Patagonia, especially around Península Valdés, has dense and viewable concentrations of marine fauna, including southern right whales, sea lions, southern elephant seals, Magellanic penguins and orcas.

National Parks

Argentina has a good range of national and provincial parks. A wide variety of climates is represented, including swamps, deserts and rainforest. Highlights include giant trees, waterfalls and glaciers.

Some of Argentina's best parks include the following:

Parque Nacional Iguazú (p110) World-renowned for its waterfalls.

Parque Nacional Los Alerces (p165) Site of ancient *alerce* (false larch) forests.

Parque Nacional Los Glaciares (p179) Awesome for its glaciers and alpine towers.

Parque Nacional Nahuel Huapi (p162) Offers vivid alpine scenery.

Parque Nacional Tierra del Fuego (p185) Amazing beech forests and fauna.

Parque Provincial Aconcagua (p148) Boasts the continent's highest peak.

Reserva Faunística Península Valdés (p170) Famous for coastal fauna.

Reserva Provincial Esteros del Iberá Home to swamp-dwelling wildlife.

SURVIVAL GUIDE

ℹ️ Directory A–Z

ACCOMMODATIONS

There's an excellent range of affordable hostels throughout Argentina. Most hostels are friendly and offer tours and services. All include kitchen access and sheets; most have towel rental, internet access, free wi-fi, luggage storage, light breakfast and double rooms (book these ahead). Hostel organizations include Hostelling International

---

ℹ️ ELECTRONICS WARNING

Note that most electronic products are more expensive in Argentina and can be hard to get hold of. If you bring your smart phone, don't flash it around unnecessarily or leave it unprotected. The same goes for tablets and laptop computers.

(www.hihostels.com) and HoLa (www.holahostels.com); membership is not required to stay at any hostel, but members get around a 10% discount.

Residenciales are small hotels, while *hospedajes* or *casas de familia* are usually family homes with extra bedrooms and shared bathrooms. Hotels can range from one to five stars, and rooms usually come with private bathroom and a light breakfast (coffee, tea and bread or croissants). In Buenos Aires, apartment rentals are popular and can be a money-saver if you're staying a long time.

Camping is cheap and popular, though sites aren't always near the center of town. National parks usually have organized sites, and some offer distant *refugios* (basic shelters for trekkers).

Peak tourist months in Buenos Aires are November to January, when accommodation prices are at their highest. Patagonia is busiest during the summer (November to February), though ski resort towns fill up fast in July and August. Northern destinations and the Atlantic beach towns attract the most travelers in December and January (the latter are practically ghost towns the rest of the year). In peak season it's wise to make reservations ahead of time.

ACTIVITIES

Argentina has plenty for the adventure-seeking traveler. A multitude of beautiful national parks offer awesome summer hiking and trekking, especially around Bariloche and Patagonia's Fitz Roy range. For the highest peak outside Asia there's lofty Aconcagua, at 6962m.

Skiing is world-class, with major resorts at Cerro Catedral, near Bariloche; Las Leñas, near Malargüe; Los Penitentes; and Chapelco, near San Martín de los Andes. The ski season runs from about mid-June to mid-October. In summer, these mountains turn into activity centers for mountain biking.

Cycling is a popular activity in Mendoza, the Andean northwest, the Lake District and Patagonia (where winds are fierce!). Mountain bikes are best for pedaling the sometimes remote and bad roads, many of which are gravel. Many tourist cities have bike rentals, though the quality is not up to Western standards.

The Lake District and Patagonia have some of the world's best fly-fishing, with introduced trout and landlocked Atlantic salmon reaching epic proportions. The season in these areas runs from November to mid-April. It's almost always catch-and-release.

Whitewater rafting can be enjoyed near Mendoza (as well as in the Lake District) and horseback riding and paragliding are popular in many tourist areas.

ELECTRICITY

Argentina's electric current operates on 220V, 50Hz. Most plugs are either two rounded prongs (as in Europe) or three angled flat prongs (as in Australia).

EMBASSIES & CONSULATES

Australian embassy (☑ 011-4779-3500; www.argentina.embassy.gov.au; Villanueva 1400; ⊙8:30am-5pm Mon-Fri; Ⓢ Línea D Olleros)

Bolivian embassy (☑ 011-4394-1463; www.embajadadebolivia.com.ar; Av Corrientes 545; ⊙9:30am-5:30pm Mon-Fri; Ⓢ Línea B Florida); **La Quiaca consulate** (☑ 03885-422283; www.consuladoboliviano.com.ar; 9 de Julio 109; ⊙7am-6:30pm Mon-Fri); **Salta consulate** (☑ 0387-421-1040; www.embajadadebolivia.com.ar; Boedo 34; ⊙8am-1pm Mon-Fri); **San Salvador de Jujuy consulate** (☑ 0388-424-0501; www.consuladobolivia.com.ar; Ramírez de Velasco 145; ⊙8:30am-2pm & 5-8pm Mon-Fri)

Brazilian embassy (☑ 011-5246-7400; http://buenosaires.itamaraty.gov.br; Cerrito 1350; ⊙9am-6pm Mon-Fri; Ⓢ Línea C San Martín); **Paco de Los Libres consulate** (☑ 03772-425444; Mitre 894; ⊙8am-1pm); **Puerto Iguazú consulate** (☑ 03757-420192; https://scedv.serpro.gov.br; Córdoba 278; ⊙visas 8am-1:30pm Mon-Fri)

Canadian embassy (☑ 011-4808-1000; www.embassy-canada.com; Tagle 2828; ⊙8:30am-12:30pm & 1:30-5:30pm Mon-Thu, 8:30am-2pm Fri; 🚌130, 62, 33)

Chilean embassy (☑ 011-4808-8601; www.chile.gob.cl/argentina; Tagle 2762; ⊙9am-1pm & 2-5pm Mon-Fri; Ⓢ Línea H Las Heras); **Bariloche consulate** (☑ 0294-443-1680; https://chile.gob.cl/bariloche; España 275; ⊙9am-2pm Mon-Fri); **Esquel consulate** (☑ 02945-451189; Molinari 754; ⊙ by appointment); **Mendoza consulate** (☑ 0261-425-5024; www.chile.gob.cl; Belgrano 1080); **Neuquén consulate** (☑ 0299-442-2447; La Rioja 241; ⊙8am-1pm Mon-Fri); **Río Gallegos consulate** (☑ 02966-422364; Moreno 148; ⊙8am-1pm Mon-Fri); **Salta consulate** (☑ 0387-421-5757; https://chile.gob.cl/salta; Santiago de Estero 965; ⊙9am-1pm Mon-Fri); **Ushuaia consulate** (☑ 02901-430909; Jainén 50)

Dutch embassy (☑ 011-4338-0060; www.paisesbajosytu.nl/su-pais-y-los-paises-bajos; Olga Cossettini 831, 3rd fl; ⊙9am-5pm Mon-Thu, to 1pm Fri; Ⓢ Línea B Alem)

French embassy (☑ 011-4515-7030; www.embafrancia-argentina.org; Cerrito 1399; ⊙9am-noon Mon-Fri; Ⓢ Línea C San Martín)

German embassy (☑ 011-4778-2500; www.buenosaires.diplo.de; Villanueva 1055; ⊙8-11am Mon-Fri; Ⓢ Línea D Olleros)

New Zealand embassy (☑ 011-5070-0700; www.nzembassy.com/argentina; Carlos Pellegrini 1427, 5th fl; ⊙9am-5pm Mon-Fri; Ⓢ Línea C San Martín)

UK embassy (☑ 011-4808-2200; www.ukinargentina.fco.gov.uk; Dr Luis Agote 2412; ⊙9am-1pm Mon-Fri; 🚌63, 130, 93)

US embassy (☑ 011-5777-4533; https://ar.usembassy.gov; Colombia 4300; ⊙9am-5:30pm Mon-Fri; Ⓢ Línea D Plaza Italia)

FOOD

The following price ranges refer to a standard main course.

$ less than AR$220

$$ AR$220–AR$350

$$$ more than AR$350

HEALTH

Argentina requires no vaccinations. In 2017 there was a dengue outbreak in Misiones and Formosa provinces. Dengue usually causes flu-like symptoms, including fever, muscle aches, joint pains, headaches, nausea and vomiting, often followed by a rash. The body aches may be quite uncomfortable, but most cases resolve in a few days.

In the high Andes, watch for signs of altitude sickness and use more sunscreen. For more information see http://wwwnc.cdc.gov/travel/destinations/argentina.htm.

Urban water supplies are usually potable, making salads and ice safe to consume. Many prescription drugs are available over the counter. Seek out an embassy recommendation if you need serious Western-type medical services.

INTERNET ACCESS

➡ Wi-fi is available at many (if not most) hotels and cafes, restaurants and airports, and it's generally good and free.

➡ Internet cafes and *locutorios* (telephone centers) with very affordable internet access can be found in practically all Argentine towns and cities.

➡ To find the @ *(arroba)* symbol on keyboards, try holding down the Alt key and typing 64, or typing AltGr-2. You can also ask the attendant *'¿Cómo se hace la arroba?'* ('How do you make the @ sign?').

> ### SLEEPING PRICE RANGES
>
> The following price ranges refer to the cost of a double room during high season. Unless otherwise stated, double rooms include bathroom, and breakfast is included in the price.
>
> **$** less than US$75
>
> **$$** US$75–US$150
>
> **$$$** more than US$150
>
> Many hotels take payment in US dollars and may also change them at a rate close to the official.

TWO-TIER COSTS IN ARGENTINA

A few upscale hotels, some museums and tango shows, most national parks and one major airline have adopted a two-tier price system. Rates for foreigners can be double (or more) the local prices.

➔ In remote spots like El Chaltén and other parts of Patagonia wi-fi may be uniformly poor.

LANGUAGE

Besides flamboyance, the unique pronunciation of *castellano* – Argentina's Italian-accented version of the Spanish language – readily identifies an Argentine elsewhere in Latin America or abroad. In Buenos Aires you'll also hear *lunfardo*, the capital's colorful slang.

Quechua speakers, numerous in the northwest, tend to be bilingual in Spanish. Many Mapuche speakers live in the southern Andes, while most Guaraní speakers live in northeastern Argentina.

Argentina is a good destination in which to learn Spanish, and there are dozens of schools (and private instructors) to choose from in Buenos Aires. Other large cities, such as Bariloche, Mendoza and Córdoba, also have Spanish schools.

LEGAL MATTERS

Police can demand identification at any moment and for whatever reason, though it's unlikely to happen. Always carry photo ID or a copy of your passport, and – most importantly – *always* be courteous and cooperative.

Drugs and most other substances that are illegal in the US and many European countries are also illegal here, though marijuana has been somewhat decriminalized in Argentina (and is legal in Uruguay).

If arrested, you have the constitutional right to a lawyer, to a telephone call and to remain silent (beyond giving your name, nationality, age and passport number). Don't sign anything until you speak to a lawyer. If you don't speak Spanish, a translator should be provided for you.

LGBT TRAVELERS

In 2010 Argentina was the first country in Latin America to legalize same-sex marriage. The country has become increasingly gay-friendly over recent years. Buenos Aires is one of the world's top gay destinations – with dedicated hotels and B&Bs, bars and nightclubs. The capital is home to South America's largest annual gay pride parade.

Although Buenos Aires (and, to a lesser extent, Argentina's other large cities) is becoming increasingly tolerant, most of the rest of Argentina still feels uncomfortable with homosexuality. Homophobia rarely takes the form of physical violence, however, and gay people regularly travel throughout the country to return home with nothing but praise.

When it comes to public affection, Argentine men are more physically demonstrative than their North American and European counterparts. Behaviors such as kissing on the cheek in greeting or a vigorous embrace are innocuous even to those who express unease with homosexuality. Lesbians walking hand in hand should attract little attention, since heterosexual Argentine women frequently do so, but this would be very conspicuous behavior for men. When in doubt, it's best to be discreet.

MONEY

Carrying a combination of US dollars, Argentine pesos and ATM or credit cards is best.

ATMs

Cajeros automáticos (ATMs) are found in nearly every city and town in Argentina and can also be used for cash advances on major credit cards. They're the best way to get money, and nearly all have instructions in English. Limits on withdrawal can be very low – sometimes as low as US$115, though the withdrawal fee can be relatively high (not including charges by your home bank). You can withdraw several times per day, but beware these charges – which are per transaction. Banelco ATMs tend to allow larger withdrawals.

Not all foreign cards work in ATMs. Bring more than one option and be sure to alert your home bank that you are traveling in Argentina.

INFLATION WARNING

Lonely Planet aims to give its readers as precise an idea as possible of what things cost. Rather than just slapping hotels or restaurants into vague budget categories, we publish the actual rates and prices that businesses quote to us during research. The problem is that Argentina's inflation was running at an official rate of around 26% at the time of writing, and some unofficial estimates are more than double this. But we've found that readers prefer to have real numbers in their hands and do compensatory calculations themselves.

Argentina remains a decent-value destination, but don't expect our quoted prices to necessarily reflect your own experience. Our advice: call or check a few hotel or tour-operator websites before budgeting for your trip, just to make sure you're savvy about current rates.

In Patagonia, places like El Calafate and El Chaltén quickly run out of cash in high season.

Bargaining

Unlike many other South American countries, bargaining is generally not the norm in Argentina.

Cash

Notes come in denominations of two, five, 10, 20, 50, 100, 200, 500 and 1000 pesos. One peso equals 100 *centavos*. Coins come in five, 10, 25 and 50 *centavos* as well as one, two, five and 10 pesos. US dollars are accepted by many tourist-oriented businesses, but always carry some pesos.

US dollars are the easiest currency to exchange, though euros are also widely accepted at *cambios* (exchange houses). In Buenos Aires especially, beware fake bills; see www.landing padba.com/ba-basics-counterfeit-money.

Credit Cards

The larger a hotel is, the greater the chance it will accept credit cards. Ditto for stores and other services like bus tickets. Some businesses add a *recargo* (surcharge) of up to 10% to credit-card purchases; ask beforehand. Note that restaurant tips (10%) can't be added to the bill and must be paid in cash.

MasterCard and Visa are the main honchos, but American Express is also commonly accepted. Limited cash advances are possible (try Banco de la Nación) but are difficult, involving paperwork and fees.

Money Changers

➤ US dollars are by far the preferred foreign currency, although Chilean and Uruguayan pesos can be readily exchanged at the borders.

➤ Cash dollars and euros can be changed at banks and *cambios* (exchange houses) in most larger cities, but other currencies can be difficult to change outside Buenos Aires.

➤ You'll need your passport to change money; it might be best to avoid any sort of street-tout money changer.

OPENING HOURS

Banks 8am to 3pm or 4pm Monday to Friday; some till 1pm Saturday

Bars 8pm or 9pm to between 4am and 6am nightly

Cafes 6am to midnight or much later; open daily

Clubs 1am to 2am to between 6am and 8am Friday and Saturday

Office business hours 8am to 5pm

Post offices 8am to 6pm Monday to Friday, 9am to 1pm Saturday

Restaurants Noon to 3:30pm and 8pm to midnight or 1am (later on weekends)

Shops 9am or 10am to 8pm or 9pm Monday to Saturday

POST

The often unreliable Correo Argentino (www. correoargentino.com.ar) is the government postal service. Essential overseas mail should be sent *certificado* (registered).

You can send packages less than 2kg from any post office, but anything heavier needs to go through *aduana* (a customs office). In Buenos Aires, this office is called Correo Internacional (p84) and located near Retiro bus terminal. Take your passport and keep the package open, as you'll have to show its contents to a customs official.

Domestic couriers, such as Andreani (www. andreani.com.ar) and OCA (www.oca.com.ar), and international couriers, such as DHL and FedEx, are far more dependable than the post office. But they're also far more expensive. The latter two have offices only in the largest cities, while the first two usually serve as their connections to the interior of the country.

PUBLIC HOLIDAYS

Government offices and businesses are closed on Argentina's numerous public holidays. If the holiday falls on a midweek day or weekend day, it's often bumped to the nearest Monday; if it falls on a Tuesday or Thursday, then the in-between days of Monday or Friday are taken as holidays.

Public-transportation options are more limited on holidays, when you should reserve tickets far in advance. Hotel booking should also be done ahead of time.

The following list does not include provincial holidays, which may vary considerably.

January 1 Año Nuevo; New Year's Day.

February/March Carnaval. Dates vary; a Monday and Tuesday become holidays.

March 24 Día de la Memoria; Memorial Day. Anniversary of the day that started the 1976 dictatorship and subsequent Dirty War.

March/April Semana Santa; Easter week. Dates vary; most businesses close on 'Good Thursday' and Good Friday; major travel week.

April 2 Día de las Malvinas; honors the fallen Argentine soldiers from the Islas Malvinas (Falkland Islands) war in 1982.

May 1 Día del Trabajador; Labor Day.

May 25 Día de la Revolución de Mayo; commemorates the 1810 revolution against Spain.

June 20 Día de la Bandera; Flag Day. Anniversary of the death of Manuel Belgrano, creator of Argentina's flag and military leader.

July 9 Día de la Independencia; Independence Day.

August (third Monday in August) Día del Libertador San Martín; marks the anniversary of José de San Martín's death in 1850.

October 12 (second Monday in October) Día del Respeto a la Diversidad Cultural; a day to respect cultural diversity.

November 20 (fourth Monday in November) Día de la Soberanía Nacional; Day of National Sovereignty.

December 8 Día de la Concepción Inmaculada; celebrates the immaculate conception of the Virgin Mary.

December 25 Navidad; Christmas Day.

Note that Christmas Eve and New Year's Eve are treated as semi-holidays, and you will find some businesses closed for the latter half of those days.

SAFE TRAVEL

Despite occasional crime waves, Argentina remains one of the safest countries in Latin America. Most alert tourists who visit Buenos Aires leave happy and unscathed. Outside the big cities, serious crime is not common. Lock your valuables up in hostels, where, sadly enough, your own fellow travelers are occasionally to blame for thefts.

In general, the biggest dangers in Argentina are speeding cars and buses: *never* assume you have the right of way as a pedestrian. If you're sensitive to cigarette smoke, be aware that smoking remains prevalent in Argentina, and tobacco rules are looser here than in some other countries.

TELEPHONE & TEXTING

➔ *Locutorios* are common in any city; you enter private booths, make calls, then pay at the front counter. These are a better choice than street phones (which are relatively rare) as they offer privacy and quiet, and you won't run out of coins.

➔ Calling the US, Europe and Australia from *locutorios* is best on evenings and weekends, when rates are lower. Least expensive is buying credit phone cards at kiosks or calling over the internet via Skype or another system.

➔ Cell phone numbers in Argentina always start with 15. If you're calling a cell phone number from a landline, you'll have to dial 15 first. But if you're calling a cell phone from another cell phone, you don't need to dial 15.

➔ To call someone in Argentina from outside Argentina, dial your country's international access code, then Argentina's country code (54), then the city's area code (leaving out the first 0), then the number itself. When dialing an Argentine cell phone from outside Argentina, dial your country's international access code, then 54, then 9, then the area code without the 0, then the number – leaving out the 15.

➔ Argentina operates mainly on the GSM 850/1900 network. If you have an unlocked, tri- or quad-band GSM cell phone, you can buy a prepaid SIM chip in Argentina and insert it into your phone, adding credits as needed. You can also buy cell phones in Argentina. This is a fast-changing field, so research ahead of time.

➔ You don't need to dial 15 to send text messages. WhatsApp is a popular way of sending free texts in Argentina, providing both parties have it installed.

TOILETS

Argentina's public toilets are better than in most other South American countries, but not quite as good as those in the West. Head to restaurants, fast-food outlets, shopping malls and even large hotels to scout out a seat. Carry toilet paper and don't expect hot water, soap or paper towels to be available. In smaller towns, some public toilets charge a small fee for entry.

TOURIST INFORMATION

Argentina's national tourist board is the **Ministerio de Turismo** (www.turismo.gob.ar); its main office is in Buenos Aires.

Almost every destination city or town has a tourist office, usually on or near the main plaza or at the bus terminal. Each Argentine province also has its own representation in Buenos Aires. Most of these are well organized, often offering a computerized database of tourist information, and can be worth a visit before heading for the provinces.

VISAS

Nationals of the US, Canada, most Western European countries, Australia and New Zealand do not need a visa to visit Argentina. Upon arrival, most visitors get a 90-day stamp in their passport.

For visa extensions (90 days, AR$2700), visit *migraciones* (immigration offices) in the provincial capitals. There's also an immigration office (p83) in Buenos Aires.

VOLUNTEERING

There are many opportunities for volunteering in Argentina, anywhere from food banks to *villas miserias* (shantytowns) to organic farms. Some ask just for your time (or a modest fee) while others charge hundreds of dollars (with not necessarily a high percentage of money going directly to those in need). Before choosing an organization, it's good to talk to other volunteers about their experiences.

Aldea Luna (www.aldealuna.com.ar) Work on a farm in a nature reserve.

Anda Responsible Travel (www.andatravel. com.ar/en/volunteering) Buenos Aires travel agency supporting local communities.

Conservación Patagonica (www.conservacion patagonica.org) Help to create a national park.

Eco Yoga Park (www.ecoyogavillages.org/ volunteer-programs) Work on an organic farm, construct eco-buildings and teach skills to local communities.

Fundación Banco de Alimentos (www.banco dealimentos.org.ar) Short-term work at a food bank.

Habitat for Humanity Argentina (www.hpha.org.ar) Building communities.

WWOOF Argentina (www.wwoofargentina.com) Organic farming in Argentina.

WOMEN TRAVELERS

Being a woman traveler in Argentina is not difficult, even if you're alone. In some ways Argentina is a safer place for a woman than Europe, the USA and most other Latin American countries. Argentina is a *machismo* culture, however, and some men will feel the need to comment on a woman's appearance. They'll try to get your attention by hissing, whistling or making *piropos* (flirtatious comments). Much as you may want to kick them where it counts, the best thing to do is completely ignore them – like Argentine women do.

WORK

In Argentina, casual jobs are limited for foreigners. Teaching English is your best bet, especially in Buenos Aires and other major cities. However, most teachers make just enough to get by. A TESOL or TESL certificate will be an advantage in acquiring work. Foreigners also find work in traveler-oriented bars and hostels.

Many expats work illegally on tourist visas, which they must renew every three months (in BA this usually means hopping to Uruguay a few times per year). Work schedules drop off during the holiday months of January and February.

For job postings, check out http://buenosaires.en.craigslist.org or look at the classifieds in www.baexpats.org.

🛈 Getting There & Away

AIR

Cosmopolitan Buenos Aires is linked to most of the capitals in South America. Argentina's main international airport is Buenos Aires' Aeropuerto Internacional Ministro Pistarini (known as Ezeiza). Aeroparque Jorge Newbery (known as Aeroparque) is the capital's domestic airport. A few other Argentine cities have 'international' airports, but they mostly serve domestic destinations. The national airline is Aerolíneas Argentinas.

BOAT

There are several river crossings between Uruguay and Buenos Aires that involve ferry or hydrofoil, and often require combinations with buses.

Buenos Aires to Colonia Daily ferries (one to three hours) head to Colonia, with bus connections to Montevideo (an additional three hours).

Buenos Aires to Montevideo High-speed ferries carry passengers from downtown Buenos Aires to the Uruguayan capital in only 2¼ hours.

Tigre to Carmelo Regular passenger launches speed from the Buenos Aires suburb of Tigre to Carmelo in 2½ hours (services also go to Montevideo from Tigre).

BUS

It's possible to cross into Argentina from Bolivia, Paraguay, Brazil, Uruguay and Chile.

🛈 Getting Around

AIR

The airline situation in Argentina is in constant flux; minor airlines go in and out of business regularly. Ticket prices are unpredictable, though they are always highest during holiday times (July and late December to February). Certain flights in extensive Patagonia are comparable to bus fares when you consider time saved.

At the time of research, a spate of new low-cost airlines including Jetsmart (https://jetsmart.com/ar/es), Norwegian Air Argentina (www.norwegian.com) and Lasa (http://www.aerolineaslasa.com) were in the process of implementing regional flights between provinces, a service that is changing travel patterns throughout Argentina.

The major airlines in Argentina are **Aerolíneas Argentinas** (www.aerolineas.com.ar) and **LATAM** (www.latam.com). Each airline has a principal office, as well as regional offices in various cities.

There may be special air-pass deals available; check with a travel agency specializing in Latin America, since deals come and go regularly. These passes may need to be purchased outside Argentina (sometimes in conjunction with an international ticket); you need to be a foreign resident to use them, and they're often limited to travel within a certain time period.

BICYCLE

Cycling around the country has become popular among travelers. Beautiful routes in the north include the highway from Tucumán to Tafí del Valle and the Quebrada de Cafayate. Around Mendoza, there's touring that includes stops at wineries. The Lake District also has scenic roads, like the Siete Lagos route.

Drawbacks include the wind (which can slow progress to a crawl in Patagonia) and reckless motorists. Less-traveled secondary roads with little traffic are good alternatives.

Rental bikes are common in tourist areas and a great way to get around.

BUS

➡ Long-distance buses are modern, fast, comfortable and usually the best budget way to get around Argentina. Journeys of more than six hours or so will either have pit stops for refreshments or serve drinks, sweet snacks and sometimes simple meals. All have bathrooms, though they're often grungy, lack water (bring toilet paper/wet wipes) and are sometimes for 'liquids only.'

➡ The most luxurious companies offer more expensive *coche-cama, ejecutivo* or *suite* seats, most of which can lay flat. But even regular buses are usually comfortable enough, even on long trips.

➡ Bus terminals usually have kiosks, restrooms, cheap eats and luggage storage. In small towns you'll want to be aware of the timetable for your next bus out (and possibly buy a ticket), since some routes run infrequently.

➡ In summer there are many more departures. During holiday periods like January, February or July, buy advance tickets. If you know your exact traveling dates, you can often buy a ticket from any departure point to any destination, but this depends on the bus company.

➡ To get an idea of bus ticket prices from Buenos Aires, check www.omnilineas.com.

CAR

Renting a car in Argentina is not cheap, but it can get you away from the beaten path and start you on some adventures. The minimum driving age in Argentina is 18. To rent a car in Argentina you must be 21 years old and have a credit card and valid driver's license from your country. An International Driving Permit is not necessary.

The **Automóvil Club Argentino** (ACA; ☑ 011-4808-4040; www.aca.org.ar; Av del Libertador 1850; ☺ 9am-4pm Mon-Fri; ☒ 130, 62, 93) has offices, service stations and garages in major cities. If you're a member of an overseas affiliate (like AAA in the US) you may be able to obtain vehicular services and discounts on maps – bring your card. The ACA's main headquarters is in Buenos Aires.

Forget driving in Buenos Aires; traffic is unforgiving and parking is a headache, while public transport is great.

HITCHHIKING

➡ Along with Chile, Argentina is probably the best country for hitchhiking *(hacer dedo)* in all of South America. The major drawback is that Argentine vehicles are often stuffed full with families and children, but truckers will sometimes pick up backpackers. A good place to ask is at *estaciones de servicio* (service stations) on the outskirts of large Argentine cities, where truckers gas up their vehicles.

➡ In Patagonia, where distances are great and vehicles few, hitchers should expect long waits and carry warm, windproof clothing and refreshments.

➡ Having a sign will improve your chances for a pickup, especially if it says something like *visitando Argentina de Canada* ('visiting Argentina

from Canada'), rather than just a destination. Argentines are fascinated by foreigners.

➡ Be aware that hitchhiking is never entirely safe in any country, and we don't recommend it. Travelers who decide to hitch should understand that they are taking a small but potentially serious risk. People who do choose to hitch will be safer if they travel in pairs. Always let someone know where you are planning to go.

LOCAL TRANSPORTATION

Even small towns have good bus systems. A few cities, including Buenos Aires, use magnetic fare cards, which can be bought at kiosks and small stores.

Taxis have digital-readout meters. Tipping isn't expected, but you can leave extra change. *Remises* are taxis that you book over the phone, or regular cars without meters; any hotel or restaurant can call one for you. They're considered more secure than taxis since an established company sends them out. Ask the fare in advance.

Buenos Aires is the only city with a subway system, which is known as Subte.

TOURS

Most of Argentina can be seen independently, but in certain destinations it can be more informative and cost-effective to take a tour. Visiting the Moreno Glacier outside El Calafate is one place; Peninsula Valdés and Punta Tombo, both near Puerto Madryn, are two others.

Whitewater rafting, whale-watching and other adventures often require signing up for tours. Buenos Aires is full of interesting tours that give you deeper insight into that great city – these include biking tours, graffiti tours and even food tours.

TRAIN

For many years there were major reductions in long-distance train services in Argentina, but recent years have seen some rail lines progressively reopened. Good sources for information are www.seat61.com/southamerica.htm and www.sofse.gob.ar.

Trains serve most of Buenos Aires and some surrounding provinces. During the holiday periods, such as Christmas or national holidays, buy tickets in advance. Train fares tend to be lower than comparable bus fares, but trains are slower and there are fewer departure times and destinations. Long-distance trains have sleepers.

Train buffs will want to take the narrow-gauge *La Trochita,* which runs 20km between Esquel and Nahuel Pan. Another legendary ride is Salta's touristy but spectacular Tren a las Nubes (p127), which at one point spans a desert canyon at an altitude of 4220m – though it's famously unreliable. And finally, the scenic *Tren Patagónico* connects Bariloche to Viedma.

Bolivia

POP 11.14 MILLION

Best Places to Eat

➡ Gustu (p213)

➡ Popular Cocina Boliviana (p212)

➡ Ali Pacha (p212)

➡ El Fogón de Gringo (p248)

➡ Clementina (p254)

Best Places to Stay

➡ Hostal Sol y Luna (p228)

➡ Casona Señorial Gloria (p247)

➡ Atix (p209)

➡ Las Olas (p221)

Why Go?

Bolivia is not for the faint of heart. Whether your tools are crampons and an ice axe for scaling 6000m Andean peaks, or a helmet and bravado for jumping into the abyss on a glider, Bolivia's rocks, rivers and ravines will challenge you into pushing your own personal limits.

On the wild side, Bolivia is so biodiverse that unique species are being discovered to this day. Tiptoe into caves of tube-lipped nectar bats, tread lightly on the terrain of the poisonous annellated coral snake, and listen for the cackling call and response of a dozen different macaw species. Multi-hued butterflies flit at your feet in the jungle; lithe alpacas and vicuñas stand out in the stark altiplano. Deep in the forest live jaguars, pumas and bears.

Superlative in its natural beauty, rugged, vexing and complex, Bolivia is one of South America's most diverse and intriguing nations.

When to Go

La Paz

Feb Carnaval dance troupes take over the streets of Oruro, Santa Cruz, Sucre and Tarija.

Mar Pujllay celebrations in Tarabuco include ritual dancing, song and *chicha* (fermented corn) drinking.

Jul Outrageous costumes and hard partying mark the Fiesta de Moxos in Beni.

FAST FACTS

Currency Boliviano (B$)

Visas US citizens need a visa; citizens of Australia, Canada and most European countries do not.

Money ATMs and credit cards accepted in cities and many towns.

Capital Sucre (constitutional), La Paz (de facto)

Emergency 110/911 (police)

Languages Spanish, Quechua and Aymará

Exchange Rates

Australia	A$1	B$5.03
Canada	C$1	B$5.22
Europe	€1	B$7.86
Japan	¥100	B$6.25
New Zealand	NZ$1	B$4.55
UK	£1	B$8.81
US	US$1	B$6.91

For current exchange rates, see www.xe.com.

Daily Costs

➡ Dorm/budget beds: B$40–70; double room in a midrange hotel: B$160–400

➡ Bread for breakfast, set lunch, dinner supplies from local market: B$50; hotel breakfast, lunch and dinner in a restaurant: B$200

Resources

Bolivia.com (www.bolivia. com, in Spanish)

Bolivian Express (www. bolivianexpress.org)

Bolivia Online (www. bolivia-online.net)

Lonely Planet (www.lonely planet.com/bolivia)

Entering the Country

Bolivia has land borders with Argentina (at Villazón, Yacuiba and Bermejo); Brazil (via Quijarro on the main highway from Santa Cruz, and a smaller crossing at San Matías), Chile (at Tambo Quemado, Hito Cajón and Ollagüe); Paraguay (the trans-Chaco crossing) and Peru (at Kasani and Desaguadero).

TWO-WEEK ITINERARY

Start with a day of acclimatization in La Paz, visiting the markets. History buffs can take a side trip to Tiwanaku. From La Paz, head to Lake Titicaca. Allow up to three days on the lake to take in the sites of Copacabana and Isla del Sol and continue acclimatization. From there, circle down the altiplano (via La Paz) to the Salar de Uyuni for a bone-chatteringly cold three-day jeep tour. Extend your trip to the former territory of Butch Cassidy in the pleasant cowboy town of Tupiza.

Swing up to Potosí, a starkly beautiful Unesco World Heritage city, situated at 4070m, where you can visit the mint and mines. After a day or two, head to the white city of Sucre to hang out with students in grand plazas. Return to La Paz via Cochabamba, taking in the views along the way. On your last day in La Paz, consider a day of museum-hopping or take a mountain-bike ride down the World's Most Dangerous Road to Coroico.

Essential Food & Drink

Mamá qonqachi Frisbee-like cheese bread.

Salteñas Pastry shells stuffed with chicken or mince.

Sonso Comfort in the form of grilled yucca and cheese.

Chicha Parties start with this fermented-corn drink.

Pique a lo macho The ultimate hangover cure: beef, sausage, eggs, peppers and onions piled over potato fries.

Top Tips

➡ Allow yourself plenty of time to acclimatize to the altitude. Go up slowly and take it easy when you reach new heights.

➡ Even a little Spanish will be a huge help in Bolivia. If you can, take some classes before you travel.

➡ Prepare yourself for sometimes challenging but always rewarding travel experiences. Your trip will go more smoothly if you are patient and flexible.

➡ Allow time in your schedule for unexpected delays. Keep an eye on the news and ask locals about potential bloqueos (road closures cause by protesters) that might affect your travel plans.

➡ Stay away from political protests. They might pique your interest, but clashes could happen at any time.

➡ Be respectful of local people and don't take photographs without asking permission.

LA PAZ

🎵 2 / POP 757,000 / ELEV 3660M (12,007FT)

A mad carnival of jostling pedestrians, honking, diesel-spewing minivans, street marches, and cavalcades of vendors, La Paz surrounds you: you'll love it, you'll hate it, but you can't ignore it. The city seems to reinvent itself at every turn – a jaw-dropping subway in the sky brings you from the heights of El Alto to the depths of Zona Sur in the blink of an eye. Standing hotels are remodeled at a manic pace, and new boutique hotels are springing up like rows of altiplano corn.

Coming from the Bolivian countryside, you'll be struck by the gritty city reality. It's the urban jungle, baby: diesel, dust, and detritus; blinding altiplano sun, cold cavernous corners of Dickensian darkness. Sharp-suited businessmen flank machine-gun-toting bank guards and balaclava-camouflaged shoeshine boys. Lung-busting inclines terminate in peaceful plazas. A maze of contradictions, where cobblestones hit concrete, and Gothic spires vie with glassine hotels, La Paz amazes and appalls all who enter.

◎ Sights

La Paz has a decent collection of museums and notable buildings, but the main attraction here is getting lost in its bustling markets, frenetic commercial streets and stunning hilltop lookouts. Most official sights, including museums, are closed during the Christmas holiday period (December 25 to January 6).

◎ West of El Prado

The areas west of El Prado include the fascinating markets around Rosario, Belén and San Pedro, the cemetery and the sophisticated Sopocachi neighborhood, with some of La Paz's best restaurants and nightspots. You can spend a few hours people-watching on **Plaza Eduardo Avaroa**, before hoofing up to the wonderful views from **Montículo Park**.

★ Mercado de las Brujas   MARKET

(Witches' Market; La Hechiceria; Map p206) The city's most unusual market lies along Calles Jiménez and Linares between Sagárnaga and Av Mariscal Santa Cruz, amid lively tourist *artesanías* (stores selling locally handcrafted items). What is on sale isn't witchcraft as depicted in horror films; the merchandise is herbal and folk remedies, plus a few more unorthodox ingredients intended to supplicate the various spirits of the Aymará world.

Iglesia de San Francisco   CHURCH

(Map p206; Plaza San Francisco, Rosario) The hewed stone basilica of San Francisco was founded in 1548 by Fray Francisco de los Ángeles. The original structure collapsed under heavy snowfall around 1610, but it was rebuilt between 1743 and 1772. The second building is made of stone quarried at nearby Viacha. The facade is decorated with carvings of natural themes such as *chirimoyas* (custard apples), pine cones and tropical birds.

Museo de Instrumentos Musicales   MUSEUM

(Museum of Musical Instruments; Map p206; Jaén 711, Casco Viejo; B\$5; ⊙9:30am-1:30pm & 2:30-6:30pm) This museum is a must for musicians. The brainchild of *charango* master Ernesto Cavour Aramayo displays all possible incarnations of the *charango* (a traditional Bolivian ukulele-type instrument) and other Bolivian folk instruments. You can also arrange *charango* and wind instrument lessons here for around B\$50 per hour.

La Paz Cemetery   CEMETERY

(http://cementerio.lapaz.bo; Av Baptista, Tacagua; ⊙8:30am-5pm) As in many Latin American cemeteries, bodies are first buried in the Western way or are placed in a crypt. Then, within 10 years, they are disinterred and cremated. After cremation, families purchase or rent glass-fronted spaces in the cemetery walls for the ashes, they affix plaques and mementos of the deceased, and place flowers behind the glass door.

◎ East of El Prado

★ Museo Nacional del Arte   MUSEUM

(National Art Museum; Map p206; www.facebook.com/museonacionaldeartebolivia; cnr Comercio & Socabaya, Casco Viejo; B\$20; ⊙9:30am-12:30pm & 3-7pm Tue-Fri, 10am-5:30pm Sat, 10am-1:30pm Sun) This colonial building was constructed in 1775 of pink sandstone and has been restored to its original grandeur, in *mestizo* (mixed) baroque and Andino baroque styles. In the center of a huge courtyard, surrounded by three stories of pillared corridors, is a lovely alabaster fountain. The various levels are dedicated to different eras, with an emphasis on religious themes.

★ Museo de Etnografía y Folklore   MUSEUM

(Ethnography & Folklore Museum; Map p206; 📞240-8640; www.musef.org.bo; cnr Ingavi & Sanjinés,

BOLIVIA LA PAZ

Bolivia Highlights

1 **Potosí** (p264) Exploring the silver city of contrasts.

2 **Parque Nacional & Área de Uso Múltiple Amboró** (p274) Making your way through this extraordinary park for spectacular biodiversity and landscapes.

3 **Sucre** (p257) Diving into history with a walking tour of the town, where architecture and culture come to light.

4 **Jesuit Mission Circuit** (p274) Discovering the living history of Chiquitania.

5 **Samaipata** (p273) Kicking back in the village before exploring the nearby El Fuerte ruins.

6 **Parque Nacional Madidi** (p281) Trekking through the jungle for ecotourism, howlers, birds and bugs at their best.

7 **Cordillera Real** (p230) Enjoying trekking, biking, climbing and rafting.

8 **Lake Titicaca** (p219) Worshipping the sun and sand with visits to the ruins and lost coves and minitreks around the lake.

9 **Salar de Uyuni** (p242) Exploring the vast crystalline perfection of this surreal salt flat.

10 **Coroico** (p226) Challenging yourself to some extreme hammocking.

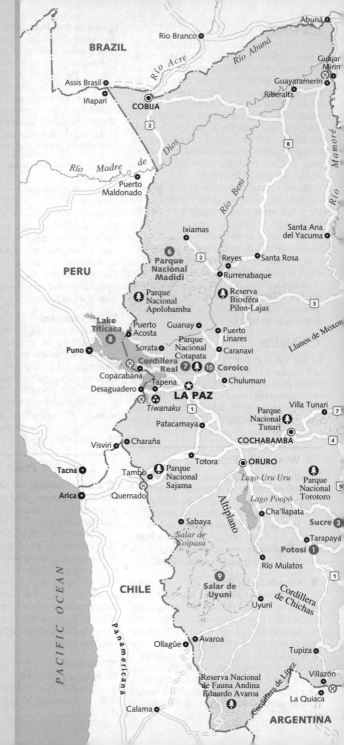

0 ———————— 200 km
0 ———————— 100 miles

Rio Guaporé (Iténez)

Costa Marques

San Joaquín

Magdalena

BRAZIL

Parque Nacional Noel Kempff Mercado

Serranía Huanchaca

Perseverancia

TRINIDAD

9

Rio Ichilo

Puerto Villarroel

Buena Vista

SANTA CRUZ

Parque Nacional & Área de Uso Múltiple Amboró

Samaipata

Concepción

San Javier

San Ignacio de Velasco

Jesuit Mission Circuit

4

Santa Ana de Velasco

San Miguel de Velasco

San Rafael de Velasco

4

Puerto Pailas

San José de Chiquitos

Pantanal

Rio Grande o Guapay

Llanos de Chiquitos

Serranía de San José

Serranía de Santiago

Roboré

Puerto Suárez

Corumbá

Quijarro

Tarabuco

Bañados del Izozog

Gran Chaco

Camiri

Boyuibe

6

Fortín General Eugenio A Garay

Rio Paraguay

Villamontes

TARIJA

Yacuiba

Pocitos

PARAGUAY

Filadelfia

Aguas Blancas

Tartagal

Rio Pilcomayo

Casco Viejo; B$20, with photography B$40; ☺9am-12:30pm & 3-7pm Mon-Fri, 9am-4:30 Sat, 9am-12:30pm Sun) Anthropology buffs should check out the Museo de Etnografía y Folklore. This museum is one of the city's best. The building, itself a real treasure, was constructed in 1720 and was once the home of the Marqués de Villaverde. Highlights include an awe-inspiring collection of ritualistic masks and an exhibition of stunning weavings from around the country. A guided tour is available by calling ahead.

★ **Museo de Textiles Andinos Bolivianos**   MUSEUM
(MUTAB; ☎224-3601; www.museodetextiles.org; Plaza Benito Juárez 488, Miraflores; B$15; ☺9:30am-noon & 3-6:30pm Mon-Sat) Fans of Bolivia's lovely traditional weaving consider this small textile museum a must-see. Examples of the country's finest traditional textiles (including pieces from the Cordillera Apolobamba, and the Jal'qa and Candelaria regions of the Central Highlands) are grouped by region and described in Spanish and English. The creative process is explained from fiber to finished product. The gift shop sells museum-quality originals; 90% of the sale price goes to the artists.

★ **Calle Jaén Museums**   MUSEUM
(Map p206; Calle Jaén, Casco Viejo; 4 museums B$20; ☺9am-12:30pm & 3-7pm Tue-Fri, 9am-1pm Sat & Sun) La Paz's best-preserved colonial street is home to four small museums. They are all clustered together and can generally be bundled into one visit. Buy tickets at the **Museo Costumbrista** (Map p206; cnr Jaén & Sucre, Casco Viejo; ☺9am-12:30pm & 3-7pm Tue-Fri, 9am-1pm Sat & Sun) and continue to the **Museo de Metales Preciosos** (Museum of Precious Metals; Map p206; Jaén 777, Casco Viejo; ☺9am-12:30pm & 3-7pm Tue-Fri, 9am-1pm Sat & Sun), **Museo del Litoral** (Museo de la Guerra del Pacífico; Map p206; Jaén 798, Casco Viejo; ☺9am-12:30pm & 3-7pm Tue-Fri, 9am-1pm Sat & Sun) and **Casa de Murillo** (Map p206; Jaén 790, Casco Viejo; ☺9am-12:30pm & 3-7pm Tue-Fri, 9am-1pm Sat & Sun).

Catedral Metropolitana   CATHEDRAL
(Map p206; Plaza Murillo, Casco Viejo) Although it's a relatively recent addition to La Paz's religious structures, the 1835 cathedral is impressive – mostly because it is built on a steep hillside. The main entrance is 12m higher than its base on Calle Potosí. The cathedral's sheer immensity, with its high dome, hulking columns, thick stone walls and high ceilings, is overpowering, but the altar is relatively simple.

◉ El Alto

La Ceja   AREA
(El Alto) In the lively La Ceja (Eyebrow) district, which commands one of the highest real-estate prices in El Alto for its commercial value, you'll find a variety of electronic gadgets and mercantile goods. For an excellent market experience, don't miss the massive **Mercado 16 de Julio** (El Alto; ☺6am-3pm Thu & Sun), which stretches for many blocks along the main thoroughfare and across Plaza 16 de Julio.

🏃 Activities

You'll get plenty of exercise hoofing up and down El Prado but you don't have to head far out of town for a real adrenaline rush. Note that the **Asociación de Guías de Montaña** (www.agmtb.org, in Spanish) certifies guides in Bolivia, and it's worth checking out their information before deciding on an operation.

Mountain Biking

There are tons of mountain-biking options just outside of La Paz. Intermediate riders can take on a thrilling downhill ride on the World's Most Dangerous Road (p227), while advanced riders may wish to go for the less-traveled **Chacaltaya to Zongo** route or the rides near Sorata (p231). Beginners not quite ready for the death road may want to check out the **Balcón Andino** descent near the Zona Sur, a 2400m roller coaster on a wide dirt road.

★ **Gravity Assisted Mountain Biking**   MOUNTAIN BIKING
(Map p206; ☎231-0218, cell 7721-9634; www.gravitybolivia.com; Linares 940, Rosario; ☺9am-7pm Mon-Fri, 10am-3pm Sat, 2-6pm Sun) This knowledgeable, highly regarded and professional outfit has an excellent reputation among travelers and tip-top Kona downhill bikes. Their Dangerous Road Trip (B$850 per person) ends with hot showers, an all-you-can-eat buffet and an optional tour of the Senda Verde animal refuge (p227).

Xtreme Downhill   CYCLING
(Map p206; ☎cell 7775-1587; www.xtremedownhill.com; Sagárnaga 392, Rosario; ☺10am-8pm) A recommended and safety-focused outfitter

La Paz

for Death Road cycle trips (B\$400 to B\$600, depending on the bike).

Hiking

Except for the altitude, La Paz and its environs are made for hiking. Many La Paz tour agencies offer daily 'hiking' tours to Chacaltaya, a rough 30km drive north of La Paz, and an easy way to bag a high peak without having to do any really hard-core hiking. Head to **Valle de la Luna** (Valley of the Moon; B\$25; ⊗ dawn to dusk), Valle de las Ánimas or **Muela del Diablo** for do-it-yourself day hikes from La Paz.

⭐**La Paz on Foot**   ECOTOUR
(Map p210; ☎ cell 7154-3918; www.lapazonfoot. com; Av Ecuador 2022, Sopocachi; ⊗ 10:30am-6:30pm Mon-Fri) This tip-top operation, run by the passionate English-speaking ecologist Stephen Taranto, offers a range of activities, including walks in and around La Paz, Apolobamba, the Yungas, Chulumani,

Madidi and Titicaca. The interactive La Paz urban treks (half-day or full-day, fee depending on group size) venture from the heights of El Alto to the depths of the historic center.

Climbing

La Paz is the staging ground for most of the climbs in the Cordilleras. From here novice climbers can arrange trips to Huayna Potosí (p230), two to three days for B\$900 to B\$1200. More experienced climbers may look to climb Illimani (p230) or Sajama, each about four to five days for roughly US\$485.

⭐**Climbing South America**   CLIMBING
(Map p206; ☎ cell 7190-3534; www.climbingsouth america.com; Linares 940, 2nd fl, Rosario; ⊗ 9am-6:30pm Mon-Fri, 10am-3pm Sat) A reputable English-speaking operator for climbing, mountaineering and trekking in the nearby mountains. Also sells great topography and trekking maps.

BOLIVIA LA PAZ

Central La Paz - The Prado

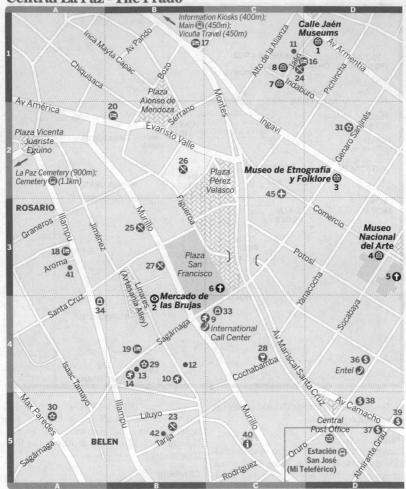

Andean Expeditions Dirninger

CLIMBING, HIKING

(Map p206; ☑ 241-4235, cell 7755-0226; www.andean-expeditions.com; Sagárnaga 189, Galería Doryan, 3rd fl, Oficina 32, Rosario; ⊙ 9am-12:30pm & 2-5:30pm Mon-Fri) Andean Expeditions Dirninger is an Austrian-founded company that offers mountain treks in Bolivia and neighboring countries, and uses guides certified by the International Federation of Mountain Guides Associations (IFMGA). More than 10 years in Bolivia, and not the same old run-of-the-mill tours.

Andean Summits

CLIMBING

(☑ 242-2106; www.andeansummits.com; Muñoz Cornejo 1009, Sopocachi; ⊙ 9am-noon & 3-7pm Mon-Fri, 9am-12:30pm Sat) Offers a variety of outdoor activities from mountaineering and trekking to 4WD tours in Bolivia and beyond. The owners are professional IFMGA mountain guides.

Paragliding

★ AndesXtremo

PARAGLIDING

(Map p210; ☑ 7358-3349; www.andesxtremo.com; Francisco Bedregal 2962, Sopocachi; ⊙ 8:30am-12:30pm & 2:30-6:30pm Mon-Fri, to 12:30pm Sat)

If the teleférico (p214) isn't enough for you, then these guys will get you higher than you've ever been in La Paz on a tandem-paragliding adventure. They also offer rock climbing, mountaineering, canyoning and caving.

🎒 Courses

Pico Verde Languages   LANGUAGE
(Map p206; 📞 231-8328; www.pico-verde.com; Sagárnaga 363, 2nd fl, Rosario; group lessons from per hour B$35) Offers flexible schedules for Spanish classes and can set you up with a homestay.

🐾 Tours

★ HanaqPacha Travel   TOURS
(Map p206; 📞 cell 6980-3602; www.hanaqpacha travel.com; Jaén 765, Casco Viejo; ⊙ 9am-6:30pm) Runs recommended daily tours to El Alto (B$140) to step inside the prismatic *cholets* of Aymará architect Freddy Mamani. Also has a daily Tastes of Bolivia tour (B$140) to learn about typical food. Uyuni, Tiwanaku and Rurrenabaque are the focus of longer tours.

Banjo Tours   ADVENTURE
(Map p210; 📞 cell 6716-5394; www.banjotours. com; Pedro Salazar 623, Oficina 2, Sopocachi; ⊙ 8am-noon & 2-6pm Mon-Fri, to noon Sat) Banjo doesn't offer the same cookie-cutter tours as its competitors; it's a highly-recommended outfit for quality small-group adventures off the beaten path.

Madidi Travel   ECOTOUR
(Map p206; 📞 231-8313; www.madidi-travel.com; Linares 947, Rosario; ⊙ 9am-7pm Mon-Fri, to 5pm Sat & Sun) Specializing in trips to Madidi, this tour operator's 40-sq-km private reserve east of the park (Eco Reserve Serere) adds another layer of protection.

🎉 Festivals & Events

Alasitas   CULTURAL
(⊙ Jan 24) During Inca times the Alasitas (Aymará for 'buy from me') fair coincided with the spring equinox (September 21), and was intended to demonstrate the abundance of the fields. The little god of abundance, Ekeko ('dwarf' in Aymará), made his appearance. Modern Alasitas traditions are now celebrated throughout the city in January.

La Festividad de Nuestro
Señor Jesús del Gran Poder   RELIGIOUS
(⊙ late May/early Jun) El Gran Poder has developed into a unique La Paz festival, and an elaborate display of economic power; embroiderers prepare lavish costumes and upwards of 25,000 performers practice for weeks in advance. A number of dances are featured, such as the *suri sikuris* (in which the dancers are bedecked in ostrich feathers), the lively *kullawada*, *morenada*, *caporales* and the *inkas*, which duplicates Inca ceremonial dances.

🛏 Sleeping

Most backpackers head for central La Paz to find a bed. The area around the Mercado de las Brujas (p201) is a true travelers' ghetto. To

BOLIVIA LA PAZ

Central La Paz - The Prado

be closer to a wider array of restaurants and a bar or two, consider Sopocachi. For more upmarket luxury, look along the lower Prado and further south in the Zona Sur.

West of El Prado

★ Onkel Inn
HOSTEL $

(Map p210; ☏ 249-0456; www.onkelinn.com; Colombia 257, San Pedro; dm/s/d/tr incl breakfast B$77/139/271/299; @ 🖘) A bright, HI-affiliated place in a convenient spot between San Pedro and El Prado. It's less of a scene than the hostels up by the terminal, good for *tranquilo* (quiet) travelers. The dorms are the nicest in town, with crisp sheets, orange bedcovers and a bright modern feel. Some bunks will leave you with vertigo; nice common areas and even a sauna!

3600 Hostel
HOSTEL $

(Map p210; ☏ 212-0478; www.3600hostel.com; Av Ecuador 1982, Sopocachi; dm incl breakfast B$90-105, d with private bathroom B$300, tr with shared bathroom B$280; 🖘) Named for the altitude in which it lies, this lovingly restored 1840s-era home has a stone-floored interior patio, funky furniture and gorgeous stained-glass windows. The dorms are spacious with privacy curtains, though the top bunks are seriously high. It's one of the few places in town with a women-only dorm.

Hotel Sagárnaga
HOTEL $$

(Map p206; ☏ 235-0252; www.hotelsagarnaga. com; Sagárnaga 326, Rosario; s/d incl breakfast B$147/270; @ 🖘) The knight in shining armor at the front desk (and no, we're not talking about the receptionist, although he *is* friendly) welcomes you to this renovated gem in the heart of Sagárnaga. East-facing rooms are the best, though all offer good value for money with safes, TVs and parquet floors.

Rendezvous   GUESTHOUSE **$$**
(Map p210; ☑ 291-2459; www.rendezvouslapaz. com; Pasaje M Carranza 461, Sopocachi; r incl breakfast from US$30; @) A great mid-range bet for couples in search of privacy, peace and quiet. The 11 rooms are each unique, with local artwork and refurbished antiques. Guests also rave about the on-site restaurant.

★ Hotel Rosario   BOUTIQUE HOTEL **$$$**
(Map p206; ☑ 245-1658; www.hotelrosario.com; Illampu 704, Rosario; d/tr/q incl breakfast US$93/ 115/148; @ ☎) The professional, English-speaking staff at La Paz's best three-star hotel pamper you with five-star treatment. The ultraclean rooms in the well-maintained colonial residence all have solar-powered hot showers, cable TV and heaters. There is free internet and a generous breakfast buffet. Groups love it, so reserve ahead. There's a sister hotel at Copacabana (p221).

🛏 East of El Prado

★ Loki Hostel   HOSTEL **$**
(Map p206; ☑ 245-7300; www.lokihostel.com/ la-paz; Av América 120, Plaza Alonso de Mendoza; dm B$62-72, d B$205; @☎) This party hostel has a gilded bar, several sunny hangout areas with games and TVs, and more than 180 beds. The rooftop terrace is dope. One of a chain of 'Lokis' throughout Peru and Argentina.

Wild Rover   HOSTEL **$**
(Map p206; ☑ 211-6903; www.wildroverhostel.com; Comercio 1476, Casco Viejo; dm B$57-92, r with shared bathroom B$230; @☎) Your best bet to meet fellow travelers, the Wild Rover has a high-octane, take-no-prisoners vibe that 20-somethings will love and 30-somethings and older might loathe. The rooms at some other hostels are better, and the dorm rooms are too tightly packed, but you'll be spending most of your day at the boisterous Irish pub anyway.

Arthy's Guesthouse   GUESTHOUSE **$**
(Map p206; ☑ 228-1439; arthyshouse@gmail. com; Ismael Montes 693; dm B$76, r per person with shared bathroom B$100; ☎) This clean and cozy place hidden behind a bright orange door deservedly receives rave reviews

as a 'tranquil oasis,' despite its location on one of La Paz's busiest roads. The friendly, English-speaking owners will do all they can do to help you. Kitchen facilities are available. Note, though, that there is a midnight curfew.

★ Ananay Hostal   HOSTEL **$$**
(Map p206; ☑ 290-6507; hostal.ananay@gmail. com; Jaén 710, Casco Viejo; r per person incl breakfast B$145, with shared bathroom B$110; ☎) A brightly painted courtyard centers this historic home, a former *peña*, in the heart of Jaén's museum district. The place includes rooftop city views and several comfortable common areas, including a beanbag-chair lounge with TV. The name, which fits, means 'how nice' in Quechua.

Casa Prado   BOUTIQUE HOTEL **$$**
(Boutique Hotel; Map p210; ☑ 231-2094; www. casapradolapaz.com.bo; Av 16 de Julio 1615, Prado; r/ste incl breakfast US$60/80; ☎) Another of the boutique options springing up in downtown, this historic home was once owned by the Prado family. All the bells and whistles of modernity (wi-fi and ironing boards) with the whiff of colonial grandeur. The floorboards creak with history, and you're steps from sights and eats. A Prado view might be a bit noisy.

Altu Qala   BOUTIQUE HOTEL **$$$**
(Map p206; www.altuqala.com; Plaza Tomás Frías 1570, Casco Viejo; r from US$300; ☎) The design concept at this stunning 10-room boutique hotel, opened in late 2018, is mid-century meets neoclassical, and the minutest of details do not go unnoticed (the floor tiles alone arc like a mesmerizing optical illusion!). It's located in the same revamped early-1900s building as Hb Bronze Coffeebar (p213) and boasts a rooftop terrace with 360-degree views over the city.

🛏 Zona Sur

★ Atix Hotel   DESIGN HOTEL **$$$**
(☑ 277-6500; www.atixhotel.com; Calle 16 No 8052, Calacoto; r from US$150; P ✱ @ ☎) La Paz finally has a world-class design hotel in this Zona Sur stunner. Nearly everything you see – from the specially-commissioned art on the walls to the wooden headboards and stone sinks – comes from Bolivian artisans. The on-site restaurant, Ona, also champions Bolivian goods, while the glassed-in rooftop pool and bar offer sweeping views of distant hills.

Sopocachi

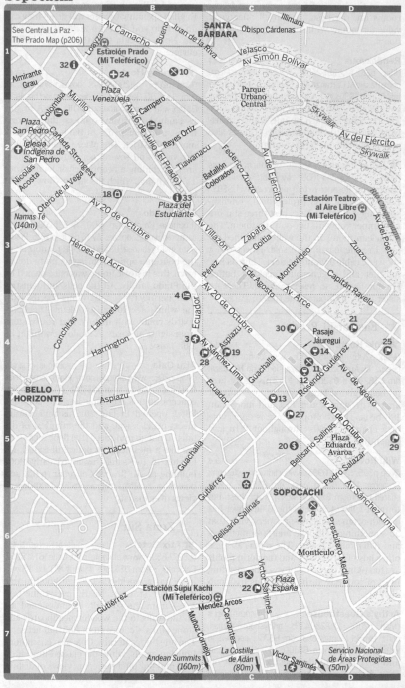

See Central La Paz -
The Prado Map (p206)

SANTA
BÁRBARA

Estación Prado
(Mi Teleférico)

Plaza
Venezuela

Plaza
San Pedro

Iglesia
Indígena de
San Pedro

Namas Té
(140m)

Parque
Urbano
Central

Estación Teatro
al Aire Libre
(Mi Teleférico)

Plaza del
Estudiante

BELLO
HORIZONTE

Pasaje
Jáuregui

Plaza
Eduardo
Avaroa

SOPOCACHI

Montículo

Estación Súpu Kachi
(Mi Teleférico)

Plaza
España

Andean Summits
(160m)

La Costilla
de Adán
(80m)

Servicio Nacional
de Áreas Protegidas
(50m)

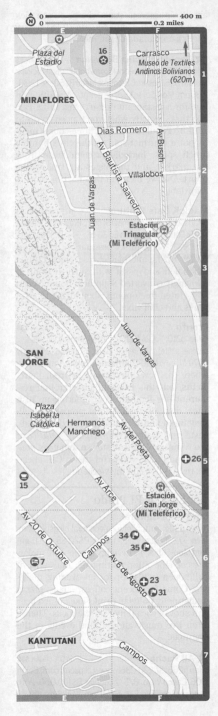

Sopocachi

Activities, Courses & Tours

Sleeping

Eating

Drinking & Nightlife

Entertainment

Shopping

Information

Eating

La Paz is a real treat if you're looking to spoil yourself after the culinary minefields of rural Bolivia. A newfound gastronomic renaissance means you can now find creative vegan fare, homemade pastas, fresh sushi and, most importantly, inventive takes on traditional fare from the Amazon to the Andes. You won't eat better anywhere else in Bolivia, guaranteed.

West of El Prado

★ Namas Té   VEGETARIAN $
(www.namastebolivia.com; Zoilo Flores 1334, San Pedro; mains B$12-30; ⊙8:30am-7pm Mon-Fri, to 4pm Sat; 🖋) Tea lovers take note: the tea menu at this lovable lime-green veggie restaurant is a staggering four pages long! There's also plenty of quinoa in all forms (falafel, soup, tabbouleh salad) and even a raved-about tofu pad thai. Smoothies, juices and sandwiches round out the well-priced menu.

La Espinita   SEAFOOD $
(Map p210; Quintín Barrios 712, Sopocachi; mains B$20-30; ⊙noon-2:30pm Tue-Sun) Get down to 'the bones' with a hearty Andean lunch of four favorite fried fish in a delicious home-made batter, all served with crispy *ispi* (little sardine-sized dudes) on top, and sides of potato and *mote* (big corn). Wash it down with fresh juices, and it's no wonder locals are flocking to this pint-sized eatery. Don't mind the eyes!

Anticafé Chukuta   CAFE $
(Map p206; www.facebook.com/anticafe.chukuta; Tarija 328, Rosario; mains B$25-30; ⊙2-9pm Tue-Sat, 9:30am-3pm Sun; 🛜) With its exposed stone walls, pallet furniture, hanging basket lamps and colorful art, this new cafe (opened in late 2016) could not be cuter. You can build your own granola, salads and sandwiches, then stick around for an afternoon coffee. There are plenty of board games and books to keep you stimulated.

Hay Pan   CAFE, WINE BAR $
(Map p206; www.facebook.com/haypanlapaz; Murillo 764, Rosario; mains B$20-30; ⊙7-11am & 7-11pm Mon-Sat) This cozy little cafe with colorful Andean decor does bountiful breakfasts that include strong coffees and fresh-baked breads. It doubles as a vino bar in the evening with soothing tunes spinning on the record player, a wide-ranging Bolivian wine list and make-your-own charcuterie boards.

Mercado Lanza   MARKET $
(Map p206; Rosario; snacks B$5-25; ⊙6am-8pm) Between Plaza Pérez Velasco and Calle Figueroa is Mercado Lanza, one of La Paz's main food markets – the other major one is **Mercado Camacho** (Map p210; cnr Av Camacho & Bueno, Casco Viejo; snacks B$5-25; ⊙7am-9pm Mon-Fri, to 6pm Sat & Sun). It sells all manner of fruits, vegetables, juices, dairy products, breads and canned foods. There are also numerous stalls where you can pick up a sandwich, soup, *salteña* (filled pastry shells), empanada or full meal.

★ Popular Cocina Boliviana   BOLIVIAN $$
(Map p206; www.facebook.com/popularlapazbolivia; Murillo 826, Rosario; 3-course lunch B$50; ⊙12:30-2:30pm Mon-Sat) The concept of waiting in line for a restaurant doesn't exist in La Paz, but that's exactly what you'll need to do to get into Popular. Seasonal three-course menus put a gourmet spin on the city's humble lunch spots. Ingredients come fresh from the market, and the plates are true works of art. Did we mention that it's ridiculously affordable?

MagicK Cafe Cultural   INTERNATIONAL $$
(Map p210; www.cafemagick.com; Presbítero Medina 2526, Sopocachi; mains B$30-55; ⊙4-11:30pm Tue-Sat; 🛜🖋) This funky pescatarian restaurant serves up fig-and-blue-cheese pizza, quinoa tabbouleh and pasta with smoked trout in a lovingly converted Sopocachi home. Vegan and gluten-free options abound, as do good tunes and chill vibes.

Pronto   ITALIAN $$$
(Map p210; ☎244-1369; http://prontodalicatessen.business.site; Jáuregui 2248, Sopocachi; mains B$70-110; ⊙6:30-11pm Mon-Sat) We don't know where (or how) they get their fresh ingredients, but this candlelit underground restaurant has figured it out, offering up dish after dish of thoughtfully prepared, well-structured and delicately balanced antipasti, pasta and mains. The *antipasta della casa* is a remarkable mix of stewed tomatoes, walnuts and other wonderful treats. Call ahead for reservations on the weekends.

East of El Prado

Etno Café Cultural   CAFE $
(Map p206; http://etnocafecultural.blogspot.com; Jaén 772, Casco Viejo; mains B$20-35; ⊙11am-2am Mon-Sat; 🛜) This edgy scarlet cafe makes a great stop after visiting the museums of Calle Jaén (p204) or for an evening nightcap. Come for decent coffees, salads, pizzas or distinctly Bolivian drinks like quinoa beer or a shot of coca liquor on the rocks. There's often live music and cultural events in the evenings.

★ Ali Pacha   VEGETARIAN $$$
(Map p206; ☎220-2366; www.alipacha.com; Colón 1306, Casco Viejo; 3/5/7 courses B$100/150/200; ⊙noon-3pm Tue-Sat & 7-10pm Wed-Sat; 🛜🖋)

PEÑAS

Typical of La Paz (and most of Bolivia) are folk-music venues known as *peñas*. Most present traditional Andean music, rendered on *zampoñas* (pan flutes), *quenas* (cane flute) and *charangos* (ukulele-style instrument), but also often include guitar shows and song recitals.

Jallalla (p214)

Peña Huari (Map p206; ☑231-6225; Sagárnaga 339, Rosario; cover B$105; ⊗ show 8pm)

Peña Jamuy (Map p206; ☑cell 7676-7817; www.facebook.com/jamuybolivia; Max Paredes, near Sagárnaga, Rosario; cover B$25-50; ⊗9pm-7am Fri & Sat)

Locals thought it absurd on so many levels to open a high-end vegetarian restaurant with degustation menus in La Paz's downtrodden Casco Viejo neighborhood. And it is absurd. Fantastically so! Even carnivores will swoon over the creative plant-based creations and herbaceous cocktails. You're guaranteed to taste the flavors of Bolivia like never before.

🍴 Zona Sur

Los Qñapés BOLIVIAN $
(www.facebook.com/losqnapes; René Moreno 1283, San Miguel; snacks B$6-15; ⊗3:30-10pm) 🥖 Snack on Bolivian favorites like *cuñapé* (a cheesy yuca bread), *humitas* (a steamed corn pie) and *masacos* (plantains or yucca mashed with meat or cheese) at this always-busy cafe. All of the ingredients are organic and come from within the country.

★Gustu BOLIVIAN $$$
(☑211-7491; www.gustu.bo; Calle 10 No 300, Calacoto; almuerzo B$95, dinner tasting menu B$430-560, à la carte mains B$95-130; ⊗noon-3pm & 6:30-11pm; P🛜) Credited with sparking La Paz's culinary renaissance, and launched by the Danish culinary entrepreneur Claus Meyer (of Noma fame), this groundbreaking restaurant works to both rescue and showcase underutilized Bolivian ingredients. It's located in a gorgeous building rich with Andean textiles, and offers everything from Andean grains to caiman from the Amazon. Even the wine pairings come from within Bolivia.

🍷 Drinking & Nightlife

While dive bars and flashy clubs are ubiquitous in Casco Viejo, there are also many elegant bars in La Paz. Local, gilded youth mingle with expats at clubs along **20 de Octubre** in Sopocachi and in Zona Sur, where US-style bars and discos are spread along **Av Ballivián**

and **Calle 21**. The faux-Irish and British bars in Rosario aren't worth your time.

★Hb Bronze Coffeebar COFFEE
(Map p206; http://hb-bronze.com; Plaza Tomás Frías 1570, Casco Viejo; ⊗8:30am-midnight Mon-Sat, 1-9pm Sun; 🛜) Sleek, earthy and architecturally inspiring – coffee shops don't get much cooler than Hb Bronze! This sorely needed addition to the Casco Viejo neighborhood offers the strongest brews in the city, and it doubles as a bar by night with 100% Bolivian cocktails, beers and wines. The food (including bountiful shared plates) is equally memorable.

★La Costilla de Adán COCKTAIL BAR
(☑cell 7207-4518; Armaza 2974, Sopocachi; ⊗9pm-4am Wed-Sat) Take a dive down the rabbit hole into the warped mind of owner Roberto Cazola at this supremely surreal speakeasy. Prepare yourself for hundreds of creepy dolls, a dozen hanging bicycles and a night full of wonder next to the roaring fire. There's no sign out front. Simply ring the bell, wait, and let the magic begin.

★Typica COFFEE
(Map p210; www.facebook.com/typica.cafe; Av 6 de Agosto 2584, Sopocachi; ⊗7am-10:30pm Mon-Sat, 8am-8pm Sun; 🛜) Pick one of four Bolivian roasts and then choose your brew method (Chemex, V60, AeroPress or siphon) at this delightfully bohemian coffeehouse with mismatched antique furnishings and great tunes. Stick around for cakes, empanadas and sandwiches.

Diesel Nacional BAR
(Map p210; ☑cell 7015-5405; Av 20 de Octubre 2271, Sopocachi; ⊗7pm-3am Mon-Sat) Indulge your metal fetish with a trip to this dark, smoky and oh-so-industrial steampunk bar. The music is as edgy as the clientele, and the cocktails are as strong as the recycled vehicle, plane and train parts that make up the decor.

MI TELEFÉRICO

Designed by Austrian company Doppelmayr, the **teleférico** (Aerial Cable Car System; www.miteleferico.bo; ticket B$3, plus B$2 per line transfer; ⊙ 6am-11pm Mon-Sat, 7am-9pm Sun) has been an apple in the eye of Bolivian politicians for decades. Opposition to the project faded under Evo Morales' presidency, and the initial red, green and yellow lines – the colors of the national flag – debuted in May 2014. Seven lines were operating in mid-2018, with four more set to open by the end of 2019.

Andean Culture Distillery   DISTILLERY

(Map p206; ☑ cell 7655-8691; www.facebook.com/andeanculturedistillery; Murillo 826, Rosario; ⊙ tours 4pm Mon-Fri) You've no doubt seen it on menus across town, so why not stop by the first craft distillery in Bolivia to learn more about its Killa Andean Moonshine. Tours include a shot and a cocktail.

Hallwright's   WINE BAR

(Map p210; www.facebook.com/hallwrightsbar; Av Sánchez Lima 2235, Sopocachi; ⊙ 5-11pm Mon-Sat) Want to taste some of Bolivia's high-altitude wines? Make a beeline for this cozy wine bar where the bartender will introduce you to the best local vino. There's a very appetizing selection of tapas, and an unmissable two-for-one happy hour from 6pm to 7:30pm.

Reineke Fuchs   BEER HALL

(Map p210; www.reinekefuchs.com; Pasaje Jáuregui 2241, Sopocachi; ⊙ noon-3pm & 7pm-late Mon-Fri, 7pm-late Sat) This woodsy Sopocachi *brewhaus* features imported German beers, *schnappsladen* and hearty sausage-based fare. They also make their own Pilsner, dunkel and amber ales, based on centuries-old Deutschland traditions – heady concoctions, indeed.

☆ Entertainment

Pick up a copy of the free monthly booklet *Jiwaki* (available in bars and cafes) for a day-by-day rundown of what's on. Otherwise, watch hotel noticeboards for bar and live-music posters, or check the newspapers.

★ Jallalla   LIVE MUSIC

(Map p206; Indaburo 710, cnr Jaén, Casco Viejo; cover incl cocktail B$30-70; ⊙ 9pm-1am Tue, Thu, Fri & Sat) Just above the **Mamani Mamani Gallery** (Fundación Mamani Mamani; Map p206; ☑ 290-6294; www.mamani.com; Indaburo 710, cnr Jaén, Casco Viejo), and with a veritable Sistine Chapel of Mamani Mamani's art on the ceiling, this is the one *peña* you won't want to miss. Not only is there top-tier live music, but also authentic Bolivian tapas (from ex-Gustu chefs!) and creative local libations like the Luka Quivo (Vodka 1825, fresh orange juice, ginger and *airampo* cactus).

★ Estadio Hernando Siles   STADIUM

(Estadio Olímpico La Paz; Map p210; Miraflores; tickets B$40-120) The popularity of *fútbol* (soccer) in Bolivia is comparable to that in other Latin American countries. Matches are played at Estadio Hernando Siles. Sundays are the big game days, and there are typically matches on Wednesdays and Saturdays, too. Prices vary according to seats and whether it's a local or international game. Get tickets at www.todotix.com, in Spanish.

Las Flaviadas   CLASSICAL MUSIC

(Fundación Flavio Machicado Viscarra; Map p210; ☑ 241-1791; www.flaviadas.org; Av Ecuador 2448, Sopocachi; by donation; ⊙ 6:30-8:30pm Sat) Flavio Machicado opened his home to music lovers in 1922 and the *paceña* tradition is continued by his son, Eduardo. Enter the genteel Sopocachi home and listen to two hours of classical music, from Bach to Bolivian artists like Piraí Vaca, while a crackling fire warms you. Start your Saturday *suavamente* (smoothly).

Teatro NUNA   THEATER

(www.teatronuna.com; Calle 21 No 8509, Calacoto) Since opening its doors in 2013, this intimate theater in Zona Sur has fast become one of the most dynamic and lauded in the city. It hosts shows for many of the city's theater, dance and music festivals.

Teatro Municipal
Alberto Saavedra Pérez   THEATER

(Map p206; cnr Sanjinés & Indaburo, Casco Viejo; tickets B$20-50) The municipal theater has an ambitious program of folkloric shows, folk-music concerts and foreign theatrical presentations. It's a great old restored building with a round auditorium, elaborate balconies and a vast ceiling mural.

🔒 Shopping

La Paz is a shopper's paradise; not only are prices very reasonable, but the quality of what's offered can be astounding. The main tourist shopping area lies along the very steep and literally breathtaking Calle Sagárnaga between Av Mariscal Santa Cruz and Tamayo, and adjoining streets. Head to the San Miguel neighborhood in the Zona Sur for stunning designer goods.

★**Walisuma** ARTS & CRAFTS
(www.facebook.com/walisuma.org; Aliaga 1231, San Miguel; ⊙10am-8pm Mon-Fri, to 7pm Sat) 🌿 For a one-of-a-kind souvenir head to Walisuma, which works with 59 different Bolivian artisans. Star items include gorgeous (and ultrasoft) alpaca and vicuña textiles made with natural dyes. There are also quinoa soaps, flavored Uyuni salts and designer sweaters. Prices match the quality.

The Writer's Coffee BOOKS
(Map p206; www.thewriterscoffee.com; Comercio 1270, Casco Viejo; ⊙8.30am-7:30pm Mon-Fri, 9am-12:30pm Sat; 🛜) A gorgeous old-school bookstore with floor-to-ceiling shelves and great titles on local art and history. There's a chilled-out coffee shop in the front corner where you can dig in to your purchases or catch up on wi-fi.

El Ceibo FOOD & DRINKS
(Map p210; www.elceibo.com; cnr Cañada Strongest & Castrillo, San Pedro; ⊙9am-1pm & 2-6:30pm Mon-Fri, 9am-12:30pm Sat) 🌿 Chocoholics mustn't miss El Ceibo, an ecologically friendly producer of fantastic local chocolates.

**Mistura Manifestación
Creativa** ARTS & CRAFTS
(Map p206; www.misturabolivia.com; Sagárnaga 163, Rosario; ⊙9:30am-8pm Mon-Sat) Stop by this lovely little concept store for silver jewelry, bowler hats, alpaca sweaters or local wine and gin.

**Sampaya Outdoor
Equipment** SPORTS & OUTDOORS
(Map p206; www.facebook.com/sampayaoutdoor; Illampu 803, Rosario; ⊙10am-8pm) The best of Illampu's many outdoor stores, with backpacks, tents, hiking shoes, coats, pants and other trekking gear.

ℹ️ Information

DANGERS & ANNOYANCES

La Paz is a big city, and if you're a gringo, you stand out a bit. Especially at night, exercise caution and keep your wits about you. In all likelihood your stay in La Paz will be safe and problem free, but a little common sense goes a long way.

You should avoid El Alto, San Pedro, the cemetery and higher-elevation neighborhoods altogether at night. Use special caution in the bus terminals.

EMERGENCY & IMPORTANT NUMBERS

Tourist police (Policía Turística; Map p210; ☑800-140-071, 800-140-081; Puerta 22, Plaza del Estadio, Miraflores; ⊙24hr) Next to Disco Love City, and English-speaking. Report thefts to obtain a *denuncia* (affidavit) for insurance purposes – they won't recover any stolen goods. They also have a kiosk in front of the bus terminal (p217). Insist on getting the paperwork!

IMMIGRATION OFFICE

Migración (Map p206; ☑211-0960; www.migracion.gob.bo; Camacho 1468; ⊙7:30am-3:30pm Mon-Fri) Some travelers call this place 'Migraine-ation' but this is where you must obtain your visa extensions (free for most nationalities).

LAUNDRY

Lavanderías (laundries) are the cheapest and most-efficient way of ensuring clean clothes in La Paz. Higher-end hotels charge per piece (10 times the price), while budget digs may charge a fair per-kilo rate.

Illampu, at the top of Sagárnaga, is lined with laundries. For quick, reliable same-day, machine-wash-and-dry services, expect to pay B$10 to B$15 per kilo.

Lavandería Maya (Map p206; Sagárnaga 339, Hostal Maya, Rosario; per kilo B$10; ⊙9am-7pm Mon-Sat)

Laverap (Map p206; Aroma 730, Rosario; per kilo B$10; ⊙9am-1:30pm & 3:30-7:30pm Mon-Sat)

Limpieza y Lavandería la Familia (Map p206; ☑290-0557; Tarija 352; per kilo B$10; ⊙9am-6:30pm Mon-Fri, to 2pm Sat)

ℹ️ STAYING SAFE IN LA PAZ

➡ Travel in groups.

➡ Take cabs to go longer distances after 9pm. Make sure it's a radio taxi with a bubble on top.

➡ Don't walk down dark alleys.

➡ Carry small amounts of cash, and leave the fancy jewelry and electronics at home or in the hotel safe.

➡ If physically threatened, it is always best to hand over valuables immediately.

➡ Remember that you likely don't know anybody in Bolivia. It's sad to say, but you should be wary of strangers here.

MEDICAL SERVICES

For serious medical emergency conditions, contact your embassy for doctor recommendations.

Doctors

Dr Ebert Orellana Jordán (☎ 242-2342, cell 6516-9407; Clínica Médica Lausanne, cnr Av Los Sargentos & Costanera) English-speaking doctor often recommended by embassies.

Dr Fernando Patiño (☎ 279-8525, cell 7722-5625; curare27@gmail.com; Los Manzanos 400 cnr Calle 10, Calacoto) English-speaking doctor. Call the cell phone number on weekends for emergencies.

Medical Centers

Clínica Alemana (Map p210; ☎ 243-3676; www.clinicaalemana.com.bo; Av 6 de Agosto 2821; ⊕24hr) Offers German efficiency.

Clínica Médica Lausanne (☎ 278-5775; assistmedbolivia@hotmail.com; cnr Av Los Sargentos & Costanera; ⊕24hr) Across from Club Hípico. Some travelers have complained about prices.

High Altitude Pulmonary & Pathology Institute (Map p210; ☎ 224-5394, cell 7325-8026; www.altitudeclinic.com; Av Copacabana Prolongación 55, Miraflores) Offers medical checkups and can help with high-altitude problems. English spoken.

Hope Centro Médico Internacional (CMI; ☎ 277-2118; www.cmihope.com; Las Retamas 8482; ⊕8am-6pm Mon-Fri) English-speaking doctors and top-notch treatment.

Techno Vision (Map p206; ☎ 240-9637; Comercio 844, Casco Viejo; ⊕10:30am-9:30pm Mon-Fri) Glasses and eye care.

Pharmacies

Farmacias Bolivia (Map p210; Av 16 de Julio 1473; ⊕24hr) A good pharmacy on El Prado.

MONEY

Cash withdrawals of bolivianos and US dollars are possible at numerous **ATMs** (Map p210; Av Sánchez Lima; ⊕24hr) at major intersections around the city.

Banco Mercantil (Map p206; cnr Mercado & Ayacucho; ⊕24hr)

Banco Nacional de Bolivia (Map p206; cnr Colón & Camacho; ⊕24hr)

Casas de cambio (exchange bureaux) in the city center can be quicker and more convenient than banks. Most places open from 9am to 6pm weekdays, and on Saturday mornings.

Be wary of counterfeit US dollars and bolivianos, especially with *cambistas* (street money changers) who loiter around the intersections of Colón, Camacho and Av Mariscal Santa Cruz. Traveler's checks can be virtually impossible to change, except at money changers and banks.

Casa de Cambio América (Map p206; Camacho 1233, Casco Viejo; ⊕9am-6pm Mon-Fri, 9:30am-noon Sat)

BUSES FROM MAIN TERMINAL

DESTINATION	COST (B$)	TIME (HR)
Arequipa (Peru)	140	14
Arica (Chile)	80-180	10
Buenos Aires (Argentina)	800-1200	48-50
Camargo	70-100	16
Cochabamba	40-50	8
Copacabana	30	3-4
Cuzco (Peru)	160-180	14
Iquique (Chile)	100-180	13-15
Juliaca	120	7
Lima (Peru)	450-550	28
Oruro	30-40	3½
Potosí	50-90	9
Puno (Peru)	70-120	7-8
Santa Cruz	110	17-18
Sucre	180	12
Tarija	80	18
Tupiza	100-175	17-18
Uyuni	110	11-12
Villazón	90-175	18

Casa de Cambio Metropoli (Map p206; cnr Colón & Camacho, Casco Viejo; ☻8:45am-6:30pm Mon-Fri, 9am-1pm Sat)

POST

Central Post Office (Ecobol; Map p206; cnr Av Mariscal Santa Cruz & Oruro, Prado; ☻8:30am-6:30pm) *Lista de correos* (poste restante) mail is held for three months for free here – bring your passport. A downstairs customs desk facilitates international parcel posting. Note that most official post offices beyond La Paz have closed in recent years, with local transport syndicates now running the show. If you need to send something internationally, do it here.

TELEPHONE

You can buy cell-phone SIM cards (known as *chips*) for about B$10 from any carrier outlet. If you plan on heading to more remote areas of Bolivia, **Entel** (Map p206; Ayacucho 267, Casco Viejo; ☻8am-7:30pm Mon-Fri, 9am-1pm Sat & Sun) is your best bet.

Convenient *puntos* (privately run phone offices) of various carriers – Entel, Tigo, Viva etc – are also scattered throughout the city, and some cell phone services now have wandering salesmen who will allow you to make a call from their cell phone. Street kiosks, which are on nearly every corner, also sell phone cards, and offer brief local calls for about B$1 per minute. International calls can be made at low prices from the **international call center** (Map p206; cnr Sagárnaga & Murillo; ☻8:30am-8pm Mon-Sat).

TOURIST INFORMATION

Information Kiosks (Main Bus Terminal, cnr Avs Perú & Uruguay) These kiosks at the main bus terminal have maps and standard bus prices, for reference. The attendants, if they happen to be around, may help you find a hotel.

Ministerio de Culturas y Turismo (Map p206; ☎2-220-0910; www.minculturas.gob.bo; Palacio Chico, cnr Ayacucho & Potosí, La Paz; ☻8:30am-6:30pm Mon-Fri) Provides a register of official operators in the tourist industry.

Servicio Nacional de Áreas Protegidas (Sernap; ☎242-6272; www.sernap.gob.bo; Francisco Bedregal 2904, 3rd fl, Sopocachi) Provides limited information on Bolivia's 22

protected national areas. There are offices close to all the major parks, but attention is sometimes erratic. That said the website is informative if you read Spanish.

Tourist Information (Map p210; cnr Av Mariscal Santa Cruz & Colombia, Prado; ☻8:30am-7pm Mon-Fri) Stop by to grab some maps and get detailed information. English is spoken by some staff.

Tourist Information (Map p210; www.facebook.com/GamlpTurismo; Plaza del Estudiante, Prado; ☻8:30am-7pm Mon-Fri) Maps, flyers and some English-speaking staff.

❶ Getting There & Away

AIR

El Alto International Airport (LPB; Héroes Km 7, El Alto) is 10km via toll road from the city center on the altiplano. At 4062m, it's the world's highest international airport.

Airport services include oxygen tanks in the international arrivals area, a newsstand, ATMs, internet, souvenir stores, a small 'sleepbox' hotel with bunkbeds paid by the hour, coffee shops, fast food, a bistro and a duty-free shop in the international terminal. The currency-exchange desk outside the international arrivals area gives poor rates on traveler's checks – if possible, wait until you're in town.

Times and schedules for flights change often. Check your airline's website or call.

The domestic departure tax is B$15, while the international departure tax is US$20 (payable in cash only in the airport lobby, though most international airlines include it in the ticket price).

BUS

Main Bus Terminal (Terminal de Buses; cnr Avs Perú & Uruguay, Challapampa) This services all domestic destinations south and east of La Paz, as well as international destinations. It is a 15-minute uphill walk north of the city center. Fares are relatively uniform among companies.

Villa Fátima Bus Terminal (Av Castillo s/n, Villa Fátima) Services Coroico, Chulumani, Guanay and numerous other Yungas and Amazon destinations. In general, the *micros*

BUSES FROM VILLA FÁTIMA

DESTINATION	COST (B$)	TIME (HR)
Caranavi	25-60	5-7
Chulumani	30	4
Coroico	20-35	3
Guanay	100	6
Rurrenabaque	70-190	12-16
Yolosita	20-35	3

are more expensive with faster and more-direct service, while the *flotas* (buses) offer cheaper, longer and more comfortable trips. The terminal is about 2km uphill from Plaza Gualberto Villarroel.

Cemetery Bus Terminal (Av Baptista) Offers cheap buses to Copacabana, Tiwanaku, Titicaca and Sorata, most of which leave when full. This area is especially hairy at night, and you should watch your bags while boarding.

TRAIN

Empresa Ferroviaria Andina (FCA; ☑212-9774.; www.ferroviaria-andina.com.bo/turismo; Av Arica s/n; tickets B$40-80) runs occasional round-trip tourist trains from El Alto to Tiwanaku (1½-hour stop) and on to Guaqui on Lake Titicaca (2½-hour stop). The train departs El Alto on the second Sunday of the month at 8am. Check the website or call ahead. Trains for the Argentine border, via Uyuni and/or Tupiza, leave from Oruro.

⊙ Getting Around

TO & FROM THE AIRPORT

There are two access routes to El Alto International Airport (p217): the *autopista* toll road (B$3), and the sinuous free route, which leads into Plaza Ballivián in El Alto.

Minibus 212 runs frequently between Plaza Isabel la Católica and the airport between around 7am and 8pm (B$3.80). Look for the sign that says 'Minibus Cotranstur' just outside arrivals. Heading into town from the airport, this service will drop you anywhere along El Prado.

Radio taxis (up to four passengers, around B$70) will pick you up at your door; confirm the price with the dispatcher, or ask the driver to verify it. For a fifth person, there is an additional B$10 charge.

MICRO & MINIBUS

La Paz's sputtering and smoke-spewing *micros*, the older three-quarter-sized buses, charge about B$2 per trip. Minibuses service most places as well, for a slightly higher cost. In addition to a route number or letter, *micros* plainly display their destination and route on a signboard posted in the front window. Minibuses usually

have a young tout screaming the stops. Wave to catch the bus. They stop at signed *paradas* (official stops), or, if the cops aren't watching, whenever you wave them down.

TAXI

Radio taxis (with roof bubbles advertising their telephone numbers) are recommended. Charges are a little higher after 11pm. Normal taxi services (with just a taxi sign, no phone number and no bubble) are best avoided as they've been used in the past for (rare) express kidnappings.

Ask your hotel or restaurant to ring for a taxi for you. Otherwise they can be waved down anywhere, except near intersections or in cordoned off areas. Always confirm the fare before you leave.

A newer solution to safe taxis is to use the **Easy Taxi app** (www.easytaxi.com/bo, in Spanish). **Uber** (www.uber.com) is also available now in La Paz, and you can review the driver's rating before booking a ride.

TRUFI

Trufis are shared cars or minibuses that ply set routes. Destinations are identified on placards on the roof or windscreen. They charge approximately B$3 around town and B$4 to Zona Sur.

AROUND LA PAZ

Tiwanaku

ELEV 3870M (12,696FT)

The ruins of Tiwanaku (sometimes spelled Tiahuanaco or Tihuanaco) make for a good day trip from La Paz for those who want to view a few carved monoliths, archways and arcades, and two decent museums. It's no Machu Picchu or Tikal, but history buffs will love diving into the myths and mysteries of this lost civilization.

Little is actually known about the people who constructed this ceremonial center on the southern shore of Lake Titicaca more than a thousand years ago. However, evidence of their influence, particularly in religion, has

BUSES FROM CEMETERY

DESTINATION	COST (B$)	TIME (HR)
Copacabana	20-25	3-4
Desaguadero	15	2
Huarina (for Cordillera Apolobamba)	15	2
Sorata	20	3½
Tiwanaku	15	1½

been found throughout the vast area that later became the Inca empire.

In the eponymous village nearby, there are a number of hotels, restaurants, a fun little plaza with excellent sculptures inspired by Tiwanaku styles, and a 16th-century church, built, no doubt, with stones from the Tiwanaku site.

Visiting the Ruins

Entrance to the complex is paid at the **ticket office** (Av Puma Punku s/n; B$100; ⊙ tickets 9am-4pm, site 9am-5pm) opposite the museums. If you go on your own, start your visit in the museums to get a basic understanding of the history, then head to the ruins.

Guided **tours** (⏀ 7724-9572; walipini.tiwanacu @gmail.com; Av Ferrocarril s/n; tour for up to 6 people in Spanish/English/French B$150/180/180) are available in English, French and Spanish, and are highly recommended.

The local guides can also arrange onward walking, boating or bus tours from here to Lake Titicaca (just 12km away), which will include camping or stays with local families.

❶ Getting There & Away

Many La Paz agencies offer reasonably priced, guided, full- and half-day Tiwanaku tours (B$80 to B$150 per person), including transportation and a bilingual (English and Spanish) guide. These tours are well worth it for the convenience; most travelers visit Tiwanaku this way.

Diana Tours (Map p206; www.diana-tours. com; Sagárnaga 326, Rosario; trips from B$80) and **Vicuña Travel** (⏀ 228-0140; http://vicuna-travel.com; Main Bus Terminal, cnr Avs Perú & Uruguay, Challapampa) have round-trip guided trips to Tiwanaku from La Paz, leaving daily at 8:30am and returning around 4pm.

For those who prefer to go it alone, minibuses from La Paz's cemetery leave when full and cost B$15 for the 1½-hour drive. Taxis to Tiwanaku from La Paz cost from B$210 to B$280 for the round trip.

LAKE TITICACA

Everything – and everyone – that sits beside this impressive body of water, from the traditional Aymará villages to the glacier-capped peaks of the Cordillera Real, seems to fall into the background in contrast with the shimmering opal jewel set into the spare altiplano earth. It is not hard to see how Inca

AYMARÁ NEW YEAR AT TIWANAKU

Locals don colorful ceremonial dress and visitors are invited to join the party, drink *singani* (distilled grape liquor), chew coca and dance until dawn at celebrations that take place on fall and spring equinox, when the rays of the rising sun shine through the temple entrance on the eastern side of Kalasasaya. The largest celebration is **Aymará New Year** (Machaq Mara; ⊙ Mar 21, Jun 21, Sep 21) on June 21, when as many as 5000 people, including a large contingent of New Agers, arrive from all over the world. Special buses leave La Paz around 4am to arrive in time for sunrise.

legends came to credit Lake Titicaca with the birth of their civilization.

Set between Peru and Bolivia at 3808m, the 8400 sq km lake offers enough activities to keep you busy for at least a week. There are trips to the many islands that speckle the shoreline, hikes to lost coves and floating islands, parties in the tourist hub of Copacabana and encounters with locals that will provide insight into the traditions of one of Bolivia's top attractions.

Copacabana

⏀ 2 / POP 15,000 / ELEV 3808M

Nestled between two hills on the southern shore of Lake Titicaca, Copacabana is a small, bright and enchanting town. It's long been a religious mecca, and local and international pilgrims still flock to its raucous fiestas, but lakeside strolls and meanderings up El Calvario will get you far from the madding crowd. Copa is the launching pad for visiting Isla del Sol and Isla de la Luna, and makes a pleasant stopover between La Paz and Puno or Cuzco.

◉ Sights

Copacabana's central attractions can be visited in one long but relaxed day, but there are some great trips further afield. Much of the action in Copa centers on Plaza 2 de Febrero and Av 6 de Agosto, the main commercial drag, which runs from east to west. At its western end is the lake and a walkway (*costañera*) that traces the shoreline. The transportation hub is in Plaza Sucre.

Lake Titicaca

Map labels: Parque Nacional Apolobamba (10km); Pumasani Pass; Lago Arapa; Huancané; 108; Charazani; Taraco; Moho; Ayata; Juliaca; Tilali; Conima; Aeropuerto Juliaca; Isla Soto; Puerto Acosta; BOLIVIA; Ancoma; Isla Amantani; Escoma; Quiabaya; Illampu (6360m); Isla Campanario; Carabuco; Sorata; Isla Taquile; Chaguaya; Ancohuma (6429m); Puno; Chimu; Lake Titicaca; Ancoraimes; Chucuito; Isla del Sol; Warisata; Acora; Isla de la Luna (Koati); Achacachi; Ilave; Yampupata; Estrecho de Tiquina; Huatajata; Copacabana; Chúa; Huarina; Kasani; San Pedro de Tiquina; San Pablo de Tiquina; Yunguyo; Puerto Pérez; Batallas; PERU; 32; 3; 113; Juli; Pomata; Isla Taquiri; Isla Suriqui; Isla Kalahuta; La Paz (40km); Lago de Wiñaymarka; Isla Pariti; Zepita; Tiwanaku; Desaguadero; Guaqui; Tiwanaku; Tacna (275km); Río Suches; 50 km; 25 miles

★ Cathedral

CHURCH

(Plaza 2 de Febrero) FREE The sparkling white *mudéjar* (Moorish–style) cathedral, with its colorful *azulejos* (blue Portuguese-style ceramic tiles) and domes, dominates the town. Check the noticeboard in front of the entrance for the mass schedule.

The cathedral's black Virgen de Candelaria statue, **Camarín de la Virgen de Candelaria**, carved by Inca Emperor Tupac-Yupanqui's grandson, Francisco Yupanqui, is encased above the altar upstairs in the *camarín* (shrine); visiting hours can be unreliable.

⚜ Festivals & Events

Fiesta de la Virgen de Candelaria

RELIGIOUS

(⊙ Feb 2-5) Honors the patron saint of Copacabana and Bolivia. Copacabana holds an especially big bash, and pilgrims and dancers come from Peru and around Bolivia. There's much music, traditional Aymará dancing, drinking and feasting. On the third day, celebrations culminate with the gathering of 100 bulls in a stone corral along the Yampupata road.

Fiesta de la Cruz

RELIGIOUS

(Feast of the Cross; ⊙ May) This fiesta is celebrated over the first weekend in May all around the lake, but the biggest festivities are in Copacabana. Expect elaborate costumes and traditional dancing.

🛏 Sleeping

A host of budget options abound, especially along Jáuregui, charging about B$30 to B$40 per person. There are also several midrange options that are well worth the extra bolivianos. During fiestas accommodations fill up quickly and prices increase up to threefold.

Hostal Sonia

HOTEL $

(☎ 862-2019, cell 7196-8441; hostalsoniacopacabana @gmail.com; Murillo 256; r per person with/without bathroom B\$50/40; @ 🛜) This lively spot has bright and cheery rooms, great views from the upstairs rooms and a top-floor terrace, making it one of the top budget bets in town. The proprietors own the swankier (and newer) **Hotel Lago Azul** (📞 862-2581; cnr Costañera 13 & Jáuregui; s/d B\$130/260; @ 🛜), if you want to upgrade.

Hotel Mirador HOTEL $

(www.titicacabolivia.com; cnr Av Busch & Costañera; r per person incl breakfast B\$50; 🛜) Stunning value for the impressive view of the lake that shines like a beacon from the end of the long rooms. The common areas are dated – and the hotel seems in a perpetual state of being half-open – but its sprawling size gives it the charm of a Los Angeles motel.

★**Las Olas** BOUTIQUE HOTEL $$

(📞 862-2112, cell 7250-8668; www.hostallasolas.com; Pérez 1-3; s/d/tr/q US\$41/52/68/79; @ 🛜) To say too much about this place is to spoil the surprise, so here's a taste: quirky, creative, stylish, ecofriendly, million-dollar vistas. Plus there are kitchens, private terraces with hammocks and a solar-powered Jacuzzi. A once-in-a-lifetime experience and well worth the splurge.

Hotel La Cúpula HOTEL $$

(📞 cell 7708-8464; www.hotelcupula.com; Pérez 1-3; s/d/tr from US\$17/29/54, s/d/tr ste from US\$32/48/60; 🛜) International travelers rave about this inviting oasis, marked by two gleaming-white domes on the slopes of Cerro Calvario, with stupendous lake views. The rooms are basic but stylish. The gardens, hammocks, shared kitchen and friendly atmosphere add to the appeal. The helpful staff speak several languages, and you can even buy the artwork in your room. Best to reserve ahead.

★**Hotel Rosario del Lago** HOTEL $$$

(📞 245-1658, in La Paz 2-277-6286; www.gruporosario.com; Paredes, near Costañera; s/d incl breakfast US\$89/99; @ 🛜) One of the smartest places in town, the hacienda-styled, three-star sister of Hotel Rosario in La Paz has charming modern rooms with solar-heated showers, double-glazed windows and lake views. The polite staff also provide excellent service. The altiplano light streams on a pleasant sun terrace.

✖️ Eating & Drinking

Some of the best Titicaca fish is served at **beachfront stalls** (Costanera; trout from B\$25;

🕗 8am-9pm), though hygiene is questionable. The bargain basement is the market *comedor* (dining hall), where you can eat a generous meal of *trucha* (river trout) for a pittance, or an 'insulin shock' breakfast of hot *api morado* (corn drink; B\$4) and syrupy *buñuelos* (doughnuts or fritters; B\$3).

Several tourist-oriented cafes are situated along Av 6 de Agosto.

El Condor & the Eagle Cafe CAFE $

(www.facebook.com/elcondorandtheeaglecafe; Av 6 de Agosto s/n; mains B\$30; 🕗 7am-1pm Mon-Fri; 🛜📶) Make this cheery traveler's cafe your breakfast spot with great veggie options, French-press coffee and owners who are more than happy to offer advice on Bolivia. There's also a small bookstore and a great collection of journals where fellow travelers offer tips for onward journeys.

★**La Cúpula Restaurant** INTERNATIONAL $$

(www.hotelcupula.com; Pérez 1-3; mains B\$24-59; 🕗 7:30am-3pm & 6-10pm, closed lunch Tue; 📶) An inventive use of local ingredients makes up the extensive international and Bolivian menu here. The vegetarian range includes a tasty lasagna and there's plenty for carnivores, too. Dip your way through the cheese fondue with authentic Gruyère – it's to die for...which leaves the Bolivian chocolate fondue with fruit platter beyond description.

★**La Orilla** INTERNATIONAL $$

(📞 862-2267; Av 6 de Agosto s/n; mains B\$36-60; 🕗 9:30am-2pm & 5-9:30pm; 📶) Some say this cozy maritime-themed restaurant is the best in town, with fresh, crunchy-from-the-vine vegetables and interesting trout creations that incorporate spinach and bacon. They might just be right. Even the high-altitude falafels are pretty good.

Gourmet Ali INTERNATIONAL $$

(📞 7124-6336; Av 6 de Agosto s/n; mains B\$40-60; 🕗 7am-11pm; 🛜) An unassuming and brightly lit restaurant with seriously good food, including fresh takes on trout (stuffed, in a lasagna), as well as pizzas, pastas and filets of llama.

Waykys Disco Bar BAR

(www.facebook.com/waykysdiscoteca; cnr Avs 16 de Julio & 6 de Agosto; 🕗 9pm-late Mon-Sat) Looking for a dark, black-lit bar with loud music, dingy bathrooms and graffiti-covered walls? The kind of place you might make poor decisions at? This is the spot. Be sure to try Evo, a lightning-bolt of a cocktail with *singani*

Copacabana

Copacabana

(distilled grape liquor), lemon juice, coca leaves and liquor de coca.

ⓘ Information

DANGERS & ANNOYANCES

Radiation The thin air, characteristically brilliant sunshine and reflection off the water mean scorching levels of ultraviolet radiation. Wear a hat and sunscreen in this region, and drink lots of water to avoid dehydration.

Crowds Be especially careful during festivals. Stand well back during fireworks displays, when explosive fun seems to take priority over crowd safety, and be wary of light-fingered revelers.

MEDICAL SERVICES

You'll likely get the best care at the tourist-friendly **Medical Health Home** (✆ cell 7727-8510; www.medicalhome.com.pe; cnr Baptista & Costañera). For serious situations don't think twice – head straight to La Paz.

MONEY

ATMs dot Plaza Sucre. Shops on Av 6 de Agosto will exchange foreign currency (clean dollar bills preferred). Most *artesanías* (crafts stores) sell Peruvian soles.

ℹ️ Getting There & Away

AIR

A new airport opened in 2018. At the time of research it was not yet complete, but was planned to have domestic flight connections to La Paz, Rurrenabaque, Trinidad and Uyuni.

BOAT

Buy your tickets for boat tours to Isla de la Luna and Isla del Sol from agencies on Av 6 de Agosto or from beachfront kiosks. If you're traveling in a big group, consider renting a private boat for B$600 to B$900 per day. Separate return services are available from both islands.

BUS

Most buses leave from near Plazas 2 de Febrero or Sucre. The more comfortable nonstop tour buses from La Paz to Copacabana – including those operated by **Titicaca Tourist Transportation** (✆ 862-2160; www.titicacabolivia.com; cnr Avs 6 de Agosto & 16 de Julio) – cost about B$30 and are well worth the investment. They depart from La Paz at about 8am and leave Copacabana at 1:30pm and 6:30pm (four hours). You will need to exit the bus at Estrecho de Tiquina (Tiquina Straits) to cross via **ferry** (per person B$2, per car B$30-$40; ⏰ 5am-9pm) between the towns of San Pedro de Tiquina and San Pablo de Tiquina (15 minutes).

Buses to Peru depart and arrive in Copacabana from Av 16 de Julio. You can also get to Puno by catching a public minibus from Plaza Sucre to Kasani (B$4, 15 minutes). Across the border there's frequent, if crowded, onward transportation to Yunguyo (five minutes) and Puno (2½ hours).

A new player in the bus game, Irish-run **Bolivia Hop** (Map p206; www.boliviahop.com; Linares 940, Rosario; ⏰ office 8:30am-7pm) offers services between Lima, Arequipa, Copa and La Paz, and helps travelers with customs and *hostal* arrangements.

Isla del Sol

☎ 2 / POP 3000 / ELEV 3808M

Easily the highlight of any excursion to Lake Titicaca, Isla del Sol is a large island with several traditional communities, decent tourist infrastructure including restaurants

BOLIVIA ISLA DEL SOL

ℹ️ GETTING TO PERU

Most travelers enter/exit Peru via Copacabana (and the Tiquina Straits) or the scruffy town of Desaguadero (avoiding Copacabana altogether). Note that Peruvian time is one hour behind Bolivian time. Always keep your backpack with you when crossing the border.

Via Copacabana

Micros to the Kasani/Yunguyo border leave Copacabana's Plaza Sucre regularly, usually when full (B$4, 15 minutes). At Kasani you obtain your exit stamp at passport control and head on foot across the border. On the Peruvian side, a taxi or mototaxi can ferry you to Yunguyo (about Peruvian S3, five minutes). From here, you can catch a bus heading to Puno.

An efficient alternative is to catch a tourist bus from La Paz to Puno via Copacabana (from B$60) or vice versa; some allow you a couple of days' stay in Copacabana. Note, though, that even if you've bought a ticket to Cuzco or elsewhere in Peru, you'll change buses in Puno. Buses to Cuzco depart from Puno's international terminal, located about three blocks from the local terminal.

Via Desaguadero

A quicker, if less interesting, route is via Desaguadero on the southern side of the lake. Several bus companies head across this border from/to Peru. The crossing should be hassle-free: you obtain your exit stamp from the **Bolivian passport control** (Desaguadero; ⏰ 8:30am-12:30pm & 2-8:45pm), walk across a bridge and get an entry stamp at *migración* in Peru. Buses head to Puno at hourly intervals (about 3½ hours).

Isla del Sol

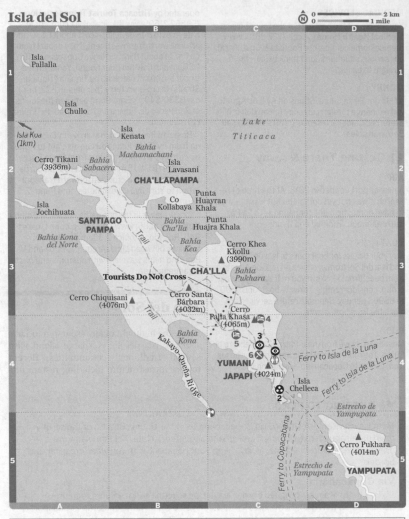

Isla del Sol

and hotels, a few worthy pre-Columbian ruins, amazing views, excellent hikes through terraced hills and, well, lots and lots of brilliant sunshine.

The island's permanent residents – a mix of indigenous peoples and émigrés – are distributed between the main settlements of **Cha'llapampa**, near the island's northern end; **Cha'lla**, which backs onto a lovely sandy beach on the central east coast; and Yumani, which straddles the ridge above Escalera del Inca in the south and is the biggest town on the island. Unfortunately, due to a conflict between island communities, it is currently only possible for travelers to visit Yumani.

Extensive networks of walking tracks make exploration fairly easy, though the altitude and sun may take their toll: carry lunch and ample water. The sun was born here and is still going strong.

◉ Sights

Yumani   VILLAGE
Yumani is the main village at the south end of the island. Most boats drop you at the village's dock, about 200m downhill from the town proper. The small church, **Iglesia de San Antonio**, serves the southern half of the island. Nearby you'll find an exploding cluster of guesthouses and fabulous views over the water to Isla de la Luna.

Pilko Kaina   RUINS
(B$10) This prominent ruins complex near the southern tip of the island is about 30 minutes (2km) south by foot from Yumani. It sits well camouflaged against a steep terraced slope. The best-known site is the two-level **Palacio del Inca**, thought to have been constructed by the Incan emperor, Túpac Inca Yupanqui.

Escalera del Inca   GARDENS
(Yumani; B$10) Just uphill from the ferry dock at Yumani, along the beautifully reconstructed Escalera del Inca (Inca stairway), you'll pass plenty of terraced gardens, small shops and hotels. It's a lung-buster that gains almost 200m in elevation over less than 1km, so take your time – or hire donkeys (B$30) to carry your pack.

☐ Sleeping

Inti Kala Hostal   HOTEL $
(☑ cell 7151-6293; hotelintikala@gmail.com; Yumani; r per person incl breakfast US$20; ☎) This place has a massive deck and remodeled rooms with solar-heated showers, fluffy bedspreads and Andean motifs. The terrace is a hit.

Hostal Jallalla   HOTEL $$
(☑ mobile 6816-5404; Yumani; r incl breakfast B$300; ☎) Known for having strong wi-fi, Hostal Jallalla is clean and perfectly located

near both the restaurants at Yumani and the turnoff to Mirador Palla Khasa. It's banana yellow; you can't miss it.

Hostal Puerta del Sol   HOTEL $$
(☑ cell 7350-6995; Yumani; s with/without bathroom B$150/40, cabin per person B$150, d B$250) Located on the promontory on top of the hill, this friendly option has good views from most rooms (number 14 is awesome), clean sheets and a nice terrace. The rooms with bathrooms are much better, and the Andean textiles add a nice touch. Passive solar heating in the cabins helps keep you warm at night.

★La Estancia Ecolodge   LODGE $$$
(☑ 2-244-0989; www.ecolodge-laketiticaca.com; La Estancia; s/d incl breakfast & dinner US$120/154; ☎) ♥ Magri Turismo's delightful adobe cottages are set above pre-Inca terraces facing snowcapped Illampu. They are authentically ecological with solar-powered showers, sun-powered hot-boxes for heaters and Aymará thatched roofs. Staff can arrange hiking, boat trips and mystic ceremonies.

★Palla Khasa   CABIN $$$
(☑ cell 7321-1585; www.pallakhasalodgeandtours.com; Yumani; bungalows incl breakfast B$570-750) About 300m north of Yumani proper, this top choice has beautifully manicured grounds and 14 circular stone bungalows with gas-heated showers, tiled bathrooms and great views. The restaurant is highly recommended for regional cuisine cooked in an earthen oven.

✕ Eating

There are more pizzerias in Yumani than Titicaca has *trucha*. Many midrange and top-end accommodation options have good restaurants, most of which are blessed with good views – those on the ridge in particular are special for the sunset. Nearly all menus are identical; *almuerzos* (set lunches) and set dinners cost between B$25 and B$30.

★Las Velas   INTERNATIONAL $$
(lasvelassunisland@gmail.com; Yumani; mains B$50-70; ⊙ 4-11pm; ☑) Want a candlelit dinner of organic vegetarian pizza at 4000m? Head to this beloved hilltop restaurant with wonderful westerly views. There are also pastas and traditional Bolivian fare like trout and kingfish. Perfect for a beer or wine at sunset, too.

THE DARK CLOUD OVER SUN ISLAND

Trekking the length of Isla del Sol from the north to the south was once one of the great joys of visiting Lake Titicaca. That's no longer possible. Tourists have been restricted from traveling north of Yumani (and its satellite village of La Estancia) due to an ongoing conflict between the communities of Cha'lla, in the middle, and Cha'llapampa, to the north.

In theory there should be someone at a guard post stopping you if you walk too far from Yumani. In practice, this doesn't always happen. Either way, do not be tempted to test your fate. A Korean tourist was stabbed and strangled under mysterious circumstances in early 2018 shortly after a heated exchange between the two communities to the north. No one was charged with the murder, but it was suspected at the time that she had unwittingly crossed into the northern half of the island.

These unfortunate events should by no means stop you from visiting Isla del Sol. Stick to Yumani or La Estancia and your trip will likely be perfectly safe and conflict-free. As with any conflict, it's best to check with hotels and tour operators in the region (namely Copacabana) before you depart for Isla del Sol to find out the latest, as everything may have been resolved by the time you read this.

❶ Getting There & Away

You can reach Isla del Sol by ferry from either Copacabana or Yampupata, or with a guided tour.

Ferry tickets may be purchased at the **Asociación Unión Marines** (Costañera, Copacabana; one-way/round-trip B$20/30; ☺ departs Copacabana 8:30am & 1:30pm) ticket kiosks on the beach in Copacabana or from town agencies (save yourself the trouble and buy direct). Boats land at either Pilko Kaina or Escalera del Inca near Yumani. Return trips leave Yumani at 10:30am and between 3pm and 4pm (one-way B$25).

Titicaca Tours (Costañera, Copacabana; round-trip B$30; ☺ departs Copacabana 8:30am) will take you to both Isla del Sol and Isla de la Luna in half a day – two hours to explore the former and one hour at the latter. However, it's highly recommended to stay overnight or longer on one of the islands.

Asociación Transport Yampu Tour Lacustre (☏ cell 7525-4675; Yampupata; ☺ 8am-6pm) runs boats between Yampupata and Isla del Sol for B$130. Prices are per boat.

THE CORDILLERAS & YUNGAS

Caught between the Andes and the Amazon, this rugged region has got just about everything you could ask for from your Bolivian adventure.

For the vertically inspired, there are glacier-capped 6000m peaks and adrenaline-charged mountain-bike descents. Nature lovers can seek out the cloud forests and hillside semitropical Yungas towns of Chulumani, Coroico and Sorata, where you can hike to nearby waterfalls, start your river trip into the Amazon, go mountain biking or simply enjoy the breeze from a mountain hideaway.

Far off the tourist trail, the areas around the Quimsa Cruz and Cordillera Apolobamba offer large swaths of wilderness, a few lost ruins and some great opportunities for adventure.

Everywhere in between you'll find treks along preserved Inca trails, plenty of good wildlife-watching opportunities, warm weather, cool breezes and a pervading air of hard-won tranquility.

Coroico & Yolosa

☏ 2 / POP 19,330 / ELEV 1750M (5741FT)

With warm weather, plenty of spectacular views, good resort-style hotels for all budgets and something of an infectious laid-back air, Coroico is the most visited tourist town in the Yungas. It's perched eyrie-like on the shoulder of Cerro Uchumachi and commands a far-ranging view across forested canyons, cloud-wreathed mountain peaks, patchwork agricultural lands, citrus orchards, coffee plantations and dozens of small settlements.

Coroico is derived from the Quechua word *coryguayco*, meaning 'golden hill.' The town's biggest attraction is its slow pace, which allows plenty of time for swimming, sunbathing and hammock-swinging.

The village of Yolosa is located about 7km from Coroico along the World's Most Dangerous Road. It has a few cool hangouts, an animal refuge, and a steady stream of dust-caked Dangerous Road bikers who generally end their rides here.

◉ Sights & Activities

The **Río Coroico** flows through the Nor Yungas about three hours north of Coroico. This is the country's most popular commercially rafted river, and is the most convenient to La Paz.

The white water is great, but unfortunately the high tourist season coincides with the dry season. Several agencies in La Paz and around Coroico's plaza offer day-long rafting trips for B$250 to B$350 per person.

★ La Senda Verde
Wildlife Sanctuary   ANIMAL SANCTUARY
(www.sendaverde.org; Yolosa; B$100, bear visit extra B$20; ⊙10am-4pm) At 12-hectare La Senda Verde, there's a new concept: humans are 'caged' while most of the 200-plus monkeys run free. This protects people and monkeys alike (adult monkeys can be aggressive, and sick humans can infect their simian cousins). Toucans, caimans, Andean bears, ocelots and margays are among the other wild residents. There's a nice buffet-style

restaurant on-site. It's located 500m north of Yolosa (B$40 taxi or B$10 minibus from Coroico).

El Calvario   WALKING
For pretty views, El Calvario is an easy 20-minute hike from town. Here, the **Stations of the Cross** lead to a grassy knoll and chapel. You can continue to **Cerro Uchumachi** (a five-hour round-trip), which affords terrific valley views.

Zzip the Flying Fox   ADVENTURE
(☑231-3849; www.facebook.com/ziplinebolivia; Yolosa; single trips B$220; ⊙9am-5pm) Three zipline sections take you flying at speeds of up to 85km/h through the forest canopy near Yolosa. The 1500m zipline can be combined with trips down the World's Most Dangerous Road. Book your ticket at agencies in La Paz or Coroico.

Cafe Munaipata   TOUR
(☑7129-8379; www.cafemunaipata.com; Rincon Munaipata; tours B$120-350) This beautifully manicured coffee plantation 4km from the plaza in Coroico has professional tours that cover everything from picking beans to roasting and taste-testing. It also has on-site lodging (B$200 per person) and a small cafe (the llama filet in a coffee sauce is unmissable). Reserve at least a day ahead.

BOLIVIA COROICO & YOLOSA

THE WORLD'S MOST DANGEROUS ROAD

Before a new replacement road opened in 2007, the road between La Paz and Coroico was identified as the World's Most Dangerous Road (WMDR) by an Inter-American Development Bank (IDB) report. The moniker was well deserved: an average of 26 vehicles per year disappeared over the edge into the great abyss.

The WMDR is now used almost exclusively by cyclists, support vehicles and the odd tourist bus. The gravel road is narrow (just over 3.2m wide), with precipitous cliffs, up to 600m drops and few safety barriers. Some 27 cyclists have died doing the 64km trip, which has a 3600m vertical descent, and readers have reported close encounters and nasty accidents.

Unfortunately, there are no minimum safety standards in place for operators of this trip. As such the buyer has to beware; this is one activity where you don't want to be attracted by cheaper deals.

Nuts & Bolts

The trip begins around 7am in La Paz. Your agency will arrange a hotel pickup. From there, you'll bus it up to the *cumbre* (summit), about 45 minutes outside La Paz. Trips cost anywhere from B$325 to B$850, but you get what you pay for. Most operations provide a solid buffet lunch in Yolosa, and some even have arrangements with hotels for showers and swimming pool access. There is a B$50 surcharge to use the old road. Bring sunscreen, a swimsuit and a dust-rag (if they don't provide one), and ask about water allotments. The bus takes you back up in the early evening; expect to arrive back in La Paz around 9pm.

🛏 Sleeping

Hostal El Cafetal   HOTEL $

(📞 7193-3979; Miranda s/n; r per person with/without bathroom B$90/55; 🛜🏊) Out of town by the hospital, this French-owned hotel has a lot of potential – tremendous views, a nice pool and large grounds. The rooms with private bathrooms are worth the price, while those without have soft beds and are slightly unkempt. French is spoken.

⭐ Hostal Sol y Luna   RESORT $$

(📞 7156-1626; www.solyluna-bolivia.com; Apanto Alto; campsites B$50, s B$220-275, d B$380-440, s/d without bathroom B$100/160; 🛜🏊) Set on a jungle-covered hill, this inspiring spot offers appealingly rustic accommodations in a variety of *cabañas* (cabins), simple rooms and camping spots (dry season only). The rambling grounds over 5 hectares include two pools and a small hot tub. There are yoga classes, secluded bungalows and enchanted forests. A 20-minute uphill walk from town, or a B$20 taxi, provides some reprieve for the non-party set.

Many cabins have kitchens, and there's a top-tier on-site **restaurant** (mains B$20-40; ⏱8am-9pm; 🖊). Email reservations require a two-night minimum.

Hotel Bella Vista   HOTEL $$

(📞 213-6059; coroicohotelbellavista@hotmail.com; Héroes del Chaco 7; s/d without bathroom B$90/180, incl breakfast B$170/250; 🛜) The views truly are something to behold – tropical-bird-filled gardens, coffee and orange plantations in the distance – and while the new management can be a bit inconsistent, you'll love the bright colors, firm mattresses (an oddity in Coroico), cast-iron furniture and…oh yeah, the views!

Hotel Esmeralda   HOTEL $$

(📞 213-6017; www.hotelesmeralda.com; Julio Suazo s/n; s/d B$360/440, dm/s/d without bathroom B$90/160/280; @🛜🏊) A top pick for the party set, this resort-style hotel on the hillside has amazing grounds, tremendous views and a swimming pool. There are rooms for all tastes, from cheap dorms to larger digs with balconies and private bathrooms. The rooms with shared bathrooms can be a bit dark. A book exchange and on-site restaurant mean you may never leave the hotel.

🍴 Eating & Drinking

Coroico Star   SOUTH AMERICAN $

(www.facebook.com/coroicostar; Tomás Monje s/n; mains B$25-30; ⏱10am-10pm; 🛜) A few steps down from the main plaza, this popular travelers' meeting point might serve the best *pique a lo macho* (sausages and french fries in sauce) you'll encounter on your entire trip. The owners also organize a very popular and respected bike ride down the Camino del Muerte. A nice spot to sit on the steps and relax with fellow *mochileros* (backpackers).

Villa Bonita   INTERNATIONAL $

(📞 7191-8298; Héroes del Chaco s/n; mains B$12-35; ⏱8:30am-5:30pm Wed-Sun; 🖊) This peaceful garden cafe is just 600m from town but seems like a world away. The personable owners offer delicious homemade ice creams bursting with fresh fruit, tasty sundaes with unusual local liqueurs (try the

---

SACRED COCA?

Coca in Bolivia is largely reserved for traditional uses such as chewing the leaf, drinking it in *mate* and using it in religious ceremonies. Its mild alkaloids are said to provide an essential barrier against altitude sickness and fatigue for farm workers and miners in the highlands. In the 2009 new constitution, President Evo Morales declared coca an intrinsic part of Bolivia's heritage and Andean culture. However, it is also used to produce the drug cocaine.

For most Bolivians, the white powder snorted by partygoers worldwide has nothing to do with their sacred plant, and they resent the suggestion that they should be held responsible for anyone else's misuse of it. Morales, a former *cocalero* (coca grower) himself, has vowed to continue the war against drug-trafficking, but not at the expense of the country's coca industry. Critics argue that his policies have enabled a huge black market for illegal cocaine production in Bolivia. Visitors will no doubt notice that drug money is pouring into the Chapare region, Morales' former home.

Regardless of its status in Bolivia, coca is illegal in most of the world and travelers should not attempt to take any coca leaves home.

THE SLOW BOAT TO RURRENABAQUE

River travel was once the only lifeline connecting remote Amazonian communities to the rest of Bolivia. While new roads mean it's harder than ever to find regular boats navigating these magnificent waterways, the journey between Guanay and Rurrenabaque is one shining exception.

Though rarely used by local commuters these days, this route is frequented by several La Paz–based tour operators who market it as a more picturesque alternative to the 15-hour bus ride or 45-minute plane trip to Rurrenabaque. Most tours involve wild camping on riverside beaches, fishing for basic camp meals and treks into some of the more remote stretches of Parque Nacional Madidi in search of wildlife.

yungueña, an elixir of orange, maracuya and lemon), and an eclectic range of vegetarian dishes.

★ Toto   ITALIAN $$
(☑7151-2707; Tomás Monje s/n; mains B$40-60; ☺6-11pm Mon, Tue & Thu-Sat) Homemade tagliatelle, gnocchi and ravioli pastas with delicious sauces, not to mention the best pizza in town, make this a must for those wanting a little Italian comfort food. The soft lighting, warm service and soothing music are oh-so inviting.

Carla's Garden Pub   GERMAN $$
(Back-Stübe Konditorei; ☑7207-5620; Pasaje Linares; mains B$20-60; ☺1-10pm Wed-Fri, from noon Sat & Sun; ☎) A Dutch pub owner has combined her thatched-roof beer hall with an established German restaurant and moved it to the bottom of the plaza's steep stairs (check for the 'Open' sign). They've maintained the same tasty breakfasts, tempting cakes and pastries, as well as pasta and memorable *sauerbraten* (marinated pot-roast beef) with *spätzle* (German noodles).

M&M Coffee   COFFEE
(www.facebook.com/cielo.recien.tostado.coroico. bolivia; Pando s/n; ☺9am-12:30pm & 3-9pm Wed-Sun) Wrap your hands around a mug of some high-quality (and low-priced) local coffee at this small 2nd-story cafe a block east of the plaza. Inquire about tours to a nearby coffee plantation to dig deeper into the local coffee culture.

❶ Information

MONEY
There are three ATMs on the main plaza. **Prodem** (Plaza García Lanza; ☺8:30am-4pm Tue-Fri, 8am-3pm Sat & Sun) changes dollars at a fair rate and does cash advances for 5% commission.

MEDICAL SERVICES
There's a basic regional **hospital** (☑213-6002; Miranda s/n; ☺24hr) near Hostal El Cafetal, but for serious medical treatment you'll be better off in La Paz.

❶ Getting There & Away

BUS
Buses and *micros* (three-quarter-size buses) from La Paz arrive either at the **bus terminal** (Av Manning; during peak travel times) or Plaza García Lanza. It's a steep walk uphill to the plaza from the terminal, or you can hop in a taxi (B$5).

From the Villa Fátima area in La Paz, buses and *micros* leave for Coroico (B$25, 3½ hours) at least hourly from 7:30am to 8:30pm, more on weekends and holidays. En route they stop in Yolosita, a dusty crossroads where you can connect with buses heading north to Rurrenabaque (B$100, 12 to 13 hours) and further into the Bolivian Amazon.

For Chulumani, the quickest route is to backtrack to La Paz. Although the junction for the Chulumani road is at Unduavi, few passing *micros* have spare seats at this point.

The road to Caranavi was only open from 4pm to 6am at the time of writing. Buses from Coroico will take you there (and on to other Amazon destinations) for B$30, departing at 2pm, 3pm and 6pm.

TAXI
Turbus Totaí (☑289-5573; Plaza García Lanza) runs comfortable taxi services to La Paz, leaving when full (B$25, two hours).

Chulumani
☑2 / POP 2000 / ELEV 1700M (5577FT)

Perched scenically on a hillside, this peaceful little burg has a friendly town square, a bustling market and tropical attitude. And with far fewer international visitors than tourist-center Coroico, it's way more tranquil.

CLIMBING IN THE CORDILLERA REAL

Bolivia's Cordillera Real has more than 600 peaks over 5000m, most of which are relatively accessible and many of which are just a few hours' drive from La Paz. The best season for climbing is May to September. You should be fully acclimatized to the altitude before attempting any of the ascents.

By far the easiest way of tackling these mountains is to go on a guided climb. Several La Paz agencies (p205) offer trips that include transportation, *refugio* (mountain hut) accommodations, equipment hire and a guide. Prices start at around B$900 to B$1400 for an ascent of Huayna Potosí.

Huayna Potosí This is Bolivia's most popular major peak because of its imposing beauty and ease of access, as well as the fact that it's 88m over the magic 6000m figure (but 26ft under the magic 20,000ft figure). While most people come here to climb, you can also stay at the mountain lodge, and head out for some fun hikes or mountain biking.

Condoriri Massif Condoriri Massif is actually a cluster of 13 peaks ranging from 5100m to 5648m. The highest of these, Cabeza del Cóndor (Head of the Condor) has twin wing-like ridges flowing from either side of the summit. Known as Las Alas (The Wings), these ridges cause the peak to resemble a condor lifting its wings.

Illimani Illimani, the 6438m giant overlooking La Paz, was first climbed in 1898 by a party led by WM Conway, a pioneer 19th-century alpinist. Although it's not a difficult climb technically, the combination of altitude and ice conditions warrants serious consideration and caution.

Chulumani is a paradise if you're into birds and butterflies – there are clouds of the latter, and several endemic species of the former. At a tropically warm and often wet altitude, the town makes a great trekking base camp and a relaxing weekend retreat with great views. The only time its pervasive tranquility is interrupted is during the week following August 24, when Chulumani stages the riotous **Fiesta de San Bartolomé**.

🛏 Sleeping

Hostal Dion   HOTEL $
(☑ 289-6034; Bolívar s/n; r per person with/without bathroom incl breakfast B$80/60) Half a block south of Plaza Libertad, this is the best of the central options. The homey setting includes extremely clean rooms, cable TV, electric showers and sparkling tile floors. Enjoy the courtyard garden, but be sure to ask about the curfew.

★ **Country House**   HOTEL $$
(☑ 7528-2212; Tolopata 13; r per person incl breakfast B$150; ❄) Easily your best bet in town, this welcoming home is 10 minutes west of the plaza, by the basketball court. Lovingly decorated rooms have hot-water showers and plant-packed patios. Great breakfasts, abundant birdlife and delicious home-cooked dinners (killer quinoa pie!). Owner Javier is a gregarious host who can organize many local excursions.

ⓘ Information

Chulumani's tourist office is in a kiosk on the main plaza, but it's rarely open. If you are thinking of exploring the region it is worth seeking out hotel owners such as English-speaking Javier Sarabia at the Country House.

There's no ATM in Chulumani. Prodem (two blocks west of the plaza on Pando) changes US dollars and gives cash advances on credit cards (5% commission).

ⓘ Getting There & Away

Since the original La Paz–Coroico road closed, the nail-biting route from La Paz to Chulumani, which extends on to Irupana, has claimed the title of the World's Most Dangerous Road (p227). If you can keep your nerves in check, it is actually an exceptionally beautiful route.

From Villa Fátima in La Paz (Minasa Terminal), various bus companies depart when full for Chulumani (B$30, four hours) from 8am to 4pm. From Chulumani, La Paz–bound buses wait around the *tranca* (police post). Theoretically, there are several departures before 10am and after 4pm.

Coming from Coroico, get off at Unduavi and wait for another vehicle.

Sorata

🎵2 / POP 23,020 / ELEV 2670M (8759FT)

Knocked back a peg in the early 2000s by social unrest, Sorata is making a slow recovery, and in fact is a bit of a Yungas gem. While it doesn't have the shiny digs of its arch-nemesis Coroico, this semi-tropical village sitting high above a verdant agricultural valley does offer great weather, access to some of Bolivia's best treks, kick-ass downhill mountain biking and an atavistic air that may just become intoxicating.

In colonial days Sorata (from the Aymará *shuru-ata* or 'shining peak') provided a link to the Alto Beni's goldfields and rubber plantations, and a gateway to the Amazon Basin. These days, mining is the main source of employment in the region. But it really is worth your while to pick up a guide in La Paz – or better yet, hire a local one from the **Asociación de Guías de Sorata** (Sorata Guides & Porters Association; 🎵213-6672; http://guiasorata.com; Plaza) – and explore this under-appreciated mountain playground.

👁 Sights & Activities

⭐ Gruta de San Pedro   CAVE

(B$20; ⏱9am-5pm) A popular excursion, San Pedro Cave, known in the Aymará language as Chussek Uta (House of Owls), is approximately 500m deep, with an enclosed lagoon that can be crossed in pedal boats (B$5 per person, and recommended). Guides with the necessary lamps will help you find your way around. PCMB, the Bolivian program to conserve bats, has identified three nectar- and insect-eating bats in the pitch-black surroundings.

Mirador Wila Kollu   VIEWPOINT

(Camino a Laripata) This vertigo-inducing lookout 3035m above Sorata is, quite literally, breathtaking. To reach it, walk (or hire a taxi, B$80) up the road to Laripata. Just before Laripata you'll see a small trail off to the left leading to a railed-in platform.

Laguna Chillata   HIKING

Laguna Chillata is a popular hike from Sorata. It's a pretty spot with great views of the surrounding sierra and Lake Titicaca. The former trail is now mostly a road, so you can take a taxi to La Mina and hike one hour up to the lagoon. On the right-hand side of the lagoon are ruins of a small Incan stone village. It's worthwhile taking a guide, as it's easy to get lost.

🛏 Sleeping

Hostal Las Piedras   HOTEL$

(🎵7191-6341; soratalaspiedras@yahoo.com; Villa Elisa Calle 2 s/n; s/d/tr B$120/160/195, s/d without bathroom B$70/110) Hostal Las Piedras has amazing views from most rooms, clean sheets, a shared kitchen and a fun common area. Breakfast (B$30 to B$46) is an optional extra.

HIKING & BIKING IN SORATA

Hiking

Sorata is a convenient base for hikers and climbers pursuing some of Bolivia's finest high-mountain landscapes. Ambitious adventurers can do the seven-day **El Camino del Oro** trek, an ancient trading route between the altiplano and the Río Tipuani goldfields. Otherwise there's the challenging seven-day **Illampu circuit.**

While it's possible to hike independently, it is best to hook up with a guide, mainly because of the need to be aware of local sensibilities and the difficulty of finding passable routes. The most economical, authorized option is to hire an independent Spanish-speaking guide from the Asociación de Guías de Sorata.

Mountain Biking

With its thrillingly steep descents and spectacular mountain scenery, the Sorata area makes a top two-wheel destination.

One of the best trips around is the descent into town from the mountains astride Lake Titicaca. Throughout the ride you're presented with superb views of towering snow-capped peaks, plunging valleys and tiny rural villages. La Paz–based **Gravity** (🎵7670-3000; www.gravitybolivia.com; Linares 940, La Paz; ⏱9am-7pm Mon-Fri, 10am-3pm Sat, 2-6pm Sun) and local company **Sorata Xtreme** (🎵7157-2302; soratxtremebike@gmail.com; Plaza; ⏱9am-noon & 2-6pm) offer guided rides here.

★**El Encanto Sorata** HOTEL $$
(☑7709-2511; Villa Elisa Calle 2 s/n; r per person B$112) This new brick building down past the soccer field has the cleanest, smartest and sunniest rooms in town, all with private bathrooms and valley views. The flowery garden below makes it an extremely tranquil oasis.

★**Altai Oasis** LODGE $$
(☑7151-9856; www.altaioasis.com; Camino a la Gruta, Zona Quincirka; campsites B$30, cabins B$750-900, s/d B$300/500, dm/s/d without bathroom B$100/125/290; ☜☒) This really does feel like an oasis, with a lush garden, hammocks and a pretty balcony cafe. The riverside retreat offers grassy campsites, comfortable rooms and romantically rustic *cabañas* (cabins), intricately and fancifully painted. The English-speaking owner can offer great local tips.

✕ Eating

★**Helados El Oso Goloso** ICE CREAM $
(☑7208-1805; Camino a la Gruta; 1 scoop B$5; ☺7am-7pm) Dig in to some seriously good artisanal ice cream under the watchful eye of rescued rheas at this eccentric outdoor *heladería* (ice cream shop) on the road to Gruta de San Pedro (p231). Try local flavors such as *chirimoya* (custard apple), *chilto* (Peruvian groundcherry) or *karicari* (wild blackberry). Also serves traditional Bolivian food and fresh fruit juices.

La Casona BOLIVIAN $
(Plaza; almuerzo B$10-15; ☺7:30am-8:30pm) For a good *almuerzo* (set lunch) at a great price and with fantastic service, do as the locals do and head to this old-school eatery on the plaza.

Cafe Illampu CAFE $
(Camino a la Gruta, Zona Quincirka; sandwiches B$28; ☺9am-6pm Wed-Mon, closed Jan & Feb) This small open-air cafe with a wild and rickety lookout tower serves sandwiches (using homemade bread), cakes and espresso coffees. It has a great lending library of books and board games, as well as a grassy field for camping (B$18 per person).

Altai Oasis INTERNATIONAL $$$
(www.altaioasis.com; Camino a la Gruta, Zona Quincirka; mains B$50-150; ☺8am-7:30pm Tue-Sat, to 2pm Sun; ☑) The peaceful balcony restaurant at this lovely retreat 20 minutes' walk from town serves coffee, drinks and a range of vegetarian dishes. There are T-bone steaks and, for an Eastern European touch, Polish borscht and tasty goulash. It's a great place to just sit with a drink, too, absorbing views over the valley and the tinkle of wind chimes.

❶ Information

Prodem (Villaricencio s/n; ☺12:30-4pm Mon, 8:30am-4pm Tue-Fri, 8am-3pm Sat) changes US dollars, does credit-card cash advances for a 5% commission and has Western Union facilities, but there are no ATMs. Be sure to bring all the cash you'll need.

Sunday is market day. Tuesday, when many businesses are closed, is considered *domingo sorateño* (Sorata's Sunday).

There's a small **tourist information** (☑7910-0320; Plaza; ☺8am-noon & 2-6pm Tue-Fri, to noon Sat) center on the plaza.

❶ Getting There & Away

Sorata is a long way from other Yungas towns, and there's no road connecting it directly with Coroico, so you must go through La Paz via a paved road.

Buses leave for Sorata from near La Paz's cemetery regularly between 4am and 5:30pm (B$20, 3½ hours). From Sorata, La Paz–bound *micros* depart when full and *flotas* (long-distance buses) leave on the hour between 4am and 5pm. **Sindicato Mixto de Sorata** (☑7321-9976; Samuel Tejerina s/n) offers services to Copacabana (B$45) and Coroico (B$50) when there is demand. It also runs regular trips to Achacachi (B$15) and Haurina (B$20).

SOUTHERN ALTIPLANO

The harsh and sometimes almost primeval geography of the Southern Altiplano will tug at the heartstrings of visitors with a deep love of bleak and solitary places. Stretching southwards from La Paz, this high-plains wilderness is framed by majestic volcanic peaks, endless kilometers of treeless stubble and the white emptiness of the eerie *salares* (salt deserts), which are almost devoid of life. At night the stargazing is spectacular, but it's as cold as you could ever imagine.

The area around Parque Nacional Sajama offers some breathtaking scenery and climbing, while revelers may wish to hit up Carnaval (p236) celebrations in the gritty, straight-talking mining city of Oruro (p234). Further south Salar de Uyuni (p242) is the star attraction, and a three-day jeep tour

Southwest Bolivia

0 — 100 km
0 — 50 miles

Lake Titicaca
Sorata
Caranavi
Beni
Río Secure
Isla del Sol
Copacabana
Huayna Potosí (6088m)
Parque Nacional Cotapata
Coroico
Parque Nacional Isiboro-Securé
Río Isiboro
Puno (35km)
Lago de Huyñaymarka
Tiwanaku
Milluni
LA PAZ
La Paz
Desaguadero
Guaqui
Viacha
Nevado Illimani (6439m)
Cochabamba
PERU
Río Desaguadero
Comanche
Caquiaviri
Parque Nacional Tunari
Villa Tunari
Corocoro
Patacamaya
Cochabamba
Parque Nacional Carrasco
Calacoto
Charaña
Ciudad de Piedra
Callapa
Totora
Capachos
Oruro
Obrajes
Visviri
Volcán Sajama (6542m)
Curahuara de Carangas
Lago Uru Uru
Vinto
Calacala
Negro Pabellon
Tambo Quemado
Putre
Cosapa
Turco
Toledo
Chullpas de Chusa K'eri
Parque Nacional Torotoro
Arica (45km)
Parque Nacional Lauca
Parque Nacional Sajama
Pumiri (Ciudad Pétrea de Pumiri)
Corque
Llallagua
Volcán Guallatire (6061m)
Huachacalla
Escara
Oruro
Lago Poopó
Cha'llapata
Sabaya
Chipaya
Orinoca
Cordillera de los Frailes
Sucre
Pisiga
Villa Vitalina
Laguna Coipasa
Santuario de Quillacas
Tarapaya
Coipasa
Salar de Coipasa
Salinas de Garci-Mendoza
Volcán Tunupa (5400m)
Río Mulatos
Potosí
Iquique (35km)
Llica
Tahua
Coquesa
Salar de Uyuni
Tomave
Pulacayo
CHILE
Salar de Empexa
Isla Incahuasi (Isla del Pescado)
Ojos del Salar
Colchani
Toja
Uyuni
Cerro Chorloque (5630m)
Colcha K (Villa Martín)
Isla Cáscara de Huevo
Atocha
Huaca Huañusca
San Juan
Chiguana
Comunidad Amor
San Cristóbal
Portugalete
Oro Ingenio
Salar de Chiguana
Ollagüe
Avaroa
Alota
San Vicente
Tupiza
Volcán Ollagüe (5865m)
Potosí
Calama
Valles de Rocas
Cordillera de Lípez
San Pablo de Lípez
Laguna Cañapa
Laguna Amarilla
Laguna Guinda
Campamento Ende
Sol de Mañana Geyser Basin
Laguna Colorada
Laguna Celeste
Laguna Blanca
Villazón
Yavi
Reserva Nacional de Fauna Andina Eduardo Avaroa
La Quiaca
Termas de Polques
Salar de Chalviri
Volcán Licancábur (5930m)
Laguna Verde
ARGENTINA
Antofagasta (75km)
San Pedro de Atacama
Hito Cajón

of the region is at the top of most travelers' itineraries. From here, you can head to the warmer cactus-studded valleys around Tupiza (p243) for horseback riding and mountain biking.

Oruro

📞 2 / POP 265,000 / ELEV 3706M (12,158FT)

Oruro's Carnaval (p236) celebrations are famous throughout South America for their riotous parties, lavish costumes and elaborate parades. The culmination of the city's rich dance and musical heritage, the festivities attract bands, dance troupes and revelers from across Bolivia and beyond. Outside Carnaval season, there are some worthwhile museums to visit in the city and plenty to see in the surrounding area.

At first glance Oruro is a sprawl of sunbaked buildings in shades of terracotta and dusty tan, but there's something about this gritty miners' city that endears it to visitors. In many ways Oruro (which means 'where the sun is born') is an intriguing place, where 90% of the inhabitants are of indigenous heritage. *Orureños* (Oruro locals) refer to themselves as *quirquinchos* (armadillos), after the carapaces of their *charangos* (traditional Bolivian

Oruro

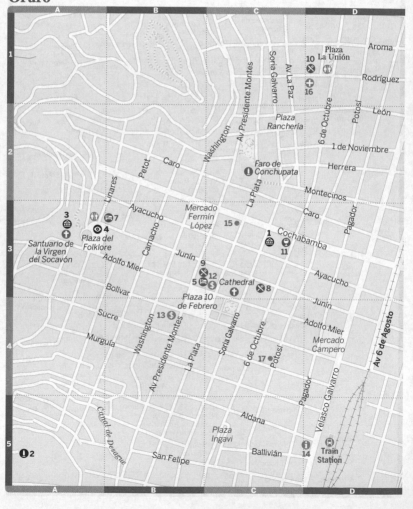

ukulele-like instruments). The city makes for an oddly atavistic experience that some may find intoxicating.

◉ Sights

Museo Sacro, Folklórico, Arqueológico y Minero — MUSEUM

(Plaza del Folklore; B$12; ◉ 9-11:45am & 3:15-6pm) An excellent double museum attached to Santuario de la Virgen del Socavón. Access is by guided tour only, beginning with a descent down from the church to a mining tunnel lined with tools and representations of El Tío, spirit of the underground. Upstairs are a variety of archaeological and folklore exhibits, from Wankarani-period stone llama heads to Carnaval costumes.

Monumento Escultérico Virgen del Socavón — MONUMENT

(Cerro Santa Bárbara; B$10; ◉ 9am-5pm) Oruro's **teleférico** (Plaza del Folklore; one-way/return B$10/15, during Carnaval B$20/30; ◉ 11am-7pm Wed, Sat & Sun) zips passengers on a three-minute journey from Plaza del Folklore up to the towering statue of Virgen del Socavón, perched atop Cerro Santa Bárbara (3883m), from where there are impressive views of the city and beyond. Inside the monument, stairs lead to viewing platforms and a small exhibition of carnival posters and photographs, some dating back to 1910.

Casa de la Cultura Simón Patiño — MUSEUM

(Soria Galvarro 5755; B$10; ◉ 8:30-11:30am & 3-6:30pm Mon-Fri, 9am-3pm Sat) The grand former residence of tin baron Simón Patiño is now a museum, displaying his furniture,

BOLIVIA ORURO

0 — 200 m
0 — 0.1 miles

Av Villarroel

Nueva Terminal de Omnibuses (2.5km)

Velasco Galvarro
Av 6 de Agosto
Rodríguez
Buenos Aires
Av Brasil
1 de Noviembre
Montecinos
Caro
Av del Ejército
Tacna
Buenos Aires
Ayacucho
Junín
Tarapaca
Av Brasil
Tejerina
Bolívar
Sucre
Tacna
Murguía

personal bric-a-brac, musical instruments and fine toys (you're not allowed to play with them though). Entry is by guided tour only.

Tours

Charlie Tours
TOURS

(📞 524-0666; charlietours@yahoo.com) Run by the knowledgeable Juan Carlos Vargas, Charlie Tours is a real specialist in the region. In addition to city tours, mine visits and excursions to nearby attractions such as **Cala Cala** (B$20; ⊙ 9am-5pm Mon-Fri) and **Termas de Obrajes** (B$15; ⊙ 7am-4pm), it offers trips to places further afield, including the Chipaya, Salar de Coipasa and Sajama. The offices are outside town, so call or email.

Festivals & Events

Carnaval
FESTIVAL

(⊙ Feb or Mar) During the spectacular 10-day Carnaval, which starts from the Saturday before Ash Wednesday, the city explodes with parades, folk dances and parties. Revelers pitch water at each other and anyone who comes in their way – it's best to just embrace it. Several parades, including **Entrada** and **La Diablada**, feature dancers in intricately garish masks and costumes.

Sleeping

Hostal Graciela
HOSTEL $

(📞 525-2082; www.facebook.com/OruroHostal Graciela; Herrera 47; dm/s/d/tr incl breakfast B$56/85/140/180; 🛜) Colorful murals and friendly, English-speaking staff make for a warm welcome at Graciela, though the unheated rooms are pretty cold at night. Dorms are small and rather dank; the street-facing private rooms are brighter. The top-floor common area with a small kitchen and bar is a good place to meet with other travelers.

The hostel runs a free city walking tour at 10am daily, and offers a number of cycling and hiking tours in the surrounding area.

⭐Flores Plaza Hotel
HOTEL $$

(📞 525-2561; www.floresplazahotel.com; Adolfo Mier 735; s/d/tr incl breakfast B$300/450/550; 🅿🖲🛜) A top midrange choice right on the main plaza, this eight-story, three-star hotel offers nicely renovated rooms, good city views, an ample breakfast buffet and friendly management. Request a room on a higher floor for better views.

Hotel Virgen del Socavón
HOTEL $$

(📞 528-2184; Junín 1179; s/d/ste incl breakfast B$300/400/480; 🅿🛜) This modern option has rooms looking right onto Plaza del Folklore, making it the most sought-after hotel in town come Carnaval time when prices spike. Outside Carnaval season, it's still a worthwhile option, with fresh bedspreads, contemporary decor and excellent balconies overlooking the action on the plaza.

Eating & Drinking

Local specialties include *thimpu de cordero* (a mutton-and-vegetable concoction smothered with *llajua*, a hot tomato-based sauce) and *charquekan* (sun-dried llama meat with corn, potatoes or beans, eggs and cheese).

Govinda
VEGETARIAN $

(Junín, btwn Soria Galvarro & Calle 6 de Octubre; mains B$6-19; ⊙ noon-2pm & 4-10pm Mon-Sat; 🖋) Forget you're in Bolivia at this Hare

BUSES FROM ORURO

DESTINATION	COST (B$)	TIME (HR)
Arica (Chile)	140	8
Calama (Chile)	150	14
Cochabamba	30	5
Iquique (Chile)	70-100	8
La Paz	35	3
Potosí	30	5
Sucre	50-80	8
Tarija	60-80	12
Tupiza	50-60	10-12
Uyuni	25-35	4½
Villazón	70-120	12

Krishna–devoted restaurant behind a modern glass front, where vegetarian meals are fresh, cheap and creative, the decor light, and the music ambient. Good juices and milkshakes too, some with soya milk, of course.

La Casona   ITALIAN $$
(Av Presidente Montes 5969; mains B$21-40; ⊙9am-1pm & 4-11pm) Straight-out-of-the-oven *salteñas* (meat and vegetable pasties) for lunch and Oruro's best pizzas for dinner keep this little place buzzing, especially at night when it gets really busy and warm.

★ Las Delicias   BARBECUE $$$
(⌨527-7256; Rodríguez, btwn Calle 6 de Octubre & Av La Paz; almuerzo B$20, mains B$45-90; ⊙9am-10:30pm) This is arguably the best *churrasquería* (grilled-meat restaurant) in town, with attentive service, sizzling tableside *parrilladas* (plates of mixed grilled meats), great *almuerzos* (set lunches) and top-notch Argentine-imported beef.

★ Dali   BAR
(cnr Calle 6 de Octubre & Cochabamba, 2nd fl; ⊙3pm-1am Mon-Sat, 4pm-midnight Sun) The closest place you'll find to a hip hangout in Oruro is this chilled cafe-bar that caters to the city's young set. Come for the drinks, not the food. It's a perfect launchpad for a night out on the town.

❶ Information

There are several banks with ATMs in town, particularly around Plaza 10 de Febrero.
Banco Bisa (Plaza 10 de Febrero)
Banco de Crédito (Plaza 10 de Febrero)
Caseta de Información Turística (Tourist Information Office; cnr Velasco Galvarro & Aldana; ⊙8:30am-noon & 2:30-7pm Mon-Fri)
Migraciónes (⌨527-0239; www.migracion. gob.bo; cnr Cochabamba & La Plata; ⊙8:30am-12:30pm & 2:30-6:30pm Mon-Fri)
Policlínica Oruro (⌨527-5082; Rodríguez 579)

❶ Getting There & Away

AIR
Domestic flights leave from Oruro's **Aeropuerto Juan Mendoza** (⌨527-8333), 5km east of the city center. **Boliviana de Aviación** (BoA; ⌨511-2473; www.boa.bo; Potosí, btwn Sucre & Bolívar; ⊙8:30am-12:30pm & 2:30-6:30pm Mon-Fri, 9am-1pm Sat) flies at least once daily to Cochabamba (30 minutes, from B$296) continuing on to Santa Cruz (2½ hours, from B$458). A taxi from the airport to Oruro city center costs B$30.

BUS
Long-distance buses use the **new bus terminal** (Gregorio Reynolds), 5km east of the city center. To get here, take any minibus marked 'nueva terminal' traveling north along Av 6 de Agosto. There's a luggage storage office (B$5) on the ground floor of the terminal.

Buses to La Paz depart every half-hour, and there are departures throughout the day for Cochabamba, Potosí, Sucre and Uyuni. Trans Copacabana and Chino Bus offer services to Santa Cruz via Cochabamba, departing in the late afternoon (B$100). There are daily services to Arica, Calama and Iquique in Chile, which depart in the evening.

TRAIN
Trains run south from Oruro to Villazón on the border with Argentina, passing through Uyuni, Atocha and Tupiza along the way. At the time of research, no trains were running south of Uyuni due to damage to the track caused by flooding in the Tupiza area. Repairs were underway to the section north of Tupiza, which suffered less damage. The section from Tupiza to Villazón is expected to take longer to repair.

Expreso del Sur is slightly more luxurious with heating, departing Oruro at 2:30pm on Tuesdays and Fridays. Cheaper service is available on the Wara Wara line, which leaves Oruro on Wednesdays and Sundays at 7pm. There is a return service on Expreso del Sur arriving at 7:10am on Thursdays and Sundays, and on the Wara Wara line arriving at 9:10am on Tuesdays and Fridays.

Buy tickets at least a day ahead from the **train station** (⌨527-4605; www.fca.com.bo; Velasco Galvarro; ⊙ticket office 9am-noon & 2:30-5:30pm Mon, Wed, Thu & Sun, 8am-5pm Tue & Fri). Don't forget to bring your passport. On train days, there's a left-luggage kiosk here.

Uyuni
⌨2 / POP 10,300 / ELEV 3669M (12,037FT)
Standing in defiance of the desert-like landscape that surrounds it, Uyuni occupies a desolate corner of southwestern Bolivia. Mention Uyuni to a Bolivian and they will whistle and emphasize *harto frío* (extreme cold). Yet despite the icy conditions, the town has a cheerful buzz about it, with hundreds of travelers passing through every week to kick off their tour of Salar de Uyuni or the Southwest Circuit.

Founded in 1889 by Bolivian president Aniceto Arce, Uyuni remains an important military base. Tourism and mining are the other major sources of employment in the town. The world's largest lithium reserve –

Uyuni

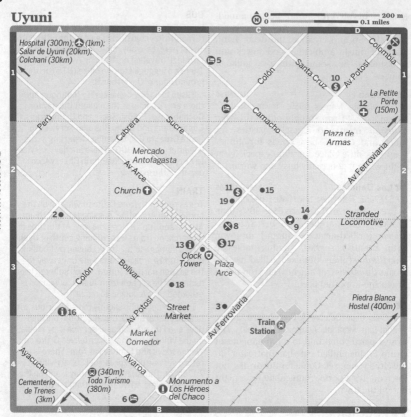

Hospital (300m); ♨ (1km);
Salar de Uyuni (20km);
Colchani (30km)

Plaza de Armas

La Petite Porte (150m)

Mercado Antofagasta

Church

Stranded Locomotive

Clock Tower

Plaza Arce

Piedra Blanca Hostel (400m)

Street Market

Train Station

Market Comedor

Cementerio de Trenes (3km)

(340m); Todo Turismo (380m)

Monumento a Los Héroes del Chaco

Uyuni

🟢 Activities, Courses & Tours
1 Hidalgo Tours...............................D1
2 Quechua Connection.......................A2
3 Salty Desert Aventours.....................C3

🛏 Sleeping
4 Hostal La Magia de Uyuni................C1
5 Tambo Aymará................................C1
6 Toñito Hotel...................................B4

🍴 Eating
Minuteman Revolutionary Pizza....(see 6)
7 Tika...D1
8 Wiphala Pub...................................C3

🍷 Drinking & Nightlife
9 Extreme Fun Pub.............................C3

ℹ Information
10 Banco Mercantil Santa Cruz.............D1
11 Banco Nacional de Bolivia................C2
Banco Unión.............................(see 11)
12 Clínica las Carmelitas.....................D1
13 Infotur...B3
14 Lavarap..C2
15 Migración.......................................C2
16 Office of Reserva Nacional de
Fauna Andina Eduardo Avaroa..........A3
17 Prodem..C3

ℹ Transport
18 Amazonas.......................................B3
19 Boliviana de Aviación......................C2

about 100 million tons – lies beneath the neighboring salt flat, and could potentially fuel all the smart phones and electric cars the world could build over the next century.

While work on building extraction and processing facilities has been proceeding slowly, expect more and more mining activity near Uyuni in the coming years.

◉ Sights

Cementerio de Trenes
HISTORIC SITE

(Train Cemetery) `FREE` The only real attraction in Uyuni, Cementerio de Trenes is a rusty collection of historic steam locomotives and rail cars dating back to the 19th century, when there was a rail-car factory here. Today they sit decaying in the yards about 3km southwest of the modern-day station along Av Ferroviaria.

☞ Tours

Theoretically, you can visit Salar de Uyuni and the attractions of the Southwest Circuit independently, but it's extremely challenging due to unreliable transport and the remoteness of the area. It's best to take an organized tour from either Uyuni or Tupiza, which probably works out cheaper than doing it alone anyway. From the end of December to the end of March, the salt flat floods and many tour agencies shut down, which means that you can only visit the edges of the salt flat at this time.

Costs

Tours cost B$800 to B$1200 for three days at a standard agency, and B$1200 to B$1500 at a high-end operation. The cheapest tours do not include English-speaking guides. It's cheaper to book in Uyuni; you'll pay more if you book elsewhere. Tours include a driver (who also serves as your guide, mechanic and cook), two nights' accommodation (quality varies depending on the agency), three meals a day and transport. You'll also pay a B$30 entrance fee to Isla Incahuasi (p242) and a B$150 fee to enter Reserva Nacional de Fauna Andina Eduardo Avaroa (p243). Those traveling on to Chile will need B$20 to B$50 for the border crossing. Most agencies don't accept credit cards.

What to Bring

You'll want to bring several liters of water, snacks, a headlamp, sunscreen, sunglasses, a sunhat, warm clothes, a camera and chargers, and a plastic dinosaur (for photos, of course). Bring cash for entry to the national parks, and small change for bathroom fees (usually B$5). A sleeping bag is also highly recommended. Some agencies provide sleeping bags for no extra fee; check when booking if a sleeping bag is included.

Choosing an Agency

Generally, it doesn't matter which agency you book with (other than the high-end ones), as most run the same routes, share drivers and sort travelers into groups of five or six people (don't accept more!). The high-end agencies have better hotels, can customize tours and have more reliable cars.

Though things are improving, a number of travelers have died on this trip, mostly in drunk-driving accidents. Ask to see the car you will be traveling in and to meet the driver ahead of time.

Standard Tours

The most popular tour is the three-day circuit taking in Salar de Uyuni, Laguna Colorada, Sol de Mañana, Laguna Verde and points in between.

The quality of food varies, though many agencies use the same caterers. Vegetarians should make arrangements with the operator ahead of time (and bring plenty of snacks just in case). Higher-end operators offer nicer hotels – with heaters and down comforters – and better food.

Many tours do the Isla Incahuasi trip on the first day and spend the night in the handful of salt hotels around the village of Chuvica that sits on the eastern edge of the salt flat.

After entering the remote and beautiful region of Los Lípez (p243) on the second day, many tour groups spend the second night in the dormitory accommodation at Laguna Colorada, or a little further on in the village of Huayajara, for the coldest night on the trip. On day three of the standard tour, you wake at dawn to visit the large geyser field dubbed Sol de Mañana (p243).

BOLIVIA UYUNI

ⓘ SALAR TOURS WARNING

Operators are piled high in Uyuni: there are currently more than 100 legal agencies offering trips to the *salar*. While the competition may mean more choice, remember that cost-cutting leads to operators corner-cutting – at the expense of your safety and the environment.

The results of this have included deadly accidents. At least 26 people have been killed in jeep accidents on the Salar de Uyuni salt plains since May 2008, including an accident in 2016 in which five tourists died. There have been alarming reports of ill-equipped vehicles without seat belts, speeding tour operators, a lack of emergency equipment, breakdowns, drunk drivers and disregard for the once-pristine environment of the *salar*.

If you're not heading to Chile, the final afternoon drive back to Uyuni has a few potential worthwhile stops in Valles de Rocas and San Cristóbal.

Salty Desert Aventours TOURS
(☑7237-0444; www.saltydesert-uyuni.com; Av Ferroviaria, btwn Av Arce & Bolívar; ⊙10am-12:30pm & 2:30-7:30pm) This operator gets good reviews. Tours with an English-speaking guide are available for an extra cost.

Quechua Connection TOURS
(☑693-3923; www.quechuaconnection4wd.com; cnr Bolívar & Cabrera; ⊙7:30am-noon & 3-8pm) This company offers salt-flat tours with English-speaking guides. Its best-sellers are tours that include the chance to cycle 3km across the salt flats.

Hidalgo Tours TOURS
(☑693-2989; www.salardeuyuni.net; Av Potosí 113, Hotel Jardines de Uyuni; ⊙7am-7:30pm) This upscale agency offers high-end, private tours with accommodations at luxury salt hotels.

🛏 Sleeping

★Piedra Blanca Hostel HOSTEL $$
(☑7643-7643; www.piedrablancabackpackers. hostel.com; cnr Loa & Tomás Frías; dm B$77, d with/ without bathroom B$290/220) This appealing hostel is in a modern building featuring plenty of concrete and wood, a bright central courtyard and sociable common areas. The private rooms are simple but cozy, and dorms have large pine bunks, comfy mattresses, lockers and thick comforters; all rooms are heated. There's a bar and a well-equipped kitchen, and breakfast is included in the room rates.

Tambo Aymará HOTEL $$
(☑693-2227; www.hoteltamboaymara.com; Camacho, near Cabrera; s/d incl breakfast B$390/500; 🛜) This homely option has terrific common areas and rooms decorated with Bolivian textiles, huge beds and handmade wooden furniture. There are also flannel sheets and electric heaters to keep you warm. Some rooms are a bit dark but there's reliable hot water and service is friendly. Touch the ring to get in.

Hostal La Magia de Uyuni HOTEL $$
(☑693-2541; www.hostalmagiauyuni.com; Colón 432; s/d in old section B$210/350, in new section B$280/490; @🛜) One of the pioneers of Uyuni tourism, this choice hacienda-inspired

hotel is a solid midrange choice. The rooms in the older wing have fewer creature comforts and are smaller and darker, while the newer rooms have nice antique furniture, new beds, thick comforters and heaters. Breakfast is included.

★La Petite Porte BOUTIQUE HOTEL $$$
(☑7388-5960; www.hotel-lapetiteporte-uyuni.com; Av Ferroviaria 742; s/d B$620/725; @🛜) This gorgeous boutique hotel oozes with understated class and pizzazz. Rooms have a unique ceiling heating system that ensures they are toasty and warm even when it's freezing outside, and little touches like free tea and coffee make you feel at home.

🍴 Eating & Drinking

★Minuteman Revolutionary Pizza PIZZA $$
(☑693-3186; Av Ferroviaria 60; mains B$55-65; ⊙8-10am & 5-9pm) This convivial spot inside **Toñito Hotel** (www.tonitouyuni.com; s/d incl breakfast B$400/500; 🅿🛜) is run by Chris from Boston and his Bolivian wife Sussy, and is a travelers' favorite. Sample the best pizzas in town as well as tasty gourmet salads. It's also a cozy spot for a beer, glass of Tarija wine or a hearty breakfast (B$20 to B$50).

★Tika BOLIVIAN $$
(☑693-2989; www.tikarestaurante.com.bo; Av Potosí 113; mains B$40-92; ⊙4-10pm; 🛜) Tika's chic, modern dining room is an appealing setting to sample contemporary takes on traditional Bolivian dishes, such as *charque lipeño* (sun-dried llama meat with potatoes, cheese and corn) and *k'alaphurka*, a gurgling corn soup served with a hot volcanic stone. There's also a well-stocked bar and a lengthy wine list.

Wiphala Pub PUB FOOD $$
(☑693-3545; Av Potosí 325; mains B$35-50; ⊙2-11pm) Named after the multicolored indigenous flag, this place has a traditional atmosphere and welcoming feel with its wooden tables, earthy vibe and board games. It serves pizza and tasty Bolivian dishes, specializing in llama meat and quinoa, and has quinoa beer (B$35). Service can be slow.

Extreme Fun Pub PUB
(La Llamita; Sucre 23; ⊙2:30pm-1am) For a night of extreme fun head to Uyuni's top drinking spot. The extensive cocktail list features concoctions such as Sexy Llama Bitch and Sensual Llama's Navel, as well as hot cocktails to

warm you up on cold nights. There are salt floors, drinking games, friendly service and beautiful *salar* photos. Guitars are on hand for impromptu music sessions.

ℹ Information

DANGERS & ANNOYANCES

Watch your cash, especially around the train and bus stations. There have been reports of groups of young men pretending to help buy tickets or transfer luggage to a bus, and then taking off with backpacks. If you are robbed, you can get a police report from the **Tourist Police** (cnr Avs Potosí & Arce) at their office in the clock tower.

IMMIGRATION

Migración (☑ 7307-9328; www.migracion.gob. bo; Av Potosi, near Sucre; ⊙ 8:30am-12:30pm & 2:30-6:30pm Mon-Fri, 8:30am-12:30pm Sat) Visa extensions only. Get your visas and exit/entry stamps at the border.

LAUNDRY

Most hotels offer some sort of laundry service, but it can be pricey.
Lavarap (Av Ferroviaria, btwn Sucre & Camacho; per kilo B$20; ⊙ 8am-8pm) Handy and efficient.

MEDICAL SERVICES

Hospital Obrero (Caja Nacional de Salud; ☑ 693-2025; Av Arce, btwn Fernando Alonzo & Calvimontes)
Clínica las Carmelitas (☑ 693-3539; Santa Cruz, btwn Avs Potosí & Ferroviaria)

MONEY

There are several cash machines in town. Several places on Av Potosí between Arce and Bolívar buy Chilean and Argentine pesos.
Banco Mercantil Santa Cruz (cnr Av Potosí & Santa Cruz)
Banco Nacional de Bolivia (cnr Av Potosí & Sucre)
Banco Unión (cnr Sucre & Av Potosí)

Prodem (Plaza Arce; ⊙ 8am-4pm Mon-Fri, 9am-noon Sat)

TOURIST INFORMATION

Infotur (☑ 693-3666; cnr Avs Potosí & Arce; ⊙ 8am-noon & 2:30-6:30pm Mon-Fri) Well stocked with leaflets on Uyuni and the rest of Bolivia. At research time the office was located in the bus terminal while the office on Avenida Arce was being renovated.
Office of Reserva Nacional de Fauna Andina Eduardo Avaroa (REA; ☑ 693-2225; www.boliviarea.com; cnr Colón & Avaroa; ⊙ 9am-6pm Mon-Fri) Administrative office for the park in Uyuni. You can buy your park entry (B$150) here if going under your own steam.

ℹ Getting There & Away

AIR

The quickest way to get to Uyuni is by flying direct from La Paz to Aeropuerto Joya Andina, 1km north of town.
Amaszonas (☑ 693-3333; www.amaszonas. com; Av Potosí s/n; ⊙ 8:30am-7pm Mon-Fri) and **Boliviana de Aviación** (BoA; ☑ 693-3674; www.boa.bo; Av Potosí, near Sucre; ⊙ 8:30am-12:30pm & 2:30-6:30pm Mon-Fri, 8:30am-12:30pm Sat) both operate two flights a day to La Paz (from B$700, one hour).

BUS

At the time of research, Uyuni's gleaming new **bus terminal** (Avaroa) was complete and awaiting the official sign-off for bus companies to begin operating here. All long-distance buses will no doubt depart from the new terminal. There's a choice of companies to most destinations, so ask around to get the best price, time and service.

Potosí buses leave hourly; for Sucre it's easiest to head to Potosí and change there.

The highway between Uyuni and Oruro is now fully paved, making for quicker and more comfortable journeys as well as a more frequent bus service to Oruro and further north to La Paz.

The safest and most comfortable terrestrial transport to La Paz is with **Todo Turismo**

BUSES FROM UYUNI

DESTINATION	COST (B$)	TIME (HR)
Cochabamba	130	10
La Paz	100-250	8-9
Oruro	30	4½
Potosí	30	4
Sucre	60	7
Tupiza	40	5
Villazón	50	6

> ### ⓘ GETTING TO CHILE
>
> Most tour agencies now offer cross-border connections to **San Pedro de Atacama** by arrangement with Chilean operators. You'll make the connection around 9am not long after visiting Laguna Verde, giving you limited time to enjoy the hot springs. Arrange this ahead of time with your operator. The Hito Cajón border post charges an exit tax of B$15 to B$30 here (B$21 is the standard).

(☑ 693-3337; www.todoturismo.bo; Avaroa; one-way B$250), which runs a heated bus service, departing daily at 8pm.

At research time, the road south to Tupiza and Villazón was nearly completely paved, cutting journey times. Buses leave at 6am and 8pm daily.

For Calama, Chile, Cruz del Norte buses depart at 5am (B$130, nine hours).

TRAIN

Uyuni has a modern, well-organized **train station** (☑ 693-2153; www.fca.com.bo; Av Ferroviaria s/n). Trains take you north to Oruro and south to Villazón. Seats often sell out, so buy your ticket several days in advance or get an agency to do it for you. There are numerous reports of slow trains, cancelled trains and large gaps in service – but that's all part of the adventure.

At research time, no trains were running south of Uyuni due to damage to the track caused by flooding in the Tupiza area. Repairs were underway to the section north of Tupiza, which suffered less damage. The section from Tupiza to Villazón is expected to take longer to repair.

Depending on size, you may have to check your backpack/suitcase into the luggage compartment. Look out for snatch thieves on the train just before it pulls out.

Southwest Circuit

Bolivia's southwestern corner is an awe-inspiring collection of diverse landscapes ranging from the blinding white Salar de Uyuni salt flat to the geothermal hotbed of Los Lípez, one of the world's harshest landscapes and a refuge for Andean wildlife. The ground here literally boils with minerals, and the spectrum of colors is extraordinary. A circuit from Uyuni takes you through unforgettable landscapes and is the highlight of a visit to Bolivia.

Although it gets plenty of visitors, Bolivia's southwest is still oddly remote, with rough dirt roads, scattered mining settlements, quinoa-producing villages and little public transportation. The main town, Uyuni (p237), is a military outpost with a frontier feel. It's the launching point for expeditions into the region, from the desolate expanses of the *salares* to the craggy hills of Los Lípez, which rise into the high Andean peaks along the Chilean frontier.

Salar de Uyuni

An evocative and eerie sight, the world's largest **salt flat** (guided tour only from Uyuni, Tupiza or San Pedro de Atacama across the border in Chile) measures 12,106 sq km and sits at 3653m (11,984ft). When the surface is dry, the *salar* is a pure white expanse of the greatest nothing imaginable – just blue sky, white ground and you. When there's a little water, the surface perfectly reflects the clouds and the blue altiplano sky, and the horizon disappears. If you're driving across the surface at such times, the effect is surreal; it's hard to believe that you're not flying through the clouds.

Salar de Uyuni is now a center of salt extraction and processing, particularly around the settlement of Colchani. The estimated annual output of the Colchani operation is nearly 20,000 tons, 18,000 tons of which is for human consumption while the rest is for livestock. And beneath the surface, massive lithium deposits should fuel Bolivia's economy for the next 100 years.

◉ Sights

★ Isla Incahuasi   ISLAND
(B$30) One of the highlights of a Salar de Uyuni tour is a hike around the spectacular Isla Incahuasi, otherwise known as Inkawasi. It's located in the heart of the *salar*, 80km west of Colchani. This hilly outpost is covered in *Trichocereus* cactus and surrounded by a flat white sea of hexagonal salt tiles.

Playa Blanca Salt Hotel   NOTABLE BUILDING
Although it is now closed to overnight visitors, you can still check out the salt sculptures inside and the **Dakar Rally** and **Flag Monuments** outside (add your flag if you've brought one). Find your own isolated piece of salt desert to enjoy and take out your props – it's here that plastic dinosaurs come out, as photographers play with the bizarre perspective caused by the bright blue skies

and super-flat landscape. Many tour groups stop for lunch here.

Los Lípez

Wild and otherworldly, Los Lípez is the kind of place where you can feel like you and your companions are the only people on earth. Though tours leave Uyuni in convoys, by the time you reach the military checkpoint of Colcha K (*col*-cha-*kah*) the other groups are well dispersed across this vast region, allowing you to enjoy the scenery and ponder your own insignificance.

◎ Sights

★ **Reserva Nacional de Fauna Andina Eduardo Avaroa**   NATIONAL PARK
(REA; www.bolivia-rea.com; B$150) Tucked away in the southwestern corner of Los Lípez near the Chilean border is the remote Reserva Nacional de Fauna Andina Eduardo Avaroa. It's a rough bumpy road through marvelous Martian landscapes to get there, but worth every bang of the head along the way.

The park headquarters is located opposite **Laguna Colorada**, where you can pick up informative materials, pay your fee, and learn more about local flora and fauna.

Sol de Mañana   GEYSER
Most tour groups wake at dawn to visit the large geyser field dubbed Sol de Mañana. This 4850m-high geyser basin has bubbling mud pots, hellish fumaroles and a thick and nauseating aroma of sulfur fumes. Approach the site cautiously; any damp or cracked earth is potentially dangerous and cave-ins do occur, sometimes causing serious burns.

Termas de Polques   HOT SPRINGS
(B$6) At the foot of **Cerro Polques** lies Termas de Polques, a small 29.4°C hot-spring pool, and an absolute paradise after the chilly *salar* nights. Although they're not boiling by any means, they're suitable for bathing, and the mineral-rich waters are thought to relieve the symptoms of arthritis and rheumatism. There's a restaurant here, and changing sheds with toilet facilities.

Desierto de Dalí   NATURAL FEATURE
Where the route splits about 20km south of Sol de Mañana, the more scenic left fork climbs up and over a 5000m pass, then up a stark hillside dotted with enormous rocks, which appear to have been meticulously placed by the surrealist master Salvador Dalí.

Laguna Verde   LAKE
The stunning blue-green Laguna Verde (4400m) is tucked into the southwestern corner of Bolivian territory, 52km south of Sol de Mañana. The incredible green color comes from high concentrations of lead, sulfur, arsenic and calcium carbonates. Most tours visit this in the morning, but it's at its most dramatic during the afternoon when incessant icy winds have whipped the water into a brilliant green-and-white froth.

ⓘ Getting There & Away

The best way to explore this area is on a tour from Uyuni or Tupiza. In winter (June to August) the roads in this area may become impassable due to snow, and the Reserva Nacional de Fauna Andina Eduardo Avaroa and Hito Cajón border crossing may be closed.

Tupiza

📞 2 / POP 22,233 / ELEV 2950M (9678FT)
The pace of life in tranquil Tupiza seems a few beats slower than in other Bolivian towns, making this a great place to relax for a few days, head out for a rip-romping cowboy adventure like Butch Cassidy and Sundance did more than 100 years ago, or trundle off on the back road to Salar de Uyuni.

Set in a spectacular 'Wild West' countryside, the capital of the southern Chichas region is in a corner of Río Tupiza Valley, surrounded by rugged scenery – cactus-studded slopes and eroded rainbow-colored rocks cut by gravelly *quebradas* (ravines, usually dry).

The climate is mild year-round, with most of the rain falling between November and March. From June to August, days are hot, dry and clear, but nighttime temperatures can drop to below freezing.

◎ Sights

Tupiza's main attraction is the surrounding countryside, which is best seen on foot or horseback.

Cañón del Duende   CANYON
This canyon, located 9km outside Tupiza, can be reached from the town on a great half-day hike through towering red rock formations of the nearby Quebrada de Santa Elena; ask any of the tour agencies in Tupiza for a map and directions.

Quebrada Palmira   NATURAL FEATURE
Cañon del Inca, 8km west of Tupiza, makes a great destination for a half-day hike via

ℹ️ GETTING TO ARGENTINA

The Bolivian side of the main border crossing to Argentina is the town of **Villazón**, a sprawling, dusty, chaotic sort of place. The **Argentine consulate** (☑ 597-2011; http://villazon.consulado.gob.ar; cnr Tarija & Calle 20 de Mayo, Villazón; ⊘ 8am-1pm Mon-Fri) is on the main square.

All northbound buses depart from the **Villazón bus terminal** (Av Tumusla), 3km north of the border. All except those bound for Tarija pass through Tupiza (B$15 to B$20, two hours). It's slightly quicker and no more expensive to take a *rapidito* (minibus or van). Regular bus services also head to Potosí (B$30, seven hours), La Paz (B$50, 15 hours), Uyuni (B$40, 6½ hours) and Oruro (B$50, 12 hours).

Argentine bus companies have ticket offices at Villazón's terminal, but all Argentine buses leave from the La Quiaca bus terminal, across the border. The first bus south to Salta from La Quiaca is at 8:30am Argentine time (7:30am Bolivian time).

The **Villazón train station** (☑ 597-2565; www.fca.com.bo; Calle 20 de Mayo) is 1.5km north of the border crossing – a taxi costs B$5. Trains run north to Tupiza (B$14 to B$60, three hours), Uyuni (B$38 to B$180, eight to nine hours) and Oruro (B$67 to B$279, 16 to 18 hours) at 3:30pm on Monday, Wednesday, Thursday and Saturday.

On the north side of the international bridge, **Bolivian customs and immigration** (Av JM Deheza, btwn Junín & Tupiza; ⊘ 6am-11pm) issues exit and entry stamps (valid for 30 days). There is no official charge for these services, but a 'service fee' is sometimes leveraged. Argentine immigration and Argentine customs are open from 7am to 11pm. Formalities are minimal but the wait and exhaustive custom searches can be very long. In addition, those entering Argentina may be held up at several control points further south of the border by more customs searches.

Quebrada Palmira, a normally dry wash flanked by tall and precarious fin formations. The route leads past the **Puerta del Diablo** rock formation, 5km outside Tupiza. The right fork of the wash is rather comically known as **Valle de los Machos** (Valley of Males); the name stems from the clusters of exceptionally phallic pedestal formations.

El Sillar   VIEWPOINT

El Sillar (the Saddle), located 17km northwest of Tupiza, is where a road straddles a narrow ridge between two peaks and two valleys. Throughout this area, rugged amphitheaters have been gouged out of the mountainsides and eroded into spires that resemble a stone forest. The easiest way to get here is on the 3:30pm Tupiza Tours bus (B$70); it's possible to hire a bike and cycle back to Tupiza for an extra B$80.

🕝 Tours

An increasing number of operators in Tupiza offer trips through the Southwest Circuit (p239) ending in Uyuni or back in Tupiza. Tupiza is a great place to start this trip, as you get to explore the lesser-known wild lands of Sud Lípez as well as seeing the well-established highlights at different times to the large convoys of 4WDs that visit them out of Uyuni. Tours out of Tupiza often kick off

with a visit to El Sillar or **Quebrada Palala**, before heading on to the Sud Lípez lakes, including several that aren't visited on standard circuits that start from Uyuni. The *salar* itself is visited on the final day, with the option to see the sunrise over the salt well worth getting out of bed for.

The downside is that you may have to wait a while in Tupiza to get a group together (although the larger outfits have departures almost daily). While the standard *salar* tour starting in Uyuni is three days, Tupiza to Uyuni tours require four days, and therefore cost a little more. Expect to pay between B$1200 and B$1600 per person for the standard four-day trip, based on four people in a jeep, during the high season.

Tupiza Tours   TOURS

(☑ 694-3003; www.tupizatours.com; Av Regimiento Chichas 187, Hotel Mitru; ⊘ 8am-8pm) This outfit pioneered many of the Tupiza-area routes now also offered by competitors. As well as tours to Uyuni via the *salar*, it runs a useful daily bus service to nearby sights, including La Poronga, Puerta del Diablo, El Cañón del Duende (p243) and el Sillar.

La Torre Tours   TOURS

(☑ 694-2633; www.latorretours-tupiza.com; Av Regimiento Chichas 220, Hotel La Torre; ⊘ 7am-8pm)

Run by a friendly couple, this agency offers personalized tours of Tupiza's surroundings and the *salar*. It rents bikes at B$80 for three hours.

🛏 Sleeping

★ Hostal Butch Cassidy
HOSTEL $

(📞 7944-8880, 7183-3271; hostalbutch@hotmail.com; Av Jose Luis San Juan Garcia s/n; s/d/tr incl breakfast B$120/160/240; 📶) Located across the river from town and a 10-minute walk from the bus station, this hostel has 13 spacious rooms with gleaming tiled floors, bright and comfortable common areas and a well-equipped kitchen. It's run by Franklin, who can also arrange tours of the surrounding area and to Uyuni via the *salar*.

Hotel La Torre
HOTEL $

(📞 694-2633; www.latorretours-tupiza.com; Av Regimiento Chichas 220; s/d incl breakfast B$80/150, r per person with shared bathroom B$60; @📶) Run by a retired nurse and doctor, this hotel offers clean rooms with good beds and smart bathrooms with gleaming tiles. Rooms at the front of the rambling colonial-era home receive more daylight but are chillier, and the beds can be a bit lumpy. Guests have use of a kitchen, roof terrace and TV lounge – the latter is a good place to meet other travelers.

★ Hotel Mitru
HOTEL $$

(📞 694-3001; www.hotelmitru.com; Av Regimiento Chichas 187; s B$280-380, d B$380-480, s/d with shared bathroom B$90/160; @📶🏊) The best and most reliable hotel in town, Mitru has been run by the same family for generations and is a relaxing choice built around a swimming pool that's just the ticket after a dusty day on horseback. It has a variety of rooms in two sections: the older 'garden' part and the newer 'cactus' area. Breakfast is included.

🍴 Eating

★ Salteñas Especiales
Marianita
BOLIVIAN $

(📞 7917-8578; Florída; per salteña B$4; ☉ 8am-5pm) Get these hot-from-the-oven chicken and beef *salteñas* (savory pies) to eat in or take away. They're some of Bolivia's best.

★ Milan Center
PIZZA $$

(cnr Av Regimiento Chichas & Chuquisaca; mains B$25-55, pizza B$33-35; ☉ 9am-10pm Mon-Sat, 4-10pm Sun; 📶) For the best pizza in town, head over to Milan Center, which serves crispy thin-crust pizzas with a variety of topping options. The covered back patio is a nice break from the streets of Tupiza. It's also a good place to come for a coffee.

Alamo
MEXICAN $$

(cnr Av Regimiento Chichas & Avaroa; snacks B$10-30, mains B$30-60; ☉ noon-2pm & 6-10pm Mon-Sat) A saloon-style spot where locals and tourists mingle in the fun two-story space with a Hollywood vibe and lots of knick-knacks. The menu features mainly meat dishes, like *pique a lo macho* (beef chunks and sausages over french fries with lettuce, tomatoes, onions and spicy *locote* peppers), and comes in huge tasty portions.

ℹ Information

Banco Union (cnr Florída & Santa Cruz)

Banco Fie (Plaza Independencia)

Latin America Cambio (Avaroa 160; ☉ 8am-9pm Mon-Sat) Changes many currencies but not always at the best rates.

Hospital Eduardo Eguía (Suipacha 22)

Super Clean Laundry (Florída, cnr Av Serrano; ☉ 8am-8pm)

ℹ Getting There & Away

BUS

The **bus station** (Av Pedro Arraya) has buses to most major destinations or hubs in the region.

BUSES FROM TUPIZA

DESTINATION	COST (B$)	TIME (HR)
Cochabamba	80	15
La Paz	50-100	14
Oruro	50-80	10
Potosí	30-70	5
Tarija	50	7
Uyuni	40	4½
Villazón	15-22	2

There are services throughout the day, though the majority of buses leave in the evening.

For Villazón and the border crossing to Argentina, take a *rapidito* (minibus or van), which leave when full (B$20, one hour). The **boarding point** (Av Pedro Arraya) is next to the bus terminal.

Rapiditos also run to Potosí (B$80, 3½ hours) and Uyuni (B$80, three hours), and get there much faster than the bus.

TRAIN

The ticket window at the **train station** (694-2529; www.fca.com.bo; Av Serrano) opens irregularly on days when there's a train, so it can be easier to have a tour agency buy your tickets for a small surcharge.

At the time of research, no trains were running to or from Tupiza due to damage to the track caused by flooding. Repairs were underway to the section north of Tupiza, which suffered less damage. The section from Tupiza to Villazón is expected to take longer to repair.

Expreso del Sur is the most comfortable service. Southbound trains to Villazón leave on Wednesday and Saturday at 3:10am. Northbound services to Uyuni and Oruro leave on the same days at 6:25pm. The cheaper Wara Wara heads south to Villazón on Monday and Thursday at 9:05am, with the northbound service departing Tupiza at 7:05pm.

Tarija

4 / POP 205,300 / ELEV 1905M

With its pleasantly mild climate and easily walkable colonial center, you may find yourself lingering in Tarija longer than expected on your way to or from Argentina or Paraguay. Despite the fact that many Bolivians from bigger cities regard South Central Bolivia as a backwater, Tarija's palm-lined squares, tight streets, laid-back feel and lively restaurants feel just the right amount of cosmopolitan and sophisticated. After an afternoon with a glass of local vino on the central plaza you might consider relocating.

Tarija is also the base for excursions further afield, especially to the vineyards on its doorstep in El Valle de la Concepción and to surrounding villages and nature reserves.

Chapacos – as *tarijeños* (Tarija locals) are otherwise known – are culturally distinct from other parts of the country.

Sights & Activities

Half a dozen or so companies offer standard packages to area sights, including tours to the wineries (p250) from B$130 for a half-day trip (four hours). Most of the full-day options,

for around B$230, involve adding on either a city tour or, more recommended, spots like San Lorenzo (p249), Coimata (p250) and Tomatitas (p250) not far to the north. They're pleasant trips in a minibus with generally well-informed guides (some are English speaking) and can often be arranged at the last minute with hotel pickups. Most have morning (8:30am or 9:30am) and afternoon (2:30pm) departures.

Basílica de San Francisco CHURCH

(cnr Campos & La Madrid; museum 8am-6pm Mon-Fri) FREE This basilica was founded in 1606 as the Jesuit 'base camp' in Bolivia and is now a national monument. The 16th-century convent library and archives, which may be reminiscent of *The Name of the Rose*, can be used only by researchers who have been granted permission by the Franciscan order; it holds an important archive of baroque music compositions. Inside the basilica, the free **Museo Franciscano Fray Francisco Miguel Mari** displays ecumenical paintings, sculptures and artifacts.

★ Valle de los Condores WILDLIFE WATCHING

(7023-2025; www.valledeloscondores.com; Virginio Lema 284; by appointment) This pioneering company runs two- to four-day treks in what it describes as the 'Yungas of Tarija' in order to spot majestic condors gliding over and around high-altitude cliffs. Most of the hiking is done between 2000m and 3000m, and nights are spent in traditional adobe homes.

Viva Tours TOURS

(663-8325; vivatours.turismo@gmail.com; Bolívar 251, 2nd fl; 8am-12:30pm & 3-7pm Mon-Fri, 8am-12:30pm Sat) For wine tours and adventurous ecotrips to Tarija's hinterlands – including nearby national reserves – it's tough to beat Viva Tours.

Bolivian Wine Tours OUTDOORS

(7187-1626; viviugarte@gmail.com; Méndez 175, btwn Avaroa & La Américas) Does all the standard wine tours and also runs highly recommended two-day tours to Reserva Biológica Cordillera de Sama (B$390 per person). It also has one-day tours (B$295 per person), but it's a lot of driving and you miss out on the experience of spending the night and stargazing. Costs per person go up for groups smaller than five.

Sleeping

Casa Blanca HOSTEL $

(664-2909; www.hostelcasablancatarija.com; Ingavi 645; dm B$60;) The whitewashed

LOCAL KNOWLEDGE

TARIJA SPECIALTIES

You'll need to be brave to try *sopa la poderosa* (soup with vegetables, rice and bull's penis), *ranga ranga* (tripe with onion, tomato and chili) and *chan faina* (diced lamb guts with potatoes and greens), but even delicate stomachs will enjoy *guiso de karas* (stew of pork skin, potatoes and mote, a corn-like grain), *chancao de pollo* (spicy chicken), *sopa de maní* (peanut soup) or *saice* (spicy ground beef and vegetables with rice or noodles), which is just as commonly eaten for breakfast as dinner. Don't forget to sample the desserts too – *dulce de lacayote* (caramelized squash), *pepitas de leche* (cinnamon fudge) and *tojori* (pancakes with cloves and aniseed) are all favorites.

The best places to try these are the **Mercado Central** (cnr Sucre & Bolívar; mains B$7-15; ⊙6am-10pm Mon-Sat), **El Mercado de los Campesinos** and **El Puente Night Market** (Av Estenssoro; dishes B$5-12; ⊙4-11pm).

colonial-era facade and shady courtyard make Casa Blanca easily the most attractive of the city's budget accommodations. Three dorm rooms have two bunk beds each, and the bathrooms are kept clean and have reliably hot showers. It's on a quiet block a short walk to the central plaza; however, the soundness of your sleep depends on other guests.

Kultur Berlin Guesthouse   HOSTEL $
(☑186-2725; Ballivián 367; dm B$75, s/d/tr B$110/160/230; ☜) Good-value place with a friendly owner, comfortable beds, a pleasant courtyard and sort of a roof patio; the basic bathrooms could use an upgrade. An especially good breakfast for this price bracket of homemade yogurt and granola, fruit, eggs and freshly made bread is served at a large communal table. Knock loudly even if it looks closed from the outside.

★**Casona Señorial Gloria**   BOUTIQUE HOTEL $$
(☑7824-5070; www.sites.google.com/view/casona gloria; Trigo 0680; B$280-385; ❀☜☜) Worthy of an upscale design magazine, five-room family-run Casona Gloria is a mix of historic colonial cra architecture and contemporary boutique stylings. The cherry on top, as it were, is its location: above and behind the owner's ice-cream shop. Rooms have high ceilings, brick walls, paintings by Bolivian artists and luxurious bedding, not to mention spa-quality bathrooms.

Hostal del Sol   HOTEL $$
(☑666-5259; www.hoteldelsol.com.bo; Sucre 782; s/d incl breakfast B$230/350; ❀@) Good value and conveniently located only two blocks from the central plaza, Hostal del Sol is a reliable choice for its sunny street-facing rooms with minibalconies and breakfasts served in a similarly light-filled 2nd-floor

dining room. Interior rooms are darker and less preferred but all have flat-screen TVs and sparkling-clean marble floors.

★**Hotel Los Ceibos**   HOTEL $$$
(☑663-4430; www.hotellosceibos.com; Av Panamericana 612; r B$550; ❀@☜☒) The downtown area's largest hotel is only a little more than a half-dozen blocks from the central plaza and delivers the most bang for your bolivianos. Several towering palm trees give the pool area a tropical resort vibe. Guests have complimentary access to **Nivel Fitness Club** (La Madrid 1030; ⊙6am-10:30pm Mon-Fri, 8am-noon & 3-7pm Sat, 9am-1pm Sun), a fabulous gym attached to the hotel.

✖ Eating

★**Entre Frutas**   HEALTH FOOD $
(Calle 15 de Abril 142; mains B$15-40; ⊙8am-noon & 4-9pm Mon-Fri) Açaí bowls and fruit smoothies are the specialties here, with salads and ceviches rounding out the healthy menu. A few front seats are good for watching passersby, and the enclosed cobblestone back patio is nice for a longer stay.

Belén   BOLIVIAN $
(Colón; mains B$17-36; ⊙7am-10pm Mon-Sat, to 3pm Sun; ☜✐) A US- and Australian-trained chef/owner created this homey, eclectically decorated restaurant serving artisan sandwiches, excellent burgers and a lightly seasoned trout dish for lunch. Equally good for breakfast of poached eggs and the yogurt and granola bowl.

★**Pappillon**   SEAFOOD $$
(☑7189-8676; E-1005 Arce; mains B$50; ⊙12:30-4pm Sat) Popular with locals, especially older men who come here for *cacho* (a dice game), guitar strumming and fish like *pacu* (from

the Amazon around Beni), *sabalu* (from Villamontes) and *surubí*. It's located on a road commonly referred to as Av Pescado for the number of fish restaurants. Pappillon (also the owner's nickname) is tough to find without some help.

★**Macondo de
Pizza Pazza Restaurant**   PIZZA $$$
(☑664-2107;   macondopizzapazza@gmail.com;
Sucre 508; mains B$55-110, pizza B$60-110;
☺3:30pm-midnight Mon-Thu, to 3am Fri, 9am-midnight Sat, 9am-2:30pm & 6-11pm Sun; 🖥) Exuberant host Edith Paz Zamora and her son Hector have put together a really unique blend of art and, you guessed it, pizza, on the ground floor of the Club Social Tarija. But the homemade pastas are equally good (the all-you-can-eat Sunday pasta buffet for B$70 is excellent) and the menu also includes steak and fish dishes.

★**El Fogón de Gringo**   STEAK $$$
(La Madrid 1051; mains B$70-100; ☺7-11pm Mon-Fri, noon-3pm & 7-11pm Sat, noon-3pm Sun; 🖥) The quality and value of El Fogón's choice steaks equal the appeal of its warm ambience, which echoes the casual sophistication of a southern Spanish bodega's restaurant. All mains come with a tasty buffet of salad, rice, potatoes and pasta and there's an excellent wine selection.

🍷 Drinking & Nightlife

Tarija's bar and cafe scene is vibrant and many of the popular restaurants transform into drinking dens after dark. The Friday bohemian night at **Macondo de Pizza Pazza Bar** (☑7022-2022; https://macondopizzapazza. negocio.site; cnr Sucre & Calle 15 de Abril; ☺6:30pm-midnight, to 3am Fri; 🖥) is worth planning your trip around.

🛍 Shopping

La Vinoteca (☑7299-6486; lavinoteca@hotmail. com; Ingavi 371; ☺9am-12:30pm & 3-7pm Mon-Fri, to 1pm Sat) is the best place to sample and then pick up a bottle of wine from any of the area bodegas. It also sells other locally produced foodstuffs. Bodegas **Aranjuez** (☑664-5651; www.vinosaranjuez.com; Calle 15 de Abril 254; ☺8am-noon & 2:30-6:30pm Mon-Fri, 8am-12:30pm Sat), **Kohlberg** (☑663-6366; www.kohlberg. com.bo; 15 de Abril E-275; ☺8am-noon & 2:30-6:30pm Mon-Fri, 8am-12:30pm Sat), **La Concepción** (☑663-2250; www.bodegaslaconcepcion. com; Colón 585; ☺8am-noon & 2:30-6:30pm Mon-Fri, 8am-12:30pm Sat) and **Campos de Solana** (☑664-5498; www.camposdesolana.com; Calle 15 de Abril E-259; ☺8am-noon & 2:30-6:30pm Mon-Fri, 8am-12:30pm Sat) all have shops near one another just off Plaza Sucre. For cloyingly sweet artisan wines, hit one of the shops lining Calle Sucre between Domingo Paz and Cochabamba.

ℹ Information

Infotur (☑666-7701; www.tarijaturismo.com; cnr Calles 15 de Abril & Sucre; ☺8am-noon & 2:30-6:30pm Mon-Fri, 9am-noon & 4-7pm Sat & Sun) distributes basic town maps and is reasonably helpful with queries regarding sights in and around town – Spanish-speaking only. Also, check out the excellent www.brujulaturistica. com/tarija for transportation, food and other helpful tourist information.

Head to the **migración** (☑664-3450; cnr La Paz & Oruro; ☺8:30am-12:30pm & 2:30-6:30pm Mon-Fri) office in front of Parque Bolívar for entry/exit stamps or to extend your stay.

Conduct all your business in the morning or you'll have to wait until after the siesta because Tarija becomes a virtual ghost town between 1pm and 4pm.

The **Protección del Medioambiente del Tarija** (Prometa; www.prometa.org.bo; Tarija) works in the Gran Chaco region on a series of social and conservation initiatives.

Hospital San Juan de Dios (☑664-5555; Santa Cruz s/n) For medical emergencies.

There are numerous banks with ATMs around the plaza and at the airport.

Several **casas de cambio** (Bolívar; ☺8am-1pm & 3-8pm Mon-Fri, 8am-1pm Sat), which change US dollars, euros and Argentine pesos, are conveniently located on Bolívar between Sucre and Daniel Campos. Most are open from 8am to 1pm and 3pm to 8pm Monday to Friday and only in the morning on Saturday.

ℹ Getting There & Away

AIR

The **Capitán Oriel Lea Plaza Airport** (☑664-2195; Av Victor Paz Estenssoro) is 3km east of town off Av Jaime Paz Zamora. **TAM** (☑664-5899; www.tam.bo; La Madrid 0-470; ☺8:30am-1pm & 3-7pm Mon-Fri, 8:30am-1pm Sat), **BOA** (☑611-2787; www.boa.bo; Trigo, btwn Alejandro del Carpio & Lema; ☺8:30am-12:30pm & 2:30-6:30pm Mon-Fri, 9am-noon Sat), **Ecojet** (☑611-3427; www.ecojet.bo; cnr Colón & Madrid; ☺8:30am-1pm & 3-7pm Mon-Fri, 8:30am-1pm Sat) and **Amaszonas** (www. amaszonas.com) service La Paz, Santa Cruz, Sucre and Cochabamba (tickets for all these

ℹ GETTING TO ARGENTINA

These days, Bermejo/Aguas Blancas is the most convenient crossing to Argentina for those coming directly from Tarija or Salta in Argentina; the border is open from 8am to 5pm. The bus company Trans Tours Juarez C (www.facebook.com/juarezcinfo) has highly recommended Tuesday, Thursday and Sunday departures (B$320 to B$400, 10 hours, 7pm) via this crossing; it helps expedite the process and you don't have to change buses.

Otherwise, it's a more complicated and inconvenient ordeal. Bermejo's bus terminal is eight blocks southeast of the main plaza. Buses leave every couple of hours from Tarija to Bermejo (B$20, three hours) between 7:30am and 9pm, but you'll need to get a morning service (last departure 10:30am) if you want to cross the border the same day; *colectivos* (B$45) are more frequent and leave when full. It's a quick B$3 *chalana* (ferry) ride across the river frontier to Aguas Blancas in Argentina (be sure to pick up an exit stamp before crossing). From here, buses to Orán (US$2, one hour) depart hourly from the terminal opposite the immigration office. From Orán, you can connect to Argentina's Salta, Jujuy and Tucumán.

destinations range from B$220 to B$450; for La Paz and Sucre it can sometimes involve a stop in Cochabamba). TAM and Amaszonas also make the short hop to Yacuiba (B$300 to B$500) one to two days a week.

Syndicate taxis from the airport to the center cost B$20 to B$25, but if you walk 100m past the airport gate (visible from outside the terminal), you'll pay as little as B$12 per person for a normal taxi. Otherwise, cross the main road and take a passing *micro A* or *trufi*, which run by the old bus terminal and the Mercado Central.

BUS
The new, modern and very large **bus terminal** is 7km south of town. Most long-haul services leave in the afternoon between 4:30pm and 8:30pm. Lince and Platinum's daily 7pm buses (B$195 to B$265) offer the most luxurious service to La Paz; expect 180-degree reclining seats, wi-fi, USB outlets, private video screens with headphones and clean bathrooms, plus snacks and water.

Services to Santa Cruz pass through Villamontes from where there are connections to Yacuiba and Asunción in Paraguay.

The bus company Trans Tours Juarez C has Tuesday, Thursday and Sunday departures direct all the way to Salta in Argentina (B$320 to B$400, 10 hours, 7pm) via the Bermejo crossing (p249); it's highly recommended for fairly luxurious buses (every *cama* seat has its own TV) and expediting the border-crossing process.

Micros for northern destinations like Camargo and Potosí leave from **Parada del Norte**. **Micros to Padcaya** (Hwy 1, btwn Avs Sossa & Moreno, Parada del Chaco) leave from the Parada del Chaco.

Trufis to San Jacinto (Ingavi, btwn Campos & Colón; B$3, 10 minutes) run every 20 minutes from the corner of Ingavi and Campos (outside the Palacio de la Justicia) in Tarija.

DESTINATION	COST (B$)	TIME (HR)
Bermejo	50	3½
Camiri	60	11
Cochabamba	130-256	15
La Paz	120-260	18
Oruro	60-103	12
Potosí	60-70	5-6
Sucre	80-180	12
Santa Cruz	90-254	12-13
Tupiza	50-80	7
Villamontes	60-100	8
Villazon	45	6
Yacuiba	60	6

TAXIS
Colectivos in all shapes and sizes, though primarily Subaru station wagons and minivans, service every regional destination (for either Villamontes or Yacuiba it's B$100 and six hours) and some further afield. They are in general a little more expensive, though arguably more comfortable than buses (depending on your seat). However, they leave when full so waits vary. *Colectivos* to Bermejo (B$45, three hours) on the Argentinian border leave frequently.

Around Tarija

San Lorenzo, 14km north of Tarija along the Tupiza road, is a quaint village with freshly whitewashed adobe facades, cobblestone streets, carved balconies, a church

VISITING WINERIES IN EL VALLE DE LA CONCEPCIÓN

The region south of Tarija, the Concepción Valley or simply 'El Valle,' is the heart of Bolivian wine production. Most people breeze on through on organized day trips from Tarija (advertisements for 'Ruta del Vino' trips are everywhere), but the village of **La Concepción**, with picturesque colonial architecture, a plaza sporting lovely flowering ceibo trees and a sleepily prosperous feel, is worth lingering over.

Winery visits usually involve a quick tour of the production facilities, which vary from the basement of a suburban-style home to larger operations with industrial-size equipment. The main wineries are **Campos de Solana** (☑466-4549; www.camposdesolana.com; ⊗9-11am & 1-4pm Mon-Fri, 9-11am Sat), **Bodega Kuhlmann** (☑664-4346; www.bodegakuhlmann.com), **Kohlberg** (☑663-6366; www.kohlberg.com.bo; Av Jorge Paz; ⊗8am-noon & 2:30-6:30pm Mon-Fri), Casa Real (a distillery), **Bodega La Concepción** (☑664-5040; www.bodegaslaconcepcion.com; ⊗8am-5pm Mon-Fri, to noon Sat) and Aranjuez (at the time of research this one was due to open to visitors in September 2018). Most tours include visits to two of these, plus a smaller artisan bodega.

If you go on your own, you'll pay around B$5, plus the cost of whatever bottle you like for a 'tasting.' Keep in mind, most places are open from 9am to 11am and 2pm to 4pm Monday to Friday and only in the mornings Saturday. For lunch in La Concepción, try **Bodega Casa Vieja** (☑666-2605; www.lacasavieja.info; mains B$20-60; ⊗10am-6pm), an atmospheric winery and restaurant with beautiful mountain views.

built in 1709 and a charming plaza shaded by towering palm trees.

Just to the north is the former home of erstwhile Bolivian president Jaime Paz Zamora. Only a few kilometers north of here, you can arrange in advance for a guided tour of **El Picacho** (near Lajas Merced), Zamora's beautiful estate – he'll likely be on hand to regale visitors with stories. Contact **Macondo de Pizza Pazza Hotel** (☑666-3566; cnr Sucre & Calle 15 de Abril; s/d B$245/290; ❋🏠) in Tarija for tour information.

Micros (cnr Domingo Paz & Rojas) and *trufis* (B$3, 30 minutes) to San Lorenzo leave from the corner of Av Domingo Paz and Calle Rojas in Tarija approximately every 20 minutes during the day. All of the tour companies in Tarija include a stop in San Lorenzo on at least one of their designated itineraries.

Tomatitas, with its natural swimming holes, three lovely rivers (the Sella, Guadalquivir and Erquis) and happy little eateries serving *cangrejitos* (soft-shelled freshwater crabs), is popular with day-trippers from Tarija 5km to the south.

From here you can walk the 9km to **Coimata,** where there are more swimming holes and the two-tiered **Coimata Falls**, which has a total drop of about 60m. The twin 40m waterfalls at **Chorros de Jurina**, 26km northwest of Tarija, also make an agreeable destination for a day trip.

Micros A and B to Tomatitas leave every 20 minutes from the corner of Domingo Paz

and Saracho in Tarija (B$2), some continuing on to Jurina (B$7) via San Lorenzo.

The **Sama Biological Reserve** protects sandy Sahara-like dunes, tens of thousands of flamingos and startling clear night skies, all within several hours of Tarija. On the cold and windy *puna* (high open grasslands) portion of the reserve (3400m above sea level, nearly the same altitude as La Paz), you can visit the **Tajzara Lagoons**, a Ramsar site of international importance for aquatic birds.

Entry to the reserve costs B$100; the fee is not usually included in prices quoted by tour companies.

CENTRAL HIGHLANDS

Geographically – and some would say metaphorically – the heart and soul of the country, the Central Highlands are a mix of lively urban centers and vast pastoral and mountainous regions dotted with remote villages. Gorgeous whitewashed Sucre, where independence was declared in 1825, is the gateway to trekking the Cordillera de los Frailes. Potosí is a powerful symbol of the natural wealth of the country, built on the silver deposits extracted from nearby Cerro Rico. Much-lower-altitude Cochabamba is one of Bolivia's most pleasant cities, with a perfect climate and modern vibe.

Throughout, there are lovely, little-known colonial towns; it's well worth eschewing the city-to-city mode of travel to explore them. A more distant past is evoked by the Inca ruins in the Cochabamba Valley, but Parque Nacional Torotoro has the last laugh on the age front: it's bristling with dinosaur footprints and fossils, some of which date back 300 million years.

Cochabamba

🕿 4 / POP 1.24 MILLION / ELEV 2553M

Busy, buzzy Cochabamba is one of Bolivia's boom cities and has a distinct, almost Mediterranean vitality that perhaps owes something to its clement climate. While much of the city's population is typically poor, parts of town have a notably prosperous feel. The spacious, ever-expanding new-town avenues have a wide choice of restaurants, eagerly grazed by the food-crazy *cochabambinos*, and the bar scene is lively, driven by students and young professionals. It's also the base for outdoor adventures further afield, including trips to Parque Torotoro. You could easily find yourself staying a lot longer than planned.

The city's name is derived from the Quechua *khocha pampa*, meaning 'swampy plain'. Cochabamba lies in a fertile green bowl, 25km long by 10km wide, set in a landscape of fields and low hills. To the northwest rises Cerro Tunari (5050m), the highest peak in central Bolivia.

◉ Sights & Activities

There's no shortage of outdoor activities within a couple of hours' drive from Cochabamba. Rock climbing, trekking, canyoning, whitewater rafting and paragliding are best done with one of two recommended tour companies: **Andes Xtremo** (🕿 036-5816; www.andesxtremo.com; La Paz 138) and **El Mundo Verde Travel** (🕿 534-4272; www.elmundoverdetravel.com).

★ Palacio Portales   PALACE
(c.pedagogicocultral@fundacionpatino.org; Potosí 1450; incl guide B$25; ⊙ gardens 3-6:30pm Tue-Fri, 9:30-11:30am Sat & Sun, palace guided tours in English 2pm, 5pm & 6pm Tue-Fri, 10:30am & 11:30am Sat, 11:30am Sun) Nothing symbolizes Bolivia's gilded mineral age like tin baron Simón Patiño's European-style Palacio Portales. Though he never actually inhabited this opulent mansion completed in 1927, it was stocked with some of the finest imported materials available at the time – Carrara

marble, French wood, Italian tapestries and delicate silks. The gardens and exterior were inspired by the palace at Versailles, the games room is an imitation of Granada's Alhambra and the main hall takes its design inspiration from Vatican City.

★ Convento de Santa Teresa   CONVENT
(🕿 452-5765; cnr Baptista & Ecuador; guided tour B$50; ⊙ tours hourly 9-11am & 2:30-4:30pm Mon-Sat) The noble, timeworn Convento de Santa Teresa is straight out of a Gabriel García Márquez novel. Guided tours (around 45 minutes) of this gracefully decaying complex allow you to see the peaceful cloister, fine altarpieces and sculptures (from Spanish and Potosí schools) and the convent church. However, it's not so much the quality of the architecture or art that's noteworthy, but rather the challenge to your imagination in picturing and conceiving what life was like for the cloistered nuns here.

★ Cristo de la Concordia   LANDMARK
(Innominada, Zona la Chimba; ⊙ 10am-6pm Tue-Sat, 9am-6pm Sun) This immense Christ statue standing atop Cerro de San Pedro (2800m) behind Cochabamba is the second largest of its kind in the world. It's 44cm higher than the famous *Cristo Redentor* in Rio de Janeiro, which stands 33m high, or 1m for each year of Christ's life. *Cochabambinos* justify the one-upmanship by claiming that Christ actually lived '33 años y un poquito' (33 years and a bit). Fantastic 360-degree panoramic views of the city and valley are worth the trip.

La Cancha   MARKET
(Av Aroma; ⊙ 9am-8pm) Sprawling, chaotic and claustrophobic, Cochabamba's main market, while lacking an attractive mise-en-scène, is nevertheless a colorful place to wander. The largest and most accessible area is **Mercado Cancha Calatayud**, which spreads across a wide area along Av Aroma and south toward the former railway station. It's your best opportunity to see local dress, which differs strikingly from that of the altiplano.

Villa Albina   HOUSE
(🕿 401-0470; Pairumani; B$10; ⊙ 8am-4pm Mon-Fri, 9am-1pm Sat) 🌿 If you haven't already had your fill of Simón Patiño's legacy in Oruro and Cochabamba, you can visit Villa Albina in the village of Pairumani and tour the home the tin baron occupied. This enormous

Cochabamba

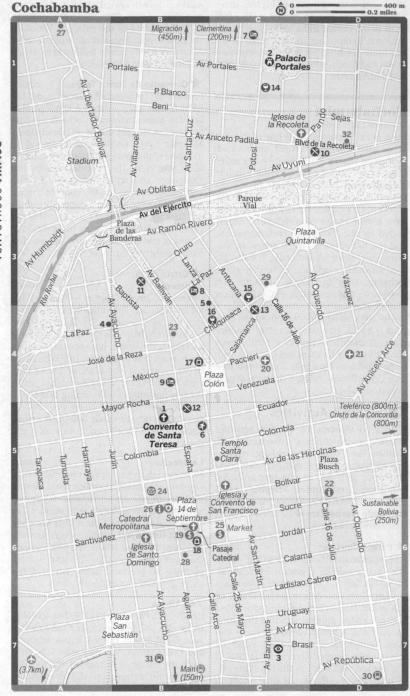

0 — 400 m
0 — 0.2 miles

Migración (450m)
Clementina (200m)
7

2 Palacio Portales

14

Portales

Av Portales

P Blanco

Beni

Av Libertador Bolívar

Av Villarroel

Av Santa Cruz

Av Aniceto Padilla

Iglesia de la Recoleta

Sejas

32

Blvd de la Recoleta

10

Potosí

Pando

Av Uyuni

Stadium

Av Humboldt

Río Rocha

Av Oblitas

Av del Ejército

Plaza de las Banderas

Av Ramón Rivero

Parque Vial

Plaza Quintanilla

Oruro

Lanza

La Paz

Antezana

Av Ballivián

29

Av Oquendo

Vázquez

11

Baptista

8

15

5

16

Chuquisaca

13

Calle 16 de Julio

4

Av Ayacucho

La Paz

23

Salamanca

José de la Reza

17

Paccieri

20

21

Av Aniceto Arce

México

9

Plaza Colón

Venezuela

Mayor Rocha

1

12

Ecuador

Teleférico (800m);
Cristo de la Concordia (800m)

Tarapaca

Tumusla

Hamiraya

Junín

Convento de Santa Teresa

6

Colombia

España

Templo Santa Clara

Av de las Heroínas

Plaza Busch

24

22

Achá

Santivañez

26

19

18

28

Plaza 14 de Septiembre

Iglesia y Convento de San Francisco

25 Market

Bolívar

Sucre

Jordán

Calama

Sustainable Bolivia (250m)

Calle 16 de Julio

Av Oquendo

Catedral Metropolitana

Iglesia de Santo Domingo

Pasaje Catedral

Av San Martín

Ladislao Cabrera

Plaza San Sebastián

Av Ayacucho

Aguirre

Calle Arce

Calle 25 de Mayo

Av Barrientos

Uruguay

Av Aroma

Brasil

3

Av República

31

Main (150m)

30

(3.7km)

Cochabamba

BOLIVIA COCHABAMBA

white mansion, with its long palm-tree-lined entrance roadway, was named after Simón's wife, Albina. She was presumably as fussy as her husband when it came to the finer things in life, and the elegant French decor of the main house seems fit for royalty.

Teleférico　　　　　　　　　CABLE CAR
(return B$12; ⊗ closed Mon) The quickest, most scenic and comfortable way to the top of Cristo de la Concordia (p251) is riding the cable car.

🍃 Courses

**Instituto Cultural
Boliviano Alemán**　　　　　　LANGUAGE
(ICBA; ☑ 412-2323; www.icbacbba.org; Lanza 727) Offers group Spanish lessons.

🎎 Festivals & Events

Fiesta de la Virgen de Urkupiña　RELIGIOUS
(⊗ mid-Aug) For four or so days in Quillacollo, basically a district of Cochabamba 13km to the east, the *chicha* flows liberally (as does *garapiña*, a strong blend of *chicha*, cinnamon, coconut and *ayrampo*, a local mystery ingredient from a cactus that colors the drink red). Folkloric musicians and dancers from around the country perform amid large cheering and intoxicated crowds.

🛏 Sleeping

★ **Running Chaski Hostal**　　　HOSTEL $
(☑ 425-0559; www.runningchaski.com.bo; España 449; dm B$75-89, s/d/tr B$130/250/300; ❋ @ 🛜) Easily the best choice for budget-minded travelers, Running Chaski is justifiably busy – reserve in advance, especially for weekends. The handsome colonial-style entryway leads to a small grassy back garden. Woodfloored rooms have modern furnishings and the extremely helpful staff can provide travel advice.

★ **Las Lilas Hostel**　　　　　　HOSTEL $
(☑ 7740-1222; www.hostellaslilas.com; Zona Linde, Tiquipaya; dm from B$57, r with shared/private bath B$70/85; 🛜 ⊞) With relatively quick access to Cochabamba (it depends on traffic), but in a lovely rural setting, Las Lilas is a stately looking adobe home in front with an arts-and-craft-style patio out the back. There are several dorm rooms of varying configurations, and basic private rooms as well. Hammocks and lounge chairs are provided in the large back garden.

Hotel Luxor　　　　　　　　　HOTEL $$
(☑ 452-4048; luxoraparthotel@hotmail.es; La Paz 439; s/d incl breakfast B$270/380; ❋ 🛜) On a leafy and quiet residential street only a block

from Av Ballivián, this multistory tower has no-frills, spick-and-span rooms with faux-wood floors, excellent light and old TVs.

★**Hotel Aranjuez** HOTEL $$$
(📞428-0076; www.aranjuezhotel.com; Av Buenos Aires E-563; r from B$630; ❋ @ ❄) As you walk around the wonderfully decorated salons in this elegantly furnished hotel on a quiet street in the wealthy Recoleta district, you could be forgiven for thinking you were staying in one of Patiño's palaces. In fact, the Palacio Portales (p251) is just a half block away. This is old-world luxury, so not the place for those seeking contemporary style.

✖ Eating

Cochabambinos pride themselves on being the most food-loving of Bolivians and their city's reputation as the culinary capital of the country is deserved. The highest concentration of good restaurants is in La Recoleta, an upscale neighborhood north of the center; there are several recommended Argentinian-style *churrasquerías* in a pedestrian plaza here.

★**Vainilla** INTERNATIONAL $
(cnr Salamanca & Antezana; mains B$25-36; ☺8am-10:30pm Mon-Sat, to 9:30pm Sun; 🛜) This contemporary, bright and airy restaurant has the look, feel and healthy menu choices of a southern California cafe. The umbrella-shaded outdoor patio is an ideal place for a breakfast of eggs, a fruit smoothie and a cappuccino.

★**Clementina** INTERNATIONAL $$
(📞425-2151; www.clementina.com.bo; mains B$38-48; ☺7-11pm Tue-Sat) A corrugated shipping container facade conceals this intimate and sophisticated scene. Dishes include creative salads, like quinoa with tandoori chicken, burgers and a dozen pasta dishes (gluten-free upon request). Lamps hanging in mason jars and a dimly lit back patio give it a romantic vibe.

★**Casa de Campo** LATIN AMERICAN $$
(Pasaje del Blvd 618; mains B$43-70; ☺11:30am-midnight; 🛜) A Cochabamba classic, this loud and cheerful partly open-air restaurant is a traditional spot to meet, eat and play *cacho* (dice). There's a big range of Bolivian dishes and grilled meats; the food is fine (and piled high on the plates), but the lively, unpretentious atmosphere is better.

★**Menta** VEGETARIAN $$
(España; mains B$29-45; ☺noon-3pm & 6:30-10pm Mon-Sat) A sparsely designed white-brick space with several long picnic-style tables and a menu of Bolivian-style vegetarian dishes and good fruit juices.

Drinking & Nightlife

Cochabamba is famous for its *chicha*, a fermented corn drink that is the locals' favorite tipple.

★**Muela del Diablo** BEER GARDEN
(Potosí 1392; ☺5:30pm-2am; 🛜) The central patio of this exceptionally charming place, wonderfully lit up at night by candles and glowing heat lamps, is surrounded by archways and columns. The feel is of a cool hideaway in an abandoned villa in a European city. Indoors, the bar is more downtown trendy and has live music some weekend nights.

★**Suassuna por Cafe Fragmentos** BEER GARDEN
(Chuquisaca, btwn Lanza & Valdiviezo; ☺5-11:30pm Mon-Sat) Lively on weekend nights when the outdoor garden tables lit with candles are filled with young couples and small groups of friends enjoying cheap drinks (B$20 for two Cuba Libres), snacks and small dishes.

Novecento BAR
(Chuquisaca 711; ☺noon-late Mon-Fri, 6pm-late Sat, noon-5pm Sun; 🛜) Live performance space, cultural center, bar and restaurant all in one; but true to its name, film is the inspiration and movies are shown in a small screening room most nights at 8:30pm. There's also live jazz Wednesdays at 9pm. But it's always a good spot to hang out, and the menu is large and eclectic.

🔒 Shopping

Try **Asarti** (www.asarti.com; cnr Calle México & Av Ballivián, edificio Colon; ☺10am-1pm & 3-8pm Mon-Fri, 10am-4pm Sat), which makes expensive export-quality alpaca clothing. Cheaper alpaca- and llama-wool *chompas* (sweaters) are found in the markets. Check out **Sombreros Boston** (Arce, near Jordán) for handmade straw hats, and you can scour the *artesanía* stalls behind the main post office for inexpensive souvenirs. The city's largest and most modern mall with relatively upscale shops, Hupermall, opened in 2017 in la Recoleta.

ⓘ Information

DANGERS & ANNOYANCES

➡ According to locals, the streets south of Av Aroma are dangerous at night and are best avoided. The bus station is around here, so don't be surprised if, when arriving in the early hours of the morning, you're strongly discouraged from leaving until sunrise.

➡ Pickpocketing and petty theft aren't uncommon in the markets.

➡ The parkland areas Colina San Sebastián and Coronilla Hill near the bus station are both considered dangerous throughout the day – avoid them.

➡ As in any large city, it's best to travel with others late at night and keep your wits about you.

➡ **Tourist Police** (☑450-3880, emergency 120; Plaza 14 de Septiembre; ⊙24hr)

LAUNDRY

Most hotels offer laundry services, but they tend to be pricey and charge per piece. The two hostels are more affordable and charge per kilo. For commercial *lavanderías* try **Limpieza Superior** (España 616; ⊙8:30am-1pm & 2-7pm Mon-Fri, 8am-1pm & 2-5pm Sat), which charges B$18 per kilo.

MEDICAL SERVICES

Centro Médico Quirúrgico Boliviano Belga (☑422-9407; Antezana N-455; ⊙24hr) Private clinic.

Hospital Viedma (☑453-3240; Venezuela; ⊙24hr) Full-service public hospital.

MONEY

Moneychangers gather along Av de las Heroínas and near the market at **Calle 25 de Mayo**; some only accept US cash. **Amanda Casa de Cambio** (Pasaje de la Catedral 340; ⊙8:30am-5:30pm) is quick and professional. You're never far from an ATM, with clusters on Av Ballivián, including five separate ones in front of the **Hipermaxi** (Ballivián 1185; ⊙7:30am-10:30pm) supermarket and at the corner of Avs Heroínas and Ayacucho.

POST

The main **post office and Entel** (cnr Avs Ayacucho & de las Heroínas; ⊙6:30am-10pm) are together in a large complex. Downstairs from the main lobby is an express post office.

TOURIST INFORMATION

The **tourist office** (☑425-8030; www.cochabambaturistica.com.bo; Plaza 14 de Septiembre; ⊙8am-noon & 2:30-6:30pm Mon-Fri) hands out good city material. There are several information kiosks, which also open Saturday mornings, including at the bus station and airport.

Cochabamba has a superb website for visitors (www.brujulaturistica.com/cochabamba), with details and information about places of interest, links to flight information, hotel listings, photos and local events.

Visit the **Instituto Geográfico Militar** (IGM; ☑425-5563; Calle 16 de Julio S-237; ⊙8am-noon & 2-6pm Mon-Fri) for topographic maps (useful for hikers) of Cochabamba department. The **Sernap office** (Servicio Nacional de Áreas Protegidas; www.sernap.gob.bo) has limited information about national parks. Private tour companies are usually better equipped to answer questions.

Head to the **Migración** (☑452-4625; Av Rodríguez Morales, btwn Santa Cruz & Potosí; ⊙8.30am-12:30pm & 2:30-6:30pm Mon-Fri) office for visa and length-of-stay extensions.

ⓘ Getting There & Away

AIR

The flight between La Paz and Cochabamba's **Jorge Wilstermann International Airport** (☑412-0400; Av Killman s/n) – only 4km southwest of the center – must be one of the world's most incredible (sit on the left coming from La Paz, the right from Cochabamba), with fabulous views of the dramatic Cordillera Quimsa Cruz and a (disconcertingly) close-up view of the peak of Illimani. Most flights between Santa Cruz and La Paz touch down briefly at Cochabamba and the city also connects them with flights to Sucre.

BoA (☑414-0873; www.boa.bo; cnr Jordán & Aguirre; ⊙8:30am-7pm Mon-Sat), **Ecojet** (www.ecojet.bo; Plazuela Constitución 0879, cnr 16 de Julio; ⊙8:30am-7:30pm), **Amazonas** (☑479-4200; www.amazonas.com; Av Bolívar 0-1509; ⊙8:30am-12:30pm & 2:30-6pm Mon-Fri, 8:30am-12:30pm Sat) and **TAM** (☑458-0547, www.tam.bo; Av Aniceto Padilla 755; ⊙8:30am-1pm & 2:30-7pm Mon-Fri, 8:30am-1pm Sat) combined, run a bunch of daily flights between Santa Cruz and La Paz via Cochabamba and a couple of daily flights to Sucre. There are also daily flights to Oruro, Trinidad and Tarija, the latter continuing on to Yacuiba a couple of days a week (the schedule changes). Flights to Uyuni generally connect via La Paz.

Micro B (B$2) shuttles between the airport and the main plaza. Taxis to or from the center cost B$25 to B$30. To Quillacollo or Tiquipaya it's B$50.

BUS

Cochabamba's **main bus terminal** (☑422-0550; Ayacucho; terminal fee B$4), just south of the center, has an information kiosk, a branch of the tourist police, ATMs, luggage storage and a *casa de cambio*. The traffic around the terminal is a mess; if bags are small and light and it's daytime, it might be worth walking a few blocks to hail a taxi.

Trufis and micros to eastern Cochabamba Valley villages leave from a variety of spots south of the center, along Av República at the corners of Barrientos, Av 6 de Agosto and Mairana.

Torotoro micros (B$35) with **Sindicato de Transporte Mixto Toro Toro Turistico** (⌨ 7144-2073; Mairana, near Av República) depart daily, when full, from around 7am until late in the afternoon, but waits can vary; 1½ hours isn't unusual. Arrive around 7am or go with a group and it should be quick. Services to the western part of the valley leave from the corner of Avs Ayacucho and Aroma. For Villa Tunari, micros to **Chapare** (Av Oquendo, near Av República) leave from the corner of Avs República and Oquendo.

Expreso Campero (⌨ in Aiquile 695-1569, in Cochabamba 453-7046; Mairana) runs minivans to Aquile and Peña Colorada leaving Cochabamba at noon, 4pm and 6pm.

Departures to La Paz and Santa Cruz leave frequently throughout the day. Oruro and Potosí are mostly nighttime trips.

Bolívar and Trans Copacabana generally have the most qualified drivers and so are the most recommended bus lines.

Best to buy your tickets in the morning the day of your trip. If you turn up in the evening, shortly before departure, we've heard stories of people being scammed.

DESTINATION	COST (B$)	TIME (HR)
Buenos Aires	900	54
La Paz	40-100	9
Oruro	20-50	5
Potosí	80-120	12
Santa Cruz	95-130	12
Sucre	65-95.	8-9
Villa Tunari	bus 15, trufi 35	bus 4, trufi 3

ⓘ Getting Around

BUS

Convenient lettered micros and trufis display their destinations and run to all corners of the city (B$2). Micros to **Quillacollo, Pahirumani & Sipe Sipe** (cnr Avs Aroma & Ayacucho) leave from the intersection of Avs Ayacucho and Aroma near the bus terminal.

TAXI

The taxi fare around the center of Cochabamba is B$6 per person. An extra boliviano is charged if you cross the river or go far to the south. At night, a taxi to La Recoleta runs around B$10.

Drivers will ask for B$15 from the center to various micro stops south of Av 6 de Agosto. To accommodations around Quillacollo it's B$35 to B$40. For a radio taxi, ring **Radio Taxi SJ** (⌨ 428-0002).

Around Cochabamba

Parque Nacional Tunari

This easily accessible 3090 sq km park was created in 1962 to protect the forested slopes above Cochabamba and the wild summit of Cerro Tunari. It encompasses a wide diversity of habitats, from dry inter-Andean valleys to the more humid and highly endangered Polylepis forests of the Cordillera Tunari; because of habitat destruction the endemic Cochabamba mountain finch is also endangered.

Coming from Cochabamba take trufi 109 (B$2) along Av Ayacucho to the last stop, which will drop you close to the park entrance. You may have to show ID and sign in to the park. From the gate turn right, then left after 100m; the road winds up past the playground to some mountain lakes.

Parque Nacional Torotoro

One of Bolivia's most memorable national parks surrounds the remote and tranquil colonial village of Torotoro. The area's geography can seem like a practical demonstration of geology on an awe-inspiring scale. Beds of sedimentary mudstone, sandstone and limestone, bristling with marine fossils and – from drier periods – dinosaur footprints, have been muscled and twisted into the sharp, inhospitable hillscapes of the Serranías de Huayllas and de Cóndor Khaka. In places, the immensity of geological time is showcased, with exposed layers revealing fossils below a hundred meters or more of sedimentary strata.

◉ Sights & Activities

In order to protect the park's geological wonders, it is compulsory to take a guide on any excursion outside the village. Entry tickets (B$100 for four days) are purchased at the **park office** (⌨ 7149-4473; Olvido; ⊙ 7am-noon & 1:30-5pm) next door to the office where you arrange **guides** (⌨ 7435-9152; Olvido; ⊙ 7am-noon & 1:30-4:30pm). Hang on to your ticket at all times as it will be inspected by park rangers. Guides are unlikely to speak English, but their knowledge of the surroundings greatly enhances your visit and contributes positively to the local community.

The going rate for a guide is about B$80 to B$100 per person for a full day of excursions for groups of no more than six (ie for a full day to Ciudad de Itas and Caverna Umajallta it's B$106 in a group of five). Most people go to **Caverna de Umajalanta** (guide B$150, transportation B$150, equipment rental B$12), **Ciudad de Itas** (guide B$150, transportation B$300, entrance fee B$5) and **Cañon de Torotoro & El Vergel** (guide B$180, optional transportation B$70), combining Ciudad de Itas with one of the other two sights on one day and doing the remaining one in the afternoon of their arrival or morning of departure.

If on your own, the easiest and most affordable sight to visit is Cañon de Torotoro and El Vergel.

Turn up at the guides office around 7:30am to book morning and full-day trips; if you're just looking to join with others for the afternoon, it's best to hang out there starting at around 1:30pm.

🎉 Festivals & Events

Fiesta del Señor Santiago RELIGIOUS
(⊙ Jul) From July 24 to 27, the village stages the Fiesta del Señor Santiago, which features sheep sacrifices, dynamite explosions, colorful costumes, lots of *chicha* and some light *tinku* (traditional Bolivian fighting). An interesting time to visit, with more public transportation than usual, but the natural attractions are crowded.

🛏 Sleeping

★ Villa Etelvina HOSTAL $$
(☏ 7073-7807; www.villaetelvina.com; Sucre s/n; camping B$50, s/d B$180/240, 5-person bungalow B$780; ☎) A welcoming oasis with simple, comfortable accommodations, nice bathrooms with good hot water pressure, and delicious home cooking, including tasty vegetarian fare, available on request. Books, board games and DVDs are available for guests to pass the time. The owners can organize transfers from Cochabamba and professional tours of nearby attractions. It's a five-minute walk south of the plaza.

ℹ Information

Bring all the cash you'll need. There are no ATMs and no money changers, but you might be able to change dollars or euros in a pinch at a restaurant or hotel. Villa Etelvina and **Hotel El**

Molino (☏ 424-3633; www.elmolino torotoro.com; s/d/tr B$100/180/250) accept credit cards.

ℹ Getting There & Away

Parque Nacional Torotoro is 135km southeast of Cochabamba in Potosí department. The road is very slowly being improved, but much of the way is along a rough rocky and sandy road, muddy in the rainy season (November to February), when access can be problematic. Once it's completely paved, the driving time should be only around 2½ hours (or so we're told optimistically).

Trans Mixto, **Sindicato Mixto Torotoro** (☏ 7147-7601) or Trans del Norte minivans (B$35, four to six hours in the dry season from May to September) depart Cochabamba throughout the day, when full, from the corner of Avs República and Mairana. They generally seat 11, so if you have a group you can rent the entire vehicle for around B$400. Minivans return to Cochabamba from near the plaza in Torotoro. Best to get a group together to shorten wait times.

Sucre

⟁ 4 / POP 278,000 / ELEV 2750M

Proud, genteel Sucre is Bolivia's most beautiful city and the symbolic heart of the nation. It was here that independence was proclaimed, and while La Paz is the seat of government and treasury, Sucre is recognized in the constitution as the nation's capital. Set in a valley surrounded by mountains with a glorious ensemble of whitewashed buildings sheltering pretty patios, it's a spruce place that preserves a wealth of colonial architecture. Sensibly, there are strict controls on development and it was declared a Unesco World Heritage Site in 1991. Both the city and its university enjoy reputations as focal points of progressive thought within the country.

With a selection of excellent accommodations, a mild and comfortable climate, a wealth of churches and museums, and plenty to see and do in the surrounding area, it's no surprise that visitors end up spending much longer in Sucre than they bargained on.

⊙ Sights

Sucre is overflowing with impressive museums and architecture. For the best view in town, inquire about climbing the cupola at the national police office inside the **Prefectura de Chuquisaca** (State Government Building; cnr Estudiantes & Arce), next to the cathedral.

Sucre

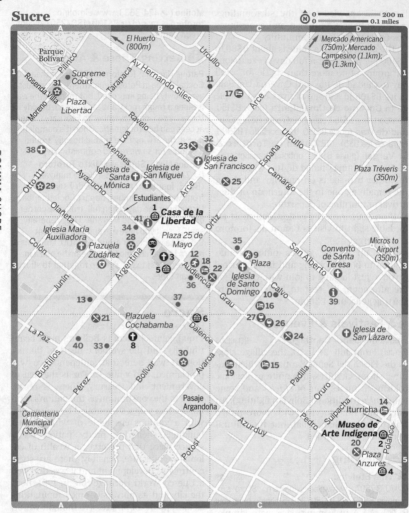

Note the murals depicting the struggle for Bolivian independence as you go upstairs.

⭐ **Museo de Arte Indígena**　MUSEUM
(☑645-6651; www.asur.org.bo; Pasaje Iturricha 314; B$22; ⊙9am-12:30pm & 2:30-6pm Mon-Fri, 9am-noon & 2:30-6pm Sat) This superb museum of indigenous arts is a must for anyone interested in the indigenous groups of the Sucre area, focusing particularly on the woven textiles of the Jal'qa and Candelaria (Tarabuco) cultures. It's a fascinating display and has an interesting subtext: the rediscovery of forgotten ancestral weaving practices has contributed to increased community pride and revitalization. Information in English is available and you can observe the weavers patiently at work.

⭐ **Casa de la Libertad**　MUSEUM
(www.casadelalibertad.org.bo; Plaza 25 de Mayo 11; admission incl optional guided tour B$15; ⊙9am-noon & 2:30-6:30pm Tue-Sat, 9am-noon Sun) For a dose of Bolivian history, it's hard to beat this museum where the Bolivian declaration of independence was signed on August 6, 1825. It has been designated a national memorial and is considered the birthplace of the nation. Spanish-speaking guides are top flight – you'll likely applaud at the end of your guided tour.

Sucre

BOLIVIA SUCRE

**Templo Nuestra
Señora de la Merced** CHURCH
(Pérez 1; B$10; ⊙9am-noon & 3-5pm Mon-Fri)
After several years of restoration work (the
completion date was still unknown at the
time of research), this church's interior is
still mostly bare, but the views from the bell
tower are splendid. Because the order of La
Merced left Sucre for Cuzco in 1826, taking
its records with it, the church's founding date
is uncertain, but it's believed to be sometime
in the 1540s.

Museos Universitarios MUSEUM
(📞645-3285; www.usfx.bo/museos-universitarios;
Bolívar 698; B$20; ⊙9am-noon & 2:30-6:30pm
Mon-Fri, 9am-12:30pm Sat) Housed in a beautifully restored 17th-century building with a
picture-perfect colonial courtyard, the Museos Universitarios consist of three separate
halls housing colonial relics, anthropological artifacts and modern art. Most interesting are the cases filled with dolls dressed
in traditional ethnic fiesta clothing and, for
the more macabre, a collection of skulls and
mummified remains. The permanent gallery
of paintings are mostly dark and dour portraits of generals and politicians; the quality of the contemporary exhibitions varies.
Spanish and English text.

Museo de la Recoleta MUSEUM
(Plaza Anzures; B$15; ⊙9-11:30am & 2:30-4:30pm
Mon-Fri, 3-5pm Sat) Overlooking the city from
the top of Calle Polanco, La Recoleta was established by the Franciscan Order in 1601.
It has served not only as a convent and
museum, but also as a barracks and prison.
The highlight is the church choir and its
magnificent wooden carvings dating back
to the 1870s, each one intricate and unique,
representing the martyrs who were crucified
in 1595 in Nagasaki.

Cementerio Municipal CEMETERY
(entrance on Calle José Manuel Linares; ⊙8-
11:30am & 2-5:30pm Mon-Fri, 8am-5:30pm Sat)
Sucre's immaculately maintained cemetery
is evidence that inequality doesn't die when
we do. Mausoleums of wealthy colonial families and their descendants, interspersed with
arches carved from poplar trees, as well as
picturesque palms, are larger and certainly
more elaborate than most living residents'
homes. At weekends it's jam-packed with
families. You can walk the eight blocks from

Plaza 25 de Mayo south along Junín, or take a taxi or *micro A*.

Catedral CHURCH
(Plaza 25 de Mayo; ⊙ Mass 9am Thu & Sun) Sucre's cathedral dates from the middle of the 16th century and is a harmonious blend of Renaissance architecture with later baroque additions. It's a noble structure, with a bell tower that is a local landmark. Inside, the white single-naved space has a series of oil paintings of the apostles, as well as an ornate altarpiece and pulpit. If you are not attending Mass, you can enter as part of a visit to the **Museo Eclesiástico de Sucre** (Ortiz 31; B$30; ⊙ 9am-noon & 2:30-6:30pm Mon-Fri, 2:30-6:30pm Sat) next door.

🏃 Activities

★**Condor Trekkers** HIKING
(📱 7289-1740; www.condortrekkers.org; cnr Calvo & Bolívar; ⊙ 8:30am-6:30pm Mon-Sat) Popular and recommended tour agency, housed in the cafe of the same name, which organizes a variety of multiday hikes in the surrounding region. You can put your name on the whiteboard and hope to find other takers to share the cost. The agency has very high-quality guides and can customize any trip. A portion of earnings go toward social development projects.

★**Off Road Bolivia** OUTDOORS
(📱 7033-8123; www.offroadbolivia.com; Audiencia 44) These are the safest and best-quality quad-biking, mountain-biking and motorcycle tours in Sucre. For newbies, they even offer lessons on riding off-road motorbikes.

📖 Courses

Instituto Cultural Boliviano Alemán LANGUAGE
(ICBA; 📱 645-2091; www.icba-sucre.edu.bo; Calvo 217; ⊙ 9:30am-12:30pm & 3-9pm Mon-Fri, 10am-noon Sat) Offers recommended Spanish lessons with homestay options and also runs Quechua classes. ICBA has a German-language library and listings of rooms for rent.

South American Spanish School LANGUAGE
(📱 7033-5141; www.sas-school.com; Plazuela San Francisco 107) Group or private conversational Spanish classes, plus salsa and folkloric dancing and cooking classes. The school can also help organize homestays and volunteer opportunities.

Me Gusta Spanish LANGUAGE
(📱 645-8689; www.megustaspanish.com; Junín 333, 2nd fl) Can tailor lessons to subjects of interest such as sports, cooking or walking tours of the city; can also help arrange homestays.

🎭 Festivals & Events

Fiesta de la Virgen de Guadalupe RELIGIOUS
(⊙ Sep) On the weekend closest to September 8, people from all over the country flock to join local *campesinos* in a celebration of the Fiesta de la Virgen de Guadalupe with songs, traditional dances and poetry recitations. The following day, they dress in colorful costumes and parade around Plaza 25 de Mayo carrying religious images and silver arches.

🛏 Sleeping

★**Kultur Berlin** HOSTEL $
(📱 646-6854; www.kulturberlin.com; Avaroa 326; 4-/8-bed dm B$75/55, s/d incl breakfast B$85/200; @ 🛜) Sprawling and social, this is easily the best hostel for those looking to meet up with other gringo travelers. It's a big operation housed in a colonial-era building, but couples or those just interested in quiet aren't excluded – ask for one of the uniquely configured and furnished upper-floor rooms in the back building.

La Dolce Vita GUESTHOUSE $
(📱 691-2014; www.dolcevitasucre.com; Urcullo 342; s/d/tr B$90/140/195, s/d without bathroom B$55/100; @ 🛜) A newly whitewashed facade makes this traveler-friendly guesthouse on a quiet street more appealing. Offers basic rooms for a variety of budgets. The kitchen is somewhat shabby, but the terrace is a good spot to catch some sun. Discounts offered for long-term stays.

★**Casa Verde** B&B $$
(📱 645-8291; www.casaverdesucre.com; Potosí 374; s/d/ste B$145/260/340; @ 🛜 🏊) Immaculate Casa Verde is a home away from home. It's deservedly popular and frankly underpriced given the quality of service: Belgian owner Rene almost bends over backwards to help his guests. Rooms, arranged around a small courtyard with a pool, are named after Rene's children and grandchildren. If you visit in winter you'll be thankful for the thick duvets.

Casa Kolping HOTEL $$
(📱 642-3812; www.casakolpingsucre.com; Pasaje Iturricha 265; s/d B$300/360; @ 🛜) High on

a hill by Plaza Anzures, with great views over Sucre, this excellent hotel caters mostly for conferences, but is an appealing place to stay. It boasts clean, comfortable, well-equipped (if somewhat generic) rooms, plus efficient service and a good restaurant. It's also a good place for kids, with family apartments, plenty of space and a ping-pong table.

★ **Samary**
Boutique Hotel   BOUTIQUE HOTEL $$$
(☑ 642-5088; www.samaryhotel.com; Dalence 349; s/d from B$380/500; ✷ @ 🛜 ♨) Samary has an ambitious concept – reproducing a traditional Chuquisaca village in hotel form – and it pulls it off surprisingly well. There's a plaza, a chapel and even a *chichería* selling authentic home-brew liquor. Rooms are of the highest standard, adorned with Yamparaez textiles and replica rock carvings.

★ **La Posada**   BOUTIQUE HOTEL $$$
(☑ 646-0101; www.hotellaposada.com.bo; Audiencia 92; s/d B$345/552; @ 🛜) This comfortable and classy property has charming, tastefully furnished and comfortable rooms with an appealing colonial ambience and wooden trimmings. There are views over town, a stylish and intimate feel, and a good family suite. The courtyard restaurant is recommended and a great spot for your breakfast. Service is professional.

✖ Eating

Mercado Central   MARKET $
(cnr Ravelo & Junín; ⊘ 7am-7.30pm Mon-Sat, to 11am Sun) Don't miss the fresh juices (B$7) – the vendors and their blenders always come up with something indescribably delicious; try *jugo de tumbo* (unripe passion-fruit juice). Upstairs, above the clothing vendors, tasty, cheap meals are fried up and served at picnic tables from morning to night. Sensitive stomachs might want to pass.

El Paso de los Abuelos   FAST FOOD $
(Bustillos 216; salteñas B$8; ⊘ 8am-1pm) Come early to get your *salteñas* (meat and vegetable pasties) from this *salteñería* bakery – the tasty treats sell out fast.

Prem   VEGAN $
(San Alberto 54; set lunch B$25; ⊘ 11am-3pm & 7-9pm Mon-Sat; ☑) Tiny, crowded spot where locals crowd the few tables for a tasty vegan set lunch. Good juices, smoothies and cupcakes as well.

★ **Om**   INTERNATIONAL $$
(cnr Potosí & Grau; mains B$30-70; ⊘ 8:30am-10pm) The tapas-style plates are equal to the beautifully sophisticated Mediterranean-like courtyard patio here, which, since it's one of the most pleasant places to eat in the city, is no small compliment. The menu ranges from blue-cheese-and-walnut-stuffed dates wrapped in bacon to Cajun shrimp and mains like mesquite-smoked trout with rosemary foam. Heaters on hand for cool nights; hours may vary.

★ **Café Gourmet Mirador**   CAFE $$
(Pasaje Iturricha 297, Mirador de la Recoleta; mains B$25-45; ⊘ 9am-8pm; 🛜) Settled in a lounge chair looking out over the city's rooftops and surrounding mountains, you'll likely be inspired to scour the classifieds for Sucre real estate. No matter the time (though bring a hat and sunscreen during the day) it feels quite Edenic – catching up on your reading, sipping an espresso or smoothie and snacking on a sandwich or tortilla.

★ **Florín**   INTERNATIONAL $$
(Bolívar 567; mains B$35-45; ⊘ 10am-2am Mon-Fri, 8:30am-late Sat & Sun; 🛜) This atmospheric bar-restaurant serves a mixture of typical Bolivian food and international dishes (the latter, such as chicken tandoori, pad thai or moussaka, are generally pale imitations), including a 'full English' breakfast. Popular with locals and gringos alike, who line up along the enormous 13m-long bar at night to swill down the beers.

★ **El Huerto**   INTERNATIONAL $$$
(☑ 7612-3300, 645-3587; www.elhuertorestaurante.net; Av Cabrera 86; mains B$65-95; ⊘ noon-4pm Mon, Tue & Sun, noon-4pm & 7-10pm Wed-Sat) Set in a lovely secluded garden, El Huerto has the atmosphere of a classy lawn party, with sunshades and grass underfoot. There's great service and stylishly presented traditional plates (especially the chorizo) that don't come much better anywhere in the country. Other specialties are the prawns, Peruvian- and Bolivian-caught fish and chateaubriand, plus an excellent wine selection.

🍷 Drinking & Nightlife

La Quimba   BAR
(Grau 238; ⊘ 7:30pm-late Tue-Sat) Somehow, in this postage-stamp-sized spot, there's space made for musicians (of the jazz and world-music variety) to perform most Friday nights. There are drinks, of course, a

laid-back bohemian vibe, and a menu of vegetarian dishes such as lentil and quinoa burgers (B$20).

Goblin Brew Pub BAR
(Grau 246; ⊙8pm-late Thu-Sat) This high-ceilinged family-run place resembles a Spanish taverna and offers a good selection of its own craft beers.

Kulturcafé Berlin BAR
(www.kulturberlin.com; Avaroa 326; ⊙8am-12:30am; 🖘) Most gringo backpackers end up at this spacious and happening bar for a night or two. There's outdoor patio seating, sports on the TV, regular game nights and even folkloric dancing and live music. There's also a menu of the usual Bolivian fare, plus Mexican and German specialties and good desserts.

☆ Entertainment

There's a monthly brochure detailing Sucre's cultural events; look for it at tourist offices or in bars and restaurants. Art centers **La Guarida Espacio Cultural** (☑7756-7432; www.facebook.com/laguaridaespaciocultural; Azurduy 118) and **El Mercado** (☑644-3154; Olañeta 277; ⊙hours vary Thu-Sat) draw a local bohemian crowd. Other establishments provide language courses and host cultural events.

Teatro Gran Mariscal de Ayacucho THEATER
(Plaza Libertad) This opulent old opera house today hosts a wide range of live performances – the tourist office and the **Casa de la Cultura** (☑643-9621; sucrecultural@hotmail.com; Argentina 65) both distribute a monthly calendar of events.

🔒 Shopping

The best place to learn about traditional local weavings is the Museo de Arte Indígena (p258), but to buy them you are best off going direct to the villages. Prices are steep by Bolivian standards, but the items are high quality. Several shops near the central plaza sell locally made clothing, from high-quality alpaca sweaters to cheap ponchos.

A trip to the **Mercado Americano** (⊙8am-7pm), around the junction of Mujía and Reyes, will keep clothes lovers busy for hours, while the enormous and maze-like **Mercado Campesino** (⊙6am-7pm) is a fascinating mix of stalls selling traditional and authentic food and everyday housewares and junk. Take *micro* 7 or *G* northbound from the center.

ℹ Information

DANGERS & ANNOYANCES
Sucre has long enjoyed a reputation as one of Bolivia's safest towns, but if you have a problem, report it to the **tourist police** (☑648-4811; Dalence 1, Plazuela Zudáñez).

LAUNDRY
There are a handful of *lavanderías*, including **Laverap** (Ortiz; per kg B$9; ⊙8am-8pm Mon-Sat, to noon Sun) and **Superlimp** (Estudiantes 26; per kg B$12; ⊙8:30am-8pm Mon-Sat) that charge per kilo around town; most need a half-day or more. All but one or two are closed Sundays.

MEDICAL SERVICES
For medical emergencies try **Hospital Santa Bárbara** (☑643-5240; cnr Ayacucho & René Moreno, Plazuela Libertad; ⊙24hr).

MONEY
ATMs are located all around the city center, but not at the bus station.

TOURIST INFORMATION
Infotur (☑645-5983; San Alberto 413; ⊙8am-noon & 4-6pm Mon-Sat, 9am-noon & 2:30-6pm Sun) has a moderately helpful office in town and has booths at the airport, bus terminal and Plaza Libertad. The **Oficina Universitaria de Turismo** (☑644-7644; Estudiantes 49; ⊙4-7pm Mon-Sat, 2-7pm Sun), run by university students, sometimes offers guides for city tours.

The **Migración** (☑645-3647; www.migracion. gob.bo; Bustillos 284; ⊙8:30am-12:30pm & 2:30-6:30pm Mon-Fri) office is a no-fuss place to extend visas and lengths of stay.

Stop by the **Instituto Geográfico Militar** (☑645-5514; Arce 110; ⊙8:30am-noon & 2:30-6pm Mon-Fri) for topographic maps of the Chuquisaca department.

ℹ Getting There & Away

AIR
You can fly internationally between Sucre and Buenos Aires, Madrid, Salta and São Paulo on **BoA** (☑691-2360; www.boa.bo; Audiencia 21; ⊙8:30am-12:30pm & 2:30-6:30pm Mon-Fri, 8:30am-12:30pm Sat).

BoA, **Ecojet** (☑691-4711; www.ecojet.bo; Dalence 138; ⊙8:30am-12:30pm & 2:30-6:30pm Mon-Fri) and **Amazonas** (☑643-7000; www.amazonas.com; Calvo 90; ⊙8:30am-12:30pm & 2:30-6:30pm Mon-Fri) offer several flights a day to Cochabamba, La Paz and Santa Cruz; Amazonas also flies to Uyuni (around B$374 one-way) daily Monday, Wednesday and Friday. There are direct flights on BoA to Tarija several days a week. TAM also serves Sucre, La

Paz and Santa Cruz; however, the location of its local office was in flux when we last visited.

The city's new airport, named **Alcantarí International Airport**, located in Yamparáez, 30km south of the city, is still a work in progress. The space feels mostly vacant, with few shops or eateries open, especially for night flights. There is an ATM, but no money exchange. Compared to the old airport, however, it's less vulnerable to bad weather and certainly isn't in danger of being overrun by housing developments. Departure tax is B$11.

The airport is a 40-minute taxi ride (B$50) from the city at night (longer during the day when there's more traffic). Or you can grab a shared one, minimum two people (B$60), from **Plaza Tréveris** or a *micro* that leaves when full from a **spot** near Plaza Camargo (B$8).

BUS

The **bus terminal** (☑ 644-1292; Av Ostria Gutiérrez) is a 3km uphill walk from the center along Av Gutierrez and most easily accessed by *micros* A or 3 (B$1.50) from along Ravelo, or by taxi (as the *micros* are too crowded for lots of luggage). You can also walk and get there quicker in midday gridlock. Unless you're headed for Potosí, it's wise to book long-distance buses a day in advance in order to reserve a seat. There's a terminal tax of B$2.50; services include an information kiosk, but no ATM. To save the trip to the bus station, many centrally located travel agents also sell tickets on selected services for a small commission.

There are plans to build a new bus station in the next couple of years.

Take an early evening bus to La Paz, as opposed to an afternoon one, so you don't arrive at an ungodly hour. A new company called El Mexicano (leaves 6pm) is the best for the Santa Cruz route, and Andes Bus to Oruro or Tarija is like flying 1st class on a plane.

If you are headed to Tarija or Villazón, you'll have more luck going to Potosí; the quickest and comfiest (if not the cheapest) way to get there is in a shared taxi (B$50, two hours), which can be arranged through your hotel or by calling direct. Try **Super Movil** (☑ 645-2222).

For Uyuni, we recommend 6 de Octubre buses (either *cama*, ie fully reclining, or *semi-cama*), which leave at 9am and 8pm daily.

DESTINATION	COST (B$)	TIME (HR)
Camiri	120	18
Cochabamba	80-90	10
La Paz	150-260	12
Oruro	40-70	7-8
Potosí	30-50	3
Santa Cruz	94-105	12
Uyuni	80-90	8½

Around Sucre

Tarabuco

☑ 4 / POP 19,500 / ELEV 3284M

The small, predominantly indigenous village of **Tarabuco**, 65km southeast of Sucre, is famous for its textiles, which are among the most renowned in all of Bolivia. To travelers though, Tarabuco is best known for its annual **Pujllay** (☺ Mar) celebrations in March and its colorful, sprawling **Sunday market** (☺ 7am-4pm), a popular day trip from Sucre. Look out for high-quality *artesanías* such as pullovers, *charangos*, coca pouches, ponchos and weavings that feature geometric and zoomorphic designs.

Micros to Tarabuco (B$10, 1½ hours) leave when full from the intersection of Avs de las Américas and Mendoza in Sucre on Sunday between 6:30am and 9:30am. Returns to Sucre leave between 11am and 3:30pm from just outside the **tourist office** (cnr Calle 1° de Mayo & Potosí) in Tarabuco.

Many tourists arrive by 'chartered' minivans (B$40 round-trip, two hours each way) from Sucre. Tickets must be bought in advance from bigger hotels or any travel agent.

Bring all the cash in bolivianos you'll need. There are no ATMs and credit cards aren't accepted.

Cordillera de los Frailes

The imposing serrated ridge forming Sucre's backdrop creates a formidable barrier between the departments of Chuquisaca and Potosí. Only a short drive heading northwest out of Sucre, roads turn rough, carving their way around forested mountains, leaving modern Bolivian urban life far behind. Home to the Jal'qa people, this region of bizarrely shaped and multi-hued rocks and deceptively tall and remote peaks is a trekker's dream.

🏃 Activities

We strongly recommend taking a guided hiking tour to increase your enjoyment of the region and to communicate with the Quechua-speaking *campesinos* (subsistence farmers). A responsible guide will help you avoid local hostility, minimize your impact and get a better feel for the local culture.

Almost every Sucre travel agency advertises jaunts into the Cordillera, including one-day trips to see the rock paintings of Incamachay and Pumamachay or a two-day circuit from Chataquila to Incamachay and Chaunaca. It's important to go with a responsible operator committed to contributing to the communities you visit. In general, guided trips run in and around B$650 for three days and B$800 for four days per person. Condor Trekkers (p260) in Sucre comes highly recommended.

🛏 Sleeping

⭐ **Samary Wasi** HOSTAL **$$**
(📞 693-8088; Maragua; s/d/tr B$152/207/276) A kilometer from the village of Maragua, in Irupampa, is this lovely stone and red-tile-roofed *hostal* with three bedrooms, heaps of heavy blankets for cool nights, a toilet and shower, and a little sitting area for meals. There are electrical outlets for charging devices.

Potosí

📞 2 / POP 190,000 / ELEV 4070M

The conquistadors never found El Dorado, the legendary city of gold, but they did get their hands on Potosí and its Cerro Rico, a 'Rich Hill' full of silver. Indeed, the city was founded in 1545 as soon as the ore was discovered and pretty soon the silver extracted here was bankrolling the Spanish empire. Even today, something very lucrative is said to *vale un Potosí* (be worth a Potosí).

During the boom years, when the metal must have seemed inexhaustible, Potosí became the Americas' largest and wealthiest city. Once the silver dried up, however, the city went into decline and its citizens slipped into poverty. The ore, plus tin, lead and other minerals, is still being extracted by miners in some of the most abysmal conditions imaginable. But the rest of Potosí – its grand churches and ornate colonial architecture – is also worth getting to know.

◉ Sights

⭐ **Casa Nacional de la Moneda** MUSEUM
(📞 622-2777; www.casanacionaldemoneda.bo; Ayacucho, near Bustillos; admission by guided tour B$40, photo permit B$20; ⊙ tours 9am, 10:30am, 2:30pm & 4:30pm Tue-Sat, 9am & 10:30am Sun) The National Mint is Potosí's star attraction and one of South America's finest museums. Potosí's first mint was constructed on the present site of the Casa de Justicia in 1572 under orders from the Viceroy of Toledo. This, its replacement, is a vast and strikingly beautiful building that takes up a whole city

block. You don't have to be a numismatist to find the history of the first global currency fascinating.

⭐ **Museo y Convento de Santa Teresa** MUSEUM
(www.museosantateresa.blogspot.com; cnr Santa Teresa & Ayacucho; admission by guided tour B$21, photo permit B$10; ⊙ 9am-12:30pm & 2:30-6pm Mon & Wed-Sat, 2:30-6pm Tue, 3-6pm Sun) The fascinating Santa Teresa Convent was founded in 1685 and is still home to a small community of Carmelite nuns who have restored the sizable building and converted part of it into a museum. The excellent guided tour (1¾ hours; in Spanish and English) explains how girls from wealthy families entered the convent at the age of 15, getting their last glimpse of parents and loved ones at the door.

Museo y Convento de San Francisco MUSEUM
(📞 622-2539; cnr Tarija & Nogales; admission by guided tour B$15; ⊙ tours 9:30am, 11am, 3pm & 4pm Mon-Fri, 9am & noon Sat) This convent, founded in 1547 by Fray Gaspar de Valverde, is the oldest monastery in Bolivia. Owing to its inadequate size, it was demolished in 1707 and reconstructed over the following 19 years. The museum has a fine collection of religious art, including paintings from the Potosí school, such as *The Erection of the Cross* by Melchor Pérez de Holguín, various mid-19th-century works by Juan de la Cruz Tapia and 25 scenes from the life of St Francis of Assisi.

Torre de la Compañía de Jesús CHURCH
(Ayacucho, near Bustillos; mirador B$10; ⊙ 8-11:30am & 2-5:30pm Mon-Fri, 8am-noon Sat) The ornate and beautiful bell tower, on what remains of the former Jesuit church, was completed in 1707 after the collapse of the original church. Both the tower and the doorway are adorned with examples of *mestizo* baroque ornamentation. Also the location of the Potosí tourist office (p267).

La Catedral ARCHITECTURE
(Cathedral; Plaza 10 de Noviembre; ⊙ 3-6:30pm Mon-Fri, hours subject to change) Construction of La Catedral was initiated in 1564 and finally completed around 1600. The original building lasted until the early 19th century, when it mostly collapsed. Most of what is now visible is the neoclassical construction, and the building's elegant lines represent one of Bolivia's best exemplars of that style.

Potosí

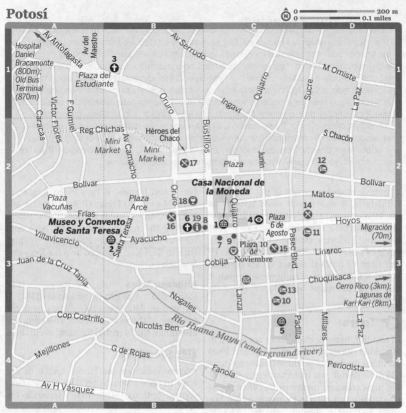

The interior decor represents some of the finest in Potosí. You can visit the **bell tower** (Junín; B$15; ☉9am-noon & 3-6pm Mon-Fri) for nice views of the city.

**La Capilla de Nuestra
Señora de Jerusalén**   CHURCH
(Plaza del Estudiante; ☉9am-7pm Sun) This is a little-known Potosí gem. Originally built as

ℹ️ MINE TOURS WARNING

The cooperatives are not museums, but working mines that are fairly nightmarish places. Anyone planning to take a tour needs to realize that there are risks involved. People with medical problems – especially claustrophobia, asthma and other respiratory conditions – should avoid them. While medical experts including the NHS note that limited exposure from a tour lasting a few hours is extremely unlikely to cause any lasting health impacts, if you have any concerns whatsoever about exposure to asbestos or silica dust, you should not enter the mines. Accidents can also happen – explosions, falling rocks, runaway trolleys etc. For these reasons, all tour companies make visitors sign a disclaimer absolving them completely from any responsibility for injury, illness or death. If your tour operator does not, choose another. Visiting the mines is a serious decision. If you're undeterred, you'll have an eye-opening and memorable experience.

a humble chapel in honor of the Virgen de Candelaria, it was rebuilt more lavishly in the 18th century. There's a fine gilt baroque *retablo* (portable box with depictions of religious and historical events) – the Virgin has pride of place – and a magnificent series of paintings of biblical scenes by anonymous Potosí school artists. The impressive pulpit has small paintings by Melchor Pérez de Holguín.

☞ Tours

In addition to mine tours, there are a variety of guided offerings by over two dozen local agencies, including a three-hour city tour (B$70 to B$100, not including entry fees) of the museums and monuments. Other popular options include the Tarapaya (p268) hot springs (B$50 to B$100); guided trekking trips around the Lagunas de Kari Kari (p268; B$160 to B$280); and tours of colonial haciendas around Potosí (B$150). Many outfits also book Salar de Uyuni tours for those heading in that direction. You can generally book tours at your hotel, too, as most properties either run their own tours or work with the agencies.

Big Deal Tours   TOURS
(☑623-0478; www.bigdealtours.blogspot.com; Bustillos 1092; mine tours B$150; ⊘8am-8pm Mon-Sat) The specialty of this outfit run by current and former miners is, of course, mine tours. Guides are informative, passionate and have a good sense of humor, plus clearly have a good relationship with the mine workers encountered along the way.

Koala Tours   TOURS
(☑622-2092; www.koalabolivia.com.bo; Ayacucho 5) Ground floor of the similarly named **cafe** (mains B$15-45; ⊘7am-10pm) and popular with backpackers, partly because it also operates

two Potosí hostels. It runs twice-daily mine tours Monday to Friday (B$130; 8:45am and 1:30pm), and a small portion of the profits goes to the mining community. Also runs trips to Tarapaya (p268; B$150) and trekking trips to Kari Kari, and can help book onward bus tickets.

Altiplano Tours   TOURS
(☑622-5353; Ayacucho 19; mine tours B$140) At the end of Altiplano's mine tours, you can try some of the work yourself. This company also offers *tinku* (ritual fighting) excursions.

🛏️ Sleeping

Accommodations in Potosí aren't of the kind to tempt you to prolong a visit. Only central options (other than Hacienda Cayara) should be considered. Usually only the midrange to top-end hotels have heating, and they sometimes need to be persuaded to use it. There may be blanket shortages in the cheapies, so you'll want a sleeping bag.

★La Casona Hostal   HOSTEL $
(☑623-0523; www.hotelpotosi.com; Chuquisaca 460; dm B$40, s/d/tr/q B$100/140/200/240, without bathroom B$70/90/135/180; @ 🖋) Housed in an attractively crumbling 18th-century colonial house in the center of town with an equally handsome yellow and stone slab inner atrium. The private rooms have nice wood floors, heavy blankets and clean, hot-water showers. Backpackers give the dorms mixed reviews, in part because of the state of the shared bathrooms.

Casa Blanca   HOSTEL $
(☑7142-4313; luiszilvetiali@gmail.com; Tarija 35; dm B$40, d B$100) The graffiti-painted walls of the inner courtyard give this otherwise whitewashed place a splash of color. Rooms are otherwise ordinary and the bathrooms

could use a bit of work. Staff are friendly and helpful.

★ Hostal Colonial
HOTEL $$

(622-4265; www.hostalcolonialpotosi.com.bo; Hoyos 8; s/d/tr B$320/420/505; @ 🛜) In a well-kept colonial building near the main plaza, this warm whitewashed retreat has smallish rooms with windows onto a central courtyard; all rooms have minibars and cable TV, and some have bathtubs. It's a longstanding favorite with midrange travelers and boasts very helpful English-speaking staff and a great location.

Hotel Coloso Potosí
HOTEL $$$

(622-2627; www.potosihotel.com; Bolívar 965; s/d/tr B$530/670/920, ste B$707-884; @ 🛜 🌐) Luxurious for Potosí, the city's only five-star option wouldn't beat out your average Holiday Inn, at least as far as room features and design go. But there's a pool, restaurant, sauna and room service, if slightly stuffy formality. Some rooms have great city views.

✗ Eating & Drinking

★ Café la Plata
CAFE $

(Plaza 10 de Noviembre; mains B$14-45; 1:30-11pm Mon, 10am-11pm Tue-Sat) The city's most sophisticated cafe by far, this handsome, high-ceilinged place is comfortable and chic in a restored sort of way, and a good place to hang out, especially at one of the window seats with plaza views. There are rich espressos, magazines to read and wine served by the glass. Pastas, cakes, salads, sandwiches – it's all done well.

Mercado Central
MARKET $

(Oruro; snacks B$6; 6am-7pm) Stalls in the *comedor* (dining hall) serve inexpensive breakfasts of bread, pastries and coffee. Downstairs there are some excellent juice stands. Cheese or meat empanadas are sold around the market until early afternoon, and in the evening, street vendors sell *humitas* (cornmeal filled with cheese, onion, egg and spices, baked in the oven or boiled).

El Fogón
INTERNATIONAL $$

(cnr Oruro & Frías; almuerzo B$30, mains B$30-70; 10am-10pm) This spacious, colorful and brightly lit central restaurant is popular for its range of international and Bolivian food, including llama steaks. In truth though, portions aren't huge and the service is slow and less than attentive.

★ 4.060
INTERNATIONAL $$$

(622-2623; www.cafepub4060.com; Hoyos 1; mains B$45-90; 4-11:30pm Mon-Sat) Potosí's most au courant restaurant, 4.060 is popular with groups of travelers looking for a comfortable and familiar night out. This spacious contemporary cafe-bar has earned plenty of plaudits for its pizzas, burgers and Mexican food (and paella, if you order it in advance) as well as being a sociable spot for a drink. There's a good beer selection.

La Casona Pub
PUB

(Frías 41; 6pm-12:30am Mon-Sat) This atmospheric pub is tucked away in the historic 1775 home of the royal envoy sent to administer the mint. It's a friendly watering hole with pub grub. On Friday it stages live music performances.

❶ Information

ATMs are common in the center of town. Lots of businesses along Bolívar, Sucre and in the market change US dollars at reasonable rates; stalls along Héroes del Chaco also change euros and Chilean and Argentine pesos. Many hotels now accept credit cards, primarily Visa and Mastercard.

InfoTur de Potosí (622-7404; http://info turpotosi.blogspot.com; Ayacucho; 8am-noon & 2-6:30pm) has quite helpful Spanish-speaking staff, good city maps and loads of brochures on city sights; it's located at the entrance to the Torre de la Compañía de Jesús (p264). Another useful site is www.brujulaturistica.com/potosi.

The **tourist police** (Plaza 10 de Noviembre; 8am-noon & 2-6pm) on the ground floor of the Gobernación building can be helpful; there's also a branch at the new bus terminal.

Head to the **Migración** (622-2745; Linares 136; 8:30am-12:30pm & 2:30-6:30pm Mon-Fri) office for visa extensions.

There's a **Post Office** (cnr Lanza & Chuquisaca; 8am-8pm Mon-Fri, to 5:30pm Sat, 9am-11:30pm Sun) in town.

The **Hospital Daniel Bracamonte** (624-4960; Italia s/n; 24hr) has some English-speaking doctors.

❶ Getting There & Away

All road routes into Potosí are quite scenic, and arriving by day will always provide a dramatic introduction to the city. The **new bus terminal** (Av Circunvalación) is about 2km north of the center on Av Las Banderas and nearly all *flotas* (long-distance buses; except for Uyuni) depart from here. *Micros I* or *A* run between the bus terminal and the cathedral.

There are direct *flotas* to La Paz, but in many cases it can be quicker to look for a connection in Oruro. Similarly for Sucre shared taxis (B\$50, 2¼ hours) are pricier than the *flotas*, but are faster and more comfortable and can pick you up at your hotel. Try **Cielito Express** (📞 624-6040) or **Correcaminos** (📞 624-3383); if solo, it's quicker to go to their offices behind the **old bus terminal** (Av Universitaria) as they won't depart without a full car.

For Uyuni (B\$40, five hours) buses depart from the old terminal 15 minutes downhill on foot from the center on Av Universitaria roughly every half-hour from 7am to noon and then several more in the early evening. The rugged 210km route is quite breathtaking. *Micros* to Tarija also depart from this location.

Autobuses Quirquincho (www.autobuses quirquincho.com) and two other companies service Buenos Aires, Argentina

DESTINATION	COST (B\$)	TIME (HR)
Cochabamba	52-120	10
La Paz	52-135	9-10
Oruro	25-40	4
Sucre	20	3
Tarija	100	5-6
Tupiza	40-100	6
Villazón	50-90	8-9

❶ Getting Around

Micros and minibuses (B\$1.50) shuttle between the center and the Cerro Rico mines, as well as to the old and new bus terminal (p267). Taxis charge B\$4 per person around the center, slightly more at night, and B\$10 or so to the new bus terminal.

Around Potosí

The **Lagunas de Kari Kari** are artificial lakes (ranging from an elevation of 4500m to 5025m) constructed in the late 16th and early 17th centuries by 20,000 indigenous slaves to provide water for Potosí and for hydropower to run the city's 82 *ingenios* (smelters). Of the 32 original lakes only 25 remain and all have been abandoned – except by waterfowl, which appreciate the incongruous surface water in this otherwise stark region. The easiest way to visit Lagunas de Kari Kari is with a Potosí tour agency, which charge about B\$180 per person per day based on a group of three.

Belief in the curative powers of **Tarapaya** (3600m), the most frequently visited hot-springs area around Potosí (21km northwest of the city), dates back to Inca times. The most interesting sight is the 30°C Ojo del Inca, a perfectly round, green lake in a low volcanic crater, 100m in diameter. *Camiones* leave for Tarapaya (B\$4, 30 minutes) from Mercado Chuquimia near the old bus terminal in Potosí on Av Antofagasta roughly every half hour from 6am to 7pm. Taxis cost about B\$70 one-way. The last *micro* from Tarapaya to Potosí leaves between 5pm and 6pm.

For a peaceful retreat or some comfortable hill walking, visit **Hacienda Cayara** (📞 740-9024; www.hotelmuseocayara.com/en; r per person B\$180) which lies 25km down the valley northwest of Potosí.

SANTA CRUZ & GRAN CHIQUITANIA

The Bolivian Oriente is not what you generally see in Bolivian tourist brochures. This tropical region, the country's most prosperous, has a palpable desire to differentiate itself from Bolivia's traditional highland image. The region's agriculture boom has brought about a rise in income and a standard of living unequaled by any other Bolivian province.

Santa Cruz is Bolivia's most populous city, with a cosmopolitan population, yet it retains a small-town atmosphere. From here you can visit charming Jesuit mission towns with the country's loveliest examples of Jesuit architecture, tour pre-Inca ruins near the village of Samaipata or embark on a revolutionary pilgrimage to where Che Guevara met his maker around Vallegrande. Prefer nature? There are miles of hikes and tons of wildlife at Parque Nacional & Área de Uso Múltiple Amboró (p274), the so-called 'elbow of the Andes' where the ecosystems of the Chaco, the Amazon Basin and the Andes meet.

Santa Cruz

📞 3 / POP 1.4 MILLION / ELEV 417M (1368FT)

Santa Cruz may surprise you with its small-town feeling, colonial buildings and relaxed tropical atmosphere. Bolivia's largest city oozes modernity yet clings stubbornly to tradition. The city center is vibrant and thriving, its narrow streets crowded with suited businesspeople sipping *chicha* (a fermented-corn drink) at street stalls. Locals still lounge on benches in the main square listening to *cam-*

ba (eastern lowlands) music, restaurants close for siesta and stores line the porch-fronted houses selling cheap, local products.

This is not the Bolivia that you see on postcards, but it is the place with the greatest population diversity in the country – from the overall-wearing Mennonites strolling past goth kids, to the Japanese community, altiplano immigrants, Cuban doctors, Brazilian settlers and fashionable *cruceños* (Santa Cruz locals) cruising the tight streets in their SUVs. It's worth spending a few days here, eating at the international restaurants and checking out the nightlife.

◎ Sights & Activities

Though the city has no standout sights, there is plenty to see and do around town. If the heat saps your energy though, you may prefer to just stroll around, sip a fruit juice in one of the city's many cafes or do some people-watching in the shade of the buzzing **Plaza 24 de Septiembre**.

★ Jardín Botánico   GARDENS
(☑ 362-3101; Carretera a Cotoca KM 8½; adult/child B$10/5; ◎ 8am-6pm) Santa Cruz's lush botanical gardens, 12km east of the city center, make for a tranquil escape from the urban scene. Covering more than 200 hectares, the gardens feature woodland trails, a lake, a cactarium (cactus garden) and plenty of exotic plants. Climb the wooden viewing platform for vistas across the treetop canopy to the city skyline. The gardens are teeming with wildlife, too; look out for tortoises and sloths.

To get here, take the green minibus marked Cotoca from the corner of Suárez Arana and Barrón and ask the driver to drop you at the entrance to the Jardín Botánico (B$2.50, 25 minutes).

Basílica Menor de San Lorenzo   CATHEDRAL
(Plaza 24 de Septiembre; ◎ 7:30am-noon & 3-8pm Mon-Sat, 6:30am-1pm & 5-9pm Sun) **FREE** Although the original cathedral on Plaza 24 de Septiembre was founded in 1605, the present structure dates from 1845 and wasn't consecrated until 1915. Inside, the decorative woodwork on the ceiling and silver plating around the altar are worth a look. There are good views of the city from the **bell tower** (Plaza 24 de Septiembre; B$3; ◎ 8am-noon & 3-6pm Tue, Thu, Sat & Sun).

Biocentro Güembé   OUTDOORS
(☑ 370-0700; www.biocentroguembe.com; Km 5, Camino Porongo, Zona Urubó; adult/child B$150/50; ◎ 8:30am-6pm) A great day trip from Santa Cruz, Biocentro Güembé (12km west of the city) has a butterfly farm, orchid exhibitions, 15 natural pools and sports facilities. You can go fishing and hiking in the surrounding forest. There's a restaurant with international cuisine, so you won't go hungry, and there are cabins and a campsite if you wish to stay the night.

☞ Tours

Tour agencies can arrange day trips to **Lomas de Arena** (☑ 327-0963; B$10; ◎ 8:30am-5pm) and longer tours to Parque Nacional Amboró, the Jesuit missions and the jaguar conservation area of San Miguelito.

Nick's Adventures   TOURS
(☑ 334-1820; www.nicksadventuresbolivia.com; Celia Salmón, Edificio Isuto, office 208) Excellent tour company with a strong ethos of social responsibility and promoting conservation through tourism. Especially good for wildlife tours, including tours to the San Miguelito Jaguar Reserve and the Pantanal.

Bird Bolivia   BIRD-WATCHING
(☑ 356-3636; www.birdbolivia.com) Professional birding and wildlife tours with expert guides for those with a special interest in nature. Based in Santa Cruz but without a public office; arrange tours by phone or email.

⌂ Sleeping

Nomad Hostel   HOSTEL $
(☑ 7530-8001;   www.facebook.com/nomad316; René Moreno 44; dm/d B$50/180) Still a work in progress at research time, Nomad opened in 2018 and is sure to become one of the city's best budget options. It's right on the edge of Plaza 24 de Septiembre; the hostel's roof terrace overlooks the cathedral. Dating from 1895, the building has been carefully restored to create a homey feel. Beds have thick mattresses.

★ Jodanga
Backpackers Hostel   HOSTEL $$
(☑ 339-6542; www.jodanga.com; El Fuerte 1380, Zona Parque Urbano; dm B$85-100, d/tr B$300/340, d without bathroom B$210; ❋ @ ☆) This superbly equipped hostel has a pool, pool table and seriously groovy, air-conditioned rooms, as well as a party atmosphere inspired by its own bar. A quieter complex across the road houses three well-appointed rooms (with private bathroom) in converted shipping containers. Jodanga is near Parque Urbano in a leafy

neighborhood, a 25-minute walk from the city center.

Backpacker Bar & Suites   HOSTEL $$

(☏ 339-8027; www.facebook.com/bedbarback packers; cnr Monseñor Salvatierra & Velasco; dm B$55-65, r B$190-250, r without bathroom B$150; ❖❂) Occupying a prime corner plot near the city center, Backpacker is a solid option. Rooms are spacious and equipped with cable TV; some have a balcony. Facilities include a kitchen, book exchange, lockers, a bar (of course) and a terrace that's perfectly positioned for sunset views. Breakfast is included.

★ Cosmopolitano   BOUTIQUE HOTEL $$$

(☏ 332-3118; www.cosmopolitano.com.bo; Pari 70; r incl breakfast B$450-600; ❖@❂) An oasis of contemporary design in the city center, the Cosmopolitano has just eight spacious rooms arranged on two levels around a central courtyard with a small pool. The aesthetic here is sleek lines, wood and concrete, with splashes of color and carefully chosen furniture, including modern and antique pieces. Staff are beyond helpful.

★ CasaPatio
Hotel Boutique   BOUTIQUE HOTEL $$$

(☏ 333-1728; www.casapatio-hotelboutique.com; Av Ibérica Calle 5, Las Palmas; s/d incl breakfast B$450/580, restaurant almuerzo B$30, mains B$39-46; ❖❂❂) Out by the fourth *anillo* (ring), this boutique hotel is worth every boliviano. The rooms have a delicate, understated appeal, as well as quirky names such as the 'No se lo digas a nadie habitación matrimonial' ('Don't tell anybody matrimonial suite'). The owners are warm, welcoming hosts and the patio is exquisite. You'll need to take taxis into town.

✕ Eating

Vegelin   VEGAN $

(www.facebook.com/vegelinhouse; Fray del Pilar 143; per kilo B$65; ⊙11:30am-2:30pm) Pile your plate high at this vegan buffet, which charges by weight (about B$20 to B$35 per plate). The dishes have a range of international influences and include vegan sushi, Italian pastas and Chinese-style stir-fries.

El Aljibe   BOLIVIAN $$

(Ñuflo de Chávez; mains B$35-65; ⊙noon-3am & 7-11:30pm Mon-Sat) A cute little restaurant in a charming old colonial house. It specializes in *comida típica* (typical food), which is increasingly difficult to find in cosmopolitan Santa Cruz.

★ Sach'a Rest   PERUVIAN $$$

(www.facebook.com/sacharest; Av Profesor Noel Kempff 761, 3er anillo; mains B$75-150; ⊙6:30pm-midnight Mon-Fri, noon-4pm & 6:30pm-midnight Sat, noon-4pm Sun; ❂) Lip-smackingly good Peruvian food served in a bright and modern dining room, decorated with fab wall murals. The ceviches are made with fresh paiche, a local river fish, and come with a range of sauces including a killer *leche de tigre* (citrus marinade). The Pisco sours might be the best you'll find this side of Lima.

★ Jardín de Asia   FUSION $$$

(☏ 342-1000; www.jardindeasia.com; Av San Martín 455, Hotel Los Tajibos; mains B$110-179; ⊙noon-3pm & 7:30pm-1am Mon-Sat; ❂) The chefs at Jardín de Asia fuse Bolivian ingredients with Asian flavors and culinary techniques to create original dishes with plenty of local flair, served in a candlelit setting. This stylish and atmospheric restaurant is the hottest ticket in town, so book ahead. Kick things off with a perfectly prepared cocktail.

☕ Drinking & Nightlife

The hippest nightspots are along Av San Martín, between the second and third *anillos* (rings) in **Barrio Equipetrol** (B$15 to B$20 taxi from the center). Hot spots change frequently so it's best to dress to impress, cruise the *piranhar* (strip) and see what catches your fancy. Cover charges cost B$20 to B$70. Most places don't warm up until 11pm.

★ Patrimonio Cafetería SCZ   CAFE

(www.facebook.com/patrimoniocafescz; Sucre 50; ⊙8am-11:30pm) The best lattes in town can be found at Patrimonio, a third-wave coffee shop serving brews made with beans from the Yungas, as well as sandwiches and cakes (B$27 to B$32). It's inside **Casa Melchor Pinto** (Sucre 50; ⊙9am-10pm Mon-Fri, 3-10pm Sat, 11am-7pm Sun) **FREE**, a beautifully renovated former home which is now a cultural center and gallery. Drink your flat white in the breezy central patio.

★ Duda Bar   BAR

(www.facebook.com/dudapub; Flórida 228, 2nd fl; ⊙9:30pm-2am Tue & Wed, to 3am Thu-Sat) There's a cool vibe to this colorful bar occupying the 1st floor of an elegant old building in the city center. Under plaster arches and between pillars you'll find retro furniture, badminton rackets and the odd garden gnome. Come for cocktails or beers.

⭐ Entertainment

Cafe Lorca LIVE MUSIC
(www.facebook.com/cafelorcasc; Sucre 8; ⏲ 9am-midnight Mon-Thu, to 3am Fri & Sat, 6pm-midnight Sun) A meeting point for the city's arty and diversity-loving crowd, Lorca is perfect for a chilled caipirinha or mojito while you enjoy the live music (B$40 cover).

ℹ Information

DANGERS & ANNOYANCES
Beware of bogus immigration officials, and carefully check the credentials of anyone who demands to see your passport or other ID. No real police officer will ever ask to see your documents in the street; be especially wary of 'civilian' police, who will most certainly turn out to be fraudsters.

Tourist Police (☎ 800-14-0099; Plaza 24 de Septiembre)

IMMIGRATION
Migración (☎ 351-9579; cnr Sucre & Quijarro, Edificio Guapay; ⏲ 7:30am-3pm Mon-Fri) Visa extensions are available here.

MEDICAL SERVICES
Clínica Foianini (☎ 336-2211; www.clinica foianini.com; Av Irala 468) Hospital used by embassies, but be aware that some travelers have complained that it can be pricy.

Clínica Kamiya (☎ 336-3400; Av Monseñor Rivero 265)

Hospital San José de Dios (☎ 335-2866; Cuellar)

Hospital Universitario Japonés (☎ 346-2038; 3er anillo interno) On the third *anillo*, east side; recommended for inexpensive and professional medical treatment.

MONEY
ATMs line Junín and most major intersections. Street money changers shout '¡Dóares!' on the main plaza, but make sure you know the value of what you are changing, or use an official office (there are plenty nearby).

Casa de Cambio Alemán (Plaza 24 de Septiembre; ⏲ 8:45am-12:30pm & 2:45-6:30pm Mon-Fri, 9am-12:30pm Sat) The easiest place to change cash. On the east side of the plaza.

POST
Main Post Office (Junín; ⏲ 8am-8pm Mon-Sat, 9-11:30am Sun)

TOURIST INFORMATION
Online information about the city of Santa Cruz and the main attractions of the Oriente region can be found at www.visitbolivia.org.

Armonía Office (☎ 356-8808; www.armonia bolivia.org; Lomas de Arenas 400; ⏲ 8:30am-12:30pm & 2:30-6pm Mon-Fri) Visit the Armonía office in Santa Cruz for more information about conservation programs and details on visiting the lodges.

Casa de Gobierno (Plaza 24 de Septiembre, Palacio Prefectural; ⏲ 9am-5pm Mon-Fri) A small information kiosk on the north side of the plaza is good for quick inquiries, but has little printed information.

Fundación Amigos de la Naturaleza (FAN; ☎ 355-6800; www.fan-bo.org; Carr a Samaipata, Km 7.5; ⏲ 8am-4:30pm Mon-Thu, to 2pm Fri) A good source of national parks information. It's west of town off the old Cochabamba road.

Infotur (☎ 336-9581; www.gmsantacruz.gob. bo; Sucre; ⏲ 9am-noon & 3-7pm) Within the Museo de Arte Contemporáneo, this office provides information for the whole region and the rest of the country.

Servicio Nacional de Áreas Protegidas (Sernap; ☎ 339-4311; www.sernap.gob.bo; Calle Efesios 4, near Av Nueva Jerusalen; ⏲ 8:30am-6:30pm Mon-Fri) Theoretically provides information on national parks, especially Amboró.

ℹ Getting There & Away

AIR
Viru-Viru International Airport (☎ 338-5000), 15km north of the center, handles some domestic and most international flights. International destinations served by direct flights include Asunción, Buenos Aires, Lima, Madrid, Miami, Panama City, São Paulo and Santiago de Chile.

The smaller **Aeropuerto El Trompillo** (☎ 352-6600), in the southeast of the city, receives some domestic flights.

Flights to national destinations leave frequently and it's easy enough to find a seat to anywhere, or at least a suitable connection via Cochabamba.

Aerolíneas Argentinas (☎ 333-9776; Junín 22; ⏲ 8am-noon & 2:30-6:30pm Mon-Fri)

Amaszonas (☎ 311-5393; Av Las Ramblas, Edificio ALAS 2, 4th fl, btwn Los Cedros & Av San Martín; ⏲ 8:30am-12:30pm & 2:30-6:30pm Mon-Fri)

American Airlines (☎ 800-100-541; www. aa.com; Calle 15 No 8054, San Miguel; ⏲ 9am-6pm Mon-Fri, to 1pm Sat); **Av San Martín office** (☎ 800-100-541; Av San Martín, Comercial Fidalga; ⏲ 9am-6pm Mon-Fri, to 1pm Sat)

Boliviano de Aviación (BOA; ☎ 312-1343; www.boa.bo; Aroma, Edificio Casanova, 1st fl, office 7; ⏲ 8:30am-12:30pm & 2:30-6:30pm Mon-Fri, 9am-1pm Sun)

BOLIVIA SANTA CRUZ

TAM (☑ 353-2639; Aeropuerto el Trompillo; ☺ 8am-6:30pm Mon-Fri, to 1pm Sat)

BUS

The full-service **bimodal terminal** (☑ 348-8482; terminal fee B$3), the combined long-distance bus and train station, is 1.5km east of the center, just before the third *anillo* at the end of Av Brasil. For departmental destinations turn right on entering; for national and international destinations turn left.

The main part of the terminal is for *flotas* (long-distance buses) and the train; on the other side of the tunnel is the *micro* (minibus) terminal for regional services. Most *flotas* leave in the morning before 10am and in the evening after 6pm. Taking a series of connecting *micros* or taxis can be a faster, if more complicated way, of reaching regional destinations, rather than waiting all day for an evening *flota*.

To the Jesuit missions and Chiquitania, *flotas* leave in the morning and early evening (after 8pm). *Micros* run throughout the day, every two hours or so, but only go as far as Concepción. Buses to San Rafael, San Miguel and San Ignacio (B$60 to B$70, eight hours) run via San José de Chiquitos and depart between 6:30pm and 8pm.

Smaller *micros* and *trufis* (shared car or minibus) to regional destinations in Santa Cruz department leave regularly from outside the old bus terminal and less regularly from the *micro* platforms at the bimodal terminal. **Trufis to Buena Vista** (Izozog; B$23, two hours), wait on Izozog (Isoso), near the old bus terminal. **Trufis to Samaipata** (☑ 333-5067; cnr Av Grigota & Aruma, 2do anillo; B$30, three hours), leave from Calle Aruma near Av Grigota, one block past the 2do anillo. **Trufis to Vallegrande** (Doble Vía La Guardia, Km 6, behind the Shopping del Automóvil; B$60, five hours) depart from behind the shopping center 'Shopping del Automovil' at Km 6 on Doble Vía La Guardia, beyond the sixth *anillo*. *Flotas* to Vallegrande (B$35) leave from the same place at 9am, 1pm, 3pm, 6:30pm and 7:30pm.

DESTINATION	COST (B$)	TIME (HR)
Camiri	30-40	5
Cochabamba	80-131	10
Concepción	35	5
La Paz	100-220	17-18
Quijarro	70-150	9
San Xavier	35	4
San José de Chiquitos	50	4
San Matías	120-150	15
Sucre	70-120	13
Tarija	80-100	11-14
Trinidad	49-140	10-11
Yacuiba	70-100	8

TRAIN

Trains (☑ 338-7000; www.fo.com.bo; Av Internacional, Terminal Bimodel; ☺ ticket office 8am-12:30pm & 2:30-6pm Mon-Thu, to 4pm Fri, 8am-noon Sat, 4-6pm Sun) depart from the bimodal terminal bound for Yacuiba on the Argentine border and Quijarro on the Brazil border. For access to the platform you need to buy a platform ticket and show your passport to the platform guard.

The Yacuiba train departs at 3:30pm on Thursday (B$47, 18 hours) and returns on Friday at 5pm, arriving back in Santa Cruz at 9:55am. It runs via Villamontes (B$38, 14 hours) – the connection point for buses to Paraguay – arriving inconveniently at 5:13am.

With the recent completion of the road paving all the way from Santa Cruz to Quijarro, the relevance of the Trans-Chiquitano train has declined sharply. No longer the harrowing journey that once earned this line the nickname 'Death Train,' these days it's a nice lazy route, and is more comfortable than the bus if you have time on your hands.

Two types of train run this line via San José de Chiquitos and Roboré (for Santiago de Chiquitos). The slowest and cheapest service is the Expreso Oriental, departing Santa Cruz at 1:20pm on Monday, Wednesday and Friday, which operates a single comfortable Super Pullman class. The fastest, comfiest and priciest is the Ferrobus, departing Santa Cruz at 6pm on Tuesday, Thursday and Sunday. There is rarely a problem getting a seat from Santa Cruz or Quijarro, but if joining the service midway along the line then tickets are best bought in advance – only a limited number of seats are allotted for these stations. Hot and cold food and drinks are available during daylight hours.

ⓘ Getting Around

BUS

Santa Cruz's system of city *micros* connects the transportation terminals and all the *anillos* with the center. *Micros* 17 and 18 circulate around the first *anillo*. To reach Av San Martín in Barrio Equipetrol, take *micro* 23 from anywhere on Vallegrande. **Buses to the Jardín Botánico** (cnr Suárez Arana & Barrón) leave from the corner of Suárez Arana and Barrón. A *Guía de Micros* documenting all the city routes is available from bookstores and kiosks (B$25 to B$50).

TAXI

Taxis are cheap but there is no rigid price structure. Typically the price is higher if you are in a group, are carrying lots of luggage or wish to travel after 10pm, and drivers will quote a fee that they consider fair for the journey. If you think it is too much, refuse, and try the next one:

there are plenty to choose from. Typically a trip for one person within the first *anillo* during the day is about B$15, rising to B$20 if you stray to the second *anillo*. Agree on your price in advance to avoid arguments.

Samaipata

📍 3 / POP 4400 / ELEV 1650M (5413FT)

Samaipata has developed into one of the top Gringo Trail spots in eastern Bolivia, but don't let that put you off. This sleepy village in the foothills of the Cordillera Oriental has held on to its tranquil vibe, and since it's now brimming with well-run hostels and restaurants, you can enjoy a decent coffee as well as stunning views of the verdant landscape.

Visitors come to see the pre-Inca site of El Fuerte; some come searching for a dose of the ancient site's supposed mystical energy. Increasingly Samaipata is the main jumping-off point for forays to Parque Nacional Amboró. It's also a popular weekend destination for *cruceños* (Santa Cruz locals) seeking to escape the city. The Quechua name, meaning 'Rest in the Highlands,' could hardly be more appropriate.

◎ Sights

★ El Fuerte   RUINS
(B$50; ⊘9am-4:30pm) The mystical site of El Fuerte exudes such pulling power that visitors from all over the world come to Samaipata just to climb the hill and see the remains of this pre-Inca site. A designated Unesco World Heritage Site since 1998, El Fuerte occupies a hilltop about 10km from Samaipata and offers breathtaking views across the valleys.

Allow at least two hours to fully explore the complex, and take sunscreen and a hat with you.

⛵ Tours

Jukumari Tours   TOURS
(📱7576-0013; www.facebook.com/jukumaritours; Av del Estudiante) An excellent locally run agency; in addition to the local attractions it offers packages to the Che Trail and the Jesuit Mission Circuit.

Roadrunners   TOURS
(📱944-6294; Bolivar) Visit Olaf and Frank at German- and English-speaking Roadrunners for guided hikes to Amboró's waterfalls, cloud forests and El Fuerte.

🍴 Sleeping & Eating

El Jardín   HOSTEL $
(📱7311-9461; www.eljardinsamaipata.blogspot.com; Arenales; camping per person B$25, s/d B$35/80, cupola r B$130) Hippie-style hangout squirreled away in a wild garden in the southeast corner of town. Chilled music, basic digs and a relaxed scene for those who like to take it easy. There is a kitchen for guest use and a pair of unique cupola rooms if you can't abide the idea of a room with corners.

★ Nómada   HOSTEL $$
(📱944-6446, cell 7782-8132; www.facebook.com/nomadahostelresto; Avaroa, Plaza del Estudiante; incl breakfast, camping per person B$45, dm/s/d B$77/195/305, s/d without bathroom B$130/191; ⊘cafe 8am-4pm Thu, to 9pm Fri & Sat) Care has been taken to make this hostel a welcoming and relaxing place. Rooms are cozy and decorated with local fabrics and original artwork, and there are gorgeous gardens with fruit trees. The on-site cafe has a changing menu of local dishes and pizzas (B$40 to B$90); on public holidays, the Argentine owners fire up the barbecue.

Finca La Víspera   CABIN $$
(📱944-6362; www.lavispera.org; campsite per person B$40, d B$350, cabins for 2/3/7 people B$480/520/1100) 🍃 This relaxing organic farm and retreat is a lovely place on the outskirts of Samaipata. The attractive rooms with shared kitchen, and five self-contained guesthouses (for two to seven people), enjoy commanding views across the valley. The campsite includes hot showers and kitchen facilities. It's an easy 15-minute walk southwest of the plaza.

Guests can eat breakfast and lunch at **Café Jardín** (mains B$40-60; ⊘8am-3pm; 🍃) 🍃 and help themselves to vegetables from the garden for dinner.

★ El Pueblito   RESORT $$$
(📱944-6383; www.elpueblitoresort.com; Carr Valle Abajo 1000; s/d incl breakfast B$400/550, house d/tr/q B$700/850/1000; 🅿🛜🏊) This four-star resort is arranged like a little village complete with its own church and plaza. Each room is uniquely styled after a village shop and positively dripping with creativity. There's a swimming pool (B$40 for nonguests), *artesanía* shops and an excellent **restaurant-bar** (mains B$20-70; ⊘noon-2:30pm & 6:30-8:30pm). The resort is set on a hillside with marvelous views of Samaipata in the valley below.

★**Latina Café**   INTERNATIONAL **$$**
(🖉944-6153; www.facebook.com/latinacafesamai
pata; Bolívar 3; mains B$35-70; ⊗6-10pm Mon &
Wed-Fri, noon-2:30pm & 6-10:30pm Sat, noon-3pm
& 6-10pm Sun) This bar-restaurant serves
some of the best food in town: juicy steak,
tempting pasta, vegetarian delights and gor-
geous brownies. The lighting is intimate and
the sunsets beautiful. Happy hour is from
6pm to 7pm.

ℹ Information

Banco Union (Campero) Samaipata's only ATM.
Accepts Visa, but not all foreign cards.

Co-operativa Merced (🖉944-6171; Sucre;
⊗8am-noon & 2:30-6pm Mon-Fri, 8:30am-
12:30pm Sat) If the ATM on Campero is down
you can draw cash on a credit card with your
passport here.

ℹ Getting There & Away

Trufis (p272; shared car or minibus) run
throughout the day when full between Santa
Cruz and Samaipata (B$30, three hours). From
Samaipata, services depart from the main
plaza.

The quickest and easiest way to get to Val-
legrande is to organize a group and take a *trufi*
(around B$300 for a carload to Vallegrande).

For Cochabamba buses leave from nearby
Mairana (15km west of Samaipata) at 8am and
3pm (seven hours, B$80). A taxi to Mairana
costs B$7 per person.

Buses to Sucre leave at 8pm from opposite
the gas station on the main road. Buy tickets
in advance from Nueva Turista cafe (10 hours,
B$100).

Parque Nacional & Área de Uso Múltiple Amboró

This 4300-sq-km park lies in a unique geo-
graphical position at the confluence of three
distinct ecosystems: the Amazon Basin, the
Chaco and the Andes.

The park's range of habitats means that
both highland and lowland species are found
here. Mammals include elusive spectacled
bears, jaguars, tapirs, peccaries and various
monkeys, while more than 800 species of
birds have been documented. The park is
the stronghold of the endangered horned
curassow, known as the unicorn bird.

Samaipata sits just outside the southern
boundary of the Área de Uso Múltiple Am-
boró and provides the best access point for
the Andean section of the park. The best

guides to the region are available in Sa-
maipata. One popular day hike is through
a nearby cloud forest known for its giant
ferns.

🛏 Sleeping

★**Refugio los Volcánes**   LODGE **$$$**
(🖉7316-6677;   www.refugiolosvolcanes.com;
Bermejo; s/d incl meals B$700/1200; 🅿🛜) 🗲
Folks rave about this place in the breathtaking Los Volcánes region, 5km up a dirt
track off the Santa Cruz–Samaipata road,
near Bermejo. Accommodations are in ecofriendly, solar-powered *cabañas* (cabins)
with hot showers. Activities on offer include
bird-watching and guided hikes through
wonderfully wild landscapes, with pools for
swimming. It's popular, so book well ahead.

Jesuit Mission Circuit

The seven-town region of *Las Misiones
Jesuíticas* has some of Bolivia's richest cultural and historic sites. Forgotten by the
world for more than two centuries, the region and its history captivated the world's
imagination when the 1986 Palme d'Or
winner *The Mission* spectacularly replayed
the last days of the Jesuit priests in the region (with Robert de Niro at the helm). The
growing interest in the unique synthesis of
Jesuit and native Chiquitano culture in the
South American interior resulted in Unesco
declaring the region a World Heritage Site
in 1991. Thanks to 25 years of painstaking
restoration work, directed by the late architect Hans Roth, the centuries-old mission
churches have been restored to their original splendor.

If you wish to travel the mission circuit
on public transportation, the bus schedules
synchronize better going counterclockwise:
that is starting the circuit at San José de
Chiquitos. A much less time-consuming way
is by taking a guided tour from Santa Cruz
(around US$500 per person for a four-day
package), taking in all the major towns. **Mi-
sional Tours** (🖉332-7709; www.misionaltours.
com; Av Beni, 9th fl, Edificio Top Center, office 9-E;
⊗9am-12:30pm & 2-7pm Mon-Fri, 9am-1pm Sat) is
a recommended operator.

San Xavier
🖉3 / POP 15,400
San Xavier, founded in 1691, is the oldest
mission town in the region. It's also a fa-

vorite holiday destination for wealthy *cruceño* (people from Santa Cruz) families. The village sits on a lovely forested ridge with a great view over the surrounding low hills and countryside.

Concepción

☑ 3 / POP 20,380

'Conce' *(Conchay)*, as Concepción is known here, is a dusty village with a friendly, quiet atmosphere in the midst of an agricultural and cattle-ranching area. It stands some 182km west of San Ignacio de Velasco and is the center for all the mission restoration projects.

San Ignacio de Velasco

☑ 3 / POP 52,400

San Ignacio de Velasco is a thriving commercial center and the largest town on the mission circuit. There's a real buzz about the place, and it's worth planning your route to include an overnight stop here. The church here is a modern reconstruction.

San Miguel de Velasco

☑ 3 / POP 11,400

Sleepy San Miguel hides in the scrub, 37km south of San Ignacio. Its church was founded in 1721 and is, according to the late Jesuit priest and Swiss architect Hans Roth, the most accurately restored of all the Bolivian Jesuit missions.

Santa Ana de Velasco

☑ 3 / POP 680

Of all the villages on the mission circuit, tiny Santa Ana de Velasco is the most peaceful and perhaps the most charming. Reached by a bumpy dirt road from San Ignacio, it feels barely connected to the modern world.

San Rafael de Velasco

☑ 3 / POP 7500

San Rafael de Velasco, a dusty little village 132km north of San José de Chiquitos, was founded in 1696. Its church was constructed between 1743 and 1747.

San José de Chiquitos

☑ 3 / POP 16,600

An atmospheric place, San José de Chiquitos has the appeal of an old Western film set.

🛈 GETTING TO BRAZIL

The main border crossing to Brazil is at **Quijarro** at the end of the train line, with a second, minor crossing at **San Matías**, the access point to the northern Brazilian Pantanal.

You'll more than likely arrive in **Puerto Quijarro** by bus or by train between 6am and 7am to be greeted by a line of taxi drivers offering to take you the 3km to the border (B$20). **Immigration offices** (Ruta Nacional 4; ⊙ 8am-6pm) are on opposing sides of the bridge. Bolivian officials have been known to charge an unofficial fee for the entry stamp (usually around B$18). Crossing this border you are generally asked to show a yellow-fever vaccination certificate. On the Brazilian side of the border buses or taxis will take you into Corumbá. Brazilian entry stamps are given at the border.

With an enormous and handsome plaza shaded by *toboroche* (thorny bottle) trees, the most accessible Jesuit mission town is also arguably the most appealing.

AMAZON BASIN

The Amazon Basin is one of Bolivia's largest and most mesmerizing regions. The rainforest is raucous with wildlife, and spending a few days roaming the sweaty jungle is an experience you're unlikely to forget. But it's not only the forests that are enchanting: it's also the richness of the indigenous cultures, traditions and languages that exist throughout the region.

Mossy hills peak around the town of Rurrenabaque, most traveler's first point of entry into the Amazon Basin and the main base camp for visits to the fascinating Parque Nacional Madidi (p281). This is home to a growing ethno-ecotourism industry established to help local communities. The village of San Ignacio de Moxos (p283) is famous for its wild fiesta held in late July; Trinidad, the region's cosmopolitan hub, is encased by buzzing wetlands and is the transit point toward Santa Cruz. North of here the frontier towns of Riberalta and Guayaramerín are in remote regions few travelers dare to tread.

The Amazon Basin

Rurrenabaque

📋 3 / POP 10,000 / ELEV 229M (751FT)

The gentle whisking of brooms on the plaza serves as a wake-up call in sleepy Rurre, a gringo crossroads sliced by the deep Río Beni and surrounded by mossy green hills. Mesmerizing sunsets turn the sky a burnt orange, and a dense fog sneaks down the river among the lush, moist trees. Once darkness falls, the surrounding rainforest comes alive with croaks, barks, buzzes and roars. This is civilization's last stand.

Backpackers fill the streets, and restaurants, cafes and hotels cater mainly to Western tastes. Some travelers spend their days relaxing in the ubiquitous hammocks, but at some stage the majority go off on riverboat adventures into the rainforest or pampas.

The area's original people, the Tacana, are responsible for the curious name of 'Rurrenabaque,' which is derived from 'Arroyo Inambaque,' the Hispanicized version of the Tacana name 'Suse-Inambaque,' the 'Ravine of Ducks.'

👁 Sights & Activities

Though there isn't really that much to do in town, Rurrenabaque's appeal is in its surrounding natural beauty. It's easy to pass

a day or three here while waiting to join a tour. Scramble up a 295-step staircase two blocks from the plaza, and then up a dirt-and-stone pathway to a *mirador* (lookout), and finally to a big cross (La Cruz) overlooking town and the Beni. Bring your hiking boots!

San Buenaventura   VILLAGE
Sleepy San Buenaventura sits across the Río Beni from Rurrenabaque, watching all the busy goings-on, but content with its own slower pace. The **Centro Cultural Tacana** (892-2394; San Buenaventura; ⊙8am-noon & 2:30-6pm Mon-Fri) has a handicrafts store on

the southwest side of the plaza and celebrates the Tacana people's *cosmovision* (world view). The official Sernap office (p280) for Parque Nacional Madidi is also here, near the market.

Canopy Zip Line
Villa Alcira   ADVENTURE SPORTS
(cell 7284-3874; http://ziplinevillalcira.com; Comercio, near Santa Cruz; trip B$350) A series of *tranquilo* (quiet/low-key) community-run tourism projects operate in Parque Nacional Madidi – but if you need more adrenaline, try the company formerly known as Biggest Canopy in Bolivia. It's a forest-canopy zipline for those with a head for heights, a strong stomach and a need for speed. Book at the Rurrenabaque office.

El Chorro   SWIMMING
El Chorro is an idyllic waterfall with a series of pools apt for swimming. You'll find it at the end of Calle Santa Cruz, following a well-worn trail 500m upstream into the jungle. It's popular with local families, but you should still be sure to watch your belongings.

⛟ Tours

Bala Tours   TOURS
(cell 7112-2053; www.balatours.com; cnr Santa Cruz & Comercio; ⊙7:30am-7pm Mon-Sat, 7:30am-noon & 4-6pm Sun) Has its own jungle camp, Caracoles, a comfortable pampas lodge on Río Yacumo and a forest lodge in Tacuaral.

🛏 Sleeping

★Hostal El Lobo   HOSTEL $
(cell 6770-7582; hostalellobo@gmail.com; Comercio; dm per person B$60, r B$140; 🖥🌊) Two hundred meters from the main plaza, this updated spot is now a buzzing playground for backpackers. A complete makeover includes crafty *tacuara* (bamboo) doors, a kidney-shaped swimming pool overlooking the Beni and a sweet hammock-filled terrace with pool tables and a bar. Dorms have screened windows and catch a cool breeze. Private rooms have river-facing balconies.

Hotel Oriental   HOTEL $
(892-2401; www.facebook.com/hoteloriental rurre; Plaza 2 de Febrero; s/d/tr B$100/150/210; 🖥) If you meet people who are staying at the Oriental, right on the plaza, they'll invariably be raving about what an excellent place it is – and it really is. Comfy rooms, great showers, garden hammocks for snoozing and big breakfasts are included in the price.

Rurrenabaque

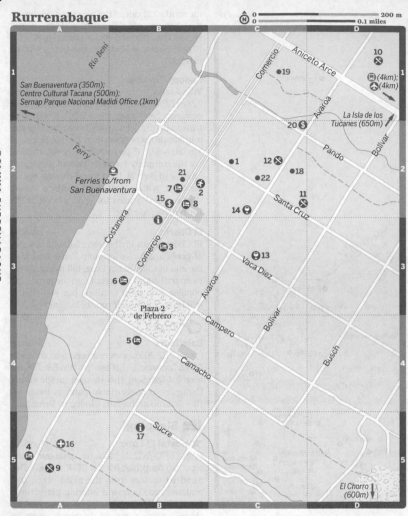

Hotel Takana   HOTEL **$$**
(☎892-2118, cell 7205-1565; Plaza 2 de Febrero; s/d with air-con B$230/250, s with fan B$180; P❄🛜🏊) This newer joint on the main plaza is a cut above the rest with hefty wooden furnishings and Jacuzzi tubs in some rooms. It's worth paying a bit extra for air-con, although you can get away with the ceiling fans. Nice view from the back pool to the Río Beni.

La Isla de los Tucanes   CABIN **$$**
(☎892-2127; www.islatucanes.com; Bolívar; s/d B$280/380; ❄🛜🏊) An ecological cabin complex 1km north of town with thatched bungalows designed to make you feel even further away. With pool tables, an international restaurant and two clean swimming pools there is no real reason to leave – unless, of course, you are going into the jungle proper.

🍴 Eating & Drinking

Eating options are varied, from quick chicken to fresh fish along the riverfront and fantastic international cooking. In addition to the Beni standard, *masaco* (mashed yuca or plantains, served with dried meat, rice, noodles, thin soup and bananas), try the excellent *pescado en dunucuabi* (fish

Rurrenabaque

BOLIVIA RURRENABAQUE

wrapped in a rainforest leaf and baked over a wood fire).

The Sunday **feria** along the riverfront attracts local farmers with all their wild and wonderful produce.

Pizza al Paso PIZZA $
(La Bella Italia; cell 6728-5349; Avaroa near Pando; pizzas B$25-80; 5-10pm Wed-Mon) This popular (and incredibly friendly) street-side pizzeria offers four thin-crust pie sizes and an unlimited choose-your-own toppings menu at fixed prices. Toss in cheap juices and beers and it adds up to a great value for groups.

El Nomádico INTERNATIONAL $$
(cell 7284-3850; Avaroa, near Aniceto Arce; mains B$50-65; 10am-10pm Fri-Wed) Set down a long brick alleyway in a candlelit courtyard, this 'hidden' upscale eatery has a hearty menu of delicious steaks, veggie pastas, chicken wings and curries. The fish curry, in particular, is legendary.

Juliano's EUROPEAN $$
(Santa Cruz, btwn Avaroa & Bolívar; mains B$45-90; 5-11pm) Fusion in the jungle! This Tunisian emigre to Bolivia, via Paris, makes some awesome fish dishes (*pescado Juliano* is particularly tasty) and has the only imported Peruvian shellfish in town. Save some room for the crème brûlée. The red lighting is *très chic!*

Casa de Campo HEALTH FOOD $$
(cell 7199-3336; Comercio; mains B$25-75; 7:30am-2pm & 5-10pm) Healthy food is the name of the game here, with all-day breakfasts, homemade pastries, vegetarian dishes, soups and salads on a breezy terrace across from Hostel El Lobo. Hospitable Adela is keen to make her guests happy (and give local hiking advice). Her 'tropical breakfast' with fresh-ground coffee and a crispy croissant is heavenly.

Jungle Bar Moskkito BAR
(Vaca Diez, near Avaroa; 4pm-3am) Peruvian-run, but English is spoken here. There's a positive vibe, cheery service and the foliage that hangs from the roof makes you feel like you're in the jungle, whether there are 'moskkitos' or not. Throw some darts, shoot some pool and choose your own music by request.

Luna Lounge BAR
(Avaroa, near Santa Cruz; 10am-2:30pm & 6pm-2am) One of Rurre's longest-standing bars, with a bouncing atmosphere, good pizza and great cocktails. There's also a pool table, foosball and, occasionally, live bands.

Information

A couple of 'per kilo' laundries, including **Laundry Number One** (Avaroa, Edificio Candelaria; 8am-noon & 2-8pm Mon-Sat, 11am-noon & 4-7pm Sun) and **Laundry Service Garfield** (Comercio, near Aniceto Arce; 6am-10pm), offer a next-day service (per kilo B$8), a same-day service (per kilo B$10) and a four-hour service (per kilo, B$15) if you are in a hurry.

Clínica El Puerto (Comercio; 24hr) is used to handling tourists with stomach problems. For anything more serious, make your way back to La Paz.

For visa extensions, head to **immigration** (892-2241; cnr Sucre & Avaroa; 8:30am-12:30pm & 2:30-6:30pm Mon-Fri).

The most convenient of the two ATMs in town is a block north of the plaza at **Banco Unión** (cnr Comercio & Vaca Diez; ⏱ 24hr). You can get cash advances at **Prodem** (cnr Avaroa & Pando; ⏱ 8am-4pm Mon-Fri, to noon Sat), but only on Visa and MasterCard (including Visa debit cards). It also does Western Union transfers and changes cash.

Workers at the **tourist office** (☎ cell 7138-3684; cnr Vaca Diez & Comercio; ⏱ 8am-noon & 2:30-6pm Mon-Fri) are happy to answer questions and keen to advise on responsible tourism, but they're short on material. For information on Parque Nacional Madidi, head to the **Sernap office** (☎ 892-2540, cell 6822-6337; Libertad, San Buenaventura; ⏱ 7am-3pm) in San Buenaventura.

ⓘ Getting There & Away

AIR

Rurre's **airport** is 4km north of town. **Amaszonas** (☎ 892-2472; Comercio, near Santa Cruz; ⏱ 7am-7pm) has daily flights to La Paz (B$480 and up) but at the time of research only one plane – you're out of luck if that's 'in maintenance.' **TAM** (☎ 892-2398; www.tam.bo; Santa Cruz) sporadically offers flights between La Paz and Rurre.

The brief flight to La Paz is an affordable way of avoiding the arduous bus journey. Flights sell out fast and are frequently cancelled during bad weather. You will be refunded only 75% of the ticket value if your flight is cancelled and you're not prepared to wait around for the next one.

Be sure to reconfirm your ticket the day before flying, otherwise you may find yourself without a seat.

If you wish to fly to Riberalta or Guayaramerín, you need to go to Trinidad.

BOAT

The boat journey from Guanay to Rurre (p229) down Río Kaka and Río Beni is – for fans of slow travel – certainly the most scenic way to reach town from La Paz. Thanks to the Guayaramerín road, there's little cargo transportation further down the Río Beni to Riberalta these days. You'll need a dose of luck to find something and will have to negotiate a fair price for the boat (about B$4,000). The trip may take as long as three days.

BUS

The main **bus terminal** is across from the airport and a B$5 moto-taxi ride from town. All buses leave from here, though shared taxis to San Borja and Caranavi also depart when full from the **old terminal** by the cemetery. Prices do not vary between companies.

Several daily services make the daunting trip from Rurrenabaque to La Paz (B$70, 13 to 15 hours), via Yolosa (B$60, 12 hours), the hop-off point for Coroico. If you find the narrow, twisting Andean roads and sheer drops a harrowing experience on a bus, another option is to bus it as far as Caranavi (B$70, five to seven hours) and take a shared taxi from there, the rest of the trip being the most scary, or picturesque, depending on your point of view.

ⓘ CHOOSING A JUNGLE OR PAMPAS TOUR

Jungle and pampas tours are Rurrenabaque's bread and butter, but quality of service provided by the numerous tour agencies varies considerably; in the name of competition, some operators are less responsible than they ought to be.

➡ Cheaper most definitely does not mean better. Local authorities have set minimum prices at B$1,200 for a three-day, two-night excursion; be suspicious of any company that undercuts those rates, and do not barter for a lower price.

➡ There are no guarantees of spotting wildlife. Any company that offers them is likely to be breaking the rules. Guides are forbidden from feeding, handling or disturbing animals.

➡ Use only Sernap-authorized operators, as these are the only ones allowed to legally enter Parque Nacional Madidi.

➡ Foreigners must be accompanied by a local guide, but not all speak good English.

Jungle Tours
Most trips are by canoe upstream along the Río Beni, and some continue up the Río Tuichi, taking shore and jungle walks along the way, with plenty of swimming opportunities and hammock time. Accommodations are generally in agencies' private camps.

Pampas Tours
It's easier to see wildlife in the wetland savannas northeast of town, but the sun is more oppressive, and the bugs can be worse, especially in the rainy season.

The route to Trinidad (B$130, 10 to 13 hours) via San Borja (taxi/bus B$80/50, three hours) and San Ignacio de Moxos (B$100, seven hours) was once one of the worst in the country, but is now paved for much of the way. Buses currently run year-round on this route, as well as to Riberalta (B$120, 13 to 14 hours) and Guayaramerín (B$130, 14 to 15 hours), but you need a healthy dose of stamina, insect repellent and food if you're going to attempt trips in the wet season. Departure times are erratic for these long-distance destinations and change day to day, so it's best to check at the station in advance.

Parque Nacional Madidi

The 18,000-sk-km Parque Nacional Madidi is one of South America's most intact ecosystems, taking in a range of habitats from steaming lowland rainforests to 6000m Andean peaks. This little-trodden utopia is home to an astonishing variety of Amazonian wildlife: 44% of all mammal species in North and South America, 38% of neotropical amphibian species and more than 1000 species of bird. Some scientists call it the most biodiverse place on earth.

The populated portions of the park along the Río Tuichi have been accorded a special Unesco designation permitting indigenous inhabitants to utilize traditional forest resources, but the park has also been named as a site for a major hydroelectric scheme. Illicit logging has damaged several areas around the perimeter and the debate continues over road building and oil exploration. With President Morales opening all Bolivian parks to oil and gas exploration, environmentalists are holding their collective breath.

🛏 Sleeping

★ **Chalalán Ecolodge**   LODGE $$$
(☏892-2419; www.chalalan.com; 4-day/3-night all-inclusive program per person US$500-544, per day US$145) 🍃 This is Bolivia's oldest and most successful community-based ecotourism project. Chalalán provides the opportunity to amble through relatively untouched rainforest and appreciate the diversity of the native wildlife. The lodge's simple and elegant huts surround the idyllic oxbow lake, Laguna Chalalán. There is a booking office in **Rurrenabaque** (☏892-2419; www.chalalan.com; Comercio, near Campero; ⊙7am-7pm) and also in **La Paz** (Map p206; ☏231-1451; www.chalalan.com; Sagárnaga 189, Galería Doryan, 2nd fl, Office 23, Rosario).

WORTH A TRIP

PARQUE NACIONAL NOEL KEMPFF MERCADO

The wonderfully remote and globally important **Noel Kempff Mercado National Park** is home to a broad spectrum of Amazonian flora and fauna and has a wide range of dwindling habitats, from open *cerrado* (savanna) to dense rainforest. The park lies in the northernmost reaches of Santa Cruz department, between the banks of the Ríos Verde, Guaporé (Río Iténez on Bolivian maps) and Paraguá.

Due to the lack of infrastructure, visits are best done with a Santa Cruz–based tour agency. Nick's Adventures (p269) and **Amboró Tours** (☏339-0600, cell 7261-2515; www.amborotours.com; Libertad 417, 2nd fl; ⊙9am-noon & 2:30-6pm Mon-Wed, 9am-5pm Thu & Fri) both run tours.

★ **Sadiri**   LODGE $$$
(☏cell 7162-2567; http://sadirilodge.com; all-inclusive per person per day US$135) 🍃 One of the newest kids on the community-project block is wonderful Sadiri: six luxury cabins in dense foothill rainforest in the Serranía Sadiri. Community members staff the lodge, which has the best-trained wildlife guides in the Rurrenabaque area. Email bookings are preferred at sadirilodge@gmail.com. Rates include full board and return transfer to Rurrenabaque.

San Miguel del Bala   LODGE $$$
(☏892-2394; www.sanmigueldelbala.com; per person per day B$520) 🍃 A glorious community ecolodge in its own patch of paradise right on Madidi's doorstep, 40 minutes upstream by boat from Rurrenabaque. This Tacana community will be happy to show you their traditional agricultural methods, weaving and wood carving. Accommodations are in cabins with mahogany wood floors, separate bathrooms and beds covered by silky mosquito nets. The **booking office** (☏892-2394; www.sanmigueldelbala.com; Comercio; ⊙7am-noon & 2-6pm) is in Rurrenabaque.

Trinidad

☏3 / POP 122,000 / ELEV 158M (520FT)
Trinidad is the place you'll come to if you're after a trip down the long and deep Río

Mamoré, or on your way between Santa Cruz and Rurrenabaque. Despite its colonial architecture and colonnaded streets, it's a modern city that is growing rapidly. Yet, it's surprisingly easy to trade the hum of motorbikes for the sounds of blue-throated macaws or pink river dolphins in the surrounding wetlands.

The city of La Santísima Trinidad (the Most Holy Trinity) was founded in 1686 by Padre Cipriano Barace as the second Jesuit mission in the flatlands of the southern Beni. It was originally constructed on the banks of the Río Mamoré, 14km from its present location, but floods and pestilence along the riverbanks forced relocation. In 1769 it was moved to the Arroyo de San Juan, which now divides the city in two.

⊙ Sights

★**Santuario Chuchini**   NATURE RESERVE
(Jaguar's Lair; ☑cell 7284 2200; www.chuchini.org; B$20, half-day visit incl meal & boat ride B$100, all-inclusive two-day stay from B$1120; ⊙8am-6pm Wed-Mon) The Santuario Chuchini (Jaguar's Lair) is one of the few easily accessible Paitití sites. This wildlife sanctuary and camp sits on an 8-hectare *loma* (artificial mound) of the ancient civilization. From the camp, you can take short walks in the rainforest to lagoons with caimans, other larger animals and profuse birdlife.

WORTH A TRIP

SERERE ECO RESERVE

Named after a bird with a blue face and punk-rock hair, this 40-sq-km refuge has four lagoons, a week's worth of hiking trails, and enough monkeys, birds and reptiles to please the pickiest of wildlife watchers. It is the private reserve of Rosa María Ruiz, a towering figure in Bolivian conservation.

When you visit Serere you create your own itinerary based on your specific interests, with the help of indigenous guides. The income earned by the ecolodge gets pumped back into local conservation efforts. You can book a trip to the reserve at the **Madidi Travel** (☑cell 6821-6580; www.madidi-travel.com; Comercio near Vaca Diez; all-inclusive 3-day, 2-night trip B$1899; ⊙8am-noon & 2-8pm) office in Rurrenabaque.

★**Museo Etnoarqueológico Kenneth Lee**   MUSEUM
(Kenneth Lee Ethno-Archaeological Museum; Av Ganadera; ⊙8am-noon & 2:30-6:30pm Mon-Fri) **FREE** Named for the *gringo querido del Beni*, the beloved white man of the Beni, this small museum north of the center is considered the city's top cultural attraction. It exhibits artifacts from the Trinidad region, including traditional instruments and tribal costumes.

⊂ᵧ Tours

★**La Ruta del Bufeo**   BOATING
(ECOterra; ☑cell 7281-8317; https://bolivia-natura.com/en; half-day/full-day/2-day tours from B$195/375/690) This tour company specializes in *la ruta del bufeo*, a one- or two-day boat journey through the **Área Protegida Municipal Ibare-Mamoré** to view the pink Amazon river dolphins. Departures are typically from Puerto Ballivián (8km from Trinidad). English-language guides cost extra.

Conservación Loros Bolivia   WILDLIFE WATCHING
(CLB; ☑cell 7112-6506; https://fclbolivia.org; 18 de Noviembre 278; ⊙8am-noon & 2-6pm Mon-Fri, to noon Sat) 𝄞 This foundation doesn't actually sell tours, but executive director José Antonio Díaz is so passionate about the region and its wildlife that he can set you up with guides (any money you pay will serve as a donation to support CLB's conservation work). Stop by for information on bird-watching in the **Reserva Barba Azul** or **Área Protegida Municipal Gran Mojos**.

Bici Tour   CYCLING
(☑cell 7114-7183; www.facebook.com/bicitourlyliam; Av 18 de Noviembre 278; bike rentals hr/day B$15/80) Bike rentals and English-language city tours. Also offers nature-focused bike trips to Laguna Suárez, Laguna La Bomba and destinations further afield.

🛌 Sleeping

Residencial Santa Cruz   PENSION $
(☑462-0711; Av Santa Cruz 537; s/d B$80/150, s/d without bathroom B$70/130; ☎) A budget place that's a bit beat up, but makes a real effort to cheer up its rooms with colorful decor, hand-painted wall hangings and bright bedclothes. Rooms on the top floor are airier. All rooms have cable TV. Nice old couple also offer a shared kitchen (but won't help you cook!).

WORTH A TRIP

EXPLORING MORE OF THE AMAZON

San Ignacio de Moxos is a friendly, tranquil indigenous Moxos village, 92km west of Trinidad, with an ambience quite distinct from any other Bolivian town. The people speak an indigenous dialect known as *ignaciano*, and their lifestyle, traditions and food are unique. The best time to visit is during the **annual festival** (Fiesta del Santo Patrono de Moxos) on July 30 and 31. This is when the villagers let their hair down and get their feather headgear up, and don't stop drinking, dancing and letting off fireworks for three days.

San Ignacio is located smack-bang in the middle of the notoriously poor (though increasingly asphalted) Trinidad–San Borja road. From April to October, it's three to four hours from Trinidad to San Ignacio by van (B\$60), including the *balsa* crossing of the Río Mamoré, but this route is sporadically closed during the rainy season.

★ **Casa Lucia Hotel Boutique** BOUTIQUE HOTEL **\$\$**
(☑ cell 7828-8146; www.facebook.com/CasaLucia HotelBoutique; El Palmar 42; s/d/tr incl breakfast B\$280/350/450; ❄ ≋ ☒) Slightly removed from town on a secluded residential street near the Kenneth Lee museum, this gorgeous hideaway is Trinidad's finest, with seven antique-filled rooms clustered around lush gardens and a kidney-shaped pool.

Hotel Colonial HOTEL **\$\$**
(☑ 462-2864; www.facebook.com/hotelcolonial trinidad; Vaca Diez 306; s/d B\$200/250, ste B\$250/350; ❄ ≋ ☒) Hotel Colonial is a few blocks from the plaza and is a superb midrange option with well-appointed rooms, extremely friendly service and a lovely centerpiece pool surrounded by tropical plants.

✗ Eating & Drinking

Sabor Brazil BRAZILIAN **\$**
(www.facebook.com/saborbrasilTdd; Av 6 de Agosto 164; mains B\$25-35; ⊗ 4-11pm Sat-Thu; ☎) This tiny cafe is a real belly-pleaser with its selection of fresh juices, bountiful açaí bowls, jumbo-sized calzones and delectable desserts (the passion-fruit cheesecake is a tropical dream). Oh, and it's the only place in town with real espresso coffees. We only wish it was open in the mornings.

★ **Churrasquería La Estancia** STEAK **\$\$**
(www.facebook.com/ChurrasqueriaLaEstancia; Ibare, near Velarde; mains B\$45-75; ⊗ 11am-3pm & 7pm-midnight; ☎) Ask anybody in Trinidad where to get a good bit of beef and you will be sent to Churrasquería La Estancia. With its palm roof and coal-fire barbecue hamming up the ranch-house setting, the succulent and juicy cuts will make you wonder how other restaurants even dare to call

themselves *churrasquerías* (grilled-meat restaurants).

★ **El Tábano** SEAFOOD **\$\$**
(Villavicencio, near Néstor Suárez; mains B\$40-65; ⊗ 11:30am-2:30pm & 7pm-midnight) With cool beers and cocktails served in the courtyard, this grass-roofed resto-pub is a popular place with Trinidad's young crowd on account of its great atmosphere (thanks to live bands) and excellent food. The menu consists of inventive variations of fish and caiman dishes.

Palo Diablo BAR
(☑ 462-7254; Av Santa Cruz 825; ⊗ 6pm-1am) Dark lights, rock videos on the flat-screen TV and the largest cocktail menu in town make this the bar of choice for the karaoke-averse. There's live music on Friday and Saturday nights at 10pm.

ℹ Information

For visa extensions, head to the **immigration office** (cnr Vaca Diez & Av Santa Cruz; ⊗ 8:30am-12:30pm & 2:30-6:30pm Mon-Fri).

Several ATMs near the main plaza accept international cards – this is a good spot to get some cash before heading out to the Amazon proper. **Prodem** (Vaca Diez s/n; ⊗ 8:30am-12:30pm & 2:30-6:30pm Mon-Fri, 9am-noon Sat) is just off the plaza for cash advances.

The municipal **tourist office** (☑ 462-1322; Vaca Diez, near 18 de Noviembre; ⊗ 8am-12:30pm & 2:30-6:30pm Mon-Fri) offers flyers and limited info, but if you're planning a trip into the countryside you're better off chatting with English-speaking José Antonio Díaz at Conservación Loros Bolivia.

There are only a handful of laundry shops, mostly on the outskirts of town. The most central option is **Lavandería Industrial Burbujas** (☑ mobile 6938-0072; La Paz 259; ⊗ 8am-noon

& 2-7pm Mon-Sat), which charges B$22 per dozen items.

❶ Getting There & Away

AIR

Departing air travelers must pay B$11 for use of the **Teniente Jorge Henrich Arauz airport** (Av José Chávez Suárez), which is just outside the northwest corner of town (taxi/moto-taxi B$20/10).

BOA (Boliviana de Aviación; ✉ 901-105-010; www.boa.bo; cnr Sucre & Cipriano Barace; ⊘ 8:30am-12:30pm & 2:30-6:30pm Mon-Fri, 9am-1pm Sat) has six flights weekly (not Sunday) to La Paz, and daily flights to Santa Cruz and Cochabamba. **EcoJet** (✉ 465-2617, 901-105-055; www.ecojet.bo; cnr Avs 6 de Agosto & Santa Cruz; ⊘ 8:30am-12:30pm & 2:30-6:30pm Mon-Fri, 8:30am-12:30pm Sat) has daily flights to Cochabamba, Guayaremerín and Riberalta, and regular flights to La Paz (three weekly) and Santa Cruz (six weekly).

There are also flights to Sucre via Santa Cruz (four weekly) and Tarija via Cochabamba (two weekly). **Amazonas** (✉ 462-7575; www.amaszonas.com; Teniente Jorge Henrich Arauz Airport, Av José Chávez Suárez; ⊘ 7:30am-4:30pm Mon-Fri) connects Trinidad with Riberalta and Santa Cruz daily. **TAM** (✉ 462-2363; cnr Avs Bolívar & Santa Cruz; ⊘ 8am-noon & 2-6:30pm Mon-Fri, to 1pm Sat) has an irregular schedule with occasional flights to Santa Cruz, Guayaremerín and Riberalta.

BUS & VAN

The rambling, disorderly **bus terminal** (Beni btwn Martiniano Fuentes & Rómulo Mendoza) is a 1km walk or B$20 taxi ride east of the center. Several *flotas* (long-distance buses) depart nightly between 6pm and 10pm for Santa Cruz (B$50, 10 to 12 hours); a bus *cama* (sleeper bus) costs B$80. A number of companies theoretically serve Rurrenabaque (B$130, 10 to 13 hours) daily via San Borja (B$80, six to eight hours), though from November to May these services can be temporarily suspended (or greatly enlarged).

There are also daily departures to Riberalta (B$200) and Guayaramerín (B$200) which can take either 12 or 24 hours depending on whether they pass through Puerto Siles (when it's dry) or Rurrenabaque (when it rains).

Across from the terminal, there are a few van and car services to nearby cities which only depart when they've sold all seats. Vans depart for San Borja (B$100, six to seven hours), Rurrenabaque (B$180, nine to 11 hours) and Santa Rosa (B$230, 13 to 15 hours). Vans run to San Ignacio de Moxos (B$60, three to four hours) when full from a separate **parada** at Pedro Ignacio Muiba and Jarajorechi.

UNDERSTAND BOLIVIA

Bolivia Today

In Bolivia, protests, poverty and inequality have long been a part of everyday life. But since Evo Morales was elected president in 2006, he has transformed Bolivia with a radical new constitution, economic reforms and social policies. What Bolivians make of Morales depends on who you ask, but to the outside observer these changes add up to one of the most interesting chapters in Bolivian history.

Economically, the nationalization of energy and mining interests was applauded by Bolivia's poor, but it has soured relations with foreign investors and some foreign governments. Bolivia has sought closer ties with Brazil, Russia, India and China (the BRIC powers) and has distanced itself more from the USA. While this has been welcomed in some parts of society, others, particularly in the Santa Cruz region, have reacted negatively. Of the BRIC countries, it is China that has established the most powerful economic presence in Bolivia.

An improving economy has allowed for investment in social projects that have made a positive impact on poverty levels and have succeeded in reframing Bolivia's social structure. There is now a spark of self-awareness and hope that's never been more evident among the nation's indigenous majority. The role of women is also slowly evolving, as they step out of their traditional roles, emerging as business people and community leaders.

However, conflict and struggle remain a way of life in a country where historically you only got what you were willing to fight for. People protest against poor working conditions, mining operations that contaminate rivers, and roads that displace communities and affect ecosystems. Protests regularly shut down Bolivia's roads and have a knock-on effect on the economy. Violence stemming from the ever-evolving drug trade is also simmering under the surface, throughout the region.

History

Bolivia's living history is evident in every corner of daily life. And the significant events that shaped the past – from the rise of Tiwanaku and the Pax Incaica to the Spanish Conquest, independence movement, discovery of vast mineral wealth, loss of territories to neighbors on all sides, economic twists, flips and flops, and coup after coup after coup – have piled on top of each other to create the Bolivia you see today.

You can connect with the artistic threads of history in the country's pre-Hispanic ruins, colonial-era churches and in the museums, galleries and chaotic markets of the city centers. The cultural imprint that dates back more than 6000 years is seen in the language, dress, customs and traditions of native peoples, and in the unique dual society that is only now being challenged with the rise of the country's first self-declared indigenous president.

The economic wake from this dual society is viscerally palpable in the underclasses and indigenous majority, and in the sky-scraping edifices of La Paz and the broad haciendas around Santa Cruz.

From a purely economic standpoint, Bolivia is a country that never should have been. The country has vast natural resources, but a small, sparse population, meaning the country primarily produces raw goods. Politically, it has been pushed and pulled and bent out of shape by the stronger spheres of influence centering in Cuzco, Madrid, Lima, Buenos Aires and Washington, DC. And while much of Bolivia's history follows the macro-trends of the rest of South America, the country's spirit, character and context have come together to form a complex and intricate story unique unto itself.

Pre-Colonial Times

Advanced civilizations first developed along the Peruvian coast and in the valleys in the early AD period. Highland civilizations developed a little later on. Some archaeologists define the prehistory of the Central Andes in terms of 'horizons' – Early, Middle and Late – each of which was characterized by distinct architectural and artistic trends.

The so-called Early Horizon (1400–400 BC) was an era of architectural innovation and activity, most evident in the ruins of Chavín de Huantar, on the eastern slopes of the Andes in Peru. Chavín influences resounded far and wide, even after the decline of Chavín society, and spilled over into the Early Middle Horizon (400 BC–AD 500).

The Middle Horizon (AD 500–900) was marked by the imperial expansion of the Tiwanaku and Huari (of the Ayacucho Valley of present-day Peru) cultures. The Tiwanakans produced technically advanced work, most notably the city itself. They created impressive ceramics, gilded ornamentation, engraved pillars and slabs with calendar markings, and designs representing their bearded white leader and deity, Viracocha.

The period between AD 900 and 1475 is known as the Late Intermediate Horizon. After the fall of Tiwanaku, regionalized city-states like Chan-Chan in Peru and the Aymará kingdoms around the southern shores of Lake Titicaca came to power. But it was the rise and fall of the Inca empire that would truly define the pre-Columbian period.

Around 1440 the Inca started to expand their political boundaries. The eighth Inca king, Viracocha (not to be confused with the Tiwanaku deity of the same name), believed the mandate from their Sun God was not just to conquer, plunder and enslave, but to organize defeated tribes and absorb them into the realm of the benevolent Sun God.

Between 1476 and 1534 the Inca civilization was able to extend its influence over the Aymará kingdoms around Lake Titicaca.

By the late 1520s internal rivalries began to take their toll on the empire, with the sons of Inca Huayna Capac – Atahualpa and Huáscar – fighting a bloody civil war after the death of their father. Atahualpa (who controlled the northern reaches of the empire) won the war.

Conquistadors

The Spanish conquest of South America was remarkably quick. The power vacuum left by the Inca Civil War helped, as did the epidemics caused by European diseases.

Alto Perú (the area we now know as Bolivia) was aligned with Huáscar during the Inca Civil War, making its conquest rather easy for Diego de Almagro.

In 1544, Diego Huallpa revealed his discovery of silver at Cerro Rico in Potosí. By this time, Spanish conquerors had already firmly implanted their customs on the remnants of the Inca empire.

Potosí was officially founded in 1545, and in 1558 Alto Perú gained its autonomy from Lima with the placement of an Audiencia (Royal Court) in Sucre. Spider-webbing out from Potosí, transportation hubs, farming communities and other support centers sprung up. Due to the world's most prolific mine, Potosí's silver underwrote Spain's international ambitions – enabling the country to fight the Counter-Reformation in Europe – and also supported the extravagance of its monarchy for at least two centuries.

Independence

The early part of the 19th century was a time of revolution and independence in Bolivia (and much of the world for that matter). Harvest failures and epidemics severely affected the Bolivian economy between 1803 and 1805. And when the economy is bad, the conditions are good for revolution. To top it off, with the French Revolution, Napoleon's wars in Europe and British support for Latin America independence movements, the colonists of the Americas were finally able to perceive what the world without royalty would look like.

By May 1809, Spanish America's first independence movement had gained momentum, and was well underway in Chuquisaca (later renamed Sucre), with other cities quick to follow suit.

By the early 1820s, General Simón Bolívar had succeeded in liberating both Venezuela and Colombia from Spanish domination. In 1822 he dispatched Mariscal (Field Marshall) Antonio José de Sucre to Ecuador to defeat the Royalists at the battle of Pichincha. In 1824, after years of guerrilla action against the Spanish and the victories of Bolívar and Sucre in the battles of Junín (August 6) and Ayacucho (December 9), Peru finally won its independence.

With both Argentina and Peru eying the prize of the Potosí mines, Sucre incited a declaration of independence from Perú and, in 1825, the new Republic of Bolivia was born. Bolívar (yep, the country was named after him) and Sucre served as Bolivia's first and second presidents, but after a brief attempt by the third president, Andrés Santa Cruz, to form a confederation with Peru, things began to go awry. Chilean opposition eventually broke up this potentially powerful nation, and thereafter Bolivia was relegated to a more secondary role in regional affairs, with a period of *caudillo* (strongman) rule dominating national politics until the 1880s. Thereafter Bolivia was ruled by a civilian oligarchy divided into liberal and conservative groups until the 1930s, when the traditional political system again fell apart, leading to constant military intervention until the 1952 Revolution.

Shrinking Territory

At the time of independence Bolivia's boundaries encompassed well over 2 million sq km. But its neighbors soon moved to acquire its territory, removing coastal access and much of the area covered by its ancient Amazonian rubber trees.

The coastal loss occurred during the War of the Pacific, fought against Chile between 1879 and 1884. Many Bolivians believe that Chile stole the Atacama Desert's copper- and nitrate-rich sands and 850km of coastline from Peru and Bolivia by invading during Carnaval. Chile did attempt to compensate for the loss by building a railroad from La Paz to the ocean and allowing Bolivia free port privileges in Antofagasta, but Bolivians have never forgotten this devastating *enclaustramiento* (landlocked status).

The next major loss was in 1903 during the rubber boom, when Brazil hacked away at Bolivia's inland expanse. Brazil and Bolivia had both been ransacking the forests of the Acre territory – it was so rich in rubber trees that Brazil engineered a dispute over sovereignty and sent in its army. Brazil then convinced the Acre region to secede from the Bolivian republic and promptly annexed it.

There were two separate territory losses to Argentina. First, Argentina annexed a large slice of the Chaco in 1862. Then, in 1883, the territory of Puna de Atacama also went to Argentina. It had been offered to both Chile and Argentina, the former in exchange for return of the Litoral (coastal strip), the latter in exchange for clarification over Bolivia's ownership of Tarija.

After losing the War of the Pacific, Bolivia was desperate to have the Chaco, an inhospitable region beneath which rich oilfields were mooted to lie, as an outlet to the Atlantic via the Río Paraguay. Between 1932 and 1935, a particularly brutal war was waged between Bolivia and Paraguay over the disputed territory (more than 80,000 lives were lost).

Though no decisive victory was reached, both nations had grown weary of fighting, and peace negotiations in 1938 awarded most of the disputed territory to Paraguay.

Continuing Political Strife

During the early 20th century wealthy tin barons and landowners controlled Bolivian farming and mining interests, while the peasantry was relegated to *pongueaje*, a feudal system of peonage. Civil unrest brewed, with the most significant development being the emergence of the Movimiento Nacionalista Revolucionario (MNR) political party. It united the masses behind the common cause of popular reform, sparking friction between peasant miners and absentee tin bosses. Under the leadership of Víctor Paz Estenssoro, the MNR prevailed in the 1951 elections, but a last-minute military coup prevented it from actually taking power.

What ensued was a period of serious combat, which ended with the defeat of the military and Paz Estensorro's rise to power in what has been called the April Revolution of 1952. He immediately nationalized the mines, evicted the tin barons, put an end to *pongueaje* and set up Comibol (Corporación Minera de Bolivia), the state entity in charge of mining interests. The MNR remained in power for 12 years but even with US support it was unable to raise the standard of living or increase food production substantially.

The '60s and '70s were decades of military coups, dictators, brutal regimes of torture, arrests and disappearances, as well as a marked increase in cocaine production and trafficking.

In 1982 Congress elected Hernán Siles Zuazo, the civilian left-wing leader of the Communist-supported Movimiento de la Izquierda Revolucionaria (MIR), which began one of the longest democratic periods in Bolivian history. His term was beleaguered by labor disputes, government overspending and huge monetary devaluation, resulting in a staggering inflation rate that at one point reached 35,000% annually.

When Siles Zuazo gave up after three years and called general elections, Paz Estenssoro returned to politics to become president for the fourth time. He immediately enacted harsh measures to revive the shattered economy, including ousting labor unions, imposing a wage freeze and eliminating price subsidies, then deployed armed forces to keep the peace. Inflation was curtailed within weeks, but spiraling unemployment threatened the government's stability.

Chaos Prevails

The early '90s were characterized by political apathy, party politics and the struggle between *capitalización* (the opening of state companies to international investment) and populist models. The free market won with the election of Gonzalo 'Goni' Sánchez de Lozada, the MNR leader who had played a key role in the curtailing of inflation through 'shock therapy' during the Estenssoro government.

Economic reforms saw state-owned companies and mining interests opened up to overseas investment in the hope that that privatization would bring stability and make the enterprises profitable. Overseas investors were offered 49% equity, total voting control, license to operate in Bolivia and up to 49% of the profits. The remaining 51% of the shares were distributed to Bolivians as pensions and through Participación Popular, a program meant to channel spending away from cities and into rural schools, clinics and other local infrastructure.

In late 1995 reform issues were overshadowed by violence and unrest surrounding US-directed coca eradication in the Chapare. In the late '90s the government faced swelling public discontent with the coca eradication measures, and protests in response to increasing gas prices, a serious water shortage and economic downturn in the department of Cochabamba.

Following a successful campaign advised by a team of US political consultants that he hired, 'Goni' was again appointed president in August 2002. The following year his economic policies were met with widespread demonstrations, which resulted in the loss of 67 lives during a police lockdown in La Paz. In October 2003, Goni resigned amid massive popular protests and fled to the US. He currently faces charges related to the deaths during the demonstrations, both in the US and Bolivia, and a long-winded formal extradition process has been underway since 2008.

Protests, rising fuel prices and continued unrest pushed Goni's successor, Carlos Mesa, to resign in 2005.

The Morales Era

In December 2005 Bolivians elected their country's first indigenous president. A former *cocalero* (coca grower) and representative from Cochabamba, Evo Morales Ayma of Movimiento al Socialismo (MAS) won nearly 54% of the vote, having promised to change the traditional political-class system and to empower the nation's poor (mainly indigenous) majority. After the election, Morales quickly grabbed the spotlight, touring

BOLIVIA'S INDIGENOUS GROUPS

Highlands

Aymará The Aymará culture emerged on the southern shores of Titicaca after the fall of Tiwanaku. Today, Aymará live in the areas surrounding the lake and in the Yungas, calling La Paz' El Alto the capital of Aymará culture.

Quechua Descended from the Inca, there are some 9 to 14 million Quechua speakers in Bolivia, Peru, Ecuador, Chile, Colombia and Argentina today.

Chipaya Perhaps the direct descendants of Tiwanaku.

Kallawaya A remote ethnic group from the mountains north of La Paz.

Lowlands

Chiquitano Living primarily in the Chiquitania tropical savanna outside Santa Cruz, but also in Beni and into Brazil. There are about 180,000 Chiquitanos in Bolivia. About a quarter of them speak Chiquitano.

Guaraní This ethnic group shares a common language and lives in Paraguay, Brazil and parts of Uruguay and Bolivia.

Mojeño From the Beni department, this significant ethnic group was quite large before the 17th century, with over 350,000 people.

the world and meeting with Venezuela's Hugo Chávez, Cuba's Fidel Castro, Brazil's Luiz Inácio Lula da Silva and members of South Africa's African National Congress. Symbolically, on May Day 2006, he nationalized Bolivia's natural gas reserves and raised taxes on energy investors in a move that would consolidate Bolivian resources in Bolivian hands.

In July 2006, Morales formed a National Constituent Assembly to set about rewriting the country's constitution. In January 2009, the new socially focused constitution was approved by 67% of voters in a nationwide referendum. The first Bolivian constitution to be approved by popular vote, it gave greater power to the country's indigenous majority, made official the role of indigenous languages and religions in the new 'plurinational' state and allowed Morales to seek a second five-year term, which he won that same year. The constitution also limited the size of landholdings in order to redistribute Bolivia's land from large ranchers and landowners to poor indigenous farmers.

While Evo Morales enjoys widespread support among the indigenous people of Bolivia, his radical social changes aren't without their opponents. In the eastern part of the country – the four departments known as La Media Luna (Half Moon, for their geographic shape) – where much of the natural resources lie, a strong right-wing opposition has been challenging Morales, accusing him of being an ethnocentric despot. In 2016, a referendum proposing to change the constitution to allow Morales to run for a fourth consecutive term delivered a shock no vote. Undeterred, Morales looked to the courts, who overruled the constitution, scrapping limits on terms altogether, and in 2017 Morales announced his intention to stand for reelection in 2019.

Culture

The National Psyche

Bolivia is a remarkably stratified society. And while the archetypes defined by 500 years of Spanish-descent rule are starting to slowly fade, who you are – where you fit in society and what opportunities you will have throughout life – is still largely defined by the color of your skin, the language you speak, the clothes you wear and the money you have.

Attitude depends on climate and altitude. *Cambas* (lowlanders) and *kollas* (highlanders) enjoy expounding on what makes them different (ie better) than the other. Lowlanders are said to be warmer, more casual and more generous to strangers; highlanders are supposedly harder-working but less open-minded. While the jesting used to be good-natured, Bolivians are acutely aware of the economic disparity between the two regions and tensions are occasionally brought to a head, when Santa Cruz threatens secession from the republic due to disagreements with the political script.

Lifestyle

Life in this fiercely self-reliant nation begins with the family. No matter what ethnic group or class you come from, it's likely that you have close ties to your extended family. In the highlands, the concept of *ayllu* (the traditional peasant system of communal land ownership, management and decision making) that dates back to the Inca times is still important today.

Day-to-day life varies: many *campesinos* (subsistence farmers) live without running water, heat or electricity, although rural amenities and living conditions continue to improve. In the cities, thousands of people enjoy the comforts of contemporary conveniences and live very modern lifestyles.

Homosexuality is legal in Bolivia but isn't often openly displayed in this society where machismo is common. Despite a growing number of gay bars in some larger cities, gay culture remains fairly subtle.

Religion

Roughly 77% of Bolivia's population professes Roman Catholicism and practices it to varying degrees. The remaining 23% are Protestant or agnostic or belonging to other religions. Strong evangelical movements are rapidly gaining followers with their fire-and-brimstone messages of the world's imminent end, and in some areas are also putting paid to centuries of traditional cultural practices. Despite the political and economic strength of Christianity, it's clear that most religious activities have incorporated some Inca and Aymará belief systems. Doctrines, rites and superstitions are commonplace, and some *campesinos* still live by a traditional lunar calendar.

Population

Bolivia is a multi-ethnic society with a remarkable diversity of linguistic, cultural and artistic traditions. It is a fact that the country has the largest population of indigenous peoples in South America, with most sociologists and anthropologists stating that over 60% of the population is of indigenous descent.

Bolivia has 36 identified indigenous groups. The vast majority of those who identify themselves as indigenous are Aymará (about 25%) and Quechua (about 30%), many of whom live in the highlands. The remaining groups (including Guaraní and Chiquitano) are located almost entirely in the lowlands.

Mestizos (a person of mixed indigenous and Spanish descent), make up a substantial portion of the population.

Arts

Music & Dance

While all Andean musical traditions have evolved from a series of pre-Inca, Inca, Spanish, Amazonian and even African influences, each region of Bolivia has developed distinctive musical traditions, dances and instruments.

The instrument Bolivia is most known for, and understandably proud of, is the *charango*, considered the king of all stringed instruments. Modeled after the Spanish *vihuela* and mandolin, it gained initial popularity in Potosí during the city's mining heyday. Another instrument commonplace in the gringo markets is the *quena*, a small flute made of cane, bone or ceramic. The instrument pre-dates Europeans by many centuries and the earliest examples, made of stone, were found near Potosí. A curious instrument known as a jaguar-caller comes from the Amazon region. This hollowed-out calabash, with a small hole into which the player inserts his hand, seems to do the trick in calling the big cats to the hunt.

Traditional altiplano dances celebrate war, fertility, hunting prowess, marriage and work. With Spanish arrival came also European and African dance traditions, resulting in the hybrid dances that now characterize many Bolivian celebrations.

Oruro's Carnaval draws huge local and international crowds. Potosí is famed for its re-creations of the region's *tinku* fight tradition, while La Paz is renowned for La Morenada, which reenacts the dance of African slaves brought to the courts of Viceroy Felipe III.

Weaving

Bolivian textiles come in diverse patterns displaying a degree of skill resulting from millennia of artistry and tradition. The most common piece is a *manta* or *aguayo*, a square shawl made of two handwoven strips joined edge to edge. Also common are the *chuspa* (coca pouch), *chullo* (knitted hat), *falda* (skirt), woven belts and touristy items such as camera bags made from remnants.

Regional differences are manifested in weaving style, motif and use. Weavings from Tarabuco often feature intricate zoomorphic patterns, while distinctive red-and-black designs come from Potolo, northwest of Sucre. Zoomorphic patterns are also prominent in the wild Charazani country north of Lake Titicaca and in several altiplano areas outside La Paz, including Lique and Calamarca.

Some extremely fine weavings originate in Sica Sica, one of the many dusty and nondescript villages between La Paz and Oruro, while in Calcha, southeast of Potosí, expert spinning and an extremely tight weave – more than 150 threads per inch – produce Bolivia's finest textiles.

Vicuña fibers, the finest and most expensive in the world, are produced in Apolobamba and in Parque Nacional Sajama.

Sports

Like many of its Latin American neighbors, Bolivia's national sport is *fútbol* (soccer). La Paz' Bolívar and The Strongest usually participate (albeit weakly) in the Copa Libertadores, the annual showdown of Latin America's top clubs. Professional *fútbol* matches are held every weekend in big cities, and impromptu street games are always happening. While small towns lack many basic services, you can be sure to find a well-tended *cancha* (football field) almost everywhere you go – and you'll be welcome to join in. Some communities still bar women from the field, but in the altiplano, women's teams have started popping up.

In rural communities, volleyball is a sunset affair, with mostly adults playing a couple of times a week. Racquetball, billiards, chess and *cacho* (dice) are also popular. The unofficial national sport, however, has to be feasting and feting – the competition between dancers and drinkers knows no bounds.

Environment

When people think of Bolivia it generally conjures up images of somewhere high (La Paz), dry (altiplano) and salty (Uyuni salt plains). While this may be true for large areas of the country, there's much more to the Bolivian landscape than just mountains. The range of altitude – from 130m above sea level in the jungles of the Amazon Basin to 6542m on the peaks of the rugged Andes – has resulted in a huge variety of ecological and geological niches supporting a bewildering variety of nature. Environmentally it is one of the most diverse countries on the continent.

The country's 1415 bird species and 5000 described plant species rank among the highest numbers in the world. It's also among the neotropical countries with the highest level of endemism (species which exist only in Bolivia), with 21 birds, 28 reptiles, 72 amphibians and 25 mammals found nowhere else on earth.

But while it may seem obvious that Bolivia's natural resources are one of its greatest assets, not everybody values assets that don't have a direct monetary value. From the lush tropical forests of Parque Nacional e Área de Uso Múltiple Amboró to the wetlands of the Pantanal, the scrub that obscures the Chaco gas fields and the Polylepis woodlands of the Andes, the Bolivian environment is under constant threat from destruction for economic exploitation.

The Land

Two Andean mountain chains define the west of the country, with many peaks above 6000m. The western Cordillera Occidental stands between Bolivia and the Pacific coast. The eastern Cordillera Real runs southeast, then turns south across central Bolivia, joining the other chain to form the southern Cordillera Central.

The haunting altiplano (altitude 3500m to 4000m) is boxed in by these two great cordilleras. It's an immense, nearly treeless plain punctuated by mountains and solitary volcanic peaks. At the altiplano's northern end, straddling the Peruvian border, Lake Titicaca is one of the world's highest navigable lakes. In the far southwestern corner, the land is drier and less populated. The salty remnants of two vast ancient lakes, the Salar de Uyuni and the Salar de Coipasa, are there as well.

East of the Cordillera Central are the Central Highlands, a region of scrubby hills, valleys and fertile basins with a Mediterranean-like climate. North of the Cordillera Real, the rainy Yungas form a transition zone between arid highlands and humid lowlands.

More than half Bolivia's total area is in the Amazon Basin, with sweaty tropical rainforest in the western section, and flat *cerrado* savannas and extensions of the Pantanal wetland in the east. In the country's southeastern corner is the nearly impenetrable scrubland of the Gran Chaco, an arid, thorny forest that experiences the highest temperatures in the country.

Wildlife

The distribution of wildlife is dictated by the country's geography and varies considerably from region to region. The altiplano is home to vicuñas, flamingos and condors; the Chaco to secretive jaguars, pumas and peccaries; the Pantanal provides refuge for giant otters, marsh deer and waterbirds; while the Amazon Basin contains the richest density of species on earth, featuring an incredible variety of reptiles, parrots, monkeys, hummingbirds, butterflies, fish and bugs (by the zillions!).

Of course the animals that steal the show are the regional giants. The majestic jaguar, the continent's top predator; the elephant-nosed tapir (*anta*); and the walking vacuum cleaner that is the giant anteater. The continent's biggest bird is here too, the ostrich-like rhea or *ñandú,* and it can be surprisingly common in some areas. You may even be lucky enough to spot the breathtaking Andean condor, unsurprisingly revered by the Inca, soaring on mountain thermals.

River travelers are almost certain to spot capybaras (like giant aquatic guinea pigs) and caiman (similar to alligators). It's not unusual to see anacondas in the rivers of the department of Beni and a spot of piranha fishing is virtually an obligation for anybody spending time in the Amazon.

Overland travelers frequently see armadillos, foxes, *jochis* (agoutis) and the grey-faced, llama-like guanaco. Similar, but more delicately proportioned, is the fuzzy vicuña, once mercilessly hunted for its woolly coat but now recovering well. You won't have to work quite as hard to spot their domesticated relatives, the llama and the alpaca.

Many nonprofit groups are working on countrywide environmental conservation efforts. Besides the international conservation organizations, the following local groups are having a positive impact:

Asociación Armonía (www.armonia-bo.org) Everything you need to know about birding and bird conservation.

Fundación Amigos de la Naturaleza (www.fan-bo.org) One of the most active of the local conservation groups, working at the national level.

Protección del Medio Ambiente Tarija (http://prometa.org.bo) Works in the Gran Chaco region on a series of social and conservation initiatives.

National Parks & Reserves

Our favorite national parks and protected areas (there are 22 in total) and what you'll see:

Amboró Near Santa Cruz, home to rare spectacled bears, jaguars and an astonishing variety of birdlife.

Apolobamba Excellent hiking in this remote mountain range abutting the Peruvian border, with Bolivia's densest condor population.

Cotapata Most of the Choro trek passes through here, midway between La Paz and Coroico in the Yungas.

Madidi Protects a wide range of wildlife habitats; more than 1000 species of birds have been identified in Madidi.

Noel Kempff Mercado Remote park on the Brazilian border; contains a variety of wildlife and some of Bolivia's most inspiring scenery.

Reserva Nacional de Fauna Andina Eduardo Avaroa A highlight of the Southwest Circuit tour, including wildlife-rich lagoons.

Sajama Adjoining Chile's magnificent Parque Nacional Lauca; contains Volcán Sajama (6542m), Bolivia's highest peak.

Tororo Enormous rock formations with dinosaur tracks from the Cretaceous period, plus caves and ancient ruins.

Tunari Within hiking distance of Cochabamba; features lovely nature trails through mountain scenery.

SURVIVAL GUIDE

ℹ️ Directory A–Z

ACCESSIBLE TRAVEL
The sad fact is that Bolivia's infrastructure is ill equipped for travelers with disabilities. You will, however, see locals overcoming myriad obstacles and challenges while making their daily

BOLIVIA DIRECTORY A–Z

rounds. If you encounter difficulties yourself, you'll likely find locals willing to go out of their way to lend a hand. Download Lonely Planet's free Accessible Travel guides from http://lp travel.to/AccessibleTravel.

ACCOMMODATIONS

Bolivian accommodations are among South America's cheapest, though price and value are hardly uniform.

The Bolivian hotel-rating system divides accommodations into *posadas* (inns), *alojamientos, residenciales, casas de huéspedes, hostales* (hostels) and *hoteles* (hotels). Rock-bottom places are usually found around the bus and train stations, though this area is often the most dangerous in town. Room availability is only a problem at popular weekend getaways like Coroico and during fiestas (especially Carnaval in Oruro and festivals in Copacabana), when prices double.

In the altiplano, heat and hot water often make the difference in price, while in lowland areas, air-con and fans are common delimiters.

Warning: several readers have alerted us to improper use of propane heaters in Bolivia. These are sometimes offered in cheaper accommodations but are not meant to be used in enclosed spaces so refrain from using them if supplied.

Bolivia offers excellent camping, especially along trekking routes and in remote mountain areas. Gear (of varying quality) is easily rented in La Paz and at popular trekking base camps like Sorata. It's always a good idea to ask for permission if somebody is around. Theft and assaults have been reported in some areas – always inquire locally about security before heading off to set up camp.

ACTIVITIES

Bolivia is like a theme park for grown-up adventurers. It offers multiday treks, relatively easy day hikes, mountain biking that'll leave your teeth chattering, climbs to lost Andean peaks, rivers for rafting and rugged 4WD journeys over stones that once paved the Inca empire.

ELECTRICITY

Electricity Most electricity currents are 220V AC, at 50Hz. Most plugs and sockets are the two-pin, round-prong variety, but a few anom-

---

alous American-style two-pin, parallel flat-pronged sockets exist.

EMBASSIES & CONSULATES

Argentine Embassy (Map p210; ☑241-7737; www.ebolv.cancilleria.gov.ar; Aspiazu 475, Sopocachi; ☺8:30am-1:30pm Mon-Fri)

Argentine Consulate (☑03-332-4153; www. cscrs.cancilleria.gov.ar; Junín 22, 3rd fl; ☺8:30am-5pm Mon-Fri)

Australian Consulate (☑cell 7676-8787; https://dfat.gov.au/about-us/our-locations/missions/Pages/australian-consulate-in-la-paz-bolivia.aspx; Av Montenegro 961, Torre Olimpo, San Miguel; ☺9am-noon Mon-Fri)

Brazilian Embassy (Map p210; ☑244-1273; http://lapaz.itamaraty.gov.br/pt-br; Av Arce s/n, Edificio Multicentro, Sopocachi; ☺9am-1pm & 2-5pm Mon-Fri)

Brazilian Consulate (☑03-344-7575; http://santacruz.itamaraty.gov.br; Av Banzer 334; ☺8am-2pm Mon-Fri)

Canadian Embassy (Map p210; ☑241-5141; www.international.gc.ca; Victor Sanjinés 2678, 2nd fl, Sopocachi; ☺8:30am-1:30pm Mon-Fri)

Ecuadorian Embassy (☑211-5869; https://bolivia.embajada.gob.ec; Calle 14 No 8136, Calacoto; ☺9am-5pm Mon-Fri)

French Embassy (☑214-9900; https://bo.ambafrance.org; Calle 8 No 5390, Obrajes; ☺8:30am-12:30pm Mon-Fri)

German Embassy (Map p210; ☑244-0066; www.la-paz.diplo.de; Av Arce 2395, Sopocachi; ☺9am-noon Mon-Fri)

Irish Honorary Consul (☑2241-3949, 2242-1408; consulbolivia@gmail.com; Pasaje Gandarillas 2667, cnr Macario Pinilla, Sopocachi, La Paz)

Italian Embassy (☑cell 7155-4805; https://amblapaz.esteri.it; cnr Av Hernando Siles & Calle 5, Obrajes; ☺8:30am-noon Mon-Thu)

Japanese Embassy (Map p210; www.bo.emb-japan.go.jp; cnr Av Sánchez Lima & Gutiérrez; ☺8:30-11:30am & 1:30-5pm Mon-Fri)

Netherlands Consulate General (Map p210; ☑2242-2542; lapaz@nlconsulate.com; 7th fl, Edificio, Rosario, Sopocachi, Av Sanchez Lima 2061, La Paz; ☺3:30-6pm Mon & Wed)

Paraguayan Embassy (Map p210; ☑243-2201; Pedro Salazar 351, Edificio Illimani II, Sopocachi; ☺9am-4pm Mon-Fri)

Peruvian Embassy (Map p210; ☑244-1250; www.embaperubolivia.com; Fernando Guachalla 300, Sopocachi; ☺9:30am-1:30pm & 3:30-6:30pm Mon-Fri)

Spanish Embassy (Map p210; ☑243-4180; www.exteriores.gob.es/Embajadas/LaPaz; Av 6 de Agosto 2827, Sopocachi; ☺9am-1pm Mon-Fri)

SLEEPING PRICE RANGES

The following price ranges refer to a double room with bathroom.

$ less than B$180

$$ B$180–B$500

$$$ more than B$500

Spanish Consulate (📞03-312-1349; cnr Av Cañoto & Perú; ⏰8:30am-12:30pm Mon-Fri)

UK Embassy (Map p210; 📞243-3424; www. gov.uk/world/bolivia; Av Arce 2732, Sopocachi; ⏰8:30am-12:30pm & 1:30-5pm Mon-Thu, 8:30am-12:30pm Fri)

UK Honorary Consulate (📞3-353-5035; silvanag@scis-bo.com; Santa Cruz International School)

US Embassy (Map p210; 📞216-8000; https:// bo.usembassy.gov; Av Arce 2780, Sopocachi; ⏰8am-5pm Mon-Thu, 9am-12:30pm Fri)

US Consulate (📞3-351-3477; Radial Castilla, 3ero anillo, in front of Santo Tomas School soccer field; ⏰8am-3pm Mon & Tue, from 8:30am Wed & Thu, 9am-noon Fri)

FOOD

Meat invariably dominates Bolivian cuisine and it is usually accompanied by rice, a starchy tuber (usually potato) and shredded lettuce. Often, the whole affair is drowned by *llajhua* (a fiery tomato-based salsa). The soups are a specialty.

Desayuno (breakfast) consists of little more than coffee and a bread roll, and is often followed by a mid-morning street snack such as a *salteña* (meat and vegetable pasty), *tucumana* (an empanada-like pastry) or empanada.

Almuerzo (lunch) is the main meal of the day. The best-value meals are found in and around markets (often under B$10) and at no-frills restaurants offering set lunches (usually between B$15 and B$40). *Cena*, the evening meal, is mostly served à la carte.

Vegetarian options are on the rise, but you might be stuck with over-cooked vegetables, rice, potatoes, pizza and pasta. Quinoa is a super-grain, perfect for vegetarians.

HEALTH

Sanitation and hygiene are not Bolivia's strong suits, so pay attention to what you eat. Most tap water isn't safe to drink; stick to bottled water if your budget allows (your bowels will thank you). Carry iodine if you'll be trekking.

The altiplano lies between 3000m and 4000m, and many visitors to La Paz, Copacabana and Potosí will have problems with altitude sickness. Complications like cerebral edema have been the cause of death in otherwise fit, healthy travelers. Diabetics should note that only the Touch II blood glucose meter gives accurate readings at altitudes over 2000m.

Yellow fever is a risk in certain parts of Bolivia. Vaccination is recommended if visiting yellow fever risk areas, and proof of vaccination may be required for onward travel (such as to Brazil). Anyone coming from a yellow-fever-infected area needs a vaccination certificate to enter Bolivia. Take precautions against malaria in the lowlands.

While medical facilities might not be exactly what you're used to back home, there are decent hospitals in the biggest cities and passable clinics in most towns (but *not* in remote parts of the country).

INTERNET ACCESS

➡ Nearly every corner of Bolivia has a cyber cafe, and wi-fi is now standard in most midrange and top-end hotels (and many cafes).

➡ Rates run from B$4 to B$6 per hour.

➡ In remote areas, internet access is sometimes only possible via a cell-phone signal. Consider buying a local chip/SIM with data.

LEGAL MATTERS

➡ The biggest legal problems affecting travelers include trafficking and possession of cocaine and other drugs, minor traffic violations and sex-related crimes.

➡ If you are arrested, contact your embassy immediately. Note however that they don't have the power to resolve the legalities (or illegalities) if you break the law.

➡ Be aware that incidences of fake police have been on the rise.

LGBT+ TRAVELERS

➡ Bolivia's 2009 constitution is one of the first in the world to expressly ban discrimination on the basis of sexual orientation or gender identity. However, homosexuality is still not widely accepted by the populace and gay marriage and same-sex unions are illegal.

➡ LGBT+ bars and venues are limited to larger cities, especially Santa Cruz and La Paz – check out **Open Mind Club** (Map p206; www.facebook.com/omc.openmindclub; Cochabamba 100, Rosario; ⏰9pm-4am Fri & Sat) – but these are still somewhat clandestine affairs. Sharing a room is no problem – but discretion is suggested.

➡ LGBT+ rights lobby groups are active in La Paz, Cochabamba and most visibly in progressive Santa Cruz, which held Bolivia's first Gay Pride march in 2001.

➡ La Paz is known for La Familia Galán, the capital's most fabulous group of cross-dressing queens, who aim to educate Bolivians around issues of sexuality and gender through theater performances.

BOLIVIA DIRECTORY A–Z

BOLIVIA DIRECTORY A–Z

→ Mujeres Creando (www.mujerescreando.org) is a feminist activist group based in La Paz that promotes the rights of oppressed groups.

MAPS

Maps are available in **La Paz** (Map p206; Ballivián 1273; ⊙ 9am-12:30pm & 3-7:30pm Mon-Fri, 9:30am-12:30pm Sat), Cochabamba and **Santa Cruz** (☑ 336-0709; Ballivián 145; ⊙ 9am-1pm & 3-10pm Mon-Sat) through Los Amigos del Libro and some bookstores. Government 1:50,000 topographical and specialty sheets are available from the **Instituto Geográfico Militar** (IGM; Map p206; Av Diagonal Juan XXIII No 100, Edificio Murillo, San Pedro; ⊙ 8:30am-12:30pm & 2:30-6:30pm Mon-Thu, 8:30am-12:30pm Fri), with offices in most major cities.

MONEY

→ Bolivia uses the boliviano (B$), divided into 100 centavos.

→ Most prices are pegged to the US dollar.

→ Often called pesos (the currency was changed from pesos to bolivianos in 1987).

→ Only crisp US dollar bills are accepted (they are the currency for savings).

→ Boliviano notes: 10, 20, 50, 100 and 200.

→ Coins: one, two and five bolivianos as well as 10, 20 and 50 centavos.

→ Bolivianos are extremely difficult to unload outside the country. Change them before you leave.

→ Counterfeit bolivianos and US dollars are less common than they used to be, but it still happens more often than you'd like.

→ If a bill looks excessively tatty don't accept it, because nobody else will.

→ Torn notes are still legal tender, but unless both halves of a repaired banknote bear identical serial numbers, the note is worthless.

ATMs

→ All sizeable towns have cajeros automáticos (ATMs) – usually Banco Nacional de Bolivia, Banco Fassil, Banco Mercantil Santa Cruz and Banco Unión.

→ They dispense bolivianos in 50 and 100 notes (sometimes US dollars as well) on Visa, MasterCard, Plus and Cirrus cards.

→ In smaller towns, the local bank Prodem is a good option for cash advances on Visa and MasterCard (3% to 6% commission charged) but the service is sometimes unreliable.

→ Don't rely on ATMs; always carry some cash with you, especially if venturing into rural areas.

Credit Cards

→ Brand-name plastic – such as Visa, MasterCard and (less often) American Express – may be used in larger cities at the better hotels, restaurants and tour agencies.

Money Changers

→ Currency may be exchanged at casas de cambio (exchange bureaux) and at some banks in larger cities. Occasionally travel agencies, hotels and sometimes tourist stores will change money, but at a price.

→ Visitors fare best with US dollars; it's hard to change euros or British pounds, and rates are poor.

→ Cambistas (street money changers) operate in most cities but only change cash dollars, paying roughly the same as casas de cambio. They're convenient but beware of rip-offs and counterfeit notes.

→ The rate for cash doesn't vary much from place to place, and there is no black-market rate.

→ Currencies of neighboring countries may be exchanged in border areas and at casas de cambio in La Paz.

International Transfers

To transfer money from abroad use the following.

Western Union (www.westernunion.com).

MoneyGram (www.moneygram.com).

Your bank can also wire money to a cooperating Bolivian bank; it may take a couple of business days.

PayPal (www.paypal.com) Increasingly used to make bank transfers to pay for hotels.

Tipping

Restaurants Service is not usually included in the bill; leave 10% to 15%.

Tours Guides are grateful for tips (10% to 20% is the norm); remember that their wage is often much lower than the tour price.

Taxis Tipping is not expected, though it's common to round up.

OPENING HOURS

Take care of business on weekdays. Nearly all businesses close for lunch, usually from noon to 2:30pm.

Banks Standard hours 9am–4pm or 6pm Monday to Friday, and 10am–noon or 5pm Saturday.

Shops Weekdays 10am–7pm but sometimes close for lunch noon–2pm. Open 10am–noon or 5pm Saturdays.

Restaurants Hours vary, but are generally open for breakfast (8am–10am), lunch (noon–3pm) and dinner (6pm–10pm or 11pm) daily.

PHOTOGRAPHY

Lonely Planet's Guide to Travel Photography is full of helpful tips for photography while on the road.

→ Some Bolivians are willing photo subjects; others may be suspicious of your camera and/or your motives. Ask permission to photograph; if permission is denied, you should neither insist nor snap a picture. Be sensitive to the wishes of locals.

➡ Many children will ask for payment, often after you've taken their photo. A few bolivianos will suffice.

➡ Avoid taking photographs of political rallies, military facilities or police – they are not noted for their sense of humor or understanding.

POST

In 2018 the Bolivian post service Ecobol (Empresa Correos de Bolivia) was closed (with a backlog of post left undelivered) and the government created the Agencia Nacional de Correos (www. oopp.gob.bo/agbc). Mail sent from bigger cities is more reliable than that sent from small towns. Expect delays.

➡ To mail an international parcel take it open to the post office so that the contents can be inspected. After inspection close it yourself (take what you need with you) before handing it over.

➡ You may be asked to fill in some official forms detailing the contents of the package. Avoid being too detailed, and don't explicitly mention items that might be attractive to thieves.

➡ The cost of sending the package depends on its weight. If you are offered the chance to 'register' the package for a small cost, take it; it doesn't guarantee much, but at least it gives you some kind of leg to stand on if it subsequently disappears.

➡ Avoid sending anything valuable by standard mail. Use an international courier, such as DHL (www.dhl.com). It's more expensive, but it will get to where you send it.

PUBLIC HOLIDAYS

Public holidays vary from province to province. The following are celebrated nationally.

Año Nuevo (New Year's Day) January 1
Día del Estado Plurinacional (Celebrates new constitution) January 22
Carnaval February/March
Semana Santa (Good Friday) March/April
Día del Trabajo (Labor Day) May 1
Corpus Christi May/June
Año Nuevo Andino Amazónico y del Chaco (Andean New Year) June 21
Día de la Independencia (Independence Day) August 6
Día de los Muertos (All Souls' Day) November 2
Navidad (Christmas) December 25

SAFE TRAVEL

➡ Crime against tourists is on the increase in Bolivia, especially in La Paz and, to a lesser extent, Cochabamba, Copacabana and Oruro.

➡ There is a strong tradition of social protest in Bolivia and demonstrations are a regular occurrence. While generally peaceful, they can turn threatening in nature: agitated protesters throw stones and rocks and police occasionally use force and tear gas to disperse crowds.

➡ Note that the mine tours in Potosí, bike trips outside La Paz and 4WD excursions around Salar de Uyuni can be dangerous. Some agencies are willing to compromise safety, so choose carefully.

Scams & Bribes

Scams are commonplace and fake police, false tourist police and 'helpful' locals are on the rise. Be aware, too, of circulating counterfeit banknotes.

Bribes are illegal in Bolivia, but common. People stopped for minor traffic violations or more serious infractions sometimes ask if they can 'pay the fine now.' Watch out for false police – authentic police officers will always wear a uniform and will never force you to show them your passport, insist you get in a taxi with them, or search you in public.

TELEPHONE

Bolivia's country code is 591. The international direct-dialing access code is 00.

Local SIM cards should work in cell phones that are not tied to a single network. Make sure your phone has triband network capabilities. Roaming rates can be high. Kiosks often have telephones that charge B$1 for brief local calls.

When buying a local SIM card, activate the number and check that the phone works before purchasing. To top up your call amount, buy cards (ask for *crédito*, ie credit) from the numerous kiosks or *puntos* (local call centers with public phones) in any city or town.

TOILETS

➡ Toilet humor becomes the norm in Bolivia. First and foremost, you'll have to learn to live with the fact that facilities are nonexistent on nearly all buses (except for a few of the luxury ones).

➡ Smelly, poorly maintained *baños públicos* (public toilets) abound and charge about B$1 in populated areas and B$5 in the wilderness, such as near the Salar de Uyuni.

➡ Toilet paper isn't flushed down any Bolivian toilet – use the wastebaskets provided.

➡ Use the facilities at your hotel before heading out.

➡ Carry toilet paper with you wherever you go, at all times! Some budget hotels and hostels can be stingy with toilet paper. It's best to always come armed with your own.

TOURIST INFORMATION

➡ Bolivian tourism has really taken off in recent years, but the industry and its associated infrastructure is still in its formative stages.

→ InfoTur (www.visitbolivia.org) offices are found in most of the major tourist destinations. The amount of printed material available and the level of attention from staff can vary from place to place, and from visit to visit. Don't expect a lengthy conversation if you go just before lunch for example. Note that the posted opening hours are not always followed.

→ Ministerio de Culturas y Turismo (p217) Provides a register of official operators in the tourist industry.

→ There is plenty of competition between tourist operators in the most popular destinations and this is often reflected in their website content, which often features abundant information to make the company more attractive. This can be a useful research tool, provided you remember the context the information is provided in!

VISAS

→ Your passport must be valid for six months beyond the date of entry.

→ Charging of unofficial 'administration fees,' particularly at remote borders, is not unusual. The path of least resistance is to just pay and go.

→ US citizens need a visa to visit Bolivia (a 90-day visa valid for 10 years costs US$160). Theoretically it is possible to obtain the visa upon arrival in Bolivia, but some airlines will not let you board your flight without one and the US embassy advises to get a visa before traveling.

→ Citizens of Australia, Canada, New Zealand, most European countries and most South American countries do not need a visa and will be granted an entry stamp valid for 30 days.

→ If you want to stay longer, you can get a free 30-day extension at the immigration office in any major city. The maximum time travelers are permitted to stay is 90 days.

→ Overstayers can be forced to pay a fine – payable at the immigration office or airport – and may face ribbons of red tape at the border or airport when leaving the country.

→ In addition to a valid passport and visa, citizens of some African, Middle Eastern and Asian countries may require 'official permission' from the Bolivian Ministry of Foreign Affairs before a visa will be issued.

→ Personal documents – passports and visas – must be carried at all times, especially in lowland regions. It's safest to carry photocopies rather than originals, but if you are going anywhere near a border area (even if you don't actually cross) you should have your real passport with you.

VOLUNTEERING

→ There are hundreds of voluntary and non-governmental organizations (NGOs) working in Bolivia, making this a popular spot to volunteer.

→ Many of the opportunities follow the pay-to-volunteer model, and often include room and board, costing anywhere from US$200 to US$1000 per month. Options to do free volunteer work are more limited.

→ Research your placement carefully. Be aware that some profit organizations offer 'internship' or 'volunteer' opportunities, when in reality it's unpaid work in exchange for free trips or activities.

→ Government-sponsored organizations or NGOs offer longer-term programs for which you receive an allowance, predeparture briefings and ongoing organizational support.

→ Church-affiliated or religious organizations offer short-term opportunities, often on a group basis.

→ Smaller volunteer organizations (sometimes profit-based) offer independent travelers the opportunity to work on community projects. These usually have a two- or four-week minimum for which you pay.

→ **Animales SOS** (📞 230-8080; www.animalessos.org; Av Chacaltaya 1759, Achachicala) An animal-welfare group caring for mistreated or abused stray animals.

→ **Sustainable Bolivia** (📞 423-3783; www.sustainablebolivia.org; Julio Arauco Prado 230) Cochabamba-based not-for-profit with a variety of volunteering programs, both short- and long-term, through 22 local organizations. Also offers Spanish language classes.

→ **Volunteer Bolivia** (📞 7171-2491; www.volunteerbolivia.org; Ecuador E-0342) Arranges short- and long-term volunteer work, Spanish language classes in Cochabamba and homestay programs throughout Bolivia.

→ **WWOOF Latin America** (www.wwooflatinamerica.com) Sets you up with volunteer opportunities on organic farms.

WORK

→ Teachers can try for private-school positions, with the greatest demand in math, science or social studies. New or unqualified teachers must forfeit two months' salary in return for their training.

→ Other travelers find work in bars, hostels or with tour operators.

→ **Centro Boliviano-Americano** (www.cba.edu.bo) For paid work, qualified English-language teachers can try the professionally run Centro Boliviano-Americano in La Paz, with branches in other cities. Accredited teachers can expect to earn up to US$500 per month for a full-time position.

ℹ️ Getting There & Away

A landlocked country, Bolivia has numerous entry/exit points, and you can get here by boat, bus, train, plane, bike and on foot. Some places are easier to travel through and more accessible than others.

Flights, cars and tours can be booked online at lonelyplanet.com/bookings.

AIR

There are direct services to most major South American cities, and the flights to/from Chile and Peru are the cheapest. Santa Cruz is an increasingly popular entry point from European hubs. Due to altitude-related costs, it is more expensive to fly into La Paz than Santa Cruz. High season for most fares is from early June to late August, and from mid-December to mid-February.

Airports & Airlines

Bolivia's principal international airports are La Paz's El Alto International Airport (p217), formerly known as John F Kennedy Memorial, Santa Cruz's Viru-Viru International Airport (p271) and Cochabamba's Jorge Wilstermann International Airport (p255).

The national airline is the state-owned **Boliviana de Aviación** (BOA; ☑ 901-105-010; www.boa. bo), which has international flights to Madrid, Barcelona and Miami.

Aerolíneas Argentinas (☑ 800-100-242; www. aerolineas.com.ar) Daily flights from Santa Cruz to Buenos Aires.

Amaszonas (☑ 901-105-500; www.amaszonas. com) Flights to Asunción, Buenos Aires, Cuzco, Iquique and Montevideo.

American Airlines (☑ 800-100-541; www. aa.com) Daily flights from Santa Cruz to Miami.

Avianca (☑ 1-866-998-3357; www.avianca. com) Flights from La Paz to Bogotá and Lima.

Copa (☑ 800-102-672; www.copaair.com) Flights from Santa Cruz to Panama, with onward connections.

Gol (☑ 800-122-201; www.voegol.com.br) Flights from Santa Cruz to Rio de Janeiro and other destinations.

LAND

Bus

Depending on which country you enter from, some intercountry buses booked through an agency might cover your entire route; at other times you'll switch to an associated bus company once you cross the border. If traveling by local bus, you'll usually need to catch onward buses once you've made your border crossing.

Car & Motorcycle

You can enter Bolivia by road from any of the neighboring countries. The Trans-Chaco road from Paraguay is in a dreadful state, especially beyond the town of Mariscal Estigarribia, and should be considered only if you are driving a 4WD. The main routes from Argentina, Brazil, Chile and Peru pose no significant problems.

Foreigners entering Bolivia from another country need a *hoja de ruta* (circulation card, www. dgsc.gob.bo/hoja-ruta.php), available from the Servicio Nacional de Tránsito/Aduana at the border. This document must be presented and stamped at all police posts – variously known as *trancas, tránsitos* or *controles* – which are found along highways and just outside major cities. *Peajes* (tolls) are often charged at these checkpoints and vehicles may be searched for contraband.

❶ Getting Around

Transportation to most places in Bolivia is covered by small bus, boat, train and airline companies. Over the past few years Bolivia's roads have vastly improved as the government has invested in paving major roads. However road closures caused by protests, construction or landslides are common, as are flooded roads and rivers with too little water to traverse. Air transit is also getting easier and slightly more cost effective and prevalent, especially in the lowlands.

AIR

Air travel within Bolivia is inexpensive and the quickest and most reliable way to reach out-of-the-way places. It's also the only means of transportation that isn't washed out during the wet season. When weather-related disruptions occur, planes eventually get through, even during summer flooding in northern Bolivia. Schedules tend to change often and cancellations are frequent, so plan ahead.

Amaszonas Domestic connections to La Paz, Santa Cruz, Uyuni, Sucre, Cochabamba, Rurrenabaque, Trinidad and Riberalta.

Boliviana de Aviación Flights to La Paz, Santa Cruz, Cochabamba, Potosí, Sucre, Oruro, Uyuni, Tarija, Trinidad, Chimore, Cobija and Yacuiba.

TAM (☑ 2-268-1111; www.tam.bo) Flights to La Paz, Santa Cruz, Tarija, Rurrenebaque, Riberalta, Sucre, Cochabamba and Cobija.

BOAT

The only public ferry service in Bolivia operates between San Pedro and San Pablo, across the narrow Estrecho de Tiquina (Straits of Tiquina) on Lake Titicaca. You can travel by launch or rowboat to any of Lake Titicaca's Bolivian islands. Boats and tours are available from Huatajata to the Huyñaymarka islands in the lake's southernmost extension.

There's no scheduled passenger service on the Amazon, so travelers almost invariably wind up on some sort of cargo vessel. The most popular route is from Guanay to Rurrenabaque. Thanks to the Guayaramerín road, there's little cargo transportation further down the Río Beni to Riberalta these days.

BUS

Bus travel is cheap and relatively safe in Bolivia, but can also be quite uncomfortable and nerve-wracking at times. Buses are the country's most popular type of transport, and come in various forms.

Types Long-distance bus services are called *flotas*, large buses are known as *buses*, three-quarter (usually older) ones are called *micros*, and minibuses are just that.

Terminals If looking for a bus terminal, ask for *la terminal terrestre* or *la terminal de buses*. Each terminal charges a small fee (a couple of bolivianos), which you pay to an agent upon boarding or when purchasing a ticket at the counter.

Theft There have been numerous reports of items disappearing from buses' internal overhead compartments and luggage holds. Put any valuables into your day pack and keep them close to you in the bus. Try to watch as your luggage is loaded – there have been instances of bags becoming 'lost' or 'disappearing.' You will be given a baggage tag, which you must show when reclaiming your bag. A lock is a good idea: very occasionally belongings are stolen from within bags while they are in the hold.

Departures Except on the most popular runs, most companies' buses depart at roughly the same time to the same destinations, regardless of how many companies are competing for the same business. Between any two cities, you should have no trouble finding at least one daily bus. On the most popular routes, you can choose between dozens of daily departures.

Safety It's always a good idea to check the vehicles of several companies before purchasing your ticket. Some buses are ramshackle affairs with broken windows, cracked windshields and worn tires; it's best to stay away from these and look for a better vehicle, even if it means paying a little more. Don't try to save on safety.

The only choices you'll have to make are on major, long-haul routes, where the better companies offer *coche* (or 'bus'), *semicama* (half-sleeper, with seats that recline a long way and footrests) and *cama* (sleeper) services. The cost can be double for sleeper service, but is often worth it for the comfort. Tourist buses to major destinations such as Copacabana and

Uyuni are twice the price of standard buses, but are safer and more comfortable.

The DVD player on the newest buses will be in better shape than the reclining seats (expect Van Damme all night), heaters *may* function, snacks *may* be served and toilets (yes, toilets) *may* work. Be prepared.

Prices vary according to the different standard of bus (from the more luxurious *bus cama* service to the ancient Bluebird-style buses) and the length of trip (whether overnight or short day hop).

CAR & MOTORCYCLE

The advantages of a private vehicle include flexibility, access to remote areas and the chance to seize photo opportunities. Most major roads have now been paved but some (especially in the Amazon) are in varying stages of decay, making high-speed travel impossible and inadvisable.

Preparation The undaunted should prepare their expeditions carefully. Bear in mind that spare parts are a rare commodity outside cities. A high-clearance 4WD vehicle is essential for off-road travel. You'll need tools, spare tires, a puncture repair kit, extra gas and fluids, and as many spare parts as possible. For emergencies, carry camping equipment and plenty of rations. You'll also need to purchase a good travel insurance policy back home (check with your credit card to see if it covers rental insurance in Bolivia).

Fuel types Low-grade (85-octane) gasoline (*nafta*) and diesel fuel (*gasoil*) is available at *surtidores* (gas stations) in all cities and major towns, but in more remote areas these can sometimes run out. Before embarking on any long journeys make sure you know where you can get fuel and, if necessary, take it with you. Gasoline costs about B$8.68 per liter for foreigners (the price of fuel is subsidized for Bolivians, who pay about half the price) and more in remote areas.

Motorcycles In lowland areas where temperatures are hot and roads are scarce, motorbikes are popular for zipping around the plazas, as well as exploring areas not served by public transportation. They can be rented from about B$100 per day from moto-taxi stands. Note that many travel insurance policies will not cover you for injuries arising from motorbike accidents.

HITCHHIKING

Thanks to relatively easy access to *camiones* and a profusion of buses, hitchhiking isn't really necessary or popular in Bolivia. Still, it's not unknown and drivers of *movilidades* – *coches* (cars), *camionetas* (pickup trucks), NGO vehicles, gas trucks and other vehicles – are usually happy to pick up passengers when they have room. Always ask the price, if any, before climbing aboard, even for short distances. If they do charge, it should amount to about half the bus fare for the same distance.

Hitching is never entirely safe, and we don't recommend it. Travelers who hitch should understand that they are taking a small but potentially serious risk.

LOCAL TRANSPORTATION
Micro, Minibus & Trufi

Micros (half-size buses) are used in larger cities and are Bolivia's least expensive form of public transportation. They follow set routes, with the route numbers or letters usually marked on a placard behind the windshield. There is also often a description of the route, including the streets taken to reach the end of the line. They can be hailed anywhere along their route, though bus stops are starting to pop up in some bigger cities. When you want to disembark, move toward the front and tell the driver or assistant where you want them to stop.

Minibuses and *trufis* (which may be cars, vans or minibuses), also known as *rapiditos* or *colectivos,* are prevalent in larger towns and cities, and follow set routes that are numbered and described on placards. They are always cheaper than taxis and nearly as convenient if you can get the hang of them. As with *micros,* you can board or alight anywhere along their route.

Taxi

In cities and towns, taxis are relatively inexpensive. Few are equipped with meters, but in most places there are standard per-person fares for short hauls. In some places, taxis are collective and behave more like *trufis,* charging a set rate per person. However, if you have three or four people all headed for the same place, you may be able to negotiate a reduced rate for the entire group.

TOURS

Many organized tours run out of La Paz or towns closest to the attractions you're likely to wish to visit. Tours are a convenient way to visit a site when you are short of time or motivation, and are frequently the easiest way to visit remote areas. They can also be relatively cheap, depending on the number of people in your group and the mode of transport.

There are scores of companies offering trekking, mountain climbing and rainforest-adventure packages around Bolivia. For climbing in the Cordilleras, operators offer customized expeditions and can arrange anything from guide and transportation to equipment, porters and a cook. Some also rent trekking equipment.

It's best to check an agency's website first, before making contact and bookings.

TRAIN

Train fares range from B$11 to B$240, depending on the class and distance. Prices are competitive with bus fares and trains are more comfortable, but typically they are quite a bit slower.

Empresa Ferroviaria Andina (www.fca.com.bo) Operates the western network from Oruro to Villazón on the Argentinian border. Note that at research time trains were not running south of Uyuni due to track damage.

Ferroviaria Oriental (www.fo.com.bo) Covers eastern Bolivia, operating a line from Santa Cruz to the Brazilian frontier at Quijarro, where you can cross to the Pantanal. An infrequently used service goes south from Santa Cruz to Yacuiba on the Argentine border.

Tren Turístico Guaraní (www.ferroviaria-andina.com.bo/tren_turistico_fca) A tourist service departing every second Sunday of the month between El Alto and Tiwanaku.

Brazil

POP 208 MILLION

Best Places to Eat

➜ Maní (p337)

➜ Taypá (p363)

➜ Ostradamus (p354)

➜ Flor do Luar (p424)

➜ Rocka Beach Lounge (p329)

Best Places to Stay

➜ Mirante do Gavião Amazon Lodge (p423)

➜ Parador Casa da Montanha (p353)

➜ Bonito Paraiso Beach House (p330)

➜ Toca da Coruja (p395)

➜ Hotel Emiliano (p313)

Why Go?

Brazil. The mere whisper of its name awakens the senses with promises of paradise: cerulean waters giving way to over 7000km of sun-kissed sands; music-filled metropolises and idyllic tropical islands; enchanting colonial towns and rugged red-rock canyons; majestic waterfalls and crystal-clear rivers; lush rainforests and dense jungles; gorgeous people and the Beautiful Game. It's all here in spectacular cinematic overload.

The country has enthralled for centuries for good reason: every bit of the hyperbole is unequivocally true. It all climaxes in Brazil's most famous celebration, Carnaval, which storms though the country's cities and towns like a best-of blitz of hip-shaking samba, dazzling costumes and carefree lust for life, but Brazilians hardly check their passion for revelry at Lent. The Brazilian Way – O Jeito Brasileiro – embodies the country's lust for life, and will seize you in its sensational clutches every day of the year.

When to Go
Rio de Janeiro

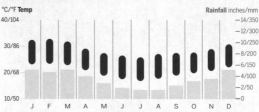

Dec–Feb Summer sizzles in the lead-up to Carnaval. Rainy season in the Amazon.

Sep–Nov Crowds dissipate as spring brings serenity and pleasant temperatures.

Mar–Jun Low season offers good-value travel, moderate temperatures and a sunny Northeast.

Entering the Country

There are many places to cross into Brazil, with some borders quite remote (eg in the Amazon and the northern reaches of the country), while others see a great deal of traffic. The most popular and easiest crossings are near Foz do Iguaçu (to reach Argentina) and in Chuy (for Uruguay). Make sure you have your proper documents in order *before* you reach the border – namely your Brazilian visa (if entering Brazil) and your Bolivian visa if heading that way.

ONE-WEEK ITINERARY

Start off in the Cidade Maravilhosa, aka Rio de Janeiro. Spend two days taking in grand views from the forested mountaintops overlooking the city (atop Pão de Açúcar and Cristo Redentor), leaving time for relaxing on Ipanema Beach, biking along Copacabana Beach and strolling through the historic center. One night, take in a samba club in Lapa. On days three and four, fly up to Salvador for a heady dose of Afro-Brazilian culture. Check out the brightly painted colonial buildings of the Pelourinho, take in a dazzling dance performance of the Balé Folclórico da Bahia and feast on seafood at Pelô Bistrô. On your fifth day, make a day trip out to Morro de São Paulo for a slice of tropical, car-free paradise. Beat the sunrise for an early-morning flight down to Iguaçu Falls (via São Paulo). Spend the first day exploring the Brazilian side of the majestic waterfalls. On your last day, cross to the Argentine side for a walk through rainforest and a boat trip near the thundering falls

Essential Food & Drink

Feijoada Rich stew of black beans and pork traditionally served on Saturday or Sunday.

Petiscos (appetizers) The perfect match to a cold *cerveja* (beer).

Agua de coco (coconut water) Sometimes served straight from the nut.

Sucos (juices) Available in myriad flavors at the corner juice bar.

Top Tips

➡ Brazil is massive! Rather than trying to see it all, focus on one or two regions.

➡ Download WhatsApp and set up your profile. Tour operators, guides, restaurants, guesthouses and everyone else uses it.

➡ Using a ride-sharing app (like Uber, 99Taxis or Easy Taxi) to get around major towns and cities is generally faster and cheaper than using a traditional taxi.

FAST FACTS

Currency Real (R$)

Visas Required for Americans, Australians, Canadians and various other nationalities.

Money ATMS are widespread in Brazil. Credit cards are accepted at most restaurants, shops and hotels.

Capital Brasília

Emergency 190 (police)

Language Portuguese

BRAZIL

Exchange Rates

Australia	A$1	R$2.68
Canada	C$1	R$2.80
Euro	€1	R$4.27
New Zealand	NZ$1	R$2.53
UK	UK£1	R$4.76
US	US$1	R$3.71

For current exchange rates, see www.xe.com.

Daily Costs

➡ Dorm bed: R$40–80; standard double room in a hotel: R$160–300

➡ Sandwich and drink in a juice bar: R$18–25; dinner for two in a midrange restaurant: R$80–160

Resources

Embratur (www.visitbrasil. com)

Rio Times (www.riotimes online.com)

What About São Paulo (http://whataboutsao paulo.com)

Lonely Planet (www.lonely planet.com/brazil)

Brazil Highlights

1 Rio de Janeiro (p304) Falling under the seductive spell of Rio amid the whirlwind of wild samba clubs, sizzling sands and soaring peaks.

2 Iguaçu Falls (p358) Feeling the breath of Mother Nature's ferocious roar at these jaw-dropping waterfalls.

3 Fernando de Noronha (p392) Digging into some of the world's most pristine sands.

4 Amazon Jungle (p424) Spying pointy-toothed piranhas and glowing caiman eyes while cruising the mighty Amazon.

5 Ouro Prêto (p344) Meandering along cobblestones in the cinematic colonial mountain town.

6 Salvador (p375) Following delirious drumbeats through the colonial center during regular evening street parties.

7 Pantanal (p364) Shutter-stalking spectacular animals in the home to some of Brazil's best wildlife watching.

8 Bonito (p371) Snorkeling in crystal-clear rivers, hiking through forests, cave exploring and relaxing in waterfalls.

9 Parque Nacional da Chapada Diamantina (p381) Hiking surreal landscapes in this dramatic national park.

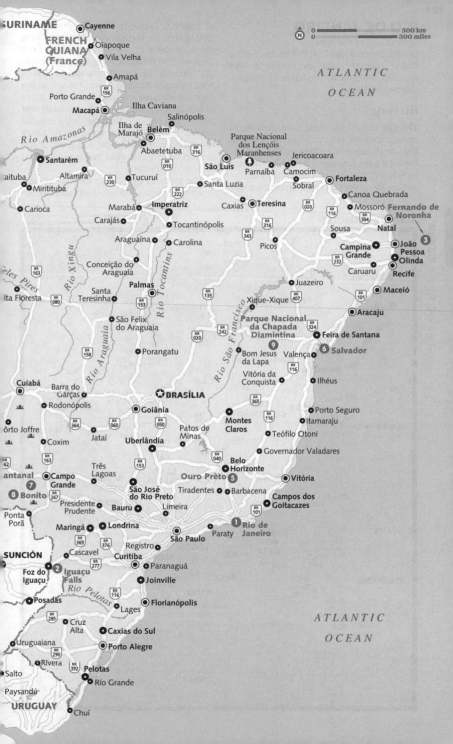

RIO DE JANEIRO

0XX21 / POP 6.5 MILLION

Golden beaches and lush mountains, samba-fueled nightlife and spectacular football matches: welcome to the Cidade Maravilhosa (Marvelous City).

History

The city earned its name from early Portuguese explorers, who entered the huge bay, Baía de Guanabara, in January 1502, and believing it a river, named it Rio de Janeiro (January River). The French were actually the first settlers along the bay, establishing the colony of Antarctic France in 1555. The Portuguese, fearing that the French would take over, gave them the boot in 1567 and remained from then on. The Portuguese supported their colony through the horrific practice of slavery, with captured Africans brought to toil on the sugar plantations and later in the gold mines of Minas Gerais. In 1763, with a population of 50,000, Rio replaced Salvador as the colonial capital. By 1900, after a coffee boom, heavy immigration from Europe and internal migration by working-class residents, Rio had 800,000 inhabitants.

The 1920s to 1950s were Rio's golden age, when it became an exotic destination for in-

Rio de Janeiro

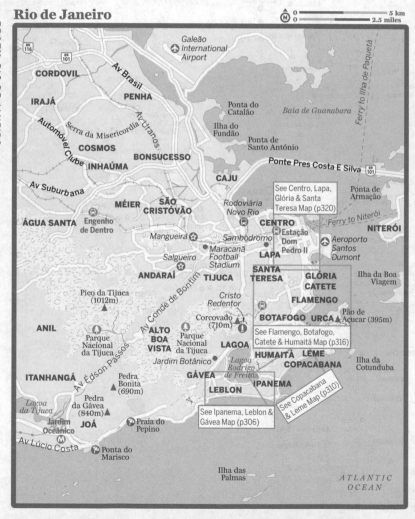

ternational high society. But by the time the capital was moved to Brasília in 1960, Rio was already grappling with problems that continue to this day. Immigrants poured into *favelas* (slums; informal communities) from poverty-stricken areas of the country, swelling the number of urban poor and increasing the chasm between the haves and have-nots.

Things were looking up at the turn of the 21st century as Rio's economy boomed, and the city played a starring role in both the 2014 FIFA World Cup and the 2016 Olympic Games – the first South American city to host the event. Sadly, the good times came crashing to an end by 2017, with a big recession, soaring unemployment and rising crime rates. Despite the challenges, Rio has seen major improvements, notably a new metro line to Barra da Tijuca and a revitalized swath of downtown – with new museums and a mural-lined promenade near Praça Mauá.

◎ Sights

◎ Ipanema & Leblon

Boasting magnificent beaches and pleasant tree-lined streets, Ipanema and Leblon are Rio's loveliest destinations and the favored residence for young, beautiful (and wealthy) *cariocas*. Microcultures dominate the beach, often centering around *postos* (elevated stands where lifeguards sit). **Posto 9** (Map p306; off Vieira Souto), off Vinícius de Moraes, is the gathering spot for the beauty crowd; nearby, in front of Farme de Amoedo, is the gay section; **Posto 11** (Map p306; off Delfim Moreira) in Leblon attracts families.

◎ Gávea, Jardim Botânico & Lagoa

The northern border of Ipanema and Leblon is formed by the Lagoa Rodrigo de Freitas, a saltwater lagoon fronted by the high-rent districts of Gávea, Jardim Botânico and Lagoa. The lake is encircled by a 7.2km walking and cycling path, with bikes and paddleboats available for hire along the east side of the lake. Verdant botanical gardens lie to the west.

★**Jardim Botânico**   GARDENS
(☑21 3874-1808; www.jbrj.gov.br; Jardim Botânico 920; R$15; ⊙noon-6pm Mon, 8am-6pm Tue-Sun) This exotic 137-hectare garden, with more than 8000 plant species, was designed by order of the Prince Regent Dom João (later to become Dom João VI) in 1808. The garden is

quiet and serene on weekdays and blossoms with families on weekends. Highlights of a visit here include the row of palms (planted when the garden first opened), the Amazonas section, the lake containing the huge Vitória Régia water lilies, and the enclosed **orquidário**, home to 600 species of orchids.

Parque Lage   PARK
(☑21 2334-4088; www.eavparquelage.rj.gov.br; Jardim Botânico 414; ⊙8am-5pm Apr-Nov, to 6pm Dec-Mar) FREE This beautiful park lies at the base of the Floresta da Tijuca, about 1km from Jardim Botânico. It has English-style gardens, little lakes, and a mansion that houses the **Escola de Artes Visuais** (School of Visual Arts), which hosts free art exhibitions and occasional performances. The park is a tranquil place and the cafe here offers a fine setting for a coffee or a meal.

◎ Copacabana & Leme

The scalloped beach of Copacabana begins northeast of Ipanema. Once a destination for international jet-setters, Copacabana is the city's somewhat ragged tourist magnet, with dozens of oceanfront hotels and sidewalk restaurants. The population density is high here and mixes old-timers, favela kids and tourists, and high and low culture.

◎ Botafogo & Urca

Just north of Copacabana, Botafogo and Humaitá are desirable neighborhoods with vibrant nightlife and cutting-edge restaurants. East of Botafogo, Urca retains a peaceful vibe, and is famed for Pão de Açúcar (Sugarloaf Mountain), which shadows its quiet streets.

★**Pão de Açúcar**   MOUNTAIN
(Sugarloaf Mountain; Map p316; ☑21 2546-8400; www.bondinho.com.br; Av Pasteur 520, Urca; adult/child R$85/42; ⊙8am-8pm) Seen from the peak of Pão de Açúcar, Rio is undoubtedly a *Cidade Maravilhosa* (Marvelous City). There are many good times to make the ascent, but sunset on a clear day is the most rewarding. Two cable cars connect to the summit, 395m above Rio. At the top, the city unfolds beneath you, with Corcovado mountain and Cristo Redentor (Christ the Redeemer) off to the west, and Copacabana Beach to the south.

◎ Flamengo & Around

To the north of Botafogo, residential neighborhoods include low-key Flamengo, leafy

Ipanema, Leblon & Gávea

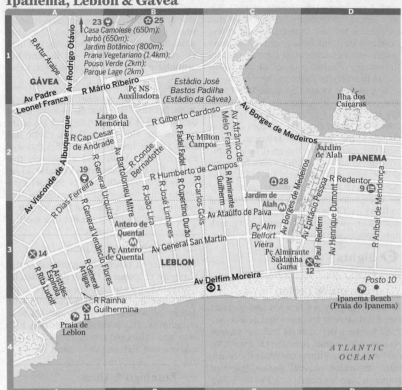

Ipanema, Leblon & Gávea

BRAZIL RIO DE JANEIRO

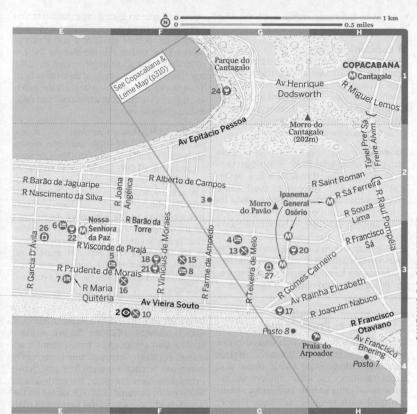

Laranjeiras and, further west, Cosme Velho, above which looms Cristo Redentor (Christ the Redeemer) atop Corcovado. Following the curve of the bay north is **Parque do Flamengo** (Map p316; Av Infante Dom Henrique), home to cycling trails, sports fields, and several monuments and museums.

★**Cristo Redentor**   MONUMENT
(Christ the Redeemer; ☑21 2558-1329; www.tremdo corcovado.rio; cog train station, Cosme Velho 513; adult/child R$75/49; ⊙8am-7pm) Standing atop Corcovado (which means 'hunchback'), Cristo Redentor gazes out over Rio, a placid expression on his well-crafted face. The mountain rises straight up from the city to 710m, and at night the brightly lit 38m-high open-armed statue – all 1145 tons of him – is visible from nearly every part of the city.

Museu da República   MUSEUM
(Map p316; ☑21 2127-0324; http://museuda republica.museus.gov.br; Rua do Catete 153; R$6,

Wed & Sun free; ⊙10am-5pm Tue-Fri, 11am-6pm Sat & Sun) The Museu da República, located in the Palácio do Catete, has been wonderfully restored. Built between 1858 and 1866, and easily distinguished by the bronze condors on its eaves, the palace was home to the president of Brazil from 1896 until 1954, when President Getúlio Vargas committed suicide here. The museum has a good collection of art and artifacts from the Republican period, and it is also home to a small cafe, an art-house cinema and a bookstore.

👁 Santa Teresa & Lapa

On the southwestern edge of Centro, Lapa is a ramshackle district that's also the epicenter of Rio's nightlife, with dozens of samba-filled bars and clubs, and late-night street parties. Uphill from Lapa, Santa Teresa is a picturesque neighborhood of winding streets and old mansions that have been

BRAZIL RIO DE JANEIRO

restored by the many artists and bohemian characters who have settled there.

★ Escadaria Selarón   LANDMARK

(Map p320; btwn Joaquim Silva & Pinto Martins, Lapa) One of Rio's best-loved attractions, the steps leading up from Joaquim Silva became a work of art when Chilean-born artist Jorge Selarón decided to cover them with colorful mosaics. A dedication to the Brazilian people, the 215 steps are a vivid riot of color.

Bonde   CABLE CAR

(Map p320; return ticket R$20; ⊙ 9am-5pm Mon-Fri, 10am-5:30pm Sat, 11am-4:30pm Sun; Ⓜ Carioca) The *bonde* is the last of the historic streetcars that once crisscrossed the city. Its romantic clatter through the cobbled streets is the archetypal sound of bohemian Santa Teresa. Currently the *bonde* travels every 15 to 20 minutes from the cable-car station in **Centro** (Map p320; Lélio Gama 65) over the scenic **Arcos da Lapa** (Map p320; Lapa) and as far as Largo do Guimarães in the heart of Santa Teresa.

⊙ Centro & Praça Mauá

Centro is Rio's business hub and also one of the city's oldest areas; it houses baroque churches, historic sites, scenic plazas and lavish theaters. Its wide boulevards are crisscrossed with narrow pedestrian streets sprinkled with colonial buildings. History aside, Centro has atmospheric open-air cafes and bars that draw the happy-hour crowd. North of Centro, Praça Mauá is the center of Rio's revitalized port district and has some outstanding new museums.

Boulevard Olímpico   AREA

(Map p320) Rio's formerly derelict port district has been reborn as a wide promenade lined with massive street art. A handful of renowned artists have painted spectacular murals on the old warehouses, though Brazilian artist Eduardo Kobra (www.eduardo kobra.com) deserves special mention for his jaw-dropping work entitled *Etnias* (Ethnicities). The massive mural stretches for 190m and features photogenic portraits of indigenous people from around the globe.

★ Museu de Arte do Rio   MUSEUM

(MAR; Map p320; ☑ 21 3031-2741; www.museudearte dorio.org.br; Praça Mauá 5; adult/child R$20/10, Tue free; ⊙ 10am-5pm Tue-Sun) Looming large over Praça Mauá, the MAR is an icon for the rebirth of Rio's once derelict port. The huge museum hosts wide-ranging exhibitions that focus on Rio in all its complexity – its people, landscapes, beauty, challenges and conflicts. Start off by taking the elevator to the top (6th) floor, and absorbing the view over the bay. There's also an excellent restaurant here. Then work your way down through the galleries, taking in a mix of international and only-in-Rio exhibitions.

★ Museu Histórico Nacional   MUSEUM

(Map p320; ☑ 21 3299-0324; http://mhn.museus. gov.br; off General Justo, near Praça Marechal Âncora; adult/child R$10/5, Sun free; ⊙ 10am-5:30pm Tue-Fri, 1-5pm Sat & Sun) Housed in the colonial arsenal, which dates from 1764, the impressive Museu Histórico Nacional contains relics relating to the history of Brazil from its founding to its early days as a republic. Highlights include gilded imperial coaches, the throne of Dom Pedro II, massive oil paintings depicting the horrific war with Paraguay and a full-sized model of a colonial pharmacy.

Museu do Amanhã   MUSEUM

(Map p320; www.museudoamanha.org.br; Rodrigues Alves 1; adult/child R$20/free, Tue free; ⊙ 10am-6pm Tue-Sun) Designed by famed Spanish architect Santiago Calatrava, this thoughtfully conceived science museum has interactive exhibitions on outer space, the earth and its biodiversity, humans (and our impact on the world), and the major global trends and challenges that lie in the future. In all, the museum takes a somewhat pessimistic view of the human species and its long-ranging impact on everything around it.

Activities

The fantastic hang glide off 510m Pedra Bonita, one of the giant granite slabs towering over the city, is a highlight of any trip to Brazil. Recommended operators include **Tandem Fly** (☑ 21 9996-6341, 21 2422-0941; www.riotandemfly.com.br; flight R$500), **Just Fly** (☑ 21 3593-4362; www.justflyinrio.blogspot.com; R$520) and **Asa Delta Flight in Rio** (☑ 21 99693-8800; www.facebook.com/asadeltaflightrio; tandem flight R$490).

⮌ Courses

Cook in Rio   COOKING

(Map p310; ☑ 21 98894-9857; www.cookinrio.com; 2nd fl, Belfort Roxo 161, Copacabana) Run by Simone Almeida, Cook in Rio is a hands-on one-day course that shows you how to prepare either *moqueca* (seafood stew) or *feijoada* (black bean and pork stew). You'll also learn how to make other sides and drinks including *aipim frito* (fried cassava slices), a perfect pot of rice, dessert and a masterful caipirinha (the secret's in the slicing of the lime).

Rio Samba Dancer DANCING
(☑21 98229-2843; www.riosambadancer.com; group/private class US$20/60, private class for 2/3 people US$65/90) English-speaking dance instructor Hélio Ricardo offers private and group dance classes in samba or *forró* (a popular music of the Northeast). To try out your new moves, take a samba class and night tour combo: you'll get a one-hour crash course, then head out to Lapa for a night of dancing in a club (US$60 per person, including guide, transportation and club admissions).

☞ Tours

Eat Rio Food Tours WALKING
(www.eatrio.net; tours from US$75) On these highly recommended small-group tours, you'll visit markets, snack bars and other foodie hot spots to taste a wide range of fruits, juices and street food little known outside Brazil. The English-speaking guides are excellent and provide culinary as well as cultural insights. The cost of the tour covers all food, including snacks and a big meal at the end.

Jungle Me HIKING
(☑21 4105-7533; www.jungleme.com.br; tours from R$195; ☀) This top-notch outfit offers excellent hiking tours through Parque Nacional da Tijuca led by knowledgeable guides. The eight-hour Tijuca Circuit (Peaks & Waterfalls tour) offers challenging walks up several escarpments with stunning views of Rio, followed by a refreshing dip in a waterfall. The Prainha & Grumari tour consists of a hike between scenic beaches in Rio's little-visited western reaches.

Rio by Bike CYCLING
(Map p310; ☑21 96871-8933; www.riobybike.com; Av NS de Copacabana 1085, Copacabana; tours R$100-135) Two Dutch journalists operate this biking outfit, and their excellent pedaling tours combine scenery with cultural insight. It's a great way to get an overview of the city, with guides pointing out landmarks and describing key events that have shaped Rio. Tours generally last three to four hours and travel mostly along bike lanes separated from traffic.

Rio Street Art Tour CULTURAL
(☑21 99762-8083; www.riostreetarttour.com; tours R$60-120) Nina Chini Gani's street-art tours

PARQUE NACIONAL DA TIJUCA

The Tijuca Forest is all that's left of the Atlantic rainforest that once surrounded Rio de Janeiro. This 39-sq-km tropical-jungle preserve is an exuberant green, with beautiful trees, creeks and waterfalls, mountainous terrain and high peaks. It has an excellent, well-marked trail system. Serious hikers climb the 1012m to the summit of Pico da Tijuca. It's hard to reach without a car. Numerous outfits lead hiking tours, including Jungle Me (p309) and **Rio Adventures** (☑21 3587-3282; www.rioadventures.com; hiking/climbing/rafting tours from R$180/370/450).

take small groups on foot or by van to explore Rio's vibrant urban-art scene. Tours last two to four hours, and cover Zona Sul, Zona Norte and the revitalized Port Zone. Nina's encyclopedic knowledge of Rio's urban artists gives guests a deeper understanding of the artworks while providing an alternative introduction to the city.

Brazil Expedition TOURS
(☑21 99998-2907; www.brazilexpedition.com; all-day city tours R$160) Friendly English-speaking guides run a variety of traditional tours around Rio, including trips to Cristo Redentor, hikes in Parque Nacional da Tijuca, game-day trips to Maracanã football stadium, street-art tours and favela (slum, informal community) tours.

Crux Eco CLIMBING
(☑21 3322-8765, 21 99392-9203; www.cruxeco.com.br; ☀) This reputable outfit offers a huge range of excursions and outdoor adventures. You can arrange a mountaineering adventure up Pão de Açúcar (R$470) or climb Corcovado, go rappelling (abseiling) down waterfalls, head off on full-day hikes through Floresta da Tijuca, or go on cycling and kayaking trips.

Free Walker Tours WALKING
(Map p320; ☑21 97101-3352; www.freewalkertours.com) This well-organized outfit runs a free walking tour that takes in a bit of history and culture in downtown Rio. You'll visit the Travessa do Comércio, Praça XV (Quinze) do Novembre, Cinelândia, the Arcos da Lapa and the Selarón steps, among other places. Although it's free, the guide asks for tips at

Copacabana & Leme

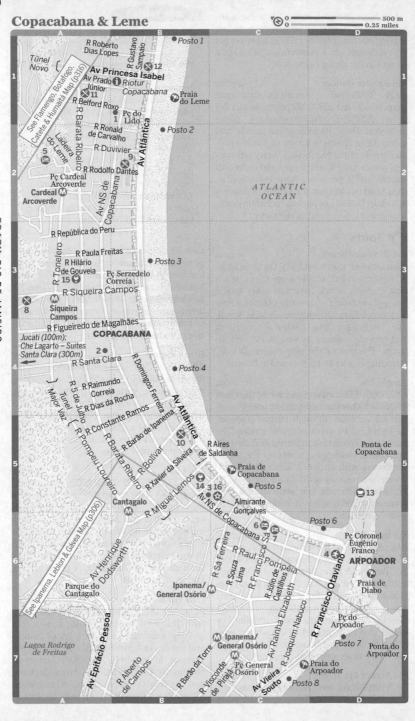

Map labels:

R Roberto Dias Lopes
R Gustavo Sampaio
Posto 1
Túnel Novo
Av Princesa Isabel
Av Prado Júnior
Riotur Copacabana
Praia do Leme
R Belford Roxo
Pç do Lido
R Ronald de Carvalho
Posto 2
R Duvivier
R Barata Ribeiro
R Rodolfo Dantés
Av Atlântica
See Flamengo, Botafogo, Catete & Humaitá Map (p316)
Ladeira do Leme
Pç Cardeal Arcoverde
Cardeal Arcoverde
Av NS de Copacabana
R República do Peru
R Paula Freitas
R Hilário de Gouveia
R Toneleiro
Posto 3
Pç Serzedelo Correia
R Siqueira Campos
Siqueira Campos
R Figueiredo de Magalhães
COPACABANA
Jucati (100m); Che Lagarto – Suites Santa Clara (300m)
R Santa Clara
R Raimundo Correia
R 5 de Julho
R Dias da Rocha
Tunel Maior Vaz
R Constante Ramos
R Pompeu Loureiro
R Barata Ribeiro
R Domingos Ferreira
Posto 4
Av Atlântica
R Barão de Ipanema
R Bolívar
R Aires de Saldanha
R Xavier da Silveira
R Miguel Lemos
Praia de Copacabana
Posto 5
Cantagalo
Almirante Gonçalves
See Ipanema, Leblon & Gávea Map (p306)
Av Henrique Dodsworth
Av NS de Copacabana
Ponta de Copacabana
Posto 6
Parque do Cantagalo
R Sá Ferreira
R Souza Lima
R Raul Pompéia
R Francisco Sá
R Júlio de Castilhos
Pç Coronel Eugénio Franco
ARPOADOR
Ipanema/General Osório
Praia de Diabo
Lagoa Rodrigo de Freitas
Av Epitácio Pessoa
R Alberto de Campos
R Barão da Torre
R Visconde de Pirajá
Pç General Osório
Ipanema/General Osório
Av Rainha Elizabeth
Av Joaquim Nabuco
Pç do Arpoador
Posto 7
Ponta do Arpoador
R Francisco Otaviano
Praia do Arpoador
Av Vieira Souto
Posto 8

ATLANTIC OCEAN

Scale: 0 — 500 m / 0 — 0.25 miles

Copacabana & Leme

the end: R$50 is fair for the insightful three-hour walk.

Fruit Brazil TOURS
(www.fruitbrazil.com; tours per person R$105) This outfit focuses on the tropical fruits of Brazil, taking small groups on an in-depth, 90-minute tasting tour through a local market in Ipanema. The market varies depending on the day of the week.

✨ Festivals & Events

One of the world's biggest and wildest parties, Carnaval in all its colorful, hedonistic bacchanalia is virtually synonymous with Rio. Although Carnaval is ostensibly just five days of revelry (Friday to Tuesday preceding Ash Wednesday), *cariocas* begin partying months in advance. The parade through the Sambódromo (samba parade ground), featuring elaborate floats flanked by thousands of pounding drummers and twirling dancers, is the culmination of the festivities, though the real action is at the parties about town.

Nightclubs and bars throw special costumed events. There are also free live concerts throughout the city (Largo do Machado, Arcos do Lapa, Praça General Osório), while those seeking a bit of decadence can head to various balls about town. *Bandas*, also called *blocos*, are one of the best ways to celebrate *carioca*-style. These consist of a procession of drummers and vocalists followed by anyone who wants to dance through the streets of Rio. Check Riotur for times and locations. *Blocos* in Santa Teresa and Ipanema are highly recommended.

The spectacular main parade takes place in the **Sambódromo** (www.sambadrome.com; Marques do Sapuçaí) near Praça Onze metro station. Before an exuberant crowd of some 30,000, each of 12 samba schools has its hour to dazzle the audience. Top schools compete

on Carnaval Sunday and Monday (February 23 and 24 in 2020, February 14 and 15 in 2021, and February 27 and 28 in 2021). The safest way of reaching the Sambódromo is by taxi or metro, which runs round the clock during Carnaval.

Liesa (Map p320; 📲 21 3213-5151; http://liesa. globo.com; Av Rio Branco 4, Centro; ⊙10am-4pm Mon-Fri Sep-Carnaval), the official samba school league, begins selling tickets in December or January, most of which get immediately snatched up by travel agencies then later resold at higher prices. Check with Riotur about where you can get them, as the official outlet can vary from year to year. At face value, tickets run R$190 to R$500. By Carnaval weekend, most tickets are sold out, but there are lots of scalpers. If you buy a ticket from a scalper (no need to worry about looking for them – they'll find you!), make sure you get both the plastic ticket with the magnetic strip and the ticket showing the seat number. The tickets for different days are color-coded, so double-check the date as well.

If you haven't purchased a ticket but still want to go, during Carnaval you can show up at the Sambódromo at around midnight. This is when you can get grandstand tickets for about R$50 from scalpers outside the gate. Make sure you check which sector your ticket is for. Most ticket sellers will try to pawn off their worst seats.

🛏 Sleeping

Zona Sul is the chic Rio zone where all the tourist action happens. Ipanema and Leblon are the most appealing Zona Sul neighborhoods to base yourself. The historic hillside bohemian quarter of Santa Teresa also appeals, and it's close to nightlife-centric Lapa, though it's far from the beaches. Other northern neighborhoods along the metro line (Botafogo, Flamengo and Catete) often

BRAZIL RIO DE JANEIRO

have cheaper options than the beachside southern neighborhoods.

Ipanema & Leblon

Mango Tree
HOSTEL $

(Map p306; ☑21 3083-5031; www.mangotree hostel.com; Prudente de Morais 594, Ipanema; dm R$40-55, d with/without bathroom R$220/160; ✴☎) In a cheery yellow house in Ipanema, this well-run hostel offers rooms with two-toned wood floors and a welcoming atmosphere. The back terrace with a bar provides open-air space for unwinding, and it's a great spot to meet other travelers. There's a kitchen, surfboard rental and plenty of activities on offer (including boat parties, surf outings and street art tours).

El Misti
HOSTEL $

(Map p306; ☑21 2246-1070; www.elmistihostel ipanema.com; Joana Angélica 47; dm/d from R$45/250; ✴☎) An excellent base in Ipanema, the friendly El Misti has simple, well-maintained dorm rooms (sleeping four to 12) as well as a few private rooms (two with balcony). All rooms have bathrooms. There's a pleasant cafe-bar on the ground floor where you can meet other travelers. Great location just a block from the beach, with a Bike Rio kiosk in front.

Thoughtful extras include a communal shower-bathroom, so you can still spend the day at the beach after you check out and have a chance to clean up before you fly home.

Bonita
HOSTEL $$

(Map p306; ☑21 2227-1703; www.bonitaipanema. com; Barão da Torre 107, Ipanema; dm from R$60, d with/without bathroom R$360/230; ✴@☎☷) This brightly painted, palm-fringed house has history: it's where bossa nova legend Tom Jobim lived from 1962 to 1965 and wrote some of his most famous songs. Rooms are clean but simply furnished, and most open onto a shared deck overlooking a small pool and patio.

Ipanema Beach House
HOSTEL $$

(Map p306; ☑21 3202-2693; www.beachhouse ipanema.com; Barão da Torre 485, Ipanema; dm R$60-85, d with/without bathroom from R$270/220; ☎☷) The location is fabulous, in a converted two-story house with a beautiful pool and yard, just a short stroll to the beach. The private rooms, while small, are bright and attractively furnished, and the common areas are quite enticing. On the downside, space is tight in the dorms (with three-tiered

bunk beds), and the wait for the communal bathrooms can be long.

Margarida's Pousada
POUSADA $$

(Map p306; ☑21 2239-1840; www.margaridas pousada.com; Barão da Torre 600, Ipanema; d from R$280, apt from R$360; ✴☎) Those seeking something smaller and cozier than a high-rise hotel should try this superbly located Ipanema pousada (guesthouse). You'll find 11 simply furnished rooms scattered about the low-rise building; the best have small verandas. Margarida also rents out several private, fully equipped apartments nearby.

Ipanema Inn
HOTEL $$$

(Map p306; ☑21 2523-6092; www.ipanemainn. com.br; Maria Quitéria 27, Ipanema; d R$580-720; ✴☎) Located just a short stroll from the beach, the Ipanema Inn is a simple hotel whose rooms have off-white ceramic tile floors and simple wood furnishings; some rooms are disappointingly small. *Superiores* (front-facing rooms) don't have ocean views.

Despite its shortcomings, the Ipanema Inn earns high marks for its friendly service and excellent on-site restaurant.

Gávea, Jardim Botânico & Lagoa

Pouso Verde
GUESTHOUSE $$

(☑21 2529-2942; www.pousoverde.com; Caminhoá 14, Jardim Botânico; s/d from R$260/300) On a quiet cobblestone street in a charming corner of Jardim Botânico, Pouso Verde has elegant, comfortably furnished rooms, the best of which have views of Cristo Redentor (Christ the Redeemer). The historic house, dating back to the 1890s, is packed with artwork, and the owners go out of their way to make guests feel at home. Excellent breakfasts.

Copacabana & Leme

Cabana Copa
HOSTEL $

(Map p310; ☑21 97154-9473; www.cabanacopa. com.br; Travessa Guimarães Natal 10, Copacabana; dm R$40-60, d R$150-180; ✴@☎) Top hostel honors go to this Greek-Brazilian-run gem in a colonial-style '50s house tucked away in a Copacabana cranny. Four- to 10-bed dorms prevail throughout the home, which is chock-full of original architectural details and a hodgepodge of interesting floorings. There's a lively bar and common areas.

The hostel also runs a brand-new all-suites building next door: a great option for travelers who want a private room without missing out on the social interaction of a hostel.

Marta Rio Guesthouse B&B $$
(Map p310; ☑21 2521-8568; www.martarioguest house.com; Francisco Sá 5, Copacabana; d R$350-580; ※☎) Marta, a gracious host with an innate sense of hospitality, opens up her home and rents out six comfortable rooms at this split-level penthouse overlooking the beach. The highlight is undoubtedly the outdoor veranda, which has gorgeous views over Copacabana.

**Che Lagarto –
Suites Santa Clara** HOSTEL $$
(☑21 3495-3133; www.chelagarto.com; Santa Clara 304, Copacabana; r with/without bathroom from R$260/180; ※@☎) On a tree-lined street in Copacabana's Bairro Peixoto neighborhood, this converted house has clean, simple and well-maintained rooms (all private, no dorms), and a small downstairs lounge where you can meet other travelers. The friendly staff gives out helpful advice, and can direct you to loads of activities.

Jucati APARTMENT $$
(☑21 2547-5422; www.edificiojucati.com.br; Tenente Marones de Gusmão 85, Copacabana; d/q from R$240/300; ※※) On a tranquil street overlooking a small park, Jucati has large, simply furnished serviced apartments with tile floors and small but serviceable kitchens. Most apartments have just one bedroom with a double bed, and a living room with either a bunk bed (*beliche*) or pull-out sofa bed. The small covered courtyard is a fine spot to unwind.

★Hotel Emiliano LUXURY HOTEL $$$
(Map p310; ☑21 3503-6600; www.emiliano.com. br; Av Atlântica 3804; d R$1600-2300; ※☎❄)
🌿 Rio's loveliest new hotel sits on a prime spot fronting Copacabana's southern shore. The rooms have a modernist aesthetic, with jacaranda wood furniture, artful lighting and tropical photographs by the artist Leonardo Finotti. The small rooftop pool and bar (for guests only) is a fabulous retreat, and the ground-floor restaurant serves outstanding cuisine – including a decadent weekend brunch (R$195 including drinks).

Other thoughtful touches include high-end bath products by Santapele, a free pair of Havaianas flip-flops, plus fruit and a free cocktail (enjoy it on the roof) upon arrival.

🛏 Botafogo & Urca

★Yoo2 BOUTIQUE HOTEL $$
(Map p316; ☑21 3445-2000; www.yoo2.com; Praia de Botafogo 242; d from R$350; ※☎❄) Yoo2, which opened in 2016, has taken a generic high-rise and transformed it into a captivating 138-room hotel with an avant-garde style. Glass elevators ascend up an interior adorned with street art, while the rooftop pool and bar offer 360° vistas over a jaw-dropping stretch of the city. Rooms are spacious and most have alluring views.

You can hire bikes, and the ground-floor restaurant is a fine place to try local microbrews while dining on creative Brazilian fusion fare (mains R$58 to R$77).

Injoy Hostel GUESTHOUSE $$
(Map p316; ☑21 3593-6662; www.injoyhostel.com; Estácio de Coimbra 80, Botafogo; dm R$43-59, d R$160-250; ※@☎) Despite the name, this place feels less like a hostel and more like a small guesthouse. Injoy has a mix of private doubles and cozy dorms set in a lovely house at the end of a tree-lined lane. Rooms are modern, very clean and well maintained, and each is named after a major city, with iconic photos from the destination decorating one wall. Friendly staff.

🛏 Flamengo & Around

★Maze Inn GUESTHOUSE $
(Map p316; ☑21 2558-5547; www.jazzrio.com; Casa 66, Tavares Bastos 414, Catete; s/d R$120/140, with panoramic view R$160/180) Set in the Tavares Bastos favela, the Maze Inn is a fantastic place to overnight for those looking for an alternative view of Rio. The rooms are uniquely decorated with original artworks by English owner and Renaissance man Bob Nadkarni, while the veranda offers stunning views of the bay and Pão de Açúcar (Sugarloaf Mountain).

Don't miss the jazz parties held on the first Friday of every month, or the **Sunday curry feasts** (Map p316; ☑21 97967-8270; www.themazerio.com/en/hoje-tem-curry; Casa 66, Tavares Bastos 414; buffet R$59; ⊙12:30-3:30pm Sun), when Bob's son cooks up delicious Indian curries.

🛏 Centro & Praça Mauá

Belga Hotel HOTEL $$
(Map p320; ☑21 2263-9086; www.belgahotel. com.br; Rua dos Andradas 129; d R$130-320) In a

beautifully restored building from the 1920s, this classy hotel is helping to breathe new life into an overlooked corner of downtown. The Belgian-owned pioneer has simple but comfortably priced rooms that are excellent value for the money (the best are the 'executive' rooms with French doors opening onto decorative balconies).

The **Belgian bistro** (Map p320; www.belga hotel.com.br; Rua dos Andradas 129; mains R$48-64; ⏱6:30am-10pm Mon-Fri, 7am-3pm Sat; 🛜🅿) on the ground floor is not to be missed.

🛏 Santa Teresa & Lapa

Books Hostel HOSTEL $
(Map p320; ☑21 3437-3783; www.bookshostel. com; Francisco Muratori 10, Lapa; dm R$45-75; ✳@🛜) In the heart of Lapa and true to the nature of the neighborhood, this party hostel is the appetizer for your crazy night out. Dorms have eye-catching graffiti art and there's a social bar styled like a *barraca* (stall) – rooms overlooking it don't allow for much sleep. All bathrooms are shared, and only some rooms have air-conditioning.

★Casa Beleza POUSADA $$
(Map p316; ☑21 98288-6764; www.casabeleza. com; Laurinda Santos Lobo 311, Santa Teresa; r R$290-470, villas R$650; ✳🛜🏊) This lovely property dates to the 1930s and was once a governor's mansion. Tropical gardens overlook the picturesque pool, and you can sometimes spot toucans and monkeys in the surrounding foliage. It's a small and peaceful operation, with just four guest rooms and one peacefully set villa (complete with rooftop deck offering panoramic views).

The kind multilingual family that runs the pousada lives on-site.

Mama Shelter BOUTIQUE HOTEL $$
(Map p320; ☑21 3980-0300; www.mamashelter. com; Paschoal Carlos Magno 5, Santa Teresa; r R$320-650; ✳🛜) Part of a budget-minded boutique-hotel chain, Mama Shelter has 55 colorful rooms, each with whimsical touches and bursting with personality. Lush greenery surrounds the property, and the various terraces make fine places to enjoy the tropical setting. The airy restaurant serves a mix of Brazilian classics and creatively topped pizzas, and the stylish bar is a destination in its own right.

Mama Shelter is in a good location within walking distance of Santa Teresa's epicenter, about 400m from Largo de Guimarães.

🍴 Eating

Leblon's Rua Dias Ferreira is home to Rio's densest concentration of quality restaurants (which transform into festive drinking dens as the evening progresses). Self-caterers should look out for the ubiquitous Rio grocery chain, Zona Sul – named after the city's most coveted zone.

🍴 Ipanema & Leblon

Joana PIZZA $
(Map p306; ☑21 98201-8044; www.facebook.com/joanapizzabar; Joana Angélica 47; pizzas R$24-30; ⏱6pm-midnight Tue-Sun; 🛜🅿) One block up from Ipanema Beach, this hip little spot with a small terrace fires up some of the best thin-crust pizzas in the Zona Sul. The creative toppings steal the show: grilled pumpkin and eggplant with cherry tomatoes (the Veggie), or thin slices of marinated steak with fresh goat cheese and mint (the Churrasco Turco).

You can match the pizzas with a range of excellent cocktails shaken up at the small side bar.

Vero ICE CREAM $
(Map p306; ☑21 3497-8754; Visconde de Pirajá 229; ice creams R$11-16, pizza slices R$13-16; ⏱10am-12:30am; 🅿) This artisanal Italian-run gelateria whips up Rio's best ice cream. You'll find more than two dozen rich and creamy temptations, including *gianduia* (chocolate with hazelnut), *caramelo com flor de sal* (caramel with sea salt), *figo com amêndoas* (fig with almond) and classic flavors such as *morango* (strawberry).

A counter out back serves delicious thin-crust pizzas, with creative options like caramelized pear or a cheese-free vegan option, as well as the classic margherita.

Quitéria BRAZILIAN $$
(Map p306; ☑21 2267-4603; www.ipanemainn. com.br/en/quiteria; Maria Quitéria 27; mains around R$53, lunch buffet weekday/weekends R$39/53; ⏱7am-11pm) Inside the Ipanema Inn (p312), this humble-looking place serves delectable contemporary Brazilian cooking. Seasonal, high-quality ingredients feature in the extensive lunch buffet, which draws mostly locals. By night the à la carte menu offers hits such as nicely turned out pork ribs with mashed baroa potatoes and cashew sauce, or grilled catch of the day with creamy rice and black-eyed beans.

SEASIDE VIEWS

Beachfront dining kiosks, rooftop bars and alfresco cafes secreted away in an old military fort are among some of the best places to enjoy a drink or a bite while taking in Rio's enchanting seascape.

Café de la Musique (Map p306; ✆21 97273-7467; www.facebook.com/cafedelamusique beach; Av Delfim Moreira; mains R$32-64; ◷8am-10pm Sun-Thu, to midnight Fri & Sat) Rio's most stylish kiosk is the go-to spot for high-end cocktails (R$35 to R$40) while watching the surf roll in. You can also dine alfresco on salads, sandwiches and seafood – or breakfast fare.

Espaço 7zero6 (Map p306; ✆21 2141-4992; www.espaco7zero6.com.br; Av Vieira Souto 706; set brunch R$100; ◷noon-midnight Mon-Thu, 8am-2pm & 6pm-midnight Fri-Sun) From its location on the top floor of the Hotel Praia Ipanema, this place has a jaw-dropping view of Ipanema Beach. Serves great Brazilian classics and a celebrated weekend brunch.

Cafe 18 do Forte (Map p310; ✆21 2523-0171; www.cafe18doforte.com.br; Av Atlântica & Francisco Otaviano; ◷10am-8pm Tue-Sun) Far removed from the hustle and bustle of Av Atlântica, this cafe has magnificent views of Copacabana Beach. At the outdoor tables you can sit beneath shady palm trees, enjoying craft brews and Brazilian fare. To get here, you'll have to pay admission to the Forte de Copacabana.

Espetto Carioca (✆21 3514-2111; off Av Atlântica, near Praça Almirante Júlio de Noronha; snacks R$16-32; ◷9am-midnight) At the northeast end of Leme, elevated over the beach, this peacefully set kiosk serves *espettos* (kebabs or skewers) and refreshing drinks. Nearby, you can watch fearless *carioca* kids diving off the seawall.

Barraca do Uruguai (Map p306; Posto 9, Ipanema Beach; sandwiches R$14-20; ◷noon-5pm) There's no need to leave the sands for a satisfying bite. Uruguai is a long-term favorite *barraca* (food stall) that serves scrumptious grilled chicken sandwiches, plus *agua de côco* (coconut water), caipirinhas and other refreshments. Look for the blue-and-white striped Uruguayan flag flying high over Ipanema beach.

Frontera BUFFET $$
(Map p306; ✆21 3289-2350; www.frontera.com.br; Visconde de Pirajá 128; food per kg R$65-70; ◷11:30am-11pm) Run by a Dutch chef, Frontera offers more than 60 plates at its lunch buffet, which features a mouthwatering assortment of grilled meats, baked casseroles and seafood pastas, plus grilled vegetables, salads, fresh fruits and desserts. Sushi and the dessert counter costs extra. Dark woods and vintage travel posters give it a cozier feel than most per-kilo places.

After 6pm Frontera offers all-you-can-eat pizzas (served *rodizio*-style), for R$20 to R$30, depending on the day (it's cheapest on Wednesdays).

Stuzzi ITALIAN $$
(Map p306; ✆21 2274-4017; www.stuzzibar.com.br; Dias Ferreira 48; sharing plates R$29-55, mains R$52-76; ◷7pm-1am Tue, to 3am Wed-Sat, to midnight Sun) This buzzing, uberpopular Leblon spot specializes in creative Italian tapas (such as roast lamb croquettes, and goat cheese, fig and honey bruschetta) and expertly mixed cocktails. The lively, candelit

tables on the sidewalk are the place to be; come early to score one.

★Zazá Bistrô Tropical FUSION $$$
(Map p306; ✆21 2247-9101; www.zazabistro.com.br; Joana Angélica 40; mains R$65-87; ◷7pm-midnight Mon-Thu, from noon Fri-Sun) Inside an art-filled and whimsically decorated converted house, Zazá serves beautifully prepared dishes with Asian accents, and uses organic ingredients when possible. Favorites include chicken curry with jasmine rice, flambéed prawns with risotto, and grilled fish served with caramelized plantain. Don't miss brilliantly creative cocktails like the Caramba Carambola, with Amazonian gin (or vodka), *carambola* (star fruit), ginger, mint and lemon.

✖ Gávea, Jardim Botânico & Lagoa

★Casa Camolese BRAZILIAN $$
(✆21 3514-8200; www.casacamolese.com.br; Jardim Botânico 983; mains R$42-70; ◷noon-midnight Mon-Sat, to 11pm Sun; ✆) One of the

Flamengo, Botafogo, Catete & Humaitá

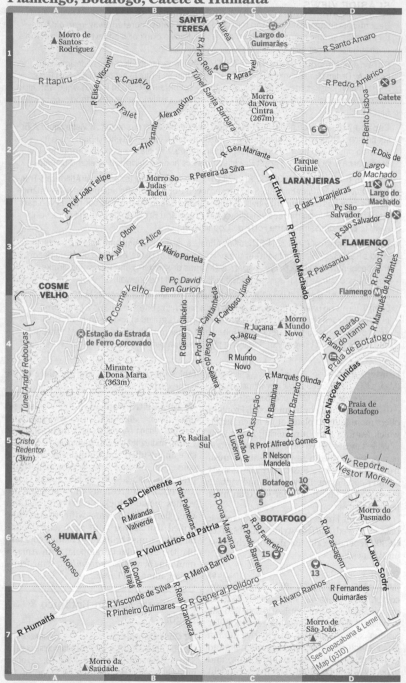

SANTA TERESA

R Áurea

Largo do Guimarães

R Santo Amaro

Morro de Santos Rodriguez

R Eliseu Visconti

R Cruzeiro

R Ar ao Reis

R Itapiru

Túnel Santa Barbara

R Falet

R Almirante Alexandrino

R Apraz´vel

R Pedro Américo

Catete

Morro da Nova Cintra (267m)

R Gen Mariante

Parque Guinle

R Dois de

Largo do Machado

R Pref João Felipe

R Pereira da Silva

Morro So Judas Tadeu

LARANJEIRAS

R Erfurt

R das Laranjeiras

Pç São Salvador

R São Salvador

FLAMENGO

R Dr Julio Otoni

R Alice

R Mário Portela

R Pinheiro Machado

R Paissandu

R Paulo IV

COSME VELHO

R Cosme Velho

R General Glicério

Pç David Ben Gurion

R Prof. Luis Cantanheda

R Cardoso Júnior

R Osvaldo Seabra

R Juçana

R Jaguá

Morro Mundo Novo

R Barão do Itambi

R Farani

R Marquês de Abrantes

Flamengo

Estação da Estrada de Ferro Corcovado

R Mundo Novo

Praia de Botafogo

Túnel André Rebouças

Mirante Dona Marta (363m)

R Marquês Olinda

Praia de Botafogo

Cristo Redentor (3km)

R Assunção

R Bambina

R Muniz Barreto

Av dos Nações Unidas

Pç Radial Sul

R Barão de Lucerna

R Prof Alfredo Gomes

R Nelson Mandela

Av Reporter Nestor Moreira

Botafogo

R São Clemente

R das Palmeiras

R Dona Mariana

BOTAFOGO

Morro do Pasmado

R Miranda Valverde

R 19 Fevereiro

R Paolo Barreto

R da Passagem

Av Lauro Sodré

HUMAITÁ

R Voluntários da Pátria

R João Afonso

R Conde de Irajá

R Mena Barreto

R Visconde de Silva

R Real Grandeza

R General Polidoro

R Álvaro Ramos

R Fernandes Quimarães

R Pinheiro Guimares

R Humaitá

Morro de São João

Morro da Saudade

See Copacabana & Leme Map (p310)

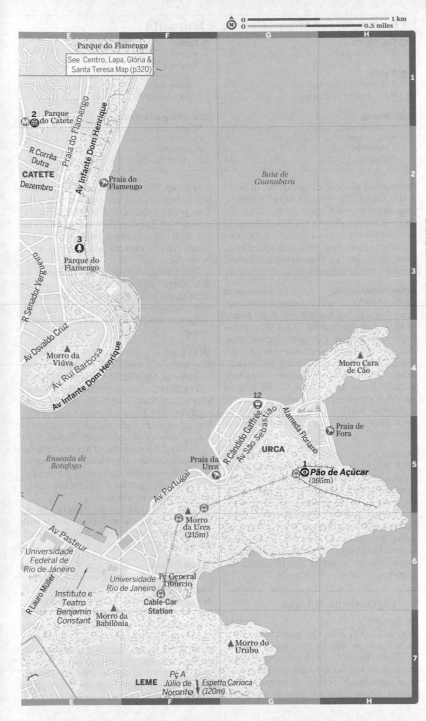

0   1 km
0   0.5 miles

Parque do Flamengo

See Centro, Lapa, Glória & Santa Teresa Map (p320)

2 Parque do Catete

R Corrêa Dutra

Av Infante Dom Henrique

Praia do Flamengo

CATETE

Dezembro

Baía de Guanabara

3 Parque do Flamengo

R Senador Vergueiro

Av Osvaldo Cruz

Morro da Viúva

Av Rui Barbosa

Av Infante Dom Henrique

Morro Cara de Cão

12

R Cândido Gaffrée

Av São Sebastião

Alameda Floriano

Praia de Fora

Praia da Urca

URCA

Enseada de Botafogo

Av Portugal

1 Pão de Açúcar (395m)

Morro da Urca (215m)

Av Pasteur

Universidade Federal de Rio de Janeiro

Universidade Rio de Janeiro

Pç General Tibúrcio

Instituto e Teatro Benjamin Constant

Cable-Car Station

R Lauro Müller

Morro da Babilônia

Morro do Urubu

LEME

Pç A Júlio de Noronha

Espetto Carioca (120m)

Flamengo, Botafogo, Catete & Humaitá

BRAZIL RIO DE JANEIRO

most talked-about openings in recent years is this beautifully designed eating, drinking and entertainment space overlooking the Jockey Club Brasileiro. Camolese is home to a microbrewery, a cafe, a live-music spot and a spacious restaurant, with soaring ceilings, glass walls and an elegant plant-trimmed terrace – the best place to be on clear nights.

Prana Vegetariano   VEGETARIAN $$
(☑21 2245-7643; www.pranavegetariano.com; Lopes Quintas 37, Jardim Botânico; mains around R$40; ⊙noon-4pm Mon-Sat; ☑) A short stroll from the Jardim Botânico's north exit, this very friendly vegetarian restaurant has garnered quite a following for its deliciously healthy meat-free plates. The small menu changes daily (check the website to see what's cooking), and features creative and filling lunch combinations, as well as great juices and smoothies, and decadent desserts.

Jarbô   FRENCH $$
(☑21 2259-2924; www.jarbocafe.com; Jardim Botânico 1008; mains R$38-67; ⊙noon-6:30pm Mon, 8am-6:30pm Tue-Sun; 🛜☑) Just outside the entrance to the Jardim Botânico (but inside the gates off the busy roadway), Jarbô is a great anytime favorite, with a wide-ranging menu encompassing tartines (open-faced sandwiches), eggs Benedict, Gorgonzola-topped salads or fancier fare like beet and goat cheese ravioli or duck confit.

✗ Copacabana & Leme

★Salomé   BISTRO $$
(Map p310; ☑21 2541-2416; www.facebook.com/salomebistro; Av Atlântica 994; mains R$48-65; ⊙6:30pm-midnight Tue-Thu, noon-midnight Fri-Sun; ☑) Run by the same people behind Ipanema's enormously popular Canastra (p321), Salomé brings a dash of style to the Leme beachfront. The easygoing open-sided bistro has vintage mirrors and curious wall hangings, potted palms and atmospheric lighting – though on fine days, the outdoor tables are the best place to enjoy high-quality small plates, grilled meats and seafood, and wines by the glass.

While small, the menu has plenty of variety, from grilled octopus to Moroccan lamb tagine with couscous. You'll also find seafood linguine, duck breast with eggplant caviar and salads with warm Saint-Marcellin cheese.

★El Born   SPANISH $$
(Map p310; ☑21 3496-1780; www.barelborn.com.br; Bolívar 13-57, sandwiches R$25-31; ⊙5pm-2am Mon-Fri, from 4pm Sat & Sun) Named after Barcelona's hippest, foodie-loving neighborhood, El Born fires up some of Rio's best tapas plates, such as Galician-style octopus, spicy prawns and tender Iberian ham. The setting channels a bit of old-world Spain, with rustic stone and brick walls, outdoor tables on the sidewalk, and ample bar seating, which is a fine spot for watching the dexterous bartenders in action.

Don't order too much. Waiters emerge from the kitchen and make the rounds with freshly cooked tapas plates; if you see something you like, take it!

Adega Pérola   TAPAS $$
(Map p310; ☑21 2255-9425; www.facebook.com/adegaperolariodejaneiro; Siqueira Campos 138; sharing plates R$24-46; ⊙11am-1am Mon-Thu, to 2am Fri & Sat) Going strong since 1957, this atmospheric bottle-lined eating and drinking den serves outstanding Spanish and Portuguese small plates, including marinated octopus, whole sardines, stuffed olives, codfish balls, fried squid and marinated shrimp. Just step inside and check out the culinary bounty on the long front counter.

Outdoor tables are a fine spot for an afternoon pick-me-up.

Galeto Sat's
BRAZILIAN $$
(Map p310; ✎ 21 2275-6197; Barata Ribeiro 7; mains R$30-76, lunch specials R$34; ⊘ 11am-5am) One of Rio's best roast-chicken spots, laid-back Galeto Sat's has earned many fans since it opened back in 1962. Grab a seat along the mirrored, tiled wall, order a *chope* (draft beer) and enjoy the scent of grilled spit-roasted birds before tucking into a filling meal. Price-wise you can't beat the *galeto completo*, a R$55 chicken feast for two.

★Churrascaria Palace
CHURRASCARIA $$$
(Map p310; ✎ 21 2541-5898; www.churrascaria palace.com.br; Rodolfo Dantas 16; all you can eat R$140; ⊘ noon-midnight; ✍) This elegantly set dining room is one of the best *churrascarias* (traditional barbecue restaurants) in town. Aside from juicy, high-quality cuts of meat, the included buffet nearly steals the show with fresh oysters, grilled heart of palm, sushi and sashimi, rice with wild mushrooms and goji berries, codfish casseroles, smoked fish, grilled prawns and octopus and amazing salads.

Waiters make frequent rounds with the goods; don't be shy about saying no, otherwise you'll end up with more than you could possibly eat.

🍴 Botafogo & Urca

Marchezinho
CAFE $$
(Map p316; www.facebook.com/marchezinho; Voluntários da Pátria 46, Botafogo; sandwiches R$28-38; ⊘ 9am-1am Mon-Wed, to 2am Thu & Fri, 10am-2am Sat) ✐ This multipurpose space operates as a cafe, bar and minimarket. The owner's French roots show through on the menu and store shelves, with the excellent cheese, bread and coffee. The carefully selected ingredients and produce are exclusively Brazilian, however, with most coming from small local producers. Come for creative tapas, delectable sandwiches, craft beers and first-rate cocktails.

🍴 Flamengo & Around

Sírio Libaneza
MIDDLE EASTERN $
(Map p316; ✎ 21 2146-4915; Largo do Machado 29, Loja 16-19; snacks R$6-28; ⊘ 8am-11pm Mon-Sat; ☎) Always packed, this bustling place serves tasty and cheap Syrian-Lebanese cuisine and great juices. Try the hearty *kibe de forno* (an oven-baked ground-beef dish with spices), a hummus platter or *kafta* (spiced meat patty), followed by baklava and other sweets. It's inside the Galleria Condor on Largo do Machado.

★Ferro e Farinha
PIZZA $$
(Map p316; Andrade Pertence 42; pizzas R$40-50; ⊘ 7-11:30pm Tue-Sat, from 6:30pm Sun) Sei Shiroma, an expat from NYC, and a dexterous team of dough handlers serve Rio's best pizza at this atmospheric and delightfully ramshackle spot in Catete. Seats are few, with just a handful of bar stools crowding around the pizza makers and oven at center stage, plus a few outdoor tables, so go early to try to beat the crowds.

Brou
BRAZILIAN $$
(Map p316; ✎ 21 2556-0618; www.facebook.com/ casa.brou; Senador Vergueiro 2, Flamengo; mains lunch R$18-30, dinner R$32-56; ⊘ 11:30am-3pm & 6pm-midnight) A brilliant new addition to Flamengo, this bright and attractive eating and drinking spot features a daytime menu of creative salads topped with grilled veggies, salmon or roast meat, as well as quiches and soups. By night, crowds come for nicely prepared prime rib, grilled octopus and thin-crust pizzas fired up in a wood-burning oven.

🍴 Centro & Praça Mauá

Confeitaria Colombo
BRAZILIAN $
(Map p320; ✎ 21 2505-1500; www.confeitaria colombo.com.br; Gonçalves Dias 34; pastries R$11-16, sandwiches R$22-46; ⊘ 9am-7pm Mon-Fri, to 5pm Sat) Stained-glass windows, brocaded mirrors and marble countertops create a lavish setting for coffee or a meal here. Dating from the late 19th century, the Confeitaria Colombo serves desserts – including a good *pastel de nata* (custard tart) – befitting its elegant decor.

ℹ BEACH BLANKET BURY IT!

Rio's beaches are targets for thieves and there has been an alarming rise in *arrastãos* of late – waves of bandits robbing everyone in their path across broad swaths of sand. Don't take anything valuable to the beach. Ever! But if you must, locals in the know bury their valuables in a plastic bag in the sand and cover it with their beach towel. Out of sight, out of mind!

BRAZIL RIO DE JANEIRO

Centro, Lapa, Glória & Santa Teresa

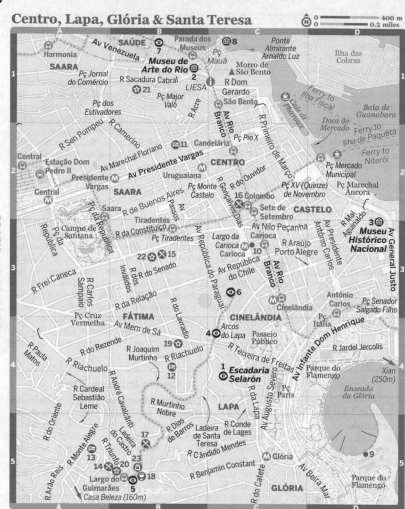

The restaurant above, **Cristóvão** (Map p320; Gonçalves Dias 34; buffet per person R$100; ⏱11:30am-4pm), spreads an extensive buffet of Brazilian dishes for those wanting to further soak up the splendor.

⭐**Xian**　　　　　　　　　　ASIAN $$
(☐21 2303-7080; www.xianrio.com.br; top fl, Almirante Silvio de Noronha 365, Bossa Nova Mall; mains R$65-90; ⏱noon-11pm Mon-Thu, to midnight Fri & Sat, noon-10pm Sun; 🛜) One of Rio's loveliest new additions is this spacious, theatrically decorated dining room, open-air cocktail bar and nightclub, all set rather dramatical-

ly on the edge of the bay. Come for mouth-watering seafood and tender meats with Asian accents, such as fresh oysters with ponzu sauce, salmon truffle tartar or marinated pork ribs with miso.

✖ Santa Teresa & Lapa

⭐**Casa Momus**　　　　MEDITERRANEAN $$
(Map p320; ☐21 3852-8250; www.casamomus.com.br; Rua do Lavradio 11, Lapa; mains R$42-58; ⏱11:30am-5pm Mon, to midnight Tue & Wed, to 2am Thu-Sat) One of the best and loveliest restaurants in Lapa, Casa Momus has a small but

Centro, Lapa, Glória & Santa Teresa

◉ **Top Sights**
1 Escadaria Selarón...................................C4
2 Museu de Arte do Rio..........................B1
3 Museu Histórico Nacional D3

◎ **Sights**
4 Arcos da Lapa C4
5 Bonde...B5
6 Bonde Station C3
7 Boulevard Olímpico...............................B1
8 Museu do Amanhã.................................C1

✪ **Activities, Courses & Tours**
9 Bem Brasil D5
10 Free Walker Tours C3

🛏 **Sleeping**
11 Belga Hotel B2
12 Books Hostel B4
13 Mama Shelter.......................................A5

✖ **Eating**
14 Bar do Mineiro A5
   Belga ....(see 11)
15 Casa Momus B3
16 Confeitaria Colombo...........................C2
   Cristóvão ....(see 16)
17 Espírito Santa B5

◐ **Drinking & Nightlife**
18 Explorer Bar B5

✪ **Entertainment**
19 Carioca da Gema..................................B4
20 Favela Hype..B5
21 Pedra do Sal...B1
22 Rio Scenarium B3

🛍 **Shopping**
   Favela Hype................................(see 20)
23 La Vereda B5

very well-executed menu of Mediterranean-influenced dishes. Start with prawn croquettes, fried polenta with spicy Gorgonzola or a Moroccan lamb *kafta* (spiced meat patty) with tabbouleh and yogurt sauce, then feast on oxtail risotto with watercress, seared tuna with couscous, grilled beef tenderloin, and other rich main courses.

Bar do Mineiro BRAZILIAN **$$**
(Map p320; 🗹 21 2221-9227; Paschoal Carlos Magno 99, Santa Teresa; mains R$65-125, weekday lunch special R$22-35; ⊘ noon-2am Tue-Sat, to midnight Sun) Black-and-white photographs of legendary singers cover the walls of this old-school *boteco* (small open-air bar) in the heart of Santa Teresa. Lively crowds have been filling this spot for years to enjoy traditional Minas Gerais dishes. The *feijoada* (bean-and-meat stew served with rice) is tops, and served every day, along with appetizers, including *pasteis* (savory pastries).

★Espírito Santa AMAZONIAN **$$$**
(Map p320; 🗹 21 2507-4840; www.espiritosanta.com.br; Almirante Alexandrino 264, Santa Teresa; mains R$55-98; ⊘ noon-11pm) At this beautifully restored mansion, you can sit on the back terrace with its sweeping views or in the charming, airy dining room, and feast on rich, expertly prepared meat and seafood dishes from the Amazon and Northeast. Top picks include the *moqueca* (fish stew), made with pintado (a delicious river fish), and the slow-roasted pork ribs served with sweet potato.

🍸 Drinking & Nightlife

Ipanema, Leblon and Copacabana offer flashy nightspots as well as old-school watering holes. A youthful bar scene draws revelers to Gávea, while scenic Lagoa draws mostly couples. The narrow pedestrian streets of Centro near Praça XV attract drinkers during weekday cocktail hours, while Santa Teresa is a laid-back spot for cocktails. Lapa, with its samba clubs and frenetic outdoor bars, becomes a late-night street party on weekends.

Rio's numerous juice bars are a must. For coffee culture and people-watching, head to the sidewalk cafes scattered about Ipanema and Leblon.

🍸 Ipanema & Leblon

★Canastra WINE BAR
(Map p306; Jangadeiros 42; ⊘ 6:30pm-1am Tue-Sat) Run by a trio of Frenchmen, Canastra has become one of the top nightlife destinations in Ipanema. Most nights, the crowd spills out onto the streets, and plenty of socializing *cariocas* never even make it inside. This, however, would be a mistake, as the food (cheese and charcuterie plates, grilled squid and octopus) and drinks (Brazilian wines, sangria, creative caipirinhas) are outstanding.

Nosso COCKTAIL BAR
(Map p306; 🗹 21 99619-0099; www.facebook.com/nossoipanema; Maria Quitéria 91, Ipanema; ⊘ 7pm-1am Tue-Thu, to 2am Fri & Sat, 6-11pm Sun) Located in the heart of Ipanema, this supremely stylish cocktail bar and restaurant, complete

with swanky rooftop terrace, feels like it has been plucked directly from downtown Manhattan. The meticulously crafted cocktails are made with high-quality spirits and often arrive adorned with foams and dehydrated fruit slices. The menu offers equally intricate yet delicious dishes.

Bar Astor
BAR

(Map p306; ☑21 2523-0085; www.barastor.com.br; Av Vieira Souto 110, Ipanema; ⊙6pm-1am Mon-Thu, 1pm-2am Fri, noon-2am Sat, noon-10pm Sun) Not visiting São Paulo? No problem. One of Sampa's best bars has now become a mainstay of post-beach revelry on prime real estate along the Ipanema shorefront. This gorgeous art deco bar does meticulously prepared caipirinhas, as well as Astor's own creative cocktails – try a Tiki Brasil, featuring mango, rangpur and Brazil nut syrup, plus *cachaça* (sugarcane alcohol).

Barzin
BAR

(Map p306; www.facebook.com/barzinriolive; Vinícius de Moraes 75; ⊙noon-1am Sun, Mon, Wed & Thu, noon-4am Tue, Fri & Sat) Barzin is a popular spot for post-beach drinks; its open-sided ground-floor bar fills with animated chatter at all hours. Upstairs you can catch a changing lineup of bands playing surf rock, hip-hop and other popular Brazilian music (cover charge from R$30 to R$80). The Tuesday night parties hosted by **Bem Brasil** (Map p320; www.bembrasilrio.com; Marina da Glória, Glória; cruises from R$75) are all the rage.

Belmonte
BAR

(Map p306; ☑21 2294-8249; Dias Ferreira 521; ⊙11am-2am) An icon in Leblon, Belmonte always draws huge crowds: it's pretty much a massive street party every night, with beer-drinking revelers spilling onto the sidewalk from 8pm onward. If you can score a table, don't miss the delicious, well-priced *pasteis* (dough that's filled then deep-fried), stuffed with crab, jerked beef with cheese, shrimp, heart of palm and other tasty ingredients.

Garota de Ipanema
BAR

(Map p306; ☑21 2523-2787; www.bargarotade ipanema.com; Vinícius de Moraes 49; ⊙noon-1am) During its first incarnation, this small, open-sided bar was called the Bar Veloso. Its name and anonymity disappeared once two scruffy young regulars – Tom Jobim and Vinícius de Moraes – penned the famous song, 'The Girl from Ipanema.' It changed history, and the name of the street, too.

🍸 Gávea, Jardim Botânico & Lagoa

★ Palaphita Kitch
LOUNGE

(Map p306; ☑21 2227-0837; www.palaphitakitch. com.br; Av Epitácio Pessoa s/n; ⊙6pm-midnight Mon-Fri, from 10am Sat & Sun) A great spot for a sundowner, Palaphita Kitch is an open-air, thatched-roof wonderland with rustic bamboo furniture, flickering tiki torches and a peaceful setting on the edge of Lagoa Rodrigo de Freitas. It's a popular spot with couples, who come for the view and the creative (but pricey) cocktails: the caipirinhas, made from unusual fruits from the Northeast and Amazonia, are a hit.

Palaphita Gávea
BAR

(Map p306; ☑21 3114-0853; www.palaphitakitch. com.br; Bartolomeu Mitre 1314; ⊙6pm-1am Mon, 8pm-4am Thu, 9pm-4am Fri & Sat, 5pm-1am Sun) Overlooking the **Jockey Club Brasileiro** (Hipódromo da Gávea; Map p306; ☑21 3534-9001; www.jcb.com.br; Jardim Botânico 1003, Gávea; ⊙6-11pm Mon & Tue, 2-8pm Sat & Sun), this sprawling open-air bar and party space is a wonderful mess of rustic wooden structures, thatch-roofed bars and scattered-about handmade furniture. It draws a young, animated crowd most evenings and is a great place at which to end the night. On racing days, you can even place bets here and watch the horses thunder past.

🍸 Copacabana & Leme

Escondido
BAR

(Map p310; ☑21 2522-9800; Aires de Saldanha 98, Copacabana; ⊙6pm-1am Tue-Sun) One of the top beer bars in Copacabana, Escondido has a rotating selection of microbrews such as American pale ales (IPAs), stouts and ciders, including about two dozen on draft at any one time. It's a laid-back spot to head to with friends to sample a few brews and nibble on pub grub (including huge burgers).

Pavão Azul
BAR

(Map p310; ☑21 2236-2381; Hilário de Gouveia 71, Copacabana; ⊙noon-midnight Mon-Sat, to 8pm Sun) A Copacabana classic, Pavão Azul is a simple open-sided bar where huge crowds gather on the sidewalk out front to drink ice-cold *chope* (draft beer) and chat late into the night. It's been so successful in fact that the owners have opened a similar *boteco,* Pavãzinho, across the street. Don't miss the fantastically good, inexpensive *pataniscas* (codfish fritters).

☕ Botafogo & Urca

CoLAB
BAR

(Map p316; ☎21 3592-0470; www.colab-rio.com; Fernandes Guimarães 66; ⊙10am-1am Tue-Sat) CoLAB is one of Botafogo's increasing number of lively bar/restaurants attracting a predominantly young crowd with a combination of international cuisine, cocktails and craft beers. The menu features curries (both Indian and Thai) as well as samosas, falafel sandwiches, burgers and other temptations. Calm by day, CoLAB picks up in the evenings – with DJs and the occasional band keeping things lively.

Comuna
BAR

(Map p316; ☎21 3579-6175; www.facebook.com/comunacc; Sorocaba 585, Botafogo; ⊙noon-1am Tue-Fri, 6:30pm-1:30am Sat, 6:30pm-midnight Sun) This creative space is equal parts bar, art gallery and independent bookseller (and indie publishing house). There's always something afoot in the delightfully off-the-beaten-path locale, with workshops, music sessions, readings, exhibitions and fashion shows. It's also just a great spot for a local microbrew and a bite (try one of the award-winning burgers).

Hocus Pocus
BAR

(Map p316; ☎21 4107-3107; www.facebook.com/HocusPocusDNA; Dezenove de Fevereiro 186; ⊙6pm-midnight Mon-Wed, to 2am Thu-Sat) Helping to lead Rio's craft-beer revolution, Hocus Pocus opened this beer hall in 2016 to provide its fans with easy access to its brews. There are over a dozen drafts here – including HP's finest (try the Magic Trap, a Belgian-style golden ale) as well as a few beers from other microbrewers. The buzzing barn-like setting is a great place to while away the evening.

Bar Urca
BAR

(Map p316; ☎21 2295-8744; Cândido Gaffrée 205, Urca; ⊙6:30am-11pm Mon-Sat, 8am-8pm Sun) This much-loved neighborhood bar and restaurant has a marvelous setting near Urca's bayside waterfront. At night, young and old crowd along the seaside wall to enjoy cold drinks, appetizers and fine views.

☕ Santa Teresa & Lapa

Explorer Bar
COCKTAIL BAR

(Map p320; ☎21 3264-9665; www.explorerbar.com; Almirante Alexandrino 399, Santa Teresa; ⊙5pm-midnight Tue-Fri, from 2pm Sat & Sun) A gorgeous multilevel garden with fairy lights is the centerpiece of this charming cocktail bar. Beautifully conceived cocktails (around R$30) showcase exotic flavors in elixirs like TLV, with orange, tamarind, ginger foam and grated nutmeg. The first-rate food menu features an eclectic mix of Sicilian seafood pasta, *sabich* (a roasted eggplant and hummus sandwich) and other globally inspired dishes (mains R$32 to R$56).

☆ Entertainment

Live Music

Rio Scenarium
SAMBA

(Map p320; ☎21 3147-9000; www.rioscenarium.art.br; Rua do Lavradio 20, Lapa; R$35-60; ⊙7pm-4am Tue-Sat) One of the city's most photogenic nightspots, Rio Scenarium has three floors, each lavishly decorated with antiques. Balconies overlook the stage on the 1st floor, where dancers keep time to the jazz-infused samba, *choro* (romantic, improvised, samba-related music) or *pagode* (popular samba music) filling the air. Rio Scenarium receives much press outside Brazil, and attracts about twice as many foreigners as locals. Bring ID.

Carioca da Gema
SAMBA

(Map p320; ☎21 2221-0043; www.barcariocadagema.com.br; Av Mem de Sá 79, Lapa; R$20-40; ⊙7:30pm-1:30am Sun-Tue & Thu, to 3am Fri, from 9pm Sat) Although it's now surrounded by other clubs, Carioca da Gema was one of Lapa's pioneers when it opened in 2000. This small, warmly lit club still attracts some of the city's best samba bands, and you'll find a festive mixed crowd filling the dance floor most nights.

Pedra do Sal
SAMBA

(Map p320; Largo João da Baiana, Gamboa; ⊙8pm-midnight Mon & Fri) The Monday- and Friday-night street parties here are major draws for lovers of samba, whether they're Brazilian or foreign, rich or poor. The lively *samba da mesa* features a handful of changing players who belt out well-known songs to swaying, joyful crowds surrounding the tiny plaza.

★ Bip Bip
LIVE MUSIC

(Map p310; ☎21 2267-9696; www.facebook.com/barbipbip; Almirante Gonçalves 50, Copacabana; ⊙7pm-midnight Sun-Fri) For years Bip Bip has been one of the city's favorite spots to catch a live *roda de samba* (informal samba played around a table), despite it being just a storefront with a few battered tables. As the evening progresses the tree-lined neighborhood becomes the backdrop to serious jam

MARACANÃ STADIUM

For a quasi-psychedelic experience, go to a futebol match at **Maracanã** (☑21 2334-1705; www.suderj.rj.gov.br/maracana.asp; Av Maracanã, São Cristóvão), Brazil's temple to football (soccer). Matches here rate among the most exciting in the world, particularly during a championship game or when local rivals Flamengo, Vasco da Gama, Fluminense or Botafogo go head-to-head. Games take place year-round and generally happen on a Wednesday, Thursday, Saturday or Sunday. For a behind-the-scenes look inside the stadium, take the **Maracanã Tour** (☑21 98341-1949; www.tourmaracana.com.br; Av Maracanã, São Cristóvão; tour guided/unguided R$60/50; ⊙9am-4:30pm), available daily.

sessions, with music and revelers spilling into the street.

Samba Schools

Starting in August or September, the big Carnaval schools open their rehearsals to the public. These are lively but informal affairs where you can dance, drink and join the party. The schools are mostly in dodgy neighborhoods, so go by taxi, but by all means go.

Salgueiro SAMBA
(☑21 2238-9226; www.salgueiro.com.br; Silva Teles 104, Andaraí; ⊙10pm Sat) One of the best samba schools for foreigners to visit, Salgueiro hosts big Saturday-night parties from late August until Carnaval. Expect live music, ever-flowing caipirinhas and lots of fiery footwork.

Mangueira SAMBA
(☑21 2567-3419; www.mangueira.com.br; Visconde de Niterói 1072, Mangueira; ⊙10pm Sat) One of Rio's most famous samba schools, Mangueira has many followers all across the city. They come out en masse in their green and pink (Mangueira's colors), when the school parades on Carnaval weekend.

🛍 Shopping

★**Hippie Fair** MARKET
(Map p306; Praça General Osório; ⊙9am-6pm Sun) The Zona Sul's most famous market, the Hippie Fair (aka Feira de Arte de Ipanema) has artwork, jewelry, handicrafts, clothing and souvenirs for sale. Stalls in the four corners of the plaza sell tasty plates of *acarajé*

(croquettes made from mashed black-eyed peas, with a sauce of *vatapá* – manioc paste, coconut and *dendê* oil – and shrimp), plus excellent desserts. Don't miss it.

Gilson Martins FASHION & ACCESSORIES
(Map p306; ☑21 2227-6178; www.shop.gilsonmartins.com.br; Visconde de Pirajá 462; ⊙9am-8pm Mon-Fri, to 7pm Sat) 🖉 Designer Gilson Martins transforms the Brazilian flag and silhouettes of Pão de Açúcar (Sugarloaf Mountain) and Corcovado into eye-catching accessories in his flagship store in Ipanema. This is the place for unique glossy handbags, wallets, passport covers, key chains and iPad covers. Products are durable and use recycled and sustainable materials – and are not available outside Rio.

Favela Hype FASHION & ACCESSORIES
(Map p320; www.facebook.com/favelahype; Paschoal Carlos Magno 103, Santa Teresa; ⊙10am-11pm Tue-Sun) This ultrahip but very friendly gathering spot is part fashion boutique, part restaurant and (at certain times) all party space. The art-filled shop sells swimwear, dresses, jewelry, sunglasses, ecofriendly flip-flops, floral-print button-downs (for the guys) and original artworks. Most products are made by local designers. Favela Hype also serves creative Brazilian fare, including an excellent *feijoada* (bean-and-meat stew).

La Vereda ARTS & CRAFTS
(Map p320; ☑21 2507-0317; www.lavereda.art.br; Almirante Alexandrino 428, Santa Teresa; ⊙10am-8pm) La Vereda stocks a colorful selection of handicrafts from local artists and artisans in a spot near Largo do Guimarães. Handpainted clay figurines by Pernambuco artists, heavy Minas ceramics, delicate sterling-silver jewelry and loosely woven tapestries cover the interior of the old store.

Shopping Leblon SHOPPING CENTER
(Map p306; ☑21 2430-5122; www.shoppingleblon.com.br; Av Afrânio de Melo Franco 290; ⊙10am-10pm Mon-Sat, 1-9pm Sun) This glittering multistory shopping center packed with top-name Brazilian and foreign labels is the best shopping destination in Leblon. It has plenty of tempting stores that will drain your vacation funds, as well as good restaurants and a cinema.

ℹ Information

DANGERS & ANNOYANCES

There's no point sugarcoating it: the security situation in Rio has deteriorated since the Olympics in 2016, and crime is on the rise. That said, if you take some basic precautions, you'll greatly minimize your risk of becoming a target.

➜ Dress down and leave expensive (or even expensive-looking) jewelry, watches and sunglasses at home. Copacabana and Ipanema beaches have a police presence, but robberies still occur on the sands, even in broad daylight. Don't take anything of value with you to the beach. Late at night, don't walk on any of the beaches.

➜ Buses are sometimes targets for thieves. Avoid taking buses after dark, and keep an eye out while you're on them. Take taxis at night to avoid walking along empty streets and beaches.

➜ Don't walk around deserted areas – Centro is barren and can be unsafe on Sunday (and on Saturday in some parts). Get into the habit of carrying only the money you'll need for the day, so you don't have to flash a wad of reais when you pay for things. Cameras and backpacks attract a lot of attention. Plastic shopping bags nicely disguise whatever you're carrying. If headed to Maracanã football stadium, take only your spending money for the day and avoid the crowded sections.

➜ Many formerly secure favelas are no longer safe to visit. Several tourists have been killed in the favelas in recent years by being in the wrong place at the wrong time. Before going on a favela tour, or lodging or dining in a favela, make sure you find out the latest information.

➜ If you have the misfortune to be robbed, calmly hand over the goods. Thieves in the city are only too willing to use their weapons if provoked.

EMERGENCY

Report robberies to the **tourist police** (☎21 2332-2924; cnr Afrânio de Melo Franco & Humberto de Campos, Leblon; ⊙24hr); you will get a police form to give to your insurance company.

Ambulance	192
Fire Department	193
Police	190

MEDICAL SERVICES

Clinica Galdino Campos (☎21 2548-9966; www.galdinocampos.com.br; Av NS de Copacabana 492, Copacabana; ⊙24hr) The best hospital for foreigners, with high-quality care and multilingual doctors (who even make outpatient calls). The clinic works with most international health plans and travel-insurance policies.

MONEY

ATMs are the handiest way to access money in Rio. Unfortunately, there has been an alarming rise in card cloning, with travelers returning home to find unauthorized withdrawals on their cards. This has been especially problematic with Bradesco ATMs, which you should avoid at all costs.

Banco do Brasil has branches with ATM in **Centro** (Av Ataúlfo de Paiva 980, Leblon), **Copacabana** (Av NS de Copacabana 1274, Copacabana; ⊙10am-4pm Mon-Fri) and **Galeão international airport** (1st fl, Terminal 1, Galeão international airport).

TOURIST INFORMATION

Riotur's multilingual website (www.visit.rio) is a good source of information. Its offices distribute maps and guides about major events; the main branch is in **Copacabana** (Map p310; ☎21 2541-7522; Av Princesa Isabel 183; ⊙9am-6pm Mon-Fri).

❶ Getting There & Away

AIR

Most international flights arrive at Aeroporto Internacional Antônio Carlos Jobim (p441), also called Galeão, located 15km north of the city center.

Aeroporto Santos Dumont (☎21 3814-7222; www4.infraero.gov.br; Praça Senador Salgado Filho), used by some domestic flights, is by the bay, in the city center, 1km east of Cinelândia metro station. It has ATMs, a few shops and an internet cafe.

GETTING TO RIO

From the international airport (Galeão), Premium Auto Ônibus 2018 (R$16) runs approximately every 30 to 40 minutes to Flamengo, Copacabana, Ipanema, Leblon and other neighborhoods. The bus also stops at the bus station and Santos Dumont Airport. The trip takes one to two hours depending on traffic; though you can also transfer to the metro at Carioca station. Radio taxis charge a set fare of R$130 to Copacabana and Ipanema (45 to 90 minutes). Less-expensive metered yellow-and-blue *comum* (common) taxis cost between R$82 and R$100. Ride-sharing services cost around R$60. There's also shuttle service (R$25).

If you arrive in Rio by bus, it's a good idea to take a taxi to your hotel, as the bus station is in a seedy area. To arrange a cab, go to the small booth on the 1st floor of the bus station. Average fares are R$50 to the international airport and R$50 to Copacabana or Ipanema.

BUS

Buses leave from the sleek **Rodoviária Novo Rio** (☏21 3213-1800; www.novorio.com.br; Av Francisco Bicalho 1), 2km northwest of Centro. You can consult the schedule and buy tickets online at www.clickbus.com. There's a dedicated pickup booth in the front of the bus terminal.

❶ Getting Around

BIKE

Rio has many kilometers of bike paths along the beach, around Lagoa and along Parque do Flamengo. In addition to the public bike-sharing scheme, **Bike Rio** (www.bikeitau.com.br/bike rio), you can rent bikes from stands along the east side of Lagoa Rodrigo de Freitas for around R$20 per hour and at various bike shops near the bike path between Copacabana and Ipane-ma, including **Velô Bike Store** (Map p310; ☏21 2523-4315; Francisco Otaviano 20; per hr/day R$10/70, electric bike per hr R$50; ☺9am-7pm Mon-Fri, to 4pm Sat, to 3pm Sun).

BUS

Rio's new BRS (Bus Rapid System) features dedicated public-transportation corridors in Copacabana, Ipanema, Leblon and Barra. Fares on most buses are around R$3.50.

Every bus has its key destination displayed on the illuminated signboard in front. If you see the bus you want, hail it by sticking your arm straight out (drivers won't stop unless flagged down).

METRO

Rio's **metro system** (www.metrorio.com.br; 1 ride R$4.30; ☺5am-midnight Mon-Sat, 7am-11pm Sun) is an excellent way to get around. Its three

BUSES FROM RIO

DESTINATION	TIME (HR)	COST (R$)	FREQUENCY (PER DAY)	BUS COMPANY
International				
Buenos Aires, Argentina	46	540	1	Crucero del Norte (www.crucerodelnorte.com.ar)
Santiago, Chile	64	560	1	JBL Turismo (www.jblturismo.com.br)
National				
Belém	52-60	500-700	2	Rápido Marajó (www.rapidomarajo.com.br), Itapemirim (www.itapemirim.com.br)
Belo Horizonte	7	110-205	15-30	Util (www.util.com.br), Cometa (www.via caocometa.com.br)
Brasília	17-20	220-392	3-4	Util (www.util.com.br), Kaissara (www.kaissara.com.br)
Buzios	3	60-85	9-18	Viação 1001 (www.autoviacao1001.com.br)
Curitiba	14	230-300	3-4	Penha (www.nspenha.com.br), Kaissara (www.kaissara.com.br)
Florianópolis	17-19	300	1	Kaissara (www.kaissara.com.br)
Foz do Iguaçu	24-27	260-430	3-5	Pluma (www.pluma.com.br), Catarinense (www.catarinense.net), Nordeste (www.expnordeste.com.br)
Ouro Prêto	7-8	110-140	2	Util (www.util.com.br)
Paraty	4½	80	5-12	Costa Verde (www.costaverdetransportes.com.br)
Petrópolis	1½	28	25	Única-Fácil (www.unica-facil.com.br)
Porto Alegre	28	395-520	1-2	Penha (www.nspenha.com.br)
Recife	40	365-560	1	Itapemirim (www.itapemirim.com.br)
São Paulo	6½	130-230	every 30min	Viação 1001 (www.autoviacao1001.com.br), Expresso Brasileiro (www.expressobrasileiro.com), Kaissara (www.kaissara.com.br)
Salvador	28-31	330-380	1-2	Aguia Branca (www.aguiabranca.com.br), Kaissara (www.kaissara.com.br)
Vitória	8	145-310	8-11	Aguia Branca (www.aguiabranca.com.br), Kaissara (www.kaissara.com.br)

lines are air-conditioned, clean and efficient. Line 1 goes from Ipanema-General Osório to Uruguai in the north zone. Line 2, which partly overlaps line 1, travels from Botafogo to Pavuna (passing Maracanã football stadium en route). Line 3 travels between Ipanema-General Osório and the eastern end of Barra da Tijuca at Jardim Oceânico.

You can purchase a *cartão pré-pago* (prepaid card) from a kiosk in any metro station using cash (no change given) with a minimum of R$5. You can then recharge the card at any kiosk. Free subway maps are available from most ticket booths.

TAXI & RIDE-SHARING

Rio's yellow taxis are plentiful, and easy to hail, particularly by using free apps like 99Taxis or Easy Taxi. The flat rate is around R$5.50, plus around R$2.50 per kilometer (R$3 per kilometer at night and on Sunday).

Uber is available in Rio de Janeiro, and service is widespread and generally quite good; it costs about 30% less than a traditional taxi. Lyft was not available at the time of writing.

THE SOUTHEAST

Those who manage to tear themselves away from Rio's charming clutches will find some of Brazil's most endearing attractions right in its backyard. Coastal highlights include the Costa do Sol (Sun Coast) north of Rio, home to the upscale beach resort of Búzios – a weekend city escape for hot-to-trot *cariocas*; and the spectacular Costa Verde (Green Coast), stretching south from Rio to São Paulo, boasting rainforest-smothered islands (Ilha Grande), beautifully preserved colonial villages (Paraty) and postcard perfect beaches (the whole stretch).

Or head inland to the convivial state of Minas Gerais, famous throughout Brazil for its hearty cuisine and friendly population. Here time has frozen colonial-era gold-mining towns such as Ouro Prêto or sleepy villages like Tiradentes, where magical historical delights beckon around every corner.

It all culminates in South America's cultural capital, São Paulo, where you'll find some of the best museums, nightclubs and restaurants in South America.

❶ Getting There & Around

Rio de Janeiro is the major gateway to the coastal regions, though if coming from the south or west you can reach the Costa Verde via São Paulo. Belo Horizonte, Brazil's third-largest city,

is the gateway to the old gold-mining towns in Minas Gerais.

Numerous flights connect the three major cities of the Southeast – Belo Horizonte, Rio and São Paulo – with plenty of bus links covering southeastern destinations. Ilha Grande is reached by ferry from Angra dos Reis, Mangaratiba or Conceição de Jacareí.

Búzios

0XX22 / POP 32,260

Beautiful Búzios sits on a jutting peninsula scalloped by 17 beaches. A simple fishing village until the early '60s, when it was 'discovered' by Brigitte Bardot and her Brazilian boyfriend, it's now one of Brazil's most upscale and animated seaside resorts, littered with boutiques, fine restaurants, villas, bars and posh pousadas. The Mediterranean touch introduced by the Portuguese has not been lost – indeed, the narrow cobblestone streets and picturesque waterfront contribute to Búzios' image as Brazil's St Tropez.

Búzios is not a single town but rather three settlements on the same peninsula – Ossos, Manguinhos and Armação de Búzios. Ossos (Bones), at the northern tip of the peninsula, is the oldest and most attractive. It has a pretty harbor and yacht club, plus a few hotels and bars. Manguinhos, on the isthmus, is the most commercial. Armação, in between, is the heart of town, with the most tourist amenities.

🏃 Activities

The biggest draws in Búzios are the natural setting plus its endless array of opportunities for relaxation, nightlife, shopping and ocean sports.

Several operators, including **Tour Shop Búzios** (22 2623-4733; www.tourshop.com.br; Orla Bardot 550; tours from R$60), offer tours to local beaches and islands. If you'd rather explore at your own pace, Búzios' *taxis marítimos* (water taxis) are an attractive alternative, charging R$10 to R$30 per person to individual beaches around the peninsula; rates are posted on a board at Armação's **water taxi & boat tour dock** and elsewhere around town.

🛏 Sleeping

Lodgings in Armação dos Búzios and along the Orla Bardot waterfront towards Ossos offer the easiest walking access to restaurants and nightlife.

Southeast Brazil

N
0 — 200 km
0 — 100 miles

★**The Search House Búzios**　　HOSTEL **$**
(✆22　2623-6628;　www.thesearchhouse.com.
br/buzios;　Vila das Aroeiras 221, Manguinhos;
dm R$60-75, d R$175-350; ❄🛜) With clean
white air-conditioned dorms and doubles,
comfortable beds, and a dreamy backyard
opening directly onto Manguinhos beach,
the Search House is Búzios' best new hostel in years. The on-site bar, movie room,
ping-pong table, beachside lounge chairs
and sports equipment (surfboards, SUP and
kite surfing gear) create a seductively festive
atmosphere.

★**Bamboo Búzios Hostel**　　HOSTEL **$**
(✆22　98835-0085, 22　2620-8085;　www.bamboo
buzioshostel.com; Rua das Pedras 25; dm R$85-120,
d R$260-400; ❄@🛜) Boasting a seaside perch
in the thick of the Rua das Pedras nightlife
zone, Búzios' most centrally located hostel
offers four- to 13-bed dorms complemented
by a dozen-plus private doubles and family
rooms. The best units enjoy gorgeous full-on

ocean views, as do the light-filled breakfast
area and the deck chairs and lounging bed on
the waterfront terrace.

Cesar Apartamentos　　APARTMENT **$$**
(✆22　2623-1349;　www.cesarbuzios.com;　Orla
Bardot 974; r R$180-200, apt R$350-380, apt with
sea view R$400-420; ❄🛜) One of Búzios' rare
beachfront bargains, this family-run clus-
ter of three modest rooms and seven more
spacious upstairs apartments sleeping up
to four boasts a prime Orla Bardot location.
Budget-minded travelers will appreciate the
motel-like cheapies downstairs; those with
extra reais to spend should reserve ahead for
one of the two oceanfront quads with pri-
vate terraces directly overlooking the water.

🍴 Eating & Drinking

Chez Michou Crêperie　　CRÊPES **$**
(✆22　2623-2169; www.chezmichou.com.br;　Rua
das Pedras 90; crepes R$19-32; ⊙noon-late Thu-
Tue, from 5pm Wed) Crowds flock here not only

for the sweet and savory crepes, but also for mixed drinks at the outdoor bar, sports events on the big screen TVs and the weekend DJ mixes (from 9pm).

★ **O Barco** SEAFOOD $$
(②22 2629-8307; Orla Bardot 1054; mains per person R$28-45; ⊙11am-11pm Wed-Mon) This down-to-earth waterfront joint stakes its reputation on well-made, reasonably priced fish dishes – from fried fish with rice and salad to full-on seafood stews. Eight tables on a cute little terrace plus a few extra sidewalk seats offer excellent people-watching and ocean views. Solo diners will appreciate the menu's wealth of *pratos individuais* (individual dishes), a rarity in couples-oriented Búzios.

★ **Rocka Beach Lounge** SEAFOOD $$$
(②22 2623-6159; www.rockafish.com.br; Praia Brava; mains R$79-86; ⊙9:30am-6:30pm daily mid-Dec–mid-Mar, to 5pm Wed-Mon rest of year) Prime people-watching and some of Búzios' most creative cuisine are the twin draws at this casual-chic seafood eatery perched directly above Praia Brava. Rocka is a full-day event for most visitors, who linger long after lunchtime on the lounge chairs and beds spread out on terraced hillsides overlooking the beach. Reserve ahead for weekends, when things fill up fast.

❶ Information

Búzios' two tourist offices – at the **town entrance portal** (②22 2623-4254; www.buzios.rj.gov.br/informacoes_turisticas; Av José Bento Ribeiro Dantas; ⊙8am-8pm) and on the **main square** (②22 2623-2099; Praça Santos Dumont, Armação; ⊙8am-8pm) in Armação – distribute city maps and hotel information.

❶ Getting There & Away

The Búzios **bus station** (Estrada da Usina 444) is a simple covered bus stop with no building attached, five blocks south of the Armação waterfront. **Viação 1001** (②22 2623-2050; www.autoviacao1001.com.br; Estrada da Usina) runs buses from Búzios to Rio's Novo Rio bus station (R$70, 2¾ hours, eight daily between 6am and 8:30pm); the same company offers direct buses to Rio's Galeão airport (R$72, six daily). The ticket office is on the northern side of Estrada da Usina, diagonally across from the Rio-bound bus stop.

Municipal buses between Búzios and Cabo Frio (R$5.55; 45 minutes) travel along Av José Bento Ribeiro Dantas and Estrada da Usina; there's a convenient **stop** (Estrada da Usina) just outside the Viação 1001 ticket office. Buy tickets on board the bus.

Ilha Grande

②0XX24 / POP 5000

The fabulous island retreat of Ilha Grande owes its pristine condition to its unusual history. For centuries, the island's unsavory reputation – first as a pirate's lair, then as a leper colony and penitentiary – kept developers at bay. Consequently, beautiful tropical beaches and virgin Atlantic rainforest (now protected as state parkland) abound, and the island still has only a handful of settlements.

Vila do Abraão, Ilha Grande's main town, was just a sleepy fishing village until the mid-1990s, when the infamous prison was destroyed and tourism began in earnest. Despite the influx of outsiders, Abraão, with its palm-studded beachfront and tidy orange church, remains small by mainland standards, and the prevailing rhythm is agreeably slow, thanks in large part to the absence of motorized vehicles. By day, life is all about exploring the island's dozens of trails and beaches, while evening brings half the town down to socialize by the waterfront.

◎ Sights & Activities

Posted around town are maps showing 16 different signposted trails leading through the lush forest to several of the island's 102 beaches. When visiting some beaches, it's possible to hike one way and take a boat the other.

Before hitting the trail, let people at your pousada know where you're going and when you'll be back, stock up on water and bug repellent, and bring a flashlight, as darkness comes swiftly under the jungle canopy. Guides are advisable for exploring beyond the most heavily traveled routes; poorly marked trails and poisonous snakes can make things challenging.

★ **Praia Lopes Mendes** BEACH
Facing the Atlantic, this seemingly endless beach with good surfing waves (shortboard/longboard rentals available on-site) is considered by some the most beautiful in Brazil. It's accessible by Ilha Grande's most popular walking trail, a three-hour, 6.1km trek that starts at the eastern end of Abraão's town beach, crosses the hills to **Praia de Palmas**, then follows the coast to **Praia do Pouso**. Alternatively, take a boat from Abraão to Pouso. From Pouso, it's a 15-minute walk to Lopes Mendes.

🍴 Sleeping & Eating

Vila do Abraão is swarming with pousadas, hostels and other accommodations for every budget. Prices drop by as much as 50% between April and November. Restaurants abound along Rua da Praia, Rua Getúlio Vargas and the small pedestrian street Travessa Buganville.

★ Che Lagarto   HOSTEL $

(☑24 3361-9669; www.chelagarto.com; Praia do Canto; dm R$70-90; @🛜) Unbeatable location at the far eastern end of Abraão's main beach, a panoramic waterfront deck and a bar with free-flowing caipirinhas are the prime attractions at this hostel, part of South America's largest chain. Some boats from Conceição de Jacareí will drop you at the Aquário hostel next door; otherwise, it's a 10-minute walk from Abraão's town center.

★ Pousada Lagamar   POUSADA $$

(☑24 99904-6623, 24 99997-7219; www.pousada lagamar.com.br; Praia Vermelha; d with garden/sea view R$270/350, chalet R$400; ☺closed mid-May–Jun) Owners Ezequiel and Luciana have created this family-friendly pousada at beautiful Praia Vermelha on Ilha Grande's northwestern shore. It's a perfect place to kick back in nature for a few days and settle into a simpler rhythm: swimming, snorkeling, walking the nearby trails, lounging with a good book in your hammock, and enjoying dinners of freshly caught fish.

★ Pousada Manacá   POUSADA $$$

(☑24 3361-5404; www.ilhagrandemanaca.com.br; Rua da Praia 333; d R$360-400, tr R$440-480; 🌬🛜) It's worth reserving ahead and paying the small surcharge for a front room with balcony and hammock at this French-run beachfront pousada. The ample breakfast is accompanied by sea views from the pleasant front terrace; other nice touches include in-room fridges, dependable solar hot water and a central patio for lounging. Septuagenarian owner Gerard speaks five languages.

★ Bonito Paraiso Beach House   POUSADA $$$

(☑24 99907-0307; www.bonitoilhagrande.com; Praia Abraãozinho; r R$430-570; 🌬🛜) A five-minute boat ride or a 30-minute hike from Abrão brings you to this idyllic hideaway at the end of Abraãozinho beach. Argentine owners Juan and Paolina have transformed the original beach house into a delightful pousada, with an open seaside porch where meals are served, a breezy family unit upstairs, and several doubles in a modern structure up the hill.

★ The Secret   INTERNATIONAL $$

(☑24 99921-1124; www.facebook.com/thesecret gourmetclub; mains R$38-65; ☺7:30-11pm) Every evening, Argentine expats Cris and Nel invite up to 10 prereserved guests into their secret garden in Abraão village for wonderful home-cooked dinners accompanied by chilled-out music and convivial conversation. Contact them via WhatsApp to check out the nightly changing offerings (typically Mediterranean, South American or vegetarian), reserve a time, get directions and learn the secret (shh!) password.

Café do Mar   BRAZILIAN $$

(☑24 3361-9446; www.cafedomar.com; Getúlio Vargas 719; mains R$42-72; ☺10am-11pm) This candlelit beach bar and lounge is perfect for sundown cocktails, with reasonably priced (by Ilha Grande standards!) *pratos do dia* (daily specials) and frequent barbecue nights.

ℹ Information

Note that there are no ATMs on the island, and although many places accept credit cards, it's still advisable to bring cash from the mainland; in a pinch, some businesses will accept foreign cash.

Health Center (Serviço de Pronto Atendimento; ☑24 3361-5523; Getúlio Vargas; ☺24hr) Provides first aid and emergency care.

ℹ Getting There & Away

Most boats from the mainland arrive at Vila do Abraão, the island's biggest town.

The quickest and most hassle-free way to reach the island from Rio is with a door-to-door shuttle service such as **Easy Transfer** (☑21 99386-3919; www.easytransferbrazil.com). This will pick you up at any hostel, hotel or pousada in Rio and deliver you to the island (R$95, 3½ to 4½ hours), with a synchronized transfer from van to speedboat in the coastal town of Conceição de Jacareí. Easy Transfer offers a similar service to Ilha Grande from Paraty (R$85, 3½ hours).

Reaching the island via public transport is slightly cheaper but more complicated, as you have to choose from multiple routes and buy two separate tickets (one for the bus, one for the boat).

Costa Verde (p332) runs buses from Rio to the three ports where boats for Ilha Grande depart: Conceição de Jacareí (R$56, 2½ hours, four daily), Mangaratiba (R$39, 2½ hours, four daily) and Angra dos Reis (R$56, three hours, hourly).

The most frequent boat crossings are from Conceição de Jacareí, where speedboats (R$40,

20 minutes) and schooners (R$25, 50 minutes) leave every hour or two between 8:30am and 6pm, returning from Abraão between 8am and 5:30pm. From Angra dos Reis, similar service is available by speedboat (R$50, 30 minutes) and schooner (R$25, 80 minutes). Boat companies operating along one or both routes include **Objetiva** (☑ 24 98112-4730, 24 3370-5584; www.objetivatour.com; Rua da Praia 677; ⊙ 8am-10pm), **Angra Flex** (☑ 24 3365-2125; www.facebook.com/angraflex; Terminal Rodoviário, Av Caravelas, Angra dos Reis; ⊙ 7am-5pm), **Doce Atitude** (☑ 24 99954-9477, 24 3367-1281; www.doceangraturismo.com; Av Júlio Maria 74, Angra dos Reis; ⊙ 7am-7pm Mon-Sat, to 1pm Sun) and **Água Viva** (☑ 24 99978-4932; www.aguavivatour.com.br; Rua da Praia 26; ⊙ 8am-8pm).

More affordable but less frequent are the daily ferries to Ilha Grande operated by **CCR Barcas** (☑ 0800-721-1012; www.grupoccr.com.br/barcas/linhas-horarios-tarifas; Cais do Abraão; ⊙ 9:30-10am & 5-5:30pm), leaving from Angra dos Reis and Mangaratiba (R$17, 80 minutes from either port). Ferries depart Angra at 3:30pm weekdays and 1:30pm weekends, returning from Abraão at 10am daily. From Mangaratiba, ferries leave at 8am daily and 10pm Friday, returning from Abraão at 5:30pm daily. Extra ferries are sometimes added during high season; confirm locally before departure.

Angra is the most useful port for those traveling west from Ilha Grande. Colitur buses for Paraty (R$15, two hours, at least hourly from 6am to 11pm) leave Angra's bus station, 1.5km east of the boat docks.

Paraty

☑ 0XX24 / POP 41,454

Backed by steep, jungled mountains plunging into an island-studded bay, Paraty enjoys one of Brazil's most spectacular settings and an exquisitely preserved colonial center, recognized as a National Historic Site since 1966. The area surrounding Paraty is really a nature-lover's paradise, offering some of southeastern Brazil's prettiest coastal and mountain scenery.

☉ Sights & Activities

Paraty has some 65 islands and 300 beaches in its vicinity. To visit the less accessible beaches, take an organized schooner tour. Multiple boats depart daily from the **Cais de Turismo** at the southeastern edge of the historic center; tickets average about R$65 per person.

Alternatively, you can hire one of the small motorboats at the port for a private tour. Local captains know some great spots and will take you out for around R$100 per hour, which can be a good deal if you have a large enough group.

★**Paraty Explorer** OUTDOORS
(☑ 24 99952-4496; www.paratyexplorer.com; Praia do Jabaquara) ✎ This agency on Jabaquara beach, run by outdoors enthusiasts Paddy (from Ireland) and Rodrigo (from Brazil), specializes in sea kayaking tours of Paraty Bay (from R$170), stand-up paddle boarding, and hiking adventures to destinations including Cachoeira Melancia, a spectacular waterfall in Serra da Bocaina National Park (R$200), the dramatic Pão de Açúcar do Mamanguá (R$300), and remote Costa Verde beaches.

★**Cachoeira Tobogã** SWIMMING
In the hills 8km inland from Paraty, this natural waterslide is a blast. The slick rock-face sends swimmers plunging into an idyllic pool surrounded by jungle. Tourists who value their skulls should heed the posted warnings against surfing (ie standing instead of sitting), although local teenagers have mastered the technique and it's exciting (if terrifying!) to watch. Afterwards, grab a caipirinha at Bar do Tarzan, across the swinging bridge above the falls.

From Paraty, take a local Colitur bus to Penha (R$4.25, 30 minutes), get off at the church and follow signs 100m downhill.

🛏 Sleeping

From December to February, and during festivals, hotels fill up and room prices double, so reservations are advisable. The rest of the year, finding accommodations is relatively easy.

Budget-minded travelers will find several campgrounds and hostels along the Pontal and Jabaquara beachfronts (north of town, across the pedestrian bridge).

★**Happy Hammock** HOSTEL $
(☑ 24 99994-9527; www.facebook.com/happyhammockparaty; Ponta Grossa; dm/d R$55/200) This Swiss-run waterfront hostel sits on isolated Ponta Grossa, a 15-minute boat ride from Paraty. With no road access, limited generator-fueled electricity and gorgeous sea views, it's a dreamy end-of-the-line getaway where guests can lounge in hammocks, swim in phosphorescent waters or hike to nearby beaches before the tour boats arrive. Book

dinners (R$25) and boat transfers (R$20) in advance.

Canguru Hostel
HOSTEL $

(📱 24 3371-1477; www.canguruhostel.com.br; Avenida Vera Cruz 46, Praia do Jabaquara; dm R$38-65; 🛜) A block inland from Jabaquara beach, friendly Canguru offers a varied collection of doubles, six- to 12-bed dorms and campsites surrounding a sprawling enclosed yard. Barbecues, dance parties with live bands, and shots of *gabriela* (*cachaça* with cloves and cinnamon) from the in-house bar keep things hopping, while the free laundry service is one of several homey touches.

Hotel Solar dos Gerânios
INN $$

(📱24 3371-1550; www.paraty.com.br/geranio; Praça da Matriz 2; s/d/tr R$120/180/240; @🛜) Run by the same family for decades, this rustic place on lively Praça da Matriz is by far the best budget hotel deal in Paraty's colonial center. Wood and ceramic sculptures, stone walls and floors, columns and beamed ceilings, and a courtyard full of plants, cats and dogs all add character. Several rooms have balconies overlooking the square.

🍴 Eating & Drinking

Maria Fulô Bistrô
Natural & Tapiocaria
VEGETARIAN $

(📱24 3371-5036; www.facebook.com/mariafulobistro; Rua Presidente Pedreira; mains R$15-28; ⊙noon-11pm Mon-Sat; 🥢) This cheerfully painted little restaurant just outside the historic center is a welcome refuge for both wallet and taste buds. At lunchtime, reasonably priced, healthy *pratos feitos* (set meals; R$26) rule the day; come evening, the menu shifts over to *tapiocas*, the spongy manioc-flour pancakes stuffed with various fillings that have long been a Brazilian budget staple.

Quiosque Dito e Feito
SEAFOOD $$

(Praia do Pontal; mains per person from R$30; ⊙10am-6pm) Ask locals where to find reasonably priced fresh seafood and they'll send you to this simple beachfront kiosk on Praia do Pontal. From straightforward fried fish to *moqueca* to the *caldeirada do mar* (a seafood stew for three), dishes are huge, but half-portions are available upon request.

⭐ Entertainment

Margarida Café
LIVE MUSIC

(📱24 3371-6037; www.margaridacafe.com.br; Praça do Chafariz; ⊙noon-midnight) This cavernous yet cozy bar with checkerboard tile floors and massive stone columns has great drinks and live music nightly, including MPB (Musica Popular Brasileira), bossa nova, jazz, *forró* and tango.

Paraty 33
LIVE MUSIC

(📱24 3371-1630; www.paraty33.com.br; Rua da Lapa 357; ⊙noon-1am Sun-Thu, to 4am Fri & Sat) With an early evening happy hour featuring MPB and bossa nova, and a late-night weekend mix of DJs and live acts, Paraty 33 is the historic center's liveliest nightspot.

ℹ️ Information

CIT (📱24 3371-1222; www.visiteparaty.tur.br; Av Roberto Silveira 1; ⊙9am-9pm) Paraty's tourist office is perfectly positioned at the entrance to the historic center.

Bradesco (Av Roberto Silveira 73-77) has multiple ATMs two blocks north of the bus station; more at Banco do Brasil next door.

ℹ️ Getting There & Away

The bus station (Rua Jango Pádua) is 500m west of the old town. Costa Verde (📱21 3907-3900; www.costaverdetransportes.com.br) offers frequent services to Rio de Janeiro (R$76, 4¾ hours, 12 daily). Colitur has buses to Angra dos Reis (R$15, two hours, hourly from 5am to 8pm) and Reunidas (📱18 2102-4420; www.reunidaspaulista.com.br) buses head to São Paulo (R$78, six hours, six daily).

São Paulo

📍0XX11 / POP 11.3 MILLION (CITY), 19.9 MILLION (METRO) / ELEV 760M

São Paulo is home to 20 million fiercely proud *paulistanos* (as residents are known), all of whom will happily tell you at length to you how they'd never live elsewhere. Spend time with them and the reasons will soon unfold. Maybe they will introduce you to the city's innumerable art-house cinemas and experimental theaters. If they're gourmands, they'll focus on the smart bistros and gourmet restaurants that make the city a world-renowned foodie haven. If they're scenesters, follow them on a raucous tour of underground bars and the 24/7 clubbing scene. Whatever pleasures you might covet, *Sampa* (the city's affectionate nickname) probably has them in spades.

Of course, it's also enormous, intimidating and, at first glance at least, no great beauty (to say nothing of the smog, the traffic, the crumbling sidewalks and the gaping divide between poor and rich).

A beautiful mess, if you will? And Brazil's city of dreams.

◉ Sights & Activities

The atmospheric old center of São Paulo lies between Praça da Sé, Luz metro station and Praça da República. Cleverly titled Centro Velho, it's a pedestrianized maze offering a fascinating cornucopia of architectural styles (always look above the ground floors, which have all lost their charm to everyday shops). Other interesting neighborhood strolls are found in Liberdade, Sampa's Japan town (also home to other Asian communities); and Vila Madalena, the artistic quarter. Both host lively weekend street markets, the former at Praça da Liberdade on Sunday, the latter at Praça Benedito Calixto on Saturday.

★ Mercado Municipal   MARKET
(Mercadão; Map p334; www.oportaldomercadao. com.br; Rua da Cantareira 306, Centro; ⊙6am-6pm Mon-Sat, to 4pm Sun) This covered market is a belle epoque confection of stained glass and a series of vast domes. Inside, a fabulous urban market specializes in all things edible. It's also a great place to sample a couple of classic Sampa delights: mortadella (Italian sausage) sandwiches at **Bar do Mané** or **Hocca Bar**, and *pasteis* (fried, stuffed pastries).

★ Edifício Copan   HISTORIC BUILDING
(Map p334; www.copansp.com.br; Av Ipiranga 200, República; ⊙15-min tour 10:30am & 3:30pm Mon-Fri) FREE Copan was designed by late modernist master Oscar Niemeyer. The building, with its serpentine facade and narrow *brises soleil* (permanent sunshades), is Sampa's most symbolic structure. You can visit its snaking, sloping ground-floor shopping arcade anytime; its spectacular rooftop opens only on weekdays at 10:30am or 3:30pm, however. The 15-minute visit is no frills – there's barely a railing! – and feels wonderfully unrushed. Checkin at Bloco F (space limited – arrive at least 30 minutes in advance).

★ Pina_Luz   MUSEUM
(Map p334; www.pinacoteca.org.br; Praça da Luz 2, Luz; adult/student R$6/3, Sat free; ⊙10am-6pm Wed-Mon) This elegant neoclassical museum, formerly known as Pinacoteca do Estado but modernly rebranded 'Pina_Luz' (*with* the underline!) in 2017, houses an excellent collection of Brazilian – and especially Paulista – art from the 19th century to the present.

Works include big names such as Portinari and Di Cavalcanti, and it has an excellent permanent collection of modernist Brazilian art. There is a lovely cafe that faces adjacent Parque da Luz.

★ Museu Afro-Brasil   MUSEUM
(www.museuafrobrasil.org.br; Av Pedro Alvares Cabral s/n, Parque Ibirapuera, Gate 10; adult/student R$6/3, Sat free; ⊙10am-5pm Tue-Sun) This hugely important, absolutely fascinating Parque Ibirapuera museum features a permanent 3rd-floor collection chronicling five centuries of African immigration (and a nod to the 10 million African lives lost in the construction of Brazil) and hosts a rotating array of contemporary Afro-centric exhibitions on its bottom two floors.

★ Museu de Arte de São Paulo   MUSEUM
(MASP; www.masp.art.br; Av Paulista 1578, Bela Vista; adult/student R$35/17, free Tue; ⊙10am-6pm 10am-8pm Tue, to 6pm Wed-Sun) Sampa's pride, the Museu de Arte de São Paulo possesses Latin America's most comprehensive collection of Western art. Hovering above a concrete plaza that turns into an antiques fair on Sunday (and acts as a protest gathering point almost always!), the museum, designed by architect Lina Bo Bardi and completed in 1968, is considered a classic of modernism by many and an abomination by a vocal few.

★ Museu Xingu   MUSEUM
(www.casaamarela.art.br/espacos/museu-xingu; José Maria Lisboa 838, Jardins; ⊙10am-4pm Mon-Fri) FREE Relatively unknown and blissfully uncrowded, the unassuming Casa Amarela is part **NGO handicraft shop** (www.pontosol idario.org.br; José Maria Lisboa, Jardins; ⊙10am-7pm Mon-Fri, to 4pm Sat) 🍴, part two-table romantic cafe and part tiny Museu Xingu. The last of these has one the world's best collections of artifacts from Irmãos Villas-Bôas, a three-brother Brazilian activist team who were the first white men to come in contact with upper Xingu river indigenous communities of the Amazon.

★ Beco do Batman   PUBLIC ART
(Map p337; Gonçalo Afonso s/n, Vila Madalena; ⊙24hr) One of São Paulo's premiere street-art locations, 'Batman's Alley' has slowly risen from a secret location for band promotional shots and Brazilian films to a bonafide tourist attraction – even school kids visit nowadays. The open gallery, tucked away in

Central São Paulo

Parque da Luz

Estação Júlio Prestes

★ 8

Praça Júlio Prestes

Estação da Luz

R Mauá

LUZ

R Conselheiro Nébias

Praça Princesa Isabel

R dos Andradas

R Santa Efigênia

R Washington Luís

Av Duque de Caxias

D-Edge (2km)

R General Osório

R dos Gusmões

R Vitória

Av Rio Branco

Av Ipiranga

R Aurora

Av Casper Líbero

Largo do Arouche

R Timbiras

Av São João

Viaduto Santa Efigênia

Cervejaria Dogma (550m)

R Aurora

R 24 de Maio

Largo de Paiçandú

R Cap Salomao

Praça da República

República M

R Dom José de Barros

Praça Antonio Prado

Parque do Anhangabaú

R Marquês de Itu

C.I.T. ℹ ● 4

R Barão de Itapetininga

R Conselheiro Crispiniano

● 9

Praça Ramos

R Libero Badaró

R São Bento

R Rego Freitas

R Araújo

Av Ipiranga

R 7 de Abril

Viaduto de Chá

🏛 Edifício Copan
1

Av São Luís

7 🏧

Praça Dom José Gaspar

Anhangabaú M

Praça do Patriarca

CENTRO

Praça Franklin Roosevelt

R da Consolação

R Direita

Av Radial Leste Oeste

R Martin Fontes

✕ 6

Largo de São Francisco

R Benjamin Constant

Praça da Bandeira

R Senador Feijó

Av 9 de Julho

🏧 5

R Avanhandava

R Santo Antônio

R Major Diogo

R da Abolição

Viaduto Jacarei

Speranza (1.5km)

Praça Carlos Gomes

Lamen Kazu (650m)

Museu de Arte de São Paulo (1.4km); C.I.T. (1.6km); Capim Santo (2km); Museu Xingu (2km); Ponto Solodário (2km)

BRAZIL SÃO PAULO

artsy Vila Madalena, is covered head-to-toe in cutting-edge street art by local and international artists.

Museu do Futebol　MUSEUM
(www.museudofutebol.org.br; Praça Charles Miller s/n, Pacaembu; adult/student R$12/6, Tue free; ⊙9am-6pm Tue-Sun; ☍) Tucked under the bleachers of colorfully art deco Pacaembu Stadium, this fantastic museum is devoted to Brazil's greatest passion – football (soccer). Its multimedia displays over two floors manage to evoke the thrill of watching a championship game, even for nonfans.

★**SP Free Walking Tour**　WALKING
(Map p334; www.spfreewalkingtour.com; Praça da República, República; tips only; ⊙11:30am Mon, Wed, Fri & Sat) FREE Condenses over 450 years of Sampa history into a long but fascinating 'Old Downtown' walk four times a week at 11:30am. The tour meets next to the CIT (tourist booth) at Praça da República and ends 3½ hours later at Largo São Bento; and there's walk-exclusive discounts to be had along the way. Reservations unnecessary – just show up 20 minutes prior.

🎊 Festivals & Events

São Paulo Gay Pride Parade　LGBT
(www.paradasp.org.br; Av Paulista; ⊙Jun) Av Paulista morphs into a come-all, free-for-all for São Paulo's annual gay pride parade, often considered the biggest in the world (both the 2016 and 2017 events drew three million people).

🛏 Sleeping

Vila Madelena is the most traveler-friendly neighborhood for leisure visitors and is home to the majority of hostels. The city's top boutique hotels sit in the leafy, upscale district of Jardins.

★ We Hostel Design   HOSTEL $
(🖉11 2615-2262; www.wehostel.com.br; Morgado de Mateus 567, Vila Mariana; dm R$60-77, d without bathroom R$145-205; ✳@🅰) Simply gorgeous, São Paulo's best hostel sits inside a beautiful historic 1926 white mansion on a quiet Vila Mariana residential corner. From the guest kitchen to the hammock-strewn, quasi-wraparound porch to the kitschy living room, everything here has been designed with expert connoisseurship of retro furniture and coveted antiques.

Ô de Casa   HOSTEL $
(Map p337; 🖉11 3063-5216; www.odecasahostel.com; Inácio Pereira da Rocha 385, Vila Madelena; dm R$45-60, r R$150-200, r without bathroom R$120-150; ✳🅰) This artsy and colorful hostel is one of the neighborhood's oldest, with a sociable bar and rooftop terrace that gives way to shotgun-style lodging in four-, six- and eight-bed mixed dorm configurations and well-kept bathrooms. A newer annex houses spiffier private rooms with lofts and private bathrooms, but you won't escape the noise from the imbibing nighttime crowds.

Sampa Hostel   HOSTEL $
(Map p337; 🖉11 3031-6779; www.hostelsampa.com.br; Girassol 519, Vila Madelena; dm from R$40, s/d/tr/q R$90/140/210/280; @🅰) This newly remodeled veteran of Vila Madelena's hostel scene is one of its best, offering four-, six- and eight-bed dorms (the last of these a bit cramped), a few sparse privates, kitchen facilities and a sun deck.

★ Guest Urban   BOUTIQUE HOTEL $$
(Map p337; 🖉11 3081-5030; www.guesturbansp.com.br; Lisboa 493, Pinheiros; d R$259-309; ✳✳🅰) This 1930s mansion, opened in late 2015, holds 14 suites reeking of industrial-chic (exposed brick and beams, unfinished steel and concrete) offset by a sunny open patio and cutting-edge art (reprints for sale in the lobby). It's one block from Praça Benedito Calixto in the heart of hip Pinheiros.

155 Hotel   BOUTIQUE HOTEL $$
(Map p334; 🖉11 3150-1555; www.155hotel.com.br; Martinho Prado 173, Consolação; d/tr/ste R$160/240/270; ✳@🅰) This gay-friendly, 76-room affordable boutique hotel is located between Centro and the alterna-hipster bars of Baixo Augusta. Ultrasleek suites are steeped in minimalist blacks and grays; regular rooms aren't quite as hip but are still top value all things considered, with tight bathrooms but hardwood floors and writing desks.

🍴 Eating

★ Estadão   FAST FOOD $
(Map p334; www.estadaolanches.com.br; Viaduto 9 de Julho 193, Centro; specialty sandwiches R$7-33; ⊘24hr) This classic Centro *lanchonete* (snack bar) serves working folk's meals at all hours, but its signature *pernil* (pork loin) sandwich, smothered in the cheese of your choice (provolone!) and sautéed onions, is one of Sampa's gastronomic musts.

★ Capim Santo   BRAZILIAN $$
(🖉11 3089-9500; www.capimsanto.com.br; Alameda Ministro Rocha Azevedo 471, Jardins; dinner mains R$56-123, lunch buffet weekday/weekends R$63/96; ⊘noon-3pm & 7-11pm Tue-Fri, 12:30-4:30pm & 8pm-midnight Sat, 12:30-4:30pm Sun; 🅰) 🍃 Top chef Morena Leite turns out excellent regional Brazilian fare, with an emphasis on local and organic ingredients, served in a relaxed, beautifully Brazilian indoor-outdoor space. The excellent weekday buffet is the affordable way into this higher-end spot.

★ Tordesilhas   BRAZILIAN $$
(🖉11 3107-7444; www.tordesilhas.com; Alameda Tietê 489, Jardins; mains R$63-87; ⊘6pm-1am Tue-Fri, noon-5pm & 7pm-1am Sat, noon-5pm Sun; 🅰) Chef Mara Salles creates some of the best contemporary Brazilian cuisine in the city at Tordesilhas. There's a palpable lean on specialties from the Amazon such as *pato no tucupí* (roasted duck flavored with juice of the manioc plant and *jambu,* a mouth-numbing indigenous herb) and grilled Amazonian fish, as well as Brazil-wide regional dishes.

★ Futuro Refeitório   FUSION $$
(Map p337; 🖉11 3085-5885; www.futurorefeitorio.com.br; Cônego Eugênio Leite 808, Pinheiros; small plates R$11-43, mains R$32-41; ⊘8am-10:30pm Mon-Thu, to 11pm Fri, 9am-4pm & 7-11pm Sat, 9am-4pm Sun; 🅰🍴) 🍃 A former Pinheiros parking lot has been transformed into this unapologetically trendy canteen that bills itself as the future of eating. Indeed, low-key chef Gabriela Barretto has a vision: scale back on meat-derived and processed foods, and muck about less with things. Vegans flip over the plant-based lunch menu (R$34),

Vila Madalena

Vila Madalena

while dinner mostly focuses on small plates and sandwiches.

★ Lamen Kazu   JAPANESE $$

(www.lamenkazu.com.br; Tomás Gonzaga 51, Liberdade; mains $29-47; ⊙11am-3pm & 6-10:30pm Mon-Sat, 11am-3pm & 6-9pm Sun; 🛜) It's not as famous (or cheap) as its nearby rival Aska, but take the hint: the 99% Japanese clientele should tell you something. The fiery Kara Misso Lamen (spicy broth and spiced pork in addition to the usual condiments; R$42), doused with the house-made chili sauce, is a revelation; as is everything on the menu. Veg options as well. Get slurpin!

★ Maní   BRAZILIAN $$$

(Map p337; ☏11 3085-4148; www.manimanioca. com.br; Joaquim Atunes 210, Jardim Paulistano; mains R$51-110; ⊙noon-3pm & 8-11:30pm Tue-Thu, noon-3pm & 8pm-midnight Fri, 1-4pm & 8pm-midnight Sat, 1-4pm Sun; 🛜) Rustic-chic Maní will astound you. Run impeccably by the 2014

PIZZA PAULISTANA

Forget New York and Chicago (or even Naples, for that matter): one of the world's best kept secrets is São Paulo's excellent *pizza paulistana*. Locals say the city's pizza is so good, even the Italians are jealous. It shouldn't be a surprise, though, as swarms of Italian immigrants settled here in the late 19th century, giving the city one of the largest Italian populations in the world outside Italy. Do not depart without trying one of the following.

Bráz Pizzaria (Map p337; ☑ 11 3037-7975; www.brazpizzaria.com.br; Vupabussu 271, Pinheiros; pizza R$43-88; ⊙ 6:30pm-12:30am Sun-Tue, noon-3pm & 6:30pm-midnight Wed-Thu, to 1am Fri & Sat; 🕾 🖶) This Pinheiros pizza Paulistana warrior will leave you questioning if pizza ever originated elsewhere. Keep the Brahma draft beer (*chope*) coming while engaging in a warm sausage bread (*pão de calabresa*) appetizer (dip it in spiced olive oil) followed by your pie of choice.

Leggera Pizza Napoletana (☑ 11 3862-2581; www.pizzerialeggera.com.br; Diana 80, Vila Pompeia; pizza R$34-42; ⊙ 7-11pm Tue-Thu, to 11:30pm Fri & Sat, to 10pm Sun; 🕾) Brazilian-Italian-American pizzaiolo Andre Guidon imports everything humanly possible from Italy – and this small, family-run affair epitomizes the Brazilian-Italian diaspora. The 20 individual-sized, uncut pies here are some of Sampa's best.

Carlos Pizza (Map p337; ☑ 11 3813-2017; www.carlospizza.com.br; Harmonia 501, Vila Madalena; pizzas R$36-56; ⊙ 6pm-midnight; 🕾) This intimate Vila Madalena pizzeria has been scooping up citywide pizza awards, and its novel concept makes for a quick explanation: Neapolitan-style tradition and sensibility but forged with farm-to-table Brazilian ingredients from small producers.

Speranza (☑ 11 3288-3512; www.pizzaria.com.br; Rua 13 de Maio 1004, Bixiga; pizza R$57-100; ⊙ 6:30pm-12:30am Sun-Thu, to 1am Fri & Sat; 🖶) One of the oldest and most traditional pizzerias in the Italian neighborhood of Bixiga, where the Tarallo family has been serving serious pizza since 1958.

Veuve Cliquot World's Best Female Chef, Helena Rizzo, it's often rightfully touted as Sampa's best Brazilian restaurant. The inventive slow-cooked egg (1½ hours at 63°C) is more famous, but the house-cooked potato chips topped with filet mignon, or hearts of palm taglierini with creamed Tulha cheese are true culinary coups.

🍷 Drinking & Nightlife

Traditional bar neighborhoods include *boteco*-filled Vila Madalena (mainstream); along Rua Mario Ferraz in Itaim Bibi (rich, bold and beautiful); and Baixo Augusta, where the GLS scene (Portuguese slang for Gay, Lesbian and Sympathetics) mingles with artsy hipsters in the city's edgiest-nightlife district. Artists, journalists and upper middle-class bohemians have claimed Pinheiros, immediately southeast of Vila Madalena. Current rage: rooftop bars!

⭐**Bar da Dona Onça**   BAR
(Map p334; ☑ 11 3129-7619; www.bardadonaonca. com.br; Av Ipiranga 200, lojas 27/29, Edifício Copan, República; cocktails; ⊙ noon-11:30pm Mon-Wed, to 12:30am Thu-Sat, to 5:30pm Sun; 🕾) In the

striking Edifício Copan (p333), Dona Onça is one of downtown's best bars, not only for the packed crowds and excellent drinks, but for lauded chef Janaina Rueda's kitchen that churns out extraordinary Brazilian-heartland fare. Commence with the *caju amigo* – a *cachaça*-based Paulistano cocktail with cashew fruit (R$33).

⭐**Cervejaria Dogma**   MICROBREWERY
(www.facebook.com/pg/cervejariadogma; Fortunato 236, Santa Cecília; ⊙ 5-11pm Wed-Fri , noon-11pm Sat, 2-9pm Sun) Dogma routinely dominates the top 10 ranked beers in Brazil on *Untappd*, and this no-frills taproom near Santa Cecília metro station is Sampa's best microbrewery by a considerable margin – especially for hopheads. You can count on the 20 taps here including plenty of strong IPAs, imperial stouts and so on. Choices marked 'local' are brewery exclusive.

⭐**Ambar**   CRAFT BEER
(Map p337; www.barambar.com.br; Cunha Gago 129, Pinheiros; ⊙ noon-3pm Mon, to midnight Tue & Wed, to 1am Thu-Sat, 1-7pm Sun; 🕾) Cozy and convivial, Ambar's long, welcoming bar is

probably the single best spot in town to sip on juicy IPAs or a humidity-retreating pilsner or weiss. The craft beer on the 15 taps here is impossibly fresh, and good relationships with Rio de Janeiro, Rio Grande do Sul and Santa Catarina breweries mean you see suds here you don't easily find elsewhere.

★**Guilhotina** COCKTAIL BAR
(Map p337; www.guilhotinabar.com.br; Costa Carvalho 84, Baixa Pinheiros; ⊙6pm-1am Wed-Sat) Pages of in-house-created cocktails are the calling at this hip den of mixology. At the helm, *Veja* magazine's 2017 bartender of the year, Márcio Silva, a SubAstor alum. Silva shakes and stirs 15 years of European experience into his fine concoctions, which actually come out cheaper (R$29) than classic preparations (R$31). Try Vitriol, a boozy and refreshing bourbon bombshell.

★**SubAstor** COCKTAIL BAR
(Map p337; ☑11 3815-1364; www.subastor.com.br; Delfina 163, Vila Madalena; ⊙8pm-3am Tue-Sat) This dark and speakeasy-sexy bar sits below a *boteco* called Astor (extraordinarily great as well for food and caipirinhas), hence the name: SubAstor. Sincere mixology goes down here, from creative takes on classics such as *caju amigo* (*cachaça* and cashew juice) to far more cutting-edge liquid art.

★**D-Edge** CLUB
(☑11 3665-9500; www.d-edge.com.br; Av Auro Soares de Moura Andrade 141, Barra Funda; ⊙11pm-late Mon & Wed-Sat) With one of the city's most remarkable sound systems and a roster of world-famous DJs, this mixed gay-straight club is a well-established venue for the club scene and remains a 'don't miss' for fans of electronica; one of South America's best.

Love Story CLUB
(Map p334; ☑11 3231-3101; www.danceterialove story.tur.br; Araújo 232, República; ⊙11:45pm-8am Tue-Wed, to 9am Thu, to 10am Fri & Sat) Nick Cave was once a regular, celebrity chef Alex Atala oversees the menu; legendary Love Story has seen it all! It doesn't get going until 3am, and is the late-night stomping grounds of math rock maniacs, off-duty sex workers, edgier celebrities and deep-pocketed rich kids. Get in line and dance until breakfast.

☆ Entertainment

São Paulo is home to the world-class theater at **Theatro Municipal** (Map p334; ☑11 3223-3022; www.theatromunicipal.org.br; Praça Ramos de Azevedo, Centro; ⊙box office 10am-7pm Mon-Fri, to 5pm Sat & Sun) and classical music at **Sala São Paulo** (Map p334; ☑11 3223-3966; www.sala saopaulo.art.br; Praça Júlio Prestes 16, Centro; ⊙box office 10am-6pm Mon-Fri, to 4:30pm Sat); in addition to live samba, which is prevalent across a wide range of bars, *botecos* and other venues around town.

São Paulo's three biggest football teams are **Corinthians** (www.corinthians.com.br), who play at the **Arena Corinthians** (☑11 3152-4099; www.arenacorinthians.com.br; Av Miguel Ignácio Curi 111, Artur Alvim), 24km east of Centro (a 2014 FIFA World Cup venue); **Palmeiras** (www.palmeiras.com.br), who play in the modern 43,600-capacity **Allianz Parque** (☑11 4800-6670; www.allianzparque.com.br; Francisco Matarazzo 1705, Água Branca) near Barra Funda; and **São Paulo FC** (www.saopaulofc. net), who play at the 67,428-capacity **Estádio do Morumbi** (Estádio Cícero Pompeu de Toledo; Praça Roberto Gomes Pedrosa 1, Morumbi) – a 2016 Olympic Games venue.

BRAZIL SÃO PAULO

GETTING TO SÃO PAULO

Passaro Marron (www.passaromarron.com.br) operates two airport bus options: the flashier **Airport Bus Service** (☑0800-770-2287; www.airportbusservice.com.br; btwn Terminal 2 East & West, GRU Airport; one-way from R$50), which is one of the most efficient ways to/from GRU Airport, making stops at Aeroporto Congonhas, Barra Funda, Tiête, Praça da República and various hotels around Av Paulista and Rua Augusta; and the cheaper and more crowded suburban Airport Service line 257 to/from Metrô Tatuapé (R$6.15, 30 to 45 minutes; every 15 minutes between 5am and 12:10am). It's easy to confuse the two from the airport – they depart right next to each other outside the terminals.

For Congonhas, catch bus 875A-10 'Perdizes-Aeroporto' from Metrô São Judas or catch an Uber (R$45 to R$65) to/from most neighborhoods of interest (or get there for under R$20 if you catch an Uber from Metrô Jabaquara).

★ **Barretto** LIVE MUSIC

(☑ 11 3896-4000; www.fasano.com.br; Vittorio Fasano 88, Jardins; cover R$60; ⊙ 7pm-3am Mon-Fri, from 8pm Sat) Hands down one of the best places to see live music in the world, this intimate bar inside the Hotel Fasano recalls prewar Milan and attracts top jazz and popular Brazilian musicians who normally play far larger venues.

★ **Vila do Samba** SAMBA

(☑ 11 3858-6641; www.viladosamba.com.br; João Rudge 340, Casa Verde; ⊙ 8pm-3am Tue, 9-11pm Fri, 2-11pm Sat, 5pm-midnight Sun) A 'can't miss' stalwart in São Paulo's live samba scene, Vila do Samba – named as such due to its location inside a charming set of town-house villas – is worth a trip to the northern district of Casa Verde, which is said to be where samba's origins lie. It swarms with connoisseurs at least four nights a week.

Information

DANGERS & ANNOYANCES

Crime is an issue in São Paulo, though the majority is limited to the city's periphery and tourists aren't often targeted unless they're the unlucky victim of an *arrastão*, when armed bandits rob an entire restaurant of patrons. Be especially careful in the center and elsewhere at night and on weekends (when fewer people are about). Watch out for pickpockets on buses, around Praça da Sé and on Linhas 1 (blue) and 3 (red) of the metro.

EMERGENCY

Ambulance	192
Police	190
Fire	193

MEDICAL SERVICES

Einstein Hospital (☑ 11 2151-1233; www.einstein.com.br; Av Albert Einstein 627, Morumbi)

MONEY

ATMs are widely available throughout the city. Bradesco and Banco do Brasil are feeless and the most foreign-friendly. Note that most are closed from 10pm to 6am for security reasons. Always use ATMs inside banks to avoid cloning.

TOURIST INFORMATION

Useful CIT offices include **Av Paulista** (Central de Informação Turística; www.cidadedesaopaulo.com; Av Paulista 1853; ⊙ 9am-6pm), **Praça da República** (Central de Informação Turística; Map p334; ☑ 11 3331-7786; www.cidadedesaopaulo.com; Praça da República, República; ⊙ 9am-6pm), **Rodoviário Tietê** (Central de Informação Turística; www.cidadedesaopaulo.com; Av Cruzeiro do Sul 1800,

BUSES FROM SÃO PAULO

DESTINATION	STARTING FARE (R$)	DURATION (HR)	BUS COMPANY
Angra dos Reis	84	7½	Reunidas Paulista (www.reunidaspaulista.com.br)
Asunción (PY)	250	20	Pluma (www.pluma.com.br)
Belo Horizonte	121	8	Cometa (www.viacaocometa.com.br)
Brasília	189	15	Real Expresso (www.realexpresso.com.br)
Buenos Aires (AR)	467	44	JBL (www.jblturismo.com.br)
Curitiba	89	6¾	Cometa (www.viacaocometa.com.br)
Florianópolis	149	11	Catatrinense (www.catarinense.net)
Foz do Iguaçu	220	17½	Catatrinense
Montevideo (UY)	490	32	JBL
Paraty	65	6	Reunidas Paulista
Pantanal (Cuiabá)	395	27½	Andorinha (www.andorinha.com)
Pantanal (Campo Grande)	261	14	Andorinha
Recife	379	45	Itapemirim (www.itapemirim.com.br)
Rio de Janeiro	96	6	1001 (www.autoviacao1001.com.br)
Salvador	375	26½	Gontijo (www.gontijo.com.br)
Santos	27	1¼	Cometa
Santiago (CH)	465	57	JBL

Rodoviário Tietê, Santana; ⊙6am-10pm) and **Congonhas Airport** (Central de Informação Turística; www.cidadedesaopaulo.com; Av Washington Luis s/n, Congonhas Airport, Vila Congonhas; ⊙7am-10pm).

ℹ️ Getting There & Away

AIR

GRU Airport (Aeroporto Guarulhos; ☑11 2445-2945; www.gru.com.br; Rod Hélio Smidt s/n), the international airport, is 25km northeast of the center.

Most domestic flights depart from Terminal 2 East or West; but Azul and Passaredo operate out of the newer Terminal 1 located 2km to the southwest, among others.

Most international flights operate out of the newer Terminal 3 (connected to T2 by corridor and people-mover) an impressive world-class terminal that opened in 2014. Exceptions include mid-haul flights from Central and South America and the Caribbean (Aerolíneas Argentinas/ Austral, Aeromexico, Avianca/Taca, Copa, Tame etc), and a few stragglers from Africa (Ethiopian, Royal Air Maroc, TAAG) and Europe (Air Europa) – but check ahead.

Frequent free shuttles connect the terminals 24 hours a day.

The domestic-only airport, **Congonhas** (Aeroporto de São Paulo-Congonhas; www.aeroporto congonhas.net; Av Washington Luís s/n), 14km south of the center, services many domestic destinations, including the majority of flights to Rio (Santos Dumont Airport), which depart every half-hour (or less).

BUS

South America's largest bus station, **Terminal Tietê** (☑11 3866-1100; www.terminalrodoviar iodotiete.com.br; Av Cruzeiro do Sul 1800, Santana) is 4.5km north of Centro and accessible by metro. Avoid bus arrivals during early morning or late afternoon – traffic jams are enormous.

ClickBus (www.clickbus.com.br) is a good app for consulting departures times, fares and purchases and there's a dedicated pickup booth on the eastern side of Tietê bus terminal in front of Bradesco bank.

ℹ️ Getting Around

You can reach many places on the excellent **Metrô São Paulo** (☑0800-770-7722; www. metro.sp.gov.br; fare R$4), the city's rapidly expanding subway system, which is integrated with its commuter rail counterpart, **CPTM** (Companhia Paulista de Trens Metropolitanos; www. cptm.sp.gov.br; fare R$4). The metro is cheap, safe and fast, and runs from 4:40am to midnight on most lines. A single ride costs R$4.

Belo Horizonte

☑0XX31 / POP 2.5 MILLION / ELEV 858M

Known to locals as Beagá (pronounced 'bay-ah-gah', Portuguese for BH), Belo Horizonte was named for its beautiful view of nearby mountains. Urban sprawl may make it a little more challenging to appreciate the natural setting nowadays, but Brazil's third-largest city still has considerable charm.

Walk down the buzzing cosmopolitan streets of the Savassi neighborhood on a Saturday evening, eat at one of the fine restaurants in Lourdes, stroll through the densely packed stalls at Mercado Central, attend the exuberant weekend street fair alongside leafy Parque Central, and you'll see that Belo Horizonte has countless dimensions.

👁️ Sights

Fans of modernist architect Oscar Niemeyer won't want to miss his creations dotted around a huge artificial lake in the Pampulha district, north of downtown. Over the last decade Belo Horizonte has opened several worthwhile museums and cultural attractions in the former government buildings surrounding Praça da Liberdade; for information on all of these, visit www.circuitoliberdade.mg.gov.br/pt-br/visite-br.

🛌 Sleeping

For easier walking access to the city's main attractions, stay near Praça da Liberdade or elsewhere within the central zone delineated by the Av do Contorno ring road.

★ Hostel Savassi HOSTEL $

(☑31 3243-4771; www.hostelsavassi.com.br; Antônio de Albuquerque 626; dm R$45-55; 🛜) This small and cozy hostel enjoys a dream location on a pedestrianized street in the heart of Savassi. The trio of four- to 10-person dorms (two for women, one mixed) offers thoughtful features such as individual reading lights and power outlets for every bed, while the bright upstairs guest kitchen and spacious downstairs lounge and TV area invite travelers to mingle.

Adrena Sport Hostel HOSTEL $

(☑31 3657-9970; www.adrenasporthostel.com.br; Av Getúlio Vargas 1635A; dm R$52-55, with HI card R$47-50, d with shared/private bathroom R$125/145; 🛜) This homey HI-affiliated hostel in a 1950s Savassi town house is the brainchild of Belo Horizonte local Pedro, who also owns the adventure-sports store downstairs. Six- to

ESSENTIAL BELO HORIZONTE EXPERIENCES

For a quintessential taste of the city, seek out at least one or two of the following during your visit:

→ Stroll through the cheerful chaos of market stalls and restaurants at **Mercado Central** (☑ 31 3274-9497; www.mercadocentral.com.br; Av Augusto de Lima 744; ⊙ 7am-6pm Mon-Sat, to 1pm Sun).

→ Spend a Sunday morning at the open-air **Hippie Fair** (Feira da Afonso Pena; Feira de Arte e Artesanato; Av Afonso Pena; ⊙ 8am-2pm Sun).

→ Explore the 23 art galleries and magnificent grounds at the **Instituto de Arte Contemporânea Inhotim** (☑ 31 3571-9700; www.inhotim.org.br; Rua B, 20, Brumadinho; adult/reduced R$44/22, Wed free; ⊙ 9:30am-4:30pm Tue-Fri, to 5:30pm Sat & Sun).

→ Take a stadium tour and visit the football museum at **Mineirão** (☑ 31 3499-4300; www.estadiomineirao.com.br/museu-e-visita; Av Antônio Abrahão Caram 1001; adult/child stadium tour R$8/4, incl football museum R$14/7; ⊙ 9am-5pm Tue-Fri, to 1pm Sat & Sun).

→ Attend a performance or stop in for an evening drink at **Centro Cultural Banco do Brasil** (☑ 31 3431-9400; www.bb.com.br/cultura; Praça da Liberdade 450; ⊙ 9am-9pm Wed-Mon) **FREE**.

→ Praça da Liberdade's standout cultural attraction, the supremely cool contemporary **Memorial Minas Gerais – Vale** (☑ 31 3308-4000; www.memorialvale.com.br; Praça da Liberdade 640; ⊙ 10am-5:30pm Tue, Wed, Fri & Sat, to 9:30pm Thu, to 3:30pm Sun) museum chronicles Minas culture from the 17th to 21st centuries via three floors of cutting-edge interactive galleries and audiovisual installations.

10-bed sport-themed dorms with paragliding, skateboard and climbing wall decor are complemented by a small sitting area, a welcoming kitchen-dining space and a back room where guests can linger over billiards and a beer.

Royal Savassi Hotel　　　　HOTEL **$$**
(☑ 31 2138-0000; www.royalsavassi.com.br; Alagoas 699; r R$200-320; ❈@✿) Well positioned just east of Praça da Liberdade, this business-oriented hotel offers good online deals year-round, especially on weekends, when prices can get slashed nearly in half. Amenities include plush beds, big flat-screen TVs, minibars, a rooftop Jacuzzi and the **Amadeus** (☑ 31 3261-4292; per kg lunch weekday/weekend R$50/68, dinner R$95; ⊙ 11:30am-3pm & 6pm-12:30am Mon-Sat, noon-4pm Sun) restaurant downstairs with its sumptuous lunch buffet. Weak links include lackadaisical customer service and inconsistent wi-fi.

✗ Eating & Drinking

The area between Praça Sete and Praça da Liberdade is best for cheap eats, with countless *lanchonetes* (snack bars), self-serve *por kilo* restaurants and fast-food places. Further south, the Lourdes and Savassi neighborhoods constitute the epicenter of the city's fine-dining scene.

Casa Amora　　　　BUFFET **$**
(☑ 31 3261-5794; www.casaamora.com.br; Paraiba 941, Savassi; meals R$24-32; ⊙ 11:30am-3pm Mon-Fri, noon-3:30pm Sat) The concept is simple at this health-conscious lunch spot, founded by a trio of women: select one of the three daily specials (including one vegetarian option), add two or three side dishes of your choice, grab a glass of juice and decamp to the sunny outdoor patio or one of the cheery yellow tables up front.

★ Xapuri　　　　MINEIRA **$$**
(☑ 31 3496-6198; www.facebook.com/Restaurante Xapuri; Mandacarú 260, Pampulha; mains per person R$48-75; ⊙ noon-11pm Tue-Sat, to 6pm Sun) Run by the affable Dona Nelsa, this long-standing local institution 15km northwest of Belo Horizonte is renowned for its fabulous *comida mineira* (typical Mineira cuisine). Everything is served at picnic tables under a thatched roof, with children's entertainment and hammocks close at hand for post-meal relaxation. The traditional wood stove blazes up front, while colorful desserts are attractively displayed in two long cases.

Wäls Gastropub MICROBREWERY

(📋31 3582-5628; Levindo Lopes 358, Savassi; ⊙11:30am-2:30pm & 6pm-midnight Mon-Thu, noon-2am Fri & Sat) Locals flock to this retail branch of Belo Horizonte's popular Wäls microbrewery for weekday lunch specials (R$20 to R$30) and late-night weekend carousing. The high-ceilinged, industrial-chic space serves over a dozen varieties on tap, from the bargain-priced X-Wäls lager to Hop Corn IPA to the intensely strong Quadruppel Belgian ale.

Jângal BAR

(📋31 3653-8947; www.jangalbh.com; Outono 523; ⊙6pm-1am Tue-Fri, 2pm-1:30am Sat, 2-10pm Sun) This cool and colorfully lit garden bar draws regular crowds for its creative mixed drinks and nightly musical offerings that run the gamut from samba to electronica.

★Café com Letras CAFE

(📋31 3225-9973; www.cafecomletras.com.br; Antônio de Albuquerque 781, Savassi; ⊙noon-11:30pm Mon-Wed, to midnight Thu, to 1am Fri & Sat, 5-11pm Sun; 🛜) With live jazz on Sundays, DJs Thursday through Saturday, and a bohemian buzz between sets, this bookstore-cafe is a fun place to kick back over light meals (R$25 to R$56) and drinks, browse the shelves and enjoy the free wi-fi. There's a second branch in the **Centro Cultural Banco do Brasil** (Praça da Liberdade 450, lower level; ⊙10am-9pm) and it sponsors jazz performances citywide at the annual **Savassi Festival** (www.savassi festival.com.br; ⊙Aug).

ℹ Information

Belo Horizonte's municipal tourist bureau, Belotur (www.belohorizonte.mg.gov.br), is among the best in Brazil. Several branches are located around town.

Alô Turismo (📋from Belo Horizonte 156, from elsewhere 31 3429-0405; ⊙24h) Belotur's tourist-inquiry hotline.

Belotur Mercado Central (📋31 3277-4691; www.belohorizonte.mg.gov.br; Av Augusto de Lima 744; ⊙8am-4:20pm Mon & Tue, to 5:20pm Wed-Sat, to 1pm Sun) On the ground floor of Belo's famous indoor market.

Belotur Pampulha Lakeshore (📋31 3277-9987; www.belohorizonte.mg.gov.br; Av Otacílio Negrão de Lima 855, Pampulha; ⊙8am-5pm Tue-Sun) On the lakeshore in the northern suburb of Pampulha.

Belotur Rodoviária (📋31 3277-6907; www. belohorizonte.mg.gov.br; Praça Rio Branco 100; ⊙8am-5pm) On the main floor of the bus station, near the entrance.

Centro de Informação Circuito Cultural (www.circuitoliberdade.mg.gov.br/visite-br; Av Bias Fortes 50, Praça da Liberdade; ⊙9am-6pm Tue-Sun, to 9pm Thu) Information center for the museums and other cultural attractions surrounding Praça da Liberdade.

ℹ Getting There & Away

Belo Horizonte has two airports. International flights and many domestic flights use the renovated and expanded **Aeroporto Internacional de Belo Horizonte** (CNF; Aeroporto Tancredo Neves; Aeroporto Confins; 📋0800-037-1547; www. bh-airport.com.br; Rodovia LMG 800, Km 7.9, Confins), 40km north of the city. The **Aeroporto da Pampulha** (PLU; Aeroporto Carlos Drummond de Andrade; 📋31 3490-2000; www4.infraero. gov.br/aeroportos/aeroporto-de-belo-horizonte-pampulha-carlos-drummond-de-andrade; Praça Bagatelle, Pampulha), 10km north of the city center, is more conveniently located but only has limited domestic flights. Between them, the two airports serve most locations in Brazil.

Expresso Unir (📋31 3689-2415; www.conexao aeroporto.com.br) runs frequent, comfortable Conexão Aeroporto buses between downtown and Belo's two airports. The *convencional* bus (R$12.70 to either airport) leaves Belo's bus

BRAZIL BELO HORIZONTE

BUSES FROM BELO HORIZONTE

DESTINATION	COST (R$)	TIME (HR)	COMPANY
Brasília	168-230	11-12	União (www.expressouniao.com.br), Kaissara (www.kaissara.com.br)
Diamantina	97	5	Pássaro Verde (www.passaroverde.com.br)
Ouro Prêto	34	2	Pássaro Verde
Rio de Janeiro	81-166	6-7	Útil (www.util.com.br), Cometa (www.viacaocometa.com.br)
Salvador	298	25	Gontijo (www.gontijo.com.br)
São João del Rei	60	3½	Viação Sandra (www.viacaosandra.com.br)
São Paulo	146-256	8-9	Cometa
Vitória	120-161	9-10	São Geraldo (www.saogeraldo.com.br), Kaissara

station every 15 to 30 minutes between 4am and 10:30pm (slightly less frequently on weekends). Travel time is approximately 30 minutes to Pampulha airport, 70 minutes to Confins. Buses return from Confins between 5:15am and 12:20am.

Belo's long-distance **bus station** (📞 31 3271-8933, 31 3271-3000; Praça Rio Branco 100) is at the northern end of downtown.

TRAIN
Companhia Vale do Rio Doce (📞 0800-285-7000; www.vale.com/tremdepassageiros; Aarão Réis s/n; ⊘ 6am-4pm Tue-Sat, to noon Sun; 🛜) operates a daily train to Vitória (*econômica/executiva* class R$73/105) in Espírito Santo state, departing at 7:30am from Belo Horizonte's **train station** (Praça da Estação), just north of Parque Municipal, and arriving at Cariacica/Pedro Nolasco train station on Vitória's western outskirts at 8:30pm. The return run leaves Vitória at 7am, reaching Belo Horizonte at 8:10pm.

Ouro Prêto
📍 0XX31 / POP 74,659 / ELEV 1179M

Of all the exquisite colonial towns scattered around Minas Gerais, Ouro Prêto is the jewel in the crown. Built at the feet of the Serra do Espinhaço, Ouro Prêto's colonial center is larger and has steeper topography than any other historical town in Minas. The narrow, crooked streets of the upper and lower towns tangle together and in places are too rough and precipitous for vehicles. Navigating the vertiginous cobblestone slopes on foot can be exhausting, but the views of 23 churches spread out across the hilly panorama are spectacular. The city is a showcase of outstanding *mineiro* art and architecture, including some of Aleijadinho's finest works.

☉ Sights & Activities
There are virtually no 20th-century buildings in this colonial town. As you wander, watch for informative historical plaques that have been placed on 150 houses around town to heighten visitors' curiosity and expand their knowledge of the city's treasures – part of a citywide cultural initiative known as Museu Aberto/Cidade Viva.

★ Igreja de São Francisco de Assis `CHURCH`
(www.museualeijadinho.com.br; Largo de Coimbra s/n; adult/reduced R$10/5; ⊘ 8:30-11:50am & 1:30-5pm Tue-Sun) This exquisite church is Brazil's most important piece of colonial art, after Aleijadinho's masterpiece **The Prophets** (Praça do Santuario) in Congonhas. Its entire exterior was carved by Aleijadinho himself, from the soapstone medallion to the cannon waterspouts to the Franciscan two-bar cross. The interior was painted by Aleijadinho's long-term partner, Manuel da Costa Ataíde.

Matriz NS do Pilar `CHURCH`
(Praça Monsenhor Castilho Barbosa; adult/reduced R$10/5; ⊘ 9-10:45am & noon-4:45pm Tue-Sun) On the southwestern side of town, this is Brazil's second most opulent church (after Salvador's São Francisco). It has 434kg of gold and silver and is one of the country's finest showcases of artwork. Note the wild-bird chandelier holders, the scrolled church doors and the hair on Jesus (the real stuff, donated by a penitent worshipper).

Museu da Inconfidência `MUSEUM`
(www.museudainconfidencia.gov.br; Praça Tiradentes 139; adult/child R$10/5; ⊘ 10am-6pm Tue-Sun) This historical museum is housed in Ouro Prêto's old municipal headquarters and jail, an attractive building built between 1784 and 1854 on the southern side of Praça Tiradentes. It contains the tomb of Tiradentes, documents of the Inconfidência Mineira (an unsuccessful separatist movement in the 18th century), torture instruments and important works by Manuel da Costa Ataíde and Aleijadinho. Last admission is at 5pm.

Igreja de Santa Efigênia dos Pretos `CHURCH`
(📞 31 3551-5047; Santa Efigênia 396; adult/reduced R$5/2.50; ⊘ 8:30am-4:30pm Tue-Sun) Financed by gold from Chico-Rei's mine and built by the slave community, this mid-18th-century church honors Santa Efigênia, princess of Nubia. The exterior image of NS do Rosário is by Aleijadinho. Slaves legendarily contributed to the church coffers by washing their gold-flaked hair in baptismal fonts, or smuggling gold powder under fingernails and inside tooth cavities.

Casa dos Contos `MUSEUM`
(São José 12; ⊘ 10am-5pm Tue-Sat, to 3pm Sun) `FREE` This 18th-century treasury building still retains its historic foundry, where gold was melted down and formed into bars under the watchful eye of the Portuguese crown. It doubled as a prison for members of the Inconfidência. The renovated mansion now houses informational displays about the history of money in Brazil. The grand rooms upstairs command sweeping

Ouro Prêto

Ouro Prêto

◎ **Top Sights**

◎ **Sights**

🛌 **Sleeping**

🍽 **Eating**

views over Ouro Prêto's streets, while the dank, cobblestoned former *senzala* (slave quarters) below exhibits harrowing instruments of imprisonment and torture.

🛌 Sleeping

⭐ **Goiabada com Queijo** HOSTEL **$**
(☎31 3552-3816, 31 99435-1813; www.facebook.com/HostelGoiabadacomQueijo; Rua do Pilar 44; dm R$40-50; 🛜) Midway between Praça Tiradentes and the train station, this sweet and simple three-room hostel is a labor of love for well-traveled owner Lidiane, who makes guests feel at home with her solid command of German and English and her enthusiasm for showing off Ouro Prêto's hidden treasures.

Pousada São Francisco HOSTEL, GUESTHOUSE **$**
(☎31 3551-3456; www.pousadasaofranciscodepaula.com.br; Padre Pena 201; dm R$50, s R$80-100, d R$120-200, tr R$200-250, q R$250-300; @🛜) Hidden away on a leafy hillside full of chirping birds, this old-school hostel-like guesthouse has friendly multilingual staff and a guest kitchen. The two upstairs rooms with panoramic terraces are the best of the bunch. From the bus station, follow signs five minutes downhill, turning left opposite Igreja

RIDING THE VINTAGE RAILS

On weekends, the Vale mining company operates a renovated historic **tourist train** (www.vale.com/brasil/PT/business/logistics/railways/trem-turistico-ouro-preto-mariana; one-way/round trip R$46/66, air-conditioned panoramic car R$70/90) between Ouro Prêto and Mariana, leaving Ouro Prêto's **train station** (☑31 3551-7705; Praça Cesário Alvim) at the south edge of town once daily on Thursday and twice daily Friday, Saturday and Sunday. The 18km, one-hour journey is pretty, but slow, snaking along a river gorge the whole way. Best views are from the right side leaving Ouro Prêto. Mariana has an attractive, compact historical center that's easier to navigate than Ouro Prêto's, not only because of its smaller size, but also because the hills are less steep.

São Francisco de Paula. After-dark arrivals can phone for an escort to help find it.

⭐**Pouso do Chico Rei** POUSADA $$
(☑31 3551-1274; www.pousodochicorei.com.br; Brigadeiro Musqueira 90; s R$210-250, d R$240-290, tr R$310-370, q R$400-450, s/d/tr without bathroom from R$100/175/260; ✳@🛜) Ouro Prêto's best midrange option, this beautifully preserved 18th-century mansion directly opposite the Carmo church is all charm, with creaky wood floors and a breakfast room full of hand-painted antique cupboards. Each room is unique, and most have period furniture and wonderful views. The three least-expensive rooms share a bathroom.

✗ Eating & Drinking

⭐**Casa do Ouvidor** MINEIRA $$
(☑31 3551-2141; www.casadoouvidor.com.br; Direita 42; mains per person R$29-69; ⊙11am-3pm & 7-10pm) Just downhill from Praça Tiradentes, Ouvidor has garnered numerous awards for its authentic *comida mineira* over the past four decades, with specialties like *tutu à mineira* (mashed beans with roast pork loin, crackling, collard greens and boiled egg). At night, low lighting enhances the rustic charm of the ancient wood-beamed upstairs dining room. Bring an empty stomach – portions are immense!

⭐**O Passo** ITALIAN $$
(☑31 3552-5089; www.opassopizzajazz.com; São José 56; pizzas R$50-69, mains R$33-79;

⊙11:30am-midnight Sun-Thu, to 1am Fri & Sat) In a lovely 18th-century building with intimate candlelit interior, this local favorite specializes in pizza, pasta and salads complemented by a good wine list. Outside, the relaxed creekside terrace is ideal for an after-dinner drink. On Tuesday nights, don't miss the *rodizio de pizzas* (all-you-can-eat pizza; R$42). There's live jazz on Thursday and Friday evenings, and during Sunday lunch.

Cervejaria Ouropretana –
Loja da Fábrica MICROBREWERY
(☑31 98818-0646; www.ouropretana.com.br; Benedito Valadares 250; ⊙3-9pm Tue-Fri, noon-9pm Sat) The recently launched brewpub affiliated with Ouro Prêto's favorite microbrewery is a festive place for bar snacks and glasses of Ouropretana's trademark coffee lager or passion fruit and ginger IPA. It's especially boisterous on Tuesday evenings, when pint prices get slashed in half.

ℹ Information

Centro Cultural e Turístico da FIEMG (☑31 3551-3637; turismo@ouropreto.mg.gov.br; Praça Tiradentes 4; ⊙8:15am-7pm) Ouro Prêto's underfunded tourist office can provide general information about the city, but if you want a map, you'll need to snap a photo of the dog-eared copy on the countertop.

Look for banks with ATMs on Praça Tiradentes and Rua São José including **Banco do Brasil** (São José 189) and **Bradesco** (São José 201).

ℹ Getting There & Away

Long-distance buses leave from Ouro Prêto's main **bus station** (☑31 3559-3252; Padre Rolim 661), a 10-minute uphill walk from Praça Tiradentes at the northwest end of town. During peak periods, buy tickets a day in advance.

Pássaro Verde (☑31 3551-1081; www.gabrasil.com.br) provides service to Belo Horizonte (R$34, two hours, hourly from 6am to 8pm); **Útil** (☑31 3551-3166; www.util.com.br) goes to Rio (R$100 to R$123, eight hours, 10am and 9:30pm daily) and São Paulo (R$154, 11 hours, 7pm daily).

Tiradentes

☑0XX32 / POP 7807 / ELEV 927M

Perhaps nowhere else in Minas do the colonial architecture and picturesque natural setting blend so harmoniously as in Tiradentes. Quaint historic houses, fringed by exuberant wildflowers, stand out against a backdrop of pretty blue mountains threaded with hiking trails. If you can, visit midweek, when the town's abundant attractions are most easily appreciated. On weekends, the swarms of visitors who come to gawk at Tiradentes' antique stores and boutiques can make the place feel a bit like a theme park, and the sudden increase in horse-drawn carriages creates some strong aromas!

◉ Sights

★**Igreja Matriz de Santo Antônio** CHURCH
(Padre Toledo s/n; admission R$5; ☺9am-5pm) Named for Tiradentes' patron saint, this gorgeous church is one of Aleijadinho's last designs. The dazzling gold interior is rich in Old Testament symbolism. Noteworthy elements include the polychrome organ, built in Portugal and brought here by donkey in 1798, and the seven golden phoenixes suspending candleholders from long braided chains. The famous sundial out front dates back to 1785.

★**Mazuma Mineira** DISTILLERY
(☑32 3353-6654; www.mazuma.com.br; São Bento 300, Bichinho; ☺9:30am-5pm Thu-Sat, Mon & Tue, to 2:30pm Sun) **FREE** If you've ever wondered how *cachaça* (Brazil's famous sugarcane alcohol) is made, this is a perfect place to learn. This small-scale *alambique* (distillery) with a focus on sustainable production offers free guided tours demonstrating every stage of the process, from harvesting and milling of sugarcane, to filtering and separation of the juice, to distillation at high heat in elegant copper cooling towers, to aging in casks of oak, Brazil nut or local pink jequitibá wood. It's located 7km northeast of Tiradentes.

Igreja NS Rosário dos Pretos CHURCH
(Praça Padre Lourival; admission R$3; ☺10am-4pm Wed-Mon) This beautiful stone church, with its many images of black saints, was built in 1708, by and for slaves. Since they had no free time during daylight hours, construction took place at night – note the nocturnal iconography in the ceiling paintings of an eight-pointed black star and a half-moon.

Museu de Sant'Ana MUSEUM
(☑32 3355-2798; www.museudesantana.org.br; cnr Cadeia & Direita; adult/reduced R$5/2.50; ☺10am-7pm Wed-Mon) This innovative museum in Tiradentes' former town jail was conceived by Belo Horizonte–based Angela Gutierrez, creator of Ouro Prêto's **Museu**

do Oratório (☑31 3551-5369; www.museudo oratorio.org.br; Adro da Igreja do Carmo 28; adult/reduced R$5/2.50; ☺9:30am-5:30pm Wed-Mon) and Belo Horizonte's **Museu de Artes e Ofícios** (☑31 3248-8600; www.mao.org.br; Praça Rui Barbosa 600; ☺9am-9pm Tue, to 5pm Wed-Sun) **FREE**. The simple but beautifully presented collection features 270 images of St Anne in wood, stone and terracotta, from the 17th century to the present. Bilingual exhibits trace the importance of St Anne imagery throughout Brazil and its evolution through the baroque and rococo periods.

❶ Getting There & Away

Tiradentes' **bus station** (São Francisco de Paula 71) is just north of the main square, across the stream. Two companies, Presidente (R$3.80, 20 minutes) and Porto Real (R$4.20, 30 minutes), run regular buses between Tiradentes and São João del Rei.

Tiradentes' **train station** (Praça da Estação s/n; ☺ticket office 9am-4pm Thu-Sat, to 1pm Sun) is located about 700m southeast of the main square. A tourist train connects Tiradentes with São João del Rei.

THE SOUTH

Spectacular white-sand beaches, pristine subtropical islands and the thunderous roar of Iguaçu Falls are a few of the attractions of Brazil's affluent South. While often given short shrift by first-time visitors, the states of Paraná, Santa Catarina and Rio Grande do Sul offer a radically different version of what it means to be Brazilian. Here *gaúchos* still cling to the cowboy lifestyle on the wide plains bordering Argentina and Uruguay, while old-world architecture, European-style beer, blond hair and blue eyes reveal the influence of millions of German, Italian, Swiss and Eastern European immigrants.

❶ Getting There & Around

The major air gateways are Curitiba, Florianópolis, Porto Alegre, and Iguaçu Falls, which borders both Argentina and Paraguay. All these cities have good bus connections to São Paulo.

❶ Getting Around

Short flights and longer bus journeys connect the four major cities of the South. If you're heading to Ilha do Mel, don't miss the scenic train ride from Curitiba through the Serra do Mar to Morretes.

BRAZIL THE SOUTH

South Brazil

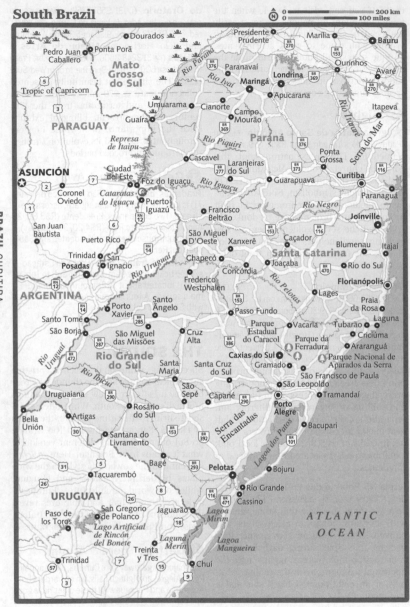

Curitiba

☑ 0XX41 / POP 1.75 MILLION

Known as Brazil's eco-evolved capital and famous for its efficient urban planning, Curitiba is one of Brazil's metropolitan success stories, with pleasant parks, well-preserved historic buildings, little traffic congestion and a large university population.

◉ Sights & Activities

★ **Museu Oscar Niemeyer**   MUSEUM
(MON; ☑ 413350-4400; www.museuoscarniemeyer.
org.br; Marechal Hermes 999; adult/child R$20/10,

free Wed 10am-6pm & 1st Weds of the month until 8pm; ☉10am-6pm Tue-Sun) Designed by and named for the architect responsible for much of Brasília, this striking museum features an iconic eye-shaped tower painted with whimsical dancing figures in shadowy black. Rotating exhibits highlight Brazilian and international artists of the 20th and 21st centuries. Permanent exhibitions include a photographic time capsule of the museum's construction (housed in the tower) and an excellent presentation on Niemeyer himself, the highlight of the space.

There's a nice shop for those into Niemeyer's signature style. Bus 505 from Passeio Público stops right at the museum.

Curitiba Free Walking Tour WALKING
(☑41 98875-7721; www.curitibafreewalking.com; ☉11am Sat) FREE This recommended walking tour meets on the steps of the Federal University of Paraná every Saturday at 11am for a 2½-hour jaunt through the historic *centro*. Tipping is encouraged (R$10 to R$15 is fine).

🛏 Sleeping

★**Motter Home** HOSTEL $
(☑41 3209-5649; www.motterhome.com.br; Desembargador Motta 3574; dm R$40-54, d/tr R$150/200; @🛜) In leafy Mercês, Curitiba's top hostel inhabits a canary-yellow, turret-style mansion from the '50s, with striking art, retro-sophisticated common areas, original hardwood floors and funky door handles. It's a 15-minute walk from Largo da Ordem.

Curitiba Casa HOSTEL $
(☑41 3044-7313; www.curitibacasahostel.com; Brasílio Itiberê 73; dm R$46-52, r R$135; @🛜) Despite its odd location 15 minutes east of the *rodoferroviária* (bus and train station), this hostel has more fans than *futebol*. Clean, colorful and classy.

🍴 Eating & Drinking

Rua 24 Horas, near Praça General Osório, is a street that's now an atmospheric enclosed food court (and no, it's not open 24 hours). On warm nights, revelers spill out of pubs and cafes onto the streets around Praça Garibaldi and Largo da Ordem. You'll find the city's most happening nightlife along Av Vincent Machado in hip Batel.

Mercado Municipal MARKET $
(www.mercadomunicipaldecuritiba.com.br; 7 de Setembro 1865; ☉7am-2pm Mon, to 6pm Tue-Sat, to 1pm Sun) 🥬 Curitiba's excellent urban market, full of food stalls, cafes, gourmet emporiums and Brazil's first organic food court.

★**Rause Cafe + Vinho** CAFE
(www.rausecafe.com.br; Carlos de Carvalho 696; coffee from R$6.50; ☉9am-11pm Mon-Fri, 9am-7pm Sat; 🛜) At its heart, this is a retro coffeehouse (choose from specialty Bahia and Minas coffees, brewed in a variety of pour-over methods), but there's a great selection of eats as well (wild boar and gorgonzola risotto, fig confit and brie crepes), plus wine.

★**Hop'N Roll** BAR
(☑41 3408-4486; www.hopnroll.com.br; Mateus Leme 950; ☉5:30pm-1am Mon-Thu, to 2am Fri & Sat; 🛜) The hophead assault on this excellent craft beer bar's 32 draft options – served in proper pints – is relentless. Aficionados will find the lion's share of local and southern Brazil's artisanal beers either on draft or on the 120+ bottle menu – and Hop'N Roll brews its own, too. Book ahead if you want a seat.

ℹ Information

Helpful tourist offices:

CAT Jardim Botânico (Centro de Atendimento ao Turista; ☑41 3362-3831; www.turismo.curitiba.pr.gov.br; Ostoja Roguski 690, Jardim Botânico; ☉9am-6pm)

PIT Aeroporto Internacional Afonso Pena (Posto de Informações Turísticas; ☑41 3381-1153; www.turismo.curitiba.pr.gov.br; Av Rocha Pombo, Aeroporto Internacional Afonso Pena, Arrivals Hall; ☉7am-11pm Mon-Fri, to 6pm Sat & Sun)

PIT Oi Torre Panorâmica (Posto de Informações Turísticas; ☑41 3339-7613; www.turismo.curitiba.pr.gov.br; Castro Vellozo 191, Oi Torre Panorâmica; ☉10am-7pm Tue-Sun)

PIT Rodoferroviária (☑41 3225-4336; Av Affonso Camargo 330, Rodoferroviária; ☉9am-6pm)

ℹ Getting There & Away

AIR

There are direct flights from **Aeroporto Internacional Afonso Pena** (CWB; ☑41 3381-1515; www.aeroportocuritiba.net; Av Rocha Pombo s/n, São José dos Pinhais), 18km southeast of Centro, to cities throughout Brazil.

BUS

Curitiba's long-distance bus and train stations form a single three-block complex called the **rodoferroviária** (☑41 3320-3000; www.urbs.curitiba.pr.gov.br/comunidade/rodoferroviaria; Av Pres Affonso Camargo 330), which sits 2km

BRAZIL CURITIBA

southeast of downtown and received a World Cup 2014 makeover. Access to the departures areas are restricted to ticket holders. Ticket counters for interstate bus travel (*interestadual*) sit on the second floor of the first block; bus companies for destinations within Paraná (*estadual*) are located on the second floor of the second block. The train station block sits behind the two bus station blocks.

TRAIN

The **Serra Verde Express** (☏ 41 3888-3488; www.serraverdeexpress.com.br; Estação Ferroviária) train between Curitiba and Morretes via the Serra do Mar is one of the marvels of travel in Brazil.

ℹ Getting Around

URBS (www.urbs.curitiba.pr.gov.br) runs Curitiba's space-age bus system, made up of integrated station pods, known as *tubos*. City buses, several of which are electric/biodiesel (Hibribuses), cost R$4.25.

The classy, wi-fi-enabled **Aeroporto Executivo** (☏ 41 99817-9666; www.aeroportoexecutivo. com.br; one way R$15) runs direct every 15 minutes from 5:25am to midnight (from 6am Sunday) between the airport and well-marked Centro stops, including: **Teatro Guaíra** (XV de Novembro), Receita Federal, **Bibiloteca Nacional** (Cândido Lopes 133) and **Rua 24 Horas** (Visconde de Nacar). From the *rodoferroviária* (bus/train station), buses run from 4:40am to 11:11pm (5:30am to 11:24pm Sunday). An express bus follows the same schedule but only goes between the airport, *rodoferroviária* and Estação Shopping.

Paranaguá

☏ 0XX41 / POP 140,500

Paranaguá is the embarkation point for ferries to idyllic Ilha do Mel. Colorful but now faded buildings along the colonial waterfront create a feeling of languid tropical decadence.

Hostel Continente (☏ 41 3423-3224; info@ hostelcontinente.com.br; General Carneiro 300; dm R$50, s/d/tr R$80/140/180; ❄ ☎) has clean if cramped dorms and doubles in an enviable location across from the ferry dock

From the **bus station** (☏ 41 3420-2925; Ponta do Caju) on the waterfront, **Viação Graciosa** (☏ 41 3423-1215; www.viacaograciosa.com. br; Ponta do Caju, Rodoviária de Paranaguá) has 13 buses per day to Curitiba (R$30.87, 1½ hours) and frequent departures on a bus that circulates between Paranaguá, Antonina and Morretes (R$6.45, one hour). You can also continue south without heading back to Curitiba – two buses per day leave for Joinville (R$30.45, two hours, 6am & 4pm).

Ilha do Mel

☏ 0XX41 / POP 1100

This hourglass-shaped island at the mouth of the Baía de Paranaguá is the most picturesque beach resort in all of southern Brazil, offering mostly wild beaches, good surfing waves and scenic coastal walks. Accessible only by boat, Ilha do Mel is traversed by sandy paths and has not a single car, so traffic jams through-

BUSES FROM CURITIBA

DESTINATION	STARTING FARE (R$)	DURATION (HR)	COMPANY
Buenos Aires* (AR)	385	32	JBL (www.jblturismo.com.br)
Florianópolis	56	5	Catarinense (www.catarinense.net)
Foz do Iguaçu	193	10	Catarinense
Joinville	31	2	Catarinense
Montevideo** (UY)	415	25	TTL (www.ttl.com.br)
Morretes	27	1½	Graciosa (www.viacaograciosa.com.br)
Paranaguá	33.50	1¾	Graciosa
Rio de Janeiro	172	14	Penha (www.nspenha.com.br), Kaissara (www.kaissara.com.br)
Santiago (CL)***	455	50	JBL
São Paulo	65	7	Kaissara (www.kaissara.com.br), Cometa (www.viacaocometa.com.br)

* Departs Tuesday, Thursday and Saturday at 4am.

** Departs Tuesday at 5:30am.

*** Departs 8pm on Sunday.

out the island's scenic sandy lanes consist of surfboard-toting Brazilians on bicycles and bedazzled foreigners in their new Havaianas (flip-flops).

◉ Sights & Activities

Ilha do Mel has no shortage of beaches. **Praia da Fora** and **Praia Grande** are a 20-minute walk (2km) from Nova Brasília and a 40-minute walk (4km) from Encantadas. **Praia do Farol** is the long stretch of sand between the Nova Brasília dock and the Farol das Conchas (an 1872 lighthouse that's a great spot for watching the sunset). Surfers congregate at the base of the hill and ride the legendary **Ondas das Paralelas**.

If you didn't bring your surfboard, you might prefer the calmer, warmer waters of the beaches that face the shallow bay. In the north, **Praia da Fortaleza**, often nearly deserted, allows you to bathe in the shadow of the 18th-century Portuguese fort. The best beach near the settlement of Encantadas is **Praia da Fora**, which has big waves and a few stalls selling *cervejas* (beers) and *sucos* (fruit juices).

🛏 Sleeping & Eating

★ **Pousada das Meninas**   POUSADA $$
(☑41 3426-8023; www.pousadadasmeninas.com. br; Vila do Farol s/n, Nova Brasília; s/d without bathroom from R$180/360, with bathroom from R$280/400, chalets R$210-550; ❋ 🛜) 🅿 Built from driftwood and recycled material, this pousada has the charm of a guesthouse and a family welcome. Hung with hammocks and chock-full of cutesy kitsch, the simple but tasteful rooms are set around a cozy garden.

★ **Bob Pai e Bob Filho**   POUSADA $$
(☑41 3426-9006; joelsonbobpai@yahoo.com. br; Praia de Encantadas s/n; r R$270; ❋ 🐾 @ 🛜) 'Father Bob and Son Bob' easily wins the island's personality contest with eight unadorned but well-equipped rooms (flat-screen TVs, minibars, beach kits – some with hammock-strewn patios) surrounding the atmospheric Captain's Bar and knick-knack-peppered gardens.

★ **Mar e Sol**   SEAFOOD $$
(www.restaurantemaresol.com.br; Praça Felipe Valentim, Farol dos Conchas; meals R$29-38; ⏰11am-10pm; 🛜) En route to the lighthouse, Mar e Sol serves spectacular fish, shrimp and crab *moquecas* (seafood stews; R$109 to

R$255 for two), seafood risottos, and cheaper daily specials in individual portions. Junior, the local pet parrot, gives recommendations.

ℹ Information

There are no banks, ATMs or pharmacies on the island, so plan ahead. Most services are clustered near the ferry dock in Nova Brasília.

Ilha do Mel's tourist information booths are handily located at each arrival dock.

CIT (Centro de Informações Turística; ☑41 3426-9112; Arrival Dock, Nova Brasília; ⏰8am-7pm, to 8pm Nov-Mar)

CIT (Centro de Informações Turística; Encantadas; ⏰8am-noon & 2-6pm Wed-Sun)

ℹ Getting There & Away

Abaline-PR (☑41 3455-6325; www.abaline. com.br; General Carneiro 258) runs boats (R$53 return) at 8:30am, 9:30am, 11am, 1pm, 3pm, 4:30pm and 6pm in summer (these dwindle to 9:30am and 3:30pm in low season) from the jetty opposite Paranaguá's tourist office, stopping first in Nova Brasília (1½ hours), and then in **Encantadas** (Praia das Encantadas; two hours). Returning to the mainland, boats depart Nova Brasília for Paranaguá in summer at 8am, 10am, 1:30pm, 3:30pm, 4:30pm, 6:30pm and 7pm. In low season, departures are 8am and 5pm during the week and 10:30am and 5pm on weekends. All boats leave a half-hour earlier from Encantadas.

Alternatively, **Viação Graciosa** (www.viacao graciosa.com.br) runs four to six daily buses to/from Curitiba to Pontal do Sul (R$42.74, 2½ hours), on the mainland opposite Encantadas, where you can embark for the 30-minute crossing to Nova Brasília or Encantadas (R$35 return). In high season, boats leave every half hour from 8am to 8pm from Pontal and from Ilha do Mel; in low season, every hour until 6pm.

ℹ Getting Around

It's a 4.5km tide-dependent walk from Nova Brasília to Encantadas – do not set out without checking with tide charts and/or locals; otherwise, grab the island ferry from one village to the other (R$15, 20 minutes, hourly, 8am to 7:30pm).

Florianópolis & Ilha de Santa Catarina

Ilha de Santa Catarina has a vibrant and varied coastline, from the calm, crowded bays of the north, to the wild, cliff-hugging beaches south. But it's not just the beaches that make this island so enchanting. A forest of

Ilha de Santa Catarina

0 — 10 km
0 — 5 miles

Ponta do Rapa

Ponta das Canas
Ponta das Canas

Praia da Lagoinha
Lagoinha
Praia Brava

Ilha do Francês

Ilha Mato-Fame

Praia de Canasvieiras
Cachoeira do Bom Jesus

Ponta do Magalhães

Ponta dos Currais

Praia de Jurerê

Canasvieiras

Praia dos Ingleses

Baía de São Miguel

Ponta da Cruz
Ponta Grossa

Ingleses do Rio Vermelho

Praia do Santinho

Daniela
Pontal

SC 402
SC 403
TICAN

Rio Ratones
SC 401

Muquém

SC 406

Ilha do Ratones Grande

Ponta de Sambaqui

São João do Rio Vermelho

Ilha do Ratones Pequeno

Sambaqui

Ratones

Ilhas das Aranhas

Biguaçu

Santo Antônio de Lisboa

Baía Norte

Ponta do Forte

Cacupé

Praia do Moçambique

Ilha de Santa Catarina

Costa da Lagoa

Parque Flor do Rio Vermelho

Ponta Três Henriques

Praia do Saco Grande

Lagoa da Conceição

Praia Barra da Lagoa

Itacorubi

Ponta da Galheta

TICEN
SC 404
TILAG

Barra da Lagoa

Florianópolis

Ponta do Caçador

BR 282

Lagoa da Conceição

Praia Mole

São José

Ilha das Vinhas

Saco dos Limões

Canto da Lagoa
SC 406

Ponta da Gravatá

Ilha do Xavier

Praia da Joaquina

Ponta Pirajubaé

Palhoça

Ponta Coroa Grande

Carianos
SC 405

Praia do Campeche

Florianópolis-Hercílio Luz International Airport
TIRIO
Rio Tavares

Baía Sul

Tapera
Alto Ribeirão
SC 405

Campeche

Ilha do Campeche

Ilha Maria Francisca

Reserva Ecológica e Arqueológica

Ribeirão da Ilha

Morro das Pedras

Lagoa do Peri

Ponta do Constantino

Armação

SC 405
Parque da Lagoa do Peri

Praia da Armação

Ponta do Cuaiaguçu
Caiaguçu

Matadeiro
SC 406

Enseado do Brito

Costa de Dentro

Pântano do Sul

Ponta da Lagoinha
Lagoinha do Leste

ATLANTIC OCEAN

Tapera
Solidão

Praia dos Açores

Ponta da Andorinha

Caieiras da Barra do Sul

Praia Solidão
Saquinho

Praia dos Naufragados

BR 101

Ilhas das Três Irmãs

PARQUE NACIONAL DE APARADOS DA SERRA

This magnificent national park is 18km from the town of Cambará do Sul, approximately 200km northeast of Porto Alegre. The most famous attraction is the Cânion do Itaimbezinho, a fantastic narrow canyon with dramatic waterfalls and sheer escarpments of 600m to 720m.

Two easy self-guided trails, Trilha do Vértice (2km return) and Trilha Cotovelo (6km return), lead from the park's visitor center to waterfalls and canyon vistas; the more challenging Trilha do Rio do Boi follows the base of the canyon for 7km; it also requires a guide and is closed during rainy season. For guided trips, try the excellent eco-agency **Cânion Turismo** (☑ 54 3251-1027; www.canionturismo.com.br; Getúlio Vargas 876; ⊘ 8am-7pm) ✐. Midway between Cambará and Itaimbezinho, the stunning **Parador Casa da Montanha** (☑ 54 3295-7575; www.paradorcasadamontanha.com.br; Estrada do Faxinal, RS-429; d incl afternoon tea R$450-2500; @⟨⟩) is modeled after luxurious African safari camps, and overlooks araucária forest and a rushing waterfall.

Citral (www.citral.tur.br) offers one bus from Porto Alegre for Cambará do Sul (R$48, 5½ hours) at 6am Monday to Saturday. Returning, you must catch a 7am or 1:30pm bus to São Francisco de Paula (R$20, one hour) and switch there for Porto Alegre (from R$30, three hours), Canela (from R$11, one hour) or Gramado (from R$12, one hour). From Cambará do Sul, a taxi to the national park costs around R$100 round trip.

protected pines shelters the east coast, while the dunes near Praia da Joaquina create a lunar landscape. The spine of mountains, luxuriant with the Mata Atlântica (Atlantic rainforest), drops precipitously down to the lovely Lagoa da Conceição.

Though technically speaking, the whole island is Florianópolis, it's downtown Floripa, known as Centro, that is both the political capital of Santa Catarina, the cultural capital of southern Brazil and the gateway to the rest of the island. The island's *bairros* (districts) can feel like completely different towns, with their own distinct personalities and infrastructure.

🏃 Activities

Surfing, kitesurfing and diving outfits line the beach at Barra da Lagoa, on the island's eastern shore. A few kilometers south, try your hand at sand boarding on the dunes at Praia da Joaquina or stand-up paddling at Lagoa da Conceição.

The island's southern tip offers excellent hiking, including the one-hour trek through lush forest from Pântano do Sul to pristine Lagoinha do Leste beach, and whale-watching from June to November.

🛏 Sleeping & Eating

Our favorite places are around the rowdy and social Lagoa da Conceição and the more tranquil south island, but the island has many more nooks and crannies of surf and sand spread throughout its 42 beaches. Prices drop between 15% and 40% outside high season.

★ Tucano House   HOSTEL $
(☑ 48 3207-8287; www.tucanohouse.com; Rua das Araras 229; dm R$55-75, d with/without bathroom from R$260/240; ⊘ closed Mar 15-Nov; ❄@⟨⟩⟨⟩) ✐ Siblings Lila and Caio are your hospitality wizard hosts at this eco-forward hostel in the heart of Lagoa. Their childhood home now features solar-heated showers, a recycled rainwater cistern and amenities like bike and surfboard rentals. Dorms have personal USB ports, and the revamped outdoor bar is killer for a cold one. Island adventures are in a decked-out VW van.

★ Barra Beach Club   HOSTEL $$
(☑ 48 3232-3336; www.barrabeachclub.com; Servidão da Prainha 122; dm R$80-90, d with/without bathroom R$250/220; ⊘ closed May-Aug; ❄⟨⟩) This American-run hostel earns top honors across the pedestrian bridge. Three-, four- and 10-bed dorm facilities are spread across several buildings, all with spectacular seaview terraces. It's popular with surfers (wetsuits, short and longboards, and bodyboards are all available for free) who are content to kick back here with Asian and Italian meals, veranda massages and post-wave beers at the bar.

★ **Café Cultura** CAFE $$
(www.cafeculturafloripa.com.br; Severino de Ol-
iveira 635; mains R$9-46.50; ⊙8:30am-11:30pm
Mon-Sat, to 10pm Sun; 🕿) Breakfast until 1pm,
waffles, salads, panini (really bruschetta,
but who's paying attention?), sophisticated
mains and specialty java served by various
methods. Floripa's best cafe is brought to
you by a Californian ex-Starbucks barista
and his Brazilian coffee-heiress wife. The
expanded location is gorgeous, with cof-
fee sacks as lampshades and cushy couch
seating.

★ **Ostradamus** SEAFOOD $$$
(✆48 3337-5711; www.ostradamus.com.br; Rod
Baldicero Filomeno 7640; oysters R$35-45, mains
for 2 people R$135-195; ⊙noon-11pm Tue-Sat,
to 5pm Sun; 🕿) Atmospheric tables line the
glass-enclosed deck at this incredibly cinematic seafood restaurant. You can slurp
oysters served over a dozen ways, but don't
fill up on those – the outstanding and incredibly presented seafood dishes here are
a vacation highlight.

❶ Information

'Floripa' has four government-run tourist info
booths of interest to tourists, one at the airport,
three in Centro and another near Armacão (open
seasonally).

CAT (Centro de Atendimento ao Turista; ✆48
3228-1095; www.vivendofloripa.com.br; Rodoviária; ⊙8am-6pm)

CAT (Centro de Atendimento ao Turista; ✆48
3337-5040; www.santur.sc.gov.br; Florianópolis-Hercílio Luz International Airport;
⊙7am-midnight)

CAT (Centro de Atendimento ao Turista; ✆48
3240-4407; www.vivendofloripa.com.br; Conselheiro Mafra 255, Mercado Público; ⊙9am-
6pm Mon-Fri, to noon Sat)

CAT (Centro de Atendimento ao Turista; ✆48
3348-3554; www.vivendofloripa.com.br; Portal
Turístico de Florianópolis; ⊙8am-6pm)

❶ Getting There & Away

Floripa Airport (Florianópolis-Hercílio Luz
International Airport; ✆48 3331-4000;
www.floripa-airport.com/contato.html; Rod
Deputado Diomício Freitas 3393, Bairro Carianos), 12km south of Centro, and **Terminal
Rodoviário Rita Maria** (✆48 3212-3508; Av
Paulo Fontes 1101), Florianópolis' long-distance
bus station, are the main gateways in and out
of the island, while **TICEN** (Terminal de Inte-
gração Centro; www.consorciofenix.com.br; Av
Paulo Fontes s/n), Centro's integrated local bus
terminal, is the transport hub for local buses to
the rest of the island.

To reach the airport, buses 183 'Corredor
Sudoeste' (35 minutes) and 186 'Corredor
Sudoeste Semi-Direto' (25 minutes) leave from
TICEN (p354) terminal frequently between 5am
and 12:30am. Uber fares are around R$18 or so
to Centro, R$26 or so to Lagoa da Conceicão and
R$36 or so to Barra da Lagoa.

❶ Getting Around

Local buses run on an integrated scheme called
SIM – *Sistema Integrado de Mobilidade*. Buses
leave from the TICEN (p354) terminal, one block
east of Florianópolis' long-distance bus station.
Connections to the island's beaches are made
via three outlying terminals: **TIRIO** (Terminal Rio
Tavares; www.consorciofenix.com.br; SC-405
630), **TILAG** (Terminal Lagoa da Conceição;
www.consorciofenix.com.br; Av Afonso Delam-

BUSES FROM FLORIANÓPOLIS

DESTINATION	STARTING FARE (R$)	TIME (HR)	BUS COMPANY
Asunción (Paraguay)	104	22	Nordeste (www.expnordeste.com.br)
Blumenau	53	3	Catarinense (www.catarinense.net)
Buenos Aires (Argentina)	458	25	JBL (www.jblturismo.com.br)
Curitiba	51	5	Catarinense
Foz do Iguaçu	179	14	Catarinense
Garopaba	27	2	Santo Anjo (www.santoanjo.com.br)
Joinville	63	2½	Catarinense
Montevideo (Uruguay)	350	18	EGA (www.ega.com.uy)
Porto Alegre	115	6	Eucatur (www.eucatur.com.br)
Rio de Janeiro	214	17	Itapemirim (www.itapemirim.com.br)
Santiago (Chile)	440	44	JBL (www.jblturismo.com.br)
São Paulo	122	12	Catarinense

BRAZIL FLORIANÓPOLIS & ILHA DE SANTA CATARINA

bert Neto 51) and **TICAN** (Terminal Canasvieiras; www.consorciofenix.com.br; Francisco Faustino Martins 877).

For southern beaches, including Armação, Pântano do Sul and Costa de Dentro, catch bus 410 'Rio Tavares' (Platform B), then transfer at TIRIO to bus 563.

For eastern beaches, catch bus 330 'Lagoa da Conceição' (Platform A), then transfer at TILAG for a second bus to your final destination, for example bus 360 to Barra da Lagoa.

For Canasvieiras and northern beaches, catch bus 210 'Canasvieiras Direto' (Platform B) from TICEN to TICAN.

A single fare of R\$4.20 (paid at the TICEN ticket booth) covers your initial ride plus one transfer.

Floripanoponto (www.floripanoponto.com.br) is a handy trip planner. It's available both online and as an app (Android/iOS).

Porto Alegre

📝 0XX51 / POP 1.4 MILLION

Porto Alegre is a good introduction to progressive Rio Grande do Sul. Built on the banks of the Rio Guaíba, this lively, modern port has a well-preserved neoclassical downtown, with handsome plazas, good museums, and a vibrant arts and music scene.

👁 Sights

Praça 15 de Novembro, site of the 1869 Mercado Público (p356), is the centerpiece of the city. The old building bustles during daytime hours, when vendors sell fresh produce, meats and seafood, as well as the all-important *erva maté* for *chimarrão* (tea).

Three blocks south, the picturesque Praça da Matriz is dominated by the early 20th-century neoclassical **Catedral Metropolitana** (www.catedralportoalegre.com.br; Duque de Caxias 1047; ⏲ 7am-7pm Mon-Fri, from 9am Sat, from 8am Sun) FREE. On the northern side, you'll find the elegant mid-19th-century edifice of the **Teatro São Pedro** (📝 51 3227-5100; www.teatrosaopedro.com.br; Praça Mal Deodoro s/n; ⏲ box office 1-6:30pm Mon-Fri, to 3pm Sat & Sun) and the sculpted facade of the **Biblioteca Público** (📝 51 3224-5045; www.bibliotecapublica.rs.gov.br; cnr Riachuelo & General Câmara; ⏲ 9am-7pm Mon-Fri, 2-6pm Sat).

🛏 Sleeping

Most travelers stay in Cidade Baixa, where a hostel and nightlife scene thrive, or the leafy northern districts of Moinhos de Vento, Rio Branco and Bom Fim.

★ **Porto Alegre Eco Hostel** HOSTEL $
(📝 51 3377-8876; www.poaecohostel.com.br; Luiz Afonso 276; dm R\$43, s/d from R\$80/145; @ 🛜 🎐) Down a quiet residential street in the heart of Cidade Baixa, this excellent hostel, chock-full of demolition wood furniture and eco-awareness, has a lovely backyard garden in a pristine '30s-era home.

Brick Hostel HOSTEL $
(📝 51 3028-3333; www.brickhostel.com; Cabral 217; dm R\$46-58, r R\$150; ✳ 🛜) ∅ This Rio Branco hostel is walking distance from Parque Farroupilha, Moinhos de Vento and Centro but is a quiet respite from both the latter and the more rambunctious Cidade Baixa. There's an artsy common area (local

BRAZIL PORTO ALEGRE

WORTH A TRIP

JESUIT MISSIONS

In the 16th century, the Portuguese and Spanish kings authorized Catholic orders to create missions to convert the natives. The Jesuits were the most successful order, establishing a series of reductions (missions) across Paraguay, Bolivia, Brazil and Argentina. At its height in the 1720s, this prosperous 'nation' claimed 30 mission villages inhabited by more than 150,000 Guarani people.

Today, all 30 missions are in ruins. Together, they form the Rota Missões, or 'Missions Route,' a network of pilgrimage sites for the faithful and the curious. Seven are in Brazil (in the northwestern part of Rio Grande do Sul), eight are in southern Paraguay and 15 are in northeastern Argentina.

The town of Santo Ângelo is the main jumping-off point for the Brazilian missions; the most interesting and intact site is **Sítio Arqueológico São Miguel Arcanjo** (adult/child R\$14/7, incl Museu das Missões; ⏲ 9am-noon & 2-8pm Oct-Mar, 9am-noon & 2-6pm Tue-Sun, 1:30-6pm Mon Apr-Sep), 53km southwest of Santo Ângelo in São Miguel das Missões. Several buses daily run from Porto Alegre to Sânto Angelo, where you can make onward connections to São Miguel das Missões (R\$13.25, 1½ hours, two to three daily).

Porto Alegre

BRAZIL PORTO ALEGRE

Porto Alegre

art for sale) and dorms with individual lockers, reading lights and electrical outlets, plus a few minimalist private rooms.

✗ Eating & Drinking

While here, don't miss an opportunity to try a Brazilian *churrascaria* (or *rodízio*) – this is where the all-you-can eat meat fest originated.

★ Agridoce Café
CAFE **$**

(Sarmento Leite 1024; mains R$16-29; ⊙ noon-10pm Tue-Sun; 🛜🅿) Don't judge a cafe by its facade! Enter the fascinating Victorian-vintage world of Agridoce and you'll quickly learn which Southern Brazilian cafe is hogging all of the personality. With walls adorned with a dissected chest of drawers, well-traveled suitcases and other retro paraphernalia, each room is a different dive into a kaleidoscope of detail and design.

Mercado Público
MARKET **$$**

(www.mercadopublico.com.br; Galeria Mercado Público Central s/n; ⊙ 7:30am-7:30pm Mon-Fri, to 6:30pm Sat) Porto Alegre's bustling public market has a wealth of eats. Recommended options include **Banca 40** (www.banca40.com.br; light bites & sweets R$2-24), home of the incomparable *super bomba royal* (a showy ice cream and fruit salad concoction; R$15); **Gambrinus** (📞 51 3226-6914; www.gambrinus.com.br; mains R$38-99; ⊙ 11am-9pm Mon-Fri, to

4pm Sat), an old-world seafood restaurant; and **Café Do Mercado** (www.cafedomercado. com.br; ⊙8am-7:30pm Mon-Fri, 9:30am-5pm Sat), one of the city's best cafes.

★ **Bier Markt Vom Fass**　　　　　BAR
(www.biermarkt.com.br; Barão de Santo Ângelo 497; ⊙6-11:30pm Mon-Sat; 🛜) With its 38 taps and 100 international labels by the bottle, this Moinhos de Vento drinking den has won the city's Best Beer List honors every year since 2010. There's is a strong emphasis on local breweries — including Seasons, Tupiniquim and Irmãos Ferraro — and the music supervisor unearths some real toe-tapping gems.

ℹ Information

Both the municipality and the state have tourist information booths in Porto Alegre, the former at the **Mercado Público** (Centro de Informações Turísticas; ☎51 3211-5705; www2.portoalegre. rs.gov.br/turismo; Mercado Público; ⊙8am-6pm Mon-Sat) and the main **Linha Turismo bus stop** (Centro de Informações Turísticas; ☎51 3289-6765; www2.portoalegre.rs.gov.br/ turismo; Travessa do Carmo 84; ⊙8am-6pm); the latter at the **airport** (Centros de Atenção ao Turista; ☎51 3374-0294; www.turismo.rs.gov. br; Arrivals Hall, Terminal 1, Porto Alegre Airport; ⊙8am-10pm) and the **bus station** (Centro de Atenção ao Turista; ☎51 3225-0677; www. turismo.rs.gov.br; Rodoviária; ⊙8am-6pm).

ℹ Getting There & Away

The city's airport – privatized and renamed **Porto Alegre Airport** (POA; ☎51 3358-2000; www. portoalegre-airport.com.br; Av Severo Dulius 90.010) in 2017 – is 6km northeast of downtown, with two terminals connected by a free shuttle. The majority of airlines operate out of Terminal 1, but Azul departs from the older Terminal 2. In addition to major destinations throughout Brazil, international destinations include Buenos Aires, Lima, Montevideo and Panama City.

Prepaid **Cootaero** (☎51 3358-2500; www. cootaero.com.br; Arrivals Hall, Porto Alegre Airport) taxis from the arrivals hall run R$33 or so to Centro and R$38 or so to Cidade Baixa. An Uber is considerably less.

The busy **long-distance bus station** (☎51 3210-0101; www.rodoviaria-poa.com.br; Largo Vespasiano Julioveppo 70), 1.5km northeast of Centro, is accessible by metro; alternatively, a taxi downtown costs R$10 to R$20 or so from the pre-paid **Ponte do Taxi** (☎51 3221-9371; Estação Rodoviária de Porto Alegre). If your baggage is considered large, they will tack on

BRAZIL PORTO ALEGRE

BUSES FROM PORTO ALEGRE

DESTINATION	STARTING FARE (R$)	DURATION (HR)	BUS COMPANY
Buenos Aires (Argentina)	335	21	Flecha Bus (www.flechabus.com.ar), JBL (www.jblturismo.com.br)
Cambará do Sul	46.75	6	Citral (www.citral.tur.br)
Canela	37.60	3	Citral
Chuí	124	8	Planalto (www.planalto.com.br)
Curitiba	192	13	Penha (www.passagempenha.com.br), Catarinense (www.catarinense.net)
Florianópolis	89	6	Santo Anjo (www.santoanjo.com.br), Eucatur (www.eucatur.com.br)
Gramado	35	3	Citral
Montevideo (Uruguay)	267	12	TTL (www.ttl.com.br), EGA (www.ega. com.uy)
Pelotas	61	3½	Expresso Embaixador (www.expresso embaixador.com.br)
Rio de Janeiro	358.50	26	Penha
Rio Grande	77.50	5	Planalto
Santiago (Chile)	486	40	JBL
Sânto Angelo	127	7	Ouro e Prata (www.ouroeprata.com)
São Francisco de Paula	28	3	Citral
São Paulo	180	19	Penha, Eucatur
Torres	49	3	Unesul (www.unesul.com.br)

an additional R\$7.27. An Uber to Centro runs around R\$10 or so off-peak; to Cidade Baixa around R\$15 or so.

ⓘ Getting Around

Porto Alegre's metro, **Trensurb** (www.trensurb. gov.br; one-way R\$3.30; ⊙ 5am-11:25pm), has convenient stations at Estação Mercado (by the port), Estação Rodoviária (the next stop) and the airport (three stops beyond). For Cidade Baixa, catch bus T5/T51/T52 from the airport or 282, 282.1, 244, 255, 272 or 343 from the bus station (R\$4.30).

Both the metro and the bus stop sit between Terminals 1 and 2 (closer to 2). The free **Aeromóvel** (Brazil's first atmospherically powered people mover) connects the metro with Terminal 1 every 10 to 15 minutes. Terminal 2 is accessed by a 400m footbridge from the metro.

Foz do Iguaçu

🗗 0XX45 / POP 263,500

The stupendous roar of 275 waterfalls crashing 80m into the Rio Iguaçu seems to create a low-level buzz of excitement throughout the city of Foz, even though the famed Cataratas (falls) are 20km southeast of town. Apart from the waterfalls, you can dip into the forests of Paraguay or check out Itaipu Dam, one of the world's largest hydroelectric power plants.

◉ Sights & Activities

Hotels and agencies in Foz do Iguaçu offer tours to the Argentine park for around R\$50 to R\$120 (transport only). It's possible to save a bit of cash and a few hours if you opt to go independently.

★ Cataratas do Iguaçu   WATERFALL

(www.cataratasdoiguacu.com.br; Parque Nacional do Iguaçu) Once you're in the park and ready to visit the falls, take the Parque Nacional do Iguaçu bus to the third stop at Belmond Hotel das Cataratas. Here you can pick up the main waterfall observation trail, Trilha das Cataratas ('Waterfall Trail'), a 1200m trail following the shore of the Iguaçu River, terminating at the Garganta do Diabo.

★ Macuco Safari   OUTDOORS

(🗗 45 3529-6262; www.macucosafari.com.br; Av das Cataratas, Km 25, Parque Nacional do Iguaçu; boat trip R\$215, excursions R\$61-515) Under concession from the national park, Macuco is the designated adventure operator on the Brazilian side of the falls. The main event is

the namesake safari, which involves a wet-and-wild boat ride on rapids and waterfalls, but they also offer trekking, bird-watching, whitewater-rafting and other nature-centric activities. To reach Macuco, get off the double-decker bus at the second stop.

★ Parque das Aves   BIRD SANCTUARY

(Bird Park; 🗗 45 3529-8282; www.parquedasaves. com.br; Av das Cataratas, Km 17.1; R\$45; ⊙ 8:30am-5pm) This 5-hectare bird park, located 300m from the entrance to **Parque Nacional do Iguaçu** (🗗 45 3521-4400; www.cataratasdoiguacu. com.br; Hwy BR-469, Km 18; adult foreigners/Mercosur/Brazilians R\$62/49/36, child R\$10; ⊙ 9am-5pm), is home to 800-plus species of birds, including red ibis, bare-throated bellbird, and flamingos galore. They live in 8m-high aviaries that are constructed right in the forest, some of which you can walk through. Kids and adults freak out alike. Well worth it.

★ Itaipu Binacional   DAM

(🗗 45 3576-7000; www.turismoitaipu.com.br; Tancredo Neves 6702; panoramic/special tour R\$38/82; ⊙ tours 8:30am-4:45pm) With a capacity of 14 million kilowatts, this binational dam is the world's second-largest hydroelectric power station, and the one that produces the most electricity per year. The impressive structure, at some 8km long and 200m high, is a memorable sight, especially when the river is high and a vast torrent of overflow water cascades down the spillway.

🛏 Sleeping

★ Tetris Container Hostel   HOSTEL \$

(🗗 45 3132-0019; www.tetrishostel.com.br; Av das Cataratas 639; dm R\$50-65, d from R\$140; 🅿 @ 🛜 🏊) 🌿 Brazil's coolest hostel is crafted from 15 shipping containers – even the pool is a water-filled shipping container – and makes full use of other industrial by-products as well, like sinks made from oil drums. Colorful bathrooms brighten the dorms (a four-bed female plus 10- and 12-bed mixed) and the patio/bar area is tops. Adorable staff to boot.

★ Hostel Nature   HOSTEL \$

(🗗 45 99116-0979; www.hostelnature.com.br; Alameda Buri 333; camping/dm per person R\$32/70, s/d/tr R\$100/150/200; 🅿 @ 🛜 🏊) This hostel is set on a gorgeous piece of land planted with sugarcane, bananas and mandarins and is a delightful escape just 12km from the entrance to Parque Nacional do Iguaçu. Pleasant and tidy rooms – six privates are a

Foz do Iguaçu

step up in comfort – pair with ample outdoor lounge space, a restaurant and a fun bar.

Pousada Sonho Meu   GUESTHOUSE **$$**
(☑45 3573-5764; www.facebook.com/Pousada SMFoz; Mem de Sá 267; s/d/tr/qd R$150/200/ 250/380; ✺🛜⛱) Located just 50m from the local bus terminal, this administrative-looking building is actually a delightful oasis on the inside. Upgraded rooms are simply decorated with rustic wood bricks and colorful faux *azulejos* (decorative tiles); there's also a standout pool with a mini-waterfall, breakfast area and outdoor guest kitchen.

🍴 Eating & Drinking

Tropicana   CHURRASCARIA **$**
(www.facebook.com/tropicanafoz; Av Juscelino Kubitschek 228; buffet R$35; ☺11am-11pm; 🛜) This all-you-can-eat shoestring savior offers absolutely ridiculous taste for money. Expect a madhouse.

★**Vó Bertila**   PIZZA **$$**
(www.facebook.com/vobertila; Bartolomeu de Gusmão 1116; pizza R$27-82, pasta for 2 people R$58-86; ☺6:30-11:30pm Tue-Sun) This informal, family-run cantina churns out wood-fired pizza – even in personal sizes – and reasonably authentic pasta in heaping portions. This is the kind of down-home Italian spot Brazil does so very well. Don't expect Bologna or Napoli, but expect it to be packed.

★**Zeppelin Old Bar**   LIVE MUSIC
(www.facebook.com/ZeppelinFoz; Raul Mattos 222; ☺7pm-midnight Tue, 9pm-2am Wed-Sat; 🛜) Outstanding bar serving up excellent cocktails and live music that spans the gamut from grunge to reggae. The beautiful people congregate from Thursday onwards.

ℹ Information

The region's tourist board has an excellent website, a toll-free English-speaking information line, maps and detailed info about the area. The main office is in **Vila Yolanda** (📞 45 3521-8128; www.pmfi.pr.gov.br/turismo; Av das Cataratas 2330, Vila Yolanda; ⊙ 8am-8pm), out of town toward the falls, reachable on bus 120. Other branches are at the **airport** (📞 45 3521-4276; www.pmfi.pr.gov.br/turismo; Hwy BR-469, Km 16.5, Aeroporto Internacional de Foz do Iguaçu/Cataratas; ⊙ 9am-8:30pm), **long-distance bus station** (📞 45 3522-1027; www.pmfi.pr.gov.br/turismo; Av Costa e Silva 1601, Rodoviária Internacional de Foz do Iguaçu; ⊙ 7am-6pm) and **local bus station** (📞 45 3523-7901; www.pmfi.pr.gov.br/turismo; Juscelino Kubitschek 1385, TTU; ⊙ 7:30am-6pm).

❶ Getting There & Away

AIR

Daily flights link **Foz do Iguaçu/Cataratas International Airport** (IGU; 📞 45 3521-4200; Hwy BR-469, Km 16.5) to Lima and several major Brazilian cities. Sit on the left-hand side of the plane on arrival for good views of the falls.

BUS

The **long-distance bus station** (📞 45 3522-2590; Av Costa e Silva 1601) is 4.5km northeast of the center of town. **Central de Passagens** (📞 45 99819-0303; www.centraldepassagens.com; Av Juscelino Kubitschek 526; ⊙ 8am-7pm Mon-Fri, to 3pm Sat) sells tickets downtown for the same price as the bus companies.

TO PUERTO IGUAZÚ, ARGENTINA

If traveling by bus, at Brazilian immigration in either direction, most bus drivers won't wait around while you finish formalities unless the number of foreigners exceeds locals. Officially, you should get a pass from the driver, get your passport stamped, then wait and reboard the next bus *from the same bus company*. The reality is that some wait, some don't; some give you a pass, some don't (most folks just pay again, rather than wait out the hour for the same company to come through again). On the Argentine side, drivers wait, so with luck and patience you can do this for R$5/AR25, and if you are prone to the blues, it could run you R$10/AR50. Welcome to tri-border anarchy!

It's important you pay attention as drivers ask if anyone needs to stop at immigration on the Brazilian side – but in Portuguese (or Spanish), if at all. Many travelers miss it and end up with serious immigration hassles later (ie hefty fines).

At Argentine immigration, the bus always stops and usually waits for everyone to be processed. Both borders are open 24 hours but bus service ends around 7:15pm. The last bus you can catch is the second-to-last bus back to Brazil (around 6:45pm). If you make the mistake of opting for the final bus, there will be no bus coming after yours to scoop you up after you finish with border formalities.

TO CIUDAD DEL ESTE, PARAGUAY

To get to the border, take a bus (R$5.50/10,000G, 30 minutes, 6am-6pm) from **Av Juscelino Kubitschek** (Av Juscelino Kubitscheck) across from TTU (p361), or any bus inside TTU signed 'Ponte da Amizade' (101, 102, 103 etc), which pass by Ponte da Amizade, or a taxi – buses also leave regularly from the bus station (p360). At the border, get your passport stamped, then catch the next bus or taxi to Ciudad del Este, or walk across the Ponte da Amizade ('Friendship Bridge'). If traveling further into Paraguay, you'll need to complete formalities (p360) with Brazil's **Polícia Federal** (www.pf.gov.br; Hwy BR-277; ⊙ 24hr) and the Paraguayan immigration authorities at the consulate.

For Paraguay, Americans ($160), Australians ($135) and Canadians ($150) need a visa – though not unless you go beyond Ciudad del Este. Get this in advance at home or from the **Paraguayan Consulate** (📞 45 3523-2898;

BUSES FROM FOZ

DESTINATION	STARTING FARE (R$)	DURATION (HR)	COMPANY
Asunción*	59	6½	NSA (www.nsa.com.py)
Buenos Aires**	286	18	Crucero del Norte (www.crucerodelnorte.com.ar)
Campo Grande	114	13	Eucatur (www.eucatur.com.br)
Curitiba	192	10	Catarinense (www.catarinense.net)
Florianópolis	179	16	Catarinense, Nordeste (www.expnordeste.com.br)
Rio de Janeiro	299	24	Catarinense, Nordeste
São Paulo	213	16	Catarinense, Pluma (www.pluma.com.br)

* Departs at 6:30pm (*convencional*) and midnight (*leito*).

** Departs at 10:30am

fozconsulpar@mre.gov.py; Marechal Deodoro da Fonseca 901; ⊙ 9am-1pm Mon-Fri) in Foz.

❶ Getting Around

Local bus fare is R$3.55. The local transport terminal, the **Urban Bus Terminal** (TTU; Terminal de Transporte Urbano; ☏ 2105-1385; Av Juscelino Kubitschek 1385), is referred to colloquially as 'terminal.'

Bus 120 'Aeroporto/Parque Nacional' runs to the airport (R$3.55, 30 minutes) and the Brazilian side of the waterfalls (40 minutes) every 22 to 30 minutes from 5:25am to 12:10am (from 5:10am Sunday). Catch it at the local bus terminal or any stop along Av Juscelino Kubitschek south of Barbosa. Bus 120 'Centro/TTU' goes from the airport to Centro (exit to the far left end and look for the multilingual 'Parada de Ônibus' sign).

Taxis run around R$20 to R$25 to the falls and R$50 to R$60 to Centro (Uber runs around R$7 to R$8 to the falls and R$20 to R$25 to Centro). If you want to dump your bags, there is a self-service luggage deposit at the airport for R$30 for 24 hours.

City buses 105 and 115 (R$3.55) cover the 6km between the long-distance bus station and the local terminal downtown.

THE CENTRAL WEST

A land of breathtaking panoramas and exceptional wildlife, Brazil's Central West is a must-see for nature lovers and outdoor enthusiasts. The Pantanal, one of the planet's most important wetland systems, is the region's star attraction. Its meandering rivers, savannas and forests harbor one of the densest concentrations of plant and animal life in the New World. Other regional attractions include dramatic *chapadas* (tablelands), which rise like brilliant red giants from the dark-green cerrado (savanna), punctuated by spectacular waterfalls and picturesque swimming holes; Bonito, where crystal-clear rivers teeming with fish highlight one of the world's most unusual natural destinations;

BRAZIL FOZ DO IGUAÇU

Central West Brazil

and Brazil's surreal, master-planned capital, Brasília.

Brasília

🖉 0XX61 / POP 3.1 MILLION / ELEV 1172M

Brasília, conceived as a workable, utopian answer to urban chaos, replaced Rio as capital in 1960 and remains an impressive monument to national initiative. The purpose-built city is lauded by many for its avant-garde design. It's not only a pilgrimage for architecture buffs but also foodies, night owls and those seeking a unique travel experience.

⦿ Sights

Brasília's major edifices are spread along a 5km stretch of the Eixo Monumental and are listed in northwest–southeast order. Further south, in the 'cockpit' of the airplane ground plan, are the most interesting government buildings: **Palácio do Itamaraty** (Palácio dos Arcos; 🖉 61 2030-8051; www.itamaraty.gov.br; Esplanada dos Ministérios, Bloco H; ⊘ hourly visits 9am-11am & 2-5pm Mon-Fri, 9am, 11am, 2pm, 3pm, 5pm Sat & Sun) FREE, **Palácio da Justiça** (🖉 61 2025-3000; www.justica.gov.br; Esplanada dos Ministérios) and **Congresso Nacional** (Parliament; 🖉 61 3216-1771; www.congressonacional.leg.br; Praça dos Três Poderes; ⊘ 9am-5:30pm Thu-Mon) FREE. To visit them, you can combine local buses 104 and 108 with some long walks or, most conveniently, take a city tour.

★ Santuário Dom Bosco   CHURCH
(🖉 61 3223-6542; www.santuariodombosco.org.br; SEPS 702, Bloco B; ⊘ 7am-8pm) FREE Santuário Dom Bosco is made of 80 concrete columns that support 7400 pieces of illuminated Murano glass, symbolizing a starry sky, which cast a blue submarine glow over the pews. The central chandelier weighs 2.5 tons and adds an amazing 435 light bulbs' worth of energy to the monthly electricity bill.

★ Catedral Metropolitana   CATHEDRAL
(Nossa Senhora Aparecida; 🖉 61 3224-4073; www.catedral.org.br; Esplanada dos Ministérios; ⊘ 8am-4:30pm Wed, Thu & Sat-Mon, 10:30am-4pm Tue & Fri) FREE The 16 curved ribs rising to the crown of the iconic exterior coupled with the light-filled circular interior, which sits under a dome of wavy stained-glass, make this cathedral a heavenly sight. At the entrance are Ceschiatti's haunting *Four Disciples* statues; he also created the aluminum angels hanging inside. Wearing shorts and visiting during Mass are not encouraged.

★ Centro Cultural
Banco do Brasil   ARTS CENTER
(CCBB; 🖉 61 3108-7600; www.culturabancodobrasil.com.br; SCES, Trecho 2, Conjunto 22; ⊘ 9am-9pm Tue-Sun) FREE Brasília's most important contemporary museum houses temporary exhibitions in two galleries, an indie cinema, a cafe and a bookstore. Buses 0.103 and 103.2 run here from the center.

★ Museu Nacional   MUSEUM
(Museu Honestino Guimarães; 🖉 61 3325-5220; www.cultura.df.gov.br; Esplanada dos Ministérios; ⊘ 9am-6:30pm Tue-Sun) FREE This landmark white dome, gleaming in the sun, was opened to the public on the 100th birthday of architect Oscar Niemeyer. The inside is softer in grays but equally spectacular, featuring a discreet mezzanine mostly held up by columns suspended from the roof. A signature curved ramp juts out from its base and runs around the outside like a ring of Saturn. Good-quality temporary art exhibitions fill the interior.

🛏 Sleeping

Hostel 7   HOSTEL $
(🖉 61 3033-7707; www.hostel7.com.br; SCLRN 708, Bloco I, Loja 20; dm R$50-80; 🏵@🤶) This excellent hostel has tightly packed but decent dorms with lockers, air-con and bathrooms, plus a couple of private rooms sleeping up to four. Common spaces are limited, but there's a nice covered courtyard and bar in the back. Rooms named after Brasília's key founders and historic photos add a local touch; you've gotta love the Kombi-van reception and car couch.

★ Brasília Palace Hotel   HOTEL $$
(🖉 61 3306-9000; www.brasiliapalace.com.br; SHTN, Trecho 1, Lote 1; d R$320-650; 🏵@🤶🏊) Near the presidential palace, this emblematic hotel is a marvelous spot for architecture fans. Designed by Oscar Niemeyer in 1957, common spaces are a living midcentury modern treasury, with furniture and art by Niemeyer, Athos Bulcão and others around every turn, all shaded by an exterior blanketed with massive movable shutters. The whole experience screams: this is Brasília!

🍴 Eating & Drinking

The best restaurant selections are in the Asa Sul, around SCLS 209/210, 409/410 and 411/412, which forms a sort of 'gourmet triangle' (it is also home to some of the city's most lively nightlife). Another good selection

Central Brasília

10pm (food court) Sun; 🛜), **Pátio Brasil** (📞61 2107-7400; www.patiobrasil.com.br; Asa Sul, W3 SCS; ⏱10am-10pm Mon-Sat, 2-8pm Sun) and **Conjunto Nacional** (www.conjuntonacional. com.br; SDN CNB, Conjunto A; ⏱9am-10pm Mon-Sat, food only noon 8pm Sun) – all have food courts with enough variety to cater to most tastes.

Boteco do Juca
BOTECO **$**

(📞61 3242-9415; www.botecodojuca.com.br; CLS 405, Bloco A; petiscos R$17-55; ⏱11:30am-midnight; 🛜) Deservedly popular, this sprawling Rio-style outdoor bar has icy draft beer and on-the-ball service. All-you-can-eat evening pizza (R$26 to R$28) draws crowds, and there is also a nice range of skewers, grilled meats and shared finger-food plates that are excellent value.

★ Taypá
PERUVIAN **$$$**

(📞61 3248-0403; www.taypa.com.br; SHIS QI 17, Bloco G, Loja 208; mains R$60-110; ⏱noon-3pm & 7pm-midnight Mon-Fri, noon-4pm & 7pm-1am Sat, noon-5pm Sun; 🛜) It's worth a trip to the edges of Lago Sul – a R$40 or so taxi fare – for Marco Espinoza's authentic upscale Peruvian fare. His whole team hails from Peru and it shows: the fabulous ceviche *criollo,* drowning in creamy *leche de tigre* (citrus marinade), and decadent *suspiro de limeño* (milk caramel and meringue) were the best we've had outside Peru. Great *pisco* cocktails.

★ Ernesto Cafés Especiais
CAFE

(📞61 3345-4182; SCLS 115, Bloco C, Loja 14; ⏱7am-10pm; 🛜) Easily Brasília's best coffee experience, this serious java joint has specialty microlot coffees from Minas Gerais and is hopping with locals day or night, whether over breakfast (fresh baked bread, good tapiocas) or simply losing an afternoon

of restaurants is clustered in SCLS 405 and SCLN 412/413.

Elsewhere, Brazilians in need of sustenance head to the shopping malls. Three centrally located oases – **Brasília Shopping** (www.brasiliashopping.com.br; Quadra 5, Asa Norte SCN; ⏱10am-10pm Mon-Sat, 1-7pm (shops), noon-

BRAZIL BRASÍLIA

entrenched in conversation on the pleasant back patio. Non-dairy milks are available; there's also a bakery.

Bar Beirute – Asa Sul BOTECO
(☑ 61 3244-1717; www.barbeirute.com.br; SCLS 109, Bloco A; ⊘ 11am-1am Sun-Wed, to 2am Thu-Sat) This Brasília institution has a massive outdoor patio packed with an edgier crowd than most. It's a GLS point (the clever Brazilian acronym for gays, lesbians and sympatheticos) but it's really a free-for-all and a great spot for a mug of teeth-numbing cold Beira – Beirute's own brand of beer. There's Lebanese food to soak it up.

❶ Information

The city's two most helpful tourist information booths are on the Praça de Três Poderes and at the airport:

CAT (Centro de Atendimento ao Turista; ☑ 61 3226 0153; www.turismo.df.gov.br; Praça dos Três Poderes; ⊘ 9am-noon & 1-6pm)

CAT Aeroporto (Centro de Atendimento ao Turista; www.turismo.df.gov.br; Presidente Juscelino Kubitschek International Airport; ⊘ 9am-noon & 1-6pm)

❶ Getting There & Away

Brasília's shiny **Aeroporto Presidente Juscelino Kubitschek** (BSB; ☑ 61 3364-9000; www.bsb.aero) is 12km south of the center.

The easiest way to and from the airport is **Ônibus Executivo Aeroporto** (Bus 113; ☑ 61 3344-2769; www.tcb.df.gov.br; fare R$12; ⊘ 6:30am-11:55pm), which runs from the far right of the arrivals hall (as you arrive) into the center (20

to 40 minutes). Bus 0.102/102.1 runs between the **local bus station** (☑ 61 3327-4631) and the airport for R$3.50 (40 minutes). Taxis to the airport cost around R$60.

From the flashy long-distance bus station **Rodoviária Interestadual** (☑ 61 3234-2185; www.rodoviariabrasilia.com; SMAS, Trecho 4, Conjunto 5/6), 3km southwest off the edge of Asa Sul, buses go almost everywhere in Brazil.

❶ Getting Around

The **Metrô DF** (www.metro.df.gov.br; R$5; ⊘ 6am-11:30pm Mon-Sat, 7am-7pm Sun) only covers the south side of the city but is useful for access to restaurants and bars in the Asa Sul as well as to the intercity bus station (stop: Shopping). It runs from the city bus station to the huge suburbs of Ceilândia and Samambaia, with a predictably named station (102 Sul, 104 Sul, etc) every two blocks or so from the central station.

The key point for the city's complex series of bus routes, run by DFTrans (www.dftrans.df.gov.br), is the central local bus station, Rodoviária Plano Piloto.

The Pantanal

This vast natural paradise, covering an estimated 210,000 sq km and stretching into Paraguay and Bolivia, is Brazil's major ecological attraction and offers a density of exotic wildlife found nowhere else in South America. During the rainy season (December to April), the Rio Paraguai and lesser rivers of the Pantanal inundate much of this low-lying region, creating *cordilheiras* (vegetation is-

BUSES FROM BRASÍLIA

DESTINATION	STARTING FARE (R$)	DURATION (HR)	COMPANY
Belém	255	35	Satélite Norte (www.satelitenorte.com.br), Rápido Marajó (www.rapidomarajo.com.br)
Campo Grande	238-261	23-25	Motta (www.motta.com.br), Viação São Luiz (www.viacao saoluiz.com.br)
Cuiabá	208-232	23	Expresso São Luiz (www.expressosaoluiz.com.br), Eucatur (www.eucatur.com.br), Andorinha (www.andorinha.com)
Goiânia	40-62	3-4	Araguarina (www.araguarina.com.br), Viação Goiânia (www.viacaogoiania.com.br), Expresso São Luiz, Catedral Turismo (www.catedralturismo.com.br)
Porto Velho	512	43	Andorinha, Eucatur
Rio de Janeiro	220	18	Viação Util (www.util.com.br), Kaissara (www.kaissara.com.br)
Salvador	270-310	25	Catedral Turismo, Real Expresso (www.realexpresso.com.br)
São Paulo	228	17	Catedral Turismo, Real Expresso, Emtram (www.emtram.com.br)

NATURE CALLS!

You're in cerrado country, the South American savanna. Nature lovers approaching urban overdose in Brasília should seek refuge in the surrounding grasslands. A Brazilian National Heritage site backed by lovely mountains, Pirenópolis attracts weekend escapees from Brasília (165km east) for some of the country's most picturesque 18th-century architecture and abundant waterfalls. Within 20km of town, **Parque Estadual da Serra dos Pireneus** (62 3265-1320; www.secima.go.gov.br; 8am-5pm, 9am-8pm summer) and **Reserva Ecológica Vargem Grande** (62 99652-6857; www.vargemgrande.pirenopolis.tur.br; Estrada Parque dos Pirineus, Km 9; R$35; 9am-4:30pm) both have beautiful waterfalls and swimming holes; while **Santuário de Vida Silvestre Vagafogo** (Vagafogo Farm Wildlife Sanctuary; 62 99115-0376; www.vagafogo.com.br; Estrada O Morro do Frota; guided walk R$20; 9am-5pm) offers a self-guided forest walk (R$20) and a delicious weekend brunch (R$55). Goianésia (www.viacaogoianesia.com.br) has four daily buses from Brasília (R$48, three hours).

The spectacular **Parque Nacional da Chapada dos Veadeiros** (62 3455-1116; www.icmbio.gov.br; 7am-5pm, last entry noon Tue-Sun, also Mon in Jul) FREE, 220km north of Brasília, showcases the high-altitude cerrado, a sublime landscape where maned wolves, giant anteaters and 7ft-tall rheas roam amid big skies, canyons, waterfalls and oasis-like stands of wine palms. The closest towns to the park are the new-age Alto Paraíso de Goias (40km east) and tranquil São Jorge (2km south), both offering an abundance of comfy and charming accommodations. Real Expresso (www.realexpresso.com.br) has three daily buses from Brasília to Alto Paraíso (R$52, 4 hours).

lands above the high-water level). The waters here in the world's largest freshwater wetlands rise as much as 3m above low-water levels around March in the northern Pantanal and as late as June further south.

This seasonal flooding, while severely limiting human occupation of the area, provides an enormously rich feeding ground for wildlife, including 650 bird species and 80 mammal species, such as jaguars, ocelots, pumas, maned wolf, deer, anteaters, armadillos, howler and capuchin monkeys, and tapirs. The waters teem with fish; birds fly in flocks of thousands and gather in enormous rookeries. In dry season (July to November), when animals concentrate around limited water sources, the wildlife spotting is nothing short of spectacular. For nature and animal lovers, the Pantanal is Brazil's Eden.

Tours

Tours generally include transportation, accommodations, meals, hikes, horse-riding excursions and boat rides.

The principal access towns where you can arrange tours are Cuiabá in the north (for the Transpantaneira) and Campo Grande in the south (for the Estrada Parque), with Corumbá on the Bolivian border more of a sideshow these days.

Tours from Cuiabá tend to be slightly more expensive, but more professional, with smaller groups and better-trained guides than those from either Campo Grande or Corumbá. They also go deeper into the Pantanal.

Northern Pantanal

★ Pantanal Nature   WILDLIFE
(65 99925-2265, 65 3322-0203; www.pantanalnature.com.br; Av Historiador Rubens de Mendonça 1856, Cuiabá; 4-day nature tour per person R$4150, jaguar tour R$5800; office hours 7-11:30am & 1:30-5pm Mon-Thu, 8am-noon Fri & Sat) Superb agency run by Ailton Lara that has a sterling reputation for its professional tours and expert guides. It runs Pantanal nature tours and, in season, jaguar tours from the **Pantanal Jaguar Camp** (65 99925-2265; www.pantanaljaguarcamp.com.br; Transpantaneira, Km 145, Porto Jofre; d with meals & excursion R$1035, camping per person R$60, with own tent R$45;) in Porto Jofre. You can also go for a five- or six-day combination. Tours are cheaper off-season and if you opt to camp. Single supplement is 20%.

Ecoverde Tours   WILDLIFE
(65 99638-1614; www.ecoverdetours.com.br; Pedro Celestino 391, Cuiabá; 4-day nature tour s/d R$2400/4000, jaguar tour R$3000/5000) This relaxed budget company has decades of service and experienced guides. Working with local pousadas toward an ecofriendly approach, Joel Souza can guide you in several

The Pantanal

0 / 0 — 100 km / 60 miles

BRAZIL THE PANTANAL

Parque Nacional da Chapada dos Guimarães
Portão do Inferno
Cidade de Pedra
Salgadeira
Mirante de Geodésia
Chapada dos Guimarães
Cuiabá
Cachoeira Véu de Noiva
BR 70
Aeroporto Internacional
BR 70
Santo Antônio do Leverger
BR 364

Mato Grosso

Cáceres
Corixio
San Matías
BR 174
Poconé
Barão de Melgaço
Baía Chacororé
Rodonópolis
BR 364

Pousada Rio Clarinho
Transpantaneira
Rio Cuiabá
Rio São Lourenço

Pantanal Jaguar Camp
Rio Piquiri
Porto Jofre Pantanal Pousada & Camping
Porto Jofre
Rio Correntes

Laguna Uperaba
Parque Nacional do Pantanal Matogrossense
Rio São Lourenço
BR 163

Lagoa Gaiba

BOLIVIA

Lagoa Mandiorê
Rio Taquari

Serranía de Sunsas
Coxim

Santa Ana de Chiquitos
El Carmen
Puerto Suárez
Corumbá
Puerto Quijarro
Porto da Manga
Aeroporto Internacional
Curva do Leque
Estrada Parque
Pantanal Jungle Lodge
Pousada & Camping Santa Clara
Passo do Lontra
Buraco das Piranhas
Rio Negro

The Pantanal

São Gabriel do Oeste

Bandeirantes
BR 163

Forte Coimbra
Rio Paraguai

Miranda
BR 262
Bodoquena
Aquidauana

Campo Grande
Aeroporto Internacional

PARAGUAY

Rio Miranda
Sidrolândia

Fuerte Olimpo

Parque Nacional da Serra da Bodoquena
Bonito

Mato Grosso do Sul

Pôrto Murtinho
Jardim
Guia Lopes da Laguna

Rio Apa
Bela Vista
Dourados

Puerto Valle Mí
Pedro Juan Caballero
Ponta Porã

languages. You can find him at Hostel Pousada Ecoverde. He runs Pantanal nature tours year-round and jaguar-spotting tours from June to October.

☞ Southern Pantanal

Pantanal Discovery   WILDLIFE
(☑67 99163-3518; www.gilspantanaldiscovery. com.br; Hotel Mohave, Afonso Pena 602, Campo Grande; 3-day, 2-night package hammock/dm/s/d R$1000/1200/1550/2800) Owner Gil is a perennial operator with a polished sales pitch. He's assertive, very helpful and the pick of budget operators in town. He's used to dealing with short notice or tight schedules and has his own transportation.

Pantanal Viagens   WILDLIFE
(☑67 3321-3143; www.pantanalviagens.com.br; Room 9, Old Bus Terminal, Joaquim Nabuco 200, Campo Grande) A nice agency working with Pousada Passo do Lontra and other Pantanal lodgings that has worked hard to maintain its excellent reputation. Caters to mid- to high-end budgets and has professional and reliable packages.

🛏 Sleeping & Eating

🛏 Northern Pantanal

Pousada Rio Clarinho   POUSADA $
(☑65 99637-0516; www.pousadarioclarinho.com. br; Transpantaneira, Km 40; s/d/tr incl full board & excursions R$290/460/690; ❄) An avian symphony is your wake-up call at this rustic *fazenda* right on the Rio Clarinho (there's a river platform for swimming). There is an extensive area of forested trails, and more than 260 species of birds on the property, as well as capybaras and giant otters. The food is authentic *pantaneiro* and the owners' warmth transcends the language barrier.

Porto Jofre Pantanal
Pousada & Camping   POUSADA, CAMPING $$
(Pousada de Neco; ☑65 99971-3699; www.porto jofrepantanal.com.br; Transpantaneira, Km 145, Porto Jofre; s/d incl full board R$350/660, camping R$40; ❄🛜) Turn left at the end of the Transpantaneira to reach this budget favorite that is better known hereabouts as Pousada de Neco. It's a genuinely welcoming place with a wonderful riverfront location – ideal for wildlife-spotting boat tours, as well as tasty food, spartan but air-conditioned rooms, and clean showers for campers. Meals are included in the room price (campers pay extra).

🛏 Southern Pantanal

Pantanal Jungle Lodge   LODGE $$
(☑67 3242-1488; www.pantanal-jungle-lodge. com; Estrada Parque, Km 8; 3-day, 2-night package dm/s/d R$910/1380/2310; ❄🛜❄) This boardwalk lodge is a backpacker favorite, thanks to its enviable riverside location as well as its well-organized activities – from canoeing and piranha fishing to night safaris on the river and wildlife-spotting treks. Lodge either in one of the breezy dorms or in a private room with air-conditioning. All have an insect-screened porch to relax in.

Pousada & Camping
Santa Clara   POUSADA, CAMPGROUND $$
(☑67 99939-3570; www.pantanalsantaclara.com. br; Estrada Parque, Km 22; 3-day, 2-night package incl full board & excursions camping/dm/s/d R$580/860/1220/1980; ❄🛜❄) This working ranch is enthusiastically run and has a host of activities (hikes, piranha fishing, night safaris, horseback riding), accommodations to suit all budgets and hearty *pantaneiro* cooking. It is deservedly popular; expect large groups. Rooms are compact but OK, dorms have decent spacing, there's a plunge pool and games, and macaws and peccaries are about.

Cuiabá

☑0XX65 / POP 590,100

Cuiabá is a boomtown basking in the relentless Mato Grosso sun. It's actually two sister cities separated by the Rio Cuiabá: Old Cuiabá and Várzea Grande (where the airport is located).

🛏 Sleeping & Eating

★Hostel
Pousada Ecoverde   POUSADA $
(☑65 99638-1614; www.ecoverdetours.com.br; Celestino 391; s/d without bathroom R$50/100; 🛜) This rustic pousada is in a 100-year-old house with a tranquil, hammock-hung minijungle out back and a notable collection of antique radios, record players and telephones. Affable owner, music lover and local wildlife expert Joel Souza is a founder of ecotourism in the area; the accommodation consists of five fan-cooled rooms that share four external bathrooms.

ℹ CHOOSING A GUIDE IN THE PANTANAL

Pantanal tourism is big business and in the past some companies have been guilty of employing underhand tactics in the race to hook clients. Though measures have finally been taken to clamp down on the worst offenders, it is still worth bearing a few suggestions in mind to have a safe and enjoyable trip:

➡ Resist making a snap decision, especially if you've just climbed off an overnight bus.

➡ Do not make your decision based on cost. Cheaper very rarely means better, but even expensive tours can be a letdown.

➡ Go on forums. Read online reviews. Speak to other travelers. What was their experience like? In Campo Grande some of the tour companies are quick to badmouth others. Get your advice straight from the horse's mouth. Be aware that operators often run each other down in online reviews too.

➡ Compare your options, but remember that the owner or salesperson is not always your guide, and it's the guide you're going to be with in the wilderness for several days. Ask to meet your guide if possible. Ascertain your guide's linguistic abilities.

➡ Don't hand over your cash to any go-betweens or buy bus tickets that somebody other than the person you give your money to is going to give you.

➡ If you are even remotely concerned about sustainable tourism, do not use operators and lodges that harm this fragile environment. That means no picking up the animals for photographs or touching them whatsoever.

➡ Group budget tours focus squarely on the spectacular and easy-to-see species. Serious wildlife-watchers should be prepared to pay more for a private guide.

Dom Bosco Hostel   HOSTEL $

(☑ 65 99245-1007; www.domb<!---->oscohostel.com.br; Cândido Mariano 1390; dm R$62, breakfast R$8; ❈ ☎) Very handy for restaurants and night-life, Dom Bosco occupies an unmarked purple house on a quiet street. Dorms are tight but have an excellent lockable wardrobe space and en-suite bathrooms. Air-con is nighttime only. Attractive common areas include a proper kitchen, and it is run in a calm, welcoming fashion.

Lélis Peixaria   SEAFOOD $$

(☑ 65 3322-9195; www.lelispeixaria.com.br; Marechal Mascarenhas de Morães 36; rodízio lunch/dinner R$60/90; ⊙ 11:30am-3pm & 6:30-11pm Mon-Sat, 11:30am-3pm Sun) You'll be gobbling up river fish like a caiman at this quality *rodízio* (all-you-can-eat), which features several dozen preparations of pintado, pacu and other denizens of the local waterways, including caiman itself. À la carte options include great stews for two.

★ Choppão   BAR

(www.choppao.com.br; Praça 8 de Abril 44; ⊙ 11am-2am Sun, Mon, Wed & Thu, from 5:30pm Tue, 11am-5am Fri & Sat; ☎) If you like your beer *bem gelada* (nice and cold) and it's another baking Cuiabá day, the Choppão is heaven. Ice-insulated tankards keep the *chope* (draft beer) glacial the whole way down. A wide range of traditional Mato Grosso fare is on hand in generous quantities, including a legendary chicken soup that locals rate the city's best hangover cure.

ℹ Information

Sedtur (☑ 65 3613-9300; www.cultura.mt.gov.br; Voluntários da Pátria 118; ⊙ 1-7pm Mon-Fri) Has some helpful maps and brochures in Portuguese.

ℹ Getting There & Away

Cuiabá's **international airport** (CGB; ☑ 65 3614-2511; Av João Ponce de Arruda, Várzea Grande) is in Várzea Grande, 7km from central Cuiabá. There are flights all over Brazil, principally operated by Azul. Gol, LATAM and Avianca also have some routes, mainly to São Paulo and Brasília.

Cuiabá's **bus station** (Jules Rimet) is 3km north of the center.

ℹ Getting Around

From the airport, bus 7 (R$3.85) runs to town and on to the bus station. A taxi costs around R$40. Buses back to the airport run along Av Isaac Póvoas and Rua Barão de Melgaço.

From inside the bus terminal, you can get a Centro bus to Praça Alencastro (R$3.85). More frequent buses marked 'Centro' leave from outside the bus station and drop you along Av Isaac Póvoas. A taxi from inside the bus station costs around R$35.

Referência (☑ 65 3682-6689; www.referencia. com.br; Av Governador João Ponce de Arruda 1034, Várzea Grande; ☺ 7am-11pm) and **Localiza Hertz** (☑ 65 3925-9250; www.localizahertz. com; Av Governador João Ponce de Arruda 820, Várzea Grande) are a couple of reliable car rental companies with offices at the airport. The best car for the Pantanal is one with high clearance, though any car can make it during dry season. In the wet season (November to March) you'll need a 4x4 and off-road driving experience, and some sections may be impassable anyway.

Around Cuiabá

Parque Nacional da Chapada dos Guimarães

☑ 0XX65

This high plateau 60km northeast of Cuiabá is a beautiful region reminiscent of the American Southwest. Its three exceptional sights are the 60m falls **Cachoeira Véu de Noiva** (Bridal Veil; ☺ 9am-5pm, last entry 4pm) FREE, the Mirante de Geodésia lookout (South America's geographical center) and the colorful rocky outcrops known as **Cidade de Pedra** (Stone City; www.icmbio.gov.br/parnaguimaraes/ guia-do-visitante.html; entry only with authorized guide; ☺ 9am-5pm Sun-Fri, from 3pm Sat) FREE, providing Guimarães' most transcendent moment. Véu de Noiva is the only part of the park you can visit independently. Otherwise, a certified guide is required. Access is split among three day-trip circuits: **Circuito das Cachoeiras** (Waterfall Circuit; www.icmbio.gov. br; entry only with authorized guide; ☺ 8:30am-5pm, last entry noon) FREE, which takes in six waterfalls; **Circuito Vale do Rio Claro** (Rio Claro Valley; ☺ 8am-5pm, last entry 1pm) and its lush valley views and forest-pool snorkeling; and the **Roteiro da Caverna Aroe Jari e Lagoa Azul** (Aroe Jari Cave Circuit; from R$250 per person), which includes Brazil's largest sandstone cave.

Trips typically begin by 9am and return by 6pm and should be reserved in advance. Figure on around R$150 to R$250 per person for a half- to full-day excursion. The website www.ecobooking.com.br has a list of guides for each attraction, together with contact details and languages spoken. **Chapada Explorer** (☑ 65 3301-1290; www.chapadaexplorer.com.br; Praça Dom Wunibaldo 57; ☺ 8-11am Mon-Sat) ✎ is a great agency to get you into the park.

ℹ️ Getting There & Away

CMT buses (☑ 65 3301-2679) leave Cuiabá's bus station for Chapada town (R$17, 1¼ hours, nine daily) between 6am and 7:40pm. The miraculous views are on the right-hand side from Cuiabá.

BUSES FROM CUIABÁ

DESTINATION	COST (R$)	TIME (HR)	FREQUENCY	COMPANY
Alta Floresta	223	14	6 daily	Verde Transportes (www.verdetransportes.com. br), Viação Novo Horizonte (65 3056-1256)
Brasília	208-232	23	7 daily	Expresso São Luiz (www.expressosaoluiz.com. br), Eucatur (www.eucatur.com.br), Andorinha (www.andorinha.com)
Bom Jardim	41	4	daily al 2pm	GM Tur (65 3625-1287)
Campo Grande	147-170	11-14	20 daily	Andorinha, Eucatur, Motta (www.motta.com. br), Nova Integração (www.eucatur.com.br), Viação São Luiz (www.viacaosaoluiz.com.br)
Chapada dos Guimarães	17	1¼	10 daily	CMT (65 3046-6151)
Goiânia	160-200	18	9 daily	Expresso São Luiz, Eucatur, Satélite Norte (www.satelitenorte.com.br)
Poconé	29	2¾	5 daily	CMT
Porto Velho	206-324	23-26	15 daily	Eucatur, Gontijo (www.gontijo.com.br), Expresso Itamarati (www.expressoitamarati.com. br), Roderotas (www.roderotas.com)
São Paulo	220-350	28-30	12 daily	Andorinha, Roderotas, Eucatur, Gontijo, Viação Util (www.util.com.br)

In the other direction, the first bus leaves Chapada town at 5:30am and the last at 7:40pm. Chapada's **bus station** (Fernando Correa) is two blocks from the main plaza.

Poconé

🖉 0XX65 / POP 32,200

This dusty frontier town is a place travelers invariably have to pass through on their way to the Transpantaneira 'highway.' It's so sleepy that, as one local put it, 'In Poconé, even the restaurants close for lunch!' This place is unlikely to detain you for longer than a meal stop, though those driving themselves to a lodge along the Transpantaneira might consider overnighting here to get an early start and catch sight of the wildlife in action on the way.

Pousada Pantaneira (🖉 65 3345-3357; www.pousadapantaneira.com.br; Rodovia Transpantaneira, Km 0; rodizio R$40, per kg R$40; ☀🏠) is a justifiably popular *churrascaria* (barbecue restaurant) that sits at the top of the Transpantaneira.

There are five daily CMT buses between Cuiabá and Poconé (R$29, 2¾ hours). Arriving in Poconé, they first stop at the bus station, about 10 blocks from the center of town, then continue on to Praça da Matriz; behind the Matriz church is the road that leads to the beginning of the Transpantaneira.

Campo Grande

🖉 0XX67 / POP 874,200 / ELEV 592M

Gateway to the southern Pantanal, Campo Grande is a vast, modern metropolis, where high-rises tower above the shopping malls and streets are lined with restaurants.

Built on the site of a Bororo burial ground, the **Museu das Culturas Dom Bosco** (🖉 67 3326-9788; www.mcdb.org.br; Parque das Nações Indígenas, Av Afonso Pena; R$10; ☉ 8am-4:30pm Tue-Sat) is a superb museum that provides an unmissable introduction to the indigenous people as well as the flora and fauna of the Mato Grosso region.

🛏 Sleeping

Turis Hotel HOTEL $

(🖉 67 3382-2461; www.turishotel.com.br; Allan Kardec 200; s R$90-112, d R$155-180; ☀🏠) Modern and minimalist, this excellent option is entirely too hip for its location and is very good value. Great breakfast, and the staff go out of their way to be helpful in spite of limited English.

Hauzz Hostel HOSTEL $

(🖉 67 98118-7270; www.hauzzhostel.wixsite.com/hostel; Piratininga 1527; dm R$50-60, s/d R$80/150; ☀🏠) A quiet, secure hostel with snug, fancooled rooms that share several bathrooms, in a pretty bungalow with floorboards underfoot. There's also an air-conditioned private room. Towels are R$10 extra. It's a short walk to Shopping Campo Grande and it is handy for visiting Parque das Nações.

🍴 Eating & Drinking

Ceará SEAFOOD $$

(🖉 67 3022-6404; www.facebook.com/peixariaceara; Dom Aquino 2249; meals for two R$86-105, lunch buffet weekday/weekend R$58/68; ☉ 11am-2:30pm Tue-Sun) One of the city's best *peixarias* (fish restaurants). The pintado in a tomato stew with banana *mandioca* (cassava) incites tears of culinary joy.

Bar Mercearia BOTECO

(🖉 67 3384-9622; www.merceariabar.com.br; 15 de Novembro 1064; ☉ 5pm-midnight Mon-Fri, from noon Sat & Sun; 🏠) A handsome corner bar decked out in historic style to resemble São Paulo *botecos* of the 1930s. Football shirts and beer posters reflect the main two obsessions here, but it's the wraparound exterior seating under the awning that's the real charmer.

ⓘ Information

There are small tourist kiosks at the **bus station** (🖉 67 3314-4448; www.campogrande.ms.gov.br; Rodoviária; ☉ 8am-10pm) and **airport** (🖉 67 3363-3116; www.campogrande.ms.gov.br; ☉ 7:30-11:30am, 1-5pm & 6-10pm Mon-Fri) and a larger one at the central **Morada dos Bais** (🖉 67 3314-9968; www.campogrande.ms.gov.br; Av Noroeste 5140; ☉ 2-8pm Mon-Fri, noon-6pm Sat & Sun).

Central banks with ATMs and exchange facilities:

Banco do Brasil (www.bb.com.br; Av Afonso Pena 2202; ☉ 11am-4pm Mon-Fri)

Bradesco (www.banco.bradesco; Av Afonso Pena 1828; ☉ 11am-4pm Mon-Fri)

ⓘ Getting There & Away

Aeroporto Internacional de Campo Grande (CGR; 🖉 67 3368-6000; Av Duque de Caxias) is 7km west of town. To reach the center, walk out of the airport to the bus stop on the main road and catch the 409 (R$3.75, buy ticket from the airport). A taxi costs around R$30 to R$40.

Campo Grande's **bus station** (🖉 67 3026-6789; Av Gury Marques 1215) is inconveniently located 6km south of the center on the road to

São Paulo. Buses coming from the north may make a stop in the center first.

Vanzella ([📱] 67 3255-3005; www.vanzella transportes.com.br) and **Terra Transportes** ([📱] 67 3255-1001; www.terratransportes.com. br) run door-to-door bus and van services between Campo Grande and Bonito, with several daily departures for R$80.

ℹ Getting Around

Local buses 61 and 87 (R$3.75) connect the long-distance bus station to the city center. To use city buses you need to buy a *passe de ônibus* (bus pass) from newsstands, pharmacies or bus stop kiosks. They come as one-time use (*unitário*) or rechargeable (*recarregável*). A taxi to the center will cost around R$30.

Bonito & Around

[📍] 0XX67 / POP 21,000

This small aquatic playground in the southwestern corner of Mato Grosso do Sul has few attractions of its own, but the natural resources of the surrounding area are spectacular, and local authorities have taken the high road in their regulation and maintenance. There are caves with lakes and amazing stalactite formations, beautiful waterfalls and incredibly clear rivers surrounded by lush forest where it's possible to swim eyeball to eyeball with hundreds of fish.

Bonito's long main street, Coronel Pilad Rebuá, is a 3km stretch that is home to everything you are likely to need during your stay.

⊙ Sights & Activities

Prices of attractions are regulated by their owners, so it makes no difference who you book your tour with. However, transportation is usually only included in the cost when you book through a hotel, not an agency.

In the high season, the most popular tours must be booked in advance, preferably months in advance in the case of small-capacity attractions like Abismo Anhumas. You'll need several days to take in the best of Bonito.

★**Abismo Anhumas**   ADVENTURE
(www.abismoanhumas.com.br; rappelling plus floating R$910, with scuba diving R$1270) Rappel into a gigantic, beautiful cave that culminates in an underground lake. After you make it down the 72m, it's time for a spin around the lake to admire the beautiful rock formations. Then you dive (license required) or snorkel in the frigid underwater world (visibility 30m), with phallic pinnacles rising from the depths, before climbing back out. A heart-stopping experience.

★**Rio da Prata**   SNORKELING
(www.riodaprata.com.br; 5-hour trip incl lunch R$280; ⊙7:30am-5pm) ✐ The marvelous Rio da Prata, 50km south of Bonito, includes a hike through rainforest and some great snorkeling. The latter involves a 3km float downstream along the Rio Olha d'Agua, amazingly crystal clear and full of fish, and Rio da Prata, a little

BRAZIL BONITO & AROUND

BUSES FROM CAMPO GRANDE

DESTINATION	COST (R$)	TIME (HR)	FREQUENCY	COMPANY
Bonito	63	6	3 daily	Cruzeiro do Sul (www.cruzeirodosulms.com.br)
Brasília	238-261	23 25	4 daily	Motta (www.motta.com.br), Viação São Luiz (www.viacaosaoluiz.com.br)
Corumbá	124	7	8 daily	Andorinha (www.andorinha.com)
Cuiabá	147-170	11-14	20 daily	Andorinha, Eucatur (www.eucatur.com.br), Motta, Nova Integração (www.eucatur.com.br), Viação São Luiz
Foz do Iguaçu	235-290	16-20	No direct buses, change in Cascavel or Toledo, several daily options.	Nova Integração, Eucatur, UneSul (www.unesul.com.br), Ouro e Prata (www.viacaoouroeprata.com.br)
Ponta Porã	85-97	6	7 daily	Expresso Queiroz (www.expresso queiroz.com.br), Cruzeiro do Sul
Rio de Janeiro	427	24	2 daily	Andorinha (www.andorinha.com)
São Paulo	249-304	15½	7 daily	Andorinha, Motta

GETTING TO BOLIVIA

Bus 102 (R$3.25, 15 minutes) goes from Corumbá's Praça Independência to the Bolivian border hourly (at minimum) from 6am to 7pm. A taxi from the center to the border is around R$45; groups of two or fewer traveling light are better off using a moto-taxi (R$25).

All Brazilian exit formalities must be completed with the **Polícia Federal** (✆67 3234-7822; www.pf.gov.br; ◷8am-6pm) at the border. There are often lengthy queues. Bolivian immigration is open the same hours as Brazilian immigration; prepare to overnight in Corumbá if you are crossing outside of them. To enter Bolivia, most countries do not need a visa, but citizens of the United States must obtain a visa (US$160) from abroad, via online application or at the **Bolivian Consulate** (✆67 3231-5605; www.cancilleria.gob.bo; 7 de Setembro 47; ◷visas 8:30-9:30am Mon-Fri) in Corumbá.

In Bolivia *colectivos* (B$5) and taxis (around B$15 to B$25) run the 3km between the border and Quijarro train station for onward travel to Santa Cruz. There are two train options (www.fo.com.bo): the faster and more comfortable *Ferrobus* which departs at 6pm on Monday, Wednesday and Friday (B$235, 13 hours), arriving at 7am, and the cheaper *Expreso Oriental* that leaves at 1pm on Tuesday, Thursday and Sunday (B$100, 16¾ hours), arriving at 5:40am. Buy tickets in advance if you can.

foggier but still fantastic for viewing massive pacu and big, scary dourado.

Buraco das Araras   BIRD-WATCHING
(✆67 3255-4344; www.buracodasararas.com.br; R$75) 🚶 A sunset visit to Buraco das Araras, one of the world's largest sinkholes, is usually tagged on to a day out at Rio da Prata and Laguna Misteriosa. It's a 1km walk, complete with two viewpoints, that allows you to watch dozens of scarlet macaws flying home to roost, their metallic cries piercing the air. An impressive spectacle.

🛌 Sleeping

Bonito HI Hostel   HOSTEL $
(✆67 3255-1022; www.bonitohostel.com.br; Dr Pires 850; dm R$45, d with/without air-con R$150/100; ❄@☎≋) 🚶 One of Brazil's top HI hostels, this well-oiled backpacker haunt is a bit far from the action, but perks include hammocks, a pool, large lockers, kitchen, laundry and multilingual staff. Dorms come with private bathrooms, and the private en-suite rooms with air-con (a must in summer) are hotel quality. The hostel runs tours to all local attractions.

Papaya Hostel   HOSTEL $
(✆67 3255-4690; www.papayahostelbonito.com; Vicente Jacques 1868; dm R$35-55, d R$120-160; ❄@☎≋) This papaya-colored hostel, handily located near the bus station, is the kind of place where backpackers find themselves delaying their departure, seduced by the poolside chill-out area, communal barbecues, fellow travelers to chat with and a

plethora of tours organized by the English-speaking owner.

Pousada Muito Bonito   POUSADA $$
(✆67 3255-1645; www.pousadamuitobonito.com.br; Coronel Pilad Rebuá 1444; d/tr R$280/340; ❄☎≋) On the main street, a flashy facade fronts a simple but pleasing pousada with well-appointed, inexpensive rooms in brick around a small courtyard with plunge pool. These folk also run one of the most popular tour agencies in town and are happy to provide plenty of information on the area.

🍴 Eating & Drinking

Local freshwater fish is the highlight and served everywhere; farmed caiman meat is also common, including in snack-sized portions if you just want to sample it.

★ Juanita   SEAFOOD $$
(✆67 3255-1924; www.facebook.com/juanita restaurante; Nossa Senhora da Penha 854; portions for 2 people R$65-95; ◷11:30am-2:30pm & 6:30-10:30pm Wed-Mon) There are a few fish dishes at this likable rustic restaurant, but the star of the show is the chargrilled boneless pacu served with plump capers and sides. It's really delicious. Half-portions are available if you ask, and would still serve two. Tables on the sunny front deck are at a premium on warm days; inside, a harpist accompanies your meal.

Zapi Zen   PIZZA $$
(✆67 3255-2455; www.facebook.com/zapizen bonitoms; Filinto Müller 573; wraps R$23-27, pizzas

R$28-64; ☺6-11:30pm; 🖊) Just off the main drag, this warm-hearted spot serves top-notch pizzas with mostly – but not exclusively – vegetarian toppings. All are brimming with goodness, and you can choose between white or wholewheat crusts. There are also wraps: pick from the menu or create your own.

Bonito Beer   MICROBREWERY
(www.facebook.com/bonitobeer; Coronel Pilad Rebuá 2052; ☺5-11pm Mon-Sat) This tiny microbrewery is in the heart of things. You buy a refillable token, grab a glass and pour your own from the selection of taps out front (our favorite was the American pale ale). Minimum charge is R$30, which gets you just under a liter, but you can always come back if you don't spend it all. There's also G&T on tap.

ℹ Information

ATMs are available at **Banco do Brasil** (www.bb.com.br; Luiz da Costa Leite 2279; ☺bank 9am-2pm Mon-Fri) and **Bradesco** (Coronel Pilad Rebuá 1942; ☺bank 9am-2pm Mon-Fri), both near the main square.

ℹ Getting There & Away

There are two weekly flights with **Azul** (www.voeazul.com.br) between Bonito and São Paulo (Campinas) airport on Sundays and Wednesdays (1½ hours); more operate during high season. Some services go via Corumbá.

The bus station is handily located three blocks south of the main street.

ℹ Getting Around

Most of Bonito's attractions are a fair hike from town, and there's no public transport. Some guesthouses lend their guests bicycles, or you can rent a decent mountain bike along the main street for around R$30 per day. Hotels and agencies can arrange transport for an extra R$40 to R$80 per excursion. Vanzella (p371)

also runs some scheduled departures to popular excursion points and can be chartered.

If you are part of a group, it might end up being more economical to hire a taxi for the full day (R$80 to R$180 depending on the distance). Moto-taxis can also be a good option for solo travelers.

Corumbá
📋 0 X X 67 / POP 109,900

'Corumbaly' (old Corumbá) is a gracefully aging river-port city close to the Bolivian border. Known as Cidade Branca (White City), it is 403km northwest of Campo Grande by road. The city sits atop a steep hill overlooking the Rio Paraguai; on the far side of the river, a huge expanse of the Pantanal stretches out on the horizon. One of Brazil's biggest and best Carnaval celebrations really makes this hot, sleepy backwater come to life.

On the waterfront, the excellent **Museu de História do Pantanal** (MUHPAN; 📋67 3232-0303; Manoel Cavassa 275; ☺1-5:30pm Tue-Sat) FREE tells the story of the formation of the Pantanal and 10,000 years of human habitation in the region. The **Porto Geral** (Manoel Cavassa) is a charming locale with colorful historic facades opposite bobbing boats, some of which offer boisterous pleasure cruises on the Paraguai.

The **Hostel Roadriders** (📋67 3232-8143; www.hostelroadriders.com.br; Firmo de Matos 1; dm/d R$50/130; ❄🖥) makes a great base for exploring the area.

From the **long-distance bus station** (Porto Carreiro) near the center, regular buses run to Campo Grande. It pays to buy your ticket in advance as services fill up with those crossing the border. Corumbá **international airport** (CMG; 📋67 3231-3322; Santos Dumont) has an Azul flight that links the city with São Paulo twice a week, once via Bonito.

BRAZIL CORUMBÁ

BUSES FROM BONITO

DESTINATION	COST (R$)	TIME (HR)	FREQUENCY
Campo Grande (bus)	63	6	three daily
Campo Grande (minibus)	80	5	four daily (Vanzella); three daily (Terra)
Corumbá (bus)	102	6	one Mon-Sat
Corumbá (minibus; call 67 99809-2397)	100	5	one daily
Foz do Iguaçu (via Dourados or Campo Grande)	210-250	21-24	three daily
Ponta Porã (bus)	78	5½	one daily

THE NORTHEAST

Year-round warm climate, physical beauty and sensual culture rich in folkloric traditions all make Brazil's Northeast a true tropical paradise. More than 2000km of fertile coastline is studded with idyllic white-sand beaches, pockets of lush rainforest, sand dunes and coral reefs. A spectrum of natural environments creates the perfect backdrop for a wide variety of outdoor activities.

The picturesque urban centers of Salvador, Olinda and São Luís are packed with

Northeast Brazil

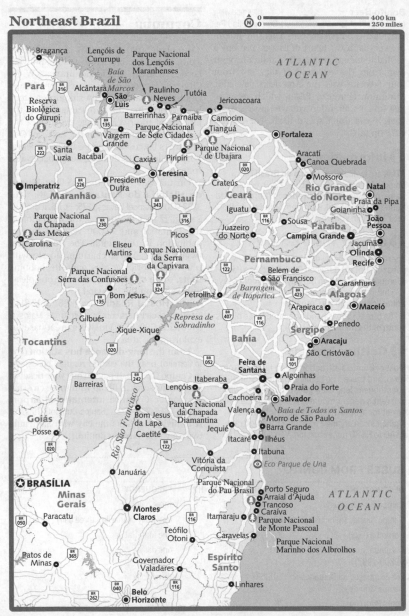

beautifully restored and satisfyingly decaying architecture. Add to this the lively festivals, myriad music and dance styles, and exotic cuisine loaded with seafood, and you will find Brazil's most culturally diverse region.

Salvador

◢ 0XX71 / POP 2.9 MILLION

Salvador da Bahia has an energy and unadorned beauty that few cities can match. Once the magnificent capital of Portugal's New World colony, today Salvador is the pulsating heart of the country's Afro-Brazilian community. Its brilliantly hued center is a living museum of 17th- and 18th-century architecture and gold-laden churches. Wild festivals happen frequently, with drum corps pounding out rhythms against the backdrop of colonial buildings almost daily. Elsewhere in town, a different spirit flows as crowds of religious adherents celebrate and reconnect with African gods at Candomblé ceremonies. In fact, there's no other place in the world where the culture of those brought as slaves from Africa has been preserved as it has been in Salvador – from music and religion to food, dance and martial-arts traditions. Aside from the many attractions within Salvador, a gorgeous coastline lies right outside the city – a suitable introduction to the tropical splendor of Bahia.

◉ Sights

The Cidade Alta (the Pelourinho and Carmo) is packed with the city's most impressive sights, though you'll also find worthwhile museums in Vitória, a wonderfully scenic lighthouse in Barra and other fascinating attractions scattered about the city.

◉ Cidade Alta

★Pelourinho   AREA

The centerpiece of the Cidade Alta is the Pelourinho, a Unesco-declared World Heritage site of colorful colonial buildings and magnificent churches. As you wander the cobblestone streets, gazing up at the city's oldest architecture, you'll realize that the Pelô is not just for tourists. Cultural centers and schools of music, dance and capoeira pack these pastel-colored 17th- and 18th-century buildings.

Museu Afro-Brasileiro   MUSEUM

(◢71 3283-5540; www.facebook.com/museuafro2; Terreiro de Jesus; adult/child R$6/3; ☺9am-5pm Mon-Fri, 10am-5pm Sat) Holding one of Bahia's most important collections, the Museu Afro-Brasileiro exhibits wood carvings, baskets, pottery and other artwork and crafts linking Brazilian and African artistic traditions. The highlight of the museum is a room lined with 27 huge, breathtaking carved wooden panels depicting *orishas* (spirits common in Afro-Brazilian spirituality) by Argentine-born Carybé, who is perhaps Salvador's most renowned 20th-century fine artist.

Igreja e Convento São Francisco   CHURCH

(Cruzeiro de São Francisco; R$5; ☺10am-5pm) One of Brazil's most magnificent churches, the baroque Igreja e Convento São Francisco is filled with displays of wealth and splendor. An 80kg silver chandelier dangles over ornate wood carvings smothered in gold leaf, and the convent courtyard is paneled with hand-painted *azulejos* (Portuguese tiles). The complex was finished in 1723.

Elevador Lacerda   HISTORIC BUILDING

(◢71 3322-7049; fare R$0.15; ☺6am-11pm) The beautifully restored, art deco Elevador Lacerda connects the Cidade Alta with Comércio via four elevators traveling 72m in 30 seconds. The Jesuits installed the first manual rope-and-pulley elevator around 1610 to transport goods and passengers from the port to the settlement. In 1868 an iron structure with clanking steam elevators was inaugurated, replaced by an electric system in 1928.

◉ Cidade Baixa, Barra & the Coast

Forte de Santo Antônio da Barra   HISTORIC BUILDING

(Largo do Farol da Barra s/n) Built in 1698, Bahia's oldest fort is more commonly called the Farol da Barra for the lighthouse (South America's oldest) within its walls. In addition to having superb views, the fort houses an excellent nautical **museum** (Nautical Museum of Bahia; ◢71 3264-3296; www.museunautico dabahia.org.br; Largo do Farol da Barra s/n, Forte de Santo Antônio da Barra; adult/student & senior R$15/7.50; ☺9am-6pm Tue-Sun, daily Jan & Jul), with relics and displays from the days of Portuguese seafaring, plus exhibits on the slave trade.

BRAZIL SALVADOR

Salvador

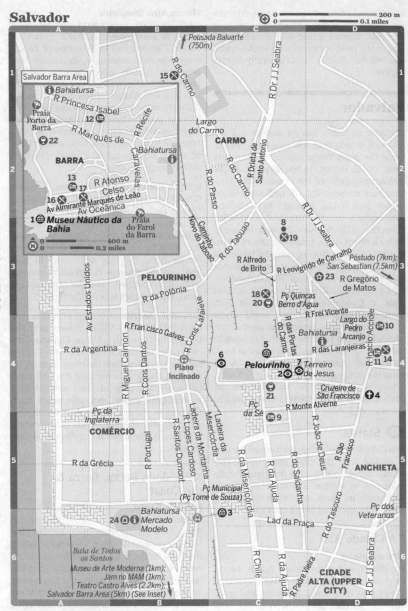

⊙ Itagipe Peninsula

★ **Igreja NS do Bonfim** CHURCH
(☎71 3316-2196; www.santuariosenhordobonfim.
com; Praça Senhor do Bonfim; ⊙6:30am-6.30pm
Mon-Thu & Sat, from 5:30am Fri & Sun) This famous
18th-century church, located a few kilometers
north of Comércio on the Itapagipe Peninsula,
is the source of the *fitas* (colored ribbons) you
see everywhere in Salvador, a souvenir of the
church and a symbol of Bahia itself. Bonfim's
fame derives from its power to effect miraculous cures, making it a popular shrine.

Salvador

🕾 Courses

Classes in capoeira, African dance and percussion are easily arranged through hostels and pousadas (guesthouses) in the Pelourinho. Course prices vary depending on season, availability and the number of people in your party, but generally you can expect to pay anywhere from R$55 to R$120 per hour for a class.

✿ Festivals & Events

Carnaval CULTURAL
(⊙ Feb/Mar) Salvador's Carnaval is Brazil's second largest and, for many, the best. It's characterized by parades of *axé* and *pagode* bands atop creeping *trios electricvs* (long trucks loaded with huge speakers). A *trio* or drum corps, together with its followers grouped in a roped-off area around it, form a *bloco*.

People pay hundreds of reais for the *abadá* (outfit) for their favorite band, mostly for prestige and the safety of those ropes. Choosing to *fazer pipoca* (be popcorn) in the street is still a fine way to spend Carnaval. There are three main areas: the beachside Barra to Rio Vermelho circuit (most touristy), the narrow Campo Grande to Praça and Castro Alves circuit and the Pelourinho (no *trios* here, mostly concerts and drum corps). Check www.carnaval.salvador.ba.gov.br.

Lavagem do Bonfim RELIGIOUS
(⊙ 2nd Thu Jan) Salvador's biggest festival outside of Carnaval honors the saint with Bahia's largest following – Senhor do Bonfim, associated with Candomblé. A procession of *baianas* (women dressed as Bahian 'aunts') in ritual dress carrying buckets of flowers walk 6km from Cidade Baixa to Igreja NS do Bonfim.

Festa de Iemanjá RELIGIOUS
(⊙ Feb 2) Perhaps Candomblé's most important festival, the event pays homage to the *orixá* (deity) Iemanjá, goddess of the sea and fertility. Devotees descend on Praia Rio Vermelho in the morning, where ceremonies are held to bless offerings of flowers, cakes, effigies and perfume bottles. The ensuing street festival goes until night and is packed with people and some of Salvador's best bands.

⎓ Sleeping

Staying in the Pelourinho means being close to the action, but the beach suburbs are mellower (and just a short bus or taxi ride away). Reservations during Carnaval are essential.

⎓ Cidade Alta

★ **Hostel Galeria 13** HOSTEL $
(📱 71 3266-5609; www.hostelgaleria13.com; Inacio Acciole 23, Historic Center; dm/d from R$40/135; ❄ 🕸 ⛱) Located in an old colonial house complete with a swimming pool and a Moroccan-style lounge (rarities at any hostel), but especially in one at such a great location in the middle of the historic center – Galeria 13 is a huge hit with backpackers. Breakfast is served till noon, and nonguests are welcome to hang out.

BRAZIL SALVADOR

Laranjeiras Hostel
HOSTEL $

(📞 71 3321-1366; www.laranjeirashostel.com.br; Rua da Ordem Terceira 13; dm/d R$44/98; ❄ @ 🛜) This cheerful, yellow colonial mansion-turned-hostel is one of the best budget options in the Pelô. High-ceilinged rooms range from dorms to comfortable suites – save cash by choosing a room with a fan instead of air-conditioning. Perks include kitchen access, laundry facilities and an on-site crêperie.

Bahiacafé Hotel
BOUTIQUE HOTEL $$

(📞 71 3322-1266; www.bahiacafehotelsalvador.com; Praça da Sé 22; s/d/tr from R$179/233/287; ❄❄🛜) This chic but low-key boutique hotel has fashionably outfitted rooms and an excellent location close to the center of the action in the Pelourinho. The lobby cafe, filled with locally produced artwork and open to the public, is the perfect spot for a quick cappuccino during an afternoon of sightseeing.

Pousada Baluarte
POUSADA $$

(📞 71 3327-0367; Ladeira do Baluarte 13; d with/without bathroom R$155/200; ❄🛜) Run by a friendly French-Brazilian couple, Baluarte feels like a B&B, with a welcoming, homelike ambience and just five rooms with hardwood floors and beautiful block prints by a local artist. A delicious breakfast is served on the veranda. It's right off the trendy Praça de Santo Antonio and a 10-minute walk from the Pelourinho.

🛏 Cidade Baixa, Barra & the Coast

★ Open House Barra
POUSADA $

(📞 71 99142-1285; www.openhousebarra.com; Bernardo Catarino 137, Barra; dm from R$44, r with/without bathroom from R$118/69; 🛜) This fantastically colorful and homey place is run by professional artists with deep connections to the local music, dance and film community. Musicians and capoeira demonstrations periodically take place at the hostel, especially during Carnaval, when the guesthouse offers one of Salvador's most memorable party experiences. Special packages and classes, including Portuguese language, can be booked through the hostel.

Pousada Estrela do Mar
POUSADA $$

(📞 71 3022-4882; www.estreladomarsalvador.com; Afonso Celso 119, Barra; d from R$220; ❄🛜) This white stucco house with dark-blue shutters – very Portugal-meets-the-tropics – is surrounded by greenery, while inside plain white walls set off bright Bahian paintings and vibrant blue tilework. The location is close to the beach on a mellow, tree-shaded street.

✖ Eating

Dining out is a delight in Salvador. Traditional Bahian cuisine has a heavy African influence, featuring ingredients like coconut cream, tomato, seafood, bell pepper and spices of ginger, hot peppers and coriander. You'll also find cuisines from many other nationalities well represented.

✖ Cidade Alta

★ Bar Zulu
INTERNATIONAL $

(Rua das Laranjeiras 15; mains R$22-56; ⏱ 11am-10pm; 🛜) This laid-back corner bar and restaurant has outdoor tables and serves a wide range of Spanish tapas, Bahian classics and international dishes, plus Argentine wine by the glass and strong cocktails. Try the grilled veggie sandwich, one of the famous burgers, or one of the rice-based dishes – like a lighter take on *moqueca* (fish stew).

★ Cafélier
CAFE $

(📞 71 3241-5095; www.cafelier.com.br; Rua do Carmo 50; mains R$15-40; ⏱ 2-9pm Mon, Tue & Thu-Sat, to 8pm Sun) This quaint hideaway cafe, located inside an antique house that's positioned dramatically on a cliff top over the ocean, is one of a kind. Come for the views, plus beautifully prepared cappuccino, rich chocolate cake, delicious sandwiches and wines by the glass.

★ Restaurante do Senac
BUFFET $$

(📞 71 3324-8101; www.ba.senac.br; Largo do Pelourinho 13; buffet per kg R$50, típico per kg R$51.90; ⏱ buffet a quilo 11:30am-3:30pm Mon-Fri, buffet típico 11:30am-3:30pm Mon-Sat; 🅿) The best Bahian buffet in town. The cooking school SENAC (📞 71 3186-4000; from R$180; ⏱ 9-11am & noon-4:30 Mon-Fri) spreads a tempting array of regional dishes, including several varieties of seafood, *moqueca* (fish stew), and traditional desserts. The impressive *buffet típico* (traditional Bahian food) is on the top floor, not to be confused with the more general street-level *buffet a quilo*, which is also good for a quick lunch.

✖ Cidade Baixa, Barra & the Coast

In the Comércio, cheap *lanchonetes* (snack bars) and self-service restaurants abound. For something more memorable, head south along the bay, where there are several fine (if expensive) restaurants with views over the water.

A NIGHT OUT IN RIO VERMELHO

The coastal neighborhood of Rio Vermelho has always been culturally significant to the city of Salvador: Portuguese sailors wrecked their ship offshore in 1510, famed writer Jorge Amado lived here and the important Candomblé festival Festa da Iemanjá (p377), honoring the goddess of motherhood and fertility, takes place on its shores. But in recent years, the neighborhood has also emerged as a hub of nightlife.

Arrive around sunset and take your pick from the sea of plastic tables and chairs set up on the lively plaza of **Largo de Santana**. Several casual bars serve cold beer to these outdoor tables, but the real attraction is the traditional street food prepared by colorfully dressed Bahian women at stands around the square. Particularly legendary are the *acarajé* (balls of dough fried in *dendê* oil and served with spicy sauces and shrimp).

On any given evening, there are cultural events and free concerts in the square, at the cultural center **Casa de Lemanjá** (☑71 3334-3041; Guedes Cabral 81, Rio Vermelho; ⏰hours vary), and around the waterfront market **Mercado do Peixe**. Afterwards, go for drinks at nearby **Póstudo** (☑71 3015-8800; João Gomes 87, Rio Vermelho; ⏰noon-2am), then catch some live music at **Commons Studio Bar** (☑71 3022-5620; www.facebook.com/commonsstudiobar; Doutor Odilon Santos 224, Rio Vermelho; from R$20; ⏰10pm-5am Thu-Sat). After midnight, hit the dance floor at **San Sebastian** (☑71 3012-5013; www.sansebastianoficial.com.br; Rua da Paciência 88, Rio Vermelho; ⏰midnight-5am Fri & Sat).

Rio Vermelho is a short bus ride from Barra on any bus marked 'Orla' (waterfront).

Light House BUFFET $
(Afonso Celso s/n, Barra; per kg R$39; ⏰11am-3:30pm Mon-Sat, 11:30am-4pm Sun; ☑) Tucked away on a quiet block around the corner from the beach, this laid-back place does a self-serve lunch buffet with a range of seafood and vegetarian dishes; there's appealing outdoor seating under the shade of tall trees.

Du Chef Arte e Gastronomia SEAFOOD $$
(☑71 3042-4433; www.facebook.com/duchefartegastronomia; Afonso Celso 70, Barra; mains R$45-90; ⏰noon-11pm Tue-Thu, to 1am Fri & Sat, to 5pm Sun; ☑) Fresh seafood and upscale plating make the dishes at this swish Barra restaurant pop. You're likely to make the acquaintance of the chef, Lucius Gaudenzi, while you dine on tender shrimp or one of the vegan dishes on the menu.

 Drinking & Nightlife

The Pelourinho is Salvador's nightlife capital: bars with outdoor tables and live music spill onto the cobbled streets.

In Barra, find relaxed ambience and music along Av Almirante Marques de Leão and the waterfront around the Farol da Barra.

★**Pereira** BAR
(☑71 3264-6464; www.pereirarestaurante.com.br; Sete de Setembro 3959, Barra; ⏰noon-4pm & 5pm-midnight Tue-Fri & Sun, noon-4pm & 5:30pm-1am Sat) Up a staircase from the seaside road that curves around the tip of Barra, Pereira is a stylish restaurant and wine bar. Excellent *chope* (draft beer) is on tap and the sunset views over the ocean are beautiful.

Casa do Amarelindo Bar COCKTAIL BAR
(☑71 3266-8550; www.casadoamarelindo.com; Rua das Portas do Carmo 6, Hotel Casa do Amarelindo; ⏰noon-late) The chic tropical-style bar at the lovely **Pelô Bistrô** (mains R$45-90; ⏰11:30am-10:30pm; ☑) at Casa do Amarelindo is the ideal spot for a nightcap; better still is the panoramic terrace where a skilled bartender shows up after dark to mix classic cocktails.

O Cravinho BAR
(☑71 99314-6022; www.ocravinho.com.br; Terreiro de Jesus 3; ⏰11am-11:30pm) This friendly neighborhood bar specializes in flavored shots of *cachaça* (sugarcane alcohol), including its trademark clove-infused variety. Decorated with barrels and packed with a vibrant mix of locals and tourists and featuring live music many evenings of the week, it's an atmospheric place to stop in for a quick drink while sightseeing in the Pelourinho.

☆ **Entertainment**

Salvador is the pulsing center of an incredible music scene. During the high season, there are almost nightly concerts in the inner courtyards of the Pelourinho, with cover charges ranging from free to R$50. Take a stroll by the following places and find out what's on for the evening: Largo de Tereza

Batista, Largo do Pedro Arcanjo and Praça Quincas Berro d'Água (all usually free). There are also occasional concerts on the **Terreiro de Jesus** (Praça 15 de Novembro) and you can frequently hear drum corps, which rehearse by walking through the Pelourinho, blocking traffic and gathering a following as they go.

Traditional groups (characterized by strong Afro drum corps) to look out for include Ilê Aiyê (the first exclusively black Carnaval group), the all-female Dida, Muzenza and Male Debalê. More pop, and with strong percussion sections, are world-famous Olodum (a Tuesday-night Pelourinho institution) Araketu and Timbalada, brainchild of master composer and musician Carlinhos Brown. The queens of Salvador pop music – Margareth Menezes, Ivete Sangalo and Daniela Mercury – also often 'rehearse' publicly.

★ **Balé Folclórico da Bahia**   PERFORMING ARTS
(☑ 71 3322-1962; www.balefolcloricodabahia.com. br; Gregório de Mattos 49, Teatro Miguel Santana; R$60; ☺ shows 8pm) The most astounding professional show is put on by this world-renowned folkloric ballet company.

★ **Jam no MAM**   LIVE MUSIC
(www.jamnomam.com.br; Av Contorno s/n, Museu de Arte Moderna; adult/child R$8/4; ☺ 6-9pm Sat) Saturday-evening jazz and bossa nova at MAM (☑ 71 3117-6139; www.jamnomam.com. br/mam; Av do Contorno s/n; ☺ 1-6pm Tue-Sun) **FREE** is a must for music lovers. Go early to see the museum first and catch the views at sunset. Though the venue is within walking distance of the Pelourinho, muggings are common along this quiet stretch; taking a taxi is recommended.

Teatro Castro Alves   LIVE MUSIC
(www.tca.ba.gov.br; Praça 2 de Julho, Campo Grande) For the biggest acts, keep your eye on Salvador's finest venue, the Teatro Castro Alves. Its Concha Acústica (amphitheater) has weekly concerts throughout summer.

🛍 Shopping

Mercado Modelo   ARTS & CRAFTS
(Praça Cayru, Cidade Baixa; ☺ 9am-6pm Mon-Sat, to 2pm Sun) In Salvador's unpleasant past the **Mercado Modelo** (www.mercadomodelo bahia.com.br; Praça Visconde de Cayru) was the site where slaves coming into the city were detained. Now the building houses dozens of tourist-oriented stalls selling local handicrafts, as well as food stalls and restaurants.

ℹ Information

TOURIST INFORMATION

Bahiatursa The tourism authority is friendly if not terribly organized. The **Pelourinho office** (☑ 71 3321-2463; www.bahiatursa. ba.gov.br; Rua Francisco Muniz Barreto 12, Pelourinho; ☺ 8:30am-9pm Mon-Thu, to 10pm Fri-Sun), which has maps and listings of what's happening around town, is your best bet. There are also desks at the **bus station** (☑ 71 3450-3871; www.bahiatursa.ba.gov.br; Av Antônio Carlos Magalhães, Iguatemi; ☺ 9am-6pm Mon-Sat) and the **airport** (☑ 71 3204-1244; www.bahiatursa.ba.gov.br; Praça Gago Coutinho s/n; ☺ 7:30am-11pm), at **Shopping Barra** (☑ 71 3264-4566; www.bahiatursa. ba.gov.br; Av Centenário 2992, Barra, SAC, Shopping Barra; ☺ 9am-6pm Mon-Sat), **Mercado Modelo** (☑ 71 3241-0242; www. bahiatursa.ba.gov.br; Praça Cayru, Mercado Modelo; ☺ 9am-6pm Mon-Sat) and a **Barra office** (☑ 71 3264-5440; www.bahiatursa. ba.gov.br; Av 7 de Setembro, Instituto Mauá, Porto da Barra; ☺ 9am-6pm Mon-Sat). Also see www.bahia.com.br.

EMERGENCY & IMPORTANT NUMBERS

Any crime involving a tourist must be handled by the city's **tourist police** (Tourist Police; ☑ 71 3116-6817; Cruzeiro de São Francisco 14, Pelourinho). A few speak English or French.
Pronto Socorro (Ambulance) ☑ 192

DANGERS & ANNOYANCES

Crime in the Pelô increases during the high season (especially around Carnaval) and on crowded Tuesday nights, and pickpocketing is common on buses and in congested places where tourists are easily singled out. To minimize risks, dress down, keep smartphones out of sight, carry just enough cash for your outing and only a photocopy of your passport, and try to be roughly oriented before you set out. The Pelourinho shifts quickly into sketchy areas, so avoid wandering off the beaten path. Cidade Baixa is deserted and unsafe at night and on weekends, and the *ladeiras* (steep roads) should be used with caution.

ℹ Getting There & Away

AIR

Aeroporto Deputado Luis Eduardo do Magalhães (SSA; ☑ 71 3204-1010; Praça Gago Coutinho s/n, São Cristóvão) is served by domestic airlines like **GOL** (☑ 0300 115-2121; www.voegol.com.br; airport), **LATAM** (☑ 1-866-435-9526; www.latam.com), and **Azul** (☑ 1-888-587-2985; www.voeazul.com.br). There are several direct flights to/from foreign cities such as Miami and Lisbon via **TAP** (Air

Portugal; ☑1-800-221-7370; www.flytap.com), and Buenos Aires via **Aerolíneas Argentinas** (☑1-800-333-0276; www.aerolineas.com.ar), but generally speaking, flights to international destinations go via São Paulo or Rio.

BUS

Terminal Rodoviario de Salvador is 8km east of the center. Buy tickets online through sites like www.clickbus.com.br or www.busbud.com.

Note that, in addition to the fares, for many bus tickets out of Salvador, you are also required to buy an Interestadual card (R$6) at the time of ticket purchase. Swipe it at the departure gates for access to the bus platforms.

ⓘ Getting Around

To reach Barra or Cidade Alta from the airport (30km east of the center), catch a local 'Praça da Sé' bus (R$3.70, one to 1½ hours) or the plush First Class executive bus (www.firstclassbus. com.br, R$25).

From Salvador's long-distance bus station, cross the footbridge to Shopping Bahia and catch any bus marked 'Praça da Sé'.

Regular city buses connect Praça da Sé and Barra. Linking the lower and upper cities in the center is the fabulous art-deco Elevador Lacerda (p375), and the **Plano Inclinado Gonçalves** (Praça da Sé & Guindaste dos Padres, Comércio; R$0.15; ⊙7am-7pm Mon-Fri, to 1pm Sat) funicular railway.

Lençóis

☑0XX75 / POP 11,400

Lençóis is the prettiest of the old diamond-mining towns in the Chapada Diamantina, a mountainous wooded oasis in the dusty *sertão* (backlands of the Northeast).

The surrounding area is the real attraction: caves, waterfalls, idyllic rivers and panoramic plateaus set the stage for some fantastic adventures.

◉ Sights & Activities

Numerous local agencies offer a wide range of outdoor activities, including hiking, rappelling, climbing, kayaking, mountain biking and horseback riding, in **Parque Nacional da Chapada Diamantina** (www.guiachapada diamantina.com.br) FREE. There are also great hikes leaving from town that the adventurous can undertake without a guide.

Walking & Swimming

One lovely hike is a 3km walk out of town, following the Rio Lençóis upstream. You first pass a series of rapids known as **Cachoeira Serrano**; off to the right is the **Salão de Coloridas Areias** (Room of Colored Sands), where artisans gather material for bottled-sand paintings. You then pass **Poço Halley** (Swimming Hole), and the **Cachoeirinha** and **Cachoeira da Primavera** waterfalls. The second walk follows Rua São Benedito 4km southeast out of town to Ribeirão do Meio, a series of swimming holes with a natural waterslide.

Hiking

Southwest of Lençóis, Parque Nacional da Chapada Diamantina comprises 1520 sq km of breathtaking scenery, waterfalls, rivers, monkeys and striking geology. Standout sights near Lençóis include **Poço Encantado**, a cave filled with stunningly beautiful blue water, **Lapa Doce**, another cave with impressive formations, **Cachoeira da Fumaça**,

BRAZIL LENÇÓIS

BUSES FROM SALVADOR

DESTINATION	DURATION (HR)	COST (R$)	FREQUENCY (DAILY)	BUS COMPANY
Aracaju	4-6	72-105	8	various
Ilhéus	8	108-231	4	Águia Branca
Lençóis	7-8	86	3	Real Expresso
Maceió	11	93-145	6	various
Natal	25	250-262	2	Gontijo
Penedo	10	104	1	Águia Branca
Porto Seguro	11	144	1	Águia Branca
Recife	16	130-171	2	various
Rio de Janeiro	30	330-410	2	Águia Branca & Kaissara
São Paulo	32	199-462	2	Kaissara & Catedral Turismo
Vitória	21	281	1	Águia Branca

Brazil's highest waterfall (420m), and **Morro do Pai Inácio**, a mesa-style peak affording an awesome view over a plateau-filled valley.

The park has little infrastructure (trails are unmarked) and bus services are infrequent; your best bet is to go with an organized tour or a certified guide.

☞ Tours

Lençóis' many agencies organize a rotating schedule of half and full-day car trips (from R$190 per person depending on group size and destination) and hikes with certified guides, ranging from a couple of hours to a week or longer. Agencies pool customers and rent out necessary gear. Multiday hikes usually involve a combination of camping or staying in local homes and pousadas.

Chapada Adventure David   OUTDOORS
(☑75 3334-1933; www.chapadaadventure.com; Praça Horácio de Matos 114; hiking tours per person from R$150; ⊙8am-10pm) A friendly agency that offers hiking tours throughout the park with multilingual staff.

H2O Travel Adventures   OUTDOORS
(☑75 3334-1229; www.h2otraveladventures.com; tours from R$40) Both day trips and treks are offered; the website has detailed descriptions of each excursion's attractions and level of difficulty. It no longer has an office, so book online or over the phone.

🛏 Sleeping

★**Pousada Lua de Cristal**   POUSADA $
(☑75 3334-1658; Rua dos Patriotas 27; r R$140-375; 🔊) Run by an exceptionally kind owner, this charming guesthouse offers sweet, simple rooms with antique stained-glass windows, many opening to views over the town. Outdoor breakfast tables are an added bonus.

★**Pouso Da Trilha**   POUSADA $$
(☑75 3334-1192; www.pousodatrilha.com.br; Rua dos Mineiros 60; d with/without air-con R$170/280; ❄🔊) Conveniently located on the edge of the historic center, this guesthouse has simple rooms with homey design flourishes and a tranquil patio area with hammocks and a small garden. A great breakfast spread and friendly staff give it an edge over some of the other accommodations in town.

Villa Justen   POUSADA $$
(☑75 3334-2135; www.villajusten.com; Sao Felix 44; d/tr R$240/340) Villa Justen features a handful of smartly outfitted chalets, each with a pa-

tio and hammock, plus a kitchen that's better equipped than the usual: a full-sized refrigerator, pots and pans, even a couple of wine glasses. It's tucked away on the hill behind the bus station, about a 10-minute walk away.

✖ Eating & Drinking

Cozinha Rição   BAHIAN $
(www.facebook.com/pfdoricao; Praça Horácio de Matos 100; mains R$14-30; ⊙noon-10:30pm) One of the more popular spots on the main square in the historic center. The food is fairly standard but very tasty. You'll see people gathered here all afternoon enjoying a few beers after a long hike.

Burritos y Taquitos   MEXICAN $
(☑75 99288-1437; José Florencio 3; mains R$15-42; ⊙6-10pm Tue-Sun) This is a rare chance to get your Mexican fix in rural Bahia: popular with locals, this casual restaurant does burritos, tacos and guacamole, and has a back patio overlooking the river. The food isn't exactly authentic, but it's delicious nonetheless.

★**Lampião**   BRAZILIAN $$
(☑75 3334-1157; www.facebook.com/lampiaofood; Rua da Baderna 51; mains R$34-53; ⊙4-11pm Tue-Sun; 🍴) This popular eatery specializes in cuisine from Brazil's Northwest – think grilled meats, fish and chicken, served at cute alfresco tables for two. It's also a popular drinking spot.

❶ Information

The online portal of Guia Lençóis (www.guia lencois.com.br) is a great resource for tourist information.

Banco do Brasil (Praça Horácio de Matos 56), located on the main square once you cross the bridge into the old town, has ATMs.

❶ Getting There & Away

The **bus station** (Av Sr dos Passos s/n) is north of the center. **Real Expresso** (☑75 3334-1112; www.realexpresso.com.br) runs a few buses daily from Salvador (R$85, seven to eight hours). Bring a jacket: these buses are notorious for blasting the air-conditioning.

Morro de São Paulo

☑0XX75 / POP 4000

Trendy, isolated Morro, across the bay from Salvador and reached by boat, is known for nightlife but still has a tranquil charm along its pedestrianized main street running between three jungle-topped hills.

The beaches, with their shallow, warm water, disappear with the tides, liberating you for a hike to the waterfall, a round-the-island boat trip, a visit to the quieter neighboring island of Boipeba or sunset-watching from the fort. A short climb from the boat dock brings you to Morro's main square. From here, follow Caminho da Praia down to the beaches, which are named in numerical order; most of the action is around Segunda (Second) and Terceira (Third) Praias, a 10- to 15-minute walk from the Praça.

🛏 Sleeping

Book well ahead during high season (December to March).

Che Lagarto Hostel HOSTEL $
(📷75 3652-1018; www.chelagarto.com; Rua da Fonte Grande 11; dm/d from R$75/226; ❇🛜) Convenient to the ferry dock and local nightlife, yet with a middle-of-the-jungle feel thanks to its forest-shrouded wooden sundeck, this chain hostel is geared to those looking for a youthful party vibe.

★Porto de Chima Surf Hostel POUSADA $$
(📷75 99810-3242; www.portodecimahostel.com; Porto de Cima 56; dm/d from R$69/279; ❇🛜) This former pousada (guesthouse), now a chill hostel catering to surfers, sits along the path to Porto de Cima Beach. Watching electric-blue hummingbirds and the occasional monkey from the vantage point of one of the porch hammocks is about as relaxing as it gets, and the breakfast is downright picturesque.

Pousada O Casarão POUSADA $$
(📷75 3652-1022; www.pousadaocasarao.com; Praça Aureliano Lima 190; d/bungalow from R$135/158; ❇🛜🏊) Reigning over the main plaza, this beautifully renovated colonial mansion – dating from 1906 – has lovely rooms with classic furnishings and large windows, plus hillside bungalows with private balconies. Amenities include two swimming pools: one, with a bar, for adults, and another for children. Note that the rooms overlooking the square have great views, but can be noisy at night.

🍴 Eating & Drinking

At night, Segunda Praia is alive with restaurants competing for your business – it's a prime opportunity to dine with the sand between your toes.

Café das Artes BRAZILIAN $$
(📷75 3652-1057; www.solardasartes.net; Praça Aureliano Lima; mains R$30-53; ⊘noon-11pm) This pretty cafe-restaurant doubles as an art space; the patio overlooking the square is a sweet spot for a little night music. House specialties include seafood risotto and shrimp cooked in green coconut sauce. It's located at a popular pousada (guesthouse), Solar das Artes.

★Portaló Bar & Restaurante COCKTAIL BAR
(📷75 3652-1375; www.hotelportalo.com; Hotel Portaló; ⊘noon-10pm) This hotel's terrace is the place to be at sunset for glorious views over the harbor, a DJ-spun soundtrack and festive drinks served with the flourish of tropical flowers. There's a full dinner menu, too, if you want to make an evening of it (mains R$24–R$46). Look for it when you're stepping off the boat upon arrival on the island.

ℹ Information

There are a few ATMs on the island, at **Banco do Brasil** (Praça Aureliano Lima) and **Brandesco** (Caminho da Praia), but it's wise to bring necessary funds with you from the mainland, especially during high season, when tourists deplete the ATMs' cash supplies. Many establishments also accept credit cards.

ℹ Getting There & Away

Catamarans and small ferries (around R$100, two hours) cross between Morro and Salvador's Terminal Marítimo Turístico five to seven times daily. For reservations, contact **Biotur** (📷75 3641-3327; www.biotur.com.br), **Farol do Morro** (📷71 3319-4570; www.faroldomorrotour.com), **IlhaBela** (📷 in Salvador 71 3326-7158; www.ilhabelatm.com.br) or **Lancha Lulalu** (📷75 9917-1975), or stop into a travel agency on the Island. Note that the ride can be rough. Come with travel-sickness medication. Also keep in mind it's common for passengers to get wet on smaller boats.

There are also daily boats to Valença (R$25–R$27, 40 minutes), convenient if you're heading to Boipeba, the Peninsula Marau or points south.

If you're heading directly to Salvador's airport from Morro, contact **Cassi Turismo** (📷71 99121-1111; www.cassiturismo.com.br), which has a boat-plus-bus transfer package (R$95 to R$125, five daily) to the airport.

Itacaré

📷 0XX73 / POP 13,100
Beautiful Itacaré has long been sought out by hippies and surfers mesmerized by wide stretches of virgin Atlantic rainforest, picturesque beaches and reliable surf breaks.

Countless pousadas (guesthouses) and restaurants now pack the streets; still, a mellow, youthful vibe prevails, surf culture reigns supreme, and many establishments in the area are committed to environmentally friendly practices (look for the Carbon Free Tourism sign proudly posted around town).

🏃 Activities

Brazil Trip Tour   ADVENTURE
(☑73 9996-3331; www.braziltriptour.com; Pedro Longo 235) One of several reliable agencies offering excursions, surf lessons, transfers and tours, Brazil Trip Tour specializes in English-speaking guides and eco-minded tours.

Easy Drop   SURFING
(☑73 3251-3065; www.easydrop.com; João Coutinho 140; 1-day class R$213, 1-week package from R$1926) This well-established surf camp, offering a weeklong surfing experience with classes and accommodations, gets great reviews from travelers.

🛌 Sleeping

The majority of guesthouses are scattered along Rua Pedro Longo/Pituba. For a quieter stay that's still close to the action, try a pousada (guesthouse) on a side street or in the Condomínio Conchas do Mar area instead of one that's located right on the main drag.

Pousada Casa Tiki   POUSADA $
(☑73 99804-8901; www.pousadacasatiki.com.br; Rua C, Praia da Concha; d with/without bathroom from R$150/120; 🐀) The home-away-from-home vibe is what makes this small guesthouse special: there are only four rooms, leisurely breakfasts happen around a communal table, and the owners, a young English-speaking couple, mix potent cocktails and offer travel advice.

Casarão Verde Hostel   HOSTEL $
(☑73 3251-2037; http://casaraoverdehostel.com.br; Castro Alves s/n; dm from R$35, d without bathroom from R$80; 🌐🐀) Budget travelers rave about the friendly reception and pristine, spacious rooms at this lovely colonial house – painted pale green, as the name suggests – that's been smartly converted into a hostel.

★ Pousada Ilha Verde   POUSADA $$
(☑73 3251-2056; www.ilhaverde.com.br; Ataíde Setúbal 234; s/d from R$210/240, chalet for 4 R$439; 🌐🐀🐀) 🏆 In a lush setting, Ilha Verde has uniquely decorated rooms inspired by the owners' world travels. Features include private patios, an inviting swimming pool, abundant outdoor lounge space for luxuriating in the greenery, and a fair-trade shop with handicrafts made from Brazilian straw and shells.

🍴 Eating & Drinking

★ Agua   BISTRO $
(☑73 99950-9548; Pedro Longo 147; mains R$25-28; ⊙4-11pm Tue-Sun; 🍴) Itacaré's Agua is a blast of modern cool in Itacaré's beach-bum-centric dining scene. The regular menu features exquisitely cooked dishes inspired by Brazilian and Asian cuisine (including some good vegan and vegetarian options), but you'll want to make sure to go on Wednesday evening when the restaurant features a menu of various curries.

Alamaim   MIDDLE EASTERN $
(☑73 3251-3462; www.restaurantealamaim.com.br; Pedro Longo 204; mains R$24-39; ⊙2:30-10pm Mon-Sat; 🍴) Get your hummus fix here: this cool but casual eatery specializes in vegetarian Arabic food, from falafel to couscous, and has a relaxing lounge space where you can kick back after a day of surfing or swimming.

Mar e Mel   BAR
(☑73 3251-2358; www.maremel.com.br; Alpínia s/n; mains R$28-60; ⊙5pm-midnight) This is the place to hear (and dance to) live *forró* three nights a week (Tuesday, Thursday and Saturday at 9pm). There's a spacious wooden deck and abundant seafood and drink choices.

ℹ Getting There & Away

Itacaré's **bus station** (☑73 3251-2181; Rua da Rodoviário) is just out of the center (a $15–20 taxi ride to most pousadas). To the south, **Rota** (☑73 3251-2181; http://rotatransportes.com.br) has around 15 daily departures to Ilhéus (R$15, 1¾ hours) and one 7am bus to Porto Seguro (R$87, eight hours). For northbound travelers, **Cidade Sol** (www.viacaocidadesol.com.br) runs five daily buses to Bom Despacho (R$49), from where ferries continue across to Salvador.

Ilhéus

☑0XX73 / POP 142.210

Bright, early-20th-century architecture and oddly angled streets lend a vibrant and rather whimsical air to slightly rough-around-the-edges Ilhéus. The town's fame comes from its history as a prosperous cocoa port, as well as being the hometown of Jorge Amado, the celebrated Brazilian novelist, who used it as the setting for one of his best novels, *Gabriela, Cravo e Canela (Gabriela, Clove and Cinnamon)*. The city's reputation as a tourist destination has been rising in the past few years, with plenty of visitors from elsewhere in Brazil stopping through to tour the historic center and lounge on the beaches south of the city.

◉ Sights

Casa de Jorge Amado   MUSEUM
(🖉71 99168-0571; Jorge Amado 20; R$5; ☺9am-12:30pm & 2-6pm Mon-Fri, 9am-1pm Sat) The Casa de Jorge Amado, where the eponymous writer lived with his parents while working on his first novel, has been restored and turned into a lovely and informative museum honoring Amado's life. Not many writers can boast this sort of recognition while still alive, but he became a national treasure well before his death in 2001.

🛏 Sleeping & Eating

Lagoa Encantada II   POUSADA $
(🖉73 3632-5675; Italia 156, Pontal; d R$100; ❄ 🛜) Located south of the center, near the airport and the beach, this quiet guesthouse is ideal for budget travelers, if a bit hard to find. It's about 5km from the historic center, but the walk is mostly along the waterfront and is lovely during the day.

Pousada Pier do Pontal   POUSADA $$
(🖉73 3221-4000; www.pierdopontal.com.br; Lomanto Junior 1650, Pontal; s/d from R$206/222; ❄🛜🏊) Despite needing some upgrades to the decor, this pleasant guesthouse is on the waterfront and has a swimming pool. From here you can head north to check out Ilheus' historic center, or south for the beaches.

★ Bataclan   BRAZILIAN $$
(🖉73 3634-0088; www.bataclan.com.br; Av 2 de Julho 77; mains R$22-59, per kg R$54.90; ☺11am-5pm Mon & Tue, to 4pm Sat, to late Wed-Fri, event times vary) Once a cabaret frequented by cocoa tycoons (and one of the settings for Amado's *Gabriela*), this colonial building was restored to its original brilliance in 2004. Now it serves as a restaurant and cultural center. There's a lunch buffet from 11:30am to 2:30pm. You can tour the house while you wait for your food or visit without eating for R$5.

ℹ Getting There & Away

The **long-distance bus station** (Rodoviaria Ilheus; 🖉73 2102-5335; Av Roberto Santos 15) is located 4km west of the center. Rota (www.rota transportes.com.br) buses go to Porto Seguro (R$63 to R$85, six hours, four daily), and Aguia Branca (www.aguiabranca.com.br) has buses to Salvador (R$95 to R$231, eight hours, seven daily) making a long sweep around the Baía de Todos os Santos.

Porto Seguro

🖉0XX73 / POP 145,531

Historically, Porto Seguro is significant: it's the point where Portuguese sailors first set foot on the land now known as Brazil. But apart from its small historic center and colorful colonial houses, the city is more a popular destination for hordes of Brazilian and Argentinian package tourists, here for beach action and nightlife. It's also favored by rowdy high schoolers on school-break holidays. Many travelers linger in town only long enough to catch the ferry toward the lovely coastline and mellow village of nearby Arraial d'Ajuda.

◉ Sights

Cidade Histórica   HISTORIC SITE
Motivation is required to climb the stairs to Porto Seguro's old town. Rewards include colorful historic buildings and sweeping views over the coastline. Warning: the area is beautifully illuminated at night, and definitely worth a look, but the steps are not safe after dark. Take a taxi.

🏖 Beaches

North of town is one long bay dotted with *barracas* (food stalls) and clubs creating the Orla Norte (North Coast): **Praia Curuípe** (3km), **Praia Itacimirim** (4km), **Praia Mundaí** (6km), **Praia de Taperapua** (7km) and **Praia do Mutá** (10km.) The sands are white and fluffy, backed by green vegetation lapped by a tranquil sea, dotted with big beach clubs like **Tôa-Tôa** (🖉73 3679-1714; www.portaltoatoa.com.br; Av Beira Mar, Km 5, Praia de Taperapuã; ☺8am-6pm), where MCs and dancers lead Brazilian crowds through popular dances.

🛏 Sleeping & Eating

Most dining and drinking options are found around the Passarela do Álcool (Alcohol Walkway). At night, the passarela has craft stalls and street performers, with live music spilling onto the plazas.

Pousada Brisa do Mar POUSADA $

(📞73 3288-1444; Praça Coelho 180; s/d/tr R$55/75/95; ❄️🀫) This basic guesthouse, in a long, narrow house near the waterfront, is nothing fancy. But as Porto Seguro accommodations go, the location is good: it's close to restaurants, the Passarela do Álcool (Alcohol Walkway) and the ferry to Arraial.

★**Rabanete** BUFFET $$

(📞73 3288-2743; www.restauranterabanete.com. br; Saldanha Marinho 33; per kg R$61; ⊘noon-4:30pm) One of the classiest per-kilo eateries around, Rabanete puts out a mouthwatering buffet of gourmet dishes, from pasta with sun-dried tomatoes and basil to fresh fish fillets. Both the leafy patio tables and the stylish rustic interior offer plenty of atmosphere. Look out for its locations in Arraial d'Ajuda and Trancoso too.

Ilha dos Aquários CLUB

(📞73 3268-2828; www.ilhadosaquarios.com.br; Ilha Pacuío; adult/child under 10 R$75/free; ⊘8pm-late Fri) Ilha dos Aquários is traditionally a good party, probably because of the novelty of the aquariums and its river-island setting (reachable by boats from the port on party nights). The beginning of the evening is family-friendly and the party begins once the kids head home. You'll see lots of places to get tickets around town, including most hotels.

❶ Getting There & Away

Porto Seguro's airport (BPS), served by several domestic carriers, is 1.5km west of the bus station and 3km northwest of the port. From the bus station, 500m west of the Cidade Histórica, Rota (www.rotatransportes.com.br) runs four daily buses to Ilhéus (R$63 to R$75, six hours) and one to Itacaré (R$87, eight hours). Águia Branca (www.aguiabranca.com.br) offers overnight service to Salvador (R$176, 11 hours) and Rio de Janeiro (R$306, 22 hours, via Vitória).

Arraial d'Ajuda

📞0XX73 / POP 17,000

Perched on a bluff above long sandy beaches, Arraial has a curious blend of upmarket tourism and chilled backpackers. Squat buildings painted bright colors surround a traditional plaza; roads lined with pousadas, bars and restaurants slope down to the beaches. Arraial caters to both partiers and those looking to unwind in the tropics.

The closest beach to town is crowded **Praia Mucugê**, but a short walk south

brings you to dreamy **Praia de Pitinga** and other gorgeous beaches beyond. Several ATMs cluster around the center.

🛏️ Sleeping & Eating

Head to the main square at night for inexpensive crepes, tapioca, caipirinhas (cocktails) and traditional Bahian plates of rice, beans and grilled steak; or stop at one of the gourmet ice-cream stands along Rua do Mucugê.

Arraial d'Ajuda Hostel HOSTEL $

(📞73 3575-1192; www.arraialdajudahostel.com. br; Manoel Crescêncio Santiago 94; dm/d from R$60/140; ❄️@🀫🏊) This colorful HI hostel offers well-equipped private rooms as well as dorm-style accommodations in a funky Greco-Bahian-style building with a courtyard swimming pool. Travelers like the communal outdoor kitchen and the location near the beach.

★**Pousada Erva Doce** POUSADA $$

(📞73 3575-1113; www.ervadoce.com.br; Rua do Mucugê 200; d from R$240; ❄️🀫🏊) Squarely in the center of the village on a cobblestone plaza lined with boutiques and cafes, this peaceful guesthouse has spacious, thoughtfully designed rooms with roomy showers and mosquito-net canopies. Surrounding the small swimming pool is a leafy tropical garden with an open-air bar and hammocks, ideal for lazing away the afternoon.

★**Portinha** BUFFET $

(📞73 3575-1882; www.portinha.com.br; Shopping d'Ajuda, Rua do Mucugê 333; per kg R$59.50; ⊘11am-4:30pm Tue-Sun; 🖋️) Portinha is several steps up from most per-kilo restaurants you'll find. There is a plethora of meat and seafood dishes on offer, most of which are inspired by traditional Bahian cuisine and taste like they were made to order in an upscale bistro. It's located on a pleasant patio in the Shopping d'Ajuda complex.

🍷 Drinking & Nightlife

Arraial has lively nightlife options throughout the summer, when beach clubs host huge parties (cover R$25 to R$50).

Morocha Club CLUB

(📞73 3575-2611; www.morochaclub.com; Rua do Mucugê 260; cover generally free; ⊘5pm-late, event times vary) In town, Morocha is ground zero for nightlife, particularly in summer and around Carnaval. This popular local hangout and restaurant serving pizza, steaks, sand-

CARAÍVA

For end-of-the-road tranquility, head south from Trancoso to captivating Caraíva, a sandy hamlet tucked between a mangrove-lined river and a long churning surf beach. It's all the more peaceful given the absence of cars. In low season, Caraíva all but shuts down. There are no ATMs – bring cash.

Boat trips upriver, to the spectacular beaches north of town or south to Parque Nacional de Monte Pascoal, are easily organized through local pousadas, as are horse rides or walks to Barra Velha, an indigenous Pataxó village 6km from Caraíva. A 14km walk, boat trip or bus ride north brings you to celebrated Praia do Espelho, widely regarded as one of Brazil's top 10 beaches.

To fully appreciate Caraíva's magic, stay overnight. Accommodations range from simple campsites to high-end ocean-front cottages. The Aruanda Hostel has simple dorm rooms set amid lush grounds near the village center, while the Pousada Lagoa is an eco-minded spot with stylish bungalows and an enticing restaurant-bar.

Two daily buses run by **Aguia Azul** (☑73 3575-1170; www.viacaoaguiaazul.com.br) travel between Caraíva and the ferry in Arraial d'Ajuda (R$20, two hours) stopping in Trancoso along the way. From Caraíva's bus stop, canoes (R$5, five minutes) ferry you into town.

wiches and Tex-Mex (mains R$22–R$55) has a lounge-like vibe earlier in the evening. Things get rowdy late at night, with concerts, dancing, DJs and theme parties.

❶ Getting There & Away

The *balsa*, a quick car and passenger **ferry**, connects Porto Seguro to Arraial d'Ajuda (R$4.50, 10 to 15 minutes). From the boat dock, jump on a bus or Kombi van to the center of Arraial d'Ajuda (R$3.25).

Trancoso

☑0XX73 / POP 9860

Perched atop a grassy bluff overlooking the ocean, this small tropical paradise centers on the utterly picturesque Quadrado, a long grassy expanse with a white church flanked by low colorful houses, rooted in the town's history as a Jesuit mission. At night everyone turns out to lounge at outdoor restaurants surrounding the twinkling square. The beaches south of Trancoso are gorgeous, especially **Praia do Espelho** (20km south), off the road to Caraíva. ATMs are readily available.

🛏 Sleeping & Eating

Baianeiro Hostel   HOSTEL $
(☑73 99160-3065; Carlos Chagas 851; dm R$70; 🛜) Things are simple at Baianeiro Hostel: three dorm-style rooms, two shared bathrooms, a kitchen and ample indoor and outdoor communal space. What makes it special is the familial atmosphere cultivated by hosts Maria Luiza and Adriano. It is a 15-minute

walk from the Quadrado, making it a better choice for those who value affordability and tranquility over convenience.

⭐**Pousada Jacarandá**   POUSADA $$
(☑73 3668-1950; www.pousadajacaranda.com.br; Jovelino Rodrigues Vieira 91; bungalows for 2 from R$279; 🅿❄🛜📶) 🏄 This ecofriendly guesthouse features six freestanding bungalows built with natural, locally sourced materials, plus a lovely swimming pool and art-filled interiors. It's a short walk from both the Quadrado and the beach, but the quiet location is a benefit if you're looking to relax.

⭐**Rabanete**   BUFFET $$
(☑73 3668-1835; Quadrado s/n; per kg R$69.99; ◷noon-5:30pm) This Trancoso classic, formally known as Portinha, woos diners with a sumptuous buffet (don't miss the dessert spread) and atmospheric seating at tree-shaded picnic tables on the Quadrado. It's one of only a few places open for lunch in town.

❶ Getting There & Away

Hourly buses (R$11) and Kombi vans connect Trancoso with Arraial d'Ajuda (50 minutes) and its ferry dock (one hour); some continue to Porto Seguro. At low tide, the 13km walk along the beach from Arraial makes a scenic alternative.

Maceió

☑0XX82 / POP 1M

Maceió, bustling high-rise-dotted capital of Alagoas state, offers reef-sheltered swimming in an emerald sea along its lengthy waterfront. The swaying palms of the city shoreline are seductive, but the real beach jewels are out of town, just an hour away.

◉ Sights & Activities

Picturesque *jangadas* (traditional wooden fishing boats of Northeastern Brazil) sail 2km out from **Praia de Pajuçara**, offering opportunities to snorkel in natural pools formed by the reef. **Praia de Ponta Verde** and **Jatiúca** are good city beaches with calm water. Pretty **Praia do Francês** (24km), lined with beach bars, is Maceió's major weekend destination and has lots of pousadas. Further south, **Praia do Gunga** sits across a river from Barra de São Miguel (34km). Less crowded beaches north of town include **Garça Torta** (12km), **Riacho Doce** (14km) and **Ipioca** (23km). Another worthwhile excursion is to **Pontal da Barra** (8km south of Maceió), a popular spot to purchase traditional Alagoan *filé* (crochetwork) and embark on scenic four-hour lagoon cruises.

Marcão Turismo TOURS
(☑82 3231-0843; www.turismomaceio.com.br; 2nd fl, Hotel Expresso R1, Avenida João Davino 386) This well-established outfitt runs a number of tours and transfers, including tours to the Nove Ilhas (R$90), Dunas de Marape (R$100) and the Foz do São Francisco (R$110), all including lunch and boat ride. They also run a day trip to Praia do Gunga and Praia do Francês (R$25) and one-way transfers to Maragogi (R$40).

⌂ Sleeping

Maceió Hostel e Pousada HOSTEL $
(☑82 3231-7762; www.maceiohostel.com.br; Jangadeiros Alagoanos 1528, Pajuçara; dm/d from R$55/129; ▩🕈) A budget option a few blocks from the beach, this HI hostel is small – shared quads don't leave much room for your backpack – but the staff are friendly and the place is efficiently run. Doubles are basic, with good showers and large lockers.

Gogó da Ema POUSADA $
(☑82 3231-2117; www.hotelgogodaema.com.br; Francisco Laranjeiras 97, Ponta Verde; s/d/tr from R$100/120/160; ▩🕈) On a quiet street near two lovely beaches, reliable budget pick Gogó da Ema (named for a famous old palm tree that fell in the city in 1955 and has come to symbolize Maceió itself) is a five-story guesthouse with a tropical theme. The 24-hour front desk is particularly helpful if you're arriving late or catching an early plane.

🍴 Eating & Drinking

Villa Maceio Food Park FOOD TRUCK $
(☑82 99937-7174; www.facebook.com/villamaceio foodpark; Lourenço Moreira da Silva 203-245, Ponta Verde; mains R$20-40; ☺6-11pm Tue & Wed, to midnight Fri & Sat, 5-11pm Sun; ☑) You'll find both post-beach tourists and post-work locals flocking to this collection of food trucks at night. Everything from Brazilian favorites to gourmet hamburgers are represented and there is (of course) a beer-keg cart that dispenses several varieties of craft brew.

★Lopana BAR
(☑82 3231-7484; www.lopana.com.br; Av Silvio Carlos Viana 27, Ponta Verde; ☺10am-midnight Tue-Fri, 9am-1am Sat & Sun) Maceió's best beachfront bar is always buzzing: when an acoustic guitarist is playing and a good-looking crowd is drinking beer and caipirinhas under the sky-high palm trees, the place looks straight out of a movie.

❶ Getting There & Away

Maceió's Zumbi dos Palmares International Airport (MCZ), 23km north of the center, has domestic connections. The long-distance bus station is 4km north of the center. Real Alagoas (www.realalagoas.com.br) offers service to Recife (R$50 to R$78, six hours, seven daily); Rota (www.rotatransportes.com.br) goes to Salvador (R$117 to R$145, 11 hours, four daily).

Van-like municipal buses (from R$3.50) run to all northern and southern beaches.

Recife

☑0XX81 / POP 1.63 MILLION
Recife ('heh-*see*-fee'), one of the Northeast's major ports and cities, is renowned throughout Brazil for its dance and musical heritage. The bustling, decidedly gritty commercial center, with water on all sides, is busy during the day but deserted at night and on Sunday. Quieter Recife Antigo, on Ilha do Recife, has picturesque colonial buildings. Most travelers stay in Boa Viagem – an affluent suburb south of the center backing a long golden beach – or in Recife's more peaceful sister city, Olinda.

◉ Sights & Activities

The old city has many restored noble buildings with explanatory panels in English.

Recife

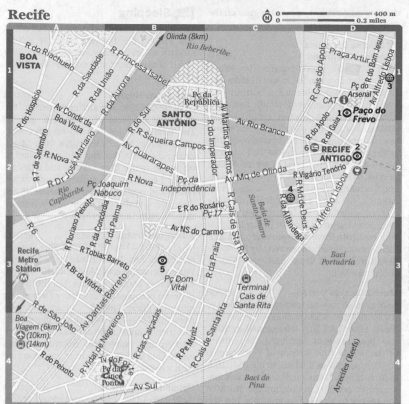

Recife

◎ Top Sights
1 Paço do Frevo...D1

◎ Sights
2 Marco Zero...D2
3 Museu Cais do Sertão.........................D1
4 Paço Alfândega....................................C2
5 Pátio de São Pedro.............................B3

◎ Sleeping
6 Azul Fusca Hostel...............................D2

◎ Drinking & Nightlife
7 Armazéns do Porto.............................D2

Strolling through Recife Antigo, you can admire the colorful houses and historic synagogue on Rua Bom Jesus and the customs-building-turned-shopping-mall **Paço Alfândega** (www.pacoalfandega.com.br; Rua da Alfândega 35, Recife Antigo; ⊙9am-9pm Mon-Sat, 11-8pm Sun). A key old city landmark is

Marco Zero (Praça Rio Branco, Recife Antigo), a small 'Km 0' marker near the waterfront, designating the place where the Portuguese founded Recife in 1537. Across in Centro, **Pátio de São Pedro** (Santo Antônio) is a pretty cobbled square lined with characterful buildings under the gaze of a handsome baroque church.

★ **Paço do Frevo**   ARTS CENTER
(☑81 3355-9500; www.pacodofrevo.org.br; Praça do Arsenal, Recife Antigo; adult/child R$8/4; ⊙9am-5pm Tue-Fri, 2-6pm Sat & Sun) This strikingly red museum is a small and modern house of worship for *frevo*, the quintessential dance of the Recife Carnaval that is easily identified by its use of colorful small umbrellas. There is a great energy about the place, which offers beautifully designed exhibits together with performances and classes of *frevo*. Highlights include a permanent top-floor exhibit that features giant Carnaval insignias from Recife's famous *blocos* (drumming and

dancing processions), encased in glass on the floor. Signage is bilingual.

★ Oficina Cerâmica Francisco Brennand
MUSEUM

(☑ 81 3271-2466; www.brennand.com.br; Várzea; R$20; ⊗ 8am-5pm Mon-Thu, to 4pm Fri, 10am-4pm Sat & Sun) Francisco Brennand, born in 1927 into an Irish immigrant family and now considered Brazil's greatest ceramicist, revitalized his family's abandoned tile factory to create his own line of decorative ceramic tiles. The expansive indoor and outdoor space in Várzea, 11km west of central Recife, is now mostly dedicated to his enormous and fascinating oeuvre, which ranges across painting, tile work and hundreds of highly original sculptures. It's best reached by taxi from Boa Viagem and visited in combination with **Instituto Ricardo Brennand** (☑ 81 2121-0352; www.institutoricardobrennand.org.br; Alameda Antônio Brennand, Várzea; adult/child R$30/15; ⊗ 1-5pm Tue-Sun).

Museu Cais do Sertão
MUSEUM

(www.facebook.com/caisdosertao; Av Alfredo Lisboa, Recife Antigo; adult/child R$10/5; ⊗ 9am-5pm Tue-Fri, 1-5pm Sat & Sun) Inaugurated in 2014, this bold museum highlights the culture of the *sertão* (the interior of Pernambuco state), especially as it relates to the godfather of *forró* music, Luiz Gonzaga, who was a major player not only in bringing the music of the region to national prominence but the culture as well.

Olha Recife
OUTDOORS

(www.olharecife.com.br) A wonderful initiative of the forward-thinking local government, Olha Recife organizes free outings around town with a cultural slant. Activities change regularly but include boat trips up the Rio Capibaribe to get to know the city from the water, and walking tours through the historic center. Check the website for the program; some tours require advanced registration.

🎉 Festivals & Events

Carnaval
CARNAVAL

(www.carnavalrecife.com) Recife holds one of Brazil's most colorful and folkloric Carnavals. Groups and spectators deck themselves out in elaborate costumes such as *maracatu* (headpieced warrior), harlequin, bull and *frevo* (crop tops with ruffled sleeves for both genders and a tiny umbrella) and shimmy for days to frenetic *frevo* and African-influenced *maracatu* beats.

🛏 Sleeping

The high-rise, middle-class beach suburb of Boa Viagem has the best range of accommodations and restaurants. It begins 3km south of the center and extends about 5km along the coast.

Azul Fusca Hostel
HOSTEL $

(☑ 81 97906-6338; www.azulfuscahostel.com; Mariz e Barros 328, Recife Antigo; dm R$45; ❄ @ 🛜) The 'Blue Beetle' (as in Volkswagen Beetle) is an intriguing hostel mere steps from Marco Zero. All spartan chic and minimalist steel, it offers two sparse 12-bed dorms and a design-forward common area with mid-century furniture and quality kitchen appliances. If you have just one day to take in Recife Antigo's cultural attractions, stay here.

Albergue Piratas da Praia
HOSTEL $

(☑ 81 99776-4949, 81 3326-1281; www.piratasdapraia.com; Av Conselheiro Aguiar 2034, Boa Viagem; dm with air-con R$40-50, r R$140; ❄ @ 🛜) You'd never know it was here, but this friendly hostel occupies the 3rd floor of a building named Edifício Barão de Camaçari (entered from Rua Osias Ribeiro). It's a bit like staying in a friend's apartment, as it has a good clean kitchen and wonderfully colorful common areas. One of the two private rooms comes with a hammock.

Pousada Casuarinas
POUSADA $

(☑ 81-3325-4708; www.pousadacasuarinas.com.br; Antônio Pedro Figueiredo 151, Boa Viagem; s/d/tr R$110/140/170, with veranda R$120/150/180; ❄ @ 🛜 ⛱) A tranquil former family home run by two sisters (who speak English, Italian and German), Casuarinas is a marvelous retreat from the heat and bustle outside. Spotless rooms are set around a shady courtyard, where regional folk art and knickknacks spice up the decor. Recife's best-value stay.

🍴 Eating & Drinking

Recife is justly proud of its nightlife and the variety of music that can be found in the city. Many venues are in Boa Viagem, but the streets behind Recife Antigo's Paço Alfândega also have lively bars.

★ Chica Pitanga
BUFFET $$

(www.chicapitanga.com.br; Petrolina 19, Boa Viagem; per kg lunch weekday/weekend R$77.40/82.10, dinner R$65.50; ⊗ 11:30am-3:30pm & 6-10pm Mon-Fri, 11:30am-4pm & 6-10pm Sat & Sun; ✍) As near as *por kilos* restaurants can get to a gourmet experience, Chica Pitanga offers a changing array of diverse dishes every day. The dozen or so salad options might, for example, include tabbouleh or mango salad, while duck rice or shrimp in spinach sauce might appear among the hot dishes. Most dangerous pay-by-weight restaurant in Brazil!

Haus Lajetop & Beergarden　　BAR
(☑81 3039-6304; Galeria Joana D'Arc, Av Herculano Bandeira 513, Pina; cocktails R$15-30; ☺6pm-midnight Sun-Wed, to 2am Thu-Sat; ☎) Tucked away in the back of the artsy Galeria Joana D'Arc, this boxy bar and beer garden gets the balance right: a smart, industrial-chic atmosphere marrying unfinished concrete walls with reclaimed wooden doors and shutters on the ceiling; cool tunes; and an extensive cocktail, beer and wine list that is perfect for washing down the range of bar eats.

It's just north of and walkable from Boa Viagem.

Armazéns do Porto　　BAR
(www.armazensdoporto.com.br; Av Alfredo Lisboa, Recife Antigo; ☺10am-late) This modern dining and harborside entertainment complex next to Marco Zero houses a series of bright and inviting cafes, restaurants and bars that come alive in the evening.

❶ Information

Delegacia do Turista (Tourist Police; ☑81-3322-4867; www.policiacivil.pe.gov.br; Arrivals Hall, Guararapes International Airport; ☺24hr) Recife's tourist police is (perhaps unhelpfully) located in the airport only, down a hallway to the left of Luck Receptivo.

Police Boa Viagem (☑81-3184-3327, emergency 190; Av Domingos Ferreira 4420, Boa Viagem) Local police office.

TOURIST INFORMATION
Most Recife tourist offices have helpful English-speaking staff:

Airport (Centro de Atendimento ao Turista; ☑81 3182-8299; www.turismonorecife.com.br; Arrivals Hall, Guararapes International Airport; ☺24hr)

Bus Station (Centro de Atendimento ao Turista; ☑81 3182-8298; Terminal Integrado de Passageiros; ☺7am-7pm)

Praça do Arsenal (Centro de Atendimento ao Turista; ☑81 3355-3402; www.turismono recife.com.br; Praça do Arsenal, Rua da Guia s/n, Recife Antigo; ☺8am-6pm)

Praça de Boa Viagem (Centro de Atendimento ao Turista; ☑81 3182-8297; www.turismono recife.com.br; Praça de Boa Viagem, Boa Viagem; ☺8am-8pm)

❶ Getting There & Away

AIR
Recife's **Guararapes International Airport** (REC; ☑81 3322-4188) is at the south end of Boa Viagem, 2km inland.

BUS
Recife's bus station is the large **Terminal Integrado de Passageiros** (TIP/Rodoviária; ☑81 3207-1088; Av Prefeito Antônio Pereira s/n, Várzea), generally known as the Rodoviária, 17km west of the center. TIP handles all interstate buses and many destinations within the state of Pernambuco.

❶ Getting Around

Recife is spread out and some of the buses (R$3.20; R$1.60 on Sundays) take circuitous, confusing routes. Taxis will save you time and stress, while Uber has a big presence here and is often significantly cheaper.

Routes and schedules for Recife's buses (R$3.20, R$1.60 on Sundays) are online at www.granderecife.pe.gov.br (click Serviços then Atendimento ao Usuário then Itinerário). Recife also has a two-line metro (R$3) that is handy for the bus station, airport and football matches at Arena Pernambuco.

BUSES FROM RECIFE

DESTINATION	COST FROM (R$)	TIME (HR)	COMPANY
Caruaru	26-28	2	Progresso (www.progressoonline.com.br)
Fortaleza	165	13	Expresso Guanabara (www.expressoguanabara.com.br)
João Pessoa	41	2	Progresso
Maceió	58	4-5	Real Alagoas (www.realalagoas.com.br)
Natal	83	4½	Progresso
Rio de Janeiro	490-600	38	Gontijo (www.gontijo.com.br), Itapemirim (www.itapemirim.com.br)
Salvador	182	18	Catedral Turismo (www.catedralturismo.com.br), Kaissara (www.kaissara.com.br)

FERNANDO DE NORONHA

A one-hour flight from Recife or Natal is Brazil's greenest destination **Parque Nacional Marinho de Fernando de Noronha** (Fernando de Noronha National Marine Park; www.parnanoronha.com.br; Brazilian/foreigner R$97/195; ⊗8am-6:30pm) ✦, an idyllic 21-island archipelago that's home to the country's most postcard-perfect beaches and staunchly protected marine life. It's a sea-turtle sanctuary, and also the world's best place to see spinner dolphins. Throw in Brazil's best surfing and diving and you're rewarded with an unforgettable paradise.

Noronha only opened for tourism in 1988 (it was formerly a military installation and prison). Since then, no new construction has been allowed on its beaches, giving floury patches of sand such as **Baía do Sancho** and Praia do Leão a dreamlike quality. There are restrictions on vehicles, boats and people as well – Brazilians aren't even allowed to live here unless they were born here (all others get hard-to-secure temporary residence permits). No condos, no chain hotels, no beach vendors, no people. In short, it's an environmental success story and a true treat to visit.

But paradise comes at a price. Round-trip flights from Recife (with Azul and Gol airlines) or Natal (with Azul) cost between R$700 and R$1200, and all visitors must pay a daily island tax of R$71 plus a one-time national-park entrance fee of R$195/97 for foreigners/Brazilians. Contact **Your Way** (☑81 99949-1087; www.yourway.com.br) ✦ for English assistance with accommodations and activities on the island.

The 032 Setúbal/Conde da Boa Vista connects Boa Viagem with Recife Antigo. From Recife's central metro station to Boa Viagem, catch the Setúbal/Príncipe bus.

There are convenient public bicycle stations throughout Boa Viagem, Pina and Recife Antigo; visitors need a credit card to rent one but the process is fairly straightforward.

TO & FROM THE AIRPORT

Air-conditioned bus 042 (R$4) leaves from outside the arrivals hall and heads to Boa Viagem (20 minutes) and the city center (40 minutes) but you need a transit card to board and it takes a convoluted route, which slows it considerably. A faster option for downtown Recife is the metro (R$3, 15 minutes), directly across the busy road in front of the airport.

Coopseta (☑81 3322-4153; Arrivals, Guararapes International Airport) prepaid taxis from the airport cost between R$23 and R$39 to Boa Viagem, and R$87 to Olinda or the bus station. During high traffic times prepaid taxis can be a better-value option then metered taxis; at other times it's cheaper to go with metered rivals **Coopstar** (☑81 3072-4433; Arrivals, Guararapes International Airport). Booths for both taxi companies are located just outside the baggage-claim area.

Olinda

☑0XX81 / POP 390,770

Pretty Olinda, set around a tree-covered hill 6km north of Recife, is the artsy, colonial counterpart to the big city's hubbub. It's an artist colony full of creative types and brimming with galleries, artisans' workshops, museums, lovely churches and music in the streets. With twisting streets of colorful old houses and gorgeous vistas over treetops, church towers and red-tile roofs, this is one of the best-preserved and prettiest colonial towns in Brazil.

⊙ Sights & Activities

The historic center is easy to navigate and delightful to wander. Climb up to Alto da Sé, which affords superb views of both Olinda and Recife. The area is peppered with food, drink and craft stalls.

Worthwhile churches include the newly restored **Igreja NS do Carmo** (Praça do Carmo; entry by donation; ⊗9am-noon & 1-5pm Tue-Sat, 9am-12:45pm Sun) in the town center; baroque **Mosteiro de São Bento** (São Bento; ⊗8-11:30am & 2:15-5:30pm Mon-Sat, 8-9:30am & 2:30-5pm Sun), with an elaborate gilt altarpiece and a 14th-century Italian painting of St Sebastian; and **Convento de São Francisco** (Rua de São Francisco 280; R$2; ⊗9am-11:30pm & 2-5:30pm Mon-Sat), with a memorable tiled cloister.

If you're not around for Carnaval, pay a visit to the **Casa dos Bonecos Gigantes** (Prudente de Morais 440; R$5; ⊗1-9pm Tue-Thu, to 9:30pm Fri & Sat, to 8:30pm Sun), which houses a collection of the giant puppets used in Olinda's biggest annual event.

✨ Festivals & Events

Carnaval CARNAVAL

(www.carnaval.olinda.pe.gov.br) Traditional, colorful and with an intimacy and security not found in big-city Carnavals, Olinda's street party is hugely popular. Fast and frenetic *frevo* music sets the pace, balanced by the heavy drumbeats of *maracatu*, while costumed *blocos* and spectators dance through the streets in this inclusive, playful and lewd festival.

🛌 Sleeping

Mameluco Hostel HOSTEL $

(☎81 3493-6864; Saldanha Marinho 206, Amparo; dm/r R$40/100; ❄☎) The best budget bet in the center of the old town, this arty hostel has spacious air-conditioned private rooms with polished concrete floors and a large dorm with windows overlooking a lush garden.

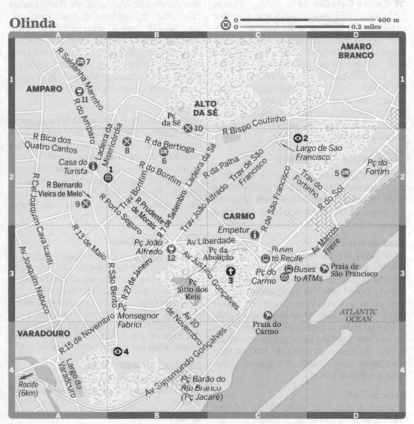

Olinda

◉ Sights
1 Casa dos Bonecos Gigantes.................B2
2 Convento de São Francisco C2
3 Igreja NS do Carmo.............................C3
4 Mosteiro de São Bento.........................B4

🛏 Sleeping
5 Albergue de Olinda...............................D2
6 Cama e Cafe Olinda..............................B2
7 Mameluco Hostel..................................A1

◈ Eating
8 Casa de Noca.......................................B2
  Estação Café................................(see 1)
9 Patuá...A2
10 Tapioca Stands....................................B1

◉ Drinking & Nightlife
11 Bodega de Véio....................................A1
12 Casbah...B3

Albergue de Olinda   HOSTEL **$**

(☑81 3439-1913; www.alberguedeolinda.com.br; Rua do Sol 233; dm/s/d R$55/105/120; ❋🐕🛜) Olinda's excellent HI hostel isn't on a colorful street, but offers modern amenities; spotless no-frills rooms; gender-separate fan-cooled dorms; and a sizable garden with a lovely pool, loungers, outdoor kitchen, barbecue and plenty of hammocks. Some private rooms have air-con.

★ **Cama e Cafe Olinda**   B&B **$$**

(☑81 98822-9083; www.camaecafeolinda.com; Rua da Bertioga 93; r R$165; ❋@🛜) Austrian Sebastian and his Brazilian wife, Yolanda, are the hospitality gatekeepers at this signless B&B with just two rooms. It's chock-full of local art, lazy-day hammocks and views of both the sea and Recife. You'll encounter extraordinary care and character here; breakfast on the terrace, with fresh juices and fruits picked straight from the property, is just one of many highlights.

🍴 Eating & Drinking

A great way to start an evening is with a tasty tapioca snack and a beer or caipirinha from the myriad **tapioca stands** (Praça da Sé; snacks R$3-11; ⊙ approx 6-11pm) and food stalls overlooking Recife from Alto da Sé.

Casa de Noca   BRAZILIAN **$**

(☑81 3439-1040; Rua da Bertioga 243; meals for 2/3/4/5 people R$60/80/100/120; ⊙11am-4pm & 6-11pm) For simple Northeastern food at its best, you can't beat this backyard restaurant that offers just one dish: chunks of grilled *queijo coalho* (a salty white cheese that's grillable) and slabs of surprisingly tender *carne de sol* (salted, grilled meat) atop a mountain of steamed cassava. If you're still hungry, they offer more *queijo coalho* for dessert – this time covered in honey.

Estação Café   CAFE **$**

(Prudente de Morais 440; dishes R$7-30; ⊙1-9pm Tue-Thu, to 9:30pm Fri & Sat, to 8:30pm Sun; 🛜) This artsy cafe is a perfect little pit stop for a coffee hit and light bites such as salad, soup, gourmet sandwiches and pasta. There's free bossa nova and *chorinho* (samba-related instrumental music) at 8pm on Fridays and Saturdays.

Patuá   BRAZILIAN **$$**

(☑81 3055-0833; www.restaurantepatua.com.br; Rua da Ribeira 79; mains R$39-75; ⊙11am-3pm Tue, Wed & Sun, 11am-3pm & 6-10pm Thu-Sat; 🛜) Humble, local and a kitchen magician, chef Alcindo Queiroz has produced a creative menu of regional *moquecas* and seafood at this sleeper. While the flavor combinations are interesting, dishes can be hit and miss in the execution. Start with the Taperoá appetizer – flambéed shrimp over a fried banana drizzled with a pink-peppercorn and star-anise sauce.

★ **Bodega de Véio**   BAR

(www.facebook.com/bodegadoveio; Rua do Amparo 212; ⊙10am-11:30pm Mon-Sat) Also a small and very eclectic general store, this wonderful little bar serves ice-cold bottled beer, shots of *cachaça* (potent sugarcane liquor) and great charcuterie plates (R$10 per 100g), while doing its best to manage the crowds of locals and tourists congregating on the street.

Casbah   BAR

(Praça João Alfredo 7; ⊙7-11pm Wed-Thu, to 1am Fri-Sat, 4-10pm Sun) If drinking in historic places is your thing, head down to this bar on Praça João Alfredo, set in a lovely old building that is one of the best examples of Moorish architectural influences remaining in Olinda. It's said the Emperor Dom Pedro II stayed here when visiting the town. It hosts exhibitions and frequent concerts.

ℹ️ Information

Casa do Turista (☑81 3305-1060; Prudente de Morais 472; ⊙8am-6pm Mon-Fri, from 9am Sat & Sun) The municipal tourist-information office has helpful staff, but little English.

Empetur (Empresa de Turismo de Pernambuco; ☑81 3182-8294; www.pe.gov.br/orgaos/empetur-empresa-de-turismo-de-pernambuco; Av Liberdade s/n; ⊙8am-6pm) The state tourist info office has lovely English-speaking staff.

DANGERS & ANNOYANCES

Crime (mostly petty) exists, especially during Carnaval. Don't walk alone along deserted streets at night.

MONEY

There are no ATMs in the historic center. The nearest ATMs are Banco do Brasil and Bradesco, close to each other on Av Getúlio Vargas about 2km north, reachable on any of several northbound **buses** (1983, 1973, 910, 881) from the **post office** (www.correios.com.br; Rua do Farol; ⊙9am-5pm Mon-Fri), opposite Praça do Carmo.

ℹ️ Getting There & Away

Bus 910 Piedade/Rio Doce runs about every half-hour from Boa Viagem (any stop on Av

Conselheiro Aguiar) in Recife to Olinda and back. The 1983 Rio Doce/Princesa Isabel and 1992 Pau Amarelo buses run from **Terminal Cais de Santa Rita** (Cais de Santa Rita s/n, São José) in central Recife to Olinda and back. All cost R$3.20. Olinda's main **bus stop** is on Praça do Carmo.

Taxis to Olinda cost around R$60 from Boa Viagem, R$70 from Recife bus station and R$75 from the airport.

Praia da Pipa

◢ 0XX84 / POP 6500

Pipa is one of Brazil's magical destinations: pristine beaches backed by tall cliffs, dreamy lagoons, decent surfing, dolphin- and turtle-filled waters, a great selection of pousadas, hostels, global restaurants and good nightlife. During high season, tiny Praia da Pipa attracts partygoers from Natal, João Pessoa, Recife and beyond, but remains appealingly low key at other times.

⊙ Sights & Activities

Guiana dolphins rest and frolic in Baía dos Golfinhos, accessible via Pipa's main beach about two hours on either side of low tide.

Several other worthwhile beaches are easily accessed by walking or van, including surfer favorite **Praia do Amor** just south of town; rental boards and lessons are readily available. Another popular destination is Lagoa de Guarairas, 8km north of town; **Bicho do Mangue** (☑84 98176-5736; www.bichodomangue.blogspot.com.br; per person R$35) offers 2½-hour kayak excursions around the lagoon, and the dockside **Creperia Marinas** (☑84 3246-4111; www.hotelmarinas.com.br; Av Governador Aluizio Alves 301; crepes R$16-45; ⊙11am-8pm) is a brilliant sunset-viewing spot.

Praia do Madeiro curves northward from the headland at the far end of Baía dos Golfinhos and is perhaps Pipa's most enchanting stretch of sand.

**Santuário
Ecológico de Pipa** NATURE RESERVE
(☑84 99982-8044; Baia dos Golfinhos s/n; R$15; ⊙7am-5pm) ◢ This small, privately owned reserve, 2km west along the main road from the town center, does a valuable job of protecting at least some of the Pipa coast from development. Well-marked trails lead through secondary forest to impressive lookouts over Baía dos Golfinhos and Praia do Madeiro, from which you can often see large green turtles at high tide.

🛏 Sleeping

Pipa Hostel HOSTEL $
(☑84 3246-2151; www.pipahostel.com.br; Arara 105; dm/d R$40/120; ❄@🛜🏊) More sedate than some hostels, this HI hostel has good air-conditioned facilities with tidy private bathrooms. Separate-sex, six- or eight-bed dorms and private rooms overlook a large grassy garden with a pool. The pleasant and well-traveled staff speak English and are a good source of information for further adventures around Brazil. Rents bicycles for getting around town.

Media Veronica Hostel HOSTEL $
(☑84 3246-2607; www.mediaveronicahostel.com; Rua da Albacora 267; dm R$33-38, r with/without bathroom from R$133/95, all excl breakfast; ❄🛜) This relaxed hostel is a labor of love for Argentine Juan Pablo, who impresses with reasonable prices and an emphasis on cleanliness, security and information for guests. Dorms come in four-, six- and eight-bed configurations (the latter is cramped) and a few private rooms have sea and floral garden views.

Paraíso das Tartarugas POUSADA $$
(☑84 99455-5183; www.paraisodastartarugas.net; Praia do Amor; r from R$200; 🛜) If you've dreamt of staying in a wooden shack inches from the ocean, 'Turtle Paradise' is your place. The seven rooms and apartments are rustic but clean and pleasant, and four have decks almost on top of the waves. While it's just a short walk from town, here there is nothing but nature.

★ **Toca da Coruja** POUSADA $$$
(☑84 3246-2226; www.tocadacoruja.com.br; Av Baía dos Golfinhos; r R$995-1605; ❄@🛜🏊) ◢ One of Brazil's most charming luxury pousadas, Toca da Coruja is an eco- and community-conscious place wrapped in sprawling tropical gardens with sagui monkeys, birds and two gorgeous pools. All rooms are huge, but the deluxe bungalows are gigantic, with breezy wraparound verandas in the style of old Northeast ranch houses.

🍴 Eating & Drinking

★ **Cruzeiro do Pescador** SEAFOOD $$
(☑84 3246-2026; www.cruzeirodopescador.com.br; cnr Av Baía dos Golfinhos & Concris; mains R$65-85, for 2 people R$125-230; ⊙1-4pm & 7-10:30pm; 🛜) On the southeast edge of town, about 1.5km from the center, what looks like a typical mess of a house hides a don't-miss culinary

experience. Chef Daniel does everything with homemade and homegrown finesse, from the poetically handwritten menus and the romantic candlelit setting to the products from his own garden. The flavors of his cooking – some pinched from India and Bahia – are delicious.

Garagem SEAFOOD **$$**
(Praia do Centro; plates R$28-38, mains R$38-65; ☺10:30am-sunset; 🐟) With superb views of Pipa's cliffs, Garagem got its start as a famous bar, and is still good for sundowners; but it's also the best spot in Pipa proper for a beach lunch, such as excellent Argentine *picanha* (rump steak), fresh fish, sandwiches and salads and a Bohemia to wash it down. It's the westernmost bar on the main beach.

Orishas BAR
(📩84 9815-26547; Rua da Praia 9; cocktails R$8-20; ☺9am-10pm) All by itself at the far end of the main beach away from the crowds, this colorful bar set on wooden decks right above the sea is easily Pipa's best place to drink. Come early for the fantastic views across the bay to the cliffs and stick around in the evening for the live music.

ℹ Information

There's a brand new tourism **information office** (📩84 99608-9999; ☺8am-6pm) at the beginning of Av Baía dos Golfinhos at the entrance to town.

Praia da Pipa is also extraordinarily well endowed with helpful, informative websites. Take your pick from www.pipa.com.br or www.pipa.tur.br.

MONEY
Cash is king in Pipa – many places do not accept cards, and the only ATMs are high-fee-charging Banco 24-horas, which has six ATMs around town, including near the **bus stop** (Av Baía dos Golfinhos 234; ☺8am-10pm), the central plaza, and the town **center** (Vila Pipa Shopping, Av Baía dos Golfinhos 647).

ℹ Getting There & Away

Riograndense (📩84 3205-4388; Rodoviária Nova; R$19) has 10 daily buses (six on Sundays) from Natal's Rodoviária Nova (p398) to Pipa (R$19, 1½ hours) and back. Alternatively, **Opcional** (📩84 3205-6868; Rua dos Cajueiros) runs microbuses from the Rodoviária Nova to Pipa several times a day (R$18, 2½ hours).

If you're coming from Recife and points south, get off at Goianinha (1½ hours from João Pessoa),

and catch a minibus (nicknamed 'Dolphin van') to Pipa (R$4.50, 50 minutes) from behind the faded pale-blue church, 250m off the main road.

Natal

📩 0XX84 / POP 885,180
Rio Grande do Norte's capital is a clean, bright and rather bland city that has swelled as a hub for coastal package tourism, much of it catering to Brazilian families. Its main attractions are touristic beaches, buggy rides and other organized excursions. Most visitors stay in the beach neighborhood of Ponta Negra, about 12km southeast of the city center; it's a striking location, overlooked by fantastic dunes, with steady surf and some lively nightlife.

◉ Sights & Activities

You can rent surfboards and stand-up paddleboards (SUPs) at many places on Praia de Ponta Negra for R$30 per hour.

Forte dos Reis Magos FORT
(☺8am-4pm Tue-Sun) FREE The fort that got Natal started in 1598 still stands in its original five-pointed star shape on the reef at the tip of the peninsula at the north end of town. The views of the city, the Ponte Nova and the dunes across the Rio Potengi are fantastic.

Praia de Ponta Negra BEACH
Praia de Ponta Negra, at the far south end of town, is the nicest stretch of sand in Natal and one of the most appealing big-city beaches in the Northeast. Framed by tall dunes at both ends, it's 3km long and lined with beach bars, with the city's best selection of hotels, pousadas and restaurants in the streets behind. The surf here is consistent, if small.

◉ Dunas de Genipabu

Feeling adventurous? Try a popular and exciting outing to the spectacularly high and steep dunes about 10km north of the city near Genipabu, where you can be driven up and down the sand mountains for an hour or so in a beach buggy. A number of operators are recommended: **Natal Vans** (📩84-3642-1883; www.natalvans.com.br; Av Praia de Ponta Negra 8822, Ponta Negra; ☺7am-10pm Mon-Fri, to 9pm Sun) and **Marazul** (📩84-3219-6480, 84-99608-8000; www.marazulreceptivo.com.br; Vereador Manoel Sátiro 75, Ponta Negra; ☺8am-noon & 3-7pm) offer several fairly standardized out-of-town trips, easily booked through your accommodation.

Festivals & Events

Carnatal
PARADE, MUSIC
(www.carnatal.com.br; ⏱Dec) Natal's out-of-season Carnaval, Carnatal, takes to the streets of the Lagoa Nova district over four days in early December, with Salvador-style *trios elétricos* (bands playing atop huge trucks) and *blocos* (parade groups) sporting names such as Burro Elétrico (Electric Donkey) and Cerveja & Coco (Beer & Coconut). It's the wildest out-of-season Carnaval in Brazil.

Sleeping

Republika Hostel
HOSTEL $
(☑84 3236-2782; www.republikahostel.com.br; Porto das Oficinas 8944, Ponta Negra; dm R$30-45, r R$80-120; ❄@🛜) Housed in a converted family home that evokes Santorini, Republika has a low-lit bar, comfy hammock and TV areas, and a big, clean kitchen and eating area that create a cozy atmosphere for mingling with fellow travelers. Rooms are just OK – some lack good ventilation – but the multilingual staff, decent information and positive energy make it a fine base.

Casa Grande Apart-Hotel
HOTEL $
(☑84 3236-3401; www.aparthotelcasagrande.com; Pedro da Fonseca Filho 3050, Alto de Ponta Negra; r R$130, with kitchen R$220-240; ❄🛜🏊) Casa Grande offers exceptional rates (especially in low season, when they can go for less than half) for spacious rooms and apartments just three blocks from the beach. Most have hammock-strung balconies and some have sea views.

Eating & Drinking

The Alto de Ponta Negra neighborhood in the upper part of Ponta Negra, around Rua MA Bezerra de Araújo and Rua Aristides Porpino Filho, is dense with a variety of bars, and packed from Wednesday to Saturday nights. Petrópolis, in the city center, is the best neighborhood for hip local bars and *botecos* (open-air bars).

Casa de Taipa
BRAZILIAN $
(www.facebook.com/casadetaipatapiocariaecuscuzeria; Av Praia de Ponte Negra 8868, Ponta Negra; dishes R$12-36; ⏱6-11pm, closed Wed; 🛜🚭) What is probably Brazil's most famous *tapiocaria* flips the script on a traditional street food and turns it into a gourmet treat fit for foodies. Droves of visitors and locals alike swarm this colorful and festive place for lightly pan-grilled tapioca 'pancakes' stuffed with sweet and savory goodies (vegetables, cheeses, grilled salted meats, prawns – even a *moqueca* version).

Bar 54
BAR
(www.facebook.com/54bar; Pôrto Mirim 8995, Ponta Negra; ⏱6pm-2am; 🛜) One of Ponta Negra's best bars, especially if you want to mingle with the cool kids away from the rowdier, tourist-geared places. A breezy patio flush with vintage furniture and tables of reclaimed wooden cable spools sets the vibe.

❶ Information

There's a central **Banco do Brasil** (www.bb.com.br; Av Engenheiro Roberto Freire & JM Vasconcelos) ATM to the north of Ponta Negra, plus the airport, **Praia Shopping** (www.praiashopping.com.br; Av Engenheiro Roberto Freire 8790, Ponta Negra; ⏱10am-10pm; 🛜) and **Natal Shopping** (Av das Brancas Dunas, Candelária;

BRAZIL NATAL

BUSES FROM NATAL

DESTINATION	COST FROM (R$)	DURATION (HR)	COMPANY
Aracati (Canoa Quebrada)	70	6	Expresso Guanabara (www.expressoguanabara.com.br), Viação Nordeste (www.viacaonordeste.com.br)
Belém	522	36	Expresso Guanabara
Fortaleza	98	8	Viação Nordeste, Expresso Guanabara
João Pessoa	44	3	Viação Nordeste, Autoviação Progresso (www.progressoonline.com.br)
Recife	96	4½	Autoviação Progresso
Salvador	250	21	Gontijo (www.gontijo.com.br)
São Miguel de Gostoso	18	2½	Expresso Cabral (www.expressocabral.com.br),

◎10am-10pm) malls all have ATMs that should accept non-Brazilian cards.

ⓘ Getting There & Away

AIR

Natal's **Aeroporto de Natal** (Aeroporto Internacional Governador Aluízio Alves; ☑ 84 3343-6060; www.natal.aero; Av Ruy Pereira dos Santos 3100, São Gonçalo do Amarante) is around 35km west of Ponta Negra. It has scheduled flights to many international cities in addition to services to all over Brazil.

BUS

Long-distance buses go from the **Rodoviária Nova** (☑ 84 3205-2931; Av Capitão Mor Gouveia 1237), northwest of Ponta Negra, which received a facelift for the 2014 World Cup.

ⓘ Getting Around

Natal's airport at São Gonçalo do Amarante is quite a haul, 35km west of Ponta Negra. **Trampolím da Vitória** (☑ 84-3343-5151; www.trampolimdavitoria.com; R$4.20; ◎5:10am-11:10pm) runs a public bus that's hardly worth the hassle from Ponta Negra. Most travelers opt for the far more convenient shared van services such as **24 Horas Turismo** (☑ 84 3343-6430, 84 3086-1349; www.24horasturismo.com. br; R$30) and **Van Service** (☑ 84-3278-3013, 84-4141-2848; www.vanservice.com.br; airport transfer R$40; ◎8am-10pm), which run shared vans to Natal ($40) and Praia da Pipa (R$60) usually leaving after each flight. A **taxi** (☑ 84 3343-6429; www.coopcon.com.br; Aeroporto de Natal, Av Ruy Pereira dos Santos 3100) from the airport costs about R$100 to Ponta Negra and R$240 or so to Praia da Pipa.

From the bus station to Ponta Negra (Av Engenheiro Roberto Freire), catch bus 66 (R$3.35) from the stop opposite the Petrobras gas station next to the Rodoviária Nova; a taxi costs R$35 to R$50 depending on time of day and location in Ponta Negra.

Canoa Quebrada

☑ 0XX88 / POP 4000

Easily reached from Fortaleza, this fishing village turned hippie hangout has become upmarket, but still represents a relaxing seaside spot for a few days of downtime. Hard-packed beaches backed by rust-colored cliffs are pleasant, and outdoor adventures abound, including beach-buggy tours to Ponta Grossa and nearby dunes (R$250 to R$350 for up to four people) or tandem paragliding jaunts with **Parapente Canoa Quebrada** (☑ 88 99911-9285, 88 99810-2433; Francisco Caraco; 10-15min flight R$158). From July to December, you can also go kitesurfing; lessons are available through **Extreme KiteSchool Canoa Quebrada** (☑ 88 98819-3632, 88 99960-6070; extremekitedaniel@hotmail.com; Dragão do Mar).

For a cheap sleep, check out Hostel Pousada Ibiza, whose smallish en suite dorms and doubles are complemented by a balcony lounge-bar overlooking the action in the heart of town. Numerous midrange pousadas offer considerably more comfort, such as the friendly **Pousada Dolce Vita** (☑ 88 3421-7213; www.canoa-quebrada.it; Descida da Praia s/n; r from R$220; ❋ 🛜 ❄), with bungalows set around a palm-fringed garden and swimming pool.

At lunchtime, don't miss the BBQ fish – simply but perfectly garnished with salt, lime and chimichurri – at **Lazy Days** (Praia; mains R$25-40; ◎9am-5pm, closed Mon), the best of the beach *barracas* that rub up against Canoa's picturesque red cliffs. Nightlife revolves around **Regart Bar** (Dragão do Mar s/n; ◎3pm-2am) and similar venues along 'Broadway,' Canoa Quebrada's main street. In high season, **Freedom Bar** (Praia; ◎9am-6pm Sun-Thu, 9am-6pm & 11pm-4am Fri & Sat) hosts weekend reggae parties on the beach.

The post office and a multi-card 24-hour ATM – which charges exorbitant fees – are both in a small shopping plaza near the west end of Dragão do Mar.

São Benedito (www.gruposaobenedito. com.br) runs six daily buses (R$25, 3¼ hours) between Canoa and Fortaleza. Alternatively, **Oceanview** (☑ 85-3219-1300; www.oceanviewturismo.com.br) offers faster door-to-door van service (R$55, 2½ hours) from hotels on Fortaleza's Meireles strip.

If arriving by bus from Natal or other points south, disembark at Aracati, 13km southwest of Canoa, then hop aboard São Benedito's Fortaleza–Canoa bus (R$1.85, 20 minutes), a half-hourly *topique* minibus (R$3) or a taxi (R$35 to R$40) for the quick Aracati–Canoa run.

Commercial flights were approved in 2015 for the new airport at Aracati, but at time of writing its runways remained unused.

Fortaleza

☑ 0XX85 / POP 2.6 MILLION (METROPOLITAN AREA 3.6 MILLION)

Considering its isolation, Fortaleza is a surprisingly large and sprawling place. It's one of Brazil's biggest cities, and an economic magnet for people from Ceará and beyond. It's also a draw for tourists from Brazil and overseas, who come for its beaches, party atmosphere and the spectacular smaller beach spots, rolling dunes and fishing villages accessible from here.

◉ Sights

Centro Dragão do Mar de Arte e Cultura ARTS CENTER
(📞 85 3488-8600; www.dragaodomar.org.br; Dragão do Mar 81; ⊙ 8am-10pm Mon-Thu, to 11pm Sat & Sun) **FREE** This excellent, extensive complex includes cinemas, performance spaces, a good cafe, a planetarium and two good museums: the **Museu de Arte Contemporânea** (MAC; ⊙ 9am-7pm Tue-Fri, 2-9pm Sat & Sun) **FREE** and the **Memorial da Cultura Cearense** (MCC) **FREE**, which features exhibits on Ceará's traditional life and culture. Elevated walkways join blocks on different streets; it all blends well with the surrounding older buildings, many of which have been restored to house bars, restaurants and artisans' workshops. It's a successful social focus for the city, and is very popular with locals.

🐾 Beaches

Praia do Meireles has an attractive waterfront promenade with homey beer *barracas* (stalls) on the sand side and smart restaurants with air-conditioning and hotels across the street. The fish market and evening craft fair are also draws. Further east, **Praia do Futuro** is the cleanest and most popular of the city beaches. Local agencies offer longer-distance 4WD or beach-buggy tours along Ceará's glorious coastline, as far afield as Jericoacoara.

🛏 Sleeping

★ Refugio Hostel Fortaleza HOSTEL $
(📞 85 3393-4349; www.refugiohostelfortaleza. com; Deputado João Lopes 31, Centro; dm from R$30, r R$120-130; ❄@🛜) ✈ Easily Fortaleza's best hostel. German owner Karl has whipped an old mansion into shape, following an eco-ethos with breezy natural ventilation and solar-heated showers. The bathrooms and kitchen are astonishing for a hostel, while other design-forward common spaces of note include a sunny patio/ BBQ area and various terraces. Dorms feature colorful lockers, original tiling and hardwood floors.

Albergaria Hostel HOSTEL $
(📞 85 3032-9005; www.albergariahostel.com.br; Antônio Augusto 111, Praia de Iracema; dm with fan/air-con R$40/45, d/tr/q R$140/180/270; ❄@🛜❄) This cheerful, well-located, well-run hostel has very good facilities, including a backyard with a pool, plus a sociable atmosphere helped along by the friendly English-speaking owner. There are separate-sex and mixed four-bed dorms (with privacy curtains and lockers with electrical outlets) and four good private rooms with bathroom, although some are cold water only. Breakfast is plentiful. Reservations only.

✕ Eating

★ 50 Sabores ICE CREAM $
(📞 85 3023-0050; www.50sabores.com.br; Av Beira Mar 2982, Meireles; 1/2 flavors R$14/20; ⊙ 10am-11:45pm) One of Brazil's most famous ice cream shops, though with a terribly misleading name: there are actually *150* flavors here, including caipirinha (made with *cachaça* sugarcane liquor – you must be 18 to purchase!) and beer, plus loads of Brazilian fruits and more classic options. There's another a branch in **Mucuripe** (Av Beira Mar 3958, Mucuripe; 1/2 flavors R$14/20; ⊙ 7am-midnight).

Santa Clara Café Orgânico CAFE $
(Centro Dragão do Mar, Praia de Iracema; items R$8-23; ⊙ 3-10pm Tue-Sun; 🛜✈) Santa Clara is one of the city's happening *pontos de encontros*; loosely translated, this means where hot people go to mingle (and cool down in the icy air-con). It's a wonderful little cafe on an upper level of Dragão do Mar, and serves organic coffee, sandwiches, crepes, omelets, waffles, tapiocas and a plethora of fancier coffee drinks.

Cantinho do Frango GRILL $$
(www.cantinhodofrango.com; Torres Câmara 71, Aldeota; mains for two R$65-70; ⊙ 10am-4pm Mon-Thu, 10am-10:30pm Fri, 9am-7pm Sat & Sun) Hugely popular with local families, this grill restaurant has a fabulous main dining room covered in old movie posters; it houses a collection of hundreds of LPs – pick one out and hand it to the DJ to hear your selection. The house specialty is grilled chicken but there's a wide selection of other meats too.

🍸 Drinking & Entertainment

Fortaleza is famed for its nightlife. The Dragão do Mar area is one of the best places to go out.

Fortaleza

Fortaleza

⊙ Sights
1 Centro Dragão do Mar de Arte e Cultura...B1
2 Memorial da Cultura Cearense............B2
3 Museu de Arte Contemporânea..........B2
4 Praia do Meireles...................................G2

🛏 Sleeping
5 Albergaria Hostel....................................D1
6 Refugio Hostel Fortaleza......................B2

✖ Eating
7 50 Sabores..G2
8 Santa Clara Café Orgânico...................B1

🍷 Drinking & Nightlife
9 Boteco Praia..E2
10 Turatti...H3

🛍 Shopping
11 Ceart..D3

Boteco Praia BAR
(☏85 3248-4773; www.botecofortaleza.com.br; Av Beira Mar 1680, Meireles; ⊙5pm-midnight Mon-Fri, noon-3am Sat & Sun; 🛜) The number-one spot for evening drinks and conversation, Boteco Praia attracts all ages to its long arcaded hall and its terrace facing the seafront promenade. Live music nightly. It's a fine place to knock back cold *chope* (draft beer).

Turatti MICROBREWERY
(☏85 3099-2829; www.cervejariaturatti.com.br; Rua Ana Bilhar 1178; small beer R$8-14; ⊙5pm-midnight) Locals descend on this enormous open-air microbrewery in hordes to beat the heat with artisanal draft beer brewed right on the premises. There are six varieties on tap; you can buy it by the glass but pretty

much everyone goes for the 3.5-liter towers (R$69 to R$120).

🛍 Shopping

Ceart ARTS & CRAFTS
(Av Santos Dumont 1589, Aldeota; ⊙9am-8pm Mon-Sat, 2:30-8:30pm Sun) The main showroom of this beautiful, state-run craft store, which sells lace, ceramics, wood carvings, textiles, and baskets and bags of sisal and *carnaúba* palm. There's another branch at Centro Dragão do Mar (p399).

ℹ Information

The city tourism department operates information booths around town; staff may or may not speak English but you'll find useful maps and guides.

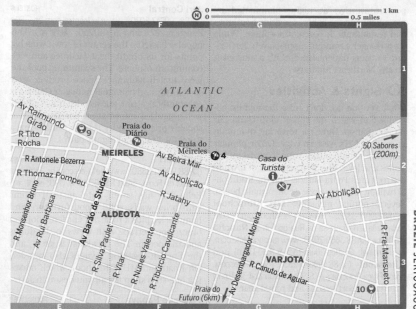

Meireles (SETFOR; ☑ 85 3105-2670; https://turismo.fortaleza.ce.gov.br; Av Beira Mar, Meireles; ⊙ 9am-5pm)

Mercado Central (SETFOR; ☑ 85 3105-1475; https://turismo.fortaleza.ce.gov.br; Basement level, Mercado Central, Av Nepomuceno 199; ⊙ 9am-5pm Mon-Fri, 9am-noon Sat)

Aeroporto Pinto Martins (☑ 85 3488-5869; https://turismo.fortaleza.ce.gov.br; Av Carlos Jereissati 3000, Aeroporto Pinto Martins; ⊙ 8am-8pm)

DANGERS & ANNOYANCES

Beware of pickpocketing and snatch-and-grab robberies in the city center, on the beaches and along Av Beira Mar.

MONEY

Banco do Brasil (Av Beira Mar; ⊙ 8am-10pm) ATM on the waterfront.

Banco do Brasil (Av Abolição 2308, Meireles; ⊙ 8am-10pm) Convenient ATM.

Bradesco (www.bradesco.com.br; Av da Abolição 1810, Meireles; ⊙ 8am-10pm) Visa/Mastercard ATM.

Bradesco (www.bradesco.com.br; Av Pessoa Anta 274; ⊙ 8am-10pm) Visa/Mastercard ATM.

ⓘ Getting There & Away

Aeroporto Pinto Martins (☑ 85 3392-1030; Av Carlos Jereissati 3000) has direct flights to/from Amsterdam, Bogotá, Buenos Aires, Cabo Verde, Lisbon, Miami, Milan, Orlando and Paris as well as domestic flights throughout Brazil. A fixed-rate taxi from the airport to Meireles or Praia de Iracema is R$47 during the day and R$70 at night.

BUS

Fortaleza's **bus station** (☑ 85 3256-5786, 85 3256-2200; Av Borges de Melo 1630) is 5.5km south of Meireles.

ⓘ Getting Around

Local buses cost R$3.40 (R$2.80 on Sundays and holidays). Bus 013 'Aguanambi I', outside the bus station, runs north up Av Dom Manoel to the Centro Dragão do Mar, while route 078 'Siqueira/Mucuripe' connects the bus station to the beaches at Iracema and Meireles.

Jericoacoara

☑ 0XX88 / POP 3000

Jericoacoara, known to its many friends simply as 'Jeri,' is one of Brazil's most cinematic destinations. Lodged between a magnificent national park and the sea, it enchants travelers with its perfect combination of hard-to-reach location (access is by unpaved tracks through the dunes), stunning coastal scenery, exciting activities, excellent pousadas (guesthouses) and restaurants, and fun nightlife. During the day, its beaches, dunes and lagoons are

BRAZIL JERICOACOARA

postcard-worthy; at night, illuminated by moonlight and the lights of inviting boutiques and restaurants, it oozes atmosphere. While it's no longer a tranquil hippie haven, Jeri's allure remains undeniable and it's a must-visit on any Northeast itinerary.

◉ Sights & Activities

Whatever you do, don't miss the nightly pilgrimage to watch the sunset atop Duna Pôr do Sol (Sunset Dune), a towering mountain of sand at Jeri's western edge. Other popular activities include buggy trips to surrounding dunes and lakes, the 3km walk east of town to the rock arch Pedra Furada, and the traditional twilight capoeira circle on Jeri's main beach. Several outfits, including **MH Kiteschool** (☑88-99971-3330; www.mhkiteschool.com; Pousada Bella Jeri, Travessa da Rua do Forró), **Rancho do Kite** (☑88 3669-2080; www.ranchodokite. br; Principal; ⊙shop 10am-1pm & 3:30-11pm) and **Kiteiscool** (☑88 99670-2330; www.kiteiscool. com; Praça Principal; ⊙8:30am-noon & 4:30-11pm) offer wind-sport lessons and rental gear.

🛏 Sleeping

Some hotels close during May, the low point of Jeri's season. The high seasons are July and January.

Villa Chic   HOSTEL $
(☑88 99968-5980; www.villachicjeri.com; Principal; dm R$65, r/t/q R$260/320/410; ✻@🛜🐾) If you've outgrown the hostel party scene, the excellent dorms here are Jeri's best, but exist within the environment of a boutique pousada (guesthouse). Each eight-bed dorm (one mixed, one male, one female) boasts one-and-a-half bathrooms (the 'half' has no shower), which are some of the most fashionable you'll come across at these prices.

Jeri Central   HOSTEL $
(☑88 99747-8070; www.jericentral.com.br; São Francisco 222; dm/r R$60/250; ✻🛜🐾) This popular hostel in the center of town wins big points for its bright, neat facilities and welcoming atmosphere. The swimming pool and large thatch hammock space promote easy socializing, and trilingual manager Gaúcho is constantly assisting guests with travel advice, well-organized information boards and reasonably priced laundry service – and keeps a watchful, anti-shenanigans patrol.

Bella Jeri   POUSADA $$
(☑88 99971-3330; www.bellajeri.com.br; Travessa da Rua do Forró; s/d/t R$260/290/390; ✻🛜🐾) Bella Jeri has seven cute, tasteful rooms with brick walls, solid wood furniture and hammocks, plus a pleasant garden, pool and breezy roof terrace with views to the dunes and the ocean. The breakfast is great, and the English-speaking owners also run Jeri Off Road and MH Kiteschool, which makes it a one-stop shop for all you desire in Jeri.

Pousada Papaya   POUSADA $$
(☑88 3669-2219, 88 99651-8015; www.jeripapaya. com.br; Dunas II 74; r R$260-380; ✻🛜🐾) Tucked away inside this walled oasis are 11 neat, comfy rooms with colorful bedspreads, a pool in a flowery front garden, and attractive common areas inside and out. These features and a great breakfast make this a deservedly popular choice, although service could be better at times. Room 10 with its dune views is the pick of the bunch.

✕ Eating

Cheap local eateries where simple meals start from R$10 cluster on the eastern end of Rua São Francisco.

BUSES FROM FORTALEZA

DESTINATION	COST FROM (R$)	DURATION (HR)	COMPANY
Belém	170	24	Guanabara (www.expressoguanabara.com.br), Itapemirim (www.itapemirim.com.br)
Natal	98	9	Viação Nordeste (www.viacaonordeste.com.br)
Parnaíba	75	9	Guanabara
Piripiri	54	8	Guanabara
Recife	100	14	Guanabara
Rio de Janeiro	565	48	Itapemirim
São Luís	160	19	Guanabara
Teresina	60	11	Guanabara
Ubajara	46	7	Guanabara

FROM JERICOACOARA TO THE LENÇÓIS MARANHENSES

The trip west from Jericoacoara to Parque Nacional dos Lençóis Maranhenses is one of South America's epic journeys. Depending on how you do it, the route can take anywhere from seven to 24 hours; in its most adventurous incarnation, it involves substantial stretches rattling along a rugged track between sand dunes, along deserted beaches, past isolated communities and gorgeous scenery.

The fastest and most costly option is a straight one-day transfer from Jericoacoara to the Lençóis Maranhenses. **Jeri Off Road** (☑88 99971-3336, 88 99971-3330; www.jeri.tur.br; Pousada Bella Jeri, Travessa da Rua do Forró) 🏍 can get you there in seven to nine hours for around R$1000 to R$1200 (up to four people). The trip heads to Paulino Neves by car, then on to Caburé along the coast by 4WD (40 minutes), then to Barreirinhas by a scenic boat ride (must be reserved in advance), with optional sightseeing in the Delta do Parnaíba.

The best combination of speed and economy is on shuttles organized by **Global Connection** (☑88 99900-2109; Rua do Forró; ⊘9am-10pm) in Jericoacoara. They also sell a combination ticket from Jericoacoara to Barreirinhas using two local van services (R$260) but it requires an overnight stay in Parnaíba, which adds to the price.

To reach the Lençóis with local transport, take a 4WD passenger truck (R$20 one-way), known as D-20 from Jeri to Jijoca. From Jijoca, take a Fretcar bus (p404) to Camocim (R$12.15, 1½ to 2¼ hours) and then the daily 3pm Expresso Guanabara (www.expressoguanabara.com.br) bus from Camocim to Parnaíba (R$22, two hours). It's necessary to spend the night in Parnaíba before taking the 5:30am bus to Tutóia (R$20, 2½ hours), from where there is a bus to Barreirinhas (R$16, two hours) at noon.

Heading eastbound from the Lençóis to Jeri, public transportation schedules along the coast are less convenient, so a direct 4WD transfer is well worth considering.

Naturalmente BRAZILIAN $
(Praia de Jericoacoara; crepes R$16-39; ⊘noon-11pm) Tasty crepes, great açaí and fresh juices served with sea views in a breezy thatched hut right on the beach make this one of Jeri's best places to chill out after a long tour or a night of too many caipirinhas.

Gelato & Grano ICE CREAM $
(Praça Principal 1; 1/2/3 scoops R$10/12/16; ⊘noon-midnight) If there's one thing you'll eventually crave in this heat, it's ice cream. This wildly popular, farmhouse-chic gelato shop on the main square serves up 20 flavors and is constantly swarmed by sweet-toothed vacationers and locals. Belgian chocolate and pistachio are the most popular, but Brazilian staples such as açaí and tapioca are here as well.

★**Bistro Caiçara** BRAZILIAN $$
(☑88 99916-0072; Principal 16; mains R$38-95; ⊘5-11pm Mon-Sat; 🐾) Right in the center of town, this place is a real crowd-pleaser for Chef Apolinário's more-creative-than-most menu which includes plenty of seafood: robalo (sea bass) in soy, ginger and honey; fish in passion-fruit or cashew-fruit sauces; and sweet-and-spicy octopus are standouts. Service is top-notch and it all goes down very romantically on a candlelit 2nd-floor open-air patio overlooking Rua Principal.

🍷 Drinking & Entertainment

Everything starts at the foot of Rua Principal at the barracas (carts) selling caipirinhas and caipifrutas with tropical fruits (R$7 to R$16). Jeri has loads of nightspots with live music, including the legendary forró nights at **Restaurante Dona Amélia** (Rua do Forró; cover R$5; ⊘8pm-midnight Wed, Thu & Sat) and **Maloca** (☑88-99810-6347; Igreja), and Friday-night samba at **Pousada Solar de Malhada** (www.solardamalhada.com; Rua da Matriz; cover R$20; ⊘10pm-late).

Samba Rock Cafe BAR
(www.sambarockcafe.com; Principal; Cover R$8; ⊘6pm-1am) Sitting on prime corner real estate across from the main square, this is easily Jeri's most atmospheric drinking spot. Rustic wooden seating is arranged under a massive, illuminated acacia tree. There are often bands playing sertanejo, rock, samba, forró (popular music of the Northeast), or MPB (Música Popular Brasileira); at other times, DJs spin an eclectic mix.

BRAZIL'S NORTH COAST: WIND SPORTS PARADISE

Brazil's north coast gets steady, sustained winds from at least July to December, creating ideal conditions for windsurfing and kitesurfing. Wind-sports schools and rental outlets abound along the Atlantic shores of Ceará and Rio Grande do Norte, making this a great place to learn or hone your skills. Aside from the hot spots listed below, other locations worth checking out are Canoa Quebrada and Praia Cumbuco near Fortaleza.

Jericoacoara

The granddaddy of Brazilian wind-sports destinations, 'Jeri' is a magical spot, with towering dunes and pristine beaches stretching on forever. Steady trade winds averaging 23 to 30 knots blow across from Africa from late June through February, creating dreamy conditions for beginners and experts alike. Add in a vibrant social scene and a slew of kitesurfing and windsurfing schools and you have paradise.

Icaraí de Amontada

Backed by a beautiful, palm-lined curve of bay, with a few fishing boats, high dunes and only a handful of people in sight, Icaraí de Amontada, 200km northwest of Fortaleza, is reminiscent of Jericoacoara 25 years ago. Take classes and rent equipment at Club Ventos, and stay at **Casa Zulu** (☑ 88 3636-3016; www.casazulu.com; Francisco Gonçalves de Sousa 194; r/bungalow from R$300/350; ❀ ❐ ❆), a rustic-stylish pousada run by a young French windsurfer.

São Miguel do Gostoso

Surrounded by empty white-sand beaches 110km north of Natal, São Miguel do Gostoso has not yet been discovered by package tourism, but windsurfers and kitesurfers in the know head for windswept Ponta de Santo Cristo, where **Clube Kauli Seadi** (☑ 84 99197-1297; www.clubekauliseadi.com; Praia do Cardeiro; ❍ 9am-5:20pm) offers lessons and rents equipment.

Cachaçaria Gourmet   BAR
(www.facebook.com/cachacariagourmetjeri; Travessa Ismael; cachaça R$8-12; ❍ 6pm-midnight) If you'd like a stiff drink without a soundtrack, this cute, tiny bar specializes in Brazil's national firewater, *cachaça*. There are around 90 labels, many of which come from Minas Gerais (as does the owner); around 30 labels are available at any given time. The liquor is even mixed into frozen caipirinhas (a rarity, despite the obviousness of the idea!).

Also sells microbrews made locally in Jeri.

❶ Information

Many pousadas (guesthouses) and restaurants will accept Visa or Mastercard, but Jeri has no international-friendly ATMs. It is recommended to stock up with cash at Banco do Brasil in Jijoca, 23km southeast.

❶ Getting There & Away

AIR

Jericoacoara's **airport** (☑ 85 2181-6277), some 30km southeast of town outside the boundaries of the national park, now receives direct flights from São Paulo and Recife.

Collective transport in pickups from the airport into town costs R$75 to R$80 per passenger; a private transfer costs R$250.

BUS

Fretcar (☑ 88 99700-7373; www.fretcar.com.br; São Francisco; ❍ 6-6:15am, 8-11am, noon-5pm & 6-10:30pm) runs a service to Fortaleza (R$74 to R$97, six to seven hours), leaving at 6:15am, 2:55pm, 4:55pm and, the most comfortable, at 10:30pm. You travel by *jardineira* (open-sided 4WD truck) as far as Jijoca, then by bus. The trip begins at Fretcar's office on Rua São Francisco, across from Jeri Central (p402) hostel. Buy tickets at least one day in advance.

You can also travel to Fortaleza in the tour vans of companies such as **Girafatur** (☑ 85 3219-3255; www.girafatur.com.br) and **Vitorino** (☑ 85 3047-1047; www.vitorinotur.com.br; office 503, Av Beira Mar & Oswaldo Cruz; ❍ 8am-noon & 2-7pm), which drop off at Fortaleza hotels (R$80 to R$100, five hours). Most accommodations can book these for you. The vans usually leave about 9am and some stop for 2½ hours at Lagoa Paraíso, near Jijoca, en route.

A private transfer to Fortaleza runs from R$500 to R$600.

The most exciting way of reaching Jericoacoara from Fortaleza is by 4WD along the coast – an option offered by agencies such as Jeri Off Road (p403), which charges R$850 for up to four people.

São Luís

☑ 0XX98 / POP 1.09 MILLION

The World Heritage-listed historical center of São Luís is an enchanting neighborhood of steamy cobbled streets and pastel-colored colonial mansions, some handsomely restored, many crumbling. It's a charming area with a unique atmosphere and one of the Northeast's best concentrations of museums, galleries and craft stores. Unfortunately, a general sketchiness pervades some of its streets after dark.

The city as a whole has a markedly Afro-Brazilian tinge to its culture, from a lively reggae scene to its highly colorful festivals.

São Luís sits at the northwest corner of the 50km-long Ilha de São Luís, which is separated from the mainland only by narrow channels.

◎ Sights & Activities

The center of São Luís has the best-preserved colonial neighborhood in the Northeast; it's full of 18th- and 19th-century mansions covered in colorful 19th-century European *azulejos* (decorative ceramic tiles; often blue, or blue and white). The historical center has been under piecemeal restoration under Pro-

jeto Reviver (Project Revival) since the late 1980s, following many decades of neglect and decay. Many of the restored buildings house interesting museums, galleries, craft shops and restaurants.

Casa do Maranhão   MUSEUM

(Rua do Trapiche; ⊗10am-6pm Tue-Sun) FREE Set in the former customs house built right on the river mouth, this informative and colorful museum is dedicated to Maranhense culture and features a great collection of costumes and props from Carnaval and Bumba Meu Boi. There are also displays on river-going boats of the region and explanations of Maranhão's different kinds of drums. Some displays are accompanied by English text.

Casa do Nhôzinho   MUSEUM

(Portugal 185; ⊗9am-6pm Tue-Sun) FREE At the eclectic and fascinating Casa do Nhôzinho, you can see a collection of ingenious fish traps, rooms featuring Maranhão indigenous artisanry, and hosts of colorful, delicate Bumba Meu Boi figurines made by the 20th-century master artisan Mestre Nhôzinho. It was closed for electrical work when we visited but was due to reopen imminently.

🎋 Festivals & Events

São Luís has one of Brazil's richest folkloric traditions, evident in its many festivals,

---

WORTH A TRIP

ALCÂNTARA

Across the Baía de São Marcos from São Luís is the colonial town of Alcântara. Built using slave labor between the 17th and 19th centuries, Alcântara was once the preferred residence of Maranhão's rich plantation owners. In decline since the latter half of the 19th century, Alcântara today is an atmospheric amalgam of ruined, maintained and restored mansions, houses and churches set along streets of artistic crisscrossed cobblestones.

Don't miss the broad, hilltop Praça da Matriz, where the best-preserved *pelourinho* (whipping post) in Brazil stands beside the shell of the 17th-century Igreja de São Matias. Two 18th-century mansions on the square's west side have been turned into museums – **Museu Histórico de Alcântara** (Largo de São Matias; admission R$2; ⊗9am-3pm Tue-Fri, to 1pm Sat & Sun) and the **Casa Histórica** (Largo de São Matias; ⊗9:30am-4:30pm Tue-Fri, to 2:30pm Sat & Sun) FREE – exhibiting the lifestyle of Alcântara's privileged families of yore, including a wealth of period furnishings and memorabilia.

Alcântara is a straightforward day trip from São Luís, but an overnight stay here is enjoyable and allows more time for exploring and for excursions to colonies of red ibis.

Run by the family of one of Alcântara's most famous local guides, Pousada Bela Vista has simple, clean rooms (some with sea views), a good patio restaurant, a pool and an inviting lookout tower. It's about a 30-minute walk or R$5 moto-taxi ride from the dock.

Two or three boats to Alcântara (R$15, 1¼ hours) leave daily from the Cais da Praia Grande in São Luís. Times vary with tides but there are usually two departures between 7am and 9am and one later.

São Luís

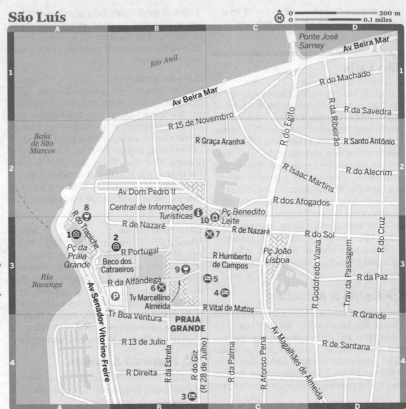

including Carnaval. For two to three weeks between early May and early June the city celebrates the **Festa do Divino Espírito Santo**, which has a strong Afro-Brazilian influence. São Luís' famous festival **Bumba Meu Boi** (☉ Jun) lasts through the second half of June. The **Tambor de Mina** festivals in July are important events for followers of the Afro-Brazilian religions.

⌂ Sleeping

★ Palma Hostel
HOSTEL **$**

(☎98 3182-8787; Rua da Palma 142; dm/s/d R$50/80/110; ❋ 🔊) Long overdue in the historical center, this bright and well-run hostel is the perfect base for budget travelers. It offers spotless colorful dorms with single beds – no bunks – and neat private rooms with good bathrooms. The fantastic common areas have plenty of comfy seating, and there are elegant decorative touches throughout. Breakfast is served in the courtyard.

Casa Frankie
POUSADA **$**

(☎98 3222-8198; www.casafrankie.com; Rua do Giz 394; s/d/tr without bathroom R$80/100/120, ste R$140; ❋ @ 🔊 ⚡) The historical center's best deal is overseen by a low-key Dane, who has restored this colonial mansion – a former brothel – into simple but superb budget sleeps. Rooms are huge but it's the common spaces – including a breezy veranda with fine original shutters, a lovely pool and a patio that wraps around a very giving mango tree – that set it apart.

Pousada Portas da Amazônia
POUSADA **$**

(☎98 3182-8787; www.portasdaamazonia.com.br; Rua do Giz 129; s/d/tr R$115/140/170, ste s/d/t R$145/185/225; ❋ 🔊) Rambling, creaky old corridors in this restored mansion lead around two patio-gardens to attractive and comfortable rooms with good mattresses and modern air-con. The master suites are way roomier and have much more character than the rather poky regular rooms. Street-side

São Luís

rooms can be noisy. You can take the good buffet breakfast in one of the courtyards.

✖ Eating

São Luís's specialty is *arroz de cuxá* (rice with shrimp, toasted sesame and the slightly bitter herb *vinagreira*). Unfortunately the culinary scene in the historical center is rather sparse (and almost nonexistent on Sundays), and foodies must head out to the northern beaches for most of the best options.

O Rei de Beiju Recheado   FAST FOOD $
(Rua da Estrêla & Alfândega; beijus R$5-8; ⊙6-10pm, to 2am Fri & Sat) The best cheap eats in the historical center can be found at this friendly roadside stand on the Largo do Comércio that serves delicious savory and sweet filled *beijus* (cassava flour pancakes). They're all good, but the shrimp in coconut milk with cheese is outstanding. Also makes a mean hamburger.

★Restaurante Senac   BUFFET $$
(Rua de Nazaré 242; lunch buffet R$42; ⊙noon-3pm Mon-Sat; 🖥) Showpiece for the São Luís branch of Brazil's best-known cooking school, this place gets packed at lunchtime for its superb all-you-can-eat buffet, which includes a big salad bar and eight or 10 hot meat and seafood dishes, plus rice, vegetables, yummy desserts – and a piano man.

🍷 Drinking & Entertainment

Evenings in the historical center, things get lively around Largo do Comércio; on Fridays, young locals turn it into one massive block party. Hot spots include the stairs in front of **Cafofinho da Tia Dica** (Beco da Alfândega; ⊙11am-midnight), and along Rua da Trapiche near the water.

Ask locals or tourist offices about what's hot, and check www.kamaleao.com/saoluis. There's a vibrant LGBT scene here.

Bar do Nelson   CLUB
(📞98 98840-3196; www.facebook.com/bardonelsonreggaeroots; Av Litorânea 135, Calhau; admission R$5-20; ⊙9pm-3am Thu-Sat) With its favela clubhouse feel, Bar do Nelson is the most famous reggae spot in town, and it's good for live music and dancing. A second **location** (Rua da Trapiche 39; ⊙10pm-3am) has opened among the lively bars of Rua da Trapiche in the historical center.

Casa das Dunas   LIVE MUSIC
(📞98 3227-8695; Av Litorânea s/n; ⊙7pm-2am Fri & Sat, to midnight Sun) The biggest thing to happen in São Luís since sliced *picanha* (steak), this massive, architecturally stunning entertainment complex opened in 2015. Overlooking Praia do Calhau, it's equal parts bar and live-music venue, and a good bet for DJs, MPB (Música Popular Brasileira) and *forró* (popular Northeastern music). Attracts national acts as well.

🛍 Shopping

São Luís is the place to find Maranhão handicrafts such as painted tiles, woodcarvings, basketry, lace, ceramics and leatherwork. There are plenty of shops around Rua Portugal and Rua da Estrela in the historical center.

Feirinha São Luís   MARKET
(Praça Benedito Leite; ⊙10am-3pm Sun) Every Sunday the Praça Benedito Leite in the historical center hosts this market fair. Stalls selling traditional meals, cheese, fresh vegetables, dry goods and handicrafts set up on the plaza, while vans selling fast food and microbrews park around the perimeter. Live music and dance performances on the big stage create a party-like atmosphere.

ℹ Information

Central de Informações Turísticas (SETUR; 📞98 3212-6210; www.saoluis.ma.gov.br/setur; Praça Benedito Leite; ⊙8am-6pm Mon-Fri, to noon Sat & Sun) The main information office of Setur, the city tourism department, and also the most helpful; English and French were spoken when we visited.

BRAZIL SÃO LUÍS

Maranhão Tourist Information (📞 98 3256-2585; www.turismo.ma.gov.br; São Luís airport; ⏱24hr) Maranhão's official state tourist information office, located in the Arrivals hall of the airport. English isn't a strong point, but the bilingual tourism site has helpful descriptions.

❶ Getting There & Away

Aeroporto Internacional de São Luís – Marechal Cunha Machado (📞 98 3217-6100; Av dos Libaneses, Tirirical), 12km southeast of the center, is served by major domestic airlines. A taxi to the centro histórico costs R$53. Alternatively, Bus 901 (São Cristóvão Aeroporto) runs between the airport – just outside the terminal and to the left – and Praça Deodoro, which is about 1km east of most of the *centro histórico* accommodations; note this is not a safe option at night.

The bus station, located 8km southeast of the historical center, is reached by taxi (R$40 to R$50) or by the Socarrão II–Rodoviária bus, which goes to the Terminal Praia Grande in the *centro histórico*. Night buses to Belém have a history of being robbed, so consider flying, which can be cheaper in any case.

Parque Nacional dos Lençóis Maranhenses

📞 098

This spectacular national park is made up of 1550 sq km of rolling white dunes. It's best visited from May to September, when rainwater forms crystal-clear lakes between the sandy hills. The main access point is the rather unprepossessing town of Barreirinhas, set on a bend of the picturesque Rio Preguiças near the park's southeast corner.

If you have at least two nights to spend in the area, there are two other access points well worth the effort. The remote village of Atins is sandwiched between dunes, river and ocean at the mouth of the Rio Preguiças. Santo Amaro is on the park's western border, where the dunes come right to the edge of the village. There are sandy river beaches for bathing here even when the lagoons among the dunes are dry. Both villages are far more charming than Barreirinhas.

Numerous local agencies – including **Caetés Turismo** (📞 98 3349-0528; www.caetes turismo.com.br; Av Brasília 40B; ⏱8am-6pm) 🌊 and **São Paulo Ecoturismo** (📞 98 3349-0079; www.saopauloecoturismo.com.br; Av Brasília 108; ⏱7am-8pm) – offer trips into the park. A common excursion from Barreirinhas is

a half-day 4WD truck tour to Lagoa Azul (R$70 to R$80) and Lagoa Bonita (R$80 to R$90), two of the park's biggest lagoons. There is also a wonderful seven-hour boat tour (R$80 to R$90) to the mouth of the Rio Preguiças, stopping to hike the dunes at Vassouras, climb the lighthouse at Mandacaru and eat at the day-trippers' beach of Caburé.

If you want to venture further into the park, you can organize memorable multiday hikes with outfits such as **Terra Nordeste** (📞98 3221-1188; www.terra-nordeste.com; Miquerinos 1, Golden Tower, Sala 416, Renascença II; ⏱9am-6pm Mon-Fri) and **Sandwalkers** (📞98 98864-0526; sandwalkers.ma@gmail.com; Atins; 2/3-day treks per hiker R$600/800).

Good budget lodging options include **Casa do Professor Hostel** (📞98 98808-2546; www.casadoprofessorhostel.com.br; Projetada 33; campsite/hammock/dm R$15/25/40; @🛜) in Barreirinhas, **Pousada Irmão Atins** (📞98-98864-4288; www.pousadairmaoatins.com.br; Principal, Atins; s/d/t R$190/230/310; ✳@🛜) in Atins and **Rancho Cajueiro** (📞98-98750-0045; tent/hammock R$45) in Santo Amaro. For a splurge, book a chalet at the **Ciamat Camp** (📞98 99604-5824; www.ciamatcamp.com; MA-320 s/n; r/tr/q R$306/374/436; ✳🛜) in Santo Amaro.

Cisne Branco runs four buses daily between São Luís and Barreirinhas (R$53, five hours). Alternatively, vans (R$60) operated by BRTur offer more efficient door-to-door service.

To get to Atins from Barreirinhas, you can take a scheduled boat service (R$40, 1½ hours; 11:30am daily) down the Rio Preguiças from the Beira Rio dock. Alternatively take a Toyota 4WD (R$25, two hours), leaving from the corner of Rua Major Galas and Monsenhor Gentil. Air-conditioned door-to-door vans by **Cito** (📞98 98784-4044, 98 99903-3282) and **Lisboa** (📞98 98702-0178) run from São Luís to Santo Amaro three or four times a day.

Barreirinhas can also be a jumping-off point for Jericoacoara.

THE NORTH

The Amazon conjures up something of a romantic, near-mythical image in our minds, but nowadays also an urgently real one. The future of this immense expanse of rivers and jungle, a vital lung for the world, is of huge importance.

RIVER TRAVEL

Riverboat travel is a unique Amazonian experience. Be warned that boats are always slow and crowded, often wet and smelly, sometimes dull and never comfortable. Do you like *forró* music? You won't after this trip! Luckily, Brazilians are friendly and river culture is interesting.

➡ Downstream travel is considerably faster than upstream, but boats heading upriver travel closer to the shore, which is more scenic.

➡ Boats often moor in port a few days before departing – check boat quality before committing.

➡ Fares vary little between boats. Tickets are best bought onboard or at official booths inside port buildings. Street vendors may offer cheaper prices but you run the risk of being cheated.

➡ *Camarotes* (cabins) are usually available and afford additional privacy and security.

➡ Ensure that yours has a fan or air-con. *Camarotes* are usually the same price as flying.

➡ Put up your hammock (available at any market from R$35; don't forget rope!) several hours before departure. There are usually two decks for hammocks; try for a spot on the upper one (the engine is below), away from the smelly toilets. Others are likely to sling their hammocks above and/or below yours. Porters may offer to help you tie yours for a small tip: well worth it if knots aren't the ace in your pack.

➡ Bring a rain jacket or poncho, sheet or light blanket, toilet paper and diarrhea medication.

➡ Meals (included) are mainly rice, beans and meat, with water or juice to drink. It's advisable to bring a few liters of bottled water, fruit and snacks. There is usually a snack bar on the top deck.

➡ Watch your gear carefully, especially just before docking and while at port. Lock zippers and wrap your backpack in a plastic bag. Keep valuables with you. Get friendly with people around you, as they can keep an eye on your stuff.

The numbers alone are mind-boggling: the Amazon Basin contains six-million sq km of river and jungle, and just over half is in Brazil. It contains 17% of the world's fresh water, and the main river-flow at its mouth is 12 billion liters per minute.

While you can still have amazing wildlife experiences in the vastness of the forest here, it's important to realize that pouncing jaguars and bulging anacondas are rare sightings. Nevertheless, a trip into the jungle ecosystem is deeply rewarding, both for wildlife-watching and the chance to appreciate how local communities have adapted to this water world. Manaus is a popular base for river trips, but there are other good possibilities. The main city, Belém, is an appealing launchpad to the region, while the tranquil white sands of Alter do Chão make a peaceful stopover on your way upriver.

ⓘ Getting There & Around

Bus travel is limited to a few routes in the North, so rivers serve as highways. Competing airlines occasionally offer fares cheaper than hammock boat prices; check for specials.

Belém

♫ 0XX91 / POP 1.44 MILLION

The eastern gateway to the Amazon region and a destination in its own right, Belém is worth at least a couple of days of your life. It's a rewarding city, with streets and parks shaded by mango trees, the pastel facades of once-decadent mansions now fading in the tropical sun, as well as a number of fascinating museums, pungent markets and decent restaurant-bars. It's also a launchpad for overnight trips to Algodoal and Ilha de Marajó, both appealing coastal destinations.

The compact Comércio business district, roughly between Av Presidente Vargas and Av Portugal, is noisy by day and deserted by night. The quieter Cidade Velha (Old City) contains Belém's historical buildings. East of the center, prosperous Nazaré has some chic shops and restaurants.

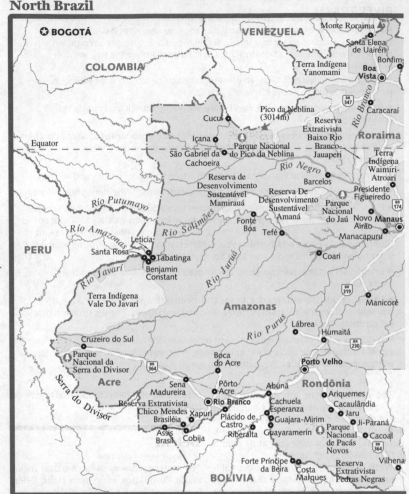

⊙ Sights & Activities

The 'Old City' has most of Belém's museums and galleries, fronting the river and four nearly adjoining plazas.

★ Mercado Ver-o-Peso   MARKET

(Blvd Castilhos França; ⊙7:30am-6pm Mon-Sat, to 1pm Sun) The name of this waterfront market, with its iconic four-turreted structure at its southwestern end, comes from colonial times, when the Portuguese would *ver o peso* (check the weight) of merchandise in order to impose taxes. The display of fruit, animals, medicinal plants and more is fascinating; go early to see fishing boats unloading their catch.

★ Estação das Docas   MARKET

(☎91 3212-5525; www.estacaodasdocas.com.br; Blvd Castilho França; ⊙9am-1am) An ambitious renovation project converted three down-at-heel riverfront warehouses into a popular gathering spot, with restaurants, bars, shops and even an art-house theater. There are river views and displays about Belém's history, plus a post office and numerous ATMs. Enjoy live music most nights, performed from a moving platform in the rafters, rolling slowly the length of the dining area.

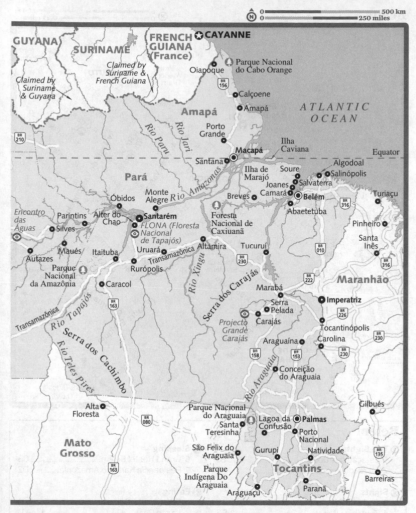

Teatro da Paz   HISTORIC BUILDING

(Praça da República; R$6, free Wed; ⊙ guided visits 9am-noon & 2-6pm Tue-Fri, 9am-noon Sat & Sun) Overlooking Praça da República, the Teatro da Paz is one of Belém's finest buildings. Completed in 1874 and built in the neoclassical style, the architecture has all the sumptuous trappings of the rubber-boom era: columns, busts, crystal mirrors and an interior decorated in Italian theatrical style. Half-hour tours are a mildly interesting trip to the city's former glory years.

Forte do Presépio   FORTRESS

(Praça Fr Brandão; R$4, free Tue; ⊙10am-6pm Tue-Fri, to 2pm Sat & Sun) The city of Belém was founded in 1616 with the construction of this imposing fort, which was intended to protect Portuguese interests upriver from incursions by the French and Dutch. Today it houses a small but excellent museum, primarily about Pará state's indigenous communities (displays in Portuguese only), and has great river and city views from atop its thick stone walls.

Belém

Belém

◉ Top Sights
1 Estação das Docas	B1
2 Mercado Ver-o-Peso	A2

◉ Sights
3 Forte do Presépio	A3
4 Teatro da Paz	D3

✦ Activities, Courses & Tours
5 Valeverde	B2

⊜ Sleeping
6 Grand Hostel Belém	C3
7 Residencia Karimbo Amazônia	D2

✖ Eating
Estação das Docas	(see 1)
La em Casa	(see 1)
8 Rei Do Bacalhau	B2

⊙ Drinking & Nightlife
9 Amazon Beer	B2

Valeverde   BOATING
(☑ 91 3218-7333; www.valeverdeturismo.com.br; Estação das Docas) Runs a variety of short tours on the river (per person R$50 to R$175), including sunrise trips and pleasant evening cruises. Valeverde has an office and daily schedule at the pier at Estação das Docas; in most cases you can simply show up.

✦ Festivals & Events

Círio de Nazaré   RELIGIOUS
(⊙ 2nd Sun in Oct) During the Círio de Nazaré, a million people accompany the image of the Virgin of Nazaré from the cathedral to the Basílica de NS de Nazaré. Two weeks of serious partying follow.

🛏 Sleeping

Grand Hostel Belém
HOSTEL $

(📞91 3355-8889; www.grandhostelbelem.com; Av Presidente Vargas 646; dm R$50, d with shared/private bathroom R$90/120; ✳🛜) This central hostel overlooks Praça da República and has brightly painted rooms with a mix of dorms and private rooms. It has a fun vibe and staff are clued in to travelers' needs. It gets a lot of repeat visitors, which is the best recommendation we can make.

Residencia Karimbo Amazônia
GUESTHOUSE $

(📞91 3298-1373; www.rkamazoniabrasil.sitew.com; Travessa Piedade 391; d/tr R$145/185) A true guesthouse, the French-Brazilian owners live in the front part of the house, while visitors stay in five comfortable rooms, with bright artful decor, well-appointed bathrooms and new bedding. A VIP room (first come, first served) has a private balcony overlooking the hotel's garden area, with a small pool and attractive wood patio.

★OVibe Hostel & Arts
HOSTEL $$

(📞91 3349-0008; www.ovibe.com.br; Travessa Benjamin Constant 1374; dm/f R$75/450; ✳@🛜) This snazzy hostel has wonderful decor and a real artsy vibe. The rooms feature lovely wrought-iron furnishings and daring artistic flourishes at every turn. The location is ideal, in a relatively quiet corner of town but within walking distance of just about everywhere.

🍴 Eating

Belém is known for *pato no tucupí* (duck in manioc juice and tongue-tingling jambu leaf sauce), *Tacacá* (a gummy soup made from manioc root, dried shrimp and jambu leaves) and *maniçoba* (black beans, pork and manioc leaves).

★Rei Do Bacalhau
SEAFOOD $

(📞91 3241-5824; Travessa Campos Sales 216; mains from R$15; ⊘8am-6pm) The 'King of Cod' is a Belém classic, with cheap and cheerful service and fresh street-food staples straight from the nearby fish market. It's no-frills, which makes us love it all the more.

★Estação das Docas
FOOD HALL $$

(www.estacaodasdocas.com.br; Blvd Castilho França; ⊘noon-midnight Sun-Wed, noon-3am Thu-Sat) One of the best places in Belém to eat, no matter what you're hungry for.

The bustling complex has almost a dozen restaurants, most with indoor and outdoor seating, open for lunch, dinner and late-night feasting. Favorites include **Lá em Casa** (📞91 3212-5588; www.laemcasa.com; Av Marechal Hermes, Estação das Docas; mains R$28-70, set menu for 1/2 people R$72/120), serving pricey but outstanding regional food, and **Amazon Beer** (📞91 3212-5400; www.amazonbeer.com.br; Av Marechal Hermes, Estação das Docas; ⊘5pm-1am), with delectable pub grub to accompany its artisanal beer.

Mango
CAFE $$

(📞91 3199-2731; www.mangoalimentacaosaudavel.com.br; Av Brás de Aguiar 593; mains R$14-45; ⊘11:30am-4pm Tue-Sun & 6-10pm Tue-Sat; 🍴) Wildly popular with Belém's hip young crowd, Mango is devoted to the art of healthy eating, with fab dishes such as duck burger, and grilled mango for dessert. Terrific juices, salads, light quiches and sandwiches round off a fine choice, with plenty of options for vegetarians.

🍷 Drinking & Entertainment

Bar Fiteiro
BAR

(📞91 3224-0075; www.facebook.com/Fiteiro Belem; Av Visconde de Souza Franco 555, at Senador Lemos; ⊘5pm-1am Sun-Fri, from noon Sat) This spacious, colorful bar has a fun, irreverent air and a commitment to not let its customers go hungry – in fact, the bar's tagline is 'We Have Food.' There's live music on offer most nights, often paired with a dish or drink, like 'Feijoada com Samba' on Saturday afternoons.

★Casa do Gilson
LIVE MUSIC

(📞91 3272-7306; www.facebook.com/casadogilson; Travessa Padre Eutíquio 3172; ⊘8pm-3am Fri, from noon Sat & Sun) Come here for Belém's best live music. Opened in 1987, Gilson's attracts crowds with first-rate samba, *choro* (improvised samba-like genre) and other music, and terrific food and atmosphere. It's between ruas Nova and Tamběs.

ℹ Information

SETUR (📞91 3212-0575; www.paraturismo.pa.gov.br; Praça Waldemar Henrique; ⊘8am-2pm Mon-Fri) A reasonably helpful branch office of the state tourism department.

Tourist Police (CIPTUR; 📞91 3222-2602; 28 de Setembro) City-center police station.

Hospital Adventista de Belém (📞91 3084-8686; www.hab.org.br; Av Almirante Barroso 1758) One of the better private hospitals.

DANGERS & ANNOYANCES

Pickpocketing is a problem in Mercado Ver-o-Peso and the Comercio districts. Take care during the day and avoid both at night. Take a cab if you're returning late.

ⓘ Getting There & Away

AIR

Belém's **Aeroporto Internacional Val-de-Cans** (☑ 91 3210-6000; www.infraero.gov.br) is 8km north of the center on Av Júlio César. The 'Pratinha – Pres Vargas' bus (638) runs between the airport and Av Presidente Vargas (R$3, 40 minutes). Taxis cost R$50.

BOAT

All long-distance boats leave Belém from the handsomely renovated **Terminal Hidroviária** (Av Marechal Hermes). You can purchase tickets inside the terminal, or from the multilingual **Amazon Star Turismo** (☑ 91 3212-6244; www.amazonstar.com.br; Henrique Gurjão 56; ⊙ 8am-6pm Mon-Fri, to noon Sat). Boats to Santarém (hammock/cabin R$230/800, four days) and Manaus (hammock/cabin R$370/1000, six days) depart on Wednesday and Saturday.

BUS

Belém's **long-distance bus station** (Av Almirante Barroso) is 3km east of the center. To get downtown, catch the 316 'Guamá–P Vargas' bus from across the road. Going to the bus station, take the same bus from Av Presidente Vargas. Taxis to points along Av Presidente Vargas cost between R$20 and R$25.

Sample travel times and fares from Belém include the following:

Algodoal

☑ 0XX91 / POP 1500

The small fishing village of Algodoal on Ilha de Maiandeua exchanges cars and paved roads for expansive views over firm, wind-swept beaches and a sometimes turbulent sea. A popular getaway for young *belenenses*, Algodoal is jam-packed during a few frenetic months in the summer and over certain holidays, and virtually abandoned during down periods. If you catch it when it's quiet, it's one of northern Brazil's best hideaways. It's 180km northeast of Belém.

Algodoal has various options for do-it-yourself excursions. Renting a canoe (ask at your hotel) and combining it with hiking are the most common ways to get active.

Hotel Bela Mar (☑ 91 3854-1128; www.facebook.com/pousadabelamar; Magalhães Barata; s/d with fan R$65/90, with air-con R$80/120; 🅿🛜) is a clean, reliable choice and the first hotel you reach from the boat drop-off. At the far end of town (near Praia do Farol), **Pousada Marhesias** (☑ 91 9112-3461, 91 3854-1129; www.marhesias.com; Bertoldo Costa 47; s R$120-150, d R$150-180; 🅿🛜🛁) is a well-run hotel, restaurant and bar with artfully designed guestrooms, a leafy garden, and a deck with beach views. Nearby, the **Pousada Ponta do Boiador** (☑ 91 99215-9939; Bertoldo Costa 44; d standard/ste from R$150/180; 🅿🛜) has well-appointed suites and breezy patios with hammocks.

There are no ATMs, and not all hotels accept credit cards. Bring cash from Belém.

Access to Algodoal is via the mainland village of Marudá. From Belém's bus station, buses (R$21.50, four hours, four daily) go to Marudá's port, where boats for Algodoal (R$10, 40 minutes) leave five times daily. Vans from Belém only go as far as the bus station, which is five long blocks away, or R$15 in a taxi. At Algodoal, donkey-cart drivers greet arriving boats, vying for the chance to take you to your hotel (per person R$12); alternatively, it's only a 10-minute stroll into the village.

Ilha de Marajó

☑ 0XX91 / POP 48,000

The 50,000-sq-km Ilha de Marajó, slightly larger than Switzerland, lies at the mouth of the Amazon River and is generally con-

BUSES FROM BELÉM

DESTINATION	COST FROM (R$)	DURATION (HRS)	COMPANY
Altamira	197	14	Boa Esperança (www.viajeboaesperanca.com.br)
Brasília	255	35	Rápido Marajó (www.rapidomarajo.com.br)
Fortaleza	170	24	Guanabara (www.expressoguanabara.com.br), Itapemirim (www.itapemirim.com.br)
Salvador	489	35	Itapemirim (www.itapemirim.com.br)
São Luís	146	13	Boa Esperança (www.viajeboaesperanca.com.br), Rápido Marajó (www.rapidomarajo.com.br)

sidered to be the largest river island in the world. It was the ancient home of the Marajoaras indigenous culture, notable for their large ceramic burial urns. Marajó remains a world apart, where bicycles outnumber cars and water buffalo graze around town.

Only the island's eastern shore is accessible to tourists, with three small towns: Joanes (the smallest), Salvaterra (with the best beach but not much else) and Soure (the laid-back 'capital' of Marajó). The island's interior is wetland, home to thousands of birds, including the graceful *guará* (scarlet ibis). Be aware that Marajó is very wet from January to June.

Joanes

It may be just across the river from Belém, but sleepy Joanes is all about total and complete isolation. The essence of its appeal is simple: a lovely hotel and beach, the remains of a 17th-century Jesuit church and hardly a soul in sight (aside from the grazing livestock). Attractive **Pousada Ventania do Rio-Mar** (☑ 91 3646-2067; www.pousadaventania.com; Quarta Rua; s/d R$165/203; ☎) is atop a breezy headland overlooking the shore. The beach is just steps away, and the staff can arrange a variety of excursions, including canoeing and fishing with local guides. Cash only.

Salvaterra

About 18km north of Joanes, Salvaterra has more of a town feel and the island's best and longest beach, Praia Grande. On an ocean-front lot shaded by mango trees, **Pousada Bosque dos Aruãs** (☑ 91 3765-1115; Segunda Rua; s/d R$90/110, ste R$165-190; ✻☎) offers simple wooden cabins on stilts overlooking the water. It's somewhat shabby, but very peaceful, with a good restaurant. Praia Grande is a 10-minute walk away.

Soure

Located on the far side of the Rio Paracauari, Soure is the biggest town on the island. Nevertheless, it has a very laid-back vibe, with horses and water buffalo grazing on the soccer fields and double-wide streets, many of them dirt or grass with a bike path weaving down the middle. **Banco do Brasil** (Rua 3, btwn Travessas 17 & 18; ⊙10am-3pm Mon-Fri) and **Bradesco** (Rua 2, btwn Travessas 15 & 16; ⊙10am-3pm Mon-Fri) have ATMs. **Bimba** (Rua

4, btwn Travessas 18 & 19; per hour/day R$4/25) rents bikes from his house.

A 4.5km bike ride north of Soure leads to Praia Barra Velha, where shacks sell drinks and seafood. Beyond lies Praia de Araruna, a long, starkly beautiful and practically deserted beach. Alternatively, follow Rua 4 inland to Praia do Pesqueiro (12km), another popular weekend beach. A moto-taxi there costs R$15 each way, while cabs charge R$40 for up to four people.

❶ Getting There & Around

Arapari Navigação (☑ 91 3241-4977; Siqueira Mendes 120) and **Rodofluvial BANAV** (☑ 91 3269-4494; www.banav.com.br) leave Belém's main boat terminal at 6:30am and 2:30pm Monday to Saturday and 10am on Sunday, arriving at a port south of Joanes called Foz do Rio Camará, or Camará for short (deck/air-con VIP lounge R$25/40, three hours). They return from the same port at 6:30am and 3pm Monday to Saturday, and 3pm Sunday. Waiting buses and air-con minivans whisk passengers from Camará's dock to Joanes (R$8), Salvaterra (R$8) and Soure (R$11 to R$18).

The centers of Salvaterra and Soure are linked by a boat (R$2, 15 minutes) that leaves when full (this can take a while). Moto-taxis are common in all three towns, and cost R$5 around town, R$5 to R$15 to outlying beaches, and R$30 between Joanes and Salvaterra.

Santarém

☑ 0XX93 / POP 296,302

Most travelers rush between Belém and Manaus, skipping over the very thing they are desperate to see: the Amazon. A stop in riverfront Santarém not only breaks up a long boat trip, but also provides a chance to investigate the jungle and communities seen from your hammock. Santarém itself is rather bland, but the lovely river beaches and beautiful rainforest preserves nearby may entice you to prolong your stay.

◉ Sights

Santarém's waterfront provides a nice perspective on the meeting of the waters between the tea-colored Rio Tapajós and the café-au-lait Rio Amazonas. The two flow side by side for a few kilometers without mingling.

★**Lago Maicá**   LAKE
The floodplains east and southeast of Santarém are among the Amazon's most rewarding excursions. Flooded for much of

the year, the plains are home to fabulous birdlife (including toucans and macaws), pink dolphins, howler monkeys, sloths and anacondas. The sunrise and sunset views are pure magic and there's a real sense of tranquility out here. Take an overnight boat trip, go canoeing through the flooded forest and relax far from the tourist hordes. Gil Serique (p417) organizes especially enjoyable excursions here.

🛏 Sleeping & Eating

Don't miss the much-loved Amazonian soup, Tacacá (made from wild manioc, dried shrimp and lip-tingling jambu). The **Quiosque da Praça** (Praça Barão de Santarém; from R$8; ☺ 7am-1pm & 4-11pm) serves some of the best *tacacá* in Brazil. For sunset drinks, the open-air waterfront restaurant **Massabor** (☑ 93 3522-0509; Av Tapajós; pizza R$33-43, mains R$15-50; ☺ 5-11pm) is tops.

Hotel Sandis Mirante   HOTEL $
(☑ 93 99239-2488; www.hotelsandismirante.com.br; Coronel Joaquim Braga 180; s/d/tr R$130/145/180) This attractive place up on the hill just back from the waterfront has clean, modern rooms, some with river views, although why they built such small windows we'll never understand. It's an otherwise excellent choice.

★ **Restaurante Piracema**   BRAZILIAN $$
(☑ 93 3522-7461; www.restaurantepiracema.com.br; Av Mendonça Furtado 73; R$25-80; ☺ 11am-11:30pm Tue-Sat, to 3pm Sun) Considered by many to be the best restaurant in town, Piracema uses regional ingredients and flavors to create dishes you'll find nowhere else. The specialty is the *peixe á Piracema,* a spherical construction of layered smoked *pirarucú* (a freshwater fish), banana and cheese. It's strange but delicious, and large enough for two.

ℹ Information

Santarém Tur (☑ 93 3522-4847; www.santaremtur.com.br; Adriano Pimentel 44; ☺ 8am-6pm Mon-Fri, to noon Sat) Arranges plane tickets, tour packages (including city tours), day trips to Alter do Chão by boat or car, and overnight riverboat tours to FLONA.

ℹ Getting There & Away

AIR
Aeroporto de Santarém – Maestro Wilson Fonseca is 14km west of town. It handles

flights to/from Manaus and Belém. Buses (R$3.50, 30 minutes) run to the city every half-hour or so between 6:15am and 6:45pm on weekdays, with reduced service on weekends. Taxis cost R$60. Going to the airport, catch the 'Aeroporto' (but not 'Aeroporto Velho') on Av Rui Barbosa near Av Barão do Rio Branco.

BOAT
Boats to Manaus (hammock/double cabin R$180/600, 40 to 48 hours, noon Monday to Wednesday, Friday and Saturday, 11am Thursday) and Belém (hammock/double cabin R$180/800, 48 hours, 10am Friday and 11am Monday) leave from Docas do Pará, 2.5km west of the center.

The 'Orla Fluvial' minibus (R$3) connects the downtown waterfront with both ports every 20 to 30 minutes until 7pm. Taxis and mototaxis to Docas do Pará cost R$15 and R$4, respectively.

BUS
Hourly buses to Alter do Chão (R$3.50, 60 minutes) stop on **Av Rui Barbosa** near Av Barão do Rio Branco.

Around Santarém

Floresta Nacional do Tapajós

One of the last and most accessible stretches of primary rainforest in the region, this 5440-sq-km protected area is the Amazon rainforest you always imagined. Wildlife includes numerous species of birds, elusive cats (including jaguar and ocelot), as well as howler monkeys, squirrel monkeys and capuchins. It's recommended to visit with a guide and it's likely to be one of your most memorable experiences.

The riverside villages of Maguarí and Jamaraquá have been hosting travelers the longest and have the most established accommodations, tours and other services. A third village, São Domingo, is at the entrance to the reserve as well. Primary rainforest is about a two-and-a-half-hour hike away from these villages.

All three villages have well-maintained forest trails. There are some lovely *igarapés* (inlets), too, with good canoeing and possibly animal-spotting when the water is high. Tour prices include: a four- to five-hour hike and a one- to two-hour canoe trip costs R$100 to R$150 per group (up to six people).

In Jamaraquá, you can overnight at the riverside **Pousada Jamaraquá** (☑ 93 99124-5750, 93 99179-9569; Transtapajós s/n; d incl meals R$125), which has a deck for hammocks but very basic rooms and bathrooms located away from the main house. The bus stops in front. Also in Jamaraquá, **Pousada Floresta do Tapajós** (☑93 99113-8458; www.pousadaflorestadotapajos.wordpress.com; Transtapajós S/N; per person R$50), aka 'Pousada de Bata', has a knowledgeable owner and tour guide, with an airy hammock area and a welcoming family atmosphere. It's about 500m past the main village center; ask the bus driver to drop you here.

Buses to Maguarí and Jamaraquá (R$12, two to three hours, 11am Monday to Saturday, 6:30am Sunday) depart from downtown Santarém. Return buses depart Jamaraquá at 4:30am and 6am Monday to Saturday, 4:30pm Sunday.

You can also get to FLONA by boat, leaving from Alter do Chão. Freelance boatmen do day trips for around R$100 per person, but it's a tiring three hours each way in a small motorized canoe, and does not include guide service. Tour agencies in Alter do Chão like **Mãe Natureza** (☑93 3527-1264, 93 99131-9870; www.maenaturezaecoturismo.com.br; Praça 7 de Setembro; ☺8:30am-1pm & 4-11pm) and **Areia Branca Ecotour** (☑93 3527-1386, 93 99121-5646; www.areiabrancaecotour.com.br; Lago Verde; ☺8am-noon & 2-7pm Mon-Fri, to 1pm Sat & Sun) charge R$200 to R$250 per person, including a local guide and using faster and more comfortable motorboats.

To experience the primary rainforest, as opposed to the river villages, we recommend the tours by Gil Serique, whose family once lived in the forest. Tours (from US$150 per person per day) can be day tours or overnight versions where you sleep in a camp deep in the forest.

ICMBio (☑93 3522-0564; www.icmbio.gov.br/flonatapajos; Av Tapajós 2267, Santarém) oversees the reserve and has an office in Santarém as well as a base station in São Domingo.

Alter do Chão
☑0XX93 / POP 7500

Alter do Chão, 33km west of Santarém, is an appealing, languid riverside town that's popular with visitors from Santarém on weekends and during holiday periods. It's best known for its Ilha do Amor (Island of Love), a picturesque island ringed by a white-sand beach directly in front of town.

But Alter do Chão is much more than a beach town. The lagoon it fronts (Lago Verde) can be explored by canoe or stand-up paddle board. It's also the departure point for boat tours to nearby forest reserves and isolated communities, and has one of the best indigenous art stores in the Amazon region.

🏃 Activities

Adventure sports are a natural fit for many visitors here. Rewarding options include stand-up paddling (SUP), windsurfing, kayaking, mountain biking and tree climbing (*arbolismo* in Portuguese). Ask at Mãe Natureza, Areia Branca Ecotour or Gil Serique for prices and availability.

★**Gil Serique**   ECOTOUR
(☑93 99130-5298; www.gilserique.com; Av Copacabana 45, at PA-457; per person per day US$150) Gil is a true character, a lithe teller of tales and one of the area's top naturalists. Born and raised nearby, Gil's tours are part history, part ecology and part family lore, related with infectious enthusiasm and near-perfect English. Visits to Lago Maicá (p415), a gorgeous floodplain teeming with birds and other wildlife, are especially memorable. Pricier than others, but worth it.

🔖 Tours

Besides short trips around Alter do Chão (Lago Verde, Ponta do Cururú, beach-hopping) there are some great options for longer multiday tours. These include canoeing the animal-rich **Canal do Jarí**, hiking and visiting villages in **Floresta Nacional (FLONA) do Tapajós** (FLONA do Tapajós) and the Reserva Extrativista (RESEX) Tapajós-Arapiuns (p422), river trips up the **Rio Arapluns**, and adventure routes into the **Parque Nacional da Amazônia**. Discuss details with tour agencies in town; prices range from R$180 to $300 per person per day, all-inclusive.

🎉 Festivals & Events

Festa do Cairé   RELIGIOUS
(☺2nd week Sep) The Festa do Çairé is the major folkloric event in western Pará. The Çairé is a standard held aloft to lead a flower-bedecked procession; its origins may go back to symbols used by early missionaries to help convert indigenous groups.

🛏 Sleeping & Eating

★**Pousada Vila Alter**   POUSADA$
(☑93 99173-9772; Everaldo Martins 603; s/d/tr R$80/120/140; ❄🖢) The pick of the many

new pousadas opening around town, the welcoming Vila Alter has a colorful little garden and tidy rooms. The whole feel here is one of intimacy and warmth, and the price is terrific value. It's far enough up the hill to avoid the evening noise, but it's just five minutes away on foot.

Pousada do Tapajós Hostel HOSTEL $
(📞93 99210-2166; www.pousadatapajos.com.br; Lauro Sodré 100; dm R$50, d/tr/q R$180/190/200; 🏵️ 🛜) Dorms here are clean and comfortable, though a bit cramped, with sturdy bunks and large lockers. Private rooms are sparkling, modern and well removed from the dorm area. There's an ample breakfast, open kitchen and large backyard with hammocks. It's five blocks west of the center.

★**Siria** VEGETARIAN $
(📞93 99217-2034; Travessa Agostinho Lobato s/n; mains R$20-30; ⏰noon-4pm; 🍴) The lovely chef-owner, Betania, prepares just one dish per day, announced on a sandwich board out front. From chickpea omelets to vegetable tarts, count on it being outstanding, served with brown rice, fresh salad and creative drinks, like hibiscus and *maracujá* (passion fruit) iced tea, plus dessert. Dishes are vegan or vegetarian, depending on the day. Attractive outdoor dining area.

★**Espaço Gastronômico** BRAZILIAN $$
(📞93 98401 6144; www.espacoalter.com.br; Lauro Sodré 74; mains R$25-60; ⏰7-11pm; 🛜) 🍴 What a fabulous place! It's made almost entirely from recycled wood and other materials, with a commitment to using local ingredients and indigenous sauces, which might include Brazil nuts, honey and manioc, or ceviche with mango. Upstairs is the place to be, with diaphanous curtains blowing in the sea breeze. Joana is a marvelous host.

☆ Entertainment

★**Espaço Gastronômico** LIVE MUSIC
(📞93 98401 6144; www.espacoalter.com.br; Laura Sodré 74; cover from R$20; ⏰10pm-4am Sat Jul-Feb; 🛜) There's always something worth seeing at this cool music-restaurant space at the east end of the waterfront promenade. There's live *carimbó* on Saturday nights in season, and guest bands play rock, *forró*, samba, reggae and more; check Facebook or the chalkboard out front for the latest.

🛍️ Shopping

★**Araribá Cultura Indígena** ARTS & CRAFTS
(📞93 3527-1324; www.araribah.com.br; Travessa Antônio Lobato; ⏰9am-9pm Mon-Sat, to 7:30pm Sun) Arguably the best indigenous art store in the region, representing communities throughout the Amazon Basin. Items range from inexpensive necklaces to museumquality masks and ceremonial costumes. Shipping available; credit cards accepted.

🛈 Getting There & Away

Buses from Alter do Chão to Santarém (R$3.50, one hour) depart hourly from the **bus station** (Everaldo Martins) 5:30am to 11pm, except on Sunday, when services end around 6pm. There is no bus to the Santarém airport from Alter do Chão. A taxi to the airport (or to Santarém or the riverboat ports) costs a painful R$100.

Manaus

📞0XX92 / POP 2.2 MILLION
Manaus is the Amazon's largest city, an incongruous urban metropolis in the middle of the jungle and a major port for seafaring vessels that's 1500km from the ocean. The Amazonian rainforest has a population density half that of Mongolia, but the journey there invariably begins in (or passes through) this gritty, bustling city. Don't be surprised if you feel a little out of whack.

Manaus is no architectural gem, but does have some genuinely rewarding sights, including a leafy zoo and an interesting beach-and-museum combo. It's a place to stock up on anything you forgot to pack, make reservations and begin your journey out into the jungle, or refill your tank with beer and internet after a week in the forest.

Another bit of advice: don't get stuck here! Manaus is best enjoyed as a starting point for your Amazon adventure, not the end of your road into the Amazon.

⊙ Sights

★**Encontro das Águas** RIVER
(Meeting of the Waters) Just beyond Manaus, the warm dark Rio Negro pours into the cool creamy Rio Solimões, but because of differences in temperature, speed and density, their waters don't mix, instead flowing side by side for several kilometers. The bicolor phenomenon occurs throughout the Amazon, but nowhere as dramatically as here. Day trips always include a stop here,

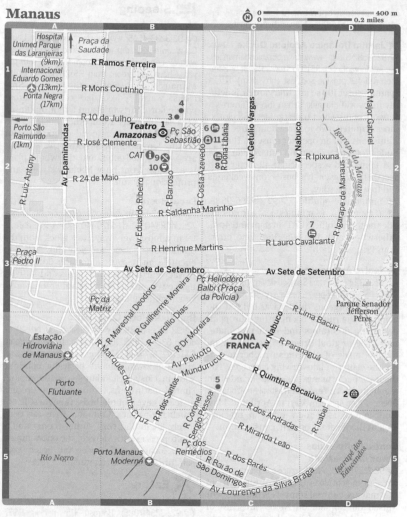

Manaus

◎ Top Sights
1 Teatro Amazonas B2

◎ Sights
2 Centro Cultural Usina
   Chaminé.. D4

✈ Activities, Courses & Tours
Amazon Antonio
   Jungle Tours.................................... (see 7)
3 Amazon Eco Adventures B1
4 Amazon Gero Tours B1
5 Amazonas Indian Turismo C4

🛏 Sleeping
6 Boutique Hotel Casa Teatro C2
7 Hostel Manaus...D3
8 Local Hostel C2

🍴 Eating
9 Casa da Pamonha B2

🍸 Drinking & Nightlife
10 Mao Bar B2

🛍 Shopping
11 Galeria Amazônica C2

and many tour operators at least pass by en route to their lodges. Never disappoints.

★ **Jardim Botânico Adolpho Ducke** PARK
(☑92 3582-3188; www.jardimbotanicodemanaus. org; Av Margarita s/n; R$10, incl tower R$30; ⊙8am-noon & 1-4:30pm Tue-Sun, last entry 4pm) FREE
Spanning over 100 sq km, this 'garden' is actually the world's largest urban forest. There's a network of five short trails (guides and closed shoes required, two to three hours, free with admission) and an open-air museum that includes rotating exhibits on Amazonian flora and fauna and a spectacular 42-meter-high observation tower. It's busier on weekends and free on Tuesday.

Comfortable shuttles (☑92 99286-9888, R$30 roundtrip, 45 minutes) leave from outside the tourist office (CAT) at 9am and 4pm. Otherwise, catch Bus 676 (R$3, one hour) from Praça da Matriz.

★ **Teatro Amazonas** THEATER
(☑92 3232-1768; Praça São Sebastião; guided tour R$20; ⊙9:15am-5pm, tours every 30 mins until 4pm) This gorgeous theater was built at the height of the rubber boom, using European designers, decorators and even raw materials. The original driveway was Brazilian, though, made of Amazonian rubber to soften the clatter of late-arriving carriages. The theater's performance schedule includes an excellent opera festival (Festival Amazonas de Ópera; ⊙late Apr–early May) in April and May. Hour-long guided tours offer an up-close look at the theater's opulent construction.

Centro Cultural dos Povos da Amazônia MUSEUM
(☑92 2123-5300; Praça Francisco Pereira da Silva s/n; ⊙9am-4pm Mon-Fri) FREE At the heart of this massive cultural complex is the excellent Museu do Homem do Norte (Museum of Northern Man), which contains an incredible array of artifacts and multimedia exhibits on Amazonian indigenous groups. From the center, buses 625, 711 and 705 all pass by, or ask a taxi to take you to the 'Bola da Suframa.'

Centro Cultural Usina Chaminé MUSEUM
(☑92 3633-3026; Av Lourenço da Silva Braga; ⊙8am-2pm Tue-Fri, 9am-1pm Sat) FREE Also known as the Museu dos Cinco Sentidos (Museum of the Five Senses), this innovative museum uses the five senses to evoke and illustrate indigenous and Caboclos life and culture. You can hear recordings of native languages, smell Amazonian spices, admire indigenous folk art and more.

🛏 Sleeping

★ **Hostel Manaus** HOSTEL $
(☑92 3233-4545; www.hostelmanaus.com; Lauro Cavalcante 231; dm with fan/air-con R$46/52, s with air-con & shared bathroom R$65, d with private/shared bathroom from R$121/93; ❋@🛜) Manaus' first hostel is still its best. Spacious, warmly decorated common areas with colorful artworks and a rooftop dining area set it apart from other hostels, and there's a highly recommended tour operator on site. Large dorms and tidy private rooms are well looked after, and the whole place is a refuge from busy Manaus streets and professionally run.

Local Hostel HOSTEL $
(☑92 3213-6079; www.localhostel.com.br; Marçal 72; dm R$40-50, d R$120-140; ❋) A great hostel in almost every way: it's a block from the opera house, there are youthful staff and clientele, and clean, comfortable dorms with privacy curtains, reading lights and individual power outlets. Spiffy private rooms are a worthwhile splurge.

Boutique Hotel Casa Teatro HOTEL $$
(☑92 3633-8381; www.casateatro.com.br; 10 de Julho 632; s/d R$210/250, with shared bathroom R$120/150; ❋🛜) Rooms are modern and cute, but really small – basically, boutique walk-in closets. Standards have bunks and shared bathrooms, while en-suite rooms at least have double beds, though still not much floor space. Common areas are truly lovely, including cozy sitting rooms and a rooftop patio with views of the opera house. Great location and service, but brace yourself for the sardine treatment.

🍴 Eating

Casa da Pamonha VEGETARIAN $
(☑92 3234-7086; Barroso 375; per kg R$37; ⊙7am-7pm Mon-Fri, to 2pm Sat; 🍴) Cool and artsy, this vegetarian place has soy burgers, Spanish tortillas, fresh juices, delicious cakes and more during its popular lunchtime buffet, plus light snacks in the morning and early evening.

★ **Amazônico Peixaria Regional** SEAFOOD, BRAZILIAN $$
(☑92 3236-0546; www.amazonico.com.br; Av Darcy Vargas 222; mains R$36-98; ⊙noon-3pm & 6:30-11pm Mon-Sat, 11:30am-4pm Sun) However you get your tambaqui (perhaps the tastiest of all Amazonian fish) prepared here – stewed, grilled, ribs – the execution is perfect. They

serve all manner of other fish and steak dishes, and fab desserts too. The atmosphere is casual, the service attentive and the cooking top-notch. It will be one of the best meals you'll have in the Amazon.

 Drinking & Entertainment

Mao Bar BAR
(☑92 3345-4550; Barroso; ⊙5pm-late Tue-Sat) This bar is super-cool – a moodily lit, semi-subterranean spot on the basement level with great music and drinks and a laid-back backpacker vibe. Occasional live music and movie screenings.

 Porão do Alemão LIVE MUSIC
(☑92 3239-2976; www.poraodoalemao.com.br; Av São Jorge 1986; R$30; ⊙10:30pm-late Wed-Sat) This longtime bar and club features Brazilian and international rock and pop, and has a safe, lively scene popular with tourists and locals alike. There's a VIP area upstairs (R$40).

 Shopping

★**Galeria Amazônica** ARTS & CRAFTS
(☑92 3203 3633; galeria@waimiriatroari.org.br; Costa Azevedo 272; ⊙8am-8pm Mon-Sat) Right on Praça São Sebastião, this is Manaus' top shop for genuine-article Amazonian handiwork, including gorgeous basketwork, pottery and folk art, as well as T-shirts, jewelry and a handful of Portuguese-language books. Prices are on the high side, but so is the quality.

ⓘ Information

Banco do Brasil (Guilherme Moreira 315; ⊙9am-3pm Mon-Fri) Has an ATM.
Bradesco (Av Eduardo Ribeiro 475, at Saldanha Marinho; ⊙9am-3pm Mon-Fri) Reliable ATM in the town center.
CAT (☑92 3182-6250; www.visitamazonas.am.gov.br; Av Eduardo Ribeiro 666; ⊙8am-5pm Mon-Fri, to noon Sat & Sun) Branch of the state tourism agency, located on the southwest corner of Praça São Sebastião. Doesn't have a lot to offer, with no brochures.
Fundação de Medicina Tropical (Tropical Medicine Foundation; ☑92 2127-3555; Av Pedro Teixeira 25) Also known as Hospital de Doenças Tropicais, this well-regarded hospital specializes in tropical diseases. Free yellow fever vaccines available.
Hospital Unimed Parque das Laranjeiras (☑0800-702-9088, 92 3633-4431; www.unimedmanaus.com.br; Av Professor Nilton Lins 3259) One of the best private hospitals in the city.

ⓘ Getting There & Away

AIR
The main airport, **Aeroporto Internacional Eduardo Gomes** (☑92 3652-1210; www4.infraero.gov.br/aeroportos/aeroporto-internacional-de-manaus-eduardo-gomes/; Av Santos Dumont 1350), is located 13km north of the city center. Charter planes and smaller regional airlines may use a separate terminal (known as 'Eduardinho'), about 600m east of the main one.

BOAT
Large passenger boats plying the Rio Solimões use Manaus' main passenger port, **Estação Hidroviária de Manaus** (☑92 3233 7061; www.portodemanaus.com.br; Porto Flutuante). Boats going downstream to Belém usually stop at Itacoatiara, Parintins, Santarém and Monte Alegre. Headed up the Rio Solimões, boats call at Tefé, Benjamin Constant and Tabatinga. Boats up the Rio Madeira to Porto Velho stop at Manicoré and Humaitá.

The main port's ticket office sells passage for most long-distance riverboats. Avoid the hawkers on the sidewalk out front; although they're slightly cheaper, you're the first to be bumped if the boat is full.

Speedboats use the smaller **Porto Manaus Moderna** (behind Mercado Municipal Adolfo Lisboa). These go to **Tefé** (R$270, 13 hours) at 6am on Tuesdays; and to **Tabatinga** (R$600, 36 hours) at 6am on Tuesdays, Thursdays, Fridays and Sundays.

 GETTING TO GUYANA

The capital of Roraima state, Boa Vista is a spot without great traveler thrills, but it's a useful gateway to Guyana. It's linked to Manaus by five daily buses (R$170 to R$230, 10 to 12 hours). From Boa Vista, there are four daily buses to little Bonfim (R$25, 1½ hours) on the Guyanese border.

For Guyana, get an exit stamp from the Polícia Federal near the river, which forms the international border. From there, walk (an hour) or hire a Guyanese taxi (around R$30) for the drive to immigration (where they'll stop and wait for you) then into downtown Lethem another 5km further.

Boats heading up the Rio Negro to **Novo Airão** use **Porto São Raimundo** (Coração de Jesus), a seedy port about 1.5km northwest of the center. These depart at 8pm on Tuesdays and Thursdays (R$48, 9 to 10 hours).

BUS

Eucatur (☑ 92 3301-5800; www.eucatur.com.br) and Asatur have buses to Boa Vista (R$170 to R$230, 10 to 12 hours).

❶ Getting Around

Buses 306 'Aeroporto' (R$3.80) and the air-conditioned bus 813 'Aeroporto-Ejecutivo' (R$8) run half-hourly between the airport and Praça da Matriz. In town, the most convenient stops are Praça da Matriz and on Av Getúlio Vargas near Rua José Clemente.

These same two buses also stop near the bus station (which is small and easy to miss, so keep your eyes peeled).

Taxis at the airport charge a fixed R$75 for the 20-minute ride into town, while the return trip costs around R$65. In either case, be sure to agree on a price before setting off.

Novo Airão

☑ 0XX92 / POP 18,600

On the other side of the Rio Negro from Manaus, Novo Airão has become an increasingly popular gateway for ecotours on the Rio Negro and its tributaries, including some of the Amazon's most rewarding destinations, such as the Reserva Extrativista Baixo Rio Branco-Jauaperi and the Anavilhanas Archipelago. As a town, Novo Airão is also a smaller, more manageable alternative to Manaus, with a handful of good lodging, eating and shopping possibilities.

⊙ Sights & Activities

Typical excursions near Novo Airão run to neighboring riverside communities, the **Parque Nacional de Anavilhanas**, and a series of local caves (more like rocky overhangs). For something multiday and further afield,

consider the **Reserva Extrativista Baixo Rio Branco-Jauaperi** (Xixuaú-Xipariná).

★ **Visit Amazônia**   ECOTOUR

(☑ 92 99114-6038, 92 99215-1648; www.visitamazonia.org; Av Presidente Getulio Vargas) This agency's owner, Chris Clark, a no-nonsense Scotsman, has spent decades helping to protect – and establish responsible ecotourism in – the gorgeous animal-rich Reserva Extrativista Baixo Rio Branco-Jauaperi, also known as Xixuaú-Xipariná. He still specializes in highly recommended trips there but also runs tours from Novo Airão to the Anavilhanas Archipelago and elsewhere.

Plan on at least a week if going to the Xixuaú, two weeks for the Xipariná.

Em Cantos da Amazônia   ECOTOUR

(☑ 92 3365-1023, 92 9229-6667; www.emcantosdaamazonia.com; Pousada Bela Vista, Av Presidente Getulio Vargas 47, at Av Ajuricaba) Day trips with this amiable operator based out of the Pousada Bela Vista explore the islands and waterways of the Anavilhanas Archipelago, the Madada Caves and nearby riverside villages, while more expensive excursions, including multiday trips, go as far as **Jaú National Park**.

Ama Boto   WILDLIFE

(☑ 93 99337-6510; Antenor Carlos Frederico; adult/child R$15/7.50; ⊙ 8am-5pm) This dolphin-feeding operation helped put Novo Airão on the map. Such is its popularity that now, thankfully, swimming with the dolphins has been stopped, but watching them feed makes for a fine photo opportunity. Visits begin on the hour (except 1pm) with a 15-minute, Portuguese-only presentation on pink dolphins, followed by the feeding.

Located 500m upriver from Pousada Bela Vista, just past the marina.

🛏 Sleeping & Eating

★ **Pousada Bela Vista**   POUSADA $$

(☑ 92 99229-6667, 92 3365-1023; www.pousadabelavista.com; Av Presidente Getulio Vargas 47; s/d/

BOATS FROM MANAUS

DESTINATION	DEPARTURE	DURATION	HAMMOCK/CABIN (R$) FROM
Belém	11am Wed & Fri	4 days	350/1100
Porto Velho	6pm Tue	4 days	240/660
Santarém	11am Mon-Sat	36 hrs	180/800
Tefé	5-6am Tue-Thu, Sat & Sun	36 hrs	175/650
Tabatinga	noon Wed, Fri & Sat	7 days	400/1620

TRIPLE FRONTIER

On the Amazon's northeast bank – about 1100km west of Manaus – Tabatinga (Brazil) and Leticia (Colombia) are separated by an invisible international border. The opposite bank of the river and the islands in the middle of it are part of Peru. Santa Rosa, Peru's border settlement, is on an island. This 'triple frontier' has travel routes linking all three countries and is a good base for jungle trips. Leticia is the largest and most pleasant of the three border towns and has the best services. Tabatinga is linked by air with Manaus. Slow boats to Manaus (hammock R$400, seven days) leave from Tabatinga's Porto Fluvial every Wednesday and Saturday, plus some Tuesdays, between 8am and 2pm. Arrive early to stake out good hammock space, as boats can be quite crowded. Speedboats operated by **Ajato** (☑ 92 3412-2227, in Manaus 92 3622-6047; ☺ 8am-5pm Mon-Fri, to noon Sat) leave Tabatinga for Manaus (R$600, 36 hours) on Tuesday, Thursday, Saturday and Sunday mornings.

To Colombia

You are free to move between Tabatinga and Leticia as much as you like, but if you plan to travel onward, even to Amacayacu National Park, you should clear immigration for both countries before leaving town. There's a **Colombian Consulate** (☑ 97 3412-2104; http://tabatinga.consulado.gov.co; Sampaio 623; ☺ 7am-1pm Mon-Fri) in Tabatinga. **Brazilian immigration** (☑ 97 3412-2180; Av da Amizade 26; ☺ 8am-6pm) is 100m south of Rua Duarte Coelho, a few blocks from the waterfront.

To Peru

High-speed passenger boats between Tabatinga and Iquitos (Peru) are operated by Transtur (p657) and Transportes Golfinho (p657). Boats depart Tabatinga's Porto da Feira daily around 5am, Brazilian time (boarding begins an hour earlier) arriving in Iquitos about 10 hours later; fares are US$75 each way. Be sure to get a Brazilian exit stamp (p423) the day before; you'll stop first at the island community of Santa Rosa, where the Policía Internacional Peruviano (PIP) handles Peruvian border control. There are slower, cheaper boats to Iquitos, but they are not comfortable and some are unsafe.

If you just want to get to Santa Rosa, small motorboats go back and forth frequently from Porto da Feria (R$4, five minutes) from around 6am to 6pm.

---

tw/tr incl breakfast R$210/260/310/360; ❄ ☎ ⊠) Easily Novo Airão's best midrange guesthouse and a wonderful place to take a break from life on the road, Pousada Bela Vista is run by a German-Brazilian couple and features comfortable rooms adorned with richly colorful paintings by a local artist, as well as a swimming pool and the town's best Rio Negro views. It has great meal and bar service too.

There's outdoor gym equipment or hammocks, depending on your needs, as well as colorfully painted children's playground equipment.

An in-house tour operator, Em Cantos da Amazônia, runs day trips and multiday excursions.

★ **Mirante do Gavião Amazon Lodge** LODGE $$$
(☑ 92 3365 1181; www.mirantedogaviao.com.br; Francisco Cardoso; s incl breakfast R$1031-1526,

d incl breakfast R$1788-2662; ❄ ☎ ⊠) 🌿 This lodge at Novo Airão's northern end is a real stunner. Everything here is architecturally striking, from its tree-house rooms to those that resemble the upturned hulls of local fishing boats, which maximize natural airflow. Rooms are large and supremely comfortable; tree-house rooms are the smallest, but have the best Rio Negro views. There's an outstanding opensided **restaurant** (☑ 92 3365 1181; www.mirantedogaviao.com.br; Francisco Cardoso; mains R$45-78; ☺ noon-9pm; 🍴) by the water.

Everything here is built from sustainable local wood, and there's an observation tower and riverside games room. A planned expansion will only bring the number of rooms to ten, ensuring that the sense of personal service remains.

The lodge's in-house tour operator, **Expedição Katerre** (☑ 92 3365-1644; www.katerre.

com; Francisco Cardoso), is similarly excellent, and all-inclusive packages are possible.

★ Flor do Luar BRAZILIAN $$

(☑93 99418-0865; Av Presidente Getulio Vargas; mains R$26-45; ☺9am-5pm Fri-Sun) One of the Amazon's best restaurants, Flor do Luar sits on a floating pontoon on the Rio Negro and serves fabulous food and cold beers. The specialty is the *banda de tambaqui assada,* a local fish cooked on the grill with plantains, but start with the brilliant *dadinho de tapioca* (deep-fried tapioca croquettes). You can even swim from the waterfront platform.

If only they opened for other days of the week and for dinner, we'd never leave. There's an art gallery attached.

❶ Getting There & Away

BOAT

Riverboats travel a few times a week between Novo Airão and Manaus (R$48, nine to ten hours). From Manaus, they leave around 8pm on Tuesday and Friday. Going the other way, they depart Novo Airão's impressive (albeit rather under-used) port around 8pm on Sunday, Monday and Thursday.

BUS & SHARED TAXI

Collective taxi services (referred to locally as *taxi lotação*) are quick and plentiful, zipping between Manaus and Novo Airão ($60, 2½ hours) many times per day. The taxi stop in Manaus is on the westbound side of AM-070, about 700m before the bridge; taxis depart as soon as there are four passengers, from roughly 6am to 5pm, and will drop you at your hotel. Leaving **Novo Airão** (Av Ajuricaba), the stop is on the main drag at the northern (river) end of town; hotel drop-off in Manaus costs an extra R$40. Alternately, **Arauná buses** (☑92 3615-1110, Manaus 92 3642-5757; Av Ajuricaba) leave Manaus' bus station at 11:30am and 4pm, and leave Novo Airão at 5:30am and 4pm (R$50, four hours).

The Amazon

POP 21 MILLION

Named after female warriors of Greek mythology, the Amazon is itself a place of near-mythical status. What traveler drawn to the wild places of the planet hasn't imagined a trip to the Amazon, not only to admire the towering trees, secretive wildlife and awesome river, but to enter, in a real sense, the very life spring of the planet? Expecting a Discovery Channel–like experience (jaguars in every tree, anacondas on every shore) is a recipe for disappointment. In fact, the Amazon's quintessential experiences are more sublime than superlative: canoeing through a flooded forest, dozing in a hammock on a boat chugging upriver, waking to the otherworldly cry of howler monkeys. On a river whose size is legendary, it's actually the little things that make it special. Give it some time, and the Amazon is all this and more.

Planning a Jungle Trip

While anything's possible, the most common trip is three to five days based at a jungle lodge or on a riverboat, with day trips for hiking, canoeing, fishing for piranha, spotting caiman at night and visiting local villages. Sleeping in hammocks in the forest for a night or two is usually possible, but not required. Some operators also offer so-called survival tours, which are spent mostly or entirely in forest camps.

'White' rivers, such as the Lago Mamorí region, tend to have a higher density of wildlife than 'black' ones, like the Rio Negro. But they also have more mosquitoes and somewhat thicker vegetation, which inhibits wildlife-viewing.

You'll need sturdy shoes or boots, long pants, a long-sleeved shirt, a raincoat, insect repellent, a flashlight, a water bottle. Binoculars are also highly recommended. Leave whatever you don't need at your hotel in Manaus – virtually all offer free, secure luggage storage.

❶ Dangers & Annoyances

Most travelers to the Amazon have a wonderful time. But Manaus is teeming with scammers and touts, and it helps to know how to avoid them. Cut-rate tours might have awful accommodations and/or surly guides in damaged forests free of wildlife. Here are some tips and pointers to avoid getting scammed:

➡ Don't be naive. The smooth-talking guy who approaches you with promises of an epic adventure at a rock-bottom price, is scamming you. Period.

➡ No legitimate tour agency 'fishes' for clients at the airport.

➡ Never pay for a tour anywhere except at the agency's main office.

➡ Above all, don't risk your life to save a little time or money.

Tours

Most agencies have a small lodge or jungle camp where guests stay and activities such as canoeing, hiking and fishing are launched. Many have amenities such as electricity and flush toilets, but not all. Prices usually include meals, lodging, transport and guides, and range between R$150 to R$350 per person per day. Prices vary primarily by the type of accommodations: hammocks with shared toilets are the cheapest option, followed by dorms and private rooms, then riverboats and specialized tours.

★ Amazon Antonio Jungle Tours
ECOTOUR

(✆ 92 3234-1294, 92 99961-8314; www.antoniojungletours.com; Hostel Manaus, Rua Lauro Cavalcante 231) Taking travelers to the wildlife-rich, scenic (and, in the north, mosquito-free) Rio Urubu, Antonio Gomes runs some of the region's best tours. Depending on water levels, you can hike deep into primary forest, canoe quietly through the flooded forest, visit local communities, fish for piranhas and spend time out on the Amazon itself.

★ Amazon Eco Adventures
ECOTOUR

(✆ 92 98831-1011; www.amazonecoadventures.com; 10 de Julho, at Tapajós) Amazon Eco Adventures is an excellent choice, offering tours with small groups, comfortable speedboats, their own overnight boat and top guides. You'll go swimming at the meeting of the waters, and activities like visiting indigenous villages don't have a voyeuristic feel. Their trips to Presidente Figueiredo are equally rewarding, forgoing the touristy waterfalls for caves and falls where few visitors go.

★ Amazônia Expeditions
ECOTOUR

(✆ 92 3671-2731; www.amazoniaexpeditions.com. br; Rua Miguel Ribas 1339) This experienced operator has decades of experience leading tour groups as well as prestigious scientific expeditions. They're one of few groups that goes up the Rio Negro to the Reserva Extrativista Baixo Rio Branco-Jauaperi (p422), and guides are professional and knowledgeable about wildlife and botany.

Amazonas Indian Turismo
ECOTOUR

(✆ 92 99240-5888; amazonasindian@hotmail.com; Andradas 311) This longtime budget agency has a rustic camp on the Rio Urubu, with latrine toilets and no electricity. You won't spend much time there, though, as the operator specializes in multiday hikes through the forest, sleeping in makeshift camps, with hammocks slung between two trees. It's notable for being indigenous-owned and operated; most guides are Wapixano, and all speak English.

Amazon Gero Tours
ECOTOUR

(✆ 9299983-6273,9299198-0111; www.amazongero tours.com; Tapajós 27) The effusive Gero Mesquita, an all-round good guy, runs a popular lodge in the Juma-Mamori area with comfortable dorms and private rooms, and a cadre of skilled guides (several former guides have opened agencies of their own). Besides standard tours, Gero arranges multiday treks into untouched forest and organizes 'social sustainability' programs where travelers work on much needed community projects.

Amazon Tree Climbing
ECOTOUR

(✆ 92 8195-8585; www.amazontreeclimbing. com; Caravelle 22a, Tarumã) Yellow-shirted guides lend a youthful vibe to this outfit, whose tours range from half-day trips near Manaus with views of the Meeting of the Waters to all-day excursions that may also include visiting an indigenous village. Getting to the top of the massive trees can be quite challenging physically, but the experience is unforgettable.

Porto Velho

⌖ 0XX69 / POP 448,000

Porto Velho is a vital link in Brazil's agricultural economy, as soybeans and other products are shipped on huge barges from here down the Rio Madeira and transferred directly to ocean liners headed abroad. That same ride – albeit on a boat not a barge – draws some travelers up from Cuiabá and the Pantanal on the slow route to Manaus and the Amazon. The city itself has a few bright spots, but mostly serves as a transfer point.

Well positioned sleeping options include **Vitória Palace Hotel** (✆ 69 3221-9232; Duque de Caxias 745; s/d R$60/75; ❋ 🖥), with aging but tidy, high-ceilinged rooms. For cheap eats, check out the buffet at **Caffé Restaurante** (✆ 69 3224-3176; Av Carlos Gomes 1097; per kg from R$40; ⊙ 11am-3pm Mon-Sat), and for nightlife, hit the cluster of boisterous bars near Av Pinheiro Machado and Av Presidente Dutra.

Domestic flights leave from Porto Velho's Jorge Teixeira de Oliveira International Airport (PVH), 7km north of the center. A taxi into town costs R$40, or catch a local bus (to your right when exiting the terminal).

Boats to Manaus (hammock R$290, double cabin with fan/air-con R$790/1020, 2½ days) leave three times weekly from the river port in the center. Buy tickets from authorized brokers such as **Agência Monte Sinai** (☑69 99346-7101, 69 3223-1987; transportes montesinai@hotmail.com; ☺8am-6pm Mon-Sat).

Buses and collective taxis (R$120, four hours) run to Guajará-Mirim. Buses also serve Rio Branco (R$115, nine to 10 hours, nine daily) and Cuiabá (R$220 to R$370, 26 hours, eight daily). From the bus station to the center (3km), take bus 201 or a cab (R$15).

Guajará-Mirim

☑0XX69 / POP 44,700

In this pleasant backwater of a border town just opposite Guayaramerín (Bolivia), bushy trees shade red-earth-stained sidewalks from the relentless sun.

Hotel Mine-Estrela (☑69 3541-1206; Av 15 de Novembro 460; s/d R$60/100; ❄☎) offers aging but adequate rooms on the main street between the bus station and the port. Nearby restaurants include **Oásis** (☑69 3541-1621; Av 15 de Novembro 460; per kg R$39; ☺11am-3pm Wed-Mon), whose worthwhile lunch buffet features freshly grilled meats.

Bradesco (Av Costa Marques 430; ☺9am-2pm Mon-Fri) has ATMs. Change bolivianos and reais with the money changers at Guayaramerín's port.

Buses (R$80, six to seven hours, seven daily) and *colectivos* (R$120, four hours) run from the bus station, 2km east of the port, to Porto Velho. Taxis between the station and the center cost R$30 to R$40; mototaxis R$18.

ℹ GETTING TO BOLIVIA FROM GUAJARÁ-MIRIM

Motorboats (R$10, 10 minutes) to Guayaramerín, Bolivia depart 24 hours a day from the port at the end of the main street 15 de Novembro. Get your Brazilian exit stamp at the **Polícia Federal** (☑69 3541-0200; cnr Avs Presidente Dutra & Bocaiúva; ☺7am-9pm). Bolivian entry visas (US$160, generally required for US citizens only) can normally be issued the same day at the **Bolivian Consulate** (☑69 3541-8622; 15 de Novembro 255; ☺8am-noon & 2-6pm Mon-Fri) near the riverfront.

Rio Branco

☑0XX68 / POP 370,000

Rio Branco, the capital of Acre, was founded in 1882 by rubber-tappers on the banks of the Rio Acre. Once a brash, uneasy town, Rio Branco has transformed itself into a genuinely pleasant place, with several excellent cultural outlets and easy access to some interesting sites, including Xapuri, the hometown of the environmentalist Chico Mendes.

Beige-green **Palacio Rio Branco** (Praça Povos da Floresta; ☺8am-6pm Tue-Fri, 4-6pm Sat & Sun) FREE is a restored art-deco masterpiece holding a historical exhibition. Banks with ATMs are nearby. The **Museu da Borracha** (Rubber Museum; ☑68 3223-1202; Av Ceará 1441; ☺8am-6pm Tue-Fri) FREE is housed in a restored mansion, with exhibits on the history of rubber-tapping, and the life and work of Chico Mendes.

Service is amiable and the rooms are cozy at the small, central **AFA Hotel** (☑68 3224-1396; Ribeiro 109; s/d R$100/150; ❄☎). The riverside **Mercado Velho** (Praça Bandeira; dishes from R$6; ☺7am-10pm) is a great place for a meal or late-afternoon beer. It also hosts evening and weekend cultural events.

The small **Aeroporto de Rio Branco** (☑68 3211-1000; www4.infraero.gov.br/aeroportos/aeroporto-de-rio-branco-placido-de-castro; Av Plácido de Castro), 22km northwest of town, has flights to Brasília and Porto Velho. Bus 304 (signed 'Custódio Freire') runs between the airport and town roughly every 45 minutes (R$3.50, 45 minutes, 5am to 11:30pm).

Long-distance buses leave from the Rodoviária Internacional de Rio Branco, 8km southwest of town. Buses run to Xapuri (R$38, 3½ hours, 6am and 1:45pm), Brasiléia (R$48, four hours, 6am, noon and 2:45pm) and Porto Velho (R$115, nine to ten hours, three daily). From the bus terminal catch a 'Norte-Sul,' 'Parque Industrial' or 'Jacarandá' bus (R$3.50, 20 to 30 minutes, every 15 minutes).

Xapuri

☑0XX68 / POP 11,670

This tidy little town of neat wooden houses along broad streets is one of the more rewarding spots in the Brazilian Amazon. It was home to Brazil's great environmental and labor hero, whom you can learn about in the **Casa Chico Mendes** (Batista de Moraes 494; ☺8:30am-4:30pm Tue-Fri, 9am-1pm Sat)

> **ℹ GETTING TO BOLIVIA & PERU**
>
> West of Xapuri, the town of Brasiléia sits across the Rio Acre from considerably more hectic Cobija, Bolivia. Brasiléia has ATMs, money changers and a Bolivian consulate. **Pousada Las Palmeras** (☑ 68 3546-3302; www.facebook.com/pousadalaspalmeras.brasileia; Odilon Pratagi 125, at Geny Assis; s/d R$60/80; ✷ 🌐) is an appealing sleeping option with an excellent breakfast. Buses run to Rio Branco (R$35, four hours) and Xapuri (R$15, two hours). Collective taxis do the same trips for double the money and half the time.
>
> You can freely cross the bridge between Brasiléia and Cobija, but if you're heading further into Bolivia, get an exit stamp from the **Polícia Federal** (☑ 68 3546-3204; ⊘ 8am-7pm) in Brasiléia's neighboring town, Epitaciolândia, just across the main international bridge. Buses from Rio Branco or Xapuri will drop you there. Cobija has places to stay, an airport and arduous bus connections.
>
> For Peru, get an exit stamp in Epitaciolândia, catch a bus to Assis (R$15, two hours) and cross the Rio Acre to Iñapari (Peru). Assis has better accommodations than Iñapari if you need to spend the night. Buses from Rio Branco to Assis theoretically stop at the Polícia Federal en route – check beforehand.

FREE. The simple house is where Mendes and his family lived until his murder in 1988. Tours include a graphic description of the moment he was shot, with bloodstains still on the walls. Across the street, the Chico Mendes Foundation center has poster-sized photos of Mendes and a collection of personal items and international awards.

A short walk from the bus terminal is **Pousada das Chapurys** (☑ 68 3542-2253; www.facebook.com/pousadachapurys; Sadala Koury 1385; s/d/tr R$80/120/150; ✷ 🌐), an old standby whose friendly owners were close friends of Chico Mendes. A park near the plaza on Rua Brandão has laid-back spots to sit outdoors with a pizza or beer. To experience the natural setting where Mendes first tapped rubber trees and collected Brazil nuts, head 32km outside Xapuri to **Pousada Ecológica Seringal Cachoeira** (☑ 68 99943-4747; www.facebook.com/seringalcachoeira; dm R$75, d R$150, all incl breakfast; ✷), a cozy ecolodge with dorms, chalets, meals (lunch and dinner R$30), guided hikes and activities.

Buses run to Rio Branco (R$38, 3½ hours) and Brasiléia (R$15, two hours, 10am).

UNDERSTAND BRAZIL

Brazil Today

Even a people accustomed to Brazil's widespread corruption were shocked at the vast size of the scandals that have rocked the country in the last few years. The magnitude of the scandal exposed by Operação Lava Jato (Operation Car Wash), which first came to light in 2014, boggles the imagination. This colossal kickback scheme was tied to Petrobras, Brazil's state-run oil company, as well as Odebrecht, the massive multinational construction firm headquartered in Brazil. The money laundering involved more than US$5 billion in bribes, and led to the convictions of over 200 of the country's top executives and politicians – including former president Lula and Rio state governor Sergio Cabral.

The repercussions from the scandal have sent shockwaves rippling through the county, and beyond, with at least 10 other countries involved. Brazil was already reeling from a crippling recession (in part brought on by overspending on the 2014 World Cup and 2016 Olympics), and the scandal only made things worse – undermining investor confidence and leading to mass layoffs by the scandal-plagued industries. The economy contracted by more than 3.5% in both 2015 and 2016 – its longest recession in history. As unemployment surged and the currency collapsed, the number of Brazilians living in poverty grew by a whopping 33% (an estimated six million people fell below the poverty line between 2014 and 2018). With prices rising and wages falling, workers have taken to the streets in mass protests; in 2018 one trucker strike left the country paralyzed for nearly two weeks. Huge budget cuts to schools, hospitals and other public institutions have also had devastating effects; a raging fire destroyed most of the collection inside Brazil's National History Museum, a 200-year-old icon that housed some of the most important archeological collections in South America.

The good news is that after three years of crisis, Brazil's economy was finally climbing out of the red by late 2018. Business investment was on the rise as the political scandal (somewhat) subsided, and production rose significantly across many sectors (agriculture, electronics and the automotive industry, among them).

Meanwhile, Brazil has continued to invest in renewable energy, and today sustainable sources meet more than 70% of the country's energy needs (some months reaching above 86% of Brazil's domestically produced electricity). Recent years have seen the opening of massive solar farms – including two in 2017 that are among the largest on the continent. Wind power has also grown in leaps and bounds, with installed capacity of 13.1MW in 2018 – a 35% increase from just three years prior. That said, oil production remains a huge part of the Brazilian economy, and finding the balance between green energy and petroleum will be one of the hot political topics in the years ahead – along with the challenge of preserving Brazil's natural environment (particularly the Amazon) amid relentless economic pressures, driven in part by the agriculture lobby.

History

Brazil's Indigenous Peoples

Little is known of Brazil's first inhabitants, but from the few fragments left behind (mostly pottery, trash mounds and skeletons), archaeologists estimate that the first humans may have arrived 50,000 years ago, predating any other estimates in the whole American continent.

The population at the time of the Portuguese landing in 1500 is also a mystery, and estimates range from two to six million. There were likely more than 1000 tribes living as nomadic hunter-gatherers or in more settled, agricultural societies.

When the Portuguese first arrived, they had little interest in the natives; and the heavily forested land offered nothing for the European market. All that changed when Portuguese merchants expressed interest in the red dye from brazilwood (which later gave the colony its name), and slowly colonists arrived to harvest the land.

The natural choice for the work, of course, was the indigenous people. Initially the natives welcomed the strange, smelly foreigners and offered them their labor in exchange for the awe-inspiring metal tools and the fascinating Portuguese liquor. But soon the newcomers abused their customs, took their best land and ultimately enslaved them.

When colonists discovered that sugarcane grew well in the colony, the natives' labor was more valuable than ever and soon the sale of local slaves became Brazil's second-largest commercial enterprise. It was an industry dominated by *bandeirantes,* brutal men who hunted the indigenous people in the interior and captured or killed them. Their exploits, more than any treaty, secured the huge interior of South America for Portuguese Brazil.

Jesuit priests went to great lengths to protect the indigenous community. But they lacked the resources to stymie the attacks (and the Jesuits were later expelled from Brazil in 1759). Natives who didn't die at the hands of the colonists often died from introduced European diseases.

Sugar & Slavery

During the 17th century African slaves replaced indigenous prisoners on the plantations. From 1550 until 1888 about 3.5 million slaves were shipped to Brazil – almost 40% of the total that came to the New World. The Africans were considered better workers and were less vulnerable to European diseases, but they resisted slavery strongly. *Quilombos,* communities of runaway slaves, formed throughout the colonial period. They ranged from *mocambos,* small groups hidden in the forests, to the great republic of Palmares, which survived much of the 17th century. Led by the African king Zumbí, it's thought Palmares had between 11,000 and 20,000 residents at its height (scholars debate the population).

According to Comissão Pró-Índio in São Paulo, an estimated 2000 to 3000 villages that formed as *quilombos* remain in Brazil today, their growth only stopped by abolition itself (1888).

Survivors on the plantations sought solace in their African religion and culture through song and dance. The slaves were given perfunctory instruction in Catholicism and a syncretic (combined) religion rapidly emerged. Spiritual elements from many African tribes, such as the Yorubá, were preserved and made palatable to slave masters by adopting a facade of Catholic saints. Such were the roots of modern Candomblé (Afro-Brazilian religion of Bahia) and Macumba (religion of African origin), prohibited by law until recently.

Life on the plantations was miserable, but an even worse fate awaited many slaves. In the 1690s, gold was discovered in present-day Minas Gerais, and soon the rush was on. Wild boomtowns such as Vila Rica de Ouro Prêto (Rich Town of Black Gold) sprang up in the mountain valleys. Immigrants flooded the territory, and countless slaves were brought from Africa to dig and die in Minas.

The Colony Under the King

For years, the ruling powers of Portugal viewed the colony of Brazil as little more than a money-making enterprise. That attitude changed, however, when Napoleon marched on Lisbon in 1807. The prince regent (later known as Dom João VI) immediately transferred his court to Brazil. He stayed on even after Napoleon's Waterloo in 1815, and when he became king in 1816 he declared Rio de Janeiro the capital of a united kingdom of Brazil and Portugal, making Brazil the only New World colony to serve as the seat of a European monarch. In 1821, Dom João finally returned to Portugal, leaving his son Pedro in Brazil as regent.

The following year the Portuguese parliament attempted to return Brazil to colonial status. According to legend, Pedro responded by pulling out his sword and shouting out '*Independência ou morte!*' (Independence or death!), crowning himself Emperor Dom Pedro I. Portugal was too weak to fight its favorite colony, so Brazil won independence without bloodshed.

Dom Pedro I ruled for nine years. He scandalized the country by siring a string of illegitimate children, and was finally forced to abdicate in favor of his five-year-old son, Dom Pedro II. Until the future emperor reached adolescence, Brazil suffered a period of civil war. In 1840 Dom Pedro II ascended the throne with overwhelming public support. During his 50-year reign he nurtured an increasingly powerful parliamentary system, went to war with Paraguay, meddled in Argentine and Uruguayan affairs, encouraged mass immigration, abolished slavery and ultimately forged a state that would do away with the monarchy forever.

The Brazilian Republic

During the 19th century, coffee replaced sugar as Brazil's primary export, at one time supplying three-quarters of world demand. With mechanization and the building of Brazil's first railroads, profits soared and the coffee barons gained enormous influence.

In 1889 a coffee-backed military coup toppled the antiquated empire, sending the emperor into exile. The new Brazilian Republic adopted a constitution modeled on the US, and for nearly 40 years Brazil was governed by a series of military and civilian presidents through which the armed forces effectively ruled the country.

Coffee remained king until the market collapsed during the global economic crisis of 1929. The weakened planters of São Paulo, who controlled the government, formed an opposition alliance with the support of nationalist military officers. When their presidential candidate, Getúlio Vargas, lost the 1930 elections, the military seized power and handed him the reins.

Vargas proved a gifted maneuverer, and dominated the political scene for 20 years. At times his regime was inspired by the Italian and Portuguese fascist states of Mussolini and Salazar: he banned political parties, imprisoned opponents and censored the press. He remained in and out of the political scene until 1954, when the military called for him to step down. Vargas responded by writing a letter to the people of Brazil, then shooting himself in the heart.

Juscelino Kubitschek, the first of Brazil's big spenders, was elected president in 1956. His motto was '50 years' progress in five.' His critics responded with '40 years of inflation in four.' The critics were closer to the mark, owing to the huge debt Kubitschek incurred during the construction of Brasília. By the early 1960s, inflation gripped the Brazilian economy, and Castro's victory in Cuba had spread fears of communism. Brazil's fragile democracy was crushed in 1964 when the military overthrew the government.

Brazil stayed under the repressive military regime for almost 20 years. Throughout much of this time the economy grew substantially, at times borrowing heavily from international banks. But it exacted a heavy toll on the country. Ignored social problems grew dire. Millions of people came to the cities, and favelas (informal communities) spread at exponential rates.

Recent Decades

The last few decades have been very good to Brazil. After Fernando Collor de Mello, its first democratically elected president in 30 years, was removed from office on charges of corruption in 1992, widespread economic growth stabilized and blessed the South American workhorse.

Collor's replacement, Itamar Franco, introduced Brazil's present currency, the real. This sparked an economic boom that continues to this day, though it was his successor, former finance minister Fernando Henrique Cardoso, who presided through the mid-1990s over a growing economy and record foreign investment. He is most credited with laying the groundwork that put Brazil's hyperinflation to bed, though often at the neglect of social problems.

In 2002, socialist Luiz Inácio Lula da Silva won the presidency under a promise of social reform. From a humble working-class background, Lula rose to become a trade unionist and a strike leader in the early 1980s. He later founded the Workers Party (PT), a magnet for his many followers seeking social reform. Lula ran one of the most financially prudent two-term administrations in years while still addressing Brazil's egregious social problems. Unfortunately, Lula's administration had some setbacks, most notably the wide-reaching *Mensalão* corruption scandal that broke in 2005, causing a number of his PT party members to resign in disgrace, and ended in 2012 in a sensational Supreme Court trial that captivated the country.

Lula's successor and fellow party member, Dilma Rousseff, was elected Brazil's first female president in 2011. A former Marxist guerrilla who was allegedly tortured by the former military regime (who also imprisoned her for several years), her past radicalism proved an appropriate résumé for her administration's hard line on corruption. But ill-fated economic policies amid a billion-dollar corruption scandal surrounding Brazilian oil giant Petrobras aligned to ensure Brazil's eyebrow-lifting economic growth did an about-face.

With huge protests rocking the country, and the country in the grip of its largest recession in history, Rousseff was headed for a fall, and in 2016 she was impeached and removed from office for budgetary violations.

The presidential election in 2018 brought to power an unlikely roster of candidates, including Jair Bolsonaro, a right-wing extremist often described as the Brazilian Donald Trump. A former military officer, Bolsonaro praised strong-arm rulers like Augusto Pinochet and promised to bring law and order back to Brazil. His fiery rhetoric earned him many enemies. He was stabbed during a campaign rally in Minas Gerais, but went on to win the election, garnering over 55% of the vote.

Culture

Brazilian culture has been shaped by the Portuguese, who gave the country its language and religion, and also by the indigenous population, immigrants and Africans. The influence of the latter is particularly strong, especially in the Northeast where African religion, music and cuisine have all shaped Brazilian identity.

Population

In Brazil the diversity of the landscape is matched by that of the people inhabiting it. Indigenous people, Portuguese, Africans (brought to Brazil as slaves) and their mixed-blood offspring made up the population until the late 19th century. Since then there have been waves of immigration by Italians, Spaniards, Germans, Japanese, Russians, Lebanese and others.

Lifestyle

Even though Brazil has the world's eighth-largest economy, with abundant resources and developed infrastructure, the living standard varies wildly. Brazil has one of the world's widest income gaps between rich and poor.

Since the mass urban migration in the mid-19th century, the poorest have lived in favelas that surround every city. Many dwellings consist of little more than a few boards pounded together, and access to clean water, sewage and healthcare are luxuries few favelas enjoy. Drug lords rule the streets and crime is rampant.

The rich often live just a stone's throw away, sometimes separated by nothing more than a highway. Many live in modern fortresses, with security walls and armed guards, enjoying a lifestyle similar to upper classes in Europe and America.

But the beauty of Brazil is when these crowds come together – at a samba club, a football match, a Carnaval parade or on the beach – and meld together seamlessly in celebration. Brazilians love a party, and revelries go on year-round. But it isn't all samba and caipirinhas in the land of the tropics. Brazilians suffer from *saudade*, a nostalgic, often deeply melancholic longing for something. The idea appears in many works by Jobim, Moraes and other great songwriters, and it manifests itself in many forms – from the dull ache of homesickness to the deep regret over past mistakes.

Kindness is both commonplace and expected, and even a casual introduction can lead to deeper friendships. This altruism comes in handy in a country noted for its bureaucracy and long lines. There's the official way of doing things, then there's the *jeitinho*, or the little way around it, and a little kindness – and a few friends – can go a long way.

Religion

Brazil is the world's largest Catholic country, but it embraces diversity and syncretism. Without much difficulty you can find churchgoing Catholics who attend spiritualist gatherings or appeal for help at a *terreiro* (the house of an Afro-Brazilian religious group).

Brazil's principal religious roots comprise the animism of the indigenous people, Catholicism, and African religions introduced by enslaved peoples. The latest arrival is evangelical Christianity, which is spreading all over Brazil, especially in poorer areas.

The Afro-Brazilian religions emerged when the colonists prohibited enslaved people from practicing their native religions. Not so easily deterred, they simply gave Catholic names to their African gods and continued to worship them. The most orthodox of the religions is Candomblé. Rituals take place in the Yoruba language in a *casa de santo* or *terreiro*, directed by a *pai de santo* or *mãe de santo* (literally, 'a saint's father or mother' – the Candomblé priests).

Candomblé gods are known as *orixás* and each person is believed to be protected by one of them. In Bahia and Rio, followers of Afro-Brazilian cults turn out in huge numbers to attend festivals at the year's end – especially those held during the night of December 31 and on New Year's Day. Millions of Brazilians go to the beach at this time to pay homage to Iemanjá, the sea goddess, whose alter ego is the Virgin Mary.

Arts

Architecture

Brazil's most impressive colonial architecture dazzles visitors in cities like Salvador, Olinda, São Luís, Ouro Prêto and Tiradentes. Over the centuries, the names of two architects stand out: Aleijadinho, the genius of 18th-century baroque in Minas Gerais mining towns and Oscar Niemeyer, the 20th-century modernist-functionalist who was chief architect for the new capital, Brasília, in the 1950s and designed many other striking buildings around the country. Niemeyer passed away in 2012 at the age of 104.

Cinema

Brazil's large film industry has produced a number of internationally successful films over the years. In the last decade, the Brazilian industry has continued to produce thought-provoking films and documentaries. Felipe Barbosa's *Casa Grande* (2014) is a coming-of-age story set in Rio about a privileged high-school student who is suddenly thrust into a life of poverty when his father's business collapses. *Laerte-Se* (2017) is a documentary about the triumphs and struggles of one of Brazil's top cartoonists, Laerte Coutinho, who after living as a man for over 50 years decides to reintroduce herself to the world as a woman.

The 2007 hit *Tropa de Elite* (Elite Squad), delves into Rio's crime and corruption from the viewpoint of its most elite police force, BOPE (Special Police Operations Battalion). The same director, José Padilha, initially garnered Brazilian cinema attention with the 2002 *Ônibus 174* (Bus 174), which tells the story of a lone gunman who hijacked a Rio bus in 2000 and held passengers hostage for hours live on national TV.

One of Brazil's top directors, Fernando Meirelles, earned his credibility and an Oscar nomination with the 2002 *Cidade de Deus* (City of God), which showed the brutality of a Rio favela.

Walter Salles, one of Brazil's best-known directors, won much acclaim (and an Oscar) for *Central do Brasil* (Central Station; 1998), the story of a lonely woman accompanying a young homeless boy in search of his father.

For a taste of the dictatorship days see Bruno Barreto's *O Que É Isso Companheiro* (released as *Four Days in September* in the US, 1998), based on the 1969 kidnapping of the US ambassador to Brazil by leftist guerrillas.

Another milestone in Brazilian cinema is the visceral film *Pixote* (1981), which shows life through the eyes of a street kid in Rio. When it was released, it became a damning indictment of Brazilian society.

It was preceded by Carlos Diegues' *Bye Bye Brasil* (1980), which chronicles the adventures of a theater troupe as it tours the country, witnessing the profound changes in Brazilian society in the second half of the 20th century.

Literature

Joaquim Maria Machado de Assis (1839–1908), the son of a freed slave, is one of Brazil's early great writers. Assis had a great sense of humor and an insightful – though cynical – take on human affairs. His major novels were *Quincas Borba, The Posthumous Memoirs of Bras Cubas* and *Dom Casmurro*.

Jorge Amado (1912–2001), Brazil's most celebrated contemporary writer, wrote clever portraits of the people and places of Bahia, notably *Gabriela, Clove and Cinnamon* and *Dona Flor and her Two Husbands*.

Paulo Coelho is Latin America's second-most-read novelist (after Gabriel García Márquez). His new-age fables *The Alchemist* and *The Pilgrimage* launched his career in the mid-1990s.

Music

Samba, a Brazilian institution, has strong African influences and is intimately linked to Carnaval. The most popular form of samba today is *pagode*, a relaxed, informal genre whose leading exponents include singers Beth Carvalho, Jorge Aragão and Zeca Pagodinho.

Bossa nova, another Brazilian trademark, arose in the 1950s, and gained the world's attention in the classic song *The Girl from Ipanema*, composed by Antônio Carlos (Tom) Jobim and Vinícius de Moraes. Bossa nova's founding father, guitarist João Gilberto, still performs, as does his daughter Bebel Gilberto, who has sparked renewed interest in the genre, combining smooth bossa sounds with electronic grooves.

Tropicalismo, which burst onto the scene in the late 1960s, mixed varied Brazilian musical styles with North American rock and pop. Leading figures such as Gilberto Gil and Caetano Veloso are still very much around. Gil, in fact, was Brazil's Minister of Culture from 2003 to 2008.

The list of emerging talent gets longer each day, topped by actor/musician Seu Jorge, who starred in *Cidade de Deus*. Jorge earned accolades in 2005 for the release of *Cru*, an inventive hip-hop album with politically charged beats, as well as the 2010 *Seu Jorge & Almaz*, a critically acclaimed soul, samba and rock collaboration with drummer Pupillo and guitarist Lucio Maia, both members of the legendary rock/hip-hop hybrid Nação Zumbi. His latest, *Músicas Para Churrasco, Vol 2* surfaced in 2015.

Rising stars in the music scene include BaianaSystem, a Salvador-based group who channel traditional Northeastern rhythms with accents from West Africa, the Caribbean and beyond on albums like *Outras Cidades* (2017). Another Salvadoran to be reckoned with is the singer and composer Lucas Santtana, whose 2017 album *Modo Avião* has earned him comparisons with João Gilberto and other legendary Brazilian artists from the past.

Brazilian rock (pronounced 'hock-ey') is also popular. Groups and artists such as Zeca Baleiro, Kid Abelha, Jota Quest, Ed Motta and the punk-driven Legião Urbana are worth a listen.

Wherever you go in Brazil you'll also hear regional musical styles. The most widely known is *forró* (foh-hoh), a lively, syncopated Northeastern music, which mixes *zabumba* (an African drum) beats with accordion sounds. *Axé* is a label for the samba-pop-rock-reggae-funk-Caribbean fusion music that emerged from Salvador in the 1990s, popularized especially by the flamboyant Daniela Mercury and now worshipped stadiums over by Ivete Sangalo. In the Amazon, you'll encounter the rhythms of *carimbo*, and the sensual dance that accompanies it.

Sertanejo, Brazilian country music, catapulted to international fame in 2011 when Michel Teló unleashed the phenomenon that was *Ai Se Eu Te Pego* – perhaps the most famous Brazilian song since *The Girl from Ipanema*.

Sports

Brazil may be the world's largest Catholic country, but *futebol* (soccer) is its religion. And Brazilians are such a devout bunch for good reason. Most people acknowledge that Brazilians play the world's most creative, artistic and thrilling style of football (Brazil is the only country to have won five World Cups – 1958, 1962, 1970, 1994 and 2002), but the national team has bailed out on the early side of recent World Cups and Olympic Games.

The national team's excruciating 7-1 pounding at the hands of Germany in the 2014 FIFA World Cup semifinal on home soil goes down as the most humiliating sporting moment in the country's history. Germany's relentless blitzkrieg – four goals in six minutes! – not only scarred the population for life, but was Brazil's worst-ever defeat at home. It broke their 62-match streak in competitive home matches going back to 1975. Brazil went on to lose to the Netherlands 3-0 in the third-place match, embarrassingly crashing out of their own World Cup in fourth place. Not a soul was caught dead in a national team jersey for the rest of the year.

Since the heartbreaking summer of 2014, things haven't exactly been looking up for the *Seleção* (the nickname for the national side, meaning 'the squad'), despite being led by Neymar, one of the most dynamic young superstars in the game. The 2018 World Cup started off promisingly for Brazil, but they was knocked out of the competition by Belgium in the quarterfinals.

Environment

The Land

The world's fifth-largest country after Russia, Canada, China and the US, Brazil borders every other South American country except Chile and Ecuador. Its 8.5 million sq km area covers almost half the continent.

Brazil has four primary geographic regions: the coastal band, the Planalto Brasileiro, the Amazon Basin as well as the Paraná-Paraguai Basin.

The narrow, 7400km-long coastal band lies between the Atlantic Ocean and the coastal mountain ranges. From the border with Uruguay to Bahia state, steep mountains often come right down to the coast. North of Bahia, the coastal lands are flatter.

The Planalto Brasileiro (Brazilian Plateau) extends over most of Brazil's interior south of the Amazon Basin. It's sliced by several large rivers and punctuated by mountain ranges reaching no more than 3000m.

The thinly populated Amazon Basin, composing 42% of Brazil, is fed by waters from the Planalto Brasileiro to its south, the Andes to the west and the Guyana shield to the north. In the west the basin is 1300km wide; in the east, between the Guyana shield and the Planalto, it narrows to 100km. More than half the 6275km of the Rio Amazonas lies not in Brazil but in Peru, where the river's source is also found. The Amazon and its 1100 tributaries contain an estimated 20% of the world's freshwater. Pico da Neblina (3014m) on the Venezuelan border is the highest peak in Brazil.

The Paraná-Paraguai Basin, in the south of Brazil, extends into Paraguay and Argentina, and includes the large wetland area known as the Pantanal.

Wildlife

Brazil is the most biodiverse country on Earth. It has more known species of plants (56,215), freshwater fish (3000) and mammals (578) than any other country in the world; and isn't far behind in birds (1721) and reptiles (651). Many species live in the Amazon rainforest, which occupies 3.6 million sq km in Brazil and 2.4 million sq km in neighboring countries. It's the world's largest tropical forest and most biologically diverse ecosystem, with 20% of the world's bird and plant species and 10% of its mammals.

Other Brazilian species are widely distributed around the country. For example the biggest Brazilian cat, the jaguar, is found in Amazon and Atlantic rainforests, the cerrado (savanna) and the Pantanal.

Many other Brazilian mammals are found over a broad range of habitats, including five other big cats (puma, ocelot, margay, oncilla and jaguarundi); the giant anteater; 77 primate species, including several types of howler and capuchin monkey, the squirrel monkey (Amazonia's most common primate) and around 20 small species of marmosets and tamarin; the furry, long-nosed coati (a type of raccoon); the giant river otter; the maned wolf; the tapir; peccaries (such as wild boar); marsh and pampas deer; the capybara (the world's largest rodent at 1m long); the pink dolphin, often glimpsed in the Amazon and its tributaries; and the Amazon manatee, an even larger river dweller.

Birds form a major proportion of the wildlife you'll see. The biggest is the flightless, 1.4m-high rhea, found in the cerrado and the Pantanal. The brilliantly colored parrots, macaws, toucans and trogons come in dozens of species. In Amazonia or the Pantanal you may see scarlet macaws and, if you're lucky, blue-and-yellow ones.

In Amazonia or the Pantanal you can't miss the members of the alligator family. One of Brazil's five species, the black caiman, grows up to 6m long. Other aquatic life in the Amazon includes the pirarucu fish, which grows 3m long – its red and silvery-brown scale patterns are reminiscent of Chinese paintings. The infamous piranha comes in about 50 species, found in the river basins of the Amazon, Orinoco, Paraguai and São Francisco, and the rivers of the Guianas.

National Parks

Brazil is home to 73 national parks, managed by **ICMbio** (www.icmbio.gov.br), 26 of which are open to the public.

Parque Nacional da Chapada Diamantina (p381) is in a mountainous region in the Northeast. There's excellent trekking with rivers, waterfalls, caves and swimming holes.

Parque Nacional da Chapada dos Guimarães (p369) is a canyon park with breathtaking views and impressive rock formations on a rocky plateau northeast of Cuiabá.

Parque Nacional da Chapada dos Veadeiros (p365), 200km north of Brasília, is a hilly national park set among waterfalls and natural swimming holes, and featuring an array of rare flora and fauna.

Parque Nacional da Serra dos Órgãos is set in the mountainous terrain of the Southeast; this park is a mecca for rock climbers and mountaineers.

Parque Nacional de Aparados da Serra (☑ 54 3251-1227; www.icmbio.gov.br/parna aparadosdaserra/guia-do-visitante.html; RS-429, Km 18; Brazilian/foreigner R$25/45; ⊙ 8am-6pm Tue-Sun) in the Southeast is famous for its narrow canyon with 700m escarpments.

It features hiking trails with excellent overlooks.

Parque Nacional dos Lençóis Maranhenses (p408) in the Northeast has spectacular beaches, mangroves, dunes and lagoons.

Parque Nacional Marinho de Fernando de Noronha (p392) is Brazil's island Eden with pristine beaches, cerulean waters, world-class diving and snorkeling. It's one of the world's best spots to view spinner dolphins.

Environmental Issues

Sadly, while Brazil is renowned for its forests, it is also notorious for destroying them. At last count more than one-fifth of the Brazilian Amazon rainforest had been completely destroyed. Cutting down forests for cattle ranches and for growing crops (namely soybeans) and for illegal logging are among the chief threats to the Amazon. The rate of deforestation has had ups and downs in recent years, falling year-on-year from 2005 to 2015. It surged again in the last few years, with the rate of deforestation rising by 22% from mid-2017 to mid-2018.

Big development projects are also affecting the Amazon. The government has some 30 large hydroelectric dams in the works for the Amazon region. The biggest is the massive Belo Monte dam on the Rio Xingu in Pará, which flooded nearly 500 sq km of rainforest, and displaced at least 20,000 people, including thousands of indigenous people who have resided along the river for centuries. At the time of writing, half of its 24 turbines were operational. It's expected to be fully operational by 2020.

The Pantanal wetlands also face serious threats, including the rapid spread of intensive soy, cotton and sugarcane farming on Brazil's central plains, which are the source of most of the Pantanal's water. The sugarcane is the raw material of ethanol motor fuel, the international growth of which has led to the creation of dozens of new ethanol distilleries in Mato Grosso do Sul. Herbicides, fertilizers and other chemicals from the plantations drizzle their way into Pantanal waters, and forest clearance on the plains leads to erosion and consequent silting of Pantanal rivers. The growing cities around the Pantanal (many of which lack adequate waste-treatment plants) and ongoing industrial development also pose serious risks to this region.

On Brazil's coasts, growth of cities and burgeoning tourism developments threaten many delicate coastal marine ecosystems, despite the creation of protected areas on extensive tracts of land and sea.

Jair Bolsonaro's rise to power portends more bad news for the environment: hours after being sworn in as president in 2019, he issued an executive order transferring the regulation of new indigenous reserves to the agriculture ministry. This is keeping in line with his campaign promises to open up indigenous lands to mining and commercial farming - a move decried by indigenous leaders and environmentalists.

SURVIVAL GUIDE

ℹ Directory A–Z

ACCESSIBLE TRAVEL
Wheelchair users don't have an easy time in Brazil, but in the large cities there is a concerted effort to keep people mobile. Problems you'll encounter include immensely crowded public buses, and restaurants with entrance steps. It pays to plan your trip through contact with some of the relevant organizations.

Rio is probably the most accessible city in Brazil for travelers with disabilities to get around in, but that doesn't mean it's always easy. The metro system has electronic wheelchair lifts, but these aren't always operational. The streets and sidewalks along the main beaches have curb cuts and are wheelchair accessible, but most other areas do not have cuts. For transport around Rio, contact **Especial Coop Taxi** (☑ 21 3295-9606, WhatsApp 21 99776-5347; www.facebook.com/especialcoop). In São Paulo, contact the the government's **Central de Atendimento do Táxi Acessível** (☑ 11 3740-5544).

Most newer hotels have wheelchair-accessible rooms, and some cable TV is closed captioned.

ACCOMMODATIONS
Brazilian accommodations are simple yet usually clean and reasonably safe, and nearly all come with some form of *café da manha* (breakfast).

Brazil has loads of hostels around the country. A dormitory bed costs between R$40 and R$80 per person.

Brazil hotels are among South America's priciest; a far more charming and local option is a pousada, which typically means a small

family-owned inn, though some hotels call themselves pousadas to improve their charm quotient. Pousadas can cost as little as R$160 for a rustic double, but more than R$600 for the country's most lavish.

ACTIVITIES
Popular activities for adrenaline-fueled adventure include canyoning, paragliding, kitesurfing, wakeboarding, rafting, surfing, trekking, diving and mountain climbing.

Hiking and climbing activities are best during the cooler months, from April to October. Outstanding hiking areas include the national parks of Chapada Diamantina in Bahia, Serra dos Órgãos in Rio de Janeiro state, Chapada dos Veadeiros in Goiás and the Serra de São José near Tiradentes in Minas Gerais.

The best surfing is in Fernando de Noronha between December and March. Also good are the beaches in the South and Southeast: Saquarema, Ilha de Santa Catarina, São Francisco do Sul, Ilha do Mel, Búzios and Rio de Janeiro. In the Northeast, head to Itacaré and Praia da Pipa. The waves are best in the Brazilian winter (June to August).

Búzios in Rio state has good windsurfing and kitesurfing conditions, and access to rental equipment. But Brazil's hardcore windsurfing hot spot is the Ceará coast northwest of Fortaleza, from July to December. Here, Jericoacoara and Canoa Quebrada are the most popular spots.

ELECTRICITY
The electrical current is not standardized in Brazil and can be almost anywhere between 110V and 220V. The most common power points have two sockets, and most will take both round and flat prongs. Carry a converter and use a surge protector with electrical equipment.

SLEEPING PRICE RANGES

The following price ranges refer to a double room with bathroom in high season (December to March). Unless otherwise stated, breakfast is included in the price.

$ less than R$160

$$ R$160–R$350

$$$ more than R$350

The price range for Rio, São Paulo and Brasília is higher:

$ less than R$200

$$ R$200–R$500

$$$ more than R$500

EMBASSIES & CONSULATES

The embassies are all in Brasília, but many countries have consulates in Rio and São Paulo, and often other cities as well. For addresses in Brasília, SES stands for Setor de Embaixadas Sul.

Argentine Embassy (☎ 61 3212-7600; www.ebras.cancilleria.gov.ar; SES Quadra 803, Lote 12, Brasília); **Foz do Iguaçu consulate** (☎ 45 3574-2969; http://cfdig.cancilleria.gov.ar; Travessia Bianchi 26; ☺10am-3pm Mon-Fri); **Porto Alegre consulate** (☎ 51 3321-1360; http://caleg.cancilleria.gov.ar; Coronel Bordini 1033); **São Paulo consulate** (☎ 11 3897-9522; www.cpabl.mrecic.gov.ar; Av Paulista 2313, Jardins)

Australian Embassy (☎ 61 3226-3111; www.brazil.embassy.gov.au; SES, Quadra 801, Lote 7, Brasília); **Rio consulate** (☎ 21 3824-4624; www.dfat.gov.au; 23rd fl, Av Presidente Wilson 231, Centro; ☺10am-4pm Mon-Fri)

Bolivian Consulate (☎ 61 3366-4448; www.embolivia.org.br; SES, Quadra 809, Lote 34, Brasília); **Brasiléia consulate** (☎ 68 3546-5760; Hilário Meireles 236; ☺8am-noon & 2-4pm Mon-Fri); **Corumbá consulate** (p372); Guajará-Mirim consulate (p426); **Rio consulate** (☎ 21 2552-5490; www.consuladodebolivia enrio.org.br; No 101, Av Rui Barbosa 664, Flamengo; ☺9am-2pm Mon-Fri)

Canadian Embassy (☎ 61 3424-5400; www.brazil.gc.ca; SES, Quadra 803, Lote 16, Brasília); **Rio consulate** (☎ 21 2543-3004; www.brasil.gc.ca; 13th fl, Av Atlântica 1130, Copacabana; ☺8am-12:30pm & 1:30-5pm Mon-Thu, 8am-12:30pm Fri); **São Paulo consulate** (☎ 11 5509-4321; www.canadainternational.gc.ca; Av das Nações Unidas 12901, 16th fl, Torre Norte, Brooklin Paulista)

Colombian Embassy (☎ 61 3214-8900; http://brasil.embajada.gov.co; SES, Quadra 803, Lote 10, Brasília); Tabatinga consulate (p423)

Dutch Embassy (☎ 61 3961-3200; www.holandaevoce.nl; SES, Quadra 801, Lote 05, Brasília); **Rio consulate** (☎ 21 2157-5400; www.nederlandenu.nl; 6th fl, Av Ataúlfo de Paiva 204, Leblon; ☺8:30am-4pm Mon-Thu, to noon Fri)

French Embassy (☎ 61 3222-3999; www.br.ambafrance.org; SES, Quadra 801, Lote 04, Brasília); **Rio consulate** (☎ 21 3974-6699; http://riodejaneiro.ambafrance-br.org; Av Presidente Antônio Carlos 58, Centro; ☺8:30am-12:30pm Mon-Fri by appointment, 2:30-4pm Tue & Wed)

German Embassy (☎ 61 3442-7000; www.brasilia.diplo.de; SES, Quadra 807, Lote 25, Brasília); **Rio consulate** (☎ 21 3380-3700; www.rio-de-janeiro.diplo.de; Av Presidente Antônio Carlos 58, Centro; ☺8:30-11:30am Mon, Tue, Thu & Fri, 1-3pm Wed)

Guyanese Embassy (☎ 61 3248-0874; www.embguyana.org.br; SHIS, QI 5, Conjunto 19, Casa 24, Brasília)

Irish Embassy (☎ 61 3248-8800; www.embaixada-irlanda.org.br; SHIS QI 12 Conjunto 5, Casa 9, Brasília)

Israeli Embassy (☎ 61 2105-0500; www.embassies.gov.il; SES, Quadra 809, Lote 38, Brasília)

New Zealand Embassy (☎ 61 3248-9900; www.mfat.govt.nz; SHIS QI 9, Conjunto 16, Casa 1, Brasília); **New Zealand Consulate** (☎ 11 3898-7400; www.mfat.govt.nz/en/countries-and-regions/latin-america; 12th fl, Bela Paulista Bldg, Av Paulista 2421)

Paraguayan Embassy (☎ 61 3242-3020; www.mre.gov.py; SES, Quadra 811, Lote 42, Brasília); Foz do Iguaçu consulate (p360)

Peruvian Embassy (☎ 61 3242-9933; www.consulado.pe; SES, Quadra 811, Lote 43, Brasília); **Rio consulate** (☎ 21 2551-9596; www.consuladoperurio.com.br; 2nd fl, Av Rui Barbosa 314, Flamengo; ☺9am-3pm Mon-Fri)

UK Embassy (☎ 61 3329-2300; www.reinounido.org.br; SES, Quadra 801, Lote 08, Brasília); **Rio consulate** (☎ 21 2555-9600; www.reinounido.org.br; 2nd fl, Praia do Flamengo 284, Flamengo; ☺8:30am-12:30pm & 1:30-4:30pm Mon-Fri); **São Paulo consulate** (☎ 11 3094-2700; www.gov.uk/world/organisations/british-consulate-general-sao-paulo; Ferreira de Araújo 741, 2nd fl, Pinheiros)

Uruguayan Embassy (☎ 61 3322-1200; www.emburuguai.org.br; SES, Quadra 803, Lote 14, Brasília); **Porto Alegre consulate** (☎ 51 3325-6200; cgportoalegre@mrree.gub.uy; Av 24 de Outubro 850; ☺9am-3pm Mon-Fri); **Rio consulate** (☎ 21 2553-6030; www.emburuguai.org.br; 12th fl, Praia de Botafogo 210, Botafogo; ☺10am-4pm Mon-Fri)

US Embassy (☎ 61 3312-7000; https://br.usembassy.gov; SES, Quadra 801, Lote 3, Brasília); **Rio consulate** (☎ 21 3823-2000; www.brazil.usembassy.gov; Av Presidente Wilson 147, Centro; ☺8am-5pm Mon-Fri); **Salvador consulate** (☎ 71 3113-2090; Room 1401, Av Tancredo Neves 1632, Salvador Trade Center, Caminho das Árvores); **São Paulo consulate** (☎ 11 3250-5000; https://br.usembassy.gov/embassy-consulates/saopaulo; Henri Dunant 500, Chácara Santo Antônio)

FOOD

Brazilian restaurants serve huge portions, and many plates are designed for two – not great for single travelers, as the bill can cost 60% to 70% of the price for two when a portion for one is ordered (though often portions for two can feed three – trios beat Brazil at its own illogical math game). The basic Brazilian diet revolves around *arroz* (white rice), *feijão* (black beans) and *farofa/farinha* (flour from the root of manioc or corn). The typical Brazilian meal, called *prato feito* (set meal, often abbreviated 'pf') or *refeição*, consists of these ingredients plus either meat, chicken or fish and costs R$12 to R$20 in most eateries.

Another good option are *por kilo* (per kilogram) lunch buffets. Here you serve yourself and pay by the weight: typically between R$45 and R$80 per kilogram, with a big plateful weighing around half a kilo. Per-kilo places are good for vegetarians too. The fixed-price *rodízio* is another deal, and most *churrascarias* (meat BBQ restaurants) offer *rodízio* dining, where they bring endless skewers of different meat to your table. Overcharging and shortchanging are almost standard procedure. Check your bill carefully.

Regional variations include *comida baiana* from Bahia's northeastern coast, which has a distinct African flavor, using peppers, spices and the potent oil of the *dendê* palm tree. Both the Pantanal and the Amazon region have some tasty varieties of fish. Rio Grande do Sul's *comida gaúcha* is meat-focused. Minas Gerais is legendary for its hearty, vein-clogging fare, often involving chicken and pork (Brazilians also say any dish in Brazil tastes better in Minas); while São Paulo, home to large populations of Italians, Japanese and Arab immigrants, is Brazil's foodie mecca.

The incredible variety of Brazilian fruits makes for some divine *sucos* (juices). Every town has plenty of juice bars, offering 30 or 40 different varieties at around R$12 to R$20 for a good-sized glass.

Cafezinho puro (coffee), as typically drunk in Brazil, is strong, hot and often sickly presweetened in rural or less sophisticated locales, usually served without milk (*leite*). *Refrigerantes* (soft drinks) are found everywhere. *Guaraná*, made from the fruit of an Amazonian plant, is as popular as Coke.

The two key alcoholic drinks in Brazil are *cachaça* (also called *pinga*), a high-proof sugarcane spirit, and *cerveja* (beer). *Cachaça* ranges from off-puttingly raw to exquisite and smooth, and is the basis of that celebrated Brazilian cocktail, the *caipirinha*. Of the common beer brands, Colorado, Bohemia, Original and Serramalte are generally the best, but the craft-beer scene has exploded since 2013, especially in São Paulo, Paraná, Rio Grande do Sul and Minas Gerais.

HEALTH

➡ Malaria is a concern in certain areas of the Amazon and Northwest Brazil. Travelers should weigh the risks of an appropriate malaria preventative (chloroquine is not effective here), and cover up as much as possible to prevent mosquito bites.

EATING PRICE RANGES

The following price indicators refer to a standard main course (including tax but excluding 10% service charge):

$ less than R$30

$$ R$30–R$75

$$$ more than R$75

➡ Dengue Fever is present in many areas, and there have been outbreaks in the past, including in and around Rio state and Bahía. If you are in an area where mosquitoes are biting during the day, you are at risk and should consider repellent.

➡ The Zika virus, transmitted by mosquitoes, causes flu-like symptoms in some infected victims. It's also linked to microcephaly (abnormally small head size with possible brain damage) in babies born to women who were infected while pregnant.

➡ Tap water is safe but can taste unpleasant in most urban areas. In remote areas, filter your own or stick to bottled water.

➡ The sun is powerful here and travelers should be mindful of heatstroke, dehydration and sunburn. Drink plenty of water, wear a strong sunscreen and allow your body time to acclimatize to high temperatures before attempting strenuous activities. A good drink when dehydrated is *agua de côco* (coconut water), which contains electrolytes.

➡ A yellow fever immunization certificate is no longer compulsory to enter Brazil, but highly recommended. At most Brazilian borders and major airports there are vaccination posts where you can have the jab (free for foreigners) and get the certificate immediately. But it's wise to do this in advance.

INTERNET ACCESS

Most hostels and hotels, as well as many cafes and restaurants, provide wi-fi access. It's usually free, although pricier hotels sometimes charge for it.

Internet cafes have largely disappeared from the Brazilian landscape. If you do manage to find one, expect to pay between R$5 and R$10 an hour.

LANGUAGE COURSES

Most language institutes charge high prices for group courses, and you can often find a private tutor for less. Hostels are a good place to troll for instructors, with ads on bulletin boards posted by native-speaking language teachers available for hire.

Rio is one of the easiest places to find Portuguese instruction. The **Caminhos Language**

Centre (Map p306; ☑ 21 2267-6552; www.
caminhoslanguages.com; Farme de Amoedo
135, Ipanema; private class per hour R$90,
4-week 80hr course R$1800) offers intensive
group classes with profits going toward orphan-
ages in Brazil. Also in Rio is the respected **Instituto Brasil-Estados Unidos** (IBEU; Map p310;
☑ 21 2548-8430; http://portuguese.ibeu.org.
br; 5th fl, Av NS de Copacabana 690, Copacabana; intensive 36hr course R$2300), which has
three different levels of classes.

LEGAL MATTERS

Be wary but respectful of Brazilian police – you
can be arrested in Brazil for shouting, cursing or
otherwise losing your temper while interacting
with any person of authority or public official.

Stiff penalties are in force for use and possession of drugs; the police don't share most
Brazilians' tolerant attitude toward marijuana.
Police checkpoints along the highways stop
cars at random. Don't even think about drinking and driving – Brazil introduced a zero-
tolerance law in 2008 and roadblocks (called
'blitz') are common in major cities, especially
Rio and São Paulo.

A large amount of cocaine is smuggled out of
Bolivia and Peru through Brazil. If you're entering Brazil from one of the Andean countries and
have been chewing coca leaves, be careful to
clean out your pack first.

LGBT TRAVELERS

Brazilians are pretty laid-back when it comes
to most sexual issues, and homosexuality is
more accepted here than in any other part of
Latin America. That said, the degree to which
you can be out in Brazil varies greatly by region,
and in some smaller towns discrimination is
prevalent.

Rio is the gay capital of Latin America, though
São Paulo and to a lesser extent Salvador also
have lively scenes. Gay and lesbian bars are
disappearing (blame it on dating/hooking-up
apps like Grindr). Those still around are all-
welcome affairs attended by GLS (Gays, Lesbians e Simpatizantes), a mixed heterosexual and
homosexual crowd far more concerned with
dancing and having a good time than anything
else.

There is no law against homosexuality in Brazil, and the age of consent is 18.

Useful resources include the following:

Mix Brasil (www.mixbrasil.org.br) The largest
Brazilian LGBT site.

ABGLT (Associação Brasileira de Lésbicas,
Gays, Bissexuais, Travestis, Transexuais e
Intersexos; www.abglt.org)

ACAPA (Associação Brasileira de Gays, Lésbicas, Bissexuais, Travestis e Transexuais; www.
disponivel.uol.com.br/acapa)

MAPS

The Quatro Rodas series, which includes good
regional maps (Norte, Nordeste etc), are the
best available maps of Brazil and can be found
throughout the country. Quatro Rodas also
publishes the Atlas Rodoviário, useful if you're
driving, as well as excellent street atlases for the
main cities.

MONEY

The Brazilian currency is the real (hay-ow; often
written R$); the plural is reais (hay-ice). One real
is made up of 100 centavos.

It might be handy to keep cash in reserve,
though you'll want to be exceptionally cautious
when traveling with it. Cash should be in US
dollars or euros.

ATMs

ATMs are the easiest way of getting cash in big
cities and are common. In many smaller towns,
ATMs exist but don't always work for non-
Brazilian cards. Make sure you have a four-digit
PIN (longer PINs may not work). In general,
Citibank, Banco do Brasil and Bradesco are the
best ATMs to try.

Credit Cards

You can use credit cards for many purchases
and to make cash withdrawals from ATMs and
banks. Visa is the most widely accepted card,
followed by MasterCard. Amex and Diners Club
cards are less useful. Visa cash advances are
widely available, even in small towns with no
other currency-exchange facilities; you'll need
your passport, and the process can be time-
consuming, especially at the ubiquitous but
bureaucratic Banco do Brasil.

OPENING HOURS

Banks 9am–3pm Monday–Friday

Bars 6pm–2am

Cafes 8am–10pm

Nightclubs 10pm–4am Thursday–Saturday

Post offices 9am–5pm Monday–Friday; some
open Saturday morning

Restaurants Noon–2:30pm and 6–10:30pm

Shops 9am–6pm Monday–Friday and 9am–
1pm Saturday

PUBLIC HOLIDAYS

April 19, the Dia do Índio (Indigenous Day), is not
a national holiday but is nevertheless marked
by festivities in indigenous villages around the
country.

New Year's Day January 1

Carnaval February/March (the two days before
Ash Wednesday)

Good Friday & Easter Sunday March/April

Tiradentes Day April 21

May Day/Labor Day May 1

ⓘ FRAUD WARNING!

Credit-card and ATM fraud is widespread in Brazil, especially in the Northeast. Card cloning (*clonagem* in Portuguese) is the preferred method: an entrepreneurial opportunist sticks a false card reader into an ATM that copies your card and steals the PIN when you come along and withdraw money. Shazam! A few hours later, $1500 disappears from your account in Recife while you and your card are safe and sound sipping caipirinhas on the beach in Natal!

To combat fraud, restaurants will bring the credit-card machine to your table or ask you to accompany them to the cashier to run a credit-card transaction. Never let someone walk off with your card. Other tips:

➡ Use high-traffic ATMs inside banks during banking hours only.

➡ Always cover the ATM keypad when entering personal codes.

➡ Avoid self-standing ATMs whenever possible and never use an ATM that looks tampered with.

Corpus Christi Late May/June (60 days after Easter Sunday)
Independence Day September 7
Day of NS de Aparecida October 12
All Souls' Day November 2
Proclamation of the Republic November 15
Christmas Day December 25

RESPONSIBLE TRAVEL

We all have an obligation to protect Brazil's fragile environment. You can do your bit by using environmentally friendly tourism services wherever possible and avoiding those that aren't proactively taking steps to avoid ecological damage (this includes Pantanal operators who encourage touching animals).

Using the services of local community groups will ensure that your money goes directly to those who are helping you, as does buying crafts and other products directly from the artisans or their trusted representatives.

SAFE TRAVEL

Brazil receives plenty of bad press about its violence and high crime rate. Use common sense and take general precautions applicable throughout South America:

➡ Carry only the minimum cash needed plus a fat-looking wad to hand over to would-be thieves.

➡ Dress down, leave the jewelry at home and don't walk around flashing iPhones, iPads and other expensive electronics.

➡ Be alert and walk purposefully. Criminals home in on dopey, hesitant, disoriented-looking individuals.

➡ Use ATMs inside buildings. Before doing so, be very aware of your surroundings.

➡ Check windows and doors of your room for security, and don't leave anything valuable lying around.

TELEPHONE

Cell Phones

Brazil uses the GSM 850/900/1800/1900 network, which is compatible with North America, Europe and Australia, but the country's 4G LTE network runs on 2500/2690 (for now), which is not compatible with many North American and European smartphones.

Cell phones have nine-digit numbers starting with a 9. Mobiles have city codes, just like landlines, and if you're calling from another city, you have to use them. Tim (www.tim.com.br), Claro (www.claro.com.br), Oi (www.oi.com.br) and Vivo (www.vivo.com.br) are the major operators.

Foreigners can purchase a local SIM with a passport instead of needing a Brazilian CPF (tax ID number) – a major bureaucratic roadblock dismantled. Local SIM cards can be used in unlocked European and Australian phones, and in US phones on the GSM network.

TOILETS

Public toilets are not common but can be found at every bus station and airport in most cities and towns; there's usually a charge of around R$1 to R$2. People will generally let you use the toilets in restaurants and bars. As in other Latin American countries, toilet paper isn't flushed. There's usually a basket next to the toilet to put paper in.

TOURIST INFORMATION

Tourist offices in Brazil are a mixed bag. Some offices have dedicated, knowledgeable staff, while others have little interest in helping tourists.

Embratur (www.visitbrasil.com), the Brazilian tourism institute, provides limited online resources.

VISAS

Brazil has a reciprocal visa system, so if your home country requires Brazilian nationals to secure a visa, then you'll need one to enter Brazil. US, Canadian and Australian citizens need visas, but UK, New Zealand, French and German citizens do not. You can check your status with the Brazilian embassy or consulate in your home country.

If you do need a visa, arrange it well in advance. Visas are not issued on arrival; and you won't be permitted into the country without one. Applying for a visa got easier in 2018, however, when Brazil rolled out its new e-visa system, which is available to citizens from the US, Canada, Australia and Japan. The application fee is US$40, plus an online service fee of US$4.25. The service is valid for both tourists and business travelers.

To apply, visit the official website endorsed by Brazil's Ministry of Foreign Affairs: VFS Global (www.vfsglobal.com/Brazil-eVisa). You will need to upload a passport photograph and a scanned image of your passport bio page, and fill in other required details on the application. E-visas are valid for two years, for stays of up to 90 days per year.

Once all the documents have been submitted, the processing time for the visa is around five business days. Unfortunately, the online application process does not currently run very smoothly. Many applicants have had problems uploading photos – or having their photos rejected – or have experienced website crashes. It's wise to apply well in advance of your departure.

After your visa has been approved, you will receive a pdf of your e-visa. Print this out and take it with you on your trip. Without the printed copy, you may not be allowed to board your flight, and may also be denied entry into the country.

Old-fashioned consular visas are also still available. These are pricier and you'll have to apply in person to a Brazilian consulate in your home country.

Applicants under 18 years of age wanting to travel to Brazil must also submit a notarized letter of authorization from a parent or legal guardian.

Entry/Exit Card

On entering Brazil, all tourists must fill out a *cartão de entrada/saida* (entry/exit card); immigration officials will keep half, you keep the other. They will also stamp your passport and, if for some reason they are not granting you the usual 90-day stay in Brazil, the number of days you are allowed to stay will be written in your passport.

When you leave Brazil, the second half of the entry/exit card will be taken by immigration officials. Don't lose your card while in Brazil, as it could cause hassles and needless delays when you leave.

Visa Extensions

Brazil's Polícia Federal, who have offices in the state capitals and border towns, handle visa extensions for those nationalities allowed to extend (Schengen-region passport holders, for example, must leave for 90 days before reentering for a second 90-days – extending is not an option).

VOLUNTEERING

Atados (Map p337; www.atados.com.br; Rua Teçaindá 81, Pinheiros) Supports several hundred volunteer organizations involved in social work, the environment and health care. Headquartered in São Paulo.

Iko Poran (📞 21 3217-1474; www.ikoporan.org) Rio-based service linking volunteers with needy organizations. Iko Poran also provides housing for volunteers.

Regua (www.regua.org; Reserva Ecológica de Guapi Assu) Accepts volunteers from all over the world for reforestation and other conservation work.

Task Brasil (www.taskbrasil.org.uk) UK-based organization that places volunteers in Rio.

WOMEN TRAVELERS

Depending on the region, women traveling alone will experience a range of responses. In São Paulo, for example, where there are many people of European ancestry, foreign women without traveling companions will scarcely be given a sideways glance. In the more traditional rural areas of the Northeast, where a large percentage of the population is of ethnically mixed origin, blonde-haired and light-skinned women, especially those not traveling with a male, will certainly arouse curiosity.

If you encounter unwelcome attention, you should be able to stop it by merely expressing displeasure.

Although most of Brazil is nearly as safe for women as for men, it's a good idea to keep a low profile in the cities at night and to avoid going alone to bars and nightclubs.

Similarly, women should not hitchhike alone or even in groups (men or couples should also exercise caution when hitching). Most importantly, the roughest areas of the North and West, where there are lots of men but few local women, should be considered off-limits by lone female travelers.

WORK

Visitors who enter the country as tourists are not legally allowed to take jobs. It's not unusual for foreigners to find English-teaching work in language schools, though. It's always helpful to speak some Portuguese, although some schools insist that only English be spoken in class. Private language tutoring may pay a little more, but you'll have to do some legwork to get students.

ℹ️ Getting There & Away

Most travelers start their Brazilian odyssey by flying into Rio, but the country has several other gateway airports, as well as land borders with every country in South America except Chile and Ecuador. Flights and tours can be booked online at lonelyplanet.com/bookings.

AIR

The most popular international gateways are Rio de Janeiro's **Galeão International Airport** (Aeroporto Internacional Antônio Carlos Jobim; ☑ 21 3004-6050; www.riogaleao.com; Domestic Arrival Hall, Av Vinte de Janeiro) and São Paulo's GRU Airport (p341). From both, connecting flights leave regularly to airports throughout the country. Salvador and Recife receive a few direct scheduled flights from Europe.

Though headquartered in Chile, **LATAM** (☑ 0300-570-5700; www.latam.com) is Brazil's largest international carrier, with flights to New York, Miami, Paris, London, Lisbon and seven South American cities. The US Federal Aviation Administration has assessed LATAM as Category 1, which means it is in compliance with international aviation standards.

LAND

Argentina

The main border point used by travelers is Puerto Iguazú–Foz do Iguaçu, a 20-hour bus ride from Buenos Aires. Further south, you can cross from Paso de los Libres (Argentina) to Uruguaiana (Brazil), which is also served by buses from Buenos Aires.

Direct buses run between Buenos Aires and Porto Alegre (R$335, 21 hours) and Rio de Janeiro (R$550, 42 hours). Other destinations include Florianópolis (R$458, 25 hours), Curitiba (R$385, 32 hours) and São Paulo (R$467, 44 hours).

Bolivia

Brazil's longest border runs through remote wetlands and forests, and is much used by smugglers. The main crossings are at Corumbá, Cáceres, Guajará-Mirim and Brasiléia.

The busiest crossing is between Quijarro (Bolivia) and Corumbá (Brazil), which is a good access point for the Pantanal. Quijarro has a daily train link with Santa Cruz (Bolivia). Corumbá has bus connections with Bonito, Campo Grande, São Paulo, Rio de Janeiro and southern Brazil.

Cáceres, in Mato Grosso (Brazil), has a daily bus link with Santa Cruz (Bolivia) via the Bolivian border town of San Matías.

Guajará-Mirim (Brazil) is a short river crossing from Guayaramerín (Bolivia). Both towns have onward bus links into their respective countries (Guayaramerín also has flights), but from late December to late February heavy rains can make the northern Bolivian roads a very difficult proposition.

Brasiléia (Brazil), a 4½-hour bus ride from Rio Branco, stands opposite Cobija (Bolivia), which has bus and plane connections into Bolivia. Bolivian buses confront the same wet-season difficulties.

Chile

Although there is no border with Chile, direct buses run via Argentina between Santiago and Brazilian cities such as Porto Alegre (R$486, 40 hours), São Paulo (R$465, 57 hours) and Rio de Janeiro (R$560, 63 hours).

Colombia

Leticia, on the Rio Amazonas in far southeast Colombia, is contiguous with Tabatinga (Brazil). You can cross the border on foot or by Kombi van or taxi. From within Colombia, Leticia is only really accessible by air. Tabatinga is a quick flight (or a several-day Amazon boat ride) from Manaus or Tefé.

French Guiana

The Brazilian town of Oiapoque, a rugged 560km bus ride from Macapá, stands across the Rio Oiapoque from St Georges (French Guiana). A road connects St Georges to the French Guiana capital, Cayenne, with minibuses shuttling between the two. (Get there early in the morning to catch one.)

Guyana & Suriname

From Boa Vista, there are daily buses to Bonfim, in Roraima state (R$26, 1½ hours), on the Guyanese border, a short motorized-canoe ride from Lethem in southwest Guyana.

Overland travel between Suriname and Brazil involves first passing through either French Guiana or Guyana.

Paraguay

The two major border crossings are Ciudad del Este (Paraguay)–Foz do Iguaçu (Brazil) and Pedro Juan Caballero (Paraguay)–Ponta Porã (Brazil). Direct buses run between Asunción and Brazilian cities such as Florianópolis (R$340, 22 hours), Curitiba (R$270, 14 hours), São Paulo (R$250, 20 hours) and Foz do Iguaçu (R$80, 6½ hours).

Peru

There is at least one daily bus connecting Rio Branco (Brazil) to Puerto Maldonado (Peru) via the border at Assis (Brazil)–Iñapari (Peru) on the US$2.75-billion Interoceanic Hwy. You can also reach Assis on daily buses from Epitáciolândia (R$20, two hours) and cross the Rio Acre to Iñapari.

Uruguay

The crossing most used by travelers is Chuy (Uruguay)–Chuí (Brazil). This is actually one town, with the international border running down the middle of its main street. Other crossings are Río Branco (Uruguay)–Jaguarão (Brazil), Isidoro Noblia (Uruguay)–Aceguá (Brazil), Rivera (Uruguay)–Santana do Livramento (Brazil), Artigas (Uruguay)–Quaraí (Brazil) and Bella Unión (Uruguay)–Barra do Quaraí (Brazil). Buses run between Montevideo and Brazilian cities such as Porto Alegre (R$267, 12 hours), Florianópolis (R$290, 18 hours) and São Paulo (R$490, 32 hours).

RIVER

Fast passenger boats make the 400km trip (around US$75, 10 hours) along the Amazon River between Iquitos (Peru) and Tabatinga (Brazil). From Tabatinga you can continue 3000km down the river to its mouth.

From Trinidad in Bolivia you can reach Brazil by a boat trip of about five days down the Río Mamoré to Guayaramerín, opposite the Brazilian town of Guajará-Mirim.

Getting Around

AIR

Because of the great distances in Brazil, the occasional flight can be a necessity, and may not cost much more than a long-haul bus journey. If you intend to take more than just a couple of flights, a Brazil Airpass will probably save you money. Book ahead if traveling during busy travel times: from Christmas to Carnaval, around Easter, and July and August. Always reconfirm your flights, as schedules frequently change.

Airlines

Brazil has two major national carriers, Gol and LATAM (a merger between the Chilean LAN and Brazilian TAM airlines), and a handful of smaller regional airlines. Brazil's main carriers:

Avianca (AV; ☑ 0300-789-8160; www. avianca.com)

Azul (☑ 0800-887-1118; www.voeazul.com.br)

Gol (☑ 0300-115-2121; www.voegol.com.br)

LATAM (p441)

Air Passes

A Brazil Airpass is a good investment if you're planning on covering a lot of ground in 30 days or less. Gol offers an air pass involving four/five domestic flights anywhere on its extensive network with prices starting at US$505/638, plus taxes and fees; each additional flight costs around US$120. Azul's air pass gives you up to four flights within a 21-day period for US$500.

Either of these passes must be purchased before you get to Brazil, and you have to book your air-pass itinerary at the time you buy it – or possibly pay penalties for changing reservations. Many travel agents sell the air pass, as does the Brazilian travel specialist Brol (www. brol.com).

If for any reason you do not fly on an air-pass flight you have reserved, you should reconfirm all your other flights. Travelers have sometimes found that all their air-pass reservations had been scrubbed from the computer after they missed, or were bumped from, one flight.

BOAT

The Amazon region is one of the last great bastions of passenger river travel in the world. Rivers still perform the function of highways throughout much of Amazonia, with vessels of many shapes and sizes putt-putting up and down every river and creek that has anyone living near it.

BUS

Bus services in Brazil are generally excellent. Departure times are usually strictly adhered to, and most of the buses are clean, comfortable and well-serviced Mercedes, Volvo and Scania vehicles.

All major cities are linked by frequent buses – one leaves every 15 minutes from Rio to São Paulo during peak hours – and there is a surprising number of long-distance buses. Every big city, and most small ones, has at least one main long-distance bus station, known as a *rodoviária* (ho-do-vi-*ah*-ree-ya).

Brazil has numerous bus companies and the larger cities have several dozen rival agencies. ClickBus (www.clickbus.com.br) is a good app for consulting departures times, fares (which can be expensive) and purchases. Another good resource for searching national bus routes is Busca Ônibus (www.buscaonibus.com.br).

There are three main classes of long-distance bus. The ordinary *convencional* or *comum* is indeed the most common. It's fairly comfortable and usually has a toilet on board. An *executivo* or *semi-leito* is more comfortable (with reclining seats), costs about 25% more and stops less often. A *leito* (overnight sleeper) can cost twice as much as a *comum* and has fully reclining seats with blankets and pillows, air-con and sometimes an attendant serving sandwiches, coffee, soda and *água mineral* (mineral water).

With or without toilets, buses generally make pit stops for food and bathroom breaks every three or four hours.

Air-con on buses is sometimes strong; carry a light sweater or jacket to keep warm.

CAR & MOTORCYCLE

Brazilian roads can be dangerous, especially busy highways such as the Rio to São Paulo corridor. There are tens of thousands of motor-vehicle fatalities every year. Driving at night is particularly hazardous because road hazards are less visible. Drink-driving is still an issue despite a recent crackdown.

That said, driving can be a convenient (if expensive) way to get around Brazil. A small four-seat rental car costs around R$100 to R$120 a day with unlimited kilometers (R$140 to R$160 with air-con) and basic insurance. Ordinary gasoline/petrol costs around R$2.80 to R$4 per liter. Ethanol (known as *álcool* and produced from sugarcane) is about 50% less but goes around 30% quicker (most cars take both, known as Flex).

Driver's License

Your home-country driver's license is valid in Brazil, but because local authorities probably won't be familiar with it, it's a good idea to carry an International Driving Permit (IDP) as well. This gives police less scope for claiming that you are not driving with a legal license. IDPs are issued by your national motoring association and usually cost the equivalent of about US$15. It is illegal for foreigners to drive motorbikes in Brazil unless they have a Brazilian license.

HITCHHIKING

Hitchhiking is never entirely safe in any country, and is not recommended. Travelers who decide to hitchhike should understand that they are taking a small but potentially serious risk. People who do choose to hitchhike will be safer if they travel in pairs and let someone know where they are planning to go.

Hitchhiking in Brazil, with the possible exception of the Pantanal and several other areas where it's commonplace among locals, is difficult. The Portuguese word for 'lift' is *carona*, so ask '*Pode dar carona?*' (Can you give us a lift?). The best way to hitchhike – practically the only way if you want rides – is to ask drivers when they're not in their vehicles; for example, by waiting at a gas station or truck stop. It's polite to offer to pay for your share of the gas in return for your lift.

LOCAL TRANSPORTATION
Bus

Local bus services tend to be decent. Since most Brazilians take the bus to work, municipal buses are usually frequent and their network of routes are comprehensive. One-way fares range from R$3 to R$4.50.

In most city buses, you get on at the front and exit from the back, though occasionally the reverse is true. Usually there's a money collector sitting at a turnstile just inside the entrance.

Crime can be a problem: don't take valuables onto the buses, and think twice about taking informal minibuses in Rio and other urban areas, which have seen a recent increase in attacks.

Metro

Both Rio and São Paulo have excellent metro systems, with Rio's system expanded for the 2016 Olympics. These metros are a safe, cheap and efficient way of exploring the cities. One-way fares are R$4.30 in Rio and R$4 in São Paulo.

Taxi & Ride-sharing Apps

Taxi rides are reasonably priced, and a taxi is the best option for getting around cities at night. Taxis in cities usually have meters that start around R$5.50 and rise by something like R$2.50 per kilometer (more at night and on weekends).

In small towns, taxis often don't have meters, and you'll have to arrange a price – beforehand.

If possible, orient yourself before taking a taxi, and keep a map handy in case you find yourself being taken on a wild detour.

The preferred app for local taxi drivers is 99Taxis (www.99app.com), and is more convenient and safer than calling for a taxi or hailing one in the street. Ride-share services like Uber (www.uber.com) and Cabify are widely available.

TOURS

Both the Amazon and the Pantanal are the two most popular areas for organized tours in Brazil. You will certainly enrich your experience with the services of a trained guide as well as gain the transport upperhand for reaching difficult-to-access spots for the best wildlife viewing. In many of Brazil's national parks, such as Lençóis Maranhenses, Chapada dos Guimarães and Chapada Diamantina, guides are a necessity, if not required by regulation.

TRAIN

There are very few passenger trains in service. One remaining line well worth riding runs from Curitiba to Morretes, descending the coastal mountain range.

Chile

POP 18 MILLION

Best Places to Eat

➡ Cotelé (p531)

➡ Anita Epulef Cocina Mapuche (p518)

➡ Chinchinero Sabor Propio (p469)

➡ Just Delicious (p517)

Best Places to Stay

➡ Casa Chueca (p504)

➡ La Joya Hostel (p468)

➡ Happy House Hostel (p453)

➡ Vinn Haus (p549)

Why Go?

Preposterously thin and unreasonably long, Chile stretches from the belly of South America to its foot, reaching from the driest desert on earth to vast southern glacial fields. Diverse landscapes unfurl over a 4300km stretch: parched dunes, fertile valleys, volcanoes, ancient forests, massive glaciers and fjords. There's wonder in every detail and nature on a symphonic scale. For the traveler, it's mind-boggling how so much has stayed intact for so long. Adventure travelers will find themselves wholly in their element.

In Chile, close borders foster backyard intimacy. Bookended by the Andes and the Pacific, the country averages just 175km in width. No wonder you start greeting the same faces. The easy, relaxing ritual, so integral to the fabric of everyday life in this far corner of the world, proves addictive. Pause long enough and Chile may feel like home.

When to Go
Santiago

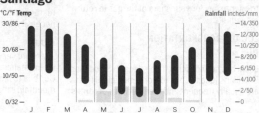

Nov–Feb Patagonia is best (and most expensive) but beaches are often crowded.

Mar–May, Sep & Oct Grape harvests in wine regions; pleasant Santiago temperatures.

Jun–Aug Fine weather in the north; Chileans go on winter vacation in July.

Entering the Country

Chile's northern border touches Peru and Bolivia, while its vast eastern boundary hugs Argentina, with numerous border crossings over the Andes. Note that many passes close in winter.

Popular Argentine crossings include Santiago to Mendoza and Buenos Aires, Calama to Jujuy and Salta, La Serena to San Juan, Temuco to San Martín de los Andes, and the bus-ferry combination between Puerto Varas and Bariloche. Other international crossings include Arica to Tacna (Peru), and Iquique to Oruro (Bolivia).

TWO-WEEK ITINERARY

Spend a day exploring the museums and cafes of Santiago, then escape to the picturesque port of Valparaíso. From central Chile, you'll have to decide whether to venture north – to San Pedro de Atacama and its mystical desertscapes, adventure sports and starry skies – or to the glaciers and trekking paradise of Torres del Paine and Patagonia in the south.

In the second week, choose your own adventure: taste wine in the Colchagua Valley, hike the Andes or go skiing at a resort like Portillo, seek out a surf break in Pichilemu, venture to the end of the earth in Tierra del Fuego, or tour the *pisco* distilleries outside La Serena.

Essential Food & Drink

Pisco This grape brandy is mixed with lemon juice and sugar to make the famous *pisco* sour.

Seafood Chile's long coastline means a bounty of fresh *pescados* (fish) and *mariscos* (shellfish).

Pasteles Traditional baked casserole made with corn, meat, crab or potatoes.

Wine Chile's wine regions are rightfully world-famous.

Top Tips

➜ Install WhatsApp on your phone for easy wi-fi contact with hotels and local businesses.

➜ Seasonality plays a big part in Patagonia. If going in low season, research what's open first and the transportation options. Be sure to plan extra days for poor weather.

➜ For multiday treks in Torres del Paine, book lodgings and campsites as soon as you have travel dates, as reservations are mandatory and very difficult to get in high season.

➜ If you're using a smartphone, be sure to download map data for the areas in which you'll be traveling.

➜ In summer, take advantage of the Fiestas Costumbristas, festivals celebrating local traditions held in small towns around the country.

FAST FACTS

Currency Chilean peso (CH$)

Visas Generally not required for stays of up to 90 days.

Money ATMs widespread; credit cards widely accepted.

Time GMT minus three hours

Capital Santiago

Emergency 133

Language Spanish

Exchange Rates

Australia	A$1	CH$475
Canada	C$1	CH$485
Euro zone	€1	CH$750
Japan	¥100	CH$585
New Zealand	NZ$1	CH$440
UK	UK£1	CH$850
US	US$1	CH$650

CHILE

Daily Costs

➜ Inexpensive *hospedaje* room/dorm bed: CH$10,000; double room in midrange hotel: CH$50,000

➜ Budget-restaurant dinner main: CH$5000; midrange-restaurant dinner main: CH$8000

Resources

Lonely Planet (www.lonelyplanet.com/chile)

Sernatur (www.chile.travel)

Santiago Times (http://santiagotimes.cl)

Visit Chile (www.visitchile.com)

CHILE SANTIAGO

Chile Highlights

❶ **Torres del Paine** (p552) Hiking to the rugged spires of Chile's finest national park.

❷ **Colchagua Valley** (p502) Swirling, sniffing and sipping your way through Chile's best vineyards.

❸ **Valparaíso** (p465) Wandering steep passageways lined with urban art in the hills of this bohemian town.

❹ **Atacama Desert** (p491) Drinking in the wild starscape above the driest desert in the world.

❺ **Chiloé** (p532) Encountering penguins, misty seascapes and mythical lore on this otherworldly archipelago.

❻ **Patagonia** (p546) Trekking, camping, kayaking and horseback riding in a wildly beautiful landscape.

❼ **Easter Island** (p556) Gazing up at the enigmatic *moai* (statues).

❽ **Iquique** (p493) Catching a wave in this surf capital of the north coast.

❾ **Tierra del Fuego** (p555) Escaping to the quiet end of the earth.

SANTIAGO

🎵 2 / POP 7.04 MILLION

Surprising, cosmopolitan, energetic, sophisticated and worldly, Santiago is a city of syncopated cultural currents, madhouse parties, expansive museums and top-flight restaurants. With a growing economy, renovated arts scene and plenty of eccentricity to spare, Santiago is an old-guard city on the cusp of a modern-day renaissance.

History

Santiago was founded by Pedro de Valdivia in 1541, and its site was chosen for its moderate climate and strategic location for defense. It remained a small town until the nitrate boom in the 1880s; Gustave Eiffel designed its central station. In 1985 an earthquake shook down some of downtown's classic architecture; thanks to smart design and strict building codes, the February 2010 quake caused comparatively minimal damage to Chile's capital city.

⊙ Sights

The wedge-shaped Centro is the oldest part of Santiago, and the busiest, bounded by the Río Mapocho and Parque Forestal in the north, the Vía Norte Sur in the west, and Av General O'Higgins (the Alameda) in the south. North and east of the center is Barrio Bellavista, with Cerro San Cristóbal (Parque Metropolitano). To the west is Barrio Brasil, the bohemian enclave of the city. At the tip of this triangle and extending east are the wealthy *comunas* (sectors) of Providencia and Las Condes, accessed via the Alameda. Nuñoa is a residential neighborhood south of Providencia.

⊙ Centro

⭐**Museo Chileno de Arte Precolombino**   MUSEUM
(Chilean Museum of Pre-Columbian Art; Map p454; 🎵 2-2928-1500; www.precolombino.cl; Bandera 361, Centro; CH$6000; ⊙10am-6pm Tue-Sun; Ⓜ Plaza de Armas) Exquisite pottery from most major pre-Columbian cultures is the backbone of Santiago's best museum, the Museo Chileno de Arte Precolombino. As well as dozens of intricately molded anthropomorphic vessels, star exhibits include hefty Maya stone columns, towering Mapuche totems and a fascinating Andean textile display.

Plaza de Armas PLAZA
(Map p454; cnr Monjitas & 21 de Mayo, Centro; M Plaza de Armas) Since the city's founding in 1541, the Plaza de Armas has been its symbolic heart. In colonial times a gallows was the square's grisly centerpiece; today it's a fountain celebrating *libertador* (liberator) Simón Bolívar, shaded by more than a hundred Chilean palm trees.

Catedral Metropolitana CHURCH
(Map p454; Plaza de Armas, Centro; ☺ Mass 12:30pm & 7pm; M Plaza de Armas) Towering above the Plaza de Armas is the neoclassical Catedral Metropolitana, built between 1748 and 1800. Bishops celebrating Mass on the lavish main altar may feel uneasy: beneath them is the crypt where their predecessors are buried.

Barrio París-Londres AREA
(Map p454; cnr París & Londres; M Universidad de Chile) This pocket-sized neighborhood developed on the grounds of the Franciscan convent of Iglesia de San Francisco is made up of two intersecting cobblestone streets, París and Londres, which are lined by graceful European-style town houses built in the 1920s. Look for the memorial at **Londres 38** (Map p454; www.londres38.cl; Londres 38, Barrio Paris-Londres; ☺ 10am-1pm & 3-6pm Tue-Fri, 10am-2pm Sat; M Universidad de Chile) FREE, a building that served as a torture center during Augusto Pinochet's government.

Palacio de la Moneda HISTORIC BUILDING
(Map p454; https://visitasguiadas.presidencia.cl; cnr Morandé & Moneda, Centro; ☺ 9am-5pm Mon-Fri; M La Moneda) FREE Chile's presidential offices are in the Palacio de la Moneda. The ornate neoclassical building was designed by Italian architect Joaquín Toesca in the late 18th century and was originally the official mint. The inner courtyards are generally open to the public; schedule a guided tour by filling out the online form a few days in advance.

Centro Cultural
Palacio La Moneda ARTS CENTER
(Map p454; ☎ 2-2355-6500; www.ccplm.cl; Plaza de la Ciudadania 26, Centro; exhibitions from CH$3000; ☺ 9am-9pm, exhibitions to 7:30pm; ♿; M La Moneda) Underground art takes on a new meaning in one of Santiago's newer cultural spaces: the Centro Cultural Palacio La Moneda beneath Plaza de la Ciudadanía. A glass-slab roof floods the vaultlike space with natural light, and ramps wind down through the central atrium past the Cineteca Nacional, a state-run art-house movie theater, to two large temporary exhibition spaces that house some of the biggest touring shows to visit Santiago.

◉ **Barrios Lastarria & Bellas Artes**

Home to three of the city's best museums and the center of Santiago cafe culture,

CHILE SANTIAGO

SANTIAGO IN...

Two Days
Start at the bustling Plaza de Armas (p447). Peer into the old train-station-turned-cultural-center Estación Mapocho (p459), or have a coffee and check out contemporary art and fair-trade crafts at the Centro Cultural Palacio La Moneda (p447). Have a seafood lunch at the Mercado Central (p457), then hike up Cerro Santa Lucía (p449) to see the city from above. Head to Bellavista for a classic Chilean dinner at Galindo (p457). On your second day, tour Pablo Neruda's house, La Chascona (p450), then ride the funicular to the top of Cerro San Cristóbal (p450). After an excellent seafood lunch at quirky Peluquería Francesa (p458), check out the cultural calendar and bookstore at Centro Gabriela Mistral (p448). Later, have a *rica rica sour* (*pisco* sour with desert herbs) at **Opera Catedral** (Map p454; ☎ 2-2664-3048; www.operacatedral.cl; cnr JM de la Barra & Merced, Barrio Bellas Artes; ☺ 12:30pm-3am Mon-Thu, to 5am Fri & Sat; M Bellas Artes).

Four Days
On your third day, go hiking in the **Cajón del Maipo** or taste-test local varietals at a winery. Spend your fourth day admiring street art in **Barrio Brasil**, stopping for steaks at **Las Vacas Gordas** (Map p448; ☎ 2-2697-1066; Cienfuegos 280, Barrio Brasil; mains CH$7000-13,000; ☺ noon-midnight Mon-Sat, to 5pm Sun; M Ricardo Cumming). Toast your stay in Santiago with dinner and drinks at Providencia's Liguria (p458).

Santiago

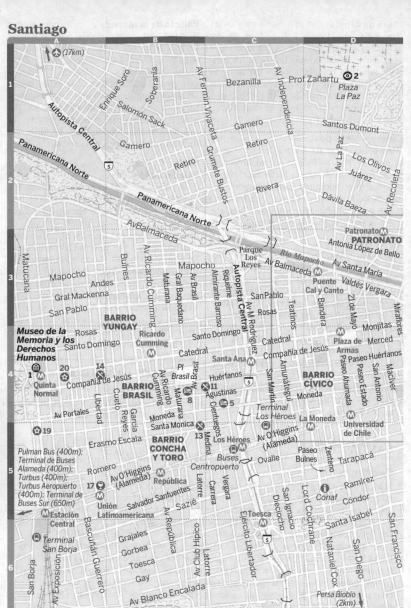

CHILE SANTIAGO

these postcard-pretty neighborhoods are Santiago's twin hubs of hip.

★ **Centro Gabriela Mistral**   ARTS CENTER
(GAM; Map p454; ☎ 2-2566-5500; www.gam.cl;
Av O'Higgins 227, Barrio Lastarria; ⊙ plazas 8am-10pm, exhibition spaces 10am-9pm Tue-Sat, from 11am Sun; Ⓜ Universidad Católica) **FREE** This striking cultural and performing-arts center – named for Chilean poet Gabriela Mistral, the first Latin American woman to win the Nobel Prize in Literature – is an exciting addition to Santiago's art scene, with concerts and performances most days. Drop by to

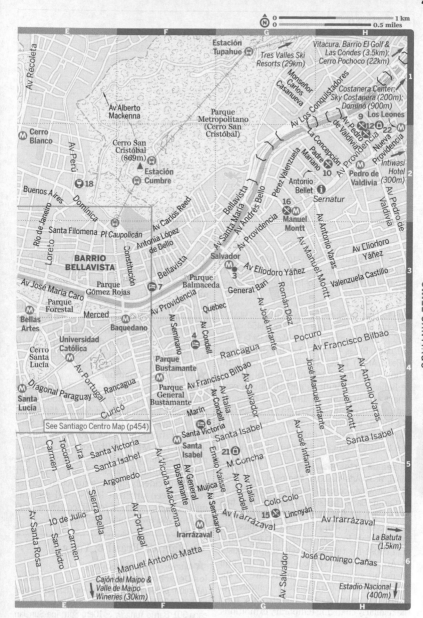

See Santiago Centro Map (p454)

check out the rotating art exhibits on the bottom floor, the iconic architecture that vaults and cantilevers on the inside and looks like a giant rusty cheese grater from the street, the little plazas, murals, cafes and more.

Cerro Santa Lucía
PARK

(Map p454; entrances cnr Av O'Higgins & Santa Lucía, cnr Santa Lucía & Subercaseaux, Bellas Artes; ⊙9am-6:30pm Mar-Sep, to 8pm Oct-Feb; ⓂSanta Lucía) FREE Take a break from the chaos of the Centro with an afternoon stroll through this lovingly manicured park. It was just a

Santiago

rocky hill until 19th-century mayor Benjamín Vicuña Mackenna had it transformed into one of the city's most memorable green spaces.

Museo Nacional de Bellas Artes MUSEUM
(National Museum of Fine Art; Map p454; ☎2-2499-1600; www.mnba.cl; José Miguel de la Barra 650, Barrio Bellas Artes; ◎10am-6:45pm Tue-Sun; ⓂBellas Artes) FREE This fine art museum is housed in the stately neoclassical Palacio de Bellas Artes, built as part of Chile's centenary celebrations in 1910. The museum features an excellent permanent collection of Chilean art. There are free guided tours starting at 10:30am daily (except January and February, when they begin at noon).

Museo de Artes Visuales MUSEUM
(MAVI, Visual Arts Museum; Map p454; ☎2-2664-9337; www.mavi.cl; Lastarria 307, Plaza Mulato Gil de Castro, Barrio Lastarria; CH$1000, Sun free; ◎11am-7pm Tue-Sun; ⓂUniversidad Católica) Exposed concrete, stripped wood and glass are the materials local architect Cristián Undurraga chose for the stunningly simple Museo de Artes Visuales. The contents of the four open-plan galleries are as impressive as the building: top-notch modern engravings, sculptures, paintings and photography form the regularly changing temporary exhibitions.

◎ Bellavista

★**La Chascona** HISTORIC BUILDING
(Map p454; ☎2-2777-8741; www.fundacionneruda.org; Fernando Márquez de La Plata 0192, Barrio Bellavista; adult/student CH$7000/2500; ◎10am-7pm Tue-Sun Jan & Feb, to 6pm Tue-Sun Mar-Dec; ⓂBaquedano) When poet Pablo Neruda needed a secret hideaway to spend time with his mistress Matilde Urrutia, he built La Chascona (loosely translated as 'Messy Hair'), the name inspired by her unruly curls. Neruda, of course, was a great lover of the sea, so the dining room is modeled on a ship's cabin and the living room on a lighthouse.

★**Cerro San Cristóbal** PARK
(Map p454; www.parquemet.cl; Pio Nono 450; funicular adult/child 1-way from CH$1500/1000; ◎funicular 10am-6:45pm Tue-Sun, 1-6:45pm Mon; ⓘ; ⓂBaquedano) The best views over Santiago are from the peaks and viewpoints of the **Parque Metropolitano**, better known as Cerro San Cristóbal. At 722 hectares, the park is Santiago's largest green space, but it's still decidedly urban: a funicular carries you between different landscaped sections on one side, while a *teleférico* (cable car) swoops you away on the other.

◎ Barrios Brasil & Yungay

★**Museo de la Memoria y los Derechos Humanos** MUSEUM
(Museum of Memory & Human Rights; Map p448; ☎2-2597-9600; www.museodelamemoria.cl; Matucana 501, Barrio Yungay; ◎10am-8pm Tue-Sun Jan & Feb, to 6pm Tue-Sun Mar-Dec; ⓂQuinta Normal) FREE Opened in 2010, this striking museum isn't for the faint of heart: the exhibits expose the terrifying human rights violations and large-scale 'disappearances' that took place under Chile's military government between 1973 and 1990.

PARQUE POR LA PAZ

During Chile's last dictatorship, some 4500 political prisoners were tortured and 266 were executed at Villa Grimaldi by the now-disbanded DINA (National Intelligence Directorate). The compound was razed to conceal evidence but since the return of democracy it has been turned into a powerful memorial park known as **Parque por la Paz** (☑ 2-2292-5229; www.villagrimaldi.cl; Av Jose Arrieta 8401, Peñalolén; ⊙ 10am-6pm) **FREE**. Each element of the park symbolizes one aspect of the atrocities that went on here. Visits are fascinating but harrowing – be sensitive about taking pictures as other visitors may be former detainees or family members. Check the website ahead of time to arrange a guided tour. Take Transantiago bus D09 (you need a Bip! card) from outside the Av Vespucio exit of Plaza Egaña metro station; it drops you opposite.

⊙ Las Condes, Barrio El Golf & Vitacura

Glittering skyscrapers, security-heavy apartment blocks, American chain restaurants and spanking-new malls: these neighborhoods are determined to be the international face of Chile's phenomenal economic growth.

★ Museo Ralli   MUSEUM
(☑ 2-2206-4224; www.museoralli.cl; Alonso de Sotomayor 4110, Vitacura; ⊙ 10:30am-5pm Tue-Sun, closed Feb) **FREE** This little-visited museum on a quiet residential street in Vitacura boasts a stunning collection of contemporary Latin American art mixed in with familiar European masters. Don't miss the gallery dedicated to 20th-century Chilean art on the basement level or the surrealist works by Salvador Dalí and René Magritte on the top floor.

Museo de la Moda   MUSEUM
(Museum of Fashion, ☑ 2-2219-3623; www.museode lamoda.cl; Av Vitacura 4562, Vitacura; adult/student & senior/child CH$3000/1500/free; ⊙ 10am-6pm Tue-Fri, 11am-7pm Sat & Sun; Ⓜ Escuela Militar) This slick, privately operated fashion museum comprises a vast and exquisite permanent collection of Western clothing – 20th-century designers are particularly well represented.

Costanera Center   NOTABLE BUILDING
(☑ 2-2916-9226; www.costaneracenter.cl; Av Andrés Bello 2425, Providencia; ⊙ 10am-10pm; Ⓜ Tobalaba) The four skyscrapers that make up Costanera Center include **Gran Torre Santiago**, the tallest building in Latin America (300m). The complex also contains offices, a high-end hotel and the largest shopping mall in South America. Head to **Sky Costanera** (www. skycostanera.cl; adult/child CH$15,000/10,000; ⊙ 10am-10pm) for panoramic views from the top of Gran Torre.

⊙ Barrio Recoleta

Bustling Korean eateries, a happening marketplace overflowing with ripe fruit, a colorful jumble of street vendors – this burgeoning barrio is just a slight detour off the beaten path.

Cementerio General   CEMETERY
(Map p448; www.cementeriogeneral.cl; Av Profesor Alberto Zañartu 951, Barrio Recoleta; ⊙ 8:30am-6pm; Ⓜ Cementerios) **FREE** More than just a graveyard, Santiago's Cementerio General is a veritable city of tombs, many adorned with works by famous local sculptors. The names above the crypts read like a who's who of Chilean history: its most tumultuous moments are attested to by Salvador Allende's tomb and the **Memorial del Detenido Desaparecido y del Ejecutado Político**, a memorial to the 'disappeared' of Pinochet's dictatorship.

Patronato   AREA
(Map p454; bordered by Av Recoleta, Loreto, Bellavista & Dominica; Ⓜ Patronato) This barrio within a barrio, roughly bordered by Recoleta, Loreto, Bellavista and Dominica streets, is the heart of Santiago's immigrant communities, particularly Koreans, Chinese and Arabs. The colorful, slightly run-down blocks are lined with antique buildings and illuminated by neon signs; a soundtrack of cumbia always seems to keep the beat in the background.

La Vega Central   MARKET
(Map p454; www.lavega.cl; cnr Nueva Rengifo & Antonia López de Bello, Barrio Recoleta; ⊙ 6am-6pm Mon-Sat, 7am-2pm Sun; Ⓜ Patronato) Raspberries, quinces, figs, peaches, persimmons, custard apples...if it grows in Chile you'll find it at La Vega Central, which is bordered by Dávila Baeza, Nueva Rengifo, López de

CHILE SANTIAGO

CHILENISMOS 101

Chilean Spanish fell off the wagon: it is slurred, sing-song and peppered with expressions unintelligible to the rest of the Spanish-speaking world. *¿Cachay?* (You get it?) often punctuates a sentence, as does the ubiquitous *pues*, said as *'po.' Sípo*, all clattered together, actually means, 'well, yes.' Country lingo is firmly seeded in this former agrarian society that refers to guys as *cabros* (goats) and complains *'es un cacho'* ('it's a horn,' meaning a sticking point). Lovers of lingo should check out John Brennan's *How to Survive in the Chilean Jungle*, available in Santiago's English-language bookstores. *¿Cachay?*

Bello and Salas. Go early to see the hollering vendors in full swing.

Activities

Outdoor access is Santiago's strong suit. For a quick hiking fix, hoof it up Cerro San Cristóbal (p450).

Santiago is flat and compact with a small network of *ciclovias* (bike lanes). You can rent bikes and helmets from tour operator La Bicicleta Verde. Each Sunday many of the city's main streets turn into bike-only thoroughfares between 9am and 2pm, thanks to CicloRecreoVía (www.ciclorecreovia.cl).

Excellent **skiing** is just a stone's throw from Santiago – the closest resort is **Farellones** (www.parquesdefarellones.cl; Camino a Farellones s/n; day pass CH$27,000; ☺ lifts 9am-5pm). **Rafting** enthusiasts head to Cascada de las Animas (p463) from October to March for Class III descents of the Río Maipo; the company also organizes hiking and horse-trekking trips at reasonable rates.

Courses

Tandem Santiago LANGUAGE
(Escuela de Idiomas Violeta Parra; Map p448; ☎ 2-2236-4241; www.tandemsantiago.cl; Triana 853, Providencia; enrollment fee US$55, 45min lesson US$22, 20-lesson course US$190; ☺ 9am-9pm Mon-Thu, to 7pm Fri; Ⓜ Salvador) Combines an outstanding academic record with a friendly vibe and cultural activities. Accommodations (optional) are in shared or private apartments. Check the website for special courses like 'Spanish for Lawyers' or 'Medical Spanish.'

Natalislang LANGUAGE
(Map p454; ☎ 2-2222-8685; www.natalislang.com; Arturo Bürhle 047, Centro; intensive 3-day traveler crash course from CH$150,000; Ⓜ Baquedano) Great for quick, intense courses. The website has an extensive list of options.

Tours

★ **La Bicicleta Verde** TOURS
(Map p454; ☎ 2-2570-9939; https://labicicleta verde.com; Loreto 6, Barrio Recoleta; bike tours from CH$25,000, rentals half-/full-day from CH$5000/9000; Ⓜ Bellas Artes) You can rent bikes and helmets here or choose from highly recommended guided tours of morning markets, shady green spaces, hip barrios or nearby vineyards in the Maipo Valley.

Free Tour Santiago WALKING
(Map p454; ☎ cell 9-9236-8789; www.freetour santiago.cl; Catedral Metropolitana, Plaza de Armas, Centro; ☺ departs 10am & 3pm; Ⓜ Plaza de Armas) A free four-hour English-language walking tour of downtown Santiago: guides work for tips only, so be prepared to offer gratuity. No booking necessary, just look for the guides wearing red shirts in front of Catedral Metropolitana (p447).

Happy Ending Tours TOURS
(☎ cell 9-9710-7758; www.happyendingtour.com; tours from CH$30,000) These tours really do make visiting backpackers happy, though not in the way you might be thinking. Reserve ahead for pub crawls, winemaking workshops and high-end clubbing trips that kick off with a glass of champagne at the top of Sky Costanera (p451), the city's tallest building. The price includes drinks and door-to-door service from your hotel.

Festivals & Events

Santiago a Mil PERFORMING ARTS
(www.fundacionteatroamil.cl/en/santiagoamil; ☺ Jan) This major performing-arts festival draws experimental companies from all over the world to the stages of Santiago each January. Expect more than 1000 shows to take place over three weeks, with many staged for free in parks and plazas across town. It's truly the most exciting time to be in Santiago.

Festival de Jazz de Providencia MUSIC
(www.providencia.cl; Parque de las Esculturas; ☺ Jan) Some of the world's top jazz performers converge on Providencia's Parque de las Esculturas for one weekend each January. Pick up free tickets from the Fundación Cultural de

CHILE SANTIAGO

Providencia (Nueva Providencia 1995) and arrive early to get a spot with a view. Alternatively, set out a blanket and picnic dinner on the far side of Río Mapocho and watch the jumbotron (big-screen TV).

Lollapalooza Chile MUSIC
(www.lollapaloozacl.com; ⊘ Mar) Santiago was the first city outside of the US to stage this famous music festival. Big-name national and international acts roll into Parque O'Higgins, generally sometime in March.

🛏 Sleeping

🛏 Centro

Hostel Plaza de Armas HOSTEL $
(Map p454; ☑ 2-2671-4436; www.plazadearmas hostel.com; Compañía de Jesus 960, Apt 607, Plaza de Armas, Centro; dm CH$7000-10,000, d with/without bathroom CH$25,000/15,000; 🛜; Ⓜ Plaza de Armas) You'll think you're in the wrong place when you show up to this busy apartment building on Santiago's main square. Take the elevator to the 6th floor to reach the hostel, which sports tiny dorms and a well-equipped communal kitchen. Great balconies with views over Plaza de Armas make up for the run-down facilities.

Ecohostel HOSTEL $
(Map p454; ☑ 2-2222-6833; www.ecohostel.cl; General Jofré 349B, Centro; dm/s/d without bathroom CH$10,000/20,000/29,000; @🛜; Ⓜ Universidad Católica) Backpackers and families looking to chill love this hostel's personalized service, cozy couches and sunny patio (complete with hammock). Eight-bed dorms in the converted old house can be dark, but bunks and lockers are both big and there are plenty of well-divided bathrooms. There's a women-only dorm.

CasAltura Boutique Hostel HOSTEL $
(Map p454; ☑ 2-2633-5076; www.casaltura.com; San Antonio 811, Centro; dm/d CH$13,000/40,000, s/d without bathroom CH$20,000/30,000; @🛜; Ⓜ Puente Cal y Canto) This sophisticated 'boutique hostel' is a travelers' favorite thanks to kitchen access, fine linens, a newly renovated terrace overlooking Parque Forestal and a location near Mercado Central.

🛏 Barrios Lastarria & Bellas Artes

Poker Hostal GUESTHOUSE $
(Map p454; ☑ 2-2633-3979; www.pokerhostal.com; Luis de Valdivia 361, Barrio Lastarria; s/d/f from

CH$19,000/35,000/35,000; 🛜; Ⓜ Universidad Católica) As eclectic and arty as the neighborhood, this great-value guesthouse offers the cheapest private rooms you'll find in Lastarria. There's a shared kitchen for cooking, and some rooms have private balconies for people-watching.

🛏 Bellavista

Bellavista Hostel HOSTEL $
(Map p454; ☑ 2-2732-3146; www.bellavistahostel. com; Dardignac 0184, Barrio Bellavista; dm US$13-17, s/d without bathroom US$30/50; @🛜; Ⓜ Baquedano) This highly social hostel is a Bellavista classic. Brightly painted walls crammed with colorful paintings and graffiti announce the relaxed, arty vibe. There's a supercool terrace and two kitchens. We only wish it was a bit cleaner. The city's best bars and clubs are on your doorstep and so, sometimes, are their patrons.

La Chimba HOSTEL $
(Map p454; ☑ 2-2732-9184; www.lachimba.com; Ernesto Pinto Lagarrigue 262, Barrio Bellavista; dm CH$11,000-15,000, s/d without bathroom CH$20,000/27,000; @🛜; Ⓜ Baquedano) A massive mural announces your arrival at this party hostel. There's a cool 1950s-style throwback lounge perfectly mismatched with a glowing chandelier and other odds and ends that span the decades. The rooms feel punk-rock beat – it's a bit grungy, but quite flavorful. And you'll love swapping stories at the rambling back plaza.

Hotel Boutique Tremo BOUTIQUE HOTEL $
(Map p448; ☑ 2-2732-4882; www.tremohotel.cl; Alberto Reyes 32, Barrio Bellavista; r CH$45,000; ❄🛜; Ⓜ Baquedano) For those looking for a boutique experience on a realistic budget, this is your best bet. The lovely converted mansion on a quiet street has a terrific patio lounge, fresh art deco stylings, decent service and a chilled-out air.

🛏 Barrios Brasil & Yungay

★ **Happy House Hostel** HOSTEL $
(Map p448; ☑ 2-2688-4849; www.happyhouse hostel.com; Moneda 1829, Barrio Brasil; dm CH$14,000, s/d CH$40,000/45,000, without bathroom CH$30,000/35,000; @🛜❄; Ⓜ Los Héroes) The best hostel in Barrio Brasil is happy news for weary travelers. This 1910 mansion has a fabulous molded ceiling, funky modern touches and incongruous art deco stylings. There's a pool, bar and patio out back, a few

Santiago Centro

Cementerio
General (1.3km)

Patronato M Santa Filomena

Av Independencia

Av La Paz

Antonia López de Bello ● 9

Av Santa María

Cal y
Canto
Bridge

Parque
Los Reyes

Av Balmaceda

40 ★

M

Puente Cal
y Canto

Av Recoleta

Manzur

Bellavista

Av Santa María

General Mackenna

Parque
Venezuela

Av José María Caro

San Pablo

31 34
✕   ✕

Diagonal Cervantes

Valdés Vergara

21 📍

Esmeralda

Morandé

Bandera

Amunátegui

Teatinos

Rosas

Santo Domingo

Santo Domingo

Paseo Puente

21 de Mayo

Maciver

Plaza de
Armas

M

19 ✉

Monjitas

Catedral

🛈 6

16

● 15

Merced

Portal Fernández Concha

24 🛏

Compañía de Jesús

Tribunales
de Justicia

🏛 Museo
4 Chileno de Arte
Precolombino

Paseo Huérfanos

Miraflores

27 ✕

✕ 29

BARRIO CÍVICO

Agustinas

41 ★

Maciver

Tenderini

Huérfanos

Agustinas

Dirección de Fronteras
y Límites

🛈

Pl de la
Constitución

✕ 36

Bandera

Matías Cousiño

Paseo Estado

Moneda

San Antonio

Biblioteca
Nacional

Moneda

Amunátegui

Amanda Labarca

Teatinos

Morandé

13 🏛

La Bolsa

Nueva York

Paseo Ahumada

Av O'Higgins (Alameda)

Av Santa Rosa

Pl de la
Ciudadanía

📍 7

Universidad
de Chile

M

Universidad
de Chile

5 ●

BARRIO
PARÍS
LONDRES

● 10

París

San Francisco

San Martín

Lord
Cochrane

La Moneda M

Nataniel
Cox

Paseo
Bulnes

Zenteno

San Diego

Arturo
Prat

Londres

Ovalle

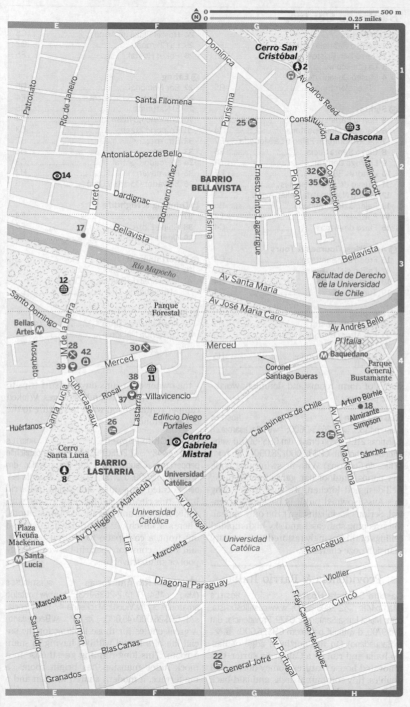

CHILE SANTIAGO

0
N
0   500 m
0.25 miles

Cerro San Cristóbal

Cerro San Cristóbal

Dominica

Av Carlos Reed

Santa Filomena

Purísima

25

Constitución

La Chascona 3

AntoniaLópezde Bello

Ernesto Pinto Lagarrigue

Pío Nono

32
35
20

33

Mallinkrodt

Constitución

BARRIO BELLAVISTA

14

Loreto

Dardignac

Bombero Núñez

Purísima

17

Bellavista

Río Mapocho

Bellavista

12

Av Santa María

Facultad de Derecho de la Universidad de Chile

Santo Domingo

JM de la Barra

Parque Forestal

Av José María Caro

Av Andrés Bello

Bellas Artes

Mosqueto

28
42
39

30

Merced

Merced

Pl Italia

Baquedano

Parque General Bustamante

Coronel Santiago Bueras

Arturo Bürhle

38
11

Rosal

37

Villavicencio

Edificio Diego Portales

Carabineros de Chile

Av Vicuña Mackenna

18
Almirante Simpson

Huérfanos

Santa Lucía

Subercaseaux

Lastarria

26

1 **Centro Gabriela Mistral**

23

Sánchez

Cerro Santa Lucía

BARRIO LASTARRIA

8

Universidad Católica

Av Portugal

Av O'Higgins (Alameda)

Lira

Universidad Católica

Plaza Vicuña Mackenna

Santa Lucía

Marcoleta

Universidad Católica

Rancagua

Fray Camilo Henríquez

Marcoleta

Diagonal Paraguay

Viollier

Curicó

San Isidro

Carmen

Blas Cañas

Av Portugal

Granados

22
General Jofré

Santiago Centro

stories of dorm rooms and definitely worthwhile privates.

La Casa Roja
HOSTEL $

(Map p448; 2-2695-0600; www.lacasaroja.cl; Agustinas 2113, Barrio Brasil; dm CH$9500, d with/without bathroom CH$32,000/28,000; @ 🖵 🗲; M Ricardo Cumming) With its swimming pool, airy patios, outdoor bar, garden and a huge, well-designed kitchen, it's easy to see why this Aussie-owned outfit is backpacker central. Serious socializing isn't the only appeal: the sweeping staircases and sky-high molded ceilings of this lovingly restored 19th-century mansion ooze character.

Providencia & Barrio Italia

Castillo Surfista Hostel
HOSTEL $

(Map p448; 2-2893-3350; www.castillosurfista.com; Maria Luisa Santander 0329, Providencia; dm CH$9700, d without bathroom CH$26,000; @ 🖵; M Baquedano) On the northern edge of Barrio Italia and run by a California surfer, this renovated house features homey dorms and doubles, tidy communal areas and laid-back hosts who can help you access the surf scene

– the owner even runs daylong surf trips to lesser-known breaks and arranges Wicked camper rentals if you want to venture to the beaches alone.

Hostal Chile Pepper
HOSTEL $

(Map p448; 2-2501-9382; www.hostalchilepepper.com; Claudio Arrau 251, Barrio Italia; dm CH$8000-10,000, d CH$22,000; 🖵; M Santa Isabel) Located on a quiet side street of Barrio Italia, this clean hostel has nine rooms with a mix of dorms and private accommodations. There's a kitschy Astroturf lawn to sun on out front, a cozy patio to grill on out back, and ample common space in-between to play pool or share travel tips.

★ Hostal Río Amazonas
GUESTHOUSE $

(Map p454; 2-2635-1631; www.hostalrioamazonas.cl; Av Vicuña Mackenna 47, Providencia; s/d CH$26,000/45,000; @ 🖵; M Baquedano) A great choice for those looking for the social life of a hostel without having to share a room. This long-running guesthouse in a mock-Tudor mansion has bright rooms, a big terrace, a modern shared kitchen and a large collection of art.

Intiwasi Hotel BOUTIQUE HOTEL **$$**
(☑ 2-2985-5285; www.intiwasihotel.com; Josue Smith Solar 380, Providencia; r US$60-90; ✲ @ 🛜; Ⓜ Los Leones) This cozy, centrally located hotel is more like a boutique hostel for grown-ups. The proud owners are eager to help you plan your travels, and the look is native Chilean, with indigenous textiles, dark wood and bright hues of red and orange throughout. Rooms have LCD televisions.

🍴 Eating

Cheap lunches abound in the center; barrios Bellavista, Lastarria and Providencia are better suited for dinner.

🍴 Centro

Mercado Central SEAFOOD **$**
(Central Market; Map p454; www.mercadocentral.cl; cnr 21 de Mayo & San Pablo, Centro; ☺ food stands & restaurants 9am-5pm Mon-Fri, 7am-3:30pm Sat & Sun; Ⓜ Puente Cal y Canto) Santiago's wrought-iron fish market is a classic for seafood lunches (and hangover-curing fish stews like the tomato- and potato-based *caldillo de congrio*). Skip the touristy restaurants in the middle and head for one of the tiny low-key stalls around the market's periphery.

Emporio Zunino BAKERY **$**
(Map p454; www.empanadaszunino.com; Puente 801, Centro; empanadas CH$1000; ☺ 9:30am-8pm Mon-Fri, to 3pm Sat; Ⓜ Puente Cal y Canto) Founded in 1930, this classic bakery makes fantastic empanadas – Chilean food journalists recently voted them among the top 10 in a contest for the best empanadas in Santiago.

El Naturista VEGETARIAN **$**
(Map p454; ☑ 2-2696-1668; www.elnaturista.cl; Paseo Huérfanos 1046, Centro; meals CH$3400-5000; ☺ 8:30am-9pm Mon-Fri, 9am-4pm Sat; 🍴; Ⓜ Plaza de Armas) A downtown vegetarian classic, El Naturista does simple but filling soups, sandwiches, salads, tarts and fresh-squeezed juices, plus light breakfasts.

Bar Nacional CHILEAN **$**
(Map p454; ☑ 2-2695-3368; Paseo Huérfanos 1151, Centro; mains CH$2000-10,000; ☺ 7:30am-11pm Mon-Fri, to 5pm Sat; Ⓜ Plaza de Armas) From the chrome counter to the waitstaff of old-timers, this *fuente de soda* (soda fountain) is as vintage as they come. It has been churning out Chilean specialties like *lomo a lo pobre* (steak and fries topped with fried egg) for years. To save a buck (or a few hundred pesos) ask for the sandwich menu.

★ **Salvador Cocina y Café** CHILEAN **$$**
(Map p454; www.facebook.com/salvadorcocinay cafe; Bombero Ossa 1059, Centro; mains CH$7700; ☺ 8am-8:30pm Mon-Fri; Ⓜ Universidad de Chile) This no-frills two-story lunch spot packs a surprising punch with market-focused menus that change daily and highlight unsung dishes (and exotic meats) from the Chilean countryside. Chef Rolando Ortega won Chile's coveted chef of the year award in 2015 and the tables have been packed ever since.

🍴 Barrios Lastarria & Bellas Artes

Café Bistro de la Barra CAFE **$**
(Map p454; www.cafedelabarra.cl; JM de la Barra 455, Barrio Bellas Artes; sandwiches CH$4000-5500; ☺ 8am-8pm Mon-Fri, 10am-8pm Sat & Sun; 🍴; Ⓜ Bellas Artes) Worn old floor tiles, a velvet sofa, a 1940s swing and light fittings made from cups and teapots make a quirky-but-pretty backdrop for some of the best lunches and *onces* (afternoon teas) in town. The rich sandwiches include salmon-filled croissants or Parma ham and arugula on flaky green-olive bread, but make sure you save some room for the berry-drenched cheesecake.

Emporio La Rosa ICE CREAM **$**
(Map p454; ☑ 2-2638-9257; www.emporiolarosa. com; Merced 291, Barrio Lastarria; ice creams CH$2000, salads & sandwiches CH$4000-6000; ☺ 9am-9:30pm Mon-Thu & Sun, to 10:30pm Fri & Sat; 🍴; Ⓜ Bellas Artes) Choco-chili, rose petal and Thai pineapple are some of the fabulous flavors of this extra-creamy handmade ice cream, which has been known to cause addiction. Flaky *pains au chocolat* and squishy *marraqueta* (a type of bread) sandwiches are two more reasons to plonk yourself at the chrome tables. Ever-expanding, there are now a dozen branches across town.

🍴 Bellavista

Galindo CHILEAN **$**
(Map p454; ☑ 2-2777-0116; www.galindo.cl; Dardignac 098, Barrio Bellavista; mains CH$3000-6000; ☺ 12:30pm-1am; Ⓜ Baquedano) Retro signs adorn the wood-backed bar at this long-running local favorite, usually packed with noisy but appreciative crowds. It's easy to see why: unlike the precious restaurants around it, Galindo is all about sizzling *parrilladas* (mixed grills) and hearty Chilean staples like

CHILE SANTIAGO

chorrillana (french fries topped with grilled onions and meat).

Etniko FUSION $$
(Map p454; ☑ 2-2732-0119; www.etniko.cl; Constitución 172, Barrio Bellavista; mains CH$5900-11,000; ☻ 7:30pm-2am Mon-Sat; Ⓜ Baquedano) With an airy transcendental energy, gigantic sushi platters and a sprinkling of other culinary offerings from Japan, Thailand and Chile, this hip eatery is fashionable and friendly. It stretches a long way back with a mix of stone, metal, bamboo, light and sound.

★ Peumayen CHILEAN $$$
(Map p454; www.peumayenchile.cl; Constitución 134, Barrio Bellavista; tasting menu CH$12,500; ☻ 1-3pm & 7pm-midnight Tue-Sat, 1-4pm Sun; Ⓜ Baquedano) Without a doubt one of the most unusual culinary experiences in Chile, this upstart is innovating Chilean cuisine by looking back to the culinary roots of the Mapuche, Rapa Nui and Atacameños.

🍴 Barrios Brasil & Yungay

Palacio del Vino CHILEAN $
(Map p448; ☑ cell 9-8855-1922; www.palaciodelvino.cl; Av Brasil 75, Barrio Brasil; mains CH$5000-8000; ☻ 11am-6pm Mon-Sat, by reservation only for dinner) This down-to-earth 'wine palace' gets high marks for both atmosphere and price. Not only is it located in a character-rich heritage building in Barrio Brasil, but you can get a glass of *gran reserva* wine for CH$3000 and a seafood dish to go with it for less than CH$6000.

Peluquería Francesa FRENCH $$
(Map p448; ☑ 2-2682-5243; www.boulevardlavaud.cl; Compañía de Jesús 2789, Barrio Yungay; mains CH$8500-13,000; ☻ 9am-1am Mon-Sat, 11am-5pm Sun; Ⓟ 🛜; Ⓜ Ricardo Cumming) This is one of Santiago's more innovative dining experiences. The name means 'French Barbershop,' and that's exactly what this elegant corner building, dating from 1868, originally was. Decorated with quirky antiques, it still has turn-of-the-century charm; it gets crowded on weekend evenings with hip Santiaguinos who come for the well-prepared French-inflected dishes.

🍴 Providencia & Barrio Italia

Voraz Pizza PIZZA $
(Map p448; ☑ 2-2235-6477; www.vorazpizza.cl; Av Providencia 1321, Providencia; pizzas CH$4000-5000; ☻ 12:30-11:30pm Mon-Sat, 5:30-11:30pm Sun; 🗹; Ⓜ Manuel Montt) This hole-in-the-wall spot serves great-value thin-crust pizzas and craft beers at sidewalk tables; it will happily deliver too. An added bonus for non-meat-eaters: this pizzeria has a few tasty vegetarian options and will also cater to vegans.

★ Silabario CHILEAN $$
(Map p448; ☑ 2-2502-5429; www.facebook.com/Silabariofficial; Lincoyan 920, Barrio Italia; mains CH$6000-9500; ☻ 7-11:30pm Tue-Fri, 1-4:30pm & 7pm-midnight Sat, 1-4:30pm Sun; Ⓜ Irarrázaval) Tucked away in an old home just south of Barrio Italia's main drag, this intimate restaurant re-envisions staples from the Chilean countryside as gourmet dishes. From northern quinoa salads to hearty Mapuche stews from the south, each culinary journey ends with a complimentary homemade *bajativo* (digestif).

El Huerto CAFE $$
(Map p448; ☑ 2-2231-4443; www.elhuerto.cl; Orrego Luco 054, Providencia; mains CH$6000-8000; ☻ noon-11pm Mon-Sat, 12:30-4:30pm Sun; 🗹; Ⓜ Pedro de Valdivia) This earthy restaurant's healthy, vegetarian fare is a big hit with both hip young things and ladies who lunch. Come for seaweed ceviches, fresh fruit juices, quinoa salads and wonderfully rich desserts.

Holm CAFE $$
(Map p448; ☑ cell 9-4227-4411; https://holmcomidafeliz.cl; Padre Mariano 125, Providencia; meals CH$5000-7500; ☻ 9am-10pm Mon-Fri, 10am-4pm Sat & Sun; 🗹; Ⓜ Pedro de Valdivia) Santiaguinos flock to this homey Providencia cafe each weekend for the best brunches in town. Fresh-baked breads and jams, yogurt and granola or scrambled eggs with crispy bacon are but a few of the offerings. Salads, sandwiches and fresh fruit juices round out the midweek fare.

Liguria Bar & Restaurant MEDITERRANEAN, CHILEAN $$
(Map p448; ☑ 2-2334-4346; www.liguria.cl; Av Pedro de Valdivia 47, Providencia; mains CH$7000-12,000; ☻ 10am-1:30am Mon-Sat; Ⓜ Pedro de Valdivia) A mainstay on the Santiago restaurant circuit, Liguria mixes equal measures of bar and bistro perfectly. Stewed rabbit and other specials are chalked up on a blackboard, then dapper old-school waiters place them on the red-checked tablecloths with aplomb.

✕ Las Condes, Barrio El Golf & Vitacura

Dominó   SANDWICHES $
(www.domino.cl; Isidora Goyenechea 2930, Barrio El Golf; sandwiches CH$1800-6000; ⊗8am-9pm Mon-Fri, noon-9pm Sat, noon-4:30pm Sun; Ⓜ Tobalaba) This location of Dominó – a contemporary take on the traditional *fuente de soda* – is hopping at lunchtime with good-looking young office workers. The cool black-and-white interior, plus budget-friendly sandwiches and *completos* (glorified hot dogs) equal stylish fast food, Chilean-style. You'll see other locations throughout the city.

🍷 Drinking & Nightlife

★**Bocanáriz**   WINE BAR
(Map p454; ☑2-2638-9893; www.bocanariz.cl; Lastarria 276, Barrio Lastarria; ⊗12:30pm-midnight Mon-Sat, 7-11:30pm Sun; Ⓜ Bellas Artes) You won't find a better wine list anywhere in Chile than this homey restobar with servers who are trained sommeliers. Try creative wine flights (themed by region or style) or sample several top bottles by the glass. There are also meat and cheese plates, as well as hearty Chilean dishes (mains CH$8000 to CH$12,000). Reservations recommended.

★**Blondie**   CLUB
(Map p448; www.blondie.cl; Av O'Higgins 2879, Centro; cover CH$2000-6000; ⊗from 11:30pm Thu-Sat; Ⓜ Union Latinoamericano) The '80s and '90s still rule at least one floor of Blondie, while the other could have anything from goth rock and techno to Britpop or Chilean indie. A favorite with both Santiago's student and gay communities, it's usually packed.

★**Chipe Libre**   COCKTAIL BAR
(Map p454; ☑2-2664-0584; Lastarria 282, Barrio Lastarria; ⊗12:30pm-12:30am Mon-Wed, to 1am Thu-Sat; Ⓜ Bellas Artes) Learn about the big sour over *pisco* – and who made it first – at the only bar in Santiago dedicated to the South American brandy. There are as many *piscos* from Peru as Chile on the menu and you can try them in flights of three or within an array of flavored sours. Reserve ahead for tables on the interior patio.

★**Restobar KY**   LOUNGE
(Map p448; ☑2-2777-7245; www.restobarky.cl; Av Perú 631, Barrio Recoleta; ⊗8pm-2am Tue-Sat; Ⓜ Cerro Blanco) Taking inspiration from Barrio Recoleta's Southeast Asian flavor is this stunning cocktail bar. The photographer owner has done wonders with a rambling old house – the interior is otherworldly, glowing with Chinese lanterns and the soft light of antique chandeliers, and filled with a fascinating mix of vintage chairs, exotic plants, carved wooden furnishings and vibrant artwork.

☆ Entertainment

Note that Santiago's excellent cultural centers – especially Centro Gabriela Mistral (p448), Centro Cultural Palacio La Moneda (p447) and **Estación Mapocho** (Mapocho Station; Map p454; www.estacionmapocho.cl; Plaza de la Cultura, Centro; ⊗event times vary, check website; Ⓜ Puente Cal y Canto) – are some of the city's best venues to catch live music, performing arts and entertainment. Admission to cultural events is often free: check the centers' websites or www.cstoy.cl for listings.

★**El Huaso Enrique**   TRADITIONAL MUSIC
(Map p448; ☑2-2681-5257; www.elhuasoenrique.cl; Maipú 462, Barrio Yungay; cover CH$2500-3000; ⊗7pm-2am Wed-Sun; Ⓜ Quinta Normal) On weekend nights at this traditional *cueca* venue, watch proud Chileans hit the dance floor – performing their national dance, a playful, handkerchief-wielding ritual that imitates the courtship of a rooster and hen – to traditional live music.

La Batuta   LIVE MUSIC
(www.batuta.cl; Jorge Washington 52, Ñuñoa; cover CH$3000-6000; ⊗7pm-4am Sun-Thu, to 5am Fri & Sat; Ⓜ Ñuñoa) Enthusiastic crowds jump to ska, *patchanka* (think: Manu Chao) and *cumbia chilombiana*; rockabilly and surf; tribute bands and goth rock...at Batuta, just about anything alternative goes.

Club de Jazz   JAZZ
(☑2-2830-6208; www.clubdejazz.cl; Av Ossa 123, La Reina; cover CH$5000-7000; ⊗8:30pm-3am Tue-Sat; Ⓜ Plaza Egaña) One of Latin America's most established jazz venues (Louis Armstrong and Herbie Hancock are just two of the greats to have played here), this venerable club hosts local and international jazz, blues and big-band performers.

★**Municipal de Santiago – Ópera Nacional de Chile**   THEATER
(Municipal Theater of Santiago; Map p454; ☑2-2463-1000; www.municipal.cl; Agustinas 794, Centro; tickets from CH$3000; ⊗box office 10am-7pm Mon-Fri, to 2pm Sat & Sun; Ⓜ Santa Lucía) This exquisite neoclassical building is the most prestigious performing-arts venue in the

CHILE SANTIAGO

city. Home to the Ópera Nacional de Chile, it also hosts world-class ballet, classical music and touring acts. Guided tours of the theater (CH$7000) run Monday, Wednesday and Friday at noon and 4:30pm. Reserve ahead at visitasguiadas@municipal.cl to arrange a tour in English.

Centro Cultural Matucana 100   ARTS CENTER
(Map p448; 2-2964-9240; www.m100.cl; Matucana 100, Barrio Estación Central; galleries free, show prices vary; galleries noon-6pm Tue & Wed, to 9pm Thu-Sun; Quinta Normal) One of Santiago's hippest alternative-arts venues, the huge red-brick Centro Cultural Matucana 100 gets its gritty industrial look from its previous incarnation as government warehouses. Renovated as part of Chile's bicentennial project, it now contains a hangar-like gallery and a theater for art-house film cycles, concerts and fringe productions.

Estadio Nacional   SOCCER
(National Stadium; 2-2238-8102; Av Grecia 2001, Ñuñoa; Estadio Nacional) On the whole, Chileans are a pretty calm lot – until they step foot in a *fútbol* (soccer) stadium. The most dramatic matches are against local rivals like Peru or Argentina, when 'Chi-Chi-Chi-Lay-Lay-Lay' reverberates through the Estadio Nacional.

🛍 Shopping

For clothes, shoes and department-store goods, hit downtown's pedestrian streets like Ahumada; for even cheaper goods, cross the river to Patronato.

Santiago's posh super-malls, a long haul from the center and often more popular with locals than visitors, include **Parque Arauco** (www.parquearauco.cl; Av Kennedy 5413, Las Condes; 10am-9pm Mon-Sat, 11am-9pm Sun; Manquehue) and **Alto Las Condes** (www.altolascondes.cl; Av Kennedy 9001, Las Condes; 10am-10pm).

★ Artesanías de Chile   ARTS & CRAFTS
(Map p454; 2-2697-2784; www.artesaniasdechile.cl; Plaza de la Ciudadanía 26, Centro Cultural Palacio La Moneda, Centro; 9:30am-7:30pm Mon-Fri, 10:30am-7pm Sat & Sun; La Moneda) Not only does this foundation's jewelry, wood carvings, ceramics and naturally dyed textiles sell at reasonable prices, most of what you pay goes directly to the artisans who made them. Look for other locations at Los Dominicos and the airport, as well as towns throughout Chile.

★ La Tienda Nacional   BOOKS
(Map p454; 2-2638-4706; www.latiendanacional.cl; Merced 369, Barrio Lastarria; 11am-8pm Mon-Fri, noon-9pm Sat; Bellas Artes) Much more than a bookstore, this two-floor shop sells Chilean movies, documentaries, records, toys, shirts and more. A must-visit to purchase unique gifts for someone special back home.

★ Pueblito Los Dominicos   ARTS & CRAFTS
(Los Dominicos Handicraft Village; www.plosdominicos.cl; Av Apoquindo 9085, Las Condes; 10:30am-7pm Tue-Sun; Los Dominicos) The best place in Santiago to buy quality gifts that were actually made in Chile. This mock village houses dozens of small stores, art galleries and traditional cafes. Look for lapis lazuli jewelry, Andean textiles, carved wooden bowls and ceramics with indigenous motifs.

Estacion Italia   SHOPPING CENTER
(Map p448; www.estacionitalia.cl; Av Italia 1439, Barrio Italia; 11am-7pm Sun & Mon, to 8pm Tue-Sat; Santa Isabel) This hub of commerce houses more than two-dozen independently owned boutiques selling everything from art supplies (Arte Nostro) to graphic novels (Pánico Ediciones) and hand-crafted leather shoes made in Chile (Blasko). Think of it like a mini mall for the mall-averse.

Galería Drugstore   FASHION & ACCESSORIES
(Map p448; www.drugstore.cl; Av Providencia 2124, Providencia; shops 11am-8pm Mon-Fri, to 6:30pm Sat; Los Leones) Head to this cool three-story independent shopping center for clothes no one back home will have – it has tiny boutiques of several up-and-coming designers, arty bookstores and cafes.

Persa Biobío   MARKET
(www.persa-biobio.com; Barrio Franklin; 10am-5pm Sat & Sun; Franklin) Antiques, collectibles and fascinating old junk fill the cluttered stalls at this famous flea market that sprawls across several blocks between Bío Bío and Franklin. Sifting through the jumble of vintage sunglasses, antique brandy snifters, cowboy spurs, old-fashioned swimsuits and discarded books is an experience.

ℹ Information

DANGERS & ANNOYANCES
Violent crime is relatively rare in Santiago, which regularly ranks as the safest big city in Latin America. Pickpocketing and bag-snatching, however, remain a problem, and tourists are often targets. Keep your eyes open and your bags

close to you around Plaza de Armas, Mercado Central, Cerro San Cristóbal and all bus stations.

EMERGENCY

Ambulance	131
Drugs hotline	135
Fire	132
Police Emergency	133
Police Information	139

INTERNET ACCESS

Cybercafes are a dying breed. Most cafes and hotels now have free wi-fi for their clients.

MEDICAL SERVICES

Consultations are cheap at Santiago's public hospitals but long waits are common and English may not be spoken. For immediate medical or dental assistance, go to a *clínica* (private clinic), but expect hefty fees – insurance is practically a must.

Clínica Alemana (☑ 2-2210-1111; www.alemana.cl; Av Vitacura 5951, Vitacura) One of the best – and most expensive – private hospitals in town with English- and German-speaking staff.

Clínica Las Condes (☑ 2-2210-4000; www.clinicalascondes.cl; Estoril 450, Las Condes) A recommended clinic in Las Condes for international-level care.

Clínica Universidad Católica (Red de Salud UC; ☑ 2-2354-3000; http://redsalud.uc.cl/ucchristus/Hospital/hospital-clinico; Marcoleta 367, Centro; M Universidad Católica) A well-respected university hospital conveniently located in Santiago Centro.

Farmacia Salcobrand (https://salcobrand.cl; Av Portugal 174, Centro; ⊗ 24hr; M Universidad Católica) A 24-hour pharmacy.

Hospital de Urgencia Asistencia Pública (☑ 2-2568-1100; www.huap.cl; Av Portugal 125, Centro; ⊗ 24hr; M Universidad Católica) Santiago's main emergency room.

Hospital del Salvador (☑ 2-2575-4000; www.hsalvador.cl; Av Salvador 364, Providencia; M Salvador) The nicest and best located of Santiago's public (and thus, cheaper) hospitals.

MONEY

You're never far from an ATM in Santiago. Supermarkets, pharmacies, gas stations and plain old street corners are all likely locations: look for the burgundy-and-white 'Redbanc' sign. Counterfeit currency does circulate in town; be especially wary of nonlicensed money changers.

Cambios Afex (www.afex.cl; Moneda 1140, Centro; ⊗ 9am-6:30pm Mon-Fri; M La Moneda) Reliable exchange office with branches around town.

POST

Correos Chile Santiago Centro (Map p454; ☑ 2-2956-0303; www.correos.cl; Catedral 989, Plaza de Armas, Centro; ⊗ 9am-6:30pm Mon-Fri, 10am-2pm Sat; M Plaza de Armas) A central branch of Chile's state-run postal service.

TOURIST INFORMATION

Sernatur (Map p448; ☑ 2-2731-8310; www.chile.travel; Av Providencia 1550, Providencia; ⊗ 9am-6pm Mon-Fri, to 2pm Sat; ⊙; M Manuel Montt) Gives out maps, brochures and advice; has free wi-fi.

🛈 Getting There & Away

AIR

Chile's main air hub for national and domestic flights is Aeropuerto Internacional Arturo Merino Benítez (p568). It's 16km west of central Santiago.

LATAM Airlines (☑ 600-526-2000; www.latam.com) and **Aerolíneas Argentinas** (☑ 800-610-200; www.aerolineas.com.ar) run regular domestic and regional services from here, as do low-cost Chilean carriers **Sky Airline** (www.skyairline.com) and **JetSmart** (www.jetsmart.com). Low-cost Brazilian carrier **Gol** (www.voegol.com.br) has services to major Brazilian cities, including São Paulo, Salvador and Rio. Other international airlines that fly to Chile have offices or representatives in Santiago.

BUS

A bewildering number of bus companies connect Santiago to the rest of Chile, Argentina and Peru. Services leave from several different terminals; make sure you know where you're going.

Santiago has four main bus terminals, from which buses leave for northern, central and southern destinations. The largest and most reputable bus companies are **Turbus** (☑ 600-660-6600; www.turbus.cl) and **Pullman Bus** (☑ 600-320-3200; www.pullman.cl).

Terminal San Borja (Map p448; San Borja 184, Barrio Estación Central; M Estación Central) This terminal is located behind Estación Central with buses to the beaches of the central coast and destinations north of Santiago. A few companies also operate southbound buses here. Ticket booths are on the 2nd floor, divided by region.

Terminal de Buses Alameda (cnr Av O'Higgins & Jotabeche, Barrio Estación Central; M Universidad de Santiago) Home to Turbus and Pullman Bus; both run comfortable, punctual services to destinations all over Chile, including every 15 minutes to Valparaíso and Viña del Mar.

Terminal de Buses Sur (Terminal Santiago; Av O'Higgins 3850, Barrio Estación Central; M Universidad de Santiago) Has the most services to the central coast, international and southern destinations (the Lakes District and Chiloé).

Terminal Los Héroes (Terrapuerto; Map p448; ☑ 2-2420-0099; Tucapel Jiménez 21, Centro; Ⓜ Los Héroes) Also known as Terrapuerto, this small but central terminal is the base for a handful of companies, mostly servicing Los Andes and northern destinations.

Fares between important destinations are listed in the bus-fares table, with approximate journey times and one-way fares for *semi-cama* (partly reclining seats). Fares can vary dramatically and spike during holidays.

Buses from Santiago

DESTINATION	COST (CH$)	DURATION (HR)
Antofagasta	33,000	19
Arica	44,000	28
Buenos Aires (Argentina)	66,000	24
Chillán	7900	5
Concepción	8000	6½
Copiapó	20,000	11
Iquique	40,000	25
La Serena	11,000	6
Los Andes	2500	1½
Mendoza (Argentina)	29,000	8
Osorno	21,800	11
Pucón	18,800	10
Puerto Montt	22,000	12
San Pedro de Atacama	40,600	23
Santa Cruz	6000	3½
Talca	5000	3½
Temuco	16,000	8
Valdivia	19,000	10
Valparaíso	4000	2
Viña del Mar	4000	2

TRAIN

Chile's limited train system, **TrenCentral** (EFE Ticket Office; ☑ 2-2585-5000; www.trencentral. cl; Estación Central, Barrio Estación Central; ⊙ tickets 7:15am-8pm Mon-Fri, 8am-7pm Sat; Ⓜ Estación Central), operates out of **Estación Central** (Av O'Higgins 3170, Barrio Estación Central; Ⓜ Estación Central). Train travel is generally slower and more expensive than going by bus, but wagons are well maintained and services are generally punctual. Normal trains run south to Chillán (CH$8100, five hours, twice daily), stopping along the way in Rancagua, Curicó and Talca. Special tourist trains head to the Colchagua Valley at least one Saturday each month (CH$60,000).

❶ Getting Around

TO/FROM THE AIRPORT

Two cheap, efficient bus services connect the airport with the city center: **Buses Centropuerto** (Map p448; ☑ 2-2601-9883; www.centropuerto. cl; one-way/round-trip CH$1800/3200; ⊙ 5:55am-11:30pm, departures every 15min) and **Turbus Aeropuerto** (☑ 600-660-6600; www.turbus.cl; one-way/round-trip CH$1800/3200; ⊙ 5am-2am, departures every 15min; Ⓜ Universidad de Santiago). Both leave from right outside the arrivals hall, and you can buy tickets on board. The total trip takes about 40 minutes. All buses stop at metro station Pajaritos on Línea 1 – you avoid downtown traffic by transferring to the metro here.

A pushy crew of 'official' taxi drivers tout their services in the arrivals hall. Although the ride to the city center should cost around CH$18,000, drivers may try to charge much more. A simpler bet is to approach the desk of **Transvip** (☑ 2-2677-3000; www.transvip.cl; one-way from CH$7000), which offers shared shuttles (from CH$7000) to the Centro. Trips to Providencia and Las Condes cost slightly more.

BUS

Transantiago buses are a cheap and convenient way of getting around town, especially when the metro shuts down at night. Green-and-white buses operate in central Santiago or connect two areas of town. Each suburb has its own color-coded local buses and an identifying letter that precedes route numbers (eg routes in Las Condes and Vitacura start with a C and vehicles are painted orange). Buses generally follow major roads or avenues; stops are spaced far apart and tend to coincide with metro stations. There are route maps at many stops, and consulting them (or asking bus drivers) is usually more reliable than asking locals.

On Sundays, take advantage of the **Circuito Cultural de Transantiago** (www.transantiago.cl; CH$630; ⊙ 10am-6:30pm Sun), a bus loop tour that passes the city's main attractions (museums, cultural centers) starting at Plaza Italia. You use your Bip! card to pay for one regular bus fare, and the driver will give you a bracelet that allows you to board the circuit's buses as many times as you like. The buses are clearly marked 'Circuito Cultural.'

CAR

Renting a car to drive around Santiago is stressful – if you must have your own set of wheels, the major agencies have offices at the airport. For more detailed information on driving and parking in Santiago, check out the helpful English-language section at **Car Rental in Chile** (www.mietwagen-in-chile.de); they'll also rent you a vehicle.

METRO

The city's ever-expanding **metro** (www.metro.cl; per ride from CH$630; ☺ 6am-11pm Mon-Fri, from 6:30am Sat, from 8am Sun) is a clean and efficient way of getting about. Services on its six interlinking lines are frequent, but often painfully crowded. A seventh line is slated to open in 2019. To get on the trains, head underground. You can use your Bip! card or purchase a one-way fare. Pass through the turnstiles and head for your line. It's a fine way to get around during the day, but during the morning and evening rush, you may prefer to walk.

TAXI

Santiago has abundant metered taxis, all black with yellow roofs. Flagfall costs CH$300, then it's CH$150 per 200m (or minute of waiting time). For longer rides – from the city center out to the airport, for example – you can sometimes negotiate flat fares. It's generally safe to hail cabs in the street, though hotels and restaurants will happily call you one, too. Most Santiago taxi drivers are honest, courteous and helpful, but a few will take roundabout routes, so try to know where you're going. *Taxis colectivos* are black with roof signs indicating routes (you'll share the ride, which generally costs CH$1500 to CH$2000).

AROUND SANTIAGO

National parks, sleepy villages, snowy slopes (in winter) and high-altitude hiking trails (in summer) all make easy escapes from the city.

Valle de Maipo

Just south of the center of Santiago lies Valle de Maipo, a major wine region specializing in big-bodied reds. You can go it alone: the wineries described here are within 1½ hours of the city center on public transportation. But if you'd rather hit the wine circuit with a knowledgeable guide, try the specialized tours at **Uncorked Wine Tours** (☑ 2-2981-6242; www.uncorked.cl; full-day tour US$195) – an English-speaking guide will take you to three wineries, and a lovely lunch is included. Also recommended is the winery bike tour with La Bicicleta Verde (p452), which takes you pedaling around the countryside to wineries within 10km of Santiago.

Worthwhile wineries include **Viña Cousiño Macul** (☑ 2-2351-4100; www.cousinomacul.com; Av Quilín 7100, Peñalolen; tours CH$14,000-24,000; ☺ English-language tours 11am, 12:15pm, 3pm & 4:15pm Mon-Fri, 10:15am & 11:30am Sat), where tours take in the production process

as well as the underground *bodega* (a storage area for wine), which was built in 1872. It is a 2.25km walk or a quick taxi ride from the metro.

Set at the foot of the Andes is the lovely **Viña Aquitania** (☑ 2-2791-4500; www.aquitania.cl; Av Consistorial 5090, Peñalolén; tours CH$13,000-22,000; ☺ by appointment only 9am-6pm Mon-Fri, 10am-2pm Sat). From Grecia metro station (Line 4), take bus D07 south from bus stop 6 and get off at the intersection of Av Los Presidentes and Consistorial (you need a Bip! card). Aquitania is 150m south.

Famous for the premium Casa Real Cabernet, **Viña Santa Rita** (☑ 2-2362-2520; www.santarita.com; Camino Padre Hurtado 0695, Alto Jahuel; tours CH$14,000-40,000; ☺ tours 10am-5pm Tue-Sun) offers bike and wine trips – through **Turistik** (Map p454; ☑ 2-2820-1000; https://turistik.com; Municipal Tourist Office, Plaza de Armas s/n, Centro; day pass from CH$23,000; ☺ 10am-6pm Mon-Fri; Ⓜ Plaza de Armas) – as well as picnics, tastings and tours of its stunning winery. There's also a jaw-dropping pre-Columbian art collection on display at the on-site Museo Andino with pottery, textiles and gold Incan jewelry. To get here, take the Santiago metro to Las Mercedes station, where you can catch bus MB81 toward Alto Jahuel and the vineyard entrance.

Cajón del Maipo

Rich greenery lines the steep, rocky walls of this stunning gorge, which the Río Maipo flows through. Starting only 25km southeast of Santiago, it's popular on weekends with Santiaguinos. November through March is rafting season, ski bums and bunnies flock here June through September, and horseback riding is popular year-round.

The river itself is made up of a series of mostly Class III rapids with very few calm areas – indeed, rafters are often tossed into the water. **Rutavertical Rafting** (☑ cell 9-9435-3143; www.rutavertical.cl; Camino al Volcán 19635, San José de Maipo; trips CH$17,000; ☺ daily departures at 11am, 2pm & 4:30pm) offers one-hour rafting trips led by enthusiastic multilingual guides, taking in some lovely gorges before ending up back in San José de Maipo. Allot about 2½ hours in total for the briefing, outfitting and drive upriver to the starting point. Helmets, wetsuits and life-jackets are provided, and there are lockers to store your belongings. The private nature reserve and working horse ranch Cascada

CHILE VALLE DE MAIPO

SKI RESORTS AROUND SANTIAGO

Chilean ski and snowboard resorts are open from mid-June to late September or early October, with lower rates available early and late in the season. Most ski areas are above 3300m and treeless; the runs are long, the season is long and the snow is deep and dry. Three major resorts are barely an hour from the capital, while a fourth is about two hours away on the Argentine border.

Santiago's four most popular ski centers – El Colorado/Farellones, La Parva and Valle Nevado – are clustered in three valleys in the Mapocho river canyon, hence their collective name, **Tres Valles**. They're only 30km to 40km northeast of Santiago, and the traffic-clogged road up can be slow going. All prices given here are for weekends and high season (usually early July to mid-August). Outside that time, there are hefty mid-week discounts on both ski passes and hotels. The predominance of drag lifts means that lines get long during the winter holidays, but otherwise crowds here are bearable. Ask about combination tickets if you're planning on skiing at multiple resorts.

El Colorado and **Farellones**, located approximately 45km east of the capital, are close enough together to be considered one destination, with 18 lifts and 22 runs from 2430m to 3330m in elevation. The eating and after-ski scenes are scanty here, so locals tend just to come up for the day. **El Colorado** (www.elcolorado.cl; El Colorado s/n; day ski pass adult/child CH$49,000/37,000; ☺lifts 9am-5pm) has the latest information on snow and slope conditions.

Only 4km from the Farellones ski resort, exclusive **La Parva** is oriented toward posh Chilean families and features 30 runs from 2662m to 3630m. For the latest information, contact **La Parva** (www.laparva.cl; Los Clonquis s/n; day pass adult/child CH$47,500/32,500; ☺lifts 8am-5pm).

Another 14km beyond Farellones, the vast **Valle Nevado** (☎2-2477-7705; www.valle nevado.com; Camino a Valle Nevado s/n; day pass adult/child CH$49,500/37,500; ☺lifts 9am-5pm) boasts about 28 sq km of skiable domain – the largest in South America. It's also the best maintained of Santiago's resorts and has the most challenging runs, ranging from 2805m to 3670m, and some up to 3km in length.

In a class of its own, the ultrasteep **Portillo**, 145km northeast of the capital on the Argentine border, is one of Chile's favorite ski resorts. The US, Austrian and Italian national teams use it as a base for summer training, and the 200km/h speed barrier was first broken here. Portillo has 14 lifts and 20 runs, from 2590m to 3310m; the longest run measures 3.2km. The on-site **Inca Lodge** (☎2-2263-0606; www.skiportillo.com; r per person per week incl meals & lift pass US$1365; P☎☒) accommodates young travelers in dorms. Tickets are included in the price and low season offers some deals. Contact **Portillo** (☎2-2263-0606; www.skiportillo.com; daily ski pass adult/child CH$46,000/30,000; ☺lifts 9am-5pm) for the latest details.

Shuttles to the resorts abound. **KL Adventure** (☎2-2217-9101; www.kladventure.com; Augo Mira Fernández 14248, Las Condes, Santiago; round-trip to Tres Valles CH$38,000, incl hotel pickup CH$50,000) goes to Tres Valles at 8am and returns at 5pm. **SkiTotal** (☎2-2246-0156; www.skitotal.cl; Av Apoquindo 4900, Local 39-42, Las Condes, Santiago; round-trip CH$17,000-19,500) arranges cheaper transportation to the Tres Valles, also with 8am departures and 5pm returns. SkiTotal can rent you equipment and runs transportation to Portillo (CH$27,000) Wednesdays and Saturdays.

de las Animas (☎2-2861-1303; www.cascadadel asanimas.cl; Camino al Volcan 31087) also offers rafting trips, alongside any number of hiking and riding options. Many travelers opt to spend the night at the rustic-chic Cascada Lodge, which features gorgeous bungalow suites, wood cabins and a shady campsite. Cascada de las Animas also runs private van transportation to and from Santiago (one to two people round-trip CH$70,000).

Only 93km from Santiago, 30-sq-km **Monumento Natural El Morado** (www.conaf. cl/parques/monumento-natural-el-morado; adult/child CH$5000/2500; ☺must enter 8:30am-1pm & leave by 6pm Oct-Apr, enter 8:30am-12:30pm & leave by 5:30pm May-Sep) rewards hikers with views of 4490m Cerro El Morado at Laguna El Morado, a two-hour hike from the humble hot springs of Baños Morales.

Refugio Lo Valdés (☎cell 9-9230-5930; www.refugiolovaldes.com; Refugio Alemán, Ruta G-25

Km77; dm/d from CH$27,600/57,500), a mountain chalet with simple, wood-clad rooms and a stunning view over the Cajón, is a popular weekend destination. The on-site restaurant is renowned for its hearty meals and *onces* (afternoon tea). About 11km on, **Termas Valle de Colina** (☑ 2-2985-2609; www.termas valledecolina.com; entrance incl camping adult/child CH$8000/4000) features a campground and terraced hot springs overlooking the valley.

Valparaíso

☑ 32 / POP 300,000

Poets, painters and would-be philosophers have long been drawn to this frenetic port city. Along with the ever-shifting population of sailors, dockworkers and sex workers, they've endowed gritty and gloriously spontaneous Valparaíso with an edgy air of 'anything goes.' Add to this the spectacular faded beauty of its chaotic *cerros* (hills), some of the best street art in Latin America, and a maze of steep, sinuous streets, alleys and *escaleras* (stairways) piled high with crumbling mansions, and it's clear why some visitors are spending more time here than in Santiago.

History

The leading merchant port along the Cape Horn and Pacific Ocean routes, Valparaíso was the stopover for foreign vessels, including whalers, and the export point of Chilean wheat destined for the California gold rush. Foreign merchants and capital made it Chile's financial powerhouse. Its decline began with the 1906 earthquake and the opening of the Panama Canal in 1914. Today 'Valpo' is back on the nautical charts as a cruise-ship stop-off, and Chile's growing fruit exports have also boosted the port. More significantly, the city has been Chile's legislative capital since 1990 and was voted the cultural capital in 2003. Unesco sealed the deal by giving it World Heritage status, prompting tourism to soar.

◉ Sights & Activities

Wandering through Valpo's streets admiring its murals and architecture is one of the city's best activities. Don't miss a trip or two on one of the six rattling *ascensores* (funiculars), built between 1883 and 1916, that crank you up into the hills and meandering back alleys (several more are currently being repaired).

Beach lovers should head north to Viña and Zapallar.

◉ El Plan & El Puerto

Valparaíso's flat commercial zone, El Plan, isn't as atmospheric as the hills that rise above it, but it contains a few monuments.

Plaza Sotomayor   PLAZA
(El Plan) Plaza Sotomayor is dominated by the palatial blue-colored **Edificio Armada de Chile** (Plaza Sotomayor s/n, El Plan). In the middle of the square lies the **Monumento a los Héroes de Iquique** (Plaza Sotomayor s/n, El Plan), a subterranean mausoleum paying tribute to Chile's naval martyrs.

Congreso Nacional   LANDMARK
(www.congreso.cl; cnr Av Pedro Montt & Rawson; ☺ library only open 9:30am-1pm & 2:30-5:30pm Mon & Fri) One of Valpo's only modern landmarks is the controversial horseshoe-shaped Congreso Nacional, located in the eastern section of El Plan. Its roots lie in Pinochet's presidency both literally and legislatively: it was built on one of his boyhood homes and mandated by his 1980 constitution (which moved the legislature away from Santiago).

◉ Cerros Concepción & Alegre

Ascensor Reina Victoria   FUNICULAR
(CH$100; ☺ 7am-11pm) This funicular dates back to 1902 and connects Av Elias to Paseo Dimalow.

Ascensor Concepción   FUNICULAR
(Prat (El Plan) & Paseo Gervasoni (Cerro Concepción); CH$300; ☺ 7am-10pm) The city's oldest funicular, Ascensor Concepción takes you to Paseo Gervasoni, at the lower end of Cerro Concepción. Built in 1883, it originally ran on steam power. At the time of research it was closed for renovations.

Museo de Bellas Artes   MUSEUM
(Palacio Baburizza, Fine Arts Museum; ☑ 32-225-2332; http://museobaburizza.cl; Paseo Yugoslavo 176, Cerro Alegre; CH$4000; ☺ 10:30am-6pm Tue-Sun) The rambling art nouveau building at the western end of Cerro Alegre is called Palacio Baburizza; it houses the Museo de Bellas Artes, which has a decent permanent collection plus plenty of details on the original palace owners. The funicular **Ascensor El Peral** (Plaza de Justicia (El Plan) & Paseo Yugoslavo (Cerro Alegre); CH$100; ☺ 7am-11pm) runs here from just off Plaza Sotomayor.

CHILE VALPARAÍSO

Valparaíso

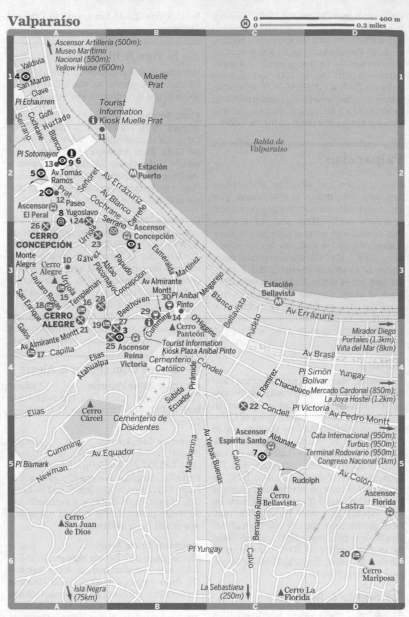

0 ─── 400 m
0 ─── 0.2 miles

Ascensor Artilleria (500m);
Museo Marítimo
Nacional (550m);
Yellow House (600m)

Valdivia

4
San Martín
Clave
Pl Echaurren
Goñi
Cochrane
Serrano
Hurtado
Blanco

Muelle
Prat

Bahía de
Valparaíso

Tourist
Information
Kiosk Muelle Prat

11

Pl Sotomayor
13
5
Av Tomás
Ramos
2
12
Prat
Paseo
Yugoslavo
Ascensor
El Peral
8
26
24
CERRO
CONCEPCIÓN
Senoret
Av Errázuriz
Cochrane
Serrano
Carrello
Av Blanco
Estación
Puerto
Ascensor
Concepción
1
23
Urriola
Monte
Alegre
Cerro
Alegre
10
Gálvez
Abtao
Picomayo
Concepción
Papudo
Esmeralda
Martínez
Estación
Bellavista
Lautaro Rosas
Urriola
Templeman
Av Almirante
Montt
30
Pl Aníbal
Pinto
Beethoven
Blanco
Melgarejo
Av Errázuriz
San Enrique
18
15
16
28
29
14
O'Higgins
Bellavista
Pudeto
Mirador Diego
Portales (1.3km);
Viña del Mar (8km)
Galos
CERRO
ALEGRE
19
27
3
Cumming
Cerro
Pantéon
Av Almirante Montt
21
17
Capilla
25
Ascensor
Reina
Victoria
Tourist Information
Kiosk Plaza Aníbal Pinto
Cementerio
Católico
Pirámide
Condell
F Ramírez
Chacabuco
Pl Simón
Bolívar
Yungay
Mercado Cardonal (850m);
La Joya Hostel (1.2km)
Elias
Atahualpa
Subida
Ecuador
Pl Victoria
Av Pedro Montt
Elias
Cerro
Cárcel
Cementerio de
Disidentes
Mackenna
22
Condell
Cata Internacional (950m);
Turbus (950m);
Terminal Rodoviario (950m);
Congreso Nacional (1km)
Cumming
Pl Bismark
Newman
Av Equador
Av Yerbas Buenas
Calvo
Ascensor
Espíritu Santo
7
Aldunate
Av Colón
Ascensor
Florida
Lastra
Rudolph
Cerro
San Juan
de Dios
Bernardo Ramos
Cerro
Bellavista
Isla Negra
(75km)
Pl Yungay
Calvo
La Sebastiana
(250m)
Cerro La
Florida
20
Cerro
Mariposa

CHILE VALPARAÍSO

Cerro Bellavista

Artists and writers have long favored this quiet residential hill; today a steady stream of hotels and eateries are opening in this neighborhood.

★ La Sebastiana
HISTORIC BUILDING

(☏ 32-225-6606; www.fundacionneruda.org; Ferrari 692; adult/child CH$7000/2500; ⓧ 10am-7pm Tue-Sun Jan & Feb, to 6pm Tue-Sun Mar-Dec) Bellavista's most famous resident writer was Pablo Neruda, who made a point of watch-

Valparaíso

◎ Sights

1	Ascensor Concepción	B3
2	Ascensor El Peral	A2
3	Ascensor Reina Victoria	B4
4	Barrio El Puerto	A1
5	Edificio Armada de Chile	A2
6	Monumento a los Héroes de Iquique	A2
7	Museo a Cielo Abierto	C5
8	Museo de Bellas Artes	A2
9	Plaza Sotomayor	A2

◉ Activities, Courses & Tours

10	Chilean Cuisine	A3
11	Harbor Boat Tours	A2
12	Natalis Language Center	A2
13	Tours 4 Tips	A2
14	Valpo Street Art Tours	B3

⊜ Sleeping

15	Hostal Cerro Alegre	A3

16	Hostal Jacaranda	A3
17	La Nona	A4
18	Mm 450	A3
19	Vía Vía Hotel	A4
20	WineBox Valparaiso	D6

⊗ Eating

21	Café Vinilo	A4
22	Casino Social J Cruz	C4
23	Chinchinero Sabor Propio	A3
24	Delicias Express	A2
25	El Internado	B4
26	El Peral	A3
27	Fauna	B4
28	Norma's	A3
	Viá Viá Restaurant	(see 19)

⊕ Drinking & Nightlife

29	Bar del Tio	B3
30	Máscara	B3

ing Valparaíso's annual New Year's fireworks from his house at the top of the hill, La Sebastiana. Entry operates on a first-come, first-served basis; it's recommended that you get here in the morning.

Getting here involves a hefty uphill hike, and the climbing continues inside the house – but you're rewarded on each floor with evermore heart-stopping views over the harbor. You can wander around La Sebastiana at will, lingering over the chaotic collection of ships' figureheads, glass, 1950s furniture and artworks by his famous friends.

Alongside the house, the Fundación Neruda has built the **Centro Cultural La Sebastiana**, containing a small exhibition space and souvenir shop.

To get here, walk 800m uphill along Héctor Calvo from Ascensor Espíritu Santo. Alternatively, take green bus O on Serrano near Plaza Sotomayor in El Plan, or from the plaza at the top of Templeman on Cerro Alegre and get off at the 6900 block of Av Alemania.

Museo a Cielo Abierto   AREA
(Open-Air Museum; cnr Rudolph & Ramos; ⊘ 24hr) Twenty classic, colorful murals are dotted through this *cerro's* lower streets, forming the Museo a Cielo Abierto, an open-air museum with works from famed Chilean artists such as Mario Toral and Roberto Matta. Sadly, many are now in very poor shape. The **Ascensor Espíritu Santo** takes you from behind Plaza Victoria to the heart of this art.

◉ Cerro Artillería

Clear views out over the sea made this southwestern hill a strategic defense spot.

Museo Marítimo Nacional   MUSEUM
(National Maritime Museum; ☑ 32-253-7018; www.mmn.cl; Paseo 21 de Mayo 45, Cerro Artillería; adult/child CH$1000/300; ⊘ 10am-5:30pm Tue-Sun) Cannons still stand ready outside this naval museum. Much space is devoted to Chile's victory in the 19th-century War of the Pacific. Other exhibits include historical paintings, uniforms, ships' furniture, swords, navigating instruments and medals, all neatly displayed in exhibition rooms along one side of a large courtyard. Rattling **Ascensor Artillería** brings you here from Plaza Aduana.

⛶ Courses

★ **Chilean Cuisine**   COOKING
(☑ cell 9-6621-4626; www.chileancuisine.cl; Pasaje Galvez 25, Cerro Concepcion; course per person from CH$40,000; ⊘ daily courses) An energetic chef takes you to shop for ingredients at the local market, then teaches you to make *pisco* sours, taste local wines and cook – then eat – a menu of Chilean classics.

Natalis Language Center   LANGUAGE
(☑ 32-225-4849; www.natalislang.com; Plaza Justicia 45, 6th fl, Oficina 602, El Plan; 3-day crash course CH$180,000) Language school with a good reputation for quick results.

CHILE VALPARAÍSO

⏚ Tours

★ Tours 4 Tips   WALKING

(www.tours4tips.com; Plaza Sotomayor, El Plan; ⏲10am & 3pm) Just show up at Plaza Sotomayor, look for the guides with the red-and-white shirts in the middle of the plaza, and head off for a friendly introduction to the city that focuses on street art, cultural history and politics. You only tip if you like the tour. We think CH$5000 to CH$10,000 is a good tip if you enjoy yourself.

Harbor Boat Tours   BOATING

(Muelle Prat; 30min tour CH$3000; ⏲9:30am-6:30pm) Pass alongside giant cruise vessels or naval battleships, or spot sea lions frolicking in the harbor. Several companies operate boats; ask around for the best price and group up for savings.

✸✸ Festivals & Events

Año Nuevo   NEW YEAR

(⏲Dec 31) Fantastic fireworks displays over the harbor draw hundreds of thousands of spectators to the city each December 31. Book accommodations well in advance.

🛌 Sleeping

★ La Joya Hostel   HOSTEL $

(☑cell 9-3187-8552; www.lajoyahostel.com; Quillota 80; dm CH$10,000, d from CH$39,000; P@⏾) La Joya is almost too posh to be called a hostel, with impeccably clean quarters, seriously comfy beds and the aesthetic of a Brooklyn

---

TOP FIVE VALPO VIEWS

Paseo 21 de Mayo on Cerro Artillería to survey the cranes and containers of the port.

Plaza Bismark on Cerro Cárcel for a panoramic take of the bay.

Mirador Diego Portales (top of Ascensor Barón, Cerro Barón) **on Cerro Barón** for a sweeping perspective of Valpo's colorful house-cluttered central views.

The viewpoint at the end of **Calle Merlet on Cerro Cordillera** to see the rusting roofs of **Barrio El Puerto** (www.barriopuertovalparaiso.cl) and the civic buildings of Plaza Sotomayor (p465) from above.

Paseo Atkinson on Cerro Concepción for views of typical Valpo houses during the day, and a twinkling sea of lights on the hills at night.

---

loft. Attached is a hip bar and burger joint that's worth the visit even if you aren't staying. Friendly staff are eager to help with city info, and they occasionally organize barbecues on the rooftop deck.

La Nona   B&B $

(☑cell 9-6618-6186; www.bblanona.com; Galos 660-662, Cerro Alegre; s/d/tr incl breakfast CH$36,000 /40,000/60,000; ⏾) The English-speaking owners of this B&B are mad about Valpo, and love sharing insider tips with their guests. Rooms are simple but highly passable. Stained glass and skylights add an open air, and the central location on Cerro Alegre is a serious selling point. Ask for a room with a view.

Yellow House   B&B $

(☑32-233-9435; www.theyellowhouse.cl; Capitán Muñoz Gamero 91, Cerro Artillería; r CH$33,000-55,000, without bathroom CH$25,000-32,000, all incl breakfast; @⏾) Oh-my-God views over the old port set this quiet B&B apart, as does the friendly care lavished on guests by the Chilean owner. Cozy, pastel-painted rooms come with thick white comforters. The Oceano has by far the best views. The only drawback: you're quite far removed from the action, dining and nightlife of the more popular *cerros*.

Hostal Jacaranda   HOSTEL $

(☑32-327-7567; www.hostaljacaranda.blogspot.com; Urriola 636, Cerro Alegre; dm/d from CH$8000/25,000; ⏾) Small but very welcoming (and perfectly located in a lively section of Cerro Alegre), this cheerful, family-style hostel features a terrace that's romantically illuminated at night. The owners have a wealth of knowledge; if you ask nicely, they might even show you how to make Chilean specialties including *pisco* sours and empanadas.

Hostal Cerro Alegre   B&B $

(☑32-327-0374; www.hostalcerroalegre.cl; Urriola 562, Cerro Alegre; dm CH$14,000, r with/without bathroom CH$59,000/36,000; ⏾) Funky antiques, original oil paintings by the former owner, and an eclectic mix of colors, styles and design sensibilities make this a good bet for the boho crowd. There's a shared kitchen and smallish living area, and the dorm sleeps just four. You can also rent bikes here (day/half-day CH$11,000/6000).

Vía Vía Hotel   GUESTHOUSE $

(☑32-319-2134; www.viaviacafe.cl; Almirante Montt 217, Cerro Alegre; r US$50-70; ⏾) 🗲 Run by a friendly Ecuadorian-Belgian couple,

DON'T MISS

VALPARAÍSO'S MURALS

Wandering up and down the winding hills of Valparaíso, you'll see colorful public art everywhere, from dreamlike wall paintings of glamorous women to political graffiti-style murals splashed across garage doors. Top spots to view street art are Cerros Concepción, Alegre and Bellavista, including the unmissable Pasaje Galvez. Explore this area with **Valpo Street Art Tours** (🤙cell 9-4021-5628; www.valpostreetart.com; Pasaje Galvez 25, oficina 2; ⏱10:30am & 3:30pm) to gain a better appreciation for the art and artists.

Cerro Polanco was 'bombed' by graffiti artists from across Latin America at the First Latin American Graffiti-Mural Festival, with 80-plus murals going up in just a few days. The neighborhood is great for wandering by day, but avoid it at night as tourists regularly report pickpockets in the area.

As you cruise the streets, keep your eyes peeled for Chilean artist Inti. His large-scale mural, painted across the surface of several neighboring buildings and visible from Cerro Concepción, was unveiled in early 2012. The vibrant sideways image shows a mysterious, partially fragmented figure draped with exotic jewelry.

this round-walled art deco boutique is a favorite with the arts-poetry-and-chunky-glasses set. With just five rooms, it's a cozy affair. The rooms are sparse but quite airy, and the bathrooms have solar showers and elegant stone accents. There is a fun cafe on the main floor, making this a good spot for night owls.

⭐**WineBox Valparaiso** DESIGN HOTEL $$
(🤙cell 9-9424-5331; wineboxvalparaiso@gmail.com; Baquedano 763, Cerro Mariposas; r CH$53,000-180,000; 🅿🛜🎱) 🍴 Built from 25 decommissioned shipping containers and home to Valparaíso's first urban winery, WineBox is primed to change the face of tourism in the city. If all goes according to plan, it will open a wine bar and shop in 2019 with 320 labels and 30 wines offered by the glass (including those made in the basement).

Mm 450 BOUTIQUE HOTEL $$$
(🤙32-222-9919; www.mm450.cl; Lautaro Rosas 450, Cerro Alegre; r incl breakfast CH$70,000-120,000; 🛜) This boutique hotel has a streamlined modern look, a gorgeous interior patio and super-comfy rooms with new mattresses and gleaming white comforters. It's attached to a hip restaurant and lounge, so there's always somebody around.

🍴 Eating

⭐**Chinchinero Sabor Propio** CHILEAN $
(🤙cell 9-9821-6612; Urriola 377, Cerro Alegre; set breakfast/lunch CH$3000/6000; ⏱10am-7pm Mon-Sat, to 6pm Sun; 🛜🍴) Extremely flavorful and very filling set breakfasts or lunches make this funky 10-table cafe the best value

in town. There are also delicious cakes, coffees and empanadas.

Delicias Express CHILEAN $
(🤙32-223-7438; Urriola 358, Cerro Alegre; empanadas CH$1000-2400; ⏱10am-6pm Mon-Fri, from 11am Sat & Sun) Boasting 81 varieties of empanadas, friendly service and a crispy crust you'll love, this is one of the best empanada joints on the coast.

Norma's CHILEAN $
(🤙32-222-3112; Av Almirante Montt 391, Cerro Alegre; set lunch $6900-9900; ⏱11am-6pm Thu-Tue) Don't let the name (or the nondescript entryway) throw you off: just climb the tall stairway into this cheerful, casually elegant restaurant for a surprisingly well-prepared set lunch that's friendlier on your wallet than most others in the area. The restored house still has the grand dimensions, polished wood and charming antique window frames of the original structure.

Mercado Cardonal MARKET $
(http://elcardonal.cl; Mercado Cardonal, 2nd fl, El Plan; mains CH$3500-5000; ⏱6am-6:30pm) There's a good selection of seafood stands at Valparaíso's main food market.

Casino Social J Cruz CHILEAN $
(🤙32-221-1225; www.jcruz.cl; Condell 1466, El Plan; mains CH$6500; ⏱noon-1:30am) Graffiti covers the walls at this tiny cafe, tucked away down a narrow passageway in El Plan. Forget about menus, there's only one essential dish to try: it's said that *chorrillana* (a mountain of French fries under a blanket of fried pork, onions and egg) was invented here. Folk singers may serenade you into the wee hours.

ISLA NEGRA

The spectacular setting on a windswept ocean headland makes it easy to understand why **Casa de Isla Negra** (Pablo Neruda's House; ☑035-247-5156; www.fundacionneruda.org; Poeta Neruda s/n; adult/child CH$7000/2500; ☺10am-6pm Tue-Sun Mar-Dec, to 7pm Tue-Sun Jan & Feb) was Pablo Neruda's favorite house. Built by the poet when he became rich in the 1950s, it was stormed by soldiers just days after the 1973 military coup when Neruda was dying of cancer. The house includes extraordinary collections of bowsprits, ships in bottles, nautical instruments and wood carvings. Neruda's tomb is also here, alongside that of his third wife, Matilde. (Note that despite the name, Isla Negra is not an island.)

Isla Negra is an easy half-day trip from Valparaíso: **Pullman Bus Lago Peñuelas** (☑032-222-4025) leaves from Valparaíso's bus terminal (CH$3200, 1½ hours) every 30 minutes. From Santiago, **Pullman Bus Costa Central** (☑032-246-9398; www.pullman costa.cl) comes here direct from Terminal de Buses Alameda (CH$4000 to CH$6000, 1½ hours, hourly).

★**El Internado**　CHILEAN **$$**
(☑32-335-4153; www.elinternado.cl; Pasaje Dimalow 167, Cerro Alegre; CH$4500-8000; ☺noon-12:30am Sun-Thu, from 12:30pm Fri & Sat; ☜) Soaring Valpo views, well-priced Chilean sandwiches and silky-smooth *pisco* sours make this funky new spot on Pasaje Dimalow a favorite among locals. Head to the basement level in the evenings for art shows, poetry readings, film screenings, live music and more.

★**El Peral**　CHILEAN **$$**
(☑32-336-1353; El Peral 182, Cerro Alegre; almuerzos CH$8000, mains CH$8000-10,000; ☺noon-4:30pm, to midnight Fri & Sat Dec-Apr) The menu at this beloved cafe above Ascensor El Peral (p465) is written on chalkboards each morning and typically includes the freshest ingredients from the sea. Pair your food with invigorating fruit juices, local craft beers or *pisco* sours in intriguing flavors. Reserve ahead for a table on the leafy terrace, which offers a shaded view over the port below.

Fauna　CHILEAN **$$**
(☑32-212-1408; www.faunahotel.cl; Pasaje Dimalow 166, Cerro Alegre; mains CH$6500-13,000; ☺12:30-10:30pm) One of the best decks in town is found at this hip lounge and restobar (with a sophisticated attached hotel). It's a top spot for locals to suck down craft beers, cocktails and wine, and boasts an alluring seafood-heavy menu. Reserve a table in advance.

Café Vinilo　CHILEAN **$$**
(☑32-223-0665; Av Almirante Montt 448, Cerro Alegre; mains CH$5000-13,000; ☺9am-1:30am Sun-Thu, to 3:30am Fri & Sat; ☜) The retro-chic atmosphere matches (and perfectly mismatches) the colors and rhythms of the city. Dinner plates feature fresh albacore (longfin tuna) and other local catches with inventive presentations and delicious flavor combinations. As the last plates are licked, the record player gets turned up and things slip into bar mode.

Viá Viá Restaurant　CAFE **$$**
(☑32-319-2134; www.viaviacafe.cl; Av Almirante Montt 217, Cerro Alegre; mains CH$5500-10,500; ☺1-11pm Tue-Sat, to 6pm Sun, closed Mon-Wed May-Oct; ☜☑) ☙ Set below a precipitous stairway and looming three-story mural, this garden cafe brims with creativity and serendipitous energy. There's occasional live music in summer, simple dining options, and a good mix of Belgian beers and Chilean wines on tap. It's a must-stop on any mural or pub crawl.

🍷 **Drinking & Nightlife**

★**Máscara**　CLUB
(www.mascara.cl; Plaza Aníbal Pinto 1178, El Plan; cover CH$2500-4000; ☺10pm-late Mon-Sat) Music-savvy clubbers in their 20s and 30s love this gay-friendly club: the beer's cheap, there's plenty of room to move and hardly any teenyboppers. There are typically drink specials and cheaper entry fees before 1am.

Bar del Tio　BAR
(☑32-259-9352; www.facebook.com/bardeltio; Av Almirante Montt 67; ☺6pm-1am Tue-Thu, to 3am Fri, 8pm-3am Sat) Jazz music bounces off exposed-brick walls in this classy cocktail bar with dangerously good libations. Soak up the liquor with tasty tapas.

ℹ️ **Information**

DANGERS & ANNOYANCES
Petty street crime and muggings are often reported in the old port area of Valparaíso, so keep a

close watch on your belongings, especially cameras and other electronics. The rest of Valparaíso is fairly safe, but stick to main streets at night and avoid sketchy stairways and alleyways.

INTERNET ACCESS

Most lodgings and tourist-friendly restaurants have free wi-fi.

MEDICAL SERVICES

Hospital Carlos Van Buren (☑ 32-236-4000; www.hospitalcarlosvanburen.cl; San Ignacio 725, El Plan; ⊙ 24hr) A large public hospital.

POST

Post Office (Correos de Chile; www.correos.cl; Prat 856, El Plan; ⊙ 9am-6pm Mon-Fri, 10am-1pm Sat) Centrally located post office.

TOURIST INFORMATION

There are several helpful tourist information stands around town, including one **kiosk** (www.ciudaddevalparaiso.cl; cnr Wagner & Cumming, El Plan; ⊙ 10am-6pm) by Plaza Aníbal Pinto and another **kiosk** (www.ciudaddevalparaiso.cl; Muelle Prat, El Plan; ⊙ 10am-6pm) by Muelle Prat.

USEFUL WEBSITES

Ciudad de Valparaíso (www.ciudaddevalparaiso.cl) Helpful, comprehensive listings of services in the city.

El Mercurio de Valparaíso (www.mercuriovalpo.cl) The city's main newspaper.

Qué hacer en Valpo (www.facebook.com/quehacerenvalpo) The latest on local events and happenings.

❶ Getting There & Away

All major intercity bus services arrive and depart from the **Terminal Rodoviario** (Av Pedro Montt 2800, El Plan), across from the Congreso Nacional, about 20 blocks east of the town center. Be aware, especially if you're arriving at night, that taxis often aren't waiting around the terminal; if you need a ride to your hotel or hostel, you might have to call one or arrange a pick-up ahead of time. If you're walking between the bus station and the center, play it safe by sticking to a major thoroughfare like Pedro Montt.

Turbus (☑ 32-213-3104; www.turbus.cl; Av Pedro Montt 2800, Terminal Rodoviario) runs frequently between Santiago and Valparaíso every day (from CH$3000, 1½ hours); from Santiago, it's easy to connect to Chilean destinations north, south and east.

You can reach Mendoza in Argentina (CH$22,000, eight hours) with Turbus or **Cata Internacional** (☑ 800-835-917; www.catainternacional.com; Av Pedro Montt 2800, Terminal Rodoviario).

The city transportation network, **Transporte Metropolitano Valparaíso** (TMV; ☑ 32-259-

4689; www.tmv.cl; one-way within El Plan CH$250, El Plan to Cerro CH$400), has services to Viña del Mar (CH$450 to CH$500, depending on the hour of departure) and the northern beach towns. For Reñaca, take the orange 607, 602 or 605. The 602 and 605 continue to Concón.

❶ Getting Around

Walking is the best way to get about central Valparaíso and explore its *cerros* – you can cheat on the way up by taking an *ascensor* or a *taxi colectivo* (CH$500). Countless local buses run by TMV run along Condell and Av Pedro Montt, Av Brasil and Yungay, connecting one end of El Plan with the other.

Taxis are much more expensive in Valparaíso than other Chilean cities.

If you're willing to brave the hills on a bike, you'll see a few outfitters around town renting bicycles (generally CH$6000 per half-day).

Viña del Mar

☑ 32 / POP 334,300

Clean and orderly Viña del Mar is a sharp contrast to the charming jumble of neighboring Valparaíso. Manicured boulevards lined with palm trees, stately palaces, a sprawling public beach and beautiful expansive parks have earned it the nickname of Ciudad Jardín (Garden City). Its official name, which means 'Vineyard by the Sea,' stems from the area's colonial origins as the hacienda of the Carrera family. Not many foreign travelers stay here, opting instead for a day trip from Valparaíso. Nevertheless, Viña remains a popular weekend and summer destination for well-to-do Santiaguinos – and the *carrete* (partying) here is first rate.

◉ Sights

Museo de Arqueología e Historia Francisco Fonck MUSEUM

(☑ 32-268-6753; www.museofonck.cl; 4 Norte 784; adult/child CH$2800/500; ⊙ 10am-2pm & 3-6pm Mon, 10am-6pm Tue-Sat, 10am-2pm Sun) The original *moai* (an Easter Island statue) standing guard outside the Museo de Arqueología e Historia Francisco Fonck is just a teaser of the beautifully displayed archaeological finds from Easter Island within, along with Mapuche silverwork and anthropomorphic Moche ceramics. Upstairs are old-school insect cases and taxidermied Chilean fauna.

Parque Quinta Vergara PARK

(Errázuriz 563; ⊙ 7am-7pm) Nowhere is Viña's nickname of the 'Garden City' better justified than at the magnificently landscaped Parque Quinta Vergara, which you enter from Errázuriz at the south end of Libertad (here called Eduardo Grove). It once belonged to one of the city's most illustrious families, the Alvares-Vergaras.

Cerro Castillo
AREA

A fantastic barrio for an afternoon stroll, with lovingly restored mansions, great city lookouts, a small 'castle' and the summer palace of the President of Chile. To reach the top of the hill, take the Bajada Britania (near Castillo Wulff) or Vista Hermosa (off Calle Valparaíso).

🛏 Sleeping

Not Found Hostel
HOSTEL $

(☑cell 9-3054-8854; www.notfoundrooms.com; Paseo Cousiño s/n; dm/d incl breakfast without bathroom CH$15,000/35,000; 🛜) Follow the cryptic yellow markings to the 3rd floor of a once-abandoned building on Paseo Cousiño to find Not Found Hostel. With hearty breakfasts, fluffy comforters on every bed and a sleek minimalist look, it's one of the best hostels in town.

Columba Hostel
HOSTEL $

(☑32-299-1669; www.columbahostel.com; Calle Valparaíso 618; dm CH$10,000-15,000, d with/without bathroom incl breakfast CH$35,000/30,000; 🛜) This vibrant hostel contains stylish dorms and doubles with colorful linens, hardwood floors and urban art. It's not always the cleanest, but the central location is great and there's a communal kitchen, a female-only dorm and a chillout room with a TV. The private rooms are actually pretty passable.

Eco-Hostal Offenbacher-hof
B&B $$

(☑32-262-1483; www.offenbacher-hof.cl; Balmaceda 102; r incl breakfast CH$55,000-68,000; 🛜) 🏵 There are fabulous views over the city from this commanding chestnut-and-yellow mansion atop quiet Cerro Castillo. Sweeping views, newly renovated bathrooms and antique furnishings make this your best buy in Viña del Mar. It's spotless, the owner is charming and there's an amazing patio for afternoon tea.

🍴 Eating & Drinking

Most of Viña's cheap eats are clustered on and around busy Calle Valparaíso in the town center. Paseo Cousiño is home to convivial pubs, some featuring live music.

Panzoni
ITALIAN $

(☑32-271-4134; Paseo Cousiño 12B; mains CH$4000-7000; ⏱1-4pm daily, 8-10pm Thu-Sat) One of the best-value eateries in central Viña, Panzoni's well-prepared Italian pastas and friendly service reel in the lunchtime diners. The location is slightly hidden on an out-of-the-way passageway.

Samoiedo
SANDWICHES $

(☑32-268-4316; www.samoiedo.cl; Calle Valparaíso 639; mains CH$3000-7000; ⏱8am-10:30pm Mon-Sat, 10am-10pm Sun) For half a century the old boys have been meeting at this *confitería* (tearoom) for lunchtime feasts of steak and fries or well-stuffed sandwiches. The outdoor seating is greatly preferable to the interior, which is open to a busy shopping mall.

★ Sativo
CHILEAN $$

(☑cell 9-8219-1025; www.sativorestaurant.com; 4 Poniente 630, Local 18; mains CH$8000-13,000; ⏱12:30-4pm Wed-Sun, 8-11:30pm Tue-Sat; 🛜) Don't let the simple storefront fool you: the plates here are works of art, the ingredients are fresh, the wine list is intriguing and the service is sublime. From the herb-filled butters and breads you get when you arrive to the free digestif offered when you leave, this will no doubt be a memorable dining experience. Try the octopus carpaccio.

★ Café Journal
CLUB

(www.facebook.com/cafejournal1999; cnr Agua Santa & Alvares; cover free-CH$3000; ⏱noon-3:30am Sun-Thu, to 4:30am Fri & Sat) Electronic music is the order of the evening at this boomingly popular club, which has two heaving dance floors, a lively terrace and an attached concert hall where emerging bands play on Friday and Saturday nights.

La Flor de Chile
BAR

(☑32-268-9554; www.laflordechile.cl; 8 Norte 601; mains CH$4000-10,000; ⏱noon-midnight Mon-Sat) For nearly 40 years, Viñamarinos young and old have downed their *schops* (draft beer) over the closely packed tables of this gloriously old-school bar.

Barbones
BAR

(☑cell 9-6434-2200; www.barbones.cl; 7 Norte 444; mains CH$5000-9000; ⏱12:30pm-3am; 🛜) Gourmet Chilean sandwiches and *chorrillanas* (fries slathered in meat, eggs and onions), well-priced cocktails you can order by the pitcher and an extensive list of craft beers on tap make this open-air restobar a one-stop spot for dinners that segue into late-night fun.

ℹ Information

Several banks have ATMs on Plaza Vergara, the main square.

Conaf (☑ 32-232-0210; www.conaf.cl; 3 Norte 541; ⊘ 9am-2pm Mon-Fri) Provides information on nearby parks, including **Parque Nacional La Campana** (☑ 33-244-1342; www.conaf.cl/parques/parque-nacional-la-campana; adult/child CH$4000/2000; ⊘ 9am-5pm Sat-Thu, to 4:30pm Fri).

Hospital Gustavo Fricke (☑ 32-257-7602; www.hospitalfricke.cl; Alvares 1532; ⊘ 24hr) Viña's main public hospital, located east of downtown.

Municipal Tourist Office (☑ 32-218-5712; www.visitevinadelmar.cl; Av Arlegui 715; ⊘ 9am-2pm & 3-7pm Mon-Fri, 10am-2pm & 3-6pm Sat & Sun) Stop by for maps, pamphlets and English-language tourist assistance.

Post Office (Correos de Chile; Plaza Vergara s/n; ⊘ 9am-7pm Mon-Fri, 10am-1pm Sat) Centrally located post office off the main plaza.

ℹ Getting There & Away

All long-distance services operate from the orderly **Rodoviario Viña del Mar** (☑ 32-275-2000; www.rodoviario.cl; Av Valparaíso 1055). There's tourist information here and luggage storage downstairs (CH$1000).

There are frequent departures for northern coastal towns from Reñaca to Papudo through several local bus lines through the **Transporte Metropolitano Valparaíso** (TMV; www.tmv.cl; short-distance trips CH$440), plus privately run line **Sol del Pacífico** (☑ 32-275-2008; www.soldelpacifico.cl). To catch one, go to Plaza Vergara and the area around Viña del Mar's metro station; expect to pay between CH$1200 and CH$2200 one-way, depending on your final destination. For Reñaca, take the orange 607, 601 or 605. The 601 continues to Concón, or take the 302 instead.

ℹ Getting Around

Frequent local buses run by Transporte Metropolitano Valparaíso connect Viña and Valparaíso. Some routes run along the waterfront following Av Marina and Av San Martín; others run through the town center along Av España and Av Libertad. Destinations are usually displayed in the windshield. The commuter train **Metro Valparaíso** (☑ 32-252-7633; www.metro-valparaiso.cl; ⊘ 6am-11pm Mon-Fri, from 7:30am Sat & Sun) also runs between Viña and Valpo every six to 12 minutes during the day.

Around Viña del Mar

North of Viña del Mar, a beautiful road snakes along the coast, passing through a string of beach towns that hum with holidaying Chileans from December to February. Towering condos overlook some, while others are scattered with rustic cottages and the huge summer houses of Chile's rich and famous.

Come to **Reñaca**, just north of Viña, for a sunset hike with incredible views on **Roca Oceanica**, a rocky hill looking out over the Pacific. Continue to **Concón**, 15km from Viña, for its unpretentious seafood restaurants. **Las Deliciosas** (☑ 32-281-1448; Av Borgoño 25370; empanadas CH$1500-2800; ⊘ 9:30am-9pm) does exquisite empanadas; the classic is cheese and crab.

Further north, **Horcón** was Chile's first hippie haven. Brightly painted, ramshackle buildings clutter the steep main road down to its small, rocky beach where fishing boats come and go. These days there's still a hint of peace, love and communal living – note the happy-go-lucky folks gathering on the beach at sunset with dogs, guitars and bottles of liquor in paper bags.

About 21km north of Horcón, the long, sandy beaches of **Maitencillo** stretch for several kilometers along the coast. **Escuela de Surf Maitencillo** (☑ cell 9-9238-4682; www.escueladesurfmaitencillo.cl; Av del Mar 1450; group class per person CH$16,000; ⊘ classes at noon & 4pm Mar-Dec, extended hours Jan & Feb) is a relaxed place to learn how to surf. A favorite restaurant, bar and cabin complex is **Cabañas Hermansen & La Canasta** (☑ 32-277-1028; www.hermansen.cl; Av del Mar 592; mains CH$7500-15,000; ⊘ 12:30pm-midnight Thu-Sat, to 4pm Sun) for wood-baked pizzas and – of course – fresh fish.

The small, laid back town of **Cachagua**, 13km north of Maitencillo, sits on the northern tip of a long crescent beach. Just across the water is the **Monumento Nacional Isla de Cachagua** (www.conaf.cl/parques/monumento-natural-isla-cachagua; Cachagua), a guano-stained rocky outcrop that's home to roughly 2000 Humboldt penguins, as well as a colony of sea lions.

Continue north 3km to reach **Zapallar**, the most exclusive of Chile's coastal resorts, with still-unspoiled beaches flanked by densely wooded hillsides. Everyone who's anyone in Zapallar makes a point of lunching at **El Chiringuito** (☑ cell 9-9248-3139; Francisco de Paula Pérez s/n, Zapallar; mains CH$12,500-20,000; ⊘ 12:30-6pm Sun-Wed, to midnight Thu-Sat, extended hours Jan & Feb; Ⓟ), where terrace tables look out over the rocks and pelicans fishing for their dinner.

Several bus companies visit Zapallar direct from Santiago, including Turbus (p461) and Pullman (p461). Sol del Pacífico (p473) comes up the coast from Viña.

NORTHERN CHILE

Traveling inland, the balmy coast of sunbathers and surfers shifts to cactus scrub plains and dry mountains streaked in reddish tones. Mines scar these ore-rich mammoths whose primary reserve, copper, fuels Chile's economic engine. But there's life here as well, in the fertile valleys producing *pisco* grapes, papayas and avocados. Clear skies mean exceptional celestial observation – it's no wonder many international telescopic, optical and radio projects are based here. The driest desert in the world, the Atacama is a refuge of flamingos on salt lagoons, sculpted moonscapes and geysers ringed by snow-tipped volcanoes.

The Norte Chico, or 'region of 10,000 mines,' is a semiarid transition zone from the Valle Central to the Atacama. Ancient South American cultures left enormous geoglyphs on barren hillsides. Aymara peoples still farm the precordillera (the foothills of the Andes) and pasture llamas and alpacas in the highlands. You can diverge from the desert scenery to explore the working mine of Chuquicamata or brave the frisky surf of arid coastal cities.

Take precautions against altitude sickness in the mountains and avoid drinking tap water in the desert reaches.

La Serena

📵 051 / POP 218,000

Blessed with neocolonial architecture, shady streets and golden shores, peaceful La Serena turns trendy beach resort come summer. Founded in 1544, Chile's second-oldest city is a short jaunt from character-laden villages, sun-soaked *pisco* vineyards and international observatories for stargazing. Nearby Coquimbo is more rough-and-tumble, but lives and breathes a hearty nightlife.

⦿ Sights & Activities

Excursions in the region range from national-park visits to nighttime astronomical trips and *pisco*-tasting tours. Agencies in town offer full-day trips through the Elqui Valley, boat trips in the Reserva Nacional Pingüino de Humboldt (Islas Damas; www.conaf.cl/parques/reserva-nacional-pinguino-de-humboldt; adult/child CH$6000/3000; ⊙9am-3pm Dec-Mar, 9am-3pm

Wed-Sun Apr-Nov) and nighttime stargazing in the valley's observatories; try Ecoturismo La Serena (📵 cell 9-7615-2371; www.ecoturismolaserena.cl; Francisco de Aguirre 76; full-day tours CH$50,000) or Tembeta Tours (📵 51-221-5553; www.tembeta.cl; Andres Bello 870; day tours from CH$34,000).

La Serena has a whopping 29 churches: on the Plaza de Armas is the 1844 Iglesia Catedral (Plaza de Armas; ⊙10am-1pm & 4-8pm), and two blocks west is the mid-18th-century Iglesia Santo Domingo (cnr Cordovez & Muñoz; 9am-6pm). The stone colonial-era Iglesia San Francisco (Balmaceda 640; ⊙9am-6pm) dates from the early 1600s.

Observatorio Collowara OBSERVATORY
(📵 cell 9-7645-2970; www.collowara.cl; Urmeneta 675, Andacollo; CH$5500) Like Mamalluca (p479), the shiny hilltop Observatorio Collowara in Andacollo is built for tourists; no serious interstellar research is conducted here. Two-hour tours run in summer at 9:30pm, 11pm and 12:30am; in winter they are at 8pm and 10:30pm. The facility boasts three viewing platforms and a 40cm telescope – slightly larger than that at Mamalluca. There are also three smaller telescopes available, so you won't have to wait for long.

Museo Arqueológico MUSEUM
(www.museoarqueologicolaserena.cl; cnr Cordovez & Cienfuegos; ⊙9:30am-5:50pm Tue-Fri, 10am-1pm & 4-7pm Sat, 10am-1pm Sun) FREE Inside a crescent-shaped building with a leafy patio, this museum makes an ambitious attempt to corral Chile's pre-Columbian past. Its highlights include an Atacameña mummy, a hefty 2.5m-high *moai* (large anthropomorphic statue) from Easter Island and interesting Diaguita artifacts such as a dinghy made from sea-lion hide.

Museo Histórico Casa
Gabriel González Videla MUSEUM
(www.museohistoricolaserena.cl; Matta 495; ⊙10am-6pm Mon-Fri, to 1pm Sat) FREE Although richly stocked with general historical artifacts, this two-story museum in an 18th-century mansion concentrates on one of La Serena's best-known (and most controversial) sons. González Videla was Chile's president from 1946 to 1952. Ever the cunning politician, he took power with communist support but then promptly outlawed the party, driving poet Pablo Neruda out of the Senate and into exile. Controversy aside, González Videla was the world's first head of state to visit Antarctica (in 1948).

Northern Chile (Norte Chico)

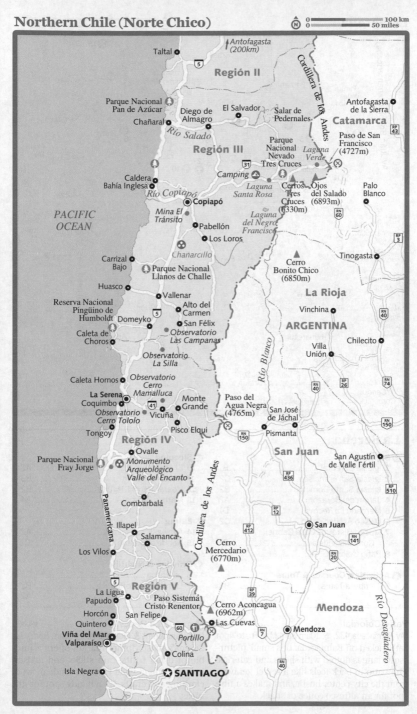

0 — 100 km
0 — 50 miles

CHILE LA SERENA

La Serena

La Serena

◎ Sights
1	Iglesia Catedral	B1
2	Iglesia San Francisco	C2
3	Iglesia Santo Domingo	B2
4	Jardín del Corazón	A2
5	Mercado La Recova	D1
6	Museo Arqueológico	C2
7	Museo Histórico Casa Gabriel	
	González Videla	B1
8	Patio Colonial	C1

⊕ Activities, Courses & Tours
9	Tembeta Tours	B3

⊨ Sleeping
10	El Arbol	A2
11	Hostal El Punto	B3
12	Hostal Tierra Diaguita	B2
13	Maria's Casa	A4

⊗ Eating
14	Ayawasi	A2
15	Donde el Guatón	D1

⊜ Drinking & Nightlife
16	La Rocca	C2
17	Lighthouse Coffee	B2
18	Moscatel	A2

Patio Colonial   AREA
(Av Balmaceda 432; ⊙10am-8pm Mon-Fri, to 4pm Sat) Tucked off Balmaceda, this small, picturesque lane is dotted with shops and eateries. The patio in back feels like a secret getaway from the city-center bustle, and makes a fine spot for an alfresco coffee or snack.

Mercado La Recova   MARKET
(cnr Cantournet & Cienfuegos; ⊙10am-8pm) La Serena's most vibrant market offers a jumble of dried fruits, rain sticks and artisan jewelry, plus a wide range of Andean wool clothing and crafts. It's a handy spot for gift ideas.

Jardín del Corazón PARK
(Parque Japonés Kokoro No Niwa; Eduardo de la Barra; adult/child CH$1000/300; ☺10am-7:40pm daily Dec-Mar, to 5:40pm Tue-Sun Apr-Nov) With its trickling brooks, drifting swans and neatly manicured rock gardens, this Japanese garden makes an idyllic escape from the city bustle. Don't miss the greenhouse collection of adorable bonsai trees in diminutive forms of *ciruela* (cherry), *higuera* (fig) and ficus trees.

🛏 Sleeping

Hostal El Punto HOSTEL $
(☑51-222-8474; www.hostalelpunto.cl; Bello 979; d/tr from CH$32,000/40,000, dm/s/d/tr without bathroom from CH$11,000/19,000/22,000/32,000; @☎) This is La Serena's best hostel, with a wide range of rooms, a bunch of sunny terraces, bright mosaics and tree-trunk tables. The staff speak German and English, and provide travel tips, tours, bike rental, nice cakes, laundry, book exchange...you name it. You'll want to book months ahead, especially in high season.

El Arbol HOSTEL $
(☑51-221-6053; www.hostalelarbol.cl; Eduardo de la Barra 29; dm/d without bathroom from CH$9000/22,000; ☎) Near the lush Parque Japones, this converted colonial house has just a handful of rooms, all sunny and well maintained. There's a pretty bougainvillea-clad garden in front and English-speaking staff on hand, and guests can make themselves at home and use the lounge area, kitchen and barbecue.

Maria's Casa GUESTHOUSE $
(☑cell 9-7466-7433; www.hostalmariacasa.cl; Las Rojas 18; d CH$28,000, s/d without bathroom CH$20,000/25,000; ☎) This family-run spot features cottage-style rooms that are simple and cozy, and there's a garden in back where you can camp (CH$5000 per person). Other backpacker-friendly amenities include well-scrubbed shared bathrooms, a quaint country kitchen with free tea and coffee, laundry service and bike rental.

★Hostal Tierra Diaguita HOSTAL $$
(☑51-221-6608; www.terradiaguita.cl; Eduardo de la Barra 440; incl breakfast s/d CH$46,000/55,000, without bathroom CH$40,000/46,000; ☎) Inside a colonial house and leafy patio sprinkled with pre-Columbian designs and artwork, you'll find a mix of attractively designed rooms, all with comfy furniture and modern bathroom. Guests can relax in the verdant back garden, complete with small open fires on cold nights. There's also an inside lounge area, where the excellent breakfast is served.

🍴 Eating

Ayawasi VEGETARIAN $
(Pedro Pablo Muñoz 566; mains CH$4000-9500; ☺9am-10pm Mon-Wed & Fri, to 4pm Thu, noon-5pm Sat; ☑) A short walk from the plaza, this little vegetarian oasis serves some fantastic set lunches, delicious fresh juices and innovative sandwiches and salads in a shady garden setting or laid-back dining room.

Lemongrass ASIAN $$
(☑cell 9-9760-6361; Las Rojas Peniente 261; mains CH$7000-10,500; ☺12:30-5pm Mon-Sat; ☑) Tucked away in a residential neighborhood 1.5km south of the plaza, Lemongrass has a loyal local following for its delicious pan-Asian cooking – a rarity in these parts. Grab a table on the small front terrace and fire up your taste buds with massaman curry (a Thai coconut curry), Malaysian-style rice noodles with shrimp, or wok stir-fried vegetables.

Donde el Guatón CHILEAN $$
(Brasil 750; mains CH$6200-13,000; ☺12:30-11pm Mon-Sat, 1-6pm Sun) One of La Serena's best restaurants, Donde el Guatón has a covered courtyard with beautifully tiled floors and an aesthetic of rustic elegance – a fine setting for grilled meats and seafood, plus traditional hits like *pastel de choclo* (beef and corn casserole). The dapper, hat-wearing waitstaff deserve special mention for the friendly service.

La Mia Pizza ITALIAN $$
(☑51-221-2232; Av del Mar 2100; mains CH$7000-12,000; ☺noon-midnight Mon-Sat, to 4:30pm Sun) Out on La Serena's oceanfront, La Mia Pizza has a solid reputation among locals for its excellent Italian fare (pizzas, pastas), plus top-notch seafood. It's a classy spot with big windows and a deck overlooking the shore – though a busy road separates it from the sands.

🍷 Drinking & Nightlife

The happening part of town is the area around the corner of Eduardo de la Barra and O'Higgins, where you'll find boho student crowds. Nightclubs sparkle along the seafront, past the lighthouse and all the way to Barrio Inglés in Coquimbo; they're especially hot during summer.

CHILE LA SERENA

CLOUD FORESTS & HOT SPRINGS

An ecological island of lush Valdivian cloud forest in semi-desert surroundings, **Parque Nacional Bosques de Fray Jorge** (Parque Nacional Fray Jorge; www.conaf.cl/parques/parque-nacional-bosque-fray-jorge; off Ruta 5; adult/child CH$6000/3000; ⊙ 9am-5:30pm daily Dec-Mar, 9am-5:30pm Thu-Sun Apr-Nov) is 80km west of Ovalle. Of Fray Jorge's 100 sq km, there remain only 400 hectares of its truly unique vegetation – enough, though, to make it a Unesco World Biosphere Reserve. There's no public transportation, but agencies in La Serena and Ovalle offer tours.

Stop in at **Termas de Socos**, a tiny spring hidden 1.5km off the Panamericana at Km370. Private tubs cost CH$5000 for a half-hour soak in steamy baths; access to the cool public swimming pool also costs CH$5000 for nonguests. Stay at the delightful on-site **Hotel Termas Socos** (☑ 53-198-2505; www.termassocos.cl; s/d incl full board CH$67,000/123,000; P ⊠), with lush surroundings and private thermal baths. Nearby **Camping Termas de Socos** (☑ 53-263-1490; www.campingtermassocos.cl; campsites per person CH$7000; ⊠) also offers its own springs and bike rentals.

Lighthouse Coffee
CAFE
(www.lighthousecoffee.cl; Matta 570; ⊙ 9am-9pm Mon-Fri, 10am-10pm Sat) This hip, art-filled cafe serves the best coffee in town. Linger over Chemex brews and V60 pour-overs whipped up by friendly baristas. If you're craving something sweet, cast your eye over the strawberry-topped cheesecake, pumpkin pie and other decadent desserts to the right of the counter.

Moscatel
COCKTAIL BAR
(www.moscatel.cl; Pedro Pablo Muñoz 580; ⊙ 9am-11pm Mon-Wed, to 1am Thu & Fri, 7pm-2am Sat) This stylish, upscale *pisco* bar serves more than 40 varieties, including rare types you won't find elsewhere. You can enjoy it straight or in beautifully made cocktails like the Sangre del Elqui with *horchata* (a rice and cinnamon drink) and grenadine, or a classic *pisco* sour. Quality craft beers and ample sharing plates (empanadas, ceviche, charcuterie, vegetarian carpaccio) round out the menu.

La Rocca
BAR
(www.facebook.com/publarocca; Eduardo de la Barra 569; ⊙ 2:30pm-3am Mon-Sat) Stay out late drinking on the interior patio at this popular student hangout with occasional live music.

❶ Information

Banks with 24-hour ATMs line the plaza.
Hospital Juan de Diós (☑ 51-233-3312; www.hospitalserena.cl; Balmaceda 916; ⊙24hr) The emergency entrance is at the corner of Larraín Alcalde and Anfión Muñóz.
Sernatur (☑ 51-222-5199; www.turismoregiondecoquimbo.cl; Matta 461; ⊙10am-8pm Mon-Fri, to 6pm Sat & Sun Dec-Mar, 9am-6pm Mon-Fri, 10am-2pm Sat Apr-Nov) Excellent

tourist info offered at this office by the Plaza de Armas.
Cámara de Turismo Kiosk (Prat; ⊙10am-6pm Mon-Fri, to 2pm Sat Dec-Feb) In summer the municipal tourist office runs an information kiosk by Iglesia La Merced.

❶ Getting There & Away

AIR
La Serena's **Aeropuerto La Florida** (LSC; ☑ 51-227-0353; www.aeropuertodelaserena.cl) is around 5km east of downtown along Ruta 41.
LATAM (☑ 600-526-2000; Balmaceda 406; ⊙9am-2pm & 3-6pm Mon-Fri, 10:30am-1:30pm Sat) flies daily to Santiago (from CH$25,000, one hour) and to Antofagasta (from CH$19,000, 1½ hours). Sky (www.skyairline.com) also flies to Santiago (from CH$11,000) and Antofagasta (from CH$12,000).

BUS
Terminal de Buses (☑ 51-222-4573; cnr Amunátegui & Av El Santo), just southwest of the center, has dozens of carriers plying the Panamericana from Santiago north to Arica, including **Turbus** (☑ 51-221-3060; www.turbus.cl) and **Pullman Bus** (☑ 51-221-8879; www.pullman.cl; Eduardo de la Barra 435).

Typical destinations and fares are as follows:

DESTINATION	COST (CH$)	DURATION (HR)
Antofagasta	18,000-36,000	12
Arica	38,000-51,000	22
Calama	17,000-39,000	14
Copiapó	9000-18,000	5
Iquique	27,000-43,000	19
Santiago	8000-18,000	6
Vallenar	5000-10,000	3

To get to Vicuña (CH$2700, 1½ hours), Ovalle (CH$2700, two hours), Montegrande (CH$4000, two hours) or Pisco Elqui (CH$4000, 2½ hours), try **Via Elqui** (☑ 51-231-2422; cnr Juan de Dios Peni & Esmeralda). You can even do Elqui Valley as a day trip; the first bus to Vicuña departs at 6:40am and the last returns at 9pm. **Hector Galleguillos** (☑ 51-225-3206; Aguirre s/n) offers bus service from La Serena to Punta de Choros.

For Argentine destinations, **Cata Internacional** (www.catainternacional.com) departs on Sundays at 7am for Mendoza (from CH$30,000, 12 hours). In summer **Covalle Bus** (☑ 51-222-1751; Infante 538) also goes to Mendoza (CH$45,000, 12 hours) and San Juan (CH$45,000, 18 hours) via the Libertadores pass every Wednesday and Friday, leaving at 11pm.

❶ Getting Around

Private taxis to Aeropuerto La Florida, 5km east of downtown on Ruta 41, cost CH$6000; try **Radio Taxi Florida** (☑ 51-221-2122; http://radiotaxila florida.cl). Women traveling alone should be wary in La Serena; sexual assaults have been reported. Only take company cabs.

For car hire, try **Avis** (☑ 51-254-5300; Av Francisco de Aguirre 063; ⊙ 8am-6:30pm Mon-Fri, 9am-2pm Sat), **Hertz** (☑ 51-222-6171; Av Francisco de Aguirre 0220; ⊙ 8:30am-6:30pm Mon-Fri) or **Econorent** (☑ 51-222-0113; Av Francisco de Aguirre 0141; ⊙ 8:30am-6:40pm Mon-Fri, 9am-1pm Sat). They all have stands at the airport as well as downtown offices.

Elqui Valley

The heart of Chilean *pisco* production, the Elqui Valley is carpeted with a broad cover of striated green. Famous for its futuristic observatories, seekers of cosmic energies, frequent UFO sightings, poet Gabriela Mistral and quaint villages, this is a truly enchanting and enchanted area, and one of the must-visit places in Norte Chico.

Vicuña

☑ 051 / POP 27,800

The spirit of Gabriela Mistral's somnambulist poetry seeps from every pore of snoozy little Vicuña. Just 62km east of La Serena, the town, with its low-key plaza, lyrical air and compact dwellings, is worth a visit for a day or two before you head out into the countryside to indulge in fresh avocados and papayas – not to mention the famous grapes that are distilled into *pisco*.

◉ Sights & Activities

Museo Gabriela Mistral   MUSEUM
(☑ 51-241-1223; www.mgmistral.cl; Av Gabriela Mistral 759; ⊙ 10am-5:45pm Tue-Fri, 10:30am-6pm Sat, 10am-1pm Sun) **FREE** The town's landmark Museo Gabriela Mistral, between Riquelme and Baquedano, celebrates one of Chile's most famous literary figures. Gabriela Mistral was born Lucila Godoy Alcayaga in 1889 in Vicuña. The museum charts her life (in Spanish only), from a replica of her adobe birthplace to her Nobel Prize, and has a clutch of busts making her seem a particularly strict schoolmarm.

Cervecería Guayacan   BREWERY
(☑ cell 9-4042-0947; www.cervezaguayacan.cl; Calle Principal 33, Diaguitas; ⊙ noon-8pm) **FREE** You won't get far in the Elqui Valley without someone offering you a Guayacan, and if you're even vaguely interested in beer, you should accept. This little craft brewery's reputation is growing fast, and brief tours of the facilities are accompanied by a generous sampling of its products.

The brewery is in the small village of Diaguitas, about 7km east of downtown Vicuña, and there's an inviting beer garden serving up tasty pizzas and burgers (mains CH$5000 to CH$7000) from Wednesday to Sunday.

Planta Pisco Capel   DISTILLERY
(☑ 51-255-4337; www.centroturisticocapel.cl; tours from CH$4000; ⊙ 10am-7:30pm Jan & Feb, to 6pm Mar-Dec) Capel distills *pisco* at this facility and has its only bottling plant here. Located about 2km (a 20-minute walk) southeast of town, this large *pisco* maker offers 45-minute tours of the facilities, which includes an on-site museum and a few skimpy samples (CH$15,000 gets you the premium tour, with snacks and tastings of six top-shelf *piscos*). To get here, head southeast of town and across the bridge, then turn left.

Observatorio Cerro Mamalluca   OBSERVATORY
(☑ 51-267-0330; www.observatoriomamalluca.cl; adult/child CH$7000/2500) The star of the stargazing show, the purpose-built Observatorio Cerro Mamalluca, 9km northeast of Vicuña, is Elqui Valley's biggest attraction. So big, in fact, that you're likely to share the tour with hordes of other tourists, all looking for their chance to goggle at distant galaxies, star clusters and nebulae through a 30cm telescope.

Bilingual guided two-hour tours take place nightly every hour between 8:30pm and

WORTH A TRIP

EXPLORING THE ELQUI VALLEY

Drive a car or rent a bicycle to explore the charming villages around Pisco Elqui. Highlights include tasting *pisco* and touring the artisanal *pisquera* **Fundo Los Nichos** (📞 51-245-1085; www.fundolosnichos.cl; Ruta 485; tours from CH$1000; ⊙ 11am-6pm), established in 1868. It's 3km south of Pisco Elqui.

Moving on from here you'll reach **Horcón Artisanal Market** (Horcón Artisanal Market; 📞 51-245-1015; Ruta D-393, Horcón Bajo; ⊙ noon-7:30pm summer, 1-6:30pm Tue-Sun rest of year), in the valley of its namesake village. Browse the gorgeous handmade arts and crafts, and local natural food and cosmetic products. With an enchanting setting for a meal, El Bosque Horcón lies 1km north of the market.

From Horcón, the paved road turns into a dusty dirt track leading to the adorable village of **Alcoguaz**, 14km beyond Pisco Elqui. Note its yellow and red wooden church and, if you wish to stay, move on to **Casona Distante** (📞 cell 9-9226-5440; www.casonadistante.cl; Fundo Distante, Alcohuaz; r CH$78,000-120,000; 🅿 ✉), a big wooden 1930s farmhouse beautifully restored into a rustic eight-room ecolodge.

2:30am in summer and between 6:30pm and 11:30pm in winter.

Make reservations through the **Mamalluca office** (Av Gabriela Mistral 260; ⊙ 9am-2pm & 3pm–last tour Mon-Fri, 11am-2pm & 4pm–last tour Sat & Sun) in Vicuña; advance booking is recommended. There is no public transportation, but a minivan takes visitors from the Vicuña office (reserve in advance, per person CH$3000). Some La Serena tour agencies arrange trips, or you can hire a taxi in Vicuña.

★ **Alfa Aldea Astronomical Tours**　TOURS
(📞 51-241-2441; www.alfaaldea.cl; Parcela 17, La Viñita; adult/child CH$15,000/5000) If you tire of getting herded around in the large observatories, you may like these small, personalized astronomical tours (in English or Spanish). Held in the on-site amphitheater, tours start with a short video exploring the basics of astronomy, followed by a listen to interstellar sounds via radio telescopes; you'll then get up close with the celestial bodies via scientific-grade telescopes.

It's largely an open-air event – after the introduction the whole thing takes place under the star-filled sky and small group sizes mean plenty of telescope time for everybody – but it can get frosty. Dress warmly (although the blankets, wine and vegetable soup that come with the tour help cut the chill). Reserve ahead; free transportation is included.

Elki Magic　ADVENTURE SPORTS
(📞 cell 9-6877-2015; www.elkimagic.com; San Martin 472; ⊙ 10am-8pm) Run by an enthusiastic Chilean-French couple, this agency offers guided downhill bike jaunts (from CH$15,000), half-day van tours to valley highlights (from CH$15,000) and all-day 4WD trips to the lagoons near Argentina (CH$40,000 including lunch). It also rents bikes (CH$7000 per day) and can provide a map of the 18km trail around the surrounding villages.

🛏 Sleeping

La Elquina　HOSTAL $
(📞 51-241-1317; www.laelquina.cl; O'Higgins 65; campsites per person CH$6000, d CH$30,000, s/d without bathroom CH$15,000/25,000; 🅿 🛜) The best of Vicuña's budget options, La Elquina is a friendly family-run spot with simply furnished rooms set around several spacious courtyards. There are also nicely shaded campsites and a kitchen that's open 24 hours. The outdoor tables on the grass are fine places to unwind in the afternoon.

Alfa Aldea　HOSTAL $
(📞 51-241-2441; www.alfaaldea.cl; La Vinita; s/d CH$20,000/35,000; 🅿 🛜) It's worth the CH$2000 taxi ride (or 15-minute walk) to the outskirts of town to stay in this low-key family-run *hostal*. Nestled in the vineyards and with priceless valley and mountain views, the rooms are simple but extremely comfortable. The stars (sorry) of the show, however, are the excellent astronomical tours held on site.

Hostal Valle Hermoso　HOSTAL $
(📞 51-241-1206; www.hostalvallehermoso.com; Av Gabriela Mistral 706; s/d/tr CH$20,000/40,000/54,000; 🛜) Great lodging choice with eight airy and immaculately clean rooms around a sun-drenched patio inside an old adobe *casona* with Oregon-pine beams and walnut floors. Staff are warm and friendly and the ambience laid-back – as if staying with old friends.

✗ Eating

Govinda's
VEGETARIAN $

(Prat 234, 2nd fl; lunch special CH$3500; ⊙1-5pm Mon-Sat; 🖉) In an airy upstairs space across from the plaza, Govinda's serves up delicious and hearty vegetarian fare, with a menu that changes daily. Spaghetti with vegetables, flavor-packed paella and juicy veggie burgers are recent selections, with homemade desserts topping things off.

Frida
INTERNATIONAL $

(Prat btwn Mistral & Chacabuco; mains CH$3000-4000; ⊙10am-10pm) Vicuña's most colorful cafe is whimsically decorated with Mexican knickknacks and serves up spice-lacking goat's-cheese sandwiches, quesadillas and fajitas, but surprisingly little else in the way of Mexican fare. It's a better spot for afternoon drinks with snacks.

★ Chivato Negro
INTERNATIONAL $$

(www.chivatonegro.com; Mistral 565; mains CH$3000-8500; ⊙9am-11pm Sun-Wed, to 1am Thu-Sat; 🖉) Two blocks east of the plaza, Chivato Negro has a bohemian, vintage vibe with a spacious patio hidden in back. There's a wide-ranging menu of sandwiches, pizzas and regional dishes (like grilled trout), plus a three-course *menú del día* for CH$5000. The cozy setting (with a roaring fire in the evening) invites lingering, whether over coffee or cocktails.

❶ Information

Gather a bit of info on the town's past and present at the municipal **tourist office** (🖉51-267-0308; www.turismovicuna.cl; San Martín 275; ⊙8:30am-8pm Jan & Feb, 8:30am-5:30pm Mon-Fri, 9am-6pm Sat, 9am-2pm Sun Mar-Dec), a few steps west of the main plaza.

❶ Getting There & Around

A block south of the plaza, the **bus terminal** (cnr Prat & O'Higgins) has frequent buses to La Serena (CH$2000, one hour), Pisco Elqui (CH$1500, 50 minutes) and Montegrande (CH$2000, 40 minutes). There's a wider choice of destinations in La Serena.

Pisco Elqui

Renamed to publicize the area's most famous product, the former village of La Unión is a laid-back hideaway in the upper drainage area of the Río Claro, a tributary of the Elqui. It has become the area's most popular backpacker draw in recent years, and while it can get overcrowded, it's well worth a couple of days' stay.

◉ Sights & Activities

Distileria Pisco Mistral
DISTILLERY

(🖉51-245-1358; www.destileriapiscomistral.cl; O'Higgins 746; tours from CH$6000; ⊙noon-7pm Jan & Feb, 11:30am-4:30pm Tue-Sun Mar-Dec) The star attraction in Pisco Elqui is the Distileria Pisco Mistral, which produces the premium Mistral brand of *pisco*. The hour-long 'museum' tour gives you glimpses of the distillation process and includes a free tasting of two *piscos* and a drink at the adjacent restaurant, which hosts occasional live music.

Turismo Dagaz
OUTDOORS

(🖉cell 9-7399-4105; www.turismodagaz.com; Prat s/n; ⊙9am-8pm) Based out of El Tesoro de Elqui (p481), this operator offers numerous tours, from downhill bike tours (CH$20,000) to starlit astro tours (CH$15,000). You can also go for all-day 4WD trips to beautiful and remote corners of Chile (CH$50,000), as well as arrange horseback-riding excursions and treks.

🛏 Sleeping

Refugio del Angel
CAMPGROUND $

(🖉cell 9-8245-9362; www.campingrefugiodelangel.cl; Calle El Condor; campsites per person CH$10,000, day use CH$4000) This idyllic spot by the river has swimming holes, bathrooms and a little shop. The turnoff is 200m south of the plaza off Carrera.

Hostal Triskel
HOSTEL $

(🖉cell 9-9419-8680; www.hostaltriskel.cl; Baquedano s/n; r without bathroom per person CH$15,000; 🛜) Up the hill from town, this lovely adobe and wood house has seven clean rooms with four shared bathrooms and a shared kitchen. A giant fig tree provides shade for the patio and there's a fruit orchard with lots of nooks, crannies and hammocks, plus laundry services.

★ El Tesoro de Elqui
HOTEL $$

(🖉51-245-1069; www.tesoro-elqui.cl; Prat s/n; s CH$30,000-40,000, d CH$45,000-55,000; 🛜🐾) Up the hill from the center plaza, this tranquil oasis dotted with lemon trees, lush gardens and flowering vines has 10 appealing wooden bungalows with terraces. There's a restaurant that serves great coffee and cake, and you can also arrange guided excursions on site.

✖ Eating & Drinking

El Durmiente Elquino
INTERNATIONAL $

(Carrera s/n; mains CH$5000-7500; ⊘1-10pm Tue-Sun) Sample the tasty tapas, pizzas and interesting mains, like quinoa risotto, in the all-natural interior of this restobar full of wood, bamboo, clay and pebbles. Sip an artisanal beer or a glass of organic wine on the small patio out back, with nice mountain views.

La Escuela
CHILEAN $$

(Prat s/n; mains CH$6500-12,000; ⊘12:30-11:30pm) For a memorable night out, head to this polished restaurant on the main road leading south of town. Grab a fireside seat in the courtyard and linger over grilled salmon, oven-baked kid or tender lamb raised locally, which pair nicely with wine and well-mixed cocktails. There are quinoa salads, quiche and at least one vegetarian plate of the day.

Rustika
BAR

(Carrera s/n; ⊘7pm-2am) Just south of the plaza, Rustika is a welcoming spot for an evening libation, with outdoor tables set beside a gurgling brook, and warming fires by starlight. Cocktails aside, Rustika also serves up pizzas, quesadillas, sharing platters and fresh juices.

ℹ Getting There & Away

Pisco Elqui has no gas station so fill up before leaving Vicuña.

Frequent buses travel between Pisco Elqui (CH$1500, 50 minutes) and Vicuña.

Copiapó

☑ 052 / POP 154,000

Welcoming Copiapó has little to hold travelers, but it does offer a handy base for the remote mountains bordering Argentina, especially the breathtaking Parque Nacional Nevado Tres Cruces, Laguna Verde and Ojos del Salado, the highest active volcano in the world. The discovery of silver at nearby Chañarcillo in 1832 provided Copiapó with several firsts, including Chile's first railroad, telegraph and telephone lines.

◉ Sights

Museo Regional de Atacama
MUSEUM

(www.museodeatacama.cl; Atacama 98; ⊘9am-5:45pm Tue-Fri, 10am-12:45pm & 3-5:45pm Sat, 10:30am-1:15pm Sun) FREE This catch-all museum provides an overview of the region's natural and human history, its min-

eral wealth, and key events that have shaped history over the centuries. Among the wide-ranging displays, you'll find ancient zoomorphic vessels for preparing hallucinogens used by indigenous shamans, pottery from the El Molle period (c AD 700) and weaponry from the War of the Pacific when Copiapó was a base of operations for the Chilean invasion of Peru and Bolivia.

★ Mina San José
MINE

(off Carretera C-327; visitor center free, guided tour CH$5000; ⊘10am-6pm Thu-Sun) In 2010, 33 miners were trapped more than 700m underground after a devastating collapse within the mountain where they'd been working. Following a Herculean effort – which pulled resources from a number of countries – all the men were successfully rescued. Televised before a global audience of an estimated one billion, the survivors emerged one by one from the specially built rescue capsule to the cheers of friends, family and assorted onlookers – including the president of Chile, Sebastián Piñera.

Although the mine was closed following the accident, the government reopened the site as a tourist attraction in 2015. At the entrance, you'll pass a hillside with 33 flags (one for each miner, including one Bolivian), which lies near the former site of Campamento Esperanza (Cape Hope), where family and loved ones held a round-the-clock vigil until the men were rescued. Indeed, without the relentless pressure by the miners' spouses, girlfriends and family, rescuers might have given up on the men before they ever made contact (a harrowing 18 days after their ordeal began).

Overlooking the site is a small visitor center that gives details of what the men endured during their 10-week imprisonment deep below the surface. You can watch videos of the unfolding saga and the miners' rescue, including some powerful reunions with men who were taken for dead. The highlight is the tour (in Spanish only) of the site led by Jorge Galleguillos, one of the original 33.

The mine is around 50km northwest of Copiapó. It's reachable by normal vehicle, though most tour agencies in Copiapó also arrange excursions.

🛏 Sleeping & Eating

Hotel El Sol
HOTEL $

(☑52-221-5672; Rodríguez 550; s/d CH$25,000/32,000; 🅿🛜) Cheerful yellow-painted hotel

PARQUE NACIONAL NEVADO TRES CRUCES

Hard-to-reach **Parque Nacional Nevado Tres Cruces** (www.conaf.cl/parques/parque-nacional-nevado-de-tres-cruces; adult/child CH\$5000/1500; ⊗8:30am-6pm) has all the rugged beauty and a fraction of the tourists of more famous high-altitude parks further north. Quite apart from pristine peaks and first-rate climbing challenges, the park shields some wonderful wildlife: flamingos in summer, large herds of vicuñas and guanacos, giant and horned coots and even the occasional condor and puma. Located just outside the park boundaries, 6893m **Ojos del Salado** is Chile's highest peak, a mere 69m short of Argentina's Aconcagua, the continent's highest and the world's highest active volcano.

It's easy to get lost on your way to the national park, and there is no public transportation; consider taking a tour from Copiapó. **Puna de Atacama** (☐cell 9-9051-3202; www.punadeatacama.com; day trips from CH\$115,000) comes recommended for tailored 4WD trips in the region. For rustic overnight accommodations at **Refugio Laguna del Negro Francisco** (per person per night CH\$10,000), check with Conaf (p483) in Copiapó.

with a string of simple but clean rooms at a good price, just a short walk from the plaza.

★**Hotel La Casona** HOTEL **$$**
(☐52-221-7277; www.lacasonahotel.cl; O'Higgins 150; s/d from CH\$48,000/54,000; 🛜) There's airiness and charm to this wonderfully homey 12-room hotel a 10-minute walk west of the plaza, boasting bilingual owners and a series of leafy patios. All room categories have a country-casual feel, hardwood floors and cable TVs. The restaurant serves delicious dinners.

Diventare CAFE **$**
(www.facebook.com/cafeteriadiventare; O'Higgins 760; sandwiches CH\$2500-5000; ⊗8:30am-9pm Mon-Sat) A short stroll from the plaza, Diventare is a charming, sun-drenched cafe with outdoor tables perfect for enjoying quality espressos, yogurt with granola, and baguette sandwiches. The gelato counter is a big draw on hot days.

La Chingana CHILEAN **$$**
(www.facebook.com/lachingana.restopub; Atacama 271; mains CH\$7000-15,000; ⊗noon-3am Mon-Sat, 8pm-3am Sun) A lively spot for a meal or a drink, with various art-filled rooms and an inviting back terrace. Three-course daily lunch specials (CH\$5000) are good value. The cocktails are first-rate and there's live music on weekends.

❶ Information

Numerous ATMs are located at banks around the plaza.
Conaf (☐52-221-3404; Rodriguez 434; ⊗8:30am-5:30pm Mon-Thu, to 4:30pm Fri) Has information on regional parks, including brochures in English about Pan de Azúcar.

Sernatur (☐52-221-2838; Los Carrera 691; ⊗8:30am-7pm Mon-Fri, 9am-3pm Sat & Sun Jan & Feb, 8:30am-6pm Mon-Fri Mar-Dec) The well-run tourist office on the main plaza gives out a wealth of materials and information in English.

❶ Getting There & Away

The **Aeropuerto Desierto de Atacama** (☐52-252-3600; www.aeropuertodecaldera.cl; Ruta 5 Norte, Km863, Caldera) is about 50km west of Copiapó.

LATAM (☐600-526-2000; Colipí 484, Mall Plaza Real, Local A-102; ⊗9am-2pm & 3-6pm Mon-Fri, 10:30am-1:30pm Sat) Flies to Santiago daily (from CH\$54,000, 1½ hours).

Bus companies are scattered through Copiapó's southern quarter. Virtually all north–south buses stop here, as do many bound for the interior. **Pullman Bus** (☐52-221-2629; Colipí 127) has a large terminal with many departures as does **Turbus** (☐52-223-8612; Chañarcillo 680). Other companies include **Expreso Norte** (☐52-223-1176; Chañarcillo 655), **Buses Libac** (☐52-221-2237; Chañarcillo 655) and **Condor Bus** (☐52-221-3645; www.condorbus.cl; Chañarcillo 631), all located in a common terminal on Chañarcillo. Note that many buses to northern desert destinations leave at night.

Standard destinations and common fares are shown in the following table:

DESTINATION	COST (CH$)	DURATION (HR)
Antofagasta	15,000	8
Arica	25,000	18
Calama	20,000	10
Iquique	26,000	15
La Serena	10,000	5
Santiago	30,000	12
Vallenar	7000	2

BAHÍA INGLESA

With rocky outcrops jutting out of turquoise waters and a long white-sand beach, this sweet seaside resort offers ideal beachside frolicking. The name originates from the British pirates who anchored here in the 17th century. Today, it's one of the north's most popular vacation spots, hectic in summer and mellow (and much cheaper) in the off season. There's a cool Mediterranean feel and a lovely beachfront promenade. Locally harvested scallops, oysters and seaweed sweeten the culinary offerings.

Even if you can't afford to stay at the swanky **Coral de Bahía** (📱 cell 9-8434-7749; www.coraldebahia.cl; Av El Morro 559; d with/without view CH$90,000/65,000; P 🛜), it's worth dining on its delectable seafood while enjoying the beachfront views.

From Copiapó, bus first to Caldera (CH$2500, one hour). From Caldera's bus terminal and main square, fast *colectivos* run to Bahía Inglesa (CH$1000, 10 minutes).

Buses Casther (📱52-221-8889; www.casther.cl; Buena Esperanza 557) goes every 30 minutes to Caldera (CH$2500).

Parque Nacional Pan de Azúcar

The cold Humboldt Current flows up the desert coastline, bringing with it its peppy namesake penguin and abundant marine life. The worthwhile 440-sq-km **Pan de Azúcar** (www.conaf.cl/parques/parque-nacional-pan-de-azucar; Ruta C-120; adult/child CH$5000/1500) includes white-sand beaches, sheltered coves, stony headlands and cactus-covered hills.

Hired boats cruise around **Isla Pan de Azúcar** to view its 2000 Humboldt penguins, as well as cormorants, gulls, otters and sea lions. Launches charge CH$6000 to CH$12,000 per person (depending on the number of passengers, with a 10-person minimum) from Caleta Pan de Azúcar; with a lack of visitors in the low season, it can be difficult to go on a trip, unless you're willing to hire the entire boat yourself. Round-trips take 1½ hours, and run from 10am to 6pm in summer, and to 4pm in winter.

Hike the 2.5km **El Mirador** trail to see sea cacti, guanacos and chilla foxes. Next up is **Las Lomitas**, an easy 4km path.

Camping is available at Playas Piqueros and Soldado, from CH$5000 per person, with toilets, water, cold showers and tables. Lovely adobe cabins at the eco-minded **Pan de Azúcar Lodge** (📱cell 9-9844-7375; www.pandeazucarlodge.cl; campsites per person CH$8500, cabins for 2/6/8 people CH$75,000/100,000/120,000) are fully equipped.

Pan de Azúcar is 30km north of Chañaral via a well-maintained paved road. Most people reach it by tour or transfer from Caldera/Bahía Inglesa or Copiapó.

Antofagasta

📱 055 / POP 361,900

The largest city in the Atacama, a rough-and-ready jumble of one-way streets, modern mall culture and work-wearied urbanites, is low on travelers' lists. Founded in 1870, the city earned its importance by offering the easiest route to the interior.

⦿ Sights

Nitrate-mining heydays left their mark with Victorian and Georgian buildings in the **Barrio Histórico** between the plaza and old port. The British-influenced **Plaza Colón** features Big Ben replica **Torre Reloj**. Sea lions circle Antofagasta's busy fish market **Terminal Pesquero.**

The oft-photographed national icon **La Portada** is a gorgeous natural arch located offshore, 22km north of Antofagasta.

Ruinas de Huanchaca   HISTORIC SITE
(📱55-241-7860; http://ruinasdehuanchaca.cl; Ave Angamos 01606; museum adult/child CH$2000/1000; ⊘10am-1pm & 2:30-7pm Tue-Sun) What at first glance looks like the ruins from some ancient indigenous settlement in fact dates only from the turn of the 20th century. Created by Bolivian Hunachaca Company (one of the richest silver-mining operations of the late 1800s), the site was used as a foundry and refinery for raw material shipped in from the Pulacayo mine in Bolivia, and once employed more than 1000 workers. You can take photos of the ruins, but are not allowed to enter.

The small **museum** in front of the site has exhibits on natural history, mining and indigenous culture, as well as a four-wheeled vehicle dubbed 'Nomad' (an early prototype for the Mars Rover) thrown in for good measure. To get there take bus 102 or 103 from the center to Calle Sangra (CH$500).

🛏 Sleeping & Eating

Sleeping options are few, and reduced by the numbers of traveling miners occupying hotels.

Hotel Licantay   HOTEL $$
(☑55-228-0885; www.licantay.cl; 14 de Febrero 2134; r CH$43,000-68,000; 🛜) This friendly small-scale hotel has bright, cheerfully painted rooms with wood furnishings and artwork on the walls. Everything is meticulously clean. On the downside, the bathrooms are tiny in the less expensive rooms.

Marisquería D&D   SEAFOOD $
(Terminal Pesquero; mains CH$3000-6000; ⊙8am-5pm Mon-Fri, to 6pm Sat & Sun) Inside the fish market, this eatery draws crowds for its tasty fish sandwiches, fried fish platters and *paila marina* (seafood soup). Grab a seat at the corner and tuck into the seafood delights.

★Cafe del Sol   CHILEAN $$
(www.cafedelsolchile.com; Esmeralda 2013; set lunch CH$4000, mains CH$4000-13,000; ⊙1-4pm & 7pm-3am Mon-Fri, 7pm-4am Sat) On weekend nights, this ramshackle corner restobar comes alive with live Andean music and dancing (CH$3000 cover after 11pm). Other nights, it serves a good range of mains in the cozy wooden interior with dim lighting. Plus it does a good set lunch for around CH$4000.

ℹ Information

Conaf (☑55 238 3320; Av Argentina 2510; ⊙8:30am-1:30pm & 3-5:30pm Mon-Thu, 8:30am-1:30pm & 3-4:15pm Fri) Information on the region's natural attractions.

Hospital Regional (☑55-265-6602; www.hospitalantofagasta.gob.cl; Av Argentina 1962)

Sernatur (☑55-245-1818; Arturo Prat 384; ⊙8:30am-6pm Mon-Fri, 10am-2pm Sat) The city tourist office is conveniently located by the plaza. Has lots of brochures.

ℹ Getting There & Away

AIR

Antofagasta's Aeropuerto Cerro Moreno (airport) is located 25km north of town. **LATAM** (☑600-526-2000; www.latam.com; Arturo Prat 445; ⊙9am-6:15pm Mon-Fri, 10am-1pm Sat) and **Sky** (☑600-600-2828; www.skyairline.cl) have daily flights to Santiago (from CH$44,000, two hours).

BUS

Terminal de Buses Cardenal Carlos Oviedo (☑55-248-4502; Av Pedro Aguirre Cerda 5750) serves most intercity destinations. It's about 4km north of the center (reachable by bus No 111, 103, 119 or 108). Here you'll find operators like **Condor/Flota Barrios** (☑55-223-4626; www.condorbus.cl; Av Pedro Aguirre Cerda 5750). A few major long-distance bus companies, including **Turbus** (☑55-222-0240; www.turbus.cl; Latorre 2751) and **Pullman Bus** (www.pullmanbus.com; Latorre 2805), still operate also out of their own terminals near downtown. To reach the **Monumento Natural La Portada** (⊙museum 10:30am-1:30pm & 3-5:30pm Sat & Sun) take a **Megatur** (www.megatur.cl; Latorre 2748) bus, located 1½ blocks southeast of the plaza.

Nearly all northbound services now use coastal Ruta 1, via Tocopilla, en route to Iquique and Arica.

DESTINATION	COST (CH$)	DURATION (HR)
Arica	12,000	9
Calama	5000	3
Copiapó	10,000	9
Iquique	10,000	6
La Serena	15,000	12
Santiago	23,000	18

CHILE CALAMA

Calama

☑055 / POP 165,700

Gritty Calama is a powerhouse pumping truckloads of copper money into the Chilean economy each year. Its existence is inextricably tied to the colossal Chuquicamata mine. For travelers, this murky city makes a quick stopover before San Pedro de Atacama. With inflated service prices and *schops con piernas* (like *cafés con piernas,* but with beer) it clearly caters to miners.

🛏 Sleeping

Hostería Calama   HOTEL $$
(☑55-234-2033; www.hosteriacalama.cl; Latorre 1521; s/d/tr from CH$45,000/52,000/60,000; P@🛜🏊) Calama's fanciest downtown h tel features spacious carpeted rooms de out in a classic style, some with leaf It has all the conveniences of an u tel, including a gym, restauran

Front rooms are noisy, but have tree-shaded balconies.

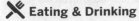 Eating & Drinking

Mercado Central   MARKET $
(Latorre; set meals CH$3500) For quick filling eats, take advantage of the *cocinerías* (greasy spoons) in this busy little market between Ramírez and Vargas.

Pasión Peruana   PERUVIAN $$
(cnr Abaroa & Ramirez; mains CH$9000-14,000; ⊗noon-11pm Mon-Sat, to 6pm Sun) One of Calama's top dining spots, this great catch-all place serves up a variety of Peruvian and Chilean fare. It's on one edge of the plaza.

Maracaibo Cafe   CAFE
(Latorre, near Mackenna; ⊗10am-9pm Mon-Fri) A charming sun-filled cafe with Venezuelan soul (and delicious *arepas*) located in a small shopping complex. Stop for strong coffee, dessert and filling lunch specials (CH$5000 to CH$6000).

ℹ Information

Several banks with ATMs are in the city center; some also change currency.
Hospital Carlos Cisternas (☑55-265-5721; http://hospitalcalama.gob.cl; Carlos Cisternas 2253) Five blocks north of Plaza 23 de Marzo.

ℹ Getting There & Away

AIR
LATAM (☑600-526-2000; www.latam.com; Latorre 1726; ⊗9am-1pm & 3-6:30pm Mon-Fri, 10am-1pm Sat) flies daily to Santiago (from CH$56,000, two hours) from **Aeropuerto**

El Loa (☑55-234-4897; www.cacsa.cl); **Sky** (☑600-600-2828; www.skyairline.cl) often has cheaper fares.

BUS
Bus companies are scattered throughout the town but are mostly concentrated along Av Balmaceda and Antofagasta. Major companies include **Condor Bus/Flota Barrios** (☑55-234-5883; www.condorbus.cl; Av Balmaceda 1852) and **Expreso Norte** (☑55-255-6845; www.expresonorte.cl; Balmaceda 1902). Those with services northbound and southbound on the Panamericana include the following:

DESTINATION	COST (CH$)	DURATION (HR)
Antofagasta	6000	3
Arica	15,000	10
Iquique	13,000	7
La Serena	23,000	14
Santiago	32,000	22

Turbus (☑55-268-8812; www.turbus.cl; Ramírez 1852) provides regular services to San Pedro de Atacama (CH$3000 to CH$4000, 1½ hours) from the main **Terminal de Calama** (Av Granaderos 3051). **Buses Frontera** (☑55-282-4269; Antofagasta 2046) also has daily buses to San Pedro (CH$3000, 1½ hours, three daily) as does Buses Atacama 2000.

International buses are invariably full, so reserve as far in advance as possible. To get to Uyuni, Bolivia (CH$12,000, nine hours) via Ollagüe (CH$9000, three hours), ask at Frontera and Buses Atacama 2000; services go only several times per week so buy ahead.

Service to Salta and Jujuy, Argentina, is provided by **Pullman Bus** (☑55-234-1282; www.pullmanbus.cl; Balmaceda 1974) and **Géminis** (☑55-289-2043; www.geminis.cl; Antofagasta 2239) several times weekly.

CHUQUI THROUGH THE EYES OF CHE

Chuqui was already a mine of monstrous proportions when visited by a youthful Ernesto 'Che' Guevara more than 50 years ago. The future revolutionary and his traveling buddy Alberto Granado were midway through their iconic trip across South America, immortalized in Che's *Motorcycle Diaries*. An encounter with a communist during his journey to Chuqui is generally acknowledged as a turning point in Che's emergent politics, so it's especially interesting to read his memories of the mine itself (then in gringo hands).

Chuquicamata

Slag heaps as big as mountains, a chasm deeper than the deepest lake in the USA, and trucks the size of houses: these are some of the mind-boggling dimensions that bring visitors to gawk into the mine of Chuquicamata (or 'Chuqui'). This awesome abyss, gouged from the desert earth 16km north of Calama, is one of the world's largest open-pit copper mines.

First run by the US Anaconda Copper Mining Company, starting in 1915, Chuqui is now operated by state-owned Corporación del Cobre de Chile (Codelco). The mine, which employs 20,000 workers, spews up a perpetual plume of dust visible for many

Northern Chile (Norte Grande)

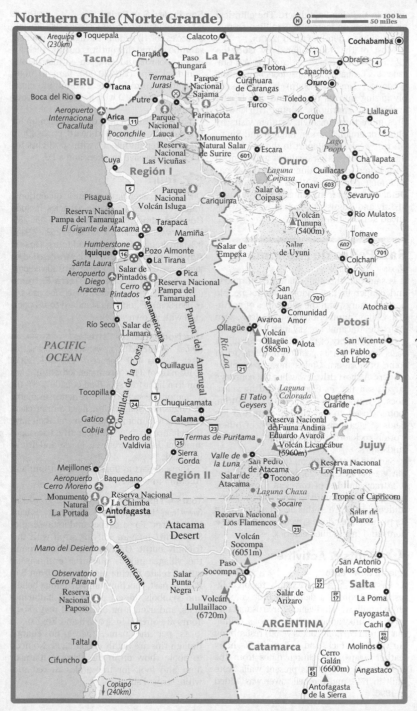

miles in the cloudless desert. The elliptical pit measures an incredible 8 million sq meters and has a depth of up to 1250m.

Most of the 'tour' offered by **Codelco** (📞 55-232-2122; visitas@codelco.cl; cnr Avs Granaderos & Central Sur, Calama; tours by donation; ⏰ bookings 9am-5pm Mon-Fri) is spent simply gazing into its depths and clambering around an enormous mining truck with tires more than 3m high. Arrange visits by phone or email. Tours in English and Spanish run weekdays. Report to the *oficina* on the corner of Avs Granaderos and Central Sur; bring identification, closed footwear and long pants. Donations are voluntary. Demand is high from January to March and in July and August, so book at least a week ahead at these times.

San Pedro de Atacama

📞 055 / POP 11,000

It is said that the high quantities of quartz and copper in the region gives its people positive energy, and the good vibes of northern Chile's number-one tourist draw, San Pedro de Atacama, are sky high.

The popularity of this adobe precordillera oasis stems from its position in the heart of some of northern Chile's most spectacular scenery. A short drive away lies the country's largest salt flat, its edges crinkled by volcanoes (symmetrical Licancábur, at 5916m, looms closest to the village). Here too are fields of steaming geysers, a host of otherworldly rock formations and weird layer-cake landscapes.

San Pedro itself, 106km southeast of Calama via paved Chile 23, is quite small, but it attracts hordes of travelers. Despite the high prices and tourist-agency touts, there's undeniable allure to this desert village with its picturesque adobe streets, laid-back residents and music-filled eateries.

👁 Sights & Activities

Iglesia San Pedro   CHURCH
(Le Paige s/n) FREE The recently restored Iglesia San Pedro is a delightful little colonial church built with indigenous or artisanal materials: chunky adobe walls and roof, a ceiling made from *cardón* (cactus wood) resembling shriveled tire tracks and, in lieu of nails, hefty leather straps. The church dates from the 17th century, though its present walls were built in 1745, and the bell tower was added in 1890.

Sandboard San Pedro   ADVENTURE
(📞 cell 9-8135-1675; www.sandboardsanpedro.com; Caracoles 362-H) Among the agencies offering sand-boarding, this outfit is our top pick for its pro boards and experienced instructors. Standard trips (CH$20,000, 9am to noon or 4pm to 7pm) involve a 20-minute class, plus you get a DVD with a video clip of your escapade.

For something a little different sign up for the Saturday-night sand-board party (9pm till just after midnight), with spotlights for the dune, massive speakers and a DJ.

🧭 Tours

Dozens of agencies operate conventional tours. The most reputable agencies include **CosmoAndino Expediciones** (📞 55-285-1069; www.cosmoandino.cl; Caracoles 259; ⏰ 9am-9:30pm), known for higher-end tours; **Desert Adventure** (📞 cell 9-9779-7211; www.desertadventure.cl; cnr Caracoles & Tocopilla; ⏰ 9:30am-9pm), with bilingual guides; and **Terra Extreme** (📞 55-285-1274; www.terraextreme.cl; Toconao s/n; ⏰ 9am-9pm) 🚗, offering standard tours operated with its own vehicles.

Una Noche con las Estrellas   STARGAZING
(📞 cell 9-5272-2201; www.unanocheconlasestrellas.cl; Calama 440; astronomy tour CH$20,000; ⏰ 10am-11pm) This recommended outfit takes you to a light-free spot 6km outside town for a memorable stargazing experience, available in English or Spanish. You'll get a brief 'class' covering astronomical phenomena, then have the chance to peer through five telescopes aimed at different features. Snacks and drinks included.

Tours depart at 9pm and 11pm (8pm and 10:30pm in winter).

Tours 4 Tips   WALKING
(www.tours4tips.com; Plaza de Armas; ⏰ tours 10am & 3pm) For a deeper understanding of San Pedro, take an edifying stroll with this friendly outfit. On two-hour walks around the village and its outskirts, enthusiastic guides relate fascinating episodes from San Pedro's past, touching on indigenous beliefs and symbols, desert plants and hallucinogens, and even a bit of celestial mythology. Tours are offered in Spanish and English.

As per the name, there's no charge, though tips are highly encouraged. No need to book; show up in the plaza at 10am or 3pm and look for the guides in red-and-white striped shirts.

San Pedro de Atacama

San Pedro de Atacama

⊙ Sights

⊕ Activities, Courses & Tours

🛏 Sleeping

🍴 Eating

Vulcano Expediciones ADVENTURE
(☎ cell 9-5333-6021; www.vulcanochile.com; Caracoles 317; 10am-8pm Tue-Sun) Runs treks to volcanoes and mountains, including day climbs to Sairecabur (5971m, CH$110,000), Lascar (5592m, CH$85,000) and Tocco (5604m,

CH$670,000). Two-day climbs take in Licancábur (CH$250,000) and other mountains. It can also hook you up with motorbike tours offered by **On Safari** (☎ cell 9-7215-3254; www.onsafariatacama.com; 4hr motorbike tour CH$170,000).

CHILE SAN PEDRO DE ATACAMA

ATACAMA DESERT ADVENTURES

A few off-the-beaten-track tours around Atacama are becoming increasingly popular, such as jaunts to **Laguna Cejar** and **Ojos de Salar** (you can swim in both, and in Cejar you can float just like in the Dead Sea), **Valle del Arcoíris**, with its rainbowlike multicolored rock formations, and **Salar de Tara**. The last is one of the most spectacular, if back-breaking. Trips from San Pedro, involving a round-trip journey of 200km, reach an altitude of 4300m.

Note that these tours don't leave regularly and have a higher price tag than the bestsellers in the area.

Rancho La Herradura HORSEBACK RIDING
(☑ 55-285-1956; www.atacamahorseadventure. com; Tocopilla 406; ⊙ 9am-8pm) Sightseeing from the saddle is available from several places, including Rancho La Herradura. Tours vary from two hours for CH$23,000 to epic 10-day treks with camping in the desert. English-, German- and French-speaking guides are available.

🛏 Sleeping

Water is scarce (and not potable) in San Pedro, so buy your own drinking water and limit your shower time. Note that prices are high here, even outside high season.

Hostal Pangea HOSTEL $
(☑ 55-320-5080; www.hostalpangea.cl; Le Paige 202; dm/d CH$13,000/43,000; 🛜) Pangea is a traveler favorite for its excellent central location, welcoming staff and budget-friendly prices. The spacious and colorfully decorated patio is a great place to meet other travelers. It can be noisy at night, and it's definitely more a place to socialize than relax.

Hostal Sonchek HOSTEL $
(☑ 55-285-1112; www.hostalsonchek.cl; cnr Paige & Calama; dm CH$12,000, d CH$44,000, s/d without bathroom CH$16,000/27,000; 🛜) Thatched roofs and adobe walls characterize the rooms at this lovely, good-value hostel. It's centered on a small courtyard, and there's a shared kitchen, luggage storage and a garden out back with table tennis and a few tables. The common bathrooms with solar-heated showers are kept quite clean.

Hostal Edén Atacameño HOSTEL $
(☑ 55-259-0819; http://cdenatacameno.cl; Toconao 592; s/d incl breakfast CH$25,000/40,000, without bathroom or breakfast CH$12,000/24,000; 🅿️@🛜) This laid-back hostel has rooms around a couple of sociable, hammock-strung patios with plentiful seating. Guests can use the kitchen, and there's laundry service and luggage storage. The shared bathrooms are clean.

Hostelling International HOSTEL $
(www.hostellingsanpedro.cl; Caracoles 360; dm/d CH$14,000/45,000, d/tr/q without bathroom CH$30,000/38,000/45,000; 🛜) This convivial spot offers dorms – with some bunks nearly 3m up – and a few doubles around a small patio. It has a shared kitchen and lockers, and staff will book tours. HI members get a CH$2000 to CH$5000 discount.

★Hostal Quinta Adela B&B $$
(☑ 55-285-1272; www.quintaadela.com; Toconao 624; r from CH$73,000; @🛜) This friendly family-run place, just a quick walk from town, has seven character-filled rooms (each with its own individual style) and a shady terrace and is situated alongside a sprawling orchard with hammocks. There's luggage storage and the hostel is flexible with check-in and checkout.

Hotel Loma Sanchez GUESTHOUSE $$
(☑ cell 9-9277-7478; www.lomasanchez.cl; Caracoles 259-A; d/tr CH$55,000/75,000, s/d without bathroom from CH$25,000/30,000; 🛜) Sitting right in the middle of the Caracoles strip, Loma Sanchez has a backyard full of small yurts with adobe walls and thatch roofs that make for an atmospheric (if somewhat chilly) stay. The guesthouse also has more traditional rooms, with pleasing touches like wooden floorboards and local weavings for decorations.

Takha Takha Hotel & Camping HOTEL, CAMPGROUND $$
(☑ 55-285-1038; www.takhatakha.cl; Caracoles 151-A; campsites per person CH$13,000, s/d CH$54,000/62,000, without bathroom CH$21,000/41,000; 🛜🏊) A popular catch-all outfit that's got decent campsites, plain budget rooms and spotless midrange accommodations set around a sprawling flowery garden with a swimming pool. A great location and friendly service add to the value.

✕ Eating & Drinking

San Pedro welcomes tourism but not late-night revelers. There's only one bar and no alcohol is sold after 1am.

Babalú   ICE CREAM $
(Caracoles 140; ice creams CH$1900-3900; ☺ 10am-10pm) One of several ice-cream shops on the main street, Babalú serves up rich flavors you won't find at home. Try ice creams made from desert fruits like *chañar* or *algarrobo,* and sample *pisco* sour, *hoja de coca* (coca leaf) and delightful surprises such as quinoa. You can't go wrong.

Franchuteria   BAKERY $
(www.lafranchuteria.com; Le Paige 527; croissants CH$1100-2500; ☺ 7am-8:30pm) About 500m east of the plaza, you'll find San Pedro's best bakery. Run by a talented young Frenchman, Franchuteria has beautifully baked goods, including perfect baguettes with rare combinations of fillings like fig and Roquefort cheese, or goat's cheese and oregano, and buttery-rich croissants – also available stuffed with unusual things like *manjar* (dulce de leche).

Cafe Peregrino   CAFETERIA $
(Gustavo Le Paige 348; mains CH$3500-6000; ☺ 9am-9pm; 🛜 ✍) Overlooking the plaza, this well-placed cafe has a few shaded cafe tables strategically placed for people-watching. Foodwise, you'll find pizzas, quesadillas, sandwiches, pancakes (for breakfast) and nice cakes and pastries. And, yes, real espressos and cappuccinos!

Las Delicias de Carmen   CHILEAN $$
(www.lasdeliciasdecarmen.cl; Calama 370; lunch specials CH$4000-7000, mains CH$8000-14,000; ☺ 8:30am-10:30pm; 🛜 ✍) Great breakfasts, delicious cakes and empanadas, brick-oven pizzas (choose your own toppings) and different dishes daily are churned out at this light-flooded restaurant with leafy views. Daily specials – such as *cazuela* (stew) or carrot-ginger soup – and a filling *menú del día* (three-course lunch) always bring in the crowds.

La Casona   CHILEAN $$
(☎ 55-285-1337; Caracoles 195; mains CH$9000-14,000; ☺ noon-midnight Wed-Mon; 🛜) A high-ceilinged dining room with dark wood

---

DESERT STARGAZING

The flats of Chajnantor plateau, at 5000m altitude 40km east of San Pedro de Atacama, host the most ambitious radio telescope the world has ever seen. The Atacama Large Millimeter/submillimeter Array (ALMA; meaning 'soul' in Spanish) consists of 66 enormous antennae, most with a diameter of around 12m. This field of interstellar 'ears' simulates a telescope an astonishing 16km in diameter, making it possible to pick up objects in space as much as 100 times fainter than those previously detected.

Contact the **ALMA Visitor Center** (☎ in Santiago 2-2467-6100; www.almaobservatory.org; Hwy 23, Km121; free with online registration; ☺ Sat & Sun) **FREE** to visit. It's free but guest numbers are limited; register online. A free shuttle from Tumisa near Ave Pedro de Valdivia provides transportation to the facility, leaving at 9am and returning at 1pm Saturday and Sunday.

ALMA is just the latest of northern Chile's cutting-edge astronomical facilities. Climatic conditions in the Atacama Desert make it an ideal location for stargazing. This is not only thanks to cloudless desert nights, but also the predictable winds that blow steadily in from the Pacific Ocean, causing minimal turbulence – a crucial requirement for observatories to achieve optimal image quality.

Other major facilities in northern Chile include the European Southern Observatory (ESO) at Cerro Paranal. Norte Chico has **Observatorio Interamericano Cerro Tololo** (☎ 51-220-5200; www.ctio.noao.edu; Cerro Tololo) **FREE** and the nearby Cerro El Pachón. Another ESO site is at **La Silla** (☎ emergencies 9-9839-5312; www.eso.org/public/teles-instr/lasilla) – which also has free public tours each Saturday at 2pm – while the Carnegie Institution's Observatorio Las Campanas is just north of La Silla.

If all that whets your appetite for astronomy, consider taking a 'Tour of the Night Sky' from San Pedro, where there's a range of astronomical tours available, including with reputable outfits like **San Pedro de Atacama Celestial Explorations** (☎ 55-256-6278; www.spaceobs.com; Caracoles 400-2; 2½hr tours CH$25,000; ☺ 11am-9pm Dec-Mar, to 7pm Apr-Nov) and Una Noche con las Estrellas (p488).

WORTH A TRIP

4X4 TO UYUNI, BOLIVIA

Colorful altiplano lakes, weird rock playgrounds worthy of Salvador Dalí, flamingos, volcanoes and, most famously of all, the blindingly white salt flat of Uyuni: these are some of the rewards for taking an excursion into Bolivia northeast of San Pedro de Atacama. Be warned that this is no cozy ride in the country, and for every five travelers that gush about Uyuni being the highlight of their trip, there is another declaring it a waking nightmare.

The standard trips take three days, crossing the Bolivian border at Hito Cajón, passing Laguna Colorada and continuing to the Salar de Uyuni before ending in the town of Uyuni. The going rate of around CH$115,000 includes transportation in crowded 4WD jeeps, basic and often teeth-chatteringly cold accommodations, plus food; bring an extra CH$15,000 to CH$25,000 will get you back to San Pedro on the fourth day (some tour operators drive through the third night). Bring drinks and snacks, warm clothes and a sleeping bag. Travelers clear Chilean immigration at San Pedro and Bolivian immigration on arrival at Uyuni. Certain nationalities (including US citizens) require visas (US$160) to visit, so be prepared. Note that entrance fees to Bolivian parks are not included, and cost approximately CH$20,000.

None of the agencies offering this trip gets consistently glowing reports. **Cordillera Traveler** (📞55-320-5028; www.cordilleratraveller.com; Tocopilla 429-B; ⊘9am-9pm) generally gets positive feedback from travelers.

paneling and an adobe fireplace in the middle, classic La Casona serves up sizzling *parrilladas* (mix of grilled meats) and Chilean staples such as *pastel de choclo* (maize casserole). There's a long list of Chilean wines and a small patio for alfresco lunches.

El Toconar INTERNATIONAL **$$**
(cnr Toconao & Caracoles; mains CH$5000-12,000; ⊘noon-1am) El Toconar has one of the best garden setups in town, complete with bonfires for those chilly desert nights. Also on offer is a wide menu and a superb selection of cocktails (including *pisco* sours infused with desert herbs).

ℹ Information

There are three ATMs in town (two on Caracoles and the other opposite the museum) but they do not always have money, so bring a big wad of cash, just in case. Many establishments take plastic, but some prefer the real stuff.

There's free wi-fi on the main plaza (when it's working).

Oficina de Información Turística (📞55-285-1420; cnr Toconao & Le Paige; ⊘9am-9pm) s a helpful tourist office offering advice and doling out town maps and brochures. Check the annual book of comments for up-to-date traveler feedback on tour agencies, hostels, restaurants, transportation providers and more.

Posta Médica (📞55-285-1010; Le Paige 377) is the local clinic, just off the plaza.

ℹ Getting There & Around

Buses Atacama 2000 (Tumisa s/n; ⊘8am-7pm) has regular departures to Calama (from CH$3000) where you can connect to its Uyuni bus. **Buses Frontera del Norte** (Tumisa s/n) goes to Calama as well as Arica (from CH$18,000) and Iquique (CH$15,000). **Turbus** (📞55-268-8711; Licancábur 154) has hourly buses to Calama (CH$3000 to CH$4000), from where you can connect to all major destinations in Chile. **Andesmar** (📞55-259-2692; www.andesmar.com; Tumisa s/n) serves Salta and Jujuy, Argentina, several times a week (from CH$24,000, 13 hours with border time). **Géminis** (📞55-289-2049; www.geminis.cl; Tumisa s/n) also goes to Salta.

Several agencies in town offer transfer services to Calama airport; expect to pay around CH$16,500 per person.

Buses stop right near the plaza and the whole town can be explored on foot.

Around San Pedro de Atacama

There's always more to see around San Pedro de Atacama. It's worthwhile visiting some tour agencies and asking other travelers about their experiences. The most popular attractions are listed here:

The crumbly 12th-century ruins of fortress **Pukará de Quitor** (CH$3000; ⊘8:30am-7pm), 3.5km northwest of town and accessible by rental bike, afford great views of town and the oasis expanse. Another 3km on the right, **Quebrada del Diablo** (Devil's Gorge) offers a serpentine single track that mountain bikers dream of.

At 4300m above sea level, the famous **El Tatio** (95km north of town; CH$10,000; ☉ 6am-6pm) is the world's highest geyser field. Visiting at dawn is like walking through a gigantic steam bath, ringed by volcanoes and fed by 64 gurgling geysers and a hundred gassy fumaroles striking against the azure clarity of the altiplano. Swirling columns of steam envelop onlookers in a Dantesque vision, and the soundtrack of bubbling, spurting and hissing sounds like a field of merrily boiling kettles. As dawn wears on, shafts of sunlight crown the surrounding volcanoes and illuminate the writhing steam. Dress in layers: it's extremely cold at dawn.

Watching the sun set from the exquisite **Valle de la Luna** (CH$3000; ☉ 9am-6pm) is an unforgettable experience. As you sit atop a giant sand dune, panting from exertion, a beautiful transformation occurs: the distant ring of volcanoes, rippling Cordillera de la Sal and surreal lunar landscapes of the valley are suddenly suffused with intense purples, pinks and golds. The 'Valley of the Moon' is named after its lunar-like landforms, eroded by eons of floods and wind. It's 15km west of San Pedro at the northern end of the Cordillera de la Sal.

The jagged crust of the **Salar de Atacama** looks for all the world like god went crazy with a stippling brush. But in the midst of these rough lifeless crystals is an oasis of activity: the pungent **Laguna Chaxa** (CH$2500; ☉ 8am-8pm), 67km south of town is home to three species of flamingo (James, Chilean and Andean), as well as plovers, coots and ducks.

The volcanic hot springs of **Termas de Puritama** (https://termasdepuritama.cl; adult/child CH$19,500/9100; ☉ 9:30am-5:15pm), 30km northeast of town, are accessible by taxi or tour. The temperature of the springs is about 91°F (33°C), and there are several falls and pools.

Iquique

☑ 057 / POP 192,000

Jutting into the sea and backed by the tawny coastal range, Iquique sits like a stage. And, in fact, the city is no stranger to drama. It first lived off guano reserves, grew lavish with 19th-century nitrate riches, then lost momentum, and now stakes its future on commerce and tourism, manifested in the duty-free mega-zone, the sparkly glitz of the casino and ubiquitous beach resort development. The real gems of this coastal city are the remainders of lovely Georgian-style architecture, Baquedano's fanciful wooden sidewalks, thermal winds and a ripping good surf.

◉ Sights & Activities

Museo Corbeta Esmeralda   MUSEUM
(www.museoesmeralda.cl; Paseo Almirante Lynch; CH$3500; ☉ 10am-12:15pm & 2-5pm Tue-Sun) This replica of sunken *Esmeralda,* a plucky little Chilean corvette that challenged ironclad Peruvian warships in the War of the Pacific, is Iquique's new pride and glory. The original ship was captained by Arturo Prat (1848–79), whose name now graces a hundred street maps, plazas and institutions. Guided tours (reserve ahead for a tour in English) take you inside the staff quarters, past the orange-lit engine, and on to the ship's deck.

Book ahead or come on Sunday when it is first come, first served.

Plaza Prat   PLAZA
The city's 19th-century swagger is hard to miss on Iquique's central square. Pride of place goes to the 1877 **Torre Reloj** (Plaza Prat) clock tower, seemingly baked and sugar-frosted rather than built. Jumping fountains line the walkway south to the marble-stepped **Teatro Municipal**, a neoclassical building that has been hosting opera and theater since 1890. A handsomely restored **tram** (Baquedano, btwn Tarapaca & Thompson) sits outside and occasionally jerks its way down Av Baquedano in high season.

Centro Cultural
Palacio Astoreca   HISTORIC BUILDING
(O'Higgins 350; ☉ 10am-2pm & 3-6pm Tue-Fri, 11am-2pm Sat) **FREE** Originally built for a nitrate tycoon, this 1904 Georgian-style mansion is now a cultural center, which exhibits contemporary work produced by local artists. It has a fantastic interior of opulent rooms with elaborate woodwork and high ceilings, massive chandeliers, a gigantic billiard table and balconies.

Playa Cavancha   BEACH
Iquique's most popular beach is worth visiting for swimming and body-boarding. Surfing and body-boarding are best in winter, when swells come from the north, but are

CHILE IQUIQUE

Iquique

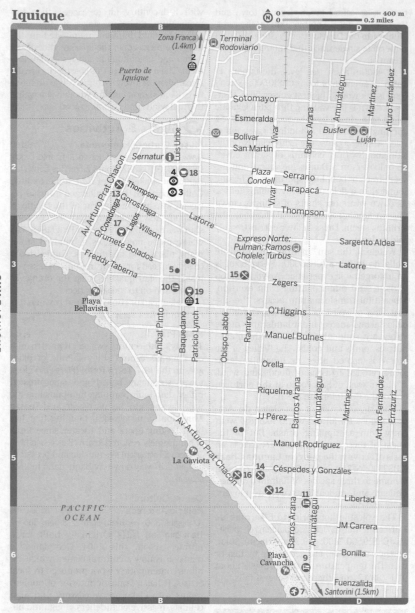

N
0 ————————— 400 m
0 ————————— 0.2 miles

Zona Franca
(1.4km)

2 Terminal
Rodoviario

*Puerto de
Iquique*

Sotomayor

Esmeralda

Bolívar
San Martín

Busfer
Luján

Amunátegui
Martínez
Arturo Fernández

Barros Arana

Vivar

Luis Uribe

Sernatur

4 **18**
3

Thompson
13 Gorostiaga

Coradinga

Lagos Wilson

17

Grumete Bolados

Freddy Taberna

Av Arturo Prat Chacon

Plaza
Condell

Serrano
Tarapacá

Thompson

Latorre

Vivar

Sargento Aldea

Expreso Norte;
Pulman; Ramos
Cholele; Turbus

Latorre

5 **8**

10 **19**
1

15

Zegers

O'Higgins

Manuel Bulnes

Orella

Anibal Pinto

Baquedano

Patricio Lynch

Obispo Labbé

Ramírez

Playa
Bellavista

Riquelme

JJ Pérez

Barros Arana

Amunátegui

Martínez

Arturo Fernández

Errázuriz

6

Manuel Rodríguez

La Gaviota

14 Céspedes y Gonzáles

16

12

11

Libertad

JM Carrera

Barros Arana

Amunátegui

Bonilla

Playa
Cavancha

9

PACIFIC
OCEAN

Av Arturo Prat Chacón

7

Fuenzalida

Santorini (1.5km)

CHILE IQUIQUE

possible year-round. There's less competition for early-morning breaks at the north end of Playa Cavancha.

Vertical   SURFING
(☎ 57-237-6031; Av Arturo Prat 580) This is Iquique's surfer central, which sells and

rents equipment. Wetsuit and board will set you back CH$12,000 for two hours; one or the other costs CH$8000. Private lessons start at CH$24,000 for 1½ hours, and it runs surf trips outside the city and sand-boarding trips to Cerro Dragón (CH$25,000 for three hours).

Iquique

⌕ Tours

Public transportation to many surrounding attractions is tricky, so tours are worth considering. In summer, agencies set up streetside tables on Prat and along Baquedano. Popular options include a day trip to the oasis towns of **Pica**, **La Tirana** and **Matilla**, taking in the nitrate ruins at **Humberstone** and **Santa Laura** en route (around CH$25,000). Another fun excursion takes you for a dip in the thermal waters of **Mamiña** (CH$27,000).

Magical Tour Chile   TOURS
(☑ 57-276-3474; www.magicaltour.cl; Baquedano 997; per person Ruta del Sol CH$23,000, Aventura Isluga CH$45,000; ☺ 10:30am-8pm Mon-Sat) Offers the full range of trips, including one full-day Ruta del Sol excursion to the Gigante de Atacama geoglyph, Humberstone ghost town and Pica Oasis. Other trips take you to geysers (Aventura Isluga) and photogenic lakes in the altiplano.

Mistico Outdoors   OUTDOORS
(☑ cell 9-9541-7762; www.chileresponsibleadventure.com; Fleuterio Ramírez 1535; full-day tour from CH$61,000) This small outfitter has a solid reputation for its customized tours and excursions, ranging from half a day to three weeks. Among the offerings: six-day trips in Parque Nacional Lauca, 10-day climbing trips to Ojos del Salado and full-day trips to Altos de Pica.
  Reserve at least four days in advance.

Show Travel   ADVENTURE
(☑ cell 9-7264-1556; www.showtravel.cl; Baquedano 1035; ☺ 9:30am-8pm Mon-Fri, 10:30am-5pm Sat) In addition to the usual tours, this is a good bet for active trips to places off the beaten track, including the El Huarango eco-camp near La Tirana.

⌸ Sleeping

Taxi drivers earn commission from some *residenciales* and hotels; be firm in your decision or consider walking.

Backpacker's Hostel Iquique   HOSTEL $
(☑ cell 9-6172-6788; www.hosteliquique.com; Amunátegui 2075; dm from CH$8000, d CH$28,000, s/d/tr without bathroom CH$15,000/23,000/24,000; ☏) One of Iquique's best budget options, this buzzing hostel has much to recommend: nicely outfitted rooms, friendly staff and a great location near Playa Cavancha. There's a cafe-bar as well as a small front terrace where you can meet other travelers. The hostel also organizes activities and excursions (sand-boarding, paragliding, surf lessons).

Virgilio B&B   GUESTHOUSE $
(☑ cell 9-7513-8035; saavedra.ivan@hotmail.fr; Libertad 825; dm/s/d without bathroom CH$14,000/18,000/33,000; ☏) In a good location within easy strolling distance of the beach, this small, welcoming guesthouse has tidy rooms, a roofed-in front terrace and a lounge where you can relax after a day of exploring. Keep in mind that the cheapest rooms are quite small, and none have private bathrooms.

Plaza Kilantur   HOTEL $
(Hotel de la Plaza; ☑ 57-241-7172; Baquedano 1025; s/d CH$25,000/35,000; ☏) One of the best deals in its category, this Georgian-style building fronts the pedestrian strip. There is a welcoming lobby with a big skylight and comfortable, medium-sized rooms arranged around a slender patio dominated by a towering pine tree.

CHILE IQUIQUE

✕ Eating

El Guru
CHILEAN $

(Libertad 732; lunch specials around CH$3000, mains CH$4000-6000; ⊙noon-4pm & 7:30-11pm Mon-Fri, noon-4pm Sat) Locals flock to this homey spot for its good-value, classic cooking. Come early for changing lunch specials of grilled fish, steak or pork served up with all the sides. It's outdoor dining only in front of the simple eatery.

Monorganiko
CAFE $

(Prat 580; sandwiches CH$3000-4000; ⊙9am-2:30pm & 4-9pm Mon-Sat; 🖊) This tiny cafe secreted away inside a surf shop serves some of Iquique's best coffees. The barista will prepare it any way you like – V60, Aeropress, Chemex etc – or you can get a flat white, latte or espresso. At the adjoining counter, order tasty acai bowls, smoothies, wraps, sandwiches and desserts.

M.Koo
SWEETS $

(Ramírez 949; snacks from CH$600; ⊙9am-8:30pm Mon-Sat) Colorful corner shop famous for its crumbly *chumbeques* – sweet biscuits filled with mango, lemon, guava, passion fruit, *manjar* (dulce de leche) and other flavors. A big pack costs CH$1500.

La Mayor Sandwicheria
BURGERS $

(Céspedes y González 717; mains CH$4500-7800; ⊙6:30pm-1am Mon-Thu, from 1:30pm Fri & Sat; 🖊) This small rock-music-loving joint dishes up sizzling gourmet burgers and frothy craft brews to a postsurf crowd near the beach. The draw: delectable toppings (Iberian ham, fried egg, caramelized onions), excellent fries, a huge beer list and a respectable vegetarian option (a quinoa patty). Portion sizes are generous – cutlery is required.

★Santorini
FUSION $$

(☎57-222-5392; www.santorinirestobar.cl; Aeropuerto 2808; mains CH$8000-14,000; ⊙6:30-11pm Mon, 1-3:30pm & 7-11:30pm Tue-Fri, 1pm-1am Sat, 1-5pm Sun; 🖊) A surprising find in Iquique, Santorini serves up a huge menu of authentic Greek fare, best enjoyed in the bougainvillea-draped back patio. Aside from *saganaki* (fried cheese) and souvlaki, you'll also find pastas, whole grilled fish, delectable thin-crust pizzas and slow-roasted tender lamb cooked in a wood-burning oven. Finish with a creamy dessert (like Greek yogurt) and strong Greek coffee.

It's about 4km southeast of the Plaza Prat.

★El Wagón
CHILEAN $$$

(☎57-234-1428; Thompson 85; mains CH$9000-17,000; ⊙1-4pm & 8pm-2am Mon-Sat) Almost single-handedly taking on the task of preserving the region's culinary traditions, this rustically decked-out dining hall serves up a fantastic collection of seafood plates, with inspiration for recipes coming from everywhere from grandma's classics to port-workers' and miners' staples. It's pricey, but worth it.

Drinking & Nightlife

Iquique has a fun-filled nightlife, with a few laid-back restobars in the center and clubs and pubs lining the seafront south of town.

Radicales
BAR

(Baquedano 1074; ⊙4pm-2:30am Mon-Thu, to 5am Fri & Sat) Set on the pedestrian drag of Baquedano, this vibrant two-story bar has a warren of creatively adorned rooms you can explore with a well-made tropical cocktail in hand. There's an upstairs balcony and outdoor seating on the lane in front – both fine spots for starting off the night.

Club Croata
CAFE

(Serrano 343; ⊙10am-6pm Mon-Sat; 🛜) Plaza-side restaurant with arched windows, Croatian coats of arms and a clutch of tables outside. It's a fine spot for an afternoon pick-me-up.

Bar the Clinic
BAR

(www.facebook.com/barthecliniciquque; Lagos 881; ⊙12:30-5pm Mon, to 1am Tue-Thu, to 4am Fri, 8pm-4am Sat) An all-wood interior lends this place a chalet-like charm, and makes a fine backdrop to drinks and snacks. There's live music most weekends, with bands kicking off around 10pm. Usually no cover.

ⓘ Information

There are many ATMs downtown and at the *zona franca*. Several *cambios* exchange foreign currency and traveler's checks.

Hospital de Iquique Dr Ernesto Torres Galdames (☎57-240-5700; www.hospitaliquique.cl; Av Héroes de la Concepción 502) Ten blocks east of Plaza Condell.

Post Office (Bolívar 458; ⊙9am-6pm Mon-Fri, 10am-noon Sat)

Sernatur (☎57-241-9241; www.sernatur.cl; Pinto 436; ⊙9am-6pm Mon-Fri, 10am-2pm Sat) This office has tourist information, free city maps and brochures.

ℹ Getting There & Away

AIR

The local airport, **Aeropuerto Diego Aracena** (☑ 57-247-3473; www.aeropuertodiegoaracena. cl), is 41km south of downtown via Ruta 1.

LATAM (☑ 600-526-2000; www.latam.com; Pinto 699; ⊘ 9am-1:30pm & 3:30-6:15pm Mon-Fri, 10:30am-1pm Sat) has several flights a day to Santiago (from CH\$55,000, 2½ hours), as does **Sky** (☑ 600-600-2828; www.skyairline.cl; from CH\$30,000). **Amaszonas** (www.amaszonas.com) offers several flights each week to the Bolivian cities of La Paz and Santa Cruz, as well as Salta in Argentina.

BUS

Most buses leave from the **Terminal Rodoviario** (☑ 57-242-7100; Lynch); most companies also have ticket offices clustered around Mercado Centenario. Several bus companies, including **Expreso Norte** (☑ 57-242-3215; www.expreso norte.cl; Barros Arana 881), **Pullman** (☑ 57-242-6522; www.pullman.cl; Barros Arana 825), **Ramos Cholele** (☑ 57-247-1628; Barros Arana 851) and **Turbus** (☑ 57-273-6161; www.turbus. cl; Barras Arana 869, Mercado Centenario), offer services to northern Chile and Santiago.

For La Paz, Bolivia, **Busfer** (☑ cell 9-9561-8050; Esmeralda 951) has four departures daily (CH\$6000 to CH\$10,000, 14 hours). **Luján** (Esmeralda 999) also has several daily departures. For Peru, connect with international departures via Arica.

Buses from Iquique

DESTINATION	COST (CH\$)	DURATION (HR)
Antofagasta	16,000	6
Arica	7000	4
Calama	10,000	6
Copiapó	30,000	14
La Serena	35,000	18
Santiago	45,000	24

East of Iquique

Ghost towns punctuate the desert as you travel inland from Iquique; they're eerie remnants of once-flourishing mining colonies that gathered the Atacama's white gold – nitrate. Along the way, pre-Hispanic geoglyphs recall the presence of humans centuries before. Further inland the barren landscape yields up several picturesque hot-spring villages.

If you only see one attraction outside Iquique, make it **Humberstone** (www.museo delsalitre.cl; adult/child incl Oficina Santa Laura CH\$4000/2000; ⊘ 9am-7pm Dec-Mar, to 6pm Apr-Nov), 45km east of the city. With the spark of the nitrate boom long gone, the ghost town remains a creepy shell. Built in 1872, the town's opulence reached its height in the 1940s: the theater drew Santiago-based performers, workers lounged about the massive cast-iron pool molded from a scavenged shipwreck, and amenities still foreign to most small towns abounded. The development of synthetic nitrates forced the closure of the *oficina* by 1960. Today some buildings are restored, but others are unstable; explore them carefully. A Unesco World Heritage site, it makes its list of endangered sites for the fragility of the existing constructions. The skeletal remains of **Oficina Santa Laura** are a half-hour walk southwest. To get to Humberstone, catch a *colectivo* for Pozo Almonte from the eastern side of Iquique's Mercado Centenario. To return, stand at the bus stop outside the entrance of Humberstone and flag down any bus marked 'Iquique' (CH\$2200).

The whopping pre-Columbian geoglyph **El Gigante de Atacama** (Giant of the Atacama), 14km east of Huara on the slopes of Cerro Unita is, at 86m, the world's largest archaeological representation of a human figure. Representing a powerful shaman, its blocky head emanates rays and its thin limbs clutch an arrow and medicine bag. Experts date it to around AD 900. The best views are from several hundred meters back at the base of the hill. To visit, go in a taxi or on a tour.

Amid Atacama's desolate pampas you'll find straggly groves of resilient tamarugo (*Prosopis tamarugo*) lining the Panamericana south of Pozo Almonte. The forest once covered thousands of square kilometers until clear-cutting for the mines nearly destroyed it. The trees are protected within the **Reserva Nacional Pampa del Tamarugal**, which also features 420 restored geoglyphs of humans, llamas and geometric shapes blanketing the hillside at **Pintados** (adult/child CH\$4000/2000; ⊘ 9:30am-5pm Tue-Sun). A derelict nitrate railyard of ruined buildings and rusting rolling stock, the site lies 4.5km west of the Panamericana via a gravel road, nearly opposite the eastward turnoff to Pica.

The oasis of **Pica** is a green-hued patch on a dusty canvas, 113km southeast of Iquique. Its fame hails from its pica limes, the key ingredient of the tart and tasty *pisco* sour. Day-trippers can enjoy splashing around the freshwater pool, **Cocha Resbaladero**

(Termas de Pica; General Ibáñez; CH$3000; ⊘ 8am-8pm), fresh fruit drink in hand.

Mamiña, 125km east of Iquique (not on the same road to Pica) is a terraced town with **thermal baths** (Cruce A-653; CH$3000; ⊘ 9am-4pm), a 17th-century church and a pre-Columbian fortress, **Pukará del Cerro Inca**. The village huddles into upper and lower sectors, the former clustered around the rocky outcrop where the 1632 **Iglesia de San Marcos** stands, while the latter lies low in the valley, near the hot springs.

Arica

⏿ 058 / POP 221,000

The pace of Arica is simply delightful. It's warm and sunny year-round, there's a cool pedestrian mall to wander around come sunset, and decent brown-sugar beaches are just a short walk from the town center. Top this off with some kick-ass surf breaks and a cool cliff-top War of the Pacific battlefield at El Morro, and you may just stay another day or two before you head up to nearby Parque Nacional Lauca or take an afternoon off from 'beach duty' to visit the Azapa Valley, home to some of the world's oldest-known mummies.

◉ Sights & Activities

★ **Museo de Sitio Colón 10**   MUSEUM
(Colón 10; adult/child CH$2000/1000; ⊘ 10am-7pm Tue-Sun Jan & Feb, to 6pm Tue-Sun Mar-Dec) See the 32 excavated Chinchorro mummies in situ at this tiny museum below El Morro. They were discovered when an architect bought this former private home with the intention of converting it into a hotel. You can gape at the glass-protected bodies as they were found, in the sand below the floors, in different positions, complete with their funerary bundles, skins and feathers of marine fowl.

Ferrocarril Arica-Poconchile   TRAIN
(http://trenturistico.fcalp.cl; Av Brasil 117; adult/child return CH$9000/7000; ⊘ ticket office 9am-2pm & 3-6:30pm Mon-Fri) One part of the old rail line that linked Arica with La Paz, Bolivia, has been restored, allowing you to ride a tourist train that runs once a week between Arica and the Lluta Valley town of Poconchile, some 37km to the northeast. The 1950s vintage train cars currently depart Saturdays at 10:30am and arrive back in Arica at 3:30pm, after a one-hour stop in Poconchile.

The train departs from the station in Chinchorro, about 3km northeast of the center. Call ahead or confirm with the tourist office that the train is running. Outside high season (December to mid-March) it tends to run only twice a month.

El Morro de Arica   VIEWPOINT
This imposing coffee-colored shoulder of rock looms 110m over the city. It makes a great place to get your bearings, with vulture-eye views of the city, port and Pacific Ocean. This lofty headland was the site of a crucial battle in 1880, a year into the War of the Pacific, when the Chilean army assaulted and took El Morro from Peruvian forces in less than an hour.

Catedral de San Marcos   CHURCH
(San Marcos 260, Plaza Colón; ⊘ 8:30am-9pm Mon-Fri, 11am-1pm Sat, 9am-1pm & 7:30-9pm Sun) This Gothic-style church has a threefold claim to fame. First, it was designed by celebrated Parisian engineer Alexandre Gustave Eiffel, before his success with the Eiffel Tower. Second, it was prefabricated in Eiffel's Paris shop in the 1870s (at the order of the Peruvian president) then shipped right around the world to be assembled on site. Still more curious is the construction itself: the entire church is made of stamped and molded cast iron, coated with paint.

Cuevas de Anzota   NATURAL FEATURE
(Av Comandante San Martín) About 10km south of the center, the serene beaches give way to an area of jagged cliffs, rocky shorelines and caves that were used by the Chinchorro culture some 9000 years ago. A new coastal walk takes you through the area, with staircases leading up to lookout points, and fine vantage points over the dramatic coastline. Keep an eye out for sea lions, *chungungo* (a marine otter) and a host of marine birds.

There's no public transportation down this way. Take a taxi.

Museo Arqueológico San Miguel de Azapa   MUSEUM
(http://masma.uta.cl; Camino Azapa, Km12; adult/child CH$2000/1000; ⊘ 9am-8pm Jan & Feb, 10am-6pm Mar-Dec) This museum, 12km east of Arica, is home to some of the world's oldest-known mummies. There are superb local archaeological and cultural-heritage displays and a handy audio guide in English. *Colectivos* (CH$1200) at the corner of Chacabuco and Patricio Lynch provide transportation.

☞ Tours

Raíces Andinas ECOTOUR
(Ecotour Expediciones; ☑9-5111-7797; www.eco tourexpediciones.cl; Héroes del Morro 632; ⊗9am-noon & 3-6pm Mon-Sat) This well-run outfit is recommended for encouraging better understanding of the local people. It specializes in trips of two or more days, and offers expeditions to Sajama in Bolivia via Lauca as well as adventures into Salar de Uyuni.

Mayuru OUTDOORS
(☑9-8582-1493; www.mayurutour.com; Baquedano 411, Putre) Mayuru has a strong reputation for its high-quality tours around the region. If time allows, skip the one-day blitz to Lauca, and do one of Mayuru's multi-day trips, taking in the natural wonders of the altiplano.

The office is in Putre, so call or email before you arrive.

🛏 Sleeping

Sunny Days GUESTHOUSE $
(☑58-224-1038; http://sunny-days-arica.cl; Tomas Aravena 161; s/d CH$20,000/32,000, dm/s/d without bathroom CH$11,000/17,000/28,000; ⓟ@⏚) If you don't mind being outside the center, this welcoming, easygoing guesthouse near Playa de Chinchorro is an appealing option. Pleasant rooms, friendly English-speaking staff, a spacious lounge area, and access to kitchens, laundry and bike hire (CH$8000 per day) draw a wide mix of travelers.

Arica Surfhouse HOSTEL $
(☑58-231-2213; www.aricasurfhouse.cl; O'Higgins 661; dm CH$10,500, s/d CH$25,000/33,000, without bathroom CH$20,000/27,000; @⏚) Doubling as Arica's surfer central, this is one of the town's top hostels, with a variety of clean rooms, a great open-air communal area, 24-hour hot water and laundry service. There's a shuttle service to the beaches in winter, and staff will hook you up with surf classes and equipment rental.

Hostal Jardín del Sol HOTEL $
(☑58-223-2795; www.hostaljardindelsol.cl; Sotomayor 848; s/d CH$23,000/$30,000; ⏚) It's been here for ages but still lives up to its reputation as one of Arica's best budget hotels, with small but spotless rooms, fans included. Guests mingle on the leafy patio, and in the shared kitchen and lounge room. There's a book exchange and lots of tourist info.

Petit Clos GUESTHOUSE $
(☑58-232-3746; www.lepetitclos.cl; Colón 9; d CH$32,000-36,000) Near the steps leading up to Morro de Arica, this Belgian-run guesthouse makes a great base for exploring the city. The rooms are pleasantly furnished, there's a terrace with lovely views (where breakfast is served) and tea and coffee are always available.

🍴 Eating & Drinking

Look for traditional seafood lunches on **Muelle Pesquero**, the fishing jetty. Tap water here is chemical-laden; buy your own bottles. Many of the hippest bars and discos are strung along Playa Chinchorro.

Mata-Rangi SEAFOOD $
(Muelle Pesquero; mains CH$5000-7000; ⊗12:30-4pm Thu-Tue) Superb seafood is served at this adorable spot hanging over the harbor by the fishing jetty. A wooden shack-style place packed with wind chimes, it has a breezy dining room and a small terrace above the ocean. Get here early to grab a seat or be prepared to wait.

Cafe del Mar CAFETERIA $
(https://cafedelmararica.cl; 21 de Mayo 260; mains CH$4200-6000; ⊗9am-11pm Mon-Sat; ⏚) On the lively pedestrian lane, the ever-popular Cafe del Mar has a big range of salads, crepes, burgers and sandwiches, plus first-rate coffee. Grab a table out front for prime people-watching.

★Los Aleros de 21 CHILEAN $$
(☑58-225-4641; 21 de Mayo 736; mains CH$8000-13,500; ⊗noon-3:30pm & 8-11:30pm Mon-Sat; ⏚) One of Arica's best restaurants serves up excellent grilled meat and seafood dishes amid wood paneling and an old-fashioned ambience. Service is generally quite good, and there's a decent wine list too.

Baristta Coffee CAFE
(18 de Sepiembre 295, 2nd fl; ⊗8:30am-11pm Mon-Fri, from 11am Sat; ⏚) Arica's best coffee is poured at this hip upstairs cafe with a spacious outdoor patio made of reclaimed wood. You choose the preparation style – V60, Chemex, Syphon or Aeropress – or straight-up espresso. There are also lunch specials (CH$4000), croissant sandwiches and breakfast fare.

Así Sea Club BAR
(San Marcos 251; ⊗9pm-late Fri & Sat) This swank hideaway inside a rambling historic

town house has a set of sleek rooms featuring original detail, and a back patio. It serves cocktails and all-Chilean wines, paired with loungey tunes.

ℹ Information

There are numerous 24-hour ATMs as well as *casas de cambio* (which change US dollars, Peruvian, Bolivian and Argentine currency, and euros) along the pedestrian mall (21 de Mayo).

While Arica is a very safe city, it has a reputation for pickpockets. Be especially cautious at bus terminals and beaches.

Hospital Dr Juan Noé (☑ 58-220-4592; 18 de Sepiembre 1000) A short distance east of downtown.

Post Office (Prat 305; ⊙ 9am-6pm Mon-Fri, 10am-12:30pm Sat) On a walkway between Pedro Montt and Prat.

Sernatur (☑ 58-225-2054; infoarica@sernatur. cl; San Marcos 101; ⊙ 9am-6pm Mon-Fri, 10am-2pm Sat) Helpful office with info on Arica and the surrounding region.

ℹ Getting There & Away

AIR

Aeropuerto Internacional Chacalluta (☑ 58-221-3416; www.chacalluta.cl; Av John Wall) is 18km north of Arica. **LATAM** (☑ 600-526-2000; www.latam.com; Arturo Prat 391) has direct daily flights to Santiago (from CH$46,000, 2½ hours), as does **Sky** (☑ 600-600-2828; www.skyairline.cl) – from CH$40,000, 2½ hours.

BUS

Arica has two main bus terminals. **Terminal Rodoviario de Arica** (Terminal de Buses; ☑ 58-222-5202; Diego Portales 948) houses most companies traveling south to destinations in Chile. Next door, **Terminal Internacional de Buses** (☑ 58-224-8709; Diego Portales 1002) handles international and some regional destinations. To reach the terminals, take *colectivo* 8

from Maipú or San Marcos; a taxi costs around CH$3000.

Various companies with destinations south to Santiago have offices in Terminal Rodoviario de Arica. Some major ones are Pullman, Flota Barrios, Ramos Cholele and Turbus.

For Putre, **Buses La Paloma** (☑ 58-222-2710; www.translapaloma.cl; Diego Portales 948) has a direct bus at 7am (CH$4500, 1½ hours). To get to Tacna, Peru, buses leave the international terminal every half-hour (CH$2000); *colectivos* charge CH$4000. To get to La Paz, Bolivia (from CH$9000, nine hours), the comfiest and fastest service is with **Chile Bus** (☑ 58-226-0505; Diego Portales 1002), but cheaper buses are available with **Trans Salvador** (☑ 58-222-8547; www.trans-salvador.com; Diego Portales 1002) in the international bus terminal. Buses on this route will drop passengers in Parque Nacional Lauca, but expect to pay full fare to La Paz. **Buses Géminis** (☑ 58-235-1465; www.geminis.cl; Diego Portales 948), in the main terminal, goes to Salta and Jujuy in Argentina via Calama on Tuesday, Friday and Sunday.

Buses from Arica

DESTINATION	COST (CH$)	DURATION (HR)
Antofagasta	18,000	10
Calama	15,000	10
Copiapó	24,000	18
Iquique	7000	5
La Paz, Bolivia	9000	9
La Serena	25,000	23
Santiago	30,000	27

TRAIN

Trains to Tacna (CH$3800, 1½ hours) depart near the port from **Estación Ferrocarril Arica-Tacna** (☑ cell 9-7633-2896; Av Máximo Lira, opposite Chacabuco) at 9am and 7:15pm every day.

Remember to set your clock back: there's a one-hour time difference in Peru.

Route 11 & Putre

About 10km north of Arica, the Panamericana intersects paved Chile 11, which ushers traffic east up the valley of the Río Lluta to Poconchile and on to Putre and Parque Nacional Lauca. The road features a clutch of worthy stops, if you want to break up the journey. Note that this heavily trafficked, winding route toward La Paz, Bolivia, gets about 500 trucks per day.

The barren slopes of the valley host hillside geoglyphs, **Poconchile** and its quake-ridden 17th-century church, candelabra cacti (consider yourself blessed if you see it in bloom, which happens one 24-hour period per year), and the chasm-side ruins of the 12th-century fortress **Pukará de Copaquilla**.

Detour in Poconchile to **Eco-Truly** (cell 9-9776-3796; http://vrindaarica.cl/eco-truly-arica; Sector Linderos, Km29; campsites/cabins per person CH$4000/8000, r incl breakfast CH$8000), a slightly surreal Hare Krishna 'ecotown' and yoga school, for an abundant vegetarian sampler lunch (CH$4000).

Aymara village **Putre** (population 1450; altitude 3530m) is 150km northeast of Arica and an appealing stop for visitors to acclimatize. There's a post office and call center in town, but only one bank – bring cash from Arica. Baquedano is the main strip.

Take advantage of the excellent hikes among ancient stone-faced terraces of alfalfa and oregano and tranquil village ambience. Colonial architecture includes the restored adobe **Iglesia de Putre** (1670). During the frivolously fun **Carnaval** (Feb), exploding flour balloons and live music rule the day.

Flavio of **Terrace Lodge & Tours** (58-223-0499; www.terracelodge.com; Circunvalación 25) runs a range of wonderful guided tours to some hidden spots, both in the immediate area around Putre as well as farther up north. The stylish and eco-friendly **Terrace Lodge & Cafe** (58-223-0499; www.terracelodge.com; Circunvalación 25; s/d CH$37,000/43,000; @) is a lovely place to spend a few nights as well. Budget lodgings are found at **Pachamama Hostel** (cell 9-6353-5187; www.hostal pachamama.cl/serv.php; off Baquedano; dm/s/d without bathroom CH$10,000/14,000/25,000, apt CH$40,000;), with tidy adobe-walled rooms set around a sunny courtyard.

On the main plaza, **Cantaverdi** (Canto 339; mains CH$4000-7500; 10am-3pm & 6:30-10pm;) is a casual eatery featuring *humitas* (corn dumplings) and home cooking, a roaring fireplace and wi-fi. On a corner of the plaza, **Rosamel** (cnr Carrera & Latorre; mains CH$4500-7500, 3-course lunch CH$4000; 8am-10pm;) has a big menu of Andean dishes, including *lomo de alpaca con papas fritas* (alpaca meat with fries).

Note that things seriously wind down in Putre from mid-December through February, the rainy season.

Buses La Paloma (p500) serves Putre daily; buses depart Arica at 7am and return at 2pm (CH$4500). Note that some international buses between Arica and La Paz stop near Putre; to make the connection into Bolivia, you'll have to coordinate with the ticketing offices in Arica's bus terminal.

Parque Nacional Lauca

At woozy heights with snow-dusted volcanoes, remote hot springs and glimmering lakes, Lauca, 160km northeast of Arica, is an absolute treasure. Herds of vicuña, viscachas (rabbit-like rodents) and bird species including flamingos, giant coots and Andean gulls inhabit the park (1380 sq km; altitude 3000m to 6300m) alongside impressive cultural and archaeological landmarks.

Lauca's crown jewel, the glittering **Lago Chungará** (4517m above sea level), is a shallow body of water formed by lava flows damming the snowmelt stream from **Volcán Parinacota** (6350m), a beautiful snowcapped cone that rises immediately to the north. **Laguna Cotacotani** has been partially drained by the national electricity company but you will still see diverse birdlife along its shores and scattered groves of queñoa, one of the world's highest-elevation trees. Wander around beautiful **Parinacota**, a tiny Aymara village of whitewashed adobe and stone streets. If you're lucky, the guide will procure the key for the town's undisputed gem, its 17th-century colonial church, reconstructed in 1789.

At the park's western entrance, **Las Cuevas** has a viewing point marked by a sculpture resembling *zampoña* (panpipes) balanced on a garish staircase. Some tours include a quick dip in **Termas Jurasi** (adult/child CH$2500/1000; dawn-dusk), a pretty cluster of thermal and mud baths huddled amid rocky scenery, 11km northeast of Putre.

Many tour agencies offer one-day blitzes from sea-level Arica – a surefire method to get *soroche* (altitude sickness). These tours leave around 7:30am and return about

8:30pm. It is common to become very sick when ascending to high altitudes without proper acclimatization. Avoid overeating, smoking and alcohol consumption the day before and while on tour. Tours that include at least a night in Putre are a wiser option, allowing more time to acclimatize. If you are renting a car, or have your own, carry extra fuel and antifreeze.

MIDDLE CHILE

Chile's heartland, covered with orchards and vineyards, is often skipped by travelers scrambling further afield. But if this region existed anywhere else in the world, it would be getting some serious attention. The harvests of the fertile central valley fill produce bins from Anchorage to Tokyo. Come for wine-tasting, unspoiled national parks and excellent skiing and surfing.

Colchagua Valley

With around 20 wineries open to the public, the Colchagua Valley is Chile's biggest and best-established wine region. Its deep loamy soils, abundant water, dry air, bright sunshine and cool nights nurture some of the country's best reds. Many travelers who come here to taste wine book hotel rooms in Santa Cruz.

Santa Cruz

📞 72 / POP 37,900

Ground zero of Chile's winemaking and wine-touring scene is a fairly sleepy place with a picturesque main square. The place perks up during the lively **Fiesta de la Vendimia de Colchagua** (Plaza de Armas; ⊙ Mar), celebrating the grape harvest.

While in town, check out the vast **Museo de Colchagua** (📞 72-282-1050; www.museocolchagua.cl; Errázuriz 145; adult/child CH$7000/3000; ⊙10am-7pm); the collection features pre-Columbian anthropomorphic ceramics from all over Latin America, weapons, religious artifacts, Mapuche silver, and *huasos* (cowboy) gear. For many Chileans, the headlining exhibit here is *El Gran Rescate* (The Big Rescue), showing objects, photos and films related to the October 2010 rescue of the 33 miners trapped 700m underground near Copiapó.

An extremely helpful resource on the main square is **Ruta del Vino** (📞72-282-3199; www.rutadelvino.cl; Plaza de Armas 298; ⊙9am-7pm). In addition to providing information about the region's wineries, it offers tasting tours (note that transportation to the wineries isn't included in the basic price; for a full tour with lunch and transportation, you'll be paying upwards of CH$66,000). If you're fine sticking with the wineries closer to town, you can pay for taxi rides. Car rental isn't available in Santa Cruz; one option is renting a car in Santiago and driving yourself around the wine country – even if you're planning on joining a guided tour.

The **bus terminal** (Rafael Casanova 478) sits four blocks west of the town plaza. **Buses Nilahue** (www.busesnilahue.cl; Rafael Casanova 478, Terminal de Buses Santa Cruz) and other lines offer hourly departures from Santa Cruz to Pichilemu (CH$3000, two hours) and Santiago (CH$5000, three hours).

Colchagua Valley Wineries

Visit top wineries on a guided tour with Ruta del Vino (p502) or via reservations with the wineries ahead of time. Visits to **Viu Manent** (📞2-2379-0020; www.viumanent.cl; Carretera del Vino, Km37; tastings CH$13,000, tours CH$16,000; ⊙tours 10:30am, noon, 3pm & 4:30pm), near Santa Cruz, involve a carriage ride through vineyards. In addition to tastings and 'make-your-own-wine' workshops (12:30pm daily, CH$33,000), award-winning **MontGras** (📞72-282-2845; www.montgras.cl; Camino Isla de Yáquil s/n, Palmilla; tastings from CH$9000, tours from CH$15,000; ⊙9am-5:30pm Mon-Fri, to 5pm Sat, open to 5pm Sun Nov-Apr only; 🚴) offers horseback riding, hiking and mountain biking. **Viña Casa Silva** (📞72-291-3117; www.casasilva.cl; Hijuela Norte s/n, San Fernando; tastings by the glass CH$1500-6000, tours from CH$16,000; ⊙10am-6pm), one of the country's oldest wineries, features insightful tours and an excellent restaurant set alongside a polo pitch.

Pichilemu

📞72 / POP 16,400

Wave gods and goddesses brave the icy waters of Chile's unofficial surf capital year-round, while mere beach-going mortals fill its long black sands December through March. Pichilemu's laid-back vibe and great waves make it easy to see why it's so popular with visiting board-riders.

The westernmost part of 'Pichi' juts out into the sea, forming **La Puntilla**, the closest surfing spot to town. **Escuela de Surf**

Middle Chile

Manzana 54 (☎ cell 9-9574-5984; www.manzana 54.cl; Eugenio Díaz Lira 5; board & gear hire per day CH$7000-8000, 2hr group classes CH$10,000) offers surf rentals and classes here. Fronting the town center to the northeast is calm **Playa Principal** (main beach), while south is the longer and rougher **Infiernillo**, known for its more dangerous waves and fast tow. The best surfing in the area is at **Punta de Lobos**, 6km south of Pichi proper, which you need to drive to.

In town, **Eco Camping La Caletilla** (☎72-284-1010; www.campingpichilemu.cl; Eugenio Suarez 905; campsites per person CH$7000-8000; ☎) is a groovy campground with hot showers and wind-sheltered pitches made from repurposed materials. Cheap *residenciales* (budget accommodations) pop up around town in summertime, too. Woodsy **Surf Lodge Punta De Lobos** (☎ cell 9-8154-1106; www.surflodgepuntadelobos.com; Catrianca s/n; d/tr/q from CH$56,000/60,000/64,000; ☎☀) oozes youthful energy with a hip design and

ample leisure toys for adults (think: board games, hammocks and swings).

Down by the surf breaks, several hostels compete for business, including **Pichilemu Surf Hostal** (☎ cell 9-9270-9555; www.surfhos tal.com; Eugenio Diaz Lira 164; dm/s/d incl breakfast CH$15,000/30,000/45,000; ☎). Also on site, **El Puente Holandés** (☎ cell 9-9270-0955; Eugenio Díaz Lira 167; mains CH$8000-10,000; ⊙1-4pm & 7-11pm) is great for seafood ravioli and grilled sea bass – the terrace is spot-on for a beer.

Back in town, **Pulpo** (☎72-284-1827; Ortúzar 275; mains CH$4000-8000; ⊙noon-1am Tue-Sat, 1-4:30pm Sun, 7:30pm-12:30am Mon; ☎☀) serves up crispy thin pizzas. **La Casa de las Empanadas** (Aníbal Pinto 268; empanadas CH$1800-2500; ⊙11am-11pm) is a cheerful takeaway counter serving up huge gourmet empanadas like *machas y queso* (razor clams and cheese).

From the **Terminal de Buses** (☎72-298-0504; cnr Av Millaco & Los Alerces) on Pichilemu's outskirts, buses run frequently to Santiago (CH$7000, four hours), Santa Cruz (CH$3000, two hours) and San Fernando (CH$5000, 3½ hours), where there are connections north and south.

Curicó

☑ 75 / POP 147,000

Attracting visitors interested in local vineyards and the exquisite Reserva Nacional Radal Siete Tazas, Curicó is a laid-back city, best known for its postcard-perfect **Plaza de Armas**, complete with monkey-puzzle trees and palms, a striking early-20th-century wrought-iron bandstand, and a wooden statue of the Mapuche chief Toqui Lautaro. Very sadly, up to 90% of the older buildings in Curicó's historic center fell in the February 2010 earthquake.

Curicó bursts into life for the **Fiesta de la Vendimia de Curicó** (Wine Harvest Festival; http://vendimiachile.cl; Plaza de Armas; ☺Mar), celebrating the wine harvest. **Ruta del Vino Curicó** (☑75-232-8972; www.rutadelvinocurico.cl; Carmen 727, Hotel Raíces; tours CH$87,000; ☺10am-1pm & 3:30-7pm Mon-Fri) arranges tours to area vineyards.

The English-speaking host of guesthouse **Homestay in Chile** (☑75-222-5272; www.homestayinchile.cl; Argomedo 448; s/d/tr US$65/85/108; ℗�☞), one block south of the Plaza de Armas, offers the warmest welcome in Curicó. Pillows are cloud-like, wi-fi is fast and breakfast includes real coffee and fresh juice.

The **Terminal de Buses** (cnr Prat & Maipú) and the **train station** (☑600-585-5000; www.trencentral.cl; Maipú 657; ☺ticket office 9:30am-2:30pm Mon-Fri, 9am-1pm Sat, 12:30-8:30pm Sun) are five blocks west of the Plaza de Armas. There are three trains a day to Santiago (CH$8100, 2¼ hours) and Chillán (CH$9100, 2½ hours). **Andimar** (☑75-231-2000; www.andimar.cl; Terminal de Buses) has frequent bus services to Santiago (CH$5000, 2½ hours, every 15 minutes). **Pullman del Sur** (☑2-2776-2424; www.pdelsur.cl; Terminal de Buses) has a cheaper service (CH$3500), but there are only three daily departures.

To get to Reserva Nacional Radal Siete Tazas, catch a bus to Molina (CH$600, 35 minutes, every five minutes) with **Aquelarre** (☑75-232-6404; Terminal de Buses Rurales, opposite the main bus terminal) from the Terminal de Buses Rurales, opposite the main bus terminal. From Molina there are frequent services to the park in January and February.

Maule Valley

The Maule Valley, a hugely significant wine-producing region for Chile, is responsible for much of the country's export wine. The specialty here is full-bodied cabernet sauvignon, though intriguing bottles of old-vine Carignan and País are the real stars.

Many visitors use Talca as a base for exploring the wineries and the nearby Reserva Nacional Altos de Lircay. Ask for the free *Región del Maule* booklet at Sernatur (p504) in Talca for great information (in English) on recommended treks, local tips and a guide to regional flora and fauna.

Talca

☑ 71 / POP 220,400

Founded in 1690, Talca is steeped in history; Chile's 1818 declaration of independence was signed here. These days, it's mainly known as a convenient base for exploring the gorgeous Reserva Nacional Altos de Lircay and the Maule Valley wine country. You'll find a decent range of traveler's services, including dining and lodging options, plus lovely views of the Andes when you're strolling down the sunbaked pedestrian thoroughfare at noon.

Four blocks from the Plaza de Armas, **Cabañas Stella Bordestero** (☑71-223-6545; www.turismostella.cl; 4 Poniente 1 Norte 1183; s/d cabin incl breakfast CH$30,000/48,000; ❋☞☒) offers cozy, well-equipped clapboard cabins in a leafy garden. In the countryside outside of town, the lovely **Casa Chueca** (☑71-197-0097; www.casa-chueca.com; Viña Andrea s/n, Sector Alto Lircay; dm CH$13,500, d CH$49,000-75,000, 4-person cabins CH$122,000; ☞☒) ✿ is a destination in its own right; the knowledgeable owners can help you plan trekking and horseback riding in Altos de Lircay. Contact ahead for pick-up information.

Centrally located **La Buena Carne** (www.parrilladaslabuenacarne.cl; cnr 6 Oriente & 1 Norte; mains CH$3500-7500; ☺noon-11pm Mon-Sat) is a contemporary steakhouse with friendly service, wines by the glass and classic Chilean platters.

For travel information, consult helpful **Sernatur** (☑71-222-6940; www.chile.travel; 1 Oriente 1150; ☺8:30am-5:30pm Mon-Fri, extended hours Dec-Feb) on the main square.

North–south buses stop at Talca's main **bus station** (☑71-220-3992; 2 Sur 1920, cnr 12 Oriente), 11 blocks east of the plaza, or the nearby **Turbus terminal** (☑600-660-6600;

www.turbus.cl; 3 Sur 1960). Destinations include Chillán (CH$4000, 2½ hours), Puerto Montt (CH$14,000, 12 hours) and Santiago (CH$5000, three hours). To connect to Pichilemu, take the bus to Curicó (CH$1800).

Buses Vilches (📞 cell 9-5703-0436; 2 Sur 1920, Terminal de Buses de Talca) has at least three daily services to Vilches Alto (CH$1900, two hours), the gateway to the Reserva Nacional Altos de Lircay. From the TrenCentral **train station** (📞 600-585-5000; www.trencentral.cl; 11 Oriente 900; ⊙ ticket office 7am-noon & 3-8pm), there are three trains a day to Santiago (CH$8100, 3½ hours) and south to Chillán (CH$9100, two hours).

Maule Valley Wineries

You can visit many of the vineyards independently or through one of the tours run by **Ruta del Vino** (www.valledelmaule.cl; Talca). There's more to do at boutique **Viña Gillmore** (📞 73-197-5539; www.gillmore.cl; Camino Constitución, Km20; tour incl 2 pours CH$6000, tasting only CH$2000; ⊙ 9am-5pm Mon-Sat) 🍴, which is converting to an organic system, than sip and swirl (though its Vigno Carignan is indeed fantastic). It also features beautiful trails, a vino-themed lodge (rooms from CH$140,000) and a spa offering various wine-based therapies. Visitor-friendly **Viña Balduzzi** (📞 73-232-2138; www.balduzzi.com; Av Balmaceda 1189, San Javier; tour incl 4 pours CH$9000, tasting only CH$4500; ⊙ 9am-6pm Mon-Sat; 🚌 San Javier Directo) is a fourth-generation winery surrounded by spacious gardens and colonial buildings.

Chillán

📞 42 / POP 184,700

Earthquakes have battered Chillán throughout its turbulent history; the 2010 quake was yet another blow. While this perpetually rebuilding city isn't especially interesting, it is a gateway to amazing skiing and summer trekking in the nearby mountains.

In response to the devastation caused by a 1939 quake, the Mexican government donated the **Escuela México** (Av O'Higgins 250; donations welcome; ⊙ 10am-12:30pm & 3-6pm Mon-Fri) to the city. At Pablo Neruda's request, Mexican muralists David Alfaro Siqueiros and Xavier Guerrero painted spectacular tributes to indigenous and post-Columbian figures in history; today it's a working school, and visitors' donations are encouraged.

Mercado de Chillán (Maipón 773; set lunches from CH$2500; ⊙ 7:30am-8pm Mon-Fri, to 6pm Sat, to 3pm Sun), among Chile's best markets, is also an excellent locale for a budget lunch – *longaniza* (pork sausage) is a local delicacy.

🛏 Sleeping & Eating

Hotel Canadá GUESTHOUSE $
(📞 42-232-9481; Bulnes 240; s/d CH$30,000/ 40,000; 🅿 🛜) A row of eight clean and comfy rooms set back from the road amid a peaceful garden.

Arcoiris VEGETARIAN $
(📞 42-233-0722; El Roble 525; buffet CH$7000, mains CH$4000; ⊙ 9am-5pm Mon-Sat; 🛜 🍴) A good vegetarian restaurant in provincial Chile? We'll take it. Filling lentil-and-bulgur-style buffet lunches are served at the back, while a cafe upfront does sandwiches and cakes, all to the tune of wind-chime and whale music.

★ Fuego Divino STEAK $$
(📞 42-243-0900; www.fuegodivino.cl; Gamero 980; mains CH$8000-15,000; ⊙ 12:30-3:30pm & 7:30-10:30pm Tue-Thu, to midnight Fri & Sat) Stylish restaurants are thin on the ground in Chillán – perhaps that's why the gleaming black tables here are always booked up on weekends. Or maybe it's because the expertly barbecued prime cuts of Osorno beef taste so delicious.

ℹ Information

ATMs abound. There's free wi-fi on the pedestrian walkways downtown.

Hospital Herminda Martín (📞 42-258-6400; www.hospitaldechillan.cl; Francisco Ramírez 10; ⊙ 24hr) Public hospital on the corner of Av Argentina.

Sernatur (www.biobioestuyo.cl; 18 de Sepiembre 455; ⊙ 9am-1pm & 3-6pm Mon-Fri, 10am-2pm Sat) Friendly staff provide city maps and information on accommodations and transport.

ℹ Getting There & Away

Chillán has two long-distance bus stations. The most central is **Terminal del Centro** (Av Brasil 560), five blocks west of the Plaza de Armas. From here, **Línea Azul** (www.buseslineaazul.cl; Av Brasil 560, Terminal del Centro) has regular services to Santiago (CH$8000, six hours) and Concepción (CH$3000, two hours).

All other long-distance carriers use the **Terminal María Teresa** (O'Higgins 010), north of Av Ecuador. These include **Turbus** (📞 600-660-6600; www.turbus.cl; O'Higgins 010, Terminal María Teresa), which has services to Talca (CH$4000, three hours), Santiago (CH$8000, six hours), Valparaíso (CH$10,000, eight hours) and Temuco (CH$8000, five hours).

CHILE CHILLÁN

WORTH A TRIP

SIETE TAZAS & ALTOS DE LIRCAY

Clear water ladles into seven basalt pools in the lush **Reserva Nacional Radal Siete Tazas** (☑ 71-222-4461; www.conaf.cl/parques/parque-nacional-radal-siete-tazas; adult/child CH$5000/2500; ⊙ 9am-7:30pm Jan & Feb, to 5:30pm Mar-Dec), with the spectacle ending at a 50m waterfall. Two well-marked hiking trails loop from **Camping Los Robles** (☑ 75-222-8029; parque.radalsietetazas@conaf.cl; campsites per person CH$3000): the 1km **Sendero el Coigüe** and 7km **Sendero Los Chiquillanes**, which has great views of the Valle del Indio (plan on about four hours in total). Conaf runs two cold-water **campsites** (☑ 75-222-8029; parque.radalsietetazas@conaf.cl; Parque Inglés; campsites per person CH$3000) at Parque Inglés. The park is 65km from Curicó. During January and February Buses Hernández operates four services from the Terminal de Buses in Molina to the Parque Inglés sector of the park (CH$3000, 2½ hours).

In the Andean foothills, 65km east of Talca, **Reserva Nacional Altos de Lircay** (☑ cell 9-9064-3369; www.conaf.cl/parques/reserva-nacional-altos-de-lircay; adult/child CH$5000/2500; ⊙ 9am-1pm & 2-5pm) offers fabulous trekking under a chattery flutter of tricahues and other native parrots. A helpful team of Conaf rangers who run the park give detailed advice about hiking and camping within it. Arguably the best hike in the whole of Middle Chile, the full-day **Sendero Enladrillado** takes you to the top of a unique 2300m basaltic plateau with stunning views. Alternatively, the shorter **Sendero Laguna** leads uphill to the gorgeous Laguna del Alto, a mountain-ringed lake 2000m above sea level. Casa Chueca (p504) outside Talca offers excellent guided day hikes.

Conaf runs the excellent **Camping Antahuara** (☑ cell 9-9064-3369; campsites per person CH$3000) about 500m beyond the *administración* (headquarters), next to Río Lircay. From Talca, Buses Vilches goes several times daily to Vilches Alto, 5km from the *administración*. It takes about 1½ hours to drive to the reserve from Talca.

Local and regional services leave from the **Terminal de Buses Rurales** (Terminal Paseo La Merced; Maipón 890), also known as Terminal Paseo La Merced.

Nevados de Chillán & Valle Las Trancas

The southern slopes of the 3122m Volcán Chillán are the stunning setting of the **Nevados de Chillán Ski Center** (☑ 42-220-6100; www.nevadosdechillan.com; Camino Termas de Chillán, Km85; ski pass per day adult/child CH$48,000/38,000). With 40 runs, superlatives abound here: it has the longest piste in South America (13km Las Tres Marías), the longest chairlift and some of the biggest and best off-piste offerings. Hikers come out on summer weekends, but it's quiet on a weekday in the off season – bring your own picnic and don't count on hotels being open. Bring cash from Chillán.

Soak in the thermal springs at **Valle Hermoso** (www.nevadosdechillan.com; Camino Termas de Chillán, Km83; thermal springs adult/child CH$8000/6000, campsite for up to 5 people CH$30,000; ⊙ thermal springs 8:30am-5pm Mon-Thu, to 9pm Fri-Sun). Ski-lodge-style **Chil'in**

Hostel (☑ cell 9-9368-2247; www.chil-in.com; Camino Termas de Chillán, Km72; dm/d without bathroom CH$10,500/32,000; ⚇⚇) is both hostel and pizzeria. The stunning shipping containers of **Ecobox Andino** (☑ 42-242-3134; www.ecoboxandino.cl; Camino a Shangri-Lá, Km0.2; 2- to 5-person cabins CH$40,000-130,000, d incl breakfast CH$40,000-80,000; ⚇⚇) ☑ offer an upscale option, while the après-ski scene is happening at **Snow Pub** (☑ 42-221-3910; Camino Termas de Chillán, Km71; mains CH$5000-7000; ⊙ 1pm-late Mon-Sat, to 8pm Sun).

From Chillán's Terminal de Buses Rurales, **Rembus** (☑ 42-222-9377; www.busesrembus.cl; Maipón 890, Terminal de Buses Rurales) has at least 10 daily departures for Valle Las Trancas (CH$2200, 1½ hours), with some services continuing to Valle Hermoso (CH$3300, 1½ hours).

Concepción

☑ 41 / POP 223,600

Concepción is an important and hard-working port city known for its universities and musical acts (many of Chile's best rock groups got their start here). There's an energetic, youthful and left-leaning arts, music and culture scene. 'Conce' sits on the northern bank of the Río Biobío, Chile's only significant navigable waterway. The metropolis seems to go on forever, with an estimated 950,000 people living in the greater area.

⊙ Sights

La Casa del Arte   MUSEUM
(📞41-220-3835;http://extension.udec.cl/pinacoteca; cnr Avs Chacabuco & Paicaví, Barrio Universitario; 🕙10am-6pm Tue-Fri, 11am-5pm Sat, 11am-2pm Sun) **FREE** The massive, fiercely political mural *La Presencia de América Latina* is the highlight of the university art museum La Casa del Arte. It's by Mexican artist Jorge González Camarena, a protégé of the legendary muralist José Clemente Orozco, and celebrates Latin America's indigenous peoples and independence from colonial and imperial powers.

🛏 Sleeping & Eating

Hostal B&B Concepción   GUESTHOUSE $
(📞41-318-9308;   www.hostalboutiqueconcepcion. com; Ongolmo 62; s/d/tr incl breakfast CH$18,500/ 32,500/40,000;   📶🛜) Exceptionally clean rooms with comfy beds in a prime location near Plaza Peru. We only wish the breakfast was more generous, given how yummy the cakes and coffees are at the hip on-site cafe.

Hotel Alborada   BOUTIQUE HOTEL $$
(📞41-291-1121; www.hotelalborada.cl; Barros Arana 457; d incl breakfast from CH$56,000; 📶🛜) A surprisingly stylish addition to Concepción's hotel scene is this centrally located, coolly minimalist hotel. The public spaces – outfitted with all-white furnishings, glass and mirrors – are sleeker than the guest rooms themselves, which are spacious and comfortable, but standard.

Deli House   INTERNATIONAL $
(www.delihouse.cl; Av Diagonal Pedro Aguirre Cerda 1234; mains CH$3500-6500; 🕙9:30am-11:30pm Mon-Fri, from noon Sat, 12:30-4:30pm Sun; 🛜) These leafy sidewalk tables are a relaxed place to kick back for coffee, empanadas, gourmet pizza or happy hour while watching the bohemian university set pass by.

★Lo que más quiero   CHILEAN $$
(📞41-213-4938; Lincoyán 60; mains CH$6000-11,000; 🕙11am-3pm & 6:30pm-midnight Mon-Fri) Conce's top restaurant is as unstuffy as the city itself, with a whimsical woodsy aesthetic and a secret garden out back. The menu includes the largest list of salads we've seen in Chile, as well as creative meat-heavy mains, delicious sandwiches and fresh juices. Don't even think about coming without a reservation.

❶ Information

Conaf (📞41-262-4046; www.conaf.cl; Rengo 345; 🕙8:30am-4:30pm Mon-Thu, to 3:30pm Fri) Limited information on nearby national parks and reserves.

CHILE CONCEPCIÓN

WORTH A TRIP

LAGUNA DEL LAJA & NAHUELBUTA

The sparkling centerpiece of **Parque Nacional Laguna del Laja** (📞cell 9-6642-6899; www.conaf.cl/parques/parque-nacional-laguna-del-laja; adult/child CH$3000/1500; 🕙8:30am-8pm Dec-Apr, to 6:30pm May-Nov) is the towering snowcone of Volcán Antuco (2985m). A fantastic trek, **Sendero Sierra Velluda**, circles its skirt, taking three days, or you can go for a day hike to get a taste of the action. The privately run **Centro Turístico** (📞cell 9-8221-2078; www.parqueantuco.cl; 1km past park entrance; campsites per person CH$5000, 4-/6-/7-person cabins CH$45,000/60,000/70,000; 🅿) complex has well-equipped two-story A-frame cabins that are built of wood and stone and lie in a valley at the entrance to the park, offering humbling views of the mountains above. Departing from Los Ángeles' Terminal de Buses Rurales, local buses (CH$2000, two hours, six daily) go to the village of El Abanico, 11km from the park entrance. The last bus back to Los Ángeles leaves Abanico at 8pm.

Amazing araucaria (monkey-puzzle trees) grow up to 50m tall and 2m in diameter on the green slopes of **Parque Nacional Nahuelbuta** (www.conaf.cl/parques/parque-nacional-nahuelbuta; adult/child CH$5000/3000; 🕙8:30am-6pm), a fine destination for hiking and mountain biking. You can pitch your tent at **Camping Pehuenco** (www.conaf.cl/parques/parque-nacional-nahuelbuta; 6-person campsites CH$16,000). From Angol, 35km to the east, the Terminal de Buses Rurales has buses to Vegas Blancas (CH$1700, 1½ hours). Some lines go on Monday, Wednesday and Friday, others on alternate days. Buses generally return from Vegas Blancas at 6pm – confirm these times so you don't get stranded.

Hospital Regional (☑ 41-272-2500; www.
hospitalregional.cl; cnr San Martín & Av Roosevelt; ⊙ 24hr) Public hospital.

Sernatur (☑ 41-274-1337; www.biobioestuyo.
cl; Pinto 460; ⊙ 9am-8pm Mon-Fri, to 4pm
Sat Jan & Feb, 8:30am-1pm & 3-6pm Mon-Fri
Mar-Dec) On Plaza Independencia with info and
brochures on the region.

❶ Getting There & Away

Long-distance buses go to **Terminal de Buses
Collao** (Tegualda 860), 3km east of central
Concepción. The separate **Terminal Camilo
Henríquez** (Camilo Henríquez 2565) is north-
east along the extension of Bulnes.

There are dozens of daily services to Santiago
(CH$8000, 6½ hours) with companies including
Eme Bus (☑ 41-232-0094; www.emebus.cl;
Tegualda 860, Terminal de Buses Collao), **Pull-
man Bus** (☑ 600-320-3200; www.pullmanbus.
cl; Tegualda 860, Terminal de Buses Collao)
and **Turbus** (☑ 600-660-6600; www.turbus.cl;
Tucapel 530), which also goes to Valparaíso and
south to Temuco (CH$8500, four hours), Val-
divia (CH$12,000, six hours) and Puerto Montt
(CH$10,000, eight hours). **Línea Azul** (☑ 42-
203-800; www.bueslineaazul.cl; Tegualda 860,
Terminal de Buses Collao) runs frequently to
Chillán (CH$2500, two hours).

Los Ángeles
☑ 43 / POP 202,300

A useful base for visiting Parque Nacional
Laguna del Laja, Los Ángeles is an otherwise
unprepossessing agricultural and industrial
service center 110km south of Chillán.

Unless you really need to catch an early
morning bus from here, rural guesthouses
just out of town make for a more pleasant
stay. In the town center there are plenty of
casual cafés; try **Cafe Francés** (☑ 43-223-
4461; www.facebook.com/cafefrances; Colo Colo
696; mains CH$3000-4500; ⊙ 10am-9pm Mon-
Sat; 🖘).

With its gorgeous rural setting 19km north
of Los Ángeles, the American-run **Residencial El Rincón** (☑ cell 9-9082-3168; www.
elrinconchile.cl; Sector El Olivo s/n; r incl breakfast
CH$48,000-61,000, without bathroom CH$38,000;
🖘) is a relaxing place to take time out from
traveling.

Long-distance buses leave from the **Terminal Santa María** (Av Sor Vicenta 2051), on the
northeast outskirts of town. The terminal for
Turbus (☑ 43-240-2003; www.turbus.cl; Av Sor
Vicenta 2061, Turbus Terminal) is nearby. For service to the village of El Abanico, 11km from
the entrance of Parque Nacional Laguna del

Laja, go to the **Terminal de Buses Rurales**
(Terminal Vega Techada; Villagrán 501).

THE LAKES DISTRICT

The further south you go, the greener it gets,
until you find snow-clad volcanoes rising
over verdant hills and lakes. This bucolic region makes a great escape to a slower pace.
The Araucanía, named for the monkey-puzzle
tree, is the geographical center of Mapuche
culture. Further south, the Lakes District was
colonized by Germans in the 1850s and still
retains some Teutonic touches.

Outside the shingled homes, many adventures await: from rafting to climbing,
from hiking to hot-springs hopping, from
taking *onces* in colonial towns to sipping
maté with rural settlers. Hospitality is the
strong suit of *sureños* (southerners); take
time to enjoy it. Though they love the malls,
rural roots still mark most city dwellers
(about half the population), who split wood
and make jam as part of their daily routine.
Seek out the green spaces bursting beyond
the city limits.

The recent eruptions of Volcán Villarrica
and Volcán Calbuco may have affected some
of the activities on offer around Pucón and
Ensenada.

Temuco
☑ 045 / POP 282,400

With its leafy, palm-filled plaza, its pleasant
Mercado Municipal and its intrinsic link to
Mapuche culture, Temuco is the most palatable of Sur Chico's blue-collar cities to visit.
The city is the former home of Pablo Neruda, one of most influential poets of the 20th
century, who once called it the Wild West.
Although it's not a high-value destination in
itself, most folks do spend some time here if
for no other reason than transport logistics.

⊙ Sights

Museo Regional de La Araucanía   MUSEUM
(www.museoregionalaraucania.cl;   Av   Alemania
084;   ⊙ 9:30am-5:30pm Tue-Fri, 11am-5pm Sat,
11am-2pm Sun) FREE Housed in a handsome
frontier-style building dating from 1924,
this small but excellent regional museum
is one of Sur Chico's best. There are permanent exhibits recounting the history of the
Araucanian peoples before, during and since
the Spanish invasion in its newly renovated

basement collection, including an impressive Mapuche dugout canoe.

Monumento Natural
Cerro Ñielol
HISTORIC SITE
(www.conaf.cl/parques/monumento-natural-cerro-nielol; Calle Prat; adult/child Chilean CH$1000/free, foreigner CH$2000/1000; ☺8am-7pm) Cerro Ñielol is a hill that sits among some 90 hectares of native forest – a little forested oasis in the city. Chile's national flower, the copihue (*Lapageria rosea*), grows here in abundance, flowering from March to July. Cerro Ñielol is also of historical importance, since it was here in 1881, at the tree-shaded site known as La Patagua, that Mapuche leaders ceded land to the colonists to found Temuco.

🛏 Sleeping & Eating

Cheap digs around the train station and Feria Pinto can be sketchy, especially for women; the neighborhood between the plaza and university is preferable.

Hospedaje Tribu Piren
GUESTHOUSE $
(☎45-298-5711; http://tribupiren.com; Prat 69; r per person without bathroom CH$20,000; P@☎) A tragic and untimely death has taken the extreme-sport enthusiast who ran this welcoming guesthouse for a decade, but his father humbly carries on his legacy at Tribu Piren. The English infrastructure is unfortunately gone, but everything remains clean and polished, and rooms, some of which open out onto a small terrace, offer cable TV and central heating.

Hospedaje Klickmann
GUESTHOUSE $
(☎45-274-8292; www.hospedajeklickmann.cl; Claro Solar 647; r per person with/without bathroom CH$20,800/16,800; P@☎) This clean and friendly family-run *hospedaje* boasts new, modern bathrooms and is close to several bus companies.

★Tradiciones Zuny
CHILEAN $
(Tucapel 1374; meals CH$5000; ☺12:30-5pm Mon-Sat) Temuco's best-kept secret is an underground locals' haunt specializing in the fresh, simple food of the countryside served out of an indigenous-themed home. It's hard to find – look for the colorful duck/basketball mural – but the cheap, Chilean-Mapuche organic fusion cuisine is a showstopper. You're welcome.

Feria Pinto
MARKET $
(Av Barros Arana; meals CH$2000-3000; ☺7:30am-5:30pm Mon-Sat, 8am-3pm Sun) Feria Pinto is a colorful Mapuche produce-and-food market taking up several blocks along Barros Arana. Along the streets more practical wares are sold, while in the *feria* itself vendors hawk everything from apples and artisan cheeses to honey and bags of *merkén* (Mapuche spice-smoked chili).

🛈 Information

ATMs and exchange houses are plentiful all around Plaza de Armas Aníbal Pinto.

Banco de Chile (www.bancochile.cl; Plaza de Armas Aníbal Pinto) ATM.

BBVA (www.bbva.cl; cnr Claro Solar & Vicuña MacKenna) ATM.

CorreosChile (www.correos.cl; cnr Diego Portales & Prat; ☺9am-7pm Mon-Fri, to 1pm Sat)

Hospital Hernán Henríquez Aravena (☎45-255-9000; www.hhha.cl; Manuel Montt 115; ☺24hr) Six blocks west and one block north of Plaza de Armas Aníbal Pinto.

Sernatur (☎45-240-6214; www.sernatur.cl; cnr Bulnes & Claro Solar; ☺9am-2pm & 3-5:30pm Mon-Thu, 9am-2pm & 3-4:30pm Fri) Well-stocked national tourist info.

Tourist Information Kiosk (☎cell 9-6238-0660; www.temuco.cl; Plaza de Armas; ☺9am-6pm Mon-Fri, to 2pm Sat, shorter hours winter) Free city tours leave from this kiosk on Tuesday, Friday and Saturday at 9:45am – reservations recommended (ofiturplaza@gmail.com).

Tourist Information Kiosk (☎45-297-3628; www.temuco.cl; Centro Mercado Modelo; ☺9am-6pm Mon-Sat, 10am-2pm Sun, shorter hours winter)

🛈 Getting There & Away

AIR

Temuco's shiny and modern **Aeropuerto de la Araucanía** (☎45-220-1900; www.aeropuerto araucania.cl; Longitudinal Sur, Km692, Freire) is located near Freire, 20km south of the city.

LATAM (☎600-526-2000; www.latam.com; Bulnes 687; ☺9am-1:30pm & 3-6:30pm Mon-Fri, 10am-1pm Sat), Sky Airline (www.skyairline.com) and JetSmart (www.jetsmart.com) service the airport from Santiago.

BUS

Long-haul bus services run from the **Terminal Rodoviario** (☎45-222-5005; Pérez Rosales 01609), located at the northern approach to town. Bus companies usually have ticket offices downtown. **Terminal de Buses Rurales** (☎45-221-0494; Av Pinto 32) serves local and regional destinations. For Parque Nacional Conguillío, **Nar-Bus** (☎45-240-7740; www.igillaima.cl; Balmaceda 995) goes to Melipeuco (CH$1900, two hours) five to eight times daily. **Buses JAC** (☎45-246-5463;

The Lakes District

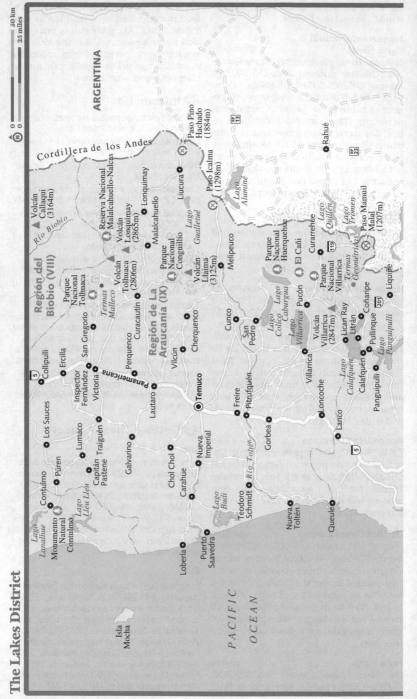

50 km
25 miles

ARGENTINA

Cordillera de los Andes

Paso Pino Hachado (1884m)

RP 13

Rahué

RP 23

▲ Volcán Callaqui (3164m)

Río Biobío

Reserva Nacional Malalcahuello-Nalcas

Volcán Lonquimay (2865m)

Lonquimay

Malalcahuello

Liucura

Lago Gualletué

Paso Icalma (1298m)

Lago Alumné

Región del Biobío (VIII)

Parque Nacional Tolhuaca

▲ Volcán Tolhuaca (2806m)

Termas Malleco

San Gregorio

Curacautín

Parque Nacional Conguillio

▲ Volcán Llaima (3125m)

Melipeuco

Parque Nacional Huerquehue

El Cañi

Curarrehue

Lago Quillén

Lago Tromen

Paso Mamuil Malal (1207m)

Collipulli

5

Ercilla

Inspector Fernández

San Gregorio

Perquenco

Panamericana

Victoria

Curacautín

Cherquenco

Vilcún

Cunco

San Pedro

Lago Colico

Lago Caburgua

Pucón

Parque Nacional Villarrica

Termas Geométricas

Liquiñe

119

Región de La Araucania (IX)

Lautaro

● Temuco

Freire

Pitrufquén

Lago Villarrica

Villarrica

Volcán Villarrica (2847m)

Lican Ray

Litrán

Coñaripe

Pullinque

205

Panguipulli

Lago Panguipulli

Los Sauces

Púren

Lumaco

Capitán Traiguén

Pastene

Galvarino

Chol Chol

Nueva Imperial

Gorbea

Loncoche

Lanco

5

Lago Calafquén

Calafquén

Contulmo

Monumento Natural Contulmo

Lago Lanalhue

Lago Lleu Lleu

Carahue

Teodoro Schmidt

Lago Budi

Río Toltén

Nueva Toltén

Loberia

Puerto Saavedra

Queule

PACIFIC OCEAN

Isla Mocha

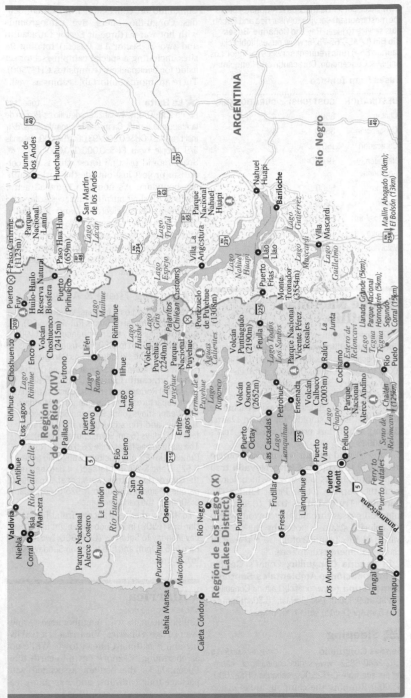

www.jac.cl; cnr Av Balmaceda & Aldunate) offers the most frequent service to Villarrica and Pucón, plus service to Lican Ray and Coñaripe. **Buses Bio Bio** (☐ 45-265-7876; www.busesbiobio.cl; Lautaro 854) runs frequent services to Angol, Los Ángeles, Concepción, Curacautín and Lonquimay.

Buses from Temuco

DESTINATION	COST (CH$)	DURATION (HR)
Chillán	8500	4
Concepción	8500	4½
Curacautín	1500	2
Neuquén, Argentina	19,000	9
Osorno	5500	4
Pucón	2900	2
Puerto Montt	6500	5
Santiago	12,000	9
Valdivia	4000	3

Parque Nacional Conguillío

A Unesco Biosphere Reserve, **Parque Nacional Conguillío** (www.conaf.cl/parques/parque-nacional-conguillio; adult/child Chilean CH$4000/2000, foreigner CH$6000/3000) protects the lovely araucaria and also shelters more than 600 sq km of alpine lakes, deep canyons and native forest. It includes a tiny ski area, but its centerpiece is the smoldering Volcán Llaima (3125m), which last erupted on New Year's Day, 2008.

To see solid stands of monkey-puzzle trees, hike the superb **Sierra Nevada trail** (7km, three hours one-way), which leaves from the parking lot at Playa Linda. The **Cañadon Truful-Truful trail** (0.8km, 30 minutes) passes through the canyon, where the colorful strata, exposed by the rushing waters of Río Truful-Truful, are a record of Llaima's numerous eruptions.

In **Laguna Conguillío**, Conaf's **Centro de Informaciónes Ambientales Santiago Gómez Luna** (www.conaf.cl; Laguna Conguillío; ☺8:30am-9:30pm Dec 16-Mar, 8:30am-1pm & 2:30-6pm Apr-Dec 15) sells trail maps.

🛏 Sleeping

Sendas Conguillío CAMPING, CABAÑAS $
(☐ 2-2840-6852; www.sendasconguillio.cl; camping per site from CH$23,000, cabañas CH$87,000-115,000) Running the camping areas inside Conguillío on concession from Conaf, Sendas Conguillío offers five campgrounds with hot water (three at Sector Curacautín and two at Sector La Caseta) totaling 98 sites, including a special camping sector set aside for backpackers (campsites CH$7500). There are more comfortable cabins as well.

★**La Baita** LODGE $$$
(☐ 45-258-1073; www.labaitaconguillio.cl; Región de la Araucanía, Km18, Camino a Laguna Verde; s/d/tr incl breakfast CH$60,000/93,000/96,000, cabañas 5/9 people from CH$60,000/120,000; ☺) 🍴 Spaced amid pristine forest, this is an ecotourism project just outside the park's southern boundary. It's home to eight attractive cabins with slow-burning furnaces, solar- and turbine-powered electricity and hot water. There's also a very cozy, incense-scented lodge and restaurant with six rooms complete with granite showers and design-forward sinks, along with a pleasant massage room, outdoor hot tub and sauna.

❶ Getting There & Away

To reach Sector Los Paraguas, Vogabus, at Temuco's Terminal de Buses Rurales (p509), runs six times daily to Cherquenco (CH$1400, 1½ hours, 1:30pm to 8:30pm), from where it's a 17km walk to the ski lodge at Los Paraguas.

For the northern entrance at Laguna Captrén, **Buses Curacautín Express** (☐ 45-225-8125; Av Manuel Rodríguez, Terminal Curacautín) has three departures from Curacautín on Mondays and Wednesdays (6am, 9am and 6pm), two on Tuesdays and Thursdays (6am and 6pm) and four on Fridays (6am, 9am, 2pm and 6pm). The bus goes as far as mile 26.5 on the Ruta Curacautín–Parque Nacional Conguillío (where R-925-S and S-297-R intersect), 4.8km before the **Guardería Captrén** (www.conaf.cl/parques/parque-nacional-conguillio; R-925-S; ☺8:30am-6:30pm) at the park's entrance.

For the southern entrance at Truful-Truful, Nar-Bus (p509) in Temuco runs eight times per day Monday to Saturday (CH$1900, two hours, 8am to 6:30pm) and five times on Sunday (9am to 6:30pm).

Villarrica

☐ 045 / POP 52,000

Unlike Pucón, its wild neighbor across windswept Lago Villarrica, Villarrica is a real living and breathing Chilean town. While not as charming, it's more down-to-earth than Pucón, lacks the bedlam associated with package-tour caravans, and has more reasonable prices and a faded-resort glory that attracts travelers of a certain lax disposition.

The newish *costanera* (lakeshore board-walk), a post-2010 Concepción earthquake project, is impressive and they have done a fine job with the new artificial black-sand beach, Chile's first (the city's main street, Aviador Acevedo, also received a 2017 make-over). Considering you can book all the same activities here as in Pucón, it makes for an agreeable alternative for those seeking less in-your-face tourism and a more culturally appropriate experience.

🏃 Activities

★ Aurora Austral
Patagonia Husky   DOG SLEDDING
(📱 cell 9-8901-4518; www.auroraaustral.com; Camino Villarrica–Panguipulli, Km19.5) Located about 19km from Villarrica on the road to Lican Ray is this German-run husky farm, where you'll find around 55 of the cutest Siberian and Alaskan huskies you ever did see, ready to take you on the ride of your life. In winter there are day trips (CH$80,000), multiday tent-/cabin-based trips and a seriously epic seven-day Andean crossing (all-inclusive CH$2,400,000).

In summer there are 6km rides with an optional barbecue (CH$33,000 to CH$39,000) and husky trekking on Volcán Villarrica (CH$48,000). True dog lovers can sleep out here as well in four extremely nice cabins (CH$40,000 to CH$70,000).

Four- to 12-week volunteers are also accepted.

🛌 Sleeping

More than half a dozen campgrounds can be found along the road between Villarrica and Pucón.

La Torre Suiza   HOSTEL $
(📱 45-241-1213; Bilbao 969; dm CH$11,000, s/d from CH$20,000/25,000; P 🛜) Formerly Villarrica's mainstay traveler hostel, this wooden chalet has evolved over the years. Once a traveler utopia with Swiss bike-enthusiast owners, it is now a Chilean-owned guesthouse that can often fill with visiting work teams. But the old-school feel of the place has its charms – creaky old floors, simple rooms – and the friendly owners are doing their best to cultivate traveler camaraderie.

Hostal Don Juan   INN $
(📱 45-241-1833; www.hostaldonjuan.cl; General Körner 770; s/d CH$34,000/44,000, without

bathroom CH$25,000/34,000; P 🛜) Don Juan wins travelers over around a large *parrilla* (outdoor grill), which was designed by the friendly owner, and offers fabulous volcano views from some rooms on the 2nd floor. Rooms are basic but homey – and service is friendly. Breakfast runs CH$3500 extra.

🍴 Eating & Drinking

★ Travellers   INTERNATIONAL $
(www.facebook.com/travellersrestobar; Letelier 753; mains CH$4950-7950; ⊙ noon-2am Mon-Sat; 🛜) Chinese, Mexican, Thai, Indian, Italian – it's a passport for your palate at this gay-friendly restobar that is ground zero for foreigners. The food isn't fantastic, but it's not bad. A postfire makeover marries a pop-culture potpourri with postcards and beer coasters from amigos the world over and a bright-light NYC skyline motif above the bar.

El Sabio   PIZZA $
(www.elsabio.cl; Zegers 393; pizzas CH$6700-7600; ⊙ 1-4pm & 7-10:30pm Mon-Sat; 🛜) A friendly Argentine couple runs the show here, creating fantastic, uncut oblong pizzas served on small cutting boards. Forget everything you thought you knew about pizza in Chile.

Delirium Tremens   CRAFT BEER
(Bravía Villarrica; www.facebook.com/cerveceriadtrb; Letelier 836; pints CH$2990; ⊙ 5:30pm-4am Tue-Thu, to 5am Fri & Sat) Traverse through doors between an inviting patio and several living-room-like spaces at Villarrica's one spot for craft beer, a five-tap brewpub that's serious about local brews. House-brewed Bravía comes in American amber, dry stout and blonde options while invitees often feature the excellent Alásse from Catripulli.

🛍 Shopping

There is a high concentration of *artesanías* (handicrafts) in Villarrica – look out for Mapuche figures, bowls and other items carved from laurel and raulí wood. **Mercado Fritz** (www.facebook.com/Mercadofritz; Acevedo 612; ⊙ 10am-7pm) and **Centro Cultural Mapuche** (Feria Wenteche Map; cnr Pedro de Valdivia & Zegers; ⊙ 10am-11pm) are two of the better markets.

ℹ Information

Banks with ATMs are plentiful near the corner of Pedro Montt and Av Pedro de Valdivia.

Banco de Chile (www.bancochile.cl; cnr Pedro Montt & Av Pedro de Valdivia) ATM.

BCI (www.bci.cl; cnr Alderete & Av Pedro de Valdivia) ATM.

Hospital de Villarrica (https://villarrica.ara ucaniasur.cl; San Martín 460; ⊘24hr)

Información Turística (☑45-220-6618; www. visitvillarrica.cl; Av Pedro de Valdivia 1070; ⊘8:30am-11pm Jan & Feb, 8:30am-6pm Mon-Fri, 9am-1pm & 2:30-5:30pm Sat & Sun Mar-Dec) Municipal office that has helpful staff and provides many brochures. A secondary office operates out of **Plaza de Armas** (☑45-241-9819; www.visitvillarrica.cl; Plaza de Armas; ⊘8:30am-1pm & 2:30-6pm Mon-Fri).

🛈 Getting There & Away

Villarrica has a main **bus terminal** (Av Pedro de Valdivia 621), though a few companies have separate offices nearby.

Buses JAC (☑45-246-7775; www.jac.cl; Bilbao 610; ⊘6am-9:40pm Mon-Fri, from 6:30am Sat, from 7:30am Sun) goes to Pucón (CH$900, 45 minutes) and Temuco (CH$1800, one hour) every 15 minutes. **Buses Coñaripe** (☑cell 9-6168-3803; Av Pedro de Valdivia 621, Terminal Villarrica; ⊘8am-9pm) has departures throughout the day to Lican Ray (CH$1500, 45 minutes) and Coñaripe (CH$2100, one hour). Several other lines make the journeys from the main terminal.

For Argentine destinations, **Igi Llaima** (☑45-241-2753; www.igillaima.cl; Av Pedro de Valdivia 621, Terminal Villarrica; ⊘9am-1:30pm & 5:30-8pm Mon-Fri, 9am-7pm Sat, noon-9pm Sun), in the main terminal, leaves every morning for San Martín de los Andes (CH$13,000, five hours), where you can make connections north or south.

Pucón

☑045 / POP 22,100

Pucón is firmly positioned on the global map as a center for adventure sports; its setting on beautiful Lago Villarrica under the smoldering eye of the volcano of the same name seals its status as a world-class destination for adrenaline junkies. Once a summer playground for the rich, Pucón is now a year-round adventure machine catering to all incomes, especially in February (a time to avoid, if possible), when it is absolutely overrun. The town receives alternating floods of package tourists, Santiago holidaymakers, novice Brazilian snowboarders, adventure-seeking backpackers, new-age spiritualists and mellowed-out ex-activists turned eco-pioneers.

While its popularity can be off-putting for some, Pucón boasts the best small-town tourism infrastructure south of Costa Rica. That means quality accommodations, efficient tourism agencies, hundreds of activities and excursions, vegetarian restaurants, falafel, microbrews and hundreds of expat residents from the world over.

🏃 Activities

Hiking

Summiting Volcán Villarrica is far and away the number-one excursion in Pucón, but it's not without its risks. Volcano ascensions were suspended in the immediate aftermath of a dramatic fireworks show put on by Pucón's definitive landmark on March 3, 2015. Around 3am, Villarrica briefly roared to life, spitting lava spectacularly up to 3km skyward for all the town to see.

Ascents were back on at the time of writing, but it's best to check on the current situation ahead of your visit, both with the recommended agencies as well as **Sernageomin** (www.sernageomin.cl), the official government agency for monitoring volcanic activity. If Villarrica is out of commission, summits are possible on nearby volcanoes Quetrupillán, Llaima and Lanín.

If summiting is allowed during your visit, by all means, do it! But be prudent: there are about 30 agencies now going up – and only about six we would recommend. If anyone tells you it's super-easy, or that you can try your boots on the morning of the walk, keep on walking. Those are two tell-tale signs of agencies we would avoid.

Reaching the summit is never a guarantee and if the weather turns, responsible agencies will always turn back, no questions asked. (The agency association was working on a bylaw that says if 50% of the agencies deem conditions unsafe to continue, everyone must turn back.) Anyone who presses on is risking fatal consequences. Nearly 20,000 people climb the volcano per year, which some local experts say is far too many.

Moral of the story: summiting this roaring monster is a truly unforgettable experience, but choosing your agency wisely is key. Fundamentally, you will get what you pay for and it is worth spending CH$5000 to CH$10,000 more for extra safety and insurance. If you have any doubts about commitment to safety, walk on. And don't hesitate to peruse the 'Libro de Reclamos' (tourist complaint book) on offer at the Oficina de Turismo (p517) in Pucón.

Pucón

Pucón

⊙ Activities, Courses & Tours
1 Aguaventura	B1
2 Bike Pucón	A3
3 Kayak Pucón	B2
4 Politur	C2
5 Summit Chile	C1

⊜ Sleeping
6 Chili Kiwi	A2
7 iécole!	C1

⊗ Eating
8 Just Delicious	C1
9 La Picada	B3
10 Latitude 39°	B1
11 Lider Express	D2
12 Menta Negra	D1
13 Trawen	B2

⊙ Drinking & Nightlife
Madd Goat Coffee Roasters	(see 8)
14 Mama's & Tapas	C2

Rock Climbing

Cerduo, at the foot of Volcán Villarrica, offers 40 climbing routes graded from 5.8 to 5.12d. There's sport climbing as well as traditional, all surrounded by native forest. For more intense and physically demanding routes, head to pristine **Las Peinetas** near the Argentine border, where climbs consist of five to six pitches and can last up to 12 hours (guide recommended). It is a three-hour hike-in to where the climbing commences. For experienced and certified guides, check out **Summit Chile** (☑45-244-3259; www.summitchile.org; Urrutia 585; ⊙10am-8pm Nov-Mar, to 6pm Apr-Oct), where, in addition to advanced options, owner Claudio Retamal has opened up five routes at Cerduo for all skill levels.

Mountain Biking

Mountain bikes can be rented all over town. Daily rental prices are negotiable but shouldn't be more than CH$10,000 to CH$14,000 (unless it is a brand-new bike with full suspension).

The most popular route is the **Ojos de Caburgua Loop**. Take the turnoff to the airfield, about 4km east of town and across Río Trancura.

Rafting & Kayaking

Pucón is known for both its river sports and the quality of the rafting and kayaking infrastructure. The rivers near Pucón and their corresponding rapids classifications are: Lower Trancura (III), Upper Trancura (IV), Liucura (II–III), the Puesco Run (V) and Maichín (IV–V).

Hot Springs

Hot springs are everywhere you turn around Pucón and La Araucanía, none more fantastic (or expensive) than **Termas Geométricas** (☑ cell 9-7477-1708; www.termasgeometricas. cl; Acceso a Termas Geométricas; adult/child before noon & 6-9pm CH$25,000/12,000, noon-6pm CH$28,000/12,000, 9-11pm CH$20,000/12,000; ⊙11am-8pm Sun-Thu, to 11pm Fri & Sat). Technically in Los Ríos, but sitting 82km south by road from Pucón, it's most often visited from La Araucanía's adventure capital). Other popular hot spots to catch a soothing soak in the area include the new agey and low-key **Termas de Panqui**, 56km east of Pucón; the upscale **Termas Peumayén**, 30km east; and the traditional **Termas de Huife**, 35km east. Pucón tour operators offer day trips (including transportation) to the most popular hot springs for between CH$20,000 and CH$25,000 (Termas Geométricas runs CH$35,000 to CH$45,000), and a few are reachable on public transportation.

☞ Tours

★ Aguaventura   OUTDOORS
(☑ 45-244-4246; www.aguaventura.com; Palguín 336; ⊙ 8:30am-10pm Dec-Mar, to 8pm Apr-Nov) This friendly French-owned agency is your one-stop shop, offering highly skilled volcano guides (beer after!) and also specializing in snow sports and kayaking, but it can book it all. It also rents everything for the mountain, water and snow (including Go-Pro). Co-owner Vincent was the president of the agency association when we visited and there's an emphasis on safety.

Bike Pucón   MOUNTAIN BIKING
(☑ cell 9-9579-4818; www.bikepucon.com; cnr Caupolicán & Perú; half-day tours incl bike rental from CH$75,000; ⊙ 10am-2pm & 5-9 pm Dec-Mar) Offers thrilling 17km to 20km downhill rides spread among six trails of very slippery volcanic terrain, single-track and old fire roads. It's not for novices – you can make it on limited experience, but expect to kiss some ash at one point or another.

Antilco   HORSEBACK RIDING
(☑ cell 9-9713-9758; www.antilco.com; Carhuello, Km7) Highly recommended outfitter that runs half- to 12-day horse treks in Liucura Valley, Parque Nacional Huerquehue, Mapuche reservations and on to Argentina. They're designed for both beginners and experts, with English-speaking guides.

Politur   RAFTING
(☑ 45-244-1373; www.politur.com; Av O'Higgins 635; ⊙ 8am-11pm Nov-Apr, 9am-8pm May-Oct) The go-to agency for rafting.

Kayak Pucón   KAYAKING
(☑ cell 9-9716-2347; www.kayakpucon.com; Av O'Higgins 211; ⊙ 9am-9pm Nov-Feb; ♠) This well-regarded kayak operator offers three-day kayak courses (CH$240,000) as well as multiday expeditions for more experienced boaters. Half-day ducky (one-person inflatable boats) tours on Class III rapids are a good option for those with less kayak experience (CH$25,000). There's rafting for kids and more adventurous tours for advanced kayakers. Also rents all kayak equipment.

🛏 Sleeping

★ iécole!   HOSTEL $
(☑ 45-244-1675; www.ecole.cl; Urrutia 592; r CH$32,000-58,000, s/d without bathroom CH$20,000/24,000, dm with/without bedding CH$12,000/9000; ℗@♠) ✿ Eco-conscious iécole! is a travel experience in itself. It's a meeting point for conscientious travelers and a tranquil and artsy hangout that has long been Pucón's most interesting place to stay. Rooms are small, clean and comfortable, but walls are thin and voices carry within the leafy grounds, so it's not a wild party hostel.

Chili Kiwi   HOSTEL $
(☑ 45-244-9540; www.chilikiwihostel.com; Roberto Geis 355; dm from CH$10,000; r without bathroom from CH$34,000; ♠) ✿ Sitting on prime lakeside real estate, this is Pucón's most sociable hostel. It's run by an enthusiastic Kiwi-Dutch partnership packing years of globetrotting experience from which to draw their traveler-centric ideas. There are various dorms and private options (converted vans, tree houses, cabins, Quonset-style huts, with top-quality bedding), an overload of design-detailed kitchens/bathrooms and up to two outlets per dorm bed.

French Andes II   HOSTEL $
(☑ 45-244-3324; www.french-andes.com; Pasaje Luck 795; dm 1/2 people CH$14,000/24,000, r without bathroom CH$45,000; ℗@♠) ✿ This French-owned hostel has a lot going for it: Japanese-style capsule dorms (both single and double) actually offer more privacy than a standard dorm room (luggage is stored outside in lockboxes or cages) and shared bright-red bathrooms have a touch of personality. The backyard – firepit and all – is a real coup.

There are impressive Villarrica views and recycling too.

Co-owner Vincent runs Aguaventura (p516), so you're in good hands for any excursion. The original **French Andes I** is just down the street, but we prefer II (though the shipping-container apartment over there is fun).

Eating

Just Delicious MIDDLE EASTERN $
(www.facebook.com/JDpucon; O'Higgins 717, Local 7, Patagonia Blvd; ⊙1-10pm Mon-Sat, 5-10pm Sun; 🕾🍴) Israeli transplant Tal makes everything from scratch – often with ingredients straight from the motherland – at this fantastic, cash-only Middle Eastern haven for hummus, falafel, *shakshuka* (eggs with spicy tomato sauce), baba ghanoush, baklava and more. The falafel sandwich (hummus, pickled cabbage, tahini and spicy *mathukha* in house-made pita) is a revelation. Even Tal's house-cured pickled veggies are memorable.

La Picada CHILEAN $
(Paraguay 215; set lunch CH$4500; ⊙noon-4pm, closed Sun Mar-Nov) This locals' secret is out: an underground eatery in someone's living room (or outside on the new terrace) serving fuss-free set lunches: salads, *pastel de choclo* (maize casserole), *cazuelas* (stews), pasta. No sign. Knock to gain entrance.

Latitude 39° AMERICAN $
(Urrutia 436, Local 2; mains CH$5900-7800; ⊙noon-11:30pm, shorter hours winter; 🕾) The California-transplant owners of this spot fill a clearly appreciated gringo niche at this homesick-remedy of a restaurant. Juicy American-style burgers are a huge hit: try the Grand Prix (caramelized onions, bacon, peanut butter) or the Buddha (sriracha mayo, Asian slaw, popcorn shrimp), but there's also a fat breakfast burrito (available for lunch), fish tacos, buffalo chicken wraps and everything else you might miss.

Menta Negra CAFE $
(www.facebook.com/emporiomentanegra; O'Higgins 772; set meals CH$6900; ⊙9am-midnight, closed Sun Apr-Nov; 🕾) On a sunny day, it's hard to beat plopping yourself down on this artsy emporium's patio for good home-cooked meals and views of a rare breed in Pucón: to nature, not development.

Lider Express SUPERMARKET $
(www.lider.cl; Pasaje Las Rosas 635; ⊙8:30am-10pm Mon-Sat, 9am-9pm Sun) Pucón's best-stocked supermarket for international brands.

★**Trawen** CHILEAN, FUSION $$
(🖳45-244-2024; www.trawen.cl; Av O'Higgins 311; mains CH$6200-16,800; ⊙8:30am-midnight; 🕾) 🍃 This time-honored favorite does some of Pucón's best gastronomic work for the price, boasting innovative flavor combinations and fresh-baked everything. Highlights on the menu include excellent smoked-trout ravioli in spinach-cream sauce, bacon-wrapped venison, *merkén* octopus risotto and salads from the restaurant's own certified-organic gardens, the first in southern Chile. To accompany, biodynamic and natural wines. Creative types tend to congregate here.

Drinking & Nightlife

Mama's & Tapas BAR, CLUB
(Av O'Higgins 597; cocktails from CH$5500; ⊙10am-4am Dec-Mar, from 6pm Apr-Nov) Known simply as 'Mama's,' this is Pucón's long-standing bar of note. It boasts an all-wood wall and ceiling space designed by an acoustic engineer to sonically seize your attention. It doesn't get going until the wee hours, when it morphs into a club.

Madd Goat Coffee Roasters CAFE
(www.facebook.com/patagoniaroast; O'Higgins 717, Local 3, Patagonia Blvd; coffee CH$1600-4000; ⊙9am-9pm Mon-Fri, 10am-7pm Sat; 🕾) Pucón may have got hip to good coffee two decades after everyone else, but it finally has a third-wave coffeehouse to satiate the masses dying from Nescafé overdose. American owner Scott Roberts roasts Latin American-sourced beans in-house and pulls his espresso from a stylish Pavoni machine from Italy.

ℹ Information

Petty theft is on the rise in Pucón, especially in the areas around the beach. Bikes and backpacks are the biggest targets, but you can't leave any thing in your vehicle overnight. Use prudence.

There are several banks with ATMs up and down Av O'Higgins. Banco do Estado's withdrawal fees are the cheapest.

CorreosChile (www.correos.cl; Fresia 183; ⊙9am-1pm & 2:30-6pm Mon-Fri, 9am-12:30pm Sat)

Hospital San Francisco (www.hospitalpucon.cl; Uruguay 325; ⊙24hr)

Oficina de Turismo (🖳45-229-3001; cnr Av O'Higgins & Palguín; ⊙8:30am-10pm, to 7pm Apr-Oct) Has stacks of brochures and usually an English-speaker on staff. There is a seasonal **kiosk** (Plaza de Armas; ⊙11:30am-7pm holiday weekends & Jul, 8:30am-10pm mid-Dec–mid-Feb) on Plaza de Armas as well.

❶ Getting There & Away

Frequent buses go to/from Santiago (CH$13,000 to CH$25,000, 9½ hours) – **Turbus** (☑ 45-268-6119; www.turbus.com; Av Bernardo O'Higgins 448B; ⏰7:30am-9:30pm), east of town, and **Pullman Bus** (☑ 45-244-3331; www.pullman.cl; Palguín 555; ⏰7:30am-9:30pm), in the center, are your best bets, with many Chilean destinations.

Buses JAC (☑ 045-299-3183; www.jac.cl; cnr Uruguay & Palguín; ⏰7am-7pm Mon-Sat, 9am-9pm Sun) goes to Puerto Montt (CH$9800, five hours), Valdivia (CH$4700, three hours) and every 30 minutes to Temuco (CH$3500, two hours). From the same station, **Buses Vipu-Ray** (☑ cell 9-6835-5798; Palguín 550) and **Trans Curarrehue** (☑ cell 9-9273-1043; Palguín 550) have continuous services to Villarrica (CH$1000, 30 minutes). Buses JAC and **Buses Caburgua** (☑ cell 9-9838-9047; Palguín 555) go to Parque Nacional Huerquehue (CH$2000, 45 minutes). For San Martín de los Andes, Argentina, **Buses San Martín** (☑ 45-244-2798; Uruguay 627; ⏰9am-1pm & 3:30-7:45pm Mon-Fri, 9am-noon Sat, 4:30-7:45pm Sun) departs at least twice weekly (CH$14,000, five hours), stopping in Junín. **Igi Llaima** (☑ 45-244-4762; www.igillaima.cl; cnr Palguín & Uruguay; ⏰7am-1:30pm & 3-9pm) also makes the trip.

Around Pucón

Río Liucura Valley

East of Pucón, the Camino Pucón–Huife cuts through a lush valley hosting myriad hot springs, a nature sanctuary and views of the silver ribbon Río Liucura.

Formed by citizens to nip logging interests in this spectacular swath of native forest, the nature sanctuary **Santuario El Cañi** (www.santuariocani.cl; Pichares, Km21; with/without guide CH$15,000/4000; ⏰enter 8am-noon only) protects some 500 hectares of ancient araucaria forest. A three-hour, 9km hiking trail ascends a steep trail to gorgeous views. Camp in the park at **La Loma Pucón** (☑ cell 9-8882-9845; www.tocatierra.cl/tocatierra4.html; Santuario El Cañi; campsites per person CH$5000). You can also make arrangements to visit El Cañi at ¡école! (p516) in Pucón.

Curarrehue

The Mapuche stronghold of Curarrehue, 40km west of the Argentine border, isn't much to look at, but it has begun a slow rise to fame for its Mapuche cultural museum and wealth of *etnoturismo* opportunities.

The small pueblo – and its fancy new Plaza de Armas – counts 80% of the population as Mapuche and is the last town of note before the Paso de Mamuil Malal (Paso Tromen) border with Argentina.

The small but interesting **Museo Intercultural Trawupeyüm** (Héroes de la Concepción 21; CH$1000; ⏰9am-8pm Mon-Fri, from 11am Sat & Sun Jan & Feb, 9:30am-5:30pm Mon-Fri, 10am-5pm Sat Mar-Dec) explores Mapuche culture. Curarrehue's real attraction, though, is **Anita Epulef Cocina Mapuche** (Mapu Lyagl; ☑ cell 9-8788-7188; anita.epulef@gmail.com; Camino al Curarrehue; menú CH$7500; ⏰1:30-5:30pm Dec-Feb, by reservation only Apr-Nov; 🖉), where a Mapuche chef turns seasonal ingredients into adventurous vegetarian tasting menus.

Stop overnight in town at **Hostal Quechupehuén** (☑ cell 9-8505-7438; www.quechupehuen.cl; O'Higgins 470; r per person without bathroom CH$18,000; P 🛜), or head 5km north of town to **Ko Panqui** (☑ cell 9-9441-5769; www.facebook.com/kopanqui; Camino a Panqui, Km4.9; cabañas/ste CH$76,000/102,000; P 🛜❄) 🖉. This sustainable lodge and artistic retreat, the brainchild of Claudio Ansorena (the grandson of Pucón's founder) is an idyllic, gay- and pet-friendly escape surrounded by bucolic bliss.

For info, stop by the (small and signless – but helpful) **Tourism Office** (☑ 45-292-2059; www.curarrehue.cl; O'Higgins s/n; ⏰9am-7pm Mon-Fri) on the main road through town.

Parque Nacional Huerquehue

Rushing rivers, waterfalls, monkey-puzzle trees and alpine lakes adorn the 125-sq-km **Parque Nacional Huerquehue** (☑ cell 9-6157-4089; www.conaf.cl/parques/parque-nacional-huerquehue; adult/child Chilean CH$3000/1500, foreigner CH$5000/3000), only 35km from Pucón. Stop at Conaf's **Centro de Informaciones Ambientales** (☑ cell 9-6157-4089; www.conaf.cl; ⏰10:30am-2:30pm & 4:30-7:30pm) for maps and information at the entrance.

The **Los Lagos trail** (7km, four hours round-trip) switchbacks through dense lenga forests to monkey-puzzle trees surrounding a cluster of pristine lakes. **Cerro San Sebastián** (16km, seven hours round-trip) is considered the best trek in all of La Araucanía. From the park entrance, climb from 700m to 2000m. From the top, on a clear day, you can see eight volcanoes and 14 lagoons.

Conaf offers camping at **Lago Tinquilco** (☑cell 9-6157-4089; parque.huerquehue@conaf.cl; campsites Chileans/foreigners CH$15,000/18,000) or **Renahue** (☑cell 9-6157-4089; parque.huer quehue@conaf.cl; campsites CH$15,000). The excellent **Refugio Tinquilco** (☑cell 9-9539-2728; www.tinquilco.cl; all incl breakfast campsites CH$20,000, dm CH$16,000, d with/without bathroom CH$42,900/34,900, cabins CH$75,000; ☺closed Jun-Aug) is a luxurious lodge with amenities like French-press coffee and a forest sauna. It's at the base of the Lago Verde trailhead. Meals are available (CH$10,500), or you can cook for yourself.

Buses Caburgua (p518) serves Pucón three times daily (CH$2000, one hour). Many agencies offer organized excursions, too.

Parque Nacional Villarrica

This glorious spread of volcanoes and lakes is one of Chile's most popular parks. The highlights of the 630-sq-km park are the three volcanoes: 2847m Villarrica, 2360m Quetrupillán and, along the Argentine border, a section of 3747m Lanín.

Lago Calafquén

Black-sand beaches and gardens draw tourists to this island-studded lake, to fashionable **Lican Ray** (30km south of Villarrica) and the more down-to-earth **Coñaripe** (22km east of Lican Ray). Out of season, it's dead. Lican Ray is tiny, with campgrounds surrounding the town. In Coñaripe, look for a friendly tourist kiosk on the main square. The road heading north of Coñaripe leads to a number of hot springs, including the standout Termas Geométricas (p516).

Buses JAC (p518) has several buses daily from Villarrica to Coñaripe (CH$1200, 1½ hours) via Lican Ray (CH$700, 30 minutes).

Valdivia

☑ 063 / POP 166,100

Valdivia was crowned the capital of Chile's second newest region, Región XIV (Los Ríos), in 2007, after years of defection talk surrounding its inclusion in the Lakes District despite its geographical, historical and cultural differences. It is the most important university town in southern Chile and, as such, offers a strong emphasis on the

arts, student prices at many hostels, cafes, restaurants and bars, southern Chile's best craft-beer culture and a refreshing dose of youthful energy and German effervescence.

◉ Sights & Activities

Av Costanera Arturo Prat is a major focus of activity, but the most important public buildings are on Plaza de la República.

Cervecería Kunstmann   BREWERY
(☑63-229-2969; www.cerveza-kunstmann.cl; Ruta T-350 950; pints CH$3100-3500, mains CH$6600-10,600; ☺noon-midnight Mon-Sat, to 10pm Sun) On Isla Teja at Km5 on the road to Niebla, you'll find the south's best large-scale brewery. Standard 45-minute tours leave hourly from 12:15pm to 8pm (CH$8000) and include a takeaway glass mug and a 300mL sampling of the Torobayo unfiltered, available only here, straight from the tank. A more elaborate 90-minute tour (CH$12,000), which includes a five-beer sampling and a ride to the factory in an electric Kombi, goes four times a day (12:15pm, 2pm, 4pm, 6pm; hours can vary).

Feria Fluvial   MARKET
(Av Prat s/n; ☺7am-3:30pm) A lively riverside market south of the Valdivia bridge, where vendors sell fresh fish, meat and produce. Waterfront sea lions have discovered the promised land here – a place where they can float around all day and let tourists and fishmongers throw them scraps from the daily catch. A fresh ceviche here runs CH$1500.

Museo Histórico y Antropológico   MUSEUM
(www.museosaustral.cl; Los Laureles s/n; adult/child CH$1500/300; ☺10am-8pm Jan & Feb, 10am-1pm & 2-6pm Tue-Sun Mar-Dec) Housed in a fine riverfront mansion on Isla Teja, this museum is one of Chile's finest. It features a large, well-labeled collection from pre-Columbian times to the present, with particularly fine displays of Mapuche Indian artifacts, and fine silverware and household items from early German settlements.

Reina Sofía   CRUISE
(☑63-220-7120; CH$20,000; ☺cruise 1:30pm) A recommended (albeit a bit pushy) outfitter for Valdivia's standard boat cruises. It departs from Puerto Fluvial at the base of Arauco.

✦ Festivals & Events

Bierfest   BEER
(http://bierfestkunstmann.cl; Parque Saval; ☺Feb) Kunstmann-organized suds festival.

CHILE PARQUE NACIONAL VILLARRICA

Valdivia

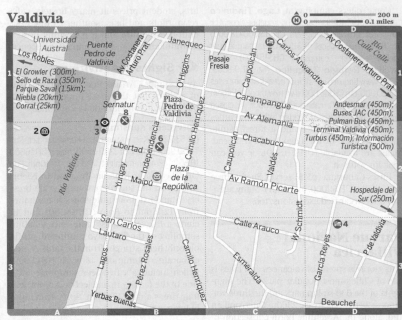

Valdivia

Noche de Valdivia   CULTURAL
(www.nochevaldiviana.cl; ⊙ 3rd Sat Feb) The largest happening is Noche de Valdivia, which features decorated riverboats and fireworks.

🛏 Sleeping

During the school year the university crowd monopolizes the cheap sleeps; summer has better options.

★ Airesbuenos Hostel & Permacultura   HOSTEL $
(☎63-222-2202; www.airesbuenos.cl; García Reyes 550; incl breakfast dm CH$10,000-12,000, r CH$32,000-38,000; @🛜) 🏅 Valdivia's best hostel is run by a friendly northern Californian who has turned this long-standing traveler mainstay into one of Sur Chico's most ecofriendly sleeps. Solar-heated showers,

rainwater catchment, permaculture, vertical gardens, compost, Egyptian bamboo towels – it's all here. Besides the sustainability, you'll find comfy, colorful dorm rooms and simple, well-done private rooms that are a little on the small side.

Hospedaje del Sur   B&B $
(☎ cell 9-8391-3169; franco.silvacampos@gmail.com; José Martí 301; s/d/tr incl breakfast CH$22,000/36,000/50,000; P🛜) On the 3rd floor of an apartment building attached to the bus terminal, you'll find astounding value and Chilean-spun hospitality with young lawyer Franco and family. Three rooms in summer (one otherwise) are spacious, with large flat-panel Samsung TVs with cable and homey hardwood ceiling. Breakfast will surprise you: real bread, pastries, cheese and cold cuts.

Hostal Totem GUESTHOUSE $
(☑ 63-229-2849; www.turismototem.cl; Carlos Anwandter 425; s/d/tr incl breakfast CH$28,000/33,000/39,000; @ 🛜) Of the ample choices along residential thoroughfare Carlos Anwandter, this 11-room guesthouse is the best bang for the peso. Clean rooms, a friendly French- and English-speaking start-up owner and a sunny breakfast room make up for the lack of antiquated character, though the hardwood floors in this old house squeak with the best of 'em.

🍴 Eating & Drinking

Isla Teja across the river from the city is the latest ubertrendy neighborhood for restaurants. For inexpensive seafood, head to the top floor of the **Mercado Municipal** (Prat s/n; mains CH$300-8000; ⊙9am-9pm), where you'll find hearty homespun meals between CH$3000 and CH$8000.

La Última Frontera SANDWICHES $
(Pérez Rosales 787; sandwiches CH$3000-5300; ⊙10am-2am Mon-Sat; 🛜 🥗) You'll find one-stop traveler nirvana at this restobar with a distinctly bohemian vibe. Hidden quietly away in a restored mansion, it has a load of outside-the-box sandwiches, fresh juices and local craft beer – 15 or so on draft (Cuello Negro, Totem, Valtare, Duende) and a few more in bottles.

Café Moro CHILEAN $
(Paseo Libertad 174; menú CH$3900; ⊙9:30am-10pm Mon-Fri, 11am-10pm Sat; 🛜) An excellent spot for a super-value set-menu lunch. It draws an age-defying and eclectic mix of intellectual hipsters and WWF (World Wildlife Fund) think-tank scientists from Valdivia's Centro de Estudios Científicos, and turns to drinking as evenings progress.

Sello de Raza CHILEAN $$
(☑ 63-222-6262; www.restaurantselloderaza.cl; Las Encinas 301; mains CH$8900-15,900; ⊙7pm-1am Tue-Fri, 12:30pm-1am Sat, 12:30-5pm Sun; 🛜) Classy Sello de Raza holds its own as a *parrilla* (steakhouse), but it does a wonderful job with typical Chilean dishes as well. The *pastel de choclo* (maize casserole) is one of the best you'll find and there's good *chupe de jaiba* (crab casserole), *guatitas a la chilena* (tripe stew) etc.

⭐ **El Growler** CRAFT BEER
(www.elgrowler.cl; Saelzer 41; pints CH$2800-4000; ⊙noon-midnight Mon-Thu, to 2am Fri & Sat, to 11pm Sun; 🛜) Sur Chico's best craft-beer destination, El Growler is a collaboration between an Oregonian brewer and his Chilean partner. There are 15 taps, more or less split evenly between house-brewed IPAs, red ales, stouts, porters and experimental brews (and always one cider), along with invitees from the region and occasionally the USA. Weather permitting, the outdoor patio is always packed.

ℹ️ Information

Downtown ATMs are abundant, as are internet cafes.

Clínica Alemana (http://portal.alemana.cl; Beauchef 765; ⊙24hr) Better, faster and closer than the public hospital.

CorreosChile (www.correos.cl; O'Higgins 575; ⊙9am-7pm Mon-Fri, 9:30am-1pm Sat)

Información Turística (☑ 63-222-0498; www.valdiviaturismo.cl; Anfión Muñoz 360, Terminal Valdivia; ⊙8am-10pm) At the bus terminal, Zone B.

Sernatur (☑ 63-223-9060; www.turismolosrios.cl; Prat s/n; ⊙9am-9pm) Provides very helpful advice.

ℹ️ Getting There & Away

AIR

Aeropuerto Pichoy (☑ 63-227-2294; San José de la Mariquina, Mariquina) is situated 32km northeast from Valdivia on Ruta 5. **LATAM** (☑ 600-526-2000; www.latam.com; Maipú 271; ⊙9:30am-1:30pm & 3:30-6:30pm Mon-Fri, 10am-1pm Sat) has one flight per day from Santiago. **JetSmart** (www.jetsmart.com) and **Sky Airline** (www.skyairline.com) also serve the airport.

BUS

Terminal Valdivia (☑ 63-222-0498; www.terminalvaldivia.cl; Anfión Muñoz 360) has frequent service to destinations between Puerto Montt and Santiago. **Turbus** (☑ 63-221-2430; www.turbus.cl; Anfión Muñoz 360, Terminal Valdivia) and **Pullman Bus** (☑ 63-220-4669; www.pullman.cl; Anfión Muñoz 360, Terminal Valdivia) are just two of the bus companies to choose from. **Buses JAC** (☑ 63-233-3343; www.busjac.cl; Anfión Muñoz 360, Terminal Valdivia) accesses Villarrica, Pucón and Temuco. **Andesmar** (☑ 63-220-7948; www.andesmarchile.cl; Anfión Muñoz 360, Terminal Valdivia) travels to Bariloche, Argentina.

Buses from Valdivia

Sample travel times and starting fares are as follows. Note that prices fluctuate with the quality of bus, seating classes and season:

DESTINATION	COST (CH$)	TIME (HR)
Bariloche, Argentina	23,000	8
Castro (Chiloé)	9300	7
Osorno	4000	2
Panguipulli	3300	1¾
Pucón	4700	3
Puerto Montt	5000	3½
Santiago	20,600	12
Temuco	3800	2¼
Valparaíso/Viña del Mar	27,400	13
Villarrica	4500	1¾

Osorno

064 / POP 161,000

Osorno (the city, not the volcano) is a bustling place and the commercial engine for the surrounding agricultural zone. Though it's an important transportation hub on the route between Puerto Montt and Santiago and the Huilliche communities of the Osorno coast, most visitors spend little time here, despite evidence of a blossoming hipsterization – once a town in dire need of quality eats and drinks, Osorno now harbors a handful of cool cafes, good restaurants and quality bars that could distract you for a day or two if necessary.

Sleeping & Eating

Hostel Vermont
HOSTEL $

(64-224-7030; www.hostelvermont.cl; Toribio Medina 2020; incl breakfast dm CH$15,000, s/d without bathroom CH$25,000/37,000, cabins CH$50,000; closed Apr-Oct;) Osorno's first decent hostel is run by a bilingual snowboarder who named the hostel after her stint near Burlington, Vermont. It's everything you want in a hostel: friendly, clean and well equipped (as well as some things you don't want: creaky old floors mixed with rowdiness means it can get sleep-deprivingly loud).

Hotel Villa Eduviges
HOTEL $$

(64-223-5023; www.hoteleduviges.cl; Eduviges 856; s/d/tr from CH$28,000/48,000/58,000;) Midrange and comfortable, Eduviges wins props for being in the minority in Región X, allowing singles to sleep in a double bed without paying for a double. The relaxed setting in a residential area south of the bus terminal bodes well, with spacious, somewhat old-fashioned rooms, private bathrooms and kind management.

Café Central
CAFE $

(O'Higgins 610; sandwiches CH$1950-6500; 8am-midnight Mon-Sat, noon-10pm Sun) This bi-level plaza hot spot is more or less a Chilean diner, crowded for its decent coffee, colossal burgers, ridiculous sandwiches and hot dogs *completísimo* (sauerkraut, avocado, mayo). There's also a counter – convenient for solo travelers.

Mercado Municipal
CHILEAN $

(cnr Prat & Errázuriz; 6am-9pm) Large and modern Mercado Municipal has an array of *cocinerías* (lunch stalls) serving good and inexpensive food.

★ El Galpón
STEAK $$$

(64-223-4098; www.hotelwaeger.cl; Cochrane 816; steaks CH$13,000-18,500; 12:30-3pm & 7:30-11pm Mon-Sat;) Tucked away around the side of Hotel Waeger, you'll find dark flooring and a rustic, barnyard vibe (old-school metallic buckets as lampshades) complementing the main event: perfectly grilled steaks for devout carnivores, on a *parrilla* piled high with wood like a fireplace. The fillets are superthick and the potent *pisco* sours often outrun the wine.

Getting There & Away

AIR

Aeródromo Cañal Bajo – Carlos Hott Siebert (ZOS; 64-224-7555; off Ruta CH-215) is 7km east of downtown. **LATAM** (600-526-2000; www.latam.com; Eleuterio Ramírez 802; 9am-1pm & 3-6:30pm Mon-Fri, 9:30am-1pm Sat) flies once daily to Santiago only on Tuesday, Friday and Sunday.

BUS

Long-distance and Argentine-bound buses use the main **Terminal de Buses de Osorno** (64-221-1120; Errázuriz 1400), five blocks from Plaza de Armas. Companies include **Pullman Bus** (64-223-0808; www.pullman.cl) and **Turbus** (64-220-1526; www.turbus.cl), among many others. Most services going north on the Panamericana start in Puerto Montt, departing hourly, with mainly overnight services to Santiago.

Try **Queilen Bus** (64-226-0025; www.queilenbus.cl) for Coyhaique or Punta Arenas. **Andesmar** (64-223-5186; www.andesmar.com) and **Via Bariloche** (64-226-0025; www.viabariloche.com.ar) have daily service to Bariloche and other Argentine destinations.

Other local and regional buses use the **Terminal Mercado Municipal** (Errázuriz btwn Prat & Colón), two blocks west of the main terminal.

THE INDIGENOUS COAST

The indigenous Huilliche communities of Osorno's gorgeous coast are sitting on an *etnoturismo* gold mine and have only started to realize it in the last few years. Fresh off an idea planted by a decade of sustainable tourism research by the World Wildlife Fund (WWF), these communities are embracing visitors.

You can immerse yourself in their way of life over multiday trips that involve some of Chile's most stunning beaches, Valdivian forest treks, and rural homestays around San Juan de la Costa and **Territorio Mapa Lahual**, an indigenous protected zone that stretches south into Río Negro province and includes Caleta Cóndor, one of Chile's most stunning off-the-beaten path destinations.

In San Juan de la Costa, a series of five magnificent *caletas* (bays) are accessible by car and can be visited as day trips from around Osorno for those short on time. **Bahía Mansa**, **Pucatrihue** and **Maicolpué** are villages where dolphins and sea lions practically swim to shore and women scramble about wild and rugged beaches collecting *luga* and *cochayuyo*, two types of seaweed that help fuel the local economy. On either side are the two best *caletas*, **Manzano**, 20km north of Bahía Mansa, and **Tril-Tril**, 7km south of Bahía Mansa.

Expreso Lago Puyehue (☑ cell 9-8838-9527; www.expresolagopuyehue.wix.com/buses-expreso) goes hourly to Termas Puyehue/Aguas Calientes (CH$2200, 1½ hours). **Buses Río Negro** (☑ 64-223-6748) goes to Caleta Cóndor (CH$1200, 45 minutes).

To get to the Huilliche communities of San Juan de la Costa (CH$1800, 1¾ hours) – Bahía Mansa, Pucatrihue and Maicolpué – minibuses depart every hour from the **Feria Libre Rahue** (cnr Chillán & Temuco). Catch bus 1, 6 or 10 from the northeast corner of Errázuriz and Cristóbal Colón (CH$400).

Buses from Osorno

DESTINATION	COST (CH$)	DURATION (HR)
Ancud	6200	4
Bariloche, Argentina	17,000	5
Concepción	17,000	9
Coyhaique	40,000	20
Pucon	8400	4
Puerto Montt	2000	1¼
Punta Arenas	35,000	28
Santiago	30,000	12
Temuco	5500	3½
Valdivia	3600	1¾

Parque Nacional Puyehue

Volcán Puyehue (2240m) blew its top the day after the 1960 earthquake, turning its dense, humid evergreen forest into a stark landscape of sand dunes and lava rivers. In 2011, nearby Cordon Caulle erupted, sending ash as far as Buenos Aires. Today, **Parque Nacional Puyehue** (www.conaf.cl/parques/parque-nacional-puyehue; Ruta Internacional 215, Puyehue; Anticura CH$1500) FREE protects 1070 sq km of this cool, contrasting environment. **Termas Aguas Calientes** (☑ 64-233-1785; www.termasaguascalientes.cl; Ruta 215, Camino Antillanca Km76; day use indoor/open-air pool from CH$11,000/4500, with lunch CH$17,000/10,500) is an unpretentious hot-springs resort. Or access the free **Pocitos Termas** about 80m across the Colgante bridge from the Conaf parking lot.

Small ski resort **Centro de Esquí Antillanca** (☑ 64-261-2070; www.antillanca.cl; Ruta U-485; lift tickets CH$35,000, full rentals adult/child CH$33,000/22,000) is 18km beyond Aguas Calientes on the flanks of 1990m-high Volcán Casablanca. In summer a trail leads to a crater outlook with views of the mountain range.

Trails abound at **Anticura**, 17km northwest of the Aguas Calientes turnoff. Pleasant, short walks lead to a lookout and Salto del Indio waterfall. The private **El Caulle**, 2km west of Anticura, accesses the southern entrance for the **Puyehue Traverse,** an iconic three- to four-day hike. **Patagonia Expeditions** (☑ cell 9-9104-8061; www.anticura.com; Ruta Internacional 215, Km90) runs guided treks and operates **Camping Catrué** (☑ cell 9-9104-8061; www.anticura.com; Ruta Internacional, 215 Km90; camping s/d CH$5000/9000, cabañas for 2/4/6 CH$45,000/CH$52,000/60,000; ☏), with 15 campsites and fully equipped cabins.

CHILE PARQUE NACIONAL PUYEHUE

Frutillar

065 / POP 18,400

The mystique of Frutillar is its Germanness, a 19th-century immigrant heritage that the village preserved. To come here is to savor this idea of simpler times, float in the lake, eat home-baked pies and sleep in rooms shaded by lace curtains. For many it is simply too still to linger; for others, it remains a serene alternative to staying in more chaotic Puerto Varas.

The town has two sectors: Frutillar Alto is a no-frills working town, while Bajo fronts the lakes and has all of the tourist attractions. Don't miss **Teatro del Lago** (Teatro del Lago; 65-242-2900; www.teatrodellago.cl; Av Philippi 1000; box office 10am-6pm), a world-class performing arts center built on stilts over the water, hosting excellent live music. **Museo Histórico Alemán** (www.museosaustral.cl; cnr Pérez Rosales & Prat; CH$2500; 9am-5:30pm) features reconstructions of a mill, smithy and mansion set among manicured gardens.

Many visit as a day trip from Puerto Varas; budget options are scarce. On a lavender farm just outside town, **Lavanda Casa de Té** (cell 9-9458-0804; www.lavandacasadete.cl; Camino a Quebrada Honda, Km1.5; menú CH$15,000; 1-8pm Dec-Mar) is a favorite for tea, gourmet lavender products and farm-fresh lunches. Steakhouse **Cocina Frau Holle** (65-242-1345; www.frauholle-frutillar.cl; Varas 54; steaks CH$9400-11,500; 1-3:30pm & 7:30-10:30pm, closed May;) focuses on serious cuts of beef, perfectly fired over Chilean oak-fed flames.

Minibuses to Puerto Varas (CH$1200, 30 minutes), Puerto Montt (CH$1600, 45 minutes) and Osorno (CH$1500, 45 minutes) leave from a small parking lot on Pedro Montt near Av Philippi.

Puerto Varas

065 / POP 44,600

Two snowcapped volcanoes stand sentinel over picturesque Puerto Varas like soldiers of adventure. Just 23km from Puerto Montt but worlds apart in charm, scenery and options for the traveler, Puerto Varas has been touted as the 'next Pucón.' There's great access to water sports here – rafting and sea kayaking in particular – as well as climbing, fishing, hiking and even skiing, making it a top choice for an extended stay. Note that while it gets packed in summer, it is quiet in winter.

◉ Sights & Activities

Visitors can stroll around town to take in the 19th-century German architecture. In summer, stand-up paddleboards and kayaks are rented on the lake. Grab a city map at the tourist information office, which highlights the **Paseo Patrimonial**, a suggested walking tour of 10 houses classified as national monuments.

☞ Tours

La Comarca
Puelo Adventure MOUNTAIN BIKING
(cell 9-9799-1920; www.pueloadventure.cl; Av Vicente Pérez Rosales 1621) Specializes in dramatic and custom-tailored adventure trips to less-explored areas of the Río Puelo Valley, Río Cochamó Valley and beyond. Highlights include extensive mountain-bike and road-cycling holidays in Chile and Argentina (including an epic 12-day single-track ride from Bariloche to Puerto Varas); beer-sluggin' and biking; and a wine-and-cheese excursion to the 900m viewpoint at Arco Iris in La Junta.

The Bike & Beer tour is a good-fun 30km bike ride along the lake, culminating in a craft-brew tasting at Chester Beer (p527). Groups are never more than 12 strong and everyone here is dedicated to giving travelers a unique off-the-beaten-path experience. Also rents road bikes, full-suspension mountain bikes and e-bikes.

Ko'Kayak RAFTING, CANYONING
(65-223-3004; www.kokayak.cl; San Pedro 311; 8:30am-7pm) A long-standing favorite, offering half-day rafting trips for CH$35,000 with two departures daily and one-/two-day sea kayaking trips for CH$70,000/165,000.

TurisTour OUTDOORS
(65-222-8440; www.turistour.cl; Del Salvador 72; 7:30am-8pm Mon-Sat, to 5pm Sun) Runs the CruceAndino, a bus-and-boat combo transport trip through the majestic lakes and mountains of the Pérez Rosales Pass to Bariloche, Argentina, and vice versa. The total fare is US$280 (backpacker/cyclist US$120), although there are seasonal discounts and a 50% discount for children. There are daily departures throughout the year. Also runs numerous day trips in the region.

Reservations must be made at least a day in advance. You may also purchase tickets at the Petrohué dock. Consider bringing your own food for the first part of the trip, as some feel meals aboard the catamaran to Peulla and in Peulla are expensive and dull. You

Puerto Varas

Puerto Varas

🟢 Activities, Courses & Tours
1 Ko'Kayak	C3
2 TurisTour	D4

🛏 Sleeping
3 Compass del Sur	B1
4 Galpón Aire Puro	B1
5 Hostel Melmac Patagonia	C4
6 Mapatagonia	A4

🍴 Eating
7 Costumbrista	B4
8 El Humedal	D2
9 Mesa Tropera	D2

🍷 Drinking & Nightlife
10 Caffé El Barista	D3
11 Pub Puerto Varas	D3

must also pay an AR$23 boarding fee (cash only in Argentine pesos, Chilean pesos, US dollars, euros or Brazilian reais) for Parque Nacional Nahuel Huapi in Argentina.

🛏 Sleeping

Hostel Melmac Patagonia HOSTEL $
(☎ 65-223-0863; www.melmacpatagonia.com; Santa Rosa 608, Interior; dm CH$10,000-14,000, s/d from CH$35,000/42,000; ℗@🛜) This intimate hostel in elevated digs perfectly positioned

above downtown is decked out with all the modern fixings – right down to the artisanal home-brew beer fridge, which goes down nicely on the front porch (first beer free!), an outdoor hot tub (per person CH$10,000) and Wall-E, the Roomba cleaning robot.

Mapatagonia HOSTEL $
(☎ 65-223-7695; www.mapatagonia.com; Purísima 681; dm CH$7500-12,000, s/d without bathroom CH$24,000/32,000; ℗@🛜) This spacious and historic 1932 home is on the town's list

WORTH A TRIP

PARQUE TAGUA-TAGUA

Carved out of virgin Valdivian rainforest 15km east of Puelo, **Parque Tagua-Tagua** (📞65-256-6646; www.parquetaguatagua.cl; adult/child CH$5000/3500) is southern Chile's latest park. A private initiative funded by Universidad Mayor in Santiago, the park preserves 30 sq km of previously unseen alerce (a towering Andean tree) forest along with two lakes, Lago Alerce and Lago Quetrus, bounded by granite mountains. Trekking and climbing are big draws here.

There are three basic but well-made alerce *refugios* (rustic shelters) with bathrooms, solar panels and wood-burning stoves.

Note that visits are possible by reservation only. To get here, catch the once-a-day Lago Tagua-Tagua–bound bus from Puerto Montt (7:45am) or Puerto Varas (8:20am), which meets the ferry at the edge of Lago Tagua-Tagua. Make sure you have called ahead to park officials, who will meet you on the other side of the ferry crossing for the final 10-minute boat ride to the park.

of patrimonial heritage sites. It's the nicest hostel in town, offering quieter, much larger rooms and bathrooms for better prices than most spots and a whole lot of French-Chilean hospitality. Big, bright dorms hold nine beds only.

Casa Azul HOSTEL $
(📞65-223-2904; www.casaazul.net; Manzanal 66; dm CH$10,000, d CH$37,000, s/d without bathroom CH$20,000/29,000; P@🛜) It's hard to find a fault with this impeccably kept German-Chilean operation set in a quieter residential neighborhood just outside downtown. The superbly tranquil garden and koi pond (with bonsai trees) immediately calm your nerves, in any case. Rooms are spacious, bathrooms recently retiled and there's an expansive guest kitchen and common area with cool furniture fashioned from tree branches.

Compass del Sur B&B $
(📞65-233-2044; www.compassdelsur.cl; Klenner 467; campsites CH$10,000, dm CH$14,000, s/d CH$34,000/46,000, without bathroom CH$29,000/39,000; P🛜) 🍽 This charming colonial house with Scandinavian touches and very friendly staff sits above the main area of town, accessed by a staired pedestrian street. It has comfortable beds and some rain-style showers that please the flashpacker crowd who dominate the scene here.

Galpón Aíre Puro GUESTHOUSE $$
(📞cell 9-9979-8009; www.galponairepuro.cl; cnr Decher&Independencia;s/dinclbreakfastCH$39,000/58,000, ste CH$78,000; P@🛜) American expat Vicki Johnson – chef, chocolatier and purveyor of life's finer things – has transformed this massive 1920s potato-storage barn into her very own den of good taste. She expanded and

moved her artisan chocolate shop and cafe here, and offers eight spacious guest rooms for more independently minded travelers above a hip commercial-office space.

🍴 Eating

★**Costumbrista** CHILEAN $
(📞cell 9-6237-2801; Del Salvador 547B; mains CH$5000-6000; ⏱1-4pm & 7-9:30pm Mon-Sat; 🛜) This little, unassuming Chiloé-inspired eatery is Puerto Varas' secret gourmet *cocinería* (kitchen). It's a two-man, eight-table show among aqua clapboard walls with a limited menu of fish and heartier dishes – a perfect pork chop, osso buco, a beautiful salmon or *meluza* (hake) – and is executed with skill and results that completely outshine its extraordinary-value price range.

★**La Gringa** AMERICAN $
(Imperial 605; mains CH$4800-11,900; ⏱8am-11pm Mon-Fri, 9am-11pm Sat; 🛜) 🍽 Evoking the rainy-day cafes of the American Pacific Northwest, this charming spot run by an adorable Seattleite dishes up scrumptious house-produced bread and pastries, hearty sandwiches (such as pulled pork with cabbage) and refreshing main courses (barbecue baby back ribs with spicy austral-pepper mash) along with stand-out CH$7300 *menús* (fixed-price menus; 1pm to 4pm except February).

Puelche BURGERS $
(www.hotelpuelche.cl; Imperial 695; burgers CH$6500-7500; ⏱12:30-4pm & 7:30-11pm Tue-Sun; 🛜) A savvy manager has helped turn this hipster hotel burger joint into the best spot in town for an age-old classic combination: burger, fries and a beer. Forget about vast Chilean portions; these 160g beef bo-

nanzas don't require manhandling but are still a beautiful mess. Stellar house-cut fries, in-house pickling and cold craft beer round out the experience.

El Humedal

FUSION $$

(☑ 65-223-6382; www.humedal.cl; Turismo 145; mains CH$7000-11,000; ⊘ 12:30-11pm Tue-Sat, to 5pm Sun; 🔊) In an adorable and cozy home perched on a hilltop over town, El Humedal (oddly, it means 'Wetland') serves up one of the best lunches in Puerto Varas with its interpretations of Asian curries and stir-fries, Mexican enchiladas and burritos, ramen bowls, and fish and chips, among others. Desserts are scrumptious as well.

Mesa Tropera

PIZZA $$

(www.mesatropera.cl; Santa Rosa 161; mains CH$6200-7900; ⊘ 10am-2am Mon-Sat; 🔊) This wildly popular Coyhaique brewery/pizzeria transplant merges a jovial mix of families and hopheads. It's majestically located, jutting out over Lago Llanquihue, framing three volcanos on a clear day. Skip the pizza, but house-specialty tartars on toast are excellent (beef, octopus, salmon, artichoke). The 12 taps of house-brewed craft beer (CH$2000 to CH$3700) – including seldom-seen double IPAs, brown ales and Belgian-style ales – are PV's best.

🍷 Drinking & Nightlife

★ Chester Beer Brewing Company

MICROBREWERY

(www.chesterbeer.cl; Línea Nueva 93, Campo Molino Viejo; pints CH$2500; ⊘ 10am-5pm Mon-Fri, noon-7pm Sat) American nanobrewer 'Chester' (real name Derek Way) has been at it since 2006, long before 'craft' was a thing in Chile. His rustic but epic countryside brewery – fashioned from shipping containers – is a true makeshift beervana, with four taps dedicated to experimental one-offs and all of his staples in bottles (IPA, summer ale, APA and stout).

The brewery isn't reachable by public transportation but there's a 50% discount for bike arrivals, or catch the Beer Bus (2pm and 4pm), which runs Thursday to Saturday from December to March from the old train station in Puerto Varas.

In 2019, Derek plans to move his operation 1.5km northeast on Línea Nueva (Llanquihue) to a new 220-sq-meter barn and brewery with pub grub, rotating food trucks and *parrilla*-equipped picnic tables (bring your own beef!).

★ Caffé El Barista

CAFE

(www.elbarista.cl; Martínez 211; coffee CH$1400-3200; ⊘ 8am-1am Mon-Thu, to 2am Fri & Sat, noon-1pm Sun, shorter hours winter; 🔊) This stylish Italian-style coffeehouse serves Sur Chico's best espresso from its La Marzocco machine, and draws a healthy breakfast and lunch crowd for cast-iron eggs, excellent CH$6800 *menús del dia* and a selection of tasty sandwiches (CH$3600 to CH$6200). As night falls, it morphs into a fine spot for a drink as well.

Pub Puerto Varas

BAR

(www.facebook.com/pubpuertovaras; Santa Rosa 068, 2nd fl; pints CH$3000; ⊘ noon-2am Mon-Sat, 1pm-1am Sun; 🔊) Two veteran hostelers opened this obviously named bar in 2017, finally giving the town what it lacked for decades: a drinking establishment dedicated to *drinking* (hence the motto 'Drink & Drink,' not 'Food & Drink'!). There are 12 taps of mostly craft-driven local beers (Chester and Morchela), cocktails mixed with Latin American craft spirits and wines-by-the-glass decanted by a Vinturi aerator.

ℹ Information

There are numerous ATMs downtown.

Clínica Puerto Varas (www.clinicapv.cl; Otto Bader 810; ⊘ 24hr) Near Del Salvador's southwest exit from town.

Parque Nacional Pumalín Office (☑ 65-225-0079; www.parquepumalin.cl; Klenner 299; ⊘ 9am-6pm Mon-Fri) Though the park is found in northern Patagonia, this is the official tourism office for Parque Nacional Pumalín. The sign says 'Tompkins Conservation.'

Tourist Office (☑ 65-236-1175; www.ptovaras.cl; Del Salvador 320; ⊘ 8:30am-9pm Mon-Fri, 9am-9pm Sat & Sun Dec-Feb, 8:30am-7pm Mon-Fri, 10am-2pm & 3-7pm Sat & Sun Mar-Nov)

ℹ Getting There & Away

Most long-distance buses originate in Puerto Montt. Buses leave from two terminals. **Cruz del Sur** (☑ 65-223-6969; www.buscescruzdelsur.cl; San Francisco 1317; ⊘ office 7am-10pm) is best for Chiloé and Punta Arenas, and also serves Bariloche, Argentina with **Bus Norte** (☑ 65-223-4298; www.busnortechile.cl; Andrés Bello 304, 2nd fl, office; ⊘ office 10am-1pm & 3-9pm Mon-Fri, 11am-1pm & 2:30-9pm Sat & Sun). **Terminal Turbus** (☑ 65-223-3787; www.turbus.cl; Del Salvador 1093; ⊘ office 7am-10:30pm Mon-Fri, 7am-2pm & 4-10:30pm Sat & Sun) also houses JAC and Condor bus lines, with many departures north, including to Santiago.

Minibuses to and from Ensenada (CH$1200, one hour), Petrohué (CH$2500, 1½ hours), Puerto Montt (CH$800, 15 minutes), Cochamó (CH$2500, 1½ hours) and Río Puelo (CH$4000, three hours) all leave from near the corner of Walker Martínez and San Bernardo. For Frutillar (CH$1200, 30 minutes), buses depart from Av Gramado near San Bernardo.

BUSES FROM PUERTO VARAS

DESTINATION	COST (CH$)	DURATION (HR)
Ancud	5000	2½
Bariloche, Argentina	18,000	6
Castro	6500	4½
Osorno	2000	1¼
Pucón	9300	5½
Punta Arenas	50,000	18
Santiago	25,000	12
Temuco	6500	6
Valdivia	4500	3½

Ensenada

Rustic Ensenada, 45km along a picturesque shore-hugging road from Puerto Varas, is really nothing more than a few restaurants, *hospedajes* and adventure outfitters, but for those looking for more outdoors and fewer hardwood floors, it's a nice natural setting in full view of Volcán Osorno and Volcán Calbuco. A great base is the cozy **Hamilton's Place** (📱 cell 9-8466-4146; www.hamiltonsplace. com; Camino a Ensenada, Km42; dm CH$17,000, s/d CH$40,000/50,000, without bathroom CH$30,000/35,000, closed Apr-Oct; P📶), run by a welcoming Brazilian-Canadian family who also offer delicious dinners. If you plan to climb or ski Osorno, you can get an extra hour's sleep by overnighting here instead of in Puerto Varas.

The eruption of Volcán Calbuco in April 2015 altered its profile and covered the area in ash and cinder, though tourist operations are back up and running.

Parque Nacional Vicente Pérez Rosales

In this park of celestial lakes and soaring volcanoes, Lago Todos Los Santos and Volcán Osorno may be the standouts, but they're actually just part of a crowd. One lake leads to the next and volcanoes dominate the skyline on all sides of this storied pass through the Andes range.

Parque Nacional Vicente Pérez Rosales protects 2510 sq km, including snow-tipped volcanoes Osorno (2652m), Puntiagudo (2190m) and Monte Tronador (3554m). Ruta 225 ends in Petrohué, 50km east of Puerto Varas, where there's park access. Minibuses from Puerto Varas are frequent in summer, but limited to twice daily the rest of the year.

Waterfalls boom over basalt rock at **Saltos del Petrohué** (www.conaf.cl/parques/ parque-nacional-vicente-perez-rosales; adult/child Chilean CH$2000/1000, foreigner CH$4000/2000; ⏲9am-6pm), 6km before the village. **Petrohué** has beaches, trailheads and the dock for Cruce de Lagos departures to Peulla. From Conaf's woodsy Camping Playa Petrohué just beyond the paid parking area (you can park for free here), a dirt track leads to **Playa Larga**, a long black-sand beach, from where **Sendero Los Alerces** heads west to meet up with **Sendero La Picada**. The sandy track climbs to Volcán Osorno's Paso Desolación, with scintillating panoramas of the lake and volcanoes. There is no road around the lake, making the interior trails only accessible by boat.

Access to climb or ski **Volcán Osorno** is near Ensenada. **Centro de Ski y Montaña Volcán Osorno** (📱 cell 9-9158-7337; www.volcanosorno.com; Ruta V-555, Km12, Volcán Osorno; half-/full-day lift tickets CH$20,000/26,000; ⏲10am-5:30pm) has two lifts for skiing and sightseeing, plus ski and snowboard rentals. Off-season, ride the ski lift (CH$16,000) up for impossibly scenic views, or take a hike.

Downhill from the ski slopes, the spruced-up **Refugio Teski** (📱 065-256-6622; www.teski.cl; Ruta V-555, Km12, Volcán Osorno; dm with bedding/sleeping bag CH$17,000/15,000, r with/without bathroom CH$54,000/42,000; 📶) offers unparalleled access to the mountain. With 24 hours' notice, rent out a mountainside hot tub (CH$40,000 for three hours, including a *pisco* sour and finger food), take advantage of two-for-one happy-hour drinks at sunset and make a night of it.

There is no public transportation to or from the slopes outside of package tours. To reach the ski area and *refugio* if driving, take the Ensenada–Puerto Octay road to a signpost about 3km from Ensenada and continue 10km up the lateral.

Puerto Montt

☑065 / POP 245,900

The capital of the Lakes District, Puerto Montt is also the region's traffic-choked, fast-growing commercial and transportation hub, with its most redeeming quality its plethora of exit points. Via plane, ferry, bus or rental car, you can get whisked away to a near-endless inventory of memorable locales. Otherwise, travelers have occasionally grown to love the unpolished working-class Chilean atmosphere here.

⊙ Sights

Catedral de Puerto Montt CHURCH
(Urmeneta s/n) Built entirely of alerce in 1856, this church, located on the Plaza de Armas, is the town's oldest building and one of its few attractive ones.

Casa del Arte Diego Rivera GALLERY
(www.culturapuertomontt.cl; Quillota 116; ⊙9am-1pm & 3-6:30pm Mon-Fri) FREE A joint Mexican-Chilean project finished in 1964, the upstairs Sala Hardy Wistuba specializes in works by local artists, sculptors and photographers. Also houses a small cafe and an excellent boutique.

Av Angelmó Street Stalls MARKET
(Av Angelmó) Along busy, diesel-fume-laden Av Angelmó is a dizzying mix of streetside stalls (selling artifacts, smoked mussels, *cochayuyo* – an edible sea plant – and mysterious trinkets), craft markets and touristy seafood restaurants with croaking waiters beckoning you to a table. Enjoy the frenzy, but keep on going...

The best-quality crafts and food are found at the end of the road at the picturesque fishing port of **Angelmó**, 3km west of downtown. It's easily reached by frequent local buses and *colectivos*.

⎘ Sleeping

Hospedaje Vista al Mar GUESTHOUSE $
(☑65-225-5625; www.hospedajevistaalmar.cl; Vivar 1337; s/d CH$23,000/35,000, without bathroom CH$16,000/30,000; @⑨) This family-run favorite is one of the nicest of the residential guesthouses, decked out in great-condition hardwoods with spick-and-span bathrooms, rooms with cable TV and wonderful bay views. Eliana fosters a family-friendly atmosphere – helpful to the nth degree – and breakfast goes a step beyond for Chile: yogurt, whole-wheat breads, cakes, muffins and filtered coffee.

Casa Perla GUESTHOUSE $
(☑65-226-2104; www.casaperla.com; Trigal 312; incl breakfast campsites per person CH$7000, dm CH$11,000, r without bathroom CH$26,000; @⑨) This welcoming family-home's matriarch, Perla, will have you feeling like a sibling. English and German are spoken. All bathrooms are shared and guests can use the kitchen, where Perla makes jam and sometimes bread on the wood-burning stove. It's the coziest, knick-knack-filled choice in this neighborhood.

★**Tren del Sur** DESIGN HOTEL $$
(☑65-234-3939; www.trendelsur.cl; Santa Teresa 643; s/d CH$39,900/53,200; P@⑨) This boutique hotel in the old neighborhood of Modelo is full of furniture (headboards, wardrobes) fashioned from rescued railway trestles. The high-style lobby is cozy and follows the principles of feng shui. The 17 rooms, a step down from the high-design common areas, offer central heating and are entered from a skylighted hallway visible through installed windows.

✖ Eating & Drinking

El Bosque CAFE, BAR $
(Rancagua 293; sandwiches CH$5600-6400; ⊙8am-9pm; ⑨) Beaming with personality, this artsy and bohemian 2nd-floor cafe and bar touts rustic design schemes often forged from recycled materials. The daily lunch *menú* (four or so choices; CH$4000 to CH$6000) draws a hip, in-the-know crowd and there are fantastic sandwiches too, including satisfying quinoa or mushrooms burgers for veggies. Cool tunes to boot.

Puerto Fritos SEAFOOD $
(Av Presidente Ibáñez 716, Mercado Municipal Presidente Ibáñez; mains CH$5300-9900; ⊙10am-5:30pm Wed-Mon; ⑨) Forget touristy Angelmó! All of Puerto Montt is laid out before you at this cute and unassuming locals' secret with the best views in town. It's well worth the CH$2000 Uber for excellent *caldillo de mariscos* (seafood soup; CH$5300 to CH$9900) and ceviches (CH$5500 to CH$7600), all of which are served fresh directly from the colorful market downstairs.

★**Chile Picante** CHILEAN $$
(☑cell 9-8454-8923; www.chilepicanterestoran.cl; Vicente Pérez Rosales 567; menú CH$10,500; ⊙11:30am-3:30pm & 7:30-10:30pm Mon-Sat; ⑨) Owner Francisco Sánchez Luengo is on to something at this intimate and playful gourmet hot spot that's an ambitious (uphill)

Puerto Montt

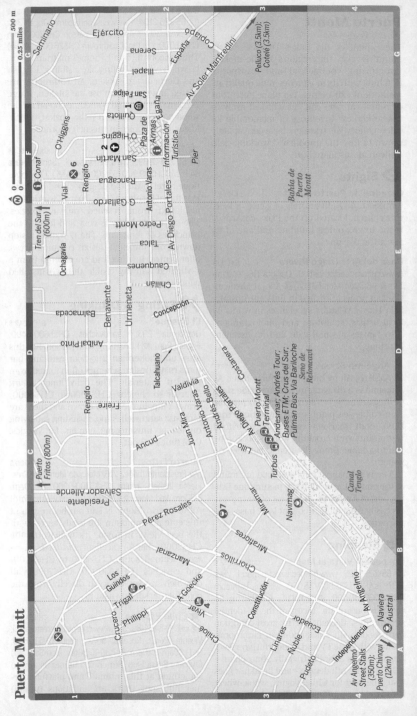

Puerto Montt

⊙ **Sights**
1 Casa del Arte Diego Rivera F2
2 Catedral de Puerto Montt F1

⊜ **Sleeping**
3 Casa Perla B2
4 Hospedaje Vista al Mar A2

⊗ **Eating**
5 Chile Picante A1
6 El Bosque F1

⊖ **Drinking & Nightlife**
7 Cirus Bar B3

walk from most of the budget sleeps. With expansive city and sea views as the backdrop, Luengo offers just a few choices in his always-changing, three-course menu, all delicately presented yet bursting with the flavors of the market that day.

★ **Cotelé** STEAK $$$
(☑ 65-227-8000; www.cotele.cl; Av Soler Manfredini 1661, Pelluco; steaks CH$11,000-15,000; ⊘ 1-3:30pm & 8-11:30pm Mon-Sat; ☜) This *quincho* (barbecue hut) steakhouse has a long-standing reputation for its meticulous grillmen, who honor the meat with Picasso-level focus. Grill maestro Julio Elgueta, who has been manning the open hearth here through various changes since 2002, isn't shy about letting you know he has skills. Fair enough: the top-end Angus cuts (sirloin, rib eye and filet) are stunning.

Cirus Bar BAR
(Miraflores 1177; ⊘ 10am-midnight Mon-Thu, to 1am Fri & Sat; ☜) By day, it's one of Puerto Montt's best-value lunch destinations. By night, 'it's a great place to find some sinister personalities!' It draws a mix of lawyers, sex workers, artists, writers and poets – local color in spades! – in a room packed with a bohemian potpourri of antiques and discarded memorabilia. Nightly folk music keeps the soundtrack lively.

ⓘ Information

Internet cafes and ATMs abound. At night the area around the bus terminal harbors petty crime; take precautions and don't walk alone here or along the waterfront.

Clínica Puerto Montt (☑ 65-248-4800; www.clinpmontt.cl; Panamericana Sur 400; ⊘ 24hr) A recommended private hospital.

Conaf (☑ 65-248-6115; www.conaf.cl; Ochagavía 458; ⊘ 9am-1pm & 2:30-5:45pm Mon-Thu, to 4:30pm Fri) Can provide details on nearby national parks.

Información Turística (Sernatur; ☑ 65-222-3016; www.sernatur.cl; San Martín 80; ⊘ 9am-1pm & 3-6pm Mon-Fri, 9am-2pm Sat) On the west side extension of Plaza de Armas at arrivals in the **airport** (Sernatur; www.sernatur.cl; El Aeropuerto Internacional El Tepual, Arrivals Hall, San Antonio; ⊘ 9am-5:50pm Mon-Fri). Stocks a wealth of brochures, but little English spoken.

ⓘ Getting There & Away

AIR

Aeropuerto El Tepual (PMC; ☑ 65-229-4161; www.aeropuertoeltepual.cl; V-60, San Antonio) is located 16km west of the city and is served by **LATAM** (☑ 600-526 2000; www.latam.com; O'Higgins 167, Local 1-B; ⊘ 9am-1:15pm & 3-6:30pm Mon-Fri, 10am-1:30pm Sat), which flies two to four times daily to Punta Arenas, twice daily to Balmaceda/Coyhaique and up to 10 times daily to Santiago. (Flights to Castro, Chiloé, are from Santiago only.) The airport is also served by local low-cost airlines **JetSmart** (www.jetsmart.com) and **Sky Airline** (www.skyairline.com).

Andrés Tour (☑ cell 9-9647-2210; www.andrestur.com; cnr Av Diego Portales & Lillo, Puerto Montt Terminal, box 38) services the airport from the bus terminal (CH$2500).

BOAT

Puerto Montt is the main departure port for Patagonia. At the **Terminal de Transbordadores** (www.empormontt.cl; Av Angelmó 2187), you can find ticket offices and waiting lounges for both **Navimag** (☑ 2-2869-9900; www.navimag.com; Av Diego Portales 2000, office; ⊘ 9am-1pm & 2:30-6:30pm Mon-Fri, 3-6pm Sat) and **Naviera Austral** (☑ 65-227-0430; www.navieraustral.cl; Av Angelmó 1673; seat CH$17,300, vehicle CH$95,100; ⊘ 9am-2:45pm & 3-6:45pm Mon-Fri, 10am-12:45pm Sat), housed inside the same building. The most popular trip is Navimag's ferry **Evangelistas**, which sails on Fridays from Puerto Montt to Puerto Natales and then back on Tuesdays. It's a popular three-night journey through Chile's fjords; book passage at Navimag offices in Santiago, Puerto Montt, Puerto Natales or via the website.

High season is from November to March and low season is April to October. Prices for the trip include full board (vegetarian meals can be requested). Per-person fares vary according to the view and whether it is a private or shared bathroom (ranging from the upper-deck AAA room with an en-suite bathroom for US$2100 based on double occupancy, to the least-attractive C class, with no views and shared bathrooms, for US$400). An additional US$10 departure tax is charged. Cars are extra; bicycles and motorcycles can also be carried along for an additional cost. The southern

CHILE PUERTO MONTT

route includes passage by the glacier Pio XI, the largest in South America (it's as big as Santiago), and there are more beautiful and photogenic glaciers along the way.

BUS

Puerto Montt's renovated waterfront **bus terminal** (☑ 65-228-3000; www.terminalpm.cl; cnr Av Diego Portales & Lillo) is the main transportation hub. Summer trips to Punta Arenas and Bariloche (Argentina) sell out, so book in advance.

Minibuses go to Puerto Varas (CH$900, 25 minutes) and Frutillar (CH$1600, one hour). Buses also go to Cochamó (CH$3000, 2½ hours) three times daily, and all carry on to Río Puelo (CH$4500).

Cruz del Sur (☑ 65-248-3144; www.buses cruzdelsur.cl) has frequent buses to Chiloé. **Turbus** (☑ 65-249-3402; www.turbus.cl; Boletería 4) has daily buses to Valparaíso/Viña del Mar. Both of these, plus **Buses ETM** (☑ 65-225-6253; www.etm.cl; Boletería 14) and **Pullman Bus** (☑ 65-225-4399; www.pullman.cl; Boletería 30), go to Santiago, stopping at various cities along the way.

For Bariloche and Cruz del Sur, **Via Bariloche** (☑ 65-223-3633; www.viabariloche.com.ar; Boletería 47) and **Andesmar** (☑ 65-228-0999; www.andesmar.com; Boletería 46) go daily.

Buses from Puerto Montt

DESTINATION	COST (CH$)	DURATION (HR)
Ancud	4000	2½
Bariloche, Argentina	18,000	6
Castro	6000	4
Concepción	17,100	10
Coyhaique	40,000	22
Osorno	2200	1½
Pucón	9800	5½
Punta Arenas	35,000	32
Quellón	8000	6
Santiago	11,900	13
Temuco	6700	5
Valdivia	5200	3½
Valparaíso/ Viña del Mar	12,000	15

CHILOÉ

When the early morning fog shrouds misty-eyed and misunderstood Chiloé, it's immediately apparent something different this way comes. Isla Grande de Chiloé is South America's fifth-largest island and is home to a fiercely independent, seafaring people.

Immediately apparent are changes in architecture and cuisine: *tejuelas*, the famous Chilote (of Chiloé) wood shingles; *palafitos* (houses mounted on stilts along the water's edge); the iconic wooden churches (16 of which are Unesco World Heritage sites); and the renowned meat, potato and seafood stew, *curanto*. A closer look reveals a rich spiritual culture that is based on a distinctive mythology of witchcraft, ghost ships and forest gnomes.

All of the above is weaved among landscapes that are wet, windswept and lush, with undulating hills, wild and remote national parks, and dense forests, giving Chiloé a distinct flavor unique in South America.

Ancud

☑ 65 / POP 39,000

Bustling and weathered, urban Ancud offers an earthy base to explore the penguin colonies and walk or sea kayak the blustery, dazzling north coast.

◉ Sights

★**Centro de Visitantes Inmaculada Concepción** MUSEUM
(www.iglesiasdechiloe.cl; Errázuriz 227; suggested donation CH$500; ◷ 9:30am-7pm Jan & Feb, 9:30am-1pm & 2:30-6pm Mon-Fri Mar-Nov) Don't even think about visiting Chiloé's Unesco-listed churches without first stopping in at this excellent museum housed in the former Convento Inmaculada Concepción de Ancud (1875). It's home to wooden scale models of all 16 churches, which show the workings of the intricate interior woodwork of each.

★**Museo Regional de Ancud Aurelio Bórquez Canobra** MUSEUM
(Museo Chilote; www.museoancud.cl; Libertad 370; ◷ 10am-7:30pm Jan & Feb, 10am-5pm Tue-Fri, to 1:30pm Sat & Sun Mar-Dec) FREE This worthwhile museum, casually referred to as Museo Chilote, offers interesting displays tracking the history of the island, including a full-sized replica of the *Ancud* – which sailed the treacherous fjords of the Strait of Magellan to claim Chile's southernmost territories – and a massive intact blue-whale skeleton.

Fuerte San Antonio FORTRESS
(cnr Lord Cochrane & Baquedano; ◷ 8:30am-9pm Mon-Fri, 9am-8pm Sat & Sun) FREE During the

wars of independence, Fuerte San Antonio was Spain's last Chilean outpost. At the northwest corner of town, late-colonial cannon emplacements look down on the harbor from the early-19th-century remains of the fortress. There's a somewhat secluded beach, **Playa Gruesa**, behind the north wall.

☞ Tours

Many folks around town run minibus tours to see the penguins at Monumento Natural Islotes de Puñihuil costing CH$15,000 to CH$17,000.

Austral Adventures   OUTDOORS
(📞 65-262-5977; www.austral-adventures.com; Av Costanera 904) 🏖 This is the go-to agency for English-speaking tours from Ancud, including extended nature-centric jaunts to see penguins, kayaking on the bay and bird-watching – always with a fierce eco-slant and more elaborate than the cookie-cutter tours. US owner Britt Lewis is impossibly nice and knowledgeable.

🛌 Sleeping

★**13 Lunas Hostel**   HOSTEL $
(📞 65-262-2106; www.13lunas.cl; Los Carrera 855; dm from CH$11,500; s/d CH$22,000/30,000; 🅿@🛜) 🏖 The best option for migrating backpackers, 13 Lunas is situated directly opposite the main bus terminal. Owner Claudio and his multicultural staff are young, enthusiastic and speak English, while the hostel itself oozes coziness with bright hardwoods, plenty of natural light, hotel-standard bathrooms, a grassy lawn and a wonderful terrace with views. Solar-heated water and active recycling give it an eco-edge.

Chiloé Turismo Rural   ACCOMMODATION SERVICES $
(www.chiloeturismorural.cl) 🏖 Chiloé's agro-tourism association organizes excursions to farming and fishing communities, as well as private homes that offer meals and lodging in several small towns and rural outposts. Pick up a catalog at the Sernatur tourism office in Ancud.

Camping Arena Gruesa   CAMPGROUND $
(📞 65-262-3428; www.hotelarenagruesa.cl; Av Costanera Norte 290; campsites per person CH$7000; s/d incl breakfast from CH$38,000/49,000; @🛜) City campsites don't get much better views than this one, located atop a bluff on the north side of town. The area is grassy and decently maintained, with electricity, hot

Chiloé

water at night, tiny *refugios* (rustic shelters) for rainy days and bright, surprisingly clean bathrooms. It's also a minute's walk to the beach.

Hostal Mundo Nuevo   HOSTEL $$
(📞 65-262-8383; www.newworld.cl; Costanera 748; dm/s/d/q CH$14,000/39,000/52,000/64,000, s/d without bathroom CH$29,000/42,000; @🛜) This Swiss-owned midrange hotel masquerading as a hostel is just a hop, skip and a jump from the Cruz del Sur bus station. It boasts postcard-perfect sunset views over the Bay of Ancud from a big, comfortable bench on its naturally lit front porch, and also from its 13 privates (including two new, larger rooms) and a six-bed dorm.

🍴 Eating & Drinking

Café Blanco   CAFE $
(www.facebook.com/cafeblancoancud; Ramírez 359; mains CH$3700-6900; ⏱9:30am-8:30pm Mon-Sat, 4:30-7:30pm Sun; 🛜) A very welcome

addition to the Ancud dining scene, this cozy Castro transplant occupies a colorful and rambling old Chilote home and is a requisite stop for sandwiches, salads, and sweet-tooth-satiating cakes and pies (CH$1500 to CH$3100). Locally produced provisions are available in the organic shop as well.

Café Amaranthine CAFE $
(www.amaranthinechiloe.com; Lord Cochrane 412; ⊙10am-9pm Mon-Sat Dec-Feb, 3-9pm Mon-Sat Mar-Nov; 🛜🖊) 🌿 Well-regarded Peruvian chef Sandra Echegaray opened this drop-dead adorable cafe, Chiloé's first organic and vegetarian option, in 2017. Rustic-chic touches like colorful wrought-iron chairs and mismatched retro couches have upped the cutesy vibe ante in Ancud, and the wonderful coffees, teas, smoothies and more substantial plates (quinoa burgers, veggie *pichangas, maqui* berry cheesecake) are a nice change from Chilean staples.

Cocinerías Mercado Gastronómico MARKET $
(Dieciocho; meals CH$2500-7000; ⊙9am-9pm) Tucked away off Dieciocho is a series of down-home market stalls dishing up *cazuela* (meat and vegetable stew), *chupe* (fish casserole) and set lunch menus for around CH$2500 to CH$7000.

Club Social Baquedano BAR
(Baquedano 469; beers CH$2000-3000; ⊙1pm-1am Mon-Thu, to 2am Fri & Sat; 🛜) Ancud's classiest bar is housed in a restored shingled Chilote house that hosted a social club of the same name in the 1960s and '70s. There's craft beer on tap – Cuello Negro and Kross – and Victorian-like sofas to lounge on.

ℹ Information

There's a **Banco de Chile ATM** (Libertad 621) on Libertad.

Conaf (🖉65-262-7520; www.conaf.cl; Errázuriz 317; ⊙8:30am-12:50pm & 2:30-5:30pm Mon & Wed, 8:30am-12:50pm & 2:30-6:30pm Fri) For national park info.

Hospital de Ancud (www.hospitalancud.gov.cl; Almirante Latorre 301; ⊙24hr) Located at the corner of Pedro Montt.

Informaciones Turísticas (www.muniancud. cl; Ruta 5; ⊙10am-5pm) Helpful city tourism office at the entrance to town.

Sernatur (🖉65-262-2665; www.sernatur.cl; Libertad 669; ⊙8:30am-7pm Mon-Fri, 9:30am-7pm Sat & Sun Dec-Feb, 8:30am-5:30pm

Mon-Thu, to 4:30pm Fri Mar-Nov; 🛜) Chiloé's only national tourism office; very helpful staff, brochures, town maps, lists of accommodations and wi-fi.

ℹ Getting There & Away

Cruz del Sur (🖉65-262-2265; www.busescruz delsur.cl; cnr Los Carreras & Cavada, Terminal de Buses; ⊙6am-11pm Mon-Sat, 7am-11pm Sun) owns and operates the main **Terminal de Buses**, which offers nearly hourly departures to Chiloé's more southerly towns, and to cities on the Panamericana to the north, including two daily departures to Santiago (CH$30,000, 16 hours). It's a five-minute walk from the waterfront and downtown.

Chiloé's more rural destinations to the east are serviced by buses that leave from the small inter-rural bus station on Colo Colo above the Bigger supermarket (buy tickets on the bus).

Castro

🖉065 / POP 43,800

Castro is the attractive, idiosyncratic capital of Chiloé. With the last decade's salmon boom, this working-class town transformed its homespun island offerings with modern mega-supermarkets and boutique hotels. At times loud and boisterous, the capital of the archipelago somehow retains its local Chilote character side by side with a comfortable tourism infrastructure. Located in the dead center of the island, Castro is a perfect base for exploring attractions further afield.

◉ Sights

Don't miss the distinctive *palafitos* houses, which testify to Castro's heritage of humble beginnings in 1567. From the street, they resemble any other houses in town, but their backsides jut over the water and, at high tide, serve as piers with boats tethered to the stilts. They're mostly along Costanera Pedro Montt, north of town.

★**Iglesia San Francisco de Castro** CHURCH
(San Martín; ⊙9:30am-10pm Jan & Feb, 9:30am-12:30pm & 3:30-8:30pm Mar-Dec) Italian Eduardo Provasoli chose a marriage of neo-Gothic and classical architecture in his design for the elaborate Iglesia San Francisco, one of Chiloé's Unesco gems and finished in 1912 to replace an earlier church that burned down (which had replaced an even earlier church that had also burned down).

Museo Regional de Castro   MUSEUM

(Esmeralda 255; 🕙9:30am-7pm Mon-Fri, to 6:30pm Sat, 10:30am-1pm Sun Jan & Feb, 9:30am-1pm & 3-6:30pm Mon-Fri, 9:30am-1pm Sat Mar-Dec) **FREE** This museum, half a block south from Plaza de Armas, houses a well-organized collection of Huilliche relics, musical instruments, traditional farm implements, Chilote wooden boat models, and exhibits on the evolution of Chiloé's towns. Its black-and-white photographs of the 1960 earthquake help you to understand the impact of the tragic event.

Feria Alcalde José
Sandoval Gomez   MARKET

(Feria Yumbel; Yumbel 863; 🕙8am-8pm, to 6pm in winter) Castro's well-conceived fresh market, new in 2017, is located a bit off the beaten path but is worth a trip for its colorful architecture and wide range of island treats (fresh cheeses, local potatoes, fish etc) arranged in a very pleasant and orderly fashion. On the 2nd floor, half a dozen *cocinerías* serve up home-cooked meals (CH$2500 to CH$5500).

Take bus 1B, 2 or 4 from the center to Galvarino Riveros.

👉 Tours

★ Chiloétnico   ADVENTURE, CULTURAL

(📞65-263-0951, cell 9-4042-1505; www.chiloetnico.cl; Los Carrera 435; 🕙9am-8pm, reduced hours winter) This highly recommended trilingual (fluent English and German) agency is doing the right things in the right places. It runs great mountain-biking (with e-bike options) and hiking trips to Parque Nacional Chiloé, Parque Tantauco and nearby islands; flora-and-fauna-focused nature trips; and cultural trips to some of Chiloé's more obscure churches on the less trampled secondary islands.

Also rents camping gear and bikes.

★ Chiloé Natural   KAYAKING

(📞65-253-4973, cell 9-6319-7388; www.chiloenatural.com; Blanco Encalada 100; 🕙10am-9pm Mon-Sat, to 2pm Sun, shorter hours winter) 🦎 This extremely friendly, environmentally conscious agency specializes in sea-kayak tours and outside-the-box excursions (cooking classes, knife forging). Half-/multiday trips around Castro and further afield (from CH$55,000 per person based on two people) include the magnificent kayak at dawn in Chepu (CH$265,000 per person; a Chiloé must!) and a Unesco-listed-churches tour (three days; CH$240,000 including lunch).

🛏 Sleeping

Hostal Cordillera   GUESTHOUSE $

(📞65-253-2247; www.hostalcordillera.cl; Barros Arana 175; s/d/tr CH$18,000/36,000/54,000, r per person without bathroom CH$15,000; @🛜) Weather dragging you down? The firecracker owner at this travelers' hub will smother you with motherly love and put a big smile on your face. You'll get some sea views, large bathrooms (two newly renovated ones upstairs), comfy beds, electric heaters and cable TV.

Palafito Waiwen   HOSTEL $$

(📞65-263-3888; www.palafitowaiwen.com; Riquelme 1236; dm/s/d incl breakfast CH$15,000/45,000/55,000; @🛜) This *palafito* haven strikes a number of balances: affordable yet stylish, hostel-like yet family friendly. The ground floor houses two four-bed dorms with lockers, central heating and private bathrooms, a communal kitchen and sea-view terrace with BBQ. Upstairs are hotel-quality private rooms hung with local art. Peppered with rescued antiques (theater seats, transistor radios), the hostel represents one of Castro's best style-for-value ratios.

Palafito Hostel   HOSTEL $$

(📞65-253-1008; www.palafitohostel.com; Ernesto Riquelme 1210; dm/s/d incl breakfast CH$17,000/42,000/58,000; P@🛜) This flashpacker hostel sitting on Palafitos Gamboa revolutionized Castro when it opened in 2008 and was the catalyst for turning the city into a hip destination. You pay more for a dorm here, but the quality outweighs the difference (as do the lockers), with great breakfasts, dreamy views and a cabin-cool feel throughout.

Palafito del Mar   BOUTIQUE HOTEL $$

(📞65-263-1622; www.palafitodelmar.cl; Pedro Montt 567; r incl breakfast from CH$60,000; 🛜) Of all the stylish *palafito* options in Castro, this minimalist, seven-room hotel along the town's northern stretch of the distinctive houses boasts an important bonus: all rooms have pleasant terraces with full or partial sea views, ready for you to kick your feet up on while enjoying a bottle of Carmenere. Cozy showers and bright *mañio* and *tepú* hardwoods throughout give it a stylish edge as well.

🍴 Eating & Drinking

Sanguche Patito   SANDWICHES $

(www.facebook.com/sanguchepatito; San Martín 718; sandwiches CH$2500-3200; 🕙1-9:30pm Mon-Sat) There's a whole lotta culinary love coming out of this divey sandwich joint near the municipal bus terminal. You choose your base (chicken, beef, pork, smoked pork or mushrooms), then build your own sandwich by choosing three options from a long list of 18 ingredients and nine sauces. It's all piled on toasted bread, becoming a gastronomic revelation!

Hostalomera
CHILEAN $

(www.hostalomera.cl; Blanco Encalada 159; set menu CH$3500; ⊙10am-6pm Mon-Thu, to 3am Fri, 8:30pm-3am Sat; 🛜) This arty lunch spot offers three exceptional home-cooked set-menu choices per day, including an appetizer and juice. An à la carte menu (mains CH$4500 to CH$5500) of Chileanized pastas like ravioli with *cochayuyo* (an algae) and more elaborate meat and fish dishes is also available. Bar open until 3am Friday and Saturday.

★ Cazador
CHILEAN $$

(☎65-253-1770; www.facebook.com/marycanela chiloe; Ernesto Riquelme 1212; mains CH$7000-14,000; ⊙1-3pm & 8-10pm Mon-Sat, 8-10pm Sun, shorter hours winter; 🛜) Formerly the excellent and innovative Mar y Canela, the restaurant's same chef, and her wine-savvy new partner, have actually managed to improve this groundbreaking *palafito* bistro, which now specializes in heartier dishes and game, many of which arrive in cast-iron skillets.

Mercadito
CHILEAN $$

(☎65-253-3866; www.elmercaditodechiloe.cl; Pedro Montt 210; mains CH$7200-10,000; ⊙1-3:30pm & 7:30-10:30pm Mon-Sat; 🛜) This wonderfully whimsical spot is one of Castro's havens for gastronomes. Creative takes calling on the wares of local farmers produce outstanding dishes, from tuna with potato and yellow-pepper puree to coriander-crusted hake with chickpea curry, as well as local oysters. Seafood isn't served out of season and tables are set with proper Laguiole cutlery.

★ Palafito Patagonia
CAFE

(www.facebook.com/palafitopatagonia; Pedro Montt 651; ⊙noon-9pm, reduced hours winter; 🛜) This wonderful cafe-gallery takes coffee very seriously – Intelligentsia and Blue Bottle are served, two of North America's best, along with Santiago-roasted Lama and We Are Four – and is a pristine spot for a caffeine jolt (espresso, V60, Chemex), light bites and postcard views from its naturally lit lounge and breezy patio. It's set along Castro's increasingly stylish northern *palafitos*.

Almud Bar
BAR

(www.facebook.com/almudbar; Serrano 325; ⊙6:30pm-1am Tue-Thu, 7:30pm-3:30am Fri, 8:30pm-3:30am Sat) The best proper bar in Castro – named after Chiloé's unit of measurement for potatoes – offers a wide range of cocktails (CH$3000 to CH$7500), craft beers (CH$3000 to CH$4500) and sparkling wines, and some bar grub to soak it up.

ℹ Information

ATMs are found around the plaza.

Conaf (☎65-253-2501; www.conaf.cl; Gamboa 424; ⊙9am-1pm & 2-5:45pm Mon-Fri) The official Chilean national parks department has a limited amount of information in Spanish and English on Parque Nacional Chiloé.

Hospital de Castro (www.hospitalcastro.gov. cl; Freire 852)

Información Turística (☎65-254-7706; www. visitchiloe.cl; Plaza de Armas; ⊙10am-9pm Jan & Feb, to 6pm Mar-Dec) A large kiosk stocking some helpful brochures and maps.

Parque Tantauco Office (☎65-263-3805; www.parquetantauco.cl; Panamericana Sur 1826; ⊙9am-6pm Jan & Feb, to 6pm Mon-Fri Mar-Dec)

ℹ Getting There & Away

AIR

Castro's Aerodrómo Mocopulli, located 20km north of town, offers commercial flights. **LATAM** (☎600-526-2000; www.latam.com; Blanco 180; ⊙9am-1:15pm & 3-6:30pm Mon-Fri, 10am-1:15pm Sat) flies from Santiago via Puerto Montt.

BOAT

Naviera Austral (☎65-263-5254; www.navier austral.cl; Chacabuco 498) runs ferries to/from Chaitén departing Quellón on Sundays (6:30pm) and Thursdays (5:15am). Seat-only fares cost CH$13,000. Vehicles cost CH$71,000.

BUS

Centrally located Castro is the bus hub for Chiloé. **Terminal de Buses Municipal** (San Martín) has the most services to smaller destinations around the island and some long-distance services. Buses to Mocopulli (CH$800), Dalcahue (CH$800), Chonchi (CH$800), Isla Quinchao (CH$1800) and Tenaún (CH$1600) all leave from here. The **Cruz del Sur terminal** (☎65-263-5152; www.busescruz delsur.cl; San Martín 486) focuses on transportation to Quellón and Ancud, and has more long-distance services. Fares include Ancud (CH$2000,1½ hours), Puerto Montt (CH$6200, four hours) and Temuco (CH$12,000, 10 hours).

Dalcahue & Isla Quinchao

Dalcahue, 20km northeast of Castro, has a 19th-century Unesco church, **Nuestra Señora de Los Dolores**, and a famous **crafts fair** (Pedro Montt; ⊙9am-6pm Dec-Feb, 9am-5pm Sun Mar-Nov) where you can buy the island's most authentic arts and crafts – sweaters, socks and hats woven from *oveja* (wool) and dyed with natural pigments made from roots, leaves and iron-rich mud. It's best on Sundays. **Hostal Encanto Patagon** (☑65-264-1651; www.hostalencantopatagon.blogspot.com; Freire 26; dm per person CH$10,000, r without bathroom per person CH$12,000; ℙ@?) offers rooms in an enchanting, century-old Chilote home, with home cooking.

Midway between Dalcahue and Achao, **Curaco de Vélez** dates from 1660 and has a treasure of Chilote architecture, plus an outstanding **open-air oyster bar** at the beach. Buses between Achao and Dalcahue stop in Curaco.

Isla Quinchao, southeast of Dalcahue, is one of the most accessible islands, and worth a day trip. Isla Quinchao's largest town, **Achao**, features Chiloé's oldest church. Wooden pegs, instead of nails, hold together **Iglesia Santa María de Loreto**. Stay at **Hospedaje Plaza** (☑65-266-1283; Amunátegui 20; s/d incl breakfast CH$9000/18,000, d without bathroom CH$16,000; ?), a friendly family home. A block back from the pier, **Restaurante El Medan** (Serrano; meals CH$2800; ⊙12:30-4pm Mon-Sat, closed Fri Apr-Nov) has no menu – you get what's procured fresh at the fish market across the street. The **bus terminal** (cnr Miraflores & Zañartu) is a block south of the church. Buses run daily to Dalcahue (CH$1400) and Castro (CH$1800) every 15 to 30 minutes.

Parque Nacional Chiloé

Gorgeous, evergreen forests meet taupe stretches of sand and the boundless, thrashing Pacific in this 430-sq-km **national park** (☑65-297-0724; www.conaf.cl/parques/parque-nacional-chiloe; adult/child Chilean CH$2000/1000, foreigner CH$4000/2000; ⊙9:30am-7:30pm Mon-Thu, to 6pm Fri-Sun Dec-Mar, 9:30am-5:30pm Mon-Thu, to 4:30pm Fri-Sun Apr-Nov), 54km west of Castro. The park protects diverse birds, Chilote fox and the reclusive pudú (the world's smallest deer). Visitors are at the mercy of Pacific storms, so expect lots of rain.

Access the park through **Cucao**, a minute village with growing amenities, and park sector **Chanquín**, where Conaf runs a **visitor center** (www.conaf.cl/parques/parque-nacional-chiloe; ⊙9:30am-7:30pm Mon-Thu, to 6pm Fri-Sun Dec-Mar, 9:30am-5:30pm Mon-Thu, to 4:30pm Fri-Sun Apr-Nov) with information. **Sendero Interpretivo El Tepual** winds 1km along fallen tree trunks through thick forest. The 2km **Sendero Dunas de Cucao** leads to a series of dunes behind a long, white-sand beach. The most popular route is the 25km **Sendero Chanquín–Cole Cole**, which follows the coast past Lago Huelde to Río Cole Cole. The hike continues 8km north to Río Anay, passing through groves of red myrtles.

🛏 Sleeping & Eating

Most accommodations and restaurants are past the bridge from Cucao.

Camping y Cabañas del Parque   CAMPGROUND $
(www.parquechiloe.cl; campsites per person CH$5000, cabins from CH$35,000; ℙ?) This well-equipped camping and cabin complex lies about 100m beyond the visitor center and into the park. The cabins are surprisingly nice, with stylish furnishings, running water, hot showers, firewood and all the mod cons. Dorms are low season only. Depending on whether or not the National Forest Corporation (Conaf) secures a concessionaire, it may or may not be up and running.

There is a small **cafe** (Parque Nacional Chiloé, Sector Chanquín; mains CH$1500-7900; ⊙9am-6:30pm Dec 15-Mar, 10am-6pm Apr-Dec 14; ?) on site that is not only great for fueling up for a hike but normally handles reception as well.

★**Palafito Cucao Hostel**   HOTEL $$
(☑65-297-1164; www.hostelpalafitocucao.cl; Camino Rural Cucao, Sector Chanquín; dm/s/d/tr incl breakfast CH$18,000/52,000/65,000/77,000; ℙ@?) This equally chic sister hotel of Castro's Palafito hotels, situated on the Lago Cucao, offers the best and most comfortable beds in Cucao, whether you lay your head in one of the 11 stylish private rooms or in the equally fashionable six-bed dorm. Facilities include a cozy common area, a kitchen, and a wraparound terrace with outstanding views and a hot tub.

ⓘ Getting There & Away

There is regular bus transportation between Castro and Cucao. Schedules vary, but there are usually numerous buses daily (CH$2000, one hour).

Quellón

☑ 065 / POP 27,200

Those imagining a pot of gold and rainbows at the end of the Carretera Panamericana will be surprised by this shabby port – most travelers only head this way to make ferry connections to Chaitén. Perched above town, **Patagonia Insular** (☑ 65-268-1610; www.hotel patagoniainsular.cl; Av Juan Ladrilleros 1737; s/d incl breakfast from CH$62,000/68,000; P @ 🛜) is not luxurious by any means, but is modern, friendly and perfectly agreeable – and recommended options in town are limited. Fill up on gourmet sandwiches at **Isla Sandwich** (Av Juan Ladrilleros 190; sandwiches CH$4000-7000; ☺ 10am-10pm, reduced hours winter; 🛜) or **Sandwichería Mitos** (www.mitoschiloe.cl; Jorge Vivar 235; sandwiches CH$4000-9000; ☺ 8:30am-10pm Mon-Fri, 11am-10pm Sat, 11am-4pm Sun; 🛜).

Cruz del Sur and Transchiloé buses leave from the **bus terminal** (☑ 65-268-1284; www. busescruzdelsur.cl; Pedro Aguirre Cerda 052) for Castro frequently (CH$2000, two hours). **Naviera Austral** (☑ 65-268-2207; www.navier austral.cl; Pedro Montt 355; ☺ 9am-1pm & 3-7pm Mon-Sat, 3-6:30pm Sun) sails to Chaitén on Sundays (6:30pm) and Thursdays (5:15am). Seat-only fares cost CH$13,000; vehicles cost CH$71,000.

NORTHERN PATAGONIA

A web of rivers, peaks and sprawling glaciers long ago provided a natural boundary between northern Patagonia and the rest of the world. Dictator Augusto Pinochet's **Carretera Austral** (Hwy 7) was the first road to effectively link these remote regions in the 1980s. Isolation has kept the local character fiercely self-sufficient and tied to nature's clock. '*Quien se apura en la Patagonia pierde el tiempo,*' locals say ('Those who hurry in Patagonia lose time'). Weather decides all in this nowhere land beyond the Lakes District. So don't rush. Missed flights, delayed ferries and floods are routine to existence; take the wait as locals would – another opportunity to heat the kettle and strike up a slow talk over maté.

Starting south of Puerto Montt, the Carretera Austral links widely separated towns and hamlets all the way to Villa O'Higgins, a total of just over 1200km. High season (from mid-December through February) offers considerably more travel options and availability. Combination bus and ferry circuits afford visitors a panoramic vision of the region. As well as Parque Pumalín to Lago General Carrera, there's plenty more to see in this region. Don't hesitate to tread off the beaten track: the little villages along the road and its furthest hamlets of Cochrane, Caleta Tortel and Villa O'Higgins are fully worth exploring.

Parque Nacional Pumalín

Verdant and pristine, this 2889-sq-km **park** (www.parquepumalin.cl) 【FREE】 encompasses vast extensions of temperate rainforest, clear rivers and seascapes. A remarkable forest-conservation effort, stretching from near Hornopirén to south of Chaitén, Parque Nacional Pumalín attracts international visitors in great numbers. Created by American philanthropist Doug Tompkins, it was one of the largest private parks in the world prior to its donation to Chile in 2017. For Chile it's a model park, with well-maintained roads and trails, extensive infrastructure and minimal impact. There's no entry fee as the park bisects the Carretera Austral and it would be difficult to distinguish the park users from those traveling through.

The park closed for several years after the dramatic 2008 eruption of Volcán Chaitén. Now there is a trail leading to a spectacular viewpoint of the smoking crater.

Currently the only way to access some of the isolated northern reaches of the park is by boat. A few Puerto Varas–based operators organize boating and kayaking trips through the fjords and to otherwise-inaccessible hot springs. In Chaitén, **Chaitur** (☑ 65-273-7249, cell 9-7468-5608; www.chaitur.com; O'Higgins 67; ☺ hours vary) has information on local guides who take hiking groups to the volcano.

Information centers and the **park website** (www.parquepumalin.cl) have details on all of the campgrounds and cabins, some of which are at trailheads. Fires are prohibited in the park.

🛈 Information

There's almost no cell service in the park. The **Centro de Visitantes Caleta Gonzalo** (www. parquepumalin.cl; Caleta Gonzalo; ☺ 9am-7pm Mon-Sat, 10am-4pm Sun) and **Centro de Visitantes El Amarillo** (www.parquepumalin.cl; El Amarillo; ☺ 9am-7pm Mon-Sat, 10am-4pm Sun) have park brochures, photographs and environmental information as well as regional artisan goods for sale.

Carretera Austral

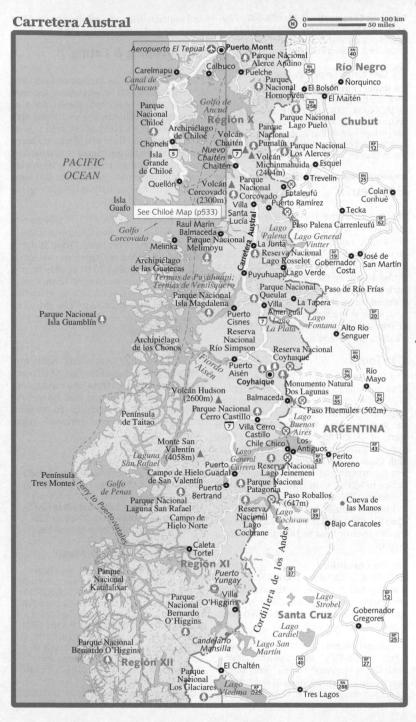

Tompkins Conservation (✆ in USA 1-415-229-9339; www.tompkinsconservation.org) has information on all the conservation projects under the Tompkins umbrella.

❶ Getting There & Away

The **Naviera Austral** (✆ 65-221-7266; www.taustral.cl; ferry dock; passenger/car CH$6000/34,000) ferries sail from Caleta Gonzalo to Hornopirén (five to six hours) twice daily in high season. Bus-boat combos from Puerto Montt can drop visitors in the park on the way to Chaitén.

Futaleufú

✆ 65 / POP 2600

The Futaleufú River's wild, frosty-mint waters have made this modest mountain town famous. A small 20-block grid of pastel-painted houses 155km southeast of Chaitén, it's not just a mecca for kayaking and rafting, it also boasts fly-fishing, hiking and horseback riding. Improved roads and growing numbers of package-tour visitors mean it isn't off the map anymore – just note the ratio of Teva sandals to woolen mantas. That said, it's still a fun place to be.

☞ Tours

The 'Futa' or 'Fu,' as it's known, is a technical, demanding river, with some sections only appropriate for experienced rafters. Depending on the outfitter you choose and the services included, rafting the Futaleufú starts at CH$50,000 per person for a half-day section known as Bridge to Bridge, with Class IV and IV-plus rapids. A full-day trip for experienced rafters only goes from Bridge to Macul, adding two Class V rapids, starting at CH$60,000.

Ideal for families, there's rafting on the Class III Río Espolón. Novice kayakers can try this river or head to Lago Espolón for a float trip.

Bio Bio Expeditions   OUTDOORS
(✆ 2-2196-4258, US toll free 1-800-246-7238; www.bbxrafting.com) A pioneer in the region, this ecologically minded group offers river descents, horse treks and more. It is well established but may take walk-ins.

Carpintero Negro   HIKING
(✆ cell 9-5825-4073; www.carpinteronegro.com; Cerda 439; ◷ hours vary) There's plenty of gorgeous hiking around Futaleufú but little information on how to do it. Offering half-day

and multiday trips, this guiding service fills a much-needed niche. Contact via WhatsApp.

🛏 Sleeping & Eating

Las Natalias   HOSTEL $
(✆ cell 9-6283-5371; www.hostallasnatalias.cl; dm/tr CH$15,000/50,000, d with/without bathroom $36,000/32,000; ◷ Nov-Apr) Named for four generations of Natalias, this welcoming spot is a great deal for backpackers, with tips on outdoor options. There are plenty of shared bathrooms, a large communal area, mountain views and a guest kitchen. It's a 10-minute walk from the center. Follow Cerda and signs for the northwest outskirts of town; it's on the right after the hill climb.

Aldea Puerto Espolón   CAMPGROUND $
(✆ cell 9-5324-0305; www.aldeapuertoespolon.cl; Ruta 231; campsites per person CH$7000, domes CH$9000; ◷ Jan-Mar; 🛜) A gorgeous setting on a sandy riverbank flanked by mountains, just before the Chilean entrance to town. Campers have hot showers and a sheltered kitchen for cooking with gas. Groups can also sleep in geodesic domes on platforms; bring your own sleeping bag.

Pizzas de Fabio   PIZZA $$
(✆ cell 9-6485-1412; Carnicer 280; pizzas from CH$7500; ◷ noon-3pm & 6:30-10pm; ✐) There's no going wrong with these thin-crust, gooey pizzas made by Argentine chef Fabio, who gave up cooking haute cuisine to open his own grungy-fun takeout business. Vegan options.

❶ Information

Bring all the money you'll need; **BancoEstado** (cnr O'Higgins & Manuel Rodríguez; ◷ 9am-2pm Mon-Fri) has the only ATM, and it only takes Mastercard. The helpful **tourist office** (✆ 65-223-7629; www.futaleufu.cl; O'Higgins 536; ◷ 9am-9pm) has information on local treks.

❶ Getting There & Away

Buses Becker (✆ 65-272-1360; www.busesbecker.com; cnr Balmaceda & Prat; ◷ 9am-1pm & 3-7pm) goes to Coyhaique (CH$24,000, 10 hours) every Sunday via Villa Santa Lucía (1½ hours), La Junta and Puyuhuapi. To Chaitén, **Bus D&R** (✆ 65-238-0898, cell 9-9883-2974; http://busesdyr.cl; Manuel Rodríguez s/n; ◷ 9am-noon & 3-7pm) goes almost daily at 6am (CH$2200, three hours). **Buses Jerry** (Lautaro s/n) goes to Palena (CH$2500, two hours) three times per week.

Buses Apsa goes to Puerto Montt (CH$18,000, 10 hours) on Tuesday and Friday at 7:30am; buy the ticket at the **post office** (☑ 65-223-7629; Balmaceda 501; ⊙ 9am-1pm & 3-7pm Mon-Fri).

International buses (☑ 65-272-1458; Cerda 436; CH$2500) to the Argentine border leave at 9am and 7pm on Monday and Friday. The **Futaleufú border post** (Ruta Internacional s/n; ⊙ 8am-8pm) is far quicker and more efficient than the crossing at Palena, opposite the Argentine border town of Carrenleufú.

Puyuhuapi

In 1935 four German immigrants settled this remote rainforest outpost, inspired by explorer Hans Steffen's adventures. The agricultural colony grew with Chilote textile workers, whose skills fed the success of the 1947 German **Fábrica de Alfombras** (☑ cell 9-9359-9515; www.puyuhuapi.com; Aysen s/n; ⊙ 9am-noon & 3-6:30pm Mon-Fri), still weaving carpets today. Located 6km south of Puyuhuapi, **Termas del Ventisquero** (☑ cell 9-7966-6805; www.termas ventisqueropuyuhuapi.cl; CH$18,000; ⊙ 9am-11pm Dec-Feb, reduced hours winter) is a peaceful hot-springs complex. Contact **Experiencia Austral** (☑ cell 9-8744-8755, cell 9-7766-1524; http://experienciaustral.com; Av Otto Uebel 36; ⊙ 9am-1pm & 2-7pm) to kayak the fjord, rent bikes or take a guided hike in Parque Nacional Queulat.

The best bargain accommodations option is **Los Mañíos del Queulat** (☑ cell 9-9491-1920; www.losmaniosdelqueulat.cl; Circunvalación s/n; d incl breakfast with/without bathroom CH$45,000/35,000; ☎). The historic **Casa Ludwig** (☑ 67-232-5220; www.casaludwig.cl; Av Otto Uebel 202; s/d CH$28,000/54,000, without bathroom from CH$20,000/30,000; ⊙ Oct-Mar) is elegant and snug. **El Muelle** (☑ cell 9-7654-3598; Av Otto Uebel s/n; mains CH$8000; ⊙ noon-10pm Tue-Sun) does big lunches of fresh seafood.

For information, stop by the helpful **tourist office** (Av Otto Uebel s/n; ⊙ 9am-9pm). Buses that run between Coyhaique and Chaitén will drop passengers in Puyuhuapi. Buy your return ticket as far ahead as possible. **Buses Becker** (☑ 67-223-2167; www.busesbecker.com; Av Otto Uebel s/n) goes to Chaitén and Futaleufú a few days per week. **Terra Austral** (☑ 67-225-4335; Av Otto Uebel s/n, Nido de Puyes supermarket) leaves at 6am daily for Coyhaique.

Parque Nacional Queulat

The 1540-sq-km **Parque Nacional Queulat** (www.conaf.cl/parques/parque-nacional-queulat; adult/child CH$5000/2500; ⊙ 8:30am-5:30pm)

is a wild realm of rivers winding through forests thick with ferns and southern beech. Its steep-sided fjords are flanked by creeping glaciers. From Conaf's **Centro de Información Ambiental** (⊙ 8:30am-5:30pm) there is a 3km hike to a lookout with views of **Ventisquero Colgante**, a chalk-blue hanging glacier.

Just north of the southern entrance at Pudú (Km170), a damp trail climbs the valley of the **Río de las Cascadas** through a dense forest to a granite bowl where half a dozen waterfalls drop from hanging glaciers.

Coyhaique

☑ 67 / POP 57,800

The cow town that kept growing, Coyhaique is the regional hub of rural Aysén, urbane enough to house the latest techie trends, mall fashions and discos. All this is plopped in the middle of an undulating mountain range, with rocky humpback peaks and snowy summits in the backdrop. For the visitor, it's the launchpad for far-flung adventures, be it fly-fishing, trekking the ice cap or rambling the Carretera Austral to its end. For those fresh from the rainforest wilderness of northern Aysén, it can be a jarring relapse into the world of semitrucks and subdivisions. Rural workers come to join the timber or salmon industries and add to the growing urban mass.

⊙ Sights & Activities

Lago Elizalde   LAKE
One of many serene mountain lakes surrounding Coyhaique and great for trout fishing, kayaking or simply time at the beach. It's just 33km from Coyhaique. Buses depart from the bus terminal (p543).

Reserva Nacional Coyhaique   NATURE RESERVE
(☑ 67-221-2109; www.conaf.cl/parques/reserva-nacional-coyhaique; adult/child CH$3000/1500; ⊙ 8:45am-5pm) Draped in lenga, ñire and coigue, the 21.5-sq-km Reserva Nacional Coyhaique has small lakes and Cerro Cinchao (1361m). The park is 5km from Coyhaique (about 1½ hours on foot), with views of town and Cerro Mackay's enormous basalt columns in the distance. Take Av General Baquedano north, across the bridge, then go right at the gravel road, a steep climb best accessed by 4WD.

CHILE PUYUHUAPI

☞ Tours

GeoSur Expediciones ADVENTURE
(☑ cell 9-9264-8671; www.geosur.com; Simón Bolívar
521; ⊘ 9am-5pm Mon-Fri) These recommended
adventure and regional-culture specialists
offer tailored trips on the Carretera Austral,
kayaking, hiking or country day trips at their
adventure center located 57km south of Coyhaique. They also do multiday treks to Cerro
Castillo or Jeinimeni-Chacabuco.

🛏 Sleeping

Huella Patagónica HOSTEL $
(☑ 67-223-0002, cell 9-4410-1571; www.huella
patagonica.cl; Serrano 621; dm/d incl breakfast
CH$18,000/49,000; ℗ 🛜) A welcome addition
to Coyhaique, this three-story corrugated-tin
hostel has attractive, modern dorms with
radiant floor heating plus lights and outlets
for each bunk. The owners, Mauricio and Ga-
briella, have long worked in regional tourism
and it shows. The on-site cafe, open to the
public, serves espresso and snacks.

Patagonia House BOUTIQUE HOTEL $$$
(☑ 67-221-1488, cell 9-7659-9963; www.patagonia-
house.com; Campo Alegre s/n; s/d/ste US$110/
120/160, 3-person cottage US$160; 🛜) 🍴 Set
apart from the bustle of downtown Coyhai-
que, this comfortable countryside lodging
has a sustainable approach and understat-
ed modern style. Spacious rooms feature
garden views and beautiful photographs.
Breakfasts are extensive and gourmet din-
ners (CH$17,000) are a godsend after a long
day on dusty roads. There's also an open-air
hot tub. It's 3km from the center.

✗ Eating

Mamma Gaucha PIZZA $
(☑ 67-221-0721; www.mammagaucha.cl; Paseo
Horn 47; mains CH$5000-10,000; ⊘ 10am-1:30am
Mon-Sat) Fusing Patagonian lore with a so-
phisticated palate and reasonable prices,
Mamma Gaucha could please the fussiest
road warrior. Cane ceilings and whitewashed
barn-board walls create a down-home set-
ting. Start with fresh-mint lemonade, organic
wine or a pint of La Tropera. The mainstays
are clay-oven pizzas, but the homemade pas-
tas and salad bowls featuring local produce
are just as worthy.

Café de Mayo CAFE $
(☑ 67-227-3020; 21 de Mayo 543; mains CH$4000-
6000; ⊘ 9am-10pm; 🛜✏) A meeting spot
specializing in espresso drinks, farm-egg

breakfasts or filling staples like *pastel de
choclo* (maize casserole). There are also
sandwiches, cheese boards and homemade
cakes. Choose from shady outdoor tables or
a cozy indoors with hanging teapots and
fireplace.

Café Holzer CAFE $
(www.holzer.cl; Dussen 317; cakes CH$2000;
⊘ 9:30am-9pm Tue-Fri, 10am-9pm Sat & Sun; 🛜)
This tiny cafe with a grassy front patio is a
local favorite for sweets and caffeine. Cakes
and tarts are flown in from a reputable San-
tiago bakery. Real coffee and noteworthy hot
chocolate are served. Or sample a gourd of
maté to see what all the buzz is about.

Adobe BURGERS $
(☑ 67-224-0846; Av General Baquedano 9; mains
CH$7000; ⊘ 1pm-1am Mon-Wed, to 2am Thu-Sat)
Oversized bacon-cheese burgers served on
pillowy rolls, lamb sandwiches and surpris-
ingly tasty roasted-vegetable burgers rule
this roadhouse-style eatery. It's also a good
place to watch Chilean soccer with a beer or
pisco infused with maqui berries. Good at-
mosphere and food available until 1am.

Carnes Quelat PARRILLA $$
(☑ 67-225-0507; Ramón Freire 327; mains
CH$6000-9000; ⊘ 1-3:30pm & 7:30-11pm)
Tucked away down a gravel alleyway, this
friendly plain-Jane place happens to serve
the best steaks in the region. *Carne a las
brasas* – meat attentively grilled over a
wood fire – is the worthy house specialty,
best matched with some piping-hot homemade empanadas and the secret-recipe *pisco* sour.

ℹ Information

Banks with ATMs and internet cafes line Condell.
Get cash here; it is one of the few stops on the
Carretera Austral with Visa ATM access.

Conaf (☑ 67-221-2109; Av Ogaña 1060;
⊘ 8:30am-1pm & 2:30-5:30pm Mon-Fri) Provides information on area parks and reserves.

Hospital Regional (☑ 67-221-9100; www.
hospitalregionalcoyhaique.cl; Ibar 68; ⊘ 24hr)
Emergency is open 24 hours.

Post Office (☑ 67-223-0013; Lord Cochrane
226; ⊘ 9am-6:30pm Mon-Fri, 9:30am-1:30pm
Sat) Near Plaza de Armas.

Sernatur (☑ 67-224-0298; www.recorreaysen.
cl; Bulnes 35; ⊘ 9am-6:30pm Mon-Fri, 10am-
6pm Sat; 🛜) A helpful office with lists of
activity, lodging and transportation options and
costs. Regional information is also available.

ℹ Getting There & Away

AIR

LATAM (📱 600-526-2000; General Parra 402; ⏰ 9am-1pm & 3-6:30pm Mon-Fri, 9:30am-1pm Sat) has several daily flights (most leaving in the morning) to Puerto Montt (CH$60,000) and Santiago (CH$180,000) from the **Balmaceda Airport** (Balmaceda), 57km south of the city; note that rates can be deeply discounted if purchased in-country.

Flights with **Sky Airline** (www.skyairline.cl; Balmaceda Airport) from Santiago stop at Balmaceda Airport on the way to Punta Arenas.

BUS

Buses operate from the **bus terminal** (📱 67-225-8203; Lautaro 109; ⏰ 8am-7pm) and separate offices. Schedules change continuously; check with Sernatur (p542) for the latest information. The following leave from the terminal.

For northern destinations, companies include **Águilas Patagónicas** (📱 67-221-1288; www.aguilaspatagonicas.cl; Lautaro 109, Bus Terminal; ⏰ 8:30am-1pm & 2:15-5pm Mon-Sat), **Transaustral** (📱 67-223-2067; Lautaro 109, Bus Terminal; ⏰ 8:30am-1pm & 3-6pm), **Buses Becker** (📱 67-223-2167; www.busesbecker.com; General Parra 335), **Transportes Terra Austral** (📱 67-225-4355; Lautaro 109, Bus Terminal; ⏰ 9:30am-1pm & 3:30-5:30pm) and **Queilen Bus** (📱 67-224-0760; www.queilenbus.cl; Lautaro 109, Bus Terminal; ⏰ 11:30am-1:30pm & 2:30-6:30pm Mon-Sat). For southern destinations, try **Acuario 13/Buses Sao Paulo** (📱 67-224-0990; Lautaro 109, Bus Terminal; ⏰ 8:30am-6pm Mon-Fri, to 10am Sat) or **Buses Don Carlos** (📱 67-223-1981; Cruz 63).

Buses from Coyhaique

DESTINATION	COST (CH$)	DURATION (HR)
Chaitén	15,000	9-11
Chile Chico	6000	3½ with ferry
Cochrane	14,000	7-10
Futaleufú	20,000	8-9
Puerto Montt	40,000	23
Puyuhuapi	8000	5

Lago General Carrera

Shared with Argentina (where it's called Lago Buenos Aires), this massive 2240-sq-km lake is a wind-stirred green-blue sea in the middle of sculpted Patagonian steppe. Its rough and twisty roads dwarf the traveler: you'll feel like you're crawling through the landscape. An excellent journey follows

PATAGONIA NATIONAL PARK

Parque Nacional Patagonia (Patagonia National Park; www.parquepatagonia.org; Valle Chacabuco) **FREE**, 18km north of Cochrane, is a reformed *estancia* (grazing ranch) home to flamingo, guanaco, huemul (endangered Andean deer), puma, viscacha and fox. Conservacion Patagonica, the NGO behind the Patagonia National Park project, began this initiative in 2004. Now dubbed the Serengeti of the Southern Cone, the 690-sq-km Valle Chacabuco features Patagonian steppe, forests, mountains, lakes and lagoons. The park stretches from the Río Baker to the Argentine border. In a private vehicle, it's possible to cross here at Paso Roballos.

the Carretera Austral south from Coyhaique, around the lake's western border.

Just before reaching Balmaceda from Coyhaique, a right-hand turnoff (the sign points to Cochrane) heads toward **Parque Nacional Cerro Castillo**. The spires of glacier-bound Cerro Castillo tower over some 1800 sq km of southern-beech forest, an excellent trekking destination. In nearby Villa Cerro Castillo, **Senderos Patagonia** (📱 cell 9-6224-4725; www.aysensenderospatagonia.com; Carretera Austral s/n; campsites per person CH$5000; dm CH$8000-10,000, horseback rides CH$40,000; 🐎) has great bilingual guide services and a new hostel.

Along the western shore, **Puerto Río Tranquilo** is the launch point for day-long tours to the stunning Glaciar San Rafael with **Destino Patagonia** (📱 cell 9-9158-6044; www.destinopatagonia.cl; Flores 208; per person full day from CH$150,000; ⏰ 10am-9pm). Boat tours visit the gorgeous caves of **Capilla de Mármol** (Marble Chapel; 5 passengers CH$50,000) when the water is calm. North of town a glacier-lined road to **Parque Nacional Laguna San Rafael** bumps toward the coast. Adventure base camp **El Puesto** (📱 cell 9-6207-3794; www.elpuesto.cl; Pedro Lagos 258; s/d/tr/q incl breakfast US$127/168/225/266; 🐎) 🍴 is a lovely B&B owned by a professional adventure guide. **Camping Pudu** (📱 cell 9-8920-5085; https://es-la.facebook.com/campingpudu; campsites per person CH$8000; ⏰ mid-Nov–Mar) offers excellent waterfront sites.

About 13km east of Cruce El Maitén, **Puerto Guadal** has gas and provisions. With rave reviews, ecocamp and hostel

Destino No Turístico (📱cell 9-7392-5510; www.destino-noturistico.com; Camino Laguna La Manga, Km1.5; campsites per person CH$5500, dm/d CH$25,000/60,000) 🍴 provides a lovely countryside getaway.

Chile Chico

📱67 / POP 4600

Gold and silver mines dot the roller-coaster road from Puerto Guadal, ending in Chile Chico, a sunny oasis of wind-pummeled poplars and orchards. From here, buses connect to Los Antiguos and Ruta 40 leading to southern Argentine Patagonia. **Reserva Nacional Lago Jeinimeni**, 60km away, is a treasure of flamingos and turquoise mountain lagoons. Aside from a few tours, there's little transportation; try **Patagonia Xpress** (📱cell 9-9802-0280; www.patagoniaxpress.com; O'Higgins 333, Galería Municipal No 8; all-day trek US$80; ⏰9am-1pm & 3-7pm).

There is a helpful **Oficina de Información Turística** (📱67-241-1751; www.chilechico.cl; cnr O'Higgins & Blest Ghana; ⏰8am-1pm & 2-5pm Mon-Thu, to 4pm Fri) and a **BancoEstado** (González 112; ⏰9am-2pm Mon-Fri) for money exchange; the ATM only takes Mastercard.

Stay at **Ñandu Camp** (📱cell 9-6779-3390; www.nanducamp.com; O'Higgins 750; dm CH$14,000, s/d without bathroom CH$20,000/30,000, q CH$45,000; 📶), with helpful trekking information, or Belgian farmhouse **Hostería de la Patagonia** (📱67-241-1337, cell 9-8159-2146; www.hosteriadelapatagonia.cl; Camino Internacional s/n; campsites per person CH$5000, incl breakfast r per person without bathroom CH$20,000, s/d/tr CH$45,000/62,000/76,000, cabins CH$50,000; 📶) 🍴, with charming rooms among the gardens.

❶ Getting There & Away

An almost-daily ferry run by **Somarco** (📱67-241-1093; www.barcazas.cl/barcazas/wp/region-de-aysen/lago-general-carrera; Muelle Chile Chico; passenger/automobile CH$2300/19,750) crosses Lago General Carrera to Puerto Ingeniero Ibáñez, a big shortcut to Coyhaique.

At the time of writing, no buses crossed the border to Los Antiguos, Argentina, just 9km east, because of new tariffs charged by Argentine authorities. Inquire locally as this situation could change. For now, you can take a taxi to the Chilean border (CH$6000), but have to walk 1km to the Argentine border. From there, it's 1.5km to Los Antiguos, which has connections to El Chaltén.

Bus providers and schedules vary from year to year. To Puerto Guadal (CH$8000, 2½ hours),

Seguel (📱67-243-1214; Av O'Higgins s/n) and **Buses Eca** (📱67-243-1224; Av O'Higgins s/n, Bus Station) go Monday to Friday at 4pm or 5pm. To Puerto Río Tranquilo (CH$15,000, four hours), **Costa Carrera** (📱cell 9-8739-2544; Av O'Higgins s/n, Bus Station) has service twice a week.

Buses Acuña (📱67-225-1579; Rodríguez 143) and **Buses Carolina** (📱67-241-1490; ferry office) go to Coyhaique (CH$5000) with a ferry-bus combination (4½ hours including ferry) via Puerto Ibáñez. The ferry is not included in the ticket.

South to Villa O'Higgins

Cochrane is a languorous old ranching outpost and the southern hub of the Carretera Austral. Though oblivious to tourism, Cochrane is the gateway to the new Parque Nacional Patagonia. Stay at **Residencial Cero a Cero** (📱67-252-2158, cell 9-7607-8155; http://residencialceroace.wixsite.com/residencialceroacero; Lago Brown 464; incl breakfast s/d CH$25,000/40,000, r per person without bathroom CH$13,000; 📶), a log home that has ample space. **Café Tamango** (📱cell 9-9158-4521; Esmeralda 464; mains CH$5000; ⏰9am-9pm Mon-Sat; 🍴) prepares good sandwiches, hearty vegetarian fare like lentil burgers, and homemade chestnut ice cream. To check out nearby Calluco Glacier, contact **Lord Patagonia** (📱cell 9-8425-2419; www.lordpatagonia.cl; full-day trek CH$50,000) for guide services. The **tourist kiosk** (www.municochrane.cl; Plaza de Armas; ⏰9am-1pm & 2-9pm Jan & Feb) on the plaza has bus schedules, if little else.

You could spend a whole day exploring the network of creaky boardwalks of fabled **Caleta Tortel**, perched over the milky waters of the glacier-fed sound. Dedicated as a national monument, this fishing village cobbled around a steep escarpment is seated between two ice fields at the mouth of Río Baker. The road stops at the edge of town at the helpful **tourism kiosk** (📱cell 9-6230-4879; www.municipalidaddetortel.cl; ⏰10am-10pm Tue-Sun), with maps, bus information and lodging.

Brisas del Sur (📱cell 9-5688-2723; valerianderos@hotmail.com; Sector Playa Ancha; incl breakfast d CH$45,000, r per person without bathroom CH$20,000; 📶) offers snug rooms, but if you can splurge, go for the stylish lodge **Entre Hielos** (📱cell 9-9579-3779; www.entrehielostortel.cl; s/d incl breakfast US$118/150; 📶), which also arranges private boat trips to the glaciers. Cheaper boat taxis do tours of the bay (CH$10,000) from the Rincon sector.

ⓘ SLOW ROAD TO ARGENTINA

Keen travelers can skirt Campo de Hielo Sur to get from Villa O'Higgins to Argentina's Parque Nacional Los Glaciares and El Chaltén. The one- to three-day trip can be completed between November 1 and April 30. Bring all of your provisions, cash (in both currencies), plus your passport and rain gear. Travel delays due to bad weather or boat problems do happen so travel with extra food and extra pesos. The trip goes as follows:

➡ Take the 8am bus from Villa O'Higgins to Puerto Bahamondez (CH$2500).

➡ Take **Robinson Crusoe** (☑ 67-243-1811; www.robinsoncrusoe.com; Carretera Austral s/n; glacier tour CH$103,000; ⊘ 9am-1pm & 3-7pm Mon-Sat Nov-Mar) catamaran *La Quetru* (CH$36,000, four hours) from Villa O'Higgins' port, Puerto Bahamondez, to Candelario Mansilla on the south edge of Lago O'Higgins. Expect one to three times a week, with departures mostly on Monday, Wednesday and Saturday.

➡ Or, **Ruedas de la Patagonia** (☑ cell 9-7604-2400; www.turismoruedasdelapatagonia. cl; Padre Antonio Ronchi 28; transfer CH$35,000; ⊘ 9am-9pm) uses a smaller, faster boat to shuttle between Candelario Mansilla and Puerto Bahamondez (one hour 40 minutes, CH$35,000), including transfer to Villa O'Higgins. Usually operates on the days the ferry does not.

➡ Candelario Mansilla has basic lodging, horseback riding and pack-horse rental (riding or pack horse CH$30,000). Pass through Chilean customs and immigration here.

➡ Trek or ride to Laguna Redonda (two hours). Camping is not allowed.

➡ Trek or ride to Laguna Larga (1½ hours). Camping is not allowed.

➡ Trek or ride to the north shore of Lago del Desierto (1½ hours). Camping is allowed. Pass through Argentine customs and immigration here.

➡ Take the ferry from the north to the south shores of Lago del Desierto (US$60, 2¼ hours). Another option is to hike the coast (15km, five hours). Camping is allowed. Check current ferry schedules with Argentine customs.

➡ Grab the shuttle bus to El Chaltén, 37km away (US$27, one hour).

For more information, consult Rancho Grande Hostel (p174) on the Argentine side. In Chile, Robinson Crusoe also offers the whole trip for a package price.

From Cochrane, buses go daily to Coyhaique (CH$14,000, 10 hours). Chile Chico is served three days per week, with stops in Puerto Guadal. There are several buses daily between Caleta Tortel (CH$10,000, three hours) and Cochrane.

For Villa O'Higgins (CH$8000, six hours), **Águilas Patagónicas** (☑ 67-252-2020; www. aguilaspatagonicas.cl; Las Golondrinas s/n, Bus Terminal; ⊘ 10am-1pm & 3-8pm) departs at 8am on Monday, Wednesday and Saturday.

Villa O'Higgins

Wild stretches of rushing rivers and virgin forest flank the curvy road south of Caleta Tortel. At **Puerto Yungay** a free government ferry (www.barcazas.cl) hauls passengers and cars across the Mitchell fjord to the final 100km stretch of the Carretera Austral. This famed road ends at the remote village of Villa O'Higgins, stopped by the massive glacial barrier of the Southern Ice Field. That doesn't stop hardy adventurers from tackling the ferry-trek-ferry combination to El Chaltén, Argentina.

On the outskirts of town, **Entre Patagones** (☑ cell 9-9498-0460; www.entrepatagones.cl; Carretera Austral s/n; domes CH$90,000, 2-/4-person cabins CH$35,000/45,000) boasts geodesic domes replete with private wooden hot tubs on the deck. In town, **El Mosco** (☑ 67-243-1819, cell 9-7658-3017; Carretera Austral, Km1240; campsites per person CH$5000, dm CH$12,000, incl breakfast d CH$45,000, s/d without bathroom CH$18,000/30,000, 4-person cabins CH$55,000; ☏) offers friendly lodgings and the lowdown on local hikes.

Guided horseback riding, trekking trips and bike rental are available with advance bookings through **Villa O'Higgins Expediciones** (☑ 67-243-1821, cell 9-8210-3191; www. villaohiggins.com; Teniente Merino s/n). There's no ATM here so bring all the cash you'll need.

Águilas Patagónicas (p545) goes to Cochrane (CH$8000, six hours) on Tuesday, Thursday and Sunday at 8am. Frequency changes in low season.

SOUTHERN PATAGONIA

Pounding westerlies, barren seascapes and the ragged spires of Torres del Paine – this is the distilled essence of Patagonia. The provinces of Magallanes and Última Esperanza boast a frontier appeal perhaps only matched by the deep Amazon and remote Alaska. Long before humans arrived on the continent, glaciers chiseled and carved these fine landscapes. Now it's a place for travelers to hatch their greatest adventures, whether hiking through rugged landscapes, seeing penguins by the thousands or horseback riding across the steppe.

Parque Nacional Torres del Paine is the region's star attraction. Among the finest parks on the continent, it attracts hundreds of thousands of visitors every year, even some towing wheeled luggage (though we don't recommend that). Throughout the region, it's easy and worthwhile to travel between Argentina and Chile.

Punta Arenas

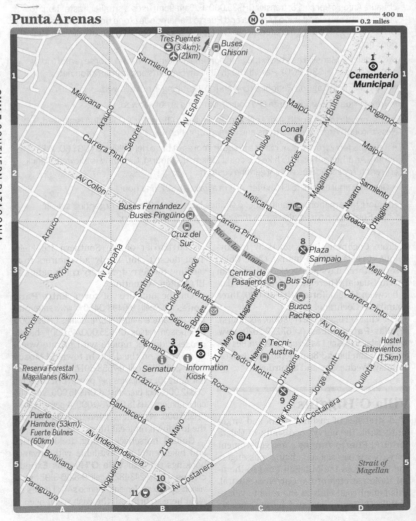

Punta Arenas

📱 061 / POP 131,600

If these streets could talk: this wind-wracked former penitentiary has hosted tattered sailors, miners, seal hunters, starving pioneers and wealthy dandies of the wool boom. Exploitation of one of the world's largest reserves of hydrocarbon started in the 1980s and has developed into a thriving petrochemical industry. Today's Punta Arenas is a confluence of the ruddy and the grand, geared toward both tourism and industry.

◉ Sights

Plaza Muñoz Gamero   PLAZA

A central plaza of magnificent conifers surrounded by opulent mansions. Facing the plaza's north side, **Casa Braun-Menéndez** (📱 61-224-1489; ⊙ 10:30am-1pm & 5-8:30pm Tue-Fri, 10:30am-1pm & 8-10pm Sat, 11am-2pm Sun) FREE houses the private Club de la Unión, which also uses the tavern downstairs (open to the public). The nearby **monument** commemorating the 400th anniversary of Magellan's voyage was donated by wool baron José Menéndez in 1920. Just east is the former **Sociedad Menéndez Behety**, which now houses Turismo Comapa. The **cathedral** sits west.

Museo Regional de Magallanes   MUSEUM

(Museo Regional Braun-Menéndez; 📱 61-224-4216; www.museodemagallanes.cl; Magallanes 949; ⊙ 10:30am-5pm Wed-Mon, to 2pm May-Dec) FREE This opulent mansion testifies to the wealth and power of pioneer sheep farmers in the late 19th century. The well-maintained interior houses a regional historical museum (ask for booklets in English) and original exquisite French-nouveau family furnishings, from intricate wooden inlaid floors to Chinese vases. In former servants' quarters, a downstairs cafe is perfect for a *pisco* sour while soaking up the grandeur.

★ Cementerio Municipal   CEMETERY

(main entrance at Av Bulnes 949; ⊙ 7:30am-8pm) FREE Among South America's most fascinating cemeteries, with both humble immigrant graves and flashy tombs, like that of wool baron José Menéndez, a scale replica of Rome's Vittorio Emanuele monument, according to author Bruce Chatwin. See the map inside the main entrance gate.

It's an easy 15-minute stroll northeast of the plaza, or catch any *taxi colectivo* (shared taxi with specific route) in front of the Museo Regional de Magallanes.

☞ Tours

Worthwhile day trips include tours to the town's first settlements at Fuerte Bulnes and Puerto Hambre. If you have the time, visit the thriving Magellanic penguin colonies of Monumento Natural Los Pingüinos.

Kayak Agua Fresca   KAYAKING

(📱 cell 9-5411-2369; www.kayakaguafresca.com; 4½hr tour CH$70,000) On the rare day in Punta Arenas when winds are calm and the sea is glass, the sea kayaking can be spectacular. This company also does Zodiac boat excursions. There's no office; see the website for information.

Solo Expediciones   TOURS

(📱 61-271-0219; http://soloexpediciones.com; Nogueira 1255; ⊙ 9am-6pm Mon-Fri) This agency offers several tours: an Isla Magdalena penguin tour with faster, recommended semi-rigid boats (other tours take the ferry) and whale-watching day trips in the Parque Marino Francisco Coloane.

🛏 Sleeping

Hostel Entrevientos   HOSTEL **$**

(📱 61-237-1171; www.hostelentrevientos.cl; Jorge Montt 0690; incl breakfast dm US$18, d/tr US$66/80; 🛜) Near the sparkling waterfront,

CHILE PUNTA ARENAS

Punta Arenas

this spacious A-frame has commanding sea views from an ultra-cozy 2nd-floor living room. There's an ample guest kitchen, and dorm rooms and snug private rooms downstairs. It's warmly attended by the owners, who also rent bikes (CH$7000 per day). The downside: it's a 25-minute walk to the center, but buses also go.

Hospedaje Magallanes B&B $$
(☑61-222-8616; www.hospedaje-magallanes.com; Magallanes 570; d CH$60,000, dm/d without bathroom CH$20,000/45,000; @ 🐱) A great inexpensive option run by a German-Chilean couple who are also Torres del Paine guides with an on-site travel agency. With just a few quiet rooms, there are often communal dinners or backyard barbecues by the climbing wall. Breakfast includes brown bread and strong coffee.

✗ Eating & Drinking

Local seafood is an exquisite treat: go for *centolla* (king crab) or *erizos* (sea urchins).

La Mesita Grande PIZZA $
(☑61-224-4312; O'Higgins 1001; mains CH$4000-9000; ☺noon-11pm Mon-Sat, 1-8pm Sun) If you're homesick for Brooklyn, La Mesita Grande might do the trick. This mod exposed-brick pizzeria serves them up thin and chewy, with organic toppings and pints of local brew. Also has awesome Caesar salads. Save room for its homemade ice cream. The original outlet is in **Puerto Natales** (☑61-241-1571; www.mesitagrande.cl; Arturo Prat 196; pizza CH$4000-9000; ☺1-3:30pm & 7-11:30pm).

Mercado Municipal MARKET $
(21 de Mayo 1465; mains CH$3000-6000; ☺8am-3pm) Fish and vegetable market with cheap 2nd-floor *cocinerías* (eateries), a great place for inexpensive seafood dishes.

La Marmita CHILEAN $$
(☑61-222-2056; www.marmitamaga.cl; Plaza Sampaio 678; mains CH$8000-12,000; ☺12:30-3pm & 6:30-11:30pm Mon-Sat; ✍) This classic bistro enjoys wild popularity for its playful ambince and tasty fare. Besides fresh salads and bread, hearty dishes such as casseroles afood hark back to grandma's cooking, n style. With good vegetarian options eout service.

za 87 BAR
57; 21 de Mayo 1469; ☺8pm-1:30am 30am Fri & Sat) A fine addition to neighborhood bar is friendly

and bubbling with life. There are memorable craft cocktails and local beer. Try a not-too-sweet calafate mojito.

❶ Information

Internet access is widely available and ATMs are common.

The **post office** (Bories 911; ☺9am-6:30pm Mon-Fri, 10am-1pm Sat) is located one block north of Plaza Muñoz Gamero.
Conaf (☑61-223-0681; Av Bulnes 0309; ☺9am-5pm Mon-Fri) Has details on the nearby parks.
Hospital Regional (☑61-229-3000; http://hospitalclinicomagallanes.cl; Av Los Flamencos 1364; ☺24hr) Large regional hospital.
Information Kiosk (☑61-220-0610; Plaza Muñoz Gamero; ☺8am-7pm Mon-Sat, 9am-7pm Sun Dec-Feb) Tourist information on the south side of the plaza.
Sernatur (☑61-224-1330; www.sernatur.cl; Fagnano 643; ☺8:30am-6pm Mon-Fri, 10am-4pm Sat) With friendly, well-informed, multilingual staff and lists of accommodations and transportation. Reduced hours in low season.

❶ Getting There & Away

The tourist offices distribute a useful brochure that details all forms of transportation available.

AIR
Punta Arenas' airport (PUQ) is 21km north of town.

From November to March, **Aerovías DAP** (☑61-261-6100; www.aeroviasdap.cl; Ignacio Carrera Pinto 1015) flies to Porvenir (CH$55,000 round-trip) Monday through Saturday several times daily, and to Puerto Williams (CH$143,000 round-trip) Monday through Saturday at 10am. Luggage is limited to 10kg per person.

Sky Airline (www.skyairline.cl), **LATAM** (☑600-526-2000; www.latam.com; Montalva 1110, Local 3; ☺10:30am-8:30pm) and **JetSmart** (www.jetsmart.com) serve Puerto Montt and Santiago. At the time of writing, LATAM was expected to add flights to Ushuaia. **Aerolineas Argentinas** (www.aerolineas.com.ar) sometimes has flights to Argentina.

BOAT
Transbordador Austral Broom (☑61-272-8100; www.tabsa.cl; Av Bulnes 05075) operates three ferries to Tierra del Fuego. The car and passenger ferry to/from Porvenir (CH$6200/39,800 per person/vehicle, 2½ to four hours) usually leaves at 9am but has some afternoon departures; check the current online schedule. From Punta Arenas, it's faster to do the Primera Angostura crossing (CH$1700/15,000 per person/vehicle, 20 min-

utes), northeast of town, which sails every 90 minutes between 8:30am and 11:45pm. Broom sets sail for Isla Navarino's Puerto Williams (reclining seat/bunk CH$108,000/151,000 including meals, 30 hours) about six times per month, including every Thursday (with a return journey on Saturday).

BUS

Buses depart from company offices, most within a block or two of Av Colón. Buy tickets several hours (if not days) in advance. The **Central de Pasajeros** (61-224-5811; cnr Magallanes & Av Colón) is the closest thing to a central booking office.

For Puerto Natales, try **Buses Fernández** (61-224-2313; www.busesfernandez.com; Sanhueza 745) or **Bus Sur** (61-261-4224; www.bus-sur.cl; Av Colón 842).

For Argentina, try **Buses Ghisoni** (61-224-0646; www.busesbarria.cl; Av España 264), **Buses Pacheco** (61-224-2174; www.buses pacheco.com; Av Colón 900) or **Tecni-Austral** (61-222-2078; Navarro 975).

For Chile's Lakes District, try **Cruz del Sur** (61-222-7970; www.busescruzdelsur.cl; Sanhueza 745).

Daily destinations include the following:

DESTINATION	COST (CH$)	DURATION (HR)
Osorno	35,000	30
Puerto Natales	7000	3
Río Gallegos	20,000	5-8
Río Grande	30,000	7
Ushuaia	35,000	10

Getting Around

Taxi colectivos, with numbered routes, are only slightly more expensive than buses (about CH$500, or a bit more late at night and on Sundays), but far more comfortable and much quicker.

Cars are a good option for exploring Torres del Paine, but renting one in Chile to cross the border into Argentina gets expensive due to international insurance requirements.

Puerto Natales

61 / POP 21,500

A pastel wash of corrugated-tin houses shoulder to shoulder, this once dull fishing port on Seno Última Esperanza has become the hub of Gore-Tex-clad travelers headed to the continent's number-one national park. While not a destination in itself, the town is pleasant, the austral light is divine and visitor services are getting ever more savvy.

Sights & Activities

Museo Histórico MUSEUM
(61-241-1263; Bulnes 285; CH$1000; 8am-7pm Mon-Fri, 10am-1pm & 3-7pm Sat & Sun, reduced hours May-Nov) Worth a quick visit, this is a crash course in local history, with archaeological artifacts, a Yaghan canoe, Tehuelche bolas (throwing weapon) and historical photos.

Mirador Dorotea HIKING
(Ruta 9; CH$5000) A day hike through a lenga forest on private land to splendid views of Puerto Natales and the glacial valley. Less than 10km from Natales. Dorotea is the large rocky outcrop just off Ruta 9.

Tours

Antares/Big Foot Patagonia ADVENTURE
(61-241-4611; www.antarespatagonia.com; Costanera 161, Av Pedro Montt; Lago Grey kayaking CH$66,000) Specializing in Torres del Paine, Antares can facilitate climbing permits and made-to-order trips. Its sister company Big Foot has the park concession for Lago Grey activities, including Glacier Grey ice-trekking and kayak trips, with a base in the park.

Baqueano Zamora HORSEBACK RIDING
(61 261-3530; www.baqueanozamora.cl; Baque dano 534; 10am-1pm & 3-7pm) Runs recommended horseback-riding trips and wild-horse viewing in Torres del Paine.

Erratic Rock ADVENTURE
(61-241-4317; www.erraticrock.com; Baquedano 955; 10am-1pm & 2-11pm) Guides bare-bones Torres del Paine trips plus alternative options and rents gear. Alternative treks include Cabo Froward, Isla Navarino and lesser-known destinations. Also provides excellent information sessions on Torres del Paine at 3pm daily.

Sleeping

Hostels often rent equipment and help arrange park transportation.

Vinn Haus BOUTIQUE HOTEL $
(cell 9-8269-2510; http://vinnhaus.com; Bulnes 499; dm/d incl breakfast US$24/80; Sep-May;) Taking dormliving to a new level, this Chilean-Finnish enterprise employs a gorgeous vintage concept with old suitcases, antique tiles and pleated leather. Each bunk has its own USB outlet, and outlets for various plug designs. The wine bar and cafe serves some of the best coffee this side of Colombia. With buffet breakfast and a cute courtyard.

Puerto Natales

Puerto Natales

★ **Wild Patagonia**   HOSTEL $

(📱 cell 9-7715-2423; www.wildhostel.com; Bulnes 555; incl breakfast d US$85, dm/d without bathroom US$21/70; 🕐 Sep-Apr; 🛜) Emanating happy vibes, this hostel has pleasant rooms, with tin-clad cabins around a courtyard with a firepit. Breakfast includes fresh bread, yogurt and jam. Open to the public from 3pm on, the cafe serves great local beef burgers and often features live music at night. The owners speak a heap of languages and orient guests on park services.

Singing Lamb   HOSTEL $

(📱 61-241-0958; www.thesinginglamb.com; Arauco 779; incl breakfast dm US$23-28, d US$80; @🛜) 🍃 A clean and green hostel with compost, recycling, rainwater collection and linen shopping bags. Dorm rooms are priced by the number of beds (maximum nine) and shared spaces are ample. Nice touches include central heating and homemade breakfasts. To get here, follow Raimírez one block past Plaza O'Higgins.

We Are Patagonia
B&B $

(☑ cell 9-7389-4802; www.wearepatagonia.com; Barros Arana 155; dm incl breakfast US$25; 🛜) A lovely art hostel with minimalist Nordic charm and a grassy backyard. The small house has mixed dorms with 30 beds with down duvets, four bathrooms and a small open kitchen. Reception is 24-hour and it rents bikes (CH$2000 per hour).

🍴 Eating & Drinking

La Forestera
BURGERS $

(☑ cell 9-7389-4802; Barros Arana 155; mains CH$6900; ⊙ 1-3pm & 7:30-11pm Mon-Sat) These gorgeous gourmet burgers do disappear fast. Tasty regular and lamb burgers or lentil and beet alternatives are served on airy brioche buns. It also does super-spicy wings and crisp onion rings, well matched with a local brew. There are just a few tables but also takeout service.

Cafe Kaiken
CHILEAN $$

(☑ cell 9-8295-2036; Baquedano 699; mains CH$7800 11,000; ⊙ 1-3:30pm & 6:30-11pm Tue-Sun) With just five tables and one couple cooking, serving and chatting up customers, this is as intimate as it gets. The owners moved here to get out of the Santiago fast lane, so you'd best follow their lead. Dishes such as mushroom ceviche, slow-roasted lamb or homemade ravioli are well worth the wait. Arrive early to claim a spot.

La Guanaca
PIZZA $$

(☑ 61-241-3245; Magallanes 167; mains CH$5000-16,000; ⊙ 12:30-10pm Mon-Sat; 🍴) From crisp oven-fired pizzas to crepes and marinated mushroom appetizers, this homespun restaurant delivers warming and satisfying meals. Oversized salads, like the quinoa with roasted vegetables, are abundant and varied. There's craft beer and several wines to choose from.

★ Last Hope
DISTILLERY

(☑ cell 9-7201-8585; www.lasthopedistillery.com; Esmeralda 882; ⊙ 5pm-2am Wed-Sun Dec-Mar, 8pm-2am Sat & Sun Apr-Nov) Two Australians on vacation tossed in their day jobs to distill whiskey and gin at the end of the world. With bonhomie to spare, their bar caters to locals and travelers alike with a rotating menu of gorgeous cocktails. The signature drink is a calafate berry gin and tonic. It's tiny and the overflow waits outside – wear your down jacket.

Base Camp
BAR

(☑ 61-241-4658; Baquedano 731; ⊙ 6pm-2am Nov-Apr) Debut your park tall tales at this happening gringo hideout. With pub trivia nights, good pub grub and occasional live music.

ℹ Information

Most banks in town are equipped with ATMs.

The best bilingual portal for the region is www.parquetorresdelpaine.cl.

Conaf (☑ 61-241-1438; www.parquetorresdel paine.cl; Baquedano 847; ⊙ 8:30am-12:45pm & 2:30-5:30pm Mon-Fri) National parks service administrative office. Contact online to book Torres del Paine campgrounds under park administration; advance reservations are required.

Municipal Tourist Office (☑ 61-261-4808; Bus Terminal; ⊙ 8:30am-12:30pm & 2:30-6pm Tue-Sun) With region-wide lodgings listings.

Sernatur (☑ 61-241-2125; infonatales@serna tur.cl; Costanera 19, Av Pedro Montt; ⊙ 9am-7pm Mon-Fri, 9:30am-6pm Sat & Sun) With useful city and regional maps and a second plaza location in high season.

ℹ Getting There & Away

BOAT

For many travelers, a journey through Chile's spectacular fjords aboard the **Navimag Ferry** (☑ 61-241-1421, Rodoviario 61-241-1642; www.navimag.com; Costanera 308, Av Pedro Montt; ⊙ 9am-1pm & 3-7pm Mon-Fri) becomes a highlight of their trip. This four-day and three-night northbound voyage has become so popular it should be booked well in advance. To confirm when the ferry is due, contact **Turismo Comapa** (☑ 61-241-4300; www.comapa.com; Bulnes 541; ⊙ 9am-1pm & 3-7pm Mon-Fri, 10am-2pm Sat) or Navimag a couple of days before your estimated arrival date. There is a second Navimag office in the Rodoviario (p552) bus terminal.

Transbordador Austral Broom (TABSA) runs the 41-hour **Puerto Yungay Ferry** (Cruz Australis; ☑ 61-241-5966; www.tabsa.cl; Costanera s/n; passenger/bicycle CH$125,000/10,500). This new ferry option between Puerto Natales and Puerto Yungay, via Puerto Eden, links two areas of Patagonia with no road connections. Frequency varies month to month, but high season offers around 10 departures per month.

Travelers should note that under the current schedule it usually arrives in Puerto Eden and Puerto Yungay late at night, so reserve Puerto

Eden hotels in advance and bring a headlamp to get around.

BUS

Buses arrive at the **Rodoviario** (Bus Terminal; ☑ 61-241-2554; Av España 1455; ☺ 6:30am-midnight), a bus terminal on the town outskirts, though companies also sell tickets at their downtown offices. Book at least a day ahead, especially for early-morning departures. Services are greatly reduced in the low season. Several lines go to Punta Arenas. For Argentina, try **Turismo Zaahj** (☑ 61-241-2260; www.turismozaahj.co.cl; Arturo Prat 236/270), **Cootra** (☑ 61-241-2785; http://cootra.com.ar; Baquedano 244), **Bus Sur** (☑ 61-242-6011; www.bus-sur.cl; Baquedano 668) or **Buses Pacheco** (☑ 61-241-4800; www.busespacheco.com; Ramírez 224).

Torres del Paine–bound buses include **Buses Fernández** (☑ 61-241-1111; www.busesfernandez.com; cnr Esmeralda & Ramírez), **Buses Gomez** (☑ 61-241-5700; www.busesgomez.com; Arturo Prat 234), **Buses JBA** (☑ 61-241-0242; Arturo Prat 258) and Turismo Zaahj. Buses leave for Torres del Paine two to three times daily at around 7am, 8am and 2:30pm. If you are headed to Mountain Lodge Paine Grande in the low season, take the morning bus to meet the catamaran. Tickets may also be used for transfers within the park, so save your stub. Schedules change, so double-check them before heading out.

Destinations include the following:

DESTINATION	COST (CH$)	DURATION (HR)
El Calafate	17,000	5
Punta Arenas	7000	3
Torres del Paine	8000	2
Ushuaia	38,000	13

❶ Getting Around

Many hostels rent bikes. Car rental is expensive and availability is limited; you'll get better rates in Punta Arenas or Argentina.

Parque Nacional Torres del Paine

Soaring almost vertically more than 2000m above the Patagonian steppe, the granite pillars of Torres del Paine (Towers of Paine) dominate the landscape of what may be South America's finest **national park** (www.parquetorresdelpaine.cl; high/low season CH$21,000/11,000). A Unesco Biosphere Reserve since 1978, the park covers 1810 sq km. Most visitors come for the park's greatest hit but, once here, realize that other (less crowd-

ed) attractions offer equal wow power: azure lakes, trails that meander through emerald forests, roaring rivers to cross on rickety bridges and one big, radiant blue glacier.

The park is home to flocks of ostrich-like rhea (known locally as the *ñandú*), Andean condor, flamingo and many other bird species. Its star success in conservation is undoubtedly the guanaco, which grazes the open steppes where pumas cannot approach undetected. After more than a decade of effective protection from poachers, these large and growing herds don't even flinch when humans or vehicles approach.

When the weather is clear, panoramas are everywhere. However, unpredictable weather systems can sheath the peaks in clouds for hours or days. Some say you get four seasons in a day here, with sudden rainstorms and knock-down gusts part of the hearty initiation. Bring high-quality foul-weather gear, a synthetic sleeping bag and, if you're camping, a good tent. If you want to sleep in hotels or *refugios* (rustic shelters), you must make reservations in advance. Plan a minimum of three to seven days to enjoy the hiking and other activities.

At the end of 2011, a raging fire burned over 160 sq km, destroying old forest, killing animals and burning several park structures. An international visitor was charged with accidentally setting the fire while trying to start an illegal campfire. The affected area, mostly between Pehoé and Refugio Grey, is essentially the western leg of the 'W' trek. The panoramic views remain, but it may take centuries for the forest to recover. Be conscientious and tread lightly – you are among hundreds of thousands of annual guests.

🏃 Activities

Hiking

Torres del Paine's 2800m granite peaks inspire a mass pilgrimage of hikers from around the world. Most go for the Circuit or the 'W' to soak in these classic panoramas, leaving other incredible routes deserted. The Circuit (the 'W' plus the backside of the peaks) requires seven to nine days, while the 'W' (named for the rough approximation to the letter that it traces out on the map) takes four to five. Add another day or two for transportation connections.

Tour operators in Puerto Natales offer guided treks, which include all meals and accommodations at *refugios* or hotels. For a day hike, walk from Guardería Pudeto, on the

Parque Nacional Torres del Paine

Parque Nacional Torres del Paine

main park highway, to **Salto Grande**, a powerful waterfall between Lago Nordenskjöld and Lago Pehoé. Another easy hour's walk leads to **Mirador Nordenskjöld**, an overlook with superb views of the lake and mountains.

The 'W'   HIKING

The park highlights of **Mirador Las Torres**, **Valle Francés** and **Lago Grey** are included in this iconic multiday trek. To start the 'W'

from the west, catch the catamaran across Lago Pehoé to Mountain Lodge Paine Grande and do the first 'W' leg to Lago Grey before doubling back east. From this direction, the hike is roughly 71km in total.

Paine Circuit   HIKING

For solitude, stellar views and bragging rights over your compadres doing the 'W', this longer, one-way 112km trek is the way to go. This loop takes in the 'W,' plus the backside between Refugio Grey and Refugio Las Torres via challenging Paso John Gardner (1214m; closed seasonally). The landscape is desolate, yet beautiful.

Kayaking

A great way to get up close to glaciers. **Big Foot Patagonia** (☑ 61-241-4611; www.bigfoot patagonia.com; kayaking CH$66,000, ice hike CH$105,000; ☺ Oct-Apr) leads 2½-hour tours of the iceberg-strewn Lago Grey in summer.

Horseback Riding

Baqueano Zamora (p549) runs excursions to Laguna Azul, Valle Frances, Dickson glacier and more remote locations; to ride the Torres area, contact the activities desk at **Hotel Las Torres** (☑ 61-271-0050; www.lastorres.com; Estancia Cerro Paine).

Ice Trekking

A fun walk through a sculpted landscape of ice, and you don't need experience to go. Antares' Big Foot Patagonia (p554) is the sole company with a park concession for ice hikes on Glacier Grey, using the Conaf house (former Refugio Grey) as a starting point. The five-hour excursion is available from October to April, in high season three times per day.

🛏 Sleeping

The park has both fee camping, with some services, and free camping. Conaf allows visitors to stay just one night in free campsites. According to new regulations, all must be reserved in advance or hikers will not be permitted to hike sections of the trail that are not day hikes.

Refugios and some *domos* (yurts) rent equipment – tent (US$25 per night), sleeping bag (US$17) and mat/pad (US$7) – but quality may be inferior to your own gear. Small kiosks sell expensive pasta, soup packets and butane gas, and cooking shelters (at some campgrounds) prove useful in foul weather.

Refugio rooms have four to eight bunk beds each, kitchen privileges (during specific hours only), hot showers and meals. Should a *refugio* be overbooked, staff provide all camping equipment. Most *refugios* close by the end of April. Another expanding option is *domos*.

For bookings, Vertice Patagonia (www.vertice patagonia.com) looks after **Camping Paine Grande** (campsites per person US$10, incl full board US$60), **Camping Grey** (campsites per person US$8, incl full board US$58), **Campamento Lago Dickson** (campsites per person US$8; ☺ around Nov-Mar), and **Campamento Los Perros** (campsites per person US$8; ☺ around Nov-Mar). Fantastico Sur (www.fantasticosur.com) owns **Camping Las Torres** (campsites per person from CH$13,000, s/d deluxe platform camping US$50/80, incl full board US$130/240), **Camping Chileno** (s/d deluxe platform camping incl full board US$130/240), **Camping Francés** (campsites per person CH$13,000, s/d deluxe platform camping US$50/80, incl full board US$130/240; ☺ Oct-Apr), **Camping Los Cuernos** (campsites per person incl full board from CH$70,000) and **Campamento Serón** (campsites per person from CH$13,000; ☺ Oct-Apr).

Sites on the trekking routes that are administered by Conaf (www.parquetorres delpaine.cl) are free but very basic. They do not rent equipment or offer showers. These include: **Campamento Británico** FREE, **Campamento Italiano** FREE, **Campamento Paso** FREE, **Campamento Torres** FREE and **Camping Guardas**. Other private campgrounds include **Camping Pehoé** (☑ in Punta Arenas 61-224-9581; http://campingpehoe. com; campsites per person CH$11,000, s/d dome incl breakfast CH$60,000/90,000) and **Camping Río Serrano** (☑ toll free 600-510-0000; www.caja losandes.cl/turismo-y-recreacion/centros-turisticos/ rio-serrano; 6-person campsites from CH$3000, motorhomes CH$50,000).

Bring your passport or a copy for check-in. Rodents lurk around campsites, so don't leave food in packs or in tents – hang it from a tree instead.

ℹ Information

The main entrance where fees are collected is **Portería Sarmiento** (☺ dawn-dusk). **Conaf Centro de Visitantes** (☺ 9am-8pm Dec-Feb), located 37km from Portería Sarmiento, has good information on park ecology and trail status. **Administración** (☑ 61-236-0496; Villa Monzino; ☺ 8:30am-8pm) is also here. Erratic Rock (p549) has a good backpacker equipment list.

ℹ Getting There & Around

Shuttles (CH$4000) drop off and pick up passengers at Laguna Amarga, the Pudeto catamaran launch and Administración.

Catamaran **Hielos Patagónicos** (☑ 61-241-1133; www.hipsur.com; Pudeto; one-way/round-trip US$30/50; ☺ Sep-Apr) connects Pudeto with Mountain Lodge Paine Grande.

Hikers can take advantage of **Navegación Glaciar Grey** (Glacier Grey Cruise; ☑ 61-271-2100; www.lagogrey.com; adult/child round-trip CH$80,000/40,000, one-way CH$70,000/35,000; ☻Oct-Apr), a cruise that links Refugio Grey to Hotel Lago Grey with glacier viewing.

TIERRA DEL FUEGO

Foggy, windy and wet, Chile's slice of Tierra del Fuego includes half of the main island of Isla Grande, the far-flung Isla Navarino, and a group of smaller islands, many of them uninhabited. Only home to 8500 people, this is the least populated region in Chile. Porvenir is considered the main city, though even that status could be considered an overstatement. These parts exude a rough and rugged charm, and those willing to venture this far can relish the end-of-the-world emptiness.

Isla Navarino

Forget Ushuaia – the end of the world starts here. With more than 150km of trails, Isla Navarino is a rugged backpackers' paradise, with remote slate-colored lakes, mossy lenga forests and the ragged spires of the **Dientes de Navarino**. The only town, **Puerto Williams** (population 1680), is a naval settlement and the official port of entry for vessels en route to Cape Horn and Antarctica.

☉ Sights & Activities

Museo Martín Gusinde   MUSEUM
(☎61-262-1043; www.museomartingusinde.cl; cnr Araguay & Gusinde; donation requested; ☻9:30am-1pm & 3-6:30pm Tue-Fri, 2:30-6:30pm Sat & Sun, reduced hours low season) A well-crafted museum named for the Austrian priest and ethnographer who worked among the Yaghans from 1918 to 1923. Focuses on ethnography and natural history. Spanish-only signs. Public wi-fi is available in the library. See its Facebook page for visiting shows.

★Explora Isla Navarino   ADVENTURE SPORTS
(☎cell 9-9185-0155; www.exploraislanavarino.com; Centro Comercial 140B; ☻10am-1pm & 3-7pm Mon-Fri) ✈ This excellent outfitter runs kayak trips in a protected bay, trail running, biking and more, using a cool refurbished bus as base camp. There are also day-long and multiday trekking trips to the Dientes circuit, and others with bilingual guides with sat-phone and first-aid training. Works with small groups and incorporates local history into tours.

Dientes de Navarino   HIKING
This trekking circuit offers impossibly raw and windswept vistas under Navarino's toothy spires. Beginning at the Virgin altar just outside of town, the five-day, 53.5km route winds through a spectacular wilderness of exposed rock and secluded lakes. Fit hikers can knock it out in four days in the (relatively) dry summer months. Markings are minimal: GPS, used in conjunction with marked maps, is a handy navigational tool.

🛏 Sleeping & Eating

Lodgings often offer meals and can arrange tours of the island or airport transfers; expensive provisions are available at a few supermarkets in town.

Hostal Pusaki   GUESTHOUSE $
(☎cell 9-9833-3248; pattypusaki@yahoo.es; Piloto Pardo 222; incl breakfast d US$75, r per person without bathroom US$28) Patty welcomes travelers into this cozy home with legendary warmth and comfortable, carpeted rooms. Her excellent group dinners with fresh seafood are also available to nonguests.

Refugio El Padrino   HOSTEL $
(☎61-262-1136, cell 9-8438-0843; Costanera 276; campsites per person US$25, dm incl breakfast US$13) Friendly and conducive to meeting others, this clean, self-service hostel doubles as a social hub hosted by the effervescent Cecilia. The small dorm rooms are located right on the channel. Marked with flags, the camping area features a nice living room, a kitchen and hot showers, and is located in an alley near the waterfront Copec gas station several blocks away.

Diente de Navarino   COLOMBIAN $$
(☎cell 9-7586-7840; Centro Comercial s/n; mains CH$4000-12,000; ☻11am-midnight Tue-Sat) Pulsing with tropical beats, this Colombian cafe serves up big sandwiches, *arepas* (cornmeal cakes) and stews. The *bandeja paisa* feeds big appetites with flavorful beans and rice, fried plantains, egg and shoe-leather meat.

❶ Information

Tourist Information (www.ptowilliams.cl/turismo.html; Centro Comercial; ☻9am-1pm & 2:30-6pm Mon-Fri, 9am-1pm Sat) Offers city maps, day trek maps, as well as weather and route conditions for Lago Windhond and Dientes de Navarino treks. Located in a small kiosk.
Turismo Shila (☎cell 9-7897-2005; www.turismoshila.cl; O'Higgins 220; ☻9am-1:30pm & 4-8pm Mon-Sat) Outdoor store that sells

WORTH A TRIP

PARQUE NACIONAL BERNARDO O'HIGGINS

Virtually inaccessible, Parque Nacional Bernardo O'Higgins remains an elusive cache of glaciers. It can be entered only by boat. From Puerto Natales, full-day excursions (CH$90,000, lunch included) to the base of Glaciar Serrano are run by **Turismo 21 de Mayo** (☑ 61-261-4420; www.turismo21demayo.com; Eberhard 560; ☺8am-10pm Oct-Mar).

Ushuaia boat tickets and can arrange boating trips for glacier viewing.

❶ Getting There & Away

Puerto Williams is accessible by plane or boat. **Aerovías DAP** (☑ 61-262-1052; www.aeroviasdap.cl; Centro Comercial s/n; one-way CH$75,000; ☺9am-1pm & 2:30-6:30pm Mon-Fri, 10am-1:30pm Sat) flies to Punta Arenas (CH$75,000, 1¼ hours) daily Monday to Saturday from November to March, with fewer winter flights.

Transbordador Austral Broom (☑ 61-272-8100; www.tabsa.cl; reclining seat/bunk incl meals CH$108,000/151,000, 32hr) sails from the Tres Puentes sector of Punta Arenas to Puerto Williams about six times a month.

Porvenir

For a slice of home-baked Fuegian life, this is it. Spending a night in this rusted village of metal-clad Victorian houses affords you an opportunity to explore the nearby bays and countryside and absorb the laid-back local life. The king-penguin colony is usually accessed as a day tour from Punta Arenas. Stay at the wonderful **Yendegaia House** (☑61-258-1919; http://yendegaiahouse.com; Croacia 702; s/d/tr incl breakfast US$67/100/120; ☎) in a historic Magellanic home. Expect an abundant breakfast, views of the strait and spacious rooms with thick down duvets.

RAPA NUI (EASTER ISLAND)

Easter Island (Rapa Nui to its native Polynesian inhabitants) is like nowhere else on earth. Historically intriguing, culturally compelling and scenically magical, this tiny speck of land looks like it's fallen off another

planet. In this blissfully isolated, unpolished gem it's hard to feel connected even to Chile, over 3700km to the east, let alone the wider world. It's just you, the indigo depths and the strikingly enigmatic *moai* (giant statues) scattered amid an eerie landscape.

Dutch admiral Jacob Roggeveen landed here on Easter Sunday, 1722, creating the name. Designated Chilean territory in 1888, the island was run as a sheep *estancia*, confining indigenous Rapa Nui people to Hanga Roa until 1953. Finally, in the 1960s they regained access. Today's islanders speak Spanish and Rapa Nui, an eastern Polynesian dialect. Essential expressions include *iorana* (hello), *maururu* (thank you), *pehe koe?* (how are you?) and *riva riva* (fine, good).

Each February island culture is celebrated in the elaborate and colorful **Tapati Rapa Nui festival**. Peak tourist season coincides with the hottest months from January to March; off-season is comparatively quiet. Allow at least three days to see the major sites. Rapa Nui is two hours behind mainland Chile, six hours behind GMT (five in summer).

❶ Getting There & Away

The only airline serving Easter Island is **LATAM** (☑ 600-526-2000; www.latam.com; Av Atamu Tekena s/n; ☺9am-4:30pm Mon-Fri, to 12:30pm Sat). It has daily flights to/from Santiago and one weekly flight to/from Pape'ete (Tahiti). A standard economy round-trip fare from Santiago can cost US$450 to US$900.

❶ Getting Around

Insular Rent a Car (☑ 32-210-0480; www.rentainsular.cl; Av Atamu Tekena s/n; bicycles/motorbikes/cars from CH$15,000/30,000/50,000; ☺9am-8pm) rents scooters and motorcycles.

Hanga Roa

☑ 32 / POP 7750

Hanga Roa is the island's sole town, home to nearly all the Rapa Nui's hotels, restaurants, shops and services.

◉ Sights

Museo Antropológico Sebastián Englert   MUSEUM

(☑ 32-255-1020; www.museorapanui.cl; Sector Tahai; ☺9:30am-5:30pm Tue-Fri, to 12:30pm Sat & Sun) **FREE** This well-organized museum makes a perfect introduction to the island's

Rapa Nui (Easter Island)

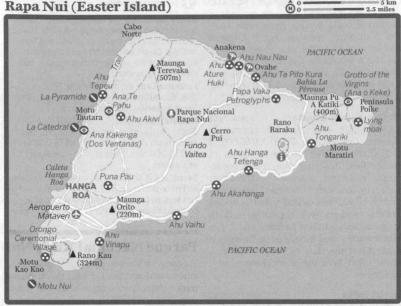

history and culture. It displays basalt fish-hooks, obsidian spearheads and other weapons, petroglyphs, circular beehive-shaped huts, funerary cists and a rare female *moai*. It also features replica Rongorongo tablets, covered in rows of tiny symbols resembling hieroglyphs.

Caleta Hanga Roa
BAY

Your first encounter with the *moai* will probably take place at **Ahu Tautira** (Av Policarpo Toro), which overlooks Caleta Hanga Roa, the fishing port in Hanga Roa at the foot of Av Te Pito o Te Henua. Many dive outfits operate out of here, and there are some ocean-kissed restaurants and cafes.

Activities

Opportunities abound for hiking, sailing and cycling. There's also excellent diving on Easter Island, with gin-clear visibility and a dramatic seascape. Try **Mike Rapu Diving Center** (☎32-255-1055; www.mikerapu.cl; Caleta Hanga Roa s/n; ⊗8:30am-7pm Mon-Sat, extended hours Dec-Mar). All operators also offer snorkeling trips to Motu Nui.

A network of trails leading to some of the most beautiful sites can be explored on horseback – expect to pay about CH$30,000 for a half-day tour. One reliable operator is **Cabalgatas Pantu** (☎32-210-0577; www.

pikerauri.com; Sector Tahai s/n; half-/full day CH$40,000/85,000; ⊗daily by reservation).

Tours

Plenty of operators do tours of the major sites, typically charging CH$45,000 for a full day and CH$25,000 for a half-day. Reputable agencies include **Aku Aku Turismo** (☎32-210-0770; www.akuakuturismo.cl; Av Tu'u Koihu s/n; ⊗8:30am-5pm) and **Kia Koe Tour** (☎32-210-0852; www.kiakoetour.cl; Av Atamu Tekena s/n; half-/full-day CH$15,000/20,000; ⊗8am-6pm Mon-Fri, 9-11am Sat & Sun).

★ Kava Kava Tours
CULTURAL

(☎cell 9-1066 9236; www.kavakavatours.com; full-day tours per person from US$90) Run by a young, knowledgeable Rapanui lad who offers private, customized tours as well as highly recommended hiking tours of Poike. Kava Kava's website is also a handy tool for researching the island.

Sleeping

Book well ahead for high season. Lodgings usually provide transportation from the airport.

Tipanie Moana
CAMPGROUND, HOSTEL $

(www.camping-tipaniemoana.cl; off Tu'u Koihu; campsite with/without tent CH$7000/6500, dm

CH$14,500, d with/without bathroom CH$35,000 /25,000; 🛜) If only all camping grounds in the world could be this clean, with spotless bathrooms, spacious shared kitchens and even racks to dry your clothes. There are also a few dorms and some great-value budget digs. The vibe here is quite lively, and while it's great for meeting fellow travelers, it may not be ideal for early risers.

★ **Cabañas Christophe** BUNGALOW $$
(📞 32-210-0826; www.cabanaschristophe.com; Av Policarpo Toro s/n; d CH$60,000-90,000, f CH$150,000; 🛜) The best-value option in Hanga Roa, this charming venue seduces those seeking character and comfort with four handsomely designed bungalows that blend hardwoods and volcanic stones. They're spacious, well appointed – think king-size beds, kitchen facilities and a private terrace – and inundated with natural light. It's at the start of the Orongo trail, about 1.5km from the center. Reserve well in advance.

★ **Hostal Tojika** GUESTHOUSE $$
(📞 cell 9-9215-2167; www.tojika.com; Av Apina s/n; d/tr/q CH$55,000/65,000/75,000; 🛜) A decent bet for budgeteers, Hostal Tojika has several rooms that are all different as well as a communal kitchen in a single building overlooking the sea. Some rooms lack privacy but get the job done. No breakfast is served but there's a small eatery at the entrance of the property.

 Eating

For self-caterers, there are a couple of supermarkets on Av Atamu Tekena.

★ **Ariki o Te Pana – Tia Berta** CHILEAN $
(Av Atamu Tekena s/n; mains CH$3000-10,000; ⊙10am-10pm Mon-Sat) Surrender to some melt-in-your-mouth seafood empanadas prepared mamma-style in this no-frills den.

★ **Te Moai Sunset** SEAFOOD, CHILEAN $$$
(📞 cell 9-4241-8603; www.facebook.com/temoai sunset; Sector Tahai; mains CH$12,000-16,000; ⊙12:30-10:30pm Mon-Sat; 🛜) Make this chic new restaurant your go-to spot in the late afternoon when the *moai* of Tahai are silhouetted against the setting sun just below your table. Dine alfresco on the hanging wicker chairs or next to one of the 2nd-floor windows for the best views. The chef puts a creative twist on Chilean staples; the ceviche is tangy perfection!

ℹ️ **Information**

Banco Santander (Av Policarpo Toro; ⊙8am-1pm Mon-Fri) Currency exchange (until 11am), and has two ATMs that accept Visa and MasterCard. Credit-card holders can also get cash advances at the counter during opening hours (bring your passport).

Farmacia Cruz Verde (Av Atamu Tekena; ⊙8:30am-10pm Mon-Sat, 9:30am-9pm Sun) Large and well-stocked pharmacy.

Hospital Hanga Roa (📞 32-210-0215; Av Simón Paoa s/n) Recently modernized. Emergency room visits cost a flat CH$25,000 to CH$30,000 plus the cost of any necessary procedures.

Sernatur (📞 32-210-0255; www.chile.travel/en; Av Policarpo Toro s/n; ⊙8:30am-5pm Mon-Fri) Has various brochures, maps and lists of accommodations. Some staff speak good English.

Parque Nacional Rapa Nui

Teeming with caves, *ahu* (stone platforms), fallen *moai* and petroglyphs, this **national park** (https://parquenacionalrapanui.cl; adult/child CH$54,000/27,000) encompasses much of Rapa Nui and all the archaeological sites. The admission fee can be paid in Hanga Roa or at the airport upon arrival. Respect the sites: walking on the *ahu* and removing or relocating rocks of archaeological structures are strictly taboo. Handle the land gently and the *moai* will smile upon you.

Near Hanga Roa, **Ahu Tahai** is a short hike north of town, lovely at sunset, with three restored *ahu*. About 4km north of Tahai, **Ahu Tepeu** has several fallen *moai* and a village site. On the nearby coast, **Ana Kakenga** has two windows open to the ocean. **Ahu Akivi** is the site of seven *moai*, unusual because they face the sea, though like all *moai* they overlook the site of a village. At the equinoxes their gaze meets the setting sun.

With white sands, clear water and leggy palms, Anakena beach is a stunning destination that abuts two major archaeological sites: **Ahu Nau Nau** and **Ahu Ature Huki**, the latter re-erected by Norwegian ethnographer Thor Heyerdahl and a dozen islanders.

Dazzling in scale, **Ahu Tongariki** has 15 *moai* along the largest *ahu* built against the crashing surf. A 1960 tsunami demolished several *moai* and scattered topknots, but the Japanese company Tadano re-erected *moai* in the early 1990s.

An ethereal setting of half-carved and buried *moai*, **Rano Raraku** is known as 'the nursery,' where *moai* were quarried from the slopes of this extinct volcano. It's worth a wander through the rocky jigsaw patterns of unfinished *moai*. There are 600, with the largest 21m tall. The crater holds a reedy lake under an amphitheater of handsome heads.

Visitors shouldn't miss **Rano Kau** and its crater lake, a cauldron of *tortora* reeds. Along a sea cliff 400m above, the fragile **Orongo Ceremonial Village** (◷9:30am-5:30pm) is where bird-cult rituals were performed. A cluster of boulders with petroglyphs depict Tangata Manu (the birdman) and Make Make (their god). Walking (7km) or biking is possible; take water.

UNDERSTAND CHILE

Chile Today

Modern Chile has gone through some seismic shifts, and we don't mean an earthquake. Change, ranging from lifestyle to globalization, arrives at record speed in the country with the highest average household income in Latin America. At the end of 2017, billionaire and former President Sebastián Piñera was elected for the second time to the country's highest office, with promises to bootstrap the economy by modernizing infrastructure and slashing taxes for businesses. By shifting to the right, Chile also has stepped in line with the latest regional trend.

The Changing Face of Chile

Drive the furthest reaches of Chile to the back roads of Patagonia and chances are that you will encounter a Haitian shop clerk and a Venezuelan running the popular roadside cafe. Far from the cosmopolitan capital, the country is undergoing a sea change. In the span of a decade, Chile has gone from a country with little immigration to one taking on similar proportions as the UK, relative to its population. Chile's half a million migrants add up to just 3% of its total. Yet, they do represent a cultural shift that makes some Chileans uneasy.

During the 2017 election campaign, nationalist sentiments were stoked on both sides. Both the right and left agree that Chile's 1970s-era immigration laws are well out of date. Outgoing president Michelle Bachelet posited that newcomers can fill needed roles as the country's aging population leaves the job market. Many of the country's immigrants are fleeing poverty and economic collapse.

Social progress is on the national agenda. Chile legalized civil unions for both same-sex and unmarried couples in January 2015. A bill recognizing transgender rights is in the works. Women have also taken to the streets to protest injustice, in areas ranging from femicide to abortion. Evolving from some of the most draconian abortion laws in the world, in 2017 Chile decriminalized abortion in cases of rape, fetal inviability and life-threatening pregnancies. While many would like to see women's rights go further, it has not been easy to shake this Catholic country from its staunchly conservative mores.

History

Early History

The discovery of a single 12,500-year-old footprint in Monte Verde, near Puerto Montt, marks Chile's earliest tangible roots. In the north, Aymara and Atacameño farmers and herders predated the Inca. Other early peoples include the El Molle and the Tiwanaku, who left their mark with geoglyphs; Chango fisher folk on the northern coast; and Diaguita who inhabited inland river valleys.

Shifting cultivators from the southern forests, the Mapuche were the only indigenous group to successfully hold off Inca domination. Meanwhile, the Cunco fished and farmed Chiloé and the mainland. In the south, groups such as Selk'nam and Yaghan long avoided contact with Europeans, who would eventually bring them to the brink of extinction.

Colonial Times

Conquistador Pedro de Valdivia and his men crossed the harsh Atacama Desert to found Santiago in the fertile Mapocho Valley in 1541. They set up the infamous *encomiendas:* forced labor systems exploiting the north's relatively large, sedentary population. In the south there was no such assimilation – the Mapuche fought European colonization for over three centuries. When the *encomiendas* lost value, agricultural haciendas or *fundos* (farms) run by South American–born Spanish took their place. These *latifundios* (estates) became the dominant force in Chilean society, with many remaining intact into the 1960s.

Revolutionary Wars & the Early Republic

Spain's trade control over the Viceroy of Peru provoked discontent among the colonies. Independence movements swept South America, with Argentine José de San Martín liberating Santiago in 1818. Under San Martín's tutelage, Chilean Bernardo O'Higgins, the illegitimate son of an Irishman, became 'supreme director' of the Chilean republic.

O'Higgins dominated politics for five years after independence, decreeing political, social, religious and educational reforms, but landowners' objections to these egalitarian measures forced his resignation. Businessman Diego Portales, spokesman for the landowners, became de facto dictator until his execution in 1837. His custom-drawn constitution centralized power in Santiago and established Catholicism as the state religion.

Expansion & Development

Chile's expansion began with its triumph over Peru and Bolivia in the War of the Pacific (1879–83), which added the nitrate-rich Atacama Desert, and treaties with the Mapuche, which added the southern Lakes District. In 1888 Chile annexed remote Rapa Nui (Easter Island).

British, North American and German capital turned the Atacama into a bonanza; nitrate prosperity also funded the government. The nitrate ports of Antofagasta and Iquique boomed until the Panama Canal (1914) reduced traffic around Cape Horn and the development of petroleum-based fertilizers made mineral nitrates obsolete.

Mining also created a new working class and nouveau riche, both of whom challenged the landowners. Elected in 1886, President José Manuel Balmaceda tackled the dilemma of unequally distributed wealth and power, igniting congressional rebellion in 1890 and a civil war that resulted in 10,000 deaths, including his own suicide.

The Struggle to Form & Reform

As late as the 1920s, up to 75% of Chile's rural population still depended on haciendas, which controlled 80% of prime agricultural land. As industry expanded and public works advanced, urban workers' welfare improved, but that of rural workers declined, forcing day laborers to the cities. The period from 1930 to 1970 saw a multifaceted struggle for agrarian reform.

During this period, the copper mines, a future cornerstone of Chile's economy, were North American–run. Elected in 1964, reformist president Eduardo Frei Montalva advocated the 'Chileanization' of the industry, giving the government 50% ownership of US-controlled mines.

Too reformist for the right and too conservative for the left, Frei's Christian Democratic administration faced many challenges, including from violent groups like the MIR (the Leftist Revolutionary Movement), which found support among coal miners and urban laborers. Activism also caught on with peasants, who agitated for land reform. As the 1970 election grew near, the Christian Democratic Party, unable to satisfy society's expectations for reform, grew weaker.

Allende Comes to Power

Socialist candidate Salvador Allende's Unidad Popular (Popular Unity or UP) coalition offered a radical program advocating the nationalization of industry and the expropriation of *latifundios*. Elected in 1970 by a small margin, Allende instituted state control of many private enterprises, creating massive income redistribution. Frustrated with slow reforms, peasants seized land and the country became increasingly unstable. Declining harvests, nationalization and the courting of Cuba provoked US hostility and meddling. By 1972 Chile was paralyzed by strikes supported by the Christian Democrats and the National Party.

After a failed military coup in June 1973, the opposition gathered force and a *golpe de estado* by relative unknown General Augusto Pinochet took place on September 11, 1973. The coup resulted in the death of Allende (an apparent suicide) and thousands of his supporters. Thousands of leftists, suspected leftists and sympathizers were apprehended. In Santiago's National Stadium, many detainees suffered beatings, torture and execution. Hundreds of thousands went into exile.

The Pinochet Dictatorship

From 1973 to 1989, General Pinochet headed a durable junta that dissolved congress, prohibited nearly all political activity and ruled by decree. In 1980, voters supported a new constitution that ratified Pinochet's presidency until 1989. Progress came in the form of a stabilized and prosperous economy. Nonetheless, voters rejected Pinochet's 1988 bid to extend his presidency until 1997. In 1989, 17 parties formed the Coalition of Parties for Democracy (Concertación de los Partidos por la Democracia; CPD), whose candidate Patricio Aylwin easily won the election that year. Aylwin's presidency suffered the constraints of the new constitution, but it did see the publication of the Rettig report, which documented thousands of deaths and disappearances during the Pinochet dictatorship.

In September 1998 General Pinochet was put under house arrest in London following investigation of the deaths and disappearances of Spanish citizens in the 1973 coup aftermath. Despite international uproar, both the Court of Appeals (in 2000) and the Supreme Court (2002) ruled him unfit to stand trial. Pinochet returned to Chile, where he died in 2006. His legacy remains extremely controversial among Chileans.

Resetting the Compass

The 21st-century governments across South America became increasingly left-leaning. In Chile the trend resulted in the 2000 election of moderate leftist Ricardo Lagos, followed by his 2005 successor, Michelle Bachelet. A watershed event, it marked Chile's first woman president, a single mother who had been detained and tortured under the Pinochet regime. Suddenly, conservative Chile looked a lot more progressive.

The first Bachelet presidency was plagued by divisions within her coalition (CPD), which made pushing through reforms difficult. Emerging crises like the chaotic institution of a new transportation system in Santiago, corruption scandals and massive student protests made her tenure a difficult one.

After 20 years of rule by the liberal CPD, in 2010 Chile elected as president the conservative billionaire businessman Sebastián Piñera from the center-right Alianza por Chile. Though Piñera enjoyed early popularity for his successful handling of the operation to rescue 33 trapped miners near Copiapó, his approval rating dipped sharply after the student-led educational protests (the 'Chilean Winter') in 2011. At one point, a 26% approval rating was the lowest of any post-dictatorship administration.

A Seismic Shift

In the early hours of February 27, 2010, one of the largest quakes ever recorded in history struck off the coast of central Chile. The 8.8-magnitude earthquake caused massive destruction, triggering tsunamis on the coast and Archipiélago Juan Fernández and claiming 525 lives. Many homes and highways were destroyed and insurance companies estimated billions of dollars' worth of damages. After some initial looting in affected areas, order returned quickly. Chile's Teletón, an annual charity fundraising event, raised an unprecedented US$39 million for the cause. Overall, the government was praised for its swift action in initial reparations, and the outpouring of solidarity demonstrated by the Chilean people was a boost to national pride.

Brave New World

In the first decade of the millennium Chile rose as an economic star, boosted by record prices for its key export, copper. When the world economic crisis hit, Chile remained in good standing. It was the first Latin country to enter into a free trade agreement with the US, though China is now its main trading partner. As hard as Chile tries to diversify, copper still accounts for a whopping 60% of exports. Yet, with diminishing demand for copper in China, the once-bulletproof Chilean peso is finally slipping in value.

Chile closed out 2013 by electing Michelle Bachelet once again to the presidency. Voter turnout was notably low for the first presidential election in Chile in which voting was no longer mandatory. The elections also brought young reform candidates to congress, such as Camila Vallejo and Giorgio Jackson, the former undergraduate leaders of the student protests.

Finding its way through financial highs and domestic snags, Chile may have to reset its compass to navigate its mounting social, ecological and economic issues; such complications are inevitable on the path to progress. In December 2017, Piñera was voted back in.

Culture

Centuries with little outside exposure, accompanied by an especially influential Roman Catholic Church, fostered a high degree of cultural conformity and conservatism in Chile. The Pinochet years of repression and censorship compounded this isolation. But the national psyche is now at its most fluid, as Chile undergoes radical social change.

The Catholic Church itself has gotten more progressive. Society is opening up, introducing liberal laws and challenging conservative values. Nowhere is this trend more evident than with the urban youth, with Generations Y and Z – the first to grow up without the censorship, curfew or restrictions of dictatorship – far more questioning and less discouraged by theoretical consequences. Authorities may perceive it as a threat, but Chile's youth is taking a stand.

The momentum has also influenced the provinces, particularly Magallanes and Aysén, to protest higher costs and general neglect by the central government.

Population

While the vast majority of the population is of Spanish ancestry mixed with indigenous groups, several moderate waves of immigrants have also settled here – particularly British, Irish, French, Italians, Croatians and Palestinians. Germans also began immigrating in 1848 and left their stamp on the Lakes District. The northern Andes is home to around 69,200 indigenous Aymara and Atacameño peoples. Almost 10 times that amount (around 620,000 people) are Mapuche. About 3800 Rapa Nui, of Polynesian ancestry, live on Easter Island. Over a third of the country's nearly 18 million people reside in the capital and its suburbs.

Lifestyle

Travelers crossing over from Peru or Bolivia may wonder where the stereotypical 'South America' went. Chilean lifestyle superficially resembles its European counterparts. A yawning gulf separates the highest and lowest incomes in Chile, resulting in a dramatic gap of living standards and an exaggerated class consciousness. Lifestyles are lavish for Santiago's *cuicos* (upper class), with swish apartment blocks and a couple of maids, while at the other end of the scale people live in precarious homes without running water.

Chileans have a strong work ethic, but are always eager for a good *carrete* (party). Young people usually remain dependent on their parents through university years and live at home through their twenties.

Generally, the famous Latin American machismo (masculine pride) is subtle in Chile and there's a great deal of respect for women. For gays and lesbians, Chile is still quite a conservative culture, with little public support for alternate lifestyles.

Arts

Literature

This land of poets earned its repute with Nobel Prize winners Gabriela Mistral and Pablo Neruda. Vicente Huidobro is considered one of the founders of modern Spanish-language poetry and Nicanor Parra continued the tradition until his death in 2018.

Chile's best-known export, contemporary writer Isabel Allende, bases much of her fiction in her native country. Other key literary figures include José Donoso, whose novel el *Curfew* narrates life under dictatorship through the eyes of a returned exile, and Antonio Skármeta, who wrote the novel *Burning Patience*, upon which the award-winning Italian film *Il Postino* (The Postman) is based. Luis Sepúlveda (1949–) has made outstanding contributions such as *Patagonia Express* and the novella *The Old Man Who Read Love Stories.*

Marcela Serrano (1951–) is praised as the best of current Latina authors. Pedro Lemebel (1952–2015) wrote of homosexuality, transgender issues and related subjects with top-notch shock value. Worldwide, Roberto Bolaño (1953–2003) is acclaimed as one of Latin America's best. The posthumous publication of his encyclopedic *2666* sealed his cult-hero status.

Cinema

Chilean cinema has proved dynamic and diverse in recent years. Addressing class stratification, Sebastián Silva's *La nana* (The Maid) won two Sundance awards in 2009. Then-twentysomething director Nicolás López used dark humor and comic-book culture to the delight of youth audiences with *Promedio rojo* (2005). Alex Bowen's *Mi mejor enemigo* (My Best Enemy, 2004) tells of not-so-distant enemies in a 1978 territorial dispute with Argentina in Tierra del Fuego. Andrés Wood's hit *Machuca* (2004) chronicles coming-of-age during class-conscious and volatile 1973. Acclaimed documentarian Patricio Guzmán explores the social impact of the dictatorship; his credits include the fascinating *Obstinate Memory* (1997).

The documentary-style film *180° South* (2010) uses a surfer's quest to explore Patagonia to highlight environmental issues. In 2012, two Chilean films won notable Sundance awards: *Violeta se fue a los cielos*, another Andrés Wood film, about the life of folk artist Violeta Parra, and *Joven y aloca-da*, a provocative coming-of-age story that was the cinematic debut of director Marialy Rivas.

The 2015 film *The 33* tells the story of 'Los 33' – the trapped Chilean miners – courtesy of producer Michael Medavoy of *Black Swan* fame. Sebastián Lelio's *A Fantastic Woman* took home the Academy Award for Best Foreign Language Film in 2018, with its star, Daniela Vega, becoming the first openly trans presenter in Oscar history.

Cuisine

Food

Chilean cuisine is built around fantastic raw materials: in the market you can get anything from goat cheese to avocados, fresh herbs and a fantastic variety of seafood. Though breakfast is meager – instant coffee or tea, rolls and jam – food and drink options get more appealing as the day progresses. At lunch, fuel up with a hearty *menú del día* (inexpensive set meal), with soup and a main dish of fish or meat with rice or vegetables. Central markets are an ideal place for these cheap and traditional meals; even the most basic eateries offer plenty of fresh lemon wedges and spicy sauces you can use to doctor up your plate.

Favorite sandwiches include the prolific *completo* (hot dog with mayo, avocado and tomato) and *churrasco* (steak with avocado and tomato). Empanadas are everywhere, from the classic *pino* (beef) to the gourmet seafood-stuffed varieties in coastal towns. Indeed, some of Chile's most delicious specialties are found at the beach, from *machas a la parmesana* (razor clams baked in Parmesan cheese and white wine) to aromatic seafood stews like *paila marina* and *caldillo de congrio* – the latter was famously Pablo Neruda's favorite. *Chupe de mariscos* is shellfish baked in a medley of butter, bread crumbs and cheese.

Everywhere in Chile, you'll find hearty classics like *lomo a lo pobre* (steak topped with fried eggs and french fries), *pastel de choclo* (baked corn casserole) and the artery-clogging *chorrillana* (a mountain-high platter featuring fries topped with onions, fried eggs and beef).

Drink

Chile and Peru both claim authorship of *pisco*, a potent grape brandy, and the famous *pisco* sour cocktail, in which *pisco* is mixed with fresh lemon juice and sugar. Many Chileans indulge in the citrusy aperitif at the start of a leisurely lunch or dinner. Young Chilenos drink *piscolas* (*pisco* and Coca-Cola) at parties.

With ample sunshine and moderate temperatures, Chile also has the ideal terroir for growing and producing wine. While cabernet sauvignon still reigns supreme, many foreigners fall in love with another red: Carmenere, originally produced in France and now produced almost exclusively in Chile. Check out www.winesofchile.org to learn more about Chilean wine regions and labels.

Kunstmann and Austral are Chile's best beers. A draft beer is called *schop*. *Bebidas* (soft drinks) are universally adored. Street vendors sell *mote con huesillo*, a refreshing nectar made with barley and peaches – it's a unique liquid snack you should try at least once.

Instant Nescafé is a national plague, though more cafes are starting to offer *cafe en grano* ('real' coffee).

Sports

Fútbol (soccer) is the most rabidly popular spectator sport. Most recently, the Chilean national team made an excellent showing at the 2014 World Cup. Tennis has gained ground, thanks to Nicolás Massú and Fernando González winning Olympic gold medals in 2004, and González' silver medal in 2008. Most young Chileans who can afford it go big on individual sports like surfing, skiing and mountain biking. Chilean rodeos proliferate in the summer, when flamboyantly dressed *huasos* (cowboys) compete in half-moon stadiums.

Environment

The Land

Continental Chile stretches 4300km from Peru to the Strait of Magellan. Less than 200km wide on average, the land rises from sea level to above 6000m in some areas, pocked with volcanoes and with a narrow depression running through the middle.

Mainland Chile, dry-topped and glacier-heavy, has distinct temperate and geographic zones, with the length of the Andes running alongside. Norte Grande runs from the Peruvian border to Chañaral, dominated by the Atacama Desert and the altiplano (Andean high plain). Norte Chico stretches from Chañaral to Río Aconcagua, with scrubland and denser forest enjoying increased rainfall. Here, mining gives way to agriculture in the major river valleys.

Middle Chile's wide river valleys span from Río Aconcagua to Concepción and the Río Biobío. This is the main agricultural and wine-growing region. The Araucanía and Lakes District go south of the Biobío to Palena, featuring extensive native forests and lakes. Chiloé is the country's largest island, with dense forests and a patchwork of pasturelands. Patagonia has indeterminate borders: for some it begins with the Carretera Austral, for others it starts in rugged Aysén, running south to the Campos de Hielo (the continental ice fields), and ending in Magallanes and Tierra del Fuego.

Flora & Fauna

Bounded by ocean, desert and mountain, Chile is home to a unique environment that developed much on its own, creating a number of endemic species.

In the desert north, candelabra cacti grow by absorbing water from the fog (*camanchaca*). Animals include guanaco (a large camelid), vicuña (found at high altitudes), and their domestic relatives llama and alpaca. The gangly ostrich-like rhea (called ñandú in Spanish) and the plump, scraggly-tailed viscacha (a wild relative of the chinchilla) are other unusual creatures. Birdlife is diverse, from Andean gulls and giant coots to three species of flamingo.

Southern forests are famed for the monkey-puzzle tree (araucaria or *pehuén*) and alerce, the world's second-oldest tree. Abundant plant life in Valdivian temperate rainforest includes the *nalca*, the world's largest herbaceous plant. Puma roam the Andes, along with a dwindling population of huemul (Andean deer) in the south. The diminutive pudú deer inhabits thick forests, *bandurrias* (buff-necked ibis) frequent southern pastures and *chucao* tweet trailside. Humboldt and Magellanic penguins seasonally inhabit the northwestern coast of Chiloé.

From the Lakes District to Magallanes, you'll find verdant upland forests of the widespread genus *Nothofagus* (southern beech). Decreased rainfall on the eastern plains of Magallanes and Tierra del Fuego creates extensive grasslands. Protected guanaco have made a comeback within Torres del Paine, and Punta Arenas hosts colonies of Magellanic penguins and cormorants. Chile's long coastline features diverse marine mammals, including sea lions, otters, fur seals and whales.

National Parks

Roughly 29% of Chile is preserved in over 100 national parks, national monuments, reserves and conservation areas. Among Chile's top international attractions, the parks receive over three million visitors yearly. Visits have doubled in the last decade. But while scene-stealing parks such as Torres del Paine are annually inundated, the majority of Chile's protected areas remain underutilized and wild. Parks and reserves are administered by the underfunded Corporación Nacional Forestal, with an emphasis on forestry and land management, not tourism. Visit **Conaf** (Corporación Nacional Forestal; Map p448; ☑ 2-2663-0000; www.conaf.cl; Paseo Bulnes 265, Centro; ⊙ 9:30am-5:30pm Mon-Thu, to 4:30pm Fri; Ⓜ La Moneda) in Santiago for inexpensive maps and brochures.

Chile has around 133 private reserves, covering almost 4000 sq km. Highlights include El Cañi near Pucón (the country's first) and Parque Tantauco on Chiloé (created by current president Sebastián Piñera).

Here are some popular and accessible national parks and reserves:

Alerce Andino Preserves stands of alerce trees near Puerto Montt.

Altos del Lircay A reserve with views of the Andean divide and a loop trek to Radal Siete Tazas.

Chiloé Features broad sandy beaches, lagoons and myth-bound forests.

Conguillío Mixed forests of araucaria, cypress and southern beech surrounding the active, snowcapped Volcán Llaima.

Huerquehue Near Pucón, hiking trails through araucaria forests, with outstanding views of Volcán Villarrica.

Lauca East of Arica, with active and

dormant volcanoes, clear blue lakes, abundant birdlife, altiplano villages and extensive steppes.

Los Flamencos In and around San Pedro de Atacama, a reserve protecting salt lakes and high-altitude lagoons, flamingos, eerie desert landforms and hot springs.

Nahuelbuta In the high coastal range, preserves the area's largest remaining araucaria forests.

Nevado Tres Cruces East of Copiapó, with a 6330m-high namesake peak and 6893m-high Ojos del Salado.

Puyehue Near Osorno, with fancy hot springs and a family ski resort. Has a popular hike through volcanic desert, up the crater, to thermals and geyser fields.

Queulat Wild evergreen forest, mountains and glaciers stretch across 70km of the Carretera Austral.

Torres del Paine Chile's showpiece near Puerto Natales, with an excellent trail network around the country's most revered vistas.

Vicente Pérez Rosales Chile's second-oldest national park includes spectacular Lago Todos los Santos and Volcán Osorno.

Villarrica Volcán Villarrica's smoking symmetrical cone attracts trekkers, snowboarders and skiers.

Environmental Issues

With so much recent growth in industry, Chile is facing a spate of environmental issues. Santiago is among the Americas' most polluted cities. Further afield, Chile's forests continue to lose ground to plantations of fast-growing exotics, such as eucalyptus and Monterey pine. Caught in a tug of war between their economic and ecological value, native tree species have also declined precipitously due to logging.

In the south of Chile, an area considered ideal for dams due to its many rivers and heavy rains, there's an ongoing battle between construction companies and environmental groups, with the government in the middle.

The continued expansion of southern Chile's salmon farms is polluting water, devastating underwater ecology and depleting other fish stocks. In 2017, Chile experienced the worst wildfires in its history, losing half a million acres of forest, with 11 people killed. Some attribute the extent of wildfires

to the deregulation of the forestry industry under the Pinochet regime.

SURVIVAL GUIDE

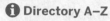 **Directory A–Z**

ACCOMMODATIONS

Chile has accommodations to suit every budget. Listings are organized in order of our preference considering value for cost. All prices listed are high-season rates for rooms that include breakfast and a private bathroom, unless otherwise specified. Room rates may be the same for single or double occupancy, yet there may be a price difference between a double with two beds and one matrimonial bed (often with the shared bed more expensive). Wi-fi is common.

In tourist destinations, prices may double during the height of high season (late December to mid-March), and extra high rates are charged at Christmas, New Year and Easter week. If you want to ask about discounts or cheaper rooms, do so at the reservation phase. Bargaining for better accommodation rates once you have arrived is not common and frowned upon.

At many midrange and top-end hotels, payment in US dollars (either cash or credit) legally sidesteps the crippling 19% IVA (*impuesto de valor agregado*; value-added tax). If there is any question as to whether IVA is included in the rates, clarify before paying. A hotel might not omit the tax from your bill without your prodding. In theory, the discount is strictly for those paying in dollars or with a credit card.

If trying to reserve a room, note that small lodgings in Chile are not always responsive to emails. Call them instead to make bookings more quickly.

ACTIVITIES

Climbers intending to scale border peaks like the Pallachatas or Ojos del Salado must have permission from Chile's **Dirección de Fronteras y Límites** (Difrol; Map p454; ☎2-2827-5900; www.difrol.cl; Teatinos 180, 7th fl). It's possible to request permission prior to arriving in Chile on the agency's website.

EMBASSIES & CONSULATES

All are located in Santiago, unless otherwise stated.

Argentine Embassy (☎2-2582-2606; http://csigo.cancilleria.gov.ar; Av Vicuña Mackenna 41, Centro; ⊗9am-2pm Mon-Fri; ⓜBaquedano)

Bolivian Embassy (☎2-2520-1704; www.consuladodebolivia.cl; Av Santa María 2796, Providencia; ⊗8:30am-12:30pm Mon-Fri; ⓜTobalaba)

SLEEPING PRICE RANGES

The following price ranges refer to high-season rates for rooms with breakfast and a private bathroom.

$ less than CH$50,000

$$ CH$50,000–CH$78,000

$$$ more than CH$78,000

Brazilian Consulate (📞2-2820-5800; http://cgsantiago.itamaraty.gov.br/pt-br; Los Militares 6191, Las Condes; ⏰9:30am-1pm Mon-Fri; Ⓜ Manquehue) Handles visas for Brazil; schedule an appointment online.

Canadian Embassy (📞2-2652-3800; www.canadainternational.gc.ca/chile-chili; Nueva Tajamar 481, 12th fl, Barrio El Golf; ⏰8:30am-12:30pm & 1:30-5:30pm Mon-Thu, 8:30am-1pm Fri; Ⓜ Tobalaba)

French Embassy (📞2-2470-8000; https://cl.ambafrance.org; Av Condell 65, Providencia; ⏰9am-noon Mon, Tue, Thu & Fri; Ⓜ Salvador)

German Embassy (📞2-2463-2500; www.santiago.diplo.de; Las Hualtatas 5677, Vitacura; ⏰9am-noon Mon-Fri)

Israeli Embassy (📞2-2750-0500; http://embassies.gov.il; Av Alonso de Córdova 5320, Las Condes; ⏰9am-4pm Mon-Thu, to 1pm Fri; Ⓜ Tobalaba)

New Zealand Embassy (📞2-2616-3000; www.nzembassy.com/chile; Isidora Goyenechea 3000, 12th fl, Barrio El Golf; ⏰10am-1pm Mon-Fri; Ⓜ Tobalaba)

Peruvian Consulate (📞2-2860-6700; www.consulado.pe/es/santiago; Antonio Bellet 444, Oficina 104, Providencia; ⏰8:30am-2:30pm Mon-Fri; Ⓜ Pedro de Valdivia)

UK Embassy (📞2-2370-4100; www.gov.uk/government/world/chile; Av El Bosque Norte 0125, Barrio El Golf; ⏰9am-1pm & 2-5:30pm Mon-Thu, 9am-1pm Fri; Ⓜ Tobalaba)

US Embassy (📞2-2330-3000; https://cl.usembassy.gov; Av Andrés Bello 2800, Las Condes; Ⓜ Tobalaba) You must schedule an appointment online prior to visiting the embassy for all non-emergency situations.

FOOD

The following price ranges refer to a standard main course.

$ less than CH$7000

$$ CH$7000–CH$12,000

$$$ more than CH$12,000

GAY & LESBIAN TRAVELERS

Chile is a very conservative, Catholic-minded country, yet strides in tolerance are being made. In 2015, Chile legalized same-sex civil unions.

Santiago has an active gay scene, concentrated in Barrio Bellavista. Movil H (Movement for the Integration and Liberation of Homosexuals; www.movilh.cl) advocates for gay rights. Guia Gay Chile (www.guiagay.cl) lists some Santiago clubs.

HEALTH

Medical care in Santiago and other cities is generally good, but it may be difficult to find assistance in remote areas. Public hospitals in Chile are reasonable but private *clínicas* are your best option. Outside of the Atacama Desert, tap water is safe to drink. Altitude sickness and dehydration are the most common concerns in the north, and sunburn in the ozone-depleted south – apply sunscreen and wear sunglasses. Chile does not require vaccinations.

INSURANCE

Signing up for a travel-insurance policy is a good idea. For Chile, a basic theft/loss and medical policy is recommended – note that some companies exclude adventure sports from coverage.

Worldwide travel insurance is available at www.lonelyplanet.com/travel-insurance. You can buy, extend and claim online anytime – even if you're already on the road.

INTERNET ACCESS

Most regions have excellent internet connections, wi-fi access and reasonable prices. Wi-fi may be slow in rural areas.

LEGAL MATTERS

Chile's *carabineros* (police) have a reputation for being professional and polite. Don't *ever* make the error of attempting to bribe the police, whose reputation for institutional integrity is high. Penalties for common offenses are similar to those given in much of Europe and North America. However, the possession, use or trafficking of drugs – including soft drugs such as cannabis – is treated very seriously and results in severe fines and imprisonment. Police can demand identification at any time, so carry your passport. Throughout the country, the toll-free emergency telephone number for the police is 133.

MAPS

In Santiago, the **Instituto Geográfico Militar** (📞2-2410-9300; www.igm.cl; Santa Isabel 1651, Centro; ⏰8:30am-1pm & 2-5pm Mon-Fri; Ⓜ Toesca) near Toesca metro station sells 1:50,000 regional topo maps; you can also buy them online. These are the best maps for hikers, though some are outdated. Conaf in Santiago allows photocopying of national park maps. JLM Mapas publishes regional and trekking maps at scales ranging from 1:50,000 to 1:500,000. While helpful, they don't claim 100% accuracy.

Drivers might find Copec maps by Compass (www.mapascompass.cl) useful, available in Copec gas stations.

MONEY

The Chilean unit of currency is the peso (CH$). Bank notes come in denominations of 1000, 2000, 5000, 10,000 and 20,000 pesos. It can be difficult to change bills larger than CH$5000 in rural areas. Solicit change with an apologetic face and the words *¿Tiene suelto?'* (Do you have change?).

Santiago has the best exchange rates and a ready market for European currencies. Chile's currency has been stable in recent years, with the value of the US dollar lower during peak tourist season. It's best to pay all transactions in pesos.

ATMs

Chile's many ATM machines, known as *redbanc*, are the easiest and most convenient way to access funds. Transaction fees can be as high as US$10, so withdraw larger sums to rack up fewer fees. Most ATMs have instructions in Spanish and English. Choose the option *tarjeta extranjera* (foreign card) before starting the transaction. You *cannot* rely on ATMs in San Pedro de Atacama, Pisco Elqui, Bahía Inglesa or in small Patagonian towns.

Cash

A few banks will exchange cash (usually US dollars only); *casas de cambio* (exchange houses) in Santiago and more tourist-oriented destinations will also do so.

Credit Cards

Plastic (especially Visa and MasterCard) is welcome in most established businesses; however, many businesses will charge up to 6% extra to cover the charge they have to pay for the transaction. Credit cards can also be useful to show 'sufficient funds' before entering another South American country.

Tipping

Restaurants It's customary to tip 10% of the bill in restaurants (the bill may include it under 'servicio').

Taxis Drivers do not require tips, although you may round off the fare.

OPENING HOURS

Hours given are generally for high season. In many provincial cities and towns, restaurants and services are closed on Sunday and tourist offices close in low season.

Banks 9am–2pm weekdays, sometimes 10am–1pm Saturday

Government offices & businesses 9am–6pm weekdays

Museums Often close Monday

Post Offices 9am–6pm Monday to Friday, to noon Saturday

Restaurants Noon–11pm, many close 4–7pm

Shops 10am–8pm, some close 1–3pm

POST

Correos de Chile (📞 600-950-2020; www.correos.cl), Chile's national postal service, has reasonably dependable but sometimes slow postal services. To send packages within Chile, sending via *encomienda* (the bus system) is much more reliable and efficient.

PUBLIC HOLIDAYS

National holidays, when government offices and businesses are closed, are listed here:

Año Nuevo (New Year) January 1

Semana Santa (Easter Week) March or April

Día del Trabajo (Labor Day) May 1

Glorias Navales Commemorating the naval Battle of Iquique; May 21

Corpus Christi May/June; dates vary

Día de San Pedro y San Pablo (St Peter and St Paul's Day) June 29

Asunción de la Virgen (Assumption) August 15

Día de Unidad Nacional (Day of National Unity) First Monday of September

Día de la Independencia Nacional (National Independence Day) September 18

Día del Ejército (Armed Forces Day) September 19

Día de la Raza (Columbus Day) October 12

Todo los Santos (All Saints' Day) November 1

Inmaculada Concepción (Immaculate Conception) December 8

Navidad (Christmas Day) December 25

SAFE TRAVEL

Compared with other South American countries and much of North America, Chile is remarkably safe. Petty theft is a problem in larger cities and bus terminals and at beach resorts in summer, so always keep a close eye on all belongings. Photographing military installations is strictly prohibited.

TELEPHONE

Call centers with private cabins are rapidly being replaced by internet cafes with Skype.

Chile's country code is 56. All telephone numbers in Santiago and the Metropolitan Region have eight digits; all other telephone numbers have seven digits except for certain toll-free and emergency numbers.

Cell-phone numbers have nine digits, starting with 9. The '9' is required when dialing from another cell phone, but not when dialing from a landline. If calling cell-to-landline, use the landline's area code. A '0' needs to be added to the beginning of an area code when dialing landlines from another landline, but not from a cell.

Cell phones have a 'caller pays' format. Calls between cell and landlines are expensive and quickly eat up prepaid card amounts.

Purchase a new SIM card from a Chilean operator such as Entel or Movistar. Then purchase phone credit from the same carrier in kiosks, pharmacies or supermarket check-outs. In Patagonia, Entel has much better coverage than other companies.

TIME

For most of the year, Chile is four hours behind GMT, but from mid-December to late March, because of daylight-saving time (summer time), the difference is three hours. The exact date of the changeover varies from year to year. Note that Southern Patagonia uses the summer time for the entire year. Easter Island is two hours behind Santiago.

TOILETS

Used toilet paper should be discarded in trash bins. Public toilets rarely provide toilet paper, so carry your own wherever you go.

TOURIST INFORMATION

The national tourist service, **Sernatur** (www.sernatur.cl) has offices in Santiago and most cities. Many towns have municipal tourist offices, usually on the main plaza or at the bus terminal.

VISAS

➨ Nationals of the US, Canada, Australia and the EU do not need a visa to visit Chile. Australian citizens must pay a US$117 'reciprocity fee' when arriving by air.

➨ Passports are obligatory and are essential for cashing traveler's checks, checking into hotels and other routine activities.

➨ Always carry your passport: Chile's police can demand identification at any moment, and many hotels require you to show it at check-in.

➨ If your passport is lost or stolen, notify the police, ask them for a police statement, and advise your consulate as soon as possible.

VOLUNTEERING

Experiment Chile (www.experiment.cl) organizes 14-week language-learning/volunteer programs. Language schools can often place students in volunteer work as well. The nonprofit organization Un Techo Para Chile (www.untechoparachile.cl) builds homes for low-income families throughout the country.

ⓘ Getting There & Away

ENTERING THE COUNTRY

Most short-term travelers touch down in Santiago, while those on a South American odyssey come via bus from Peru, bus or boat from Argentina, or 4WD trip from Bolivia. Entry is generally straightforward as long as your passport is valid for at least six months beyond your arrival date.

Chile's northern border touches Peru and Bolivia, while its vast eastern boundary hugs Argentina. Of the numerous border crossings with Argentina, only a few are served by public transportation. Most international buses depart from Terminal de Buses in Santiago.

Crossing the border into Argentina is the easiest option. Buses with international routes simply cross – no changing, no fees. Border outposts are open daylight hours, although a few long-haul buses cross at night.

Flights, cars and tours can be booked online at lonelyplanet.com/bookings.

AIR

Chile has direct connections with North America, the UK, Europe, Australia and New Zealand, in addition to neighboring countries. International flights within South America tend to be fairly expensive, but there are bargain round-trip fares between Santiago and Buenos Aires and Lima.

Santiago's **Aeropuerto Internacional Arturo Merino Benítez** (Santiago International Airport, SCL; ☎2-2690-1796; www.nuevopudahuel.cl) is the main port of entry. Some regional airports have international services to neighboring countries. Only LATAM flies to Rapa Nui (Easter Island). DAP Airlines flies between Patagonia and Tierra del Fuego.

BUS

Argentina

There are 19 crossings between Chile and Argentina. Popular crossings include:
➨ Calama to Jujuy and Salta
➨ La Serena to San Juan
➨ Santiago or Valparaíso to Mendoza and Buenos Aires
➨ Temuco to San Martín de los Andes
➨ Osorno to Bariloche via Paso Cardenal Samoré
➨ Puerto Ramírez to Esquel
➨ Puerto Natales to Río Turbio and El Calafate

Bolivia

Road connections between Bolivia and Chile have improved, with a paved highway running from Arica to La Paz. The route from Iquique to Colchane is also paved – although the road beyond to Oruro is not. There are buses on both routes, but more on the former.

Brazil

Long-haul buses leave from Santiago. The São Paulo–Santiago trip takes a punishing 55 hours.

Peru

Tacna to Arica is the only overland crossing, with a choice of bus, colectivo, taxi or train.

Car & Motorcycle

In order to drive into Argentina, special insurance is required (try any insurance agency; the cost is about CH$20,000 for seven days). There can be additional charges and confusing paperwork if you're taking a rental car out of Chile; ask the rental agency to talk you through it.

ⓘ Getting Around

AIR

Time-saving flights have become more affordable in Chile and are sometimes cheaper than a comfortable long-distance bus. LATAM (p461) and Sky (www.skyairline.com) are the two principal domestic carriers; the latter often offers cheaper fares.

BICYCLE

To pedal your way through Chile, a *todo terreno* (mountain bike) is essential – find them for rental in more touristy towns and cities. For cyclists, the climate can be a real challenge. Chilean motorists are usually courteous, but on narrow two-lane highways without shoulders, cars passing can be a hazard. Most towns outside the Carretera Austral have bike repair shops.

BOAT

Passenger/car ferries and catamarans connect Puerto Montt with points along the Carretera Austral, including Caleta Gonzalo (Chaitén) and Coyhaique. Ferries and catamarans also connect Quellón and Castro, Chiloé to Chaitén.

A highlight is the trip from Puerto Montt to Puerto Natales on board Navimag ferries. Book with Navimag (p531) far in advance. Note that this is a cargo vessel outfitted for tourism, not a cruise ship.

Known as the **Cruce de Lagos**, a 12-hour scenic boat/bus combination travels between Petrohué, Chile, and Bariloche, Argentina.

BUS

The Chilean bus system is fabulous. Tons of companies vie for customers with *ofertas* (seasonal promotions), discounts and added luxuries like movies. Long-distance buses are comfort-able, fast and punctual, with safe luggage holds and toilets.

Chile's biggest bus company is the punctual Turbus (p461), with an all-embracing network of services around the country. Its primary competitor is Pullman Bus (p461), with extensive services around Chile.

CAR & MOTORCYCLE

Having wheels gets you to remote national parks and most places off the beaten track. This is especially true in the Atacama Desert, Carretera Austral and Rapa Nui (Easter Island). Security problems are minor, but always lock your vehicle and remove valuables.

Driver's License

While an International Driving Permit (IDP) is not required, if you have one, bring it in addition to the license from your home country. Some rental-car agencies don't require an IDP.

LOCAL TRANSPORTATION

Towns and cities have taxis, which are metered or have set fees for destinations. *Colectivos* are taxis with fixed routes marked on signs. Rates are about CH$400 per ride. *Micros* are city buses, clearly numbered and marked with their destination. Santiago's quick and easy-to-use metro system connects the most visited neighborhoods.

TOURS

Adventure-tour operators have mushroomed throughout Chile; most have offices in Santiago and seasonal offices in the location of their trips. **Chilean Travel Service** (CTS; ☏ 2-2251-0400; www.chileantravelservices.com; Antonio Bellet 77, Oficina 101, Providencia; Ⓜ Pedro de Valdivia) has well-informed, multilingual staff and can organize accommodations and tours all over Chile through your local travel agency.

TRAIN

Chile's railroads blossomed in the late 19th century, but now most tracks lie neglected or abandoned. There is service throughout Middle Chile, however, and a *metrotren* service goes from Santiago as far as San Fernando. For details and prices check the website of TrenCentral (p462).

Colombia

POP 49,464,700

Best Places to Eat

➜ Mini-Mal (p580)
➜ Leo (p581)
➜ Platillos Voladores (p642)
➜ El Boliche (p615)
➜ Gringo Mike's (p595)
➜ Restaurante Itaca (p627)

Best Places to Stay

➜ San Pedro Hotel Spa (p614)
➜ Casa de François (p649)
➜ Hotel Click-Clack (p579)
➜ Casa del Farol (p601)

Why Go?

Soaring Andean summits, unspoiled Caribbean coast, enigmatic Amazon jungle, cryptic archaeological ruins and cobbled colonial communities. Colombia boasts all of South America's allure, and more.

The country's varied terrain is fertile ground for outdoor adventurers to dive, climb, raft, trek and soar. San Gil is the undisputed adventure capital, but Colombia boasts alfresco pleasures in all corners.

A wealth of ancient civilizations left behind a fascinating spread of archaeological and cultural sites throughout Colombia. Ciudad Perdida (the one-time Tayrona capital), built between the 11th and 14th centuries, is one of the continent's most mysterious ancient cities, arguably second only to Machu Picchu.

Equally alluring is the historical architecture. Led by Cartagena's extraordinarily preserved old city, Colombia offers an off-the-radar treasure trove of wonderfully photogenic cobblestoned towns and villages that often feel like they hail from a different century.

When to Go
Bogotá

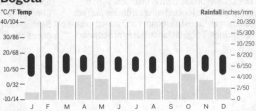

Dec–Feb Dry everywhere but the Amazon, but prices country-wide are at their highest.

Mar–Sep Bogotá, Medellín and Cali have suffer a rainy season in April/May.

Oct–Nov Low water levels in the Amazon mean excellent hiking. Prices everywhere are at their lowest.

Entering the Country

Major land crossings include the borders with Venezuela at Maicao, in the arid Guajira, and Cúcuta, on the far side of the Cordillera Oriental. The main crossing point to Ecuador is at Ipiales in the southern region of Nariño. Heading further south, there are adventurous river crossings into Brazil and Peru from Leticia in the Amazon.

While there is no land crossing to Panama, it is possible to cross via ship or private yacht from Cartagena or the idyllic Caribbean town of Capurganá.

TWO WEEK ITINERARY

Take a day or two in Bogotá, Colombia's Gotham City, admiring La Candelaria, the best of myriad museums, and world-class food and nightlife. Shake off the hangover a few hours north in the calming colonial villages of Villa de Leyva and Barichara, both miraculously preserved and picturesque. Take a day to walk the historic El Camino Real to Guane. Bus to San Gil to pick up the long bus ride to Santa Marta, from where you can access Parque Nacional Natural (PNN) Tayrona – linger on the park's otherworldly beaches for a few days. Continue southwest along the Caribbean coast to Cartagena, a postcard-perfect old city chock-full of colonial romance. It's another long bus ride to Medellín, where again you're faced with Colombia on overdrive: culture, cuisine and beer, *paisa*-style. Raise a toast to El Dorado and exit via Bogotá, bowled over by Colombia's hospitality.

Essential Food & Drink

Ajiaco Andean chicken soup with corn, many kinds of potatoes and a local herb known as *guasca*.

Aguardiente Alcoholic spirit flavored with anise.

Bandeja paisa Artery clogging tray of various meats, avocado, egg, plantains and rice.

Santafereño A cup of hot chocolate served with a chunk of cheese and bread.

Tamale Chopped pork with rice and vegetables folded in a maize dough and steamed in banana leaves.

Top Tips

➡ Don't book tight connections in Colombia – planes frequently get cancelled from smaller airports.

➡ Always check flight prices as well before booking a long-distance bus – sometimes there's not much difference.

➡ Don't be afraid to eat on the street – some of Colombia's freshest fruit and most tasty arepas (corn cakes) can be found curbside.

➡ Get a Colombian SIM card for cheap and fast data almost anywhere in Colombia.

FAST FACTS

Currency Colombian peso (COP$)

Visas Nationals of many countries don't need a visa. Otherwise, expect a nominal fee.

Money ATMs are widely available. Credit cards are accepted in many hotels and restaurants.

Capital Bogotá

Emergency 123

Languages Spanish; English in San Andrés & Providencia

Exchange Rates

Australia	A$1	COP$2140
Brazil	R$1	COP$804
Eurozone	€1	COP$3467
Japan	¥100	COP$2678
New Zealand	NZ$1	COP$1950
UK	£1	COP$3953
USA	US$1	COP$3032

For current exchange rates, see www.xe.com.

Daily Costs

➡ Dorm bed: COP$25,000–50,000; double room in a midrange hotel: COP$80,000–120,000

➡ *Comida corriente* (set meal): COP$8000–15,000; main dish in decent local restaurant: COP$20,000–30,000

Resources

This is Colombia (www.colombia.co/en)

Proexport Colombia (www.colombia.travel/en)

Colombia Reports (www.colombiareports.co)

Lonely Planet (www.lonelyplanet.com/colombia)

COLOMBIA

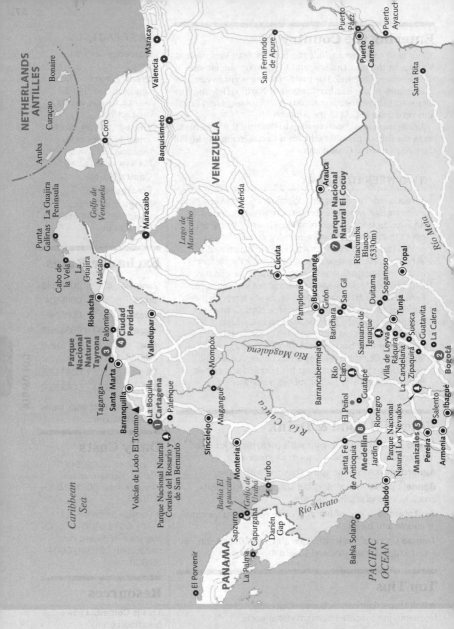

Colombia Highlights

1 Cartagena
(p610) Wandering the enchanting, perfectly preserved streets of this colonial city.

2 Bogotá (p574)
Visiting excellent museums, cozy bars and vibrant discos.

3 Parque Nacional Natural Tayrona
(p603) Soaking up the sun on the spectacular jungle-lined beaches.

4 Ciudad Perdida
(p606) Hiking through the dense jungle of the Sierra Nevada to these mysterious ruins.

5 Manizales
(p635) Trying your hand picking fresh coffee beans on a working farm in the Zona Cafetera.

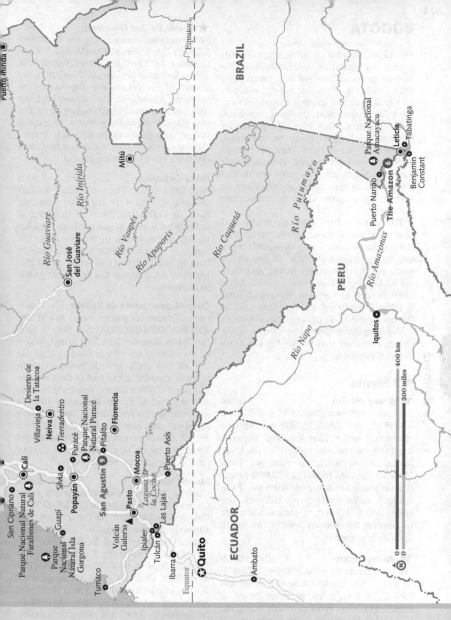

BRAZIL

PERU

ECUADOR

Puerto Inírida

Mitú

Río Inírida

Río Guaviare

San José del Guaviare

Río Vaupés

Río Apaporis

Río Caquetá

Río Putumayo

Parque Nacional Amacayacu

Leticia
Tabatinga
Benjamín Constant

The Amazon 6

Puerto Nariño

Río Amazonas

Iquitos

Río Napo

Equator

Desierto de la Tatacoa

Villavieja ● Neiva ●

Tierradentro ★

Puracé ●

Parque Nacional Natural Puracé

Florencia ●

Pitalito ●

Mocoa ●

Puerto Asís ●

Cali ●

Silvia ●

Popayán ●

Guapi ●

Parque Nacional Natural Farallones de Cali

Parque Nacional Natural Isla Gorgona

Tumaco ●

San Agustín 9

Pasto ●

Laguna de la Cocha

Volcán Galeras

Ipiales ● Las Lajas

Tulcán ●

Ibarra ●

Quito ★

Ambato ●

Equator

San Cipriano ●

400 km
200 miles

6 **Amazon** (p654)
Paddling through flooded forests and spotting pink dolphins.

7 **Parque Nacional Natural El Cocuy**
(p592) Enjoying a crisp day hike within sight of the glaciers.

8 **Medellín** (p623)
Soaring high above the city in a cable car before sampling its many bars and restaurants.

9 **San Agustín**
(p647) Galloping around the glorious countryside peppered with ancient sites and statues.

BOGOTÁ

1 / POP 7.4 MILLION / ELEV 2640M

Bogotá is Colombia's beating heart, an engaging and vibrant capital cradled by chilly Andean peaks and steeped in sophisticated urban cool. The city's cultural epicenter is La Candelaria, the cobbled historic downtown to which most travelers gravitate. Here, a potpourri of carefully preserved colonial buildings is home to museums, restaurants, hotels and bars, peppered amid 300-year-old houses, churches and convents. Nearly all of Bogotá's traditional attractions are here, radiating from Plaza de Bolívar, and gorgeous Cerro de Monserrate is just east.

The city's grittier sides sit south and southwest, where working-class barrios continue to battle their (sadly, deserved) reputations for drugs and crime. In the ritzier north you'll find boutique hotels, and well-heeled locals piling into chic entertainment districts such as the Zona Rosa and Zona G. Here, rust-tinted sunsets dramatically bounce off the bricks of upper-class Bogotá's Andes-hugging residential buildings – a cinematic ceremony that begins the city's uproarious evenings.

◎ Sights

★ Museo del Oro   MUSEUM
(www.banrepcultural.org/museo-del-oro; Carrera 6 No 15-88; adult/child COP$4000/free, Sun free; ◎9am-6pm Tue-Sat, 10am-4pm Sun) Bogotá's most famous museum and one of the most fascinating in South America, the Gold Museum contains more than 55,000 pieces of gold and other materials from all of Colombia's major pre-Hispanic cultures. The collection is laid out in logical, thematic rooms over three floors; descriptions are in Spanish and English.

★ Museo Botero   MUSEUM
(www.banrepcultural.org/museo-botero; Calle 11 No 4-41; ◎9am-7pm Mon & Wed-Sat, 10am-5pm Sun) FREE Even if you've never heard of Fernando Botero, you'll probably recognize some of his highly distinctive paintings of oversized (read: chubby) characters, including dodgy dictators, fleet-footed dancers, dogs and birds. Colombia's most famous living artist is also a prolific sculptor and his curvaceous bronze statues display equally generous girth.

★ Iglesia de San Francisco   CHURCH
(www.templodesanfrancisco.com; cnr Av Jiménez & Carrera 7; ◎6:30am-10:30pm Mon-Fri, 6:30am-12:30pm & 4-6:30pm Sat, 7:30am-1:30pm & 4:30-7:30pm Sun) Built between 1557 and 1621, the Church of San Francisco is Bogotá's oldest surviving church. In the atmospherically dark interior, with its extravagant pews and steady trickle of praying pilgrims, your eye is immediately drawn to the gilded, U-shaped 17th-century altarpiece, the largest and most elaborate of its kind in the capital.

Plaza de Bolívar   PLAZA
(btwn Calles 10 & 11) The usual place to start discovering Bogotá is the giant concrete Plaza de Bolívar, the heart of the original town. What it lacks in green foliage it makes up for in grandiosity. In the middle of the square is a bronze statue of Simón Bolívar (cast in 1846), the work of Italian artist Pietro Tenerani. This was the city's first public monument.

Casa Museo Quinta de Bolívar   MUSEUM
(www.quintadebolivar.gov.co; Calle 20 No 2-91 Este; adult/child COP$4000/2000, Sun free; ◎9am-5pm Tue-Fri, 10am-4pm Sat & Sun) Bringing a bit of the country into the middle of high-rise Bogotá, this lovely historic home-museum is set in a garden at the foot of the Cerro de Monserrate. The mansion was built in 1800 and donated to Simón Bolívar in 1820 in gratitude for his liberating services. Bolívar spent 423 days here over nine years. Rooms are filled with period pieces, including the liberator's sword. Less is said about its later days as a psychiatric institution.

Museo Nacional   MUSEUM
(National Museum; www.museonacional.gov.co; Carrera 7 No 28-66; adult/child COP$4000/2000, Sun free; ◎10am-6pm Tue-Sat, to 5pm Sun) Housed in the expansive, Greek-cross-shaped building called El Panóptico (designed as a prison by English architect Thomas Reed in 1874), the Museo Nacional explores Colombia's past via archeology, history, ethnology and art. The collection is spread across 17 galleries that will eventually be themed by floor – the museum is undergoing a major modernization that will last through to 2023.

Museo Santa Clara   CHURCH
(www.museocolonial.gov.co; Carrera 8 No 8-91; adult/child COP$4000/2000; ◎9am-5pm Tue-Fri, 10am-4pm Sat & Sun) One of Bogotá's most richly decorated churches, the Santa Clara

CERRO DE MONSERRATE

Bogotá's proud symbol – and convenient point of reference – is the white-church-topped 3150m **Monserrate peak**. It flanks the city's east, about 1.5km from La Candelaria, and is visible from most parts across the Sabana de Bogotá (Bogotá Savannah; sometimes called 'the valley'). The top has gorgeous views of the capital's 1700-sq-km sprawl. On a clear day you can even spot the symmetrical cone of Nevado del Tolima, part of the Parque Nacional Natural (PNN) Los Nevados volcanic range in the Cordillera Central, 135km west.

The **church** up top is a major mecca for pilgrims, due to its altar statue of the Señor Caído (Fallen Christ), dating from the 1650s, to which many miracles have been attributed. The church was erected after the original chapel was destroyed by an earthquake in 1917. You'll also find two restaurants (Santa Clara and San Isidro) and a cafe – make a day of it.

The steep **1500-step hike** – past snack stands – to the top (60 to 90 minutes' walk) is open from 5am (closed Tuesday). It's a popular weekend jaunt for *bogotanos*; on weekdays it used to be dangerous, as thefts occurred all too regularly, but an increase in police presence in recent years has curbed that considerably. If you're traveling solo or don't feel like walking, the regular *teleférico* (cable car) and funicular alternate schedules up the mountain from **Monserrate Station** (www.cerromonserrate. com; Sendero Peatonal Monserrate; round trip Mon-Sat from COP$20,000, Sun COP$12,000; ⏰5:30am-11:30pm Mon-Fri, to 6:30pm Sun). Generally, the funicular goes before noon (3pm on Saturday), the cable car after.

The funicular base station is a 20-minute walk up from the Iglesia de las Aguas (along the brick walkways with the fountains – up past the Universidad de los Andes), at the northeastern edge of La Candelaria. Safety along this route has also improved, although you're still best advised to make the trip at weekends, particularly in the morning, when many pilgrims are about.

is also its oldest (along with Iglesia de San Francisco). Deconsecrated in 1968, it was acquired by the government and is now run as a museum, with paintings by some of Colombia's most revered baroque artists. The church was once part of an adjoining Franciscan convent that was demolished in the early 20th century.

Plazoleta del Chorro de Quevedo PLAZA (cnr Carrera 2 & Calle 12B) No one agrees exactly where present day Bogotá was founded – some say by the Catedral Primada on the Plaza de Bolívar; others say here, in this wee plaza lined with cafes, a small white church and many boho street vendors (or hackysack players).

🎓 Courses

International House Bogotá LANGUAGE (☎1-744-1993; www.ihbogota.com; Carrera 13 No 72-23; ⏰7am-8pm Mon-Fri, to 1pm Sun) Offers group Spanish-language courses (US$230 per week for five four-hour morning classes, plus US$40 for materials) in its new location just north of Chapinero. Courses start

every Monday. Private tutors are US$30 per hour.

👉 Tours

⭐**Breaking Borders** CULTURAL (☎Diana 321-279-6637, Jaime 304-686-0755; Plaza del Chorro del Quevedo) Bogotá's most fascinating tour is through the Barrio Egipto with members of La 10ma gang, who have given up a life of crime in favor of this cultural-tourism initiative, started by the Universidad Externado de Colombia in cooperation with Impulse Travel (p578).

⭐**Bogotá Bike Tours** CYCLING (☎312-502-0554; www.bogotabiketours.com; Carrera 3 No 12-72; tours from COP$40,000, bike rental per hour/day COP$9000/45,000) In what is probably the best cycling city in South America, this is the best bike outfit. You can rent your own and take advantage of 375km of dedicated trails or choose from an array of tours that, on occasion, pedal into neighborhoods that would otherwise be no-go. Tours leave daily at 10:30am and 1:30pm from the La Candelaria office.

Bogotá

1
2
3
4

G

F

Carrera 3

Parque de la Independencia

Plaza de Toros de Santamaría (300m); La Macarena (350m)

Chapinero (4km); Zona Rosa (7km)

Universidades Station

Casa Museo Quinta de Bolívar (350m); Monserrate Station (400m)

Carrera 3

Calle 24

Calle 23

Calle 22

Calle 21

Calle 20

Carrera 5

Carrera 4

Calle 19 (Av 19)

Carrera 4A (Av 19)

CITY CENTER

Calle 18

E

See Inset

Carrera 7

Carrera 5

Carrera 7

D

Cine Tonalá (1.5km)

Carrera 8

27

Carrera 9

Carrera 10

Calle 22

Carrera 12

Calle 20

Carrera 13

Carrera 13A

Chía (30km)

Calle 22 Station

Calle 21

Av Caracas (Carrera 14)

Carrera 16

Av 19

Carrera 8

Calle 16

Carrera 9

Calle 15

Carrera 17

Calle 14

C

Inset:

200 m
0.1 miles
0

Carrera 3

Carrera 3A

Carrera 4

Carrera 4A

Carrera 5

Carrera 6

Carrera 7

Carrera 9

Calle 30

Calle 29

LA MACARENA

Calle 28

Calle 27

Calle 27 Bis

Calle 28

CENTRO INTERNACIONAL

Calle 13

Plaza de Toros de Santamaría

Parque de la Independencia

Punto de Información Turística

Av Jiménez Station

Sabana Station (1km)

Steps

4

23

61

A

B

1
2
3
4

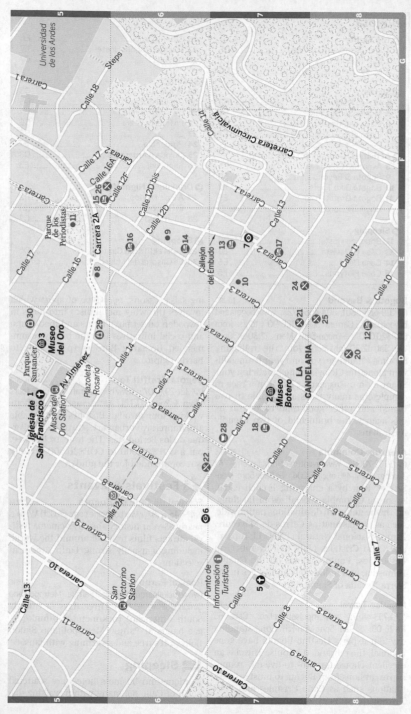

COLOMBIA BOGOTÁ

Universidad de los Andes

Carrera 1

Calle 18

Steps

Carretera Circunvalar

Calle 14

Calle 1

Calle 17

Carrera 2

Calle 16A

Calle 12F

15 26

Calle 17

Calle 16

Parque de los Periodistas

11

Carrera 2A

16

Calle 12D bis

Calle 12D

9

14

Callejón del Embudo

13

7

Carrera 2

17

Calle 13

Calle 17

Calle 16

8

Carrera 3

Calle 11

30

Museo del Oro

3

29

Carrera 3

10

24

Calle 10

Museo del Oro Station

Av Jiménez

Parque Santander

Iglesia de San Francisco

1

Carrera 4

21

25

LA CANDELARIA

12

Calle 14

Calle 13

Carrera 5

20

Calle 13

Plazoleta Rosario

Carrera 6

Calle 12

2

Museo Botero

Calle 11

28

18

Carrera 7

Calle 10

Calle 13

Carrera 8

Calle 12A

22

Carrera 9

Calle 9

Carrera 5

Carrera 10

San Victorino Station

6

Calle 11

Carrera 7

Punto de Información Turística

Calle 9

5

Carrera 8

Calle 8

Carrera 9

Calle 13

Carrera 10

Bogotá

Bogota & Beyond TOURS
(☎ 319-686-8601, 304-455-9723; www.bogotaand beyond.com; Carrera 3 No 12C-90; tours from COP$20,000; ⊙ noon-5pm Mon, 12:30-9:30pm Wed-Sat, 12:30-7pm Sun) Join the rollicking Septima Challenge (you and your team gallivant along the Ciclovía route practicing your Spanish on unsuspecting locals in a race to complete as many tasks as possible in two hours) and other good-time tours run by this agency, the brainchild of two friendly Australians.

Aventure Colombia TOURS
(☎ 1-702-7069; www.aventurecolombia.com; Av Jiménez No 4-49, oficina 204; ⊙ 8am-5pm Mon-Sat) ✎ Run by a charming French expat, Aventure Colombia specializes in far-flung, off-the-beaten-path destinations nationwide, such as the fascinating Cerros de Mavecure, Parque Nacional Natural (PNN) El Tuparro and Caño Cristales (July to November) in Los Llanos; Punta Gallinas on the Guajira Peninsula; and indigenous homestays in the Sierra Nevada of Santa Marta.

Impulse Travel TOURS
(☎ 1-753-4887; www.impulsetravel.co; Calle 65 No 16-09; ⊙ 9am-5pm Mon-Fri) Long-standing city-tour experts Destino Bogotá have gone national: the rebranded Impulse Travel is an excellent choice for two- to-five-day round-trip excursions from Bogotá to must-see destinations such as Caño Cristales and PNN Tayrona; playful city and area tours, includ-

ing salsa lessons, *tejo* (type of sport which involves throwing metal discs into holes in a wooden target box) nights and food tours; and social initiatives like the highly recommended Breaking Borders (p575) tour to Barrio Egipto.

Bogotá Graffiti Tour TOURS
(☎ 321-297-4075; www.bogotagraffiti.com; ⊙ tours 10am & 2pm) **FREE** A fascinating 2½-hour walking tour through Bogotá's considerable and impressive urban art, starting from Parque de los Periodistas. The tour itself is free, but a COP$20,000 to COP$30,000 gratuity is recommended for the guide.

✾ Festivals & Events

Festival de Cine de Bogotá FILM
(☎ 1-545-6987; www.bogocine.com; ⊙ Oct) With a nearly 35-year history, the city's cinema festival attracts films from all around the world, including a usually strong Latin American selection.

Rock al Parque MUSIC
(www.rockalparque.gov.co; Parque Metropolitano Simón Bolívar; ⊙ Aug) Three days of (mostly South American) rock/metal/pop/funk/reggae bands at Parque Metropolitano Simón Bolívar. It's free and swarming with fans.

⌂ Sleeping

Boutique and business hotels are scattered north of Calle 65, many within walking distance of the lively scenes of Zona G, Zona Rosa or Parque 93. La Candelaria is where most of Bogotá's attractions and budget lodgings are located – including many excellent hostels.

★**Masaya Bogotá Hostel**   HOSTEL $
(☑1-747-1848; www.masaya-experience.com; Carrera 2 No 12-48; dm from COP$40,000, r with/without bathroom from COP$170,000/120,000; @ 🛜) Taking flashpacker luxury to a new level, this large French-owned hostel has notably comfortable dorms, with privacy curtains, beanbags, and fluffy pillows and duvets, while the hotel-quality private rooms are very spacious and exhibit first-rate wardrobes and flat-screen TVs. You'll also find great common areas, piping-hot high-pressure showers and a wealth of cultural activities, including cooking classes.

★**Cranky Croc**   HOSTEL $
(☑1-342-2438; www.crankycroc.com; Calle 12D No3-46; dmCOP$36,000-54,000, s/dCOP$110,000/140,000, without bathroom COP$75,000/110,000; @ 🛜) 🏄 Perennial favorite the Cranky Croc, run by a friendly Aussie and styling itself as a backpacker hostel, has kept up with the times and doesn't lack space or natural light, which hits you as soon as you enter the brightly tiled lobby. The four- to 10-bed dorms feature lockers, reading lamps and individual electric outlets for device charging.

Casa Bellavista   HOSTEL $
(☑1-334-1230; www.bellavistahostelbogota.com; Carrera 2 No 12B-31; incl breakfast dm from COP$25,000, s/d from COP$70,000/80,000; @ 🛜) Shoehorned into hippy-dippy Callejón de Embudo, this small hostel in a historic house has plenty of antiquated character. Creaky hardwood floors lead to six- to nine-bed dorms that have their own bathrooms, and the three spacious private rooms are chock-full of detail such as original tile flooring – the standout is loft-style with a spiral staircase.

Botanico Hostel   HOSTEL $
(☑313-419-1288; www.botanicohostel.com; Carrera 2 No 9-87; dm COP$27,000, r with/without bathroom COP$130,000/110,000; @ 🛜) In a rambling, creaky wooden-floored house once called home by notable Colombian painter Gonzalo Ariza, this new-in-2017 Candelaria offering oozes colonial character and charm. Original touches like wood-beamed ceilings and optimal hang spaces (fire-lit lounge, jungly garden, supreme rooftop with city and mountain views) make leaving difficult; a

spacious private room with wood-burning stove doesn't help, either.

★**12:12 Hostel**   HOSTEL $$
(☑1-467-2656; www.1212hostels.com; Calle 67 No 4-16; dm incl breakfast COP$35,000-48,000, r/ste COP$98,000/138,000; @ 🛜) 🏄 This artsy hostel epitomizes the cutting-edge Chapinero Alto scene: recycled materials such as discarded bikes, which are mounted like fun-house art installations, and tossed-aside books, which pepper the walls instead of wallpaper, are the backbone of this design-forward choice.

The colorful dorm beds are some of Bogotá's most comfortable, with reading lamps, privacy curtains and cozy bedding; the big, modern communal kitchen and slate bathrooms are above and beyond for a hostel.

Casa Platypus   GUESTHOUSE $$
(☑1-281-1801; www.casaplatypusbogota.com; Carrera 3 No 12F-28; dm/s/d/tr COP$55,000/160,000/182,000/220,000; @ 🛜) Looking like a colonial home brought over from Villa de Leyva, this upscale guesthouse is an ideal flashpacker choice right in the heart of Bogotá. The interior patio exudes charm, the common areas (a handsome breakfast room and a relaxing terrace) invite guest interaction, and the small but tidy rooms come with comfy beds equipped with deluxe headboards.

★**Hotel Click-Clack**   BOUTIQUE HOTEL $$$
(☑1-743-0404; www.clickclackhotel.com; Carrera 11 No 93-77; r incl breakfast COP$379,000-688,000; ❄ @ 🛜) This high-design haven, the boutique hotel of choice for Colombia's trendsetters, has a sophisticated aesthetic vaguely based around vintage TVs and photographic equipment. The best of the five room sizes (extra small to large) are the 2nd-floor mediums, which open onto spacious patios with small patches of grass and a vertical garden.

There's no spa or fitness center: everything here – from Apache, the high-class miniburger bar on the roof, with stupendous views, to 100 Grams, the trendy basement restaurant where everything is served in 100g portions (like larger-size tapas) – is focused on a good time, not on R & R. There's a Lust kit and a Hangover kit in each room, depending on how things go.

Casa Legado   BOUTIQUE HOTEL $$$
(☑318-715-9519; www.casalegadobogota.com; Carrera 8 No 69-60; r incl breakfast COP$650,000-1,300,000; Ⓟ @ 🛜) Find your way to this

renovated 1950s art deco home in Quinta Camacho and you'll fall in love with your host, Helena, and her seven-room dream pad. An exotic fruit garden, a communal dining room and a guest-use kitchen, plus an ivy-draped courtyard, are perfect companions to stylish rooms, decked out according to the personalities of Helena's nieces and nephews.

Orchids
BOUTIQUE HOTEL **$$$**

(📱1-745-5438; www.theorchidshotel.com; Carrera 5 No 10-55; r/ste incl breakfast COP$360,000/680,000; @🖥) Behind a mauve facade hides La Candelaria's most discerning and upscale choice, an intimate six-room boutique hotel bursting with historic character. Every generously proportioned room has a different design scheme: period furniture (some original to the historic mansion), four-poster beds, porcelain sinks and thick wooden writing desks are just some of the features.

Casa Deco
BOUTIQUE HOTEL **$$$**

(📱1-282-8640; www.hotelcasadeco.com; Calle 12C No 2-36; s/d incl breakfast from COP$210,000/ 252,000; @🖥) A 22-room gem run by an Italian emerald dealer, this discerning option is a serious step up from the sea of hostels surrounding it.

Rooms come in seven bright colors and are laced with bespoke hardwood art deco–style furniture, desks, futon beds and newly installed soundproof doors and windows.

🍴 Eating

Fusion is the watchword of many Bogotá restaurateurs, who are running Mediterranean, Italian, Californian or pan-Asian influences through typical Colombian dishes, but reinvented homegrown cuisine is on the rise.

The best dining destinations include Zona Rosa, Nogal and Zona G; also recommended is the slightly boho scene in La Macarena, just north of La Candelaria.

Arbol de Pan
BAKERY **$**

(www.facebook.com/panaderiaarboldelpan; Calle 66 No 4A-35; pastries COP$2500-7800; ⊙8am-8pm Mon-Fri, to 6pm Sat; 🖥) You'll feel like your sweet nighttime dreams have extended into breakfast at this all-natural bakery and pastry shop that has an array of just-baked breads and a slew of delectable pastries. There's also heartier breakfast fare (COP$9000 to COP$15,000), such as lovely prosciutto-wrapped asparagus and that old hipster standby: avocado and poached egg on toast.

La Puerta Falsa
FAST FOOD **$**

(www.restaurantelapuertafalsa.inf.travel; Calle 11 No 6-50; snacks COP$6000-8000; ⊙7am-9pm Mon-Sat, 8am-7pm Sun) If it ain't broke, don't fix it. Maybe that's why, after two centuries, the 'False Door' is still successfully knocking out the same one-page menu, dominated by two epoch-spanning snacks: *tamales,* and the practically sacred *chucula y almojábanas,* a simple plate of sweet bread and soft cheese accompanied by a cup of steaming hot chocolate. On an average morning you'll have to wait patiently for a table outside this diminutive two-story cafe–pastry shop just off the Plaza de Bolívar. Inside, pull up a small stool at an even smaller table and partake in a tasty piece of Bogotá history.

Canasto Picnic Bistró
COLOMBIAN **$$**

(www.facebook.com/canastopicnicbistro; Calle 88 No 13A-51; breakfast COP$4100-15,900, mains COP$16,100-34,000; ⊙noon-10pm Mon, 7am-10pm Tue-Sat, 7am-6pm Sun; 🖥🍴) 🌿 This artistically driven and sustainably minded bistro near Parque El Virrey is all the rage in the city. Breakfast items like avocado toast with smoked trout and a long and colorful list of organic egg dishes are perfectly accompanied by strong espresso served in gorgeous blue ceramic cups from Chía's Santa Paloma.

⭐ Mini-Mal
COLOMBIAN **$$**

(📱1-347-5464; www.mini-mal.org; Carrera 4A No 57-52; mains COP$27,900-38,000; ⊙noon-3pm & 7-10pm Mon-Thu, noon-11pm Fri & Sat; 🖥) 🌿 You'll be hard-pressed to find a more creative Colombian menu than at this excellent Chapinero Alto hot spot, which has resurrected some of the country's more interesting regional ingredients – sustainably sourced and fiercely artisan – and breathed new life into contemporary Colombian cuisine. The menu is an intriguing triumvirate of Caribbean, Altiplano and jungle-sourced food.

Sant Just
FRENCH **$$**

(📱314-478-1460; www.santjustbogota.com; Calle 16A No 2-73; mains COP$20,000-37,000; ⊙11am-4pm Mon-Wed, to 8pm Thu & Fri, 11:30am-4:30pm Sat; 🖥) 🌿 The wonderful French-owned cafe Sant Just serves a daily changing menu of Colombian-leaning French fare. Whatever the kitchen makes that day – fresh juices, sustainably caught seafood, wonderful lamb served alongside previously out-of-favor veggies such as *cubio* (an Andean root) – it nails it, both in presentation and in the comfort-food stakes. Expect a wait.

De Una Travel Bar SOUTH AMERICAN **$$**
(📱1-806-6791; www.deunatravelbar.com; Calle 11 No 2-98; mains COP$15,000-23,000; ⏱10:30am-10pm Mon-Sat, to 8pm Sun; 🛜📷) With a menu written on a suitcase hung on the door and well-thumbed travel books scattered within, it's no surprise that this cafe is a travelers' favorite. The diminutive space has an open prep area that rustles up a pleasant sampling of South American food, supported by cold beer, fine cocktails and outstanding service.

Quinua y Amaranto VEGETARIAN **$$**
(www.quinuayamaranto.com.co; Calle 11 No 2-95; set lunch COP$17,000; ⏱8:30am-7pm Tue-Fri, to 4pm Mon & Sat; 📷) This sweet spot – run by women in an open-front kitchen – offers tasty set lunches, as well as empanadas, salads and coffee. Fare is all vegetarian during the week, but there's often *ajiaco* (chicken, corn and potato soup) on weekends. A small selection of coca leaves, baked goods and tempting chunks of artisanal cheese (on Saturday) rounds out the cozy offerings.

Capital Cocina COLOMBIAN **$$**
(Calle 10 No 2-99; mains COP$23,000-34,000; ⏱12:15-3pm & 6:45-9pm Mon, to 10pm Tue-Fri, 12:15-3pm & 6-10pm Sun; 🛜) Prepare to fight for tables at this quaint cafe serving a few takes on simple Colombian comfort food – fish of the day, pork chop, steak, grilled chicken – that are in fact anything but simple. The daily menu (COP$20,500) is a three-course steal considering the quality of chef Juan

Pablo's food; and there are artisanal beers, decent wines and single-origin coffee.

⭐**Leo** COLOMBIAN **$$$**
(📱1-286-7091; http://restauranteleo.com; Calle 27B No 6-75; mains COP$52,000-87,000; ⏱noon-3:30pm & 7-11pm Mon-Sat; 🛜) Chef Leo Espinosa is the culinary priestess for innovative Colombian fine dining. Her epic 12-course tasting menu (COP$210,000) paired with wine and artisanal beverages (COP$280,000) is a belt-loosening, multihour journey through exotic regional ingredients, many of which are ignored by most Colombian kitchens. A meal here is revelatory, with bold colors and striking flavors unlike those of anything previously plated.

In 2018 Leo crept into the prestigious World's Best Restaurants list (sponsored by *Restaurant* magazine) at No 99, the only Colombian restaurant to do so.

⭐**Andrés Carne de Res** COLOMBIAN **$$$**
(📱1-861-2233; www.andrescarnederes.com; Calle 3 No 11A-56, Chía; steaks COP$49,600-59,000, cover Fri & Sat COP$21,000; ⏱11am-3am Thu-Sat, to midnight Sun; 🛜) This legendary steakhouse blows everyone – even repeat visitors – away with its all-out fun atmosphere. The 75-page menu of classics like *arepas* (corn cakes) and ceviches, and pages of succulent steaks (some portioned to serve as many as seven) is totally overwhelming; *al trapo* (chargrilled beef tenderloin) is recommended if you need some help narrowing things down.

COLOMBIA BOGOTÁ

BOGOTÁ CHAINS

Bogotá has some surprisingly worthy chain eateries, many of which once dominated their speciality before the rise of movements like Third Wave coffee, gourmet burgers and craft beer. The best of the lot by a landslide is **Wok** (www.wok.com.co; Calle 93B No 12-28, Parque 93; mains COP$15,900-34,900; ⏱noon-10:30pm Mon-Sat, to 9pm Sun; 🛜); its excellently executed, sustainably sourced Asian-fusion food is some of the best you'll find in South America. Other Bogotá-born staples to keep an eye out for include **El Corral** (www.elcorral.com; Calle 85 No 13-77; burgers from COP$19,900; ⏱24hr; 🛜), with excellent fast-food hamburgers; **Crepes & Waffles** (www.crepesywaffles.com.co; Carrera 9 No 73-33; mains COP$10,900-28,400; ⏱11:45am-9:30pm Mon-Thu, to 10pm Fri & Sat, to 9pm Sun; 🛜), a do-it-all, diner-like chain; **Bogotá Beer Company** (www.bogotabeercompany.com; Calle 85 No 13-06; pints COP$16,900; ⏱12:30pm-2am Sun-Wed, to 3am Thu-Sat; 🛜), with corporate craft-beer pubs; and **Juan Valdez** (www.juanvaldezcafe.com; Centro Cultural Gabriel García Márquez, Carrera 6 No 11-20; coffee COP$3600-7900; ⏱8am-8pm Mon, 7am-8pm Tue-Sat, 9am-6pm Sun; 🛜), a Starbucks-like coffee chain – and there are more where those came from (La Hamburguesería for burgers, Julia for authentic Italian pizza, Tostao' for coffee and bakery items – you get the idea.)

You'll find branches in most neighborhoods, particularly in the north, and a few have even gone international. They're a solid bet for a quick, dependable and consistent bite, pint or pick-me-up.

DON'T MISS

CICLOVÍA - BOGOTÁ'S BIKING BONANZA

If there's one area in which Bogota is a world leader, it's urban cycling. The metropolis is credited with initiating the world's first **ciclovía** (www.idrd.gov.co) in 1974, a weekly closedown of 120km of arterial city streets to motorized traffic between 7am and 2pm on Sunday. The much-copied two-wheeled happening regularly attracts around two million participants – 25% of Bogota's population!

Today, the *ciclovía* has evolved into Bogota's biggest street party, with thoroughfares brimming with fruit-juice carts, food vendors (*obleas! majorca! canelazo!*), performers, bike-repair stands, kids' cycling schools and literally hundreds of bicycles of all shapes and sizes.

Aside from bikes, the *ciclovía* is open to strollers, wheelchairs, scooters, skateboards, pedestrians and anything else without a motor.

★**Prudencia** INTERNATIONAL **$$$**
(📱1-394-1678; www.prudencia.net; Carrera 2 No 11-34; prix fixe COP$45,000-56,000; ⊘noon-4pm Mon-Sat; 🐿🍽) 🍴 This doozy of dining and design is run by Colombian-American husband-and-wife team Mario and Meghan. The sunlit canopy, an unorthodox marriage of bamboo and steel designed by noted architect Simón Vélez, is a striking setting for the weekly changing four-course menus (vegetarian or non), forged with local ingredients and an often wood-fired international flair.

Agave Azul MEXICAN **$$$**
(📱315-277-0329; www.restauranteagaveazul.blog spot.com.co; Carrera 3A No 26B-52; tasting menu COP$75,000; ⊘noon-3pm & 6:30-10pm Tue-Fri, 1-4pm & 7-10pm Sat; 🐿) This outstanding restaurant is a trip, both literally and figuratively, through truly authentic Mexican cuisine by way of Chicago, New York and Oaxaca. Chef Tatiana Navarro has no set menu – just a daily open-ended tasting menu – and no sign. Agave Azul is hidden inside a residential La Macarena home, offering a handful of tables and highly personalized service. Advance reservations essential.

🍷 Drinking & Nightlife

Atmospheric 300-year-old homes with corner fireplaces and old tile floors dot La Candelaria. Watering holes turn up the trend as you head north: especially in Chapinero Alto, Zona Rosa and Parque 93. Bohemian barrios west of Av Caracas, such as Parkway in La Soledad, have become stomping grounds for craft brewing and other hipster trends in the last few years.

★**Azahar Café** CAFE
(www.azaharcoffee.com; Calle 93B No 13-91; coffee COP$4000-16,000; ⊘7am-8pm Mon-Fri,

9am-8pm Sat & Sun; 🐿) 🍴 Possibly the finest shrine to coffee in Colombia, the recently amplified Azahar exudes taste, expertise and an undying passion for the country's second-most-famous homegrown product (after cocaine). Busy baristas work behind a huge counter like alchemists in a chemistry lab, experimenting with French press, Chemex, pour-over and espresso. The attention to detail jumps out of the cup.

★**El Mono Bandido** PUB
(www.elmonobandido.com; Carrera 10A No 69-38; pints COP$9500-10,500; ⊘4pm-midnight Mon-Wed, to 1am Thu-Sat, noon-8pm Sun; 🐿) Having commandeered a Quinta Camacho mansion and flipped it into one of Bogotá's most cinematic pubs, El Mono Bandido has atmosphere in spades. Enjoy house-brewed craft suds inside the two-floor space teeming with exposed, loose-end pipes illuminated with Edison lighting, or at one of a handful of oil-candle-lit tables in the surrounding garden.

★**Cine Tonalá** CLUB
(www.cinetonala.co; Carrera 6A No 35-37; films COP$7000; ⊘noon-2:30am Tue & Thu-Sat, to 8pm Wed; 🐿) Bogotá's only independent cinema champions Latin and Colombian films and international cult classics, but this Mexico City import refuses to be categorized. The multifaceted cultural center, set in a renovated 1930s La Merced mansion, is a shelter for artistic refugees, who retreat here for a very hip bar scene, excellent Mexican food and rousing club nights from Thursday to Saturday.

Amor Perfecto CAFE
(www.amorperfectocafe.net; Carrera 4 No 66-46; ⊘8am-9pm Mon-Sat, 10am-7pm Sun; 🐿) Pick your single-origin regional Colombian specialty bean, select your method of preparation (Chemex, Siphon, AeroPress or French

press), and let the highly knowledgeable and national-champion baristas at this hip Chapinero Alto coffeehouse do the rest. You can also pop in for tastings and courses.

Theatron
GAY

(www.theatron.co; Calle 58 No 10-32; ☉9pm-5am Thu-Sat) On a small road between Carreras 9 and 13 in the heart of Chapinero, the classic Theatron is carved from a huge film house. It draws a gay and straight crowd – some 3000 people on weekends – spread between its eight environments. Some areas are men-only.

Taller de Té
TEAHOUSE

(www.tallerdete.com; Calle 60A No 3A-38; tea COP$4000-10,000; ☉10am-8pm Mon-Sat; 🛜) 🍃 This adorable cafe is unique in Bogotá for serious tea. Owner Laura sources more than 70 teas and infusions from plantations around the world and blends them with local herbs, flowers, spices, teas and traditional plants. There are organic, vegetarian and vegan light bites from trusted culinary artisans around Colombia to pair with them.

A Seis Manos
BAR

(www.aseismanos.com.co; Calle 22 No 8-60; ☉noon-11:30pm Mon-Sat; 🛜) This cool, contemporary cultural venue and bar lures the artistically inclined, who mingle at communal tables in the industrial, warehouse-like space. People eat, drink, work, read, flirt and unwind with good mojitos and a menu of Franco-Colombian food. A versatile events program includes live music, stand-up comedy and book launches.

El Bembe
BAR

(www.facebook.com/elbembebar; Calle 27B No 6-73; cover Fri & Sat COP$25,000; ☉noon-9pm Mon-Wed, to 1am Thu, to 3am Fri & Sat) Cuba and Colombia share a loose cultural alliance, especially when it comes to music, as this little piece of *tropicalia* ably demonstrates. Head up the multicolored stairs off a cobbled street in La Macarena for rum and salsa, live bands and potent mojitos (COP$25,000 to COP$42,000), all of which seem to flow more freely on Friday. Skip the food.

WORTH A TRIP

ZIPAQUIRÁ

Far and away the most popular day trip from Bogotá is to head 50km north of the city to the **Salt Cathedral** (☎315-760-7376; www.catedraldesal.gov.co; Parque de la Sal; foreigners/Colombians COP$55,000/34,000; ☉9am-5:45pm) of Zipaquirá. This underground cathedral carved out of salt is one of only three such structures in the world (the other two are in Poland).

In the mountains about 500m southwest of Zipaquirá there are two salt cathedrals: the first opened in 1954 and was closed in 1992 for safety reasons, but you can visit its stunning replacement. Between 1991 and 1995, around 250,000 tons of salt were cleared away to carve out the moody, ethereal underground sanctuary, hailed as one of Colombia's greatest architectural achievements. You'll descend to 180m below ground through 14 small chapels representing the Stations of the Cross (Jesus' last journey), each an evocatively lit triumph of both symbolism and mining. But nothing prepares you for the trail's culmination in the main nave, where a mammoth cross (the world's largest in an underground church) is illuminated from the base up. The tradition of mixing religion with salt has logical roots: work in the mines was dangerous, so altars were made.

All visitors must join regularly departing groups on hour-long tours – you can leave the tour once you're inside if you want.

To reach Zipaquirá, hop on a frequent bus from the Portal del Norte TransMilenio station at Calle 170, which is about a 45-minute ride from the city center. From here, buses to Zipaquirá (COP$5400, 45 minutes) leave every four minutes or so until 11:30pm from Portal's Buses Intermunicipales platform. You can also catch an hourly direct bus from *módulo 3* (red) at Bogotá's bus station (COP$5400, 1½ hours). Alternatively, take the **Turistren** (☎1-316-1300; www.turistren.com.co; Parque la Esperanza; round trip adult/child COP$58,000/50,000; ☉Sat & Sun), which runs Saturday and Sunday from Bogotá to Zipaquirá. The train departs Bogotá's main train station, **Sabana Station** (Estación de la Sabana; Calle 13 No 18-24), at 8:15am, stops briefly at Usaquén Station at 9:05am and reaches Zipaquirá at 11:05am.

Armando Records CLUB
(www.armandorecords.org; Calle 85 No 14-46; cover
Thu-Sat COP$17,000-30,000; ⊘8:30pm-2:45am
Tue-Thu, from 8pm Fri & Sat) Still a Bogotá hot
spot after several years, this multilevel den of
nocturnal delight features the 2nd-floor Armando's All Stars, which skews younger for
crossover tunes and includes a back garden
packed with patrons; and the 4th-floor retro
rooftop, where the likes of LCD Soundsystem
and Empire of the Sun guide your evening.

☆ Entertainment

Bogotá is home to a well-established arts,
theater and music scene. The city's best
theaters are found in La Candelaria, while
live-music venues dot the north, from grittier/
trendier Chapinero to more mainstream venues in the Zona Rosa.

Estadio El Campín STADIUM
(☑1-315-8728; Carrera 30 No 57-60) The principal soccer venue in Bogotá is the Estadio El
Campín, shared home of Categoría Primera
A teams Independiente Santa Fe and its big
rival, Millonarios FC. Games are played on
Wednesday night and Sunday afternoon.
Tickets can be bought at the stadium before
the matches.

🔒 Shopping

Locals love malls – **Centro Comercial El
Retiro** (www.elretirobogota.com; Calle 81 No 11-84; ⊘10am-8pm Mon-Thu, 10am-9pm Fri & Sat,
noon-7pm Sun) and **Centro Comercial Andino** (www.centroandino.com.co; Carrera 11 No 82-71;
⊘8am-10pm Mon-Thu, 7am-3am Fri-Sun) are the
best – but Sunday flea markets are more inviting attractions. Also look along Carrera
9, south of Calle 60, for Chapinero's antique
shops. For cutting-edge Colombian fashion,
there are boutiques in Chapinero on Carrera
7 between Calles 54 and 55.

★ Artesanías de Colombia ARTS & CRAFTS
(www.artesaniasdecolombia.com.co; Calle 86A No
13A-10; ⊘10am-7pm Mon-Sat, 11am-5pm Sun) 🌱
This classy shop has higher-end crafts (lots of
home accessories, plus bags, toys, hammocks
and some clothing), and 70% of the profits
go directly back to the village artisans. It has
seven sales outlets, three of them in Bogotá.

La Casona del Museo ARTS & CRAFTS
(www.facebook.com/LaCasonaDelMuseo; Calle 16
No 5-24; ⊘9am-7pm Mon-Sat, 10am-5pm Sun)
This old building near the Museo del Oro
doubles as a kind of colonial-style mall, filled

with a convenient and cheerful collection of
souvenir stands purveying everything from
emeralds to soccer scarfs. For refreshments,
there are two open-sided cafes; La Fuente,
on the upper level beside a trickling fountain, does the best coffee.

ℹ Information

EMERGENCY

Ambulance	125
Police	112
Fire	119

MONEY

There are two exchange houses in the **Emerald
Trade Center** (Av Jiménez No 5-43; ⊘7:30am-7pm Mon-Fri, 8am-5pm Sat), but it's best to use
one of the plentiful ATMs.

Banco de Bogotá (Calle 11 No 5-60)
Bancolombia (Carrera 8 No 12B-17; ⊘9am-4pm Mon-Fri)
Western Union (www.westernunion.com; Calle
28 No 13-22, local 28; ⊘9am-5:30pm Mon-Fri,
to 1pm Sat)

POST

Colombia's postal service is **4-72** (www.4-72.
com.co).
4-72 (Carrera 8 No 12A-03; ⊘8am-6pm Mon-Fri, 9am-noon Sat)
4-72 (cnr Av Chile & Carrera 15; ⊘8am-6pm
Mon-Fri, 9am-1pm Sat)

TOURIST INFORMATION

Colombia's energetic **Instituto Distrital de
Turismo** (☑1-800-012-7400; www.bogota
turismo.gov.co; Carrera 24 No 40-66; ⊘7am-4:30pm Mon-Fri) is making visitors feel very
welcome, with a series of Puntos de Información
Turística (PIT) branches opening at key locations around Bogotá, operated by very friendly
English-speaking staff. A couple of locations
offer free walking tours (scheduled separately
in English or Spanish). There are PITs at each of
the airport terminals as well as other locations
around the city, including the following:
Casa de Las Comuneros (PIT; ☑1-555-7627;
www.bogotaturismo.gov.co; Carrera 8 No 9-83,
Casa de Las Comuneros; ⊘8am-6pm Mon-Sat,
to 4pm Sun)
Centro Internacional (PIT; ☑1-800-012-7400;
www.bogotaturismo.gov.co; Carrera 7 No 26-07; ⊘9am-5pm Mon-Thu & Sat, 1-8pm Fri)
Terminal de Transportes (PIT; ☑1-800-012-7400; www.bogotaturismo.gov.co; Diagonal
23 No 69-60, La Terminal, módulo 5; ⊘7am-7:30pm Mon-Sat, 8am-4pm Sun)

ℹ️ SAFETY IN BOGOTÁ

Since the mid-'90s Bogotá has made many significant advances, among them reducing its homicide rate from 80 murders per 100,000 residents in 1993 to 15.8 in 2016 (mobile-phone theft fell by 20% from the previous year as well). These statistics mirror the downward trend of the overall Colombian murder rate for the same year (it was the lowest in four decades). Today Bogotá is one of the safest urban areas in Latin America – so safe, in fact, that Pope Francis visited in 2017.

In 2016 the Colombian government and the Fuerzas Armadas Revolucionarias de Colombia (FARC; Revolutionary Armed Forces of Colombia) signed a historic cease-fire deal, so Bogotá potentially sees fewer bombings than it did at the height of Colombia's armed conflict, but that doesn't mean the bombings have stopped entirely: an explosion at Centro Comerical Andino killed three people in 2017. (The bomb was attributed to members of a smaller urban guerrilla group known as the Movimiento Revolucionario del Pueblo, or MRP; this was its first attack to cause fatalities). Also in 2017, a bomb injured 29 (26 were police officers) in La Macarena. Though no arrests have been made, known members of the National Liberation Army (ELN) are wanted for the attack. While tourists are not specifically targeted, it's easy to be in areas where these things happen. Thankfully, the Colombian government announced a cease-fire with ELN in late 2017, and wavering peace talks in Havana, Cuba, continued through 2018; Bogotà – and Colombia – breathed a sigh of relief.

Hostel owners report a considerable drop in robberies in La Candelaria, which is generally safe during the day but can still be dicey at night. Always be aware of your surroundings. Be wary of handling your phone near the edge of streets, as thieves on motorcycles and bikes have been known to ride by and snatch them. If you opt to stay in La Candelaria, choose accommodations based not only on your general criteria but also on security. Avoid walking alone or with anything valuable after dark – these days the area has more of a police presence at night, though it's still a far cry from the show of force during the day.

Muggings are common around Calle 9 up the hill nearer the poorer neighborhood of Barrio Egipto, which remains a notable hot spot. Although tours of the barrio are now offered, under no circumstances should you wander there on your own. Do not stray beyond Carrera 1. At the Barrio Egipto's northern end there's private security in Parque de los Periodistas (you'll see personnel walking around with dogs) hired by the universities, so this once-sketchy area is now a lot safer. Solo travelers should always exercise caution on the road between the Universidad de Los Andes and Monserrate, though a police presence on the mountainside trails from 6am has curbed incidents here dramatically.

Police presence has been stepped up in La Macarena as well, though it's still a good idea to take a taxi and stick to the main restaurant streets – La Perseverancia barrio, just north of La Macarena, has a very dodgy reputation and it's not difficult to stray into it if you're unfamiliar with the area.

ℹ️ Getting There & Away

AIR

Bogotá's shiny airport, Aeropuerto Internacional El Dorado (p670), which handles nearly all domestic and international flights, is located 13km northwest of the city center. It received a massive US$900-million face-lift in 2014, and an expansion in 2017 to accommodate an additional 12 million passengers annually.

Terminal T1, which replaced the old El Dorado terminal, serves all international flights, Avianca's main domestic routes (Barranquilla, Cali, Cartagena, Medellín and Pereira) and domestic routes from other airlines.

Terminal T2 (commonly referred to as Puente Aéreo), 1km west of T1 and reached by airport shuttle, serves the remainder of Avianca's domestic routes (Armenia, Barrancabermeja, Bucaramanga, Cúcula, Florencia, Ibagué, Leticia, Manizales, Montería, Neiva, Pasto, Popayán, Riohacha, San Andrés, Santa Marta, Valledupar, Villavicencio and Yopal).

BUS

Bogotá's main bus terminal, **La Terminal** (☎1-423-3630; www.terminaldetransporte.gov.co; Diagonal 23 No 69-11), about 5km west of the city center in the squeaky-clean planned neighborhood of Salitre, is one of South America's

BOGOTÁ BUSES

DESTINATION	PRICE (COP$)	DURATION	MÓDULO (NO)	COMPANIES
Armenia	43,000-68,000	7hr	yellow (1)	Bolivariano, Magdalena, Velotax
Barranquilla	80,000-100,000	17-20hr	red (3) & blue (2)	Brasilia, Continental Bus, Ochoa
Bucaramanga	60,000-70,000	8-9hr	red (3)	Autoboy, Berlinas, Copetran & others
Cali	60,000-70,000	8-10hr	yellow (1)	Bolivariano, Magdalena, Palmira, Velotax
Cartagena	100,000-110,000	12-24hr	red (3)	Autoboy, Berlinas, Brasilia, Copetran
Cúcuta	90,000-115,000	15-16hr	red (3) & blue (2)	Berlinas, Bolivariano, Copetran, Cotrans, Ormeño
Ipiales	148,000	22hr	yellow (1) & red (3)	Bolivariano, Brasilia, Continental Bus, Ormeño
Manizales	50,000-64,000	8-9hr	yellow (1), blue (2) & green (4)	Bolivariano, Palmira, Tax La Feria, Tolima
Medellín	60,000-80,000	9hr	blue (2)	Arauca, Bolivariano, Brasilia, Magdalena
Neiva	30,000-50,000	5-6hr	yellow (1)	Bolivariano, Coomotor, Cootranshuila, Magdalena, Taxis Verdes, Tolima
Pasto	120,000-140,000	18-20hr	yellow (1) & blue (2)	Continental Bus, Cruz del Sur
Pereira	50,000-75,000	7-9hr	yellow (1)	Bolivariano, Magdalena, Velotax
Popayán	95,000-110,000	12hr	yellow (1)	Continental Bus, Cruz del Sur, Velotax
Ráquira	22,000	3-4hr	red (3)	El Carmen, Coflonorte, La Verde
Riohacha	100,000-107,000	18-19hr	red (3)	Copetran
San Agustín	65,000	9-10hr	yellow (1)	Coomotor, Taxis Verdes
San Gil	50,000	6-7hr	red (3)	Omega
Santa Marta	80,000-90,000	16-17hr	red (3)	Berlinas, Brasilia, Copetran
Tunja	22,000	3hr	red (3) & green (4)	Autoboy, Los Muiscas, Nueva Flota Boyaca
Villa de Leyva	25,000	4hr	blue (2) & red (3)	Aguila, Alianza, El Carmen, Cundinamarca & others
Villavicencio	26,000	3hr	blue (2)	Arimena, Autollanos, Bolivariano, Macarena, Velotax

best and most efficient, and it's shockingly un-sketchy. It's housed in a huge, arched red-brick building divided into five *módulos* (units). South-bound buses leave at the western end from *módulo 1* (color-coded yellow); east- and westbound buses from *módulo 2* (blue); and northbound buses from *módulo 3* (red). *Colectivo* vans leave for some nearby towns such as Villavicencio from *módulo 4* (green), while all arrivals come into *módulo 5* (at the station's eastern end).

ℹ Getting Around

TO/FROM THE AIRPORT
The most economical and efficient route from the airport is the TransMilenio (p587). You'll need to buy a *tarjeta tullave* from the attendants in blue-and-yellow jackets outside Puerta 8 of the arrivals area next to where the buses depart.

Taxi Imperial (🖉 317-300-3000; www.taxi imperial.com.co) manages a fleet of white air-port taxis – look for the folks in orange jackets – which are pricier (more comfortable! working seat belts!), but regular yellow taxis are fine as well. Estimated fares from the airport are La Candelaria COP$30,000 to COP$32,000, Chapinero COP$35,000 to COP$37,000 and Zona Rosa COP$35,000 to COP$38,000.

BICYCLE
Bogotá has one of the world's most extensive bike-route networks, with more than 375km of separated, clearly marked bike paths called CicloRuta. Free Bogotá maps from PIT information centers show the CicloRuta paths.

TAXI
Bogotá's impressive fleet of Korean-made yellow taxis are a safe, reliable and relatively inexpensive way of getting around. In mid-2018 the city was in the process of changing from traditional taxi meters to a digital-pricing scheme similar to those implemented by taxi apps like Uber.

TRANSMILENIO
The ambitiously named **TransMilenio** (www. transmilenio.gov.co), modeled after a similar groundbreaking system in Curitiba, Brazil, revolutionized Bogotá's public transportation when it opened in 2000.

The system is, in essence, a bus network masquerading as a subway. Covering 112km with a fleet of over 2000 buses, the TransMilenio has 12 lines and approximately 147 self-contained stations, which keeps things orderly and safe (and some stations have wi-fi). Buses use dedicated lanes, which keeps them free from car traffic.

A frequent-rider smart card, the **tarjeta tullave** (www.tullaveplus.com; COP$5000, rechargeable up to COP$322,000), is used to enter the system. The card is sold at all portals as well as some stations; it can be recharged at all stations as well as some grocery stores, pharmacies and *papelerías* (stationary shops); check for locations at www.tullaveplus.com/web/public/puntos-de-recarga).

On maps posted in stations, routes are color coded, with different-numbered buses corresponding to various stops.

NORTH OF BOGOTÁ

Villa de Leyva
📲 8 / POP 17,500 / ELEV 2140M

One of the most beautiful colonial villages in Colombia, Villa de Leyva is a city frozen in time. Declared a national monument in 1954, the photogenic village has been preserved in its entirety, with cobblestone roads and whitewashed buildings.

Villa's physical beauty and mild, dry climate have long attracted outsiders. The town was founded in 1572 by Hernán Suárez de Villalobos, and early on it was mainly a retreat for military officers, clergy and the nobility.

In recent years an influx of wealthy visitors and expats has slowly transformed this once-hidden gem. Boutique hotels, gourmet restaurants and tacky tourist shops are replacing many of the old family *hosterías* (inns) and cafes, and the authenticity. On weekends the narrow alleys can get downright crammed with day-trippers from Bogotá. But, thankfully, on weekdays it reverts to a peaceful, bucolic village.

◉ Sights

Villa de Leyva is a leisurely place made for wandering – roam the charming cobblestone streets, listen to the church bells and enjoy the lazy rhythm of days gone by. It's also famous for its abundance of **fossils** from the Cretaceous and Mesozoic periods, when this area was underwater. Look closely and you'll notice that fossils have been used as construction materials in floors, walls and pavements.

As you stroll around, pop into the **Casa de Juan de Castellanos** (Carrera 9 No 13-15), **Casona La Guaca** (Carrera 9 No 13-57) and **Casa Quintero** (cnr Carrera 9 & Calle 12), three meticulously restored colonial mansions just off the plaza that now house quaint cafes, restaurants and shops.

Villa de Leyva

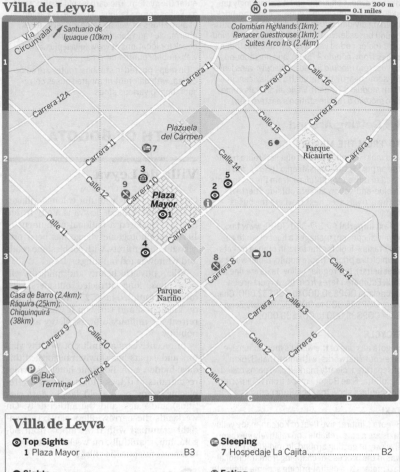

Villa de Leyva

★ Plaza Mayor   PLAZA

At 120m by 120m, Plaza Mayor is one of the largest town squares in the Americas. It's paved with massive cobblestones and surrounded by magnificent colonial structures and a charmingly simple parish church. Only a small, central Mudejar fountain, which provided water to the villagers for almost four centuries, interrupts the vast expanse. In most Colombian cities the main square is named after a historic hero, but this one is traditionally and firmly called Plaza Mayor.

Casa Museo de
Luis Alberto Acuña   MUSEUM

(📞 8-732-0422; Plaza Mayor; adult/child COP$6000/4000; ⊙ 9am-6pm) Villa de Leyva's best museum features works by one of Colombia's most influential painters, sculptors, writers and historians, Luis Alberto Acuña

(1904–93), who was inspired by sources ranging from Muisca mythology to contemporary art. Set up in the mansion where Acuña lived for the last 15 years of his life, this museum is the most comprehensive collection of his work in Colombia.

🏃 Activities

Activity options around Villa de Leyva include hiking, cycling, horseback riding and swimming, along with more extreme sports such as rappelling, canyoning and caving.

👉 Tours

Taxis at the bus terminal offer round trips to the surrounding sights – expect to pay COP$25,000 to COP$30,000 per attraction including waiting time. However, as many of the sights are located only 12km or less from the town center, you'll save money by walking or renting a bike.

If you want to learn more about the attractions, consider taking a tour. The standard routes offered by local operators include El Fósil (p591), **Estación Astronómica Muisca** (El Infiernito; adult/child COP$8000/6000; ⊙ 8am-5pm Tue-Sun) and Convento del Santo Ecce Homo (p591; COP$145,000). Prices, which include transportation, guide and insurance (but not entrance fees), are per person based on two people and drop with larger groups.

Ciclotrip CYCLING
(📞 320-899-4442; www.ciclotrip.com; Carrera 9 No 14-101; ⊙ 9am-6pm Mon-Fri, 8am-8pm Sat & Sun) This highly recommended bike outfitter and tour agency gets you out on two wheels to all the popular attractions but also to more obscure waterfalls and mountain trails. Owner Francisco is trained in first aid and mountain rescue. Guided day trips run COP$120,000 to COP$300,000. The half-day trip to the Periquera waterfall (COP$130,000) is also popular.

If you want to go it alone, Ciclotrip also rents bikes (COP$90,000 per day) that are a step up from those found elsewhere around town. Staff will help you plan a route and give you a marked-up map to follow and even a cell phone so you can call for mechanical support if you run into difficulties.

Colombian Highlands ECOTOUR
(📞 310-552-9079, 8-732-1201; www.colombianhighlands.com; Av Carrera 10 No 21-Finca Renacer) 🏃 Run by biologist and Renacer Guesthouse (p589) owner Oscar Gilède, this agency runs a variety of offbeat tours, including ecotours, mountain trips, bird-watching, nocturnal hikes, rappelling/abseiling, canyoning, caving and hiking. It also rents bikes and horses. English spoken.

🛏 Sleeping

Villa de Leyva has a large selection of hotels in all price ranges. Note that prices increase on weekends, when it may be hard to find a room. During the high seasons, including Semana Santa and December 20 to January 15, prices can more than double. Plan ahead. Camping around the area runs about COP$20,000 per person.

★ Renacer Guesthouse HOSTEL $
(📞 8-732-1201, 311-308-3739; www.renacerhostel.com; Av Carrera 10 No 21-Finca Renacer; campsites per person from COP$18,000, dm from COP$32,000, s/d from COP$70,000/90,000; @ 🛜 ♨) Located 1.2km northeast of Plaza Mayor, this delightful 'boutique hostel' is the creation of biologist and tour guide extraordinaire Oscar Gilède of Colombian Highlands (p589). Everything about this place feels like home – hammocks surrounding an immaculate garden, a communal, open-air kitchen with brick pizza oven, and spotless dorms and rooms. Staff will even donate herbs from the garden toward your cooking needs.

Hospedaje La Cajita B&B $$
(📞 310-618-2819; Calle 13 No 10-80; d/tr/q COP$140,000/260,000/280,000; 🛜) Operated by delightful Leyva couple Julio and Julia, La Cajita is a secure little homestay a block from the main square. The good-size rooms, decorated in clean whites and punchy oranges, are embellished with red-tile floors and funky art; some rooms have bunks. There's strong wi-fi, perfectly balanced fruity breakfasts and a nice atmosphere of quiet congeniality.

★ Suites Arco Iris BOUTIQUE HOTEL $$$
(📞 311-254-7919; www.suitesarcoiris.com; Km2 Vila la Colorada; r mountain/village view incl breakfast from COP$260,000/280,000; 🛜) Perched on a hilltop above town and surrounded by a fine garden, this romantic 26-room hotel tops the charts in Villa de Leyva for personality. The massive rooms, each unique but all equally drenched in color, art and character, are snazzy affairs, with Jacuzzis, terraces, fireplaces and kaleidoscopically tiled bathrooms. Views, be they mountain or town, are stupendous.

✖ Eating & Drinking

Villa is the most sophisticated foodie destination in Boyacá. There are a few gourmet food courts in the village, with Casa Quintero (p587) and Casona La Guaca (p587) offering the best and most diverse options.

During low season a lot of higher-end restaurants offer discount lunch menus, but these all but disappear once the crowds arrive.

★ **Mercado Municipal**　　　COLOMBIAN $$$
(☑ 318-363-7049; Carrera 8 No 12-25; ☺ 1-10pm Mon-Sat, to 9pm Sun) On its way to becoming Boyacá's most interesting dining experience, this chef-driven restaurant in the gardens of a colonial house (1740) has resurrected ancient techniques of cooking meat in a 1m-deep underground wood-burning *barbacoa* (barbecue). Among the specialties are rich pork ribs in apricot barbecue sauce – the tender meat slides effortlessly off the bone.

Tavolo Hamburguesería　　　BURGERS $$
(☑ 320-337-3761; Carrera 10 No 12-09; burgers COP$17,000-29,000; ☺ 7:30-10pm Mon-Tue, Thu & Sun, to 11pm Fri & Sat) A newborn gourmet-burger joint on the main square, the Tavolo enables diners to enjoy their innovatively adorned patties (served on mini bread boards) with equally satisfying plaza views. If in doubt, go for the *'de la tierrita'*, a multidecker amalgamation of fried egg,

long sausage and beef. Nonburger choices include trout, ribs and pork tenderloin.

Café Los Gallos　　　CAFE
(☑ 300-851-4714; Carrera 8 No 13-2; ☺ 8am-8pm Thu-Tue) Los Gallos serves the finest joe in town, a smooth, sophisticated brew that you can spike with something sweet from the cake display, like the apple-and-*arequipe* (sweet milk-based caramel) pie, a gem of a dessert that deserves a culinary Oscar.

❶ Information

There are several ATMs on the southwestern side of the plaza, including at **Banco de Bogota** (Carrera 9 No 11-2) and **Bancolombia** (Carrera 9 No 11-25; ☺ 8-11:30am & 2-4:30pm Mon-Fri, 9am-1pm Sat).

Oficina de Turismo (☑ 8-732-0232; Carrera 9 No 13-11; ☺ 8am-noon & 2-6pm) Helpful official tourism office just off the plaza. Provides free maps, brochures and information in Spanish.

❶ Getting There & Away

The **bus terminal** (cnr Carrera 9 & Calle 9) is three blocks southwest of Plaza Mayor, on the road to Tunja. Minibuses run between Villa de Leyva and Tunja (COP$7000, 45 minutes) every 15 minutes from 5am to 7:45pm. Around a dozen direct buses travel daily to Bogotá (COP$25,000, four hours) between 4:30am and 5pm; otherwise, take any bus to Tunja and change there.

WORTH A TRIP

TUNJA

The capital of Boyacá and a bustling student center, Tunja was founded by Gonzalo Suárez Rendón in 1539 on the site of Hunza, the pre-Hispanic Muisca settlement. Almost nothing is left of the indigenous settlement, but much colonial architecture remains. Tunja is particularly noted for its colonial churches; several imposing examples dating from the 16th century stand almost untouched by time. The town also has an imposing central square, the Plaza de Bolívar, and elegant mansions adorned with some of South America's most unique artwork.

Several colonial mansions in Tunja, including the **Casa del Fundador Suárez Rendón** (Carrera 9 No 19-68; ☺ 8am-noon & 2-5pm Tue-Sun) **FREE** and the **Casa de Don Juan de Vargas** (☑ 313-208-6176; Calle 20 No 8-52; COP$3000; ☺ 9-11:30am & 2-4:30pm Tue-Fri, 9am-3:30pm Sat & Sun), have ceilings adorned with paintings featuring a strange mishmash of motifs taken from very different traditions. They include mythological scenes, human figures, animals and plants, coats of arms and architectural details.

The well-priced, slightly monastic **Hotel Casa Real** (☑ 8-743-1764; www.hotelcasareal tunja.com; Calle 19 No 7-65; s/d/tw COP$66,000/80,000/85,000; ☎) near the bus station offers a friendly welcome.

The bus terminal is on Av Oriental, a short, hilly walk southeast of Plaza de Bolívar. Buses to Bogotá (COP$19,000, 2½ to three hours) depart every 10 to 15 minutes. Minibuses to Villa de Leyva (COP$7000, 45 minutes) depart regularly between 6am and 7pm.

For San Gil, it's easiest to connect in Tunja; while traveling via Arcabuco cuts some distance off the route, you may wait a while by the side of the road for a pull-in.

Buses from Villa to Santa Sofía (COP$4000, one hour) leave at 6:45am, 8am, 9am, 10am, 1:15pm, 3pm, 4:15pm and 5:45pm.

Around Villa de Leyva

Archaeological relics, colonial monuments, petroglyphs, caves, lakes and waterfalls are among the attractions surrounding the picturesque colonial village of Villa de Leyva. Endowed with gentle pastoral fields and crisscrossed by quiet country lanes, the area is ideal for walking and cycling.

◉ Sights

Casa de Barro
ARCHITECTURE
(Casa Terracotta; Via Sáchica; adult/child COP$10,000/5000; ◷9am-6pm) One of Villa de Leyva's most magnificent buildings is the Gaudí-esque Casa de Barro, an artistic house made from entirely handworked clay fired in stages to produce one continuous terracotta structure. It's decorated with ornamental flourishes throughout, with delightful wrought-iron features on the windows. The garden hosts surrealistic sculptures, some of them made of recycled metal.

Convento del Santo Ecce Homo
CHURCH
(COP$5000; ◷8am-5pm Tue-Sun) Founded by the Dominican fathers in 1620, this convent is a large stone-and-adobe construction with a huge, faintly regal courtyard. The floors are paved with stones quarried in the region, so they contain ammonites and fossils, including petrified corn and flowers. There are also fossils in the base of a statue in the chapel.

Centro de Investigaciones Paleontológicas
MUSEUM
(CIP; ☑321-978-9546, 314-219-2904; info@ centropaleo.com; adult/child COP$9000/5000; ◷8am-noon & 2-5pm Tue-Thu, 8am-5pm Fri-Sun) Just across the main road from the famed El Fósil (p591) site, this sleek center combines an open-window research facility with a collection of impressive fossils, including an amazing full-body plesiosaurus (a Jurassic sea dragon), the oldest known turtle fossil and the only tooth of a saber-tooth tiger ever discovered in Colombia. Everything is signed in English.

El Fósil
ARCHAEOLOGICAL SITE
(☑310-629-1845; adult/child COP$8000/5000; ◷8am-6pm) This impressive 120-million-year-old baby-kronosaurus fossil is the world's most complete specimen of this prehistoric marine reptile. The fossil is 7m long – the creature was about 12m in size, but the tail did not survive – and it remains in place exactly where it was found in 1977. Museum staff can explain how the fossil was found and direct you around several other paleontological specimens in the same museum.

❶ Getting There & Away

You can walk from Villa de Leyva to some of the nearest sights, or go by bicycle (highly recommended) or on horseback. You can also go by taxi or arrange a tour with Villa de Leyva's tour operators. If you choose to go by taxi, make sure you confirm with the driver all the sights you want to see and agree on a price before setting off. A round-trip taxi (for up to four people) from Villa de Leyva to El Fósil (p591), Estación Astronómica Muisca (p589) and Ecce Homo (p591) should cost about COP$75,000, including waiting time.

Local buses pass close to some of the attractions but are not particularly regular, so it's important to check timetables before heading out.

Santuario de Iguaque

High above the surrounding valley and shrouded in mist is a pristine wilderness that Muiscas consider to be the birthplace of humankind. According to Muisca legend, the beautiful goddess Bachué emerged from the Laguna de Iguaque with a baby boy in her arms. When the boy became an adult they married, bore children and populated the earth. In old age the pair transformed into serpents and dove back into the sacred lake.

◉ Sights

Santuario de Flora y Fauna de Iguaque
NATIONAL PARK
(foreigners/Colombians COP$46,500/17,500; ◷8am-5pm) Covering 67.5 sq km, this unique *páramo* (high-mountain plains) neotropical ecosystem contains hundreds of species of flora and fauna but is most noted for the frailejón, a shrub typical of the highlands. There are eight small mountain lakes in the reserve, sitting at an altitude of between 3550m and 3700m, although the only one accessible to visitors is **Laguna de Iguaque**.

Only 50 people are allowed to enter the sanctuary per day. Note that entry to the park is only permitted until 10am – even if you have a reservation for accommodations – after which point you'll be turned around at the gate.

The well-signposted hike from the **visitors center** (dm COP$50,000, campsites per person COP$10,000; ⊘8am-5pm) to Laguna de Iguaque is 4.7km long and climbs 800m. It's easily done solo and takes about three hours. A leisurely round trip takes five to six hours. A rather fastidious 10-minute briefing is given to all hikers before they set out. Optional guides can be hired for COP$150,000.

ⓘ Getting There & Away

To get to the park from Villa de Leyva, take the Arcabuco-bound bus (departs 6am, 7am and 8am) and tell the driver to drop you at Casa de Piedra (also known as Los Naranjos; COP$4000) at Km12, from where it's a 3km hike up the rough road to the visitors center (p592). The 6am service is the best choice, as it passes closer to the access road.

Returning to Villa, make sure you're at Casa de Piedra no later than 4pm in order to catch the last bus. Colombian Highlands (p589) runs full-day tours from Villa de Leyva for COP$170,000 per person for two people (less for larger groups). Alternatively, you can negotiate a rate with a taxi driver in Villa de Leyva.

Parque Nacional Natural El Cocuy

Covering an enormous 306,000 hectares, **Parque Nacional Natural El Cocuy** (foreigners/Colombians COP$61,000/30,500) is home to some of Colombia's most impressive landscapes and is the main attraction of the Sierra Nevada del Cocuy region. It has 15 peaks that are at least 5000m, the highest of which is Ritacuba Blanco at 5330m.

Once off-limits because of the security situation, the park is now safe to visit, but access can still be complicated. In 2013 the main attraction, the Güicán–El Cocuy Circuit Trek, was closed to visitors indefinitely, and in 2016 the park was closed completely while the government negotiated with local indigenous communities. The park reopened in early 2017 but with even more restrictions. It's no longer possible to touch any of the glaciers, making climbing the peaks impossible, and overnight stays are no longer permitted. Check ahead to see if the situation has changed by the time you visit.

🏃 Activities

The mountains of PNN El Cocuy are relatively compact and easy to reach. The complete Güicán–El Cocuy Circuit Trek, which traverses passes that top out at Boquerón de la Sierra (4650m) and takes in the park's most transcendent attraction, Laguna de la Plaza, was indefinitely closed at research time. However, there are three shorter day hikes in operation that take visitors to the edge of the glaciers. The hike to the snow line is only about three hours from the northern park boundary.

No special experience is required. However, due to the elevation and the terrain, park officials now require that all visitors hire the services of a local guide. It's recommend that hikers have at least some previous trekking experience and be in good health. Park entry is prohibited to children under 10 years, and is not recommended for pregnant women and people with heart or lung ailments.

The starting points for hiking PNN El Cocuy are the archrival villages of Güicán and El Cocuy. All visitors to the park must first report to the PNN El Cocuy offices in either **Güicán** (🖉8-789-7280; cocuy@parque nacionales.gov.co; Transversal 4A No 6-60; ⊘7am-11:45am&1-4:45pm) or **El Cocuy** (🖉8-789-0359; cocuy@parquesnacionales.gov.co; Calle 5A No 4-22; ⊘7-11:45am & 1-4:45pm), register their itineraries, provide the name and phone number of their guide, prove insurance coverage and pay the park admission fee (foreigners/Colombians COP$61,000/30,500). You'll be given a document authorizing park access, which you'll need to present at the ranger checkpoints at the beginning of the trails. The document is valid for four days from the first entry, so it's possible to hike all three open trails while paying just one fee.

Don't forget to check back in after your hike; if you don't show up by your return date, park officials will launch search-and-rescue operations.

Aseguicoc HIKING
(Asosciacion de Servicios Turisticos de Guican y El Cocuy; 🖉311-255-1034, 314-252-8977; aseguicoc@gmail.com) 🖋 This is a highly recommended community-driven concession of guides and services that also operates the closest cabañas to the park boundaries, at Laguna Pintada. In addition to arranging trekking guides and

MONGUÍ

Once voted the most beautiful village in Boyacá, Monguí is just 14km east of Sogamoso but feels far removed from the latter's industrial landscapes. The first missionaries appeared in the region around 1555, but the town wasn't founded until 1601. It later became a catechetic center of the Franciscan monks – as evidenced by one of Monguí's most striking buildings, the **Convento de los Franciscanos** (Plaza Principal; foreigner/Colombian COP$12,000/7000; ☺10am-noon & 2-4pm Tue-Fri, 9am-4pm Sat & Sun), which dominates the gorgeous plaza.

Today this idyllic Christmas-colored village boasts uniform green-and-white colonial architecture only interrupted by the occasional newer brick construction that evokes the English countryside. Either way, the beautiful facades drip with colorful red-rose-scented geraniums and ivy. It's a truly lovely pueblo adhering to a fiercely authentic ethos.

Monguí is the base for some satisfying but little-trodden high-altitude hikes. It's the main starting point for the 18km journey on foot through the unique alpine tundra of **Páramo de Ocetá**. Due to disputes with local landowners, for this hike it is important to hire a local guide who knows which lands are open. **Monguí Travels** (☎313-424-8207; www.monguitravels.com; Plaza Principal, cnr Carrera 4 & Calle 5; ☺7am-8pm) offers great itineraries for hikes.

In a prime position on the main square, the **Mongui Plaza Hotel** (☎313-209-0067; monguiplaza@gmail.com; Carrera 4 No 4-13; s/d incl breakfast from COP$60,000/120,000;) is housed in a colonial mansion decked out in the town's characteristic green, red and gold trim.

Minibuses to Sogamoso (COP$4000, every 20 minutes) depart from the northwestern corner of Monguí's plaza. There are two daily buses to Bogotá, but a *super directo* from Sogamoso is a much quicker bet.

porters for trips into the park, it can also organize a range of activities outside the park, including horseback riding and overnight hikes with accommodations in tents.

It doesn't have a physical office, but the concession works with most local hotels.

❶ Getting There & Away

There are direct buses into the region from Bogotá via Tunja. All buses call at El Cocuy first and then continue to Güicán.

San Gil

☑7 / POP 44,600 / ELEV 1110M

For a small city, San Gil packs a lot of punch. This is the outdoors capital of Colombia and a mecca for extreme-sports enthusiasts. The area is best known for white-water rafting, but other popular pastimes include paragliding, caving, rappelling and trekking. San Gil has a handsome 300-year-old town square and Parque El Gallineral (p593), a beautiful nature reserve on the banks of the Río Fonce.

San Gil may not be the prettiest town in Colombia, but dig beneath the exterior and you'll discover a wonderful city of natural beauty and friendly, welcoming residents.

San Gil definitely lives up to its motto, 'La Tierra de Aventura' (The Land of Adventure).

◉ Sights

Parque El Gallineral　　PARK
(☎7-724-4372; cnr Malecón & Calle 6; with/without swimming COP$10,000/6000; ☺8am-6pm) San Gil's showpiece is the salubrious Parque El Gallineral, a 4-hectare park set on a triangular island between two arms of the Quebrada Curití and Río Fonce. Many of the 1900 trees are covered with long, silvery tendrils of moss called barbas de viejo (old man's beard), hanging from branches to form translucent curtains of foliage and filtered sunlight. It's like a scene set in JRR Tolkien's Middle Earth.

Cascadas de Juan Curi　　WATERFALL
(COP$9000; ☺6am-5pm) Take a day trip to this spectacular 180m-high waterfall where you can swim in the natural pool at its base or relax on the rocks. Adventure junkies can rappel the sheer face of the falls; book this activity with one of the tour companies. Juan Curi is 22km from San Gil on the road to Charalá. Charalá buses (COP$6300, one hour) depart twice hourly from the local bus terminal.

🏃 Activities

Several tour agencies in San Gil run white-water rafting on local rivers. A 10km run on Río Fonce (Class I to III) costs COP$45,000 per person and takes 1½ hours; experienced rafters can tackle the rapids of the Río Suárez (COP$130,000, up to Class V). Most operators also offer paragliding, caving, horseback riding, rappelling/abseiling, mountain biking, bungee jumping and ecowalks.

Macondo Adventures   ADVENTURE SPORTS
(📋 7-724-8001; www.macondohostel.com; Carrera 8 No 10-35) A one-stop adventure shop, this professional tour desk inside the Macondo hostel (p594) organizes the full gamut of adventure activities. The helpful staff have tried all the activities themselves and can recommend a variety of options depending on your interests and sanity. Choose from rafting, paragliding, mountain biking, kayaking and caving.

🧭 Tours

★ Colombian
Bike Junkies   MOUNTAIN BIKING
(📋 316-327-6101; www.colombianbikejunkies.com; day trips from COP$270,000) Modeled after Gravity in Bolivia, this Colombian-Ecuadorean-owned extreme-mountain-bike operation offers a 50km downhill adrenaline overdose on two wheels through the Cañón del Río Suárez (with a stop in Barichara) or the equally spectacular Cañón de Chicamocha. It's an all-day affair that takes in absolutely epic countryside. Lunch is included; a celebratory beer is de rigueur.

Colombia Rafting Expeditions   RAFTING
(📋 7-724-5800; www.colombiarafting.com; Carrera 10 No 7-83; rafting from COP$130,000; ⊙8am-5pm) The rafting specialist for the Río Suárez; also offers hydrospeeding and kayaking.

🛏 Sleeping

San Gil has plenty of downtown budget and moderately priced lodgings. Private rooms in most hostels are so comfortable that it's not usually necessary to splurge on midrange accommodations. There are many basic cheapie hotels on Calle 10, but if you're looking for luxury, check out the resorts on the outskirts of town along Vía Charalá or Vía Mogotes; alternatively, head to Bogotá.

★ Macondo Guesthouse   HOSTEL $
(📋 7-724-8001; www.macondohostel.com; Carrera 8 No 10-35; dm COP$22,000-28,000, d COP$100,000, without bathroom COP$65,000; @🛜) The original San Gil hostel is still easily the best in town. It's a laid-back but secure place (with CCTV) that feels a bit like crashing at a friend's. There's a wonderful leafy courtyard with a 10-person Jacuzzi and a variety of dorm and room options, including three upgraded private rooms that punch above their hostel weight class.

Hostal de la Nueva Baeza   GUESTHOUSE $
(📋 7-724-2606; hostaldelanuevabaeza@hotmail.com; Calle 9 No 8-49; r with/without air-con COP$50,000/40,000; ❄🛜) Early risers looking for a very comfortable room in a quiet house should consider this 10-room guesthouse, a relatively new construction skilfully done in old-colonial style. Service is limited, but rooms feature vaulted bamboo ceilings, new flat-screen TVs and very nice bathrooms. It's a step up from other budget options.

Sam's VIP   HOSTEL $$
(📋 7-724-2746; www.samshostel.com; Carrera 10 No 12-33; dm COP$30,000, s/d COP$85,000/110,000, without bathroom COP$65,000/90,000; @🛜🏊) There aren't many hostels that claim VIP status, but Sam's does, at least, make you feel like a VIB (very important backpacker). The dark garage entry off the main square doesn't promise much, but things get infinitely brighter when you climb the two flights of stairs to enter a sunny, plaza-facing lounge-lobby-terrace.

La Posada Familiar   GUESTHOUSE $$
(📋 301-370-1323, 7-724-8136; laposadafamiliar@hotmail.com; Carrera 10 No 8-55; r per person COP$40,000; @🛜) Señora Esperanza dotes on her guests at this most Colombian of choices, a lovely six-room guesthouse wrapped around a plant-jammed courtyard with a gurgling fountain. Well-maintained rooms are unembellished but offer modern bathrooms and hot water, and there's a small but pleasant guest kitchen with a hardwood sink.

🍴 Eating

San Gil isn't a gourmet destination, but it does have a collection of restaurants serving home-cooked local cuisine alongside some good international fare. For self-catering there's **Autoservice Veracruz** (Calle 13 No

9-24; ⊘8am-9pm Mon-Sat, to 2pm Sun) on the plaza (better for fresh fruit and veggies) and **Metro** (⊘8am-9pm Sun-Fri, to 10pm Sat) – San Gil's biggest; better for dry goods – inside **Centro Comercial El Puente** (www.elpuente. com.co; Calle 10 No 12-184; ⊘9am-9pm), San Gil's modern shopping center.

⭐**El Maná** COLOMBIAN $
(Calle 10 No 9-42; set meals COP$15,000; ⊘11am-3pm & 6-8:30pm Mon-Sat, to 3pm Sun) This popular, word-of-mouth favorite is the best Colombian restaurant in town. You can taste the extra love in the fantastic set meals – seven or so to choose from daily – featuring traditional dishes like chicken in plum sauce, *estofado de pollo* (chicken stew) and grilled mountain trout. The bummer is that it closes early – no good if you're out all day.

Coffee House CAFE $
(Calle 10 No 8-44; breakfast COP$6200-10,900; ⊘7:30am-12:30pm & 4-9pm Mon-Sat, 7:30am-12:30pm Sun; 🖉) Fairly new, the simply named Coffee House has elevated itself into one of San Gil's best places for breakfast (available all day), with everything from granola and yogurt and fruit salads to bacon sandwiches. Come back in the evening for burritos, quesadillas and burgers, along with a variety of vegetarian options.

⭐**Gringo Mike's** AMERICAN $$
(🖉7-724-1695; www.gringomikes.net; Calle 12 No 8-35; burgers COP$18,500-24,500; ⊘8am-11pm; 🛜🖉) What *isn't* good here? In a moody, candlelit courtyard you'll find this US-UK operation thrilling homesick travelers with a surplus of American-portioned gourmet burgers, bacon-heavy sandwiches, breakfast burritos and French-press coffee. You may need a knife and fork to dismember the spicy jalapeño burger and the Mexican beef-fillet burrito.

🍷 **Drinking & Nightlife**

La Habana BAR
(🖉300-407-5138; Calle 8 No 10-32; ⊘3pm-midnight Mon-Thu, to 1am Fri & Sun, 9am-1am Sun) With a wall display that pays homage to Che Guevara and The Beatles and an agreeably unkempt location overlooking the *malecón* (jetty/promenade), this unpretentious 2nd-floor bar is where San Gil's extreme adventurers go to wind down (or up). If you've been sitting on too many Colombian buses listening to local radio, you'll appreciate the edgy reggae, rock and blues soundtrack.

🛈 **Information**

MONEY
There are several ATMs in and around the plaza (avoid the problematic Banco Agrario one).
Bancolombia (Calle 12 No 10-44)
BBVA (Carrera 10 No 12-23)
Davivienda (cnr Carrera 10 & Calle 11)

TOURIST INFORMATION
For listings of hotels and adventure companies, check out www.sangil.com.co.
Punto Información Turística (Malecón contiguo a Parque Gallineral; ⊘10am-5pm)

COLOMBIA SAN GIL

TEJO

Gunpowder, lead weights, alcohol? That's a dream mix anywhere, and in Colombia it's perfectly legal. *Tejo*, a rural tradition with roots in Boyacá, is a loud and rambunctious pre-Columbian game in which 2kg puck-like weights (once made of solid gold called *zepguagoscua*, nowadays made of lead) are tossed to a clay pit to hit a metal ring known as a *bocin*, which is surrounded by ready-to-explode gunpowder-filled triangular pieces of wax paper called *mechas*.

Staff at Macondo Guesthouse (p594) in San Gil run a *tejo* night every Tuesday at 8pm. They block out a few lanes at **Comite Municipal de Tejo** (🖉7-724-4053; Carrera 18 No 26-70; ⊘4-10:30pm) and organize a guide to help explain the rules and make sure you don't blow anything up that isn't meant to be blown up! The *tejo* is free for hostel guests; nonguests are welcome when space permits and pay COP$10,000 each for the guide. Cheap beers are usually delivered courtside by the crate.

Although well-behaved foreigners are welcome other days of the week (Wednesday and Friday are best for getting a court), it's not recommended unless you're educated in all things *tejo*.

ℹ Getting There & Away

San Gil has two bus stations with numerous names, but you'll most likely arrive at the **inter-city bus terminal** (terminal principal; Vía San Gil-Bogotá), located 3km west of downtown on the road to Bogotá. Local buses shuttle regularly between the terminal and the city center, or you can take a taxi (COP$4000).

Minibuses leave for Bucaramanga (COP$16,000, 2½ hours) via Parque Nacional del Chicamocha every half-hour from 4am to 8pm, after which time you can also jump on passing long-distance services.

Frequent buses depart to Bogotá (COP$35,000, seven hours) via Tunja (COP$25,000, four hours). Less frequent direct services call at Barranquilla (COP$70,000, 13 hours), Cartagena (COP$80,000, 15 hours), Santa Marta (COP$70,000, 12 hours) and Medellín (COP$80,000, 12 hours).

The **Cotrasangil Terminal** (Terminalito; 📞7-724-2155; www.cotrasangil.com; cnr Calle 17 & Carrera 10) has frequent buses to Barichara (COP$5000, 45 minutes) from 6am to 6:45pm.

Barichara

📞7 / POP 7100 / ELEV 1336M

Barichara is the kind of town that Hollywood filmmakers dream about. A Spanish colonial town saturated with atmosphere, it boasts cobblestone streets and whitewashed buildings with red-tiled roofs that look almost as new as the day they were constructed some 300 years ago. It's no wonder that many Spanish-language films and *telenovelas* are shot here. Granted, the movie-set appearance owes a debt to considerable reconstruction efforts made since the town was declared a national monument in 1978.

The town is located 20km northwest of San Gil, high above the Río Suárez. Founded in 1705, its natural beauty, temperate climate and bohemian lifestyle have long attracted visitors. In recent years Barichara has become a magnet for affluent Colombians. Compared to Villa de Leyva, Baricharas is more upscale but less touristy. It is, without a doubt, one of the most beautiful small colonial towns in Colombia.

🏃 Activities

Don't miss the spectacular hike to the hamlet of Guane on the historic El Camino Real. This ancient stone-paved road was built by the indigenous Guane people and rebuilt continuously over the centuries. It was declared a national monument in 1988.

From Barichara the easy 9km hike takes about two hours to complete. The trail is mostly downhill, occasionally crossing over the modern highway to Guane. You'll begin the hike by climbing down the rim of a canyon and then traversing a valley filled with cacti and trees, occasionally encountering grazing goats or cows but rarely other humans. Notice the many fossils embedded in the stone road.

While most visitors just hike the short leg between Barichara and Guane, it's possible to extend the trek into a multiday adventure by continuing to Villanueva and down into the Cañon de Chicamocha to the tiny town of Jordán at the bottom of the canyon, before climbing up to Mesa de los Santos.

In Barichara, El Camino Real begins at the northern end of Calle 4, where a sign marks the beginning of the trail. If you plan to hike the full trail, leave your luggage in storage in San Gil or Baricharas – you don't want extra weight in the canyon. Bring a hat, sunscreen and plenty of water.

🛏 Sleeping & Eating

⭐ **Tinto Hostel**   HOSTEL $

(📞7-726-7725; www.tintohostel.com; Carrera 4 No 5-39; dm COP$23,000-27,000; s/d from COP$80,000-120,000; @🛜🏊) Baricharas's best hostel occupies a great multilevel home with a productive fruit garden. There are three dorms and five private rooms with good bathrooms, vaulted ceilings and hot water. The common areas – guest kitchen with artsy ceramic pottery, lounge, hammock space, terrace and small pool – are all wonderful, and the latter has views over the red roofs of Baricharas.

Color de Hormiga Hostel   HOSTEL $$

(📞315-297-1621; Carrera 7 No 7-78; dm COP$38,000, d COP$135,000-160,000; 🅿🛜) With a name referencing Baricharas's ant obsession, this well-run place has recently moved into new 'olde' digs in a handsome colonial home in the town center. The building has red-tile floors, heavy dark-wood furnishings and beautiful, thick whitewashed walls.

There's a five-bed dorm and several private rooms.

7 Tigres   PIZZA $$

(📞312-521-9962; Calle 6 No 10-24; pizzas COP$19,000-21,000; ⊗noon-3pm & 6-10pm) Colombians love their crispy thin-crust 'pita' pizzas, and the pies at this semi-alfresco place with its open kitchen and exclamation marks of artsy decor are piled with fresh ingredients sautéed immediately before they're slung in the oven. Great lasagna, too.

Shambalá
VEGETARIAN $$
(Carrera 7 No 6-20; mains COP$20,000-30,000; ☺12:30-4pm & 6-9:30pm Thu-Tue; ☎🖉) An extremely popular and consciously retro cafe doing made-to-order, mostly vegetarian dishes. Choose from wraps, rice and pasta in Mediterranean, Indian or Thai styles (you can add chicken or shrimp), and accompany your meal with an excellent juice or tea.

Restaurante Las Cruces
COLOMBIAN $$
(☎7-726-7577; www.tallerdeoficiosbarichara.com; Carrera 5 No 4-26; mains COP$20,000-40,000; ☺noon-3pm Mon-Thu, noon-3pm & 7-9:30pm Fri-Sun; 🖉) Encased in one of Barichara's larger colonial mansions, this venerable cooking school offers its student-prepared food in a spacious garden patio with tables laid out both alfresco and in little nooks in a sheltered wraparound porch. The menu often changes but is perennially anchored by Colombian food with some minor international variations.

This is the place to try Santander specialties like *carne oreada* (sun-dried steak), *mute santandereano* (a broth-like meat and vegetable soap) and that Barichara classic, meat cooked in *salsa de hormigas colunas* (sauce of big-bottom ants). Service can be slow but is always conscientious, and the food, inspired by the inventive young chefs, rarely falters. There's also a small cafe.

ℹ Information

Punto Información Turística (☎315-630-4696; Carrera 5, Salida San Gil; ☺9am-5pm Wed-Mon)

ℹ Getting There & Away

Buses shuttle between Barichara and San Gil (COP$5000, 45 minutes) every 30 minutes from 5am to 6:45pm. They depart from the **Cotrasangil office** (☎8-726-7132; www.cotrasangil.com; Carrera 6 No 5-70) on the main plaza. There are 10 buses to Guane (COP$2300, 15 minutes) between 5:30am and 5:45pm.

Cañon del Chicamocha

Halfway between San Gil and Bucaramanga is the spectacular canyon of Río Chicamocha, an arid landscape of majestic mountains standing guard over the cappuccino-colored river way down below. The cliff-hugging road between the two cities is one of the most wonderful (and windy) drives in Santander.

⊙ Sights

Parque Nacional del Chicamocha
AMUSEMENT PARK
(☎7-639-4444; www.parquenacionaldelchicamocha.com; Km4, Vía Bucaramanga-San Gil; adult/child COP$25,000/18,000; ☺10am-6pm Wed-Fri, 9am-7pm Sat & Sun; 🖼) Don't be fooled by the name: Parque Nacional del Chicamocha, or 'Panachi' as it's known by locals, isn't a national park in the conventional sense. It's really a slightly tacky amusement park built atop some spectacular mountains. There are no hiking trails here, but there is a *mirador* (lookout) offering magnificent 360 degree views. The highlight of the park is the 6.3km-long, 30-minute **teleférico** (return ticket incl park entrance adult/child COP$50,000/32,000; ☺10:30-11am, 12:30-1pm, 2:30-3pm & 4:30-5pm Wed-Fri, 9am-6pm Sat & Sun; 🖼), which descends to the base of the canyon, then ascends to the top of the opposite rim.

Other activities include an extreme swing and a zipline. The park also houses the mildly diverting **Museum of Guane Culture** (full of pre-Colombian Guane ceramics), several restaurants, a 4D cinema, a children's playground, a forgettable ostrich farm and the strange but striking *Monumento a la Santandereanidad,* a huge multistatue sculpture (with running commentaries in Spanish and English) commemorating the revolutionary spirit of santanderians (inhabitants of Santander province).

The most recent addition is an incongruous US$6-million water park (admission including national park adult/child COP$38,000/32,000) – an interesting thing to build on the top of an arid mountain range that regularly suffers from severe drought. The park is accessed via an underground road tunnel.

ℹ Getting There & Away

Any bus between San Gil (COP$10,000, one hour) and Bucaramanga (1¾ hours, COP$12,000) will drop you off at the entrance to Parque Nacional del Chicamocha. To get back to either city, just flag a passing bus from the bus stop on the highway.

In other areas of the canyon along the main highway there are few safe places to disembark: there's no footpath and there are sheer drops on the side of the road.

The paragliding site is located just off the main highway south of the park, but the companies include private transportation with the purchase of a flight.

Bucaramanga

📍7 / POP 528,500 / ELEV 960M

Dubbed 'The City of Parks,' Santander's capital has some fine green spaces and is a suitable spot to recharge your batteries. It comes to life at night, when dozens of clubs, hundreds of bars and the students of 10 universities don their party hats.

Buca, as it's known to locals, is one of Colombia's major cities. It has a greater-metropolitan population of about a million; it's packed with skyscrapers and surrounded by mountains. While it may not be the most interesting city in the country, it's not overrun with visitors and is a pleasant place to get a taste of the region's culture.

The city was founded in 1622 and developed around what is today the Parque García Rovira, but most of its colonial architecture is long gone. Over the centuries the city center moved east, and today Parque Santander is Bucaramanga's heart. Further east are newer, posh neighborhoods with hotels and nightspots.

👁 Sights & Activities

Museo Casa de Bolívar   MUSEUM
(📍7-630-4258; www.academiadehistoriade santander.org; Calle 37 No 12-15; COP$2000; ⏰8am-noon & 2-6pm Mon-Fri, 8am-noon Sat) Another piece in the historical jigsaw of Simón Bolívar's life (Colombia is full of them), this slightly musty museum is housed in a colonial mansion where the *libertador* stayed for two months in 1828. One room is dedicated to Bolívar and his exploits, while the rest of the suites tell the story of Santander province and the Guane people who once inhabited it. Take your time to peruse archaeological exhibits, weapons, yellowed documents, faded paintings, and frighteningly real mummies.

Colombia Paragliding   PARAGLIDING
(📍312-432-6266; www.colombiaparagliding. com; Km2 Via Mesa Ruitoque; 15/30min tandem rides COP$80,000/150,000) Try Bucaramanga's most popular sport on a tandem ride, or go all out and become an internationally

licensed paragliding pilot: 12-day courses including lodging begin at COP$3,400,000. Rides and courses are held atop the Ruitoque mesa, Buca's paragliding hub.

🛏 Sleeping

Kasa Guane Bucaramanga   HOSTEL $
(📍7-657-6960; www.kasaguane.com; Calle 11 No 26-50, Barrio Universidad; dm COP$35,000, s/d from COP$65,000/75,000; @🛜) Bucaramanga's best hostel has bright rooms with Guane-themed murals, cable TV and hot-water bathrooms alongside cheery dorms. Management is great for information and organizing all kinds of guest activities, including paragliding, but the real star here is the ample rooftop bar, which is a good place to hang out with locals.

Nest   HOSTEL $$
(📍7-678-2722; www.thenesthostel.com; Km2 Vía Mesa Ruitoque; dm COP$40,000, s/d from COP$60,000/90,000; @🛜🏊) This fly-site hostel is perched on a hilltop with amazing views of the city; it's next to one of Bucaramanga's best paragliding launch pads, 20 minutes' drive from downtown. The majority of guests are paragliding students (p598), but it's also a good choice for anyone seeking peace and quiet.

🍴 Eating & Drinking

⭐Penelope Casa
Gastronómica   INTERNATIONAL $$
(📍7-643-1235; Carrera 27A No 48-15; mains COP$20,000-35,000; ⏰11:30am-10:30pm) A diverse selection of gourmet plates from faraway lands awaits at this small but seriously hip restaurant run by talented young chefs. Among the options are naan bread topped with lamb and baked vegetables, *causa limena* (savory Peruvian potato cakes), and chicken tikka served with almond rice and chickpeas. All plates are spectacularly presented and combine many subtle flavors.

⭐Mercagán   STEAK $$
(📍7-632-4949; www.mercaganparrilla.com; Carrera 33 No 42-12; steak COP$21,500-47,500; ⏰11:30am-11pm Mon & Thu-Sat, to 3pm Tue & Wed, to 4pm Sun) Often touted as serving the best steak in the whole of Colombia, this traditional *parrilla* (grilled-meat restaurant) run by a team of brothers is all it's cracked up to be. Perfect slabs of meat from the brothers' own farm come in 200g, 300g or 400g (good luck!) sizes, served on sizzling iron plates.

Vintrash BAR

(Calle 49 No 35A-36; cover Fri & Sat COP$10,000; ⊙4-11pm Mon-Wed, to midnight Thu, to 3am Fri & Sat; 🛜) Among vintage oil barrels, hanging bicycles and a wisp of street cred, this bar sucks in the indie cool kids and those drawn to them for great music and alternative attitude. Electronica is the main sound, decent food plates are served and dancing is de rigueur. Entry is for those 21 and over.

ℹ️ Information

MEDICAL SERVICES

Clínica Foscal (📞7-638-2828; www.foscal. com.co; Av El Bosque No 23-60) Best private hospital in the region.

MONEY

There's no shortage of ATMs; many are clustered near Parque Santander along Calle 35, and in Sotomayor on Carrera 29.

Bancolombia (Carrera 18 No 34-28; ⊙24hr)

BBVA (cnr Carrera 19 & Calle 36; ⊙24hr)

Davivienda (cnr Calle 49 & Carrera 29)

TOURIST INFORMATION

Oficina de Turismo (📞7-634-1132, ext 112; www.imct.gov.co; Calle 30 No 26-117, Biblioteca Pública Gabriel Turbay, Piso 4; ⊙8am-noon & 1-5pm Mon-Fri) Main tourism office.

ℹ️ Getting There & Away

AIR

The **Palonegro airport** (BGA; Lebrija) is on a *meseta* (plateau) high above the city, 20km west in Lebrija. The landing here is quite breathtaking. The airport has direct flights to Bogotá, Barranquilla, Medellín, Cali and Cartagena, and international services from Panama City.

Colectivo taxis (Parque Santander; ⊙6am-6pm Mon-Sat) to the airport (COP$11,000) park off Parque Santander on Carrera 20 and leave every 15 minutes between 5am and 6pm. A taxi from the city center is a fixed COP$32,000.

Coming from San Gil, get off the bus at the Papi Quiero Piña bus stop to pick up a taxi to the airport.

BUS

Bucaramanga's **Terminal TB** (📞7-637-1000; www.terminalbucaramanga.com; Transversal Central Metropolitana) is situated southwest of the city center, midway to Girón; frequent city buses marked 'Terminal' go there from Carrera 15 (COP$2100), or take a taxi (COP$10,000).

Copetran (📞7-644-8167; www.copetran.com. co; Terminal de Transporte) is the big bus company here, serving most major destinations, such as Bogotá (COP$60,000 to COP$80,000, 10 hours), Cartagena (COP$80,000, 13 hours), Medellín (COP$95,000, eight hours) and Santa Marta (COP$70,000, 12 hours). There's a convenient **ticket office** (📞7-685-1389; Calle 49 No 28-64; ⊙8am-noon & 2-6pm Mon-Sat) in the center of town.

Cootrasangil (www.cotrasangil.com; Terminal de Transporte) heads to San Gil (COP$16,000, three hours) via Parque Nacional del Chicamocha (COP$10,000, 1½ hours). It's usually quicker to pick up San Gil buses at the Papi Quiero Piña bus stop at the edge of town near Floridablanca rather than going all the way to the terminal.

CARIBBEAN COAST

Sun soaked and rich in culture, Colombia's dramatic Caribbean coastline is its dazzling crown, capping the country with myriad ecosystems, from the dense jungles of the Darién Gap on the border with Panama to the hauntingly atmospheric desert of La Guajira near Venezuela.

The jewel along the coast is the colonial city of Cartagena, its beauty and romance unrivaled anywhere in Colombia despite the enormous number of visitors it attracts. A yet-undiscovered version can be enjoyed by journeying inland to find gorgeously isolated Mompós, a sleepy colonial hamlet lost in the jungle whose star is truly in the ascendant. Other attractions are more natural: the PNN Tayrona, a wonderful stretch of perfect beach and virgin rainforest, and the thrilling and arduous Ciudad Perdida (Lost City) trek, which will satisfy adventurers keen to discover the remnants of an ancient civilization against a stunning mountain backdrop.

Santa Marta

📞5 / POP 450,000

Santa Marta is South America's oldest European-founded town and the second-most-important colonial city on Colombia's Caribbean coast. Despite its long history and charming center, it gets a bad rap from many travelers, who cite its unlovely urban sprawl and terrible traffic as reasons not to hang about here. The secret to Santa Marta is to use it for what it does well: hotels, restaurants and bars, and then

Santa Marta

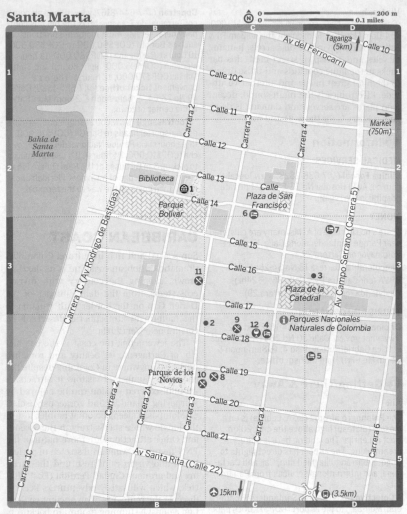

Santa Marta

⊙ Sights
1 Museo del Oro B2

✪ Activities, Courses & Tours
2 Expotur C4
3 Magic Tours D3

🛏 Sleeping
4 Casa del Farol C4
5 Casa Verde D4
6 La Brisa Loca C2

7 Masaya Santa Marta D3

✘ Eating
8 Ikaro C4
9 La Canoa C4
10 Ouzo B4
11 Restaurante LamArt B3

🍸 Drinking & Nightlife
12 Crabs C4

601

get out to the slew of superb nearby destinations during the daytime. That said, following an impressive sprucing up of its colonial heart, Santa Marta has gained a bit more of its own charm, and you might well find yourself spending more time here than you imagined. The climate is hot, but the heat here is drier than in Cartagena, and the evening sea breeze keeps the city cool after dark.

⊙ Sights

★Quinta de San
Pedro Alejandrino   MUSEUM
(☑5-433-1021; www.museobolivariano.org.co; Av Libertador; foreigners/Colombians COP$21,000/ 15,000; ⊙9am-4:30pm) This hacienda is where Simón Bolívar spent his last days in 1830 before succumbing to either tuberculosis or arsenic poisoning, depending on whom you believe. The hacienda was owned by a Spanish supporter of Colombia's independence who invited Bolívar to stay and take a rest before his journey to exile in Europe, but Bolívar died before he could complete the journey.

Museo del Oro   MUSEUM
(Calle 14 No 1-37; ⊙9am-5pm Tue-Sat, 10am-3pm Sun) FREE Oro (gold) is only half of what this fabulous museum is about. Housed in the impressively renovated Casa de la Aduana (Customs House), which features in the Gabriel García Márquez novel No One Writes to the Colonel, the displays lure you in with ceramics and jewelry from the Nahuange and Tayrona periods, backed by a comprehensive history of metalwork in the pre-Columbian Sierra Nevada.

⟆ Tours

Santa Marta's tour market revolves around Ciudad Perdida treks, but the same agencies that offer these can also arrange various other hiking trips, plus bird-watching, mountain biking and visits to Minca and PNN Tayrona. Highly recommended agencies for local tours include **Magic Tours** (☑5-421-5820, 317-679-2441; www.magictourcolombia.com; Calle 16 No 4-41) and **Expotur** (☑5-420-7739; www.expotur-eco.com; Carrera 3 No 17-27).

🛏 Sleeping

★Masaya Santa Marta   HOSTEL $
(☑5-423-1770; www.masaya-experience.com; Carrera 14 No 4-80; dm COP$40,000-50,000, r incl breakfast COP$120,000-200,000; ❉@🛜🛏)

This fabulous hostel in the town center takes some beating. A clever and stylish multi-level conversion of an old mansion, it has superb-value dorms and gorgeous private rooms. Dorm beds have individual curtains for increased privacy; private rooms are adorned with interesting art. There are three plunge pools, a busy rooftop bar, a large outdoor kitchen, billiards and a cinema room.

La Brisa Loca   HOSTEL $$
(☑317-585-9598, 5-431-6121; www.labrisaloca. com; Calle 14 No 3-58; dm with/without air-con from COP$45,000/30,000, r with/without bathroom COP$150,000/120,000; ❉@🛜🛏) The 'Crazy Breeze' is the choice of a young, festive crowd, who pack out the 100 or so beds. Dorms sleep four to 10, and there's an array of private rooms, too, all with firm mattresses, high ceilings, ancient tile work, and in-room lockers that allow you to charge your phone securely while you're out.

★Casa del Farol   BOUTIQUE HOTEL $$$
(☑5-423-1572; www.lacasadelfarol.com; Calle 18 No 3-115; r/ste incl breakfast from COP$275,000/ 330,000; ❉🛜🛏) A superb hotel that could almost be recommended as a city highlight, the Farol hides a wealth of little luxuries behind its plain red facade. The large, funky-modern rooms are named and decorated after various cities (the Beijing and NYC rooms stand out), and the polite, courteous staff members are as helpful as tour guides.

Casa Verde   HOTEL $$$
(☑313-420-7502, 5-431-4122; www.casaverde santamarta.com; Calle 18 No 4-70; d/ste incl breakfast COP$254,000/315,000; ❉🛜🛏) If you're what the relaxed and attentive live-in owner calls 'a retired backpacker,' then this cute nine-room spot – with pebble-lined walls and floors, smart bathrooms, crisp bed linen, and intelligently designed, pristine whitewashed rooms – is for you. Lounge in the refreshing pool near the lobby or enjoy city views on the new roof terrace.

🍴 Eating

Santa Marta has some of the best food on the coast. An influx of Latin and North American restaurateurs has simplified menus and moved the focus to ambience, classic cooking and stylish presentation. Parque de los Novios is the heart of Santa Marta's eating scene.

★Ikaro   VEGETARIAN $$
(☑5-430-5585; www.ikarocafe.com; Calle 19 No 3-60; mains COP$12,000-28,000; ⊙8am-9pm

COLOMBIA SANTA MARTA

Mon-Sat, 9am-9pm Sun; 🛜🅿) 🍴 Ikaro draws you in with its micro-roasted coffee and freshly baked bread then entreats you to stay with its giant lounging 'beds' (ideal for sprawling with your headphones) and interior green wall dripping with foliage. The cafe menu is vegetarian, but carnivores will also find it appealing, and there are vegan options and craft beer, too.

La Canoa
FRENCH $$

(📋 5-421-7895; www.canoacafe.com; Calle 18 No 3-75; mains COP$15,000-37,000; ⊙9am-9pm Mon, Wed & Fri, to 10pm Thu, to 11pm Sat, 11am-11pm Sun; ❄🛜🅿) A fusion spot with French pretensions that doesn't come across as at all pretentious, La Canoa is a Franco-Colombian marriage made in heaven that's ideal if you're craving cool air (strong air-con), a jolting caffeine hit (strong coffee) and a quick connection to the worldwide web (strong wi-fi).

Restaurante LamArt
INTERNATIONAL $$

(📋 5-431-0797; www.lamart.com.co; Carrera 3 No 16-36; breakfast COP$16,000, dinner COP$25,000-36,000; ⊙9am-10:30pm Mon-Fri, 11am-11:30pm Sat, 5-10:30pm Sun) Santa Marta's charismatic Callejón del Correo (Carrera 3) sucks you in, especially in the evening, and there's no better doorway to the melee than LamArt, where spicy ceviche meets homemade pasta over potent coffee. The ambitious menu pulls off the near-impossible task of pleasing practically everyone, from Thai-curry lovers to Spaniards missing their Galician octopus.

Ouzo
MEDITERRANEAN $$

(📋 5-423-0658; www.ouzosantamarta.com; Carrera 3 No 19-29; mains COP$26,000-44,000; ⊙noon-10:30pm Mon-Thu, to 11pm Fri & Sat; 🛜) Ouzo offers a stripped-back, classic Greek and Italian menu that includes superb pizza from a wood-fired oven and a good wine list. The octopus is slow-cooked for two hours in a garlicky broth, then slammed on the coals to sear and seal in the flavor. There's great service, and the superbly designed interior means the heat stays in the kitchen.

🍷 Drinking & Nightlife

Crabs
BAR

(Calle 18 No 3-69; ⊙8pm-3am Wed-Sat) Less to do with crustaceans and more to do with rock and roll, the whimsically decorated Crabs is considered one of Colombia's best rock and blues bars, with cold beer, friendly staff and live sounds most nights. There are plenty of icons on the wall, a pool table, and even a bath to sit in.

COLOMBIA MINCA

❶ Information

Aviatur (📋 5-423-5745; www.aviatur.com; Calle 15 No 3-20; ⊙8am-noon & 2-4pm Mon-Fri) A place to reserve accommodations run by the agency inside PNN Tayrona.

Parques Nacionales Naturales de Colombia (📋 5-423-0758; www.parquesnacionales.gov.co; Calle 17 No 4-06) This office of the national-park service gives some basic information about PNN Tayrona.

❶ Getting There & Away

AIR

The **Aeropuerto Internacional Simón Bolívar** (📋 5-438-1360; http://smr.aerooriente.com.co; Vía Ciénaga Santa Marta, Km18) is 16km south of the city on the Barranquilla–Bogotá road and must be one of the few airports in the world right on the beach. City buses marked 'El Rodadero Aeropuerto' will take you there in 45 minutes from Carrera 1C. Flight destinations include Bogotá and Medellín.

BUS

The **bus terminal** (Calle 41 No 31-17) is on the southeastern outskirts of the city. Frequent minibuses go there from Carrera 1C in the center, or you can take a cab (COP$6000).

The main bus companies all offer several daily connections to the following destinations.

DESTINATION	FARE (COP$)	DURATION (HOURS)
Barranquilla	14,000	2
Bogotá	80,000-90,000	16-17
Bucaramanga	70,000	9-12
Cartagena	35,000	4
Medellín	126,000	15
Riohacha	20,000	2½
Tolú	51,000	7

For Palomino, take the Mamatoco bus from the market in Santa Marta (COP$9000, two hours).

Minca

🎫 5 / POP 1200

Perched 600m high up in the Sierra Nevada above Santa Marta, Minca is a small mountain village famous for its organic coffee, incredibly varied birdlife and – perhaps more importantly – much cooler temperatures than on the scorching coast below. The town, which until a few years ago could only be reached via a dirt road, is delightful, surrounded by thick cloud forest and soaring mountain peaks. Despite being recognized by Unesco as a biosphere reserve since 1980, it's only in the last few years that Minca has grown as a traveler destination, with a slew of new hostels and hotels.

It's now well and truly on the map, however, and specializes in ultraremote traveler retreats scattered amid the surrounding steep mountainsides. A great base for mountain biking, bird-watching and hiking, Minca also offers delightfully warm locals who seem genuinely happy to see visitors.

⊙ Sights

Finca La Candelaria   FARM
(📞 321-588-7985; www.fincacarpediem.com/activities/finca-la-candelaria; tours COP$20,000; ⊙9am-5pm) 🍃 This small coffee, cacao and fruit farm is a family-run, organic business that visitors are welcome to tour to see the various stages of growth, harvest and preparation. Each themed tour lasts around an hour. It's a COP$20,000 moto-taxi ride from town, plus a 10-minute walk.

☞ Tours

Bird-watching, hiking and mountain biking are the most popular activities in Minca, and can be organized by almost any hostel or hotel. Minca is also well located for the Ciudad Perdida (p606) trek, and makes for a good place to relax and unwind afterwards.

Jungle Joe
Minca Adventures   TOURS
(📞 317-308-5270; www.junglejoeminca.com) If you haven't got much time or are just keen to immerse yourself in Minca's diversity, English-speaking Joe Ortiz can organise an excellent tour incorporating a coffee farm, cacao production, hiking, a local lunch and a swim near a waterfall, all for a very reasonable COP$130,000. There are also more specialised tubing and bird-watching trips.

🛏 Sleeping & Eating

Minca has blossomed in recent years and now has some of the best hostels along the coast – and certainly many of those with the best views. There are many hostels in the town itself, but the very best options are in the mountains, often involving a motorbike ride to get there.

★ Casa Elemento   HOSTEL $
(📞 313-587-7677, 311-655-9207; www.casaelemento.co; hammocks/dm COP$25,000/40,000,

cabañas from COP$150,000; 📶) When they say the location here is 'above Minca' they're not kidding – just getting here is an adventure and ensures that only the intrepid arrive. Created and run by an international crew, Casa Elemento has an incredible position with extraordinary views and is the perfect place to escape the world. It's a 30-minute, COP$25,000 motorbike ride from Minca.

Minca Ecohabs   CABAÑAS $$
(📞 317-586-4067; www.mincaecohabs.com; r incl breakfast from COP$196,000; 🅿🛜) 🍃 On a steep hillside with views toward the Caribbean and Santa Marta, this long-standing hotel was recently taken over by a Santa Marta hotelier who has attempted to reinvigorate the place. The two-story rooms are made of entirely natural fibers, have screened windows, balconies, fans, electricity and fridges. It's a wonderful place to really drink in Minca's unique location.

Lazy Cat   INTERNATIONAL $
(Calle Principal Diagonal; mains COP$13,000-20,000; ⊙9am-9pm; 🛜✏) You can slink into the Lazy Cat at any time of day for all kinds of hunger relief, from breakfasts (COP$8000 to COP$10,000) to superb local coffee, smoothies, sandwiches, burgers and quesadillas. There's a lovely balcony overlooking the valley below, and the eponymous cat can usually be found lounging around the place somewhere.

ℹ Getting There & Away

Colectivos (shared taxis, minivans, or midsize buses) and shared taxis to/from Santa Marta arrive at and depart from the center of Minca throughout the day (COP$8000, 30 minutes), and you'll rarely have to wait longer than 20 minutes for them to fill up and depart. A taxi to Santa Marta is around COP$40,000.

In Santa Marta, Minca-bound *colectivos* and shared taxis leave from outside the market at the corner of Calle 11 and Carrera 12. A faster option for the same price is the moto-taxi to Minca. However, these depart from Yucal, a barrio on the outskirts of town, so you'll need to take a COP$6000 taxi from anywhere in Santa Marta to get there.

Parque Nacional Natural Tayrona

Parque Nacional Natural Tayrona (www.parquetayrona.com.co; foreigners/Colombians COP$54,500/23,000; ⊙8am-5pm) is a magical slice of Colombia's Caribbean coast, with stunning stretches of golden sandy beach

Parque Nacional Natural Tayrona

backed by coconut palms and thick rainforest. Behind it all rise the steep hillsides of the Sierra Nevada de Santa Marta, the world's highest coastal mountain range. The park stretches along the coast from the Bahía de Taganga near Santa Marta to the mouth of the Río Piedras, 35km east, and covers some 12,000 hectares of land and 3000 hectares of coral-rich sea.

The park gets extremely crowded in high season (December and January), and vicious currents mean that most of the gorgeous beaches aren't suitable for swimming, though you can take a dip and snorkel (with great care) at a select, safer few. Despite these issues, Tayrona is an immensely attractive place and one that's rewarding and exciting to explore.

◉ Sights

From El Zaíno, a 4km paved side road goes northwest to **Castilletes**, the longest beach in the park and the first place you can turn in for the night. A van plies the route constantly and charges just COP$3000. A few more kilometers down the road is **Cañaveral**, also on the beach. Here you'll find a campground, upscale cabañas and a restaurant. You can then continue to walk along to all the beaches and even up to **Pueblito**, a small indigenous village in the middle of the jungle.

★ **Cabo San Juan del Guía** BEACH
Cabo San Juan del Guía is a beautiful cape with a knockout beach. It's also by far the most crowded area of the park, although lack of road access deters casual day-trippers.

The area has a **restaurant** and a **campsite** (☑ 333-356-9912; www.cabosanjuantayrona.com; Cabo San Juan del Guía; campsites COP$20,000, hammocks COP$40,000-50,000, rent-a-tents COP$60,000, cabins COP$200,000), with hammocks and cabins, in a spectacular lookout on a rock in the middle of the beach. It's possible to spend a very atmospheric night here. Swimming is also possible most of the time, but don't go in too deep.

🛏 Sleeping

There are multiple options for spending a night or two in the park, though they are either exceptionally expensive or very basic. **Castilletes** (☑ 300-405-5547, 313-653-1830; www.campingcastilletespnntayrona.blogspot.com; campsites/tents per person COP$20,000/30,000, hammocks COP$25,000, cabins COP$110,000; 🅿), the first point reached after entering from El Zaíno, offers peaceful camping with sea views; Cañaveral (p604) is where the fancier options are, while **Arrecifes** and Cabo San Juan del Guía (p604) are the most popular spots for backpackers.

★ **Ecohostal Yuluka** HOSTAL **$$**
(☑ 310-361-9436; www.aviatur.com; Via Santa Marta, Km28; incl breakfast dm COP$40,000, r from COP$160,000; 🛜❄) This gorgeous place very stylishly caters for discerning backpackers who want to explore the park without giving up all comforts. It's very rustic but supremely comfortable, with large private bathrooms, spacious dorms and even a slide into the pool. All beds come with mosquito nets, and the food is great.

entrance and Cañaveral (COP$3000, 10 minutes) or walk the 2.5km.

It's located on the main road just before the main El Zaíno park entrance if you're coming from Santa Marta.

★ Finca Barlovento　　　　　HOTEL $$$

(☏ 314-626-9789; http://barloventotayrona.com; Via Riohacha, Km33; s/d/tr incl half board from COP$330,000/450,000/695,000) Finca Barlovento may be the single most beautiful spot in the area, and it's located just outside PNN Tayrona right on the beach at Playa Los Naranjos. Here, where the Río Piedras bursts out of the Sierra Nevada and empties into the Caribbean, you'll find this architecturally unique home, clinging to a cliff face.

The property consists of the original house and the *maloka*, an indigenous-style thatched structure divided into private rooms. Both feature open-air beds that jut out on a deck over the sea, and the food is simply sensational.

❶ Information

PNN Tayrona can be entered at several points, but wherever you enter, you'll need to pay the entrance fee (foreigners/Colombians COP$54,500/23,000). This fee is valid for as long as you care to stay inside the park, and you can also leave the park and reenter at another entrance until 5pm on the day of purchase. Upon entering you may be searched for alcohol and glass bottles, neither of which are permitted.

❶ Getting There & Away

You can get to El Zaíno (COP$7000, one hour) on Palomino-bound buses that depart regularly from Santa Marta's market; just let the driver know where you want to get out. From El Zaíno, catch the jeep that shuttles between the park

Palomino

♪ 5 / POP 6000

Palomino doesn't look like much as you pass through on the main Santa Marta–Riohacha highway, but lurking on one side of its urban sprawl is one of Colombia's most perfect beaches, while on the other are the dramatic Sierra Nevada mountains, a place the local indigenous people still guard carefully from outsiders. Palomino makes a wonderful base from which to explore both, with a number of great accommodations options and a backpacker vibe you'll not find in many other places along the coast.

Along Palomino's palm-backed beach you'll also find fishers using traditional nets, while in its mountainous hinterland indigenous tribes live as they have done for centuries. With seven ecosystems between the beach and the glaciers of the Sierra Nevada, it's no surprise that ecotourism has slowly come into its own here, making Palomino an almost obligatory stop for Colombia travelers.

🛏 Sleeping

Palomino has some of the best traveler hostels and most laid-back beach hotels in the country. Most listings are on the beach, but all can arrange trips into the mountains for activities, including hiking, tubing or white-water rafting.

★ Tiki Hut Hostel Palomino　　　　HOSTEL $

(☏ 314-794-2970; www.tikihutpalomino.co; dm/d incl breakfast COP$40,000/160,000; 🛜🏊) Like a backpacker hostel relocated to a tropical beach setting, Tiki Hut is paradise on a budget, a beautifully designed place set around a large pool, with charming staff and comfortable, rustic rooms that feature mosquito nets and artsy splashes of color. Less brilliant are the not-fully-enclosed toilets in the big dorms.

Finca Escondida　　　　　　HOSTEL $

(☏ 310-456-3159, 315-610-9561; www.finca escondida.com; hammocks COP$30,000, dm COP$40,000, d COP$170,000-210,000; 🛜) The football pitch, outdoor gym, yoga classes and surf school suggest that this large beachfront complex is run by a bunch of fitness fanatics, but it also rewards guests in search of tranquility, with inviting hammocks, relaxing gardens and largish rooms complete with

TAGANGA

Once a tiny fishing village, Taganga seemed to have hit the jackpot when it became a big backpacker destination in the early 2000s. It drew a diverse crowd of locals and travelers, and quietly boomed. Hostels and restaurants prospered with the endless stream of visitors.

Taganga today is something of a cautionary tale about the overdevelopment of small towns, though, and in the past few years the village has gone from a near-obligatory backpacker stop to a rather depressing place where poverty is rife and much of what originally attracted visitors has disappeared. That said, some travelers still come here for cheap accommodations, partying and diving; there are also those who love being so close to Parque Nacional Natural (PNN) Tayrona, just a short boat ride away. The town's hostel owners are a determined bunch and are doggedly fighting to restore Taganga to its former glory.

One of the best reasons to visit Taganga is to dive. **Poseidon Dive Center** (☑5-421-9224, 314-889-2687; www.poseidondivecenter.com; Calle 18 No 1-69) offers minicourses allowing beginners to dive up to 12m (COP$300,000), Professional Association of Diving Instructors (PADI) Open Water courses (COP$1,150,000) and two-tank dives (COP$240,000). Boats leave most mornings for the pristine waters in and around PNN Tayrona.

Taganga is easily accessible; there are frequent minibuses (COP$1600, 15 minutes) from Carreras 1C and 5 in Santa Marta. A taxi costs COP$10,000. From Taganga there's a daily boat to Cabo San Juan del Guía (p604) in PNN Tayrona (COP$50,000 one way, one hour).

beautiful heavy beds and psychedelic murals. The feel is rustic, with wooden buildings set in grounds full of fruit trees.

Dreamer Hostel HOSTEL $$
(☑300-609-7229, 320-556-7794; www.thedreamerhostel.com; dm/d incl breakfast from COP$45,000/180,000; ☞☀) Like a resort for backpackers, the Dreamer has a kidney-shaped pool, a large, florid garden and a restaurant with good pizzas. The supersocial ambience is reminiscent of a refined beach party, and there are plenty of activities on offer. The tile-floored, fan-cooled, thatched-roofed dorms are spacious, if lacking in luxury touches.

Aité Eco Hotel HOTEL $$$
(☑321-782-1300; www.aite.com.co; d/cabañas/bungalows incl breakfast from COP$511,000/430,000/610,000; ❄☞☀) Compared to Palomino's other backpacker-oriented spots, Aité is a bit more grown up and manicured. Set on a secluded hillside with closely cropped grass and well-tended plants, this 15-room pleasure garden has common areas perched atop a small ridge, though the loveliest rooms are arguably the beachside cabañas, which open onto the sea.

❶ Getting There & Away

There's no bus station in Palomino, but regular buses in both directions run along the main road.

Destinations include Santa Marta (COP$9000, two hours), PNN Tayrona (COP$6000, one hour) and Riohacha (COP$8000, 1½ hours). The best place to pick them up is at the top of Carrera 6.

If you're arriving in Palomino, you can walk down to the beach or grab a moto-taxi to drive you the 500m there (COP$2000). Buses and motorbikes run all day and until late at night – not a bad option if you have luggage.

Ciudad Perdida

What could be more intriguing than an ancient abandoned city? Ciudad Perdida (Lost City) disappeared into the jungle around the time of the Spanish Conquest and was only 'discovered' again in the 1970s. Deep in the Sierra Nevada de Santa Marta mountains, it remains accessible only on foot in what is easily one of Colombia's most exciting and breathtaking hikes. Known locally by its indigenous name Teyuna, the city was built by the Tayrona people on the northern slopes of the Sierra Nevada de Santa Marta. Today it's one of the largest known pre-Columbian towns in the Americas, and the focus of Colombia's most popular multiday hike. Doing the hike is a fantastic experience, and you don't need to be particularly strong or experienced to do it. The landscapes and the sense of remoteness will stay with you long after you return.

🏃 Activities

After meeting your tour group (obligatory) in Santa Marta in the morning, you'll be driven to the village of El Mamey (also known as Machete), the end of the road from Santa Marta, where you'll have a leisurely lunch before setting off. The walk normally takes 1½ days uphill to Ciudad Perdida, with a half-day at the site on the morning of the third day, then one full day's walking back downhill that is split over two days. The round trip is just shy of 45km, but it feels like a lot more as you scramble uphill, slide through mud downhill and generally exhaust every leg muscle you have. In the dry season the schedule can vary. Ask your tour company for a detailed itinerary. You walk in and out along the same route; travel agencies are continuing to negotiate with the indigenous Wiwa people to grant access to a different route out, but the Wiwa understandably remain extremely protective of their lands.

The normal hike is challenging but not mercilessly so; although each day covers only 5km to 8km, it's nearly all very steep ascent or descent. If you've never hiked before in your life, you'll find it tough, but even unfit first-timers complete the journey. At times you'll be scrambling alongside vertiginous river banks, clutching onto vines, and most people find that carrying a stick helps with balance. The rainy season brings its own challenges, such as surging rivers; heavy, boot-caking mud; and collapsed walkways.

There are significant uphill slogs that can be brutal in the scorching jungle heat. When the sun isn't blazing, it's likely to be muddy, so you'll trade sweat for loose traction. The driest period is from late December to February or early March. Depending on the season, on day three you might have to cross the Río Buritaca multiple times, at times going in up to your waist, and finally you'll have to slog up Ciudad Perdida's mystical but slippery, moss-strewn rock steps – all 1260 of them – that lead to the site.

Along the way, the food is surprisingly good and the accommodations are comfortable, often located by rivers, where you can cool off in natural swimming pools. The scenery is (obviously) nothing short of astonishing: this is a walk that is done at least as much for the journey as for the destination.

The site itself, a high plateau surrounded by blindingly brilliant jungle, is fascinating, and you'll likely only be sharing it with your group and the few Colombian soldiers stationed there when you arrive.

It's important to be aware that the mountains are sacred to all the indigenous people who live there, so it's essential to leave absolutely no litter (and by all means pick up any you find on the route), and behave with respect within the Ciudad Perdida site.

ℹ Information

Previously, just the one agency, Turcol, had access to Ciudad Perdida. However, in 2008 the Colombian military cleared out the paramilitaries in the area, which has effectively opened up the route to Ciudad Perdida to healthy competition. There are now six licensed agencies, all based in Santa Marta (p601), guiding groups of travelers on the four- to six-day hike to the ancient ruins. You cannot do the trip on your own or hire an independent guide. If you're not sure about the legitimacy of your guide or agency, be sure to ask for the Operación de Programas Turísticos (OPT) certificate, the essential document needed by any guide.

Once the market opened in 2008, the race to the bottom began, and prices and quality fell. The government intervened by regulating prices and service, and the official price of the tour is now set at COP$950,000.

The price includes transportation, food, accommodations (usually mattresses with mosquito nets, though some agencies still use hammocks on one night), porters for your food, non-English-speaking guides and all necessary permits. The price does not go down if you complete the walk in fewer days. Most groups tend to do the trek in four days, but less fit walkers and those who want to take their time often do it in five. Six-day trips are the maximum and are only really necessary for the very slow and easily exhausted; the four-day version is recommended.

Take the strongest mosquito repellent you can find and reapply it every few hours. Local brand Nopikex is excellent and will protect you better than many stronger foreign brands. Take some long pants and a long-sleeved T-shirt, both of which are advisable at Ciudad Perdida itself, where the mosquitoes are particularly hungry.

Tours are in groups of four to 15, and depart year-round as soon as a group is assembled. In high season expect a tour to set off every day. In low season the agencies tend to form a joint group, even if each agency still has its own guides. Other companies are agents for these outfits and there's really no reason to use them.

Note that all access to Ciudad Perdida is closed (and thus no hikes depart) for much of September, when indigenous peoples meet to perform cleansing ceremonies at the site.

COLOMBIA CIUDAD PERDIDA

La Guajira Peninsula

English pirates, Dutch smugglers and Spanish pearl hunters have all tried to conquer the Guajira Peninsula – a vast swath of barren sea and sand that is Colombia's northernmost point – but none were able to overcome the indigenous Wayuu people, who wisely traded with, or waged war upon, the invaders. The Wayuu's complex and autonomous political and economic structures meant they were ready to mount a staunch defense of their lands – on horseback and with firearms.

Even today, this is a diesel-and-dust landscape with more than a whiff of *Mad Max*–like lawlessness. Sadly, the roadsides around the small towns in the west are littered with rubbish – indeed, the symbol of modern-day Guajira might well be a plastic bag caught in a leafless bush. Fortunately, as you head east the litter fades away until you fall upon the end-of-the-world paradise of Punta Gallinas, an immaculate collision of desert dunes and crashing waves.

ℹ Getting There & Away

Access to La Guajira is normally via Riohacha, and to Middle and Upper Guajira via the small town of Uribia, the transport hub for the peninsula proper. There are no scheduled buses, and transportation is always in 4WD jeeps that leave when full. In general, it's never a good idea to rely on public services in this part of Colombia; it is recommended to travel on a tour that includes transportation.

Riohacha

📋 5 / POP 278,000

Riohacha, traditionally the end of the line, is the gateway to the northern, semiarid desert region of La Guajira and retains more than a little frontier-town feeling. As tourism in the peninsula has developed in recent years, Riohacha has become an unlikely traveler hub of sorts and you may find yourself spending the night here on the way to or from more isolated and beautiful parts of Colombia. The town isn't teeming with things to do, but it's pleasant enough; there's a 5km-long beach strewn with palm trees, and the long pier, constructed in 1937, makes for a lovely evening stroll. Despite Riohacha's oppressive daytime heat, there's generally a cool breeze coming in off the Caribbean, and the town is friendly and welcoming.

🛏 Sleeping & Eating

Bona Vida Hostel Tercera   HOSTEL **$**
(📋 314-637-0786; www.bonavidahostel.com; Calle 3 No 10-10; dm incl breakfast COP$30,000-38,000, d with/without bathroom COP$110,000/95,000; ❄ 🛜) La Bona Vida is so good that it had to add a second branch in 2017, only a year after opening the first. Behind the turquoise colonial facade lies a diminutive, well-laid-out interior sporting dorms (with curtained bunks and personal fans) and private doubles (with air-con and – drumroll – Netflix!).

Lima Cocina Fusión   FUSION **$$**
(📋 5-728-1313; Calle 13 No 11-33; mains COP$15,000-35,000; 🛜 ✐) The cool interior of this polished place exerts a magnetic force on hungry walk-by traffic. While the name's a little misleading (there's not much gourmet Peruvian cuisine to be had), the food quality and service are certainly worthy of comparisons to Lima. The menu revolves around a selection of 'pitas' (thin-crust mini-pizzas), backed by some of the best salads in Colombia.

ℹ Getting There & Away

The **bus terminal** (cnr Calle 15 & Carrera 11a) is about 1km from the center. A taxi from the center is COP$5000.

Expreso Brasilia (📋 5-727-2240; Terminal de Transporte Riohacha) has buses to Santa Marta (COP$20,000, 2½ hours) and Barranquilla (COP$31,000, five hours) every 30 minutes; hourly services to Cartagena (COP$42,000, seven hours); and services every 45 minutes to Maicao (COP$10,000, one hour), on the border with Venezuela. There's a daily bus to Bogotá (COP$100,000 to COP$107,000, 18 hours) at 3pm, which also passes through Valledupar (COP$30,000, four hours).

Cootrauri (📋 5-728-0000; Terminal de Transporte Riohacha) runs *colectivos*, leaving as they fill up, every day from 5am to 6pm to Uribia (COP$14,000, one hour), where you switch for the final leg to Cabo de la Vela (COP$12,000 to COP$18,000, 2½ hours).

Cabo de la Vela

📋 5 / POP 1500

The fishing village of Cabo de la Vela, 180km northwest of Riohacha, was until recently little more than a remote rural community, its Wayuu inhabitants living in traditional huts made from cactus right up against the sea. But in the last couple of years Cabo has become a hotbed of ecotourism and kitesurfing and now boasts a wealth of indigenous-style accommodations. Nevertheless, the village still has electricity by generator only, and there are few fixed phone lines. Internet access is sporadic at best.

The surrounding area is a highlight of the Upper Guajira and one of the most starkly beautiful spots in Colombia. The cape for which it's named is full of rocky cliffs above and sandy beaches below, all set against a backdrop of stunning desert ochres and aquamarines.

If you're looking for peace and quiet, Cabo is best avoided around Easter, December and January.

◉ Sights & Activities

Playa del Pilón   BEACH
Playa del Pilón, far and away the most beautiful beach in Cabo, is a vivid orange-sand beach lapped by surprisingly cool waters and framed by low, rocky cliffs. Spectacular at any time of day, the colors are especially impressive at sunrise and sunset. In the wet season add lush desert flora to the mix and the whole scene is rather cinematic.

Pilón de Azúcar   VIEWPOINT
Pilón de Azúcar looms over the eponymous beach and provides the area's most telescopic viewpoint, with the whole of Alta Guajira displayed before you and the Serranía del Carpintero mountain range in the distance. A statue of La Virgen de Fátima, erected here in 1938 by Spanish pearl hunters, stands at the top of the viewpoint as the patron saint of Cabo.

Awalayúu Kite School   KITESURFING
(☎314-439-9427; board rental per hour/day COP$100,000/300,000) Runs personalized courses with one-on-one tuition and all equipment (COP$150,000 per hour). Gear rental also available. Find it on the seafront near the **Posada Pujuru** (☎310-659-4189, 300-279-5048; posadapujuru@gmail.com; hammocks/chinchorros COP$15,000/20,000, r per person COP$30,000) in a typical fenced Wayuu corral.

🛏 Sleeping

A government-sponsored ecotourism project has resulted in more than 60 rustic posadas (hotels) in Cabo. Lodging is generally in Wayuu huts fashioned from *yotojoro*, the core of the cardon cactus that grows in the desert here. Choose between smaller hammocks, larger and warmer traditional *chinchorros* (locally crafted hammocks) or

beds with private bathrooms (note: running water is scarce). Bring your own towel.

Ranchería Utta   GUESTHOUSE $
(☎312-678-8237, 313-817-8076; www.rancheria utta.com; hammocks/chinchorros/cabañas per person COP$20,000/30,000/45,000) On the far side of the village, within walking distance of El Faro lighthouse, is the best *ranchería* in town. The adjoining rooms, fashioned from the traditional Wayuu cactus, have a few splashes of color, with hung blankets and the like. Bonuses are a large, clean restaurant and an owner who's happy to greet his guests.

Punta Gallinas
📞5 / POP 20

Punta Gallinas is South America's most northerly point and offers one of the continent's most dazzling landscapes. Its access point, Bahía Hondita, is where burnt-orange cliffs surround an emerald bay with a wide and wild beach, beyond which is a large colony of pink flamingos. Otherwise the bay is home to just eight Wayuu families, who dwell in an exceptionally harsh environment peppered with vibrant green vegetation and shared only with herds of goats and locusts.

As the continent gives way to the Caribbean, sand dunes topping 60m high push right up against the turquoise sea, like a five-story sand tsunami in reverse. This is Playa Taroa, perhaps Colombia's most beautiful and certainly its least trampled-upon beach, accessed by sliding down a towering sand dune right into the water.

Barranquilla
📞5 / POP 1.2 MILLION / ELEV 10M

Colombia's fourth-largest city, the hardworking port town of Barranquilla is located on the delta of the massive Río Magdalena and laid out in a tangled ribbon along mangroves and the Caribbean Sea, sweltering and hustling in the blinding sun. The birthplace of Colombian pop goddess Shakira, Barranquilla is actually most famous for its Carnaval, when the town clocks off, puts on its glad rags and goes wild as it throws the country's biggest street party.

While Barranquilla attracts big crowds for Mardi Gras, at any other time of the year there are very few visitors, and most travelers skip the town altogether (there's very little to see compared with elsewhere on the coast). If you do come, you'll find a city proud to be the home of *costeño* (people from the coast) culture, and one with plenty of excellent restaurants, lively bars and a smattering of decent museums.

🍴 Sleeping & Eating

⭐ Pizzeria the Meeting Point PIZZA $$

(📞 5-310-8581; Carrera 61 No 68-100; pizzas COP$12,000-32,000; ⊙ 5:30-11pm; 📶🍴) With its simple stools and tables on an enclosed porch, Italian-run Meeting Point looks more fast-food joint than promising pizzeria. But don't be too quick to judge. These are hands down Barranquilla's best pies: fresh, tangy and Naples authentic, from the simple margherita to the rich *disco volante* piled high with roast beef and an array of vegetables.

Service is lightning fast, and the place does a fly-off-the-shelf takeout service, too. A namesake **hostel** (📞 320-502-4459, 5-318-2599; www.themeetingpoint.hostel.com; Carrera 61 No 68-100; dm/r from COP$30,000/90,000; ❄🌐) sits right next door.

ⓘ Getting There & Away

The **bus terminal** (www.ttbaq.com.co; cnr Carerra 14 & Calle 54, Soledad) is located 7km from the city center. It's not convenient: it may take up to an hour to get to the terminal by urban bus. It's much faster to go by taxi (COP$25,000, 30 minutes). From here, there are at least hourly buses to Bogotá (from COP$89,000, 18 hours), Medellín (from COP$118,000, 12 hours), Santa Marta (COP$14,000, two hours), Riohacha (COP$31,000, four hours) and Cartagena (from COP$14,000, two hours). Other services include daily buses to Tolú (COP$40,000, five hours, hourly every morning) and Mompós (COP$38,000, six hours, 7:30am).

For speedy and more convenient travel to Cartagena and Santa Marta, head to the far more central terminals of **Berlinas** (📞 5-385-0030; www.berlinasdelfonce.com; cnr Calle 93 & Carrera 47) or **Marsol** (📞 5-369-0999; www.transportesmarsol.net; cnr Calle 93 & Carrera 47), both located on Calle 93 between Carreras 47 and 49C. From here, zippy shuttle buses make fast journeys with no stops to both cities, and you'll rarely wait more than 15 minutes for a departure.

Cartagena

📞 5 / POP 971,500

Cartagena de Indias is the undisputed queen of the Caribbean coast, a historic city of superbly preserved beauty lying within an impressive 13km of centuries-old colonial stone walls. Cartagena's Old Town is a Unesco World Heritage Site – a maze of cobbled alleys, balconies covered in bougainvillea, and massive churches that cast their shadows across leafy plazas.

This is a place to drop all sightseeing routines. Instead of trying to tick off all the sights, just stroll through the Old Town day and night. Soak up the sensual atmosphere, pausing to ward off the brutal heat and humidity in one of the city's many excellent bars and restaurants.

Holding its own against Brazil's Ouro Preto and Peru's Cuzco for the continent's most enthralling and impressively preserved historic city, Cartagena is hard to walk away from – it seizes you in its aged clutches and refuses to let go.

⊙ Sights

Without a doubt, Cartagena's **old city** is its principal attraction, particularly the inner walled town consisting of the historical districts of El Centro and San Diego. El Centro in the west was traditionally home to the upper classes, and San Diego in the northeast was previously occupied by the middle classes. Both sections of the Old Town are packed with perfectly preserved colonial churches, monasteries, plazas, palaces and mansions, with balconies and shady patios that overflow with bright flowers.

With its modest architecture, the outer walled town of Getsemaní is less obviously impressive, but as it's far more residential and less sanitized, it offers plenty of atmosphere and is well worth exploring. In recent years it has become a backpacker hub, and gentrification has come astonishingly quickly – the area is full of trendy restaurants, packed cocktail bars and salsa clubs, and almost as many boutique hotels as the inner walled town. A beautiful walkway alongside the **Muelle Turístico de los Pegasos** links Getsemaní with the Old Town.

The Old Town is surrounded by **Las Murallas**, the thick walls built as protection against enemies. Construction began toward the end of the 16th century, after a siege by Francis Drake; until that time Cartagena was almost completely unprotected. The project took two centuries to complete due to repeated damage from storms and pirate attacks. It was finally finished in 1796, just 25 years before the Spaniards were eventually expelled.

★ Castillo de
San Felipe de Barajas   FORTRESS

(Av Arévalo; adult/child COP$25,000/10,500; ⊘8am-6pm) The greatest fortress ever built by the Spaniards in any of their colonies, the Castillo de San Felipe de Barajas still dominates an entire section of Cartagena's cityscape. It should definitely be the first fortress you visit. The original edifice was quite small. It was commissioned in 1630, and construction began in 1657 on top of the 40m-high San Lázaro hill. In 1762 an extensive enlargement was undertaken, which resulted in the entire hill being covered with this powerful bastion.

Palacio de la Inquisición   MUSEUM

(Plaza de Bolívar; adult/child COP$20,000/17,000; ⊘9am-6pm Mon-Sat, 10am-4pm Sun) The Palace of the Inquisition may today be one of the finest buildings in the city, but in the past it housed the notoriously grisly Inquisition, whose bloody task it was to stamp out heresy in colonial Cartagena. The palace is now a museum, displaying the inquisitors' instruments of torture, some of which are quite horrific. The museum also houses pre-Columbian pottery and plots a historical trajectory of the city using armaments, paintings, furniture and even church bells.

Catedral   CHURCH

(Calle de los Santos de Piedra) Work on Cartagena's cathedral began in 1575, but in 1586, while still under construction, it was partly destroyed by the cannons of Francis Drake. The structure known officially as the Basílica Santa Catalina de Alejandría wasn't completed until 1612, although the distinctive terracotta dome visible all over town was added later. Further alterations were carried out in the early 20th century by Cartagena's first archbishop, who covered the church with stucco and painted it to look like marble.

Convento & Iglesia
de San Pedro Claver   MUSEUM

(⊋5-664-4991; Plaza de San Pedro Claver; adult/child COP$13,000/8000; ⊘8am-5:30pm) Founded by Jesuits in the first half of the 17th century as Convento San Ignacio de Loyola, this convent later changed its name to honor Spanish-born monk Pedro Claver (1580–1654), who lived and died here. Called the 'Apostle of the Blacks' or the 'Slave of the Slaves,' the monk spent his life ministering to enslaved people brought from Africa. A series of lucid paintings inside the building relates his life story.

Plaza de Bolívar   PLAZA

Formerly the Plaza de Inquisición, this leafy and shaded plaza is surrounded by some of the city's most elegant balconied colonial buildings. It's one of Cartagena's most alluring plazas and offers wonderful respite from the Caribbean heat. A **statue** of the eponymous Simón Bolívar stands in the middle of the square.

Puerta del Reloj   GATE

Originally called the Boca del Puente, this was the main gateway to the inner walled town and was linked to Getsemaní by a drawbridge over the moat. The side arches of the gate, which are now open as walkways, were previously used as a chapel and armory. The republican-style tower, complete with a four-sided clock, was added in 1888.

Convento de la Popa   CHURCH

(adult/child COP$11,000/8000; ⊘8am-6pm) On a 150m-high hill, the highest point in Cartagena, stands this convent. The views from here are outstanding and stretch all over the city. The convent's name literally means the 'Convent of the Stern,' after the hill's similarity to a ship's back end. Founded by Augustine fathers in 1607, it was initially just a small wooden chapel, but when the hill was fortified two centuries later it was replaced by a stouter construction.

🏃 Activities

Cartagena has grown into an important scuba-diving center, taking advantage of the extensive coral reefs along its coast. La Boquilla, just outside town, is also popular for kitesurfing.

Diving Planet   DIVING

(⊋310-657-4926, 320-230-1515; www.diving planet.org; Calle Estanco del Aguardiente No 5-09; ⊘8am-6pm Mon Sat) This five-star PADI diving school offers two-tank dives in the Islas del Rosario, including transportation, equipment, lunch and instructors, for COP$408,000. Discounts of 10% are available if you pay in cash.

Sico   CYCLING

(⊋300-339-1728; www.sicobikerental.com; Calle Puntales 37-09; ⊘9am-10pm) This friendly outfit in the middle of the Old Town offers two-hour guided bicycle tours of the city and its surroundings. It also rents out good-quality hybrids and mountain bikes (COP$24,000 per half-day). Multilingual two-hour city tours depart at 8am and 4:30pm daily.

Cartagena Old Town

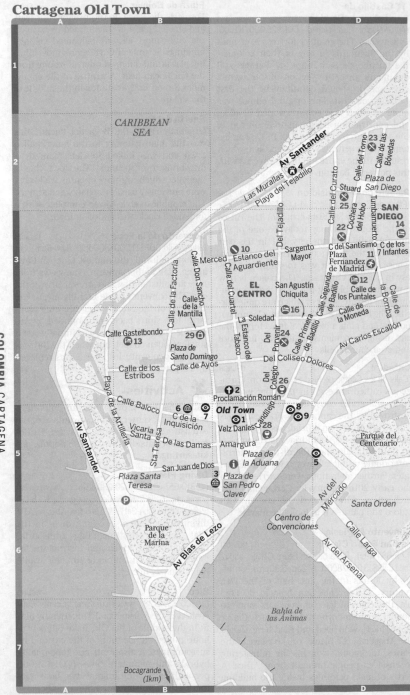

CARIBBEAN
SEA

Av Santander

Las Murallas
Playa del Tejadillo

Calle del Torno
Calle de las Bóvedas
23

Plaza de
San Diego

Calle del Curato
Stuard
25
Cochera
del Hobo

Turbamuerto

SAN
DIEGO
14

Del Tejadillo

Merced
Estanco del
Aguardiente
10

Sargento
Mayor

C del Santísimo
Plaza
Fernandez
de Madrid
11

C de los
7 Infantes

Calle de la Factoria

Calle Don Sancho

Calle del Cuartel

Calle
de la
Mantilla

EL
CENTRO

San Agustín
Chiquita

La Soledad
16

Calle Segunda
de Badillo

Calle Primera
de Badillo

12
Calle de
los Puntales

Calle de
la Moneda

Calle de
la Bomba

Calle de
la Moneda

Estanco del
Tabaco

Del
Porvenir
24

Av Carlos Escallón

Calle Gastelbondo
13

29

Plaza de
Santo Domingo

Calle de Ayos

Del Coliseo Dolores

Calle de los
Estribos

Del
Colegio
26

Playa de la Artillería

Calle Baloco

6
C de la
Inquisición
7

2
Proclamación Román

Old Town
1
Velz Daníes

Candilejo

8
9

Vicaria
Santa

Sta Teresa

De las Damas

Amargura

28

Parque del
Centenario

Av Santander

San Juan de Dios

3
Plaza de
San Pedro
Claver

Plaza de
la Aduana

5

Av del Mercado

Plaza Santa
Teresa

P

Santa Orden

Parque
de la
Marina

Av Blas de Lezo

Centro de
Convenciones

Av del Arsenal

Calle Larga

Bahía de
las Ánimas

Bocagrande
(1km)

Cartagena Old Town

COLOMBIA CARTAGENA

🛏 Sleeping

Cartagena has a huge choice of places to sleep, though you'll pay a pretty penny for anything above a hostel or a very simple midrange hotel. Catering to wealthy Colombian and US weekenders, the town's top-end accommodations have truly stratospheric rates, and there's an enormous number of beautifully restored boutique colonial options to choose from. Getsemaní, especially Calle de la Media Luna, is the main place to find budget accommodations.

El Viajero Cartagena
HOSTEL $$

(📞5-660-2598; www.elviajerohostels.com; Calle de los 7 Infantes No 9-45; incl breakfast dm COP$50,000-56,000, d COP$220,000, without bathroom COP$175,000; 🕸🛜) This backpacker blockbuster is the most centrally located hostel and one of the most social pads in the city. All rooms have air-con – an absolute dream in this heat and at this price. The beds are firm, the kitchen is well organized and spotless, and there's a very friendly, social vibe in the lovely open courtyard.

Media Luna Hostel
HOSTEL $$

(📞5-664-3423; www.medialunahostel.com; Calle de la Media Luna No 10-46; dm/r incl breakfast COP$45,000/160,000; 🕸@🛜🌊) Cartagena's ultimate party hostel is paradise for some and rather too much noise for others. Etched with a grand colonial feel, it's undoubtedly the hub of the backpacking scene in Getsemaní and a good place to meet the international bus set. Standout features include a big courtyard, a pool table and a roof terrace where fiestas kick off on Wednesday nights.

Friends to Be
BOUTIQUE HOTEL $$

(📞5-660-6486; www.friends-to-be.hotels-cartagena colombia.com; Calle del Espíritu Santo No 29-101; dm COP$40,000, s/d incl breakfast COP$160,000/ 180,000; 🕸🛜🌊) One of Getsemaní's best midrange deals, this charming place is like an urban hacienda, with a large, rustic wooden courtyard hidden behind the walls of a colonial mansion. The most impressive rooms are the two at the front of the house, both of which are spread over two floors, and one of which has a private roof terrace and sleeps four.

★San Pedro Hotel Spa
BOUTIQUE HOTEL $$$

(📞5-664-5800; www.sanpedrohotelspa.com.co; Calle San Pedro Mártir No 10-85; r incl breakfast from COP$460,000; 🕸🛜🌊) An arresting seven-room boutique hotel wrapped in a handsome colonial mansion, the San Pedro manages to balance authentic historical touches with genuine modern luxury. Excitement mounts with the mosaic-tiled atrium pool and extends through large bedrooms beautified with Chinese screens, antique bed chests and elegant chairs. The rooftop terrace with plunge pool and quiet bookish lounge is spectacular, as is the service.

Hotel Casa San Agustin
LUXURY HOTEL $$$

(📞5-681-0621; www.hotelcasasanagustin.com; Calle de la Universidad; r incl breakfast from COP$1,350,000; 🕸🛜🌊) Firmly established as Cartagena's finest hotel, the Casa San Agustin enjoys a central location that would be wonderful for any establishment. However, it's the unique building (through which the city's former aqueduct cuts over an angular swimming pool) that creates such an unusual and atmospheric space, not to mention its superengaged and polite staff and club-like atmosphere.

Bantú
HOTEL $$$

(📞5-664-3362; www.bantuhotel.com; Calle de la Tablada No 7-62; s/d incl breakfast COP$550,000-630,000; 🕸@🛜🌊) Two wonderfully restored 15th-century homes make up this lovely 28-room, open-air boutique hotel, replete with exposed-brick archways, original stone walls and lush vegetation. Smartly appointed rooms are full of local artistic touches that blend sympathetically with the building. There's also a rooftop pool, as well as a musical fountain and a swing hanging from the towering courtyard mango tree.

Casa Gastelbondo
BOUTIQUE HOTEL $$$

(📞5-660-8978; www.casagastelbondo.com; Calle Gastelbondo No 2-101; r incl breakfast from COP$400,000; 🕸🛜🌊) At this adults-only, made-for-romance hotel in a restored colonial building where old and new features seamlessly meld, guests can enjoy both opulence and authenticity. Cleverly decorated, uncluttered rooms accentuate the ample space, two pools and air-con deaden the humidity, and professional staff offer friendly but discreet service (with only four rooms, they have time for everyone).

🍴 Eating

Cartagena is strong on street food: plenty of snack bars all across the Old Town serve local snacks such as *arepas de huevo* (fried maize dough with an egg inside), *dedos de queso* (deep-fried cheese sticks), empanadas and *buñuelos* (deep-fried maize-and-cheese balls). Try the region's sweets at confectionery stands lining El Portal de los Dulces on the Plaza de los Coches.

Beer & Laundry
PIZZA $

(www.beerandlaundry.com; Calle de la Media Luna No 10-113; pizzas from COP$12,000; ⏰8am-7pm Mon-Sat; 🛜) The bane of every backpacker is where to get your laundry done with minimal fuss. Here's the answer: deposit it with the friendly English-speaking staff at this Getsemaní laundry-bar and enjoy beer and a pizza while you wait (two hours max). It's possibly the best pizza in Cartagena – and definitely the best laundry!

Espíritu Santo
COLOMBIAN $

(Calle del Porvenir No 35-60; mains COP$16,000; ⊙11:30am-3:30pm) In a city full of tourists, Espíritu Santo is where you come to meet the locals – hundreds of 'em in one sitting. (The restaurant is small from the outside but deceptively large within.) Choose your protein plus three sides and, in the true spirit of *comida corriente* (set menu of the day), it'll arrive in the blink of an eye.

Caffé Lunático
TAPAS $$

(☑320-383-0419; Calle Espíritu Santo No 29-184; tapas COP$12,000-20,000, mains COP$26,000-53,000; ⊙11am-3pm & 7-11pm; 🛜🍽) There's nothing remotely looney about this artsy little spot in the hosteling hub of Getsemaní that pays homage to Amy Winehouse in a head-and-shoulders mural that takes up a whole wall. The perfect solution to minor lunchtime hunger pangs, midafternoon cake yearnings or early-evening cocktail urges, the Lunático does a full range of small plates and desserts exceedingly well.

Beiyu
CAFE $$

(Calle del Guerrero No 29-75; breakfast COP$10,000-13,000; ⊙7am-9pm Mon-Sat, 9am-6pm Sun; 🛜🍽) 🥢 A simple little cafe plying excellent Colombian coffee, fresh juices, full breakfasts and an innovative selection of lunch and dinner dishes, Beiyu is a slice of organic, sustainable heaven in the heart of Getsemaní. It's top pick as the place to slowly eat off the effects of a late night. Portions are supergenerous. Don't miss the açai bowl.

★El Boliche
CEVICHE $$$

(☑5-660-0074, 310-368-7908; Cochera del Hobo No 38-17; mains COP$48,000-60,000; ⊙12:30-3pm & 7-11pm Mon-Sat; 🛜) Small, delightful and not so well known that it's inundated, El Boliche basks in its relative obscurity. If you're reticent about raw fish, Boliche offers hot and cold ceviche daubed with bold and adventurous ingredients such as tamarind, coconut milk and mango. The handsome six-table interior features a glass waterfall and a bar that dispatches spot-on mojitos.

La Cevichería
SEAFOOD $$$

(☑5-664-5255; Calle Stuart No 7-14; mains COP$39,000-120,000; ⊙noon-11pm Wed-Mon; 🛜) A once little-known spot prized by locals, La Cevichería was given ample publicity in an episode of Anthony Bourdain's *No Reservations* in 2008. Cue the crowds but, thankfully, no real slide in the excellent quality of the food. Each dish is prepared

with panache; the octopus in peanut sauce is incredible, as is the black-squid-ink rice and Peruvian ceviche.

El Santísimo
COLOMBIAN, FUSION $$$

(☑5-660-1531, 314-541-2117; www.elsantisimo.com; Calle del Torno No 39-62; mains COP$45,000-60,000; ⊙noon-11pm) A family-friendly restaurant that won't scare off romantic couples, Santísimo indulges in a bit of creative recycling. The chandeliers are made from empty wine bottles, while wood from rescued packing cases lines the walls and ceiling. There's nothing secondhand about the food, though; it's a trip through Colombian cuisine, combining ingredients and reinventing classics as it goes.

🍸 Drinking & Nightlife

There's a long-standing bar scene centered on the **Plaza de los Coches** in El Centro for salsa and vallenato, while most of the hotter and hipper action can be found in thumping Getsemaní, where the venues are bigger and the crowd younger. Weekends are best, though the action doesn't really heat up until after midnight.

★Alquímico
COCKTAIL BAR

(☑318-845-0433; www.alquimico.com; Calle del Colegio No 34-24; ⊙5pm-2am Sun-Thu, to 3:30am Fri & Sat) Anyone remotely hip ultimately gravitates to this Old Town bar with a pharmaceutical theme. Occupying a gorgeous colonial building, the bar is spread over three floors: the ground floor is a sleek, low-lit lounge perfect for an aperitif, while upstairs there's a kitchen and pool table. One more floor up is the always-packed roof-terrace bar, serving imaginative aguardiente cocktails.

★Café Havana
CLUB

(cnr Calle del Guerrero & Calle de la Media Luna; cover COP$30,000; ⊙8:30pm-4am Thu-Sat, 5pm-2am Sun) Havana has it all: live salsa from horn-blowing Cubans, strong drinks, a gorgeous horseshoe-shaped bar surrounded by brilliant eccentrics, wood-paneled walls and a ceiling full of whirring fans. While it's no secret these days, it's still worth a pilgrimage. Expect sweaty crowds and the odd elbow in the ribs when you're trying out your salsa moves at 1am. No shorts.

Donde Fidel
BAR

(☑5-664-3127; El Portal de los Dulces No 32-09; ⊙11am-2am) Old salts meet salsa-seekers at this usually packed and always loud Old Town bar characterized by glaring florescent lighting and busy walls covered with photos of owner Fidel posing with a Wikipedia's worth of Latin celebrities from A-list to D-list. Order a bottle of rum along with an ice bucket and some mixers and hunker down.

🛍 Shopping

Ábaco
BOOKS

(🖉 5-664-8338; cnr Calle de la Iglesia & Calle de la Mantilla; ⊙ 8am-10pm Mon-Sat, 10am-8pm Sun; 🕿) An erudite-looking bookshop-cafe that's short on space but big on atmosphere, with the obligatory ladder to reach the higher shelves. Search carefully and you'll encounter Cervantes tomes, English-language titles and pretty much everything Gabriel García Márquez ever wrote. There's also Italian beer, Spanish wine and strong espresso.

ℹ Information

MEDICAL SERVICES

Hospital Naval de Cartagena (🖉 8-655-4306; Carrera 2 No 14-210; ⊙ 24hr) Has a hyperbaric chamber.

MONEY

Casas de cambio (currency exchanges) and banks are ubiquitous in the historic center, especially around Plaza de los Coches and Plaza de la Aduana. Compare rates before buying. There are many street 'money changers' around Cartagena offering fantastic rates; they are all, without exception, expert swindlers, so don't even think of changing money on the street. There's a real lack of ATMs in El Centro and San Diego; however, there's a proliferation on Av Venezuela.

TOURIST INFORMATION

The city's main **tourist office** (Turismo Cartagena de Indias; 🖉 5-660-1583; Plaza de la Aduana; ⊙ 9am-noon & 1-6pm Mon-Sat, 9am-5pm Sun) can be found on Plaza de la Aduana. There are also small booths in Plaza de San Pedro Claver and Plaza de los Coches.

ℹ Getting There & Away

AIR

All major Colombian carriers operate flights to and from Cartagena's **Aeropuerto Internacional Rafael Núñez** (🖉 5-693-1351; www.sacsa.com.co; Calle 71 No 8-9), 3km from the city, in Crespo. There are flights to Bogotá, Cali, Medellín, San Andrés and many other major cities with **Avianca** (🖉 5-655-0287; www.avianca.com; Av Venezuela No 8B-05; ⊙ 8am-12:30pm & 2-6pm Mon-Fri, 8am-1pm Sat). **Copa** (🖉 5-655-0428; www.copaair.com; Calle 71 No 8-9; ⊙ 8am-6pm Mon-Fri, to 5pm Sat & Sun) connects to Panama City, American Airlines

to Miami and JetBlue Airways to New York. Air Canada Rouge has seasonal flights to Toronto.

The terminal has four ATMs, a *casa de cambio* (currency exchange; in domestic arrivals) and multiple car-hire agencies in the terminal building or immediately nearby.

BOAT

Sailboat is a great way to get to Panama and also a unique way to experience the San Blas Islands. Various boats leave Cartagena for Panama via the San Blas Archipelago and vice versa; the schedule is set a few months ahead and has boats departing almost every day in both directions. The trip normally takes five days and includes three days in San Blas for snorkeling and island-hopping. Trips cost around US$550 per person but can range from US$450 to US$650, as there are many factors involved.

Most boats arrive at the Panamanian ports of Porvenir, Puerto Lindo or Portobello. It's easy to connect to Panama City from all three.

The industry has been transformed in recent years by **Blue Sailing** (🖉 310-704-0425, 300-829-2030; www.bluesailing.net; Calle San Andrés No 30-47; 5-day trips US$450-650; ⊙ 9am-5pm Mon-Sat), a Colombian-American-run agency that has sought to legalize what had been an unregulated business. Blue Sailing currently represents more than 22 boats and ensures that all have proper safety equipment for open-sea navigation. It monitors boats' locations and uses licensed captains. It's therefore highly recommended that you find your boat through Blue Sailing to ensure a safe and legal crossing.

Other agencies and hostels in Cartagena offer boat crossings, but do ask about safety equipment and the captain's license. Ideally, check online for reviews of the boat and crew before you commit to anything.

Different boats depart each week, even in low season; email an operator with your preferred departure dates and the staff will hook you up with a boat that best fits your needs. It's important to book ahead, especially December through March, as boats tend to book out weeks before departure.

The sailboat trip is a popular way to visit San Blas even for those who didn't originally plan to travel to Panama. A few airlines offer cheap flights back to Colombia from Panama City; try Wingo, Air Panama and Avianca.

For those passengers traveling with vehicles, various shipping companies offer container sharing or 'roll on, roll off' services between Cartagena and Colón (US$700 to US$1200, six to eight days including loading/unloading). Passengers can take the sailboat across to meet their vehicle. It's easy and inexpensive to reach Colón from Puerto Lindo or Portobello.

Visas are not generally required for stays of up to 90 days in Panama.

DAY TRIPS FROM CARTAGENA

Playa Blanca

Playa Blanca lives up to its name – it is indeed a lovely stretch of sugary white sand and one of the finest beaches around Cartagena. However, encroaching development and incessant hawkers mean that it can feel extremely overcrowded during high season and at weekends, so it's best to visit during the week and outside of December and January.

The beach is located about 20km southwest of Cartagena, on the Isla de Barú. It's usually a stop for boat tours heading to the Islas del Rosario (p617). Beware: when the boats arrive, peddlers descend in their droves, offering everything from beach chairs to massages (most of them ridiculously overpriced). Keeping these folks at bay can be an irksome challenge. The only thing worth buying is *cocada*, a sweet coconut treat available in a variety of flavors. Playa Blanca is also good for snorkeling – if you can see past the Jet-skis.

Islas del Rosario

An archipelago about 35km southwest of Cartagena, the Islas del Rosario consist of 27 small coral islands, including some tiny islets. The islands are surrounded by coral reefs, where the color of the sea is an incredible combination of cerulean and turquoise. The whole area has been declared a national park, the PNN Corales del Rosario y San Bernardo. Sadly, warm-water currents have eroded the reefs, and the diving isn't as good as it once was. But water sports are still popular, and the two largest islands, Isla Grande and Isla del Rosario, have inland lagoons and some tourist facilities, such as hotels and a resort. The islands can be visited in a day trip from Cartagena, although to really appreciate them and to avoid the crowds, consider spending a night or two here.

Volcán de Lodo El Totumo

About 50km northeast of Cartagena, a few kilometers off the coast, is an intriguing 15m **mound** (mud bath COP$10,000; ⊙dawn-dusk) that looks like a miniature volcano. However, instead of erupting with lava and ashes, it spews forth lukewarm mud that has the consistency of cream. You can climb into the crater and frolic in a refreshing mud bath; the mud contains minerals acclaimed for their therapeutic properties. Once you've finished you can wash off in the lagoon, just 50m away.

Bring plenty of small bills to tip (COP$5000) the various locals who will wait on you during your time here – massaging you rather inexpertly, rinsing you off, holding your camera and taking photos. All in all, it's a lot of fun and a rightly popular day trip from Cartagena.

BUS

If you're heading to Barranquilla or Santa Marta, the easiest option is to leave from the **Berlinastur Terminal** (☑318-724-2424, 318-354-5454; www.berlinastur.com), a short taxi ride from the Old Town. Air-conditioned minibuses depart from here every 20 minutes from 5am to 8pm, stopping first in Barranquilla (COP$20,000, two hours) and then in Santa Marta (COP$40,000, four hours).

An even better, but pricier, option for this route is the **MarSol** (☑5-656-0302; Carrera 2 No 43-111) bus to Santa Marta (COP$50,000, three hours). There are two buses a day; call a day ahead to reserve your seats.

Several bus companies serve Bogotá and Medellín throughout the day. Among them, Copetran (www.copetran.com) heads to Bogotá (from COP$110,000, 21 hours, six buses daily). **Unitransco** (☑5-663-2067, 5-663-2665; Terminal de Transportes de Cartagena, Calle 1A No 3-89) serves Barranquilla (COP$14,000,

2½ hours, hourly), with continuing services to Santa Marta (COP$35,000, four hours, hourly). There's also a 7:30am service to Mompós (COP$46,000, six hours, daily) and an hourly service to Montería (COP$40,000, five hours, daily). For Riohacha on La Guajira Peninsula, Expreso Brasilia and **Rápido Ochoa** (☑312-843-1249, 5-693-2133; Terminal de Transportes de Cartagena, Calle 1A No 3-89) both have hourly departures (COP$42,000, eight hours). The latter also has four daily departures to Medellín (COP$125,000, 13 hours).

On overland trips to Panama, take one of the hourly buses to Montería (COP$40,000, five hours), where you can switch to one of the hourly buses to Necoclí (COP$25,000, 2½ hours) and Turbo (COP$35,000, 3½ hours).

Buses to Playa Blanca (Calle de la Magdalena Concolón; COP$1500, 70 minutes), for those who aren't keen to take the boat excursion (p617) there, leave throughout the day.

Mompós

📍 5 / POP 44,000 / ELEV 33M

Mompós is one of Colombia's most perfectly preserved colonial towns. Remotely located deep inland on the banks of the Río Magdalena, the town (also known by its original Spanish name of Mompox) has essentially been in decline since river transport patterns changed in the mid-19th century, leaving it – quite literally – a backwater. Its similarities to García Márquez' fictional town of Macondo are striking, and Mompós, ironically, is a far better place to soak up the atmosphere of *One Hundred Years of Solitude* than García Márquez' nearby hometown of Aracataca. The 21st century finds this forgotten gem rising again, with a steady proliferation of boutique hotels and restaurants in recent years. It's easily the most charming town in northern Colombia, its decaying facades and multicolored churches reminiscent more of Havana's old town than of polished-and-buffed Cartagena.

🛏 Sleeping & Eating

★ **Casa Amarilla** BOUTIQUE HOTEL $$
(📞 310-606-4632, 5-685-6326; www.lacasaamarilla mompos.com; Carrera 1 No 13-59; r incl breakfast COP$135,000-250,000; ❄🎧) This beautiful hotel was developed by a British journalist and his *momposina* wife inside a restored 17th-century mansion overlooking the river. It has several wonderfully atmospheric rooms, as well as a couple of roomy upstairs suites that are perfect for romantic stays. Breakfast is a communal affair served up on a large dining table overlooking the courtyard garden.

El Fuerte San Anselmo EUROPEAN $$$
(📞 5-685-6762, 314-564-0566; www.fuerte mompox.com; Carrera 1 No 12-163; mains from COP$40,000; ⏱6:30-11pm) With its beautifully crafted interior and spacious, airy garden overlooked by a towering banana tree, El Fuerte really is a highlight of Mompós. Try the excellent pizza cooked in a wood-fired oven, one of its lovingly prepared pasta dishes or the excellent gazpacho. Come in good time to ensure you get an outdoor table.

❶ Getting There & Away

Mompós is remote, there's no denying that, but it can be reached by direct bus from Cartagena and several other major towns. Most travelers arrive from Cartagena with Ulnitransco (www. unitransco.co), which runs a daily bus at 7:30am (COP$46,000, six hours).

It's also possible to travel to Mompós from Bucaramanga (COP$65,000, seven hours, 10am and 9:45pm) and from Bogotá (COP$90,000, 15 hours, three times daily). All these services are operated by Copetran.

There are direct door-to-door services from Mompós to Barranquilla, Cartagena and Santa Marta, all taking between five and six hours, with a cost ranging from COP$75,000 to COP$85,000. If you want to use these services, ask your hotel to book you a pickup.

Golfo de Urabá

Necocli

📍 4 / POP 15,400

With a small grid of wood and concrete buildings dusted with a quiet Afro-Caribbean sensibility, Necocli is undergoing a renaissance in the wake of its new daily boat service to Capurganá, the Darién jungle town formerly only accessible via the rough port of Turbo. Necocli is a thoroughly pleasant place to spend the night before catching the morning boat across the Golfo de Urabá.

🛏 Sleeping & Eating

Hotel Punta de Águila HOTEL $$
(📞 4-821-5500; www.hotelpuntadeaguila.co; Calle 50 No 46-10; s/d/tr incl breakfast COP$70,000/ 100,000/140,000; 🎧) Safe, friendly and reliable, these simple digs are all you need for a snug pre- or postferry stop in Necocli. As a bonus, the staff will reserve your boat ticket in advance and cook up an early breakfast on the day of departure.

Zion Beach Bar SEAFOOD $$
(📞 321-642-6522; cnr Calle 51 & Carrera 51; mains COP$20,000; ⏱noon-10pm) Grilled fish on your plate, sand between your toes, a cold beer within easy reach and Bob Marley on the sound system: sit outside this Caribbean-style beach shack a couple of blocks from Necocli's main square and absorb the languid spirit of Colombia's Caribbean coast.

❶ Getting There & Away

There are regular buses between Necocli and Montería (COP$35,000, 2½ hours, hourly), with several per day carrying on to Cartagena (COP$80,000, eight hours).

In the other direction, a dozen daily buses head to Turbo (COP$10,000, one hour) and Medellín (COP$56,000, 10 hours).

Buses leave from where the main road, Hwy 90, intersects with Calle 51.

You can purchase boat-bus combo tickets from the office of **El Caribe SAS** (☑ 315-687-4284; www.maritimaelcaribe.com; Calle 46 No 43-44; ⊙ 6am-6pm).

Capurganá & Sapzurro

☑ 4 / POP 2200

Colombia ends its desert-to-jungle Caribbean coastline with a flourish: the idyllic, laid-back villages of Capurganá and Sapzurro, and their surrounding beaches, are hidden in a half-forgotten corner of Colombia's northwest, just a stroll from the Panamanian border. Hemmed in by jungle-covered mountains and washed by fabulously azure waters, the villages are littered with the colorful quirks that characterize wild, isolated settlements. Cars are banned, electricity gets turned off almost daily and ATMs remain a distant urban rumor.

Part of the adventure is just getting here: both villages are only accessible by a choppy 1½- to 2½-hour boat ride from Turbo or Necoclí, or by a tiny plane from Medellín. Consequently, the beaches remain pleasantly unkempt and the jungle deliciously impenetrable. While in-the-know Colombians and a trickle of foreign backpackers might have discovered the area, the vibe is still decidedly casual, unhurried and locally led.

🏃 Activities

Sendero Ecoturístico
Capurganá-Sapzurro   HIKING
The only traffic you might see on the 'main road' between Capurganá and Sapzurro are toucans, howler monkeys and thousands of giant ants. This long-established jungle trail has recently been made more accessible, with wooden staircases (to ascend and descend the steep ridges), proper toilet blocks, and interpretative signs highlighting the abundant bird and animal life.

Although still muddy and steep in places, the walk is a joy, ending at a newly constructed lookout tower at the halfway point. From it you can catch a glimpse of Panama in the distance and admire the bushy canopy of the Darién jungle in all its dark, green mystery.

The trail runs for 3.6km (4km if you continue through Sapzurro to the Panama border) and is well signposted. Wear good shoes and take plenty of water – the heat and humidity make the trail seem longer than it is. At the Sapzurro end, follow the shoreline to the village center (a tiny church facing the jetty). Should the jungle heat sap your

energy, a couple of local vendors sell drinks (including beer!) out of a small shack just below the lookout tower.

Dive & Green   DIVING
(☑ 316-781-6255, 311-578-4021; www.diveandgreen.com; Capurganá; 1/2 dives COP$140,000/210,000) 🤿 The only PADI diving center in the area, Dive & Green is right by Capurganá's arrivals jetty. It offers a full range of courses and certification, with open-water courses from COP$950,000 and one-day discovery-school diving from COP$190,000. The outfit has been awarded a PADI green star for its environmentally friendly practices.

☞ Tours

San Blas Adventures   TOURS
(☑ 321-505-5008; www.sanblasadventures.com; Capurganá) Offers highly recommended four-day tours of the San Blas Islands that will deposit you in Carti, Panama, from where it's possible to catch a jeep on to Panama City. Trips cost from US$400 and depart from Sapzurro. You'll need to arrive in Capurganá at least a day ahead.

Professional, English-speaking guides will meet you at the dock in Capurganá (where the company maintains a small office).

🛏 Sleeping & Eating

Capurganá

Hostal Capurganá   HOSTEL $
(☑ 318-206-4280, 316-482-3665; www.hostalcapurgana.net; Calle de Comercio; s/d/f incl breakfast COP$75,000/125,000/225,000; 🛜) On the main street, just back from the dock, this excellent option has six private rooms and a couple of six-berth family rooms, each with fan, private bathroom and access to a charming courtyard garden. This is the only place in town that takes credit cards. Delightful owners Silvio and Beatriz run a local **travel agency** (☑ 4-824-3173) from the hostel.

US dollars can also be exchanged here.

★Posada del Gecko   GUESTHOUSE $$
(☑ 314-525-6037, 314-629-1829; www.posadadelgecko.com; Capurganá; s/d/tr/q COP$30,000/80,000/110,000/140,000; ❋🛜) Megapopular Gecko has simple wooden rooms that are great value; smarter options include rooms with air-con and private bathroom. The place is known for its garden bar-restaurant serving authentic Italian pizzas and pastas. It's a fine place for a drink, too, with a soundtrack

ℹ GETTING TO PANAMA

It's not possible to drive from Colombia to Panama – the Pan-American Hwy does not extend through the swamps of the Darién Gap. Various foolhardy maniacs have ignored the dangers and attempted to cross the 87km distance in all-terrain vehicles and even on foot, risking encounters with guerrillas, paramilitaries or drug traffickers – don't attempt this.

It is possible and fairly safe, however, to reach Panama (mostly) overland, with just a few sea trips and a short flight. At research time the following route was secure and calm, but always check ahead for security updates before setting out, and stick to the coast.

First, make your way to Turbo or (far better) Necoclí. The Medellín–Turbo bus route (COP$70,000, eight hours) is now safe, but daytime travel is still advised. From Cartagena, you'll have to go to Montería (COP$50,000, five hours) and change there for Necoclí (COP$35,000, 2½ hours). Buses run regularly from 7am to 5pm. Ensure you leave Cartagena before 11am to avoid getting stuck overnight in Montería. You'll have to spend the night in either Turbo or Necoclí, as boats only depart for Capurganá in the mornings. Necoclí is the more pleasant town by far.

Next, catch a boat from Turbo or Necoclí to Capurganá. The cost for each is COP$70,000, although the Necoclí crossing is an hour shorter (taking 1½ hours total). Arrive at the dock at least an hour early to secure a ticket. Hang onto your hat: this can be a bumpy ride. There's a 10kg baggage limit – a COP$1000-per-kilogram excess charge applies – and a COP$2600 port tax.

Then, take a boat from Capurganá to Puerto Obaldía in Panama (COP$35,000, 30 minutes). The day before you depart, get your Colombian exit stamp at **Migración Colombia** (☎311-746-6234; www.migracioncolombia.gov.co; Capurganá; ⊙8am-5pm Mon-Fri, 9am-noon Sat & Sun), near Carpuganá's harbor (the office will not be open in time on the day you leave). Boats depart Capurganá daily at 7:30am; be at the docks for 7am. This is another bumpy journey, depending on sea conditions. Note: the boat journey costs a minimum of COP$100,000, so you'll have to pay the full amount if you're the only passenger.

Obtain your Panama entry stamp at Panamanian immigration in Puerto Obaldía, though you might be asked for two copies of your passport. (There's a copy place here if you need it.) Then fly to Panama City's domestic Albrook terminal. There are flights on Tuesday, Thursday and Sunday (US$115, one hour). Puerto Obaldía has very little to offer tourists: avoid spending any more time here than necessary, and head straight to Panama City.

that's a little more subtle than Capurganá's default skull-splitting reggaeton.

★Josefina's
SEAFOOD $$
(Capurganá; mains COP$22,000-40,000; ⊙noon-9:30pm) Scour the coast and you won't find better seafood – or a warmer welcome – than at Josefina's. Her medium-sized *pargo* (red snapper) practically fills the plate and is a succulent joy, supported by coconut rice, tangy salad and crispy *patacones* (plantain chips); the *crema de camerón* (cream-of-shrimp soup) isn't far behind.

Sapzurro

★La Posada
HOSTEL $$
(☎310-410-2245; www.sapzurrolaposada.com; r per person incl breakfast COP$75,000-95,000; campsite or hammocks per person COP$15,000-20,000; ❋𝕒) The most comfortable, well-run spot in Sapzurro has beautiful gardens with flourishing guava, coconut and mango trees; open-air showers for campers; and beautiful, airy rooms with wooden floors, exposed beams and hammocks on the balconies. Owner Mario speaks great English, and his wife, Lena, prepares meals (mains COP$20,000 to COP$35,000 – call ahead if you plan to eat).

Zíngara Hospedaje
GUESTHOUSE $$
(☎320-687-4678, 313-673-3291; www.hospedaje sapzurrozingara.com; r per person incl breakfast COP$45,000-55,000; 𝕒) Owner Clemencia will make you feel instantly welcome at this rustic wooden guesthouse. The two rooms are on the jungle-covered mountainside and have private bathrooms, mosquito nets and balconies surrounded by fruit trees. The best is the top room: it sleeps five and has a huge balcony with gorgeous views.

ℹ Information

Be aware that there are no ATMs in either Capurganá or Sazurro, so it's important to bring as much cash as you'll need for your stay in town. In a pinch, you can get cash advances on a credit card from Hostal Capurganá (p619). The same place (and a few others) also change US dollars, but both transactions will cost you.

ℹ Getting There & Away

AIR

ADA (📞1-800-051-4232; www.ada-aero.com) operates daily flights from Medellín to the town of Acandí (COP$140,000 to COP$320,000 one way), from where it's easy to take a boat to Capurganá (COP$30,000 per person, 20 minutes), though you'll want to hire a donkey (COP$5000) to take you to the docks from the airport if you have luggage. For assisstance booking flights or transfers, contact Capurganá Tours (p619).

Otherwise, the nearest airports are in Montería (followed by a bus-boat combo via Necocli) and Apartado (bus-boat combo via Turbo).

BOAT

There are two main ways of getting to Capurganá by boat.

Coming from **Necocli** (COP$70,000, 1½ hours) is by far the best method. The trip is relatively brief, the boats are fast and efficient, and Necocli is a pleasant beach town with plenty of decent accommodations. A daily boat leaves Necocli year-round at 8am, returning from Capurganá at 10am. Several more daily departures are offered in high season. It's best to reserve a day ahead at the Caribe SAS office. Crossings can be rough in January and February. Local vendors sell bin bags (COP$1000) to keep your bag dry.

Coming from **Turbo** (COP$70,000, 2½ hours) is less advisable, especially if you're starting in Cartagena. The boat takes an hour longer than the Necocli crossing and the town of Turbo is a shady, far less desirable place to spend the night. It's also further by bus from Montería and Cartagena (but closer to Medellín). Daily boats leave Turbo at 7am and Capurganá at 8am, with more departures in high season.

You'll have to overnight in Necocli or Turbo on the outward journey, as the boats leave early in the morning. It's possible to reach Cartagena or Medellín in one day on the return trip. Boat-and-bus combo tickets can be booked through Capurganá Tours (p619).

As well as your boat fare, you'll need to pay a COP$2600 port tax and COP$1000 per kilogram for excess luggage.

SAN ANDRÉS & PROVIDENCIA

The archipelago of San Andrés and Providencia is geographically located near Nicaragua, historically tied to Great Britain and politically part of Colombia. Here you'll find isolated beaches, unspoiled coral reefs and an alluring island flavor, and with just a little digging the 300-year-old English-Creole-speaking Raizal culture.

San Andrés, the largest island in the archipelago and its commercial and administrative hub, attracts many Colombian tourists seeking duty-free shopping sprees. The crowds, however, are not difficult to escape.

Providencia offers the same turquoise sea and extensive coral reefs but is much less commercialized. Its colonial heritage is thriving in hamlets of colorful wooden homes peppered about the island.

Both islands offer a total change of pace to the mainland and are well worth the effort of getting to.

San Andrés

📞8 / POP 70,000

Just 150km east of Nicaragua and some 800km northwest of mainland Colombia, the seahorse-shaped island of San Andrés is best known as Colombia's favorite weekend getaway, where mainlanders love to come to drink, tax-free shop, sunbathe and party. San Andrés Town, the focus of the action, won't be splashed across postcards any time soon, though it does boast an attractive beach promenade and has in recent years begun to address what might be charitably termed its beauty gap.

San Andrés is best appreciated outside the downtown hubbub. Whether you take a boat trip to one of the idyllic offshore cays, check out the excellent scuba-diving and snorkeling opportunities or head down the scenic 30km road encircling the rest of the island, this quirky place – where Anglo-Caribbean Raizal culture grinds up against the far more recently imported Colombian one – often manages to charm visitors in the end.

🏊 Activities

Due to the beautiful coral reefs all around it, San Andrés is an important diving center, with more than 35 dive spots. Otherwise, most visitors are focused on beach-hopping, day trips to various islands, water sports and partying in San Andrés Town.

Banda Dive Shop
DIVING

(☑8-513-1080, 315-303-5428; www.bandadive shop.com; Hotel Lord Pierre, Av Colombia, San Andrés Town; ☺8am-6pm Mon-Sat) Extra-friendly dive shop offering two-tank dives for COP$235,000 and PADI Open Water certification for COP$1,300,000. One of the most professional outfits on the island.

🛏 Sleeping & Eating

★Cocoplum Hotel
HOTEL $$$

(☑8-513-2121; www.cocoplumhotel.com; Via San Luis No 43-39; s/d incl breakfast COP$362,000/500,000; ✳☎➹) On a gorgeous private white-sand beach shaded with palms, this multicolored, low-key beach resort sports Caribbean architecture. The restaurant, serving fresh meals all day, is also open to nonguests. Rocky Cay, a good spot for snorkeling, is nearby.

Donde Francesca
SEAFOOD $$$

(San Luis; mains COP$30,000-60,000; ☺10am-6pm; ☎) Right on the beach, this breezy place may be little more than a shack, but it serves up delicious traditional Caribbean food, such as *langostinos al coco* (breaded crayfish deep-fried with coconut), *pulpo al ajillo* (octopus cooked in garlic) and tempura calamari. Even better, showers and changing facilities mean you can combine a meal with a swim.

Restaurante La Regatta
SEAFOOD $$$

(☑317-744-3516; www.restaurantelaregatta.com; Club Náutico, Av Newball, San Andrés Town; mains COP$30,000-100,000; ☺noon-3pm & 6.30-11pm; ☎) The island's best restaurant, La Regatta is housed on a wooden pontoon over the sea at Club Náutico. Despite a healthy dose of pirate kitsch, it has a formal, white-linen-tablecloth atmosphere and the food is heavenly. The *langosta regatta* (lobster tails with three sauces) is nothing short of perfection. Book a table for the evenings.

ℹ Information

Tourist office (Secretaría de Turismo; ☑8-513-0801; Av Newball, San Andrés Town; ☺8am-noon & 2-6pm Mon-Fri) The staff here speak English and are very helpful. There's also a **tourist information booth** (cnr Avs Colombia & 20 de Julio; ☺8am-6pm) by the beach.

ℹ Getting There & Away

AIR

Gustavo Rojas Pinilla International Airport (☑8-512-6112) is right in the town center and the runway ends at the beach. You must buy a tourist card (COP$105,000) on the mainland before boarding your San Andrés–bound flight, but the cards are sold at the gate and there's no chance you'll be allowed to board without one. Airlines that connect to San Andrés (and that are located at the airport) include **Avianca** (☑8-512-3216; www.avianca.com), **Latam** (☑1-800-094-9490; www.latam.com) and **Copa** (☑8-512-7619; www.copaair.com), and cities with direct flights here include Bogotá, Barranquilla, Cali, Cartagena, Medellín and Panama City.

Satena (☑8-512-1403; www.satena.com) operates two flights per day between San Andrés and Providencia in low season (round trip from COP$600,000) and up to six per day in high season.

BOAT

Conocemos Navegando (☑toll free 01-8000-111-500; www.conocemosnavegando.com; Centro Comercial New Point L.111, Av Providencia; 1 way/return COP$213,000/378,000; ☺8am-12:30pm & 2-6pm Mon-Fri, 8am-1pm Sat) provides pricey catamaran services between San Andrés and Providencia daily, except Tuesday, in both directions. Services depart from **Muelle Toninos** (Tonino Marina) at 8am and return at 2:30pm the same day. You're supposed to arrive a full hour and a half before departure for registration. The journey takes three hours, and can be extremely rough. It's possible to visit Providencia on a day trip with this service, but it would be very rushed. Seats often sell out, even in low season, so it's important to book ahead.

Providencia

☑8 / POP 5000

Providencia, 90km north of San Andrés, is a wonderfully remote and traditional Caribbean island with breathtaking scenery, gorgeous golden-sand beaches, friendly locals and superb diving. Best of all, it's a pain to get to, ensuring that you'll only have to share this slice of paradise with the other intrepid travellers happy to fly here in a rickety 20-seater plane or brave the often-rough three-hour catamaran ride.

Without a direct connection to the Colombian mainland, Providencia hasn't seen nearly the same levels of cultural invasion as San Andrés, leaving its traditions and customs more or less intact. You'll still hear the local English Creole spoken all over the island, and road signs direct you using the old English town names rather than their Spanish counterparts. All this, combined with beautiful topography standing sentinel over swaths of turquoise-blue sea, gives Providencia no small claim to being a quirky paradise.

◉ Sights

The main activity in Providencia is enjoying the beaches. The very best are **Bahía Suroeste** (Southwest Bay), **Bahía Aguadulce** (Freshwater Bay), and **Bahía Manzanillo** (Manicheel Bay) at the southern end of the island, but there are several other lovely places to swim.

⌶ Sleeping & Eating

Mr Mac CABAÑAS $$
(🖉316-567-6526, 318-695-9540; posadamister mack@hotmail.com; Aguadulce; bungalows/apt per person COP$100,000/110,000; ✳) The island's cheapest option is also one of its friendliest, where host Laudina warmly welcomes guests. The green-painted timber house is over the water, with hammocks strewn along the veranda. Rooms are large and the enormous apartments have kitchenettes. It's possible to swim in the sea from the garden here, though the beach is a five-minute walk away. No wi-fi.

★Café Studio SEAFOOD $$$
(🖉8-514-9076; Bahía Suroeste; mains COP$30,000-60,000; ⊗11am-10pm Mon-Sat) Providencia's most popular restaurant is operated by a Canadian–Raizal couple and the food is generally delightful, both memorable and reasonably priced given where you are. It gets fearsomely crowded come evening – not least with mosquitoes, making repellent a must – so get here in good time to secure a table, or try visiting at lunch to avoid the rush.

❶ Getting There & Away

Satena (p622) flies between San Andrés and Providencia (round trip from COP$600,000) twice daily in low season, with several more flights in high season. Buy your ticket in advance in high season. Note that, due to the small planes used on this route, the luggage allowance is 10kg; you'll need to pay for any extra, though it's not expensive and generally no issue to do so.

The Conocemos Navegando (p622) catamaran connects Providencia to San Andrés daily, except Tuesday, in both directions (COP$378,000 return, three hours).

NORTHWEST COLOMBIA

Medellín

🖉4 / POP 2 MILLION / ELEV 1495M

Situated in a narrow valley, Medellín packs the punch of a city twice its size. Its skyline reaches for the heavens, setting high-rise apartments and office buildings against a backdrop of jagged peaks in every direction. Its pleasant climate gives it its nickname – the City of Eternal Spring – and the moderate temperatures put a spring in the locals' steps, at work and at play. It's a bustling place of industry and commerce, especially in textile manufacturing and exported cut flowers. On weekends Medellín lets its hair down, its many discos attracting the beautiful people.

The city sprawls north and south along the valley floor; slums hug the upper reaches of the hills. True to its *paisa* (people of Antioquia) roots, Medellín affects an indifference to the rest of Colombia, putting on metropolitan airs and looking overseas for inspiration for its next great public-works projects.

◉ Sights

Plazoleta de las Esculturas PLAZA
(Plaza Botero; Map p624; Plazoleta de las Esculturas) This public space in front of the Museo de Antioquia (p623) is home to 23 large, curvaceous bronze sculptures by renowned local artist Fernando Botero, including some of his most iconic works.

Cerro Nutibara VIEWPOINT
(🖉4-260-2416, 4-385-8017; ⊗6am-11pm; 🚌1, 2) On top of this 80m-tall hill, 2km southwest of the city center, sits the kitschy **Pueblito Paisa**, a miniature version of a typical Antioquian township, complete with tacky gift stalls. Views across the city from the adjacent platform are stunning on a good day. Take a taxi to the top (or a Metroplus bus to the Nutibara stop) and check out the Parque de las Esculturas – a handful of modern abstract sculptures by South American artists – on the way down.

Next to the lookout you'll find the **Museo de la Ciudad** (COP$2000; ⊗10am-6pm; 🚌1, 2), a small museum dedicated to the history of Medellín, which often showcases old photographs of the city.

★Museo de Antioquia MUSEUM
(Map p624; 🖉4-251-3636; www.museode antioquia.co; Carrera 52 No 52-43; adult/student COP$18,000/9000; ⊗10am-5:30pm Mon-Sat, to 4:30pm Sun) In the grand art deco Palacio Municipal, Colombia's second-oldest museum (Museo Nacional in Bogotá is the oldest) houses one of the country's most important art collections. The permanent collection spans 19th-century and contemporary

COLOMBIA MEDELLÍN

Medellín

N 0 ——————————— 200 m
0 ——————————— 0.1 miles

Medellín

◎ Top Sights
1 Museo de Antioquia B1

◎ Sights
2 Plazoleta de las Esculturas B2

◉ Drinking & Nightlife
3 Salon Malaga B4

★ Entertainment
4 Teatro Lido D2

Colombian art, as well as pre-Columbian pieces. The highlight is the 3rd floor, where there are many sculptures and paintings by native son Fernando Botero as well as other artists' work from his personal collection. Look out for the wonderful Pedro Nel Gómez murals around the building.

Parque Arví   PARK
(www.parquearvi.org; Veredas Mazo & Piedras Blancas, Santa Elena; Metrocable Línea L) Accessible by the fantastically scenic Metrocable Línea L from the Santo Domingo interchange (COP$4850 one way, 15 minutes), Parque Arví is a big chunk of countryside in Santa Elena, popular with city residents, particularly on weekends. Inside the boundaries of the 17.61-sq-km reserve are hiking trails running through the pine and eucalyptus forest and past lakes and lookout points, canopy lines, and a mariposario (butterfly enclosure). Attractions are spread out so it's best to arrive early.

Jardín Botánico   GARDENS
(www.facebook.com/JardinBotanicoMedellin; Calle 73 No 51D-14; ⊙9am-4:30pm; Ⓜ Universidad) FREE One of Medellín's nicest green spaces, the botanic gardens cover 14 hectares, showcase 600 species of trees and plants, and in-

clude a lake, a herbarium and a butterfly enclosure. Events often take place beneath the **Orquideorama** – an organically expanding meshwork of wooden flowers.

Museo Casa de la Memoria MUSEUM
(☑ 4-385-5555; www.museocasadelamemoria.gov.co; Calle 51 No 36-66; ⊙ 9am-6pm Tue-Fri, 10am-4pm Sat & Sun) FREE This harrowing museum dedicated to the urban conflict in Medellín is a must-visit for travelers wanting to fully understand the city (and Colombia). There are interesting displays on the geopolitical origins of the conflict, but the most moving parts are the life-size video screens, where survivors recount their experiences as if they were standing in front of you, and the Wall of Memory outside, which pays homage to local residents killed in the violence, their names etched onto the bricks.

La Comuna 13 AREA
(🖺 221i, 225i) Once one of the most dangerous neighborhoods in Medellín, the Comuna 13, which clings to the mountainside above the San Javier metro station, has undergone an impressive transformation in recent times and is now considered safe to visit. The focal point of a trip to the *comuna* is the area around the *escaleras electricas,* the outdoor escalators that provide access to homes in marginalized barrios that were formerly isolated from the city below. A taxi from the metro costs COP$5500.

🏃 Activities

Dance Free DANCING
(Map p626; ☑ 4-204-0336, WhatsApp 316-288-7063; www.dancefree.com.co; Calle 10A No 40-27; individual classes per hour COP$65,000, group classes per month COP$100,000) A hugely popular school offering salsa and bachata classes in a large space in El Poblado. Teachers are enthusiastic and professional and both private and group classes are available. At night it turns into a disco so you can practice your moves.

Zona de Vuelo PARAGLIDING
(☑ 4-388-1556, 301-535-8330; www.zonadevuelo.com; Km5.6 Via San Pedro de los Milagros) Experienced operator Zona de Vuelo offers 15- and 20-minute tandem flights (COP$130,000/160,000) and photos/videos of your flight for an extra COP$40,000. Also on offer are 15-day courses (COP$3,500,000). It also provides round-trip transportation to the launch point in San Felix from Medellín (COP$90,000 for up to four passengers).

Courses

Universidad EAFIT LANGUAGE
(☑ 4-261-9500; www.eafit.edu.co; Carrera 49 No 7 Sur-50; 38hr course COP$1,250,000-1,600,000) A private university offering intensive and semi-intensive Spanish study in a group setting. Individual tuition is also available.

☞ Tours

★ Bicitour CYCLING
(Map p626; ☑ 312-749-2581, 312-512-0690; www.bicitour.co; Carrera 36 No 7-10, Casa Kiwi; tours COP$70,000) Bicitour offers in-depth cycle tours of Medellín, visiting a variety of interesting sights pertinent to local history, politics and culture, on a 19km route through diverse neighborhoods. They're a healthy and ecological way to see a side of the city you might otherwise miss. Tours begin and end in El Poblado.

★ Real City Tours WALKING
(☑ 319-262-2008; www.realcitytours.com) Run by enthusiastic young locals, this company offers a free walking tour through the city center, with detailed explanations in English of the stories behind the main points of interest. Tips for the guides are expected. You need to reserve online to secure your spot.

Comuna 13 Graffiti Tour WALKING
(Map p626; www.comuna13tours.com; Calle 10, COP$70,000; ⊙ 10am & 4pm) This highly informative and entertaining walking tour takes you through the notorious former barrio of La Comuna 13, with the guide explaining the barrio's troubled history when it was run by drug gangs, and showing off its remarkable transformation, along with some astounding graffiti works.

⚜ Festivals & Events

Feria de las Flores CULTURAL
(www.feriadelasfloresmedellin.gov.co; ⊙ Aug) This weeklong festival is Medellín's most spectacular event, with numerous parades and concerts. The highlight is the Desfile de Silleteros, when up to 400 *campesinos* (peasants) come from the mountains to parade along the streets with flowers on their backs.

⌂ Sleeping

El Poblado is the preferred place to stay for most travelers. It's close to the bars and restaurants, and is usually safe, even late at night.

El Poblado

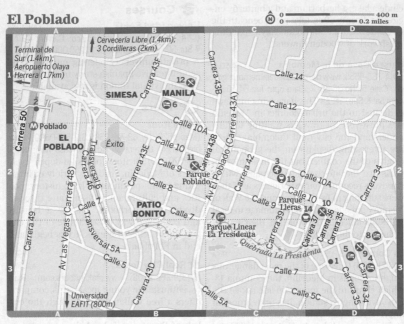

0 — 400 m
0 — 0.2 miles

El Poblado

Activities, Courses & Tours
1 Bicitour	D3
2 Comuna 13 Graffiti Tour	A1
3 Dance Free	C2

Sleeping
4 Garden of Blues Hostel	D3
5 In House Hotel	D3
6 Los Patios	B1
7 Rango	C2
8 YOLO Hostel	D3

Eating
9 Arte Dolce	D3
10 Bao Bei	D2
Betty's Bowls	(see 8)
11 Osea	B2
12 Tal Cual	B1

Drinking & Nightlife
13 Cervecería Maestre	C2
14 Pergamino	D2

Those who want a less sanitized experience of Medellín may prefer the more rough-and-tumble center, although you'll want to take taxis after dark.

A middle-of-the road option is the area around Laureles/La Setenta, which is less flashy than Poblado yet more orderly than the center.

El Poblado has several different sub districts with different kinds of accommodation options. Most hostels in the blocks around Parque Lleras tend to be 'party hostels' so be sure to bring ear plugs. The Patio Bonito area close to the metro has more relaxed accommodations and a quieter vibe. Another option is Manila, where there are several good hostels dotted among hip restaurants and bars.

Wandering Paisa HOSTEL $
(☎4-436-6759; www.wanderingpaisahostel.com; Calle 44A No 68A-76; dm COP$25,000-29,000, r COP$75,000; @☎) Right by the bars and restaurants of La 70, this dynamic hostel is a great choice for those wanting to find a middle ground between the bright lights of El Poblado and downtown. There is a small bar and roof terrace and the enthusiastic management is constantly arranging social events and group outings. Bikes are available to explore the neighborhood.

YOLO Hostel HOSTEL $$
(Map p626; ☎4-583-1373; www.facebook.com/yolohostelmedellin; Carrera 32D No 7a-77; dm/s/d/tr COP$38,000/70,000/110,000/150,000; ☎) Well located on the edge of El Poblado, this

hostel get the thumbs up for the wonderfully warm welcome from staff, the comfy bunks in the fan-cooled dorms, the breakfast bowls at Betty's Bowls (p627) next door, group events, such as barbecues, that make solo guests feel included, and a variety of interesting city tours. YOLO, indeed.

Garden of Blues Hostel
HOSTEL **$$**

(Map p626; ☑300-736-2160; Carrera 34 No 7-46; dm COP$35,000-39,000, r COP$80,000; 🛜) The owners of this delightful little hostel have decided to run with a garden theme. There's an Edenesque, greenery-festooned courtyard for chilling out, tendrils of vegetation sprout from the ceilings and tree murals snake their way up walls. Beds are comfy, the staff are superhelpful and the El Poblado location is ideal for city exploration.

Rango
HOSTEL **$$**

(Map p626; ☑4-480-3180; www.hostelrango.com; Calle 8 No 42-25; dm COP$59,000-64,000, tw/d COP$236,000/247,000; 🛜) An industrial-chic hostel-hotel hybrid overlooking Parque La Presidenta, with polished concrete floors and wood features throughout. It offers comfortable dorms with top facilities including big solid lockers and hotel-class private rooms complete with minibars. There's no guest kitchen but the fusion restaurant downstairs earns accolades from locals and visitors alike.

In House Hotel
HOTEL **$$**

(Map p626; ☑4-444-1786; www.inhousethe hotel.com; Carrera 34 No 7-109; s/d/tr incl breakfast COP$156,500/174,000/258,000; 🛜) This excellent-value small hotel stands out from the crowd in busy El Poblado. Its stylish, bright rooms feature pine furniture, work desks and big windows. Service is friendly and professional, and a continental breakfast is included. Rooms at the front have private balconies while those at the rear are quieter.

★Los Patios
HOSTEL **$$$**

(Map p626; ☑305-323-9897; www.lospatioshb. com; Carrera 43E No 11-40; dm COP$62,400-71,400, r/tr COP$195,000/234,000; 🛜) Setting the standard for flashpacker comfort, this large hostel in Manila features slick industrial-chic design and some of the best common areas you'll find on your travels. The open kitchen offers great views over town, but the panoramas are even better from the upstairs lounge and phenomenal rooftop. Modern dorms are equipped with privacy curtains and male/female bathrooms.

✗ Eating

El Poblado is full of restaurants covering a wide range of tastes and budgets. The Provenza area up the hill from Parque Lleras is home to many high-end options, while Manila, on El Poblado's northern edge, is a hip dining spot packed with cafes and eateries.

Southwest of the center, the Laureles neighborhood around Av Nutibara has many unpretentious eateries.

★Betty's Bowls
VEGETARIAN **$**

(Map p626; ☑305 469 6582; www.bettysbowls. com; Carrera 32D No 7a-77; mains COP$10,000-12,000; ⊙8am-6pm Mon-Sat, to 2pm Sun; 🛜🍴) Betty's Bowls has been making waves among locals, expats and El Poblado's backpacker contingent. It's a simple concept: beautifully presented granola bowls with different fruit combos, each one brimming over with color like a miniature Garden of Eden, plus fresh juices and tostadas – with avo, with cheese, with honey. Great coffee and service, too.

★Arte Dolce
GELATO **$**

(Map p626; ☑4-352-0881; www.facebook.com/artedolcemde; Carrera 33 No 7-167; gelati COP$4500-8000; ⊙noon-8pm Mon, 8:30am-9:30pm Tue-Sat, 8:30am-7pm Sun) Swing by this little corner cafe to try some of the fabulous gelato made right on the premises. Lorenzo the confectioner manages to evoke the tastes and texture of Italian gelato; our favorite flavor is the Mediterranean, which blends pistachios, caramelized almonds, lemon, orange and olive oil.

★Restaurante Itaca
COLOMBIAN **$**

(☑4-581-8538; www.facebook.com/Restaurante Itaca; Carrera 42 No 54-60, Boston; set lunch COP$14,000, mains COP$16,000-33,000; ⊙noon-3pm & 6-10pm Mon-Sat, noon-5pm Sun; 🍴) This tiny hole-in-the-wall restaurant on the outskirts of downtown prepares fantastic, fairly priced gourmet plates bursting with flavor. At lunch there are a couple of set options while in the evening there is no menu – the friendly chef Juan Carlos will tell you what he has; go for a *picada* (mixed grill) if you can.

Osea
FUSION **$$**

(Map p626; ☑4-268-3964; www.oseamed.co; Calle 9 No 43B-28, El Poblado; mains COP$28,000-40,000; ⊙noon-2:30pm & 7-10pm Tue-Sat, 7-10pm Mon) Offering a small, changing menu of inventive modern cuisine at reasonable prices, this neat little restaurant just off Parque Poblado is a real winner. A team of young chefs work away in the open kitchen preparing interesting dishes, such as grilled octopus with salsa verde. It only has six tables so it's best to make a reservation.

Bao Bei ASIAN $$
(Map p626; ☑ 304-396-2418; www.facebook.com/baobeicolombia; Carrera 36 No 8A-123; mains COP$23,000-27,000; ⊙ noon-3pm & 6-10pm Tue-Sun) You might have to wait for a table at this tiny place run by a Filipino chef and his Colombian wife, but it's worth it. Dishes are an eclectic Chinese-Korean-Japanese mélange, but their specialty, *bao* – filled steamed buns – are light and fluffy and moreish, and their Korean chicken wings set your mouth on fire in a most welcome way.

⭐ **Tal Cual** FUSION $$$
(Map p626; ☑ 316-478-4555; www.talcualrestaurante.com; Calle 12 No 43D-12, Manila; mains COP$27,000-56,000; ⊙ noon-3pm & 6-10pm; ☑) An unpretentious place in Manila with a casual arty vibe, Tal Cual serves creative fusion cuisine at reasonable prices. The varied menu features a lot of seafood, including some great Peruvian dishes, alongside pastas, risottos, steak and ribs. It's all delicious and well presented, but the ceviches and tuna *tataki* are outstanding. The service is also excellent.

🍷 Drinking & Nightlife

The city's *zona rosa* (nightlife zone) is around Parque Lleras in El Poblado, a dense tangle of upscale restaurants, bars and clubs. Some of Medellín's most exclusive bars are located along Av El Poblado. Less showy are the bars around the Laureles neighborhood. For a more bohemian experience, check the options around Parque del Periodista in the center.

⭐ **Salon Malaga** BAR
(Map p624; ☑ 4-231-2658; www.salonmalaga.com; Carrera 51 No 45-80; ⊙ 8am-1am) A Medellín institution, Salon Malaga is more than just a bar, it's a cultural experience. With walls decked out in black-and-white images of long-dead singers and an amazing collection of gramophones, it is a visual feast. But Malaga is all about the tunes, with the senior DJ spinning classic tango and boleros from a collection of old vinyl.

⭐ **Pergamino** COFFEE
(Map p626; ☑ 4-268-6444; https://us.pergamino.co; Carrera 37 No 8A-37; ⊙ 8am-9pm Mon-Fri, 9am-

9pm Sat, 10am-7pm Sun) It's worth the effort to wait in line for a drink at this popular cafe, which serves the best coffee in Medellín. There is a full range of hot and cold beverages, all made with top-quality beans sourced from small farms around the country. You can also buy coffee in bags to take home.

Cervecería Libre MICROBREWERY
(☑ 314-615-4688; www.cervecerialibre.com; Carrera 44 No 25-31; ⊙ 5pm-midnight Wed & Thu, to 2am Fri & Sat) Started by four friends with a passion for beer, this microbrewery still brews small batches, with four of its own beers on tap at any one time – their award-winning Pasión (with a hint of passion fruit), an APA, an IPA and a stout. Guest craft beers include Espiga and Aburra Valley, and there's a rock soundtrack and football on TV.

3 Cordilleras MICROBREWERY
(☑ 4-444-2337; www.3cordilleras.com; Calle 30 No 44-76; ⊙ 5:30-9pm Thu, 6:30-11pm Fri; Ⓜ Industriales) Cerveza connoisseurs shouldn't miss out on an entertaining brewery tour at 3 Cordilleras, going strong for a decade now. The tour culminates in a flight of its five brews – an APA, a sweet stout, a wheat beer, an amber ale and a delicate rosé – and excellent live bands to round off the evening.

Cervecería Maestre PUB
(Map p626; ☑ 313-626-0281; www.facebook.com/cerveceriamaestre; Carrera 40 No 10-47; ⊙ 4pm-midnight Tue-Thu, to 3am Fri & Sat) This friendly brewpub joined the Medellín scene in 2017. Beers include contributions from the local Madre Monte, Sierra Blanca, Libre, 4 Sur and other local microbreweries; owner Mario also plans to brew his own.

Son Havana CLUB
(☑ 311-339-7175; www.facebook.com/sonhavana; Carrera 73 No 44-56; cover charge COP$8000; ⊙ 8pm-3am Wed-Sat) The bar of choice for serious *son*, *la timba* and *la charanga* fans, this popular Cuban-themed place just off La 70 has a great tropical vibe. The small dance floor fills up fast, so most patrons end up dancing around the tables. It's pretty dark so you don't need to worry too much if you lack the moves.

☆ Entertainment

Medellín has the liveliest theater scene outside of Bogotá, with venues concentrated in the center and the Boston neighborhood. Dance fans will want to attend a performance at one of the city's tango centers. Once the preferred dance of the we're-not-really-Colombian *paisas*, it now lingers on in the memories of the older generation, and those with a taste for nostalgia.

Teatro Lido   CINEMA, THEATER
(Map p624; ☑ 4-251-5334; www.facebook.com/LidoTeatroMedellin; Carrera 48 No 54-20) On Parque de Bolívar, this refurbished theater sometimes has free screenings of documentaries and films, as well as concerts and other events.

🛍 Shopping

**Artesanías Caballo
de Troya**   GIFTS & SOUVENIRS
(☑ 4-448-3479; www.artesaniascaballodetroya.com; Km16 Via Las Palmas; ⊙ 8am-7pm) An excellent one-stop gift shop conveniently located on the road to the airport (if you take the Las Palmas route). It sells quality handicrafts from artisans all over the country that you won't find in the more mainstream souvenir shops.

ℹ Information

DANGERS & ANNOYANCES
➡ While Medellín is for the most part a safe city for visitors, robberies are not unheard of. Take care especially after dark in the center when office workers and retailers head home and the streets empty fast.

➡ Pickpockets have been reported on buses and the metro – keep a close eye on your belongings.

MEDICAL SERVICES
Clínica Las Vegas (☑ 4-315-9000; www.clinicalasvegas.com; Calle 2 Sur No 46-55; ⊙ 24hr) This professional private medical facility is your best option if you need a doctor in a hurry. Staff speak some English.

MONEY
Banco Popular (Carrera 50 No 50-14) Downtown ATMs.

Bancolombia (Carrera 39 No 8-100) ATM near Parque Lleras.

TOURIST INFORMATION
Medellín makes it easy to get tourist information through a network of Punto Información Turísticas (PIT) offices, operated by courteous and knowledgeable bilingual staff.

PIT Cerro Nutibara (Calle 30A No 55-64; ⊙ 8:30am-6pm Mon-Fri)

PIT Parque Arví (⊙ 9:30am-5:30pm Tue-Sun)

PIT Parque de Las Luces (Map p624; cnr Calle 44 & Carrera 54; ⊙ 9am-5:30pm Mon-Sat)

PIT Plaza Mayor (☑ 4-261-7277; www.medellin.travel; Calle 41 No 55-80; ⊙ 8am-6pm Mon-Fri)

There are also branches in each of the airports and bus terminals.

ℹ Getting There & Away

AIR
Medellín has two airports. All international flights (to Miami, Fort Lauderdale, Lima, Madrid, Panama City, Caracas) and most domestic flights to major destinations (Bogotá, Cartagena, Santa Marta, San Andrés) depart from **Aeropuerto Internacional José María Córdova** (☑ 4-402-5110; www.aeropuertorionegro.co; Rionegro), 35km southeast of the city near the town of Rionegro.

Buses shuttle between the city center and the airport every 15 minutes (COP$9500, one hour, 5am to 9pm). The **bus stop** (Map p624; Carrera 50A No 53-13) in town is behind the Hotel Nutibara, but you can also get onboard near the Centro Commercial San Diego. **Acoa Taxi** (☑ 2-261-1616; www.acoataxiaeropuerto.com.co) – with blue-and-white-striped vehicles – serves the airport; it's COP$70,000 there and COP$60,000 coming from the airport.

The smaller **Aeropuerto Olaya Herrera** (EOH; ☑ 4-403-6780; http://aeropuertoolayaherrera.gov.co; Carrera 65A No 13-157) is in town, next door to the Terminal del Sur bus station. Regional domestic flights leave from here, including services to Bogotá, Armenia, Manizales and Pereira.

BUS
Medellín has two bus terminals. **Terminal del Norte** (www.terminalesmedellin.com; Autopista Norte; Ⓜ Caribe), 3km north of the city center, handles buses to the north, east and southeast. It is easily reached from El Poblado by metro (alight at Caribe) or by taxi (COP$15,000). Destinations include the following:

DESTINATION	PRICE (COP$)	DURATION (HR)
Bogotá	66,000-70,000	9-10
Cartagena	139,000-149,000	13½-14
Neiva	80,000-100,000	11-12¼
Santa Fe de Antioquia	11,000-15,000	1½-2
Santa Marta	11,000-15,000	16

Terminal del Sur (www.terminalesmedellin.com; Carrera 65 No 8B-91), 4km southwest of the center, handles all traffic to the west and south. From El Poblado it's a quick taxi ride (COP$6500). Destinations include the following:

DESTINATION	PRICE (COP$)	DURATION (HR)
Armenia	45,000-49,000	6
Cali	63,000	8
Ipiales	123,000-132,000	22
Manizales	37,000-40,000	5
Pasto	100,000	22-24
Pereira	40,000	5
Popayán	70,000	10

❶ Getting Around

BICYCLE

Medellín has a functional and widespread free public bicycle system called Encicla (www.encicla.gov.co). You'll need to register first and pick up a 'Civica' card in any one of these metro stations: Niquía, San Antonio, Itagüí or San Javier. A network of bicycle paths links many of the stations.

BUS

Medellín is well serviced by buses, although most travelers will find the metro and taxis sufficient for their needs. The majority of routes originate on Av Oriental and from Parque Berrío. Buses stop running around 10pm or 11pm.

METRO

Medellín's **metro** (www.metrodemedellin.gov.co; single ticket COP$2400; ☉ 4:30am-11pm Mon-Sat, 5am-10pm Sun) is Colombia's only commuter rail line. It opened in 1995 and consists of a 23km north–south Linea A, which connects El Centro to El Poblado, and a 6km east–west Linea B. Trains run at ground level except for 5km through the central area where they use elevated tracks.

The metro company also operates four cable-car lines, called Metrocable, built to service the impoverished barrios in the surrounding hills and Parque Arví in Santa Elena, with two more under construction at the time of research.

TAXI

Taxis (☑ 4-444-4444) are plentiful and all are equipped with meters. The minimum charge is COP$5500. A taxi from the center to El Poblado will cost around COP$10,000 to COP$12,000. Alternatively, use a ride-share app.

Jardín

☑ 4 / POP 14,200 / ELEV 1750M

The self-proclaimed most beautiful town in Antioquia, Jardín lives up to its name. Festooned with greenery, its brightly painted two-story houses are surrounded by small coffee farms that cling impossibly to the slopes of majestic green mountains.

At the center of town life is the breezy cobblestone plaza dominated by the immense neo-Gothic Basilica Menor de la Inmaculada Concepción. It is chock-full of colorful wooden tables and chairs where fruit sellers hawk delicious cocktails and old-timers converse between measured sips of coffee. In the evenings it seems like the entire community comes out to socialize over a drink. While on weekends the town is flooded with visitors from Medellín, the rest of the week it's still full of ye olde colonial charm.

Beyond the small-town Colombia of Jardín lies spectacular countryside with hidden caves, waterfalls and top-notch bird-watching, as well as a wide variety of adventure-sport opportunities.

◎ Sights

★Cueva del Esplendor   CAVE

(☐ 316-515-2000; entry COP$7000) Located at 2200m amid beautiful landscapes, this spectacular cave has a 10m waterfall gushing through a large hole in the roof and is Jardín's most famous attraction. The cave is only accessible by foot along muddy, sometimes-narrow mountain paths. The entrance is around a three-hour hike from Jardín, and since 2017 there's been a daily limit of 40 visitors to prevent further damage to the cave. Only one operator is now allowed to lead hiking tours; book ahead.

★Cerro Cristo Rey   VIEWPOINT

(Via Jardín-Tamesis) You'll spot this lookout point with its white Christ statue from the center of Jardín. Take the modern cable car (round trip COP$5000) up for fantastic views of town and the mountains beyond. There is a shop at the top selling cold beers and snacks.

Cueva de los Guácharos   CAVE

A less visited cave and a great alternative to the Cueva El Esplendor excursion, Cueva de los Guácharos is reachable via a six-hour round trip from Jardín. First, your guide drives you to the Cerro de Cuchillion, from where it's a 90-minute, moderately difficult, muddy trek through splendid rainforest that arrives at a spectacular waterfall that thunders through a rocky gorge past the cave. Ask your lodgings to recommend a good trekking guide.

RESERVA NATURAL CAÑON DE RÍO CLARO

Set 2km south of the Medellín–Bogotá highway, three hours east of Medellín and five hours west of Bogotá, is the **Reserva Natural Cañon de Río Claro** (☑ 4-268-8855, 313-671-4459; www.rioclaroelrefugio.com; Km152, Autopista Medellín-Bogotá; COP$15,000; ⊙ 8am-6pm), a small reserve that should be on anyone's list of Colombia highlights. Here the crystalline Río Claro rushes through a stunning marble canyon surrounded by lush forest. The two must-do activities here are visiting the **Caverna de los Guácharos** (guided tour COP$20,000), a spectacular cave next to the river, and rafting on the river itself.

Bring a swimsuit, towel and flashlight (torch). On weekends the reserve is often full of Colombian holidaymakers; coming during the week guarantees a peaceful experience.

The reserve is 24km west of Doradal, where you will find a couple of budget hotels near the main plaza, as well as ATMs.

☞ Tours

Condor de los Andes   ADVENTURE
(☑ 310-379-6069; condordelosandes@colombia. com; Calle 10 No 1A-62) This dynamic adventure company inside the hostel of the same name offers a range of high-adrenaline activities around town, including canyoning in **Cascada La Escalera** (Via Jardín-Tamesis; for COP$80,000).

🛏 Sleeping & Eating

★ Condor de los Andes   HOSTEL $
(☑ 310-379-6069;www.facebook.com/Condordelos andesHostalViajesyAventuras; Calle 10 No 1A-62; dm with/without breakfast COP$32,000/27,000, s/d incl breakfast COP$65,000/99,000; ☜) Offering amazing views and total tranquility in a colonial-style house just a block from Jardín's plaza, this superb hostel is the best choice in town for budget travelers. There's a variety of comfortable rooms with hot water surrounding a stone terrace that overlooks the majestic mountains. Guests have access to the kitchen and a fine open-air common area.

Cafe Europa   ITALIAN $$
(☑ 302-235-3100; www.facebook.com/cafeeuropa colombia; Calle 8 No 4-02; pasta from COP$15,000, pizzas COP$16,000-20,000; ⊙ 5-10pm; ✐) You might have to wait a while for a table at this great-value corner cafe serving a small menu of delicious pizzas and pasta dishes at bargain prices. It's a cozy place, owned by a German travel writer and photographer, with the walls lined with European newspaper clippings and Colombian photographic exhibits. It serves wine by the glass or bottle.

🍷 Drinking & Nightlife

★ Cafe Macanas   COFFEE
(☑ 313-657-5979; www.facebook.com/Macanas jardin; Parque Principal; ⊙ 8am-8:30pm) Grab a cup of fantastic locally grown coffee and a pastry, and head out the back to the flower-filled patio right next to the church at this exceptional cafe on the main plaza. There are also cozy spaces inside the colonial building to sit and chill out when the rains come down. Also sells bags of Don Darío's coffee to go.

❶ Information

Punto Informacion Turistica (☑ 350-653-6185; piteljardin@gmail.com; cnr Carrera 3 & Calle 10; ⊙ 8am-noon & 2-5pm) Helpful tourist office around the corner from the church.

❶ Getting There & Away

Around a dozen buses (COP$22,000 to COP$26,000, three hours) head daily to Jardín from Medellín's southern bus terminal. In Jardín the buses depart from the offices on Calle 8, where both **Rapido Ochoa** (☑ 4-845-5051, 312-286-9768; www.rapidoochoa.com; Calle 8 No 5-24) and **Transportes Suroeste Antioqueño** (☑ 4-845-5505; Calle 8 No 5-21) operate. Seats sell out during peak periods, so make sure to purchase your round-trip ticket in advance.

If you are continuing south to the Eje Cafetero (Coffee Axis) in the Zona Cafetera, **Cotransrio** (☑ 311-762-6775; Calle 8 No 5-24) has a direct service from Jardín to Manizales (COP$42,000, six hours) at 6:30am. Alternatively, take the bus to Ríosucio (COP$20,000, three hours) at 8am or 3pm (noon on Saturdays) and pick up a connection to Manizales there.

COLOMBIA JARDÍN

Santa Fe de Antioquia

📶 4 / POP 25,300 / ELEV 550M

This sleepy colonial town, founded in 1541 by Jorge Robledo, is the region's oldest settlement and was once the capital of Antioquia. The clock stands still at 1826, the year the government moved to Medellín. Because it was eclipsed for so long by its neighbor 80km southeast, its colonial center never fell to the wrecking ball and today it looks very much like it did in the 19th century. The narrow streets are lined with single-story, whitewashed houses, many arranged around beautiful courtyards. You'll also see elaborately carved, typically Antioquian woodwork around windows and doorways.

It makes a great day trip from Medellín. Don't miss sampling *pulpa de tamarindo*, the beloved sour-sweet candy made with tamarind from the surrounding valley.

◉ Sights

Puente de Occidente   BRIDGE
(Km5, Via Santa Fe de Antioquia-Liborina) This unusual 291m bridge over the Río Cauca is 5km east of town. When completed in 1895, it was one of the first suspension bridges in the Americas. José María Villa, its designer, was also involved in the creation of New York's Brooklyn Bridge. It's a boring 45-minute walk downhill here. You're best to cycle or take a moto-taxi (round trip COP$15,000). The driver will wait while you walk across.

Iglesia de Santa Bárbara   CHURCH
(cnr Calle 11 & Carrera 8; ⊘ 7-8:30am & 6-7:30pm Mon-Sat, 6-7:30am & 6-7:30pm Sun) Built by Jesuits in the mid-18th century, Santa Fe's most interesting church has a fine baroque facade. The interior has an impressive, if time-worn, retable over the high altar.

Museo Juan del Corral   MUSEUM
(📞 4-853-4605; Calle 11 No 9-77; ⊘ 9am-noon & 2-5:30pm Mon, Tue, Thu & Fri, 10am-5pm Sat & Sun) FREE This perfectly preserved colonial mansion hosts exhibits dedicated to the history of the region, from prehistory to independence from the Spanish. Temporary displays of contemporary Colombian art are also showcased here, and it hosts regular cultural events.

✦✦ Festivals & Events

Fiesta de los Diablitos   CULTURAL
(⊘ Dec 22-31) The town's most popular festival runs annually over the last week of the year and has been held continuously since 1653. It includes musical performances, bullfights, dance, parades and – like almost every party in the country – a beauty contest.

🛏 Sleeping & Eating

★**Hotel Mariscal Robledo**   HOTEL $$$
(📞 4-853-1563; www.hotelmariscalrobledo.com; cnr Carrera 12 & Calle 10; r incl breakfast COP$335,000-390,000; 🅿 ❄ @ 🛜 ☲) Occupying a privileged place on Parque de la Chinca, Santa Fe's finest hotel oozes character. The spacious rooms are packed with antiques, most of which are for sale, and reflect a simple colonial elegance. There is a rooftop viewpoint, a fantastic large swimming pool and a pretty interior courtyard. The biggest negative is the electric showers.

★**La Casa Solariega**   INTERNATIONAL $$$
(📞 4-853-1530; cnr Calle 11 & Carrera 8; mains COP$32,000-42,000; ⊘ 9am-5pm Fri, 11am-10pm Sat & Sun) Part art gallery, part restaurant, this greenery-festooned colonial house serves the likes of chicken and mushroom lasagna, pizza and pasta dishes, along with a superb beer selection (including many Belgian brews). Gregarious owner Oliver speaks five languages and this is a 'slow food' restaurant: prepare for a leisurely meal.

ℹ Getting There & Away

There are hourly buses (COP$11,000, two hours) and minivans (COP$15,000, 1½ hours) to/from Medellín's Terminal del Norte. The last van back to Medellín from the **bus terminal** (Carretera Medellín-Urabá) leaves around 7:30pm, but after this time you can always flag down a passing intercity service from Turbo (in Urabá) on the highway.

Guatapé

📶 4 / POP 5500 / ELEV 1925M

The pleasant holiday town of Guatapé is located on the shores of the Embalse Guatapé, a sprawling artificial lake. It is known for the fresco-like adornment of its traditional houses. Brightly painted bas-relief depictions of people, animals and shapes cover the lower half of many dwellings.

Guatapé makes a great day trip from Medellín, a two-hour bus ride away, but there is enough outdoor adventure here to keep you entertained a bit longer if you fancy a peaceful break from the city. Visit on the weekend if you want to experience the festival atmosphere when the town is packed with Colombian tourists, or come during the week to explore the surrounding nature at a more relaxed pace.

◎ Sights & Activities

A hydraulic **canopy ride** (Calle 32; per ride COP$15,000; ⊙1-6pm Mon-Fri, 9am-6pm Sat & Sun) runs along the lakeshore from a large hill near the entrance to town. Rock climbing on the southern side of the Piedra del Peñol is another popular activity; paragliding and kayaking are other fun things to do. Most hostels and hotels can hook you up with local guides.

★**Piedra del Peñol**   VIEWPOINT
(off Via El Peñol; per climb COP$18,000; ⊙8am-6pm) Also known as El Peñon de Guatapé, thanks to the fierce rivalry between the towns it straddles, this 200m-high granite monolith rises from near the edge of the Embalse Guatapé. A brick staircase of 659 steps rises up through a broad fissure in the side of the rock. From the top there are magnificent views of the region, the fingers of the lake sprawling amid a vast expanse of green mountains. Medellín–Guatape buses can drop you off at 'La Piedra.'

🛏 Sleeping & Eating

There's a good range of hostels and hotels. The most inviting places to rest are in the countryside outside town. Many rural hotels have fine views of Piedra del Peñol.

★**Hostal Casa de Mamá**   HOSTEL $
(Mom's House Hostel; ☏320-207-0707; www.facebook.com/momshousehostel; Calle 32 Carrera 23-27, Vereda El Roble; dm COP$20,000; 🛜) Painted in psychedelic colors and watched over by motherly Gloria, who makes the hostel live up to its name, this is a tranquil hideaway a 10- to 15-minute walk from Guatapé. The cat joins the guests as they do yoga, the bunks have privacy curtains and travelers swap tales over communal dinners.

★**Oak Tree House**   GUESTHOUSE $$
(☏320-417-2497; Vereda El Roble; r COP$114,000-230,000, tr/f COP$300,000/360,000; 🛜) Some 10 minutes' walk across the bridge from Guatapé proper, this delightful place really stands out due to the warmth of its staff, who go above and beyond the call of duty. Add to it a clutch of spotless rooms (some with mountain views, others overlooking the garden) and inviting common areas with swings and hammocks, and it's a winner!

★**Pizzeria de Luigi**   PIZZA $$
(☏320-845-4552; Calle 31 No 27-10; pizzas COP$22,000-30,000; ⊙6:30-10:30pm Wed-Sat, 12:30-2:30pm & 6:30-10:30pm Sun; 🍴) A friendly Italian-run place near the sports field serving up the best pizzas in Guatapé, nay – the region! Freshly baked, fluffy crusts, high-quality ingredients as toppings, good wine, wonderful service...an immensely satisfying experience overall.

❶ Getting There & Away

If you're coming on a day trip from Medellín, it makes sense to climb Piedra del Peñol before venturing onward to Guatapé, as it can get cloudy and rainy in the afternoon. Buses to and from Medellín (COP$13,500, two hours) run about once an hour. *Colectivos* shuttle frequently between the turnoff to Piedra del Peñol and Guatapé (COP$2000, 10 minutes) or you can take a moto-taxi to the entrance (COP$10,000).

The last bus back to Medellín is at 6:30pm on weekdays and at 7:45pm on weekends and other peak periods. If returning to Medellín from Guatapé on the weekend, be sure to buy your return ticket immediately upon arrival as buses fill up fast. The ticket office is at the **Terminal de Transporte** (cnr Carrera 30 & Calle 32) on the waterfront.

Manizales

📍6 / POP 357,800 / ELEV 2107M

The northern point of the Eje Cafetero (Coffee Axis), Manizales is a pleasantly cool, midsized university town with hilly streets, surrounded on all sides by green mountain scenery. The capital of the Caldas department, Manizales was founded in 1849 by a group of Antioquian colonists looking to escape the civil wars of that time. The town's early development was hindered by two earthquakes in 1875 and 1878 and a fire in 1925, which is why there's not a lot of historical interest left – the real attractions are the surrounding nature activities and the town's vibrant nightlife.

◎ Sights

★**Monumento a**
Los Colonizadores   MONUMENT
(Av 12 de Octobre, Chipre; ⊙10am-6pm) **FREE** Located atop a hill in the neighborhood of Chipre, this massive monument to the city's founders was crafted from 50 tonnes of bronze (including keys and other implements

donated by local residents). It's a very impressive work, but an even bigger attraction is the spectacular view over town and to PNN Los Nevados. Catch a bus marked 'Chipre' along Carrera 23 to get here.

★ **Catedral de Manizales** CHURCH
(☑320-683-5618; Carrera 22 No 22-15; tour incl tower access adult/child COP$10,000/7000; ☺9am-8pm) Plaza de Bolívar's south side is dominated by the odd but impressive Catedral de Manizales. Begun in 1929 and built of reinforced concrete, it is among the first churches of its kind in Latin America. Its main tower is 106m high, making it the highest church tower in the country. You can climb the seemingly endless spiral staircase to the top for great views of the city, but only as part of a guided tour (these last around 75 minutes).

↻ Tours

Ecosistemas ADVENTURE
(☑312-705-7007, 6-880-8300; www.ecosistemas travel.com.co; Carrera 20 No 20-19; ☺8am-noon & 2-6pm Mon-Fri, 8am-noon Sat) An experienced and professional outfitter offering excursions and multiday tours to PNN Los Nevados, including hikes to the summits of Nevado de Santa Isabel and Nevado del Tolima. It is one of the only operators with regular day trips into the park (COP$160,000). It also specializes in visits to local coffee farms.

🛏 Sleeping & Eating

★ **Finca Mirador Morrogacho** B&B $$
(☑317-661-6117; www.miradorfincamorrogacho. com; Morrogacho Villa Jordan, enseguida Padres Salvatorianos, Calle 2; incl breakfast dm/s/d from COP$42,000/110,000/140,000, apt from COP$198,000; 🛆) Located on a mountainside on the outskirts of town, this fantastic small hotel with phenomenal views has a variety of spacious, classy accommodations with polished-wood highlights and loads of natural light; some have guest kitchens. To get here take bus 601 or 619 marked 'Morrogacho' from central Manizales (COP$2000, 20 minutes). A taxi from Cable Plaza costs around COP$10,000.

The breakfast is hearty, and vegetarian meals (COP$20,000) are available.

The enchanting grounds are full of flowers and hummingbirds.There's a path beside the property that winds down through coffee farms to a waterfall and a panoramic yoga space.

★ **Mirador Andino** HOSTEL $$
(☑310-609-8141, 6-882-1699; www.miradorandino-hostel.com; Carrera 23 No 32-20; dm/r COP$52,000/170,000; 🛆) Perched on the side of the ridge on the edge of downtown, right next to the cable-car station, this hostel is a superb budget-traveler choice. Rooms are spotless, views from the fine rooftop bar are amazing, and the staff are wonderfully accommodating and superhelpful. Even the dorms come with private bathrooms.

La Condesa Cantina MEXICAN $
(☑300-613-2218; www.facebook.com/LaCondesa CantinaManizales; Carrera 23 No 73-09; items COP$12,000-15,000; ☺noon-3pm & 5-10pm Mon-Thu, to 11pm Fri, noon-11pm Sat; 🍴) A bright little Mexican spot on the edge of the Milan dining strip serving tacos, quesadillas and *elotes* (Mexican grilled corn) with brilliance, flourish and seriously punchy salsa. Wash your meal down with a cold *cerveza michelada* or a margarita the size of a small bathtub.

★ **El Jardín**
de las Delicias INTERNATIONAL $$
(☑313-658-8991; www.facebook.com/eljardindelas delicias.rest; Carrera 25 No 68-19; mains COP$27,000-36,000; ☺noon-9:30pm Mon-Thu, to 10pm Fri & Sat) Worth every penny of your hard-earned money, this place serves modern Colombian dishes with an international twist, lovingly crafted by chef Pablo who blends cooking techniques learned in Paris with local ingredients. Take your meals (trout wiith *patacones,* veal osso buco, or dark chocolate mousse with salted caramel) out onto the sunny terrace. They roast their own coffee, too.

❶ Getting There & Around

AIR
Aeropuerto La Nubia (☑6-874-5451; Carrera 37) is 8km southeast of the city center, with several daily flights to Bogotá and a couple to Medellín. Take the urban bus to La Enea, then walk for five minutes to the terminal, or grab a taxi (COP$14,000). Delays and cancellations are common because of fog, so don't count on making a tight connection.

BUS & CABLE CAR
Manizales' sparkling modern **bus terminal** (☑6-878-7858; www.terminaldemanizales. com.co; Carrera 43 No 65-100) is located south of the center and is linked to the downtown area by an efficient **cable car** (www.cableaereo

manizales.gov.co; Carrera 23; per trip
COP$1800; ☺ 6am-10pm) that offers great
views of the city. A second cable-car line runs
from the terminal across to Villa María on the
far side of the valley. If you are staying by Cable
Plaza, it is easier to take a taxi direct from the
terminal (COP$7000).

Buses depart regularly to Cali (COP$40,000,
4½ hours), Bogotá (COP$56,000 to COP$70,000,
eight hours) and Medellín (COP$40,000 to
COP$50,000, four to five hours).

Minibuses to Pereira (COP$11,000, 1¼ hours)
and Armenia (COP$17,500, 1½ hours) run every
15 minutes or so.

Around Manizales

The lush mountainous countryside surrounding Manizales is home to some of Colombia's most beautiful landscapes and does not lack opportunities for adventure and relaxation. Here you'll find hot thermal baths, volcanic craters, working coffee farms and nature reserves full of birdlife all within a one-hour drive of the city.

⊙ Sights

★**Hacienda Venecia**   PLANTATION
(☑ 6-870-3034, 320-636-5719; www.hacienda
venecia.com; Vereda el Rosario, San Peregrino; tours
adult/child 12-15yr COP$50,000/40,000; ☺ tours
9:30am) This hacienda has won numerous awards for its coffee. It offers a tour in English that includes an informative presentation about Colombian coffee, an introduction to coffee cupping, a class in coffee preparation and a walking tour through the plantation. You can use the pool afterwards, and a typical lunch is available for COP$15,000. The tour price includes transportation to/from your hotel in Manizales. Barista workshops are available.

Hacienda Guayabal   PLANTATION
(☑ 314-772-4856, 317-280-4899; www.hacienda
guayabal.com; Km3 Via Peaje Tarapacá, Chinchiná;
tours Spanish/English COP$35,000/40,000; ☺ tours
8am-5pm) This slow-paced working coffee farm near Chinchiná is a great place to come and unwind while surrounded by *cafetero* culture. It runs an excellent tour that follows the coffee process from the plant to the cup and includes a tasting workshop at the end. To get here, take an Autolujo bus from Manizales to Chinchiná (COP$3500, 30 minutes). A taxi from Chinchiná direct to the door costs COP$10,000.

Recinto del Pensamiento   NATURE RESERVE
(☑ 6-889-7073; www.recintodelpensamiento.com;
Km11 Via al Magdalena; COP$17,000; ☺ 9am-4pm
Tue-Sun) Set in the cloud forest 11km from Manizales, this nature park has a fine mariposario (butterfly enclosure), several short walks through an impressive orchid-populated forest, and a medicinal herb garden. You'll also see plantations of *guadua* and *chusqué* (two kinds of Colombian bamboo). There's even a *telesilla* – a kind of chairlift that takes you up the mountain slope on which the park sits. To get here, take the bus marked Sera Maltería from Cable Plaza in Manizales or take a taxi (COP$12,000).

🛌 Sleeping

★**Termales del Ruiz**   SPA HOTEL $$$
(☑ 310-455-3588; www.hoteltermalesdelruiz.com;
Paraje de Termales, Villa Maria, Caldas; s/d incl
breakfast from COP$315,000/335,000; ☺ ☒) Amid stunning landscapes just outside the boundaries of PNN Los Nevados at 3500m, this thermal-baths complex is the place to go for total relaxation. Rooms have the feel of a classic alpine lodge and while not huge they're comfortable. Outside there's a large thermal pool set among otherworldly *páramo* (high-mountain plain) plants. You'll need your own wheels to get here.

Parque Nacional Natural Los Nevados

ELEV 2600-5325M

Following a spine of snow-covered volcanic peaks, this **national park** (☑ 6-887-1611; www.parquesnacionales.gov.co; foreigners/Colombians COP$43,500/15,500, south of park COP$29,500/10,500; ☺ 8am-3:30pm) sits between Manizales, Pereira and Ibagué and provides access to some of the most stunning stretches of the Colombian Andes. Its varied altitude range encompasses everything from humid cloud forests and *páramo* (high-mountain plains) to glaciers on the tallest peaks.

Thirty-seven rivers are born here, providing water to 3.5 million people in four departments. The glaciers in the park have been receding, however, and research is underway to measure the impact on the environment.

Highlights include visits to the beautiful Laguna del Otún, and the ascents of the three snowcapped volcanoes: Nevado del Ruiz, Nevado de Santa Isabel and Nevado del Tolima.

COLOMBIA AROUND MANIZALES

The best months to see snow in Los Nevados are October and November and from March to May. Outside of those times you're more likely to get the dry, windy conditions favorable to trekking and clear views.

Pereira

6 / POP 440,100 / ELEV 1410M

Hardworking Pereira is not your typical tourist destination. In fact it's not really a tourist destination at all. Almost all visitors to Pereira come for one thing – to do business. Founded in 1863, Pereira is the capital of Risaralda and the economic powerhouse of the Zona Cafetera – a hot commercial center most noted for its throbbing nightlife. Pereira doesn't offer much in the way of attractions, but if you want to experience a fast-paced yet friendly Colombian city away from the gringo trail and with a good dining scene, it certainly fits the bill. Pereira is also the gateway to Parque Ucumarí and Santuario Otún Quimbaya, a pair of top nature reserves, and the relaxing thermal springs of Santa Rosa and San Vicente.

🛌 Sleeping & Eating

★ **Kolibrí Hostel** HOSTEL $
(📞 321-646-9275, 6-331-3955; www.kolibrihostel. com; Calle 4 No 16-35; dm from COP$23,000, r with/without bathroom COP$90,000/60,000; 🛜) With a great location just off the main *zona rosa,* this top hostel is sociable without being a party place. Besides comfortable rooms, there's a great terrace with mountain views, a chilled streetside bar area, and coffee from the family *finca* (farm) of one of the owners; the Dutch-Colombian couple is happy to arrange coffee tours, paragliding and cycling excursions.

★ **Leños y Parrilla** GRILL $$
(📞 6-331-4676; www.facebook.com/lenosyparrilla; Carrera 12 No 2-78; mains COP$24,000-34,000; 🕐 noon-10pm) Just off the Circunvalar, this hugely popular altar to things that go moo delights the carnivorously inclined with its wide selection of both thin- and thick-cut steaks. They're smoky and seared to perfection over hot coals, and the T-bones have crisped ribbons of fat... It's a big place but still gets full so come early or make a reservation.

❶ Getting There & Around

The **bus terminal** (📞 6-321-5834; www.terminal pereira.com; Calle 17 No 23-157) is 1.5km south of the city center. Many urban buses will take you there in less than 10 minutes. It's a minimum fare by taxi (COP$4500) from the center or the Av Circunvalar.

There are regular departures to Bogotá (COP$48,000 to COP$69,000, nine hours). A number of buses go to Medellín (COP$34,000 to COP$46,000, six hours) and Cali (COP$25,000 to COP$32,000, four hours). Minibuses run every 15 minutes to Armenia (COP$6000 to COP$8000, one hour) and Manizales (COP$11,000, 1¼ hours).

Armenia

6 / POP 315,300 / ELEV 1483M

Armenia feels more like a big town than a departmental capital, and is far more slow-paced than its coffee-country rivals Manizales and Pereira. Originally named Villa Holguín when founded in 1889, Armenia was renamed in the early 20th century in solidarity with the Armenian victims of genocide perpetuated by the Ottoman Empire. Devastated by an earthquake in 1999 that flattened much of the city center, Armenia has never fully recovered. The center of the city is makeshift – check out the hastily reconstructed cathedral, made of prefab concrete slabs – and the de facto center has moved north of downtown, along Av Bolívar.

Most travelers will pass through Armenia only long enough to change buses; however, the city has a couple of sights, which make it interesting enough for a day or so.

◉ Sights

The city has the fine Museo del Oro Quimbaya and excellent **Parque de la Vida** (cnr Av Bolívar & Calle 7N; COP$1500; 🕐 7am-7pm).

This excellent **Museo del Oro Quimbaya** (📞 6-749-8169; www.banrepcultural.org/armenia/ museo-del-oro-quimbaya; Av Bolívar 40N-80; 🕐 9am-5pm Tue-Sun) FREE showcases the fine work of indigenous pre-Columbian Quimbaya goldsmiths, as well as fine ceramics and ceremonial items. There are thorough explanations in English about the culture of the Quimbaya. It's in the Centro Cultural, 5km northeast of Armenia's center. Grab bus 8 or 12 northbound on Av Bolívar.

🛌 Sleeping

Wanderlust Hostel HOSTEL $$
(📞 314-588-0182, 6-735-8686; www.wanderlust armenia.com; Carrera 14 No 1-24; dm COP$25,000-30,000, r COP$90,000; 🛜) A friendly hostel with top facilities and excellent service from

TERMALES SAN VICENTE

Nestled in a narrow valley surrounded by imposing mountains, 18km east of Santa Rosa de Cabal, **Termales San Vicente** (☑320-693-3707; www.sanvicente.com.co; Km17 Via Laguna del Otún y Parque Natural Los Nevados; adult/child 3-10yr COP$50,000/22,000; ⊙8am-midnight) is a thermal bath complex that has seven pools, including the small, two-person *pozos de amor*, and a spa offering a full range of treatments, including mud therapy, facials, peels and massage. Come on a weekday to avoid the crowds.

Day trips from Pereira, including round-trip transportation, cost COP$80,000/55,000 per adult/child aged three to 10 years. They run on Fridays and weekends (or daily on demand), departing from the **Termales San Vicente Office** (☑6-333-6157; Av Circunvalar No 15-62; ⊙8am-6pm Mon-Sat, to noon Sun) at 9am and returning at 6:30pm; call in advance to reserve. Day-trip prices include admission, lunch and a refreshment.

Most visitors hang around in the main pools near the restaurant building, but the natural **Piscina de las Burbujas**, surrounded by greenery near the main gate, is well worth checking out. A short walk further down the valley lies the invigorating **Rio Termal**, where the thermal waters mix with the rushing stream to create amazing natural spas surrounded by thick forest.

The complex also has natural saunas built over 80°C to 90°C hot springs. There are adventure activities, including a canopy line high above the valley (COP$25,000) and abseiling in a waterfall (COP$40,000), plus two scenic walking trails.

On-site accommodations range from comfortable, wood-paneled rooms (singles/doubles including breakfast from COP$188,000/288,000) to camping with access to the thermal pools (COP$88,000 per person).

English-speaking staff. Dorms are bright and comfortable with high-quality bedding, but the best features of the place are the attractive common areas, including a large courtyard out the back with hammocks and a modern lounge/work area. The private rooms at the front of the building are susceptible to street noise.

ⓘ Getting There & Away

Pereira's **MegaBús** (www.megabus.gov.co; s ticket COP$2000) runs crosstown and out to Dosquebradas. It's similar to Bogotá's Trans Milenio and Cali's MIO, but on a smaller scale. It's not hugely useful for travelers staying around the Av Circunvalar, however.

Salento

☑6 / POP 7250 / ELEV 1895M

Set amid gorgeous green mountains 24km northeast of Armenia, this small town survives on coffee production, trout farming and tourists, the last drawn by its quaint streets, typical *paisa* architecture and its proximity to the spectacular Valle de Cocora. It was founded in 1850, and is one of the oldest towns in Quindío.

The main drag is Calle Real (Carrera 6), which is full of *artesanías* (local craft stalls) and restaurants. At the end of the

street stairs lead up to Alto de la Cruz, a hill topped with a cross. From here you'll see the verdant Valle de Cocora and the mountains that surround it. If the skies are clear (usually only early in the morning), you can spot the snowcapped tops of the volcanoes on the horizon.

🏃 Activities

★**Mountain Bike**
Salento Colombia   MOUNTAIN BIKING
(☑311-333-5936, 316-535-1792; www.salentocycling.com; Calle 7 No 1-04, Plantation House; rides COP$130,000-250,000) Offers excellent full-day mountain-biking adventures that take you up to the Andean divide, from where you'll cruise down the far side to the biggest wax palm forest in the region, before being brought back up to the peak in a truck for the ride all the way back down the mountain to Salento. Includes a picnic lunch with amazing views.

➲ Tours

★**Finca El Ocaso**   TOURS
(☑310-451-7329, 310-451-7194; www.fincael ocasosalento.com; Km3.8 Vereda Palestina; tours COP$15,000-65,000) The most polished coffee tour around Salento is set on an expansive farm with fine coffee bushes and a pretty farmhouse. You'll visit the plantation and

then follow the process of preparing the beans for market. Tours run for 90 minutes and are offered hourly from 9am to 4pm. To get here, catch an hourly jeep from the plaza (COP$3000).

🛏 Sleeping

★ El Mocambo Hostel   HOSTEL $
(📞 312-660-0371; www.facebook.com/elmocamboboquia; Km1.5 Camino Nacional, Via a Toche Antigua Finca Pilones; dm COP$23,000, r with/without bathroom COP$74,000/57,000; 🛜) A 15-minute walk south of Salento, this peaceful place is run by hospitable Soledad, a mother figure who makes her guests feel really at home. It's hard to decide what we love more: her hospitality, the fiery sunsets, the evening silence punctuated by firefly sparks, or the queen-size beds in the dorms. Jeeps run past here hourly (COP$3000).

★ Coffee Tree Hostel   HOSTEL $$
(📞 318-390-4415; www.coffeetreebh.com; Carrera 9 No 9-06; dm/r from COP$38,000/230,000; 🛜) Coffee Tree well and truly earns its 'boutique hostel' label, with three floors of spacious, well-decorated rooms offering great mountain views alongside a bright social area with high ceilings. Staff are friendly and speak great English and the extensive breakfast spread provides fuel for outdoor adventures.

★ Reserva El Cairo   BOUTIQUE HOTEL $$$
(📞 321-649-3439; www.reservaelcairo.com; Km 3, Via Cocora, Vereda La Playa; r/f from COP$222,000/400,000) Coffee-country accommodations don't get much better than this. The elegant and comfortable rooms here are set in a charming traditional farmhouse in lush gardens, and the surrounding nature reserve contains some of the last tracts of primary forest in the valley. It's great for both bird-watching and more adventurous pursuits, such as paragliding. It's 3km from Salento, towards Valle Cocora.

🍴 Eating & Drinking

★ Rincón del Lucy   COLOMBIAN $
(Carrera 6 No 4-02; breakfast COP$7000, lunch & dinner COP$9000; ⊙ 7am-8pm) We love Lucy for her gut-busting, best-value-in-town meals: fish, beef or chicken served with rice, beans, plantain and soup, consumed at busy communal tables next to strangers who may become friends. It's a great spot for a filling breakfast before a hike.

★ Café Bernabé Gourmet   FUSION $$
(📞 315-596-1447; cnr Carrera 6 & Calle 3; mains COP$17,000-36,000; ⊙ 1-10pm; 🍴) There's a lot to love about a place that pushes the culinary boundaries of a small-town dining scene, with its ambitious pairings of flavors (salmon with coffee and passion-fruit reduction), beautifully seared steaks, cocktails (the best in town, or perhaps the region!) and excellent coffee. Our compliments to the chef.

★ Café Jesús Martín   COFFEE
(📞 300-735-5679;   www.cafejesusmartin.com; Carrera 6 No 6-14; ⊙ 7:30am-9pm Mon, 7am-9pm Tue-Sun) Expert baristas at this cafe serve top-quality espresso, drips and filtered brews from beans roasted and prepared in the owner's factory. It's got a distinctly upper-crust feel to it; don't expect to see too many local farmers drinking here. It also serves wine, beer and light meals. Ask about the high-end coffee-tasting tours.

❶ Getting There & Away

Minibuses run to/from Armenia every 20 minutes (COP$4500, 45 minutes, 5:20am to 8pm). Armenia buses run along a route through the town and pass the plaza before leaving from the **Salento Transport Office** (Carrera 2 No 4-30), though on weekends you'll have to go direct to the bus office. You can also take a taxi direct from Armenia (30 minutes, COP$85,000).

There is a direct bus service from the terminal in Pereira to Salento (COP$6500, 1½ hours). **Flota Occidental** (📞 310-449-4444; www.flotaoccidental.com; Carrera 2 No 4-40) runs four express vans per day direct between Medellín and Salento (COP$47,000, seven hours).

Valle de Cocora

In a country full of beautiful landscapes, Cocora is one of the most striking. It stretches east of Salento into the lower reaches of PNN Los Nevados, with a broad green valley framed by sharp peaks. Everywhere you'll see the palma de cera (wax palm), the largest palm in the world (up to 60m tall): it's Colombia's national tree. Set amid the misty green hills, they are breathtaking to behold, and the valley is protected as part of Unesco's Coffee Cultural Landscape of Colombia Heritage Site.

The most popular walk in the area is the four- to five-hour loop hike from the hamlet of Cocora to the **Reserva Natural Acaime** (📞 321-636-2818; incl refreshment COP$5000) and on to the Unesco-protected valley of the palma de cera. The hike is done anticlockwise. Sure, you can go clockwise and reach the wax palms first, but where's the fun in that?

🛈 Getting There & Away

Willys jeeps leave Salento's main square for Cocora (COP$3800, 30 minutes) at 6:10am, 7:30am, 9:30am, 11:30am, 2pm and 4pm, coming back an hour later. There are sometimes additional services on weekends. You can also contract a jeep privately for COP$35,000.

SOUTHWEST COLOMBIA

Cali

📱 2 / POP 2.4 MILLION / ELEV 969M

Cali is a hot, gritty city with a real zest for life that draws you in and stays with you long after you leave town. Beyond a handful of churches and museums, Cali is light on sights – but the city's main attraction is its beguiling, electrifying atmosphere. If you make the effort you will find great nightlife, good restaurants and plenty to do, especially in the evening, when a cool mountain breeze dissipates the heat of the day.

Cali is rich in Afro-Colombian heritage; nowhere is the nation's racial diversity and harmony more apparent. From the impoverished barrios to the big, slick clubs, everyone is moving to one beat, and that beat is salsa. Music in the world's salsa capital is more than entertainment: it is a unifying factor that ties the city together.

⊙ Sights

Museo de Arte
Moderno La Tertulia   GALLERY
(📱 2-893-2939; www.museolatertulia.com; Av Colombia No 5 Oeste-105; adult/student COP$10,000/7000; ⊙10am-7pm Tue-Sat, 2-6pm Sun) Presents changing exhibitions of contemporary painting, sculpture and photography from both local and South American artists. Look out for works by contemporary Colombian artists such as Hugo Zapata and Beatriz Gonzáles. It's Cali's most important cultural space, too, with regular art-house film screenings, poetry readings and music performances. Located a 15-minute walk from the city center along the Río Cali.

Museo Arqueológico la Merced   MUSEUM
(📱 2-885-4665; Carrera 4 No 6-59; adult/child COP$4000/2000; ⊙9am-6pm Mon-Sat, 10am-

4pm Sun) Housed in an 18th-century annex to La Merced, this interesting museum contains a collection of pre-Columbian pottery left behind by the major cultures from central and southern Colombia, such as the Tierradentro, Tolima and San Agustín. Among the highlights are figurines from the Tumaco culture and intricately painted Quimbaya vessels.

★Iglesia de la Merced   CHURCH
(cnr Carrera 4 & Calle 7; ⊙6:30-10am & 4-7pm) Founded in 1545, this is Cali's oldest church. It's a lovely whitewashed building in the Spanish-colonial style, with a long, narrow nave, and humble wood and stucco construction. Inside, a heavily gilded baroque high altar is topped by the Virgen de las Mercedes, the patron saint of the city.

Iglesia de la Ermita   CHURCH
(cnr Av Colombia & Calle 13; ⊙hours vary) Overlooking the Río Cali, this striking neo-Gothic church houses the 18th-century painting of *El señor de la caña* (Lord of the Sugarcane) that survived major earthquakes. Many miracles (including its own survival) are attributed to the image.

Museo del Oro Calima   MUSEUM
(📱 2-684-7755; Calle 7 No 4-69; ⊙9am-5pm Tue-Fri, 10am-5pm Sat) **FREE** One block east from Iglesia de la Merced, this excellent museum displays more than 600 pieces of intricate gold jewelry, as well as ceramics used in shaman rituals and everyday life. They belong to the ancient Calima culture that inhabited the valley northwest of Cali from around 200 BC to 400 AD.

Cerro de las Tres Cruces   VIEWPOINT
(Av 10 Norte) The views are spectacular at these three crosses high in the mountains overlooking the city, and the hike up here is a popular outdoor activity among health-conscious *caleños* (residents of Cali). It's best to come early on weekends when there's a crowd and don't bring any valuables – the area is isolated and robberies are not uncommon.

🡒 Courses

★Sabor Manicero   DANCING
(📱 315-289-4040; https://salsa-classes-in.cali-colombia.co; Calle 5 No 39-71, 3er Piso; ⊙salsa classes 4:30-6:30pm & 7-9pm Mon-Fri, 2-4pm Sat) One of Colombia's largest dance schools, offering cheap group salsa classes for all ability levels.

COLOMBIA CALI

Cali

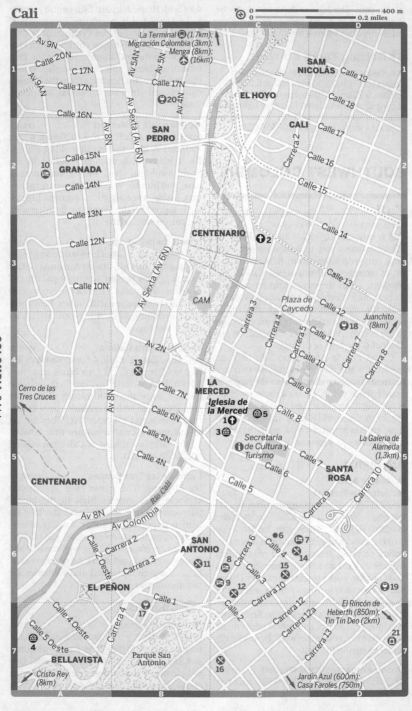

0   400 m
0   0.2 miles

A

Av 9N
Calle 20N
C 17N
Av 9AN
Calle 17N
Calle 16N

Av 5AN
Av 5N
Calle 17N

B

La Terminal (1.7km);
Migración Colombia (3km);
Menga (8km);
(16km)

Av 4N
20

EL HOYO

C

SAM
NICOLÁS   Calle 19

Calle 18

CALI   Calle 17

Carrera 2   Calle 16

Calle 15

D

1

Av Sexta (Av 6N)

SAN
PEDRO

2

10
GRANADA

Calle 15N

Calle 14N

Calle 13N

Calle 12N

Calle 10N

Av 8N

Av Sexta (Av 6N)

CENTENARIO   2

CAM

Calle 14

Calle 13

3

Carrera 3

Carrera 4

Plaza de
Caycedo   Calle 12

Calle 11

Carrera 5

Calle 10

18

Carrera 7

Juanchito
(8km)

Carrera 8

4

Cerro de las
Tres Cruces

Av 2N

N8 Av

13

Calle 7N

Calle 6N

LA
MERCED

Iglesia de
la Merced   5
1

3

Calle 9

Calle 8

Secretaría
de Cultura y
Turismo

Calle 7

La Galería de
Alameda
(1.3km)

Carrera 10

5

CENTENARIO

Río Cali

Av 8N

Av Colombia

Calle 5N

Calle 4N

Calle 6

Calle 5

SANTA
ROSA

Carrera 9

6

EL PEÑON

Calle 2 Oeste

Carrera 2

Carrera 3

SAN
ANTONIO

11

8

9   12

Carrera 6

Calle 4

Calle 3

6

7

14

15

Carrera 10

Carrera 12

19

El Rincón de
Heberth (850m);
Tin Tín Deo (2km)

7

4

Calle 4 Oeste

Calle 5 Oeste

Carrera 4

BELLAVISTA

Cristo Rey
(8km)

Calle 1

17

Calle 2

Parque San
Antonio

16

Carrera 12a

Carrera 13

Jardín Azul (600m);
Casa Faroles (750m)

21

COLOMBIA CALI

Cali

◉ **Top Sights**

◉ **Sights**

◉ **Activities, Courses & Tours**

◉ **Sleeping**

◉ **Eating**

◉ **Drinking & Nightlife**

◉ **Shopping**

You can also learn to shake your hips to the rhythms of bachata and merengue here.

Salsa Pura DANCING
(☎310-493-9660; www.facebook.com/salsapura bailesinfronteras; Calle 4 No 6-61; ☉9am-8pm Mon-Fri, 10am-6pm Sat) This salsa school in the heart of San Antonio has experienced and enthusiastic instructors offering private and group classes for dancers of all levels. They're very responsive to inquiries, making them popular with travelers.

✷ Festivals & Events

Festival Petronio Álvarez MUSIC
(https://petronio.cali.gov.co; Calle 9C, Canchas Pan-americanas; ☉Aug) A festival of Pacific music, heavily influenced by the African rhythms brought by the many slaves that originally populated the Pacific coast. *Caleños* turn up en masse for nonstop dancing, competitive outdoor gigs and copious amounts of *arrechón* (a sweet artisanal alcohol).

Festival Mundial de Salsa DANCE
(www.mundialdesalsa.com; ☉Sep) Amazing dancers of all ages from Cali and around the world take to the stage in colorful costumes during this hugely competitive salsa event. Finals take place in the Plaza de Toros.

⌂ Sleeping

For a taste of Cali's colonial origins and a plentitude of hostels, lay your head in laid-back San Antonio; nearby residential area Miraflores is calmer but still within walking distance of the action. If you're after high-end accommodations and nightlife head for Granada.

★ **El Patio Hostel** HOSTEL $
(☎316-617-5276; www.facebook.com/elpatio hostel; Carrera 5 No 2-1; dm COP$27,000-32,000, s with/without bathroom COP$63,500/48,000, d with/without bathroom COP$75,000/65,000; ☎) Smack bang in the middle of the San Antonio neighborhood, this hostel deserves every ounce of praise it gets for the warmth and hospitality of owners Adriana and Fabio. It's a colorful house with a delightful courtyard to chill out in, a good ratio of guests per bathroom, a kitchen and plenty of local tips.

La Casa Café HOSTEL $
(☎2-893-7011; www.lacasacafecali.blogspot.com; Carrera 6 No 2-13; dm COP$25,000, s/d COP$50,000/80,000, without bathroom COP$40,000/60,000; ☎) For an old-school, no-frills backpacking experience head to this cafe-bar, which rents good-value dorm beds and private rooms on the 2nd floor of its colonial building. Major bonus points for lovely owner Paola, who does a great job of looking after her guests. The cafe serves real coffee from small local farms around Valle de Cauca.

★ **Casa Alegre Art Gallery** BOUTIQUE HOTEL $$
(☎2-893-8444; www.casaalegreartgallery.com; Carrera 9 No 4-28; s/d from COP$120,000/150,000; ❋☎❀) ✐ In a handy San Antonio location for dining out and taking salsa classes, this is a characterful, converted colonial house with a greenery-filled courtyard and oasis-like pool. Spacious rooms have dark-wood furniture, really comfortable beds and high-quality bedding, colorful tiled floors and quiet air-con, with solar panels supplying some of the electricity. Staff are full of helpful advice, too.

COLOMBIA CALI

★ La Sucursal Hostel HOSTEL $$

(☑ 301-576-2474; www.facebook.com/lasucursal hostel; Av 9AN No 14-61; dm COP$23,000-25,000, s/d COP$80,000/160,000) Very sociable without being a party place, this large, colorful hostel is run by the awesome José, who goes above and beyond the call of duty for his guests. Expect free salsa lessons, a great open-air bar area with hammocks and lounges, lots of local tips and a variety of tidy, brightly painted rooms spread over several floors.

★ Jardín Azul BOUTIQUE HOTEL $$

(☑ 2-556-8380; www.jardinazul.com; Carrera 24A No 2A-59; r/tr from COP$96,000/150,000; 🐱 🐞) In a converted house on a hill near the colonial sector east of the center, this spotless small hotel has spacious, bright rooms with big beds and imported cotton sheets. Some rooms have private balconies and views of the city. Breakfast is served around a small pool set in an appealing garden.

Casa Faroles HOTEL $$

(☑ 2-376-5381; www.facebook.com/HotelFaroles; Carrera 24B No 2-48 Oeste; r COP$86,000-105,000; 🐱) You'll receive a warm welcome at this excellent-value little hotel run by an affable ex-NYC cop and his *caleña* wife. Rooms are spacious, spotless and well equipped and there's a fine terrace with sweeping views. Set on a hill in a quiet part of town, it's still within walking distance of San Antonio and Parque del Perro.

✕ Eating

The best cheap eats in town are in and around **La Galeria de Alameda** (cnr Calle 8 & Carrera 26; meals from COP$7000; ⏱ 7am-3pm), a colorful local market with plenty of small lunch counters serving seafood and *comidas típicas* (typical food). Cali's largely Colombian dining scene has recently acquired several creative international restaurants that have raised the culinary stakes considerably.

Zea Maiz COLOMBIAN $

(Arepas Cuadradas; ☑ 311-846-2774; Carrera 12 No 1-21 Oeste; arepas COP$2000-9000; ⏱ 5:30-10:30pm Tue-Sun; 🐞) Is it just us, or do *arepas* (corn cakes) taste better when they come in a square shape? This colorful basement restaurant in San Antonio stuffs them with all kinds of goodness and serves them with four homemade sauces, the *mango picante* being particularly satisfying. Ardent anti-*arepa* crusaders have been known to change their tune after eating here.

Zahavi BAKERY $

(☑ 2-893-8797; www.zahavigourmet.com; Carrera 10 No 3-81; breakfast COP$7400-13,000, sandwiches COP$10,500-23,000; ⏱ 8am-7:30pm Mon-Sat, to 6pm Sun; 🐞) This posh bakery in San Antonio serves good coffee, rich gooey brownies and delicious gourmet sandwiches. It's also popular with ladies (and gentlemen) that brunch.

★ Waunana COLOMBIAN $$

(☑ 2-345-0794; www.waunana.com; Calle 4 No 9-23; mains COP$25,000-37,000; ⏱ noon-10pm Mon-Thu, to 11pm Fri, 5-10pm Sat; 🐞) We could say that the chef's creativity puts the 'wau' in 'Waunana,' but better yet, we'll mention the brave and often spectacular pairings of local ingredients (the seabass ceviche with tropical fruit stands out), flawless presentation, excellent cocktails and the original spin on Colombian cuisine. Opt for the four-course tasting menu (that can accommodate vegetarians) and prepare to be surprised.

Pargo Rojo SEAFOOD $$

(☑ 2-893-6949; www.facebook.com/elpargorojo cali; Carrera 9 No 2-09; set meal COP$13,000, mains from COP$20,000; ⏱ noon-3:30pm Mon-Sat, plus 5-10pm Fri & Sat) Excellent typical seafood dishes, such as a lightly grilled tilapia with crisp *patacones* (fried plantains) and a dollop of punchy, spicy salsa, are prepared at this simple corner restaurant with just six tables. Set lunches come with a tasty fish soup and a big jug of lemonade.

El Buen Alimento VEGETARIAN $$

(☑ 2-375-5738; www.facebook.com/elbuenalimento vegetariano; Calle 2 No 4-53; set meal COP$12,000, mains COP$15,000-25,000; ⏱ 8am-5pm Sun & Mon, to 10pm Tue-Sat; 🐞) A busy vegetarian restaurant serving hearty meat-free versions of Colombian classics, as well as ambitious fusion dishes such as Mexican lasagna, which is interesting rather than lovely. While the falafel wraps and the like are prepared with more enthusiasm than culinary skill, the fresh juices are great and come in glasses the size of soup tureens. It's all good value.

★ Platillos Voladores FUSION $$$

(☑ 2-668-7750; www.platillosvoladores.com.co; Av 3N No 7-19; mains COP$30,000-55,000; ⏱ noon-3pm & 7-11pm Mon-Fri, 1-4pm Sat; 🐞) Cali's best fine-dining experience, Platillos Voladores offers an interesting and varied menu of beautifully presented gourmet dishes that feature a glorious interplay of Asian, European and Afro-Colombian influences and largely local ingredients. Mains run the gamut from *ceviche mixto* to tofu in green curry and Mexican *sopa de tortilla*.

Drinking & Nightlife

Many *caleños* don't really go out drinking, they go out to dance. For a low-key night out head to Parque del Perro, home to numerous small bars. Just north of Cali is Menga, with many large discos. Further afield, several large *salsatecas* (salsa dance clubs) cluster in legendary Juanchito, although the area no longer attracts crowds like it once did.

★Zaperoco
CLUB

(☑315-520-1370; www.facebook.com/zaperocobar; Av 5N No 16-46; cover charge COP$20,000; ⊘8pm-4am Thu-Sat) If you only visit one salsa bar in Cali, make sure it's Zaperoco. Here the veteran DJ spins *salsa con golpe* (salsa with punch) from old vinyl while industrial fans try in vain to keep the place cool. Somewhere under the mass of moving limbs there is a dance floor – but we've never worked out exactly where it is.

El Rincón de Heberth
BAR

(☑310-409-7229; www.facebook.com/elrincon.de heberth; Carrera 24 No 5-32; ⊘8pm-4am Thu-Sat) In a shopfront in a strip mall, this local institution of a salsa bar attracts a lively *caleño* crowd who come for the great music and laid-back vibe. Most people sit outside and drink in the fenced-in sidewalk area where it's fresher, until a particular song inspires them to take to the steamy dance floor. There's usually no cover.

Topa Tolondra
BAR

(☑323-597-2646; www.facebook.com/Latopa bar; Calle 5 No 13-27; cover charge COP$10,000; ⊘7pm-1am Mon-Wed, 8pm-4am Thu-Sat) Popular with locals and travelers alike, this large salsa bar near Loma de la Cruz is always buzzing. The tables are pushed right up against the walls, leaving plenty of floor space to get your groove on. There's frequent live music.

La Colina
BAR

(Calle 2 Oeste No 4-83; ⊘6pm-midnight) This is a friendly neighborhood shop-bar hybrid in San Antonio that's been around for over 70 years. Cheap beer accompanies classic salsa and bolero and it's a favorite *caleño* gathering spot before heading off elsewhere to dance till the wee hours.

Pérgola Clandestina
CLUB

(www.lapergola.co; Carrera 6 No 11-48; ⊘9pm-late Fri & Sat) Located on the top floor of a tower block in downtown, this open-air bar has DJs spinning quality crossover music, plus great cocktails made from high-quality ingredients, and even a swimming pool. It's popular with young and well-heeled *caleños*, but unfortunately there are often lines and the door staff can be less than welcoming. Dress nicely.

Tin Tin Deo
CLUB

(☑315-594-4712; www.facebook.com/tintindeo cali; Calle 5 No 38-71; cover charge COP$15,000; ⊘8pm-3am Thu-Sat) This large, iconic, unpretentious 2nd-floor *salsateca* features a large dance area overseen by posters of famous salsa singers. While it sometimes feels like an expat hangout (especially on Thursdays), it's an excellent place for novice dancers to get on the floor and learn to salsa, Cali-style. Saturday is *pachanguero* ('party till dawn') night.

☆ Entertainment

★Delirio
PERFORMING ARTS

(☑2-893-7610; www.delirio.com.co; Carrera 26 No 12-328; tickets COP$115,000-240,000; ⊘every other Friday) You'll need to plan well in advance to see Cali's legendary salsa circus but it's well worth the effort. Think street circus meets flashy dance club and you'll have some idea of what to expect from this explosive celebration of *caleña* culture that takes place twice monthly in a big top on the Cali–Yumbo highway. Admission is restricted to adults.

🛍 Shopping

Parque Artesanal Loma de la Cruz
MARKET

(Loma de la Cruz; ⊘10am-8pm) This is one of Colombia's better *artesanía* (local craft stall) markets. You'll find handmade goods from the Amazon, Pacific coast, southern Andes and even Los Llanos, but you have to know what you're looking for to pick them out among the tide of dream catchers and other mass-produced tat.

ℹ Information

DANGERS & ANNOYANCES
During the day, the city center is alive and buzzing with street vendors and crowds, but after dark and on Sundays it can get dodgy. Avoid the area east of Calle 5 and along the Río Cali at night. It's best to catch a taxi. Be aware of your surroundings and take extra care with your belongings.

COLOMBIA CALI

MEDICAL SERVICES

Centro Medico Imbanaco (☎2-682-1000, 2-382-1000; www.imbanaco.com; Carrera 38bis No 5B2-04; ⊘24hr) One of the top private hospitals in the country.

MONEY

Banco de Bogotá (Carrera 5 No 10-39) ATM.

TOURIST INFORMATION

Secretaría de Cultura y Turismo (☎2-885-6173; www.cali.gov.co/turista; cnr Calle 6 & Carrera 4; ⊘8am-noon & 2-5pm Mon-Fri, 10am-2pm Sat) City tourist information office.

❶ Getting There & Away

AIR

Aeropuerto Alfonso Bonilla Aragón (Aeropuerto Palmaseca; www.aerocali.com.co; Via Palmira) is 16km northeast of the city, off the road to Palmira. Minibuses between the airport and the bus terminal run every 10 minutes until about 8pm (COP$10,000, 45 minutes), or you can take a taxi (around COP$55,000). There are direct international flights from Cali to Miami, Panama City and Lima, plus numerous daily flights to Bogotá as well as some to Cartagena, Medellín, Pasto and other domestic destinations.

BUS

Terminal de Transporte (La Terminal; www.terminalcali.com; Calle 30N No 2AN-29), the main bus terminal, is 2km north of the center. It's a sweaty walk in Cali's heat – take a taxi (COP$8000) instead.

Buses run regularly to Bogotá (COP$49,000 to COP$81,000, 10 to 12 hours), Medellín (COP$42,000 to COP$64,000, eight to nine hours) and Pasto (COP$45,000 to COP$85,000, seven to nine hours).

There are frequent minibuses to Popayán (COP$15,000 to COP$28,000, two to three hours), as well as regular departures to Armenia (COP$20,000 to COP$36,000, three hours), Pereira (COP$24,000 to COP$32,000, 2½ to four hours) and Manizales (COP$40,000 to COP$47,000, four to six hours).

❶ Getting Around

Cali's air-conditioned bus network, the **MIO** (www.mio.com.co; per ride COP$1900; 🛜), will remind many of Bogotá's TransMilenio. The main route runs from north of the bus terminal along the river, through the center and down the entire length of Av Quinta (Av 5). Other routes spread out across the city. You need a MIO card (purchased at the main stations) to use the public-transit system and it's only useful if you're

staying around the Granada neighborhood and visiting central sights.

Taxis are plentiful and fairly cheap. The minimum fare is COP$5000 and there is a COP$1100 surcharge at night. It's best to use an app such as Uber, Easy Taxi or Tappsi for safety reasons.

Popayán

☎2 / POP 285,700 / ELEV 1760M

A small colonial city famous for its chalk-white facades (its nickname is La Ciudad Blanca, or 'the White City'), Popayán is second only to Cartagena as Colombia's most impressive colonial settlement. Perched beneath towering mountains in the Valle de Pubenza, it was the capital of southern Colombia for centuries, before Cali overtook it.

Founded in 1537 by Sebastián de Belalcázar, Popayán became an important stopping point on the road between Cartagena and Quito. Its mild climate attracted wealthy families from the sugar haciendas of the hot Valle de Cauca region. In the 17th century they began building mansions, schools, churches and monasteries. In March 1983, moments before the much-celebrated Maundy Thursday religious procession was set to depart, a violent earthquake shook the town, caving in the cathedral's roof and killing hundreds.

Popayán is now home to numerous universities, and the streets of its old center are filled with students in the daytime.

◉ Sights & Activities

On the last Friday of the month Popayán hosts the Noche de Museos (Night of Museums), when food and handicrafts stands line the streets, and the historic center is closed to traffic. Many of the city's museums stay open late and are free to visit.

★**Casa Museo Negret & MIAMP** MUSEUM (☎2-824-4546; www.facebook.com/casamuseo negret; Carrera 9 No 4-29; COP$3000; ⊘8am-noon & 2-6pm, 2-6pm only Tue & Thu) This 18th-century house is the home of world-renowned Colombian artist Edgar Negret, whose vast abstract iron sculptures dot plazas around the country. The Museo Iberoamericano de Arte Moderno de Popayán (MIAMP) section showcases notable works by Colombian and South American artists from the period 1940–1990.

★**Iglesia de San Francisco** CHURCH (cnr Carrera 9 & Calle 4; ⊘hours vary) Dating back to the late 18th century, Popayán's largest colonial church is also its most beautiful. Inside are a fine high altar and a collection of seven unique side altars. The 1983 earthquake cracked open the ossuary, revealing six unidentified mummies. Two are left; ask in the office to the right of the entrance to have a look at them.

Casa Museo Mosquera MUSEUM
(Calle 3 No 5-38; adult/child COP$2000/1000; ⏱9am-noon & 2-6pm Tue-Sun) This interesting museum is housed in an 18th-century mansion that was once home to General Tomás Cipriano de Mosquera, who was Colombia's president on four occasions between 1845 and 1867. The original French crystal chandelier in the dining room was transported from the Caribbean to Popayán by mule. Note the urn in the wall: it contains Mosquera's heart. A short tour in English is possible.

Popayán Tours ADVENTURE SPORTS
(☑2-831-7871; www.popayantours.com) A professional outfit, run by Scots Kim and Tony, offering a variety of adventurous tours in the countryside, including coffee-farm tours, a downhill mountain-bike run from the Coconuco thermal springs, guided outings to the Silvia market, night visits to the nearby hot springs (COP$60,000), ascents of the volcano in PNN Puracé (COP$130,000) and multiday trips to Tierradentro.

🖝 Tours

Get Up and Go Colombia WALKING
(☑301-701-6240; www.getupandgocolombia.org; Parque Caldas) A free walking tour through the historic center run by enthusiastic university students. It leaves from Parque Caldas in front of the tourist office at 10am and 4pm. Tips are appreciated. In the evenings they offer free salsa, merengue and bachata dancing lessons, as well as hikes on Sundays (10am) and mountain-biking tours (COP$60,000), the last by reservation only.

🛏 Sleeping

Popayán has a good range of hostels, guesthouses and hotels, many inside atmospheric colonial buildings. Most accommodations in Popayán are in the center of town within a few blocks of Parque Caldas.

★ Le Soleil Hostel HOSTEL $
(☑310-611-6037; www.facebook.com/lesoleil hostel; Calle 1 No 2-29; dm/r/tr COP$27,000/ 62,000/103,000; ☎) A block and a half from the Parque del Morro, this supercozy hostel gets a lot of things right: comfortable beds, spotless, tiled rooms, funky common areas, bilingual staff, occasional communal dinners and a good ratio of guests per bathroom. A decent breakfast spread costs COP$6000.

Hostal Casona Tulcán HOSTEL $
(☑304-337-5442; www.casonatulcan.com; Calle 1N No 2-25; dm/s/d/tr COP$40,000/50,000/70 ,000/90,000; ☎) Owner Santiago has put a lot of love and care into this hostel, and it shows. The rooms sparkle, the beds are comfy and covered with colorful comforters, and the free yoga and salsa lessons really make the guests feel like part of the family. It's a great place to meet companions if you're a solo traveler.

Hostel Trail HOSTEL $
(☑2-831-7871; www.hosteltrailpopayan.com; Carrera 11 No 4-16; dm COP$27,000, s/d COP$55,000/75,000, without bathroom COP$40,000/62,000; @☎) This popular budget choice is a friendly, modern place on the edge of the colonial center with everything weary travelers need. There's fast internet, express laundry, a fully equipped kitchen, staff with a wealth of local know-how and free coffee. There's no real common area, though.

Hotel Los Balcones HOTEL $$$
(☑2-824-2030; www.hotellosbalconespopayan. com; Carrera 7 No 2-75; s/d COP$130,000/207,000; ☎) Climb 200-year-old stone stairs to your spacious room in this regal 18th-century abode. The place has an almost-medieval feel, with antique furniture, stuffed eagles and a maze of corridors. In the lobby, MC Escher sketches hang next to a case of ancient pottery and plush leather sofas. The rooms on the top floor are quieter. Wi-fi struggles.

🍴 Eating

Look out for typical local snacks and drinks such as *empanadas de pipián* (fried potato pastries served with a spicy satay-style peanut sauce), *champus* (a maize beverage with *lulo* and pineapple) and *salpicón payanese* (an icy blackberry concoction). Popayán's dining scene is a mix of local and international restaurants.

★ Carmina MEDITERRANEAN $
(☑310-515-4934; Calle 3 No 8-58; mains COP$8000-20,000; ⏱noon-3pm & 6:45-10pm

Popayán

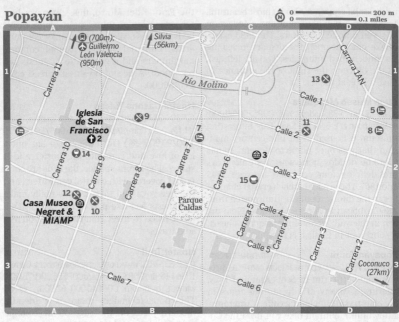

Popayán

◎ Top Sights

◎ Sights

◈ Activities, Courses & Tours

⊜ Sleeping

⊗ Eating

⊝ Drinking & Nightlife

Mon-Sat; 🖉) A cute little Catalan-run cafe in a less busy part of the historic center, serving a fantastic spread of mostly Mediterranean dishes. Expect Spanish omelettes, pasta, lasagna, crepes filled with Nutella and other tasty treats. The desserts, such as the tiramisu, are top-notch.

★ **Mora Castilla**   CAFE $
(🖉 2-838-1979; www.moracastilla.com; Calle 2 No 4-44; snacks COP$2400-4000; ◷10am-7pm) This upstairs cafe is always busy with chatting locals and prepares excellent fresh juices and traditional snacks, including *salpicón payanese, champus, tamales* and *carantantas* (a kind of toasted corn chip). If

you're still hungry, pop next door to sample some of Doña Chepa's famous *aplanchados* (flat pastries).

La Fresa   CAFE $
(Calle 5 No 8-89; snacks COP$400-3000; ◷7am-7pm) A grimy corner store with a few plastic tables, La Fresa is famed throughout Popayán for its delicious *empanadas de pipián* (potato empanadas with a spicy peanut sauce). Most locals wash them down with a *malta* (malt-based soda).

Tienda Regional del Macizo   COLOMBIAN $
(Carrera 4 No 0-42; meals COP$6000; ◷8am-4pm) This small cafe is part of an organiza-

tion that works to develop markets for farmers in the Macizo Colombiano. Needless to say the absurdly cheap lunches are made with the freshest ingredients. Buy your bags of coffee beans here, too.

Tequila's MEXICAN $$
(📞 2-822-2150; Calle 5 No 9-25; mains COP$15,000-25,000; ⊘ 3-10pm Mon-Sat; 🍴) Run by a Mexican expat and his local wife, this small restaurant in the center prepares good-value homestyle Mexican dishes. While some authentic ingredients are hard to find in small-town Colombia, their salsas pack real heat and their *enchiladas de mole poblano* are deeply satisfying.

🍷 Drinking & Nightlife

★ **Togoima Café Ancestral** COFFEE
(📞 310-257-1219; Carrera 5 No 3-34; ⊘ 8am-7:30pm Mon-Fri, 9am-7pm Sat, 10am-6pm Sun) One of the best cafes in town, preparing a wide variety of hot and cold beverages using high-quality beans from around the country. There are so many combinations you'll never have to try the same drink twice.

La Iguana Afro Video Bar BAR
(📞 316-281-0576; www.facebook.com/Lalguana AfroVideoBar; Calle 4 No 9-67, ⊘ 7pm-1am Mon-Wed, to 3am Thu-Sat) The place to go in the center to show off your salsa moves on the little dance floor. It sometimes has live bands, but can be hit or miss, depending on the night. 'Carousing not conversation' should be its motto.

ℹ Information

There are many ATMs around Parque Caldas.
Banco de Bogotá (Parque Caldas)
Banco de Occidente (Parque Caldas)

ℹ Getting There & Away

AIR
Aeropuerto Guillermo León Valencia (Panamericana) is 1km north of the city center. There are up to four flights daily to Bogotá with Avianca (www.avianca.com) and EasyFly (www.easyfly.com.co).

BUS
The **Terminal de Transporte Popayán** (www.terminalpopayan.com; Panamericana) is 1km north of the city center. There are frequent services to Cali (COP$23,000, three to four hours). Direct buses to Bogotá (COP$110,000,

12 to 14 hours) and Medellín (COP$98,000, 11 hours) depart in the evenings.

There are regular minibuses to San Agustín (COP$37,000, five hours); most companies require a change of vehicle but **Sotracauca** (📞 319-7170-503) offers a direct service four times daily.

Buses to Tierradentro (COP$26,000, five hours) leave at 5:30am, 8:30am, 10:30am, 1pm and 3pm. The 10:30am service takes you all the way to the Museo Arqueológico entrance.

Hourly buses connect to Pasto (COP$37,000, six hours) and Ipiales (COP$42,000, eight hours). It's best to travel during the day if possible, when you'll also be able to admire the amazing views.

San Agustín

🔢 8 / POP 9500 / ELEV 1695M
This small, attractive colonial town basks in refreshing, springlike weather year-round and is the gateway to one of the most important pre-Columbian archaeological sites on the continent.

Five thousand years ago, two indigenous cultures lived in the adjacent river valleys of the Magdalena and the Cauca. Divided by uncrossable peaks, the rivers were their highways, and here, near San Agustín, those two civilizations met to trade, to worship and to bury their dead.

The volcanic rocks thrown great distances by the now-extinct nearby volcanoes proved irresistible to the local sculptors, who transformed them into more than 500 fantastic statues, scattered over the surrounding green hills.

Little else is known about the peoples of San Agustín. They didn't have a written language and had disappeared many centuries before the Europeans arrived. But their legacy is a mystical place in a spectacular landscape that is well worth making a detour for.

👁 Sights & Activities

★ **Parque**
Arqueológico ARCHAEOLOGICAL SITE
(📞 1-444-0544; www.icanh.gov.co; Via San Agustín; adult/student COP$25,000/10,000; ⊘ 8am-4pm) This 78-hectare archaeological park is 2.5km west of the town of San Agustín. There are over 130 statues in the park in total, either found in situ or collected from other areas, including some of the best examples of San Agustín statuary, with human or animal features, or a mixture of the two. Don't miss the

San Agustín

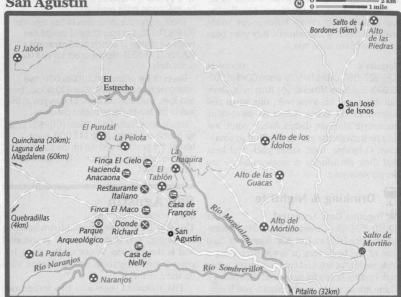

carved tombs either. Reputable guides congregate around the museum.

At the entrance to the park is the **Museo Arqueológico**, which features smaller statues, pottery, utensils, jewelry and other objects, along with interesting background information about the San Agustín culture.

Beyond the entrance, you'll stroll along the statue-lined **Bosque de las Estatuas** before ascending the four funeral hills – *mesitas* A, B, C1 and C2 with their respective tombs and clusters of statues. Many of them are anthropomorphic figures, some realistic, others resembling masked monsters. There are also sculptures depicting sacred animals such as the eagle, jaguar and frog. Archaeologists have also uncovered a great deal of pottery. Mesita B's statues are the best known.

Besides the *mesitas* is the **Fuente de Lavapatas**. Carved in the rocky bed of the stream, it is a complex labyrinth of ducts and small, terraced pools decorated with images of serpents, lizards and human figures. Archaeologists believe the baths were used for ritual ablutions and the worship of aquatic deities.

From here, the path winds uphill to the **Alto de Lavapatas**, the oldest archaeological site in San Agustín. You'll find a few tombs guarded by statues, and get a panoramic view over the surrounding countryside.

★ **Francisco 'Pacho' Muñoz**　HORSEBACK RIDING

(☎ 311-827-7972; Finca El Maco) A highly recommended horseback-riding guide who can take you around the archaeological sites and beyond. A day trip for one person costs around COP$70,000 and the horses are sweet-natured and suitable for beginners. You can usually find Pacho hanging around at Finca El Maco (p648); he's the resident guide there.

Magdalena Rafting　RAFTING

(☎ ph & WhatsApp 311-271-5333; www.magdalena rafting.com; Calle 5 No 15-237) The Río Magdalena offers challenging white-water rafting through some phenomenal landscapes. Magdalena Rafting offers 1½-hour tours (COP$65,000 per person) with Classes II to III rapids for novices, and full-day, Class V tours for experienced pros. Minimum four people per group. It also offers kayaking classes.

🛌 Sleeping

★ **Finca El Maco**　HOSTEL $$

(☎ 320-375-5982; www.elmaco.ch; Vereda El Tablón via Parque Arqueológico; dm COP$27,000, s/d/ste from COP$67,000/92,000/293,000; 🅿@🛜) This tranquil hostel has comfortable cabins set amid a pretty garden – all with piping-hot water and comfortable beds – while the dorm is inside a traditional *maloka* (earthen dwelling).

To reach the hostel, take the road to the Parque Arqueológico and turn right at the Hotel Yalconia. From here it's a 400m walk uphill (COP$7000 in a taxi).

★**Casa de François**   HOSTEL **$$**
(☑ 314-358-2930, 8-837-3847; www.lacasade francois.com; Via El Tablón; dm COP$30,000, r COP$80,000-85,000, cabaña COP$130,000-160,000; ☎) ✐ Set in a lovely garden just above town overlooking the hills, this creative, ecological hostel is constructed of natural materials, with wood, stone and glass bottles embedded in rammed-mud walls. The breezy, elevated dormitory has fantastic views and there's a spacious shared kitchen. Excellent private cabañas with wooden floors, large bathrooms and porches affording mountain views are spread around the property.

★**Hotel Monasterio**   BOUTIQUE HOTEL **$$$**
(☑ 311-277-5901; www.monasteriosanagustin.com; Vereda La Cuchilla; r/ste incl breakfast COP$290,000/485,000; ✿☎) This German-owned monastery-themed boutique hotel outside town is San Agustín's plushest option. Rooms are characterful, with heavy wooden beams and superb bathrooms, plus porches with hammocks and views of the coffee plantations. All have their own fireplaces – an attendant will come and light your fire in the evenings. The restaurant serves Colombian-Mediterranean fusion and the breakfast buffet is excellent.

✖ **Eating**

★**Humusapiens**   MIDDLE EASTERN **$$**
(☑ 317-733-6465; Carrera 13 No 3-06; mains from COP$15,000; ⊗noon-10pm Fri-Wed; ✐) On the main square, this little place tantalizes with the smells, sights and sounds of the Middle East. Thick, savory beetroot hummus. Cilantro hummus! The sizzle of shakshuka eggs on a skillet filled with a flavorful concoction of tomatoes and herbs. Warm, spicy falafel. It's all present and correct here – a boon for vegetarian and nonveggie foodies alike.

★**Donde Richard**   COLOMBIAN **$$**
(☑ 312-432-6399; Via Parque Arqueológico; mains COP$25,000; ⊗8am-6pm Wed-Mon) This grill restaurant on the road to the Parque Arqueológico serves some of the best food in town, with the beguiling scent of roasting meat and the savory crunch of *patacones* luring in diners on their way back from the park.

ℹ **Information**

Tourist office (☑ 320-486-3896; cnr Calle 3 & Carrera 12; ⊗8am-noon & 2-5pm Mon-Fri) There are numerous tour agencies masquerading as 'tourist offices,' but this office in the *Alcaldía* (town hall) is the real thing and can assist with organising activities in the area.

ℹ **Getting There & Away**

Bus-company offices are located on the corner of Calle 3 and Carrera 11 (known as Cuatro Vientos). There are regular minibuses to Popayán (COP$37,000, five hours) and Cali (COP$42,000, eight hours). For Popayán the best service is provided by **Sotracauca** (☑ 314-721-2243; www.sotracauca.com; Cuatro Vientos; COP$30,000). Do not travel on this route at night as security remains an issue in remote mountainous areas.

Coomotor (☑ 315-885-8563; www.coomotor.com.co; Cuatro Vientos) and **Taxis Verdes** (☑ 314-330-0518; www.taxisverdes.net; Cuatro Vientos) have several early-morning and evening buses to Bogotá (COP$65,000 to COP$87,000, nine to 9½ hours). Coomotor also offers a direct service to Medellín (COP$120,000, 17½ hours) at 3pm in a large, comfortable bus.

For Tierradentro, go to Pitalito and change for La Plata (COP$25,000, 2½ hours), where you can get a bus or *colectivo* to San Andrés (COP$13,000, two hours).

Arriving from Popayán, buses with few passengers will drop you at the crossroads 5km from town and pay your taxi fare to San Agustín. The taxi drivers often take you directly to a hotel they work with – be firm about where you want to go.

ℹ **Getting Around**

Around a dozen taxis service San Agustín. The rates are fixed but confirm what you'll pay before you get in.

A bus runs the 2km to the archaeological park every 15 minutes (COP$1500) from the corner of Calle 5 and Carrera 14.

Tierradentro

☑2 / ELEV 1750M

Tierradentro is the second-most-important archaeological site in Colombia (after San Agustín) but gets surprisingly few visitors. Located well off the beaten track down some rough dirt roads, it is a peaceful place with friendly locals and awe-inspiring archaeological wonders. While San Agustín is noted for its statuary, the Unesco World Heritage Site of Tierradentro is remarkable for its elaborate underground tombs, created by those who lived here from AD 500 to AD

COLOMBIA TIERRADENTRO

900. So far, archaeologists have discovered about 100 of these unusual funeral temples, the only examples of their kind in the Americas. There is a fabulous walk you can follow that takes in all the major tomb sites amid gorgeous mountain scenery.

☉ Sights

★ **Parque Arqueológico** ARCHAEOLOGICAL SITE
(Archaeological Park; ☎ 311-390-0324; www.icanh.gov.co; adult/student/child under 12yr COP$25,000/10,000/free; ⊙ 8am-4pm, closed 1st Tue of month for maintenance) Scattered across the hills around the little town of San Andrés de Pisimbalá, Tierradentro's Parque Arqueológico includes four tomb sites, an aboveground statuary and two museums. Tickets for the Parque Arqueológico are inside the museum complex, a 25-minute walk from the town. You're given a 'passport,' valid for two consecutive days, enabling entrance to all sites, accessible via a 14km walk. Visit the museums before the tombs, as there's not much in the way of explanation at the sites themselves.

Measuring from 2m to 7m in diameter, the tombs are scooped out of the soft volcanic rock that forms the region's undulating hillsides. They vary widely in depth; some are just below ground level, others are as deep as 9m, reachable via knee-killing stone steps. The domed ceilings of the largest tombs are supported by pillars. Many are painted with riotous red and black geometric motifs on white backgrounds, others with inquisitive human faces and animal forms.

Little is known about the people who built the tombs and the statues – the Páez (or Nasa) indigenous group that lives in the area today is not thought to be connected to the ruins. Most likely they were of different cultures, and the people who scooped out the tombs preceded those who carved the statues. Some researchers place the 'tomb' civilization somewhere between the 7th and 9th centuries AD, with the tombs reserved for the elite, and shallow pits holding the bodies of their servants, while the 'statue' culture appears to be related to the later phase of San Agustín development, estimated to have taken place some 500 years later.

🛏 Sleeping

There are six basic lodgings clustered within the 500m stretch uphill from the Parque Arqueológico, many run by endearing senior citizens. The budget options charge around COP$18,000 to COP$25,000 per person.

For more creature comforts and better dining, you may prefer to stay in San Andrés de Pisimbalá, a 25-minute walk uphill from the Parque Arqueológico entrance.

★ **La Portada** GUESTHOUSE **$$**
(☎ 310-405-8560, 311-601-7884; http://laportadahotel.com; San Andrés de Pisimbalá; s/d COP$70,000/90,000, without bathroom COP$45,000/70,000; ☎) Right by where the bus stops in town, this simple, elegant lodge features plenty of bamboo and has spacious, clean rooms with hot-water bathrooms downstairs and cheaper rooms with shared cold-water bathrooms upstairs. Its breezy restaurant (meals COP$6000 to COP$11,000) also serves the best food in town, and it's the only local hotel with wi-fi.

ⓘ Getting There & Away

Arriving at Tierradentro, most buses will drop you at El Crucero de San Andrés, from where it's a 25-minute walk uphill to the Tierradentro museums and another 25-minute walk to San Andrés. Very irregular *colectivos* (COP$1500) make the trip. Moto-taxis are hard to find but the trip costs COP$3500 if you get lucky.

A direct bus from Popayán (COP$26,000, four hours) to San Andrés de Pisimbalá departs at 10:30am and passes in front of the museums, making the return journey at 6am. There are return buses to Popayán (typically at 8am, 1pm and 4pm). Timetables are subject to change due to the poor road conditions.

From San Augustín you can take the 6am Bogotá bus, get off in Garzón (two hours), transfer to a La Plata bus (arriving there around 10:30am), then take the 10:30am bus to San Andrés de Pisimbalá (2½ hours).

If you prefer a guided visit with your own 4WD transport, Popayán Tours (p645) in Popayán can make arrangements.

Desierto de la Tatacoa

Halfway between Bogotá and San Agustín lies the Tatacoa Desert, a striking landscape of eroded red cliffs and gullies, sculpted by the infrequent rain.

Tatacoa isn't really a desert, although the thermometer says otherwise – it sometimes hits 50°C (122°F). It's technically semi-arid dry tropical forest, averaging 1070mm of rain annually. Surrounded by mountains, the peaks around Nevado de Huila (5750m) grab most of the incoming precipitation, leaving 330-sq-km Tatacoa arid. The result is an ecosystem unlike anywhere else in Colom-

SILVIA

A picturesque mountain town 53km northeast of Popayán, Silvia is the center of the Guambiano region. The Guambiano people don't live in Silvia itself, but in the small mountain villages of Pueblito, La Campana, Guambia and Caciques. The whole community numbers about 12,000.

The Guambiano are considered one of the most traditional indigenous groups in Colombia. They speak their own language, dress traditionally and still use long-established farming techniques. On Tuesday, market day, members of the Guambiano community come down from their surrounding villages to Silvia to sell fruit, vegetables and handicrafts. This is the best time to visit the town. It is not a tourist market – fruit and vegetables, raw meat, discount clothing and household items dominate – but you may find a poncho or woven backpack that takes your fancy. The main attraction is seeing the Guambiano themselves in traditional dress.

Almost all the Guambiano dress up; men in blue skirts with a pink fringe and bowler hats, women in handwoven garments and beaded necklaces, busily spinning wool. They travel in *chivas* (colorful traditional buses) and congregate around the main plaza. The Guambiano don't like cameras and may be offended if you take their picture; always ask before photographing someone and respect their wishes if they say no.

Buses (COP$6000, 1½ hours) and *colectivos* (COP$7000, one hour) depart Popayán roughly every hour, with extra early-morning services on Tuesday. From Cali, take a Popayán-bound bus as far as Piendamó (COP$15,000, two hours), from where you can pick up an onward bus to Silvia (COP$3000, 30 minutes).

---

bia – there are scorpions and weasels, fruit-bearing cacti, and at least 72 bird species.

To get to Tatacoa, you'll have to pass through **Neiva**, the capital of the Huíla department and a port on the Río Magdalena. From there take a *colectivo* one hour northwest to Villavieja. You can spend the night in Villavieja or in the desert.

Bring sturdy shoes (there are cactus spines on the ground) and a flashlight (torch).

⊙ Sights

Desierto de Tatacoa   DESERT
Technically not a desert but a landscape of red and gray rock, sculpted by ancient waterways, the Desierto de Tatacoa is one of Colombia's most unique ecosystems. It lies 4km east of Villavieja and can be explored on foot or by bicycle.

As you leave Villavieja you'll pass through **Bosque del Cardón**, a small cactus forest. Around 4km from Villavieja is El Cusco, where you'll find the **Observatorio Astronómico de la Tatacoa** (☑ 313-319-5106; www.facebook.com/oatastrotatacoa; El Cusco; viewings COP$10,000).

A lookout point across the road from the observatory has impressive views, and is a fine place to watch the sunset. Below the lookout are the **Laberintos del Cusco** (Cusco Labyrinths), in a striking mazelike landscape of undulating red-rock formations that seem totally out of place in tropical Colombia.

Ventanas (the Windows), 4km past the observatory, is a lookout point, named for its commanding views of the desert, with rock formations carved into the shapes of animals. Another 5km takes you to **Los Hoyos**, where there is a swimming pool fed by a natural spring deep in a barren, gray valley.

★ **Observatorio
Astronómico Astrosur**   OBSERVATORY
(☑ 310-465-6765; www.tatacoa-astronomia.com; Tigre de Marte, Tatacoa; viewings adult/child under 10yr COP$5000/3000; ◷ 7-9pm) Former Tatacoa Observatory resident astronomer Javier Rua Restrepo now runs his own observatory around 1km further away from town. He is a dynamic teacher who clearly loves his work and he has a number of high-quality telescopes for visitors to use. Talks at 6:30pm daily are in Spanish only.

❶ Getting There & Away

Moto-taxis in Villavieja charge COP$16,000 to take up to three people to the Observatorio Astronómico de la Tatacoa and nearby guesthouses. One place in Villavieja, **Tatacoa Bicitour** (☑ 300-287-6696, 316-748-2213; www.tatacoabicitour.com; Calle 7 No 2-59; ◷ rental per hour COP$10,000), rents bicycles, or you could walk the 4km, but take note that there's no shade, shelter or water on the way.

ⓘ ECUADOR BORDER CROSSING: IPIALES

Getting to the border Frequent shared taxis (COP$3000, 15 minutes) travel the 2.5km from Ipiales to Rumichaca from around 5am to 8pm, leaving from the bus terminal and the market area near the corner of Calle 14 and Carrera 8. A private taxi is COP$10,000.

At the border Passport formalities are processed at the border in Rumichaca, situated 3km southwest of Ipiales and 8km east of Tulcán in Ecuador. The border is always open and the procedure is relatively straightforward. However, due to the current humanitarian crisis in Venezuela, and Venezuelan refugees fleeing to Ecuador, it may take 15 minutes to leave Colombia but five hours or so to enter Ecuador.

Moving on After crossing the border on foot, take another *colectivo* to Tulcán (COP$2000, 6km). Colombian and Ecuadorean currency is accepted. From Tulcán's Terminal Terrestre, long-distance buses run to numerous Ecuadorian destinations.

Pasto

🚍 2 / POP 382,200 / ELEV 2527M

Just two hours from Ecuador, Pasto is a pleasant city nestling in a fertile valley, and the logical jumping-off point for the border. There are several fine colonial buildings and museums, and nature lovers might consider a longer stay, as Pasto is surrounded by some spectacular countryside and makes a good base for visiting Laguna de la Cocha, Laguna Verde and the restless Volcán Galeras.

The weather here is cool – so cool, in fact, you'll see *helado de paíla* being prepared fresh on the streets; it's traditional ice cream made in a copper tub sitting on a platform of ice.

🛏 Sleeping

★ Lucho Libre   HOSTEL $$
(📱 ph & WhatsApp 321-375-7079; www.lucho-libre.com; Calle 8 No 22-20; s/d/tr COP$35,000/79,000/119,000; 🛜) Ten minutes' walk to the center of Pasto, this hostel is a superb addition to the backpacker scene. Whether you're surveying the city from the lofty rooftop terrace, bedding down in a handmade *guadua* bunk bed, or sharing travel tales with other wanderers in the guest kitchen over free coffee, this place makes a terrific base for exploring the area.

★ Hotel Casa Lopez   HOTEL $$$
(📞 2-720-8172; hcasalopez@gmail.com; Calle 18 No 21B-07; r/tr/q from COP$214,000/249,000/284,000; 🛜) In a perfectly restored colonial home in the center, this family-run hotel is in a league of its own in terms of comfort, service and attention to detail. Set around a pretty, flower-festooned courtyard, the charming rooms have polished wooden floors and antique furnishings.

ⓘ Getting There & Away

AIR

Aeropuerto Antonio Nariño (Chachagüí, Panamericana), 33km north of the city on the road to Cali, has several daily flights to Bogotá and a single one to Cali. *Colectivos* (COP$11,000, 45 minutes) for the airport leave from Plaza de Nariño at the corner of Calle 18 and Carrera 25. A taxi will cost around COP$40,000.

BUS

The **bus terminal** (📞 2-730-8955; www.terminal depasto.com; Carrera 6) is 2km south of the city center. Frequent buses, minibuses and *colectivos* go to Ipiales (COP$9000, 1½ to two hours); sit on the left for better views. Pickups and *colectivos* also run to Mocoa via the spectacular and sometimes frightening Trampolín de la Muerte (COP$35,000, six hours); get an early morning ride. Plenty of buses ply the spectacular road to Cali (COP$32,000 to COP$40,000, nine hours). These buses will also drop you off in Popayán (COP$30,000, six hours). More than a dozen direct buses depart daily to Bogotá (COP$140,000, 20 hours).

LOS LLANOS

Caño Cristales

🚍 8 / POP 33,000 / ELEV 233M

Caño Cristales, a series of remote rivers, waterfalls and streams inside the wilderness of Parque Nacional Natural Sierra de La Macarena (p653), has been called everything from 'The River of Five Colors' to 'The Liquid Rainbow.' This is due to a unique biological phenomenon that takes place for a couple of months between July and November when an eruption of algae forms an underwater blanket of bright red. This transforms the crystal-clear water into a river of cabernet that contrasts magically with the lunarscape of ancient, hollowed-out riverbed rock and the surrounding savannah landscape.

Coming here involves some expense, a lot of sweaty hiking and some fairly unexciting meals in the town of **La Macarena**, but the payoff is immense. Until 2009, the entire region was closed off due to Fuerzas Armadas Revolucionarias de Colombia (FARC; Revolutionary Armed Forces of Colombia) activity. Yet, despite an influx of tourists in the 2010s, visiting this kaleidoscopic eco-park still feels like a rare privilege.

◉ Sights

Parque Nacional Natural
Sierra de La Macarena   NATIONAL PARK
(www.parquesnacionales.gov.co; foreigners/Colombians COP$92,000/60,000) The near-pristine PNN Sierra de La Macarena is one of Colombia's best-protected national parks and contains the fabulous rivers, streams and waterfalls collectively known as Caño Cristales. The main waterfalls and swimming holes are **Piscina del Turista**, **Piscina de Carol Cristal**, **Cascada del Aguila**, **Cascada de Piedra Negra** and **Caño la Virgen**. All access to the park is from the town of La Macarena, which sits just south of the park on the other side of the Río Guayabero. You will be guided throughout the park, and to keep tourism impact low, groups are divided up into different parts of Caño Cristales.

☞ Tours

You cannot visit Caño Cristales on your own – you are obligated to go into the national park with one of the official local guides, even if you do make it to La Macarena under your own steam. Most tours include air transportation to La Macarena, hotels, meals and guide services, and you'll normally be in a group of up to 12 people with a couple of local guides. You'll sleep in La Macarena and spend the days inside the national park.

★Cristales Aventura Tours   OUTDOORS
(☑300-693-9988, 313-294-9452; www.cano-cristales.com; Calle 5 No 7-35, La Macarena) Friendly English-speaking experts Cristales Aventura Tours are very used to dealing with foreign visitors and offer a flexible range of packages to suit all interests. You can make your own way to La Macarena where they will meet you, or it's possible to buy an all-inclusive package from Bogotá, Medellín, Calí or Villavicencio.

Cristales Macarena   OUTDOORS
(☑313-499-6038; www.viajescristalesmacarena.com; Carrera 7 No 8-50, La Macarena) Doris Mora runs her own travel company offering tours to Caño Cristales. As well as organizing the usual Caño Cristales itineraries and travel from elsewhere in Colombia, Doris can arrange camping and bird-watching in the national park.

Doris has an office in **Hotel La Fuente** (☑313-496-7701, 312-365-5107; www.hotellafuentejn.com; Carrera 7 No 8-50, La Macarena; per person COP$80,000; ❄️☎️).

🛏 Sleeping

There are numerous hotels in the town of La Macarena where all visitors to Caño Cristales stay overnight. These range from comfortable midrange options to fairly basic guesthouses, but as you'll be out in the national park all day, they're all absolutely fine and generally assigned to groups quite randomly. If you want a specific hotel, do be sure to request it.

Hotel Punto Verde   HOTEL $$
(☑310-341-8899; Carrera 9 No 4-12, La Macarena; per person COP$90,000; ❄️☎️🌊) This is the best hotel in town, but you'll need to travel with **Ecoturismo Sierra de La Macarena** (☑8-664-8400, 311-202-0044; www.ecoturismomacarena.com; Aeropuerto Vanguardia, Villavicencio; ⊙8am-6pm Mon-Fri, to 1pm Sat) to stay here, as it leases the entire property during the tourist season between June and November. There's a large pool, gorgeous tropical garden and good cafe to boot.

ⓘ NATIONAL-PARK RULES

Access to the Parque Nacional Natural (PNN) Sierra de La Macarena is closely controlled by the park authorities and there are several unusually strict rules that all visitors must follow. Most important of these is that sun cream and mosquito spray cannot be used on the body prior to entry into the park, as the introduction of chemical compounds to the water could pollute the otherwise-pristine waters and adversely affect the unique ecosystem that produces the rivers' extraordinary colors. Visitors are also banned from bringing in plastic bottles, from walking in sandals and from wearing shorts. There are checks by park rangers when you enter the park to ensure that these rules are not broken.

JUNGLE IMMERSION

With just six gorgeously designed cabins, the tiny jungle lodge **Calanoa Amazonas** (☎350-316-7210; www.calanoaamazonas.com; per person per night campsite/cabin US$135/165) truly is a slice of paradise, and one of the few in the Amazon Basin that allows visitors to relax in style. Two activities per day are included, ranging from long jungle hikes to night walks, canoe trips and visits to nearby indigenous communities that the lodge supports.

If you want an even more immersive jungle experience, then you can sleep in a hanging tent with a protective vine roof and shared bathing facilities open to the elements. The delicious meals are comprised largely of ingredients grown right in the lodge's own garden.

For non-Spanish-speakers, a translator costs an extra US$70 per group per day, while one-way/round-trip private speedboat transfer from Leticia costs US$150/300 for up to four guests, including the pickup from Leticia's airport; alternatively, take the public boat.

❶ Getting There & Away

Most package tours include transportation to **La Macarena Airport** by charter or scheduled flight from Bogotá, Medellín or Villavicencio, though it's perfectly possible to book your own transportation and arrange your tour to begin at the airport.

Easy Fly (☎Bogotá 1-414-8111; www.easyfly.com.co) offers direct flights from Bogotá three times a week (COP$300,000) in high season (July to November). Alternatively, get yourself to Villavicencio (an easy bus ride from Bogotá) and then take one of the daily flights to La Macarena from there (COP$250,000).

Ecoturismo Sierra de La Macarena (p653) arranges daily flights from Villavicencio (COP$520,000 to COP$550,000), including rather adventurous Saturday outings in an aged 16-person DC-3.

Barely anyone tries to reach La Macarena by an overland route. However, there are several 4x4s that make the journey from San José del Guaviare several times a week (COP$80,000, seven hours). Ask around in San José del Guaviare.

AMAZON BASIN

Amazon. The very word evokes images of pristine jungle, incredible wildlife and, of course, one world-famous river. The region known to Colombians as Amazonia is a vast 643,000-sq-km slice of rainforest accounting for a third of Colombia's total area – about the size of California – and spread over some eight of the country's departments. There are no roads here, just fast-flowing waterways and vast tracts of wilderness where, for now at least, humans have had relatively little impact on nature, and indigenous groups deep in the jungle have managed to keep their cultures intact.

Tourism is still relatively undeveloped here, and what little there is can be found in and around the towns of Leticia and Puerto Nariño. Yet precisely because of the lack of development, a visit here remains a transcendent experience, from thrilling rainforest treks to simple hammock siestas alongside the sounds of the jungle.

Leticia

☎8 / POP 29,700 / ELEV 95M

The capital city of the Amazonas province, Leticia is the largest settlement for hundreds of kilometers and yet still looks and feels very much like the small frontier town it is. Located on the Amazon River where Colombia, Brazil and Peru meet, Leticia is some 800km from the nearest Colombian highway. It's a bustling town abuzz with fleets of motorcycles, with a few minor sights to entertain you for a day or two.

Notwithstanding the oppressive heat, stultifying humidity and ferocious mosquitoes, Leticia is a pleasant enough town but not a destination in itself: it's a stepping stone for visiting the tropical rainforest that's right on your doorstep, with remote jungle lodges and indigenous communities just a short boat ride away along the Río Amazonas.

Leticia lies right on the Colombia–Brazil border. Just south across the frontier is Tabatinga, a Brazilian town of similar size.

❍ Sights & Activities

★ **Mundo Amazónico** GARDENS

(☎8-592-6087, 321-472-4346; www.mundoamazonico.com; Km7.7, Via Tarapacá; tours COP$10,000;

Leticia

⊙ 8am-3pm Mon-Sat) 🌿 This 29-hectare reserve works as a center for environmental education and makes for a great place to get to know something of the plants, trees and inhabitants of the jungle before you set out on an expedition. The extensive botanical gardens boast some 700 species of flora that can be visited on four differently themed tours (the botanical garden, sustainable processes, cultural presentations and the aquarium), each lasting between 30 and 45 minutes and leaving every hour until 2pm.

Museo Etnográfico Amazónico　MUSEUM
(📞 8-592-7783; Carrera 11 No 9-43; ⊙ 8:30am-6pm Mon-Fri, 9am-1pm Sat) **FREE** This little museum has a small but thorough collection of indigenous artifacts. Learn about *malocas* (ancestral longhouses) and *chagras* (indigenous production systems) and peruse the musical instruments, textiles, tools, pottery, weapons and many ceremonial masks. La-

beled in English, the exhibits make a good introduction to the indigenous cultures of the region, such as the Huitotos, Yukunas and Ticunas.

↩ Tours

The real jungle begins well off the Amazon proper, along its small tributaries. The deeper you go, the more chance you have to observe wildlife in relatively undamaged habitats and to visit indigenous settlements. This involves time and money, but can be immensely rewarding, and there are numerous tour agencies and guides waiting to take you out here.

Amazon Jungle Trips   TOURS
(📞321-426-7757; www.amazonjungletrips.com.co; Av Internacional No 6-25) With more than 25 years of experience catering to backpackers, Amazon Jungle is one of the oldest and most reliable tour companies in Leticia. Owner Antonio Cruz Pérez speaks fluent English and can arrange individually tailored tours, including trips to the two very different reserves the company runs: **Zacambú** (COP$290,000 per person per day all inclusive) and **Tupana Arü Ü**.

Selvaventura   TOURS
(📞8-592-3977, 311-287-1307; www.selvaventura. org; Carrera 9 No 6-85) Owner Felipe Ulloa speaks English, Spanish and Portuguese and can arrange a variety of trips into the jungle (including day trips on Río Amazonas) to both high-forest and *igapó* (flooded) ecosystems. He also sells tickets for various river trips into Peru and Brazil. The agency uses the Maloka jungle camp and the less remote Agape (at Km10).

🛏 Sleeping

★ Pirañita Hostel   HOSTEL $
(📞313-209-2671; Calle 8 No 6-42; dm/s/d COP$24,000/65,000/75,000; ❄️🛜) Sociable without being a crush-your-beer-can-against-your-forehead party hostel, the 'Little Piranha' features the eponymous fish motif throughout its spotless rooms and greenery-festooned common areas. Air-con is a boon in sweaty Leticia and the friendly bilingual owners are happy to organize group activities, from guest barbecues to jungle trips. Walls are on the thin side.

★ Hostel Casa de las Palmas   HOSTEL $
(📞321-435-2114; www.casadelaspalmasleticia.com; Carrera 11 No 13-110; dm/r COP$25,000/65,000; 🛜🏊) Designed with the comfort of backpackers in mind, this friendly hostel consists of a clutch of snug, spotless rooms, with a wonderful pool and garden area round back, fresh fruit and coffee for breakfast and plenty of helpful advice from the staff. Its jungle tours get glowing reports from the guests, too.

★ Amazon B&B   B&B $$$
(📞8-592-4981; www.amazonbb.com; Calle 12 No 9-30; s/d incl breakfast COP$165,000/228,000, cabaña d/tr/f COP$280,000/350,000/420,000; ❄️🛜) Leticia's most charming and stylish option, this hotel comprises six cabañas and four rooms surrounding a gorgeous tropical garden. The cabañas are spacious and come with high ceilings, well-stocked minibars and small, enclosed terraces with hammocks. Big discounts are available out of season, but note that only two rooms have air-con; the others are fan-cooled.

🍴 Eating

There are a number of good restaurants in Leticia, although they mostly open only in the evenings. Leticia's specialty is fish, including the delicious *gamitana* and *pirarucú*, which is best avoided out of season as some locals ignore bans on catching the species when spawning. Prices can be higher than in 'mainland' Colombia, but many restaurants serve cheap set meals.

Donut Company   CAFE $
(📞321-318-3444; Calle 8 No 7-35; donuts COP$2200-3500; ⊙1-9pm Mon-Sat) This wonderful little cafe serves good, reliable coffee, and if you thought it was impossible to get freshly baked donuts in the Colombian jungle, 'donut' underestimate their baking skills! Run by an American evangelist couple, the cafe donates its profits to supporting an orphanage in Benjamin Constant.

★ El Cielo   AMAZONIAN $$
(📞320-454-4569; Av Internacional No 6-11; mains COP$17,000-33,000; ⊙4-11pm Mon & Wed-Sat, 11am-5pm Sun; 🛜) The pinnacle of culinary sophistication in Leticia, this cool, creative space serves *casabes* (mini-pizzas made from yuca instead of flour) with imaginative toppings, including *pirarucú* (a popular local fish) and *tucupi* (a cassava extract). Despite the busy location on the main road, its pleasantly lit gravel garden is a lovely place for a meal.

★ El Santo Angel   INTERNATIONAL $$
(📞8-592-3866; www.facebook.com/elsantoangeld; Carrera 10 No 11-119; mains COP$15,000-37,000; ⊙4pm-midnight Tue-Sun; 🛜) With one of the most varied and interesting menus in town, Santo Angel is a popular place for an

evening meal. Diners spill out all over the street, and there's often live (but not ear-splitting) musical entertainment. On offer are wraps, nachos, salads, grills, pita bread, burgers and pizza, as well as German beers.

Information

DANGERS & ANNOYANCES

A long-standing military presence in the region has tried to keep Leticia/Tabatinga and the surrounding region safe, but there are issues. Former drug traffickers, guerrillas, paramilitaries and *raspachines* (coca-plant harvesters), reinserted into mainstream society and now living on the outskirts of Leticia and Puerto Nariño, run poker houses, brothels, dubious bars and the like. Don't wander outside these urban areas on your own at night, especially on Leticia's infamous 'Los Kilometros' road. In Peru, drug traffickers remain in business in this wayward corner of the country and have harassed tourists who've wandered off the beaten track. Tour operators and lodges in the region have been issued warnings about where they can and cannot bring tourists, so don't stray on your own beyond areas where local tourism guides normally operate.

MEDICAL SERVICES

San Rafael de Leticia Hospital (☑ 8-592-7826; www.esehospitalsanrafael-leticia-amazonas.gov.co; Carrera 10 No 13-78) Basic medical services; for anything serious, it's best to fly to Bogotá.

A yellow-fever vaccination is recommended 10 days before arrival; make sure to bring your yellow-fever certificate with you.

MONEY

There are ATMs in the town center, especially along Carrera 10 between Calles 7 and 10, and *casas de cambio* on Calle 8 between Carrera 11 and the market. Shop around; exchange rates vary.

TOURIST INFORMATION

Leticia's small **tourist office** (Secretaría de Turismo y Fronteras; ☑ 8-592-4162; Calle 8 No 9-75; ⊗ 8am-noon & 2-5pm Mon-Fri, 8am-1pm Sat) is helpful and friendly.

Fonturama (Fondo de Promoción y Desarrollo Turístico del Amazonas; ☑ 8-592-4162; www.fonturamazonas.org; Carrera 11 No 9-04; ⊗ 9am-noon & 2-7pm Mon-Sat) has info on sustainable tourism in the region.

ⓘ GETTING TO BRAZIL & PERU

Brazil

Slow boats depart from Tabatinga's Porto Fluvial for Manaus (Brazil) on Wednesday and Saturday at around 2pm. A hammock space (buy your own hammock in Leticia) costs R$400, while a stuffy, cramped cabin for two costs R$1620 for the three-day, four-night journey. Bag your hammock space early for the best spot: ventilation is important. Buy your ticket directly from the boat a day or two before departure. Basic meals are included in the price but the quality leaves much to be desired; bring your own bottled water and plenty of snacks. Don't want to go slow? Take an Ajato speedboat to Manaus (R$600, 36 hours) on Tuesday, Thursday, Saturday or Sunday morning. It's not as atmospheric, but has reasonably comfy airplane seats and TV entertainment.

Peru

High-speed passenger boats between Tabatinga and Iquitos (Peru) are operated by **Transtur** (☑ in Iquitos 51 6529-1324; www.transtursa.com; Jirón Raymondi 384) and **Transportes Golfinho** (☑ in Iquitos 51 65-225-118; www.transportegolfinho.com; Marechal Mallet 306, Tabatinga). Boats leave from Isla Santa Rosa daily at around 5am (Brazilian time!), arriving in Iquitos about 10 hours later. Don't forget to get your Colombian exit stamp at Leticia airport's office of Migración Colombia (p658) the day before departure. You can buy tickets through Selvaventura (p656) in Leticia, as neither company has an office in town.

The journey costs US$75 in either direction, including breakfast and lunch (mint-condition banknotes only; or COP$225,000).

Note there are no roads out of Iquitos into Peru. You have to fly or continue by river to Pucallpa (five to seven days), from where you can go overland to Lima.

If you need a Peruvian visa, there's a **Peruvian consulate** (☑ 8-592-7755; Calle 11 No 5-32; ⊗ 8am-noon & 2-4pm Mon-Fri) in Leticia.

❶ Getting There & Around

AIR

All foreigners must pay a COP$32,000 tourist tax upon arrival at Leticia's airport, **Aeropuerto Internacional Alfredo Vásquez Cobo** (Carrera 10), to the north of town. Taxis into town cost around COP$10,000; if traveling light, hop on a moto-taxi.

Avianca (www.avianca.com) and Latam (www.latam.com) have several daily flights to Bogotá.

Tabatinga International Airport has flights to Manaus daily with Azul (www.voeazul.com.br). The airport is 4km south of Tabatinga; *colectivos* (shared taxis, minivans, or midsize buses) marked 'Comara' from Leticia will drop you nearby. Don't forget to get your Colombian exit stamp at Leticia's airport and, if needed, a Brazilian visa before departure.

When departing Leticia's airport, all foreigners must check in at **Migración Colombia** (☑ 8-592-7189; www.migracioncolombia.gov.co; Aeropuerto Internacional Alfredo Vásquez Cobo; ⊙ 7am-6pm Mon-Fri, 7am-4pm & 7-10pm Sat & Sun) before proceeding through airport security, regardless of whether they're leaving Colombia or not; you'll be directed there after check-in if you haven't done it already – it's a painless and free procedure that takes a matter of seconds.

BOAT

Buy tickets for Puerto Nariño and other points upriver from one of the three agencies at **Transportes Fluviales** (☑ 311-486-9464, 311-532-0633; Malecon Plaza, Carrera 12 No 7-36). Boats to Puerto Nariño depart from Leticia's **Muelle Turístico** at 7am, 9am, noon and 2pm daily (COP$31,000, two hours). Arrive in good time for your boat, as the dock can be hard to find. You'll need your passport when buying tickets.

If you're departing from Tabatinga, be aware that it is one hour ahead of Leticia. Don't miss your boat!

Parque Nacional Natural Amacayacu

Sprawling across almost 3000 sq km, **Parque Nacional Natural Amacayacu** (☑ 8-520-8654; www.parquesnacionales.gov.co) is an ideal spot from which to observe the Amazonian rainforest up close, with extraordinary biodiversity and lots of wildlife. Catastrophic flooding in 2012 heavily damaged the park infrastructure and the park facilities remain closed, though it is still possible to enter the park and arrange tours with local indigenous people. Contact a tour operator in Leticia to arrange a visit.

Puerto Nariño

☑ 8 / POP 5500 / ELEV 110M

The Amazonian village of Puerto Nariño, 75km upriver from Leticia, is an inspiring example of human coexistence with nature. Here, cars are banned (the only two vehicles are an ambulance and a truck for collecting recyclables), rainwater is pooled in cisterns for washing and gardening, and electricity comes from the town's fuel-efficient generator, which runs only until midnight. Every morning, citizen brigades fan out to tidy up the town's landscaped sidewalks, and Puerto Nariño's ambitious recycling and organic-waste management programs would put most world cities to shame. As a contrast to dirty and polluted Leticia, it couldn't be more stark.

The majority of Puerto Nariño's residents are indigenous Ticuna, Cocoma and Yagua peoples. Their community experiment in ecological living has made ecotourism an important source of income, and this tranquil place is a great base from which to visit beautiful Lago Tarapoto and the Amazon in general.

◎ Sights & Activities

Communing with nature is the main activity here. You can rent a kayak for around COP$15,000 and go in search of river dolphins, and jungle guides can take you on day treks and night walks. Your accommodations can help organize any of these.

★ Lago Tarapoto   LAKE

Lago Tarapoto, 10km west of Puerto Nariño, is a beautiful jungle lake fed by the Río Amazonas, and is home to pink dolphins, a tiny population of manatees and massive water lilies. A half-day trip to the lake in a *peque-peque* (a low-slung wooden boat) from Puerto Nariño (around COP$50,000 for up to four people for around four hours) is the main draw for visitors, who usually take a dip in the gorgeously clear water. Piranha fishing is also possible here.

🛏 Sleeping & Eating

★ Alto de Aguila – Cabañas del Fraile   CABAÑAS $

(☑ 314-201-3154, 311-502-8592; altodelaguila@hotmail.com; dm COP$20,000, r per person with/

without bathroom COP$30,000/25,000) In the jungle outside the village, friar Hector José Rivera and his delightful monkeys run this hilltop oasis overlooking the Amazon. The complex includes several simple huts, shared facilities and a lookout tower. Between the monkeys, turkeys, dogs and macaws roaming about, there's a real menagerie to enjoy, along with utter isolation and free use of canoes on the Amazon.

★**Maloca Napü**   GUESTHOUSE $
(📞 314-437-6075, 315-607-4044; www.maloca napu.com; Calle 4 No 5-72; dm COP$20,000, r per person with/without balcony COP$30,000/25,000; @) Perhaps the most charming guesthouse in Puerto Nariño, Maloca Napü has the look and feel of a tree-house fort, surrounded as it is by a thickly forested garden. The rooms are simple but comfortable, with fans, shared bathroom with super-refreshing rain-style showers, and fully equipped kitchen. Everyone who works here is above-and-beyond friendly.

Las Margaritas   COLOMBIAN $$
(📞 311-276-2407; Calle 6 No 6-80; set-price meals COP$15,000; ⊙noon-3pm) Under a huge *palapa* (thatched roof) just beyond the soccer pitch, lunch-only Las Margaritas is the best restaurant in Puerto Nariño, even if it's rather pricey by local standards and aimed almost entirely at visiting tour groups. The all-you-can-gobble buffet-style meals are delicious, though, and involve fish, chicken, *patacones* (fried plantains) and salad.

❶ Information

There are no banks or ATMs in Puerto Nariño, and credit cards are not accepted anywhere, so bring plenty of cash from Leticia if you plan to do excursions into the jungle from here, as costs can add up quickly.

Tourist office (cnr Carrera 6 & Calle 5; ⊙8am-noon & 2-5pm Mon-Fri) Located inside the *Alcaldía* (town hall building).

❶ Getting There & Away

High-speed boats to Puerto Nariño depart from Leticia's dock at 7am, 9am, noon and 2pm daily (COP$30,000, two hours); return-trip boats to Leticia depart at 7am, 10am, 1:30pm and 3:30pm.

You can purchase tickets at **Transportes Fluviales** (📞8-592-6752; Muelle Turistico). In Leticia boats can get very full, so buy your tickets early or the day before.

UNDERSTAND COLOMBIA

Colombia Today

Colombia has largely overcome the instability and violence that has blighted it since the mid-20th century, and is now one of the most dynamic and fast-growing economies in Latin America. Having avoided the recessions that have hit many Latin American countries in recent years, and also due in part to the high price of its main natural resources (oil and coal), Colombia looks set to continue its economic growth at an impressive pace in the near future.

While it's undeniable that for many rural poor life has yet to improve, Colombia today is racing ahead to become one of the hottest, most exciting destinations on the continent, and tourism is playing an increasingly large role in that. Colombian confidence hasn't been as high in living memory.

The journey has been an arduous one, of course, and Colombia remains a nation beset by the demons of its past: memories of the Fuerzas Armadas Revolucionarias de Colombia (FARC; Revolutionary Armed Forces of Colombia) insurgency, paramilitary groups and violent drug cartels are never far from the minds of locals. But as the healing process begins and the Colombian government remains committed to ensuring long-term peace, there has never been such an occasion for optimism in the country's history.

History

Pre-Columbian Times

Colombia's original inhabitants have left behind three main prehistoric sites: San Agustín, Tierradentro and Ciudad Perdida, along with the continent's finest goldwork. They were highly skilled goldworkers and metalsmiths. Their efforts can be seen throughout Colombia in *museos del oro* (gold museums). Bogotá's is the best.

Scattered throughout the Andean region and along the Pacific and Caribbean coasts, the pre-Columbian cultures of Colombia developed independently. The most notable were the Calima, Muisca, Nariño, Quimbaya, San Agustín, Sinú, Tayrona, Tierradentro, Tolima and Tumaco.

The Conquistadores Arrive

In 1499 Alonso de Ojeda was the first conquistador to set foot on Colombian soil and to see its people using gold objects. Several short-lived colonial towns were founded, but it was not until 1525 that Rodrigo de Bastidas laid the first stones of Santa Marta, the earliest surviving town. In 1533 Pedro de Heredia founded Cartagena, which soon became the principal center of trade.

In 1536 a general advance toward the interior began independently from both the north and south. Jiménez de Quesada set off from Santa Marta and founded Santa Fe de Bogotá two years later. On the way he conquered the Muisca, a blow that would foretell the ultimate ruin of civilizations throughout the New World.

Meanwhile, Sebastián de Benalcázar deserted from Francisco Pizarro's army, which was conquering the Inca empire, and mounted an expedition from Ecuador. He overpowered the southern part of Colombia, founding Popayán and Cali along the way, before reaching Bogotá in 1539.

Independence Wars

As the 18th century closed, disillusionment with Spanish domination matured into open protests and rebellions. When Napoleon Bonaparte invaded Spain and placed his own brother on the throne in 1808, the colonies refused to recognize the new monarch. One by one Colombian towns declared their independence.

In 1812 Simón Bolívar, who was to become the hero of the independence struggle, arrived in Cartagena to attack the Spanish. In a brilliant campaign to seize Venezuela, he won six battles, but was unable to hold Caracas and had to withdraw to Cartagena. By then Napoleon had been defeated at Waterloo, and Spain set about reconquering its colonies. Colonial rule was reestablished in 1817.

Bolívar doggedly took up arms again. After assembling an army of horsemen from the Venezuelan Llanos, strengthened by a British legion, he marched over the Andes into Colombia. Independence was won at Boyacá on August 7, 1819.

Independence & Civil War

Two years after declaring independence, revolutionaries sat down in Villa del Rosario (near Cúcuta) to hash out a plan for their new country. It was there that the two opposing tendencies, centralist and federalist, came to the fore. Bolívar, who supported a centralized republic, succeeded in imposing his will. The Gran Colombia (which included modern-day Ecuador, Colombia, Venezuela and Panama) came into being and Bolívar was elected president.

From its inception, the state started to disintegrate. It soon became apparent that a central regime was incapable of governing such a vast and diverse territory. The Gran Colombia split into three separate countries in 1830.

The centralist and federalist political currents were both formalized in 1849 when two political parties were established: the Conservatives (with centralist tendencies) and the Liberals (with federalist leanings). Colombia became the scene of fierce rivalries between the two forces; chaos ensued. During the 19th century the country experienced no less than eight civil wars. Between 1863 and 1885 there were more than 50 antigovernment insurrections.

In 1899 a Liberal revolt turned into a full-blown civil war – the so-called War of a Thousand Days. That carnage resulted in a Conservative victory and left 100,000 dead. In 1903 the US took advantage of the country's internal strife and fomented a secessionist movement in Panama (at that time a Colombian province). By creating a new republic, the US was able to build a canal across the Central American isthmus.

La Violencia

After a period of relative peace, the struggle between Liberals and Conservatives broke out again in 1948 with La Violencia, the most destructive of Colombia's many civil wars, which left a death toll of some 300,000. Urban riots broke out on April 9, 1948 in Bogotá following the assassination of Jorge Eliécer Gaitán, a charismatic populist Liberal leader. Liberals soon took up arms throughout the country.

By 1953 some groups of Liberal supporters had begun to demonstrate a dangerous degree of independence. As it became evident that the partisan conflict was taking on revolutionary overtones, the leaders of both the Liberal and Conservative parties decided to support a military coup as the best means of retaining power and pacifying the countryside. The 1953 coup of General Gustavo Rojas Pinilla was the only military intervention the country experienced in the 20th century.

The dictatorship of General Rojas was not to last. In 1957 the leaders of the two parties signed a pact to share power. The party leaders, however, repressed all political activity that remained outside the scope of their parties, thus sowing the seeds for the appearance of guerrilla groups.

Birth of FARC & the Paramilitaries

During the late 1950s and early 1960s Colombia witnessed the founding of many guerrilla groups, each with its own ideology and its own political and military strategies. The most significant – and deadly – movements included FARC, Ejército de Liberación Nacional (ELN; National Liberation Army) and Movimiento 19 de Abril (M-19; April 19 Movement).

Until 1982 the guerrillas were treated as a problem of public order and persecuted by the army. President Belisario Betancur (r 1982–86) was the first to open direct negotiations with the guerrillas in a bid to reincorporate them into the nation's political life. Yet the talks ended in failure, and the M-19 guerrillas stormed the capital's Palacio de Justicia in November 1985, leaving more than 100 dead.

The Liberal government of President Virgilio Barco (r 1986–90), succeeded in getting M-19 to lay down its arms and incorporated it into the political process.

Another group emerging in the 1980s was the Autodefensas Unidas de Colombia (AUC; United Self-Defense Forces of Colombia). The AUC, paramilitary groups formed by rich Colombians looking to protect their lands, was responsible for dozens of massacres. This group supposedly disbanded in Uribe's second term (2006–2010), but many observers including Human Rights Watch say the disarmament was a sham.

All sides have committed and continue to commit atrocities, and the UN High Commissioner for Refugees says Colombia has more than 7 million internally displaced people, with the rural poor caught in the crossfire between the guerrillas, the neo-paramilitaries and the army.

White Gold

The cocaine mafia started in a small way in the early 1970s but, within a short time, the drug trade developed into a powerful industry with its own plantations, laboratories, transportation services and protection.

The boom years began in the early 1980s. The Medellín Cartel, led by Pablo Escobar, became the principal mafia and its bosses lived in freedom and luxury. They even founded their own political party and two newspapers, and in 1982 Escobar was elected to congress.

In 1983 the government launched a campaign against the drug trade, which gradually turned into an all-out war. The war became even bloodier in August 1989 when Luis Carlos Galán, the leading Liberal contender for the 1990 presidential election, was assassinated.

The election of the Liberal President César Gaviria (r 1990–94) brought a brief period of hope. Following lengthy negotiations, which included a constitutional amendment to ban extradition of Colombians, Escobar and the remaining cartel bosses surrendered and the narco-terrorism subsided. However, Escobar escaped from his palatial prison following the government's bumbling attempts to move him to a more secure site. An elite 1500-man special unit hunted Escobar for 499 days, until it tracked him down in Medellín and killed him in December 1993.

Despite this, the drug trade continued unaffected. The Cali Cartel, led by the Rodríguez Orejuela brothers, swiftly moved into the shattered Medellín Cartel's markets and became Colombia's largest trafficker. Although the cartel's top bosses were captured in 1995, the drug trade continued to flourish, with other regional drug cartels, paramilitaries and the guerrillas filling the gap left by the two original mafias.

In 1999 then-President Andrés Pastrana launched Plan Colombia with US backing. The plan called for the total eradication of the coca plant from Colombia by spraying fields with herbicide. While the program achieved some initial success on paper (in the early stages cultivated land was cut by around half), it has also generated dire environmental effects, as impoverished growers moved their crops into national parks, where the spraying is banned.

The job of eradicating cocaine from Colombia appears Sisyphean. Despite US aid of around US$8 billion, latest figures show that cocaine production has soared once again and Colombia is still the world's largest producer.

President Álvaro Uribe

Right-wing hard-liner Álvaro Uribe was elected president in 2002. He inherited a country on the brink of collapse, a pariah state plagued by security problems, with many highways in the country roadblocked and controlled by the rebels. Uribe promised decisive military action against the guerrillas – and he delivered. Suddenly, the country's roads were open, swamped with military, and safe.

Hugely popular, Uribe took a second term in 2006 after a constitutional amendment allowed him to run for power again. Uribe was viewed as a national hero but his presidency was ultimately tainted by scandal. By 2008, 60 congressmen had been arrested or questioned for alleged 'parapolitics' (links with paramilitaries).

The biggest scandal broke in October 2008, when journalists discovered that the army was killing civilians, dressing them in rebel uniforms and claiming them as combat kills in order to gain promotions or days off. It is estimated that during Uribe's presidency the Colombian army killed 3000 young, uneducated, so-called 'false positive' *campesinos* (peasant farmers), in a strategy described by Philip Alston, UN Special Rapporteur on extrajudicial, summary or arbitrary executions, as 'systemic.' When the scandal hit, Uribe launched a purge of the army, but prosecutions remain rare.

Yet more embarrassment for the Uribe regime came in early 2009, when the magazine *Semana* reported that the country's secret police, the Departamento Administrativo de Seguridad (DAS), had been tapping the phones of judges, opposition politicians, journalists and human-rights workers.

FARC: Negotiations & Peace

The last decade has been a disastrous period for FARC. The armed group has lost as many as half of its fighters and several key leaders through a combination of combat deaths and demobilizations.

In 2008 the rebels' chief bargaining pawn, French-Colombian presidential candidate Ingrid Betancourt, kidnapped six years earlier, was snatched in an audacious and legally questionable jungle raid by army forces.

But the biggest blow to the organization was delivered in November 2011 when army troops shot dead FARC leader and chief ideo-logist Alfonso Cano in rural Cauca. Within days of the death of Cano, new leader Rodrigo Londoño Echeverry, alias Timochenko, took control of the organization, announcing that FARC would continue to battle on all fronts, but behind the scenes the seriously weakened FARC entered preliminary talks with the government and within a year was sitting at the table in formal peace negotiations.

When Harvard-educated President Juan Manuel Santos began overseeing highly controversial negotiations with representatives of the FARC rebels in Havana in 2012, Colombian society was simultaneously floored and outraged. Santos, who had defined himself in the 2010 election campaign as passionately anti-FARC, was heavily criticized for the bold move, not least by his mentor and predecessor, Álvaro Uribe.

In 2016 a final agreement with FARC was rejected by the narrowest of margins in a referendum: 50.2% against versus 49.8% in favor. Santos returned to the negotiating table and made some 50 amendments to the agreement that would allow it to be passed directly by Congress. This was duly done so on 30 November 2016, when both the Congress and the Senate approved the bill unanimously.

Under the terms of the agreement, the FARC gave up their weapons, a process they completed in August 2017. In return – and the biggest issue most people had with the agreement – the FARC leaders entered politics and formed a political party under the same name.

Culture

Every traveler you meet who comes to Colombia with an open mind says the same thing: the people are genuinely friendly and helpful.

With a population of 49.5 million people, Colombia is the third-most-populous country in Latin America after Brazil and Mexico, and the figure is rising fast. Each city in Colombia has its own unique cultural mix, making traveling here as satisfyingly varied as a rich *sancocho* (soup). Many European immigrants populated Medellín, while much of the population of Cali is descended from former enslaved people. Bogotá and the surrounding areas saw much intermarriage between European colonists and indigenous people, while Cali and the Caribbean and Pacific coasts have a high proportion of African-Colombians. Colombia's indigenous population speaks about 65 languages and nearly 300 dialects belonging to several linguistic families.

The divide between rich and poor in Colombia remains large. The wealthiest 10% of the country controls some 45% of the country's wealth, while the poorest 10% control around 1%. The nation's rapidly growing economy has seen some reduction in poverty, but almost one in three Colombians still live below the poverty line.

Colombian families are tight-knit and supportive and, in common with most Latin Americans, children are adored. Most couples that live together are married, though this is beginning to change.

The majority of Colombians are Roman Catholic. However, over the past decade there has been a proliferation of various Protestant congregations, which have succeeded in converting millions of Colombians, especially in rural areas.

Arts

Literature

During the independence period and up to WWII, Colombia produced few internationally acclaimed writers other than José Asunción Silva (1865–96), perhaps the country's best poet, and considered the precursor of modernism in Latin America.

A postwar literary boom thrust many great Latin American authors into the international sphere, including Colombian Gabriel García Márquez (aka Gabo; 1927–2014). Gabo's novel *Cien años de soledad* (One Hundred Years of Solitude), published in 1967, immediately became a worldwide best seller. It mixed myths, dreams and reality, and amazed readers with a new form of expression that critics dubbed *realismo mágico* (magic realism). In 1982 García Márquez won the Nobel Prize in Literature.

There are several contemporaries who deserve recognition, including poet, novelist and painter Héctor Rojas Herazo, and Álvaro Mutis, a close friend of Gabo. Of the younger generation, seek out the works of Fernando Vallejo, a highly respected iconoclast who has claimed in interviews that García Márquez lacks originality and is a poor writer. Popular young expat Santiago Gamboa has written travel books and novels; Mario Mendoza writes gritty, modern urban fiction; and Laura Restrepo focuses on how violence affects the individual and society – they are prolific writers who have each produced major works in recent years.

Music

Colombians love music and it is ever present in any journey through the country. From first thing in the morning sound systems are turned up to full to play a variety of music as diverse as the country itself.

The Caribbean coast is the birthplace of vallenato, based (some might say excessively) on the European accordion. This is the most popular Colombian musical genre today and is played nonstop at earsplitting volume on long-distance buses. The region also vibrates with African-inspired rhythms including cumbia (Colombia's most famous musical export), *mapalé* and *champeta* (an Afro-electronic fusion).

The music of the Pacific coast, such as *currulao,* is even more influenced by African elements and features a strong drum pulse with melody supplied by the *marimba de chonta,* also known as the 'piano of the jungle.'

Salsa is adored by everyone here, and nowhere is it more popular than in Cali, which has adopted the genre as its own and produced more than its share of great *salseros.*

Colombian Andean music has been strongly influenced by Spanish rhythms and instruments, and differs notably from its Peruvian and Bolivian counterparts.

Visual Arts

The colonial period in Colombia was dominated by Spanish religious art. The most renowned colonial artist was Bogotá-born Gregorio Vásquez de Arce y Ceballos, who painted more than 500 works that are now distributed among churches and museums across the country.

Since the end of WWII, the most distinguished artists have been Pedro Nel Gómez (known for his murals, oils and sculptures), Luis Alberto Acuña (a painter and sculptor who used motifs from pre-Columbian art), Alejandro Obregón (a painter tending to abstract forms), Rodrigo Arenas Betancourt (Colombia's most famous monument creator) and Fernando Botero (the most internationally renowned Colombian artist). Spot a fat statue or portrait in Colombia and it's likely Botero's.

The recent period has been characterized by a proliferation of schools, trends and techniques. Artists to watch out for include Bernardo Salcedo (conceptual sculpture and photography), Miguel Ángel Rojas (painting and installations), Lorenzo Jaramillo (expressionist painting), María de la Paz Jaramillo (painting), María Fernanda Cardozo (installations), Catalina Mejía (abstract painting) and Doris Salcedo (sculpture and installations).

Sports

Soccer (*fútbol*) and cycling are Colombia's most popular spectator sports. Colombia regularly takes part in international events in these two fields, such as the World Cup and the Tour de France, and has recorded some successes. The national soccer league has matches most of the year. Baseball is limited to the Caribbean coast.

Tejo is a truly Colombian sport that involves throwing large metal discs at paper bags filled with gunpowder that let off a loud bang when you hit the target. It is usually accompanied by copious amounts of beer drinking.

Environment

Colombia covers 1,138,910 sq km, roughly equivalent to the combined area of California and Texas (or France, Spain and Portugal). It occupies the northwestern part of the continent and is the only South American country with coasts on both the Pacific (1448km long) and the Caribbean (1760km). Colombia is bordered by Panama, Venezuela, Brazil, Peru and Ecuador.

The physical geography of Colombia is extremely diverse. Most of the population live in the western part, which is mountainous with three Andean chains – the Cordillera Occidental, Cordillera Central and Cordillera Oriental – running roughly parallel north–south. More than half of the territory lies east of the Andes and is a vast lowland, which is divided into two regions: the savanna-like Los Llanos in the north and the rainforest-covered Amazon in the south.

There are more plant and animal species per unit area in Colombia than any other country in the world. This abundance reflects Colombia's numerous climatic zones and microclimates, which have created many different habitats and biological islands in which wildlife has evolved independently.

Colombia is home to the jaguar, ocelot, peccary, tapir, deer, armadillo, spectacled bear and numerous species of monkey, to mention just a few of the 350-odd mammal species. There are 1870 recorded bird species (nearly a quarter of the world's total), ranging from the huge Andean condor to the tiny hummingbird. Colombia's flora is equally impressive and includes some 3500 species of orchid alone. The national herbariums have classified more than 130,000 plants.

SURVIVAL GUIDE

❶ Directory A–Z

ACCESSIBLE TRAVEL

Colombia is taking strides toward improving accessibility but unfortunately, it remains a somewhat-challenging destination for travelers with disabilities. Forward-thinking Medellín is perhaps the easiest place for travelers with reduced mobility, followed by other major cities like Bogotá, Bucaramanga and Cali.

Sidewalks are often uneven and while more and more ramps are being added they are far from being universal. Motorists also are used to flying around corners without stopping for those crossing the road.

Many restaurants and hotels do not have ramps for visitors with impaired mobility. Large chain hotels are more likely to have accessible rooms – usually just a couple – and public areas. Larger shopping malls also usually have ramps and elevators.

Most major integrated public-transport systems, including the TransMilenio in Bogotá and the metro in Medellín, have accessible stations and vehicles but overcrowding can make travel difficult and unpleasant. The majority of Colombia's taxis are small hatchback vehicles that are not particularly easy to get in or out of and often have little space for wheelchairs or other bulky items.

ACCOMMODATIONS

Colombia's backpacker market is growing daily, and with it comes the huge growth in facilities familiar to the continent. Even smaller, less visited cities now have hostels with dormitories, internet, wi-fi, laundry services and travel advice. See www.colombianhostels.com for some of the most popular hostels in each city.

While dormitories are usually the cheapest option for budget travelers, private rooms in hostels in Colombia are often fancier and more expensive than local-oriented budget options. It's usually possible to find cheaper rooms, albeit with less facilities at your disposal, at local *hospedajes*, *residencias* and posadas.

A hotel generally suggests a place of a higher standard, and almost always has private bathroom, while *residencias*, *hospedajes* and posadas often have shared facilities.

Motels rent rooms by the hour. They're found on the outskirts of the city and usually have garish signs. Many Colombians live at home until marriage, so couples check in here for a few hours of passion and privacy.

Camping is gaining in popularity as the country's safety improves. Note that army-style kit is forbidden for private use.

ACTIVITIES

Any hikers planning to visit remote national parks, including PNN El Cocuy, need to register their itineraries with the local Parques Nacionales (www.parquesnacionales.gov.co) office beforehand.

ELECTRICITY

Colombia uses two-pronged US-type plugs that run at 110V, 60Hz.

EMBASSIES & CONSULATES

Most of the countries that maintain diplomatic relations with Colombia have their embassies and consulates in Bogotá. Some countries also have consulates in other Colombian cities.

In Barranquilla:

Panamanian Consulate (📞5-360-1870; Carrera 57 No 72-25, Edificio Fincar 207-208)

Venezuelan Consulate (📞5-368-2207; www.barranquilla.consulado.gob.ve; Carrera 52 No 69-96; ⏲8am-noon & 1:30-3:30pm Mon-Thu, 8am-noon Fri)

In Bogotá:

Australian Embassy (📞1-657 7800; www.colombia.embassy.gov.au; Av Carrera 9 No 115-06, edificio Tierra Firme, oficina 2002)

Brazilian Embassy (📞1-635-1694; http://bogota.itamaraty.gov.br; Calle 93 No 14-20, piso 8)

Canadian Embassy (📞1-657-9800; www.colombia.gc.ca; Carrera 7 No 114-33)

Ecuadorian Consulate (📞1-212-6512; www.colombia.embajada.gob.ec; Calle 89 No 13-07)

French Embassy (📞1-638-1400; www.ambafrance-co.org; Carrera 11 No 93-12)

German Embassy (📞1-423-2600; www.bogota.diplo.de; Calle 110 No 9-25, edificio Torre Empresarial Pacífic, piso 11)

Netherlands Embassy (📞1-638-4200; www.nederlandwereldwijd.nl; Carrera 13 No 93-40, piso 5)

ℹ️ ACCESSIBLE TRAVEL GUIDES

Download Lonely Planet's free Accessible Travel guides from http://lptravel.to/AccessibleTravel.

Panamanian Embassy (📞1-257-5067; www.embajadadepanama.com.co; Calle 92 No 7A-40)

Peruvian Embassy (📞1-746-2360; www.embajadadelperu.org.co; Calle 80A No 6-50)

UK Embassy (📞1-326-8300; www.ukincolombia.fco.gov.uk; Carrera 9 No 76-49, piso 8)

US Embassy (📞1-275-2000; https://co.usembassy.gov/es; Carrera 45 No 24B-27)

Venezuelan Embassy (📞1-644-5555; http://colombia.embajada.gob.ve; Carrera 11 No 87-51, edificio Horizonte, piso 5)

In Cali:

Panamanian Consulate (📞2-486-1116; Av 6 No 25-58, Piso 3)

In Cartagena:

Panamanian Consulate (📞5-655-1055; Carrera 1 No 10-10)

Venezuelan Consulate (📞5-665-0382; Edificio Centro Executivo, Carrera 3 No 8-129, piso 14)

In Medellín:

Panamanian Consulate (📞4-312-4590; Calle 10 No 42-45, Oficina 266; ⏲9:30-11:30am Mon-Fri)

Venezuelan Consulate (📞4-444-0359; www.consulvenemedellin.org; Calle 32B No 69-59; ⏲8-11:30am Mon-Fri)

FOOD

While you probably didn't come to Colombia for the food, it's fairly easy to eat well, especially if you seek out some of the varied regional specialties.

Variety does not, unfortunately, apply to the *comida corriente* (basic set meal). It is a two-course meal with *sopa* (soup) and *bandeja* (main plate). A *seco* (literally 'dry') is just the

---

SLEEPING PRICE RANGES

The following price ranges refer to a standard double room before discounts or taxes.

$ less than COP$75,000

$$ COP$75,000–COP$175,000

$$$ more than COP$175,000

EATING PRICE RANGES

The following price ranges refer to the cost of main dishes for lunch and dinner.

$ less than COP$15,000

$$ COP$15,000–30,000

$$$ more than COP$30,000

main course without soup. At lunchtime (from noon to 2pm) it is called *almuerzo*; at dinnertime (after 6pm) it becomes *comida*, but it is identical to lunch. The *almuerzos* and *comidas* are the cheapest way to fill yourself up, usually costing between COP$7000 and COP$10,000. Breakfasts are dull and repetitive, normally *arepa* (grilled cornmeal patty) and eggs.

Typical food along the Caribbean coast tends to involve fish, plantains and rice with coconut, while in the interior, meat, potatoes and beans are the norm.

Colombian food generally doesn't involve too many vegetables. However, many towns have dedicated vegetarian restaurants, and local markets are full of great fresh produce, including amazing fruits, some of which you won't find anywhere else. Try *guanábana* (soursop), *lulo, curuba, zapote, mamoncillo* (Spanish lime), *uchuva, granadilla, maracuyá* (passion fruit), *tomate de árbol, borojó* (tamarillo), *mamey* and *tamarindo* (tamarind).

Coffee is the number-one drink – though the quality in most establishments will not impress aficionados. *Tinto,* a small cup of (weak) black coffee, is served everywhere. Other coffee drinks are *perico* or *pintado,* a small milk coffee, and *café con leche,* which is larger and uses more milk.

Beer is popular, cheap and generally not bad. Colombian wine is vile. In rural areas, try homemade *chicha* and *guarapo* (alcoholic fermented maize or sugarcane drinks).

HEALTH

Colombia has some of the best medical facilities in South America, but they are not cheap. Many private clinics will not begin treatment (other than emergency stabilization) until your insurance has cleared or a deposit is made. Keep your travel-insurance details handy. Public hospitals are generally overcrowded and should be considered only as a last resort.

Tap water in the large cities is safe to drink, but in rural areas water should be boiled or disinfected with tablets.

Yellow-fever vaccinations are required for those visiting several national parks and may be required by your next destination after a visit to Colombia.

INTERNET ACCESS

➜ Colombia is a wired country. Internet is everywhere and while internet cafes have died out in large cities, some of the remoter places still retain one or two.

➜ In smaller towns and more remote destinations, the government's ambitious and heralded Plan Vive Digital has brought free wi-fi to almost everywhere. You can usually stop by the local library, park or cultural center to get online.

➜ Almost all hostels and hotels offer free wi-fi. Shopping centers often have free wi-fi and so do most restaurants and cafes. Major airports offer wi-fi although it's usually very poor.

LANGUAGE COURSES

Colombia can be a good place to study Spanish. The Spanish spoken in Colombia is clear and easy to understand and there are language schools in the big cities.

The most intense option is to enroll in a specialist language course at one of Colombia's major universities. They are able to organize long-term visas. Private language centers are often more costly but require less of a commitment.

LEGAL MATTERS

If arrested you have the right to an attorney. If you don't have one, one will be appointed to you (and paid for by the government). There is a presumption of innocence and you can expect a speedy trial.

The most common legal situation that travelers find themselves in involves drugs. In 2012 Colombia's Constitutional Court decriminalized the possession of small amounts of cocaine (1g or less) and marijuana (20g or less) for personal use, and in 2016 it removed the cap on the legal amount of drugs for personal use, but that doesn't mean it's a good idea. Although you cannot be criminally prosecuted, police may still give you a hard time and you may be ordered to receive physical or psychological treatment depending on your level of intoxication.

LGBT TRAVELERS

➜ Compared to some Latin American countries, homosexuality is well tolerated in Colombia (it was declared legal by the government in 1981).

➜ There is a substantial gay undercurrent in the major cities and as long as you don't broadcast the fact in public you are unlikely to be harassed.

➜ With popular apps like Grindr for men, most contact is initiated online these days.

➜ In 2011 Colombia's Constitutional Court ordered Congress to pass legislation addressing same-sex marriage by June 2013; if they did not, the ruling dictated same-sex couples would automatically receive all marital rights from that date forward. Congress failed to act and

Colombia's first gay wedding was performed on July 24, 2013. Full legal rights were confirmed in 2016 when the country's Constitutional Court ruled that the constitution required the state to process and recognize same-sex marriages.

➡ For LBGT-specific listings see the website www.guiagaycolombia.com.

MAPS

The widest selection of maps of Colombia is produced and sold by the **Instituto Geográfico Agustín Codazzi** (IGAC; ☎1-369-4000; www.igac.gov.co; Carrera 30 No 48-51), the government mapping body, which has its head office in Bogotá and branch offices in departmental capitals.

MONEY

➡ The Colombian peso (COP$) is the unit of currency in Colombia.

➡ There are paper notes of COP$1000, COP$2000, COP$5000, COP$10,000, COP$20,000, COP$50,000 and COP$100,000. The coins you will use are primarily the COP$100, COP$200, COP$500 and COP$1000; the COP$50 is rarely seen outside of supermarkets, and some people may refuse to accept it.

➡ Counterfeit pesos are a major problem in Colombia and you'll notice cashiers everywhere vigorously checking notes before completing transactions. While it is difficult for visitors to identify dud bills, if you are given one that is old, battered or just doesn't seem right, hand it back and ask for another.

ATMs

Almost all major banks have ATMs, and they usually work fine with cards issued outside Colombia (Bancolombia being the ornery exception for some folks). Cash machines affiliated with Banco de Bogotá/ATH and BBVA are good bets.

Credit Cards

Credit cards are common in Colombia and used extensively in the major cities and larger towns.

Money Changers

➡ You are better off using your ATM card in Colombia, as you will get a much better exchange rate.

➡ The US dollar is the only foreign currency worth trying to change in Colombia; expect dismal rates for euros, pounds sterling, Australian dollars etc.

➡ Many but not all banks change money; in major cities and in border regions there are usually several casas de cambio (currency exchanges).

OPENING HOURS

Banks 9am to 4pm Monday to Friday, 9am to noon Saturday

Bars 6pm to around 3am

Cafes 8am to 10pm

Nightclubs 9pm until very late Thursday to Saturday

Restaurants Breakfast from 8am, lunch from noon, dinner until 9pm or 10pm

Shops 9am to 5pm Monday to Friday, 9am to noon or 5pm Saturday; some shops close for lunch

POST

Colombia's official postal service is the terribly named **4-72** (www.4-72.com.co), which has turned the debilitating pension liabilities and inefficiency of Colombia's former government postal service, Adpostal (shut down in 2006), into a profitable and efficient business.

PUBLIC HOLIDAYS

The following days are observed as public holidays in Colombia.

Año Nuevo (New Year's Day) January 1

Los Reyes Magos (Epiphany) January 6*

San José (St Joseph) March 19*

Jueves Santo & Viernes Santo (Maundy Thursday and Good Friday) March/April (Easter). The following Monday is also a holiday.

Día del Trabajo (Labor Day) May 1

La Ascensión del Señor (Ascension) May*

Corpus Cristi (Corpus Christi) May/June*

Sagrado Corazón de Jesús (Sacred Heart) June*

San Pedro y San Pablo (St Peter and St Paul) June 29*

Día de la Independencia (Independence Day) July 20

Batalla de Boyacá (Battle of Boyacá) August 7

La Asunción de Nuestra Señora (Assumption) August 15*

Día de la Raza (Discovery of America) October 12*

Todos los Santos (All Saints' Day) November 1*

Independencia de Cartagena (Independence of Cartagena) November 11*

Inmaculada Concepción (Immaculate Conception) December 8

Navidad (Christmas Day) December 25

When the dates marked with an asterisk do not fall on a Monday, the holiday is moved to the following Monday to make a three-day long weekend, referred to as the puente (bridge).

RESPONSIBLE TRAVEL

When visiting national parks, hire guides from the closest local community; not only are you creating jobs, you'll learn a whole lot more about the area than with a tour from the city.

Respect indigenous culture and beliefs – ask permission before taking pictures and only enter

ETIQUETTE

Colombians rarely talk politics with anyone but friends and you should follow their lead. The country is polarized by the conflict and many Colombians have first-hand experience of the violence. You never really know who you are talking to, or who is listening to your conversation, and it can be quite easy to offend someone if you start ranting about the government or guerrillas.

communities if you have been explicitly invited. Support local artisans by purchasing crafts direct at the source, but avoid those made from coral, turtles or fossils.

SAFE TRAVEL

Keep your wits about you, avoid dodgy parts of town and be extravigilant after dark, and Colombia should offer you nothing but good times.

➡ Avoid wandering off the grid, especially without checking the security situation on the ground.

➡ Be cautious when using ATMs after dark; avoid doing so entirely on deserted streets.

➡ Carry a quickly accessible, rolled bundle of small notes in case of robbery.

➡ Avoid drug tourism.

➡ Be very wary of drinks or cigarettes offered by strangers or new 'friends.'

➡ Beware of criminals masquerading as plainclothes police.

➡ The border towns of Cúcuta and Maicao are best avoided at present due to the ongoing crisis in Venezuela.

Drugs

Cocaine and marijuana are cheap and widely available in Colombia's major cities. Purchasing and consuming drugs, however, is not a good idea. Many Colombians find Colombian drug tourism very offensive, especially in smaller towns. It's important to note the majority of Colombians don't consume drugs and many believe the foreign drug trade is responsible for Colombia's decades of violent conflict. So, asking after drugs, or openly using drugs, could land you in a lot of trouble (note: it's illegal to buy or sell drugs in any quantity).

A recent rise in travelers coming to Colombia to use ayahuasca (or yagé as it's often known in Colombia) is another worrying trend. The hallucinogenic drug, derived from various rainforest plants and used by Colombia's indigenous peoples in ceremonies for centuries, causes purging and vomiting alongside incredibly strong hallucinations. In 2014 a 19-year-old British backpacker died near Putumayo while trying the drug, and we strongly recommend that you avoid it.

Sometimes you may be offered drugs on the street, in a bar or at a disco, but never accept these offers. The vendors may well be setting you up for the police, or their accomplices will follow you and stop you later, show you false police documents and threaten you with jail unless you pay them off.

There have been reports of drugs being planted on travelers, so keep your eyes open. Always refuse if a stranger at an airport asks you to take their luggage on board as part of your luggage allowance.

Guerrilla & Paramilitary Activity

Despite the peace deal between the government and the Fuerzas Armadas Revolucionarias de Colombia (Revolutionary Armed Forces of Colombia; FARC), there remain isolated pockets of guerrilla activity in remote parts of Colombia, with dissident FARC soldiers operating in some areas and the Ejército de Liberación Nacional (National Liberation Army; ELN) – who are locked in peace negotiations with the government – yet to disarm.

Of perhaps more concern are neo-paramilitary groups engaged in drug trafficking who have extended their operations around the country following the withdrawal of the FARC, and whose areas of influence are more difficult to identify.

Going off the beaten track should be done with great caution, if at all. While most armed groups no longer specifically target tourists, most are very suspicious of unannounced visitors in their territory – and cases of mistaken identity have led to kidnapping and deaths.

Large swaths of Colombia are not currently covered by Lonely Planet, as the security situation remains dubious and tourist infrastructure simply does not exist: this is the case for much of the west of the country, remote areas bordering Venezuela and chunks of the Amazon region (though the area of the Amazon we cover is extremely safe).

TELEPHONE

The telephone system in Colombia is modern and works well for both domestic and international calls. Cell (mobile) phone coverage is extensive and inexpensive.

Cell Phones

Colombians love their cell phones, and in urban areas almost everyone has at least one. The three major providers are Claro (www.claro.com.co), Movistar (www.movistar.co) and Tigo (www.tigo.com.co). Claro has the best nationwide coverage, though all networks now have competitive data and call packages. Of the smaller providers, ETB is regarded as having the best internet speed. Cell phones are cheap, and many travelers end up purchasing one – a basic, no-frills handset will set you back around COP$130,000.

Alternatively you could bring your own cell phone from home and buy a Colombian SIM card, which usually costs between COP$2000 and COP$5000. You will need to take ID to buy a SIM from one of the phone companies; you can also buy them from third parties but eventually you'll need to register with the company or risk having your handset blocked.

Colombian cell-phone companies do not charge you to receive calls, only to make them.

Phone Codes

Many Colombian landlines are barred from making calls to cell phones.

Landline from cell (mobile) phone	03 + area code + 7-digit number
Colombian landline from abroad	57 + area code + 7-digit number
Colombian cell phone from abroad	57 + 10-digit number

TOURIST INFORMATION

➡ Almost all towns and cities that are frequented by tourists have a Punto Información Turística (PIT) – an information kiosk or office identifiable by the red 'i' logo. They're often located near the central plaza as well as at transport terminals.

➡ Colombia has a number of good regional and national websites offering information (sometimes in English) about what to do and where to stay.

➡ The country's principal portal is the excellent www.colombia.travel.

VISAS

Canadian travelers do not need a visa but will be charged a Colombian equivalent of C$85 reciprocity fee upon arrival at the airport or land border crossing. It can be paid in cash in Colombian pesos or with an international debit or credit card. It is waived for travelers under 14 or over 79. At international airports there is a special immigration line to pay the fee, marked with a Canadian flag.

All visitors get an entry stamp in their passport upon arrival and receive a 90-day tourist visa. Double-check your stamp immediately; errors are sometimes made.

If traveling overland, make sure you get an entry stamp or you'll have troubles later. Overstaying your welcome can result in heavy fines, and in some cases can result in being barred entry in the future. Similarly, make sure you get your departure stamp or there will be trouble the next time around.

Visa Extensions

Migración Colombia (Centro Facilitador de Servicios Migratorios; www.migracion colombia.gov.co; Calle 100 No 11B-27; ⊘7:30am-3:30pm Mon-Fri) handles visa extensions for tourists via Centros Facilitadores de Servicios Migratorios offices around the country. Visitors on a tourist visa may extend up to an additional 90 days at the discretion of the officer. To apply for an extension, known as a 'permiso temporal de permanencia,' you'll be asked to submit your passport, two photocopies of your passport (picture page and arrival stamp) and two passport-sized photos, along with an air ticket out of the country in most cases. The fee of COP$96,000 can be paid by debit or credit card at Migración Colombia offices.

If you're paying in cash it must be deposited into the government bank account, which is often Banco de Occidente but depends on the city in which you are applying. Show up first to fill out forms, then they'll direct you to a nearby bank to pay the fee.

You can also complete the process and pay online and once it's approved pop into a Migración Colombia office to get the stamp.

If you apply for the extension in the office, expect the process to take an entire morning or afternoon. It can be done at any of the Centros Facilitadores de Servicios Migratorios offices in Colombia, which are present in all the main cities and some smaller towns (there's a list on the Migración Colombia website). You'll usually (but not always) get the extension on the spot.

Fines for overstaying range from half of to up to seven times the minimum salary (depending on the length of overstay): travelers in 2018 were charged at least COP$450,000 for overstaying a few days.

VOLUNTEERING

Colombia offers a decent array of volunteering opportunities in education, the environment and social fields. Most major international volunteer boards have in-country listings.

One worthwhile local organization is Goals for Peace (www.goalsforpeace.com) in Bucaramanga where volunteers can help out giving English classes, sports training, arts and crafts workshops or with homework assistance.

While some hostels will offer travelers 'volunteer' positions in exchange for food and board, this is technically illegal as it takes jobs away from Colombians.

WOMEN TRAVELERS

➡ Women traveling in Colombia are unlikely to encounter any problems.

* The usual caveats apply: bring your street smarts, don't wander alone in dodgy neighborhoods after dark, and keep an eye on your drink.

* Female travelers are also more likely to be victims of a bag-snatching or mugging attempt, as you will be perceived as less likely to fight back.

* Also be careful taking taxis alone after dark – while rare, there have been reports of taxi drivers raping single female passengers.

WORK

* In order to take part in any paid employment in Colombia it's necessary to apply for the appropriate visa through Migración Colombia; your employer will need to sponsor the application, which is more likely if you have formal qualifications and are willing to commit to a longer contract.

* There is a growing demand for qualified English-language teachers in Colombia. Some schools may be willing to pay cash-in-hand for a short period of time, but for longer-term employment you will have to find a school willing to organize a work visa. Don't expect to get rich teaching English: you're unlikely to make more than a few million pesos a month, and usually much less.

* As a general rule, the more popular the city is among travelers, the harder it will be to find employment.

❶ Getting There & Away

It's possible to arrive in Colombia by air, road, river and sea. The majority of visitors fly in through the major gateway airports of Bogotá, Medellín, Cartagena and Cali.

Colombia borders Panama, Venezuela, Brazil, Peru and Ecuador, but has road connections with Venezuela and Ecuador only. These are the easiest and most popular border crossings, although the political crisis in Venezuela has led to the borders operating irregularly.

You can also cross the border to Santa Rosa in Peru and Tabatinga in Brazil at the three corners near Leticia. There are privately run charter yachts to and from Panama and regular local boats running to Ecuador from Tumaco.

Flights, cars and tours can be booked online at lonelyplanet.com/bookings.

AIR

Colombia's biggest international airport is Bogotá's newly renovated **Aeropuerto Internacional El Dorado** (☑1-266-2000; www. eldorado.aero; Av El Dorado). A second phase of its expansion project is under way.

Other major airports servicing international flights:

Aeropuerto Internacional José María Córdova (p629) Serving Medellín.

Aeropuerto Internacional Rafael Núñez (p616) In Cartagena.

Aeropuerto Alfonso Bonilla Aragón (p644) Serving Cali.

Colombia's national carrier is **Avianca** (☑1-8000-953 434, 5-330-2030; www.avianca. com), which is one of the better airlines in the region both in terms of service and reliability.

LAND

Almost all travelers crossing between Ecuador and Colombia use the Carretera Panamericana border crossing through Ipiales and Tulcán.

There are several crossings between Colombia and Venezuela although recent political tensions have seen the borders closed on occasion – check the latest before setting out.

The most popular crossing with travelers is the route via Cúcuta and San Antonio del Táchira, on the main Bogotá–Caracas road. Another major border crossing is at Paraguachón, on the Maicao–Maracaibo road. There are shared taxis between Maicao and Maracaibo, and direct buses between Cartagena and Caracas.

AIRLINE	WEBSITE	MAIN DESTINATIONS
Avianca	www.avianca.com	26 major destinations all over the country
Easyfly	www.easyfly.com.co	Armeia, Bogotá, Bucaramanga, Cali, Cartagena, Cúcuta, Ibague, Manizales, Medellín, Neiva, Pereira, Popayán, Quibdó, Valledupar, Yopal
Latam	www.latam.com	Barranquilla, Bogotá, Bucaramanga, Cali, Cúcuta, Leticia, Medellín, Pereira, San Andrés, Santa Marta, Valledupar, Yopal
Satena	www.satena.com	Bahía Solano, Bogotá, Cali, Guapi, Ipiales, La Macarena, Medellín, Nuquí, Pasto, Pitalito, Providencia, Puerto Asis, San Andrés, San José del Guaviare
Viva Colombia	www.vivaair.com	Bogotá, Bucaramanga, Cartagena, Leticia, Medellín, Montería, Pereira, San Andrés, Santa Marta
Wingo	www.wingo.com	Barranquilla, Bogotá, Cali, Cartagena, San Andrés

COLOMBIA GETTING THERE & AWAY

There is no overland route between Colombia and Panama, but it is possible to deliver a car between the two countries on a cargo ship. The pick-up and drop-off points are Colón and Cartagena.

RIVER & SEA

Regular riverboat services connect Leticia in the Colombian Amazon with Iquitos (Peru) and Manaus (Brazil).

There is one passenger ship and many private sailboats running between Colón in Panama and Cartagena in Colombia. It's also possible to cross from Colombia to the San Blas region in Panama via small boat from Capurganá/Sapzurro.

Getting Around

AIR

Colombia has several main passenger airlines and many smaller carriers and charter airlines. Busy routes are operated with modern jet aircraft while flights in remote areas can be in anything from tiny single-propellor three-seaters to Soviet jets and even WWII-era DC-3s!

Satena (☑1-8000-912-034, 1-605-2222; www.satena.com), the commercial carrier of the FAC (Colombian Air Force) services flights to the vast areas of the Amazon, Los Llanos and the Pacific coast; it lands at numerous small towns and villages that would be otherwise virtually inaccessible.

BUS

The main way to get around Colombia, buses range from tightly packed *colectivos* (shared minibuses or taxis) to comfortable, air-conditioned, long-distance buses, and connect nearly every town in the country. Buses are the principal means of intercity travel, and go just about everywhere. Most long-distance intercity buses are more comfortable than your average coach-class airplane seat, and the overnight buses sometimes have business-class-sized seats. Wi-fi is now pretty much standard on nicer buses (though it's often patchy or doesn't work at all). A word of warning: many Colombian bus drivers turn the air-con up to arctic temperatures. Wear a sweater, a beanie and gloves, or better yet, bring a blanket. Bus drivers also tend to crank up the music and/or action movie

(dubbed in Spanish) on the TV, even in the middle of the night. Earplugs are a boon.

It is common for buses to stop at *requisas* (military checkpoints), even in the dead of night. The soldiers at checkpoints will ask everyone to get off the bus, check everyone's identification, and then pat people down. They may look through your bags but often ignore foreigners altogether.

CAR & MOTORCYCLE

➡ Useful for traveling at your own pace, or for visiting regions with minimal public transport. Cars can be hired in major cities, but they're generally not cheap.

➡ What's more, the security situation remains dodgy in remote and rural parts of the country, increasing the risk of vehicle theft and pushing up insurance prices. Check government websites for warnings before setting out anywhere remote.

➡ In the cities, on the other hand, traffic is heavy, chaotic and mad. Driving 'manners' are wild and unpredictable. It takes some time to get used to the local style of driving. This goes without saying for motorcycle travel as well.

➡ Colombians drive on the right-hand side of the road and there are seatbelt requirements, so buckle up or risk a fine. The speed limit is 60km/h in the city and 80km/h on the highway. The nationwide highway police telephone number is 767.

➡ If you do plan to drive in Colombia, bring your driver's license. The driver's license from your country will normally do unless it's one of non-Latin-alphabet origin, in which case, you'll need an International Driving Permit as well.

Ecuador

POP 16.9 MILLION

Best Places to Eat

➡ Seaflower Lateneus (p737)

➡ Moliendo Café (p719)

➡ Tiki Limbo (p746)

➡ El Jardín (p734)

Best Places to Stay

➡ Hostería Mandála (p742)

➡ Pepe's House Hostal (p719)

➡ Masaya Hostel (p682)

➡ Casa Blanca (p759)

Why Go?

Postcard-pretty colonial centers, waves splashing white-sand beaches, Kichwa villages, Amazonian rainforest and the breathtaking Andes – a dazzling array of wonders is squeezed into this compact country.

The historic centers of Quito and Cuenca are lined with photogenic plazas, 17th-century churches and monasteries, and beautifully restored mansions. Beyond the cities, the Ecuadorian landscape unfolds in all its startling variety. There are Andean villages renowned for their colorful textiles and sprawling markets, Afro-Ecuadorian towns where days end with meals of fresh seafood and memorable sunsets, and remote settlements in the Amazon where shamans still harvest the traditional rainforest medicines of their ancestors.

The famous Galápagos Islands, with their volcanic, otherworldly landscapes, are a magnet for wildlife lovers. The Amazon rainforest offers a different wildlife-watching experience, while Mindo's cloud forest is considered a birder's paradise.

When to Go

Quito

[Climate chart showing Temperature (°C/°F) and Rainfall (inches/mm) by month J F M A M J J A S O N D]

°C/°F Temp — Rainfall inches/mm
40/104
30/86
20/68
10/50
0/32
-10/14

20/350
15/300
10/250
8/200
6/150
4/100
2/50
0

Jun Swig *chicha* (indigenous corn beer) at the indigenous festival of Inti Raymi in the northern highlands.

Sep Processions, costumes, fireworks, dancing and Andean music at Latacunga's Fiesta de la Mamá Negra.

Dec A week of parties in the capital commemorates the founding of Quito.

Entering the Country

Major border crossings into Peru are at busy Tumbes–Aguas Verdes (near the coast), Macará and La Balsa (a few hours south of Vilcabamba); hardy travelers with heaps of time can also go by river via Nuevo Rocafuerte. To Colombia, the safest crossing (and the only one we recommend) is at Tulcán–Ipiales, a few hours northwest of Ibarra.

TWO WEEK ITINERARY

Begin the trip in Quito. Spend two days soaking up the architectural gems of the Old Town, then go 2½ hours north to Otavalo for its famous market (best on Saturdays). Spend the night there and squeeze in a hike out to the stunning lakes Laguna de Cuicocha or Lagunas de Mojanda. On the fourth day, go west (via Quito) to the lush cloud forests of Mindo. Overnight in a riverside or mountaintop lodge, then return to Quito for a flight to Cuenca, the colonial jewel of the south. Spend two days exploring 500-year-old churches and visiting the fairy-tale-like setting of Parque Nacional Cajas, 30km to the west. If time allows, visit the Inca ruins of Ingapirca before continuing to Guayaquil for a flight to the Galápagos. Spend four days there, wildlife-watching and island-hopping. For the final part of the Ecuadorian adventure, fly back to Guayaquil and onward (via Quito) to Coca, gateway to the Amazon. Spend three nights at a jungle lodge on the Lower Río Napo, one of the best places to see Ecuador's Amazonian wildlife.

Essential Food & Drink

Canelazo *Aguardiente* (sugarcane alcohol) with hot cider and cinnamon, distilled and warmed, just right for Andean nights.

Ceviche Ecuador's take on sushi, but cooked a bit.

Chifle Because who doesn't love banana chips?

Chugchucara Too much pork for just one fork?

Pajaro Azul Herb-infused *aguardiente* that will have you seeing stars.

Top Tips

➜ Acclimatize properly before attempting any high-altitude hikes. Spend a few days in Quito to allow your body to adapt.

➜ Most Ecuadorians eat their main meal at lunchtime. Look for excellent-value *almuerzos* (set lunches), for just a few dollars.

➜ When traveling on buses, keep your belongings on your lap in front of you and use a money belt for important documents and cash. Put larger items in the storage compartment underneath the bus and get a claim ticket.

➜ Alert the driver to where you want to get off if your bus does not enter the terminal for your town; some only stop alongside the highway for certain destinations.

FAST FACTS

Currency US dollar ($)

Visas Not required for most nationalities.

Money ATMs in cities and larger towns; credit cards accepted only at higher-end places.

Capital Quito

Emergency 911 (major cities only); 101 (police)

Language Spanish

Exchange Rates

Australia	A$1	US$0.74
Canada	C$1	US$0.76
Europe	€1	US$1.17
Japan	¥100	US$0.90
New Zealand	NZ$1	US$0.68
UK	UK£1	US$1.32

For current exchange rates see www.xe.com.

Daily Costs

➜ Budget guesthouse per person: $10–20; double room in a midrange hotel: $40–90

➜ Set lunch: $2.50–3.50; dinner for two in a good restaurant: $20–30

Resources

Lonely Planet (www.lonely planet.com)

Ministry of Tourism Ecuador (http://ecuador.travel)

Latin American Network Information Center (http://lanic.utexas.edu/la/ecuador)

Life in Ecuador (www.life-in-ecuador.com)

Ecuador Highlights

1 Quito (p676)
Delving into the picturesque Old Town, its cobblestone streets crisscrossing one of Latin America's finest colonial centers.

2 La Oriente (p727) Staying in a jungle lodge, taking wildlife-watching excursions and visiting indigenous villages.

3 Galápagos Islands (p753) Snorkeling with sea lions, spotting penguins, and coming face to face with gigantic tortoises.

4 Otavalo (p698) Haggling over handmade treasures in one of South America's biggest open-air markets.

5 Mindo (p696) Hiking in cloud forests, cooling off in waterfalls and going ziplining over the canopy.

6 Quilotoa Loop (p706) Trekking past topaz lakes and peaceful villages high up in the Andes.

7 Parque Nacional Machalilla (p743) Spotting massive humpback whales on their annual migration.

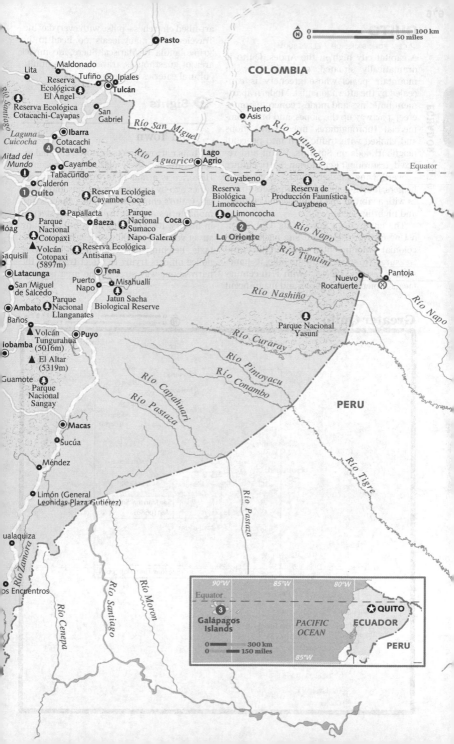

QUITO

02 / POP 1.6 MILLION / ELEV 2800M

A capital city high in the Andes, Quito is dramatically situated, squeezed between mountain peaks whose greenery is concealed by the afternoon mist. Modern apartment buildings and modest concrete homes creep partway up the slopes, and busy commercial thoroughfares lined with shops and choked with traffic turn into peaceful neighborhoods on Sundays. Warm and relaxed, traditional Ecuadorian Sierra culture – overflowing market stands, shamanistic healers, fourth-generation hatmakers – mixes with a vibrant and sophisticated culinary and nightlife scene.

The city's crown jewel is its 'Old Town,' a Unesco World Heritage Site packed with colonial monuments and architectural treasures. No sterile, museum mile, its handsomely restored blocks – with 17th-century facades, picturesque plazas and magnificent art-filled churches – pulse with everyday life. Travelers, and many locals too, head to the 'gringolandia' of Mariscal Sucre, a compact area of guesthouses, travel agencies, multicultural eateries and teeming bars.

⊙ Sights

⊙ Old Town

With its narrow streets, restored colonial architecture and lively plazas, Quito's Centro Histórico is a marvel to wander. Built centuries ago by indigenous artisans and laborers, Quito's churches, convents, chapels and monasteries are cast in legend and steeped in history. It's a bustling area, full of yelling street vendors, ambling pedestrians, tooting taxis, belching buses and whistle-blowing police officers trying to direct traffic in the narrow one-way streets. The area is magi-

Greater Quito

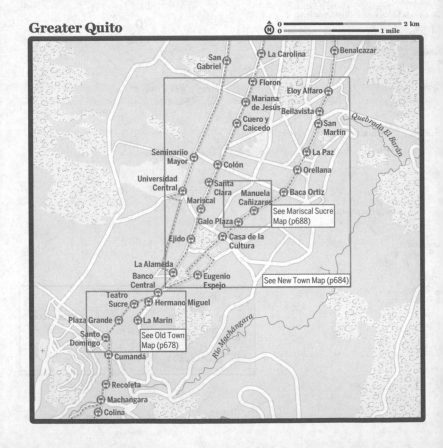

cal; it's a place where the more you look, the more you find.

★ **Iglesia de la**
Compañía de Jesús CHURCH
(Map p678; www.fundacioniglesiadelacompania.
org.ec; García Moreno & Sucre, Old Town; adult/
student $5/2.50; ⊙9:30am-6:30pm Mon-Thu, to
5:30pm Fri, to 4pm Sat, 12:30-4pm Sun) Capped
by green-and-gold domes, La Compañía de
Jesús is Quito's most ornate church and a
standout among the baroque splendors of
the Old Town. Free guided tours in English
or Spanish highlight the church's unique
features, including its Moorish elements,
perfect symmetry (right down to the *trom-
pe l'oeil* staircase at the rear), symbolic elements (bright-red walls are a reminder of
Christ's blood) and its syncretism (Ecuadorian plants and indigenous faces are hidden
along the pillars).

Plaza Grande PLAZA
(Map p678; Old Town) While wandering around
colonial Quito, you'll probably pass through
the Plaza Grande several times. Its benches
are great for soaking up the Andean morning sun and watching the bustle all around.
On Monday, the changing of the guards
takes place on the plaza at 11am.

The white building on the plaza's northwest
side with the national flag flying atop is the
Palacio de Gobierno (Carondelet Palace; Map
p678; www.presidencia.gob.ec/palacio-de-gobierno;
cnr Espejo & García Moreno, Plaza Grande; ⊙guid-
ed tours 9am-6pm Tue-Fri, to 8pm Sat, to 9pm Sun)
FREE, the seat of the Ecuadorian presidency.
On the southwest side stands Quito's **cathedral** (Map p678; Plaza Grande, Old Town; cathedral
adult/child $3/2, cathedral & dome, adults only, $6;
⊙9am-5pm Mon-Sat).

Casa del Alabado MUSEUM
(Map p678; ☑02-228-0940; www.alabado.org;
Cuenca N1-41 near Bolívar, Old Town; adult/child
$6/1; ⊙9:30am-5:30pm) Housed in an elegant
colonial-era home, this privately owned museum with contemporary displays showcases
an impressive collection of pre-Columbian
artifacts. Thematically organized around
subjects such as shamans, pigmentation and
the afterlife, explanations in English and
Spanish (audio guides are available) explore
the indigenous beliefs represented by the
finely crafted ceramic pieces and jewelry.

Museo de la Ciudad MUSEUM
(Map p678; ☑02-228-3883; www.museociudad
quito.gob.ec; García Moreno S1-47 near Rocafuerte,

Old Town; adult/child $3/1.50; ⊙9am-5pm Tue-
Sun) This first-rate museum depicts daily
life in Quito through the centuries, with
displays including dioramas, model indigenous homes and colonial kitchens. The 1563
building itself (a former hospital) is a work
of art. There are also a number of temporary
exhibitions. Entry is free on the last Sunday
of the month.

Plaza San Francisco PLAZA
(Map p678) Walking from the Old Town's narrow colonial streets into this open plaza reveals one of the finest sights in all of Ecuador:
a sweeping cobblestone plaza backed by the
mountainous backdrop of Volcán Pichincha,
and the long, whitewashed walls and twin bell
towers of Ecuador's oldest church.

Museo Franciscano MUSEUM
(Museo Fray Pedro Gocial; Map p678; www.museo
fraypedrogocial.com; Cuenca 477 near Sucre, Plaza
San Francisco, Old Town; adult/child $3/1; ⊙9am-
5:30pm Mon-Sat, to 1pm Sun) To the right of the
Iglesia de San Francisco's main entrance,
and within the Convent of St Francis, this
museum contains some of the church's finest artwork, including paintings, sculpture
and 16th-century furniture, some of which
is fantastically wrought and inlaid with
thousands of pieces of mother-of-pearl. The
admission fee includes a guided tour in English or Spanish.

Parque Itchimbia PARK
(Map p678; Old Town; ⊙5am-6pm) Sitting high
on a hill above the Old Town, this grassy park
boasts magnificent views of the city, running
and cycle tracks and a children's playground.
It's the perfect spot to spread out a picnic
lunch, soak up the sun and take in the panorama. It's a steep climb up here from the San
Blas neighborhood; walk up Elizalde, from
where steps lead up to the park.

El Panecillo VIEWPOINT
(General Melchor Aymerich, Old Town; monument
interior adult/child $1/0.50; ⊙9am-6pm Mon-Thu,
to 9pm Fri-Sun) Topped by a 41m-tall aluminum mosaic statue of La Virgen de Quito
(Virgin of Quito; completed in 1976), with a
crown of stars, angelic wings and a chained
dragon, the hill to the south of the Old Town
called El Panecillo (the Little Loaf of Bread)
is a major Quito landmark. From the summit
there are marvelous views of the sprawling
city and the surrounding volcanoes. Climb
steps up to the base of the Virgin statue for
an even loftier outlook.

Old Town

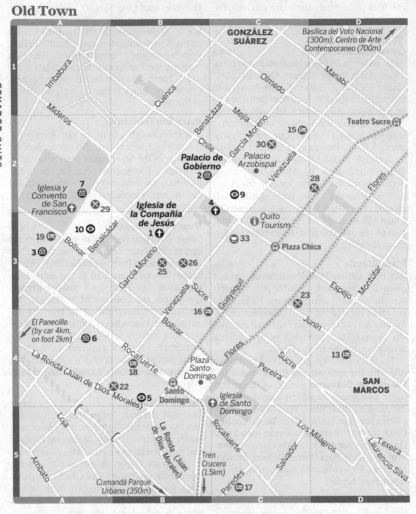

La Ronda
STREET

(Map p678; Old Town; ⊙24hr) La Ronda is a colorful cobblestone street featuring colonial houses mostly given over to souvenir shops, bars and restaurants, and carefully restored for the purposes of tourism. The architecture is mostly 17th century, and signs on the walls describe aspects of the street's history.

Cumandá Parque Urbano
CULTURAL CENTER

(☑02-257-3645; www.facebook.com/quitocumanda; Av 24 de Mayo, Old Town; ⊙7am-8pm Tue-Fri, 8am-6pm Sat & Sun) FREE The Old Town's old bus terminal has been converted into a sparkling covered cultural center and sports complex with a volleyball court, soccer pitch, climbing wall, yoga studios and several small swimming pools – all free of charge. Those not interested in getting their heart rate up can take in the temporary art exhibitions, theater performances, live music and other cultural events that are now held here. It's accessed from La Ronda.

Centro de Arte Contemporáneo
MUSEUM

(CAC; www.centrodeartecontemporaneo.gob.ec; Dávila & Venezuela, Old Town; ⊙10am-6pm Tue-Sun) FREE Inside a beautifully restored former military hospital, this excellent museum showcases cutting-edge multimedia exhibits

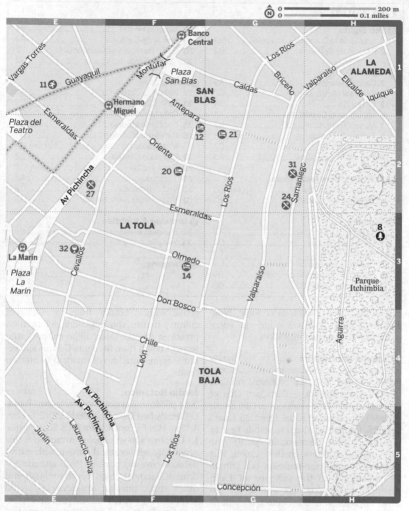

as well as top modern-art shows that travel to the city.

New Town

★ TelefériQo
CABLE CAR

(https://teleferico.com.ec; Av Occidental near Av La Gasca, New Town; adult/child $8.50/6.50; ⊙9am-8pm Tue-Thu, 8am-8pm Fri-Mon) For spectacular views over Quito's mountainous landscape, hop aboard this sky tram, one of the world's highest aerial lifts, that takes passengers on a 2.5km ride (10 minutes) up the flanks of Volcán Pichincha to the top of Cruz Loma. Once you're at the top (a mere 4100m), you can hike to the summit of Rucu Pichincha (4680m), a 4km (five-hour) round-trip – ask about the safety situation before attempting the climb and bring warm clothes.

★ Casa Museo Guayasamín
MUSEUM

(www.guayasamin.org; Calvache E18-94 & Chávez, Bellavista; adult/child incl Capilla del Hombre $8/4; ⊙10am-5pm) In the former home of the legendary painter Oswaldo Guayasamín (1919–99), this wonderful museum houses the most complete collection of the artist's work. Guayasamín was also an avid collector, and the museum displays his outstanding

Old Town

collection of pre-Columbian ceramic, bone and metal pieces. Admission includes entry to the Capilla del Hombre gallery.

★**Capilla del Hombre** GALLERY
(Chapel of Man; www.guayasamin.org; Calvache E18-94 & Chávez, Bellavista; adult/child incl Casa Museo Guayasamín $8/4; ☉10am-5pm) One of the most important works of art in South America, Ecuadorian artist Oswaldo Guayasamín's Capilla del Hombre stands next to the Casa Museo Guayasamín (p679). The fruit of Guayasamín's greatest vision, this giant monument-cum-museum is a tribute to humankind, to the suffering of Latin America's indigenous poor and to the undying hope for something better. It's a moving place and tours (in English, French and Spanish, included in the price) are highly recommended. Admission includes entrance to the Casa Museo.

Museo Nacional MUSEUM
(Map p684; http://muna.culturaypatrimonio.gob.ec; cnr Avs Patria & 12 de Octubre, Eugenio Espejo, New Town; ☉9am-6pm Tue-Sun) **FREE** Located in the circular, glass-plated, landmark building of the Casa de la Cultura is one of the country's largest collections of Ecuadorian art, with magnificent works of pre-Hispanic and colonial religious art. The museum collection includes more than 1000 ceramic pieces dating from 12,000 BC to AD 1534, with highlights

being 'whistle bottles' from the Chorrera culture, figures showing skull deformation practiced by the Machalilla culture, wild serpent bowls from the Jama-Coaque and ceramic representations of *tzantzas* (shrunken heads).

Jardín Botánico GARDENS
(Map p684; www.jardinbotanicoquito.com; Parque La Carolina, New Town; adult/child $3.50/2; ☉8am-4:45pm Mon-Fri, 9am-4:45pm Sat & Sun) Parque La Carolina's most popular attraction is this peacefully set botanical garden with native habitats covering *páramo* (high-altitude Andean grasslands), cloud forest, wetlands and other areas, plus an *orquideario* (orchid greenhouse), ethnobotanical garden (exploring the plants used by indigenous groups) and Amazonian greenhouse. Accessed by a bridge, there's also a kids' play/discovery area, a Japanese garden and a collection of more than 100 bonsai trees.

Mindalae – Museo Etnográfico de Artesanía de Ecuador MUSEUM
(Map p684; www.mindalae.com.ec; Reina Victoria N26-166 near La Niña, Colón, New Town; adult/child $3/1.50; ☉9:30am-5:30pm Mon-Sat) Just north of Mariscal Sucre, this worthwhile museum has displays on the spiritual beliefs and practices, artwork, clothing and utensils of Ecuador's indigenous people. Start at the top with the 4th-floor shamanism exhibi-

tion and make your way down via the spiral staircase at the center of the unusual curved building. It's run by the fair-trade organization Fundación Sinchi Sacha, and there's an excellent shop selling indigenous crafts from across Ecuador.

Quito Observatory MUSEUM
(Map p684; ☏02-257-0765; http://oaq.epn.edu.ec; Parque La Alameda, Eugenio Espejo, New Town; adult/child $2/1; ◷9am-5pm Mon-Sat) Opened by President García Moreno in 1864, this four-sided observatory is the oldest on the continent. It houses a museum of 19th-century pendulums, sextants, chronometers and other historical instruments. From February to May and July to August, stargazing sessions are held on Tuesday, Wednesday and Thursday nights ($3; reserve ahead). It sits inside the small Parque La Alameda.

Santuario de Guápulo CHURCH
(Plaza de Guápulo, Guápulo, New Town; adult/child $2/1; ◷8-11:30am & 2:30-5:30pm Mon-Fri) In an elegant square in Guápulo stands the neighborhood's centerpiece, the 17th-century Santuario de Guápulo, surrounded by sheer valley sides. It has an excellent collection of Quito School art and sculpture, and a stunning 18th-century pulpit carved by master wood-carver Juan Bautista Menacho.

🏃 Activities

Cycling
Local mountain-biking companies rent bikes and offer excellent tours, including one-day rides through the *páramo* (high-altitude Andean grasslands) of Parque Nacional Cotopaxi as well as downhill descents, and trips incorporating a stop at Papallacta hot springs. Two-day trips take in Cotopaxi and Chimborazo or Cotopaxi and Quilotoa. Single day trips cost about $60. Compare prices and trips before committing to a particular operator.

Biking Dutchman CYCLING
(Map p684; ☏02-256-8323; www.bikingdutchman. com; La Pinta E-731 near Reina Victoria, New Town; 1-day tours from $59; ◷office 9:30am-5:30pm Mon-Fri) Ecuador's pioneer mountain-biking operator has good bikes and guides, and an outstanding reputation. It offers one- to eight-day tours. The office is just north of Mariscal Sucre.

Arie's Bike Company CYCLING
(☏02-238-5712; www.ariesbikecompany.com) Owned by a Dutch-Ecuadorian couple, Arie's

organizes multiday mountain-biking trips throughout Ecuador.

📣 Courses

Language
Ecuador is a great place to study Spanish, with homestays, organized activities and volunteer opportunities typically on offer. Some of our favorites include **Colourful Ecuador** (Map p688; ☏02-223-1595; www.colour fulecuador.com; García E6-15 near Mera, Mariscal Sucre, New Town), **Vida Verde** (Map p684; ☏02-252-4333; www.vidaverde.com; Madrid E13-137 near Lugo, La Floresta, New Town) and **Simon Bolivar** (Map p688; ☏02-254-4558; www.simon-bolivar. com; Foch E9-20 near Av 6 de Diciembre).

Salsa
Quito is also a good spot to hone (or learn) those salsa moves. Some of the best include **Academia Salsa & Merengue** (Map p688; ☏02-222-0427; www.facebook.com/tropicaldanc ing; Foch E4-256 near Av Amazonas, Mariscal Sucre, New Town; group lessons per hour $10; ◷10am-8pm Mon-Fri) and **Ritmo Tropical** (Map p688; ☏02-255-7094; www.ritmotropicalsalsa.com; Av Amazonas N24-155 near Calama; private/group lessons $10/6; ◷9am-8pm Mon-Fri).

🧭 Tours

Quito is one of the easiest places in Ecuador to arrange a guided tour, be it a Galápagos cruise, mountain climbing, Amazon lodge, biking tour or white-water rafting. Itineraries ranging from one day to several weeks can be customized for small groups. Many agencies offer standard tours to nearby places such as Mitad del Mundo, Pululahua and further afield to Otavalo, Mindo, Cotopaxi and Baños. Be sure to stop by on weekdays (many offices close on weekends), and for longer trips try to meet your guides in advance.

CarpeDM Adventures TOURS
(Map p678; ☏02-295-4713; www.carpedm.ca; Antepara E4-70 near Los Rios, San Blas, Old Town; day tours per person $50) CarpeDM earns high marks for its affordable prices and wide range of tours, though it's the excellent service that makes this agency stand out from many others. Day trips to Cotapaxi, Otavalo and Mindo for those short on time.

Condor Trekk ADVENTURE
(Map p688; ☏02-222-6004; https://condortrekk expeditions.com/; Reina Victoria N24-281 near Rodriguez, Mariscal Sucre, New Town; ◷9:30am-6pm

Mon-Fri, to noon Sat & Sun) Reputable climbing operator offering single- and multiday guided climbs and tough hikes up and around most of Ecuador's peaks. It is best to pop into its office to discuss what you are looking for.

Happy Gringo   TOURS

(☑02-512-3486; www.happygringo.com; Aldaz N34-155 near Portugal, Edificio Catalina Plaza, 2nd fl, La Carolina, New Town; ⊙9am-6pm Mon-Fri) A British- and Dutch-owned company catering to a midrange market, Happy Gringo can organize week- to month-long customized itineraries throughout the country, from the Galápagos all the way to the Amazon. Professionally run with English-speaking guides and private drivers available, it's one of the best all-around tour companies in the city.

Eos Ecuador   TOURS

(Map p688; ☑02-601-3560; www.eosecuador. travel; Av Amazonas N24-66 near Pinto, Mariscal Sucre, New Town) ✔ Eos offers a full range of climbing, trekking, Galápagos and Amazon trips, as well as stays in community-oriented tourism initiatives.

Gulliver   TOURS

(Map p688; ☑02-252-9297; www.gulliver.com.ec; Foch E7-38 near Reina Victoria, Reina Victoria Bldg, Mariscal Sucre, New Town; 4-day Ecuador tour from $1699; ⊙8:30am-5:30pm Mon-Fri) Well-regarded operator offering hiking, climbing, mountain-biking and horseback-riding trips in the Andes. Daily departures.

Sierra Nevada Expeditions   ADVENTURE

(Map p688; ☑02-255-3658; http://sierranevada. ec; Pinto E4-150 near Cordero, Mariscal Sucre, New Town) Long in the business, Sierra Nevada offers an array of climbing and river-rafting trips. The owner Freddy Ramirez is a well-established and very reputable mountain guide.

🎊 Festivals & Events

Carnaval   CARNIVAL

(www.quitocultura.info; ⊙Feb) Held in the days leading up to Ash Wednesday, Carnaval is centered around La Mascarada Andina, a colorful masked parade with music and dancing along the streets of the Old Town. There are intense water fights across the city too – no one is spared – and even tourists join in with water pistols and foam.

La Floresta Summer Festival   FOOD & DRINK

(Festival Verano de La Floresta; La Floresta, New Town; ⊙Aug) Held over the first weekend of August, La Floresta showcases its food, drink and crafts with stalls stationed along the street, alongside live music.

🛏 Sleeping

The Old Town is an obvious choice: a Unesco-listed area of architectural jewels. Several hostels are in the Old Town neighborhood of San Blas, an ordinary, working-class area on the east side of the Av Pichincha that you'll need to taxi to and from at night.

International chains, including Marriott, Best Western, Swissôtel and Hilton, are well represented throughout the city, but particularly in the modern and massive New Town. Whilst most foreigners who stay here do so in Mariscal Sucre – replete with hostels, touristy bars and restaurants – the most appealing area of the New Town is the quiet and refined La Floresta neighborhood.

🛏 Old Town

Masaya Hostel   HOSTEL $

(Map p678; ☑02-257-0189; www.masaya-experience.com/en/hostel-quito; cnr Rocafuerte & Venezuela; 8-/4-person dorm $11/14, d incl breakfast from $55; ☎) ✔ Occupying the best part of a city block, Masaya Hostel outclasses almost all the city's top hotels with its spacious wood-floored rooms, beautiful public spaces and enclosed courtyard garden strung with hammocks and centered around a ceiba tree with a wraparound stage. That it offers such exemplary accommodations *and* some of the Old Town's cheapest beds can scarce be believed.

Blue House Old Town   HOSTEL $

(Map p678; Antepara e4-27 near Leon, San Blas; dm/s/d/tr incl breakfast from $9/20/25/36) The Mariscal's famous **Blue House** (Map p688; ☑02-222-3480; www.bluehousequito.com; Pinto E8-24 near Almagro, Mariscal Sucre, New Town; dm/s/d/tr from $9/20/25/36; @☎) comes to the Old Town in a quiet, chilled form. Expect clean, wood-floored rooms and a pleasant roof terrace. The free breakfast is substantial and it offers a free walking tour.

Secret Garden   HOSTEL $

(Map p678; ☑02-295-6704; www.secretgarden quito.com; Antepara E4-60 near Los Ríos, San Blas; dm $10-12, d with/without bathroom $38/28; @☎) This perennially popular hostel has an undeniably social vibe, and wallflowers or those seeking privacy will want to head elsewhere. Long-term travelers getting by on bartending jobs in Quito and others on the South America circuit swap stories over a beer on the rooftop terrace with magical views over the Old Town. You'll also find simple but clean wood-floor rooms.

La Posada Colonial   GUESTHOUSE **$**
(Map p678; ☎02-228-2859; www.laposada colonial.com; Paredes S1-49 near Rocafuerte; s/d from $14/27, tr without bathroom $35; @ 🛜) A no-brainer for those looking for low-key, low-budget nonhostel accommodations in the Old Town. It's even within stumbling distance of La Ronda. The rooms have high ceilings and wood floors, and most have several beds, making it good value for groups. Bathrooms, however, are compact. It has a small rooftop with good views and a kitchen for guests' use.

Quito Backpacker Guesthouse   GUESTHOUSE **$**
(Map p678; ☎995-157-338 02-316-0264; www. quitobackpackerguesthouse.com; Oriente E3-108 near Léon, San Blas; dm/r without bathroom incl breakfast from $9/20; 🛜) A good choice for those seeking hostel prices with a family-run-guesthouse vibe, this large converted colonial home in the San Blas neighborhood has several floors of spacious, high-ceilinged, wood-floor rooms. There are kitchens on every floor and an expansive rooftop terrace with views of the Old Town. There's also table tennis, table football, a pool table, a barbecue and a movie-screening area.

Colonial House   HOSTEL **$**
(Map p678; ☎02-316-1810; www.colonialhouse quito.com; Olmedo E-432 near Los Ríos, La Tola; dm $10, r with/without bathroom $25/20; @ 🛜) The colonial facade leads travelers into a warren of 13 brightly painted rooms, both dorms and doubles with shared or private bathrooms. There is a games room with a pool table, and a backyard garden with hammocks, a barbecue and pet rabbits. The guest rooms are variously shaped and variously appealing, though all have (sloping) wood floors.

Hotel San Francisco de Quito   HOTEL **$$**
(Map p678; ☎02-228-7758; www.sanfrancisco dequito.com.ec; Sucre Oe3-17 near Guayaquil; s/d incl breakfast $45/73; @ 🛜) No exaggerating, stepping through the medieval-looking doorway into the bright, plant-filled inner courtyard of this historic hotel is like being transported to another century. Specifically, to 1698 when the bones of this house were originally built. There's a variety of differently configured and sized rooms, though all have wood floors and cozy furnishings.

Portal de Cantuña   BOUTIQUE HOTEL **$$**
(Map p678; ☎02-228-2276; www.portalde cantunaquito.com; Bolívar OE6-105 near Cuenca; r incl breakfast $79; 🛜) 🐾 Hidden down an alleyway, this beautifully restored mid-19th-century building once housed an order of nuns. No doubt they would have been distracted by the charming stained-glass window covering the inner courtyard, the gold leaf and baroque decorations, and an overall feeling of warmth and comfort. Wi-fi is generally only available in the lobby area.

Casa San Marcos   BOUTIQUE HOTEL **$$$**
(Map p678; ☎02-228-1811; www.casasanmarcos. com; Junín E1-36 & Montúfar; s/d incl breakfast from $70/92; 🛜) This beautifully restored colonial mansion has 10 rooms replete with antique furnishings, 18th- and 19th-century oil paintings and luxurious fittings. The larger doubles with better views can cost up to $100 more than the listed prices. There's also an art gallery and antiques shop here, and a lower-level breakfast room with picturesque views of El Panecillo.

Hotel El Relicario del Carmen   GUESTHOUSE **$$$**
(Map p678; ☎02-228-9120; www.hotelrelicario delcarmen.com; Venezuela 1041 near Olmedo; s/d/ste incl breakfast $89/110/130; @ 🛜) This delightful 18-room guesthouse is set in a converted colonial mansion sprinkled with colorful paintings and stained-glass windows. Rooms are even sweeter, with polished wood floors and beamed ceilings (but small bathrooms); most face an interior courtyard. There is a tiny restaurant for dinner.

🛏 New Town

La Casona de Mario   GUESTHOUSE **$**
(Map p684; ☎02-254-4036; www.casona demario.com; Andalucía N24-115 near Galicia, La Floresta; r per person with/without bathroom

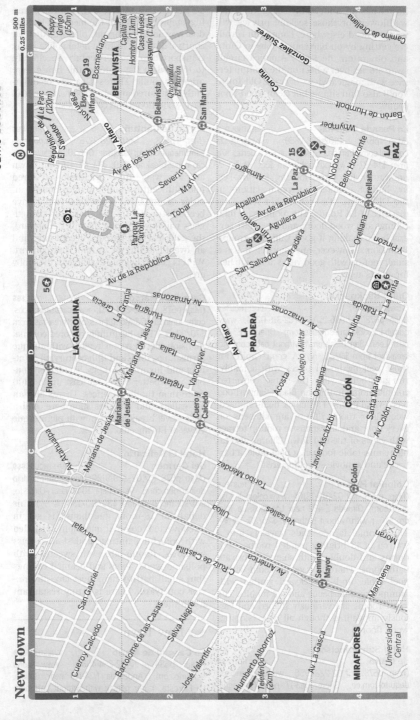

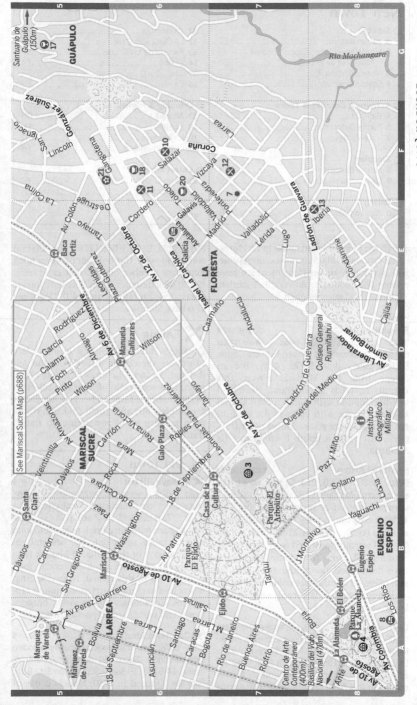

GUÁPULO

Santuario de Guápulo (150m)

17

Río Machangara

San Ignacio

Lincoln

González Suárez

Coruña

10

Salazar

18

1

Vizcaya

12

La Colina

Galoteria

21

Destruge

Av Colón

Tamayo

Plaza Gutierrez

Leonidas

García Gutiérrez

20

Toledo

Galavis

Andaluela

Ponteveldra

11

Cordero

Valladolid

Madrid

Baca Ortiz

Av 12 de Octubre

Isabel La Católica

Galicia

9

LA FLORESTA

Caamaño

Valladolid

Lérida

Lugo

Ladrón de Guevara

Iberia

13

La Coruña

Callas

Av 12 de Octubre

Rodríguez

García

Calama

Foch

Pinto

Wilson

Manuela Cañizares

Wilson

Av 6 de Diciembre

Andrade

Ladrón de Guevara

Av Libertador Simón Bolívar

Coliseo General Rumiñahui

La Concamine

Queseras del Medio

Instituto Geográfico Militar

See Mariscal Sucre Map (p688)

Almagro

Veintimilla

Azuay

Mera

Roca

Dávalos

Reina Victoria

Carrión

MARISCAL SUCRE

Tamayo

Robles

Leonidas plaza Gutiérrez

Galo Plaza

Paz y Miño

Solano

Llona

Santa Clara

Páez

9 de Octubre

18 de Septiembre

Casa de la Cultura

3

Parque El Arbolito

Yaguachi

EUGENIO ESPEJO

Av Patria

Washington

Av 10 de Agosto

Mariscal

San Gregorio

Av Pérez Guerrero

LARREA

J Larrea

Salinas

Santiago

Caracas

Bogotá

Buenos Aires

Río de Janeiro

Centro de Arte Contemporáneo (400m); Basílica del Voto Nacional (470m)

Parque El Ejido

Tarqui

Borja

Ejido

Río frío

Ante

M Larrea

Eugenio Espejo

J Montalvo

El Belén

Parque La Alameda

4

8

La Alameda

Av 10 de Agosto

Av Colombia

Los Ríos

Márquez de Varela

Márquez de Varela

Bolivia

18 de Septiembre

Larrea

Asunción

New Town

$15/12; 🛜) In a lovely old house in La Floresta, La Casona de Mario is outstanding value, with six homey rooms (four of which have private bathrooms), a flower-filled garden, TV lounge and guest kitchen.

Hostel Revolution GUESTHOUSE $
(Map p684; 📞02-254-6458; www.hostel revolutionquito.com; Los Ríos N13-11 near Castro, Eugenio Espejo; dm/d $9/25; @🛜) For an escape from the Mariscal circus, this friendly hostel is an excellent, clean and laid-back option with comfy rooms, shared kitchen, terrace with views and a colorful bar/lounge where you can meet other travelers. Just a block uphill from Parque La Alameda.

Hostal El Arupo GUESTHOUSE $$
(Map p688; 📞02-255-7543; www.hostal elarupo.com; Rodríguez E7-22 near Reina Victoria, Mariscal Sucre; s/d/tw incl breakfast $30/45/48; @🛜) A cozy and homey refuge from nearby Plaza Foch's madness, El Arupo is a spotless and warmly decorated converted house with a small, lovely front patio. The rooms have dark wood floors and firm beds. It also offers an immaculate communal kitchen where breakfast is served, and a small lounge.

Le Parc BUSINESS HOTEL $$$
(📞02-227-6800; https://en.leparc.com.ec; cnr Av República de El Salvador N34-349 & Irlanda, Parque La Carolina; ste incl breakfast from $174; P@🛜) If you want modern, stylish and as far removed in feel from Quito's Centro Histórico as possible, Le Parc hotel is for you. 'Beyond stars' and with the bold aim of becoming Ecuador's number one lodging experience, the 30 slick designer suites here have lounge areas, desks, minibars and LED TVs; some also have hydro-massage tubs.

✗ Eating

Ecuador's culinary capital is a great place to explore the classic dishes from the Andes and beyond. The city's rich and varied restaurant scene also offers a fine selection of international fare. All budgets and tastes are catered for, and you'll find everything from modern sushi restaurants to Italian trattorias.

✗ Old Town

★ Masaya Bistro BISTRO $
(Map p678; www.masaya-experience.com/en/ hostel-quito; cnr Venezuela & Rocafuerte; mains $3-8; ⏱7am-midnight; 🛜📶) This large, inviting space with bare brick pillars and long wooden tables spills onto the peaceful enclosed garden of the affiliated Masaya Hostel (p682). Ecuadorian-international food is served up in this casual, relaxed setting, where beef in chimichurri sauce, quinoa croquettes, Ecuadorian-style ceviche, burgers, wraps and pastas are all possibilities.

★ Cafetería Modelo ECUADORIAN $
(Map p678; www.facebook.com/cafeteriamodelo centrohistorico; Sucre 391 near García Moreno; mains $4-6.25; ⏱8am-7:30pm Mon-Sat, 9am-6pm Sun) Opened in 1950, Modelo is one of

the city's oldest cafes and a great spot to try traditional snacks such as *empanadas de verde* (empanadas made with plantain dough), *quimbolitos* (sweet, cake-like corn dumplings) and tamales. It's also a popular spot for ice cream. The fun, slightly kitsch Ecuador-of-yore trappings make the wait for the food interesting.

Nearby **Cafetería Modelo II** (Map p678; Sucre OE4-48, near Venezuela; mains $4-6.25; ☺9am-6:30pm Mon-Thu, to 7:30pm Fri & Sat, to 5:30pm Sun) offers a similar environment plus live music on Friday afternoons from 5pm to 7pm.

Bohemia Cafe & Pizza   PIZZA $

(Map p678; www.facebook.com/bohemia.pizzeria; La Ronda Oe3-108 near Venezuela; pastas $6-8, pizzas $14-16; ☺noon-midnight Mon-Thu, to 3am Fri & Sat) Feel like a local at this welcoming low-key spot where the wonderfully energetic owner will greet you like family on repeat visits.

The menu includes excellent pizza (*albondigas* – meatballs – being our fave topping) and layered nachos cooked with homemade corn chips. Wash it down with a giant *michelada*, a mix of beer, lime and salt, accompanied by various salsas.

Mercado Central   MARKET $

(Map p678; Av Pichincha near Esmeraldas, La Tola; meals $1.50-4; ☺7am-5pm) For stall after stall of some of Quito's most traditional (and cheapest) foods, head straight to the Mercado Central, located between Esmeraldas and Manabí. Here you'll find everything from *locro de papas* (potato soup served with avocado and cheese) and seafood, to *yaguarlocro* (potato and blood-sausage soup) and *fritada* (fried chunks of pork, served with hominy).

San Agustín   ECUADORIAN $$

(Map p678; ☏02-228-5082; http://heladeria sanagustin.net; Guayaquil N5-59 near Mejia; mains $5.50-12.50; ☺restaurant 10am-3pm, ice-cream shop 10am-5pm; 🕾) Kitschy religious icons and old-fashioned radios decorate this old-school classic serving Ecuadorian fare to bustling workday crowds.

Opt for first-rate *seco de chivo* (goat stew), *corvina* (sea bass) or *arroz marinero* (seafood rice) – there are so many options the menu takes an age to peruse. Follow these up with old-fashioned *helados de paila:* ice cream handmade in big copper bowls.

Café Dios No Muere   CAJUN $$

(Map p678; cnr Junín & Flores; mains $7.50-12.50; ☺8:30am-10pm Mon-Sat) The Louisiana native who owns this eccentrically designed restaurant attached to a 17th-century monastery takes pride in the quality of the ingredients cooked up in a kitchen that's squeezed into a corner on the ground floor. Space fills up fast, as there are only a handful of tables on two tiny floors, plus a few alleyway tables.

Tianguez   ECUADORIAN $$

(Map p678; Plaza San Francisco; mains $9-14.50; ☺9am-6:30pm; 🕾) Tucked into the stone arches beneath the Iglesia y Convento de San Francisco, this excellent cafe prepares tasty Ecuadorian appetizers (tamales, soups, quinoa salads) as well as heartier mains. The breakfasts, and particularly the coffee, are excellent, and tables on the plaza are perfect for people-watching. The handicrafts outlet of Tianguez (p692) is alongside.

Café Mosaico   INTERNATIONAL $$$

(Map p678; ☏02-254-2871; https://cafemosaico ecuador.com; Samaniego N8-95 near Antepara, Parque Itchimbia; mains $15-17; ☺4-11pm Mon-Wed, 1-11pm Thu-Sat, 1-10:30pm Sun) Serving up a mix of Ecuadorian, Greek and Mexican fare near Parque Itchimbia, vine-covered Mosaico is famed for its magnificent views. The open-sided terrace is great for a sundowner and there's one of the city's best selections of picking platters to go with the view-gazing. There are vegan options available, too, and live music on Fridays and Saturdays from 8:30pm.

Vista Hermosa   INTERNATIONAL $$$

(Map p678; ☏02-295-1401; http://vista hermosa.ec; Mejía 453, 5th fl; mains $13-28; ☺1pm-midnight Mon-Sat, noon-8pm Sun) A much-loved spot in El Centro, Vista Hermosa (Beautiful View) delivers the goods with a magnificent 360-degree panorama over the Old Town from its open rooftop terrace. Ecuadorian specials include *seco de chivo* (goat stew). Live music on Friday and Saturday from 10pm adds to the magic. Arrive early to beat the crowds.

There is another **Vista Hermosa** (Map p678; https://vistahermosa.ec/; Samaniego s/n, Parque Itchimbia; mains $13-28; ☺3pm-midnight Mon-Sat) up by Parque Itchimbia serving up similar food and impressive views (truth be told, the views are still loftier here).

✗ La Mariscal

Fried Bananas   ECUADORIAN $

(Map p688; 📱02-223-5208; www.newfried bananas.com; Foch E4-150, Mariscal Sucre, New Town; mains $6-10; ⊘12:30-8pm Mon-Sat) For innovative Ecuadorian food at a reasonable price close to Mariscal Sucre, check out this atmospheric restaurant where the namesake bananas help shape dishes such as delectable shrimps with fried bananas and vodka, and flambéed bananas with honey and cinnamon. The pastas and salads are good, too.

El Maple   VEGETARIAN $

(Map p688; 📱02-290-0000; www.elmaple.com; Pinto E7-68 near Almagro, Mariscal Sucre, New Town; mains $4.50-8.50; ⊘11am-10pm Mon & Tue, to 10:30pm Wed-Sat, 10am-6pm Sun; 🖉) This well-loved restaurant serves good vegetarian food with global influences (burritos, *thali*, Asian noodle dishes, creamy pastas, burgers, sandwiches and salads). There's a cheery

dining room with a maple-tree mural on the wall and shelves of books, and outdoor tables in a pretty courtyard.

El Cafecito   CAFE $

(Map p688; 📱02-223-4862; www.cafecito.net; Cordero 1124, Mariscal Sucre, New Town; snacks & light lunches $3-8; ⊘8am-10pm Mon-Sat, to 8pm Sun; 🛜) Inside a yellow colonial house, this cafe is known for its charm, serving breakfasts, sandwiches and great homemade desserts. The coffee served here is produced in Mindo and roasted on-site; other specialty coffees are also available to sample.

La Union   BAKERY $

(Map p688; cnr Reina Victoria & Av Colón, Mariscal Sucre, New Town; sandwiches & cakes $2-4; ⊘6am-10pm) Bustling La Union always packs a crowd, with its glass displays of croissants, berry tarts and ice cream, plus filling sandwiches.

Mariscal Sucre

Cosa Nostra
ITALIAN $$

(Map p688; ☑02-252-7145; https://pizzeria cosanostra.ec; cnr Baquerizo Moreno & Almagro, Mariscal Sucre, New Town; mains $11-18; ⊙12:30-3:30pm & 6-11pm Mon-Wed, 12:30-4pm & 6-11pm Thu & Sat, 12:30-4pm & 6-11:30pm Fri, 12:30-3:30pm & 6-10pm Sun; 🛜) Italian-owned Cosa Nostra has a pleasant front patio, cozy dining room and nearly three-dozen varieties of pizza piled with generous toppings and fired up in a brick oven – we consider it the best in town. It has good gnocchi and other pastas, and tiramisu for dessert.

Magic Bean
INTERNATIONAL $$

(Map p688; ☑02-256-6181; www.facebook. com/TheMagicBeanQuito; Foch E5-08 near Mera, Mariscal Sucre, New Town; breakfasts $3-9, mains $8-15; ⊙8am-10pm; 🛜) Magic Bean packs a crowd with its ample American-style breakfasts and lunches, plus frothy juices, coffees and desserts, best enjoyed on the covered front terrace. Particularly recommended for the smoothies, fruit salad with granola and the great range of burgers.

Baalbek
MIDDLE EASTERN $$$

(Map p688; ☑02-255-2766; http://restaurant baalbek.com/wp/; Av 6 de Diciembre N23-103 near Wilson, Mariscal Sucre, New Town; mains $7-25; ⊙noon-5pm Sun-Tue, to 10:30pm Wed-Sat) Authentic, although expensive, Lebanese fare served up quickly in a comfortable and contemporary dining room with a Middle Eastern soundtrack and aesthetic. Most of the menu items can be ordered as a half or full plate, which makes family-style sharing,

perhaps with a mezze platter ($15 to $25) between two, the way to go.

Achiote
ECUADORIAN $$$

(Map p688; ☑02-250-1743; http://achiote.com. ec; Rodriguez 282 near Reina Victoria, Mariscal Sucre, New Town; mains $12.50-30; ⊙noon-9:45pm) Ecuadorian dishes with an upscale twist in a warmly lit contemporary setting. Empanadas, ceviches, rich seafood stews and *llapingachos* (fried pancakes of mashed potatoes with cheese) are all first-rate. Live music Friday to Monday nights.

🍴 La Floresta & Around

Parque de las Tripas
STREET FOOD $

(Parque Navarro Food Stalls; Map p684; cnr Ladrón de Guevara & Iberia, La Floresta, New Town; mains $2-4; ⊙4-11pm) To sample some of Quito's most authentic and traditional cooking, head to this attractive park in La Floresta where every evening food stalls are set up selling freshly prepared *tripa mishqui* (grilled cow intestines), *seco de pollo* (chicken stew), empanadas and *morocho* (a kind of spiced corn porridge). Stall holders are happy to let you taste before you buy.

Jürgen Cafe
DUTCH $$

(Map p684; www.jurgencafe.com; cnr Coruña & Valladolid, La Floresta, New Town; mains $3.75-19; ⊙7am-8pm Mon-Sat, to 2:30pm Sun) Owned and operated by fourth-generation baker from Holland Jürgen Spelier, this casually sophisticated restaurant with clean lines and blond-wood decor does especially good breakfasts and brunches; traditional Dutch pancakes

---

Mariscal Sucre

and chicken and waffles are among the highlights. The coffees and eclectic line of bakery products could tempt you to linger here.

Zao
ASIAN $$
(Map p684; ☏02-252-3496; www.zaoquito.com; Rivet N30-145 near Whymper, New Town; mains $8-22, menú $15; ☺12:30-4pm & 7-11:30pm Mon-Sat, 12:30-3:30pm Sun) Adorned with carved wooden screens and statues resembling samurai, Zao is a buzzing spot serving up quality Asian fusion dishes such as sushi, rice noodles, spring rolls and Thai-style curries.

La Cleta Bici Café
CAFE $$
(Map p684; ☏02-223-3505; www.facebook.com/lacleta.bicicleta; Lugo N24-250 near Guipuzcoa, La Floresta, New Town; pizzas $6-14; ☺11am-11pm Mon-Thu, to 11:45pm Fri, 5:30-11pm Sat; ☎) Bicycle lovers shouldn't miss this small, cleverly designed cafe-restaurant, where nearly everything (chairs, bar stools, tables, hanging lamps) is fabricated from bicycle parts. The wheel-shaped menu includes pizzas, sandwiches, great coffee, wine and other drinks.

La Briciola
ITALIAN $$
(Map p684; ☏02-254-5157; http://labriciola.com.ec; cnr Isabel La Católica & Salazar, La Floresta, New Town; mains $11-17; ☺noon-midnight) This longtime favorite occupies a huge but attractively laid-out space and has an outstanding varied menu of pastas and pizzas, plus other Italian faves. The portions are large, and the wine selection from Italy, Chile and Argentina is fairly priced. Reservations recommended.

Z(inc)
INTERNATIONAL $$$
(Map p684; ☏02-256-2846; www.zincquito.com; Rivet N30 near Whymper, New Town; mains $13-22; ☺noon-midnight Tue-Thu, noon-2am Fri, 7pm-2am Sat, 10:30am-3:30pm Sun) Equal parts restaurant and bar, Z(inc) has a multilevel industrial-chic interior of untreated timber, dark metals and exposed brick. It's frequented by a well-dressed clientele. Sip a lychee-infused cocktail on the front patio before heading inside for brick-oven flatbread pizza, burgers, tempura prawns and other dishes ideal for sharing.

✖ La Pradera

★ Zazu
FUSION $$$
(Map p684; ☏02-254-3559; www.zazuquito.com; Aguilera 331, La Pradera, New Town; mains $13-25, tasting menu $70; ☺12:30-3:30pm & 6:30-11pm Mon-Fri, 6:30-11pm Sat) One of Quito's best restaurants, Zazu serves beautifully prepared seafood dishes, grilled meats and ceviches in a stylish setting of light brick, ambient electronica and an inviting, backlit bar. The menu showcases the best of Ecuadorian cuisine with dishes such as Andean grains and veg, confit guinea pig empanada and seafood tamale.

🍷 Drinking & Nightlife

Most of the *farra* (nightlife) in Quito is concentrated in and around Mariscal Sucre. A weekend night wandering La Ronda, a cobblestone lane lined with bars and restaurants in the Old Town, shouldn't be missed. For more relaxed, low-key hangouts, head to one of the sophisticated spots in La Floresta, Guápulo or Benalcázar. A spate of microbreweries have opened recently in the city.

Isveglio
CAFE
(Map p684; www.isveglio.com; Isabel La Católica N24-682 near La Coruña, La Floresta, New Town; coffee & snacks $2-6; ☺9am-8:30pm Mon-Fri, 11am-8:30pm Sat, 2-8pm Sun) ✐ The standard of artisan coffee has been on an upward trajectory in Quito and Isveglio is at the forefront of the movement. Cafe, coffee education center and barista training school, it serves up organic brews from Ecuador's various coffee-growing regions, plus some beans from further afield.

Baristas invite you to smell and taste the beans they are using, and tell you about the origins. All this in a bustling, modern space with a patio out front. There is another branch of **Isveglio** (Map p678; Venezuela N3-157 near Espejo, Old Town; ☺9:30am-7:30pm Mon-Sat, 10:30am-6pm Sun) in the Old Town too.

Ochoymedio
CAFE
(Map p684; www.ochoymedio.net; cnr Valladolid N24-353 & Vizcaya, La Floresta, New Town; drinks & snacks $2-6; ☺3-9pm) This colorful cafe with its flower-filled terrace on a quiet street junction is La Floresta's most buzzing, so it must be doing something right. Attached to the cinema of the same name, this place is primarily for drinks, whether that be an espresso or liqueur coffee (the coffee comes from their own organic farm) or a prefilm glass of wine.

Bandido Brewing
MICROBREWERY
(Map p678; http://bandidobrewing.com; Olmedo E1-136 near Cevallos, San Blas, Old Town; ☺4-11pm

Mon-Fri, 2-11pm Sat) These guys from Oregon produce their own creative brews such as La Gran Calabaza Imperial Pumpkin Ale (made with cinnamon, cloves and pumpkin spice) and La Gua.Pa (an American Pale Ale flavored with *guayusa*, a tea leaf native to the Ecuadorian Amazon). The bar has a vaguely Gothic feel, with stone walls, wooden benches and even a small chapel. The menu includes freshly baked pizzas and bar snacks, and there's live music on Tuesdays from 7pm. Happy hour is from 4pm to 7pm.

Q   BAR
(Map p688; Foch E6-11 near Reina Victoria, Plaza Foch, Mariscal Sucre, New Town; ⊙4pm-midnight Mon-Thu, to 3am Fri & Sat, noon-10pm Sun; 🛜) Fashion types gather for midweek cocktails at this hip bar and restaurant, where the ceiling is decorated to resemble Amazonian vegetation ('Q' stands for *quinde*, Spanish for 'hummingbird'). The service is great, there's live music most nights and a DJ plays lounge-style beats on Saturdays.

Ananké   BAR
(Map p684; www.anankeguapulo.com; Camino de Orellana 781, Guápulo, New Town; ⊙6pm-midnight Mon-Thu, to 1am Fri & Sat) Well worth the trip out here, Ananké is a stylish and warmly lit bar/pizzeria with small, colorfully decorated rooms spread out over an old two-story house. It has a small terrace (complete with fireplace) and several good nooks for hiding away with a beer and a few friends. When the fog clears, the views over Guápulo are superb.

Dirty Sanchez   LOUNGE
(Map p688; www.dirtysanchezbar.com; Pinto E7-38 near Reina Victoria, Mariscal Sucre, New Town; ⊙3pm-midnight Mon-Wed, to 2:30am Thu-Sat) The cheekily named Dirty Sanchez is a small art-filled lounge with a bohemian vibe. Decent cocktails (and coffee), better music and a laid-back crowd make this place a standout.

Bungalow 6   CLUB
(Map p688; www.bungalow6ecuador.com; Almagro N24-151 & Calama, Mariscal Sucre, New Town; ⊙8pm-3am Wed-Sat) A popular nightspot among foreigners and locals alike, Bungalow 6 often features long lines on weekends and Wednesday ladies' night (gals drink for free until 10pm). It plays a good mix of beats, and has a small but lively dance floor and a warren of colorfully decorated rooms (with table football, pool table and small outdoor terrace) upstairs.

La Reserva   CRAFT BEER
(Map p684; cnr Roca & Bosmediano, Bellavista, New Town; ⊙5pm-midnight Tue-Sat) Some 30 of Ecuador's top microbrews are served at La Reserva, backed up by a range of sharing platters ($6 to $9).

☆ Entertainment

Quito's theaters stage a variety of dramas, dance performances and concerts, so check ahead to see what's on. Look out too for performances by local musicians playing everything from salsa and merengue to rock, jazz and blues. Several bars and restaurants in the Old Town and Mariscal Sucre have regular live-music nights.

★Ochoymedio   CINEMA
(Map p684; 📞02-292-4720; www.ochoymedio. net; cnr Valladolid N24-353 & Vizcaya, La Floresta, New Town) This Floresta film house shows art films (often in English) and has occasional dance, theater and live music. There's a great cafe (p690) attached.

La Juliana   LIVE MUSIC
(Map p684; www.lajuliana.com.ec; Av 12 de Octubre N24-722 near Coruña, La Floresta, New Town; admission incl drink $25; ⊙9pm-2:30am Fri & Sat) In an old converted house, La Juliana is a colorfully decorated space with a good mix of bands (rock, salsa, merengue) lighting up the dance floor most weekend nights.

Café Libro   LIVE MUSIC
(Map p688; 📞02-250-3214; www.cafelibro.com; Leonidas Plaza Gutiérrez N23-56 near Wilson, Mariscal Sucre, New Town; cover charge $5-10; ⊙12:30-2:30pm Mon, 12:30-2:30pm & 5pm-midnight Tue-Thu, 12:30-2:30pm & 6pm-2am Fri, 6pm-2am Sat) Live music, poetry readings, discussions, contemporary dance, tango, jazz and other performances draw an arts-loving crowd to this long-running venue. There are regular tango classes ($10) and *milongas* (tango

---

GOING TO A GAME

Located in the northern part of the city near the shopping mall Quicentro, **Estadio Olimpico Atahualpa** (cnr 6 de Diciembre & Naciones Unidas) is the city's main soccer stadium and seats 37,750. Ecuador's national team, Deportivo Quito (www.deportivoquito.com) and El Nacional (www.elnacional.ec) play here. Take an Ecovia bus to the Estadio stop.

dance sessions) on Wednesday and Saturday nights.

Shopping

There are some excellent crafts stores in Mariscal Sucre. If buying from street stalls, you should bargain; in the fancier stores, prices are normally fixed. Note that souvenirs are a little cheaper outside Quito, if you have the time and inclination to search them out.

Centros comerciales (shopping malls) are similar to their North American counterparts, and sell international brands.

★ Tianguez   ARTS & CRAFTS
(Map p678; www.tianguez.org; Plaza San Francisco, Old Town; ⏲ 9am-6pm) Next to Tianguez cafe (p687), this fair-trade shop sells a wide selection of quality handmade crafts from across Ecuador. Items are arranged by region, with information on the techniques used to produce them.

Ag   JEWELRY
(Map p688; Mera 614 near Carrión, Mariscal Sucre, New Town; ⏲ 10am-1:30pm & 2:30-9:30pm Mon-Fri, 2:30-6:30pm Sat) Ag's selection of rare, handmade silver jewelry from throughout South America is outstanding. You'll also find antiques.

Librería del Fondo Carlos Fuentes   BOOKS
(Map p688; ☎ 02-254-9817; www.fce.com.ec; Av 6 de Diciembre N24-04 near Wilson, Mariscal Sucre, New Town; ⏲ 10am-8pm Mon-Fri, to 7pm Sat, to 2pm Sun) One of Ecuador's best bookshops is located in the former mansion of Galo Plaza Lasso, Ecuadorian president from 1948 to 1952. An excellent selection of titles is displayed beneath the original wood-paneled ceiling and chandeliers, and even the fireplaces have been retained. Up a sweeping staircase there's a gallery space, and there's also a peaceful garden cafe.

Casa Mariscal   ARTS & CRAFTS
(Map p688; Mera N23-54 near General Baquedano, Mariscal Sucre, New Town; ⏲ 10am-7pm Mon-Sat) An artists' collective selling beautiful handmade jewelry, prints, bags, textiles and other handicrafts.

Galería Latina   ARTS & CRAFTS
(Map p688; www.galerialatina-quito.com; Mera N23-69 near General Banquedano, Mariscal Sucre, New Town; ⏲ 10am-7pm Mon-Sat, 11am-6pm Sun) One of the finest handicraft and clothing shops in the city, Galería Latina has a huge selection of beautifully made pieces: tagua carvings, colorful Andean weavings, textiles, jewelry, sweaters and handmade items from across Latin America. Prices are high, but so is the craftsmanship.

Mercado Artesanal La Mariscal   ARTS & CRAFTS
(Map p688; Washington btwn Mera & Reina Victoria, Mariscal Sucre, New Town; ⏲ 8am-7pm Mon-Sat, to 6pm Sun) Half a city block filled by more than 200 crafts stalls, with good prices and mixed quality. It's great for souvenirs.

ℹ Information

DANGERS & ANNOYANCES
Quito has its share of robberies and petty crime, but the dangers can be minimized by taking a few precautions.

➡ Mariscal Sucre remains a target for muggers and pickpockets, though Plaza Foch and the surrounding streets now have a visible police presence. Take a taxi after dark when traveling more than a few blocks.

➡ Because most of the shops and restaurants in the Old Town close in the evening, it can feel sketchy wandering some of its outlying dimly lit blocks alone. Pickpocketing, the old-fashioned mustard scam and snatch-and-run robberies do happen here, so keep your wits about you.

➡ Use ATMs in the daytime, choose locations with other people about (shopping malls, banks etc) and stay alert upon exiting.

➡ Pickpockets are a problem on the trolley bus system – keep an eye out while riding, and avoid taking it during rush hour and after dark. Always keep your bag close (on your lap); the slicing open of bags (even while between your legs/under your seat, or on your back) is common practice.

EMERGENCIES
Police Station (☎ 02-244-7070; Amazonas N35-115, Parque La Carolina, New Town; ⏲ 24hr) On the west edge of Parque La Carolina

Servicio de Seguridad Turística (Tourist Security Service; ☎ 02-295-5785; Chile btwn Moreno & Venezuela, Plaza Grande, Old Town; ⏲ 10am-6pm)

MEDICAL SERVICES
Take out overseas health insurance before you travel to cover any medical expenses. Many doctors and hospitals will expect payment in cash.

Hospital Metropolitano (☎ 02-399-8000; www.hospitalmetropolitano.org; Mariana de Jesús near Arteta, San Gabriel, New Town)

ℹ️ GETTING INTO TOWN FROM THE AIRPORT

Taxi prices into the city center are fixed and cost $26 to Mariscal Sucre or the Old Town. After exiting customs there's a small kiosk with the rates conveniently posted. Depending on the time of day and traffic, the trip takes between 45 minutes and one hour 15 minutes.

Every half-hour, the **Aeroservicios** (📞 02-604-3500; www.aeroservicios.com.ec; cnr Av Amazonas s/n & Av La Prensa; 1 way $8; ⏰ 3:30am-11:30pm Mon-Fri, 4am-10:30pm Sat & Sun) shuttle bus makes the 30-minute trip between the airport and Parque Bicentenario (the old airport) at the northern end of Avenida Amazonas. From here, taxis are cheaper into Mariscal Sucre or the Old Town, respectively only 9km or 15km away.

The least expensive and least convenient alternative is to take a public bus ($2) to or from the **Río Coca bus terminal** (Río Coca near Las Hiedras) north of the Mariscal.

Hospital Voz Andes (📞 02-397-1000; www.hospitalvozandes.org; Villalengua Oe2-37 near Av 10 de Agosto, La Carolina, New Town)

Dr John Rosenberg (📞 099-973-9734, 02-252-1104; rosenberg.john@gmail.com; Foch 476 near Almagro)

MONEY

There are a few *casas de cambio* (currency-exchange bureaus) in the New Town, along Avenida Amazonas between Avenida Patria and Orellana, and there are dozens of banks throughout town.

Banco de Guayaquil (Av Amazonas near Veintimilla, Mariscal Sucre, New Town)

Banco de Guayaquil (Av Colón near Reina Victoria, Mariscal Sucre, New Town)

Banco del Pacífico (cnr Guayaquil & Chile, Old Town)

Banco del Pacífico (cnr Av 12 de Octubre & Coruña, La Floresta, New Town)

Banco del Pichincha (Guayaquil near Manabí, Old Town)

Western Union (Av de la República 450 near Martin Carrión, La Pradera, New Town)

Western Union (Av Colón 1333 near Foch, Colón, New Town)

POST

Post office (Map p688; www.correosdelecuador.gob.ec; cnr Reina Victoria & Av Colón, Mariscal Sucre, New Town; ⏰ 8am-6pm Mon-Fri, to noon Sat & Sun)

TOURIST INFORMATION

Instituto Geográfico Militar (IGM; Map p684; 📞 02-397-5100; www.igm.gob.ec; Seniergues E4-676 near Gral Telmo Paz y Miño, Eugenio Espejo, New Town; ⏰ map sales room 7:30am-4:30pm Mon-Thu, 7am-3pm Fri) Good for getting maps of different areas of Ecuador.

Quito Tourism (Corporación Metropolitana de Turismo; Map p678; 📞 02-257-2445; www.quito-turismo.gob.ec; Venezuela near Espejo, Plaza Grande, Old Town; ⏰ 9am-6pm Mon-Sat, 9:30-4:30pm Sun; 📶)

Tourist Information (📞 02-281-8363; aeropuerto@quito-tourism.gob.ec; Aeropuerto Internacional Mariscal Sucre) At the airport.

Tourist Information (📞 02-382-4815; quitumbre@quito-turismo.gob.ec; Terminal Terrestre Quitumbre) At Terminal Terrestre Quitumbre.

Tourist Information (Map p688; cnr Reina Victoria & Foch; ⏰ 9am-6pm Mon-Sat) Small booth on Plaza Foch in Mariscal Sucre.

ℹ️ Getting There & Away

AIR

Quito's **Aeropuerto Internacional Mariscal Sucre** (📞 02-395-4200; www.aeropuertoquito.aero) is 37km northeast of the city in a broad valley near Tababela. It's a modern facility with the longest runway in Latin America and the second-highest control tower (after Cancun); however, the terminal is significantly smaller than Guayaquil's. There is a tourist information booth (p693) in the arrivals hall, and the terminal also has a hotel, **Wyndham Quito Airport** (📞 02-395-8000; www.wyndhamquito.com; Terminal Aeropuerto Internacional Mariscal Sucre; r from $120; 📶).

BUS

Quito has two main bus terminals (and a smaller third terminal) that handle arrivals and departures to destinations nationwide, and they are all a long way from the center (allow at least an hour by public transport, 30 minutes or more by taxi).

Terminal Terrestre Quitumbe

Located 10km southwest of the Old Town, **Terminal Terrestre Quitumbe** (cnr Cóndor Ñan & Sucre) handles the Central and Southern Andes, the coast, and the Oriente (ie Baños, Cuenca, Guayaquil, Coca and – aside from Otavalo and Mindo – most destinations of interest to travelers). It can be reached by Trole bus south to the last stop. A taxi costs about $12 to $15. There is a tourist information office located here.

Terminal Terrestre Carcelén

Located in the north, **Terminal Terrestre Carcelén** (Av Eloy Alfaro s/n) services Otavalo, Ibarra, Mindo, Santo Domingo, Tulcán and other northern destinations. To get here, take the Trole bus north to Carcelén at the end of the line. A taxi costs about $10 to $15.

Terminal Terrestre La Ofelia

Located in the north, **Terminal Terrestre La Ofelia** (cnr Vásquez de Cepeda & de los Arupos) services destinations to the northwest of Quito such as Nanegalito and Mindo, as well as Cayambe. To get here take the Metrobus north to the end of the line. A taxi costs around $10.

TRAIN

After massive investment, the country's **train network** (☑1-800-873-367; http://tren-ecuador.com; cnr Guayllabamba & Sincholagua,

Estación de Ferrocarril Chimbacalle, Chimbacalle) is once again ferrying passengers on slow-motion journeys through breathtaking high-altitude scenery. Routes include the **Tren de los Volcanes** (☑1-800-873-637; www.trenecuador.com; adult/child $53/37; ⊙8am-5:30pm Fri-Sun), which makes the round-trip to El Boliche in Cotopaxi National Park, and the luxurious **Tren Crucero** (Train of Wonders; ☑1-800-873-637; www.trenecuador.com; adult/child $1650/1485; ⊙Tue-Fri), a four-day, four-night luxury train tour from Quito to Guayaquil.

Trains depart from Quito's beautifully renovated **Estación de Ferrocarril Chimbacalle** (Chimbacalle Train Station; cnr Guayllabamba & Sincholagua) 2km south of the Old Town. Book tickets online or at the booking desk at Quito Tourism (p693).

BUSES FROM QUITO

DESTINATION	COST ($)	DURATION (HR)	FREQUENCY (DAILY)
Ambato	3-4	2½	every 10min
Atacames	9-10	7	6
Baños	4-5	3-4	every 30min or change in Ambato
Cayambe	2-3	2	every 10min
Coca	11-12	6 (via Jondachi), 9-10 (via Lago Agrio)	5 direct or change in Lago Agrio
Cuenca	11-13	9-10	every 30min
Esmeraldas	9	6-7	every 30min
Guayaquil	10-14	8	hourly
Huaquillas	17	11	hourly
Ibarra	4	2½-3	every 15min
Lago Agrio	10	7-8	every 45min
Latacunga	2	2	every 10min
Loja	18-21	14-15	hourly or change in Cuenca
Machala	13-14	10	hourly
Manta	12	8-9	hourly
Mindo	3	2	5 departures Mon-Fri, 9 Sat & Sun
Otavalo	3	2	hourly
Portoviejo	11	7	hourly
Puerto López	12-13	10-11	3
Puyo	8-9	5½	24
Riobamba	5-6	4	every 20min
San Lorenzo	10-11	6½	5
Santo Domingo	5-6	3	every 15min
Tena	7-8	5	every 1½hr
Tulcán	7-8	5	every 30min

ℹ Getting Around

BICYCLE

The city's bike-share program, **BiciQuito** (Map p684; ☎ 02-395-2300; www.biciquito.gob.ec; Av Amazonas N33-299 near Inglaterra, 1st fl, Agencia Metropolitana de Tránsito, Parque La Carolina, New Town; ⊗ 7am-7pm Mon-Fri, 8am-3pm Sat & Sun), is free but you'll need to register at the Agencia Metropolitana de Tránsito on Avendia Amazonas with a completed application form (downloaded from the website) and a color photocopy of your passport photo ID page and Ecuador entry stamp. Once you've registered you can pick up a bike from any of the rental stations.

Quito also has Sunday *ciclopaseos* when key streets are closed to car traffic.

BUS

Local buses ($0.25) operate from 6am to 9pm and are convenient since, despite designated stops, you can usually get on and off at any street corner. No route numbers, but the primary and final stops are posted in the front window. Keep a close watch on your bags and pockets. The green buses serve outlying districts and suburbs.

METRO

The first line of Quito's new underground rail transport system, the Metro de Quito (www.metrodequito.gob.ec), was under construction at the time of writing. The metro will connect Quitumbe in the south with El Labrador in the north in just 34 minutes, with 15 stops along the way, including Plaza San Francisco, La Almeda, El Ejido and La Carolina.

TROLE, ECOVÍA & METROBUS

Quito has three electric, wheelchair-accessible bus routes ($0.25): the Trole, the Ecovía and the Metrobus. Each runs north–south along one of Quito's three main thoroughfares, and each has designated stations and car-free lanes, making them speedy and efficient.

Trole Runs through the middle of the city, along Maldonado and Avenida 10 de Agosto. It links Carcelén bus terminal in the north with the Quitumbe bus terminal, southwest of the Old Town. In the Old Town, southbound trolleys take the west route along Guayaquil, while northbound trolleys take Flores and Montúfar.

Ecovía Runs along the eastern side, Avenida 6 de Diciembre, between Río Coca (from where you can connect to a bus to the airport) in the north and Quitumbe bus terminal in the south.

Metrobus This route runs along Avenida América between La Ofelia bus terminal in the north to Quitumbe bus terminal in the south.

AROUND QUITO

📷 02

Quito makes a great base for exploring the region's striking geography and biodiversity, with excellent day trips available to volcanoes and remote forest reserves. South America's most fabled market (Otavalo), the sublime Cotopaxi volcano, the cloud forests around Mindo and the Papallacta hot springs (en route to the Oriente) can also be visited in a long day trip.

La Mitad del Mundo

Appealing perhaps to our childish belief that there is an actual line painted around the world and that an equatorial visit should be checked off a bucket list like skydiving or a boat trip to Antarctica, the area around the so-called 'Middle of the World' has developed into a touristy, circus-like environment. There are food and handicraft stalls, bustling weekend crowds and an assortment of sights and attractions, few of which relate to the equator.

◉ Sights

Mitad del Mundo   LANDMARK
(Middle of the World City; www.mitaddelmundo. com; Av Galarza Km13.5; adult/child $5/2.50; ⊗ 9am-6pm) At the center of the Mitad del Mundo stands the centerpiece of the park: a 30m-high, stone trapezoidal **monument** topped by a brass globe containing a viewing platform and a museum, which provides a good introduction to the *indígena* peoples of Ecuador through dioramas, clothing displays and photographs. On the lower floors are new interactive exhibits examining the science behind the myths of the equator.

Museo Solar Inti Ñan   MUSEUM
(http://museointinan.com.ec/en/; adult/child $4/2; ⊗ 9:30am-5pm) A few hundred meters north of the entrance to the main Mitad del Mundo complex, this amusing museum has meandering outdoor exhibits of astronomical geography and explanations of the importance of Ecuador's geographical location. One of the highlights is the 'solar chronometer,' a unique instrument made in 1865 that shows precise astronomical and conventional time, as well as the month, day and season – all by using the rays of the sun.

ECUADOR LA MITAD DEL MUNDO

WORTH A TRIP

PAPALLACTA

Slip into this tiny village's steamy, therapeutic waters to soothe sore muscles or combat the high-altitude chill. At Termas de Papallacta, more than a dozen sparkling pools offer the country's most luxurious thermal-baths experience. The main spa complex is 3km above the village of Papallacta and is a good day trip from Quito, 67km (two hours) away. Be prepared for cold nights and intense sun.

The **Termas de Papallacta** (📞 06-289-5060; www.termaspapallacta.com) 🏊 is the main event here, but the following places (in order up from the Quito–Baeza road junction in Papallacta village) also have thermal pools: **La Choza de Don Wilson** (📞 06-289-5027; www.hosteriachozapapallacta.com; mains $5-9; ⏰ 8am-10pm; 📶), **Hostería Pampallacta Thermales** (📞 06-289-5014; www.pampallactatermales.com; s/d incl breakfast from $36/75; 🅿 📶 🏊) and **Hostal Antisana** (📞 06-289-5016; s/d incl breakfast $20/40; 🅿 📶 🏊).

Any of the buses from Quito heading toward Baeza, Tena or Lago Agrio can drop you off in Papallacta, as can the occasional Papallacta bus.

ℹ Getting There & Away

Quito sprawls almost the entire 22km north to La Mitad del Mundo. It's easy to get here on public transportation: take a metrobus ($0.25) from the city north to the last stop, Ofelia station, and then transfer to the Mitad del Mundo bus (another $0.40), which is clearly marked. The entire trip takes one to 1½ hours.

Volcán Pululahua

The 3383-hectare **Reserva Geobotánica Pululahua** (cnr Kingman & Galarza; ⏰ 8am-5pm) FREE lies about 4km northwest of La Mitad del Mundo. The most interesting part of the reserve is the volcanic crater of the extinct Pululahua. This was apparently formed in ancient times, when the cone of the volcano collapsed, leaving a huge crater some 400m deep and 5km across. The crater's flat and fertile bottom is used for agriculture. The crater is open to the west side, through which moisture-laden winds from the Pacific Ocean blow dramatically; it is sometimes difficult to see the crater because of the swirling clouds and mist. The moist winds, combined with the crater's steep walls, create a variety of microclimates, and the vegetation on the fertile volcanic slopes is both rampant and diverse. There are many flowers and a variety of bird species.

The easiest way to reach the Reserva Geobotánica Pululahua entrance, just before Mirador de Ventanillas, is by inexpensive organized tour. Most arrange this from Quito, including a look around the Mitad del Mundo complex, although you can arrange tours at Mitad del Mundo. Taxis from Mitad del Mundo are around $5. Public buses bound for San Miguel de los Bancos drop you within a 20-minute walk of the entrance.

NORTHERN HIGHLANDS

Follow the snaking Panamericana past florid Cayambe to the vibrant market town of Otavalo and surrounding indigenous villages. As the spine of the Andes bends north from Quito, volcanic peaks punctuate valleys blanketed by flower farms and sugarcane fields. This is Ecuador's beating heart and a cradle of Andean culture: artisans produce their wares using methods unaltered for generations, and visitors find some of the country's best deals here, on everything from leather goods to traditional weavings.

High-altitude landscapes surrender to steamy lowlands in the west, a rich transitional zone where coffee plantations flourish in the spectacular but politically contested Intag Valley. Further south, laid-back Mindo is a base for bird-watching, hiking and river romps. Remote jungle lodges are scattered around the region for those looking to retreat deeper into nature. Wherever you go, off-the-beaten-path adventures, sustainable community-tourism initiatives and volunteering opportunities are close by.

Mindo

📞 02 / POP 4000 / ELEV 1250M

If there's anything Mindo's about, it's the birds. Perhaps you noticed the Andean cock-of-the-rock statue at the town entrance? Or the giant painted hummingbird in the central plaza? Birders come from around the globe to revel in the species density present in and around this very special valley.

With its lovely setting surrounded by forested mountains, this pint-sized *pueblo* (small town) has become a deservedly popular destination for backpackers. It's conveniently located just off the main highway between Quito and Esmeraldas, with a curvy road that descends to the rather ramshackle yet immensely likable town center. It's become a site of sensual sensations, from aromatic coffees to chocolates that dazzle the taste buds and tickle your nose (several tours of each process are available). Hikers and weekenders from Quito and beyond flock here, and locals have created an impressive range of activities (rafting, tubing, ziplining) for enjoying the surrounding cloud forest.

◉ Sights & Activities

Tarabita   CABLE CAR
(road to Cascada de Nambillo; $5; ⊘ 8:30am-4pm Tue-Sun) This unique, small motor-powered (2002 Nissan!) cable car takes you soaring across a lush river basin over thick cloud forest to the Bosque Protector Mindo-Nambillo, where you can hike to a number of waterfalls. Not for the acrophobic, the wire basket on steel cables glides 152m above the ground. Your ticket includes a map with routes; while the Cascada Nambillo is the closest (2km), it's the series of six waterfalls (Ondinas, Guarumos, Colibrí, Madre, Maderos, Reina) that's really worth it.

Mariposario de Mindo   BUTTERFLY FARM
(☑ 099-920-2124; www.mariposasdemindo.com; Via al Mariposario; $7.50; ⊘ 9am-4pm; P ⚑) Mindo's best butterfly garden is like walking through a paint factory with the fans set to slow – a stunning kaleidoscope. Visit in the warmest part of the day, around 11am, when butterflies are most active. If it's raining, the butterflies are dormant and you can use your ticket another day. Kids will love scaling the observation towers, and feeding the giant koi.

Mindo Canopy
Adventure   ADVENTURE SPORTS
(☑ 099-453-0624; www.mindocanopy.com; Via las Cascadas Km 2.5; 2½hr circuit per adult/child $20/$12) Halfway up the road to the *tarabita* (cable car), this long-running Costa Rican-owned operation has 10 different cables ranging from 20m to 400m in length, enabling you to fly above the trees – an activity that gets faster in the rain.

Bird-Watching
With more than 500 bird species, the area around Mindo has become a major

destination for bird-watching. If you don't know your rufous-headed chachalaca from your rufous-fronted wood-quail and your interest is casual, you can access trails on your own from Casa Amarilla (Yellow House), located a couple of blocks from the *parque central*. In addition to a wide variety of birds, locals claim to have spotted pumas, spectacled bears and monkeys here.

Keep in mind that bird-watching is an activity for early risers, generally taking place from 6am to 10am. And the majority of the top flight bird-watching doesn't happen in Mindo itself but in privately owned reserves (most have admission costs) scattered throughout the area, anywhere from a hike to a two-hour drive away.

Locally there are many competent, professional guides. Most charge a minimum of $50 to $75, and depending on the number in the group and the particular reserve, that could go up to $100 or more per day.

Irman Arias (☑ 099-170-8720; www.mindo birdguide.com)

Julia Patiño (☑ 098-616-2816; www.mindo birdwatching.wordpress.com)

Danny Jumbo (☑ 099-328-0769; www.mindo birding.com)

🛏 Sleeping & Eating

Caskaffesu   GUESTHOUSE $
(☑ 099-386-7154, 02-217-0100; www.caskaffesu. net; Sixto Duran Ballen near Av Quito; r per person incl breakfast $25-30; ☎) Run by a kind Ecuadorian, Caskaffesu is a lovely low-key refuge just off the main road in the center of town. The two stories of brightly painted adobe rooms have a vaguely Mediterranean/colonial feel and surround a small, leafy courtyard. The complex features one room which is fully compatible for people with a disability, with access ramp and shower.

★ El Monte
Sustainable Lodge   LODGE $$$
(☑ 02-217-0102, 099-308-4675; www.ecuador cloudforest.com; cabins per person incl meals & activities $140; P ☎ ⊠) ✔ Run by a warmhearted and knowledgeable American-Ecuadorian couple, El Monte is a lush ecofriendly retreat with six lovely, private riverside cabins. The aesthetic is contemporary, with lots of wood and natural tones. Three cabins sleep up to four people and have bathtubs. Located 3km south of Mindo along a winding dirt road, it's reached by a *tarabita* over the Río Mindo.

★**Casa Divina**   CABIN $$$
(☎ 099-172-5874; www.mindocasadivina.com; s/d
incl breakfast & dinner $140; 🅿 🛜) 🏄 Highly
recommended for seclusion and tranquility
with a splash of luxury is this small complex
of two-story wooden cabins 2km from town.
Porches with hammocks provide roosts for
bird-watching, and on-site trails expand the
observation territory. The owners are lead-
ers in the local sustainable-tourism effort,
but don't skimp on comfort, as the delicious
breakfasts (banana pancakes, yuca bread)
prove.

✖ Eating

★**Mishqui Quinde Heladería**   CAFE $
(Vicente Aguirre cnr Gallo de la Peña, 'Gourmet Av-
enue'; ice creams $2; ⊙ 11:30am-7pm Wed-Mon)
Oswaldo has moved from the old van to a
more permanent site, but it's still all quinoa,
all the time: in burgers ($4 to $5), pudding,
homemade sorbet and shakes where you
can mix it with other flavors like blackberry,
chocolate and passion fruit. The five-juice
Cuicocha Lake drink is a surefire hit, but the
chocolate liqueur shouldn't be missed.

★**Yumbo's Chocolate**   CAFE $
(☎ 098-000-4417, 099-063-6345; www.yumbos
chocolate.com; Av Quito; ⊙ 8am-9pm) Own-
er Claudio Ponce works with an all-female
cooperative of cacao growers near Timbiré,
Mujeres Para El Futuro (Women for the
Future), bringing the heat from the Pacif-
ic Coast straight to your Mindo mug, with
the best-tasting *chocolate caliente* in town.
There's also a short Spanish-English in-store
chocolate tour ($8), a store, and even a choc-
olate stout from Quito's Pileus Brewery.

El Quetzal   ECUADORIAN $$
(www.elquetzaldemindo.com; Av 9 de Octubre;
mains $7-12; ⊙ 8am-9pm; 🛜) This laid-back
coffee shop and restaurant, easily the
largest in town (for better or worse), has
excellent coffee plus locally grown beans
and chocolate for sale (with a handy tasting table), a selection of breakfasts and
sandwiches, and some Ecuadorian main
courses. The American owner's pride is her
famous brownie.

ℹ Information

The San Miguel de los Bancos ATM accepts
most cards on the Mastercard and Maestro
networks but not Visa. The Banco Pichincha
ATM on the plaza does accept Visa and most
other foreign cards.

ℹ Getting There & Away

There are several daily buses to Quito ($3.10,
2½ hours, 6:30am, 11am, 1:45pm, 3pm and 5pm
Monday to Friday), run by Cooperativa Flor de
Valle, which leave from the terminal a few blocks
uphill on Av Quito from the main plaza – you
can hop out at Nanegalito ($1.50) to grab a
camioneta (pickup or light truck) to other area
destinations.

Taxis, regulated with fixed prices, line up on
the main plaza, right near the giant hummingbird. To Quito it's $60, to the airport $80, and
to skip Quito altogether and head northeast to
Otavalo, it's $150.

Otavalo

📍 06 / POP 48,700 / ELEV 2550M

Otavalo's market is legendary, but it
shouldn't be the only reason you come to
this charming Andean minicity. The buzzing
little burg, whose sidewalks are embossed in
red, yellow and blue (the colors of the national flag), is a perfect jumping-off point for
regional hikes (Cotacachi, Peguche) or train
trips (Ibarra, Salinas), and has enough interesting restaurants and cafes to sate your
taste buds for a few days. Two days a week
the cemetery springs to life as residents
honor their dead with vibrant flowers and
hearty meals. There's a brewpub in town
and a few fun weekend bars too. And, oh
yes, that market.

◉ Sights

The **market** (Plaza de Ponchos) is the reason
everyone comes to town. For centuries,
Otavalo has hosted one of the most important markets in the Andes, a weekly fiesta
that celebrates the gods of commerce. Vendors hawk a dizzying array of traditional
crafts as well as an ever-increasing number
of slyly disguised imports. Saturday is the
big day, but the market runs all week.

Crafts Market   MARKET
(Plaza de Ponchos; 🔆) Plaza de Ponchos, the
nucleus of the crafts market, is filled every
day with vendors selling woolen goods,
such as rugs, tapestries, blankets, ponchos,
sweaters, scarves, gloves and hats, as well
as embroidered blouses, hammocks, carvings, beads, paintings, woven mats and
jewelry made from tagua nut (also known
as vegetable ivory). But it metastasizes on
Saturday, official market day, swelling into
adjacent roads and around half of the town
center.

Otavalo

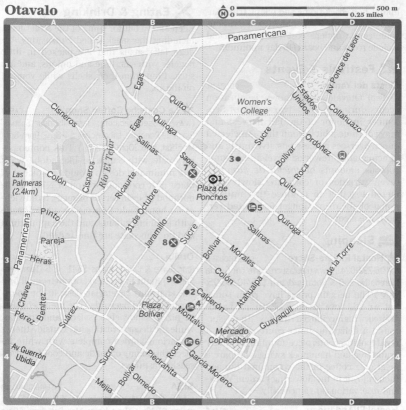

Otavalo

◎ Sights
1 Crafts Market....................................C2

⊕ Activities, Courses & Tours
2 Mundo Andino B3
3 Runa Tupari Native Travel C2

⬢ Sleeping
4 Hostal Doña Esther............................B3
5 Hostal El Andariego C2
6 Hostal Riviera-Sucre.........................B4

⊗ Eating
Árbol de Montalvo ....(see 4)
7 La Cosecha Coffee Shop B2
8 Oraibi B3
9 SISA B3

⊕ Drinking & Nightlife
Cava Caran ....(see 7)

⊚ Shopping
Market ....(see 1)

🎓 Courses

Mundo Andino LANGUAGE
(📞06-2921-864; www.mandinospanishschool.com; Bolívar No 816 near Calderon, 3rd fl; individual/group lessons per hour $7.75/5.75) This excellent language school offers classes Monday through Friday, homestays with local families and long-term volunteer opportunities where your Spanish will really get a workout. It will also take you on excursions around Otavalo.

👉 Tours

**★ Runa Tupari
Native Travel** CULTURAL, OUTDOORS
(📞06-292-2320, 099-728-6756; www.runatupari.com; Sucre No 14-15 btwn Quito & Quiroga; ⊗Mon-Sat) 🖉 Deservedly renowned and respected, Runa Tupari have partnered with indigenous, mestizo (person of mixed indigenous and Spanish descent) and Afro-Ecuadorian rural communities to offer a range of sightseeing,

hiking, horseback-riding and biking trips. Rural homestays are $35 per night, while various volunteering options cost $15 per day and include room and board (15-day minimum).

Festivals & Events

Fiesta del Yamor   CULTURAL
(⊙Sep) Otavalo's best-known celebration occurs during the first two weeks of September in honor of the fall harvest and may continue a bit beyond that. An elected queen oversees processions, live music and dancing, and fireworks. Revelers consume copious amounts of *chicha de yamor* – seven varieties of corn are slowly simmered together to produce this unusual nonalcoholic drink (longer-fermented versions are alcoholic).

Sleeping

★ Hostal Riviera-Sucre   GUESTHOUSE $
(☏06-292-0241; www.rivierasucre.com; cnr García Moreno No 380 & Roca; s/d/tr/q $25/40/60/75; @🛜) The bargain prices have risen some, but we still love Freddy's charming wood-floored, high-ceilinged rooms that surround a delightful inner courtyard with a regal-looking centerpiece fountain, a lovely arupa tree and hammock swings. Prepare a meal or a coffee in the communal kitchen then enjoy it in the flowering garden. Weekend reservations are a necessity.

Hostal El Andariego   HOSTAL $
(☏62-924-510, 099-594-1029; Bolívar, btwn Salinas & Quiroga; r with/without bathroom $13/11; 🛜) Could you feel more secure than in a *hostal* (small, reasonably priced hotel) above the Red Cross office? This new entry to Otavalo is clean, compact and friendly. Smooth cedar floors can be a bit slippery, but guests love the comfy beds and warm showers. The kitchen and common area make this one a winner, but book early – there are only five rooms.

★ Hostal Doña Esther   GUESTHOUSE $$
(☏06-292-0739; www.otavalohotel.com; Montalvo No 4-44; s/d/tr $34/49/61; @🛜) This small, Dutch-owned colonial-style hotel is cozy, with attractive rooms surrounding a courtyard ornamented with ceramics and ferns. The service is personable; there's a popular book exchange and a **recommended restaurant** (Montalvo No 4-44; mains $9-12; ⊙6-9pm Mon-Thu, noon-10pm Fri-Sun; 🍴). Just a half-block walk to Plaza Bolívar.

✕ Eating & Drinking

Keep an eye out for some of the street food, including the snack called *churo:* tiny Andean lake snails that are packed in little baggies with salt, lime and onions, and are sucked out from their shells while you are on the go.

★ La Cosecha Coffee Shop   CAFE $
(www.lacosechaec.com; Jaramillo near Salinas, Plaza de Ponchos; sandwiches $4-8; ⊙9am-8pm Mon-Sat, to 6:30pm Sun; 🛜) This contemporary cafe with Santa Fe–like adobe walls and minimalist design wouldn't look out of place in a cool outer-borough NYC neighborhood (it even serves bagels!). Sandwiches on homemade focaccia bread are made with local ingredients, and the cappuccinos and hot chocolate are fine, indeed.

Oraibi   VEGETARIAN $
(cnr Sucre & Colón; mains $5-11; ⊙5-11pm Wed-Sat; 🍴) Right in the heart of town you'll find this charming vegetarian oasis in the courtyard of an old hacienda. The menu consists of pizza, sandwiches, salads and tortillas, while the decor is rustic-chic. Outside there's a spacious garden complete with white tablecloths, plenty of shade and cool fossilized seashell ashtrays.

SISA   INTERNATIONAL $$
(☏06-292-5624; Calderón No 4-9 near Sucre; mains $5-12; ⊙9am-10pm Mon-Sat, from 10am Sun; 🛜) An attractive three-story complex: the ground floor has local handicrafts, the 2nd floor sandwiches and the top floor standard international fare, plus up-to-date live folk and jazz in the window-stage on Fridays and Saturdays. Rockers of a certain age will dig the publicity shots of musicians from Yanni to Ray Charles, and from Andean icons to Dire 'Streets.'

Cava Caran   MICROBREWERY
(☏099-189-7959; www.caran.ec; Plaza de Ponchos, Jaramillo near Salinas; flight of 5 beers $5; ⊙5pm-midnight Tue-Fri, from 11am Sat) This funky little brewpub, with a magic formula that relies on Ibarra's deep underground springs, is a breath of fresh air on the Otavalo scene. White adobe walls, intricate murals and minimalist wood furniture make this a cool hangout for locals and tourists alike, and every couple of weeks there's a 'rave Andino' to get your spirits flowing.

ⓘ Getting There & Away

Otavalo is well connected to Quito, as well as being a major transport hub for smaller towns and villages in the northern highlands. The busy **bus terminal** (cnr Atahualpa & Ordóñez) is on Atahualpa and Ordóñez, only a few blocks from the Plaza de Ponchos.

To get to Tulcán and the Colombian border, travel to Ibarra and change buses there.

Around Otavalo

📍 06 / POP 48,700

Green-checkered farmland creeps up the steep flanks of the mountains surrounding Otavalo, a rewarding combination for visitors seeking heart-pounding exercise and long views. Hikers shouldn't miss the spectacular **Lagunas de Mojanda**. Located 17km south of Otavalo, the area acquired protected status in 2002 and has since become a popular spot for Sunday family outings. If you've come to camp, set up on the south side of the biggest lake, Laguna Grande, or in the basic stone refuge (bring a sleeping bag and food). Otavalo tour companies can arrange kayaking trips here. But hiking around the sparkling waters is what seems to draw most people.

Hidden haciendas, once-grandiose epicenters of colonial society, now invite travelers to enjoy their sprawling grounds. Then there's Ecuador's largest lake, **Laguna de San Pablo**, a more domesticated setting with paddleboats and groomed shoreline hotels. We've received rave reviews about horseback riding and horse therapy at German-owned **4 Volcanoes** (www.4volcanoes.com; San Pablo del Lago).

Northeast of Otavalo, the villages of Peguche, Agato and Ilumán are known for their weaving workshops; Ilumán is also notable for its 120-member shaman association. Only 6km further, Atuntaqui is worth visiting solely for the **El Museo Fábrica Textil Imbabura** (📞 06-253-0240; Abdon Calderon cnr Junin, La Parroquia de Andrade Marín; adult/child $3/1.50; ⏱ 9am-5pm Wed-Fri, 10am-6pm Sat & Sun). A convenient way to explore these villages is with a tour operator in Otavalo, as tour prices are not much more than a long taxi rental. Most are also easily reachable by public bus.

🛏 Sleeping

⭐ La Luna   GUESTHOUSE $$

(📞 099-829-4913, 099-315-6082; www.laluna ecuador.info; camping $8, dm $14, s/d $30/47, without bathroom $22/38; 🅿🛜) Past rows of cornfields 4.5km south of Otavalo on the long uphill to the Lagunas, La Luna has million-dollar views for budget-minded travelers. Guests dine in the cozy main house, where the fireplace is the nexus of evening activity. Showers are hot and two of the doubles have a private bathroom and fireplace. Lunchboxes can be arranged for hikes.

⭐ Hostería La Mirage   HOTEL $$$

(📞 06-291-5237; www.mirage.com.ec; 10 de Agosto Prolongacion; r/ste incl breakfast & dinner $295/350; 🅿🛜🏊) One of Ecuador's finest hotels lies beyond an unpaved entry road, past iron gates, white cupolas and columned entrances where peacocks stroll the green. This place is hard to beat if you're looking for serious pampering in a beautiful Andean setting. The decor is Louis XIV-exquisite, with original paintings, canopy beds, flower bouquets and luxurious linens.

⭐ Casa Mojanda   CABIN $$$

(📞 098-033-5108, 06-304-9253; www.casa mojanda.com; Via Lagunas de Mojanda; s/d/ tr/q incl breakfast $115/134/164/176, fireplace +10%; 🅿🛜) 🌿 On the road to Lagunas de Mojanda is this lovely inn with gorgeous views of steep Andean farmland. Cheerful adobe cottages are equipped with electric heaters and hot-water bathrooms. Slip into the outdoor hot tub after a day of hiking or horseback riding. One lovely cabin is a dedicated library/den, and one is perfect for families.

ECUADOR AROUND OTAVALO

BUSES FROM OTAVALO

DESTINATION	COST ($)	DURATION
Apuela	2.50	2½hr
Cayambe	0.90	45min
Cotacachi	0.35	15min
Ibarra	0.55	30min
Quito	2	2hr

RESERVA ECOLÓGICA COTACACHI-CAYAPAS

The **Reserva Ecológica Cotacachi-Cayapas** FREE protects a huge swath of the western Andes. The range of altitudes, from Volcán Cotacachi to the lowland rainforests, means tremendous biodiversity. Crossing the park from highland areas to lowland areas is nearly impossible due to vegetation density; most visit the lowlands from San Miguel on Río Cayapas or the highlands from Cotacachi.

Less than hour's drive east are the popular **Chachimbiro hot springs**, a Disney-like complex with pools to suit all tastes and some spectacular views. A round-trip taxi from Cotacachi with a stay of several hours is $50. Further west in the *páramo* (high-altitude Andean grasslands) is **Laguna de Piñán**, with mesmerizing vistas and hiking trails; contact Runa Tupari (p699) in Otavalo for organized trips.

❶ Getting There & Away

San Miguel has a regular bus service to and from Otavalo. But some of the lodges are a bit off the beaten track and require a taxi if you don't have your own vehicle. Taxis are cheap, but these places are especially recommended if you have your own transport.

Ibarra

📞 06 / POP 156,800 / ELEV 2225M

More than any other northern population, the largest city north of Quito feels *urban*, moving to the everyday rhythms of its mix of Afro-Ecuadorians (the first Sunday of October, the city takes part in the nationwide Día Nacional del Pueblo Negro Ecuatoriano), *indígenas* and mestizos. Known as *la ciudad blanca* (the white city), most of its buildings have been turned into ordinary shops with a bustling commercial atmosphere. Several beautiful plazas with towering palms and baroque churches lend a distinctively sophisticated feel.

Volcán Imbabura looms impressively nearby and Laguna de Yahuarcocha (in Kichwa it means 'Lake of Blood' for the nearly 30,000 Caranqui warriors killed by the forces of Incan emperor Huayna Capac) is only 3km northeast. Today, joggers, cyclists and paddle-boaters occupy the lakeshore. Throw in a couple of small, interesting museums, a worthwhile train journey, good cafes and proximity to Otavalo and other *indígena* villages, and you might wonder why the tourism infrastructure is fairly lacking.

🏃 Activities

★ Tren Ecuador   RAIL

(📞 1-800-873-637, Ibarra station 06-295-0390; www.trenecuador.com; round-trip adult/child $33/29; ⊙ office 8am-5pm Mon-Sat, to 1pm Sun; 🚹) A newly restored route runs between Ibarra and the lowland Afro-Ecuadorian village of Salinas. The impressive shiny new terminal, right next to the famous Obelisk, seems to be filled mostly with railroad employees (and a cool gift shop). Service to Otavalo began in 2017, but damage to the tracks rerouted the service to nearby San Roque, still the case at the time of writing. The trip includes cultural stops and dance performances.

🛏 Sleeping & Eating

Backpackers Hostel   HOSTEL $

(📞 099-657-3989; Flores btwn Salinas & Maldonado; dm/s/d/tr/q $10/12/18/24/30; 🛜) Something new in Ibarra! We like this low-cost option with a small shared kitchen, reliable wi-fi, nicely tiled rooms, modern bunks and flat-screen televisions. The house is 150-plus years old but Nady's attention to her guests is 21st century. A beautiful courtyard is next to the kitchen. Best budget option in town.

★ Hostería Cananvalle   CABIN $$

(📞 098-260-9132; www.hosteria-cananvalle.com; s incl breakfast $50, d incl breakfast $60-70, family cabin $130; 🅿🛜) 🌿 Literally on the other side of the tracks, 5km from downtown, this family-owned working farm sits on a bucolic property with canyon and mountain views. There's a main house covered in creeping vines and several stand-alone cabins with Spanish-tile roofs and adobe walls. Some of the food served is grown here; they make their own delicious bread and coffee.

El Quinde Café   CAFE $

(Sucre btwn Flores & Garcia Moreno, Parque Pedro Moncayo; mains $2-2.50; ⊙ 11:30am-9pm Mon-Fri; 🛜) Run by a Colombian husband-and-wife team, this charming little spot on Parque Pedro Moncayo serves locally grown coffee, and cakes and pastries. The small 2nd-floor perch is a good place to settle in with a book or laptop. New-agey without being pretentious, it also features the prettiest bathroom in all of Ecuador. More veggie options (empanadas, quiche) promised soon!

☆ Entertainment

Café Arte   LIVE MUSIC, FILM
(Salinas No 5-43; ⊙5pm-midnight Thu, to 2am Fri & Sat) Surprisingly, one of the better live-music venues in Ecuador is here in Ibarra. It hosts bands from as far away as Cuba and Spain. The music ranges from jazz and flamenco to rock. Shows start Fridays and Saturdays around 10pm. Films, dance lessons and art shows are also on the program.

🛍 Shopping

Feria de Zuleta   ARTS & CRAFTS
(Feria de Bordados de Zuleta; ☑099-335-9213; main Plaza Zuleta, Community Center; ⊙8am-5pm Sat) A smaller alternative to the madness of Otavalo, about 30 families of indigenous and mestizo artisans from Zuleta and La Esperanza have teamed up to offer handmade crafts, including weavings, in this quiet village between Ibarra and Otavalo. Held twice monthly; enquire at the Ibarra Tourist Office for dates. There are buses here from Ibarra and Cayambe (30 minutes).

ⓘ Information

Tourist Office (iTur; ☑098-123-2789, 06-260-8489; www.ibarraesturismo.wordpress.com; cnr Oviedo & Sucre, Plazoleta de Coco; ⊙8am-5pm Mon-Fri, to 4pm Sat) Extremely helpful bilingual staff can organize community-tourism activities, mountaineering and hiking. Office hours may vary during festival weeks; the office closes for about 90 minutes, from 12:30pm, at lunchtime.

ⓘ Getting There & Around

Ibarra's modern bus terminal is **Terminal Terrestre** (Av Teodoro Gomez near Espejo). A taxi to/from downtown is $1. Buses to Quito leave roughly every 10 minutes.

Buses to the village of La Esperanza ($0.25, 25 minutes) leave from the north side of Parque German Grijalva in the center of town.

If you want to explore the area on your own, Ibarra's **Explorer Rentacar** (☑06-295-1668; www.rentacarecuador.net; Mariano Acosta No 10-06, across from train station) is the only option; rates start at $38 per day.

CENTRAL HIGHLANDS

The rooftop of Ecuador offers up more adventure per square meter than most places on earth. This vast region cut from fire and ice inspires the imagination and offers a remarkable journey deep into the myth and beauty of the Andes. There are heavenly volcanoes, glacier-capped peaks, high-arching grassy plains, surprisingly quaint colonial cities, bucolic haciendas and precipitous green valleys that take you from highlands down past waterfalls and indigenous villages to the heavy-aired environs of the Amazon Basin.

Most trips to the area will include a couple of days in the region's exceptional national parks and reserves, including Los Ilinizas, Cotopaxi, Llanganates, Chimborazo and Sangay. The Quilotoa Loop brings hiking travelers through traditional indigenous communities to an impossibly deep crater lake. And there are rail adventures and crafts markets, plus plenty of tropical experiences in the verdant valley leading down to the ever-popular town of Baños.

ⓘ GETTING TO COLOMBIA

The busy highland city of Tulcán is the last Ecuadorian stop for visitors headed overland to Colombia.

The Rumichaca crossing (6am to midnight daily) is 6km from Tulcán. Even day-trippers to Ipiales will need their passport stamped.

Minibuses to the border ($0.75, shared) leave as soon as they are full from the corner of Venezuela and Bolívar on Tulcán's Parque Ayora (near the bandshell).

On the Colombian side, entrance formalities are straightforward. Check with the **Colombian consulate** (☑06-298-0559, 06-225-2458; http://tulcan.consulado.gov.co; Olmedo, cnr 10 de Agosto, Edificio La Catedral Mezzanine, Plaza de Independencia; ⊙8am-1pm & 2:30-3:30pm Mon-Fri) to make sure your nationality doesn't require a visa. Visas are good for 30 to 90 days.

At the time of research, hundreds and sometimes thousands of Venezuelan refugees were crossing daily into Ecuador at Tulcan. This caused some travelers we talked to delays of several hours. Be aware of this situation if you plan to cross here from Colombia.

Parque Nacional Cotopaxi

♪ 03

Although you can see **Volcán Cotopaxi** ('Shining Peak' in Kichwa) from several provinces, its majestic bulk and symmetrical cone take on entirely new dimensions within the bounds of its namesake **national park** (Cotopaxi National Park; ☺8am-5pm, last entry 3pm). Covered in a draping glaciated skirt that gives way to sloping gold and green *páramo*, the flanks of Cotopaxi are home to wild horses, llamas, foxes, deer, Andean condors and the exceedingly rare spectacled bear.

Get here early for the best views. Hiking and mountain biking to pre-Columbian ruins around the area's lakes and along the park roads can be done with guides or on your own. And an ascent to the top of the peak is a singular experience any fit adventurer should try.

The 32,000-hectare park is easily reached on a day trip from Latacunga or Quito.

⚡ Activities

★**Volcán Cotopaxi**　　　CLIMBING
Summit attempts can be arranged in Quito and Latacunga. Although the climb is not technical – save for a few basic crevasse crossings and heart-pounding shimmies up fallen seracs – it is physically demanding, freezing and, for some people, vertigo-inducing.

Mountain Biking

Cruising around the park's circuit of relatively flat dirt roads is popular, as is a descent down from the *refugio* (mountain refuge) parking lot to the Control Caspi. Tour operators in Latacunga and Quito, such as Biking Dutchman (p681), can arrange trips.

🛏 Sleeping

★**Hacienda Los Mortiños**　　LODGE **$$**
(♪02-334-2520; www.losmortinos.com; dm/s/d/ste incl breakfast $30/80/103/151; 🛜) A wonderful place to stay not far from Control Norte on the north side of the park, this modern adobe dwelling (not an old hacienda, but newly constructed) has beautiful bathrooms, pitched ceilings, comfortable private rooms, dorms that sleep between six and 16 people, and jaw-dropping views of the neighboring volcanoes.

★**Tambopaxi**　　　GUESTHOUSE **$$$**
(♪02-600-0365; www.tambopaxi.com; camping per person $16, dm $24, s/d/tr incl breakfast $92/115/140; 🛜) 🅿 Located within the national-park boundaries, with Cotopaxi looming close by, Tambopaxi is a certified sustainable-tourism project that hires local workers. It's perfectly positioned for hikes, though you could spend all day gazing at the volcano, llamas and wild horses through the windows of the stove-heated main lodge. The restaurant here is open all day; a set lunch costs $17.50.

ℹ Information

Among the hazards here are the serious threat of altitude sickness and bulls. These problems can be avoided, the first by acclimatizing in Quito for a couple of days, drinking lots of water and donning sun protection, the second by keeping your distance.

ℹ Getting There & Away

Buses to and from Quito, Machachi and Latacunga can be flagged down or drop you off at the Control Caspi turnoff on the Panamericana. Please note that it's 15km from the highway to the park entrance. From here you can hire a pickup truck to take you to Refugio José Rivas (one way/return $30/50). Be sure to be specific if you want to go all the way to Refugio José Rivas.

Latacunga

♪ 03 / POP 77,000 / ELEV 2800M

Many travelers end up passing through Latacunga to access either the Quilotoa Loop or Parque Nacional Cotopaxi. But for those who stick around, Latacunga also offers a quiet and congenial historic center that has partially survived several Cotopaxi eruptions. You'd never know that such a charming city lies behind the loud and polluted section that greets visitors on the Panamericana.

Volcán Cotopaxi, which dominates the town on a clear day, erupted violently in 1742 and 1768, destroying most of the city both times. The indomitable survivors rebuilt, only to have an immense eruption in 1877 wreak havoc a third time. In 2015 Latacunga was once again coated in ash from Cotopaxi; luckily, no lava flows damaged the town this time.

To celebrate their rich indigenous and Catholic history, the people of Latacunga put on one of the most famous and magnificent parties in all of Ecuador, the Mama Negra festival.

☞ Tours

A number of tour operators have sprung up in recent years. Day trips to Cotopaxi and Quilotoa cost around $40 per person, with the price varying depending on the size of your group. Add a bike descent from Cotopaxi for $15. Two-day climbing trips to Los Ilinizas, Cayambe and Volcán Cotopaxi (when open) cost about $250 per person. Hostal Tiana is a good spot to form groups for your trip.

✵ Festivals & Events

Fiesta de la Mama Negra   FIESTA
(☉late Sep & early Nov) Latacunga's major annual fiesta honors La Virgen de las Mercedes. More popularly known as the Fiesta de la Mama Negra, the event features processions, costumes, fireworks, street dancing and Andean music. This is one of those festivals that, although superficially Christian, has a strong indigenous influence and is well worth seeing.

🛏 Sleeping & Eating

The classic Latacunga dish, *chugchucara* (say that 10 times fast!), is a tasty, heart-attack-inducing plate of *fritada* (fried chunks of pork, served with *mote* – hominy), *chicharrón* (fried bits of pork skin), potatoes, fried banana, *tostado* (toasted corn), popcorn and cheese empanadas. Many cheap *leñadores* (woodburning ovens) roast chicken along Amazonas between Salcedo and Guayaquil. There are two nice vegetarian options, including **Kipi** (☎099-813-7160; https://kipinaturalposta.blogspot.com/; Quijano y Ordonez 6-73 & Guayaquil; ☉6am-9pm Mon-Fri, 8am-7pm Sun; 🖊), which is close to the historic center.

Hotel Rodelu   HOTEL $
(☎03-280-0956; www.rodelu.com.ec; Quito 16-31; s/d $20/38; 🖥) Popular with the tour groups but still down-home enough to attend to independent travelers, the Rodelu (named by its proud Uruguayan owner, Republica Oriente del Uruguay) has highly fragranced Andean-style business digs with blaring orange comforters, granite-clad bathrooms and flat-screen TVs. You'll save a few bucks staying on the top floor.

Its **restaurant** (Quito 16-31; mains $10-14, set lunch $3.80, set dinner $4.90; ☉7:30am-9pm Mon-Fri, to 3:30pm Sat) serves tasty pizzas and good-value set lunches.

Hostal Tiana   HOSTEL $
(☎03-281-0147; www.hostaltiana.com; Vivero 1-31; dm/s/d incl breakfast $11/25/32, s/d without bathroom $16/25; @🖥) This good-vibes place has everything a top hostel should: common areas to swap tales, a kitchen, free internet, book exchange, clean rooms and bathrooms, luggage storage, good information and a free breakfast. The old colonial atmosphere lends an air of cool, but the old pipes may leave you wanting come hot-shower time.

Pollos Jimmy's   LATIN AMERICAN $
(Quevedo 8-85, near Valencia; mains $4-5; ☉10:30am-10pm) Pop in for delicious rotisserie chicken served with rice, potatoes and chicken soup. Half a chicken with fries and salad ($7) should be plenty for two. The place stays busy for a reason, and has since 1969.

★ El Alabado   ARGENTINE $$
(www.facebook.com/chefgustavozarate; Maldonado 41-25, near Quijano y Ordoñez; mains $4.50-12; ☉6-10pm Tue-Fri, noon-10pm Sat; 🖥) Contemporary furnishings have transformed a historic building dating from 1668 into a chic restaurant. With good-quality beef steaks and dishes such as pork in a spicy passion-fruit sauce, the Argentinian chef has infused the menu with the food of his homeland, including *choripan* (Argentine sausage sandwich) and *mate* tea. There's a decent wine list, too.

ℹ Information

Banco Guayaquil (Maldonado 7-20)
Banco Pichincha (Quito, near Salcedo)
Hospital (Hermanas Páez, near 2 de Mayo)
Post office (Quevedo, near Maldonado)

ℹ Getting There & Away

BUS

From Quito, buses drop you at the **bus terminal** (Panamericana) if Latacunga is their final destination. If the bus is continuing to Ambato or Riobamba, it'll drop you on the corner of Avenida 5 de Junio and Cotopaxi, about five blocks west of the Panamericana and 10 minutes' walk to downtown. Some, however, will just drop you at the Panamericana, where you can catch a taxi ($1 to $1.50).

Buses to Quito ($2.15, two hours) and Ambato ($1.15, one hour) leave from the bus terminal and from the corner of Avenida 5 de Junio and Cotopaxi. For Riobamba, it's easiest to catch a passing southbound Cuenca bus from the corner.

TAXI

You can hire taxis and pickup trucks in Plaza Chile (also called Plaza El Salto) for visits to Parque Nacional Cotopaxi (park interior $30, Control Caspi entrance $20).

The Quilotoa Loop

🎥 03

The Quilotoa Loop is a bumpy, ring-shaped road that travels from the Panamericana far into the backcountry of Cotopaxi province. Along the way you'll encounter colorful indigenous markets, a crystal-blue lake that the local people believe has no bottom, a community of painters who are preserving the legends of the Andes, and ancient trails that meander in the shadow of snowcapped volcanoes. The isolation of the loop brings you into contact with lots of Kichwa-speaking indigenous people and their centuries-old way of life.

Hiking the Loop

For many travelers, the Quilotoa Loop is one of the highlights of their trip to Ecuador. The hiking is fantastic, and although guides are inexpensive and a good way to support the local economy, many *hostales* (small, reasonably priced hotels) and inns also have maps on hand for solo wanderers. Llullu Llama in Isinlivi is a particularly good source of information.

The loop is shorthand for the circular route clockwise by road from the Panamericana past Tigua, Zumbahua, Quilotoa, Chugchilán, Sigchos and Saquisilí; it's also possible to start at Saquisilí and travel the route in a counterclockwise direction. Isinliví lies off the main road, between Chugchilán and Sigchos.

Hikers usually choose to walk a two- to four-day section of the loop. Sigchos is a good place to start a three-day hike, with overnight stops in Isinliví and Chugchilán, finishing the walk in Quilotoa. Bear in mind that doing the walk in this way means slightly more uphill climbs (good for acclimatization but harder on the legs). Another option is to hike from Tigua to Quilotoa and on to Chugchilán.

Transportation is infrequent, so it takes some planning if your time is limited. It's wise to travel the loop with rain gear, water and plenty of snacks for long waits and hikes, but try to leave your heavy luggage behind and hike with a day pack; Hostal Tiana (p705) in Latacunga has a luggage storage room.

Many travelers have reported problems with dogs along the way. If they charge you, don't run away. Stand your ground, grab a rock and pretend to throw it. Also, it's good to have a walking stick, for this reason.

🍴 Sleeping & Eating

There are some wonderful budget and midrange places to stay along the loop, particularly in Isinliví and Chugchilán. Accommodations can fill up, especially on weekends, so it's best to book ahead. Check with hostels for up-to-date bus times or to arrange private transport. There are no ATMs on the loop and most places only accept payment in cash, so come prepared.

Most hostels and guesthouses on the loop provide breakfast and dinner, and many can also prepare a packed lunch on request. Restaurants and shops are few and far between, so be sure to carry plenty of water and snacks.

★ **Llullu Llama** GUESTHOUSE $

(📞 098-317-7845, 099-367-8165; www.llullullama.com; dm/r/cottages per person incl breakfast & dinner from $19/24/40) 🍴 Two blocks west of the plaza, Llullu Llama is an enchanting old farmhouse with thick adobe walls, colorful rooms and a woodburning stove. The biggest attractions here are the good-time vibes, friendly hosts and spectacular surroundings. Cottages with exposed wood, fireplaces, large beds and giant showers are well worth the extra cash. Rooms in the main house share bathrooms.

Hostal Chukirawa HOSTEL $

(📞 03-305-5808; www.hostalchukirawa.com; s/d/tr incl breakfast & dinner $33/55/72; @ 🛜) Located right across from the lake viewpoint, bright and welcoming Hostal Chukirawa is one of Quilotoa's more appealing accommodations. Rooms are arranged around a central lounge area with hammocks and a woodburning stove, and there's a cozy restaurant and sprawling lounge on the 1st floor.

★ **Black Sheep Inn** LODGE $$

(📞 03-270-8077; www.blacksheepinn.com; incl full board dm $35, s/d $100/160, without bathroom $70/120; 🛜) This wonderfully rustic community-operated property sits above the valley, 100m north of Chugchilán, and offers spectacular views. Rooms have a cozy cabin feel with stove heaters, tiled floors and exposed wood, and semi-open-air bathrooms. Ecological practices here include composting toilets, rainwater collection, waste recycling and a wood-fired sauna. Three vegetarian meals a day are included in the rates.

DON'T MISS

LAGUNA QUILOTOA

The famous volcanic-crater lake of **Laguna Quilotoa** ($2) is a gasp-inducing sight. A lookout on the precipitous crater rim offers stunning views of the green mirror lake 400m below and the snowcapped peaks of Cotopaxi and Iliniza Sur in the distance. When you ask the locals how deep it is, they inevitably say it has no bottom, which seems entirely plausible given its awesomeness (the geologists say 250m).

Fit walkers can hike the crater rim trail in about six hours; another path leads down to the water on a zigzagging trail. At the bottom, you can head out in a canoe or kayak (per 30 minutes $3).

Posada de Tigua　　　　　HACIENDA **$$**
(☑ 03-305-6103, 099-161-2391; posadadetigua@yahoo.com; Vía Latacunga–La Maná, Km 46; dm/r per person incl breakfast & dinner $30/42) La Posada de Tigua is part of a working dairy ranch. The farmhouse dates to the 1890s and is now a rustic and delightfully cozy guesthouse. The rooms, with meter-thick walls, have modern bathrooms and cowhide rugs, and meals include cheese and yogurt made on the farm (you can assist!), as well as homegrown potatoes and carrots.

Shalalá　　　　　LODGE **$$**
(☑ 03-280-0215, 099-537-4750; www.quilotoashalala.com; Shalalá; camping per person $5, r per person incl breakfast $35, meals $5-7) ✑ The nicest spot on the lake, 7km north of Quilotoa road, this community-run ecolodge has just three cabins, beautifully appointed with travertine tiles and hardwood headboards. The vaulted ceilings and exposed wood beams add rustic touches to the new buildings. You'll also love the quiet and seclusion of this wooded setting.

❶ Getting There & Away

No buses go all the way around the loop. From Latacunga, they only travel as far as Chugchilán, either taking the southern road through Zumbahua and Quilotoa or the northern road via Saquisilí and Sigchos. Tigua is served by regular buses passing between Latacunga and Quevedo. If you're more adventurous, catch a *lechero* (milk truck). If speed is your need, hire a taxi in Latacunga; rates start around $60.

Baños

☑ 03 / POP 14,700 / ELEV 1800M

Baños is a mixed bag. The setting is amazing: you can see waterfalls, hike through lush forests, rest your bones in steaming thermal springs, hike down impossibly steep gorges, bike or boat all the way to the Amazon Basin, and marvel at the occasional eruption of nearby Volcán Tungurahua. The town itself is somewhat overwhelmed with garish tour operators, cut-price spas and budget accommodations, but the jigsaw-puzzle-like sidewalks in red, yellow, and blue are wide enough to stroll on, and the cathedrals, spotlit in different colors, look pretty from the plazas at night.

Look and feel aside, this is the central highlands' premiere destination for mountain biking, hiking, rafting and partying, and while some folks will have their reservations about the town's appearance, almost everybody leaves with a big smile on their face and great stories from their adventures.

The 2000 action film *Proof of Life* was filmed here.

🏃 Activities

Thermal Baths

★ **Termas de La Virgen**　　　THERMAL BATHS
(Montalvo; adult/child $2/1, after 6pm $3/1.50; ☺ 5am-4pm & 6-9:30pm) These are the only hot pools in the town proper. A community project built in 1928, they are named for the Virgin Mary, who is said to have come here to dip her own feet. Some baths are cold, others warm and one reaches an intense 42°C (118°F). The rooftop pools have lovely views of a nearby waterfall. There are two locations; the 'old' pools at the top of the street, and the newer building below, which is open Wednesday to Sunday ($6/3).

Termas El Salado　　　　THERMAL BATHS
(Salado; adult/child $3/1.50; ☺ 5am-8pm) These wonderful hot springs are located in a verdant canyon, 2.5km from town. There are hot, medium and cool pools surrounded by tree-covered hills, with the soothing sounds of a fast-flowing river close by. You'll need a swimming cap. Buses to here ($0.25, 10 minutes) depart from the stop on Rocafuerte (p711).

Baños

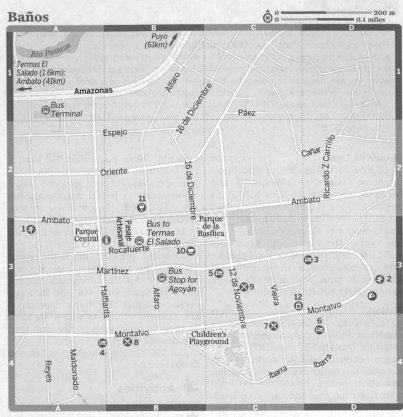

Baños

🔼 Activities, Courses & Tours
1 Andean Summit Adventure.................A3
2 Termas de La Virgen.........................D3

🛏 Sleeping
3 Hostal Chimenea................................D3
4 La Floresta..A4
5 Plantas y Blanco................................C3
6 Posada del Arte..................................D4

🍴 Eating
7 Cafe Hood...C4
8 Cafe Mariane......................................B4
9 La Tasca de Baños.............................C3

🍷 Drinking & Nightlife
10 La Tostaduria....................................B3
11 Mocambo..B2

🛍 Shopping
12 Maki Awashka....................................C3

Hiking

The tourist office (p710) provides a useful map showing some of the trails around town. Reports of assaults on nearby hikes have dropped in recent years. Nevertheless, it's advisable to bring just the cash you need and leave the expensive camera and other technology at your hotel.

Climbing

The climbing conditions on Tungurahua (5016m), an active volcano, are naturally in flux. At the time of research, climbing to the peak was allowed, but only with a licensed guide (six hours for those in optimum condition; others may be well advised to take the two-day approach and sleep at the refuge). For an experienced guide, try **Andean Sum-**

mit Adventure (☎968-959-533; www.andean
summitadventure.com; Ambato & Reyes).

Mountain Biking

Several companies rent mountain bikes
starting at about $7 per day ($15 gets you
disk brakes and suspension), but check that
the bike, helmet and lock are adequate-
ly maintained or even ask to take a quick
test ride before agreeing to rent. The most
popular ride is the dramatic descent past a
series of waterfalls on the road to Puyo, a
jungle town 61km to the east. Various other
mountain-biking options are available and
the outfitters will be happy to tell you about
them.

On the issue of safety, the Baños–Puyo
road has several narrow, long and pitch-
black tunnels. Bike riders should bypass the
tunnels by veering down on the signed trails
that swing around them.

🛏 Sleeping

Rates are highest on weekends and during
vacations, when hotels can all fill up.

Hostal Chimenea   HOSTEL $
(☎03-274-2725;   www.hostalchimenea.com;
Martínez, near Vieira; dm/s/d from $9/16/20;
@🛜🏊) From the rather dark reception
area, you wouldn't know that this hostel is
the best budget offering in town. The bright
and clean rooms and dorms come with
rainbow-colored blankets, and the upstairs
terrace has great views of the waterfall. Upstairs rooms all have balconies, and there's
a nice common kitchen with fridge for the
DIY crowd.

Plantas y Blanco   HOSTEL $
(☎03-274-0044;   www.plantasyblanco.com;
Martínez, near 12 de Noviembre; dm $9, r per person
$13; @🛜) A bit disco in the common areas,
the clean and eternally popular 'Plants and
White' (you figure it out) scores big points
for its rooftop terrace/common kitchen/
bar, outstanding breakfasts ($4.50), on-site

steam bath and overall value. There's a TV
room with Netflix and a games room with
a pool table and table tennis. Some rooms
share bathrooms. Earplugs for $1.50.

★Posada del Arte   BOUTIQUE HOTEL $$
(☎03-274-0083; www.posadadelarte.com; Ibarra,
near Montalvo; s/d/tr incl breakfast $38/72/103;
🛜) This exquisite little guesthouse has
colorful, comfortable rooms, wood floors, gi-
gantic breakfasts and art all around. Several
rooms have waterfall views, some also have
fireplaces. There's also an excellent restau-
rant here which, like the hotel, is a welcom-
ing and cozy place. It serves international
dishes, wonderful breakfasts (including
Tungurahua pancakes – they don't explode!)
and small plates for snacking.

La Floresta   HOTEL $$
(☎03-274-1824;   www.laflorestahotel.com;   cnr
Montalvo & Halflants; d/tr/ste incl breakfast
$89/125/130; @🛜) This comfortable inn
situated around a pretty interior garden
with plenty of hangout areas offers a quiet
retreat. The staff here are friendly, and the
spacious, tile-floor rooms have big windows,
modern bathrooms and comfortable beds –
though we wish they were a little brighter.

★Luna Runtún   RESORT $$$
(☎03-274-0882;   www.lunaruntun.com;   Vía
Runtún Km 6; d incl breakfast & dinner $242;
@🛜🏊) Perched at the top of a cliff
(2260m), gazing down over Baños and up
to the Tungurahua summit, Luna Runtún
is a luxurious hotel in a fabulous location.
Just laying eyes on the infinity pool (open
to nonguests for $20) will relax you. There's
a wonderful spa complete with local vol-
canic stones; a herb and vegetable garden
supplies the restaurant.

🍴 Eating

As a popular spot on the traveler trail, Baños
is full of international eateries catering to
backpackers and holidaymakers; quality

CYCLING THE RUTA DE LAS CASCADAS

Nicknamed 'La Ruta de las Cascadas' (Highway of the Waterfalls), the road from Baños
to Puyo is one of the region's most dramatic routes. It hugs the Río Pastaza canyon as it
drops steadily from Baños, at 1800m, to Puyo, at 950m, and passes more than a dozen
waterfalls on the way. The bus ride is great, but zipping down on a mountain bike is even
better. The first third of the route is mostly downhill, but there are some definite climbs,
so ready those legs (it's about 61km if you do the whole thing). Mountain bikes can be
rented in Baños.

varies. The town is famous for *melcocha,* a chewy taffy that's softened and blended by swinging it onto wooden pegs, usually mounted in the doorways of shops. Pieces of chewable *caña de azúcar* (sugarcane) and *jugo de caña* (sugarcane juice) are sold at sugarcane stalls across from the bus terminal.

Cafe Hood   INTERNATIONAL **$**
(☑03-274-1609; www.cafehoodecuador.com; Montalvo & Rafael Viera; mains $4-8; ☺noon-10pm; ☎☑) Named for owner Ray Hood, a long-standing gringo-in-residence, this excellent cafe has cheap *almuerzos* (set lunches) and a menu of Asian and South American dishes. The cafe is a welcoming place to meet with friends or just chill *solito* (alone). If you don't feel like leaving, well, there's a comfy *hostal* in back with nice views.

★La Tasca de Baños   SPANISH **$$**
(12 de Noviembre, near Montalvo; tapas $3.50-6; ☺6:30-10:30pm Wed-Fri, 12:30-4:30pm & 6:30-10:30pm Sat & Sun) It may be difficult to get a table at this tiny tapas restaurant. The selection of small dishes is excellent, ranging from perennial favorites like *tortilla española* (Spanish omelet) to Andalusian meatballs and shellfish. Order up five to share.

Cafe Mariane   FRENCH **$$**
(☑03-274-1947; Montalvo; mains $10-15; ☺1-11pm Mon-Sat) Mariane's French-Mediterranean cuisine is a real standout in Baños. The cheese-and-meat fondues are a lot – even for two people – and the pasta and meat dishes are quite elegant.

🍷 Drinking & Nightlife

Mocambo   BAR
(☑03-274-1329; Alfaro near Ambato; ☺8pm-midnight) Tired of the bus *bachata*? Guitar-hungry gringos need look no further than this joint, where the owner's laptop always has a classic playlist cued up, from Guns N' Roses to Metallica, while revisiting some classics from further back. And he takes requests. You'll likely *hear* Mocambo before you see it. Best bar sign in Ecuador: 'No wi-fi. Talk amongst yourselves.'

La Tostaduria   COFFEE
(cnr 16 de Diciembre & Rocafuerte; ☺8am-noon & 4-9pm Sun, Mon, Wed & Thu, to 10pm Fri & Sat) Java junkies can get a fix at this hole-in-the-wall coffee joint. The beans from Loja, Pichincha and Imbabura are roasted inside the small shop.

🛍 Shopping

★Maki Awashka   ARTS & CRAFTS
(Montalvo, near Santa Clara; ☺8am-7pm) The family from Salasaca who own this shop weave many of the gorgeous wool rugs and tapestries in their workshop upstairs. There's a good selection of artisan crafts for sale here, including tablecloths, scarves and blankets.

ℹ️ Information

DANGERS & ANNOYANCES
Eruptions of Tungurahua force locals to evacuate about every five years. In recent years the volcano has been quite active. This said, it's a well-monitored situation and shouldn't be a major concern. Ask your hotel staff about evacuation procedures in the event of an eruption.

Reports of robberies on the trails outside Baños have dropped. Hiring a guide is a good way to contribute to the local economy and reduce your risk.
Police Station (☑03-274-0251)

MEDICAL SERVICES
Hospital (☑03-274-0301; Montalvo) Near Pastaza; pharmacies are along Ambato.

MONEY
Banco del Pacifico (cnr Halflants & Rocafuerte)
Banco Pichincha (cnr Ambato & Halflants)

TOURIST INFORMATION
Tourist office (☑03-274-0483; www.facebook.com/gadbanosdeaguasanta; Halflants near Rocafuerte; ☺8am-noon & 2-5pm) Lots of info, free maps and emergency evacuation information.

ℹ️ Getting There & Away
The Baños **bus terminal** (Amazonas) is within easy walking distance of most hotels. Transportes Baños offers frequent buses direct to Quito ($4.45, 3½ hours). There are buses every 30 minutes to Salasaca ($0.50, 30 minutes) and Ambato ($1.10, one hour); take a Quito-bound bus for Latacunga ($2, 1½ hours). There are daily buses to Guayaquil ($9, seven hours).

The Baños–Riobamba road via Penipe has great views of the volcano along the way. There are six buses a day to Riobamba ($2, 1½ hours); change in Riobamba for buses to Cuenca, or if you miss a Guayaquil bus.

To the Oriente, buses depart regularly for Puyo ($2, two hours), Tena ($4, five hours), Coca ($10, 10 hours) and Macas ($7.50, four hours).

ℹ Getting Around

Westbound local buses leave from Rocafuerte, behind the Mercado Central. Marked 'El Salado,' they go to the Piscinas El Salado ($0.25, 10 minutes). **Eastbound local buses** go as far as the Pailón del Diablo ($0.50); they leave from Alfaro at Martínez.

Round-trip taxi tours for Pailón del Diablo ($20) leave from the bus terminal.

Guaranda

📞 03 / POP 25,000 / ELEV 2650M

Half the fun of Guaranda is getting there. The 99km 'highway' from Ambato reaches altitudes over 4000m and passes within 5km of the glacier on Volcán Chimborazo (6263m). From here, the mountain almost looks easy to climb. The capital of Bolívar province, Guaranda is a small and uneventful city – but it is a city, with accompanying traffic (auto and pedestrian). It sits amid seven steep hills that have prompted the moniker 'the Rome of the Andes' – but it certainly didn't get this nickname for its cultural offerings. The Wednesday and Saturday markets in the Plaza 15 de Mayo are worth checking out, as are the Carnaval celebrations in February, with water fights, dances, parades and a little liquor with local herbs called 'Pájaro Azul' (Blue Bird).

🛏 Sleeping & Eating

Hostal Bolívar   HOTEL **$**
(📞 03-298-0547; hbguaranda@gmail.com; Sucre 7-04, near Rocafuerte; s/d $20/35; 🅿🛜) A good option for discerning travelers, the rooms here are welcoming and clean – though slightly dated save for the flat-screen TVs (some rooms don't even have them) – and there's a pleasant courtyard. Breakfast costs $2.80. It's two blocks south of Parque Simón Bolívar.

Los 7 Santos   CAFE **$**
(Cafe y Galeria; 📞 03-298-0612; www.facebook.com/los7santosgda; Convención de 1884, near 10 de Agosto; sandwiches $1.50-3.25; ⊙10am-10pm Mon-Thu, to 2am Fri & Sat) Half a block downhill from Parque Simón Bolívar, Los 7 Santos offers all that you would expect from an artsy cafe in a much larger city. There's breakfast in the morning ($4) and small sandwiches and *bocaditos* (snacks) all day. The artwork and wall graffiti make it worth the wait for service. Live music some Fridays and Saturdays.

ℹ Information

Banco Pichincha (Azuay, near 7 de Mayo)

Clínica Bolívar (📞 03-298-3310) One of several clinics and pharmacies near Plaza Roja, south of the hospital.

Hospital Alfredo Noboa Montenegro (📞 03-298-0110; Cisneros, near Selva Alegre)

ℹ Getting There & Around

Guaranda's bus terminal is a solid 20-minute walk or a $1.25 cab ride from downtown.

Bus services depart hourly for Ambato ($2.50, two hours) and Quito ($5, five hours). Almost as frequently, there are buses for Guayaquil ($4.50, four hours). There are numerous daily buses to Riobamba ($2.75, two hours); this route passes the Chimborazo park entrance and access road to the mountain refuges, and the views of Volcán Chimborazo are amazing.

Shared taxis for Salinas ($0.50, 45 minutes) depart frequently from the Plaza Roja, waiting to fill up before they go.

Salinas

📞 03 / POP 5550 / ELEV 3550M

The remote village of Salinas, about 35km north of Guaranda, sits at the base of a dramatic and precipitous bluff surrounded by *páramo*. Famous as a model of rural development (think: cheese!), Salinas is a terrific place to see what successful community-based tourism is all about. A trail above town takes you to the top of the bluff.

🛏 Sleeping

Hostal La Minga   HOSTAL **$**
(📞 098-626-7586, 03-221-0255; www.lamingahostal.com; Guayamas, btwn Salinerito & Tomabelas, r per person incl breakfast $15; 🛜) This cheery place offers the best accommodations in the village. The bright rooms have fleece sheets and firm beds, and are arranged around a central, plant-filled atrium.

Inside, you'll also find the **Pizzeria Casa Nostra** (Guayamas, between Salinerito & Tomabelas; mains $6-10; ⊙3-10pm Mon-Fri, 11am-9pm Sat & Sun).

ℹ Information

The **Oficina de Turismo Comunitario** (📞 099-563-2095, 03-221-0234; www.salinasmatiavi.com; El Salinerito, near Guayamas; ⊙8am-5pm) is in the main plaza. It can give you the password for free wi-fi in the plaza.

There are no ATMs in the village.

ⓘ Getting There & Away

Collective taxis to Guaranda leave frequently from Calle Los Tomabelas, one block downhill from the main square ($1, 45 minutes).

Riobamba

🔊 03 / POP 156,700 / ELEV 2750M

Riobamba has a strong indigenous presence that grows to wonderfully colorful proportions during the Saturday market, but the city's layout, large arcaded plazas and architecture are imposing reminders of Spanish colonization. The colonial center is a maze of churches and narrow streets, but it also feels a bit urban and diesel-choked. The 'Americanization' of the center, with KFC and other copy-cat fast-food joints, is disconcerting.

◉ Sights

The handsome, tree-filled **Parque Maldonado** (Primera Constituyente, btwn Espejo &

5 de Junio) is flanked by Riobamba's **cathedral** on the northeastern side. A few blocks southeast, **Parque La Libertad** (Primera Constituyente, btwn Alvarado & Benalcazar) is anchored, near Alvarado, by its neoclassical **basilica** (Veloz near Velasco), famous for being the only round church in Ecuador. It's often closed, but try Sundays and evenings after 6pm. Just north of downtown, the **Parque 21 de Abril** (cnr Orozco & Ángel León) has an observation platform with views of the surrounding mountains.

☞ Tours

Thanks to Riobamba's proximity to Chimborazo, the country's highest peak, the city is home to some of the country's best climbing operators and mountain guides. Two-day summit trips start from around $260 per person and include guides, gear, transportation and meals.

One-day mountain-biking trips start at $45 per person. Descents from the refuge on

Riobamba

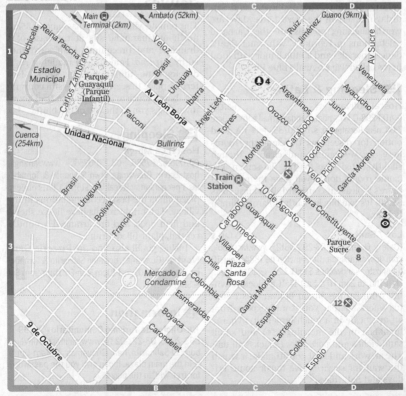

Chimborazo – an exhilarating way to take in the views – are very popular.

Julio Verne Travel ADVENTURE
(☎ 03-296-3436; www.julioverne-travel.com; Brasil 22-40, near León Borja; ⊙ office 8:30am-1pm & 3-6pm Mon-Fri) Recommended Ecuadorian-Dutch full-service operator offering affordable, two-day summit trips to Chimborazo and other peaks, as well as multiday treks. The company also offers downhill mountain biking on Chimborazo.

Pro Bici CYCLING
(☎ 03-294-1880, 03-295-1760; www.probici.com; 2nd fl, Primera Constituyente 23-51, near Larrea; ⊙ office 8:30am-8pm Mon-Sat) Located on the 2nd floor through the fabric store, this is one of the country's best-mountain bike operators, with many years of experience and excellent trip reports from clients. It offers mountain-bike rentals (per day $15 to $25), excellent maps, good safety practices

and fascinating day tours ($45 to $70) to Chimborazo, Atillo and Colta.

🛏 Sleeping

★ **Hostal Oasis** GUESTHOUSE $
(☎ 03-296-1210; www.oasishostelriobamba.com; Veloz 15-32, near Almagro; s/d $18/30; P @ 🛜) When it comes to friendliness, value and down-home cutesiness, this guesthouse is hard to beat. Rooms and apartments are grouped around a garden patrolled by friendly cats, and there's a shared kitchen. We only wish it were a little closer to the downtown action.

La Moya
Community Tourism AGROTURISMO $
(☎ 099-875-2686; Calpi, Comunidad La Moya; per person incl breakfast $15) A recent opportunity in community tourism, here you can learn about how the villagers harvest various crops (and their traditional uses), weave beautiful alpaca vestments, and survive day-to-day mountain life. Relatively new accommodations (2016) include two double rooms and one group-sized unit, all with small heaters, shiny bathroom fixtures and simple beds. Various tours run $10 per guide.

A taxi from Riobamba costs $6. There's a small artisan's gift shop and a museum dedicated to the La Moya culture.

🍴 Eating

Riobamba is not known for its foodie scene, but there are plenty of places to get a decent meal nonetheless. Head to the **Mercado La**

Merced (Mercado Mariano Borja; Guayaquil, btwn Espejo & Colón; mains $3; ☺ 7am-5:30pm Mon-Sat, to 5pm Sun) to sample the local specialty, *hornado* (whole roast pork).

★ El Delirio   ECUADORIAN $$
(☑ 03-296-6441; Primera Constituyente 28-16, near Rocafuerte; mains $8-12; ☺ noon-10pm Tue-Sun) Named for a poem by the great liberator, Simón Bolívar, this former hacienda (now in the city center) serves *comida típica* (traditional Ecuadorian food) in a candlelit dining room. The open fire, wooden booths, antiques and artwork-covered walls make for an inviting atmosphere. Service is slow but the *almuerzos* (set lunches; $10) are excellent and the patio is simply amazing. Live music weekend evenings.

Cayfruts   ECUADORIAN $$
(Casa Rubio; ☑ 03-294-1018; Veloz 18-27, near Velasco; mains $8-12; ☺ 8:30am-9:30pm Mon-Sat; ☎) This friendly restaurant is a good bet for breakfasts, lunchtime sandwiches and burgers and evening meals. It's open all day, making it a great place to drop in for an afternoon coffee with *humita* (a local snack made with corn flour), or a glass of beer or wine. The hosts' 15 years in Spain show in the decor.

🛍 Shopping

The Saturday **market** (Plaza de la Concepción; ☺ 6am-5pm Sat) is an excellent place to shop for handicrafts. As you're walking around, keep your eyes peeled for locally made *shigras* (small string bags), tagua nut carvings, and *totora* baskets and mats woven by the indigenous Colta from the reeds lining the shores of nearby Laguna de Colta.

🛈 Getting There & Away

Main Bus Terminal (Av León Borja, near Av de la Prensa) About 2km northwest of downtown, this modern terminal has hourly buses for Quito ($4.60, four hours) and intermediate points, as well as buses to Guayaquil ($5.65, 4½ hours), Cuenca ($6, six hours) and Alausí ($2.35, two hours, at least hourly between 5am and 8pm).

Flota Bolívar has morning and afternoon buses to Guaranda ($2.50, two hours); some continue on to Babahoyo. Guaranda-bound buses pass the access road to Chimborazo and the mountain refuges. There are hourly buses for Baños ($2), Puyo ($6) and Macas ($5).

Volcán Chimborazo

Called 'Taita' (Father) by indigenous people in the area, Volcán Chimborazo (6263m) is the country's tallest mountain, a hulking giant topped by a massive glacier. Because of Earth's equatorial bulge, Chimborazo is both the furthest point from the center of the earth and the closest terrestrial point to the stars.

Along with its smaller, craggier companion Volcán Carihuairazo (5020m) to the northeast, and the Río Mocha valley that connects them, Chimborazo is a remote, even desolate, place populated by only a few indigenous communities.

Chimborazo and Carihuairazo lie within the **Reserva de Producción de Fauna Chimborazo** (☑ 03-202-7358; http://areasprotegidas. ambiente.gob.ec; Vía Riobamba-Guaranda, Km 45; ☺ 8am-4pm) FREE. It is called a 'fauna-production reserve' because it is home to thousands of vicuña (a relative of the llama). Once extinct in Ecuador, they were donated by Chile and Bolivia in the 1980s. Now prospering, their elegant silhouettes are easily spotted in the mist on the bus ride between Guaranda and Riobamba.

Climbing Chimborazo or Carihuairazo is an adventure only for well-acclimatized, experienced mountaineers with snow- and ice-climbing gear (contact guides in Riobamba or Quito). From Riobamba, you can organize a day trip that takes you to Chimborazo's **Refugio Whymper** (Edward Whymper Refuge) FREE at 5000m, or just beyond, to Laguna Cóndor Cocha at 5100m.

Care should be taken to properly acclimatize if you plan to do physical activities around Chimborazo and Carihuairazo. You can arrange mountain-bike descents from the high-altitude refuges with tour operators in Riobamba.

The small indigenous community of **Pulinguí San Pablo** (3900m) on the Riobamba–Guaranda road is well worth an afternoon visit, and climbers and hikers can stay overnight in the simple **community lodge** (☑ 099-032-5984; www.geocities.ws/projet_cooperation_chimborazo/documents/Depliant_touristique_v1.5v5.pdf; Pulinguí San Pablo; per person incl breakfast & dinner $25).

Several buses go from Riobamba's main terminal to Guaranda daily via a paved road. About 45 minutes from Riobamba ($1.50), the bus passes Pulinguí San Pablo, and about 7km further it passes the signed turnoff (4370m) for the Chimborazo *refugios* at the park's entrance (p714). From the turnoff, it is 8km by road to the parking lot at **Refugio Carrel** (☑03-296-5820, 03-295-1389; refugios chimborazo@gmail.com; per person incl breakfast & dinner $30) and 1km further (on foot) to **Refugio Whymper** (☑03-295-1389, 03-296-5820; refugioschimborazo@gmail.com; per person incl breakfast & dinner $30). If you're walking up this road, allow several hours to reach the *refugios*.

Most hotels in Riobamba can arrange a taxi service to Refugio Carrel via this route. It's about $60 to hire a taxi to drop you off and pick you up on a later day. One-way trips cost around $40.

Alausí

☑03 / POP 10,200 / ELEV 3340M

Set almost dizzyingly on the edge of the Río Chanchán gorge and presided over by a giant statue of St Peter, Alausí is the jumping-on point for the Nariz del Diablo (p715) train run. Alausí is wonderfully picturesque, especially near the railway station and on the cobblestone streets, where old adobe buildings with wooden balconies take you back in time. The town is really just a whistle-stop these days, but it's a pretty place for a day trip nonetheless. Alausí lies about 97km south of Riobamba and has a busy **Sunday market**. The train station is at the north end of Avenida 5 de Junio.

Tours

★Nariz del Diablo   RAIL
(Devil's Nose; ☑1-800-873-637; www.trenecuador. com; Alausí train station; adult/child $33/21; ☺8am-10:30am & 11am-1:30pm Tue-Sun) The Nariz del Diablo is a 765m sheer cliff of solid rock traversed by a round-trip tourist train. In 1902 track engineers devised a clever way up this monster by carving a zigzag route into the side of the mountain (many lives were lost in the process). The train tugs a bit north, switches track, tugs a bit south and again switches track, slowly making its way up and down the Devil's Nose.

Sleeping

Hostería La Quinta   HOTEL $$$
(☑03-293-0247; www.hosteria-la-quinta.com; Eloy Alfaro 121; s/d/ste incl breakfast $55/92/150; ☐)

Just 300m uphill from the train station, this 120-year-old family home has beautiful wooden beams and even better views. Much of the furniture is original and rooms are decorated with family photographs and antiques. Rooms vary in size but all are charming; the best is the family suite with a private terrace.

ℹ Getting There & Away

The bus station is on Avenida 5 de Junio. Buses for Riobamba ($2.35, two hours) depart hourly; about half of them continue on to Quito, otherwise Quito-bound travelers can change buses in Riobamba. Buses for Cuenca ($6.25, four hours) depart 10 times a day.

SOUTHERN HIGHLANDS

Emerging from the shadows of the breath-sapping peaks, glaciers and active volcanoes of the north, a gentler land reveals itself. Still mountainous, but also more benign, the southern spine of the Ecuadorian Andes ushers intrepid travelers down lush valleys that hide some treats: pastel-hued colonial towns and remote villages where indigenous cultures thrive.

Veering from chilly, elfin woodland to humid lowland forest, the region is home to a huge diversity of wildlife and landscapes; make time for a trip to at least one of the region's national parks.

Most journeys begin in Cuenca, a classic South American traveler hub with one of the continent's best-preserved colonial centers. Then it's a choose-your-own adventure romp through seldom-visited ancient settlements and untrammeled wild areas toward vibrant, museum-rich Loja and balmy Vilcabamba. From here, forays begin into stark ocher hills, along verdant slopes where Ecuador's best coffee is cultivated and down into sticky semitropical forest.

Cuenca

☑07 / POP 332,000 / ELEV 2530M

After Quito, Cuenca is Ecuador's most important and beautiful colonial city. But don't say that to the locals, who insist that their laidback culture, cleaner streets and more agreeable weather outclass the capital, hands down.

Dating from the 16th century, Cuenca's historic center, a Unesco World Heritage Site with its trademark skyline of massive rotundas and soaring steeples, is a place

Cuenca

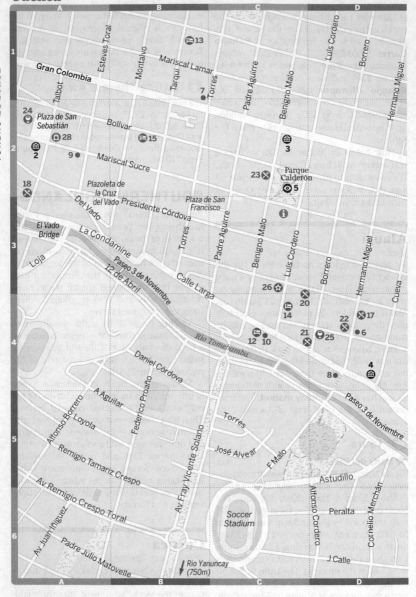

time keeps forgetting: nuns march along cobblestone streets, kids in Catholic-school uniforms skip past historic churches, and old ladies spy on promenading lovers from their geranium-filled balconies.

The city is the center of many craft traditions, including ceramics, metalwork and the internationally famous panama hat – and the nearby villages offer many more handicrafts besides.

Cuenca

◎ Sights

★ Museo del Banco Central 'Pumapungo'

MUSEUM

(☎07-283-1521; www.pumapungo.org; Larga, btwn Arriaga & Huayna Capac; ⊙8am-5:30pm Tue-Sun) **FREE** One of Ecuador's most significant museums, Pumapungo houses great modern art downstairs, but the highlight is on the 2nd floor. Here begins a comprehensive voyage through Ecuador's diverse indigenous cultures, with colorfully animated dioramas and reconstructions of typical houses of Afro-Ecuadorians from Esmeraldas province, the cowboy-like *montubios* (coastal farmers) of the western lowlands, several rainforest groups and all major highland groups.

Museo de las Culturas Aborígenes   MUSEUM
(☑ 07-284-1540; www.museodelasculturas aborigenes.com; Larga 5-24; adult/student $4/2; ⊙ 9am-6pm Mon-Fri, to 2pm Sat) This indigenous culture museum has more than 5000 archaeological pieces representing more than 20 pre-Columbian Ecuadorian cultures going back some 15,000 years. But what makes this such a gem of a museum is the informative self-guided tour – touching upon such unexpected items as combs, obsidian mirrors and cooking equipment, as well as explaining the striking designs. A peaceful courtyard cafe sells wickedly strong coffee.

Museo de Arte Moderno   MUSEUM
(cnr Mariscal Sucre & Talbot; admission by donation; ⊙ 9am-5pm Mon-Fri, to 1pm Sat & Sun) On the south side of Plaza de San Sebastián, this fun museum was once a home for the insane. It now houses a highly regarded collection of Ecuadorian and Latin American art.

Museo de la Ciudad   MUSEUM
(cnr Gran Colombia & Benigno Malo; ⊙ 8am-1pm & 3-6pm Mon-Fri, 10am-2pm Sat & Sun) FREE Housed in the former Escuela Central la Inmaculada, this beautifully preserved colonial building has been revamped with sleek, contemporary lines to house art exhibitions in its salons. Of particular interest is the fascinating and thought-provoking video art, often with controversial themes.

Parque Calderón   PLAZA
A central meeting point and generally lovely place to relax, Parque Calderón is the central park of Cuenca.

➷ Courses

Sampere   LANGUAGE
(☑ 07-282-3960; www.sampere.com; Hermano Miguel 3-43) A highly recommended and busy Spanish-owned school.

Simón Bolívar Spanish School   LANGUAGE
(☑ 07-283-2052, 07-283-9959; www.bolivar2.com; Mariscal Sucre 14-21, btwn Toral & Talbot; registration fee $35, lessons 1/2/more people per hour $9/6.50/6) Offers homestays, excursions, plus salsa (free) and cooking ($3) lessons when you sign up to a course. Weeklong courses start at $285 one-to-one with a teacher.

Centers for Interamerican Studies   LANGUAGE
(CEDEI; ☑ 07-283-9003; www.cedei.org; cnr Gran Colombia 11-02 & General Torres, 2nd fl; per semester incl homestay, meals & excursions $14,000) A nonprofit school offering drop-in and/or long-term courses in Spanish, Kichwa and Portuguese.

⌲ Tours

★ Expediciones Apullacta   ADVENTURE
(☑ 07-283-7815; www.apullacta.com; Gran Colombia 11-02, 2nd fl; ⊙ 8:30am-1pm & 2:30-6:30pm Mon-Fri, 9am-noon Sat) A big operation that organizes day tours to Ingapirca ($50), Parque Nacional Cajas ($50) and a combined Ingapirca/Chordeleg trip ($60), among other sites. It also runs a three-day/two-night Inca Trail trek package ($519), as well as canyoning day trips ($80) with internationally certified bilingual guides and excellent equipment.

Arutam Ecotours   CULTURAL
(☑ 098-197-0361; www.arutamecotours.com; cnr Vásquez & Miguel) This small company specializes in small group tours to local communities. Tours involve the local people and the company aims to make visits to nearby indigenous villages, including those inhabited by the Shuar people, as authentic and participatory as possible.

Terra Diversa Travel Center   TOURS
(☑ 07-282-3782, 099-920-4832; www.terra diversa.com; Calle Larga near Cordero) Specializes in biking (from $54) and horse-riding (from $75) day trips, as well as overnight horse-riding trips that include staying at haciendas or camping along the Inca Trail north of Ingapirca. The Ingapirca tours throw some different activities into the mix: biking there, or stopping at crafts-making villages en route. The three-hour Cuenca city walking tour is $24.

⌸ Sleeping

★ El Cafecito   HOSTEL $
(☑ 07-411-4765; www.elcafecito.net; Cueva 11-28, near Lamar; dm/s/d $10/20/30; 🛜) In a smart

and beautifully decorated building on the plaza opposite the market of Mercado 9 de Octubre, flashpackers are catered for as much as backpackers at this well-established travel hangout. There's a great roof terrace-bar, and quiet wood-floored rooms and dorms, each of which has a private bathroom.

★ **Pepe's House Hostal**　　　HOSTEL $
(📞07-283-3135; www.pepeshouse.com; Mariano Cueva 9-69; incl breakfast dm $10, s/d from 23/44; 📶) Opened in 2017, superchill and aesthetically appealing Pepe's House is Cuenca's hostel for travelers who've graduated from party mode. With a colorful but minimalist style, dorms with cushy beds are partitioned with half-walls for some privacy, while private rooms feel like guest bedrooms at a friend's place. Ample common space invites lounging, while the in-house cafe offers wholesome, tasty eats.

Hostal Yakumama　　　HOSTEL $
(📞07-283-4353; http://en.hostalyakumama.com/; Cordero, btwn Jaramillo & Vásquez; dm from $6.50, d with/without bathroom $28/20; 📶) As hostels go, the spacious Yakumama, named after the Inca water goddess, is one of Cuenca's best. From the light, roomy 10-bed dorm down through the nicely hand-painted private rooms to the cool common areas (a courtyard full of murals and plants), the owners get what a great hostel needs. There's a community bulletin board posting current activities/ events around town.

Hostal Casa del Barranco　　GUESTHOUSE $$
(📞07-283-9763; www.casadelbarranco.com; Larga 8-41, btwn Benigno Malo & Cordero; s/d/tr incl breakfast from $30/44/58; 📶) Hanging over the high cliffs of El Barranco, this colonial abode has comfortable rooms, four of which have river-facing terraces. The cafeteria – all bare stone walls, haughty furniture and more river views from its terrace – makes a good breakfast spot. Its great location puts it on the map.

Hostal Macondo　　　HOTEL $$
(📞07-282-1700; www.hostalmacondo.com; Tarqui 11-64; s/d incl breakfast $27/44; 📶) The colonial-style Hostal Macondo has spotless, slightly dark, palatial rooms in the front, older section, and small, but cozy, rooms situated around a big garden out back, making this one of the best midrange deals in town. Longer-staying guests will enjoy access to the well-equipped and spotless kitchen, and

everyone likes the continental breakfasts with bottomless cups of coffee.

★ **Mansión Alcázar**　　HISTORIC HOTEL $$$
(📞07-282-3889, 07-282-3918; http://mansion alcazar.com; Bolívar 12-55; s/d/ste incl breakfast $145/251/359; 🅿️@📶) With unrivaled service and rooms decorated with unique themes, the Alcázar is the best high-end offering in Cuenca. A water fountain spills over with fresh flowers in the interior courtyard, and the sumptuous garden, library and international restaurant all convey the management's tireless attention to detail. Five newer rooms surround a garden at the back. There are several suites, too.

🍴 Eating

★ **Moliendo Café**　　　COLOMBIAN $
(Vásquez 6-24; mains $4.50-8; ⏲9am-9pm; 📶) This is one of the best little eateries you'll find in Ecuador – and that's why Moliendo Café is always rammed. The hearty *arepas* (maize pancakes, from $4.50) come from Ecuador's northern neighbors but are a specialty here, topped with anything from beans and cheese to slow-cooked pork. The delicious and filling *almuerzos* (set lunches; $2.50) are also a smashing deal.

★ **Café Ñucallacta**　　　CAFE $
(http://cafenucallacta.com; Hermano Miguel 5-62, btwn Honorato Vasquez & Juan Jaramillo; snacks/ light meals $2-5; ⏲8am-6pm Mon-Sat, 9am-1pm Sun; 📶) The best cafe in Cuenca. Artisan Ecuadorian coffee is roasted and the resulting brews are the main reason to stop by – along with gleaning an insight into Ecuador's coffee industry from the knowledgeable owner. But they also do nice breakfasts and cakes and the tables in this dinky, welcoming little joint fill up fast in the mornings.

These guys have a second **cafe** (Talbot s/n, Plaza El Otorongo; snacks/light meals $2-5; ⏲8am-6pm Tue-Sat) on Plaza El Otorongo.

Govinda's　　　INTERNATIONAL $
(Jaramillo 7-27; mains $2.50-4; ⏲noon-4pm Mon-Sat; 📶🍴) Pizzas, lentil burgers and a little good karma to wash it down. It's one of Ecuador's nicest Hare Krishna restaurants. The buffet lunch is $2.50.

Fabiano's　　　PIZZA $$
(📞07-282-4517; cnr Presidente Córdova & Cueva; pizzas $6-18; ⏲noon-10pm Mon-Thu, to 11pm Fri & Sat; 📶) Amiable, family-friendly Fabiano's is

a tried and tested gringo hangout that garners a following among Ecuadorians too. Pizzas are generous and tasty, although the crowds of other diners sometimes means service can be below par. Try the stodge-fest that is lasagne pizza – should it prove too much, they will willingly wrap it up for you to take home.

Raymipampa ECUADORIAN $$

(Benigno Malo 8-59; mains $6.50-12; ⊙8:30am-11pm Mon-Fri, 9:30am-10pm Sat & Sun; 🛜) This Cuenca institution overlooking Parque Calderón is overwhelmingly popular with locals and travelers and stays open late. The menu hangs somewhere between Ecuadorian comfort food and diner fare. Get a pew on the upstairs deck for a view of what Ecuadorian meals are all about.

Goza Espresso Bar CAFE $$

(www.gozaespresso.com; cnr Borreo 4-11 & Larga; breakfast $4-7, mains $8-15; ⊙8am-10:30pm Sun-Wed, to midnight Thu-Sat) Goza, a trendy European-style cafe-bar on a pedestrianized section of Borreo, is equally appealing for the fabulous international breakfasts (like eggs Benedict or fruit and granola), coffee (made with aplomb) and evening drinks (cocktails such as *maracuyá* – passion fruit – daiquiri particularly tempt). The food is standard international fare (cheeseburgers, steaks, chicken nuggets).

Casa Alonso at
Mansión Alcázar INTERNATIONAL $$$

(http://mansionalcazar.com/casa-alonso; Bolívar 12-55; mains $16-30; ⊙7-10am & 12:30-3pm, 3:30-10pm) Mansión Alcazar's inviting restaurant, backing onto its beautiful internal garden, maintains the same lofty standards that the hotel does: ornately furnished and with quality service. Dinner could be sea bass in a crust of green plantain, braised duck leg or salmon in bourbon sauce. Whatever it is, it will be delicious.

🍷 Drinking & Nightlife

★ Jodoco Belgian Brew CRAFT BEER

(http://jodocobelgianbrew.com; Sucre, next to Church of San Sebastián; beers $3.90-18; ⊙4pm-midnight Tue, from 11am Wed-Sat; 🛜) Blessedly authentic Belgian beer, brewed in Cuenca and served alongside lovely bistro fare, is poured at this appealing plaza-side spot with patio seating. A jazz soundtrack and clean, moody interior set the scene for a relaxed sip of craft-beer bliss. We love the

Petit Belge: not an obvious fave, but subtly spicy and refreshing after a day's sightseeing.

La Compañía BREWERY

(☑099-887-4099; cnr Borrero & Vásquez; ⊙4-11:30pm Mon-Wed, to 2am Thu-Sat) Cuenca's first microbrewery is still one of the city's best. It caters to a young rocker crowd and offers up decent hand-crafted stouts, Irish reds and golden brews. And if you're not into beer, it does great cocktails as well.

Wunderbar BAR

(Escalinata 3-43; ⊙noon-midnight Mon-Thu, to 2am Fri, 3pm-2am Sat) This Austrian-owned place is *wunder*ful if you want a classic bar with big wooden tables to sit around with friends. Food is served, and there's a happy 'hour' from noon all the way to 6pm. It has an American pool table and big-screen sports.

☆ Entertainment

★ Jazz Society Café JAZZ

(☑in English 093-934-2714, in Spanish 099-588-8796; www.facebook.com/JazzSocietyCafe; 5-101 Cordero, near Jaramillo; ⊙6:30-10pm Wed-Sat) The performance venue of the Jazz Society of Ecuador provides soothing aural therapy with Ecuadorian musicians, as well as international artists. The Jazz Society also cultivates young local talent, and though there's rarely a cover charge, a humble donation of $5 is suggested – a bargain for the caliber of performances hosted here. The live jazz is nightly during opening hours.

La Mesa Salsoteca DANCE

(www.facebook.com/lamesasalsayson; Gran Colombia 03-35; ⊙9pm-midnight Wed, to 3am Fri) *The* place to show off or refine your salsa moves, but don't expect to get going until late.

🛍 Shopping

Mercado 9 de Octubre MARKET

(Plaza Cívica 9 de Octubre; ⊙8am-7pm) Amazing fruit and vegetable market in a covered building on Plaza Cívica 9 de Octubre (also known as Plaza Rotary).

MAKI ARTS & CRAFTS

(☑07-282-0529; maki@fairtrade.ec; Sucre 14-96, near Talbot; ⊙10am-7pm Mon-Fri, to 5pm Sat & Sun) Featuring high-quality textiles, baskets, clothing, jewelry and ceramics, this fair-trade shop is a wonderful showcase from which to scoop up souvenirs you can feel good about.

❶ Information

Banco de Guayaquil (Mariscal Sucre near Borrero) Bank with ATM.

Banco del Pichincha (cnr Solano & 12 de Abril) Big branch with ATMs.

Clínica Hospital Monte Sinaí (🕿 07-288-5595; www.hospitalmontesinai.org; cnr Av Solano & Miguel Cordero) An excellent clinic with some English-speaking staff.

Tourist Office (iTur; 🕿 07-282-1035; Mariscal Sucre, near Luís Cordero; ⊗ 8am-8pm Mon-Fri, 9am-4pm Sat, 8:30am-1:30pm Sun) Friendly and helpful; English spoken. On Parque Calederón.

❶ Getting There & Away

AIR

Cuenca's **Aeropuerto Mariscal Lamar** (🕿 07-286-7120, 07-286-2095; www.aeropuerto cuenca.ec; Av España) is 2km from the heart of town and just 500m from the Terminal Terrestre bus station. **TAME** (🕿 07-286-6400, 07-286-2193; www.tame.com.ec; Aeropuerto Mariscal Lamar; ⊗ 7am-8pm Mon-Fri, 8am-noon Sat, 6-8pm Sun) has daily flights to Quito ($99 to $131) and Guayaquil ($73 to $150).

BUS

Cuenca's main bus station is **Terminal Terrestre** (Av España), about 1.5km from downtown, across the street from the airport. It has daily buses to Ingapirca and Gualaceo, Chordeleg and Sigsig.

Two routes go to Guayaquil: the shorter via Parque Nacional Cajas and Molleturo ($8, four hours), and the longer via La Troncal and Cañar ($8, five hours).

Services are frequent on all routes.

❶ Getting Around

Taxis cost about $2 between downtown and the airport or the bus terminal – or it's a 20-minute walk. Regular buses head downtown ($0.25) from in front of Terminal Terrestre. From downtown to the terminal, take any bus marked 'Terminal' from stops on Padre Aguirre near the flower market.

Local buses for Turi ($0.25), 4km south of the center, go along Avenida Solano – or a taxi is $5.

Around Cuenca
🕿 07

Cuenca is an easy base for day trips to indigenous villages in the surrounding area. Many are invested in community-based tourism, so you can support local people by hiring local guides and buying traditional crafts. Gualaceo, Chordeleg and Sigsig can all be done together in one day, while Parque Nacional Cajas and the ruins at Ingapirca are separate day trips of their own.

Ingapirca
🕿 07 / ELEV 3150M

Ecuador's best-preserved archaeological site, **Ingapirca** (🕿 07-221-7115; http://patrimonio cultural.gob.ec/complejo-arqueologico-ingapirca; entry incl optional guided tour $2; ⊗ 8am-5:30pm), 1km above the homonymous village, pales in comparison to large archaeological sites in neighboring Peru. This said, the small site, with its semi-intact temple, grazing llamas and open fields, is definitely worth a stopover if you are headed this way. And hikers won't want to miss the three-day Camino del Inca trek.

DON'T MISS

THE INCA TRAIL TO INGAPIRCA

Though it sees only a fraction of the traffic of the Inca Trail to Machu Picchu, the three-day trek to Ingapirca is popular. For approximately 40km, it follows the original Ingañan Incan royal road that linked Cuzco with Tomebamba (at present-day Cuenca) and Quito.

The starting point for the hike is **Achupallas**, 23km southeast of Alausí. You'll need a GPS and three 1:50,000 topographical maps (*Alausí, Juncal* and *Cañar*), available at the IGM (p693) in Quito. Also be prepared for extremely persistent begging from children.

To get to Achupallas, take one of the daily midday buses from Alausí or, more reliably, hire a taxi-pickup for about $10 to $15 one way. Alternatively, south-bound Panamericana buses from Alausí can drop you at **La Moya** (also known as **Guasuntos**), where you can wait for passing trucks headed to Achupallas, 12km up a slim mountain road. You can hire guides in Achupallas for $30 to $40 per day, or Julio Verne Tour Operator (p713) in Riobamba runs trips for about $320 per person. If you want to go on your own, check out a hiking guide, such as *Ecuador: Climbing and Hiking Guide* by Rob Rachowiecki and Mark Thurber.

Cooperativa Cañar buses ($3.50, two hours) go direct from Cuenca's main bus terminal, leaving Monday to Friday at 9am and 12:20pm and returning from Ingapirca to Cuenca at 1pm and 3:45pm. On weekends, the only bus leaves Cuenca at 9am, returning at 1pm. Buses also leave every half-hour from Cuenca for El Tambo, 8km below Ingapirca. From El Tambo, buses leave about every half-hour to Ingapirca, or take a taxi (about $5).

Gualaceo, Chordeleg & Sigsig

If you start early, you could easily visit the Sunday markets at all three of these traditional towns and be back in Cuenca for happy hour. Doing this, in fact, is deservedly one of Cuenca's most popular day trips. Between them all you'll find many traditional handicrafts: woven baskets, fine gold and silver filigreed jewelry, woodwork, pottery, guitars and *ikat* textiles – made using a pre-Columbian technique of weaving tie-dyed threads.

From Cuenca's Terminal Terrestre bus terminal, buses leave every half-hour to Gualaceo ($0.90, one hour), Chordeleg ($1, one hour) and Sigsig ($1.50, 1½ hours). Buses run from town to town for $0.50 and can be flagged down from the main street. For Sigsig, you might need to change in Gualaceo.

Parque Nacional Cajas

Parque Nacional Cajas (Cajas National Park; 07-237-0126; http://areasprotegidas.ambiente. gob.ec/es/areas-protegidas/parque-nacional-cajas; 8am-4:30pm) FREE, only 30km west of Cuenca, encompasses 2854 sq km of golden-green moor-like *páramo* (mountainous Andean grasslands) dotted with hundreds of chilly lakes that shine like jewels against a rough, otherworldly countryside.

This extremely wet and foggy area feeds rivers that flow into Cuenca and is considered a major conservation area for birds, mammals and flora: in fact, this is the most biologically diverse portion of *páramo* in the entire Andes range.

Especially important are small forests of *Polylepis* trees that are found in sheltered hollows and natural depressions. *Polylepis* trees have adapted to grow at higher elevations than almost any other tree in the world, making this one of the highest forests on earth. Wandering into one of these dense dwarf forests is like entering a Brothers Grimm fairy tale.

Transportes Occidental buses ($1.25, one hour) bound for Guayaquil leave from Terminal Terrestre in Cuenca every day at 6:15am, 7am, 8am, 10am, noon, 1:30pm, 2:30pm, 4:10pm and 5:45pm. To return to Cuenca, flag any passing Cuenca-bound bus.

Buses for Soldados ($1.50, 1¼ hours) and Angas ($2, 1¾ hours) leave from the El Vado bridge in Cuenca at 6am and return in the afternoon.

Saraguro

07 / POP 9000 / ELEV 2520M

Surrounded by emerald hills that have been sown with hearty tubers and grains for thousands of years, Saraguro, 165km south of Cuenca, is the center of indigenous Saraguro culture. This prosperous and proud indigenous group originally lived near Lake Titicaca in Peru but ended up here in the 1470s as a result of the Inca Empire's system of *mitimaes* (resettlement).

Saraguro's excellent community-tourism projects are applauded across Ecuador – there are few better places in South America to go off grid and authentically experience indigenous highland culture.

Activities

The villages around Saraguro, most within a half-hour walk or 10-minute bus ride ($0.20), are full of outdoor and cultural activities. Buses to any of these places leave from the main square in front of the cathedral: get information on the best activities running from the **tourism office** (cnr 10 de Marzo & Loja; 8am-5pm Mon-Fri).

Sleeping & Eating

★**Hostal Achik Wasi**   HOTEL $$
(07-220-0058; Intiñan, Barrio La Luz; s/d incl breakfast $23/40; P) A 10-minute walk up and out of town (taxi $1), this large adobe-and-wood *hostal* is by far the best place to stay. It has comfortable, clean rooms with thick wool blankets and beamed ceilings. The great views and charming service are also big pluses. It's part of a well-run tourism project that benefits the community.

★**ShamuiCo Espai Gastronòmic**   FUSION $$
(07-220-0590; shamuicorestaurant@gmail.com; cnr Loja & 10 de Marzo; small dishes $3-8; 10am-

9pm Wed-Sun) A surprising find in Saraguro, this unpretentiously sophisticated spot is run by a local chef who trained in some of Europe's best restaurants. Bold cuisine falls somewhere along the lines of highland Ecuadorian-European tapas, inspired by the grains grown around Saraguro and straight-from-the-market fresh produce that melds into tasty but uncomplicated plates.

ℹ️ Getting There & Away

Any Loja-bound bus from Cuenca will drop you a block from Saraguro's main plaza ($5, three hours, hourly). Buses to Loja ($2 to $3, 1½ hours) leave hourly-ish during the day. In either direction, buses stop on Azuay, between El Oro and 10 de Marzo. Buy your ticket on the bus.

Loja

📃 07 / POP 181,000 / ELEV 2100M

Whilst once upon a time, Loja was the thriving base from which Spanish conquistadors set off to explore the jungle just over the mountains, now Loja's main lure is its proximity to one of Ecuador's most diverse protected areas, the vast Parque Nacional Podocarpus (p725), south of town.

But Loja's center has plenty of appeal too. Its cuisine, its musical traditions and its university are known across Ecuador and beyond. Its streets, some of which are pedestrianized, might at first seem a tad tame after Cuenca, but offer inroads into the local culture its more famous rival to the north cannot. Lying dramatically along the bottom of the Valle de Cuxibamba, Loja's surrounding slopes are fringed with the country's main coffee plantations, and several miradors (viewpoints) offer unforgettable city views.

🛏️ Sleeping

Hotel Londres HOSTEL $
(📃07-256-1936; Sucre 07-51; r without bathroom per person $6; 📶) With creaky wooden floors, saggy beds and somewhat cell-like rooms, Hotel Londres is as basic as they come, but it's a tried-and-true travelers' favorite, set far back down a corridor from the street with clean shared bathrooms and friendly owners.

Hosteria Quinta Montaña CABIN $$
(📃099-343-4739, 07-254-0851; Batalla de Tarqui, Barrio Colinas del Norte; s/d $25/45; 🅿️📶🏊) City address; countrified experience – 2km

north of the bus terminal, serene Hosteria Quinta Montaña's well-kept cabins skitter down a steep hillside. Grounds include a nice restaurant, a cold-water pool and a sauna. Swinging on a hammock might be commonplace in the jungle but in Loja, doing so with such a lush view is the preserve of guests staying here.

🍴 Eating & Drinking

El Tamal Lojano ECUADORIAN $
(cnr 18 de Noviembre 05-12 & Samaniego; dishes $1.50-4.50, set lunches from $2; ⏰8am-9pm Mon-Fri, 8:30am-noon & 3:30-8pm Sat & Sun) The *almuerzos* (set lunches) are good, but the real reason to come is for the delicious *quimbolitos, humitas, empanadas de verde* and *tamales lojanos* – all Loja region's foodie classics. Don't miss the *tigrillos* amid the scrumptious breakfast options: smashed plantains with pork scratchings and mozzarella. Order at the counter.

⭐ Riscomar SEAFOOD $$
(📃07-258-5154; www.riscomarloja.com; cnr Rocafuerte & 24 de Mayo; mains $8-16; ⏰9am-4pm & 7-10:30pm Mon-Sat, 9am-4pm Sun) Serving some of Loja's best seafood, Riscomar prepares delicious, Ecuadorian-style ceviche in a civilized dining room. A fillet of *corvina* (sea bass) in a complex *salsa de mariscos* (seafood sauce) is particularly recommended, and service is exemplary.

⭐ Zarza
Brewing Company MICROBREWERY
(📃07-257-1413; www.zarzabrewing.com; cnr Puerto Bolívar & Esmeraldas; dishes $3.50-9; ⏰4pm-midnight Mon-Wed, to 2am Thu-Sat) In the El Valle neighborhood, this brewpub is as popular with locals as with Loja expats. The owner is Texan and clearly knows a thing or two about microbrewing and Mexican food. They do unusual-for-Ecuador brews such as Lambics and Belgian wits, and on the food front an alluring range of smoked meats. A taxi here costs about $1.40.

ℹ️ Information

Banco de Guayaquil (Eguiguren, near Valdivieso) Bank with ATM.
Banco de Pichincha (cnr Bernado Valdivieso & 10 de Agosto) Has ATMs.
Clinica San Augustin (📃07-257-0314; www.hospitalclinicasanagustin.com; cnr 18 de Noviembre & Azuay; ⏰24hr) Recommended hospital for foreigners.

ℹ GETTING TO PERU

The crossing into Peru via Macará is much quieter than at Huaquillas and busier than at Zumba. Macará is 3km from the actual border crossing, or *puente internacional* (international bridge). Most people buy tickets direct to Piura (Peru) from Loja. **Transportes Loja Internacional** (☑07-269-4058; Vaca & Jaramillo) and **Unión Cariamanga** (☑07-269-4047; cnr Loja & Manuel E Rengel) leave Macará for Piura twice a day ($4, three hours). The bus stops at the border, waits for passengers to take care of exits/entries, then continues to Piura.

Ministerio del Medio Ambiente (☑ext 109 07-257-7125; Sucre 4-35, 3rd fl; ⊙8am-5pm Mon-Fri) Responsible for administering Parque Nacional Podocarpus; provides information on the park but rarely has maps available.

Police station (☑07-257-5606; Valdivieso btwn Imbabura & Quito) Just north of the city center.

Tourist office (iTur; ☑07-257-0485, 07-258-1251; cnr Bolívar & Eguiguren; ⊙8am-1pm & 3-6pm Mon-Fri, 8am-4pm Sat) Helpful, with some maps available.

ℹ Getting There & Away

Loja is served by **Aeropuerto Ciudad de Catamayo** which, as its name suggests, is in Catamayo, 35km west of Loja. Buses bound for Macará head there ($1.30).

TAME (☑07-257-0248; www.tame.com.ec; Av Ortega, near 24 de Mayo; ⊙8:30am-1pm & 2:30-6pm Mon-Fri, 9am-12:15pm Sat) flies to/from Quito and Guayaquil daily.

Almost all buses leave from the **bus terminal** (Terminal Terrestre Reina del Cisne; Av 8 de Diciembre), about 2km north of downtown. Vilcabambaturis has fast minibuses to Vilcabamba ($1.30, 1¼ hours, every 30 minutes from 5:45am to 8:45pm) from the bus terminal, to the right and at the back from the main terminal entrance. A faster way is via *taxi colectivo* (shared taxi; $2, 45 minutes), from Avenida Universitaria, about 10 blocks south of Mercadillo in Loja; ask a local taxi driver to take you to the Ruta 11 de Mayo **taxi stop** (cnr Aguirre & Mercadillo).

Huaquillas, the main border crossing to Peru, can be reached by a bus leaving from the terminal at 5pm ($10, seven hours), so you can avoid backtracking to Machala. Loja is also a departure point for buses to southern border crossings into Peru via Macará and Zumba (now connected via a direct route from Loja to Jaén, Peru).

You can go directly to Piura (Peru) from Loja without stopping in Macará. The service ($14, nine hours) is offered with **Loja International** (☑07-257-9014, 07-257-0505; bus terminal). Buy your tickets at least a day before you travel.

There are frequent services to most major destinations.

Zamora

☑07 / POP 13,400 / ELEV 970M

The hot, humid capital of the Zamora-Chinchipe province is part Oriente and part Sierra. Perched between these regions in the Andean foothills, it attracts settlers from the high-altitude communities of Saraguro and the Amazon Basin Shuar. Zamora bills itself as the 'City of Birds and Waterfalls' and whilst none are evident in the somewhat-bland city itself, tourism here is all about nearby Parque Nacional Podocarpus.

Decades of colonization by miners and growth into a provincial hub have created a city center of unremarkable, concrete structures. Zamora has, however, experienced a bit of a revival, with renovations to bridges, a spruced-up bus station and a beautiful *malecón* (waterfront) along the Río Zamora. And if you need to know what time it is, just look up: the big hill above the bus station sports a ginormous clock.

🛏 Sleeping

★**Copalinga** LODGE $$$
(☑099-347-7013, 099-710-1535, in Quito 02-250-5129; www.fjocotoco.org; Vía al Podocarpus Km 3; cabins incl breakfast, lunch & dinner from s/d $98/162) 🏞 Bird-watchers, ahem, *flock* to this tranquil reserve for sure-thing sightings of exotic avian species. Even nonbirders will love the orchid collection, hummingbird feeders, trails and secluded ambience. Take your pick of rustic or luxury cabins, and let the rushing river lull you to sleep. Hydropower runs the whole place, and meals are generous and tasty.

ℹ Information

Banco del Austro On the plaza, with a functioning ATM.

Ministerio del Ambiente (☑07-260-6606, 07-260-5318; Sevilla de Oro near Orellana; ⊙8:30am-4:30pm Mon-Fri) Information on Parque Nacional Podocarpus.

ℹ Getting There & Away

The **bus terminal** (cnr Av Heroés de Paquisha & Amazonas) is across the street from the big clock.

Buses leave almost hourly to Loja ($3, two hours) between 3am and 11pm. There are five daily buses heading north to Gualaquiza ($3.50, four hours). For Cuenca (seven hours), Guayaquil (11 hours) or Quito (16 hours), head first to Loja from where there are frequent connections to all three.

Parque Nacional Podocarpus

Podocarpus National Park (refugios $3) **FREE** fills in much of the triangle between Loja, Zamora and Vilcabamba as well as a huge swath to the southeast. Because altitude ranges so greatly within the park borders (from around 900m in the lowland sector to over 3600m in the highland sector), Podocarpus has some of the world's greatest plant and animal diversity. Perhaps 40% of its estimated 3000 plant species occur nowhere else in the world, and close to 600 bird species have been recorded. Rare mammals include foxes, deer, pumas, mountain tapirs and bears.

Highland Sector

Access to the highland sector of the park is through **Cajanuma control**, about 10km south of Loja. From here, a dirt road leads 8.5km uphill to the park office and adjacent **refugio** (cabin per person $3), which has seven basic cabañas with mattresses and a camping area.

From the *refugio,* several self-guided trails wend through the cloud forest. More strenuous and wide-ranging is the 5km **Los Miradores Loop Trail**, a four-hour hike up through the cloud forest and into the *páramo* (grasslands) – expect strong winds. Another trail that branches off the Miradores leads 14.5km to the beautiful highland lakes of **Lagunas de los Compadres**: the trail to the lakes is three days round-trip for most hikers.

Lowlands Sector

The main access to the lowland sector is the **Bombuscaro control**, 6km south of Zamora by a dirt road that follows the Río Bombuscaro. From the parking area at the end of the road it's a half-hour walk on a wide, uphill trail to the control point.

There are several short, maintained (but sometimes muddy) trails that meander into the forest, the most popular of which leads you to the **Cascada Poderosa** and **Chismosa Waterfalls**. The 6km **Los Higuerones** trail takes you into some primary forest, as does the five-hour **El Campesino** trail. The very fit can scramble uphill about an hour on the **El Mirador** trail, while another trail leads to a deep (but very swift) swimming hole called the *área fotográfica* on the Río Bombuscaro.

Another infrequently used entrance is at the tiny village of **Romerillos**, about 25km south of Zamora by a different road.

Vilcabamba

🎵 07 / POP 5000 / ELEV 1700M

Oh, Vilcabamba: where mountains soar alluringly above town, where the balmy air is synonymous with longevity (it shot to fame for its high number of centenarians after *Reader's Digest* did stories on them in 1955), where those who encounter it simply get waylaid – sometimes for months, sometimes years...

The area's beautiful scenery, mild weather and laid-back vibe attract waves of visitors: backpackers as well as North American and European retirees. Hiking, horseback riding and meditation are popular activities. The hills are dotted with big new houses, and the town plaza with expat-owned businesses. Gringo-ization has created tension and the cost of land and living, but the flip side is that jobs in tourism and construction are more plentiful than ever, and Vilcabamba is the rare Ecuadorian *pueblo* where young people have little ambition to leave for the big city.

🏃 Activities

Vilcabamba offers perfect weather for hiking and horseback riding, as well as access to remote sections of Parque Nacional Podocarpus, but it's also an excellent place to chill. Legions of specialists are ready to facilitate your relaxation with inexpensive massages, pedicures and meditation sessions.

Most naturalists and horse guides charge about $15 for one to two hours, $25 for four and $35 for the whole day.

Caballos Gavilán   HORSE RIDING
(📞 07-264-0415, 098-133-2806; gavilanhorse@ yahoo.com; Sucre 10-30; per hour from $15) Highly

recommended, Gavin is a New Zealander who has lived here for years. He guides one-hour to three-day horseback-riding trips, the latter with overnight stays in his refuge near the park.

🛏 Sleeping

★ Rumi-Wilco Ecolodge   LODGE $

(https://rumiwilco.com/; campsites per person $5, r without bathroom per person from $10, s/d cabins from $18/36; 🛜) 🌿 A 10-minute walk from the bus station up a track over the river, Rumi-Wilco has a series of remote houses, cabins and camping spaces within the evergreen confines of the 40-hectare Rumi-Wilco Nature Reserve. Adobe houses have attractive rooms with well-equipped communal kitchens (great for small groups) but our favorites are the rustic cabins on stilts – again with very impressive kitchens!

Hostería y Restaurante Izhcayluma   RESORT $

(📱 07-302-5162; www.izhcayluma.com; min 2-night stay dm $9.50, s/d from $29/38, without bathroom from $20/26, cabins s/d $39/49; 🅿🛜⛱) Located 2km above town to the south, German-owned Izhcayluma is excellent value, a refined hilltop retreat. The outdoor dining area serves German-Ecuadorian cuisine and has sweeping panoramic views. A 'holistic wellness room' offers massages and other treatments, and there is a bar and swimming pool. The cabins and rooms are quiet and spacious.

Eating

Mestizo   CAFE $

(light meals from $3.50; ⊙8am-8pm Mon-Sat, to 6pm Sun; 🛜🍽) This beautiful cafe with a people-watching terrace right on the plaza is the best spot in town for a coffee (the owner is Argentine, and knows how to make a good one), smoothies (choose the one with the ingredients related to your star sign) or a hunger-inducing range of creative sandwiches, muffins and cakes.

UFO   MIDDLE EASTERN $

(United Falafel Organization; www.facebook.com/unitedfalafel; Fernando de la Vega 09-18; mains $4-8; ⊙11am-8pm Wed, Thu & Sun, to 8:30pm Fri & Sat; 🍽) Besides the clever name and enviable location next to the church, the Turkish-run UFO gets jammed for its inexpensive and tasty breakfasts, Middle Eastern favorites, gluten-free desserts, fantastic coffee and a variety of vegetarian and vegan options. All of this brought to you with a smile, and with an attractive back garden to feast in.

La Baguette   BAKERY $

(cnr Eterna Juventud & Vaca de la Vega; snacks from $2; ⊙7am-5pm Wed-Sat, to 4pm Sun) Divine French goodies – *pain au chocolat* (chocolate croissant), quiche, and even gluten-free bread on Wednesdays – plus good coffee. Order it to go or eat in at one of the few tables.

ℹ Information

DANGERS & ANNOYANCES

There were a few muggings on the trail up Cerro Mandango around 2012, but safety is not cur-

---

ℹ GETTING TO PERU

Transportes Nambija runs a direct overnight service from Loja through Zumba to Jaén, Peru (from where you can pick up *colectivos*/buses to Chachapoyas).

Transportes Nambija ($10, six to seven hours) and Cooperativa Cariamanga buses, among others, leave Loja for Zumba; all stop in Vilcabamba one hour after leaving Loja.

From Zumba, *rancheras* (open-sided trucks) leave at 8am, 10:30am and 5:30pm for the border at La Balsa (around $3, 1½ to 2½ hours), where you get your exit stamp (or entry stamp, if coming from Peru). The condition of the road between Zumba and La Balsa varies greatly, depending on recent weather. On the other side of the 'international bridge' in Peru there are taxi *colectivos* (*combis*) to San Ignacio (S9/$3, 1½ hours), where you can spend the night. Money-changing can be done at La Balsa or, failing that, San Ignacio.

From San Ignacio, there are regular minibuses to Jaén ($3.50, three hours) beginning at 4am. Once you're in Jaén, take a *mototaxi* (motorcycle taxi) to the *colectivo* stop and then get a *colectivo* to Bagua Grande (one hour). From Bagua Grande you then get a bus to Chachapoyas (three hours), the first town of any real size.

rently an issue. Ask about the current situation at the iTur (p727) and leave valuables in your hotel as a precaution.

Police station (⏺07-264-0896; Agua de Hierro near Bolívar)

MONEY

Stock up on cash before arriving in Vilcabamba. There are a couple of ATMs here, but a lot of visitors for such a small town.

Banco de Guayaquil (Cnr Bolívar & Diego de la Vaca) ATM only.

Banco del Austro (Central Plaza) ATM on the plaza.

TOURIST INFORMATION

Tourist office (iTur; ⏺07-264-0090; cnr Bolívar & Diego Vaca de la Vega; ⏰9am-1pm & 3-6pm) Helpful, with good info and maps of area hikes.

❶ Getting There & Away

Transportes Vilcamixtos (⏺07-264-0044) is a taxi-truck cooperative on the main plaza (you can't miss the green-and-white trucks). Most charge $1.50 to $4 for nearby destinations.

Buses, minivans and taxis leave from the tiny **bus terminal** (Eterna Juventud & Jaramillo). **Taxis colectivos** ($2, 45 minutes) depart frequently to Loja after four people cram in; Vilcabambaturis minibuses ($1.30, one hour) leave on the hour.

Buses from Loja stop in Vilcabamba on their way south to Zumba ($9, four to five hours) and the Peruvian border, from where there is onward transportation to Chachapoyas, Peru.

THE ORIENTE

The vast tract of land locally known as Amazonía holds more drama than a rip-roaring flood or crackling lightning storm. Rivers churn from the Andes into the dense, sweltering rainforest on course for the Amazon basin. Along the way, ancient indigenous tribes call riverbanks home and astounding wildlife can be glimpsed. Those lucky enough to reach the remoter jungle lodges (several hours downriver from the nearest towns) will be able to fish for piranhas on silent blackwater lakes, hear the menacing boom of howler monkeys, spot the shining eyes of caiman at nighttime and – perhaps – spy one of those elusive bigger mammals such as a tapir or jaguar.

Exploring the Oriente gives you the unforgettable experience of seeing the natural world up close and personal. But this region

is not just jungle. Ecuador's best thermal spa, most spectacular waterfall, most active volcanoes and most formidable white-water rapids also await.

Lago Agrio

⏺06 / POP 57,700

This seedy, gray town pulses with the life of the oil industry, a chaotic market, dusty streets, thick traffic and gritty bars. Certain realities exist here, including a high amount of prostitution and crime related to the nearby Colombian border. Lago is mainly visited as the entry point to the spectacular Reserva de Producción Faunística Cuyabeno, which offers some of Ecuador's best wildlife-spotting opportunities.

Ongoing troubles in neighboring Colombia have made border towns such as Lago Agrio havens for Colombian guerrillas, antirebel paramilitaries and drug smugglers. Do not cross into Colombia from here. In town, bars can be risky and side streets unsafe, so stick to the main drag (especially at night) or take a taxi to restaurants further out. Tourists rarely have problems.

Flights fill up fast with jungle-lodge guests and oil workers traveling home for the weekend; book early.

TAME (⏺06-283-0982; Orellana near 9 de Octubre) has daily flights between Quito and Lago Agrio.

The airport is about 3km east of Lago Agrio; taxis there (yellow or white pickup trucks) cost about $3.

The drive from the jungle into the Andes (and vice versa) is dramatic and beautiful, and worth doing in daylight. The bus terminal, about 2km northwest of Lago Agrio center, has a wide selection of routes and options. In addition, Transportes Putumayo buses go through the jungle towns of Dureno and Tarapoa for travelers wanting access to the Río Aguarico side of the Cuyabeno Reserve – although it's far more rewarding to go with a guided tour. Services run daily and are relatively frequent.

Reserva Producción Faunística Cuyabeno

This beautiful **reserve** is a unique flooded rainforest covering 6034 sq km around Río Cuyabeno. Seasonally inundated with water, the flooded forest provides a home to diverse aquatic species and birdlife – not to mention pink river dolphins, manatees, caiman and anacondas, several monkey and cat species, tapirs, peccaries and agoutis. Macrolobium and ceiba treetops thrust out from the underwater forest, creating a stunning visual effect. The blackwater rivers, rich in tannins from decomposing foliage, form a maze of waterways that feed the lagoons.

Due to its remoteness, and to protect the communities within it, travelers should only visit the reserve on guided tours – which are significantly cheaper, and often yield richer wildlife sightings, than in Parque Nacional Yasuní.

Guided tours include transport to, from and on the river. Trips to Cuyabeno generally begin at the Lago Agrio airport.

🛏 Sleeping

Jamu Lodge   JUNGLE LODGE **$$$**
(www.jamulodge.com; s/d 4 days & 3 nights per person incl full board $501/668; 🔊) Squirrel monkeys cavort above the walkways at highly rated Jamu lodge, where the jungle feels close at hand. Dugout-canoe trips, walks through swamps knee-deep in mud to spot the likes of anacondas and pink river dolphins, swims in lagoons and memorable nighttime excursions all contribute to a vivid wilderness experience.

Cuyabeno Lodge   LODGE **$$$**
(📱in Quito 02-292-6153; www.cuyabenolodge.com.ec; s/d 4 days & 3 nights incl full board from $480/760) 🌿 This highly recommended place is run in close cooperation with the local Siona people. Thatched huts and towers with hot-water bathrooms and solar electricity are spread over its hillside location (which is never inundated). Upgraded tower rooms are more spacious and have private balconies. Bilingual naturalist guides get top reviews from guests.

Coca
📱06 / POP 45,200

The unavoidable starting point for many of Ecuador's most fascinating jungle tours, Coca has been through many transformations over the years, and its current look is a lot better than its previous ones. The capital of the Orellana province since 1999 (and officially known as Puerto Francisco de Orellana), Coca is the last real city before the Río Napo transports you deep into the

rainforest to the Parque Nacional Yasuní and beyond into the Amazon basin.

Though decidedly not a destination in itself, Coca is no longer just a charmless transport hub. An attractive little park adorns the center, and a pretty *malecón* (waterfront) runs along the riverfront, anchored by the excellent **Museo Arqueológico Centro Cultural de Orellana** (Museo Arqueológico Centro Cultural de Orellana; www.macco.ec; 9 de Octubre, btwn Espejo & Maleón Chimborazo; $3; ⊙8am-noon & 2-6pm Tue-Fri, 9am-noon & 2-5pm Sat & Sun) that opened in 2016. A stunning suspension bridge now spans the Napo, taking traffic down Via Auca toward Tiguino (another starting point for rainforest forays).

☞ Tours

Amazon Camping Expeditions   OUTDOORS
(http://amazoncampingexpeditions.com; 10-day river adventure per person $5000) Experienced guide Fausto Andi's multiday adventure boat trips start in Coca and head down the Río Napo toward Nuevo Rocafuerte and the Peruvian border, where the chances of viewing wildlife are much higher along parts of the river rarely glimpsed by foreigners. Camp along the riverbanks. Other trips, such as to Limoncocha, can be accommodated on request.

Amazon Wildlife Tours   WILDLIFE
(📱098-266-5506, 098-041-1985; www.amazonwildlife.ec; cnr Quito & Bolivar; per person per day $135-200) This outfit is the best reason to book a jungle jaunt within Coca: an experienced agency with an array of nature-watching tours, including a specialty jaguar expedition in Yasuní National Park, tours to see Amazon dolphins and general wildlife-watching in the Limoncocha Reserve. Two-night Yasuní tours start at $272 per person.

🛏 Sleeping & Eating

On Calle Quito, between Rocafuerte and Espejo, any night of the week, cheerful street vendors serve up grilled meats barbecued right in front of you – it's a fantastic and very sociable place to eat, and cheap.

Hotel La Misión   HOTEL **$$**
(📱06-288-0260; hlamision@hotmail.com; Camilo de Torrano; s/d $37/54; P❄🔊🏊) This long-time Coca staple, overall resembling an ailing beached ferry with its rusting metal stairs and public areas, makes the most of its location right by the Yasuní departure dock.

Some of the clean but scuffed rooms have Río Napo views. All come with cable TV, fridges and modern bathrooms. You can't get a more convenient location for embarking on a Yasuní trip.

Papees Grill   GRILL **$$**
(www.facebook.com/papeesgrill; off Espejo; mains $12-17; ⊙10am-11:30pm Mon-Sat, to 6pm Sun) A clean, unpretentious little place off the far western end of Espejo near where the Río Payamino meets the Río Napo, serving exquisite grilled meat. Hands down the best restaurant around for a very long way.

ℹ Information

Banco del Austro (☑06-289-1900; cnr Chimborazo & Quito; ⊙9am-4:30pm Mon-Fri) Has ATMs.

Banco del Pichincha (cnr 6 de Diciembre & Bolívar) Has ATMs.

Nuevo Hospital Francisco de Orellana (☑06-286-1521; cnr Arazá & Palmito) North of the center near the junction of Hwys E45A and E20.

Tourist Information Office (☑06-288-0532; www.orellanaturistica.gob.ec; Malecón Chimborazo 83-04; ⊙7:30am-4:30pm Mon-Fri, 8am-2pm Sat; 🕾) Helpful; on Malecón Chimborazo.

ℹ Getting There & Around

AIR

Aeropuerto Francisco de Orellana is almost 2km north of town on the left-hand side of the road to Lago Agrio. The five-minute taxi ride there costs around $2.

TAME (☑06-288-0786; cnr Quito N29-11 & Castillo; ⊙8am-1pm & 2-6pm Mon-Fri, 8am-2pm Sat & Sun) flies between Coca and Quito three times daily.

BOAT

Most Yasuní lodges use the **Puerto La Misión** dock within Hostería La Misión. You will be told about your departure point well in advance if on a guided tour.

Coop de Transportes Fluviales Orellana offers a passenger service downriver to Nuevo Rocafuerte, on the Peruvian border (and back upriver again). It departs Monday, Wednesday and Thursday at 7am for Nuevo Rocafuerte ($18.75, eight to 10 hours). It departs Nuevo Rocafuerte for Coca on Wednesday, Saturday and Sunday at 5am (12 to 14 hours).

BUS

Coca, among its growing number of boasts, has one of Ecuador's best new bus terminals; the **bus station** (Terminal Terrestre de Coca E P Francisco de Orellana; Río Guatараco s/n) is

---

ℹ GETTING TO PERU

A distant dot on the map for many people, **Nuevo Rocafuerte** on the Peruvian border is in no danger of losing its mystery. While backpackers may bubble with excitement at the idea of floating the Río Napo all the way to Peru and the Amazon, only the most intrepid travelers rise to the occasion and make the trip here.

Nuevo Rocafuerte is eight to 10 hours from Coca along the Río Napo, and a legal border crossing with Peru, although regular onward passenger-boat transport over the border is lacking and accommodations are basic

If you are continuing to Peru, inquire at the **Coop de Transportes Fluviales Orellana** (☑093-925-5654, 06-288-2582; Malecón Chimborazo, at docks; ⊙office hours 7-8am & 9am-12:45pm Mon & Thu, 7-8am, 9am-12:45pm & 3-5:45pm Wed, 7am-noon & 2-5:45pm Sun) in Coca, when you buy your ticket downstream, for phone numbers of cargo boats which may be connecting to Pantoja/Iquitos. But nothing guarantees timing; there's a good chance you'll get stuck here, so be prepared. Bring adequate supplies of water-purification tablets, insect repellent and food. Also, consider getting Peruvian currency in Quito before arriving.

To get to Iquitos, Peru (from where boats head down to Brazil and Colombia) it's best to travel downstream across the border to Pantoja. (Canoes can be hired for $60 per boatload.)

An adventurous trip like this one is made more enjoyable by enlisting the services of a guide; a guide (who will supply a boat) can also guarantee your passage from Coca beyond Nuevo Rocafuerte to Peru, thus saving you lengthy delays in Nuevo Rocafuerte.

3km north of town. A taxi here costs around $2 to $2.50. All main destinations are served.

Rancheras (open-sided buses, or trucks mounted with uncomfortably narrow bench seats, also known as *chivas*) leave from the market on Alejandro Labaka two blocks back from the river, heading for various destinations between Coca and Lago Agrio, and to Río Tiputini to the south. **Cooperativa Camionetas Río Napo** pickup trucks and taxis provide services around/outside town.

Buses run to Tena ($8.75, four hours), where you can change for Oriente destinations further to the south; Lago Agrio ($3.75, two hours); and Quito ($11 to $12, six hours via Jondachi or 10 hours via Lago Agrio).

Parque Nacional Yasuní

With a massive 9820-sq-km section of wetlands, marshes, swamps, lakes, rivers and tropical rainforest, **Yasuní National Park** ($2) is Ecuador's largest mainland park. Its staggering biodiversity led Unesco to declare it an international biosphere reserve, and it was established as a national park shortly after, in 1979. Because this pocket of life was untouched by the last ice age, a diverse pool of species has thrived here throughout the centuries, including more than 600 bird species, some previously unknown elsewhere. Resident animals include some hard-to-see jungle wildlife, such as jaguars, harpy eagles, pumas and tapirs. River lodges and tour operators include boat transport and sometimes airport transfers in their packages. Coca serves as the jumping-off point into the park, and your tour will always include return transportation to Coca.

Tena

🎵 06 / POP 23,300 / ELEV 598M

Unusually for a jungle transport hub, Tena is an attractive place where many travelers find themselves hanging around quite happily for days before or after a trip into the rainforest. While it won't win architectural prizes anytime soon, Tena has a friendly population, a gorgeous setting surrounded by jungle-covered hills, a lively *malecón* and lots of backpacker infrastructure. Whitewater fanatics from around the globe come to paddle and play on the high concentration of surrounding rivers, and the town is home to lots of experienced and highly recommended kayaking operators.

To imbibe the Tena vibe, take a turn along the *malecón* (waterfront) which runs east and west along the banks of the Río Tena for a few blocks. Tena's newer (southernmost) footbridge, connecting across to Parque Amazónico La Isla, has a futuristic-looking *mirador* (viewing tower). Cross the river on this bridge and come back on the old footbridge, just north. Market days are Friday and Saturday.

🏃 Activities

Tena is Ecuador's white-water rafting center, and rafting headlines the activities available here. Also possible are kayaking, trekking and rappelling. However, mining around the town is forcing operators to take groups further away to find unspoiled river.

★**River People**   RAFTING
(📞06-286-5197, 099-544-0234; http://riverpeople ecuador.com; Vía a Inchillaqu; per person per day $65) Run by the Dent family from England, River People is a top-notch outfitter that consistently gets rave reviews. River People has been pioneering rafting on previously untried rivers throughout the region, including the remote Río Hollín, where groups of experienced rafters camp overnight in pristine rainforest. One popular tour is the challenging two-day expedition to the nearby Río Quijos, site of the 2005 World Rafting Championships.

Raft Amazonía   RAFTING
(📞099-874-0170; www.raftamazonia.com; 15 de Noviembre & Rueda; per person per day from $55) Run by a local indigenous family, Raft Amazonía offers rafting and kayaking trips with friendly, experienced, licensed guides (who get excellent reviews from guests). They also run caving and cultural tours.

🛏 Sleeping

★**Hostal Pakay**   HOSTEL $
(📞06-284-7449; http://en.ecuadorpakaytours. com; above Av Perimetral; incl breakfast dm $14, s/d $28/34, without bathroom $22/32; 🅿🛜) 🌿
Ecofriendly Hostal Pakay is surrounded by woodland, and a stay here is more like a jungle lodge experience than a town hostel experience. Wooden rooms are clean and tidy (with private or shared eco-toilets), kayakers and backpackers love the chill-out terrace, and the on-site tour **agency** (📞06-284-7449, 099-090-6633; www.ecuadorpakaytours.

com; per person per day $30-75) is increasingly renowned. Much of the breakfast fruit is grown in the lush grounds.

La Casa Blanca
HOSTEL $

(☑099-549-8228, 06-231-0456; www.casablanca tena.com; cnr Churiyuyo & Ishpingo; dm/s/d $13/25/40; ☞) Situated 1.5km northwest of the center, laid-back, spick-and-span Casa Blanca aims to provide weary backpackers with everything they wanted to find in a hostel elsewhere, but couldn't. The wonderfully equipped kitchen, spacious rooms hung with Otavalo tapestries, 'honesty system' for chilled beers, special boot-wash area, washer-dryer, in-house tour agency ... Gary and Michelle have nailed it.

Brisa del Río
GUESTHOUSE $

(☑06-288-6208, 099-837-1578; Orellana, near Pano; s/d from $10/17; ✴☞☜) Rarely are backpacker places in the jungle so clean and well located. Right on the riverfront, there is a kitchen and a tiny plunge pool. Shared bathrooms are very clean, while rooms with private bathrooms also have air-con.

✖ Eating & Drinking

★ Café Tortuga
INTERNATIONAL $

(Orellana; snacks $2-7.25; ⊙7am-7:30pm Mon-Fri, to 8:30pm Sat, to 1:30pm Sun; ☞) Everyone in town seems to drop by this superpopular Swiss-run riverfront joint, whether it's for the wide choice of breakfasts, delicious *batidos* (fruit shakes) or range of salads, sandwiches and cakes. Tortuga is especially popular with backpackers, and is a great place to meet other travelers. There is a good book exchange.

Vagabundo
GERMAN $

(www.facebook.com/vagabundotena; cnr 9 de Octubre & Tarqui; mains $7-9; ⊙4pm-midnight) Tena's most atmospheric restaurant serves German-influenced food in an open-sided joint where a bright, well-stocked bar is the focal point. Lovely pastas, currywurst (curried sausage) and meatballs with mushroom sauce are highlights, as well as wine heralding from Chile and Argentina. But there is always a feisty salsa on hand to make even spice-accustomed Latin Americans break out in sweats.

Guayusa Lounge
LOUNGE

(Olmedo, near Sucre; cocktails $4, mains $3-7.50; ⊙5pm-midnight Tue-Sat) Inside or out, the ambience at this hip spot is invitingly chill. The interior, brightened by huge picture windows, feels spacious and jungle-industrial, while the outdoor patio is inviting too. Come here for cocktails concocted with Amazonian herbs like *guayusa* and *ishpingo* (native cinnamon), and stay for the refreshingly different rice bowls, pizzas, salads, hummus and appetizers.

La Araña Bar Coctelería
BAR

(down from main plaza; ⊙5pm-midnight Mon-Thu, to 2am Fri & Sat) The most popular place for drinking and carousing is the raucous 'spider,' across the river at the end of the footbridge. The cocktail list is varied, it's busy nightly, and rammed with locals and travelers on its riverfront patio at the weekend. Expect a hangover.

❶ Information

Banco del Austro (15 de Noviembre near Piñeda) Has an ATM.

Banco Pichincha (15 de Noviembre) Almost opposite the fuel station; has the most reliable ATMs.

Tourism Office (iTur; ☑06-268-6536; Rueda; ⊙8:15am-5pm Mon-Fri) Friendly staff.

❶ Getting There & Away

The **bus terminal** (Terminal Terrestre; 15 de Noviembre) is at the southern end of town. Café Tortuga (p731) keeps a very useful complete list of current bus times. Services to all destinations are frequent.

DESTINATION	COST ($)	DURATION (HR)
Ambato	7-8	4½
Baños	5-6	3½
Coca	8.75	4
Puyo	3.15	2
Quito via Baeza	7-8	5

Misahuallí

☑06 / POP 5100

Once an important transit point for travelers arriving by river from Coca, Misahuallí (mee-sah-wah-*yee*) sank into obscurity when the Loreto road connecting Coca to Tena was built. Positioned between two major rivers (at the literal end of the road), the town has a lovely sandy beach, a famous cadre of monkeys adept at swiping sunglasses from visitors, and little else.

However, the region's **Aeropuerto Jumandy** actually means that for those flying from Quito, you'll likely hit Misahuallí before you reach Tena. And many prefer this diminutive but spirited village over Tena as a base for exploring the Río Napo and its jungle. Traveler facilities are good, with several key tour operators stationed here.

Be aware that the surrounding area has been settled for decades, which means wildlife has diminished greatly.

⊙ Sights

Sinchi Warmi   CULTURAL CENTRE
(☑096-950-2486, 06-306-3009; www.facebook.com/SinchiWarmis) Founded, built and run by a group of Kichwa women, this community center introduces visitors to their culture through activities such as jungle walks, traditional chocolate-making demonstrations and dance performances. Enjoy Kichwa cuisine (meals $3 to $10) and consider staying here (cabañas per person from $15); your money goes toward supporting these women with sustainable work that allows them to continue a traditional lifestyle.

☞ Tours

★Teorumi   ECOTOUR
(☑06-289-0203; www.teorumitours.com; Arteaga s/n; tours per person per day from $65; ⊘7am-7:30pm) ✎ Working with local indigenous communities, Teorumi is a great choice for anyone interested in native culture as well as wildlife. Tours can be tailored to fit your interests, though most feature bird-watching, fishing, medicinal-plant demonstrations and jungle hikes. Other activities include panning for gold and horseback riding. English and French are spoken. The office is on the main square.

Ecoselva Pepe Tapia   ECOTOUR
(☑099-789-8900, 06-289-0019; http://ecoselva pepetapia.com; tours per day from $45) Pepe Tapia González takes visitors on enjoyable one- to 10-day tours, including nature walks and canoe trips, with overnight stays at his rustic lodge or jungle camps. He speaks fluent English, has a biology background and is knowledgeable about plants, birds and insects. Located on the main plaza.

Selva Verde   ECOTOUR
(☑099-821-5710, 06-289-0165; www.selvaverde misahualli.com; cnr Napo & Tandalia; tours per person per day $60-95) This recommended tour agency is run by Luís Zapata, an English-speaking

guide with years of experience in the region. He specializes in river trips and visits to indigenous villages.

🛏 Sleeping & Eating

Hotel El Paisano   GUESTHOUSE **$$**
(☑06-289-0027; www.hostalelpaisano.com; cnr Rivadeneyra & Tandalia; s/d incl breakfast $25/40; 🅿@🛜) This popular traveler haunt is one of the more charming places in town, with bright rooms, wooden floors, mosquito nets, laundry service, good coffee served with a very good breakfast, and a book exchange. The lovely owner speaks Spanish, French and English.

Río Napo Lodge   LODGE **$$**
(☑06-289-0071; www.rionapolodge.com; r per person incl breakfast $33.50; 🛜) Run by a local indigenous family who also grow cacao, this peaceful lodge on the south side of the Río Napo makes for a quiet retreat outside of town. Rooms are in wooden duplex cabins, with hammock-slung terraces and a lovely, lush garden setting. A pool may be in place by the time you read this.

Misahuallí Amazon Lodge   HOTEL **$$$**
(☑06-289-0063, in Quito 02-224-9651; www.misahualliamazonlodge.com; s/d incl breakfast from $60/90, s/d with air-con from $75/115; 🛜❄) A manicured version of a jungle camp, this hotel has a resort feel and is popular with Ecuadorian families. It has a great position overlooking the river and Misahuallí (from which you have to take the complimentary canoe to get here). Newer hotel-style rooms and cabins, arranged around a nice pool, are sophisticated, but there's little atmosphere (and few guests).

El Bijao   ECUADORIAN **$**
(Plaza; mains $5; ⊘lunch & dinner) On the main plaza, this is a great place to try *maito* – an Ecuadorian jungle specialty where tilapia (river fish) or chicken are wrapped in a jungle leaf and grilled, then served with rice, yuca and *guayusa* (Amazonian herbal tea). Stop by around lunch for the freshest ones. The cooking keeps on going until the last food has gone.

El Jardín   ECUADORIAN **$$**
(☑06-289-0219; mains $9-14; ⊘noon-4pm & 6-10pm Mon-Sat; 🅿🛜) Over the bridge about 200m up the road to La Punta, El Jardín is a beautiful addition to the local dining scene. In a flower-festooned garden, you can dine on

the huge platters of pricey but well-prepared meat, tilapia and seafood.

ℹ️ Information

There is no bank or post office in Misahuallí. Carry your passport on buses, boats and tours in the region, and have a stash of small bills for boat travel.

ℹ️ Getting There & Away

Buses leave from the plaza approximately every hour during daytime; the last bus is at 6pm. The main destination is Tena ($1, one hour), from where you need to change to destinations further afield.

You can also catch a **Compañía Trans Dumbiki** (📞 06-289-0051) *camioneta* on the plaza for nearby destinations, as well as to Tena and beyond.

Reserva Biológica Jatun Sacha

This 25-sq-km biological station and rainforest reserve is located on the south shore of the Río Napo, 23km east of Puerto Napo. It is run by **Fundación Jatun Sacha** ($6), an Ecuadorian nonprofit organization that was formed to promote rainforest research, conservation and education.

Biostation workers and other guests stay in rustic **cabins** (per person incl full board $30) with shared bathrooms just up from the entrance on the Misahuallí–La Punta road. Water is solar-heated and meals are included. The restaurant by the office at the reserve entrance serves healthy Ecuadorian and international meals.

Go bird-watching or meander through the surrounding forest trails, then check out the plant conservation center and botanical garden. You can also borrow a climbing harness and scale the vertigo-inducing 30m observation tower in the middle of the reserve. There are discounts for groups and students, and guided tours are offered for large groups for $40.

Puyo

📞 03 / POP 36,600

Puyo is an enigma: whereas most towns make efforts to spruce up their centers and leave the outskirts stagnating, this place does the opposite. While it retains some vitality as the capital of the Pastaza province, overall this is just a built-up town with little to attract you. Regardless, anyone traveling in southern Oriente is quite likely to pass through. Dense green jungle flourishes close around the town's edges, and – thanks in part to travelers from Baños making the hour-long drive down to do a rainforest reconnoiter – accommodations are good and plentiful, with some highly recommended jungle tour operators located here.

◉ Sights

Jardín Botánico las Orquídeas   GARDENS
(📞 03-253-0305; www.jardinbotanicolasorquideas. com; $5; ⊙8am-6pm) 🌱 Visitors rave about this privately run botanical garden, located 15 minutes south of Puyo, after Pindo Chico neighborhood just off the E45 road to Macas. Enthusiastic owner Omar Taeyu guides visitors through hills of lush foliage and fish ponds to see gorgeous plants and countless rare orchids. Call ahead to let them know you're coming.

Parque Etnobotánico Omaere   PARK
(https://omaere.wordpress.com; adult/child $3/1.50; ⊙9am-5pm Tue Sun) 🌱 Less than 1km north of the city center, this ethnobotanical park offers one- to two-hour guided tours (included in admission fee) of rainforest plants, indigenous dwellings and ecological waste disposal, by mostly indigenous guides. The park is run by biologist Chris Canaday, a font of knowledge about everything from jungle plants to ecological dry toilets, and the region's indigenous groups, the Shuar and Waorani.

➤ Tours

Papangu Tours   TOURS
(📞 03-288-7684, 099-550-4983; www.papangu tours.com.ec; Orellana, near Manzano; 3 day tour per person from $45; ⊙Mon-Fri) 🌱 Papangu Tours is an indigenous-run agency with a focus on community tourism. Trips go to Sarayaku (a Kichwa community) and Cueva de los Tayos (Shuar). Guides are indigenous and speak Spanish and Kichwa, and some of the fees go to participating communities. Highly recommended. It's in front of the entrance to the Hostería Turingia.

🛏️ Sleeping

Hostal Las Palmas   GUESTHOUSE $
(📞 03-288-4832; www.hostallaspalmaspuyo. com; cnr 20 de Julio & 4 de Enero; rooms s/d incl breakfast from $15/33; ❀🛜) This big yellow colonial place is aimed at an upmarket

backpacking crowd. It features attractive gardens, chattering parrots, statues of rainforest animals, hammocks and a 3rd-floor patio for sundowners. Rooms here are neat and bright. Breakfast is served in a cute cafe, and service is very friendly. Basic rooms are small; larger rooms (single/double $30/45) are significantly nicer, with oodles of space on the upper floor.

Posada Real   GUESTHOUSE $$

(✆03-288-5887; www.posadarealpuyo.com; cnr 4 de Enero & 27 de Febrero; s/d incl breakfast from $35/55; P🖥) If you don't have a well-to-do Ecuadorian grandmother to visit in Puyo, staying in this immaculately kept locale is the next best thing. Only two blocks down from the main square, Posada Real enjoys a set-back location in quiet grounds. Spacious rooms have cozy reading lamps and antique furniture; most have balconies. Breakfast in the dignified cafeteria is a pleasure.

★**Huella Verde**
Rainforest Lodge   JUNGLE LODGE $$$

(✆03-278-7035; http://huella-verde.org; s/d from $70/100; 🖥) On an isolated meander of the Río Bobonaza around 45km south of Puyo, Huella Verde puts even the bigger Yasuní lodges to shame by offering fascinating excursions in equally intact jungle for a fraction of the price: ethnobotanic jungle hikes, chocolate-making and canoe adventures with Kichwa guides (extra charges apply).

✖ Eating

EscoBar   ECUADORIAN $

(cnr Atahualpa & Marín; mains $4.50-9.50; ⊙9am-late) With panache to punch above its weight in Quito's coolest neighborhoods, EscoBar makes *palapas* (rustic, palm-thatched dwellings) seem chic. Sample Ecuadorian microbrews, cocktails and a menu of *patacones* (fried bananas), yuca (cassava) or salads served with meat within the two-floor open-sided bar-restaurant. Service is as slow as a motorless canoe heading upriver, but it's still the place to hang.

★**El Jardín**   ECUADORIAN $$

(✆03-289-2253, 099-140-9096; Paseo Turístico, Barrio Obrero; mains $8-14; ⊙noon-4pm & 6-10pm Mon-Sat; 🖥) The best food in the Oriente may be at this ambient house by the river inside the charming **hotel** (www.eljardin puyo.com; Paseo Turístico, Barrio Obrero; s/d incl breakfast from $45/78; P@🖥) of the same name, 1km north of town. Award-winning

chef-owner Sofia prepares fragrant *pollo ishpingo* (cinnamon chicken – *ishpingo* is a type of cinnamon native to the Oriente); its decadent, delicate flavors awake the palate.

❶ Information

Banco de Guayaquil (Marín, near Av 20 de Julio)
Banco del Austro (Atahualpa, near 27 de Febrero)
Hospital General Puyo (www.hgp.gob.ec; cnr 9 de Octubre & Feicán)
IESS Hospital (✆03-288-5378; cnr Marín & Curaray)
iTur (✆03-288-5937, 03-288-5122, ext 227; cnr Orellana & 27 de Febrero; ⊙8:30am-12:30pm & 3-6pm Mon-Fri) At the town hall. Either the booth downstairs or the office upstairs will be open.
iTur (✆099-426-5163; cnr Marín & Atahualpa; ⊙8am-5pm Mon-Sat) Small, central booth, by Escobar.

❶ Getting There & Away

The bus terminal is 1km southwest of town. There are several services daily to Baños ($3 to $4, two hours), Quito ($9, 5½ hours), Macas ($5, 2½ hours) and Tena ($3 to $4, two hours).

Macas & Around

✆07 / POP 19,000

Bienvenidos (welcome) to a jungle town with few tourist trappings: clamoring markets, *huecos* (basic hole-in-the-wall eateries) and glass-and-concrete houses are the first impressions of Macas. It gets much better. A couple of good hotels and restaurants make this the best base for tours into the least explored corners of the Ecuadorian rainforest – including opportunities to visit the Shuar and Achuar indigenous groups. The longest continuous stretch of white water in the country also lures kayakers. Untrammeled as the nearby nature might be, Macas itself is the brashly modern provincial capital of Morona-Santiago. Tribesmen wear traditional beads over Nike T-shirts, and trucks overloaded with jungle produce honk on traffic-clogged streets that keep thoughts of rivers at bay. It's raucous, and raw – but it's real.

⊙ Sights

Near Limón Indanza, 112km southwest of Macas, a trail leads to the extensive Coangos cave system, where there are multiple caverns spiked with stalactites and stalagmites.

Five kilometers of passageways can be explored, including the spectacular **Cueva de los Tayos**, which at 185m depth is Ecuador's largest publicly accessible cave. Some caving routes here require technical equipment, with a 65m vertical descent necessary on one route. Underground rivers await on other routes for the adventurous.

☞ Tours

Macas is the place to book trips into the southern Oriente. Services are not as comprehensive as those up north; then again, more unspoiled rainforest and lack of other tourists adds authenticity to adventures. Know that the Shuar do not want unguided visitors in their villages; certain villages refuse visitors entirely. It's therefore essential to travel with a professional guide who can arrange access and is sensitive to the Shuar's stance on tourism. Tena operators have more possibilities for rafting on rivers around Macas.

Tsuirim Viajes   TOURS
(☏ 099-737-2538, 07-270-1681; leosalgado18@gmail.com; cnr Don Bosco & Sucre; tours per person per day from $30-75) Offers a range of jungle tours including Shuar community visits, shamanic rituals, canyoning, caving, rafting, tubing and jungle-trekking. Owner Leo Salgado grew up in a Shuar community and knows the area well. His unique offerings include Shuar weddings or vow renewals and multiday caving expeditions with licensed, experienced guides.

🛏 Sleeping & Eating

★**Casa Upano B&B**   GUESTHOUSE $$
(☏ 07-252-5051; www.casaupano.com; Av la Ciudad s/n; s/d incl breakfast $50/80; P @ 🛜) 🐾
Perhaps this is an inkling of what Macas' future could hold: a serene retreat for travelers tucked away from the city mayhem. Four balconied rooms look out on a huge fruit-tree-dotted garden that falls away toward the Río Upano. The English-speaking owners rustle up a scrumptious breakfast with superlocal ingredients (ie from their garden or a nearby house).

La Maravilla   ECUADORIAN $
(Soasti, near Sucre; mains $3-9; ⏱ noon-2am Fri & Sat, to 10pm Sun, to midnight Mon, 11am-11pm Tue-Thu) Easily the most charming place in town, this blue casita is all ambience, from the twinkling porch lights to the stuffed red-leather armchairs. Come to chill with *tablas* (cutting boards) of meat and cheese and yuca (cassava) fries. There's live Andean music here at weekends, making it the town's best entertainment option, too.

❶ Getting There & Away

Bus station (Terminal Terrestre de Macas Dr Roberto Villareal V; Av Luis Felipe Jaramillo s/n) New in 2018 and Ecuador's second-most-impressive bus station after Quito's Quitumbe. Destinations include Quito ($10 to $12, eight to nine hours), Puyo ($5, 2½ hours and Riobamba ($6, four hours).

PACIFIC COAST & LOWLANDS

Ecuador, land of lively Andean markets, Amazon adventures and...palm-fringed beaches? While not a high priority for most travelers, Ecuador's coast offers a mix of surf towns, sleepy fishing villages, whale-watching in the south and Afro-Ecuadorian culture in the north. Keep in mind the weather: December to May is the rainy season, but also the sunniest; the sun blazes both before and after the afternoon downpour. June through November has mild days (and chilly nights), but it's often overcast.

Esmeraldas

☏ 06 / POP 161,900
Esmeraldas is a hot spot: literally, culturally, and figuratively. It's the urban epicenter of the nation's Afro-Ecuadorian population, and with some luck you'll find mesmerizing marimba and dance performances. A new *malecón* was built in 2016 at Las Palmas and is a breezy place to take in a few cocktails or a seafood lunch.

The **cultural center** (Bolívar 427; ⏱ 9am-5pm Tue-Fri, 10am-4pm Sat & Sun) **FREE** highlights the various indigenous cultures which pre-dated the Spanish colonial era, as well as occasional concerts featuring Afro-Ecuadorian rhythms.

☞ Tours

Mandagua Tours   TOURS
(☏ 098-130-9935, 098-145-6235; pandafinu@hotmail.com; Centro Artesanal) Javier Valencia runs tours to places all over Esmeraldas Province.

ⓘ ESMERALDAS TRAVEL WARNING

Tread carefully – the US State Department issued a travel warning in this province in April 2018 due to the kidnapping and murder of three Colombian journalists. The proximity to the border means drugs and violence are an issue, although often further north in San Lorenzo. This being said, a cautious entry into this rich cultural wellspring can yield unforgettable results.

He's a font of information on the city's Afro-Ecuadorian culture and can take you to marimba and dance rehearsals and shows, and to receive a traditional African cleansing and aura-reading ceremony, complete with cigar. If you have time, he can take you up the Río Cayapas into rural Afro-Ecuador.

🛏 Sleeping

Hotel Perla Verde   BUSINESS HOTEL $$
(☏ 099-501-2909; www.hotelperlaverde.ec; Piedrahíta, btwn Olmedo & Sucre; s/d incl breakfast $50/60; 🅿 ✳ 🛜) This is the best hotel in town, boasting spacious rooms with lots of creature comforts (as long as you don't mind some truly awful art on the walls and darkish corridors). The staff is friendly and you're in a central location. The downstairs restaurant is also recommended.

ⓘ Getting There & Around

TAME (☏ 06-272-6863; www.tame.com.ec; Centro Comercial, Av Maldonado near Manabi; ⏰ 10am-8pm Mon-Sat, to 7pm Sun) has daily flights to Quito (one way $75), and Guayaquil (one way $138, with one stop) and Cali, Colombia (one way/return $196/$240; one-way fare sold to Colombian nationals only).

The new bus terminal, Terminal Terreste, is 4km from the city center on the road to Atacames. There's frequent service to Quito ($9.25, six hours, six daily) and Santo Domingo ($4.25, three hours, 10-plus services daily). A taxi from the terminal to the city center is $3.

Atacames

☏ 06 / POP 15,500

It's hard to 'get' Atacames. The beach is just OK, the town is dirty and crowded as hell, and still *serranos* (highlanders) love it for the partying, the beachfront ceviche stalls and the easy trips to nearby beaches. If you

want to get down to all-night reggaeton and cheap drinks, this is a good spot. If not, head further south for better beaches, bigger waves and more relaxation.

All buses stop by the *taxis ecológicos* (motorcycle taxis with a two-seater carriage) on the main road to/from Esmeraldas. Buses for Esmeraldas ($1, one hour) normally begin from Súa. Most buses from Esmeraldas to Atacames continue on to Súa (10 minutes), Same (20 minutes) and Tonchigüe (25 minutes) for about $0.50. *Ecovias* (motorcycle taxis) charge $2 to Súa and $7 to Same.

Bus companies including **Transportes Occidentales** (☏ 06-276-0547; cnr Prado & Cuarta), **Trans Esmeraldas** (cnr Vargas Torres & Juan Montalvo) and **Aerotaxi** (Cuarta) operate a daily service to Quito ($9, seven hours) as well as to Guayaquil ($11 to $12, eight hours).

Súa

☏ 02 / POP 3100

Groups of scissor-tailed magnificent frigatebirds wheel over the roiling surf in Súa, a more family-oriented, quieter and less popular seaside spot than neighboring Atacames, with more-reasonable weekend hotel prices. That said, the cocktail bars along the beach still screech out music, so it's not always the place for an idyllic break. Humpback whales can be seen off the coast from June to September. You can walk here on the beach from Atacames, but watch the tide and don't do it at night (take an *ecovia*).

Nestled against the beach, the friendly, wind-battered **Hotel Chagra Ramos** (☏ 06-247-3106; hotelchagraramos@hotmail.com; north side of Malecón; r per person $13; 🅿 🛜) is the most popular guesthouse in town. Rooms are clean if a little weathered, with antiquated bathrooms, softer-than-wonderbread mattresses and pretty darned nice views. There's no hot water, but there's a good-value restaurant. Octogenarian owner Aida is an inspiration, as is the ageing French bulldog.

Bus services to and from Esmeraldas run about every 15 minutes. From Súa it takes 10 minutes to get to Atacames ($0.30) and about an hour to get to Esmeraldas ($1).

Same & Tonchigüe

☏ 06

Same (*sah*-may) is a real mixed bag of a resort town, boasting a wonderful beach and a genial atmosphere, while also being dominated by a vast resort-condo complex called Casablanca. The beach itself, while certainly beautiful, is far from pristine and would benefit from a community-wide effort to keep it clean, such as that seen in Mompiche.

The community *has* rallied and organized better private security up and down the little road which leads to the beach. Same is an unbridled delight compared to Atacames – *mucho mas tranquilo*, you might say. You can rent stand-up paddleboards (per hour $10) on the beach, and there are a surprising number of fine little dining establishments in this hidden nook. Morning winds provide decent surf.

Tonchigüe is a tiny fishing village about 3km west of Same, along the same stretch of beach. Go early in the morning to see the fisherpeople unloading their catch.

🛏 Sleeping & Eating

El Acantilado
CABIN $$
(☑06-302-7620; www.elacantilado.net; camping $20, s/d $45/90, cabanas sleeping up to 6 $120; P�'📶🌊) Perched on a cliff above the crashing waves, El Acantilado offers unobstructed sea views from its rooms, which make it great for whale-watching from June to September. Rustic suites are open to the elements, with just bug screens separating the rooms from individual private gardens and views down to the sea and beach below. Camping is available, too.

★ Seaflower Lateneus
SEAFOOD $$$
(☑06-247-0369; Same; mains $20-25; ⊙2-10pm) Boasting one of the best chefs along the north coast (born here, trained in Europe), Seaflower serves delicious grilled seafood (try the *spaghetti marinera*). It's worth reserving a table on weekends, when it's often packed with a smart crowd of cocktail-sipping weekenders – it also doubles as Same's best bar, with an array of hanging bottle decorations (watch your head!). There are rooms for rent here, too – one's even categorized as a 'suite'! You can bring up a $50 bottle of champagne from the bar.

ℹ Getting There & Away

Buses heading northeast to Esmeraldas and south to Muisne pick up and drop off passengers at both Same and Tonchigüe. *Rancheras* (open-sided buses, or trucks mounted with uncomfortably narrow bench seats – also known as *chivas*) head to Tonchigüe from Esmeraldas. To get around town, *ecovias* (tuk-tuks) await you at the entrance to town after you hop off the bus ($1.50 per ride, $5 per hour).

Mompiche
📞 05 / POP 28,000

Famed for its world-class waves and gorgeous 7km-long strip of pristine (if grayish) sand beach, this little fishing village has long been popular with backpackers and surfers for its good waves, and cheap eats and lodgings. Mompiche had barely been touched by the modern world until the creation of a good new road nearly a decade ago, but even now there's not extensive vehicular traffic, and everyone in town still knows everyone else. Besides its fabulous stretch of palm-fringed sands, Mompiche has little else (not even an ATM), and that's its beauty.

Like much of the region, Mompiche's was hit hard by the 2016 earthquake and is still rebounding. Rising sea levels have brought the high tide all the way to the sea wall, effectively eliminating beach time for a quarter of the day, and cutting off land access to the beach hotels north of here. Surprising amount of decibels per capita for a small place.

🏃 Activities

November through February sees the best surf, with waves up to 2m – the rest of the year it's pretty flat. There's a river break north of town and a steep point break (for experts) to the south. Two friendly competitors in town rent surfboards and give lessons for the same price: Jefferson Panezo at **La Peña Escuela de Surf** (☑096-727-4255; La Fosforera; ⊙8am-5pm) is one of them.

Head to the beach to arrange whale-watching tours as well as trips to Isla Portete, Muisne, nearby mangroves, and a bunch of lost beaches. Boats cost about $25 per person per hour, depending on occupancy. Ask for Ramon at the Banana Hotel (☑099-739-6244), who runs popular jungle tours.

🛏 Sleeping & Eating

Mudhouse
HOSTAL $
(☑093-911-2203; www.the-mud-house.com; Via a Mompiche; dm $9, d $25-30, family cabins $50-60; P�') This newish entry on the Mompiche scene is run by a friendly American expat couple and has both private rooms and dorms, the nicest of which have outdoor stone showers. It has capacity for singles, couples and families, and Mendy has a wealth of

information on local activities in her handy spiral notebook. Common kitchen.

La Chocolata   ARGENTINE $

(mains $6-8, desserts $3; ☺ 6-10pm) Arieceli, also Mompiche's yoga instructor par excellence, is known for her wickedly divine desserts, including lemon pie, a vegan crumble, and a chocolate mousse, peanut butter and dulce de leche bon bon: you may even see her skipping through town with a birthday cake for someone. The pastas are good, but you might want to skip ahead to the *postre* (dessert).

La Facha   INTERNATIONAL $

(www.lafachahostel.com; 100m north of T-Junction, across from La Casona; mains $5-8; ☺ 8am-10pm) A charming team of young locals (who also run the hostel in the same building, and are all keen surfers) serve up mouthwatering burgers, salads and sandwiches. It's on Calle Fosforeras, parallel to the *malecón*. You can rent a decent room here, too ($13 to $15 for shared bathroom, $20 private).

❶ Getting There & Away

Buses go to and from Esmeraldas a few times daily ($5, 3½ hours), passing Same and Atacames on the way. If you're coming from the south, you'll have to get off your bus at the Mompiche *entrada* (entrance; be sure to specify with the driver) and take a taxi into town ($1).

Canoa

📞 05 / POP 6900

A sleepy village with a heart of gold, Canoa has a lovely stretch of beach framed by picturesque cliffs to the north and a disappearing horizon to the south. Despite its growing popularity with sunseekers and surfers, the village remains a low-key place, where kids frolic on the sandy lanes at dusk and fishers head out to sea in the early hours before dawn. In the evenings the beachfront bars and guesthouses come to life as backpackers swap travel tales over rum cocktails. Not as noisy as Atacames, but on weekends you still might need earplugs at the beachfront hotels.

International surf competitions come in the high season (January to March), when waves reach over 2m and accommodations become hard to find. A once 'secret' beach break 6 miles north of Canoa can now be accessed by a dirt road.

Canoa's comeback from the 2016 earthquake, at the time of writing, is still a work in progress.

🏃 Activities

Tides are strong here, so stay close to the beach. At low tide you can reach caves at the north end of the beach, which house hundreds of roosting bats. A popular bike trip takes you on the bike path that runs from here to Bahía de Caráquez in about an hour. **Surf Shak** (Malecón; ☺ 8am-11pm Sun-Fri, to 1am Fri & Sat; 🖥) offers kayaking cave tours ($25, three hours), paragliding ($45, 20 minutes) and surfing classes ($25, 1½ hours).

🛏 Sleeping & Eating

⭐ **Hotel Bambu**   HOTEL $

(📞 05-258-8017; www.hotelbambuecuador.com; Malecón, north end; dm/s/d $13/30/50, camping $25; P 🖥) The nicest hotel in town has a great sand-floored restaurant and bar, cabins with exposed cane roofs, wood-panel windows and mosquito nets, plus delicious hot-water showers. Only a few have ocean views, but most catch a breeze and stay cool. A newer addition is the good-value, fully equipped camping spot with electricity and raised beds. There's ping-pong and billiards, too!

⭐ **Casa Shangri-La**   GUESTHOUSE $

(📞 099-146-8470; www.casashangrila.com; Antonio Aviega; camping/r per person $7.50/11; 🖥 🐾) This fantastic place is owned by a friendly Dutch guy, Jeroen, who has created a chilled-out surfer spot with a big garden, a plunge pool, very nice rooms and a super-relaxed vibe. There's a bar and a library, and surfboards to rent. It's a short,100m-walk north of town on the main road, which also means you won't hear the reggaeton from the beachfront all night.

Amalur   SPANISH $

(www.amalurcanoa.com; cnr Francisco Aviega & San Andres, inside Amalur Hotel; mains $7-12; ☺ 8am-10pm; 🖥) Owned by a Spanish chef (Amalur means 'Mother Earth' in Basque), this trim, minimalist restaurant is a major step up from your average Ecuadorian small-town restaurant.

A chalkboard lists the day's specials – recent favorites include fresh calamari *a la plancha* (grilled) *pulpo a la Gallega* (boiled octopus with paprika), homegrown, nicely seasoned eggplant in salsa and a marvelously tender sea bass.

❶ Information

There are no banks in Canoa (San Vicente has the nearest ATMs).

ⓘ Getting There & Away

Buses between Bahía de Caráquez ($1, 45 minutes) and Pedernales or Esmeraldas will all stop in Canoa. The office for Coachtur is about three blocks inland from Hotel Bambu and has hourly services to Portoviejo ($4, 2½ hours), Manta ($6, three hours) and Guayaquil ($9, six hours). For points further north of Pedernales, take a bus there or to Chamanga and transfer.

Bahía de Caráquez

📋 05 / POP 20,900

Gleaming white high-rises and red-tile roofs once filled this bustling peninsula city. With the Río Chone on one side, and the Pacific on the other, this tidy former port city basks in the sun and enjoys a wonderfully laid-back feel.

The city was devastated by the 2016 earthquake, however, with many businesses reduced to rubble. We have to admit, with two recent visits here, tourism has yet to recover. The major structures standing are redone fancy condos for visiting wealthy folks from Quito, who had the money and/ or insurance to rebuild.

It's worthwhile to visit if only for one of the country's best ceviche stands, and bird-watchers will delight in the very affordable trips on and around Isla Corazon, just 7km across the San Vicente bridge.

◉ Sights & Activities

Head to San Vicente to organize boat tours to heart-shaped Isla Corazón, and whale-watching tours (per hour $25).

Isla Corazón　　　　　　　　ISLAND
(📋 05-267-4836; www.islacorazon.com; San Vicente or Puerto Portovelo; per person incl 2hr guided tour $12-15) Bird-watchers shouldn't miss a visit to Isla Corazon, where you can take guided tours through mangroves in search of frigate birds, herons, egrets and other species. It's 7km east of San Vicente, reachable by bus ($0.50) or taxi ($5). For tours, contact Francisco Reyes (99-938-4425) or Oscar Ortiz (98-471-0814, www.sanplaya.com). Pickup at local hotels for an additional $10.

🛏 Sleeping & Eating

With Bahía's hotel scene still recovering from the 2016 earthquake, you're likely to find more options further down the coast.

Casa Ceibo　　　　　LUXURY HOTEL $$$
(📋 05-239-9399, 099-470-3622; www.casaceibo. com; Av Sixto Durán Ballén; d/ste incl breakfast from $110/240; 🅿 ❄ 🛜 🛝) If you're looking for pampering and seclusion, this gated luxury hotel 4km from central Bahía (on the road out of town, just beyond the bus terminal) is the place for you. With plush rooms that have all the creature comforts, minimalist public areas and huge manicured gardens that lead down to the river, this is definitely the smartest place in town.

Hermanacho　　　　　　　CEVICHE $
(📋 05-269-2483; Malecón; ceviches $5-12; ⊘ 8am-3:30pm) Folks drive over from Canoa to visit this long-lived and well-loved *cevicheria*. You can get half orders of Pedro Avila's *mixto* shrimp or lobster ceviche ($5 to $6) but if you're really hungry, pay for a whole one ($8 to $12). It's across the road from D'Camaron, along the waterfront.

D'Camaron　　　　　　　SEAFOOD $$
(www.dcamaron.com.ec; Bolívar btwn Plaza Acosta & Leannen; mains $8-11; ⊘ 8:30am-6pm Mon-Thu, to 7pm Fri-Sun) As the name implies (*camaron* means 'shrimp'), shrimp is the specialty at this casual open-air spot near the water. Order them grilled, with a cocktail, and enjoy the ocean breezes. For a change, try the *arroz marinera*, rice with loads of different shellfish.

ⓘ Getting There & Away

A bridge connects Bahía to San Vicente (and the rest of the north coast) over the Río Chone.

The bus terminal is 4km from the center of town on the *malecón* as you head toward Chone. From there you'll find buses that offer regular or *ejecutivo* (1st-class) services: they head to Quito (regular/*ejecutivo* $10/$12, eight hours, four daily) via Santo Domingo (regular/*ejecutivo* $5/$6), and there are services to Guayaquil ($7.50, six hours, seven daily), Manta ($3, three hours, three daily) and Canoa ($1.25, 45 minutes, half-hourly).

Manta

📋 05 / POP 217,500

The largest city in the province (and the fifth largest in Ecuador), Manta is a bustling and prosperous port town graced with high-rises, and a few urban beaches that draw mostly domestic tourists.

As an important center for the fishing and tuna-processing industries, it's the kind of place you smell before you arrive, and its quirkiest sight is a huge statue of a tuna

Manta

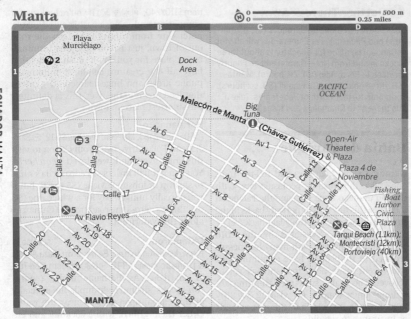

Manta

◎ Sights

1 Museo Arqueológico del Banco
   Central D3
2 Playa Murciélago A1

⬛ Sleeping

3 Hotel Balandra A2
4 Manakin A2

✖ Eating

5 Parrillada La Vacanisima A2
6 Trovador Café D3

(complete with attached tin can). Indeed, there aren't a lot of reasons to come here – the beaches are far better elsewhere on the coast – but it's an important transportation hub and has lively nightlife. You may pass through if you're visiting the handicraft town of Montecristi.

◎ Sights

Playa Murciélago   BEACH
(Malecón, btwn Calle 30 & Calle 19) This beach is less protected than most beaches in the area and has bigger waves (although they're not very big) along with a powerful undertow. It's a couple of kilometers northwest

of downtown (near Hotel Balandra) and is the town's most popular beach, backed by snack bars, restaurants and umbrella-rental spots.

Tarqui Beach   BEACH
(Malecón) The east end of this stretch of sand is a hive of activity early in the mornings, as vendors sell row upon row of shark, tuna, swordfish, dorado and other fish (the sizes of which decrease with each passing year). You'll also find the so-called Parque del Marisco here: lots of stalls serving up fresh seafood in a variety of styles right on the beach, including what locals will swear to you is the best ceviche in the country.

**Museo Arqueológico
del Banco Central**   MUSEUM
(Malecón, btwn Calle 9 & Av 2; $1; ⊘8:30am-5pm Mon-Fri) The fully modernized city Museo Arqueológico del Banco Central opened in its current location in 2009, and showcases valuable artifacts from pre-Colombian Manta culture, a selection of Ecuadorian paintings and quirky fishing paraphernalia.

🛏 Sleeping & Eating

Manakin   GUESTHOUSE $$
(📞05-262-0413; hostalmanakin@hotmail.com; cnr Calle 17 & Av 21; s/d incl breakfast $55/70;

✳🔊) Near the heart of all the nightlife, Manakin is a converted one-story house with a pleasant laid-back vibe. Narrow, well-ordered rooms are nicely furnished, and the house offers fine places to unwind – including the front patio. And it's near the mall. Truly, what more could one ask for? Cash discounts offered.

Hotel Balandra HOTEL $$$

(☑05-262-0545; www.hotelbalandra.com; Av 7 near Calle 20; s/d $124/172, deluxe r $185; ✳@🔊☀) This small but upscale hillside hotel offers pleasantly furnished deluxe rooms and two-bedroom cabins, some with balconies looking out to sea. Outside you'll find sculpted shrubbery, a small gym and sauna, a pool and a playground. Family groups can make for a less-than-relaxing experience on weekends.

Trovador Café CAFE $

(☑05-262-9376; Av 3 & Calle 10, Pasaje Hermanos Egas Miranda; mains $2-5; ◷6am-6pm Mon-Fri, to 3pm Sat) On a pleasant pedestrian lane set back just a short distance from the *malecón* (and Parque de la Madre), this amiable hole-in-the-wall offers frothy cappuccinos, sandwiches and inexpensive lunch plates. There's outdoor seating in this old colonial home.

Parrillada La Vacanisima GRILL $$

(by Oh Mar; cnr Avs 20 & Flavio Reyes; mains $9-13; ◷noon-midnight Mon-Sat) This amenable grill in the center of Manta's nightlife area is a great place for a filling *parillada* (grilled meats for one, enough for two) and a glass of good Argentinian red wine. A recent redesign brought a name change to 'Super Cow,' but the message remains the same: no vegetarians need apply, although there are several fish dishes.

❶ Getting There & Around

TAME (☑05-261-0008; Malecón de Manta btwn Avs 13 & 14, Edificio El Vigia; ◷8:30am-5:30pm Mon-Fri) has one to two flights daily to/from Quito (one way from $86, 30 minutes).

The airport is some 3km east of Tarqui, and a taxi costs about $2 for the 10-minute trip.

Most long-distance buses depart from the new **Terminal Terreste** (Terminal Luis Valdiviezo Morán; ☑05-262-1081; www.terminalmanta.gob.ec; Parque Tohali) near the airport.

Buses serve Jipijapa ($0.90, one hour), Canoa ($4, 3½ to four hours), Bahía de Caráquez ($3, three hours), Guayaquil ($5, four hours), Esmeraldas ($7, six hours) and Ambato ($8, 10 hours).

Ejecutivo buses to Quito ($10, nine hours) and Guayaquil ($7.50, four hours) leave from a smaller nearby terminal on the *malecón* throughout the day.

Montecristi

☑05 / POP 46,300

Montecristi produces the finest straw hat on the planet, even if it is mistakenly referred to as the 'Panama' hat. Ask for yours as a sombrero *de paja toquilla,* a fine, fibrous straw endemic to this region. Hat stores line the road leading into town and the plaza, but most of their wares are cheap and loosely woven.

The city was founded in around 1628, when Manteños fled inland to avoid the frequent plundering by pirates. Today its many unrestored colonial houses give the village a rather tumbledown and ghostly atmosphere. The key draw here is hat shopping, but Montecristi's main plaza has a beautiful **church** (Calle Sucre, La Madre Parque) which contains a statue of the Virgin to which miracles have been attributed as well as a statue of native son Eloy Alfaro, who was twice Ecuador's president. His tomb is in the town hall and there's a relatively new **museum** (Centro Cívico Ciudad Alfaro; ☑05-231-1210; www.ciudadalfaro.gob.ec; Prolongacion 10 de Agosto; ◷8:30am-5pm) ▣FREE▣ in his honor on the hilltop.

Montecristi can be reached during the day by frequent buses ($0.50, 45 minutes) from the Terminal Terrestre in Manta.

Puerto López

☑05 / POP 16,000

A long, wide beach and proximity to the wonders of the Parque Nacional Machalilla have turned this quiet fishing village into a traveler's base on Ecuador's coastline. During whale-watching season especially, tourists wander the spiffy new *malecón* (built from 2015 to 2017) and the dusty streets – home to a surprising number of good accommodations options, cafes and restaurants. In the wee morning hours – before tour groups escape for the day and the handful of sunbathers take up their positions on the sand – fishers gut their catch on the beach, and the air teems with frigate birds, pelicans and vultures diving for scraps.

🍴 Courses

Tentáculo Clases y Cultura   COOKING
(📞 098-336-0849; www.facebook.com/Tentaculo clasesycultura; Malecón Julio Izurieta, between Hostería Nantu & Cabañas Playa Sur) California teacher Kelly has reinvented herself in Ecuador and offers a variety of cool cultural activities – its 'tentacles' spread far and wide – including a ceviche-making class, a Spanish-language class ($8 per hour), and other community-based stuff, like the weekly Sunday beach cleanup. There is also a room to rent. Look for the octopus on the wall.

🧭 Tours

Numerous agencies offer tours to Isla de la Plata or the mainland part of the park. Hiking, horseback-riding, mountain-biking and fishing trips are also available. From June through September, whale-watching tours combined with visits to Isla de la Plata are popular (from $45). Licensed companies are found along Córdova and Malecón Julio Izurieta. Outside of the whale-watching season, similar tours to the island are offered to see birds and sea lions, and you may well see dolphins, too.

Machalilla Tours   ADVENTURE
(📞 093-984-5839; www.machalillatours.org; Malecón Julio Izurieta; tours from $45; ⏱ 9:30am-5:30pm) Runs standard tours, plus excursions for horseback riding, kayaking, mountain biking and paragliding, as well as trips to Los Frailes Beach and Agua Blanca.

Exploramar Diving   DIVING
(📞 02-256-3905; www.exploradiving.com; Malecón Julio Izurieta; 2-dive package from $140, snorkeling $40; ⏱ 8am-6pm) This PADI-certified dive center on the *malecón* runs dive sessions and snorkeling off the coast.

🛏 Sleeping

Reserve ahead during the busy whale-watching season, and during the coastal high season (end of December to April). Off-season, the rates listed will drop; ask for discounts if the place has few occupants.

Hostal Yemayá   HOSTEL $
(📞 05-230-0122, 098-864-6118; www.facebook. com/YemayaPuertoLopez; General Córdova & Cristo del Consuelo; dm $10, r per person $15-20; ❄️🛜) Good value for money, a couple of minutes from the beach. The handful of fan-cooled rooms (some have air-con) have hot water, (some) TVs and are simple and clean. There's a pleasant interior courtyard with plants, tables and chairs. Miguel, the friendly English-speaking owner, also runs **activity tours** (📞 099-957-0396, 098-864-6618; www. facebook.com/travesiasurfnbikes; 2hr lesson $30) and a tiny adjacent cafe which serves the town's best coffee.

★ **Hostería Mandála**   CABIN $$
(📞 05-230-0181; www.hosteriamandala.info; d $35-155; 🅿️🛜) Easily the nicest place to stay in town, Mandála has a beachfront location north of the *malecón* – you can't miss the giant rainbow whale tail beckoning you in. Cabins are scattered throughout a thick and lush flower garden, and the rooms are rustic and sophisticated: wood, bamboo and colorful textiles combine to make charming, cozy hideaways.

🍽 Eating

Cafe Madame   CAFE $
(📞 098-436-7851; Malecón Julio Izurieta; crepes from $2.50, mains from $5; ⏱ 8am-7pm; 🛜🍴) A beachfront bar and organic cafe with a shaded veranda and wooden tables. Order crepes, ice cream, coffee, fruit smoothies, sandwiches, omelets and salads, or enjoy a sundowner in this pretty location.

Restaurant Carmita   SOUTH AMERICAN $$
(📞 099-372-9294; Malecón Julio Izurieta; mains $6-14; ⏱ 10am-9:30pm; 🛜) The patio dining is a good people-watching spot at this popular Ecuadorian restaurant on the *malecón*. It serves well-priced fish dishes plus ceviches, mixed rice, and chicken plates. The octopus in garlic sauce has to be tried. Ask about lunch and dinner specials.

Bellitalia   ITALIAN $$
(📞 099-617-5183; Juan Montalvo; mains $9-12; ⏱ 6-10pm Mon-Sat) You won't stumble upon this delightful spot hidden in a backstreet, but you should seek it out for its high-quality Italian cooking in a romantic, garden-like setting. It's one block inland from the beach. Reserve ahead, especially on weekends.

ℹ️ Information

Banco del Pichincha (Malecón Julio Izurieta; ⏱ 9am-4pm Mon-Fri) Has a reliable ATM.

Tourism office (📞 099-480-4886; Av Machalilla & Atahualpa; ⏱ hours vary) On a side street off Ruta del Spondylus, but is often unmanned.

Alternatively, ask at guesthouses and tour operators for local info.

ℹ Getting There & Around

All buses now run out of the new **bus terminal** (Terminal Terrestre; Ruta del Spondylus), located 2.5km north of town. A moto-taxi ride to/from the town center should cost around $1.

Carlos Aray Ejecutivo Has buses to Quito ($14, 10 hours) at 5:05am, 9:15am and 7pm via Jipijapa, Portoviejo, Chone and Santo Domingo. Alternatively, you can catch the bus to Portoviejo or Manta to make connections.

Reina de Camino (☑ 05-303-6002; 🕾) Has the comfiest service to Quito ($14, 10 hours), with one first-class bus at 8pm.

Cooperativa Manglaralto Has buses heading to Santa Elena ($4, 1½ hours) every 20 minutes from 4am to 7pm, stopping in Montañita ($2.50).

Ruta Spondylus

Formerly known as the Ruta del Sol, this coastline has much more to offer than just sun and sand. The area's geography runs the gamut from dry scrub and cactus to lush mountainous cloud forests, beautiful beaches and offshore islands teeming with unique flora and fauna. It's easily accessed by buses from Guayaquil in the south to Puerto López and Manta in the north.

Parque Nacional Machalilla

☑ 05

Ecuador's only coastal national park is a reminder of what much of the Central and South American Pacific coast once looked like. Now almost entirely disappeared, it's one of the most threatened tropical forests in the world. The park, created in 1979, preserves a small part of the country's rapidly vanishing coastal habitats, protecting about 50km of beach, some 400 sq km of tropical dry forest and cloud forest, and around 200 sq km of ocean (including offshore islands, of which Isla de la Plata is the most important).

Aside from rare exotic species, the park is also home to an important archaeological site that dates from the Manta period – beginning around AD 500 and lasting until the Spanish conquest. There are also remains of the much older Machalilla and Chorrera cultures, dating from about 800 BC to 500 BC, and of the Salango culture from 3000 BC.

⊙ Sights

Plants in the park include cacti, various figs and the giant kapok tree.

The turnoff to the lovely beach of **Los Frailes** (⊙ 8am-4pm) is about 10km north of Puerto López, just before the town of Machalilla. Framed by dramatic headlands, the picturesque beach is one of Ecuador's loveliest. Buses stop near the ranger station, from which a 3km road and a 4km trail lead to the beach. Seabirds are plentiful and camping is allowed.

The barren, sun-charred **Isla de la Plata** is a highlight of the park, especially from mid-June to September when humpback whales mate offshore and sightings from tour boats are practically guaranteed. The island itself hosts nesting seabird colonies, and a hike is usually included in guided tours.

From the mainland park entrance, 6km north of Puerto López, a dirt road goes 5km to **Agua Blanca** (☑ 098-161-0095; www.comunidad aguablanca.com; $5; ⊙ 8am-5pm), a small indigenous village. Admission includes a visit to the small, intriguing **archaeological museum** (☑ 099-443-4864; www.comunidad aguablanca.com; ⊙ 8am-5pm), followed by a walk through the community to a sulfur pool where you can take a dip and cover yourself with therapeutic mud if so inclined. You can also arrange longer hiking and horse treks, including overnight trips.

ℹ Getting There & Away

Boat trips to Isla de la Plata are arranged through tour agencies in Puerto López and at hostels and hotels along the coast.

Buses run up and down the coast along Ruta de Spondylus between Puerto López and Jipijapa (hee-pee-*hah*-pah) at least every 20 minutes ($1, four minutes). The main road goes straight through the park, so you should have no difficulty getting a bus to drop you off at any point and flagging one down when you're ready to leave. However, it can be a long, hot wait. Walking roughly 5km back to town is an option if you're fit (bring water). The most sensible plan is to hire a taxi in Puerto López (round-trip around $15 to $20) or hire a guide with transport in town.

Salango, Las Tunas & Ayampe

Along the coast you'll find the sleepy towns of Salango, Las Tunas, and Ayampe – where the Río Ayampe empties into the ocean (the strong undertow here makes swimming difficult), and the luxuriant green hills close in on the beach. If you're looking to get away from people, the guesthouses in these parts offer solace, peace and quiet. Only 6km south of Puerto López is the little fishing town of Salango. From here you can hire fishing boats to buzz the 2km out to Isla Salango, a haven for birdlife (including blue-footed boobies, pelicans and frigate birds), with good snorkeling, too.

◉ Sights & Activities

Salango
Archaeological Museum
MUSEUM

(☑05-257-4304; www.salango.com.ec/museo-arqueologico-salango.php; Calle Balseros del Sur; adult/child $2.50/1.50; ⊙9am-5pm) A fascinating collection of more than 245 ceramics pieces is exhibited here. Objects date from 3000 BC to 1500 AD and account the settlements of the Valdivia, Machalilla, Chorrera Engoroy, Bahia and Guangala peoples. Archaeologists are still making discoveries in this very spot, and there's a lab for research on-site. The museum has 11 cabins (per person $15) on the beach for those wanting to stay and get involved with archaeology projects and research (by prior arrangement only).

Mirador de Salango
OBSERVATORY

(⊙dawn-dusk) FREE Awesome sunset views of Salango, Isla Salango and Río Chico from a wooden observatory jutting out over the sea on a spit of land between Las Tunas and Salango.

Ruta de Colibri
BIRDWATCHING

(Hummingbird Hike; www.fjocotoco.org/ayampe.html; btwn Ayampe & Puerto López) This nice, slightly uphill hike through the local communities allows for observation of a multitude of avian species (nearly 400 have been spotted), including, if you're lucky, the elusive, endangered Esmeraldas Woodstar, one of the world's smallest hummingbirds at 6.4cm (2.5in) in length.

The route, which is a total of 12km, crisscrosses Jocotoco Foundation's Rio Ayampe Reserve. There are also occasional bicycle races held here. Jardin de la Diversidad (☑099-033-9264; www.classicmototravel.com; per person incl breakfast $25) will rent you a basic room on the route.

Abel Muñoz
BOAT GUIDE

(Joe Salango Tour; ☑099-399-8515; www.salangotour.com; Calle Balseros del Sur; per person $15-20, whale-watching $25) Local guide and boat

driver Abel Muñoz offers 1½-hour boat trips to Isla Salango to visit the untouched beach and spot pelicans, boobies and other wildlife. Abel also has snorkeling equipment you can use (included in the price). His office is about three houses down the road from the entrance to town (Joe is his son, hence the name of the tour).

🍽 Sleeping & Eating

Finca Punta Ayampe
CABIN $$

(☑099-189-0982; www.fincapuntaayampe.com; Ayampe; r $55-60; 🖎) Surrounded by rainforest, this idyllic place feels like an end-of-the-road hideout. The high-ceilinged main house's bamboo bedrooms, as well as the cabañas, are filled with light, while a big lounge area has chunky wooden tables and spectacular sea views. Surfing, diving, kayaking and bird-watching tours can be arranged, and there's a good restaurant serving fresh ceviches, burritos, fish dishes, pastas, salads and sandwiches.

La Buena Vida
GUESTHOUSE $$

(☑099-486-3985; www.surflabuenavida.com; near Ruta del Spondylus, Ayampe; r per person incl breakfast $30-35; ✳🖎) Run by an Ecuadorian-American couple, La Buena Vida has seven colorful rooms, all with fans and ocean views. Friendly hosts, good breakfasts, and an inviting open-sided cafe-bar that's perfect for a sundowner have made this a popular spot. Surf lessons and packages are also available (from $25). A 50% deposit is required to hold a reservation.

Azuluna Eco-Lodge
LODGE $$$

(☑05-234-7093, 099,951-0542; www.azuluna-ecuador.com; off Ruta del Spondylus, Las Tunas; d from $79-109; ✳🖎) 🏊 Secluded on a hill across from Las Tunas proper are these thatch-roofed bungalows made from bamboo, wood and palm leaves. Each has a mesmerizing view of the ocean, and a balcony with a hammock from which to enjoy it. Thoughtful touches include hand-painted nature murals, windows with colored glass detailing, and bathrooms with tiled floors.

Delfin Mágico
SEAFOOD $$

(☑05-2574-4291, 09-9951-3938; www.delfinmagico.com.ec; Salango; mains $12-25; ⊙noon-8pm Mon-Fri, from 9am Sat & Sun; 🖎) In Salango, it's worth stopping in at the under-the-sea-themed Delfin Mágico, which serves outstanding seafood. Order everything from cherna and grouper to corvina, octopus, shrimp and sea bass, marinated in all manner of delicious sauces and prepared using local and Spanish techniques. Go early to avoid long waits. It sells smooth, locally roasted coffee from nearby Jipijapa under the brand Cafe Salango.

ⓘ Getting There & Away

Green Manglaralto buses speed (really!) up and down the coast along Ruta de Spondylus between Montañita and Puerto López about every 20 minutes; flag them down anywhere along the route. Alternatively, local taxis and moto-taxis between towns cost around $2 to $7.

Olón

A few kilometers north of Montañita is the coastal village of Olón, boasting a long beach (with beginner waves) and an inland landscape that marks the beginning of a dramatic departure from the dry scrubland further south. This lush cloud forest is part of the Cordillera Chongón-Colonche, which climbs over a low coastal mountain range. It's one of the few places in the world with a cloud forest and a beach in such close proximity; jaguars, howler monkeys and the endangered great green macaw all reside here.

After a day in Montañita or Guayaquil, you'll feel, dare we say, all Olón here.

⌒ Sleeping

La Mariposa HOTEL $
(☑ 04-278-8120; www.lamariposahostal.com; Calle 13 de Diciembre, near Rosa Mística; d $30-35; ❈ ❈ ❞) Two minutes from the beach, the Italian-run La Mariposa has pretty gardens with coconut trees and is a relaxing, welcoming place. Upper floors have ocean views and there's a pleasant courtyard strung with hammocks. Continental breakfast is available (from $3.50). You can pay $5 extra for air-conditioning.

Samaí Lodge GUESTHOUSE $$$
(☑ 099-462-1316; www.samailodge.com; s/d incl breakfast from $54/114; ❈ ❞ ❈) Overlooking the forest, Samaí Lodge feels like an idyllic oasis. Twelve cabins are scattered throughout the property; many with floor-to-ceiling windows and hammocks from which to enjoy views all the way to the coast – with a chance to spot both whales and monkeys in the same place.

There's also a Jacuzzi, yoga classes, a spa, pool and tasty food.

ⓘ Getting There & Away

Comfortable **CLP buses** (☑ 04-293-3001, 04-293-3009, 04-294-4322; http://libertad peninsular.com) leave from just north of Olón on the main road, headed to Guayaquil ($6.25, 2½ to three hours, five to six daily). This route also stops in Montañita.

To head north to points as far as Manta, catch a green Manglaralto bus on the highway: they run every 20 minutes – at perilous speed.

Montañita

☑ 04 / POP 1200

The beachfront village of Montañita is a party place with a surfing problem. There's a steady stream of cosmopolitan backpackers, with as many South Americans as gringos. Cheap digs and a Rasta vibe mean some travelers put down temporary roots, paying their way by hair braiding, jewelry-making or working in guesthouses. Montañita is ideal for the kind of person who, regardless of age, balks at the typical restaurant dress code: bare feet and no shirt is practically de rigueur here.

A rabbit warren of stalls crowd the center, which feels as much a Middle Eastern market as a Pacific beach town; the influence of Argentine, Peruvian and Israeli cultures is strong. The itinerant vendors never took to a riverside site set up by the government, which remains abandoned. As this miniature Babylon builds up and up (three to four stories) it feels like it's reached its breaking point, almost literally.

⚡ Activities

The beach break is rideable most of the year (best from December to May), but beginners should keep in mind that waves can be big, and riptides are common. Real surfers ride the wave at the northern end of the beach, a right hander that can reach 2m to 3m on good swells.

Machalilla Tours ADVENTURE
(☑ 099-169-4213; ⊙ 9am-6pm) On the main street near Banco Bolivariano, Machalilla Tours offers a wide range of activities, including walking tours through the rainforest ($35), cycling excursions ($35), horseback riding ($45), paragliding ($40) and parasailing ($35).

🎓 Courses

Montañita Spanish School   LANGUAGE
(📞09-9758-5207; www.montanitaspanishschool.
com; near Ruta Del Spondylus; 20hr group/private
language classes $170/240, 5-day surf classes
$80) Overlooking town, Montañita Spanish
School is *the* place to take language classes.
It offers Spanish and surf-lesson combos.
Find it on an unnamed road, east of the main
village of Montañita, off Ruta del Spondylus.
Ask a local or call the school for directions
(or just look uphill when you get off the bus).

🛏 Sleeping

Hostal Mamacucha   GUESTHOUSE $
(📞099-402-9356; dm from $7, r per person
from $10; ❋🛜) Adorned with murals and
color-saturated walls, this uberfriendly hostel
is good value, with simple rooms surrounding a small garden courtyard. Bathrooms
have hot water, there's a pool table and TV
room, mosquito nets, free tea and coffee and
guests often make dinner together like a family. Offers great deals on bike tours, surf lessons and nighttime nature walks, too.

★ Hostal Kundalini   HOSTEL $$
(📞09-5950-5007; www.hostalkundalini.com.
ec; r incl breakfast $42-105; ❋🛜) Sitting on
the beach in front of a surf break, Kunda-
lini was once nothing more than a thatch-
roofed building set out on a lawn with four
rooms. Now it's a smart tropical-themed
22-room hostel/boutique hotel, including a
top beachside restaurant and exceptionally
finished rooms with bamboo headboards.

Selina Hostal   HOSTAL $$
(www.selina.com;dm/r/stefrom$8/38/71;❋🛜🏊)
Latin America's ever-expanding boutique
hostal empire has arrived in Ecuador (with
Quito, Cuenca and Banos locales), and that's
a good thing. Setting a new standard in *mo-
chillero* (backpacker) offerings, Selina has
an on-site cinema and 'business office' that
no other *hostal* can offer, while not losing
the common touch of the traveler experience. With everything from dorms to suites,
Selina's got you covered.

🍴 Eating & Drinking

Restaurant Surf Food   ECUADORIAN $
(meal deals from $3.50; ⏰8am-midnight) Always
packed with locals, this cafe has zero atmosphere (it's very basic with simple tables and
chairs), but is *the* place to get a satisfying
and inexpensive Ecuadorian meal. Decent
plates include breaded shrimp or fish in
coconut sauce, accompanied by rice, lentils
and plantain. Meal deals include a soup and
a drink. Menus change daily.

★ Tiki Limbo   INTERNATIONAL $$
(📞099-954-0607, 04-206-0019; www.tikilimbo.
com; mains $8-15; ⏰8:30am-midnight; 🛜🍴)
In the epicenter of town, Montañita's best
restaurant has an eclectic menu of global
dishes (fajitas, falafels, homemade burgers,
sesame-crusted shrimp, seafood platters)
served in a charming setting of well-kept
bamboo furniture with crisp white cush-
ions. To finish your meal, try the milkshakes
loaded with Nutella and vanilla ice cream or
the bannoffee waffles. There's a good range
of breakfasts, too.

It's attached to the hotel of the same
name, which is modernizing by the minute,
so if you're one-stop shopping, you can stay
here, too.

**★ Montañita
Brewing Company**   BREWERY
(www.montanitabrewingcompany.com; ⏰noon-
10pm, closed Wed Jun-Jul) At the northern end
of the beach, overlooking the sand, the only
microbrewery on Ecuador's coast serves up
Amazonian IPA, chocolate stout, blackber-
ry, jalapeno and passion-fruit blondes, and
tropical ciders (mango, lime, ginger) – all
fresh out of the keg. It doesn't export these
top-notch brews, so you can only experience
them in Montañita.

ℹ Information

Women should be cautious about walking alone
along the beach at night as there have been
reports of assaults.

Banco Bolivariano, Banco de Guayaquil and
Banco Pichincha (near the taxi stand) all have
ATMs in town.

ℹ Getting There & Away

CLP (p745) buses are the most comfortable
option (in our experience, the best buses in
Ecuador, likely designed for gringo comfort
levels). They depart from Olón and stop in Mon-
tañita on their way south to Guayaquil ($6.25,
2½ to three hours, six daily). Other buses stop
on their way to Santa Elena ($3, two hours), La
Libertad ($2.50, 1¾ hours), or north to Puerto
López ($2.50, 1¼ hours) every 20 minutes or
so. These are the green Manglaralto buses,
which run at an alarming speed through the
mountain turns. The main **bus station** (📞04-

266-0203; Segundo Rosales, near Ruta Spondylus) and ticket office are on the main road.

The two local taxi companies are **Montañisol S.A** (📞093-914-0192, 098-279-5312, 04-206-0217; montanisol@gmail.com; ⊘24hr) and **Montañisol Compañía De Taxis** (📞096-891-1333; www.montanisol.com). Located just in from the highway, they offer services to destinations from Puerto López ($25) to as far away as Guayaquil ($80).

Guayaquil

📞04 / POP 2.7 MILLION

Guayaquil is not only the beating commercial heart of Ecuador but a vibrant sprawling city, growing ever more confident. A half-dozen high-rises give it a big-city profile, and several hillsides are engulfed by colorful favelas, but it's the Río Guayas' *malecón* (the riverfront town square) that defines the city's identity.

The picturesque barrio of Las Peñas, which perches over the river, anchors the city both geographically and historically, while the principal downtown thoroughfare Avenida 9 de Octubre funnels office workers, residents and shoppers into one hybrid stream. Amid revitalized squares, parks and massive urban-renewal projects, the city has a growing theater, film and arts scene and lively bars, fueled in part by several large universities.

Note that all flights to the Galápagos Islands either stop at or originate in Guayaquil, so the city is the next best place after Quito to set up a trip.

◎ Sights

◉ Center

⭐**Museo Antropológico y de Arte Contemporáneo** MUSEUM
(MAAC; 📞04-230-4000, 04-230-9385; cnr Malecón Simón Bolívar & Loja; ⊘8.30am-4.30pm Tue-Fri, 10am-4pm Sat & Sun) FREE Marking the end of the riverfront is the modern MAAC, a museum of anthropology and archaeology that hosts a superb permanent collection of pre-Colombian pieces and videos showing artistic techniques of early peoples. Changing exhibitions showcase thought-provoking works by contemporary Ecuadorian artists. MAAC also has a modern 350-seat **theater** (📞04-230-9400; www.culturaypatrimonio.gob.ec/

cartelera-maac-cine; Av Malecon & Loja, Malecon 2000; $2) for plays, concerts and films.

Malecón 2000 SQUARE
(Malecón Simón Bolívar; ⊘6am-11pm) One of the most extensive urban-renewal projects in South America, Malecón 2000 is made up of monuments, playgrounds, sculptures, gardens and river views. From its southernmost point at the Mercado Sur to Cerro Santa Ana and Las Peñas in the north, *el malecón* stretches some 2.5km along the bank of the wide Río Guayas. It's a gated, policed public space with restaurants, a museum, a performance space, a movie theater and a shopping mall.

Museo de los Equipos del Astillero MUSEUM
(📞04-207-5054; Santa Ana, Edificio Astillero # 3; ⊘10am-6pm Wed-Sun) FREE A photo- and trophy-filled tribute to Guayaquil's great rival soccer teams, Barcelona and Emelec, this museum is divided neatly into two colors: the yellow side for Barcelona and the blue for Emelec.

Balcon Mirador Cerro Paraiso VIEWPOINT
(off Jorge Perrone Galarza; ⊘6am-9:30pm) If you'd prefer to get away from the crowds at Santa Ana Hill, this little known viewpoint offers staggering views over Guayaquil, including downtown, the Río Guayas, the financial district, Urdesa and colorful favelas to the west. There's a little shop selling drinks and snacks as well as restrooms.

◉ Las Peñas & Cerro Santa Ana

These two historic neighborhoods are some of Guayaquil's oldest, with parts untouched by the many fires that have ravaged the city over the years. Perched here for more than 400 years, the streets and buildings have been restored into an idealized version of a quaint South American hillside village, with brightly painted homes and cobblestone alleyways. The views from the top are spectacular, especially at night. Small, informal, family-run restaurants and neighborhood bars line the steps and it's safe, patrolled by friendly security officers who make sure foot traffic up the steep stairway flows unimpeded.

Guayaquil – City Center

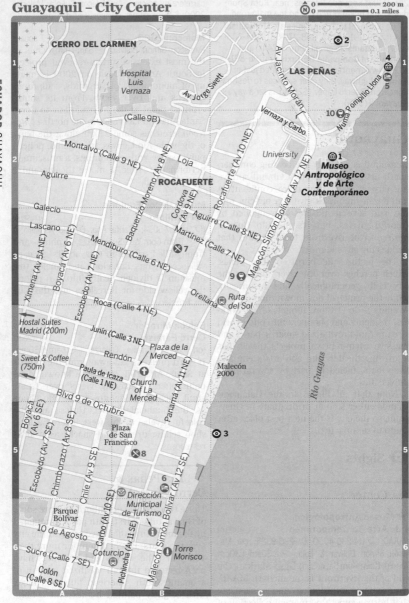

Cerro Santa Ana

AREA

One of Guayaquil's most iconic sights is this hillside enclave, which is dotted with brightly painted homes, cafes, bars and souvenir shops. Follow the winding path up the 444 steps to reach the hilltop **Fortín del Cerro** (Fort of the Hill; Cerro Santa Ana).

Cannons, which were once used to protect Guayaquil from pirates, aim over the parapet toward the river and are still fired today during celebrations.

You can climb the **lighthouse** (Cerro Santa Ana; ⏲10am-10pm) **FREE** for spectacular

Guayaquil – City Center

360-degree views of the city and its rivers, and stop in a tiny chapel across from it.

👉 Tours

Prices for Galápagos cruises are no lower here than they are in Quito; however, flights to the islands are slightly cheaper. For Guayaquil city tours and beyond, My Trip to Ecuador is highly recommended.

My Trip to Ecuador TOURS
(📞 09-8727-3727; http://mytriptoecuador.net; Victor Emilio Estrada 727 near Guayacanes, Luis Antonio Bldg, 2nd fl, office 2; tours per person from $65) Run by enthusiastic guide Mario, this could be the best tour operator in the country. Mario's enthusiasm for his home nation is addictive. He's charming, knowledgeable and flexible, running everything from quick city tours of his native city Guayaquil to weeklong Galápagos and Amazon adventures. English and Portuguese are spoken; customized tours and transfers are available.

Trips & Dreams TOURS
(📞 099-235-1335; www.tripsanddreams.com; Quísquis 305 near Rumichaca) This is an agency that shares space and management with **Hostal Suites Madrid** (📞 04-230-7804; www. hostalsuitesmadrid.com; Junín/Quisquis 305, near Rumichaca; r incl fan/air-con from $23/25; P ❄ @ 🛜). Ask for Christopher Jimenez, the extremely knowledgeable and affable manager. Can arrange all manner of trips, including to the Galápagos and Amazon.

🛏 Sleeping

⭐ **NucaPacha** HOSTEL $
(📞 04-261-0553; www.nucapacha.com; Bálsamos Sur 308; dm $11.50, s/d $22/35, without bathroom $18/29; @ 🛜 🏊) On a peaceful street in Urde-

sa, this appealing guesthouse has a pool, patio, and hammocks rimmed by mango and papaya trees and tropical foliage. Some simple rooms have colorful artworks, all have fans. There's also a clean shared kitchen (with filtered drinking water) and free walking tours. The staff are friendly and the price is right. No frills = no air-con!

⭐ **Manso Boutique Hotel** HOTEL $$
(📞 04-252-6644, in US 786-245-4973; www.manso. ec; cnr Malecón Simón Bolívar & Aguirre; dm $15, s/d/tr incl breakfast from $50/60/70, without bathroom $35/$43/51; ❄ @ 🛜) 🍃 The unrivaled *malecón* location aside, Manso is both a hostel and boutique hotel, housed in an atmospheric period property. Rooms vary in comfort and style – the best being bright, with high ceilings, framed artwork, and a splash of color. There's a bohemian vibe, with wooden sculptures, photography exhibitions and occasional readings and rooftop music, and an appealing pescatarian restaurant.

El Escalon GUESTHOUSE $$
(📞 04-238-8239; www.escalonhotel.com; Manuel Rendon 419, near Circunvalación Sur; s/d from $60/85; P ❄ 🛜) In a quiet residential street, not far from the action in Urdesa, this welcoming gated villa has immaculately finished rooms and a relaxing garden that backs on to mangroves. Rooms have TVs, hot water, desks and refrigerators. Hang out in the comfy lounge with games and books.

⭐ **Mansion del Rio** HOTEL $$$
(📞 04-256-6044; www.mansiondelrio-ec.com; Numa Pompilio Llona 120, Las Peñas; incl breakfast s $70, d from $177; ❄ @ 🛜) Housed in a lovingly restored home from the 1920s and hidden down a riverside cobblestone street in Las Peñas, the rooms at Mansion del Rio

POP UP THEATER

A growing phenomenon is one-act plays set in small bars and restaurants (*mini-teatro*, Spanish only) in places like La Bota on Malecon del Salado. Fifteen-minute works cost $5.

are handsomely designed with well-curated antique furnishings and many original details (chandeliers, vintage wallpaper, brass fixtures). The rooftop terrace offers great views, and if you're on your own, the single is a sweet deal.

 Eating

Guayaquileños love their *encebollado,* a tasty soup made with fish, yuca and onion, and garnished with popcorn and *chifles* (crispy fried banana slices). The best *encebollados* are found in cheap mom-and-pop restaurants, which usually sell out by lunchtime. *Cangrejo* (crab) is another local favorite. Many of the best restaurants are in the northwestern suburb of Urdesa, 4km northwest of downtown.

Palo Ceviches   CEVICHE $
(☑04-604-8223; Calle 11B NO; ceviches from $7.50; ☺10am-5pm Tue-Fri, 9am-5pm Sat & Sun) Fresh, tangy ceviches are served up in glass tankards (with a garnish of plantain chips) at this casual, modern spot in Urdesa. Tuck into shrimp, fish, octopus or seafood ceviche mixed in the special house sauce, at the inside or outside seating. Sides include crunchy calamari, plantain chips and hot salsa.

Zentro   FUSION $
(Cocina Agroecologico; ☑04-252-6644; cnr Malecón Simón Bolívar & Aguirre; mains $7-9; ☺8am-10pm; ☎☑) Inside the bohemian Manso Boutique Hotel (p749), this colorful cafe serves up tasty organic and vegetarian fare, including quinoa tortillas, satisfying bean burgers as well as tasty fish in coconut sauce. The name has changed recently, but it's still wonderful, healthy stuff.

Picanteria La Culata   SEAFOOD $
(Córdova, btwn Mendiburo & Martínez; mains $5-12; ☺6am-midnight Mon-Thu, to 2am Fri & Sat) Bringing a taste of the coast to the big city, La Culata serves excellent ceviches, *encocados* (shrimp or fish cooked in a rich, spiced coconut sauce) and seafood rices. It's a laid-back, open-sided joint (with beachy, cabaña-style murals on the walls) that draws crowds at all hours of the day and night.

Sweet & Coffee   CAFE $
(cnr Carbo & Luque; snacks $0.60-3.50; ☺7:30am-8:30pm Mon-Fri, from 9am Sat, noon-6pm Sun; ❋☎) Ecuador's answer to Starbucks is a popular dark-wood cafe with excellent cakes and quiches (the *torta de jamón y queso* is quite good); there are many other branches around Guayaquil, including the **branch** (cnr 9 de Octubre & José de Antepara; snacks $0.60-3.50; ☺7:30am-8:30pm Mon-Fri, from 9am Sat, noon-6pm Sun) near Oro de Verde.

Cocolon   ECUADORIAN $$
(☑04-263-4181; Av Francisco de Orellana; mains $8-14; ☺noon-11pm) Not far from the Hilton Colon Guayaquil and Mall del Sol, Cocolon has a modern, fun interior with bright-red

BUSES FROM GUAYAQUIL

DESTINATION	COMPANY	DURATION (HR)	FREQUENCY	PRICE
Chiclayo	CIVA	15	Once daily at 9pm	$25 to $32
Lima	Cruz del Sur	24	Once daily at either 9am or 2pm, rotating on various days	$90 to $100
Lima	Expreso Internacional Ormeño	26	Daily, times vary	$90
Máncora	Cruz del Sur	8	Once daily at either 9am or 2pm, rotating on various days	$41
Trujillo	Cruz del Sur	18	Once daily at either 9am or 2pm, rotating on various days	$60 to $80

chairs and photos decorating the walls. Coco-lon is well known for its Ecuadorian dishes: *La ultima cena* (grilled loin with rice, beans and all the fixings) is a classic. Adventurous palates should try *guatita* (a tripe and pota-to stew in a seasoned, peanut-based sauce).

 Lo Nuestro ECUADORIAN $$$
(☑04-462-7233; Estrada 903; mains $15-40; ⊘noon-11pm) Housed in a century-old man-sion complete with wooden shutters and pe-riod furniture, Lo Nuestro is one of the most atmospheric places in Guayaquil to feast on ceviche, sea bass with crab, and other seafood dishes. Musicians play on weekend evenings, when reservations are recommended. Leave room for some of the homemade cakes, dis-played on a trolley. Good wine selection, too.

Drinking & Nightlife

Las Peñas, the hillside to the north of down-town, is the place to enjoy a sangria or glass of wine, while more chic offerings can be found in the northern suburb of Urdesa and the Samborondón area. Adjacent to Las Penas, Puerto Santa Ana is a newer hangout with riverside views and the *malecón* to stroll; it has a bit of a yuppie, plastic–Miami Beach vibe.

La Paleta BAR
(en Las Rocas; www.facebook.com/lapaleta.enlasrocas; Numa Pompilio Llona 180; ⊘8pm-3am Tue-Sun) La Paleta is a great little lounge to while away an evening, with cave-like nooks, a hipster crowd and good ambient grooves. Serves beers and high-end cocktails, as well as tapas.

Frutabar JUICE BAR
(☑04-230-0743; www.trutabar.com; Malecón Simón Bolívar 504; juices from $1.75, mains $5-7; ⊘9am-midnight Mon-Thu, to 1am Fri & Sat, 3-10:30pm Sun) This surfer-themed eating and drinking spot serves up gourmet sand-wiches, snacks and tasty tropical fruit juices and cocktails. It's a fun spot for a drink, with a soundtrack of reggae and relaxed beats. Two other locations in the city, but this one's got the best position.

Information

DANGERS & ANNOYANCES

Guayaquil has its fair share of poverty and urban woes, but nothing to justify paranoia. The main tourist areas of Avenida 9 de Octubre, the Ma-lecón 2000, Las Peñas and the restaurant strip in Urdesa are perfectly safe. It's common to see security guards in flack jackets outside restau-rants, and tourist police on the streets, but don't be alarmed, they're always here. The area direct-ly north and south of the Parque del Centenario can feel dodgy at night, but simply use common sense and take the normal precautions for visit-ing any large city.

MEDICAL SERVICES

A number of 24-hour pharmacies can be found on Avenida 9 de Octubre. **Clínica Kennedy** (☑1-800-536-6339, 04-228-9666; www.hospikennedy.med.ec; Av del Periodista near Callejon 11A NO; ⊘24hr) hospital is also open 24 hours.

MONEY

There are major banks and stand-alone ATMs all over downtown Guayaquil, especially around the plazas.

POST

Post office (cnr Carbo & Aguirre; ⊘8am-6pm Mon-Fri, to noon Sat) For local and inter-national mail.

TOURIST INFORMATION

Dirección Municipal de Turismo (☑04-259-4800; www.turismo.gob.ec/coordinacion-zonal-5; cnr Pichincha & Ballén, Museo Nahim Isaias; ⊘9am-5pm Mon-Fri) This small office for city and regional tourist info is friendly, but usually Spanish-speaking only.

Getting There & Away

AIR

There are many internal flights to all parts of the country. The most frequent flights are to Quito (one hour) with **Avianca** (☑1-800-003-434; www.avianca.com; Av Francisco de Orellana), **LAN** (☑04-259-8500; www.lan.com; Aeropuer-to José Joaquín de Olmedo) or **Tame** (☑04-256-0728; www.tame.com.ec; Av 9 de Octubre 424, Gran Pasaje; ⊘9am-6pm Mon-Fri). One-way tickets start at $78. For the best views, sit on the right side when flying to Quito.

Tame also flies to Cuenca (return from $85, 50 minutes) and Loja (return from $96, one hour) daily. There are flights to Manta and Esmeraldas as well. Avianca, Tame and LAN fly daily to Baltra (return from $278, two hours) and San Cristóbal (return from $256, two hours) in the Galápagos.

BUS

The enormous **Terminal Terrestre** (☑04-213-0166; http://ttg.ec; Av Benjamin Rosales), just north of the airport, is as much a sprawling mall (shops, restaurants, internet cafes etc) as it is a transportation hub. There are more than 100 bus companies with small offices lined up along one side of the bottom floor of the building. The kiosks are grouped by region, and most of the destinations and departure times are clearly marked. Buses depart from the 2nd and 3rd floors.

Most bus companies sell tickets in advance, which will guarantee you a seat. Otherwise, just show up at the terminal and you'll usually find a bus to your destination leaving the same day. Departures on Friday nights and holidays can sell out.

The best services to Quito are the direct evening departures with **Panamericana** (☑04-213-0638; www.panamericana.ec; Terminal Terreste); $10, eight hours. For Cuenca, buses leave from Terminal Terrestre and run both via El Cajas ($8.25, four hours) and the more indirect route via La Troncal ($7.25, five hours).

Peru-bound buses (p754) are also available from the main Terminal Terrestre.

MINIVAN

For Salinas, **Ruta del Sol** (☑04-294-2060; www.rutadelsol.com.ec; Panama 501 near Orellana) runs direct shared minivans (around $12, 2½ hours) from behind the Hotel Ramada on the *malecón*. These leave hourly from 6am to 8pm, but it's best to reserve ahead.

For Machala, **Coturcip** (☑04-239-6439; Pichincha & Carbo) has shared minivans leaving hourly from downtown (around $10, three hours), or transfers from the airport in Machala to the airport in Guayaquil (around $60, three hours).

Machala

☑07 / POP 241,800

Machala is surrounded by banana plantations – *oro verde* (green gold), the region's moniker – and is the commercial and ad-ministrative capital of El Oro province. This dusty city is a transport hub and there's not much to see, but it's a convenient stop south from Guayaquil on the way to the Peruvian border to refuel and recharge, or for those making journeys further into the mountains directly to the east. Puerto Bolívar, only 7km away, is the local international port and sea-food center.

Parque Juan Montalvo is the main plaza at Machala's epicenter. The bus stations, most hotels and restaurants are within six blocks of here. The **World Banana Fair** (Feria Mundial del Banano; ☑07-370-0300; www.face book.com/feriabananaoec), held the third week in September, is when Machala celebrates all things banana. Its most telling public art: Monumento al Bananero (the Banana Pick-er), naturally.

🍴 Sleeping & Eating

Hotel Bolívar Internacional   HOTEL **$**
(☑07-293-0727, 02-293-887; cnr Bolívar & Colón; s $20, d $30-33; ℗❋🛜) Clean, friendly and only a short walk from several bus compa-nies. Some of the tiled rooms have windows overlooking a small park; rooms also have cable TV. There's a restaurant and confer-ence center on-site.

⭐ **Zona Refrescante**   INTERNATIONAL **$$**
(☑07-296-2977; Guayas, near Pichincha; mains $6-12; ⊙9am-10:30pm; ❋) The best dining op-tion in town is this inviting air-conditioned place specializing in grilled meats. The *seco de pollo* (passion-fruit chicken) is delightful, served with fresh avocado, rice, plantain and french fries. Other choices include Cuban sandwiches, pork and chicken grills (with salad, salsa fries and plantain), and *churras-co ecuatoriano* (steak in garlic and cumin with fries and salad).

ⓘ GETTING INTO TOWN

The **airport** (GYE; ☑04-216-9000; www.tagsa.aero; Av de las Américas) is about 5km north of downtown. A taxi (☑04-282-3333; www.fastline.com.ec) in either direction should cost around $5 and take around 20 minutes.

By bus, cross the street in front of the airport to take a green-line **Metrovia** (☑04-259-7680; http://metrovia-gye.com.ec) downtown ($0.30). The journey should take roughly 45 minutes.

The bus terminal (p751) is about 2km from the airport. A taxi between the two is approximately $3 or you can hop on a north-bound Metrovia ($0.30), which arrives at **Terminal Río Daule**, across from the bus terminal.

From the city center, there are two convenient Metrovia lines that go to Terminal Río Daule. A taxi to/from downtown is around $5.

❶ GETTING TO PERU

There are two ways to cross the border, by road (bus/car) and by foot (using a pedestrian bridge), but only the road route has official offices.

The easiest way to cross over to Peru is by road with one of the international lines that depart from Guayaquil's main bus terminal. The following companies have daily departures for Lima: **Cruz del Sur** (www.cruzdelsur.com.pe), **CIVA** (http://civa.com.pe), **Expreso Internacional Ormeño** (☑04-214-0487; www.grupo-ormeno.com.pe/contacto.html; Centro de Negocios El Terminal, Bahia Norte, Office 34, Bloque C; ☺8am-6pm Mon-Sat, to 1pm Sun) and **Rutas de America** (☑04-265-5373; La Garzota, Camilo Nevarez Vasquez, behind large RTS antenna). These services are very convenient because the bus goes to the Ecuadorian Immigrations Office and waits for you to take care of border formalities.

Alternatively, the pedestrian border crossing is in the center of Huaquillas at Río Zarumilla. An international footbridge goes over a mostly dry riverbed linking Huaquillas to Aguas Verdes in Peru. The bridge guards and police won't bother you with formalities. You can walk back and forth as you please, but remember that without an exit stamp from Ecuador and entry stamp into Peru you will have problems leaving Peru at any other official border crossing or airport.

The official **Ecuadorian Immigrations Office** (☺24hr) and the Peruvian Immigration Office are in new complexes, some 4km north of the bridge on the North Panamerica Hwy. All entrance and exit formalities (including passport stamps) are carried out here. If you're coming by non-international bus, it's easiest to disembark in Huaquillas and hire a taxi to take you to the immigration office. Taxis ask around $5 there and back.

Across the footbridge you will find *colectivos* (shared minivans; $3) in Aguas Verdes, plus moto-taxis ($5) running to Tumbes in Peru, which has plenty of hotels, as well as transportation to take you further south. **Transportes Flores** (http://floreshnos.pe) has four daily departures from the Peruvian side of the border south to Lima ($30, 20 hours) and destinations en route. More comfortable premium bus options might be available for a few extra dollars.

If you're leaving Peru and entering Ecuador, after walking across the international bridge you'll find yourself on the main road, which is crowded with market stalls and stretches out through Huaquillas. Take a taxi ($5; double if you ask them to wait and return to the town) to the Ecuadorian and Peruvian immigration offices. For onward northbound transport you'll have to return to Huaquillas, where the buses and minivans depart.

❶ Information

A handful of major banks with ATMs are located around Parque Juan Montalvo, including **Banco Pichincha** (Guayas near Rocafuerte).

Tourist Information (cnr Av 25 de Junio & Av 9 de Mayo, Carrera Central; ☺8am-1pm & 2:30-5:30pm Mon-Sat) Has city and area maps (only Spanish spoken).

❶ Getting There & Away

Flights to Quito (from $27, 1¼ hours) with **Tame** (☑07-293-2710; www.tame.com.ec; Montalvo, near Pichincha; ☺9am-6pm Mon-Fri) depart from Santa Rosa Airport, 40 minutes south of Machala. Jump on any bus heading to Huaquillas (ask the bus driver to stop at the airport), or take a taxi ($30).

Machala has no central bus terminal, though most bus companies cluster about five blocks southeast of Parque Juan Montalvo.

Bus schedules change regularly. Reservations are recommended for international journeys and more obscure destinations.

GALÁPAGOS ISLANDS

The Galápagos Islands may just inspire you to think differently about the world. The creatures that call the islands home, many found nowhere else in the world, act as if humans are nothing more than slightly annoying paparazzi.

The Galápagos Islands

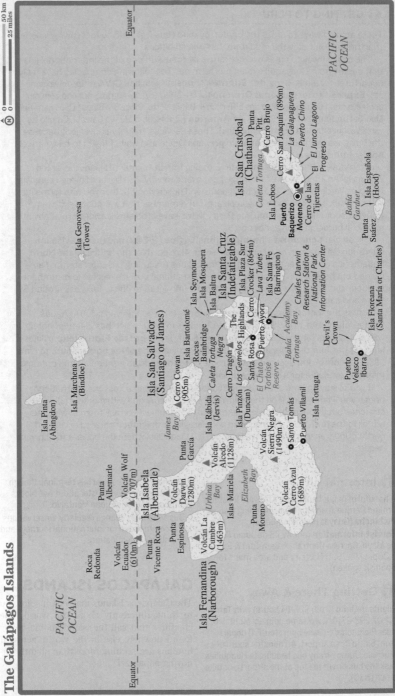

Equator

PACIFIC OCEAN

50 km
25 miles

N
0

Equator

PACIFIC OCEAN

Isla Pinta (Abingdon)

Isla Marchena (Bindloe)

Isla Genovesa (Tower)

Isla San Salvador (Santiago or James)

Cerro Cowan (905m)

James Bay

Isla Bartolomé
Rocas Bainbridge
Caleta Tortuga Negra
Isla Rábida (Jervis)
Cerro Dragón
Isla Pinzón (Duncan)

Punta Albemarle

Volcán Wolf (1707m)

Punta García

Volcán Darwin (1280m)

Isla Isabela (Albemarle)

Volcán Alcedo (1128m)

Volcán Sierra Negra (1490m)

Santo Tomás

Puerto Villamil

Isla Tortuga

Roca Redonda

Volcán Ecuador (610m)

Punta Vicente Roca

Punta Espinosa

Volcán La Cumbre (1463m)

Isla Fernandina (Narborough)

Urbina Bay

Islas Mariela

Punta Moreno

Elizabeth Bay

Volcán Cerro Azul (1689m)

Isla Seymour
Isla Mosquera
Isla Baltra

Isla Santa Cruz (Indefatigable)

Isla Plaza Sur

Cerro Crocker (864m)

Lava Tubes

Isla Santa Fe (Barrington)

The Highlands

Los Gemelos

Santa Rosa

El Chato Tortoise Reserve

Puerto Ayora

Charles Darwin Research Station & National Park Information Center

Bahía Academy

Bahía Tortuga

Devil's Crown

Puerto Velasco Ibarra

Isla Floreana (Santa María or Charles)

Isla San Cristóbal (Chatham)

Cerro San Joaquín (896m)

Punta Pitt

La Galapaguera

Puerto Chino

El Junco Lagoon

El Progreso

Cerro Brujo

Caleta Tortuga

Isla Lobos

Puerto Baquerizo Moreno

Cerro de las Tijeretas

Bahía Gardner

Punta Suárez

Isla Española (Hood)

This is not the Bahamas and these aren't typical tropical paradises; in fact, most of the islands are devoid of vegetation and some look more like the moon than Hawaii. However, more humans live here than is commonly assumed, and there's a surprising level of development in the islands' towns, mostly geared toward the thriving tourism industry.

This isolated group of volcanic islands and its extremely fragile ecosystem has taken on almost-mythological status as a showcase of biodiversity. Yet you don't have to be an evolutionary biologist or an ornithologist to appreciate one of the few places left on the planet where the human footprint is kept to a minimum.

Island Basics

The islands lie in the Pacific Ocean on the equator, about 90 degrees west of Greenwich. There are 13 major islands (ranging in area from 14 sq km to 4588 sq km), six small islands (1 sq km to 5 sq km) and scores of islets, of which only some are named.

Five of the islands are inhabited. About half the residents live in Puerto Ayora, on Isla Santa Cruz in the middle of the archipelago. Puerto Baquerizo Moreno on Isla San Cristóbal (the easternmost island) is second in importance to Puerto Ayora when it comes to tourism.

The other inhabited islands are Isla Isabela (the largest island, accounting for half the archipelago's land mass), with the small, increasingly popular town of Puerto Villamil; Isla Baltra; and Isla Floreana, with Puerto Velasco Ibarra. The remaining islands are not inhabited but are visited on tours.

Most of the islands have two, or sometimes three, names. The earliest charts gave the islands both Spanish and English names (many of these refer to pirates or English noblemen), and the Ecuadorian government assigned official names in 1892. We use the official names in most cases.

☞ Tours

There are basically three kinds of tours in the Galápagos: the most common and most recommended are boat-based trips with nights spent aboard – this is because of their relatively low environmental impact and the exposure to a variety of wildlife and geography. There are also day trips returning to the same island each night, and hotel-based trips staying on different islands.

Boat Tours

Most visitors tour the Galápagos on boat tours, sleeping aboard the boat. Tours can last from three days to three weeks, although five- to eight-day tours are the most common. It's difficult to do the Galápagos justice on a tour lasting less than a week, but five days is just acceptable. If you want to visit the outlying islands of Isabela and Fernandina, a cruise of eight days or more is recommended. On the first day of a tour, you arrive from the mainland by air before lunchtime, so this is really only half a day in the Galápagos, and on the last day, you have to be at the airport in the morning. Thus, a five-day tour gives only three full days in the islands.

Itineraries

You can find boats to go to almost any island, although it does take more time to reach any of the outlying ones. Boats have fixed itineraries, so be sure to think ahead if you want a tour that visits a specific island. Make sure the tour doesn't include more than one night or half a day in either Puerto Ayora or Puerto Baquerizo Moreno, since you can always tack on a few days at the beginning or end on your own.

The daily itinerary on almost all boats includes taking a morning *panga* (small boat used to ferry passengers from a larger boat to shore) to a site on land to observe birds and other wildlife, followed by snorkeling nearby. Lunch and snacks are served while the boat motors to another island or site for a similar combination in the afternoon. There's usually a few hours of time to rest or socialize before dinner, and there's a pre- or postmeal briefing of the next day's schedule. While the standardized routine may irk those accustomed to the flexibility of independent travel, it's exceedingly comforting to have everything planned out – in the end, it's a surprisingly tiring trip.

Hotel-Based Tours

These tours go from island to island, and you sleep in hotels on three or four different islands: Santa Cruz, San Cristóbal, Isabela and Floreana. Tours typically last five days and four nights and cost $1000 to around $3000 per person, plus airfare and park fee. Several of the travel agencies in Puerto Ayora and Puerto Baquerizo Moreno book these – **Red Mangrove Aventura Lodge** (☎05-252-6564; www.redmangrove.com; Av Darwin; r incl breakfast from $350; ❄ @ 🛜) in Puerto Ayora and **Galakiwi** (📋05-252-1770; www.facebook.com/Galakiwi; Av Darwin; ⊙9am-5pm) in Puerto Baquerizo Moreno are recommended for these trips.

Day Tours

Boat-based day trips depart from either Puerto Ayora or Puerto Baquerizo Moreno. Several hours are spent sailing to and from the day's visitor sites, so only a few central islands are feasible destinations. Some trips may involve visiting sites on other parts of Isla Santa Cruz or Isla San Cristóbal.

One of the downsides of this kind of tour is that there is no chance of visiting the islands early or late in the day. The cheapest boats may be slow and overcrowded; their visits may be too brief; the guides may be poorly informed; and the crew may be lacking an adequate conservationist attitude. Nevertheless, day trips are useful if your time and budget are extremely limited.

Companies in Puerto Ayora and Puerto Baquerizo Moreno charge from $100 to $200 per person per day, depending on the destination on offer and the quality of the boat and guides.

❶ Information

FEES & TAXES

The Galápagos national park fee is $100. It must be paid in cash at one of the airports after you arrive, or in advance through a prebooked tour. You will not be allowed to leave the airport until you pay. In addition, a transit control fee of $20 must be paid at the Instituto Nacional Galápagos window next to the ticket counter in either the Quito or Guayaquil airports; the charge is already included in the price of many prearranged boat tours. When flying to Isla Isabela, tourists must pay a $10 fee on arrival.

MONEY

Compared to the mainland, you get much less bang for your buck in the Gálapagos. Cash is preferred for most transactions – many restaurants and shops don't accept cards and some accommodations may not either.

➤ Bring cash with you from the mainland in case your credit card isn't accepted or the ATMs run out of bills.

➤ ATMs can be found in Puerto Ayora and Puerto Baquerizo Moreno only – make withdrawals before heading to Isabela or Floreana.

➤ Small bills are best – $5s and $10s are ideal; most places won't take any over $20.

➤ MasterCard and Visa are the most accepted credit cards, few businesses take American

Express; note that some establishments may charge a 5% to 10% fee.

➤ Traveler's checks aren't widely accepted, so stick to cash and credit cards.

❶ Getting There & Away

Flights from the mainland arrive at two airports: Isla Baltra just north of Santa Cruz, and Isla San Cristóbal. There are almost an equal number of flights to Baltra and San Cristóbal.

The three airlines flying to the Galápagos Islands are Tame (www.tame.com.ec), Avianca (www.avianca.com) and LAN (www.latam.com). All operate two morning flights daily from Quito via Guayaquil to the Isla Baltra airport (two hours), which is just over an hour away from Puerto Ayora by public transportation. They also provide one or two daily morning flights to the San Cristóbal airport (1½ hours). Return flights are in the early afternoons of the same days.

Round-trip flights from Guayaquil start at around $300, and round trips from Quito start around $340; the latter trips include a layover in Guayaquil, although you don't have to get off the plane. It's also possible to fly from Quito and return to Guayaquil or vice versa; it's often more convenient to fly into Baltra and out of San Cristóbal (or vice versa). If you're booked on a boat through an agency, it will likely make the arrangements for you. There is a limit of 20kg for checked luggage (per person) on the flight to the Galápagos.

❶ Getting Around

Most people get around the islands by organized boat tour, but it's very easy to visit the inhabited islands independently. Islas Santa Cruz, San Cristóbal, Isabela and Floreana all have accommodations and daily interisland boat service (one way $30). There are also pricier interisland flights between Santa Cruz, San Cristóbal and Isabela.

Isla Santa Cruz (Indefatigable)

The island of Santa Cruz has the largest and most developed town in the Galápagos; almost every visitor to the islands spends at least some time here, even if it's simply commuting from the airport on nearby Isla Baltra to a cruise ship in the harbor of Puerto Ayora. However, to anyone who stays for longer, the island of Santa Cruz is more than just a way station or place to feel connected to the modern, human-made world. It's a destination in itself, full of visitor sites, easily accessible beaches and remote highlands in the interior, and a base for adventurous activities far from the tourism trail.

Puerto Ayora

05 / POP 20,000

Clean, prosperous Puerto Ayora is the Galápagos' main population center and the heart of the tourist industry. It's a friendly place to linger for a few days and the best place in the islands to set up a cruise.

◎ Sights

Charles Darwin
Research Station   WILDLIFE RESERVE
(05-252-6146; www.darwinfoundation.org; Av Darwin; ⊙7:30am-12:30pm & 2-5:30pm) FREE Just northeast of Puerto Ayora is this iconic national-park site, where over 200 scientists and volunteers are involved with research and conservation efforts, the most well known of which involves a captive breeding program for giant tortoises. Paths leading through arid-zone vegetation take you past tortoise enclosures, where you can look at these Galápagos giants. You can also visit a **baby-tortoise house** with incubators (when the tortoises weigh about 1.5kg or are about four years old, they're repatriated to their home islands).

Tortuga Bay   BEACH
In terms of sheer white-sand beauty, this beach is the rival of any in South America. You'll find it at the end of a 2.5km paved trail southwest of Puerto Ayora. In addition to swimming (a spit of land provides protection from the strong and dangerous currents on the exposed side), surfing or just sunbathing, you can see sharks, marine iguanas, pelicans and the occasional flamingo. There's no drinking water or other facilities.

⛵ Tours

Scuba Iguana   DIVING
(05-252-6497; www.scubaiguana.com; Av Darwin; ⊙9am-noon & 3-6pm Mon-Fri, 3-6pm Sat & Sun) Run by two of the most experienced divers in the Galápagos.

Moonrise Travel   TOURS
(05-252-6402; www.galapagosmoonrise.com; Av Darwin) Run by a family of Galápagos experts and guides, who can arrange camping at their private highlands ranch, plus boat- and hotel-based tours and diving trips.

🛏 Sleeping

Hotel Sir Francis Drake   HOTEL $
(05-252-6221; www.sirfrancisdrakegalapagos. com; cnr Av Baltra & Binford; d $42-65; ❀🖷) Hidden behind a small department store, the Sir Francis Drake is one of the better-value places in town. Ask for one of the ground-floor rooms all the way in the back – these have large windows that let in lots of natural light. Common space is limited to an inner patio with no seating and a single balcony.

Galapagos Native   GUESTHOUSE $$
(05-252-4730; www.galapagosnative.com.ec; Berlanga near Av 12 de Febrero; r $25-45) This place offers decent value for its clean rooms with white adobelike walls. Three rooms (the best) are bright and airy with balconies.

Hostal Gardner   HOSTAL $$
(05-252-6979; www.hostalgardnergalapagos. com; Berlanga; s/d from $25/45; ❀🖷) The budget-minded Gardner has simple rooms and a covered rooftop patio with lounge chairs and hammocks.

🍴 Eating

More than a half-dozen popular food kiosks sell inexpensive and hearty meals – mainly seafood – along Charles Binford, just east of Avenida Baltra. It's liveliest at night, particularly on weekends, when there's a festive atmosphere among the outdoor tables set out on the street.

Galápagos Deli   DELI, PIZZERIA $$
(Berlanga; mains $4.50-10; ⊙7am-9:45pm Tue-Sun; 🖷) Tired of standard *almuerzos* (set lunches)? Head to this sleek and modern place for brick-oven pizza (small $6.50 to $9.75) and high-quality deli sandwiches ($4.70 to $8.75), as well as fish and chips, espresso and delicious gelato. Because it's on a block with few pedestrians, it feels like a secret.

Casa del Lago Café Cultural   CAFE $$
(cnr Moisés Brito & Montalvo; mains $7-11; ⊙7am-7pm Tue-Sat; 🖷🍴) This boho cafe with a few indoor and outdoor patio tables serves excellent breakfasts, sandwiches, empanadas and salads, as well as homemade cakes, fruit drinks and brewed coffee.

ⓘ Information

There are two ATMs near the pier and in front of Proinsular Supermarket.
Banco del Pacífico (Av Darwin near Isla Florena; ⊙8am-3:30pm Mon-Fri, 9:30am-12:30pm Sat) Has an ATM and changes traveler's checks.

i-Tur (Av Darwin, entrance to water-taxi pier) A small kiosk with flyers, maps and basic hotel and travel-agency info.

❶ Getting There & Away

Lanchas (speedboats) head daily to the islands of Isabela ($30, two to 2¼ hours) and San Cristóbal ($30, two hours). Boats depart to Isabela/San Cristóbal at 7am and 2pm. There's also boat service to Floreana ($30, 1¾ hours) at 8am, but this service is irregular.

Interisland Boat Pier Catch boats to other islands here – be sure to arrive 30 minutes before departure.

Interisland Boats Book speedboat tickets from one of the several offices near the pier.

Around Puerto Ayora

◎ Sights & Activities

★**El Chato**
Tortoise Reserve　　　　WILDLIFE RESERVE
($3; ◎8am-5pm) South of Santa Rosa is El Chato Tortoise Reserve, where you can observe giant tortoises in the wild. When these virtually catatonic, prehistoric-looking beasts extend their accordion-like necks to feed, it's an impressive sight. The reserve is also a good place to look for short-eared owls, Darwin's finches, yellow warblers, Galápagos rails and paint-billed crakes (these last two are difficult to see in the long grass). The reserve is part of the national park and a guide is required.

Rancho Primicias　　　　WILDLIFE RESERVE
($5; ◎8am-5pm) Next to El Chato is this private ranch, where there are dozens of giant tortoises, and you can wander around at will. The entrance is beyond Santa Rosa, off the main road – ask locals for directions. Remember to close any gates that you go through. There is a cafe selling cold drinks and hot tea, which is welcome if the highland mist has soaked you.

Lava Tunnels　　　　TUNNEL
(◎8am-5pm) **FREE** These impressive underground tunnels southwest of the village of Santa Rosa are more than 1km in length and were formed when the outside skin of a molten-lava flow solidified. When the lava flow ceased, the molten lava inside the flow kept going, emptying out of the solidified skin and thus leaving tunnels. Because they are on private property, the tunnels can be

visited without an official guide. The tunnels have electrical lighting (you can also hire flashlights/torches).

Las Grietas　　　　LAKE
For nice swimming and snorkeling, head to this water-filled crevice in the rocks. Talented and fearless locals climb the nearly vertical walls to plunge into the water below. Take a water taxi (per person US$0.80 from 6am to 7pm) to the dock for the Angermeyer Point restaurant, then walk past the Finch Bay Hotel, then past an interesting salt mine, and finally up and around a lava-rock-strewn path to the water. It's about a 700m walk from the dock.

Isla San Cristóbal (Chatham)

Some local boosters say that San Cristóbal is the capital of paradise – and, technically, it is, because its port town of Puerto Baquerizo Moreno is the political seat of the Galápagos. It's the only island with fresh water and an airport in town, and it has several easily accessible visitor sites, all of which means that its tourism profile is second only to Santa Cruz. San Cristóbal is the fifth-largest island in the archipelago and has the second-largest population. The Chatham mockingbird, common throughout the island, is found nowhere else.

Puerto Baquerizo Moreno

☎05 / POP 7000

Despite its abundance of restaurants and hotels, Puerto Baquerizo Moreno retains its sleepy, time-stands-still fishing-village feel. And though an increasing number of trips begin or end here, it remains under the shadow of Puerto Ayora, its larger and higher-profile sister city in the Galápagos. The surfing is world class, and you can explore many places on the island from here on your own.

◎ Sights & Activities

The modern and easy-to-digest **Interpretation Center** (☎05-252-0021; https://galapagos.unc.edu/gsc; Av Alsacio Northia; ◎8:30am-5:30pm Mon-Sat) **FREE** on the north side of the bay explains the history and significance of the Galápagos better than anywhere else in the islands. Exhibits deal with the biology, ecology, geology and human history of the islands, and it definitely deserves a visit even if you've already been inundated with facts from boat guides.

From the center, there are various well-marked and paved trails that wind around the scrub-covered **Cerro de las Tijeretas** (Frigate-Bird Hill, above Bahia Tijeretas). One trail leads over the hill to the small Las Tijeretas bay, which has excellent **snorkeling**; there's no beach here – just step in from the rocks. Other paths lead to **viewing points** with breathtaking panoramas, and there's also a path down to scenic **Playa Baquerizo** (2km one way from the viewing point); the last half is strewn with large, sharp rocks, so wear good shoes.

Directly in front of the Interpretation Center is **Playa Mann**, a small beach popular with locals and tourists alike, especially for lovely sunsets and on weekends. The large building across the street houses the Galápagos Academic Institute for the Arts & Sciences, which hosts semester-abroad international students and special marine-ecology and volunteer programs.

From the end of the dirt road that passes in front of the Interpretation Center, there's a short trail to **Playa Punta Carola**, a narrow beach nicknamed 'Playa del Amor' (Beach of Love) because the sheltering mangrove trees are favorite make-out spots (the sea lions here show little interest in the goings-on). Surfing off the nearby point is excellent.

Surfing

Hands down, Baquerizo Moreno has the best surfing in the Galápagos. From December to March a northern swell brings world-class waves and more than a hundred surfers, especially Brazilians, head here around January. Waves are rideable year-round, but the best time is December to April. High-quality reef breaks near town are **El Cañon** and **Tongo Reef**, both of which are accessed by walking through the military zone. If you're carrying a board and show identification (your passport), the guard will sign you through. **La Lobería** and **Punta Carola** are also excellent spots with reef breaks. **Lava Wave Surf** (☑05-252-1815; www.lavawavesurf.com; Wolf near Av Darwin) rents out boards (per day $20) and provides half-day lessons (about $60 per person).

Diving

There are several good spots for diving nearby. Eagle rays, sea turtles, sea lions, and hammerhead and white-tip sharks can be found at León Dormido (Kicker Rock). Schools of jacks, eagle rays, stingrays and seahorses are seen around Stephanie's Rock. Roca Ballena is a cave at about 23m to 24m down with corals, parrotfish and rays; strong currents mean it's for experienced divers only. There are also several wreck dives, including the *Caragua*, a 100m-long cargo ship near the site of the *Jessica* oil spill. Several companies in town offer diving.

Sharksky Tours   SNORKELING, DIVING
(☑05-252-1188; www.sharksky.com; Av Darwin near Wolf; ⊗8am-6pm Mon-Sat, to noon Sun) This outfit offers island-hopping adventure-sports tours that range from four to eight days. It can also arrange longer cruises on many of the Galápagos expedition vessels.

🛏 Sleeping

⭐**Casa de Laura Hostal**   HOSTEL $
(☑05-252-0173, 098-771-4689; hostalcasadelaura@hotmail.com; Av de la Armada Nacional; r per person $20; ❈@🛜) This friendly, family-owned hideaway is one of the best-value places in town. Located in a two-story adobe building with modern hot-water rooms, it has a nicely landscaped courtyard, and hammocks in the tiny cactus garden in front. It's just off the western end of Av Darwin.

⭐**Casa Blanca**   HOTEL $$
(☑05-252-0392; www.casablancagalapagos.com; cnr Av Darwin & Melville; incl breakfast r $70-120, ste $150; ❈🛜) There's no better place to base yourself in town: not only does this white-washed adobe building have charmingly decorated rooms and tile floors, but it sits on the *malecón* directly across from the passenger pier, meaning rooms with sea-facing balconies have great views. There's even a top-floor cupola suite, with its own private balcony.

Isla Isabela (Albemarle)

Isabela is the largest island in the archipelago at 4588 sq km, but despite its size and imposing skyline of active volcanoes, it's the delicate sights like frigate birds flying as high as the clouds or penguins making their way tentatively along the cliffs that reward visitors.

It's a relatively young island and consists of a chain of five intermittently active volcanoes, including Volcán Sierra Negra, which erupted in late 2005 and sent up a 20km-high smoke column. One of the island's volcanoes, Volcán Wolf, is the highest point in the Galápagos at 1707m (some sources claim 1646m). There's also a small, older volcano, Volcán Ecuador (610m).

In response to an ecosystem-wide threat and a dwindling tortoise population on Isabela and especially around Volcán Alcedo (1097m), the Charles Darwin Research Station and Galápagos National Park Service successfully eradicated tens of thousands of feral goats through ground and aerial hunting.

◉ Sights & Activities

There are a handful of good surf breaks for experienced surfers near town, some only reached by boat. Stop by **Isabela Discovery** (☎ 05-252-9303; jacibruns@hotmail.com; cnr Av Gil & Los Petreles; ⊙9am-7pm or by appointment) to rent a board.

Pozo Villamil   WILDLIFE RESERVE
(⊙trail 6am-6pm) Behind and to the west of the village is this lagoon, known for its **marine iguanas** and migrant birds, especially waders – more than 20 species have been reported here. A **trail** a little over 1km long begins just past the Iguana Crossing Hotel. The wooden boardwalk takes you over the lagoon, passing through mangroves and dense vegetation, eventually ending in the **Centro de Crianza de Tortugas** (Giant Tortoise Breeding Center).

★Los Túneles   SNORKELING
Around a 30- to 40-minute boat ride from Puerto Villamil is this outstanding spot for snorkeling, formed by convoluted lava formations standing between mangroves and the open sea. Look out for white-tipped sharks, manta rays, eagle rays, sea lions, turtles and even seahorses in the shallows. Tour operators in Puerto Villamil run daily five-hour trips here for around $90.

⌁ Sleeping & Eating

Some of the best beachfront hotels and guesthouses in the Galápagos can be found in Puerto Villamil. Further from the shore, there are several modest properties tucked among the town's sleepy streets.

There are several restaurants located along Avenida Antonio Gil. Seafood mains here run from $10 to $20.

ⓘ Information

There is no ATM that accepts foreign cards, so bring all the cash you'll need.

Isla Floreana (Santa María or Charles)

This, the sixth largest of the islands, is known as much for the mysterious history of its first residents – a small contingent of European settlers who became entangled in power struggles, peculiar disappearances and alleged murders – as it is for its intensely pink flamingos and top-flight snorkeling sites.

Many Santa Cruz tour operators sell Floreana as a day trip. If you're considering this, know that on a day trip, almost none of your money goes to the community, and you will be subjected to over four hours of exhausting speedboat travel. Instead it's well worth staying overnight, as the village of Puerto Velasco Ibarra has appealing lodging options, and this is a fascinating area to explore for those willing to make the effort.

UNDERSTAND ECUADOR

Ecuador Today

Ecuador, under the leadership of charismatic ex-president Rafael Correa, invested in new roads, hospitals, schools and social programs. Ecuador's vast oil and mineral wealth played a pivotal role in this infrastructure bonanza. When oil prices crashed in 2008, Correa borrowed heavily to maintain momentum, and the country is paying the price today in oil and mineral concessions to the lender nations, specifically China, to whom it owes billions. In early 2018 new president Lenin Moreno replaced the government's finance minister – twice.

The 'Citizens Revolution' is how President Correa described the big changes that swept across Ecuador, and it's hard to deny the enormous gains many citizens made during Correa's administration. Infant mortality rates are down, and with the building of new schools and universities, more students have access to education.

Given all this, it's not surprising that Correa enjoyed widespread popularity during his first term. However, his attacks on the press

GALÁPAGOS WILDLIFE GUIDE

Galápagos sea lion Nearly everyone's favorite island mammal is the widespread Galápagos sea lion, which numbers about 50,000 and is found on every island. These delightful animals lounge about on sandy beaches and will often swim with snorkelers and bathers. **Where to see** Everywhere.

Galápagos fur seal More introverted than its sea-lion cousin, the endemic Galápagos fur seal has a dense, luxuriant, insulating layer of fur. Although it was nearly hunted to extinction in the 19th century, it has made a remarkable comeback and numbers some 30,000 animals. **Where to see** Santiago (Puerto Egas), Genovesa.

Giant tortoise The archipelago's most famous reptile is the giant tortoise, or Galápagos ('saddle' in Spanish), after which the islands are named. They can live for several hundred years. **Where to see** Santa Cruz (highlands), Isabela (Urbina Bay), San Cristóbal (Galapaguera).

Darwin's finches All of the islands' finches are believed to be descendants of a common ancestor, and evolved into 13 unusual species, including the blood-sucking vampire finch. **Where to see** Santa Cruz (Los Gemelos; Media Luna), Española (Punta Suárez), Genovesa.

Frigate birds Dazzling fliers, frigates ride high on thermals above coastal cliffs, sometimes harassing smaller seabirds into dropping their catch and then swooping to snag the booty in midair. **Where to see** North Seymour, Genovesa, San Cristóbal (Punta Pitt).

Blue-footed booby These boobies, one of four booby species on the islands, perform an enchanting, if rather clownish, display during courtship. **Where to see** Española (Punta Suárez), Genovesa, San Cristóbal (Punta Pitt).

Flightless cormorant Apart from penguins, the flightless cormorant is the only flightless seabird in the world, and it is endemic to the Galápagos. About 700 pairs remain. **Where to see** Fernandina (Punta Espinoza), Isabela (Tagus Cove; Urbina Bay).

Galápagos penguin Today the Galápagos penguin is the most northerly penguin in the world and the only species that lives in the tropics. **Where to see** Isabela, Fernandina, Bartolomé.

Galápagos flamingo These striking birds are one of the largest of the world's five species of flamingo. They're spread in small groups among the islands' shallow, brackish lagoons and number no more than 500. **Where to see** Floreana (Punta Cormorant), Rábida, Isabela (Puerto Villamil).

Galápagos land iguana Despite their large size and fearsome appearance, land iguanas are harmless vegetarians. Mature males are territorial, engaging in head-butting contests to defend their terrain. **Where to see** South Plaza, Isabela, Santa Cruz (Cerro Dragón), Fernandina, Baltra and North Seymour.

Lava lizards The most commonly seen reptiles on the islands are the various species of lava lizard, which are frequently seen scurrying across rocks or even perched on the backs of iguanas. **Where to see** Everywhere.

and the environment in his second term diminished his reputation, as did a running media battle with his successor, Moreno.

After leaving office in 2017, Correa moved to Europe. He was indicted by the Ecuadorian congress in June 2018 for his alleged role in the kidnapping of his political enemy Fernando Balda in 2012. In early 2018 the nation's voters rejected a referendum which would have allowed presidents to serve more than two terms, negating Correa's possible return.

The growth in public spending was fueled by the worldwide thirst for oil. Ecuador is particularly well endowed when it comes to petroleum; it's home to the third-largest oil reserves in South America (after Venezuela and Brazil).

While oil has undoubtedly lined the nation's coffers, it has also brought greater threats to

Ecuador's ecology. Parque Nacional Yasuní, a pristine area of the Amazon, holds one of Ecuador's largest reserves – thought to contain 846 million barrels (worth an estimated $7 billion). It also contains some of the greatest biodiversity on the planet, and is home to isolated indigenous groups. Attempts by environmental groups to hold a referendum on oil exploitation in the park were rejected by the government, and the state oil company Petroamazonas began drilling in this UNESCO World Heritage Site in early 2016.

History

The land of fire and ice has certainly had a tumultuous history. Since becoming an independent nation in 1830, Ecuador has gone through countless changes in government and 20 constitutions – the most recent drafted in 2008. Fueling the nation's volatility are rivalries both internal (conservative, church-backed Quito versus liberal, secular Guayaquil) and external (border disputes with Peru and Colombia).

Early Cultures

The oldest tools found in Ecuador date back to 9000 BC, meaning people were mucking about the region in the Stone Age. The most important early societies developed along the coast, which was a more habitable landscape than the frigid highlands. Ecuador's first permanent sedentary culture was the Valdivia, which emerged along the Santa Elena Peninsula nearly 6000 years ago.

By the 11th century AD, Ecuador had two dominant cultures: the expansionist Cara along the coast and the peaceful Quitu in the highlands. These cultures merged and became known as the Quitu-Caras, or the Shyris. They were the dominant force in the highlands until the 1300s, when the Puruhá of the central highlands became increasingly powerful. The third important group was the Cañari, further south. These were the cultures the Inca encountered when they began their expansion north from present-day Peru.

Land of the Four Quarters

Until the early 15th century, the Inca empire was concentrated around Cuzco, Peru. That changed dramatically during the rule of Inca Pachacutec, whose expansionist policies set into motion the creation of the vast Inca empire, Tahuantinsuyo, meaning 'Land of the Four Quarters' in Quichua (called Quechua elsewhere in South America). By the time the Inca reached Ecuador they were under the rule of Túpac Yupanqui, Pachacutec's successor, and they met with fierce resistance, both from the Cañari and the Quitu-Caras. In one battle the Inca massacred thousands of Caras and dumped them in a lake near Otavalo, which supposedly turned the waters red and gave the lake its name, Laguna Yaguarcocha (Lake of Blood).

The subjugation of the north took many years, during which the Inca Túpac fathered a son with a Cañari princess. The son, Huayna Capác, grew up in present-day Ecuador and succeeded his father to the Inca throne. Huayna Capác had two sons: Atahualpa, who grew up in Quito, and Huáscar, who was raised in Cuzco.

When Huayna Capác died in 1527, he left his empire not to one son, as was traditional, but to two. Rivalry developed between the sons, which eventually boiled into civil war. After several years of fighting, Atahualpa defeated Huáscar near Ambato in central Ecuador. Atahualpa was thus ruling a weakened and still divided Inca empire when Francisco Pizarro landed in Peru in 1532.

The Spanish Power Play

Pizarro's advance was rapid and dramatic. He successfully exploited divisions within the Inca empire and enlisted many non-Inca ethnic groups that had been recently and reluctantly subjugated by the Inca. Most importantly, Inca warriors on foot were no match for the fully armored conquistadors on horseback who slaughtered them by the thousands. Within three years, and after betraying Inca rulers on several occasions, the Spanish controlled the former Inca empire.

Settling In

From 1535 onward, the colonial era proceeded with no major uprisings by indigenous Ecuadorians. Francisco Pizarro made his brother Gonzalo the governor of Quito in 1540. Hoping to find more gold, Gonzalo sent his lieutenant, Francisco de Orellana, to explore the Amazon. The lieutenant and his force ended up floating all the way to the Atlantic, becoming the first party to descend the Amazon and cross the continent. This feat took almost a year and is still commemorated in Ecuador.

During the first centuries of colonial rule, Lima (Peru) was the seat of Ecuador's political administration. Ecuador, originally a *gobernación* (province), became known as the Audiencia de Quito in 1563, a more important political division. In 1739 the Audiencia de Quito was transferred from the viceroyalty of Peru, of which it was a part, to the viceroyalty of Colombia (then known as Nueva Grenada).

Ecuador remained a peaceful colony during these centuries, and agriculture and the arts flourished. Churches and monasteries were constructed atop every sacred indigenous site and were decorated with unique carvings and paintings, the result of a blend of Spanish and indigenous artistic influences. This so-called Escuela Quiteña (Quito school of art), still admired by visitors today, has left an indelible stamp on both the colonial buildings of the time and Ecuador's unique art history.

Life was comfortable for the ruling colonialists, but the indigenous people – and later, the mestizos (people of mixed Spanish and indigenous descent) – were treated abysmally under their rule. A system of forced labor was not only tolerated but encouraged, and by the 18th century there were several indigenous uprisings against the Spanish ruling classes. Social unrest, as well as the introduction of cocoa and sugar plantations in the northwest, prompted landowners to import African slave laborers. Much of the rich Afro-Ecuadorian culture found in Esmeraldas province today is a legacy of this period.

Adiós, España

The first serious attempt at independence from Spain was made on August 10, 1809, by a partisan group led by Juan Pío Montúfar. The group took Quito and installed a government, but royalist troops regained control in only 24 days.

A decade later, Simón Bolívar, the Venezuelan liberator, freed Colombia in his march southward from Caracas. Bolívar then supported the people of Guayaquil when they claimed independence on October 9, 1820. It took another two years for Ecuador to be entirely liberated from Spanish rule. The decisive battle was fought on May 24, 1822, when Mariscal (Field Marshall) Sucre, one of Bolívar's best generals, defeated the royalists at Pichincha and took Quito.

Bolívar's idealistic dream was to form a united South America. He began by amalgamating Venezuela, Colombia and Ecuador into the independent state of Gran Colombia. This lasted only eight years, with Ecuador becoming fully independent in 1830. That same year a treaty was signed with Peru, establishing a boundary between the two nations.

Liberals Versus Conservatives

Following independence from Spain, Ecuador's history unfolded with the typically Latin American political warfare between liberals and conservatives. Quito emerged as the main center for the church-backed conservatives, while Guayaquil has traditionally been considered liberal and socialist. The rivalry between these groups has frequently escalated to extreme violence: conservative President García Moreno was shot and killed in 1875, and liberal President Eloy Alfaro was killed and burned by a mob in Quito in 1912. The rivalry between the two cities continues on a social level today. Over time, the military began assuming control, and the 20th century saw more periods of military than civilian rule.

War with Peru

In 1941 war broke out with Peru over border disputes. The boundary was finally redrawn by a conference of foreign-government ministers in the 1942 Protocol of Rio de Janeiro. Ecuador never recognized this border, and minor skirmishes with Peru have occurred because of it – the most serious was the short war in early 1995, when several dozen soldiers on both sides were killed. Finally, after more fighting in 1998, Peru and Ecuador negotiated a settlement in which Peru retained a majority of the land in question.

Recent Political Developments

Ecuador's most recent period of democracy began in 1979, when President Jaime Roldos Aguilera was elected. Over the next two decades, control flip-flopped democratically between liberals and conservatives.

In the 1998 elections, Jamil Mahuad, former mayor of Quito, emerged victorious and was immediately put to the test. The devastating effects of El Niño and the sagging oil market of 1997–98 sent the economy into a tailspin in 1999. The sucre, Ecuador's former currency, depreciated from about 7000 per US dollar to about 25,000 by January 2000.

When Mahuad declared his plan to dump the national currency in exchange for the US dollar, the country erupted in protest. On January 21, 2000, marches shut down the capital and protesters took over the Ecuadorian congress building, forcing Mahuad to resign. His successor, Gustavo Noboa, went ahead with 'dollarization,' and in September 2000, the US dollar became Ecuador's official currency.

Presidential Comings & Goings

President Noboa was succeeded in 2002 by former coup leader Lucio Gutiérrez. In 2004 he also tossed out most of the supreme court, which allowed him to expel his rivals from the court and change the constitution in order to drop corruption charges against his former ally, the popularly despised ex-president Antonio Bucaram.

As a consequence, protests erupted in the capital, and in April 2005 the congress finally voted Gutiérrez out, replacing him with vice president Alfredo Palacios. Ousted and exiled, Gutiérrez made a surprise return to Ecuador in 2005, claiming he was the country's rightful leader. However, his political days were over, and in 2006 Rafael Correa, a US-educated economist and former finance minister (under Palacios) was elected president.

After taking the reins, Correa ushered in a series of large-scale changes. A new constitution in 2008, approved by referendum, laid the groundwork for a new social archetype that increased spending on health care and the poor, gave more rights to indigenous groups, accorded new protections to the environment and even allowed civil unions for gay couples.

Life After Correa

Ultimately Correa's decade-long legacy will be a mixed one. While he united the country with new roads and communication lines, he accomplished much of this by borrowing billions of dollars after the price of petroleum plummeted in 2008.

Lenín Moreno, formerly Correa's vice president, was elected in May 2017. In a historic moment, Moreno became the only global head of state in a wheelchair, having been paralyzed in an armed robbery in 1998. Upon assuming office, Moreno took a stand against Correa's free-spending ways, leading to a bitter dispute between the former allies.

Culture

Population

Ecuador has the highest population density of any South American country – about 58 people per sq km. Despite this, the country still feels incredibly wild, mainly because over 30% of the population is crammed into the cities of Quito and Guayaquil, and another 30% resides in Ecuador's other urban areas. Nearly half of the country's people live on the coast (including the Galápagos), while about 45% live in the highlands. The remainder live in the Oriente, where colonization is slowly increasing.

About 72% of the Ecuadorian people are mestizos, 15% are indigenous, 6% are white and 4% are Afro-Ecuadorian. Other ethnicities account for 3%. The majority of the indigenous people speak Quichua and live in the highlands. A few small groups live in the lowlands.

Lifestyle

How an Ecuadorian lives is a matter of geography, ethnicity and class. A poor *campesino* (subsistence farmer) family that cultivates the thin volcanic soil of a steep highland plot lives very differently from a coastal fishing family residing in the mangroves of Esmeraldas province, or a family staying in the slums of Guayaquil. An indigenous Saraguro family that tends communally owned cattle in the southern highlands has a dramatically different life to that of an upper-class *quiteño* (people from Quito) family, which might have several maids, all the latest electronic gadgets and an expensive car in the garage.

An estimated 22% of Ecuadorians live below the poverty line, and paying for cooking fuel and putting food in the belly is a constant concern for most people. But, as most first-time visitors are astounded to experience, even the poorest Ecuadorians exude an openness, generosity and happiness all too rare in developed countries. Fiestas are celebrated with fervor by everyone, and you'll sometimes roll around in bed, kept awake until dawn by the noise of a nearby birthday bash.

Religion

The predominant religion (74% of the population) is Roman Catholicism, with a small minority of other churches. Indigenous people tend to blend Catholicism with their own traditional beliefs.

Arts

Music

Música folklórica (traditional Andean music) has a distinctive, haunting sound that has been popularized in Western culture by songs such as Paul Simon's version of 'El cóndor pasa' ('If I Could'). Its otherworldly quality results from the use of a pentatonic (five-note) scale and pre-Columbian wind and percussion instruments that conjure the windswept quality of *páramo* (high-altitude Andean grasslands) life. It is best heard at a *peña* (folk-music club or performance).

Northwest Ecuador, particularly Esmeraldas province, is famous for its marimba music, historically the sound of the Afro-Ecuadorian population. Today, it's becoming increasingly difficult to hear live because many Afro-Ecuadorians have swapped it for salsa and other musical forms.

If there's one music you won't escape, it's *cumbia*, with a rhythm that resembles a trotting three-legged horse. Originally from Colombia, Ecuadorian *cumbia* has a more raw (almost amateur), melancholic sound and is dominated by the electronic keyboard. Bus drivers love the stuff, perhaps because it so strangely complements those back-road journeys through the Andes.

Although most people associate Ecuador with *folklórica*, the country's most popular national music is the *pasillo*, which is rooted in the waltz. The origins of *pasillo* date back to the 19th century when Ecuador was part of Gran Colombia. These poignant songs with their melancholic melodies often touch on themes of disillusionment, lost love and unquenchable longing for the past. *Pasillo's* most famous voice was that of Julio Jaramillo (1935–78), who popularized the genre throughout Latin America.

When it comes to youth culture, Caribbean-born reggaeton (a blend of Puerto Rican *bomba,* dance hall and hip-hop) is the anthem among urban club-goers. Ecuador also has its share of Latin pop artists, with singers like teen-idol Fausto Miño filling the airwaves.

Architecture

Many of Quito's churches were built during the colonial period, and the architects were influenced by the Escuela Quiteña. In addition, churches often show Moorish influences, particularly in the decorative details of interiors. Known as *mudéjar,* this reflects an architectural style that developed in Spain beginning in the 12th century. The overall architecture of colonial churches is over poweringly ornamental and almost cloyingly rich – in short, baroque.

Many colonial houses have two storys, with the upper floors bearing ornate balconies. The walls are whitewashed and the roofs are red tile. Quito's Old Town and Cuenca are Unesco World Heritage Sites and both abound with beautifully preserved colonial architecture.

Visual Arts

The colonial religious art found in many churches and museums – especially in Quito – was produced by indigenous artists trained by the Spanish conquistadors. The artists portrayed Spanish religious concepts, yet infused their own indigenous beliefs, giving birth to a unique religious art known as the Escuela Quiteña. The Quito school died out with independence.

The 19th century is referred to as the Republican period, and its art is characterized by formalism. Favorite subjects included heroes of the revolution, important members of the new republic's high society and florid landscapes.

The 20th century saw the rise of the indigenist school, whose unifying theme is the oppression of Ecuador's indigenous inhabitants. Important *indigenista* artists include Camilo Egas (1889–1962), Oswaldo Guayasamín (1919–99), Eduardo Kingman (1913–97) and Gonzalo Endara Crow (1936–96). You can (and should!) see the works of these artists in Quito's galleries and museums. The former home of Guayasamín, also in Quito, houses a stunning showcase of his work.

Environment

Land

Despite its diminutive size, Ecuador has some of the world's most varied geography. The country can be divided into three regions: the Andes form the backbone of Ecuador; the coastal lowlands lie west of the mountains; and the Oriente, to the east, comprises the jungles of the upper Amazon Basin. In only 200km as the condor flies, you can climb from the coast to snowcaps, over 6km above sea level, and then descend to the jungle on the country's eastern side. The Galápagos Islands lie on the equator, 1000km west of Ecuador's coast, and constitute one of the country's 21 provinces.

Wildlife

Ecuador is one of the most species-rich countries on the globe, deemed a 'mega diversity hot spot' by ecologists. The country has more than 20,000 plant species, with new ones discovered every year. In comparison, there are only 17,000 plant species on the entire North American continent. The tropics, in general, harbor many more species than temperate regions do, but another reason for Ecuador's biodiversity is simply that the country holds a great number of habitat types. Obviously, the Andes will support very different species than the tropical rainforests, and when intermediate biomes and the coastal areas are included, the result is a wealth of different ecosystems, a riot of life that draws nature lovers from the world over.

Bird-watchers flock to Ecuador for the great number of bird species recorded here – some 1600, or about twice the number found in any one of the continents of North America, Europe or Australia. But Ecuador isn't just for the birds: some 300 mammal species have been recorded, from monkeys in the Amazon to the rare Andean spectacled bears in the highlands.

National Parks & Reserves

Ecuador has over 30 government-protected parks and reserves (nine of which carry the title of 'national park'), as well as numerous privately administered nature reserves. Eighteen percent of the country lies within protected areas. Ecuador's first *parque nacional* (national park) was the Galápagos, formed in 1959. Scattered across mainland Ecuador are eight other national parks, including the most visited (from north to south):

Parque Nacional Cotopaxi (p704) The towering ice-capped cone of Volcán Cotopaxi makes for spectacular year-round hiking and mountaineering.

Parque Nacional Yasuní (p730) Amazon rainforest, big rivers and caiman-filled lagoons, plus monkeys, birds, sloths and more, mean year-round forest fun.

Parque Nacional Machalilla (p743) Coastal dry forest, beaches and islands are home to whales, seabirds, monkeys and reptiles. Hiking opportunities and beaches are superb.

Parque Nacional Cajas (p722) Shimmering lakes and moorlike *parámo* make this highland park an excellent adventure from Cuenca.

Parque Nacional Podocarpus (p725) From cloud forest to rainforest, this epic southern park is best explored from Loja, Zamora or Vilcabamba.

Many parks are inhabited by native peoples who were living in the area long before it achieved park status. In the case of the Oriente parks, indigenous hunting practices (which have a greater impact as outside interests diminish their original territories and resources) have met with concern from those seeking to protect the park. The issue of how to protect these areas from interests such as oil, timber and mining industries, while recognizing the rights of indigenous people, continues to be extremely tricky.

All national parks – apart from the Galápagos (which costs $110 to enter) – are free.

Environmental Issues

Ecuador has one of South America's highest deforestation rates. In the highlands, almost all of the natural forest cover has disappeared, and only a few pockets remain, mainly in privately administered nature reserves. Along the coast, once-plentiful mangrove forests have all but vanished to make way for artificial shrimp ponds.

About 95% of the forests of the western slopes and lowlands have become agricultural land, mostly banana plantations. Although much of the rainforest in the Ecuadorian Amazon remains standing, it is being seriously threatened by fragmentation. Since the discovery of oil, roads have been laid, colonists have followed and the destruction of the forest has increased exponentially. The main drives behind the destruction are logging, cattle ranching, and oil and mineral extraction.

The rainforest's indigenous inhabitants – who depend on the rivers for drinking water and food – are also dramatically affected. Oil residues, oil-treatment chemicals, erosion and fertilizers all contaminate the rivers, killing fish and rendering formerly potable water toxic. The documentary *Crude,* which premiered in 2009, provides a disturbing portrait of the heavy toll exacted on local inhabitants.

SURVIVAL GUIDE

❶ Directory A–Z

ACCESSIBLE TRAVEL

Unfortunately, Ecuador's infrastructure for disabled travelers is limited. Wheelchair ramps are few and far between, and sidewalks are often badly potholed and cracked. Bathrooms and toilets are often too small for wheelchairs. Signs in braille or telephones for the hearing impaired are practically unheard of.

Nevertheless, Ecuadorians with disabilities get around, mainly through the help of others. It's not particularly unusual to see travelers with disabilities being carried onto a bus, for example. Buses are (legally) supposed to carry travelers with disabilities for free. Local city buses, which are already overcrowded, won't do that, but long-distance buses sometimes do. Travelers with disabilities are also eligible for 50% discounts on domestic airfares.

When it comes to hotels, the only truly accessible rooms are found at the international chain hotels in Quito and Guayaquil.

Download Lonely Planet's free Accessible Travel guides from http://lptravel.to/Accessible-Travel.

ACCOMMODATIONS

There is no shortage of places to stay in Ecuador, but during major fiestas or the night before market day, accommodations can be tight, so plan ahead. Most hotels have single-room rates, although during high season some beach towns charge for the number of beds in the room, regardless of the number of people checking in. In popular resort areas, high-season prices (running from June to August and mid-December

SLEEPING PRICE RANGES

The following price ranges refer to a double room in high season. Room prices include bathroom. Exceptions are noted in specific listings.

$ less than $40

$$ $40–$90

$$$ more than $90

to January) are about 30% higher than the rest of the year.

Ecuador has a growing number of youth hostels, as well as inexpensive *pensiones* (short-term budget accommodations in a family home). Staying with families is an option in remote villages.

ACTIVITIES

From visiting ancient historic sites and remote Amazon indigenous communities to paragliding along the coastline, surfing in laid-back beach towns, hiking volcanoes and untouched national parks, plus encountering rare wildlife in the Galápagos – diverse Ecuador has it all.

ELECTRICITY

Ecuador uses 110V, 60 cycles, AC (the same as in North America). Plugs have two flat prongs, as in North America.

EMBASSIES & CONSULATES

Hours are short and change regularly, so it's a good idea to call ahead. New Zealand does not have an embassy or consulate in Ecuador.

Australian Consulate (☑04-601-7529; www. dfat.gov.au/about-us/our-locations/missions/ Pages/ecuador.aspx; SBC Office Centre Bldg Office 1-14, 1st fl, Samborondon, Guayaquil)

Canadian Embassy (☑02-245-5499; www. canadainternational.gc.ca/ecuador-equateur; cnr Av Amazonas 4153 & Unión de Periodistas, 3rd fl, Parque La Carolina, New Town, Quito; ⊙9am-noon Mon-Fri)

Colombian Consulate (☑04-263-0674; http://guayaquil.consulado.gov.co; Francisco de Orellana 111, World Trade Center, Tower B, 11th fl, Guayaquil)

Colombian Embassy (☑02-333-0268; http:// quito.consulado.gov.co; Catalina Aldaz N34-131 near Portugal, 2nd fl, La Carolina, New Town, Quito; ⊙8am-1:30pm Mon-Sat)

French Consulate (☑04-232-8442; cnr José Mascote 909 & Hurtado; ⊙10am-1pm Mon-Fri)

French Embassy (☑02-294-3800; www. ambafrance-ec.org; cnr Leonidas Plaza 127 & Av Patria, New Town, Quito; ⊙9am-noon Mon-Fri)

German Embassy (☎ 02-297-0820; www. quito.diplo.de; Naciones Unidas E10-44 near República de El Salvador, Edificio Citiplaza, 14th fl, Parque La Carolina, New Town, Quito; ☺8am-1pm & 2-4pm Mon-Thu, 8-1pm Fri)

Irish Honorary Consul (☎ 02-380-1345; www. dfa.ie; Calle del Establo 50, tower III, office 104, Urb Santa Lucia Alta, Cumbaya, Quito; ☺10am-1pm)

Peruvian Consulate (☎ 04-263-4014, 04-263-4035, 04-228-0114; www.consulado.pe/es/Guayaquil/Paginas/Inicio.aspx; Av Francisco de Orellana 501, Kennedy Norte, 13th fl, Guayaquil; ☺9am-5pm Mon-Fri)

Peruvian Embassy (☎ 02-246-8410; www. embajadadelperu.org.ec; Av República de El Salvador N34-361 near Irlanda, Parque La Carolina, New Town, Quito; ☺9am-noon & 2-4pm)

UK Embassy (☎ 02-397-2200; www.gov.uk/world/ecuador; cnr Naciones Unidas & El Salvador, Edificio Citiplaza, 14th fl, Parque La Carolina, New Town, Quito; ☺9-11am Mon-Fri)

US Consulate (☎ 04-371-7000; https://ec.usembassy.gov/u-s-citizen-services; Santa Ana near Av José Rodriguez Bonin, Guayaquil)

US Embassy (☎ 02-398-5000; https://ec.usembassy.gov/; Av Avigiras E12-170 near Eloy Alfaro, Parque Brasilia, Quito; ☺8-12:30pm & 1:30-5pm Mon-Fri)

FOOD

Ecuador has eating options for most palates, especially in Guayaquil and Quito, where international cuisine, fast food and most styles of South American dishes can be found. Ecuadorian specialties vary depending on which region you find yourself in, but one thing's for sure – the whole country loves plantain. Typical plates include meat or fish, with a choice of carbs plus vegetables or salad. It's common to be served double carbs (commonly rice, with beans, lentils, plantain or potatoes) with most meals.

Ecuador has a diverse range of local and international dining options. Booking a table on the day is usually fine, with the exception of holidays and festivals. Book top end restaurants in advance.

EATING PRICE RANGES

We've used the following price ranges, based on the cost of a standard main course. Fancier places usually add on tax (12%) and service charge (10%) to the bill.

$ less than $8

$$ $8–$15

$$$ more than $15

Restaurants Range from streetside vendors to plush air-conditioned, security-guard-fronted venues. Mostly South American options, plus international cuisine in bigger cities.

Cafes Many places disappointingly serve instant coffee, so ask if they use real ground coffee beans before you order. Most cafes have wi-fi and are open early morning to early evening. Mostly, be patient: coffee often takes time here.

Hotels Many hotels do have restaurants, only the international brands will have superior restaurants.

HEALTH

Recommended Vaccinations

If you're traveling into the Amazon, you should consider getting the yellow-fever vaccine (highly effective and good for at least 10 years) at least 10 days prior to arrival.

Typhoid fever, hepatitis A and hepatitis B vaccines are also recommended for Ecuador. The typhoid vaccine must be administered at least two weeks prior to arrival.

Consult your health provider on which, if any, vaccines are appropriate to your situation.

Availability of Health Care

Medical care is usually available in major cities, but may be quite difficult to find in rural areas. Pharmacies in Ecuador are known as *farmácias*. It can be challenging to find imported pharmaceutical items; bring essential health and hygiene supplies since these generally cost more in Ecuador.

Altitude Sickness

Altitude sickness may develop in travelers who ascend rapidly to altitudes greater than 2500m, including those flying directly to Quito. Symptoms may include headaches, nausea, vomiting, dizziness, malaise, insomnia and loss of appetite. Severe cases may be complicated by fluid in the lungs (high-altitude pulmonary edema) or swelling of the brain (high-altitude cerebral edema). The most common cause of death related to high altitude is high-altitude pulmonary edema.

To lessen the chance of getting altitude sickness, ascend gradually to higher altitudes, avoid overexertion, eat light meals and steer clear of alcohol and caffeine.

Tap Water

It's generally advisable not to drink tap water anywhere in Ecuador. Bottled water is widely available, and some hotels and guesthouses catering to foreigners provide purified water (*agua purificada*) for guests wishing to fill their own bottles.

INTERNET ACCESS

Wi-fi is ubiquitous, with guesthouses across the country offering access (usually free). Some cities also have free wi-fi in public areas. The wi-fi symbol indicates where it is available.

Internet cafes are disappearing in Ecuador, though most larger towns have a few. These cost around $1.50 an hour. Some hotels also have a computer or two for guest use. Accommodations options that have a computer for internet access are labeled with an internet symbol.

LANGUAGE COURSES

Ecuador is one of the best places to study Spanish in South America. Ecuadorian Spanish is clear and precise, and similar to Mexican and Central American Spanish, and rates are cheap. Quito (p681) and Cuenca (p718) are the best places to study, and both have a plethora of language schools. Expect to pay around $10 per hour for private lessons. Accommodations with local families can be arranged. There are also schools in Baños and Otavalo (p699) if you want smaller-town experience.

LEGAL MATTERS

Ecuador has a zero-tolerance policy for possession of illegal drugs of any amount. Previously, possession of up to 10g of cannabis and up to 2g of cocaine did not result in criminal charges, but this is no longer the case – the use or trafficking of drugs is a punishable offense that could result in imprisonment; and a scale is used to differentiate between users, microtraffickers and large-scale traffickers when handing down prison sentences.

Drivers should carry their passport, as well as their driver's license. In the event of an accident, unless it's extremely minor, the vehicles should stay where they are until the police arrive and make a report. This is essential for all insurance claims. If the accident results in injury and you are unhurt, you should take the victim to obtain medical help, particularly in the case of a pedestrian accident. You are legally responsible for a pedestrian's injuries and will be jailed unless you pay, even if the accident was not your fault. Drive defensively.

Note that it is a jailable offense to drive without insurance in Ecuador, so unfortunately, uninsured drivers involved in accidents often keep going.

LGBT TRAVELERS

Same-sex couples traveling in Ecuador should be wary of showing affection when in public. All same-sex civil unions were enshrined in the 2008 constitution, and for most Ecuadorians gay rights remain a nonissue in a political context. But homosexuality was technically illegal until 1998, and antigay bias still exists.

Several fiestas in Ecuador have parades with men cross-dressing as women. This is all meant in fun, rather than as an open acceptance of sexual alternatives, but it does provide the public at large (both gay and straight) with a popular cultural situation in which to enjoy themselves in an accepting environment.

MONEY

Ecuador's official currency is the US dollar. Aside from euros, Peruvian soles and Colombian nuevos soles, it's very difficult to change foreign currencies in Ecuador.

ATMs

ATMs are the easiest way of getting cash. They're found in most cities and even in smaller towns, though they are occasionally out of order (or money!). Make sure you have a four-digit Personal Identification Number (PIN); many Ecuadorian ATMs don't recognize longer ones.

Credit Cards

Visa, MasterCard and Diners Club are the most widely accepted cards. Merchants accepting credit cards will often add between 5% and 10% to the bill. Paying cash is often better value.

Exchanging Money

It is best to change money in the major cities of Quito, Guayaquil and Cuenca, where rates are best. Because banks have limited hours, *casas de cambio* (currency-exchange bureaus) are sometimes the only option for changing money. They are usually open 9am to 6pm Monday to Friday and until at least noon on Saturday.

OPENING HOURS

Opening hours are provided when they differ from the following standard hours:

Restaurants 10:30am–11pm Monday to Saturday

Bars 6pm–midnight Monday to Thursday, to 2am Friday and Saturday

Shops 9am–7pm Monday to Friday, 9am–noon Saturday

Banks 8am–2pm or 4pm Monday to Friday

Post offices 8am–6pm Monday to Friday, 8am–1pm Saturday

Telephone call centers 8am–10pm daily

Note that many businesses and government offices close for one or two hours in the afternoon for lunch (noon to 2pm, approximately) and some restaurants do this between lunch and dinner hours.

POST

Ecuador's postal service is somewhat reliable but expensive (postcard to Europe: $3). Allow at least two weeks for a letter or package to reach its destination. Courier services including FedEx,

DHL and UPS are readily available in sizable towns, but the service is costly.

PUBLIC HOLIDAYS

On major holidays, banks, offices and other services close. Transportation gets crowded, so buy bus tickets in advance. Major holidays are sometimes celebrated for several days around the actual date. If an official public holiday falls on a weekend, offices may be closed on the nearest Friday or Monday.

New Year's Day January 1

Epiphany January 6

Semana Santa (Easter Week) March/April

Labor Day May 1

Battle of Pichincha May 24

Simón Bolívar's Birthday July 24

Quito Independence Day August 10

Guayaquil Independence Day October 9

Columbus Day/Día de la Raza October 12

All Saints' Day November 1

Day of the Dead (All Souls' Day) November 2

Cuenca Independence Day November 3

Christmas Eve December 24

Christmas Day December 25

SAFE TRAVEL

Don't be paranoid; most unpleasant incidents can be avoided by using common sense.

If it can be avoided, do not carry valuables on day hikes, especially in areas commonly visited by tourists.

On the off chance you are robbed, you should file a police report as soon as possible. This is a requirement for any insurance claim, although it is unlikely that the police will be able to recover the property.

While highly unlikely, there are occasional incidents of express kidnapping (secuestro exprés) in urban areas. This is when armed thieves (usually operating an unlicensed taxi) force you to withdraw money from an ATM, then abandon you on the outskirts of town. To avoid this happening, have a hotel or restaurant call a taxi for you. You can also use the Easy Taxi app to hail one.

Trouble Spots

Due to occasional armed conflict in neighboring Colombia, areas along the Colombian border (particularly in the northern Oriente) can be dangerous. Tours into the Oriente are generally safe, but there have been a few isolated incidents of armed robbery.

Northern Esmeraldas province has been hit by the double-punch of disaffected Fuerzas Armadas Revolucionarias de Colombia (FARC; Revolutionary Armed Forces of Colombia) militaries from Colombia spilling over, and the cross-border drug trade.

TELEPHONE

If you have not purchased an international plan for your mobile, it's easy to buy and install a chip with an Ecuadorian local number ($5 to $10). Look for Claro or other mobile carrier signs in storefronts.

All telephone numbers in Ecuador have seven digits (after the area code) – except for cellular phone numbers, which have 10 digits including the initial 0.

Ecuador's country code is 593. To call a number in Ecuador from abroad, call your international access code, Ecuador's country code, the area code without the 0, and the seven-digit local telephone number (or the nine-digit mobile number – again without the initial 0).

Whatsapp has changed the landscape of international calling, and many hotels and guides can be reached in this way.

TOILETS

As throughout South America, Ecuadorian plumbing has very low pressure, and putting toilet paper into the bowl is a serious no-no anywhere except in the fanciest hotels and in Quito airport. Always put your used toilet paper in the basket.

Public toilets are limited mainly to bus terminals, airports and restaurants. Lavatories are called *servicios higiénicos* and are usually marked 'SS.HH.' – there's often an attendant, whom you will pay about $0.10 or $0.15; for a ration of toilet paper it's usually $0.05 extra. You can simply ask to use the *baño* (bathroom) in a restaurant. Toilet paper is not always available, so the experienced traveler always carries a personal supply.

TOURIST INFORMATION

Ecuador's system of government-run tourist offices is hit or miss, but is getting better. Tourist information in Quito and Cuenca is excellent.

Many towns have some form of municipal or provincial tourist office; most of the time, the staff are good at answering the majority of questions.

Ministerio de Turismo (www.ecuador.travel) Responsible for tourist information at the national level.

VISAS

Visitors from most countries don't need visas for stays of less than 90 days. Residents from a handful of African and Asian countries (including China) require visas.

Visa Extensions

New regulations mean it's a real headache getting visa extensions. Unless you're from an Andean Pact country, tourist visas are not extendable. If you wish to stay longer than 90 days, you'll need to apply for a 12-IX Visa; you can also do this while in Ecuador, though it's more time-consuming than doing it in advance through an Ecuadorian consulate in your home country.

Pick up the necessary paperwork for the 12-IX Visa, and pay the $230 fee at the **Ministerio de Relaciones Exteriores y Movilidad Humana** (☑ 02-299-3200; www.cancilleria.gob.ec; Carrión E1-76 & Av 10 de Agosto, Quito). Don't wait until your visa has expired to sort out your paperwork, the fine for overstaying can be hefty ($200 to $2000).

VOLUNTEERING

Numerous organizations look for the services of volunteers; however, the vast majority require at least a minimal grasp of Spanish, a minimum commitment of several weeks or months, as well as fees (anywhere from $10 per day to $700 per month) to cover the costs of room and board. Volunteers can work in conservation programs, help street kids, teach, build nature trails, construct websites, do medical or agricultural work – the possibilities are endless. Many jungle lodges also accept volunteers for long-term stays. To keep your volunteer costs down, your best bet is to look when you get to Ecuador.

The classifieds section on Ecuador Explorer (www.ecuadorexplorer.com) has a long list of organizations seeking volunteers.

Note that Lonely Planet does not vouch for any organization that we do not work with directly, and we strongly recommend travelers research volunteer opportunities themselves to assess suitability.

AmaZOOnico (www.selvaviva.ec/en/amazoonico) Accepts volunteers for the animal-rehabilitation sector.

Andean Bear Conservation Project (www.andeanbear.org) Trains volunteers as bear trackers. Hike through remote cloud forest to track the elusive spectacled bear, whose predilection for sweet corn is altering its wild behavior. Other jobs here include maintaining trails and working with local farmers to replenish cornfields ravaged by bears (to discourage bear hunting). Volunteers can come for as little as a week, but a month ($700) is recommended.

Bosque Nublado Santa Lucia (www.santalucia ecuador.com) Community-based ecotourism project in the cloud forests of northwest Ecuador. It regularly contracts volunteers to work in reforestation, trail maintenance, construction, teaching English and more.

Jatun Sacha Foundation (www.jatunsacha. org) This foundation has four biological research stations in four zones of Ecuador: the coast, highlands, Amazonía and the Galápagos.

It accepts volunteers at each one, with a minimum commitment of two weeks.

Merazonia (www.merazonia.org) A central highlands refuge for injured animals.

New Era Galápagos Foundation (www.newera galapagos.org) Nonprofit offering volunteerships focused on community empowerment and sustainable tourism in the Galápagos. Volunteers live and work on Isla San Cristóbal.

Progreso Verde (www.progresoverde.org) Accepts volunteers for reforestation, organic farming, teaching and other areas.

Reserva Biológica Los Cedros (www.reserva loscedros.org) This biological reserve in the cloud forests of the western Andean slopes often needs volunteers.

Río Muchacho Organic Farm (☑ 05-302-0487; www.riomuchacho.com; via Canoa Jama Km 10, Troncal del Pacifico, northeast of Canoa) Guests and locals get their hands dirty learning about sustainable farming practices. There are short programs from one to three days, plus week- to month-long courses ($300 to $1200). You can volunteer here for $300 per month. Most people come here on a three-day, two-night tour costing $179 per person, with discounts for larger groups. On the accommodations front, cabins are Thoreau-approved-rustic, with shared showers and composting toilets. The coveted spot is a tree-house bunk. Lying along the river of the same name, this tropical organic farm is reached by a 7km rough, unpaved road branching inland from the road north of Canoa.

Siempre Verde (☑ ext 1460 in the US 404-262-3032; www.siempreverde.org; N 0 22' 18) Get off the road just before Santa Rosa for the two-hour walk into Siempre Verde, a small community run research station supporting tropical-conservation education with excellent hiking and bird-watching. Students and researchers are welcome with prior arrangement.

Yanapuma Foundation (Map p678; ☑ 02-228-7084; www.yanapuma.org; Guayaquil E9-59 near Oriente, Old Town) Offers a number of ways for volunteers to get involved: teaching English, building houses in remote communities, helping with reforestation projects or taking part in coastal cleanups. Stop by its Quito headquarters and language school for more information.

WOMEN TRAVELERS

Generally, women travelers will find Ecuador safe and pleasant, despite the fact that machismo is alive and well. Ecuadorian men often make flirtatious comments; the best strategy is to ignore them.

On the coast, come-ons are more predatory, and solo female travelers should take precautions such as opting for taxis over walking etc. Do not accept drinks from strangers, and don't leave your drink unattended – there are occasional reports of drugging.

Lonely Planet has received warnings in the past from women who were molested while on organized tours. If you're traveling solo, it's essential to do some research before committing to a tour: find out who's leading the tour, what other tourists will be on the outing and so on. Women-only travel groups or guides are available in a few situations.

ℹ Getting There & Away

AIR

Ecuador has two international airports. Aeropuerto Internacional Mariscal Sucre (p693) Quito's airport is located about 38km east of the center.

Aeropuerto José Joaquín de Olmedo (p752) Guayaquil's airport is just a few kilometers from downtown.

TAME (☑1-700-500-800; www.tame.com.ec) Ecuador's main airline; it has had a good safety record in recent years, with a modern fleet of Boeing, Airbus and Embraer aircraft as well as several turboprop ATRs.

LATAM (☑1-800-000-527; www.latam.com) Flies internationally to New York and various cities in Peru, Argentina, Chile, Brazil and Bolivia.

LAND

Peru and Colombia are the only countries sharing borders with Ecuador. If you are entering or leaving Ecuador, border formalities are straightforward if your documents are in order. No taxes are levied on tourists when entering or exiting overland.

If you've overstayed the allowed time on your T3 visa (90 days – consecutive or not – per year, beginning on your stamped entry date), you'll have to pay a hefty fine or you will be sent back to Quito. If you don't have an *entrada* (entrance) stamp, you will also be sent back.

At the time of research, hundreds of Venezuelan citizens were flooding the Ecuadorian border with Colombia daily: officially, 50,000 settled in the country in 2018, although the unofficial number is far greater. Some travelers we spoke with were delayed for several hours in this logjam at the border.

Busing into Ecuador from Colombia or Peru is straightforward and usually requires walking across one of the international borders and catching another bus once you're across (this is more complicated in Huaquillas, though). Some international bus companies offer direct, long-haul services from major cities such as Lima and Bogotá.

RIVER

It is possible but time-consuming to travel down the Río Napo from Ecuador to Peru, joining the Amazon near Iquitos. The border facilities are minimal, and the boats doing the journey are infrequent. It is also geographically possible to travel down Río Putumayo into Colombia and Peru, but this is a dangerous region because of drug smuggling and terrorism, and is not recommended.

ℹ Getting Around

AIR

With the exception of flying to the Galápagos Islands, internal flights are generally fairly cheap, rarely exceeding $125 for a one-way ticket. All mainland flights are under an hour and often provide you with incredible views over the Andes.

Flights to most destinations originate in Quito or Guayaquil only. The following are Ecuador's passenger airlines:

Avianca (☑1-800-003-434; www.avianca.com) Serves Quito, Guayaquil, Cuenca, Esmeraldas, Isla Baltra (Galápagos), Isla San Cristóbal (Galápagos), Manta and Coca.

Emetebe (☑in Guayaquil 04-230-1277; www.emetebe.com.ec) Galápagos-based airline that flies between Isla Baltra, Isla Santa Cruz, Isla San Cristóbal and Isla Isabela.

LATAM (p772) Flies from Quito to Cuenca, Guayaquil and the Galápagos (Isla San Cristóbal and Isla Baltra), plus New York and various cities in Peru, Argentina, Chile, Brazil and Bolivia.

TAME (p772) Serves Coca, Cuenca, Esmeraldas, Isla Baltra and Isla San Cristóbal (Galápagos), Guayaquil, Lago Agrio, Loja, Manta, Quito, Salinas, plus Bogotá and Cali (Colombia), Lima (Peru), New York and Fort Lauderdale (USA).

BOAT

The most common boat is the motorized canoe, which acts as a water taxi or bus along the major rivers of the Oriente (especially on the Río Napo) and parts of the northern coast. Most people experience this novel form of transport during a tour in the Amazon, as motorized canoes are often the only way to a rainforest lodge.

These canoes often carry as many as 36 passengers. Generally, they're long in shape and short on comfort. Seating is normally on hard, low wooden benches which accommodate two people each. Most river lodges provide bench cushions on their boats. If you're taking public-transport canoes: bring seat padding. A folded sweater or towel will make a world of difference on the trip.

In the Galápagos, you have a choice of traveling in anything from a small sailboat to a cruise ship replete with air-conditioned cabins and private bathrooms. Passenger ferries run infrequently between the islands, offering the cheapest means of interisland transport. Only folks traveling around the islands independently (ie, not on a cruise) need consider these.

In addition to the dugout canoes of the Oriente, one live-aboard riverboat, the *Anakonda,* makes relatively luxurious passages down Río Napo.

BUS

Buses are the primary means of transport for most Ecuadorians, guaranteed to go just about anywhere. They can be exciting, cramped, comfy, smelly, fun, scary, sociable and grueling, depending on your state of mind, where you're going and who's driving.

There have also been some tragic bus accidents in recent years. Most buses lack seat belts, but if you're on one that has them, do use them.

Most major cities have a main *terminal terrestre* (bus terminal), although some towns have a host of private terminals – and you'll have to go to the right one to catch the bus going where you need to go. Most stations are within walking distance or a short cab ride of the town's center. Smaller towns are occasionally served by passing buses, in which case you have to walk from the highway into town, usually only a short walk since only the smallest towns lack terminals.

Bigger luggage is stored in the compartment below and is generally safe. Theft is more of a concern for objects taken inside the bus. To avoid the risk of becoming a victim, keep whatever you bring onto the bus on your lap (not the floor or overhead).

On average, bus journeys cost a bit more than $1 per hour of travel. Remember to always have your passport handy when you're going anywhere by bus, as they are sometimes stopped for checks. This is especially true in the Oriente.

CAR & MOTORCYCLE

Driving a car or motorcycle in Ecuador presents its challenges, with potholes, blind turns, and insanely fast bus and truck drivers. The good news is that infrastructure has dramatically improved, with new roads and bridges, and better road signage, making road travel much smoother. Speed bumps ('sleeping policemen' to Ecuadorians) are sometimes painted, but often, invisible.

You are required to have a driver's license from your home country and a passport whenever you're driving. The international driver's license can also come in handy when renting a car (though it's not officially required).

HITCHHIKING

Hitchhiking is never entirely safe in any country, and we don't recommend it. Travelers who decide to hitchhike should understand that they are taking a small but potentially serious risk.

People who do choose to hitchhike will be safer if they travel in pairs and let someone know where they are planning to go.

Hitching is not very practical in Ecuador for three reasons: there are few private cars, public transportation is relatively cheap and trucks are used as public transportation in remote areas, so trying to hitch a free ride on one is the same as trying to hitch a free ride on a bus. Many drivers of *any* vehicle will pick you up, but will also expect payment, usually minimal.

TAXI

Ecuadorian taxis come in a variety of shapes and sizes, but they are all yellow. Most taxis have a lit 'taxi' sign on top or a 'taxi' sticker on the windshield. In Quito and other bigger cities, licensed taxis have an orange or orange-striped license plate, with ID numbers clearly marked on the sides.

Always ask the fare beforehand, or you may be overcharged. Meters are rarely seen, except in Quito, Guayaquil and Cuenca. A long ride in these cities should rarely go over $5 (unless traveling to Quito's bus terminals, which are quite distant from the center). The minimum fare nearly everywhere is $1.25, and you'll be required to pay $1 in Quito even if the meter only says $0.80. On weekends and at night, fares are always about 25% to 50% higher.

You can hire a taxi for a day for about $40 to $60. Hiring a taxi for a few days is comparable to renting a car, except that you don't have to drive. But you will have to pay for the driver's food and room. Some tour companies in Quito rent 4WD vehicles with experienced drivers.

In less urban areas, you're also likely to see ecotaxis (a three-wheeled bicycle with a small covered carriage that fits two people) as well as *taxis ecológicos* (motorcycle taxis with a two-seater carriage).

TOURS

If you're short on time, the best place to organize a tour is either Quito or Guayaquil. A plethora of operators for every budget offer trips including Galápagos cruises, climbing and hiking tours, horseback riding, jungle tours, mountain-biking tours, hacienda tours and more.

Tour costs vary tremendously depending on what your requirements are. The cheapest city tours start from around $60 per person; a banana and cocoa trail tour starts from $80 per person per day, while a two-night Amazon camping tour starts at $68 (per person based on two or more people). Meanwhile, the most expensive lodges can exceed $200 per person per night including meals and tours. Volcano national park hiking tours start around $75 per day per person, and start from $190 for a two-day volcano summit hike. Many tour prices reduce the more people you have in your group. Galápagos boat cruises range from $3000 up to $7000 per week ($400 to $700 per day), excluding airfare, taxes and entrance fees.

TRAIN

Much to the delight of train enthusiasts, Ecuador's rail system has finally been restored. Unfortunately, it's not useful for travel, as the routes are used for day trips designed exclusively for tourists. The trains run along short routes, typically on weekends, sometimes with return service by bus. The most famous line is the dramatic descent from Alausí along La Nariz del Diablo (The Devil's Nose), a spectacular section of train track that was one of the world's greatest feats of railroad engineering. The second is the weekend train excursion between Quito and the Area Nacional de Recreación El Boliche, near Cotopaxi.

Other routes run from Durán (near Guayaquil), Ibarra, Ambato, Riobamba and El Tambo (near Ingapirca).

For departure times, ticket prices and itinerary information, visit Tren Ecuador (www.tren ecuador.com).

TRUCK

In certain towns, especially in rural areas where there are many dirt roads, camionetas (pickup trucks) act as taxis. If you need to get to a national park, a climbers refuge or a trailhead from a town, often the best way to do so is by hiring a pickup, which is usually as easy as asking around.

In remote areas, trucks often double as buses. Sometimes these are large, flatbed trucks with a tin roof, open wooden sides and uncomfortable wooden-plank seats. These curious-looking 'buses' are called rancheras or chivas, and are seen on the coast and in the Oriente.

In the remote parts of the highlands, camionetas (ordinary trucks or pickups) are used to carry passengers; you just climb in the back. If the weather is good, you get fabulous views and the refreshing sensation of Andean wind in your face. If the weather is bad, you hunker down beneath a tarpaulin with the other passengers.

Payment is usually determined by the driver and is a standard fare depending on the distance. You can ask other passengers how much they are paying; trucks typically charge about the same as buses.

French Guiana

POP 289,000

Best Places to Eat

→ Restaurant Paris Cayenne (p779)

→ Central Market (p778)

→ La Petite Maison (p779)

→ La Goélette (p787)

→ Sunday Market (p781)

Best Places to Stay

→ Hôtel des Palmistes (p778)

→ Hôtel Le Gros Bec (p783)

→ Auberge des Îles du Salut (p784)

→ Hôtel La Tentiaire (p786)

Why Go?

French Guiana is a remote region of France covered in thick jungle and wilderness, although you'll also find colonial architecture, eerie prison-camp history and some of the world's most diverse plant and animal life here. It's a strange mix of French law and rainforest humidity where only a few destinations along the coast are easily accessed and travel can be frustratingly difficult as well as expensive.

As a department of France, it's one of South America's wealthiest corners, with funds pouring in to ensure the smooth working of the Guiana Space Center at Kourou. But not even a European superpower can tame this vast, pristine jungle: you'll find potholes in newly paved roads, and ferns sprouting between bricks, while Amerindians, Maroons and Hmong refugees live traditional lifestyles so far from *la vie métropole* that it's hard to believe they're connected at all.

When to Go
Cayenne

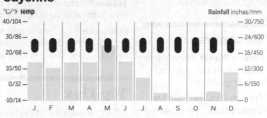

Jan–Jun Expect frequent downpours during these months, with the heaviest rains in May.

Late Jan–Mar Dates vary according to when Easter falls, but you can expect Cayenne to throw a wild and exciting carnival.

Jul–Sep It mercifully rains less during the summer dry season, although it remains hot and humid year-round.

FAST FACTS

Currency Euro (€)

Visas Not needed for 90 days for most nationalities.

Money ATMs in bigger towns; the only *cambios* (currency-exchange offices) are in Cayenne; credit cards widely accepted.

Capital Cayenne

Emergency 112

Languages French, Creole

Exchange Rates

Australia	A$1	€0.62
Canada	C$1	€0.64
New Zealand	NZ$1	€0.59
UK	UK£1	€1.14
USA	US$1	€0.81

Daily Costs

➡ Hammock space in a *carbet:* €10; double room in a midrange hotel: €85–150

➡ Pho at the Cayenne Central Market: €4; top-end meal in Cayenne: €50

Resources

Lonely Planet (www.lonelyplanet.com/the-guianas/french-guiana)

French Guiana Tourism Committee (www.guyane-amazonie.fr)

Guyane 1ère (http://guyane.la1ere.fr)

Guyane.fr (www.guyane.fr)

Entering the Country

French Guiana has a border crossing at St Georges, where the Oyapock River marks the frontier with Brazil (a new bridge to Brazil opened in 2017), and at St Laurent, where the Maroni River is the border with Suriname (crossings to Suriname are made by boat).

TWO WEEK ITINERARY

Base yourself in Cayenne for the first week and take a day trip to Cacao on a Sunday for the Laotian market. Make sure you visit the Îles du Salut and the Centre Spatial Guyanais at Kourou during that time. Then take a two-night tour of Kaw, where you'll stay on a floating lodge, and look for black caiman and a huge array of bird species including scarlet ibis. After this, head to Awala-Yalimopo to watch nesting turtles if the season is right or otherwise to enjoy some beach time in this traditional Amerindian village. Finish up with a couple of nights in St Laurent du Maroni, where you can visit two spooky abandoned prison camps and take a river tour to explore Maroon culture.

Essential Food & Drink

Pho Vietnamese soup made with beef broth, rice noodles, many fragrant herbs and meat.

Mie/nasi goreng Javanese-style fried rice/noodles.

Gibier Bush meat like capybara, wild boar and agouti is legally hunted and found widely on restaurant menus.

Pizza Find delicious thin-crust, French-style, wood-fired pizzas in most main towns.

Jamais goûté A delicate freshwater fish that's best steamed in banana leaves.

Ti'punch Literally a 'small punch' made with local rum, lime juice and sugarcane syrup – a Caribbean favorite.

Fricassee Rice, beans and sautéed meat stewed in gravy – unlike French fricassee, the Caribbean style has a brown or red sauce with a kick of cayenne pepper.

Top Tips

➡ Carry a hammock to stay in *carbet* – covered huts usually with dirt, gravel or cement floors – for the cheapest lodging. Then you can self-cater or eat at markets and street stalls to cut costs even more.

➡ To get the most of the country you'll need to splurge however, – frst on a rental car to get around without a ton of frustration, and then on a jungle tour to see one of the country's biggest assets, the rainforests.

Map labels:

Moengo

Galibi Nature Reserve

Plage les Hattes

Awala-Yalimopo

Mana

Javouhey

Organabo

Iracoubo

Pripri Yiyi Trail Head

Sinnamary

Îles du Salut

Kourou

Tonate (Macouria)

Centre Spatial Guyanais

Barrage de Petit Saut

St Élie

Albina

St Laurent du Maroní

St Jean

Apatou

Camp Voltaire

Cascades Voltaire

Langatabbetje

Montsinéry

Cayenne

Montjoly

Rémire

Matoury

Félix Eboué International Airport

Roura

Kaw Nature Reserve

Cacao

Trésor Nature Reserve

Mont Favard (200m)

Kaw

Les Nouragues Nature Reserve

Régina

Baie de L'Oyapock

Ouanary

Grand Santi

ATLANTIC OCEAN

50 km
25 miles

Mont Machoulou (782m)

Maripasoula

Saül

SURINAME

Rivière Grand Inini

Rivière Waki

Pic Coudreau (711m)

Rivière Tampok

Rivière Camopi

Camopi

Caçiporé

Litani River

Claimed by Suriname & French Guiana

Tumac - Humac Mountains

Mont St Marcel (635m)

BRAZIL

St Georges de l'Oyapock

Oiapoque

Fleuve Oyapock

Rio Uaçá

Fleuve Maroni (Marowijne River)

Fleuve Mana

Fleuve Sinnamary

Fleuve Approuague

French Guiana Highlights

1 Îles du Salut (p784) Escaping the mainland for sand, palms and a creepy, defunct penal colony.

2 Centre Spatial Guyanais (p782) Touring one of the world's busiest satellite launchers

3 Cacao (p781) Gorging on Laotian treats and admiring ornate embroidery in this remote hillside village.

4 Awala-Yalimopo (p788) Watching leatherback turtles laying their eggs on the sands of this Amerindian village.

5 Les Palmistes (p779) Sipping a cold beer and people-watching at Cayenne's quintessential cafe.

6 Camp de la Transportation (p785) Getting an eerie tour in prisoner-haunted St Laurent du Maroni.

7 Kaw Nature Reserve (p782) Spending the night in a floating lodge surrounded by jungle, caimans and flourishing birdlife.

Cayenne

POP 57,600

A crossroads of the Caribbean, South America and Europe, Cayenne is a city of myriad cultures surrounded on all sides by the sounds, smells and colors of the tropics. The streets of the town center are lined with colonial wrought-iron balconies with louvered shutters painted in now-faded tropical pinks, yellows and turquoises. Above it all sits the town's old fortress, an atmospheric wind-whipped ruin that looks down onto the palm trees of the town's elegant main square.

While undeniably run down and visibly poor in many parts, Cayenne is home to vibrant markets and excellent Brazilian, Creole, French and Chinese restaurants. Outside the city center, however, highways and urban sprawl remind you that you're still very much in the 21st century, and the encroachment of *la France métropolitaine* is never far away.

◉ Sights

Cayenne is easy to see on foot in one day. The center of the action is the Place des Palmistes, lined with colonial timber-fronted buildings and full of palm trees. To its west, Place Léopold Héder (aka Place Grenoble) is the oldest part of the city. After a siesta, cruise Av du Général de Gaulle, the main commercial street, to experience Cayenne at its bustling peak. La Place des Amandiers near the coast is the place to go to relax with *pétanque* (bowling) and dominoes.

★ Central Market   MARKET

(cnr Brassé & Ste Rose; ⊙ 6am-1:30pm Wed, Fri & Sat) Inside Cayenne's market, shoppers will find a vibrant jumble of Amerindian basketry, African-style paintings and carvings, piles of spices at great prices, and soup stalls that serve up the best Vietnamese pho (from €4) in the Guianas. Dark aisles of fruit and vegetable stands – overflowing with daikon, bok choy and bean sprouts – look more like Southeast Asia than South America. Annoyingly, it's only open three days a week.

Fort Cépérou   RUINS

(cnr Blanc & Chandon) FREE Off the gardened Place Léopold Héder are the remains of Fort Cépérou, perched on land bought in 1643 from the Galibi people by the first French colonists. Most of the site is now a restricted military zone, but you can still stroll around the ruins for good views of Cayenne and the river.

Tours

French Guiana's pristine jungles are impenetrable and dangerous without a knowledgeable guide. Licensed Cayenne-based agencies run tours, often hiring out guides throughout the country.

JAL Voyages   TOURS

(☑ 0594-316820; www.jal-voyages.com; 26 Av du Général de Gaulle; ⊙ 8:30am-noon & 3-6pm Mon-Fri, 9:30am-noon Sat) Operating throughout the country, JAL offers everything from day trips to the Îles du Salut (Salvation Islands) and a popular overnight jaunt on a floating *carbet* (open-air hut) in Kaw to four-day trips down the Maroni River and much more.

★☆ Festivals & Events

QUERCarnaval   CARNIVAL

(⊙ Feb or Mar, dates vary) Carnaval is a gigantic, colorful occasion, with festivities taking place across the region from Epiphany to several solid days of partying before Ash Wednesday.

⌇ Sleeping

In terms of accommodations, there is almost nothing on offer for the budget traveller in Cayenne. Midrange options start at €90 per night for anything decent

Oyasamaïd   PENSION $

(☑ 0594-315684, 0694-418530; www.oyasamaid. com; off Rte de la Madeleine; r €65-90; ⊙ reception 10am-3:30pm & 6-8:30pm; ✻ 🛜 ☀) A French family pension *à la Guianese*, this four-room place is warm, bright and impeccably clean. All the spacious rooms have Jacuzzi bathtubs, and a swimming pool seals the deal. It's a short drive from the town center so you'll need a car. You'll see signs for it on the Rte de la Madeleine near the roundabout and Géant supermarket.

★ Hôtel des Palmistes   HOTEL $$

(☑ 0594-300050, 0694-030598; www.palmistes. com; 12 Av du Général de Gaulle; r from €130; ✻ 🛜) Housed in a gorgeously renovated colonial building overlooking Cayenne's main square, this boutique bolt-hole has the best rooms in town (room 1, in particular, is fabulous), with high ceilings, large bathrooms and comforts including Nespresso machines and L'Occitane toiletries. Sadly, it can be noisy in the evenings due to the hugely popular downstairs restaurant, and reception is almost always deserted.

Hôtel des Amandiers HOTEL $$
(📞 0594-289728; www.hoteldesamandiers.com; Pl Auguste Horth; r €90; ❋ 🛜) A welcome midrange addition to Cayenne's generally poor-value accommodations, the Amandiers is also the only hotel in town on the seafront, even if Cayenne's brown Caribbean waters are far from postcard worthy. The rooms are on the small side, but modern and clean, with Lavazza coffee machines, fridges, safes and balconies in many. Downstairs has a charming cafe.

Central Hôtel HOTEL $$
(📞 0594-256565; www.centralhotel-cayenne.fr; cnr Molé & Becker; s/d €75/90; ❋ 🛜) The utilitarian Central isn't interesting in any particular way, but the decently comfortable and clean rooms, central location and good service make it one of the best deals in town at this price.

✖ Eating

For the best bang for your buck, you can slurp delicious noodles at Cayenne's Central Market (p778) or browse the nighttime **food stalls** (Pl des Palmistes; meals from €5) around Place des Palmistes. Small Chinese takeout joints and grocery shops make self-catering a breeze. The sit-down options in Cayenne can be outstanding, though they often come with a hefty price tag.

Les Palmistes FRENCH $$
(12 Av du Général de Gaulle; pizzas from €12, mains around €20; ⊘ 6:30am-1am Mon-Sat, 10am-11pm Sun; 🛜) The best place to people-watch on the Place des Palmistes also serves up perfect Caribbean-French ambience. Sit on the wooden terrace with its wrought-iron balustrade to dine on pleasant salads, crepes, pizzas and Franco-creole standards while sipping a cold beer. Alternatively, make a beeline for the tables in the large back courtyard. The restaurant's sheer popularity means service can be erratic.

★ Restaurant Paris Cayenne FRENCH $$$
(📞 0594-317617; www.pariscayenne.fr; 59 Lalouette; mains €23-36; ⊘ noon-3pm & 8-10:30pm Tue-Fri, 8-10:30pm Mon & Sat; 🛜) Buzzing ambience meets white-tablecloth elegance at Cayenne's chicest dining spot. Ring the buzzer to enter, and don't be put off by the initial darkness in the horseshoe wooden bar – you'll soon be conducted into the dining room at the back, which is hung with abstract art and has the feel of a private members' club. Food is sublime.

★ La Petite Maison CREOLE $$$
(📞 0594-385839; 23 Eboué; mains €17-36; ⊘ noon-2:30pm & 7-11pm Mon-Fri, 7-11pm Sat; 🛜) Easily one of Cayenne's most charming spots for lunch or dinner, La Petite Maison really lives up to its name and is an old traditional Cayenne house, homely decorated with an elegant feel and serving an innovative Creole menu. Dishes include eggplant crumble, shrimp *moqueca* (seafood stew), pork in honey sauce, and sublime ice cream made on the premises.

🍷 Drinking & Nightlife

Live music, beer and rum punch flow freely in bars and clubs throughout Cayenne. Reggae music rocks small clubs in Village Chinois, and a few Brazilian and Dominican bars dot Av de la Liberté.

Cafe de la Gare BAR
(42 Av Léopold Héder; ⊘ 7:30pm-1am Tue-Sat) A fun (if rules-heavy) spot with live music and theme nights, such as jazz, salsa and rockabilly.

Le Cosmopolitan BAR
(118 Av du Général de Gaulle; ⊘ 5pm-1am Mon-Sat) A popular nightspot with a young, mixed clientele getting down to reggaeton and other Caribbean music.

ℹ Information

MONEY
Banks and ATMs are all over the city, but traveler's checks and foreign currency can only be cashed at *cambios* (currency-exchange offices).
Global Transfer (64 Av du Général de Gaulle; ⊘ 7:30-11am & 3-6pm Mon-Fri, 7:30-11am Sat) Central location.

TOURIST INFORMATION
Comité du Tourisme de la Guyane (📞 0594-296500; www.tourisme-guyane.com; 12 Lalouette; ⊘ 7:30am-1pm Mon, Wed & Fri, 7:30am-1pm & 2-5pm Tue & Thu) Filled with pamphlets, maps and information, this tourist office, geared toward all of French Guiana rather than Cayenne specifically, is always staffed with someone to answer questions. An information desk at the airport theoretically stays open late for arriving flights.
Office du Tourisme (📞 0594-396883; 1 Rue de Rémire; ⊘ 8:30am-12.30pm & 2-5pm Mon-Fri,

Cayenne

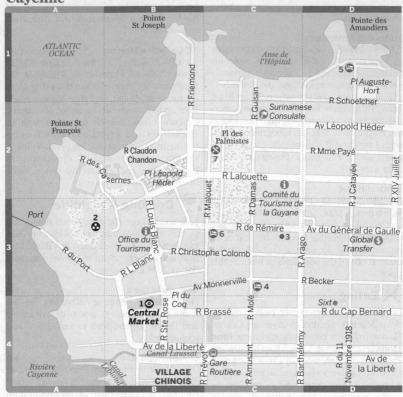

9am-1pm Sat) A tourist office with information specific to Cayenne, though the staff weren't particularly knowledgeable or helpful at the time of research.

🛈 Getting There & Away

AIR

All international and domestic flights leave from **Félix Eboué International Airport** (Rochambeau; ☎ 0594-299700), which has flights to Paris, Paramaribo, Belem and Pointe-à-Pitre.

TAXI COLLECTIF

Taxis collectifs (minibuses) leave when full from the Gare Routière (p782) on Av de la Liberté until 6pm daily. From the corner of Rue Molé, they head to Matoury (€2, 15 minutes, 10km) and St Laurent (€35, four hours, 250km). From the corner of Rue Malouet, they depart for Kourou (€8, one hour, 60km) and St Georges (€15, two hours, 100km). Settle rates in advance and show up around 8am to get a spot. Be very careful, however, as there have been reports of muggings by drivers – if possible ask a local to help

you find a reliable driver, or ask at the Office du Tourisme (p779).

🛈 Getting Around

TO/FROM THE AIRPORT

Félix Eboué International Airport (p780) is 13km southwest of downtown Cayenne. The fastest and most convenient way to or from the airport is by taxi (€35 to €50, 20 minutes), as there is no public transport serving the route. However, during the day you can save money by taking a taxi to the nearby town of Matoury and then taking a *taxi collectif* to Cayenne from there (€2, 10km, 15 minutes).

BUS

There is a comprehensive six-line bus network that serves Cayenne and the surrounding suburbs. Bus stops are clearly marked, and buses have their destination clearly displayed. Tickets cost €1.10 on lines 1 to 5, while on line 6, which connects Cayenne to Rémire-Montjoly, tickets cost €2. You can find route information at www.ville-cayenne.fr/transports-lignes-horaires-tarifs.

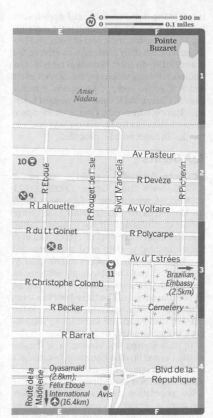

TAXI

Taxis charge a hiring fee of €2, plus €0.85 per kilometer; the per-kilometer charge increases to €1 from 7pm to 6am and on Sundays and holidays. There's a taxi stand on the southeast corner of Place des Palmistes.

Cacao

POP 950

A tiny slice of Laos in the hills of French Guiana, Cacao, about 75km southwest of Cayenne, is a village of clear rivers, vegetable plantations and wooden houses on stilts. The Hmong refugees who left Laos in the 1970s keep their town a safe, peaceful haven, and it's now a favorite weekend day trip among locals from Cayenne. Sunday (market day) is the best time for a visit if you want to shop for Hmong embroidery and weaving, and feast on a smorgasbord of Laotian treats. Don't miss the excellent **nature museum** (☑0594-270034; cleplaneurbleu@wanadoo.fr; adult/child under 12 €4/

free; ⊙9am-1pm & 2-4pm Sun, by appointment other times) here to see butterflies and arachnids, both dead and alive, or to hold live tarantulas. Walkers will also want to come here as it's the start of the excellent **Sentier Molokoï** (Cacao Molokoï Nature Trail), one of French Guiana's most accessible deep-rainforest hikes, which can be done without hiring a guide.

🛌 Sleeping & Eating

In Cacao, the activity-oriented **Quimbe Kio** (☑0596-270122; www.quimbekio.com; Cacao; hammock spaces €40, with hammock €45, d €80, all incl half board; ☞) is the best choice of accommodations. Another option, some distance from town, is the rustic-chic **Auberge des Orpailleurs** (☑0970 417855, 0594-270622; www.aubergedesorpailleurs.com; PK62, RN 2; hammock spaces per person €40, r per person from €55, all incl full board; ⊙reception 8am-6pm Fri-Mon, noon-6pm Thu, 8am-4pm Tue), on the main road heading east at the far end of the Sentier Molokoï (p781). Both guesthouses can arrange other ecotourism excursions and have good restaurants. Reserve ahead for both.

Sunday Market   MARKET **$**

(mains €3-6; ⊙8am-4pm Sun) This lively Hmong Sunday market serves up various Lao street-food dishes such as pho, and day-trippers from Cayenne often come to Cacao on a Sunday just to experience it. While it won't impress anyone who has spent much time in

Southeast Asia, it's an enjoyable option if you happen to be here.

ⓘ Getting There & Away

There is no public bus to Cacao, so you'll need your own transport or be prepared to pay for a taxi to get here.

Trésor & Kaw Nature Reserves

The **Trésor Nature Reserve** `FREE` is one of French Guiana's most accessible primary rainforest areas, and wandering its 1.75km botanical trail is a great way to experience its rich diversity and wildlife. Trésor borders the mysterious forests and swamps of the Kaw Nature Reserve, an excellent place to observe caiman and spectacular waterbirds such as the scarlet ibis.

Patawa (☑ 0972-412382; patawa2@gmail.com; Kaw; hammock space €10, hammock hire €15, s/d/tr €26/34/46; ☺ Fri-Wed) offers a well-run set of cabins in a pleasant spot, perfect for visitors wanting to explore the nearby nature reserves. It's rather fussily run, however, and all guests must take a meal plan on top of room charges, so factor in an extra €43 per person per day full board.

Kourou

POP 26,200

On a small peninsula overlooking the Atlantic Ocean and the massive Kourou River, this small city of modern apartment blocks once existed solely to serve the mainland and offshore penal colonies. Today, Kourou exists pretty much solely to serve the Centre Spatial Guyanais (Guyanese Space Center), a satellite-construction facility and launchpad that employs thousands of people, and where two-thirds of the world's commercial satellites are launched. A few beaches suitable for sunbathing line the easternmost part of town, and catamarans leave daily from here to explore the dramatic Îles du Salut (Salvation Islands), but Kourou is mostly visited for the Space Center and – if you're lucky – for seeing a rocket launch. Plan ahead to make the most of Kourou – launches mean the closure of the Space Center to tourists for three days, and boats to the Îles du Salut are also cancelled.

◉ Sights

★**Centre Spatial Guyanais**   OBSERVATORY
(CSG, Guyanese Space Center; ☑ 0594-326123, 0594-335384; www.cnes-csg.fr; €7; ☺ tours 8am & 1pm Mon-Thu, 8am Fri) `FREE` Visiting the Centre Spatial Guyanais and (if you're lucky) seeing a rocket launch are two of French Guiana's biggest highlights. Both need to be arranged in advance though, so plan carefully. Just to visit the CSG you'll need to apply online or by phone with your passport information at least 48 hours in advance. The three-hour bus tours of the space center, which include a visit to the massive launchpad, are fascinating; witnessing a launch is simply unforgettable.

In 1964 Kourou was chosen to be the site of the Centre Spatial Guyanais because it's close to the equator, is away from tropical storm tracks and earthquake zones, and has a low population density. Three launchers are now in service, increasing the number of liftoffs to more than a dozen per year; this frequency makes it that much easier to coordinate your visit with a launch.

The launch site is the only one in the world this close to the equator (within five degrees), where the earth's spin is significantly faster than further north or south; this means that the site benefits from the 'slingshot effect,' which boosts propulsion and makes launches up to 17% more energy efficient than those

BUSES FROM CAYENNE

Minibuses leave when full from the makeshift **Gare Routière** (☑ 0594-254929; Av de la Liberté) Monday to Friday, with fewer services on the weekend. In general, if you want to get anywhere reliably in French Guiana by bus, come early in the morning, when you have the most chance of finding transport.

DESTINATION	COST (€)	DURATION (HR)	FREQUENCY (DAILY)
Rémire-Montjoly	2	15 min	every 15-20min
Kourou	15	1¼	hourly
Regina	20	1½	8
Sinnamary	15	2½	5
St Georges	30	5	8
St Laurent	30	4	1

at sites further away from the equator. Since 1980 two-thirds of the world's commercial satellites have been launched from French Guiana. The center is run by Centre National d'Études Spatiales (CNES; www.cnes.fr) in collaboration with the European Space Agency (ESA; www.esa.int) and Arianespace (www.arianespace.com).

Visit the ESA website to find out the launch schedule and reserve a space at one of the observation points within the space center. Email csg-accueil@cnes.fr well ahead of time, providing your full name, address, phone number and age. It's free, but children under 16 are not permitted at sites within 6km of the launchpad and those under eight are not permitted within 12km. You can watch it, reservation-free, with locals at Kourou's beaches or at the Carapa Observation Site, 15km west of the city center.

Whether you're attending a launch or just visiting the space center for a tour, be sure to bring your passport. Tour guides at the space center sometimes speak English or German; ask when you book. Note that the space center is closed on the day before, the day of and the day after a launch. Be aware also that if a launch is postponed, then days when the space center is shut will be extended too. This makes attending a launch and visiting the CSG for the tour quite hard to combine during a short stay, so plan ahead and give yourself plenty of time to do both.

Musée de l'Espace　　　　　MUSEUM
(Space Museum; adult/child €7/4; ⊙ 8am-6pm Mon-Fri, 2-6pm Sat) Don't miss the excellent Musée de l'Espace within the Centre Spatial Guyanais (p782), with informative displays in English and French.

🍴 Sleeping & Eating

Kourou has pitifully few inexpensive options. Both of the best-value places have restricted reception hours, so plan your arrival and reserve ahead if possible.

Potholed, colorful Le Vieux Bourg, centralized along Av Général de Gaulle, is by far the most eclectic area of Kourou and the best place for cheap Indian, Creole, Chinese, Moroccan, French cuisine and more.

Hotel Ballahou　　　　GUESTHOUSE $
(✆ 0694-236237; www.hotel-ballahou.com; 1-3 Mar-tial; d/apt €57/65; ❉ 🛜) This secure complex of simple studio rooms is within easy walking distance of the beaches. The cheapest are a room only, while for a small price hike you can have a studio with its own kitchenette. There's no restaurant, but it's an easy walk to the seafront and its cafes.

★**Hôtel Le Gros Bec**　　　HOTEL $$
(✆ 0594-329191; www.hotel.legrosbec.com; 56 Rue du Docteur Floch; s/d/tr from €80/89/96; ❉ 🛜) Right next to Le Vieux Bourg, this rather hidden hotel (find its entrance behind a forbidding electric gate on a side street overlooking a creek) is actually very pleasant inside, with spacious split-level studios featuring well-equipped kitchens, spacious bathrooms and individual patio areas for each room. Reservations are advised.

ℹ️ Information

There are two tourist offices in Kourou. The main **Office de Tourisme** (✆ 0594-329833; www.tourisme-kourou.fr; Av de l'Anse; ⊙ 9am-5pm Mon-Fri) is on the seafront and has helpful English-speaking staff. A small **Point Information Tourisme** (✆ 0594-329833; Ponton des Balourous; ⊙ 8-8:45am Tue-Sat, 4:45-6pm Tue & Thu) can be found where the boats leave for the Îles du Salut (Salvation Islands).

ℹ️ Getting There & Away

There is no bus station in Kourou, but buses run hourly from 6am to 6pm between Kourou and Cayenne (€10, 1¼ hours) and four times a day to St Laurent (€25, three hours). Contact the Office de Tourisme for exact schedules. Buses pick up at the Mairie.

Alternatively, the Office de Tourisme also gives out the numbers of reliable *taxi collectif* (minibus) drivers, who charge €10 per passenger to Cayenne and €30 per passenger to St Laurent.

WORTH A TRIP

RÉMIRE-MONTJOLY

Though technically two separate towns, Rémire-Montjoly, 8km from Cayenne, functions as a single entity. Its sweeping beaches may be some of the country's better waterfront, but it's generally popular as a more laid-back and pleasant alternative to Cayenne, with large gated houses along the coast and thickly forested hillsides overlooking the sea.

It's perfectly possible to base yourself in Rémire-Montjoly if you'd rather avoid the overpriced hotels of Cayenne. You'll need a car if you plan to base yourself out here, however.

FRENCH GUIANA KOUROU

Various catamarans and sailboats leave Kourou's Ponton des Balourous each morning for day trips to the Îles du Salut. You can buy tickets at the Office de Tourisme.

Îles du Salut

Known in English as the Salvation Islands, this archipelago was anything but that for prisoners who were sent here from the French mainland by Emperor Napoleon III and subsequent French governments. The three tiny islands, 15km north of Kourou over choppy, shark-infested waters, were considered escape-proof and particularly appropriate for political prisoners. These included Alfred Dreyfus, the French military officer convicted of treason for espionage, whose notorious trial and harsh sentencing became a cause célèbre for antisemitism. From 1852 to 1947, some 80,000 prisoners died from disease, inhumane conditions and the guillotine on these sad isles.

In the elapsing seven decades, the islands have become a relaxing delight – a place to escape *to*.

◎ Sights

Surprisingly abundant wildlife includes green-winged Ara macaws, agoutis, capuchin monkeys and sea turtles.

Île Royale   ISLAND
Once the administrative headquarters of the penal settlement, Île Royale has several restored prison buildings, including a fine prisoner-built chapel and a restaurant-guesthouse where it's possible to eat an excellent lunch and even spend the night. The Centre Spatial Guyanais also has a huge infrared camera on Île Royale.

The old **director's house** (Île Royale; ⊘2-4pm Tue-Sun) FREE has an interesting English-language history display; free, two-hour guided tours of the island (usually in French) begin here.

Île St Joseph   ISLAND
With its eerie solitary-confinement cells and guards' cemetery, Île St Joseph is overgrown with coconut palms, though it does have a good white-sand beach that is perfect for swimming.

Île du Diable   ISLAND
Covered with a thick foliage of palms, rocky Île du Diable (Devil's Island) was where the most high-profile prisoners were kept, including Alfred Dreyfus. Sadly most day-trip boats don't stop here, but it's a rewarding place to wander around if you get the chance, and several of its historic buildings have been restored.

⊨ Sleeping & Eating

It's possible to camp for free along some of the paradisiacal areas along the shore of Île Royale (but bring mosquito repellent, nets and rain gear). A far more comfortable option is the Auberge des Îles du Salut, which is an atmospheric – if basic – place to bed down for the night.

★ **Auberge des Îles du Salut**   INN $$
(☑0594-321100; www.aubergedesiles.fr; hammock spaces €10, r €60-70, director's house s/d €188/299) The welcome hasn't improved much since the days of arriving convicts, but the rooms in the artfully renovated director's house are something out of a breezy Bogart film. If you want a more Papillon-like (p784) experience, you can stay in simpler rooms in old guards' quarters (some with

---

PAPILLON: ESCAPE ARTIST OR CON MAN?

Of all the prisoners who did hard time on Île du Diable (Devil's Island), only Alfred Dreyfus, the Frenchman wrongly convicted of treason in 1894, achieved anything near the fame of Henry Charrière, who became known – or notorious – for his epic tale of nine remarkable escapes from French Guiana's infamous prison camps. Nicknamed Papillon (Butterfly) for a tattoo on his chest, Charrière claims in his autobiography that after being wrongly convicted of murder he escaped from the Îles du Salut by floating toward the mainland on a sack full of coconuts and braving harsh malarial jungles to flee eastward. Fashioning himself into an international man of mystery living among native villagers, he eventually became a Venezuelan citizen and was portrayed by Steve McQueen in a Hollywood version of his life. His published story is widely believed to be a compilation of his own adventures and stories he heard about other convicts' escapades while he was in prison.

terraces) or sling a hammock in the cleaned-up prison dormitories.

Don't leave without having at least one meal (set menu €26) at the restaurant, which serves the best fish soup (€10) this side of Provence. There are no cooking facilities, but bringing picnic supplies (and plenty of water – it's not potable on the islands) can keep your costs to a minimum.

ⓘ Getting There & Away

Comfortable, fume-free catamarans and sail-boats take about 1½ to two hours to reach the islands from Kourou. They all depart around 8am from Kourou's ponton des pêcheurs (fishers' dock, at the end of Av Général de Gaulle) and return between 4pm and 6pm. Usual itineraries stay on Île Royale through lunchtime, then visit Île Saint Joseph in the afternoon before returning to Kourou. Call the Office de Tourisme (p783) in Kourou to reserve a place 48 to 72 hours in advance, or book directly with tour operators in Cayenne or Kourou:

Albatros (☑ 0694-263954; albatros@gmx.fr)

Guyavoile (☑ 0594-321132; www.guyavoile.fr; day trip/overnight €49/70)

La Hulotte (☑ 0594-323381; www.lahulotte-guyane.fr; day trip/overnight €48/63)

Tropic Alizés (☑ 0694-402020, 0594-251010; www.ilesdusalut-guyane.com; day trip/ovenight €50/66)

St Laurent du Maroni

POP 50,800

St Laurent was founded in 1857 by the French government as a penal colony modelled on Britain's use of Australia. In just under 90 years, some 70,000 prisoners were transported here from mainland France and then sent to prison camps along the Maroni basin. The camps finally closed in 1946, but the town's entire history has been informed by its brutal and sad past.

Today, St Laurent houses the country's finest colonial architecture and remains dominated by penal buildings and the ghosts of its prisoners. Along the banks of the Fleuve Maroni (Marowijne River), bordering Suriname, St Laurent is also a place to take a river trip to Maroon and Amerindian settlements. It's set up better for tourism than any other town in the country including Cayenne and, if you've been getting frustrated by the difficulty of travel in French Guiana, you'll find it refreshingly easy to organize activities here.

⊙ Sights

Time your visit for the weekend if you'd like to visit both camps in St Laurent. At present the Camp de la Relégation is only open from Friday to Sunday. Combination tickets for the Camp de la Transportation and the Camp de la Relégation can be bought at the Office du Tourisme (p787) for €12.

★**Camp de la Transportation** HISTORIC SITE
(Rue du Lieutenant-Colonel Chandon; tours per person €6, exhibition hall admission €8; ⊙ tour hours vary) The eerie Camp de la Transportation, where prisoners arrived for processing, was the largest prison in French Guiana. Convicts arrived exhausted after 20 days crossing the Atlantic and were eventually dispatched onwards from here. It's possible to visit half of the complex on your own, for which entry is free, though you'll need to stump up €8 if you'd like to visit the several exhibition halls with good interactive displays on the history of the camp in French.

The tourist office offers 1½-hour tours – some guides speak minimal English – of the complex that are highly recommended. One cell has Papillon's (p784) name engraved on it, but whether this was really his cell is up for debate.

Camp de la Relégation HISTORIC SITE
(St Jean; per person €8; ⊙ tours 3:30pm Fri, Sat & Sun) The Camp de la Relégation, aka St Jean, is another abandoned prison camp 17km from St Laurent. It's accessed via two-hour tours offered by various operators, all of which can be booked through the Office du Tourisme, but which only run on weekends. These buildings were once home to 'the crowbars' – repeat light offenders who were given more freedom. As such, the atmosphere here isn't as creepy as at other camps, but visiting is still a fascinating and atmospheric experience.

St Laurent du Maroni

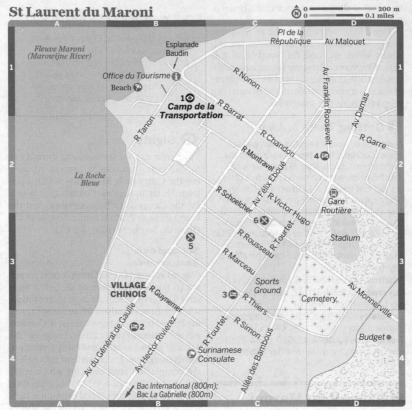

St Laurent du Maroni

Fleuve de Maroni RIVER
(half-day tours around €50) Explore the Amerindian and Maroon cultures that inhabit the shores of this great river. You'll usually also visit the island of an old leper colony (mentioned in *Papillon*) and take a jungle stroll. The Office du Tourisme will know which of the several local river-tour companies have scheduled trips and can direct you to guides who speak English. Longer trips usually involve a night or more in a hammock in a traditional Amerindian hut and a taste of local cuisine.

🛏 Sleeping

★**Hôtel La Tentiaire** HOTEL $
(☎0594-342600; tentiaire@wanadoo.fr; 12 Av Franklin Roosevelt; r from €70-85; 🅿❄🛜🏊) The best in the center, La Tentiaire has classy rooms with wood accents in a renovated administrative penitentiary building. Some rooms have balconies looking over the adjacent park and others have two levels that comfortably sleep a family of four. The breakfast buffet is of a high standard for the genre and there's a pleasant pool out back.

Amazonie Accueil LODGE $
(☎0594-343612, 0694-412350; am.ac@orange.fr; 3 Barrat; hammock spaces €10, with hammock €15; 🛜) A central and welcoming place to hang a

ℹ GETTING TO SURINAME

Getting to the Border
The **Bac International** international quay is about 2km south of central St Laurent, down Av Eboué. It's possible to walk, or you can take a taxi from town for €4. Be sure to stamp out at customs and immigration here. Note that you can now get Suriname Tourist Cards and visas from St Laurent's efficient **Surinamese Consulate** (☑0594-344968; 26 Catayée; ⊗9am-noon & 2-4pm Mon-Thu, to 3:30pm Fri), as well as at the one in Cayenne. Bring a passport and yellow-fever certificate to get a tourist card or visa here.

At the Border
Private *pirogues* (dugout canoes; €3 per person, 10 minutes) are the easiest way to cross to Suriname, and leave the quay on demand all day, dropping passengers at the Albina ferry dock on the river's far side. Otherwise, the car ferry **Bac La Gabrielle** (☑0694-411093, 0594-279129; passenger/car & driver €4/35) crosses the river four times per day in 30 minutes. Note that there are no ferry services on Wednesday afternoons or Sunday mornings.

Moving On
Across the border in Suriname, shared taxis (SR$75, two hours), minibuses (SR$30 to SR$40, 2½ hours) and public buses (SR$8.50, three hours) to Paramaribo meet the boats in Albina.

hammock (or rent one if you don't have your own). The hammock lodge has a gravel floor and room for five. There's a breakfast area and shared bathrooms.

Hotel Amazonia du Fleuve   HOTEL **$$**
(☑0594-341010; hotelamazoniadufleuve@orange.fr; 20 Thiers; r from €100; ❇🛜) This new addition to St Laurent's hotels is a bit pricey, but offers comfortable and central accommodations in clean, tiled rooms with generous bathrooms and indifferent furnishings. It does have a number of rooms for mobility-impaired travelers, though, and the staff speak English.

✖ Eating

Several small grocery stores and a midsize market provide self-catering options. Stalls at the lovely **Marché de Saint Laurent** (Food & Craft Market; Av Félix Eboué; ⊗5am-1pm Wed & Sat) offer filling *bami goreng* (fried noodles), pho and French-style quiche, all for around €5.

Chez Félicia   CREOLE **$**
(23 Av du Général de Gaulle; mains €10-15; ⊗noon-2pm & 6-11pm, closed Sun nights) This local favorite has tasty Creole cuisine (including bush meat) enjoyed in a homey, checkered-tablecloth setting with friendly staff and happy regulars. Portions are huge and sharing is encouraged.

★La Goélette   CREOLE **$$**
(☑0594-342897; mains €16-23; ⊗noon-2pm & 6:30-11pm Tue-Sun; 🛜) The best restaurant in St Laurent, 'the Schooner' is indeed built boatlike over the river and offers a selection of breezy tables with great views toward Suriname. The food is excellent, with a range of seafood and meat dishes as well as a vegetarian plate. It's a short distance from town – take a taxi.

ℹ Information

MONEY
Banks and ATMs are scattered throughout town but none of them exchange foreign currency or traveler's checks. You'll have to wait to get to Cayenne if you need to exchange money.

TOURIST INFORMATION
Office du Tourisme (☑0594-342398; www.ot-saintlaurentdumaroni.fr; Esplanade Baudin; ⊗8am-12:30pm & 2:30-6pm Tue-Sat, 2:30-6pm Mon, 8:30am-12:30pm Sun) Everything there is to do and see in St Laurent can be arranged from here, including hiring bikes, organizing tours and buying tickets for various attractions. The staff also speak English and give out free maps.

ℹ Getting There & Away

The **Gare Routière** (Gueril) is in the center of town and has two daily departures for Cayenne

ⓘ GETTING TO BRAZIL

French Guiana has a border crossing at St Georges, where the Oyapock River marks the frontier with Brazil. A brand-new bridge to Brazil opened in 2017.

If you get stuck in St Georges for a night, try the popular **Chez Modestine** (📞0694-370013; modestine@wanadoo.fr; Place du Village, Elie-Elfort; r €60; ❄) on the main square or the quieter **Caz-Calé** (📞0694-455182, 0694-125496; Elie Elfort; s/d/tr from €60/70/75; ❄🔊) just down the road. Most travelers head directly on to Cayenne or into Brazil, however.

Getting to the Border

Minibuses leave when full from Cayenne to St Georges (€30, five hours), located on the border with Brazil. You may need to transfer buses in Regina. This is the only public-transport option to the border.

At the Border

Once across the bridge on the Brazilian side, you'll stamp into Brazil before continuing into town, from where daily buses (R$160, 11–14 hours, morning and afternoon) and planes leave Oiapoque for Macapá.

(€25, four hours). The first bus leaves at 4am and the second between 11am and 1pm depending on when it fills up. For an extra €5, the bus will drop you off wherever you want in Cayenne.

If you miss the bus, a *taxi collectif* (minbus) costs €35 and can be arranged through the Office du Tourisme (p787). Alternatively, you can hire a car at **Budget** (📞0594-340294; www.budget-guyane.com; 328 Av Gaston Monnerville), which tacks on a €100 fee for one-way rentals to Cayenne. Its office is located on a road out of town toward Cayenne.

Mana & Awala-Yalimopo

POP 600

About 50km northeast of St Laurent lies the rustic village of Mana, which has a particularly scenic waterfront on the wide river of the same name. Sadly the town itself is in a fairly dire state, with its once-lovely colonial buildings now literally falling down, and a fairly unlovely collection of modern housing elsewhere.

A 22km drive northwest of Mana is the beachside Amerindian settlement of Awala-Yalimopo, which is mostly notable for Plage Les Hattes (p788), one of the world's most spectacular nesting sites for giant leatherback turtles.

⊙ Sights

★ Plage Les Hattes   BEACH

(Awala-Yalimopo) This long stretch of beach is a very important nesting ground for giant leatherback turtles, which can grow up to 600kg. The females come ashore from April to July, and their young hatch and make their way into the sea between July and September.

**Maison de la Reserve
Naturelle l'Amana**   NATURE RESERVE
(📞0594-348404; Awala-Yalimopo; adult/child €2/ free; ⊙8am-noon & 2-6pm Mon, Wed, Fri & Sat, 2-6pm Tue & Thu) The reserve has a small museum that offers information about turtle biology and has two nature trails leading from its premises.

🛏 Sleeping & Eating

There is a comfortable **hotel** (📞0594-278667; hotellesamana@orange.fr; 18 Aubert, Mana; d/ studio €60/65; 🅿❄🔊) in Mana, as well as several simple beachside guesthouses in Awala-Yalimopo, which you can find by wandering along the village's shoreline. The latter options are the best if you want to see turtles.

There are a couple of simple restaurants in both Mana and Awala-Yalimopo. Don't miss a chance to dine on French cuisine with a Guianese twist at **Le Buffalo** (📞0594-344280; 36 rue Javouhey, Mana; mains €15-25; ⊙9:30am-3pm & 7-10pm Tue-Sun). For meals in Awala-Yalimopo, try reserving a French-Amerindian lunch or dinner at **Yalimalé** (📞0594-343432; Awala-Yalimopo; mains €25; ⊙8am-2pm & 4-8pm Tue-Sat, 4-8pm Sun), although it's rarely open outside of turtle season.

ⓘ Getting There & Away

Mana and Awala-Yalimopo are only accessible by car, so you'll need to have your own or take a taxi to get here. Do note that if you're heading east to Cayenne from here, Mana has the last gas station before Kourou, so be sure you have enough fuel to get there.

UNDERSTAND FRENCH GUIANA

French Guiana Today

Developments at the Centre Spatial Guyanais (Guyanese Space Center) in Kourou tend to dominate the news in French Guiana, not least when the entire complex was taken over by a group of protestors in 2017 and a rocket launch was delayed. The group, calling itself 500 Frères (500 Brothers), was protesting both the low quality and the high cost of life in the overseas department, under the slogan *'pou lagwiyann dekole'* (Creole for 'let Guiana take off'). Many local people feel that despite huge amounts of money being invested into the space center here, there's very little concern for the average inhabitant of French Guiana, something made awkwardly apparent when President Emmanuel Macron referred to the region as an island, a gaffe that astonished and angered locals.

In a referendum in 2010, the population voted against increased autonomy from France, confirming French Guiana's long-term status as an overseas department. While this meant that European funds continued to flood in and that the region's position as the wealthiest and best developed of the Guianas was cemented, this was in stark contradiction to how many locals saw the situation. Industrial relations in French Guiana have been fraught ever since, with intermittent strikes, demonstrations and protests against social exclusion, poor education and joblessness.

Gold mining has become more prevalent around the country, particularly along the eastern Brazilian border. The government has been battling a massive illegal gold-mining industry – which involves the dumping of tons of polluting mercury into French Guiana's once-pristine rivers – with some success, but the logistics of managing so much jungle and the long, lonely borders of Suriname and Brazil make it an extremely challenging task.

History

The earliest French settlement was in Cayenne in 1643, but plantation development was limited due to tropical diseases and an Amerindian population that strongly resisted colonization. After various conflicts with the Dutch and the British and an eight-year occupation by Brazil and Portugal, the French resumed control shortly before slavery was abolished in 1848 by Paris, and many of the colony's plantations collapsed.

At about the same time, France decided that penal settlements in Guiana would reduce the cost of French prisons and contribute to the colony's development. Napoleon III sent the first convicts in 1852; those who survived their sentences had to remain there as exiles for an equal period of time. With 90% of them dying of malaria or yellow fever, this policy did little to increase the population or develop the colony. French Guiana became notorious for the brutality and corruption of its penal system, which lasted until 1953.

Guiana became an overseas department of France in 1946, and in 1964 work began on the Centre Spatial Guyanais, which brought an influx of scientists, engineers, technicians and service people from Europe and elsewhere, turning the city of Kourou into a sizable, modern town responsible for 15% of all economic activity. The first Hmong refugees from Laos arrived in 1975 and settled primarily in the towns of Cacao and Javouhey. They now make up about 1.5% of the population and have become vital agricultural producers, growing about 80% of the department's produce.

Successive French governments have provided state employment and billions of euros in subsidies, resulting in a higher standard of living in some areas, though many urban areas around Cayenne remain extremely deprived. Rural villages also suffer from poverty, while in the hinterland many Amerindians and Maroons still lead a subsistence lifestyle.

Culture

French Guiana is a tantalizing mélange of visible history, diverse cuisine and ingrained metropolitan French attitudes to how things are done, all set against the majestic canvas of the Amazon wilderness. Though Cayenne and Kourou enjoy somewhat-continental economies, the majority of the populace struggles financially and most people live modest lifestyle.

Guianese people take pride in their multicultural universe borne of multiregional influences. With 30 languages spoken in a region smaller than Iceland, around 38% of the population claims a mixed African (or Creole) heritage, 8% are French, 8% Haitian, 6% Surinamese, 5% are from the French Antilles, 5% are Chinese and 5% are Brazilian. The remainder is a smattering of Amerindian, Hmong and other South American ethnicities.

The country is predominantly Catholic, but Maroons and Amerindians follow their own religious traditions. (After the abolition of slavery in 1834, Africans refused to work on the plantations for wages, and many established their own villages in the bush and became known as Maroons.) The Hmong also tend to be Roman Catholic due to the influence of Sister Anne-Marie Javouhey, who brought them to French Guiana in the 1970s.

Environment

French Guiana borders Brazil to the east and south, while the Maroni and Litani Rivers form the border with Suriname to the west. The majority of the population lives in the Atlantic coastal zone, which has most of French Guiana's limited road network. The coast is mostly mangrove swamp with only a few sandy beaches, and the water along the coast tends to be an unappealing brown color, due to the vast number of huge rivers emptying into the Atlantic from the Amazon Basin. If that wasn't enough to keep you out of the water, in 2018 swimming was banned at beaches around Cayenne due to dangerous levels of unprocessed sewage. A beach destination this is not, though there's an active and well-protected turtle population that lays its eggs annually between April and July on the beaches around the town of Mana. The densely forested interior, the terrain of which rises gradually toward the Tumac-Humac Mountains on the Brazilian frontier, is largely unpopulated, and is home to incredible biodiversity that is nevertheless under threat from illegal gold mining and deforestation.

SURVIVAL GUIDE

ℹ Directory A–Z

ACCOMMODATIONS
Hotels in French Guiana are generally pricey but comfortable. Most hotels have some English-speaking staff. The most economical options include long-stay *gîtes* (guesthouses; inquire at tourist offices) in Cayenne, Kourou and St Laurent du Maroni, and rustic *carbets* (open-air huts) for hammocks in more rural areas.

ACTIVITIES
Bird-watching, hiking and canoeing are popular in French Guiana. Water sports – windsurfing, kitesurfing and sailing – are a major pastime on beaches at Montjoly and Kourou, but renting gear is practically impossible, so unless you know locals who enjoy these sports, you may have difficulty arranging it.

ELECTRICITY
Plugs are the three-pronged European type. Currents are 220/127V, 50Hz.

EMBASSIES & CONSULATES
French Guiana only hosts diplomatic missions from its neighbors. If you need diplomatic assistance, in most cases you'll need to contact your country's embassy in Paris.

Brazilian Embassy (☑ 0594-296010; 444 Chemin St Antoine, Cayenne)

Surinamese Consulate (☑ 0594-282160; 3 Av Léopold Héder; ⊙ 9am-2pm Mon-Fri) Often busy, but if you're lucky you can get a tourist card issued within a few minutes. There's a smaller consulate in St Laurent du Maroni (p787) that's less busy and offers the same services.

FOOD
French Guiana offers an enviable combination of culinary rigor brought by the French and an impressive variety of ingredients and spices courtesy of the other ethnic groups present in the region. Cayenne has some excellent eating options, while elsewhere things are rather less sophisticated, but you will still eat well, with fish and seafood dominating most menus.

HEALTH
Chloroquine-resistant malaria is present in the interior, and French Guiana is considered a yellow-fever-infected area. The Zika virus is present in French Guiana too, so take extreme precautions if you are pregnant, and avoid the rainforest altogether. Excellent medical care is available, but few doctors speak English. Water is fine in bigger towns; drink bottled or boiled water elsewhere.

INTERNET ACCESS

Patchy wireless is available at all urban hotels for free. Expect slow speeds and frequent disconnections, however. The easiest way to stay online as a visitor is by getting a local SIM card and buying data packages.

LANGUAGE

The official language of French Guiana is French and most people speak it fluently. Creole is spoken casually by the Creole population, while French Guianese is a mixture of Creole and other languages. Otherwise, the Hmong population speak Hmong, there are several Amerindian dialects spoken by the native population, and along the Suriname border many Maroons speak Sranan Tongo (the Creole lingua franca of Suriname).

MAPS

France's Institut Géographique National publishes a 1:500,000 map of French Guiana, with fine city maps of Cayenne and Kourou as well as more detailed maps of the populated coastal areas. Topographic maps (1:25,000) and a variety of tourist maps are available throughout the country.

MONEY

French Guiana uses the euro. The only *cambios* for currency exchange are in Cayenne, but ATMs are found in most midsized to large towns.

Credit cards are widely accepted, and you can get Visa or MasterCard cash advances at ATMs, which are on the Plus and Cirrus networks. Eurocard and Carte Bleu are also widely accepted.

OPENING HOURS

Many businesses close up shop in the heat of the day; generally hours are 8am to noon and 2pm to 6pm, while restaurants tend to serve from noon to 2pm and again from 7pm to 10pm or later. The country stops on Sunday and sometimes Monday, just about everywhere. Nightclubs and bars open at around 10pm.

POST

The postal service is very reliable, although all mail is routed through France, so it's not particularly fast to non-European destinations.

PUBLIC HOLIDAYS

New Year's Day January 1
Ash Wednesday February/March
Good Friday/Easter Monday March/April
Labor Day May 1
Bastille Day July 14
All Saints' Day November 1
All Souls' Day November 2
Armistice Day (Veterans Day) November 11
Christmas Day December 25

SLEEPING PRICE RANGES

The following price ranges refer to a double room with bathroom outside of Carnaval (which preceeds Easter and is usually in February). Unless otherwise stated, all taxes are included, but breakfast is not.

$ less than €85
$$ €85–150
$$$ more than €150

SAFE TRAVEL

➡ Larger towns warrant caution at night. Crime and drug trafficking have increased throughout the country in recent years, and you'll often find police roadblocks on coastal routes and your car and luggage may be searched.

➡ Locals hitchhike around Cayenne and west toward St Laurent, but it's riskier for travelers, who may be seen as money-laden targets. Never hitch at night or on the road between Régina and St Georges, which is more dangerous and remote. Hitchhiking is never entirely safe in any country. Travelers who decide to hitch should understand they are taking a potentially serious risk. Hitching is less dangerous if you travel in pairs and let someone know where you are planning to go.

TELEPHONE

Digicel, Orange and SFR SIM cards are available in Cayenne, Kourou and St Laurent for €15 including €5 of credit. There are no area codes in French Guiana, but all numbers have 10 digits and must begin with either 0594 (for landlines) or 0694 (for cells).

TOURIST INFORMATION

Nearly every city and town in French Guiana has a tourist office of some sort, though it may be just a small kiosk that is rarely staffed. Even tiny villages have helpful public maps with lists of businesses, sights and walking routes marked on them.

EATING PRICE RANGES

The following price ranges refer to a standard main course, including service.

$ less than €12
$$ €12–20
$$$ more than €20

VISAS

Passports are obligatory for all visitors except those from France, who may travel on their national identity cards. Visitors must also have a yellow-fever vaccination certificate. Australian, New Zealand, Japanese, EU and US nationals, among others, do not need a visa for stays up to 90 days.

Those who need visas should apply with two passport photos at a French embassy and be prepared to show an onward or return ticket. Officially, all visitors, even French citizens, should have either onward or return tickets, but this is rarely enforced.

ⓘ Getting There & Away

AIR

All international passengers must fly through Cayenne's Félix Eboué International Airport (p780). The following airlines have desks at the airport:

Air Caraïbes (☑ 0820-835835; www.air caraibes.com) Flies to Paris.

Air France (☑ 0594-298700; www.airfrance. gf) Flies to Paris, Fort-de-France, Pointe-à-Pitre and Miami.

Air Guyane (☑ 0594-293630; www.airguyane. com) Flies from Cayenne to four domestic airfields including St Laurent du Maroni.

Suriname Airways (☑ 0594-293000; www. flyslm.com) Flights to Belem and Paramaribo.

BOAT

From St Laurent du Maroni (in the west), boats and a car ferry head to Suriname, and there are boats and a massive suspension bridge (opened 2017) from St Georges de l'Oyapock (in the east) to Brazil.

ⓘ Getting Around

Getting around French Guiana without your own wheels is much more difficult and costly than in mainland France, where public trans-

port and hitchhiking are more common. Even though renting a car might blow your budget, it's probably the most cost-efficient way to see the country.

AIR

From Cayenne, small planes operated by Air Guyane (p792) fly to various small towns deep in the jungle that can't easily be reached by road.

BOAT

Tours often use river transport, but individuals can try to catch a boat at Kaw and St Laurent. Catamarans sail to the Îles du Salut from the town of Kourou.

CAR & MOTORCYCLE

Renting a car can be cheaper than public transport if two or more people are traveling together. Some companies have offices in Kourou, St Laurent du Maroni and at the airport (some have airport-pickup surcharges of up to €25). Expect to pay from €35 per day for a compact car with unlimited mileage. Cars are not allowed over the border. Be sure to leave Cayenne with a full tank, as gas stations are extremely limited in the rest of the country.

Avis (☑ 0594-302522; www.avis.fr; 58 Blvd Mandela) Also has an office at the airport.

Budget (☑ 0694-279780; www.budget-guyane. com; Félix Eboué International Airport) The office is in Zone Galmot on the Cayenne outskirts, just off Av Galmot; also has an office at the airport.

Sixt (☑ 0594-298042; www.sixt.fr; 11 Rue du Capitaine Bernard) Has a convenient downtown office, as well as an office at the airport and was planning to open an office in St Laurent du Maroni at the time of research.

TAXI COLLECTIF

Taxis collectifs (minibuses) are the second-best wheeled option. They leave when full from Cayenne, Kourou, St Laurent and St Georges, and can often be arranged by tourist offices, which keep lists of reliable drivers.

Guyana

POP 782,000

Best Places to Eat

➡ Backyard Café (p799)

➡ Aagman Indian Restaurant (p800)

➡ Shanta's (p797)

➡ Bistro Cafe & Bar (p797)

Best Places to Stay

➡ King's Hotel & Residence (p797)

➡ Iwokrama River Lodge & Research Center (p803)

➡ Rewa Eco-Lodge (p804)

➡ Pakaraima Mountain Inn (p804)

➡ Karanambu Lodge (p805)

Why Go?

Few places on the planet offer raw adventure as authentic as densely forested Guyana. Although the country has a troubled history of political instability and interethnic tension, underneath the headlines of corruption and economic mismanagement is a joyful and motivated mix of people who are slowly turning the country into the continent's best-kept ecotourism secret.

Georgetown, the country's crumbling colonial capital, is distinctly Caribbean, with an alluring vibe, happening nightlife and some great places to eat. The interior of the country is more Amazonian, with its Amerindian communities and unparalleled wildlife-viewing opportunities tucked quietly away from the capital's noise and bustle. From sea-turtle nesting grounds along the country's north coast to monkeys and jaguars in the rainforest, and giant anteaters down in the southern savannas, Guyana's natural wonders are well worth the mud, bumpy roads and sweat.

When to Go
Georgetown

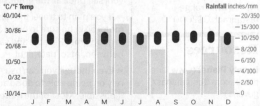

| Mid-Nov–mid-Jan Coastal rainy season and the height of tourism for expat Guyanese. | May–Aug Interior and a second coastal rainy season. Road travel becomes difficult. | Late Dec 'Cashew rains' in the interior – light showers often provide a welcome temperature drop. |

FAST FACTS

Currency Guyanese dollar (G$)

Visas A 90-day stay is granted on arrival for travelers from most countries.

Money Not all ATMs accept foreign cards; credit cards are rarely accepted outside the better hotels in Georgetown.

Capital Georgetown

Emergency 911 (police)

Language English

Exchange Rates

Australia	A$1	G$155
Canada	C$1	G$158
Eurozone	€1	G$241
New Zealand	NZ$1	G$144
UK	£1	G$276
USA	US$1	G$208
Japan	¥100	G$187

For current exchange rates, see www.xe.com.

Daily Costs

➡ Double room in a budget hotel: G$6000; in a midrange hotel G$10,000

➡ Street snack: G$200; meal in a midrange restaurant: G$2000

Resources

Lonely Planet (www.lonelyplanet.com/the-guianas/guyana)

Guyana Tourism (www.guyana-tourism.com)

Stabroek News (www.stabroeknews.com)

Explore Guyana (www.exploreguyana.org)

Entering the Country

Guyana's only legal border crossings are at South Drain (Suriname) and Bonfim (Brazil); both can be reached by minibus. Venezuela makes up much of the country's western border, but due to a long-standing border dispute, crossing anywhere is illegal and not recommended.

ONE WEEK ITINERARY

Stay in Georgetown for a night then take a day trip by plane to the outrageously scenic Kaieteur Falls. Next, fly or travel overland into the interior to stay in the Amerindian village of Surama for two nights. From here take road and river to either Caiman House, to help with caiman research, or Lethem, from where you can explore the nearby mountains, waterfalls and villages. On your final day, fly back to Georgetown from Lethem, enjoying stunning views of the rainforest.

Essential Food & Drink

Pepperpot Stewed meat flavored with cinnamon and cassareep.

Cook up rice A mixture of rice, meat, coconut milk and lots of herbs.

El Dorado rum Considered one of the world's best rums.

Roti Soft Indian flatbread.

Cow heel soup A soup made with split peas, vegetables, dumplings and cow heels.

Top Tips

➡ Don't miss Kaieteur Falls, the country's undoubted highlight, and consider staying overnight there; a real adventure that allows you to have this magical place all to yourself once all the groups have departed.

➡ If you plan to travel the Rupununi on the back of a motorbike, be sure to make arrangements to find a driver in good time. Reliable and safe drivers are few and far between. Also, pack light.

➡ Even though you can use ATMs in most towns now, never rely on being able to do so and carry a good supply of cash if possible. Most of the more remote jungle lodges are seriously far away from working ATMs.

Guyana Highlights

1 Kaieteur Falls (p802)
Standing on the ledge of the world's highest single-drop fall.

2 Rupununi Savanna (p804) Paddling past populations of giant river otters in these wildlife-rich grasslands.

3 Dadanawa Ranch (p806) Going on a cattle drive with *vaqueros* (cowboys) at this historic ranch.

4 Iwokrama Rainforest (p803) Bird-watching and animal tracking deep in the virgin rainforests of this reserve.

5 Shell Beach (p801) Passing through rice-farming villages and crossing rivers teeming with wildlife en route to Guyana's best beach.

6 Rewa Eco-Lodge (p804) Catching a glimpse of the giant arapaima, the planet's biggest freshwater scaled fish, at this remote river lodge.

7 Saddle Mountain (p806) Horseback riding and searching for giant anteaters at this beautiful corner of the South Rupununi.

Georgetown

POP 240,000

Standing proudly where the mighty Demerara River pours into the Atlantic, Georgetown is by far Guyana's biggest city and a place all visitors will spend at least some of their time. With its dilapidated architecture, unkempt parks and vibrant street life, Georgetown has a laid-back feel and considerable charm in parts, even if there's little to see beyond a smattering of museums, churches and colonial curiosities. Home today to the Caricom economic community, and thus a kind of Brussels of the Caribbean, Georgetown is no backwater, and its restaurants and nightlife reflect that, lending a distinctly cosmopolitan edge to the general chaos of a modern Guyanese city.

◉ Sights

Georgetown can be explored comfortably in a couple of days, with several interesting museums and attractive parks to explore. The best 19th-century buildings are along Main St and especially along Ave of the Republic, just east of the Demerara River.

St George's Cathedral　　ARCHITECTURE
(North Rd) The most impressive building in town is the white-painted, Gothic-style St George's Cathedral, said to be the world's tallest wooden building. It was completed in 1892 and was built with a native hardwood called greenheart. It was enjoying a renovation at the time of writing – though remains open – and will look wonderful when it's finished.

Stabroek Market　　MARKET
(Water St; ⊙24hr) One of the city's most prominent landmarks is Stabroek Market, a cast-iron building with a giant corrugated-iron clock tower. This frenetic and colorful market dates back to the late 1700s, although the current structure was built in 1880. Visiting is a must for sheer atmosphere, but don't bring any valuables and keep a grip on your bag.

Castellani House　　MUSEUM
(cnr Vlissengen Rd & Homestretch Ave; ⊙10am-5pm Mon-Fri, 2-6pm Sat) FREE This gorgeous wooden building, erected in 1877, is home to the National Art Gallery and rotating art exhibits, many by local artists. To get here from the Botanical Gardens, it's possible to take a shortcut through the military bar-racks to avoid having to walk along the main road – just ask the guard to let you through.

Promenade Garden　　GARDENS
(cnr Middle & Carmichael Sts; ⊙7.30am-6pm) During daylight hours, the Promenade Garden in Cummingsburg is a quiet place to relax, read and enjoy the flowers and tropical birdlife. Its tranquility is in stark contrast to its role in the 19th century as a public execution site during the Demerara Revolt, a slave uprising that took place in 1823. A statue of Gandhi can be found here today, as well as a very Victorian-looking bandstand.

Botanical Gardens　　GARDENS
(Regent Rd) FREE Georgetown's Botanical Garden is a pleasant open space with a huge range of tropical plants, trees and flowers in it, including the Victoria Regia Lily, Guyana's national flower. The entire place is charmingly laid out, with ponds, bandstands, walkways and gazebos. You'll also find Georgetown's small **zoo** (cnr Regent & Vlissengen Rds; adult/child G$200/100; ⊙7:30am-5:30pm) here, as well as the mausoleum of Guyana's longtime president, Forbes Burnham.

Walter Roth Museum of Anthropology　　MUSEUM
(61 Main St; ⊙8am-4:30pm Mon-Fri) FREE A small museum in a breezy old building, with lots of Amerindian items from Guyana's indigenous peoples.

Demerara Distillers　　DISTILLERY
(☏256-5019; www.theeldoradorum.com; Plantation Diamaon, East Bank Demerara; tours G$3000; ⊙tours 9am & 1pm Wed & Thu, or by appointment) This is where Guyana's most famous export, its exceptional Eldorado Rum, was originally made in 1670. It is no longer made here, but the site is now open as an excellent museum. One-hour tours take you through the distillery (where you'll see the last operating wooden Coffey still in the world), warehouse, heritage center and gift shop.

☞ Tours

★ Wilderness Explorers　　ADVENTURE
(☏227-7698; www.wilderness-explorers.com; 141 4th St; ⊙8am-5pm Mon-Fri) A long-running, reliable company with tons of itinerary choices all around the country, including specialty tours such as fishing and remote trekking, day trips to Kaieteur Falls (from G$36,700 per person), jungle expeditions and Georgetown city tours (G$10,000 per person). It can

arrange pretty much anything with notice, including transfers, flights and remote lodge stays.

Evergreen Adventures ADVENTURE
(📞 222-0264, 222-2525; www.evergreenadventures gy.com; Ogle Aerodrome, Ogle, ECD; ⊙ 8am-5pm Mon-Fri, to noon Sat) Puts together superb customized trips, and is run by the same company that owns Trans Guyana Airways (TGA), so it's a reliable choice for booking flights with lodges all around the country. Regular tours include day trips to the Essequibo River (G$20,000 per person) and Kaieteur Falls (G$30,000 per person) as well as longer Iwokrama Jungle expeditions and a Guyana Essentials tour.

Dagron Tours TOURS
(📞 227-1174, 223-7921; www.dagron-tours.com; 91 Middle St; ⊙ 8am-5pm Mon-Fri) Offers a variety of interesting Guyana day tours, including several not offered by most operators. These include a heritage cruise on the Demerara River, steel-pan tours with music pioneer Roy Geddes and a rum tour. Also on offer are Kaieteur trips (from G$40,000 per person) and tours along the Essequibo River (from G$16,000 per person).

🛏 Sleeping

Rima Guest House GUESTHOUSE $
(📞 225-7401; rima@networksgy.com; 92 Middle St; s/d/r without bathroom G$6300/8,400/10500; 🛜) This backpackers' favorite is a family-run place with 10 pleasant, homey rooms sharing one bathroom and two toilets in a large colonial house in the center of Georgetown. The owners are friendly and helpful, and provide meals by arrangement. Breakfast is US$6. Cash only.

⭐ Rainforest B&B B&B $$
(📞 227-7800; www.rainforestbbguy.com; 272 Forshaw St; s/d/t G$14,700/18,900/23,000; ✳🛜) Somewhere between an art gallery and a botanical garden, this grand home with five rooms is an oasis from Georgetown's chaos, and yet it's also conveniently located just a few minutes' walk from it all. Charming hosts Saeyeda and Jerry are dedicated to animal welfare, locals arts and crafts, and making sure their guests are fed a delicious breakfast.

Sleepin International Hotel HOTEL $$
(📞 227-3467, 227-3452; www.sleepininternational hotel.com; 24 Brickdam; r incl breakfast from G$14,300; ✳🛜✳) Sleepin has three locations

in town; this is the best midrange choice with a great pool to relax around and a restaurant. Rooms are clean, modern and bright, and service is professional, although rooms do vary quite a bit in quality.

⭐ King's Hotel & Residence HOTEL $$$
(📞 226-1684; www.kingshotel.gy; 176 Middle St; d/tw/ste from G$27,000/31,000/42,000; ✳ 🛜) This is the smartest choice in downtown Georgetown, with a sleek feel and modern furnishings, crisp white cotton sheets on all the beds and some great views over the two nearby parks. It's secure and central and staff are very kind and helpful. The suites come with kitchens, sitting areas and dining tables too, while downstairs is the **Bistro Cafe & Bar** (📞 225-8634; 176 Waterloo St; mains G$2000-3500; ⊙ 7:30am-10pm; 🛜).

Cara Lodge HOTEL $$$
(📞 225-5301; www.carahotels.com; 294 Quamina St; s/d from G$27,300/31,400; ✳🛜) This is Georgetown's most historic hotel, although in this case that also means 'aged'. There's an old-fashioned ballroom, a patio bar around a 100-year-old mango tree, and a classy, rich and-famous-worthy restaurant downstairs, but the rooms are definitely rather tired, and feature more wicker and rattan than is reasonably warranted.

🍴 Eating

⭐ Shanta's INDIAN $
(225 Camp St; mains from G$500-1000; ⊙ 8am-6pm) For more than a half century, simple Shanta's has been filling Georgetown's bellies with the best roti, curries and *chokas* (roasted vegetables) this side of India. It's unbelievably inexpensive considering how delicious the food is. Try everything.

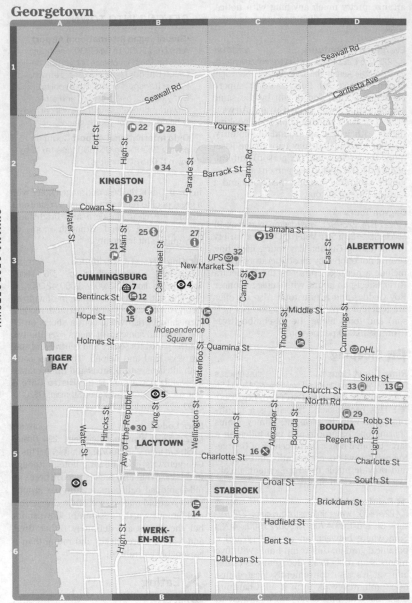

House of Flavors CARIBBEAN $
(177 Charlotte St; mains from G$250; ⊘6am-9pm Mon-Sat, to 4pm Sun; ✍) Serving only one dish – home-cooked rice, beans, veggies and mango *achar* (a spicy pickled condiment) – in a calabash, this Rastafarian (and vegetarian) res-

taurant doubles as a music store and caters to long lines of diners.

Cafe Bellvana CAFE $$
(☑231-8749; Middle St; mains G$1500; ⊘8am-5pm Mon-Fri, to 3pm Sat; ☎✍) This gleaming

Georgetown

⊙ Sights
1 Botanical Gardens F5
2 Botanical Gardens Zoo......................F5
3 Castellani House E5
4 Promenade Garden B3
5 St George's Cathedral........................B4
6 Stabroek Market A5
7 Walter Roth Museum of
   Anthropology...................................B3

⊕ Activities, Courses & Tours
8 Dagron Tours.....................................B4

⊟ Sleeping
9 Cara Lodge C4
10 King's Hotel & Residence..................B4
11 Rainforest B&B.................................E4
12 Rima Guest House B3
13 Sleepin Guesthouse..........................D4
14 Sleepin International Hotel B6

⊗ Eating
   Bistro Cafe & Bar ....(see 10)
15 Cafe Bellvana....................................B4
16 House of Flavors...............................C5
17 Shanta's..C3

⊜ Drinking & Nightlife
18 704 Sports Bar.................................E3
19 Vintage Wine Bar & Lounge...............C3

ⓘ Information
20 Brazilian Embassy.............................F4
21 British High Commission B3
22 Canadian Embassy B2
23 Iwokrama Rainforest
   Conservation and
   Development Office.........................B2
24 National Parks Commission...............E2
25 Scotiabank B3
26 Surinamese Embassy........................E3
27 Tourism & Hospitality Association
   of Guyana.......................................B3
28 US Embassy......................................B2

ⓘ Transport
29 BD Express.......................................D5
30 Caribbean Airlines............................B5
31 Carly's..E5
32 Copa Airlines....................................C3
33 P&A Bus Services.............................D4
34 Suriname Airlines.............................B2

new place offers good coffee, homemade cakes and a selection of cold drinks too. It does a good breakfast (G\$1200) and offers three filling daily specials, one of which is always vegetarian.

★ **Backyard Café**   GUYANESE \$\$\$
(☑ 663-5104; Rose St, West Ruimveldt; meals G\$3000-5000) This unique cultural experience is quickly becoming a phenomenon in Georgetown, with anyone interested in Guyanese cooking heading to eat in Delven Adam's backyard. He serves an extra

ordinarily varied and creative feast, informed by years of working in restaurants in the US before he headed back to his native Guyana. Call at least 24 hours ahead to arrange a table. Prepare yourself for a wonderful experience.

★ **Aagman Indian Restaurant** INDIAN $$$
(291-0161, 654-7693; www.aagmanrestaurant. com; 28 Sherif St, Campbellville; mains G$2000-3500; ⊙noon-3pm & 6-10.30pm; 🖥🖊) The best Indian food in town is rather a way from downtown, but it's well worth the trip by cab. The menu is huge and takes in all the classics, including tandoori dishes, vegetarian options and scores of curries. The attractive dining room is decked out like an Indian fantasy and is one of the smartest in town. Delivery available.

🍷 Drinking & Nightlife

East of Newtown, Sheriff St is a raucous parade of bars, discos and nightclubs, with an equally raucous clientele plying the streets; it might be the action you're looking for, but it's not Georgetown's safest strip.

Vintage Wine Bar & Lounge WINE BAR
(Lamaha St; ⊙5pm-2am) The most fashionable and popular joint in town during our last visit to Georgetown, this is a place where the movers and shakers of the city meet and enjoy wine and cocktails in a sophisticated lounge-bar atmosphere.

Nightcap BAR
(8 Pere St; ⊙5pm-midnight) A sophisticated yet homey place to grab a drink, be that a banana milkshake or a coffee martini, this place has a large garden area as well as a chilly and rather dark bar inside. It's run by former Miss World contestant Candace Charles and is popular with an international crowd.

704 Sports Bar BAR
(1 Lamaha St; ⊙noon-2am) Named for the lucky gold-mining claim that funded its creation, this popular hot spot has a sports bar on the 1st floor and a very popular nightclub upstairs.

ℹ Information

DANGERS & ANNOYANCES
Although Georgetown has more crime than other cities in the Guianas, you can safely explore the city by using a good dose of precaution: be aware of your surroundings, don't wear jewelry,

carry more cash than you need or use your phone when walking. Also, you should avoid deserted streets, especially on the weekends, and use taxis, which are inexpensive, to get around in at night.

MONEY
Scotiabank (104 Carmichael St; ⊙8am-6pm Mon-Fri) The most reliable bank; accepts international ATM cards and processes credit-card advances.

TOURIST INFORMATION
Tourism & Hospitality Association of Guyana (THAG; 🖊225-0807; www.exploreguyana.org; 157 Waterloo St; ⊙8am-5pm Mon-Fri) Publishes the useful *Explore Guyana* guide and has maps and pamphlets.

ℹ Getting There & Away

AIR
Forty-one kilometers from downtown Georgetown, **Cheddi Jagan International Airport** (GEO; 🖊600-7022; www.cjairport-gy.com; Timeri, East Bank Demerara) is a very outdated international airport that was undergoing upgrades at the time of writing, but is never likely to be a particularly easy place to arrive at or depart from, even when these are complete. There are simple facilities such as a couple of cafes and an ATM, but nothing else.

Eleven kilometres from downtown Georgetown, **Ogle International Airport** (OGL; Eugene F. Correira International Airport; Ogle Airstrip Road, Ogle) is a collection of small terminals abutting an airstrip only large enough for domestic and a few regional carriers to land. There is nothing else here apart from a couple of cafes and an ATM.

BUS & MINIBUS
Economical, cramped and dangerously driven minibuses to destinations along the coast depart from Stabroek Market and have no fixed schedules (they leave when full). Even getting aboard them can be a harrowing experience as six touts harass you into choosing theirs.

To travel into the interior by bus, you're limited to overnight services to Lethem, which run the entire way along the country's main road, a dirt track through the jungle. The long, loud, bumpy, dusty journey is not for the fainthearted and involves stopping to sleep at a hammock camp for a few hours (hammock rental G$500), a 6am ferry at the Kurukupari Crossing and several police checkpoints; bring warm clothes, your passport and patience. The buses stop along the main road on demand and pick up as long as they have empty seats (which they often do not – ask your lodging to call and reserve a spot ahead of time for any stops besides Lethem and Georgetown).

ⓘ GETTING TO SURINAME

Getting to the Border

For minibus service from Georgetown (G$5000, four to six hours) to the border, or all the way to Paramaribo in Suriname (G$9000, nine to 12 hours), call **Champ** (☑629-6735; G$9000; ⊘ picks up around 5am).

At the Border

The **Canawaima Ferry** (one-way/round-trip per person G$3500/4500; ⊘10:30am, journey time 30 minutes) to Suriname leaves from Moleson Creek and crosses the Corentyne River to the Suriname border at South Drain, 45 minutes south of Nieuw Nickerie. Get to the ferry no later than one hour before departure to stamp passports and go through customs control. There are no border-crossing fees and immigration remains open to coincide with boat arrivals and departures.

Most nationalities will need a Suriname Tourist Card or visa from a Surinamese consulate or embassy to enter Suriname. These cannot be obtained on the border, so plan in advance; there is a Surinamese Embassy (p810) in Georgetown.

Moving On

Minibuses to Nieuw Nickerie and Paramaribo meet the ferry on the Suriname side. It's best to change your Guyanese currency before leaving Guyana in case no one's buying across the river. Make sure you know your rates before you make the exchange.

Note that Suriname is an hour ahead of Guyana.

CAR

Dolly's Auto Rental (☑225-7126; www.dollysautorental.com; 272 Bissessar Ave) and **Sleepin Guesthouse** (☑231-7667, 223-0991; www.sleepinguesthouse.com; 151 Church St; ✳ 🛜) rent cars (from G$7000 per day), but with bad roads full of farm animals and crazy drivers, few people decide to drive themselves in Guyana. If you do decide to drive you will need a Driving Permit, available for free at Cheddi Jagan International Airport (p800) arrivals terminal.

ⓘ Getting Around

TAXI

For simplicity and safety, taxis are *the* way to get around central Georgetown; trips around the center cost G$300 to G$500 or so, even at night. Have your hotel call a reliable cab company. If you need to flag down a taxi, use only registered ones painted yellow (all registered taxi license plates start with a 'H') and try to find ones with a company logo on the side. Recommended operators include **GR Taxi Service** (☑225-7878) and **Cyril's Taxi Service** (☑227-1700).

Northwest Coast

Guyana's little-visited Northwest Coast, which begins initially on the western bank of the Demerara River across the water from Georgetown and extends way beyond the Essequibo River all the way to the border with Venezuela, has a number of interesting sights, wildlife-watching opportunities and the odd natural wonder to keep you busy should you head out this way. Beyond the Essequibo River, this is wild and largely unpopulated land with no roads or infrastructure, so it's best to travel with an experienced travel agency rather than attempt to strike out alone.

Near Bartica, the Essequibo River meets the Mazaruni River and **Marshall Falls**, a series of rapids and jungle waterfall, reached via a hike through the rainforest. Nearby is the **Arrowpoint Nature Resort** (☑225-9650; per person incl full board & activities from G$45,000; 🛜), a pricey but lovely place to base yourself in this part of the country.

Heading west from the Essequibo, a coastal road passes quaint rice-mill and farming villages to the town of Charity, about 50km away. From here you'll need a boat to go further – through bird-filled rivers, mangrove swamps and savannas – to **Shell Beach**, which extends for about 140km along the coast toward the Venezuelan border and is a nesting site for four of Guyana's eight sea-turtle species. Waini Point, near the town of Mabaruma, is a popular sighting area for the scarlet ibis.

From Georgetown you can cross the Demerara River by bridge and continue to

TRAGEDY AT JONESTOWN

On November 18, 1978, 913 people (including over 270 children) were killed in a mass suicide-murder in a remote corner of Guyana's northwestern rainforest. Since then, Guyana has been sadly associated with this horrific event that became known as the Jonestown Massacre.

In the 1950s Jim Jones, a charismatic American leader, started a religious congregation in Indiana called the Peoples Temple. With utopian ideas of an egalitarian agricultural community, Jones attracted hundreds of followers, but by the 1960s, after moving his church to San Francisco, he became increasingly paranoid and the Peoples Temple started to resemble a cult. Jones' next move took the congregation to the Guyanese bush, and by 1977 word leaked from escaped members that Jones was running the settlement in questionable ways.

California congressperson Leo Ryan, along with journalists and worried family members, visited Jonestown, where they encountered several frightened Temple members who wanted to leave. Not realizing how dangerous Jones really was, Ryan tried to take several residents with him, only to meet gunfire from Jones' followers on the Jonestown airstrip. Ryan and four others were killed. That night Jones ordered his followers to drink cyanide-laced punch; while many 'drank the Kool-Aid,' others were found shot or with slit throats. Jones either shot himself or ordered someone to do it.

the town of Parika. From there speedboats travel southward to the lively mining town of Bartica (G$2500, one hour, hourly), at the confluence of the Mazaruni and Essequibo Rivers, as well as to the west bank of the Essequibo River (G$1000, 45 minutes, leaves when full from dawn to dusk) at Supernam. Georgetown agencies can help you set up a tour through the area or arrange travel by plane or boat.

Kaieteur National Park

The 627-sq-km Kaieteur National Park is perhaps Guyana's greatest drawcard, with the magnificent Kaieteur Falls its single biggest attraction, not to mention a national icon. As well as the stunning falls, the park is home to a tiny population of Amerindians and the endless biodiversity of the Guiana Shield, a massive geological formation covered in pristine rainforest, rushing rivers and vast savanna. This is the reason you came to Guyana.

Nearly all visitors to the country visit Kaieteur on a day trip by air from Georgetown, often combined with a second stop at nearby Orinduik Falls, a place where you can actually get wet and swim. The real adventure, though – not to mention the chance to be alone here – comes with organizing an overnight stay in this staggering natural setting.

⊙ Sights

★ Kaieteur Falls   WATERFALL

You may have been to Salto Ángel or Iguazú Falls, seen Niagara or not even be particularly interested in waterfalls, but it doesn't matter: go to Kaieteur Falls. Watching 1140 metric tons of water shooting over a 250m cliff (the world's highest single-drop falls) in the middle of an ancient jungle with few tourists in sight is a once-in-a-lifetime experience.

Depending on the season, the falls are from 76m to 122m wide. The trail approaching the falls is home to scarlet Guianan cock-of-the-rock birds, and miniscule golden frogs (best seen in the rainy season and/or in the morning), which produce a potentially fatal poison.

🛏 Sleeping

There are two very basic lodges near the falls, both of which need to be booked in advance through the **National Parks Commission** (☑ 226-7974, 226-8082; Thomas Rd, Georgetown; ⊙ 8am-12.30pm & 2-5pm Mon-Fri). You'll need to bring your own hammock and bedding, but spending the night is an incredible experience, and one that allows you to have the falls and the surrounding rainforest all to yourself.

❶ Getting There & Away

Several Georgetown tour operators offer day trips via small planes; make early inquiries and be flexible. The cheapest option to Kaieteur only is to book directly with Air Services Limited (p811), which usually runs two flights per day that allow you to spend two hours, with a guide, at the falls. Return flights cost G$30,000. Most tour companies also offer charter tours where you can choose to add in Orinduik Falls (p802) or a stop at Baganara Resort (on an island with white-sand beaches in the Essequibo River), for an additional cost.

Iwokrama Rainforest

The Iwokrama Centre for Rainforest Conservation and Development is a giant 3710-sq-km slab of pristine jungle; it is a unique living laboratory for tropical forest management and socioeconomic development for Amerindians. Established as a protected reserve in 1996, this exceptional region is home to South America's largest cat, the jaguar, and the world's highest recorded number of fish and bat species, not to mention the world's largest freshwater fish, otters, river turtles, anteaters, snakes, rodents, eagles and caimans. While wildlife can be tough to spot, birders will love the **canopy walkway** (www.iwokramacanopy walkway.com; day pass G$5000) located in the middle of the reserve, and excursions run by the two big lodges here aim to get you into the jungle to see its unique inhabitants yourself.

Overnight buses (p800) between Georgetown and Lethem go through the rainforest reserve, and so one of the lodges makes for an excellent stopover to break up the journey.

🛏 Sleeping

Iwokrama River Lodge & Research Center   LODGE $$
(hammocks G$5000, cabins s/d G$24,000/30,000; 🛜) 🍴 There are three tiers of accommodations at the Iwokrama HQ. The spacious raised wooden bungalows overlook a gorgeous bend in the Essequibo River, while the cheaper accommodations share facilities,

---

RUPUNUNI BACKPACKERS TRAIL

As more options open close to the main public-transport arteries, it's becoming easier to see this amazing area on the cheap. This route, all done via the Georgetown–Lethem–Georgetown minibus, can also be done in reverse. Book lodging in advance for best results.

Georgetown–Kurukupari Crossing
After a long night on the minibus, you have two options at this ferry crossing: **Michelle's Island** (☎261-6454; experienceguyananow@gmail.com; r/hammock incl breakfast G$21,000/G$4200), the best budget choice, is right on the Essequibo River, complete with swimming hole. Otherwise, the Iwokrama River Lodge & Research Center is a quick jump across the river and offers a higher level of comfort and prices.

Kurukupari Crossing–Annai
Only 50km from the Kurukupari Crossing, Annai also has two options. **Oasis** (☎226-5412; Annai; bungalows/hammock space G$10,000/1000; 🛜) is basically a truck stop but offers cheap hammock lodging, two simple bungalows and affordable meals. You may be able to rent motorbikes here. A newer and more scenic option is Pakaraima Mountain Inn (p804).

Annai–Lethem
Lethem, the biggest settlement in the Rupununi, is 120km down the road on the Brazilian border. Here you can choose to either sling a hammock or stay in pricier rooms at the popular Takutu Hotel (p806), or try the more budget-focused Adventure Guianas Guesthouse (p806).

South Rupununi
There's plenty to do to the south of Lethem. Options include camping/trekking trips in the nearby Kanuku Mountains (from G$12,500 per person), and day or overnight Amerindian village trips, staying at lesser-visited, small, community-run lodges. Check in at **Visit Rupununi** (☎772-2228, 772-2227; www.visitrupununi.com; Conservation International Office; ⏱9am-4pm Mon-Fri) to find out what's available and to book.

lack views and are nearer to the loud generator. An even more economical hammock camp is perfect for backpackers, while a two-story octagonal timber building holds the restaurant and offices.

Mix-and-match tours include visits to Amerindian villages, forest walks and nighttime caiman-spotting, with each activity costing between G$2000 and G$20,000.

Atta Rainforest Lodge   LODGE $$$
(☑ 227-7698;   www.iwokramacanopywalkway.com; s/d incl full board & activities G$36,600/48,000; ☏) Within easy walking distance of the canopy walkway (p803), this friendly and comfortable lodge just off the main road in the middle of the rainforest is a great place to spend time doing forest walks, bird-watching and wildlife observation. The eight rooms are comfortable brick-and-thatch creations, with 24-hour solar electricity, and the staff are charming.

❶ Getting There & Away

There is an **airfield** in the village of Fairview, right next to Iwokrama River Lodge & Research Center and Michelle's Island (p805), which takes regular Trans Guyana Airways (p811) flights from Georgetown (one hour, G$33,000). These run only on Monday, Wednesday, Friday and Sunday and require a minimum of three passengers.

Otherwise, the Georgetown–Lethem overnight bus service (p800) goes through the Iwokrama Rainforest and you can ask the driver to let you off for any of the lodges here.

Iwokrama's **Georgetown office** (☑ 225-1504; www.iwokrama.org; 77 High St, Georgetown; ☺ 9am-noon & 2-5:30pm Mon-Fri) can arrange comfortable but pricey transport to its two lodges by private transfer.

North Rupununi

The North Rupununi **savannas** are Africalike plains scattered with Amerindian villages, small islands of jungle and an exceptional diversity of wildlife. Rivers full of huge caimans and the world's largest water lilies (*Victoria amazonica*) cut through plains of golden grasses and termite mounds, and a mind-boggling array of birds fly across the sky. In the background the Pakaraima Mountains loom, more verdant hillsides than vast peaks, but which nonetheless give the landscape a touch of drama. On a human level, the North Rupununi feels like a tight-knit community spread over a vast area – everyone knows everyone and strangers are warmly welcomed. The heart of the North Rupununi is the village of Annai, a crossroads for Amerindian peoples with a few sleeping options and an airstrip.

🛏 Sleeping

Pakaraima Mountain Inn   LODGE $
(☑ 644-3145, WhatsApp 662-7235; pakarminn@ gmail.com; Annai; hammocks/r without bathroom per person G$2100/6300, mountain rooms per person G$15,200; ☏) This wonderful, simple lodge is clearly signed off the main road 15km west of Annai. It offers two types of room: simple accommodations in bunk beds and hammocks, with shared bathrooms, down at the main house, and two bright and beautiful self-contained rooms half way up the mountainside, which boast magnificent views. Homemade meals (G$1500 to G$2100) are served. Activities and tours are also organized.

Rewa Eco-Lodge   LODGE $
(www.rewaguyana.com;   Rewa;   hammocks/s/d from G$5200/8400/12,100; ☏) 🌿 Deep in the jungle, 80km up the Rupununi River from the main road, this lovely lodge sits beside a river and is a short walk from the beautiful, tiny, thatched village of Rewa. The specialty here is catch-and-release fishing as well as arapaima-spotting, but there are also hikes and cultural village visits. Full board is G$9000 extra per person per day.

Caiman House   LODGE $$
(www.rupununilearners.org; Yupukari; hammocks/r per person incl full board G$14,700/24,000; ☏) 🌿 This fantastic lodge offers you the rare chance to stay in the middle of an Amerindian village, and has spacious ranch-style rooms with running water and solar power. The lodge was started as a caiman research center and uses tourism to finance its ongoing studies. In the dry season you can help with nighttime catching and tagging of caiman.

Walks and river trips are also available, as are bird-watching and anteater tours.

Rock View Lodge   LODGE $$
(☑ 614-1060, 645-9675; www.rockviewlodge.com; Annai; s/d US$14,600/25,100; ☏✖) Hummingbirds may flit through the windows of your room at this elegant hacienda-style retreat at the scenic Annai airstrip. The passion project of Colin Edwards, a Brit who has devoted decades of his life to Guyanese tourism,

Rock View has been visibly struggling since scheduled flights to Annai stopped, but it's easily one of the Rupununi's most charming spots. Colin is a mine of information about the area and can arrange walks, village visits and horseback riding in the surrounding countryside.

Karanambu Lodge   LODGE $$$
(☑643-4110; www.karanambutrustandlodge.org; s/d incl full board & activities G$52,300/94,100; 🔊) 🍃 This former ranch is now run as a ecotourism destination by an extremely welcoming team who continue the work of the legendary Diane McTurk, who worked tirelessly for giant river otters. Accommodations are in spacious ranch-meets-Amerindian-style huts, and have mosquito nets and plenty of books. Activities include bird-watching, giant otter- and anteater-spotting, and swimming in the nearby Rupununi River.

The transfer from Lethem airstrip costs US$350 per vehicle.

Surama Eco Lodge   LODGE $$$
(☑653-7160; https://suramaecolodge.com; Surama; huts per person incl full board & activities from G$39,000; 🔊) 🍃 Just outside the Amerindian village of the same name, Surama boasts thriving rainforest and rich birdlife – indeed, yellow-rumped caciques nest right outside the four simple cabins that surround the striking two-floor restaurant and birding platform here. Rooms have running water and solar power, while a number of cheaper cabins can be found a short distance away.

The village of Surama, which collectively owns the lodge, will impress you with its totem pole and innovative approach to tourism. Local guides teach guests about daily life, including cassava processing and medicinal-plant usage. There are plenty of hiking, bird-watching and dugout canoe trips on offer too.

❶ Getting There & Away

Buses leave both Georgetown (p800) and Lethem (p807) between 5pm and 6pm every evening, and both pass through the North Rupununi, including the town of Annai. The bus from Georgetown arrives in the North Rupununi the following morning, having crossed the Essequibo at the Kurukupari Crossing at 6am. The bus from Lethem arrives around 8pm.

There is an airstrip in Annai, but it currently only takes chartered services, as the scheduled TGA flight between Georgetown and Lethem, which often used to stop in Annai, now uses a plane that is too big to land here.

South Rupununi

The South Rupununi is the wildest, most remote and least developed part of the vast Rupununi grasslands, and any trip here is a guaranteed adventure. Setting out under a vast sky along red dirt tracks through the savanna, with distant hills and bluish mountains in the distance, is an unforgettable experience. You'll meet dozens of local characters out here, from Amerindian village chiefs to authentic cowboys who make their living on the vast cattle ranches that still dot the landscape. Many of these have now turned to tourism and staying on one is bound to be a highlight of your time in Guyana. In between, you'll hopefully spot giant anteaters and giant otters, be able to hike to local waterfalls, see rich birdlife, and learn the traditions and customs of those who call this wilderness home.

🏃 Activities

★ Rupununi Trails   OUTDOORS
(www.rupununitrails.com; Wichabai Ranch) This highly recommended ecotourism operator based at Wichabai Ranch (p805) has been arranging tours in Guyana for 20 years or so. Ideal for bird-watchers and wildlife photographers, Rupununi Trails specializes in river trips to remote regions, adventure tourism and bird-watching. Rates are dependent on group size and activities included, but start at around G$18,880 per person, per day.

🛏 Sleeping

Wichabai Ranch   RANCH $$
(www.wichabai.com; r incl full board per person G$16,700-33,500) This newly built ranch with three double bedrooms and plenty of hammock space is a project from the owners of Dadanawa Ranch (p806). It's one of the most comfortable options in the area, built with tourism in mind. Meals are made from the ranch livestock and gardens, while activities offered include horseback riding, bird-watching, wildlife walks, canoeing and hiking.

Best of all, there's a lake for swimming. Two independent guesthouses near to the main house are also planned.

Saddle Mountain
RANCH $$

(📞 604-5600; a.kenyon47@yahoo.com; per person incl meals & activities G$21,000; ⊘ closed May-Aug; 🛜) This small working cattle ranch 80km from Lethem has a gorgeous location at the foot of its eponymous hill, surrounded by savanna, rivers and mountains. Guest accommodations aren two brick huts with thatched roofs, each with a single and double bed. The main activity is horseback riding. Owners Tommy and Joan cook up great food and are warm and friendly company. Wildlife is everywhere and you'll quickly get pulled in to daily tasks on the ranch.

Manari Ranch
RANCH $$

(📞 668-2006; manariranch@gmail.com; per person incl meals US$25,100; 🛜) This atmospheric and stylish ranch is noticeably less rustic than others, having been renovated by dynamic owner Lisa Melville. Just a 15-minute drive north from Lethem, it's also a good alternative to staying in town. Join OJ the adopted giant otter who lives here, and enjoy the great swimming hole and a supremely laid-back vibe. Tons of activities are on offer, from horseback riding to canoe trips. The Rupununi Music & Arts festival takes place here every February. A taxi from Lethem costs G$3000.

Dadanawa Ranch
RANCH $$

(📞 668-8562; www.rupununitrails.com; hammocks/dm G$6000/14,000, r per person incl meals & activities G$36,600) 🏖 The De Frietas' remote and historic ranch is straight out of *National Geographic*, with three stilted timber guesthouses facing the distant Kanuku Mountains. Rooms are basic, with mosquito nets, but have an undeniable cowboy charm to them as well as solar power. Here you'll fill your days tracking harpy eagles, jaguars, giant anteaters, anacondas and the red siskin finch.

More adventurous types can join rangers in ranch work or even riding on a cattle drive to Lethem. Meals with the hammock/dorm option cost G$1000 for breakfast and G$2000 for dinner – a really great deal.

ℹ Getting Around

All ranches will offer guests 4WD transfers from Lethem, although these are not cheap given the high cost of gas down here. There are some minibus connections from Lethem to villages in the surrounding area, but none of them serve the ranches. Your only alternative to a transfer is to hire a motorbike and driver, which can save you some money, although not a huge amount. Ask around in Lethem at least 24 hours before you want to travel.

Lethem
POP 3000

Sleepy Lethem is the 'capital' of the Rupununi; it's where buses and flights from Georgetown arrive, and it has a decent array of services for travellers passing through on their way to the various ranches and nearby. Local *vaqueros* (cowboys) and visiting Brazilian shoppers mingle on the red dust streets that surround the airstrip, and very little goes on here, though it's an important local center in a region that is otherwise virtual wilderness. Its annual rodeo, held over the Easter weekend, is a massive event attracting thousands, and a great time to visit.

☞ Tours

Bushmasters ADVENTURE
(📞 682-4175; www.bushmasters.co.uk; Lethem) One- and two-week jungle-survival courses, as well as cowboy holidays, horse-riding tours and safaris, mostly through the Rupununi.

🛏 Sleeping & Eating

Nobody comes to Lethem for the food, though if meat is your thing, you're in the right place – the towns has several Brazilian *churrascaria* serving up plates of grilled meats. Fish is also widely available, but vegetarians will struggle.

Takutu Hotel HOTEL $
(📞 772-2034; takutuhotel@gmail.com; Takutu Dr, Lethem; d from G$6000-20,000, hammocks G$1000; ❄🛜) The best all-rounder in Lethem, the Takutu has everything from cheap and clean air-conditioned doubles to fancier suites and a *benab* (palm-thatched hut), where you can sling a hammock for G$1000. There's an on-site restaurant and a bar, which can get loud – especially on Wednesday karaoke nights.

Adventure
Guianas Guesthouse GUESTHOUSE $
(📞 227-4713, 673-0039; 3 Tabatinga Drive; r G$5000; ❄🛜) The rooms here are on the small and dark side, but they're absolutely fine, making this the best budget option in Lethem. There's a bar and restaurant on-site, and Adventure Guianas can also arrange tours and transfers.

ℹ Information

Bring all the cash you need when visiting the South Rupununi. The only place to get more money is at the **GBTI Bank** (⊘ 24hrs) in Lethem.

ⓘ GETTING TO BRAZIL

Getting to Lethem

Lethem gets several flights a day from Georgetown (G$30,000, one hour) on both Trans Guyana Airways (p811) and Air Services Limited (p811). It's also the terminus for the epic, if extremely uncomfortable and bumpy, bus ride from Georgetown (G$10,000-14,000, 15 to 20 hours). These leave both Lethem and Georgetown around 5pm–6pm each evening and go overnight, arriving around lunchtime the next day (depending on how much rain there has been). The main operators are **Carly's** (☑616-5984, 699-1339; cnr Robb & Oronoque Sts; 1-way Georgetown–Lethem G$14,000), **P&A Bus Services** (☑628-6001, 225-5058; 75 Church St) and **BD Express** (☑678-9998; 36/37 Cummings St).

Crossing the Border

A Brazilian-built bridge – with a cool lane-crossing system that switches from Guyana's left-hand driving to Brazil's right-hand driving – straddles the Takutu River from Lethem on Guyana's side to Bonfim, Brazil, on the other. Stamp out of customs and immigration at the bridge on the Guyana side and stamp into the corresponding office at the Brazil end. There are no fees at the border and the immigration office hours are 7am to 7pm daily.

Note that American, Canadian and Australian nationals need visas. These are available in Georgetown – the Brazilian consulate in Lethem does not issue them – and you should count on a week for processing.

Moving On

There are five buses to Boa Vista (R$20, 1¼ hours) between 7am and 2pm daily. The 'Federales' customs officials on the Brazilian side of the bridge are very friendly and can update you on the schedule. From Boa Vista, planes and buses connect to further destinations.

UNDERSTAND GUYANA

Guyana Today

Oil is the big topic of conversation in Guyana these days – more precisely, how efforts to extract the country's impressive deposits of the stuff will affect its moribund economy (it's currently the third-poorest country in the western hemisphere) as well as its status as one of the last real wildernesses left on earth.

In 2017 ExxonMobil announced that it had discovered offshore reserves of around 3.2 billion barrels of oil at a site 193km from the coast. Production is expected to begin in 2020, and Guyana is bracing itself for massive social change as an unprecedented source of income begins flooding the country.

The government, wary of the fate of other nations where oil has been discovered, is attempting to make sure that the oil boom will profit the country as a whole, leading to the creation of a sovereign wealth fund as well as desperately needed investment in infrastructure, rather than just the enrichment of foreign investors and a few local oligarchs. The challenge remains enormous, however, when you consider that over 60% of Guyana's population lives outside the country, and that this figure includes the vast majority of people with a higher education and skills that could prove so vital in managing the transformation of the country into a wealthy oil nation. Efforts have been made to call patriotic Guyanese back home, but have yet to bear much fruit.

The election of David A Granger to the presidency in 2015, with his anti-money-laundering, constitutional-reform and crime-fighting agenda, left many people hopeful of a better future for the country. While his presidency hasn't delivered everything it promised, there is evidence that the levels of rampant corruption a decade ago have decreased, though observers, international and domestic, agree that there is still a huge distance to go.

Guyana has been the seat of Caricom (The Caribbean Community, an economic union with 15 members who share a single market) since 1973 and has strong relations with other Caribbean nations, particularly Trinidad and Tobago, and Barbados. A long-running dispute with neighboring Venezuela over the border between the two countries is ongoing, however, so current relations are strained and there's no official border crossing. Venezuela and Guyana share a disputed border in the Guayana Esequiba region, which has been contested since the end of the 19th century. Despite efforts at mediation, an agreement between the two countries has never been made and Guyana continues to control the territory. In 2018 the dispute was referred to the International Court of Justice by the UN Secretary General, and, perhaps unsurprisingly, the Venezuelan side has become even more determined to regain control of the area since the discovery of oil was made.

Gold and bauxite mining, and logging have greatly benefited the top tier of Guyanese residents in recent years, although the wealth hasn't trickled down to the masses. Roads are still waiting to be paved and areas of extreme poverty are put in greater perspective by massive housing developments for the nouveau riche. Guyana stands on the cusp of great change today, though it remains to be seen whether it will be managed well or not.

History

Both Carib and Arawak peoples inhabited the land that is now Guyana before the Dutch arrived in the late 16th century. Running a plantation economy dependent on African slaves, the Dutch faced a widespread rebellion, known as the Berbice Slave Revolt, in 1763. The rebel leader, Kofi, remains a national hero despite the ultimate failure of the slaves to gain their freedom.

The British took control in 1796, and in 1831 the three colonial settlements of Essequibo, Demerara and Berbice merged to become British Guiana. After the abolition of slavery in 1834, Africans refused to work on the plantations for wages, and many established their own villages in the bush and became known as Maroons. Plantations closed or consolidated, but the sugar industry was resurrected with the introduction of indentured laborers from Portugal, India, China and other countries, drastically transforming the nation's demographic.

British Guiana was run very much as a colony until 1953, when a new constitution provided for home rule and an elected government. In 1966 the country became an independent member of the British Commonwealth with the new name, Guyana, and in 1970 it became a republic with an elected president.

For decades after independence, most of the important posts had been occupied by Afro-Guyanese, but in the past two decades Indo-Guyanese have been appointed to influential positions, fueling racial tensions. Cheddi Jagan, Guyana's first elected president, died in office in 1997 and was replaced by his US-born wife Janet, resulting in continued political friction. In 1999 Janet Jagan retired from the presidency on health grounds and named Bharrat Jagdeo her successor.

Delayed elections in 2001 resulted in entire blocks of Georgetown being set ablaze by opposition supporters. The police and protesters clashed in the capital for weeks. Fortunately, violence on this scale has not returned to Georgetown since, but this division continue to be a part of Guyanese politics. However, efforts at tolerance education have made a positive impact on Guyanese youth, and many people acknowledge that more cooperation to end racial conflict is needed.

Guyana's economy relies on commodities exports, especially bauxite, but also gold, sugar, rice, timber and shrimp.

Culture

Guyana's culture is a reflection of its colonialist plantation past. African slaves lived under severe conditions that destroyed much – but not all – of their culture. East Indian laborers, while still suffering horrendous treatment, managed to keep much of their heritage intact. The main groups of Amerindians, who reside in scattered interior settlements – Arawak, Carib, Makushi and Wapishana – still live significantly off the land. Ethnic discord comes out during election times and there's increasing distrust of Brazilians, who are perceived to want access to Guyana's natural resources. According to the country's last census, 40% of the population is Indo-Guyanese, 29% Afro-Guyanese,

20% mixed heritage, 10.5% Amerindian and 0.5% have other heritage.

Some 500,000 Guyanese live abroad, mostly in Canada, the UK, USA, and Trinidad and Tobago. Some Guyanese are concerned, and probably justifiably so, about 'brain drain,' as the country loses skilled workers overseas.

Most Afro-Guyanese are Christian, usually Anglican, but a handful are Muslim. The Indo-Guyanese population is mostly Hindu, with a sizable Muslim minority, but Hindu-Muslim friction is uncommon. Since independence, efforts have been made to recognize all relevant religions in national holidays.

Environment

Guyana is awash with rivers, including its three principal waterways (listed east to west): the Berbice, Demerara and Essequibo. The narrow strip of coastal lowland (with almost no sandy beaches) is 460km long and comprises 4% of the total land area, but is home to 90% of the population. The Dutch, using a system of drainage canals and seawalls, reclaimed much of the marshy coastal land from the Atlantic and made it available for agriculture.

Tropical rainforest covers most of the interior, though southwestern Guyana features extensive savannas between the Rupununi River and the Brazilian border.

Guyana is home to over 2000 animal species and the likelihood of seeing some of the bigger and more famous ones – such as the black caiman, giant anteater, howler monkey, peccary, capybara, giant river otter and tapir – are high. You'll probably see a slew of monkeys and, if you're lucky, spot a jaguar or harpy eagle.

SURVIVAL GUIDE

ℹ Directory A–Z

ACCESSIBLE TRAVEL

Guyana is a challenging destination for people with impaired mobility or who face other obstacles to getting around independently. While Georgetown is quite straightforward to navigate, trips to the interior are likely to be tough unless you are able to contact ranches, hotels or travel agencies in good time beforehand. Download Lonely Planet's free Accessible Travel guides from http://lptravel.to/AccessibleTravel.

ACCOMMODATIONS

In Georgetown you can expect clean guesthouses, with rooms that include shared bathrooms from around G$6000. Rainforest lodges and savanna ranches often seem expensive, but note that food and activities are often included. In the interior, the most budget-friendly accommodations are in a hammock, either your own or one provided by your hosts.

ACTIVITIES

The interior and coastal areas offer countless outdoor adventure possibilities, from river rafting, trekking and bird-watching to wildlife-viewing and fishing. Community tourism is growing, particularly in the Rupununi. Most folk arrange adventures through Georgetown's tour agencies, but independent travel is possible – though it really pays to plan ahead, as many lodges and ranches are simply not prepared for last-minute guests.

What you can't expect almost anywhere in Guyana, however, is marked hiking trails – you're effectively going to be in the wilderness anywhere you'll want to walk. With this in mind it's always best (and often essential) to go hiking with a local guide, rather than to strike out alone. One walk that is particularly notable is the expedition-level hike to Kaieteur Falls, which usually begins at the gold-mining town of Mahdia and takes three full days. It's a challenging but highly scenic trek through the rainforest, including several stretches by boat on the river, and can even involve swimming in parts.

One of the few marked hiking trails in the country is the Panorama Nature Trail on the edge of the village of Annai in the North Rupununi. This is a short but fairly challenging half-day hike, with some excellent bird-watching to be had on the way.

ELECTRICITY

Guyana uses American two-square-pronged plugs (also known as type A). Currents are 127V, 60Hz.

EMBASSIES & CONSULATES

Most countries' embassies and consulates are in Georgetown. However, many countries do not have embassies in Guyana at all. These include Australia and Germany, whose consulates in

---

SLEEPING PRICE RANGES

The following price ranges refer to a double room with private bathroom. Breakfast is not included unless otherwise stated.

$ less than G$12,000

$$ G$12,000–G$30,000

$$$ more than G$30,000

Trinidad and Tobago cover Guyana; New Zealand, which covers Guyana from its high commission in Barbados; and France and the Netherlands, whose embassies in Suriname are accredited to Guyana.

Brazilian Embassy (☎225-7970; http://georgetown.itamaraty.gov.br/en-us; 308-309 Church St) Visa processing takes three to seven days.

British High Commission (☎226-5881; www.gov.uk/world/organisations/british-high-commission-georgetown; 44 Main St; ⊗8am-4pm Mon-Thu, to 1pm Fri)

Canadian Embassy (☎227-2081; www.canadainternational.gc.ca/guyana; cnr High & Young Sts; ⊗8:30am-12:30pm Mon-Thu, to 11:30am Fri)

Surinamese Embassy (☎226-9844; 54 New Garden St; ⊗8am-noon & 1-3pm Mon-Thu, to 2.30pm Fri) Visa processing takes one to five days, tourist cards are issued on the same day.

US Embassy (☎225-4900; https://gy.usembassy.gov; 100 Young St; ⊗9am-noon & 2-4pm Mon-Thu, 9am-noon Fri)

HEALTH

Adequate medical care is available in Georgetown, at least at private hospitals, but facilities are few elsewhere. Costs are generally low.

Guyana is regarded as a yellow-fever-infected area, and your next destination may require a vaccination certificate, as does Guyana when you arrive. Typhoid, hepatitis A, diphtheria/tetanus and polio inoculations are recommended.

Chloroquine-resistant malaria is endemic, and dengue fever and chikungunya are both also dangers, particularly in the interior and even in Georgetown – protect yourself against mosquitoes and consider taking a malaria prophylaxis. The Zika virus is present in Guyana and pregnant women should not travel here at present. Cholera outbreaks have occurred in areas with unsanitary conditions, but precautions are recommended everywhere.

Local tap water is suspect, especially in Georgetown. Drink bottled water only.

INTERNET ACCESS

Wi-fi is widely available and is generally pretty reliable and free in Georgetown's hotels, restaurants and cafes. Outside Georgetown it's a different story, though nowadays most remote lodges and ranches have achingly slow wi-fi, even if you often need to pay for access.

LGBT TRAVELERS

Guyana is the only country in South America where homosexuality is still illegal and penalties are severe, with life sentences still potentially possible. However, attitudes are slowly changing, despite opposition from fiercely conservative religious groups in the country, and President David Granger has publicly voiced his support for decriminalization. In 2018 Guyana held its first ever Gay Pride Parade, which was attended by hundreds of marchers and went off without arrests or violence. LGBTIQ+ visitors to Guyana should be careful and discreet, but not discouraged from visiting the country, though requesting a double room might be problematic in some hotels.

MONEY

The Guyanese dollar (G$) is stable and pegged to the US dollar, which is widely accepted. You may also be able to spend your euros at Georgetown travel agencies. Credit cards are accepted at Georgetown's better hotels and restaurants (usually for a 5% service charge), although not at gas stations or, in general, anywhere else. Scotiabank is the easiest place to get cash advances, and its ATMs are the only ones that accept foreign cards.

Cash can be exchanged at banks, but *cambios* (foreign-exchange offices) offer better rates and less red tape. Sometimes hotels change cash for a small commission.

OPENING HOURS

Commerce awakens around 8:30am and tends to last until 4pm or so. Saturdays are half-days, if shops open at all, and Georgetown becomes a ghost town on Sundays. Hotels and cafes provide breakfast, and restaurants generally serve lunch from about 11:30am to 3pm and dinner from around 6:30pm to 10pm.

POST

Postal services are iffy and shouldn't be trusted with much more than the odd postcard. For important shipments, try these international shippers with offices in Georgetown businesses: **UPS** (Mercury Couriers; ☎227-1853; 210 Camp St) and **DHL** (USA Global Export; ☎225-7772; 50 E 5th St, Queenstown).

PUBLIC HOLIDAYS

Republic Day celebrations in February are the most important national cultural events of the year, though Hindu and Muslim religious festivals are also significant.

New Year's Day January 1

Republic Day (marking the slave rebellion of 1763) February 23

Phagwah/Holi (Hindu New Year) March/April

Good Friday/Easter Monday March/April

Labor Day May 1

Emancipation Day August 1

Diwali (Hindu Festival of Lights) October/November

Christmas Day December 25

Boxing Day December 26

Eid ul-Fitr End of Ramadan; dates vary

SAFE TRAVEL

Although Guyana's interior is tranquil and safe, Georgetown is well known for crime. This reputation may be exaggerated, but a good dose of caution and common sense is warranted.

➡ In urban areas, avoid flashing expensive items and jewelry, and be aware of others on the street.

➡ Use only registered airport taxis and drivers with official IDs (attached to their shirt pockets). When traveling from the airport do not let yourself be separated from your luggage or backpack.

➡ Hitchhiking is highly discouraged – the threat of robbery and physical danger is very real.

TELEPHONE

Hotels and restaurants generally allow free local phone calls. There are no area codes in Guyana. To dial nationally, simply dial the seven-digit number. To dial internationally, dial 00 then the access code of the country you want to call, plus the full number with area code, minus the initial zero.

SIM cards are available with local mobile companies Digicel and GT&T. Coverage is good in Georgetown and along the coast, but very unreliable outside bigger towns in the country's interior.

TOURIST INFORMATION

➡ Tourism and Hospitality Association of Guyana (p800) The government has no official tourism representative abroad, but this association works hard to attract visitors to Guyana and help them when they arrive.

➡ Iwokrama Rainforest Conservation and Development Office (p804) Another useful organization to contact in Georgetown.

➡ National Parks Commission (p802) Also based in Georgetown.

VISAS

Travelers from the USA, Canada, EU countries, Australia, New Zealand, Japan, the UK and most Caribbean countries do not need a visa; confirm with your nearest embassy or consulate. A 90-day stay is granted on arrival in Guyana with an onward ticket. If you do need a visa, file your application at least six weeks before you leave your home country. As well as a passport, carry an international yellow-fever vaccination certificate with you (although you probably won't be asked for this), and keep other immunizations up to date.

WOMEN TRAVELERS

Guyana's not-so-safe reputation should put women travelers on particular alert. It's best to avoid going out alone at night in towns and cities, and if you do so, taking a taxi is always the safest option. It is less risky to stick to well-peopled areas if walking alone during the day in Georgetown. In the interior, traveling alone should pose few problems. Women should be aware that the Zika virus is present in Guyana and so if there is any chance you are pregnant, take very strict precautions against mosquito bites.

ⓘ Getting There & Away

Travelers flying to Guyana arrive at Cheddi Jagan International Airport (p800), south of the capital. Some regional services arrive at Ogle International Airport (p800), which is closer to town and largely services domestic routes. There are no trans-Atlantic routes from Guyana. The following airlines serve Georgetown:

Caribbean Airlines (☑1800-744-2225; www. caribbean-airlines.com; 91-92 Ave of the Republic; ◷8am-3:30pm Mon-Fri, 8:30am-noon Sat) Three or four direct flights a day to Port-of-Spain in Trinidad and Tobago (70 minutes), with good connections onwards elsewhere in the Caribbean and to the US.

Copa Airlines (☑231-2491; www.copa.com; 212 Camp St) Connects to Panama City, Panama (3½ hours, four times a week).

Fly Jamaica (☑222-0227; www.fly-jamaica. com; Cheddi Jagan International Airport) Flies to Kingston, Jamaica (four hours, four times a week).

LIAT (☑222-1725; www.liat.com; Ogle International Airport) Flies from Ogle airport to Port-of-Spain, Trinidad and Tobago (70 minutes, daily), and Barbados (3½ hours, daily).

Suriname Airlines (☑225-4249, Cheddi Jagan airport office 261-2292; www.flyslm.com; cnr Duke & Barrack Sts) Connects to Paramaribo, Suriname (40 minutes, three times a week) and Miami, USA, (3½ hours, three times a week).

ⓘ Getting Around

AIR

Scheduled daily flights to Lethem and charter air services to interior destinations such as Annai, Kaieteur and Iwokrama are available from the Ogle International Airport (p800) in Georgetown. These tickets cannot generally be booked online and it's easiest to book through a local travel agency to arrange them. **Air Services Limited** (☑222-1234; www.aslgy. com; Ogle Aerodrome) and **Trans Guyana Airways** (TGA; ☑222-2525; www.transguyana. net; Ogle International Airport) each ply the Georgetown–Lethem–Georgetown route twice a day. A one-way ticket costs G$30,000. Both these airlines, plus **Roraima Airways** (☑225-9648; www.roraimaairways.com; Ogle Airstrip) arrange charter flights to various air strips in the country.

BOAT

Regular ferry services cross the Essequibo River between Charity and Bartica, with a stop at Parika (reached by paved highway from Georgetown). More frequent speedboats (river taxis) carry passengers from Parika to Bartica.

BUS

Buses are the main way for locals to get around the country, and while they're a fascinating cultural experience, they're also uncomfortable, overcrowded, noisy and in many cases downright dangerous, with drivers who seem to care little for the safety of passengers or pedestrians, terrible road conditions and the ever-present threat of pickpocketing.

The main hub in the country is Georgetown, and from here cheap local buses speed between points all over the city and suburbs, while minibuses to destinations along the coast cost up to G$1500.

The primary long-distance bus route through the country is the epic overnight trip along the country's only main road – the unsealed track that ploughs through the rainforest via Linden, Iwokrama and Annai to Lethem. Between Georgetown and Lethem one way is G$10,000–G$14,000 (15–20 hours, daily, 6pm, may be cancelled during the wet season). The best-known operators are Carly's (p807), P&A Bus Services (p807) and BD Express (p807), although there are many more.

CAR & MOTORCYCLE

Rental cars are available in Georgetown, though not from the airport at the time of writing. A Driving Permit (available for free at the Cheddi Jagan International Airport arrivals terminal) is required for car rental (an International Driving Permit won't suffice). Driving in Guyana is on the left.

If you're not in a group, getting around by motorcycle is a much cheaper option. This entails finding a local willing to take you (lodges will help with this), having small enough luggage to strap on the back of a motorbike or wear on your back, and having a very sturdy rear end (expect extremely bumpy rides).

Sample costs per person: Lethem to Dadanawa G$15,000; and Caiman House to Karanambu G$10,000. A full day's hire, including a driver and gas, should be around G$60,000.

TAXI

Many taxi companies travel between Georgetown and coastal destinations, although they cost significantly more than buses and minibuses. They can be good value for a group.

Paraguay

POP 6.9 MILLION

Best Places to Eat

➡ Paulista Grill (p820)

➡ La Cabrera (p820)

➡ Milord (p827)

➡ Hiroshima (p827)

Best Places to Stay

➡ Casa de la Y Bed & Breakfast (p826)

➡ Mbaracayú Eco-lodge (p833)

➡ Pro Cosara (p830)

➡ IDEAL Eco-hostel (p829)

➡ Santa María Hotel (p831)

Why Go?

Little-visited, little-known Paraguay is a country much misunderstood. Despite its location at the heart of the continent, it is all too often passed over by travelers who wrongly assume that a lack of mega-attractions means there's nothing to see. However, it's ideal for those keen to get off the gringo trail for a truly authentic South American experience.

Paraguay is a country of remarkable contrasts: it's rustic and sophisticated; it boasts spectacular natural reserves and massive human-made dams; it is a place where horses and carts pull up alongside Mercedes Benz vehicles, artisans' workshops abut glitzy shopping centers, and Jesuit ruins in rural villages lie just a few kilometers from interesting colonial towns. The steamy subtropical Atlantic Forest of the east is a stark contrast to the dry, spiny wilderness of the Chaco, the location of the isolated Mennonite colonies.

When to Go
Asunciona

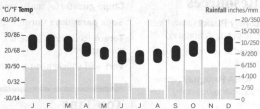

Feb Carnaval season in full swing in Encarnación.

Jun A great opportunity to try traditional foods during the Fiesta de San Juan.

Dec Thousands descend on Caacupé for the Día del Virgen celebrations.

FAST FACTS

Currency Guaraní (G)

Visas Canadians, New Zealanders and Americans need visas, others need only a valid passport.

Money ATMs widely available. Credit cards accepted in most hotels and restaurants.

Exchange Rates

Argentina	AR$1	205G
Australia	A$1	4189G
Brazil	R$1	1476G
Canada	C$1	4368G
Eurozone	€1	6654G
New Zealand	NZ$1	3920G
UK	UK£1	7606G
USA	US$1	5615G

Daily Costs

➡ Hostel bed: 80,000G; double room in a midrange hotel: 200,000G

➡ Fast-food meal: 25,000G; midrange restaurant meal: 80,000G

Resources

Lonely Planet (www.lonely planet.com/paraguay)

Senatur (www.senatur. gov.py)

FAUNA Paraguay (www. faunaparaguay.com)

Entering the Country

International arrivals by air inevitably arrive in Asunción. Paraguay's main land or river border crossings are Foz do Iguaçu (Brazil) to Ciudad del Este; Posadas (Argentina) to Encarnación; Clorinda (Argentina) to Asunción; and via the Ruta Trans-Chaco from Bolivia. Minor border crossings include a ferry between Ciudad del Este and Puerto Iguazú (Argentina) and an adventurous boat ride to remote Puerto Cano (Argentina) from Pilar. There are no charges at any Paraguayan land or river border crossings.

TWO WEEK ITINERARY

Start with a historical tour of Asunción, take day trips to Yaguarón (for the Franciscan church), Caacupé (for the basilica) and San Bernardino (to mix with high society). From here, head east to the jungle lodge at Mbaracayú Biosphere Reserve. Back in civilization at Ciudad del Este you can do some shopping, or visit the awe-inspiring Itaipú Dam nearby. It's only a short day trip to the breathtaking Salto del Monday, and you'll have time to nip across the border to Brazil and Argentina to compare it with Iguazú Falls. A night in the forest at Hotel Tirol will prepare you for another few days' bird-watching in the wilderness at Parque Nacional San Rafael. After all this moving around, you'll be glad to relax on the Paraná river beach and enjoy the top-class restaurants in trendy Encarnación. It's also a great base for visiting the nearby Jesuit missions of Trinidad and Jesús. When you're ready for a change of scene, cross the international bridge to Posadas, Argentina.

Essential Food & Drink

Asado Grilled meats are the focal point of every social event.

Chipa Cheese bread made with manioc flour.

Chipa guasú Hot maize pudding with cheese and onion.

Sopa paraguaya Cornbread with cheese and onion.

Tereré Iced yerba maté tea, drunk ubiquitously and constantly.

Vori-vori Chicken soup with cornmeal balls.

Top Tips

➡ Drinking *tereré* is the ultimate Paraguayan pasttime.

➡ National snack *chipa* is on sale throughout the country, but it is better in the south (Coronel Bogado is the *chipa* capital).

➡ It's worth paying extra for air-conditioning in steamy Paraguay. However, prepare for freezing buses as most drivers blast the air-con!

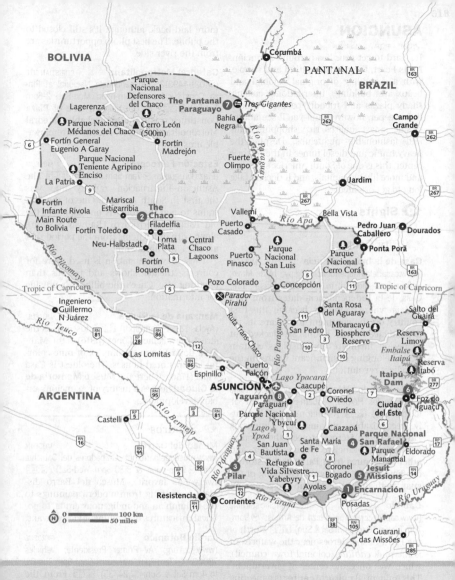

Paraguay Highlights

1 Carnaval (p823) Partying until well after dawn in hedonistic Encarnación.

2 The Chaco (p835) Watching a jaguar laze in the shade, sleeping under billions of stars.

3 Pilar (p829) Making a difference by volunteering on scientific and social projects

in the quaint, colonial City of Birds.

4 Parque Nacional San Rafael (p830) Bird-watching in Paraguay's most biodiverse reserve.

5 Jesuit Missions (p830) Exploring the picturesque remnants of a unique culture.

6 Itaipú Dam (p832) Marvelling at this damned big piece of engineering.

7 The Pantanal Paraguayo (p834) Ogling the animals in Paraguay's corner of this wet wilderness.

8 Yaguarón (p823) Admiring the ornate interior of the Franciscan church.

ASUNCIÓN

📞 021 / POP 2.2 MILLION

It's hard to get your head around Asunción. At its heart, the city is beautiful and simple, with a sprinkling of original colonial and beaux arts buildings, international cuisine, shady plazas and friendly people. Probe a little deeper, however, and you'll see another side: smart suburbs, ritzy shopping malls and fashionable nightclubs. Despite the heavy traffic and diesel fumes in the historic center, this is one of South America's greener and more likable capitals, and it doesn't take long to get oriented.

⊙ Sights

⊙ City Center

Casa de la Independencia   MUSEUM
(www.casadelaindependencia.org.py; 14 de Mayo; ⊙8am-6pm Mon-Fri, to 1pm Sat) FREE The Casa de la Independencia dates from 1772 and is where Paraguay became the first country on the continent to declare its independence in 1811. Rooms are decked out in period furniture and displays contain items belonging to significant figures in the bloodless revolution.

Panteón de los Héroes   HISTORIC BUILDING
(Plaza de los Héroes; ⊙6am-6:30pm Mon-Sat, to noon Sun) FREE Asunción's most instantly recognizable building, the imposing Panteón de los Héroes protects the remains of Mariscal Francisco Solano López and other key figures from Paraguay's historical conflicts. There is a regular changing of the guard with all the usual pomp and ceremony.

Cabildo   HISTORIC BUILDING
(www.cabildoccr.gov.py; Plaza de Armas; ⊙9am-7pm Tue-Fri, 10am-5pm Sat & Sun) FREE North of the Plaza de los Héroes near the waterfront is the pink *cabildo* (colonial town council), which was once the center of government. This influential **cultural center** is a meeting place for bohemian thinkers, hosting regular cultural events and exhibitions by local artists, historians and academics.

Palacio López   PALACE
(Paraguayo Independiente) The grand pink Palacio López is the seat of government. During the early years of independence you could be shot for merely looking at the exterior! These days, despite being the seat of government, you will find security rather more laid back, although it's still closed to the public. The best photo opportunities are from the river side.

Catedral Metropolitana   CHRISTIAN SITE
(📞021-449512; Independencia Nacional at Plaza Constitución; ⊙8am-noon Mon-Sat, 2-6pm Tue-Fri) FREE On the eastern side of Plaza Constitución is the unremarkable Catedral Metropolitana, with its equally unremarkable museum.

Estación Ferrocarril   MUSEUM
(Plaza Uruguaya; ⊙7am-5pm Mon-Fri) FREE The Asunción–Encarnación railway line was the first in South America. One of the first trains to run the route is on display at the old Estación Ferrocarril (Railway Station), along with other items from the period that are decaying decadently.

These days the station is used more for concerts, theater shows and recitals than anything else. Check the billboards outside for information.

Manzana de la Rivera   MUSEUM
(Ayolas 129; ⊙7am-9pm) FREE Just across the street from Palacio López (p816) is the Manzana de la Rivera, a complex of nine colorful and restored houses. The oldest is Casa Viola (1750), where the **Museo Memoria de la Ciudad** houses a history of Asunción's urban development.

⊙ Suburbs

Museo del Barro   MUSEUM
(www.museodelbarro.net; Grabadores del Cabichuí s/n; ⊙9am-noon & 3:30-8pm Wed-Sat) FREE Everyone's favorite, Museo del Barro displays everything from modern paintings to pre-Columbian and indigenous crafts, to political caricatures of prominent Paraguayans.

Jardín Botánico   GARDENS
(www.jbza.org; Av Primer Presidente; 7000G; ⊙7am-7pm; museums 9am-6pm Tue-Fri, to 4pm Sat & Sun; 🚌24, 35) FREE From the center, Av Artigas runs approximately 6km to the Jardín Botánico. The former estate of the ruling López dynasty, it now houses the city **zoo**, a small **nature reserve** and a couple of **historical buildings**: Carlos Antonio López humble colonial house and his son Francisco Solano López former mansion.

Take bus 24 or 35 from Cerro Corá.

Cementerio de la Recoleta   CEMETERY
(Av Mariscal López) FREE This cemetery, 3km east of the center along Av Mariscal López,

is a maze of incredible mausoleums as Asunción's wealthy try to do outdo each other in the grandeur of their resting places.

Conmebol
MUSEUM

(www.conmebol.com; Av Sudamericana Km 12, Luque; ⊙9am-noon & 3-6pm Mon-Fri) The headquarters of Conmebol, the South American football confederation, is in Luque, on the road to the airport. It houses an impressive museum depicting the sport's history on the continent.

Activities

Intercultural Experience
VOLUNTEERING

(📱021-44-3630; www.ie.org.py; Caballero 1102) Volunteer opportunities involving cultural exchange.

🎓 Courses

IDIPAR
LANGUAGE

(📱021-44-7896; www.idipar.com.py; Manduvirá 963, ⊙8am-8pm Mon-Fri, to noon Sat) Spanish and Guaraní courses with homestay options.

Centro Cultural Paraguayo-Americano
LANGUAGE

(📱021-22-4831; www.ccpa.edu.py; Av España 352) Always lots happening at the CCPA, including English- and Spanish-language courses, social events and the chance to meet Paraguayans keen to speak English.

Alianza Francesa
LANGUAGE

(📱021-21-0503; www.alianzafrancesa.edu.py; Estigarribia 1039, ⊙9am-7pm Mon-Fri, 8:30am-4pm Sat) A meeting place for those who like events of a Gallic flavor, including French-language courses.

Instituto Cultural Paraguayo Alemán
LANGUAGE

(📱021-20-9060; www.icpa-gz.org.py; Juan de Salazar 310; ⊙9am-7pm Mon-Fri, to 1:30pm Sat) This operation offers German-language courses and other events with a Germanic theme.

👉 Tours

DTP
TOURS

(📱021-22-1816; www.dtp.com.py; Brúguez 353; ⊙8am-6pm Mon-Fri) Reliable tour operator/travel agent that can organize trips around the country.

🎉 Festivals & Events

AcervaPy
BEER

(www.acervapy.com; ⊙vary) The national craftbrewers association organizes regular

---

---

beer-related events, including the annual anniversary party where brewers showcase their creative wares accompanied by live music and traditional Paraguayan food.

🛏 Sleeping

Accommodations are more expensive in Asunción than in the rest of the country, but it's unlikely to bust your budget.

🛏 City Center

Isla Francia
HOSTEL $

(📱0983-39-3424; Eligio Ayala 1036; dm/r 50,000/140,000G; ✆❄🔊🖥) How many hostels have a pool AND a solarium? This one is in a classic old building with wrought-iron balconies and something of a farmhouse feel to the decor. Excellent attention.

Palmas del Sol
HOTEL $$

(📱021-44-9485; www.hotelpalmasdelsol.com; Av España 202; s/d 170,000/231,000G; ❄@🔊🖥) Despite its location on a noisy central road, this place is a real oasis with a quiet courtyard and tastefully functional rooms. The breakfast is a treat. Relaxing on a poolside sun lounger, you'll feel a million miles from the traffic fumes outside.

El Nómada
HOSTEL $$

(📱0992-27-2946; www.hostel-asuncion-paraguay.com; Iturbe 1156; dm/s/d 55,000/106,000/157,000G; ❄🔊🖥) Colorful and cute, with a rustic, colonial style, this place has a great central location.

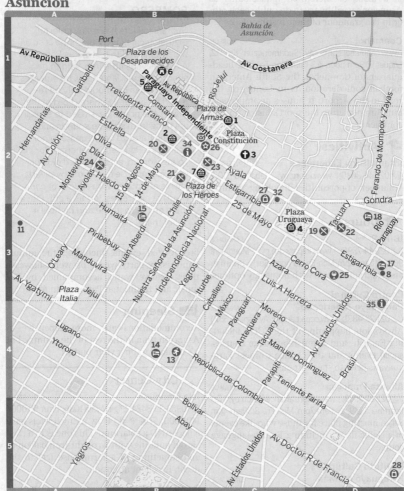

El Viajero Hostel & Suites HOSTEL $$
(☎021-44-4563; www.elviajerohostels.com; Alberdi 734; dm/s/d 60,000/150,000G/185,000G; ❄@🛜☲) Part of a successful chain of South American hostels, this old colonial mansion has air-conditioned dorms, a spacious garden and a refreshing splash pool.

Gran Hotel del Paraguay HOTEL $$$
(☎021-20-0051; www.granhoteldelparaguay. com.py; cnr De la Residenta & Pucheu; s/d 460,000/590,000G; 🅿❄@🛜☲) Dripping with the kind of colonial-era luxury that you will either love or hate, this historic hotel is said to be the place where the national anthem was first heard in July 1860. Prices drop during winter.

🛏 Suburbs

Portal del Sol HOTEL $$
(☎021-60-9395; www.portaldelsol.com; Roa 1455, c/ Sta Teresa; s/d 245,000/290,000G; 🅿❄@🛜☲) Spacious rooms, mammoth breakfast, a pleasant splash pool, good restaurant and airport pickup. Out by the Shopping del Sol in a plush residential area, this is one of the most popular hotels with tour groups, so book ahead.

Asunción

Sights
1 Cabildo	C2
2 Casa de la Independencia	B2
3 Catedral Metropolitana	C2
4 Estación Ferrocarril	C3
5 Manzana de la Rivera	B1
6 Palacio López	B1
7 Panteón de los Héroes	B2

Activities, Courses & Tours
8 Alianza Francesa	D3
9 Centro Cultural Paraguayo-Americano	E3
10 DTP	F4
11 IDIPAR	A3
12 Instituto Cultural Paraguayo Alemán	E3
13 Intercultural Experience	B4

Sleeping
14 El Nómada	B4
15 El Viajero Hostel & Suites	B3
16 Gran Hotel del Paraguay	F3
17 Isla Francia	D3
18 Palmas del Sol	D3

Eating
19 Bar San Roque	D3
20 Bellini	B2
21 Confitería Bolsi	B2
22 La Flor de la Canela	D3
23 Lido Bar	C2
24 Taberna Española	A2

Drinking & Nightlife
25 Britannia Pub	D3

Entertainment
26 Teatro Municipal	C2

Shopping
27 Folklore	C2
28 Mercado Cuatro	D5
Open-Air Market	(see 7)

Information
29 Argentine Embassy	F3
30 Brazilian Embassy	F4
31 French Embassy	F3
32 Immigration Office	C2
33 Instituto Geográfico Militar	F2
34 Senatur	B2
35 Touring y Automóvil Club Paraguayo	D4

La Misión Hotel Boutique BOUTIQUE HOTEL $$$
(☑021-62-1800; www.lamision.com.py; Estígarribia 4990, Villa Morra; r from 980,000G; ❄@🖵⏛) A charismatic Jesuit-style boutique hotel close to Shopping Mariscal López. Individually decorated rooms range from minimalist to classy and cozy, and extend to the oddly floral octagon rooms. Rooms are 25% cheaper on weekends.

Posada del Cielo HOTEL $$$
(☑021-66-4882; www.hotelposadasdelcielo.com.py; Del Maestro 1416, Villa Morra; s/d 250,000/300,000G; ❄@🖵⏛) Colorful Posada del Cielo makes you feel like you are staying in somebody's house, while packing a number of individually decorated rooms into the illusion. Some rooms are a little pokey, though, so ask to see a selection.

✖ Eating

Asunción's eating options reflect its cultural diversity: sophisticated local, Asian and international foods abound and even vegetarians are catered for. Carnivores, however, will find the ubiquitous all-you-can-eat grill restaurants hard to resist. Though there are some good pit stops in the center, Asunción's most refined restaurants are in the eastern suburbs, especially Villa Morra.

✖ City Center

For typical Paraguayan food, try out the million-and-one options south of the center along Av Figueroa, known locally as La Quinta Avenida, or sample the *asadito* stands (mini meat kebabs with mandioca; 3000G) on street corners.

Lido Bar   DELI $
(cnr Chile & Palma; mains 7000-35,000G) Asunción's historic diner is famous for its sidewalk tables opposite the Panteón de los Héroes, making it the city's most popular meeting place. Though it serves a variety of Paraguayan specialties in generous portions, the location is better than the food.

Bellini   ITALIAN $$
(Palma near 15 de Agosto; 35,000-45,000G; ⊙ noon-3pm & 7pm-midnight) Join the queue to pick your ingredients and watch while the chefs cook up a delicious plate of fresh pasta before your eyes. Hugely popular and deservedly so.

Bar San Roque   INTERNATIONAL $$
(cnr Tacuary & Ayala; mains 30,000-85,000G; ⊙ 8am-3pm & 6pm-midnight Mon-Sat, 10am-3pm Sun) An Asunción landmark, with a warm turn-of-the-20th-century atmosphere. The counter displays fresh goods from the family farm and the wine list is as impressive as the menu of fish and meat dishes. As many locals will attest, it's a culinary must, with service to match.

Confitería Bolsi   INTERNATIONAL $$
(Estrella 399; mains 25,000-85,000G; ⊙ 24hr; ✖ 🗑 🖉) More than a *confitería* (cafe/snack bar), this traditional place has been going since 1960 and serves everything from sandwiches to curried rabbit and garlic pizza. Try the *surubí cosa nostra*, a delicious fish dish.

Taberna Española   SPANISH $$$
(Ayolas 631; mains 33,000-195,000G; ⊙ 11am-2:30pm & 7-11:30pm Mon-Thu & Sun, to 1am Fri & Sat) A slice of Spain in Paraguay. The energetic ambience of this 'food museum,' with dangling bottles, cooking implements and bells, is only the backdrop for good-value tapas and paella.

La Flor de la Canela   PERUVIAN $$$
(Tacuary 167; mains 40,000-95,000G) The Peruvian food is more genuine than this smart place's faux-Inca statues. The menu is dominated by fish and *mariscos* (seafood), and the *ceviche* (marinated raw seafood) is good.

✖ Suburbs

On Sunday it's best to head to one of the large shopping centers such as Mariscal López (p821), Shopping del Sol (p821) or Paseo La Galería (p821), all with food courts.

★ Paulista Grill   BRAZILIAN $$$
(Av San Martín near Spano, Villa Morra; buffet week/weekends 85,000/100,000G) One of the city's most famous all-you-can-eat restaurants. There are more than 15 different cuts of mouthwatering meats, and salad, pasta and sushi bars to peruse, as well as creative desserts. Attentive table service.

Ciervo Blanco   BARBECUE $$$
(🖉 021-21-4514; cnr Flores & Radio Operadores del Chaco, Barrio Pinozá; meals 45,000-75,000G; ⊙ dinner Tue-Sat) If you're looking for a traditional Paraguayan experience, this place just southeast of the center has it. Juicy *asado* (barbecue), traditional music and bottle dancers will keep you entertained.

Le Sommelier   FRENCH $$$
(Roa near Av Santa Teresa; mains 55,000-90,000G) Not as pretentious as you might expect from the name (wine recommendations for each dish apart), this is a cozy little restaurant with an inventive menu.

Hacienda Las Palomas   MEXICAN $$$
(Guido Spano 1481, Villa Morra; mains 55,000-80,000G; ⊙ 7pm-midnight) Hacienda Las Palomas manages to capture the vibrant colors of Mexico in the decor as much as it captures the country's vibrant flavors on the plate. With friendly waitstaff and generous portions, it's a refined yet casual dining experience.

La Cabrera   ARGENTINE $$$
(🖉 0984-50-5178; Av Sta Teresa 2495; meats from 50,000G; ✖ 🗑) Hugely popular Argentine grill, with delicious meat dishes accompanied by an astonishing array of minisalads,

sauces and garnishes. See if you can remember what they all are! Book ahead for Sunday, especially at lunch time. It gets busy fast!

Drinking & Nightlife

Some bars and all discos charge admission for men (women usually get in free) if you arrive after 10pm. Options are limited in the center and most of the flashy clubs are a short cab ride east of downtown. For a more upmarket (and pricier) scene, head to Paseo Carmelitas off Av España.

Palo Santo Brewing Co.   CRAFT BEER
(Del Maestro; ⊙ 5pm-1am Tue-Sun) This megalithic bar in a brewery was one of the pioneers of the Paraguayan craft-beer scene, and has one of the best selections of regional beers in Asunción.

Sacramento Brewing Co.   CRAFT BEER
(Av Santísimo Sacramento 655; beer from 15,000G; ⊙ 6pm 1am Tue-Sun) Draught-only craft-beer bar selling inventive, locally brewed beers. A very lively place to sample brews.

Britannia Pub   PUB
(Cerro Corá 851; ⊙ Tue-Sun) Casually hip with an air-conditioned international ambience and outdoor patio, the Brit Pub is a favorite among foreigners and locals alike for its pub grub. It even has its own beer!

Seven   CLUB
(Shopping del Sol, Av Aviadores del Chaco; cover 30,000G) A jumping disco-bar where the young and the restless party to techno and house tunes until the sun comes up.

☆ Entertainment

Asunción has several venues for live music and theater, such as the **Teatro Municipal** (cnr Presidente Franco & Alberdi) and the Estación Ferrocarril (p816); the season is March to October. Large international music concerts usually play at the **Jockey Club** (www.jcp.com.py/index.php/galeria/27-conciertos/84-calendario-de-conciertos; Hipódromo de Asunción, Curupay).

Asunción's main shopping malls have multiscreen cinemas. Films are often in English with Spanish subtitles. Tickets start from around 25,000G, but may be more at weekends. See www.cines.com.py for schedules.

🔒 Shopping

Asunción offers Paraguay's best souvenir shopping. The typical Paraguayan souvenir is a set of *matero, bombilla* and *termo*

(gourd, straw and flask) for *tereré* (iced herbal tea) consumption. These are ubiquitous, though quality varies. The ground floor of the Senatur office (p822) has examples of local *artesanías* (handicrafts) from around the country, ranging from intricate Luque silver to fine *ñandutí* (lace).

A small **antique market** is held along Palma on a Sunday.

Paseo La Galería   MALL
(Av Sta Teresa) Paraguayan malls are more than just shopping centers, and shopping in them is seen as a status symbol. This is Asunción's newest and glitziest mall.

Mercado Cuatro   MARKET
Mercado Cuatro is a lively trading lot occupying the wedge formed by the intersection of Avs Francia and Pettirossi and stretching over several blocks. It sells everything from produce to Chinese imports.

Shopping del Sol   MALL
(cnr Aviadores del Chaco & González) Shopping del Sol is one of Asunción's biggest and most established malls.

Shopping Mariscal López   MALL
(cnr Quesada & Charles de Gaulle; ☎) A trendy mall and a major city landmark.

Folklore   ARTS & CRAFTS
(cnr Caballero & Estigarribia) A good bet for quality Paraguayan handicrafts, though not cheap.

Open-Air Market   MARKET
(Plaza de los Héroes) Stocked with *ao po'i* or *lienzo* (loose-weave cotton) garments and other indigenous crafts, it expands considerably on weekends.

ℹ Information

DANGERS & ANNOYANCES
Asunción is a comparatively safe city but, as with anywhere else, keep your eye on your belongings, particularly at the bus station. On Sunday the city center is a ghost town. Plaza Uruguaya and the streets around Palma are frequented by prostitutes after dark – you may be solicited. There are reports of occasional robberies along the *costanera* riverside road.

MEDICAL SERVICES
Medical services in private hospitals in Paraguay are surprisingly well equipped and efficient. Those in public hospitals are not.
Hospital Bautista (☑ 021-688-9000; Av República Argentina) Recommended private hospital.

ⓘ GETTING TO ARGENTINA

The San Ignacio de Ayolas bridge links Puerto Falcón with Clorinda in Argentina, and customs offices (24 hours) are found at either end. A local bus marked Falcón leaves hourly from Mercado Cuatro (p821) and passes the stop at Av República Argentina outside the Asunción bus terminal (p822). There are no organized package trips for this crossing and the ferry crossing to Clorinda is not recommended for tourists.

MONEY

Along Palma and its side streets it is hardly possible to walk a block without money changers shouting *'cambio'* at you, but rates are better in the numerous *casas de cambio* (currency exchanges) and banks that line this road. There are ATMs and money changers at the bus station and airport.

POST

Main post office (Alberdi near Constant; ⏱7am-7pm Mon-Fri) In a historical colonial mansion. Send your mail *certificado* (registered) if you want it to have a hope of arriving.

TOURIST INFORMATION

Senatur periodically produces the *Quick Guide* with information about upcoming events. It's available at hotels and the **tourist office** (☎021-45-0965; www.senatur.gov.py; Palma 468; ⏱7am-7pm).

SEAM (☎021-287-9000; www.seam.gov.py; Av Madame Lynch 3500; ⏱7am-1pm Mon-Fri) Responsible for the maintenance of national parks.

ⓘ Getting There & Away

AIR

Asunción's tiny airport, **Aeropuerto Internacional Silvio Pettirossi** (☎021-64-5600; Autopista Silvio Pettirossi, Luque; 🛜), is in the suburb of Luque, 20km to the east.

BUS

Asunción's **bus terminal** (☎021-55-1740; http://toa.asuncion.gov.py; Av República Argentina) is several kilometers southeast of downtown. City buses 8 and 31 run along Oliva to the terminal, while buses 14, 18.2 and 38 run along Haedo.

Purchase long-distance tickets at the company offices on the 2nd floor of the bus terminal. Don't be put off by the touts shouting destinations at you – take your time to choose the company you want.

Buses from Asunción

DESTINATION	COST (G)	DURATION (HR)
Buenos Aires (Argentina)	300,000-350,000	18-21
Ciudad del Este	60,000-90,000	4½-6
Concepción	55,000-70,000	4½-6
Encarnación	60,000-95,000	6-7
Filadelfia	110,000	8
Pilar	60,000-65,000	5-6
Rio de Janeiro (Brazil)	450,000	30
Santa Cruz (Bolivia)	350,000-450,000	20-24
São Paulo (Brazil)	300,000-400,000	18-20

ⓘ Getting Around

TO/FROM THE AIRPORT

Buses displaying *'Aeropuerto'* signs head out along Av Aviadores del Chaco between the airport and the center (2200G). Airport taxis are expensive (from 100,000G to the center), but if you flag one down on the road outside it's half the price.

BUS

Noisy, bone-rattling kamikaze-like city buses (2200G) go almost everywhere, but few run after 10pm. Air-conditioned services are more expensive and less frequent (3600G). Nearly all city buses start their route at the western end of Oliva and post their destinations in the front window.

TAXI

Taxis are metered and reasonable but tack on a surcharge late at night and on Sunday. A taxi from the center to the bus terminal costs about 50,000G.

AROUND ASUNCIÓN

Circuito de Oro

Prepare yourself for a taste of rural and historical Paraguay in the lazy villages that surround the capital. Though there is no set route or defined itinerary for visiting them, the historic satellite towns around Asunción are dubbed the Circuito de Oro or Circuito Central by the tourist industry. This series of communities is dominated by colonial buildings and observes long siestas, disturbed only by occasional ox- or horse-drawn carts clacking up dusty streets.

◉ Sights

★ Yaguarón Church   CHURCH
(Ruta Mariscal López) `FREE` This 18th-century Franciscan church is a landmark of colonial architecture that is not to be missed. The simple design of the exterior, with its separate wooden bell tower, belies the extraordinary beauty of the painted and carved interior, a masterpiece of religious art and one of the most ornate churches in South America.

San Buenaventura has hourly departures (5000G, one hour) to Yaguarón from Asunción bus terminal's platform 30.

Basilica de Caacupé   CHURCH
(O'Leary) `FREE` Paraguay's answer to the Vatican City, the enormous Basilica de Caacupé looks quite out of place in this otherwise quiet provincial town. Though modern, it is still impressive, and the mural-lined stairs leading up to the bell tower are quite exquisite.

Caacupé is 54km east of Asunción (7000G, two hours). Bus company Empresa Villa Serrana departs every 10 minutes from platform 35 on the ground floor of the Asunción terminal (p822).

Itauguá

Itauguá's women are famous for their unique weaving of multicolored spiderweb ñandutí (lace – ñandú means 'spider' in Guaraní). These exquisite pieces range in size from doilies to bedspreads. Smaller ones cost only a few dollars but larger ones are upward of 250,000G. In July the town celebrates its annual **Festival de Ñandutí**.

La Itaugueña buses make the 32km trip approximately hourly for Itauguá from outside Asunción bus terminal (p822).

Areguá

Areguá is renowned for its ceramics, displayed en masse along the main street. The historic cobbled lanes are lined with exquisite colonial homes, and the village atmosphere is completed with a church perched on the hill and an enviable position overlooking **Lago Ypacaraí**.

La Aregueña buses run the 27km to Areguá every half hour from outside the Asunción bus terminal (p822).

Ferries (30,000G, 25 minutes) between San Bernadino and Areguá operate in the high season.

Piribebuy

Piribebuy is a rural town that was briefly the capital of the nation during the War of the Triple Alliance (1865–70). With Asunción captured, it became the site of a famous siege in 1869, when an army of children led by the local schoolteacher bravely held off the invading Brazilians. The remarkable events are recounted in the small **museum** (Mariscal Estigarribia cnr Yegros, Piribebuy; ⊙ 7:30am-noon & 2-6pm Mon-Fri).

Empresa Piribebuy buses run 75km every 45 minutes from platform 35 in the *subsuelo* (basement) of the Asuncion bus terminal.

San Bernardino

📞 0512 / POP 9,500

Renowned as the elite escape for the privileged of Asunción, tranquil 'San Ber' is a trendy place to relax or party: pubs, discos, upmarket hotels and restaurants line the shady cobbled streets of Lago Ypacaraí's eastern shore. Despite its reputation, there's plenty for budget travelers as well. In high season a **pleasure boat** takes passengers for

---

CARNAVAL!

Paraguayan-style Carnaval might not be on the same scale or as famous as Rio's, but if you are young and looking for a wild party, then you may find it a lot more fun. More bare flesh, louder music and obligatory crowd involvement all make for a mad night out. Don't forget your *lanzanieves* (spray snow) and a pair of sunglasses (you don't want that stuff in your eyes!), pick your place in the stands and get ready to party hard with the locals – it's surprisingly infectious!

Carnaval dates vary from year to year, but usually includes at least every weekend in February. The Carnaval parade ground, Sambadromo (p825), is along Av Costanera, which is Encarnación's main strip for nightlife. Tickets (from 60,000G) can be bought in advance around the city, at the offices in front of the Sambodromo or from touts on the night at a slightly higher price. Gates open around 9pm, but the action really starts around 11pm. It's all over by 2am, when everybody piles into the local discos.

Southern & Eastern Paraguay

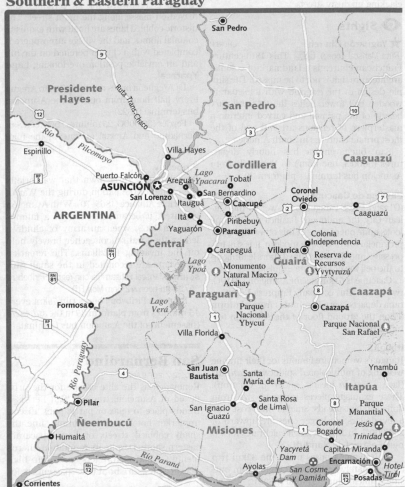

short cruises on the lake. Unfortunately, you won't want to swim in the lake – it's filthy.

AventuraXtrema (Peatonal cnr Hassler) has adrenaline-fueled adventure tours and ferry tickets.

🛏 Sleeping & Eating

Hostal Brisas del Mediterraneo HOSTEL **$$**
(📞 0512-23-2459; Callejón Brisas 7; camping 70,000G; dm/d 110,000/300,000G; ⊘ closed May-Sep; 🅿 ✳ 🕿) Perched on the edge of the lake, it has a nice location. Some rooms are better than others though, so ask to see a selection.

Hotel del Lago HOTEL **$$$**
(📞 0512-23-2201; Weiler 411; s/d 240,000/ 310,000G; 🅿 ✳ @ 🛜 🕿) On the lake side of the plaza, this hotel is worn and romantically Victorian, full of antique furniture. Each room is different and the restaurant isn't bad either.

Walterio INTERNATIONAL **$$**
(Balbuena; picadas from 45,000G) A relaxed and informal place that is popular in the summertime for its *picadas* (finger food) and craft beers.

Getting There & Away

From Asunción, Cordillera de los Altos buses run hourly from platform 35 (5000G, 1½ hours).

SOUTHERN PARAGUAY

Paraguay's southernmost region, east of the Río Paraguay, is home to some of the country's most important historical sites. The Jesuit ruins, national parks and the *locura* (madness) of Carnaval make it an eclectic and fascinating area to visit.

On the way from Asunción to Encarnación you'll pass through the town of **Coronel Bogado**. Known as the 'Capital de Chipa' (*chipa* is a bread made of manioc flour, eggs and cheese), Coronel Bogado is the best place to sample this national obsession. There's no need to get off the bus; the vendors will come to you and it's as cheap as *chipa* (2000G).

Encarnación

071 / POP 127,500

Encarnación, aka La Perla del Sur (The Pearl of the South), is Paraguay's most attractive city. It's also known as the 'Capital de Carnaval' and, following the completion of the new *costanera* (riverside promenade) with its fabulous river beach, is sometimes referred to – rather ambitiously – as Paraguay's answer to Rio de Janeiro. It has very quickly metamorphosed into the place to be seen in Paraguay during the stifling summer months.

It is rather less proud to be the birthplace of dictator Alfredo Stroessner. His former house (p826) is now a private university.

Sights & Activities

The city center is a pleasant enough place for a stroll, but there isn't much in the way of sights. Better to head for the river and hang out with the sunbathers, beer drinkers and beach-volleyball players.

★**Costanera & Beach**   BEACH
(Av Costanera) Slap on your flip-flops and jostle for a place on Encarnación's river beach, located on the flash coastal promenade. It's a hive of activity during the summer months, with events from local theater to sports events or even rock concerts. The place to be seen in Paraguay.

If you prefer to avoid the crowds, there is another quieter beach at Quiteria, a 30,000G taxi ride away.

Sambadromo Carnaval   MONUMENT
(Av Costanera) The Sambadromo (Carnival parade ground) is along Av Costanera, which is Encarnación's main strip for nightlife. Outside of Carnaval season it is used for other events.

Escalinata San Pedro   MONUMENT
(Av Costanera) FREE A Gaudí-esque ornamental stairway in a residential neighbourhood at the far end of Av Costanera.

Encarnación

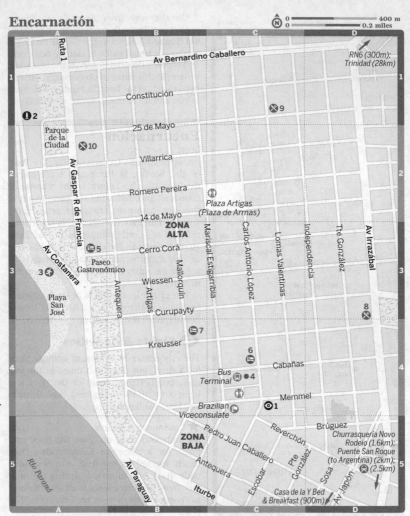

Former House of Stroessner NOTABLE BUILDING

(cnr Memmel & Carlos Antonio Lopez) The former house of dictator Alfredo Stroessner is now a private university just behind the bus terminal.

Tours

FAUNA Paraguay TOURS

(☎ 0985-74-6866; www.faunaparaguay.com; Ruta 1 Km 7.5) Best for ecotourism, national parks, Jesuit tours and wildlife-watching excursions with professional biologist guides. Reservations by email.

Karumbés TOUR

(Cabañas; per person 10,000G) Look out for *karumbés*, yellow horse-drawn carriages that once served as city taxis. Rides are free on weekends. Pick one up at the bus terminal (p828).

Sleeping

Book ahead during Carnaval: prices rise considerably and finding a cheaper room can be a challenge.

★ Casa de la Y Bed & Breakfast B&B $

(☎ 0985-77-8198; http://casadelay.wix.com/casa-de-la-y; Lara Castro 422; d/r 180,000/250,000G;

Encarnación

P ✳ @ 📶) 🍴 A tiny homestay with a warm welcome from hostess doña Yolanda and a delicious home-cooked menu of *comida típica* (local cooking, 25,000G). There are only two rooms: a tasteful, spacious double/triple with gigantic bathroom and a traditionally adorned, expansive family room. The wonderfully floral garden is a cute place to sip *tereré* in the sunshine. Reservation by email essential.

Hotel Germano HOTEL $
(☎ 071-20-3346; Cabañas; s/d 130,000/200,000G, without bathroom 50,000/100,000G; ✳ 📶) Directly opposite the bus terminal, Hotel Germano couldn't be better located for late arrivals. It's a budget spot, but they have done a decent job upgrading many of the rooms. Cheaper rooms only have a ceiling fan: you won't regret paying the extra for air-conditioning in summer!

St Mallorquín HOSTEL $$
(☎ 0984-90-0492; Mallorquín 950; dm/s/d 75,000G/140,000/200,000G) Conveniently located around the corner from the bus terminal, this hostel has a selection of different dorms in sparsely decorated rooms. Some private rooms are available, but they are a bit small. A kitchen is available for guest use.

Hotel de la Costa HOTEL $$$
(☎ 071-20-5694; cnr Av Francia & Cerro Corá; s/d/ste 220,000/400,000/620,000G; P ✳ @ 📶 ♨) A megahotel on the *costanera* with a welcoming pool and a plum location near the beach. The suite with Jacuzzi is worth splashing out on, but some of the standard rooms are quite small.

✕ Eating & Drinking

There is a concentration of good eating places on the Paseo Gastronómico, near the roundabout on Av Costanera.

Heladería Mako ICE CREAM $
(Av Caballero 590; ice cream per kg 50,000G; ✳ 📶 🍴) Delicious pastry delights, artisanal ice cream, great coffee and magazines make this well worth the trek.

Habib's FAST FOOD $
(Av Irrazáhal; lomito árabe 15,000G) Habib's is the best bet for local specialty *lomito árabe* – a Paraguayan-style kebab invented by the expat Arab community.

★Hiroshima JAPANESE $$
(cnr 25 de Mayo & Lomas Valentinas; mains 25,000-100,000G; P ✳ 📶 🍴) This place has top-notch Japanese food and is a deserved local favorite with unbelievable udon, super sushi and tempting tofu dishes. Food fit for a Japanese crown prince.

La Piccola Italia ITALIAN $$
(cnr Ruta 1 & Av Caballero; mains 12,000-40,000G; ⊘ Tue-Sun; P ✳ 🍴) Great-value pizza and pasta in huge portions served in distinctly Mediterranean surroundings. This is a good bet if you want to eat well on a tight budget.

Churrasquería Novo Rodeio BRAZILIAN $$$
(☎ 071-20-4665; Galeria San Roque, Ruta Internacional; buffet per person 95,000G) All-you-can-eat meats, salads and pastas at the most established Brazilian buffet in the city. Attentive service and music at weekends. A great feed, but discipline is required to avoid overdoing it! Located in a small shopping center on the road to Argentina.

Milord EUROPEAN $$$
(☎ 071-20-6235; www.milord.com.py; cnr Av Francia & 25 de Mayo; mains 40,000-110,000G; ✳ 📶 🍴) With a chef who studied in Paris, formal waiters and a more refined atmosphere than other Encarnación restaurants, Milord is widely regarded as the place to be seen by fine diners. The menu is varied and inventive and, despite the slightly more elevated price tag, you won't feel that you've overspent.

Peltzer Artesanal BEER GARDEN
(Av Francia; draft beers from 15,000G, sandwiches 40,000G) An attractive beer garden with

PARAGUAY ENCARNACIÓN

ℹ GETTING TO ARGENTINA

International buses (5000G) cross to Posadas in Argentina via the Puente San Roque, leaving from outside the bus terminal (p828) in Encarnación. You must get off at the immigration offices (24 hours) at both ends of the international bridge for exit and entry stamps. Buses don't always wait – take your luggage and keep your ticket to catch the next one.

An air-conditioned **train service** (Av Von Winkel; 7000G; ⊙ 6am-5:30pm daily) that departs from Av Von Winkel near the international bridge is the quickest way to cross. Entry and exit formalities take place in the same office on the Argentine side of the border.

Alternatively, picturesque ferries (5000G) cross the Río Paraná from the eastern end of the *costanera* in Encarnación to the *costanera* in Posadas.

If you're in a group, a taxi to the Paraguayan customs post will cost around 40,000G, but the price rises exponentially to take it across the bridge as long queues are frequent. The bus may be less convenient, but it has the advantage of being able to skip the lines.

delicious local craft beers on tap and monster sandwiches.

ℹ Information

Most banks are on or near the Plaza de Armas and all have ATMs. Money changers congregate around the bus terminal (p828) and at the border, but check rates before handing over any money.

For tourist information, stop by **Senatur** (☑ 071-20-5335; cnr Ruta 1 & Padre Bolik; ⊙ 8am-6pm Mon-Fri, to noon Sat & Sun), located in a large building at the western end of Av Costanera, near the entrance to town.

ℹ Getting There & Away

The **bus terminal** (☑ 071-20-2412; Cabañas) is a few blocks north of Av Costanera. Frequent buses run between Encarnación and Asunción (60,000G to 95,000G, 5½ hours) with La Encarnacena and Nuestra Señora de la Asunción providing the best service. The latter also runs an executive minibus service for the same cost. Buses run east almost hourly to Ciudad del Este (60,000G to 90,000G, six hours), though they stop frequently and the route is painfully slow.

Around Encarnación

Encarnación is a great base for exploring the south of the country. Though the Jesuit Missions are the headline grabbers, there are plenty of other activities to keep you busy in the surroundings.

🏃 Activities

Bella Vista Yerba Factories TOUR
(☑ 0767-24-0724; Mallorquín) A few days in Paraguay are all you need to grasp the importance of yerba maté (Paraguayan tea) in the local culture. For full immersion, take a yerba maté factory tour, which incorporate

plantations, production, packaging and, of course, the practice of drinking the tea. Visit the **Selecta** (25,000G) and **Pajarito** (free) factories; the former includes a visit to its **nature reserve.**

Tours are arranged through Mate Roga, the tourist office on the main road in the yerba maté capital, Bella Vista del Sur, 45km east of Encarnación. With the giant *guampa* (gourd) and *bombilla* (straw) in front, you can't miss it!

Parque Manantial RESORT
(☑ 0775-23-2250; Hohenau; entry 20,000G, pool 20,000G, camping 50,000G, s/d 150,000/250,000G; ⊙ 9am-8pm Tue-Sun) A forested oasis for travelers who like to get away from it all, Parque Manantial is located off Ruta 6, 35km outside of Encarnación near the town of Hohenau. You can camp, or there is a pleasant hotel here, and for much of the year you'll likely have the 200 hectares with swimming pools and walking trails to yourself.

Horseback riding and a zipline are available; there's also a river for paddling.

🛏 Sleeping

Hotel Tirol HOTEL $$$
(☑ 071-20-2388; www.hoteltirol.com.py; Ruta 6 Km 20, Capitán Miranda; s/d 300,000/400,000G; discounts for longer stays; P ✳ @ 🛜 🛝) A favorite with the king of Spain, the timeless red-stone Hotel Tirol is set in 20 hectares of humid forest and makes for a great day trip from Encarnación. Over 300 species of bird have been observed here and four inviting swimming pools (nonguests 10,000G) are a great way to cool off after walking the *senderos* (trails).

You'll need to book ahead in the high season (October to December), though it's often empty at other times of year. To get here take local bus 1y2 (marked Capitán Miranda) from along Av Artigas in Encarnación, which terminates at the entrance to the hotel. Any bus headed for Trinidad or Ciudad del Este also passes in front.

Pilar

☑ 0786 / POP 29,000

Squirreled away in the corner of southwestern Paraguay, surrounded by the wetlands of Ñeembucú, is the lovely colonial town of Pilar. Reborn as the City of Birds, it is a town where life is peaceful and traditional, and the word 'hurry' doesn't make it into the local vocabulary. With some fantastic river beaches nearby, great wildlife in the vicinity and a tranquil setting on the Río Paraguay, this is the kind of place where you may end up staying much longer than you had planned.

◎ Sights

Cabildo Histórico   HISTORIC BUILDING
(Plaza Mariscal López) The old seat of local government is a two-tiered wood-and-adobe building on the leafy plaza.

**Basilica Menor de
Nuestra Señora del Pilar**   CHURCH
(Plaza de los Héroes) FREE A charming little church with a marble-and-wood interior. It is the only temple officially declared a basilica in Paraguay, granting it special papal privilege.

✦ Activities

Para La Tierra   VOLUNTEERING
(☑ 0985-26-0074; www.paralatierra.org; Centro IDEAL, Estigarribia cnr Capurro; volunteer per month from US$700) Award-winning ecological, conservation and social volunteer roles.

Caminata de las Aves   WALKING
FREE Scattered around town are a series of charismatic statues of native birds by local artist Ramón Vásquez. The walk is only a few kilometers, but is a pleasant way to get to know the city, passing the major sights and taking in a series of attractive murals that depict Paraguayan history. Start on the plaza.

A booklet in Spanish is available from IDEAL Eco-hostel, explaining the cultural and ecological significance of the species depicted.

Lobope Kayaking   KAYAKING
(☑ 0972-28-7610; Mazzei; per hour 10,000G, guided trips from 50,000G) ✦ Facundo Zarnikowsky

is a local kayak guide. Text him to find out about the options.

⌖ Tours

Fábrica de Textiles   TOURS
(Mello; per person with English guide 25,000G, unguided free; ☺ by arrangement) Pilar is famous for its textiles, and while a tour of a textile factory might not sound like much fun, you will be surprised by how the mix of modern and traditional practices keeps you entertained. Tours arranged through IDEAL Eco-hostel.

✸ Festivals & Events

Hawaiana   MUSIC
(☺ early Jan) A huge music festival, the Hawaiiana all-night open-air party is one of Paraguay's best-kept secrets.

⌷ Sleeping

IDEAL Eco-hostel   HOSTEL $
(☑ 0985-26-0074; https://ecohostelideal.wixsite. com/idealeco-hostel; Centro IDEAL, Estigarribia cnr Capurro; dm/r 70,000/150,000G; @ ☎ ✸) ✦ Both international hostel and cultural center, there is always something going on at Centro IDEAL. Run by the nonprofit Para La Tierra (p829), all of its proceeds go to social and environmental projects in the local area.

Hotel Las Garzas   HOTEL $$
(☑ 0786-23-3130; Cabañas cnr Antequera; s/d 190,000/250,000G; P ✸ ☎) A comfortable midrange hotel, Las Garzas is sleek yet affordable, though some of the rooms are a little cramped.

✕ Eating & Drinking

Corona   PARAGUAYAN $
(14 de Mayo cnr Saavedra; menú del día 10,000-15,000G, mains from 20,000G; ✸) A cheap, daily set meal, and all-you-can-eat pizza on Tuesday evenings. A filling menu of oversized, carbohydrate-fuelled dishes is available for the really hungry.

Rincón Saludable   VEGETARIAN $
(Rios cnr 14 de Mayo; veggie burgers from 20,000G; ✎) Sugar-free fruit juices, oatmeal cookies, salads and veggie burgers, with outdoor seating.

Tim's Texas Cantina   TEX-MEX $$
(14 de Mayo cnr Rios; picadas 50,000G; ✸) Fusion of Texan, Mexican and (yes) Paraguayan food, based strongly around finger-food grills and tortillas.

PARAGUAY PILAR

> ### ⓘ GETTING TO ARGENTINA
>
> If you're looking for an adventurous way to get into Argentina, take the twice-daily ferry (7am and 1pm) to Puerto Cano (20,000G, 20 minutes). There isn't much to do in town except catch a bus to Corrientes, Formosa or Resistencia.

Home BAR

(Estigarribia cnr Capurro; miniburgers 5000-10,000G; ⊙7pm-2am Fri & Sat; 🛜) 🍴 A home from home in the Centro IDEAL. Pool table, inventive cocktails named after local wildlife, regional beers and some of the best miniburgers you'll try on your travels.

ⓘ Information

Tourist information is provided by Centro IDEAL which houses the IDEAL Eco-hostel (p829). This is a happening place with a young, international crowd. They have their finger on the pulse of local events and can organize trips and tours in the local area.

ⓘ Getting There & Away

Buses from Asunción run approximately every two hours (six hours, 60,000G) with Ñeembucú (7:15am, 11:15am and 23:30pm), Ciudad de Pilar (2pm, 6pm and 8:50pm) and La Encarnacena (noon and 10:30pm), among others. From Encarnación, Ñeembucú (9am) and Ciudad de Pilar (4pm) run the only direct services. All buses leaving Pilar pass through the town of San Ignacio, from where you can catch much more frequent connections to Asunción and Encarnación.

Jesuit Missions

Declared as Unesco World Heritage Sites in 1993, the best of the Jesuit-era architecture is showcased in the imposing stone churches of Trinidad and Jesús de Tavarangüe.

Set atop a lush green hill 28km northeast of Encarnación, **Trinidad** (25,000G; ⊙8am-dusk, to 9pm when light show is held) is Paraguay's best-preserved Jesuit *reducción* (settlement). Built with red stone from the nearby quarry at **Ita Cajón** (Parque Ecológico Ita Cajón; 10,000G), it is by far the most visited *reducción*. **Jesús de Tavarangüe** (25,000G; ⊙8am-8pm), 12km further north, is the near-complete structure of the Jesuit mission that was interrupted by the Jesuits' expulsion in 1767.

Stay around until dark at either site for the atmospheric light show, projecting a history in images onto the walls of the churches and accompanied by haunting religious music. Spanish-speaking guides hang around near the gates at both sites. Tip generously.

More difficult to access but well worth the effort is **San Cosme y Damián**, 27km south of the main road to Asunción at Km 308 (about 57km west of Encarnacion), which was the location of the astronomical observatory.

In Trinidad you can overnight at the **Posada María** (✆0985-76-9812; Mujer Paraguaya, Trinidad; s/d 80,000/140,000G; 🅿🛜), a charming little guesthouse that's a stone's throw from the *reducción*.

A handy website details local services for tourists: www.turismojesusytrinidad.com.py.

From Encarnación, frequent buses go to Trinidad (5000G, one hour) between 6am and 7pm, but any bus headed east along Ruta 6 to Ciudad del Este or Hohenau will drop you off nearby; get off when you see the power station on your right.

Getting to Jesús from Encarnación without your own transportation is difficult, but there are sometimes taxis hanging around (15,000G per person). Alternatively, walk 100m along the *ruta* (highway) to the crossroads – you'll see the sign to Jesús – and wait for the Jesús–Obligado bus, which theoretically passes hourly (3000G).

Parque Nacional San Rafael

Southern Paraguay's last great tract of Atlantic Forest, gorgeous San Rafael is a lush wilderness and a bird-watcher's paradise with more than 430 species recorded. Endangered species abound in this lush but easily accessible wilderness.

San Rafael is a wonderful place to get a taste of nature, with plenty of walking trails and comfortable accommodations available. You will see a lot more wildlife with a guide.

FAUNA Paraguay (p826) runs recommended all-inclusive three- to four-day bird-watching trips to the park from Encarnación, which include visits to both Pro Cosara and Kangüery.

🛏 Sleeping & Eating

Pro Cosara LODGE $

(✆0985-71-0900; http://procosara.org/en; Parque Nacional San Rafael; r per person with/without meals 180,000/90,000G; 🛜) 🍴 The Hostettler

SANTA MARÍA DE LA FE

A must-see for those interested in Jesuit history is the **museum of Jesuit art** (☑0975-62-0387; Mariscal López; 10,000G; ☺call for times) in the village of Santa María de la Fe, which houses the finest examples of religious carving. The indigenous carvers were taught their trade by a Jesuit master who carved a miniature template, which was then copied in full size by the students. The museum holds examples of both, glorious in their imperfections. To get into the museum, ask at the Santa María Hotel.

Santa María was also home to Aimé Bonpland, a famous French botanist, and a small monument in his honor stands on the plaza. Look out for howler monkeys in the trees, which are surprisingly tame!

Santa María Hotel (☑0781-28-3311; www.santamariahotel.org; Francia; s/d/tr/q 100,000G/180,000G/250,000G/320,000G, meals 35,000G; P❋☎) is a lovely little Jesuit-themed hotel on the main plaza. Atmospheric rooms contain replica Jesuit carvings and the owners are knowledgeable local guides who can show you around the museum. The hotel is involved in a number of superb community projects with a strong women's empowerment theme. They will be more than happy to tell you more.

It can be a bit of a challenge to get to Santa María on public transport; the easiest way is to take any bus between Asunción and Encarnación and get off at San Ignacio, and taxi it from there. Alternatively, there is a single direct Mariscal López bus from Asunción at 11:45am (40,000G, five hours).

family will give you a warm welcome at this charming jungle lodge on the southern tip of the park. As the HQ of local conservation group Pro Cosara, it's a wonderful source of information about the reserve. Accommodations are in comfortable wooden cabins and the surroundings are beautiful, with forest trails and a tantalizing lake for swimming.

Kangüery LODGE **$$**
(Guyra Reta; ☑021-22-9097; www.guyra.org.py; Parque Nacional San Rafael; r per person 100,000G, meals by arrangement per person 80,000G; P) 🖉
The dorm rooms in the Kangüery grasslands at Guyra Reta lodge are located deep inside San Rafael. Contact Guyra Paraguay (p845) in Asunción in advance to arrange your visit, especially if you want to be fed.

❶ Getting There & Away

Two daily buses run from Encarnación at 8am and 11:30am to Ynambú (25,000G, three hours) with Empresa Pastoreo. If you're not part of a tour, you'll need to arrange pick up from Encarnación in advance. Return trips leave around 1pm, depending on the enthusiasm of the driver.

EASTERN PARAGUAY

Corresponding to the region formerly known as Alto Paraná, this area was once the domain of ancient, impenetrable forests teeming with wildlife. The building of the world's second-largest dam, Itaipú (p832), changed all that, flooding huge areas of pristine forest and swallowing up a set of waterfalls comparable to those at Iguazú. The dam brought development to the region, leading to the founding of the city of Ciudad del Este, and an influx of farmers bent on turning what was left of the ancient forests into soy fields.

Ciudad del Este
☑ 061 / POP 294,000

Originally named Puerto Presidente Stroessner after the former dictator, the 'City of the East' is a renowned center for contraband goods, earning it the nickname 'the Supermarket of South America.' The part near the busy Brazilian border is chaotic and it can be a massive shock if it's your first experience of Paraguay, but rest assured there is nowhere else in the country quite like this. Give Ciudad del Este a chance and you'll find the rest of it is surprisingly pleasant, with some interesting attractions nearby.

🛏 Sleeping

Most accommodations in Ciudad del Este are aimed at business travelers using expense accounts. Midrange places, however, are definitely worth the extra couple of bucks, especially once you sample the megavalue breakfast buffets included in the price.

Hotel Tía Nancy HOTEL $
(☑ 061-50-2974; Cruz del Chaco; r with fan 80,000G, s/d with air-con 100,000G/120,000G; ✳) Near the bus terminal, this friendly place has dark rooms but is perfectly adequate for a tranquil transit stop if you're on a tight budget.

Hotel Austria HOTEL $$
(☑ 061-50-0883; www.hotelaustriarestaurante.com; Fernández 165; s/d 220,000/245,000G; P✳@⊚) Superclean European number with spacious rooms, big bathrooms and even bigger breakfasts. Great restaurant, too, with German and Austrian specialties.

Hotel Munich HOTEL $$
(☑ 061-50-0347; Fernández 71; s/d 200,000/240,000G; P✳@⊚) Solid midrange bet a stone's throw from the border, with comfortable and spacious rooms including cable TV.

✗ Eating

The cheapest places to eat are the stalls along Capitán Miranda and Av Monseñor Rodríguez, while Av del Lago is lined with Brazilian-style *rodízio* restaurants, where slabs of meat are brought to your table and you eat until you (almost) explode.

SAX BISTRO $$
(Av San Blás; bistro from 25,000G, pizzas from 60,000G) This unusual eatery features a triple menu (pizza, sushi and bistro) served above the trendy SAX department store.

ℹ GETTING TO BRAZIL OR ARGENTINA

The border with Brazil (Foz do Iguaçu) is at the Puente de la Amistad (Friendship Bridge). Immigration (24 hours) is at both ends of the bridge. Buses between Ciudad del Este and the local terminal in Foz do Iguaçu (R$3, every 10 minutes) run from 6am to 7:30pm. Locals don't need to stop at immigration, but travelers do, so make sure you tell the driver you want to get off.

A direct car-ferry service (10,000G, hourly 8:30am to 5pm Monday to Saturday) runs from Puerto Presidente Franco to Puerto Iguazú (Argentina). It's a short uphill walk to the town from here. Alternatively, cross to Brazil first and take the land border there – which means two sets of customs. No visa is necessary unless you are staying in Brazil.

Gugu's CHINESE $$
(cnr Boquerón & Av Jara; mains 27,000-55,000G; ☺Mon-Sat; ✳☑) If you haven't had a decent Chinese meal for a while you may go gaga over Gugu's. It's great value and pretty tasty; portions serve two.

ℹ Information

Street money changers lounge around the Pioneros del Este rotunda near the border. Banks line Av Jara and all have ATMs.

Senatur (☑ 061-50-8810; Puente de la Amistad; ☺24hr) Tourist information at a useful location at the international bridge.

ℹ Getting There & Around

The minor **Aeropuerto Guaraní** (Ruta 7, Minga Guazú) is 30km west of town on Ruta 2. Flights pass through here en route between Asunción and Brazil whenever there is enough demand.

The **bus terminal** (☑ 061-51-0421; Chaco Boreal) is about 2km south of the center. City buses (3500G) shuttle frequently between terminal and center, continuing on to the border. There are frequent buses to Asunción (60,000G–90,000G, 4½ to six hours) and Encarnación (60,000G–90,000G, six hours). Daily buses with Pluma and Sol del Paraguay run to São Paulo (Brazil, 250,000G, 17 hours).

Taxis are fairly expensive, costing around 40,000 to 50,000G to downtown.

Around Ciudad del Este

With the exception of shopping, most of Ciudad del Este's tourist attractions are just outside the city.

◉ Sights & Activities

Itaipú Dam DAM
(☑ 061-599-8040; www.itaipu.gov.py; Super Carretera Itaipú; ☺tours 7:30am-5:30pm Mon-Fri, to 4:30pm Sat & Sun) Paraguay's publicity machine is awash with facts and figures about the Itaipú hydroelectric project – the world's second-largest dam (only China's Three Gorges Dam is bigger). Itaipú's generators supply nearly 80% of Paraguay's electricity and 25% of Brazil's entire demand. While project propaganda gushes about this human accomplishment, it omits the US$25-billion price tag and avoids the mention of environmental consequences. The 1350-sq-km, 220m-deep reservoir drowned Sete Quedas, a set of waterfalls that was larger than Iguazú.

Free **tours** leave from the visitors center, north of Ciudad del Este, near the town of

Hernandarias; passports are required. Any bus marked 'Hernandarias' (3500G, every 15 minutes) passes in front of the dam. A taxi will charge around 60,000G one way or 90,000G return, including waiting time.

Monumento Bertoni   MONUMENT
(Puerto Bertoni; 20,000G; ⊙ Tue-Sun 9am-5pm) A family of Swiss immigrants led by father Moisés, the Bertonis had the idea of breeding a community of scientists deep in the Paraguayan jungle at the turn of the 20th century. With each child given a branch of the sciences to study, they made a significant impact on the (admittedly limited) Paraguayan scientific community of the time. The monument is the family home, holding a museum documenting the family's achievements, walking trails in the surrounding forest on the banks of the Río Paraná, and Moises' resting place.

Perhaps the most famous of Bertoni's offspring was his son Winkelried, a world-renowned biologist who published tirelessly until his early 30s, when he decided that science wasn't really his calling and moved to Asunción to work in a bank.

Ask at Senatur (p832) for information on how to visit.

Salto del Monday   WATERFALL
(Parque Saltos del Monday; 25,000G; ⊙ 7am-7pm) This impressive 80m-high waterfall, located 10km south of Ciudad del Este, suffers from its close proximity to Iguazú Falls on the other side of the border. If you have time on your hands, it's well worth the visit, especially as dusk falls and tens of thousands of swifts gather before zipping in to roost on the slippery rocks behind the cascades.

Plenty of adventure activities are offered by the organization Aqua Paraná Tour, which now runs the site, including zipwires, arboreal walkways and a panoramic elevator. A return taxi ride will cost around 80,000G, including waiting time. In case you're wondering, it's pronounced mon-da-OO!

Mbaracayú Biosphere Reserve

Singled out by the WWF as one of the 100 most important sites for biodiversity on the planet, the 700-sq-km hectare Mbaracayú Biosphere Reserve is one of Paraguay's natural treasures. Consisting of pristine Atlantic Forest and *cerrado* (savanna) in approximately equal quantities, it is home to more than 400 bird species and a range of large mammals. Bird-watchers will be in search of the bare-throated bellbird (Paraguay's national bird), the rare helmeted woodpecker and the endangered black-fronted piping-guan.

This model reserve is run by the Asuncion-based Fundación Moisés Bertoni (p845). You'll need a 4WD if you want to drive here yourself, or else take the 11:30am or 11:30pm Canindeyú bus from Asunción to Villa Ygatimi (70,000G, eight hours) and arrange pickup from there in advance. Return trips to Asunción depart at 7am and 7pm.

Mbaracayú Eco-lodge (✆0985-26-1080; reservasmbaracayu@gmail.com; Jejui-Mi; s/d incl meals 265,000/420,000G; P✴☎) ✐ is the best eco-lodge in Paraguay. It is part of an innovative tourism project combining education, conservation, women's empowerment and tourism. The lodge is run by female students at the on-site eco-school, who handle reception, cook, wait and clean, on their way to earning a valuable diploma in hostelry.

NORTHERN PARAGUAY

Northern Paraguay is off the radar for most travelers, but the colonial city of Concepción is the best place to catch a boat heading north along the Río Paraguay. Natural wonders abound in this remote area, and the road east from Pozo Colorado to Concepción is famed for its abundance of wildlife.

Concepción
✆0331 / POP 77,000
'La Perla del Norte' (The Pearl of the North) is an easygoing city on the Río Paraguay with poetic early-20th-century buildings and a laid-back ambience. Action around here means a trotting horse hauling a cart of watermelons or a boatload of people and their cargo arriving at the port. Indeed, river cruises are the main reason travelers come to Concepción, whether it's for an adventurous odyssey north to Brazil or just a short weekend jaunt upriver with the locals to nearby sandy beaches.

◎ Sights
Several stunning **mansions**, now municipal buildings, stand out along Estigarribia.

UP THE RÍO PARAGUAY TO THE PANTANAL

North of Concepción, the Río Paraguay wends its way slowly to the Pantanal Paraguayo. Unlike in the Brazilian Pantanal, you probably won't see another tourist here, and except for your boat mates your main companions will be the wildlife. Bring a hammock and a mosquito net for the boat trip, prepare yourself for unusual bedfellows, and claim your territory early – it gets crowded with locals. Some boats have basic cabins (100,000G per night) but they need to be booked well in advance. Bring your own food.

Typical routes leave Concepción for Vallemí, then Fuerte Olimpo (last place to obtain an exit stamp, though it's safer to get one before leaving Asunción) with some continuing on to tiny Bahía Negra, near the borders with Bolivia and Brazil. The exit stamp is only required if you're considering carrying on north into Brazil or Bolivia.

Boats heading upriver from Concepción to Vallemí (65,000G, 30 hours) or as far as Bahía Negra (110,000G, three days) include the *Aquidabán* (departs Tuesday at 11am, returns Friday). The erratic *Guaraní* leaves fortnightly on Monday afternoons but goes only as far as Fuerte Olimpo via Vallemí, and returns Thursday. Check schedules and boats in advance (☎0331-24-2435); they change frequently.

Museo del Cuartel de la Villa Real　　　　MUSEUM
(cnr Estigarribia & Carlos A. López; ⊙8am-noon Mon-Sat) FREE The museum in the beautifully restored barracks exhibits historical and war paraphernalia. The attack on Mato Grosso, Brazil, was launched from here during the War of the Triple Alliance.

🛏 Sleeping & Eating

It's not cheap to stay in Concepción and you may be a little disappointed at what you get for your money.

You are best eating at one of the hotels, unless you happen to be addicted to rotisserie chicken – in which case Calle Presidente Franco is lined with places ready to sell you a fix.

Hotel Francés　　　　HOTEL $$
(☎0331-24-2383; cnr Franco & Av López; s/d 100,000/190,000G; ❋@≋) Located in an old colonial mansion, this place has personality and is decent value at the budget end of the spectrum, even if it is aging gracefully.

Concepción Palace　　　　HOTEL $$$
(☎0331-24-1858; www.concepcionpalace.com.py; Mariscal López 399; s/d 390,000/490,000G; P❋@🗢≋) Far and away the most upmarket hotel in Concepción, the stylish wood-and-leather rooms have pretensions that reach beyond the dusty streets outside. An impressive pool and the best restaurant in town complete the effect.

ℹ Information

Banks along Presidente Franco have ATMs that accept foreign cards. If you are heading north

to the Pantanal, this is your last chance to get money.

ℹ Getting There & Away

BUS
The **bus terminal** (☎0331-24-2744; Asunción Flores) is eight blocks north of the center.

For Asunción (90,000G, 4½ to six hours), La Santaniana and La Concepciónera offer the best service. Several services head to Pedro Juan Caballero (35,000G, four hours) and Filadelfia (100,000G, six hours). There are daily departures with NASA at 12:30pm and 8pm to Ciudad del Este (100,000G, nine hours).

Bahía Negra & the Pantanal Paraguayo

The Pantanal Paraguayo (Paraguayan Pantanal) is remote and rarely visited, but if you are willing to make the effort and spend more than you would in Brazil, then it is a fantastic, adventurous, off-the-beaten track destination for those with an interest in wildlife. There is little in the way of tourist infrastructure, though, so this is very much a DIY experience. There are no local wildlife guides to show you around.

The main access town is Bahía Negra, and while there isn't much there except a military base, a visit is a necessary evil to organize your boat trips along the Río Negro. Wildlife abounds in this area, with raptors and waterbirds flushing from the riverside, marsh deer grazing in reed beds and caiman and capybara sunning themselves on exposed banks.

🛏 Sleeping & Eating

Accommodations are poor and overpriced in Bahía Negra town, a result of its remoteness. The ramshackle places along the main road charge around 50,000G per person.

Food is hard to come by (even in the stores), so bring it with you if you want anything other than greasy burgers or bad pizza.

Tres Gigantes   LODGE $$
(☎021-22-9097; s/d 120,000/240,000G, meals extra) The only place to stay in the Pantanal itself, this is an attractive wooden lodge with ceiling fans overlooking the Río Negro, an hour or so west of Bahía Negra by boat. You should reserve your visit in advance with Guyra Paraguay (p845) in Asunción to organize a boat transfer. Electricity is by generator only (25,000G per hour).

Ask Tres Gigantes about providing food; if it isn't possible you will have to bring your own, but there is at least a kitchen you can use.

❶ Getting There & Away

Tour companies provide the least complicated way to visit the Pantanal, but if you decide to do it alone there are several options.

The easiest but most expensive way to get to Bahía Negra is to fly from Asunción with Grupo de Transporte Aéreo (p847) for 580,000G return, leaving at 6am Wednesday, sometimes with additional departures Friday. An uncomfortable weekly Stel Turismo (p846) bus to Bahía Negra (200,000G, 18 hours) leaves Asunción at 7pm Thursday and returns Saturday or Sunday, weather permitting. It's a long way, but you will see animals along the route. Take food and water.

If you have time on your hands, you can come by riverboat from Concepción.

Access from Bahía Negra to the best wildlife-watching areas is by motorboat only and it's not cheap, as fuel costs in this remote area are high. Tres Gigantes offers a motorboat-transfer service that carries four people and costs 800,000G.

THE CHACO

The Chaco remains a great place to see wildlife. This vast plain – roughly divided into the flooded palm savannas of the Humid Chaco (the first 350km west of Asunción) and the spiny forests of the Dry Chaco (the rest) – encompasses the entire western half of Paraguay and stretches into Argentina and Bolivia.

Bisected by the **Ruta Trans-Chaco**, it's an animal-lover's paradise, with flocks of waterbirds and birds of prey abounding, easily spotted along the roadside. Although the Chaco accounts for more than 60% of Paraguayan territory, less than 3% of the population actually lives here. Historically it was a refuge for indigenous hunter-gatherer communities; today the most obvious settlements are the Mennonite communities of the Central Chaco.

The Mennonite Colonies

Of the three Mennonite Colonies in the Central Chaco, only two of the towns are easily accessible on public transportation – **Filadelfia** and **Loma Plata**. Many people are surprised by just how small these towns are. Although there's not much to do here except take in the unique atmosphere, they make for an interesting short break and are good bases for exploring the surrounding area.

Some 15,000 Mennonites inhabit the Chaco. According to their history, Canadian Mennonites were invited to Paraguay to settle what they believed to be lush, productive territory in return for their rights – religious freedom, pacifism, independent administration of their communities, and permission to speak German and practice their religious beliefs. The reality of the harsh, arid Chaco came as a shock, and a large percentage of the original settlers succumbed to disease, hunger and thirst as they struggled to gain a foothold.

There are other Mennonite communities elsewhere in Paraguay, but those in the Chaco are renowned for both their perseverance in the 'Green Hell' and subsequent commercial success; their cooperatives provide much of the country's dairy products, among other things.

Today there are three main colonies in the Chaco. The oldest colony, **Menno**, was founded by the original settlers in 1927, and is centered around Loma Plata. **Fernheim** (capital Filadelfia), was founded in 1930 by refugees from the Soviet Union, followed by **Neuland** (capital Neu-Halbstadt), founded by Ukrainian Germans in 1947.

❶ Getting There & Away

There is only one way into the Chaco and that is via the long, straight Trans-Chaco highway. Buses to the Mennonite towns of Loma Plata and Filadelfia leave from Asunción (110,000G, eight hours) and Concepción (100,000G, six hours).

There are two buses a day from Filadelfia to Loma Plata.

Filadelfia

📍 0491 / POP 9700 (COLONY)

The largest of the Mennonite towns and administrative center of Fernheim colony, Filadelfia resembles a suburb of Munich plonked in the middle of a sandy desert. Though dusty Av Hindenburg is the main street, the town lacks a real center; its soul is the giant dairy cooperative.

⊙ Sights

Colonists' Museum   MUSEUM

(Av Hindenburg; ⊙ 7-11:30am Mon-Fri) FREE The creaky wooden building that houses the museum is the original colony headquarters. It's filled with a bit of everything, from information about Mennonite history to handmade flamethrowers for combating locusts, and colorful Nivaclé headdresses.

Jakob Unger Museum   MUSEUM

(Av Hindenburg; ⊙ 7-11:30am Mon-Fri) FREE The natural-history museum, named after the famous Mennonite naturalist, is stuffed with taxidermied animals and is part of the impressive **Filadelfia museum complex**.

🛏 Sleeping & Eating

Hotel Florida   HOTEL $$$

(📞 0491-43-2151; www.hotelfloridachaco.com; Av Hindenburg 984; s 200,000-250,000G; d 280,000-400,000G; 🅿❄🛜) Orderly and efficient, and by far Filadelfia's nicest accommodations. Variations in room prices refer to the difference between 'new' and 'old' rooms: the newer rooms are nicer and a little larger. The restaurant isn't bad.

Meshin   CHINESE $$

(📞 0981-81-2700; Av Central; buffet per kilo 40,000G; ⊙ 11am-1:30pm & 7-11pm; 🅿❄🛜📞) A real treat and a bit of a surprise considering the location. Out near the airstrip, the Meshin serves probably the best Chinese buffet in the country.

Girasol   BRAZILIAN $$$

(Unruh; buffet 75,000G) Girasol is a good option that serves delicious all-you-can-eat Brazilian *asados* (barbecue).

🛍 Shopping

Cooperativa Fernheim   SUPERMARKET

(Unruh; ⊙ 7am-noon & 2-7pm Mon-Sat) It's worth a trip to the gigantic, well-stocked Cooperativa Mennonita supermarket. It's amazing how much you can fit under one roof, but you may find yourself the only person paying; the Mennonites deal in credit more than hard currencies.

ℹ Information

Tourist Information (📞 0491-41-7380; Av Hindenburg 131; ⊙ 7-11:30am Mon-Fri) Information in English, German and Spanish. It can organize tours in the colonies with some notice. Walter Ratzlaff is a knowledgeable, local, multilingual guide.

ℹ Getting There & Away

Buses from Filadelfia to Loma Plata leave at 7:15am and 1pm (10,000G, 30 minutes).

Loma Plata

📍 0492 / POP 5500 (COLONY)

Loma Plata is the oldest and most traditional of the Mennonite settlements, but there

---

ℹ GETTING TO BOLIVIA

Buses to Bolivia do not pass through the Mennonite towns, so if you're planning on heading there it can be less stressful to return to Asunción and take a direct bus from there. However if you are in Filadelfia or Loma Plata you have two choices. One is to catch a lift to the Ruta Trans-Chaco and wait for the Santa Cruz bus to pass – they come through in the early hours of the morning. The other is to get yourself to the town of Mariscal Estigarribia, where Paraguayan customs formalities take place (24 hours), book yourself into a hotel and wake yourself up in time to coincide with the bus service (usually somewhere between 3am and 5am).

A 5am Wednesday minibus runs from Filadelfia direct to Mariscal, leaving you with a whole day to kill. Alternatively, an uncomfortable and somewhat unpredictable daily service leaves Asunción at 6am, passing through Loma Plata around 2pm and Filadelfia around 3pm, arriving in Mariscal around 5pm (all being well). **Hotel La Estancia** (📞 0494-24-7250; opposite the military base; s/d 170,000/220,000G; 🅿❄) is the best place to stay in Mariscal, and also offers an edible evening meal.

Bolivian customs is at Ibibobo (open 24 hours theoretically), some distance from the frontier and little more than a collection of huts.

isn't a lot to do besides visit the Museo Loma Plata, a small history museum.

The rambling **Cooperativa Supermarket** (Av Central; ⊙ 7am-noon & 2-6pm Mon-Fri 7am-noon Sat) is worth a visit for an insight into Mennonite life.

🛏 Sleeping & Eating

Hotel Mora   HOTEL **$$**
(📞 0492-25-2255; Sand Strasse 803; s/d 120,000G/ 180,000G; 🅿 ❈ @ 🛜) Appealing, spotless rooms around a grassy setting. There is no such thing as budget in the Chaco, but when it comes to value for money, this is as good a bet as any.

Loma Plata Inn   HOTEL **$$**
(📞 0492-25-3235; Ayala; s/d 200,000/250,000G; 🅿 ❈ @ 🛜 ☒) Comfortable and professionally run, functional rather than snazzy. It's the best place to stay in town.

Chaco's Grill   GRILL **$$$**
(📞 0983-25-0621; Gondra; buffet per kg 97,000G; ⊙ noon-2:30pm & 7-11pm) A meat merry-go-round awaits, with the salad bar something of an afterthought. They eat well around here, and this calorific smorgasbord is not for the fainthearted.

ⓘ Getting There & Away

All buses destined for Filadelfia pass through Loma Plata. From Asunción there are five daily services (110,000G, seven hours 30 minutes).

Around the Mennonite Colonies

Unless you have your own transport or can arrange something locally, it can be difficult to explore the area around the Mennonite towns. But if you make the effort, there are some fantastic natural attractions that will make it worth your while.

◉ Sights & Activities

Chaco Lodge   WILDLIFE RESERVE
(📞 0981-22-3974; per car 100,000G) Chaco Lodge is a forest reserve around a large salt lake famous for its flamingos. It is one of the last in the area to dry out, and is accessible only during dry weather. It's a great place to camp. Norbert Epp, the owner can arrange private trips.

Fortín Boquerón   MUSEUM
(5000G, tip expected; ⊙ 8am-6pm Tue-Sat) Fortín Boquerón is the site of one of the decisive

TRANSCHACO RALLY
....
The Chaco's **Transchaco Rally** (http:// rally.com.py; ⊙ Sep) is a three-day world motorsports competition, said to be one of the toughest on the planet. Book accommodations in advance.

battles of the Chaco War (1932–35). There is an excellent museum, as well as a graveyard of the fallen and a gigantic monument constructed from the original defenses and trenches. The site is 65km south of a turnoff at Cruce Los Pioneros on the Ruta Trans-Chaco.

Look for the hollowed-out palo borracho tree once used as a sniper's nest. From the front it looks like a woodpecker hole but, despite being gutted more than 70 years ago, the tree is still alive!

Laguna Capitán   WILDLIFE WATCHING
A series of ephemeral saline lakes that form to the east of Loma Plata are a key habitat for migrating birds. Though individual lagoons may be dry for several years between good rainstorms, the birds somehow find them. Laguna Capitán is one of the most accessible.

It is best from May to September when flocks of ducks and flamingos obscure the water. From October to December and March to April they are used by waders on passage. Accommodations are available in **dorm rooms** (📞 0983-34-4463; dm 50,000G; 🅿 @ 🛜) with advance booking, and there's a kitchen is available for use (100,000G per day).

Fortín Toledo   WILDLIFE WATCHING
(www.cccipy.org; 20,000G) 🏃 Fortín Toledo preserves Chaco War trenches but is perhaps more interesting for the **Proyecto Taguá** breeding project. The Chacoan peccary (or *taguá*) is a pig-like creature that was known only from subfossil remains until its remarkable rediscovery in the 1970s. The project, initiated by San Diego Zoo, acts as a reintroduction program for this painfully shy and critically endangered species.

Herds of friendly collared peccaries and nasty white-lipped peccaries are also kept here, giving you a unique opportunity to compare all three species and their differing characters. Also look out for the rare black-bodied woodpecker.

Fortín Toledo is accessed via a turnoff from the Ruta Trans-Chaco at Km 475. Follow the peccary signs for 5km or so. **Accommodations** (☑ 0981-26-0378; per person 80,000G) are available.

Northwestern National Parks

Once the realm of nomadic Ayoreo foragers, **Parque Nacional Defensores del Chaco** is a wooded alluvial plain; isolated Cerro León (500m) is its greatest landmark. The dense thorn forest harbors large cats such as jaguars and pumas, as well as tapirs and herds of peccary. The free accommodations are dreadful, and you'll need to bring all your own food, drink and fuel for the generator. 'Defensores' is a long 830km from Asunción, over roads impassable to ordinary vehicles, and there's no regular public transportation. It's not a good idea to attempt to visit without a guide, and don't bother if you don't have a 4WD vehicle. FAUNA Paraguay (p826) runs recommended trips.

A more accessible option is **Parque Nacional Teniente Enciso**, which boasts better infrastructure, including an interpretation center and a visitors' house with kitchen and some air-conditioned rooms. Again, bring all your own food and water.

A short hop further north is **Parque Nacional Médanos del Chaco**. There are no accommodations here and it should not be attempted without a guide. The habitat is more open than at Enciso and bird-watchers should keep their eyes peeled for local species such as the quebracho crested-tinamou and spot-winged falconet.

NASA runs a single weekly minibus to Enciso (60,000G, six hours) on Wednesday, leaving at 5am from Filadelfia and passing through Mariscal Estigarribia at 7am. It returns at 3pm the same afternoon.

UNDERSTAND PARAGUAY

Paraguay Today

The run up to the 2018 elections was marred by an attempt by Horacio Cartes to change the constitutional guarantee of single-term presidencies – in place since the dictatorship – in order to stand again for election. The proposal was met with violent demonstrations in the capital. Street protests saw leading Liberal candidate Efraín Alegre shot with rubber bullets, a young Liberal campaigner shot dead by police in the party offices under mysterious circumstances, and the congress building stormed and burned by protestors.

Though Cartes eventually dropped the proposal, his chosen candidate for the Colorado pre-candidacy, the young and virtually unknown economist Santiago Peña, was widely viewed as a puppet. Peña was beaten comfortably in the Colorado internal elections by Mario Abdo Benítez (Marito), son of Stroessner's most trusted companion of the same name. In April 2018 Marito then beat Efraín Alegre to the presidency in one of the closest-fought elections in Paraguayan history, tainted by the usual accusations of electoral fraud.

Marito inherits a country that has ridden a economic boom for the last decade, but which has failed to translate economic success into sustained social development. The economy is healthy, even while some other countries in the region have plunged into crisis, and the guaraní currency has been strong and stable since the early noughties, though the cost of living has risen exponentially over the same period. Paraguay is still a reasonably cheap country to visit for foreigners, but first-time visitors may find costs to be higher than they had expected.

Paraguay is still a country split along class lines, with the most wealthy reluctant to share the spoils with the impoverished majority. Paraguayan towns often ooze modernity, but new developments generally cater for the rich while the needs of the rural poor are ignored. Indigenous rights, *campesino* (peasant farmer) land claims and environmental issues all take a back seat to the free-market ethos which dominates the Paraguayan political and social scene. Inequality continues to rise.

Environmentally Paraguay is facing crisis. The deforestation of the Chaco, the fastest-disappearing forest habitat on earth, continues apace. Tales of genetically engineered soybeans which can withstand the harsh Chaco climate are exciting the farming community, but horrifying conservationists, who see it as a potential nail in the coffin of this unique habitat. The lack of priority given to environmental issues were highlighted in proposals during 2015 to blow up the highest point in the Chaco, Cerro León, officially for rock for road-paving, but perhaps for the uranium the *cerro* is rumored to contain.

Quite apart from being the centerpoint of Parque Nacional Defensores del Chaco, the mountain is also of religious significance to the Guaraní tribes in the area and the last stronghold of the endangered Chaco peccary. The disregard for environmental law was greeted with horror by the public, who managed to stop the plans following an outcry and demonstrations, but then-president Cartes showed little sympathy for public concerns, joking that the government would put the peccary 'in a cage' to protect it.

History

The Indigenous & the Europeans

Historically Paraguay was inhabited by the indigenous Guaraní, a family of hunter-gatherer tribes, culturally close to the Tupí of Brazil. Seventeen ethnic groups belonging to five language groups inhabit Paraguay. Major groups in the Chaco are the nomadic Nivaclé, Lengua, Ayoreo and Chamacoco, whilst in eastern Paraguay the principal groups are the Aché and Mbyá.

Pedro de Mendoza's expedition founded Asunción in 1537, and the city became the most significant Spanish colonial city east of the Andes for nearly 50 years until Buenos Aires was fully established. It declined in importance once it became clear that the hostile Chaco impeded the passage toward the fabled 'City of Gold' in modern-day Peru.

In the early 17th century, Jesuit missionaries created *reducciones* where the indigenous Guaraní and Europeans developed new crafts, crops and methods of cultivation. By the time of their expulsion in 1767 (because of Madrid's concern that the Jesuits' power had become too great), the Jesuit influence had spread to what is today Bolivia, Brazil and Argentina.

Independence, Boom & Bust

The bloodless revolution of May 1811 gave Paraguay the distinction of being the first South American country to declare its independence from Spain. Since independence, however, Paraguayan history has been dominated by a cast of dictators who have influenced the direction of the country.

Dr José Gaspar Rodríguez de Francia was the first leader of independent Paraguay. Chosen as the strongest member of the Próceres de Mayo (founding fathers), 'El Supremo' was initially reluctant to take charge, insisting he would accept the role only until somebody better equipped was found. That somebody never was found, and he ruled until his death in 1840. Francia sealed the country's borders to promote self-sufficiency, expropriated the properties of landholders, merchants and even the church, and established the state as the only political and economic power. Though his rule was controversial, under it Paraguay became the dominant power on the continent.

By the early 1860s, Francia's successor, Carlos Antonio López, had ended Paraguay's isolation by building railroads, a telegraph system, a shipyard and a formidable army. Paraguay was in a strong position at the time of his death, when power passed to his son, Francisco Solano López. Seduced by his European education, Mariscal (Marshal) López longed to be seen as the Napoléan of the Americas. At his side was the Irish courtesan Eliza Lynch, who had her own fantasies about French high society. Her dream of making Asunción the 'Paris of the Americas' turned her into an unpopular Marie Antoinette figure, and the country rapidly deteriorated under their combined rule.

War of the Triple Alliance

When Brazil invaded Uruguay in 1865, López jumped at the opportunity to prove his military genius and save the smaller nation from its fate. To send his army to the rescue, permission was required to cross Argentine territory. Argentina's refusal led him to declare war on them, too. With Uruguay quickly overwhelmed by the Brazilians, Paraguay suddenly found itself at war with three of its neighbors simultaneously. The disastrous War of the Triple Alliance had begun and the course of Paraguayan history would be changed forever. Allied forces outnumbered Paraguayans 10 to one, and by the end of the campaign boys as young as 12 years old were fighting on the front lines armed only with farm implements. Paraguay eventually lost half of its prewar population and 26% of its national territory.

The Chaco War

The next war wasn't too far away. In the early 1900s and with Paraguay in political turmoil, the Bolivians began to slowly advance into the Chaco, resulting in the eruption of full-scale hostilities in 1932. The exact reasons for the Chaco War are debated, but Bolivia's desire for a sea port (via the Río Paraguay) and rumors of petroleum deposits in the area are often cited as factors.

In the punishingly hot, arid Chaco, access to water was key to military success and the war hinged on the capture and protection of freshwater sources. Paraguay further benefited from a British-built railway line, which allowed them to bring supplies to troops from Asunción. The British had earlier warned the Bolivians to not touch their railway line or risk adding another, more formidable enemy to their list. As a result the Paraguayan troops were able to overcome Bolivia's numerically stronger forces and even advance as far as the southern Bolivian town of Villamontes. With the futility of the war becoming ever more obvious, a 1935 cease-fire left no clear victor but more than 80,000 dead.

Dictatorship

Paraguay subsequently entered into a decade of disorder before a brief civil war brought the Colorado Party to power in 1949. A 1954 coup installed General Alfredo Stroessner as president. His brutal 35-year, military-dominated rule was characterized by repression and terror and is the longest dictatorship in South American history. Perceived political opponents were persecuted, tortured and 'disappeared,' elections were fraudulent and corruption became a national industry. By the time Stroessner was overthrown in yet another coup, 75% of Paraguayans had known no other leader.

The Return to Democracy

Stroessner was eventually driven into exile on 3 February 1989 and Paraguay's first democratic elections were held the same year. They were won by the Colorado candidate Andrés Rodríguez, who had masterminded the coup. The Colorados then went on to win every successive election until their grip was finally broken during the historic events of April 2008, which saw Archbishop Fernando Lugo, a man with no prior political experience, elected president of the republic. Campaigning on social reform, an end to corruption and equal opportunities for all, Lugo's power base stemmed from the numerically superior lower classes – his campaign slogan 'Paraguay Para Todos' (Paraguay for Everybody) struck the right note with voters. With the Colorado Party in turmoil, there was at last a sense that corruption and social injustice really could be consigned to the trash can of history.

President Lugo's government viewed social and economic progress as one and the same, and actively sought closer trade links with neighboring countries. Lugo's relationship with Evo Morales and the late Hugo Chávez brought criticism from his opponents, but marked improvements at the domestic level kept his critics at bay. In 2010 Paraguay had the third-fastest-growing economy in the world, a successful renegotiation of the highly unfavorable contracts for the Itaipú Dam had been completed – ensuring that Brazil would pay Paraguay a fair rate for its electricity usage – and at last the country was beginning to move away from the bottom of the international corruption tables.

Impeachment

Internal strife marred Lugo's administration, and in 2012 the Liberal party withdrew its support for Lugo and joined forces with its traditional rivals, the Colorados, to impeach the president. The official reasons given included a breakdown of security and a failure to address the problems associated with land rights. Over 80% of the land in Paraguay is owned by just 1% of the population, and Lugo had promised to address the decades-long social imbalance by providing land for landless *campesinos*. This promise had infuriated the land-owning classes, who accused him of failing to protect their interests, while a lack of progress had also led to the mobilization of *campesino* groups, pushing for their own rights to be respected. With his future in the hands of a senate dominated by the parties that sought to oust him, Lugo was declared guilty on June 22, 2012, after a shotgun trial. Vice President Franco was sworn in that same day.

The brevity of the trial process, completed in less than 24 hours, raised eyebrows internationally and resulted in accusations of an antidemocratic abuse of process from neighboring countries. The events were officially declared a coup d'état by the trade bloc Mercosur, of which Paraguay is a member, and trade partners Argentina, Brazil and Uruguay all refused to recognize the Franco government's legitimacy. Mercosur suspended Paraguay from the bloc until free elections were held in April 2013, and this position was later followed unanimously

RECOMMENDED READS: PARAGUAY

At the Tomb of the Inflatable Pig (John Gimlette; 2003) Interweaves humorous travel accounts with social commentary.

Chronicle of the Guayaki Indians (Pierre Clastres; 1972) For an anthropological slant.

Historical Dictionary of Paraguay (Andrew Nickson; 2015) For history buffs.

I, the Supreme (Augusto Roa Bastos; 1974) This thoughtful novel about the dictator Dr Francia is widely considered Roa Bastos' best work.

Land Without Evil (Matthew Pallamary; 2000) Fantasy novel about the birth of modern Guaraní culture and its struggle for survival.

The Liberation of Little Heaven and Other Stories (Mark Jacobs; 1999) Collection of Paraguayan short stories.

The News from Paraguay (Lily Tuck; 2004) Historical fiction focusing on Mariscal López and his relationship with Eliza Lynch, and the consequences for the nation.

Rebirth of the Paraguayan Republic (Harris Gaylord Warren; 1985) For more about Paraguay's notorious wars.

Son of Man (Augusto Roa Bastos; 1988) Paraguay's most famous author explores the country's conflict-strewn history.

The Stroessner Era (Carlos R Miranda; 1990) For a look at Paraguay's infamous dictator.

by the Union of South American Nations (Unasur). Defenders of the process claimed that Paraguay was exercising its democratic and sovereign rights to govern as permitted in the national constitution, and called the disapproval of its neighbors a modern-day attack by the Triple Alliance, invoking memories of the disastrous conflict that forever changed Paraguay's destiny.

Recent Developments

Franco's reign was short and marred by allegations of government misspending. Obliged by law to call elections in 2013, the Liberals, stripped of the support of the allies who had helped them to victory in the previous elections, were soundly beaten by the rejuvenated Colorados. Millionaire businessman, owner of Libertad football club and tobacco magnate Horacio Cartes became the new president.

Though a political novice, Horacio Cartes promised a 'new direction' for Paraguay by improving infrastructure, and he continued the economic upswing by inviting foreign investment. However, he raised suspicions about his intentions when he publicly invited multinationals to 'use and abuse' Paraguay. With frequent corruption scandals linking prominent politicians with the drug trade (called narcopolíticos by the press), the accelerating deforestation of the Chaco and the abandonment of many of the social policies

introduced by Lugo, the Cartes government failed to deliver on the promises it made when taking office.

People & Culture

Some 95% of Paraguayans are considered *mestizos* (of mixed indigenous and Spanish descent). Spanish is the language of business and most prevalent in the cities, while in the *campaña* (countryside), Guaraní is more common. *Jopará* (a mixture of the two) is used in some parts of the media. The remaining 5% of the population are descendants of European immigrants (mainly Ukrainians and Germans), Mennonite farmers and indigenous tribes. Small but notable Asian, Arab and Brazilian communities are found, particularly in the south and east of the country.

More than 95% of the population lives in eastern Paraguay, only half in urban areas. Unicef reports a literacy rate of 99%, an infant mortality rate of 1.8% and an average life expectancy of 72 years. The annual population growth rate is 2.6%.

Statistically, Paraguay is the second-poorest South American country, though walking around the country's cities you might find it hard to believe. Lines of souped-up Mercedes Benz whiz around, classy restaurants are full to bursting and there are houses the size of palaces. Contrast this with the lives of the rural poor, where landless *campesinos* live hand to mouth and are exploited by landowners who employ long-discredited *latifundio* (large landholding)models. This continues to represent the country's biggest social problem.

Paraguayan towns are frequently nicknamed 'Capital of ...' after their most notable features or products. Encarnación, for example, is 'Capital de Carnaval,' Coronel Bogado 'Capital de Chipa,' and Itauguá 'Capital de Ñandutí.'

Paraguayans are famously laid-back and rightly renowned for their warmth and hospitality. Sipping *tereré* (iced herbal tea) in the 40°C shade while shooting the breeze takes the better part of a day. Siesta is obligatory and in some communities extends from noon to sunset, making the early morning and dusk the busiest times of day.

Though things have improved, corruption remains a part of daily life. For visitors, corruption is most likely to manifest itself in the form of police soliciting bribes or in higher prices for gringos.

Ninety percent of the population claims to be Roman Catholic, but folk variants are common and evangelical Christianity is on the rise. Most indigenous peoples have retained their core religious beliefs, or modified them only slightly, despite nominal allegiance to Catholicism or evangelical Protestantism.

Arts

As many intellectuals and artists will tell you, the Paraguayan government gives little funding to the arts. Many artists, musicians and painters have left the country to perform or work elsewhere. Nevertheless, Paraguay boasts some well-known figures.

Paraguay's major literary figures are poet-critic and writer Josefina Plá and poet-novelist Augusto Roa Bastos, winner of the 1990 Cervantes Prize. Bastos died in 2005, aged 87. Despite many years in exile, he focused on Paraguayan themes and history, drawing from personal experience. Contemporary writers include Nila López, poet Jacobo A Rauskin, Luis María Martínez, Ramón Silva Roque Vallejos, Delfina Acosta and Susy Delgado.

Sports

Paraguayans are *fútbol*-mad. It's not uncommon to see large groups of men in bars supping Pilsen and watching the Copa Liberta-

dores on a communal TV. The most popular soccer teams, Olimpia and Cerro Porteño, have a fierce rivalry, though the national team has been in slow declines since reaching the quarterfinals of the 2010 World Cup and finishing runner-up in the 2011 Copa América. The headquarters of Conmebol (p817), the South American football confederation, is in Luque, on the road to the airport. It's home to an impressive museum depicting the history of the sport in South America.

Tennis, basketball, volleyball, hunting and fishing are also popular.

Environment

The country is divided into two distinct regions, east and west of the Río Paraguay. Eastern Paraguay historically was a mosaic of Atlantic Forest and *cerrado* (savanna), with the unique Mesopotamian flooded grasslands in the extreme south of the country. Much of the original habitat has now been converted to agriculture, especially in departments of Itapúa and Alto Paraná, but substantial tracts of these pristine but globally endangered habitats still remain. To the west is the Gran Chaco, with a lush palm savanna in its lower reaches (Humid Chaco), and a dense, arid, thorny forest (Dry Chaco) further north and west. The northeastern Chaco represents the southern extent of the great Pantanal wetland.

Wildlife

Wildlife is diverse, but the expanding rural population is putting increasing pressure on eastern Paraguay's fauna. Mammals are most abundant and easy to see in the largely unpopulated Chaco. Anteaters, armadillos, maned wolves, giant otters, lowland tapirs, jaguars, pumas, peccaries and brocket deer are all still relatively numerous here. In the mid-1970s the Chacoan peccary, a species previously known only from subfossilized remains, was found alive and well in the Paraguayan Chaco, where it had evaded discovery for centuries.

Birdlife is abundant, and Paraguay is home to 713 bird species. The national bird is the bare-throated bellbird, named for its remarkable call, but serious bird-watchers will be in search of endangered, limited-range species, such as the white-winged nightjar, saffron-cowled blackbird, lesser nothura, helmeted woodpecker and black-fronted piping-guan. Reptiles, including caiman and anaconda, are widespread. The amphibian that will most likely catch your eye is the enormous rococo toad, which is attracted to lights, even in urban areas.

National Parks

Paraguay's national parks are largely remote and typically inadequately protected. Parque Nacional Teniente Enciso and Parque Nacional Defensores del Chaco are the principal parks in the Chaco (p838), but visitor facilities are poor and you'll need to take all your food and drink with you. The most biodiverse Atlantic Forest reserve is Parque Nacional San Rafael (p830). There is also a series of excellent and well-run private reserves across the country, perhaps the best of which is the Mbaracayú Biosphere Reserve (p833), another substantial block of Atlantic Forest.

Environmental Issues

The disappearance of the eastern Atlantic Forest has been alarming; much of the rainforest has been logged for agriculture, especially soy and wheat crops, and mostly for the benefit of large-scale, wealthy farmers. The construction of the Itaipú hydroelectric plant was not without controversy, and a second dam at Yacyretá, near Ayolas, has permanently altered the country's southern coast (made up of gallery forest).

The country's most pressing environmental threat, however, now concerns the rapid deforestation of the previously pristine Chaco. With the Paraguayan economy healthy and new technological advances making it easier than ever to raise cattle in this harsh environment, wealthy ranchers are taking advantage of the low land prices in the western region to establish new *estancias* (ranches). The resulting deforestation has been rapid and has made international headlines.

Furthermore, experiments in the development of soybean strains that can withstand the harsh Chaco climate potentially pose a serious threat to the remaining natural habitats. This prospect would introduce highly profitable monocultures into this delicate ecosystem, threatening to tip the ecological balance permanently.

SURVIVAL GUIDE

ℹ Directory A–Z

ACCESSIBLE TRAVEL
Infrastructure for travelers with disabilities is negligible. Irregular pavements can be a serious problem.

Download Lonely Planet's free *Accessible Travel* guides from http://lptravel.to/AccessibleTravel.

ACCOMMODATIONS
City hotels and hostels are generally good value, with air-conditioning, private bathrooms and wi-fi access. *Residenciales* (guesthouses) and *hospedajes* (basic hotels) are at the lower end and can attract suspect clientele – it's worth spending more. Camping facilities are rare. Most land is privately owned, so you can't pitch a tent without permission. In the Chaco, outside of the main towns you will need your own food, drink and bed sheets.

ACTIVITIES
Extraordinary biodiversity makes Paraguay a notable destination for ecotourism, in particular bird-watching. Hot spots for bird- and wildlife-watching include Parque Nacional San Rafael (p830), Mbaracayú Biosphere Reserve (p833) and the Laguna Capitán area (p837) of the Chaco.

Despite the large open spaces, hiking and camping are difficult. Much of the land is privately owned, and even the national parks usually only have a limited trail system. You are strongly advised to not attempt to camp in the Chaco unless accompanied by a local guide. People go missing every year.

ELECTRICITY
Use plugs with two round or flat pins and no grounding pin – 220V, 50Hz.

EMBASSIES & CONSULATES
A full, updated list of diplomatic offices in Paraguay is available at www2.mre.gov.py/index.php/representaciones/representaciones-extranjeras-acreditadas-en-paraguay2.

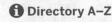

PARAGUAY DIRECTORY A–Z

SLEEPING PRICE RANGES

The following price ranges refer to a double room with bathroom in high season. Unless otherwise stated, breakfast is included in the price.

$ less than 150,000G

$$ 150,000–300,000G

$$$ more than 300,000G

Argentine Embassy (☎ 021-21-2320; Av España cnr Perú, Asunción; ⊙ 9am-5pm Mon-Fri)

Bolivian Embassy (☎ 021-21-1430; Israel 309 near Rio de Janeiro, Asunción; ⊙ 9am-5pm Mon-Fri)

Brazilian Embassy (☎ 021-24-8400; cnr Irrazábal & Eligio Ayala, Asunción; ⊙ 8am-5pm Mon-Fri)

Brazilian Consulate (☎ 061-50-0984; Pampliega 205, Ciudad del Este; ⊙ 7am-noon Mon-Fri)

Brazilian Viceconsulate (☎ 071-20-6335; Memmel 452, Encarnación; ⊙ Mon-Fri 8am-3pm)

French Embassy (☎ 021-21-3840; Av España 893, Asunción)

German Embassy (☎ 021-21-4009; Av Venezuela 241, Asunción; ⊙ 8-11am Mon-Fri)

UK Embassy (☎ 021-328-5507; Av Mariscal López 3794, Edificio Citicenter, 5th fl, Asunción; ⊙ 9am-5:30pm Mon-Thu, to 1pm Fri)

US Embassy (☎ 021-21-3715; Av Mariscal López 1776, Asunción; ⊙ 8am-5pm Mon-Fri)

FOOD

Beef here is succulent, abundant and easily rivals that of Argentina. The best cuts are *tapa de cuadril* (rump steak) and *corte americano* (T-bone), though the most common (and cheapest) are fatty *vacío* (flank) and chewy-but-flavorsome *costillas* (ribs).

Grains, particularly maize, are common ingredients in traditional foods, while *mandioca* (manioc) is the standard accompaniment for every meal. *Chipa* (a type of bread made with manioc flour, eggs and cheese) is sold everywhere but is best in the southern town of Coronel Bogado. Empanadas are great wherever you buy them. However, it can be hard to find typical dishes in restaurants: locals tend to eat them only at home where recipes are passed from generation to generation.

Paraguayans consume massive quantities of yerba maté (a type of tea), most commonly as refreshing ice-cold *tereré* (iced maté) and generously spiked with *yuyos* (medicinal herbs). The national obsession can be bought in any general store, but you will need to get your *guampa* (gourd) and *bombilla* (drinking straw) first. There are countless brands and brews of yerba available in the supermarket,

EATING PRICE RANGES

The following price ranges refer to a standard main course.

$ less than 15,000G

$$ 15,000–55,000G

$$$ more than 55,000G

and the most refreshing for *tereré* are those flavored with mint or citrus. Kurupí, Campesino, Selecta and Pajarito are among the most popular brands.

HEALTH

Paraguay presents relatively few health problems for travelers.

➡ There are occasional minor outbreaks of dengue fever, but no malaria.

➡ Carry sunscreen, a hat and plenty of bottled water to avoid becoming dehydrated.

➡ Avoid cheap condom brands.

Water is drinkable in the cities, but avoid it in the countryside. In the Chaco it is positively salty.

Availability & Cost of Health Care

Private hospitals are better than public hospitals, and those in Asunción, Ciudad del Este and Encarnación are the best. If you need treatment, get yourself to one of those cities rather than using a clinic in a smaller town.

INTERNET ACCESS

Internet is widely available in cities, but limited in smaller towns. An hour of use costs around 3000G to 6000G. Wi-fi is common in the cities, and all hotels and most restaurants and bars have it, though it is often password protected.

LANGUAGE COURSES

Ask at the cultural centers for private language classes. See p817 for language courses.

LGBT TRAVELERS

Paraguay is an old-fashioned country, with conservative views. Despite a growing LGBT movement in the country, high-ranking government officials (including the outgoing president) have expressed views that suggest that reviewing equality laws is not high on their agenda. Public displays of affection between same-sex couples are unknown. Gay bars are appearing in Asunción, but on the whole homosexuality is not yet widely accepted.

MAPS

For more detailed maps of Paraguay's interior, the **Instituto Geográfico Militar** (☎ 021-20-6344; Artigas 988, Asunción; ⊙ 7am-5:30pm Mon-Fri) sells topographical maps that cover most of the country.

The **Touring y Automóvil Club Paraguayo** (☎ 021-217-0000; www.tacpy.com.py; 25 de Mayo near Brasil, Asunción; ⊙ 8am-5pm Mon-Fri) produces a series of road and town maps for tourists that are often available in gas stations.

MONEY

Banknote values are 2000G, 5000G, 10,000G, 20,000G, 50,000G and 100,000G; increasingly useless coins come in denominations of 50G, 100G, 500G and 1000G. Keep plenty of change and small notes as you travel.

ATMs & Credit Cards

➡ ATMs in major cities and towns are connected to Visa, MasterCard and Cirrus networks but often incur usage charges (25,000G).

➡ Outside of the Mennonite Colonies there are no ATMs in the Chaco.

➡ Plastic is rarely accepted outside the major cities, and sometimes comes with a surcharge.

➡ Most ATMs have a daily withdrawal limit of 1,500,000G.

Exchanging Money

➡ *Casas de cambio* (currency exchanges) are abundant in major cities, but shop around for the best rates.

➡ Street money changers give slightly better rates for cash and can be lifesavers at weekends, but do your calculations in advance!

➡ Rates for changing pounds sterling are poor outside of Asunción.

➡ Change your unwanted guaraníes before you leave Paraguay. If you don't, you risk being stuck with them!

OPENING HOURS

Banks 8am to 1pm Monday to Saturday; *casas de cambio* keep longer hours

Government offices 7am to 1pm or 2pm Monday to Friday

Restaurants Noon to 3pm & 6pm to 11pm. Many close on Monday.

Shops 8am to noon & 2pm to 7pm Monday to Friday, and Saturday morning

POST

The Paraguayan *correo* (postal service) claims to be the best on the continent, but in reality things are regularly lost en route. Essential mail should be sent *certificado* (registered) for a small additional fee. Take packages to the post office unsealed so the contents can be verified, then close them up with your own materials after inspection.

The central post office (p822) is in Asunción.

PUBLIC HOLIDAYS

Government offices and businesses in Paraguay are closed for the following official holidays.

Año Nuevo (New Year's Day) 1 January

Cerro Corá (Heroes' Day) 1 March

Semana Santa (Easter) March/April

Día de los Trabajadores (Labor Day) 1 May

Independencia (Independence Day) 15 May

Paz del Chaco (End of Chaco War) 12 June

Fundación de Asunción (Founding of Asunción) 15 August

Victoria de Boquerón (Battle of Boquerón) 29 September

Día de la Virgen (Immaculate Conception Day) 8 December

Navidad (Christmas Day) 25 December

RESPONSIBLE TRAVEL

➡ Avoid buying crafts made from native woods (such as *lapacho* and *palo santo*) or wild animals.

➡ Visitors interested in natural history and conservation should contact Para la Tierra (p829), the **Fundación Moisés Bertoni** (📞 021-60-8740; www.mbertoni.org.py; Argüello 208, Villa Morra), FAUNA Paraguay (p826) or **Guyra Paraguay** (📞 021-22-9097; www.guyra.org. py; Bobeda, Parque Ecológico Capital Verde, Asunción).

SAFE TRAVEL

Despite what you may hear from people who have never been, Paraguay is one of the continent's safest countries for travelers.

➡ With the exception of Ciudad del Este and the *costanera* (riverside road) in Asunción, cities are quite safe to walk around, even at night.

➡ The Chaco environment is hostile and desolate with limited infrastructure – it is highly recommended that you go with a guide.

➡ Beware of strong currents when swimming in rivers.

TELEPHONE

Private *locutorios* (telephone offices) are less common than before, though most have internet service as well. International calls are expensive.

Cell Phones

Local rates are low. Free SIM cards, or those with *saldo* (credit) charged to them are available for a small fee. Local SIM cards are much cheaper than roaming, but do not allow international calls to be made, only received.

The best cell-phone companies are Tigo, Personal and Claro; their *tarjetas* (cards) for charging credit to your phone are sold at every newsagent or you can charge credit over the counter via *minicarga*, where you see signs. Claro SIM cards can also be formatted to work in both Brazil and Argentina. Cell-phone prefixes usually start 09.

TOILETS

➡ Toilets in hotels, restaurants and service stations are typically well maintained.

➡ Public toilets are thin on the ground. Most bus terminals have one – for a small fee you get a smelly loo and an (often insufficient) wad of paper.

→ Carry your own toilet paper and use the bin, don't flush it.

→ Most buses have an on-board toilet (liquid only, please!) but cheaper services and those in more remote areas do not.

TOURIST INFORMATION

The government tourist ministry Senatur (p822) has picked up its game in the last few years, and there are good tourist offices in Asunción and other major cities.

SEAM (p822) Responsible for the maintenance of national parks.

FAUNA Paraguay (p826) Provides information about ecotours and visiting national parks.

VISAS

Canadians, New Zealanders and Americans need visas, others need only a valid passport. Visas are available on arrival at the airport, but complications sometimes arise.

Visas may be requested and obtained on the same day at most Paraguayan consulates abroad, but requirements and cost depend where you are applying. Typically you will need two passport photos and two copies of each of the following: your passport, proof of onward travel and proof of sufficient funds.

Visit the **immigration office** (☑ 021-44-2840; cnr Ayala & Caballero, Asunción; ⏱7am-2:30pm Mon-Fri) for information about immigration points, entrance or exit stamps, or visa paperwork.

Entering and exiting Paraguay is straightforward and hassle-free provided you get your passport stamps. Note that buses that cross country borders often do not stop at customs because locals don't need to. You do, however, so make sure you tell the driver!

VOLUNTEERING

Volunteering is a comparatively new concept in Paraguay, but the idea is starting to take root. Para la Tierra (p829), based in Pilar, is a pioneer of the idea, offering an award-winning volunteer and intern program for socially aware, eco-minded visitors. Those interested in women's empowerment should contact the Santa María Education Fund (p831) in Santa María de Fe. Intercultural Experience (p817) is based out of Asunción.

WOMEN TRAVELERS

Paraguay is a reasonably safe country for women, but young unaccompanied women are likely to be hit on by Paraguayan men, especially if they are drinking alcohol. If it is unwelcome, be firm but polite in your response. Paraguayan women tend not to show much skin, and acting contrary to custom risks misinterpretation.

ⓘ Getting There & Away

AIR

Paraguay's Aeropuerto Internacional Silvio Pettirossi (p822) is in Luque, a satellite town of Asunción, and is the main international arrival and departure point. The Aeropuerto Guaraní (p832) in Ciudad del Este connects Asunción and major Brazilian destinations. All airlines have offices at Silvio Pettirossi.

International airlines flying to/from Asunción:

Aerolíneas Argentinas (☑ 021-23-3000; www.aerolineas.com.ar; Av España 2028, Asunción) Serves Buenos Aires only.

Air Europa (☑ 021-66-0777; www.aireuropa.com; Av San Martín 1672, Asunción) Serves Madrid four times a week.

Amazonas (☑ 021-60-5905; www.amazonas.com; Senador Long 515, Asunción) Multiple destinations in Brazil and Argentina, plus Santa Cruz (Bolivia).

Avianca (www.avianca.com; cnr Av España & Feliciángeli, Asunción) Direct flight to Lima Wednesday, Thursday and Friday.

Copa Airlines (☑ 021-61-4300; www.copaair.com; cnr Nudelmann & Boggiani, Asunción) Serves Panama City.

Gol (☑ 021-23-3000; www.voegol.com.br; Av España 2028, Asunción) Flies to São Paulo and onward to other Brazilian destinations via Ciudad del Este.

LATAM (☑ 021-45-1535; www.latam.com; Av Venezuela, Asunción) Flights to Lima, Miami, Buenos Aires, São Paulo and Santiago (Chile).

RIVER

Ferries cross into Ciudad del Este and Encarnación from Argentina. With patience, stamina, some negotiation and likely a fair amount of expense, unofficial river travel from Bahía Negra into Brazil or Bolivia is possible. Adventurers may want to try the crossing from colonial Pilar to the one-horse town of Puerto Cano, Argentina.

LAND

Negotiating Paraguayan borders can be harrowing; on the bus, off the bus, on the bus...Pay special attention when crossing from Brazil or Argentina. Ask the driver to stop at immigration (locals don't always need to) and be sure your papers are in order. Get your passport stamped on entering the country or face a fine upon leaving.

Stel Turismo (☑ 021-551-647; cnr Avs República Argentina & de la Mora, Asunción) runs a daily 8pm service from Asunción to Santa Cruz (Bolivia). The Friday service is in a newer, better bus, and is correspondingly more expensive.

ℹ Getting Around

Buses dominate transportation, offering reasonable fares and usually efficient service. Journeys between Paraguayan cities typically take less than eight hours, depending on the start and end points.

AIR

Paraguay is a relatively small country and internal flights are thin on the ground. Perhaps the most useful service for travelers is the **Grupo de Transporte Aéreo** (☎ 0983-11-7964; Aeropuerto Internacional Silvio Pettirossi, Autopista Silvio Pettirossi) flight to Bahía Negra and the Pantanal Paraguayo.

The new Encarnación airport, **Aeropuerto Teniente Amín Ayub González** (Capitán Miranda), receives infrequent **Sol del Paraguay** (☎ 021-22-4555; www.viajaconsol.com; Aeropuerto Internacional Silvio Pettirossi, Autopista Silvio Pettirossi) charter flights from Asunción, but is inconveniently located some distance outside of the city, near the town of Capitán Miranda. Flights link Asunción with Ciudad del Este en route to/from Brazilian destinations.

BOAT

You can travel by boat up the Río Paraguay to Concepción and Bahía Negra. You will need to hire a local boatman if you plan on exploring the Pantanal region. Costs can be high.

BUS

Bus quality varies from luxury services with TV, air-conditioning and comfortable reclining seats to bumpy sardine cans with windows that don't open and aisles crammed with people picked up along the way. Typically you get what you pay for – the best services are only slightly more expensive, so there's no need to scrimp.

Larger towns have central terminals with separate offices for each company. You can expect to be approached by touts shouting potential

> ### DEPARTURE TAX
> There is a US$40 airport tax on all departing flights. It is almost always included in the ticket; if it isn't, pay at the desk adjacent to the departure-lounge entrance and get a sticker on your ticket to prove it.

destinations at you. Take your time and pick your company wisely.

CAR & MOTORCYCLE

Car Rental

It is not cheap to rent (or buy!) a car in Paraguay, but it can be worth it if there are a few of you. Flexibility is your main advantage, although buses go most places accessible to an ordinary car. Anywhere away from the main *rutas* and you'll need a 4WD (around US$100 per day). Companies often charge extra mileage for distances above 100km and gas costs about 50% more than in neighboring countries. Better deals are available for longer rentals. Remember to keep your headlights on at all times.

Driver's License

Most rental agencies accept a home-country driver's license, but it's wise to back it up with an International Driving Permit – the lack of one is a favorite scam for soliciting bribes.

TAXI

In Asunción, taxi fares are metered; don't get in the taxi if it's not. In other cities they often are not metered, but no trip within city limits should cost more than 50,000G in Ciudad del Este and 40,000G elsewhere (usually less). Drivers in Asunción legally levy a 30% *recargo* (surcharge) between 10pm and 5am, and on Sunday and holidays.

Peru

POP 31.8 MILLION

Includes ➜

Best Places to Eat

➜ Central (p863)

➜ Maido (p866)

➜ Inti-Mar (p869)

➜ La Patarascha (p941)

➜ Cicciolina (p896)

Best Places to Stay

➜ Villa Barranco (p861)

➜ La Xalca (p938)

➜ Hotel Casona Solar (p880)

➜ Sol y Luna (p902)

Why Go?

Peru is as complex as its most intricate and exquisite weavings. Festivals mark ancient rites, the urban vanguard beams innovation and nature bestows splendid diversity.

Visitors flock to the glorious Inca citadel of Machu Picchu, yet this feted site is just a flash in a 5000-year history of peoples. Welcome to a place of mythical beliefs where ancient pageants unwind to the tune of booming brass bands. Peru's rich cultural heritage is never more real and visceral than when you are immersed streetside in the swirling madness of a festival.

Save time for adventure too. Giant sand dunes, chiseled peaks and Pacific breaks a few heartbeats away from rush-hour traffic: this vast country translates to paradise for the active traveler. Take it in small bites and don't rush. Festivals can swallow you whole for days. And that's when you realize: in Peru the adventure usually lies in getting there.

When to Go

Lima

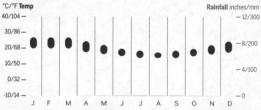

Jun–Aug Dry (and high) season in Andean highlands and eastern rainforest. Best time for festivals and highland sports.

Sep–Nov & Mar–May Ideal for less-crowded visits. September to November are good for rainforest trekking.

Dec–Feb Rainy season in the highlands. High season for the coast and beach activities.

Entering the Country

Border crossings include Arica (Chile) via Tacna; Huaquillas, Guayaquil and Macará (all in Ecuador), reached from the northern coast and highlands at Tumbes, La Tina or Jaén; Copacabana and Desaguadero (Bolivia) along Lake Titicaca; and multiple Brazilian and Bolivian towns and river ports in the Amazon.

ONE WEEK ITINERARY

Start your journey in Lima; sleep in at cozy Barranco lodgings and find a ceviche restaurant for a leisurely seafood lunch with a touch of pisco (grape brandy). Follow it up by visiting museums in Lima Centro or by renting bikes to pedal the clifftops via the parks of Miraflores.

Fly early the next day to Cuzco, transferring immediately to the lower Sacred Valley to acclimatize for several days. Explore the market and ruins of Pisac. With ancient Ollantaytambo as your base, take the train to Aguas Calientes for a day of exploration in the world-famous Inca citadel Machu Picchu. From here, take the train to Estación Poroy so you can spend your last day tripping the cobblestones of wonderful Cuzco, with museum visits, arts and crafts shops and great restaurants.

Fly back to Lima for your final hurrah, with perhaps a food tour before checking out the club scene before you head back home.

Essential Food & Drink

Arroz chaufa Fried rice is ubiquitous.

Ceviche Raw fish and seafood marinated in lime with onions, hot pepper slivers and other additions.

Chicha Drink usually made from fermented blue corn and consumed before it ferments.

Cuy Guinea pig is a common Andean delicacy.

Potatoes With surprising diversity and varied presentations.

Top Tips

➡ When visiting the Cuzco area, start in the lower Sacred Valley and Machu Picchu and work your way up to Cuzco and higher attractions to aid your acclimatization.

➡ Book sightseeing flights over Nazca Lines in advance. Try to get an early slot when conditions are calmer.

➡ Shop around for ATMs as fees vary.

➡ Take altitude seriously. When you go to higher altitudes, don't book tours for the first few days; take hiking ascents gradually.

➡ Fly into Cuzco in the morning since afternoon flights can be cancelled due to high winds.

➡ Avoid the cheapest buses as they often have safety issues.

FAST FACTS

Currency Nuevo sol (S)

Visas Generally not required for travelers entering Peru.

Money ATMs widely available in larger towns and cities. Credit cards accepted in most establishments.

Capital Lima

Emergency 105 (police)

Languages Spanish, Quechua, Aymara

Exchange Rates

Australia	A$1	S2.37
Canada	C$1	S2.54
Europe	€1	S3.85
Japan	¥100	S3.00
New Zealand	NZ$1	S2.17
UK	UK£1	S4.33
USA	US$1	S3.31

PERU

For current exchange rates, see www.xe.com.

Daily Costs

➡ Inexpensive hotel room or dorm bed: S28–165; double room in a midrange hotel: S85–435

➡ Set lunches: less than S15; main dish at a midrange restaurant: S40

Resources

Lonely Planet (www.lonely planet.com/peru)

Living in Peru (www.living inperu.com)

Peruvian Times (www. peruviantimes.com)

Expat Peru (www.expat peru.com)

Peru Highlights

1 Machu Picchu
(p906) Trekking a breathless rite of passage to awe-inspiring ancient Inca ruins hidden in cloud forest.

2 Cuzco (p890)
Pounding colonial Andean cobblestone streets, taking in historical museums, and trekking humbling Inca hillsides.

3 Arequipa
(p875) Exploring this historical city, surrounded by imposing volcanoes and sunken canyons.

4 Huaraz (p927)
Using this trekking metropolis as a base to tackle the Cordillera Blanca, one of South America's most spectacular mountain ranges.

200 miles
400 km

Equator

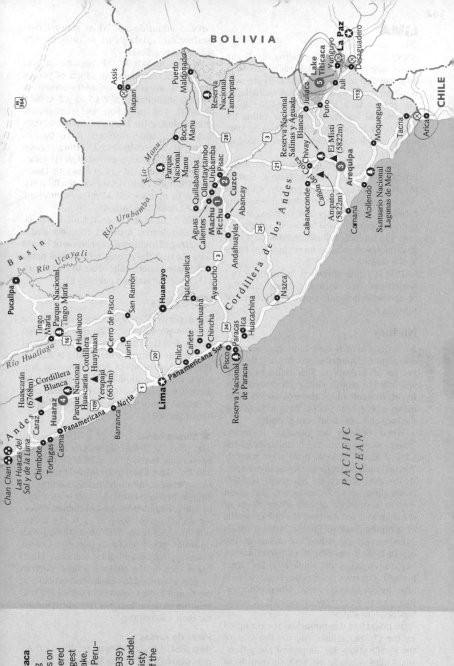

BOLIVIA

CHILE

PACIFIC OCEAN

LIMA

⏱ 01 / POP 9.75 MILLION

After Cairo, this sprawling metropolis is the second-driest world capital, rising above a long coastline of crumbling cliffs. To enjoy it, climb on the wave of chaos that spans high-rise condos built alongside pre-Columbian temples and fast Pacific breakers rolling toward noisy traffic snarl-ups. Think one part southern Cali doused with a heavy dose of *America Latina*.

But Lima is also sophisticated, with a civilization that dates back millennia. Stately museums display sublime pottery; galleries debut edgy art; solemn religious processions recall the 18th century and crowded nightclubs dispense tropical beats. No visitor can miss the capital's culinary genius, part of a gastronomic revolution more than 400 years in the making.

This is Lima. Shrouded in history (and sometimes fog), gloriously messy and full of aesthetic delights. Don't even think of missing it.

History

As ancient as it is new, Lima has survived apocalyptic earthquakes, warfare and the rise and fall of civilizations. This resilient city has welcomed a rebirth after each destruction. In pre-Hispanic times, the area served as an urban center for the Lima, Wari, Ichsma and the Inca cultures in different periods.

When Spanish conquistador Francisco Pizarro sketched out the boundaries of his 'City of Kings' in 1535, there were roughly 200,000 indigenous people living in the area. By the 18th century, the Spaniards' tumbledown village of adobe and wood had given way to a viceregal capital, where fleets of ships arrived to transport the golden spoils of conquest back to Europe. After a disastrous earthquake wiped out much of the city in 1746, it was rebuilt with splendorous baroque churches and ample *casonas* (large houses). The city's prominence began to fade after independence in 1821, when other urban centers were crowned capitals of newly independent states.

In 1880 Lima was ransacked and occupied by the Chilean military during the War of the Pacific (1879–83). As part of the pillage, the Chileans made off with thousands of tomes from the National Library (they were returned in 2007). Postwar expansion meant that by the 1920s Lima was crisscrossed by a network of broad boulevards inspired by Parisian urban design. When another devastating earthquake struck in 1940, the city again had to rebuild.

By the mid-1900s the population was growing exponentially. An influx of people from rural areas took the metro area from 661,000 inhabitants in 1940 to 8.5 million by 2007. The migration was particularly intense during the 1980s, when armed conflicts in the Andes displaced many people. Shantytowns mushroomed, crime soared and the city fell into a period of steep decay. In 1992 the terrorist group Sendero Luminoso (Shining Path) detonated deadly truck bombs in middle-class Miraflores, marking one of Lima's darkest hours.

Today's Lima has been rebuilt to an astonishing degree. A robust economy and a vast array of municipal improvement efforts have repaved the streets, refurbished parks and created safer public areas to bring back a thriving cultural and culinary life.

◉ Sights

The majority of museums are located in the busy downtown area of Central Lima. If you have a few days here, try visiting them on a weekend morning when traffic is calmer. The neighborhoods of Miraflores and Barranco can be walked in their entirety, and there are pleasant parks and seaside walks to retreat to when you've had your fill of urban attractions.

★ Museo Larco   MUSEUM

(Map p853; ⏱ 01-461-1312; www.museolarco.org; Bolívar 1515, Pueblo Libre; adult/child under 15 S30/15; ⏱ 9am-10pm) In an 18th-century viceroy's mansion, this museum offers one of the largest, best-presented displays of ceramics in Lima. Founded by pre-Columbian collector Rafael Larco Hoyle in 1926, the collection includes more than 50,000 pots, with ceramic works from the Cupisnique, Chimú, Chancay, Nazca and Inca cultures. Highlights include the sublime Moche portrait vessels, presented in simple, dramatically lit cases, and a Wari weaving in one of the rear galleries that contains 398 threads to the linear inch – a record.

Plaza de Armas   PLAZA

(Map p854) Lima's 140-sq-meter Plaza de Armas, also called the Plaza Mayor, was not only the heart of the 16th-century settlement established by Francisco Pizarro, it was a center of the Spaniards' continent-wide empire. Though not one original building remains,

Metropolitan Lima

0 — 2 km
0 — 1 mile

Cerro San ▲
Cristóbal
(409m)

RÍMAC

EL AGUSTINO

Vía de
Evitamiento

Internacional
Jorge Chávez
(9.5km)

Av Grau

US Embassy

Av El Polo

SAN
LUIS

Av Canada

Av Panamericana Sur

See Centro
Histórico
Map (p854)

Av 28 de Julio

Av Nicolas Arriola

LIMA
CENTRO

LA
VICTORIA

Av México

Cruz
del Sur

SAN BORJA

Av Aviación

Pachacamac
(32km)

LIMA

See Lima District
& La Victoria
Map (p856)

Paseo de la
República
(Vía Expresa)

Av Javier Prado Este

Av Primavera

Río Surco

Av Arica

Av Arequipa

German
Embassy

BREÑA

LINCE

LC Perú

Av Tingo María

Av Brasil

Israeli
Embassy

SURQUILLO

Av Santiago de Surco

JESÚS
MARÍA

French Embassy

Oltursa

Av Aramburu

Av República de Panama

PUEBLO
LIBRE

Av Bolívar

Italian
Embassy

See San Isidro
Map (p864)

SAN ISIDRO

Av Benavides

Museo
Larco

Av S. Carrión

Barra
Chalaca

Av República de Panama

Av Sucre

Av Salaverry

See Barranco
Map (p862)

Av Universitaria

Swiss
Embassy

See Miraflores
Map (p859)

Av Jose Pardo

MAGDALENA
DEL MAR

Playa
Costa Verde

Circuito de Playas

PACIFIC OCEAN

PERU LIMA

at the center of the plaza is an impressive
bronze fountain erected in 1650.

Monasterio de San Francisco   MONASTERY

(Map p854; ☎01-426-7377, ext 300; www.museocata
cumbas.com; cnr Lampa & Ancash; adult/child under 15 S15/3; ☻9am-8pm) This bright-yellow
Franciscan monastery and church is most
famous for its bone-lined **catacombs** (containing an estimated 70,000 remains) and its
remarkable **library** housing 25,000 antique
texts, some of which pre-date the conquest.
Admission includes a 30-minute guided tour
in English or Spanish. Tours leave as groups
gather.

★ El Circuito Mágico del Agua   FOUNTAIN

(Map p856; Parque de la Reserva, Av Petit Thouars,
cuadra 5; S4; ☻3-10:30pm Wed-Sun) This indul-
gent series of illuminated fountains is so over
the top it can't help but induce stupefaction
among even the most hardened travel cynic.
A dozen different fountains are capped, at the

end, by a laser light show at the 120m-long
Fuente de la Fantasía (Fantasy Fountain).
The whole display is set to a medley of tunes
comprising everything from Peruvian waltzes to ABBA. It has to be seen to be believed.

★ Fundación Museo Amano   MUSEUM

(Map p858; ☎01-441-2909; www.museoama
no.org; Retiro 160; ☻10am-5pm) **FREE** The
well-designed Fundación Museo Amano
features a fine private collection of ceramics,
with a strong representation of wares from
the Chimú and Nazca cultures. It also has
a remarkable assortment of lace and other
textiles produced by the coastal Chancay
culture. There's an optional 1.5-hour guided
tour in English, Portuguese or Spanish.

★ Iglesia de Santo Domingo   CHURCH

(Map p854; ☎01-427-6793; cnr Camaná & Conde
de Superunda; church free, convent S7; ☻9am-
1pm & 5-7:30pm Mon-Sat) One of Lima's most
historic religious sites, the Iglesia de Santo

Centro Histórico

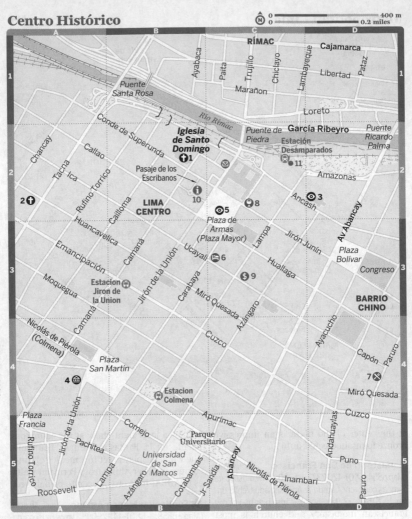

Centro Histórico

⊚ Top Sights
1 Iglesia de Santo Domingo....................B2

⊚ Sights
2 Iglesia de las Nazarenas A2
3 Monasterio de San Francisco D2
4 Museo Andrés del Castillo...................A4
5 Plaza de Armas C2

🛏 Sleeping
6 Hotel Maury C3

🍴 Eating
7 Wa Lok D4

🍷 Drinking & Nightlife
8 Museo del Pisco.....................................C2

ℹ Information
9 Banco de Crédito del Perú C3
10 Municipal Tourist Office B2

ℹ Transport
11 Ferrocarril Central Andino C2

Domingo and its expansive **convent** are built on land granted to the Dominican friar Vicente de Valverde, who accompanied Pizarro throughout the conquest and was instrumental in persuading him to execute the captured Inca Atahualpa. Originally completed in the 16th century, this impressive pink church has been rebuilt and remodeled at various points since.

Impakto
GALLERY

(Map p858; 📞 01-368-7060; www.galeria-impakto.com; Av Santa Cruz 857, Miraflores; ⊗ noon-8pm Mon-Fri, 9am-5pm Sat) Located on the 1st floor of a towering and dark office building, this contemporary-art museum has a glass facade that reveals just enough of the stark white interior to pique your interest. Both national and international artists are continually exhibited here to provide diverse yet always fresh perspectives.

★ Monumental Callao
CULTURAL CENTER

(www.monumentalcallao.com; Jirón Constitución 250; ⊗ 11am-6pm) Superstar graffiti artists are helping to revive the rough neighborhood surrounding Casa Ronald, a 1920 architectural masterpiece. Now a center for creatives, Monumental Callao incorporates restaurants and artists' studios, as well as galleries, with tenants intermittently donating their time to the surrounding community. Every weekend you can find rooftop parties with DJs or live salsa concerts, and even fashion shows using the colorful Spanish-style tiling as the catwalk.

Museo Andrés del Castillo
MUSEUM

(Map p854; 📞 01-433-2831; www.madc.com.pe; Jirón de la Unión 1030; S10; ⊗ 9am-6pm Mon-Sat, 10am-6pm Sun) Housed in a pristine 19th-century mansion with Spanish tile floors, this worthwhile private museum showcases a vast collection of minerals, as well as breathtakingly displayed Nazca textiles and Chancay pottery, including some remarkable representations of Peruvian hairless dogs.

★ Museo de Arte de Lima
MUSEUM

(MALI; Map p856; 📞 01-204-0000; www.mali.pe; Paseo Colón 125; adult/child S30/15; ⊗ 10am-7pm Tue, Thu & Fri, to 5pm Sat & Sun) Known locally as MALI, Lima's principal fine-art museum is housed in a striking beaux-arts building that was renovated in 2015. Subjects range from pre-Columbian to contemporary art, and there are also guided visits to special exhibits. On Sunday entry is just S1. A satellite museum is under construction in Barranco.

Huaca Pucllana
RUINS

(Map p858; 📞 01-617-7138; cnr Borgoño & Tarapacá; adult/child S12/6; ⊗ 9am-4:30pm; 🔊) Located near the Óvalo Gutiérrez, this huaca is a restored adobe ceremonial center from the Lima culture that dates back to AD 400. In 2010 an important discovery of four Wari mummies, untouched by looting, was made. Though vigorous excavations continue, the site is accessible by regular guided tours in Spanish (for a tip). In addition to a tiny on-site **museum**, there's a celebrated **restaurant** (Map p858; 📞 01-445-4042; www.resthuacapucllana.com; Gral Borgoño cuadra 8; mains S24-72; ⊗ 12:30-4:30pm & 7pm-midnight Mon-Sat, to 4pm Sun) that offers incredible views of the illuminated ruins at night

🏃 Activities

Cycling

Bike paths along the coast and designated lanes in Miraflores make the area great for cycling. Popular excursions from Lima include the 31km ride to **Pachacamac** (📞 01-321-5606; http://pachacamac.cultura.pe; Antigua Carr Panamericana Sur Km 31.5, Lurín; adult/child S15/5; ⊗ 9am-5pm Tue-Sat, to 4pm Sun), where there are good local trails open between April and December. Expert riders can inquire about the stellar downhill circuit from Olleros to San Bartolo south of Lima. For general information on cycling (in Spanish), try **Federación Deportiva Peruana de Ciclismo** (Map p858; 📞 01-480-7390; www.fedepeci.pe; Av Aviación s/n puerta 13, La Videna San Luis; ⊗ 9am-1pm & 3-5pm Mon-Fri) or the Facebook page of Ciclismo Sin Fronteras Miraflores.

Mirabici
CYCLING

(Map p858; 📞 01-673-3908; www.mirabiciperu.pe; Costaneras/n. Miraflores; rentals per hour S23; ⊗ 9am-7pm) On the coastal paths, this is a convenient stop for bicycle rentals (including tandems) and offers tours of Barranco, Miraflores and San Isidro.

Paragliding

From the Miraflores cliff tops, tandem flights (S260 for 10 minutes) take off from the cliff-top 'paraport' at the Parque Raimondi to soar over coastal skyscrapers and gaze down at the surfers.

Peru Fly
PARAGLIDING

(Map p858; 📞 959-524-940, 01-444-5004; www.perufly.com; Parque del Amor, Miraflores; ⊗ 10am-6pm) A paragliding school that also offers tandem flights in Miraflores.

PERU LIMA

Lima District & La Victoria

Lima District & La Victoria

Swimming & Water Sports

Despite the newspaper warnings about pollution, *limeños* (inhabitants of Lima) hit the beaches in droves in summer (January through March). **Playa Costa Verde** in Miraflores (nicknamed Waikiki) is a favorite of local surfers and has good breaks year-round. Barranco's beaches have waves that are better for longboards. There are seven other beaches in Miraflores and four more in Barranco. Serious surfers can also try **Playa La Herradura** in Chorrillos, which has waves up to 5m high during good swells. Do not leave your belongings unattended, as theft is a problem.

☞ Tours

Andean Photo Expeditions   TOURS
(☏ 960-724-103; www.andeanphotoexpeditions.com)
Excellent photography tours of Lima led by French and Peruvian photographers, with tailor-made options. There's no office, meet ups are in Parque Kennedy or Central Lima.

✷ Festivals & Events

El Señor de los Milagros   RELIGIOUS
(Lord of Miracles; ⊙ Oct) The city drapes itself in purple during this massive religious procession through Centro Historico on October 18 in honor of the Christ from the **Iglesia de las Nazarenas** (Map p854; ☏ 01-423-5718; cnr Tacna & Huancavelica; ⊙ 7am-1pm & 4-8:30pm); smaller processions on occur other Sundays in October.

🛏 Sleeping

From family *pensións* to glass towers, Lima has every type of accommodations. Though it's one of the most expensive destinations in the country, an overflow of lodgings means there's some good value, particularly in the midrange.

If arriving at night, it's worth contacting hotels in advance to arrange for airport pick-up; even budget hostels can arrange this – sometimes for a few dollars less than the official airport service.

Lima Centro

Offerings in the congested city center lag behind other neighborhoods. Central Lima has seen its high-end business slip away as upscale establishments have shifted to San Isidro and Miraflores.

1900 Backpackers HOSTEL $

(Map p856; ☎01-424-3358; www.1900hostel.com; Av Garcilaso de la Vega 1588; dm S26-43, s/d incl breakfast S86/112; @ 📶) A downtown hot spot, this old mansion designed by Gustavo Eiffel is revamped with modern design touches, though it maintains the marble floors and other turn-of-the-century flourishes. For a hostel it's downright gorgeous. Rooms are smart and simple, with bunks side by side. There's a tiny kitchen and cool common spaces, such as a pool room with a bar and a red chandelier.

Hotel Maury HOTEL $$

(Map p854; ☎01-428-8188; www.hotelmaury.hoteles; Ucayali 201; d/tr incl breakfast S227/263; ❄ @ 📶) A longtime Lima outpost renowned for cultivating a new-fangled cocktail known as the pisco sour (grape brandy cocktail) back in the 1930s. While public areas retain flourishes such as gilded mirrors and Victorian-style furniture, the 76 simple rooms are more modern, and some feature Jacuzzi tubs and lockboxes. Credit cards accepted.

Miraflores

The favored neighborhood for travelers is Miraflores, which offers plenty of hostels, inns and upscale hotel chains and vigilant neighborhood security.

Overlooking the ocean, this area's streets are pedestrian-friendly and teem with cafes, restaurants, hotels, high-rises, shops and nightclubs that pump out everything from disco to *cumbia* (Colombian salsa-like dance music). There are many quiet blocks, too.

★Quinta Miraflores BOUTIQUE HOTEL $

(Map p858; ☎01-446-5147; www.quintamiraflores.com; Av 28 de Julio 844; r incl breakfast S120-180; 📶) Run by an effervescent Italian, this lovely Mediterranean-style home welcomes visitors to enjoy a real retreat in the heart of busy Miraflores. There are just four elegant rooms, each decked out with fun period pieces and thoughtful touches like thick robes, large desks and a cheat sheet of city tips. Breakfast is served in the garden or in your room.

Pariwana HOSTEL $

(Map p858; ☎01-242-4350; http://pariwana-hostel.com/hostels/lima; Av Jose Larco 189; dm S40-62, d with/without bathroom S160/140, all incl breakfast; @ 📶) This well-heeled and central party hostel has proved a hit with the international backpacker crowd. It's full service, with tours on offer, an on-site cafe and a lovely roof deck with shady seating. Doubles with hairdryers feel all grown up. The complimentary earplugs are an unsubtle tip-off, but you probably didn't come here to rest. There are some women-only dorms.

★Casa Cielo BOUTIQUE HOTEL $$

(Map p858; ☎01-242-1127; www.hotelcasacielo.com; Berlin 370; s/d/ste incl breakfast S198/333/396; P 📶) A beautiful option that's centrally located, offering top-notch service and great value. The look is modern Andino, with ceramic bulls and Mario Testino photographs set against a neutral palette. Rooms feature hypoallergenic pillows, double-pane windows and safe boxes. À la carte breakfasts are served at a top-floor cafe.

IFE Boutique Hotel BOUTIQUE HOTEL $$

(Map p858; ☎01-677-2229; www.ifeboutique.com; San Ignacio de Loyola 646; d incl breakfast S324; ❄ 📶) A little, service-oriented boutique hotel in a convenient neighborhood. It's stylish and elegant, with eight rooms, with styles ranging from classical to pop art. King- and queen-size beds have luxuriant linens. Staff is helpful and amenities include LCD televisions, minibar, iPod docks and safe boxes.

Tryp DESIGN HOTEL $$

(Map p858; ☎01-571-8100; www.melia.com/en/hotels/peru/lima/tryp-lima-miraflores; Av Ernesto Diez Canseco 344; d/ste S310/450; P ❄ 📶 🏊) This Melia property updates the international chain hotel with hipster sensibilities: a smart, contemporary style, bicycles to borrow and bluetooth speakers. The 140 rooms are spread over 10 floors, each with a safe, minibar and huge flatscreen TV. There's also 24-hour room service, a gym and heated rooftop lap pool. There is a restaurant in the glass lobby.

Miraflores

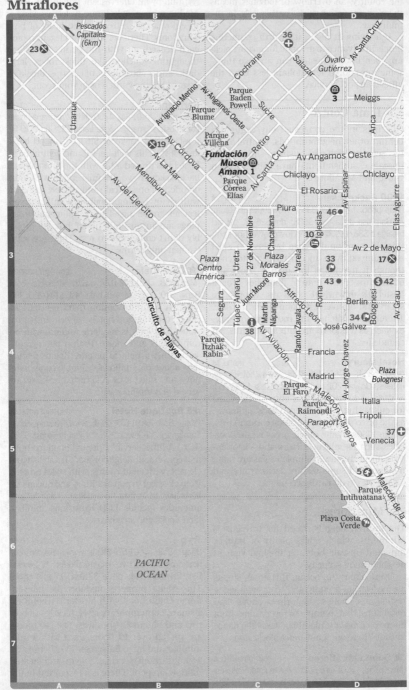

Pescados Capitales (6km)

23

36

Cochrane

Salazar

Óvalo Gutiérrez

Av Santa Cruz

Unanue

Av Ignacio Merino

Av Angamos Oeste

Parque Baden Powell

Sucre

3

Meiggs

Parque Blume

Arica

19 Av Córdova

Parque Villena

Retiro

Av La Mar

Mendiburu

Fundación Museo Amano 1

Av Santa Cruz

Av Angamos Oeste

Parque Correa Elías

Chiclayo

Chiclayo

Av del Ejército

El Rosario

Av Espinar

Piura

46

27 de Noviembre

Iglesias

Chacaltana

10

Av 2 de Mayo

Plaza Centro América

Ureta

Plaza Morales Barros

Varela

33

17

43

42

Tupac Amaru

Juan Moore

Alfredo León

Roma

Berlin

Bolognesi

Av Grau

Segura

Martín Napanga

Ramón Zavala

34

José Gálvez

Parque Itzhak Rabin

38

Av Aviación

Francia

Circuito de Playas

Madrid

Av Jorge Chavez

Plaza Bolognesi

Parque El Faro

Malecón Cisneros

Italia

Parque Raimondi

Tripoli

Paraport

37

Venecia

5

Malecón de la

Parque Intihuatana

Playa Costa Verde

PACIFIC OCEAN

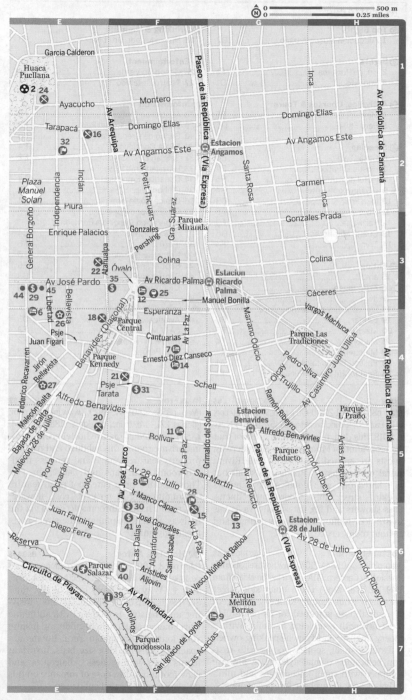

Miraflores

Libre
DESIGN HOTEL **$$**

(Map p858; ☎01-209-0900; https://librehotel.pe; Av La Paz 730; s/d incl breakfast S345/414; 🛜) New in 2018, this design hotel is further proof that the renovation of Miraflores is well underway. Guests are greeted by a playful Jade Rivera mural upon entering. Rooms are small but well kitted out, with double-pane windows blocking street noise, coordinated linens, glass showers and big flat-screen TVs. It has an 8th-floor rooftop terrace, a restaurant and 24-hour room service.

Hostal El Patio
GUESTHOUSE **$$**

(Map p858; ☎01-444-2107; www.hostalelpatio.net; Ernesto Diez Canseco 341A; s/d/tr incl breakfast from S149/182/248; @🛜) On a quiet side street just steps from Parque Kennedy, this gem of a guesthouse is named for its plant-filled courtyard with a trickling fountain. With a cheery English- and French-speaking owner, it features small, spotless rooms with cast-iron beds and colonial-style art. A few are equipped with small kitchenettes and mini-fridges. Check the website for special offers.

Inka Frog
HOTEL **$$**

(Map p858; ☎01-445-8979; www.inkafrog.com; Iglesias 271; s/d/tr incl breakfast S188/228/264; @🛜) Targeted at mature hostel-goers wanting private rooms, this subdued and friendly property features ample and spotless modern rooms with fans and flat-screen TVs. Those located on a cute roof patio feature air-conditioning at no extra cost. Beware: two rooms have bathrooms accessed via the hallway. Staff is helpful and the street is refreshingly quiet.

★ Hotel de Autor
B&B **$$$**

(Map p858; ☎01-681-8074; http://autor.pe; Av 28 de Julio 562B, Quinta Bustos; d incl breakfast S545; 🅿✳🛜) Why can't every hotel be like this? Service is personal, breakfasts are satisfying, and the style is modern, with authentic travel memorabilia to help guide and inspire your journey throughout Peru. Rooms are spacious, all with king-size beds, luxuriant linens and writing desks. Balconies and claw-foot tubs add a dose of romance on this quiet, centrally located cul-de-sac.

🛏 Barranco

At the turn of the 20th century, this was a summer resort for the upper crust. In the 1960s it was a center of bohemian life. Today, it is cluttered with restaurants and bustling bars, its graceful mansions converted into boutique hotels. It is certainly one of the most walkable areas, with lots of gardens and colonial architecture.

Casa Nuestra   B&B $$
(Map p862; ☎01-248-8091; www.casanuestraperu.com; Jirón Tumbes 270; s/d/tr incl breakfast S132/165/198; @ 🛜) With cool decor, murals and retro poster art, this sweet home sits on a peaceful, shady side street. It provides a great base for exploring Barranco, and offers discounts for long stays. The 2nd-floor rooms are best – 1st floor digs remain a step behind in terms of renovation. There's kitchen access and a lovely roof deck. By reservation only.

★ Second Home Perú   B&B $$$
(Map p862; ☎01-247-5522; www.secondhomeperu.com; Domeyer 366; d/ste incl breakfast S446/545; @ 🛜 🏊) With a fairy-tale feel, this lovely five-room Bavarian-style *casona* has claw-foot tubs, sculpted ironworks, a swimming pool and breathtaking views of the ocean. Run by the children of artist Victor Delfín, it features private gardens with his taurine sculptures, works of other artists and a sculpting studio that's available for rent. Credit cards accepted.

★ Villa Barranco   BOUTIQUE HOTEL $$$
(Map p862; ☎01-396-5418; www.ananay-hotels.com/branches/villa-barranco; Calle Carlos Zegarra 274; d incl breakfast S1706; 🛜) The kind of effortlessly beautiful but comfortable old house that instantly feels like home. This Barranco boutique hotel is brimming with style, from the clever decor to the garden with hummingbirds dive-bombing the honeysuckle. Rooms are spacious, some with claw-foot tubs, and garden access. The best feature is a gorgeous rooftop bar for enjoying pisco sours with friends.

Hotel B   BOUTIQUE HOTEL $$$
(Map p862; ☎01-206-0800; www.hotelb.pe; Sáenz Peña 204; d S990-1584; @ 🛜) This refurbished mansion mixes modern with classical to dramatic effect. There are 17 eclectic rooms (some can feel a bit overstuffed) surrounding a courtyard planted with a living wall of figs. Popular with nonguests, the lovely bar specializes in

G&Ts and Gatsby moments. You can also visit the rooftop, which has ocean views.

🍴 Eating

🍴 Lima Centro

Wa Lok   CHINESE $$
(Map p854; ☎01-447-1314; Paruro 878; mains S15-80; ⊙9am-11pm Mon-Sat, to 10pm Sun; 🍴) Serving seafood, fried rice as light and fresh as it gets, and sizzling meats that come on steaming platters, Wa Lok is among the best *chifas* (Chinese restaurants) in Chinatown. The 16-page Cantonese menu includes dumplings, noodles, stir-fries and a good selection of vegetarian options (try the braised tofu casserole). Portions are enormous; don't over-order.

🍴 San Isidro

★ Barra Chalaca   CEVICHE $$
(Map p853; ☎01-422-1465; Av Camino Real 1239; mains S14-39; ⊙11am-5pm) This casual ceviche and seafood bar combines masterful cooking and playful rapport for the win. Watching the prep cooks from your bar stool, order *curatado* (cures everything) – a fishbowl of tropical juices and fresh herbs. There's mouthwatering *tiradito chichuito* (sashimi with capers,

PERU LIMA

Barranco

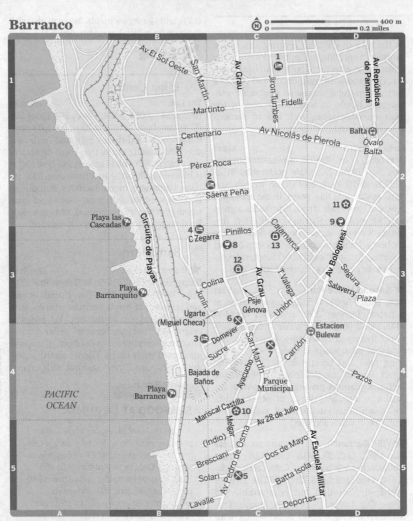

avocado and garlic); crisp, lightly battered *pejerrey* (silverside fish), and seafood fried rice that you can't put down.

★ Astrid y Gastón
Casa Moreyra   FUSION $$$

(Map p864; ☎01-442-2775; www.astridygaston. com; Av Paz Soldan 290; mains S53-89; ☻1-3pm & 7-11pm Mon-Sat) The standard-bearer of *no-voandina* cooking in Lima, Gastón Acurio's flagship French-influenced restaurant, run by Lima native Diego Muñoz, remains a culinary tour de force. The seasonal menu features traditional Peruvian fare, but it's the exquisite fusion specialties that make this a sublime

fine-dining experience. The 28-course tasting menu showcases the depth and breadth of possibility here – just do it.

✕ Miraflores

La Lucha Sanguachería   SANDWICHES $

(Map p858; ☎01-241-5953; Benavides 308; sandwiches S12-21; ☻8am-1am Sun-Thu, to 3am Fri & Sat) This all-hours corner sandwich shop is the perfect fix for the midnight munchies. *Lechón a la leña* (roasted pork) is its specialty, but there's also roast chicken or ham served in fluffy rolls, and juices are blended on the spot.

Barranco

Manolo CAFE $

(Map p858; ☏01-444-2244; www.manolochurros.com; Av José Larco 608; churros S4; ⊙7am-1am Sun-Thu, to 2am Fri & Sat) This thriving all-hours sidewalk cafe is best known for its piping-hot churros, which go smashingly well with a *chocolate caliente espeso* (thick hot chocolate) – perfect for dipping. Of course, there's also typical cafe fare.

★ **ámaZ** AMAZONIAN $$

(Map p858; ☏01-221-9393; www.amaz.com.pe; Av La Paz 1079; mains S20-65; ⊙12:30-11:30pm Mon-Sat, to 4:30pm Sun; ☏) Chef Pedro Miguel's wonder is wholly dedicated to the abundance of the Amazon. Start with oversized *tostones* (plantain chips) and tart jungle-fruit cocktails. Banana-leaf wraps, aka *juanes,* hold treasures such as fragrant Peking duck with rice. There's excellent *encurtido* (pickled vegetables) and the generous vegetarian set menu for two is a delicious way to sample the diversity.

★ **El Bodegón** BISTRO $$

(Map p858; ☏01-444-4704; www.elbodegon.com.pe; Av Tarapaca 197; mains S28-39; ⊙noon-midnight Mon-Sat, 11am-9pm Sun) Dimly lit with polished hardwood and offering snappy service, this corner taverna feels more Buenos Aires than Lima; we're just thankful it's here. This Gastón Acurio enterprise recaptures home-style Peruvian eating. It's worth sharing several dishes to spread your good fortune. Standouts include a creamy roasted cauliflower served whole and an ultradelectable *rocoto relleno* (stuffed pepper) with a nutty, rich sauce.

Matsuei JAPANESE $$

(Map p858; ☏981-310-180; www.matsueiperu.com.pe; Atahualpa 195; mains S16-70; ⊙12:30-3:30pm & 7:30-11pm Mon-Sat) Venerated Japanese superchef Nobu Matsuhisa once co-owned this sushi bar. Its new location is posh and atmospheric. Diners come to try some of the most spectacular sashimi and *maki* (sushi

rolls) in Lima. A must-have: the *acevichado,* a roll stuffed with shrimp and avocado, then doused in a house-made mayo infused with ceviche broth. Your brain will tingle.

★ **Central** PERUVIAN $$$

(Map p862; ☏01-242-8515; www.centralrestaurante.com.pe; Av Pedro de Osma 301; mains S52-95; ⊙seating 12:45-1:15pm & 7:45-8:30pm Mon-Sat) ☏ Part restaurant, part laboratory, Central reinvents Andean cuisine and rescues age-old Peruvian ingredients not used elsewhere. Dining is an experience, evidenced by tender native potatoes served in edible clay. Chef Virgilio Martinez wants you to taste the Andes. He paid his dues in Europe and Asia's top kitchens, but it's his work here that dazzles.

La Mar SEAFOOD $$$

(Map p858; ☏01-421-3365; www.lamarcebicheria.com; Av La Mar 770; mains S39-79; ⊙noon-5pm Mon-Fri, 11:45am-5:30pm Sat & Sun) A good-time *cevichería* (restaurant serving ceviche) with outstanding service and wonderful ceviche and *tiraditos* (Japanese version of ceviche), alongside a light and fresh *chifon chaufa* (fried rice). This Gastón Acurio outpost is not much more than a polished cement patio bursting with VIPs. Try the delicious riff on a bloody Mary – the sublime bloody *locho,* seafood shells and all. Desserts deliver too. It does not take reservations.

IK PERUVIAN $$$

(Map p858; ☏01-652-1692; www.ivankisic.pe; Elías Aguirre 179; mains S45-75; ⊙6-11pm Mon-Sat) Combining ancestral traditions with the Peruvian vanguard of molecular gastronomy is a tall order, but most feel that IK pulls it off with style. The restaurant is a tribute to a well-known local chef and its restorative atmosphere of living plants, natural sounds and light projections bring something new to the dining experience. Dishes are well balanced and meticulously presented.

PERU LIMA

San Isidro

San Isidro

😮 Eating
1 Astrid y Gastón Casa Moreyra D2

ℹ️ Information
2 Bolivian Embassy A2
3 Chilean Embassy C1
4 Colombian Embassy C2
5 Ecuadorian Embassy C2
6 iPerú C2
7 Scotiabank B1
8 Spanish Consulate D2

Pescados Capitales CEVICHE **$$$**
(Map p858; ☏ 01-421-8808; www.pescadoscapitales. com; Av La Mar 1337; mains S39-70; ⊙12:30-5pm) On a street once lined by clattering auto shops, this industrial-contemporary destination serves some of the finest ceviche around. Try the 'Ceviche Capital,' a mix of flounder, salmon and tuna marinated with red, white and green onions, bathed in a three-chili crème. A nine-page wine list offers a strong selection of Chilean and Argentinean vintages.

🍴 Barranco

La Panetteria BAKERY **$**
(Map p862; ☏ 01-469-8260; www.facebook.com/ lapanetteriabarranco; Av Grau 369; mains S8-22; ⊙8am-9pm Tue-Sun; 🛜) One of the neighborhood favorites, this bakery serves up a wide variety of breads, from traditional baguettes and French rolls, to playful experiments such as pesto or *aji* (Peru's slightly spicy pepper) loaves and gorgeous pastries. It's busy on weekends with the brunch crowd (eggs aren't on the menu but are available).

⭐ **Isolina** PERUVIAN **$$$**
(Map p862; ☏ 01-247-5075; www.isolina.pe; Av San Martín 101; mains S35-78; ⊙noon-10pm Mon & Tue, to 11pm Wed-Fri, 9am-5pm Sat, 9am-11pm Sun) Go old school. This is home-style *criollo* (spicy Peruvian fare with Spanish and African influences) food at its best. Isolina doesn't shy away from tripe and kidneys, but also offers loving preparations of succulent ribs, *causa escabechada* (whipped potato dishes with marinated onions) and vibrant green salads on the handwritten menu. Family-sized portions come in old-fashioned tins, but you could make a lighter meal of starters such as marinated clams or ceviche.

🍸 Drinking & Nightlife

⭐ **Dada** COCKTAIL BAR
(Map p862; www.dada.com.pe; Av San Martín 154; ⊙7pm-1am Tue & Wed, to 3am Thu-Sat) This chic mansion with themed rooms and a gorgeous patio is Barranco's newest hot spot. You know those locales that are described not as a place but a feeling, perhaps like hugging a friend? That's Dada. Come well dressed and well funded. The cocktails here are not cheap, but they are delicious. Live performances of calypso, jazz and rock.

⭐ **Museo del Pisco** BAR
(Map p854; ☏ 99-350-0013; www.museodelpisco. org; Jirón Junin 201, Lima Centro; ⊙10am-midnight) The 'educational' aspect of this wonderful bar might get you in the door, but it's the congenial atmosphere and outstanding original cocktails that will keep you here. We loved the *asu mare* – a pisco martini with ginger, cucumber, melon and basil. A sister bar to the

popular original in Cuzco, this one occupies the Casa del Oidor, a 16th-century *casona*.

Nuevo Mundo Draft Bar CRAFT BEER

(Map p858; ☑01-241-2762; Calle Manuel Bonilla 103, Miraflores; ☺noon-1am Mon-Thu, to 3am Fri & Sat, 5pm-1am Sun) Nuevo Mundo was one of the first craft breweries to come out of Lima, and it's now a major player on the pub scene, with a wide range of national craft brews on tap. Heavily decorated in what locals call *'chicha'* art (think neon palettes and loud phrases), this is a casual place for happy hour or to catch a soccer game.

Red Cervecera BEER GARDEN

(Map p862; ☑01-396-7944; www.redcervecera.com; Av Francisco Bolognesi 721, Barranco; ☺11am-8pm Mon, to 1am Tue-Thu, to 3am Fri & Sat; 🐕🎲) An all-encompassing stop for beer connoisseurs and amateurs alike. A well-stocked store at the entrance provides all the ingredients and equipment you'll need to brew up your own craft beer, while the bar toward the back serves up house brews and other domestic beers on tap.

☆ Entertainment

Brisas del Titicaca
Asociacion Cultural TRADITIONAL MUSIC

(Map p856; ☑01-715-6960; www.brisasdeltiticaca. com; Heroes de Tarapacá 168, Lima Centro; admission from S30; ☺noon-3pm & 9pm-12:30am) A lauded *folklórica* show near Plaza Bolognesi downtown, in an enormous venue.

Centro Cultural de España ARTS CENTER

(CCELIMA; Map p856; ☑01-330-0412; www.ccelima. org; Natalio Sánchez 181, Plaza Washington; ☺noon-10pm Tue-Sun) A full range of offerings, including a roomy 1st-floor gallery that puts on some of Lima's most intriguing contemporary-art exhibits. Also has a library (closes 7pm).

Cocodrilo Verde LIVE MUSIC

(Map p858; ☑01-444-2381; www.cocodriloverde. com; Francisco de Paola 226; ☺7pm-3am Mon-Sat) With great bands that range from popular music to jazz and bossa nova, this hip lounge is good for a night out. Minimum tab S25.

Microteatro Lima THEATRE

(Map p862; ☑01-252-8092; www.microteatrolima. com; Jirón Batallón Ayacucho 271) The theater is anything but dry or about high society, at least as far as this tiny space is concerned. A rotating roster of directors and actors changes weekly, offering up plays of just 15 minutes, performed in a 15-sq-meter room in front of 15

audience members. A lively bar makes this a great and unique outing. Plays are in Spanish.

Sargento Pimienta CLUB

(Map p862; ☑01-247-3265; www.sargentopimienta. com.pe; Av Bolognesi 757, Barranco; admission from S15; ☺10pm-4am Tue & Thu-Sat) A reliable spot in Barranco with a name that means 'Sergeant Pepper.' The barnlike club hosts various theme nights and occasional live bands.

Teatro Británico THEATRE

(Map p858; ☑01-615-3636; www.britanico.edu.pe; Bellavista 527, Miraflores) This theater hosts a variety of worthwhile productions, including plays in English.

🔒 Shopping

Clothing, jewelry and handicrafts from all over Peru can be found in Lima. Shop prices tend to be high, but bargain hunters can haggle their hearts out at craft markets. Credit cards and traveler's checks can be used at some spots, but you'll need photo ID.

Quality pisco can be bought duty-free at the airport prior to departure.

★ Las Pallas ARTS & CRAFTS

(Map p862; ☑01-477-4629; Cajamarca 212, Barranco; ☺10am-7pm Mon-Sat) For special gifts, check out this handicrafts shop featuring a selection of the highest-quality products from all over Peru; it's even on the radar of Sotheby's. Ring the bell if the gate is closed during opening hours.

★ El Cacaotal CHOCOLATE

(Map p862; ☑937-595-812; www.elcacaotal.com; Colina 108, 2nd fl; ☺11am-8pm Mon-Thu & Sat, to 7pm Fri, to 6pm Sun) 🍃 A sustainable chocolate shop with delicious bars and connoisseur expertise. It's the perfect opportunity to appease friends and family back home, and it offers fair-trade compensation for small-scale farmers around Peru. Products are organized by region and portraits of the farmers themselves grace the walls. It also does tastings and excellent workshops in English with an adjacent chocolate lab.

ℹ Information

DANGERS & ANNOYANCES

Like any large Latin American city, Lima is a land of haves and have-nots, which has made stories about crime here the stuff of legend. Yet the city has greatly improved since the lawless 1980s and most travelers have a safe visit. Nonetheless, stay aware.

DON'T MISS

NIKKEI NIRVANA

True artistry and exquisite flavors make **Maido** (Map p858; 01-446-2512; www.maido.pe; San Martín 399; mains S26-110; 12:30-4pm & 7:30-11pm Mon-Sat, 12:30-4pm Sun) an excellent stop for top-notch *nikkei* (Japanese-Peruvian) fare that has put it on World's Best lists. The menu of chef Mitsuharu 'Micha' Tsumura ranges from sushi to tender 50-hour ribs, okonomiyaki (Japanese savory pancake) and ramen, with a Peruvian accent. Desserts – such as the yucca mochi or a white-chocolate egg with sorbet yolk – delight. It supports sustainable fishing.

EMERGENCY

Ambulance	117
Police	105
Fire	116

MEDICAL SERVICES

Clínica Anglo-Americana (Map p858; 01-616-8990; www.clinicaangloamericana.pe; Calle Alfredo Salazar 350; 24hr) A renowned (but expensive) hospital in San Isidro.

Clínica Good Hope (Map p858; 01-610-7300; Malecón Balta 956; 8:30am-8pm Mon-Fri, to 1pm Sun) Quality care at good prices; there is also a dental unit.

MONEY

For extra security use ATMs inside banks (as opposed to on the street or in supermarkets); cover the key pad as you enter your password; and graze the whole keypad to prevent infrared tracing of passwords. Avoid making withdrawals late at night.

Banco de Crédito del Perú (BCP; Map p858; www.viabcp.com; cnr Av José Larco & José Gonzales) Has 24-hour Visa and Plus ATMs; also gives cash advances on Visa, and changes Amex, Citicorp and Visa traveler's checks. The **Central Lima** (Map p854; 01-427-5600; www.viabcp.com; cnr Lampa & Ucayali) branch has incredible stained-glass ceilings. There's another branch at **José Pardo** (Map p858; 01-445-1259; www.viabcp.com; Av José Pardo 491).

BBVA Continental (Map p858; 01-595-0000; www.bbvacontinental.pe; Av José Larco 631) A representative of Visa; its ATMs also take Cirrus, Plus and MasterCard.

Citibank (Map p858; 01-215-2000; www.citibank.com.pe; Av José Pardo 127) Has 24-hour ATMs in Miraflores operating on the Cirrus, Maestro, MasterCard and Visa systems; it cashes Citicorp traveler's checks.

Scotiabank (Map p864; 01-311-6000; www.scotiabank.com.pe; Av 2 de Mayo 1510-1550) ATMs (24-hour) operate on the MasterCard, Maestro, Cirrus, Visa and Plus networks and dispense soles and US dollars. There are also branches at **Miraflores Larco** (Map p858; 01-311-6000; www.scotiabank.com.pe; Av José Larco 1119, Larco) and **Miraflores Pardo** (Map p858; 01-311-6000; www.scotiabank.com.pe; cnr Av José Pardo & Bolognesi, Pardo).

POST

Main post office (Map p854; 01-511-5000; www.serpost.com.pe; Pasaje Piura, Lima Centro; 8am-9pm Mon-Sat) Poste restante mail can be collected here, though it's not 100% reliable. Bring ID.

TOURIST INFORMATION

Federación Deportiva Peruana de Ciclismo (p855) Has general information (in Spanish) on cycling and events.

iPerú (01-574-8000; www.peru.travel/iperu; Aeropuerto Internacional Jorge Chávez; 24hr) The government's reputable tourist bureau dispenses maps, offers good advice and can help handle complaints. The **Miraflores office** (Map p858; 01-445-9400; www.peru.travel/iperu; LarcoMar; 11am-1pm & 2-8pm) is tiny but is very useful on weekends. There's another branch in **San Isidro** (Map p864; 01-421-1627; www.peru.travel/iperu; Jorge Basadre 610; 9am-6pm Mon-Fri).

Municipal Tourist Office (Map p854; 01-632-1300; www.munlima.gob.pe; Pasaje de los Escribanos 145, Lima Centro; 9am-5pm Mon-Fri, 11am-3pm Sat & Sun) Of limited use; check the website for a small number of listings of local events and info on free downtown tours.

🛈 Getting There & Away

AIR

Lima's **Aeropuerto Internacional Jorge Chávez** (01-517-3500, schedules 01-511-6055; www.lima-airport.com; Callao) is stocked with the usual facilities plus a pisco boutique, a post office and luggage storage. Internet access is available on the 2nd floor.

All departure taxes are included in ticket prices. You can get flight information, buy tickets and reconfirm flights online or via telephone, but for ticket changes or problems, it's best to go to the airline office in person.

The following airlines service Lima:

Avianca (Map p858; 01-511-8222; www.avianca.com; Av José Pardo 831, Miraflores; 8:30am-7pm Mon-Fri, 9am-2pm Sat) Flies to Cuzco, Arequipa, Juliaca, Puerto Maldonado and Trujillo.

LATAM (p962) Goes to Arequipa, Chiclayo, Cuzco, Iquitos, Juliaca, Piura, Puerto Maldonado, Tacna, Tarapoto and Trujillo. Additionally it offers link services between Arequipa and Cuzco, Arequipa and Juliaca, Arequipa and Tacna, Cuzco and Juliaca, and Cuzco and Puerto Maldonado. It offers international services as well.

LC Perú (p963) Flies from Lima to Andahuaylas, Ayacucho, Cajamarca, Huánuco, Huaraz, Iquitos and Huancayo (Jauja) on smaller turbo-prop aircraft.

Peruvian Airlines (p963) Flies to Arequipa, Cuzco, Piura, Iquitos, Jauja, Pucallpa, Tarapoto, Tacna and internationally to La Paz, Bolivia.

Star Perú (p963) Flies to Ayacucho, Cuzco, Huanuco, Iquitos, Pucallpa, Puerto Maldonado and Tarapoto.

Viva Air (p963) This budget airline flies to Arequipa, Cuzco, Iquitos, Piura and Tarapato.

BUS

There is no central bus terminal; each company operates its ticketing and departure points independently. Some companies have several terminals, so always clarify from which point a bus leaves when buying tickets. The busiest times of year are Semana Santa (the week before Easter Sunday) and the weeks surrounding Fiestas Patrias (July 28–29), when thousands of *limeños* make a dash out of the city and fares double. At these times, book well ahead.

Near the airport, the **Gran Terminal Terrestre** (Terminal Plaza Norte; ☎ 945-018-248; www.granterminalterrestre.com; cnr Av Tomás Valle & Av Túpac Amaru, Plaza Norte Panamericana Norte; ⊙ 6am-midnight), the city's largest bus terminal, has buses to international destinations as well as smaller subsidiaries to northern and southern Peru.

Some stations are in rough neighborhoods. If possible, buy your tickets in advance and take a taxi when carrying luggage.

Civa (Map p856; ☎ 01-418-1111; www.civa.com.pe; Paso de la Republica 569) For Arequipa, Cajamarca, Chachapoyas, Chiclayo, Cuzco, Ilo, Máncora, Nazca, Piura, Puno, Tacna, Tarapoto, Trujillo and Tumbes. The company also runs a more luxurious sleeper line to various coastal destinations called Excluciva (www.excluciva.com).

Cruz del Sur (Map p853; ☎ 01-225-3748; www.cruzdelsur.com.pe; Av Javier Prado Este 1109) One of the biggest companies, serving the coast – as well as inland cities such as Arequipa, Cuzco, Huancayo and Huaraz – with three different classes of service: the cheaper Ideal, and the more luxurious Imperial and Cruzero.

Móvil Tours (Map p856; ☎ 01-716-8000; www.moviltours.com.pe; Paseo de la República 749) For Chachapoyas, Chiclayo, Huancayo, Huaraz and Tarapoto.

Oltursa (Map p853; ☎ 01-708-5000; www.oltursa.pe; Av Aramburu 1160, Surquillo) A short distance from San Isidro lies the main terminal for this very reputable company, which travels to Abancay, Arequipa, Chiclayo, Ica, Máncora, Nazca, Paracas, Piura, Tacna, Trujillo and Tumbes.

Lima Buses

DESTINATION	COST* (S)	DURATION (HR)
Arequipa	80/170	16-18
Ayacucho	75/110	9-11
Cajamarca	90/150	16
Chiclayo	50/130	12-14
Cuzco	110/185	22-23
Huancayo	40/80	7-8
Huaraz	30/150	8
Ica	30/85	4½-5½
Nazca	50/120	6-8
Piura	90/150	16
Puno	150/170	22
Tacna	120/180	18-22
Trujillo	40/125	9-10
Tumbes	100/200	20

*prices are general estimates for normal/luxury buses

TRAIN

The **Ferrocarril Central Andino** (Map p854; ☎ 01-226-6363; www.ferrocarrilcentral.com.pe; Estación Desamparados; round-trip adult/child 12 & under tourist class S600/300, standard class S450/225) railway line runs from **Estación Desamparados** (Map p854; ☎ 01-263-1515; Ancash 203) in Lima inland to Huancayo, climbing from sea level to 4829m – the second-highest point for passenger trains in the world – before descending to Huancayo at 3260m.

❶ Getting Around

TO & FROM THE AIRPORT

The airport resides in the port city of Callao, about 12km west of downtown or 20km northwest of Miraflores. In a private taxi, allow at least an hour to the airport from San Isidro, Miraflores or Barranco; by *combi* (minibus), expect the journey to take at least two hours – with plenty of stops in between. Traffic is lightest before 6:30am.

BUS

The trans-Lima electric express bus system, El Metropolitano (www.metropolitano.com.pe), is the fastest and most efficient way to get into the city center. Routes are few, though coverage is expanding to the northern part of the city. Ruta

Troncal (S2.50) goes through Barranco, Miraflores and San Isidro to Plaza Grau in the center of Lima. Users must purchase a *tarjeta inteligente* (smart card; S4.50) that can be credited for use.

Alternatively, traffic-clogging caravans of minivans hurtle down the avenues with a *cobrador* (ticket taker) hanging out the door and shouting out the stops. Look for the destination placards taped to the windshield. Your best bet is to know the nearest major intersection or landmark close to your stop (eg Parque Kennedy) and tell that to the *cobrador* – they'll let you know whether you've got the right bus. *Combis* are generally slow and crowded, but startlingly cheap: fares run from S1 to S3, depending on the length of your journey.

The most useful bus routes link Central Lima with Miraflores along Av Arequipa or Paseo de la República. Minibuses along Garcilaso de la Vega (also called Av Wilson) and Av Arequipa are labeled 'Todo Arequipa' or 'Larco/Schell/Miraflores' when heading to Miraflores and, likewise, 'Todo Arequipa' and 'Wilson/Tacna' when leaving Miraflores for Central Lima. Catch these buses along Av José Larco or Av Arequipa in Miraflores. To get to Barranco, look for buses along Av Arequipa labeled 'Chorrillos/Huaylas/Metro' (some will also have signs that say 'Barranco'). You can also find these on the Diagonal, just west of Parque Kennedy, in Miraflores.

The principal bus routes connecting Central Lima with San Isidro and Miraflores run along broad avenues such as Tacna, Garcilaso de la Vega and Av Arequipa. These neighborhoods are also connected by the short highway Paseo de la República or Vía Expresa, known informally as *el zanjón* (the ditch).

TAXI

Lima's taxis lack meters, so negotiate fares before getting in. Fares vary depending on the length of the journey, traffic conditions, time of day (evening is more expensive) and your Spanish skills. Registered taxis or taxis hailed outside a tourist attraction charge higher rates. As a (very) rough guide, a trip within Miraflores costs around S8 to S10. From Miraflores to Central Lima is S20 to S25, to Barranco from S10 to S12, and San Isidro from S15 to S20. You can haggle fares – though it's harder during rush hour.

SOUTH COAST

This wild and lonely coast entrances visitors with teetering sand dunes, verdant desert oases, forgotten fishing villages, ancient earth drawings, and plenty of rugged open space for the imagination to run wild.

It's a stark, dry corner of earth – caught between the Andes and the sea – that only comes to life in the fertile river valleys that produce wine and fruit, providing visitors with a fleeting relief from the relentless beat of the brown desolate desert.

Most adventures take you on a tried-and-true trail that begins with rafting in Lunahuaná, wildlife-watching in the Islas Ballestas, sandboarding out of Huacachina and a requisite stop at the mysterious lines and odd geoglyphs that decorate the blank desert canvas outside Nazca. Step beyond the outlines of this Gringo Trail to discover unspoiled surf spots, vibrant agricultural villages and spirited and unassuming cultural beats.

Paracas & the Islas Ballestas

⌀ 056 / POP 7000

The Paracas Peninsula's main village, El Chaco – often referred to as 'Paracas' – is the primary embarkation point for trips to the Islas Ballestas and the Reserva Nacional de Paracas. New condos and luxury hotels are found north and south of the village proper. It's a fun place with a lively traveler scene. Most of the action centers on the *malecón* (boardwalk), where you'll find a pretty wide selection of restaurants and bars. Its natural attractions and long beaches stand out from many south-coast destinations, and many travelers end up spending at least two or three nights here, allowing for a day tour to the islands, beach time and an extended foray across the peninsula.

◉ Sights & Activities

The region's essential business is the de rigueur boat tour of the Islas Ballestas and the one-day sojourn around the bald, deserted Paracas Peninsula. Birds and sea mammals are the lures here, but, lest we forget, this is also one of Peru's most important archaeological sites, thanks primarily to the pre-Inca treasures unearthed by one of the country's most important archaeologists, Julio Tello, in the 1920s.

Islas Ballestas   ISLAND
(tours S35-40, park entrance islands only S11, islands & peninsula S17) Grandiosely nicknamed the 'poor man's Galápagos,' the Islas Ballestas make for a memorable excursion. The only way to get here is on a boat tour, offered by many tour agencies, touts and hotels. Tours leave at 8am, 10am and noon from the **Marina Turística de Paracas** (Malecón s/n, El

Chaco), The 8am tour usually has the calmest seas and best wildlife-viewing.

While the two-hour tours do not disembark onto the islands, they do get you startlingly close to an impressive variety of wildlife.

Reserva Nacional de Paracas PARK
(Carr Punta Pejerrey, Km 27; peninsula only S11, islands & peninsula S17) This vast desert reserve occupies most of the Península de Paracas and houses remote beaches backed by dramatic arid landscapes and plenty of wonderful wildlife. In front of the **Centro de Interpretación** (Reserva Nacional de Paracas; ⊙7am-6pm) **FREE** near the park entrance there is a lookout from which it's possible to spot Chilean flamingos in the bay below. Further south, **La Mina** (Reserva Nacional de Paracas) is the best beach in the reserve with gentle waters perfect for swimming. To the west of La Mina, Punta Arquillo hosts a significant sea-lion colony.

🖒 Tours

Paracas Explorer TOURS
(☑056-53-1487; www.paracasexplorer.com; Av Libertadores s/n; ⊙7am-7pm) This busy local travel agency has two offices on the same block and offers the usual island and reserve tours, as well as tours to Tambo Colorado (S200) and multiday trips that take you to Ica and Nazca (from US$200 per person). Can also book flights over the Nazca Lines leaving from Pisco or Ica airports.

🛏 Sleeping & Eating

Paracas Backpackers House HOSTEL $
(☑056-53-6700; www.paracasbackpackershouse.com.pe; Av Libertadores s/n; dm S20-30, s without bathroom S45, d with/without bathroom S85/55; ☎) Of the several 'backpackers hostels' on this strip, this is the original and still the most popular. Most rooms have private baths and look onto the terrace, with hammock and chill area. Dorms sleep seven to 10 people.

★Hotel Paracas RESORT $$$
(☑056-58-1333; www.luxurycollection.com/hotel paracas; Av Paracas 178; r S2221-2421, ste S2555-3122, all incl breakfast; P🅿🌡@🛜🏊) A dreamscape plucked from a tourist brochure, with puffed cushions, permanently smiling staff, excellent kids facilities and a luxuriously raked beach, this Starwood resort offers the best high-end rooms in town. The *cabaña*-style rooms have private balconies and massive bathrooms. Unfortunately, ocean views are limited from many rooms. There are three hotels, two pools and a private dock on-site.

★Inti-Mar SEAFOOD $$
(www.inti-mar.com; Contiguo Puerto General San Martín, Punta Pejerrey; mains S25-45; ⊙10:30am-3:30pm) One of our favorite places to eat on the entire coast, this breezy spot on the far side of the bay is a working scallop farm with a handful of tables right next to the water. It serves a bunch of different seafood dishes but the fresh scallops served *natural* with lemon and olive oil are phenomenal.

ℹ Information

iPerú (☑056-638-216; iperunasca@promperu.gob.pe; Av Libertadores s/n; ⊙9am-4pm Wed-Sun) Inside the municipal building, this information desk is useful for impartial travel advice for destinations in Paracas and beyond.

ℹ Getting There & Away

The fastest way to get to Paracas is via the new **airport** at Pisco although at the time of press Cusco was the only destination with regular flights.

Several buses run daily between Lima and the El Chaco beach district of Paracas (S45 to S68, 3½ hours) before continuing to other destinations south.

Cruz del Sur (☑056-53-6636; www.cruzdelsur.com.pe; Av Libertadores s/n, Ingreso El Chaco) Departs from its flash terminal on the northern edge of town and has the most frequent services with departures at 7:30am, 12:30pm, 1:30pm, 3pm, 4pm and 7:10pm. Also runs buses from Paracas to Ica and Nazca at 7:25am, 10:30am, 10:40am, 11:10am, 5:10pm and 5:40pm.

Oltursa (☑056-53-0726; www.oltursa.com.pe; Av Libertadores s/n) Has one comfortable bus a day to Lima leaving the office on the main boulevard at 9:50am, and one bus south to Ica, Nazca and Arequipa at 10:15am.

Peru Bus (☑056-22-3687; www.perubus.com.pe; Av Libertadores s/n) Has the cheapest daily services to Lima at 10:25am and 4:40pm.

Most agencies in El Chaco sell bus tickets, including Paracas Explorer.

Ica

☑056 / POP 131,000 / ELEV 420M
Just when you thought the landscape was dry enough for martians, out jumps Ica, Peru's agricultural 'miracle in the desert' that churns out bumper crops of asparagus, cotton and fruits, as well as laying claim to being the nation's leading (and best) wine producer. Ica, like Pisco, sustained significant earthquake damage in 2007 – the graceful cathedral and two other churches were significantly damaged and are undergoing lengthy repairs.

Most people who make it this far bed down in infinitely more attractive Huacachina 4km to the west, but Ica has reasons to be cheerful too: the south coast's best museum (outside Arequipa) resides here, plus – arguably – the finest winery in Peru. If Nazca seems too much of a circus, it's also possible to organize Nazca Line excursions from Ica – the desert etchings lie 1½ hours to the south.

◉ Sights & Activities

Museo Regional de Ica   MUSEUM
(Ayabaca cuadra 8; S7.50; ⊘8am-7pm Mon-Fri, 8:30am-6:30pm Sat & Sun) In the suburban neighborhood of San Isidro, Ica pulls out its trump card: a museum befitting a city three times the size. While it might not be the Smithsonian in terms of layout and design, this understated gem catalogs the two key pre-Inca civilizations on Peru's southern coast, namely the Paracas and Nazca cultures, the former famed for its intricate textiles and the latter for its instantly recognizable ceramics.

Bodega Lazo   WINE
(☏056-40-3430; San Juan de Bautista; ⊘9am-1pm Mon-Fri, to 3pm Sat & Sun) FREE One of the best wineries to visit near Ica, Bodega Lazo still uses an artisanal winemaking process to make its traditional piscos, and visitors can observe the entire process before tasting the products.

Bodega Tacama   WINE
(☏056-58-1030; www.tacama.com; Camino Real s/n, Tinguiña; ⊘9:30am-4:30pm Tue-Sun) FREE Possibly the most professional and lauded of Ica's wineries, Tacama is run out of a sprawling hacienda backed by striped fields lined by vines. Eschewing Peru's penchant for sickly sweet wines, Tacama produces some rather good chardonnays and malbecs that might one day give the Chileans a run for their money.

⊨ Sleeping

★ El Carmelo   HISTORIC HOTEL $$
(☏056-23-2191; www.elcarmelohotelhacienda.com; Carr Panamericana Sur Km 301; s/d/tr/q from S135/190/280/350; @⊜❄) This romantic roadside hotel on the outskirts of town inhabits a delightful 200-year-old hacienda that has undeniable rustic charm. Rooms exude a classic elegance but also boast mod-cons and are very comfortable. However, the stars of the show are the grounds with courtyards, a wonderful wood and cane gazebo and an open fire for the chilly desert nights.

There's a good restaurant plus a winery on-site. Take a taxi from the city center (S5).

Hotel Sol de Ica   HOTEL $$
(☏056-23-6168; www.hotelsoldeica.com; Lima 265; s/d/tr incl buffet breakfast S199/249/299; @⊜❄) This five-story central hotel is hidden down a long, dark passage behind reception that delivers more than it initially promises. Fairly small rooms have natural wood touches and calm beige curtains and bedspreads, but don't really sparkle. However, it does boast a large garden and swimming pool which is a bit of an oasis from the bustle outside.

✕ Eating

Helena   PERUVIAN $
(☏056-22-1844;www.helena.pe;Cajamarca139;items S4; ⊘9:30am-8pm) Stop in at this shop half a block from the plaza that is famed around the country for its chocolates and traditional sweets. Try the *tejas* (caramel-wrapped candies flavored with fruits, nuts etc.)

El Cordón y La Rosa   PERUVIAN $$
(☏056-21-8012; Los Maestros, Frente Hotel Real; mains S35-55; ⊘11am-11pm, to 7pm Sun) It's worth the short taxi ride from the center to dine at this modern Peruvian bistro which specializes in seafood but has a wide-ranging menu. It's very popular so tables are a little crammed in. The spotless open kitchen area looks like something straight out of *Masterchef* with neatly uniformed cooks wearing headsets and knocking out plates at lightning speed.

❶ Information

DANGERS & ANNOYANCES
Ica experiences some petty theft. Take the normal precautions, particularly around the bus terminals and market areas.

MEDICAL SERVICES
Hospital Regional de Ica (☏056-23-4798; www.hrica.gob.pe; Prolongación Ayabaca s/n; ⊘24hr) For emergency services.

MONEY
Banco de la Nación (Grau 161) Fee-free ATM.
BCP (Plaza de Armas) Has Visa/MasterCard ATMs and changes US dollars.

❶ Getting There & Away
Ica is a main destination for buses along the Panamericana Sur, so it's easy to get to/from Lima or Nazca. Most of the bus companies are clustered in a high-crime area at the west end of Salaverry, and also Manzanilla west of Lambayeque.

Soyuz (☎ 056-22-4138; www.soyuzonline.com. pe; Manzanilla 130), which is sometimes branded Peru Bus, runs to Lima via Chincha and Cañete with services leaving every 15 minutes. It also has frequent buses south to Nazca via Palpa. Watch your belongings on Soyuz, especially when people get on and off the bus, as petty theft is common.

Flores (☎ 056-21-2266; Manzanilla 152) also runs economic buses to Lima and has services to Nazca. Note that southbound buses leave from a different terminal a block away.

Cruz del Sur (☎ 0801-11111; www.cruzdelsur. com.pe; Fray Ramon Rojas 189) offers more luxurious services going north and south.

Huacachina

☑ 056 / POP 200

Imagine... It's 6pm and you're sitting atop a giant wind-sculpted sand dune watching the sun set psychedelically over a landscape of golden yellows and rusty reds. Two hundred meters below you lies a dreamy desert lagoon ringed by exotic palm trees and furnished with a clutch of rustic yet suitably elegant hotels. It took you an exhausting 20 minutes to climb up to this lofty vantage point, but with a well-waxed sandboard wedged beneath your belly you'll be down in less than one.

While not as famous as Nazca to the south, Huacachina, an aesthetically perfect desert oasis 4km west of Ica, is a firmly established stopover on southern Peru's well-trampled Gringo Trail, and with good reason. Sandboarding, dune-buggie rides and good-old romantic idling are the orders of the day here. This is backpacker central, so expect plenty of late-night parties and international flavors. Many people just make it here for a quick overnight and dune trip the next day, but a few days of relaxed strolls and dune climbs may just channel your inner chi.

🏃 Activities

You can rent basic sandboards all over town for S5 to S8 an hour to slide, surf or ski your way down the dunes, getting sand lodged into every bodily orifice. Snowboarding this isn't. There are no tow ropes or chairlifts here. Instead you must stagger up the sugary dunes for your 45-second adrenaline rush. Make sure you are given wax (usually in the form of an old candle) when you rent your board as they are pretty useless without regular rubdowns. Start on the smaller slopes and don't be lulled into a false sense of security – several people have seriously injured themselves losing control of their sandboards.

Most riders end up boarding belly down with their legs splayed out behind as emergency brakes. Don't forget to keep your mouth shut.

🛏 Sleeping & Eating

Huacachina is pretty much just a collection of hotels and hostels so there is a wide range of beds to choose from. It's a popular destination, though, so be sure to make advance reservations.

Hostería Suiza   HOTEL $$
(☎ 056-23-8762; www.hosteriasuiza.com.pe; Balneario de Huacachina; s/d/tr incl breakfast S152/249/309; ✳ 🛜 ▧) This formal hotel on the northwest end of the lagoon offers tranquility and some of the best value in Huacachina, with high-ceilinged rooms and Moorish-meets-hacienda architectural features. The rooms looking onto the backyard garden and pool area are the best, with textured green bedspreads and newly remodeled modern bathrooms.

★**Banana's Adventure**   HOSTEL $$
(☎ 056-23-7129; bananasadventure@hotmail.com; Av Perotti s/n; r per person incl breakfast & excursion S75-110; 🛜 ▧) This peaced-out crash pad on the north side of the lagoon only offers packaged stays. They include a room for the night – four-bed dorms with superfirm mattresses or elegant private rooms with glass on all sides and modern fixings – plus a dune-buggy and sandboarding excursion the next day.

Desert Nights   INTERNATIONAL $
(Blvd de Huacachina; mains S15-25; 🛜) The menu might have been ripped off from anywhere else on the banana-pancake trail, but the cafe restaurant at the front of the hostel of the same name has fantastic views from its rooftop terrace and is somewhere you're guaranteed to meet other travelers.

ℹ Information

Though safer than Ica, Huacachina is not a place to be lax about your personal safety or looking after your property. Some guesthouses have reputations for ripping off travelers and also harassing young women with sexual advances. Check out all of your options carefully before accepting a room. Also, the few small stores around the lagoon offer plenty of souvenirs but are often out of the basics; come prepared!

ℹ Getting There & Away

The only way to get to Huacachina from Ica is by taxi (S8 to S10 one way).

Nazca & Around

📞 056 / POP 26,700 / ELEV 590M

'Nazca Lines' refers to the ancient geometric lines that crisscross the Nazca desert and the enigmatic animal geoglyphs that accompany them. Like all great unexplained mysteries, these great etchings on the pampa, thought to have been made by a pre-Inca civilization between AD 450 and 600, attract a variable fan base of archaeologists, scientists, history buffs, New Age mystics, curious tourists, and pilgrims on their way to (or back from) Machu Picchu.

Questions still hang over how they were made and by whom, and the answers are often as much wild speculation as pure science (aliens? prehistoric balloonists?). Documented for the first time by North American scientist Paul Kosok in 1939 and declared a Unesco World Heritage Site in 1994, the lines today are the south coast's biggest tourist attraction, meaning the small, otherwise-insignificant desert town of Nazca can be a bit of a circus.

◎ Sights

Nazca Lines

The best-known lines are found in the desert 20km north of Nazca, and by far the best way to appreciate them is to get a bird's-eye view from a *sobrevuelo* (overflight). Prices for a standard 30-minute flight taking in 12 of the figures are normally around US$90 but can rise and fall depending on demand. Extended flights taking in more of the lines and including detours to other archaeological sites in the area including the Aqueductos de Cantalloc are also offered.

During high season it's a good idea to reserve flights well in advance – either online or through an agency – as they can get booked out. In low season it's possible to just turn up at the airport and shop around.

Outlying Sights

Aqueductos de Cantalloc   ARCHAEOLOGICAL SITE

(S10; ⊙9am-6pm) About 4km southeast of town are the 30-plus underground Cantalloc Aqueducts, many of which are still in working order and are essential in irrigating the surrounding fields. The impressive series of stone and wood channels and spiraling access ways were built by the Nazca between AD 200 and 900 and are considered one of the finest examples of pre-Hispanic engineering. Locals say the water here is still good to drink.

OVERFLIGHTS OVERVIEW

Bad publicity wracked the Nazca Lines in 2010 when two small aircraft carrying tourists on *sobrevuelos* (overflights) crashed within eight months of each other causing a total of 13 fatalities. The crashes followed an equally catastrophic 2008 accident that killed five French tourists, along with another incident when a plane was forced to make an emergency landing on the Panamericana Sur in 2009. In reaction to the incidents some changes have been made. All planes now fly with two pilots, more thorough safety inspections have been implemented, and prices have gone up to ensure that companies don't cut corners with poorly maintained aircraft or overfilled flights.

Nonetheless, it still pays to put safety before price when choosing your overflight company. Question anyone who offers prices significantly lower than the other companies and don't be afraid to probe companies on their safety records and flight policies. **Aeroparacas** (📞016-41-7000; www.aeroparacas.com; Lima 169) is one of the better airline companies. Other long-standing operators include **Aerodiana** (📞014-47-6824; www.aerodiana.com.pe; Aeropuerto Maria Reiche Neuman) and **Alas Peruanas** (📞056-52-2444; www.alasperuanas.com; Lima 168). Some countries, including the UK, still place warnings about overflights on their foreign-office websites.

If you do opt for a flight, bear in mind that because the small aircraft bank left and right it can be a stomach-churning experience, so motion-sickness sufferers should consider taking medication. Looking at the horizon may help mild nausea. It's generally best to fly in the morning when there is less wind.

Most airline companies use **Aeropuerto Maria Reiche Neuman** (NZC; 📞56-52-3731; Panamericana s/n), 4km southwest of Nazca, although you can also depart from Pisco and Ica if you are not keen on the long bus ride down to Nazca. On top of the tour fee the airport in Nazca normally charges a departure tax of S30.

Nazca

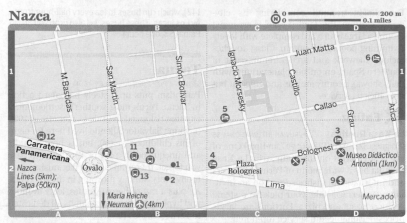

Nazca

⊙ Activities, Courses & Tours

🛏 Sleeping

❌ Eating

Chauchilla Cemetery ARCHAEOLOGICAL SITE
(S8; ⊙8am-5:30pm) The most popular excursion from Nazca, this cemetery, 28km south of Nazca, will satisfy any urges you have to see ancient bones, skulls and mummies. Dating back to the Ica-Chincha culture around AD 1000, the mummies were originally scattered haphazardly across the desert, left by ransacking tomb-robbers. Now they are seen carefully rearranged inside a dozen or so tombs, though cloth fragments and pottery and bone shards still litter the ground outside the demarcated trail.

🛏 Sleeping

★ Hotel Oro Viejo HOTEL $$
(☎056-52-2284; www.hoteloroviejo.net; Callao 483; s/d/tr incl buffet breakfast S150/200/240/450; P❄@🛜🏊) There's a decidedly oriental feel to this excellent midrange hotel with its open gardens and glistening swimming pool. Occasional farming artifacts grace the common areas and lounge, while the well-fragranced rooms deliver comfort, quiet and relaxation. The rooms on the ground floor of the original buildling are a bit poky; ask for a new room out back.

Kunan Wasi Hotel HOTEL $$
(☎056-52-4069; www.kunanwasihotel.com; Arica 419; s/d/tr S70/90/120; @🛜) Very clean and bright with each room conforming to a different color scheme. Kunan Wasi is English-speaking, superfriendly, and immaculately clean. Tours can be arranged on-site and travelers will love the top-floor terrace. Welcome to a perfectly packaged Nazca bargain.

Casa Andina HOTEL $$$
(☎012-13-9718; www.casa-andina.com; Bolognesi 367; s/d incl buffet breakfast S396/451; ❄@🛜🏊) This Peruvian chain hotel, poised between the bus stations and the Plaza de Armas, offers contemporary Andean touches like leather lampshades and textile bed runners, creating a solid-value proposition in the upmarket hotel category. The palm-filled courtyard and adjacent pool area are small but tasteful.

DM Hoteles Nazca HOTEL $$$
(☎016-14-3900; www.dmhoteles.pe; Bolognesi 147; d/tr/ste incl breakfast S474/507/697; P❄@🛜🏊)

PERU NAZCA & AROUND

Exceedingly tranquil considering its city-center location, this lauded hotel is arranged around a large courtyard complete with lovely swimming pool and fountain. Classy touches include tilework and arches reminiscent of southern Spain, an on-site planetarium (with daily shows), a comfy lounge, and efficient but not officious service.

✖ Eating

La Kasa Rustika   PERUVIAN, INTERNATIONAL **$$**
(Bolgnesi 372; mains S18-40; ⊙7am-11pm) One of the best eateries on the main strip, La Kasa Rustika has a wide menu of Peruvian flavors and international dishes served on an inviting open terrace. Take your pick from steak, seafood, pasta and pizza. Portions are large, prices reasonable and service top-notch.

La Encantada Cafe   INTERNATIONAL **$$**
(📞056-52-4216; Bolgnesi 282; mains S20-60; ⊙10am-10:30pm) A top spot on the 'Boulevard' (Bolgnesi), La Encantada sparkles in Nazca's dusty center with bright and modern dining areas, great coffee, and courteous and friendly waitstaff. The menu mixes Europhile flavors (pasta etc) with Peruvian favorites.

ℹ Information

MONEY

Banco de la Nacion (Lima 465) Fee-free ATMs in the center of town.

TOURIST INFORMATION

iPerú (📞016-16-7300, ext 3042; Aerodromo Maria Reiche Neuman; ⊙7am-4pm) A government-run tourism desk at the airfield.

ℹ Getting There & Away

There are no scheduled flights to Nazca as the small airport (p872) does not have the facilities to receive larger commercial operations.

Nazca is a major destination for buses on the Panamericana Sur and is easy to get to from Lima, Ica or Arequipa. Bus companies cluster at the west end of Calle Lima, near the óvalo (main roundabout). Buses to Arequipa often originate in Lima, and to get a reserved seat you may have to pay the Lima fare.

Most long-distance services leave in the late afternoon or evening. **Cruz del Sur** (📞0801-11111; www.cruzdelsur.com.pe; Av Los Incas) and **Civa** (📞056-52-4390; www.civa.com.pe; Lima 155; ⊙6am-2am) have a few luxury buses daily to Lima. Intermediate points such as Ica and Pisco are more speedily served by smaller, económico (cheap) bus companies, such as **Flores** (Panamericana s/n) and **Soyuz** (📞056-52-1464; San Martín

142), which run buses to Ica every half-hour from Av Los Incas. These buses will also drop you at Palpa (S3, one hour).

Tacna
📞052 / POP 262,700 / ELEV 460M

Patriotism puts up a steely rearguard action in Tacna, Peru's most southerly settlement, a city that belonged to Chile as recently as 1929 (a young Salvador Allende lived here for eight of his childhood years), but is now proudly and unequivocally part of Peru. Just in case you forget, there's an earnest flag-raising ceremony every Sunday morning in the main plaza, plus a raft of heroic statues, leafy avenues and hyperbolic museum exhibits all dedicated to Peru's glorious past.

🛏 Sleeping & Eating

Dorado Hotel   HOTEL **$$**
(📞052-41-5741; www.doradohoteltacna.com; Av Arias Aragüez 145; s/d/tr incl breakfast from S144/187/230; @ 🛜 ☒) Posing as Tacna's grandest hotel, the Dorado is the sort of place where the curtains are heavy, the lobby has shiny fittings, and a bellhop will carry your bags to your room. While it can't emulate the classy exclusivity of a big-city hotel, it makes a good job of trying.

★Muelle Sur   SEAFOOD **$$**
(📞052-24-5106; www.muellesur.com; Los Alamos 1995; mains S29-70) Widely regarded as Tacna's best restaurant, this bustling open-air seafood affair fulfills the hype. It gets crowded with Chilean visitors on weekends who come for their ceviche fix. While the ceviche and *tiraditos* (Japanese version of ceviche) are the stars here there's also whole fish, rice dishes and reasonably priced whole lobster in addition to beef from the grill. Reservations are advisable.

ℹ Information

IMMIGRATION

Oficina de Migraciones (Immigration Office; 📞052-24-3231; Circunvalación s/n, Urb Él Triángulo; ⊙8am-4pm Mon-Fri)

MONEY

Banco de la Nacion (San Martín 321) Fee-free ATMs in the center.

TOURIST INFORMATION

iPerú (📞052-42-5514; San Martín 491; ⊙8:30am-6pm Mon-Sat, to 1pm Sun) National tourist office, providing free information and brochures. There are additional branches at the border, airport and bus station.

ⓘ Getting There & Away

Most long-distance departures leave from the **Terminal Terrestre** (Hipólito Unánue), at the northeast edge of town, with the exception of some buses to Juliaca, Desaguadero and Puno, which leave from **Terminal Collaysuyo** (Av Emancipación), located in the district of Alta Alianza to the north of town.

Frequent buses (S12) to Arica, Chile, leave between 5am and 7pm from the **international terminal** across the street from the *terminal terrestre* where a S2 terminal tax must also be paid.

San Martín (🖉 952-524-252; Terminal Collaysuyo s/n) runs overnight *económico* and luxury bus services to Puno via Desaguadero on the Bolivian border, finally ending up in Cuzco. These mostly leave in the evening from Terminal Collaysuyo.

The usual suspects head to all destinations north including Cruz del Sur, Civa Oltursa and more economical Flores.

ⓘ GETTING TO CHILE VIA TACNA

Border-crossing formalities are relatively straightforward. There are three main transport options: train, public bus or *colectivo* (shared taxi), with the last proving to be the most efficient. The five-passenger taxis are run by professional companies with desks inside Tacna's international bus terminal. They charge around S25 to take you the 65km to Arica in Chile with stops at both border posts. Most of the paperwork is done before you get in the car. On a good day the trip should take little more than an hour. The public bus is cheaper (S12), but slower, as you have to wait for all the passengers to disembark and clear customs.

Both border posts are open 24 hours.

AREQUIPA & CANYON COUNTRY

Arequipa province is Peru's big combo ticket, with authentic historical immersion and white-knuckle Andean adventure inhabiting the same breathing space. Imagine the cultural riches of one of South America's finest historic cities just a few hours' drive from the world's two deepest canyons and you'll get a hint of the dramatic contrasts here. Ample urban distractions can be found in Arequipa, the arty, audacious, unflappably resilient metropolis that lies in the shadow of El Misti volcano. Beckoning to the northwest are the Colca and Cotahuasi canyons, whose impressive depth is a mere statistic compared to the Andean condors, epic treks and long-standing Spanish, Inca and pre-Inca traditions that lurk in their midst. Other unusual apparitions include the lava-encrusted Valle de los Volcanes, the haunting Toro Muerto petroglyphs, and the barren Paso de Patopampa where a main road ascends to 4910m, higher than any point in Western Europe or North America.

Arequipa

🖉 054 / POP 969,300 / ELEV 2350M

Other Peruvians joke that you need a different passport to enter Peru's second-largest city. One-tenth the size of Lima, Arequipa is its pugnacious equal in terms of cuisine, historical significance and confident self-awareness.

Guarded by three dramatic volcanoes, the city's resplendent setting makes an obvious launchpad for trekking, rafting and visiting the Cañón del Colca. The Unesco World Heritage-listed city center is dressed in baroque buildings carved from *sillar* (white volcanic rock) stone, giving Arequipa the nickname 'Ciudad Blanca' (White City). Its centerpiece, a majestic cathedral with the ethereal **El Misti** rising behind it, is worth a visit alone.

Pretty cityscapes aside, Arequipa has played a fundamental role in Peru's gastronomic renaissance and dining here – in communal *picantería* eateries or tastebud-provoking fusion restaurants – is a highlight.

The city has produced one of Latin America's most influential novelists, Mario Vargas Llosa. Juanita, the ice-preserved, sacrificed Inca mummy, is another Arequipan treasure.

⊙ Sights

The city's architecture, an ensemble of baroque buildings grafted out of the local *sillar* (white volcanic rock), shows its resilience by thus far withstanding most of the seismic activity thrown at it. Colonial *sillar* churches around the city center include Iglesia de San Francisco, Iglesia de San Agustín, Iglesia de La Merced and Iglesia de Santo Domingo.

★**Monasterio de Santa Catalina**   MONASTERY
(🖉054-22-1213; www.santacatalina.org.pe; Santa Catalina 301; S40; ⊙9am-5pm, to 7:30pm Tue &

Arequipa

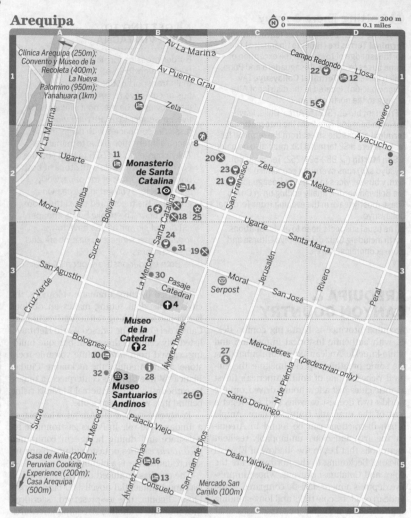

Wed, last entry 1hr before closing) This convent shouldn't be missed, even if you've overdosed on colonial edifices. Occupying a whole block and guarded by imposing high walls, it is one of the most fascinating religious buildings in Peru. Nor is it just a religious building – the 20,000-sq-meter complex is almost a citadel within the city. It was founded in 1580 by a rich widow, doña María de Guzmán. Enter from the southeast corner.

⭐**Museo Santuarios Andinos**   MUSEUM
(☎054-28-6613; www.ucsm.edu.pe/museo-santuarios-andinos; La Merced 110; adult S20, child 5-17 S10; ☺9am-6pm Mon-Sat, to 3pm Sun) There's

an escalating drama to this theatrically presented museum, dedicated to the preserved body of a frozen 'mummy', and its compulsory guided tour (free, but a tip is expected at the end). Spoiler: the climax is the vaguely macabre sight of poor Juanita, the 12-year-old Inca girl sacrificed to the gods in the 1450s and now eerily preserved in a glass refrigerator. Tours take about an hour and are conducted in Spanish, English and French.

⭐**Museo de la Catedral**   BASILICA
(☎054-21-3149; www.museocatedralarequipa.org. pe; Santa Catalina, Plaza de Armas; admission & tour S10; ☺10am-5pm Mon-Sat) A must for visitors

Arequipa

who want to see more of Arequipa's **cathedral** (☎054-23-2635; ⏱7-10am & 5-7pm Mon-Sat, 11am-noon Sun) **FREE**, the included 45-minute bilingual tour of this 'museum' is actually a peek at the inner workings of the basilica, with an explanation of the impressive 1000-pipe church organ and the symbology and colors employed in religious paintings and ornaments. The rooftop views of Arequipa and its *sillar* buildings are a bonus.

**Convento y Museo
de la Recoleta** MONASTERY
(☎054-27-0966; La Recoleta 117; S10; ⏱9am-5pm daily, to 8pm Wed & Fri by appointment) Bibliophiles will delight in this musty monastery's huge library, which contains more than 20,000 dusty books and maps; the oldest volume dates to 1494. Scholarship was an integral part of the Franciscans' order; the library is open for supervised visits, just ask at the entrance.

Also on the premises is a well-known museum of Amazonian artifacts (including preserved jungle animals) collected by the missionaries, and an extensive collection of pre-conquest artifacts and religious art of the *escuela cuzqueña* (Cuzco school).

🏃 Activities

Arequipa is the center for a slew of outdoor activities dotted around the high country to the north and east of the city. Trekking, mountaineering and river running are the big three, but there are plenty more.

Trekking & Mountaineering
The Association of Mountain Guides of Peru warns that many guides are uncertified and untrained, so climbers are advised to go well-informed about medical and wilderness-survival issues. Most agencies sell climbs as packages that include transportation, so prices vary widely depending on the size of the group and the mountain, but the cost for a guide alone is around US$85 per day.

Trekking solo in the well-traveled Cañón del Colca area is popular and easy, but if you're nervous about hiking without guides or want to tackle more untrammeled routes, there are dozens of tour companies based in Arequipa that can arrange guided treks.

⭐ **Naturaleza Activa** ADVENTURE SPORTS
(☎968-969-544; naturactiva@yahoo.com; Santa Catalina 211; ⏱office 11am-7pm Mon-Sat) With a full range of trekking, mountain-biking and climbing options on offer, this is a favorite of those seeking adventure tours. A major advantage of going here rather than an agency is that the people you speak to at Naturaleza Activa are actually the qualified guides, not salespeople, so can answer your questions

Arequipa's Canyon Country & Lake Titicaca

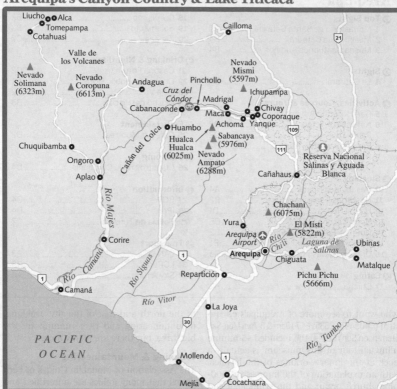

with genuine knowledge. Guides speak English, French and German.

Carlos Zárate Adventures ADVENTURE SPORTS (☑054-20-2461; www.zarateadventures.com; Jerusalén 505A) This highly professional company offers various treks, and climbs all the local peaks. Founded in 1954 by Carlos Zárate, the great-grandfather of climbing in Arequipa, it's now run by one of his sons, experienced guide Carlos Zárate Flores. Another of Zárate's sons, Miguel, was responsible, along with archaeologists, for unearthing 'Juanita the Ice Maiden' atop Nevado Ampato in 1995.

Pablo Tour TREKKING (☑054-20-3737; www.pablotour.com; Jerusalén 400 AB-1; ⊙office 8:30am-8pm) Consistently recommended by readers, Pablo Tour's guides are experts in trekking and cultural tours in the region, and can furnish trekkers with all the necessary equipment and topographical maps.

River Running

Arequipa is one of Peru's premier bases for river rafting and kayaking. Many trips are unavailable during the rainy season (between December and March), when water levels can be dangerously high. For more information and advice, consult www.peru whitewater.com.

The **Río Chili**, about 7km from Arequipa, is the most frequently run local river, with a half-day trip suitable for beginners leaving almost daily from April to November (from US$40). Further afield, you can also do relatively easy trips on the **Río Majes**, into which the Río Colca flows. The most commonly run stretches include class II and III rapids.

Mountain Biking

The Arequipa area has numerous mountain-biking possibilities. Many of the companies that offer mountain-climbing or trekking trips also organize downhill volcano mountain-biking trips at **Chachani** and **El Misti**

The standard two-day tour of the Cañón del Colca (p883) costs S65 to S225 per person, depending on the season, group size and comfort level of the hotel you stay at in Chivay. Different agencies may sell you tickets for the same tours, so shop around. All tours leave Arequipa between 7am and 9am. Stops include the Reserva Nacional Salinas y Aguada Blanca, Chivay, **La Calera Hot Springs** (admission S5-15; ⊙ 5am-6pm), an evening *peña* (bar or club featuring live folkloric music; at an additional fee) trip plus a visit to the Cruz del Cóndor (p884).

While a one-day tour of the Cañón del Colca (really mainly the Cruz del Cóndor) is heavily touted, you will spend most of your time cooped up in a van, missing out on spending significant time in any of the canyon towns and wind up exhausted by the time you return to Arequipa the same day. Departures are at the unholy hour of around 2am.

🥾 Courses

Peruvian Cooking Experience COOKING
(☑ 054-213-975; www.peruviancookingexperience.com; San Martín 116, Vallecito; 3hr course US$23.50; ⊙ 11am & 3pm Mon-Sat) A popular option for Peruvian cooking lessons, where you can study the art of ceviche preparation or even opt for vegetarian recipes. Courses are available in Spanish and English. Maximum group size is six. It's based out of the Casa de Avila (p880) hotel four blocks southwest of Plaza de Armas.

Rocio LANGUAGE
(☑ 054-22-4568; www.spanish-peru.com; Ayacucho 208) This language school with accommodations options charges US$6 per hour for an individual Spanish class, while small group lessons cost US$116 per 20-hour week. Ring bell number 21 at the communal entrance.

🎎 Festivals & Events

Semana Santa RELIGIOUS
(Holy Week; ⊙ Mar or Apr) *Arequipeños* claim that their Semana Santa celebrations leading up to Easter are similar to the very solemn and traditional Spanish observances held in Seville. The Maundy Thursday, Good Friday and Holy Saturday processions are particularly colorful and sometimes end with the burning of an effigy of Judas.

🛌 Sleeping

Stay near the Plaza de Armas for convenience, though away from the bars of San

or can arrange tailor-made tours. If you have the experience and wherewithal, these agencies can also rent you high-end bikes and offer expert trip-planning advice to help get you started on your own. **Peru Adventures Tours** (☑ 054-22-1658; www.peruadventurestours.com; Zela 209; ⊙ 8am-5pm Mon-Sat) organizes cycling tours around El Misti for US$50 (half day) including transportation, big-name bikes, helmet, gloves and snacks, with oxygen and first-aid available.

🕮 Tours

Dozens of travel agencies line Santa Catalina and Jerusalén offering near-identical excursions to the canyon country, most with daily departures; ho-hum city tours are also pushed. Some agencies are professional, but there are also plenty of carpetbaggers muscling in on the action, so shop carefully. Never accept tours from street touts and, where possible, tours should be paid for in cash, as occasional credit-card fraud is reported.

LOCAL KNOWLEDGE

YANAHUANA

This tranquil **neighborhood** (cnr Cuesta del Angel & Av Lima) makes for a pleasant, walkable excursion, with a *mirador* (lookout) as its centerpiece providing excellent views of Arequipa and El Misti through arches inscribed with poetry. To get here, go west on Puente Grau over the namesake bridge, and take the first right along Francisco Bolognesi hugging the park. Take the first left on Cuesta del Ángel and continue four blocks to Plaza Yanahuara with its church and *mirador*.

Francisco on weekends if you want quiet. Many accommodations inhabit attractive *sillar* (white volcanic rock) buildings, the thick walls of which often weaken wireless signals. Cable TV and free wi-fi are pretty much a given, as is breakfast – usually merely bread, jam and coffee at cheaper joints. Prices can fluctuate greatly even during high season (June to August).

Hostal Núñez HOSTEL $

(☑ 054-21-8648; www.hotel-nunez.de; Jerusalén 528; s/d/tr S59/79/156; 🛜) On a street full of not-so-great guesthouses, this secure, friendly hostel is always stuffed with gringos. The colorful rooms sport yesteryear orange decor and cable TV. Note that the singles are a bit of a squeeze.

★Casa Arequipa BOUTIQUE HOTEL $$

(☑ 054-28-4219; www.arequipacasa.com; Av Lima 409, Vallecito; r incl breakfast from US$70; 🛜) Inside a cotton-candy-pink colonial mansion in the gardens of suburban Vallecito, this gay-friendly B&B offers more than half a dozen guest rooms with fine design touches such as richly painted walls, pedestal sinks, antique handmade furnishings and alpaca-wool blankets. There's a sociable cocktail bar in the lobby.

Casablanca Hostal HOTEL $$

(☑ 054-22-1327; www.casablancahostal.com; Puente Bolognesi 104; s/d/tr incl breakfast S111/190/235; 🖥🛜) You might marvel at what you get for your money at this hotel. It has a prime corner location on the main plaza (though with accompanying street noise), beautiful exposed *sillar* (white volcanic rock) brickwork and rooms large enough to keep a horse (or two) in. Service is discreet and breakfast is taken in a lovely sun-filled cafe.

Casa de Avila HOTEL $$

(☑ 054-21-3177; www.casadeavila.com; San Martín 116, Vallecito; s/d/tr incl breakfast S151/188/271; 🖥🛜) If the spacious courtyard garden doesn't swing it for you, the congenial personalized service ought to – this is not some 'yes sir, no sir' chain hotel. The brown decor and comfy beds emphasize the homey feel. Casa de Avila also hosts Spanish-language courses and a cooking course in the sunny garden three times a week.

Hostal las Torres de Ugarte HOTEL $$

(☑ 054-28-3532; www.torresdeugarte.com; Ugarte 401A; s/d/tr incl breakfast S163/196/232; 🖥🛜) This friendly hostel in a quiet location behind the Monasterio de Santa Catalina has small, bright modern rooms with blackout curtains, colorful woolly bedspreads and flat-screen TVs. You'll just have to ignore the cacophonous echoing hallways, or head to the rooftop deck chairs. Rates drop considerably in low season.

Orkkowasi Casa de Montaña HOSTEL $$

(☑ 054-21-4518; Álvarez Thomas 208; dm S29, d/tr S88/130, d without bathroom 72; 🛜) Don't let the cramped entrance at this hostel near the Plaza de Armas put you off. The quiet rooms upstairs are clean and spacious with sofas, desks, flat-screen TVs and comfy beds – no springs digging into your ribs! – and modern where it counts, in the (small) bathrooms and speedy wi-fi. There is a kitchen and rooftop lounging space.

★Hotel Casona Solar HOTEL $$$

(☑ 054-22-8991; www.casonasolar.com; Consuelo 116; s/d/ste S199/319/389; 🛜) This gorgeous 'secret garden' is situated – incredibly given its tranquility – only three blocks from Arequipa's main square. Grand 18th-century rooms are crafted from huge *sillar* (white volcanic rock) stones, some with mezzanine bedrooms. The service (same-day laundry, bus reservations, free airline check-in) is equally dazzling. One of the city's best places to stay.

★Hotel La Posada del Monasterio HOTEL $$$

(☑ 054-40-5728; www.hotelessanagustin.com.pe; Santa Catalina 300; s/d/tr incl buffet breakfast from S377/429/514; 🖥🛜🏊) On a prime corner, this hotel gracefully inhabits an architectural mix-and-match building combining the best of the European and South American style. The comfortable modern rooms have all the expected facilities. The rooftop balcony peers into the Santa Catalina convent across the street. Ask to access the laundry terrace for impressive volcano vistas. It's especially popular with European tour groups.

★ **La Hostería**   HOTEL $$$
(☑ 054-28-9269; www.lahosteriaqp.com.pe; Bolívar 405; s/d/tr incl breakfast US$66/75/83; ☎) Worth every sol is this picturesque colonial hotel with a flower-bedecked courtyard, light and quiet rooms (with minibar), carefully chosen antiques, a sunny terrace and a lounge. Some rooms do suffer from street noise, so request one in the back. Apartment-style suites on the upper floors have stellar city views.

✖ Eating

Arequipa has a reputation for tasty local dishes like *rocoto relleno* (stuffed spicy red peppers), best enjoyed in the traditional, communal *picantería* restaurants. Trendy upscale spots line San Francisco north of the Plaza de Armas, while touristy outdoor cafes huddle together on Pasaje Catedral. Good, local eateries are in the busy Mercado on San Camilo southeast of the plaza.

Crepísimo   CAFE $
(www.crepisimo.com; Alianza Francesa, Santa Catalina 208; mains S15-34; ☺ 8am-11pm; ☎ ☑) All the essential components of a great cafe – food, setting, service, ambience – come together at Crepísimo, located inside Arequipa's French cultural center. In this chic colonial setting, the simple crepe is offered with 100 different types of filling, from Chilean smoked trout to South American fruits and ample vegetarian options, while casual waitstaff serve you Parisian-quality coffee.

★ **La Nueva Palomino**   PERUVIAN $$
(☑ 054-25-2393; Leoncio Prado 122; mains S22-69; ☺ noon-5pm Mon-Sat, 7:30am to noon Sun; ☎ ☑ ▣) An unmissable local favorite, this long-running *picantería* has old-world formal service but a casual atmosphere that turns boisterous even during the week when family groups descend to eat generous servings of local specialties and drink copious amounts of *chicha de jora* (fermented corn beer) in the courtyard. Solo diners will get full on the excellent *ricoto relleno* (meat-stuffed peppers) alone.

★ **Zig Zag**   PERUVIAN $$
(☑ 054-20-6020; www.zigzagrestaurant.com; Zela 210; mains S36-50; ☺ noon-11pm; ☑) Upscale but not ridiculously pricey, Zig Zag is a Peruvian restaurant with European inflections. It in-

habits a two-story colonial house with an iron stairway designed by Gustave Eiffel (wow, that man must have been busy). The menu classic is a meat selection served on a unique volcano-stone grill with various sauces. The fondues are also good.

★ **Salamanto**   PERUVIAN $$$
(☑ 979-394-676; www.salamanto.com; San Francisco 211; mains S48-57, 5-course tasting menus S85; ☺ 12:30-3:30pm & 6:30-10:30pm Mon-Sat; ☎) The innovative, wonderfully plated contemporary Peruvian creations at Salamanto bolster Arequipa's reputation as a foodie destination. The five-dish degustation is unmissable with mushroom and pistachio mousse, trout carpaccio, and alpaca steak with pisco (Peruvian grape brandy) mustard dazzling on artful slabs of stone. There are only three wines (Argentinian and Peruvian) to choose from but they have been carefully chosen.

★ **Chicha**   PERUVIAN, FUSION $$$
(☑ 054-28-7360; www.chicha.com.pe; Santa Catalina 210; mains S44-69; ☺ noon-11pm Mon-Sat, to 8pm Sun; ☎ ☑) Peru's most famous chef, Gastón Acurio, owns this experimental place where the menu closely reflects Peru's Inca-Spanish roots. River prawns are a highlight in season (April to December), but Acurio prepares Peruvian staples with equal panache, along with tender alpaca burgers and earthy pastas. Staff can help pair food with pisco (Peruvian grape brandy) cocktails and wines by the glass.

♬ Drinking & Nightlife

★ **Chelawasi Public House**   MICROBREWERY
(www.facebook.com/chelawasi; Campo Redondo 102; beers S15-18; ☺ 4-11pm Mon-Fri, from noon Sat) Arequipa's first craft-beer bar is a modern but unpretentious pub in the village-like San Lázaro area. The burgers, wings and hand-cut fries are excellent for pacing yourself. New to craft beer? Chelawasi's friendly Canadian-Peruvian owners will step you through the best beers from Peru's microbreweries, with bonus local travel advice, or a chat with other solo drinkers.

Déjà Vu   COCKTAIL BAR
(San Francisco 319B; ☺ 9am-late; ☎) This eternally popular haunt has a rooftop terrace overlooking the Iglesia de San Francisco, a long list of crazy cocktails and a lethal happy hour every evening. Some of Arequipa's best DJs play electro and house here nightly, but only draw crowds on weekends.

PERU AREQUIPA

Casona Forum   CLUB
(www.casonaforum.com; San Francisco 317; ☺nightclubs 9pm-late Thu-Sat, bars & restaurant from 7pm daily) A seven-in-one excuse for a good night out in a *sillar* (white volcanic rock) building incorporating a pub (Retro), pool club (Zero), sofa bar (Chill Out), restaurant (Terrasse) and nightclubs (Forum, Club 80s and Latino Salsa Club).

Museo del Pisco   COCKTAIL BAR
(www.museodelpisco.org; cnr Santa Catalina & Moral; drinks S16-32, tastings per person S37; ☺5pm-midnight Sun-Thu, to 1am Fri & Sat) The name says 'museum,' but the designer slabs of stone and glass, plus the menu of more than 100 pisco (Peruvian grape brandy) varieties, says cocktail bar. Identify your favorite with a tasting of three mini craft piscos, explained in English by knowledgeable staff. Then mix your own (S26) behind the bar. Pace yourself with gourmet burgers and hummus.

☆ Entertainment

Café Art Montréal   LIVE MUSIC
(Ugarte 210; ☺6:30pm-midnight Mon-Wed, to 2am Thu-Sat) This intimate little bar with live bands playing (Thursday to Saturday) on a stage at the back would be equally at home as a bohemian student hangout on Paris' Left Bank.

🛍 Shopping

Claustros de la Compañía   SHOPPING CENTER
(118 General Morán; ☺most stores 9am-9pm) One of South America's most elegant shopping centers, with a wine bar, ice-cream outlet, numerous alpaca-wool shops and chic cafes and restaurants. Its ornate double courtyard is ringed by cloisters held up by *sillar* (white volcanic rock) columns, etched with skillful carvings. Couples dot the upper levels enjoying the romantic setting and southerly views.

ℹ Information

DANGERS & ANNOYANCES
➡ Petty theft is often reported in Arequipa, so hide valuables and keep your stuff in sight while in bars, cafes and restaurants.

➡ Take great care in Parque Selva Alegre, north of the city center, as muggings have been reported there.

➡ Don't hail taxis from the street. Ask your accommodations or tour operator to call you an official taxi; the extra time and money are worth the added safety.

➡ Only pay for tours at a recognized agency and never trust touts in the street – they bamboozle cash out of a surprisingly high number of travelers.

EMERGENCY
Policía de Turismo (Tourist Police; ☑054-28-2613; Jerusalén 315-317; ☺24hr) May be helpful if you need an official theft report for insurance claims. English speakers available.

MEDICAL SERVICES
Clínica Arequipa (☑054-599-000; www.clinicarequipa.com.pe; Bolognesi, near Puente Grau; ☺8am-8pm Mon-Fri, to 12:30pm Sat) Arequipa's best and most expensive medical clinic. A 24-hour pharmacy is available.

MONEY
BCP (San Juan de Dios 123; ☺9am-6pm Mon-Fri, to 1pm Sat & Sun) Changes US dollars; has a 24-hour Visa ATM.

POST
Serpost (Moral 118; ☺8am-8pm Mon-Fri, to 7pm Sat) Main Arequipa branch of the national postal service.

TOURIST INFORMATION
Indecopi (☑054-42-7495; www.indecopi.gob.pe; cnr Calle 1 & Cultura Tiahuanaco, Urb La Esperanza; ☺8:30am-4:30pm Mon-Fri) National tourist-protection agency.

iPerú (☑054-22-3265, 24hr hotline 574-8000; iperuarequipa@promperu.gob.pe; Portal de la Municipalidad 110, Plaza de Armas; ☺9am-6pm Mon-Sat, to 1pm Sun) English-speaking staff give excellent information on local and regional attractions. Also has an office at the **airport** (☑054-44-4564; 1st fl, Main Hall, Aeropuerto Rodríguez Ballón; ☺10am-7:30pm).

ℹ Getting There & Away

AIR
Arequipa's **Rodríguez Ballón International Airport** (Aeropuerto Internacional Alfredo Rodríguez Ballón, AQP; ☑054-34-4834; Cerro Colorado) is about 8km northwest of the city center.

LAN (☑054-20-1100; Santa Catalina 118C; ☺office 9am-7pm, to 2pm Sat) has daily flights to Lima and Cuzco. **LCPeru** (☑054-21-4746; www.lcperu.pe; Moral 225; ☺office 9am-7pm Mon-Fri, to 1pm Sat) also offers daily flights to Lima. **Sky Airline** (☑054-28-2899; www.skyairline.cl; La Merced 121) flies to Santiago in Chile.

BUS
Most bus companies have departures from the Terminal Terrestre or the smaller Terrapuerto bus terminal, located together on Av Andrés Avelino Cáceres, less than 3km south of the city center (take a taxi for S7). Check in advance which terminal your bus leaves from and keep a close watch on your belongings while you're

waiting there. There's a S1.50 departure tax from either terminal, paid separately at a booth. Both terminals have shops, restaurants and left-luggage facilities. The more chaotic Terminal Terrestre also has a global ATM.

Dozens of bus companies have desks at the Terminal Terrestre so shop around. Prices range between superluxury **Cruz del Sur** (☑ 054-42-7375; www.cruzdelsur.com.pe) and **Ormeño** (☑ 054-42-3855; www.grupo-ormeno.com.pe/destinos.html; Terminal Terrestre) with 180-degree reclining 'bed' seats, and no-frills **Flores** (Transportes Flores Hermanos; ☑ 054-43-2228, 01-480-0725; www.floreshnos.pe; Terminal Terrestre) which travels to a greater variety of destinations including Mollendo, Moquegua and Ilo.

Arequipa Buses

DESTINATION	COST (S)	DURATION (HR)
Cabanaconde	17	5
Camaná	12-55	2.5
Chivay	13	3½
Cotahuasi	30	10
Cuzco	25-135	10
Ica	75-160	11-15
Juliaca	20-80	5
Lima	50-140	14-17
Mollendo	12-15	2-2½
Moquegua	20-30	6½
Nazca	50-120	10-12
Pisco	40-144	15
Puno	20-82	5
Tacna	30-40	6

❶ Getting Around

Combis (minibuses) go south along Bolívar and Cruz Verde to the Terminal Terrestre (S1, 20 minutes), next door to the Terrapuerto bus terminal, but make sure to ask if they are going *directo* (direct) or it'll be a slower 35-minute trip via the market area. A taxi costs about S7.

Cañón Del Colca

It's not just the vastness and depth of the Colca that make it so fantastical, it's the shifts in its mood. There are more scenery changes along the river canyon's 100km passage than there are in most European countries; from the barren steppe of Sibayo, through the ancient terraced farmland of Yanque and Chivay toward the cruising condors riding warm air currents, into the steep-sided canyon proper beyond Cabanaconde that wasn't

❶ BOLETO TURÍSTICO

To access sites in the Cañón del Colca you need to purchase a *boleto turístico* (tourist ticket; S70) from a booth on the Arequipa road just outside Chivay. If you are taking an organized tour, the cost of the tour usually does not include this additional fee, and you will be asked for this in cash by your guide at the booth. If you are traveling alone, tickets can be purchased on most public buses entering or leaving Chivay, or in the town of Cabanaconde. You will likely also be accosted as you enter the Cruz del Cóndor. Half of the proceeds from this ticket go to Arequipa for general maintenance and conservation of local tourist attractions, while the other half goes to the national agency of tourism.

thoroughly explored until the 1980s. The Colca is the world's second-deepest canyon, a smidgeon shallower than its near neighbor, the Cotahuasi, and twice as deep as the more famous Grand Canyon in the US. But, more than that, it is replete with history, culture, ruins, tradition and – rather like Machu Picchu – intangible Peruvian magic.

❶ Getting There & Away

Most people race through the region on the classic two-day tours, with a night in Chivay, and not passing Cruz del Condor. From Arequipa, it's easy to take a large, comfortable bus to Cañón del Colca stopping at Chivay (S13, 3½ hours) or all the way to Cabanaconde (S17, five hours). There are frequent departures with **Andalucía** (☑ 054-44-5089), from Terrapuerto, and **Reyna** (☑ 054-43-0612; www.reyna.com.pe), from Terminal Terrestre; neither make any stops but do have toilets aboard. Note that buses get cold as they ascend to high altitudes.

Chivay

☑ 054 / POP 7700 / ELEV 3630M

Behold the most accessible and popular segment of the Cañón del Colca, a landscape dominated by agriculture and characterized by some of the most intensely terraced hillsides on earth. The greenery and accessibility has led to this becoming the canyon's busiest region, with the bulk of the business centered in the small town of Chivay. The canyon's unashamedly disheveled nexus, this traditional town has embraced tourism without (so far) losing its unkempt high-country identity. Long may it continue!

Around the market area and in the main square are good places to catch a glimpse of the decorative clothing worn by local Colca women. The town itself affords enchanting views of snowcapped peaks and terraced hillsides, and serves as a logical base from which to explore smaller towns further up the valley.

🏃 Activities

Hiking

Chivay is a good starting point for canyon hikes, both short and long. The view-embellished 7km path to **Corporaque** on the north side of the canyon starts on the north edge of town. Fork left on the La Calera Hot Springs road, cross the Puente Inca, and follow the fertile fields to the village. Rather than retracing your steps, you can head downhill out of Corporaque past some **small ruins** and descend across the orange bridge across the Río Colca toward Yanque. From Yanque, on the southern bank, you can catch a passing bus or *colectivo* (shared transportation) for the 7km return to Chivay (or you can walk along the road). For a quicker sojourn rent a mountain bike in Chivay.

To penetrate further west it's possible to continue on up the northern side of the canyon from Corporaque to the villages **Ich-upampa**, **Lari** and, ultimately, **Madrigal**. Occasional *combis* (minibuses) run to these villages from the streets around the main market area in Chivay. Another option is to pitch northeast from near the Puente Inca and follow a path along the river to the villages of Tuti and Sibayo.

Ziplining

Want to dangle terrifyingly over the Río Colca while entertaining bathers relaxing below in La Calera Hot Springs? Then try the canyon's most modern sport – zip-lining. The start point is just past the hot springs, 3.5km from Chivay, but you can organize rides with one of the agencies in town or directly with **Colca Zip-Lining** (☑95-898-9931; www.colcaziplining.com; 2/4/6 rides S50/100/150; ⏱ from 9am Mon-Sat, from 10:30am Sun).

🛏 Sleeping & Eating

⭐ **La Casa de Anita** HOTEL **$$**
(☑958-911-869; www.facebook.com/hotellacasade anitacolca; Plaza de Armas 785; s/d/tr S80/120/160; @🖥) Just what Chivay needed: a hotel right on the Plaza de Armas where you can rest in clean, spacious rooms with very comfy cotton bedding, spotless modern bathrooms and portable heaters to keep you warm. With the attached restaurant serving good set meals and free tea, and knowledgeable staff (including Chivay's former mayor!), you'd swear you were staying somewhere fancier.

El Balcon De Don Zacarias BUFFET **$$**
(cnr Av 22 de Agosto & Trujillo; buffet S35; ⏱11am-3pm; 🖥🍴) There are buffets galore catering to captive tour-group diners but this large restaurant on a corner of the Plaza de Armas stands out for the freshness of dishes such as alpaca steaks and the abundance of meat-free options such as *pastel de papa andina* (potato lasagna) and stuffed eggplant.

Cruz del Cóndor

The famed **Cruz del Cóndor** (Chaq'lla; Carr al Colca; admission with boleto turístico) viewpoint is for many the highlight of their trip to the Cañón del Colca. A large family of Andean condors nests by the rocky outcrop and, with lots of luck, they can occasionally be seen gliding effortlessly on thermal air currents rising from the canyon, swooping low over onlookers' heads. It's a mesmerizing scene, heightened by the spectacular 1200m drop to the river below and the sight of **Nevado Mismi** on the other side of the ravine.

Some much-hyped travel sights are anti-climactic in the raw light of day, but this is not one of them. Recently it has become more difficult to see the condors, mostly due to air pollution, including from travelers' campfires and tour buses. The condors are also less likely to appear on rainy days so it's best to visit during the dry season; they are unlikely to emerge at all in January and February. Expect a couple of hundred people for the 8am 'show' in season.

If you are not part of a tour, large Milagro buses (S8) travel here on the way to Cabanaconde, departing at 7:30am from Chivay's bus station. Afterward, the only public transportation to Cabanaconde is with the minivan (S5) that transports the women selling *artesanías* (handicrafts) at about 11am, otherwise it's a long 12.5km walk or a long wait until the next return bus from Cabanaconde materializes.

Cabanaconde

☑054 / POP 2400 / ELEV 3290M

The narrow lower canyon that runs roughly from Cabanaconde down to Huambo is the Colca at its deepest. Only approximately 20%

of Cañón del Colca visitors get as far as ramshackle Cabanaconde (most organized itineraries turn around at the Cruz del Cóndor). For those who make it, the attractions are obvious – fewer people, more authenticity and greater tranquility. Welcome to the *true* canyon experience.

The Colca is significantly deeper here with steep, zigzagging paths tempting the fit and the brave to descend 1200m to the eponymous river. Fruit trees can be found around Tapay and Sangalle, but otherwise the canyon supports no real economic activity.

You've only half-experienced Colca if you haven't descended into the canyon by foot (the only method anywhere west of Madrigal). The shortest route is the spectacular two- to three-hour hike from Cabanaconde down to flower-filled **Sangalle** (known as 'the Oasis') at the canyon's base.

Alternative, and equally distant, options include serene and authentic **San Juan de Chuccho, Tapay** or **Lluhar**.

As upmarket as Cabanaconde gets, **Hotel Kuntur Wassi** (☑054-66-4016; www.arequipacolca.com; CruzBlancas/n; s/d/ste incl breakfast S121/140/250; @ ☎) is rather charming. It's built into the hillside above town, with stone bathrooms, trapezoidal windows overlooking the gardens and a nouveau-rustic feel. Suites have enormous bathtubs. There's also a bar, restaurant, library, laundry and foreign-currency exchange. It serves top-notch city-standard food.

There are no ATMs in Cabanaconde; be sure to bring some cash.

LAKE TITICACA

In Andean belief, Titicaca is the birthplace of the sun. Set between Peru and Bolivia, it's the largest lake in South America and the highest navigable body of water in the world. Bright days contrast with bitterly cold nights. Enthralling, deep-blue Lake Titicaca is the unifying, longtime home of highland cultures steeped in the old ways.

Pre-Inca Pukara, Tiwanaku and Collas all left their mark on the landscape. Today the region is a mix of crumbling cathedrals, desolate altiplano (Andean plateau) and checkerboard fields backed by rolling hills and high Andean peaks. In this world, crops are still planted and harvested by hand. *Campesinos* (farmers) wear sandals recycled from truck tires, women work in petticoats and bowler hats, and llamas are tame as pets.

It might at first appear austere, but ancient holidays are marked with riotous celebrations where elaborately costumed processions and brass bands start a frenzy that lasts for days.

Juliaca

☑051 / POP 245,700 / ELEV 3826M

The region's only commercial airport makes Juliaca, the largest city on the altiplano, an unavoidable transit hub. The city bustles with commerce (and contraband) due to its handy location near the Bolivian border. Daytime muggings and drunks on the street are not uncommon. Since Juliaca has little to offer travelers, it is advisable to while away some hours in nearby Lampa or move on to Puno.

Hotels, restaurants, *casas de cambio* and internet cafes abound along San Román, near Plaza Bolognesi.

An excellent, if pricey, choice, the towering **Royal Inn Hotel** (☑051-32-1561; www.royalinnhoteles.com; San Román 158; s/d/tr incl breakfast S315/330/420) boasts well-maintained, modern rooms with hot showers, heating and cable TV, plus one of Juliaca's best restaurants with an extensive buffet breakfast (mains from S20).

ATMs and banks are nearby on Nuñez.

The **airport** (Inca Manco Capac International Airport, JUL; ☑051-32-4248) is 2km west of town. **LAN** (☑051-32-2228; San Roman 125; ☺ office 8am-7pm Mon-Fri, to 4pm Sat) has daily flights to/from Lima, Arequipa and Cuzco. **Avianca** (☑051-827-4951; www.avianca.com; Centro Comercial Real Plaza, Tumbes 391, Local LC-105; ☺ 11am-8pm Mon-Fri, to 6pm Sat & Sun) also flies to Lima.

The **Terminal Terrestre** (San Martin at Av Miraflores) houses long-distance bus companies. Buses leave for Cuzco every two hours from 5am to 11pm, and for Arequipa every two hours from 2:30am to 11:30pm.

Puno

☑051 / POP 149,100 / ELEV 3830M

With a regal plaza, concrete-block buildings and crumbling bricks that blend into the hills, Puno has its share of both grit and cheer. It serves as the jumping-off point for Lake Titicaca and is a convenient stop for those traveling between Cuzco and La Paz. But it may just capture your heart with its own rackety charm.

Puno is known as Peru's *capital folklórica* (folkloric capital) – its Virgen de la Candelaria (p887) parades are televised across the nation – and the associated drinking is the

Puno

Puno

0 _____ 200 m
0 _____ 0.1 miles

PERU PUNO

Puno

⊙ Sights
1 Casa del Corregidor B3
2 Museo Carlos Dreyer B4

✪ Activities, Courses & Tours
3 Edgar Adventures B2

🛏 Sleeping
4 Casona Plaza Hotel C3
5 Inka's Rest C2
6 Intiqa Hotel B2
7 Puma Hostel Puno C4

✖ Eating
8 La Casa del Corregidor B3
9 La Choza de Oscar B3
10 La Table del Inca B4

11 Mareas Ceviche y Más B4
12 Mojsa B4

ℹ Information
13 BCP B3
14 Bolivian Consulate B4
15 Botica Fasa B2
16 iPerú B3
17 LAN C2
18 Medicentro Tourist's Health
    Clinic C2
19 Oficina de Migraciónes B3

ℹ Transport
20 Rossy Tours C3
21 Tour Perú C2
22 Turismo Mer C3

stuff of legend. Its urban center can feel contaminated and cold. But Puno's people are upbeat, cheeky and ready to drop everything if there's a good time to be had.

As a commercial (and contraband) hub, its colonial and naval identity can be glimpsed in its spots of old architecture, the colorful traditional dress worn by many inhabitants and the scores of young cadets in the streets.

◉ Sights

Museo Carlos Dreyer   MUSEUM
(Conde de Lemos 289; admission with English-speaking guide S15; ⊙ 9am-7pm Mon-Fri, to 1pm Sat) This small museum houses a fascinating collection of Puno-related archaeological artifacts and art from pre-Inca, Inca, colonial and the Republic periods. Upstairs there are three mummies and a full-scale fiberglass *chullpa* (funerary tower).

It's around the corner from Casa del Corregidor (p887). Guides tend to leave an hour before closing.

Casa del Corregidor   HISTORIC BUILDING
(☑ 051-35-1921; www.casadelcorregidor.pe; Deustua 576; ⊙ 9am-9pm Mon-Sat) FREE An attraction in its own right, this 17th-century house is one of Puno's oldest residences. A former community center, it now houses a small fair-trade arts-and-crafts store and a cafe.

☞ Tours

It pays to shop around for a tour operator. Agencies abound and competition is fierce, leading to touting in streets and bus terminals, undeliverable promises, and prices so low as to undercut fair wages. Several of the cheaper tour agencies have reputations for ripping off the islanders of Amantaní and Taquile, with whom travelers stay overnight and whose living culture is one of the main selling points of these tours.

Island-hopping tours, even with the better agencies, are often disappointing: formulaic, lifeless and inflexible, the inevitable result of sheer numbers and repetition. If you only have a day or two though, a reputable tour can give a good taster and insight you might not otherwise get. If you have time, seeing the islands independently is recommended – you can wander around freely and spend longer in the places you like.

Edgar Adventures   CULTURAL
(☑ 051-35-3444; www.edgaradventures.com; Lima 328; ⊙ office 7am-8pm) Longtime agency with positive community involvement. More unusual activities include kayaking on Lake Titicaca and visiting remote areas.

✱ Festivals & Events

La Virgen de la Candelaria   RELIGIOUS
(Candlemas; ⊙ Feb 2-18) The region's most spectacular festival spreads out for several days around the actual date (Candlemas), depending upon which day of the week Candlemas

falls. If it falls between Sunday and Tuesday, things get underway the previous Saturday; if it occurs between Wednesday and Friday, celebrations will get going the following Saturday.

🛏 Sleeping

Inka's Rest   HOSTEL $
(☑ 051-36-8720; www.fb.me/inkasrestpuno; Pasaje San Carlos 158; dm/d incl breakfast S16.50/60; ◙ 🗢) Tucked into a small alley, this hostel earns high marks for service. Very clean, it features bunks with down duvets, and tile and parquet floors. There's a cute breakfast area as well as a guest kitchen and huge flat-screen TV. Private rooms are less attractive. There is intercom entry; take a taxi if arriving at night.

Puma Hostel Puno   HOSTEL $
(☑ 051 36-5300; Cajamarca 154; dm/d/tr incl breakfast S23/47/60; 🗢) The fake 'wood paneling' might make Puma resemble a 1980s business hotel with family beds thrown in, but it's clean, comfortable and excellent value for a hostel near the plaza.

★ Casa Panq'arani   B&B $$
(☑ 051-36-4892, 951-677-005; www.casapanqarani.com; Jr Arequipa 1086; s/tw/d incl breakfast S80/135/145; 🗢) This delightful traditional Puno home has a flower-filled courtyard and inviting rooms lining a 2nd-floor balcony. But the real draw is the sincere hospitality of owners Edgar and Consuelo. Rooms are spacious, with comfortable beds with crocheted bedspreads and fresh flowers. There are ample sunny spots for lounging. Don't miss Consuelo's gourmet altiplano cooking (meals S35 with advance request).

★ Intiqa Hotel   HOTEL $$
(☑ 051-36-6900; www.intiqahotel.com; Tarapacá 272; d/tr incl breakfast S247/313; 🗢) A midrange Puno hotel with a sense of style, the 33 large, heated rooms feature duvets, extra pillows, desks, flat-screen TVs and a safe box. The elevator is a rarity in Puno. Offers free pickups from the Terminal Terrestre. Credit cards are accepted.

Casona Plaza Hotel   HOTEL $$
(☑ 051-36-5614; www.casonaplazahoteles.com; Jr Puno 280; d/ste incl breakfast from S135/297; ◙ 🗢) This well-run, central hotel with 64 rooms is one of the largest in Puno, but is often full. All rooms are modern and neutral, and the bathrooms are great. They offer *matrimoniales* (matrimonial suites) especially for lovers – most are big enough to dance the *marinera* (Peru's national dance) between the bed and the lounge suite.

✕ Eating

La Choza de Oscar CHICKEN $
(☏ 051-35-1199; www.lachozadeoscar.com; Libertad 354; chicken plate S11; ⊙ 2-10pm Mon-Sat) Peruvian *pollo a la brasa* (roast chicken) has a spiced, crispy exterior and this eatery at the back of a restaurant creates wonders. Vegetarians can opt for a popular nightly salad buffet, and you can even sit in the main restaurant and enjoy the dance show (7.30pm to 9pm), but tips are encouraged.

La Casa del Corregidor CAFE $$
(http://cafebar.casadelcorregidor.pe; Deustua 576; mains S24-34, drinks S6.50-14; ⊙ 9am-10pm Mon-Sat; 🐾🅿) It's just off the plaza but feels like a world and era away. Vinyl records of Peru's yesteryear decorate the walls, while board games and clay teapots are ready to adorn the tables, and a happy yellow courtyard shows off the historical building. Try the good fresh infusions or alpaca BBQ sticks.

★ La Table del Inca FUSION $$
(☏ 994-659-357; www.fb.me/latabledelinca; Ancash 239; mains S26-40, 3 courses with wine S80; ⊙ noon-2pm & 6-9.30pm Mon-Thu, 6-9.30pm Sat & Sun; 🐾) If you need a reason to dress up, this fusion restaurant, a little away from the noise, shows off paintings by local artists on its walls, with colorful plating. Peruvian dishes like *lomo saltado* (stir-fried beef with potatoes and chili) hold their own against Euro-Peruvian twists such as quinoa risotto, alpaca carpaccio with *huacatay* (a local aromatic herb), and French desserts.

Mareas Ceviche y Más CEVICHE $$
(www.fb.me/mareassocialpage; Cajamarca 448; mains S13-35; ⊙ 9am-4pm; 🐾) There are dozens of ways to do ceviche and seafood in this family-filled courtyard restaurant. If you can't decide between seafood pasta, squid fried rice, trout ceviche or ceviche *palteado* (with avocado), try a *combinado* (set combo) of ceviche, *chaufa* (fried rice) and battered fried fish.

★ Mojsa PERUVIAN $$
(☏ 051-36-3182; Lima 635; mains S22-30; ⊙ noon-9.30pm; 🐾🅿) The go-to place for locals and travelers alike, Mojsa lives up to its name, which is Aymara for 'delicious.' Overlooking the plaza, it has a thoughtful range of Peruvian and international food, including innovative trout dishes and a design-your-own salad option. All meals start with fresh bread and a bowl of local olives. In the evening crisp brick-oven pizzas are on offer.

ℹ Information

DANGERS & ANNOYANCES
There are scenic lookouts (Inca, Condor) on the hills above town, but as assaults and robberies have been reported (even by groups), it's not recommended to visit them unless there is a drastic improvement in security.

IMMIGRATION
Bolivian Consulate (☏ 051-20-5400; www.consuladopuno.simplesite.com; Cajamarca 664; ⊙ 8am-4pm Mon-Fri) Can help issue visas for Bolivia.

Oficina de Migraciónes (Immigration Office; ☏ 051-35-7103; www.migraciones.gob.pe; Ayacucho 270-280; ⊙ 8am-1pm & 2-4pm Mon-Fri) Helps organize student and business visas but can't arrange extensions on tourist cards.

MEDICAL SERVICES
Botica Fasa (☏ 051-36-6862; Arequipa 314; ⊙ 24hr) A well-stocked, 24-hour pharmacy – knock loudly late at night.

Medicentro Tourist's Health Clinic (☏ 951-62-0937, 051-36-5909; Moquegua 191; ⊙ 24hr) The 'house' doctors can attend you at your accommodations, and include English- and French-speakers.

MONEY
BCP (Lima 444) BCP has branches and ATMs on Lima.

TOURIST INFORMATION
iPerú (☏ 051-36-5088; Plaza de Armas, Lima at Deustua; ⊙ 9am-6pm Mon-Sat, to 1pm Sun) Patient, English-speaking staff offer good advice here. An excellent first port of call on arrival in Puno. Other useful iPerú offices are at the Terminal Terrestre and Juliaca airport.

ℹ Getting There & Away

AIR
The nearest airport is in Juliaca, about an hour away. Hotels can book you a comfortable, safe shuttle bus for S15 or you can book directly with **Rossy Tours** (☏ 051-36-6709; www.rossytours.com; Tacna 308; ⊙ office 9am-8pm). The earliest bus is timed to give you just enough time to check in for the earliest flight, so there is no need to stay in Juliaca. There is a **LAN** (☏ 051-36-7227; Tacna 299) office in Puno.

BUS
The **Terminal Terrestre** (☏ 051-36-4737; Primero de Mayo 703), three blocks down Ricardo Palma from Av El Sol, houses Puno's long-distance bus companies. The terminal has an ATM, and there is a departure tax of S1.50, which you must pay in a separate booth before departure.

ⓘ GETTING TO BOLIVIA

There are two viable routes from Puno to Bolivia along Lake Titicaca. The north-shore route is very much off the beaten track and rarely used. There are two ways to go via the south shore: through either Yunguyo or Desaguadero. The only reason to go via Desaguadero is if you're pressed for time. The Yunguyo route is safer, prettier and far more popular; it passes through the chilled-out Bolivian lakeshore town of Copacabana, from where Isla del Sol – arguably the most significant site in Andean mythology – can be visited.

US citizens have to pay US$160 cash for a tourist visa to enter Bolivia.

Note that Peruvian time is one hour behind Bolivian time.

Via Yunguyo

The quickest and easiest way is with a cross-border bus company such as Tour Perú. Purchase tickets at the Terminal Terrestre, or the more convenient Tour Perú ticket office in central Puno, at least one day in advance.

The alternative is catching local transportation – *micros* (small buses) – from the Terminal Zonal. Yunguyo is the end of the line. Catch a *triciclo* (three-wheeled cycle) to Kasani or cross on foot. First visit the Peruvian police, followed by the Control Migratorio (Immigration Office) on the left. A *combi* (minibus) to Copacabana is B$3.

Via Desaguadero

If you're going straight from Puno to La Paz, unsavory Desaguadero is faster, slightly cheaper and more direct than Yunguyo.

In Desaguadero, visit the Peruvian Dirección General de Migraciones y Naturalización to get stamped out of Peru. Then head to the building that says 'Migraciones Desaguadero,' to the left of the bridge, to complete Bolivian formalities.

Catch a *triciclo* (three-wheeled cycle) to the Bolivian-side transportation terminal, from where you can get to La Paz in 3½ hours by *combi* (minibus; B$30/S16).

Buses leave for Cuzco every two to three hours from 4am to 10pm, and for Arequipa every three to four hours from 2am to 10pm. **Cruz del Sur** (☑ in Lima 01-311-5050; www.cruzdelsur.com.pe; Terminal Terrestre) has the best services to both. **Turismo Mer** (☑ 051-36-7223; www.turismomer. com; Tacna 336; ⊙ office 8am-1pm & 3-8pm) buses to Cuzco are also comfortable. **Civa** (☑ 051 365-882; www.civa.com.pe; Terminal Zonal) goes to Lima and Arequipa. **Tour Perú** (☑ 051-35-2991; www.tourperu.com.pe; Tacna 285 No 103) goes to Cuzco at 10pm and also has a daily 7am service crossing to La Paz, Bolivia, via Copacabana

TRAIN

There are two train services. The sumptuous Belmond Andean Explorer train is an overnight sleeper service with three meals and cocktails included, coming at a hefty cost for five-star-hotel-like pampering. The cheaper PeruRail Titicaca service is a day trip.

Reservations can be made online at www. perurail.com.

Andean Explorer trains depart from Puno's **train station** (☑ 051-36-9179; www.perurail. com; Av La Torre 224; ⊙ train station office 6.30am-noon & 4-6pm Mon-Fri, 6.30am-2.30pm Sat) at noon on Wednesdays, arriving at Cuzco around 7:40am the next day. Tickets cost from US$480 per person.

PeruRail Titicaca trains do not include sleeping and depart Mondays, Thursdays and Saturdays at 7:30am, and arrive in Cuzco at 5:50pm the same day. Tickets are US$260.

Around Puno

Sillustani

Sitting on rolling hills on the Lago Umayo peninsula, the chullpas (funerary towers) of **Sillustani** (adult/child S15/2) stand out for miles against a desolate altiplano landscape. The ancient Colla people who once dominated the Lake Titicaca area were a warlike, Aymara-speaking tribe, who later became the southeastern group of the Incas. They buried their nobility in these towers, which can be seen scattered widely around the hilltops of the region.

Lake Titicaca's Islands

Lake Titicaca's islands are world famous for their peaceful beauty and the living tradition of their agrarian cultures, which date to pre-Columbian times.

The ever-popular, human-made reed islands of the Islas Uros are the most visited. Isla Taquile is a sleepy island with a unique culture that can suddenly turn festive by night in local dances. **Isla Amantaní** is the least visited as it requires an overnight stay with a family but also can be the most insightful and rewarding. Luxurious **Isla Suasi**, the only privately owned island, is home to a boutique resort.

Be aware that not all islanders welcome tourism, which only stands to reason since not all benefit from it and may see the frequent intrusions into their daily life as disruptive. It's important to respect the privacy of islanders and show courtesy.

Islas Uros

Just 7km east of Puno, these unique floating islands are Lake Titicaca's top attraction. Their uniqueness is due to their construction. They have been created entirely with the buoyant *totora* reeds that grow abundantly in the shallows of the lake. The lives of the Uros people are interwoven with these reeds. Partially edible (tasting like non-sweet sugarcane), the reeds are also used to build homes, boats and crafts. The islands are constructed from many layers of the *totora*, which are constantly replenished from the top as they rot from the bottom, so the ground is always soft and springy.

Getting to the Uros is easy – there's no need to go with an organized tour, though you'll miss out on the history lesson given by the guides and be saving just S10 on the cheapest tours, which include admission. Ferries leave from **Puno port** (Puerto de Puno; Av Titicaca) – east of the Plaza de Armas along Jirón Puno, which becomes Avenida Del Puerto – for Uros (return trip S10) when full – at least once an hour from 6am to 4pm. The community-owned ferry service visits two islands, on a rotation basis. Ferries to Taquile and Amantaní can also drop you off in the Uros.

Isla Taquile

Inhabited for thousands of years, the lovely scenery on Isla Taquile is reminiscent of the Mediterranean. In the strong island sunlight, the deep, red-colored soil contrasts with the intense blue of the lake and the glistening backdrop of Bolivia's snowy Cordillera Real on the far side of the lake. Several hills boast Inca terracing on their sides and small ruins on top.

Ferries (round-trip S25; admission to island S5) leave from the Puno port (east of the Plaza de Armas along Av Del Puerto) for Taquile from 7:35am, via Islas Uros. As the ferry stops in Islas Uros, you will also have to pay the admission there. A ferry from Taquile to Puno leaves at 2pm, but this can change so confirm the time with the captain as you arrive on Taquile.

CUZCO & THE SACRED VALLEY

For Incas, Cuzco was the belly button of the world. A visit to this city and its nearby ruins tumbles you back into the cosmic realm of ancient Andean culture – knocked down and fused with the colonial imprint of Spanish conquest, only to be repackaged as a thriving tourist center. The capital of Cuzco is only the gateway. Beyond lies the Sacred Valley, Andean countryside dotted with villages, high-altitude hamlets and ruins linked by trail and railway tracks to the continent's biggest draw – Machu Picchu.

Old ways are not forgotten here. Colorful textiles keep the past vivid, as do the wild fiestas and carnivals where indigenous tradition meets solemn Catholic ritual. A stunning landscape careens from Andean peaks to orchid-rich cloud forests and Amazon lowlands. Explore it on foot or by fat tire, rafting wild rivers or simply braving the local buses to the remote and dust-worn corners of this far-reaching, culturally rich department.

Cuzco

✈ 084 / POP 427,000 / ELEV 3326M

The undisputed archaeological capital of the Americas, Cuzco is the continent's oldest continuously inhabited city and the gateway to Machu Picchu. Cosmopolitan Cuzco (also Cusco, or Qosq'o in Quechua) thrives with a measure of contradiction. Ornate cathedrals squat over Inca temples, massage hawkers ply the narrow cobblestone passages, a rural Andean woman feeds bottled water to her pet llama while the finest boutiques sell pricey alpaca knits.

Visitors to the Inca capital get a glimpse of the richest heritage of any South American city. Married to 21st-century hustle, Cuzco can be a bit disconcerting (note the McDonald's set in Inca stones). Soaring rents on the Plaza de Armas and in trendy San Blas are increasingly pushing locals to the margins. Foreign guests undoubtedly have the run of the roost, so showing respect toward today's incarnation of this powerhouse culture is imperative.

History

According to legend, in the 12th century, the first *inca* (king), Manco Capac, was ordered by the ancestral sun god Inti to find the spot where he could plunge a golden rod into the ground until it disappeared. At this spot – deemed the navel of the earth (*qosq'o* in the Quechua language) – he founded Cuzco, the city that would become the thriving capital of the Americas' greatest empire.

The Inca empire's main expansion occurred in the hundred years prior to the arrival of the conquistadors in 1532. At that point, the empire ranged from Quito in Ecuador to south of Santiago in Chile. Shortly before the arrival of the Europeans, Huayna Cápac had divided his empire, giving the northern part to his son Atahualpa and the southern Cuzco area to another son, Huascar.

Meanwhile, Francisco Pizarro landed in northern Peru and marched southward. Atahualpa had been too busy fighting a civil war to worry about a small band of foreigners, but by 1532 a fateful meeting had been arranged with the Spaniard in Cajamarca. It would radically change the course of South American history: Atahualpa was ambushed by a few dozen armed conquistadors, who succeeded in capturing him, killing thousands of indigenous tribespeople and routing tens of thousands more.

In an attempt to regain his freedom, Atahualpa offered a ransom of a roomful of gold and two rooms of silver, including gold stripped from the temple walls of Qorikancha. But after holding Atahualpa prisoner for a number of months, Pizarro murdered him anyway, and soon marched on to Cuzco.

Pizarro entered Cuzco on November 8, 1533, by which time he had appointed Manco, a half-brother of Huascar and Atahualpa, as the new puppet leader. After a few years of toeing the line, however, the docile puppet rebelled. In 1536 Manco Inca set out to drive the Spaniards from his empire, laying siege to Cuzco with an army estimated at well over a hundred thousand people. A desperate last-ditch breakout and violent battle at Sacsaywamán saved the Spanish from complete annihilation.

Manco Inca was forced to retreat to Ollantaytambo and then into the jungle at Vilcabamba. After Cuzco was safely recaptured, looted and settled, the seafaring Spaniards turned their attentions to the newly founded colonial capital, Lima. Cuzco's importance quickly waned to that of another colonial backwater.

◉ Sights

While the city is sprawling, areas of interest to visitors are generally within walking distance, with some steep hills in between. The center of the city is the Plaza de Armas, while traffic-choked Av El Sol nearby is the main business thoroughfare. Walking just a few blocks north or east of the plaza will lead you to steep, twisting cobblestone streets, little changed for centuries. The flatter areas to the south and west are the commercial center.

★**Cusco Planetarium** MUSEUM
(☑ 974-877-776,084-23-1710; www.planetariumcusco. com; Carr Sacsayhuamán, Km 2; per person with transport S75; ☉ presentations 6pm) An excellent way to explore the Inca cosmovision. They defined constellations of darkness as well as light, used astronomy to predict weather patterns, and designed Cuzco's main streets to align with constellations at key moments. After an indoor presentation in English and Spanish there's high-powered telescope viewings outside. Reservations are essential; price varies with group size, and includes pickup and drop-off. The planetarium van picks up visitors at 5:40pm from Plaza Regocijo.

Iglesia de La Compañía de Jesús CHURCH
(Plaza de Armas; S10; ☉9am-5pm Mon-Sat, 9-10:30am & 12:45-5pm Sun) Built upon the palace of Huayna Cápac, the last *inca* to rule an undivided, unconquered empire, the church was built by the Jesuits in 1571 and reconstructed after the 1650 earthquake. Two large canvases near the main door show early marriages in Cuzco in wonderful period detail. Local student guides are available to show you around the church, as well as the grand view from the choir on the 2nd floor, reached via rickety steps. Tips are gratefully accepted.

La Catedral CHURCH
(Plaza de Armas; adult/student S25/12.50; ☉10am-5:45pm) A squatter on the site of Viracocha Inca's palace, the cathedral was built using blocks pilfered from the nearby Inca site of Sacsaywamán. Its construction started in 1559 and took almost a century. It is joined by the 1536 **Iglesia del Triunfo** (Triunfo s/n) to

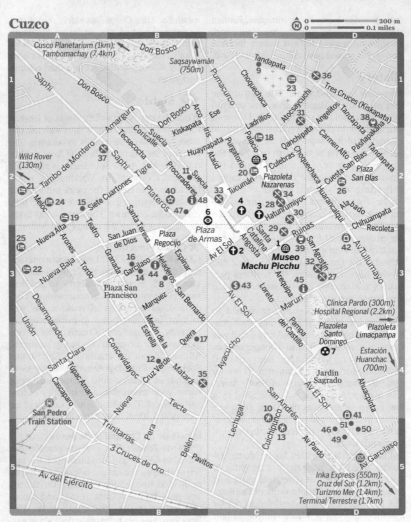

its right and the 1733 **Iglesia de Jesús María** to the left.

Museo de Arte Precolombino MUSEUM
(☎ 084-23-3210; www.map.museolarco.org/museo. html; Plazoleta Nazarenas 231; S20; ☺ 8am-10pm) Inside a Spanish colonial mansion with an Inca ceremonial courtyard, this dramatically curated pre-Columbian art museum showcases a stunningly varied, if selectively small, collection of archaeological artifacts previously buried in the vast storerooms of Lima's Museo Larco. Dating from between 1250 BC and AD 1532, the artifacts show off the artistic and cultural achievements of many of Peru's an-

cient cultures, with exhibits labeled in Spanish, English and French.

★**Museo Machu Picchu** MUSEUM
(Casa Concha; ☎ 084-25-5535; Santa Catalina Ancha 320; adult/child S20/10; ☺ 8am-7pm Mon-Fri, 9am-5pm Sat) This newish museum exhibits 360 pieces from Machu Picchu taken by Hiram Bingham's expeditions and recently returned by Yale University, including stone tools and metals, ceramics and bones. The collection shows the astounding array of fine handicrafts and ceramics acquired from throughout the vast Incan empire. There's also good background on the Bing-

Cuzco

ham expeditions with informative documentaries (subtitled). Signs are in English and Spanish.

Plaza de Armas   PLAZA
In Inca times, the plaza, called Huacaypata or Aucaypata, was the heart of the capital. Today it's the nerve center of the modern city. Two flags usually fly here – the red-and-white Peruvian flag and the rainbow-colored flag of Tahuantinsuyo. Easily mistaken for an international gay-pride banner, it represents the four quarters of the Inca empire.

Qorikancha   RUINS
(☎084-24-9176; Plazoleta Santo Domingo; admission S15 or boleto turístico; ⊙8:30am-5:30pm Mon-Sat, 2-5pm Sun) If you visit only one Cuzco site, make it these Inca ruins forming the base of the colonial church and convent of Santo Domingo. Once the richest temple in the Inca empire, all that remains today is the masterful stonework. The temple was built in the mid-15th century during the reign of the 10th *inca*, Túpac Yupanqui. Postconquest, Francisco Pizarro gave it to his brother Juan who bequeathed it to the Dominicans, in whose possession it remains.

🏃 Activities

Scores of outdoor outfitters in Cuzco offer trekking, rafting and mountain-biking adventures, as well as mountaineering, horseback riding and paragliding. Price wars can lead to bad feelings among locals, with underpaid guides and overcrowded vehicles. The cheaper tours usually take more guests and use guides with a more basic skill set.

Hiking

The department of Cuzco is a hiker's paradise. Ecosystems range from rainforest to high alpine environments in these enormous mountain ranges. Trekkers may come upon isolated villages and ruins lost in the undergrowth. Altitudes vary widely, it is essential to acclimatize properly before undertaking any trek.

Of course, most visitors come to hike the famed Inca Trail to Machu Picchu. Be aware that it's not the only 'Inca trail.' What savvy tourism officials and tour operators have christened the Inca Trail is just one of dozens of footpaths that the Incas built to reach Machu Picchu, out of thousands that crisscrossed the Inca empire. Some of these overland routes are still being dug out of the jungle by archaeologists. Many more have been developed for tourism, and an ever-increasing number of trekkers are choosing them.

Closer to Cuzco, multiday Sacred Valley trekking itineraries go well off the beaten track to little-visited villages and ruins.

Further afield, recommended treks include Lares and Ausangate and, for archaeological sites, Choquequirao and Vilcabamba.

River Running

Rafting isn't regulated in Peru – literally anyone can start a rafting company. On top of this, aggressive bargaining has led to lax safety by many cheaper rafting operators. The degree of risk cannot be stressed enough: there are deaths every year. Rafting companies that take advance bookings online are generally more safety conscious (and more expensive) than those just operating out of storefronts in Cuzco.

When choosing an outfitter, it's wise to ask about safety gear and guide training, ask about the quality of the equipment used (ie how old are the flotation devices) and check other traveler comments. It's essential to book a top-notch outfitter employing highly experienced rafting guides with first-aid certification and knowledge of swift-water rescue techniques. Be wary of new agencies without a known track record.

In terms of locations, there are a number of rivers to choose from. Rivers further from Cuzco are days away from help in the event of illness or accident.

Mountain Biking

Mountain-biking tours are a growing industry in Cuzco, and the local terrain is superb. Rental bikes are poor quality and it is most common to find *rígida* (single suspension)

models, which can make for bone-chattering downhills. Good new or secondhand bikes are not easy to buy in Cuzco either. If you're a serious mountain biker, consider bringing your own bike from home. Selling it in Cuzco is eminently viable.

Courses

Marcelo Batata Cooking Class COOKING
(☑984-384-520; www.cuzcodining.com; Calle Palacio 135; 4hr course S297; ⊙2pm) If you've fallen for Peruvian cooking, this four-hour course is a worthwhile foray. A fully stocked market pantry demystifies the flavors of the region and the kitchen setup is comfortable. Includes appetizers, a pisco tasting and a main course. In English, Spanish or Portuguese. Accommodates vegetarians, and there's a private-course option.

Proyecto Peru LANGUAGE
(☑084-24-0278; www.proyectoperucentre.org; Seite Cuartones 290; ⊙8am-6pm Mon-Fri) Offers Quechua and business or medical Spanish, with the option of homestays.

Excel Language Center LANGUAGE
(☑084-23-5298; www.excelspanishperu.info; Cruz Verde 336; ⊙8am-1pm & 4-9pm Mon-Fri, 9am-noon Sat) A Spanish-language program that has been highly recommended for its professionalism. Also offers lodging.

Tours

Cuzco has hundreds of registered travel agencies, so ask other travelers for recommendations. Many of the small agencies clustered around Procuradores and Plateros earn commissions selling trips run by other outfitters, which can lead to organizational mix-ups. If the travel agency also sells ponchos, changes money and has an internet cabin in the corner, chances are it's not operating your tour.

Alpaca Expeditions HIKING
(☑084-25-4278; www.alpacaexpeditions.com; Heladeros 157, piso 2 No 24; ⊙9am-7:30pm Mon-Fri, 4:30-7:30pm Sat & Sun) A popular outfitter for the Inca Trail, Sacred Valley treks, Salkantay and Choquequirao, this is one of the few companies to prioritize hiring female guides and porters. Also uses portable bathrooms, plants trees and participates in trail cleanup.

Apus Peru HIKING
(☑084-23-2691; www.apus-peru.com; Cuichipunco 366; ⊙9am-1pm & 3-7pm Mon-Sat) A recommended outfitter for the Inca Trail and others,

also offering conventional tours. Responsible and popular with travelers. The company joins the Choquequirao trek with the Inca Trail for a total of nine days of spectacular scenery and an ever-more-impressive parade of Inca ruins, culminating in Machu Picchu.

Alain Machaca Cruz
TOURS

(☑984-056-635; www.alternativeincatrails.com; Belen s/n, Paruro) This independent guide based outside Cuzco leads Laguna Yanahuara and multiday hikes to Choquequierao, Vilcabamba and other areas. He also makes recommended tours to the village of Paruro where you can make *chicha* (fermented corn beer) or see *cuy* (guinea pig) farms. Quechua and English spoken. No set office hours, contact ahead.

🎆 Festivals & Events

Inti Raymi
CULTURAL

(Festival of the Sun; ☉ Jun 24) This is Cuzco's most important festival. Visitors from throughout Peru and the world join the whole city celebrating in the streets with dancing and parades. The festival culminates in a reenactment of the Inca winter-solstice festival at Sacsaywamán. Despite its commercialization, it's still worth seeing the pageantry in the city and at Sacsaywamán.

Q'oyoriti
CULTURAL

(Ausangate; ☉ May/Jun) Less well-known than June's spectacular Inti Raymi are the more traditional Andean rites of this festival, which is held at the foot of Ausangate the Tuesday before Corpus Christi, in late May or early June.

🛏 Sleeping

Cuzco has hundreds of lodgings of all types and prices, with some of Peru's highest room rates. Book ahead in peak season (between June and August) especially the 10 days before Inti Raymi on June 24 and Fiestas Patrias (Independence Days) on July 28 and 29.

Prices vary dramatically according to the season and demand. Lonely Planet lists high-season rates.

With advance notice, most hotels offer free airport pickups.

⭐ Wild Rover
HOSTEL $

(☑084-22-7546; www.wildroverhostels.com; Cuesta Santa Ana 782; dm S28-50, d/ste S120/160, all incl breakfast; @☎) In its new, highly fortified hilltop location, Wild Rover is an island – or bubble – unto itself and it's wildly popular. It certainly brings Cusco hostels to a whole new standard, with a brand-new resort-style compound featuring 201 beds and a separate, soundproof Irish pub. Forget culture shock with these top-notch, modern standards, frequent parties and strict security.

Mama Simona
HOSTEL $

(☑084-26-0408; www.mamasimona.com; Ceniza 364; dm S36-46, d with/without bathroom S126/102; @☎) Styled for hipsters, with a crushed-velvet sofa and oddball decor. Beds have nice down covers and the shared kitchen with picnic tables is undoubtedly cute. There's also a cute on-site cafe with an excellent, good-value breakfast menu. Stylish, comfortable and clean, it's two blocks northeast of Plaza San Francisco.

Intro Hostel
HOSTEL $

(☑084-22-3860; www.introhostels.com; Cuesta Santa Ana 515; dm S28-48, d without bathroom S112, all incl breakfast; ☎) From the owners of 1900 Backpackers in Lima, this old colonial offers a clean look and good service, an ample courtyard and nice rooms. The mixed stall bathrooms are in good shape. There's a covered outdoor cooking area, billiards and travel-agent services. The reception operates 24 hours; take a taxi if it's late.

⭐ Niños Hotel
HOTEL $$

(☑084-23-1424; www.ninoshotel.com; Meloc 442; s without bathroom S99, d with/without bathroom S198/182; @☎) Long beloved and highly recommended, this hotel is run by a Dutch-founded nonprofit foundation that serves underprivileged children in Cuzco. It is a rambling colonial with sunny courtyard. Refurbished rooms are bordered with bright trim and feature plaid throws and portable heaters. In the coldest months there are hot-water bottles to tuck in bed. A second branch is located at Fierro 476.

Ñawin Cusco
APARTMENT $$

(☑968-586-106; www.nawincusco.com; Tandapata 357; d S215-248; ☎) Located on the quiet side of Tandapata, these small garden-level apartments are a home away from home. Cozy rooms with kitchenettes feature plump bedding, Andean weavings, handmade soaps and teas. There are also space heaters, TV and good wi-fi. The attentive owners leave you a map of the city with their own favorite haunts.

Reservation only, no walk-ins.

Tambo del Arriero
HOTEL $$

(☑084-26-0709; www.tambodelarriero.com; Nueva Alta 484; s/d/ste incl breakfast S297/396/495;

PERU CUZCO

@ 🛜) A spacious and quiet courtyard hotel. Rooms are bordered with floral accents, with heated towel racks and down duvets. Some feature bathtubs. Breakfast comes buffet-style, and the hotel also offers free walking tours. If you like your space it's good value, though the neighborhood remains up-and-coming.

★ **Casa Cartagena** BOUTIQUE HOTEL $$$
(📞 in Lima 01-242-3147; www.casacartagena.com; Pumacurco 336; ste incl breakfast from S825; @ 🛜 🌊) Fusing modern with colonial, this Italian-owned boutique hotel is dripping in style. Its 16 suites feature walls with oversized stripes, king-sized beds, iPod docks, bouquets of long-stemmed roses and enormous bathtubs lit by candles. There's a lovely on-site spa and room service is free.

★ **Inkaterra La Casona** BOUTIQUE HOTEL $$$
(📞 Lima 01-610-0400; www.inkaterra.com/inkaterra/inkaterra-la-casona; Atocsaycuchi 616; ste incl breakfast from S1779; @ 🛜) Hitting the perfect balance of cozy and high style, this renovated grand colonial in tiny Plazoleta Nazarenas is simply debonair. Rustic meets majestic with original features like oversized carved doors; rough-hewn beams and stone fireplaces are enhanced with radiant floors, glittering candelabras, plush divans and gorgeous Andean textiles.

★ **Tocuyeros**
Boutique Hotel BOUTIQUE HOTEL $$$
(📞 084-26-2790; www.tocuyeros.com; Tocuyeros 560; d incl breakfast from S825; 🛜) A fine addition to San Blas, this hidden treasure sits far off the street, accessed via a long stone tunnel. With only nine rooms, this boutique hotel shines with modern Andean style. Each has double-pane windows, central heating, coffee makers and Netflix on the flat-screen TV. There's also a gorgeous rooftop terrace and low-key on-site restaurant and bar.

El Mercado DESIGN HOTEL $$$
(📞 084-42-1777; www.elmercadohotel.com; Seite Cuartones 306; d/ste incl breakfast S594/772; @ 🛜) Modern meets colonial in this hotel adorned with painted rocking horses and market carts. Activity centers on an open courtyard with loungers and evening bonfires. Large 2nd-story rooms feature radiant heat – a luxury in these parts – as well as fireplaces. Breakfasts are varied, with made-to-order juices from an old-fashioned cart. With elevator access.

✗ Eating

Cuzco's restaurant scene caters for a wide range of tastes and budgets, thanks to its international appeal. Due to its location, Cuzco has access to diverse crops from highland potatoes and quinoa to avocados, jungle fruit and *ají picante* (hot chiles).

For self-caterers, small, overpriced grocery shops are located near the Plaza de Armas, including **Gato's Market** (📞 084-23-4026; Santa Catalina Ancha 377; ⏰ 9:30am-11pm) and **Mega** (cnr Matará & Ayacucho; ⏰ 10am-8pm Mon-Sat, to 6pm Sun).

★ **Monkey Cafe** CAFE $
(📞 084-59-5838; Tandapata 300; mains S15-20; ⏰ 8am-8pm Wed-Mon) Cuzco's finest coffee shop is shoehorned into a tiny locale at the top of San Blas hill. All espresso drinks feature double shots made with Peruvian-origin roasts. There are also very tasty sweets and hearty breakfasts ranging from healthy to heart-stopping.

La Bohème Crepería CRÊPES $
(📞 084-23-5694; www.labohemecusco.com; Carmen Alto 283; mains S10-17; ⏰ 8am-10pm; 🛜 📞) You can't go wrong with the authentic crepes in this Marseillaise-owned cafe, crafted with fusion ingredients. There's a little patio with great views and firelit evening ambience. The set menu is a great deal. For dessert, try its signature crepe with salted butter and caramel.

★ **Bojosan** JAPANESE $$
(📞 084-24-6502; San Agustin 275; mains S20-26; ⏰ 12:30-10pm; 🛜 📞) This Tokyo-style noodle shop does right in so many ways. Take a stool and watch the cooks prepare your udon noodles from scratch. Oversized bowls have flavorful broth, you add the protein (duck, chicken and vegetarian options) and a dash of authentic pepper mix. With bottled local artisan beers on offer. Run by the highly regarded Le Soleil (p897) next door.

★ **Cicciolina** INTERNATIONAL $$
(📞 084-23-9510; www.cicciolinacuzco.com; Triunfo 393, 2nd fl; mains S38-59; ⏰ 8am-11pm) On the 2nd floor of a colonial courtyard mansion, Cicciolina may be Cuzco's best restaurant. The eclectic, sophisticated food is divine, starting with house-marinated olives, and continuing with polenta squares with cured rabbit, huge green salads, charred octopus and satisfying mains like red trout in coconut milk, beetroot ravioli and tender lamb. With impeccable service and warmly lit seating.

★ La Bodega 138
PIZZA $$

(☎ 084-26-0272; www.labodega138.com; Herrajes 138; mains S26-37; ☺11am-10:30pm Mon-Fri, from 10am Sat & Sun; ✐) Sometimes you are home-sick for good atmosphere, uncomplicated menus and craft beer. In comes La Bodega, a fantastic laid-back enterprise run by a fami-ly in what used to be their home. Thin-crust pizzas are fired up in the adobe oven, organic salads are fresh and abundant and the prices are reasonable. With weekend brunch. A true find. Cash only.

★ Limo
SEAFOOD $$

(☎ 084-24-068; www.cuscorestaurants.com/res taurant/limo; Portal de Carnes 236, 2nd fl; mains S20-60; ☺11am-11pm Mon-Sat) If you fancy sea-food, make your way to this elegant Nikkei (Japanese-Peruvian) restaurant. Don't skip the house pisco sour, tinged with ginger and garnished with a whole chili. *Tiraditos* (raw fish in a fragrant sauce) simply melt on the tongue. Other hits are the creamy potato *cau-sas* and crunchy shrimp rolls with avocado and smoked pepper. With attentive service.

★ Marcelo Batata
PERUVIAN $$

(☎ 084-22-2424; www.cuscodining.com/marcelo-batata; Palacio 121; mains S43-56; ☺12:30-11pm) A sure bet for delectable Andean cuisine with a twist. Marcelo Batata innovates with traditional foods to show them at their best – like the humble *tarwi* pea, which makes a mean hummus. The chicken soup with *hier-ba Luisa* (a local herb), is exquisite, alongside satisfying beet *quinotto* (like risotto), tender alpaca and twice-baked Andean potatoes that offer crispy-creamy goodness.

Mr Soup
INTERNATIONAL $$

(☎ 084-38-6073; Saphi 448; mains S20-28; ☺noon-10pm Tue-Sun) Sometimes you just want a huge bowl of soup. Serving fairly authentic udon curry, Thai *tom kha* (coconut soup), Andean quinoa soup and others, this tiny shop does the trick. Recipes were sourced from families, which helps gives them a homespun taste. For a bargain, go for the soup of the day (S15).

★ Le Soleil
FRENCH $$$

(☎ 084-24-0543; www.restaurantelesoleilcusco.com; San Agustín 275; mains S38-89; ☺12:30-3pm & 7-11:30pm Thu-Tue) Cuzco's go-to spot for tradi-tional French cooking, this romantic white-linen restaurant delivers with cool precision. Start with trout in a tart mango ginger confit. The duck à l'orange cooked two ways is sim-ply divine. You can also go for a tasting menu

(from S145). There's a wonderful selection of French wines and lovely desserts – chocolate fondant being the obvious, happy choice.

Drinking & Nightlife

Cuzco has some lively nightlife offerings, ranging from the tame dinner show to late-night clubs. Bars are plentiful and cater to a spectrum of tastes. The European pubs are good places to track down those all-important soccer matches, with satellite TVs more or less permanently tuned to sports.

★ Limbus
ROOFTOP BAR

(☎ 084-43-1282; www.limbusrestobar.com; Pasñapa-kana 133; ☺8am-1am Mon-Sat, noon-midnight Sun) Billed as the best view in Cuzco, it's all that (even after climbing to the top of San Blas). Don't worry, if you come during peak hours you'll have plenty of time to catch your breath while you queue to get in. With gorgeous cocktails and glass-walled panoramas, this was the hottest city spot when we visited.

★ Museo del Pisco
BAR

(☎ 084-26-2709; www.museodelpisco.org; Santa Catalina Ancha 398; ☺noon-1am) When you've had your fill of colonial religious art, investi-gate this pisco museum, where the wonders of the national drink are extolled, exalted and – of course – sampled. Opened by an enthu-siastic expat, this museum-bar is Pisco 101, combined with a tapas lounge. Grab a spot early for show-stopping live music (9pm to 11pm nightly).

☆ Entertainment

★ Ukuku's
LIVE MUSIC

(☎ 084-24-2951; Plateros 316; ☺6pm-2am) The most consistently popular nightspot in town, Ukuku's plays a winning combination of crowd-pleasers – Latin and Western rock, reg-gae, *reggaetón*, salsa and hip-hop – and often hosts live bands. Usually full to bursting after midnight with as many Peruvians as foreign tourists, it's good, sweaty, dance-a-thon fun. Happy hour is 8pm to 10:30pm.

🛍 Shopping

The neighborhood of San Blas – the plaza itself, Cuesta San Blas, Carmen Alto and Tandapata – offers Cuzco's best shopping. Traditionally an artisan quarter, it still has some remain-ing some workshops and showrooms of local craftspeople. Jewelry shops and quirky, one-off designer boutiques are a refreshing re-minder that the local aesthetic is not confined

PERU CUZCO

to stridently colored ponchos and sheepskin-rug depictions of Machu Picchu.

Center for Traditional
Textiles of Cuzco
ARTS & CRAFTS

(☑84-228-117; Av El Sol 603; ⏰7:30am-8pm) This nonprofit organization, founded in 1996, promotes the survival of traditional weaving. You may be able to catch a shop-floor demonstration illustrating different weaving techniques in all their finger-twisting complexity. Products for sale are high end.

Inkakunaq Ruwaynin
ARTS & CRAFTS

(☑084-26-0942; inside CBC, Tullumayo 274; ⏰9am-7pm Mon-Sat) This weaving cooperative with quality goods is run by 12 mountain communities from Cuzco and Apurimac; it's at the far end of the inner courtyard.

ℹ Information

DANGERS & ANNOYANCES

➡ Bags may be stolen from the backs of chairs in public places or from overhead shelves in overnight buses.

➡ Walk around with a minimum of cash and belongings. If you keep your bag in your lap and watch out for pickpockets in crowded streets, transport terminals and markets, you are highly unlikely to be a victim of crime in Cuzco.

➡ Avoid walking by yourself late at night or very early in the morning. Revelers returning late from bars or setting off for the Inca Trail before sunrise are particularly vulnerable to 'choke and grab' attacks.

MEDICAL SERVICES

Clinica Pardo (☑084-24-0997; Av de la Cultura 710; ⏰24hr) Well equipped and expensive – perfect if you're covered by travel insurance.

Hospital Regional (☑084-23-9792, emergencies 084-22-3691; Av de la Cultura s/n; ⏰24hr) Public and free, but wait times can be long and good care is not guaranteed.

MONEY

BCP (☑01-458-1230; Av El Sol 189; ⏰9am-6:30pm Mon-Thu, to 7:30pm Fri, to 1pm Sat) With an ATM.

POST

Serpost (☑084-22-5232; Av El Sol 800; ⏰8am-8pm Mon-Sat) General delivery (poste restante) mail is held here at the main post office; bring proof of identity.

TOURIST INFORMATION

iPerú (☑084-59-6159; www.peru.travel; Portal de Harinas 177, Plaza de Armas; ⏰9am-7pm Mon-Fri, to 1pm Sat) Efficient and helpful. Excellent source for tourist information for both the region and entire country. There's an adjoining section of guarded ATMs. Also has a branch at the **airport** (☑084-23-7364; ⏰6am-5pm).

ℹ Getting There & Away

AIR

Cuzco's **Aeropuerto Internacional Alejandro Velasco Astete** (CUZ; ☑084-22-2611) receives national and international flights. Most arrivals are in the morning, as afternoon conditions make landings and takeoffs more difficult.

Avianca (☑0800-18-2222; www.avianca.com; Av El Sol 602; ⏰8:30am-7pm Mon-Fri, 9am-2pm Sat) Service to/from Lima Monday to Saturday and direct flights to Bogota, Colombia.

LATAM (☑084-25-5555; www.latam.com; Av El Sol 627B; ⏰9am-7pm Mon-Fri, to 1pm Sat) Direct flights to Lima, Arequipa, Juliaca and Puerto Maldonado, as well as Santiago, Chile.

Peruvian Airlines (☑084-25-4890; www.peruvianairlines.pe; Av El Sol 627-A; ⏰9am-7pm Mon-Sat, to noon Sun) To Lima and La Paz, Bolivia.

Star Perú (☑01-705-9000; www.starperu.com; Av El Sol 627, oficina 101; ⏰9am-1pm & 3-6:30pm Mon-Sat, 9am-12:30pm Sun) Service to Lima.

Viva Air (☑call center 084-64-4004; www.vivaair.com) Low-cost airline with online booking.

BUS & TAXI
International

All international services depart from the **Terminal Terrestre** (☑084-22-4471; Vía de Evitamiento 429), about 2km out of town toward the airport. Take a taxi (S30) or walk via Av El Sol. After it turns into Alameda Pachacutec, pedestrians can walk on the median. Straight after the tower and statue of Pachacutec, turn right, and follow the railway lines into a side street that reaches the terminal in five minutes.

To Bolivia, the following companies offer offer daily services to Copacabana (10 hours) and La Paz: **Transporte Copacabana** (☑084-40-2953; www.transcopacabanasa.com.bo; Vía de Evitamiento 429, Terminal Terrestre; ⏰9am-6pm), **Tour Peru** (☑084-23-6463; www.tourperu.com.pe; Vía de Evitamiento 429, Terminal Terrestre; ⏰9am-6pm), **Transzela** (☑084-23-8223; www.transzela.com; Vía de Evitamiento 429, Terminal Terrestre; ⏰9am-7pm) and **Titicaca** (☑084-22-9763; Vía de Evitamiento 429, Transporte Terrestre; ⏰10am-5pm).

Long Distance

Buses to major cities leave from the Terminal Terrestre. Buses for more unusual destinations leave from elsewhere, so check carefully in advance.

The most enjoyable way to get to Puno is via luxury tourist buses that take the Ruta del Sol. **Inka Express** (☑084-63-4838; www.inkaexpress.

com; Av Alameda Pachacuteq 499; S165; ☉ 9am-1pm & 3-7pm Mon-Fri, 9am-1pm & 4-6pm Sat) and **Turismo Mer** (☑ 084-24-5171; www.turismomer. com; El Óvalo, Av La Paz A3; tourist service with entry fees S198; ☏) go every morning. The service includes lunch and an English-speaking tour guide, who talks about the four sites that are briefly visited along the way: Andahuaylillas, Raqchi, Abra la Raya and Pucará. The trip takes about eight hours. Check to see if rates include your site entrance fees.

Departures to Arequipa cluster around 6am to 7am and 7pm to 9:30pm. **Ormeño** (☑ 969-933-579; Vía de Evitamiento 429, Terminal Terrestre; ☉ 9am-7pm) offers a deluxe service at 9am.

Cruz del Sur (☑ 084-74-0444; www.cruz delsur.com.pe; Av Industrial 121) and **CIVA** (☑ 084-24-9961; www.civa.com.pe; Vía de Evitamiento 429, Terminal Terrestre; ☉ 9am-6pm) offer relatively painless services to Lima.

Julsa (☑ 951-298-798; Vía de Evitamiento 429, Terminal Terrestre) offers direct buses to Tacna, near the Chilean border.

Cuzco Buses

DESTINATION	COST* (S)	DURATION (HR)
Abancay	30/50	5
Arequipa	40/135	10
Ayacucho	65/95	16
Copacabana (Bolivia)	60/90	10
Ica	100/155	16
Juliaca	35/40	5
La Paz (Bolivia)	80/120	12
Lima	100/160	21
Nazca	100/150	13
Puerto Maldonado	50/90	10
Puno	40/70	6
Quillabamba	25/35	4½
Tacna	80/120	15

*Prices are general estimates for normal/luxury buses

TRAIN

Cuzco has two train stations. **Estación Huanchac** (Wanchaq; ☑ 084-58-1414; Av Pachacutec s/n; ☉ 7am-5pm Mon-Fri, to midnight Sat & Sun), near the end of Av El Sol, serves Juliaca and Puno on Lake Titicaca. **Estación Poroy** (Calle Roldan s/n, Carr Cuzco-Urubamba), 20 minutes east of town, serves Ollantaytambo and Machu Picchu.

An exercise in old-fashioned romance, the **Belmond Andean Explorer** (☑ 084-58-1414; www. perurail.com; Estación Huanchac; to Puno/Arequipa from S5754/13,393; ☉ 7am-5pm Mon-

Fri, to noon Sat) is a gorgeous luxury sleeper train with a glass-walled observation car. It travels across the altiplano to Puno and on to Arequipa. Weekly departures leave Thursdays, arriving at Puno the same evening and Arequipa on Saturday.

Peru Rail (☑ 084-58-1414; www.perurail. com; Estación Poroy; ☉ 7am-5pm Mon-Fri, to noon Sat) also has regular service to Puno on the Titicaca train (S859, 10½ hours). Its flagship service to Aguas Calientes has multiple departures daily from Estación Poroy. There are three service categories: Expedition (from S232 one way), Vistadome (from S347 one way) and the luxurious Hiram Bingham (from S1736 one way).

Inca Rail (☑ 084-25-2974; www.incarail. com; Portal de Panes 105, Plaza de Armas; 1 way S231-330; ☉ 8am-9pm Mon-Fri, 9am-7pm Sat, to 2pm Sun) has three departures daily from Ollantaytambo and four levels of service.

❶ Getting Around

Local rides on public transportation cost only S1, though it's easier to walk or just take a taxi than to figure out where any given *combi* is headed.

TO & FROM THE AIRPORT

The airport is about 6km south of the city center. The *combi* lines Imperial and C4M (S0.80, 20 minutes) run from Av El Sol to just outside the airport. A taxi to or from the city center to the airport costs S30. An official radio taxi from within the airport costs S40. With advance reservations, many hotels offer free pickup.

TAXI

There are no meters in taxis, but there are set rates. At the time of research, trips within the city center cost S8 and destinations further afield, such as El Molino, cost S12.

AloCusco (☑ 084-22-2222) is a reliable company to call.

Around Cuzco

Saqsaywamán

Saqsaywamán (boleto turístico adult/student S130/70; ☉ 7am-5:30pm), the immense ruin of both religious and military significance, is the most impressive in the immediate area around Cuzco. The long Quechua name means 'Satisfied Falcon,' though tourists will inevitably remember it by the mnemonic 'sexy woman.' Today's visitor sees only about 20% of the original structure. Soon after conquest, the Spaniards tore down many walls and used the blocks to build their own houses in Cuzco, leaving the largest

Around Cuzco

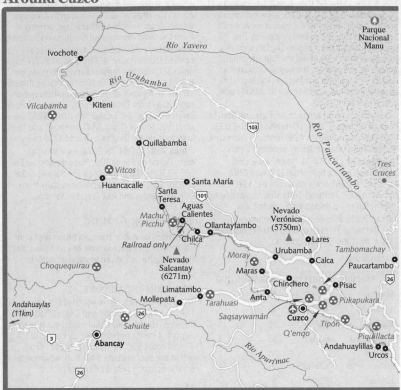

and most impressive rocks, especially those forming the main battlements.

In 1536 the fort was the site of one of the most bitter battles of the Spanish conquest. More than two years after Francisco Pizarro's entry into Cuzco, the rebellious Manco Inca recaptured the lightly guarded Sacsaywamán and used it as a base to lay siege to the conquistadors in Cuzco. Manco was on the brink of defeating the Spaniards when a desperate last-ditch attack by 50 Spanish cavalry led by Juan Pizarro, Francisco's brother, succeeded in retaking Sacsaywamán and putting an end to the rebellion. Manco Inca survived and retreated to Ollantaytambo, but most of his forces were killed. Thousands of dead littered the site after the Incas' defeat, attracting swarms of carrion-eating Andean condors. The tragedy was memorialized by the inclusion of eight condors in Cuzco's coat of arms.

The site is composed of three different areas, the most striking being the magnificent three-tiered zigzag fortifications. One stone, incredibly, weighs more than 300 tons. It was the ninth *inca*, Pachacutec, who envisioned Cuzco in the shape of a puma, with Sacsaywamán as the head, and these 22 zigzagged walls as the teeth of the puma. The walls also formed an extremely effective defensive mechanism that forced attackers to expose their flanks when attacking.

Opposite is the hill called Rodadero, with retaining walls, polished rocks and a finely carved series of stone benches known as the Inca's Throne. Three towers once stood above these walls. Only the foundations remain, but the 22m diameter of the largest, Muyuc Marca, gives an indication of how big they must have been. With its perfectly fitted stone conduits, this tower was probably used as a huge water tank for the garrison. Other buildings within the ramparts provided food and shelter for an estimated 5000 warriors. Most of these structures were torn

down by the Spaniards and later inhabitants of Cuzco.

Between the zigzag ramparts and the hill lies a large, flat parade ground that is used for the colorful tourist spectacle of Inti Raymi (p895), held every June 24. To walk up to the site from the Plaza de Armas takes 30 to 50 minutes, so make sure you're acclimatized before attempting it. Arriving at dawn will let you have the site almost to yourself, though solo travelers shouldn't come alone at this time of day.

Tambomachay

Tambomachay (☑ 84-227-037; boleto turístico adult/student S130/70; ⊙ 7:30am-5:30pm), also called El Baño del Inca (The Bath of the Inca), is a ceremonial stone bath with spring water through fountains that was created in Inca times. It is thought to be part of an Inca water cult. It's located 8km northeast of Cuzco.

The Sacred Valley

Tucked under the tawny skirts of formidable foothills, the beautiful Río Urubamba Valley, known as El Valle Sagrado (the Sacred Valley), is about 15km north of Cuzco as the condor flies, via a narrow road of hairpin turns. It's worth exploring this peaceful, fetching corner of the Andes with attractive colonial towns and isolated weaving villages. Star attractions are the markets and the lofty Inca citadels of Pisac and Ollantaytambo, but it's also packed with other Inca sites. Its myriad trekking routes are deservedly gaining in popularity. Adrenaline activities range from rafting to rock climbing.

A multitude of travel agencies in Cuzco offer whirlwind tours of the Sacred Valley, stopping at markets and the most significant ruins. It's also worth an in-depth visit. The archaeological sites of Pisac, Ollantaytambo and Chinchero can be visited with a *boleto turístico*, which can be bought directly on-site.

Pisac

☑ 084 / POP 9440 / ELEV 2715M

Welcome to the international airport for the cosmic traveler, according to one seasoned local. It's not hard to succumb to the charms of sunny Pisac, a bustling and fast-growing colonial village at the base of a spectacular Inca fortress perched on a mountain spur. Its pull is universal and recent years have seen an influx of expats and New Age followers in search of an Andean Shangri-la. The local tourism industry has responded by catering to spiritual seekers, offering everything from yoga retreats and cleanses to guided hallucinogenic trips. Yet it's also worthwhile for mainstream travelers, with ruins, a fabulous market and weaving villages that should not be missed. Located just 33km northeast of Cuzco by a paved road, it's the most convenient starting point to the Sacred Valley.

◉ Sights

Pisac Ruins   RUINS
(boleto turístico adult/student S130/70; ⊙ 7am-6pm) A truly awesome site with relatively few tourists, this hilltop Inca citadel lies high above the village on a triangular plateau with a plunging gorge on either side. Allow several hours to explore. Taking a taxi up and walking back (4km) is a good option. The most impressive feature is the agricultural terracing, which sweeps around the south and east

PERU THE SACRED VALLEY

flanks of the mountain in huge and graceful curves, almost entirely unbroken by steps.

🛏 Sleeping

★ Pisac Quishu   GUESTHOUSE $$
(📞 084-509-106, 942-664-132; www.pisacinca.com; Calle Huayna Picchu F-5; s/d incl breakfast S130/210; 🛜❄) Talk about sibling rivalry: this excellent new property is next door to the Pisac Inca Guesthouse, which is run by the same family. This one, run by the effervescent sisters Tatiana and Libertad, is slightly more design-conscious, with beautiful, bold-hued rooms around a tranquil courtyard garden. Breakfast includes fruit as well as vegan and gluten-free options. They're adding an on-site ceramic workshop you can visit.

La Casa del Conde   GUESTHOUSE $$
(📞 084-78-7818; Andenes de Chihuanco s/n; s/d incl breakfast S205/264; 🛜) Guests rave about this lovely country house, nestled into the foothills with blooming flower patches. Family-run and brimming with personality, its lovely rooms feature down duvets, heat and cable TV. There's no car access. It's a 15-minute walk uphill from the plaza, but a *mototaxi* (three-wheeled motorcycle rickshaw taxi) can leave you at the chapel that's five minutes away.

Pisac Inca Guesthouse   GUESTHOUSE $$
(📞 084-50-9106; www.pisacinca.com; Huayna Picchu s/n; s/d incl breakfast 153/198; 🛜) A few blocks away from the center, this ample guesthouse is a find. Rooms are smart and simple, centered around a large, grassy area with lounge chairs. Some have kitchenettes. There's also a roof deck with views and a glass breakfast room. It's run by the same hospitable family that runs Pisac Quishu.

🍴 Eating

Doña Clorinda   PERUVIAN $$
(📞 084-20-3051; Urb San Luis, La Rinconada; mains S18-35; ⊙9am-5pm) In a lovely colonial home, this longtime Pisac mainstay serves up hearty Andean fare. Order some homemade *chicha morada* (blue corn juice) to go with heaping plates of *arroz chaufa* (Peruvian fried rice), trout, beef and *rocoto relleno* (stuffed peppers) with *kapchi*. A classic.

Mullu   FUSION $$
(📞 084-20-3073; www.mullu.pe; San Francisco s/n, 2nd fl, Plaza Constitución; mains S30-56; ⊙9am-9pm) The balcony of this chill and welcoming place may be the best spot to watch market-day interactions in the plaza below. The menu is fusion (think Thai meets Amazonian while flirting with highland Peruvian). Traditional lamb is tender to falling-off-the-bone; soups, alpaca burgers and blended juices also satisfy. It can also cater for special diets. With homemade chocolates and all-day breakfast (S29).

ℹ Getting There & Away

Buses to Urubamba (S5 to S7, one hour) leave frequently from the downtown bridge between 6am and 8pm. **Minibuses to Cuzco** (Amazonas s/n; S5, one hour) leave from Calle Amazonas when full. Many travel agencies in Cuzco also operate tour buses to Pisac, especially on market days.

For the Pisac ruins, minivans (S60 round-trip) near the plaza leave regularly, or hire a **taxi** from near the bridge into town to drive you up the 7.5km paved road.

Urubamba

📞 084 / POP 17,800 / ELEV 2870M

A busy and unadorned urban center, Urubamba is a transport hub surrounded by bucolic foothills and snowy peaks. The advantages of its lower altitude and relative proximity to Machu Picchu make it popular with both high-end hotels and package tours. While there is little of historical interest, nice countryside and great weather make it a convenient base from which to explore the extraordinary salt flats of Salineras and the terracing of Moray.

🏃 Activities

★ Cusco for You   HORSE RIDING
(📞 987-417-250, 987-841-000; www.cuscoforyou.com; Carr a Salineras de Maras, Pichingoto; 1hr ride S238) Highly recommended for horseback-riding and trekking trips from one to eight days long. Horseback-riding day trips go to Moray and Salineras and other regional destinations. Ask about special rates for families and groups. With an optional transportation service to the ranch, which also has accommodation and dining.

🛏 Sleeping & Eating

★ Sol y Luna   BOUTIQUE HOTEL $$$
(📞 084-20-1620; www.hotelsolyluna.com; Fundo Huincho lote A-5; d/tr incl breakfast from S1492/1848; @🛜❄) A living fairy tale, this luxury Relais & Chateaux property runs wild with whimsy. Fans of folk art will be overwhelmed – its 43 *casitas* (cabins) feature original murals

and comic, oversized sculptures by noted Peruvian artist Federico Bauer. The playful feel spills over to bold tropical hues and a decor of carved wooden beds, freestanding tubs and dainty chandeliers.

Tambo del Inka
LUXURY HOTEL $$$

(☑084-58-1777; www.libertador.com.pe; Carr Urumbamba a Ollantaytambo; d incl breakfast from S1000; @☎❄) ✎ Just like Hogwarts, Tambo del Inka features its own train station – handy for a morning jaunt to Machu Picchu. Stark and commanding, this LEED-certified hotel (with its own water-treatment plant and UV air filters) occupies an immense riverside spread with giant eucalyptus trees. The eucalyptus is a staple of interior decor and even spa treatments.

Tierra Cocina Artesanal
PERUVIAN $$

(☑980-728-604; Av Berriozabal 84; mains S35-42; ⊙noon-8pm Thu-Tue; ✐) ✎ The gorgeous smells wafting in from the kitchen will lure you into this unassuming restaurant serving hearty country-style Andean dishes in the warm ambience of a small Spanish-tile home. There's slow-cooked beef simmering in the kitchen, homemade alpaca sausage, trout ceviche and corn *pepian* (stew). With organic meats and good vegetarian options.

ⓘ Getting There & Away

Urubamba serves as the valley's principal transportation hub. The bus terminal is about 1km west of town on the highway. Buses leave every 15 minutes for Cuzco (S7, two hours) via Pisac (S5, one hour) or Chinchero (S5, 50 minutes). Buses (S1.50, 30 minutes) and *colectivos* (S3, 25 minutes) to Ollantaytambo leave often.

Colectivos to Quillabamba (S40, five hours) leave from the *grifo* (gas station).

A standard *mototaxi* ride around town costs S2.

Ollantaytambo

☑084 / POP 2848 / ELEV 2800M

Dominated by two massive Inca ruins, the quaint village of Ollantaytambo, also called Ollanta, is the best surviving example of Inca city planning, with narrow cobblestone streets that have been continuously inhabited since the 13th century. After the hordes passing through on their way to Machu Picchu die down around late morning, Ollanta is a lovely place to be. It's perfect for wandering the mazy, narrow byways, past stone buildings and babbling irrigation channels, pretending you've stepped back in time. It also offers access to excellent hiking and biking.

⊙ Sights

Ollantaytambo Ruins
RUINS

(boleto turístico adult/student S130/70; ⊙7am-5pm) Both fortress and temple, these spectacular Inca ruins rise above Ollantaytambo, making a splendid half-day trip. (Admission is via the *boleto turístico* tourist card, valid for 10 days and for 16 other sites across the region.) The huge, steep terraces that guard Ollantaytambo's spectacular Inca ruins mark one of the few places where the Spanish conquistadors lost a major battle.

🛏 Sleeping

★ Mama Simona
HOSTEL $

(☑084-436-757; www.mamasimona.com/es/ollanta.php; Av Quera Uqllo s/n; dm/s/d incl breakfast S46/117/124) As locations go, this is one of Ollanta's finest, with riverside garden hammocks and papaya trees. Dorms feature individual bed lights and attached bathrooms, with space heaters for rent (S10). There's a large, inviting guest kitchen, cozy TV area and filtered water for drinking. Service, however, could be more enthusiastic. It's on the outskirts of the center.

★ Apu Lodge
INN $$

(☑084-79-7162; www.apulodge.com; Lari s/n; s/d/q incl breakfast S215/248/330; @☎) ✎ Backed against the ruins, this modern lodge with a sprawling lawn is a real retreat, thanks to the welcoming staff, big breakfasts and the helpful attention of its Scottish owner. It's great for families. Ample, cozy rooms feature powerful hot showers that melt your muscle aches. The common area has wi-fi and filtered water to fill up on.

★ El Albergue Bed & Breakfast
B&B $$

(☑084-20-4014; www.elalbergue.com; Estación de Tren; d/tr incl breakfast from S359/393; @☎) On the train platform, this romantic pit stop exudes Andean charm. Surrounded by green lawns with lush flowerbeds, tasteful tile rooms feature a dark-hardwood trim, tapestries and quality linens in an early-20th-century building. There are portable heaters, games for kids and sauna access. It's 800m (all uphill) from the village center but there's an excellent on-site restaurant (p904).

Samanapaq
INN $$

(☑999-583-243, 084-20-4042; www.samanapaq.com; cnr Principal & Alameda de las Cien Ventanas; s/d incl breakfast S254/277, d superior S340; ☎) This complex features lawns for the kids to run on, comfortable shared spaces and 20

PERU THE SACRED VALLEY

motel-style rooms with massage-jet showers. With buffet breakfast and wi-fi in the common areas, and a pottery workshop on-site.

✗ Eating

★ El Albergue Restaurante   INTERNATIONAL $$

(☏084-20-4014; Estación de Tren; mains S29-45; ☺5:30-10am, noon-3pm & 6-9pm; ☝) ☝ This whistle-stop cafe serves elegant and well-priced Peruvian fare. It's inviting, with an open kitchen bordered by heaping fruit bowls and candles adorning linen-topped tables. Start with the *causas* (potato dish) or organic greens from the garden. Lamb medallions with *chimichurri* (herb sauce) is a standout, as is as the molle-pepper steak spiced from the tree outside. Access via the train platform.

Chuncho   PERUVIAN $$

(☏084-20-4014; www.chuncho.pe; Ventidierio; mains S27-47; ☺noon-11pm) This concept restaurant connects visitors to the bounty of ancestral Andean foods, admittedly, most of them tubers. It's a great idea, with traditional soups, rehydrated potato dishes, *tarwi* bean salads, tasty alpaca and *cuy*. Sample all with a banquet, the half-portion (S65) easily feeds two. But the real standout is the craft cocktails made with Caña Alta, a locally produced sugarcane spirit.

❶ Getting There & Away

Frequent *combis* and taxi *colectivos* shuttle between Urubamba and Ollantaytambo (S2 and S3, respectively, 30 minutes) from 6am to 5pm. **Buses** are located outside the fruit and vegetable market.

To Cuzco, it's easiest to change in Urubamba, though occasional departures go directly from the Ollantaytambo train station to Cuzco's Puente Grau (*combis* S15, two hours; *colectivos* S15, 1½ hours).

Aguas Calientes

☏084 / POP 1600 / ELEV 2410M

Also known as Machu Picchu Pueblo, this town lies in a deep gorge below the ruins. A virtual island, it's cut off from all roads and enclosed by stone cliffs, towering cloud forest and two rushing rivers. Despite its gorgeous location, Aguas Calientes has the feel of a gold-rush town, with a large itinerant population, slack services that count on one-time customers and an architectural tradition of rebar and unfinished cement. With

merchants pushing the hard sell, it's hard not to feel overwhelmed. Your best bet is to go without expectations.

🛏 Sleeping

Lodgings here are consistently overpriced – probably costing two-thirds more than counterparts in less-exclusive locations. There's a variety of midrange accommodations, alongside some luxury offerings and budget options. Book well ahead for the best selection.

★ Mama Simona   HOSTEL $

(☏936-579-801; www.mamasimona.com; Calle Amuraypa Tikan 104; dm S46-52, tw/d S146/163, all incl breakfast; ☞) Your best bet for hostel digs, this stylish newcomer in a brand-new building features mixed and female dorms with raw wood furnishings, lockers, attached bathrooms and TVs. Dorms house up to six. It's spotless and well attended, with filtered water, breakfast from 4am and a well-equipped guest kitchen. Also stores luggage.

Gringo Bill's   HOTEL $$

(☏084-21-1046; www.gringobills.com; Colla Raymi 104; d/tr incl breakfast from S268/471; @☞☒) One of the original Aguas Calientes lodgings, friendly Bill's features smart rooms in a multitiered construction. Beds are covered in thick cotton quilts, and bathrooms are large. Suites feature massage-jet tubs and TVs. The mini pool only has space for two. Larger suites easily accommodate families.

★ Machu Picchu Pueblo Hotel   LODGE $$$

(☏in Lima 01-610-0400; www.inkaterra.com; d casitas from US$838, villas from US$1036; ✳@☞☒) ☝ Luxuriant and set amid tropical gardens, these Andean-style cottages (many with their own private pool) connected by stone pathways are pure indulgence. The devil is in the details: iPod docks, subtle, classy decor and showers with glass walls looking out onto lush vegetation. The on-site spa features a bamboo-eucalyptus sauna, but the best feature is the (included) guided excursions.

✗ Eating

Restaurants range from basic eateries to fine dining. Touts on the street will try to herd you into their restaurant, but take your time making a selection. Standards are not very high in most restaurants – if you go to one that hasn't been recommended, snoop around to check the hygiene first. Since refrigeration can be a problem, it's best to order vegetarian if you're eating in low-end establishments.

Aguas Calientes

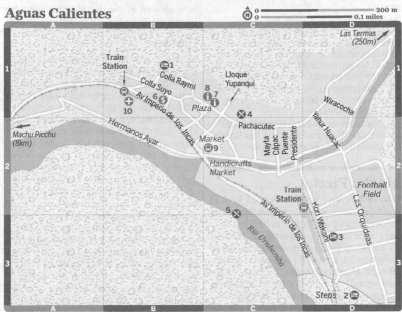

Aguas Calientes

Sleeping
1 Gringo Bill's..B1
2 Machu Picchu Pueblo Hotel....................D3
3 Mama Simona..D3

Eating
4 Indio Feliz...C1
5 Mapacho..C2

Information
6 Banco La Nacion..B1
7 Centro Cultural...C1
8 iPerú..C1
9 Machu Picchu Bus Tickets &
   Bus Stop...C2
10 Medical Center..B1

★ **Indio Feliz**   FRENCH $$
(☑ 084-21-1090; Lloque Yupanqui 4; mains S34-48; ⊗ 11am-10pm) Hospitality is the strong suit of French cook Patrik at this multi-award-winning restaurant, but the food does not disappoint. Start with *sopa a la criolla* (mildly spiced, creamy noodle soup with beef and peppers). There are also nods to traditional French cooking – Provençal tomatoes, crispy-perfect garlic potatoes and a melt-in-your-mouth apple tart.

Mapacho   CAFE $$
(☑ 984-759-634; Av Imperio de los Incas 614; mains S20-48; ⊗ 10am-10pm) This friendly streetside cafe is popular with the backpacking set. Perhaps it's all the craft beer and burgers on offer. It's worth checking out the *arroz chaufa* (fried rice) and *lomo saltado* (strips of beef stir-fried with onions, tomatoes, potatoes and chili).

ℹ Information

MEDICAL SERVICES
Medical Center (☑ 084-21-1005; Av Imperio de los Incas s/n; ⊗ emergencies 24hr) Located by the train tracks.

MONEY
Banco La Nacion (⊗ 24hr) ATM.

TOURIST INFORMATION
iPerú (☑ 084-21-1104; Av Pachacutec, cuadra 1; ⊗ 9am-6pm Mon-Sun) A helpful information center for everything Machu Picchu.

ℹ Getting There & Away

BUS
There is no road access to Aguas Calientes. The only buses go from the **bus stop** (where you can purchase tickets) up the hill to Machu Picchu (round-trip S80, 25 minutes) from 5:30am to 4pm; buses return until 6pm.

TRAIN

Buy a return ticket to avoid getting stranded in Aguas Calientes – outbound trains sell out much quicker than their inbound counterparts. All train companies have ticket offices in the train station, but you can check their websites for up-to-date schedules and ticket purchases.

To Cuzco (three hours), Peru Rail (p899) has service to Poroy and taxis connect to the city, another 20 minutes away.

To Ollantaytambo (two hours), both Peru Rail and Inca Rail (p899) provide service. Inca Rail offers a ticket with connecting bus service to Cuzco.

Machu Picchu

Shrouded by mist and surrounded by lush vegetation and steep escarpments, the sprawling Inca citadel of Machu Picchu lives up to every expectation. In a spectacular location, it's the most famous archaeological site on the continent, a must for all visitors to Peru. Like the *Mona Lisa* or the pyramids, it has been seared into our collective consciousness, though nothing can diminish the thrill of being here. This awe-inspiring ancient city was never revealed to the conquering Spaniards and was virtually forgotten until the early part of the 20th century.

In the most controversial move in Machu Picchu since Hiram Bingham's explorations, the Peruvian authorities changed entries from daily visits to morning and afternoon turns in 2018. Visitors must plan more carefully than ever to seize the experience. Though an expanded limit of 5940 people are now allowed in the complex (including the Inca Trail) daily, demand remains insatiable.

History

Machu Picchu is not mentioned in any of the chronicles of the Spanish conquistadors. Apart from a couple of German adventurers in the 1860s, who apparently looted the site with the Peruvian government's permission, only the local Quechua people knew of Machu Picchu's existence until American historian Hiram Bingham was guided to it by locals in 1911. You can read Bingham's own account of his 'discovery' in the classic book *Inca Land: Explorations in the Highlands of Peru,* first published in 1922 and now available as a free download from Project Gutenberg (www.gutenberg.org).

Bingham was searching for the lost city of Vilcabamba, the last stronghold of the Incas, and he thought he had found it at Machu Picchu. We now know that the remote ruins at Espíritu Pampa, much deeper in the jungle, are actually the remains of Vilcabamba. The Machu Picchu site was initially overgrown with thick vegetation, forcing Bingham's team to be content with roughly mapping the site. Bingham returned in 1912 and 1915 to carry out the difficult task of clearing the thick forest, when he also discovered some of the ruins on the so-called Inca Trail. Peruvian archaeologist Luis E Valcárcel undertook further studies in 1934, as did a Peruvian-American expedition under Paul Fejos in 1940 and 1941.

ⓘ BUYING MACHU PICCHU TICKETS

You would think accessing the continent's number-one destination might be easier. Get ready. Currently, Machu Picchu tickets can be purchased online (www.machupicchu.gob.pe), though not all foreign credit cards go through. If you reserve online, can't get your card to work and happen to be in Cuzco, you can deposit the amount due at a Banco de la Nación outlet within a three-hour window; later check in via the website to print your ticket.

In Cuzco, you can also purchase tickets from the **Dirección Regional de Cultura Cusco** (DIRCETUR; ☏ 084-58-2030; www.dirceturcusco.gob.pe; Maruri 340; ⊙ 7:15am-6:30pm Mon-Sat) or the **DIRCETUR outlet** (☏ 084-58-2030, ext 2000; www.dirceturcusco.gob.pe; Garcilaso s/n, Museo Historico Regional; ⊙ 7am-7:30pm Mon-Sat) in the Museo Histórico. Both outlets accept Peruvian soles, Visa or Mastercard. If you want to risk waiting, you can also purchase them from the **Centro Cultural** (☏ 084-21-1196; Av Pachacutec s/n; ⊙ 5:30am-8:30pm) in Aguas Calientes, but only in Peruvian soles. Note that Aguas Calientes ATMs frequently run out of cash. Student tickets must be purchased in person with valid photo ID from the institution. For a reasonable fee, travel agencies can also obtain tickets, which some readers recommend.

Entry to Machu Picchu requires a valid photo ID.

Lastly, ticketing procedures can change, but iPeru (p898) can offer the latest updates. Good luck.

Machu Picchu

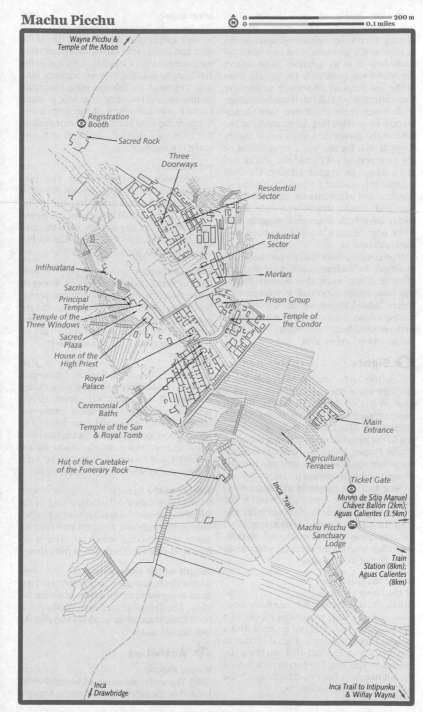

0   200 m
0   0.1 miles

Wayna Picchu &
Temple of the Moon

Registration
Booth

Sacred Rock

Three
Doorways

Residential
Sector

Industrial
Sector

Intihuatana

Mortars

Sacristy
Principal
Temple

Prison Group

Temple of the
Three Windows

Temple of
the Condor

Sacred
Plaza

House of the
High Priest

Royal
Palace

Ceremonial
Baths

Main
Entrance

Temple of the Sun
& Royal Tomb

Agricultural
Terraces

Hut of the Caretaker
of the Funerary Rock

Ticket Gate

Inca Trail

Museo de Sitio Manuel
Chávez Ballón (2km);
Aguas Calientes (3.5km)

Machu Picchu
Sanctuary
Lodge

Train
Station (8km);
Aguas Calientes
(8km)

Inca
Drawbridge

Inca Trail to Intipunku
& Wiñay Wayna

Despite scores of more recent studies, knowledge of Machu Picchu remains sketchy. Even today archaeologists are forced to rely heavily on speculation and educated guesswork as to its function. Some believe the citadel was founded in the waning years of the last Incas as an attempt to preserve Inca culture or rekindle their predominance, while others think that it may have already become an uninhabited, forgotten city at the time of the conquest. A more recent theory suggests that the site was a royal retreat or the country palace of Pachacutec, abandoned at the time of the Spanish invasion. The site's director believes that it was a city, a political, religious and administrative center. Its location, and the fact that at least eight access routes have been discovered, suggests that it was a trade nexus between Amazonia and the highlands.

It seems clear from the exceptionally high quality of the stonework and the abundance of ornamental work that Machu Picchu was once vitally important as a ceremonial center. Indeed, to some extent, it still is: Alejandro Toledo, the country's first indigenous Andean president, impressively staged his inauguration here in 2001.

⊙ Sights

Unless you arrive via the Inca Trail, you'll officially enter the ruins through a ticket gate on the south side of **Machu Picchu** (www.machupicchu.gob.pe; adult/student S152/77; ⊙6am-6pm). About 100m of footpath brings you to the mazelike main entrance of Machu Picchu proper, where the ruins lie stretched out before you, roughly divided into two areas separated by a series of plazas.

Note that the names of individual ruins speculate their use – in reality, much is unknown. To get a visual fix of the whole site and snap the classic postcard photograph, climb the zigzagging staircase on the left immediately after entering the complex, which leads to the Hut of the Caretaker.

Hut of the Caretaker
of the Funerary Rock   RUINS
(Machu Picchu Complex) An excellent viewpoint to take in the whole site. It's one of a few buildings that has been restored with a thatched roof, making it a good shelter in the case of rain. The Inca Trail enters the city just below this hut. The carved rock behind the hut may have been used to mummify the nobility, hence the hut's name.

Intihuatana   RUINS
(Machu Picchu Complex) This Quechua word loosely translates as the 'Hitching Post of the Sun' and refers to the carved rock pillar, often mistakenly called a sundial, at the top of the Intihuatana hill. The Inca astronomers were able to predict the solstices using the angles of this pillar. Thus, they were able to claim control over the return of the lengthening summer days. Its exact use remains unclear, but its elegant simplicity and high craftwork make it a highlight.

Intipunku   GATE
(⊙checkpoint closes around 3pm) The Inca Trail ends after its final descent from the notch in the horizon called Intipunku (Sun Gate). Looking at the hill behind you as you enter the ruins, you can see both the trail and Intipunku. This hill, called Machu Picchu (Old Peak), gives the site its name.

Principal Temple   RUINS
(Machu Picchu Complex) The 'temple' derives its name from the massive solidity and perfection of its construction. The damage to the rear right corner is the result of the ground settling below this corner rather than any inherent weakness in the masonry itself.

Sacristy   RUINS
(Machu Picchu Complex) Behind and connected to the Principal Temple lies this famous small building. It has many well-carved niches, perhaps used for the storage of ceremonial objects, as well as a carved stone bench. The Sacristy is especially known for the two rocks flanking its entrance; each is said to contain 32 angles, but it's easy to come up with a different number whenever you count them.

Temple of the Sun   RUINS
(Machu Picchu Complex) Just above and to the left of the ceremonial baths is Machu Picchu's only round building, a curved and tapering tower of exceptional stonework. This structure is off-limits and best viewed from above.

Temple of the Three Windows   RUINS
(Machu Picchu Complex) Important buildings flank the remaining three sides of the Sacred Plaza. The Temple of the Three Windows features huge trapezoidal windows that give the building its name.

Activities

Wayna Picchu   HIKING
(S48) The steep mountain of Wayna Picchu, located at the far end of the ruins, is featured

in the most iconic shots of Machu Picchu. Thanks to excellent Inca engineering, the trail is not as hard as it looks but sturdy footwear and good fitness are recommended. It requires a separate ticket obtained with your entrance ticket purchase. These spots sell out a week ahead in low season and a month ahead in high season, so plan accordingly.

❶ Getting There & Away

From Aguas Calientes, frequent buses for Machu Picchu (S80 round-trip, 25 minutes) depart from a ticket office along the main road from 5:30am to 3:30pm. Buses return from the ruins when full, with the last departure at 5:45pm. There's a proposal for a tram to eventually replace the bus system, still in the preliminary stages of consideration.

Otherwise, it's a steep walk (8km, 1½ hours) up a tightly winding mountain road. First there's a flat 20-minute walk from Aguas Calientes to Puente Ruinas, where the road to the ruins crosses the Río Urubamba, near the museum. A breathtakingly steep but well-marked trail climbs another 2km up to Machu Picchu, taking about an hour to hike (but less coming down!).

The Inca Trail

The most famous hike in South America, the four-day Inca Trail is walked by thousands every year. Although the total distance is only about 39km, the ancient trail laid by the Incas from the Sacred Valley to Machu Picchu winds its way up and down and around the mountains, snaking over three high Andean passes en route, which have collectively led to the route being dubbed 'the Inca Trail.' The views of snowy mountain peaks, distant rivers and ranges, and cloud forests flush with orchids are stupendous – and walking from one cliff-hugging pre-Columbian ruin to the next is a mystical and unforgettable experience.

The Hike

Most trekking agencies run buses to the start of the trail, also known as Piscacucho or Km 82 on the railway to Aguas Calientes.

After crossing the Río Urubamba (2600m) and taking care of registration formalities, you'll climb gently alongside the river to the trail's first archaeological site, **Llactapata** (Town on Top of the Terraces), before heading south down a side valley of the Río Cusichaca. (If you start from Km 88, turn west after crossing the river to see the little-visited site of **Q'ente** (Hummingbird), about 1km away, then return east to Llactapata on the main trail.)

The trail leads 7km south to the hamlet of **Wayllabamba** (Grassy Plain; 3000m), near which many tour groups will camp for the first night. You can buy bottled drinks and high-calorie snacks here, and take a breather to look over your shoulder for views of the snowcapped **Nevado Verónica** (5750m).

Wayllabamba is situated near the fork of Ríos Llulucha and Cusichaca. The trail crosses the Río Llullucha, then climbs steeply up along the river. This area is known as **Tres Piedras** (Three White Stones; 3300m), though these boulders are no longer visible. From here it is a long, very steep 3km climb through humid woodlands.

The trail eventually emerges on the high, bare mountainside of **Llulluchupampa** (3750m), where water is available and the flats are dotted with campsites, which get very cold at night. This is as far as you can reasonably expect to get on your first day, though many groups will actually spend their second night here.

From Llulluchupampa, a good path up the left-hand side of the valley climbs for a two- to three-hour ascent to the pass of **Warmiwañusca**, also colorfully known as 'Dead Woman's Pass.' At 4200m above sea level, this is the highest point of the trek,

PERU THE INCA TRAIL

BOOKING YOUR TRIP

It is important to book your Inca Trail trip at least six months in advance for dates between May and August. Outside these months, you may get a permit with a few weeks' notice, but it's very hard to predict. Only licensed operators can get permits, but you can check general availability at www.camino-inca.com.

Consider booking a five-day trip to lessen the pace and enjoy more wildlife and ruins. Other positives include less-crowded campsites and being able to stay at the most scenic one – Phuyupatamarka (3600m) – on the third evening.

Take some time to research your options – you won't regret it. It's best to screen agencies for a good fit before committing. Also make sure you have international travel insurance that covers adventure activities.

Inca Trail

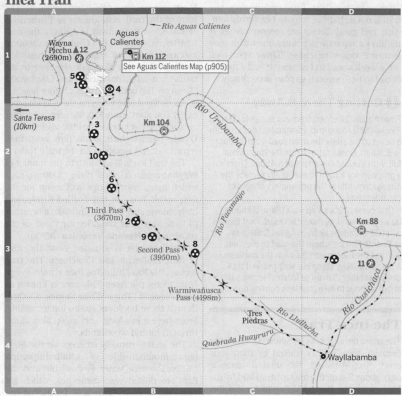

and leaves many a seasoned hiker gasping. From Warmiwañusca, you can see the Río Pacamayo (Río Escondido) far below, as well as the ruin of Runkurakay halfway up the next hill, above the river.

The trail continues down a long and knee-jarringly steep descent to the river, where there are large campsites at **Paq'amayo**. At an altitude of about 3600m, the trail crosses the river over a small footbridge and climbs toward **Runkurakay** (Egg-Shaped Building); at 3750m this round ruin has superb views. It's about an hour's walk away.

Above Runkurakay, the trail climbs to a false summit before continuing past two small lakes to the top of the second pass at 3950m, which has views of the snow-laden Cordillera Vilcabamba. You'll notice a change in ecology as you descend from this pass – you're now on the eastern, Amazon slope of the Andes and things immediately get greener. The trail descends to the ruin of **Sayaqmarka** (Dominant Town), a tightly constructed complex perched

on a small mountain spur, which offers incredible views. The trail continues downward and crosses an upper tributary of the Río Aobamba (Wavy Plain).

The trail then leads on across an Inca causeway and up a gentle climb through some beautiful cloud forest and an **Inca tunnel** carved from the rock. This is a relatively flat section and you'll soon arrive at the third pass at almost 3600m, which has grand views of the Río Urubamba Valley, and campsites where some groups spend their final night, with the advantage of watching the sun set over a truly spectacular view, but with the disadvantage of having to leave at 3am in the race to reach the Sun Gate in time for sunrise. If you are camping here, be careful in the early morning as the steep incline makes the steps slippery.

Just below the pass is the beautiful and well-restored ruin of **Phuyupatamarka** (Place Above the Clouds), about 3570m above sea level. The site contains six beautiful ceremonial

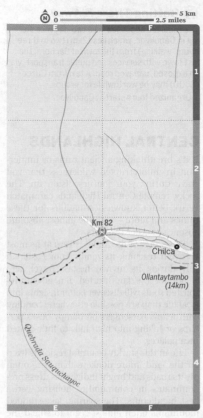

```
        0              5 km
        0          2.5 miles
```

Km 82

Chilca

Ollantaytambo
(14km)

Quebrada Sauquchayoc

baths with water running through them. From Phuyupatamarka, the trail makes a dizzying dive into the cloud forest below, following an incredibly well-engineered flight of many hundreds of Inca steps (it's nerve-racking in the early hours, use a headlamp). After two or three hours, the trail eventually zigzags its way down to a collapsed red-roofed white building that marks the final night's campsite.

A 500m trail behind the old, out of use, pub leads to the exquisite little Inca site of **Wiñay Wayna** (Huiñay Huayna), which is variously translated as 'Forever Young,' 'To Plant the Earth Young' and 'Growing Young' (as opposed to 'growing old'). Peter Frost writes that the Quechua name refers to an orchid *(Epidendrum secundum)* that blooms here year-round. The semitropical campsite at Wiñay Wayna boasts one of the most stunning views on the whole trail, especially at sunrise. A rough trail leads from this site to another spectacular terraced ruin, called

Intipata, best visited on the day you arrive to Wiñay Wayna: consider coordinating it with your guide if you are interested.

From the Wiñay Wayna guard post, the trail winds without much change in elevation through the cliff-hanging cloud forest for about two hours to reach **Intipunku** (Sun Gate) – the penultimate site on the trail, where it's tradition to enjoy your first glimpse of majestic Machu Picchu while waiting for the sun to rise over the surrounding mountains.

The final triumphant descent takes almost an hour. Trekkers generally arrive long before the morning trainloads of tourists, and can enjoy the exhausted exhilaration of reaching their goal without having to push past enormous groups of tourists fresh off the first train from Cuzco.

Choquequirao

Remote, spectacular, and still not entirely cleared, the ruins of Choquequirao are often described as a mini–Machu Picchu. This breathtaking site at the junction of three rivers currently requires a challenging two-day hike each way, though you will be happy if you budget more time for it.

Many see it as 'the next big thing' in Inca ruins tourism. In fact, the Peruvian government has already approved controversial plans to put in a tramway, the country's first, with a capacity of 3000 visitors daily. It would bring this remote attraction to within 15 minutes of the nearby highway. Conservationists worry about its potential impact.

For now, you can still go without the crowds. Most Cuzco trekking operators go. Travelers can also organize the walk on their own, but it is remote and its steepness makes it very challenging, especially if you're carrying a heavy pack.

◉ Sights

The many features of this sprawling site take a while to explore. Archaeology fans will not be content with the half-day allotted by a four-day trek.

Take special care exploring these ruins as the site's popularity can cause a huge impact on the infrastructure and there is little funding for its conservation.

Trail guides don't always offer detailed information. It's well worth bringing a copy of *Machu Picchu's Sacred Sisters: Choquequirao & Llactapata* by Gary Ziegler. Peter Frost's *Exploring Cusco* is also useful.

🏃 Activities

Hiking

Outfitters from Cuzco offer a guided, four-day trek (averaging US$500 to US$750 per person). Reputable outfitters include Alpaca Expeditions (p894), Apus Peru (p894), **Journey Experience** (JOEX; ☑ 084-24-5642; www.joextravel.com; Av Tupac Amaru V-2-A, Progreso; ⊕ 9am-6pm), **Llama Path** (☑ 084-24-0822; www.llamapath.com; Cuichipunco 257; ⊕ 9am-1pm & 3-8pm Mon-Sat, 4-8pm Sun), **Peru Eco Expeditions** (☑ 084-60-7516, 957-349-269; www.perueco expeditions.com; Urb San Judas Chico II D-13; ⊕ 9am-4pm Mon-Fri) 🖉, **SAS Travel** (☑ 084-24-9194; www.sastravelperu.com; Calle Garcilaso 270; ⊕ 8am-8pm Mon-Sat) and **Wayki Trek** (☑ 084-22-4092; www.waykitrek.net; Quera 239; ⊕ 9am-7pm Mon-Fri, to 1pm Sat) 🖉. Costs for an independent guide can be comparable. Packhorses can be hired in Cachora (per day S50 horse or mule, and S50 for muleteer); make sure that they will be in good condition for the trip, since not all are. Trekking poles are highly recommended.

Independent hikers will find rest stops with organized campgrounds with toilets and some cold showers, expensive bottled water, drinks and basic meals or provisions (such as pasta or instant soup). Bring a water filter, as the water found along the way is not potable. Always carry plenty of water, as sources are infrequent.

ℹ️ Getting There & Away

The ruins are accessed via a two-day hike starting in Capuliyoc, which lies 12km (two to three hours' walking) from the town of Cachora, the last town with services and public transport, via an exposed, unpaved road. A taxi from Cuzco (S300) may be worthwhile for groups.

Organized tours start at Capuliyoc.

CENTRAL HIGHLANDS

If it's breathtaking ancient ruins or immersion in uninterrupted wilderness that you crave during your journey, listen up. The rocky, remote Central Highlands can match Peru's better known destinations for these things and more – with the almost absolute absence of other travelers.

This sector of the Andes is Peru at its most Peruvian reaching its zenith from Easter to July during its myriad fiestas. Travel here is not for the fainthearted. But adventure-spirited souls will discover better insights into local life than are possible elsewhere: bonding with fellow passengers on bumpy buses perhaps or hiking into high hills to little-visited Inca palaces.

Life in this starkly beautiful region is lived off the land: more donkeys than cars often ply its roads and bright indigenous dress predominates in communities housing Peru's best handicrafts. The soaring, lake-studded mountains often almost seem to shield the Central Highlands from the 21st century.

Ayacucho

☑ 066 / POP 181,000 / ELEV 2750M

Travelers are only just rediscovering Ayacucho's treasures. Richly decorated churches dominate the vivid cityscape alongside peach- and pastel-colored colonial buildings hung with wooden balconies. Among numerous festivities, Ayacucho boasts Peru's premier Semana Santa celebrations, while in the surrounding mountains lie some of the country's most significant archaeological attractions.

◉ Sights

The **Plaza de Armas** (Plaza Mayor de Huamanga; Plaza de Armas) in Ayacucho is one of Peru's most beautiful, and should be a starting point for your explorations. The four sides of the plaza, clockwise from the east, are Portal Municipal, Portal Independencia, Portal Constitución and Portal Unión. Around here, you'll find many gorgeous colonial mansions, including the **Prefectura** (Jirón 28 de Julio) FREE. Ask at the tourist office for details on how to visit these buildings.

Other sights in Ayacucho are mostly churches and museums.

★**Cathedral** CHURCH
(Portal Municipal; ⊙10am-noon & 4-6pm) FREE This spectacular 17th-century cathedral on the Plaza de Armas has a religious-art museum inside. The moody facade doesn't quite prepare you for the intricacy of the interior, with its elaborate gold-leaf altar being one of the best examples of the baroque-*churrigueresque* style (in which cornices and other intricate, Spanish-influenced workmanship mingled with Andean influences, often evinced by the wildlife depicted).

★**Museo de Arte Popular** MUSEUM
(Portal Independencia 72; ⊙8am-1pm & 2-4:15pm Mon Fri) FREE Displays popular art covering the *ayacucheño* (natives of Ayacucho) spectrum – silverwork, rug- and tapestry-weaving, stone and woodcarvings, ceramics (model churches are especially popular) and the famous *retablos* (ornamental religious dioramas). The latter are colorful wooden boxes varying in size and containing intricate papier-mâché models: Peruvian rural scenes or the nativity are favorites, but interesting ones with political or social commentary can be seen here. Photographs show how Ayacucho changed during the 20th century. Opening hours here change almost as frequently.

★**Museo de la Memoria** MUSEUM
(Prolongación Libertad 1229; S2; ⊙9am-1pm & 3-6pm Mon-Fri, 9am-1pm Sat) Ayacucho's most haunting museum, remembers the impact the Sendero Luminoso (Shining Path) had on Peru in the city that was most deeply affected by the conflict. Its simple displays (in Spanish) are moving: there are eyewitness accounts of the horrors that occurred and a particularly poignant montage of photos by mothers whose children were killed in the fighting.

Wari Ruins RUIN
(S3; ⊙8am-5:30pm) Sprawling for several kilometers along a cactus-forested roadside are the extensive ruins of Wari, the capital of the eponymous empire, which predated the Incas by five centuries. The site occupies a beautiful, peaceful hilltop location. A small **museum** (information in Spanish only) explains, using artifacts, the relevance and importance of this pre-Inca culture. Look out for the distinctive **Wari ceramics**. Don't leave the site too late to look for return transport – vehicles get hopelessly full in the afternoon.

★ Festivals & Events

Semana Santa RELIGIOUS
(⊙Mar or Apr) Held the week before Easter, this is Peru's finest religious festival and attracts visitors from all over the country. Each succeeding day sees solemn yet colorful processions and Catholic religious rites. Ayacucho's Semana Santa celebrations also include art shows, folk-dancing competitions, local music concerts, street events, sporting events (especially equestrian ones), agricultural fairs and the loving preparation of traditional meals.

🛏 Sleeping

Hostal Tres Máscaras GUESTHOUSE $
(☑066-31-2921; hoteltresmascaras@yahoo.com; Tres Máscaras 194; s/d S60/80, without bathroom S30/50) The pleasing walled garden and friendly owner render this an enjoyable place to stay, and garden-facing rooms are generously sized. Hot water is on in the morning and later on request. A room with TV is S5 extra. Continental and American breakfasts are available for S8 and S10, respectively. All these things have made it a longtime backpacker favorite.

Hostal Florida GUESTHOUSE $
(☑066-31-2565; Cuzco 310; s/d S40/70) This traveler-friendly *hostal* (guesthouse) has a relaxing courtyard garden and clean rooms (those on the upper level are better) with bathrooms and TV, hot water in the morning and later on request. There is a basic cafeteria too, and a laundry service.

Via Via Alameda HOTEL $$
(☑066-31-7040; http://viavia.world/en/south-america/ayacucho; Bolognesi 720, Parque Alameda; s/d incl breakfast S100/130; ℗) This colonial building in a quiet, lovely location has rooms with beautiful furniture, and there's a grassy garden-courtyard where you can sit outside and enjoy the on-site restaurant's wonderful cooking. Now under ownership of the city center's famous Via Via company, the hotel is about 700m from the center; the walk back at night involves passing some dark neighborhoods.

Hotel La Crillonesa HOTEL $$
(☑066-31-2350; www.hotelcrillonesa.com; Nazareno 165; s/d from S60/85; 🛜) A popular hotel with helpful staff, La Crillonesa offers a rooftop terrace with photogenic views, a TV room, tour

information and 24-hour hot water. Its rather small, clean rooms have comfy beds and generally functioning cable TV. The best rooms are right at the top.

★ **Via Via Plaza** ⬩ HOTEL $$
(📞 066-31-2834; http://viavia.world/en/south-america/ayacucho; Portal Constitución 4; s/d S130/190; 📶) One of the more imaginative sleeping options in central Ayacucho is Via Via, with an enviable plaza location and cool, vibrantly decorated rooms themed around different countries and continents. Travelers will feel like they've landed in a veritable oasis, all centered on a plant-filled courtyard. English and Dutch are spoken, and there's a popular 2nd-floor restaurant hangout alongside.

DM Hoteles Ayacucho ⬩ HOTEL $$$
(📞 066-31-2202; fax 066-31-2314; 9 de Diciembre 184; d/ste incl breakfast S345/511; 🅿️📶) The interior of this impressive-looking colonial building exudes a certain kind of charm, but for what you pay, the rooms are oh-so-plain and merely adequate. Better rooms have balconies (request one); some have plaza views. It was once considered the best in town, and few centrally located top-end hotels have yet given it a run for its money in scale or in facilities.

Eating

Standards are high, with many regional specialties on offer. There are some quality restaurants on the Plaza de Armas and atmospheric, if slightly touristy, dining within the **Centro Turístico Cultural San Cristóbal** (Jirón 28 de Julio 178). Meanwhile, **Plaza Moré** (Jirón 28 de Julio 262) offers eateries that are positively gourmet: signs of the changing Ayacucho, perhaps. After all, how many Andean towns can boast their own 'Barrio Gastronómico' (Gastronomic Neighborhood)?

🍷 Drinking & Nightlife

Yaku ⬩ BAR
(Portal Unión 30; ⊙11am-11:30pm) First things first: enthusiastically run Yaku is not just a bar with a lovely balcony overlooking the Plaza de Armas: it's a live-music venue, it's a restaurant, it brews its own beer, it has table football – and its owners are ever-developing more plans. There are some of Ayacucho's best burgers (S15 to S20) here, too: wolf down a 'Cancún' (with guacamole).

Museo ⬩ COCKTAIL BAR
(cnr 9 de Diciembre & Av Cáceres; ⊙6pm-3am) An intriguing mix of cocktails are served, DJs

provide the music (*reggaetón*, salsa) most nights and the atmosphere is buzzing.

Shopping

Ayacucho is a renowned handicraft center: a visit to the Museo de Arte Popular (p913) will give you an idea of local products. The tourist office (p914) can recommend local artisans who will welcome you to their workshops. The Santa Ana *barrio* (neighborhood) is particularly well known for its crafts.

There is a rather tamer **craft market** (Quinua s/n) close to the city center.

ℹ️ Information

MEDICAL SERVICES
Clínica de la Esperanza (Hospital Regional de Ayacucho; 📞 066-31-7436; www.hospital regionalayacucho.gob.pe; Independencia 355; ⊙8am-8pm) English is spoken.

MONEY
BBVA Banco Continental (Portal Unión 28)

TOURIST INFORMATION
iPerú (📞 066-31-8305; cnr Cusco & Asamblea; ⊙9am-6pm Mon-Sat, to 1pm Sun) Helpful advice; English spoken.

ℹ️ Getting There & Around

AIR
The **airport** is 3.5km from the town center. Taxis charge about S10. Flight times and airlines can change without warning, so check airline websites for the latest schedules. Daily flights to Lima are with **LC Peru** (📞 066-31-2151; Jirón 9 de Diciembre 139; ⊙9am-7pm Mon-Fri, to 1pm Sat), with departures alternating between early morning and mid-afternoon depending on the day. There are morning and afternoon departures on Sundays.

BUS
Most buses (to long-distance north- and southbound destinations, including Lima) arrive and depart from the grandiosely named **Terrapuerto Libertadores de America** (Terminal Terrestre; end of Perez de Cuellar) bus terminal to the north of the city center, although you can still buy tickets at the downtown offices.

Transport connections with Lima are via the relatively fast and spectacular Hwy 24 that traverses the Andes via Rumichaca to Pisco.

Heading north to Huancayo (S30 to S40, seven hours), the road is poor, featuring vertiginous drops with precious little protection: a heart-in-mouth, spectacular old-school Andean bus ride.

For Cuzco, buses run from Terrapuerto Libertadores de America, but for Andahuaylas the best option is to take a *combi* (minibus) from Pasaje Cáceres in central Ayacucho. These trips boast fantastic scenery, and are worth doing in daylight.

Cruz del Sur (📋 information only 066-31-2813, reservations 01-311-5050; www.cruzdelsur.com.pe; Cáceres s/n, btwn Libertad & Sucre) Top-notch, executive-style service to Lima, with comfortable seats and meals thrown in. Departs from its own terminal, with a bakery across the way to stock up on snacks. Prices vary depending on when and how you purchase the ticket, but start around the S70 mark.

Expreso Molina (📋 066-31-9989; Universitaria 160) A good company to know about, with departures from its own terminal not too far from the center. Not tops for comfort, but serves Lima (two daily departures and no less than seven night departures), Huancayo (one daily, five night departures) and Huancavelica (nightly departures).

Expreso Turismo Los Chankas (📋 066-31-2391; Terrapuerto Libertadores de America) Currently one of the only through services to Cuzco (otherwise, you need to change in Andahuaylas); departures are at 7:30am (Monday to Saturday) and 8:30pm (daily). Even though the road is now paved, breaking this long journey in Andahuaylas is a good idea.

Turismo Libertadores (📋 962-889-142; Manco Cápac, btwn Calle de la Vega & 9 de Diciembre) One of the best of the cheap options to Lima: the one daytime and four nightly departures cost S40 to S60.

NORTH COAST

This savage shore has some of the world's best surfing and plenty of tanned travelers to keep you company. It's also home to a jaw-dropping array of archaeological sites, colonial cities and evocative desertscapes straight out of *Mad Max*. In this land of rock and desert sand, you'll also find a few verdant valleys, while Peru's only mangrove forests cling for their lives up north.

There's a lot of hyperbole to be had – one of the world's longest left breaks challenges surfers in Puerto Chicama, South America's oldest civilization vexes archaeological explorers at Caral, and the massive pre-Columbian adobe complex at Chan Chan was once the largest city in the Americas.

The backpacker hubs of Máncora and Huanchaco kick into full party mode from November to March, while those seeking tranquility can go lo-fi and seek out unique adventures in fishing villages such as Zorritos and Cabo Blanco.

Trujillo

📋 044 / POP 709,500

Stand in the right spot and the glamorous streets of old Trujillo look like they've barely changed in hundreds of years. Well, there are more honking taxis now, but the city still manages to put on a dashing show with its profusion of colonial-era churches and polychrome buildings. Most people come here to visit the remarkable pre-Incan archaeological sites nearby, spending just a short time wandering the compact city center.

The Chimú capital of Chan Chan (p919) is nearby. It was the largest pre-Columbian city in the Americas, making it the top attraction in the region. Other Chimú sites bake in the surrounding desert, among them the immense and impressive Huacas del Sol y de la Luna (p919), which date back 1500 years. Beach bums may consider staying in the laid-back surfer village of Huanchaco (p920), just 20 minutes up the road.

◉ Sights

Trujillo's spacious and spit-shined main square, surely the cleanest in the Americas and definitely one of the prettiest, hosts a colorful assembly of preserved colonial buildings and an impressive statue dedicated to work, the arts and liberty. Elegant mansions abound, including Hotel Libertador (p917).

Museo de Arqueología MUSEUM
(Junín 682; S5; ⊙9am-2:30pm Mon, to 4:30pm Tue-Sat) This well-curated museum features a rundown of Peruvian history from 12,000 BC to the present day, with an emphasis on Moche, Chimú and Inca civilizations as well as the lesser-known Cupisnique and Salinar cultures. It's also worth popping in for the house itself: a restored 17th-century mansion known as La Casa Risco, which features striking cedar pillars and gorgeous painted courtyard walls.

Casa de Urquiaga HISTORIC BUILDING
(Pizarro 446; ⊙9:15am-3:15pm Mon-Fri, 10am-1pm Sat) FREE Owned and maintained by Banco Central de la Reserva del Perú since 1972, this colonial mansion dates to 1604, though the original house was completely destroyed in the earthquake of 1619. Rebuilt and preserved since, it now houses exquisite period furniture, including a striking writer's desk used by Simón Bolívar, who organized much of his final campaign to liberate Peru from the Spanish empire from Trujillo in 1824.

Trujillo

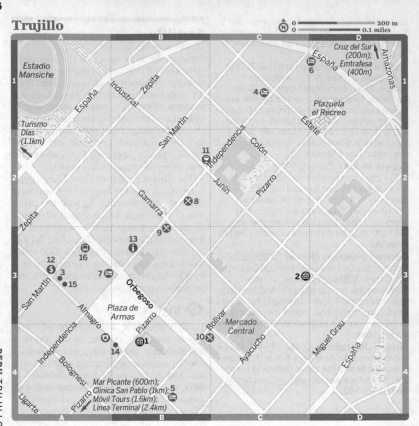

Trujillo

◎ Sights

1 Casa de Urquiaga	B4
2 Museo de Arqueología	C3

✪ Activities, Courses & Tours

3 Trujillo Tours	A3

🛏 Sleeping

4 Hospedaje El Mochilero	C1
5 Hotel Chimor	B4
6 Hotel El Brujo	D1
7 Hotel Libertador	A3

✕ Eating

8 Casona Deza	B2

9 El Celler de Cler	B3
10 Jugería San Augustín	B4

◉ Drinking & Nightlife

11 Café Bar Museo	B2

ℹ Information

12 Banco de la Nacion	A3

ℹ Transport

13 iPerú	B3
14 LATAM	B4
15 LC Perú	A3
16 Línea Booking Office	A3

☞ Tours

Trujillo Tours CULTURAL
(📞 044-23-3091; www.trujillotours.com; Almagro
301; ⊕ 7:30am-1pm & 4-8pm) This friendly operation has three- to four-hour tours to Chan
Chan, Huanchaco and Huacas del Sol y de la
Luna, as well as city tours. Tours are available
in English, French, Portuguese and German.

🛏 Sleeping

Some travelers prefer to stay in the nearby
beach town of Huanchaco. Many budget

and midrange hotels can be noisy if you get streetside rooms. For a city of its size and history, Trujillo lags way behind when it comes to design and boutique hotels.

Hospedaje El Mochilero   HOSTEL $
(☑ 044-29-7842; elmochileroperu@gmail.com; Independencia 887; dm/s/d from S25/35/50; 🛜) It feels more like a youth hostel than anything else in Trujillo. It has hammocks out back, three big dorm rooms that sleep 10 to 12 (bring your earplugs), a guest kitchen and cool common areas for chillaxing megathons. There are basic cane cabins out back if you want to sleep in the open air. All in all, good vibes.

Hotel Chimor   HOTEL $$
(☑ 044-20-2252; www.hotelchimor.com; Almagro 631; s/d/tr S110/160/220; 🛜) This is a very solid midrange choice for comfort and modernity. The contempo rooms can get a little hot, but they are quite sharp, with built-in desks and flat-screen TVs. It's friendly and central, and borders on boutique cool.

Hotel El Brujo   HOTEL $$
(☑ 044-20-8120; www.elbrujohotel.com; Independencia 978; s/d/tr incl breakfast S151/201/251; ❄@🛜) This is a solid (though slightly boring) midrange option. It is clean and quiet, and its location close to several northern bus stations adds to the convenience factor. It's very businesslike, with spacious modern rooms and all the requisite amenities (minibar, cable TV and writing desk).

★Hotel Libertador   HISTORIC HOTEL $$$
(☑ 044-23-2741; www.hotellibertador.com.pe; Independencia 485; r incl breakfast from S442; P❄@🛜 🏊) The classy dame of the city's hotels, the 79-room Libertador is in a beautiful building that's the Audrey Hepburn of Trujillo – it wears its age with refined grace. It earns its four stars with a beautiful and lush courtyard pool, archways aplenty and modern rooms with all expected amenities.

🍴 Eating

The 700 *cuadra* (block) of Pizarro is where Trujillo's power brokers hang out and families converge, and they're kept well fed by a row of trendy yet reasonably priced cafes and restaurants. Some of the best eateries in Trujillo are found a short taxi ride outside the town center.

If you're here on Monday look out for *shambar,* a traditional soup made with wheat, legumes, onions, pork and herbs and served all over town.

Jugería San Augustín   SANDWICHES $
(Bolívar 526; sandwiches S3.50-7.50; ⊗ 8:30am-1pm & 4-8pm Mon-Sat, 9am-1pm Sun) You can spot this place by the near-constant lines snaking around the corner in summer as locals queue for the drool-inducing juices. But don't leave it at that. The chicken and *lechón* (suckling pig) sandwiches, slathered with all the fixings, are what you'll be telling friends back home about.

★El Celler de Cler   PERUVIAN $$
(☑ 044-31-7191; cnr Gamarra & Independencia; mains S38-58; ⊗ 6pm-1am) This atmospheric spot is the only place in Trujillo to enjoy dinner (coupled with an amazing cocktail) on a 2nd-floor balcony – the wraparound number dates to the early 19th century. The food is upscale, featuring pasta and grills, and delicious. Antiques fuel the decor, from a 1950s-era American cash register to an extraordinary industrial-revolution pulley lamp from the UK.

★Mar Picante   PERUVIAN $$
(www.marpicante.com; Húsares de Junín 412; mains S20-40; ⊗ 10am-5pm) This hugely popular place has recently undergone an overhaul and is now all polished concrete and industrial metal beams, but the food remains outrageously good. If you come to Trujillo without sampling its *ceviche mixto* (mixed ceviche) ordered with a side of something spicy, you haven't lived life on the edge.

Casona Deza   PERUVIAN $$
(Independencia 630; mains S23-46; ⊗ 5:30-11:30pm Mon-Sat; 🛜) 🌿 Expect excellent espresso, house-made desserts and tasty pizzas and pasta, often sourced organically, at this spacious cafe that occupies one of the city's most fiercely preserved colonial homes.

🍷 Drinking & Nightlife

★El Tragsu   BAR
(Las Hortencias 588; ⊗ 9pm-4am Mon-Sat) This popular place south of the center is one of the best pubs in Peru, with a themed front room complete with elf decorations and an elegant wooden bar for those who want to converse. There's also a steamy split-level band room where the dial is stuck on 'full party' mode.

Café Bar Museo   BAR
(cnr Junín & Independencia; ⊗ 5pm-late Mon-Sat) This locals' favorite shouldn't be a secret. The tall, wood-paneled walls covered in artsy posters and the classic marble-top bar feel like a

PERU TRUJILLO

cross between an English pub and a Left Bank cafe. Hands down the most interesting place to drink in Trujillo. There's a limited menu of bar snacks if you want to make a night of it.

ℹ Information

EMERGENCY

Policía de Turismo (☎ 044-29-1705; Almagro 442; ⊗ 8am-11pm) Shockingly helpful. Tourist police wear white shirts around town and some deputies speak English, Italian and/or French.

MEDICAL SERVICES

Clinica San Pablo (☎ 044-48-5244; www. sanpablotrujillo.com.pe; Húsares de Junin 690; ⊗ 24hr) This modern clinic is considered one of the best in town and offers outpatient and emergency services.

MONEY

Banco de la Nacion (cnr San Martin & Almagro) Bank with fee-free ATMs.

TOURIST INFORMATION

iPerú (☎ 044-29-4561; www.peru.travel; Independencia 467, oficina 106; ⊗ 9am-6pm Mon-Sat, to 1pm Sun) Provides tourist information, maps and a list of certified guides and travel agencies.

ℹ Getting There & Away

AIR

The **airport** (TRU) is 10km northwest of town. **LATAM** (☎ 044-22-1469; www.latam.com; Almagro 480) has three daily flights between Lima and Trujillo. **Avianca** (☎ 080-01-8222; www.avianca. com; Real Plaza, César Vallejo Oeste 1345; ⊗ 10am-9pm) flies the same route twice a day, while **LC Perú** (☎ 044-29-0299; www.lcperu.com; Almagro 305; ⊗ 9am-8pm) has one evening flight.

BUS

Buses often leave Trujillo full, so booking a little earlier is advised. Several companies that go to southern destinations have terminals on the Panamericana Sur, the southern extension of Moche, and Ejército; check where your bus actually leaves from when buying a ticket.

Línea has services to most destinations of interest to travelers and is one of the more comfortable bus lines.

Cruz del Sur (☎ 080-11-1111; www.cruzdelsur. com.pe; Amazonas 437) One of the biggest and priciest bus companies in Peru. It goes to Lima six times a day and has evening buses to Guayaquil from Monday to Saturday.

Emtrafesa (☎ 044-48-4120; www.emtrafesa. com; Tupac Amaru 185) Regular departures to Chiclayo and points further north.

Línea (☎ 044-29-7000; www.linea.pe) The company's **booking office** (☎ 044-24-5181; www.linea.pe; cnr San Martín & Obregoso; ⊗ 8am-9pm Mon-Sat) is conveniently located in the historic center, although all buses leave from its **terminal** (☎ 044-29-9666; Panamerica Sur 2857) on Panamericana Sur, a S6 taxi ride away. Línea goes to Lima nine times daily between 9am and 10:45pm; to Piura at 1:30pm and 11pm; to Cajamarca at 10:30am, 1pm, 10pm, 10:30pm and 10:40pm; and to Huaraz at 9:30am and 9:30pm.

Móvil Tours (☎ 017-16-8000; www.moviltours. com.pe; Panamerica Sur 3955) Specializes in very comfortable long-haul tourist services. It has a 10pm service to Lima, and 9:40pm and 10:10pm departures to Huaraz, the first of which continues on to Caraz. There's a bus at 4pm to Chachapoyas and a 3pm bus to Tarapoto. A taxi to the station is S6, or catch a *combi* (California/Esperanza) on Av España and hop off at Ovalo Larco.

Turismo Días (☎ 044-20-1237; www.turdias. com; Nicolás de Piérola 1079) Has four departures to Cajamarca (10am, 1:15pm, 10pm and 11pm) and two to Cajabamba (8pm and 9pm).

Trujillo Buses

DESTINATION	COST (S)	DURATION (HR)
Cajabamba	25-35	12
Cajamarca	25-80	6-7
Caraz	50-65	8
Chachapoyas	70-90	15
Chiclayo	20-45	3-4
Chimbote	12-60	2
Guayaquil (Ecuador)	130-200	18
Huaraz	45-65	5-9
Lima	30-120	8-9
Máncora	40-90	8-9
Otuzco	8	2
Piura	35-80	6
Tarapoto	90-120	18
Tumbes	40-95	9-12

ℹ Getting Around

The airport is 10km northwest of Trujillo and reached cheaply on the Huanchaco *combi*, though you'll have to walk the last 1km. It takes around 30 minutes. A taxi from the city center costs S20.

A short taxi ride around town costs about S4. For sightseeing, taxis charge about S30 (in town) to S40 (out of town) per hour.

Around Trujillo

Five major archaeological sites can be easily reached from Trujillo by local bus or taxi. Two of these are principally Moche, dating from about 200 BC to AD 850. The other three, from the Chimú culture, date from about AD 850 to 1500. The relatively recently excavated Moche ruin of **La Huaca el Brujo** (www.elbrujo.pe; admission to site & museum S10; ⊙ 9am-5pm) can also be visited, but it's not as convenient.

The Moche and Chimú cultures left the greatest marks on the Trujillo area, but they were by no means the only cultures in the region. In a March 1973 *National Geographic* article, Drs ME Moseley and CJ Mackey claimed knowledge of more than 2000 sites in the Río Moche valley and many more have been discovered since.

Chan Chan

Built around AD 1300 and covering 20 sq km, **Chan Chan** (www.chanchan.gob.pe; admission S10, guide for groups of 1-5 S40; ⊙ 9am-4pm, museum closed Mon) is the largest pre-Columbian city in the Americas and the largest adobe city in the world. Although it must have been a dazzling sight at one time, devastating El Niño floods and heavy rainfall have severely eroded much of the city's outer portions. You can still visit the impressive restored Palacio Nik An complex and revel in the broad plazas, royal burial chamber and intricate designs that remain.

At the height of the Chimú empire, Chan Chan was home to an estimated 60,000 people and contained a vast wealth of gold, silver and ceramics. The wealth remained more or less undisturbed after the Incas conquered the city, but once the Spaniards hit the stage, the looting began. Within a few decades little but gold dust remained. Remnants of what was found can be seen in museums nearby.

The Chimú capital consisted of 10 walled citadels, also called royal compounds. Each contained a royal burial mound filled with vast quantities of funerary offerings, including dozens of sacrificed young women and chambers full of ceramics, weavings and jewelry.

The **Palacio Nik An** (also called the Tschudi Complex, after a Swiss naturalist) is the only section of Chan Chan that's partially restored. Parts of the site are covered with tentlike structures to protect from erosion. It is possible that other areas will open in the future, but until they are properly policed and signed, you run the risk of being mugged if you visit them.

At the Palacio Nik An you'll find an entrance area with tickets, souvenirs, guides, bathrooms and drinks, but there's no longer a cafe so bring snacks. Guides hang around next to the ticket office.

The best option for a visit is with an organized guided tour from Trujillo or with a local site tour guide, as signage is extremely limited. There are usually English-, French-, German- and Italian-speaking guides available here. If you want to go it alone, the path is marked out with fish-shaped pointers and you can purchase a small booklet for S2 at the ticket checkpoint with descriptions of the different areas of the complex and a map.

The site **museum** (www.chanchan.gob.pe; admission free with Chan Chan ticket; ⊙ 9am-4pm Tue-Sun) is out on the main road, about 500m before the main Chan Chan turnoff, and contains exhibits explaining Chan Chan and the Chimú culture. It has a few signs in Spanish and English, but a guide is still useful. The aerial photos and maps showing the huge extension of Chan Chan are fascinating, as tourists can only visit a tiny portion of the site.

Combis and buses to Chan Chan (S1.50) leave Trujillo every few minutes, passing the corners of España and Ejército, and España and Industrial. They'll drop you off at the turnoff, from where it's a 10-minute walk down to the ticket office. From Huanchaco take any Trujillo-bound transport.

A taxi from Trujillo or Huanchaco runs around S12.

Las Huacas del Sol y de la Luna

The Temples of the Sun and the Moon, attributed to the Moche period, are more than 700 years older than Chan Chan, yet parts of the **complex** (www.huacasdemoche.pe; ⊙ 9am-4pm) are remarkably well preserved. Located on the south bank of the Río Moche, the main attraction here is the **Huaca de la Luna** with its phenomenal multicolored friezes. The entrance price includes an English-speaking guide; individual travelers need to wait for a group to fill. The larger **Huaca del Sol** is closed to visitors.

Archaeologists believe the Huaca de la Luna was the religious and ceremonial center of the Moche capital, while the Huaca del Sol was the administrative center. The two edifices are separated by 500m of open desert that once contained the dwellings and other buildings of the common residents.

While Huaca de la Luna is smaller than its neighbor, it proves that, in Moche pyramids at least, size isn't everything. The structure is riddled with rooms that contained ceramics and precious metals and are adorned with some of the beautiful polychrome friezes for which the Moche were famous. The *huaca* was built over six centuries to AD 600, with six succeeding generations expanding on it and completely covering the previous structure.

Archaeologists onion-skinning selected parts of the *huaca* have discovered that there are friezes of stylized figures on every level, some of which have been perfectly preserved by the later levels built around them.

If there's one must-see archaeological site in the region, this is it. Enthusiastic local guides will walk you through different parts of the complex and explain the richly colored motifs depicting Moche gods and zoomorphic figures, before leading you to the spectacular finale: the magnificent, richly decorated external wall. Don't even think of dropping out early. Many of the guides are volunteers, so tips are appreciated.

From the Huaca de la Luna site there are good views of the Huaca del Sol, which is the largest single pre-Columbian structure in Peru, though about a third of it has been washed away.

Around 600m from the Huaca de la Luna car park, the excellent **Museo Huacas de Moche** (☑ 044-60-0457; admission S5; ☺ 9am-4pm) is a fascinating and well-planned museum with three rooms of objects excavated from the site and explanations in Spanish and English. Visitors need to check in here to buy a ticket and schedule a tour before heading over to the Huaca de la Luna. Entry to the museum costs an additional S5, and it's well worth popping in while you wait for your tour departure.

Combis (S1.50) for the Huacas del Sol y de la Luna leave from Av Los Incas in Trujillo every 15 minutes or so. It's also possible to take a taxi (S15).

Huanchaco

☑ 044 / POP 68,100

This once-tranquil fishing hamlet, 12km outside Trujillo, woke up one morning to find itself a brightly highlighted paragraph on Peru's Gringo Trail. Its fame came in large part from the long, narrow reed boats you'll see lining the *malecón*. A small number of local fishers still use these age-old crafts, and you may even sight some surfing in with the day's catch. Though you can almost picture Huanchaco on postcards of days gone by, the beach is distinctly average. Nevertheless, the slow pace of life attracts a certain type of beach bum and the town has managed to retain much of its villagey appeal.

Today Huanchaco is happy to dish up a long menu of accommodations and dining options, and great waves for budding surfers. Come summertime, legions of local and foreign tourists descend on its lapping shores, and this fast-growing resort town makes a great base for exploring the ruins surrounding Trujillo.

🏃 Activities

The curving, gray-sand beach here is fine for swimming during the December to April summer, but expect serious teeth chatter during the rest of the year. The good surf, perfect for beginners, draws its fair share of followers and you'll see armies of bleached-blond surfer types ambling the streets with boards under their arms. Expect decent waves year-round.

You can rent surfing gear (S35 per day for a wetsuit and surfboard) from several places along the main drag. Lessons cost about S70 for a 1½-hour to two-hour session.

Muchik Surf School   SURFING
(☑ 044-63-3487; www.escueladetablamuchik.com; Independencia 100) Muchik is Huanchaco's longest-running surf school and is said to be the most reliable. It offers an 'if you don't stand, you don't pay' guarantee.

🛏 Sleeping

Most guesthouses are located at the southern end of town in the small streets running perpendicular to the beach. You can get discounts of up to 50% outside festival and holiday times, so be sure to ask.

★ Naylamp   GUESTHOUSE $
(☑ 044-46-1022; www.hostalnaylamp.com; Larco 1420; camping with/without tent rental S18/15, dm/s/d from S20/40/60; @ 🖥) At the northern end of Huanchaco, and top in the budget stakes, Naylamp has one building on the waterfront and a second, larger building behind the hotel. Great budget rooms share a spacious seaview patio, and the lush camping area has perfect sunset views. Kitchen, laundry service, hammocking zone and a cafe all included.

Moksha
HOSTEL $

(📞 973-713-628; La Ribera 224; dm/s/d from S15/45/50; 🛜) Right across the road from the water, this spacious hostel run by a hip young couple is a great place to hang out. Rooms are basic but homey and there are plenty of public places to chill, including a sea-view terrace and rear courtyard with open kitchen for guests. Offers surf and yoga classes and there's a vegetarian cafe.

Hotel Bracamonte
HOTEL $$

(📞 044-46-1162; www.hotelbracamonte.com.pe; Los Olivos 160; s/d incl breakfast from S120/165; @ 🛜 🏊) Popular, friendly, welcoming and secure behind high walls and a locked gate, the Bracamonte is one of the oldest of Huanchaco's nicer hotels and it remains one of the top choices. Nice gardens, a games room, barbecue, restaurant, bar and toddlers' playground make it great for families, and the executive rooms are probably the best maintained in Huanchaco.

Hotel Caballito de Totora
BOUTIQUE HOTEL $$

(📞 044-46-2636; www.hotelcaballitodetotora.com. pe; La Ribera 348; s/d/tr incl breakfast S145/205/290; ❄ @ 🛜 🏊) Bright modern rooms surrounding an inviting pool area make this professionally run place a top choice. The suites are the best single rooms in Huanchaco, decked in modern motifs that wouldn't be out of place in Miami. They offer perfect sea views, Jacuzzis, 100cm TVs and private patios to boot.

🍴 Eating

Not surprisingly, Huanchaco has oodles of seafood restaurants, especially near the *caballitos de tortora* (traditional indigenous reed boats) stacked at the north end of the beach.

Umi Sushi
SUSHI $

(📞 976-361-624; Las Orquideas 317; sushi S10.50-23; ⏰ 7-11pm Tue-Sun) Many of Huanchaco's better restaurants close early, but fortunately this great little sushi place, tucked away on a quiet road at the southern end of town, is here to cater to visitors looking for something different. It serves gourmet *makis* with a Peruvian twist – try the Spicy Kani made with avocado and shrimp covered in crab sauce.

★Restaurante Mococho
PERUVIAN, SEAFOOD $$

(www.facebook.com/restaurantemococho; Bolognesi 535; mains S36, whole fish per 1kg S110; ⏰ 1-3pm, closed Mon) This tiny place sits secluded in a walled garden where the legend of chef don Victor is carried on by his widow and son, Wen. It's not cheap, but it's fresh and excellent. The specialty is steamed whole fish in sauce, which is big enough to serve three. Come early – it closes once the fresh fish runs out.

★Restaurante Big Ben
PERUVIAN $$$

(📞 044-46-1378; www.bigbenhuanchaco.com; Larco 1184; mains S49-70; ⏰ 11:30am-5:30pm; 🛜) This sophisticated seafooder at the far north end of town specializes in lunchtime ceviches and is the best place in town for top-notch seafood. Though ceviche is the main draw, the menu is also heavy on fresh fish, *sudados* (seafood stews) and prawn dishes, all of which go down best on the 3rd-floor patio with ocean views.

🛈 Getting There & Away

Some bus companies have ticket agents in Huanchaco, but buses depart from Trujillo. *Combis* and yellow and red *micro* buses to Huanchaco frequently leave from Trujillo (S2). To return, just wait on the beachfront road for the bus as it comes back from the north end.

A taxi from Trujillo to Huanchaco should cost S18 to S20, and returning you should be able to get a cheaper ride as drivers are keen to get back to where the action is.

Chiclayo
📞 074 / POP 553,200

Spanish missionaries founded a small rural community on this site in the 16th century. Either by chance or through help from above, Chiclayo has prospered ever since. In one of the first sharp moves in Peruvian real estate, the missionaries chose a spot that sits at the hub of vital trade routes connecting the coast, the highlands and the deep jungle. Chiclayo's role as the commercial heart of the district has allowed it to overtake other once-vital organs of the region.

La Ciudad de la Amistad (The City of Friendship) holds a friendly, outstretched hand to the wayward venturer. While it's shaking hands in greeting, it will probably slip in a bold mix of unique regional dishes to tickle your taste buds. The town itself is pretty light on tourist attractions, but the dozens of tombs with Moche and Chimú archaeological booty surrounding the area should not be missed.

🛏 Sleeping

Hostal Sicán
HOTEL $

(📞 074-20-8741; hsican@hotmail.com; Izaga 356; s/d/tr incl breakfast S45/70/100; 🛜) This appealing pick has lots of polished wood and wrought iron, creating an illusion of grandeur. The rooms are small, comfortable and cool. All feature wood paneling as well as tasteful bits of art and a TV. A great choice, sitting on one of Chiclayo's most charming brick-lined streets.

Hotel Mochiks BOUTIQUE HOTEL **$$**
(📞074-20-6620; www.hotelmochiks.com; Tacna 615; s/d incl breakfast S165/210; ❄@🛜) This polished upstart made an immediate impression on the city's hotel scene, owing much of its success to a sense of style that was previously MIA. Tall and narrow, the lobby, cafe and 2nd-floor bar are decked out in chromes and moody reds, which contrast perfectly with the smallish but soothing beige-toned rooms.

Casa Andina Select Chiclayo HOTEL **$$$**
(📞074-23-4911; www.casa-andina.com; Villarreal 115; r/ste incl breakfast S803/1071; P❄@🛜🏊) The Peruvian boutique chain Casa Andina swooped in and gobbled up this aging relic, formerly the Gran Hotel Chiclayo. It's like a business hotel with an Andean pulse. There's a pleasant terrace and pool area, spa, fitness center and restaurant, plus modern, clean rooms that are sparkly new.

🍴 Eating

Chiclayo is one of the best places to eat on the North Coast. *Arroz con pato a la chiclayana* (duck and rice cooked in cilantro and beer) and *tortilla de manta raya* (Spanish omelet made from stingray) are endless sources of culinary pride. For dessert try the local street sweet called King Kong – a large cookie filled with a sweet caramel cream made of milk and sugar. It's available everywhere.

El Pescador SEAFOOD, PERUVIAN **$**
(San José 1236; mains S15-20; ⏰11:30am-5:30pm) This little locals' secret packs in the droves for outstanding seafood and regional dishes at fantastic prices. The ceviches are every bit as good as places charging double or even triple the price, and weekend specials such as *cabrito con frijoles* (goat with beans; Saturday) and *arroz con pato* (duck with rice; Sunday) are steals.

Mi Tia BURGERS **$**
(Aguirre 662; burgers S2-5, mains S13-44; ⏰8am-10pm) Lines run deep at this no-frills Peruvian haunt, where the burger stand draws legions of céntimo pinchers for burgers and sandwiches that are practically free if you take them away. Inside, sandwiches are pricier (S5 to S12), but you get them on a plate with salad and chips. Smiling staff also serve a long list of country staples.

⭐**Cafe 900** PERUVIAN **$$**
(www.cafe900.com; Izaga 900; mains S25-32; ⏰8am-11pm Mon-Thu, 1pm-1am Fri & Sat; 🛜) Live music, slowly spinning ceiling fans, exposed wood and adobe that connects you with the elements are the hallmarks of the best bar-cafe-restaurant in Chiclayo. It's certainly tops on ambience, and the food is simple, direct, unpretentious and affordable.

Fiesta Chiclayo Gourmet PERUVIAN **$$$**
(📞074-20-1970; www.restaurantfiestagourmet.com; Salaverry 1820; mains S40-90) Few things are as satisfying as scraping those last bits of slightly charred rice off the bottom of an iron-clad pan and savoring all that's great about a rice dish such as *arroz con pato a la chiclayana*, made here with farm-raised duck that must be a black-feathered quacker not a day over three months of age.

ℹ️ Information

EMERGENCY
Policía de Turismo (📞074-23-8658; Saenz Peña 830; ⏰24hr) Useful for reporting problems.

MONEY
BCP (Balta 630) Has 24-hour Visa and Master-Card ATMs.

TOURIST INFORMATION
iPerú (Edificio Municipal, cnr San José & Balta; ⏰9am-6pm Mon-Sat, to 1pm Sun) The best spot for tourist info in town; there's an additional office at the airport and one at the Museo Tumbas Reales de Sipán (p923) in Lambayeque. If it's closed, hit up the tour agencies.

ℹ️ Getting There & Around

AIR
The airport (CIX) is 1.5km east of town; a taxi ride there is S6. **LATAM** (📞074-27-4875; www.latam.com; Izaga 770) has five daily flights in each direction between Lima and Chiclayo, while **LC Peru** (📞074-27-1478; www.lcperu.pe; Tacna 578; ⏰9am-7pm Mon-Fri, to 1pm Sat) has fewer flights but can often be cheaper.

BUS
Cruz del Sur, Móvil Tours, Línea, Ittsa and Oltursa usually have the most comfortable buses and have their own terminals.

Cruz del Sur (📞080-11-1111; www.cruzdelsur.com.pe; Bolognesi 888) Has four departures to Lima between 8am and 8pm.

Línea (☑ 074-23-2951; Bolognesi 638) Has a comfortable Lima service at 7:30pm and regular services every couple of hours to Piura, in addition to buses to Cajamarca and Jaén.

Móvil Tours (☑ 01-716-8000; www.moviltours. com.pe; Bolognesi 199) Has three good Lima buses at 6:20pm, 6:30pm and 7pm; Tarapoto buses at 5pm and 6:30pm; a Cajamarca bus at 10:30pm; a Jaen bus at 11pm; and a Chachapoyas bus at 9pm.

Around Chiclayo

The countryside around Chiclayo is home to an immense wealth of archaeological sites, many of which have yet to be fully excavated. While many of the ruins are not as impressive as some other sites elsewhere in the north, the riches recovered from the tombs are absolutely magnificent and are now housed in several fantastic museums.

While busy Chiclayo is the most convenient base from which to explore the region, there are several more tranquil options, including a string of three peaceful beach towns – Puerto Etén, Santa Rosa and Pimentel – just a short drive away.

Lambayeque

☑ 074 / POP 47,900

About 11km north of Chiclayo, Lambayeque was once the main town in the area, but now plays second fiddle to Chiclayo. It's a pleasant enough town with narrow streets and some crumbling colonial buildings, but the main reason to stop is for a visit to the town's world-class museums, which are among the best in Peru.

Opened in November 2002, the **Museo Tumbas Reales de Sipán** (Museum of the Royal Tombs of Sipán; ☑ 074-28-3978, 074-28-3977; www.museotumbasreales.com; Vizcardo y Guzman 895; S10; ☺ 9am-5pm Tue-Sun) is the pride of northern Peru – as well it should be. With its burgundy pyramid construction rising gently out of the earth, it's a world-class facility specifically designed to showcase the marvelous finds from **Sipán** (Huaca Rajada; ☑ 978-977-622; museohrsipan@gmail.com; S8; ☺ 9am-5pm). Photography is not permitted and all bags must be checked.

The **Brüning Museum** (☑ 074-28-2110; www.museobruning.com; Huamachuco Cuadra 7; S8; ☺ 9am-5pm Tue-Sun), once the regional archaeological showcase, is now overshadowed by the Museo Tumbas Reales de Sipán, but it still houses an excellent collection of artifacts

from the Inca, Chimú, Moche, Lambayeque, Vicus and Chavín cultures, amassed by Hans Heinrich Brüning, after whom the museum is named. It is a good place to get an overview of the different groups that have inhabited the region.

Ferreñafe

The splendid **Museo Nacional Sicán** (☑ 074-28-6469; Av Batangrande Cuadra 9, ; S8; ☺ 9am-5pm Tue-Sun) displays replicas of the 12m-deep tombs found at the Sicán site at Batán Grande, among the largest tombs found in South America. Enigmatic burials were discovered within – the Lord of Sicán was buried upside down, in a fetal position, with his head separated from his body. Beside him were the bodies of two women and two adolescents, as well a sophisticated security system – the red *sinabrio* dust, toxic if inhaled – to ward off grave robbers.

Túcume

The **Túcume** (www.tucume.com; single/combined circuit S8/12; ☺ 8am-4:30pm) archaeological site, around 30km north of Lambayeque on the Panamericana, is not particularly well known, but it's the most impressive collection of ruins in the region. A vast area, with more than 200 hectares of crumbling walls, plazas and 26 pyramids, it was the final capital of the Sicán culture, who moved their city from nearby Batán Grande around AD 1050 after that area was devastated by the effects of El Niño.

Piura

☑ 073 / POP 755,500

After several hours of crossing the vast emptiness of the Sechura Desert, Piura materializes like a mirage on the horizon, enveloped in quivering waves of heat. It's hard to ignore the sense of physical isolation forced on you by this unforgiving environment – the self-sufficiency imposed upon early settlers may explain why they identify as Piuran rather than Peruvian.

Being so far inland, the scorching summer months will have you honing your radar for air-conditioning, as you seek out chilled venues in which to soothe sweltering skin. It's not a hugely attractive city, a fact not helped by severe flooding in 2017 that damaged some urban areas, but remnants of narrow cobbled streets and some charismatic colonial houses make up for the fact that there's little else for visitors to do here.

Its role as a hub for the northern towns means you'll probably end up spending some time here.

◎ Sights

Jirón Lima, a block east of the Plaza de Armas, has preserved its colonial character more than most areas in Piura.

🛏 Sleeping & Eating

Los Portales   HISTORIC HOTEL **$$$**
(📞 073-32-8887; www.losportaleshoteles.com.pe/hotel-piura; Libertad 875; r incl breakfast S440-660; 🅿@🛜🛝) This beautiful and fully refurbished colonial building on the Plaza de Armas delivers with its exquisite details. Handsome public areas with iron grillwork and black-and-white checkered floors lead to a poolside restaurant and rooms with large cable TV, minibar and great beds.

★ Bottega Capuccino   CAFE **$$**
(Santa Maria 287, Santa Isabel; breakfast S11-21, mains S18-40; ⊙ 9am-11pm Mon-Sat, 5-10pm Sun; 🛜) The real deal. This bright, modern cafe in bustling Santa Isabel, a 10-minute taxi from the center, offers wholesome breakfasts and gourmet sandwiches and salads that are great for lunch. It also serves more sophisticated fare for a fine night out with a bottle of wine at dinner and, for caffeine freaks, one of the best espressos (S6.50) in Piura.

ℹ Getting There & Around

AIR

The airport (PIU) is on the southeastern bank of the Río Piura, 2km from the city center. Schedules change often. An official taxi into town costs S15. Those hanging around outside charge about S10, although we don't recommend taking an unofficial taxi.

LATAM (📞 073-39-4379; www.latam.com; Centro Commercial Open Plaza, Tienda 51, 1era Nivel; ⊙ 10am-10pm Mon-Fri, to 2pm Sat) flies from Lima to Piura six times daily from 5am to 7:40pm, with return flights from 7am to 10pm. Often cheaper is **Peruvian Airlines** (📞 073-32-4206; www.peruvian.pe; Libertad 777; ⊙ 9am-7pm Mon-Fri, to 2pm Sat), which has a morning and afternoon flight between the two cities.

BUS

Several companies have offices on *cuadra* 1100 of Sánchez Cerro, though for Cajamarca and across the northern Andes, it's best to go to Chiclayo and get a connection there.

Civa (📞 073-33-1944; www.civa.com.pe; Loreto 1400) Has 4:15pm, 5pm and 5:30pm buses to Lima, frequent buses to Chulucanas and buses to Huancabamba at 10am and 6pm, the latter two leaving from **Terminal Terrestre Castilla** (Terminal El Bosque; Av Guardia Civil).

Cruz del Sur (📞 073-33-7094; www.cruzdelsur.com.pe; cnr Bolognesi & Lima) Comfortable Lima buses at 3pm, 5:30pm, 6:30pm and 7:30pm, as well as a lone shot to Trujillo at 3pm.

Eppo (📞 073-30-4543; www.eppo.com.pe; Panamericana Manzana 243) Services to Máncora every half hour from 5:30am to 7:15pm from its huge private station behind Real Plaza on the Panamericana.

Linea (📞 073-30-3894; www.linea.pe; Cerro 1215) Hourly buses to Chiclayo between 5am and 8pm, and a 1:30pm and 11pm bus to Trujillo.

Oltursa (📞 073-32-6666; www.oltursa.pe; Bolognesi 801) Runs some of the most comfortable buses to Lima, with regular departures between 4pm and 9:15pm from its centrally located terminal.

Máncora

📞 073 / POP 12,600

Máncora is *the* place to see and be seen along the Peruvian coast – in summer foreigners flock here to rub sunburned shoulders with the Peruvian jet set. It's not hard to see why – Peru's best sandy beach stretches for several kilometers in the sunniest region of the country, while dozens of plush resorts and their budget-conscious brethren offer up rooms just steps from the rolling waves. On shore most of the action is focused on the noisy main street, with plenty of good seafood restaurants and international flavors from which to choose.

The bathtub-warm waters and consistently good surf draw a sun-bleached, board-toting bunch, and raucous nightlife keeps visitors busy after the sun dips into the sea in a ball of fiery flames.

Year-round sun means this is one of the few resort towns on the coast that doesn't turn into a ghost town at less popular times.

🏄 Activities

Surf here is best from November to February, although good waves are found year-round and always draw dedicated surfers.

You can rent surfboards (per hour/day S10/20) from several places at the southern end of the beach in Máncora – in front of

ⓘ GETTING TO ECUADOR

La Tina

The border post of La Tina lacks accommodations, but the Ecuadorean town of Macará (3km from the border) has adequate facilities. La Tina is reached by *colectivos* (shared transportation; S12, 2½ hours) leaving from Sullana, 40km north of Piura, throughout the day. A better option is **Transporte Loja** (☑ 073-33-3260; Loreto 1241, Adentro Terminal Ronco), which has two daily buses from Piura (1pm and 9pm) that conveniently go straight through the border and on to Loja (S48, eight hours).

The border is the international bridge over the Río Calvas and is open 24 hours. Formalities are relaxed as long as your documents are all in order. There are no banks, though you'll find money changers at the border or in Macará. The Peruvian and Ecuadorean immigration offices share the same building on the bridge, which makes the crossing easy peasy.

Travelers entering Ecuador will find taxis (US$1) and *colectivos* (US$0.50) to take them to Macará.

Aguas Verdes

There are two integrated border facilities 3km apart on either side of the border at Pocitos/Huaquillas called Centro Binacional de Atención de Frontera (CEBAF). When leaving Peru you do not need to stop at the Peruvian facility, but rather go direct to the **CEBAF Ecuador office** (🕙 24hr) across the river (where guest Peruvian officials will give an exit stamp) then step a few metres over to have your passport stamped for Ecuador.

Very few nationalities need a visa, but exit tickets out of Ecuador and sufficient funds (US$20 per day) are legally required, although rarely asked for. Tourists are allowed only 90 days per year in Ecuador without officially extending their stay at a consulate.

You are strongly advised to take a direct bus across the border with a long-distance bus company such as **Cruz del Sur** (☑ 072-52-6200; www.cruzdelsur.com.pe; Tumbes 319), **Civa** (☑ 072-52-5120; www.civa.com.pe; Tumbes 518) or **Cifa** (☑ 972-894-619; www.cifainternacional.com; Tumbes 572). The slightly cheaper option is to take a *colectivo* or local bus to the border and switch busses after passing immigration.

Del Wawa is the most convenient. Classes are offered around town for S50 to S60 per hour, including equipment.

May through September offers the best kitesurfing in Máncora and there are several schools at the southern end of town.

★**Pacífico Adventures** WHALE WATCHING
(☑ 998-391-428; www.pacificoadventures.com; Rivera del Mar, 150m Sur del Muelle, Los Organos) A professionally run outfit that operates whale-watching tours leaving from Los Organos, a short drive south of Máncora. It uses good boats and carries submarine audio equipment to listen to the cetacean calls. Also offers bird-watching tours.

🛏 Sleeping

★**Loki del Mar** HOSTEL $$
(☑ 073-25-8484; www.lokihostel.com; Piura 262; dm S28-39, r S96, all incl breakfast; ❋@🛜🏊) Social butterflies flock to this mother of all beach hostels, which is really a self-contained resort masquerading as a backpackers' hangout. Tucked away in the whitewashed building

are spacious dorm rooms with extrawide beds and minimalist private rooms for those seeking a hostel vibe without the communal snoring.

Aloha Lina GUESTHOUSE $$
(☑ 982-732-284; linamollehuanca@gmail.com; 8 de Noviembre s/n; r S50-100; 🛜) Offering excellent value down a quiet alley just steps from the main beach, this small guesthouse has 11 spotless, fan-cooled rooms with fresh paint jobs set over two floors around a central courtyard. Rooms 6 to 8 on the top floor are the best, with windows on both sides that let in a breeze and glimpses of the sea.

★**Sunset Hotel** BOUTIQUE HOTEL $$$
(☑ 073-25-8111; www.sunsetmancora.com; Antigua Panamericana 196; r/tr incl breakfast S320/480; ❋🛜🏊) The intimate, boutique-styled Sunset wouldn't be out of place on the cover of a glossy travel mag. It has beautifully furnished interiors and great aqua-themed rock sculptures, while the good-sized rooms supply solid mattresses, hot showers, balconies and views of the seascape.

COLÁN

If you want to lose a few days in an authentic Peruvian beach town that foreigners haven't yet embraced, look no further than Colán, 15km north of Paita, Piura's main port.

Paita itself is a dusty, crumbling and unattractive port town that looks like it sprouted organically from the desert and has a roguish, Wild West feel to it, but as soon as Colán comes into view after you've turned off the main highway, you'll feel that often-lost sense of discovery.

Colán is home to the oldest colonial church in Peru (it looks like something out of a Cormac McCarthy novel), and the long beach is a trendy summer destination for the Peruvian jet set – and is practically deserted the rest of the year. The curving bay has a shallow beach that's excellent for swimming.

Casa de Playa   RESORT $$$

(☑073-25-8005; www.casadeplayamancora.net; Antigua Panamericana Km 1217, Playa Los Pocitas; r incl breakfast S495-560; P 🛜 🏊) This elegant and friendly place is popular with well-to-do Peruvians and offers up modern, slick dwellings with bamboo ceilings and warm tones opening onto private balconies. Half the room interiors are dressed in smoothed exposed concrete, which contrasts well with the plethora of colorful common areas – all are reached along lush corridors strewn with all manner of vibrant plants.

✖ Eating

Seafood rules the culinary roost in Máncora. Other ingredients tend to be pricier due to transportation costs. There are several mini-markets for self-caterers along the strip.

Green Eggs & Ham   BREAKFAST $

(The Bird House Centro Comercial, Pasaje 8 de Noviembre; meals S12-18; ⊙7:30am-4:30pm) There's nothing silly about this Dr Seuss–inspired breakfast spot, which counts a battalion of gringo fans for its homesick-remedy breakfasts (pancakes, French toast, hash browns). Yes, you'll like them Sam I Am, but the real coup is the 2nd-floor patio – with a view through a thatch of tall palms to the crashing waves.

★ Donde Teresa   PERUVIAN $$

(☑073-25-8702; Antigua Panamericana Km 1217, Hotelier; mains S28-38; ⊙noon-9pm; 🛜) Before Gastón Acurio there was Teresa Ocampo, Peru's most recognizable celebrity chef (famous before Peruvian food was even famous). She lives in Texas now, but her son, Javier, keeps the dream alive with gourmet takes on Peruvian classics served overlooking Los Pocitas Beach.

★ La Sirena d'Juan   PERUVIAN $$

(☑073-25-8173; Piura 316; mains S40-45; ⊙noon-3pm & 6-11pm Wed-Mon; 🛜) Local boy done good Juan has turned his intimate little main-drag seafooder into northern Peru's best restaurant. Yellowfin tuna fresh from Máncora's waters is the showstopper, whether it's prepared as a *tiradito* (a sort of Peruvian sashimi) in yellow curry or grilled with a mango-*rocoto*-red pepper chutney.

ℹ Information

Oficina de Turismo (Piura s/n, Edificio Municipal; ⊙8am-3:45pm) Lacks resources and isn't as useful as the government-run iPerú tourist centers, but this office run by the local government will try to answer your questions if possible.

ℹ Getting There & Away

Many bus offices are in the center, though most southbound trips originate in Tumbes.

Cifa (☑941-816-863; www.cifainternacional.com; Grau 313) Cheap daily buses to Guayaquil (S65) and Cuenca (S65) in Ecuador.

Civa (☑014-18-1111; www.excluciva.pe; Piura 472) Has an economical 3:30pm service to Lima, as well as nicer buses at 5:30pm and 6:30pm. Also has a midnight bus to Guayaquil.

Cruz del Sur (☑0-801-11111; www.cruzdelsur.com.pe; Grau 208) Has *bus-cama* (bed bus) services to Lima at 5pm and 5:30pm; buses to Trujillo and Chimbote on Tuesday, Wednesday, Friday and Saturday at 10:30pm; and you can catch its Guayaquil-bound bus from Lima at 9am on Monday, Tuesday, Thursday and Saturday.

El Dorado (☑073-25-8161; www.transportes eldorado.com.pe; Grau 198) Six buses a day to Piura between 9:30am and 9:30pm, as well as buses for Chiclayo (9:30am, 9:30pm, 11:30pm and midnight) and Trujillo (9:30am, 9:30pm and 11pm). A Tumbes-bound bus also grabs passengers seven times a day.

Oltursa (☐017-08-5000; www.oltursa.pe; Grau 505; ☎) Lima *bus-cama* (with wi-fi) at 5pm and 5:30pm. Has a direct bus to Trujillo at 10pm.

HUARAZ & THE CORDILLERAS

Ground zero for outdoor-adventure worship in Peru, the Cordilleras are one of the preeminent hiking, trekking and backpacking spots in South America. Wherever you throw your gaze, perennially frozen white peaks razor their way through expansive mantles of lime-green valleys. In the recesses of these prodigious giants huddle scores of pristine jade lakes, ice caves and torrid springs. The Cordillera Blanca is one of the highest mountain ranges in the world outside the Himalayas, and its 18 ostentatious summits of more than 6000m will not let you forget it for a second.

Huaraz

☐043 / POP 127,000 / ELEV 3091M

Huaraz is the restless capital of this Andean adventure kingdom and its rooftops command exhaustive panoramas of the city's dominion: one of the most impressive mountain ranges in the world. Nearly wiped out by the earthquake of 1970, Huaraz isn't going to win any Andean-village beauty contests anytime soon, but it does have personality – and personality goes a long way.

This is first and foremost a trekking metropolis. During high season the streets buzz with hundreds of backpackers and adventurers freshly returned from arduous hikes or planning their next expedition as they huddle in one of the town's many fine watering holes. Dozens of outfits help plan trips, rent equipment and organize a list of adventure sports as long as your arm. An endless lineup of quality restaurants and hopping bars keep

Huaraz & the Cordilleras

the belly full and the place lively till after the tents have been put away. Mountain adventures in the off-season can be equally rewarding, but the vibe is more subdued and some places go into hibernation once the rains set in.

◉ Sights

Monumento Nacional Wilkahuaín RUINS
(adult/student S5/2; ⊙9am-5pm Tue-Sun) This small Wari ruin about 8km north of Huaraz is remarkably well preserved, dating from about AD 600 to 900. It's an imitation of the temple at Chavín done in the Tiwanaku style (square temples on raised platforms). Wilka-

huaín means 'grandson's house' in Quechua. The three-story temple has seven rooms on each floor, each originally filled with bundles of mummies. The bodies were kept dry using a sophisticated system of ventilation ducts. A one-room museum gives some basic background information in English and Spanish.

⋀ Activities

Trekking & Mountaineering

Whether you're arranging a mountain expedition or going for a day hike, Huaraz is the place to start – it is the epicenter for

Huaraz

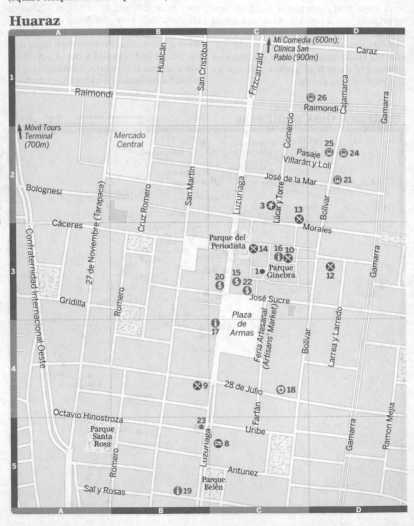

planning and organizing local Andean adventures. Numerous outfits can prearrange entire trips so that all you need to do is show up at the right place at the right time. Many visitors go camping, hiking and climbing in the mountains without any local help and you can too if you have the experience. Just remember, though, that carrying a backpack full of gear over a 4800m pass requires much more effort than hiking at low altitudes.

★ **Quechuandes** TREKKING
(☎ 943-386-147; www.quechandes.com; Santa Gadea 995; ⊙ 9am-8pm Mon-Sat, from 11am Sun) A very well organized agency that gets rave

reviews for its quality guides and ethical approach to treks. Management will assess your level before sending you out into the mountains or renting gear, to ensure you are up to the task. In addition to offering treks, summit expeditions and mountaineering courses, its staff are experts in rock climbing and bouldering.

★ **Eco Ice Peru** TREKKING
(www.ecoice-peru.com; Figueroa 1185; 3- to 4-day treks from US$240; ⊙ 8am-6pm) Run by a gregarious and passionate young guide, this agency gets top reviews from travelers for its customer service, guides, *arrieros* (mule drives) and food. Treks often end with a dinner at the owner's pad in Huaraz.

Huaraz

PERU HUARAZ

Andean Kingdom ADVENTURE

(☎944-913-011; www.andeankingdomhuaraz.com; Parque Ginebra; climbing trips from S120; ⊙9am-9pm Mon-Sat) A laid-back but enthusiastic agency offering day courses for aspiring climbers, logistical support for experts and the usual day excursions, with an obvious bias toward climbing trips (Los Olivos and Hatun Machay feature highly).

Rock Climbing

Rock climbing is one of the Cordillera Blanca's biggest pastimes and its popularity is growing. Huaraz is an ideal place to plan excursions, rent gear and set off from on day trips. There are good climbs for beginners at Chancos, while the Los Olivos area has the most varied routes and is located conveniently close to Huaraz. Avid climbers will find some gnarly bolted sport climbs at Recuay and Hatun Machay, located 30km and 70km south of Huaraz respectively. For some big-wall action that will keep you chalked up for days, head to the famous Torre de Parón, known locally as the Sphinx. Most trekking tour agencies offer climbing trips, for both beginners and advanced climbers, as part of their repertoire. Many also rent gear. No serious climber should leave base camp without a copy of *Huaraz: The Climbing Guide* (2014) by David Lazo and Marie Timmermans, with detailed descriptions of over 1000 climbing routes backed up with photos and color-coded maps.

Mountain Biking

★ Mountain Bike Adventures MOUNTAIN BIKING

(☎972-616-008; www.chakinaniperu.com; Lúcar y Torre 530, 2nd fl; 2-day tours from US$380; ⊙9am-1pm & 3-8pm) Mountain Bike Adventures has been in business for well over a decade and receives repeat visits from mountain bikers for its decent selection of bikes, knowledgeable and friendly service, and good safety record. It offers guided tours, ranging from an easy five-hour cruise to 12-day circuits around the Cordillera Blanca.

Involved owner, Julio, is a lifelong resident of Huaraz who speaks English and will tailor-make a trip for your specific requirements. No one knows the region's single-track possibilities better than he does.

☞ Tours

All activity within Parque Nacional Huascarán – whether mountaineering or hiking – technically requires that you are accompanied by a certified guide, although in practice this is not enforced at most park entrances. Even so, it is well worth taking a guide even for nontechnical activities as conditions change rapidly in the mountains and altitude sickness can seriously debilitate even experienced hikers. Furthermore, a good guide will ensure you see things you otherwise may have missed.

All guides must be licensed by the Peruvian authorities and registered with the national-parks office. Mountaineers and trekkers should check out Casa de Guías (p932), the headquarters of the Mountain Guide Association of Peru. It maintains a list of its internationally certified guides, all of whom are graduates of a rigorous training program. Bear in mind that international certification is not necessary to work in the park; there are also some excellent independent guides from other associations certified to work in the region.

Many agencies arrange full trekking and climbing expeditions that include guides, equipment, food, cooks, porters and transportation. Depending on the number of people, the length of your trip and what's included, expect to pay from under S100 for an easy day out to up to S750 for more technical mountains per person per day. Try not to base your selection solely on price, as you often get what you pay for. Do your research; things change, good places go bad and bad places get good.

One of the best resources for guides in Huaraz is other travelers who have just come back from a trek and can recommend (or not recommend) their guides based on recent experience. The South American Explorers Club in Lima is also an excellent source of information and maps.

🛏 Sleeping

El Jacal Backpacker HOSTAL $

(☎043-23-2924; www.eljacalhostel.com; 28 de Julio 1066; dm S40, dS130, s/d without bathroom S65/100; P🐾🗐) A kind of cross between a *hostal* (guesthouse) and hostel, the 'Backpacker' is run by the same family as the wonderful El Jacal Classic (☎043-42-4612; José Sucre 1044; s/d incl breakfast S80/105; 🗐), meaning you get warm welcomes, ultraclean rooms and simple but very comfortable decor. There are dorm rooms available here, but also some doubles with private bathroom, plus a lovely lounge, modern kitchen and free parking.

★ Albergue Churup HOSTEL $$

(☎043-42-4200; www.churup.com; Figueroa 1257; dm S45, s/d incl breakfast S120/185; @🗐) This immensely popular family-run hostel has spick-and-span rooms with sharp color accents and plenty of bright space, plus invitingly comfortable lounging areas on *every* floor. The building is topped by a massive, fireplace-warmed lounge space with magnificent 180-degree views of the Cordillera.

Hotel San Sebastián HOTEL $$
(☑043-42-6960; www.sansebastianhuaraz.com; Italia 1124; s/d incl breakfast S180/218; @ 🛜) A fetching white-walled and red-roofed urban sanctuary, this four-story hotel is a neocolonial architectural find. Balconies and arches overlook a grassy garden and inner courtyard with a soothing fountain, and all rooms have a writing desk, good beds, hot shower and cable TV. Most have balconies too. If you want something more stylish than your typical posthiking Huaraz crash pad, indulge here.

La Aurora HOTEL $$
(☑043-42-6824; www.hotelaurorahuaraz.com; Luzuriaga 915; s/d/tr incl breakfast from S120/220 /310; 🛜) A midrange traveler's favorite, the Aurora makes a pleasant bookend to a trekking trip where you can wash the dust from your hair (with hot water) and sink deservedly into a soft, comfortable bed. Bright upgraded rooms feature wooden floors, luxurious bathrooms with marble sinks, and flourishes of local flavor such as straw lampshades and woven bedspreads.

★**Cuesta Serena** BOUTIQUE HOTEL $$$
(☑981-400-038; www.cuestaserena.pe; via Carhuaz, Anta; r incl 2 meals from S870) Out near the airport, this high-end hotel is a great place to stay to avoid the noise of Huaraz while remaining accessible to transportation and local attractions. The elegant rooms with subtle Peruvian touches are set in lovely manicured gardens, which offer fantastic views of Huascarán and its Cordillera siblings. The balance between luxury and homeliness is perfectly maintained.

★**Lazy Dog Inn** LODGE $$$
(☑943-789-330; www.thelazydoginn.com; Km 3, Cachipampa Alto; s US$79-139, d US$99-159, all incl breakfast & dinner; @ 🛜) 🐾 Run by rugged and proud Canadians Diana and Wayne, this deluxe ecolodge steeped in sustainable and community tourism is at the mouth of the Quebrada Llaca, 8km east of Huaraz. It's made entirely of adobe and built by hand. You can either stay in comfortable double rooms in the main lodge or in fancier private cabins, with fireplaces and bathtubs.

 Eating

★**Manka** PERUVIAN, ITALIAN $
(☑043-23-4306; Bautista 840; menú S10; ☺8:30am-11pm) If you were curious about what happens when Peruvian *cocina* (cuisine) collides with Italian *cucina* then, let us tell you, it's a taste worth savoring. For proof, head straight to this simply decorated restaurant whose mix-and-match menu can deliver bruschetta for starters, *lomo saltado* (strips of beef stir-fried with onions, tomatoes, potatoes and chili) for a main and a delectable chocolate mousse for desert.

California Café BREAKFAST $
(www.huaylas.com; Jiron 28 de Julio 562; breakfast S15-25; ☺7:30am-6:30pm, to 2pm Sun; 🛜 🍴) Managed by a Californian, this hip traveler magnet does breakfasts at any time, plus light lunches and salads. It's a funky, chilled space to while away many hours with a library of ancient guidebooks, well-used sofas, a sublime world-music collection and usually plenty of backpacks spread across the floor.

★**Mi Comedia** ITALIAN $$
(☑043-58-7954; Centenario 351; mains S22-38; ☺5-11pm Mon-Sat) Many restaurants claim great pizzas with some even uttering the word 'Naples' blasphemously in the description. But at Mi Comedia the Italian boasts are no exaggeration. This is about as Neapolitan as a pizza can get in Peru without the DOC Campania ingredients.

Café Andino CAFE $$
(www.cafeandino.com; Lúcar y Torre 530, 3rd fl; breakfast S8-24, mains S18-35; ☺9am-10pm; 🛜 🍴) This modern top-floor cafe has space and light in spades, comfy lounges, art, photos, fireplace, books and groovy tunes – it's the ultimate South American traveler hangout. You can get breakfast anytime (Belgian waffles, huevos rancheros), and snacks you miss (nachos). It's also the best place in town for information about trekking in the area.

Trivio INTERNATIONAL $$
(☑043-22-0416; Parque del Periodista; mains S21-37; ☺8am-midnight) 🐾 Cementing a three-way marriage of craft beer, micro-roasted coffee and food made with local ingredients, Trivio joins a few Huaraz restaurants that wouldn't be alien in Lima. The decor is North America hip, the clientele predominantly gringo, and the food clever enough to excite the taste buds but filling enough to cover the hole left by your recent four-day trek.

PERU HUARAZ

Chili Heaven
INDIAN, THAI **$$**

(Parque Ginebra; mains S17-35; ⊘noon-11pm) Whether you send your appetite to India or Thailand, the fiery curries at this hot spot will seize your taste buds upon arrival, mercilessly shake them up and then spit them back out the other side as if you've died and gone to chili heaven (hence the name).

Rinconcito Mineiro
PERUVIAN **$$**

(Morales 757; menú S8-16, mains S12-35; ⊘7am-11pm; 🛜) This popular place is *the* spot to tuck into homey and cheap Peruvian daily *menús* (set meals). The daily blackboard of 10 or so options includes an excellent *lomo saltado* (strips of beef stir-fried with onions, tomatoes, potatoes and chili), plus grilled trout, *tacu-tacu* (a Peruvian fusion dish of rice, beans and a protein) and the like.

La Casona Huaracina
PERUVIAN **$$$**

(📞43-39-6420; Campos 735; mains S22-42; ⊘11am-10pm) The colonial architectural style is noticeably absent in Huaraz until you step into the sparkling new Huaracina, the clever designers of which have drawn inspiration from the graceful buildings of Arequipa. The business is split into three interconnecting spaces: a smart lounge bar, a *pasteleria* (pastry shop) and the restaurant, all decked out with astute attention to detail.

🍷 Drinking & Nightlife

★ Los 13 Buhos
BAR

(Parque Ginebra; ⊘11am-2am) Halfway up some monstrous Andean pass with a 15kg pack on your back, it's not uncommon to start dreaming of 13 Buhos with its Luchos craft beer, pool table and delectable afternoon 'snacks'.

ℹ️ Information

DANGERS & ANNOYANCES

Time to acclimatize is important. The altitude here will make you feel breathless and may give you a headache during your first few days, so don't overexert yourself. The surrounding mountains will cause altitude sickness if you venture into them without spending a few days acclimatizing in Huaraz first.

Huaraz is a generally safe city that experiences little crime. However, there has been a small spike in robberies of tourists on the periphery of town in recent years, especially in the area of the Mirador de Retaqeñua and the Wilkahuaín ruins. Stay alert in these areas and walk with a group or hire a taxi to avoid problems.

Always check for safety updates when you arrive in town. The **Policìa de Turismo** (📞043-42-1341; Luzuriaga 724; ⊘24hr) and iPeru offices are good places to inquire.

EMERGENCY
National Police (28 de Julio)

MEDICAL SERVICES
Clínica San Pablo (📞043-42-8811; Huaylas 172; ⊘24hr) North of town, this is the best medical care in Huaraz. Some doctors speak English.

MONEY
These banks have ATMs and will exchange US dollars and euros.

Banco de la Nación (Luzuriaga 653; ⊘8am-5:30pm Mon-Fri, 9am-1pm Sat)

BCP (Luzuriaga 691; ⊘9am-6pm Mon-Fri, to 1pm Sat)

Interbank (José Sucre 320; ⊘9am-6pm Mon-Fri, to 1pm Sat)

TOURIST INFORMATION
Casa de Guías (📞043-42-1811; www.agmp. pe; Parque Ginebra 28G; ⊘9am-1pm & 4-8pm Mon-Fri, 8am-noon Sat) Runs mountain safety and rescue courses and maintains a list of internationally certified guides. Also mounts rescue operations to assist climbers in emergencies. If you are heading out on a risky ascent, it's worth consulting with them first.

iPerú (📞043-42-8812; iperuhuaraz@promperu. gob.pe; Pasaje Atusparia, Oficina 1, Plaza de Armas; ⊘9am-6pm Mon-Sat, to 1pm Sun) Has general tourist information but little in the way of trekking info.

ℹ️ Getting There & Away

AIR
The Huaraz **airport** (ATA) is actually at Anta, 23km north of town. A taxi will cost about S40.

LC Perú (📞043-42-4734; www.lcperu.pe; Luzuriaga 904; ⊘9am-7pm Mon-Fri, to 6pm Sat) is currently the only company offering service, with flights to/from Lima (US$120, one hour) on Tuesdays, Thursdays and Saturdays. Flights leave in the morning, but they are often cancelled at short notice.

BUS
Huaraz has no central bus station. Rather buses leave from different company offices, most of which are located in and around Raimondi and Bolívar streets a couple of blocks north of the Plaza de Armas.

A plethora of companies have departures for Lima. The top four for comfort and reliability are Cruz del Sur, Oltursa, Linea and Movil Tours.

Many small companies with well-used, beat-up buses cross the Cordillera Blanca to the towns east of Huaraz.

LAGUNA PARÓN

Silent awe enters people's expressions when they talk of **Laguna Parón** (S5). Nestled at 4185m above sea level, along a bumpy road 25km east of Caraz, and surrounded by spectacular snow-covered peaks, this lake is heralded by many as the most beautiful in the Cordillera Blanca. It is certainly the largest, despite its water levels being lowered from 75m to 15m in the mid-1980s to prevent a collapse of Huandoy's moraine.

Ringed by formidable peaks, Parón offers close-up views of Pirámide de Garcilaso (5885m), Huandoy (6395m), Chacraraju (6112m) and several 1000m granite rock walls. The challenging rock-climbing wall of Torre de Parón, known as the Sphinx, is also found here.

A trail rambles along the lake's north shore on flat terrain for about two hours and then up the valley to another smaller lake and the foot of Artesonraju. There is also a steep climb to a mirador that could prove difficult if you haven't acclimatized to the thin air. If you go on your own, note that it's not possible to circumnavigate the lake – the northern side is fine, but on the southern side there is a very dangerous section where the path disappears and slippery vegetation grows flush against the mountain surface. The potential for falls is huge and foreigners have died attempting to cross here.

Most people see the lake as part of an organized tour out of Huaraz or Caraz (from S50). Going solo, you can organize a taxi in Caraz for around S150 round-trip with wait. The journey from Caraz takes 1½ hours on an unpaved road.

Despite being inside the national park, Parón falls under a separate justification and is run by a local community group who charge S5 admission.

Cruz del Sur (☑ 043-42-8726; Bolívar 491) Has 11am and 10pm luxury nonstop services to Lima (S35 to S75, eight hours). Arguably, the most comfortable and reliable buses.

Línea (☑ 043-42-6666; Bolívar 450) Has excellent buses to Lima (S35 to S80, eight hours, twice daily) and Trujillo (S30 to S55, seven hours, once daily).

Movil Tours (www.moviltours.com.pe; Bolívar 452) Buses to Lima (S35 to S135, eight hours, 10 daily), Chimbote (S40 to S60, five hours, one daily) and Trujillo (S45 to S75, seven hours, two daily). They leave from a **terminal** (☑ 043-42-2555; www.moviltours.com.pe; Confraternidad Internacional Oeste 451) 1.5km northwest of the Plaza de Armas.

Oltursa (☑ 043-42-3717; www.oltursa.pe; Raimondi 825) One daily ultracomfortable Lima-bound bus at 12:15pm (S60 to S90, eight hours).

Parque Nacional Huascarán

Peruvian mountaineer César Morales Arnao first suggested protecting the flora, fauna and archaeological sites of the Cordillera Blanca in the early 1960s, but it didn't become a reality until 1975, when the national park was established. This 3400-sq-km park encompasses practically the entire area of the Cordillera Blanca above 4000m, including more than 600 glaciers and nearly 300 lakes, and protects such extraordinary and endangered species as the giant *Puya raimondii* plant, the spectacled bear and the Andean condor.

Visitors to the park can register (bring your passport) and pay the park fee at the **park office** (☑ 043-42-2086; www.sernanp.gob.pe; Sal y Rosas 555; ⊙ 8:30am-1pm & 2:30-6pm Mon-Fri) in Huaraz, although most of the main entrances to the park also sell tickets. Fees are S30 per person for a day visit, S60 for a three-day visit and S150 for a month.

Note, the park doesn't include the Cordillera Huayhuash, which are protected in a separate reserve.

🏃 Activities

⭐ **Santa Cruz Trek** TREKKING
(national park pass S60) The Santa Cruz is one of South America's classic multiday treks: lightly trodden, spectacular from start to finish, and achievable by anyone of decent fitness who's had adequate time to acclimatize. Running for 45km through the Cordillera Blanca between the villages of Vaqueria and Cashapampa, the trek takes hikers along the verdant Quebrada Huarípampa, over the (literally) dizzying Punta Union Pass (4760m) and down through the deeply gouged Quebrada Santa Cruz Valley.

Unlike the Inca trail, no permit system exists for the Santa Cruz, plus you can undertake it solo without a guide (although many Huaraz agencies offer the trip). The trail can be hiked in either direction but the easiest and recommended route is to head east–west from Vaqueria to Cashapampa. By starting in Vaqueria, you avoid a grueling, hot and dusty ascent at the very beginning of the hike. Finishing in Cashapampa leaves you with more transport options at the end.

Head-turning sights along the way include emerald lakes, sensational views of many of the Cordillera's peaks, beds of brightly colored alpine wildflowers and stands of red *qeñua* (Polylepis) trees.

★ Laguna Churup   HIKING
The hamlet of Pitec (3850m), just above Huaraz, is the official start for this six-hour 7km round-trip hike to drop-dead gorgeous Laguna Churup (4450m) at the base of Nevado Churup.

Laguna 69   HIKING
This vivid blue lake surrounded by snow-covered peaks is the jewel of the Cordilleras. Set at 4600m, it's a challenging acclimatization hike (we recommend working up to it with an easier hike at altitude). 'Sixty-nine' is most commonly visited as a day trip from Huaraz and has become increasingly popular in recent years. Don't expect to have the place to yourself. Swimming in the lake is prohibited.

Los Cedros-Alpamayo   TREKKING
This is one of the more dazzling and demanding treks of the Cordillera Blanca and an alternative to the epic Huayhuash circuit further south. There are numerous variations, from seven- to 14 day itineraries, measuring 90km to 120km in length, so study the options carefully before you set out.

NORTHERN HIGHLANDS

Vast tracts of unexplored jungle and mist-shrouded mountain ranges guard the secrets of the Northern Highlands like a suspicious custodian. Here, Andean peaks and a blanket of luxuriant forests stretch from the coast all the way to the deepest Amazonian jungles. Interspersed with the relics of Inca kings and the jungle-encrusted ruins of cloud-forest-dwelling warriors, connections to these outposts are just emerging from their infancy.

Cajamarca's cobbled streets testify to the beginning of the end of the once-powerful Inca Empire, and remnants of the work of the famed Andean masons still remain. The hazy forests of Chachapoyas have only recently revealed their archaeological bounty: witness the staggering stone fortress of Kuélap, which clings for dear life to a craggy limestone peak. At the jungle gateway of Tarapoto, the Amazon waits patiently on the periphery, as it has for centuries, endowed with a cornucopia of wildlife and exquisite good looks.

Cajamarca

♫ 076 / POP 249,000 / ELEV 2750M

A dainty but strong-willed metropolis, Cajamarca is cradled in a languid valley and stonewalled by brawny mountains in every direction. The most important town in the Northern Highlands, its mushroom field of red-tile-roofed abodes surely confesses a secret desire to cling to its village roots. Fertile farmland carpets the entire valley and Cajamarca's streets belong as much to the wide-brimmed-hat-wearing *campesinos* (peasants) bundled in brightly colored scarves as they do to the young city slickers who frequent the town's boutique restaurants and bars.

In the colonial center, majestic churches border the capacious Plaza de Armas. From here, once-decadent baroque mansions spread out along the narrow streets, many housing elegant hotels and fine restaurants. Cajamarca is famous for its cheese, gold (one of the world's largest mines lies nearby), baroque churches – and as the place where Inca emperor Atahualpa faced off against the Spanish conquistadors. It's a potent brew.

⊙ Sights

El Complejo de Belén   HISTORIC BUILDING
(cnr Belén & Comercio; S5; ⊙ 9am-1pm & 3-8pm Tue & Wed, 9am-8pm Thu-Sat, 9am-1pm Sun) Construction of this sprawling colonial complex, comprising a church and hospital made entirely from volcanic rock, occurred between 1627 and 1774. The hospital was run by nuns and 31 tiny, cell-like bedrooms line the walls of the T-shaped building. The baroque church next door is one of Cajamarca's finest and has a prominent cupola and a well-carved pulpit. Art exhibitions usually adorn the interior.

El Cuarto del Rescate   RUINS
(Ransom Chamber; Puga; S5; ⊙ 9am-1pm & 3-8pm Tue & Wed, 9am-8pm Thu-Sat, 9am-1pm Sun) The Ransom Chamber, the only Inca building still standing in Cajamarca, is where Inca ruler Atahualpa was imprisoned. The small room has three trapezoidal doorways and a few similarly shaped niches in the inner walls –

Cajamarca

Cajamarca

⊙ Sights
1 El Complejo de Belén................................B3
2 El Cuarto del Rescate C3
3 Iglesia de San Francisco.........................C2

⊜ Sleeping
4 Hospedaje los Jazmines.........................C2
5 Hotel Cajamarca B3
6 Hotel Sol de Belén C3

⊗ Eating
7 Cascanuez Café Bar B2

8 El Marengo...B3
9 Paprika B2

⊙ Drinking & Nightlife
10 Usha-Usha..A1

ⓘ Information
11 iPerú A3
12 LC Perú..B3
13 Scotiabank..C2

signature Inca construction. Visitors are not permitted to enter the room, but from outside it's possible to observe the red line marking the original ceiling of the structure – the point to which it was to be filled with treasure to secure Atahualpa's release.

Iglesia de San Francisco   CHURCH, MUSEUM
(Calle 2 de Mayo; S5; ⊙ museum 10am-2pm & 4-6pm, church 10am-2pm & 5-8pm) Outgunning the cathedral on Plaza de Armas is this elaborate church with striking stone carvings and decadent altars. Unlike other illustrious Cajamarca churches, the San Francisco has two belfries. It houses the slightly dog-eared **Museo de Arte Religioso** full of 17th-century religious paintings by indigenous artists. The

museum includes some creepy catacombs – in one room you'll see the orderly tombs of monks, and in another are skeletons recovered from indigenous graves found at the site, lying bare and without ceremony.

🎊 Festivals & Events

Carnaval   FESTIVAL
The Peru-wide pageantry of Carnaval is celebrated at the beginning of Lent, usually in February. Not all Carnavals are created equal, however. Ask any Peruvian where the wildest celebrations are, and Cajamarca will invariably come up trumps. The festival here is nine days of dancing, eating, singing, partying, costumes, parades and general rowdy mayhem.

DAY TRIPS FROM CAJAMARCA

Plaza de Armas is ringed by tour agencies all offering pretty much the same full- and half-day trips. Many companies claim to have English-speaking guides, but, as most tourism in these parts is Peruvian, the reality is a little different.

Tours (S20) to Cumbemayo run from 9am to 1:30pm daily, meaning you can squeeze in a 3:30pm to 7pm tour (S17) to the Ventanillas de Otuzco in the afternoon. Tours (S70) to the ruins of Kuntur Wasi take all day, but run less frequently. Check ahead of time.

There are several other half-day tours to cheese factories, mini zoos (containing most- ly domesticated animals) and local lakes, all costing in the vicinity of S20.

Ventanillas de Otuzco (S5; ⊙ 9am-6pm) This pre-Inca necropolis has scores of funer- ary niches built into the hillside, hence the name *ventanillas* (windows). Set in alluring countryside, 8km northeast of Cajamarca, the site is easily walkable from either Caja- marca or Los Baños del Inca (ask for directions). Alternatively, *combis* (minibuses) to Ventanillas de Otuzco (S1, 20 minutes) leave frequently from the corner of Jirón Los Gladiolos and Jirón Tayabamba, north of the Plaza de Armas in Cajamarca.

Kuntur Wasi (adult/child S5/1; ⊙ 9am-5:30pm Tue-Sun) Perched on a mountaintop over- looking the small town of San Pablo, these seldom-visited pre-Inca ruins are well worth the trip from Cajamarca. The site is considered one of the cradles of Andean culture; four distinct cultures used the area for their ceremonies, with the first constructions taking place around 1100 BC. The main structure is a large U-shaped temple consisting of three elevated platforms around which are located numerous tombs.

Cumbemayo (S8) Cumbemayo (derived from the Quechua *kumpi mayo*, meaning 'well-made water channel') is an astounding feat of pre-Inca engineering. These perfectly smooth aqueducts were carved around 2000 years ago and zigzag at right angles for 9km, for a purpose that is as yet unclear, since Cajamarca has an abundant water supply. Other rock formations are carved to look like altars and thrones. Nearby caves contain petro- glyphs, including some that resemble woolly mammoths. The site is located about 20km southwest of Cajamarca.

🛏 Sleeping

Hotel Sol de Belén   HOTEL $$

(☎ 076-36-2196; www.hotelsoldebelen.com; Belén 636; s/d incl breakfast S100/135; 🅿 🕸 🛜) The 'Sol' mixes smart rooms with an old-town Ca- jamarca feel – and a perfect location on a pedestrian street opposite the Complejo de Belén (p934). Quiet rooms are set back from the road and come with good lighting along with customized sheets and towels. Bonus: there's a small gym on the top floor.

Hospedaje los Jazmines   HOTEL $$

(☎ 076-36-1812; Amazonas 775; s/d/tr S60/90/120, without bathroom S50/70/90; @ 🛜) 💋 In a land of ubiquitous colonial court- yards, this friendly inn is a value standout. Compared to Cajamarca's grander man- sions, the Jazmines appears a little quaint- er, more intimate and more lived-in. Small rooms set around a lush garden are simple but comfortable. The hotel's profits help sus- tain an orphanage for special-needs children in Los Baños del Inca.

Hotel Cajamarca   HISTORIC HOTEL $$$

(☎ 076-36-2532; www.hotelcajamarca.com.pe; Calle 2 de Mayo 311; s/d incl breakfast S180/250; @ 🛜) The grand covered courtyard with its soft set- tees makes a perfect introduction, while the sleek rooms with parquet floors, crisp duvets and shiny bathrooms give an encouraging second impression. Obviously designed by someone with an eye for function *and* history, the Cajamarca strikes a good balance between modernity and colonial character.

🍴 Eating

★ Cascanuez Café Bar   CAFE $

(☎ 076-36-6089; Puga 554; cakes S7.50; ⊙ 7:30am-10pm; 🛜) Every city needs a Cas- canuez, where you can go at 4pm for your tea or *merienda* (afternoon snack) and have a bow-tied waiter serve you a hot drink and a sweet treat. In Cajamarca this means *cafe pasado* (coffee made by mixing thick coffee essence with boiling water) and a choice of nine varieties of *tres leches* (a cake made with three types of milk).

El Marengo
PIZZA $

(Junín 1201; pizzas S11-20; ⊙ 7-11pm) Marengo is the smallest, hottest and most fun of the melee of pizza places in the blocks west of Plaza de Armas. With six wooden tables and a brick pizza oven squeezed into a space the size of a dentist's waiting room, it feels more like a blacksmith's forge than a restaurant. Choose from 14 pizza flavors.

Paprika
PERUVIAN $$$

(☑ 076-36-2472; www.costadelsolperu.com; Cruz de Piedra 707; mains S25-50; ⊙ noon-11pm) Cajamarca's poshest restaurant is located in its fanciest hotel and – no surprise – offers the most inventive food in the city. Large windows look out onto the main plaza, starched white tablecloths lend a formal edge and food arrives artistically arranged on a variety of slates, boards, spoons and sometimes even plates.

🍷 Drinking & Nightlife

★Usha-Usha
BAR

(Puga 142; cover S5; ⊙ 9pm-late) For an intimate local experience head to this hole-in-the-wall dive bar run by eccentric local musician Jaime Valera, who has cultivated a heap of charisma in a small space. He sings his heart out with his musician friends and you walk out with an unforgettable travel memory.

ℹ Information

MONEY

Scotiabank (Amazonas 750; ⊙ 8am-6pm Mon-Fri, 9am-noon Sat) Useful Canadian-run bank with ATM.

TOURIST INFORMATION

iPerú (☑ 076-36-5166; Cruz de Piedra 601; ⊙ 9am-6pm Mon-Sat, to 1pm Sun)

ℹ Getting There & Away

AIR

The **airport** is 4km outside town off the road to Otuzco.

LC Perú (☑ 076-36-3115; www.lcperu.pe; Jirón del Comercio 1024; ⊙ 9am-7pm Mon-Fri, to 1pm Sat) Most economical but least reliable operator with two daily flights to Lima (US$100, 1¼ hours) leaving at 7:15am and 5pm.

LATAM (www.latam.com; Centro Commercial El Quinde; ⊙ 10am-10pm) Has two to three daily flights from Cajamarca to Lima (US$135, 1¼ hours)

BUS

Cajamarca continues its ancient role as a crossroads, with buses heading to all four points

of the compass. Most bus terminals are close to *cuadra* (block) 3 of Atahualpa, about 1.5km southeast of the center (not to be confused with the Atahualpa in the town center), on the road to Los Baños del Inca.

Cruz del Sur (☑ 076-36-2024; Atahualpa 884) Nice *bus-cama* (bed bus), with seat-back screens, to Lima (S100 to S120, 16 hours) at 6:30pm.

Línea (☑ 076-34-0753; www.linea.pe; Atahualpa 316) Has a comfortable Lima-bound *bus-cama* (S120 to S140, 15 hours) with a departure at 6pm. There are departures to Chiclayo (S25 to S46, six hours) at 10:45am, 1:30pm, 10:50pm and 11pm, and Trujillo (S25 to S50, six hours) at 10:30am, 1pm, 10pm, 10:15pm, 10:30pm and 10:40pm.

Movil Tours (☑ 076-28-0093; www.moviltours.com.pe; Av Atahualpa 686) Daily bus to Lima (S90 to S110, 15 hours) at 3:50pm. Also a daily bus to Piura (S50 to S70, eight hours) via Chiclayo at 8:45pm.

Chachapoyas

☑ 041 / POP 29,000 / ELEV 2335M

Isolated for centuries in the cloud forests of northern Peru, mellow Chachapoyas appears to be a town on the cusp of wider discovery. For vintage travelers, the ignition of interest will come as no surprise. Straddling the transitional zone between the high Andes and the Amazon Basin, 'Chacha' and its surroundings have long felt like a box of hidden treasure waiting to be dug up.

Founded early in the Spanish conquest as the base from which the exploitation of the Amazon region was launched, contemporary Chacha is a relatively unremarkable town, a tight grid of whitewashed houses with red-tiled roofs whose individualistic history means that few of the populace speak Quechua. Instead, Chacha's jewels lie scattered across the surrounding countryside: a crinkled web of cloud-enveloped mountains and valleys, inhabited by colossal waterfalls, remarkable birdlife and a mysterious raft of pre-Columbian, pre-Inca ruins, half of them still covered by tangled undergrowth.

🏃 Activities

Trekking to the numerous impressive sights and ruins around Chachapoyas is becoming increasingly popular and is easy to arrange in town. The most popular outing is the four- or five-day **Gran Vilaya** trek, from Choctámal to the Marañón canyon, through pristine cloud forest and past several ruins and the heavenly Valle de Belén. Another popular adventure heads out to the **Laguna de los Cóndores**, a three-day trip on foot and horseback from Leimebamba.

Potential DIY day hikes include the Gocta waterfall (p939), the **Inca trail** to or from Levanto (and **Yalape** FREE), the old Camino Herradura (p940) up to Kuélap (p939), and the long hike from Yerbabuena to **Revash** (admission S10; ☉ ticket office 8am-1pm & 2-5pm).

☞ Tours

All the budget tour agencies are found near or on the Plaza de Armas. Ask around for other travelers' experiences before you choose an agency. Expect to pay S100 to S150 per person for multiday treks (a little more for groups of less than four) and between S50 and S80 for day tours.

Standard day tours include Kuélap for S100, **Karajía** (admission S10) to **Caverna de Quiocta** (admission S5; ☉ 8am-5pm) for S100, Gocta for S60 and Revash to Leimebamba for S120. Prices might vary.

Turismo Explorer   TOURS
(☑ 041-47-8162;   www.turismoexplorerperu.com; Grau 549) This company has a great reputation among travelers and offers short trips and multiday treks. It has professional guides who speak excellent English.

🛏 Sleeping

★ Chachapoyas Backpackers   HOSTEL $
(☑ 041-47-8879;   www.chachapoyasbackpackers. com; Calle 2 de Mayo 639; d S70, dm/s/d without bathroom S20/35/45; @ ☎) A godsend in a region not overflowing with hosteling options, this travelers' nexus doesn't just go through the motions, it excels. Offering clean, uncluttered rooms and dorms ignited by splashes of color plus a well-stocked communal kitchen and hot showers, it doubles up as a local information portal masterfully overseen by keen multilingual staff.

★ La Xalca   HOTEL $$$
(☑ 041-47-9106; www.laxalcahotel.com; Grau 940; s/d/tr incl breakfast S290/360/530; P ☎) It's hard to believe that this drop-dead-handsome colonial edifice was built from scratch only a few years ago – the elegant wood and adobe walls and balconies are gloriously authentic. Melding modern minimalism with sturdy tradition, the hotel abounds with inviting communal spaces decked out with comfy sofas, hand-carved furniture and curious art. Best hotel in town, hands down.

 Eating

Café Fusiones   CAFE $
(www.cafefusiones.com; Ayacucho, Plaza de Armas; breakfasts S8-11, light meals S6-17; ☉ 7am-10pm; ☎ 🍴) 🌿 One of those comfortable 'Gringo Trail' cafes that offer everything necessary to keep a peanut-butter-deprived backpacker happy – vegetarian omelets, multilingual book exchange, Pearl Jam on repeat, organic coffee and leaflets advertising the nearest yoga studio. If you're dying to meet a gringo, this is where they'll be. It's also one of the few Chacha cafes that stays open all day.

★ Amazonas 632   CAFE, INTERNATIONAL $$
(☑ 979-877-031; Amazonas 632; mains S10-22; ☉ 7:30am-2:30pm & 5-11pm; ☎) This smart new coffee shop and casual dining spot attracts a mix of laptop campers (free wi-fi and power outlets) and locals tucking into the thick, juicy burgers – the best in town. Strong coffee, gigantic fruit salads, and small but unusually flavored artisanal pizzas, too. The underlying owl motif lends the place a warm quirkiness despite the otherwise Starbucks-y decor.

Candela   PIZZA $$
(☑ 961-867-428; Calle 2 de Mayo 728; pizzas S14-28; ☉ 6-11pm) Colorful Chachapoyas culture (indigenous-style murals adorn the walls) is married with decent Italian-influenced food at this spot. The focus is the giant pizza oven stoked industriously by a hard-working chef who turns out crunchy thin-crust pies with generous toppings. A theatrical sideshow is provided by the wait staff, some of whom appear to have a talent for dancing.

★ El Batan de Tayta   AMAZONIAN $$
(☑ 959-865-539; La Merced 604; mains S20-46; ☉ 11am-11pm Sun-Thu, to midnight Fri & Sat) Exotic is the word here, from the decor (Amazonian creepers, bamboo table umbrellas and furry seat covers), to the food ('drunk' guinea pig, duck and edible ants in a vanilla and cognac cocktail!) and the implements it's served on (model boats, mini-drums, or if you're lucky, a terra-cotta roof tile). Despite the theatrics, the food is plentiful and well executed.

Try the *arroz shutito con bife y chica de jora* (creamy rice with tenderloin and a touch of maize liquor) or house specialty *cuy borracho* (literally 'drunk guinea pig' with Andean potatoes and herb sauce).

There's even a few boring dishes (eg pasta) on the menu if you don't happen to like insects or inebriated rodents.

THE MIGHTY FALLS OF GOCTA

The 771m **Catarata de Gocta** (1/both falls S10/20; ☺8am-5pm) somehow escaped the notice of the Peruvian government, international explorers and prying satellite images until 2005, when German Stefan Ziemendorff and a group of locals put together an expedition to map the falls. Various claims ranging from the third-loftiest waterfall on earth to the 15th highest resulted in an international firestorm. Whatever its rank, Gocta is mighty impressive and, thanks to a web of well-signposted, forested trails, it's now pretty accessible, too.

To get to the falls from Chachapoyas, catch an **ETSA** (☎950-046-809; Terminal Terrestre) combi (minibus) heading toward Pedro Ruíz (S3, 45 minutes) and get off at Cocahuayaco (a bridge on the main road). Mototaxis (three-wheeled motorcycle rickshaw taxis) usually wait here offering to take hikers up to the villages of Cocachimba (5.3km) or San Pablo (6km) for S10. Alternatively, you can hike up to either village. San Pablo provides best access to the upper falls. Cocachimba is the start of the trail to the lower falls. Both villages have community tourist offices where you must pay your entrance fee. Cocachimba has more in the way of places to stay and eat.

For a full day out, it's possible to visit both the upper and lower falls on one 15km circuit. Start in San Pablo village, from where a 6km trail leads to the base of the 231m-high upper cascade. Double back on the same path for 1.8km and then turn left heading down the mountain to a fantastic lookout with a clear view of both cascades, and then across a suspension bridge to the base of the taller 540m-high lower falls. From here you exit along the main trail to Cocachimba (6.2km), where you can catch a mototaxi back to Cocahuayco. From the road bridge, combis for Chachapoyas pass every 30 minutes.

For die-hard athletes wanting to do the full circuit, starting and finishing in Cocahuaycos, you're looking at a 26km hike over hilly, sometimes-muddy terrain. Start early.

❶ Information

MONEY

Banco de la Nación (cnr Ayacucho & Calle 2 de Mayo; ☺8am-5:30pm Mon-Fri, 9am-1pm Sat) Has a Visa/MasterCard ATM.

BCP (Plaza Burgos; ☺9am-6pm Mon-Fri, to 1pm Sat) Changes US dollars and has an ATM.

TOURIST INFORMATION

iPerú (☎041-47-7292; Ortiz Arrieta 582; ☺9am-6pm Mon-Sat, to 1pm Sun) Extremely helpful like most iPerú offices, this place on Plaza de Armas hands out excellent maps, transportation information and brochures.

❶ Getting There & Away

All local and regional transport leaves from Chachapoyas' scruffy beehive of a **bus terminal** (Triunfo cuadra 2), 1km east of Plaza de Armas. Note that long-distance express buses leave from private terminals around the city.

The very comfortable **Movil Tours** (☎041-47-8545; www.moviltours.com.pe; La Libertad 464) has buses to Lima (S130 to S165, 22 hours) at 4pm, Chiclayo (S55 to S75, nine hours) at 8pm, Trujillo (S65 to S85, 14 hours) at 7:30pm, and Jaén (S50, four hours) at 4:30am.

Continuing into the Amazon Basin is **Turismo Selva** (☎961-659-443; Terminal de Transporte), running less-comfortable minivans to Tarapoto (S35, eight hours) via Moyobamba (S24, six hours) at 6:30am, 8:30am, 10:30am and 12:30pm.

Turismo Kuélap (Terminal Terrestre) runs frequent minibuses from Chachapoyas' main bus terminal to the base of the cable-car station in Nuevo Tingo (S7, one hour). Buses leave when full, approximately every half-hour.

Kuélap

The 700m-long oval fortress of **Kuélap** (adult/child S20/10; ☺8am-5pm), made up of millions of cubic feet of remarkably preserved stone, was constructed between AD 900 and 1100, and rediscovered in 1843. Shaped like an ocean liner atop a 3000m-high limestone ridge, it is surrounded by an imposing, near-impenetrable wall that towers up to 20m high in places. Entrance into this stronghold is via three deep, narrow gates designed like funnels – an ingenious security system that forced attacking parties into easily defeated single files.

The main entrance, **Acceso 3**, is reached by walking along the east side of the fortress. A wooden boardwalk takes visitors on a winding route inside with newly installed panels giving basic explanations in Spanish and English. You'll be directed first to the raised **Pueblo Alto**, site of the 7m-high **Torreón** (Tower) which sits like a sentry guarding Kuélap's northern bows. Despite its name, the tower's role was probably ritualistic rather than military – burials have been unearthed in its entrails. Nearby is the **Callanca**, one of the complex's few rectangular buildings, thought to have been a hostel and ritualistic center, where pieces of Inca-influenced ceramics have been found.

The center of the fort is scattered with the remnants of more than 400 circular dwellings. Some are decorated with zigzag and rhomboid friezes, and all were once topped by soaring thatched roofs. A variety of trees grow in and around the ruins, many heavy with epiphytes that attract hundreds of hungry hummingbirds.

The most impressive and enigmatic structure, named the **Templo Mayor** or El Tintero (Inkpot), sits near the south end of Kuélap and has been fashioned in the shape of a large inverted cone. Inside, an underground chamber houses the remains of animal sacrifices, leading archaeologists to believe that it was a religious building of some kind. Kuélap resident archaeologist Alfredo Narvez has now excavated graves and llama skeletons around El Tintero to further support this theory. A 1996 hypothesis by a team from the University of San Diego suggests it may have also been a solar calendar.

Since 2017 access to the ruins has been made infinitely easier by the building of a cable car, or **Telecabinas** (www.telecabinaskuelap.com; S20 round-trip; ⊙ 8am-3:30pm). Eight-berth cabins take visitors on a 20-minute journey across a V-shaped river valley and up a steep treeless hillside to within a 20-minute walk of the ruins. The bottom station is located just above the village of Nuevo Tingo. From here minibuses shuttle visitors up a 3km road to where the cable-car ride starts. At the top station there is a **cafeteria** (snacks S7-10; ⊙ 8am-5pm), interpretation center and a ticket office for the site itself. A stone path leads 1½ km directly to the ruins from the top station. Community guides can be hired for S50 from the top station. Bank on two hours to view the ruins properly.

Tour groups usually arrive at the ruins around 11:30am and leave by 3pm, so consider setting off from Chachapoyas at around 8am to avoid the rush.

It is still possible to hike down (or up) the 9km-long **Camino Herradura** between the ruins and Tingo Viejo. Pick up the path by the old ticket office outside Acceso 1 (if going down), or by the river bridge in Tingo Viejo (if going up).

ⓘ Getting There & Away

Getting to Kuélap is now easy in a day trip from Chachapoyas arriving either independently or as part of an organized group.

Several bus companies, including Turismo Kuélap (p939), run frequent minibuses from Chachapoyas' main bus terminal to the base of the cable-car station in Nuevo Tingo (S7, one hour). Buses leave when full about every half hour.

Tarapoto

♪ 042 / POP 144,200 / ELEV 356M

Hot, noisy, *mototaxi*-infested Tarapoto straddles the base of the Andean foothills, providing an unlikely entry ticket into the vast jungles of eastern Peru. A sweltering rainforest metropolis, it dips its toe into the Amazon Basin while managing to cling to the rest of Peru by the umbilical cord of a long paved road back to civilization. People come here more for the sights that surround the town than the town itself – although it's by no means an unpleasant place. From Tarapoto you can take the plunge deeper into the Amazon, or just enjoy the easily accessible jungle-lite, with plenty of places to stay and eat, and reliable connections to the coast. There's a bunch of natural sights to explore nearby, from waterfalls to lagoons, while river-running opportunities will entertain the adventure-seeking contingent.

ⓒ Tours

There are dozens of licensed agencies selling almost identical tours mostly catering for national (Peruvian) tourists. Prices are low and pretty generic, but don't expect your guide to speak anything but Spanish.

Popular half-day tours include outings to **Lamas** and the **Cataratas de Ahuashiyacu** (Carr Yurimaguas, Km 13). Both cost around S35 and run most days. Full-day tours include **Laguna Azul** (S85) and trips on the **Alto Mayo River** (S120).

Martín Zamora Tours   TOURS
(✆ 042-52-5148; Morey 247; ⊙ 8am-1pm & 4-7:30pm) Tarapoto's go-to operator for day tours, cultural trips and longer excursions to local lakes and waterfalls.

🛌 Sleeping

You don't need to go far from town to find lush jungle surrounds. There are a string of nature lodges on the banks of the Rio Shilcayo just north of the center.

In town, expect your digs to be a little less exotic.

El Mirador
GUESTHOUSE $

(☑042-52-2177; www.elmiradortarapoto.com; San Pablo de la Cruz 517; s/d incl breakfast S60/80, with air-con S100/150; 🕸🛜) Travelers swoon over this budget spot. Maybe it's because the family owners offer up the warmest welcome in Tarapoto; or perhaps it's about the excellent breakfast served on the terrace with hammocks and jungle views? Rooms in the main house are basic, with fans and white decor; those in the newer annex are bright, air-conditioned and sport very yellow bathrooms.

Sol de Selva
HOTEL $$

(☑042-52-4817; Pedro de Urzúa 161; s/d/tr incl breakfast S80/100/150; 🕸🛜) Cross the threshold of calm, collected and clean Sol de Selva and you'll feel instantly freed from the noisy, dusty streets outside. Rooms have modern air-con units, shampoos restocked every day and furnishings colored by pale yellows and subtle oranges. The family operators extend a warm welcome and the breakfast sandwiches are substantially tastier than your average Peruvian omelets.

Tucan Suites
HOTEL $$$

(☑042-52-8383; www.tucansuites.com; Calle 1 de Abril 315; apt from S439; 🕸@🛜🕸) This chic apartment-hotel in the *barrio* (neighborhood) of Banda de Shilcayo is Tarapoto's only four-star accommodations. Spacious one- and two-bedroom suites feature chrome-tiled kitchenettes and soundproof glass, another city first (and wholly welcomed). Eight of the duplex rooms have open-air kitchenettes and the restaurant drops out onto a tri-level pool terrace. You'll sleep no sounder in town than here.

🍴 Eating

Don't leave Tarapoto without trying *inchicapi* (chicken soup with peanuts, cilantro and yucca) or *juanes* (banana leaves stuffed with chicken or pork and rice).

There's a growing band of experimental restaurants in town including new gourmet offering **Natural** (☑042-60-1741; Lamas 142; meals S35-56; ⊗6-11pm Mon-Sat) – Tarapoto's first.

Café Plaza
CAFE $

(San Martín 109; small plates S6-12; ⊗7:30am-11pm; 🛜) Classic central-plaza corner cafe stocked full of people sipping espressos, breaking the no-smoking policy, and discussing 'deals' hunched over wooden tables. Open to the street, it offers a front-row seat into the film that is Tarapoto. Good for coffee, cakes, snacks and milkshakes.

Suchiche
AMAZONIAN $$

(☑042-52-7554; www.lapatarashca.com; Lamas 245, La Patarashca Hotel; mains S11-20; ⊗7am-11pm) A relatively new addition to Tarapoto's colony of bars and clubs on and around Jirón Lamas, Suchiche positions itself as a restobar, with good food, from Peruvian-Japanese (Amazonian sushi, aka *maki*) to Peruvian-Italian (pasta with *lomo saltado*). The long, handsome bar dispatches coffee, craft beer, pisco sours or freshly blended juice.

⭐ La Patarashca
AMAZONIAN $$

(www.lapatarashca.com; Lamas 261, La Patarashca Hotel; mains S26-44; ⊗noon-11pm; 🛜) Come to Patarashca for an Amazonian culinary awakening. Outstanding regional cuisine is on tap at this woody open-sided restaurant replete with pre-Columbian iconography. Don't miss the salad of *chonta*, thin strips of local hearts of palm, with avocados; or the namesake *patarashcas,* fish served in a warm bath of tomatoes, peppers, onions, garlic and cilantro wrapped in a *bijao* leaf.

ℹ Information

MEDICAL SERVICES

Clínica San Martín (San Martín 274; ⊗24hr) The best medical care in town.

MONEY

Scotiabank (Hurtado 215; ⊗9:15am-6pm Mon-Fri) Cashes traveler's checks and has an ATM.

TOURIST INFORMATION

Tourist Information Office (☑042-52-6188; Hurtado s/n; ⊗7:30am-11pm) The municipal tourist office on Plaza Mayor.

ℹ Getting There & Away

AIR

The **airport** (TPP; ☑042-53-1165) is 3km southwest of the center, a S5 *mototaxi* ride or a 30-minute walk.

LATAM (☑042-52-9318; www.latam.com; Hurtado 183) has four to five daily flights to Lima (US$60, 1¼ hours).

PERU TARAPOTO

Star Perú (⌨ 042-52-1056; www.starperu.com; Plaza Mayor 325; ⏰9am-7pm Mon-Fri, to 5pm Sat) has one daily flight to Lima (US$60, 1¼ hours) and another to Iquitos (US$80, one hour).

Peruvian (www.peruvian.pe; Hurtado 277; ⏰9am-7pm) has three daily flights to Lima (US$50, 1¼ hours).

BUS

Several companies head west on the paved road to Lima via Moyobamba, Chiclayo and Trujillo, generally leaving between 8am and 4pm. All these companies can be found along the same *cuadra* (block) of Salaverry and its cross streets in the Morales district, an S3 *mototaxi* ride from the town center.

Civa (⌨ 042-52-2269; www.civa.com.pe; Salaverry 840) Has a comfortable 12:45pm bus to Lima (S100 to S120, 30 hours), stopping at Chiclayo and Trujillo.

Movil Tours (⌨ 042-52-9193; www.moviltours. com.pe; Salaverry 880) Top-end express buses to Lima (S120 to S170, 29 hours) leave at 8am and 1pm, with a 3pm departure to Trujillo (S90 to S120, 17 hours), a 4pm bus to Chiclayo (S80 to S105, 13 hours), a 5pm bus to Piura (S80 to S105, 14 hours) and a 3:45pm bus to Pucallpa (S75 to S95, 11 hours).

Turismo Selva (⌨ 042-52-5682; Alfonso Ugarte 1130) Runs frequent minivans to Yurimaguas (S15, 2¾ hours), Moyobamba (S10, two hours) and Chachapoyas (S35, eight hours).

AMAZON BASIN

ELEV 0–1800M

The best-protected tract of the world's most biodiverse forest, the strange, sweltering, seductive country-within-a-country that is Peru's Amazon Basin is changing. Its vastness and impenetrability have long protected its indigenous communities and diverse wildlife from external eyes. Tribes exist here that have never had contact with outside civilization, and more flora and fauna flourish in one rainforest hectare than in any European country.

But as the 21st century encroaches on this enticing expanse of arboreal wilderness, exploitation of the rainforest's abundant resources threatens to irreversibly damage it. Sure: the Peruvian Amazon offers phenomenal wildlife-spotting, dalliances into untamed forest from the jungle's best selection of lodges and raucous city life. But it also begs for ongoing protection. Remember that as, forging through it by rough road and raging river, you emulate the explorers who first brought international attention to this region.

To maximise wildlife-viewing, visit during the dry season (July to October).

Puerto Maldonado

⌨082 / POP 56,000 / ELEV 250M

Visibly blossoming from its road connection to the outside world, Puerto Maldonado, capital of the southern jungle, has an increasingly smart sheen to the bedlam of its central streets, abuzz with tooting *mototaxis* (three-wheeled motorcycle rickshaw taxis).

The city's money-spinning proximity to the most easily visited animal-rich jungle in the entire Amazon Basin is its blessing but also its curse: travelers arrive, yet quickly leave again to the lodges and wildlife on the nearby rivers.

Yet Puerto Maldonado's languid laid-back ambience invites you to linger. Although a shock to the system, with its sweltering climate and mosquitoes aplenty, its beautiful plaza, burgeoning accommodation options and lively nightlife provide reason enough to hang around.

It remains of foremost importance to travelers, however, as a jumping-off point for voyaging on Ríos Tambopata and Madre de Dios, converging here: watery wonderlands that offer the most accessible primary jungle-locales in the country.

🤝 Tours

Most visitors arrive with prearranged tours and stay at a jungle lodge – convenient, but by no means the only possibility. You can also arrange a tour upon arrival by going to the lodge offices in town, where you'll likely get a significant discount on a tour that would cost more in Lima or Cuzco.

You can, too, look for an independent guide. However, to enter the Reserva Nacional Tambopata (including Lago Sandoval, and anywhere upriver of Puesto Control El Torre on the Río Tambopata) all guides need licenses which are only issued if they are affiliated with a lodge or registered tour operator (this is an important thing to check).

Almost all of the best guides with official licenses granted by the Ministerio de Industria y Turismo work full time for one of the area's jungle lodges. Guides charge from S120 to S200 per person per day, depending on the destination and number of people.

Most tours, either with a lodge or with an independent guide, leave from the **Río Madre de Dios ferry dock** (Puerto Capitanía), heading downriver on the Río Madre de Dios or upriver on the Río Tambopata (meaning a large expense on a jungle trip is the fuel the boat will expend).

Puerto Maldonado

PERU PUERTO MALDONADO

🛏 Sleeping

Wasai Hostel HOSTEL $
(📞082-57-2290; www.wasai.com; cnr Billinghurst & Arequipa; dm S39-52, r incl breakfast S98-117; ☰) It's quite expensive as hostels go, but it's quite nice, too, with a prime central location with the benefit of the on-site pool and tour agency offering jungle tours, as well as the lovely El Faro (p944) restaurant. Breakfast is included with the rooms but not with the dorms.

★ Anaconda Lodge LODGE $$
(📞982-611-039, 082-79-2726; http://anaconda junglelodge.com; cnr Prolongación La Joya/ Av Aeropuerto & Elmer Faucett; s/d/tr 100/160/80 /220, s/d without bathroom S50/80; ₧🛜☰) The most original airport hotel in South Ameri-ca? Cocooned in its own tropical garden on the edge of town, and with its own Thai res-taurant, too, this lodge has a more remote feel than its location would suggest. There are eight double-room bungalows with shared bathroom and four luxury bunga-lows with private facilities; all are mosquito netted.

Paititi Hostal HOTEL $$
(📞082-57-4667; Prada 290; s S90-120, d S120-140, all incl breakfast; ✦🛜) A relatively flash, central place, the Paititi has a series of spacious, airy rooms, many full of attractive old wooden furniture, along with telephones and cable TV. A continental breakfast is included, and there's even hot water at night – very un-Amazon. Higher tariffs are for air-con.

✗ Eating

Regional specialties include *juanes* (banana leaves stuffed with chicken or pork and rice), *chilcano* (a broth of fish chunks flavored with cilantro) and *parrillada de la selva* (barbecued marinated meat, often game, in a Brazil-nut sauce). *Plátano* (plantain) is served as an accompaniment to many meals.

Other culinary options are Wasai Lodge's restaurant, El Faro, or delicious Thai food at Anaconda Lodge.

★ La Semilla   VEGETARIAN $
(Arequipa, btwn Carrión & Loreto; light meals S10-20; ⊙ 10am-1pm & 4-9pm Mon-Sat, 10am-1pm Sun; ☑) Clamber up three flights of stairs to this welcoming open-sided vegetarian restaurant with views over the Plaza de Armas. Here you can get about the best coffee in town, *pie de maracuya* (like lemon meringue pie with a fruit change) and lovingly prepared salads.

★ Burgos's Restaurante   PERUVIAN $$
(cnr 26 de Diciembre & Loreto; mains S19-38; ⊙ 11am-11pm; ☑) This has quickly developed into Puerto Maldonado's standout restaurant. It calls itself an exponent of Novo Amazonica cuisine – that's like Novo Andino, only making those bold culinary adaptations to jungle dishes – but this is still more about dependable Peruvian Amazon staples, cooked to perfection rather than with particular innovation.

El Faro at Wasai Lodge   PERUVIAN $$
(cnr Billinghurst & Arequipa; mains S25; ⊙ 7am-9:30pm) A pleasing and popular little spot that charges above-average prices for way-above-average Amazonian food, with a few surprises such as the divine ceviche with camu camu fruit. It overlooks the little plaza with the statue of the *faro* (lighthouse).

�iₓ Drinking & Nightlife

Discoteca Witite   CLUB
(Velarde 151; ⊙ 9pm-late Fri & Sat) Well, we preferred Witite with the gaudy clapboard but the smartened-up version is still the classic place to party, jungle-style – a party that goes on all night. It's on the pedestrianized street near the plaza.

❶ Information

iPeru (☑ 082-57-1830; Loreto 390; ⊙ 9am-6pm Mon-Sat, to 1pm Sun) Central tourist information office.

Sernanp (☑ 082-57-1247; www.sernanp.gob. pe; Cajamarca, btwn Ancash & Madre de Dios)

The national park office gives information and collects entrance fees (in nearly all cases, guides sort this out); standard entrance to the Reserva Nacional Tambopata's reserve zone is S30 for the day, increasing to S65 for two or three days. The website is in Spanish only.

❶ Getting There & Away

AIR
The **airport** (PEM) is 7km outside town. Scheduled flights leave every day to/from Lima via Cuzco with **LAN** (LATAM; ☑ 082-57-3677; Velarde 503; ⊙ 9am-7pm Mon-Fri, to 1pm Sat) and **Star Perú** (☑ 082-57-3564; Velarde 505; ⊙ 8:30am-7pm Mon-Sat). Schedules and airlines change from one year to the next, but the airline offices, as well as numerous travel agents in the town center, have the latest details.

BUS
Terminal Terrestre (Av Circunvalación Nte s/n) is 6km northwest of the center; from there, buses ply the Carr Interocéanica (Transoceanic Hwy) southwest to Cuzco and northeast to Rio Branco, Brazil. Numerous companies leave either during the morning or at night (around 8pm) to Cuzco (S35 to S70, 10 hours). Top tariffs are for fully reclining seats. Other options heading southwest include Juliaca (S35, 12 hours) and Arequipa (S50, 17 hours), both destinations being served by **Transportes Julsa** (☑ 951-751-246; Terminal Terrestre). Options from Terminal Terrestre to Río Branco (S100, nine to 10 hours) are more scant and do not depart every day. It's advisable to buy your ticket as far in advance of travel as you possibly can.

Parque Nacional Manu

This vast **national park** (entry per 1/2-3/4+ days S30/60/150) 🌿 in the Amazon Basin covers almost 20,000 sq km and is one of the best places in South America to see a stunning variety of tropical wildlife. Progressive in its emphasis on preservation, Unesco declared Manu a Biosphere Reserve in 1977 and a World Natural Heritage Site in 1987. Entry is only with guide and permit.

One reason the park is so successful in preserving such a large tract of virgin jungle and its wildlife is that it's remote and relatively inaccessible to people, and therefore has not been exploited by rubber tappers, loggers, oil companies or hunters.

At **Cocha Salvador**, one of the park's largest and most beautiful lakes, you'll find camping and guided hiking possibilities, as well as wonderful wildlife-viewing.

MANU GUIDED TOURS

It is illegal to enter the park's *zona reservada* (reserved area) without a guide, and difficult to arrange a tour independently that will get you good wildlife sightings even in the *zona cultural* (cultural area). Going with an organized group can be arranged in Cuzco or with international tour operators.

It's an expensive trip; budget travelers should arrange their trip in Cuzco and be flexible with travel plans. Travelers often report returning from Manu several days late. Don't plan an international airline connection the day after a Manu trip!

Tour operators include the following:

Amazon Trails Peru (☑084-43-7374; www.amazontrailsperu.com; Tandapata 660; 2 nights & 3 days from US$540) 🏷

Bonanza Tours (☑084-50-7871, 985-371-500; www.bonanzatoursperu.com; Suecia 343; 3 nights & 4 days per person from US$510; ☺8am-5pm) 🏷

InkaNatura (☑084-25-5255, 084-23-1138, 984-691-838; www.inkanatura.com; Ricardo Palma J1 Urb Santa Mónica & Plateros 361)

Pantiacolla Tours (☑084-23-8323; www.pantiacolla.com; Garcilaso 265 interior, 2nd fl, Cuzco; ☺8am-6pm Mon-Sat) 🏷

Permits, which are necessary to enter the park, are arranged by tour agencies. Transportation, accommodations, food and guides are also part of tour packages. Most visits are for a week, although three-night stays at a lodge can be arranged.

With patience, wildlife is seen in most areas. During a one-week trip, you can reasonably expect to see scores of different bird species, several kinds of monkey and a few other mammals.

The best time to go is during the dry season (June to November); much of Manu may be inaccessible or closed during the rainiest months (January to April). Going with an organized group is best arranged in Cuzco, from where trips depart almost daily, or with international tour operators.

Pucallpa

☑061 / POP 205,000 / ELEV 154M

The busy port of Pucallpa is enjoying something of a renaissance. It has an attractive pedestrianized boulevard, and is a starting point for a spectacular river adventure north to Iquitos – and, if time and inclination allow, on to Brazil and the Atlantic.

However, the city has a distinctly less junglelike appearance than other Amazonian towns. Although this is an important distribution center for goods along the broad, brown Río Ucayali, which sweeps past the city en route to join the Río Amazonas, the rainforest feels far away. After all those miles of tropical travel to get here, Pucallpa seems underwhelming, and hasty modern development in the center barely disguises the shantytown simplicity a few blocks further out.

But beyond the city sprawl, there is reason for the traveler to linger: the lovely, more traveler-friendly oxbow lake of Yarinacocha, with river lodges to relax at and interesting indigenous communities to visit.

🛏 Sleeping & Eating

★**Manish Hotel Ecológico**　　CABINS $$
(☑061-57-7167; www.manishhotel.com.pe; Jirón Vargas Guerra s/n; s/d/ste incl breakfast S180/230/270, 4-person bungalows incl breakfast S420; P✳🛜☀) Escape Pucallpa's dusty thoroughfares in this serene expanse of leafy grounds, dotted with terra-cotta-roofed cabins. For families, taking one of the bungalows can mean downtime on the terrace for the grown-ups while the kids can safely run wild betwixt the palms and the pool.

La Plaza Bar & Grill　　AMAZONIAN $$
(Sucre 198, cnr Atahualpa; mains S20-30; ☺6am-11pm) While quiet outside of prime hotel guest eating hours, the hotel restaurant at **Casa Andina Select** (☑061-58-6600; P✳🛜☀) is a slick, modern eatery offering delicious ceviche and other tasty Peruvian Amazonian classics.

❶ Getting There & Away

AIR

Pucallpa's decent-sized **airport** is 5km west of town. The best connection is with **Star Perú** (☑061-59-0585; 7 de Junio 865; ☺8:30am-6:30pm Mon-Fri, to 5pm Sat) with a direct flight

ⓘ GETTING TO BRAZIL & BOLIVIA

Brazil

A good paved road, part of the Transoceanic Hwy, goes 170km from Puerto Maldonado to **Iberia** (with very basic hotels) and then another 70km on to the village of **Iñapari**, on the Brazilian border.

Peruvian border formalities can be carried out in Iñapari. Stores around the main plaza accept and change both Peruvian and Brazilian currency; if leaving Peru, it's best to get rid of any nuevos soles here. From Iñapari, you can cross over the new bridge to **Assis Brasil**, which has better hotels (starting from around US$15 per room).

US citizens need to get a Brazilian visa beforehand, either in the USA or Lima. It's 325km (six to seven hours) by paved road from here to the important Brazilian city of Rio Branco, via Brasiléia (100km, two hours).

Bolivia

The easiest way of reaching Bolivia is to go to Brasiléia in Brazil and cross the Río Acre by ferry or bridge to **Cobija** in Bolivia, where there are hotels, banks, an airstrip with erratically scheduled flights further into Bolivia, and a rough gravel road with several river crossings to the city of **Riberalta** (seven to 12 hours depending on season).

Alternatively, hire a boat at Puerto Maldonado's Madre de Dios dock to take you to the Peru–Bolivia border at **Puerto Pardo**. A few minutes from Puerto Pardo by boat is **Puerto Heath**, a military camp on the Bolivian side.

---

leaving from Lima at 7:15am – the flight continues to Iquitos. For Pucallpa–Lima, the time is 12:15pm. Another option is **LAN** (LATAM; Tarapacá 805) with three daily (but pricier) flights to Lima.

BOAT

Riverboats sail the Río Ucayali from Pucallpa to Iquitos (S80 to S100, slinging your own hammock and with basic meals, three to five days).

BUS

A direct bus to Lima (S65 to S90) takes 18 to 20 hours in the dry season; the journey can be broken in Tingo María (S20, six hours) or Huánuco (S25, eight hours).

Yarinacocha

About 10km northwest of central Pucallpa, Yarinacocha is an enticing oxbow lake where you can go boating, observe wildlife and visit indigenous communities. The lake, once part of the Río Ucayali, is now landlocked, though a small canal links the two bodies of water during rainy season.

The lakeside village, **Puerto Callao,** is a welcome relief from the chaos of downtown Pucallpa. It's still ramshackle, with only a dirt road skirting the busy waterfront. Buzzards amble among pedestrians, and *peki-pekis* (canoes powered by a two-stroke motorcycle engine with a long propeller shaft) come and go to their various destinations all day. Travelers stop by, too, to check out either the wildlife

or the *ayahuasca* (derivative of a hallucinogenic jungle vine) ceremonies for which Yarinacocha area is known.

In Puerto Callao you'll find limited accommodations, as well as the Central Amazon's best food. Hire boats here to further explore the lake, too. Overall, it is worth spending a couple of days hereabouts.

ⓖ Tours

You'll be nabbed as soon as you turn up by boat touts and *peki-pekis* owners seeking to lure you to their vessel. Choose your boat carefully. Wildlife to watch out for includes freshwater pink dolphins, sloths and meter-long green iguanas, as well as birds such as the curiously long-toed wattled jacana and the metallic-green Amazon kingfisher.

A highly recommended guide is **Gilber Reategui Sangama** (messages 936-508-090; http://ayakruna.com; Puerto Callao; per hour S40), who owns the boat *La Normita* in Yarinacocha. Contact him in advance to arrange a tour.

Boat trips to the Shipibo villages of either **San Francisco** (also reached by road) or, better, **Santa Clara** (reached only by boat), are also popular. For short trips, boat drivers charge around S30 an hour for the boat; these can carry several people.

ⓘ Getting There & Away

Offer any passing *mototaxi* driver in central Pucallpa S6 and they will bring you to Puerto Callao.

Iquitos

📞 065 / POP 472,000 / ELEV 130M

Linked to the outside world by air and by river, Iquitos is the world's largest city that cannot be reached by road. It's a prosperous, vibrant jungle metropolis and the northern Amazon Basin's chief city, teeming with the usual, addictive Amazonian anomalies. Unadulterated jungle encroaches beyond town in view of the air-conditioned, elegant restaurants that flank the riverside; motorized tricycles whiz manically through the streets yet locals mill around the central plazas eating ice cream like there is all the time in the world. Mud huts mingle with magnificent tiled mansions; tiny dugout canoes ply the water alongside colossal cruise ships. You may well arrive in Iquitos for the greater adventure of a boat trip down the Amazon, but whether it's sampling rainforest cuisine, the buzzing nightlife or one of Peru's most fascinating markets in the floating shantytown of Belén, this thriving city will entice you to stay awhile.

👁 Sights

★ Belén Mercado MARKET
FREE At the southeast end of town is the floating shantytown of Belén, consisting of scores of huts, built on rafts, which rise and fall with the river. During the low-water months, these rafts sit on the river mud, but for most of the year they float on the river – a colorful and chaotic sight. Seven thousand people live here, and canoes float from hut to hut selling and trading jungle produce.

★ Historical Ships Museum MUSEUM
(Plaza Castilla; S10; ⊙8am-8pm) Moored below Plaza Castilla is the diverting Historical Ships Museum, on a 1906 Amazon riverboat, the gorgeously restored three-deck *Ayapua*. The exhibitions reflect the Amazon River's hodgepodge past: explorers, tribes, rubber barons and the filming of the 1982 Werner Herzog movie *Fitzcarraldo*. Included in the entrance price is a half-hour historic-boat ride on the river (Río Itaya out to the Río Amazonas proper).

Malecón VIEWPOINT
(Malecóns Maldonado & Tarapaca) The sight of Iquitos' sophisticated riverside walkway, edged by swanky bars and restaurants and yet cut off from the rest of the world by hundreds of kilometers of jungle river, is as spectacular as it is surreal. Tours are touted and jungle food

is served from stalls, while below are decaying old riverboats, and the lower town's huts on stilts are at the mercy of rapidly changing river levels.

☞ Tours

Cruising the Amazon is an expensive business: the shortest trips can cost over US$1000. It's a popular pastime, too, and advance reservations are often necessary (and often mean discounts). Cruises naturally focus on the Río Amazonas, both downriver (northeast) toward the Brazil–Colombia border and upriver to Nauta, where the Ríos Marañón and Ucayali converge. Beyond Nauta, trips continue up these two rivers to the Reserva Nacional Pacaya-Samiria. Trips can also be arranged on the three rivers surrounding Iquitos: the Itaya, the Amazonas and the Nanay. Operators quote prices in US dollars. A useful booking website is www. amazoncruise.net.

★ Dawn on the Amazon Tours & Cruises CRUISE
(📞065-22-3730; www.dawnontheamazon.com; Malecón Maldonado 185; day trips incl lunch per person from US$85, multiday cruises per day from US$225) This small outfit offers a great deal for independent travelers. The *Amazon I* is a beautiful 11m wooden craft with modern furnishings, available for either day trips or river cruises up to two weeks. Included are a bilingual guide, all meals and transfers.

🎊 Festivals & Events

San Juan TRADITIONAL MUSIC
(⊙ Jun 22-27) This is the big annual debauch, a festival that has grown around the saint's day of San Juan Bautista (St John the Baptist) on June 24 (the main party day). It's celebrated in most Amazon towns but Iquitos honors the saint most fervently with dancing, and above all feasting and frivolity.

Juanes are the typical food consumed. On the night of June 23 locals partake in the river dunk, as this is the day of the year when the waters of the Itaya are said to have healing properties.

🛏 Sleeping

★ Boulevard 251 Riverside Apartments APARTMENT $$
(📞965-730-491; www.iquitosapartments.com; Malecón Maldonado 251; apt S157-230; ※🛜) We'll tell it to you straight: there is no better place to stay in Iquitos, either for the exceptional

Iquitos

Clínica Ana Stahl (550m);
Al Frio y al Fuego (750km)

Pedro Rosell

Castilla

Pucallpa

Loreto

Callao

Yavari

Nanay

Tavara

Pevas

Nauta

Ocampo

Yavari

Pucallpa

Moore

Loreto

Condamine

Fitzcarrald

Putumayo

Tacna

Pevas

Nauta

Raimondi

**Historical
Ships
Museum**

5 ▣
Plaza
Castilla 1 🏛

9 📍

Araujo

Moore

📍12

Napo

●17

Araujo

Condamine

Putumayo

Plaza de
Armas

Próspero

📦4

3 ●

8

🚌2

*Río
Amazonas*

7
Lores 🍴

10 💲

16 ●

ℹ️
15

Malecón
Maldonado

Tacna

Fitzcarrald

Lores

Huallaga

📍11

Morona

Próspero

Malecón Tarapaca

Oficina de
Migraciónes
(1.8km)

Brasil

✈(6km)

📍14

Belén Mercado
(900m)

location, high above the banks of the river,
or for the chic environs that those who check
in enjoy here. There are three categories of
accommodations, but we recommend the
riverside apartments, on the upper floors
gazing out at the river.

Casa Morey BOUTIQUE HOTEL **$$$**
(☎065-23-1913; www.casamorey.com; Loreto 200;
s/d incl breakfast S230/310; ❄🛜📺) This former
mansion of the rubber baron Luis F Morey
dates from 1910 and has been renovated to
its former elegance, with 14 extravagant-
ly large suites, plenty of original *azulejos*
(handmade tiles imported from Portugal), vo-

luminous bathrooms with baths, river views,
a courtyard with a small pool and a library
with a stupendous collection of Amazon-
related literature.

✖️ Eating

★ Belén Mercado MARKET **$**
(cnr Próspero & Jirón 9 de Diciembre; menús from S5)
There are great eats at Iquitos' markets, par-
ticularly the Belén *mercado* where a *menú*,
including *jugo especial* (jungle juice) costs
S5. Look out for specialties including meaty
Amazon worms, *ishpa* (simmered sabalo fish
intestines and fat) and *sikisapa* (fried leaf-

PERU IQUITOS

Iquitos

cutter ants; abdomens are supposedly tastiest), and watch your valuables. Another good market for cheap eats is **Mercado Central** (Lores cuadra 5; snacks from S1).

★**Dawn on the Amazon Cafe** INTERNATIONAL **$$**
(http://dawnontheamazoncafe.com; Malecón Maldonado 185; mains S10-30; ☺7:30am-10pm Mon-Sat; 🛜) This traveler magnet on the Malecón, with its tempting row of street-front tables, sports a menu divided up into North American, Peruvian, Spanish and Chinese. Travel wherever your taste buds desire but bear in mind that the steamed fresh fish is very good. Ingredients are all non-MSG and those on gluten-free diets are catered for.

ChillOut Carnes y Pescados CEVICHE **$$**
(Napo 834; mains S20-32; ☺10am-5pm Sun-Tue, 7-10pm Thu-Sat; 🌐) This gets our nod for first prize in the keenly contested battle for number one in the city's *cevichería* (ceviche restaurant) contest. An air-conditioned interior, a little street-front courtyard and, most crucially of all, delicious, huge platters of ceviche.

Al Frio y al Fuego FUSION **$$**
(📱965-607-474; www.facebook.com/alfrioyalfuego restaurante; Embarcadero Av La Marina 138; mains S40-50; ☺noon-11pm Mon-Sat, to 6pm Sun; 🚤) Take a boat out to this floating foodie paradise in the middle of the mouth of the Río Itaya to sample some of the city's best food. The emphasis is on river fish (such as the delectable *doncella*), but the *parrillas* (grills) are inviting, too. The address given is the boat embarkation point.

🍷 **Drinking & Nightlife**

Arandú Bar BAR
(Malecón Maldonado 113; ☺till late) The liveliest of several thumping Malecón bars, full of funky art, great for people-watching and always churning out loud rock-and-roll classics.

Musmuqui BAR
(Raimondi 382; ☺5pm-midnight Sun-Thu, to 3am Fri & Sat) Locally popular lively bar with two floors and an extensive range of aphrodisiac cocktails concocted from wondrous Amazon plants.

ℹ **Information**

DANGERS & ANNOYANCES
Street touts and self-styled jungle guides tend to be aggressive, and many are both irritatingly insistent and dishonest. They are working for commissions, and usually for bog-standard establishments. It is best to make your own decisions by contacting hotels, lodges and tour companies directly. Exercise particular caution around Belén, which is very poor and where petty thieving is quite common. That said, violent crime is almost unknown in Iquitos.

EMBASSIES & CONSULATES
If arriving from or departing for Brazil or Colombia, get your entry/exit stamp at the border.
Brazilian Consulate (📱065-23-5151; Lores 363; ☺9am-1pm Mon-Fri)
Colombian Consulate (📱065-23-1461; Moore 249, cnr Calvo de Aurajo)
Oficina de Migraciones (📱065-23-5173; Mariscal Cáceres cuadra 18; ☺8am-4pm Mon-Fri, to noon Sat)

PERU IQUITOS

ⓘ GETTING TO THE PERU-COLOMBIA-BRAZIL BORDER ZONE

Even in the middle of the Amazon, border officials adhere to formalities and will refuse passage if documents are not in order. With a valid passport and visa or tourist card, border crossing is not a problem. It is highly advisable to check what immigration policies are for your country prior to showing up at the border.

When leaving Peru for Brazil or Colombia, you'll get an exit stamp at a Peruvian guard post just before the border (boats stop there long enough for this; ask the captain).

The ports at the three-way border are several kilometers apart, connected by public ferries. They are reached by air or boat, but not by road.

At this point, Peru occupies the south side of the river, where currents create a constantly shifting bank. Peru's border town (OK, tiny village) is Santa Rosa, which has Peruvian immigration facilities.

From here, motor canoes reach Leticia, in Colombia, in about 15 minutes. The biggest, nicest border town, Leticia boasts by far the best hotels and restaurants, and a hospital. You can fly from Leticia to Bogotá on almost-daily commercial flights.

The two small ports in Brazil are Tabatinga and Benjamin Constant; both have basic hotels. Tabatinga has an airport with flights to Manaus.

MEDICAL SERVICES

Clínica Ana Stahl (☑065-25-2535; www.facebook.com/caas.iquitos; La Marina 285; ☉24hr) Private clinic 2km north of the center.

Happydent (Putumayo 786) Dentist.

InkaFarma (Próspero 397, cnr Morona; ☉7am-midnight) Reliable.

MONEY

Several banks provide an ATM, including BCP, which has secure ATMs.

BCP (Próspero & Putumayo)

TOURIST INFORMATION

iPerú (☑065-23-6144; Napo 161; ☉9am-6pm Mon-Sat, to 1pm Sun) There's also a branch at the airport (☑065-26-0251; Main Hall, Francisco Secada Vignetta Airport; ☉when flights are arriving/departing).

ⓘ Getting There & Away

AIR

Iquitos' small **airport**, 7km from the center, receives flights from Lima, Pucallpa and Tarapoto.

Charter companies at the airport have five-seat passenger planes to almost anywhere in the Amazon, if you have a few hundred US bucks going spare.

LATAM (LAN; ☑065-23-2421; Próspero 232; ☉9am-6:30pm Mon-Fri, to 1pm Sat) Direct daily runs to Lima, plus flights to Cuzco on Mondays, Wednesdays and Saturdays.

Star Perú (☑065-23-6208; Napo 260; ☉8:30am-6:30pm Mon-Fri, to 5:30pm Sat) Star Perú operates two daily flights to and from Lima: the morning flight stops at Pucallpa and the afternoon flight at Tarapoto. Fares are about US$70 to Lima and US$60 to Pucallpa or Tarapoto.

BOAT

Puerto Masusa (Los Rosales), about 3km north of the town center, is where cargo boats depart for Yurimaguas (upriver; three to six days) and Pucallpa (upriver; four to seven days); but these trips are better undertaken in the other direction, with the current. Fares cost S80 to S100 for hammock space and S130 to S180 for a tiny (often cell-like) cabin. Boats leave most days for both places: there are more frequent departures for the closer intermediate ports en route. For Yurimaguas, the Eduardo boats have the best reputation.

Downriver boats to the Peruvian border with Brazil and Colombia leave from Puerto Masusa too. There are about two or three departures weekly for the two-day journey (per person S80). Boats will stop at Pevas (hammock space S40, about 15 hours) and other ports en route.

Closer to the center, the more organized **Henry Boats Port** (Av La Marina 1640; ☉7am-7pm) runs services along the Iquitos–Pucallpa route.

You can often sleep aboard the boat while waiting for departure, and this enables you to get the best hammock space. Never leave gear unattended – ask to have your bags locked up when you sleep.

Reserva Nacional Pacaya-Samiria

At 20,800 sq km, **Reserva Nacional Pacaya-Samiria** (per person per day S30, incl entrance fee, guide, food & accommodations S150) is the most immense of Peru's parks and reserves. Pacaya-Samiria provides local people with food and a home, and protects ecologically important habitats. An estimated 42,000 people live on and around the reserve; juggling the needs of human inhabitants while protecting wildlife is the responsibility of some 30 rangers. Staff also teach inhabitants how to best harvest the natural renewable resources to benefit the local people and to maintain thriving populations of plants and animals.

The reserve is the home of aquatic animals such as Amazon manatees, pink and grey river dolphins, two species of caiman, giant South American river turtles and many other bird and animal species.

Lagunas is the reserve's western entry point; it is also possible to access the eastern side of the reserve from Iquitos/Nauta. The area close to Lagunas has suffered from depletion: allow several days to get deep into the least-disturbed areas. With 15 days, you can reach Lago Cocha Pasto, where there are reasonable chances of seeing jaguars and larger mammals. Other noteworthy points in the reserve include Quebrada Yanayacu, where the river water is black from dissolved plants; Lago Pantean, where you can check out caimans and go medicinal-plant collecting; and Tipischa de Huana, where you can see the giant *Victoria amazonica* waterlilies, big enough for a small child to sleep upon without sinking.

Official information is available at the agencies offering Pacaya-Samiria tours in Iquitos and Lagunas.

The best way to visit the reserve is to go by dugout canoe with a guide from Lagunas and spend several days camping and exploring. Alternatively, comfortable ships visit from Iquitos.

If coming from Lagunas, Santa Rosa is the main entry point, where you pay the park entrance fee (often included in tour prices).

The best time to go is during the dry season, when you are more likely to see animals along the riverbanks. Rains ease off in late May; it then takes a month for water levels to drop, making July and August the best months to visit (with excellent fishing). September to November isn't too bad, and the heaviest rains begin in January. The months of February to May are the worst times to go. February to June tend to be the hottest months, with animal-viewing best in the early morning and late afternoon.

Travelers should bring plenty of insect repellent and plastic bags (to cover luggage), and be prepared to camp out.

UNDERSTAND PERU

Peru Today

From the happening capital of Lima to cobblestoned Andean villages, Peru leaves an indelible impression as a place of incredible diversity, bustling commerce and innovation. There are still tangles to be worked out – environmental woes, a growing drug trade and political uncertainty – but by and large, Peru is finding its way.

Over the past decade, Peru has had one of the region's fastest growing economies, averaging at a rate of 5.9%, according to World Bank data. No small feat, the national poverty rate has been halved in the mere space of a decade. However, the good times haven't trickled down to everyone: rural areas account for 44% of the population below the poverty line, with indigenous populations and the Andean highlands hit the hardest.

Between 2014 and 2017 Peru's growth slowed, largely in response to the drop in the price of its main export, copper. Many think the economy is poised to rebound, both with industry, including growing mining profits, and investments in infrastructure. Tourism is also big: the number of foreign travelers going to Peru almost tripled between 2003 and 2014 from 1.3 to 3.2 million.

When two tourist trains collided in the middle of the 2018 high season, injuring 15 people, the fever pitch of Machu Picchu visitation was finally seeing hard consequences. With 1.3 million visitors in 2016, the site visitation increased 38% over five years. Seems becoming one of the New Seven Wonders of the World has its price.

Unesco has long been pressuring for better control of the visitation at the site. In response, Machu Picchu introduced timed entry tickets in July 2017, with morning and afternoon sessions. Some responsible Cuzco tour operators have responded to the quandary by offering a more diverse portfolio of tours to disperse the overflow. Many in the tourism industry fear the eventual consequences of overexploitation.

History

Early Cultures

The Inca civilization is merely the tip of Peru's archaeological iceberg.

The country's first inhabitants were loose-knit bands of nomadic hunters, fishers and gatherers, living in caves and killing fearsome (now extinct) animals like giant sloths, saber-toothed tigers and mastodons. Domestication of the llama, alpaca and guinea pig began between 7000 and 4000 BC. Various forms of the faithful potato (Peru boasts almost 4000 varieties!) were domesticated around 3000 BC.

Roughly from 1000 to 300 BC, the Early Horizon or Chavín Period evidenced at Chavín de Huántar near Huaraz saw widespread settled communities, plus the interchange of ideas, enhanced skills and cultural complexity, although the Chavín horizon inexplicably disappeared around 300 BC. The next 500 years saw the rise and fall of the Paracas culture south of Lima, which produced some of the most exquisite textiles in the Americas.

Between AD 100 and 700, pottery, metalwork and textiles reached new heights, and the Moche built their massive pyramids near Trujillo and at Sipán near Chiclayo. Around this time, the Nazca sculpted their enigmatic lines in the desert.

From about 600 to 1000 the first Andean expansionist empire emerged, and the influence of the Wari (Huari), from north of Ayacucho, can still be seen throughout most of Peru.

During the next four centuries several states thrived, including the Chimú, who built the city of Chan Chan near Trujillo, and the Chachapoyas, who erected the stone fortress of Kuélap. Several smaller, warlike highland groups lived near Lake Titicaca and left impressive circular funerary towers, including those at Sillustani and Cutimbo.

Inca Empire & Spanish Conquest

For all its glory, incas (kings) pre-eminence only lasted around 100 years. The reign of the first eight Incas spanned the period from the 12th century to the early 15th century, but it was the ninth *inca,* Pachacutec, who gave the empire its first bloody taste of conquest. A growing thirst for expansion had led the neighboring highland tribe, the Chankas, to Cuzco's doorstep around 1438, and Viracocha Inca fled in the belief that his small empire was lost. However, his son Pachacutec rallied the Inca army and, in a desperate battle, he famously routed the Chankas.

Buoyed by victory, Pachacutec embarked upon the first wave of Inca expansion, promptly bagging much of the central Andes.

Over the next 25 years, the Inca empire grew until it stretched from the present-day border of Ecuador and Colombia to the deserts of northern Chile. During this time scores of fabulous mountaintop citadels were built, including Machu Picchu.

When Europeans came to the New World, epidemics including smallpox swept down from Central America and the Caribbean. In 1527 the 11th *inca,* Huayna Capác, died in one such epidemic. He had divided his empire between his two sons: Atahualpa, born of a Quiteña mother, who took the north, and the pure-blooded native Cuzqueñan Huáscar, who took Cuzco and the south. Civil war eventually ensued, precipitating the slow downfall of the Inca empire.

By 1526 Francisco Pizarro had started heading south from Panama and soon discovered the rich coastal settlements of the Inca empire. After going back to Spain to court money and men for the conquest, he sailed to Ecuador and marched overland toward Peru and the heart of the Inca empire, reaching Cajamarca in 1532, by which time Atahualpa had defeated his half-brother Huáscar.

This meeting was to change the course of South American history. Atahualpa was ambushed by a few dozen armed conquistadors who killed thousands of unarmed indigenous tribespeople in his capture. For his freedom, the *inca* offered a ransom of gold and silver from Cuzco, including that stripped from the walls of Qorikancha.

But after imprisoning Atahualpa for months and adding ransom requests, Pizarro had him killed anyway, and marched on Cuzco. Wearing armor and carrying steel swords, the Spanish cavalry was virtually unstoppable. Despite sporadic rebellions, the Inca empire was forced to retreat into the mountains and jungle, and never recovered its glorious prestige or extent.

Colonial Peru

In 1535 Pizarro founded the capital of Lima. Decades of turmoil ensued, with Peruvians resisting their conquerors, who were fighting among themselves for control of the rich colony. Pizarro was assassinated in 1541 by the son of conquistador Diego de Almagro, whom Pizarro had put to death in 1538. Manco Inca nearly regained control of the highlands in 1536 but by 1539 had retreated to his rainforest hideout at Vilcabamba, where he was killed in 1544. Inca Túpac Amaru also attempted to overthrow the Spaniards in 1572 but was defeated and executed.

For the next two centuries Lima was the major political, social and commercial center of Andean nations, while Cuzco became a backwater. The *encomienda* system, whereby settlers were granted land and native slaves, exploited native peoples. This system eventually spurred the 1780 uprising under the self-proclaimed ruler Inca Túpac Amaru II. The rebellion was crushed and its leaders cruelly executed.

Independence

By the early 1800s, rebellion was stirring. Colonists resisted high taxes imposed by Spain, and hoped to take control of the country's rich mineral deposits, beginning with prime *guano* (seabird droppings) used for fertilizer.

Change came from two directions. After liberating Argentina and Chile from Spain, José de San Martín entered Lima and formally proclaimed Peru's independence in 1821. Meanwhile, Simón Bolívar had freed Venezuela, Colombia and Ecuador. San Martín and Bolívar met in Ecuador and Bolívar continued into Peru. Two decisive battles were fought at Junín and Ayacucho in 1824, and the Spanish finally surrendered in 1826.

Peru also won a brief war with Spain in 1866 and lost a longer war with Chile (1879–83) over the nitrate-rich northern Atacama Desert. Chile annexed much of coastal southern Peru but returned some areas in 1929. A little over a decade later, Peru went to war with Ecuador over another border dispute. A 1942 treaty gave Peru the area north of the Río Marañón, but Ecuador disputed this and skirmishes occurred every few years. It wasn't until 1998 that a peace treaty finally put an end to the hostilities.

Modern Times

Despite periods of civilian rule, coups and military dictatorships characterized Peru's government during most of the 20th century.

In the late 1980s the country experienced severe social unrest. Demonstrations protesting the disastrous handling of the economy by President Alan García Pérez were an everyday occurrence – at one point, inflation reached 10,000%! His first term was shadowed by the disruptive activities of Maoist terrorist organization Sendero Luminoso, which waged a guerrilla war resulting in the death or disappearance of at least 40,000 people, mostly in the central Andes.

In 1990 Alberto Fujimori, the son of Japanese immigrants, was elected president. Strong, semidictatorial actions led to unprecedented improvements in the economy. Popular support propelled Fujimori to a second term in 1995 (after he amended the constitution expressly so he could run again), but that support was dwindling by 1998. In September 2000 a video was released showing Fujimori's head of intelligence bribing a congressman, causing Fujimori's 10-year presidency to spiral out of control. Amid the scandal and human-rights abuse accusations, Fujimori resigned during a state trip to Asia and hid in Japan, which refused Peru's repeated extradition requests. In 2005 he was arrested while on a trip to Chile, and extradited to Peru in 2007, when he was initially tried and convicted for ordering an illegal search and sentenced to six years in prison. In 2009 Fujimori was sentenced to an additional 25 years for crimes against humanity. He was found guilty of murder, bodily harm and two incidences of kidnapping.

Despite the blemish on the family record, Fujimori's daughter Keiko was elected to the Peruvian Congress in a landslide in 2006 and ran for president in 2011, losing in a tight runoff election to former army officer Ollanta Humala.

Humala was initially thought to be a populist in the Hugo Chávez vein (the Lima stock exchange plunged when he was first elected), but his administration turned out to be quite friendly to business. Though the economy functioned well under his governance, a botched raid on a Sendero Luminoso encampment in the highlands sent his approval rating into a tailspin by the middle of 2012. Extraordinarily, Humala's approval rebounded in August 2015, his final year in power, despite (or due to) declaring martial law on the south coast in reaction to violent conflict between local farmers and the forces of the Tía María copper mine.

Culture

With a geography that encompasses desert, highland and jungle, Peru is relentlessly touted as a land of contrasts. This also applies to the lives of its people: the country is a mix of rich and poor, modern and ancient, agricultural and urban, indigenous and white. Day-to-day existence can be difficult – but it can also be profoundly rich. For centuries, this has been the story of life in Peru.

Population

Peru is essentially a bicultural society: the part that's indigenous, and the part that's European-influenced. Peruvians who speak Spanish and adhere to *criollo* tradition (Peru-born Spaniards during the colony) are a racial mix of those who are white (15% of the population) and those who are *mestizo*, people of mixed indigenous and European heritage (another 37%).

About 45% of Peru's population is pure *indígena* (people of indigenous descent), making it one of three countries in Latin America to have such high indigenous representation. A disproportionate share of *indígenas* inhabit rural areas in the Andes and work in agriculture. Most *indígenas* speak Quechua and live in the Andean highlands, while a smaller percentage speak Aymara and inhabit the Lake Titicaca region. In the vast Amazon, various indigenous ethnicities speak a plethora of other languages.

About 3% of Peruvians are of African or Asian descent. Afro-Peruvians descend from slaves brought by Spanish conquistadors.

Lifestyle

Though the 21st-century economic boom has been good to the country, there is still a yawning disparity between rich and poor. The minimum monthly wage stands at US$284. Around 22% of the population lives below the poverty line, according to INEI, Peru's national institution for statistics and information. Though the official national unemployment rate is only 6.7%, underemployment is rampant, especially in Lima and other cities.

In rural areas, the poor survive largely from subsistence agriculture, living in traditional adobe or tin houses that often lack electricity and indoor plumbing. In cities, the extreme poor live in shantytowns, while the lower and middle classes live in concrete, apartment-style housing or small stand-alone homes. More affluent urban homes consist of large stand-alone houses, often bordered by high walls.

Across the board, homes are generally shared by more than one generation.

Religion

More than 81% of Peruvians identify as Roman Catholics, and Catholicism is the official religion. While some *indígenas* are outwardly Catholic, they often combine elements of traditional beliefs into church festivals and sacred ceremonies. Evangelicals and other Protestants are around 13% of the population.

Sports

Fútbol (soccer) inspires fanaticism in Peru, even though its national squad hasn't qualified for the World Cup since 1982. The big-boy teams mostly hail from Lima: the traditional *clásico* (classic match) pitches Alianza Lima against rivals Universitario (La U). The season is late March to November.

Bullfighting is also part of the national culture. Lima's Plaza de Acho attracts international talent. In remote Andean festivals, condors are tied to the back of the bull – representative of indigenous struggle against Spanish conquistadors.

Arts

The country that has been home to both indigenous and European empires has a wealth of cultural and artistic tradition. Perhaps the most outstanding achievements are in the areas of music (both indigenous and otherwise), painting and literature — the last of which received plenty of attention in 2010, when Peruvian novelist Mario Vargas Llosa won the Nobel Prize.

Music

Like its people, Peru's music is an intercontinental fusion of elements. Pre-Columbian cultures contributed bamboo flutes, the Spaniards brought stringed instruments and the Africans gave it a backbone of fluid, percussive rhythm. By and large, music tends to be a regional affair: African-influenced *landós* with their thumbing bass beats are predominant on the coast; high-pitched indigenous *huaynos*, heavy on bamboo wind instruments, are heard in the Andes; and *criollo* waltzes are a must at any dance party on the coast.

Over the last several decades, the *huayno* has blended with surf guitars and Colombian *cumbia* (a type of Afro-Caribbean dance music) to produce *chicha* – a danceable sound closely identified with the Amazon region. (Well-known *chicha* bands include Los Shapis and Los Mirlos.) *Cumbia* is also popular. Grupo 5, which hails from Chiclayo, is currently a favorite in the genre.

On the coast, guitar-inflected *música criolla* (*criollo* music) has its roots in both Spain and Africa. The most famous *criollo* style is the *vals peruano* (Peruvian waltz), a three-quarter-time waltz that is fast moving and full of complex guitar melodies. The most legendary singers in this genre include singer and composer Chabuca Granda (1920–83), Lucha Reyes (1936–73) and Arturo 'Zambo' Cavero (1940–2009). Cavero in particular was revered for his gravelly vocals and soulful interpretations. *Landó* is closely connected to this style of music but features the added elements of call-and-response. Standout performers in this vein include singers Susana Baca (b 1944) and Eva Ayllón (b 1956).

Visual Arts

The country's most famous art movement dates to the 17th and 18th centuries, when the native and *mestizo* artists of the Cuzco School produced thousands of religious paintings, the vast majority of which remain unattributed. *Cuzqueña* canvases are proudly displayed in many highland churches.

Traditional Crafts

Peru has a long tradition of producing extraordinarily rendered crafts and folk art. Here's what to look for:

Textiles You'll see intricate weavings with elaborate anthropomorphic and geometric designs all over Peru. Some of the finest can be found around Cuzco.

Pottery The most stunning pieces of pottery are those made in the tradition of the pre-Columbian Moche people of the north coast. But also worthwhile is Chancay-style pottery: rotund figures made from sand colored clay. Find these at craft markets in Lima.

Religious crafts These abound in all regions, but the *retablos* (3D ornamental dioramas) from Ayacucho are the most spectacular.

Literature

Peru's most famous novelist is the Nobel Prize–winning Mario Vargas Llosa (b 1936), who ran unsuccessfully for president in 1990. His complex novels including *The Time of the Hero* delve into Peruvian society, politics and culture.

Considered Peru's greatest poet, César Vallejo (1892–1938) wrote *Trilce,* a book of 77 avant-garde, existentialist poems. Vallejo was known for pushing the Spanish language to its limits, inventing words when real ones no longer served him.

Two writers noted for their portrayals of indigenous communities are José María Arguedas (1911–69) and Ciro Alegría (1909–67). Rising literary star Daniel Alarcón (b 1977) is a Peruvian-American whose 2007 debut novel *Lost City Radio* achieved wide acclaim.

Environment

Few countries have topographies as rugged, as forbidding and as wildly diverse as Peru. The third-largest country in South America (at 1,285,220 sq km), it is five times larger than the UK, almost twice the size of Texas and one-sixth the size of Australia. It lies in the tropics, south of the equator, straddling three strikingly different geographic zones: the arid Pacific coast, the craggy Andes mountain range and a good portion of the Amazon Basin.

The Land

The coastal strip is mainly desert, punctuated by cities and rivers down from the Andes forming agricultural oases. The country's best road, the Carr Panamericana, slices through coastal Peru from border to border.

The Andes rise rapidly from the coast to spectacular heights over 6000m just 100km inland. Most mountains are between 3000m and 4000m, with jagged ranges separated by deep, vertiginous canyons. Huascarán (6768m) is Peru's highest peak.

The eastern Andes get more rainfall than the dry western slopes, and so they're covered in cloud forest, merging with the rainforest of the Amazon Basin.

Wildlife

With mammoth deserts, glaciated mountain ranges, tropical rainforests and almost every imaginable habitat in between, Peru hosts a menagerie of wildlife.

Bird and marine life is abundant along the coast, with colonies of sea lions, Humboldt penguins, Chilean flamingos, Peruvian pelicans, Inca terns and the brown booby endemic to the region. Remarkable highland birds include majestic Andean condors, puna ibis and a variety of hummingbirds. The highlands are also home to camelids such as llamas, alpacas, guanacos and *vicuñas*,

TOP WILDLIFE-WATCHING SPOTS

Parque Nacional Manu (p944) The remote jungle is your best chance to see jaguars, tapirs and monkeys.

Islas Ballestas This coastal reserve is home to penguins, flamingos and sea lions.

Iquitos Canopy walkways, jungle lodges and river cruises.

Parque Nacional Huascarán Andean condors and *vicuñas*.

Puerto Maldonado Capybaras and macaws.

Cañón del Colca The easiest place to spot Andean condors.

Yarinacocha Home to pink dolphins, huge iguanas and myriad bird species.

Reserva Nacional Pacaya-Samiria (p950) Best explored by dugout canoe.

Machu Picchu (p908) More than 400 species of rare and endemic birds.

while cloud forests are the haunts of jaguars, tapirs and endangered spectacled bears.

Swoop down toward the Amazon and with luck you'll spot all the iconic tropical birds – parrots, macaws, toucans and many more. The Amazon is home to over a dozen species of monkey, plus river dolphins, frogs, reptiles, fish and insects galore. Snakes? Don't panic. Many species live here, but they're mostly shy of humans.

National Parks

Peru's wealth of wildlife is protected by a system of national parks and reserves, with 60 areas covering almost 15% of the country. Yet these areas seriously lack infrastructure and are subject to illegal hunting, fishing, logging and mining.

Some highlights include Parque Nacional Huascarán, a prime spot for trekking in the Cordillera Blanca, and Parque Nacional Manu, among the world's most biodiverse rainforests, located northwest of Cuzco. Many reserves or *reservas nacionales* and protected areas – such as Cañón del Colca and Lake Titicaca – are just as worthy of a visit.

After decades in waiting, in 2015 Sierra del Divisor Reserve Zone finally became a national park. This offers protection for its 15,000 sq km of rainforest on the Brazilian border, including unique flora, fauna and indigenous communities.

Environmental Issues

Peru faces major challenges in the stewardship of its natural resources, with problems compounded by a lack of law enforcement and its impenetrable geography. Deforestation and erosion are major issues, as is industrial pollution, urban sprawl and the continuing attempted eradication of coca plantations on some Andean slopes. In addition, the Interoceanic Hwy through the heart of the Amazon may imperil thousands of square kilometers of rainforest.

DEFORESTATION & WATER PROBLEMS

At the ground level, clear-cutting of the highlands for firewood, of the rainforests for valuable hardwoods, and of both to clear land for agriculture, oil drilling and mining has led to severe erosion. In the highlands, where deforestation and overgrazing of Andean woodlands and *puna* (Andean highlands) grass is severe, soil quality is rapidly deteriorating. In the Amazon rainforest, deforestation has led to erosion and a decline in bellwether species such as frogs. Erosion has also led to decreased water quality in this area, where silt-laden water is unable to support micro-organisms at the base of the food chain.

Other water-related problems include pollution from mining in the highlands. Sewage contamination along the coast has led to many beaches around some coastal cities being declared unfit for swimming. In the south, pollution and overfishing have led to the continued decline of the Humboldt penguin (its numbers have declined by more than a third since the 1980s).

PROTECTIVE STEPS

In late 2014 Peru signed an agreement with Norway and Germany to reduce its forest-related emissions in an effort to become carbon-neutral by 2021. Norway pledged to pay up to US$300 million for verified results.

Some positive measures are being taken to help protect the country's environment. For example, the Peruvian government and private interests within the tourism industry have come together to develop sustainable travel projects in the Amazon.

SURVIVAL GUIDE

ⓘ Directory A–Z

ACCESSIBLE TRAVEL

Peru offers few conveniences for travelers with disabilities. Features such as signs in braille or phones for the hearing-impaired are virtually nonexistent, while wheelchair ramps and lifts are few and far between, and the pavement is often badly potholed and cracked. Most hotels do not have wheelchair accessible rooms, at least not rooms specially designated as such. Bathrooms are often barely large enough for an able-bodied person to walk into, so few are accessible to wheelchairs.

Nevertheless there are Peruvians with disabilities who get around, mainly through the help of others.

Apumayo Expediciones (📞914-169-665; www.apumayo.com; Jr Ricardo Palma Ñ-11, Urb Santa Monica Wanchaq, Cuzco; ⊘9am-6pm Mon-Fri) An adventure-tour company that takes disabled travelers to Machu Picchu and other historic sites in the Sacred Valley.

Conadis (Map p856; 📞01-332-0808; www.conadisperu.gob.pe; Av Arequipa 375, Santa Beatriz, Lima; ⊘8am-5pm Mon-Fri) Governmental agency for Spanish-language information and advocacy for people with disabilities.

Emerging Horizons (www.emerginghorizons.com) Travel magazine for the mobility-impaired, with handy advice columns and news articles.

Mobility International (📞USA 541-343-1284; www.miusa.org; 132 E Broadway, Suite 343, USA; ⊘9am-4pm Mon-Fri) Advises disabled travelers on mobility issues and runs an educational exchange program.

ACCOMMODATIONS

Lima and the tourist mecca of Cuzco are the most expensive places to stay in Peru. During high season (June through August), major holidays and festivals, accommodations are likely to be full and rates can triple. At other times, the high-season rates we quote taper off. Foreign tourists normally aren't charged the 10% sales tax on accommodations. *Incluye impuesto* (IGV) means a service charge has been included in the price. At better hotels, taxes and service charges combined may total 28%. Budget hotels usually have hot (or, more likely, tepid) showers some of the time. Dormitory beds come with shared bathrooms, while single and double rooms (including those in *hostales*, which are guesthouses and not

---

SLEEPING PRICE RANGES

Lima, Cuzco & the Sacred Valley

$ less than S165

$$ S165–S435

$$$ more than S435

The Provinces

$ less than S85

$$ S85–S250

$$$ more than S250

---

the same as backpacker hostels) have private bathrooms unless otherwise noted.

ACTIVITIES

Most activities are available year-round, but certain times of year are better than others. Peak season for most outdoor activities is during the winter dry season (June to August). Trekking in the highlands is a muddy proposition during the wet season, especially December to March, when the heaviest rains fall. However, those hotter summer months are best for swimming and surfing along the Pacific Coast.

For your safety, avoid the cheapest, cut-rate tour agencies and outdoor outfitters. For specialized activities, bring high-quality gear from home.

If bird-watching gets you in a flap, head for the Amazon Basin, Islas Ballestas and Cañón del Colca for starters.

When it comes to mountain climbing, Huascarán (6768m), Peru's highest mountain, is experts-only, but easier peaks abound near Huaraz and Arequipa. Rock and ice climbing are popular around Huaraz.

Horse rentals can be easily arranged. For a real splurge, take a ride on a graceful Peruvian *paso* horse near Urubamba.

Gearing up for some downhill adventures? Easy or demanding single-track trails await mountain bikers outside Huaraz, Cuzco and Arequipa.

Paragliding is especially popular in Lima.

Whitewater-rafting (river-running) agencies in Cuzco and Arequipa offer a multitude of day runs and longer hauls (grade III to IV+ rapids). Travelers have died on these rivers, so be especially cautious about which rafting company to trust with your life. The best place for beginners is Lunahuaná.

Surfing has a big fan base in Peru. There are some radical waves up north, famously at Huanchaco, Máncora and just south of Lima. For something completely different, sandboard down humongous dunes in the coastal desert near Huacachina and Nazca.

Trekkers, pack your boots – the variety of trails in Peru is staggering. The Cordillera Blanca can't be beaten for peaks, while the nearby Cordillera Huayhuash is similarly stunning. But if you've heard of *any* trek in Peru, you'll have heard of the world-famous Inca Trail to Machu Picchu – and everyone else has, too, so consider taking an alternative route. The spectacular six-day Ausangate circuit and ancient ruins hidden in cloud forests outside Chachapoyas are a couple of other possibilities. Alternatively, get down into the world's deepest canyons – the Cañón del Cotahuasi and Cañón del Colca.

ELECTRICITY

Electrical current is 220V, 60Hz AC. Standard outlets accept round prongs, some have dual-voltage outlets which take flat prongs. Even so, your adapter may need a built-in surge protector.

EMBASSIES & CONSULATES

Most foreign embassies are in Lima, with some consular services in major tourist centers such as Cuzco.

It is important to realize what your embassy can and can't do if you get into trouble. Your embassy will not be sympathetic if you end up in jail after committing a crime, even if such actions are legal in your own country. If all your money and documents are stolen, the embassy can help you get a new passport.

Call in advance to double-check operating hours or schedule an appointment. While many consulates and embassies are staffed during regular business hours, attention to the public is often more limited. For after-hours and emergency contact numbers, check individual websites.

Oficinas de migraciónes (immigration offices) are where you'll need to go to receive an exit stamp or secure a new entry card, which can also be done online through the website.

Australian Embassy (Map p858; 01-630-0500; www.peru.embassy.gov.au; Av La Paz 1049, piso 10, Miraflores)

Belgian Embassy (Map p858; 01-241-7566; www.peru.diplomatie.belgium.be; Av Angamos Oeste 380, Miraflores; 8:30am-4pm Mon-Fri)

Bolivian Embassy (Map p864; 01-440-2095; www.boliviaenperu.com; Los Castaños 235, San Isidro; 8:30am-12:30pm Mon-Fri) There's a consulate in Puno (p888).

Brazilian Embassy (Map p858; 01-512-0830; www.embajadabrasil.org.pe; Av José Pardo 850, Miraflores; 8:15am-4pm Mon-Fri)

Canadian Embassy (Map p858; 01-319-3200; www.canadainternational.gc.ca/peru-perou; Bolognesi 228, Miraflores; 8am-12:30pm & 1:15-5pm Mon-Thu, 8am-12:30pm Fri) With a helpful website.

Chilean Embassy (Map p864; 01-710-2211; www.chile.gob.cl/peru; Javier Prado Oeste 790, San Isidro)

Colombian Embassy (Map p864; 01-201-9830; http://peru.embajada.gov.co/embajada; Av Víctor Andrés Belaúnde 340, San Isidro; 8am-1pm & 2-5pm Mon-Fri) There's a consulate in Iquitos (p949).

Ecuadorian Embassy (Map p864; 01-212-4027; www.peru.embajada.gob.ec; Las Palmeras 356, San Isidro; 8:30am-4pm Mon-Fri) There's a consulate in **Tumbes** (072-52-5949; Bolívar 129, 3rd fl, Plaza de Armas).

French Embassy (Map p853; 01-215-8400; www.ambafrance-pe.org; Av Arequipa 3415, San Isidro; 8:30am-12:15pm Mon-Thu, to noon Fri)

German Embassy (Map p853; 01-203-5940; www.lima.diplo.de; Av Dionisio Derteano 144, 7th & 8th fl, San Isidro; 8am-4:30pm Mon-Thu, to 1:30pm Fri)

Israeli Embassy (Map p853; 01-418-0500; www.embassies.gov.il/lima; Centro Empresarial Platinum Plaza II, Av Andres Reyes 437, piso 13, San Isidro; 9am-12:30pm Mon-Fri)

Italian Embassy (Map p853; 01-463-2727; www.amblima.esteri.it; Av Guiseppe Garibaldi 298, Jesús María; 8:30am-5:30pm Mon & Thu, 8am-2pm Tue, Wed & Fri)

Netherlands Embassy (Map p858; 01-213-9800; www.dutch-embassy.com/contact-details/netherlands-in-lima; Av José Larco 1301, Torre Parque Mar, 13th fl, Miraflores; 8:30am-12:45pm & 1:30-5pm Mon-Thu, 8:30am-1pm Fri)

Spanish Consulate (Map p864; 01-513-7930; www.consuladolima.com.pe; Calle Los Pinos, San Isidro; 8:30am-1pm Mon-Fri)

Swiss Embassy (Map p853; 01-264-0305; www.eda.admin.ch/lima; Av Salaverry 3240, San Isidro; 8am-1pm & 2-4:30pm Mon-Thu, 8am-2pm Fri)

UK Embassy (Map p858; 01-617-3000; www.gov.uk/world/organisations/british-embassy-peru; Av José Larco 1301, Edificio Parquemar, 22nd fl, Miraflores; 8am-1pm & 2-4:30pm Mon-Thu, 8am-1pm Fri)

US Embassy (Map p853; 01-618-2000; https://pe.usembassy.gov/embassy/lima; Av Encalada, cuadra 17, Surco; 8am-5pm) Call before showing up in person.

FOOD

Peru has long been a place where the concept of 'fusion' was a part of everyday cooking. Over the course of the last 400 years, Andean stews mingled with Asian stir-fry techniques, and Spanish rice dishes absorbed flavors from the Amazon, producing the country's famed *criollo* (creole) cooking. In the past decade, a generation of experimental young innovators has pushed this local fare to gastronomic heights.

This *novoandina* approach interprets Peruvian cooking through the lens of haute cuisine.

Food tends toward the spicy, but *ají* (chili condiment) is served separately. Conventional eaters can find refuge in a *chifa* (Chinese restaurant) or *pollería* (rotisserie restaurant). Vegetarian options are expanding, and Peru's many innovative potato dishes are worth trying. Restaurants commonly offer a *menú del día* (set meal, usually lunch), consisting of soup, main course and possibly dessert for S8 to S22. Dried corn called *canchita* is a ubiquitous table snack.

Incluye impuesto (IGV) means a service charge has been included in the price. Better restaurants add 18% in taxes and 10% in tips to the bill.

Drinks

The main soft-drink brands are available, but locals have a passion for Inca Kola – which tastes like bubble gum and comes in a spectacular shade of nuclear yellow. Fresh fruit juices are also popular, as are traditional drinks such as *chicha morada*, a refreshing, nonalcoholic beverage made from purple corn and spices.

Though the country exports coffee to the world, many Peruvians drink it instant: some restaurants dish up packets of Nescafé or an inky coffee reduction that is blended with hot water. In cosmopolitan and touristy areas, cafes serving espresso and cappuccino have proliferated. Tea and matés (herbal teas), such as *manzanilla* (chamomile), *menta* (mint) and *mate de coca* (coca-leaf tea), are also available. Coca-leaf tea will not get you high, but it can soothe stomach ailments and it's believed to help in adjusting to high altitude.

INTERNET ACCESS

→ Most regions have excellent internet connections and reasonable prices; it is typical for hotels and hostels to have wi-fi or computer terminals.

→ Family guesthouses, particularly outside urban areas, lag behind in this area.

→ Internet cafes are widespread.

LANGUAGE COURSES

Peru has schools in Lima, Cuzco, Arequipa, Huaraz, Puerto Maldonado and Huancayo. You can also study Quechua with private teachers or at one of the various language institutes in Lima, Cuzco and Huancayo.

LEGAL MATTERS

Legal assistance Your own embassy is of limited help if you get into trouble with the law in Peru, where you are presumed guilty until proven innocent. If you are the victim, the *policía de turismo* (tourist police; Poltur) can help, with limited English. Poltur stations are found in major cities.

Police Should you be stopped by a plainclothes officer, don't hand over any documents or

money. Never get into a vehicle with someone claiming to be a police officer, but insist on going to a real police station on foot.

LGBT TRAVELERS

Peru is a strongly conservative, Catholic country. While most believe that legalizing same-sex civil unions will happen soon, the initiative has met resistance from the Peruvian Congress in the past, despite the adoption of similar measures in neighboring countries in the Southern Cone. While many Peruvians will tolerate homosexuality on a 'don't ask; don't tell' level when dealing with foreign travelers, LGBT+ rights remain a struggle. As a result, many Peruvians don't publicly identify.

Public displays of affection among homosexual couples is rarely seen. Outside gay clubs, it is advisable to keep a low profile. Lima is the most accepting of gay people, but this is on a relative scale. Beyond that, the tourist towns of Cuzco, Arequipa and Trujillo tend to be more tolerant than the norm. Social-media platforms Tinder and Grindr can connect travelers to the gay scene.

FYI: the rainbow flag seen around Cuzco and in the Andes is *not* a gay pride flag – it's the flag of the Inca empire.

MAPS

The best road map of Peru is the 1:2,000,000 *Mapa Vial* published by Lima 2000 and available in better bookstores. The 1:1,500,000 *Peru South and Lima* country map, published by International Travel Maps, covers the country in good detail south of a line drawn east to west through Tingo María.

MONEY

The nuevo sol ('new sun') comes in bills of S10, S20, S50, S100 and (rarely) S200.

ATMs

➤ *Cajeros automáticos* (ATMs) proliferate in nearly every city and town in Peru, as well as at major airports, bus terminals and shopping areas.

➤ ATMs are linked to the international Plus (Visa) and Cirrus (Maestro/MasterCard) systems, as well as American Express and other networks.

➤ Users should have a four-digit PIN. To avoid problems, notify your bank that you'll be using your ATM card abroad.

➤ If your card works with Banco de la Nación, it may be the best option as it doesn't charge fees (at least at the time of writing).

➤ Both US dollars and nuevos soles are readily available from Peruvian ATMs.

➤ Your home bank may charge an additional fee for each foreign ATM transaction.

➤ ATMs are normally open 24 hours.

➤ For safety reasons use ATMs inside banks with security guards, preferably during daylight hours. Cover the keyboard for PIN entry.

Changing Money

The best currency for exchange is the US dollar, although the euro is accepted in major tourist centers. Other hard currencies can be exchanged, but usually with difficulty and only in major cities. All foreign currencies must be in flawless condition.

Cambistas (money changers) hang out on street corners near banks and *casas de cambio* (foreign-exchange bureaus) and give competitive rates (there's only a little flexibility for bargaining), but are not always honest. Officially, they should wear a vest and badge identifying themselves as legal. They're useful after regular business hours or at borders where there aren't any other options.

Credit Cards

Midrange and top-end hotels and shops accept *tarjetas de crédito* (credit cards) with a 7% (or greater) fee. Your bank may also tack on a surcharge and additional fees for each foreign-currency transaction. The most widely accepted cards in Peru are Visa and MasterCard.

OPENING HOURS

Hours are variable and liable to change, especially in small towns, where hours are irregular. Posted hours are a guideline. Lima has the most continuity of services. In other major cities, taxi drivers often know where the late-night stores and pharmacies are located.

Banks 9am–6pm Monday to Friday, some 9am–6pm Saturday

Government offices and businesses 9am–5pm Monday to Friday

Museums Often close on Monday

Restaurants 10am–10pm, many close 3pm–6pm

Shops 9am–6pm, some open Saturday

POST

The privatized postal system is run by Serpost (www.serpost.com.pe). Its service is fairly efficient and reliable, but surprisingly expensive. Most international mail will take about two weeks to arrive from Lima; longer from the provinces.

PUBLIC HOLIDAYS

Major holidays may be celebrated for days around the official date.

Fiestas Patrias (National Independence Days) is the biggest national holiday, when the entire nation seems to be on the move.

New Year's Day January 1

Good Friday March/April

Labor Day May 1

Inti Raymi June 24

Feast of Sts Peter & Paul June 29

National Independence Days July 28–29

Feast of Santa Rosa de Lima August 30

Battle of Angamos Day October 8

All Saints Day November 1

Feast of the Immaculate Conception December 8

Christmas December 25

RESPONSIBLE TRAVEL

Archaeologists are fighting a losing battle with *guaqueros* (grave robbers), particularly along the coast. Refrain from buying original pre-Columbian artifacts, and do not contribute to wildlife destruction by eating endangered animals or purchasing souvenirs made from skins, feathers, horns or turtle shells. Some indigenous communities make their living from tourism. Visiting these communities may financially support their initiatives but also weaken traditional cultures. If you go on an organized tour, make sure the company is locally owned and ask if any of the proceeds benefit the places you'll be visiting.

SAFE TRAVEL

Peru has its fair share of traveler hassles, which may often be avoided by exercising common sense.

The most common problem is theft, either stealth or snatch – theft by violent mugging is rare, though it's not to be ruled out. Watch out for 'choke and grab' attacks, especially at archaeological sites. Robberies and fatal attacks have occurred even on popular trekking trails, notably around Huaraz.

Avoid unlicensed 'pirate' taxis, as some drivers have been known to be complicit in 'express' kidnappings. Take good-quality day buses instead of cheap, overnight services to lower the risk of having an accident or possibly being hijacked.

Do *not* get involved with drugs. Gringos who have done so are being repaid with long-term incarceration in harsh Peruvian prisons. Any suspect in a crime (which includes vehicle accidents, whether or not you're the driver at fault) is considered guilty until proven innocent.

While terrorism lingers in Peru, drug trafficking is serious business. Areas to avoid are the Río Huallaga valley between Tingo María and Juanjui, and the Río Apurímac valley near Ayacucho, where the majority of Peru's illegal drug-growing takes place. Currently, it is unadvisable to visit Vilcabamba, Ivochote, Kiteni and beyond, but the situation is subject to change.

Not all unexploded ordinance (UXO) along the Ecuadorian border has been cleaned up. Use only official border crossings and don't stray off the beaten path in border zones.

Soroche (altitude sickness) can be fatal. For more information about altitude sickness, see p1052.

TELEPHONE

A few public pay phones operated by Movistar and Claro are still around, especially in small towns. They work with coins or phone cards, which can be purchased at supermarkets and groceries. Often internet cafes have 'net-to-net' capabilities (such as Skype), to talk for free.

Cell Phones

In Lima and other larger cities you can buy SIM cards for unlocked phones for about S15. Credit can be purchased in pharmacies and supermarkets. Cell-phone reception may be poor in the mountains or jungle.

Phone Codes

When calling Peru from abroad, dial the international access code for the country you're in, then Peru's country code (51), then the area code without the 0 and finally, the local number. When making international calls from Peru, dial the international access code (00), then the country code of where you're calling to, then the area code and finally, the local phone number.

In Peru, any telephone number beginning with a 9 is a cell-phone number. Numbers beginning with 0800 are often toll-free only when dialed from private phones. To make a credit-card or collect call using AT&T, dial ☑ 0800-50288. For an online telephone directory, see www.pagina samarillas.com.pe.

TOILETS

Peruvian plumbing leaves something to be desired. Even a small amount of toilet paper in the bowl can muck up the entire system – that's why a small plastic bin is routinely provided for disposing of it. Except at museums, restaurants, hotels and bus stations, public toilets are rare in Peru. Always carry toilet paper with you.

TOURIST INFORMATION

➡ The Ministry of Culture and Tourism has a network of tourist information offices throughout the country.

➡ iPeru (www.peru.travel) is a great resource for travelers. It can supply schedules for public transportation and information on lodgings and attractions.

VISAS

Tourists are permitted a 183-day, nonextendable stay, stamped into passports and onto a tourist card called a Tarjeta Andina de Migración (Andean Immigration Card). Keep it – it must be returned upon exiting the country. If you will need it, request the full amount of time to the immigration officer at the point of entry, since they have a tendency to issue 30- or 90-day stays.

Those who enter Peru via the Lima airport or cruise ship do not receive a tourist card; their visits are processed online.

If you lose your tourist card, visit the **Oficina de Migraciónes** (Immigration Office; Map p856; ☑ 01-200-1000; www.migraciones.gob.pe; Prolongación España 734, Breña, Lima; ☺ 8am-1pm Mon-Fri) or obtain a replacement copy via the website. Information in English can be found online. Extensions are no longer officially available.

Anyone who plans to work, attend school or reside in Peru for any length of time must obtain a visa in advance. Do this through the Peruvian embassy or consulate in your home country.

Carry your passport and tourist card on your person at all times, especially in remote areas (it's required by law on the Inca Trail). For security, make a photocopy of both documents and keep them in a separate place from the originals.

VOLUNTEERING

General advice for finding volunteer work is to ask at language schools; they usually know of several programs suitable for their students. Both nonprofit and for-profit organizations can arrange volunteer opportunities, if you contact them in advance.

Action Without Borders (www.idealist.org) Online database of social-work-oriented jobs, internships and volunteer opportunities.

Cross-Cultural Solutions (www.crosscultural solutions.org) Educational and social-service projects in Lima and Ayacucho; program fees include professional in-country support.

Earthwatch Institute (www.earthwatch. org) Pay to help scientists on archaeological, ecological and other real-life expeditions in the Amazon Basin and the Andes.

WOMEN TRAVELERS

Machismo is alive and well in Latin America. Most female travelers to Peru will experience little more than shouts of *mi amor* (my love) or an appreciative hiss. If you are fair-skinned with blond hair, however, be prepared to be the center of attention. Peruvian men consider foreign women to have looser morals and be easier sexual conquests than Peruvian women and will often make flirtatious comments to single women.

Unwanted attention Staring, whistling, hissing and catcalls in the streets is common and best ignored. Most men rarely, if ever, follow up on the idle chatter (unless they feel you've insulted their manhood). Ignoring all provocation and staring ahead is generally the best response. If someone is particularly persistent, try a potentially ardor-smothering phrase such as *soy casada* (I'm married). If you appeal directly to locals, you'll find most Peruvians to be protective of lone women, expressing surprise and concern if you tell them you're traveling without your family or husband.

Bricheros It's not uncommon for fast-talking charmers, especially in tourist towns such as Cuzco, to attach themselves to gringas. Known in Peru as *bricheros,* many of these young Casanovas are looking for a meal ticket, so approach any professions of undying love with extreme skepticism. This happens to men too.

First impressions Use common sense when meeting men in public places. In Peru, outside of a few big cities, it is rare for a woman to belly up to a bar for a beer, and the ones that do tend to be prostitutes. If you feel the need for an evening cocktail, opt for a restaurant. Likewise, heavy drinking by women might be misinterpreted by some men as a sign of promiscuity. When meeting someone, make it very clear if only friendship is intended. This goes double for tour and activity guides. When meeting someone for the first time, it is also wise not to divulge where you are staying until you feel sure that you are with someone you can trust.

WORK

It's increasingly difficult to obtain residence and work permits for Peru, and likewise to get jobs without a proper work visa. Some jobs teaching English in language schools may not require one, but this is illegal. Occasionally, schools advertise for teachers, but more often, jobs are found by word of mouth. Schools expect you to be a native English-speaker, and the pay is low. If you have teaching credentials, so much the better.

American and British schools in Lima sometimes hire teachers of math, biology and other subjects, but usually only if you apply in advance. They pay much better than the language schools, and might possibly be able to help you get a work visa if you want to stay. In Lima, the South American Explorers clubhouse and international cultural centers may have contacts with schools that are looking for teachers.

Most other jobs are obtained by word of mouth (eg bartenders, hostel staff, jungle guides), but the possibilities are limited. Volunteer organizations offer internships and short-term job opportunities.

❶ Getting There & Away

AIR

Located in the port city of Callao, Lima's Aeropuerto Internacional Jorge Chávez (p866) has terminals sparkling with shopping and services. A major hub, it's serviced by flights from North, Central and South America, and two regular direct flights from Europe (Madrid and Amsterdam).

BOAT

Boats ply the Amazon from Iquitos to Leticia (Colombia), Colombia, and Tabatinga (Brazil). It's difficult to reach Bolivia by river from Puerto Maldonado. It's possible, but time consuming, to travel along the Río Napo from Iquitos to Coca (Ecuador).

BUS, CAR & MOTORCYCLE

The major border crossings: Tacna to Chile; Tumbes, La Tina or Jaén to Ecuador; and Copacabana or Desaguadero at Lake Titicaca to Bolivia. Brazil is reached (but not easily) via Iñapari or multiple towns and river ports in the Amazon.

TRAIN

There are inexpensive, twice-daily trains between Tacna and Arica, Chile.

❶ Getting Around

Peru has a constant procession of flights and buses connecting the country. In particular, driving routes to the jungle have improved drastically. Note, poor weather conditions can cancel flights and buses. Strikes can be another obstacle in regional travel – consult travel experts on the routes you will be taking.

On the road keep your passport and Andean Immigration Card with you, not packed in your luggage, as overland transport goes through police checkpoints.

AIR

Most airlines fly from Lima to regional capitals, but service between provincial cities is limited. **LATAM** (Map p858; ☑01-213-8200; www. latam.com; Av José Pardo 513, Miraflores) Reliable service to Arequipa, Chiclayo, Cuzco, Iquitos, Juliaca, Piura, Puerto Maldonado, Tacna, Tarapoto and Trujillo. Additionally it offers link services between Arequipa and Cuzco, Arequipa and Juliaca, Arequipa and Tacna, Cuzco and Juliaca, and Cuzco and Puerto Maldonado. With international services as well.

LC Perú (Map p853; 📞 01-204-1300; www.lcperu.pe; Av Pablo Carriquirry 857, San Isidro; ⏰ 9am-7pm Mon-Fri, to 5pm Sat) Flies from Lima to Andahuaylas, Arequipa, Ayacucho, Chachapoyas, Chiclayo, Cajamarca, Huánuco, Huaraz, Iquitos, Trujillo and Huancayo (Jauja) on smaller turbo-prop aircraft. Gets low marks for frequent cancellations and the difficulty in obtaining a refund.

Peruvian Airlines (Map p858; 📞 01-715-6122; www.peruvianairlines.pe; Av José Pardo 495, Miraflores; ⏰ 9am-7pm Mon-Fri, to 5pm Sat) Flies to Arequipa, Cuzco, Piura, Iquitos, Jauja, Pucallpa, Tarapoto, Tacna and internationally to La Paz, Bolivia.

Star Perú (Map p858; 📞 01-213-8813; www.starperu.com; Av Espinar 331, Miraflores; ⏰ 9am-6:45pm Mon-Fri, to 1pm Sat) Domestic carrier, flying to Ayacucho, Cuzco, Huanuco, Iquitos, Pucallpa, Puerto Maldonado and Tarapoto.

Viva Air (📞 01-705-0107; www.vivaair.com; Aeropuerto Internacional Jorge Chávez; ⏰ hours vary) Budget flights to Arequipa, Piura, Cuzco, Iquitos and Tarapoto.

BOAT

There are no passenger services along the Peruvian coast. In the Andean highlands, there are boat services on Lake Titicaca. Small motorized vessels take passengers from the port in Puno to visit various islands on the lake, while catamarans zip over to Bolivia.

In Peru's Amazon Basin, boat travel is of major importance. Larger vessels ply the wider rivers. Dugout canoes powered by outboard engines act as water taxis on smaller rivers. Those called *peki-pekis* are slow and rather noisy. In some places, modern aluminum launches are used.

BUS

Buses are the usual form of transportation for most Peruvians and many travelers. Fares are cheap and services are frequent on the major long-distance routes, but buses are of varying quality. Don't always go with the cheapest option – check their safety records first. Remote rural routes are often served by older, worn-out vehicles. Seats at the back of the bus yield a bumpier ride.

Many cities do not have a main bus terminal. Buses rarely arrive or depart on time, so consider most average trip times as best-case scenarios. Buses can be significantly delayed during the rainy season, particularly in the highlands and the jungle. From January to April, journey times may double or face indefinite delays because of landslides and bad road conditions.

Fatal accidents are not unusual in Peru.

Avoid overnight buses, on which muggings and assaults are more likely to occur.

CAR & MOTORCYCLE

With the exception of the Carr Panamericana and new roads leading inland from the coast, road conditions are generally poor, distances are great and renting a car is an expensive, often dangerous hassle. Keep in mind that road signage is deficient and most major roads are also toll roads. Renting a private taxi for long-distance trips costs little more than renting a car, and avoids most of these pitfalls. Motorcycle rental is an option mainly in jungle towns, and there are a few outfitters in Cuzco.

Driver's License

A driver's license from your own home country is sufficient for renting a car. An International Driving Permit (IDP) is only required if you'll be driving in Peru for more than 30 days.

LOCAL TRANSPORTATION

Taxis are unmetered, so ask locals about the going rate, then haggle; drivers often double or triple the standard rate for unsuspecting foreigners. A short run in most cities costs S3 to S5 (in Lima S5 to S8). Be aware that street hawkers sell fluorescent taxi stickers throughout Peru, and anybody can just stick one on their windscreen. Some drivers of these unlicensed 'pirate' taxis have been known to be complicit in violent crimes against passengers, especially in Arequipa. It's safer if more expensive to take officially regulated taxis, requested by telephone.

Mototaxis (motorized rickshaws) are common in some of the smaller towns. *Colectivos* (shared minivans, minibuses or taxis) and trucks (in the Amazon) run between local and not-so-local destinations.

TOURS

Some protected areas such as the Inca Trail and Parque Nacional Manu can only be entered with a guided tour. Other outdoor activities, such as trekking in the Andes or wildlife-watching in the Amazon, may be more rewarding with an experienced guide.

TRAIN

The privatized rail system, PeruRail (www.perurail.com), has daily services between Cuzco and Aguas Calientes, aka Machu Picchu Pueblo, and services between Cuzco and Puno on the shores of Lake Titicaca three times a week. There's also luxury passenger services between Cuzco, Puno and Arequipa twice weekly. Inca Rail (p899) also offers service between Ollantaytambo and Aguas Calientes.

Suriname

POP 568,300

Best Places to Eat

➜ Souposo (p971)

➜ Bodega & Grill De Waag (p971)

➜ De Gadri (p971)

➜ Zus & Zo (p971)

Best Places to Stay

➜ Danpaati River Lodge (p974)

➜ Gunsi Resort Tei Wei (p974)

➜ Greenheart Hotel (p970)

➜ GuestHouse TwenTy4 (p970)

➜ Awarradum Jungle Lodge & Spa (p974)

Why Go?

South America's smallest country, Suriname is a warm, dense convergence of rivers that thumps with the lively rhythm of ethnic diversity. From Paramaribo, the country's effervescent Dutch-colonial capital, to the fathomless jungles of the interior, you'll get a genuine welcome to the country – whether from the descendants of escaped African slaves, Dutch and British colonialists, Indian, Indonesian and Chinese indentured laborers or indigenous Amerindians.

Charismatic Paramaribo is loaded with gorgeous architecture, party-hard night spots and some excellent restaurants, while the untamed jungle, just a few hours away by road or boat, could not be more of a contrast to Paramaribo's chaotic traffic. It's relatively easy to get around this river-heavy, forest-dense country, even if the mix of languages can make communications interesting. Best of all, sumptuous and spicy cuisines from all over the world can be found here, making mealtimes a joy.

When to Go
Paramaribo

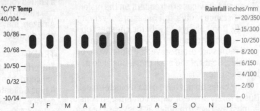

Feb–Apr The first dry season is slightly cooler than the second, and is the best time to visit.

Aug–Nov The second dry season is busier and hotter than the first.

Dec–Jan Paramaribo is known for its explosive New Year's Eve celebrations.

Entering the Country

Suriname's border crossings are at Corriverton (Guyana) and St Laurent du Maroni (French Guiana). Both crossings are made by boat across massive rivers that flow into the Caribbean. These ferries traverse the river borders from Albina (in the east of Suriname) and Nieuw Nickerie via South Drain (in the west), respectively.

ONE WEEK ITINERARY

Spend three days exploring Paramaribo and the plantations of the Commewijne River by bike or on foot. On one afternoon be sure to take a sunset dolphin-viewing tour and, if you've still got energy, get out on the town for a night of dancing, Suriname style. For your remaining days, head to the interior – either the Upper Suriname River or Brownsberg Nature Reserve – for some stellar wildlife-watching and to meet the locals.

Essential Food & Drink

Bakbana Delicious fried plantain dipped in peanut sauce.

Bojo cake A thick, damp creation made from grated cassava and coconut.

Moksi-alesi Literally 'mixed rice' cooked with salted meat, fish or shrimp.

Peanut soup Don't leave Suriname without trying this staple.

Roti Grilled flatbread stuffed with spicy meats, potato or veg.

Top Tips

➔ Make contacts with travel agencies and/or jungle lodges well in advance of your planned travel dates as trips to remote camps involve precise start dates and transfers don't always run every day.

➔ Arrange a pickup at the airport with your hotel if you're arriving by air, as neither airport is well serviced by public transport and taxis are rarely waiting for customers. Neither airport has ATMs, so ensure you have enough cash to get into town.

➔ Get your tourist card before you travel if you're arriving at one of Suriname's land borders. Tourist cards are available on arrival at both Paramaribo airports.

Daily Costs

➔ Double room in a budget hotel: SR$150–200; in a midrange hotel: SR$200–500

➔ Chicken-and-vegetable roti: SR$25; meal in a midrange restaurant: SR$50–100

FAST FACTS

Currency Suriname dollar (SR$)

Visas Tourist cards (€35) are valid for 90 days and available at any Surinamese embassy or on arrival at either airport in Paramaribo.

Money Republic Bank ATMs accept most foreign cards; credit cards rarely accepted except at hotels and upscale restaurants.

Capital Paramaribo

Emergency ☏112

Languages Dutch, Sranan Tongo (Surinaams/Taki Taki)

Exchange Rates

Australia	A$1	SR$5.65
Canada	C$1	SR$5.73
Eurozone	€1	SR$8.77
UK	UK£1	SR$9.97
USA	US$1	SR$7.47

For current exchange rates, see www.xc.com.

Resources

Lonely Planet (www.lonely planet.com/the-guianas/suriname)

Suriname Tourism Foundation (www.suriname tourism.sr)

Suriname Online Tourist Guide (www.suriname tourism.com)

Surinam.net (www.surinam.net)

ATLANTIC
OCEAN

0 ——— 100 km
0 ——— 60 miles

Rosignol
New Amsterdam
Berbice River

Mara
Corriverton
Nieuw
Nickerie
South
Drain

GUYANA

Totness
Wageningen
Caledonia
Jenny
Boskamp
Coppename
Nature Reserve

Commewijne
River
Nieuw
Amsterdam
Paramaribo
Groningen
Matapica
Alliance
Wia Wia
Nature
Preserve

Galibi
Nature
Reserve
5

Moengo
Albina

Corantijn (Corentyne) River
Wasjabo
Apura
Matapi
Avanavero

Marataka River
Bakhuis

Kabalebo
Blanche
Marie Falls

Kabalebo River

Bakhuis Mountains

Nickerie River

Coppename River

Voltzberg
(240m)
2
Central Suriname
Nature Reserve

Goliathberg
(358m)
Witagron

Johan Pengel
International
Airport
Onverwacht
Zanderij
Colakreek
Kraka
Kwakugron
Brownsberg

Palulu
Camping
1
Upper
Suriname
River

St Laurent
du Maroni
Apatou

Camp
Voltaire
Langatabbetje

Brokopondo
Afobaka Dam

French
Guiana
(France)

Brownsberg
Nature
Reserve
6

Brokopondo
6

Suriname
River

Saramacca River

Van Asch-Van Wijck Mountains

Kininipaati
Tei Wei
New Aurora
Anaula
Botapasie
Pikin Slee
Kumalu Dream Island
Djumu
Kumalu
Danpaati

Marowijne River

Grand
Santi

Drietabbetje

Maroni River

Tafelberg
Pasensie

Tafelberg
(1026m)

Julianatop
(1230m)

Coeroeni

Lucie River

Gran Rio

Awarradam

Palumeu
Tepu

Mt Kasikasima
(718m)

Boven Tapanahoni River

Litani River

Maripasoula

Corantijn (Corentyne) River

New River

Eilerts
de Haan
(986m)
Eilerts de
Haan Nature
Park

Claimed by
Suriname &
French Guiana

Claimed by
Suriname & Guyana

Sipaliwini
Nature
Reserve

BRAZIL

Rio Paru

Suriname Highlights

1 Upper Suriname River (p973) Exploring Maroon culture, swimming in jungle rivers and relaxing along the epic waterways of this vast river.

2 Central Suriname Nature Reserve (p975) Driving through jungle and savanna, then canoeing to Raleighvallen, to this huge nature reserve.

3 Paramaribo (p967) Strolling along the Unesco-listed waterfront lined with Dutch colonial architecture and superb restaurants.

4 Commewijne River (p973) Discovering historic riverside plantations by bicycle or on a boat tour, possibly spotting pink river dolphins.

5 Galibi Nature Reserve (p976) Treading lightly on the beaches where giant leatherback turtles lay eggs.

6 Brownsberg Nature Reserve & Brokopondo (p975) Marvelling at primate-filled forests surrounding an endless, eerie artificial lake in Suriname's best nature reserve.

Paramaribo

POP 250,000

Amsterdam meets the Wild West in Paramaribo, the most vivacious and striking capital in the Guianas. Black-and-white colonial Dutch buildings line grassy squares, wafts of spices escape from Indian roti shops and mingle with the chaos of the city's market, while Maroon artists sell colorful paintings outside somber Dutch forts.

The friendly, multilingual residents of the Surinamese capital, who call the city 'Parbo,' are proud of their staggering ethnic diversity and the fact that they live in a city where mosques, synagogues, churches and Hindu temples are happy neighbors. The historical inner city, a Unesco World Heritage site, is a veritable treasure trove of traditional colonial architecture, and makes a great place to relax between jaunts to Suriname's rainforest. Welcome to one of the more surprising cities in South America.

◉ Sights

Exploring this capital, with its colonial architecture and lively main streets, could fill two days. Southwest along Waterkant from Fort Zeelandia are some of the city's most impressive colonial buildings, mostly merchants' houses built after the fires of 1821 and 1832. The streets inland from here, particularly Lim-a-Postraat, have many old wooden buildings, some restored, others in picturesque decay.

Saint Peter & Paul Cathedral-Basilica   BASILICA

(Henk Arronstraat; ⊘ 6am-1:30pm Mon-Fri, 8am-1pm Sat, 8:30am-noon Sun) Commonly called 'the Cathedral,' this gorgeously restored building was designated a Minor Basilica by Pope Francis in 2014. It's said to be the largest wooden structure in the western hemisphere and is worth a peek inside for the masterful woodwork and carvings. Mass is held daily and English tours are available on demand.

Fort Zeelandia   FORT

(adult/child SR$25/5; ⊘9am-2pm Tue-Fri, from 10am Sun, tours in Dutch 10:30am & noon Sun) Inside well-restored Fort Zeelandia, a star-shaped, 18th-century fort built on the site where the first colonists alighted, is the worthwhile Stichting Surinaams Museum (p967), as well as the Baka Foto restaurant.

Mosque Keizerstraat   MOSQUE

(Keizerstraat) This is the biggest mosque in the Caribbean. The current building was completed in 1984.

Neveh Shalom Synagogue   SYNAGOGUE

(Keizerstraat; ⊘10am-4pm Mon-Thu) The expansive Dutch Israeli synagogue, which famously sits side by side with the Caribbean's largest mosque on Keizerstraat, dates from 1716, when it was founded by the Sephardic Jews. The current structure was completed in 1843 and contains a small museum about the history of Jews in Suriname.

Central Market   MARKET

(Waterkant; ⊘5am-5pm Mon-Sat) The frenzied and fascinating central market is divided into distinct areas: the meat, fish, fruit and vegetable sections on the lower floor and a less photogenic clothing area on the upper. The 'Witch's Market' (aka the Maroon Market; no photography allowed) has a separate entrance just to the west on Waterkant, and sells herbs, bones, shells and mysterious concoctions. It's best to get to these markets before noon.

Het Surinaamsch Rumhuis   DISTILLERY

(☑473-344, ext 240; www.rumhuis.sr; Cornelis Jongbawstraat 18; 1½/2hr tours SR$60/70; ⊘2hr tours 10am & 1pm Tue-Fri, or by request) Tours here begin with a 'happy shot,' then it's through the distillery, rum museum and tasting room, where you will learn to sample each variety like a pro. Finish with cocktails on the patio. Shorter tours skip the distillery.

Stichting Surinaams Museum   MUSEUM

(☑425-871; adult/child SR$25/5; ⊘9am-2pm Tue-Fri, from 10am Sun, free tours in Dutch 10:30am and noon Sun) Inside the beautifully restored Fort Zeelandia, a pentagonal 17th-century fort built on the riverbank where the first colonists alighted, is the Stichting Surinaams Museum, which features colonial-era relics, period rooms and temporary exhibitions. All labeling is in Dutch. It's an interesting visit and you can enjoy some great river views from the ramparts.

ReadyTex Art Gallery   GALLERY

(Steenbakkerijstraat; ⊘8am-4:30pm Mon-Fri, 8:30am-1:30pm Sat) FREE Step off the chaotic streets and enter these five glorious floors of colorful local sculpture and paintings, all of which are for sale. Also check out the ReadyTex craft and souvenir shop (p972) just around the corner.

Paramaribo

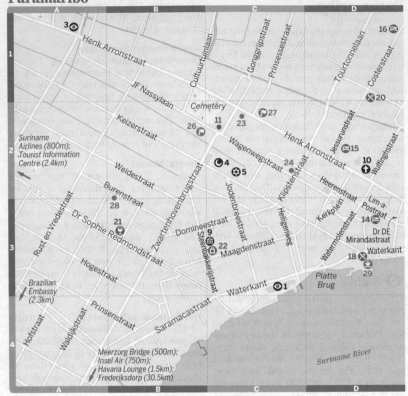

Onafhankelijkheidsplein   SQUARE

(Independence Square) Surrounding the centrally located Onafhankelijkheidsplein (Independence Sq) are the contrasting stately 18th-century Presidential Palace (p968) and aging colonial government buildings. Behind the palace is the Palmentuin (p968), where it's a pleasure to walk and escape the chaos of the city outside.

Presidential Palace   NOTABLE BUILDING

(Henk Arronstraat) Official residence of the President of Suriname, this fine white colonial house was originally built in 1730. It opens to the public on Suriname's Independence Day (November 25) each year, and otherwise can only be enjoyed from the outside.

Palmentuin   GARDENS

(Van Roseveltkade) FREE The Palmentuin is a shady haven of tall royal palms, home to some tropical birds and a troop of capuchin monkeys.

Hindu Temple   TEMPLE

(Henk Arronstraat) This is the biggest of the many Hindu temples in Paramaribo, and is a beautifully ornate structure both inside and out. Visitors are welcome.

🏃 Activities & Tours

Green Fund Suriname   VOLUNTEERING

(📞 437-533; www.greenfundsuriname.org; Geertruidastraat 24) A conservation trust that works to support Suriname's population of sloths and dolphins and helps arrange volunteer postings.

Orange Suriname   TOURS

(📞 426-409; www.orangesuriname.com; Van Sommelsdijckstraat; ⊙9am-6pm) A comprehensive and professional company with extremely knowledgeable and helpful staff, Orange offers everything from consistent big sellers, such a turtle-watching day trips (€65) to river cruises to the ruins of the old Jewish settlement of Jodensavanne (€85), zip-line

adventures and multiday jungle trips. Orange organizes car hire, and can book accommodations and flights.

Fietsen in Suriname   CYCLING
(☏ 520 781; www.fietseninsuriname.com; Zus & Zo, Grote Combéweg 13A; bike rental per day €5-25; ⊙ 8am-6pm) A slick bike-tour and rental agency based behind Zus & Zo Guesthouse (p970). Bike maps for self-guided tours are €2 and plantation day tours start at €50.

Waterproof Suriname   BOATING, ECOTOUR
(☏ 896-2927; www.waterproofsuriname.com; Venusstraat 16) Runs laid-back boat cruises to see river dolphins (€27.50; sometimes combined with walks around the Commewijne River plantations and beach visits), as well as day trips to watch sea turtles at Galibi and in French Guiana (€70). The company mainly operates by phone and online – the office can only be visited by appointment.

Cardy Adventures   CYCLING
(☏ 422-518; www.cardyadventures.com; Cornelis Jongbawstraat 31; bike rental per day €3-10; ⊙ 8am-7pm Mon-Sat) Cardy Adventures has bike tours to the nearby Commewijne plantations, as well as longer, nonbiking tours of up to 10 days to the interior. Also rents apartments in Parbo and offers various day trips, including dolphin-spotting trips (€27), Brownsberg (€65) and Jodensavanne (€85).

SUNDAY BIRDSONG

On Sunday mornings, people – mostly men – engage in peaceful yet secretly cutthroat birdsong competitions on the Onafhankelijkheidsplein. Everyone brings their favorite *twatwa* (song bird), usually a seed finch purchased from Amerindian people in the interior. The *twatwa* that can best belt out a song wins. Something of a national obsession, this competition is well worth observing if you're in Parbo on a Sunday.

METS ECOTOUR
(Movement for Eco-Tourism in Suriname; ☑ 477-088; www.mets.sr; JF Nassylaan 2; ☉ 8am-4pm Mon-Fri) 🍃 Well organized and easily the most professional and eco-minded travel agency in Suriname, METS donates proceeds to conservation and conducts a wide range of trips. It specializes in jungle expeditions to the deep interior, including Palumeu (from €399, five days) and the Gran Rio (from €600, five days).

Stinasu TOURS
(Stichting Natuurbehoud in Suriname; ☑ 476-597; www.stinasu.sr; Cornelis Jongbawstraat 14; ☉ 8am-5pm Mon-Fri) The Foundation for Nature Conservation in Suriname runs lodges (many in a bad state of repair), as well as guided trips to Brownsberg (from €65), the Galibi or Matapica turtle reserves (from €75), and Raleighvallen/Voltzberg/Foengoe Island (from €250, four days).

🛌 Sleeping

★ Guesthouse TwenTy4 GUESTHOUSE $
(☑ 420-751; www.twenty4suriname.com; Jessurunstraat 24; s/d from €25/35, without bathroom from €15/27.50; ❄ 🌐) This sparkling clean guesthouse is the best budget deal in the city. It's on a central, quiet backstreet, and the whole place has a welcoming vibe with a sleek lobby and communal areas, a chilled backyard and a cat. You can get breakfast (SR$20) and beer, and set up your activities with the help of the friendly staff.

Only some rooms have air-con; the rest are fan cooled.

Palulu Camping CAMPGROUND $
(☑ 864-5223; www.surinamecamping.com; Zanderij; per person hammock/tent SR$40/60) 🍃 Enormous, private and artistically built sites include a raised wooden hammock or 'stretcher' shelter, kitchen, fire pit and bathrooms. Look

for wildlife on DIY jungle walks or swim in the refreshingly cool black waters of the creek. It's an insanely relaxing, solar-powered spot only 3km from Johan Pengel International Airport.

Colakreek LODGE $
(☑ 472-621; www.mets.sr; hammock lodge/tent SR$90/100, cabins SR$300) Run by METS, this beautiful 'recreation center' 6km from Johan Pengel International Airport is on a sandy bank along brown Cola Creek. It offers everything from hammock space and tents to more luxurious cabins. Swimming and jungle walks are the main activities. Day passes (SR$12.50) are good for evening flight departures. It gets very busy on weekends and holidays.

Un Pied A Terre GUESTHOUSE $
(☑ 470-488, 888-9998; www.guesthouse-un-pied-a-terre.com; Costerstraat 59; hammock/s/d/tr/q from €10/20/27/38/48; ❄ 🌐) A gorgeous, classified World Heritage building with all the paint-chipped, louvered-window, creaky-wood-floor charm that entails. The staff are superfriendly and can help with ideas and bookings. Only the lower-level rooms are en suite and have air-con, but the prettiest choices are upstairs, where you'll have to share bathrooms and cope with fan-cooled rooms.

Zus & Zo GUESTHOUSE $
(☑ 520-905; www.zusenzosuriname.com; Grote Combéweg 13A; r per person from €17.50; ❄ 🌐) A backpacker's hostel, the bright and inviting Zus & Zo has five simple rooms with a shared hot-water bathroom on the top floor of a classic Paramaribo colonial-style house. There's also an excellent ground-floor restaurant. The staff can help you arrange almost any excursion in Suriname.

Guesthouse Albergo Alberga GUESTHOUSE $
(☑ 520-050; www.guesthousealbergoalberga.com; Lim-a-Postraat 13; s/d €20/26, with air-con €26/38; ❄ 🌐 🏊) This long-running guesthouse is situated on a quintessentially colonial Parbo street in an endearing yet palpably aging World Heritage–listed building. Some rooms are quite spacious, while the little pool out back is great for a dunk after a day exploring Parbo, but there's no escaping the institutional feel here, with lots of rules and ugly carpeting.

★ Greenheart Hotel HOTEL $$
(☑ 521-360; www.greenheart-hotel.com; Costerstraat 68; s/d/tr/f incl breakfast from €48/68/89/109; ❄ 🌐 🏊) A lovely hotel in a converted colonial

mansion of polished hardwoods. Many rooms have loft spaces, perfect for families, and there are lots of inviting communal spaces and friendly staff. Breakfast and meals on request are served in the open-air dining area out back, where there's also a great little pool. Rooms with air-con cost €5 extra per night.

✖ Eating

There are some fantastic dining opportunities in Parbo. Avoid, if possible, the touristy strip across from Hotel Torarica at Rietbergplein 1, and head instead for some of the more in-the-know places listed here. The cheapest city-center options are at the frenetic Central Market (p967) and the Indonesian stalls along Waterkant. Eating in Suriname (www.ctcninsuriname.com) is a useful website with information on restaurants in Paramaribo.

CY Coffee + Roasters   CAFE $
(Gompertstraat; mains SR$15-30; ☺9:30am-11pm Tue-Sun, from 6pm Mon; ☎) Excellent coffee is served in this giant wood-, glass- and concrete-heavy space that looks quite unlike anywhere else in Parbo, yet much like any coffee specialist elsewhere in the modern world. It's a good spot for a late breakfast, with a big selection of freshly baked goods, as well as a full menu of Chinese-leaning dishes. Take a taxi.

Martin's House of Indian Food   INDIAN $
(☑477-535; Hajarystraat 19; mains SR$25-60; ☺11am-11pm; ☎☑) Tasty home-cooked Indian delights from a voluminous menu await you at Martin's, located in the Rainville neighborhood and well worth the SR$10 cab ride from the old town. You don't come here for the decor or ambience particularly, but the excellent spicy cooking and warm welcome from Martin and his family makes all that irrelevant

Zus & Zo   INTERNATIONAL $
(Grote Combéweg 13A; meals from SR$30; ☺9am-11pm; ☎) This restaurant and bar serves up some of the best food and cocktails in town in a charming sand-floored garden with fairy lights. Dishes range from Surinamese soups to noodles, burgers and salads. Live music is played here on occasion and the welcome is warm and friendly.

De Gadri   CREOLE $
(Zeelandiaweg 1; mains SR$27-45; ☺11am-10pm Mon-Sat) This quiet outdoor restaurant overlooking the river has Parbo's best Creole food along with exceptionally friendly service. Try the delicious soup of the day – peanut, cassava or banana accompanied by roast chicken and *pom*, a kind of casserole.

★Souposo   FUSION $$
(Costerstraat 20A; mains SR$25-100; ☺10am-11pm Tue-Sat; ☎) From delicious daily soups to mains like duck leg confit in masala and an amazing pesto pasta topped with home-smoked *bang bang* (freshwater fish) and sundried tomatoes, the food here would stand out anywhere, but in Parbo it's exceptional. Brunch includes omelets, fresh juices and salads. The heritage-home garden setting makes the experience even more lovely.

★Bodega & Grill
De Waag   INTERNATIONAL $$$
(☑474-514; www.dewaag.sr; Waterkant 5; mains SR$75-200; ☺8am-11pm; ☎) This gorgeously realised addition to Parbo's eating choices has seen the transformation of an old waterfront building into a smart and stylish indoor-outdoor eating space and bar, with a great menu focused on (but not limited to) steaks, all of which come US Department

---

❶ GETTING TO FRENCH GUIANA

Getting to the Border
Albina is the last stop before crossing the Marowijne River to St Laurent du Maroni, French Guiana. From Paramaribo, you can take a shared taxi (SR$75, two hours), minibus (SR$30 to SR$40, 2½ hours) or public bus (SR$8.50, three hours) to Albina.

At the Border
The **La Gabrielle Ferry** (Albina; S$20; ☺8am & 10am Mon & Tue, 7:30am, 8:30am & 9:30am Wed & Fri, 7:30am & 10am Thu, 8:30am & 9:30am Sat) sails to St Laurent du Maroni two or three times each morning except Sunday. At peak travel times there are also two sailings each afternoon, but you cannot count on these.

Note that although there are banks and ATMs in St Laurent du Maroni, none of them exchange foreign currency or traveler's checks, so exchange money in advance in Albina if you need to.

WORTH A TRIP

JAVANESE FEAST

Family-run Javanese restaurants (open for dinner only) line **Blauwgrond**, a laid-back residential area about 10 minutes by taxi from downtown Paramaribo. Rena, Mirioso, Pawiro and Saoto are some of the better known spots, but any of them will serve cheap and delicious noodle, rice and soup dishes. It's worth making this trip for the ambience alone.

of Agriculture (USDA) certified and are the best in the city. Also available are good salads, tapas, soups and breakfasts.

 Drinking & Nightlife

Casinos are everywhere in Paramaribo and are extremely popular with locals and Dutch tourists. Duck inside a few to see a different side of the city. This is also a town that loves to party, with hopping nightlife from Wednesday through Saturday. For cheap drinks with locals, head to the outdoor stalls near Platte Brug on Waterkant.

Havana Lounge CLUB
(402-258; Van 't Hogerhuysstraat 13; 6pm-3am) This popular club is at its best on Thursdays when salsa plays till 1am and then switches from reggae to hip-hop. Expect a meat market and a young, up-for-it crowd.

Club Touché CLUB
(cnr Waldijkstraat & Dr Sophie Redmondstraat; 10pm-3am Wed-Sat) Dance the night away with techno downstairs and salsa upstairs. Wednesday is the biggest night.

 Shopping

Good-quality clothing knockoffs can be found for exceptionally low prices along Steenbakkerijstraat and Domineestraat. For high-quality Suriname handicrafts and jewelry, head to the gift shop at Zus & Zo (p970).

ReadyTex Craft & Souvenir Shop ARTS & CRAFTS
(Maagdenstraat 44-48; 8am-4:30pm Mon-Fri, 8:30am-1pm Sat) Get all your Suriname souvenirs, handicrafts and more at this big shop.

 Information

DANGERS & ANNOYANCES
Avoid quiet streets and secluded areas after dark; the Palmentuin and Watermolenstraat in par-

ticular are known for drug dealing and robberies at night (Watermolenstraat is central and leads from Waterkant through the Unesco area). Watch for pickpockets around the market area, even in daylight hours.

TOURIST INFORMATION
The friendly folks at the **Tourist Information Center** (532-373; www.surinametourism.sr; Kernkampweg 37) can normally welcome you in several languages, provide a walking-tour map and guide you in the right direction for most activities in Suriname, but the office was closed at the time of research and it was unclear when it would reopen.

 Getting There & Away

AIR
There are two airports in Paramaribo: nearby Zorg-en-Hoop (p973), for domestic and Guyana flights; and the larger Johan Pengel International Airport (p973), 45km south of Parbo, usually referred to as Zanderij and used for all other flights.

BUS & MINIBUS
Minibuses to Brownsberg and Atjoni (SR$50 to SR$70, three hours) leave from the corner of Prinsenstraat and Saramacastraat. Public buses to Nieuw Nickerie (SR$20 to SR$40, four hours) and other western destinations leave throughout the day from the corner of Dr Sophie Redmondstraat and Hofstraat. For a private minibus, ask your hotel for a list of prices and companies that will pick you up. To Albina, public buses (SR$8.50, 140km, three hours) leave hourly and private buses (SR$30, 3½ hours) leave when full from Waterkant at the foot of Heiligenweg.

TAXI
Taxis are fast and many work on a share system. Most share taxis are minivans that hold up to eight people and if you leave town in the morning, they fill quickly. Expect to pay SR$70 per person to Albina and SR$100 per person to Nieuw Nickerie. Ask your hotel to contact a driver for you.

 Getting Around

BICYCLE
In good Dutch fashion, many people see Parbo and its environs, including the old plantations across the Suriname River, on bicycles. Helmets are rarely worn and are hard to rent. Road and mountain bikes are available for rent from SR$15 per day.

TAXI
To get a city taxi, call 1690. Operators speak English, and fares – which use a meter system – are low.

WATER TAXI
Fast and frequent water taxis leave from Platte Brug dock on Waterkant just south of Keizerstraat. Expect to pay SR$50 to cross to the far bank.

Commewijne River

Opposite Paramaribo, the banks of the Commewijne River are lined with old plantation properties divided by canals and strewn with the remains of coffee, cacao and sugar-cane-processing facilities. The best way to explore is by renting a bike to spend a full day touring the well-defined routes past the plantations. This makes for a fascinating day trip and an impressive contrast to the chaos of the capital. The most popular route crosses the Suriname and Commewijne rivers using water taxis to reach Frederiksdorp, a plantation complex that has been lovingly restored and turned into a hotel and restaurant.

There's no need to stay overnight though, as you're never more than a short boat ride from Paramaribo, but there are several accommodations options, including the gorgeous **Plantage Resort Frederiksdorp** (☑820-0378; www.plantagefrederiksdorp.com; r per person incl full board €197; ❀ 🛜 ☒).

◉ Sights

Popular boat tours are available to the same sites you can get to by bike. Spotting friendly-faced river dolphins along the Commewijne is popular, especially at sunset, and most plantation boat tours will attempt to point them out to passengers when passing through the dolphins' feeding grounds.

Peperpot Nature Park　　　NATURE RESERVE
Beautiful Peperpot Nature Park, about 10km from Paramaribo, stands in eerie dilapidation (with poorly maintained paths) across the Meerzorg Bridge. It is a favorite bird-watchers' locale, with a well-marked 3km-long trail through the forest, from which you'll often see lots of monkeys as well. Bring your own water and mosquito repellent, and go early to see the most wildlife.

Fort Nieuw Amsterdam　　　PLANTATION
(www.fortnieuwamsterdam.sr; Wilhelminastraat, Nieuw Amsterdam; SR$15; ◷9am-5pm Mon-Fri, 10am-6pm Sat & Sun) This open-air museum is inside one of the earliest surviving Dutch structures in Suriname, a fortress built at the confluence of the Suriname and Commewijne Rivers in 1747. Inside you'll find chilling artifacts of the slave trade and a

Dutch-engineered system of locks holding back the river.

Matapica　　　BEACH
North of Fort Nieuw Amsterdam, Matapica is a tranquil and almost mosquito-free beach where sea turtles come ashore April to August. Tours generally reach it by boating through the plantation canals and a swamp rich in birdlife. Stinasu (p970) runs a small camp here.

❶ Getting There & Away

To get to this side of the Commewijne River, you can either go by car across the Meerzorg Bridge, or take a water taxi (SR$50) across the river from Paramaribo's waterfront.

Cardy Adventures (p969), Fietsen in Suriname (p969) and Paramaribo's tourist information center (p972) can provide maps and information about cycling routes, and then you can guide yourself along the river by bike. If you come on an organized tour, everything will be arranged for you from your hotel in Paramaribo.

Upper Suriname River

This jungle-locked, chocolate-brown river plows through the sweaty wilderness of the Surinamese rainforest from the Eilerts de Haan Mountains in the country's south towards the giant Brokopondo reservoir. Relatively accessible by air and boat, the Upper Suriname River is where most visitors to Suriname come to experience the wonders of the country's raw nature, magnificent wildlife and the rich Maroon cultures. Tourism here is well established but still low-key, meaning that while facilities are good and

OFF THE BEATEN TRACK

AMERINDIAN EXPERIENCE
....

The remote **Palumeu Jungle Lodge** (✆477-088; www.mets.sr; Palumeu; 4-5 day all-inclusive packages from €399) is located in the Amerindian village of Palumeu on the banks of the stunning Boven Tapanahoni River. It's managed by METS (p970) in collaboration with the locals. Stay in comfortable thatched huts and enjoy guided tours of the village and jungle walks (going off on your own is not allowed). Minimum three-night stay.

guides experienced, it's still very easy to get out into untrammeled rainforest and to feel that you've left the modern world far behind.

⊙ Sights

Maroon Museum MUSEUM
(Marronmuseum Saamaka; Kumalu; SR$20; ◷10am-3pm) Guided visits of this little museum on a large property offer great insight into the local culture, from marriage customs to dress codes, music and much more. It's an important institution for Maroon culture, and is generally visited by travelers staying in nearby lodges as part of day trips visiting Maroon villages.

⌂ Sleeping

★Gunsi Resort Tei Wei LODGE $
(✆882-8998, 856-142; bertajaiso@gmail.com; incl meals SR$90) ⊘ Operated by the tiny, very traditional and welcoming village of Gunsi, this is the best place to immerse yourself into Saamaca culture. Huts with beds and mosquito nets are basic but clean, with fantastic, hammock-strewn terraces overlooking the river. Bathrooms are shared. Activities range from village visits (SR$50) to caiman-spotting (SR$100) and even overnight jungle hiking trips.

Eco Resort Pasensie LODGE $
(✆712-4404, 811-6547; www.totomboti.nl/pasensie.html; Pikin Slee; incl meals SR$275; ☏) Ideally located just outside of Pikin Slee, this tidy riverside lodge is walking distance to the Maroon Museum and a few other villages, so visitors can really delve into the Saamaca culture. Bathrooms are shared. Museum trips (SR$40) and half-/full-day jungle tours (SR$80/150 per group) are two of the activities on offer.

Hotel Botopassie LODGE $$
(✆472-224, 896-8157; www.botopasi.com; 3 day package €175; ☏) Dutch- and Surinamese-run, this exceptionally clean and comfortable jungle lodge sits just across the river from the lively Saamaca town of Botopasi. The seven *wosu* (traditional Maroon houses) have en suite bathrooms with hot water – a true rarity in these parts – and mosquito nets. Hearty meals are taken on the main house's beautiful terrace with wonderful river views.

A 3-day/2-night package includes lodging, full board, excursions and transport.

★Awarradam Jungle Lodge & Spa LODGE $$$
(✆477-088; www.mets.sr; 4-day package from €390) This remote lodge built on an island next to the Awarradam rapids is a great place for those who want to get deep into the jungle while experiencing Saamaca culture. The wooden cabins on stilts are very comfortable and enjoy breezy terraces, and you can swim in nearby pools created by the rapids or just visit the spa.

The four-day/three-night package includes meals and activities.

★Danpaati River Lodge LODGE $$$
(✆471-113, 810-9727; www.danpaati.net; 3-day package €335; ☒) This magical spot on an island surrounded by thick rainforest is only accessible via a three-hour boat ride from Atjoni, where the road from Paramaribo ends. The accommodations are in various types of cabins, including luxury ones with big terraces that offer gorgeous river views. The setting is stunning, staff are wonderful and dozens of activities are available.

Three-day/two-night packages include meals and transportation.

Knini Paati River Resort LODGE $$$
(✆536-5002; www.knini-paati.com; ◷3-day package from €250; ☒☏☒) ⊘ Unique as the only top-end jungle lodge run by Maroon management, Knini Paati underwent a total renovation in 2017 and is now looking very fine indeed. Each of the six light-bathed cabins here can sleep up to five people, and come with traditional wooden furnishings. There's a terrific restaurant and bar with great river views too.

A 3-day/2-night package to the resort includes lodging, meals, excursions and transportation.

The resort also runs a jungle camp, a sweaty but enjoyable two-hour hike through the rainforest, where guests stay in far more rustic surroundings, sleep in hammocks, wash in the river and cook their own food.

Anaula Nature Resort   LODGE **$$$**
(☑ 410-700; www.anaulanatureresort.com; near New Aurora; 3-day package €260; 🛜 🐾) Spacious, manicured grounds, comfortable en suite cabins and even a swimming pool sit next to scenic rapids on a jungle island in the Suriname River. It's popular yet tranquil. Stay here to relax and get away from it all, but don't expect to experience Saamaca culture. The three-day/two-night package includes full board, excursions and transportation.

❶ Getting There & Away

Travel to the Upper Suriname River usually involves a combination of flights in small twin-propeller aircraft, bumpy 4WD jeep rides along dirt tracks, and far more tranquil boat travel. Most lodges fly their guests in using one of the several airstrips in the region, after which they transfer visitors by jeep and boat to their destination. This will all be included in your package price and will be organized by each lodge, most of which have a couple of transfers per week from Paramaribo.

Water taxis ply the river and can easily be hired, allowing independent travelers to move around between lodges with ease. Prices are not set and need to be agreed with the boat captains. Lodges can help you with this.

Brownsberg Nature Reserve & Brokopondo

Brownsberg Nature Reserve, named after the eponymous 560m peak at its heart, was founded in 1969 and is made up of 112 sq km of pristine jungle populated by dozens of rare species of animal, many of which are unique to Suriname. It's a stunning slice of nature covered in thick jungle and bordering the vast Brokopondo reservoir. Head here for wild tropical adventure, some superb bird-watching and endless wildlife-viewing opportunities.

Brownsberg's park headquarters are located on a high plateau overlooking the Brokopondo reservoir, about 100km south of Paramaribo along a red-dirt highway. Monkeys seem to be everywhere, whether they're red howlers growling in the canopy, or precious black-bearded sakis checking you out from a tree limb. Park operator Stinasu (p970) has rustic lodges (from SR$120) for groups, and camping (SR$50) and hammock sites (SR$30) at the headquarters.

WORTH A TRIP

KABELEBO

Way out west near the Guyana border, the remote **Kabalebo Nature Resort** (☑ 426-532; www.kabalebo.com; 3-night package from US$300; 🐾) is in the middle of pristine jungle. Accommodations here range from an economical 'jungle camp' to some of the most private and luxurious retreats in the country. Tons of activities are on offer, from fishing and wildlife-spotting to hiking and kayaking.

Brokopondo is a human-made reservoir, created in 1964 when the government dammed the Suriname River. Views of storm clouds moving in over the 1550-sq-km lake are breathtaking, but a closer look reveals a rainforest graveyard, in which dead trees stick up through the water's surface from what was once the forest floor. The park headquarters has interesting displays detailing how the dam project required relocating thousands of mostly Maroon and Amerindian people as well as hundreds of thousands of animals.

It's relatively easy to visit Brownsberg on your own: take an Atjoni-bound bus from the Saramacastraat bus station near the central market in Paramaribo and ask to be let off at the village of Brownsberg (SR$60, three hours). From here, arrange in advance for Stinasu to pick you up and drive you to the park (SR$70, 30 minutes). Several Parbo-based tour agencies also do Brownsberg as a (very) long day trip or a more relaxed overnight tour.

Central Suriname Nature Reserve

Covering 12% of Suriname's land area, the epic 16,000 sq km **Central Suriname Nature Reserve** was established in 1998 with a US$1-million donation from Conservation International. Around 40% of the plants and animals here are found only in the Guianas, and the vast majority of the reserve is dense, impenetrable wilderness. As you'd expect, visiting the park is challenging but hugely rewarding, and can only be done by guided tour.

The most commonly visited place in the park is Raleighvallen (Raleigh Falls), a low, long staircase of cascading water on the upper Coppename River, about two hours

GETTING TO GUYANA

At the Border

The **Canawaima Ferry** (☑ 212-332, 212-331; South Drain; per passenger SR$110; ☉ 10am daily; one-way/round-trip SR$48/65, 30 minutes, 10:30am daily) from South Drain crosses the Corantijn River to the dock at Moleson Creek, near the town of Corriverton, Guyana. You'll have to wait in line to stamp out of Suriname before getting on the boat. Money changers abound and tend to offer good rates. There are no fees at the border and immigration is always open to coincide with boat departures and arrivals.

Moving On

After waiting in line again to get stamped in and passing a customs check in Guyana, you'll find the minibuses to Georgetown. Guyana is an hour behind Suriname.

upriver from the nearest Maroon village. Resident wildlife includes spider monkeys, electric eels and the Guiana cock-of-the-rock, a spectacular blood-orange bird. Stinasu (p970) has well-run tourist lodges on Foengoe Island next to the falls. Nearby Voltzberg is a 240m granite dome accessible by a 2½-hour jungle trail and then a steep ascent – the 360-degree views of the jungle from the top are simply astounding.

Nieuw Nickerie

POP 13,100

This bustling border town of wide streets was once a major center for the collection of wood of the balata tree, a unique tree that produces a sap that can be made into latex. Today, Nieuw Nickerie is mostly a banana and rice production hub with a large port, and it has very little to offer visitors, although it's perfectly pleasant. As the last stop in Suriname before Guyana, the town gets its fair share of visitors passing though, and most travelers do just that – staying the night is generally done unintentionally. Nieuw Nickerie is also the departure point for exploring **Bigi Pan**, a swampy reservoir known for caimans, scarlet ibises and more than 100 other kinds of birds.

Most travelers make a point of not getting caught in Nieuw Nickerie overnight, but those who do should head to **Residence Inn Nickerie** (☑ 210-950; Bharosstraat 84; r incl breakfast SR$500; ❉ ❋). Those on a tight budget can try **Concord 2000** (☑ 232-345, 210-926; Wilhelminastraat 3; d SR$220; ❉).

All buses and minibuses arrive at and leave from the market. Government buses travel to Paramaribo (SR$15, four hours) at 6am and 1pm daily, and a private bus (SR$25) leaves when full after the first government bus leaves.

Taxis to Paramaribo (SR$100 per person) take three to four hours. Minibuses to South Drain (SR$15) for the ferry to Guyana leave at 8am, and it's best to reserve with the driver the day before; your hotel can help with this.

Galibi & Coppename Nature Reserves

On Suriname's eastern shoulder, **Galibi Nature Reserve** faces French Guiana across the Marowijne River. Here, hordes of sea turtles, including the giant leatherback, crowd the beaches during egg-laying season (April through August). You can get there from Albina with permission from members of the local Carib community and a hired canoe, or more easily from Paramaribo with the tour operator Stinasu (p970).

Just 100 sq km in size, the **Coppename Nature Reserve**, at the mouth of the Coppename River, is home to the endangered manatee and is a haven for bird-watchers who come here to see rare species of migratory shorebirds and several types of herons. Stinasu organizes trips on request.

UNDERSTAND SURINAME

Suriname Today

Suriname finds itself in a highly unusual position, even by the fairly high standards of South American politics. Its president since 2010, Desiré Bouterse, has been indicted by a Dutch court for drug trafficking and sentenced to 11 years in jail – that he'll serve if he ever sets foot in the Netherlands. He has also had a Europol warrant out for his arrest since 1999. Add to this, after a scramble for amnesty, a 2017 court recommendation in Suriname that the president be sentenced to 20 years in jail for his role in the 1982 'December Murders' (when 15 opponents of Bouterse's military coup were murdered in Paramaribo).

While Bouterse has accepted collective responsibility for the 1982 murders, which happened under his command, he claims he had no knowledge of them at the time, and that he personally played no role in them. In 2012 the Suriname parliament passed an amnesty law protecting Bouterse from any trial for the murders. As president of the country he also enjoys immunity from prosecution while he is in office.

Despite the president's efforts, the trial went ahead in 2017, and despite the amnesty law and his immunity, he took the stand and denied his involvement. This was later contradicted by his codefendant Ruben Rozendaal, who testified that Bouterse had been present and had personally killed some of the victims. Rozendaal took his own life in late 2017, having been sentenced to 10 years for the murders.

Against this extraordinary background, Bouterse remains surprisingly popular, particularly among the younger generations who weren't alive during the civil war.

Outside of politics, Suriname enjoys relatively high levels of living standards, health care and education. The country relies on bauxite for 70% of its foreign trade. Agriculture, particularly irrigated rice cultivation and bananas, is a major industry for the republic, and the fishing industry is growing.

The country is also making a conscious effort to develop ecotourism in the interior. In 2013 alone, some 60 never before seen species were discovered in the pristine rainforest-covered interior, making Suriname a dream destination for nature lovers.

History

For millennia Suriname was populated by the Arawak ethnic group, who were largely replaced by the Carib ethnic group around 2000 years ago, while dozens of smaller ethnic groups populated the interior. The Europeans arrived in 1499, when Amerigo Vespucci sailed along the country's coast, a full expedition landing the following year. However, early European attempts to colonize the land failed due to the fierce resistance of the Amerindian people. It wasn't until 1651 that a group of British planters founded the first permanent European settlement here. Shortly afterwards, the British exchanged the territory for the Dutch village of New Amsterdam, finalizing British control of Manhattan and simultaneously creating the biggest Dutch territory in the Caribbean. Suriname became home to profitable sugar plantations and during the 19th century, Indians and Indonesians (locally referred to as 'Javanese') arrived as indentured plantation workers to supplement the local population.

Despite some limited autonomy, Suriname remained a colony until 1954, when the area became a self-governing state; it gained full independence in 1975. A coup in 1980, led by Sergeant Major (later Lieutenant Colonel) Desiré Bouterse, brought a military regime to power. Bouterse was later brought to trial for ordering the execution of 15 prominent opponents in Fort Zeelandia – an event now called the 'December Murders' – in 1982.

In 1986 the government carried out a campaign to suppress Maroon rebellion, led by Ronnie Brunswijk and his Jungle Commando (the Maroon military). Many of those loyal to Brunswijk fled to French Guiana as their villages were destroyed.

In 1987 a civilian government was elected, but it was deposed by a bloodless coup in 1990. Another civilian government led by Ronald Venetiaan was elected in 1991 and signed a peace treaty with the Jungle Commando and other armed bands in 1992.

Venetiaan was re-elected in May 2000 and held office until 2010. This period was marked by economic difficulty and unrest: flooding in 2006 caused a national disaster and left up to 20,000 people homeless; and in 2009, government troops were sent to gold-mining areas near Albina to quell anti-Chinese and anti-Brazilian protests.

Culture

Suriname is a cultural free-for-all of incredibly friendly and generous people. Paramaribo's level of acceptance and unity is primarily undisturbed by religious and racial tension, which is remarkable given the intimacy of so many groups living in such a small corner of the world. However, Maroons and Amerindians in the interior live with high poverty levels and fewer educational opportunities.

Many Surinamese live or have lived in the Netherlands, either to enjoy its greater economic opportunities or to escape military repression, and are consequently knowledgeable of European trends.

About 40% of the country's well-integrated population are nominally Christian, but some also adhere to traditional African beliefs. Hindus make up 26% of the population (most of the East Indian community), while 19% is Muslim (ethnic Indonesians plus a minority of East Indian origin). A small number is Buddhist, Jewish or follow Amerindian religions. In terms of ethnicities, 37% of the population is Indian, 31% is Creole, 15% is Indonesian, 10% is Maroon, 2% is Amerindian, 2% is Chinese and 1% is Dutch, leaving 2% 'other'.

Some cultural forms – such as gamelan music, often heard at special events – derive from the Indonesian immigrant populations. Other art forms that visitors enjoy include intricate Amerindian basketry and wood carvings by Maroons, widely regarded as the best carvers in tropical America.

Environment

Suriname is divided into a coastal region and dense tropical forest and savannas. To its west, the Corantijn (Corentyne in Guyana) River forms the border, disputed in its most southerly reaches with Guyana. The Marowijne (Maroni in French Guiana) and Litani Rivers form the border with French Guiana.

The majority of Surinamese inhabit the Atlantic coastal plain, where most of the country's few roads are located. The nearby Afobaka Dam created one of the world's largest (1550 sq km) reservoirs, Brokopondo, on the Upper Suriname River.

Being mostly covered by rainforest, Suriname has diverse wildlife, from the flashy jaguar and black caiman to humble agouti and squirrel monkeys. Birders flock to see a wide range of bird species, including the red ibis and harpy eagle.

SURVIVAL GUIDE

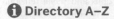 Directory A–Z

ACCESSIBLE TRAVEL

Suriname is a challenging destination for people with impaired mobility or who face other obstacles to getting around independently. While Paramaribo is quite straightforward, trips to the interior are likely to be tough unless you are able to contact hotels or travel agencies in good time to let them know exactly what physical challenges you face. Download Lonely Planet's free Accessible Travel guides from http://lptravel.to/AccessibleTravel.

ACCOMMODATIONS

Fairly affordable hotels and guesthouses are readily found in Paramaribo. Sleeping in the interior can involve more rustic accommodations, although luxurious ecolodges are also available. Due to instability of the local currency, nearly all hotels quote prices in euros or dollars. Jungle lodges tend to offer all-inclusive packages on a per person per day basis.

ACTIVITIES

Suriname's best activity is experiencing nature and indigenous cultures in the interior. Bird-watching and other wildlife-spotting adventures are once-in-a-lifetime experiences, and boating and trekking opportunities are abundant. The accessible Maroon cultures are unique, and most trips to the interior will involve visits to Maroon villages.

ELECTRICITY

Plugs are standard European with two round prongs. Currents are 110/220V, 60Hz.

EMBASSIES & CONSULATES

Most embassies and consulates are in Paramaribo, although many countries have no embassy at all in Suriname. The UK and Canada cover their citizens from their embassy in Guyana, while Australia and Germany cover their citizens from Trinidad & Tobago, and New Zealand covers its citizens from Brazil.

Brazilian Embassy (☑400-200; http://paramaribo.itamaraty.gov.br; Maratakastraat 2, Zorg-en-Hoop)

Dutch Embassy (☑477-211; www.nederlandenu.nl/uw-land-en-nederland/suriname; Van Roseveltkade 5)

French Embassy (☑475-222; www.ambafrance-sr.org; Dr JF Nassylaan 23)

Guyanese Embassy (☑477-895; guyembassy@sr.net; Henk Arronstraat 82)

US Embassy (☑556-700; https://sr.usembassy.gov; Kristalstraat 165) Also responsible for US citizens in French Guiana.

FOOD

You'll eat well in Suriname, where the mixture of cultures ensures a wide variety of cuisines, including plenty of spicy Indian and Southeast Asian influence. Paramaribo has the country's best restaurants by far, and things are inevitably rather less exciting deep in the rainforest, but you'll be unlikely to have any complaints wherever you go.

HEALTH

Recommended Vaccinations

A yellow-fever vaccination certificate is required for all travelers arriving in Suriname. Have it with you in your hand luggage for presentation at the airport or border post.

Other recommended vaccinations include DTP (diphtheria, typhoid and polio), and hepatitis A and B. Travelers planning to spend a lot of time in the interior or with mammals should also consider a rabies vaccine.

Availability & Cost of Health Care

Paramaribo has excellent health care, with modern hospitals, well-stocked pharmacies and private clinics. Health care is harder to find elsewhere along the coast and virtually nonexistent in the interior. Treatment is generally inexpensive by international standards, although prices rise sharply in private facilities.

Enviromental Hazards

The Zika virus is present in Suriname and pregnant women should exercise caution when traveling here, particularly on any trip to the interior. Typhoid and chloroquine-resistant malaria are present in the interior, as are dengue fever and chikungunya. All of these are best avoided by covering your skin and using repellent to avoid mosquito bites.

Tap Water

Tap water is safe to drink in Paramaribo but not elsewhere.

INTERNET ACCESS

Most guesthouses, hotels and some cafes offer free wi-fi.

LANGUAGE

Dutch is the official national language, but many people speak Sranan Tongo (similar to Creole and also called Taki Taki), which can be understood fairly well by English-speakers once you develop an ear for it. Other languages include Hindi, Urdu, Javanese, Mandarin, Cantonese and several dialects of both Maroon and Amerindian languages. English is also widely spoken.

LGBT TRAVELERS

Homosexuality is legal in Suriname, and LGBT people are visible in society, although they do not yet enjoy legal protection against discrimination or the right to marriage or civil partnerships. There is a very small gay scene in Paramaribo, though currently no dedicated gay bars or clubs. LGBT travelers have nothing to worry about in Suriname, and it should be no problem to request a double room at hotels anywhere in the country.

MONEY

Although the official unit of currency is the Surinamese dollar (SR$), some businesses

---

---

quote prices in euros or US dollars. Most banks will accept major foreign currencies, but you may run into difficulty trying to change Guyanese dollars and Brazilian reals. Republic Bank ATMs are the most reliable at accepting foreign cards. You can get credit-card advances at some banks and some hotels. Most hotels, better restaurants and travel agencies – but hardly anywhere else – accept credit cards, usually for a fee.

OPENING HOURS

General business hours are 7:30am to 3pm weekdays, with perhaps a few hours on Saturday. Most restaurants serve lunch from around 11am to 2:30pm, and dinner from about 6pm to 10pm. A small number of places open for breakfast at 8am. Opening hours are not listed in reviews unless they vary widely from these.

PUBLIC HOLIDAYS

New Year's Day January 1; the biggest celebration of the year

Day of the Revolution February 25

Phagwah/Holi (Hindu New Year) March/April

Good Friday/Easter Monday March/April

Labor Day May 1

National Union Day/Abolition of Slavery Day July 1

Independence Day November 25

Christmas Day December 25

Boxing Day December 26

Eid ul-Fitr (Lebaran or Bodo in Indonesian) End of Ramadan; dates vary

---

TELEPHONE

Suriname has a decent landline system. There are no area codes. Landlines have six digits, while cell phones have seven.

The national telephone company is TeleSur, which sells SIM cards, although service is considerably better at Digicel and the cost is the same (SR$20, which includes SR$5 worth of credit).

TOURIST INFORMATION

The Tourist Information Center (p972) in Paramaribo has everything to get you started, including a helpful website. You can also get lots of useful information from Stinasu (p970).

VISAS

Visitors from the US, UK, Australia, Canada, New Zealand and the EU need a tourist card. Longer stays or multiple entries will require a visa. For up-to-date info and embassy locations check www.surinameembassy.org. Allow approximately four weeks for a postal visa or tourist-card application.

The Surinamese consulates in Georgetown (Guyana) and Cayenne (French Guiana) can issue tourist cards on the spot or within a couple of hours, but visas can take up to five working days. Bring a passport-size photo and your ticket out of South America. Visitors planning to stay in Suriname for more than 30 days should register at the **Vreemdelingenpolitie** (Immigration Service; ✒403-609; Henk Arronstraat 1; ☺7am-2pm Mon-Fri) in Paramaribo within eight days of their arrival.

WOMEN TRAVELERS

Female travelers, especially if traveling alone, may encounter harassment from local men, but they are rarely physically threatening. Constant 'hissing' and 'sucking' noises can be annoying, if not truly disconcerting – ignore them if you can.

ⓘ Getting There & Away

AIR

Long-haul international flights arrive at Suriname's outdated Johan Pengel International Airport (p973), more often called Zanderij, while domestic and regional international flights arrive mostly at the similarly poor Zorg-en-Hoop Airport (p973), close to Paramaribo.

Blue Wings (✒434-393; www.bluewingairlines. com; Zorg-en-Hoop Airport) Scheduled and charter services to many domestic destinations.

Caribbean Airlines (✒520-034; www.caribbean-airlines.com; Wagenwegstraat 36) Connects Paramaribo to various Caribbean islands.

Insel Air (✒403-866; www.fly-inselair.com; Van 't Hogerhuysstraat 9-11) Service to Curaçao with connections to other Caribbean islands.

KLM (✒411-811; www.klm.com; Hofstraat 1) Four direct flights to Amsterdam per week.

Surinam Airways (✒465-700; www.flyslm. com; Dr Sophie Redmondstraat 219) Flies to many destinations, including Georgetown (Guyana), Cayenne (French Guiana), Port of Spain (Trinidad), Curaçao, Aruba, Belem (Brazil), Miami and Amsterdam.

RIVER

Suriname's border crossings are at Corriverton (Guyana) and St Laurent du Maroni (French Guiana). Both crossings are made by boat across massive rivers that flow into the Caribbean. These ferries traverse the river borders from Albina (in the east of Suriname) and Nieuw Nickerie via South Drain (in the west), respectively. While Brazil borders the country to the south, there are no roads through the impenetrable jungle into Suriname so you can't cross the border here.

ⓘ Getting Around

AIR

Small planes shuttle people between Paramaribo and remote destinations, including some nature reserves that have airstrips.

BOAT

Rivers offer scenic routes to parts of the interior that are otherwise inaccessible. Scheduled services are few, and prices are negotiable. Ferries and launches cross some major rivers, such as the Suriname and the Coppename Rivers.

BUS & MINIBUS

In order from cheapest to priciest, you can choose from scheduled government buses, private minibuses that leave from designated points when full, and minibuses that pick you up from your hotel. Trips to the interior cost significantly more than those on coastal routes.

CAR & MOTORCYCLE

Suriname's roads are limited and difficult to navigate. Passenger cars can handle the roads along the coast and to Brownsberg, but tracks into the interior are for 4WDs only. Driving is on the left. An International Driving Permit is required; your national licence will not be valid here, so plan ahead if you want to drive during your trip.

TAXI

Shared taxis cover routes along the coast. They can be several times more expensive than minibuses but are markedly faster. Local cab fares are negotiable and reasonable; set a price before getting in. Paramaribo cabs are metered.

Uruguay

POP 3.4 MILLION

Best Places to Eat

➜ Café Picasso (p1002)

➜ Don Joaquín (p994)

➜ Resto-Pub 70 (p1008)

➜ Candy Bar (p985)

➜ Escaramuza (p989)

Best Places to Stay

➜ Estancia Panagea (p1001)

➜ El Galope Horse Farm & Hostel (p993)

➜ La Posadita de la Plaza (p994)

➜ Tas D'Viaje Hostel (p1003)

➜ El Diablo Tranquilo (p1008)

Why Go?

Wedged like a grape between Brazil's gargantuan thumb and Argentina's long forefinger, Uruguay has always been something of an underdog. Yet after two centuries living in the shadow of its neighbors, South America's smallest country is finally getting a little well-deserved recognition. Progressive, stable, safe and culturally sophisticated, Uruguay offers visitors opportunities to experience everyday 'not made for tourists' moments, whether caught in a cow-and-*gaucho* (cowboy) traffic jam on a dirt road to nowhere or strolling with maté-toting locals along Montevideo's beachfront.

Short-term visitors will find plenty to keep them busy in cosmopolitan Montevideo, picturesque Colonia and party-till-you-drop Punta del Este. But it pays to dig deeper. Go wildlife-watching along the Atlantic coast, or hot-spring-hopping up the Río Uruguay, or horseback riding under the big sky of Uruguay's interior, where vast fields spread out like oceans.

When to Go
Montevideo

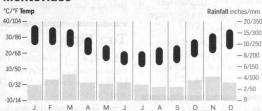

Feb Street theater and drumming consume Montevideo during Carnaval celebrations.

Mar Tacuarembó's *gaucho* festival, plus lower prices on the still-sunny Atlantic coast.

Oct Soak in Salto's hot springs, or explore Uruguay's monuments for free during Días del Patrimonio.

FAST FACTS

Currency Uruguayan peso (UR$)

Visas Not required for many nationals of Western Europe, USA, Canada or New Zealand.

Money ATMs widespread; credit cards widely accepted.

Time GMT minus three hours

Emergency 911

Language Spanish

Exchange Rates

Argentina	AR$1	UR$0.89
Australia	A$1	UR$23.36
Brazil	R$1	UR$8.81
Canada	C$1	UR$25.14
Chile	CH$100	UR$4.86
Eurozone	€1	UR$37.66
Japan	¥100	UR$29.30
New Zealand	NZ$1	UR$21.52
UK	UK£1	UR$42.80
USA	US$1	UR$32.86

For current exchange rates, see www.xe.com.

Daily Costs

➡ Hostel bed: US$15–25; double room in a midrange hotel: from US$75

➡ *Menu ejecutivo* (fixed-price lunch) US$10–15; midrange restaurant meal including drinks: US$25

Resources

Lonely Planet (www.lonelyplanet.com/uruguay)

Uruguay Tourism Ministry (www.turismo.gub.uy)

Entering the Country

Coming from Argentina, most people arrive by boat, departing either from Buenos Aires (for Montevideo and Colonia del Sacramento) or Tigre (for Carmelo). Land crossings are also possible from the Argentine towns of Colón, Gualeguaychú and Concordia. The most common point of entry from Brazil is at Chuí/Chuy.

TWO WEEK ITINERARY

With a week up your sleeve you won't see it all, but if you keep on the move you can see some of the best of what Uruguay has to offer. Start in the easygoing, picturesque historical river port of Colonia and head for the urban attractions of Montevideo, both an easy ferry ride from Buenos Aires. From Montevideo, continue north along the Atlantic coast and sample a few of Uruguay's best beaches: the 1930s vintage resort of Piriápolis, glitzy Punta del Este, isolated Cabo Polonio, surfer-friendly La Paloma or the relaxed beach-party town of Punta del Diablo. Alternatively, follow the Río Uruguay upstream toward Iguazú Falls via the quirky industrial museum at Fray Bentos and the wonderful hot springs of Salto.

Adding another week will allow you to do the above at a more leisurely pace, plus get out and explore Uruguay's scenic and little-visited interior, where the *gaucho* (cowboy) tradition lives on.

Essential Food & Drink

Asado Mixed grill featuring various cuts of meat cooked over a wood fire.

Buñuelos de Algas Savory seaweed fritters.

Chajá A sweet concoction of sponge cake, meringue, cream and fruit.

Chivito Steak sandwich piled high with toppings.

Medio y medio A refreshing blend of half white wine, half sparkling wine.

Top Tips

➡ Uruguay is a paradise for travelers who want to get off the beaten track. Look beyond the tourist hot spots and embrace Uruguay's wide-open spaces in places like Valle del Lunarejo and Cabo Polonio.

➡ Travel in Uruguay is refreshingly easy. Buses are frequent, efficient, comfortable and relatively inexpensive, while driving Uruguay's sparsely traveled back roads is considerably less stressful than in many other South American countries.

➡ If possible, visit Montevideo on the weekend, when you can enjoy some of the city's most iconic local events, like the Ciudad Vieja antiques market.

Uruguay Highlights

1 Carnaval (p989) Dancing during Montevideo's festivities.

2 Punta del Diablo (p1007) Catching a wave or beach party along the shoreline.

3 Thermal Baths (p1000) Soaking your muscles in the hot springs near Salto.

4 Valle del Lunarejo (p1001)

Getting off the beaten track in this nature preserve.

5 Colonia del Sacramento (p993) Sunbathing on the town wall, or wandering this town on the Río de la Plata.

6 Cabo Polonio (p1006) Losing yourself in the sand dunes and surveying the sea lions from atop the lighthouse.

7 Museo de la Revolución Industrial (p998) Touring Uruguay's newest Unesco World Heritage Site in Fray Bentos.

8 Punta del Este (p1003) Hitting the beaches by day and the clubs by night.

9 Tacuarembó (p1000) Discovering the simple joys of *estancia* living under the stars.

MONTEVIDEO

POP 1.3 MILLION

Uruguay's capital and largest city, Montevideo is a favorite for many travelers: small enough to walk or cycle around, but big enough to have some great museums and nightlife, plus an impressive string of beaches along the Río de la Plata. Young *montevideanos* (people from Montevideo) take genuine pride in their city, and the arts and artisan scene is particularly strong.

👁 Sights

Montevideo's most interesting buildings and museums are in the Ciudad Vieja (Old Town), west of **Plaza Independencia**, the city's largest square. Here, remnants of the colonial past such as **Puerta de la Ciudadela**, a vestigial stone gateway from Montevideo's 18th-century citadel, rub shoulders with grand 19th-century legacies of the beef boom, including the beautifully restored, neoclassical **Teatro Solís** (☑1950-3323; www.teatrosolis.org.uy; Buenos Aires 678; tours UR$90, Wed free; ⊙tours 4pm Tue & Thu, 11am, noon & 4pm Wed, Fri & Sun, 11am, noon, 1pm & 4pm Sat).

⭐**Mercado del Puerto**   MARKET

(Pérez Castellano) No visitor should miss Montevideo's old port market building, at the foot of Pérez Castellano; the building's impressive wrought-iron superstructure shelters a gaggle of bustling *parrillas* (steak restaurants). On weekend afternoons in particular, it's a lively, colorful place where the city's artists, craftspeople and street musicians hang out.

Museo del Carnaval   MUSEUM

(☑2916-5493; www.museodelcarnaval.org; Rambla 25 de Agosto 218; UR$110; ⊙11am-5pm daily Dec-Mar, Thu-Sun Apr-Nov) This museum houses a wonderful collection of costumes, drums, masks, recordings and photos documenting the 100-plus-year history of Montevideo's Carnaval (p989). Behind the museum is a cafe and a courtyard where spectators can view performances during the summer months. Touch-screen displays offer limited English-language commentary.

Museo de los Andes   MUSEUM

(☑2916-9461; www.mandes.uy; Rincón 619; UR$200; ⊙10am-5pm Mon-Fri, to 3pm Sat) Opened in 2013, this unique museum documents the 1972 Andean plane crash (made famous in the book *Alive!*) that cost 29 Uruguayans their lives and profoundly impacted Uruguay's national psyche. Using original objects and photos from the crash site, it tells the story of the 16 survivors, who battled harrowing conditions for 72 days before returning alive to a stunned nation. The museum is a labor of love for director Jörg Thomsen, a personal friend of many of the families affected.

Casa Rivera   MUSEUM

(☑2915-1051; www.museohistorico.gub.uy; Rincón 437; ⊙noon-5:45pm Wed-Sun) FREE Former home of Fructuoso Rivera (Uruguay's first president and Colorado Party founder), this neoclassical 1802 building is the centerpiece of Montevideo's National Historical Museum, with a collection of paintings, documents, furniture and artifacts that trace the history of Uruguay's 19th-century path to independence. Several other historic Ciudad Vieja homes nearby, officially part of the museum, are rarely open to visitors.

⭐**Museo del Gaucho**   MUSEUM

(☑2900-8764; Av 18 de Julio 998; ⊙10am-4pm Mon-Fri) FREE Housed in the ornate Palacio Heber, this museum eloquently conveys the deep attachments between the *gauchos,* their animals and the land. Its superb collection of historical artifacts includes horse gear, silverwork, and maté (a bitter ritual tea) and *bombillas* (metal straws with filters, used for drinking maté) in whimsical designs.

⭐**Museo Nacional de Artes Visuales**   MUSEUM

(MNAV; ☑2711-6124; www.mnav.gub.uy; Giribaldi 2283, Parque Rodó; ⊙1-8pm Tue-Sun) FREE Uruguay's largest collection of paintings is housed here in Parque Rodó. The spacious rooms are graced with works by Blanes, Cúneo, Figari, Gurvich, Torres García and other famous Uruguayans. For a closer look at some of these same artists, visit the **Museo Torres García** (☑2916-2663; www.torresgarcia.org.uy; Sarandí 683; UR$150; ⊙10am-6pm Mon-Sat), **Museo Figari** (☑2915-7065; www.museofigari.gub.uy; Juan Carlos Gómez 1427; ⊙1-6pm Tue-Fri, 10am-2pm Sat) FREE and **Museo Gurvich** (☑2915-7826; www.museogurvich.org; Sarandí 524; UR$180; ⊙10am-6pm Mon-Fri, 11am-3pm Sat) in Ciudad Vieja, or the **Museo Blanes** (☑2336-2248; www.blanes.montevideo.gub.uy; Av Millán 4015; ⊙noon-6pm Tue-Sun) FREE in the Prado neighborhood north of Centro.

Museo del Fútbol   MUSEUM

(☑2480-1259; www.estadiocentenario.com.uy/site/footballmuseum; Estadio Centenario, Av Ricaldoni s/n, Parque José Batlle y Ordóñez; UR$150; ⊙10am-5pm Mon-Fri & when no match Sat) A must-see for any *fútbol* fan, this museum displays memorabilia from Uruguay's 1930 and 1950 World Cup wins. Visitors can also tour the stands.

🏃 Activities

Hire a bicycle from **Orange Bike** (📞2908-8286; www.orangebike.com.uy; Pérez Castellano 1417; bike rental per 4/24hr UR$300/600; ⊙9am-7pm Nov-Apr, 10am-5:30pm May-Oct) and go cruising along the riverfront Rambla, a 20km walking-jogging-cycling track that leads past Parque Rodó, one of Montevideo's most popular parks, then follows the shoreline to the city's eastern beaches: Punta Carretas, Pocitos, Buceo, Malvin and Carrasco.

🎒 Courses

Academia Uruguay   LANGUAGE
(📞2915-2496; www.academiauruguay.com; Juan Carlos Gómez 1408; group classes per week US$245, individual classes per hour US$30) One-on-one and group Spanish classes with a strong cultural focus. Also arranges homestays, private apartments and volunteer work.

Joventango   DANCING
(📞2908-6813; www.joventango.com; Aquiles Lanza 1290; per class UR$250) Tango classes for all levels, from beginner to expert.

🎆 Festivals & Events

Much livelier and longer-lasting than its Buenos Aires counterpart, Montevideo's multi-week **Carnaval** is the cultural highlight of the year. Festivities begin as early as January and end as late as March, depending on the year.

At Parque Prado, north of downtown, Semana Criolla festivities during **Semana Santa** (Holy Week/Easter) include displays of *gaucho* skills, *asados* (barbecues) and other such events.

In the last weekend of September or first weekend of October, Montevideo's museums, churches and historic homes all open their doors free to the public during the **Días del Patrimonio** (National Heritage Days), celebrated throughout Uruguay).

🛏 Sleeping

★Hotel Palacio   HOTEL $
(📞2916-3612; www.hotelpalacio.com.uy; Bartolomé Mitre 1364; r without breakfast & with/without balcony US$47/42; ❄🖥) If you can snag one of the two 6th-floor rooms at this ancient family-run hotel one block off Plaza Matriz, go for it! Both feature air-conditioning and balconies with superb views of Ciudad Vieja's

rooftops. The rest of the hotel also offers great value, with wood floors, antique furniture, a vintage elevator and old-school service reminiscent of a European pension.

Ukelele Hostel   HOSTEL $
(📞2902-7844; www.ukelelehostel.com; Maldonado 1183; dm US$18-22.50, tw/d US$48/60; @🖥🏊) Attractive features at this 1920s family-home-turned-hostel include vintage architectural details and a grassy pool and patio area out back for lounging. It has a good mix of dorms and private rooms, and the inviting common areas include an on-site bar and a music room with high ceilings.

Spléndido Hotel   HOTEL $
(📞2916-4900; www.splendidohotel.com.uy; Bartolomé Mitre 1314; d US$38-55, d without bathroom US$30-45, s without bathroom US$25-35; @🖥) The faded, funky Spléndido offers decent value for budget travelers preferring privacy over a hostel-style party vibe. The better rooms have 5m-high ceilings and French doors opening to balconies; three rooms (106, 220 and 221) directly overlook Teatro Solís. Others are more cramped and considerably less inviting; survey the options before committing. Bars on the street below can get noisy.

Caballo Loco Hostel   HOSTEL $
(📞2902-6494; www.caballolocohostel.com; Gutierrez Ruiz 1287; dm US$17-26; ❄🖥) This friendly hostel in a remodeled historic building enjoys an unbeatable downtown location, only steps from leafy Plaza Cagancha and bus stops for Montevideo's bus station and beaches. Six spick-and-span four- to 10-bed dorms surround a welcoming common area with guest kitchen, pool table and TV lounge. Other pluses include on-site bike rentals.

★Casa Sarandí Guesthouse   GUESTHOUSE $$
(📞099-707068, 2400-6460; www.casasarandi.com; Buenos Aires 558, 3rd fl; r without breakfast US$85; 🖥) One block south of Plaza Matriz, two attractive guest rooms in a vintage apartment share a kitchen and comfortable living room adorned with local artwork and parquet wood floors. Reserve ahead to set a time to meet the Welsh-Argentine owners, who live off-site but provide a key and oodles of up-to-the-minute tips on eating, entertainment and transport.

🍴 Eating

★Candy Bar   TAPAS, BURGERS $
(📞2904-3179; www.facebook.com/candybarpalermo; Durazno 1402; tapas UR$150, mains

Montevideo

Bahía de Montevideo

Dársena 2

Muelle B

Puerto de Montevideo

Rambla Franklin D Roosevelt

Dársena I

Muelle A

Ciudadela

Juncal

Florida

40

Dársena Fluvial

43

Rambla 25 de Agosto de 1825

Piedras

Treinta y Tres

Ituzaingó

Bartolomé Mitre

Cerrito

28

7
1
42

Mercado del Puerto

Yacaré

Colón

Solís

27

8
13
6

Plaza Matriz
(Plaza Constitución)

18
29
19

10
12
11

37

35

4

5

32

Bacacay

Guaraní

Maciel

25 de Mayo

Plaza Zabala

9

Juan Carlos Gómez

3
Teatro Solís

Liniers

Ciudadela

15
24

CIUDAD VIEJA

Washington

Zabala

Misiones

23

17

Brecha

21

Cuestas

Sarandí

Pérez Castellano

Alzáibar

26

Reconquista

Buenos Aires

Plaza España

Rambla Gran Bretaña

Rambla Francia

Montevideo

UR$270-300; ⊘ 12:30pm-1am Tue-Sat, noon-3pm Sun) At this cool corner eatery, colorful folding chairs fill the sidewalk beneath a sycamore tree, while the chefs inside mix drinks, whip up meals and juggle fresh-baked bread behind a countertop overhung with artsy lampshades. Reasonably priced tapas and burgers (carnivorous and vegetarian) rule the menu, complemented by artisan beers and mixed drinks. Sunday brunch is especially popular.

El Club del Pan   BAKERY $
(www.facebook.com/pg/clubdelpan; cnr Pablo de María & Muller; items from UR$30; ⊘ 8:30am-7pm Tue-Fri, 10am-3pm Sat) After deriving inspiration from bakers around the world, Gonzalo Zubirí returned home to Montevideo to open this sweet corner spot, a stone's throw from Parque Rodó, in 2017. A cornucopia of sublime baked goods – croissants to focaccia to *pain au chocolat* (chocolate croissants) – emerges daily from the oven. At lunchtime, don't miss its daily sandwich specials, which range from vegan to carnivorous.

Shawarma Ashot   MIDDLE EASTERN $
(www.facebook.com/shawarmaashot; Zelmar Michelini 1295; sandwiches UR$160-250; ⊘ 11am-5pm Mon-Thu, 11am-5pm & 7:30pm-midnight Fri, noon-4pm & 7:30pm-midnight Sat) Well-prepared Middle Eastern classics such as falafel and shawarma draw loyal lunchtime crowds at this unpretentious hole-in-the-wall. For a special treat, don't miss the UR$250 Saturday special: Uruguayan lamb with rice pilaf!

Bar Tasende   PIZZA $
(☑ 2900-2970; cnr Ciudadela & San José; pizza slices UR$105; ⊘ 10am-1am Sun-Thu, to 2am Fri & Sat) This classic high-ceilinged corner bar has been wooing patrons since 1931 with its trademark *muzzarella al tacho* (simple but tasty pizza slices laden with mozzarella), a perfect snack to accompany a beer any time of day.

Mercado Agrícola de Montevideo   MARKET $
(MAM; ☑ 2200-9535; www.mam.com.uy; José Terra 2220; ⊘ 9am-10pm) One of Montevideo's newer foodie attractions, this early 20th-century market building and national historic monument

2.5km north of the center was completely renovated and reopened in 2013. It now houses more than 100 merchants, including fruit and veggie vendors, cafes, restaurants, specialty food shops and a microbrewery.

★ **Escaramuza** CAFE $$
(☎2401-3475; www.escaramuza.com.uy; Pablo de María 1185; mains UR$270-450; ⊙9am-9pm Mon-Sat) Tucked into a beautifully restored Cordón home, Escaramuza impresses on many levels. Cross the threshold to discover one of Montevideo's most attractive bookshops. A few paces further and you've entered the high-ceilinged cafe and back-patio restaurant, where patrons linger over superbly prepared, reasonably priced Uruguayan specials with health-food overtones; *milanesas* (breaded cutlets) and buttery mashed potatoes, meet kale salad!

★ **La Fonda** VEGAN, HEALTH FOOD $$
(☎2917-1559; www.facebook.com/pg/lafonday; Pérez Castellano 1422; mains UR$375-500; ⊙11am-6:30pm Mon-Thu, to 11pm Fri, noon-11pm Sat & Sun; 🖉) Grab a table on the pedestrianized street, or enter the brick-walled interior to watch the chefs bantering to cool jazz as they roll out homemade pasta, carefully lay asparagus spears atop risotto or grab ingredients from boxes of organic produce. The chalkboard menu always includes one vegan option.

★ **Estrecho** INTERNATIONAL $$
(☎2915-6107; Sarandí 460; mains UR$350-490; ⊙noon-4pm Mon-Fri) Grab a seat at the long stoveside counter and watch the chefs whip up delicious daily specials at this cozy Ciudad Vieja lunch spot. The international menu includes baguette sandwiches with steak or smoked salmon, a variety of salads, fresh fish of the day and divine desserts.

La Pulpería PARRILLA $$
(☎2710-8657; www.facebook.com/lapulperia mvdeo; cnr Lagunillas & Nuñez, Punta Carretas; mains UR$300-475; ⊙7pm-midnight Tue-Sat, noon-4pm Sun) The epitome of an intimate neighborhood *parrilla,* this corner place doesn't advertise its presence (drop by before 7pm and you won't even find a sign outside); instead, it focuses on grilling prime cuts of meat to perfection, and relies on word of mouth to do the rest. Grab a barstool by the blazing fire or a table on the sidewalk.

Sin Pretensiones CAFE $$
(☎2916-9972; www.sinpretensiones.com.uy; Peatonal Sarandí 366; mains UR$290-550; ⊙9:30am-6:30pm Mon-Fri) Enterprising Argentine owner Guillermina has created this pleasingly unique cafe-boutique on Ciudad Vieja's main pedestrian street. The wide-open space invites people to settle in over breakfast pastries, glasses of wine or *grappamiel* (honey-infused grape brandy), afternoon tea or maté, and light meals any time of day (a real boon to foreigners who still haven't adjusted to Uruguay's late-night dinner schedule).

CARNAVAL IN MONTEVIDEO

If you thought Brazil was South America's only Carnaval capital, think again! *Montevideanos* (people from Montivideo) cut loose in a big way every year, with music and dance filling the air for a solid month.

Not to be missed is the early February **Desfile de las Llamadas**, a two-night parade of *comparsas* (neighborhood Carnaval societies) through the streets of Palermo and Barrio Sur districts, just southeast of the Centro. Neighborhood rivalries play themselves out as wave after wave of dancers whirl to the electrifying rhythms of traditional Afro-Uruguayan *candombe* drumming. The heart of the parade route is Isla de Flores, between Salto and Gaboto. Spectators can pay for a chair on the sidewalk or try to snag a spot on one of the balconies overlooking the street.

Another key element of Montevideo's Carnaval are the *murgas,* organized groups of 15 to 17 gaudily dressed performers, including three percussionists, who perform original pieces of musical theater, often satirical and based on political themes. *Murgas* play all over the city, and also compete throughout February in Parque Rodó at the **Teatro de Verano** (www.teatrodeverano.org.uy).

The fascinating history of Montevideo's Carnaval is well documented in the city's Museo del Carnaval (p984). Another great way to experience Carnaval out of season is by attending one of the informal weekend *candombe* practice sessions held around town throughout the year. For a list of regular sessions (complete with links to participating *comparsas'* Facebook pages), see www.descubrimontevideo.uy/es/candombe-por-los-barrios.

WHAT'S THE BUZZ? URUGUAY'S MARIJUANA LAW

In December 2013 Uruguay became the first country in the world to fully legalize cannabis. Uruguayan citizens are now allowed to grow up to six marijuana plants for personal
use each year, and are entitled to purchase up to 40g per month at local pharmacies
through the government's national distribution system.

Meanwhile, smoking pot in public is perfectly legal – for anyone, foreigners included –
in the same places where cigarette smoking is permitted. Paradoxically, non-Uruguayans
are not allowed to purchase weed – but stick around long enough and you're bound to
find Uruguayans, whether at a hostel, a beach or a local park, who are happy to share.

🍷 Drinking & Nightlife

Montevideo offers an intriguing mix of ven-
erable cafes and trendy nightspots. Bars are
concentrated on Bartolomé Mitre in Ciudad
Vieja, south of Plaza Independencia in the
Centro, and near the corner of Canelones and
Juan Jackson where the Parque Rodó and
Cordón neighborhoods meet.

★ Café Brasilero   CAFE
(📞 2917-2035; www.facebook.com/cafebrasilerouy;
Ituzaingó 1447; ⏰ 9am-8pm Mon-Fri, to 6pm Sat)
This vintage 1877 cafe with dark wood paneling and historic photos gracing the walls
makes a delightful spot for morning coffee
or afternoon tea. It's also an excellent lunch
stop, with good-value *menus ejecutivos*
(all-inclusive daily specials for UR$425).

Baker's Bar   BAR
(📞 092-201829;   www.facebook.com/bakersbar;
Pablo de María 1198; ⏰ 7pm-1am Mon-Thu, to 3am
Fri & Sat) One of Montevideo's newer drinking hot spots, Baker's sits in the heart of
the Cordón–Parque Rodó nightlife district.
Cofounders Santiago Urquhart and Charlie
Sarli have infused the place with a cool, low-
key energy, serving up well-mixed drinks
and tasty tapas.

Chopería Mastra   MICROBREWERY
(www.mastra.com.uy; Mercado Agrícola de Montevideo, Local 17; ⏰ 11am-11pm) This convivial pub
in Montevideo's agricultural market is the
flagship outlet for Uruguay's beloved Mastra
microbrewery. With a dozen varieties to
choose from, you may prefer to opt for the
tabla degustación (a four-beer sampler,
available weekdays only). Mastra has several
other pubs around town, including near the
beach in **Pocitos** (www.mastra.com.uy; cnr 26
de Marzo & Pérez, Pocitos; ⏰ 7pm-2am Tue-Sat).

Shannon Irish Pub   PUB
(www.theshannon.com.uy;   Bartolomé Mitre 1318;
⏰ 6pm-late Mon-Fri, from 7pm Sat & Sun) Always
hopping, the Shannon features a variety of
Uruguayan microbrews plus a full comple-
ment of other beers from over a dozen countries. There's live music 365 days a year, from
rock to traditional Irish bands.

La Farmacia   CAFE
(Cerrito 550; ⏰ 9am-8pm Mon-Fri, 10am-4:30pm
Sat) Opened in 2017, this Ciudad Vieja cafe
in a 19th-century pharmacy (circa 1870)
oozes historic charm. Green marble table-
tops, ornamental tiled floors and built-in
wood cabinetry from its former incarnation
make a splendid setting for morning coffee
or midafternoon snacks.

☆ Entertainment

★ Fun Fun   LIVE MUSIC
(📞 2904-4859; www.barfunfun.com; Soriano 922,
Centro; ⏰ 8pm-2:30am Tue-Sat) Since 1895 this
intimate, informal venue has been serving
its famous *uvita* (a sweet wine drink) while
hosting tango and other live music on a tiny
stage. At the time of writing it was temporarily located on Calle Soriano, but by the
time you read this it may have returned four
blocks west to its traditional home in Mercado Central.

★ Teatro Solís   PERFORMING ARTS
(📞 1950-3323;   www.teatrosolis.org.uy;   Buenos
Aires s/n, Ciudad Vieja; tickets from UR$190) The
city's top performing-arts venue is home
to the Montevideo Philharmonic Orchestra
and hosts formal concerts of classical, jazz,
tango and other music, plus music festivals,
theater, ballet and opera.

Sala Zitarrosa   PERFORMING ARTS
(📞 1950-9241; www.salazitarrosa.com.uy; Av 18 de
Julio 1012, Centro) Montevideo's best midsize
auditorium venue for big-name music and
dance performances, including tango, rock,
flamenco, reggae and *zarzuela* (traditional
Spanish musical theater).

🔒 Shopping

Feria de Tristán Narvaja   MARKET
(Tristán Narvaja, Cordón; ⊘9am-4pm Sun) This colorful Sunday-morning outdoor market is a decades-long tradition begun by Italian immigrants. It sprawls from Av 18 de Julio northwards along Calle Tristán Narvaja, spilling over onto side streets. You can find used books, music, clothing, live animals, antiques and souvenirs in its many makeshift stalls.

Feria de Antigüedades   MARKET
(Antiques Market; Plaza Matriz, Ciudad Vieja; ⊘8am-1pm Sat) Every Saturday, vendors take over Ciudad Vieja's central square, selling antique door knockers, saddles, household goods and just about anything else you can imagine. A smaller contingent of vendors appears on the plaza some weekdays.

ⓘ Information

EMERGENCY

Ambulance	🖉105
Police	🖉911

MEDICAL SERVICES
Hospital Británico (🖉2487-1020; www.hospital britanico.com.uy; Av Italia 2420) Highly recommended private hospital with English-speaking doctors; 2.5km east of downtown.

MONEY
Banks, ATMs and exchange houses such as **Indumex** (🖉2408-4060; www.indumex.com; Terminal Tres Cruces; ⊘6am-midnight) are everywhere, including the airport and bus terminal; downtown they're concentrated along Av 18 de Julio.

TOURIST INFORMATION
The Municipal Tourist Office has city maps, general Montevideo information and a downloadable visitor's guide to the city in English, Spanish and Portuguese.

Centro (🖉1950-1830; www.descubrimonte video.uy; cnr Av 18 de Julio & Ejido; ⊘10am-4pm Mon-Sat) Downtown tourist office, on the ground floor of Montevideo's city hall.

Ciudad Vieja (🖉2916-8434; www.descubri montevideo.uy; Piedras 252; ⊘10am-4pm Mon-Sat) Next to Mercado del Puerto.

The National Tourism Ministry offers info about Montevideo and destinations throughout Uruguay.

Carrasco Airport (🖉2604-0386; www. turismo.gub.uy; Carrasco Airport; ⊘8am-8pm)

Port (🖉2188-5111; www.turismo.gub.uy; Rambla 25 de Agosto & Yacaré; ⊘9am-5pm Mon-Fri)

Tres Cruces Bus Terminal (🖉2188-5801; cnr Bulevar Artigas & Av Italia; ⊘8am-10pm Mon-Fri, from 9am Sat & Sun)

ⓘ Getting There & Away

AIR
Montevideo's **Carrasco International Airport** (🖉2604-0329; www.aeropuertodecarrasco.com. uy; Ruta 101, Km 20) is 20km east of downtown.

BOAT
Buquebus (🖉092-913123, 130; www.buque bus.com.uy) runs daily ferries direct from Montevideo to Buenos Aires on the high-speed *Francisco* boat (2¼ hours), named after Pope Francis. Full *turista*-class fares run UR$4071. Buquebus also offers less-expensive bus-boat combinations from Montevideo to Buenos Aires via Colonia (UR$1610 to UR$2580, 4½ hours). Better fares for all services above are available with online advance purchase; you can also buy direct from Buquebus counters at **Montevideo Port** (Terminal Fluvio-Marítima, Montevideo Port; ⊘9am-7:30pm) and **Tres Cruces bus terminal** (Tres Cruces Bus Terminal, ticket counters 28 & 29; ⊘5:30am-11pm Mon-Fri, to 10pm Sat, to 1am Sun).

Seacat (🖉2915-0202; www.seacatcolonia. com.uy; Río Negro 1400; ⊘9:30am-6:30pm Mon-Fri) and **Colonia Express** (🖉2401-6666; www. coloniaexpress.com; Tres Cruces Bus Terminal, ticket counter 31A; ⊘5:30am-10:30pm) both offer slightly more economical bus-boat connections from Montevideo to Buenos Aires via Colonia (ranging from UR$1510 to UR$2330, 4¼ hours).

Cacciola Viajes (🖉2407-9657; www.cacciola viajes.com; Tres Cruces Bus Terminal, ticket counter B25; ⊘8:30am-12:30am Mon-Fri, to 10pm Sat, 7:30am-12:30am Sun) runs a scenic twice- to thrice-daily bus-launch service from

---

ⓘ GETTING TO ARGENTINA

Ferries offer the most popular and convenient way to cross between Uruguay and Argentina; routes include Montevideo to Buenos Aires, Colonia del Sacramento to Buenos Aires and Carmelo to the Buenos Aires suburb of Tigre. Immigration is carried out at the port, so try to arrive an hour ahead of your departure time.

Further north, local buses run across the Río Uruguay from Fray Bentos, Paysandú and Salto (Uruguay) to their Argentine counterparts, Gualeguaychú, Colón and Concordia. Immigration procedures are often handled on the bus, and borders are generally open 24 hours.

Montevideo to Buenos Aires via the riverside town of Carmelo and the Argentine Delta suburb of Tigre. The seven-hour trip costs UR$900 one way.

BUS

Montevideo's modern **Tres Cruces Bus Terminal** (☏2401-8998; www.trescruces.com.uy; cnr Bulevar Artigas & Av Italia) is about 3km east of downtown. It has tourist information, toilets, luggage storage, ATMs and a shopping mall upstairs.

All domestic destinations are served daily, and most several times a day. A small *tasa de embarque* (departure tax) is added to the ticket prices. Travel times are approximate.

EGA (☏2402-5164; www.ega.com.uy) provides the widest range of service to neighboring countries. Destinations in Argentina include Paraná, Santa Fe and Mendoza (all once weekly, on Friday), plus Córdoba and Rosario (each four times weekly). EGA also runs buses once weekly on Sunday to Florianópolis (UR$4985, 18 hours) and São Paulo, Brazil (UR$7525, 30 hours); twice weekly on Wednesday and Saturday to Asunción, Paraguay (UR$4550 to UR$5555, 20 hours); and daily to Porto Alegre, Brazil (UR$2790 to UR$3580, 12 hours).

Service to Buenos Aires is more frequent, with **CITA** (☏2402-5425; www.cita.com.uy) and several competing companies offering multiple nightly departures (UR$1735, eight hours).

❶ Getting Around

TO/FROM THE AIRPORT

Buses, shuttle vans, taxis and *remises* (private cars) make the 20km journey from the airport into Montevideo. Cheapest are the local Copsa and Cutcsa buses (UR$63, 45 minutes) that leave from a stop directly in front of the arrivals hall, making frequent stops en route to **Terminal Suburbana** (Terminal Baltasar Brum; ☏1975; cnr Río Branco & Galicia), five blocks north of Plaza del

Entrevero. Faster and more comfortable is COT's direct bus service between the airport (UR$187, 30 minutes) and Tres Cruces bus terminal. Look for the stop to the right as you exit the arrivals hall.

Shared shuttle vans (five-person minimum) also travel from the airport to the center (UR$400 per person); buy tickets from the taxisaeropuerto. com taxi counter in the airport arrivals hall.

Fixed-rate **airport taxis** (☏2604-0323; www.taxisaeropuerto.com) charge between UR$1200 and UR$1800 (depending on neighborhood) for the 30- to 45-minute taxi ride from the airport into Montevideo. A less expensive and more comfortable way to get into the city is to pre-book a *remise* from a company like **B&B Remises** (☏096-603780; www.bybremises.com).

BUS

Montevideo's city buses, operated by **Cutcsa** (☏19333; www.cutcsa.com.uy), go almost everywhere for UR$36 per ride. For bus-connection info based on your point of origin and destination, see the Spanish-language website Como Ir (www.montevideo.gub.uy/aplicacion/como-ir).

A taxi from the bus terminal to downtown costs between UR$180 and UR$200. To save your pesos, take city bus CA1, which leaves from directly in front of the terminal (on the eastern side), traveling to Ciudad Vieja via Av 18 de Julio (UR$26, 15 minutes).

For the beach neighborhoods of Punta Carretas and Pocitos, take city buses 174 and 183, respectively, from in front of the terminal (UR$36). A taxi to either neighborhood costs between UR$180 and UR$200.

WESTERN URUGUAY

The land west of Montevideo is in many ways the 'real' Uruguay – little river towns separated by large expanses of pampas and

DOMESTIC BUSES FROM MONTEVIDEO

DESTINATION	COST (UR$)	DURATION (HR)
Carmelo	514	3¼
Colonia	375	2¾
La Paloma	514	3½
La Pedrera	535	4
Mercedes	599	4
Paysandú	814	4½
Piriápolis	216	1½
Punta del Diablo	642	5
Punta del Este	302	2¼
Salto	1071	6½
Tacuarembó	835	4½

WORTH A TRIP

ESTANCIA LIVING ON A BUDGET

What do you get when you cross a tourist *estancia* (ranch) and a hostel? Find out at the unique **El Galope Horse Farm & Hostel** (☎099-105985; www.elgalope.com.uy; Colonia Suiza; dm US$25, d with/without bathroom US$75/68; ☒), 115km west of Montevideo and 60km east of Colonia. Experienced world travelers Mónica and Miguel offer guests a chance to 'get away from it all' and settle into the relaxing rhythms of rural life for a few days.

Horseback jaunts for riders of all levels (US$50) are expertly led by Miguel himself, and there's a sauna (US$10) and small pool to soothe those aching muscles at the end of the day. Breakfast is included; other meals, from lunches (US$11) to full-fledged *asados* (barbecues) or fondue dinners (US$16) are available. Taxi pickup from the bus stop in nearby Colonia Valdense is available upon request (US$10).

wheat fields. It's far off the tourist trail, mostly, except for the region's superstar, Colonia del Sacramento, whose charms attract visitors from all over the world.

Colonia del Sacramento

POP 26,200

Take some cobbled streets and picturesque plazas, add an intriguing history and put them on a gorgeous point overlooking the Río de la Plata. What do you get? A major tourist attraction. Colonia's compact historic center, packed with atmospheric eateries and enshrined as a Unesco World Heritage Site, is a major draw every weekend, for Argentines, who visit in droves every weekend.

The Portuguese founded Colonia in 1680 to smuggle goods across the Río de la Plata into Buenos Aires. A century of sieges and battles ensued, as Colonia repeatedly changed hands between Portugal and Spain. In 1777 the Treaty of San Ildefonso gave more definitive control to the Spanish, and Colonia's commercial importance declined as foreign goods proceeded directly to Buenos Aires.

◎ Sights

Colonia's Barrio Histórico is filled with visual delights. Picturesque spots for wandering include the roughly cobbled 18th-century **Calle de los Suspiros** (Street of Sighs), lined with tile-and-stucco colonial houses, the **Paseo de San Gabriel**, on the western riverfront, the **Puerto Viejo** (Old Port) and the historic center's two main squares: sprawling **Plaza Mayor 25 de Mayo** and shady **Plaza de Armas** (the latter is also known as Plaza Manuel Lobo).

A single UR$50 ticket covers admission to Colonia's eight historical museums. All keep the same hours, but closing day varies by museum. Tickets are sold at Museo Municipal (p993).

Museo Portugués   MUSEUM

(☎4522-9240; www.museoscolonia.com.uy; Plaza Mayor 25 de Mayo 180; admission incl in historical museums ticket UR$50; ◎11:15am-4:30pm, closed Wed & Fri) In this old house on Colonia's main square you'll find Portuguese relics including porcelain, furniture, maps, Manuel Lobo's family tree and the old stone shield that once adorned the Portón de Campo.

Museo Municipal   MUSEUM

(☎4522-7031; www.museoscolonia.com.uy; Plaza Mayor 25 de Mayo 77; admission incl in historical museums ticket UR$50; ◎11:15am-4:30pm Wed-Mon) Houses an eclectic collection of treasures including a whale skeleton, a re-creation of a colonial drawing room, historical timelines and a scale model of Colonia (c 1762).

Faro   LIGHTHOUSE

(UR$25; ◎10:30am-1pm & 2pm-sunset) One of the town's most prominent landmarks, Colonia's 19th-century working lighthouse provides an excellent view of the old town and the Río de la Plata. It stands within the ruins of the 17th-century **Convento de San Francisco** (Plaza Mayor 25 de Mayo), just off the southwest corner of Plaza Mayor 25 de Mayo.

⌷ Sleeping

Colonia is short on budget hotels, but hostels offer some decent-value private rooms.

El Viajero Hostel   HOSTEL $

(☎4522-2683; www.elviajerohostels.com; Washington Barbot 164; dm US$15-19, s US$34-38, d US$45-70; ❄@☎) With bike rental, a bar for guests and air-con in all rooms, this hostel is brighter, fancier and somewhat cozier than the competition, and the location two blocks east of Plaza de Armas couldn't be better.

Colonia del Sacramento

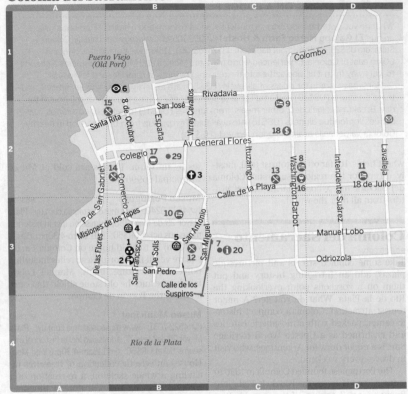

URUGUAY COLONIA DEL SACRAMENTO

Hostel del Río HOSTEL $
(☑4523-2870; www.hosteldelrio.com; Rivadavia 288; dm US$16-24, d US$70-125; ☎) Well-placed near the historic center, this hostel offers squeaky-clean four- to six-bed dorms and private rooms, along with a guest kitchen and back patio. While the overall atmosphere is rather sterile, the bright white dorms are excellent value, with thoughtful features including individual bedside reading lights on the bunk beds. Private rooms are less compelling, especially the musty back-facing units.

★**La Posadita de la Plaza** B&B $$
(☑4523-0502; www.posaditadelaplaza.com; Misiones de los Tapes 177; r US$113-180; ☎) At this whimsical guesthouse on Colonia's most historical square, Brazilian photographer Eduardo has poured his creative genius into building a magical space. Three guest rooms, an interior patio-deck with pretty old-town perspectives, and a cozy library-lounge are all decorated with objects from Eduardo's world travels. Ample breakfasts feature freshly squeezed orange juice.

Remus-Art Hostel B&B $$
(☑092-066985; www.facebook.com/remusart hostel; 18 de Julio 369; r without bathroom US$80-90) This B&B in the home of German visual artist Christiane Brockmeyer has three comfortable, colorful rooms with shared bathroom and a roof terrace where you can sunbathe, reach out and touch the overhanging sycamore leaves, or enjoy home-cooked candlelight dinners (per person US$25 including wine; specialties include raclette and fondue from Switzerland).

🍴 Eating & Drinking

★**Don Joaquín** PIZZA $
(☑4522-4388; www.facebook.com/donjoaquinpizza napoletana; 18 de Julio 267; pizzas UR$165-250; ◷8pm-midnight Tue-Sun) After 13 years in Europe, Colonia natives Yancí and Pierina returned home with a genuine Neapolitan pizza

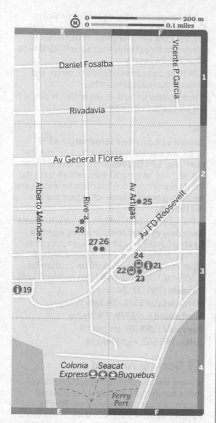

Colonia del Sacramento

oven in tow. The result is this cheerful eatery where diners can watch the pizza chef creating thin-crusted beauties with superb homemade sauce. Don't miss the carbonara with cheese, egg and delicately crunchy bacon, or the *pescatore* with mussels and shrimp.

La Bodeguita INTERNATIONAL $$
(☑ 4522-5329; www.labodeguita.net; Del Comercio 167; mini pizzas UR$180, mains UR$340-550; ⊙ 8pm-midnight Tue-Fri, 12:30-3:30pm & 8pm-midnight Sat & Sun) Nab a table out back on the sunny two-level deck and soak up the sweeping river views while drinking sangria or munching on La Bodeguita's trademark mini pizzas, served on a cutting board. The wide-ranging menu also includes pasta, salads, steaks and *chivitos* (steak sandwiches piled high with toppings).

Buen Suspiro URUGUAYAN $$
(☑ 4522-6160; www.facebook.com/bardevinosy picadas; Calle de los Suspiros 92; picadas for 2

UR$360-670; ⊙ 11am-midnight Wed-Mon) This cozy spot specializes in *picadas* (sharing boards of cheese and cold cuts). Sample local wines by the bottle or glass, accompanied by tarts, ricotta-and-walnut 'truffles', local cheese, sausage, soups and salads. Reserve ahead for a fireside table in winter, or while away a summer afternoon on the intimate back patio.

Lentas Maravillas INTERNATIONAL $$
(☑ 4522-0636; lentasmaravillas@gmail.com; Santa Rita 61; mains UR$300-395; ⊙ 12:30-7:30pm Wed-Mon) Cozy as a friend's home, this is an agreeable spot to kick back with tea and cookies, or savor a homemade lemonade accompanied by soup, sandwiches or goulash. Flip through an

art book from owner Maggie Molnar's personal library and enjoy the river views.

Barbot
MICROBREWERY

(📞 4522-7268; www.facebook.com/barbotcerveceria; Washington Barbot 160; ⊙ 6pm-2am Mon-Thu, from noon Fri-Sun; 🐱) This sleek brewpub is well worth a visit for its ever-evolving collection of 15 home brews. If you can't chose between them, go for the four-beer tasting selection.

Ganache
CAFE

(📞 4523-5895; www.facebook.com/cafeganacheuy; Real 178; ⊙ 10am-8pm, closed Thu Apr-Oct) An inviting spot for a coffee break any time of year, Ganache lays tables out on the cobblestones in warm weather. Come winter or a rainy day, you'll be tempted by its sweet interior space with flowers on every table, cushiony chairs, parquet floors and a fireplace to ward off the Río de la Plata's chill breezes.

ℹ️ Information

BBVA (Av General Flores 299; ⊙ 1-5pm Mon-Fri) One of several ATMs along Av General Flores.

BIT Welcome Center (📞 4523-7707; info@coloniaturismo.com; Odriozola 434; ⊙ 9am-6pm; 🐱) In a sparkling glass-walled building opposite the port, this modern welcome center, operated by Uruguay's national tourism ministry, has tourist information, touch-screen displays and an overpriced (UR$50) 'Welcome to Uruguay' video presentation. It also has a travel agency and left-luggage lockers.

Tourist office (📞 4522-8506; Manuel Lobo 224; ⊙ 9am-6pm Apr-Oct, to 7pm Nov-Mar) On the edge of the Barrio Histórico is Colonia's municipal tourist office, which also organizes good **walking tours** (📞 099-379167; asociacionguiascolonia@gmail.com; tour per person in Spanish/other languages UR$150/200) led by local guides.

Tourist office (cnr Manuel Lobo & Av FD Roosevelt; ⊙ 9am-6pm Apr-Oct, to 7pm Nov-Mar) There's another branch

ℹ️ Getting There & Away

BOAT

From the ferry terminal at the foot of Rivera, **Buquebus** (📞 130; www.buquebus.com.uy; ferry terminal; ⊙ 9am-10pm) runs three or more fast boats (UR$1310 to UR$2228, 1¼ hours) daily to Buenos Aires. The same company owns **Seacat** (📞 4522-2919; www.seacatcolonia.com.uy; ferry terminal; ⊙ 8am-9pm), which runs slightly faster, and often cheaper, ferry services along the same route (UR$1220 to UR$1780, one hour).

A third operator offering similar service is **Colonia Express** (📞 4522-9676; www.coloniaexpress.com; ferry terminal; ⊙ 9am-10pm), which runs three fast ferries a day (UR$1049 to UR$1349, 1¼ hours).

All three companies offer child, senior and advance-purchase discounts.

Immigration for both countries is handled at the port before boarding.

BUS

Colonia's modern **bus terminal** (📞 4523-0288; www.terminalcolonia.com.uy; cnr Manuel Lobo & Av Buenos Aires) is located near the port and an easy 10-minute walk from the Barrio Histórico. It has tourist information and luggage-storage, money-changing and internet facilities.

The following destinations are served at least twice daily by companies including **Agencia Central** (📞 4522-4734; www.agenciacentral.com.uy; bus terminal; ⊙ 5:30am-8:30pm & 11pm-midnight Mon-Fri, 5:30am-2:30pm Sat, 5:30-6am, 1:30-2:30pm & 11pm-midnight Sun):

Carmelo (UR$171, 1¼ hours)

Mercedes (UR$385, 3¼ hours)

Montevideo (UR$375, 2¾ hours)

Paysandú (UR$707, six hours)

Salto (UR$963, eight hours)

ℹ️ Getting Around

Walking is enjoyable in compact Colonia, but motor scooters, bicycles and gas-powered buggies are popular alternatives. **Thrifty** (📞 1848-8200, 4522-2939; www.thrifty.com.uy; Av General Flores 172; bicycle/scooter/golf cart per hour US$6/12/18, per 24hr US$24/40/66; ⊙ 9am-7pm) rents everything from high-quality bikes to scooters to golf carts. Several other agencies rent cars and motorbikes near the bus and ferry terminals, including the following:

Multicar (📞 4522-4893; www.multicar.com.uy; Manuel Lobo 505; ⊙ 9am-7pm)

Motorent (📞 4522-9665; www.motorent.com.uy; Manuel Lobo 505; ⊙ 9am-7pm)

Punta Car (📞 4522-2353; www.puntacar.com.uy; 18 de Julio 496; ⊙ 9am-7pm)

Avis (📞 4522-9842; www.avis.com.uy; bus terminal, cnr Manuel Lobo & Av Buenos Aires; ⊙ 24hr)

Europcar (📞 4522-8454; www.europcar.com.uy; Av Artigas 152; ⊙ 9am-7pm Tue-Sat, to 1pm Sun)

The last two offer one-way car rentals between Colonia and Montevideo.

Local COTUC buses go to the beaches and bullring at Real de San Carlos (UR$25) from along Av General Flores.

Carmelo

POP 18,000

Carmelo, dating from 1816, is a laid-back town of cobblestone streets and low old houses, a center for yachting, fishing and exploring the Paraná Delta. Surrounded by vineyards, it has also increasingly become a destination for wine tourism. The town straddles the Arroyo de las Vacas, a stream that widens into a sheltered harbor just below the Río Uruguay's confluence with the Río de la Plata. The town center, seven blocks north of the arroyo, is Plaza Independencia. South of the arroyo across the bridge lies the pleasant beach of Playa Seré, backed by a large park with open space, camping, swimming and a huge casino. Daily launches connect Carmelo to the Buenos Aires suburb of Tigre.

🛌 Sleeping & Eating

Camping Náutico Carmelo   CAMPGROUND $
(📞4542-2058; dnhcarmelo@adinet.com.uy; Arroyo de las Vacas s/n; tent sites US$12) South of the arroyo, this pleasant tree-shaded campground, with hot showers, caters to yachties but accepts walk-ins too. Sites accommodate up to four people.

Ah'Lo Hostel Boutique   HOSTEL $$
(📞4542-0757; www.ahlo.com.uy; Treinta y Tres 270; dm US$30-35, d US$90-135, d without bathroom US$75-84, q US$130-150; ❀🐾) Carmelo's best downtown option, this hostel-*posada* delivers on its 'boutique' moniker, offering a comfortable seven-bed dorm with plush duvets and immaculate shared bathroom, plus nine private rooms, a well-equipped guest kitchen and a spacious common area, all in an attractively restored colonial building seven blocks from the ferry terminal and two blocks from the main square.

Piccolino   URUGUAYAN $
(📞4542-4850; cnr Calle 19 de Abril & Roosevelt; dishes UR$150-320; ⊘10:30am-midnight Wed-Mon) This corner place has decent *chivitos* (steak sandwiches piled high with toppings) and views of Carmelo's central square.

ℹ Information

Casa de la Cultura (📞4542-2001; Calle 19 de Abril 246; ⊘9am-6pm Apr-Oct, to 7pm Nov-Mar) Tourist information on offer three blocks south of the main square and eight blocks northeast of the launch docks.

Scotiabank (Uruguay 401; ⊘1-5pm Mon-Fri) One of several ATMs opposite the main square.

ℹ Getting There & Away

BOAT

Cacciola (📞4542-4282; www.cacciolaviajes.com; Wilson Ferreyra 263; ferry Carmelo-Tigre 1-way adult/child UR$800/700, shuttle bus Tigre-Buenos Aires UR$30; ⊘ticket office 3:30-4:30am & 8:30am-8pm) Runs launches once or twice daily to the Buenos Aires suburb of Tigre. Service is sometimes expanded to thrice-daily in summer. The 2½-hour trip through the Paraná Delta is the most scenic crossing between Uruguay and Argentina.

BUS

Both main bus companies are on or near Plaza Independencia. **Berrutti** (📞4542-2504; www.berruttiturismo.com/horarios.htm; Uruguay 337) has the most frequent service to Colonia; **Chadre** (📞4542-2987; www.agenciacentral.com.uy; Calle 18 de Julio 411; ⊘3-4am & 6am-11:30pm) is the best bet for all other destinations.

Buses from Carmelo

DESTINATION	COST (UR$)	DURATION (HR)
Colonia	171	1½
Mercedes	214	2
Montevideo	514	3½
Paysandú	514	5
Salto	771	7

Mercedes

POP 42,000

Capital of the department of Soriano, Mercedes is a livestock center with cobblestone streets and a small pedestrian zone around an 18th-century cathedral on central Plaza Independencia. The town's most appealing feature is its leafy waterfront along the south bank of the Río Negro.

🛌 Sleeping & Eating

Camping del Hum   CAMPGROUND $
(📞4532-2201, ext 2501; Isla del Puerto; sites per person/tent US$1/3) Mercedes' spacious campground, one of the region's best, occupies half the Isla del Puerto in the Río Negro. Connected to the mainland by a bridge, it has swimming, fishing and sanitary facilities.

Martiniano Parrilla Gourmet   PARRILLA $$
(📞4532-2649; Rambla Costanera s/n; dishes UR$225-400; ⊘11am-3pm & 7:30pm-midnight Tue-Sun) The prime riverfront setting at the foot of 18 de Julio is complemented by a varied menu featuring homemade pasta, grilled meat, fish, gourmet burgers and *chivitos*.

WORTH A TRIP

THE LITTLE BEEF CUBE THAT CIRCLED THE GLOBE

In 1865 the Liebig Extract of Meat Company established its pioneer South American plant near the river town of Fray Bentos, 35km west of Mercedes. It soon became Uruguay's most important industrial complex. British-run El Anglo took over operations in the 1920s and by WWII the factory employed 4000 people, slaughtering 2000 cattle a day.

Looking at the abandoned factory today, you'd never guess that its signature product, the Oxo beef cube, once touched millions of lives on every continent. Oxo cubes sustained WWI soldiers in the trenches, Jules Verne sang their praises in his book *Around the Moon*, Stanley brought them on his search for Livingstone, and Scott and Hillary took them to Antarctica and Everest. More than 25,000 people from more than 60 countries worked here, and at its peak the factory was exporting nearly 150 different products.

Enshrined as Uruguay's newest Unesco World Heritage Site in July 2015, the former factory is now a museum – the **Museo de la Revolución Industrial** (www.paisajefraybentos. com/pc/museo-de-la-revolucion-industrial; Barrio Anglo; UR$50, guided tour UR$120; ⊙ 9:30am-5pm Tue-Sun). Dozens of colorful displays, ranging from the humorous to the poignant, bring the factory's history vividly to life. Note that most signs are in Spanish only.

One- to two-hour guided tours (schedule varies) grant access to the intricate maze of passageways, corrals and abandoned slaughterhouses behind the museum. At 11am on Thursdays, Saturdays and Sundays visitors can also tour the Casa Grande, a mansion that once housed the factory's manager.

The adjacent town of Fray Bentos, with its pretty riverfront promenade, is the southernmost overland crossing over the Río Uruguay into Argentina. Fray Bentos is 40 minutes by bus from Mercedes (UR$64), two hours from Paysandú ($214), four hours from Colonia (UR$471) or Buenos Aires (UR$1450), and 4½ to 6½ hours from Montevideo (UR$664).

❶ Information

Municipal Tourist Office (☑ 4532-2201, ext 2501; www.sorianoturismo.com; Plaza El Rosedal, Av Asencio, btwn Colón & Artigas; ⊙ 8am-6pm Mon-Fri, to 2pm Sat & Sun) In El Rosedal park, four blocks east of the bridge to Mercedes' campground.

Scotiabank (Giménez 719; ⊙ 1-5pm Mon-Fri) ATM on Plaza Independencia.

❶ Getting There & Around

Mercedes' modern, air-conditioned **bus terminal** (☑ 4533-0510; www.mercedesshopping.com. uy/terminal.php; Don Bosco 734) has departures to Colonia (UR$385, 3¼ hours), Montevideo (UR$599, 3½ to 4½ hours), Salto (UR$578, five hours) and Buenos Aires (UR$1450, five hours). Plaza Independencia is 10 blocks north of the bus terminal; walk straight up Colón with Plaza Artigas on your right or catch any local bus.

Paysandú

POP 76,400

On the east bank of the Río Uruguay, connected to Colón, Argentina, by the Puente Internacional General Artigas, Uruguay's third-largest city is mainly of interest as a stepping stone for travelers en route to or from Argentina. To see the city's wilder side,

visit during Easter Week for the annual **beer festival**, when there's plenty of live music, open-air cinema and a ready supply of a certain carbonated alcoholic beverage.

◉ Sights

Museo Histórico   MUSEUM
(☑ 4722-6220, ext 247; Av Zorrilla de San Martín 874; ⊙ 9am-5pm Tue-Fri, to 2pm Sat & Sun) FREE This historical museum displays evocative images from the multiple 19th-century sieges of Paysandú, including of the bullet-riddled shell of the cathedral, and women in exile watching the city's bombardment from an island offshore.

🛏 Sleeping & Eating

Hotel Rafaela   HOTEL $
(☑ 4722-4216; hrafaela@hotmail.com; 18 de Julio 1181; s/d with air-con US$39/53, with fan & without bathroom US$32/38; ❊ 🐭) A decent budget option just west of the main square. Rafaela's rooms are dark but large, and some have small patios.

Los Tres Pinos   PARRILLA $
(☑ 4724-1211; www.facebook.com/losnuevostres pinos; Av España 1474; mains UR$220-330; ⊙ 11am-3pm & 7:30pm-midnight Mon-Fri, to 1am Sat, 11am-3pm Sun) The *parrilla* here is excellent;

carnivores will be in heaven, with everything from *milanesas* (breaded cutlets) to *chivitos* to pork chops, steaks and whole roast chickens – though if you've already maxed out on meat, you can always go rogue and order up a *morrón relleno* (stuffed grilled red pepper) or veggie lasagna.

El Bar
URUGUAYAN $$

(📞 4723-7809; www.facebook.com/elbarpaysandu; cnr 18 de Julio & Herrera; mains UR$175-450; ⏱ 8am-1am) Smack in the heart of town (one block west of Plaza Constitución), this corner resto-bar is open all day long for pizza, burgers and standard Uruguayan fare. After dark it shifts smoothly into bar mode, getting especially packed on Fridays when there's live music.

ℹ️ Information

Banco Santander (18 de Julio 1139; ⏱ 1-5pm Mon-Fri) Has ATM.

Scotiabank (18 de Julio 1026; ⏱ 1-5pm Mon-Fri) Has ATM.

Tourist Office – Bus Terminal (Bl Artigas 770; ⏱ 10am-10pm Mon-Fri, to 3pm & 4-9pm Sat & Sun)

Tourist Office – Centro (📞 4724-1636; www.facebook.com/descubripaysandu; 18 de Julio 1226; ⏱ 8am-7pm Mon-Fri, 9am-7pm Sat & Sun) The main tourist office is centrally located on Plaza Constitución.

Tourist Office – Riverfront (Av de Los Iracundos; ⏱ 9am-5pm) Next to Museo de la Tradición.

ℹ️ Getting There & Away

Paysandú's **bus terminal** (📞 4724-4100; www.paysandushopping.com.uy/terminal.php; Bl Artigas 770) has buses to Colón, Argentina (UR$145, 45 minutes), Buenos Aires (UR$920, 5½ hours) and several other international destinations. Domestic departures include Montevideo (UR$814, 4½ to six hours) and Salto (UR$259, 1½ to two hours). To reach the center from the bus terminal, walk nine blocks west on Ituzaingó, then three blocks north on Zorilla de San Martín, or take any local Copay bus (UR$22).

Salto

POP 104,000

Built near the falls where the Río Uruguay makes its 'big jump' (*'salto grande'* in Spanish), Salto is Uruguay's second-largest city and the most northerly crossing point to Argentina. It's a relaxed place with some 19th-century architecture and a pretty riverfront. People come here for the nearby hot springs and

the recreation area above the enormous Salto Grande hydroelectric dam.

⊙ Sights & Activities

Museo del Hombre y la Tecnología
MUSEUM

(cnr Av Brasil & Zorrilla; ⏱ 2-7pm Mon-Fri) FREE Housed in a historic market building, this museum features excellent displays on local cultural development and history upstairs, and a small archaeological section downstairs.

🛏️ Sleeping & Eating

Accommodations at nearby hot springs offer an alternative to sleeping in town.

Gran Hotel Concordia
HOTEL $

(📞 4733-2735; www.facebook.com/granhotelconcordia; Uruguay 749; s/d US$25/49; ❄️🅿️) This faded 1860s relic, a national historical monument, remains Salto's most atmospheric downtown budget option. A life-size cutout of tango legend Carlos Gardel, who once stayed in room 32, beckons you down a marble corridor into a leafy courtyard filled with murals and sculptures, surrounded by tired and musty rooms with tall French-shuttered windows.

★ Art Hotel Deco
BOUTIQUE HOTEL $$

(📞 4732-8585; www.arthoteldeco.com; Sarandí 145; s/d/ste US$90/120/150; ❄️🅿️) Just paces from the city center, this classy boutique hotel easily outshines Salto's other downtown sleeping options. The lovingly renovated historic building abounds in period details, including high ceilings, polished wood floors, art deco door and window frames, an elegant sitting room and a lush back garden. Amenities include Egyptian-cotton sheets, cable TV, sauna and gym.

La Caldera
PARRILLA $

(📞 4732-4648; Uruguay 221; dishes UR$195-395; ⏱ noon-3pm & 8pm-1am Tue-Sun) With fresh breezes blowing in off the river and sunny outdoor seating, this *parrilla* makes a good lunch stop; at dinnertime, the cozy interior dining room, with its view of the blazing fire, is equally atmospheric.

La Trattoria
URUGUAYAN $$

(📞 4733-6660; www.facebook.com/latrattoriasalto; Uruguay 754; dishes UR$225-495; ⏱ noon-1am) Locals flock to this downtown eatery for fish, meat and pasta. Sit in the wood-paneled dining room or people-watch from a sidewalk table on busy Calle Uruguay.

ℹ Information

BBVA (Av Uruguay 602; ⊙1-5pm Mon-Fri) One of several banks at this intersection.

Tourist Office – Bus Terminal (☐4732-5194; www.turismo.salto.gub.uy; Salto Shopping Center, cnr Avs Blandengues & Batlle; ⊙8am-10pm)

Tourist Office – Centro (☐4733-4096; www. turismo.salto.gub.uy; Uruguay 1052; ⊙8am-7pm Mon-Sat)

ℹ Getting There & Around

Salto's **bus terminal** (☐4733-6200; www. saltoshopping.com.uy/terminal.php; Salto Shopping Center, Av Batlle 2265), in a spiffy modern shopping center 2km east of downtown, has a tourist-info kiosk, ATMs, internet facilities, free public restrooms and a supermarket.

From the port at the foot of Av Brasil, **Transporte Fluvial San Cristobal** (☐4733-2461; cnr Av Brasil & Rambla Costanera Norte) runs launches across the river to Concordia (UR$160, 15 minutes) Monday to Saturday.

Departures include Buenos Aires (UR$1225, seven hours) and Concordia, Argentina (UR$146, one hour) Monday to Saturday. Domestic buses go to Montevideo (UR$1071, 6½

hours) and Paysandú (UR$259, 1½ to two hours). Local bus 1 connects the bus terminal with the center of town.

Tacuarembó & Around

POP 54,800

In the rolling hills along the Cuchilla de Haedo, Tacuarembó is *gaucho* country. It's also the alleged birthplace of tango legend Carlos Gardel.

Valle Edén, a lush valley 24km southwest of Tacuarembó, is home to the **Museo Carlos Gardel** (☐099-107303; UR$25; ⊙9:30am-5:30pm Thu-Sun), which documents various facets of the singer's life, including the birth certificate which Uruguayans hold as proof of his local provenance – a claim vigorously contested by Argentina and France!

◉ Sights

Museo del Indio y del Gaucho   MUSEUM

(☐4633-1545; cnr Flores & Artigas; ⊙10am-5pm Tue-Sat) **FREE** Paying romantic tribute to Uruguay's *gauchos* and indigenous peoples, this museum's collection includes stools made

SALTO'S HOT SPRINGS

A whole slew of hot springs bubble up around Salto.

Termas San Nicanor (☐4730-2209; www.sannicanor.com.uy; Ruta 3, Km 475; campsites per person US$9, dm US$20-30, d US$110-150, 4-person cabins US$230; 🛜🏊) Surrounded by a pastoral landscape of cows, fields and water, this is the most tranquil of Salto's hot-springs resorts. It has two gigantic outdoor thermal pools, a restaurant, and accommodations for every budget, including campsites, no-frills dorms, four-person cabins and private rooms in a high-ceilinged *estancia* (ranch) house. Day use of the springs (8am to 10pm, available Friday to Sunday only) costs UR$250. The 12km unpaved access road leaves Ruta 3 10km south of Salto. With advance notice, you can arrange shuttle transport to the springs from Salto or Termas del Daymán (staff at Termas San Nicanor keep a list of drivers offering this service), but it's far more convenient to get here with your own wheels.

Termas de Daymán (☐4736-9711; www.termasdayman.com; UR$150; ⊙7am-11pm) About 8km south of Salto, Daymán is a heavily developed Disneyland of thermal baths complete with kids' water park. It's popular with Uruguayan and Argentine tourists. For comfortable accommodations adjacent to the springs, try **La Posta del Daymán** (☐camping 4736-9094, hotel 4736-9801; www.lapostadeldayman.com; Ruta 3, Termas del Daymán; campsites per person US$7-13, r per person incl breakfast US$45; 🛜🏊). Empresa Cossa runs hourly buses between Salto and the baths (UR$32), leaving Salto's port via Avenida Brasil at 30 minutes past every hour (6:30am to 10:30pm), returning hourly from 7am to 11pm.

Termas de Arapey (☐4770-5085; www.termasarapey.com; UR$150; ⊙7am-10:30pm) About 90km northeast of Salto, Uruguay's oldest hot-springs resort offers multiple pools surrounded by gardens, fountains, and paths to the Río Arapey Grande. **Hotel Municipal** (☐4768-2441; s/d/tr US$55/74/89; 🅿🛜🏊), down near the river, offers the area's best-value accommodations. **Argentur** (☐099-734003, 4732-9931; https://minibusesargentur.blogspot. com) runs one or two buses daily from Salto (UR$220, 1½ hours).

VALLE DE LUNAREJO

This gorgeous valley, 95km north of Tacuarembó, is a place of marvelous peace and isolation, with birds and rushing water providing the only soundtrack.

Visitors can spend the night at enchanting **Posada Lunarejo** (☑ 4650-6400; www. facebook.com/posada.lunarejo.7; Ruta 30, Km 238; r per person incl full board US$75), a restored 1880 building 2km off the main road, 3km from the river and a few steps from a bird colony teeming with *garzas* (cranes) and *espátulas rosadas* (roseate spoonbills). The posada organizes nearby hikes and horseback rides.

CUT (www.cutcorporacion.com.uy) offers the most convenient bus schedule to Valle del Lunarejo on its daily Montevideo–Tacuarembó–Artigas bus, leaving Montevideo at noon (UR$1006, 6½ hours) and leaving Tacuarembó at 5:10pm (UR$171, 1¼ hours). Posada Lunarejo can meet your bus if you call ahead.

from horse and cow bones, elegantly worked silver spurs and other accessories of rural life.

✦✦ Festivals & Events

Fiesta de la Patria Gaucha CULTURAL
(www.patriagaucha.com.uy; ☺ Mar) This colorful, homegrown five-day event is the planet's largest *gaucho* festival, attracting participants from Argentina, southern Brazil and all over Uruguay for exhibitions of traditional *gaucho* skills, music and other activities. It takes place in Parque 25 de Agosto, north of town.

🛏 Sleeping & Eating

Inexpensive but bland accommodation is available downtown at places such as **Hotel Internacional** (☑ 4632-3324; Ituzaingó 211; s/d US$42/59). Nearby *estancias* offer a more meaningful and memorable taste of Tacuarembó's traditional culture.

★ Estancia Panagea ESTANCIA $
(☑ 099-836149, 4630-2670; www.panagea-uruguay.blogspot.com.uy; Ruta 31, Km 189; dm per person incl full board, farm activities, horseback riding & transport US$65) For a spectacular introduction to life on the Uruguayan land, head to this 970-hectare working *estancia* 40km northwest of Tacuarembó. Juan Manuel, who was born and raised here, his Swiss wife Susanne and *gaucho* Bilinga invite guests to get fully immersed in farm activities from the mundane to the classic (herding cattle on horseback).

Guests sleep dorm-style in simple rooms, eat three home-cooked meals a day (including self-serve bacon and eggs cooked on the woodstove), hit the basketball and volleyball courts at sunset and congregate around the fireplace at night. Call ahead to coordinate dates and arrange transportation from Tacuarembó's bus station.

★ Yvytu Itaty ESTANCIA $$
(☑ 4630-8421, 099-837555; www.viviturismorural.com.uy; s/d/tr/q incl full board, farm activities & horseback riding US$85/150/225/300) 🍴 Pedro and Nahir Clariget's unpretentious ranch-style home, 50km southwest of Tacuarembó, offers a first hand look at real *gaucho* life. Guests are invited to accompany Pedro and his friendly cattle dogs around the 636-hectare working *estancia* on horseback, participate in daily *estancia* routines and sip maté on the patio at sunset in anticipation of Nahir's tasty home cooking.

Call in advance for driving directions or to arrange pickup at Tacuarembó's bus station (UR$1900 round trip for a group of up to four people).

El Mirador Resto-Pub PUB FOOD $
(☑ 4634-2491; www.facebook.com/elmiradorrestopubtacuarembo; Sarandí 349; pub food from UR$250; ☺ 7pm-3am Wed-Sun) This spiffy resto-pub pours eight varieties of Tacuarembó's homegrown Cabesas beer on tap, accompanied by *chivitos* (steak sandwiches piled high with toppings), pizza, *picadas* (shared appetizer plates) and other pub food.

La Rueda PARRILLA $
(☑ 4632-2453; W Beltrán 251; dishes UR$170-450; ☺ noon-2:30pm & 8pm-midnight Mon-Sat, noon-3pm Sun) With its thatched roof and walls covered with *gaucho* paraphernalia, this neighborhood *parrilla* is a perennial local favorite.

ℹ Information

Banco Santander (18 de Julio 258; ☺ 1-5pm Mon-Fri) One of several ATMs near Plaza Colón.
Tourist office (☑ 4632-7144; www.tacuarembo.gub.uy; cnr Ruta 5 & Av Victorino Pereira; ☺ 7am-8pm Mon-Fri, 8am-noon Sat) Inside the bus terminal.

ⓘ Getting There & Around

The **bus terminal** (☎4632-4441; Av Victorino Pereira) is 1km northeast of town. Fares include Montevideo (UR$835, 4½ hours), and Salto (UR$470 to UR$604, four to 4½ hours). A taxi to the center costs about UR$80.

EASTERN URUGUAY

This is Uruguay's playground (and, to an extent, Argentina's, Brazil's, Chile's and Spain's) – a long stretch of beaches all the way from Montevideo to the Brazilian border offering something for everyone: surfers, party animals, nature lovers and family groups.

Conflicts between Spain and Portugal, and then between Argentina and Brazil, left eastern Uruguay with historical monuments such as the imposing fortress of Santa Teresa. Just inland lies a varied landscape of palm savannas, lagoons and marshes rich in birdlife.

In midsummer prices skyrocket and these beach towns seriously pack out. During the rest of the year you might have them to yourself.

Piriápolis

POP 8800

With its grand old hotel and beachfront promenade backed by small mountains, Piriápolis is vaguely reminiscent of a Mediterranean beach town and exudes a certain old-school coastal-resort charm. It was developed for tourism in the early 20th century by Uruguayan entrepreneur Francisco Piria, who built the imposing landmark Argentino Hotel and an eccentric hillside residence known as Castillo de Piria.

Almost all the action happens in the 10-block stretch of beachfront between Av Artigas (the access road from Ruta 9) and Av Piria (where the coastline makes a broad curve southwards). Streets back from the beach quickly become residential.

The surrounding countryside holds many interesting features, including two of Uruguay's highest summits.

🛏 Sleeping & Eating

Hostel de los Colores   HOSTEL **$**
(☎4432-6188; www.hosteldeloscolores.com.uy; Simón del Pino 1137; dm/d from US$20/50; @🛜) Directly opposite Piriápolis' institutional 240-bed HI facility, this much smaller year-round hostel two blocks from the beach offers clean,

colorful four- and six-bed dorms, plus three doubles. Bikes (UR$400 per day) and a kayak (UR$500 per day) are available for rent.

★ Café Picasso   SEAFOOD **$$**
(☎4432-2597; cnr Rojas & Caseros; mains UR$290-490; ⊗noon-3:30pm Sun-Thu, noon-3:30pm & 8-11:30pm Fri & Sat May-Nov) Down a residential backstreet several blocks from the beach, septuagenarian chef-owner Carlos has converted his carport and front room into an informal, colorfully decorated restaurant with an open-air grill. Locals chat astride plastic chairs and listen to tango recordings while Carlos cooks up fresh fish and homemade pasta, along with paella (UR$930 for two) on Sundays.

ⓘ Information

Banco de la República (Rambla de los Argentinos 1405; ⊗1-6pm Mon-Fri) Convenient ATM.

Tourist office (☎4432-5055; www.costaserrana .uy; Rambla de los Argentinos, Paseo La Pasiva; ⊗10am-6pm Wed-Mon Apr-Nov, 9am-8pm daily Dec & Mar, to midnight Jan & Feb) Helpful staff and public toilets, on the waterfront near Argentino Hotel.

ⓘ Getting There & Away

The **bus terminal** (Misiones s/n) is a few blocks back from the beach. COT and Copsa run frequent buses to Montevideo (UR$216, 1½ hours) and Punta del Este (UR$125, 50 minutes).

Around Piriápolis

About 5km north of Piriápolis, hikers can climb Uruguay's fourth-highest 'peak,' **Cerro Pan de Azúcar** (389m). The trail (2½ hours round trip) starts from the parking lot of the Reserva de Fauna Autóctona, narrowing from a gradual dirt road into a steep path marked with red arrows. Across the highway you can tour **Castillo de Piria** (Piria's Castle; ☎4432-3268; Ruta 37, Km 7; ⊗9am-6pm) FREE, Francisco Piria's outlandishly opulent former residence.

Back on the Interbalnearia (coastal highway), 25km toward Montevideo from Piriápolis, the private nature reserve **Sierra de las Ánimas** (☑text only 094-419891; www.sierradelasanimas.com; Ruta 9, Km 86; UR$150; ⊗9am-sunset Sat & Sun, plus Carnaval & Easter weeks, from 10am May-Oct) ✎ has two good hiking trails, one leading to the 501m summit, the other to the **Cañadón de los Espejos**, a series of waterfalls and natural swimming holes. Coming from Montevideo by bus, ask the driver to be let off at Km 86 and cross the highway. Send an SMS in advance to verify it's open on the day you plan to visit; the site is off-limits in cold or rainy weather.

Punta del Este

POP 9300

OK, here's the plan: tan it, wax it, buff it at the gym, then plonk it on the beach at 'Punta.' Once you're done there, go out and shake it at one of the town's famous clubs.

Punta's an international beach resort, packed with celebrities and swarming with Brazilian and Argentine tourists from Christmas through Carnaval. Out of season it's a bit of a ghost town, although the surrounding beaches are still nice.

◉ Sights

★**Casapueblo** GALLERY

(☑ 4257-8041; www.casapueblo.com.uy; Punta Ballena; US$10; ☉ 10am-sunset) Cascading nine stories down a cliffside, Uruguayan artist Carlos Páez Vilaró's exuberantly whimsical villa and art gallery sits atop Punta Ballena, a jutting headland 15km west of Punta del Este. Visitors can tour five rooms, view a film on the artist's life and travels, and eat up spectacular sunset views at the upstairs cafeteria-bar. There's a hotel and restaurant adjacent. It's a 2km walk from the junction where Codesa's Línea 8 bus drops you.

Isla de Lobos ISLAND

About 10km offshore, this small island is home to the world's second-largest southern sea-lion colony (200,000 at last count), along with colonies of southern fur seals and South America's tallest lighthouse. The island is protected and can only be visited on an organized tour, which can be arranged through operators such as Dimar Tours.

Isla Gorriti ISLAND

Boats leave every half hour or so (daily from December through Carnaval, weekends rest of year) from Punta del Este's yacht harbor for the 15-minute trip to this nearby island, which has excellent sandy beaches, a couple of restaurants and the ruins of Baterías de Santa Ana, an 18th-century fortification.

🏃 Activities

Surf shops such as **Sunvalleysurf** (☑ 4248-1388; www.sunvalleysurf.com; Parada 3½, Playa Brava; ☉ 11am-7pm) rent boards and wetsuits. During summer, parasailing, waterskiing and jet skiing are possible on Playa Mansa.

LA MANO EN LA ARENA

Punta's most famous landmark is this monster-sized **sculpted hand** (The Hand in the Sand; Playa Brava) protruding from the sands of Playa Brava. Constructed in iron and cement by Chilean artist Mario Irarrázabal, it won first prize in a monumental art contest in 1982 and has been a Punta fixture ever since. The hand exerts a magnetic attraction over thousands of visitors every year, who climb and jump off its digits and pose for photos with it. Look for it just southeast of the bus station.

From Punta's port, **Dimar Tours** (☑ 094-410899; www.isladelobos.com.uy; Puerto; adult/child to Isla Gorriti UR$350/250, to Isla de Lobos US$50/30) offers excursions to Isla Gorriti (15 minutes) and Isla de Lobos (two to 2½ hours). Boats depart daily December through Carnaval (peak season), weekends rest of year. A highlight of Isla de Lobos is the chance to swim with sea lions. Other operators, including **Crucero Samoa** (☑ 099-545847; www.crucerosamoa.com; Puerto), have offices along the same boardwalk. Reserve ahead during peak season.

🛏 Sleeping

Between Christmas and Carnaval Punta is jammed with people, and prices are astronomical. Off-season visitors will find prices more in keeping with standard ranges.

★**Tas D'Viaje Hostel** HOSTEL $

(☑ 4244-8789; www.tasdviaje.com; Calle 24, btwn Calles 28 & 29; dm US$16-32, d US$52-110; ❉ @ 🛜) Just one block from Playa El Emir, Punta's best – and best-located – hostel keeps improving, thanks to thoughtful owners and regular reinvestments in infrastructure. New in 2017, all dorms are now air-conditioned, and there's a spacious new deck, thatched-roof bar area out back and pizzeria up front to go with the pre-existing guest barbecue.

Hostel Punta Ballena HOSTEL $

(☑ 4257-7665; www.hostelpuntaballena.uy; cnr San Francisco & Sierra de la Ballena, Punta Ballena; dm US$15-30; 🛜) In the hills above Punta Ballena, this secluded retreat is ideal for budget-minded travelers who prefer low-key fireside camaraderie to Punta-style partying. The dorms are pretty standard issue (and

Punta del Este

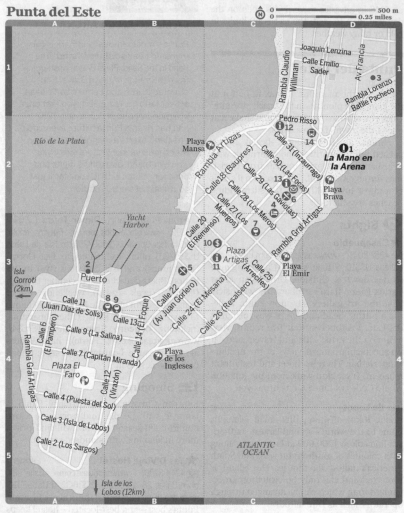

URUGUAY PUNTA DEL ESTE

the triple-decker bunks may give pause to acrophobes), but the on-site bar-restaurant invites cozy conversation by the *parrilla*, and the beach (Playa Portezuelo) is a short walk downhill.

Camping San Rafael CAMPGROUND $
(☑4248-6715; www.campingsanrafael.com.uy; Saravia s/n; campsites per person US$10-12.50, per vehicle US$2.40-3; ☺Nov-Easter) This campground, near the bridge to La Barra, has well-kept facilities on woodsy grounds, complete with store, restaurant, laundry, 24-hour hot water and other amenities.

✕ Eating & Drinking

In summer Punta is famed for its club scene, which extends 10km east along the beaches all the way to La Barra. Outside of the peak Christmas-to-Carnaval period, you can still stomp the sand until the sun comes up at **Ocean Club** (www.facebook.com/oceanclubpunta; Parada 12, Playa Brava; ☺1-7am), one of the few beachfront dance spots operating year-round. In town, the most happening nightspots are down by the port. Places such as **Soho** (☑4244-7315; www.facebook.com/sohopuntauy; Rambla Artigas, btwn Calles 10 & 12; ☺11am-6am) and **Moby Dick** (☑4244-1240; www.mobydick. com.uy; Rambla Artigas 650; ☺6pm-5am Mon-Thu, noon-5am Fri-Sun) stay open year-round as long as there's a crowd; they sometimes have live music on weekends.

Rustic INTERNATIONAL $$
(☑4243-8391, 092-007457; www.facebook.com/rusticbarpuntadeleste; Calle 29, btwn Juan Gorlero & Calle 24; mains UR$200-450; ☺11am-4pm & 8pm late Dec-Feb, 11am-4pm daily & 8pm-late Fri & Sat Mar-Nov) Rustic wood tables, exposed brick walls, retro decor, and tasty food at affordable prices make this one of the peninsula's most attractive lunch spots. Owners Luciana and Sebastian offer service with a smile, bustling from table to table with *chivitos*, *milanesas*, quesadillas, salads and fish of the day. There's a UR$200 daily lunch special (cash only).

Olivia INTERNATIONAL $$
(☑4244-5121; Calle 21, btwn Rambla Artigas & Gorlero; mains UR$390-570; ☺noon-midnight) Popular for its varied menu and moderate (by Punta standards) prices, this bright little eatery decked out with red-and-white chairs serves tacos, salads, sandwiches and more substantial fish and meat dishes, along with caipirinhas, mojitos, sangria or fresh ginger-mint

HORSING AROUND IN THE HILLS

An hour inland from La Pedrera, the Sierra de Rocha is a lovely landscape of gray rocky crags interspersed with rolling rangeland. **Caballos de Luz** (☑099-400446; www.caballosdeluz.com; horseback rides per person with/without lunch from US$72/60, s/d incl horseback ride & full board US$160/290), run by Austrian-Uruguayan couple Lucie and Santiago, offers hill-country horse treks lasting from 2½ hours to a week, complete with three delicious vegetarian meals daily and overnight accommodation in a thatched cottage, a dome or a private double room. Call for pickup at the bus station in Rocha (US$20), or drive there yourself (it's about 30 minutes off Hwy 9).

lemonade. In good weather sit on the scenic rooftop terrace overlooking the port.

Capi Bar BAR
(www.facebook.com/capipde; Calle 27, btwn Gorlero & Calle 24; ☺6pm-3am Mon-Fri, 1pm-3am Sat & Sun) Punta del Este's first artisanal brewpub serves up its own Capitán home brew along with craft beers from all over Uruguay. The classy, low-lit interior also makes a nice place to linger over reasonably priced fish and chips, *rabas* (fried squid) and other bar snacks.

ℹ Orientation

Punta sits on a narrow peninsula that divides the Río de la Plata from the Atlantic Ocean. The town has two separate grids: north of the yacht harbor is the high-rise hotel zone; the southern area is largely residential. Streets bear both names and numbers. Av Juan Gorlero (Calle 22) is the main commercial street.

East and west of town, locations along the Ramblas (waterfront boulevards) are identified by *paradas* (numbered signposts).

ℹ Information

Punta's many banks, ATMs and exchange offices are concentrated along Gorlero.

Banco de la República Oriental (cnr Gorlero & Calle 25; ☺1-6pm Mon-Fri) One of two ATMs on this corner.

Municipal Tourist Office (☑4244-6510; www. maldonadoturismo.com.uy; Plaza Artigas; ☺8am-11pm mid-Dec–Feb, 10am-6pm rest of year) Full-service office on Punta's main square, with hotel-booking desk attached.

URUGUAY PUNTA DEL ESTE

Municipal Tourist Office – Playa Mansa (Liga de Fomento; 📞 4244-6519; www.maldonado turismo.com.uy; cnr Calles 18 & 31; ⊙ 9am-10pm mid-Dec–Mar, 10am-4pm rest of year)

National Tourism Ministry (📞 4244-1218; www.uruguaynatural.com; Gorlero 942; ⊙ 10am-5pm Mon-Sat)

ℹ Getting There & Away

AIR

Punta del Este International Airport (Aeropuerto de Punta del Este; 📞 4255-9777; www. puntadeleste.aero; Ruta Interbalnearia, Km 113) is at Laguna del Sauce, 20km west of Punta del Este. Direct international flights include Aerolíneas Argentinas to Buenos Aires' Aeroparque and **Latam** (📞 000-4019-0223; www.latam.com) to São Paulo.

BUS

From Punta's **bus terminal** (📞 4249-4042; cnr Calle 32 & Bulevar Artigas), dozens of daily buses ply the coastal route to Montevideo (UR$302, 2¼ hours). COT (www.cot.com.uy) also runs two daily buses northeast up the coast to the Brazilian border, with intermediate stops at Rocha (UR$228, 1½ hours, transfer point for La Paloma, La Pedrera and Cabo Polonio) and Punta del Diablo (UR$437, three hours).

ℹ Getting Around

Door-to-door **minivan transfers** (📞 099-903433; transfer btwn airport & bus terminal or port UR$250, btwn airport & hotel UR$350) are the most convenient way to reach Punta del Este's airport. Or any Montevideo-bound bus can drop you at the airport entrance on the main highway (UR$101), 250m from the terminal building.

Bus 14, operated by **Codesa** (📞 4266-9129; www.codesa.com.uy), runs from Punta's bus terminal via the eastern beaches to La Barra (UR$35, 10 minutes) and José Ignacio (UR$74, 50 minutes); other Codesa buses run year-round to points west, including Punta Ballena.

Cabo Polonio

POP 60

Northeast of La Paloma at Km 264.5 on Ruta 10 lies the turnoff to Cabo Polonio, one of the country's wildest areas and home to its second-biggest sea-lion colony, near a tiny fishing village on a windswept point crowned by a lonely **lighthouse** (UR$25; ⊙ 10am-1pm & 3pm-sunset). In 2009 the region was declared a national park, under the protective jurisdiction of Uruguay's SNAP program (Sistema Nacional de Áreas Protegidas; www.mvotma. gub.uy/portal/snap). Despite a growing influx

of tourists (and a spiffy entrance portal), Cabo Polonio remains one of Uruguay's most rustic coastal villages. There are no banking services, and the town's limited electricity is derived from generators, and solar and wind power.

🏃 Activities

★**Cabalgatas Valiceras**   HORSEBACK RIDING
(📞 099-574685; www.cabalgatasvaliceras.com.uy; Barra de Valizas; full-day excursion US$80-95, full-moon ride US$110) Based in nearby Barra de Valizas, this excellent operator offers horseback excursions into the national park, through the dunes and along the beaches north of Cabo Polonio, including monthly full-moon rides.

Cabo Polonio Surf School   SURFING
(📞 099-212542; Playa Sur; single lesson/5-lesson series $30/125; ⊙ Christmas-Easter) Local surfing aficionados Mario and Ruben run this recommended surf school, which offers two-hour classes (equipment included) at least twice daily (11am and 5pm) from late December through Easter. Call in advance to reserve a spot, or ask directions to the school from anyone in town (it's just inland from Playa Sur).

🛌 Sleeping & Eating

Casitas de Marta y Hector   RENTAL HOUSE $
(📞 098-533427; r US$30-70, house Apr-Nov US$30, Dec-Mar US$150) Hector and Marta, a friendly local fishing couple, rent out two sweet double rooms and a self-contained house sleeping up to seven. All come with stoves, gas refrigerators and solar-powered outlets for charging phones. Look for the salmon-orange house with the green flag just north of where trucks stop (and the 'Hay Pescado' sign when they've got fish to sell!).

Cabo Polonio Hostel   HOSTEL $
(📞 099-445943; www.cabopoloniohostel.com; dm/d mid-Dec–Feb US$33/100, remaining months US$18/50; ⊙ Oct-early May) 🍃 The affable Gabi presides over this rustic beachfront hostel, expanded to include a larger, brighter kitchen and an ocean-view dorm. A Polonio classic, it also features a hammock-strewn patio and a woodstove for stormy nights. The abandoned TV in the dunes out front and the custom-designed NoFi logo epitomize owner Alfredo's low-tech philosophy: slow down and unplug!

Pancho Hostal del Cabo   HOSTEL $
(📞 099-307870; dm Jan & Feb US$30, Mar-Dec US$11) Providing bare-bones dorms on two levels, Pancho's popular hostel is impossible

LA PALOMA & LA PEDRERA

Some 225km east of Montevideo, in the pretty rural department of Rocha, the coastal towns of La Paloma and La Pedrera offer some of Uruguay's best surfing. La Paloma owes its remarkably dependable waves to its tip-of-the-peninsula location: if there's no swell on the left, it'll be coming in on the right. La Pedrera, set atop a bluff with magnificent beach views, is also famous for its lively Carnaval festivities. Both towns fill up with young Uruguayans in summertime but get downright sleepy in the off-season, with many businesses shutting down completely from April through November.

Friendly **Peteco Surf Shop** (☑ 4479-6172; www.facebook.com/petecosurfshop; Av Nicolás Solari, btwn Avs El Sirio & del Navío; ☉ 10am-8pm Thu-Mon, to 6pm Tue & Wed) in La Paloma rents all the necessary equipment (shortboards, longboards, bodyboards, sandboards, wetsuits and kayaks) and can hook you up with good local instructors. The best surfing beaches are Los Botes, Solari, Anaconda, La Aguada and La Pedrera.

Both towns have an active summer hostel scene. In La Paloma, surfer-friendly **Beach Hostel La Balconada** (☑ 091-063927; www.labalconadahostel.com.uy; Centauro s/n; dm US$20-38, tw US$40-76, d US$50-80; ⬤) has an enviable location a stone's throw from the beach, while **Hostel Arazá** (☑ 4479-9/10; www.facebook.com/hostelarazalapaloma; Orion s/n; dm US$11-20, d US$40-80; ⬤⬤) stands out for its welcoming owners. In La Pedrera, **El Viajero Hostel** (☑ 099-470542; www.elviajerohostels.com; Venteveo, btwn Pirincho & Zorzal; dm US$14-22, d US$59-74; ☉ mid-Dec–mid-Mar; ⬤⬤) is 200m from the bus stop and 500m from the waterfront.

COT, Cynsa and Rutas del Sol all run frequently from Montevideo to La Paloma (UR$514, four hours) and La Pedrera (UR$535, 4¼ hours). Additional buses run between the two towns (UR$62, 15 minutes) and northeast to the Cabo Polonio turnoff (UR$83, 30 to 45 minutes).

to miss; look for the yellow corrugated roof, labeled with giant red letters, toward the beach from the 4WD truck stop. Nice features include a spacious kitchen, a beachfront lounging area and the 2nd-floor dorm under the A-frame roof, with its small terrace looking straight out at the ocean.

El Club PARRILLA, INTERNATIONAL **$$**
(☑ 098-353165; www.facebook.com/elclubcabo polonio; mains UR$300-480; ☉ 11am-late mid-Dec–Easter) ✒ This colorful, eco-conscious eatery combines the creative efforts of Colombian artist Camila, her Uruguayan partner Fernando and various local chefs. Specialties include grilled fish, artisanal beer, wood-fired pizza and fondue cooked atop recycled tin cans. It doubles as a social club where people gather to play chess and enjoy live music. *Platos del día* (UR$420) include some vegetarian options.

Look for it 50m west of the 4WD truck stop.

Lo de Dany URUGUAYAN **$$**
(mains UR$180-450; ☉ 9am-10pm) This straightforward orange snack shack near the 4WD truck stop is run by one of Polonio's few year-round resident families. It's a welcoming, affordable spot for everything from homemade

buñuelos de algas (seaweed fritters) to *rabas* (fried squid), to *chivitos*.

ⓘ Getting There & Away

Rutas del Sol runs two to five buses daily from Montevideo to the Cabo Polonio entrance portal on Ruta 10 (UR$642, 3¾ to 4¾ hours). Here you'll pile onto a 4WD truck for the lurching, bumpy ride across the dunes into town (UR$230 round trip, 30 minutes each way).

Punta del Diablo

POP 800

Once a sleepy fishing village, Punta del Diablo has long since become a prime summer getaway for Uruguayans and Argentines, and the epicenter of Uruguay's backpacker beach scene. Uncontrolled development has pushed further inland and along the coast in recent years, but the stunning shoreline and laid-back lifestyle still exert their appeal. To avoid the crowds, come outside the Christmas-to-February peak season; in particular, avoid the first half of January, when as many as 30,000 visitors inundate the town.

From the town's traditional center, a sandy 'plaza' 200m inland from the ocean, small dirt streets fan out in all directions.

🏃 Activities

During the day you can rent surfboards or horses along the town's main beach, or trek an hour north to Parque Nacional Santa Teresa. In the evening there are sunsets to watch, spontaneous bonfires and drum sessions to drop in on...you get the idea.

🛏 Sleeping & Eating

There are a multitude of private *cabañas* (cabins) for rent in the village; ask locally or check online at www.portaldeldiablo.com.uy. For cheap eats, don't miss the Acosta sisters' **empanada stands** (Feria Artesanal, Playa de los Pescadores; empanadas UR$75; ⊙ 10am-late daily Jan & Feb, 10am-4pm Sat & Sun Mar-Dec) down near the port.

⭐ El Diablo Tranquilo   HOSTEL $
(☑ 4477-2647; www.eldiablotranquilo.com; Av Central; late Dec-Carnaval dm US$25-49, d with/without bathroom from US$149/100, rest of year dm from US$10, d with/without bathroom from US$69/39; @ 🛜) Follow the devilish red glow into one of South America's most seductive hostels, whose endless perks include inviting chill-out areas, bike and surfboard rentals, yoga and language classes, and horseback excursions. At the beachside Playa Suites annex, upstairs rooms have full-on ocean views, while the attached bar-restaurant offers meals, beach service and a late-night party scene.

La Casa de las Boyas   HOSTEL $
(☑ 4477-2074; www.lacasadelasboyas.com.uy; Playa del Rivero; dm Dec-Mar only US$15-40, d Dec-Mar US$60-150, Apr-Nov US$50-70; @ 🛜 🏊) A stone's throw from the beach and a 10-minute walk north from the town center, this hostel offers a pool, two guest kitchens, summer-only dorms, and year-round apartments and lofts equipped with en suite bathrooms, kitchenettes and satellite TV. Other enticements include restaurant, game room, bike and surfboard rentals, and horseback excursions.

⭐ Resto-Pub 70   ITALIAN $
(☑ 099-103367; www.facebook.com/pub70; Playa de los Pescadores; mains UR$275-350; ⊙ 12:30-4pm & 7:30-11pm daily late Dec-Mar, Fri-Sun rest of year) Run by an Italian family from the Veneto, this portside eatery serves divine, reasonably priced homemade pasta such as *lasagne alle cipolle* (veggie lasagna with walnuts and caramelized onions), accompanied by UR$50 glasses of house wine. Afterward, don't miss the *cantucci con vino dolce* (almond biscotti dipped in sweet wine) and *limoncino* (an artisanal liqueur made with fragrant Uruguayan lemons).

Cero Stress   INTERNATIONAL $$
(☑ 4477-2220; Av de los Pescadores; mains UR$320-490; ⊙ noon-4pm & 7-11pm; 🛜 ☑) By far the greatest asset of this laid-back eatery is its deck, which offers amazing ocean views. It's the perfect place to sip a *caipirinha* (Brazilian cocktail with sugarcane alcohol) at sunset while contemplating your evening plans. There's also occasional live music.

ℹ Information

Punta del Diablo has no cash machines other than the temporary **Redbrou ATM** (Paseo del Rivero, Calle 9) set up at Paseo del Rivero each summer. Bring cash with you; only some businesses accept credit cards, and the nearest banks are an hour away in Castillos (40km southwest) or Chuy (45km north).

ℹ Getting There & Around

Rutas del Sol, COT and Cynsa all offer service to Punta del Diablo's dreary bus terminal, 2.5km west of town. From here it's a five- to 10-minute shuttle (UR$25) or taxi (UR$100) into town.

Several direct buses run daily to Montevideo (UR$642, five hours) and Chuy (UR$107, one hour) on the Brazilian border; for other coastal destinations, you'll usually need to change buses in Castillos (UR$86, one hour) or Rocha (UR$214, 1½ hours).

Parque Nacional Santa Teresa

This army-administered **national park** (☑ 4477-2101; www.serviciodeparquesdelejercito.com.uy; Ruta 9, Km 302; ⊙ 8am-8pm Dec-Feb, 9am-6pm Mar-Nov) FREE, 35km south of the Brazilian border, attracts many Uruguayan and Brazilian visitors to its relatively uncrowded beaches, including **Playa Grande**, **Playa del Barco** and **Playa de las Achiras**.

The **Capatacía** (park headquarters), 1km east of Ruta 9, has an Antel phone office, a post office, a market, a bakery and a restaurant, along with a very small zoo and a plant conservatory.

The park's star attraction, 4km north of park headquarters on Ruta 9, is the impressive hilltop **Fortaleza de Santa Teresa** (☑ 4474-6541; UR$40; ⊙ 10am-7pm daily Dec-Feb, to 5pm Wed-Sun Apr-Nov), a fortress begun by the Portuguese in 1762 and finished by the Spaniards after they captured the site in 1793.

❶ GETTING TO BRAZIL

The rather dreary border town of Chuy (population 11,300, called Chuí on the Brazilian side) is the main gateway from Uruguay into Brazil. Av Brasil/Uruguay, a wide avenue lined with money changers and vendors of pirated CDs, forms the international border. There's no reason to linger, but if you find yourself stuck here, **Etnico Hostel** (☑4474-2281; www.facebook.com/etnicohostelchuy; Liber Seregni 299; dm/s/d US\$16/28/46; ✿@◉) is your best bet for an overnight stay.

The Uruguayan and Brazilan customs offices are a couple of kilometers apart, on opposite sides of the border. Long-distance buses operated by TTL (www.ttl.com.br) and EGA (www.ega.com.uy) stop at both offices on their international runs up the Atlantic coast from Montevideo and Punta del Este to Porto Alegre, Florianópolis, Curitiba and São Paulo.

COT and Cynsa buses for Punta del Diablo (UR\$107, one hour) and Montevideo (UR\$728, five hours) leave from near the corner of Brasil and Oliviera. Two blocks west, at the corner of Brasil and Mauro Silva, Tureste buses head inland to Treinta y Tres (UR\$333, three hours, twice daily), where you can make onward connections to Tacuarembó (via Melo).

At the park's northeastern corner is **Cerro Verde**, a coastal bluff providing important sea-turtle habitat. Directly opposite the park entrance, on the west side of Ruta 9, a 5km dead-end dirt road leads to **Laguna Negra**, a vast lagoon where flamingos, capybaras and other wildlife can be spotted.

The park offers 2000 dispersed campsites in eucalyptus and pine groves, along with a simple hostel and a variety of four- to 10-person *cabañas* for rent.

Buses from Punta del Diablo (UR\$64, 15 minutes) will drop you off at Km 302 on Ruta 9; from here, it's a flat 1km walk east to the Capatacía (park headquarters).

Or, walk north along the beach a couple of kilometers from Punta del Diablo to reach the park's southern edge at Playa Grande.

UNDERSTAND URUGUAY

Uruguay Today

Current topics of conversation in Uruguay include the continued implementation of the country's groundbreaking marijuana law, the revitalization of Montevideo's Ciudad Vieja and the bright future prospects of Uruguay's national soccer team.

Uruguay's move toward legalized marijuana, first authorized in 2013, cleared its first major hurdle in mid-July 2017 as government-approved pharmacies began selling pot to Uruguayan citizens. Some 16 pharmacies provided over 5000 registered users with their first legally approved weekly dose of 10g of government greenhouse-grown weed (the initial price tag for each 5g bag was UR\$187, or about US\$6.50). By July 2018, the number of registered pharmacy buyers had quintupled, to over 25,000. Meanwhile, thousands more Uruguayans have opted for one of the other two legal channels for obtaining marijuana: growing their own (a maximum of six plants per person) or joining a club (each club needs at least 15 members and is allowed to grow up to 99 plants). Despite the boom in domestic consumption, Uruguay's government has so far steadfastly opposed any plan that would allow foreign tourists to purchase cannabis.

Montevideo's Ciudad Vieja has seen a surge of revitalization in recent years as municipal-government efforts to eliminate petty crime in the neighborhood have begun to bear fruit. Several new restaurants and hotels have moved in, and businesses are keeping longer hours as concerns about security have waned. This has all translated into an uptick in tourism to Montevideo's historic center.

Meanwhile, Uruguayan soccer fans are jazzed about the recent success of their beloved 'Celeste,' which made it to the quarterfinals of the 2018 World Cup, losing only to eventual champions France. The team's crop of stars includes 20-something players like Rodrigo Bentancur and José María Giménez, who seem poised to continue making an impact at 2022's Qatar World Cup and well beyond.

History

Uruguay's indigenous peoples were the Charrúa along the coast and the Guaraní north of the Río Negro. The hunting-and-gathering Charrúa discouraged European colonization for more than a century by killing Spanish explorer Juan de Solís and most of his party in 1516. In any event there was little to attract the Spanish, who valued these lowlands along the Río de la Plata only as an access route to gold and other quick riches further inland.

The first Europeans to settle on the Banda Oriental (Eastern Shore) were Jesuit missionaries near present-day Soriano, on the Río Uruguay. Next came the Portuguese, who established present-day Colonia in 1680 as a beachhead for smuggling goods into Buenos Aires. Spain responded by building its own citadel at Montevideo in 1726. The following century saw an ongoing struggle between Spain and Portugal for control of these lands along the eastern bank of the Río de la Plata.

Napoleon's invasion of the Iberian peninsula in the early 19th century precipitated a weakening of Spanish and Portuguese power and the emergence of strong independence movements throughout the region. José Gervasio Artigas, Uruguay's homegrown national hero, originally sought to form an alliance with several states in present-day Argentina and southern Brazil against the European powers, but he was ultimately forced to flee to Paraguay. There he regrouped and organized the famous '33 Orientales,' a feisty band of Uruguayan patriots under General Juan Lavalleja, who, with Argentine support, crossed the Río Uruguay on April 19, 1825, and launched a campaign to liberate modern-day Uruguay from Brazilian control. In 1828, after three years' struggle, a British-mediated treaty established Uruguay as a small independent buffer between the emerging continental powers.

For several decades, Uruguay's independence remained fragile. There was civil war between Uruguay's two nascent political parties, the Colorados and the Blancos; Argentina besieged Montevideo from 1838 to 1851; and Brazil was an ever-present threat. Things finally settled down in the second half of the 19th century, with region-wide recognition of Uruguay's independence and the emergence of a strong national economy based on beef and wool production.

In the early 20th century, visionary president José Batlle y Ordóñez introduced such innovations as pensions, farm credits, unemployment compensation and the eight-hour work day. State intervention led to the nationalization of many industries, the creation of others, and a new era of general prosperity. However, Batlle's reforms were largely financed through taxing the livestock sector, and when exports faltered midcentury, the welfare state crumbled. A period of military dictatorship began in the early 1970s, during which torture became routine, and more than 60,000 citizens were arbitrarily detained, before the 1980s brought a return to democratic traditions.

The past two decades have seen remarkable developments in Uruguayan culture and politics. After nearly two centuries of back-and-forth rule between the two traditional parties, Blancos and Colorados, Uruguayans voted the leftist Frente Amplio (Broad Front) into power in 2004 and again in 2009 and 2014. Over that span, the Frente Amplio government has presided over numerous social changes, including the legalization of marijuana, abortion and same-sex marriage.

Culture

The one thing Uruguayans will tell you is that they're *not* anything like their *porteño* (people from Buenos Aires) cousins across the water. Where Argentines can be brassy and sometimes arrogant, Uruguayans tend to be more humble and relaxed. Where the former have always been a regional superpower, the latter have always lived in the shadow of one. Those jokes about Punta del Este being a suburb of Buenos Aires don't go down so well on this side of the border. There are plenty of similarities, though: the near-universal appreciation for the arts, the Italian influence and the *gaucho* (cowboy) heritage.

Uruguayans like to take it easy and pride themselves on being laid back. Sunday's the day for family and friends, to throw half a cow on the *parrilla* (grill), and to sit back and sip some maté (a bitter ritual tea). The population is well educated, and the gap between rich and poor is much less pronounced than in most other Latin American countries.

Population

With 3.4 million people, Uruguay is South America's smallest Spanish-speaking country. The population is predominately white (87.7%), with smaller percentages self-identifying as black (4.6%) or indigenous (2.4%). The average life expectancy (77.4 years) is one of Latin America's highest. The literacy rate is also high, at 98.5%, while population growth is a slow 0.27%. Population density is roughly 19 people per square kilometer.

Religion

Uruguay has more self-professed atheists and agnostics per capita (17%) than any other Latin American country. Some 47% identify themselves as Roman Catholic, with 11% claiming affiliation with other Christian denominations. There's a small Jewish minority, numbering around 20,000.

Sports

Uruguayans, like just about all Latin Americans, are crazy about *fútbol* (soccer). Uruguay has won the World Cup twice, including the first tournament, played in Montevideo in 1930. The national team has continued to excel periodically at the international level, winning the 2011 Copa America, making it to the round of 16 in the 2014 World Cup, and reaching the round of eight in the 2018 World Cup.

The most notable teams are Montevideo-based Nacional and Peñarol. If you go to a match between these two, sit on the sidelines, not behind the goal, unless you're up for some serious rowdiness.

Asociación Uruguayo de Fútbol (www.auf.org.uy) and Fanáticos Fútbol Tours (www.futboltours.com.uy), both in Montevideo, can provide information on matches and venues.

Arts

Despite its small population, Uruguay has an impressive literary and artistic tradition. Major Uruguayan writers include poet Ida Vitale (winner of the prestigious Cervantes Literature Prize in 2018), Juana de Ibarbourou, Juan Carlos Onetti, Mario Benedetti, Delmira Agustini, Eduardo Galeano and Cristina Peri Rossi. Theater and film are also popular, with director/screenwriter Beatriz Flores Silva and playwright Mauricio Rosencof among the Uruguayan artists who have achieved international recognition. The country's most famous philosopher and essayist is José Enrique Rodó, whose 1900 essay *Ariel*, contrasting North American and Latin American civilizations, is a classic of the country's literature.

Uruguay's most renowned painters include Juan Manuel Blanes, Pedro Figari and Joaquín Torres García, each of whom has a museum dedicated to their works in Montevideo. Other noteworthy figures include painter Petrona Viera, associated with Uruguay's early 20th-century Planismo movement, and sculptor José Belloni, whose life-size bronzes can be seen in Montevideo's parks,

and award-winning digital artist Agustina Casas Sere-Leguizamon.

Tango is big in Montevideo – Uruguayans claim tango legend Carlos Gardel as a native son, and one of the best-known tangos, 'La Cumparsita,' was composed by Uruguayan Gerardo Matos Rodríguez. During Carnaval, Montevideo's streets reverberate to the energetic drumbeats of *candombe,* an African-derived rhythm brought to Uruguay by slaves from 1750 onwards, and to the sounds of *murgas,* satirical musical-theater groups who perform throughout the city. On the contemporary scene, several Uruguayan musicians have won a following on both sides of the Río de la Plata, including Malena Muyala, Laura Canoura, Buitres and No Te Va Gustar.

Environment

Though one of South America's smallest countries, Uruguay is not so small by European standards. Its area of 176,215 sq km is greater than England and Wales combined, or slightly bigger than the US state of Florida.

Uruguay's two main ranges of interior hills are the Cuchilla de Haedo, west of Tacuarembó, and the Cuchilla Grande, south of Melo; neither exceeds 500m in height. West of Montevideo the terrain is more level. The Río Negro flowing through the center of the country forms a natural dividing line between north and south. The Atlantic coast has impressive beaches, dunes, headlands and lagoons. Uruguay's grasslands and forests resemble those of Argentina's pampas or southern Brazil, and patches of palm savanna persist in the east.

The country is rich in birdlife, especially in the coastal lagoons of Rocha department. Most large land animals have disappeared, but the occasional ñandú (rhea) still races across northwestern Uruguay's grasslands. Whales, fur seals and sea lions are common along the coast.

SURVIVAL GUIDE

❶ Directory A–Z

ACCESSIBLE TRAVEL

Uruguay is increasingly providing for travelers with special needs. In Montevideo, for example, you'll find newly constructed ramps and dedicated bathrooms in high-profile destinations such as Plaza Independencia and Teatro Solís, disabled access on some bus lines and a growing

number of ATMs for the visually impaired. The Uruguayan government organization Pronadis/Mides (http://pronadis.mides.gub.uy) lists Spanish-language resources for disabled travelers on its website.

ACCOMMODATIONS

Uruguay has an excellent network of hostels and campgrounds, especially along the Atlantic coast. Other low-end options include *hospedajes* (family homes) and *residenciales* (budget hotels).

Posadas are available in all price ranges and tend to be homier than hotels. Hotels are ranked from one to five stars, according to amenities.

Country *estancias turísticas* (marked with blue National Tourism Ministry signs) provide lodging on farms.

ACTIVITIES

Punta del Diablo, La Paloma, La Pedrera and Punta del Este all get excellent surfing waves, while Cabo Polonio and the coastal lagoons of Rocha department are great for whale- and bird-watching, respectively. Punta del Este's beach scene is more upmarket, with activities such as parasailing, windsurfing and jet skiing.

Horseback riding is very popular in the interior and can be arranged on most tourist *estancias*.

ELECTRICITY

Uruguay uses the same electrical plug as Argentina. Argentina's electric current operates on 220V, 50Hz. Most plugs are either two rounded prongs (as in Europe) or three angled flat prongs (as in Australia).

EMBASSIES & CONSULATES

Argentine Embassy (☎ 2902-8166; www.eurug.cancilleria.gov.ar; Cuareim 1470; ⊘10am-6pm Mon-Fri)

Argentine Consulate (☎ 2902-8623; www.cmdeo.mrecic.gov.ar; WF Aldunate 1281; ⊘1-3pm Mon-Fri)

Australian Consulate (☎ 098-451451; www.dfat.gov.au/missions/countries/uy.html; 25 de Mayo 455, 2nd fl; ⊘ by arrangement)

Brazilian Embassy (☎ 2707-2119; http://montevideu.itamaraty.gov.br; Artigas 1394; ⊘10am-1pm & 3-6pm Mon-Fri)

Brazilian Consulate (☎ 2901-2024; http://cgmontevideu.itamaraty.gov.br; Convención 1343, 6th fl; ⊘9am-3pm Mon-Fri)

Canadian Embassy (☎ 2902-2030; www.uruguay.gc.ca; Plaza Independencia 749, Oficina 102; ⊘9-11am & 2-4:30pm Mon-Thu, 9-11am Fri)

French Embassy (☎ 1705-0000; www.ambafranceuruguay.org; Av Uruguay 853; ⊘8:30am-12:30pm & 1:30-5:30pm Mon-Thu, 8:30am-4:30pm Fri)

German Embassy (☎ 2902-5222; www.montevideo.diplo.de; La Cumparsita 1435; ⊘9-11:30am Mon & Wed-Fri, 1-3:30pm Tue)

UK Embassy (☎ 2622-3630; www.gov.uk/world/uruguay; Marco Bruto 1073; ⊘9am-1pm & 2-5:30pm Mon-Thu, 9am-2pm Fri)

US Embassy (☎ 1770-2000; https://uy.us embassy.gov; Lauro Müller 1776; ⊘9am-5:30pm Mon-Fri)

FOOD

Uruguayan cuisine revolves around grilled meat. *Parrillas* (restaurants with big racks of meat roasting over a wood fire) are everywhere, and weekend *asados* (barbecues) are a national tradition. *Chivitos* are hugely popular, as are *chivitos al plato* (served with fried potatoes instead of bread). In rural Uruguay, vegetarians often have to content themselves with the ubiquitous pizza and pasta, although vegetarian- and vegan-friendly restaurants are increasingly emerging in places like Montevideo and Colonia del Sacramento. Seafood is excellent on the coast. Desserts are heavy on meringue, *dulce de leche* (milk caramel), burnt sugar and custard.

Tap water is fine to drink in most places. Uruguayan wines (especially tannats) are excellent, and a small but growing lineup of craft brews is now appearing alongside traditional mass-produced beers like Patricia, Pilsen and Zillertal.

Uruguayans consume even more maté than Argentines. If you get the chance, try to acquire the taste – there's nothing like whiling away an afternoon with new-found friends passing around the maté.

Most restaurants charge *cubiertos* – small 'cover' charges that theoretically pay for the basket of bread offered before your meal.

INSURANCE

Worldwide travel insurance is available at www.lonelyplanet.com/travel-insurance. You can buy, extend and claim online anytime – even if you're already on the road.

INTERNET ACCESS

Wi-fi zones are commonplace in cities and larger towns. Antel (state telephone company) offices sell SIM cards with reasonably priced data plans for unlocked phones, and also provide free wi-fi in many cases.

SLEEPING PRICE RANGES

The following price ranges refer to a double room with bathroom in high season (December through Easter). Breakfast is usually included in the price.

$ less than US$75

$$ US$75–US$150

$$$ more than US$150

LEGAL MATTERS

Uruguay has some of Latin America's most lenient drug laws. Possession of small amounts of marijuana or other drugs for personal use has been decriminalized, but their sale to non-Uruguayans remains illegal.

LGBT TRAVELERS

Uruguay is widely considered the most LGBT+-friendly nation in Latin America. In 2008 it became the first Latin American country to recognize same-sex civil unions, and in 2013 same-sex marriage was legalized. In Montevideo, look for the pocket-sized Friendly Map (www.friendly map.com.uy) listing LGBT-friendly businesses throughout the country.

MONEY

Prices are in Uruguayan pesos (UR$), the official Uruguayan currency. Banknote values are 20, 50, 100, 200, 500, 1000 and 2000. There are coins of one, two, five, 10 and 50 pesos.

US dollars are commonly accepted in major tourist hubs, where many accommodations quote US$ prices. In hotels that accept payment in either dollars or pesos, it pays to check the exchange rate offered. In many cases, you'll come out ahead paying in pesos. Away from the touristed areas, dollars are of limited use.

Uruguay has no black or 'blue' market offering higher exchange rates for US and European banknotes.

ATMs

In all but the smallest interior towns, getting cash with your ATM card is easy. Machines marked with the green Banred or blue Redbrou logo serve all major international banking networks. ATMs dispense bills in multiples of 100 pesos. Many also dispense US dollars, designated as US$, but only in multiples of US$100.

Credit Cards

Most upmarket hotels, restaurants and shops accept credit cards. Visa is most commonly accepted, followed by MasterCard. American Express cards are of more limited use.

Money Changers

There are *casas de cambio* in Montevideo, Colonia, the Atlantic beach resorts and border towns such as Chuy. They typically keep longer hours than banks but may offer lower rates.

Tipping

Restaurants Leave 10% of the bill.
Taxis Round up the fare a few pesos.

OPENING HOURS

Banks 1–6pm Monday to Friday
Bars, pubs and clubs 6pm–late; things don't get seriously shaking until after midnight

Restaurants noon–3pm and 8pm–midnight or later; if serving breakfast, open around 8am
Shops 9am–1pm and 3–7pm Monday to Saturday; in larger cities, many stay open at lunchtime and/or on Sunday

PUBLIC HOLIDAYS

Año Nuevo (New Year's Day) January 1
Día de los Reyes (Epiphany) January 6
Viernes Santo/Pascua (Good Friday/Easter) March/April (dates vary)
Desembarco de los 33* (Return of the 33 Exiles) April 19; honors the exiles who returned to Uruguay in 1825 to, with Argentine support, liberate the country from Brazil
Día del Trabajador (Labor Day) May 1
Batalla de Las Piedras* (Battle of Las Piedras) May 18; commemorates a major battle in the fight for independence
Natalicio de Artigas* (Artigas' Birthday) June 19
Jura de la Constitución (Constitution Day) July 18
Día de la Independencia (Independence Day) August 25
Día de la Raza* (Columbus Day) October 12
Día de los Muertos (All Souls' Day) November 2
Navidad (Christmas Day) December 25

Holidays marked with an asterisk may be celebrated on the nearest Monday to create a *puente* (long weekend).

TELEPHONE

Uruguay's country code is 598. Antel (www.antel.com.uy) is the state telephone company, with offices in every town.

All Uruguayan landline numbers are eight digits long, beginning with 2 for Montevideo or 4 for elsewhere in the country. Cell (mobile) phone numbers consist of a three-digit prefix (most commonly 099) followed by a six-digit number. If dialing internationally, drop the leading zero.

Cell Phones

Three companies – Antel (www.antel.com.uy), Claro (www.claro.com.uy) and Movistar (www.movistar.com.uy) – provide cell-phone service in Uruguay. Rather than use expensive roaming plans, many travelers bring an unlocked cell phone (or buy a cheap one here) and insert a local pay-as-you-go SIM card. SIMs can readily be purchased

URUGUAY DIRECTORY A–Z

at Antel offices and recharged at service stations, malls and streetside kiosks throughout Uruguay.

TIME

Uruguay Standard Time is three hours behind GMT, as in Argentina. Daylight-saving time was abolished in 2015.

TOURIST INFORMATION

The **National Tourism Ministry** (Ministerio de Turismo y Deporte; www.turismo.gub.uy) operates 11 *centros de informes* (information centers) around the country. It distributes excellent free maps for each of Uruguay's 19 departments, along with specialized information on *estancia* tourism, Carnaval, surfing and other subjects of interest to travelers. Most towns also have a municipal tourist office on the plaza or at the bus terminal.

VISAS

Nationals of Western Europe, Australia, the USA, Canada and New Zealand automatically receive a 90-day tourist card, renewable for another 90 days. Other nationals may require visas. For an official list of current visa requirements by nationality, see https://migracion.minterior.gub.uy.

VOLUNTEERING

Uruguayan organizations that accept volunteers generally require a minimum commitment of one month, and many also expect at least basic Spanish proficiency.

International volunteers seeking shorter-term placements (minimum eight days) can contact Karumbé (www.karumbe.org/voluntarios), which promotes sea-turtle conservation in Parque Nacional Santa Teresa.

WOMEN TRAVELERS

Women are generally treated with respect, and traveling alone is safer here than in many other Latin American countries.

ⓘ Getting There & Away

AIR

Montevideo's Carrasco International Airport (p991) is the main port of entry. A few direct flights from Argentina and Brazil also serve Punta del Este International Airport (p1006).

With the failure of former carriers the country no longer has a national airline, and there are no commercial domestic flights.

BOAT

There are several ferry routes between Argentina and Uruguay, with the most popular being the one-hour crossing of the Río de la Plata between Buenos Aires and Colonia del Sacramento. Other routes include Buenos Aires to Montevideo, Tigre to Carmelo and Concordia to Salto.

BUS

➔ Direct buses run from Montevideo to Buenos Aires via the Fray Bentos–Gualeguaychú bridge, but these are slower than bus/ferry combinations across the Río de la Plata. Two other bridges connect Uruguay with Argentina, over the Río Uruguay from Paysandú to Colón and Salto to Concordia.

➔ There are multiple crossings to Brazil – the most popular is the Atlantic coast route from Chuy to Chuí, with northbound connections to Porto Alegre, Florianópolis and São Paulo.

➔ Buses generally continue through the border and passport formalities take place on the bus.

ⓘ Getting Around

BUS

Buses are comfortable, the government-regulated fares are reasonable and distances are short. Many companies offer free wi-fi on board. In the few cities that lack terminals, all companies are within easy walking distance of each other, usually around the main plaza.

Reservations are unnecessary except during holiday periods. On peak travel dates a single company may run multiple departures at the same hour, in which case they'll mark a bus number on your ticket; check with the driver to make sure you're boarding the right bus, or you may find yourself in the 'right' seat on the wrong bus!

Most towns with central bus terminals have a reasonably priced left-luggage facility.

CAR & MOTORCYCLE

Visitors to Uruguay who are staying less than 90 days need only bring a valid driver's license from their home country. Uruguayan drivers are extremely considerate, and even bustling Montevideo is quite sedate compared with Buenos Aires.

Due to government regulation, all service stations, including the ubiquitous state-owned Ancap, charge the same price for fuel. At the time of research, regular unleaded gasoline cost UR$54.95 per liter, premium UR$57 per liter.

LOCAL TRANSPORTATION

Taxis, *remises* (private cars) and local buses are similar to those in Argentina. Taxis are metered; between 10pm and 6am, and on Sundays and holidays, fares are 20% higher. There's a small additional charge for luggage, and passengers generally tip the driver by rounding fares up to the next multiple of five or 10 pesos. Uber and similar ride-sharing services are also widely used in Montevideo. City bus service is excellent in Montevideo and other urban areas, while *micros* (minibuses) form the backbone of the local transit network in smaller coastal towns such as La Paloma.

Venezuela

Fast Facts

Area 912,050 sq km

Population 32.4 million

Capital Caracas

Emergency 171

Country Code 58

Resources

Today Venezuela (www.todayvenezuela.com)

El Universal (www.eluniversal.com)

Venezuelan Politics & Human Rights (www.venezuelablog.tumblr.com)

Introduction

Venezuela, home to some of South America's most incredible landscapes, rightly has a terrible image problem at the moment. Hyperinflation has led to a dramatic drop in living standards and issues with the supply of basic goods, while personal safety, particularly in Caracas, is worse than anywhere else on the continent. Thousands of its own citizens have fled the country and spread throughout South America (it's estimated more than two million have left since 2014). While visiting can be incredibly cheap because of the black-market value of the dollar/euro, safety is a serious concern.

Few countries in the world have this degree of natural beauty: Andean peaks, Caribbean coastline, idyllic islands, grasslands teeming with wildlife, the steamy Orinoco Delta and the world's highest waterfall, Angel Falls. We cannot recommend traveling here at present, but we hope that the future holds amazing tourist possibilities.

Travel Warning

Venezuela is a tricky place to travel at present and showing up on a whim is a bad idea. Because of security concerns, we cannot recommend traveling to Venezuela at this time. There is a basic lack of services for the ordinary citizen – food, health care and personal security – so a traveler with no knowledge of the lay of the land could find themselves seriously out of their depth in a hurry.

If you're still determined to travel, the only way we can truly recommend visiting is if you organize a trip with a Venezuela-based travel agency in advance. On the ground, do not use unofficial taxis, change money with strangers or stay in hotels you don't know to be safe. Take local advice seriously and carry a copy of your passport and entry stamp with you at all times rather than carrying your actual passport with you. Finally, be discreet about the often enormous piles of cash you're forced to carry due to the currency being so weak.

Venezuela

VENEZUELA TODAY

Since the death of former president Hugo Chávez in March 2013, Venezuela's fortunes have been decidedly poor, and the country, once a beacon for left-wing causes around the world, is now in a state of near collapse. Endemic corruption, poor governance, the world's highest inflation rate, spiraling crime levels and huge lines outside supermarkets and pharmacies at any time of day are the defining features of contemporary life here. Once one of South America's wealthiest and safest countries, it's no exaggeration to today call Venezuela one of the continent's poorest and most dangerous places. Most Venezuelans simply shake their head when the inevitable discussion about politics starts: despair tempered by the trademark Venezuelan dry humor seems to be a common reaction to the topic.

The current president is Nicolás Maduro, previously Chávez' deputy and anointed successor, who came to the presidency on his predecessor's death in 2013. He has continued most of Chávez' policies, but without any of Hugo's trademark charisma, which was always so vital to his popularity and appeal.

Indeed, Maduro has done little to define himself politically, save arresting and imprisoning several of his political enemies and starting a diplomatic spat with Colombia that dramatically backfired in 2015, sparking some in South America to publicly question his fitness for office. His steak-and-cigar dinner with celebrity chef Salt Bae in Turkey in 2018 led to more questions and outright indignation. The year before he suggested that Venezuelans raise and eat more rabbit to combat food shortages. 'Plan Conejo' (Rabbit Plan) distributed baby rabbits to poor neighborhoods, but many adopted them as pets.

In September 2015 opposition leader Leopoldo López received a 13-year sentence for inciting violence during antigovernment protests in 2014. He was first sent to prison but since 2017 has been mostly under house arrest.

On the ground life has changed enormously in recent years for the majority of Venezuelans. Many people simply earn money by lining up all day for food and other basic goods at state stores, which they resell on the black market for huge markups. You will see these so-called *bachacos* (ants) in enormous lines all over the country – today the country is divided into those who line up and those who pay others to line up for them. With state salaries now worth barely US$30 a month (estimated in late 2018 but subject to great fluctuation), corruption or moonlighting often becomes the only viable way to earn a living wage.

Even the most basic of medical services are difficult to come by as medicines and supplies are in a shortage and 20% of the doctors have left the country in the past five years.

Maduro was reelected to a new six-year term in early 2018, defeating former governor Henri Falcon, but the election was widely decried as fraudulent within and without the country. Officials reported total voting at 46% while opposition said as few as one-third of voters cast their ballots.

Maduro's government introduced a new currency – the 'bolivar sovereign' – in August 2018 to battle 32,000% inflation, basically lopping five zeros off the old bolivar fuerte. The two competing currencies, however, mainly caused confusion. The standard wage was also raised 6000%.

In September 2018, to ratchet up the pressure on Venezuela's government, the US imposed sanctions on Nicolas Maduro's wife and several other members of his political inner circle, seizing their assets in the US and preventing them from doing business there.

Five South American nations, along with Canada, called for an investigation into the Maduro government's crimes against humanity at the UN in September 2018. The alleged suicide of opposition politician Fernando Alban while in custody in October 2018 cast a wider shadow on the government, with UN calls for a full investigation.

Despite opposition from the international community, Maduro moved forward with his inauguration in January 2019. Previously under-the-radar politician Juan Guaido, a member of the socialist-democratic Popular Will party, assumed leadership of the National Assembly a few days prior to the inauguration. Guaido, actively disputing Maduro's claim to power, was then declared interim president of Venezuela at an opposition rally a few weeks later.

While several countries have officially recognized Guaido as Venezuela's leader, the country's future remains uncertain, as some internal and external support for Maduro exists. For Venezuelans, however, the main goal is restoration of social normalcy and economic stability.

HISTORY

Venezuela has always drawn adventurers, explorers and exploiters to its incredible natural riches and warm climes. Names that dot the history books – such as Columbus, Humboldt and the great liberator of South America Simon Bolivar – made their mark on the nascent republic. Later, oil wealth drew in the Rockefellers and others, and as a founder Organization of the Petroleum Exporting Countries (OPEC) nation, Venezuela established a powerful cartel that still wields global power. Its 21st-century socialist epoch under Hugo Chávez marked the rising of the 'pink tide' of left-leaning South American leadership.

Pre-Columbian Times

There is evidence of human habitation in northwest Venezuela going back more than 10,000 years. Steady agriculture was established around the first millennium, leading to the first year-round settlements. Formerly nomadic groups began to develop into larger cultures belonging to three main linguistic families: Carib, Arawak and Chibcha. By the end of the 15th century, during the Spanish conquest, some 300,000 to 400,000 indigenous people inhabited the region that is now Venezuela.

The Timote-Cuica tribes, of the Chibcha linguistic family, were the most technologically developed of Venezuela's pre-Hispanic societies. They lived in the Andes and developed complex agricultural techniques including irrigation and terracing. They were also skilled craftspeople, as we can judge by the artifacts they left behind – examples of their fine pottery are shown in museums across the country.

Spanish Conquest

Christopher Columbus was the first European to set foot on Venezuelan soil, which was also the only place where he landed on the South American mainland. On his third trip to the South American continent in 1498, he anchored at the eastern tip of the Península de Paria, just opposite Trinidad. He originally believed that he was on another island, but the voluminous mouth of the Río Orinoco hinted that he had stumbled onto something slightly larger.

A year later Spanish conquistador Alonso de Ojeda, accompanied by the Italian Amerigo Vespucci, sailed up to the Península de la Guajira, on the western end of present-day Venezuela. On entering Lago de Maracaibo, the Spaniards saw indigenous people living in *palafitos* (thatched homes on stilts above the water). Perhaps as a bit of sarcasm, they called the waterside community Venezuela, meaning 'Little Venice,' and simultaneously gave birth to the country's name. The first Spanish settlement on Venezuelan soil, Nueva Cádiz, was established around 1500 on the small island of Cubagua, just south of Isla de Margarita. The earliest Venezuelan town still in existence, Cumaná (on the mainland directly south of Isla Cubagua) dates from 1521.

Simón Bolívar & Independence

Venezuela lurked in the shadows of the Spanish empire through most of the colonial period. The country took a more primary role at the beginning of the 19th century, when Venezuela gave Latin America one of its greatest heroes, Simón Bolívar. A native of Caracas, Bolívar led the forces that put the nail in the coffin of Spanish rule over South America. He is viewed as being largely responsible for ending colonial rule all the way to the borders of Argentina.

Bolívar assumed leadership of the revolution, which had kicked off in 1806 (initially inspired and led by another national hero, Francisco de Miranda). After unsuccessful initial attempts to defeat the Spaniards at home, he withdrew to Colombia and then to Jamaica to plot his final campaign. In 1817 Bolívar marched over the Andes with 5000 British mercenaries and an army of horsemen from Los Llanos, defeating the Spanish at the battle of Boyacá and bringing independence to Colombia. Four months later in Angostura (present-day Ciudad Bolívar), the Angostura Congress proclaimed Gran Colombia a new state, unifying Colombia (which included present-day Panama), Venezuela and Ecuador – though the last two were still under Spanish rule.

The liberation of Venezuela was completed with Bolívar's victory over Spanish forces at Carabobo in June 1821, though the royalists put up a rather pointless fight from Puerto Cabello for another two years. Gran Colombia existed for only a decade before splitting into three separate countries. Bolívar's dream of a unified republic fell apart before he died in 1830.

Caudillo Country

On his deathbed, Bolívar proclaimed: 'America is ungovernable. The man who serves a revolution plows the sea. This nation will fall inevitably into the hands of the unruly mob and then will pass into the hands of almost indistinguishable petty tyrants.' Unfortunately, he was not too far off the mark. Venezuela followed independence with nearly a century of rule by a series of strongmen known as *caudillos.* It wasn't until 1947 that the first democratic government was elected.

The first of the *caudillos,* General José Antonio Páez, controlled the country for 20 years (1830–48, 1861–63). Despite his tough rule, he established a certain political stability and strengthened the weak economy. The period that followed was an almost uninterrupted chain of civil wars that was only stopped by another long-lived dictator, General Antonio Guzmán Blanco (1870–88). He launched a broad program of reform, including a new constitution, and assured some temporary stability. Nonetheless his despotic rule triggered popular opposition, and when he stepped down the country fell back into civil war. Both Páez and Blanco died in exile (New York and Paris, respectively).

Twentieth Century Oil State

The first half of the 20th century was dominated by five successive military rulers from the Andean state of Táchira. The longest lasting and most ruthless was General Juan Vicente Gómez, who seized power in 1908 and didn't relinquish it until his death in 1935. Gómez phased out the parliament and

VENEZUELAN CULTURE

Venezuela is an intensely patriotic nation that's proud of its history. The War of Independence and the exploits of Simón Bolívar are still championed throughout the country, and Venezuelans love to see themselves on the world stage. Whether it's the crowning of its most recent Miss Universe or a major league baseball shutout, you can guarantee that the folks at home will be cheering.

However, unlike some neighboring South American nations, there are few defining factors of contemporary Venezuelan culture. Many attribute this to the fact that, as a petrol state, Venezuela has spent much of its existence consuming goods from abroad and not needing or bothering to produce much at home. But just like the oil pumped out of the country, Venezuela does produce raw materials and raw talent, including a prolific number of beauty queens and baseball players (six Miss Universe winners and current American League Most Valuable Player and World Series winner Jose Altuve).

Regardless of national ills and social tensions, Venezuelans are full of life and humor. People are open, willing to talk and not shy about striking up conversations with a stranger who becomes an instant *chamo* (pal or friend). The nature of the current moribund political and economic situation is something locals are always willing to discuss – and if you can find a single person with anything good to say about the government, consider yourself to have made a serious anthropological find.

crushed the opposition on his path to monopolizing power.

The discovery of oil in the 1910s helped the Gómez regime to put the national economy on its feet. By the late 1920s, Venezuela was the world's largest exporter of oil (and later became a cofounder of OPEC in 1960), which not only contributed to economic recovery but also enabled the government to pay off the country's entire foreign debt.

As in most petrol states, almost none of the oil wealth made its way to the common citizen. The vast majority continued to live in poverty. Fast oil money led to the neglect of agriculture and development of other types of production. It was easier to just import everything from abroad, which worked temporarily but proved unsustainable, as the country is learning at present.

After a short flirtation with democracy and a new constitution in 1947, the inevitable coup took place and ushered in the era of Colonel Marcos Pérez Jiménez. Once in control, he smashed the opposition and plowed oil money into public works and modernizing Caracas – not making many friends in the process.

Coups & Corruption

Pérez Jiménez was overthrown in 1958 by a coalition of civilians and military officers. The country returned to democratic rule, and Rómulo Betancourt was elected president. He enjoyed popular support and was the first democratically elected president

to complete his five-year term in office. There was a democratic transition of power though the country drifted to the right.

Oil money buoyed the following governments well into the 1970s. Not only did production of oil rise but, more importantly, the price quadrupled following the Arab–Israeli war in 1973. The nation went on a spending spree, building modern skyscrapers in Caracas and Maracaibo, and importing all sorts of luxury goods. But what goes up must come down and by the late 1970s the bust cycle was already in full swing, and the economy continued to fall apart through the 1980s.

In 1989 the government announced IMF-mandated austerity measures, and a subsequent protest over rising transportation costs sparked the *caracazo*, a series of nationwide riots quelled by military force that killed hundreds – maybe thousands – of citizens. Lingering instability brought two attempted coups d'état in 1992. The first, in February, was led by a little-known paratrooper named Colonel Hugo Chávez Frías. The second attempt, in November, was led by junior air-force officers. The air battle over Caracas, with warplanes flying between skyscrapers, gave the coup a cinematic dimension. Both attempts resulted in many deaths.

Corruption, bank failures and loan defaults plagued the government in the mid 1990s. In 1995 Venezuela was forced to devalue the currency by more than 70%. By the end of 1998, two-thirds of Venezuela's 23 million inhabitants were living below the poverty line.

A Left Turn

Nothing is better in political theater than a dramatic comeback. The 1998 election put Hugo Chávez, the leader of the 1992 failed coup, into the presidency. After being pardoned in 1994, Chávez embarked on an aggressive populist campaign: comparing himself to Bolívar, promising help (and handouts) to the poorest masses and positioning himself in opposition to the US-influenced free-market economy. He vowed to produce a great, if vague, 'peaceful and democratic social revolution.'

Since then, however, the Chávez 'social revolution' was anything but peaceful. Shortly after taking office, Chávez set about rewriting the constitution. The document was approved in a referendum in December 1999, granting him new and sweeping powers. The introduction of a package of new decree laws in 2001 was met with angry protests and was followed by a massive and violent strike in April 2002. It culminated in a coup d'état run by military leaders and sponsored by a business lobby, in which Chávez was forced to resign. He regained power two days later, but this only intensified the conflict.

While the popular tensions rose, in December 2002 the opposition called a general strike in an attempt to oust the president. The nationwide strike paralyzed the country, including its vital oil industry and a good part of the private sector. After 63 days, the opposition finally called off the strike, which had cost the country 7.6% of its GDP and further devastated the oil-based economy. Chávez again survived and claimed victory.

Twenty-First Century Socialism

National politics continued to be shaky until Chávez survived a 2004 recall referendum and consolidated his power. He won reelection in 2006 by a comfortable margin. After an unsuccessful attempt in 2007 to eliminate presidential term limits, Chávez won a referendum to amend the constitution in 2009, positioning him to run for reelection indefinitely.

Chávez expanded his influence beyond the borders of Venezuela, reaching out to leftist leaders across the continent, oil-producing countries in the Middle East, as well as China – an increasingly important South American trade partner. He allied himself with Cuba's Fidel Castro and Bolivia's Evo Morales, and stoked a combustible relationship with the US (US and Israeli citizens today require paid visas to enter Venezuela). Bad blood continues to this day between Venezuela and neighboring Colombia over accusations that Venezuela has been supporting the Fuerzas Armadas Revolucionarias de Colombia guerrillas (FARC; Colombia's main insurgent group) and shelters its members within its borders. The border has been closed at least once since 2015 due to this.

Supporters highlighted the country's programs for the country's poor. Under Chávez, government-sponsored projects called *misiones* (missions) provided adult literacy classes, free medical care and subsidized food. Large land holdings were broken up in land redistribution programs and given to subsistence farmers. Opponents criticized the centralization of power, intolerance of political dissent, a policy of nationalization that scared away international investment and the liberal use of government funds for partisan affairs.

After Chávez

Despite presiding over the slow collapse of the national economy, and lurching from crisis to crisis, Chávez' position seemed unassailable after a decade in power, in which it essentially became impossible to rise in politics unless you were a 'Chavista'. Having abolished presidential term limits, Chávez won a third term in power in 2012, albeit by a far smaller majority than in previous elections, and despite having been diagnosed with cancer in 2011, something long rumored but never announced to the electorate before the ballot. Indeed, Chávez had barely been seen in public in the run-up to the election, instead spending months in Cuba undergoing treatment and even missing his third inauguration as president.

Chávez died on March 5, 2013. Nicolás Maduro, the vice president (who had been anointed his successor by Chávez shortly before his death), was elected to the presidency in April 2013 by a wafer-thin majority in a special election where fairness was contested by his opponent, Henrique Capriles Radonski.

Understand South America

History

South America has a long and tumultuous history. It was the birthplace of one of the world's great empires, sadly brought to ruin upon the European arrival, and the destination for millions of men, women and children who were enslaved and brought over from Africa. The drive toward independence freed the continent from foreign rule, though it did little to address the yawning divide between rich and poor. Homegrown social justice movements were later crushed in the 20th century when military dictatorships ruled much of the continent.

First Peoples

There are various competing theories about how the indigenous peoples arrived in the Americas. Until recently, it was generally believed that early inhabitants traveled from present-day Siberia to Alaska over a land bridge across the Bering Strait. Some scholars estimate this epic migration occurred around 14,000 years ago. In the last several decades, new evidence of older sites in the southern reaches of South America has challenged the land-bridge theory. Early humans may have arrived by a combination of foot and boat travel following the coastline south as early as 23,000 years ago. In Monte Verde, Chile, scientists have discovered some of the oldest undisputed evidence of human occupation in the Americas. Apparently, early peoples were seafarers (or at least seafood lovers): among the artifacts found were 10 different species of seaweed.

The earliest peoples were nomadic hunter-gatherers who lived in small groups. Agriculture likely developed around 5000 BC with the planting of wild tubers such as manioc and sweet potato under systems of shifting cultivation. About the same time, highland people began to farm seed crops, such as beans, and to domesticate animals, such as the llama. One of South America's greatest foodstuffs is the humble but versatile potato, a root crop domesticated in the Andean highlands. Today, more than 6000 varieties of potato are cultivated there.

Complex societies first developed in the valleys of coastal Peru. Their growth was unsustainable, however – it's thought that the population of some of these valleys grew until all the cultivable land was occupied. The

The Chinchorro culture began mummifying their dead some 2000 years before the Egyptians. The oldest known mummy dates from around 5050 BC.

TIMELINE	14,000-23,000 BC	1493	1494
	Humans traveling from Asia, probably across the Bering land bridge, reach the Americas in one of the greatest human migration events in history.	Inca Huayna Cápac begins his reign, pushing his vast empire north to Colombia; his untimely death in 1525 – probably from smallpox – leaves the kingdom fatally divided.	Spain and Portugal sign the Treaty of Tordesillas, dividing colonized lands in the Americas between them. The eastern half of South America will 'belong' to Portugal.

need to expand into neighboring valleys led the inhabitants to organize, innovate and conquer. Not dissimilar from what would happen after the Europeans arrived, conquerors became the rulers and the conquered became their subjects, thus developing the social and economic hierarchies of these early states and beyond.

These embryonic societies ultimately developed into major civilizations, such as the Wari empire of the Peruvian central highlands, the Tiahuanaco culture of highland Bolivia, the Chimú of northern Coastal Peru and the Inca empire of Cuzco.

Inca Empire

According to legend, the Inca civilization was born when Manco Cápac and his sister Mama Ocllo, children of the sun, emerged from Lake Titicaca to establish a civilization in the Cuzco Valley. Whether Manco Cápac was a historical figure is up for debate, but what is certain is that the Inca civilization was established in the area of Cuzco at some point in the 12th century. The reign of the first several *incas* (kings) was largely unremarkable, and for a couple of centuries they remained a small, regional state.

Expansion took off in the early 15th century, when the ninth king, Inca Yupanqui, defended Cuzco – against incredible odds – from the invading Chanka people to the north. After the victory, he took on the boastful new name of Pachacutec (Transformer of the Earth) and spent the next 25 years bagging much of the Andes. Under his reign, the Incas grew from a regional fiefdom in the Cuzco Valley into a broad empire of about 10 million people known as Tawantinsuyo (Land of Four Quarters). The kingdom covered most of modern Peru, in addition to pieces of Ecuador, Bolivia and Chile. The empire traversed the Andes with more than 8000km of highways and managed to control peoples from 100 separate cultures and 20 different language groups for about a century. This was made more remarkable by the fact that the Incas, as an ethnicity, never numbered more than about 100,000.

At the height of their empire, the Incas ruled more than 12 million people across some 1 million sq km.

SETTLEMENTS IN THE AMAZON

New discoveries are reshaping the dominant thinking about pre-Columbian societies. The Amazon, once thought to be a wilderness incapable of supporting large populations, is now viewed as home to mound-building societies with some settlements containing as many as 100,000 inhabitants. At least 12% (and probably more) of the non-flooded Amazon forest is of anthropegenic origin (directly or indirectly altered by humans). Evidence of agriculture in the rainforest exists as far back as 4000 years ago, with as many as 140 different crops grown. Anthropologists have even found proof that early peoples used complex farming techniques to enrich the earth with microorganism-rich *terra preta* (black soil).

1548	1550	1807	1819
Wine comes to Chile via missionaries and conquistadores. Jesuit priests cultivated early vineyards of rustic pais grapes; today Chile has more than 120 wineries and international distribution.	Facing a shortage of labor (as the enslaved indigenous people die from introduced European diseases), Portugal turns to the African slave trade; open-air slave markets flourish in the slowly growing colony.	Napoleon invades Portugal; the Portuguese prince regent (later known as Dom João VI) and his entire court of 15,000 flee to Brazil. The royal coffers shower wealth upon Rio.	Simón Bolívar – crossing Los Llanos with an army of Venezuelans and Nueva Granadans from present-day Colombia – defeats the Spanish army at Boyacá; the Republic of Gran Colombia is founded.

Portuguese Arrival

The Portuguese were the first Europeans to set foot on the South American continent. In 1500 a fleet of 12 Portuguese ships carrying nearly 1200 men dropped anchor near what is today Porto Seguro. There they erected a cross and held Mass in the land they baptized Terra da Vera Cruz (Land of the True Cross) before taking to the waves once again. Over the next century, the Portuguese set up coastal colonies in present-day Salvador, Rio de Janeiro and other coastal areas. There they harvested the profitable *pau brasil* (brazilwood), which gave the country its name.

Over the following centuries a four-front war was waged on the indigenous way of life. It was a cultural war, as well as a physical, territorial and biological one. Many indigenous peoples fell victim to the *bandeirantes* – groups of roaming raiders who spent the 17th and 18th centuries exploring Brazil's interior, pillaging indigenous settlements as they went. Those who escaped such a fate were struck down by the illnesses which traveled from Europe, against which they had no natural resistance. Others were worked to death on sugar plantations.

Defeat of the Incas

The vast Inca Empire was in trouble even before the Spanish arrived in present-day Peru. Smallpox and other epidemics transmitted by European soldiers were sweeping through the entire American continent. Thousands of indigenous people were killed by the disease – including, in all likelihood, that of Inca emperor Huayna Cápac, who died in 1525.

Without a clear plan of succession, the emperor's untimely death left a power vacuum. The contest turned into a face-off between two of his many children: the Quito-born Atahualpa, who commanded his father's army in the north, and Huáscar, who was based in Cuzco. The ensuing struggle plunged the empire into a bloody civil war, reducing entire cities to rubble. Atahualpa emerged as the victor in April 1532. But the vicious nature of the conflict left the Incas with a lot of enemies throughout the Andes – which is why some tribes were so willing to cooperate with the Spanish when they arrived just five months later.

While the Portuguese were battling for control over the eastern half of the continent, the Spaniards set their sights on South America's Pacific coast. Following rumors of golden splendor in the interior, Francisco Pizarro led an exploratory journey to the north coast of Peru in 1528. There, near Tumbes, a crew of welcoming indigenous people offered them meat, fruit, fish and corn beer. To their delight, a cursory examination of the city revealed an abundance of silver and gold. The group quickly returned to Spain to court royal support for a bigger expedition.

Historical Reads

1491: New Revelations of the Americas before Columbus (Charles C Mann)

Last Days of the Incas (Kim MacQuarrie)

Open Veins of Latin America (Eduardo Galeano)

Prisoner without a Name, Cell without a Number (Jacobo Timerman)

1830	1834–35	1865–70	1879–83
Gran Colombia splits into Colombia (including modern-day Panama), Ecuador and Venezuela. Bolívar sends himself into exile; he dies in Santa Marta.	HMS *Beagle* explores South America with Charles Darwin on board; the planned two-year expedition lasts five, giving Darwin fodder for his later-developed theory of evolution.	Brazil, allied with Uruguay and Argentina, wages the 'War of the Triple Alliance' on Paraguay. South America's bloodiest conflict leaves untold thousands dead, and wipes out half of Paraguay's population.	Chile wages war against Peru and Bolivia over nitrate-rich lands in the Atacama Desert; Bolivia loses its coastline and Peru loses its southernmost region of Tarapacá.

They returned in September 1532, with a shipload of arms, horses and slaves, as well as a battalion of 168 troops. Tumbes, the rich town he had visited just four years earlier, had been devastated by epidemics, as well as the recent Inca civil war. Atahualpa, in the meantime, was in the process of making his way down from Quito to Cuzco to claim his hard-won throne. When the Spanish arrived, he was in the highland settlement of Cajamarca, enjoying the area's mineral baths.

Pizarro quickly deduced that the empire was in a fractious state. He and his men charted a course to Cajamarca and approached Atahualpa with royal greetings and promises of brotherhood. But the well-mannered overtures quickly devolved into a surprise attack that left thousands of Incas dead and Atahualpa a prisoner of war. (Between their horses, their armor and the steel of their blades, the Spanish were practically invincible against fighters armed only with clubs, slings and wicker helmets.)

In an attempt to regain his freedom, Atahualpa offered the Spanish a bounty of gold and silver. Thus began one of the most famous ransoms in history – with the Incas attempting to fill an entire room with the precious stuff in order to placate the unrelenting appetites of the Spanish. But it was never enough. The Spanish held Atahualpa for eight months before executing him with a garrote at the age of 31.

The Inca empire never recovered from this fateful encounter. The arrival of the Spanish brought on a cataclysmic collapse of the indigenous society. It is estimated that the local population – around 10 million when Pizarro arrived – was reduced to 600,000 within a century.

Guns, Germs & Steel, the Pulitzer Prize–winning book by Jared Diamond is a thoughtful, biological examination of why some European societies triumphed over so many others. The battle for Cajamarca and Atahualpa's capture by the Spanish is discussed at length.

The Dark Era of Slavery

The slave trade practiced by early European traders from the 1500s to 1866 enslaved as many as 12.5 million people – with just around 10.7 million surviving the grueling journey from Africa to the Americas. Only a fraction (around half a million) ended up in North America. The rest were destined for Latin America and the Caribbean with the majority (as many as six million) ending up in Brazil, most of them working on the backbreaking sugarcane plantations. They were torn from a variety of tribes in Angola, Mozambique and Guinea, as well as the Sudan and Congo. Whatever their origins and cultures, their destinations were identical: slave markets such as Salvador's Pelourinho or Belém's Mercado Ver-o-Peso. Elsewhere, smaller numbers of Africans were taken to Peru, Colombia, the Guianas and all along the Caribbean coast.

For those who survived the ordeal of removal and transfer, arrival in the Americas meant only continued suffering. A slave's existence was one of brutality and humiliation. Kind masters were the exception, not the rule, and labor on the plantations was relentless. Slaves were required to work as many as 17 hours each day, before retiring to the

Norwegian Thor Heyerdahl explored Easter Island while crossing the Pacific in the 1950s; it became the centerpiece of his theories about the South American origins of Polynesian civilization. For more details, read Aku-Aku and The Kon-Tiki Expedition.

1888	1890s	1967	1970
Slavery is abolished in Brazil, the last country in South America to do so.	With slavery abolished, Brazil opens its borders to meet its labor needs. Over the next four decades, millions arrive from Italy, Portugal, Spain, Germany and later Japan and other countries.	Argentine revolutionary Ernesto 'Che' Guevara, having failed to foment a peasant revolt in Bolivia, is executed by a US-backed military squad in the hamlet of La Higuera.	A 7.7-magnitude earthquake in northern Peru kills almost 80,000 people, leaves 140,000 injured and another 500,000 homeless.

squalid *senzala* (slave quarters), and with as many as 200 slaves packed into each dwelling, hygiene was a concept as remote as the distant coasts of Africa. Dysentery, typhus, yellow fever, malaria, tuberculosis and scurvy were rife; malnutrition a fact of life.

Syphilis also plagued a slave population sexually exploited by its masters. Sex slavery was so common that a large mixed-race population soon emerged. Off the plantations there were greater numbers of white men than white women, and many black or indigenous women were used by white men as live-in sex slaves.

Many slaves escaped from their masters to form *quilombos,* communities of runaway slaves that quickly spread across the countryside. The most famous, the Republic of Palmares, which survived through much of the 17th century, was home to some 20,000 people before it was destroyed by federal troops.

Most countries in South America banned slavery between 1816 and 1831, but in Brazil, it wasn't until 1888 that slavery was finally outlawed. Unsurprisingly, this didn't make a huge immediate difference to the welfare of the 800,000 freed slaves, who were largely illiterate and unskilled. Thousands were cast into the streets without any kind of infrastructure to support them. Many died, while others flooded to Brazil's urban centers, desperately in search of jobs.

Critics point out that the end of slavery didn't really bring justice to newly freed people. Gross inequalities continued to plague South America up to the present day. One 2015 study in Brazil showed that people of color earn 59% of what whites earn, and that 132% more Afro-Brazilians than whites are killed by violence each year.

One of Brazil's great folk heroes is Chico Rei, an African king enslaved and brought to work in the mines, who managed to buy his freedom and later the freedom of his tribe.

The first *favela* (slum or shantytown) appeared on Rio's landscape in 1897, but it wasn't until 1994 that the communities (which today number over 600) were included on maps.

Independence

By the early 19th century, *criollos* (creoles, born in South America to Spanish parents) in many Spanish colonies had grown increasingly dissatisfied with their lack of administrative power and the crown's heavy taxes – leading to revolutions all over the continent. Argentine revolutionary José de San Martín led independence campaigns in Argentina and Chile (1818), before sailing up the coast to take Lima in 1821. From the opposite direction came Simón Bolívar, the Venezuelan revolutionary who had been leading independence fights in Venezuela, Colombia and Ecuador.

The two liberators met in Guayaquil, Ecuador, in 1822. At this famous meeting, the apolitical San Martín found himself in conflict with Bolívar, who had strong political ambitions. San Martín considered the installation of a powerful leader, even a monarch, as essential to avoid the disintegration of Peru, while Bolívar insisted on a constitutional republic. In a complicated exchange, which aroused ill-feeling in both camps, Bolívar

1970	1973–89	1976–83	1992
Chile's Salvador Allende becomes the world's first democratically elected Marxist president. Radical social reform follows; the state takes control of private enterprises and there is massive income redistribution.	Following a military coup, General Augusto Pinochet takes charge of Chile. He dissolves Congress, prohibits nearly all political activity and rules by decree.	Under the leadership of General Jorge Videla, a military junta takes control of Argentina, launching the country into the 'Dirty War.' In eight years an estimated 30,000 people 'disappear.'	Thousands of indigenous protesters seeking land reform march in Quito, Ecuador, on the 500th anniversary of Columbus' arrival. In ensuing negotiations they are granted title to 2.5 million acres in Amazonia.

won the day and San Martín returned to the south. In the long run, both were disappointed. The proliferation of *caudillos* (local warlords) set a deplorable pattern for most of the 19th century.

Ever in its own world, Brazil followed quite a different path to independence. Unlike its neighboring countries, Brazil had a European monarch living within its borders in the early 1800s. Brazil became a temporary sanctuary to the Portuguese royal family, who fled from the advance of Napoleon in Iberia in 1807. The prince regent – and future king, Dom João VI – fell in love with Rio, naming it the capital of the United Kingdom of Portugal, Brazil and the Algarves. His affection for Brazil was so strong that he didn't want to return to Portugal even after Napoleon's defeat at Waterloo in 1815. He finally returned to Europe six years later, leaving his son Pedro as prince regent. When the Portuguese parliament attempted to restore Brazil to its previous status as subservient colony, Dom Pedro rebelled and declared Brazil independent, declaring himself the country's head as Emperor Dom Pedro I. Portugal was too weak to fight its favorite son, so without spilling blood, Brazil attained its independence in 1822.

Military Dictatorships

The 20th century was a tumultuous period for South America, with political turmoil and economic crises paving the way for the rise of military dictatorships. The social unrest that followed the Great Depression of 1929 provided justification for the army to intervene in countries across the continent. In Argentina, the pro-fascist general José Félix Uriburu seized control during a military coup in 1930, ushering in the so-called Infamous Decade. Likewise the 1930s saw military coups and repressive regimes rise in Peru and Chile. In Brazil, it was the era of the autocratic Getulio Vargas, when rival political parties were banned, the press was muzzled and opponents were imprisoned.

Unfortunately, this was just the beginning, with far more horrifying dictatorships on the horizon. The 1960s and 1970s were an even darker period in South America when military dictatorships ruled in Argentina, Bolivia, Brazil, Chile, Paraguay, Peru, Suriname and Uruguay. Student- and worker-led movements crying out for social justice were met with increasing brutality.

In the late 1960s and '70s in Argentina, anti-government feeling was rife and street protests often exploded into all-out riots. Armed guerrilla organizations emerged as radical opponents of the military, the oligarchies and US influence in Latin America. In 1976, the army general Jorge Rafael Videla seized power, ushering in a bloody seven-year period known as the Dirty War. Security forces went about the country arresting, torturing and

HISTORY MILITARY DICTATORSHIPS

Robert Harvey's extremely readable *Liberators: South America's Struggle for Independence* (2002) tells the epic history of colonial Latin America through larger-than-life heroes and swashbucklers such as O'Higgins, San Martín and Lord Cochrane.

In his magic realism novel *One Hundred Years of Solitude* (1967), Gabriel García Márquez depicts the back-and-forth brutality of Liberal and Conservative rivalries and vendettas in ongoing conflicts from 1885 to 1902 in the fictional village of Macondo.

1998	2001	2010	2014
Hugo Chavez becomes president of Venezuela. He invests in social programs, while also nationalizing industries, centralizing power and crushing dissent.	Unemployment reaches 18.3% as a vast financial crisis hits Argentina. Interim president Duhalde devalues the peso and defaults on US$140 billion in debt, the biggest default in world history.	The world is captivated by the saga of 33 Chilean miners trapped for 69 days 700m underground near Copiapó - the longest entrapment in history. Chile rejoices as all are ultimately rescued.	Brazil hosts the 2014 FIFA World Cup, spending around US$12 billion in preparation for the event, which is staged at 12 different cities across the country.

killing anyone on their hit list of suspected leftists. As many as 30,000 people were 'disappeared' – that is, murdered.

In Chile, there was hope for a brighter future when socialist candidate Salvador Allende was elected in 1970. This was soon crushed, however, when Augusto Pinochet led a coup in 1973. Ruling until 1989, he would become Latin America's most notorious dictator, with thousands of suspected leftists jailed, tortured and executed, and hundreds of thousands fleeing the country.

Meanwhile in Brazil, military dictators ran the show from 1964 to 1984. Though not as brutal as the Chilean or Argentine regimes, it was still a period when dissent was crushed, political parties were banned and the media was muzzled. Things remained grim throughout South America until the early 1990s when democracy at last returned to most of the continent.

Hectór Olivera's film *Funny Dirty Little War* (1983) is an unsettling but excellent black comedy set in a fictitious town just before the 1976 military coup in Argentina.

The 21st Century

Toward the end of the 1990s and into the 21st century, things took a remarkable turn for the better in South America. A rising middle class, falling poverty rates and strong economies were hallmarks of the early 2000s. As the continent veered to the left, wage disparities fell slightly and social justice seemed to be the hot topic of the day.

Progressives like former Brazilian president Lula helped pave the way, demonstrating that you could both grow an economy and help lift people out of poverty. Machismo took a blow, with the first female presidents in South America helping to break down barriers. Cristina Kirchner of Argentina, Dilma Rousseff of Brazil and Michelle Bachelet of Chile all recently served as presidents of some of South America's largest economies. Leaders from indigenous backgrounds also emerged on the political stage, including Evo Morales of Bolivia and Alejandro Toledo of Peru.

The Falklands War is still a touchy subject in Argentina. If the subject comes up, try to call them the 'Malvinas' instead of the 'Falklands.'

On the downside, political corruption remains pervasive in South America. In Brazil, one of the largest scandals in the nation's history (a staggering US$3-billion bribery and money-laundering scheme) brought down many politicians and heads of industry, and led to the impeachment of President Dilma Rousseff in 2016.

In recent years South American economies have struggled with falling currencies and rising unemployment. Rural poverty remains a gripping problem in every country in South America, with many families still struggling with basic needs: adequate nutrition, health care and clean water. And one in seven still live in extreme poverty, subsisting on less than US$2.50 per day.

2015	2016	2018	2019
Pope Francis visits Bolivia and humbly begs forgiveness for the grave sins committed against indigenous peoples of America in the name of God.	Rio hosts the Summer Olympics, becoming the first city in South America to host the big event. The city spends US$13 billion in preparations, adding a new metro line, a downtown light rail and new museums.	Facing scandals and impeachment, Peruvian President Pedro Pablo Kuczynski resigns from office and is succeeded by Vice President Martín Vizcarra.	Right-wing Jair Bolsonaro is sworn as president of Brazil. Along with Piñera of Chile, Macri of Argentina, and Duque of Colombia, Bolsonaro represents a drastic turn to the right with the rise of ultraconservative populists.

People & Culture

There are so many layers to South American culture. Religion is a key component of life on the continent, where Christianity, indigenous beliefs and African religions have all shaped identity. South America is also the birthplace of great music including samba, tango, Andean sounds and countless other regional genres. While religion and music can be a great unifier across the socioeconomic divide, there is still a huge gulf between haves and have-nots in this highly stratified society.

Multiculturalism

South America boasts astonishing diversity. The continent has been shaped by the original indigenous inhabitants, European colonists and Africans brought over as slaves to toil in the plantations and mines. The level of intermixing varies greatly from country to country, which has led to the relative diversity or homogeneity of the population.

Immigration has also added to the complex ethnic tapestry of the continent. For decades, the US was a major destination for migrants from South America. These days, there's much more migration happening internally (ie between South American countries), with Brazil, Argentina and Chile attracting the largest numbers of migrants, largely from neighboring countries. There are also complicated dynamics at work in each of the continent's 13 countries. Ecuador for instance, with a population of just 16 million, has an estimated two million emigrants, living in the US, Italy and Spain; in the latter, they make up the largest contingent of Latin Americans. On the flipside, Ecuador has seen an influx of refugees (in the 1980s and 1990s) fleeing from conflicts in neighboring Colombia, and opportunity-seeking migrants from Peru.The situation, however, remains quite fluid. Since 2008, with improved job opportunities at home, a growing number of Ecuadorians are choosing to return home.

In the 19th century Brazil and Argentina saw mass immigration from Europe: Spaniards, Italians, Germans and Eastern Europeans were the most common immigrants moving to the Americas. Brazil also welcomed immigrants from Japan, Portugal and the Middle East. They worked in a wide variety of fields, from coffee plantations and farming to heavy industry in the continent's growing cities. The influx of new arrivals continued well into the 20th century, with tumult in Europe causing the flight of Jews fleeing persecution from the Nazis, followed by Nazis looking to avoid being put on trial for war crimes, in addition to Italians and others escaping their ravaged cities in the postwar period.

Lifestyles

No matter where you go in South America, you'll likely encounter a yawning divide between rich and poor. Modern-day South Americans inherited a highly stratified society from the slave-owning European colonists, and this dispiriting chasm persists centuries later between the haves and have-nots of both urban and rural society. At the bottom of the heap are those struggling in low-wage jobs in the city, or scraping out a meager existence in the countryside – many are barely able to put food

One of the most famous figures from the Amazon is Raoni Metuktire, chief of the Kayapó people. Born in 1930, Chief Raoni was an early advocate for indigenous rights and the preservation of the Amazon, and his hard-fought campaigns have brought worldwide attention to the plight of the rainforest and its inhabitants.

Dozens of uncontacted indigenous groups still live in the Amazon. In 2007, 89 Metyktire suddenly emerged in a village in Pará, the first time this particular group (feared dead) had been encountered since 1950.

on the table. Those who live in rural areas are practically invisible to the urban middle and upper classes.

The middle and upper class live in comfortable apartments or houses, with all the trappings of the developed world, including good health care in private clinics, cars, vacations away and easy access to the latest gadgets and trends (though iPhones and laptops are pricier here). Owing to low wages, maids are common, even among the middle class. Crime is of high concern, and those that can afford it live in high-security buildings or gated residential complexes.

The divide is greatest in struggling countries like Bolivia, where nearly half the population lives below the poverty line. There many live without running water, electricity and heat, and the threat of illness looms high over children – with the majority of childhood deaths associated with malnutrition and poverty.

Religion

Christianity

The dominant religion in South America is Roman Catholicism, a legacy from the early Spanish and Portuguese colonizers. The number of followers varies by region, with no small degree of complexity from country to country (in Argentina, for instance, 92% of the population call themselves Catholic, though less than 20% practice regularly). On average though, 70% or more of each country's population professes to be Roman Catholic. The ranks are declining from year to year, and many people (particularly in urban areas) merely turn up to church for the basics: baptism, marriage and burial. Nevertheless, the church still has a strong visible presence here. Nearly every city, town or village has a central church or cathedral, and the calendar is loaded with Catholic holidays and celebrations.

Evangelical Christianity, meanwhile, is booming. All across the continent, especially in poor communities where people are most desperate, simple, recently built churches are full of worshippers. The religion has done particularly well here, with converts from Catholicism often citing a more personal relationship with God, as well as receiving more direct guidance in the realm of health, jobs and living a moral life. The firebrand Pentecostal branch attracts many new followers, with its emphasis on divine healing, speaking in tongues and receiving direct messages from God. With the current growth of the Evangelical church, some predict that the majority of South America will be Protestant by 2050.

Indigenous Beliefs

Among indigenous peoples, allegiance to Catholicism was often a clever veneer adopted to disguise traditional beliefs ostensibly forbidden by the church. In parts of the interior, the Amazon and the Andes, shamanism and animism still flourish. There is also a strong belief in powerful spirits that inhabit the natural world – the sky, mountains, lightning and the wind. Some groups, like the Andean Aymara, practice a syncretic religion that pays equal homage to both deities and Catholic saints. They may attend mass, baptisms and saint's day celebrations, while also paying respect to Pachamama (Mother Earth) come harvest time. The old Inca celebration of Inti Raymi (Festival of the Sun) is celebrated with fervor in some parts of the Andes. It happens on the winter solstice (late June) and commemorates the mythical birth of the Inca.

African Religions

Enslaved peoples brought over ancient African religions to the Americas, which were adapted over the centuries. The best known and most orthodox is Candomblé, which arrived in Brazil via the Nago, Yoruba and

Una Mujer Fantástica (2017), directed by the Chilean filmmaker Sebastián Lelio, is a powerful film about a transgender woman navigating the deep-seated prejudices of society. It stars Daniela Vega, the first openly transgender person in history to be a presenter at the Academy Awards ceremony.

It was a Peruvian priest, Gustavo Gutiérrez, who first articulated the principles of liberation theology – the theory that links Christian thought to social justice – in 1971. He now teaches in the US.

PROTEST SONGS

South America went through a dark epoch in the 20th century, when military dictatorships controlled vast swaths of the continent. Crying out against the oppression were a handful of brave singers and songwriters who targeted the atrocities being committed, and led the call for social justice. The socially progressive folk music of *nueva canción* (literally, 'new song'), which emerged from Latin America in the 1960s, flourished in Chile during the dictatorship of Pinochet and soon spread to other countries. Singer Víctor Jara, who sang of peace and social justice, paid for his activist views with his life, when he was tortured and murdered by the Chilean military in 1973.

In Argentina, singer Mercedes Sosa was one of the leading figures of the protest movement, and became known as 'the voice of the voiceless' for her courageous performances. Antagonized by Argentina's military rulers, she was banished from the country in 1979, and returned in 1982 shortly before the collapse of the military regime.

In Brazil, one of the seminal figures of protest against the military (in power from 1964 to 1984) was Chico Buarque, considered one of the country's finest songwriters. His poetic lyrics were cleverly worded and used cryptic analogies that were often overlooked by military censors. Songs like 'A Pesar de Você' (In Spite of You) became national songs of protest for social justice.

Jeje peoples. It later found root in Bahia, where it is still practiced today. Candomblé denotes a dance in honor of the gods, and indeed trancelike dancing is an essential part of the religion. Afro-Brazilian rituals are directed by Candomblé priests, the *pai de santo* or *mãe de santo* (literally 'saint's father' or 'saint's mother'), and practiced in a *casa de santo* or *terreiro* (house of worship).

The religion centers upon the *orixás*. Like the gods in Greek mythology, each *orixá* has a unique personality and history. Although *orixás* are divided into male and female types, there are some that can switch from one sex to the other, such as Logunedé, the son of two male gods, or Oxumaré, who is male for six months of the year and female for the other six months. (Candomblé, not surprisingly, is much more accepting of homosexuality and bisexuality than other religions.)

Candomblé followers believe that every person has a particular deity watching over them, and followers give food or other offerings to their respective *orixá*.

Music

South America has given the world a rich musical heritage. This is the birthplace of tango, samba, bossa nova and haunting Andean folk music, but this is just the beginning of the dizzying soundtrack, of wide-ranging rhythms with roots in Europe, Africa and indigenous pre-Columbian villages.

Tango

Music plays a key part in festivities across the continent, and it also takes center stage when it comes to nightlife in many cities. The tango is deeply linked to Buenos Aires (though the music also has ties to lesser-known Montevideo in Uruguay). It emerged from the country's bordellos in the late 19th century, though it didn't become mainstream until Carlos Gardel helped popularize the songs in the 1920s and 1930s. Although Gardel was born in France, he was brought by his destitute single mother to Buenos Aires when he was three years old. In his youth he entertained neighbors with his rapturous singing, then went on to establish a successful performing career. He single-handedly helped bring tango out of the tenement and onto the world stage. He died tragically in a plane crash at the height of his career and was mourned around the world.

Of the infinite varieties of music that exist all over Peru, the Afro-Peruvian tunes from the coast are perhaps the grooviest. For an excellent primer, listen to the David Byrne–produced compilation *Afro-Peruvian Classics: The Soul of Black Peru*.

Another seminal figure in the tango world was Astor Piazzolla, who moved the genre from the dance halls into the concert halls. Tango nueva, as it was called when it emerged in the 1950s, was given a newfound respect, with its blend of jazz and classical elements and new forms of melodic structures. Piazzolla also paved the way for the tango fusion, which emerged in the 1970s and continues to this day with *tango electrónico* groups such as Gotan Project Bajofondo Tango Club and Tanghetto.

Samba & Bossa Nova

The birth of modern Brazilian music essentially began with the birth of samba, first heard in the early 20th century in a Rio neighborhood near present-day Praça Onze. Here, Bahian immigrants formed a tightly knit community in which traditional African customs thrived – music, dance and the Candomblé religion. Such an atmosphere nurtured the likes of Pixinguinha, one of samba's founding fathers, as well as Donga, one of the composers of 'Pelo Telefone,' the first recorded samba song (1917) and an enormous success at the then-fledgling Carnaval.

Samba continued to evolve in the homes and *botequims* (neighborhood bars) around Rio. The 1930s are known as the golden age of samba. Sophisticated lyricists such as Dorival Caymmi and Noel Rosa wrote popular songs featuring sentimental lyrics and an emphasis on melody (rather than rhythm), foreshadowing the later advent of cool bossa nova. The 1930s were also the golden age of samba songwriting for Carnaval.

In the 1950s came bossa nova (literally, 'new wave'), sparking a new era of Brazilian music. Bossa nova's founders – songwriter and composer Antônio Carlos (Tom) Jobim and guitarist João Gilberto, in association with the lyricist-poet Vinícius de Moraes – slowed down and altered the basic samba rhythm to create a more intimate, harmonic style. Bossa nova was also associated with the new class of university-educated Brazilians. Its lyrics reflected the optimistic mood of the middle class in the 1950s, and by the following decade it had become a huge international success.

Andean Sounds

The breathy, mournful songs played by groups across the western half of the continent (from Chile up to Venezuela) are all part of the legacy of Andean folk music. Its roots date back to pre-Inca times when music was largely played during religious ceremonies. It was viewed as a sacred art with connections to the divine world, and it paid homage to the spirits that were believed to inhabit the natural world.

Musical styles vary from region to region (with four-, five-, six- or seven-note scales), but the instruments are often quite similar. Panpipes are a staple: usually made of bamboo, these instruments consist of a single or double row of hollow tubes, and come in a bewildering variety of sizes. These are often accompanied by a smaller flutelike *quena,* a bass drum and a stringed instrument (an influence adopted from Europe), such as the 10-string *charango,* which is similar to a mandolin. Prior to the Spaniards, wind and percussion were the dominant sounds – fitting for a region of fiery volcanoes and bone-chilling gales that blow across the highlands.

Bossa Nova: The Story of the Brazilian Music that Seduced the World, by Ruy Castro, is an excellent book that captures the vibrant music and its backdrop of 1950s Rio.

Cumbia villera is a relatively recent musical phenomenon: a fusion of cumbia and gangsta posturing with a punk edge and reggae overtones. Born of Buenos Aires' shantytowns, its aggressive lyrics deal with marginalization, poverty, drugs, sex and the Argentine economic crisis.

Survival Guide

Directory A–Z

Accessible Travel

In general, South America is not well set up for travelers with disabilities, but the more modernized Cono Sur (Southern Cone; a collective term for Argentina, Chile, Uruguay and parts of Brazil and Paraguay) countries are more accommodating – notably Chile, Argentina and the bigger cities of Brazil. For city travel, Santiago is the most accessible city in South America. Things are slowly improving in some places, particularly in Ecuador, which now has a president who uses a wheelchair.

Unfortunately, cheap local lodgings probably won't be well equipped to deal with physically challenged travelers; air travel will be more feasible than most local buses (although this isn't impossible); and well-developed tourist attractions will be more accessible than off-the-beaten-track destinations. Start your research with the following websites:

Lonely Planet (http://lptravel. to/AccessibleTravel) Free Accessible Travel guides.

Emerging Horizons (www. emerginghorizons.com) Features well-written articles and regular columns full of handy advice.

Go Wheel the World (http://go wheeltheworld.com) Chile-based outfit that leads excellent adventure tours. Check the website for inspiring documentaries about traveling off the beaten path.

Mobility International (www. miusa.org) This US-based outfit advises travelers with disabilities and runs educational-exchange programs overseas.

Royal Association for Disability and Rehabilitation (www. disabilityrightsuk.org) Good resource for travelers from the UK.

Society for Accessible Travel & Hospitality (www.sath.org) Good, general travel information; based in the USA.

Accommodations

Costs vary from country to country, with Andean countries (especially Bolivia) being the cheapest (from around US$10 per night) and Chile, Brazil, Argentina and the Guianas the costliest (upwards of US$30).

Hostels

Albergues (hostels) have become increasingly popular throughout South America and, as throughout the world, are great places to socialize with other travelers. Across South America, there are around 110 official *albergue juveniles* (youth hostels), where you can get a small discount if you're a card-carrying member of Hostelling International–American Youth Hostel (HI-USA).

Hotels

When it comes to hotels, both terminology and criteria vary. The costliest in the genre are *hoteles* (hotels) proper. A step down in price are *hostales* (small hotels or guesthouses). The cheapest places are *hospedajes, casas de huéspedes, residenciales, alojamientos* and *pensiones*. A room in these places includes a bed with (hopefully) clean sheets and a blanket, maybe a table and chair and sometimes a fan. Showers and toilets are generally shared; there may not be hot water. Cleanliness varies widely, but many places are remarkably tidy. In some areas, especially southern Chile, the cheapest places may be *casas familiares*, family houses whose hospitality makes them excellent value.

In Brazil, Argentina and some other places, prices often include breakfast, the quality of which is usually directly related to the room price.

BOOK YOUR STAY ONLINE

For more accommodations reviews by Lonely Planet authors, check out http://lonelyplanet.com/hotels/. You'll find independent reviews, as well as recommendations on the best places to stay. Best of all, you can book online.

Hot-water supplies are often erratic, or may be available only at certain hours of the day. It's something to ask about (and consider paying extra for), especially in the highlands and far south, where it gets cold.

When showering, beware the electric shower head, an innocent-looking unit that heats cold water with an electric element. Don't touch the shower head or anything metal when the water is on or you may get shocked – never strong enough to throw you across the room, but hardly pleasant.

Dormitory prices are for rooms with shared bathrooms, while room prices include private bathrooms, unless otherwise noted.

Camping

Camping is an obvious choice in parks and reserves and is a useful budget option in pricier countries such as Chile. Bring all your own gear. While camping gear is available in large cities and in trekking and activities hubs, it's expensive and choices are usually minimal. Camping gear can be rented in areas with substantial camping and trekking action (eg the Lake District, Mendoza and Huaraz), but quality is sometimes dubious.

An alternative to tent camping is staying in *refugios* (simple structures within parks and reserves), where a basic bunk and kitchen access are usually provided. For climbers, most summit attempts involve staying in a *refugio*.

Children

In general, wherever you roam across South America, you'll find a warm welcome when traveling with children. Family culture is strong in Latin America, and locals generally do their best to accommodate young travelers. That said, infrastructure can be lacking. Baby-change facilities are rare outside of big cities. And

pushing strollers (prams) around can be a challenge amid broken pavements and missing sidewalks (a wearable baby carrier is a better idea). Public transport can often be quite crowded. For insider tips check out Lonely Planet's *Travel with Children*.

Practicalities

➡ Disposable diapers (nappies) are found in big-city supermarkets, but variety may be limited, so come prepared.

➡ Cribs (cots) aren't widely available in hotel rooms.

➡ High chairs are found in many midrange and top-end restaurants.

➡ Children get in free or half price to most major sights around South America.

➡ Baby formula isn't always available outside major cities; bring your own supply.

Customs Regulations

Customs vary slightly from country to country, but you can generally bring in personal belongings, camera gear, laptops, handheld devices and other travel-related gear. All countries prohibit the export (just as home countries prohibit the import) of archaeological items and goods made from rare or endangered animals. Avoid carrying plants, seeds, fruits and fresh meat products across borders.

Discount Cards

An HI-USA membership card can be useful in some places (particularly in Brazil, where there are dozens of HI-affiliated lodging options).

An International Student Identity Card (ISIC) can provide discounted admission to archaeological sites and museums. It may also entitle you to reductions on bus, train and air tickets. In less developed countries, student

discounts are rare, although high-ticket items such as the entrance to Machu Picchu (discounted nearly 50% for ISIC holders under 26) may be reduced. In some countries, such as Argentina, almost any form of university identification will suffice where discounts are offered.

Electricity

Electricity is not standard across South America. Voltage ranges from 100 to 240V, with the most common plug types being flat-pronged American style and rounded European style.

Embassies & Consulates

As a visitor in a South American country, it's important to realize what your own embassy – the embassy of the country of which you are a citizen – can and cannot do. Generally speaking, it won't be much help in emergencies where you're even remotely at fault. Remember that you are bound by the laws of the country you are in. Your embassy will not be sympathetic if you end up in jail after committing a crime locally, even if such actions are legal in your own country.

In genuine emergencies you may get some assistance, but only if other channels have been exhausted. For example, if you have all your money and documents stolen, it might assist in getting a new passport, but a loan for onward travel will be out of the question.

For embassy and consulate addresses and phone numbers, see each country's Directory section.

Food

South America has staggering variety when it comes to cuisine. Every country has its own specialties; and within countries you'll find a great range (with coastal recipes quite different from cooking traditions in the interior). The capitals and big cities of South America are all fertile grounds for foodies, though increasingly, you can also find fantastic meals in smaller towns. Memorable meals can sometimes be had at markets, as well.

Insurance

A travel-insurance policy covering theft, loss, accidents and illness is highly recommended. Many policies include a card with toll-free numbers for 24-hour assistance, and it's good practice to carry it with you. Note that some policies compensate travelers for misrouted or lost luggage. Baggage insurance is worth its price in peace of mind. Also check that the coverage includes worst-case scenarios: ambulances, evacuations or an emergency flight home. Some policies specifically exclude 'dangerous activities,' such as scuba diving, motorcycling or even trekking. If such activities are on your agenda, avoid this sort of policy.

There are a wide variety of policies available and your travel agent will be able to make recommendations. The policies handled by student-travel organizations usually offer good value. If a policy offers lower and higher medical-expense options, the low-expenses policy should be OK for South America – medical costs are not nearly as high here as elsewhere in the world.

If you have baggage insurance and need to make a claim, the insurance company may demand a receipt as proof that you bought the stuff in the first place. Make a list of stolen items and their value. At the police station, you complete a *denuncia* (statement), a copy of which

is given to you for your insurance claim.

Worldwide travel insurance is available at www.lonely planet.com/bookings. You can buy, claim and extend online anytime – even if you're already on the road.

Internet Access

Wi-fi access is widely available, with many hostels, cafes and guesthouses offering free wi-fi. In contrast, internet cafes are a rarity.

Language Courses

Spanish-language courses are available in many South American cities, with Cuzco and Arequipa (Peru), Quito and Cuenca (Ecuador) and Buenos Aires being some of the best. For Portuguese, Rio de Janeiro is a great place to spend some time studying. For Quechua and Aymara, try Cochabamba (Bolivia) or Cuzco.

Legal Matters

In city police stations, an English-speaking interpreter is rare. In most cases you'll either have to speak the local language or provide an interpreter. Some cities have a tourist police service, which can be more helpful.

If you are robbed, photocopies (even better, certified copies) of original passports, visas and air tickets and careful records of credit-card numbers and traveler's checks will prove invaluable during replacement procedures. Replacement passport applications are usually referred to your home country, so it helps to leave a copy of your passport details with someone back home.

LGBT+ Travelers

Buenos Aires, Rio de Janeiro, São Paulo and Santiago are the most gay-friendly cities,

though gay couples are openly out only in certain neighborhoods. Elsewhere on the continent, where public displays of affection by same-sex couples may get negative reactions, do as the locals do – be discreet to avoid problems.

Despite a growing number of publications and websites devoted to gay travel, few have specific advice on South America. One exception is Purple Roofs (www.purple roofs.com), an excellent guide to gay-friendly accommodations throughout South America.

Maps

International Travel Maps & Books (www.itmb.com) produces a range of excellent maps of Central and South America. For the whole continent, it has a reliable reference map at a 1:4,000,000 scale and a commemorative edition of its classic 1:5,000,000 map. The maps are huge for road use, but they're helpful for pretrip planning. More detailed ITMB maps are available for the Amazon Basin and every country in South America. All are available on the ITMB website.

Maps of the South American continent as a whole are widely available; check any well-stocked map or travel bookstore.

Money

Fraud
Unfortunately, ATM-card cloning is a big worry in Brazil (p439), and your account can be drained of thousands of dollars before you even realize it.

ATMs
ATMs are available in most cities and large towns, and are almost always the most convenient, reliable and economical way of getting cash. The rate of exchange

is usually as good as any bank or legal money changer. Many ATMs are connected to the Cirrus or Plus network, but many countries prefer one over the other. If your ATM card gets swallowed by a machine, generally the only thing you can do is call your bank and cancel the card. Although such events are rare, it's well worth having an extra ATM card (to a different account), should something go wrong.

If possible, sign up with a bank that doesn't charge a fee for out-of-network ATM withdrawals. Also, try to find a bank that offers a low exchange-rate fee (1% to 2%). Before hitting the road, call your bank, informing them of your travel plans – that way the bank won't put a hold on foreign withdrawals while you're on the road.

Many ATMs will accept a personal identification number (PIN) of only four digits; find out whether this applies to the specific countries you're traveling to before heading off.

Bargaining
Bargaining is accepted and expected when contracting long-term accommodations and when shopping for craft goods in markets. Haggling is a near sport in the Andean countries, with patience, humor and respect serving as the ground rules of the game. Bargaining is much less common in the Cono Sur.

Cash
It's convenient to have a small wad of US dollars tucked away (in US$20 denominations and less; US$100 bills are difficult to exchange). US currency is by far the easiest to exchange throughout South America. Of course, unlike traveler's checks, nobody will give you a refund for lost or stolen cash. When you're about to cross from one country to another, it's handy to change some cash. Trying to exchange worn notes can be a hassle, so procure crisp bills before setting out.

In some countries, especially in rural areas, *cambio* (change) can be particularly hard to come by. Businesses even occasionally refuse to sell you something if they can't or don't want to change your note. So break down those larger bills whenever you have the opportunity, such as at busy restaurants, banks and larger businesses.

Credit Cards
Visa and MasterCard are accepted at most large stores, travel agencies and better hotels and restaurants. Credit-card purchases sometimes attract an extra *recargo* (surcharge) on the price (from 2% to 10%), but they are usually billed to your account at favorable exchange rates. Some banks issue cash advances on major credit cards. The most widely accepted card is Visa, followed by MasterCard (those with UK Access should insist on its affiliation with MasterCard). American Express is accepted at fewer places.

Exchanging Money
Traveler's checks and foreign cash can be changed at *casas de cambio* (currency-exchange offices) or banks. Rates are usually similar, but *casas de cambio* are quicker, less bureaucratic and open longer hours.

It is preferable to bring money in US dollars, although banks and *casas de cambio* in capital cities will change euros, pounds sterling, Japanese yen and other major currencies. Changing these currencies in smaller towns and on the street is next to impossible.

Traveler's Checks
Traveler's checks are not nearly as convenient as ATM cards, and you may have difficulty cashing them – even at banks. High commissions (from 3% to upwards of 10%) also make them an unattractive option. If you do take traveler's checks, American Express is the most widely accepted brand, while Visa, Thomas Cook and Citibank are the next best options. To facilitate replacement in case of theft, keep a record of check numbers and the original bill of sale in a safe place. Even with proper records, replacement can be a tedious, time-intensive process.

Photography
Lonely Planet's Guide to Travel Photography is full of helpful tips for photography while on the road.

Photographing People
Ask for permission before photographing individuals, particularly indigenous people. Paying folks for their portrait is a personal decision; in most cases, the subject will tell you right off the going rate for a photo.

Restrictions
Some tourist sites charge an additional fee for tourists with cameras. Don't take photos of military installations, military personnel or security-sensitive places like police stations. Such activities may be illegal and could even endanger your life. In most churches, flash photography (and sometimes any photography) is not allowed.

Post
International postal rates can be quite expensive. Generally, important mail and parcels should be sent by registered or certified service; otherwise, they may go missing. Sending parcels can be awkward: often an *aduana* (customs) officer must inspect the contents before a postal clerk can accept them, so wait to seal your package until after it has been checked. Most post offices

have a parcels window, usually signed *encomiendas* (parcels). The place for posting overseas parcels is sometimes different from the main post office.

UPS, FedEx, DHL and other private postal services are available in some countries, but are prohibitively expensive.

Safe Travel

There are potential dangers to traveling in South America, but with sensible precautions, you are unlikely to encounter serious problems. Your greatest threats will likely be reckless drivers, pollution, fiesta fireworks and low-hanging objects (watch your head!).

Confidence Tricks & Scams

Keep your wits about you if nefarious substances (mustard, bird droppings, human excrement) are thrown upon you followed by the appearance of someone who lends a helping hand – while others steal your belongings. Other scams to be aware of involve a quantity of cash being 'found' on the street, whereby the do-gooder tries to return it to you; elaborate hard-luck stories from supposed travelers; and 'on-the-spot fines' by bogus police. Be especially wary if one or more 'plainclothes' cops demand to search your luggage or examine your documents, traveler's checks or cash. Insist that you will allow this only at an official police station or in the presence of a uniformed officer, and don't allow anyone to take you anywhere in a taxi or unmarked car. Thieves often work in pairs to distract you while lifting your wallet. Simply stay alert.

Drugs

And now a word from your mother: marijuana and cocaine are big business in parts of South America. They are available in many places but illegal everywhere, apart from Uruguay (where smoking marijuana is legal but non-Uruguayans are not allowed to buy it). Indulging can either land you in jail or worse. Unless you're willing to take these risks, avoid illegal drugs.

Beware that drugs are sometimes used to set up travelers for blackmail and bribery. Avoid any conversation with someone proffering drugs. If you're in an area where drug trafficking is prevalent, ignore it entirely, with conviction.

In Bolivia and Peru, chewing coca leaves or drinking *maté de coca* (coca-leaf-infused tea) may help alleviate some of effects of altitude. Keep in mind, though, that transporting coca leaves over international borders is illegal.

Druggings

Lonely Planet has received correspondence from travelers who were unwittingly drugged and robbed after accepting food from a stranger.

Be very careful in bars as there are occasional reports of folks being unwittingly drugged then raped or robbed. Always keep a close eye on your drink, and be cautious when meeting new friends.

Kidnappings

Be careful when taking taxis. 'Express' kidnappings occur in some cities, like La Paz (Bolivia). These incidents involve whisking travelers to far-off neighborhoods and holding them there while their ATM accounts are emptied; sometimes assaults have also occurred. We've noted in individual country chapters the known places that pose this kind of risk to travelers. To be on the safe side, have your guesthouse call you a taxi rather than hailing one on the street, and use official taxis at airports rather than those outside the gates. And never ride in a vehicle that already has a passenger in it.

Natural Hazards

The Pacific Rim 'ring of fire' loops through eastern Asia, Alaska and all the way down through the Americas to Tierra del Fuego in a vast circle of earthquake and volcanic activity that includes the whole Pacific side of South America. Volcanoes usually give some notice before blowing and are therefore unlikely to pose any immediate threat to travelers. Earthquakes, however, are not uncommon, occur without warning and can be very serious. The last big one in the region was an 7.8-magnitude quake that hit the northern coast of Ecuador in 2016, and over 600 people died. Andean construction rarely meets seismic safety standards; adobe buildings are particularly vulnerable. If you're in an earthquake, take shelter in a doorway or dive under a table; don't go outside.

Police & Military

In some places you may encounter corrupt officials who are not beyond enforcing minor regulations in the hopes of extracting a bribe.

If you are stopped by 'plainclothes policemen,' never get into a vehicle with them. Don't give them any documents or show them any money, and don't take them to your hotel. If the police appear to be the real thing, insist on going to a police station on foot.

The military often maintains considerable influence, even under civilian governments. Avoid approaching military installations, which may display warnings such as 'No stopping or photographs – the sentry will shoot.' In the event of a coup or other emergency, state-of-siege regulations suspend civil rights. Always carry identification and be sure someone knows your whereabouts. Contact your embassy or consulate for advice.

Theft

Theft can be a problem, but remember that fellow travelers can also be accomplished crooks, so where there's a backpacker scene, there may also be thievery. Here are some common-sense suggestions to limit your liability:

➡ A small padlock is useful for securing your pack zippers and hostel door, if necessary. Twist ties, paper clips or safety pins can be another effective deterrent when used to secure your pack zippers.

➡ Even if you're just running down the hall, never leave your hotel door unlocked.

➡ Always conceal your money belt and its contents, preferably beneath your clothing.

➡ Keep your spending money separate from the big stuff (credit cards, tickets etc).

➡ Be aware of the risk of bag slashing and the theft of your contents on buses. Keep close watch on your belongings – the bag isn't safe under your seat, above your head or between your legs (it's better on your lap). Be mindful in crowded markets or terminals where thefts are more likely to occur.

➡ When exploring cities, consider ditching the daypack and carrying what you need in a plastic bag to deter potential thieves.

Tours

There are loads of great adrenaline activities on offer, from rafting to mountain biking, but do your research on an agency before joining a tour. Travelers have lost their lives owing to poorly maintained equipment and reckless, ill-prepared guides. It's never wise to choose an operator based on cost alone. In Bolivia, for instance, the mine tours in Potosí, bike trips outside La Paz and the 4x4 excursions around Salar

> ### GOVERNMENT TRAVEL ADVICE
> The following government websites offer travel advisories and information on current hot spots.
> **Australian Department of Foreign Affairs** (www.smarttraveller.gov.au)
> **British Foreign Office** (www.gov.uk/foreign-travel-advice)
> **Canadian Department of Foreign Affairs** (www.travel.gc.ca/travelling/advisories)
> **US State Department** (http://travel.state.gov)

de Uyuní have become so hugely popular that some agencies are willing to forgo safety. Talk to other travelers, check out equipment and meet with guides before committing to anything.

Trouble Spots

Colombia is much safer than it has been in years, but certain regions are still off-limits. The northern border region of Ecuador, specifically in the Oriente, can be dodgy due to guerrilla activity. Travelers have been assaulted at remote and even well-touristed archaeological sites, primarily in Peru; stay informed. La Paz (Bolivia), Rio and São Paulo (Brazil) and Quito (Ecuador) are all notorious for assaults on tourists.

Smoking

Argentina Smoking is banned in workplaces, all public indoor areas, schools, hospitals, museums and theaters, and on all public transportation.

Bolivia Banned in certain public spaces, including on public transportation, in health-care facilities and government offices, but there is no law against smoking in restaurants, cafes, bars or offices. Many hotels forbid smoking in rooms.

Brazil Banned in restaurants and bars; some hotels have smoking rooms.

Chile Banned in public places (restaurants, bars), though smoking is allowed on outdoor verandas.

Colombia Forbidden in enclosed spaces, including bars and restaurants. Some hotels have ventilated smoking zones although many are smoke-free.

Ecuador Banned in restaurants and bars.

French Guiana Universal smoking ban.

Guyana Universal smoking ban.

Paraguay Banned in indoor public spaces; permitted at outdoor establishments.

Peru Permitted in designated physically separated smoking areas in hotels, restaurants, cafes and bars.

Suriname Strict universal smoking ban.

Uruguay Banned in indoor public spaces, including restaurants and bars.

Venezuela Banned in indoor public spaces, including restaurants and bars.

Telephone

Skype and other net-to-phone services are the best way to call abroad.

From traditional landlines, the most economical way of calling abroad is by using phone cards. You can also try direct-dial lines, accessed via special numbers and billed to an account at home. There are different access numbers for each telephone company in each country; get a list from your phone company before you leave.

Mobile Phones

Cell (mobile) numbers in South America often have different area codes than fixed-line numbers, even if the cell-phone owner resides in the same city. Calling a cell-phone number is always more expensive (sometimes exorbitantly so) than calling a fixed line.

If you plan to travel with a smartphone, you may want to purchase an international plan or local SIM to minimize (what could be) enormous costs. Remember it's possible to call internationally for free or very cheaply using Skype or other Voice over Internet Protocol (VoIP) systems.

Time

South America has five time zones, ranging from GMT minus two hours (Fernando de Noronha off Brazil's east coast) to GMT minus six hours (Easter Island and the Galapagos, off South America's west coast).

Toilets

There are two toilet rules for South America: always carry your own toilet paper and don't ever throw anything into the toilet bowl. Except in the most developed places, South American sewer systems can't handle toilet paper, so all paper products must be discarded in the wastebasket. Another general rule is to use public bathrooms whenever you can, as you never know when your next opportunity will be. Folks posted outside bathrooms proffering swaths of paper require payment.

Visas & Arrival Fees

Some travelers – including those from the USA – may require visas to enter several countries, including Bolivia and Brazil. Arrange these well in advance of your departure. Some countries don't generally require visas but may require a reciprocity fee (such as the $117 fee Chile charges to Australian travelers), paid upon arrival. If no visa is required, a tourist card is issued upon arrival. See individual countries for more details.

Carry a handful of passport-sized photos for visa applications. Hold onto any entry-exit cards you are given. There can be serious fines and complications if you lose them!

If you need a visa for a country and arrive at a land border without one, be prepared to backtrack to the nearest town with a consulate to get one. Airlines won't normally let you board a plane for a country to which you don't have the necessary visa. Also, a visa in itself does not guarantee entry: you may still be turned back at the border if you don't have 'sufficient funds' or an onward or return ticket.

Onward or Return Tickets

Some countries require you to have a ticket out of their country before they will admit you at the border, grant you a visa or let you board their national airline. The onward or return ticket requirement can be a major nuisance for travelers who want to fly into one country and travel overland through others. Officially, Peru, Colombia, Ecuador, Venezuela, Bolivia, Brazil, Suriname and French Guiana demand onward tickets, but only sporadically enforce it. Still, if you arrive in one of the countries technically requiring an onward ticket or sufficient funds and a border guard is so inclined, he or she can enforce these rules (yet another reason to be courteous and neatly dressed at border crossings).

While proof of onward or return tickets is rarely asked for by South American border officials, airline officials, especially in the US, sometimes refuse boarding passengers with one-way tickets who cannot show proof of onward or return travel or proof of citizenship (or residency) in the destination country. One way around this is to purchase a cheap, fully refundable ticket out of the country and cash it in after your arrival. The downside is that the refund can take up to three months. Before purchasing the ticket, you should also ask specifically where you can get a refund, as some airlines will only refund tickets at the office of purchase or at their head office.

Any ticket out of South America plus sufficient funds are usually an adequate substitute for an onward ticket. Having a major credit card or two may help.

Sufficient Funds

Sufficient funds are often technically required but rarely asked for. Immigration officials may ask (verbally or on the application form) about your financial resources. If you lack 'sufficient funds' for your proposed visit, officials may limit the length of your stay, but once you are in the country, you can usually extend your visa by producing a credit card or two.

Volunteering

If you just want to donate your hard work, there are plenty of local organizations that will take you on, though you'll have better luck looking once you're in the country. A good place to start is at a Spanish-language school (Quito, Cuenca or Cuzco are top choices); many schools link volunteers with organizations in need.

If you prefer to set something up before you go, keep in mind that most international volunteer organizations require a weekly or monthly fee (sometimes up to US$1500 for two weeks, not including airfare), which can feel a bit harsh. This is usually to cover the costs of housing you, paying the organization's staff, rent, website fees and so on.

Here are a few places to start the search:

Amerispan (www.amerispan. com/volunteer_intern) Volunteer and internship programs in Argentina, Bolivia, Brazil, Chile, Ecuador and Peru.

Cross Cultural Solutions (www.crossculturalsolutions. org) Volunteer programs with an emphasis on cultural and human interaction in Peru.

Go Abroad (www.goabroad.com) Extensive listings of volunteer and study-abroad opportunities.

Idealist.org (www.idealist.org) Action Without Borders' searchable database of thousands of volunteer positions throughout the world. Excellent resource.

Rainforest Concern (www. rainforestconcern.org) British nonprofit organization offering affordable volunteer positions in forest environments in several South American countries. Volunteers pay a weekly fee.

Transitions Abroad (www. transitionsabroad.com) Useful portal for both paid and volunteer work.

UN Volunteers (www.unv.org) The lofty international organization offers volunteer opportunities for peace and development projects across the globe.

Volunteer Latin America (www. volunteerlatinamerica.com) Worth a peek for its interesting programs throughout Latin America.

Working Abroad (www.working abroad.com) Online network of grassroots volunteer opportunities with trip reports from the field.

Note that Lonely Planet does not vouch for any organization that we do not work with directly, and we strongly recommend travelers always investigate a volunteer project themselves to assess the standards and suitability of the project.

Women Travelers

At one time or another, solo women travelers will find themselves the object of curiosity – sometimes well intentioned, sometimes not. Avoidance is an easy, effective self-defense strategy. In the Andean region, particularly in smaller towns and rural areas, modest dress and conduct are the norm, while in Brazil and the more liberal Cono Sur, standards are more relaxed, especially in beach areas.

Machista (macho) attitudes, stressing masculine pride and virility, are fairly widespread among South American men (although less so in indigenous communities). They are often expressed by boasting and in exaggerated attention toward women. Snappy putdown lines or other caustic comebacks to unwanted advances may make the man feel threatened, and he may respond aggressively. Most women find it easier to invent a husband.

There have been isolated cases of South American men raping women travelers. Women trekking or taking tours in remote or isolated areas should be especially cautious. Some cases have involved guides assaulting tour group members, so it's worth double-checking the identity and reputation of any guide or tour operator. Also be aware that women (and men) have been drugged, in bars and elsewhere, using drinks, cigarettes or pills. Police may not be very helpful in rape cases – if a local woman is raped, her family usually seeks revenge rather than calling the police. Tourist police may be more sympathetic, but it's possibly better to see a doctor and contact your embassy before reporting a rape to police.

Tampons are generally difficult to find in smaller towns, so stock up in cities or bring a supply from home.

Work

Aside from teaching or tutoring English, opportunities for employment are few, low-paying and usually illegal. Even tutoring, despite good hourly rates, is rarely remunerative because it takes time to build up a clientele. The best opportunities for teaching English are in the larger cities, and, although you won't save much, it will allow you to stick around longer. Other work opportunities may exist for skilled guides or in restaurants and bars catering to travelers. Many people find work at foreign-owned lodges and inns.

There are several excellent online resources, including the following:

Association of American Schools in South America (www.aassa.com) Places accredited teachers in many academic subjects in schools throughout South America.

Dave's ESL Café (www.eslcafe. com) Loads of message boards, job boards, teaching ideas, information, links and more.

EnglishClub.com (www.english club.com) Great resource for ESL teachers and students.

TEFL Net (www.tefl.net) This is another useful online resource for teachers from the creators of EnglishClub.com.

Transportation

GETTING THERE & AWAY

Flights, cars and tours can be booked online at lonelyplanet. com/bookings.

Entering South America

Visitors from the US and some other countries require visas (best arranged in advance) when visiting Brazil, Bolivia, Paraguay, Suriname and Venezuela. Make sure you have enough blank pages in your passport, and that it will be valid for six months beyond your proposed entry date to each country.

Air

Airports & Airlines

North American, European and Australian airlines offer regular South American connections.

Argentina The main airports are **Aeropuerto Internacional Ministro Pistarini** (Ezeiza; ☑011-5480-6111; www.aa2000. com.ar) and **Aeroparque Jorge Newbery** (Map p64; ☑011-5480-6111; www.aa2000. com.ar; Av Rafael Obligado; ☑33, 45), both in Buenos Aires. There are several other international airports around Argentina; find info online at Aeropuertos Argentina 2000 (www.aa2000. com.ar). Aerolíneas Argentinas (www.aerolineas.com.ar) is the national carrier.

Bolivia The principal international airports are La Paz' **El Alto International Airport** (LPB; Héroes Km 7, El Alto), Santa Cruz' **Viru-Viru International Airport** (☑338-5000) and Cochabamba's **Jorge Wilstermann International Airport** (☑412-0400; Av Killman s/n). The national airline is the state-owned Boliviana de Aviación (www.boa.bo), which has international flights to Madrid, Barcelona and Miami.

Brazil The most popular international gateways are **Galeão**

International Airport (Aeroporto Internacional Antô-nio Carlos Jobim; ☑21 3004-6050; www.riogaleao.com; Domestic Arrival Hall, Av Vinte de Janeiro) in Rio de Janeiro and São Paulo's **GRU Airport** (Aeroporto Guarulhos; ☑11 2445-2945; www.gru.com.br; Rod Hélio Smidt s/n). **Salvador** (SSA; ☑71 3204-1010; Praça Gago Coutinho s/n, São Cristóvão) and **Recife** (REC; ☑81 3322-4188) receive a few direct scheduled flights from Europe. Though headquartered in Chile, LATAM (www.latam. com) is Brazil's largest international carrier.

Chile Santiago's **Aeropuerto Internacional Arturo Merino Benítez** (Santiago International Airport, SCL; ☑2-2690-1796; www.nuevo pudahuel.cl) is the country's main gateway. LATAM (www. latam.com) is the chief international airline serving Chile.

Colombia Aeropuerto Internacional El Dorado (☑1-266-2000; www.eldorado. aero; Av El Dorado) in Bogotá is

---

CLIMATE CHANGE & TRAVEL

Every form of transport that relies on carbon-based fuel generates CO_2, the main cause of human-induced climate change. Modern travel is dependent on aeroplanes, which might use less fuel per kilometre per person than most cars but travel much greater distances. The altitude at which aircraft emit gases (including CO_2) and particles also contributes to their climate change impact. Many websites offer 'carbon calculators' that allow people to estimate the carbon emissions generated by their journey and, for those who wish to do so, to offset the impact of the greenhouse gases emitted with contributions to portfolios of climate-friendly initiatives throughout the world. Lonely Planet offsets the carbon footprint of all staff and author travel.

the main gateway. Avianca (www. avianca.com) is the national carrier.

Ecuador Quito (☎02-395-4200; www.aeropuertoquito. aero) and **Guayaquil** (GYE; ☎04-216-9000; www.tagsa. aero; Av de las Américas) airports are both international hubs. TAME (www.tame.com.ec) is the national carrier but Avianca (www.avianca.com), based in Quito, is close behind.

The Guianas All three of the Guianas (Guyana, French Guiana and Suriname) are difficult to reach, with **Cayenne** (Rochambeau; ☎0594-299700) the only modern airport in the region. Both Cayenne and **Paramaribo** (Zanderij; ☎032-5200; www.japi-airport.com; Zanderij) have direct flights to Europe. Suriname has the best connections to elsewhere in the Americas. The key airlines are Suriname Airways (www.flyslm. com), Air France (www.airfrance. gf) and Air Caraïbes (www. aircaraibes.com).

Paraguay Aeropuerto Internacional Silvio Pettirossi (☎021-64-5600; Autopista Silvio Pettirossi, Luque; ☎) is in Luque, a satellite town of Asunción, and is the main international arrival and departure point. Paraguay has no national carrier.

Peru Lima's **Aeropuerto Internacional Jorge Chávez** (☎01-517-3500, schedules 01-511-6055; www.lima-airport. com; Callao) is the country's major hub. LATAM (www.latam. com) has the most flights domestically and internationally.

Uruguay Montevideo's **Carrasco International Airport** (☎2604-0329; www.aeropuerto decarrasco.com.uy; Ruta 101, Km 20) is the main port of entry. Uruguay has no national airline.

Venezuela We cannot recommend traveling here at present.

Land

From North America, you can journey overland only as far south as Panama. There is no road connection onward to Colombia: the Carretera Panamericana (Pan-American Hwy) ends in the vast wilderness of the Darién Province, in southeast Panama. This roadless area between Central and South America is called the Darién Gap. In the past it has been difficult, but possible, to trek across the gap with the help of local guides, but since around 1998 it has been prohibitively dangerous, especially on the Colombian side. The region is overrun with smugglers and is positively unsafe.

Border Crossings

There are ample border crossings in South America, so you generally never have to travel too far out of your way to get where you eventually want to go. This is particularly true in Argentina and Chile, where a shared 3500km-long frontier provides many opportunities (especially in Patagonia) to slide between countries. Most crossings are by road (or bridge), but there are a few that involve boat travel (such as across the Río de la Plata between Buenos Aires and Uruguay; several lake crossings between Argentina and Chile; and across Lake Titicaca between Bolivia and Peru).

With the influx of footloose foreigners in the region, border police are used to backpackers turning up at their often-isolated corner of the globe. That said, crossing is always easier if you appear at least somewhat kempt, treat the guards with respect and make an attempt at Spanish or Portuguese. If, on the off chance, you encounter an officer who tries to extract a little *dinero* (money) from you before allowing you through (it does happen occasionally), maintain your composure. If the amount is small (and it generally is), it's probably not worth your trouble trying to fight it. Generally, border police are courteous and easy going.

Before heading to a border, be sure to get the latest information on visas – whether or not you need one – with a little on-the-ground research.

Bus

The cheapest but most time-consuming way to cross South American borders is to take a local bus to the border, handle immigration formalities and board another bus on the other side. To save a few hours, you might consider boarding an international bus that connects major towns in neighboring countries.

Sea

One of the most popular modes of travel between South and Central America is by booking passage on one of the foreign sailboats that travel between Cartagena (Colombia) and the San Blás islands, with some boats continuing to Colón (Panama). The typical passage takes about five days and costs between US$450 and US$650. A good source of information regarding schedules and available berths is at **Blue Sailing** (Map p612; ☎310-704-0425, 300-829-2030; www.bluesailing.net; Calle San Andrés No 30-47; 5-day trips US$450-650; ⏰9am-5pm Mon-Sat) in Cartagena. Do some serious research before joining any tour; there are many unsavory operators out there, and a few boats have even sunk.

A less expensive way to reach Panama from Colombia is via small boat from Capurgana to Puerto Obaldia (COP$30,000 for the 30-minute trip), from where you can take a domestic flight to Panama City (US$115, flying Tuesdays, Thursdays and Sundays) or continue up through the San Blás islands.

Officially, both Panama and Colombia require an onward or return ticket as a condition of entry. This may not be enforced in Colombia, but it's wise to get one anyway, or have lots of money and a plausible itinerary. Panama requires a visa or tourist card, an onward ticket and sufficient funds, and has been known to turn back arrivals who don't meet these requirements.

There are occasional reports of pirate attacks off the coast of South America, most of which occur in the Caribbean region.

GETTING AROUND

Air

There is an extensive network of domestic flights, with refreshingly low price tags, especially in the Andean countries (Bolivia, Ecuador and Peru). After 18-hour bus rides across mountainous terrain on atrocious roads, you may decide to take the occasional flight.

There are drawbacks to flying, however. Airports are often far from city centers, and public buses don't run all the time, so you may end up spending a bit on taxis (it's usually easier to find a cheap taxi *to* an airport than *from* one). Airport taxes also add to the cost of tickets; they are always higher for international departures. If safety concerns you, check out the 'Fatal Events by Airline' feature at www.airsafe.com.

Avoid scheduling a domestic flight with a close connection for an international flight or vice versa. Reconfirm all flights 48 hours before departure and allow ample extra time at the airport.

Air Passes

Air passes offer a number of flights within a country or region, for a specified period, at a fixed total price. Passes are an economical way to cover long distances in limited time, but they have shortcomings. Some are irritatingly inflex-

ible: once you start using the pass, you're locked into a schedule and you can't change it without paying a penalty. The validity period can be restrictive and some passes require that you enter the country on an international flight – you can't travel overland to the country and then start flying around with an air pass. Citizens of some countries are not eligible for certain air passes.

MULTICOUNTRY AIR PASSES

A few South America air passes exist and can save you a bit of money, provided you can deal with a fixed itinerary. These mileage-based passes allow travelers to fly between cities in a limited set of countries. The restrictions vary, but flights must be completed within a period ranging from 30 days to 12 months. You'll pay higher rates (or be ineligible) if you arrive in South America on a carrier other than the one sponsoring the air pass.

Gol South America Airpass (www.voegol.com.br) Includes Brazil, Argentina, Bolivia, Chile, Paraguay and Uruguay.

One World Alliance Visit South America Airpass (www.one world.com) Includes Argentina, Bolivia, Brazil, Chile, Colombia, Ecuador, Paraguay, Peru, Uruguay and Venezuela.

LATAM South American Airpass One of the most extensive networks around the continent; covers some 124 different destinations in Argentina, Bolivia, Brazil, Chile, Colombia, Ecuador, Paraguay, Peru, Uruguay and Venezuela.

SINGLE-COUNTRY AIR PASSES

Most air passes are only good within one country and are usually purchased in combination with a round-trip ticket to that country. In addition, most air passes must be purchased outside the destination country; check with a travel agent.

Argentina, Brazil and Chile all offer domestic air passes.

Bicycle

Cycling South America is a challenging yet highly rewarding alternative to public transport. While better roads in Argentina and Chile make the Cono Sur (Southern Cone; a collective term for Argentina, Chile, Uruguay and parts of Brazil and Paraguay) countries especially attractive, the entire continent is manageable by bike, or – more precisely – by mountain bike. Touring bikes are suitable for paved roads, but only a *todo terreno* (mountain bike) allows you to tackle the spectacular back roads (and often main roads!) of the Andes.

There are no multicountry bike lanes or designated routes. Mountain bikers have cycled the length of the Andes. As for road rules, forget it – except for the logical rule of riding with traffic on the right-hand side of the road, there are none. Hunt down good maps that show side roads, as you'll have the enviable ability to get off the beaten track at will.

Bring your own bicycle since locally manufactured ones are less dependable and imported bikes are outrageously expensive. Bicycle mechanics are common even in small towns, but will almost invariably lack the parts you'll need. Before setting out, learn bicycle mechanics and purchase spares for the pieces most likely to fail. A basic road kit will include extra spokes and a spoke wrench, a tire patch kit, a chain punch, inner tubes, spare cables and a cycling-specific multitool. Some folks box up spare tires, leave them with a family member back home and have them shipped to South America when they need them.

Drawbacks to cycling include the weather (fierce rains, blasting winds), high altitude in the Andes, poor roads and reckless drivers – the biggest hazard for riders. Safety equipment such as reflectors, mirrors and a helmet are highly recommended. Security is another issue: always take your panniers with you, lock your bike (or pay someone to watch it) while you sightsee and bring your bike into your hotel room overnight.

Boat

From cruises through the mystical fjords of Chilean Patagonia and riverboat chugs up the Amazon to outboard canoe travel in the coastal mangroves of Ecuador, South America offers ample opportunity to travel by boat. Safety is generally not an issue, especially for the established ferry and cruise operators in Chile and Argentina. There have been a couple of recent problems with tourist boats in the Galápagos (including a few that have sunk over the years), so do some research before committing to a cruise.

Lake Crossings

There are outstanding (but expensive) lake excursions throughout southern Chile, Argentina, Bolivia and Peru. Some of the most popular routes:

➡ Copacabana (Bolivia) to the Lake Titicaca islands of Isla del Sol and Isla de la Luna.

➡ Lago General Carrera (Chile) between Chile Chico and Puerto Ingeniero Ibáñez.

➡ Puerto Montt and Puerto Varas (Chile) to Bariloche (Argentina).

➡ Puno (Peru) to the Lake Titicaca islands.

Riverboat

Long-distance travel on major rivers such as the Orinoco or Amazon is possible, but you'll have a more idyllic time on one of the smaller rivers such as the Mamoré or Beni, where boats hug the shore and you can see and hear the wildlife. On the Amazon, you rarely even see the shore. The river is also densely settled in its lower reaches, and its upper reaches have fewer passenger boats than in the past. River travel in Bolivia is less common than it once was, with more folks opting to take short flights between destinations.

Riverboats vary greatly in size and standards, so check the vessel before buying a ticket and shop around. When you pay the fare, get a ticket with all the details on it. Downriver travel is faster than upriver, but boats going upriver travel closer to the shore and offer more interesting scenery. The time taken between ports is unpredictable, so river travel is best for those with an open schedule.

Food is usually included in ticket prices and means lots of rice and beans and perhaps some meat, but bring bottled water, fruit and snacks as a supplement. The evening meal on the first night of a trip is not usually included. Drinks and extra food are generally sold on board, but at high prices. Bring some spare cash and insect repellent.

Unless you have cabin space, you'll need a hammock and rope to sling it. It can get windy and cool at night, so a sleeping bag is recommended. There are usually two classes of hammock space, with space on the upper deck costing slightly more; it's cooler there and worth the extra money. Be on the boat at least eight hours prior to departure to get a good hammock space away from engine noise and toilet odors.

Overcrowding and theft on boats are common complaints. Don't allow your baggage to be stored in an insecure locker; bring your own padlock. Don't entrust your bag to any boat officials unless you are quite certain about their status – bogus officials have been reported.

Sea Trips

The best-known sea trip, and a glorious one at that, is the Navimag (www.navimag.com) ferry ride down the Chilean coast, from Puerto Montt to Puerto Natales. Short boat rides in some countries take you to islands not far from the mainland, including Ilha Grande and Ilha de Santa Catarina in Brazil, Isla Grande de Chiloé in Chile and Isla Grande de Tierra del Fuego in Argentina. More distant islands are usually reached by air. In parts of coastal Ecuador, outboard canoes act as public transport through the mangroves.

Bus

In general, bus transport is well developed throughout the continent. Note that road conditions, bus quality and driver professionalism vary widely. Much depends on the season: vast deserts of red dust in the dry season become oceans of mud in the rainy season. In Argentina, Uruguay, Ecuador, coastal and southern Brazil, and most of Venezuela, roads are generally better. Chile and much of Argentina have some of the best-maintained roads and most comfortable and reliable bus services in South America.

Most major cities and towns have a *terminal de autobuses* or *terminal de ómnibus* (bus terminal); in Brazil, it's called a *rodoviária*, and in Ecuador it's a *terminal terrestre*. Terminals are often on the outskirts of town, and you'll need a local bus or taxi to reach it. The biggest and best terminals have restaurants, shops, showers and other services, and the surrounding area is often a good (but frequently ugly) place to look for cheap sleeps and eats. Village 'terminals' in rural areas often amount to dirt lots flanked by dilapidated metal hulks called 'buses' and men hawking various destinations to passersby; listen for your town of choice.

Some cities have several terminals, each serving a different route. Sometimes each bus company has its own terminal, which is particularly inconvenient. This is most common in Colombia, Ecuador and Peru, especially in smaller towns.

Classes

Especially in the Andean countries, buses may be stripped nearly bare, tires are often treadless, and rock-hard suspension ensures a less-than-smooth ride, particularly for those at the back of the bus. After all seats are taken, the aisle is packed beyond capacity, and the roof is loaded with cargo to at least half the height of the bus, topped by the occasional goat or pig. You may have serious doubts about ever arriving at your destination, but the buses usually make it. Except for long-distance routes, different classes often don't exist: you ride what's available.

At the other extreme, you'll find luxurious coaches in Argentina, Brazil, Chile, Colombia, Uruguay, Venezuela and even Bolivia along main routes. The most expensive buses usually feature reclining seats, and meal, beverage and movie services. Different classes are called by a variety of names, depending on the country. In Argentina, Chile and Peru, the deluxe sleeper buses, called *coche-cama* or *bus-cama* (literally 'bus-bed') – or *leito* (sleeping berth) in Brazil – are available for most long-distance routes.

Costs

In the Andean countries, bus rides generally add up to about US$1 per hour of travel. When better services (such as 1st class or *coche-cama*) are offered, they can cost double the fare of a regular bus. Still, overnighters obviate the need for a hotel room, thereby saving you money.

Prices elsewhere average about $2 per hour, but can vary considerably within countries. Prices are highest in French Guiana (around $5 per hour).

Reservations

It's always wise to purchase your ticket in advance if you're traveling during peak holiday seasons (January through March in the Cona Sur; and around Easter week and during holiday weekends everywhere). At best, bus companies will have ticket offices at central terminals and information boards showing routes, departure times and fares. Seats will be numbered and booked in advance. In places where tickets are not sold in advance, showing up an hour or so before your departure will usually guarantee you a seat.

Safety

Anyone who has done their share of traveling in South America can tell you stories of horrifying bus rides at the mercy of crazed drivers. And there are occasionally accidents. Choosing more expensive buses is no guarantee against accidents; high-profile crashes sometimes involve well-established companies. Some roads, particularly those through the Andes, can be frightening to travel. A few well-placed flights can reduce bus anxiety.

Car & Motorcycle

Driving around South America can be mentally taxing and at times risky, but a car allows you to explore out-of-the-way places – especially parks – that are totally inaccessible via public transport. In places like Patagonia and other parts of Chile and Argentina, a short-term rental car can be well worth the expense.

There are some hurdles to driving. First off, it's a good idea to have an International Driving Permit to supplement your license from home. Vehicle security can be a problem anywhere in

South America. Avoid leaving valuables in your car, and always lock it. Drive carefully. Throughout South America, if you are in an accident that injures or kills another person, you can be jailed until the case is settled, regardless of culpability.

Bringing Your Own Vehicle

Shipping your own car or motorcycle to South America involves a lot of money and planning. Shipping arrangements should be made at least a month in advance. Stealing from vehicles being shipped is big business, so remove everything removable (hubcaps, wipers, mirrors), and take everything visible from the interior. Shipping your vehicle in a container is more secure, but more expensive.

Driver's License

If you're planning to drive anywhere, obtain an International Driving Permit or Inter-American Driving Permit (Uruguay theoretically recognizes only the latter). For about US$10 to US$15, any motoring organization will issue one, provided you have a current driver's license.

Insurance

Home auto-insurance policies generally do not cover you while driving abroad. Fender benders are generally dealt with on the spot, without involving the police or insurance agents. When you rent, be certain your contract includes *seguro* (insurance).

Purchase

If you're spending several months in South America, purchasing a car is worth considering. It will be cheaper than renting if you can resell it at the end of your stay. On the other hand, any used car can be a financial risk, especially on rugged roads, and the bureaucracy involved in purchasing a car can be horrendous.

The best countries in which to purchase cars are Argentina, Brazil and Chile, but, again, expect exasperating bureaucracies. Be certain of the title; as a foreigner, getting a notarized document authorizing your use of the car is a good idea, since the bureaucracy may take its time transferring the title. Taking a vehicle purchased in South America across international borders may present obstacles.

Officially, you need a *carnet de passage* or a *libreta de pasos por aduana* (customs permit) to cross most land borders in your own vehicle, but you'll probably never have to show these documents. The best source of advice is the national automobile club in the country where you buy the car.

Rental

Major international rental agencies such as Hertz, Avis and Budget have offices in South American capitals, major cities and at major airports. Local agencies, however, often have better rates. To rent a car, you must be at least 25 and have a valid driver's license from home and a credit card. Some agencies rent to those under 25 but charge an added fee. If your itinerary calls for crossing borders, know that some rental agencies restrict or forbid this; ask before renting.

Rates can fluctuate wildly (ranging from US$40 to US$80 per day). It's always worth getting a group together to defray costs. If the vehicle enables you to camp out, the saving in accommodations may offset much of the rental cost, especially in Cona Sur countries.

Road Rules

Except in Guyana and Suriname, South Americans drive on the right-hand side of the road. Road rules are frequently ignored and seldom enforced; conditions can be hazardous; and

many drivers, especially in Argentina and Brazil, are reckless and even willfully dangerous. Driving at night is riskier than the day due to lower visibility and the preponderance of tired and/or intoxicated nighttime drivers sharing the road.

Road signs can be confusing, misleading or nonexistent – a good sense of humor and patience are key attributes. Honking your horn on blind curves is a simple, effective safety measure; the vehicle coming uphill on a narrow road usually has the right of way. If you're cruising along and see a tree branch or rock in the middle of the road, slow down: this means there's a breakdown, rock slide or some other trouble up ahead. Speed bumps can pop up anywhere, most often smack in the center of town, but sometimes inexplicably in the middle of a highway.

Hitchhiking

Hitching is never entirely safe, and we don't recommend it. Travellers who hitch should understand that they are taking a small but potentially serious risk. Hitching is less dangerous if you travel in pairs and let someone know where you are planning to go.

Though it is possible to hitch all over South America, free lifts are the rule only in Argentina, Chile, Uruguay and parts of Brazil. Elsewhere, hitching is virtually a form of public transport (especially where buses are infrequent) and drivers expect payment. There are generally fixed fares over certain routes; ask the other passengers what they're paying. It's usually about equal to the bus fare, marginally less in some places. You get better views from the top of a truck, but if you're hitching on the *altiplano* (Andean high plain of Peru, Bolivia, Chile and Argentina) or *páramo* (humid, high-altitude grassland) take warm clothing. Once the sun goes down

or is obscured by clouds, it gets very cold.

There's no need to wait at the roadside for a lift, unless it happens to be convenient. Almost every town has a central truck park, often around the market. Ask around for a truck going your way and how much it will cost; be there about 30 minutes before the departure time given by the driver. It is often worth soliciting a ride at *servicentros* (gas stations) on the outskirts of large cities, where drivers refuel their vehicles.

Local Transportation

Local and city bus systems tend to be thorough and reliable throughout South America. Although in many countries you can flag a bus anywhere on its route, you're best off finding the official bus stop. Still, if you can't find the stop, don't hesitate to throw your arm up to stop a bus you know is going your direction. Never hesitate to ask a bus driver which is the right bus to take; most of them are very generous in directing you to the right bus.

As in major cities throughout the world, pickpockets are a problem on crowded buses and subways. If you're on a crowded bus or subway, always watch your back. Avoid crowded public transport when you're loaded down with luggage.

Taxis in most big cities (but definitely not all) have meters. When a taxi has a meter, make sure the driver uses it. When it doesn't, always agree on a fare *before* you get in the cab. In most cities, fares are higher on Sundays and after 9pm.

Train

Trains have slowly faded from the South American landscape, but several spectacular routes still operate. Ecuador has invested heavily in rehabilitating its old lines. Uruguay is also revitalizing its old rails, though it's still years from completion.

For great scenery with a touch of old-fashioned railway nostalgia, try the following routes:

Curitiba–Paranaguá (Brazil) Descending steeply to the coastal lowlands, Brazil's best rail journey offers unforgettable views.

Oruro–Uyuni–Tupiza–Villazón (Bolivia) The main line from Oruro is currently out of service going south of Uyuni owing to track damage. If it reopens, the line continues from Uyuni to Tupiza (another scenic rail trip through gorge country) and on to Villazón at the Argentine border.

Ferroviaria Oriental (Bolivia; www.fo.com.bo) Covers eastern Bolivia, operating a line from Santa Cruz to the Brazilian frontier at Quijarro, where you can cross to the Pantanal. An infrequently used service goes south from Santa Cruz to Yacuiba on the Argentine border.

Lima–Huancayo and Huancayo–Huancavelica (Peru) These memorable rail journeys are among the best on the continent. The less frequent Lima–Huancayo train travels one of world's highest rail routes.

Tren Túristico Guaraní (Bolivia; www.ferroviaria-andina.com. bo/turismo) A tourist service departing every second Sunday of the month between El Alto and Tiwanaku.

Puno–Juliaca–Cuzco (Peru) From the shores of Lake Titicaca and across a 4600m pass, this train runs for group bookings in high season. Departures are unpredictable, but when it does run, it's open to nongroup passengers.

Riobamba–Sibambe (Ecuador) One of a growing number of short tourist-train jaunts in the country, the Nariz del Diablo (Devil's Nose) is an exhilarating, steep descent via narrow switchbacks.

Salta–La Polvorilla (Argentina) The Tren a las Nubes (Train to the Clouds) negotiates switchbacks, tunnels, spirals and death-defying bridges during its ascent into the Andean *puna* (highlands). Unfortunately, schedules are extremely unreliable.

Health

Prevention is the key to staying healthy while in South America. Travelers who receive the recommended vaccines and follow common-sense precautions usually go away with nothing more than a little diarrhea.

BEFORE YOU GO

Bring medications in their original, clearly labeled containers. A signed and dated letter from your physician describing your medical conditions and medications, including generic names, is also a good idea. If carrying syringes or needles, be sure to have a physician's letter documenting their medical necessity.

Health Insurance

If your health insurance doesn't cover you for medical expenses abroad, consider getting extra insurance. Find out in advance if your insurance plan will make payments directly to providers or reimburse you later for overseas health expenditures. (In many countries doctors expect payment in cash.)

Recommended Vaccinations

Since most vaccines don't produce immunity until at least two weeks after they're given, visit a physician four to eight weeks before departure. Ask your doctor for an International Certificate of Vaccination (otherwise known as the yellow booklet), which will list all the vaccinations you've received. This is mandatory for countries that require proof of yellow-fever vaccination upon entry, but it's a good idea to carry it wherever you travel.

The only required vaccine is yellow fever, and that's only if you're arriving from a yellow-fever-infected country in Africa or the Americas. (The exception is French Guiana, which requires yellow-fever vaccine for all travelers.) However, a number of vaccines are recommended.

Medical Checklist

➡ Acetaminophen (Tylenol) or aspirin

➡ Acetazolamide (Diamox; for altitude sickness)

➡ Antibacterial ointment (eg Bactroban; for cuts and abrasions)

➡ Antibiotics for diarrhea (eg Norfloxacin, Ciprofloxacin or Azithromycin)

➡ Antihistamines (for hay fever and allergic reactions)

➡ Anti-inflammatory drugs (eg ibuprofen)

➡ Bandages, gauze, gauze rolls and adhesive or paper tape

➡ Diarrhea 'stopper' (eg loperamide)

➡ Insect repellent containing DEET for the skin

➡ Iodine tablets (for water purification)

➡ Oral rehydration salts

➡ Permethrin-containing insect spray for clothing, tents and bed nets

➡ Pocketknife

➡ Scissors, safety pins, tweezers

➡ Steroid cream or cortisone (for poison ivy and other allergic rashes)

➡ Sunblock

➡ Thermometer

Internet Resources

There is a wealth of travel health advice on the internet. The World Health Organization (www.who.int/ith) publishes a superb book called *International Travel and Health*, which is revised annually and available online (as a downloadable pdf) for $12. Another resource of general interest is MD Travel Health (www.mdtravelhealth.com), which provides complete travel health recommendations for every country in the world; information is updated daily.

It's usually a good idea to consult your government's travel health website before departure, if one is available:

Australia (www.smartraveller.
gov.au)

Canada (www.travelhealth.gc.ca)

UK (www.fco.gov.uk)

USA (wwwnc.cdc.gov/travel)

IN SOUTH AMERICA

Availability & Cost of Health Care

Good medical care may be more difficult to find in smaller cities and impossible to locate in rural areas. Many doctors and hospitals expect payment in cash, regardless of whether you have travel health insurance. If you develop a life-threatening medical problem, you'll probably want to be evacuated to a country with state-of-the-art medical care. Since this may cost tens of thousands of dollars, be sure you have insurance to cover this before you depart. You can find a list of medical-evacuation and travel-insurance companies on the US State Department website (http://travel.state.gov).

Infectious Diseases

Dengue

Dengue fever is a viral infection found throughout South America. Dengue is transmitted by Aedes mosquitoes, which bite preferentially during the daytime and are usually found close to human habitations, often indoors. They breed primarily in artificial water containers, such as jars, barrels, cans, cisterns, metal drums, plastic containers and discarded tires. As a result, dengue is especially common in densely populated, urban environments.

Dengue usually causes flu-like symptoms, including fever, muscle aches, joint pains, headaches, nausea and vomiting, often followed by a rash. The body aches may be quite uncomfortable, but most cases resolve uneventfully in a few days.

There is no treatment for dengue fever except to take analgesics such as acetaminophen/paracetamol (Tylenol) and drink plenty of fluids. Severe cases may require hospitalization for intravenous fluids and supportive care. There is no vaccine. The cornerstone of prevention is protection against insects.

Keep an eye out for outbreaks in areas where you plan to visit. A good website on the latest information is the CDC (wwwnc.cdc.gov/travel).

Hepatitis A

Hepatitis A is the second most common travel-related infection (after travelers' diarrhea). It's a viral infection of the liver that's usually acquired by ingestion of contaminated water, food or ice, though it may also be acquired by direct contact with infected persons. The illness occurs throughout the world, but the incidence is higher in developing nations. Symptoms may include fever, malaise, jaundice, nausea, vomiting and abdominal pain. Most cases resolve themselves without complications, though hepatitis A occasionally causes severe liver damage. There is no treatment.

The vaccine for hepatitis A is extremely safe and highly effective. If you get a booster six to 12 months later, it lasts for at least 10 years. You really should get it before you go to any developing nation.

Malaria

Malaria occurs in every South American country except Chile, Uruguay and the Falkland Islands (Islas Malvinas). It's transmitted by mosquito bites, usually between dusk and dawn. The main symptom is high spiking fevers, which may be accompanied by chills, sweats, headache, body aches, weakness, vomiting or diarrhea. Severe cases may involve the central nervous system and lead to seizures, confusion, coma and death.

There is a choice of three malaria pills, all of which work about equally well. Mefloquine (Lariam) is taken once weekly in a dosage of 250mg, starting one to two weeks before arrival and continuing through the trip and for four weeks after your return. The problem is that a certain percentage of people (the number is disputed) develop neuropsychiatric side effects, which may range from mild to severe. Atovaquone/proguanil (Malarone) is a newly approved combination pill taken once daily with food starting two days before arrival and continuing through the trip and for seven days after departure. Side effects are typically mild. Doxycycline is a third alternative, but may cause an exaggerated sunburn reaction.

Protecting yourself against mosquito bites is just as important as taking malaria pills, since none of the pills are 100% effective.

If you do not have access to medical care while traveling, bring along additional pills for emergency self-treatment, which you should take if you can't reach a doctor and you develop symptoms that suggest malaria, such as high spiking fevers. One option is to take four tablets of Malarone once daily for three days. However, Malarone should not be used for treatment if you're already taking it for prevention. An alternative is to take 650mg quinine three times daily and 100mg doxycycline twice daily for one week. If you start self-medication, see a doctor at the earliest possible opportunity.

If you develop a fever after returning home, see a physician, as malaria symptoms may not occur for months.

Rabies

Rabies is a viral infection of the brain and spinal cord that is almost always fatal. The rabies virus is carried in the saliva of infected animals and is typically transmitted through an animal bite, though contamination of any break in the skin with infected saliva may result in rabies. Rabies occurs in all South American countries.

Rabies vaccine is safe, but a full series requires three injections and is quite expensive. Those at high risk for rabies, such as animal handlers and spelunkers (cave explorers), should certainly get the vaccine. The treatment for a possibly rabid bite consists of rabies vaccine with rabies-immune globulin. It's effective, but must be given promptly. Most travelers don't need rabies vaccine.

All animal bites and scratches must be promptly and thoroughly cleansed with large amounts of soap and water, and local health authorities should be contacted to determine whether further treatment is necessary.

Typhoid

Typhoid fever is caused by ingestion of food or water contaminated by a species of salmonella known as *Salmonella typhi*. Fever occurs in virtually all cases. Other symptoms may include headache, malaise, muscle aches, dizziness, loss of appetite, nausea and abdominal pain. Either diarrhea or constipation may occur. Possible complications include intestinal perforation, intestinal bleeding, confusion, delirium or (rarely) coma.

Unless you expect to take all your meals in major hotels and restaurants, the typhoid vaccine is a good idea.

The drug of choice for typhoid fever is usually a quinolone antibiotic such as ciprofloxacin (Cipro) or levofloxacin (Levaquin), which many travelers carry for treatment of travelers' diarrhea. However, if you self-treat for typhoid fever, you may also need to self-treat for malaria, since the symp-

toms of the two diseases may be indistinguishable.

Yellow Fever

Yellow fever is a life-threatening viral infection transmitted by mosquitoes in forested areas. The illness begins with flu-like symptoms, which may include fever, chills, headache, muscle aches, backache, loss of appetite, nausea and vomiting. These symptoms usually subside in a few days, but one person in six enters a second, toxic phase characterized by recurrent fever, vomiting, listlessness, jaundice, kidney failure and hemorrhage, leading to death in up to half of the cases. There is no treatment except for supportive care.

Yellow-fever vaccine can be given only in approved yellow-fever vaccination centers, which provide validated International Certificates of Vaccination (yellow booklets). The vaccine should be given at least 10 days before any potential exposure to yellow fever and remains effective for approximately 10 years. Reactions to the vaccine are generally mild and may include headaches, muscle aches, low-grade fevers, or discomfort at the injection site. Severe, life-threatening reactions have been described but are extremely rare. In general, the risk of becoming ill from the vaccine is far less than the risk of becoming ill from yellow fever, and you're strongly encouraged to get the vaccine, which is required if you're arriving from a yellow-fever-infected country in Africa or the Americas, or you are visiting French Guiana.

Taking measures to protect yourself from mosquito bites is an essential part of preventing yellow fever.

Zika Virus

Zika Virus is primarily transmitted by infected mosquitoes, typically active from dawn to dusk. It can be transmitted from a pregnant woman to her fetus. Human

transmission can also occur through unprotected sex, and on occasion through saliva and urine. Symptoms include mild fever, headache, muscle and joint pain, nausea, vomiting and general malaise. Symptoms may present three to 12 days after being bitten.

The best prevention is to wear long sleeves, repellent with 20–30% DEET and avoid being outdoors at dawn and dusk when mosquitoes are most common. High-altitude destinations are not considered a risk.

Other Infections

CHAGAS DISEASE

Chagas disease is a parasitic infection that is transmitted by triatomine insects (reduviid bugs), which inhabit crevices in the walls and roofs of substandard housing in South and Central America. Chagas disease is extremely rare in travelers. However, if you sleep in a poorly constructed house, especially one made of mud, adobe or thatch, be sure to protect yourself with a bed net and a good insecticide.

GNATHOSTOMIASIS

Gnathostomiasis is an intestinal parasite acquired by eating raw or undercooked freshwater fish, including *ceviche* (marinated, uncooked seafood).

LEISHMANIASIS

Leishmaniasis occurs in the mountains and jungles of all South American countries except for Chile, Uruguay and the Falkland Islands (Islas Malvinas). The infection is transmitted by sand flies, which are about one-third the size of mosquitoes. Leishmaniasis may be limited to the skin, causing slow-growing ulcers over exposed parts of the body or (less commonly) disseminate to the bone marrow, liver and spleen. There is no vaccine. To protect yourself from sand flies, follow the same precautions as for mosquitoes, except that netting must be finer mesh (at least 18 holes to the linear inch).

Environmental Hazards

Altitude Sickness

Altitude sickness may develop in those who ascend rapidly to altitudes greater than 2500m. Being physically fit offers no protection. Those who have experienced altitude sickness in the past are prone to future episodes. The risk increases with faster ascents, higher altitudes and greater exertion. Symptoms may include headaches, nausea, vomiting, dizziness, malaise, insomnia and loss of appetite. Severe cases may be complicated by fluid in the lungs (high-altitude pulmonary edema) or swelling of the brain (high-altitude cerebral edema).

When traveling to high altitudes, it's also important to avoid overexertion, eat light meals and abstain from alcohol.

If your symptoms are more than mild or don't resolve promptly, see a doctor. Altitude sickness should be taken seriously; it can be life-threatening when severe.

Animal Bites

Do not attempt to pet, handle or feed any animal, with the exception of domestic animals known to be free of any infectious disease.

Any bite or scratch by a mammal, including bats, should be promptly and thoroughly cleansed with large amounts of soap and water, followed by application of an antiseptic such as iodine or alcohol. The local health authorities should be contacted immediately for possible postexposure rabies (p1050) treatment, whether or not you've been immunized against rabies.

Snakes and leeches are a hazard in some areas of South America. In the event of a bite from a venomous snake, place the victim at rest, keep the bitten area immobilized and move the victim immediately to the nearest medical facility. Avoid tourniquets, which are no longer recommended.

Cold Exposure & Hypothermia

Cold exposure may be a significant problem in the Andes, particularly at night. Be sure to dress warmly, stay dry, keep active, consume plenty of food and water, get enough rest, and avoid alcohol, caffeine and tobacco.

Hypothermia occurs when the body loses heat faster than it can produce it and the core temperature of the body falls. If you're trekking at high altitudes or simply taking a long bus trip over mountains, particularly at night, be prepared. In the Andes, you should always be prepared for cold, wet or windy conditions even if it's just for a few hours. It is best to dress in layers, and a hat is also important.

The symptoms of hypothermia include exhaustion, numbness, shivering, slurred speech, irrational or violent behavior, lethargy, stumbling, dizzy spells, muscle cramps and violent bursts of energy. Watch out for the 'umbles' (stumbles, mumbles, fumbles and grumbles), which are important signs of impending hypothermia.

To treat mild hypothermia, first get people out of the wind or rain, remove their clothing if it's wet and give them something warm and dry to wear. Make them drink hot liquids – not alcohol – and some high-calorie, easily digestible food. Do not rub victims – instead allow them to slowly warm themselves.

Heatstroke

To protect yourself from excessive sun exposure, you should stay out of the midday sun, wear sunglasses and a wide-brimmed sun hat, and apply sunscreen with SPF 15 or higher, with both UVA and UVB protection. Travelers should also drink plenty of fluids and avoid strenuous exercise when the temperature is high.

Insect Bites & Stings

To prevent mosquito bites, wear long sleeves, long pants, a hat and shoes (rather than sandals). Bring along a good insect repellent, preferably one containing DEET, which should be applied to exposed skin and clothing, but not to eyes, mouth, cuts, wounds or irritated skin. Products containing lower concentrations of DEET are as effective, but for shorter periods of time. In general, adults and children over 12 years should use preparations containing 25% to 35% DEET, which usually lasts about six hours. Children between two and 12 years of age should use preparations containing no more than 10% DEET, applied sparingly, which will usually last about three hours. DEET-containing compounds should not be used on children under age two.

Insect repellents containing certain botanical products, including oil of eucalyptus and soybean oil, are effective but last only 1½ to two hours. DEET-containing repellents are preferable for areas where there is a high risk of malaria or yellow fever. Products based on citronella are not effective.

For additional protection, you can apply permethrin to clothing, shoes, tents and bed nets. Permethrin treatments are safe and remain effective for at least two weeks, even when items are laundered. Permethrin should not be applied directly to skin.

Parasites

Intestinal parasites occur throughout South America. Common pathogens include Cyclospora, amoebae and Isospora. A tapeworm called Taenia solium may lead to a chronic brain infection called cysticercosis. If you exercise discretion in your choice of food and beverages, you'll sharply reduce your chances of becoming infected. Choose restaurants or market stalls that are well attended. If there's a high turnover, it means food hasn't been sitting around that long.

A parasitic infection called schistosomiasis, which primarily affects the blood vessels in the liver, occurs in Brazil, Suriname and parts of north-central Venezuela. The disease is acquired by swimming, wading, bathing or washing in fresh water that contains infected snails. It's therefore best to stay out of bodies of fresh water, such as lakes, ponds, streams and rivers, in places where schistosomiasis might occur.

A liver parasite called Echinococcus (hydatid disease) is found in many countries, especially Peru and Uruguay. It typically affects those in close contact with sheep. A lung parasite called Paragonimus, which is ingested by eating raw infected crustaceans, has been reported from Ecuador, Peru and Venezuela.

Travelers' Diarrhea

To prevent diarrhea, avoid tap water unless it has been boiled, filtered or chemically disinfected (with iodine tablets); only eat fresh fruits or vegetables if cooked or peeled; be wary of dairy products that might contain unpasteurized milk; and be highly selective when eating food from markets and street vendors.

If you develop diarrhea, be sure to drink plenty of fluids, preferably an oral rehydration solution containing salt and sugar. Gastrolyte works well for this. A few loose stools don't require treatment but you may want to take antibiotics if you start having more than three watery bowel movements within 24 hours, and it's accompanied by at least one other symptom – fever, cramps, nausea, vomiting or generally feeling unwell. Effective antibiotics include Norfloxacin, Ciprofloxacin or Azithromycin – all will kill the bacteria quickly. Note that an antidiarrheal agent (such as loperamide) is just a 'stopper' and doesn't get to the cause of the problem. Don't take loperamide if you have a fever or blood in your stools. Seek medical attention quickly if you don't respond to an appropriate antibiotic.

Tap Water

Tap water is generally not safe to drink. Vigorous boiling for one minute is the most effective means of water purification. At altitudes greater than 2000m, boil for three minutes.

Other methods of treating water include using a handheld ultraviolet-light purifier (such as a SteriPEN), iodine and water filters.

Argentina Generally safe to drink, but best to check in rural areas.

Bolivia Not safe to drink.

Brazil Generally safe to drink in major cities; not safe in rural areas.

Chile Tap water is generally safe to drink from Middle Chile down to Patagonia, but generally unwise in the Atacama Desert.

Colombia Not safe to drink, except in Bogotá and Cartagena.

Ecuador Not safe to drink.

Guyana Not safe to drink.

French Guiana Not safe to drink.

Paraguay Not safe to drink.

Peru Not safe to drink.

Suriname Not safe to drink.

Uruguay Generally safe to drink; check rural areas.

Language

Latin American Spanish is the language of choice for travelers in all of South America except Brazil (where Portuguese is the national tongue) and the Guianas (where French, Dutch or English are widely spoken).

PORTUGUESE

A characteristic feature of Brazilian Portuguese is the use of nasal vowels (pronounced as if you're trying to force the sound through the nose). In Portuguese, vowels followed by a nasal consonant (*m* or *n*) or those written with a tilde over them (eg *ã*) are nasal. In our pronunciation guides, the ng after a vowel indicates a nasal sound. The consonant sounds are very similar to those of English. Keep in mind that rr is strongly rolled, zh is pronounced as the 's' in 'pleasure', ly as the 'll' in 'million' and ny as in 'canyon'. If you read our colored pronunciation guides as if they were English, you'll be understood. The stressed syllables are in italics.

Where necessary, both masculine and feminine forms of words are included, separated by a slash and with the masculine form first, eg *obrigado/obrigada* (m/f).

Basics

Hello.	Olá.	o·*laa*
Goodbye.	Tchau.	tee·*show*
How are you?	Como vai?	ko·mo vai
Fine, and you?	Bem, e você?	beng e vo·se

WANT MORE?

For in-depth language information and handy phrases, check out Lonely Planet's *Latin American Spanish Phrasebook*. You'll find it at **shop.lonelyplanet.com**, or you can buy Lonely Planet's iPhone phrasebooks at the Apple App Store.

Excuse me.	Com licença.	kong lee·*seng*·saa
Sorry.	Desculpa.	des·*kool*·paa
Please.	Por favor.	por faa·*vorr*
Thank you.	Obrigado/ Obrigada. (m/f)	o·bree·*gaa*·do/ o·bree·*gaa*·daa
You're welcome.	De nada.	de naa·daa
Yes./No.	Sim./Não.	seeng/nowng

What's your name?
Qual é o seu nome?   kwow e o se·oo no·me

My name is ...
Meu nome é ...   me·oo no·me e ...

Do you speak English?
Você fala inglês?   vo·se faa·laa eeng·gles

I don't understand.
Não entendo.   nowng eng·*teng*·do

Accommodations

Do you have a single/double room?
Tem um quarto de solteiro/casal?   teng oom *kwaarr*·to de sol·*tay*·ro/kaa·zow

How much is it per night/person?
Quanto custa por noite/pessoa?   kwang·to koos·taa porr *noy*·te/pe·so·aa

Does it include breakfast?
Inclui café da manhã?   eeng·*kloo*·ee kaa·fe daa ma·*nyang*

campsite	local para acampamento	lo·*kow* paa·raa aa·kang·paa·meng·to
guesthouse	hospedaria	os·pe·daa·*ree*·a
hotel	hotel	o·*tel*
youth hostel	albergue juventude	ow·*berr*·ge zhoo·veng·*too*·de
air-con	ar condicionado	aarr kong·dee·syo·*naa*·do
bathroom	banheiro	ba·*nyay*·ro

| bed | cama | ka·maa |
| window | janela | zhaa·ne·laa |

Directions

Where's ...?
Onde fica ...? ong·de fee·kaa ...

What's the address?
Qual é o endereço? kwow e o eng·de·re·so

Could you please write it down?
Você poderia vo·se po·de·ree·aa
escrever num es·kre·verr noom
papel, por favor? paa·pel porr faa·vorr

Can you show me (on the map)?
Você poderia me vo·se po·de·ree·aa me
mostrar (no mapa)? mos·traarr (no maa·paa)

at the corner	à esquina	aa es·kee·naa
at the traffic lights	no sinal de trânsito	no see·now de trang·zee·to
behind ...	atrás ...	aa·traaz ...
in front of ...	na frente de ...	naa freng·te de ...
near ...	perto ...	perr·to ...
next to ...	ao lado de ...	ow laa·do de ...
opposite ...	do lado oposto ...	do laa·do o·pos·to ...
right	à direita	aa dee·ray·taa
straight ahead	em frente	eng freng·te

Eating & Drinking

I'd like the menu, please.
Eu queria o e·oo ke·ree·aa o
cardápio, por favor. kaar·daa·pyo porr faa·vorr

What would you recommend?
O que você recomenda? o ke vo·se he·ko·meng·daa

Do you have vegetarian food?
Você tem comida vo·se teng ko·mee·daa
vegetariana? ve·zhe·taa·ree·a·naa

I don't eat (red meat).
Eu não como e·oo nowng ko·mo
(carne vermelha). (kaar·ne verr·me·lyaa)

That was delicious!
Estava delicioso! es·taa·vaa de·lee·see·o·zo

Cheers!
Saúde! sa·oo·de

Please bring the bill.
Por favor traga a porr faa·vorr traa·gaa aa
conta. kong·taa

| I'd like a table for ... | Eu gostaria uma mesa para ... | e·oo gos·taa·ree·aa oo·maa me·zaa paa·raa ... |
| (eight) | (às oito) | (aas oy·to) |

KEY PATTERNS

To get by in Portuguese, mix and match these simple patterns with words of your choice:

When's (the next flight)?
Quando é (o kwaang·do e (o
próximo vôo)? pro·see·mo vo·o)

Where's the (tourist office)?
Onde fica (a ong·de fee·kaa (aa
secretaria de se·kre·taa·ree·aa de
turismo)? too·rees·mo)

Where can I (buy a ticket)?
Onde posso ong·de po·so
(comprar (kong·praar
passagem)? paa·saa zheng)

Do you have (a map)?
Você tem (um vo·se teng (oom
mapa)? maa·paa)

Is there (a toilet)?
Tem (banheiro)? teng (ba·nyay·ro)

I'd like (a coffee).
Eu gostaria de e·oo gos·taa·ree·aa de
(um café). (oom kaa·fe)

I'd like (to hire a car).
Eu gostaria de e·oo gos·taa·ree·aa de
(alugar um carro). (aa·loo·gaarr oom kaa·ho)

Can I (enter)?
Posso (entrar)? po·so (eng·traarr)

Could you please (help me)?
Você poderia vo·se po·de·ree·aa
me (ajudar), me (aa·zhoo·daarr)
por favor? por faa·vorr

Do I have to (get a visa)?
Necessito ne·se·see·to
(obter visto)? (o·bee·terr vees·to)

| o'clock | horas | aw·raas |
| (two) people | (duas) pessoas | (doo·aas) pe·so·aas |

Key Words

appetisers	aperitivos	aa·pe·ree·tee·vos
bottle	garrafa	gaa·haa·faa
bowl	tigela	tee·zhe·laa
breakfast	café da manhã	kaa·fe daa ma·nyang
children's menu	cardápio de crianças	kaar·da·pyo de kree·ang·saas
(too) cold	(demais) frio	(zhee·mais) free·o
dinner	jantar	zhang·taarr
food	comida	ko·mee·daa
fork	garfo	gaar·fo
glass	copo	ko·po

hot (warm)	quente	keng·te
knife	faca	faa·kaa
lunch	almoço	ow·mo·so
main courses	pratos principais	praa·tos preeng·see·pais
plate	prato	praa·to
restaurant	restaurante	hes·tow·rang·te
spoon	colher	ko·lyer
with	com	kong
without	sem	seng

Meat & Fish

beef	bife	bee·fe
chicken	frango	frang·go
duck	pato	paa·to
fish	peixe	pay·she
lamb	ovelha	o·ve·lyaa
lobster	lagosta	laa·gos·taa
pork	porco	porr·ko
prawn	camarão	kaa·maa·rowng
tuna	atum	aa·toong
turkey	perú	pe·roo
veal	bezerro	be·ze·ho

Fruit & Vegetables

apple	maçã	maa·sang
apricot	damasco	daa·maas·ko
asparagus	aspargo	aas·paarr·go
avocado	abacate	aa·baa·kaa·te
banana	banana	baa·na·naa
bean	feijão	fay·zhowng
beetroot	beterraba	be·te·haa·baa
cabbage	repolho	he·po·lyo
carrot	cenoura	se·no·raa
cauliflower	couve flor	ko·ve flor
cherry	cereja	se·re·zhaa
corn	milho	mee·lyo
cucumber	pepino	pe·pee·no
fruit	frutas	froo·taas
grapes	uvas	oo·vaas

lemon	limão	lee·mowng
lentil	lentilha	leng·tee·lyaa
lettuce	alface	ow·faa·se
mushroom	cogumelo	ko·goo·me·lo
nut	noz	noz
onion	cebola	se·bo·laa
orange	laranja	laa·rang·zhaa
peas	ervilha	err·vee·lyaa
peach	pêssego	pe·se·go
pepper (bell)	pimentão	pee·meng·towng
pineapple	abacaxi	aa·baa·kaa·shee
plum	ameixa	aa·may·shaa
potato	batata	baa·taa·taa
pumpkin	abóbora	aa·bo·bo·raa
spinach	espinafre	es·pee·naa·fre
strawberry	morango	mo·rang·go
tomato	tomate	to·maa·te
vegetables	legumes	le·goo·mes
watermelon	melancia	me·lang·see·aa

Other

bread	pão	powng
butter	manteiga	mang·tay·gaa
cheese	queijo	kay·zho
eggs	ovos	o·vos
honey	mel	mel
jam	geléia	zhe·le·yaa
oil	óleo	o·lyo
pasta	massas	maa·saas
pepper	pimenta	pee·meng·taa
rice	arroz	aa·hos
salt	sal	sow
sugar	açúcar	aa·soo·kaarr
vinegar	vinagre	vee·naa·gre

Drinks

beer	cerveja	serr·ve·zhaa
coffee	café	kaa·fe
(orange) juice	suco de (laranja)	soo·ko de (laa·rang·zhaa)
milk	leite	lay·te
red wine	vinho tinto	vee·nyo teeng·to
tea	chá	shaa
(mineral) water	água (mineral)	aa·gwaa (mee·ne·row)
white wine	vinho branco	vee·nyo brang·ko

SIGNS – PORTUGUESE

Banheiro	Toilet
Entrada	Entrance
(Não) Tem Vaga	(No) Vacancy
Pronto Socorro	Emergency Department
Saída	Exit

Emergencies

Help!
Socorro! so·ko·ho

Leave me alone!
Me deixe em paz! me day·she eng paas

Call the police!
Chame a polícia! sha·me aa po·lee·syaa

Call a doctor!
Chame um médico! sha·me oom me·dee·ko

I'm lost.
Estou perdido/ es·to perr·dee·do/
perdida. (m/f) perr·dee·daa

I'm ill.
Estou doente. es·to do·eng·te

I'm allergic to (antibiotics).
Tenho alergia te·nyo aa·lerr·zhee·aa
à (antibióticos). aa (ang·tee·bee·o·tee·kos)

Where are the toilets?
Onde tem um banheiro? on·de teng oom ba·nyay·ro

Shopping & Services

I'd like to buy ...
Gostaria de gos·taa·ree·aa de
comprar ... kong·praarr ...

I'm just looking.
Estou só olhando. es·to so o·lyang·do

Can I look at it?
Posso ver? po·so verr

Do you have any others?
Você tem outros? vo·se teng o·tros

How much is it?
Quanto custa? kwang·to koos·taa

That's too expensive.
Está muito caro. es·taa mweeng·to kaa·ro

Can you lower the price?
Pode baixar o preço? po·de bai·shaarr o pre·so

There's a mistake in the bill.
Houve um erro na o·ve oom e·ho naa
conta. kong·taa

ATM	*caixa*	*kai·shaa*
	automático	*ow·to·maa·tee·ko*
market	*mercado*	*merr·kaa·do*
post office	*correio*	*ko·hay·o*
tourist office	*secretaria de turismo*	*se·kre·taa·ree·aa de too·rees·mo*

Time & Dates

What time is it?
Que horas são? ke aw·raas sowng

It's (10) o'clock.
São (dez) horas. sowng (des) aw·raas

How?	*Como?*	ko·mo
What?	*Que?*	ke
When?	*Quando?*	kwang·do
Where?	*Onde?*	ong·de
Who?	*Quem?*	keng
Why?	*Por que?*	porr ke

Half past (10).
(Dez) e meia. (des) e may·aa

morning	*manhã*	ma·nyang
afternoon	*tarde*	taar·de
evening	*noite*	noy·te

yesterday	*ontem*	ong·teng
today	*hoje*	o·zhe
tomorrow	*amanhã*	aa·ma·nyang

Monday	*segunda-feira*	se·goong·daa·fay·raa
Tuesday	*terça-feira*	terr·saa·fay·raa
Wednesday	*quarta-feira*	kwaarr·taa·fay·raa
Thursday	*quinta-feira*	keeng·taa·fay·raa
Friday	*sexta-feira*	ses·taa·fay·raa
Saturday	*sábado*	saa·baa·doo
Sunday	*domingo*	do·meeng·go

January	*janeiro*	zha·nay·ro
February	*fevereiro*	fe·ve·ray·ro
March	*março*	marr·so
April	*abril*	aa·bree·oo
May	*maio*	maa·yo
June	*junho*	zhoo·nyo
July	*julho*	zhoo·lyo
August	*agosto*	aa·gos·to
September	*setembro*	se·teng·bro
October	*outubro*	o·too·bro
November	*novembro*	no·veng·bro
December	*dezembro*	de·zeng·bro

Transportation

Public Transportation

boat	*barco*	baarr·ko
bus	*ônibus*	o·nee·boos
plane	*avião*	aa·vee·owng

NUMBERS – PORTUGUESE

1	*um*	oom
2	*dois*	doys
3	*três*	tres
4	*quatro*	kwaa·tro
5	*cinco*	seeng·ko
6	*seis*	says
7	*sete*	se·te
8	*oito*	oy·to
9	*nove*	naw·ve
10	*dez*	dez
20	*vinte*	veeng·te
30	*trinta*	treeng·taa
40	*quarenta*	kwaa·reng·taa
50	*cinquenta*	seen·kweng·taa
60	*sessenta*	se·seng·taa
70	*setenta*	se·teng·taa
80	*oitenta*	oy·teng·taa
90	*noventa*	no·veng·taa
100	*cem*	seng
1000	*mil*	mee·oo

train	*trem*	treng
first	*primeiro*	pree·may·ro
last	*último*	ool·tee·mo
next	*próximo*	pro·see·mo
airport	*aeroporto*	aa·e·ro·porr·to
aisle seat	*lugar no corredor*	loo·gaarr no ko·he·dorr
bus stop	*ponto de ônibus*	pong·to de o·nee·boos
cancelled	*cancelado*	kang·se·laa·do
delayed	*atrasado*	aa·traa·zaa·do
ticket office	*bilheteria*	bee·lye·te·ree·aa
timetable	*horário*	o·raa·ryo
train station	*estação de trem*	es·taa·sowng de treng
window seat	*lugar na janela*	loo·gaarr naa zhaa·ne·laa
a ... ticket	*uma passagem de ...*	oo·maa paa·sa·zheng de ...
1st-class	*primeira classe*	pree·may·raa klaa·se
2nd-class	*segunda classe*	se·goom·daa klaa·se
one-way	*ida*	ee·daa
return	*ida e volta*	ee·daa e vol·taa

Does it stop at ...?
Ele para em ...?   e·le paa·raa eng ...

What station is this?
Que estação é esta?   ke es·taa·sowng e es·taa

What time does it leave/arrive?
A que horas sai/chega?   aa ke aw·raas sai/she·gaa

Please tell me when we get to ...
Por favor me avise quando chegarmos à ...   porr faa·vor me aa·vee·ze kwang·do she·gaarr·mos aa ...

I'd like to get off here.
Gostaria de saltar aqui.   gos·taa·ree·aa de sow·taarr aa·kee

Driving & Cycling

I'd like to hire a/an ...	*Gostaria de alugar ...*	gos·taa·ree·aa de aa·loo·gaarr ...
4WD	*um carro quatro por quatro*	oom kaa·ho kwaa·tro porr kwaa·tro
bicycle	*uma bicicleta*	oo·ma bee·see·kle·taa
car	*um carro*	oom kaa·ho
motorcycle	*uma motocicleta*	oo·ma mo·to·see·kle·taa
child seat	*cadeira de criança*	kaa·day·raa de kree·ang·saa
diesel	*diesel*	dee·sel
helmet	*capacete*	kaa·paa·se·te
hitchhike	*pegar carona*	pe·gaarr kaa·ro·naa
mechanic	*mecânico*	me·ka·nee·ko
petrol/gas	*gasolina*	gaa·zo·lee·naa
service station	*posto de gasolina*	pos·to de gaa·zo·lee·naa
truck	*caminhão*	kaa·mee·nyowng

Is this the road to ...?
Esta é a estrada para ...?   es·taa e aa es·traa·daa paa·raa ...

Can I park here?
Posso estacionar aqui?   po·so es·taa·syo·naarr aa·kee

The car has broken down.
O carro quebrou.   o kaa·ho ke·bro

I had an accident.
Sofri um acidente.   so·free oom aa·see·deng·te

I've run out of petrol/gas.
Estou sem gasolina.   es·to seng gaa·zo·lee·naa

I have a flat tyre.
Meu pneu furou.   me·oo pee·ne·oo foo·ro

SPANISH

Latin American Spanish pronunciation is easy, as most sounds are also found in English. The stressed syllables are indicated with italics in our pronunciation guides.

Note that kh is a throaty sound (like the 'ch' in the Scottish *loch*), v and b are like a soft English 'v' (between a 'v' and a 'b'), and r is strongly rolled. There are some variations in spoken Spanish across Latin America, the most notable being the pronunciation of the letters *ll* and y. In our pronunciation guides they are represented with y because they are pronounced as the 'y' in 'yes' in most of Latin America. In some parts of the continent, though, they sound like the 'lli' in 'million', while in Argentina, Uruguay and highland Ecuador they are pronounced like the 's' in 'measure', or the 'sh' in 'shut'.

Where both polite and informal options are given in this section, they are indicated by the abbreviations 'pol' and 'inf'. The masculine and feminine forms are indicated with 'm' and 'f' respectively.

Basics

Hello.	Hola.	o·la
Goodbye.	Adiós.	a·dyos
How are you?	¿Qué tal?	ke tal
Fine, thanks.	Bien, gracias.	byen gra·syas
Excuse me.	Perdón.	per·don
Sorry.	Lo siento.	lo syen·to
Please.	Por favor.	por fa·vor
Thank you.	Gracias.	gra·syas
You are welcome.	De nada.	de na·da
Yes.	Sí.	see
No.	No.	no

My name is ...
Me llamo ... — me ya·mo ...

What's your name?
¿Cómo se llama Usted? — ko·mo se ya·ma oo·ste (pol)
¿Cómo te llamas? — ko·mo te ya·mas (inf)

Do you speak English?
¿Habla inglés? — a·bla een·gles (pol)
¿Hablas inglés? — a·blas een·gles (inf)

I don't understand.
Yo no entiendo. — yo no en·tyen·do

Accommodations

I'd like a single/double room.
Quisiera una habitación individual/doble. — kee·sye·ra oo·na a·bee·ta·syon een·dee·vee·dwal/do·ble

How much is it per night/person?
¿Cuánto cuesta por noche/persona? — kwan·to kwes·ta por no·che/per·so·na

Does it include breakfast?
¿Incluye el desayuno? — een·kloo·ye el de·sa·yoo·no

air-con	aire acondicionado	ai·re a·kon·dee·syo·na·do
bathroom	baño	ba·nyo
bed	cama	ka·ma
campsite	terreno de cámping	te·re·no de kam·peeng
guesthouse	pensión	pen·syon
hotel	hotel	o·tel
youth hostel	albergue juvenil	al·ber·ge khoo·ve·neel
window	ventana	ven·ta·na

Directions

Where's ...?
¿Dónde está ...? — don·de es·ta ...

What's the address?
¿Cuál es la dirección? — kwal es la dee·rek·syon

Could you please write it down?
¿Puede escribirlo, por favor? — pwe·de es·kree·beer·lo por fa·vor

Can you show me (on the map)?
¿Me lo puede indicar (en el mapa)? — me lo pwe·de een·dee·kar (en el ma·pa)

at the corner	en la esquina	en la es·kee·na
at the traffic lights	en el semáforo	en el se·ma·fo·ro
behind ...	detrás de ...	de·tras de ...
in front of ...	enfrente de ...	en·fren·te de ...
left	izquierda	ees·kyer·da
near	cerca	ser·ka
next to ...	al lado de ...	al la·do de ...
opposite ...	frente a ...	fren·te a ...
right	derecha	de·re·cha
straight ahead	todo recto	to·do rek·to

SIGNS – SPANISH

Abierto	Open
Cerrado	Closed
Entrada	Entrance
Hombres/Varones	Men
Mujeres/Damas	Women
Prohibido	Prohibited
Salida	Exit
Servicios/Baños	Toilets

KEY PATTERNS

To get by in Spanish, mix and match these simple patterns with words of your choice:

When's (the next flight)?
¿Cuándo sale kwan·do sa·le
(el próximo vuelo)? (el prok·see·mo vwe·lo)

Where's (the station)?
¿Dónde está don·de es·ta
(la estación)? (la es·ta·syon)

Where can I (buy a ticket)?
¿Dónde puedo don·de pwe·do
(comprar un billete)? (kom·prar oon bee·ye·te)

Do you have (a map)?
¿Tiene (un mapa)? tye·ne (oon ma·pa)

Is there (a toilet)?
¿Hay (servicios)? ai (ser·vee·syos)

I'd like (a coffee).
Quisiera (un café). kee·sye·ra (oon ka·fe)

I'd like (to hire a car).
Quisiera (alquilar kee·sye·ra (al·kee·lar
un coche). oon ko·che)

Can I (enter)?
¿Se puede (entrar)? se pwe·de (en·trar)

Could you please (help me)?
¿Puede (ayudarme), pwe·de (a·yoo·dar·me)
por favor? por fa·vor

Do I have to (get a visa)?
¿Necesito ne·se·see·to
(obtener (ob·te·ner
un visado)? oon vee·sa·do)

Eating & Drinking

Can I see the menu, please?
¿Puedo ver el menú, pwe·do ver el me·noo
por favor? por fa·vor

What would you recommend?
¿Qué recomienda? ke re·ko·myen·da

Do you have vegetarian food?
¿Tienen comida tye·nen ko·mee·da
vegetariana? ve·khe·ta·rya·na

I don't eat (red meat).
No como (carne roja). no ko·mo (kar·ne ro·kha)

That was delicious!
¡Estaba buenísimo! es·ta·ba bwe·nee·see·mo

Cheers!
¡Salud! sa·loo

The bill, please.
La cuenta, por favor. la kwen·ta por fa·vor

I'd like a *Quisiera una* kee·sye·ra oo·na
table for ... *mesa para ...* me·sa pa·ra ...

(eight) *las (ocho)* las (o·cho)
o'clock

(two) people *(dos)* (dos)
personas per·so·nas

Key Words

appetisers	aperitivos	a·pe·ree·tee·vos
bottle	botella	bo·te·ya
bowl	bol	bol
breakfast	desayuno	de·sa·yoo·no
children's menu	menú infantil	me·noo een·fan·teel
(too) cold	(muy) frío	(mooy) free·o
dinner	cena	se·na
food	comida	ko·mee·da
fork	tenedor	te·ne·dor
glass	vaso	va·so
hot (warm)	caliente	kal·yen·te
knife	cuchillo	koo·chee·yo
lunch	comida	ko·mee·da
main course	segundo plato	se·goon·do pla·to
plate	plato	pla·to
restaurant	restaurante	res·tow·ran·te
spoon	cuchara	koo·cha·ra
with	con	kon
without	sin	seen

Meat & Fish

beef	carne de vaca	kar·ne de va·ka
chicken	pollo	po·yo
duck	pato	pa·to
fish	pescado	pes·ka·do
lamb	cordero	kor·de·ro
lobster	langosta	lan·gos·ta
pork	cerdo	ser·do
shrimps	camarones	ka·ma·ro·nes
tuna	atún	a·toon
turkey	pavo	pa·vo
veal	ternera	ter·ne·ra

Fruit & Vegetables

apple	manzana	man·sa·na
apricot	albaricoque	al·ba·ree·ko·ke
artichoke	alcachofa	al·ka·cho·fa
asparagus	espárragos	es·pa·ra·gos
banana	plátano	pla·ta·no
beans	judías	khoo·dee·as
cabbage	col	kol
carrot	zanahoria	sa·na·o·rya
celery	apio	a·pyo

cherry	cereza	se·re·sa
corn	maíz	ma·ees
cucumber	pepino	pe·pee·no
fruit	fruta	froo·ta
grape	uvas	oo·vas
lemon	limón	lee·mon
lentils	lentejas	len·te·khas
lettuce	lechuga	le·choo·ga
mushroom	champiñón	cham·pee·nyon
nuts	nueces	nwe·ses
onion	cebolla	se·bo·ya
orange	naranja	na·ran·kha
peach	melocotón	me·lo·ko·ton
peas	guisantes	gee·san·tes
pepper (bell)	pimiento	pee·myen·to
pineapple	piña	pee·nya
plum	ciruela	seer·we·la
potato	patata	pa·ta·ta
pumpkin	calabaza	ka·la·ba·sa
spinach	espinacas	es·pee·na·kas
strawberry	fresa	fre·sa
tomato	tomate	to·ma·te
vegetable	verdura	ver·doo·ra
watermelon	sandía	san·dee·a

Other

bread	pan	pan
butter	mantequilla	man·te·kee·ya
cheese	queso	ke·so
egg	huevo	we·vo
honey	miel	myel
jam	mermelada	mer·me·la·da
oil	aceite	a·sey·te
pasta	pasta	pas·ta
pepper	pimienta	pee·myen·ta
rice	arroz	a·ros
salt	sal	sal
sugar	azúcar	a·soo·kar

Drinks

beer	cerveza	ser·ve·sa
coffee	café	ka·fe
(orange) juice	zumo (de naranja)	soo·mo (de na·ran·kha)
milk	leche	le·che
red wine	vino tinto	vee·no teen·to
tea	té	te
(mineral) water	agua (mineral)	a·gwa (mee·ne·ral)
white wine	vino blanco	vee·no blan·ko

LANGUAGE SPANISH

Emergencies

Help! ¡Socorro! so·ko·ro
Go away! ¡Vete! ve·te
Call ...! ¡Llame a ...! ya·me a ...
  a doctor un médico oon me·dee·ko
  the police la policía la po·lee·see·a

I'm lost.
Estoy perdido/a. es·toy per·dee·do/a (m/f)
I'm ill.
Estoy enfermo/a. es·toy en·fer·mo/a (m/f)
I'm allergic to (antibiotics).
Soy alérgico/a a (los antibióticos). soy a·ler·khee·ko/a a (los an·tee·byo·tee·kos) (m/f)
Where are the toilets?
¿Dónde están los baños? don·de es·tan los ba·nyos

Shopping & Services

I'd like to buy ...
Quisiera comprar ... kee·sye·ra kom·prar ...
I'm just looking.
Sólo estoy mirando. so·lo es·toy mee·ran·do
Can I look at it?
¿Puedo verlo? pwe·do ver·lo
I don't like it.
No me gusta. no me goos·ta
How much is it?
¿Cuánto cuesta? kwan·to kwes·ta
That's too expensive.
Es muy caro. es mooy ka·ro
Can you lower the price?
¿Podría bajar un poco el precio? po·dree·a ba·khar oon po·ko el pre·syo
There's a mistake in the bill.
Hay un error en la cuenta. ai oon e·ror en la kwen·ta

| **ATM** | cajero automático | ka·khe·ro ow·to·ma·tee·ko |
| **market** | mercado | mer·ka·do |

QUESTION WORDS – SPANISH

How?	¿Cómo?	ko·mo
What?	¿Qué?	ke
When?	¿Cuándo?	kwan·do
Where?	¿Dónde?	don·de
Who?	¿Quién?	kyen
Why?	¿Por qué?	por ke

post office	correos	ko·re·os
tourist office	oficina de turismo	o·fee·see·na de too·rees·mo

Time & Dates

What time is it?
¿Qué hora es? ke o·ra es

It's (10) o'clock.
Son (las diez). son (las dyes)

It's half past (one).
Es (la una) y media. es (la oo·na) ee me·dya

morning	mañana	ma·nya·na
afternoon	tarde	tar·de
evening	noche	no·che
yesterday	ayer	a·yer
today	hoy	oy
tomorrow	mañana	ma·nya·na
Monday	lunes	loo·nes
Tuesday	martes	mar·tes
Wednesday	miércoles	myer·ko·les
Thursday	jueves	khwe·ves
Friday	viernes	vyer·nes
Saturday	sábado	sa·ba·do
Sunday	domingo	do·meen·go

NUMBERS – SPANISH

1	uno	oo·no
2	dos	dos
3	tres	tres
4	cuatro	kwa·tro
5	cinco	seen·ko
6	seis	seys
7	siete	sye·te
8	ocho	o·cho
9	nueve	nwe·ve
10	diez	dyes
20	veinte	veyn·te
30	treinta	treyn·ta
40	cuarenta	kwa·ren·ta
50	cincuenta	seen·kwen·ta
60	sesenta	se·sen·ta
70	setenta	se·ten·ta
80	ochenta	o·chen·ta
90	noventa	no·ven·ta
100	cien	syen
1000	mil	meel

January	enero	e·ne·ro
February	febrero	fe·bre·ro
March	marzo	mar·so
April	abril	a·breel
May	mayo	ma·yo
June	junio	khoon·yo
July	julio	khool·yo
August	agosto	a·gos·to
September	septiembre	sep·tyem·bre
October	octubre	ok·too·bre
November	noviembre	no·vyem·bre
December	diciembre	dee·syem·bre

Transportation

Public Transportation

boat	barco	bar·ko
bus	autobús	ow·to·boos
plane	avión	a·vyon
train	tren	tren
first	primero	pree·me·ro
last	último	ool·tee·mo
next	próximo	prok·see·mo
airport	aeropuerto	a·e·ro·pwer·to
aisle seat	asiento de pasillo	a·syen·to de pa·see·yo
bus stop	parada de autobuses	pa·ra·da de ow·to·boo·ses
cancelled	cancelado	kan·se·la·do
delayed	retrasado	re·tra·sa·do
ticket office	taquilla	ta·kee·ya
timetable	horario	o·ra·ryo
train station	estación de trenes	es·ta·syon de tre·nes
window seat	asiento junto a la ventana	a·syen·to khoon·to a la ven·ta·na

A ... ticket, please.	Un billete de ..., por favor.	oon bee·ye·te de ... por fa·vor
1st-class	primera clase	pree·me·ra kla·se
2nd-class	segunda clase	se·goon·da kla·se
one-way	ida	ee·da
return	ida y vuelta	ee·da ee vwel·ta

Does it stop at ...?
¿Para en ...? pa·ra en ...

What stop is this?
¿Cuál es esta parada?   kwal es es·ta pa·ra·da

What time does it arrive/leave?
¿A qué hora llega/sale?   a ke o·ra ye·ga/sa·le

Please tell me when we get to ...
¿Puede avisarme   pwe·de a·vee·sar·me
cuando lleguemos a ...?   kwan·do ye·ge·mos a ...

I want to get off here.
Quiero bajarme aquí.   kye·ro ba·khar·me a·kee

Driving & Cycling

I'd like to hire a ...	Quisiera alquilar ...	kee·sye·ra al·kee·lar ...
4WD	un todo-terreno	oon to·do-te·re·no
bicycle	una bicicleta	oo·na bee·see·kle·ta
car	un coche	oon ko·che
motorcycle	una moto	oo·na mo·to
child seat	asiento de seguridad para niños	a·syen·to de se·goo·ree·da pa·ra nee·nyos
diesel	petróleo	pet·ro·le·o

helmet	casco	kas·ko
hitchhike	hacer botella	a·ser bo·te·ya
mechanic	mecánico	me·ka·nee·ko
petrol/gas	gasolina	ga·so·lee·na
service station	gasolinera	ga·so·lee·ne·ra
truck	camion	ka·myon

Is this the road to ...?
¿Se va a ... por   se va a ... por
esta carretera?   es·ta ka·re·te·ra

Can I park here?
¿Puedo aparcar aquí?   pwe·do a·par·kar a·kee

The car has broken down.
El coche se ha averiado.   el ko·che se a a·ve·rya·do

I had an accident.
He tenido un   e te·nee·do oon
accidente.   ak·see·den·te

I've run out of petrol/gas.
Me he quedado sin   me e ke·da·do seen
gasolina.   ga·so·lee·na

I have a flat tyre.
Se me pinchó   se me peen·cho
una rueda.   oo·na rwe·da

AYMARÁ & QUECHUA

The few Aymará and Quechua words and phrases included here will be useful for those traveling in the Andes. Aymará is spoken by the Aymará people, who inhabit the highland regions of Bolivia and Peru and smaller adjoining areas of Chile and Argentina. While the Quechua included here is from the Cuzco dialect, it should prove helpful wherever you travel in the Andes. The exception is Ecuador, where it is known as Quichua – the dialect that's most removed from the Cuzco variety.

In the following lists, Aymará is the second column, Quechua the third. The principles of pronunciation for both languages are similar to those found in Spanish. An apostrophe (') represents a glottal stop, which is the 'nonsound' that occurs in the middle of 'uh-oh.'

Hello.	Kamisaraki.	Napaykullayki.
Please.	Mirá.	Allichu.
Thank you.	Yuspagara.	Yusulipayki.
Yes.	Jisa.	Ari.
No. Mana.		Janiwa.
How do you say ...?	Cun saña-sauca'ha ...?	Imainata nincha chaita ...?
It's called ...	Ucan sutipa'h ...	Chaipa'g sutin'ha ...
Please repeat.	Uastata sita.	Ua'manta niway.
How much?	K'gauka?	Maik'ata'g?
father	auqui	tayta
mother	taica	mama

food	manka	mikíuy
river	jawira	mayu
snowy peak	kollu	riti-orko
water	uma	yacu
1	maya	u'
2	paya	iskai
3	quimsa	quinsa
4	pusi	tahua
5	pesca	phiska
6	zo'hta	so'gta
7	pakalko	khanchis
8	quimsakalko	pusa'g
9	yatunca	iskon
10	tunca	chunca

GLOSSARY

Unless otherwise indicated, the terms listed in this glossary refer to Spanish-speaking South America in general, but regional variations in meaning are common. Portuguese phrases, which are only used in Brazil, are indicated with 'Bra.'

aduana – customs

aguardiente – sugarcane alcohol

ají – chili

albergue – hostel

alcaldía – town hall; virtually synonymous with *municipalidad*

almuerzo – fixed-price set lunch

alojamiento – rock-bottom accommodations with shared toilet and bathroom facilities

altiplano – Andean high plain of Peru, Bolivia, Chile and Argentina

apartamento – apartment or flat; in Brazil, a hotel room with private bathroom

artesanía – handicrafts; crafts shop

asado – roasted; in Argentina, a barbecue which is often a family outing

ascensor – elevator

audiencia – colonial administrative subdivision

ayahuasca – hallucinogenic brew made from jungle vines

Aymará – indigenous people of highland Bolivia, Peru and Chile (also called *Kolla*); also their language

balneario – bathing resort or beach

baños – baths

barrio – neighborhood, district or borough; in Venezuela, a shantytown; in Brazil, *bairro*

bloco (Bra) – group of musicians and dancers who perform in street parades during Brazil's Carnaval

bodega – winery or storage area for wine

bus-cama – literally 'bus-bed'; very comfortable bus with fully reclining seats; also called *coche-cama*

cabaña – cabin

cabildo – colonial town council

cachaça (Bra) – sugarcane rum, also called *pinga*; Brazil's national drink

cachoeira (Bra) – waterfall

caipirinha (Bra) – Brazil's national cocktail

calle – street

cambista – street money changer

camino – road, path, way

camión – open-bed truck; popular form of local transport in the Andean countries

camioneta – pickup or other small truck; form of local transport in the Andean countries

campamento – campsite

campesino/a – rural dweller who practices subsistence agriculture; peasant

caña – rum

Candomblé (Bra) – Afro-Brazilian religion of Bahia

capoeira (Bra) – martial art/dance developed by Bahian slaves

Carnaval – all over Latin America, pre-Lenten celebration

casa de cambio – authorized foreign-currency exchange house

casa de familia – modest family accommodations

casa de huésped – literally 'guesthouse'; form of economical lodging where guests may have access to the kitchen, garden and laundry facilities

casona – large house, usually a mansion; term often applied to colonial architecture in particular

catarata – waterfall

caudillo – in 19th-century South American politics, a provincial strongman

cazuela – hearty stew

cena – dinner; often an inexpensive set menu

cerro – hill; also refers to very high Andean peaks

certificado – registered (for mail)

cerveza – beer

ceviche – marinated raw seafood (it can be a source of both cholera and gnathostomiasis)

charango – Andean stringed instrument, traditionally made with an armadillo shell as a soundbox

chicha – in Andean countries, a popular beverage (often alcoholic) made from ingredients such as yucca, sweet potato or maize

chifa – Chinese restaurant (term most commonly used in Peru, Bolivia and Ecuador)

chiva – in Colombia, basic rural bus with wooden bench seats

churrasquería – restaurant featuring barbecued meat; in Brazil, *churrascaria*

cocalero – coca grower

coche-cama – see *bus-cama*

colectivo – depending on the country, either a bus, a minibus or a shared taxi

combi – small bus or minibus; also called *micro*

comedor – basic eatery or dining room in a hotel

comida corriente – in Colombia, basic set meal

confitería – cafe that serves coffee, tea, desserts and simple food orders

cordillera – mountain range

correo – post office; in Brazil, *correio*

costanera – in the Southern Cone, a seaside, riverside or lakeside road

costeño – inhabitant of the coast

criollo/a – Spaniard born in colonial South America; in modern times, a South American of European descent

cumbia – big on horns and percussion, a cousin to salsa, merengue and lambada

curanto – Chilean seafood stew

cuy – roasted guinea pig, a traditional Andean food

denuncia – affidavit or statement, usually in connection with theft or robbery

edificio – building

esquina – corner (abbreviated to 'esq')

estancia – extensive grazing establishment, either for cattle or sheep, with a dominant owner or manager (*estanciero*) and dependent resident labor force

FARC – Fuerzas Armadas Revolucionarias de Colombia (Revolutionary Armed Forces of Colombia); guerrilla movement

farmacia – pharmacy

favela (Bra) – slum or shanty-town

fazenda (Bra) – large ranch or farm, similar to *hacienda*

ferrobus – type of passenger train

ferrocarril – railway, railroad

ferroviária (Bra) – railway station

flota – fleet; often a long-distance bus line

fútbol – soccer; in Brazil, *fútebol*

gaucho – in Argentina and Uruguay, a cowboy, herdsman; in Brazil, *gaúcho*

golpe de estado – coup d'état

gringo/a – a foreigner or person with light hair and complexion; not necessarily a derogatory term

guanaco – undomesticated relative of the llama

guaraná – Amazonian shrub with berries believed to have magical and medicinal powers; in Brazil, a popular soft drink

Guaraní – indigenous people of Argentina, Brazil, Bolivia and Paraguay; also their language

hacienda – large rural landholding with a dependent resident labor force under a dominant owner (*hacendado*)

hidroviária – boat terminal

hospedaje – budget accommodations with shared bathroom; usually a family home with an extra guest room

hostal – small hotel or guesthouse

huaso – cowboy

humita – a sweet-corn tamale or dumpling

iglesia – church; in Brazil, *igreja*

Inca – dominant indigenous civilization of the central Andes at the time of the Spanish Conquest; refers both to the people and, individually, to their leader

indígena – native American; indigenous person

isla – island; in Brazil, *ilha*

lago – lake

laguna – lagoon; shallow lake

lanchero – boat driver

latifundio – large landholding, such as a *hacienda* or cattle *estancia*

lavandería – laundry

leito (Bra) – luxury overnight express bus

licuado – fruit shake blended with milk or water

lista de correos – poste restante

locutorio – small telephone office

machismo – exaggerated masculine pride

malecón – shoreline promenade

Mapuche – indigenous people of northern Patagonia

marisquería – seafood restaurant

maté – see *yerba maté*

mate de coca – coca-leaf tea

menú del día – inexpensive set meal

mercado – market

mercado negro – black market

mestizo/a – a person of mixed indigenous and Spanish descent

micro – small bus or minibus; also called *combi*

migración – immigration office

minuta – short-order snack in Argentina, Paraguay and Uruguay

mirador – viewpoint or lookout, usually on a hill but often in a building

moai – enormous stone statues on Easter Island

mototaxi – in Peru, three-wheeled motorcycle rickshaw; also called *motocarro*

mudéjar – a Moorish-influenced architectural style that developed in Spain beginning in the 12th century

mulato/a – person of mixed African and European ancestry

municipalidad – city or town hall

museo – museum; in Brazil, *museu*

música criolla – creole music

música folklórica – traditional Andean music

nevado – snow-covered peak

oferta – promotional fare for plane or bus travel

oficina – office (abbreviated to 'of')

onces – morning or afternoon tea; snack

Pachamama – Mother Earth, deity of the indigenous Andean people

panadería – bakery

panama – traditional lightweight straw hat, actually of Ecuadorian origin

parada/paradero – bus stop

páramo – humid, high-altitude grassland of the northern Andean countries

parque nacional – national park

parrilla/parrillada – barbecued or grilled meat; also used to refer to a steakhouse restaurant or the grill used to cook meat

paseo – avenue, promenade

patio de comidas – food court

peatonal – pedestrian mall

pehuén – the monkey-puzzle tree of southern South America

peña – club/bar that hosts informal folk music gatherings; performance at such a club

pensión – short-term budget accommodations in a family home, which may also have permanent lodgers

piropo – sexist remark, ranging from relatively innocuous to very offensive

pisco – white-grape brandy, Peruvian national drink; most frequently served as a pisco sour cocktail

Planalto – enormous plateau that covers much of southern Brazil

pollería – restaurant serving grilled chicken

por puesto – in Venezuela, shared taxi or minibus

posada – small family-owned guesthouse; term sometimes also used for a hotel; in Brazil, *pousada*

prato feito (Bra) – literally 'made plate' or 'plate of the day'; typically an enormous and very cheap, fixed-price meal

precordillera – foothills of the Andes

pucará – an indigenous Andean fortification

puna – Andean highlands, usually above 3000m

quebrada – ravine, normally dry

Quechua – indigenous language of the Andean highlands; 'Quichua' in Ecuador

quena – simple reed flute

quinoa – native Andean grain, the dietary equivalent of rice in the pre-Columbian era

rancho – rural house

recargo – surcharge; added by many businesses to credit-card transactions

reducción – in colonial Latin America, the concentration of native populations in central settlements, usually to aid political control or religious instruction; also known as *congregación*

refugio – rustic shelter in a national park or remote area

reggaeton – Caribbean-born popular music which combines Latin rhythms with rap

remise – in Argentina, taxi booked over the phone

residencial – budget accommodations, sometimes only seasonal; in general, *residenciales* are in buildings designed expressly for short-stay lodging

río – river; in Brazil, *rio*

rodoferroviária (Bra) – combined bus and train station

rodoviária (Bra) – bus station

ruta – route or highway

s/n – *sin número;* indicating a street address without a number

salar – salt lake or salt pan, usually in the high Andes or Argentine Patagonia

salsoteca – salsa club

salteña – meat and vegetable pasty, generally a spicier version of empanada

Semana Santa – celebrated all over South America, Holy Week, the week before Easter

Sendero Luminoso – Shining Path, Peru's Maoist terrorist group which led a guerrilla war in the late 1980s

serrano – inhabitant of the mountains

siesta – lengthy afternoon break for lunch and, occasionally, a nap

soroche – altitude sickness

Sranan Tongo – creole widely spoken in Suriname; also called Surinaams

suco (Bra) – fruit juice; fruit-juice bar

tasca – Spanish-style bar-restaurant

teleférico – cable car

telenovela – TV soap opera

tenedor libre – in Argentina, 'all-you-can-eat' buffet

tepui – flat-topped mountain; home to unique flora

termas – hot springs

terminal de ómnibus – bus station; also called *terminal terrestre*

tinto – red wine; in Colombia, small cup of black coffee

todo terreno – mountain bike

torrentismo – rappelling down a waterfall

totora – type of reed, used as a building material

vaquero – cowboy; in Brazil, *vaqueiro*

vicuña – wild relative of the domestic llama and alpaca, found only at high altitudes in the south-central Andes

yerba maté – 'Paraguayan tea' *(Ilex paraguariensis);* consumed regularly in Argentina, Paraguay, Uruguay and Brazil

zampoña – pan flute featured in traditional Andean music

zona franca – duty-free zone

Behind the Scenes

SEND US YOUR FEEDBACK

We love to hear from travelers – your comments keep us on our toes and help make our books better. Our well-traveled team reads every word on what you loved or loathed about this book. Although we cannot reply individually to your submissions, we always guarantee that your feedback goes straight to the appropriate authors, in time for the next edition. Each person who sends us information is thanked in the next edition – the most useful submissions are rewarded with a selection of digital PDF chapters.

Visit **lonelyplanet.com/contact** to submit your updates and suggestions or to ask for help. Our award-winning website also features inspirational travel stories, news and discussions.

Note: We may edit, reproduce and incorporate your comments in Lonely Planet products such as guidebooks, websites and digital products, so let us know if you don't want your comments reproduced or your name acknowledged. For a copy of our privacy policy visit lonelyplanet.com/privacy.

OUR READERS

Many thanks to the travelers who used the last edition and wrote to us with helpful hints, useful advice and interesting anecdotes:

Amélie Baechler, Anne Jachmann, Anouk Lubbe, Arthur Châteauvert, Bethan Phillips, Boon Quek, Cain Papettas, Carla Doyle, Catalina Tanasescu, Chris Verrill, Ciarán Ó Súilleabháin, Dominik Hofmann, Elin Lyckestam, Etienne Rompre, Hannah Wallin, Heather Monell, Lisa Howarth, Lucas Liu, Luke Porter, Manuel Gaviria, Marcus Draxler, Marta Alfonsea Zaragoza, Michael Weber, Natasha Walker, Piotr Dziadosz, Reiss Draper & Kaylie McArthur, Susanne Neuenschwander, Zak Hirsch

WRITER THANKS

Regis St Louis

Countless locals and expats provided help and friendship along the way, and I'm deeply grateful to Cristiano Nogueira, Jackki Saysell, Eduardo Cruxen, Ian Papareskos, Alberto Armendáriz, Bindu Mathur, Tom Lemesurier, German and Daniel Olano, Michael Nagy, Marcelo Esteves, André Paranhos, Toninho, Kevin Raub, Samantha Aquim, Gilson Martins, Antônia Leite Barbosa, and Lenny Niemeyer. As always heartfelt thanks to Cassandra, Magdalena and Genevieve for their continued support.

Isabel Albiston

Huge thanks to MaSovaida Morgan, Patricio Santos, Cé Martínez, Jessica Pollack, Madi Lang, Miles Lewis, Sorrel Moseley-Williams, Jazmín Arellano, Mercedes Fauda, Lorena Polo, Alan Seabright, Bárbara Poey, Patricia Franco, Nano Aznarez, Maria Elia Capella, Magda Dobrajska and my family. Your insider tips, friendship and support are greatly appreciated. Besos for Facundo, Verita, Felipe, Ciro and Lottie and Alice, and special thanks to *asadores* Marcelo Larroque and Julian Mule – *un aplauso!*

Gregor Clark

Muchísimas gracias to the many Uruguayans and resident expatriates who shared their love of the country and local knowledge with me, especially Gloria, Tino, Miguel, Monica, Alain, Cecilia, Eduardo, Aaron, Victoria, Karen, Juan Manuel, Nahir and Pedro. Back home, *besos y abrazos* to Gaen, Meigan and Chloe, who always make coming home the best part of the trip.

Mark Johanson

Muchas gracias to all the Chilean and Rapa Nui people who warmed my heart and filled my belly with so much *manjar* and Carmenere that it was often impossible to work. Thanks to Felipe Bascuñán, Megan Snedden, Vanessa Petersen and Carla Andrade for joining me for portions of the trip and offering expertise.

...aula Santa Ana, ...s, Gonzalo Silva ...being fountains

...entrusting me with ...try, to my fellow ...eryone who's helped ...ticular: Jose and ...Medellin; Tony in Popayan, ... the mountain biking folk of Salento; Ko... Hostel in Pereira; Gloria in Guatape; Finca El Maco and Pacho in San Agustín; plus the driver who successfully navigated the Trampolin de la Muerte.

Brian Kluepfel

My wife Paula Paz, who is always with me, even when we are apart. My editor Bailey, for putting up with all the silly WhatsApp photos. My *amigo para siempre* Goyo, a voice of reason in traveling tempests. My Lonely planet colleagues Neill and Cheree for overseas cheer. My family, who don't like me doing this, but nonetheless pray for me. For every bus driver in Ecuador: I wouldn't have made it without you guys!

Tom Masters

Huge thanks to the cast of colourful characters in three countries that helped me with research, but in particular to Amarylis Lewis at Wilderness Expeditions, Candace Phillips at Visit Rupununi, Charlie and Christian in Georgetown, Celeste Brash and Anna Kaminski, Oren Jarvis, Ayla Kenyon, Sebastian DeFreitas, Kayla DeFreitas, Leroy Ignacio, Colin Edwards and Erienne Hynes-Lourens.

Brendan Sainsbury

Muchas gracias to all the skilled bus drivers, helpful tourist information staff, generous hotel owners, expert *arepa* makers, and innocent passerby who helped me, unwittingly or otherwise, during my research trip. Special thanks to my wife, Liz for joining me on the road in Cartagena and Santa Marta.

Paul Smith

Thanks to my family Carol, Shawn and Ewan for their patience with me being away. Karina Atkinson and Joe Sarvary in Pilar and Irma Ramírez in Sta Maria de Fe were extremely helpful. Bailey Freeman was always quick with replies to my questions. Special thanks also for the great social and conservation work being done by Para La Tierra, Santa Maria Education Fund, Pro Cosara, Guyra Paraguay and FMB to make Paraguay a better place to live and visit.

Luke Waterson

Combining a huge capital like Quito with the Andes, Amazon and Galápagos in one research trip is an endeavour – and I couldn't have done it without the help of Mark Thurber in Quito, Fausto Andi in Coca, Matt Terry in Tena and Tony Lloyd in Cuenca. Thanks to the unnamed bus drivers, taxi drivers, speedboat and canoe operators, pilots and administrative assistants at umpteen hotels, restaurants and other businesses that eased the passage by providing me with insightful information.

ACKNOWLEDGEMENTS

Climate map data adapted from Peel MC, Finlayson BL & McMahon TA (2007) 'Updated World Map of the Köppen-Geiger Climate Classification', Hydrology and Earth System Sciences, 11, 1633-44.

Cover photograph: Llama, Peru, Agatha Kadar/ Shutterstock ©

THIS BOOK

This 14th edition of Lonely Planet's *South America* guidebook was researched and written by Regis St Louis, Isabel Albiston, Robert Balkovich, Celeste Brash, Jade Bremner, Cathy Brown, Gregor Clark, Alex Egerton, Michael Grosberg, Anthony Ham, Mark Johanson, Anna Kaminski, Brian Kluepfel, Tom Masters, Carolyn McCarthy, MaSovaida Morgan, Anja Mutić, Kevin Raub, Brendan Sainsbury, Adam Skolnick, Paul Smith, Andy Symington, Phillip Tang, Luke Waterson and Wendy Yanagihara. It was curated by Regis St Louis, Isabel Albiston, Celeste Brash, Bailey Freeman and Brendan Sainsbury. This guidebook was produced by the following:

Destination Editor Bailey Freeman

Senior Product Editor Saralinda Turner

Regional Senior Cartographer Corey Hutchison

Product Editor Sandie Kestell

Book Designer Mazzy Prinsep

Assisting Editors Sarah Bailey, Michelle Bennett, Nigel Chin, Joel Cotterell, Barbara Delissen, Carly Hall, Gabrielle Innes, Jodie Martire, Lou McGregor, Alison Morris, Lauren O'Connell, Charlotte Orr, Monique Perrin, Sam Wheeler

Assisting Cartographers Mick Garrett, Valentina Kremenchutskaya

Cover Researcher Naomi Parker

Thanks to Melanie Dankel, Amy Lynch, Claire Rourke

Malbecs + Syrahs

Buller Brewery - Recoleta

NE -

Iguazau Falls to chic

Sophisticated Rosan

wedged Uruguay + Rio Parana

"Mesopotamia

Few Hours North

Chile

Elqui Valley

Carmenere wine

pisco

Altacama desert

Index

Map Legend

Sights

- Beach
- Bird Sanctuary
- Buddhist
- Castle/Palace
- Christian
- Confucian
- Hindu
- Islamic
- Jain
- Jewish
- Monument
- Museum/Gallery/Historic Building
- Ruin
- Shinto
- Sikh
- Taoist
- Winery/Vineyard
- Zoo/Wildlife Sanctuary
- Other Sight

Activities, Courses & Tours

- Bodysurfing
- Diving
- Canoeing/Kayaking
- Course/Tour
- Sento Hot Baths/Onsen
- Skiing
- Snorkeling
- Surfing
- Swimming/Pool
- Walking
- Windsurfing
- Other Activity

Sleeping

- Sleeping
- Camping
- Hut/Shelter

Eating

- Eating

Drinking & Nightlife

- Drinking & Nightlife
- Cafe

Entertainment

- Entertainment

Shopping

- Shopping

Information

- Bank
- Embassy/Consulate
- Hospital/Medical
- Internet
- Police
- Post Office
- Telephone
- Toilet
- Tourist Information
- Other Information

Geographic

- Beach
- Gate
- Hut/Shelter
- Lighthouse
- Lookout
- Mountain/Volcano
- Oasis
- Park
- Pass
- Picnic Area
- Waterfall

Population

- Capital (National)
- Capital (State/Province)
- City/Large Town
- Town/Village

Transport

- Airport
- Border crossing
- Bus
- Cable car/Funicular
- Cycling
- Ferry
- Metro station
- Monorail
- Parking
- Petrol station
- Subway/Subte station
- Taxi
- Train station/Railway
- Tram
- Underground station
- Other Transport

Routes

- Tollway
- Freeway
- Primary
- Secondary
- Tertiary
- Lane
- Unsealed road
- Road under construction
- Plaza/Mall
- Steps
- Tunnel
- Pedestrian overpass
- Walking Tour
- Walking Tour detour
- Path/Walking Trail

Boundaries

- International
- State/Province
- Disputed
- Regional/Suburb
- Marine Park
- Cliff
- Wall

Hydrography

- River, Creek
- Intermittent River
- Canal
- Water
- Dry/Salt/Intermittent Lake
- Reef

Areas

- Airport/Runway
- Beach/Desert
- Cemetery (Christian)
- Cemetery (Other)
- Glacier
- Mudflat
- Park/Forest
- Sight (Building)
- Sportsground
- Swamp/Mangrove

Note: Not all symbols displayed above appear on the maps in this book

Kevin Raub

Brazil, Chile, Colombia Atlanta native Kevin started his career as a music journalist in New York, working for *Men's Journal* and *Rolling Stone* magazines. He ditched the rock 'n' roll lifestyle for travel writing and has written over 95 Lonely Planet guides, focused mainly on Brazil, Chile, Colombia, USA, India, the Caribbean and Portugal. Kevin also contributes to a variety of travel magazines in both the USA and UK. Along the way, the self-confessed hophead is in constant search of wildly high IBUs in local beers. Follow him on Twitter and Instagram (@RaubOnTheRoad).

Adam Skolnick

Argentina Adam's travel obsession bloomed while working as an environmental activist in the mid-1990s. These days he's an award-winning journalist and travel writer who writes about travel, culture, human rights, sports and the environment for a variety of publications, including the *New York Times, Playboy, Outside, BBC.com, Wired, ESPN.com* and *Men's Health,* and he's authored or co-authored over 35 Lonely Planet guidebooks. An avid open water swimmer and diver, he's also the author of the critically acclaimed narrative non-fiction book, *ONE BREATH: Freediving, Death and the Quest to Shatter Human Limits* and *INDOLIRIUM.* He lives in Malibu, California. IG. @adamskolnick

Paul Smith

Paraguay From an early age, and with a vague and naive ambition to be the next David Attenborough, Paul dreamed of exploring the remotest areas of South America in search of wildlife. After spending two months in Bolivia as a student, that dream started to come true, but with David Attenborough still going strong he changed his career plans, became a travel writer and moved to Paraguay permanently in 2003.

Andy Symington

Brazil Andy has written or worked on over a hundred books and other updates for Lonely Planet (especially in Europe and Latin America) and other publishing companies, and has published articles on numerous subjects for a variety of newspapers, magazines and websites. He part-owns and operates a rock bar, has written a novel and is currently working on several fiction and non-fiction writing projects. Andy, from Australia, moved to Northern Spain many years ago. When he's not off with a backpack in some far-flung corner of the world, he can probably be found watching the tragically poor local football side or tasting local wines after a long walk in the nearby mountains.

Phillip Tang

Peru Phillip grew up on a typically Australian diet of *pho* and fish'n'chips before moving to Mexico City. A degree in Chinese and Latin-American cultures launched him into travel and then writing about it for Lonely Planet's *Canada, China, Japan, Korea, Mexico, Peru* and *Vietnam* guides. See his writing at hello phillip.com; photos @mrtangtangtang; and tweets @philliptang

Luke Waterson

Ecuador, Peru Raised in the remote Somerset countryside in Southwest England, Luke quickly became addicted to exploring out-of-the-way places. Completing a Creative Writing degree at the University of East Anglia, he shouldered his backpack and vowed to see as much of the world as possible. Fast-forward a few years and he has travelled the Americas from Alaska to Tierra del Fuego and developed an obsession for Soviet Architecture and pre-Columbian ruins in equal measure.

Wendy Yanagihara

Ecuador Wendy serendipitously landed her dream job of writing for Lonely Planet in 2003, and has since spent the intervening years contributing to titles including *Southeast Asia on a Shoestring, Vietnam, Japan, Mexico, Costa Rica, Indonesia,* and *Grand Canyon National Park.* In the name of research, she has hiked remote valleys of West Papua, explored the tiny nooks and alleys of Tokyo sprawl, trekked on a Patagonian glacier, and rafted Colorado River whitewater. Wendy has also written for *BBC Travel,* the *Guardian, Lonely Planet Magazine,* lonelyplanet.com, and intermittently freelances as a graphic designer, illustrator and visual artist.

Mark Johanson
Bolivia, Chile Mark grew up in Virginia and has called five different countries home over the last decade. His travel-writing career began as something of a quarter-life crisis, and he's happily spent the past eight years circling the globe reporting for Australian travel magazines (such as *Get Lost*), British newspapers (such as the *Guardian*), American lifestyles (such as *Men's Journal*) and global media outlets (such as CNN and BBC). When not on the road, you'll find him gazing at the Andes from his home in Santiago.

Anna Kaminski
Argentina, Colombia Originally from the Soviet Union, Anna grew up in Cambridge, England. She graduated from the University of Warwick with a degree in Comparative American Studies, a background in the history, culture and literature of the Americas and the Caribbean, and an enduring love of Latin America. Her restless wanderings led her to settle briefly in Oaxaca and Bangkok and her flirtation with criminal law saw her volunteering as a lawyer's assistant in the courts, ghettos and prisons of Kingston, Jamaica. Anna has contributed to more than 30 Lonely Planet titles. When not on the road, Anna calls London home.

Brian Kluepfel
Ecuador, Venezuela Brian had lived in three states and seven different residences by the time he was nine, and he's just kept moving, making stops in Berkeley, Bolivia, the Bronx and the 'burbs further down the line. His journalistic work across the Americas has ranged from the Copa America soccer tournament in Paraguay to an accordion festival in Quebec. He has contributed to Lonely Planet titles including *Costa Rica, Belize, Guatemala, Bolivia* and *Ecuador*. Brian is an avid birder and musician and dabbles in both on the road; his singing has been tolerated at open mics from Sámara, Costa Rica, to Beijing, China.

Tom Masters
Colombia, French Guiana, Guyana, Suriname Dreaming since he could walk of going to the most obscure places on earth, Tom has always had a taste for the unknown. This has led to a writing career that has taken him all over the world, including North Korea, the Arctic, Congo and Siberia. Despite a childhood spent in the English countryside, as an adult Tom has always called London, Paris and Berlin home. He currently lives in Berlin and can be found online at www.tommasters.net.

Carolyn McCarthy
Argentina, Chile, Peru Carolyn specializes in travel, culture and adventure in the Americas. She has written for *National Geographic, Outside, BBC Magazine, Sierra Magazine,* the *Boston Globe* and other publications. A former Fulbright fellow and Banff Mountain Grant recipient, she has documented life in the most remote corners of Latin America. Carolyn has contributed to 40 guidebooks and anthologies for Lonely Planet, including *Colorado, USA, Argentina, Chile, Trekking in the Patagonian Andes, Panama, Peru* and *USA's National Parks.* For more information, visit www.carolynmccarthy.org or follow her Instagram travels @mccarthyoffmap.

MaSovaida Morgan
Ecuador MaSovaida is a travel writer and multimedia storyteller whose wanderlust has taken her to more than 40 countries and all seven continents. Previously, she was Lonely Planet's Destination Editor for South America and Antarctica for four years and worked as an editor for newspapers and NGOs in the Middle East and United Kingdom. Follow her on Instagram @MaSovaida.

Anja Mutić
Argentina Born and raised in Zagreb, Croatia, Anja has traveled the globe as a professional wanderer for decades. Her travel-writing career has taken her to more than 60 countries, taught her several languages and won her several awards. She has lived, worked and traveled on every continent (except Antarctica), including a stint of several months living in Buenos Aires. Follow her on Instagram at Everthenomad.

Robert Balkovich

Brazil Robert was born and raised in Oregon, but has called New York City home for almost a decade. When he was a child and other families were going to theme parks and grandma's house he went to Mexico City and toured Eastern Europe by train. He's now a writer and travel enthusiast seeking experiences that are ever so slightly out of the ordinary to report back on.

Jade Bremner

Ecuador Jade has been a journalist for more than a decade. She has lived in and reported on four different regions. Wherever she goes she finds action sports to try – the weirder the better – and it's no coincidence many of her favorite places have some of the best waves in the world. Jade has edited travel magazines and sections for *Time Out* and *Radio Times* and has contributed to the *Times*, *CNN* and the *Independent*. She feels privileged to share tales from this wonderful planet we call home and is always looking for the next adventure.

Cathy Brown

Argentina Cathy is a travel writer (Lonely Planet, OARS, Luxury Latin America) and editor (Matador Network). She live with her three kids in the Andes of Argentine Patagonia, where she hikes, gardens, drinks Malbec, works with medicinal herbs and indigenous cultures, and is building a straw-bale house. She's passionate about any adventure travel, including surfing, rafting, skiing, climbing or trekking, and works closely with the Adventure Travel Trade Association.

Gregor Clark

Brazil, Uruguay Gregor is a US-based writer whose love of foreign languages and curiosity about what's around the next bend have taken him to dozens of countries on five continents. Chronic wanderlust has also led him to visit all 50 states and most Canadian provinces on countless road trips through his native North America. Since 2000, Gregor has regularly contributed to Lonely Planet guides, with a focus on Europe and the Americas.

Alex Egerton

Argentina, Brazil, Peru A news journalist by trade, Alex has worked for magazines, newspapers and media outlets on five continents. Having had his fill of musty newsrooms, Alex decided to leap into travel writing in order to escape the mundane. He spends most of his time on the road checking under mattresses, sampling suspicious street food and chatting with locals. A keen adventurer, Alex has hiked through remote jungles in Colombia, explored isolated tributaries of the mighty Mekong and taken part in the first kayak descent of a number of remote waterways in Nicaragua. When not on the road, you'll find him at home in the colonial splendor of Popayán in southern Colombia.

Michael Grosberg

Argentina, Bolivia Michael has worked on over 50 Lonely Planet guidebooks. Other international work included development work on Rota in the western Pacific; and teaching in Quito, Ecuador. He has also worked in South Africa, where he investigated and wrote about political violence, and trained newly elected government representatives. He received a Masters in Comparative Literature, and has taught literature and writing as an adjunct professor.

Anthony Ham

Brazil, Colombia Anthony is a freelance writer and photographer who specializes in Spain, East and Southern Africa, the Arctic and the Middle East. When he's not writing for Lonely Planet, Anthony writes about and photographs Spain, Africa and the Middle East for newspapers and magazines in Australia, the UK and US.

OUR STORY

A beat-up old car, a few dollars in the pocket and a sense of adventure. In 1972 that's all Tony and Maureen Wheeler needed for the trip of a lifetime – across Europe and Asia overland to Australia. It took several months, and at the end – broke but inspired – they sat at their kitchen table writing and stapling together their first travel guide, *Across Asia on the Cheap*. Within a week they'd sold 1500 copies. Lonely Planet was born.

Today, Lonely Planet has offices in Franklin, London, Melbourne, Oakland, Dublin, Beijing and Delhi, with more than 600 staff and writers. We share Tony's belief that 'a great guidebook should do three things: inform, educate and amuse'.

OUR WRITERS

Regis St Louis

Brazil, Chile Regis grew up in a small town in the American Midwest – the kind of place that fuels big dreams of travel – and he developed an early fascination with foreign dialects and world cultures. He spent his formative years learning Russian and a handful of Romance languages, which served him well on journeys across much of the globe. Regis has contributed to more than 50 Lonely Planet titles, covering destinations across six continents. His travels have taken him from the mountains of Kamchatka to remote island villages in Melanesia, and to many grand urban landscapes. When not on the road, he lives in New Orleans. Regis also wrote the Plan Your Trip, Understand and Survive chapters.

Isabel Albiston

Argentina, Bolivia, Ecuador After six years working for the *Daily Telegraph* in London, Isabel left to spend more time on the road. A job as writer for a magazine in Sydney, Australia, was followed by a four-month overland trip across Asia and five years living and working in Buenos Aires, Argentina. Isabel started writing for Lonely Planet in 2014 and has contributed to 12 guidebooks. She's currently based in Ireland.

Celeste Brash

French Guiana, Guyana, Suriname Like many California natives, Celeste now lives in Portland, Oregon. However, she arrived after 15 years in French Polynesia, a year and a half in Southeast Asia and a stint teaching English as a second language (in an American accent) in Brighton, England – among other things. She's been writing guidebooks for Lonely Planet since 2005 and her travel articles have appeared in publications from *BBC Travel* to *National Geographic*. She's currently writing a book about her five years on a remote pearl farm in the Tuamotu Atolls and is represented by the Donald Maass Agency, New York.

Brendan Sainsbury

Colombia, Peru Born and raised in the UK in a town that never merits a mention in any guidebook (Andover, Hampshire), Brendan spent the holidays of his youth caravanning in the English Lake District and didn't leave Blighty until he was 19. Making up for lost time, he's since squeezed 70 countries into a sometimes precarious existence as a writer and professional vagabond. copy of Lonely Planet's *Africa on a Shoestring*. In the last 11 years, he has written over 40 books for Lonely Planet.

OVER PAGE MORE WRITERS

Published by Lonely Planet Global Limited
CRN 554153
14th edition – October 2019
ISBN 978 1 78657 488 6
© Lonely Planet 2019   Photographs © as indicated 2019
10 9 8 7 6 5 4 3 2 1
Printed in Singapore